Collins
thematic thesaurus of
The Bible

Collins
thematic thesaurus of
The Bible

A. Colin Day

Collins

Collins, part of HarperCollinsPublishers
77–85 Fulham Palace Road, London w6 8jb
www.collins.co.uk

First published in Great Britain in 2005 by
HarperCollinsPublishers

10 9 8 7 6 5 4 3 2 1

A catalogue record for this book is available
from the British Library.

ISBN 0 00 717278 8

Printed and bound in Great Britain by
Clays Ltd, St Ives plc

Contents

1
Introduction

5
List of categories

11
Abbreviations

13
The Categories

475
Index

Introduction

Thesaurus of the Bible?

This is a reference book for people studying the Bible. It may be used to find the answer to the type of question, 'What does the Bible say about . . . ?' That is to say, it groups together verses and passages of the Bible which are about the same subject.

Traditionally a Bible concordance has been used to find sets of verses or passages on the same subject, so it is necessary to understand how a thesaurus differs from a concordance.

Bible concordances enable one to find verses containing the same word. This usually works only for a particular version (or translation) of the Bible in a particular language. For example, in English, passages on faith will be found by searching for such words as 'believe', 'faith', 'trust', 'rely on' etc. Where you find particular verses depends on which word has been used when translating them.

A Bible thesaurus links together passages with similar meanings. Those passages may then be linked together irrespective of the version or the language. So, for example, passages on faith may be found grouped together under category 485 Belief.

How to use this book

Let us suppose that you want to find passages about who Jesus is. First it is necessary to think of a word which specifies the topic. You may think of the word 'identity' ('the identity of Jesus'), or simply the word 'is' ('who is this man?').

Look up the word of your choice in the index at the back of the book. If your word was 'is' you will see:

is

as is 7
does not exist 2
exists 1
identity 13
is present 189
nature 5
who is? 13

This signifies that the word 'is' may be used in different ways. One can use it to indicate that something exists ('God is!'). This meaning is dealt with in category number 1.

Another way one can use the word 'is' is to talk about someone's identity ('Who is this man?') This meaning is dealt with under category 13.

The sense in which you are interested is the latter one. Turn to the categories (the major part of the book) and look up category 13. Bible references on the theme of Identity are listed there. These references are grouped under various headings. The major divisions of category 13 are:

A Identity of God

B Identity of the Christ

C Identity of people

Obviously it is section 13B which concerns us. If you turn to this part of the Categories you should find the information you needed. The word 'is' is not the only one you could have used. Looking in the index for any of the terms 'identity', 'am', 'be', 'are', or 'who?' would also have pointed you to category 13.

Bible references

The words accompanying each Bible reference should not be taken as a formal quotation. These are merely my informal paraphrase.

Sometimes the content of several references needs to be summarised, and therefore an exact translation could not be given. The need to keep the book to a reasonable size means that the text should be as brief as possible, and an exact translation may be too long. The wording given should be enough to remind you of what the Bible says without quoting it exactly.

Browsing

You may find it useful to browse not only in the category you have reached, but also in neighbouring ones. If, for instance, you are exploring category 485 Belief, you might also find relevant material in the next category, 486 Unbelief.

Sometimes cross-references to other related categories are given. For instance, at the end of category 125 Past time there is a cross- reference to category 68 Beginning.

When you have found Bible references which appear to be promising for your search, look them up and browse in the Bible itself to see the context in which those references appear.

About this book

This book grew out of a desire to have a file of Bible verses so arranged as to group together references to the same subject. Bible concordances are often used for such a purpose, but as already mentioned, they suffer from the drawback of dealing with words (in a particular language, in a particular version) rather than meanings.

Topical concordances approach nearer to the desired result, but if the headings are words in alphabetic order the subjects may overlap. Moreover, there may be subjects which are not covered in such a work because the headings are not fully comprehensive.

The thesaurus which has descended from P. M. Roget was intended to categorise the whole field of meaning under 1000 heads (reduced in the current edition used to 990). When these heads are used as categories for Bible references, then the version or language used is immaterial providing that the meaning conveyed is the same. The heads cover all branches of meanings, and so should provide places for filing topics as diverse as one cares to list. Moreover, similar topics will often be listed near one another, to enhance browsing.

This, then, seemed to provide a suitable framework for a Bible reference book. I have in general used the categories of the 1982 Longman's revision of Roget's Thesaurus. The names of some categories seemed to be unduly abstruse or broad for my purposes, so I have in these cases chosen other names. This is not to quarrel with the basic categories, but simply to exploit them more comfortably for this particular application.

The idea of producing a thesaurus of Bible references seemed a sound one; the problem lay in the implementation. It took nearly fifteen years of trying various schemes in order to arrive at a methodology with which I am reasonably satisfied. Arranging references after a suitable methodology had been found, and then revising the work to add many more references, took the total time spent in writing this book to around twenty five years.

The first printed version of this Thesaurus (Roget's Thesaurus of the Bible, HarperCollins (1992)) had 43 756 Bible references. The full version (Collins Thesaurus of the Bible, HarperCollins (2002)) had 115 224 references. The present more concise version has 62 575 references. The spelling of proper nouns (names of people, places, rivers, mountains etc.) is that used by most modern versions. The index also includes most variant spellings of the proper nouns which appear in the King James and the New International Version.

Producing a more concise version has resulted in a number of benefits. Besides producing a smaller (and cheaper!) book, it has involved combing through the full version to pick out the references which are more likely to be of value to the reader. In finding the Bible references which you want, you do not have to climb over so many others.

The ordering

I have attempted to group references so that similar verses are recorded together. This has been attempted both by grouping like

However, these references could have been grouped in completely different ways. If my arrangements do not suit your needs, treat the references as items laid out at a rummage sale. Though the material may lack complete order, yet there is value for those who will browse.

Electronic version

I have written a suite of programs for Roget's Thesaurus of the Bible to run on an IBM-compatible PC. One program (the 'display program') takes a binary file containing all the material available in this book and displays it on the screen. The user can access the Bible references and indexes, cutting and pasting them to a word processor or printing them. Three other programs (the 'build programs') enable the user to modify the source text material and to produce a new binary file for the first program to display. All the original source text material is supplied along with the build programs.

The programs and files (for the concise version or the full version) may be downloaded from the Web site www.colinday.co.uk in the form of two installation packages. The build package is freely available to anyone. The display package is available to those who have purchased the book, and in order to install it you will need a serial number which is:

KqZ-29D-JpS4

It is hoped that those who wish to study the Bible will not want to pirate this package, or to enable others to do so.

Acknowledgements

I am very grateful to Susan M. Lloyd, editor of Roget's Thesaurus of English words and Phrases (Longman, 1982 edition) for her encouragement to use the categories of that work as a basis for my thesaurus. My wife Jean has believed in the scheme when few others did and when I nearly lost hope myself. Her quiet understanding has often been just the impetus I needed. Debra Jarzabek's emails have been a constant encouragement. My son Graham has given invaluable advice on the programming.

List of categories

Class one: Abstract relations
1 Existence
1 Existence
2 Nonexistence
3 Substantiality
4 Insubstantiality
5 Intrinsic nature
6 Extrinsic
7 State
8 Circumstance

2 Relation
9 Fellowship
10 Unrelated
11 Kindred
12 Correlation
13 Identity
14 Opposite
15 Difference
16 Uniformity
17 Non-uniformity
18 Similarity
19 Dissimilarity
20 Imitation
21 Unique
22 Copy
23 Prototype
24 Agreement
25 Disagreement

3 Quantity
26 Quantity
27 Gradually
28 Equality
29 Inequality
30 Average
31 Compensation
32 Great quantity
33 Small quantity
34 Superiority
35 Inferiority
36 Increase
37 Decrease
38 Addition
39 Subtraction
40 Adjunct
41 Remainder
42 Decrement
43 Mixture
44 Unmixed
45 Joining
46 Separating
47 Bond
48 Cohesion
49 Non-cohesion
50 Combination
51 Decomposition
52 Whole
53 Part
54 Complete
55 Incomplete
56 Composition
57 Exclusion
58 Component
59 Foreignness

4 Order
60 Order
61 Disorder
62 Arrange
63 Derange
64 Precedence
65 Sequence
66 Forerunner
67 Sequel
68 Beginning
69 End
70 Middle
71 Continuity
72 Discontinuity
73 Ranking
74 Gathering
75 Scattering
76 Meeting place
77 Class
78 Inclusion
79 Generality
80 Self
81 Principle
82 Multiplicity
83 Conformity
84 Nonconformity

5 Number
85 Number
86 Counting
87 List
88 One
89 Accompanying
90 Two
91 Double
92 Half
93 Three
94 Three times
95 Third part
96 Four
97 Four times
98 Quarter
99 Five and over
100 Multisection
101 Plurality
102 Fraction
103 Zero / nothing
104 Numerous
105 Few
106 Repetition
107 Infinity

6 Time
108 Time
109 Never
110 Period
111 Course
112 Contingent duration
113 Long duration
114 Brief
115 For ever
116 Instantly
117 Chronometry
118 Anachronism
119 First
120 Afterwards
121 Present time

122 Different time
123 Synchronism
124 Future time
125 Past time
126 Newness
127 Oldness
128 Morning. Spring
129 Evening. Autumn
130 Youthfulness
131 Age
132 Young person
133 Old person
134 Adultness
135 Earliness
136 Lateness
137 Opportunity
138 Untimeliness
139 Frequent
140 Infrequent
141 Regularity
142 Irregularity

7 Change
143 Change
144 Permanence
145 Cessation
146 Unceasing
147 Conversion
148 Returning
149 Revolutionary change
150 Substitution
151 Interchange
152 Changeableness
153 Stability
154 Present events
155 Destiny

8 Causation
156 Cause
157 Effect
158 Attribution of cause
159 Chance
160 Power
161 Impotence
162 Strength
163 Weakness
164 Making
165 Destruction
166 Reproducing
167 Reproduction
168 Destroyer
169 Parentage
170 Descendant
171 Productiveness
172 Unproductiveness
173 Agency
174 Vigour
175 Inertness
176 Violence
177 Gentleness
178 Influence
179 Tendency
180 Liability
181 Concurrence
182 Counteraction

Class two: Space
  1 Space in general
183 Space
184 Region
185 Place
186 Situation
187 Location
188 Displacement
189 Presence
190 Absence
191 Inhabitant
192 Abode
193 Contents
194 Receptacle

  2 Dimensions
195 Size
196 Littleness
197 Expansion
198 Contraction
199 Distance
200 Nearness
201 Gap
202 Contiguity
203 Length
204 Shortness
205 Breadth
206 Narrowness
207 Layer
208 Filament
209 Height
210 Lowness
211 Depth
212 Shallowness
213 Summit
214 Base
215 Vertical
216 Horizontal
217 Hanging
218 Support
219 Parallel
220 Tilting
221 Turning upside down
222 Crossing
223 Outside
224 Inside
225 Centrality
226 Covering
227 Lining
228 Dressing
229 Uncovering
230 Surroundings
231 Interposing
232 Circumscription
233 Outline
234 Edge
235 Enclosure
236 Limit
237 Front
238 Rear
239 Side
240 Opposite side
241 Right side
242 Left side

  3 Form
243 Form
244 Formlessness
245 Symmetry
246 Distortion

247 Angularity
248 Curvature
249 Straightness
250 Circularity
251 Convolution
252 Sphere
253 Convexity
254 Prominence
255 Concavity
256 Sharpness
257 Bluntness
258 Smoothness
259 Roughness
260 Notch
261 Fold
262 Furrow
263 Opening
264 Closure

  4 Motion
265 Motion
266 Stillness
267 Land travel
268 Traveller
269 Water travel
270 Mariner
271 Flying
272 Transference
273 Carrying
274 Vehicle
275 Ship
276 Aircraft
277 Swiftness
278 Slowness
279 Impact
280 Rebounding
281 Direction
282 Changing direction
283 Preceding
284 Following
285 Advance
286 Backwards
287 Propulsion
288 Pulling
289 Approach
290 Recession
291 Attraction
292 Repulsion
293 Convergence
294 Divergence
295 Arrival
296 Departure
297 Entrance
298 Emergence
299 Reception
300 Ejection
301 Food
302 Excretion
303 Insertion
304 Extraction
305 Passage
306 Overstepping
307 Shortfall
308 Ascent
309 Descent
310 Lifting up
311 Lowering
312 Leap
313 Plunge
314 Circling
315 Rotation

316 Unwinding
317 Oscillation
318 Agitation

Class three: Matter
  1 Matter in general
319 Materiality
320 Spirituality
321 Universe
322 Weight
323 Lightness

  2 Inorganic matter
324 Density
325 Tenuous
326 Hardness
327 Softness
328 Elasticity
329 Toughness
330 Brittleness
331 Structure
332 Powderiness
333 Friction
334 Lubrication
335 Liquids
336 Gaseousness
337 Liquefaction
338 Vaporization
339 Water
340 Atmosphere
341 Moisture
342 Dryness
343 Seas
344 Land
345 Gulf: inlet
346 Lake
347 Marsh
348 Plain
349 Island
350 Stream
351 Channel
352 Wind
353 Air-pipe
354 Semiliquid
355 Cloud
356 Pulpiness
357 Oiliness

  3 Organic matter
358 Organisms
359 Mineral
360 Life
361 Death
362 Killing
363 Corpse
364 Interment
365 Animals
366 Plants
367 Zoology
368 Botany
369 Animal husbandry
370 Agriculture
371 Mankind
372 Male
373 Female
374 Physical sensibility
375 Physical insensibility
376 Physical pleasure
377 Physical pain
378 Touch

379 Heat
380 Cold
381 Heating
382 Refrigeration
383 Heater
384 Refrigerator
385 Fuel
386 Taste
387 Insipidness
388 Pungency
389 Salt
390 Savouriness
391 Unsavouriness
392 Sweetness
393 Sourness
394 Odour
395 Without smell
396 Fragrance
397 Stench
398 Sound
399 Silence
400 Loudness
401 Faintness
402 Bang
403 Roar
404 Resonance
405 Nonresonance
406 Hissing
407 Squeak
408 Human cry
409 Animal sounds
410 Melody
411 Discord
412 Music
413 Musician
414 Musical instruments
415 Hearing
416 Deafness
417 Light
418 Darkness
419 Dimness
420 Light source
421 Screen
422 Transparency
423 Opacity
424 Semitransparency
425 Colour
426 Colourless
427 White
428 Black
429 Grey
430 Brown
431 Red
432 Orange
433 Yellow
434 Green
435 Blue
436 Purple
437 Variegation
438 Vision
439 Blindness
440 Defective vision
441 Spectator
442 Mirror
443 Visibility
444 Invisibility
445 Appearance
446 Disappearance

Class four: Intellect

Div. 1 Formation of ideas

1 In general
447 Intellect
448 Absence of intellect
449 Thought
450 Absence of thought
451 Idea
452 Topic

2 Precursory conditions
453 Curiosity
454 Incuriosity
455 Attention
456 Inattention
457 Carefulness
458 Negligence
459 Enquiry
460 Answer
461 Experiment
462 Comparison
463 Discrimination
464 Lack of discrimination
465 Measurement

3 Materials for reasoning
466 Evidence
467 Counterevidence
468 Qualification
469 Possibility
470 Impossibility
471 Probability
472 Improbability
473 Certainty
474 Uncertainty

4 Reasoning processes
475 Reasoning
476 Intuition
477 Sophistry
478 Proof
479 Confuting

5 Results of reasoning
480 Judgement
481 Misjudgement
482 Overestimation
483 Underestimation
484 Discovery
485 Belief
486 Unbelief. Doubt
487 Credulity
488 Assent
489 Dissent
490 Knowledge
491 Ignorance
492 Scholar
493 Ignoramus
494 Truth
495 Error
496 Maxim
497 Absurdity
498 Intelligence
499 Unintelligence
500 Wise person
501 Fool
502 Sanity
503 Insanity

504 Madman

6 Extension of thought
505 Memory
506 Forgetfulness
507 Expectation
508 Lack of expectation
509 Disappointment
510 Foreknowledge
511 Prediction

7 Creative thought
512 Supposition
513 Imagination

Div. 2 Communication of ideas

1 Nature of ideas
514 Meaning
515 Lack of meaning
516 Intelligibility
517 Unintelligibility
518 Ambiguity
519 Metaphor
520 Interpretation
521 Misinterpretation

2 Modes of communication
522 Manifestation
523 Hiding oneself
524 Informing
525 Concealment
526 Disclosure
527 Disguising
528 Publication
529 News
530 Secret
531 Communications
532 Affirmation
533 Negation
534 Teaching
535 Misteaching
536 Learning
537 Teacher
538 Learner
539 School
540 Truthfulness
541 Falseness
542 Deception
543 Untruth
544 Dupe
545 Deceiver
546 Exaggeration

3 Means of communicating
547 Indication
548 Record
549 Recorder
550 Obliteration
551 Representation
552 Misrepresentation
553 Painting
554 Sculpture
555 Engraving
556 Artist
557 Language
558 Letter
559 Word
560 Neology
561 Names

562 Misnomer
563 Phrase
564 Grammar
565 Solecism
566 Style
567 Perspicuity
568 Imperspicuity
569 Conciseness
570 Diffuseness
571 Vigour
572 Feebleness
573 Plainness
574 Ornament
575 Elegance
576 Inelegance
577 Voice
578 Voicelessness
579 Speech
580 Speech defect
581 Talkativeness
582 Not speaking
583 Addressing someone
584 Conversation
585 Soliloquy
586 Writing
587 Print
588 Correspondence
589 Book
590 Description
591 Dissertation
592 Summary
593 Poetry. Prose
594 Drama

Class five: Volition

Div. 1 Individual volition

1 Volition in general
595 Will
596 Necessity
597 Willingness
598 Unwillingness
599 Resolution
600 Perseverance
601 Irresolution
602 Obstinacy
603 Change of mind
604 Caprice
605 Choice
606 Absence of choice
607 Rejection
608 Predetermination
609 Spontaneity
610 Habit
611 Weaning
612 Motive
613 Dissuasion
614 Pretext
615 Good
616 Evil

2 Prospective volition
617 Intention
618 Nondesign. Gamble
619 Pursuit
620 Avoidance
621 Relinquishment
622 Business
623 Plan

624 Way
625 Middle way
626 Circuit
627 Requirement
628 Instrumentality
629 Means
630 Equipment
631 Materials
632 Store
633 Provision
634 Waste
635 Sufficiency
636 Insufficiency
637 Excess
638 Importance
639 Unimportance
640 Usefulness
641 Uselessness
642 Good policy
643 Inexpedience
644 Goodness
645 Badness
646 Perfection
647 Imperfection
648 Cleanness
649 Uncleanness
650 Health
651 Ill health
652 Salubrity
653 Insalubrity
654 Improvement
655 Deterioration
656 Restoring
657 Relapse
658 Remedy
659 Bane
660 Safety
661 Danger
662 Refuge
663 Pitfall
664 Warning
665 Danger signal
666 Preservation
667 Escape
668 Deliverance
669 Preparation
670 Unpreparedness
671 Attempt
672 Undertaking
673 Use
674 Nonuse
675 Misuse

3 Voluntary action
676 Action
677 Inaction
678 Activity
679 Inactivity
680 Haste
681 Leisure
682 Exertion
683 Repose
684 Fatigue
685 Refreshment
686 Worker
687 Workshop
688 Conduct
689 Guiding
690 Director
691 Advice
692 Council

693 Precept
694 Skill
695 Unskilfulness
696 Proficient person
697 Bungler
698 Cunning
699 Artlessness

4 Antagonism
700 Difficulty
701 Facility
702 Hindrance
703 Aid
704 Opposition
705 Opponent
706 Cooperation
707 Co-worker
708 Party
709 Dissension
710 Concord
711 Defiance
712 Attack
713 Defence
714 Retaliation
715 Resistance
716 Contention
717 Peace
718 War
719 Pacification
720 Mediation
721 Submission
722 Combatant
723 Weapons
724 Arena

5 Results of action
725 Completion
726 Non-completion
727 Success
728 Failure
729 Trophy
730 Prosperity
731 Adversity
732 Averageness

Div. 2 Social volition

1 General social volition
733 Authority
734 Anarchy
735 Severity
736 Leniency
737 Command
738 Disobedience
739 Obedience
740 Compulsion
741 Master
742 Servant
743 Badge of rule
744 Freedom
745 Subjection
746 Liberation
747 Restraint
748 Prison
749 Jailer
750 Prisoner
751 Commission
752 Abrogation
753 Resignation
754 Nominee

755 Deputy

2 Special social volition
756 Permission
757 Prohibition
758 Consent
759 Offer
760 Refusal
761 Request
762 Deprecation
763 Petitioner

3 Conditional social volition
764 Promise
765 Covenant
766 Conditions
767 Security
768 Observance
769 Nonobservance
770 Compromise

4 Possessive relations
771 Acquisition
772 Loss
773 Possession
774 Nonownership
775 Joint possession
776 Possessor
777 Property
778 Retention
779 Nonretention
780 Transfer (of property)
781 Giving
782 Receiving
783 Apportioning
784 Lending
785 Borrowing
786 Taking
787 Restitution
788 Stealing
789 Thief
790 Booty
791 Trade
792 Purchase
793 Sale
794 Merchant
795 Merchandise
796 Market
797 Money
798 Treasurer
799 Treasury
800 Wealth
801 Poverty
802 Credit
803 Debt
804 Payment
805 Nonpayment
806 Expenditure
807 Receipt
808 Accounts
809 Price
810 Discount
811 Dearness
812 Cheapness
813 Liberality
814 Economy
815 Prodigality
816 Parsimony

Class six: Emotion, religion and morality
1 General
817 Affections
818 Feeling
819 Sensibility
820 Insensibility
821 Excitement
822 Excitability
823 Inexcitability

2 Personal emotion
824 Joy
825 Suffering
826 Pleasurableness
827 Painfulness
828 Content
829 Discontent
830 Regret
831 Comfort
832 Aggravation
833 Cheerfulness
834 Sadness
835 Signs of joy
836 Mourning
837 Amusement
838 Tedium
839 Wit
840 Dullness
841 Beauty
842 Ugliness
843 Beautification
844 Ornamentation
845 Blemish
846 Good taste
847 Bad taste
848 Fashion
849 Ridiculousness
850 Affectation
851 Ridicule
852 Hope
853 Hopelessness
854 Fear
855 Courage
856 Cowardice
857 Rashness
858 Caution
859 Desire
860 Indifference
861 Dislike
862 Fastidiousness
863 Satiety
864 Wonder
865 Lack of wonder
866 Repute
867 Disrepute
868 Nobility
869 Common
870 Title
871 Pride
872 Humility. Humiliation
873 Vanity
874 Modesty
875 Ostentation
876 Celebration
877 Boasting
878 Insolence
879 Servility

3 Interpersonal emotion
880 Friendship
881 Enmity
882 Sociality
883 Unsociability
884 Courtesy
885 Discourtesy
886 Congratulation
887 Love
888 Hatred
889 Endearment
890 Darling. Favourite
891 Anger
892 Quick temper
893 Sullenness
894 Marriage
895 Celibacy
896 Divorce. Widowhood
897 Benevolence
898 Malevolence
899 Curse
900 Threat
901 Philanthropy
902 Misanthropy
903 Benefactor
904 Evildoer
905 Pity
906 Pitilessness
907 Gratitude
908 Ingratitude
909 Forgiveness
910 Revenge
911 Jealousy
912 Envy

4 Morality
913 Righteousness
914 Wrong
915 Dueness
916 Undueness
917 Duty
918 Undutifulness
919 Exemption
920 Respect
921 Disrespect
922 Contempt
923 Approval
924 Disapproval
925 Flattery
926 Calumny
927 Vindication
928 Accusation
929 Faithfulness
930 Unfaithfulness
931 Unselfishness
932 Selfishness
933 Virtue
934 Wickedness
935 Innocence
936 Guilt
937 Good person
938 Bad person
939 Repentance
940 Impenitence
941 Atonement
942 Temperance
943 Intemperance
944 Sensualism
945 Asceticism
946 Fasting

947 Gluttony
948 Sobriety
949 Drunkenness
950 Purity
951 Impurity
952 Libertine
953 Law
954 Illegality
955 Jurisdiction
956 Tribunal
957 Magistrate
958 Lawyer
959 Litigation
960 Acquittal
961 Condemnation

962 Reward
963 Punishment
964 Means of punishment

5 Religion
965 God
966 Deities in general
967 Pagan gods
968 Angel
969 Devil
970 Ghost
971 Heaven
972 Hell
973 Religion
974 Irreligion

975 Scriptures
976 Orthodoxy
977 Heterodoxy
978 Sectarianism
979 Holiness
980 Impiety
981 Worship
982 Idolatry
983 Sorcery
984 Occultism
985 The church
986 Priests
987 Non-priests
988 Ritual
989 Priests' garments
990 Temple

Abbreviations

Old testament

Gen.	Genesis
Exod.	Exodus
Lev.	Leviticus
Num.	Numbers
Deut.	Deuteronomy
Josh.	Joshua
Judg.	Judges
Ruth	Ruth
1 Sam.	1 Samuel
2 Sam.	2 Samuel
1 Kgs.	1 Kings
2 Kgs.	2 Kings
1 Chr.	1 Chronicles
2 Chr.	2 Chronicles
Ezra	Ezra
Neh.	Nehemiah
Esther	Esther
Job	Job
Ps.	Psalms
Prov.	Proverbs
Eccles.	Ecclesiastes
S. of S.	Song of Solomon
Isa.	Isaiah
Jer.	Jeremiah
Lam.	Lamentations
Ezek.	Ezekiel
Dan.	Daniel
Hos.	Hosea
Joel	Joel
Amos	Amos
Obad.	Obadiah
Jonah	Jonah
Mic.	Micah
Nahum	Nahum
Hab.	Habakkuk
Zeph.	Zephaniah
Hag.	Haggai
Zech.	Zechariah
Mal.	Malachi

New testament

Matt.	Matthew
Mark	Mark
Luke	Luke
John	John
Acts	Acts
Rom.	Romans
1 Cor.	1 Corinthians
2 Cor.	2 Corinthians
Gal.	Galatians
Eph.	Ephesians
Phil.	Philippians
Col.	Colossians
1 Thess.	1 Thessalonians
2 Thess.	2 Thessalonians
1 Tim.	1 Timothy
2 Tim.	2 Timothy
Titus	Titus
Philem.	Philemon
Heb.	Hebrews
Jas.	James
1 Pet.	1 Peter
2 Pet.	2 Peter
1 John	1 John
2 John	2 John
3 John	3 John
Jude	Jude
Rev.	Revelation

The Categories

1 Existence

A Existence of God
He who comes to God must believe that he exists (Heb. 11:6); God is the I AM (Exod. 3:14); there is a God in heaven who reveals mysteries (Dan. 2:28); him who is and was and is to come (Rev. 1:4, 8; 4:8); God is and was (Rev. 11:17); you who are and were (Rev. 16:5).

B Existence of Christ
The Word existed at the beginning (John 1:1); he existed before me (John 1:15, 30); before Abraham was, I AM (John 8:58); when you lift up the Son of man you will know that I AM [he] (John 8:28); that when it occurs you will believe that I AM (John 13:19); unless you believe that I AM [he], you will die in your sins (John 8:24); do not be afraid, I AM [it is I] (Matt. 14:27; Mark 6:50; Luke 24:39; John 6:20); Jesus said 'I AM [he]' (Mark 14:62; John 18:5, 8); when he said, 'I AM [he]', they fell to the ground (John 18:6).
I AM THE . . . see 13B5.

C Existence through God
God calls into existence what does not exist (Rom. 4:17); by your will they existed (Rev. 4:11); my hand made all these things and so they came into being (Isa. 66:2); in God we live and move and have our being (Acts 17:28); in the Son all things hold together (Col. 1:17); through the Word all things came into existence (John 1:3); all that came into existence found its life in him (John 1:3–4); Christ, through whom are all things and through whom we exist (1 Cor. 8:6); Christ, for whom are all things and through whom are all things (Heb. 2:10).

D Arrogant existence
God chose the things that are not, to render inoperative the things that are (1 Cor. 1:28); 'I am, with no one beside me': said by Chaldea (Isa. 47:10); said by Nineveh (Zeph. 2:15).

2 Nonexistence

A God not existing
The fool says there is no God (Ps. 14:1; 53:1); all his thoughts are, 'There is no God' (Ps. 10:4); where is your God? (Ps. 42:3, 10); where is their God? (Ps. 79:10; 115:2; Joel 2:17); where is the Lord your God? (Mic. 7:10); where is the God of justice? (Mal. 2:17); we have never even heard that there is a Holy Spirit (Acts 19:2).
WHERE IS GOD?, see 190A1.

B Idols not existing
An idol has no real existence (1 Cor. 8:4).

C People not existing
I will make them jealous with what is not a people (Deut. 32:21); once you were not a people but now you are the people of God (1 Pet. 2:10); God chose the things that are not, to render inoperative the things that are (1 Cor. 1:28); one who has never been is better off than the living or the dead (Eccles. 4:2–3); Job wished he had never been born (Job 3:1-19; 10:19); woe to me, my mother, that you bore me (Jer. 15:10); better for the betrayer if he had never been born (Matt. 26:24; Mark 14:21).
NONENTITIES, see 639.

D Passing away
The rulers of this age are passing away (1 Cor. 2:6); Rachel's children are no more (Jer. 31:15; Matt. 2:18); my children have gone from me and are no more (Jer. 10:20); those who attack you will be non-existent (Isa. 41:11-12); the wicked will be no more (Ps. 37:10; Prov. 10:25); the godly man ceases to be (Ps. 12:1); heaven and

earth will pass away (Matt. 5:18; 24:35; Mark 13:31; Luke 16:17; 21:33); the heavens will pass away (2 Pet. 3:10); the first heaven and the first earth passed away (Rev. 21:1); changed like a garment (Heb. 1:11-12); shaken and removed (Heb. 12:26-7); the form of this present world is passing away (1 Cor. 7:31); the world and its lusts are passing away (1 John 2:17); there will no longer be sea (Rev. 21:1); there will no longer be death, mourning, crying or pain (Rev. 21:4); there will no longer be night (Rev. 22:5); when the perfect comes, that which is partial will be done away (1 Cor. 13:10); old things have passed away, the new has come (2 Cor. 5:17); the beast was and is not and is to come (Rev. 17:8); the beast was and is not (Rev. 17:11).
DEATH, see 361.

3 Substantiality
The substance belongs to Christ (Col. 2:17).
MATERIAL, see 319.

4 Insubstantiality
SPIRITUALITY, see 320.

5 Intrinsic nature

A Nature of God
His invisible nature has been clearly seen in what is made (Rom. 1:20); that you may become partakers of the divine nature (2 Pet. 1:4); God's nature [seed] remains in him and he cannot go on sinning (1 John 3:9).

B Nature of Christ
What sort of man is this? (Matt. 8:27); they are not of the world just as I am not (John 17:14, 16); what do you say about him, since he opened your eyes? (John 9:17).
WHO IS JESUS?, see 13B1.

C Nature of people
Who may sojourn in your tent? (Ps. 15:1); who may ascend the hill of the Lord? (Ps. 24:3); what will this child turn out to be? (Luke 1:66); what is Apollos, what is Paul? (1 Cor. 3:5); they are not of the world just as I am not (John 17:14); are you a Roman? (Acts 22:27); I was born a citizen (Acts 22:28); I am a Pharisee (Acts 23:6); as to the law, a Pharisee (Phil. 3:5); by the grace of God I am what I am (1 Cor. 15:10-11); we were by nature children of wrath, like the rest (Eph. 2:3); you know what kind of people we were among you (1 Thess. 1:5).
NATURE OF MAN, see 371A1a.
NATURE OF FOOLS, see 501A.

D Nature of things
WHAT KIND? see 77.

D1 What is this?
What are these seven ewe lambs? (Gen. 21:29); what are these cities you have given me? (1 Kgs. 9:13); see what the land is like (Num. 13:18-19); what is that in your hand? (Exod. 4:2); what do you have in the house? (2 Kgs. 4:2); manna – what is it? (Exod. 16:15); when your children ask you, 'What is this?' (Exod. 13:14); what are you, O great mountain? (Zech. 4:7); what is this? a new teaching! (Mark 1:27); what is truth? (John 18:38).

D2 What is done?
What have God wrought? (Num. 23:23); no one can say to God, 'What are you doing?' (Dan. 4:35); what have we spoken against you? (Mal. 3:13); what shall I do with Jesus called Christ? (Matt. 27:22); what shall I do with him you call the king of the Jews? (Mark 15:12); what

shall we do with these men? (Acts 4:16); what are you doing here, Elijah? (1 Kgs. 19:9, 13); what are you doing, untying the colt? (Mark 11:5).

6 Extrinsic

FOREIGN, see 59.

7 State: absolute condition

Let each lead the life God has assigned (1 Cor. 7:17); let every one remain in the station in which he was called (1 Cor. 7:20, 24); it is good for a man to remain as he is (1 Cor. 7:26); the widow is happier if she remains as she is (1 Cor. 7:40).

8 Circumstance: relative condition

A Circumstances
Content in all circumstances (Phil. 4:11-12); give thanks in everything (1 Thess. 5:18).

B Welfare
Seek the welfare of the city to which you are exiled (Jer. 29:7); I have no one like Timothy, anxious for your welfare (Phil. 2:20); I pray that all may go well with you (3 John 2); do not pray for the welfare of this people (Jer. 14:11); Jeremiah is not seeking the welfare of this people (Jer. 38:4).

9 Fellowship

A Fellowship with God
Fellowship with the Father and his Son (1 John 1:3); the fellowship of the Holy Spirit (2 Cor. 13:14); if there is any fellowship of the Spirit (Phil. 2:1); you were called into fellowship with his Son (1 Cor. 1:9); that I may know the fellowship of his sufferings (Phil. 3:10); if we say we have fellowship with God and walk in darkness, we lie (1 John 1:6).

B Fellowship with believers
They devoted themselves to fellowship (Acts 2:42); fellowship with one another (1 John 1:7); that you may have fellowship with us (1 John 1:3); the right hand of fellowship (Gal. 2:9); thankful for your partnership in the gospel (Phil. 1:5); you are partakers with me of grace (Phil. 1:7); the fellowship of your faith (Philem. 6).

C Fellowship with sinners
Throw in your lot with us (Prov. 1:14); do not share in someone else's sin (1 Tim. 5:22).

KINDRED, see 11.

ACCOMPANY, see 89.

10 Unrelated: absence of relation

A Unrelated people
What relation can exist between a believer and an unbeliever (2 Cor. 6:15); you know how unlawful it is for a Jew to associate with a foreigner (Acts 10:28); you are not of my sheep (John 10:26); if I do not wash you, you have no part in me (John 13:8); if anyone does not have the Spirit of Christ he is not his (Rom. 8:9); once you were estranged from God (Col. 1:21); they went out from us to demonstrate that they are not of us (1 John 2:19); what more have I to do with idols? (Hos. 14:8); what have we in common?: David and the sons of Zeruiah (2 Sam. 16:10; 19:22); Elijah and the widow (1 Kgs. 17:18); Elisha and the king of Israel (2 Kgs. 3:13); demons and Jesus (Matt. 8:29; Mark 1:24; 5:7; Luke 4:34; 8:28); Jesus and his mother (John 2:4).

B Unrelated things
What has straw in common with grain? (Jer. 23:28); what relation can exist between righteousness and lawlessness (2 Cor. 6:14); what relation can exist between light and darkness (2 Cor. 6:14).

11 Kindred

A Attitudes between kin

A1 Love between relatives
It is good for brothers to live in unity (Ps. 133:1); a believer should take care of relatives (1 Tim. 5:4, 16); a brother was born for adversity (Prov. 17:17); there is a friend who sticks closer than a brother (Prov. 18:24); if any one will not provide for his family, he has denied the faith (1 Tim. 5:8); relatives should not quarrel (Gen. 13:8); you must not fight against your relatives (1 Kgs. 12:24); you are brethren, why wrong one another? (Acts 7:26).

KINSMAN-REDEEMER, see 792C2.

A2 Subject to relatives
May your mother's sons bow down before you (Gen. 27:29); I have given all his brothers to him as servants (Gen. 27:37); because you are my kinsman, should you serve me for nothing? (Gen. 29:15).

A3 Hatred between relatives
Am I my brother's keeper? (Gen. 4:9); Joseph's brothers hated him (Gen. 37:4); betrayed by kinsmen (Luke 21:16); if a relative entices you to serve other gods, kill him (Deut. 13:6-10); brother will deliver up brother to death (Matt. 10:21; Mark 13:12); a man's enemies will be his own family (Mic. 7:6; Matt. 10:36); I will raise up evil against you from your own household (2 Sam. 12:11); a prophet is not without honour except among his own relatives (Mark 6:4); whoever comes to me and does not hate his brothers and sisters (Luke 14:26); the Lord hates those who sow discord among brothers (Prov. 6:19).

A4 Separating from relatives
Go from your family (Gen. 12:1; Acts 7:3); God has estranged me from my relatives (Job 19:13-14); he who leaves brothers or sisters for Christ's sake (Matt. 19:29; Mark 10:29; Luke 18:29).

A5 Relatives also involved
Go into the ark, you and all your house (Gen. 7:1); words by which you will be saved, you and all your household (Acts 11:14); believe in the Lord Jesus and you will be saved, you and your household (Acts 16:31); they spoke the word of the Lord to him and all in his house (Acts 16:32); he was baptised with his household (Acts 16:33); he had believed in God with all his household (Acts 16:34); Lydia and her household were baptised (Acts 16:15).

B Particular blood relatives

B1 Relatives
This woman is bone of my bones and flesh of my flesh (Gen. 2:23); Jacob told Rachel he was a relative (Gen. 29:12); Boaz was a relative of Elimelech (Ruth 2:1, 3; 3:2); Eliashib the high priest was related to Tobiah (Neh. 13:4); Joseph was of the house and family of David (Luke 2:4); Elizabeth was a relative of Mary (Luke 1:36); none of your relatives is called John (Luke 1:61).

FATHER AND MOTHER, see 169.

CHILDREN, see 170.

B2 Christ's earthly family
He went to Capernaum with his mother and brothers and disciples (John 2:12); Christ's mother and brothers came to him (Matt. 12:46; Mark 3:31-2; Luke 8:19-20); his brothers James, Joseph, Simon and Judas and his sisters (Matt. 13:55-6; Mark 6:3); his brothers said, 'Leave here and go to Judea' (John 7:3); a believer as wife, as the rest of the apostles, the Lord's brothers and Cephas? (1 Cor. 9:5); James the Lord's brother (Gal. 1:19); his mother and brothers in the upper room (Acts 1:14); his family said he had lost his senses (Mark 3:21); not even his brothers believed in him (John 7:5).

B3 Brothers

Cain's brother, Abel (Gen. 4:2); Sarah said Abraham was her brother (Gen. 20:5, 13); is not Esau Jacob's brother? (Mal. 1:2); two brothers, Simon and Andrew (Matt. 4:18; 10:2; Mark 1:16; Luke 6:14; John 1:40); two other brothers, James and John (Matt. 4:21; 10:2; Mark 1:19; 3:17).

B4 Sisters

Do not uncover the nakedness of your sister (Lev. 18:9, 11; 20:17); do not uncover the nakedness of your brother's wife (Lev. 18:16); Abraham told Sarah to say she was his sister (Gen. 12:13, 19); Abraham said she was his sister (Gen. 20:2, 5, 12); Isaac said Rebekah was his sister (Gen. 26:7, 9).

C Non-blood relations

C1 God's family

The Father, from whom every family is named (Eph. 3:15); members of God's household (Eph. 2:19); the household of faith (Gal. 6:10); you are all brothers (Matt. 23:8); treat younger men like brothers (1 Tim. 5:1); warn him as a brother (2 Thess. 3:15); Onesimus is no longer a slave but a beloved brother (Philem. 16); treat younger women as sisters, in all purity (1 Tim. 5:2).

C2 Christ's true family

Christ's true relatives are those who obey God (Matt. 12:48-50; Mark 3:33-4; Luke 8:21); he calls them brothers (Heb. 2:11-12); he is the firstborn among many brothers (Rom. 8:29); made like his brothers (Heb. 2:17); as you did it to the least of my brethren you did it to me (Matt. 25:40); tell my brothers to go to Galilee (Matt. 28:10); he will receive brothers and sisters a hundredfold (Mark 10:30).

C3 Related nations

Her false sister Judah (Jer. 3:7, 8, 10); your older sister is Samaria and your younger sister Sodom (Ezek. 16:46-56); Oholah is Samaria and Oholibah her sister is Jerusalem (Ezek. 23:4); the cup of your sister Samaria (Ezek. 23:33); because of your violence to your brother Jacob (Obad. 10).

12 Correlation

A According to people

Food according to their descendants (Gen. 47:12); God set boundaries according to the number of the sons of Israel (Deut. 32:8); land according to the tribes of Israel (Ezek. 45:8; 47:21); according to the number of people: take a lamb (Exod. 12:4); gather manna (Exod. 16:16); take an inheritance (Num. 26:53-4; 33:54); give the Levites cities (Num. 35:8).

B According to things

The valuation of a field is proportional to the seed needed to sow it (Lev. 27:16); cereal offerings according to the number of sacrifices (Num. 15:12); according to the anger and envy you showed (Ezek. 35:11); according to their uncleanness and transgressions (Ezek. 39:24); according to your faith (Matt. 9:29); the disciples sent aid, each according to his ability (Acts 11:29); let everyone make a contribution as he has prospered (1 Cor. 16:2); give as the Lord has blessed (Deut. 15:14; 16:17); grace given to each according to the measure of Christ's gift (Eph. 4:7).

ACCORDING TO THE NUMBER, see 85.

C According to time

According to the number of years to the Jubilee (Lev. 25:15-16, 50-2; 27:18); according to the days spying out the land, a year for a day (Num. 14:34); make us glad according to the days you have afflicted us (Ps. 90:15).

13 Identity

A Identity of God

Who is the Lord? (Exod. 5:2; Prov. 30:9); who is the Almighty? (Job 21:15); no one knows who the Father is except the Son and those to whom the Son reveals him (Luke 10:22); I am Yahweh (Exod. 6:2-3); I am Yahweh, that is my name (Isa. 42:8); Yahweh is his name (Exod. 15:3; Jer. 33:2); I am Yahweh your healer (Exod. 15:26); I am Yahweh who sanctifies (Lev. 20:8; 21:15, 23; 22:9, 16, 32); I am Yahweh who has separated you from the peoples (Lev. 20:24); You, whose name is the Lord, are the Most High (Ps. 83:18); the Lord, he is God (Deut. 4:35; 7:9; 1 Kgs. 18:39); the Lord, he is God in heaven above and earth below (Deut. 4:39); the Lord your God is God of gods and Lord of lords (Deut. 10:17); Lord Jahweh, you are God (2 Sam. 7:28); the altar is witness that the Lord is God (Josh. 22:34); I am God Almighty [El Shaddai] (Gen. 17:1; 35:11); I am the God of Abraham (Gen. 26:24); the God of Abraham and Isaac (Gen. 28:13); the God of Abraham, Isaac and Jacob (Exod. 3:6; Acts 7:32); I am the God of your father (Gen. 46:3); I am the God of Bethel (Gen. 31:13).

I AM, see 1A.

B Identity of the Christ

B1 Who is Jesus?

Who do you claim to be? (John 8:53); who are you? (John 8:25; Acts 9:5; 22:8; 26:15); no one dared ask, 'Who are you?' (John 21:12); who is this? (Matt. 21:10; Mark 4:41; Luke 8:25; 9:9); who is the Son of Man? (John 9:36; 12:34); who is this who forgives sins? (Luke 7:49); who is this who speaks blasphemies? (Luke 5:21); who do you say that I am? (Luke 9:20); who do people say I am? (Matt. 16:13; Mark 8:27; Luke 9:18); are you he who is to come? (Matt. 11:3; Luke 7:19-20); are you the king of the Jews? (Mark 15:2; Luke 23:3); so you are a king? (John 18:37); are you the Christ? (Matt. 26:63; Mark 14:61; Luke 22:67); this can't be the son of David, can it? (Matt. 12:23); if you are the Christ, tell us plainly (John 10:24); are you the Son of God? (Matt. 26:63; Luke 22:70); if you are the Son of God . . . (Matt. 4:3, 6; 27:40; Luke 4:3, 9); no one knows who the Son is except the Father (Luke 10:22); if you knew who it is who is saying to you, 'Give me a drink' (John 4:10).

NATURE OF CHRIST, see 5B.

B2 Who he might be

They said he was John the Baptist, Elijah or one of the prophets (Matt. 16:14; Mark 8:28; Luke 9:7-8, 19); this is John the Baptist raised from the dead (Matt. 14:2); he is John the baptiser, raised from the dead (Mark 6:14); this is the prophet Jesus from Nazareth (Matt. 21:11); just the carpenter (Mark 6:3); the carpenter's son (Matt. 13:55); Joseph's son (Luke 4:22); is not this Jesus, Joseph's son (John 6:42); behold, the man! (John 19:5); he is a prophet, like one of the prophets of old (Mark 6:15); it is Elijah (Mark 6:15); this is the Prophet who is to come into the world (John 6:14).

B3 Said to be the Christ

Some said he was the Christ (John 7:41); can this be the Christ? (John 4:29); Peter confessed him to be the Christ (Matt. 16:16; Mark 8:29; Luke 9:20); Saul confounded the Jews by proving that Jesus is the Christ (Acts 9:22); this Jesus is the Christ (Acts 17:3); Paul testified to the Jews that Jesus was the Christ (Acts 18:5); demonstrating from the Scriptures that Jesus was the Christ (Acts 18:28); we have believed and come to know that you are the holy One of God (John 6:69); who is the liar but he who denies that Jesus is the Christ? (1 John 2:22); let him save himself, if he is the Christ (Luke 23:35); are you not the Christ? (Luke 23:39); this is he (John 1:15, 30); do the authorities know this is the Christ? (John 7:26); it is the Lord (John 21:7); I know who you are, the Holy One of God (Mark 1:24); the Holy One of God (Luke 4:34); unclean spirits said, 'You are the Son of God' (Mark 3:11; Luke 4:41); the Son of God (Matt. 27:54); he is the Son of God (Acts 9:20); I believe you are the Christ, the Son of God (John 11:27); my Lord and my God! (John 20:28); whoever believes that Jesus is the Christ is born of God (1 John 5:1); who overcomes the world but he who believes that Jesus is the Son of God? (1 John 5:5).

B4 Called himself the Christ

He admitted he was the Christ, the Son of God (Matt. 26:63-4; Mark 14:61-2; Luke 22:67-70); I who speak to you am the Christ (John 4:26); he made himself out to be the Son of God (John 19:7); he says he is Christ, a king (Luke 23:2); you, a man, make yourself out to be God (John 10:33); this man said, 'I am the King of the Jews' (John 19:21).

B5 I am the . . .

I am the bread of life (John 6:35, 48); the bread which came down from heaven (John 6:41, 51); I am the light of the world (John 8:12; 9:5); I am the door (John 10:7, 9); I am the good shepherd (John 10:11, 14); I am the resurrection and the life (John 11:25); I am the way, the truth and the life (John 14:6); I am the vine (John 15:1, 5).

I AM (WITHOUT AN OBJECT), see 1A.

B6 False Christs

Many will come saying 'I am the Christ' (Matt. 24:5); many will come saying 'I am he' (Mark 13:6; Luke 21:8).

C Identity of people

C1 Who is this?

Who is he who hunted game? (Gen. 27:33); who is David? (1 Sam. 25:10); whose likeness and inscription are these? (Matt. 22:20); if he were a prophet he would know who this woman is (Luke 7:39); who are these in white robes? (Rev. 7:13).

C2 Who is the one?

Who is the man who fears the Lord? (Ps. 25:12); who is the faithful and wise servant? (Matt. 24:45; Luke 12:42); who is my neighbour? (Luke 10:29); who is it you are speaking about? (John 13:24-5); on whose account has this evil come? (Jonah 1:7-8); whom shall I send and who will go for us? (Isa. 6:8); who touched me? (Mark 5:30-2; Luke 8:45); who hit you? (Matt. 26:68; Luke 22:64).

C3 Who is John the Baptist?

Who are you? (John 1:19, 22); they wondered whether John was the Christ (Luke 3:15); he was not the Christ (John 1:20; 3:28; Acts 13:25); nor the prophet (John 1:21); nor Elijah (John 1:21); except figuratively (Matt. 11:14; 17:12-13; Mark 9:13); he was not the light (John 1:8); this is he of whom it is written (Matt. 11:10); why baptise, if you are not the Christ, nor Elijah, nor the Prophet? (John 1:25).

NATURE OF PEOPLE, see 5C.

C4 This is the one

You are the man! (2 Sam. 12:7); you are Saul! (1 Sam. 28:12); behold, the man! (John 19:5).

14 Opposite

Those who create hindrances contrary to the doctrine you have learned (Rom. 16:17).

NONCONFORMITY, see 84.

15 Difference

A Different gods

You shall have no other gods before me (Exod. 20:3; Deut. 5:7); his wives turned away his heart after other

gods (1 Kgs. 11:4); speaking in the name of other gods (Deut. 18:20); you have made for yourself other gods (1 Kgs. 14:9).

B Different person

They will not build and another inhabit (Isa. 65:22); they will not plant and another eat (Isa. 65:22); please send someone else (Exod. 4:13); are you he who is to come or should we look for someone else? (Luke 7:19-20).

C Different teachings

Their laws are different (Esther 3:8); a different gospel (2 Cor. 11:4; Gal. 1:6-9); a different Jesus or spirit (2 Cor. 11:4); if anyone teaches otherwise (1 Tim. 6:3); no one can lay another foundation from what has been laid (1 Cor. 3:11).

D Differentiating

God made a distinction between Egypt and Israel (Exod. 8:22; 9:4; 11:7); God's presence made Israel distinct from other nations (Exod. 33:16); differentiating between clean and unclean animals (Lev. 11:47; 20:25); between holy and profane, between clean and unclean (Lev. 10:10); between the righteous and the wicked (Mal. 3:18); between holy and profane (Ezek. 44:23); they made no distinction between holy and profane, clean and unclean (Ezek. 22:26); have you not made distinctions and become judges with evil thoughts? (Jas. 2:4).

DISCRIMINATING, see 463.

16 Uniformity

EQUALITY, see 28.

A The same as God

Speaking of God as if he were just the same as the gods of the nations (2 Chr. 32:19); you thought that I was just like you (Ps. 50:21).

EQUALITY WITH GOD, see 28A.

B People are the same

All people are the work of his hands (Job 34:19); we also are men, of the same nature as you (Acts 14:15); God gave the Gentiles the Holy Spirit just as he did to us (Acts 11:17; 15:8); in Christ there are no distinctions between: Jew, Greek (Rom. 10:12; Gal. 3:28; Col. 3:11); slave, free, male, female (Gal. 3:28).

EQUAL TREATMENT, see 28C.

17 Non-uniformity

Flesh of different creatures differs (1 Cor. 15:39); there are heavenly bodies and earthly bodies (1 Cor. 15:40); sun, moon and stars differ in their glory (1 Cor. 15:41); limbs do not have the same function (Rom. 12:4); believers are given diverse gifts (Rom. 12:6; 1 Cor. 12:4-31); there are varieties of ministry, but the same Lord (1 Cor. 12:5); there are varieties of workings, but the same God (1 Cor. 12:6).

DIFFERENT, see 15.

INEQUALITY, see 29.

18 Similarity

IMITATING, see 20.

A Like God

A1 Christ like God

Christ is the image of God (2 Cor. 4:4; Col. 1:15); an exact representation of God's nature (Heb. 1:3).

A2 Made like God

To whom will you liken God? (Isa. 40:18); to whom will you liken me? (Isa. 40:25; 46:5); let us make man in our image according to our likeness (Gen. 1:26); God created mankind, male and female, in the image of God (Gen. 1:27); God created man in the likeness of God (Gen. 5:1); mankind was created in the image of God (Gen. 9:6; Jas. 3:9); a man [male] is the image and glory of God (1 Cor. 11:7); when you eat of the tree you will be like God (Gen. 3:5); the man has become like one of us (Gen. 3:22); I will make myself like the Most High (Isa. 14:14); I will be satisfied when I awake in your likeness (Ps. 17:15); the new man is being renewed after the image of its Creator (Col. 3:10); we are being changed into the image of God (2 Cor. 3:18).

B Like Christ
Wives, be subject to your husbands as to the Lord (Eph. 5:22, 24); husbands, love your wives, as Christ loved the church (Eph. 5:25); that I may become like him in his death (Phil. 3:10); as is the man of heaven, so are those who are of heaven (1 Cor. 15:48-9); conformed to the image of his son (Rom. 8:29); when he appears we shall be like him (1 John 3:2).

C Like people
C1 Christ like people
Christ came in the likeness of sinful flesh (Rom. 8:3); born in the likeness of men (Phil. 2:7); made like his brothers (Heb. 2:17).

C2 Like people by nature
Seth was born in the image of Adam (Gen. 5:3); we have borne the image of the man of dust (1 Cor. 15:48-9); we also are men, of the same nature as you (Acts 14:15); Elijah was a man like us (Jas. 5:17).

C3 Like people in character
We have sinned like our fathers (Ps. 106:6); like Adam they have broken the covenant (Hos. 6:7); like lender, like borrower etc. (Isa. 24:2); 'like mother, like daughter' (Ezek. 16:44); like people, like priest (Isa. 24:2; Hos. 4:9).

C4 Becoming like people
A disciple must be like his teacher (Matt. 10:25; Luke 6:40); if you become like us, circumcised (Gen. 34:15); I would that all people were like me (Acts 26:29; 1 Cor. 7:7); become like me, for I have become like you (Gal. 4:12); the gods have become like men (Acts 14:11).

C5 Like good people
May God make you like Ephraim and Manasseh (Gen. 48:20); like Rachel and Leah (Ruth 4:11); like the house of Perez (Ruth 4:12); the feeblest of them will be like David and house of David like God (Zech. 12:8); unless you are converted and become like children you will not enter (Matt. 18:3-4); they received the Holy Spirit just as we did (Acts 10:47; 11:15).

C6 Like bad people
May all your enemies be like Absalom! (2 Sam. 18:32); like the houses of Jeroboam and Baasha (1 Kgs. 21:22); like Zedekiah and Ahab (Jer. 29:22); how can I make you like Admah? (Hos. 11:8); do not answer a fool according to his folly lest you be like him (Prov. 26:4); you who judge are doing the same things (Rom. 2:1).

C7 Things like people
Mountain shadows like men (Judg. 9:36); men like trees, walking (Mark 8:24); like clay in the potter's hand (Ps. 115:8; 135:18); those who make idols will be like them (Hos. 9:10).

C8 Like the nations
They wanted a king, to be like all the nations (Deut. 17:14; 1 Sam. 8:5); we will be like the nations, serving wood and stone (Ezek. 20:32); Moab and Seir said Judah was like all the nations (Ezek. 25:8).

D Like creatures
Do not make a likeness of anything (Exod. 20:4; Deut. 4:16-18; 5:8); the Philistines made images of tumours and mice (1 Sam. 6:5); we made cakes for the queen of heaven bearing her image (Jer. 44:19); in the resurrection people are like angels in heaven (Matt. 22:30); the devil prowls like a roaring lion (1 Pet. 5:8); men like lions: Israel (Num. 23:24; 24:9; Ezek. 19:2-9);

Gad (Deut. 33:20); Dan (Deut. 33:22); Judah (Gen. 49:9); Pharaoh (Ezek. 32:2).

E Like things
Do not make an oil similar to the holy anointing oil (Exod. 30:32); do not make incense similar to the holy incense (Exod. 30:37); a land like your own (2 Kgs. 18:32; Isa. 36:17); we would have been like Sodom and Gomorrah (Isa. 1:9; Rom. 9:29); I will make this city like Topheth (Jer. 19:12).

F Similar treatment
Do as you did to Jericho (Josh. 8:2); as I have done, so it will be done to them (Ezek. 12:11); as in the days of Noah, so it will be in the days of the Son of man (Luke 17:26).

19 Dissimilarity
UNIQUE, see 21.

A Not like people
The Hebrew women are not like Egyptian women (Exod. 1:19); do not be like the Gentiles (Matt. 6:8; 1 Thess. 4:5); he taught them as one with authority, not as the scribes (Mark 1:22); I thank you that I am not like other men (Luke 18:11); not as the world gives do I give to you (John 14:27).

B Not like things
The portion of Jacob is not like these idols (Jer. 10:16; 51:19); the new patch will not match the old (Luke 5:36); the land you enter is not like the land of Egypt (Deut. 11:10); not like the covenant I made with their fathers (Heb. 8:9).
GOD IS UNIQUE, see 21A.

20 Imitation
CONFORMING, see 83.

A Imitating good
Imitate good, not evil (3 John 11); whatever the Son sees the Father doing he also does (John 5:19); be imitators of God as beloved children (Eph. 5:1); you became imitators of us and of the Lord (1 Thess. 1:6); be imitators of me as I am of Christ (1 Cor. 11:1); love one another as I have loved you (John 13:34; 15:12); walk in love, as Christ loved us (Eph. 5:2); Christ suffered leaving us an example to imitate (1 Pet. 2:21); I have given you an example [foot-washing] that you should do as I have done (John 13:15); imitate the faith of your leaders (Heb. 13:7); you know how you should imitate us (2 Thess. 3:7); follow our example (2 Thess. 3:9); be imitators of me (1 Cor. 4:16; 11:1; Phil. 3:17); the things you have seen in me, do (Phil. 4:9); you became imitators of us (1 Thess. 1:6); you followed my teaching, conduct etc. (2 Tim. 3:10); you imitated the churches of God (1 Thess. 2:14); imitators of those who inherit the promises (Heb. 6:12); go and do the same (Luke 10:37); if you were Abraham's children, do the works Abraham did (John 8:39).

B Imitating evil
Walking in the way of Jeroboam (1 Kgs. 15:34; 16:2; 22:52; 2 Kgs. 13:11; 17:22); being like the house of Jeroboam (1 Kgs. 16:7); Jehoram walked in the way of the kings of Israel (2 Chr. 21:6, 13); Ahaz walked in the way of the kings of Israel (2 Chr. 28:2); Ahaziah walked in the way of the house of Ahab (2 Chr. 22:3); Amon did evil as Manasseh his father had done (2 Kgs. 21:20-1; 2 Chr. 33:22); they imitated the nations (2 Kgs. 17:8, 15); like Rachel... Heb. 11:12); so their fathers did to the prophets (Luke 6:23, 26); you are doing as your fathers did (Acts 7:51); you do what your father did (John 8:41).

C Not imitating evil
Do not imitate evil (3 John 11); the Lord warned me not to walk in the way of this people (Isa. 8:11); do not do

what the scribes and Pharisees do (Matt. 23:3); do not be like the Gentiles (Matt. 6:8; Eph. 4:17).

21 Unique

A Unique God
Who is like me? (Isa. 44:7; Jer. 49:19; 50:44); who is like you? (Exod. 15:11; Ps. 35:10; 71:19); who is like the Lord? (Ps. 89:6, 8; 113:5); who is a God like you? (Mic. 7:18); what god is great like our God? (Ps. 77:13); there is none like the God of Jeshurun [Israel] (Deut. 33:26); there is no one else like him (Exod. 8:10; 9:14; Deut. 3:24; 1 Kgs. 8:23); there is no one like you (2 Sam. 7:22; 1 Chr. 17:20; 2 Chr. 6:14; 14:11; Ps. 86:8; Jer. 10:6, 7); there is no one like me (Isa. 46:9); their rock is not like our Rock (Deut. 32:31); there is no rock like our God (1 Sam. 2:2); there is no saviour but me (Isa. 43:11; Hos. 13:4); what god can do such mighty deeds as you? (Deut. 3:24); no one is good except God (Matt. 19:17; Mark 10:18); you alone are God (2 Kgs. 19:15; Ps. 86:10; Isa. 37:16, 20); you alone are the Most High (Ps. 83:18); you alone are the Lord (Neh. 9:6); there is no God but one (1 Cor. 8:4); the only God (John 5:44; 1 Tim. 1:17; Jude 25); God is one and there is no other but him (Mark 12:32).
NATURE OF GOD, see 5A.

B Unique people
B1 Unique Christ
If I had not done among them the works which no one else did (John 15:24); no man ever spoke like this man! (John 7:46); no other name but his by which we must be saved (Acts 4:12).
NATURE OF CHRIST, see 5B.

B2 Unique individuals
Can we find a man like this in whom is the Spirit of God? (Gen. 41:38-9); no prophet has arisen like Moses (Deut. 34:10); who is like you in Israel? (1 Sam. 26:15); what man is like Job? (Job 34:7); among them all none was found like Daniel and his companions (Dan. 1:19); I have no one like Timothy (Phil. 2:20); there was no one like Ahab (1 Kgs. 21:25); Hezekiah (2 Kgs. 18:5); Job (Job 1:8; 2:3); Josiah (2 Kgs. 23:25); Saul (1 Sam. 10:24); Solomon (1 Kgs. 3:12-13; 1 Chr. 29:25; 2 Chr. 1:12; Neh. 13:26).

B3 Unique Israel
No other nation is like Israel (Deut. 33:29; 2 Sam. 7:23; 1 Chr. 17:21); he has not dealt thus with any other nation (Ps. 147:20); what other nation has a god so near as the Lord is to us? (Deut. 4:7); what nation has such righteous statutes as we do? (Deut. 4:8); no one plays the harlot as you do (Ezek. 16:34).

C Unique creatures
I have not seen such poor cattle in all Egypt (Gen. 41:19); locusts such as your ancestors never saw (Exod. 10:6); not such a swarm of locusts before or ever again (Exod. 10:14); nothing on earth is like the crocodile (Job 41:33); who is like the beast? (Rev. 13:4).

D Unique things
Hail such as has not been seen in Egypt (Exod. 9:18, 24); no sword like Goliath's (1 Sam. 21:9); nothing like Solomon's throne (1 Kgs. 10:20; 2 Chr. 9:19); no algum wood like that had been seen (2 Chr. 9:11); no spices like those (2 Chr. 9:9); what is like the great city? (Rev. 18:18); a weight of glory beyond comparison (2 Cor. 4:17); there are no works like yours (Ps. 86:8).

E Unique events
There was no day like that before or after (Josh. 10:14); I will do among you what I have not done and will never do again (Ezek. 5:9); great tribulation such as has never been before nor ever will be (Matt. 24:21; Mark 13:19); nothing like this was ever seen (Judg. 19:30; Matt. 9:33; Mark 2:12); see if there is any pain like my

pain (Lam. 1:12); a great outcry such as has not been and never will be (Exod. 11:6); from the beginning it has never been known for a man born blind to be healed (John 9:32); a great earthquake such as had not been since man came on the earth (Rev. 16:18).

F Unique feasts
No Passover like it since the days of Solomon (2 Chr. 30:26); no Passover like it since the days of Samuel (2 Chr. 35:18); such a Passover had not been celebrated (2 Kgs. 23:22); no Feast of Booths like that since the time of Joshua (Neh. 8:17).

22 Copy
The king had to write out a copy of the law (Deut. 17:18); Joshua wrote on the stones a copy of the law (Josh. 8:32); the men of Hezekiah copied the proverbs of Solomon (Prov. 25:1); see the copy of the altar of the Lord (Josh. 22:28); Ahaz made a copy of the altar in Damascus (2 Kgs. 16:10-11); the copies of the heavenly things (Heb. 9:23); a man-made sanctuary, a copy of the true one (Heb. 9:24).

23 Prototype

A Design
The tabernacle was made according to the pattern shown to Moses (Exod. 25:9; Num. 8:4; Acts 7:44; Heb. 8:5); David gave the pattern of the temple to Solomon (1 Chr. 28:19); describe the plan of the temple (Ezek. 43:10-11).

B Foreshadowing
Adam was a type foreshadowing the One to come (Rom. 5:14); these things happened as types for us (1 Cor. 10:6, 11); they serve a copy and shadow of the heavenly tabernacle (Heb. 8:5); the festivals and sabbath are a shadow of things to come (Col. 2:17); the law has only a shadow of good things to come (Heb. 10:1); Abraham received Isaac back from the dead as a type (Heb. 11:19).

24 Agreement
If two agree about anything they ask (Matt. 18:19); do not refuse one another except by agreement for a season (1 Cor. 7:5); the three witnesses are in agreement (1 John 5:8); you have agreed together to speak lying and corrupt words (Dan. 2:9); why have you agreed together to put the Spirit of the Lord to the test? (Acts 5:9).
OF ONE HEART, see 710.

25 Disagreement

A Disagreeing
Joseph had not agreed with the council's action (Luke 23:51); what agreement has Christ with Belial? (2 Cor. 6:15); what agreement has the temple of God with idols? (2 Cor. 6:16); Paul and Barnabas had a sharp disagreement (Acts 15:39).

B Inconsistent
Their testimony was not consistent (Mark 14:56, 59).
QUARRELLING, see 709.

26 Quantity
Take handfuls of soot (Exod. 9:8); amounts of materials for the tabernacle (Exod. 38:24-9); 40 camel loads of good things (2 Kgs. 8:9).
MEASUREMENT, see 465.

27 Gradually
I will drive them out little by little (Exod. 23:30; Deut. 7:22); line upon line, here a little, there a little (Isa. 28:10, 13); he who gathers wealth little by little will increase it (Prov. 13:11).

28 Equality

UNIFORMITY, see 16.

A Equality with God

Jesus made himself out to be equal to God (John 5:18); if you knew me you would know my Father also (John 8:19); he who believes in me believes in him who sent me (John 12:44); he who sees me sees him who sent me (John 12:45); he who has seen me has seen the Father (John 14:9); he who hates me hates my Father also (John 15:23-4); he who receives me receives him who sent me (Matt. 10:40; Mark 9:37; John 13:20); he who rejects me rejects the one who sent me (Luke 10:16); he did not grasp at equality with God (Phil. 2:6).

B Equality with Christ

B1 Believers are as Christ

As he is, so are we (1 John 4:17); as is the man of heaven, so are those who are of heaven (1 Cor. 15:48); he who listens to you listens to me (Luke 10:16); he who receives me receives me (Matt. 10:40; John 13:20); receiving a believer is receiving Christ and the one who sent him (Matt. 18:5; Luke 9:48); whoever receives one such child in my name receives me (Mark 9:37); as you did it to the least of my brethren you did it to me (Matt. 25:40); you received me as Christ himself (Gal. 4:14); he who rejects you rejects me (Luke 10:16); as you did it not to the least of my brethren you did it not to me (Matt. 25:45); sinning against the brothers, you sin against Christ (1 Cor. 8:12); if they kept my word they will keep yours also (John 15:20); if they persecuted me, they will persecute you (John 15:20); I am Jesus whom you are persecuting (Acts 9:5).

B2 Work as to Christ

Be obedient to masters as slaves of Christ (Eph. 6:5-6); work heartily, as to the Lord (Col. 3:23); render service as to the Lord, not to men (Eph. 6:7).

C Equality for people

C1 Equivalent people

You are as Pharaoh (Gen. 44:18); accept him as you would me (Philem. 17); he who loves his wife loves himself (Eph. 5:28).

C2 Equality in law

One law for both you and the alien (Exod. 12:49; Lev. 24:22; Num. 9:14; 15:14-16, 29); the alien shall be as the native (Lev. 19:34).

C3 Equality of fate

One fate comes to the righteous and the wicked (Eccles. 9:2-3); God destroys the righteous and the wicked (Job 9:22); one thing happens to both wise and foolish (Eccles. 2:14-16); men and beasts all go to the same place (Eccles. 3:20).

C4 Equality in salvation

God justifies both Jew and Gentile by faith (Rom. 3:29-30); God made no distinction between Jews and Gentiles (Acts 15:9); through the grace of the Lord Jesus we are saved, just like the Gentiles (Acts 15:11); there is no difference, for all have sinned and are justified by grace (Rom. 3:22-4).

JEW AND GENTILE, see 371B2.

C5 Equality in payment

Those with the baggage share equally with those in the battle (1 Sam. 30:24); you made these latecomers equal to us (Matt. 20:12); I wish to give to this last as I do to you (Matt. 20:14); the rich shall not pay more nor the poor less (Exod. 30:15); the measure you give will be the measure you get (Luke 6:38); the aim is financial equity among believers (2 Cor. 8:13-14).

C6 Equality of punishment

Equality in injuries caused and exacted (Exod. 21:23-5; Lev. 24:17-22); eye for eye and tooth for tooth (Exod. 21:24; Lev. 24:20; Deut. 19:21; Matt. 5:38); ox for ox

(Exod. 21:36); life for life (Exod. 21:23; Lev. 24:17-18; Deut. 19:21); your life for his life (1 Kgs. 20:39; 2 Kgs. 10:24); I will do with you as you have done, says the Lord (Ezek. 16:59); do to the false witness as he intended to the one he accused (Deut. 19:19).

D Equal measure

D1 Equal parts

Equal parts of stacte, onycha, galbanum and frankincense (Exod. 30:34).

D2 Squares

The central area of the land was 25 000 cubits square (Ezek. 48:20); a wall, 500 reeds long and 500 broad, to divide holy from profane (Ezek. 42:20); the court was square, 100 cubits by 100 cubits (Ezek. 40:47); the most holy place was 20 cubits in length and breadth (2 Chr. 3:8; Ezek. 41:4); the ledge will be 14 cubits square (Ezek. 43:17); the altar hearth will be 12 cubits square (Ezek. 43:16); the side rooms were six cubits square (Ezek. 40:12); square items: the bronze altar (Exod. 27:1; 38:1; 2 Chr. 4:1); the incense altar (Exod. 30:2; 37:25); the breastpiece (Exod. 28:16; 39:9); the openings of the stands (1 Kgs. 7:31); the doorposts (Ezek. 41:21); the bronze platform (2 Chr. 6:13); the city (Rev. 21:16).

D3 Cubes

The holy of holies was 20 cubits in length, breadth and height (1 Kgs. 6:20); the length, breadth and height of the city are equal (Rev. 21:16).

29 Inequality

A Unequal with God

Am I in place of God? (Gen. 50:19); shall the potter be regarded as equal to the clay? (Isa. 29:16).

B Unequal partners

Do not plough with an ox and donkey together (Deut. 22:10); do not be misyoked with unbelievers (2 Cor. 6:14).

DIFFERENCE, see 15.

MIXTURE, see 43.

C Unequal weights and measures

Do not have large and small weights (Deut. 25:13); do not have large and small measures (Deut. 25:14).

WEIGHTS AND MEASURES, see 465A.

30 Average

You are lukewarm, neither cold nor hot (Rev. 3:15-16).

31 Compensation

RESTITUTION, see 787.

32 Great quantity

Some gathered much (Exod. 16:17); he who gathered much had nothing over (Exod. 16:18; 2 Cor. 8:15); you looked for much but it came to little (Hag. 1:9); you sowed much but harvest little (Hag. 1:6); he who is faithful in little is faithful also in much (Luke 16:10); from him who is given much, much will be required (Luke 12:48); he who is unrighteous in little is unrighteous also in much (Luke 16:10); God gave Solomon wisdom like the sand of the seashore (1 Kgs. 4:29); joy unspeakable and full of glory (1 Pet. 1:8).

33 Small quantity

A A little bit

The nations are like a drop from a bucket (Isa. 40:15); because of the smallness of your faith (Matt. 17:20); not a jot nor a tittle will pass from the law until all is fulfilled (Matt. 5:18); the mote in your brother's eye (Matt. 7:3, 4, 5); he who is faithful in little is faithful also in much (Luke 16:10); you have been faithful in a

very little (Luke 19:17); he who is unrighteous in little is unrighteous also in much (Luke 16:10).
SMALL, see 196.

B Little food
You had little before I came (Gen. 30:30); some gathered little (Exod. 16:17); you sowed much but harvest little (Hag. 1:6, 9); he who gathered little had no lack (Exod. 16:18; 2 Cor. 8:15); better a little with the fear of the Lord (Prov. 15:16); better a little with righteousness (Prov. 16:8); better a dry morsel with quiet (Prov. 17:1); we have only five loaves and two fish (Matt. 14:17); 200 denarii would not be enough for them each to get a little (John 6:7); what are they among so many? (John 6:9).

34 Superiority
IMPORTANCE, see 638.

A Greatness of God
Ascribe greatness to our God (Deut. 32:3); the Father is greater than I (John 14:28); my Father is greater than all (John 10:29); they were amazed by the greatness of God (Luke 9:43); greater works than these will he show him, that you may marvel (John 5:20); if our hearts condemn us, God is greater than our hearts (1 John 3:20); greater is he who is in you than he who is in the world (1 John 4:4).

B Greatness of Christ
Jesus would be great (Luke 1:32); greater than our father Jacob? (John 4:12); greater than our father Abraham? (John 8:53); something greater than the temple is here (Matt. 12:6); greater than Solomon (Matt. 12:42; Luke 11:31); greater than Jonah (Matt. 12:41; Luke 11:32); Christ has obtained a more excellent ministry (Heb. 8:6).

C Greatness of people
Only in the throne will I be greater than you (Gen. 41:40; 2 Cor. 12:11); Daniel was distinguished over all the commissioners and satraps (Dan. 6:3); are you not superior to the birds of the air? (Matt. 6:26); who regards you as superior? (1 Cor. 4:7); I am not inferior to these superlative apostles (2 Cor. 11:5); who is greatest in the kingdom? (Matt. 18:1; Mark 9:34; Luke 9:46; 22:24); the least among you is the one who is great (Luke 9:48); he who humbles himself is the greatest (Matt. 18:4); whoever wants to be great must be the servant (Matt. 20:26-7; 23:11; Mark 9:35; 10:43); let the greatest become as the youngest (Luke 22:26); whoever keeps the least commandment will be greatest (Matt. 5:19); he who is least in the kingdom is greater than John (Matt. 11:11; Luke 7:28); greater works than these will he believer do (John 14:12); Diotrephes loves to be first (3 John 9); John would be great before the Lord (Luke 1:15); more than a prophet (Matt. 11:9); among those born of women none is greater (Matt. 11:11; Luke 7:28); he who is least in the kingdom is greater than John (Matt. 11:11; Luke 7:28).

D Advantages
What advantage has a wise man over a fool? (Eccles. 6:8); what advantage has the Jew? (Rom. 3:1); man has no advantage over the beasts (Eccles. 3:19); it is to your advantage that I go away (John 16:7); are we any better off? (Rom. 3:9).

E More than
What more do you do than others? (Matt. 5:47); he who loves son or daughter more than me is not worthy of me (Matt. 10:37); whoever loves father or mother more than me is not worthy of me (Matt. 10:37); seven other spirits more evil than himself (Matt. 12:45); this widow put in more than all the rest (Luke 21:3).

35 Inferiority
A disciple is not above his teacher (Luke 6:40); a slave is not above his master (Matt. 10:24; John 13:16; 15:20); I am the least in my family (Judg. 6:15); the least of the apostles (1 Cor. 15:9); the least of all the saints (Eph. 3:8); the least among you is the one who is great (Luke 9:48); he who is least in the kingdom is greater than John (Matt. 11:11; Luke 7:28); whoever annuls the least commandment will be least in the kingdom of heaven (Matt. 5:19); the foremost of sinners (1 Tim. 1:15-16).
UNIMPORTANCE, see 639.

36 Increase

A Growth in body
A1 Growing up
If I had sons, would you wait until they grew up? (Ruth 1:13); wait until my son Shelah grows up (Gen. 38:11); he grew up before him like a young plant (Isa. 53:2); those who grew and became strong: Ishmael (Gen. 21:20); Samuel (1 Sam. 2:21, 26; 3:19); John the Baptist (Luke 1:80); Jesus (Luke 2:40, 52).
A2 Swelling up
Her abdomen will swell up (Num. 5:21, 22, 27); they expected him to swell up and fall down dead (Acts 28:6).
A3 Hair growing
Samson's hair grew again (Judg. 16:22); stay in Jericho until your beards grow (2 Sam. 10:5; 1 Chr. 19:5).

B Growth of plants
Let the earth sprout vegetation (Gen. 1:11); the Lord caused trees to sprout (Gen. 2:9); the seed sprouts and grows (Mark 4:27); the rod of the man I choose shall sprout (Num. 17:5); Aaron's rod had sprouted (Num. 17:8); a man called the shoot, for he will shoot up (Zech. 6:12); the seed on good soil grew up (Mark 4:8; Luke 8:8); mustard seed grows into a tree (Matt. 13:32; Mark 4:32; Luke 13:19); when the plants grew up and bore grain (Matt. 13:26); let both grow together until harvest (Matt. 13:30); the thorns grew up and choked the plants (Matt. 13:7); consider the lilies, how they grow (Luke 12:27).

C Growth of things
C1 Growth in wealth
One scatters yet increases (Prov. 11:24); Isaac grew richer (Gen. 26:13); you had little and it has increased greatly (Gen. 30:30); Jacob increased greatly (Gen. 30:43).
C2 Growth of the gospel
The word of God grew (Acts 6:7; 12:24); the word of the Lord was growing (Acts 19:20); what has happened to me has caused the gospel to progress (Phil. 1:12); in all the world the gospel is bearing fruit and growing (Col. 1:6).
C3 Growth in grace
The path of the righteous is like dawn shining brighter and brighter (Prov. 4:18); grace abounded (Rom. 5:15, 20); shall we continue in sin that grace may abound? (Rom. 6:1); desire the pure milk of the word that you may grow (1 Pet. 2:2); grow in grace and the knowledge of our Lord (2 Pet. 3:18); grow up into Christ, the head (Eph. 4:15); increasing in the knowledge of God (Col. 1:10); increase our faith! (Luke 17:5); we hope that as your faith increases our work may be enlarged (2 Cor. 10:15); your faith is growing abundantly (2 Thess. 1:3); abound in love for one another (1 Thess. 3:12); love one another more and more (1 Thess. 4:10); your love for one another is growing (2 Thess. 1:3).

C4 Growth of evil
Lawlessness increases (Matt. 24:12); the law came in to increase the transgression (Rom. 5:20); where sin increased grace abounded (Rom. 5:20).

D People multiplying
Be fruitful and multiply (Gen. 1:22, 28; 9:7); when men began to multiply on the face of the earth (Gen. 6:1); may God increase you a thousandfold (Deut. 1:11); may God add 100 times as many people (2 Sam. 24:3; 1 Chr. 21:3); I will multiply you very much (Gen. 17:2; Heb. 6:14); I will increase Israel like a flock (Ezek. 36:37); God made this people great during their stay in Egypt (Acts 13:17); you have multiplied the nation (Isa. 9:3; 26:15); multiplication conditional on obedience (Deut. 6:3; 8:1; 13:17); the more they afflicted them the more they multiplied (Exod. 1:12).

E Growth of the church
The body of Christ grows and builds itself up (Eph. 4:16); grows with a growth from God (Col. 2:19); God gives the growth (1 Cor. 3:6-7); the structure grows into a holy temple (Eph. 2:21); the churches increased in number daily (Acts 16:5).

37 Decrease: no increase

The waters abated (Gen. 8:1-5); the dove was sent out to see if the waters had abated (Gen. 8:8); Noah knew the waters had abated (Gen. 8:11); until your brother's anger subsides (Gen. 27:44-5); he must increase but I must decrease (John 3:30); wild beasts will reduce your numbers (Lev. 26:22); the city which went forth 100 strong will have 10 left (Amos 5:3); the city which went forth 1000 strong will have 100 left (Amos 5:3); their feet did not swell (Deut. 8:4; Neh. 9:21); no reduction in the workload (Exod. 5:8, 11, 19); he must not reduce food, clothing or marriage rights (Exod. 21:10).

38 Addition

A Adding to God's things
God spoke these words and added no more (Deut. 5:22); do not add to God's words (Deut. 4:2; 12:32; Prov. 30:6); if anyone adds to the words, God will add to him the plagues (Rev. 22:18); many similar words were added to Jeremiah's scroll (Jer. 36:32); nothing can be added to God's work (Eccles. 3:14).

B Adding to man's work
I have spoken once or twice, but will not add to it (Job 40:5); those who were of repute added nothing to me (Gal. 2:6); no one annuls a man's will or adds to it (Gal. 3:15).

C Adding people
Joseph, may the Lord add another son (Gen. 30:24); may the Lord add a hundred times as many people (2 Sam. 24:3; 1 Chr. 21:3); the Lord added to them day by day those who were being saved (Acts 2:47); there were added that day about 3000 people (Acts 2:41); multitudes of both men and women were added to their number (Acts 5:14).

D Adding blessing
To him who has will more be given (Matt. 13:12; 25:29; Mark 4:25; Luke 8:18; 19:26); all these things will be added to you (Matt. 6:33; Luke 12:31); more will be given to you (Mark 4:24); add to your faith virtue etc. (2 Pet. 1:5-7); length of days, years of life and peace they will add to you (Prov. 3:2).

E Adding evil
I will add to your yoke (1 Kgs. 12:11, 14); anything more than 'yes' or 'no' comes from evil (Matt. 5:37).

39 Subtraction

A Subtracting from God's things
Do not take away from God's commands (Deut. 4:2; 12:32); if anyone subtracts from the words, God will subtract his share in the tree of life (Rev. 22:19); do not omit a word (Jer. 26:2); nothing can be taken away from God's works (Eccles. 3:14).

B Subtracting from people
One tribe was taken away from Israel (Judg. 21:3); from him who has not even what he has will be taken away (Matt. 13:12).

40 Adjunct: thing added

ADDITION, see 38.

41 Remainder: thing remaining

A People remaining
A1 Survivors of Israel
God sent me to preserve a remnant (Gen. 45:7); seven thousand followers of the Lord were left (1 Kgs. 19:18; Rom. 11:4); out of Zion a remnant (2 Kgs. 19:31; Isa. 37:32); a remnant will escape (Ezek. 6:8; 12:16); survivors will be left from Jerusalem (Ezek. 14:22); the remnant who survived (Neh. 1:3); none was left except Judah (2 Kgs. 17:18); the poorest people were left (2 Kgs. 24:14; 25:12; Jer. 39:10; 40:7; 52:16); I will make the lame the remnant (Mic. 4:7);
I will take you one from a city and two from a family (Jer. 3:14); of 1000 only 100 left and of 100 only 10 left (Amos 5:3); the Lord left a few survivors (Isa. 1:9; Rom. 9:29); only a remnant (Isa. 10:21-2; Rom. 9:27).

A2 Sole survivors
Only Noah and his family were left (Gen. 7:23); Benjamin alone is left (Gen. 42:38; 44:20); not a man of them was left except Caleb and Joshua (Num. 26:65); Mephibosheth was left of Saul's family (2 Sam. 9:1-4); Elijah only was left (1 Kgs. 18:22; 19:10, 14; Rom. 11:3).

A3 Survivors favoured
By God's favour a remnant is left (Ezra 9:8); the Lord has saved the remnant of Israel (Jer. 31:7); a remnant chosen by grace (Rom. 11:5); the remnant of Judah will again take root and bear fruit (2 Kgs. 19:30; Isa. 37:31); the Lord will be a beautiful crown for the remnant of his people (Isa. 28:5); the remnant will be like dew from the Lord (Mic. 5:7).

A4 No survivors
Not one Egyptian remained (Exod. 14:28); Joshua left no survivors (Josh. 10:28, 30, 33, 37, 39; 11:8, 11, 14); a remnant will not be left of the men of Anathoth (Jer. 11:23); of those who go to Egypt there will be no survivors (Jer. 42:17; 44:14).

B Food left over
B1 Remaining food
Leftovers of manna went bad (Exod. 16:19-20); except on the sabbath (Exod. 16:23-4); 12 baskets left over from feeding the 5000 (Matt. 14:20; Mark 6:43; 8:19; Luke 9:17; John 6:13); seven baskets from the 4000 (Matt. 15:37; Mark 8:8, 20); dogs eat the crumbs that fall from the table (Matt. 15:27; Mark 7:28); the poor man wanted to eat what fell from the rich man's table (Luke 16:21).

B2 Remaining offerings
Any left from the Passover must be burned (Exod. 12:10); nothing to be left till morning (Exod. 34:25; Lev. 7:15; 22:30; Num. 9:12); anything remaining from the ram of ordination or the bread must be burned (Exod. 29:34; Lev. 8:32); remainders from the peace offering to be burned (Lev. 7:17; 19:6-7); what is left of a votive or freewill offering may be eaten the next day (Lev. 7:16);

the remainder of the offering is for the priests (Lev. 2:3; 5:13; 6:16).

B3 Gleaning
Do not gather the gleanings of your land (Lev. 19:9-10; 23:22; Deut. 24:19-21); Ruth gleaning (Ruth 2:2, 7, 17-23); let her glean among the sheaves (Ruth 2:15-16); the gleaning of Ephraim exceeds the vintage of Abiezer (Judg. 8:2-3).

B4 Lees
Wine on the lees (Isa. 25:6); Moab has settled on his lees (Jer. 48:11); I will punish the men who have settled on their lees (Zeph. 1:12).

C Remaining things
Like a tree whose stump remains (Isa. 6:13); the holy seed is its stump (Isa. 6:13); a branch from the stump of Jesse (Isa. 11:1); leave the stump with a band round it (Dan. 4:15, 23, 26); much land remains to be possessed (Josh. 13:1).

42 Decrement: thing deducted
SUBTRACTION, see 39.

43 Mixture
COMPOSITION OF MIXTURES, see 56.

A Mixing people
Israel mixed with the nations (Ezra 9:2; Ps. 106:35; Hos. 7:8); a mixed multitude went up with them from Egypt (Exod. 12:38); they separated themselves from the mixed multitude (Neh. 13:3); do not be unequally yoked together with unbelievers (2 Cor. 6:14).

B Mixing materials / animals
Do not mix: seeds planted (Lev. 19:19; Deut. 22:9); animals for ploughing (Deut. 22:10); animals for breeding (Lev. 19:19); materials for clothes (Lev. 19:19; Deut. 22:11).

C Mixed wine
Mixed wine (Prov. 23:30); foaming wine, well mixed (Ps. 75:8); mix a double draught in the cup she mixed (Rev. 18:6); they offered him wine mingled with gall (Matt. 27:34); wine mixed with myrrh (Mark 15:23).

D Mixing various things
The image had feet of iron mixed with clay (Dan. 2:33, 41-3); I will remove your alloy (Isa. 1:25); Galileans whose blood Pilate mixed with their sacrifices (Luke 13:1); combining spiritual things with spiritual (1 Cor. 2:13).

44 Unmixed

A Not mixing
Jacob did not put his flocks with those of Laban (Gen. 30:40); iron does not mix with clay (Dan. 2:43); the wine of the wrath of God, poured unmixed in the cup of his anger (Rev. 14:10).

B Singleness of heart
Singleness of eye (Matt. 6:22; Luke 11:34); obey your masters in singleness of heart (Eph. 6:5; Col. 3:22); led astray from singleness and purity towards Christ (2 Cor. 11:3); he who gives should do so with all his heart (Rom. 12:8).

PURE IN HEART, see 950B.

45 Joining

A United with God
Foreigners who join themselves to the Lord (Isa. 56:6; Zech. 2:11); they will join themselves to the Lord in an everlasting covenant (Jer. 50:5); united with him in death and resurrection (Rom. 6:5); whoever is united to the Lord becomes one spirit with him (1 Cor. 6:17).

B United with people
B1 Israel united
The Israelites were united as one man (Judg. 20:11); the people of Judah were of one heart (2 Chr. 30:12); two sticks joined to represent the union of Judah and Israel (Ezek. 37:16-22); a staff called Union (Zech. 11:7, 14).

B2 Individuals united
Now my husband will be joined to me (Gen. 29:34); he attached himself to one of the citizens of that country (Luke 15:15); with two masters, he will cling to one and despise the other (Luke 16:13); do not be unequally yoked with unbelievers (2 Cor. 6:14).

B3 Joined to the church
In him the whole building is joined together (Eph. 2:21); the body is knit together (Eph. 4:16; Col. 2:19); knit together in love (Col. 2:2); you, a wild olive, were grafted in (Rom. 11:17-24); of the rest, no one dared join them (Acts 5:13); Paul tried to join the disciples (Acts 9:26); some were persuaded and joined Paul and Silas (Acts 17:4).

C Sexual union
C1 Teaching about sex
C1a Union into one flesh
The two will become one flesh (Gen. 2:24; Matt. 19:5; Mark 10:8; 1 Cor. 6:16; Eph. 5:31); a man will leave his father and mother and be joined to his wife (Matt. 19:5; Mark 10:7; Eph. 5:31); what God has joined together, let not man separate (Matt. 19:6; Mark 10:9); he who joins himself to a prostitute becomes one body with her (1 Cor. 6:16).

C1b Sex and uncleanness
A pair having intercourse are unclean (Lev. 15:18); sex with a menstruating woman forbidden (Lev. 15:24; 18:19; 20:18; Ezek. 18:6; 22:10).

C1c Laws about sexual union
If a man goes in to his wife and finds her not a virgin (Deut. 22:13-21); if a man lies with a virgin not betrothed (Exod. 22:16; Deut. 22:28); with an engaged virgin in the city (Deut. 22:23); with a woman who is a slave (Lev. 19:20); with a married woman (Num. 4:13; Deut. 22:22); you must not lie with a male as one lies with a female (Lev. 18:22); males who lie together have committed abomination and must be put to death (Lev. 20:13); neither man nor woman shall lie with a beast (Lev. 18:23); if a man lies with an animal, he and the animal shall be put to death (Lev. 20:15-16); going in to the brother's widow (Deut. 25:5); to the captive woman (Deut. 21:13); sex forbidden with: mother (Lev. 18:7); father's wife (Lev. 18:8; 20:11); sister (Lev. 18:9; 20:17); granddaughter (Lev. 18:10); father's sister (Lev. 18:12; 20:19); mother's sister (Lev. 18:13; 20:19); uncle's wife (Lev. 18:14; 20:20); son's wife (Lev. 18:15; 20:12); brother's wife (Lev. 18:16; 20:21); a woman and her granddaughter (Lev. 18:17); a woman and her daughter (Lev. 18:17; 20:14); a woman and her sister (Lev. 18:18); your neighbour's wife (Lev. 18:20); a fellow male (Lev. 18:22).

BESTIALITY, see 951C.

HOMOSEXUALITY, see 951D.

INCEST, see 951E.

C2 Actual sexual union
C2a Potential of sexual union
One of the people might have lain with your wife (Gen. 26:10); another will lie with your wives (2 Sam. 12:11); may others bow down on my wife (Job 31:10).

C2b Sexual union intended
Go in to my maidservant (Gen. 16:2); lie with me (Gen. 39:7, 12; 2 Sam. 13:11); he came in to lie with me (Gen. 39:14); give me my wife that I may go in to her (Gen. 29:21); Samson wanted to go in to his wife (Judg. 15:1);

bring out the men that we may know them (Gen. 19:5; Judg. 19:22).

C2c Marital sex between . . .
Adam and Eve (Gen. 4:1, 25); Cain and his wife (Gen. 4:17); the sons of God and the daughters of men (Gen. 6:4); Abraham and Hagar (Gen. 16:4); Jacob and Leah (Gen. 29:23; 30:15, 16); Jacob and Rachel (Gen. 29:30); Jacob and Bilhah (Gen. 30:3, 4); Judah and Shua (Gen. 38:2); Onan and Tamar, spilling the semen (Gen. 38:8-9); Boaz and Ruth (Ruth 4:13); Elkanah and Hannah (1 Sam. 1:19); David and Bathsheba (2 Sam. 12:24); Ithra and Abigail (2 Sam. 17:25); Ephraim and his wife (1 Chr. 7:23).
MARRIAGE, see 894.

C2d Extra-marital sex between. . .
Lot's daughters and their father (Gen. 19:32-5); Reuben and Bilhah (Gen. 35:22); Judah and Tamar (Gen. 38:16-18); Eli's sons and the serving women (1 Sam. 2:22); Abner and Rizpah (2 Sam. 3:7); David and Bathsheba (2 Sam. 11:4; Ps. 51:t); Absalom and his father's concubines (2 Sam. 16:21-2).

C2e Cases of rape
Amnon and Tamar (2 Sam. 13:14); Shechem had defiled Dinah (Gen. 34:2).
RAPE, see 951G.

C3 Sex between nations
Where have you not been lain with? (Jer. 3:2); in her youth men had lain with her (Ezek. 23:8); the Babylonians came to her into the bed of love (Ezek. 23:17); they go in to her as men go in to a harlot (Ezek. 23:44).
ADULTERY, see 951B.

C4 Animals mating
Animals mating (Gen. 30:38-41; 31:10); his bull mates without fail (Job 21:10).

C5 Absence of sex
There is no man to come in to us (Gen. 19:31); if no man has lain with you (Num. 5:19); he would not listen to her to lie with her (Gen. 39:10); shall I go home to lie with my wife? (2 Sam. 11:11); Abimelech had not come near Sarah (Gen. 20:4); I did not let you touch her (Gen. 20:6); no man had known Rebekah (Gen. 24:16); David did not know Abishag (1 Kgs. 1:4); David did not go in to the concubines again (2 Sam. 20:3); Joseph did not know Mary until Jesus was born (Matt. 1:25); before Mary and Joseph came together (Matt. 1:18).
CELIBACY, see 895.

D Sewing
There is a time to sew together (Eccles. 3:7); they sewed fig leaves to make clothing (Gen. 3:7); patching clothing with unshrunk cloth (Matt. 9:16; Mark 2:21).

E Joining flesh and bones
You knit me together with bones and sinews (Job 10:11); the bones came together (Ezek. 37:6-7); the crocodile's scales are joined together (Job 41:17); the folds of his flesh are joined together (Job 41:23).

F Joined to good
Bind lovingkindness and truth around your neck (Prov. 3:3); tie the teaching around your neck (Prov. 6:21); bind the teaching on your fingers (Prov. 7:3); bind these words on your hand (Deut. 6:8; 11:18); I cling to your testimonies (Ps. 119:31).

G Joined to evil
Israel joined themselves to Baal-peor (Num. 25:3, 5; Ps. 106:28); Ephraim is joined to idols – let him alone (Hos. 4:17).

46 Separating

A Separating in general
There is a time to rend (Eccles. 3:7); God separated light from darkness (Gen. 1:4, 14, 18).

B Moral separation
B1 Separation from God
Your iniquities have separated you from God (Isa. 59:2); branches were broken off the olive tree (Rom. 11:17-19); continue in his kindness or you too will be cut off (Rom. 11:22); you who would be justified by the law are severed from Christ (Gal. 5:4); separated from Christ (Eph. 2:12); eternal destruction away from the face of the Lord (2 Thess. 1:9); having no hope and without God in the world (Eph. 2:12); who shall separate us from the love of Christ? (Rom. 8:35); nothing can separate us from the love of God (Rom. 8:38-9).

B2 Separated to God
The Nazirite took a vow of separation (Num. 6:2-21); Samson a Nazirite from the womb (Judg. 13:5; 16:17); separated from sinners, exalted above the heavens (Heb. 7:26).

B3 Separation from evil
Separate the Israelites from their uncleanness (Lev. 15:31); the world has been crucified to me and I to the world (Gal. 6:14); be separate, says the Lord (2 Cor. 6:17).

C People divided
C1 Divisions of opinion
Let there be no divisions (1 Cor. 1:10); that there should be no separation in the body (1 Cor. 12:25); a house divided against itself cannot stand (Mark 3:25); warn a man who is factious (Titus 3:10); these are the ones who cause divisions (Jude 19); they were divided about Jesus (John 7:43; 9:16; 10:19); the city was divided about the gospel (Acts 14:4); households will be divided (Luke 12:51-3); the assembly was divided (Acts 23:7); I hear there are divisions among you (1 Cor. 11:18-19).

C2 People parting
Abraham and Lot separated (Gen. 13:9, 11, 14); the Lord watch between us when we are apart (Gen. 31:49); he parted from him (Luke 24:51); Paul separated from Barnabas (Acts 15:39); you will not see my face again (Exod. 10:29; Acts 20:25); perhaps this is why he was parted from you for a while (Philem. 15).

C3 Separation from evil people
Be separate, says the Lord (2 Cor. 6:17); the Israelites had to separate themselves from the people of the land (Ezra 6:21; 9:1-2; 10:11; Neh. 13:3); God separated them from other people (Lev. 20:24-6; 1 Kgs. 8:53); I will separate my people and your people (Exod. 8:23); the Levites were separated from the other Israelites (Num. 8:14; 16:9; Deut. 10:8); separate yourselves from this congregation (Num. 16:21, 45); keep back from the tents of Korah's men (Num. 16:24-6).

C4 Separation of kingdoms
Division into the two kingdoms of Israel and Judah (1 Kgs. 12:16-20); Israel divided into two parts (1 Kgs. 16:21); the kingdom torn from you (1 Sam. 15:28; 28:17; 1 Kgs. 11:11); Israel torn from the house of David (1 Kgs. 14:8; 2 Kgs. 17:21); the nations were separated (Gen. 10:5, 32); in Peleg's time the earth was divided (Gen. 10:25; 1 Chr. 1:19); two nations will be separated (Gen. 25:23); PERES – your kingdom is divided (Dan. 5:28); it will be a divided kingdom (Dan. 2:41); his kingdom will be broken and divided to the four winds of heaven (Dan. 11:4); a divided kingdom must fall (Matt. 12:25-6; Mark 3:24-6; Luke 11:17-18).

D Separating animals
Jacob separated the lambs (Gen. 30:40); Abraham set seven ewe lambs apart by themselves (Gen. 21:28, 29); he will separate them as sheep from goats (Matt. 25:32).

E Bodies divided

E1 Bodies cut in pieces

The Levite cut up his concubine's body (Judg. 19:29; 20:6); his master will cut him in pieces (Matt. 24:51; Luke 12:46); Samuel hewed Agag to pieces (1 Sam. 15:33); I have hewn them by the prophets, slain them with my words (Hos. 6:5); some were sawn in two (Heb. 11:37); cut the ram in pieces (Exod. 29:17); Moses cut the ram in pieces (Lev. 8:20); he shall cut the sacrifice in pieces (Lev. 1:6, 12); Saul cut up the yoke of oxen (1 Sam. 11:7); cutting up the ox (1 Kgs. 18:23, 33); they cut the calf in two and passed between the pieces (Jer. 34:18).

E2 Bodies torn to pieces

Joseph has surely been torn to pieces (Gen. 37:33; 44:28); the chiliarch was afraid Paul would be torn in pieces (Acts 23:10); lest the dogs turn and tear you to pieces (Matt. 7:6); if you do not make known the dream you will be torn limb from limb (Dan. 2:5); anyone who speaks against his God will be torn limb from limb (Dan. 3:29); what was torn by wild animals I did not bring to you (Gen. 31:39); if the animal was torn to pieces, no restitution is necessary (Exod. 22:13); meat torn to pieces in the field, throw to the dogs (Exod. 22:31); do not eat flesh torn by beasts (Lev. 17:15; 22:8); Samson tore the lion (Judg. 14:6).

E3 Severing parts of the body

The Lord cuts off head and tail from Israel (Isa. 9:14); let me go cut off his head (2 Sam. 16:9); those beheaded: Dagon (1 Sam. 5:4); Goliath (1 Sam. 17:46, 51); Saul (1 Sam. 31:9); Ish-bosheth (2 Sam. 4:7); Sheba (2 Sam. 20:22); 70 sons of Ahab (2 Kgs. 10:6-8); John (Matt. 14:10; Mark 6:16); the witnesses to Jesus (Rev. 20:4); cut off the woman's hand (Deut. 25:12); if your hand or foot causes you to sin, cut it off (Matt. 5:30; 18:8; Mark 9:43); they cut off their hands and feet (2 Sam. 4:12); he who sends a message by a fool cuts off his own feet (Prov. 26:6); the head and hands of Dagon were cut off (1 Sam. 5:4); kings with thumbs and big toes cut off (Judg. 1:6-7); Peter cut off the ear of the high priest's slave (Matt. 26:51; Mark 14:47; Luke 22:50; John 18:10, 26); Zipporah cut off her son's foreskin (Exod. 4:25); beware of the mutilators (Phil. 3:2).

CASTRATION, see 172A3.

CIRCUMCISION, see 988B.

E4 Hair removed

The cleansed leper must shave off his hair, beard and eyebrows (Lev. 14:9); Paul cut his hair, for he had a vow (Acts 18:18); Hanun cut off half their beards (2 Sam. 10:4; 1 Chr. 19:4, 5); the Nazirite must not cut his hair (Num. 6:5); do not cut your hair at the sides of your head (Lev. 19:27); do not trim your beards [for the dead] (Lev. 19:27; 21:5); if a woman will not cover her head, let her have her hair cut off (1 Cor. 11:6, 6); Ezra plucked out some of his hair and beard (Ezra 9:3); I pulled out their hair (Neh. 13:25); I gave my cheeks to those who pluck out the beard (Isa. 50:6).

E5 Gashing bodies

Do not cut your bodies mourning for the dead (Lev. 19:28; 21:5; Deut. 14:1); the priests of Baal cut themselves with swords (1 Kgs. 18:28); 80 men with their bodies gashed (Jer. 41:5); gashing himself with stones (Mark 5:5); ripping up pregnant women (2 Kgs. 8:12; 15:16; Hos. 13:16); you will tear your breasts (Ezek. 23:34); for grain and wine they gash themselves (Hos. 7:14).

E6 Breaking bony parts

E6a Bones broken

A man with a broken hand or foot could not serve as priest (Lev. 21:19); a soft tongue breaks bones (Prov. 25:15); let the bones you have broken rejoice (Ps. 51:8); God shattered the bones of your besieger (Ps. 53:5); you

broke the heads of the sea monster (Ps. 74:13); I will bind up the broken (Ezek. 34:16); the broken you have not bound up (Ezek. 34:4); before they reached the bottom the lions broke their bones (Dan. 6:24); the Jews asked Pilate that their legs might be broken (John 19:31-2).

E6b Horns broken

The horns of the wicked he will cut off (Ps. 75:10); the large horn was broken (Dan. 8:8); the he-goat shattered the ram's two horns (Dan. 8:7); the horns of the altar will be cut off and fall to the ground (Amos 3:14).

E6c Teeth broken

You have shattered the teeth of the wicked (Ps. 3:7); I broke the teeth of the wicked (Job 29:17); shatter their teeth (Ps. 58:6).

E6d No bones broken

No bone of the Passover was to be broken (Exod. 12:46; Num. 9:12); none of his bones shall be broken (Ps. 34:20; John 19:36); they did not break Jesus' legs (John 19:33).

E7 Dislocating

He dislocated the hollow of Jacob's thigh (Gen. 32:25); that what is lame may not be dislocated (Heb. 12:13).

E8 Cleft hoofs

Animals with divided hoofs (Lev. 11:3, 7, 26; Deut. 14:6-8); not dividing the hoof (Lev. 11:4-6).

F Things divided

F1 Textiles severed

F1a Tearing / cutting clothes

The leper must wear torn clothes (Lev. 13:45); tearing an infected piece out of a garment (Lev. 13:56); a patch of unshrunk cloth tears away from an old garment (Matt. 9:16; Mark 2:21; Luke 5:36); tearing clothes and mourning (2 Sam. 3:31; 2 Kgs. 22:19; 2 Chr. 34:27); Saul tore the edge of Samuel's robe (1 Sam. 15:27); Hanun cut off the edge of Saul's robe (1 Sam. 24:4-5, 11); Hanun cut off their garments in the middle (2 Sam. 10:4); those who tore their clothes: the high priest (Matt. 26:65; Mark 14:63); Barnabas and Paul (Acts 14:14); Ahijah tore his cloak in 12 pieces (1 Kgs. 11:30).

F1b Not tearing clothes

The high priest must not tear his clothes (Lev. 10:6; 21:10); the king and his servants did not rend their garments (Jer. 36:24); tear your heart and not your clothes (Joel 2:13); let us not tear it (John 19:24).

F1c Other things torn

The veil of the temple was torn in two (Matt. 27:51; Mark 15:38; Luke 23:45); their nets began to break (Luke 5:6); the net was not torn (John 21:11).

F2 Breaking various artefacts

F2a Breaking containers

Ahaz cut the temple utensils in pieces (2 Chr. 28:24); Nebuchadnezzar cut up the gold vessels (2 Kgs. 24:13); the pillars, 'sea' etc. were broken up (2 Kgs. 25:13); before the golden bowl and pitcher are broken (Eccles. 12:6); you will shatter them like earthenware with a rod of iron (Ps. 2:9); they broke the pitchers (Judg. 7:19-20); they have hewn for themselves broken cisterns (Jer. 2:13); I am like a broken vessel (Ps. 31:12); she broke the jar and poured the ointment over his head (Mark 14:3); new wine bursts old wineskins (Matt. 9:17; Mark 2:22; Luke 5:37).

F2b Breaking weapons

Their bows will be broken (Ps. 37:15); he breaks the bow and the spear (Ps. 46:9); God broke all the weapons of war (Ps. 76:3).

F2c Undoing fastenings

You will break his yoke from off your neck (Gen. 27:40); Hananiah broke Jeremiah's yoke (Jer. 28:10-12); he shatters doors of bronze and cuts iron bars (Ps. 107:16); Samson broke his bindings (Judg. 15:14; 16:9,

12); he broke the chains and fetters (Mark 5:4; Luke 8:29); a threefold cord is not easily broken (Eccles. 4:12); they cut away the ropes of the ship's boat (Acts 27:32); they loosened the ropes holding the rudders (Acts 27:40); I am not fit to untie the thong of his sandals (Mark 1:7; Luke 3:16; John 1:27; Acts 13:25).

F2d Other things broken
The stern of the ship was broken up by the waves (Acts 27:41); the ship was about to break up (Jonah 1:4); they came near to breaking the door down (Gen. 19:9); the king cut pieces off the scroll and burnt them (Jer. 36:23).

F3 Breaking bread
Jesus broke the loaves (Matt. 14:19; 15:36; 26:26; Mark 6:41; 8:6; 14:22; Luke 9:16; 22:19; 24:30; 1 Cor. 11:24); he was recognised by the breaking of bread (Luke 24:35); on the first day of the week they gathered to break bread (Acts 20:7, 11); Paul gave thanks and broke bread (Acts 27:35); the bread which we break is a sharing in the body of Christ (1 Cor. 10:16).

F4 Breaking wood / sticks
F4a Cutting trees
Your servants know how to cut timber in Lebanon (2 Chr. 2:8); do not swing your axe against trees in a siege (Deut. 20:19); non-fruit trees may be felled in a siege (Deut. 20:20); felling every good tree (2 Kgs. 3:19, 25); every fruitless tree is felled and burned (Matt. 3:10; 7:19; Luke 3:9); cut it down (Luke 13:7, 9); he cuts cedars (Isa. 44:14); I felled the cedars of Lebanon (2 Kgs. 19:23); the voice of the Lord breaks cedars of Lebanon (Ps. 29:5); I cut down cedars and cypresses of Lebanon (Isa. 37:24); if you were cut off from a wild olive tree and grafted in (Rom. 11:24); every branch which bears no fruit is cut off (John 15:2); some cut branches from the trees and spread them on the road (Matt. 21:8).

F4b Breaking sticks etc.
I broke the staff called Favour (Zech. 11:10); I broke the staff called Union (Zech. 11:14); I broke the bars of your yoke (Lev. 26:13); a bruised reed he will not break (Isa. 42:3; Matt. 12:20).

F5 Dividing earth / rocks
God split rocks in the wilderness (Ps. 78:15); he split the rock and water gushed out (Isa. 48:21); is not my word like hammer which shatters the rocks? (Jer. 23:29); rocks were split when Jesus died (Matt. 27:51); I will put you in the cleft of a rock (Exod. 33:22); Samson lived in the cleft of the rock at Etam (Judg. 15:8, 11); cutting of stones and timber (Exod. 31:5); cut two stone tablets like the first (Exod. 34:1, 4); not an altar of cut stones (Exod. 20:25); a stone was cut out without hands (Dan. 2:34, 45); the ground split open (Num. 16:31); the mount of Olives will be split in two (Zech. 14:4).

F6 Division of waters
He separated waters from waters (Gen. 1:6-7); the waters of the Red Sea were divided (Exod. 14:16, 21); God divided the sea (Neh. 9:11; Ps. 74:13; 78:13; 136:13); he who divided the waters before them (Isa. 63:12); the waters of the Jordan were divided for Elijah (2 Kgs. 2:8); and for Elisha (2 Kgs. 2:14); whose land the rivers divide (Isa. 18:2, 7); you cleaved the earth with rivers (Hab. 3:9); the clouds are not burst by the water in them (Job 26:8).

47 Bond: connecting medium
A Anchors
They cast four anchors from the stern (Acts 27:29); pretending to lay out anchors from the bow (Acts 27:30); they cast off the anchors (Acts 27:40); this hope we has as an anchor of the soul (Heb. 6:19).

B Bands / cords
Leave the stump with a band of iron and bronze around it (Dan. 4:15, 23); from a thread to a sandal-thong (Gen. 14:23); I am not fit to untie the thong of his sandals (Mark 1:7; Luke 3:16; John 1:27); preserve the unity of the Spirit in the bond of peace (Eph. 4:3); love is the bond of unity (Col. 3:14); I led them with cords of a man, with bonds of love (Hos. 11:4).

C Chains
Peter was bound with two chains (Acts 12:6); as was Paul (Acts 21:33); like me, except for these chains (Acts 26:29); this chain is due to the hope of Israel (Acts 28:20); Onesiphorus was not ashamed of my chains (2 Tim. 1:16); I am an ambassador in chains (Eph. 6:20); they suffered chains and imprisonment (Heb. 11:36); his chains fell off his hands (Acts 12:7); everyone's chains were unfastened (Acts 16:26); no one could bind him any more, even with a chain (Mark 5:3); he had been bound with chains, but he tore them apart (Mark 5:4); he was bound with chains and fetters (Luke 8:29); an angel with a great chain in his hand (Rev. 20:1); he will be clothed in purple and have a necklace of gold (Dan. 5:7); they put a chain of gold around Daniel's neck (Dan. 5:29); you will have a chain of gold for your neck (Dan. 5:16).

D Clasps
D1 Hooks
Hooks for: the veil (Exod. 26:32-3); the linen curtains (Exod. 26:6; 36:13); goats' hair curtains (Exod. 26:11; 36:18); the tabernacle (Exod. 35:11).

D2 Nails
David prepared iron for nails (1 Chr. 22:3); 50 shekels of gold in the nails (2 Chr. 3:9); the words of the wise are like firmly-driven nails (Eccles. 12:11); unless I see in his hands the print of the nails (John 20:25); our bill of debt was nailed to the cross (Col. 2:14).

D3 Pegs
Jael killed Sisera with a tent peg (Judg. 4:21; 5:26); can wood of the vine be used to make a peg to hang a vessel? (Ezek. 15:3); Eliakim will be like a peg in a firm place (Isa. 22:23); the peg in a firm place will give way (Isa. 22:25); lengthen your cords, strengthen your pegs (Isa. 54:2).

48 Cohesion
A Clinging together
In the Son all things hold together (Col. 1:17); Eleazar's hand stuck to the sword (2 Sam. 23:10); cling to what is good (Rom. 12:9).

B Clinging to God
Cling to the Lord (Deut. 10:20; 13:4; Josh. 23:8); clinging to God (Deut. 11:22); Hezekiah clung to the Lord (2 Kgs. 18:6); my soul clings to you (Ps. 63:8); as a waistband clings to a man, so I made Israel and Judah cling to me (Jer. 13:11).
GRASP, see 786E.

C Clinging to people
A man will cling to his wife (Gen. 2:24); there is a friend who sticks closer than a brother (Prov. 18:24); Ruth clung to Naomi (Ruth 1:14); do not hold on to me (John 20:17); the lame man clung to Peter and John (Acts 3:11).

49 Non-cohesion
They will not adhere to one another (Dan. 2:43).
SLIPPERY, see 258B.

50 Combination
MIXTURE, see 43.
JOINING, see 45.

51 Decomposition

A People decaying

Corruptible man, birds, animals or reptiles (Rom. 1:23); a perishable body (1 Cor. 15:42, 50, 53-4); David saw corruption (Acts 13:36); our outward man is decaying (2 Cor. 4:16); their worm will not die (Isa. 66:24); where their worm does not die (Mark 9:48); Herod was eaten by worms (Acts 12:23).

B Possessions decaying

Your riches have rotted and your garments are moth-eaten (Jas. 5:2); leftovers of manna bred worms (Exod. 16:20); treasures on earth, where moth and rust devour (Matt. 6:19-20); he who sows to the flesh will reap corruption (Gal. 6:8); regulations relating to things that perish as they are used (Col. 2:22); woe to the city, the pot with the rust in it (Ezek. 24:6-12); they do it to receive a perishable wreath (1 Cor. 9:25); your gold and silver have rusted and their rust will be a witness against you (Jas. 5:3); gold is perishable (1 Pet. 1:7); you were not redeemed with perishable things like silver and gold (1 Pet. 1:18).

C No decay

For the idol he chooses wood that will not rot (Isa. 40:20); treasure in heaven, where no moth destroys (Luke 12:33); you will not allow your holy one to see decay (Ps. 16:10; Acts 2:27; 13:35); he whom God raised saw no corruption (Acts 13:37); Christ's flesh did not suffer decay (Acts 2:31); he raised him from the dead, no more to return to decay (Acts 13:34); they exchanged the glory of the incorruptible God (Rom. 1:23); the creation will be set free from its slavery to decay (Rom. 8:21); they do it to receive a perishable wreath, but we an imperishable (1 Cor. 9:25); the body is raised imperishable (1 Cor. 15:42-54); an inheritance imperishable and undefiled (1 Pet. 1:4); born again not of perishable seed but of imperishable (1 Pet. 1:23); the imperishable adorning of a gentle and quiet spirit (1 Pet. 3:4); you will receive the unfading crown of glory (1 Pet. 5:4); you may escape the corruption that is in the world through lust (2 Pet. 1:4).

52 Whole. Principal part

All the men of Sodom surrounded the house (Gen. 19:4); all the earth came to Egypt to buy grain (Gen. 41:57); all Israel stood to hear the law read (Josh. 8:33); every tongue will confess that Jesus Christ is Lord (Phil. 2:11); in his joy he goes and sells all that he has (Matt. 13:44); he sold all that he had and bought that pearl (Matt. 13:46); she out of her poverty put in all she had to live on (Luke 21:4).

53 Part

A Parts of things

Zechariah's division was on duty (Luke 1:8); come where you will only see a part of Israel (Num. 23:13); a hardening has come upon part of Israel (Rom. 11:25); Ananias brought only a part of the proceeds (Acts 5:2).

B Branches

B1 Branches in general

On the vine were three branches (Gen. 40:10-12); branches spread on the road (Matt. 21:8; Mark 11:8); they took palm branches to meet him (John 12:13); palm branches in their hands (Rev. 7:9); birds of the air nesting in its branches (Ezek. 17:23; 31:6; Matt. 13:32); what are the two branches of the olive trees beside the two golden pipes? (Zech. 4:12); six branches for the lampstand (Exod. 25:32, 35).

B2 The branch of the Lord

The branch of the Lord will be glorious (Isa. 4:2); a righteous branch will reign (Jer. 23:5; 33:15); my servant the Branch (Zech. 3:8); a man whose name is the Branch will build the temple (Zech. 6:12); a branch from the roots of Jesse (Isa. 11:1); he shall be called a Nazarene [Heb. nezer 'branch'] (Matt. 2:23).

B3 Branches of Christ

I am the vine, you are the branches (John 15:5); unfruitful branches are removed (John 15:2); if anyone does not abide in me he is thrown away as a branch (John 15:6); branches broken off and others grafted in (Rom. 11:17-24); if the root is holy, so are the branches (Rom. 11:16).

C Limbs in general

C1 Bodily limbs

Do not yield your limbs to sin (Rom. 6:13); yield your limbs as slaves to righteousness (Rom. 6:19); present your limbs to God as instruments of righteousness (Rom. 6:13); you once yielded your limbs to impurity (Rom. 6:19); put to death your earthly limbs (Col. 3:5); better that one limb perish rather than the whole body (Matt. 5:29-30); the body is not one limb but many (1 Cor. 12:14-20); if one member suffer, all suffer (1 Cor. 12:26).

C2 Christ's limbs

Believers are limbs in Christ's body (Rom. 12:4-5; Eph. 5:30); as the body is one yet has many limbs, so is Christ (1 Cor. 12:12); your bodies are limbs of Christ (1 Cor. 6:15); we are one body in Christ and limbs of one another (Rom. 12:5); we are members of one another (Eph. 4:25); shall I take the limbs of Christ and make them limbs of a prostitute? (1 Cor. 6:15); you are the body of Christ and individually members of it (1 Cor. 12:27); the body knit together by that which every joint supplies (Eph. 4:16).

C3 Hands and feet

Hand for hand, foot for foot (Exod. 21:24; Deut. 19:21); bind him hand and foot (Matt. 22:13); Lazarus was bound hand and foot with wrappings (John 11:44); Agabus took Paul's belt and bound his own feet and hands (Acts 21:11); strengthen the weak hands and feeble knees (Isa. 35:3); they pierce my hands and feet (Ps. 22:16); see my hands and feet (Luke 24:39-40).

D Upper limbs

D1 Shoulders

Aaron will bear the names on his shoulders (Exod. 28:12); when he has found it, he lays it on his shoulders (Luke 15:5); the beloved of the Lord dwells between his shoulders (Deut. 33:12); the ram's shoulder as a wave offering (Num. 6:19-20); the priest shall be given the shoulder (Deut. 18:3).

D2 Arms

By a mighty hand and an outstretched arm (Deut. 5:15; 7:19; 26:8); he has shown strength with his arm (Luke 1:51); awake, put on strength, arm of the Lord (Isa. 51:9); the Lord has bared his holy arm (Isa. 52:10); your hand and your arm brought them victory (Ps. 44:3); with uplifted arm he led them out of Egypt (Acts 13:17); underneath are the everlasting arms (Deut. 33:27); to whom has the arm of the Lord been revealed? (Isa. 53:1; John 12:38).

D3 Hands

D3a Hands in general

God is not served by human hands (Acts 17:25); a cloud as small as a man's hand (1 Kgs. 18:44); some of his disciples ate bread with defiled, unwashed, hands (Mark 7:2); why do your disciples eat with unclean hands? (Matt. 15:2; Mark 7:5); he who dips his hand in the dish with me will betray me (Mark 14:20); strengthen the weak hands (Heb. 12:12); do not let your hands grow weak (Zeph. 3:16); all hands will hang limp, all knees be like water (Ezek. 7:17); a sign on your hand (Exod. 13:9, 16; Deut. 6:8; 11:18); a mark on their right hand or forehead (Rev. 13:16); 'because I am not a hand I am not part of the body' (1 Cor. 12:15); the eye cannot say it does not need the hand (1 Cor. 12:21); The cherubim have human hands under their wings (Ezek. 1:8; 10:8, 21); on their hands they will bear you up (Luke 4:11); the angel lifted up his right hand to heaven (Rev. 10:5); idols have hands but cannot feel (Ps. 115:7).

D3b God's hands

O God, lift up your hand! (Ps. 10:12); your right hand upholds me (Ps. 18:35); my hand will help him (Ps. 89:21); men are in the hand of God (Eccles. 9:1); I have engraved you on the palms of my hands (Isa. 49:16); humble yourselves under the mighty hand of God (1 Pet. 5:6); by a mighty hand and an outstretched arm (Deut. 5:15; 7:19; 26:8); your hand and your arm brought them victory (Ps. 44:3); is the Lord's hand shortened? (Num. 11:23); the Lord's hand is not shortened (Isa. 59:1); the hand of the Lord was with them (Acts 11:21); the hand of the Lord is on you, and you will be blind (Acts 13:11); it is a terrifying thing to fall into the hands of the living God (Heb. 10:31); I will stretch out my hand (Exod. 3:20; 7:5); his hand is stretched out still (Isa. 5:25; 9:12, 17, 21; 10:4); I spread out my hands to a rebellious people (Isa. 65:2; Rom. 10:21); stretch out your hand to heal (Acts 4:30).

D3c Christ's hands

He showed them his hands and his side (John 20:20); put out your finger and see my hands (John 20:27); unless I see in his hands the print of the nails (John 20:25); in his right hand he held seven stars (Rev. 1:16); he laid his right hand on me (Rev. 1:17); the one who holds the seven stars in his hand (Rev. 2:1).

D3d Hands of indivisuals

The hands are the hands of Esau (Gen. 27:22); his hand stuck to the sword (2 Sam. 23:10); Moses' hand was leprous (Exod. 4:6); whenever Moses lifted his hand, Israel prevailed (Exod. 17:11); he stretched out his hand and it withered (1 Kgs. 13:4); a man with a withered hand (Matt. 12:10-13; Mark 3:1, 3-5; Luke 6:6-10); his hand was restored (1 Kgs. 13:6); Pilate took water and washed his hands (Matt. 27:24); not my feet only, but also my hands and my head (John 13:9); unless I put my hand in his side I will not believe (John 20:25); put your hand into my side (John 20:27); Elisha put his hands on the child's hands (2 Kgs. 4:34); Elisha put his hands on the king's hands (2 Kgs. 13:16); a viper fastened on his hand (Acts 28:3).

D4 Fingers / thumbs

My little finger is thicker than my father's loins (1 Kgs. 12:10); Jesus wrote on the ground with his finger (John 8:6, 8); the fingers of a man's hand wrote on the wall (Dan. 5:5); they will not move the loads with so much as a finger (Matt. 23:4; Luke 11:46); send Lazarus to dip the tip of his finger in water (Luke 16:24); Jesus put his fingers in the man's ears (Mark 7:33); unless I put my finger in the mark of the nails (John 20:25); put out your finger and see my hands (John 20:27); a giant with six fingers on each hand and six toes on each foot (2 Sam. 21:20); tables written with the finger of God (Exod. 31:18; Deut. 9:10); this is the finger of God (Exod. 8:19); if I cast out demons by the finger of God (Luke 11:20); cutting off thumbs and big toes (Judg. 1:6, 7); on right thumb and right big toe: blood (Exod. 29:20; Lev. 8:23, 24; 14:14, 25); oil (Lev. 14:17, 28).

E Lower limbs

E1 Legs

The Lord does not take pleasure in the legs of a man (Ps. 147:10); his legs are alabaster pillars (S. of S. 5:15); the legs of the statue were of iron (Dan. 2:33); the Jews asked Pilate that their legs might be broken (John 19:31); the soldiers broke the legs of the two crucified

with Jesus (John 19:32); they did not break Jesus' legs (John 19:33); a leg of the sacrifice set aside for Saul (1 Sam. 9:24).

E2 Thighs / hips

The man dislocated Jacob's thigh (Gen. 32:25, 32); the sons of Israel do not eat the sinew of the thigh (Gen. 32:32); the Lord will make your thigh fall (Num. 5:21, 22); her thigh will fall (Num. 5:27); putting a hand under the thigh (Gen. 24:2, 9; 47:29); water reaching to the loins (Ezek. 47:4); let your loins be girded (Luke 12:35); gird your sword on your thigh (Ps. 45:3); on his robe and on his thigh he has a name written (Rev. 19:16); the thigh will be for Aaron and his sons (Exod. 29:27-8); give the right thigh to the priest (Lev. 7:32, 33, 34; Num. 18:18); the right thigh was waved as a wave offering (Lev. 9:21; 10:15).

E3 Knees

Let her bear children upon my knees (Gen. 30:3); the sons of Machir son of Manasseh were born on Joseph's knees (Gen. 50:23); why did the knees receive me? (Job 3:12); you will be dandled on her knees (Isa. 66:12); she made him sleep on her knees (Judg. 16:19); Elijah put his face between his knees (1 Kgs. 18:42); all hands will hang limp, all knees be like water (Ezek. 7:17; 21:7); my knees are weak through fasting (Ps. 109:24); strengthen the weak knees (Isa. 35:3; Heb. 12:12); you have strengthened the feeble knees (Job 4:4); water reaching to the knees (Ezek. 47:4).

E4 Feet

E4a Feet in general

Uncovering Boaz' feet (Ruth 3:4, 7); feet partly of clay and partly of iron (Dan. 2:33, 41); she caught hold of Elisha's feet (2 Kgs. 4:27); they took hold of his feet and worshipped him (Matt. 28:9); sit at my right hand until I put your enemies beneath your feet (Matt. 22:44); he has put all things under his feet (Eph. 1:22); you have put all things in subjection under man's feet (Heb. 2:8); a woman with the moon under her feet (Rev. 12:1); if the foot should say, 'I am not a hand' (1 Cor. 12:15); the head cannot say it has no need of the feet (1 Cor. 12:21).

E4b Types of feet

Their feet were like calves' feet (Ezek. 1:7); he makes my feet like hinds' feet (2 Sam. 22:34; Ps. 18:33); his feet like burnished bronze (Rev. 1:15; 2:18); the angel's feet were like pillars of fire (Rev. 10:1); idols have feet but cannot walk (Ps. 115:7).

E4c Feet in action

Every place that the sole of your foot treads on is yours (Deut. 11:24; Josh. 1:3); the land on which your feet trod shall be your inheritance (Josh. 14:9); when the soles of the feet of the priests rest in the Jordan (Josh. 3:13, 15); with the sole of my foot I dried up the rivers of Egypt (2 Kgs. 19:24); Egypt was watered by the foot (Deut. 11:10); the feet of him who brings good news (Isa. 52:7; Nahum 1:15; Rom. 10:15); feet shod with the preparation of the gospel (Eph. 6:15); their feet run to evil (Prov. 1:16); the Lord hates feet that hasten to evil (Prov. 6:18); turn your foot from evil (Prov. 4:27); the harlot's feet do not remain at home (Prov. 7:11); the adulteress' feet go down to death (Prov. 5:5); the feet of those who have buried your husband are at the door (Acts 5:9); their feet are swift to shed blood (Rom. 3:15); the God of peace will soon crush Satan under your feet (Rom. 16:20).

E4d Feet secure

My feet have not slipped (2 Sam. 22:37; Ps. 18:36); the Lord will keep your foot from being caught (Prov. 3:26); ponder the path of your feet (Prov. 4:26); he makes my feet like hinds' feet (Hab. 3:19); to guide our feet into the way of peace (Luke 1:79); make straight paths for your feet (Heb. 12:13).

E4e Care of feet
Let water be brought to wash your feet (Gen. 18:4); wash your own feet (Gen. 19:2); he gave water to wash their feet (Gen. 24:32); washing the disciples' feet (John 13:5-14); if she has washed the saints' feet (1 Tim. 5:10); she wet his feet with tears (Luke 7:38, 44); she has not stopped kissing my feet (Luke 7:45); she has anointed my feet with ointment (Luke 7:46); may Asher dip his feet in oil (Deut. 33:24); your foot did not swell these 40 years (Deut. 8:4); if they will not hear, shake the dust off your feet (Matt. 10:14); it is better to enter life lame than with two feet to be thrown into hell (Mark 9:45); his feet and ankles were strengthened (Acts 3:7).

E4f Injury to feet
The donkey pressed Balaam's foot against the wall (Num. 22:25); a man with a broken foot could not serve as priest (Lev. 21:19); Asa was diseased in his feet (1 Kgs. 15:23; 2 Chr. 16:12); can a man walk on hot coals and his feet not be scorched? (Prov. 6:28); Mephibosheth had not seen to his feet (2 Sam. 19:24).

E4g Feet of creatures
Insects with jointed legs you may eat (Lev. 11:21); creatures with many feet are detestable (Lev. 11:42); whatever walks on its paws is unclean (Lev. 11:27); whatever divides the hoof you may eat (Lev. 11:3); not a hoof shall be left behind (Exod. 10:26); the Lord delivered me from the paw of the lion and the paw of the bear (1 Sam. 17:37).

E5 Heels
You will bruise his heel (Gen. 3:15); Jacob held Esau's heel (Gen. 25:26; Hos. 12:3); a trap takes him by the heel (Job 18:9); Dan, the snake, bites the horse's heels (Gen. 49:17); he who eats my bread has lifted his heel against me (Ps. 41:9; John 13:18).

E6 Toes
Cutting off thumbs and big toes (Judg. 1:6-7); a giant with six fingers on each hand and six toes on each foot (2 Sam. 21:20; 1 Chr. 20:6); on right thumb and right big toe: blood (Exod. 29:20; Lev. 8:23-4; 14:14); oil (Lev. 14:17).

F Fins
Water creatures with fins and scales are clean (Lev. 11:9-12; Deut. 14:9-10).

54 Complete
THE WHOLE, see 52.

A God's fullness
In him all the fullness of God was pleased to dwell (Col. 1:19); in him all the fullness of God dwells in a body (Col. 2:9); the measure of the stature of the fullness of Christ (Eph. 4:13); filled with all the fullness of God (Eph. 3:19); from his fullness we have all received (John 1:16); I will come in the fullness of the blessing of Christ (Rom. 15:29); that God may be all in all (1 Cor. 15:28); one God who is over all and through all and in all (Eph. 4:6); Christ is all and in all (Col. 3:11); Christ, for whom are all things and through whom are all things (Heb. 2:10).

B Filled with God
B1 The earth filled with God
All the earth will be filled with the glory of God (Num. 14:21); may the whole earth be filled with his glory (Ps. 72:19); do I not fill heaven and earth? (Jer. 23:24); he ascended so that he might fill all things (Eph. 4:10); the church is the fullness of him who fills all in all (Eph. 1:23); the earth is full of his glory (Isa. 6:3); the lovingkindness of the Lord fills the earth (Ps. 33:5); the earth will be filled with the knowledge of the Lord (Isa. 11:9); with the knowledge of the glory of the Lord (Hab. 2:14).

B2 Filled with the Spirit
Be filled with the Spirit (Eph. 5:18); the seven men should be full of the Spirit (Acts 6:3); those filled with the Spirit: Bezalel (Exod. 31:3; 35:31); John the Baptist – from his mother's womb (Luke 1:15); Barnabas (Acts 11:24); Elizabeth (Luke 1:41); Jesus (Luke 4:1); Paul (Acts 9:17; 13:9); Peter (Acts 4:8); Stephen (Acts 6:5; 7:55); Zechariah (Luke 1:67); the disciples in Jerusalem (Acts 2:4; 4:31); the disciples in Antioch of Pisidia (Acts 13:52).

FILLED WITH THE SPIRIT, see 965E2d.

C Full number of people
C1 All people
We will go with our young and old, sons and daughters, flocks and herds (Exod. 10:9); all Israel from Dan to Beersheba came out (Judg. 20:1); nearly the whole city gathered to hear the word of God (Acts 13:44); death spread to all because all sinned (Rom. 5:12); one act of righteousness brought justification and life to all (Rom. 5:18); one transgression brought condemnation to all (Rom. 5:18); God is the Saviour of all people (1 Tim. 4:10); that by the grace of God he might taste death for everyone (Heb. 2:9); he is the propitiation for the sins of the whole world (1 John 2:2).

C2 Fullness of the kingdom
The wedding hall was filled with guests (Matt. 22:10); that my house may be filled (Luke 14:23); when the net was full they drew it ashore (Matt. 13:48); Israel is hardened until the full number of the Gentiles come in (Rom. 11:25); they rest until the full number of their martyred brothers should be complete (Rev. 6:11); what will the fullness of Israel be! (Rom. 11:12); all Israel will be saved (Rom. 11:26); he is called the God of the whole earth (Isa. 54:5); I will bring them in until no room is found for them (Zech. 10:10); if the firstfruits are holy, so is the whole lump (Rom. 11:16).

D Filling
D1 Filling places
God commanded the creatures to fill the waters of the sea (Gen. 1:22); God commanded man to fill the earth (Gen. 1:28); Noah and his sons were to fill the earth (Gen. 9:1); the land was filled with them (Exod. 1:7); the vine filled the land (Ps. 80:9); Israel will fill the whole world with fruit (Isa. 27:6); the stone became a mountain and filled all the earth (Dan. 2:35); you have filled Jerusalem with your teaching (Acts 5:28); your houses will be filled with locusts (Exod. 10:6); the house was full of people (Judg. 16:27); the wind filled all the house where they were sitting (Acts 2:2).

D2 Filling the sanctuary
The glory of the Lord filled the tabernacle (Exod. 40:34, 35); the glory of the Lord filled the temple (2 Chr. 7:1, 2; Ezek. 43:5); the cloud filled the inner court (Ezek. 10:3); the cloud filled the temple (1 Kgs. 8:10; Ezek. 10:4); fill the courts with the slain (Ezek. 9:7); the glory of the Lord filled the house of the Lord (Ezek. 44:4); I will fill this house with glory (Hag. 2:7).

D3 Filling people
God filled Bezalel and Oholiab with skill (Exod. 35:35); I went out full, but returned empty (Ruth 1:21); open your mouth wide and I will fill it (Ps. 81:10); fill your stomach with this scroll I am giving you (Ezek. 3:3); I am filled (Phil. 4:18); you have been filled in him (Col. 2:10); already you are filled! (1 Cor. 4:8); they are full of sweet wine (Acts 2:13); filled with all unrighteousness (Rom. 1:29); asking that you may be filled with the knowledge of his will (Col. 1:9).

E Nothing missing
Not one of the animals will be missing (Isa. 34:16); by the greatness of his power not one star is missing (Isa.

40:26); how will he not with him freely give us all things? (Rom. 8:32); then I will know fully, as I have been fully known (1 Cor. 13:12); in subjecting everything to him he left nothing not subjected (Heb. 2:8).

55 Incomplete

Rivers run into the sea yet the sea is not full (Eccles. 1:7); we know in part (1 Cor. 13:9, 12); when the perfect comes, that which is partial will be done away (1 Cor. 13:10).

NON-COMPLETION, see 726.

56 Composition

A Composition of the anointing oil
500 shekels of myrrh, 250 of cinnamon, 500 of cassia, a hin of oil (Exod. 30:23-4); do not make an oil of the same composition (Exod. 30:32).

B Composition of the holy incense
Equal parts of stacte, onycha, galbanum and frankincense (Exod. 30:34); do not make incense of the same composition (Exod. 30:37).

ARRANGEMENT, see 65.

57 Exclusion

CLOSING UP, see 264.

58 Component

CITIZEN, see 191.

59 Foreignness

A Characteristics of foreigners
A1 What foreigners are like
Gentiles are concerned about food and clothing (Matt. 6:32; Luke 12:30); liars and deceitful (Ps. 144:8, 11); darkened in their minds (Eph. 4:17-18); strangers to the covenants of promise (Eph. 2:12); the Gentiles who do not know God (1 Thess. 4:5); we are Jews, not Gentile sinners (Gal. 2:15).
A2 What foreigners do
Gentiles greet their brothers (Matt. 5:47); Gentiles pray repetitiously (Matt. 6:7); kings collect tax from strangers (Matt. 17:25-6); the rulers of the Gentiles lord it over them (Matt. 20:25; Mark 10:42; Luke 22:25); why did the Gentiles rage and the peoples imagine futile things? (Ps. 2:1; Acts 4:25); let the time past suffice for doing what the Gentiles like to do (1 Pet. 4:3).
A3 Foreigners prospering
The foreigner will rise higher and higher (Deut. 28:43); the foreigner from afar will see the plagues of the land (Deut. 29:22).
A4 Reckoned as foreigners
Abraham was a sojourner (Gen. 23:4; Heb. 11:9); Abraham's descendants would be sojourners in another land (Gen. 15:13; Acts 7:6); Moses became an alien in the land of Midian (Acts 7:29); Gershom – a sojourner in a foreign land (Exod. 2:22; 18:3); does he not reckon us as foreigners? (Gen. 31:15); I am thought a foreigner by my guests and servants (Job 19:15); I have become a stranger to my brothers (Ps. 69:8); if I do not know the meaning of the language I will be a foreigner (1 Cor. 14:11); I am like a stranger to God (Ps. 39:12); God has become like a sojourner in the land (Jer. 14:8); sojourners scattered abroad (1 Pet. 1:1); all God's people are sojourners on earth (1 Chr. 29:15); foreigners and exiles in this world (Heb. 11:13; 1 Pet. 2:11); conduct yourselves with fear during the time of your sojourning (1 Pet. 1:17).

B Harm from foreigners
B1 Suffering from foreigners
I will give you into the hands of aliens (Ezek. 11:9); they will deliver him to the Gentiles (Matt. 20:19; Mark 10:33; Luke 18:32); the Jews will deliver Paul into the hands of the Gentiles (Acts 21:11); he came as an alien and is acting the judge (Gen. 19:9); you will serve strangers in a land which is not yours (Jer. 5:19).
B2 Foreigners in the holy places
Our inheritance has been turned over to foreigners (Lam. 5:2); Jerusalem will be trampled by the Gentiles (Luke 21:24); the Gentiles trample on the holy city for 42 months (Rev. 11:2); aliens have entered the holy places of the temple (Jer. 51:51); nations you forbade have entered her sanctuary (Lam. 1:10); you brought foreigners into God's sanctuary (Ezek. 44:7, 9); they thought Paul had brought Greeks into the temple (Acts 21:28-9); the name of God is blasphemed among the Gentiles because of you (Rom. 2:24); you set foreigners to keep charge of my holy things (Ezek. 44:8).
C Treatment of foreigners
C1 Attitudes towards foreigners
Behave rightly towards outsiders (1 Thess. 4:12); act wisely towards outsiders (Col. 4:5); an elder must have a good reputation with those outside (1 Tim. 3:7); maintain good conduct among the Gentiles (1 Pet. 2:12).
C2 Avoiding foreigners
The Levite would not spend the night with foreigners (Judg. 19:12); deliver me out of the hand of aliens (Ps. 144:7, 11); they separated themselves from foreigners (Neh. 9:2); do not go to the Gentiles or Samaritans (Matt. 10:5); a stranger they will not follow (John 10:5); treat an obdurate brother as you would a Gentile or tax collector (Matt. 18:17); a Jew may not associate with a foreigner (Acts 10:28); Christian workers went out, accepting nothing from Gentiles (3 John 7); what have I to do with judging outsiders? (1 Cor. 5:12).
C3 Relations with foreigners
David left his parents with the king of Moab (1 Sam. 22:3-4); David lived with the king of Gath (1 Sam. 27:2-3); Elijah was only sent to a widow of Sidon (Luke 4:26); Elisha only cleansed Naaman the Syrian of leprosy (Luke 4:27); before certain men came from James, Peter ate with the Gentiles (Gal. 2:12); Solomon loved many foreign women (1 Kgs. 11:1); Ephraim mixes with the nations and foreigners sap his strength (Hos. 7:8-9).
C4 Laws restricting foreigners
No foreigner may eat of the Passover (Exod. 12:43); a sojourner with the priest may not eat the holy things (Lev. 22:10); no Ammonite or Moabite should ever enter God's assembly (Deut. 23:3-4; Neh. 13:1-3); the king may not be a foreigner (Deut. 17:15); the children of foreigners may become your slaves (Lev. 25:45); you may give a sojourner what has died (Deut. 14:21); you may exact a debt from a foreigner in the year of remission (Deut. 15:3); you may charge a foreigner interest (Deut. 23:20).
C5 Foreigners subdued
David set foreigners to quarry stones (1 Chr. 22:2); Solomon set foreigners to labour (2 Chr. 2:17-18); delivering you from the [Jewish] people and from the Gentiles (Acts 26:17).
C6 Kindness to foreigners
God loves aliens and gives them food and clothing (Deut. 10:18); the Lord protects strangers (Ps. 146:9); why should you take notice of me, since I am a stranger? (Ruth 2:10); the sojourner had not lodged outside my door (Job 31:32); I was a stranger and you welcomed me (Matt. 25:35); if she has shown

hospitality to strangers (1 Tim. 5:10); you are faithful in serving the brethren, especially strangers (3 John 5); love the alien because you were aliens (Deut. 10:19); support the poor as you do foreigners (Lev. 25:35); do not overlook hospitality to strangers, for some have entertained angels (Heb. 13:2); give the alien: food (Deut. 14:29); firstfruits (Deut. 26:11); gleanings (Lev. 19:10; 23:22; Deut. 24:19-21); the tithe (Deut. 26:12-13).

C7 The gospel preached to foreigners
A light for the Gentiles (Isa. 42:6; 49:6; Luke 2:32; Acts 13:47); he will proclaim justice to the Gentiles (Isa. 42:1; Matt. 12:18); Christ would announce light both to the people and to the Gentiles (Acts 26:23); to bear testimony before rulers and the Gentiles (Matt. 10:18); we turn to the Gentiles (Acts 13:46); from now on I go to the Gentiles (Acts 18:6); an apostle to the Gentiles (Rom. 11:13); God sent Paul to the Gentiles (Acts 22:21; 26:17; Gal. 2:7-8); he is my chosen instrument to carry my name to the Gentiles (Acts 9:15); God chose that by my mouth the Gentiles should hear (Acts 15:7); I am a debtor both to Greeks and barbarians (Rom. 1:14); I declared to the Gentiles that they should repent (Acts 26:20); a teacher of the Gentiles in faith and truth (1 Tim. 2:7); a minister of Christ Jesus to the Gentiles (Rom. 15:16); Philip preached to the Samaritans (Acts 8:5-8); in Antioch the gospel was first preached to Greeks (Acts 11:20); this salvation of God is sent to the Gentiles (Acts 28:28).

C8 Oppressing foreigners
Do not ill-treat foreigners because you were sojourners yourselves in Egypt (Exod. 22:21; 23:9; Lev. 19:33-4; Deut. 23:7); do not pervert justice due to an alien (Deut. 24:17; 27:19); do not wrong the alien, the orphan or the widow (Jer. 7:6; 22:3; Zech. 7:10); evildoers murder strangers (Ps. 94:6); they have oppressed the alien (Ezek. 22:7, 29); I was a stranger and you did not welcome me (Matt. 25:43); I will be a witness against those who thrust aside the alien (Mal. 3:5); why compel Gentiles to live like Jews? (Gal. 2:14).

C9 Surety for foreigners
If you have given a pledge for a stranger (Prov. 6:1); he who gives surety for a stranger will suffer for it (Prov. 11:15); take the garment of one who gives surety for a stranger (Prov. 20:16; 27:13).

D Inclusion of foreigners

D1 Foreigners permitted at the feasts
Regulations for a sojourner who wants to keep the Passover (Exod. 12:48; Num. 9:14); or who wants to make a sacrifice (Num. 15:14); let the sojourner eat the Feast of Weeks with you (Deut. 16:11); invite the alien to the Feast of Booths (Deut. 16:14).

D2 Foreigners included among the people
Sojourners will join the house of Jacob (Isa. 14:1); foreigners will rebuild your walls (Isa. 60:10); foreigners will be your shepherds and farmers (Isa. 61:5); foreigners who join themselves to the Lord (Isa. 56:6); rejoice, Gentiles, with his people (Deut. 32:43; Rom. 15:10); aliens will be as native-born (Ezek. 47:22); we are no longer foreigners but fellow-citizens (Eph. 2:19).

D3 Foreigners included in the law
The sojourner shall be as the native among you (Lev. 19:34); one law for both the native and the sojourner (Exod. 12:49; Lev. 24:22; Num. 9:14; 15:14-16); cities of refuge for the Israelite and the sojourner (Num. 35:15; Josh. 20:9); a perpetual statute for Israelite and sojourner (Num. 19:10); when the Gentiles who have not the law do what the law requires (Rom. 2:14).

D4 Foreigners included in God's blessing
May the foreigner's prayer be heard (1 Kgs. 8:41-3; 2 Chr. 6:32-3); the foreigner should not think that God

will exclude him (Isa. 56:3); God will make the foreigners joyful in his house of prayer (Isa. 56:7); praise the Lord, all you Gentiles (Ps. 117:1; Rom. 15:11); I will give praise to you among the Gentiles (2 Sam. 22:50; Ps. 18:49; Rom. 15:9); amazed that the Spirit was poured out on the Gentiles (Acts 10:45); they related what signs and wonders God had done among the Gentiles (Acts 15:12); if their failure be riches for the Gentiles (Rom. 11:12); in his name will the Gentiles hope (Matt. 12:21; Rom. 15:12).

D5 Foreigners saved by faith
For the obedience of faith among all the Gentiles (Rom. 1:5); the scripture, foreseeing that God would justify the Gentiles by faith (Gal. 3:8); Gentiles attained righteousness by faith (Rom. 9:30); God had opened a door of faith to the Gentiles (Acts 14:27); the Gentiles had received the word of God (Acts 11:1); God has granted repentance to the Gentiles (Acts 11:18); Gentiles can hear the word of the gospel and believe (Acts 15:7).

D6 Foreigners included in God's people
That in Christ Jesus the blessing of Abraham might come upon the Gentiles (Gal. 3:14); the Gentiles are fellow-heirs (Eph. 3:6); the glory of this mystery among the Gentiles, Christ in you! (Col. 1:27); in Christ there is no barbarian or Scythian (Col. 3:11); the Gentiles are indebted to minister to the Jerusalem church (Rom. 15:27).

E Particular foreigners
I am the son of an alien (2 Sam. 1:13); the Samaritan had compassion on the man (Luke 10:33); the Canaanite woman's daughter was healed (Matt. 15:22-8; Mark 7:26); was there no one to give glory to God except this foreigner? (Luke 17:18); Galilee of the Gentiles (Isa. 9:1; Matt. 4:15).

60 Order
The fixed order of the universe (Jer. 31:35-6); if you can break the fixed patterns of heaven and earth (Jer. 33:25); I rejoice to see your orderliness (Col. 2:5); let all things be done in an orderly manner (1 Cor. 14:40); I say this to promote good order (1 Cor. 7:35); belts are not undone nor sandal thongs broken (Isa. 5:27); there is no straggler in the ranks (Isa. 14:31); the locusts march in order (Joel 2:7-8).
PUT IN ORDER, see 62.

61 Disorder
Where there is no vision the people run wild (Prov. 29:18); the people were running loose (Exod. 32:25); I saw a great tumult (2 Sam. 18:29); we commend ourselves in tumults (2 Cor. 6:5); they did not find me making a riot (Acts 24:12); not during the feast, or the people may riot (Matt. 26:5; Mark 14:2); Pilate saw that a riot was starting (Matt. 27:24); there arose no small disturbance about the Way (Acts 19:23); there was uproar over Paul (Acts 17:5; 19:29, 32); we are in danger of being charged with rioting (Acts 19:40); uproar at a funeral (Matt. 9:23); why make a commotion and weep? (Mark 5:39); God is not a God of disorder (1 Cor. 14:33); Paul feared there may be disorder in the church (2 Cor. 12:20); where jealousy exists there will be disorder (Jas. 3:16); admonish the unruly (1 Thess. 5:14).

62 Arrange: put in order
Abraham arranged the wood (Gen. 22:9); Elijah put the wood in order (1 Kgs. 18:33); the priest shall set in order the wood on the fire (Lev. 1:7); the sons of Aaron are to set the light in order (Exod. 27:21); Aaron is to keep the lamps in order (Lev. 24:4); they trimmed their lamps (Matt. 25:7); I say this

to promote good order (1 Cor. 7:35); Ahithophel put his house in order (2 Sam. 17:23); put your house in order for you will die (2 Kgs. 20:1; Isa. 38:1); the unclean spirit found the house swept and put in order (Matt. 12:44; Luke 11:25); I left you in Crete to set in order what remains (Titus 1:5).

ORDERLY MANNER, see 60.

63 Derange

A Confusion
God confused their language (Gen. 11:7-9).

B Perversion
You have perverted the words of the living God (Jer. 23:36); sex with an animal is perversion (Lev. 18:23).

BESTIALITY, see 951C.
HOMOSEXUALITY, see 951D.

64 Precedence

Their king goes before them, the Lord at their head (Mic. 2:13); he who comes after me ranks before me (John 1:15, 30).

FORERUNNER, see 66.
GOING BEFORE, see 283.

65 Sequence

All are raised in their own order (1 Cor. 15:23); the natural is first, then the spiritual (1 Cor. 15:46); Jacob put the maids and their children first, then Leah, then Rachel (Gen. 33:2); the order of march from the camp of Israel (Num. 2:1-34; 10:14-28); those speaking in tongues should speak in turn (1 Cor. 14:27); you can all prophesy one by one (1 Cor. 14:31); pay them, beginning with the last, up to the first (Matt. 20:8).

RANKING, see 73.

66 Forerunner

Jesus has entered the shrine as a forerunner (Heb. 6:20); I send my messenger before your face (Mark 1:2); John was a forerunner for Jesus (Matt. 3:3-12; Luke 3:3-17).

67 Sequel

Adonijah was born after Absalom (1 Kgs. 1:6); one horn was longer than the other and came up last (Dan. 8:3).

68 Beginning

FIRST, see 119.

A Beginning of all things
A1 In the beginning
In the beginning God created heavens and earth (Gen. 1:1); in the beginning the Son created the earth and the heavens (Heb. 1:10); in the beginning was the Word (John 1:1); the Word was in the beginning with God (John 1:2).

A2 Christ the beginning
Christ the beginning of God's creation (Rev. 3:14); he is before all things (Col. 1:17); Christ is the originator of our salvation (Heb. 2:10); the originator of our faith (Heb. 12:2); the beginning, the firstborn from the dead (Col. 1:18); Christ would be the first to rise from the dead (Acts 26:23); the firstfruits of those who slept (1 Cor. 15:20, 23); his goings forth [origin] are from eternity (Mic. 5:2); you killed the originator of life (Acts 3:15).

A3 From the beginning
Him who has been from the beginning (1 John 2:13-14); what was from the beginning (1 John 1:1); everything is as it was from the beginning of creation (2 Pet. 3:4); God made them male and female from the beginning (Matt. 19:4; Mark 10:6); since the creation of the world (Rom. 1:20); his works were finished from the foundation of the world (Heb. 4:3); things hidden since the foundation of the world (Matt. 13:35); the kingdom prepared for you from the foundation of the world (Matt. 25:34); God chose you from the beginning to be saved (2 Thess. 2:13); their names not written in the book of life from the foundation of the world (Rev. 17:8); the devil sinned from the beginning (1 John 3:8); the devil was a murderer from the beginning (John 8:44); tribulation not seen from the beginning of the world until now (Matt. 24:21; Mark 13:19).

A4 Before the beginning
The Father loved the Son before the foundation of the world (John 17:24); the Lamb slain before the foundation of the world (Rev. 13:8); chosen in him before the foundation of the world (Eph. 1:4); Christ was foreknown before the foundation of the world (1 Pet. 1:20); the glory which I had with you before the world was (John 17:5).

B Beginning of periods
The first month of the year, the beginning of months (Exod. 12:2); this is the beginning of the birth pangs (Matt. 24:8; Mark 13:8).

C First people
Were you the first man? (Job 15:7); from the establishment of man on earth (Job 20:4); when men began to multiply (Gen. 6:1); Amalek was the first of the nations (Num. 24:20); Adam was created first (1 Tim. 2:13); the first Adam (1 Cor. 15:45); the first man is from the earth (1 Cor. 15:47); the spiritual is not first, but the natural [material] (1 Cor. 15:46); the first will be last and the last first (Matt. 19:30; Mark 10:31); the last will be first and the first last (Matt. 20:16; Luke 13:30); if anyone is without sin let him be the first to cast a stone (John 8:7); God appointed in the church first apostles (1 Cor. 12:28).

D Beginning of wisdom
The fear of the Lord is the beginning of wisdom (Ps. 111:10; Prov. 1:7; 9:10); the beginning of wisdom is, get wisdom (Prov. 4:7); God set up wisdom at the beginning of his way (Prov. 8:22-3).

E Beginning to act
E1 Activity begun
They began to call on the name of the Lord (Gen. 4:26); Noah began farming (Gen. 9:20); start at my sanctuary (Ezek. 9:6); as Titus had made a beginning, he should complete this gracious work (2 Cor. 8:6); he appeared first to Mary Magdalene (Mark 16:9); Solomon started to build the temple (1 Kgs. 6:1; 2 Chr. 3:1); this man began to build and was not able to finish (Luke 14:30).

E2 First to act
Your hand shall be first against a relative who serves other gods (Deut. 13:9); the hand of the witnesses shall be first (Deut. 17:7); the standard of Judah set out first (Num. 10:14); the other disciple reached the tomb first (John 20:4); who should be the first to fight? (Judg. 1:1; 10:18; 20:18; 1 Kgs. 20:14); Abijah began the battle (2 Chr. 13:3); the young men went out first (1 Kgs. 20:17).

E3 Beginning of salvation
Let what you heard from the beginning remain in you (1 John 2:24); he who began a good work in you will complete it (Phil. 1:6); Christ is the originator of our salvation (Heb. 2:10); the originator of our faith (Heb. 12:2); since the day you heard and understood the grace of God in truth (Col. 1:6); the Holy Spirit fell on them, just as on us at the beginning (Acts 11:15); having begun with the Spirit, are you ending with the flesh? (Gal. 3:3); an old commandment which you have had from the beginning (1 John 2:7; 2 John 5-6); in Antioch the disciples were first called Christians (Acts 11:26); how

God first visited the Gentiles (Acts 15:14); Epaenetus was the first convert in Asia (Rom. 16:5).

E4 To the Jew first
The word preached throughout Judea, beginning from Galilee (Acts 10:37); the gospel to be preached beginning from Jerusalem (Luke 24:47; Acts 1:8); God sent his Servant to you first (Acts 3:26); the word of God to be spoken first to the Jews (Acts 13:46); the gospel is to the Jew first (Rom. 1:16); tribulation for evildoers, the Jew first and also the Greek (Rom. 2:9); glory to everyone who does good, the Jew first and also the Greek (Rom. 2:10).

F Beginning and end
I am the Alpha and the Omega, says the Lord God (Rev. 1:8); I am the Alpha and the Omega, the beginning and the end (Rev. 21:6; 22:13); I am the first and the last (Isa. 44:6; 48:12; Rev. 1:17; 2:8; 22:13); I am the first and with the last (Isa. 41:4).

69 End

BEGINNING AND END, see 68F.

A End of all things
The end of the ages has come upon us (1 Cor. 10:11); Christ has appeared at the end of the ages (Heb. 9:26); manifested in the last time (1 Pet. 1:20); in the last days I will pour out my Spirit (Acts 2:17); children, it is the last hour (1 John 2:18); you have stored up treasure in the last days (Jas. 5:3); in the last days there will be difficult times (2 Tim. 3:1); in the last days there will be scoffers (2 Pet. 3:3; Jude 18); the gospel will be preached in all the world and then the end will come (Matt. 24:14); then comes the end (1 Cor. 15:24); the end of the age (Matt. 13:39-40, 49; 24:3); the end of all things is at hand (1 Pet. 4:7); the end is not yet (Matt. 24:6; Mark 13:7; Luke 21:9); salvation to be revealed in the last time (1 Pet. 1:5); I know he will rise in the resurrection at the last day (John 11:24); he who endures to the end will be saved (Matt. 10:22; 24:13; Mark 13:13); if we hold fast our confidence until the end (Heb. 3:6); if we hold fast our assurance to the end (Heb. 3:14); I am with you to the end of the age (Matt. 28:20).

B End of periods
The Feast of Ingathering at the end of the year (Exod. 23:16); at the end of 430 years the hosts of the Lord went out of Egypt (Exod. 12:41); at the end of seven days the word of the Lord came to me (Ezek. 3:16); on the last day of the feast Jesus stood (John 7:37).

C End of people
The end of all flesh (Gen. 6:13); he will make a full end of the inhabitants of the earth (Zeph. 1:18); make me know my end (Ps. 39:4); we end our days like a sigh (Ps. 90:9); what will be the end of those who do not obey the gospel? (1 Pet. 4:17); their end will be according to their deeds (2 Cor. 11:15); their end is destruction (Phil. 3:19); its end is to be burned (Heb. 6:8); the first will be last and the last first (Matt. 19:30; Mark 10:31); the last will be first and the first last (Matt. 20:16; Luke 13:30); the camp of Dan set out last (Num. 2:31; 10:25); the last Adam became a life-giving spirit (1 Cor. 15:45).

D End of activities
Christ is the end of the law (Rom. 10:4); has his promise come to an end? (Ps. 77:8); seventy weeks to put an end to sin (Dan. 9:24); Peter sat with the guards to see the end (Matt. 26:58); last of all he appeared to me (1 Cor. 15:8); the last enemy to be destroyed is death (1 Cor. 15:26); having begun with the Spirit, are you ending with the flesh? (Gal. 3:3); seven bowls full of the seven last plagues (Rev. 21:9).

COMPLETION, see 725.

E Last words
Jacob finished charging his sons and died (Gen. 49:33); Moses finished writing the words of this law (Deut. 31:24); the last words of David (2 Sam. 23:1); the prayers of David are ended (Ps. 72:20); the words of Job are ended (Job 31:40); thus far are the words of Jeremiah (Jer. 51:64).

70 Middle

This is Jerusalem, I have set her in the centre of the nations (Ezek. 5:5); they crucified two men, one on either side and Jesus in between (John 19:18).

AVERAGE, see 30.

71 Continuity

SEQUENCE, see 65.

72 Discontinuity

SEPARATING, see 46.

73 Ranking

The brothers were positioned according to age (Gen. 43:33; 44:12); according to their birth (Exod. 28:10).

74 Gathering

A Gathering in general
He who does not gather with me scatters (Matt. 12:30; Luke 11:23); he who reaps gets wages and gathers fruit for eternal life (John 4:36); gathering where you did not scatter (Matt. 25:24, 26).

B Gathering people
B1 Assembling people
B1a Friends and neighbours gathering
The whole city gathered at the door (Mark 1:33); calling together friends and neighbours (Luke 15:6, 9); Demetrius gathered the craftsmen (Acts 19:25).

B1b Leaders assembling
Gathering the elders of Israel (Exod. 3:16; 4:29; Deut. 31:28; 2 Kgs. 23:1); Herod assembled the chief priests and scribes (Matt. 2:4); the scribes and elders had gathered (Matt. 26:57); the chief priests, elders and scribes were assembled (Mark 14:53); the council of elders gathered (Luke 22:66); Pilate called together the chief priests, rulers and the people (Luke 23:13); the rulers, elders and scribes were gathered in Jerusalem (Acts 4:5); the apostles and elders met to consider this matter (Acts 15:6).

B1c Mustering troops
Joshua mustered the people (Josh. 8:10); all Israel were mustered (2 Kgs. 3:6); they assembled them at the place called Armageddon (Rev. 16:16).

B1d Convocations
Holy convocations on days one and seven (Exod. 12:16); trumpets to signal an assembly (Num. 10:3, 7); the Lord's holy convocations are these (Lev. 23:2, 37); Moses declared the Lord's convocations (Lev. 23:44); I do not delight in your solemn assemblies (Amos 5:21); I cannot endure iniquity and solemn assembly (Isa. 1:13).

B1e Church gatherings
Where two or three are gathered together in Christ's name (Matt. 18:20); do not neglect to meet together (Heb. 10:25); at Pentecost they were all together in one place (Acts 2:1); gathered for prayer (Acts 4:31; 12:12); they were all together in Solomon's portico (Acts 5:12); on the first day of the week they gathered to break bread (Acts 20:7); they gathered the congregation together and delivered the letter (Acts 15:30); they gathered the church and declared what God had done (Acts 14:27).

B1f Gathered by God

Gather those who have made a covenant with me (Ps. 50:5); he gathered in the redeemed from all the lands (Ps. 107:2-3); I will gather my sheep (Jer. 23:3); I longed to gather your children as a hen gathers her chicks (Matt. 23:37; Luke 13:34); Jesus died to gather into one the children of God scattered abroad (John 11:52); he will gather his elect from the four winds (Matt. 24:31; Mark 13:27); bringing everything together in Christ (Eph. 1:10); our gathering together to meet him (2 Thess. 2:1); unto him shall be the assembling of his people (Gen. 49:10); you have come to the assembly of the firstborn (Heb. 12:23).

B1g Gathering Israel

Gather us from the nations (1 Chr. 16:35; Ps. 106:47); I will gather you (Mic. 2:12; Zeph. 3:20); he who scattered Israel will gather them (Jer. 31:10); the Lord gathers the dispersed of Israel (Isa. 56:8); when I gather them from the lands (Ezek. 39:27); I gathered them again to their own land (Ezek. 39:28); God will gather his people: from the nations where they have been scattered (Deut. 30:3, 4; Neh. 1:9; Isa. 11:11-12; Jer. 29:14; Ezek. 11:17); from Egypt and Assyria (Zech. 10:10); from east and west (Isa. 43:5); from the ends of the earth (Jer. 31:8).

B2 Crowds

B2a Crowds around Jesus

The crowds were seeking him (Luke 4:42); the crowd was waiting for him (Luke 8:40; 9:37); the crowd went out to meet him (John 12:18); the crowd ran up to him (Mark 9:15); great crowds brought sick people to him (Matt. 15:30); a great crowd came to him (Mark 3:8); the great crowd came, not just because of Jesus, but also to see Lazarus (John 12:9); great crowds followed Jesus (Matt. 4:25; 8:1; 14:13; 19:2; 20:29; Mark 3:7-8; 5:24; Luke 9:11; 14:25; 23:27; John 6:2); a great crowd gathered round him (Mark 5:21; Luke 8:4); the crowds were increasing (Luke 11:29); the crowds pressed round him (Luke 5:1; 8:42, 45); a crowd was sitting round him (Mark 3:32); a large crowd went with him (Luke 7:11); a large crowd around the disciples (Mark 9:14); crowds before and behind were shouting out (Matt. 21:9); the crowd tried to touch him (Luke 6:19); he was leaving Jericho with his disciples and a big crowd (Mark 10:46); the blind man heard a crowd going by (Luke 18:36); The crowds were amazed at his teaching (Matt. 7:28; 22:33; Mark 11:18); at his authority (Matt. 9:8); at his healing (Matt. 12:23; 15:31; Mark 2:12).

B2b Teaching the crowds

Seeing the crowds he had compassion on them (Matt. 9:36; 14:14; 15:32; Mark 6:34; 8:1-2); Jesus called the crowd to him (Matt. 15:10; Mark 7:14; 8:34); they came to the crowd (Matt. 17:14); Jesus spoke to the crowds (Matt. 11:7; 13:2; 23:1; 26:55; Mark 2:13; 4:1; 10:1; Luke 5:3; 7:24); crowds gathered to hear him and be healed (Luke 5:15; 6:17-18); the crowd heard him gladly (Mark 12:37).

B2c Disadvantages of crowds

So many gathered they trod on one another (Luke 12:1); so many were gathered together there was no room (Mark 2:2); they could not get near him because of the crowd (Mark 2:4; Luke 5:19; 8:19); Zaccheus could not see for the crowd (Luke 19:3); a crowd gathered so they could not even eat (Mark 3:20; 6:31); Jesus saw the crowd making a tumult (Matt. 9:23); Herod feared the crowd, who considered John a prophet (Matt. 14:5); we are afraid of the crowd (Matt. 21:26); lest the crowd press on him (Mark 3:9).

B2d Crowds avoided

When Jesus saw the crowds he went up into a mountain (Matt. 5:1); when he saw crowds he gave orders to depart (Matt. 8:18); he sent the crowds away (Matt. 14:22; 15:39; Mark 6:45; 8:10); leaving the crowd, they crossed over (Mark 4:36); when the crowd had been put outside, Jesus went in (Matt. 9:25); he left the crowds and went into the house (Matt. 13:36); Jesus took the man aside from the crowd (Mark 7:33).

B2e Evil and crowds

Do not follow a crowd to do evil (Exod. 23:2); a great crowd with swords and clubs (Matt. 26:47; Mark 14:43); the high priests and elders persuaded the crowds (Matt. 27:20; Mark 15:11); Pilate wished to satisfy the crowd (Mark 15:15).

C Other gathering

C1 Gathering creatures

It is not time to gather the cattle (Gen. 29:7); when all the flocks were gathered the sheep were watered (Gen. 29:3, 8); where the corpse is, the eagles will gather (Matt. 24:28; Luke 17:37); they gathered the frogs in heaps (Exod. 8:14).

C2 Gathering food

He who gathers in summer is a wise son (Prov. 10:5); let them gather all the food of these good years (Gen. 41:35); he gathered all the food of the seven years of plenty (Gen. 41:48); gathering manna (Exod. 16:16-27); gathering quail (Num. 11:32); he will gather the wheat into his barn (Luke 3:17); gather the wheat into my barn (Matt. 13:30); gather up the fragments left over (John 6:12).

C3 Gathering other things

A time to gather stones (Eccles. 3:5); they gathered stones to make a heap (Gen. 31:46); gathering stubble for straw (Exod. 5:7, 12); do you want us to go and collect up the weeds? (Matt. 13:28-30); the weeds are gathered and burned (Matt. 13:40); let the water under the heavens be collected together (Gen. 1:9); God called the gathering of the waters seas (Gen. 1:10); God gathers the waters of the sea as in a bottle [heap] (Ps. 33:7).

75 Scattering

A Scattering in general

He who does not gather with me scatters (Matt. 12:30; Luke 11:23); gathering where you did not scatter (Matt. 25:24, 26); one scatters yet increases (Prov. 11:24); he scatters abroad, he gives to the poor (2 Cor. 9:9).

B Scattering people

B1 Scattering the peoples

Scatter them! (Ps. 59:11); may God's enemies be scattered (Num. 10:35; Ps. 68:1); evildoers will be scattered (Ps. 92:9); he sent out his arrows and scattered them (2 Sam. 22:15; Ps. 18:14); God has scattered the proud (Luke 1:51); you scattered your enemies (Ps. 89:10); God scattered the people of Babel all over the earth (Gen. 11:4-9).

B2 Scattering followers

The people were scattering from Saul (1 Sam. 13:8); no one will be with you by tonight (2 Sam. 19:7); followers of Theudas were scattered (Acts 5:36); followers of Judas of Galilee were scattered (Acts 5:37).

B3 Scattering Israel

God would scatter disobedient Israel among the nations (Lev. 26:33; Deut. 4:27; 28:64; Ps. 106:27; Jer. 9:16; Ezek. 12:15; 20:23; Zech. 10:9); the Lord will scatter you from one end of the earth to the other (Deut. 28:64); you have scattered us among the nations (Ps. 44:11); I scattered them among the nations (Ezek. 36:19; Zech. 7:14); though I scattered them I was a sanctuary to them (Ezek. 11:16); a people scattered and dispersed (Esther 3:8); Simeon and Levi would be scattered in Israel (Gen. 49:7); the Dispersion among the Greeks (John 7:35); why should the Jews be scattered and the remnant perish? (Jer. 40:15); they have scattered my people among the nations (Joel 3:2); these are the horns which have scattered Judah, Israel and Jerusalem (Zech. 1:19).

B4 Scattered like sheep
Israel scattered like sheep without a shepherd (1 Kgs. 22:17; 2 Chr. 18:16); scattered because there was no shepherd (Ezek. 34:5); the shepherds have become stupid and their flock is scattered (Jer. 10:21); woe to the shepherds who are scattering my sheep (Jer. 23:1); you have scattered my flock (Jer. 23:2); strike the shepherd and the sheep will be scattered (Zech. 13:7; Matt. 26:31; Mark 14:27); the wolf snatches the sheep and scatters them (John 10:12).

B5 The church scattered
The church was scattered after the death of Stephen (Acts 8:1; 11:19); you will be scattered (John 16:32); those scattered preached the message (Acts 8:4); the church referred to as the Dispersion (Jas. 1:1; 1 Pet. 1:1); Jesus died to gather into one the children of God scattered abroad (John 11:52).

C Sowing seed
C1 Sowing in general
Sow your land (Gen. 47:23); sow your seed morning and evening (Eccles. 11:6); whatever a man sows, that he will reap (Gal. 6:7-8); he who sows sparingly will reap sparingly (2 Cor. 9:6); they sow the wind and reap the whirlwind (Hos. 8:7); happy you who sow beside all waters (Isa. 32:20); one sows and another reaps (John 4:37); those who sow in tears will reap with joy (Ps. 126:5-6); the treader of grapes will overtake him who sows seed (Amos 9:13); what you sow does not come to life unless it dies (1 Cor. 15:36); it is sown a perishable body and raised imperishable (1 Cor. 15:42-4).

C2 Sowing in vain
You will sow seed in vain (Lev. 26:16); the evil one snatches away what was sown in his heart (Matt. 13:19); you will sow but not reap (Mic. 6:15).

C3 Sowing good
Sow righteousness (Hos. 10:12); he who sows righteousness gets a sure reward (Prov. 11:18); the fruit of righteousness is sown in peace (Jas. 3:18); sowing spiritual good (1 Cor. 9:11); sowing as a picture of generous giving (2 Cor. 9:10).

C4 Parables of sowing
The parable of the sower (Matt. 13:3-8; Mark 4:3-9; Luke 8:5-8); with interpretation (Matt. 13:18-23; Mark 4:14-20; Luke 8:11-15); the parable of the tares (Matt. 13:24-30); interpreted (Matt. 13:37-43); the parable of the mustard seed (Matt. 13:31-2; Mark 4:31-2; Luke 13:18-19); the parable of the sprouting seed (Mark 4:26-9); while men were asleep his enemy sowed tares (Matt. 13:25); a grain of mustard seed which a man sowed in his field (Matt. 13:31); he who sows the good seed is the Son of man (Matt. 13:37); the enemy who sowed the weeds is the devil (Matt. 13:39); the sower sows the word (Mark 4:14); unless a grain of wheat falls into the ground (John 12:24).

C5 Not sowing
The Rechabites were not to sow seed (Jer. 35:7); do not sow among thorns (Jer. 4:3); he who watches the wind will not sow (Eccles. 11:4); the birds of the air neither sow nor reap (Matt. 6:26); reaping where you did not sow (Matt. 25:24-6; Luke 19:21-2).

D Sprinkling
The priest shall sprinkle the blood around the altar (Lev. 1:5); Moses sprinkled blood on the people (Exod. 24:8); sprinkling defiled people with the blood of goats and bulls (Heb. 9:13); he sprinkled the tent and the vessels with the blood (Heb. 9:21); the sprinkled blood which speaks better things than the blood of Abel

(Heb. 12:24); for obedience to Jesus Christ and for sprinkling by his blood (1 Pet. 1:2); blood sprinkled seven times: on the healed leper (Lev. 14:7); on the cleansed house (Lev. 14:51); on the propitiatory and in front of it (Lev. 16:14, 15); to cleanse the altar (Lev. 16:19); towards the front of the tent of meeting (Num. 19:4); Moses sprinkled the altar with oil (Lev. 8:11); Moses sprinkled oil and blood on Aaron and his sons and their garments (Lev. 8:30); oil sprinkled seven times before the Lord (Lev. 14:16, 27); sprinkling the water of impurity (Num. 19:13, 20-1); the water sprinkled with hyssop (Num. 19:18); sprinkling the water on the third day and on the seventh (Num. 19:19); I will sprinkle clean water on you and you will be clean (Ezek. 36:25).

76 Meeting place
SYNAGOGUE, see 192F.

77 Class
A Kinds of living things
Fish of many kinds, like the fish of the Great Sea (Ezek. 47:10); living things according to their kind: plants with their seed (Gen. 1:11-12); sea creatures (Gen. 1:21); land creatures (Gen. 1:24-5); birds (Gen. 1:21; 6:20; 7:14); beasts (Gen. 1:25; 6:20; 7:14); creeping things (Gen. 1:25; 6:20; 7:14); all creatures (Gen. 7:14); the falcon (Lev. 11:14); every raven (Lev. 11:15; Deut. 14:14); the hawk (Lev. 11:16; Deut. 14:15); the heron (Lev. 11:19; Deut. 14:18); kites (Deut. 14:13); locusts (Lev. 11:22); the lizard (Lev. 11:29).

B What kind?
What kind of men were those you killed? (Judg. 8:18); if he were a prophet he would know what kind of woman this is (Luke 7:39); Jesus indicated the kind of death by which he would die (John 12:33); what kind of a house will you build for me? (Acts 7:49).
WHAT NATURE? see 5.

78 Inclusion
IN ONE ANOTHER, see 224B.

79 Generality
On whom has not your evil come? (Nahum 3:19); no temptation has overtaken you except what is common to man (1 Cor. 10:13).
ALL, see 54.

80 Self
A Oneself
SELFISHNESS, see 932.
A1 God himself
I spread out the heavens and earth by myself (Isa. 44:24); God's own arm brought salvation (Isa. 59:16); my own arm worked salvation for me (Isa. 63:5); I myself will seek for my sheep (Ezek. 34:11); by myself I have sworn (Gen. 22:16); God swore by himself (Heb. 6:13).
A2 Acting for oneself
Looking to yourself lest you also be tempted (Gal. 6:1); the high priest makes atonement for himself (Lev. 16:6, 11, 17, 24); if you are wise, you are wise for yourself (Prov. 9:12); these hands ministered to my needs and to those with me (Acts 20:34); if I have erred, that is my business (Job 19:4); as for me and my house, we will serve the Lord (Josh. 24:15).
A3 Acting as if to oneself
Love your neighbour as yourself (Lev. 19:18; Matt. 19:19; 22:39; Mark 12:31; Luke 10:27; Rom. 13:9; Gal. 5:14; Jas. 2:8); love the sojourner as yourself (Lev. 19:34); he who loves his wife loves himself (Eph. 5:28).

A4 Speaking from oneself
Prophesy against the prophets who prophesy out of their own minds (Ezek. 13:2); woe to the foolish prophets who follow their own spirit and have seen nothing (Ezek. 13:3); what do you say about yourself? (John 1:22); he will know whether the teaching is from God or whether I speak from myself (John 7:17); he who speaks from himself seeks his own glory (John 7:18).

A5 On oneself
On me be your curse (Gen. 27:13); every one will be put to death for his own sin (Deut. 24:16).

B Not me / us
Lest Israel say, 'My own hand has saved me' (Judg. 7:2); it is not in me (Gen. 41:16); it was not revealed because I have more wisdom than any other (Dan. 2:30); a man's way is not in himself (Jer. 10:23); not to us but to your name be glory (Ps. 115:1); it is not you who speak, but the Spirit of your Father (Matt. 10:20); it is no longer I that live, but Christ lives in me (Gal. 2:20); I laboured more than all, yet not I but the grace of God with me (1 Cor. 15:10); the surpassing power is from God, not from us (2 Cor. 4:7); you are saved not of yourselves, but by the gift of God (Eph. 2:8); we do not preach ourselves but Christ Jesus as Lord (2 Cor. 4:5); it is no longer I that do it but sin which dwells within me (Rom. 7:17, 20).

UNSELFISHNESS, see 931.

81 Principle
The principle of faith (Rom. 3:27); the principle of the Spirit of life (Rom. 8:2); a principle that when I want to do good, evil is at hand (Rom. 7:21); the principle of sin (Rom. 7:23; 8:2).

82 Multiplicity
Jesus healed every kind of disease and sickness (Matt. 4:23; 9:35); he gave his disciples authority to heal every kind of disease and sickness (Matt. 10:1); men from every kind of nation (Acts 2:5); gathering fish of every kind (Matt. 13:47); they are full of all kinds of uncleanness (Matt. 23:27); sin worked in me all kinds of covetousness (Rom. 7:8); the wrath of God is against all kinds of wickedness of men (Rom. 1:18).

83 Conformity
IMITATING, see 20.

A Normal behaviour
Women exchanged natural relations for unnatural (Rom. 1:26); men abandoned natural relations with women (Rom. 1:27).

B Conforming
Conformed to the image of his Son (Rom. 8:29); conformed to his death (Phil. 3:10); conformity with the body of his glory (Phil. 3:21); all things to all men (1 Cor. 9:19-22).

C Example
C1 Christ's example
I have given you an example [foot-washing] that you should do as I have done (John 13:15); Christ suffered, leaving you an example (1 Pet. 2:21); in me Christ demonstrated his patience as an example (1 Tim. 1:16).
C2 Believers' example
Observe those who live according to my example (Phil. 3:17); we offer ourselves as a model for you (2 Thess. 3:9); you became an example to all the believers in Macedonia and Achaia (1 Thess. 1:7); the prophets were an example of suffering and patience (Jas. 5:10); these things happened as examples for us (1 Cor. 10:6).

C3 Be an example
Be an example to believers (1 Tim. 4:12); show yourself to be an example of good deeds (Titus 2:7); elders should be examples to the flock (1 Pet. 5:3).
C4 Warning examples
These things happened to them as an example (1 Cor. 10:11); Sodom and Gomorrah are an example (Jude 7).

84 Nonconformity
A Do not be conformed
Do not be conformed to this age (Rom. 12:2); do not be conformed to your former ignorant passions (1 Pet. 1:14).

B Unnatural
Women exchanged natural relations for unnatural (Rom. 1:26); they receive the penalty of their perversion (Rom. 1:27); if you were cut off from a wild olive tree and grafted in contrary to nature (Rom. 11:24).
HOMOSEXUALITY, see 951D.

C Wild
A wild donkey of a man, against everyone (Gen. 16:12); you, a wild olive shoot, grafted in (Rom. 11:17); they are wild waves of the sea (Jude 13).

85 Number
Do not reduce the number of bricks to be made (Exod. 5:8, 18); I would declare to him the number of my steps (Job 31:37); the number of the beast (Rev. 13:17; 15:2); according to the number of people: take a lamb (Exod. 12:4); gather manna (Exod. 16:16); take an inheritance (Num. 26:53-4; 33:54); give the Levites cities (Num. 35:8); God set boundaries (Deut. 32:8); Job offered burnt offerings (Job 1:5).
IN PROPORTION, see 12.

86 Counting
A Counting in general
How many loaves do you have? (Matt. 15:34; Mark 6:38; 8:5); how many baskets of broken pieces did you take up? (Matt. 16:9, 10; Mark 8:19, 20); how many times shall my brother sin and I forgive? (Matt. 18:21).

B God counting
God counts the stars (Ps. 147:4); God counts my steps (Job 14:16; 31:4); you have kept count of my wanderings (Ps. 56:8); the hairs of your head are all numbered (Matt. 10:30; Luke 12:7); God has numbered your kingdom and put an end to it (Dan. 5:26).

C Counting people
C1 Censuses
When a census is taken, each must pay a ransom (Exod. 30:12); census of the firstborn of Israel (Num. 3:40, 42-3); the people were numbered (Judg. 21:9); Saul numbered the men (1 Sam. 11:8; 13:15); Joab began the count but did not finish (1 Chr. 27:24); Joab did not number Levi and Benjamin (1 Chr. 21:6); the numbers of people returning from exile in Babylon (Ezra 2:2-67); this was the first census (Luke 2:2); everyone went to be registered in his own city (Luke 2:3); Joseph went to be enrolled with Mary (Luke 2:5); in the days of the census (Acts 5:37); censuses taken by: Moses (Exod. 38:25-6; Num. 1:2-46; 26:2-4, 63, 64); Saul (1 Sam. 15:4); David (2 Sam. 24:1-2, 4; 1 Chr. 21:1-2; 27:1-24); Solomon (2 Chr. 2:17); Amaziah (2 Chr. 25:5); Caesar Augustus (Luke 2:1-5).
C2 Counting Levites
The Levites were not counted with the others (Num. 1:47-9; 2:33); the Levites were counted (Num. 3:15-16, 22, 28, 34, 39; 4:46-9; 26:57-62; 1 Chr. 23:3, 24, 27).

C3 Counting soldiers
Soldiers being numbered off (Num. 31:49; 1 Sam. 14:17; 2 Sam. 18:1); the numbers of those equipped for war (1 Chr. 12:23-37).

D Counting things
D1 Counting money
They counted the money in the chest (2 Kgs. 12:10); count the money brought into the temple (2 Kgs. 22:4).

D2 Counting articles
Count the towers of Zion (Ps. 48:12); where is he who counted the towers? (Isa. 33:18); you counted the houses of Jerusalem (Isa. 22:10); counting materials for the tabernacle (Exod. 38:21); counting utensils for the temple (1 Chr. 9:28); counting articles from the temple (Ezra 1:8-11).

D3 Counting few things
I can count all my bones (Ps. 22:17); the trees will be so few that a child could write them down (Isa. 10:19); teach us to number our days (Ps. 90:12).

MEASUREMENT, see 465.

E Uncountable
Count the stars, if you can (Gen. 15:5); your descendants will not be able to be counted (Gen. 16:10); if one can count the dust, your descendants can be counted (Gen. 13:16); who can count the dust of Jacob? (Num. 23:10); a people who cannot be counted (1 Kgs. 3:8); their enemies could not be counted (Judg. 6:5); so many sacrifices they could not be counted (1 Kgs. 8:5; 2 Chr. 5:6); who can count the clouds by wisdom? (Job 38:37); the sand of the sea which cannot be counted (Gen. 32:12; Hos. 1:10); what is lacking cannot be counted (Eccles. 1:15); your deeds and thoughts are uncountable (Ps. 40:5).

NUMEROUS, see 104.

87 List

SEQUENCE, see 65.
WRITING, see 586.

88 One

A One God
A1 God is one
The Lord our God is one Lord (Deut. 6:4; Mark 12:29); God is one (Job 23:13; Mark 12:32; Rom. 3:30; Gal. 3:20; 1 Tim. 2:5); even the demons believe there is one God (Jas. 2:19); one God and Father (1 Cor. 8:6; Eph. 4:6); one Lord Jesus Christ (1 Cor. 8:6); by one Spirit we were all baptised into one body (1 Cor. 12:13).

A2 God alone
The only true God (John 17:3); the only God (John 5:44; 1 Tim. 1:17; Jude 25); the only wise God (Rom. 16:27); the only ruler (1 Tim. 6:15); there is no God but one (1 Cor. 8:4); I have trodden the wine press alone (Isa. 63:3); the Lord alone guided him (Deut. 32:12); him only shall you serve (Matt. 4:10; Luke 4:8); who can forgive sins but God alone? (Luke 5:21).

NO OTHER GOD, see 21A.

A3 One with God
I and the Father are one (John 10:30); that they may be one even as we are one (John 17:22).

B One person
B1 Only child
Your only son (Gen. 22:2, 12, 16); Jephthah's only child (Judg. 11:34); the only son of a widow (Luke 7:12); Jairus had an only daughter (Luke 8:42); the man's only son (Luke 9:38); the only son before my mother (Prov. 4:3); Abraham offered up his only son (Heb. 11:17).

B2 Only Son of God
Glory as of the only begotten of the Father (John 1:14); the only begotten God (John 1:18); God's only begotten Son (John 3:16; 1 John 4:9); he has not believed in the name of the only begotten Son of God (John 3:18).

B3 Only one person
When Abraham was one I called him (Isa. 51:2); Abraham was only one person, yet he inherited the land (Ezek. 33:24); from one man were born descendants as many as the stars (Heb. 11:12); I only am left (1 Kgs. 18:22; 19:10, 14; Rom. 11:3); you cross sea and land to make one proselyte (Matt. 23:15); no one shall be put to death on the evidence of one witness (Num. 35:30; Deut. 17:6; 19:15); through one man sin entered the world (Rom. 5:12); by the transgression of the one the many died (Rom. 5:15); through the transgression of the one, death reigned through that one (Rom. 5:17); by one man's disobedience many were made sinners (Rom. 5:19); the gift by the grace of that one man (Rom. 5:15); they will reign in life through the one, Jesus Christ (Rom. 5:17); by the obedience of one many will be made righteous (Rom. 5:19); one mediator between God and man, the man Christ Jesus (1 Tim. 2:5).

B4 Isolated person
The leper has to live alone (Lev. 13:46); a true widow who is left all alone (1 Tim. 5:5); Jacob was left alone (Gen. 32:24); they saw no one but Jesus alone (Matt. 17:8; Mark 9:8; Luke 9:36); when evening came Jesus was there on his own (Matt. 14:23); the boat was out on the sea and he was alone on the land (Mark 6:47); you will be scattered and will leave me alone (John 16:32); unless a grain of wheat falls into the ground and dies it remains alone (John 12:24); it is not good for the man to be alone (Gen. 2:18); God gives the lonely a home (Ps. 68:6).

ISOLATION, see 883B.

B5 Acting alone
There was no one with him when Joseph made himself known to his brothers (Gen. 45:1); rebuke your brother on his own (Matt. 18:15); why do you sit alone from morning to evening? (Exod. 18:14); why did you go to war without us? (Judg. 12:1); why are you alone? (1 Sam. 21:1); if I have eaten my morsel alone (Job 31:17); Jesus went to pray alone (Matt. 14:23; Luke 9:18); Lord, do you not care that my sister has left me to serve alone? (Luke 10:40); apart from me you can do nothing (John 15:5).

C One flesh
The two will become one flesh (Gen. 2:24; Matt. 19:5; Mark 10:8; 1 Cor. 6:16; Eph. 5:31); they are no longer two but one (Matt. 19:6).

SEXUAL UNION, see 45C.

D One group
D1 Unified people
He made from one [man] every nation of men (Acts 17:26); they are one people and all have the one language (Gen. 11:6); we will become one people with you (Gen. 34:16, 22); I will give them one heart (Jer. 32:39; Ezek. 11:19); when brothers live together in unity (Ps. 133:1); he who plants and he who waters are one (1 Cor. 3:8).

D2 A solitary people
Israel dwells by itself, not reckoned among the nations (Num. 23:9); a nation living alone (Jer. 49:31).

D3 One church
We who are many are one body (Rom. 12:5); one body (1 Cor. 10:17; 12:20; Eph. 2:16; 4:4; Col. 3:15); as the body is one yet has many limbs, so is Christ (1 Cor. 12:12-13); Jew and Gentile made one (Eph. 2:14-15); all one in Christ Jesus (Gal. 3:28); Jesus died to gather into one the children of God (John 11:52); that they may be one even as we are one (John 17:11, 21-3); one flock, one shepherd (John 10:16); eager to preserve the unity of

the Spirit in the bond of peace (Eph. 4:3); the unity of
the faith (Eph. 4:13); love is the perfect bond of unity
(Col. 3:14); the believers were of one heart and mind
(Acts 4:32).

E One thing

You lack one thing (Mark 10:21; Luke 18:22); judgement
following one trespass brought condemnation (Rom.
5:16); one act of righteousness brought justification and
life to all (Rom. 5:18); one transgression brought
condemnation to all (Rom. 5:18); one language and one
set of words (Gen. 11:1); they are one people and have
one language (Gen. 11:6); one Lord, one faith, one
baptism (Eph. 4:5).

F Only once

Once for all Christ appeared to put away sins (Heb.
9:26); the death that he died, he died to sin, once for all
(Rom. 6:10); once for all Christ offered himself as a
sacrifice (Heb. 7:27); Christ was offered once to bear
the sins of many (Heb. 9:28); an offering once for all
(Heb. 10:10); once for all Christ entered the holy place
(Heb. 9:12); one offering (Heb. 10:12, 14); contend for
the faith once for all delivered to the saints (Jude 3);
you were once for all informed (Jude 5).

89 Accompanying

A God accompanying

A1 God with Christ

The Word was with God (John 1:1); he was in the
beginning with God (John 1:2); God was with Jesus
(Acts 10:38); I am not alone, for the Father is with me
(John 16:32); no one could do these signs if God were
not with him (John 3:2); he who sent me is with me
(John 8:29); the eternal life which was with the Father
(1 John 1:2).

A2 God with people

A2a God is with you

Immanuel, God with us (Isa. 7:14; 8:10; Matt. 1:23); the
Lord is with you when you are with him (2 Chr. 15:2);
he is at my right hand (Ps. 16:8); he who is with us is
greater than the one with him (2 Chr. 32:7); you are
with me (Ps. 23:4); you know the Spirit, for he dwells
with you and will be in you (John 14:17); the kingdom
of God is in your midst (Luke 17:21); my Spirit is
among you (Hag. 2:5); God will dwell among them
(Rev. 21:3); he will declare that God is among you (1
Cor. 14:25); may the Lord be with you as he was with
Moses (Josh. 1:17); may the Lord be with you as he was
with my father (1 Sam. 20:13).

A2b God always with you

You set me in your presence for ever (Ps. 41:12); I set
the Lord continually before me (Ps. 16:8); when I
awake I am still with you (Ps. 139:18); I am always with
God (Ps. 73:23); the God of peace will be with you
(Phil. 4:9).

A2c God with you to help

God stands at the right hand of the needy (Ps. 109:31);
with us is the Lord to help us (2 Chr. 32:8); I am with
you to deliver you (Jer. 1:8, 19); when we pass through
the waters he will be with us (Isa. 43:2).

A2d God with specific people

God with: Abraham (Gen. 21:22); Asa (2 Chr. 15:9);
David (1 Sam. 16:18; 18:12, 14, 28; 20:13; 2 Sam. 5:10; 7:3,
9; 1 Chr. 11:9; 17:2); Gideon (Judg. 6:12-13, 16); Hezekiah
(2 Kgs. 18:7); Isaac (Gen. 26:28); Ishmael (Gen. 21:20);
Israel (Jer. 30:11); Jacob (Gen. 28:15, 20; 31:5; 35:3);
Jehoshaphat (2 Chr. 17:3); Jeremiah (Jer. 1:8, 19; 15:20;
20:11); Job (Job 29:5); Joseph (Gen. 39:2, 3, 21, 23; Acts
7:9); the house of Joseph (Judg. 1:22); Joshua (Deut.
31:23; Josh. 1:9; 6:27); Joshua as with Moses (Josh. 1:5;
3:7); each judge (Judg. 2:18; 2 Chr. 19:6); Mary (Luke
1:28); Paul (Acts 18:10);

Samuel (1 Sam. 3:19); Saul (1 Sam. 10:7; 20:13); Solomon
(1 Chr. 28:20; 2 Chr. 1:1); Solomon as with David (1 Kgs.
1:37).

A3 God goes with you

My presence will go with you (Exod. 33:14-16); go in
our midst (Exod. 34:9).

A4 Walking with God

Enoch walked with God (Gen. 5:22, 24); as did Noah
(Gen. 6:9); walk before me and be blameless (Gen.
17:1); the Lord before whom I walk (Gen. 24:40); God
before whom my fathers Abraham and Isaac walked
(Gen. 48:15); walk humbly with your God (Mic. 6:8).

B Christ with people

B1 Christ with people on earth

The Word became flesh and dwelt among us (John
1:14); have I been with you so long and you have not
known me? (John 14:9); among you stands one you do
not know (John 1:26); Jesus chose 12 that they might be
with him (Mark 3:14); the 12 were with him (Luke 8:1);
I desire that they may be with me (John 17:24); the
former demoniac wanted to be with him (Mark 5:18;
Luke 8:38); two thieves were crucified with him (Matt.
27:38, 44); Peter was accused of being with Jesus (Matt.
26:69, 71; Mark 14:67; Luke 22:56, 59; John 18:26); these
men had been with Jesus (Acts 4:13).

B2 Christ with people in spirit

Today you will be with me in paradise (Luke 23:43);
better to depart and be with Christ (Phil. 1:23);
preferring to be absent from the body and at home
with the Lord (2 Cor. 5:8); for ever with the Lord
(1 Thess. 4:17); I am with you always (Matt. 28:20);
where I am, there will my servant be (John 12:26); that
where I am you may be also (John 14:3); where two or
three are gathered together, there am I (Matt. 18:20).

B3 Christ going with people

Jesus took Peter, James and John with him (Matt. 17:1;
26:37; Mark 5:37; 9:2; 14:33; Luke 8:51; 9:28); Jesus took
the child's parents and those with him (Mark 5:40);
Jesus went with them to a place called Gethsemane
(Matt. 26:36); Jesus drew near and walked with them
(Luke 24:15); Jesus went with Jairus (Mark 5:24).

B4 Christ not always with people

You will not always have me with you (Matt. 26:11;
Mark 14:7; John 12:8); for a little longer I am with you
(John 7:33; 13:33); how long will I be with you? (Matt.
17:17; Mark 9:19; Luke 9:41).

C Angels accompanying

The Lord will come and all the holy ones with him
(Zech. 14:5); the Lord came with his holy myriads (Jude
14); when the Son of man comes in glory and all the
angels with him (Matt. 25:31).

D People with people

D1 Companionship

The woman you gave me to be with me (Gen. 3:12); do
two walk together without an appointment? (Amos
3:3); where you go I will go (Ruth 1:16-18); where the
king goes, there I will be (2 Sam. 15:21); I will remain
with the one this people have chosen (2 Sam. 16:18); I
will not leave you (2 Kgs. 2:2, 4, 6; 4:30); only Luke is
with me (2 Tim. 4:11); he who walks with wise men will
be wise (Prov. 13:20); Job goes in company with
evildoers (Job 34:8); bad company ruins good morals (1
Cor. 15:33); the companion of fools suffers harm (Prov.
13:20); a companion of gluttons shames his father
(Prov. 28:7); your rulers are companions of thieves
(Isa. 1:23).

D2 Living together

The land could not support them dwelling together
(Gen. 13:6); son, you are always with me (Luke 15:31);
one of the men who have accompanied us (Acts 1:21);
all who believed were together (Acts 2:44).

D3 Going together

Lot went with Abraham (Gen. 12:4; 13:1); Elijah went with Elisha (2 Kgs. 2:1, 6); we will return with you (Ruth 1:10-11); go with the men (Num. 22:20, 35; Acts 10:20; 11:12); Peter went with them (Acts 10:23); Saul wanted Samuel to return with him (1 Sam. 15:25-31); let my servants go with your servants (1 Kgs. 22:49); let us go with you, for we have heard that God is with you (Zech. 8:23); if someone forces you to go one mile, go with him two (Matt. 5:41); we will come with you (John 21:3); Barnabas wanted to take John Mark with them (Acts 15:37); Paul wanted Timothy to go with him (Acts 16:3).

D4 Not with people

Do not desire to be with evil men (Prov. 24:1); do not go with a hot-tempered man (Prov. 22:24); do not be with heavy drinkers of wine or gluttons (Prov. 23:20); he would not listen to her to lie with her or to be with her (Gen. 39:10); we forbade him because he does not follow us (Luke 9:49); Paul thought it best not to take John Mark with them (Acts 15:38).

NOT WITH, see 190.

E Not alone

They did not possess the land by their own sword (Ps. 44:3); a single witness will not do (Deut. 19:15); I do nothing of myself (John 8:28); I did not come of my own accord (John 8:42); I did not speak of my own accord (John 12:49); it is not alone [I judge], but I and he who sent me (John 8:16); he has not left me alone (John 8:29).

90 Two

A Two angels

Two cherubim of gold (Exod. 25:18; 37:7); two cherubim of olive wood (1 Kgs. 6:23); overlaid with gold (2 Chr. 3:10); the two angels came to Sodom (Gen. 19:1); two angels in white (Luke 24:4; John 20:12; Acts 1:10).

B Two people

B1 Two people in general

No one can serve two masters (Matt. 6:24; Luke 16:13); do two walk together without an appointment? (Amos 3:3); if two of you agree on earth, it shall be done (Matt. 18:19); two are better than one (Eccles. 4:9); if two lie together they keep warm (Eccles. 4:11); two men went up to the temple to pray (Luke 18:10); two men in the field, one taken and one left (Matt. 24:40; Luke 17:36); two men in one bed, one taken and one left (Luke 17:34).

B2 Two women

Lot's two daughters (Gen. 19:8, 30); Laban had two daughters (Gen. 29:16); the leech has two daughters (Prov. 30:15); two women grinding at the mill, one taken and one left (Matt. 24:41; Luke 17:35); two prostitutes came before Solomon (1 Kgs. 3:16); these women are two covenants (Gal. 4:24).

B3 Two sons

Abraham had two sons (Gal. 4:22); a man had two sons (Matt. 21:28-31; Luke 15:11); command that my two sons may sit to left and right of you (Matt. 20:21); the two sons of Zebedee (Matt. 26:37).

B4 Twins

Rebekah gave birth to twins (Gen. 25:24); Tamar bore twins to Judah (Gen. 38:27); the twin boys as figurehead (Acts 28:11); all of them bear twins (S. of S. 4:2; 6:6); twins of a gazelle (S. of S. 4:5; 7:3); Thomas called Didymus [the twin] (John 11:16; 20:24; 21:2).

B5 Two witnesses / prophets

The testimony of two men is true (John 8:17); two witnesses prophesying for 1260 days (Rev. 11:3); these two prophets had tormented those who dwell on the earth (Rev. 11:10); two sons of Belial to accuse Naboth (1 Kgs. 21:10, 13); two false witnesses accused Jesus (Matt. 26:60).

TWO OR THREE WITNESSES, see 90J.

B6 Two disciples

Jesus sent out the 12 two by two (Mark 6:7); the seventy were sent out two by two (Luke 10:1); the disciples sent two men to Peter (Acts 9:38); two going to Emmaus (Mark 16:12; Luke 24:13); two other disciples (John 21:2); two of John's disciples (Luke 7:19; John 1:35, 37).

B7 Two needy men

Two debtors (Luke 7:41); two demonised men (Matt. 8:28); two blind men (Matt. 9:27; 20:30); two thieves crucified with him (Matt. 27:38; Mark 15:27; Luke 23:32; John 19:18).

C Two animals

Two of all animals in the ark (Gen. 6:19; 7:8, 9, 15); two of unclean animals (Gen. 7:2); two lambs were sacrificed every day (Exod. 29:38-42; Num. 28:3); are not two sparrows sold for an assarion? (Matt. 10:29); five loaves and two fish (Matt. 14:17, 19; Mark 6:38, 41; Luke 9:13, 16; John 6:9).

D Two groups

Israel was divided into two parts (1 Kgs. 16:21); they will no longer be two nations (Ezek. 37:22); one new man in place of the two [Jew and Gentile] (Eph. 2:15).

E Two stone tablets

Two tablets (Exod. 31:18; 32:15; Deut. 4:13; 5:22; 9:17; 2 Chr. 5:10); two tablets of stone (Deut. 9:10, 11; 1 Kgs. 8:9); two tablets of the covenant (Deut. 9:15); two other tablets (Exod. 34:1, 4, 29; Deut. 10:1, 3).

F Two body parts

Each cherub had two faces (Ezek. 41:18); if anyone strikes you on the right cheek, turn to him the other also (Matt. 5:39); two wings to cover the face, two to cover the feet and two to fly (Isa. 6:2); two wings touching another creature and two covering their bodies (Ezek. 1:11); the woman was given the two wings of the great eagle (Rev. 12:14); a ram with two horns (Dan. 8:3, 7); a beast with two horns like a lamb (Rev. 13:11); better to enter life than thrown into hell with: two hands (Mark 9:43); two feet (Mark 9:45); two hands or feet (Matt. 18:8); two eyes (Matt. 18:9; Mark 9:47).

G Two garments

Two changes of clothes (2 Kgs. 5:22, 23); do not take two tunics (Matt. 10:10; Mark 6:9; Luke 9:3); let him who has two coats share with him who has none (Luke 3:11).

H Two intangible things

How long will you limp between two opinions? (1 Kgs. 18:21); on these two commandments depend all the law and the prophets (Matt. 22:40); I am hard-pressed between the two choices (Phil. 1:23); two unchangeable things (Heb. 6:18).

I Two and a half

The two and a half tribes have received their inheritance (Num. 34:15; Josh. 14:3).

J Two or three

The evidence of two or three witnesses needed for confirmation (Deut. 17:6; 19:15; Matt. 18:16; 2 Cor. 13:1; Heb. 10:28); an accusation against an elder requires two or three witnesses (1 Tim. 5:19); where two or three are gathered in my name (Matt. 18:20); only two, or at most three, speaking in tongues (1 Cor. 14:27); let two or three prophets speak (1 Cor. 14:29).

91 Double

A Double portion

The firstborn had a double portion (Deut. 21:17); Joseph shall have two portions (Ezek. 47:13); Hannah was given a double portion (1 Sam. 1:5); Elishah wanted a double portion of Elijah's spirit (2 Kgs. 2:9); a double portion of manna on the sixth day (Exod. 16:5, 22, 29); instead of shame you will have a double portion (Isa. 61:7); I will restore to you double (Zech. 9:12).

B Double money
Take double money (Gen. 43:12); they took double money (Gen. 43:15); elders who rule well should be given double honour [stipend] (1 Tim. 5:17).

C Double penalty
If what he stole is still alive, he shall pay double (Exod. 22:4); if a thief is caught he shall pay double (Exod. 22:7); she has received double for all her sins (Isa. 40:2); mix a double draught in the cup she mixed (Rev. 18:6); repay her double for her deeds (Rev. 18:6).
DOUBLY DEAD, see 361F2.
DOUBLE-MINDED, see 601A.

D Acting twice over
D1 Doing things twice
Do not go over the boughs of your olive tree again (Deut. 24:20); do not go over your vines again (Deut. 24:21); Pharaoh dreamed a second time (Gen. 41:5); the doubling of Pharaoh's dream (Gen. 41:32); they made Solomon king a second time (1 Chr. 29:22); the Lord appeared to Solomon a second time (1 Kgs. 9:2; 11:9); he has supplanted me twice (Gen. 27:36); Moses struck the rock twice (Num. 20:11); circumcise the people a second time (Josh. 5:2); he laid his hands upon his eyes again (Mark 8:25); this very night, before the cock crows twice (Mark 14:30); can he enter a second time into his mother's womb and be born? (John 3:4); that you might have a double benefit (2 Cor. 1:15).
D2 Speaking again
God speaks once or twice but no one notices (Job 33:14); the angel of the Lord called to him a second time (Gen. 22:15); the word of the Lord came to Jeremiah the second time (Jer. 13:3; 33:1); the word of the Lord came a second time to Haggai (Hag. 2:20); the voice came a second time (Acts 10:15); he went away and prayed for the second time (Matt. 26:42); a second time he said, 'Simon, do you love me?' (John 21:16); have nothing to do with a factious man after a first and second warning (Titus 3:10).
D3 Duplicating words
Abraham, Abraham! (Gen. 22:11); my son Absalom, Absalom my son, my son! (2 Sam. 19:4); Jacob, Jacob! (Gen. 46:2); Martha, Martha (Luke 10:41); Moses, Moses! (Exod. 3:4); Samuel, Samuel! (1 Sam. 3:10); Saul, Saul (Acts 9:4; 22:7; 26:14); my son, my son! (2 Sam. 18:33); my father, my father! (2 Kgs. 2:12; 13:14); long live the king! long live the king! (2 Sam. 16:16); Jerusalem, Jerusalem! (Matt. 23:37; Luke 13:34); altar, altar! (1 Kgs. 13:2); aha, aha! (Ps. 35:21; 40:15; 70:3); hear! hear! (2 Sam. 20:16); amen and amen (Ps. 41:13; 72:19; 89:52); my head! my head! (2 Kgs. 4:19); shall I kill them? shall I kill them? (2 Kgs. 6:21); crucify, crucify him! (Luke 23:21); away with him, away with him! (John 19:15); treason! treason! (2 Kgs. 11:14); the Lord, he is God, the Lord, he is God (1 Kgs. 18:39); grace, grace to it (Zech. 4:7).

E Two-sided
Tablets of stone written on both sides (Exod. 32:15); a scroll written on the inside and the back (Rev. 5:1); a two-edged sword (Judg. 3:16; Ps. 149:6; Prov. 5:4; Heb. 4:12; Rev. 1:16; 2:12).

92 Half

A Half the people
Half the people stood before Mount Gerizim and half before Mount Ebal (Josh. 8:33); half the people worked while half carried arms (Neh. 4:16, 21).

B Half of bodies
Abraham cut the animals in two (Gen. 15:10); they cut the calf in two and passed between the parts (Jer. 34:18-19); dividing the dead ox (Exod. 21:35); divide the child (1 Kgs. 3:25-6); some were sawn in two (Heb. 11:37).

C Half of districts
Mephibosheth and Ziba would divide the land (2 Sam. 19:29); even to half my kingdom (Esther 5:3, 6; 7:2; Mark 6:23).

D Half of things
Hanun cut the men's beards and garments in half (2 Sam. 10:4); the half was not told me (1 Kgs. 10:7; 2 Chr. 9:6); they will not live out half their days (Ps. 55:23).

93 Three
TWO OR THREE, see 90J.

A God in three persons
Baptised in the name of the Father, Son and Holy Spirit (Matt. 28:19); the grace of the Lord Jesus Christ, the love of God, the fellowship of the Spirit (2 Cor. 13:14); same Spirit . . . same Lord . . . same God (1 Cor. 12:4-6); one Spirit . . . one Lord . . . one God and Father (Eph. 4:4-6); foreknowledge of the Father, sanctification of the Spirit, to obey Jesus Christ (1 Pet. 1:2); him who is . . . the seven spirits . . . Jesus Christ (Rev. 1:4-5).

B Three men
Three men came to Abraham (Gen. 18:2); David's three mighty men (2 Sam. 23:9, 13-17, 19, 22-3; 1 Chr. 11:12, 15-19, 21, 24-5); Job's three friends (Job 2:11; 32:1, 3, 5); these three men, Noah, Daniel and Job, could only deliver themselves (Ezek. 14:14, 16, 18); was it not three men we cast bound into the fire? (Dan. 3:24).

C Three witnesses
Three witnesses, the Spirit, the water and the blood (1 John 5:8).
TWO OR THREE WITNESSES, see 90J.

D Three animals
Three kids (1 Sam. 10:3); three oxen facing each direction (1 Kgs. 7:25); three unclean spirits like frogs (Rev. 16:13).

E Three things
E1 Three cities
Three cities of refuge (Num. 35:14; Deut. 4:41; 19:2, 7, 9); three cities for the Gershonites (Josh. 21:32).
E2 Three gates
Three gates on each side, east, north, south and west (Ezek. 48:31-4; Rev. 21:13).
E3 Three other things
On the vine were three branches (Gen. 40:10); the three branches are three days (Gen. 40:12); three baskets on my head (Gen. 40:16); the three baskets are three days (Gen. 40:18); friend, lend me three loaves (Luke 11:5); yeast in three measures of meal (Matt. 13:33; Luke 13:21); Jonathan shooting three arrows (1 Sam. 20:20); Joab pierced Absalom with three spears (2 Sam. 18:14); let us make three booths (Matt. 17:4; Mark 9:5; Luke 9:33); we came to the Tres Tabernae [Three Taverns] (Acts 28:15); I offer you three things (2 Sam. 24:12; 1 Chr. 21:10).
THE THREE WOES, see 830B4.

F Three or four
Three or four things are never satisfied (Prov. 30:15); three or four things I do not understand (Prov. 30:18); three or four things make the earth quake (Prov. 30:21); three or four things are stately in their walk (Prov. 30:29); for three transgressions and for four: of Damascus (Amos 1:3); of Ammon (Amos 1:13); of Edom (Amos 1:11); of Gaza (Amos 1:6); of Israel (Amos

2:6); of Judah (Amos 2:4); of Moab (Amos 2:1); of Tyre (Amos 1:9).

94 Three times
A Communicating three times
You have deceived me three times (Judg. 16:15); you will deny me three times (Matt. 26:34, 75; Mark 14:30, 72; Luke 22:34, 61; John 13:38); he said to him for the third time, 'Simon, do you love me?' (John 21:17); he prayed for the third time, saying the same words (Matt. 26:44); Paul three times begged the Lord to remove his thorn in the flesh (2 Cor. 12:8); Peter was three times urged to eat (Acts 10:16; 11:10); the Lord called Samuel for the third time (1 Sam. 3:8); holy, holy, holy (Isa. 6:3); land, land, land (Jer. 22:29); woe, woe, woe (Rev. 8:13).
B Acting three times
The donkey turned aside three times (Num. 22:33); Balaam struck his donkey three times (Num. 22:28, 32); the king struck the arrows three times on the ground (2 Kgs. 13:18); three times Joash defeated Aram (2 Kgs. 13:19, 25); three times beaten with rods (2 Cor. 11:25); Elijah stretched himself on the child three times (1 Kgs. 17:21); this was the third time that Jesus appeared to his disciples (John 21:14); this is the third time I am coming to you (2 Cor. 12:14; 13:1); three times I was shipwrecked (2 Cor. 11:25).
C Threefold
A three-pronged fork (1 Sam. 2:13); a threefold cord is not easily broken (Eccles. 4:12); the sixth year will produce enough crops for three years (Lev. 25:21-2).

95 Third part
A One third
A third of mankind was killed by these three plagues (Rev. 9:18); burn one third of the hair at the centre of the city (Ezek. 5:2); scatter a third part of the hair to the wind (Ezek. 5:2); take one third of the hair and strike it with the sword (Ezek. 5:2); a third of the sea turned to blood (Rev. 8:8); the destruction of a third of the earth and trees (Rev. 8:7); of a third of rivers and waters (Rev. 8:10-11); of a third of stars (Rev. 12:4); of a third of sun, moon and stars (Rev. 8:12); a third of mankind (Rev. 9:15); a third of sea creatures died and a third of the ships were destroyed (Rev. 8:9); a third of the day and a third of the night were darkened (Rev. 8:12).
B Dividing into three things
Divide the land into three (Deut. 19:3); divide your hair into three parts (Ezek. 5:1-2); the great city split into three parts (Rev. 16:19).

96 Four
THREE OR FOUR, see 93F.
A Four angels
Four angels holding the four winds (Rev. 7:1); four angels bound at the Euphrates (Rev. 9:14-15); the angel cried with a loud voice to the four angels (Rev. 7:2).
B Four people
Four men carrying a paralytic (Mark 2:3); four daughters of Philip (Acts 21:9); I see four men loose, walking unharmed in the fire (Dan. 3:25); we have four men who are under a vow (Acts 21:23).
C Four groups
Abimelech's men in four companies (Judg. 9:34); Job saw four generations of his descendants (Job 42:16); Peter was guarded by four quaternions of soldiers (Acts 12:4).

D Four creatures
Four great beasts (Dan. 7:3, 17); the four living creatures (Ezek. 1:5-18; Rev. 4:6, 8; 5:6, 8; 6:1, 6; 14:3; 15:7; 19:4).
E Four things
E1 Four horns
Four horns on the corners of the altar (Exod. 27:2; 38:2); four horns projecting upward from the altar hearth (Ezek. 43:15, 20); a voice from the four horns of the golden altar (Rev. 9:13).
E2 Four cities
Four cities: of Simeon (Josh. 19:7); for the Kohathites (Josh. 21:18, 22, 24); for the Gershonites (Josh. 21:29, 31); for the Merarites (Josh. 21:35, 37, 39).
E3 Four sides / corners
The four corners of the earth (Isa. 11:12; Rev. 7:1; 20:8); make tassels on the four corners of your garment (Deut. 22:12); a sheet let down by its four corners (Acts 10:11; 11:5).
E4 Four winds
Come from the four winds and breathe on these slain (Ezek. 37:9); he will gather his elect from the four winds (Matt. 24:31; Mark 13:27); four angels holding back the four winds of the earth (Rev. 7:1).
E5 Four body parts
Each creature had four faces and four wings (Ezek. 1:6; 10:14, 21); a leopard with four wings and four heads (Dan. 7:6).

97 Four times
Fourfold restitution (2 Sam. 12:6);
if I have cheated anyone, I will repay it fourfold (Luke 19:8).

98 Quarter
A A fourth part
A quarter of a kab of dove's dung (2 Kgs. 6:25); who can number the fourth part of Israel? (Num. 23:10); there will be a wail from the Second Quarter (Zeph. 1:10).
B Rulers of a fourth
Authority over a quarter of the earth (Rev. 6:8); Herod the tetrarch (Matt. 14:1; Luke 3:19; 9:7); Herod was tetrarch of Galilee (Luke 3:1); Lysanias was tetrarch of Abilene (Luke 3:1); Philip was tetrarch of Ituraea and Trachonitis (Luke 3:1); Herod [Antipas] the tetrarch (Acts 13:1).
C Quartering
The river divided into four (Gen. 2:10); dividing Jesus' garments into four lots (John 19:23).

99 Five and over
A Five
A1 Five people
Five lords of the Philistines (Josh. 13:3; Judg. 3:3; 1 Sam. 6:4, 16, 18); five brothers presented to Pharaoh (Gen. 47:2); five husbands (John 4:18); five will chase 100 (Lev. 26:8); you will flee at the threat of five (Isa. 30:17); five foolish virgins and wise virgins (Matt. 25:2); suppose five of the 50 are lacking? (Gen. 18:28).
A2 Five animals
Five oxen for one stolen ox (Exod. 22:1); five mice (1 Sam. 6:4, 17-18); are not five sparrows sold for two assaria? (Luke 12:6); I have bought five yoke [pairs] of oxen and must try them out (Luke 14:19).
A3 Five things
Five sets of garments for Benjamin (Gen. 45:22); five tumours and mice (1 Sam. 6:4, 17-18); rule over five cities (Luke 19:19); five porticoes (John 5:2); five smooth stones (1 Sam. 17:40); five loaves (1 Sam. 21:3; Matt. 14:17, 19; 16:9; Mark 6:38, 41; 8:19; Luke 9:13, 16;

John 6:9, 13); five talents (Matt. 25:15, 16, 20); in the church I would rather speak five words with my mind (1 Cor. 14:19).

A4 Five times
Five times more for Benjamin (Gen. 43:34); five times the 39 lashes (2 Cor. 11:24).

A5 Five or six
You should have struck five or six times (2 Kgs. 13:19).

B Six
Six names on each stone (Exod. 28:10); six loaves in each row (Lev. 24:6); six stone jars (John 2:6); six fingers per hand and six toes per foot (2 Sam. 21:20; 1 Chr. 20:6); six wings for the seraphim (Isa. 6:2); the four living creatures, each having six wings (Rev. 4:8).
FIVE OR SIX, see 99A5.

C Seven
C1 Seven creatures
C1a Seven people / groups
Seven brothers (Matt. 22:25-8; Mark 12:20-3; Luke 20:29-33); seven sons of Sceva (Acts 19:14); your daughter-in-law is better than seven sons (Ruth 4:15); the barren woman has borne seven (1 Sam. 2:5); she who bore seven sons languishes (Jer. 15:9); seven kings (Rev. 17:10-11); seven churches of Asia (Rev. 1:4, 11, 20); seven women will take hold of one man (Isa. 4:1); select seven men of good reputation (Acts 6:3); Philip was one of the seven (Acts 21:8).

C1b Seven animals
Seven pairs of clean animals (Gen. 7:2); seven pairs of birds (Gen. 7:3); seven lambs at Beersheba (Gen. 21:28-31); seven fat cows (Gen. 41:2, 18, 20, 26); seven thin cows (Gen. 41:3, 19, 27); seven altars, bulls and rams (Num. 23:1, 4, 14, 29).

C1c Seven spirits
Seven spirits of God (Rev. 1:4; 3:1; 4:5; 5:6); seven angels (Rev. 1:20; 8:2, 6; 15:1, 6, 7, 8; 16:1; 17:1; 21:9); seven demons from Mary (Mark 16:9; Luke 8:2); seven spirits more evil than the first (Matt. 12:45; Luke 11:26).

C2 Seven lights
Seven lamps on the lampstand (Exod. 25:37; 37:23; Num. 8:2; Zech. 4:2); seven lampstands (Rev. 1:12, 20; 2:1); seven lamps with seven spouts for each lamp (Zech. 4:2); seven torches of fire (Rev. 4:5); seven stars (Rev. 1:16, 20; 2:1; 3:1).

C3 Seven body parts
Seven locks of Samson's hair (Judg. 16:13-14, 19); seven horns and eyes (Rev. 5:6); seven heads (Rev. 12:3; 13:1; 17:3, 7); these seven are the eyes of the Lord which range through all the earth (Zech. 4:10).

C4 Seven things
Seven plump ears of grain (Gen. 41:5, 7, 22, 24, 26); seven thin ears of grain (Gen. 41:6, 23, 27); seven loaves (Matt. 15:34, 36; 16:10; Mark 8:5, 6, 20); seven baskets left over (Matt. 15:37; Mark 8:8, 20); seven altars (Num. 23:1, 4, 14, 29); seven fresh bowstrings (Judg. 16:7-9); seven pillars for wisdom's house (Prov. 9:1); seven trumpets (Josh. 6:4, 6, 8, 13; Rev. 8:2, 6); seven bowls (Rev. 15:7; 16:1; 17:1; 21:9); seven thunders (Rev. 10:3, 4); seven seals (Rev. 5:1, 5; 6:1); seven diadems (Rev. 12:3); seven plagues (Rev. 15:1, 6, 8; 21:9); seven hills (Rev. 17:9).

C5 Seven times
Not seven times but 70 times seven times (Matt. 18:21-2); if seven times he says, 'I repent', you must forgive him (Luke 17:4); seven times: a righteous man falls and rises again (Prov. 24:16); march round Jericho (Josh. 6:4, 15); washing in Jordan (2 Kgs. 5:10, 14); Elijah sending his servant to see (1 Kgs. 18:43); the boy sneezing (2 Kgs. 4:35); silver refined (Ps. 12:6).

C6 Sevenfold
Sevenfold: vengeance on Cain's killer (Gen. 4:15, 24); punishment (Lev. 26:18, 21, 24, 28); a thief must repay (Prov. 6:31); brightness of the sun (Isa. 30:26); furnace heated (Dan. 3:19); ways your enemies will flee (Deut. 28:7); ways you will flee before your enemies (Deut. 28:25); return the taunts of our neighbours (Ps. 79:12).

D Eight
Jesse had eight sons (1 Sam. 16:10-11; 17:12); eight people saved in Noah's ark (1 Pet. 3:20); the beast which was and is not is an eighth king (Rev. 17:11).

E Nine
Were not ten cleansed? where are the nine? (Luke 17:17); nine and a half tribes (Num. 34:13; Josh. 14:2).

F Ten to ninety nine
F1 Ten
F1a Ten people / groups
Ten righteous? (Gen. 18:32); ten brothers (Gen. 42:3); ten women to bake your bread in one oven (Lev. 26:26); ten concubines (2 Sam. 15:16; 20:3); ten tribes (1 Kgs. 11:31, 35); ten kings (Dan. 7:24; Rev. 17:12); ten virgins (Matt. 25:1); ten lepers (Luke 17:12); ten servants each given one mina (Luke 19:13); am I not better than ten sons? (1 Sam. 1:8); the city which went forth 100 strong will have ten left (Amos 5:3); the ten were indignant (Matt. 20:24; Mark 10:41); were not ten cleansed? where are the nine? (Luke 17:17).

F1b Ten things
Ten commandments (Exod. 20:2-17; 34:28; Deut. 4:13; 10:4); rule over ten cities (Luke 19:17); ten shares in the king (2 Sam. 19:43); ten horns (Dan. 7:7, 20, 24; Rev. 12:3; 13:1; 17:3, 7, 12, 16); ten diadems (Rev. 13:1); a woman who loses one of her ten drachma (Luke 15:8).

F1c Ten times
Laban changed Jacob's wages ten times (Gen. 31:7, 41); ten times they put God to the test (Num. 14:22); the Jews who lived near them told us ten times (Neh. 4:12); ten times you have insulted me (Job 19:3).

F2 Eleven
11 of Jacob's children (Gen. 32:22); 11 disciples (Matt. 28:16; Mark 16:14; Luke 24:9, 33); 11 apostles (Acts 1:26; 2:14).

F3 Twelve
F3a Twelve disciples / apostles
12 disciples (Matt. 10:1; 11:1; 20:17); 12 apostles (Matt. 10:2; Mark 3:14; Luke 6:13); did I not choose you, the 12, and one of you is a devil? (John 6:70); the 12 summoned the body of disciples (Acts 6:2); he appeared to the 12 (1 Cor. 15:5); the 12 names of the 12 apostles of the Lamb (Rev. 21:14).

F3b Twelve beings / groups
12 sons of Jacob (Gen. 35:22); 12 brothers (Gen. 42:13, 32); 12 patriarchs (Acts 7:8); 12 leaders (Num. 1:44); 12 divisions of the army (1 Chr. 27:1-15); 12 angels (Rev. 21:12); 12 legions of angels (Matt. 26:53); 12 tribes of Israel (Gen. 49:28; Exod. 28:21; 39:14; Josh. 4:5, 8; 1 Kgs. 18:31; Matt. 19:28; Luke 22:30; Acts 26:7; Jas. 1:1; Rev. 21:12).

F3c Twelve things
12 pieces of Ahijah's cloak (1 Kgs. 11:30); 12 pieces of the concubine (Judg. 19:29); 12 baskets of broken pieces (Matt. 14:20; Mark 6:43; 8:19; Luke 9:17; John 6:13); 12 stones (Josh. 4:3, 5, 8, 9, 20; 1 Kgs. 18:31); 12 stars (Rev. 12:1); 12 thrones (Matt. 19:28); 12 foundations (Rev. 21:14); 12 gates of the city (Ezek. 48:30-4; Rev. 21:12); 12 gates and pearls (Rev. 21:21); 12 kinds of fruit (Rev. 22:2).

F4 Twenty to ninety-nine

F4a Twenties
20 righteous? (Gen. 18:31); 24 divisions of musicians (1 Chr. 25:9-31); 24 elders seated on 24 thrones (Rev. 4:4); the 24 elders (Rev. 4:10; 5:8; 11:16; 19:4).

F4b Thirties
30 righteous? (Gen. 18:30); 30 mighty men (2 Sam. 23:13-39; 1 Chr. 11:11, 15, 20, 25; 27:6); 100-fold, 60-fold, 30-fold (Matt. 13:8, 23); 30-fold, 60-fold, 100-fold (Mark 4:8, 20); 37 mighty men (2 Sam. 23:39).

F4c Forties
40 righteous? (Gen. 18:29); 40 stripes (Deut. 25:3); 40 stripes less one (2 Cor. 11:24); more than 40 men vowed to kill Paul (Acts 23:13, 21); 42 youths killed by the bears (2 Kgs. 2:24).

F4d Fifties
50 righteous? (Gen. 18:24, 26); leaders of 50s (Exod. 18:21, 25; Deut. 1:15); 100 prophets hidden by 50s (1 Kgs. 18:4, 13); recline in groups of 50 (Luke 9:14); they reclined in groups of 100s and 50s (Mark 6:40).

F4e Sixties
100-fold, 60-fold, 30-fold (Matt. 13:8, 23); 30-fold, 60-fold, 100-fold (Mark 4:8, 20).

F4f Seventies
70 elders (Exod. 24:1, 9; Num. 11:16, 24; Ezek. 8:11); 70 kings with thumbs and big toes cut off (Judg. 1:7); the 70 sent out (Luke 10:1); the 70 returned with joy (Luke 10:17); 70 horsemen (Acts 23:23); Lamech will be avenged 77-fold (Gen. 4:24).

F4g Nineties
99 righteous persons who need no repentance (Luke 15:7); leaving the 99 sheep (Matt. 18:12-13; Luke 15:4).

G The hundreds

G1 A hundred and above
The least of them was equal to 100 (1 Chr. 12:14); five will chase 100 and 100 will chase 10 000 (Lev. 26:8); the city which went forth 100 strong will have 10 left (Amos 5:3); the city which went forth 1000 strong will have 100 left (Amos 5:3); leaders of 100s (Exod. 18:21, 25; Deut. 1:15); they reclined in groups of 100s and 50s (Mark 6:40); 100 prophets hidden by 50s (1 Kgs. 18:4, 13); the Lord add a hundred times as many people (2 Sam. 24:3); 99 out of 100 sheep (Matt. 18:12; Luke 15:4); Isaac reaped 100-fold (Gen. 26:12); he will receive 100 times as much (Matt. 19:29; Mark 10:30); 100-fold fruit (Matt. 13:8, 23; Mark 4:8, 20; Luke 8:8); 120 brethren in the upper room (Acts 1:15); the wall was 144 cubits high (Rev. 21:17).

G2 Two hundred and above
200 soldiers (Acts 23:23); 200 spearmen (Acts 23:23); 200 large shields of beaten gold (1 Kgs. 10:16; 2 Chr. 9:15); 200 Philistine foreskins (1 Sam. 18:27); fire from the Lord consumed the 250 men (Num. 16:35; 26:10); 276 people on board ship (Acts 27:37).

G3 Three hundred and above
Gideon's 300 men (Judg. 7:16; 8:4); 300 trumpets (Judg. 7:22); 300 shields of beaten gold (1 Kgs. 10:17; 2 Chr. 9:16); Samson caught 300 foxes (Judg. 15:4).

G4 Six hundred and above
The number of the beast is 666 (Rev. 13:18).

H A thousand and above

H1 One thousand
One puts 1000 to flight (Josh. 23:10); how could one chase 1000 unless the Lord had given them up? (Deut. 32:30); the greatest of them was equal to 1000 (1 Chr. 12:14); the city which went forth 1000 strong will have 100 left (Amos 5:3); 1000 will flee at the threat of one (Isa. 30:17); 1000 men killed with the jawbone of a donkey (Judg. 15:15, 16); 1000 may fall at your side (Ps. 91:7); may the Lord increase you 1000-fold (Deut. 1:11); Saul has killed his 1000s and David his 10 000s (1 Sam.

18:7-8; 21:11; 29:5); leaders of 1000s (Exod. 18:21, 25; Deut. 1:15); the cattle on 1000 hills is mine (Ps. 50:10); where there were 1000 vines will be briars and thorns (Isa. 7:23); 1000 chariots David took from Hadadezer (1 Chr. 18:4); 1000 shields hung on the tower of David (S. of S. 4:4); he could not answer God once in 1000 times (Job 9:3).

H2 Two thousand
I will give you 2000 horses if you can put riders on them (2 Kgs. 18:23; Isa. 36:8); the herd of pigs, about 2000 in number (Mark 5:13).

H3 Three thousand
Only 2000 or 3000 need go up to Ai (Josh. 7:3); 3000 men went up to Ai (Josh. 7:4); 3000 added to the church (Acts 2:41); Solomon spoke 3000 proverbs (1 Kgs. 4:32).

H4 Four thousand to seven thousand
4000 fed (Matt. 15:38; 16:10; Mark 8:9, 20); the one who led 4000 Assassins into the wilderness (Acts 21:38); 5000 fed (Matt. 14:21; 16:9; Mark 6:44; 8:19); 5000 men (Luke 9:14; John 6:10); about 5000 men believing (Acts 4:4); 7000 left as a remnant (1 Kgs. 19:18; Rom. 11:4); 7000 people were killed in the earthquake (Rev. 11:13).

H5 Tens of thousands
100 will chase 10 000 (Lev. 26:8); how could two put 10 000 to flight unless the Lord had given them up? (Deut. 32:30); you are worth 10 000 of us (2 Sam. 18:3); 10 000 may fall at your right hand (Ps. 91:7); whether with 10 000 he is able to meet the one with 20 000 (Luke 14:31); Saul has killed his 1000s and David his 10 000s (1 Sam. 18:7-8; 21:11; 29:5); were I to write laws by the ten thousand, they would be regarded as strange (Hos. 8:12); will the Lord be please with 10 000 rivers of oil? (Mic. 6:7); five words with my mind rather than 10 000 words in a tongue (1 Cor. 14:19); tens of thousands of angels (Heb. 12:22); the Lord came with 10 000 saints (Deut. 33:2); the Lord came with myriads of his holy ones (Jude 14); 12 000 from each tribe (Rev. 7:5-8); 12 000 men of Ai killed (Josh. 8:25); 12 000 stadia (Rev. 21:16); 23 000 of them fell in a single day (1 Cor. 10:8).

H6 Hundreds of thousands
144 000 sealed (Rev. 7:4); 144 000 redeemed (Rev. 14:1, 3); 185 000 Assyrians killed by the angel of the Lord (2 Kgs. 19:35; Isa. 37:36); 200 000 women and children of Judah taken captive by Israel (2 Chr. 28:8); Judah killed 500 000 of Israel (2 Chr. 13:17); 600 000 men went up out of Egypt (Exod. 12:37; Num. 11:21).

H7 Millions
1 000 000 men with Zerah the Ethiopian (2 Chr. 14:9); 1 100 000 of Israel (1 Chr. 21:5); 200 million horsemen (Rev. 9:16); a thousand thousands served him (Dan. 7:10); return, O Lord, to the myriad thousands of Israel (Num. 10:36); be the mother of thousands of ten thousands (Gen. 24:60); ten thousand times ten thousand stood before him (Dan. 7:10); myriads of myriads and thousands of thousands of angels (Rev. 5:11).

100 Multisection
Divide the land into seven portions (Josh. 18:5); the Levite cut his concubine into 12 pieces (Judg. 19:29). FRACTION, see 102.

101 Plurality
MANY, see 104.

102 Fraction

A A fifth
Restitution to be made, paying a fifth more than the value (Lev. 5:16; 6:5; 22:14; Num. 5:7); redemption

paying a fifth more than the value (Lev. 27:13, 15, 19, 27, 31); a fifth of the produce of Egypt was taken for Pharaoh (Gen. 41:34; 47:24, 26).

B A tenth

B1 A tenth of people
A tenth of the people would supply the food (Judg. 20:10); one in ten of the people would live in Jerusalem (Neh. 11:1); a tenth will remain in it (Isa. 6:13).

B2 A tenth of things
An omer is a tenth of an ephah (Exod. 16:36); a tenth of the city fell (Rev. 11:13).

B3 Tithing for God

B3a Tithing produce
I will give you a tenth of all you give me (Gen. 28:22); a tenth of all produce of the land and of all animals is the Lord's (Lev. 27:30-2); a tenth of all flocks is holy to the Lord (Lev. 27:32); you tithe mint and dill and cummin (Matt. 23:23); Pharisees tithed garden herbs (Luke 11:42); I tithe all I get (Luke 18:12).

B3b Bringing in the tithe
Bring your tithe there (Deut. 12:6, 11); bring the whole tithe into the storehouse that there may be food in my house (Mal. 3:10); the Levites shall bring the tithe of the tithe (Neh. 10:38); you are robbing God by your tithes and offerings (Mal. 3:8).

B3c Eating the tithe
A tenth of all produce is to be eaten before the Lord with rejoicing (Deut. 12:18; 14:22-7); do not eat the tithe within your gates (Deut. 12:17).

B3d The tithe for Levites
The third year the tithe is for the Levite and the deprived (Deut. 14:28-9; 26:12-13); the tithe is for the Levites (Num. 18:21, 24); Hezekiah commanded the people to resume the tithe for the Levites (2 Chr. 31:4-10); Nehemiah had the tithes for the Levites restored (Neh. 10:37-9; 13:10-13); Levi, who receives tithes, paid tithes (Heb. 7:9).

B4 Tithing for people
Abraham gave a tenth of everything to Melchizedek (Gen. 14:20; Heb. 7:2, 4-9); a king will take a tenth of your flocks (1 Sam. 8:17); a king will take a tenth of your seed and your vineyards (1 Sam. 8:15); mortal men receive tithes (Heb. 7:8); Levi, who receives tithes, paid tithes (Heb. 7:9).

C Smaller fractions
One fiftieth of the booty was given to the Levites (Num. 31:30, 47); give them back one hundredth of what you are exacting (Neh. 5:11); a tenth of a bath from each ten baths of oil (Ezek. 45:14); a sheep from every 200 for the prince (Ezek. 45:15); a sixth of an ephah from a homer of wheat or barley (Ezek. 45:13); one in five hundred of the people and livestock as an offering to the Lord (Num. 31:28-9).

103 Zero / nothing
No carts were given to Kohath (Num. 7:9); no one gave him anything (Luke 15:16); when he dies he will carry nothing away (Ps. 49:17); we brought nothing into the world and we cannot take anything out (1 Tim. 6:7). NO IMPORTANCE, see 639.

104 Numerous

A Many people

A1 Many in the nation

A1a Many offspring
If anyone can count the dust, your offspring can be counted (Gen. 13:16); count the stars if you can – so will your seed be (Gen. 15:5); offspring as numerous as the stars and the sand (Heb. 11:12); descendants like the sand of the sea (Gen. 32:12); he makes their families like flocks (Ps. 107:41); your descendants will be many (Job

5:25); David's offspring would be numerous as the stars and the sand (Jer. 33:22-3); your offspring would have been like the sand (Isa. 48:19); the sons of the desolate will be more than those of the married (Isa. 54:1).

A1b A great nation
Abraham was to be made a great nation (Gen. 12:2; 18:18); I will make you very fruitful (Gen. 17:6); the father of many nations (Gen. 17:4, 5; Rom. 4:16-17); nations will come from you (Gen. 35:11); they will become a multitude of peoples (Gen. 48:19); Sarah would become many nations (Gen. 17:16); I will make Ishmael a nation (Gen. 21:13, 18); I will make you a great nation (Gen. 46:3); I will make you a company of peoples (Gen. 48:4); I will make you fruitful and many (Gen. 48:4); like the stars (Gen. 15:5; 22:17; 26:4; Exod. 32:13; 1 Chr. 27:23); like the dust (Gen. 13:16; 28:14; 2 Chr. 1:9); like the sand (Gen. 22:17; 32:12; Hos. 1:10); I made you numerous like plants of the field (Ezek. 16:7); too many to count (Gen. 16:10); as numerous as sheep (Ezek. 36:37); I will make Moses a great nation instead (Exod. 32:10; Num. 14:12; Deut. 9:14); God made his people very fruitful (Ps. 105:24); God made them as numerous as the stars (Deut. 1:10; 10:22; 28:62; Neh. 9:23); may you become thousands of ten thousands (Gen. 24:60); may God make you a company of peoples (Gen. 28:3); may they become many (Gen. 48:16).

A1c Many in Israel
Who can count Israel? (Num. 23:10); who can count the dust of Jacob? (Num. 23:10); the ten thousand thousands of Israel (Num. 10:36); the people are now many (Exod. 5:5); Moab feared the Israelites because they were numerous (Num. 22:3); Ephraim and Manasseh were a numerous people (Josh. 17:17); 144 000 were sealed from every tribe of Israel (Rev. 7:4); David's seed and the priests will be as the host of heaven which cannot be counted (Jer. 33:22); to us who are many the land is given (Ezek. 33:24); the Israelites are more numerous than we are (Exod. 1:9); numerous as the sand (2 Sam. 17:11; 1 Kgs. 4:20); too many to count (1 Kgs. 3:8); they will be as many as of old (Zech. 10:8); Jerusalem will be inhabited without walls because of the multitudes within (Zech. 2:4); give a larger inheritance to a large tribe (Num. 26:54; 33:54); take more cities for the Levites from a larger tribe (Num. 35:8); may Reuben's men not be few (Deut. 33:6); the sons of Joseph were a numerous people (Josh. 17:14-15); it was not because you were numerous that God loved you (Deut. 7:7); though Israel be like the sand of the sea (Isa. 10:22; Rom. 9:27); there were many lepers in Israel (Luke 4:27); there were many widows in Israel (Luke 4:25); widows more numerous than the sand (Jer. 15:8).

A2 Many before God

A2a Many seeking salvation
Many prophets and righteous men longed to see what you see (Matt. 13:17); many called but few chosen (Matt. 22:14); many enter the gate leading to destruction (Matt. 7:13); many seek in vain to enter the narrow door (Luke 13:24); a man gave a great banquet and invited many (Luke 14:16); by the transgression of the one the many died (Rom. 5:15); by one man's disobedience many were made sinners (Rom. 5:19); much more did grace abound to the many (Rom. 5:15); by the obedience of one many will be made righteous (Rom. 5:19); to give his life a ransom for many (Matt. 20:28; Mark 10:45); my blood, poured out for many (Matt. 26:28; Mark 14:24).

A2b Many in the church
Multitudes added to the church (Acts 2:41, 47; 5:14; 6:7; 9:42; 14:1); large numbers were added to the Lord (Acts

11:24); the churches increased in number daily (Acts 16:5); the disciples were increasing in number (Acts 6:1); the church was built up and multiplied (Acts 9:31); the word of God grew and multiplied (Acts 12:24); many of those who heard believed (Acts 4:4); many of the Bereans believed (Acts 17:12); they made many disciples (Acts 14:21); many believed (Acts 11:21); thousands of Jews believed (Acts 21:20); many Jews and devout proselytes followed Paul and Barnabas (Acts 13:43); many priests were obedient to the faith (Acts 6:7); I have many people in this city (Acts 18:10); many will come from east and west and recline to eat (Matt. 8:11); a great multitude which no one could count (Rev. 7:9); the loud voice of a great multitude in heaven (Rev. 19:1); I heard the voice of a great multitude (Rev. 19:6).

A2c Many deceivers and deceived
False Christs will lead many astray (Matt. 24:5); many will say, 'I am the Christ' (Matt. 24:5); many will come saying 'I am he' (Mark 13:6; Luke 21:8); many false prophets will arise (Matt. 24:11); many false witnesses came forward (Matt. 26:60; Mark 14:56); many will betray one another and hate one another (Matt. 24:10).

A3 Many enemies
When you see horses, chariots and people more numerous than yourself (Deut. 20:1); how my enemies have increased! (Ps. 3:1); many fight against me (Ps. 56:2); many are my persecutors and adversaries (Ps. 119:157); those who hate me without a cause are more than the hairs on my head (Ps. 69:4); Saul has slain his thousands and David his ten thousands (1 Sam. 18:7-8; 21:11; 29:5); five will chase 100 and 100 will chase 10 000 (Lev. 26:8).

A4 Many combatants
In the multitude of people is the glory of a king (Prov. 14:28); those with us are more than those with them (2 Kgs. 6:16); is there any number to God's armies? (Job 25:3); opposing armies like the sand (Josh. 11:4; Judg. 7:12; 1 Sam. 13:5); opposing armies like locusts (Judg. 6:5; Jer. 46:23); opposing armies without number (2 Chr. 12:3); a great multitude (1 Kgs. 20:13; 2 Chr. 20:2); the Arameans filled the country (1 Kgs. 20:27); the number of their army is like the sand (Rev. 20:8); there were too many soldiers with Gideon (Judg. 7:2, 4); his sons will assemble a multitude of great forces (Dan. 11:10); the king of the north will raise a greater multitude (Dan. 11:13); the king of the south will wage war with a large army (Dan. 11:25); his camp is very numerous (Joel 2:11).

A5 Many active
The priests were many in number (Heb. 7:23); with many counsellors plans succeed (Prov. 15:22); in abundance of counsellors there is victory (Prov. 11:14; 24:6); when a land transgresses it has many rulers (Prov. 28:2); though you have many guides in Christ (1 Cor. 4:15); many have undertaken to compile a narrative (Luke 1:1); many will give thanks for blessings granted through the prayers of many (2 Cor. 1:11).

A6 Dealing with many people
Multitudes in the valley of decision (Joel 3:14); they gather captives like sand (Hab. 1:9); many were coming and going, so they did not even have time to eat (Mark 6:31); so many thousands had gathered that they trod on one another (Luke 12:1); they brought to him many who were demonised (Matt. 8:16); he had healed many (Mark 3:10); he found many people gathered (Acts 10:27); the Jews came to him in large numbers (Acts 28:23); what you heard from me in the presence of many witnesses (2 Tim. 2:2).

B Many spiritual beings
Myriads attended him (Dan. 7:10); myriads of myriads and thousands of thousands of angels (Rev. 5:11); you have as many gods as cities (Jer. 2:28; 11:13); the name was legion because the evil spirits were many (Mark 5:9; Luke 8:30).

C Many creatures
Let the waters teem with swarms of creatures (Gen. 1:20); numerous frogs (Exod. 8:3); numerous locusts (Exod. 10:14); let our flocks produce thousands and ten thousands (Ps. 144:13); camels as numerous as the sand (Judg. 7:12); in the sea are innumerable creeping things (Ps. 104:25); a nation has invaded my land, mighty and without number (Joel 1:6); a herd of many pigs was feeding at a distance (Matt. 8:30); you are of more value than many sparrows (Matt. 10:31).

D Many tangible things
Thousands upon thousands of God's chariots (Ps. 68:17); there were very many bones in the valley (Ezek. 37:2); I will answer him myself because of the multitude of his idols (Ezek. 14:4); many slain, countless dead bodies (Nahum 3:3); the body is not one limb but many (1 Cor. 12:14); there are many members but one body (1 Cor. 12:20).

E Many intangible things
How many are your works! (Ps. 104:24); God does wonders without number (Job 9:10); that my wonders may be multiplied in Egypt (Exod. 11:9); Jesus did many other signs in the presence of his disciples (John 20:30); your thoughts to us are too numerous to count (Ps. 40:5); your thoughts are more numerous than the sand (Ps. 139:18); the Lord has caused her grief because of the multitude of her transgressions (Lam. 1:5); my iniquities are more than the hairs on my head (Ps. 40:12); the free gift following many trespasses brought justification (Rom. 5:16); her sins, which are many, are forgiven (Luke 7:47); were I to write laws by the ten thousand, they would be regarded as strange (Hos. 8:12); in many and varied ways God spoke by the prophets (Heb. 1:1); he spoke to them with many such parables (Mark 4:33); many charges against Christ (Matt. 27:13; Mark 15:3-4); you are anxious about many things (Luke 10:41); in my Father's house are many dwelling-places (John 14:2).
GOD S THOUGHTS, see 449A.

105 Few

A Few people
In the scarcity of people is a prince's ruin (Prov. 14:28); Jacob's men were few (Gen. 34:30); the men of Israel were like two little flocks of goats (1 Kgs. 20:27); you were the least numerous of people (Deut. 7:7); he went down to Egypt few in number (Deut. 26:5); when they were few in number (1 Chr. 16:19; Ps. 105:12); there was a small city with few men in it (Eccles. 9:14); if the household is too small for a lamb (Exod. 12:4); God can save by many or by few (1 Sam. 14:6).

B Few priests
The priests were too few, so the Levites helped them (2 Chr. 29:34); not enough priests had consecrated themselves (2 Chr. 30:3).

C Few in the kingdom
Will only a few be saved? (Luke 13:23); few find the narrow gate leading to life (Matt. 7:14); many are called but few are chosen (Matt. 22:14); not many wise, powerful or noble are saved (1 Cor. 1:26); the harvest is plentiful but the labourers are few (Matt. 9:37; Luke 10:2); not many of you should be teachers (Jas. 3:1); you have a few who have not soiled their clothes (Rev. 3:4).

106 Repetition

A Saying repeatedly
She spoke to Joseph day after day (Gen. 39:10); I have spoken to you repeatedly (Jer. 25:3; 35:14); I taught them again and again (Jer. 32:33); Jesus prayed again, saying the same words (Matt. 26:44; Mark 14:39).

B Doing repeatedly
Pass your hand again over the branches (Jer. 6:9); take another scroll and write on it all the former words (Jer. 36:28); God sent his prophets repeatedly (Jer. 25:4; 29:19; 35:15; 44:4); priests offer the same sacrifices daily (Heb. 7:27; 10:11); priests offer the same sacrifices yearly (Lev. 16:34; Heb. 9:25; 10:1); he would have had to suffer repeatedly since the foundation of the world (Heb. 9:26).

C Sinning repeatedly
How often they rebelled and grieved him! (Ps. 78:40); my people have forgotten me days without number (Jer. 2:32); they tested him again and again (Ps. 78:41); like a dog returning to its vomit is a fool who repeats his folly (Prov. 26:11); if your brother sins and repents repeatedly, forgive repeatedly (Matt. 18:21-2; Luke 17:4).

107 Infinity

NUMEROUS, see 104.

108 Time

PERIOD OF TIME, see 110.

A Time in general
Redeem the time, because the days are evil (Eph. 5:16); you observe days, months, seasons and years (Gal. 4:10); times which the Father has fixed (Acts 1:7); as to times and seasons, you do not need me to write (1 Thess. 5:1); my times are in your hands (Ps. 31:15); God determined the times of all the nations (Acts 17:26); until the times of the Gentiles are fulfilled (Luke 21:24).

B When?
When shall I entreat the Lord for you? (Exod. 8:9); when will you return? (Neh. 2:6); when shall I come and appear before God? (Matt. 24:3; Mark 13:4; Luke 21:7); when will this be? (Matt. 24:3; Mark 13:4; Luke 21:7); the prophets enquired what time was indicated (1 Pet. 1:11); the Pharisees asked when the kingdom of God was coming (Luke 17:20); if the householder had known what time the thief was coming (Luke 12:39).

C The right time
RIGHT TIME FOR INDIVIDUALS, see 137.

C1 The right time in general
There is a time for every matter (Eccles. 3:1, 17; 8:6); a wise man will know the time and the way (Eccles. 8:5); man does not know his time (Eccles. 9:12); the time of the end is the time appointed (Dan. 11:35); the heir is under tutors and governors until the date set by the father (Gal. 4:2); the four angels had been prepared for the hour, day, month and year (Rev. 9:15); that in due time he may exalt you (1 Pet. 5:6); be ready in season and out of season (2 Tim. 4:2).

C2 The time for particular activities
Evening, the time when women go out to draw water (Gen. 24:11); offer the offerings at the proper time (Num. 28:2); keep this ordinance at its appointed time (Exod. 13:10); like a tree bearing fruit in its season (Ps. 1:3); it was the time of the first ripe grapes (Num. 13:20); when the time came he sent a servant to the tenants (Mark 12:2; Luke 20:10); it is time to seek the Lord (Hos. 10:12); who will give the servants food at the proper time? (Matt. 24:45; Luke 12:42); when the hour came he reclined at table with the apostles (Luke 22:14).

C3 A time to . . .
A time to seek (Eccles. 3:6); a time to give birth (Eccles. 3:2); a time to die (Eccles. 3:2); a time to plant (Eccles. 3:2); a time to keep (Eccles. 3:6); a time to gather stones (Eccles. 3:5); a time to build (Eccles. 3:3); a time to heal (Eccles. 3:3); a time to uproot (Eccles. 3:2); a time to break down (Eccles. 3:3); a time to rend (Eccles. 3:7); a time for war (Eccles. 3:8); a time to kill (Eccles. 3:3); a time to throw stones (Eccles. 3:5); a time to throw away (Eccles. 3:6); a time to laugh (Eccles. 3:4); a time to dance (Eccles. 3:4); a time to mourn (Eccles. 3:4); a time to weep (Eccles. 3:4); a time to love (Eccles. 3:8); a time to embrace (Eccles. 3:5); a time to refrain from embracing (Eccles. 3:5); a time to give up as lost (Eccles. 3:6); a time to speak (Eccles. 3:7); a time to be silent (Eccles. 3:7); a time to hate (Eccles. 3:8); a time for peace (Eccles. 3:8); a time to sew together (Eccles. 3:7).

D Times of events

D1 Time of salvation
In a day of salvation I have helped you (Isa. 49:8; 2 Cor. 6:2); to proclaim the year of the Lord's favour (Isa. 61:2); the acceptable year of the Lord (Luke 4:19); now is the acceptable time (2 Cor. 6:2); the year of my redeemed ones has come (Isa. 63:4); it is time for you to awaken from sleep (Rom. 13:11); the time came when the saints received the kingdom (Dan. 7:22); eternal life manifested at the proper time (Titus 1:3).

D2 Day of the Lord
D2a The fact of that day
The day of the Lord is near (Ezek. 30:3; Joel 1:15; 3:14; Obad. 15; Zeph. 1:7, 14); the day of the Lord is coming (Joel 2:1); the great and terrible day of the Lord (Joel 2:31; Mal. 4:5); the day of the Lord is darkness (Amos 5:18, 20; Zeph. 1:15); the day of the Lord Jesus Christ (1 Cor. 1:8; 5:5; 2 Cor. 1:14; Phil. 1:6); the day of Christ (Phil. 1:10; 2:16); the day of God (2 Pet. 3:12); the great day of God (Rev. 16:14); the great day of the Lord (Acts 2:20); the day of the Lord great and awesome, who can endure it? (Joel 2:11); on that day many will say to me (Matt. 7:22).

D2b The time unknown
No one knows the day but the Father (Matt. 24:36; Mark 13:32); you do not know the time (Matt. 24:42; Mark 13:33); you know neither the day nor the hour (Matt. 25:13); when you do not expect (Matt. 24:44; Luke 12:40); you will not know at what hour I come upon you (Rev. 3:3); as when the master returns unexpectedly (Matt. 24:50; Mark 13:35; Luke 12:46); the day of the Lord will come like a thief (1 Thess. 5:2; 2 Pet. 3:10); you are not in darkness for that day to surprise you like a thief (1 Thess. 5:4); if the householder had known at what time of night the thief was coming (Matt. 24:43); do not think the day of the Lord has already come (2 Thess. 2:2).

D3 Day of judgement
The day of judgement (Matt. 10:15; 11:22, 24; 12:36; 2 Pet. 2:9; 3:7; 1 John 4:17); the hour of his judgement has come (Rev. 14:7); a day on which he will judge (Acts 17:31; Rom. 2:16); the judgement of the great day (Jude 6; Rev. 6:17); these are days of vengeance to fulfil all that is written (Luke 21:22); each man's work will be manifest, for the day will disclose it (1 Cor. 3:13); you have fattened your hearts in a day of slaughter (Jas. 5:5); the time came for the dead to be judged (Rev. 11:18).

D4 Time of restoration
The day of redemption (Eph. 4:30); the time for restoring everything (Acts 3:21).

D5 Times of the Christ
When the time had fully come, God sent his Son (Gal. 4:4); at the right time Christ died (Rom. 5:6); my time has not yet come (John 2:4; 7:6, 8); his hour had not yet come (John 7:30; 8:20); the time is at hand (Matt. 26:18, 45); the hour has come (Mark 14:41; John 17:1); the hour has come for the Son of man to be glorified (John 12:23); the hour had come for him to leave the world (John 13:1); like the lightning, so will the Son of man be in his day (Luke 17:24); as in the days of Noah, so it will be in the days of the Son of man (Luke 17:26); on the day when the Son of man is revealed (Luke 17:30); your father Abraham rejoiced to see my day (John 8:56); shall I say, 'Father, save me from this hour'? (John 12:27); for this purpose I have come to this hour (John 12:27); Christ's appearing will be at the proper time (1 Tim. 6:15).

D6 The time appointed
The time of the promise was approaching (Acts 7:17); a plan for the fullness of time (Eph. 1:10); the time is fulfilled (Mark 1:15); the vision is for the appointed time and hastens to its end (Hab. 2:3); when the day of Pentecost had come (Acts 2:1).

E Hour of day
E1 Time of sacrifice
At the time of the morning sacrifice (2 Kgs. 3:20); at the time of the evening offering (Dan. 9:21).

E2 Twilight
Kill the lamb at twilight (Exod. 12:6); Passover begins at twilight (Lev. 23:5; Num. 9:3, 5, 11); one lamb sacrificed at twilight (Exod. 29:39, 41; Num. 28:4, 8); Aaron is to burn incense at twilight (Exod. 30:8).

E3 Midnight
God acted at midnight (Exod. 11:4; 12:29); who would ask a friend for food at midnight? (Luke 11:5); at midnight Paul and Silas were praying and singing hymns (Acts 16:25); Paul spoke until midnight (Acts 20:7); at midnight the sailors thought they were nearing land (Acts 27:27).

E4 Hours o'clock
E4a 6 am
The sixth hour [Roman time] (John 19:14).
E4b 9 am
The third hour (Matt. 20:3; Mark 15:25; Acts 2:15).
E4c 10 am
The tenth hour [Roman time] (John 1:39).
E4d Midday
Where do you make your flock lie down at noon? (S. of S. 1:7); the destruction that wastes at noon (Ps. 91:6); we stumble at midday as in the twilight (Isa. 59:10); sixth hour (Matt. 20:5; Acts 10:9); at noon Elijah mocked them (1 Kgs. 18:27); at noon the boy died (2 Kgs. 4:20); darkness from the sixth hour until the ninth hour (Matt. 27:45; Mark 15:33; Luke 23:44); I will make the sun go down at noon (Amos 8:9); at noon go to the road from Jerusalem to Gaza (Acts 8:26); as I approached Damascus about noon (Acts 22:6); at noon I saw a light brighter than the sun (Acts 26:13).
E4e 3 pm
The ninth hour (Matt. 20:5; Luke 23:44; Acts 3:1; 10:3); darkness from the sixth hour until the ninth hour (Matt. 27:45); I was praying at the ninth hour (Acts 10:30); at the ninth hour Jesus cried out (Matt. 27:46; Mark 15:34).
E4f 5 pm
The eleventh hour (Matt. 20:6, 9).
E4g 6 pm
The sixth hour [Roman time] (John 4:6).
E4h 7 pm
The seventh hour [Roman time] (John 4:52).

E4i 9 pm
Prepare soldiers for the third hour of the night [9 pm] (Acts 23:23).

F Days
F1 Day 1
F1a First day of the week
The first day of creation (Gen. 1:5); the day after the sabbath the priest shall wave the firstfruits (Lev. 23:11); the first day of the week they came to the tomb (Matt. 28:1; Mark 16:2; Luke 24:1; John 20:1); the first day of the week Christ rose from the dead (Mark 16:9; John 20:19); breaking bread on the first day of the week (Acts 20:7); making a contribution on the first day of the week (1 Cor. 16:2); the Lord's day (Rev. 1:10).
DAYS OF CREATION, see 110.

F1b First day of the feast / month
On the first day hold a holy convocation (Exod. 12:16; Lev. 23:7, 35; Num. 28:18); the first day will be a sabbath (Lev. 23:39); on the first day of Unleavened Bread (Matt. 26:17; Mark 14:12).

F2 Day 3
After two days he will revive us and raise us up on the third day (Hos. 6:2); this is the third day since this happened (Luke 24:21); on the third day I complete my course (Luke 13:32); on the third day he would rise (Luke 24:46); on the third day he must be raised (Matt. 16:21; 17:23; 20:19; Luke 9:22); raised on the third day (1 Cor. 15:4).

F3 Day 7
On the seventh day God rested (Gen. 2:2, 3; Exod. 31:17); on the seventh day no one shall work (Exod. 20:10; 23:12; 31:15; 35:2; Lev. 23:3; Deut. 5:14); he has said of the seventh day (Heb. 4:4); on the seventh day: you shall rest (Exod. 34:21); hold a feast to the Lord (Exod. 13:6); hold a holy convocation (Exod. 12:16; Lev. 23:8; Num. 28:25); a solemn assembly (Deut. 16:8).
SABBATH, see 683A.

F4 Day 8
On the eighth day they came to circumcise him (Luke 1:59); circumcised on the eighth day (Phil. 3:5); on the eighth day: the cleansed person offers a sacrifice (Lev. 14:10, 23; 15:14, 29); you shall give the firstborn to me (Exod. 22:30).
DAYS OLD, see 131B1.

G Months
G1 Beginning of month
A burnt offering at the beginning of every month (Num. 28:11); the burnt offering of the new moon (Num. 29:6; Ezra 3:5); blow the silver trumpets on the first of each month (Num. 10:10); blow the trumpet at new moon (Ps. 81:3); new moon is an abomination to me (Isa. 1:13); let no one judge you with regard to a festival, new moon or sabbath (Col. 2:16).

G2 Month 1
Month 1, Abib / Nisan: this month is to be the first of the year (Exod. 12:2); Feast of Unleavened bread in the month Abib (Exod. 23:15; 34:18); in the month Abib you left Egypt (Exod. 13:4; 34:18; Deut. 16:1).

G3 Month 7
Month 7, Tishri / Ethanim: on the first day the Feast of Trumpets (Lev. 23:24; Num. 29:1); on the ninth day the Feast of Booths (Lev. 23:41); on the ninth day at evening, start of the Day of Atonement (Lev. 23:32); on the tenth day the Day of Atonement (Lev. 16:29; 23:27; Num. 29:7); on the tenth day start of the Year of Jubilee (Lev. 25:9); on the 15th day the Feast of Booths [Tabernacles] (Lev. 23:34, 39; Num. 29:12; Neh. 8:14; Ezek. 45:25).

G4 Month 12
Month 12, Adar: the 14th day to be celebrated annually
(Esther 9:21); the 15th day to be celebrated annually
(Esther 9:21).

H Years
H1 Start of year
The start of the year of Jubilee (Lev. 25:9); Feast of
Ingathering at the turn of the year (Exod. 34:22).

H2 Particular years
In the second year eat what grows of itself (2 Kgs. 19:29;
Isa. 37:30); in the third year sow, reap and plant (2 Kgs.
19:29; Isa. 37:30); at the end of every third year bring
out the tithe (Deut. 14:28); at the end of the third year
give the tithe away (Deut. 14:28; 26:12); at the end of
seven years, a remission (Deut. 15:1; 31:10); in the
seventh year a Hebrew slave shall be set free (Exod.
21:2; Deut. 15:12); the seventh year let the land rest
(Exod. 23:11; Lev. 25:4); when you sow in the eighth
year you will be eating old produce (Lev. 25:22); you
will eat the old until the ninth year (Lev. 25:22);
consecrate the 50th year (Lev. 25:10).

109 Never
Never again will a flood destroy all the earth (Gen. 9:11,
15); you will never go back to Egypt (Deut. 17:16); you
will never see Egypt again (Deut. 28:68); the God of
heaven will set up a kingdom which will never be
destroyed (Dan. 2:44); I will plant them on their land
and they will never be rooted up (Amos 9:15); whoever
drinks the water I give will never thirst again (John
4:14); they will never perish (John 10:28); he who lives
and believes in me will never die (John 11:26); you shall
never wash my feet (John 13:8); this will never happen
to you! (Matt. 16:22).
NEVER BEEN, see 2C.

110 Period
POINT IN TIME, see 108.
A LONG TIME, see 113.
HOW LONG? see 136C.

A Periods
A1 Periods in general
The day of creation (Gen. 2:4); God made sun and
moon to mark seasons, days and years (Gen. 1:14);
while the earth remains the seasons will not cease (Gen.
8:22); he made the moon for the seasons (Ps. 104:19);
this is the day which the Lord has made (Ps. 118:24); for
every day a year (Num. 14:34; Ezek. 4:5, 6); some regard
one day as better than another (Rom. 14:5-6); you
observe days, months, seasons and years (Gal. 4:10); as
to times and seasons, you do not need me to write (1
Thess. 5:1); he changes times and seasons (Dan. 2:21); I
will pay you back for the years the locust has eaten
(Joel 2:25); this is your hour and the power of darkness
(Luke 22:53).

A2 Times of people
Like the days of Noah (Isa. 54:9; Matt. 24:37); in the
days of Abraham (Gen. 26:1, 15, 18); from the time of
Joshua the son of Nun (Neh. 8:17); since the day your
fathers came out of Egypt (Jer. 7:25); in the days when
the judges judged (Ruth 1:1); from the days of the
judges (2 Kgs. 23:22; 1 Chr. 17:10); in the days of the
kings of Israel and the kings of Judah (2 Kgs. 23:22); in
the days of Elijah (Luke 4:25); in the time of Elisha
(Luke 4:27); in the days of Herod king of Judea (Luke
1:5); from the days of John the Baptist until now (Matt.
11:12); if we had lived in the days of our fathers (Matt.
23:30).

A3 Particular periods
The days of creation (Gen. 1:5, 8, 13, 19, 23, 31; 2:2); buy
and sell according to the length of time to the Jubilee
(Lev. 25:15, 16, 50, 51-2).
AGES OF PEOPLE, see 131.

B Less than a day
B1 Half an hour
For half an hour there was silence in heaven (Rev. 8:1).

B2 One hour
These have worked only one hour (Matt. 20:12); could
you not keep watch for one hour? (Matt. 26:40; Mark
14:37); after about an hour (Luke 22:59); the ten kings
receive authority with the beast for one hour (Rev.
17:12).

B3 Two hours
The Ephesians shouted for two hours (Acts 19:34).

B4 Three hours
After about three hours his wife came in (Acts 5:7).

B5 12 hours
Are there not 12 hours in the day? (John 11:9).

B6 Watches
1000 years to you are like a watch in the night (Ps.
90:4); in the fourth watch of the night [3-6 am] (Matt.
14:25; Mark 6:48); whether the second watch or the
third (Luke 12:38).

C Days
C1 One day
The sun did not hasten for a whole day (Josh. 10:13); a
day in your courts is better than 1000 [elsewhere] (Ps.
84:10); adrift at sea for a day and a night (2 Cor. 11:25);
23 000 of them fell in a single day (1 Cor. 10:8); for
every day a year (Num. 14:34; Ezek. 4:5,
6); one day is as 1000 years (2 Pet. 3:8).
IN A SINGLE DAY, see 114A1.

C2 Three days
  C2a For three days
Three days represented by three branches (Gen. 40:12);
three days represented by three baskets (Gen. 40:18);
Mary and Joseph searching for Jesus for three days
(Luke 2:46); the crowd had been with Jesus for three
days (Matt. 15:32; Mark 8:2); for three days Paul was
blind (Acts 9:9).

  C2b Three days until
Three days until Christ rose (Matt. 16:21; 20:19; 27:63;
Mark 8:31; 9:31; 10:34; Luke 9:22; 18:33; 24:7; Acts 10:40);
rebuilding the temple in three days (Matt. 26:61; 27:40;
Mark 14:58; 15:29; John 2:19-20).

  C2c Three days and nights
Jonah in the fish for three days and nights (Jonah 1:17;
Matt. 12:40); the Son of man in the heart of the earth
three days and three nights (Matt. 12:40).

  C2d Three and a half days
For three and a half days the witnesses' bodies will lie
unburied (Rev. 11:9-11); after the three and a half days
the breath of life came into them (Rev. 11:11).

C3 Six days
Six days for God to make heaven and earth (Gen. 1:1-31;
Exod. 20:11; 31:17); six days gathering manna (Exod.
16:26); six days to do all your work (Exod. 20:9; 23:12;
31:15; 34:21; 35:2; Lev. 23:3; Deut. 5:13); there are six days
on which work should be done (Luke 13:14).

C4 Seven days
Seven days eating unleavened bread (Exod. 12:15; 13:6-7;
23:15; 34:18; Lev. 23:6; Num. 28:17; Deut. 16:3, 4; 2 Chr.
30:21, 22; 35:17; Ezra 6:22; Ezek. 45:21); no leaven in your
houses for seven days (Exod. 12:19); Feast of Booths for
seven days (Lev. 23:34, 36, 39-42; Num. 29:12; Deut.
16:15; Neh. 8:18); rejoice before the Lord for seven days
(Lev. 23:40); live in booths for seven days (Lev. 23:42).

C5 Ten or more days

Tribulation for ten days (Rev. 2:10); 14 days adrift at sea (Acts 27:27, 33); 21 days Gabriel was hindered (Dan. 10:13); I, Daniel, had been mourning for three weeks (Dan. 10:2); for three weeks I did not eat tasty food or anoint myself (Dan. 10:3).

C6 Forty days

Rain for 40 days and 40 nights (Gen. 7:4, 12); the flood was on the earth for 40 days (Gen. 7:17); 40 days before Noah sent the raven (Gen. 8:6); 40 days for embalming (Gen. 50:3); Moses was on the mountain for 40 days (Exod. 24:18; 34:28; Deut. 9:9, 11, 18, 25; 10:10); the twelve men spied out Canaan for 40 days (Num. 13:25; 14:34); Goliath challenged Israel for 40 days (1 Sam. 17:16); 40 days and 40 nights Elijah fasted in Horeb (1 Kgs. 19:8); Ezekiel lay on his right side for 40 days (Ezek. 4:6); 40 days until Nineveh's overthrow (Jonah 3:4); Jesus fasted in the wilderness 40 days (Matt. 4:2; Mark 1:13; Luke 4:2); during 40 days the risen Jesus appeared to them (Acts 1:3).

D Months

D1 One month

Captive woman mourning parents for one month (Deut. 21:13); the Israelites wept for Aaron for 30 days (Num. 20:29); the Israelites wept for Moses for 30 days (Deut. 34:8); for a month you will eat meat (Num. 11:20, 21).

D2 Five months

Elizabeth hid herself for five months (Luke 1:24); locusts tormented for five months (Rev. 9:5, 10); the flood was on the earth for 150 days (Gen. 7:24); 150 days, after which the waters decreased (Gen. 8:3).

E Years

E1 One to seven years

E1a One year and more

Redemption rights in a town for one year (Lev. 25:29-30); a newly-wed at home for one year (Deut. 24:5); Barnabas and Paul taught in Antioch for one year (Acts 11:26); 12 months for beautification (Esther 2:12); we will spend a year there and trade (Jas. 4:13); I will not drive them out in a single year (Exod. 23:29); for one year and six months Paul taught in Corinth (Acts 18:11).

E1b Two years

Paul taught daily in the school of Tyrannus for two years (Acts 19:10); Paul lived in Rome for two years (Acts 28:30).

E1c Three years

Fruit from a new tree shall not be eaten for three years (Lev. 19:23); at the end of every three years bring your tithe (Deut. 14:28); famine for three years (2 Sam. 21:1; 24:13; 1 Chr. 21:12); Paul admonished them for three years (Acts 20:31); for three years I have come seeking fruit and found none (Luke 13:7).

E1d Three and a half years

Three and a half years of drought (Luke 4:25; Jas. 5:17); 1260 days (Rev. 11:3; 12:6); 42 months (Rev. 11:2; 13:5); a time, times and half a time (Dan. 7:25; 12:7; Rev. 12:14); for half of the week he will put an end to sacrifice and offering (Dan. 9:27); 1290 days after the regular sacrifice stops (Dan. 12:11); 1335 days to wait (Dan. 12:12).

E1e Five years

Five years neither ploughing nor harvesting (Gen. 45:6); five years of more famine (Gen. 45:11).

E1f Six years

Six years I served you for your flock (Gen. 31:41); a Hebrew slave to serve for six years (Exod. 21:2; Deut. 15:12, 18; Jer. 34:14); sow your land for six years (Exod. 23:10; Lev. 25:3); 2300 evenings and mornings: (Dan. 8:14).

E1g Seven years

Jacob served for Rachel for seven years (Gen. 29:18, 20); seven years twice over (Gen. 29:27, 30); seven years of plenty and of famine (Gen. 41:26-36); during the seven years of plenty (Gen. 41:47); a sabbath every seven years (Lev. 25:2-4); seven years until the Hebrew slave is freed (Jer. 34:14); at the end of every seven years grant a release (Deut. 15:1); famine for seven years (2 Kgs. 8:1); let seven times pass over him (Dan. 4:16, 23, 32); seven times will pass over you (Dan. 4:25); he will make a strong covenant with many for one week (Dan. 9:27).

E2 Ten to 99 years

E2a Ten to 39 years

A woman had had a haemorrhage for 12 years (Matt. 9:20; Mark 5:25; Luke 8:43); 14 years until Paul returned to Jerusalem (Gal. 2:1); a man in Christ who 14 years ago was caught up to the third heaven (2 Cor. 12:2); a woman had a spirit of infirmity for 18 years (Luke 13:11); a daughter of Abraham whom Satan bound for 18 years (Luke 13:16); a man had been ill for 38 years (John 5:5).

E2b 40 years and more

Moses was in Midian 40 years (Acts 7:30); Israel in the wilderness 40 years (Num. 14:33-4; 32:13; Deut. 2:7; 8:2, 4; 29:5; Josh. 5:6; Neh. 9:21; Amos 2:10; 5:25; Acts 7:36, 42; 13:18); they saw my works for 40 years (Heb. 3:9); for every day a year, 40 years (Num. 14:34); Israel ate manna for 40 years (Exod. 16:35); God was grieved with them for 40 years (Ps. 95:10); with whom was he angry for 40 years? (Heb. 3:17); 46 years to build the temple (John 2:20); seven sabbaths [of years,] 49 years, until the Day of Jubilee (Lev. 25:8); seven weeks [of years] until Messiah (Dan. 9:25).

E2c 70 years and more

70 years of exile in Babylon (2 Chr. 36:21; Jer. 25:11, 12; 29:10; Dan. 9:2; Zech. 1:12; 7:5); a typical lifetime (Ps. 90:10); lifetime of 80 years, due to strength (Ps. 90:10).

E3 100 years and more

120 years will be man's days (Gen. 6:3); Enoch walked with God for 300 years (Gen. 5:22); 390 years for the iniquity of Israel (Ezek. 4:5); enslaved and oppressed for 400 years (Gen. 15:13; Acts 7:6); 420 years till the law came (Gal. 3:17); 430 years in Egypt (Exod. 12:40, 41); 62 weeks [of years] (Dan. 9:25-6); after the 62 weeks the anointed one will be cut off (Dan. 9:26); 450 years to gain the inheritance of the land (Acts 13:19); 480 years after they came out of Egypt (1 Kgs. 6:1); 70 weeks [490 years] to make an end of sin (Dan. 9:24).

E4 1000 years and more

1000 years as one day (Ps. 90:4; 2 Pet. 3:8); though he should live 1000 years twice told (Eccles. 6:6); Satan bound for 1000 years (Rev. 20:2-3, 7); martyrs reigning for 1000 years (Rev. 20:4-6); they will reign with him for 1000 years (Rev. 20:6); the rest of the dead did not come to life until after the 1000 years (Rev. 20:5).

111 Course: indefinite duration

PERIOD, see 110.

112 Contingent duration

DURATION, see 110.

113 Long duration

A Long time

A1 Action for a long time

A discharge of blood for a long time (Lev. 15:25); for a long time you bore with them (Neh. 9:30); the king who reads the law will rule a long time (Deut. 17:20); Paul spoke for a long time (Acts 20:7, 11); for a pretence they offer long prayers (Mark 12:40); for a long time he had worn no clothes (Luke 8:27); Jesus saw him and knew he had been lying there a long time (John 5:6); soul, you have goods laid up for many years to come (Luke 12:19); these many years I have served you (Luke 15:29); for many days he appeared (Acts 13:31).

A2 After a long time
We were in our sins a long time and shall we be saved? (Isa. 64:5); a man planted a vineyard and went away for a long time (Luke 20:9); after a long time the master returned (Matt. 25:19).

A3 Staying a long time
We were in Egypt a long time (Num. 20:15); if the cloud stayed over the tabernacle for many days (Num. 9:19); they spent a long time with the disciples (Acts 14:28); they stayed there for a long time (Acts 14:3); they asked him to stay longer (Acts 18:20); I hope to stay with you for some time, if the Lord permits (1 Cor. 16:7).

A4 Long enough
You have stayed long enough at this mountain (Deut. 1:6); you have circled this mountain long enough (Deut. 2:3).

A5 Too long
I have lived too long with those who hate peace (Ps. 120:6).

ETERNAL, see 115.

SINCE YOUTH, see 130C3.

A6 Lifelong
His favour is for a lifetime (Ps. 30:5); goodness and mercy will follow me all the days of my life (Ps. 23:6); Jehoiachin ate in the presence of the king all the days of his life (Jer. 52:33-4); that we might serve him in holiness and righteousness all the days of our life (Luke 1:75); on your belly you shall go and dust shall you eat all the days of your life (Gen. 3:14); those who through fear of death were subject to lifelong bondage (Heb. 2:15).

B Long life
SHORT LIFE, see 114B.

B1 Living long
May his years endure to all generations (Ps. 61:6); he will prolong his days (Isa. 53:10); prolong the king's life! (Ps. 61:6).

B2 How to live long
Who is the man who desires many days? (Ps. 34:12); length of life as a result of obedience (Deut. 25:15; 1 Kgs. 3:14; 1 Pet. 3:10); keep God's commands, that you may live long in the land (Deut. 4:40; 5:33; 6:2; 11:9, 21; 32:47); the fear of the Lord prolongs life (Prov. 10:27); honour your father and mother so that you may live long (Exod. 20:12; Deut. 5:16; Eph. 6:3); length of days and years of life they will add to you (Prov. 3:2); long life is in Wisdom's right hand (Prov. 3:16); by me your days will be multiplied (Prov. 9:11).

B3 God gives long life
The Lord will give you many years in the land (Deut. 30:20); I will fill up the number of your days (Exod. 23:26); with long life I will satisfy him (Ps. 91:16).

B4 Not asking for long life
Solomon did not ask for long life (1 Kgs. 3:11; 2 Chr. 1:11); here we do not have a lasting city (Heb. 13:14).

114 Brief

A Short time

A1 Short time for action
The devil showed him all the kingdoms of the world in a moment of time (Luke 4:5); what does he mean by 'a little while'? (John 16:18); not many days from now you will be baptised with the Spirit (Acts 1:5); her plagues will overtake her in a single day (Rev. 18:8); in one hour your judgement has come (Rev. 18:10); in one hour this wealth has been laid waste (Rev. 18:17-19); they

disciplined us for a short time (Heb. 12:10); the other king must remain a little while (Rev. 17:10).

A2 Short time till the end
If those days had not been shortened no one would be saved (Matt. 24:22); for the sake of the elect the days have been shortened (Mark 13:20); the time has grown short (1 Cor. 7:29); the devil knows his time is short (Rev. 12:12); a little while and the coming one will come (Heb. 10:37); again a little while and you will see me (John 16:16, 17, 19); you may have to suffer for a little while (1 Pet. 1:6); suffer for a little while (1 Pet. 5:10); light affliction for a moment (2 Cor. 4:17).

B Short life
LONG LIFE, see 113B.

B1 Life is short

B1a Mankind is short-lived
Man born of woman is short-lived (Job 14:1); a mist that appears briefly (Jas. 4:14); life is soon gone and we fly away (Ps. 90:10); youth and the prime of life are fleeting (Eccles. 11:10).

B1b Life is like a breath / shadow / grass
Our days on earth are like a shadow (1 Chr. 29:15; Job 8:9); my life is a breath (Job 7:7, 16); man is like a breath, his days a passing shadow (Ps. 144:4); man withers like a flower and flees like a shadow (Job 14:2); my days are like a lengthened shadow and I wither like grass (Ps. 102:11); man's days are like grass (Ps. 103:15); man who is made like grass (Isa. 51:12); all flesh is as grass (Isa. 40:6-8; 1 Pet. 1:24); like grass sprouting in the morning and withering by evening (Ps. 90:5-6).

MAN A MERE BREATH, see 352A5.

B1c How brief is life?
Let me know how brief my life is (Ps. 39:4; 89:47); how long have I yet to live? (2 Sam. 19:34); you have made my days as handbreadths (Ps. 39:5); 120 years (Gen. 6:3); 70 years, or at most 80 (Ps. 90:10); in a few years I shall go the way of no return (Job 16:22).

B2 Long life not achieved
If you turn to other gods you will not live long in the land (Deut. 30:18); who by worrying can add a cubit to his life span? (Matt. 6:27; Luke 12:25).

B3 Life cut short
He cut short my life (Ps. 102:23); he cuts me off from the loom (Isa. 38:12); my days are swifter than a weaver's shuttle (Job 7:6); swifter than a runner (Job 9:25).

B4 Evildoers soon die
Evildoers will wither like grass (Ps. 37:2); the godless die in youth (Job 36:14); such men will not live out half their days (Ps. 55:23); the years of the wicked will be short (Prov. 10:27); the wicked will not lengthen his days like a shadow (Eccles. 8:13); a little while and the wicked will be no more (Ps. 37:10); like flowers of the pasture they will vanish (Ps. 37:20); the rich man will wither like grass (Jas. 1:10-11); if you make idols, you will not live long (Deut. 4:26); your descendants will die in the prime of life (1 Sam. 2:33); let them be like grass on the housetops (Ps. 129:6); let his days be few (Ps. 109:8); you have shortened the days of his youth (Ps. 89:45); God has numbered your reign and ended it (Dan. 5:26).

B5 Christ's short life
Made for a little while lower than the angels (Heb. 2:9); for a little while I am with you (John 13:33); I will be with you a little longer (John 7:33); the light is with you for a little longer (John 12:35); yet a little while and the world will see me no more (John 14:19); a little while and you will see me no more (John 16:16-19).

C Transient things

C1 Transient world

The things that are seen are transient (2 Cor. 4:18); grass alive today and burned tomorrow (Matt. 6:30; Luke 12:28); the joy of the wicked is short (Job 20:5).

C2 Transient wealth

Wealth sprouts wings and flies off (Prov. 23:5); riches are not for ever (Prov. 27:24); his wealth will not endure (Job 15:29); woe to him who heaps up what is not his – for how long? (Hab. 2:6); perishable things like silver and gold (1 Pet. 1:18).

C3 Transient body

The body is sown as a perishable thing (1 Cor. 15:42); the perishable does not inherit the imperishable (1 Cor. 15:50); this perishable must put on the imperishable (1 Cor. 15:53); this mortal will put on immortality (1 Cor. 15:54).

C4 Transient devotion

Your love is like the dew (Hos. 6:4); they will be like the dew (Hos. 13:3); some have no root and endure only for a while (Matt. 13:21; Mark 4:17); they believe for a while and in time of temptation they fall away (Luke 8:13).

C5 Transient hardship

His anger is but for a moment (Ps. 30:5); for a brief moment I forsook you (Isa. 54:7); the seven years seemed like a few days (Gen. 29:20).

D Hireling time

The days of a hireling (Job 7:1); according to the years of a hireling (Isa. 16:14; 21:16).

115 For ever

A Eternity in general

What is not seen is eternal (2 Cor. 4:18); he has set eternity in man's heart (Eccles. 3:11).

B Eternal God

B1 God is eternal

The eternal God (Gen. 21:33; Deut. 33:27; Isa. 40:28; Rom. 16:26); the immortal God (Rom. 1:23); from everlasting to everlasting you are God (Ps. 90:2); you are from everlasting (Ps. 93:2; Hab. 1:12); from eternity I am he (Isa. 43:13); the one who inhabits eternity (Isa. 57:15); as I live for ever (Deut. 32:40); he who lives for ever (Rev. 4:9, 10; 10:6; 15:7); the Lord who abides for ever (Ps. 9:7; 102:12); the living God who endures for ever (Dan. 6:26); the number of God's years is unsearchable (Job 36:26); your years are throughout all generations (Ps. 102:24).

B2 Christ is eternal

Jesus Christ the same yesterday, today and for ever (Heb. 13:8); without beginning or end (Heb. 7:3); his years will never end (Ps. 102:27; Heb. 1:12); you gave him length of days for ever (Ps. 21:4); may his name endure for ever (Ps. 72:17); alive for evermore (Rev. 1:18); the power of an indestructible life (Heb. 7:16); a priest for ever (Ps. 110:4; Heb. 5:6; 6:20; 7:3, 17, 21, 24); a Son who has been made perfect for ever (Heb. 7:28); we have heard that the Christ remains for ever (John 12:34); the Son remains [in the house] for ever (John 8:35); with us always (Matt. 28:20); I saw the Lord always before me (Acts 2:25); he always lives to intercede for them (Heb. 7:25); he is able for ever to save those who draw near to God through him (Heb. 7:25).

B3 The Spirit is eternal

The eternal Spirit (Heb. 9:14); another Counsellor, to be with you for ever (John 14:16).

B4 God's eternal attributes

Eternal: love (Jer. 31:1); lovingkindness (2 Sam. 22:51; 1 Chr. 16:34, 41; Ps. 103:17; Isa. 54:8); name (Exod. 3:15; Ps. 18:50; 89:2; 100:5; 106:1; 107:1; 118:1, 2, 3, 4, 29; 135:13);

136:1-26; 138:8; Isa. 63:12); power and deity (Rom. 1:20); purpose (Eph. 3:11); righteousness (Ps. 111:3; 119:142).

C Eternal dealings

C1 Eternal reign

C1a God reigns for ever

The Lord is king for ever and ever (Ps. 10:16); you, O Lord, rule for ever (Lam. 5:19); your throne is from generation to generation (Lam. 5:19); his kingdom is an everlasting kingdom (Ps. 145:13; Dan. 4:3); the Lord will reign for ever (Exod. 15:18; Ps. 146:10); he will reign for ever and ever (Rev. 11:15); king of the ages (Rev. 15:3); the Lord enthroned as king for ever (Ps. 29:10); you are on high for ever (Ps. 92:8); his dominion is an everlasting dominion (Dan. 4:34); his dominion will be for ever (Dan. 6:26); the Lord will reign over them in Mount Zion for ever (Mic. 4:7); to the King of the ages (1 Tim. 1:17); to him be dominion for ever and ever (1 Pet. 5:11).

C1b David / Christ reigns for ever

On David's house and throne may there be peace from the Lord for ever (1 Kgs. 2:33); the throne of David shall be established before the Lord for ever (1 Kgs. 2:45); David's dynasty would last for ever (Ps. 89:29, 36, 37; 132:12); David my servant will be their prince for ever (Ezek. 37:25); I will establish his kingdom for ever (2 Sam. 7:13, 16; 1 Chr. 22:10; 28:7); the kingdom given to David by an everlasting covenant of salt (2 Chr. 13:5); his throne is for ever and ever (Ps. 45:6); of the Son he says, 'Your throne, O God, is for ever' (Heb. 1:8); eternal dominion (Dan. 7:14); he will reign for ever and his kingdom will not end (Luke 1:33); this kingdom will endure for ever (Dan. 2:44); the eternal kingdom of our Lord and Saviour Jesus Christ (2 Pet. 1:11); to him be glory and dominion for ever and ever (Rev. 1:6).

C1c Believers reign for ever

The saints of the Most High will possess the kingdom for ever (Dan. 7:18); their kingdom will be an everlasting kingdom (Dan. 7:27); they will reign for ever and ever (Rev. 22:5).

C2 Eternal praise

The Creator, blessed for ever (Rom. 1:25); Christ is God over all, blessed for ever (Rom. 9:5); blessed be the Lord from everlasting to everlasting! (1 Chr. 16:36; Ps. 41:13; 106:48); blessed be the name of the Lord from this time forth and for evermore (Ps. 113:2); eternal glory to God (Rom. 11:36; 16:27; Gal. 1:5; Eph. 3:21; Phil. 4:20; Jude 25); to the King be honour and glory for ever and ever (1 Tim. 1:17); to him be glory for ever and ever (2 Tim. 4:18); Jesus Christ, to whom be glory for ever and ever (Heb. 13:21); glory and dominion are his for ever (1 Pet. 4:11); to him be glory, now and to the day of eternity (2 Pet. 3:18); to him be glory and dominion for ever and ever (Rev. 1:6); to him who sits on the throne and to the Lamb be glory for ever (Rev. 5:13); blessing and glory and wisdom be to our God for ever and ever (Rev. 7:12); let the name of God be blessed for ever and ever (Dan. 2:20); the God and Father of the Lord Jesus, who is blessed for ever (2 Cor. 11:31).

C3 Eternal laws

C3a Perpetual statutes for priests

A perpetual statute for the priests: a perpetual priesthood (Exod. 40:15; Num. 25:13); wearing linen underpants (Exod. 28:43); the priesthood (Exod. 29:9); the priests must wash (Exod. 30:21); offering the cereal offering (Lev. 6:22); eating the cereal offering (Lev. 6:18); the priests' portion (Exod. 29:28; Lev. 7:34, 36); not to drink wine when entering the tent of meeting (Lev. 10:9); blowing the trumpets (Num. 10:8); tending the light (Exod. 27:21; Lev. 24:3); having no inheritance (Num. 18:23).

C3b Perpetual statutes for all
A statute throughout your generations (Num. 35:29); a perpetual statute: not to eat fat or blood (Lev. 3:17); the Day of Atonement (Lev. 16:29, 31, 34); to gather the ashes of the red heifer (Num. 19:10, 21); not to sacrifice to goat demons (Lev. 17:7); not to eat new grain before offering the firstfruits (Lev. 23:14); not to work on the Feast of Weeks (Lev. 23:21); not to work on the Day of Atonement (Lev. 23:31); the Feast of Booths (Lev. 23:41); the Passover (Exod. 12:14, 17, 24).

C4 Eternal covenant
Eternal covenant (Gen. 9:12, 16; 17:7, 13, 19; Num. 18:19; 2 Sam. 23:5; 1 Chr. 16:17; Ps. 105:8, 10; 111:5, 9; Isa. 55:3; Jer. 32:40; 50:5; Ezek. 16:60; 37:26; Heb. 13:20); the sabbath an eternal covenant (Exod. 31:16).

C5 Eternal loyalty
I will keep your law for ever and ever (Ps. 119:44); I incline my heart to perform your statutes for ever (Ps. 119:112); may they fear you while sun and moon endure (Ps. 72:5); the slave with pierced ear will serve his master for ever (Exod. 21:6); we will walk in the name of the Lord our God for ever (Mic. 4:5).

C6 Eternal judgement
Eternal judgement (Heb. 6:2); eternal destruction (2 Thess. 1:9); eternal fire (Jude 7); some will awake to everlasting life, others to everlasting contempt (Dan. 12:2); the eternal fire (Matt. 18:8); bend their backs for ever (Rom. 11:10); angels in everlasting bonds in darkness (Jude 6); wandering stars for whom darkness has been reserved for ever (Jude 13); the smoke of their torment goes up for ever and ever (Rev. 14:11); the smoke from her goes up for ever and ever (Rev. 19:3); the devil and his companions will be tormented day and night for ever (Rev. 20:10).

C7 Eternal work
What God does is done for ever (Eccles. 3:14); his ways are everlasting (Hab. 3:6).

C8 Eternal possession
The land given as an everlasting possession (Gen. 17:8; 48:4; Exod. 32:13; Deut. 4:40); to you and your offspring I will give this land for ever (Gen. 13:15); the righteous will dwell in the land for ever (Ps. 37:29); the land your foot has trodden shall be your inheritance for ever (Josh. 14:9); we receive an imperishable wreath (1 Cor. 9:25); we have a building from God, eternal in the heavens (2 Cor. 5:1); eternal inheritance (Heb. 9:15); an inheritance imperishable and undefiled (1 Pet. 1:4); eternal habitations (Luke 16:9).

C9 Eternal evil
Blaspheming against the Holy Spirit is an eternal sin (Mark 3:29).

D Eternal things

D1 Eternal world
The earth remains for ever (Eccles. 1:4); he has established heavens and earth for ever and ever (Ps. 148:6); the earth which he has founded for ever (Ps. 78:69); the everlasting hills (Gen. 49:26; Deut. 33:15); the eternal mountains were shattered (Hab. 3:6); they may receive you into the eternal dwellings (Luke 16:9).

D2 Eternal Jerusalem / temple
Mount Zion abides for ever (Ps. 125:1); Jerusalem will be inhabited for ever (Jer. 17:25); this is my resting-place for ever (Ps. 132:14); I have put my name in this house for ever (1 Kgs. 9:3); my sanctuary will be in their midst for ever (Ezek. 37:26, 28); this is where I will dwell among the Israelites for ever (Ezek. 43:7); Judah and Jerusalem will be inhabited for ever (Joel 3:20).

D3 Eternal truth
For ever your word stands firm in heaven (Ps. 119:89); God's word remains for ever (1 Pet. 1:25); every one of your righteous ordinances endures for ever (Ps. 119:160); his precepts are established for ever and ever (Ps. 111:8); the counsel of the Lord stands for ever (Ps. 33:11); his truth is everlasting (Ps. 117:2); the truth with us for ever (2 John 2); his testimonies founded for ever (Ps. 119:152); the word of our God stands for ever (Isa. 40:8); the fear of the Lord endures for ever (Ps. 19:9); Christ's words will never pass away (Matt. 24:35; Mark 13:31; Luke 21:33).

E Eternal salvation

E1 Eternal deliverance
God's salvation is for ever (Isa. 51:6); eternal salvation (Isa. 45:17; Heb. 5:9); the righteous are preserved for ever (Ps. 37:28); an angel with an eternal gospel to preach (Rev. 14:6).

E2 Eternal existence
The body is raised imperishable (1 Cor. 15:42); the dead will be raised imperishable (1 Cor. 15:52); born again of imperishable seed, the living and abiding word of God (1 Pet. 1:23); he who does the will of God remains for ever (1 John 2:17).

E3 Eternally with God
You set me in your presence for ever (Ps. 41:12); I will dwell in the house of the Lord for ever (Ps. 23:6); let me live in your tent for ever (Ps. 61:4); God is my portion for ever (Ps. 73:26); the Lord surrounds his people for ever (Ps. 125:2); I will dwell among them for ever (Ezek. 43:9); Israel are God's people for ever (2 Sam. 7:24); with the Lord for ever (1 Thess. 4:17).

E4 Eternal life
There the Lord commanded the blessing – life for evermore (Ps. 133:3); labour for the food which endures to eternal life (John 6:27); lay hold of the eternal life to which you were called (1 Tim. 6:12); whoever believes in him will have eternal life (John 3:15-16); that every who believes in the Son should have eternal life (John 6:40); he who believes in him who sent me has eternal life (John 5:24); he who believes has eternal life (John 6:47); those who would believe in him for eternal life (1 Tim. 1:16); if any one eats of this bread he will live for ever (John 6:51, 58); he who eats my flesh and drinks my blood has eternal life (John 6:54); you have the words of eternal life (John 6:68); I give my sheep eternal life (John 10:28); authority to grant eternal life to all you have given him (John 17:2); the fruit you get is sanctification and its end, eternal life (Rom. 6:22); he who sows to the Spirit will reap eternal life (Gal. 6:8); he who hates his life will keep it for eternal life (John 12:25); this is eternal life, that they know you (John 17:3); God has given us eternal life, and this life is in his Son (1 John 5:11); that you may know that you have eternal life (1 John 5:13); this is the true God and eternal life (1 John 5:20).

E5 Eternal blessing
Eternal blessing (2 Sam. 7:29); you have blessed and it is blessed for ever (1 Chr. 17:27); eternal comfort (2 Thess. 2:16); eternal glory (2 Tim. 2:10; 1 Pet. 5:10); eternal weight of glory (2 Cor. 4:17); eternal joy (Isa. 35:10; 51:11; 61:7); eternal redemption (Heb. 9:12); his lovingkindness is on Israel for ever (Ezra 3:11); to bring in everlasting righteousness (Dan. 9:24).

F Man's eternal attributes
The righteousness [of him who fears the Lord] endures for ever (Ps. 112:3; 2 Cor. 9:9); the righteous has an everlasting foundation (Prov. 10:25).

G Not for ever
The Lord will not reject for ever (Lam. 3:31); lest men eat of the tree of life and live for ever (Gen. 3:22); my Spirit shall not remain in man for ever (Gen. 6:3); I will not live for ever (Job 7:16); you will not always have me with you (Matt. 26:11; Mark 14:7).

116 Instantly

A Suddenly

The thing happened suddenly (2 Chr. 29:36); lest he come suddenly (Mark 13:36); lest that day come upon you suddenly (Luke 21:34); they thought the kingdom of God would appear at once (Luke 19:11); God will glorify the Son of man in himself, and that at once (John 13:32); the seed on rocky ground sprang up immediately (Matt. 13:5; Mark 4:5); he hears the word and immediately receives it with joy (Matt. 13:20; Mark 4:16); immediately he falls away (Matt. 13:21); her daughter was healed instantly (Matt. 15:28).

B In a short time

Sodom was overthrown in a moment (Lam. 4:6); in a moment they go down to Sheol (Job 21:13); in a moment they die (Job 34:20); in a short time you would have me a Christian (Acts 26:28); we shall be changed in a moment, in a wink (1 Cor. 15:52).

117 Chronometry

TIME IN GENERAL, see 108A.

118 Anachronism

PREMATURE BIRTH, see 138B.

119 First

A Firstborn

A1 Firstborn of man or animal

Abel offered some of the firstborn of his flock (Gen. 4:4); every firstborn male, man or animal, belongs to God (Exod. 13:2, 12; 34:19; Num. 3:13; 8:17); every male that opens the womb shall be holy to the Lord (Luke 2:23); give me your firstborn sons (Exod. 22:29); the Levites are God's in place of the firstborn males (Num. 3:12; 8:16, 18).

A2 Particular firstborn sons

Israel is God's firstborn son (Exod. 4:22); Ephraim is my firstborn (Jer. 31:9); she gave birth to her firstborn son (Luke 2:7).

A3 Rights of the firstborn

If the firstborn is the son of an unloved wife, his rights should not be lost (Deut. 21:16, 17); it is not the custom to marry the younger before the firstborn (Gen. 29:26); the firstborn was seated according to his birthright (Gen. 43:33); Jehoram was given the kingdom because he was the firstborn (2 Chr. 21:3); Esau sold his birthright (Gen. 25:32-3; Heb. 12:16); Esau despised his birthright (Gen. 25:34); he took my birthright (Gen. 27:36); Reuben's birthright was given to the sons of Joseph (1 Chr. 5:1, 2); having one portion more than his brothers (Gen. 48:22).

A4 Death of the firstborn

The firstborn of the Egyptians killed (Exod. 4:23; 11:5; 12:12, 29; 13:15; Num. 3:13; 8:17; 33:4; Ps. 78:51; 105:36; 135:8; 136:10); the builder of Jericho will lose his firstborn (Josh. 6:26); as Hiel did (1 Kgs. 16:34); that the destroyer of the firstborn might not touch them (Heb. 11:28).

A5 Sacrificing the firstborn

The king of Moab sacrificed his firstborn son (2 Kgs. 3:27); they made their firstborn pass through the fire (Ezek. 20:26); shall I give my firstborn for my transgression? (Mic. 6:7).

A6 Christ the firstborn

I will make him the firstborn (Ps. 89:27); Christ is the firstborn of all creation (Col. 1:15); he is before all things (Col. 1:17); the firstborn from the dead (Col. 1:18; Rev. 1:5); the firstborn among many brothers (Rom. 8:29); the assembly of the firstborn who are enrolled in heaven (Heb. 12:23).

FIRSTFRUITS, see 171D.

B First actions

Seek first his kingdom and his righteousness (Matt. 6:33); first take the log out of your own eye (Matt. 7:5); first cleanse the inside of cup and dish (Matt. 23:26); the gospel must first be preached to all nations (Mark 13:10); this was the first census (Luke 2:2); let me first bury my father (Matt. 8:21; Luke 9:59); I will follow you, but first let me say goodbye (Luke 9:61); every man serves the good wine first (John 2:10); the first of his signs (John 2:11); we love because he first loved us (1 John 4:19).

BEGINNING TO ACT, see 68E.

C Before

Before me there was no god formed (Isa. 43:10); before Abraham was, I AM (John 8:58); your Father knows what you need before you ask him (Matt. 6:8); before they call I will answer (Isa. 65:24); do not be anxious beforehand about what you are to say (Mark 13:11); she has anointed my body beforehand for burial (Mark 14:8); this must take place first (Luke 21:9); do not judge before the time (1 Cor. 4:5); before Philip called you, I saw you (John 1:48).

FIRST DAY, see 108F1.

120 Afterwards

There will be no god after me (Isa. 43:10); afterward he changed his mind and went (Matt. 21:29); you did not afterwards repent (Matt. 21:32).

DAYS TO COME, see 124.

121 Present time

A Now

The hour is coming and now is when true worshippers will worship in spirit (John 4:23); the hour is coming and now is when the dead will hear (John 5:25); now is the day of salvation (2 Cor. 6:2); will you at this time restore the kingdom to Israel? (Acts 1:6).

B Today

The Lord will take away your master today (2 Kgs. 2:3, 5); today I have begotten you (Ps. 2:7); as long as it is called 'Today' (Heb. 3:13); he sets a certain day, 'Today' (Heb. 4:7); today, if you hear his voice (Ps. 95:7; Heb. 3:7, 15; 4:7); today you will be with me in paradise (Luke 23:43); give us this day our daily bread (Matt. 6:11); today in the city of David is born a Saviour (Luke 2:11); today this scripture has been fulfilled in your hearing (Luke 4:21); I cast out demons and cure today and tomorrow (Luke 13:32); I must go on my way today and tomorrow and the next day (Luke 13:33); would that even today you knew the things that make for peace! (Luke 19:42); Jesus Christ is the same yesterday, today and for ever (Heb. 13:8); today or tomorrow we will go to such and such a town (Jas. 4:13).

C Present age

Why do you not know how to interpret the present time? (Luke 12:56); Christ saves us from the present evil age (Gal. 1:4); the sufferings of the present time (Rom. 8:18); Demas, in love with this present world (2 Tim. 4:10); the tabernacle symbolises the present time (Heb. 9:9); things present cannot separate us from the love of God (Rom. 8:38); the present and the future are yours (1 Cor. 3:22); blasphemy against the Spirit will not be forgiven in this age or in that to come (Matt. 12:32); he will receive 100 times as much now in the present age (Mark 10:30); the sons of this age marry and are given in marriage (Luke 20:34); a wisdom not of this age nor of the rulers of this age (1 Cor. 2:6); training in godliness has promise for the present life (1 Tim. 4:8); why not, if there will be peace in my lifetime? (2 Kgs. 20:19).

D To this day

D1 Places to this day

To this day: the pillar of Rachel's grave (Gen. 35:20); 12 stones stand in the middle of Jordan (Josh. 4:9); a heap of stones over Achan (Josh. 7:26); a heap of stones over the king of Ai (Josh. 8:29); stones over the mouth of the cave (Josh. 10:27); the large stone is a witness (1 Sam. 6:18); the altar is in Ophrah (Judg. 6:24); Ai is a desolation (Josh. 8:28); En-hakkore is in Lehi (Judg. 15:19); no one knows where Moses is buried (Deut. 34:6); the poles of the ark are still there (1 Kgs. 8:8; 2 Chr. 5:9); it is said, 'In the mount of the Lord it will be seen' (Gen. 22:14); the waters have been healed (2 Kgs. 2:22); David's tomb is with us (Acts 2:29).

D2 Given names to this day

To this day called: Beersheba (Gen. 26:33); Sela renamed Joktheel (2 Kgs. 14:7); the valley of Beracah (2 Chr. 20:26); Havvoth-jair (Judg. 10:4); Luz (Judg. 1:26); Mahaneh-dan (Judg. 18:12); Perez-uzzah (2 Sam. 6:8; 1 Chr. 13:11); the Field of Blood (Matt. 27:8).

D3 Where people live to this day

To this day: the sons of Esau live in Mount Seir (Deut. 2:22); the Canaanites live among Ephraim (Josh. 16:10); the Geshurites and Maacathites live among Israel (Josh. 13:13); the Jebusites live at Jerusalem (Josh. 15:63; Judg. 1:21); Rahab has lived among Israel (Josh. 6:25); the Arameans live in Elath (2 Kgs. 16:6); Israel exiled to Assyria (2 Kgs. 17:23); the Simeonites live in Mount Seir (1 Chr. 4:43); Hebron belongs to Caleb (Josh. 14:14); Ziklag belongs to the kings of Judah (1 Sam. 27:6).

D4 Statutes to this day

To this day: a statute in the land of Egypt (Gen. 47:26); the Israelites do not eat the sinew of the hip (Gen. 32:32); the Levites' ministry (Deut. 10:8); hewers of wood and drawers of water (Josh. 9:27); equal sharing of booty (1 Sam. 30:25).

D5 False religion to this day

To this day: you defile yourselves with your idols (Ezek. 20:31); the Samaritans do not truly fear the Lord (2 Kgs. 17:34); they fear the Lord and serve their idols (2 Kgs. 17:41); they have provoked me to anger (2 Kgs. 21:15); they and their fathers have transgressed against me (Ezek. 2:3); this story has been spread among the Jews (Matt. 28:15); God gave them blind eyes and deaf ears (Rom. 11:8).

D6 Events unique to this day

To this day there has not been seen: such hail (Exod. 9:18); such locusts (Exod. 10:6); such almug trees (1 Kgs. 10:12).

122 Different time

PAST TIME, see 125.

123 Synchronism

A On the same day

Do not kill an animal and its young on the same day (Lev. 22:28); your two sons, Hophni and Phinehas, will die on the same day (1 Sam. 2:34).

B While still speaking

While you are still speaking I will come in and confirm it (1 Kgs. 1:14); while she was still speaking Nathan the prophet came in (1 Kgs. 1:22); while the words were still in the king's mouth, a voice came (Dan. 4:31); while he was still speaking the cock crowed (Luke 22:60); while they are still speaking I will hear (Isa. 65:24); while he was still speaking the Holy Spirit fell on them (Acts 10:44; 11:15).

124 Future time

A The future in general

Things to come cannot separate us from the love of God (Rom. 8:38); the present and the future are yours (1 Cor. 3:22); let them tell us what is to come (Isa. 41:22); that which is or is to be has already been (Eccles. 3:15); what has been is what will be (Eccles. 1:9).

B Tomorrow

B1 About tomorrow

Do not boast about tomorrow (Prov. 27:1); today or tomorrow we will go to such and such a town (Jas. 4:13); you do not know about tomorrow (Jas. 4:14); do not be anxious about tomorrow (Matt. 6:34); let us eat and drink, for tomorrow we die (1 Cor. 15:32); do not say, 'Tomorrow I will give it' (Prov. 3:28).

B2 God's action tomorrow

When? tomorrow (Exod. 8:10); at this time tomorrow (Exod. 9:18); tomorrow this sign will happen (Exod. 8:23); tomorrow the swarms will go (Exod. 8:29); tomorrow the Lord will do this thing (Exod. 9:5-6); tomorrow I will bring locusts (Exod. 10:4); in the morning the Lord will show who is his (Num. 16:5); tomorrow the Lord will do wonders among you (Josh. 3:5); tomorrow I will deliver them into your hand (Josh. 11:6); tomorrow you will have deliverance (1 Sam. 11:9); tomorrow I will send a man (1 Sam. 9:16).

C Things to come

C1 Judgement to come

The wrath to come (Matt. 3:7; Luke 3:7; 1 Thess. 1:10); future judgement (Acts 24:25); the days will come when there will not be one stone on another (Luke 21:6); the days are coming when the barren will be considered happy (Luke 23:29).

C2 Unknown future

He does not know what is to be (Eccles. 8:7); who can tell man what will be after him? (Eccles. 6:12; 10:14); who can show him what will be after him? (Eccles. 3:22); man cannot find out what will be after him (Eccles. 7:14); there will be no remembrance of things still to happen (Eccles. 1:11).

C3 Revelation of the future

As you lay in bed came thoughts of what would happen in the future (Dan. 2:29); he has made known to King Nebuchadnezzar what will happen in the latter days (Dan. 2:28); he who reveals mysteries has made known to you what will take place (Dan. 2:29); the vision is for days yet to come (Dan. 10:14); the vision pertains to many days hence (Dan. 8:26); you have spoken of the far future (2 Sam. 7:19); what this people will do to your people in days to come (Num. 24:14); in the last days the mountain of the house of the Lord will be established (Isa. 2:2; Mic. 4:1).

C4 The future age

The age to come (Matt. 12:32; Mark 10:30; Luke 18:30; Eph. 1:21); the powers of the age to come (Heb. 6:5); the world to come (Heb. 2:5); training in godliness has promise for the life to come (1 Tim. 4:8); the city to come (Heb. 13:14); blessings to come (Heb. 11:20); good things to come (Heb. 9:11); blessed is the coming kingdom of our father David (Mark 11:10); that in the ages to come he might show the riches of his kindness to us (Eph. 2:7); the hour is coming when neither on this mountain nor in Jerusalem will you worship (John 4:21); the hour is coming when all who are in the tombs will hear his voice (John 5:28).

C5 Future generations

This covenant is also with those not here this day (Deut. 29:15); they will tell his righteousness to a people yet unborn (Ps. 22:30-1); a people yet unborn will praise the Lord (Ps. 102:18); in time to come your children may say to our children (Josh. 22:24).

C6 Personal future

Plans to give you a future and a hope (Jer. 29:11); there is hope for your future (Jer. 31:17); surely there will be a future (Prov. 23:18; 24:14); storing up for themselves a good foundation for the future (1 Tim. 6:19).

KNOWING THE FUTURE, see 510.

PREDICTING THE FUTURE, see 511A.

125 Past time

A The past in general

Ask about former days (Deut. 4:32; 32:7); do not ask why former days were better (Eccles. 7:10); I remember the days of old (Ps. 143:5); I have considered the days of old (Ps. 77:5); he remembered the days of old (Isa. 63:11); remember the former things (Isa. 46:9); do not ponder the things of the past (Isa. 43:18); that which is or is to be has already been (Eccles. 3:15); what has been is what will be (Eccles. 1:9); it has existed for ages already (Eccles. 1:10); he is a prophet, like one of the prophets of old (Mark 6:15); the mystery was not made known to previous generations (Eph. 3:5).

B God of old

B1 God being of old

Before the world was formed, you are God (Ps. 90:2); your throne is established from of old (Ps. 93:2); before the Lord's acts of old he possessed Wisdom (Prov. 8:22); from everlasting I [Wisdom] was established (Prov. 8:23); his goings forth are from eternity (Mic. 5:2); Jesus Christ is the same yesterday, today and for ever (Heb. 13:8).

B2 God planning of old

Wisdom God decreed before the ages (1 Cor. 2:7); from ancient times God planned it (2 Kgs. 19:25; Isa. 37:26); you did not have regard for him who planned it long ago (Isa. 22:11); you have carried out plans formed from long ago (Isa. 25:1); grace given in Christ ages ago (2 Tim. 1:9); from of old their condemnation has not been idle (2 Pet. 2:3); long ago they were marked out for condemnation (Jude 4).

B3 God speaking of old

God spoke of old by the prophets (Luke 1:70; Acts 3:21; Heb. 1:1); the Lord has made these things known from of old (Acts 15:18); who among them can declare the former things? (Isa. 43:9); I declared the former things (Isa. 48:3); things written in former times (Rom. 15:4); it was said to men of old (Matt. 5:21, 33); eternal life which God promised ages ago (Titus 1:2); God announced it long ago (Isa. 45:21; 48:5); steadfast love which you swore to our fathers from days of old (Mic. 7:20).

B4 God acting of old

Of old you founded the earth (Ps. 102:25); our fathers have told us what you did in days of old (Ps. 44:1); I will remember your wonders of old (Ps. 77:11); awake as in days of old (Isa. 51:9); he carried them all the days of old (Isa. 63:9); in past generations he allowed all nations to walk in their own ways (Acts 14:16).

C History of people

Let the time past suffice for bad conduct (1 Pet. 4:3); you came only yesterday (2 Sam. 15:20).

126 Newness

A Unused

A heifer which has never been yoked (Num. 19:2; Deut. 21:3, 4); two milch cows, never yoked (1 Sam. 6:7); a colt which no one had ever sat (Mark 11:2; Luke 19:30); a new tomb (Matt. 27:60; Luke 23:53; John 19:41); unshrunk cloth (Matt. 9:16; Mark 2:21; Luke 5:36); unused wineskins (Matt. 9:17; Mark 2:22; Luke

5:38); these wineskins were new (Josh. 9:13); altars of uncut stones (Exod. 20:25; Deut. 27:5, 6; Josh. 8:31); the ark on a new cart (1 Sam. 6:7; 2 Sam. 6:3; 1 Chr. 13:7); Samson was bound with new ropes (Judg. 15:13; 16:11); Ahijah wore a new cloak (1 Kgs. 11:29); bring me a new jar with salt in it (2 Kgs. 2:20); you have not been this way before (Josh. 3:4).

B Renewed

The renewing of the Holy Spirit (Titus 3:5); the renewal of your mind (Rom. 12:2); renewed in the spirit of your minds (Eph. 4:23); renew our days as of old (Lam. 5:21); renewed daily (2 Cor. 4:16).

C Not known before

C1 New creation

I make all things new (Rev. 21:5); I am doing a new thing (Isa. 43:19); the Lord has created a new thing on the earth (Jer. 31:22); I declare new things (Isa. 42:9; 48:6); if anyone is in Christ he is a new creation (2 Cor. 5:17); a new creation (Gal. 6:15); old things have passed away, the new has come (2 Cor. 5:17).

C2 New things

A new commandment (John 13:34; 1 John 2:8); I am not writing you a new commandment (1 John 2:7; 2 John 5); a new covenant (2 Cor. 3:6; Heb. 8:8, 13; 9:15; 12:24); this cup is the new covenant in my blood (Luke 22:20; 1 Cor. 11:25); new heaven and earth (Isa. 65:17; 66:22; 2 Pet. 3:13; Rev. 21:1); new Jerusalem (Rev. 3:12; 21:2); a new name (Isa. 62:2; Rev. 3:12); a new song (Ps. 33:3; 40:3; 96:1; 98:1; 144:9; 149:1; Isa. 42:10; Rev. 5:9; 14:3); new teaching (Mark 1:27; Acts 17:19); if the Lord creates something new and the earth swallows them (Num. 16:30); the Athenians spent their time in nothing other than telling or hearing something new (Acts 17:21); we enter by a new and living way (Heb. 10:20); a householder with old and new in his treasure (Matt. 13:52).

NEW COVENANT, see 765A5.

C3 New life

The new man (Eph. 4:24); you have put on the new man (Col. 3:10); one new man in place of the two (Eph. 2:15); walk in newness of life (Rom. 6:4); serve in the new life of the Spirit (Rom. 7:6); the Lord's mercies are new every morning (Lam. 3:23); the new man is being renewed after the image of its Creator (Col. 3:10).

C4 New heart

I will put a new spirit within them (Ezek. 11:19); I will give you a new heart and a new spirit (Ezek. 36:26); make yourselves a new heart and a new spirit (Ezek. 18:31).

C5 Nothing new

There is nothing new under the sun (Eccles. 1:9); everything has already been (Eccles. 3:15); what has been is what will be (Eccles. 1:9); is there anything of which one could say, 'This is new'? (Eccles. 1:10).

D Fresh

As a well keeps its waters fresh so she keeps fresh her wickedness (Jer. 6:7); fresh dough with no leaven (1 Cor. 5:7); till I drink new wine with you (Matt. 26:29; Mark 14:25); no one puts new wine into old wineskins (Matt. 9:17; Mark 2:22; Luke 5:37-8); if they do this when the wood is green (Luke 23:31).

127 Oldness

OLD PERSON, see 133.

A Old things

You will eat the old and clear out the old to make way for the new food (Lev. 26:10); when you sow in the eighth year you will be eating old produce (Lev. 25:22); ask for the ancient paths (Jer. 6:16); they have stumbled from the ancient paths (Jer. 18:15); a patch of unshrunk cloth tears away from an old garment (Matt. 9:16); new wine is not put into old wineskins (Matt. 9:17; Mark 2:22; Luke 5:37); make for yourselves purses which do not grow old (Luke 12:33); we serve in the new life of the Spirit, not the old written code (Rom. 7:6); the old is good (Luke 5:39); whatever is obsolete and growing old is ready to vanish (Heb. 8:13); an old commandment which you have had from the beginning (1 John 2:7).

B Old nature
Our old self was crucified with him (Rom. 6:6); put off the old man (Eph. 4:22); you have put off the old man (Col. 3:9); old things have gone (2 Cor. 5:17); clean out the old leaven (1 Cor. 5:7).

C Traditions

C1 Traditions in general
Zealous for the traditions of my fathers (Gal. 1:14); I had done nothing against the customs of our fathers (Acts 28:17); the customs of the peoples are false (Jer. 10:3); they walked in the customs of the nations (2 Kgs. 17:8); their fear of me is a commandment of men learned by rote (Isa. 29:13); you break God's command for the sake of your tradition (Matt. 15:3, 6; Mark 7:8-9, 13); see no one deludes you by human tradition (Col. 2:8); teaching as doctrines the traditions of men (Matt. 15:9).

OLD SAYINGS, see 496B.

C2 Particular traditions
A custom: to lament Jephthah's daughter (Judg. 11:40); taking off a shoe to indicate transfer of rights (Ruth 4:7); the priests taking meat (1 Sam. 2:13-14); the sharing of booty (1 Sam. 30:25); the prophets of Baal cutting themselves (1 Kgs. 18:28); the Israelites do not eat the sinew of the thigh (Gen. 32:32); the priests of Dagon do not tread on the threshold (1 Sam. 5:5); celebrating Purim (Esther 9:27-8); the Pharisees observed the traditions of the elders by washing before eating (Mark 7:3-4); they observe many other traditions, such as the washing of cups and pots and copper vessels (Mark 7:4); the governor was accustomed to release one prisoner at the feast (Matt. 27:15; Mark 15:6; John 18:39); the body was wrapped in linen cloths, as is the burial custom of the Jews (John 19:40).

C3 Personal customs
As his custom was: Jesus taught them (Mark 10:1); Jesus went to the synagogue on the sabbath (Luke 4:16); Jesus went to the Mount of Olives (Luke 22:39); Paul went to the synagogue on the sabbath (Acts 17:2).

C4 Customs challenged
It is not our custom to marry the younger first (Gen. 29:26); such a thing is not done in Israel (2 Sam. 13:12); it is not the custom of the Romans to give up a man untried (Acts 25:16); they promote customs which it is not lawful for Romans to accept (Acts 16:21); why do your disciples transgress the tradition of the elders? (Matt. 15:2; Mark 7:5); Jesus will alter the customs Moses handed down to us (Acts 6:14); they hear you teach Jews not to observe the customs (Acts 21:21).

C5 Christian traditions
Holding to the traditions as Paul delivered them (1 Cor. 11:2); hold to the traditions (2 Thess. 2:15); those who live not according to the tradition (2 Thess. 3:6).

128 Morning. Spring. Summer

A Daybreak

A1 The dawn
How you have fallen, morning star, son of the dawn (Isa. 14:12); if I take the wings of the dawn (Ps. 139:9); have you commanded the dawn to take place? (Job 38:12); you make the dawn and the sunset sing for joy (Ps. 65:8); his going forth is sure as the dawn (Hos.

6:3); he who makes the dawn into darkness (Amos 4:13); I will awake the dawn (Ps. 57:8; 108:2); I wait for the Lord more than watchmen for the morning (Ps. 130:6); they wished for day to break (Acts 27:29).

A2 Until daybreak
A man wrestled with Jacob until dawn (Gen. 32:24); she lay at his feet until morning (Ruth 3:14); let us take our fill of love till morning (Prov. 7:18); Paul talked with them until daybreak (Acts 20:11).

A3 At daybreak
God will help her at break of day (Ps. 46:5); let me go for dawn is breaking (Gen. 32:26); at break of day the king went to the lions' den (Dan. 6:19); at dawn the concubine fell at the doorway (Judg. 19:26); you do not know when, in the evening, midnight, at cockcrow or in the morning (Mark 13:35); as it began to dawn on the first day of the week (Matt. 28:1); when the sun had risen (Mark 16:2); they came to the tomb at dawn (Luke 24:1); they entered the temple at daybreak and taught (Acts 5:21); when day came the magistrates sent to release them (Acts 16:35).

A4 Spiritual dawn
When the sunrise from on high visits us (Luke 1:78); I will give him the morning star (Rev. 2:28); Christ the morning star (Rev. 22:16); till day dawns and the morning star rises in your hearts (2 Pet. 1:19); the day is at hand (Rom. 13:12).

B Rising early

B1 About rising early
The good wife rises while it is still light (Prov. 31:15); it is in vain that you rise early (Ps. 127:2); woe to those who rise early to pursue strong wine (Isa. 5:11); I rise before dawn and cry for help (Ps. 119:147).

B2 Those who rose early
Rising early: God (Jer. 7:13, 25; 11:7; 25:3, 4; 26:5; 29:19; 32:33; 35:14, 15; 44:4); the angels (Gen. 19:2); Jesus (Mark 1:35); the people (Judg. 21:4); people wanting to hear Jesus (Luke 21:38).

C Morning

C1 About morning
If the sun has risen, killing a burglar is culpable (Exod. 22:3); Aaron is to burn incense every morning (Exod. 30:7); how you have fallen, morning star, son of the dawn (Isa. 14:12); the hind of the morning (Ps. 22:t).

C2 In the morning
Joy comes in the morning (Ps. 30:5); let me hear your lovingkindness in the morning (Ps. 143:8); satisfy us in the morning with your lovingkindness that we may rejoice (Ps. 90:14); woe to the land whose princes feast in the morning (Eccles. 10:16); in the morning you will long for evening, and at evening for morning (Deut. 28:67); he who blesses with a loud voice early in the morning is like one who curses (Prov. 27:14); in the morning it was Leah (Gen. 29:25); when morning came they took counsel how to kill Jesus (Matt. 27:1; Mark 15:1); Ezra read the law from early morning to midday (Neh. 8:3); in the morning they saw the fig tree withered (Mark 11:20); you do not know when, in the evening, midnight, at cockcrow or in the morning (Mark 13:35); early on the first day of the week (Mark 16:2); some women were at the tomb early in the morning (Luke 24:22); it was early (John 18:28); Mary Magdalene came to the tomb early while it was still dark (John 20:1).

C3 Worship in the morning
One lamb sacrificed each morning (Exod. 29:39; Num. 28:4; Ezek. 46:13); the lamb, the cereal offering and the oil, morning by morning (Ezek. 46:15); at the time of the morning sacrifice (2 Kgs. 3:20); in the early morning while still dark he went to pray (Mark 1:35); in the morning I will pray to you (Ps. 5:3); in the morning

you hear my voice (Ps. 5:3); in the morning my prayer comes to you (Ps. 88:13); I will sing of your lovingkindness in the morning (Ps. 59:16).

C4 Every morning
The Lord's mercies are new every morning (Lam. 3:23); every morning he shows forth his justice (Zeph. 3:5); morning by morning he wakens me (Isa. 50:4).

D Morning and evening
D1 At morning and evening
There was evening and there was morning (Gen. 1:5, 8, 13, 19, 23, 31); morning is coming and also the night (Isa. 21:12); to declare your lovingkindness in the morning and your faithfulness by night (Ps. 92:2); evening, morning and noon I meditate (Ps. 55:17); sow your seed morning and evening (Eccles. 11:6); Goliath issued his challenge morning and evening (1 Sam. 17:16); the ravens brought bread and meat morning and evening (1 Kgs. 17:6).

D2 From morning till evening
The people stood around Moses from morning to evening (Exod. 18:13, 14); from dawn until the stars appeared (Neh. 4:21); from sunrise to sunset the name of the Lord is to be praised (Ps. 113:3); he expounded the gospel to them from morning till evening (Acts 28:23).

E Daytime
E1 Provision of day
God called the light 'day' (Gen. 1:5); the big light to govern the day (Gen. 1:16, 18); the sun to rule by day (Ps. 136:8).

E2 During the day
A pillar of cloud by day (Exod. 13:21, 22; Neh. 9:12, 19); there was cloud in the tabernacle by day (Exod. 40:38); the cloud was over them by day (Num. 10:34); by day the heat consumed me (Gen. 31:40); another will lie with your wives in broad daylight (2 Sam. 12:11); I will do it under the sun (2 Sam. 12:12); debauchery in the daytime is counted as pleasure (2 Pet. 2:13).
NOON, see 108E4d.

E3 All day
All day long: they devise treachery (Ps. 38:12); they are a fire that burns (Isa. 65:5); they say, 'Where is your God?' (Ps. 42:10); my disgrace is before me (Ps. 44:15); they oppress me (Ps. 56:1, 2); they twist my words (Ps. 56:5); for your sake we are killed (Ps. 44:22; Rom. 8:36); in God we boast (Ps. 44:8).

E4 Using the day
We are sons of the day (1 Thess. 5:5, 8); conduct yourselves as in the day (Rom. 13:13); we must work the works of him who sent me while it is day (John 9:4); if any one walks in the day (John 11:9).

F Day and night
F1 Provision of day and night
Lights in the firmament to divide between day and night (Gen. 1:14); day and night will not cease (Gen. 8:22); if you can break my covenant with day and night (Jer. 33:20, 25); yours is the day, yours the night (Ps. 74:16); day to day pours out speech, night to night declares knowledge (Ps. 19:2).

F2 Day or night
You will not fear the terror by night or the arrow by day (Ps. 91:5); the sun will not smite you by day nor the moon by night (Ps. 121:6); your gates will not be closed day or night (Isa. 60:11); continual day, neither day nor night, known to the Lord (Zech. 14:7).

F3 By day and by night
F3a Labour day and night
The Israelites travelled by day and by night (Exod. 13:21); all day and all night gathering quail (Num. 11:32); the singers worked day and night (1 Chr. 9:33); we set a guard day and night (Neh. 4:9); day and night

they go around on her walls (Ps. 55:10); they watched the gates day and night (Acts 9:24); night and day he was crying out and gashing himself with stones (Mark 5:5); night and day for three years I did not cease to admonish you (Acts 20:31); you remember our toil, working night and day (1 Thess. 2:9); we toiled night and day (2 Thess. 3:8).

F3b Worship day and night
Meditate on this book of the law day and night (Josh. 1:8); in his law he meditates day and night (Ps. 1:2); all day and all night the watchmen will never be silent (Isa. 62:6); listen to prayer day and night (1 Kgs. 8:29; 2 Chr. 6:20); may my words be near to the Lord day and night (1 Kgs. 8:59); I pray day and night (Neh. 1:6); I cry to you day and night (Ps. 88:1); I watch day and night (Isa. 21:8); by day and night I cry but you do not answer (Ps. 22:2); Anna worshipped with fasting and prayer night and day (Luke 2:37); the 12 tribes worship night and day (Acts 26:7); night and day we pray we may see you again (1 Thess. 3:10); a true widow continues in prayers night and day (1 Tim. 5:5); I remember you in my prayers night and day (2 Tim. 1:3); they serve him day and night in his temple (Rev. 7:15).

F3c Affliction day and night
Day and night your hand was heavy on me (Ps. 32:4); you will fear night and day (Deut. 28:66); there you will serve other gods day and night (Jer. 16:13); my tears have been my food day and night (Ps. 42:3); he accuses the brethren day and night (Rev. 12:10); they have no rest day or night (Rev. 14:11).

F3d Protection day and night
The men were a wall to us by night and by day (1 Sam. 25:16); she kept away birds by day and beasts by night (2 Sam. 21:10); a pillar of cloud by day and a pillar of fire by night (Num. 14:14); with a cloud by day and a fire by night (Ps. 78:14); the Lord commands his lovingkindness in the day and his song is with me at night (Ps. 42:8).

G Spring of the year
Seedtime and harvest will not cease (Gen. 8:22); in the spring, when kings go to war (2 Sam. 11:1; 1 Chr. 20:1); the Lord gives the autumn rain and spring rain (Jer. 5:24); he has given you the latter [spring] rain (Joel 2:23); locusts when the latter [spring] crop was sprouting (Amos 7:1); ask rain from the Lord in the season of spring rain (Zech. 10:1); winter is past and plants are growing (S. of S. 2:11-13).

H Summer
H1 Summer in general
When the fig tree sprouts, summer is near (Matt. 24:32; Mark 13:28; Luke 21:30); ants prepare their food in summer (Prov. 6:8; 30:25); he who gathers in summer is a wise son (Prov. 10:5); a basket of summer fruit (Amos 8:1, 2); harvest is past, summer is ended (Jer. 8:20).

H2 Summer and winter
Summer and winter will not cease (Gen. 8:22); you have made summer and winter (Ps. 74:17).

129 Evening. Autumn. Winter
A Sunset
Sacrifice the Passover at sunset (Deut. 16:6); return a pledged cloak by sunset (Exod. 22:26); return a poor man's pledge by sunset (Deut. 24:13); pay a hired man before sunset (Deut. 24:15); at sunset, hanged bodies were taken down (Josh. 8:29; 10:27); Moses' hands were steady till the sun went down (Exod. 17:12); David would not eat until the sun went down (2 Sam. 3:35).

B Evening
MORNING AND EVENING, see 128D.

B1 Evening in general
In the evening you will long for morning (Deut. 28:67); at evening you say it will be fair weather (Matt. 16:2); at evening there will still be light (Zech. 14:7); you do not know when, in the evening, midnight, at cockcrow or in the morning (Mark 13:35); do not let the sun go down on your anger (Eph. 4:26).

B2 Particular evenings
David rose from his bed at evening (2 Sam. 11:2); at the time of the evening offering Elijah prayed (1 Kgs. 18:36); the two angels came to Sodom in the evening (Gen. 19:1); the servant came at evening (Gen. 24:11); the day is nearly over, so spend the night here (Judg. 19:9).

B3 Evenings for Jesus and his disciples
In the evening they brought the sick to Jesus (Matt. 8:16; Mark 1:32; Luke 4:40); at evening he was reclining at table (Matt. 26:20); when it was evening he came with the twelve (Mark 14:17); when evening came Nicodemus asked for Jesus' body (Matt. 27:57); when evening came Joseph asked for the body (Mark 15:42-3); stay with us, for evening is near (Luke 24:29); when it was evening on the first day of the week (John 20:19).

B4 Until evening
B4a Action until evening
Man goes to work until evening (Ps. 104:23); they wept before the Lord until evening (Judg. 20:23, 26; 21:2); Ruth gleaned until evening (Ruth 2:17).

B4b Unclean until evening
Unclean until evening: those touching unclean things (Lev. 15:5, 6, 7, 8, 10, 11, 17, 18, 19, 21, 22, 23, 27; 17:15; Num. 19:22); the priest who attends to the red heifer (Num. 19:7); he who burns the red heifer (Num. 19:8); he who gathers the ashes of the red heifer (Num. 19:10); he who sprinkles the water of impurity (Num. 19:19, 21); he who touches the carcass of an unclean animal (Lev. 11:24, 27, 31, 39); an article on which their carcass falls (Lev. 11:32); he who carries their carcasses (Lev. 11:25, 28, 40); he who eats their carcasses (Lev. 11:40); he who enters a quarantined house (Lev. 14:46); a man with an emission of semen (Lev. 15:16); a priest touching unclean things (Lev. 22:6).

C Night
DAY AND NIGHT, see 128F.
C1 Provision of night
God called the darkness 'night' (Gen. 1:5); you appoint darkness and it becomes night (Ps. 104:20); lights in the firmament to divide between day and night (Gen. 1:14); the small light to govern the night (Gen. 1:16, 18); the moon and the stars to rule by night (Ps. 136:9); while the earth remains, day and night will not cease (Gen. 8:22); morning is coming and also the night (Isa. 21:12); there shall be no night (Rev. 21:25; 22:5).

C2 By night
A pillar of fire by night (Exod. 13:21, 22; Neh. 9:12, 19); there was fire in the tabernacle by night (Exod. 40:38); they are coming at night to kill you (Neh. 6:10); one calling from Seir, 'Watchman, what of the night?' (Isa. 21:11); the day of the Lord like a thief in the night (1 Thess. 5:2); if thieves came by night would they not steal only enough? (Obad. 5); if the householder had known at what time of night the thief was coming (Matt. 24:43); shepherds keeping watch over their flock by night (Luke 2:8).

C3 Visions at night
Dreams in the night (Gen. 40:5); God appeared to Isaac at night (Gen. 26:24); God spoke to Israel in visions of the night (Gen. 46:2); the word of the Lord came to Nathan at night (2 Sam. 7:4); God appeared to Solomon at night (1 Kgs. 3:5; 2 Chr. 7:12); the mystery

was revealed to Daniel in a vision of the night (Dan. 2:19); I saw in my vision by night (Dan. 7:2); the following night the Lord stood by him (Acts 23:11); Paul had a vision during the night (Acts 16:9; 18:9).

C4 During one night
Pharaoh summoned Moses and Aaron at night (Exod. 12:31); Israel came out of Egypt during the night (Deut. 16:1); Gideon cut down the Asherah at night (Judg. 6:27); Saul came to the witch at night (1 Sam. 28:8); Nehemiah examined the walls by night (Neh. 2:12, 13, 15); Joseph fled to Egypt with Mary and the child by night (Matt. 2:14); Nicodemus came to Jesus at night (John 3:2; 19:39); his disciples came by night and stole him away while we were sleeping (Matt. 28:13); Paul was lowered down the walls in a basket by night (Acts 9:25); the brethren sent Paul and Silas away by night (Acts 17:10); Paul was brought to Antipatris by night (Acts 23:31); you will all fall away this night (Matt. 26:31); this very night you will deny me (Matt. 26:34; Mark 14:30); an angel of the Lord opened the prison in the night (Acts 5:19); the very night when Herod was about to bring him out (Acts 12:6); this night your soul is required of you (Luke 12:20).

MIDNIGHT, see 108E3.

C5 All night long
C5a Overnight
The fat of the sacrifices is not to be kept overnight (Exod. 23:18); meat of the peace offering is not to be left overnight (Lev. 7:15); meat of the Passover must not be left overnight (Deut. 16:4); a hired man's wages must not remain with you all night until morning (Lev. 19:13); a body shall not hang on a tree all night (Deut. 21:23).

C5b Acting all night
From evening to morning the sons of Aaron are to tend the light (Exod. 27:21; Lev. 24:3); the Passover is a night of watching (Exod. 12:42); her lamp does not go out all night (Prov. 31:18); we toiled all night and caught nothing (Luke 5:5); they caught nothing all night (John 21:3).

C5c Walking all night
The men of Jabesh-gilead (1 Sam. 31:12); Rechab and Baanah (2 Sam. 4:7); Joshua (Josh. 10:9); Abner and his men (2 Sam. 2:29); Joab and his men (2 Sam. 2:32).

C6 Prayer at night
I meditate on you in the night watches (Ps. 63:6); I meditate on your word in the night watches (Ps. 119:148); I remember your name in the night (Ps. 119:55); at midnight I rise to praise you (Ps. 119:62); those who serve by night in the house of the Lord (Ps. 134:1); Jesus spent all night in prayer (Luke 6:12); Samuel cried out to the Lord all night (1 Sam. 15:11); David lay on the ground all night (2 Sam. 12:16); weeping may last all night (Ps. 30:5).

C7 Spiritual night
You are not sons of night (1 Thess. 5:5); at night people sleep and get drunk (1 Thess. 5:7); night comes when no one can work (John 9:4); if any one walks in the night he stumbles because the light is not in him (John 11:10); the night is far gone (Rom. 13:12); it will be night for you with no vision (Mic. 3:6).

D Autumn
The Lord gives the autumn rain and spring rain (Jer. 5:24); he has given you the autumn [early] rain (Joel 2:23); the sluggard does not plough in autumn (Prov. 20:4); as in my autumn days (Job 29:4); trees in autumn without fruit (Jude 12).

E Winter
It was winter (John 10:23); the king was sitting in the winter house (Jer. 36:22); come before winter (2 Tim. 4:21); pray that your flight will not be in winter (Matt.

24:20; Mark 13:18); the harbour was not suitable for wintering (Acts 27:12); perhaps I will winter with you (1 Cor. 16:6); I have decided to spend the winter at Nicopolis (Titus 3:12); intending to winter at Phoenix (Acts 27:12); a ship of Alexandria had wintered in the island (Acts 28:11); the winter is past (S. of S. 2:11).
SUMMER AND WINTER, see 128H2.

130 Youthfulness

YOUNG PEOPLE, see 132.

A Benefits of youth
A1 Freshness of youth
You have the dew of your youth (Ps. 110:3); let his flesh become fresher than in his youth (Job 33:25); his bones are full of youthful vigour (Job 20:11); your youth is renewed like the eagle's (Ps. 103:5); when you were young you girded yourself (John 21:18).

A2 Youthful devotion
Remember your Creator in the days of your youth (Eccles. 12:1); I remember the devotion of your youth (Jer. 2:2); while Josiah was still a youth he sought the Lord (2 Chr. 34:3); I will remember my covenant with you in your youth (Ezek. 16:60); you did not remember the days of your youth (Ezek. 16:43); there she will answer as in the days of her youth (Hos. 2:15); rejoice in the wife of your youth (Prov. 5:18); do not be faithless to the wife of your youth (Mal. 2:15).

B Limitations of youth
Youth and the prime of life are fleeting (Eccles. 11:10); Jether was afraid because he was only a youth (Judg. 8:20); you are only a youth (1 Sam. 17:33); Goliath disdained David for he was only a youth (1 Sam. 17:42); Solomon is young and inexperienced (1 Chr. 22:5; 29:1); let no one despise your youth (1 Tim. 4:12); do not say, 'I am a youth' (Jer. 1:7); even youths grow weary (Isa. 40:30); before the child knows how to say, 'My father' or 'My mother' (Isa. 8:4); while the heir is a child he is no different from a slave (Gal. 4:1); an overseer should not be a recent convert (1 Tim. 3:6); shun youthful passions (2 Tim. 2:22).

C From young age
C1 From the womb
You have been my God from my mother's womb (Ps. 22:10); the Lord formed me from the womb to be his servant (Isa. 49:5); before I formed you in the womb I knew you (Jer. 1:5); the name given by the angel before he was conceived in the womb (Luke 2:21); a Nazirite from the womb (Judg. 13:5, 7; 16:17); set apart from the womb (Gal. 1:15); called from the womb (Isa. 49:1); filled with the Holy Spirit from the womb (Luke 1:15); God has carried you from the womb (Isa. 46:3); a man lame from the womb (Acts 3:2; 14:8); eunuchs from their mother's womb who were born that way (Matt. 19:12).

C2 From birth
On you I was cast from birth (Ps. 22:10); on you I have leaned from birth (Ps. 71:6); from birth I have carried you (Isa. 46:3); those who speak lies from birth (Ps. 58:3); you have been a rebel from birth (Isa. 48:8); the wicked go astray from birth (Ps. 58:3); a man blind from birth (John 9:1).

C3 From youth
I have feared the Lord from my youth (1 Kgs. 18:12); all these I have observed from my youth (Mark 10:20; Luke 18:21); from my youth I have never eaten what died of itself or was torn by beasts (Ezek. 4:14); my manner of life from my youth (Acts 26:4); from childhood you have known the scriptures (2 Tim. 3:15); you have taught me from my youth (Ps. 71:17); Israel has been persecuted from youth (Ps. 129:1, 2); Moab has been at ease from his youth (Jer. 48:11).

131 Age

A Lifespan
Man's lifespan shall be 120 years (Gen. 6:3); the length of our life is 70 years, or 80 (Ps. 90:10); the youth will die at 100 (Isa. 65:20); the one who does not reach the age of 100 will be considered accursed (Isa. 65:20); as the days of a tree so shall the days of my people be (Isa. 65:22); are your years as man's? (Job 10:5); a man's lifespan is predetermined (Job 14:5); who can add a cubit to his span of life ? (Matt. 6:27; Luke 12:25).

B Specific age
B1 Less than a year old
Eight days old when circumcised (Gen. 17:12; Lev. 12:3; Luke 1:59; 2:21; Acts 7:8; Phil. 3:5); Abraham circumcised Isaac when he was eight days old (Gen. 21:4); a firstborn animal sacrificed at eight days old (Exod. 22:30; Lev. 22:27).

B2 The age of Jesus
Jesus 30 (Luke 3:23); Jesus not yet 50 (John 8:57).

B3 Age ranges of Levites
Census of Levite males one month up (Num. 3:15, 22, 28, 34, 39; 26:62); census of Levites from 30 to 50 years old (Num. 4:47); the Levites from 30 upward were numbered (1 Chr. 23:3); male priests from 30 up were given the tithe (2 Chr. 31:16); Levites numbered from 20 up (1 Chr. 23:24, 27); Levites 20 and up to oversee the work (Ezra 3:8); Levites from 20 up were given the tithe (2 Chr. 31:17); Levites start work at 25 and retire at 50 (Num. 8:24-5); census of those between 30 and 50 of: Gershonites (Num. 4:23, 39); Merarites (Num. 4:30, 43); Kohathites (Num. 4:3, 35).

B4 Age ranges of others
Census of firstborn males a month up (Num. 3:40, 42-3); Herod killed the boys two and under (Matt. 2:16); valuation of people from one month to five years old (Lev. 27:6); valuation of people from five to 20 (Lev. 27:5); valuation of people from 20 to 60 (Lev. 27:3-4); census of males 20 and up (Num. 1:3, 18, 20, 22, 24, 26, 28, 30, 32, 34, 36, 38, 40, 42, 45; 26:2, 4; 2 Chr. 25:5); David did not count those under 20 (1 Chr. 27:23); 20 and up shall pay the tax (Exod. 30:14; 38:26); none of the people 20 and upward would see the land ·(Num. 32:11); from 20 and upward they would die in the wilderness (Num. 14:29); valuation of people over 60 (Lev. 27:7); widows not enrolled under 60 (1 Tim. 5:9).

C Old age
I was young and now I am old (Ps. 37:25); when you are old (John 21:18); may he be a sustainer of your old age (Ruth 4:15); each one with staff in hand because of age (Zech. 8:4); Sarah received power to conceive when she was past the age (Heb. 11:11); the heavens and the earth will grow old like a garment (Heb. 1:11).
OLD PERSON, see 133.

132 Young person / animal

YOUTHFULNESS, see 130.

A Young people
A1 Character of young people
A1a Virtues of young people
It is by his deeds that the lad makes himself known (Prov. 20:11); the beauty of young men is their strength (Prov. 20:29); I am writing to you, young men, because you are strong (1 John 2:13); I have written to you, young men (1 John 2:14).

A1b Training young people
How can a young man keep his way pure? (Ps. 119:9); train up a child in the way he should go (Prov. 22:6); to give to the youth knowledge (Prov. 1:4); do not

withhold discipline from the lad (Prov. 23:13); urge the young men to be self-controlled (Titus 2:6).

A1c Like children
Whoever does not receive the kingdom of God like a child will not enter it (Mark 10:15; Luke 18:17); unless you are converted and become like children you will not enter (Matt. 18:3-4); the kingdom of heaven belongs to such as these (Matt. 19:14; Mark 10:14; Luke 18:16); receive the word like newborn babies (1 Pet. 2:2); let the greatest become as the youngest (Luke 22:26); you were as babes in Christ (1 Cor. 3:1); those who need milk are babies (Heb. 5:13); in evil be babies (1 Cor. 14:20); I [Solomon] am only a little child (1 Kgs. 3:7); I am only a youth (Jer. 1:6); this generation is like children sitting in the market places (Matt. 11:16; Luke 7:32); do not be children in your thinking (1 Cor. 14:20); that we may no longer be children (Eph. 4:14); when I was a child, I spoke, thought, reasoned as a child (1 Cor. 13:11); I speak as to children (2 Cor. 6:13).

A2 Rules about young people
If a woman makes a vow in her youth (Num. 30:3); when a daughter is young and in her father's house (Num. 30:16); children, obey your parents (Eph. 6:1; Col. 3:20); you younger ones, be subject to the elders (1 Pet. 5:5).

A3 Dealing with young people
I will make mere boys rule over them (Isa. 3:4); youths oppress them (Isa. 3:12); receiving a child in Christ's name (Matt. 18:5); he took a child and put him in the midst of them (Matt. 18:2; Mark 9:36); Jesus took a child and stood him by his side (Luke 9:47); he who causes one of these little ones to stumble (Matt. 18:6; Mark 9:42; Luke 17:2); do not despise on one of these little ones (Matt. 18:10); it is not your Father's will that one of these little ones should perish (Matt. 18:14); as a nursing mother cares for her children (1 Thess. 2:7); treat younger men like brothers (1 Tim. 5:1); treat younger women as sisters, in all purity (1 Tim. 5:2).

A4 Young people acting
Rehoboam sought advice from the young people (1 Kgs. 12:8; 2 Chr. 10:8); the Lord will deliver Israel by the young men of the provincial chiefs (1 Kgs. 20:14); the young men of the provincial chiefs went out first (1 Kgs. 20:17, 19); your young men will see visions (Joel 2:28; Acts 2:17); the young men covered him up, carried him out and buried him (Acts 5:6); the young men carried her out and buried her beside her husband (Acts 5:10); youths jeered at Elisha (2 Kgs. 2:23).

A5 Young people suffering
Pour God's wrath on the children in the street (Jer. 6:11); death cuts off children and young men (Jer. 9:21); little ones and infants faint on the streets of the city (Lam. 2:11); the baby's tongue cleaves to the roof of its mouth with thirst (Lam. 4:4); young men grind at the mill and boys stagger under loads of wood (Lam. 5:13); the beautiful virgins and young men will faint from thirst (Amos 8:13); happy he who dashes your little ones against a rock (Ps. 137:9).

A6 Youngest child
The youngest is with our father (Gen. 42:13, 32); there is Benjamin the youngest (Ps. 68:27); David was the youngest (1 Sam. 16:11; 17:14); the rebuilder of Jericho will lose his youngest son (Josh. 6:26); Hiel rebuilt Jericho and lost his youngest son (1 Kgs. 16:34).

A7 Children and the kingdom
From the mouth of infants God established strength (Ps. 8:2); I will bring your little ones into the land (Num. 14:31); God revealed these things to babies (Matt. 11:25; Luke 10:21); children crying Hosanna in the temple (Matt. 21:15); praise from the mouths of babes and sucklings (Matt. 21:16); they brought

children to him (Matt. 19:13; Mark 10:13); they were bringing even babies to him (Luke 18:15); a little lad will lead them (Isa. 11:6); the streets of Jerusalem will be filled with boys and girls (Zech. 8:5); the toddler will put his hand on the viper's den (Isa. 11:8); the infant will play by the cobra's hole (Isa. 11:8); I am writing to you little children (1 John 2:12); I have written to you, children (1 John 2:13); my little children (1 John 2:1).

B Young animal
A newborn animal is to be left with its mother for seven days (Exod. 22:30; Lev. 22:27); you shall not kill a mother animal and its young on the same day (Lev. 22:28); do not take a mother bird with its young (Deut. 22:6-7); if you find a bird sitting on eggs (Deut. 22:6); do not boil a kid in its mother's milk (Exod. 23:19; 34:26; Deut. 14:21); two young pigeons (Luke 2:24); Jesus found a young donkey and sat on it (John 12:14); your king is coming, sitting on a donkey's colt (John 12:15).

C Young and old
We will go with young and old (Exod. 10:9); let old men and children praise the Lord (Ps. 148:12); the men of Sodom, young and old (Gen. 19:4); both young and old were destroyed in Jericho (Josh. 6:21); both young and old were struck with tumours (1 Sam. 5:9); slay old men, young men, maidens, little children and women (Ezek. 9:6).

133 Old person
OLD AGE, see 131C.

A Old persons
ELDERS, see 741E.

A1 Old individuals
Abraham would be buried at a good old age (Gen. 15:15); David died at a ripe old age, full of days (1 Chr. 29:28); Elizabeth has conceived in her old age (Luke 1:36); Anna was of a great age (Luke 2:36); they went out one by one, beginning with the eldest (John 8:9).

A2 God as an old person
The Ancient of Days (Dan. 7:9, 13, 22).

B Character of old people
Wisdom is with the aged (Job 12:12); many years should teach wisdom (Job 32:7); old people may not be wise (Job 32:9); a poor wise lad is better then an old foolish king (Eccles. 4:13); I understand more than the aged (Ps. 119:100); older men are to be temperate (Titus 2:2); older women are to be reverent (Titus 2:3); the beauty of old men is their grey hair (Prov. 20:29).

C Hope for old people
They will bring forth fruit in old age (Ps. 92:14); do not cast me off in old age (Ps. 71:9, 18); even to old age I will carry you (Isa. 46:4); your old men will dream dreams (Joel 2:28; Acts 2:17).

D Respect for old people
Respect old people (Lev. 19:32); do not despise your mother when she is old (Prov. 23:22); do not rebuke an older man (1 Tim. 5:1); treat older women a mothers (1 Tim. 5:2).

E Limitations of old people
When Solomon was old his wives turned his heart after other gods (1 Kgs. 11:4); I am too old to have a husband (Ruth 1:12); Israel's eyes were heavy with old age (Gen. 48:10); Ahijah's eyes were dim with age (1 Kgs. 14:4).

134 Adultness

A Maturity
Go on to maturity (Heb. 6:1); in thinking be mature (1 Cor. 14:20); until we reach mature manhood (Eph. 4:13); that you may stand mature (Col. 4:12); to present every man mature in Christ (Col. 1:28); solid food is for the mature (Heb. 5:14); we do speak wisdom among

those who are mature (1 Cor. 2:6); let those who are mature think like this (Phil. 3:15).

B Adult

Ask him, he is of age (John 9:21, 23); when I became a man I gave up childish things (1 Cor. 13:11); Moses when he had grown up (Heb. 11:24).

135 Earliness

RISING EARLY, see 128B.

A Near the time

The days draw near and the fulfilment of every vision (Ezek. 12:23); the day of the Lord is near (Ezek. 30:3; Joel 1:15; 2:1; 3:14; Obad. 15; Zeph. 1:7, 14); know that Jerusalem's desolation is at hand (Luke 21:20); encouraging one another all the more as you see the day drawing near (Heb. 10:25); the time is near (Rev. 1:3; 22:10); the end of all things is at hand (1 Pet. 4:7); the coming of the Lord is at hand (Jas. 5:8); he is near, at the very gates (Matt. 24:33; Mark 13:29); your redemption is drawing near (Luke 21:28); when the fig tree sprouts, summer is near (Matt. 24:32); when they put forth leaves, you know that summer is near (Luke 21:30); the laying aside of my earthly dwelling is imminent (2 Pet. 1:14); my time is at hand (Matt. 26:18); the hour is at hand (Matt. 26:45); the days drew near for him to be received up (Luke 9:51).

B God not delaying

O Lord, do not delay (Ps. 40:17; 70:5; Dan. 9:19); will God delay over his elect? (Luke 18:7); God will speedily cause it to happen (Gen. 41:32); the Lord is not slow concerning his promise (2 Pet. 3:9); he who is coming will not delay (Hab. 2:3; Heb. 10:37); my salvation will not delay (Isa. 46:13); God will soon crush Satan under your feet (Rom. 16:20); he will vindicate them speedily (Luke 18:8); salvation is nearer than when we first believed (Rom. 13:11); there would be no more delay (Rev. 10:6); I will come soon (Rev. 2:16; 3:11; 22:7, 12, 20); the great day of the Lord is near and coming quickly (Zeph. 1:14).

DELAY, see 136A.

C Others not delaying

Come to us without delay (Acts 9:38); Paul commanded Silas and Timothy to come to him as soon as possible (Acts 17:15); do your best to come to me soon (2 Tim. 4:9); the early and the latter rain (Deut. 11:14; Jer. 5:24; Hos. 6:3; Joel 2:23).

HASTE, see 680.

136 Lateness

NO DELAY, see 135B.

A God's delay

God is slow to anger (Exod. 34:6; Num. 14:18; Neh. 9:17; Ps. 86:15; 103:8; 145:8; Joel 2:13); for the sake of my name I delay my anger (Isa. 48:9); because sentence against evil is not executed promptly (Eccles. 8:11); my master is delayed (Matt. 24:48; Luke 12:45); the bridegroom was delayed (Matt. 25:5); if it is slow, wait for it (Hab. 2:3); Jesus stayed where he was two days longer (John 11:6).

B Late

It is in vain that you go to bed late (Ps. 127:2); woe to those who stay up late drinking wine (Isa. 5:11); the hour is late (Mark 6:35); it was already late (Mark 11:11); the early and the latter rain (Deut. 11:14; Jer. 5:24; Hos. 6:3; Joel 2:23).

WAITING, see 507.

C How long?

Lord, how long? (Ps. 6:3; 13:1; 35:17; 74:10; 79:5; 89:46; 90:13; Rev. 6:10); how long must I call for help? (Hab. 1:2); how long shall I endure this congregation? (Num. 14:27); how long must I endure you? (Matt. 17:17; Mark 9:19; Luke 9:41); how long shall I be with you? (Matt. 17:17; Mark 9:19); how long will you be angry? (Ps. 80:4); how long will you keep us in suspense? (John 10:24).

137 Opportunity

RIGHT TIME FOR ACTIVITIES, see 108C.

A Right time for God

The time has come to be gracious to Zion (Ps. 102:13); it is time for the Lord to act (Ps. 119:126); in a favourable time I have answered you (Isa. 49:8); now is the acceptable time (2 Cor. 6:2); at the right time Christ died for the ungodly (Rom. 5:6); in its time I will hasten it (Isa. 60:22).

B Right time for people

How good is a timely word! (Prov. 15:23); as we have opportunity, let us do good to all men (Gal. 6:10); use the opportunity to the full, because the days are evil (Eph. 5:16); making the most of the opportunity (Col. 4:5); he looked for an opportunity to betray him (Matt. 26:16; Mark 14:11; Luke 22:6); is it time for you to live in your panelled houses? (Hag. 1:4); my time has not yet come, but your time is always ready (John 7:6); happy the land whose princes feast at the proper time (Eccles. 10:17); perhaps you have come to kingship for such a time as this (Esther 4:14).

DOOR OF OPPORTUNITY, see 263B3.

138 Untimeliness

A Not the time

Is it time for you to live in panelled houses? (Hag. 1:4); is it a time to receive presents? (2 Kgs. 5:26); the time has not come to build the temple (Hag. 1:2); have you come here to torment us before the time? (Matt. 8:29); my time has not yet come (John 2:4; 7:6, 30).

B Premature birth

As to one untimely born (1 Cor. 15:8).

139 Frequent

How often I would have gathered your children together (Matt. 23:37); it has often cast him into the fire and into the water (Mark 9:22); Jesus often met there with his disciples (John 18:2).

FREQUENCY OF OCCURRENCE, see 141.

140 Infrequent

The word of the Lord and visions were rare (1 Sam. 3:1).

141 Regularity

A Per day or more often

A1 Several times a day

Daniel prayed three times a day (Dan. 6:10, 13); seven times a day I praise you (Ps. 119:164); if he sins seven times a day, forgive him (Luke 17:4).

A2 Daily

Every priest stands daily offering the same sacrifices (Heb. 10:11); a day's portion of manna every day (Exod. 16:4); give us this day our daily bread (Matt. 6:11; Luke 11:3); Jehoiachin had a daily allowance all the days of his life (2 Kgs. 25:30; Jer. 52:34); a loaf of bread daily from the bakers' street (Jer. 37:21); the king allotted them a daily ration of the rich food he ate (Dan. 1:5); the Hellenist widows were neglected in the daily distribution (Acts 6:1); examining the scriptures daily to see if these things were so (Acts 17:11); Paul reasoned daily in the school of Tyrannus (Acts 19:9).

A3 Twice a week

I fast twice a week (Luke 18:12); bring your sacrifices every morning, your tithes every three days (Amos 4:4).

B Every month
Two male lambs at the start of every month (Num. 28:11-15); the trees will bear fruit every month (Ezek. 47:12).

C Three times a year
Men must attend the feasts three times a year (Exod. 23:17; 34:23, 24; Deut. 16:16); three times a year hold a feast to me (Exod. 23:14); three times a year Solomon sacrificed on the altar he built (1 Kgs. 9:25).

D Per year or more often
D1 Every year
Atonement for the incense altar once a year (Exod. 30:10); the high priest goes into the second tent only once a year (Heb. 9:7); the same sacrifices offered year by year (Heb. 10:1); keep the Passover at the right time year by year (Exod. 13:10); every year his parents went up to the Passover (Luke 2:41); Elkanah and his family went up to Shiloh annually to sacrifice (1 Sam. 1:3, 21; 2:19); the annual feast at Shiloh (Judg. 21:19); the annual sacrifice for the family (1 Sam. 20:6); Hannah brought Samuel a new coat each year (1 Sam. 2:19); one third of a shekel yearly (Neh. 10:32).

D2 Birthdays
Pharaoh's birthday (Gen. 40:20); Herod's birthday (Matt. 14:6; Mark 6:21).

142 Irregularity
FICKLENESS, see 152A.

143 Change
CONVERSION, see 147.
CHANGEABLE, see 152.

A Universe changed
We will not fear though the earth change (Ps. 46:2); he changes times and seasons (Dan. 2:21); you would speak lies until the times change (Dan. 2:9); he will intend to change the times and the law (Dan. 7:25).

B Wages changed
Your father changed my wages ten times (Gen. 31:7); you changed my wages ten times (Gen. 31:41).

144 Permanence
STABILITY, see 153.

A God is unchanging
God is unchanging (Ps. 55:19); God is always the same (Ps. 102:27); I the Lord do not change (Mal. 3:6); the Father of lights with whom is no shifting shadow (Jas. 1:17); we have heard that the Christ remains for ever (John 12:34); Jesus Christ is the same yesterday, today and for ever (Heb. 13:8); the Son is the same and his years will never end (Heb. 1:12).

B Not passing away
This generation will not pass away till all takes place (Mark 13:30; Luke 21:32); my words will not pass away (Mark 13:31).

C Staying put
The servant with pierced ear will serve you always (Exod. 21:6; Deut. 15:17); our wives and livestock will remain in Gilead (Num. 32:26); if you stay in the land I will build you up (Jer. 42:10); they did not obey the voice of the Lord to stay in the land (Jer. 43:4); remain in Egypt until I tell you (Matt. 2:13); stay here and keep watch with me (Matt. 26:38; Mark 14:34); the boy Jesus stayed behind in Jerusalem (Luke 2:43); stay in the city until you are clothed with power from on high (Luke 24:49).

D Abiding with God
The Spirit descended and remained on him (John 1:32-3); whoever eats my flesh and drinks my blood abides in me and I in him (John 6:56); if you remain in my word you are truly my disciples (John 8:31); abide

in me and I in you (John 15:4-6); if you abide in me and my words abide in you, ask what you will (John 15:7); remain in my love (John 15:9); I have kept my Father's commandments and remain in his love (John 15:10); if you keep my commandments you will remain in my love (John 15:10); God's kindness, if you remain in his kindness (Rom. 11:22).

145 Cessation
A People stopping
A1 Stopping activity
Levites retire at 50 years old (Num. 8:25); if the sacrifices were effective they would have ceased offering them (Heb. 10:2).

A2 Stopping rejoicing
Voices of joy, of bride and bridegroom will cease (Jer. 7:34; 16:9; 25:10; Rev. 18:23); sounds of songs and harps heard no more in Tyre (Ezek. 26:13); the gaiety of the tambourines and harp ceases (Isa. 24:8).

A3 Stopping fighting
The oppressor has ceased (Isa. 14:4); Jesus said, 'Stop! No more of this!' (Luke 22:51); they stopped beating Paul (Acts 21:32).

A4 Stopping still
David stopped at the last house (2 Sam. 15:17); the bearers halted (Luke 7:14); the star stood over the place where the child was (Matt. 2:9); he commanded the chariot to stop (Acts 8:38).

A5 Stopping evil
Cease to do evil (Isa. 1:16); immediately the flow of blood ceased (Mark 5:29); Lord God, please stop! (Amos 7:5).

A6 Stopping building
They stopped building Babel (Gen. 11:8); Baasha stopped fortifying Ramah (1 Kgs. 15:21; 2 Chr. 16:5); the Jews were forced to stop building Jerusalem (Ezra 4:21-4); we will stop them working (Neh. 4:11); why should the work stop? (Neh. 6:3).

B Things stopping
The thunder and hail ceased (Exod. 9:29, 33, 34); they threw Jonah into the sea and the sea stopped its raging (Jonah 1:15); the wind stopped (Matt. 14:32; Mark 6:51); he said to the sea, 'Peace! Be still!' (Mark 4:39); will you be to me like waters that fail? (Jer. 15:18); the oil stopped flowing (2 Kgs. 4:6); the manna ceased the next day (Josh. 5:12); the plague was halted (Num. 16:48, 50; Ps. 106:30); prophecy, tongues and knowledge will cease (1 Cor. 13:8).

146 Unceasing
A God always works
The Lord's mercies are unceasing (Lam. 3:22); the Lord daily bears our burden (Ps. 68:19); Jesus Christ will sustain you to the end (1 Cor. 1:8); he who began a good work will perform it (Phil. 1:6); my Father has never stopped working (John 5:17).

B Always praying
I will call on him as long as I live (Ps. 116:2); they ought to pray at all times (Luke 18:1); pray without ceasing (1 Thess. 5:17); pray at all times in the Spirit (Eph. 6:18); do not cease to cry to the Lord for us (1 Sam. 7:8); far be it from me to sin by ceasing to pray for you (1 Sam. 12:23); night and day we pray that we may see you (1 Thess. 3:10); I remember you constantly in my prayers (2 Tim. 1:3); I pray unceasingly for you (Rom. 1:9); we have not ceased to pray for you (Col. 1:9).

C Always praising
Let them bless him all day long (Ps. 72:15); I will bless the Lord at all times (Ps. 34:1); I will sing to the Lord as long as I live (Ps. 104:33); I will praise the Lord as long as I live (Ps. 146:2); my mouth is filled with your praise

all day long (Ps. 71:8); my mouth will speak of your salvation all day long (Ps. 71:15); day by day they attended the temple together (Acts 2:46); let us continually offer up a sacrifice
of praise (Heb. 13:15); day and night they do not cease (Rev. 4:8).

D Always rejoicing
Rejoice always (1 Thess. 5:16); rejoice in the Lord always (Phil. 4:4); sorrowful yet always rejoicing (2 Cor. 6:10).

E Always active
Day after day I was in the temple teaching (Matt. 26:55; Mark 14:49; Luke 22:53); he was teaching daily in the temple (Luke 19:47; 21:37); keep watch at all times (Luke 21:36); they encouraged the disciples to continue in the faith (Acts 14:22); night and day for three years I did not cease to admonish you (Acts 20:31); what I am doing I will continue to do (2 Cor. 11:12); encourage one another every day (Heb. 3:13); let us keep to what we have attained (Phil. 3:16); let the one who is righteous still do right (Rev. 22:11); continue in the things you have learned (2 Tim. 3:14); I will keep your law continually (Ps. 119:44); always abounding in the work of the Lord (1 Cor. 15:58).

F Continual blessing
She does him good all the days of her life (Prov. 31:12); the tree of life bearing fruit every month (Rev. 22:2).

G Continual hardship
Lot's soul was tormented day after day by their lawless deeds (2 Pet. 2:8); the devil and his companions will be tormented day and night for ever (Rev. 20:10).

H Continual sin
Man's thoughts were evil all day long (Gen. 6:5); why has this people turned away in perpetual apostasy? (Jer. 8:5); shall we continue in sin that grace may abound? (Rom. 6:1); they never cease from sin (2 Pet. 2:14); let him who does wrong continue to do wrong (Rev. 22:11).

147 Conversion
CHANGE, see 143.

A People transformed
Can the Ethiopian change his skin or the leopard his spots? (Jer. 13:23); you will be changed into another man (1 Sam. 10:6); Jesus was transfigured (Matt. 17:2; Mark 9:2-3; Luke 9:29); we are being changed into his likeness (2 Cor. 3:18); be transformed by the renewing of your mind (Rom. 12:2); he will change our bodies to be like his glorious body (Phil. 3:21); we will all be changed (1 Cor. 15:51).

B People converted
Unless you are converted and become like children you shall not enter (Matt. 18:3); lest they be converted (John 12:40); they described the conversion of the Gentiles (Acts 15:3); Epaenetus, the first convert to Christ from Asia (Rom. 16:5); an overseer should not be a new convert (1 Tim. 3:6).

C Proselytes
You cross sea and land to make one proselyte (Matt. 23:15); Nicolas, a proselyte from Antioch (Acts 6:5); visitors from Rome, both Jews and proselytes (Acts 2:10); many Jews and devout proselytes followed Paul and Barnabas (Acts 13:43); Lydia was a worshipper of God (Acts 16:14); many of the devout Greeks joined Paul and Silas (Acts 17:4); Paul reasoned in the synagogue with Jews and devout [Gentiles] (Acts 17:17); Titius Justus, a worshipper of God (Acts 18:7).

D Things changed
The staff became a snake (Exod. 4:3; 7:9, 10, 15); the magicians' staffs became snakes (Exod. 7:12); the snake became a staff (Exod. 4:4); the water will become blood

(Exod. 4:9; 7:17-20); the dust became gnats (Exod. 8:16, 17); the sea was turned to dry land (Exod. 14:21).
TURNED TO BLOOD, see 335E3.

148 Returning

A Returning and God
A1 God returning
Return to me and I will return to you (Zech. 1:3; Mal. 3:7); return to the Lord that he may return to you (2 Chr. 30:6); return, O Lord (Num. 10:36); return for the sake of your servants (Isa. 63:17); they see the Lord return to Zion (Isa. 52:8).

A2 Christ coming again
I will come again and receive you to myself (John 14:3); I am going away and I will come to you (John 14:28); this Jesus will come back in the same way (Acts 1:11); like those waiting for their Lord to return (Luke 12:36).

A3 Returning to God
A3a Return!
Return to me (Isa. 44:22; Jer. 4:1; Joel 2:12-13); return to the Lord (Hos. 12:6; 14:1); let us return to the Lord (Lam. 3:40; Hos. 6:1); return, faithless Israel (Jer. 3:12); let him return to the Lord (Isa. 55:7); if you return to the Lord with all your heart (1 Sam. 7:3).

A3b Jesus returning to the Father
I am going back to the Father (John 16:28); I am ascending to my Father (John 20:17); I am going to him who sent me (John 16:5); I go to the Father (John 16:10, 17); I am coming to you (John 17:11, 13).

A3c Not returning to God
Yet you have not returned to me (Amos 4:6, 8, 9, 10, 11); they have not returned to the Lord (Hos. 7:10); they refused to return to me (Hos. 11:5); you did not return to me (Hag. 2:17).

B Returning to people
The dove returned to Noah (Gen. 8:9); return to your mistress (Gen. 16:9); let us return and visit the brethren (Acts 15:36); the unclean spirit says, 'I will return to my house' (Luke 11:24); being warned in a dream not to return to Herod (Matt. 2:12).

C People returning
C1 Going home
C1a Permission to return home
Soldiers given a chance of returning home (Deut. 20:5-8); the hired man returns home at the Jubilee (Lev. 25:41); returning home after the death of the high priest (Num. 35:28; Josh. 20:6).

C1b Go home!
Go to your homes (Ruth 1:8, 11-12, 15); rise, take up your bed and go home (Matt. 9:6; Mark 2:11; Luke 5:24); he sent him away to his home (Mark 8:26; Luke 8:38); go home to your people and tell them how much the Lord has done for you (Mark 5:19; Luke 8:39).

C1c Not going home directly
We will not return to our homes until all Israel has inherited (Num. 32:18); when your brethren occupy their land, you may return home (Deut. 3:20); Uriah did not go home (2 Sam. 11:9); why did you not go home? (2 Sam. 11:10); he was commanded not to return the way he came (1 Kgs. 13:9-10); the magi returned home another way (Matt. 2:12); let the one in the field not return for his cloak (Matt. 24:18).

C2 Returning to the old
Shall I take your son back to the land you came from? (Gen. 24:5); take care not to take my son back there (Gen. 24:6, 8); lest the people return to Egypt (Exod. 13:17); they wanted to return to Egypt (Num. 14:3-4); in their hearts they turned back to Egypt (Acts 7:39).

C3 Returning to their land
Return to the land of your fathers (Gen. 31:3); O God who said, 'Return to your land and your family' (Gen.

32:9); I will bring them back from the land of Egypt (Zech. 10:10); they would have had opportunity to return to the land they came from (Heb. 11:15).

C4 Returning after exile
The redeemed of the Lord will return to Zion (Isa. 35:10; 51:11); I will bring you back from exile (Jer. 29:14); I will save your offspring from the land of their captivity (Jer. 30:10); your offspring will return from the land of their captivity (Jer. 46:27); Manasseh was brought back to Jerusalem from Babylon (2 Chr. 33:13); the exiles returned from captivity (Ezra 1:11; 2:1); the one who goes into exile will never return (Jer. 22:10); they will not return to the land (Jer. 22:27); Shallum will never return (Jer. 22:11).

C5 People not returning
The one who goes down to Sheol will not return (Job 7:10); I will go to the land of darkness and will not return (Job 10:21); I will go the way of no return (Job 16:22); he shall not cause the people to return to Egypt (Deut. 17:16); the seller will not return to what he has sold as long as he lives (Ezek. 7:13); let him who is in the field not turn back (Luke 17:31).

D Things returning
D1 Reversion of things
Dust you are and to dust you will return (Gen. 3:19); in the year of Jubilee property reverts (Lev. 25:10, 13, 28, 31, 33; 27:24); in walled cities property does not revert in the Jubilee (Lev. 25:30); if the house is not worthy, let your peace return to you (Matt. 10:13; Luke 10:6).

D2 No vain return
Rain and snow do not return to heaven without watering the earth (Isa. 55:10); my word will not return to me empty (Isa. 55:11).

149 Revolutionary change
CONVERSION, see 147.

150 Substitution
INTERCHANGE, see 151.

A Exchange of people
In place of your fathers will be your sons (Ps. 45:16); God appointed me another child in place of Abel (Gen. 4:25); may the Lord give you children in place of the one she lent to the Lord (1 Sam. 2:20); I gave Ethiopia and Seba in exchange for you (Isa. 43:3); I give peoples in exchange for you (Isa. 43:4).

B Exchange of individuals
God breaks the mighty and sets others in their place (Job 34:24); the king made Esther queen instead of Vashti (Esther 2:17); anoint Elisha prophet in your place (1 Kgs. 19:16); his office let another take (Acts 1:20).

C Supplanting
Jacob – supplanter (Gen. 25:26); he has supplanted me twice (Gen. 27:36); in the womb he took his brother by the heel (Hos. 12:3).

D Vicarious substitution
Abraham offered the ram instead of his son (Gen. 22:13); Judah asked to be a slave instead of Benjamin (Gen. 44:33); Levites were taken instead of the firstborn (Num. 3:12, 40-5; 8:16-18); expedient that one man die for the nation, that the nation should not perish (John 11:50-1).

E Exchanging things
A votive animal must not be exchanged (Lev. 27:10); the tithe animals cannot be exchanged (Lev. 27:33); exchange the tithe for money (Deut. 14:25); they exchanged the truth about God for a lie (Rom. 1:25); they exchanged the glory of God for idols (Ps. 106:20; Rom. 1:23); has a nation changed gods? (Jer. 2:11);

women exchanged natural sexual relations for unnatural (Rom. 1:26).

151 Interchange
The harlot exchanged the children (1 Kgs. 3:20); give me your vineyard and I will give you a better one in its place (1 Kgs. 21:2, 6); what will a man give in exchange for his soul? (Matt. 16:26).
EXCHANGE, see 150.

152 Changeableness
CHANGE, see 143.

A Fickleness
A reed swayed by the wind (Matt. 11:7; Luke 7:24); tossed about by every wind of doctrine (Eph. 4:14); a double-minded man, unstable in all his ways (Jas. 1:8); I hate double-minded men (Ps. 119:113); Reuben, unstable as water (Gen. 49:4); they entice unstable souls (2 Pet. 2:14); the ignorant and unstable twist the scriptures to their own destruction (2 Pet. 3:16); Paul was not vacillating, saying yes and no (2 Cor. 1:17).

B Without root
Plants on the rocky ground had no root (Matt. 13:6; Mark 4:6); he has no root (Matt. 13:21; Mark 4:17; Luke 8:13).

C Staggering
As a drunken man staggers in his vomit (Isa. 19:14); priest and prophet reel from strong drink (Isa. 28:7); they reeled and staggered like drunken men (Ps. 107:27); you have given us wine that made us stagger (Ps. 60:3); the nations will drink and stagger (Jer. 25:16); the earth reels like a drunkard (Isa. 24:20); you have drunk the bowl of staggering (Isa. 51:17); stagger, but not with strong drink (Isa. 29:9); I have taken out of your hand the bowl of staggering (Isa. 51:22); young men grind at the mill and boys stagger under loads of wood (Lam. 5:13).

153 Stability
PERMANENCE, see 144.

A Stability of God
A1 Unshakeable God
God is one and who can turn him? (Job 23:13); heaven and earth will pass away, but God will endure (Ps. 102:26-7); heaven and earth will pass away, but the Son will endure (Heb. 1:11-12).

A2 Unshakeable words
For ever your word is established in the heavens (Ps. 119:89); the testimony of the Lord is sure (Ps. 19:7); you have founded your testimonies for ever (Ps. 119:152); till heaven and earth pass away, nothing will pass from the law (Matt. 5:18; Luke 16:17); heaven and earth will pass away, but not Christ's words (Matt. 24:35; Mark 13:31; Luke 21:33); God showed the unchangeableness of his purpose by an oath (Heb. 6:17); two unchangeable things (Heb. 6:18).

B Stability of people
B1 Security of individuals
Moses' hands were steady until sundown (Exod. 17:12); my flesh will dwell securely (Ps. 16:9); a man is not established by wickedness (Prov. 12:3); woe to those who feel secure on the mountain of Samaria (Amos 6:1); let him who thinks he stands take heed lest he fall (1 Cor. 10:12).

B2 Firm footing
He makes my feet like hinds' feet (2 Sam. 22:34; Ps. 18:33; Hab. 3:19); he set my feet on a rock (Ps. 40:2); he will not allow your foot to be moved (Ps. 121:3); establish my steps in your word (Ps. 119:133); by the Lord a man's steps are established (Ps. 37:23); his steps do not slip (Ps. 37:31); my feet have not slipped (2 Sam.

22:37; Ps. 18:36); he who walks in integrity walks securely (Prov. 10:9).

B3 Secure kingship

If a king judges justly his throne will be established for ever (Prov. 29:14); by justice a king gives stability to the land (Prov. 29:4).

B4 Not moved

The king trusts in the Lord and will not be moved (Ps. 21:7); believers are like Mount Zion, which cannot be moved (Ps. 125:1); he who does these things will never be moved (Ps. 15:5); the righteous will not be moved (Ps. 55:22; 112:6; Prov. 10:30; 12:3); I will not be moved (Ps. 62:2, 6); because he is at my right hand I will not be shaken (Ps. 16:8; Acts 2:25); we receive a kingdom which cannot be shaken (Heb. 12:28); I said in my prosperity I would not be moved (Ps. 30:6); the wicked says 'I will not be moved' (Ps. 10:6).

B5 God's people planted

I will plant my people Israel (2 Sam. 7:10; 1 Chr. 17:9); them you planted (Ps. 44:2); the vine took deep root (Ps. 80:9); Judah will again take root (2 Kgs. 19:30; Isa. 27:6; 37:31); the righteous will be planted in the house of the Lord (Ps. 92:12-13); I will plant them on their land and they shall never be rooted up (Amos 9:15).

B6 God establishes us

God will establish what you decree (Job 22:28); God establishes us in Christ (2 Cor. 1:21); Christ will establish you to the end (1 Cor. 1:8); may he establish your hearts unblameable in holiness (1 Thess. 3:13); God will establish you (1 Pet. 5:10); he is able to establish you (Rom. 16:25); his master is able to make him stand (Rom. 14:4); the Lord will be the stability of your times (Isa. 33:6); establish the righteous (Ps. 7:9); the righteous has an everlasting foundation (Prov. 10:25); they will remain because [Christ] will be great to the ends of the earth (Mic. 5:4); your offspring and your name will endure (Isa. 66:22).

B7 Standing firm in God

The people who know their God will stand firm and act (Dan. 11:32); established in the faith (Col. 2:7); you are established in the truth (2 Pet. 1:12); we sent Timothy to establish you in your faith (1 Thess. 3:2); the stability of your faith (Col. 2:5); you stand fast only through faith (Rom. 11:20); we have a secure anchor of the soul (Heb. 6:19); now we live, if you stand firm in the Lord (1 Thess. 3:8); this is the true grace of God, stand firm in it (1 Pet. 5:12).

C Secure things

The world is firmly established (1 Chr. 16:30; Ps. 93:1; 96:10); you established the earth (Ps. 119:90); I have set the pillars of the earth steady (Ps. 75:3); since the fathers fell asleep everything remains the same (2 Pet. 3:4); the new heavens and the new earth will endure (Isa. 66:22); the house did not fall because its foundation was on a rock (Matt. 7:24-5; Luke 6:48); the house of the righteous will stand (Prov. 12:7); God will establish the city of our God for ever (Ps. 48:8); the city of God will not be moved (Ps. 46:5); Eliakim will be like a peg in a firm place (Isa. 22:23-5); created things will be shaken and removed so that unshakeable things will remain (Heb. 12:27).

D Unchanging relationships

The law of the Medes and Persians cannot be changed (Dan. 6:8, 12, 15); love never fails (1 Cor. 13:8).

154 Present events

When you see these things happening, you know that he is near (Mark 13:29).

155 Destiny

LOT, see 596B.

156 Cause

WHY?, see 158.

A Caused by God

It was not you who sent me here but God (Gen. 45:8); all things are from God (1 Cor. 11:12); all this is from God (2 Cor. 5:18).

B The reason why

B1 Why God did things

It is because of these things that the wrath of God comes (Eph. 5:6); for this reason I let you stand, to show my power (Exod. 9:16; Rom. 9:17); this is why I speak to them in parables (Matt. 13:13); let us go to the next towns to preach, for this is why I came out (Mark 1:38); for this reason the Father loves me, because I lay down my life (John 10:17); the reason the Son of God appeared was to destroy the works of the devil (1 John 3:8); I was sent for this purpose (Luke 4:43); for this purpose I have come to this hour (John 12:27); for this I came into the world, to bear witness to the truth (John 18:37); I have appeared to you for this purpose (Acts 26:16).

B2 Why people did things

Cain killed his brother because his deeds were evil and his brother's righteous (1 John 3:12); for this reason the Jews persecuted Jesus, because he healed on the sabbath (John 5:16); they will do this because they have not known the Father nor me (John 16:3); for this reason a man will leave his father and mother (Matt. 19:5; Mark 10:7; Eph. 5:31).

B3 Why it happened

When tribulation or persecution arise because of the word (Matt. 13:21); I was sent for this purpose (Luke 4:43); for this purpose I have come to this hour (John 12:27); for this I came into the world, to bear witness to the truth (John 18:37); I have appeared to you for this purpose (Acts 26:16); perhaps this is why he was parted from you for a while (Philem. 15).

B4 Not for this reason

It was not because of wisdom which I have more than any other living (Dan. 2:30); not because of your righteousness (Deut. 9:6); not on account of our righteousness but on account of your mercy (Dan. 9:18); it is not because you were more in number that the Lord chose you (Deut. 7:7); you seek me, not because you saw signs, but because you ate the bread (John 6:26).

C For the sake of

C1 For God's sake

For your sake we are killed all day long (Ps. 44:22; Rom. 8:36); made themselves eunuchs for the sake of the kingdom of heaven (Matt. 19:12); those who have left things for the sake of the kingdom of God (Luke 18:29).

C2 For Christ's sake

Blessed are you when reviled because of me (Matt. 5:11; Luke 6:22); they will bring you before governors and kings for my sake (Matt. 10:18; Mark 13:9; Luke 21:12); you will be hated by all for my name's sake (Matt. 10:22; 24:9; Mark 13:13; Luke 21:17); he who loses his life for my sake will find it (Matt. 10:39; 16:25; Mark 8:35; Luke 9:24); I will show him how much he must suffer for my name's sake (Acts 9:16); we are fools for Christ's sake (1 Cor. 4:10); we are always being delivered over to death for Jesus' sake (2 Cor. 4:11); whatever was gain, I counted loss for the sake of Christ (Phil. 3:7); submit yourself for the Lord's sake to every human institution (1 Pet. 2:13); your sins have been forgiven for his name's sake (1 John 2:12).

C3 For the sake of God's people

For the sake of the elect the days will be shortened (Matt. 24:22; Mark 13:20); for the sake of the hope of Israel I am bound with this chain (Acts 28:20); they are beloved for the sake of their fathers (Rom. 11:28); it was written not for his sake only but for ours (Rom. 4:23-4); it was written for our sake (1 Cor. 9:10); all things are for your sake (2 Cor. 4:15); Christ was revealed in these last times for your sake (1 Pet. 1:20); for the sake of the one who told you and for conscience' sake (1 Cor. 10:28).

157 Effect

PEOPLE BEARING FRUIT, see 171A2.

158 Attribution of cause

CAUSE, see 156.

A Why does Jesus do this?

Why speak to them in parables? (Matt. 13:10); they asked his disciples why he ate with tax collectors and sinners (Mark 2:16); why have you treated us like this? (Luke 2:48); no one said, 'Why are you talking to her?' (John 4:27); no one knew why Jesus said this to Judas (John 13:28).

B Why do people do this?

Why do your disciples transgress the tradition of the elders? (Matt. 15:2; Mark 7:5); why do they do what is not proper on the sabbath? (Mark 2:24; Luke 6:2); why baptize, if you are not the Christ, nor Elijah, nor the Prophet? (John 1:25); why do you transgress the commandment of God for the sake of your tradition? (Matt. 15:3); why ask me about what is good? (Matt. 19:17); why call me good? (Mark 10:18; Luke 18:19); why put me to the test? (Matt. 22:18).

C Why do people not do this?

Why do John's disciples and the Pharisees' disciples fast but yours do not? (Mark 2:18); why could we not cast it out? (Matt. 17:19; Mark 9:28); why did you not believe him? (Matt. 21:25).

159 Chance

Time and chance happen to everyone (Eccles. 9:11); we will know whether it happened by chance (1 Sam. 6:9); a man drew his bow at random (1 Kgs. 22:34; 2 Chr. 18:33).

WITHOUT CAUSE, see 916B.

160 Power

STRENGTH, see 162.

A The power of God

A1 Almighty

God Almighty (Gen. 17:1; 28:3; 35:11; 43:14; 48:3; Exod. 6:3); the Almighty (2 Cor. 6:18; Rev. 1:8; 4:8; 11:17; 15:3; 16:7, 14; 19:6, 15; 21:22).

A2 Mighty One

The mighty One, God, the Lord (Josh. 22:22); the mighty One of Jacob (Gen. 49:24; Isa. 49:26; 60:16); the great, mighty and awesome God (Neh. 9:32); great and mighty God (Jer. 32:18); mighty in deed (Jer. 32:19); the mighty One has done great things for me (Luke 1:49).

A3 God of power

Wisdom and power belong to God (Dan. 2:20); power and might be to our God for ever (Rev. 7:12); salvation and glory and power be to our God! (Rev. 19:1); power belongs to God (Ps. 62:11); the voice of the Lord is powerful (Ps. 29:4); you will see the Son of man seated at the right hand of Power (Matt. 26:64; Mark 14:62; Luke 22:69); that your faith not be in the wisdom of men but the power of God (1 Cor. 2:5).

A4 God showed his power

I have made all things by my great power and outstretched arm (Jer. 27:5); you made heaven and earth by your great power and outstretched arm (Jer. 32:17); by the greatness of his power not one star is missing (Isa. 40:26); his eternal power and deity have been clearly seen in what is made (Rom. 1:20); God raised up Pharaoh to show his power (Exod. 9:16; Rom. 9:17); the Israelites saw the power of the Lord (Exod. 14:31); the power of the Most High will overshadow you (Luke 1:35); declared Son of God with power by the resurrection (Rom. 1:4); God raised the Lord and will raise us also by his power (1 Cor. 6:14); he lives by the power of God (2 Cor. 13:4); we will live with him by the power of God (2 Cor. 13:4); the grace given to me according to the working of his power (Eph. 3:7); you who are guarded by the power of God (1 Pet. 1:5); his divine power has granted us everything pertaining to life and godliness (2 Pet. 1:3); you have taken your great power and begun to reign (Rev. 11:17); God who had power over these plagues (Rev. 16:9).

A5 Querying God's power

They did not remember his power (Ps. 78:42); you do not perceive the Scriptures nor the power of God (Matt. 22:29; Mark 12:24); what can the Almighty do to us? (Job 22:17).

B The power of Christ

Christ the power of God (1 Cor. 1:24); worthy is the Lamb to receive power (Rev. 5:12); God anointed Jesus with the Spirit and with power (Acts 10:38); a prophet mighty in deed and word (Luke 24:19); the power of our Lord Jesus (1 Cor. 5:4; 2 Pet. 1:16); mightier than John (Mark 1:7); he who comes after me is mightier than I (Matt. 3:11; Luke 3:16); power to subject all things to himself (Phil. 3:21); power to heal (Luke 5:17); power went out from him (Mark 5:30; Luke 6:19; 8:46); with power and authority he commands even the unclean spirits (Mark 1:27; Luke 4:36); coming with great power and glory (Matt. 24:30; Mark 13:26; Luke 21:27); that I may know the power of his resurrection (Phil. 3:10); he upholds all things by the word of his power (Heb. 1:3); Christ is a priest by the power of an indestructible life (Heb. 7:16).

C The power of people

C1 Powerful individuals

Nimrod became a mighty man on the earth (Gen. 10:8; 1 Chr. 1:10); Reuben, preeminent in power (Gen. 49:3); no one would be able to stand before Joshua (Josh. 1:5); David became more and more powerful (2 Sam. 5:10; 1 Chr. 11:9); David's mighty men (2 Sam. 23:8-39; 1 Chr. 11:10-47); John the Baptist would go in the spirit and power of Elijah (Luke 1:17); they said Simon was the great power of God (Acts 8:10).

C2 Power through God

Why stare at us as if by our own power we made this man walk? (Acts 3:12); the surpassing power is from God, not from us (2 Cor. 4:7); his power is made perfect in weakness (2 Cor. 12:9); the power at work in us is the power which raised Christ from the dead (Eph. 1:19-20); the power at work within us (Eph. 3:20); striving according to his working which works in me in power (Col. 1:29); we commend ourselves in the power of God (2 Cor. 6:7); he is powerful among you (2 Cor. 13:3); he gave the 12 power and authority over all demons (Luke 9:1); greater works than these will he do because I go to the Father (John 14:12); with great power the apostles bore witness to the resurrection (Acts 4:33); the weapons of our warfare are powerful through God (2 Cor. 10:4); I will boast of my weaknesses that the power of Christ may rest upon me (2 Cor. 12:9); strengthened with all power according to his glorious might (Col. 1:11); suffering for the gospel in the power of God (2 Tim. 1:8).

C3 Power through the Spirit
Not by might nor by power but by my Spirit (Zech. 4:6); Jesus was anointed with the Spirit and with power (Acts 10:38); you will receive power when the Holy Spirit comes upon you (Acts 1:8); clothed with power from on high (Luke 24:49); God has given us a spirit of power (2 Tim. 1:7); Jesus returned in the power of the Spirit (Luke 4:14); the power of the Spirit (Rom. 15:13); the power of signs and wonders, the power of the Spirit (Rom. 15:19); not persuasive words but the demonstration of the Spirit and power (1 Cor. 2:4); filled with power with the Spirit of the Lord (Mic. 3:8); Stephen, full of grace and power (Acts 6:8).

C4 Power through the Spirit
Not by might nor by power but by my Spirit (Zech. 4:6); Jesus was anointed with the Spirit and with power (Acts 10:38); you will receive power when the Holy Spirit comes upon you (Acts 1:8); clothed with power from on high (Luke 24:49); God has given us a spirit of power (2 Tim. 1:7); Jesus returned in the power of the Spirit (Luke 4:14); the power of the Spirit (Rom. 15:13); the power of signs and wonders, the power of the Spirit (Rom. 15:19); not persuasive words but the demonstration of the Spirit and power (1 Cor. 2:4); filled with power with the Spirit of the Lord (Mic. 3:8); Stephen, full of grace and power (Acts 6:8).

C5 Drawbacks to man's power
Let not the mighty man boast in his might (Jer. 9:23); their might is not right (Jer. 23:10); how have the mighty fallen! (2 Sam. 1:19, 25, 27); I will find out not the words of these arrogant people but their power (1 Cor. 4:19).

POWERLESS, see 161.

D The power of other creatures
No beast could stand before the ram or rescue from his power (Dan. 8:4); he has delivered Daniel from the power of the lions (Dan. 6:27); angels are greater in might and power (2 Pet. 2:11); this hour and the power of darkness are yours (Luke 22:53); the working of Satan with all power (2 Thess. 2:9); that through death he might render impotent him who had the power of death (Heb. 2:14); power is mine [Wisdom] (Prov. 8:14).

E The power of the gospel
The gospel is the power of God (Rom. 1:16); the message of the cross is the power of God (1 Cor. 1:18); a horn of salvation (Luke 1:69); the kingdom of God is not talk but power (1 Cor. 4:20); not persuasive words but the demonstration of the Spirit and power (1 Cor. 2:4); our gospel came not in word only but in power and in the Holy Spirit (1 Thess. 1:5).

F Ability
Our God is able to deliver us from the fiery furnace (Dan. 3:17); Abraham reckoned that God was able to raise the dead (Heb. 11:19); who can forgive sins but God alone? (Mark 2:7); he is able for ever to save those who draw near to God through him (Heb. 7:25); do you believe I am able to do this? (Matt. 9:28); if you can do anything . . . (Mark 9:22-3); are you able to drink the cup I drink? (Matt. 20:22; Mark 10:38-9); he is able to do far more than all we ask or think (Eph. 3:20); I can do all things through him who strengthens me (Phil. 4:13).

161 Impotence

WEAKNESS, see 163.

A Impotence of God
I cannot do anything until you come there (Gen. 19:22); lest people say the Lord was not able to bring

them into the land (Num. 14:16; Deut. 9:28); having a form of religion but denying the power of it (2 Tim. 3:5).

IMPOSSIBLE FOR GOD, see 470A.

B Impotence of Christ
Christ could do no mighty work there (Mark 6:5); I can do nothing of myself (John 5:30); he could not be hid (Mark 7:24); he saved others, he cannot save himself (Mark 15:31).

IMPOSSIBLE, see 470.

C Impotence of people

C1 Unable to expel
We are not able to attack the people of the land (Num. 13:31); Judah could not drive out the Jebusites (Josh. 15:63); the Manassites were not able to drive out the Canaanites (Josh. 17:12); the men of Judah could not drive out the inhabitants of the valley (Judg. 1:19); the Benjaminites could not dislodge the Jebusites (Judg. 1:21); the disciples were not able to cast out the evil spirit (Mark 9:18; Luke 9:40); why could we not drive it out? (Matt. 17:19; Mark 9:28).

C2 Unable to serve God
You cannot serve the Lord (Josh. 24:19); the carnal mind cannot submit to God's law (Rom. 8:7); those who are in the flesh cannot please God (Rom. 8:8); while we were helpless Christ died (Rom. 5:6); whoever does not hate nearest kin cannot be my disciple (Luke 14:26); whoever does not take up his cross cannot be my disciple (Luke 14:27); no one can come to me unless the Father draws him (John 6:44); as the branch cannot bear fruit unless it abides in the vine, nor can you (John 15:4); without me you can do nothing (John 15:5); I can wish to do good, but the doing is not present in me (Rom. 7:18).

C3 Unable to harm
We cannot speak to you bad or good (Gen. 24:50); we have sworn to them and so we cannot touch them (Josh. 9:19); Herodias was unable to kill John (Mark 6:19); they were not able to catch him in what he said (Luke 20:26); it was not possible for him to be held by death (Acts 2:24).

C4 Physically unable
At Lystra there was a man who could not use his feet (Acts 14:8); no one was able to bind him (Mark 5:3-4); they could not haul in the net because of the multitude of fish (John 21:6); you cannot make one hair white or black (Matt. 5:36); a good tree cannot bear bad fruit nor a bad tree good fruit (Matt. 7:18); David could not go in heavy armour (1 Sam. 17:39); after he has laid a foundation and is not able to finish (Luke 14:29-30); where I am going you cannot come (John 8:21, 22; 13:33, 36).

D Impotence of Satan
He disarmed principalities and powers (Col. 2:15); the ruler of this world has nothing in me (John 14:30); some kill the body but cannot kill the soul (Matt. 10:28; Luke 12:4); that through death he might render impotent him who had the power of death (Heb. 2:14).

E Impotence of idols
Idols can neither do harm nor good (Jer. 10:5); idols cannot see or hear or walk (Rev. 9:20); have other gods been able to deliver their lands? (2 Kgs. 18:34-5).

162 Strength

POWER, see 160.

A Strength of God

A1 God is strong
God is mighty in strength (Job 9:4); with God are strength and wisdom (Job 12:16); the Lord is girded with strength (Ps. 93:1); the Lord strong and mighty (Ps. 24:8); their Redeemer is strong (Jer. 50:34); the

strength of his might (Eph. 6:10); the weakness of God is stronger than men (1 Cor. 1:25); worthy is the Lamb to receive might (Rev. 5:12); the Lord who judges her is strong (Rev. 18:8).

A2 God's strong arm / hand
God brought them out of Egypt by his mighty hand (Exod. 6:1; 13:3, 9, 14, 16; 32:11; Deut. 7:19; 26:8); with an outstretched arm (Exod. 6:6; Deut. 7:19; 9:29; 26:8); your right hand and your arm brought them victory (Ps. 44:3); with a strong hand and an outstretched arm (Ps. 136:12); awake, put on strength, arm of the Lord (Isa. 51:9); he has shown strength with his arm (Luke 1:51).

B Strength of people
B1 Be strong!
Be strong! (Deut. 31:6, 7, 23; Josh. 1:6, 7, 9, 18; 10:25; 1 Sam. 4:9; 2 Sam. 10:12; 1 Kgs. 2:2; 1 Chr. 19:13; 22:13; 28:10, 20; 2 Chr. 15:7; 25:8; 32:7; Isa. 35:4; Dan. 10:19; Hag. 2:4; Zech. 8:9, 13; 1 Cor. 16:13); be strong and let your heart take courage (Ps. 31:24); be strong in the Lord (Eph. 6:10); be strong in the grace that is in Christ Jesus (2 Tim. 2:1).

B2 Strong through God
B2a God our strength
The Lord is the strength of his people (Ps. 28:8; 37:39); the Lord is my strength (Exod. 15:2; Ps. 28:7; 118:14; Hab. 3:19); the Lord is my strength and song (Isa. 12:2); God our strength (Ps. 81:1); God is our refuge and strength (Ps. 46:1); blessed is the man whose strength is in you (Ps. 84:5); the joy of the Lord is your strength (Neh. 8:10).

B2b God gives strength
The Lord will give strength to his people (Ps. 29:11); he gives strength to the weary, to those who wait for him (Isa. 40:29-31); I will strengthen you (Isa. 41:10); God girds me with strength (Ps. 18:32); I can do all things through him who strengthens me (Phil. 4:13); when I am weak, then I am strong (2 Cor. 12:10); whoever serves, by the strength that God supplies (1 Pet. 4:11).

B2c Seeking God's strength
Seek the Lord and his strength (1 Chr. 16:11; Ps. 105:4); Samson prayed for strength just once more (Judg. 16:28); pray for strength to escape these things and to stand before the Son of man (Luke 21:36).

B2d May God strengthen you
May you be strengthened through his Spirit in the inner man (Eph. 3:16); may you be strengthened with all power (Col. 1:11); may he strengthen your hearts in every good deed and word (2 Thess. 2:17).

B2e God strengthening people
David found strength in God (1 Sam. 30:6); the Lord strengthened me (2 Tim. 4:17); the name of Jesus, by faith in his name, has made this man strong (Acts 3:16); I thank him who has strengthened me, Christ Jesus our Lord (1 Tim. 1:12); the heart needs strengthening by grace, not food (Heb. 13:9); after you have suffered for a little while, God will strengthen you (1 Pet. 5:10); as your days, so shall your strength be (Deut. 33:25).

B3 Strong people
Due to strength, life may reach 80 years (Ps. 90:10); when a strong man, fully armed, guards his own home (Luke 11:21); when one stronger than he overpowers him (Luke 11:22); not many mighty men were called (1 Cor. 1:26); we are weak but you are strong (1 Cor. 4:10); we rejoice when we are weak and you are strong (2 Cor. 13:9); I am writing to you, young men, because you are strong (1 John 2:13-14); as the man, so is his strength (Judg. 8:21); they go from strength to strength (Ps. 84:7); the glory of young men is their strength (Prov. 20:29); a wise man is strong (Prov. 24:5); love the Lord your God with all your strength (Mark 12:30);

to love God with all the strength (Mark 12:33); Abraham grew strong in his faith as he gave glory to God (Rom. 4:20); John the Baptist grew strong in spirit (Luke 1:80); Jesus grew and became strong (Luke 2:40); Saul increased in strength (Acts 9:22); my little finger is thicker than my father's loins (1 Kgs. 12:10; 2 Chr. 10:10); God chose the weak things to shame the strong (1 Cor. 1:27).

B4 Strengthening people
Strengthen the weak hands and feeble knees (Isa. 35:3; Heb. 12:12); when you have turned, strengthen your brethren (Luke 22:32); we who are strong ought to bear the failings of the weak (Rom. 15:1); wisdom strengthens a wise man more than ten rulers in a city (Eccles. 7:19); the weak you have not strengthened (Ezek. 34:4); an angel strengthened him (Luke 22:43); he took food and was strengthened (Acts 9:19); Paul and Silas strengthened the churches (Acts 15:41); the churches were being strengthened in the faith (Acts 16:5); strengthening all the disciples (Acts 14:22; 18:23); they strengthened the brethren (Acts 15:32); we sent Timothy to strengthen you (1 Thess. 3:2); that I may impart some spiritual gift to strengthen you (Rom. 1:11).

C Strength of animals
Out of the strong came something sweet (Judg. 14:14, 18); do you give the horse his strength? (Job 39:19); a horse cannot save by its strength (Ps. 33:17); increase comes from the strength of the ox (Prov. 14:4); the strength of a hippopotamus (Job 40:16); the strength of the crocodile (Job 41:12).

D Limitations of strength
A man does not prevail by strength (1 Sam. 2:9); God's delight is not in the horse's strength, nor in a man's legs (Ps. 147:10); a warrior is not saved by great strength (Ps. 33:16); the battle is not to the strong (Eccles. 9:11); wisdom is better than strength (Eccles. 9:16); when he became strong he was proud (2 Chr. 26:16); I will make the pride of the strong to cease (Ezek. 7:24); overpower the strong man and you can plunder his goods (Matt. 12:29); no one can enter a strong man's house unless he binds the strong man (Mark 3:27; Luke 11:22).
WEAKNESS, see 163.

163 Weakness
POWERLESS, see 161.

A God's weakness
The weakness of God is stronger than men (1 Cor. 1:25); Christ was crucified in weakness (2 Cor. 13:4); he took our weaknesses and carried our diseases (Matt. 8:17); is the Lord's arm shortened? (Num. 11:23; Isa. 50:2); the Lord's hand is not shortened (Isa. 59:1).

B Human weakness
B1 Weak people
B1a Weak by nature
The weakness of the children and animals (Gen. 33:13); man's frailty (Job 4:19); every high priest is beset with weakness (Heb. 5:2; 7:28); the wife as the weaker vessel (1 Pet. 3:7); the body is sown in weakness and raised in power (1 Cor. 15:43); God did what the law, weakened by the flesh, could not do (Rom. 8:3); the spirit is willing but the flesh is weak (Matt. 26:41; Mark 14:38).

B1b Reasons for weakness
If I am shaved I will become weak (Judg. 16:17); my knees are weak from fasting (Ps. 109:24); my strength fails me because of my iniquity (Ps. 31:10); a woman who had a spirit of weakness (Luke 13:11); this is why many of you are weak and ill and some have died (1 Cor. 11:30).

B1c No strength to cope
Children are brought to the birth and there is no strength to deliver them (Isa. 37:3); if you show yourself slack in the day of distress your strength is small (Prov. 24:10); let the weak say, 'I am a mighty man' (Joel 3:10).

B2 Using weakness
I will boast of my weakness (2 Cor. 11:30; 12:5, 9); I am content with weakness, for when I am weak, then I am strong (2 Cor. 12:10); they won strength out of weakness (Heb. 11:34); Christ's power is made perfect in weakness (2 Cor. 12:9).

B3 Help the weak
Help the weak (1 Thess. 5:14); strengthen the weak hands and feeble knees (Isa. 35:3; Heb. 12:12); blessed is he who considers the weak (Ps. 41:1); bear with the failings of the weak (Rom. 15:1); receive the man weak in faith (Rom. 14:1); by working hard we must help the weak (Acts 20:35); take care your liberty does not become a stumbling block to the weak (1 Cor. 8:9-11).

B4 God helps the weak
God chose what is weak (1 Cor. 1:27); the Spirit helps us in our weakness (Rom. 8:26); a high priest able to sympathise with our weaknesses (Heb. 4:15).

C Weak things
A fox would break their wall down (Neh. 4:3); no divided city or house can stand (Matt. 12:25; Mark 3:25); the members which seem to be feeble are necessary (1 Cor. 12:22); the weak and worthless elements (Gal. 4:9); the former commandment is set aside because of its weakness and uselessness (Heb. 7:18).

164 Making

A Creation
A1 The creator of all
The creator of the ends of the earth (Isa. 40:28); God is the maker of all things (Eccles. 11:5; Jer. 10:16; 51:19; Eph. 3:9); the builder of all things (Heb. 3:4); God's eternal power and deity are seen by what has been made (Rom. 1:20); did not he who made the outside make the inside also? (Luke 11:40); the new man is being renewed after the image of its Creator (Col. 3:10); everything created by God is good (1 Tim. 4:4).

A2 Creation of the heavens and earth
God created the heavens and the earth (Gen. 1:1; 2 Kgs. 19:15; 2 Chr. 2:12; Neh. 9:6; Ps. 121:2; 124:8; 134:3; 146:6; Isa. 42:5; 44:24; 45:18; 48:13; 51:13; Acts 14:15; Rev. 10:6); in six days (Exod. 20:11; 31:17); you made heaven and earth and sea and everything in them (Acts 4:24); God created the world and everything in it (Acts 17:24).

A3 Creation of life
Creation of: vegetation (Gen. 1:11-12); sea creatures and flying things (Gen. 1:20-1); great sea monsters (Gen. 1:21); land creatures (Gen. 1:24-5); beasts and birds from the ground (Gen. 2:19); I made Behemoth along with you (Job 40:15).

A4 Creation of man
A4a Creation of all mankind
God created mankind (Gen. 1:26-7; 5:1-2; Deut. 4:32; Matt. 19:4); God made them male and female (Mark 10:6); the Lord formed man from dust (Gen. 2:7); he is the maker of rich and poor (Prov. 22:2); he who made me in the womb made my slave also (Job 31:15); God made every nation of men (Acts 17:26); has not one God created us all? (Mal. 2:10).

A4b Creation of woman
I will make a helper suitable for him (Gen. 2:18); woman made from man's rib (Gen. 2:22); Adam was created first, then Eve (1 Tim. 2:13); man was not from woman but woman from man (1 Cor. 11:8); man was not created for woman, but woman for man (1 Cor.

11:9); as woman was made from man, now man is born of woman (1 Cor. 11:12).

A4c Creation of man's faculties
Who gave man his mouth? (Exod. 4:11); God has made both ears and eyes (Prov. 20:12); does he who made ear and eye not hear and see? (Ps. 94:9).

A4d Man's relationship with his Creator
Remember your Creator (Eccles. 12:1); the people I formed for myself to declare my praise (Isa. 43:21); we are the clay, you are the potter (Isa. 64:8); you are like clay in the hand of the potter (Jer. 18:6); can the pot criticise the potter? (Isa. 29:16; 45:9); will what is moulded say to the moulder, 'Why have you made me like this?' (Rom. 9:20); should what is made say to its maker, 'You did not make me'? (Isa. 29:16); God was sorry he had made man (Gen. 6:6, 7); they served the creature rather than the Creator (Rom. 1:25).

A5 How God created
A5a Earth's foundation
God hangs the earth on nothing (Job 26:7); he has founded the earth upon the seas (Ps. 24:2); God spread out the earth above the waters (Ps. 136:6).

A5b God's method in creation
By understanding he made the heavens (Ps. 136:5); he commanded and they were created (Ps. 148:5); through the Word all things came into existence (John 1:3); the world was made through him (John 1:10); all things are by Jesus Christ (1 Cor. 8:6); all things were created in him, through him and for him (Col. 1:16); through him God made the world (Heb. 1:2); he is the beginning of God's creation (Rev. 3:14); creation: by wisdom (Prov. 3:19; 8:27; Jer. 10:12); by God's word (Ps. 33:6; Heb. 11:3); by his power (Jer. 51:15); by God's will (Rev. 4:11).

A6 New creation
I create new heavens and a new earth (Isa. 65:17); if any man be in Christ he is a new creation (2 Cor. 5:17); neither circumcision nor uncircumcision counts, but a new creation (Gal. 6:15); we are his workmanship, created in Christ Jesus for good works (Eph. 2:10); the new man, created in true righteousness and holiness (Eph. 4:24).

B Building
B1 Building in general
A time to build (Eccles. 3:3); I will build you up and not tear you down (Jer. 42:10); I have appointed you to build and to plant (Jer. 1:10); I searched for a man to build up the wall (Ezek. 22:30); no one builds a tower without first sitting down and counting the cost (Luke 14:28); if I build again what I once destroyed I prove myself to be a law-breaker (Gal. 2:18).
STONES FOR BUILDING, see 344B3.

B2 Building cities
God will build the cities of Judah (Ps. 69:35); they will rebuild the ruined cities (Isa. 61:4; Amos 9:14); woe to him who builds a city with bloodshed (Hab. 2:12); let a faithless city never be rebuilt (Deut. 13:16); let us build a city and a tower (Gen. 11:4); the city with foundations, whose builder is God (Heb. 11:10); is this not great Babylon which I have made? (Dan. 4:30); cursed be the man who rebuilds Jericho (Josh. 6:26); Hiel rebuilt Jericho (1 Kgs. 16:34); David built up Jerusalem (2 Sam. 5:9; 1 Chr. 11:8); they are rebuilding that rebellious city, Jerusalem (Ezra 4:12); build up the walls of Jerusalem (Ps. 51:18); the Lord builds up Jerusalem (Ps. 147:2); the Lord will rebuild Zion (Ps. 102:16); Cyrus will say of Jerusalem, 'Let it be rebuilt' (Isa. 44:28); they will rebuild the ancient ruins (Isa. 61:4); the day for building your walls (Mic. 7:11); you build Zion with bloodshed and Jerusalem with wrong (Mic. 3:10).

B3 Building houses

When you build a house, make a parapet for the roof (Deut. 22:8); unless the Lord builds the house the builders work in vain (Ps. 127:1); by wisdom a house is built (Prov. 24:3); the wise man built his house on rock (Matt. 7:24; Luke 6:48); the foolish man built his house on sand (Matt. 7:26; Luke 6:49); woe to him who builds his house with unrighteousness (Jer. 22:13-14); the builder of the house has more honour than the house (Heb. 3:3); a palace built for David (2 Sam. 5:11; 1 Chr. 14:1); David built houses for himself (1 Chr. 15:1); a palace built for Solomon (1 Kgs. 3:1; 7:1; 9:1, 10; 2 Chr. 2:1; 8:1); Solomon built a house for Pharaoh's daughter (1 Kgs. 9:24); Ahab built an ivory house (1 Kgs. 22:39); it is not time to build houses (Ezek. 11:3); the Rechabites were not to build houses (Jer. 35:9).

B4 Building altars

Build seven altars for me here (Num. 23:1); Aaron built an altar before the gold calf (Exod. 32:5); those who built altars: Noah (Gen. 8:20); Abraham (Gen. 12:7, 8; 13:4, 18; 22:9); Isaac (Gen. 26:25); Jacob (Gen. 33:20; 35:1, 7); Moses (Exod. 17:15); Joshua (Josh. 8:30); the two and a half tribes (Josh. 22:10, 11, 16, 19, 23, 26); Gideon (Judg. 6:24, 26, 28); the Israelites (Judg. 21:4; Ezra 3:2); Samuel (1 Sam. 7:17); Saul (1 Sam. 14:35); David (2 Sam. 24:18, 21, 25; 1 Chr. 21:18, 22, 26); Solomon (1 Kgs. 9:25); Jeroboam (1 Kgs. 12:33); Ahab (1 Kgs. 16:32); Elijah (1 Kgs. 18:30-2); Urijah the priest (2 Kgs. 16:11); Ahaz (2 Chr. 28:24); Manasseh (2 Kgs. 21:3, 4, 5; 23:12; 2 Chr. 33:3, 4, 5, 15).

B5 Building the temple

David wanted to build the temple (1 Kgs. 8:17-18; 1 Chr. 28:2-3; 2 Chr. 6:7); David could not build it (1 Kgs. 5:3; 1 Chr. 22:8; 28:3); Solomon would build it (1 Kgs. 5:5; 8:19; 1 Chr. 22:9-10; 2 Chr. 6:9); Solomon built the temple (1 Kgs. 6:1-38; 2 Chr. 3:1); God appointed Cyrus to build a temple in Jerusalem (2 Chr. 36:23; Ezra 1:2); Cyrus issued a decree to rebuild the temple (Ezra 5:13); let the temple be rebuilt (Ezra 5:15; 6:3); Zerubbabel and Jeshua started to rebuild the temple (Ezra 5:2); enemies wanted to build with them (Ezra 4:2-3); the time has not yet come for the house of the Lord to be rebuilt (Hag. 1:2); I can destroy this temple and rebuild it in three days (Matt. 26:61; Mark 14:58; John 2:19-21); you who would rebuild the temple in three days! (Matt. 27:40).

B6 Building the church

B6a The foundation of the church

On this rock I will build my church (Matt. 16:18); built upon the foundation of the apostles and prophets (Eph. 2:20); you are God's building (1 Cor. 3:9); living stones built into a spiritual house (1 Pet. 2:5); I laid a foundation as a master-builder (1 Cor. 3:10); that I might not build on another man's foundation (Rom. 15:20); no one can lay a foundation other than that which has been laid, Jesus Christ (1 Cor. 3:11); Christ Jesus himself being the cornerstone (Eph. 2:20).

B6b Building up the church

Building up the body of Christ (Eph. 4:12); it upbuilds itself in love (Eph. 4:16); authority given by the Lord for building you up (2 Cor. 10:8; 13:10); I laid a foundation and another is building on it (1 Cor. 3:10); pursue the building up of one another (Rom. 14:19); seek to excel in building up the church (1 Cor. 14:12); build one another up (1 Thess. 5:11); build yourselves up in your most holy faith (Jude 20); let each of us please his neighbour to build him up (Rom. 15:2); we have been speaking for your upbuilding (2 Cor. 12:19); let your talk be good for edifying (Eph. 4:29); let all things be done to edify (1 Cor. 14:26); the word of his grace is able to build you up (Acts 20:32); love edifies

(1 Cor. 8:1); a tongue edifies the speaker but prophecy edifies the church (1 Cor. 14:3-5); rooted and built up in Christ (Col. 2:7); all things are lawful but not all things build up (1 Cor. 10:23).

C Making things

Making an ark (Gen. 6:14; Heb. 11:7; 1 Pet. 3:20); making garments for Aaron (Exod. 28:3-4); Aaron fashioned the calf with a graving tool (Exod. 32:4); the potter remade it into another vessel (Jer. 18:4).

165 Destruction

A Destruction in general

A1 About destruction

A time to break down (Eccles. 3:3); Hormah – destruction (Num. 21:2-3; Judg. 1:17); pride goes before destruction (Prov. 16:18); devastation and destruction! (Jer. 48:3); I have heard from the Lord of destruction over all the earth (Isa. 28:22); the wide gate and the broad road that leads to destruction (Matt. 7:13); destruction will come upon them suddenly (1 Thess. 5:3); destruction and misery are in their paths (Rom. 3:16); if I build again what I once destroyed I prove myself to be a law-breaker (Gal. 2:18).

A2 God destroying

God tears down and it cannot be rebuilt (Job 12:14); the Lord your God is a consuming fire (Deut. 9:3); this disaster is from the Lord (2 Kgs. 6:33); I am bringing great destruction (Jer. 4:6); what I have built I am tearing down (Jer. 45:4); the day of the Lord will come as destruction from the Almighty (Isa. 13:6; Joel 1:15); the day of the Lord is a day of destruction and devastation (Zeph. 1:15); I will destroy the wisdom of the wise (1 Cor. 1:19); food and stomach, God will destroy both (1 Cor. 6:13); God is able to save and to destroy (Jas. 4:12).

A3 Ban of destruction

Anything under a ban is most holy (Lev. 27:28); and may not be redeemed (Lev. 27:29); Jericho was under a ban of destruction (Josh. 6:17-19; 7:1); Achar [Achan] violated the ban (1 Chr. 2:7); the Israelites became a thing devoted to destruction (Josh. 7:12); I consigned Jacob to the ban (Isa. 43:28); lest I smite the land with a ban of destruction (Mal. 4:6); there will be no more ban of destruction (Zech. 14:11).

A4 Abomination of desolation

The abomination of desolation (Dan. 9:27; 11:31; 12:11; Matt. 24:15; Mark 13:14).

B Destruction of living things

B1 Destruction of all creatures

God would destroy all people (Gen. 6:7, 13); all flesh (Gen. 6:17); if I cut off from the land man and beast (Ezek. 14:13, 17, 19); to cut off man and beast from Jerusalem (Ezek. 14:21).

B2 Destruction of nations

He destroys nations (Job 12:23); with you I shatter nations (Jer. 51:20-3); God sent angels to destroy Sodom (Gen. 19:13-14); God ruined Egypt (Exod. 8:24; 10:7); I will destroy all the nations that come against Jerusalem (Zech. 12:9); God will ruin: Amalek (Exod. 17:14; Num. 24:20); Ammon (Ezek. 25:7); Assyria (Zeph. 2:13); Babylon (Jer. 51:2); Edom (Jer. 49:13; Ezek. 35:3); Egypt (Ezek. 30:12); Damascus (Isa. 17:1); Moab (Num. 21:29; 24:17; Isa. 15:1-9; Jer. 48:1); Tyre (Ezek. 26:17); Assyria intended to destroy many nations (Isa. 10:7); Moab will be destroyed from being a people (Jer. 48:42); the land of Egypt will be a desolation and a waste (Ezek. 29:9-10); utterly destroy Babylon (Jer. 50:26); every kingdom divided against itself is laid waste (Matt. 12:25).

B3 Destruction of the wicked

The Lord will destroy evildoers (Ps. 94:23); God destroys the wicked in a moment (Ps. 73:19); destruction of the ungodly (2 Pet. 3:6); vessels of wrath designed for destruction (Rom. 9:22); their end is destruction (Phil. 3:19); the punishment of eternal destruction (2 Thess. 1:9); from of old their destruction has not been asleep (2 Pet. 2:3); they will be destroyed in the same destruction (2 Pet. 2:12); the day of judgement and the destruction of ungodly men (2 Pet. 3:7); by the things they do by instinct they are destroyed (Jude 10); they distort the scriptures to their own destruction (2 Pet. 3:16); bringing swift destruction on themselves (2 Pet. 2:1).

B4 Destruction of God's people

I will destroy the Israelites (Exod. 32:10); let us wipe out Israel (Ps. 83:4); I will not destroy Ephraim again (Hos. 11:9); do not destroy the work of God for the sake of food (Rom. 14:20).

B5 Destruction of the church

Saul began to destroy the church (Acts 8:3); if any one destroys God's temple, God will destroy him (1 Cor. 3:17); the weak brother is destroyed by your knowledge (1 Cor. 8:11); authority the Lord gave me for building up, not for tearing down (2 Cor. 13:10); I tried to destroy the church of God (Gal. 1:13).

B6 Destruction of plants

The flax and barley were ruined (Exod. 9:31); the little foxes ruin the vineyards (S. of S. 2:15); the people of the east ruined the crops like swarms of locusts (Judg. 6:4-5); swarms of locusts (Joel 1:4; Amos 7:1); wail, oaks of Bashan, for the thick forest has been felled (Zech. 11:2).

C Destruction of things

C1 Destruction of the world

The heavens will pass away with a roar (2 Pet. 3:10); as the world was formerly destroyed by water (2 Pet. 3:6); created things will be removed (Heb. 12:27); seeing all these things will be destroyed (2 Pet. 3:11); the earth will be burned up (2 Pet. 3:10); the heavens will be burned up and the elements melt with fire (2 Pet. 3:12).

C2 Destruction of countries

Your land is desolate (Isa. 1:7); the whole land will be a desolation (Jer. 4:27); the Lord and his weapons of wrath, to destroy all the land (Isa. 13:5); I will make the land a desolation and a waste (Ezek. 33:28, 29); the Lord commanded me to destroy this place (2 Kgs. 18:25); Egypt will become a waste, Edom a desolate wilderness (Joel 3:19); when I make the land of Egypt desolate (Ezek. 32:15); I will make Samaria a heap of ruins (Mic. 1:6).

C3 Destruction of cities

C3a Destruction of cities in general

I will lay waste your cities (Lev. 26:31; Ezek. 35:4; Mic. 5:14); they will demolish the fortified cities in which you trusted (Jer. 5:17); he brings low the lofty city (Isa. 26:5); until cities are devastated and without inhabitant (Isa. 6:11); I planned that you should turn cities into heaps of ruins (2 Kgs. 19:25; Isa. 37:26); by the mouth of the wicked a city is torn down (Prov. 11:11).

C3b Destruction of Babylon

The Lord is going to destroy Babylon (Jer. 51:55); one tenth of the city was destroyed (Rev. 11:13); fallen, fallen is Babylon (Isa. 21:9); Babylon was destroyed (Rev. 14:8; 16:19; 18:2, 21); in one hour she has been laid waste (Rev. 18:17, 19).

C3c Destruction of Jerusalem

The angel was about to destroy Jerusalem (2 Sam. 24:16; 1 Chr. 21:15); Jerusalem will become a heap of ruins (Jer. 9:11; Mic. 3:12); I will devastate this city (Jer. 19:8, 11); I will remove this city from before my face

(Jer. 32:31); Zion will be ploughed like a field (Jer. 26:18; Mic. 3:12); know that Jerusalem's desolation is at hand (Luke 21:20); the city has fallen (Ezek. 33:21); the Chaldeans broke down the walls of Jerusalem (2 Kgs. 25:10); Jerusalem in ruins (Neh. 2:3, 17; Ps. 79:1); Jerusalem desolated for seventy years (Dan. 9:2).

C3d Destruction of other cities

God destroyed Sodom and Gomorrah (Gen. 13:10; 2 Pet. 2:6); God destroyed the cities of the valley (Gen. 19:29); yet forty days and Nineveh will be overthrown (Jonah 3:4); Nineveh is devastated, who will grieve for her? (Nahum 3:7).

C4 Destruction of houses

Tear down the diseased house (Lev. 14:45); the house of the wicked will be destroyed (Prov. 14:11); the foolish woman tears down her own house (Prov. 14:1); a wind struck the four corners of the house and it fell (Job 1:19); the house on sand fell with a great fall (Matt. 7:27); they will destroy your pleasant houses (Ezek. 26:12); I will pull down my barns and build larger ones (Luke 12:18).

C5 Destruction of the temple

This house will become a heap of ruins (1 Kgs. 9:8); Nebuchadnezzar destroyed the temple (Ezra 5:12); the temple was burned (2 Kgs. 25:9; 2 Chr. 36:19); there will not be one stone left upon another (Matt. 24:2; Mark 13:2; Luke 19:44; 21:6); destroy this temple and in three days I will raise it up (Matt. 26:61; Mark 14:58; John 2:19); you who would destroy the temple! (Matt. 27:40; Mark 15:29); Jesus of Nazareth will destroy this place (Acts 6:14).

C6 Destruction of strongholds

Our weapons are mighty through God for the destruction of strongholds (2 Cor. 10:4-5); fire will consume the strongholds of: Ben-hadad (Amos 1:4); Bozrah (Amos 1:12); Gaza (Amos 1:7); Jerusalem (Amos 2:5); Kerioth (Amos 2:2); Rabbah (Amos 1:14); Tyre (Amos 1:10).

C7 Shipwreck

Jehoshaphat's ships were wrecked (1 Kgs. 22:48; 2 Chr. 20:37); shipwrecked three times (2 Cor. 11:25); the shipwreck of Tyre (Ezek. 27:26-7); description of one shipwreck (Acts 27:14-44); some have made shipwreck of their faith (1 Tim. 1:19).

D Destruction of Satan's works

D1 God will destroy Satan's works

God will destroy: the high places and idolatrous altars of Israel (Lev. 26:30; Ezek. 6:3-4); the idols of Egypt (Ezek. 30:13); their altars and pillars (Hos. 10:2); Samaria's idols (Mic. 1:7); the idols of Nineveh (Nahum 1:14).

D2 Destroy Satan's works!

Destroy all the idols and high places (Num. 33:52); destroy the places where they worshipped their gods (Deut. 12:2); destroy their altars and their sacred pillars (Exod. 34:13; Deut. 7:5; 12:3); smash their sacred pillars (Exod. 23:24); tear down their altars (Judg. 2:2); demolish the altar of Baal and the Asherah (Judg. 6:25).

D3 Satan's works will be destroyed

Have you come to destroy us evil spirits? (Mark 1:24; Luke 4:34); the Lord Jesus will destroy the lawless one (2 Thess. 2:8); the Son of God came to destroy the works of the devil (1 John 3:8); to destroy him who had the power of death (Heb. 2:14); the time for destroying those who destroy the earth (Rev. 11:18).

E Not destroyed

The burning bush was not consumed (Exod. 3:2, 3); struck down but not destroyed (2 Cor. 4:9); the Lord does not want any to perish (2 Pet. 3:9).

166 Reproducing

REPRODUCTION, see 167.

167 Reproduction

A Genitals

A1 Private parts

Ham saw his father's nakedness (Gen. 9:22); lest your nakedness be exposed on the altar (Exod. 20:26); linen underpants to cover their nakedness (Exod. 28:42); because your nakedness was uncovered through your harlotries (Ezek. 16:36).

NAKEDNESS UNCOVERED, see 229A4.

A2 Male genitals

A man with his male member cut off (Deut. 23:1); a woman seizing an opponent's genitals (Deut. 25:11); a man with crushed testicles could not serve as priest (Lev. 21:20); an animal with crushed testicles could not be offered (Lev. 22:24); their flesh [penis] is as the flesh of donkeys (Ezek. 23:20).

A3 Foreskin

You shall be circumcised in the flesh of your foreskins (Gen. 17:11, 14; Lev. 12:3); Zipporah touched his feet with the foreskin (Exod. 4:25); 100 Philistine foreskins (1 Sam. 18:25; 2 Sam. 3:14); 200 Philistine foreskins (1 Sam. 18:27); circumcise the foreskin of your hearts (Deut. 10:16).

A4 Womb

You knit me in my mother's womb (Ps. 139:13); naked I came from my mother's womb (Job 1:21); blessings of the breasts and the womb (Gen. 49:25); blessed is the womb that bore you (Luke 11:27); can he enter a second time into his mother's womb and be born? (John 3:4); blessed are the wombs that never bore, the breasts that never nursed (Luke 23:29); he considered the barrenness of Sarah's womb (Rom. 4:19).

BREASTS, see 253.

B Bearing children

B1 Conception

The Lord enabled Ruth to conceive (Ruth 4:13); the Lord opened Leah's womb (Gen. 29:31); God opened Rachel's womb (Gen. 30:22); that which has been conceived in her is of the Holy Spirit (Matt. 1:20); a virgin will conceive and bear a son (Matt. 1:23).

B2 Pregnancy

No birth, no pregnancy, no conception (Hos. 9:11); pregnancy of: Hagar (Gen. 16:4), Bathsheba (2 Sam. 11:5); the Shunammite woman (2 Kgs. 4:17); the prophetess (Isa. 8:3); Elizabeth (Luke 1:13-14, 24, 36); Mary (Matt. 1:18; Luke 1:31; 2:5); the woman clothed with the sun (Rev. 12:2).

B3 Harming pregnant women

You will rip up pregnant women (2 Kgs. 8:12); their pregnant women will be ripped open (Hos. 13:16); woe to those with child in those days (Matt. 24:19; Mark 13:17; Luke 21:23).

B4 Giving birth

B4a About birth

There is a time to give birth (Eccles. 3:2); this is the law of childbirth (Lev. 12:7); a woman who gives birth becomes unclean (Lev. 12:2); when a woman gives birth she forgets the anguish (John 16:21); that which is born of the flesh is flesh (John 3:6); she will bear a son and you shall call his name Jesus (Matt. 1:21, 25); God sent his Son, born of a woman (Gal. 4:4); the virgin will bear a son (Isa. 7:14; Matt. 1:23); birth of Jesus (Matt. 1:18; 2:1, 4; Luke 2:6-7); many would rejoice at John's birth (Luke 1:14); the woman gave birth to a son (Rev. 12:4-5).

B4b Labour pains

Pain in childbearing would be increased (Gen. 3:16); a woman in travail has sorrow (John 16:21); Jabez was born with pain (1 Chr. 4:9); I am in travail again until Christ be formed in you (Gal. 4:19); this is but the beginning of the birth pangs (Matt. 24:8; Mark 13:8); sudden destruction like birth pangs (1 Thess. 5:3); the whole creation groans in travail (Rom. 8:22).

B4c Regretting birth

Job cursed the day of his birth (Job 3:1); let the day I was born perish (Job 3:3); why did I not die at birth? (Job 3:11); cursed be the day I was born! (Jer. 20:14); woe is me that you bore me (Jer. 15:10); why have you brought me out of the womb? (Job 10:18); why did I come forth from the womb? (Jer. 20:18); the day of death is better than the day of birth (Eccles. 7:1).

B5 Spiritual birth

B5a Birth of evil

Your origin and birth are from the Canaanites (Ezek. 16:3-4); they hatch adders' eggs (Isa. 59:5); when desire has conceived it gives birth to sin (Jas. 1:15); sin gives birth to death (Jas. 1:15).

B5b Born of God

Unless one is born again he cannot see the kingdom of God (John 3:3); you must be born again (John 3:7); by his mercy we have been born anew to a living hope (1 Pet. 1:3); he who believes Jesus is the Christ is born of God (1 John 5:1); born again through the living and abiding word of God (1 Pet. 1:23); he brought us forth by the word of truth (Jas. 1:18); born not of blood but of God (John 1:13); born of water and the Spirit (John 3:5); born of the Spirit (John 3:6, 8); whatever is born of God overcomes the world (1 John 5:4); no one born of God goes on sinning (1 John 3:9; 5:18); he cannot go on sinning because he is born of God (1 John 3:9); he who loves is born of God and knows God (1 John 4:7); you are my Son, this day I have begotten you (Ps. 2:7; Heb. 1:5; 5:5); he who was born of God keeps him and the evil one does not touch him (1 John 5:18).

168 The destroyer

He who is slack in his work is brother to him who destroys (Prov. 18:9); the thief comes only to steal, kill and destroy (John 10:10); executioners of the city, each with his destroying weapon (Ezek. 9:1); the destroyer (Exod. 12:23); that the destroyer of the firstborn might not touch them (Heb. 11:28); the man of lawlessness, the son of destruction (2 Thess. 2:3); Abaddon [Destruction] is uncovered before God (Job 26:6); Abaddon has heard a report of wisdom (Job 28:22); adultery is fire which consumes to Abaddon (Job 31:12); woe to you, destroyer who have not been destroyed! (Isa. 33:1); he will cause fearful destruction (Dan. 8:24); the time has come to destroy the destroyer (Rev. 11:18); the angel of the abyss, called Abaddon and Apollyon [Destroyer] (Rev. 9:11); they were destroyed by the destroyer (1 Cor. 10:10).

169 Parentage

A Physical parents

A1 Relationship with parents

Parents should save for their children (2 Cor. 12:14); a good man leaves an inheritance for his children's children (Prov. 13:22); obey your parents (Eph. 6:1; Col. 3:20); let your father and mother be glad (Prov. 23:25); children will rise against parents (Matt. 10:21; Mark 13:12); disobedient to parents (Rom. 1:30; 2 Tim. 3:2); put to death a son disobedient to his parents (Deut. 21:18-21); daughter rises up against her mother, daughter-in-law against her mother-in-law (Mic. 7:6); I came to set a man against his father and a daughter against her mother (Matt. 10:35); they will be divided, father against son and son against father (Luke 12:53); brother will deliver up brother to death and a father his child (Matt. 10:21); you will be delivered up even by parents, kinsmen and friends (Luke 21:16).

A2 Honouring parents
Honour your father and mother (Exod. 20:12; Lev. 19:3; Deut. 5:16; Matt. 15:4; 19:19; Mark 7:10; 10:19; Luke 18:20; Eph. 6:2); a son honours his father (Mal. 1:6); let the widow's children make some return to their parents (1 Tim. 5:4); put to death a son who curses his parents (Exod. 21:17; Lev. 20:9; Mark 7:10); he who speaks evil of father and mother, let him be put to death (Matt. 15:4); put to death a son who strikes his parents (Exod. 21:15); he will not honour his father or mother (Matt. 15:6); you no longer permit him to do anything for his father or mother (Mark 7:12); let me go up and bury my father (Gen. 50:5); let me first bury my father (Matt. 8:21; Luke 9:59); whoever loves father or mother more than me is not worthy of me (Matt. 10:37); if anyone does not hate father and mother he cannot be my disciple (Luke 14:26); Levi did not consider his father and mother (Deut. 33:9).

A3 Parting from parents
A man will leave his father and mother (Gen. 2:24; Matt. 19:5; Mark 10:7; Eph. 5:31); he who leaves father or mother for my name's sake (Matt. 19:29; Mark 10:29; Luke 18:29); my parents forsake me but the Lord takes me up (Ps. 27:10).

B Fathers
B1 Ancestors
The Lord did not make a covenant with our fathers but with us (Deut. 5:3); I stand on trial for hope in the promise God made to our fathers (Acts 26:6); Israel are beloved for the sake of their fathers (Rom. 11:28); the patriarchs belong to Israel (Rom. 9:5); if we had lived in the days of our fathers (Matt. 23:30); fill up the measure of your fathers! (Matt. 23:32); blessed is the kingdom of our father David (Mark 11:10); to show mercy to our fathers (Luke 1:72); I am the God of your fathers, of Abraham, Isaac and Jacob (Acts 7:32); God spoke to our fathers by the prophets (Heb. 1:1).

B2 Fathers teaching
Listen to your father (Prov. 23:22); hear your father's instruction (Prov. 1:8); keep your father's commandment (Prov. 6:20); our fathers have told us what you did (Ps. 44:1); things our fathers have told us (Ps. 78:3).

B3 Fathers and sons
The glory of sons is their fathers (Prov. 17:6); I will turn the hearts of fathers to their children and children to their fathers (Mal. 4:6); to turn the hearts of the fathers back to the children (Luke 1:17); the father of the righteous will rejoice (Prov. 23:24); the father of a fool has no joy (Prov. 17:21, 25; 19:13); fathers, do not provoke your children to anger (Eph. 6:4); what son is there whom his father does not discipline? (Heb. 12:7); we had earthly fathers to discipline us (Heb. 12:9).

B4 Sins of the fathers
Your first forefather sinned (Isa. 43:27); iniquities of the fathers visited on the children (Exod. 20:5; 34:7; Num. 14:18; Deut. 5:9); God stores a man's sins for his sons (Job 21:19); the fathers have eaten sour grapes and the children's teeth are set on edge (Jer. 31:29; Ezek. 18:2); you repay the guilt of fathers to their children (Jer. 32:18); fathers shall not be put to death for the children nor vice versa (Deut. 24:16; 2 Kgs. 14:6; 2 Chr. 25:4); sons shall not bear the iniquity of their fathers nor vice versa (Ezek. 18:19, 20); he will not die for his father's iniquity (Ezek. 18:17).

B5 Father Abraham
Abraham became the father of many nations (Gen. 17:4-5; Rom. 4:17); look to Abraham your father (Isa. 51:2); Abraham is our father (John 8:39); Abraham is the father of the circumcised who also believe (Rom. 4:12); Abraham is the father of us all (Rom. 4:16); do not say Abraham is your father (Matt. 3:9; Luke 3:8). SPIRITUAL FATHERS, see 169D3.

C Mothers
SPIRITUAL MOTHERS, see 169D4.
C1 One's mother
C1a Mother and child
Eve – the mother of all living (Gen. 3:20); though a woman forget her sucking child, God will not forget you (Isa. 49:15); as one whom his mother comforts, so I will comfort you (Isa. 66:13).

C1b Attitude towards the mother
Do not forsake your mother's teaching (Prov. 1:8; 6:20); let her who bore you rejoice (Prov. 23:25); a foolish son is a grief to his mother (Prov. 10:1; 17:25); do not despise your mother when she is old (Prov. 23:22); daughter rises up against her mother, daughter-in-law against her mother-in-law (Mic. 7:6); I came to set a man against his father and a daughter against her mother (Matt. 10:35); they will be divided, mother against daughter and daughter against mother (Luke 12:53); treat older women as mothers (1 Tim. 5:2); behold, your mother! (John 19:27).

C1c Jesus' mother
The mother of Jesus was there (John 2:1); is not this Jesus, whose father and mother we know? (John 6:42); the mother of my Lord (Luke 1:43); Mary, the mother of Jesus (Acts 1:14); blessed is the womb that bore you (Luke 11:27); is not his mother called Mary? (Matt. 13:55); Jesus' mother and brothers came seeking him (Matt. 12:46-50; Mark 3:31-5; Luke 8:19-21).

C2 Mothers-in-law
Orpah kissed her mother-in-law but Ruth clung to her (Ruth 1:14); Peter's mother-in-law was sick (Matt. 8:14; Mark 1:30; Luke 4:38); daughter rises up against her mother, daughter-in-law against her mother-in-law (Mic. 7:6); I came to set a daughter-in-law against her mother-in-law (Matt. 10:35); divided, mother-in-law against daughter-in-law and daughter-in-law against mother-in-law (Luke 12:53).

C3 Animal mothers
A newborn animal is to be left with its mother for seven days (Exod. 22:30; Lev. 22:27); you shall not kill a mother animal and its young on the same day (Lev. 22:28); do not take a mother bird with its young (Deut. 22:6-7); do not boil a kid in its mother's milk (Exod. 23:19; 34:26; Deut. 14:21).

D Spiritual parents
D1 God our Father
GOD THE FATHER, see 965B.
D1a God is our Father
Father in heaven (Matt. 5:16, 48; 6:9; 23:9); we have our Father, God (John 8:41); Abba! Father! (Mark 14:36); a spirit of adoption, crying, Abba! Father! (Rom. 8:15); the Spirit of his Son in our hearts, crying, Abba! Father! (Gal. 4:6); for us there is one God, the Father (1 Cor. 8:6); one God and Father of all (Eph. 4:6); I will be a Father to you (2 Cor. 6:18); you are our Father though Abraham does not know us (Isa. 63:16); my Father, the friend of my youth (Jer. 3:4); the Father from whom every family derives its name (Eph. 3:14-15); his name will be Everlasting Father (Isa. 9:6); do we not all have one Father? has not one God created us? (Mal. 2:10); God is a father to the fatherless (Ps. 68:5); the Father of spirits (Heb. 12:9); the Father of lights (Jas. 1:17); the Father of mercies (2 Cor. 1:3); the Father of glory (Eph.

1:17); as a father pities his children (Ps. 103:13); he reproves as a father his children (Prov. 3:12; Heb. 12:5-9); if you address him as Father (1 Pet. 1:17); if God were your Father you would love me (John 8:42).

D1b Attitude to God the Father
You have known the Father (1 John 2:13); our fellowship is with the Father, and with his Son, Jesus Christ (1 John 1:3); he who confesses the Son has the Father also (1 John 2:23); he who abides in the doctrine has both the Father and the Son (2 John 9); if what you heard remains in you, you will remain in the Son and the Father (1 John 2:24); Father, hallowed be your name (Matt. 6:9; Luke 11:2); to our God and Father be glory (Phil. 4:20); so that you may be sons of your Father in heaven (Matt. 5:45); be merciful as your Father is merciful (Luke 6:36); this is the antichrist who denies the Father and the Son (1 John 2:22); no one who denies the Son has the Father (1 John 2:23).

D2 Father of the Christ
D2a God is Christ's Father
Jesus Christ the Son of the Father (2 John 3); you are my Son, today I have begotten you (Ps. 2:7; Heb. 1:5); I will be his Father and he will be my son (2 Sam. 7:14; 1 Chr. 17:13; 22:10; 28:6; Heb. 1:5); the God and Father of our Lord Jesus Christ (2 Cor. 1:3; Eph. 1:3; Col. 1:3; 1 Pet. 1:3); the God and Father of the Lord Jesus, who is blessed for ever (2 Cor. 11:31); he was calling God his Father (John 5:18); glory as of the only Son of the Father (John 1:14); the only begotten Son who is in the bosom of the Father (John 1:18); my Father is greater than all (John 10:29).

D2b The Father's activity regarding Christ
The Father sent the Son to be the Saviour of the world (1 John 4:14); as the living Father sent me and as I live because of the Father (John 6:57); he whom the Father sanctified and sent into the world (John 10:36); the Father who sent me (John 8:18; 12:49); my Father glorifies me, of whom you say he is your God (John 8:54); he received honour and glory from God the Father (2 Pet. 1:17); the Son of man will come in the glory of his Father (Matt. 16:27); Father, the hour has come, glorify your Son (John 17:1); all things have been handed over to me by my Father (Matt. 11:27; Luke 10:22); this charge I received from my Father (John 10:18); as I received from my Father (Rev. 2:27); the Father has given all things into his hands (John 13:3); the Father loves the Son (John 3:35; 5:20); as my Father appointed a kingdom for me (Luke 22:29); the Father judges no one, but has committed all judgement to the Son (John 5:22); the Father has granted the Son to have life in himself (John 5:26).

D2c Christ's activity regarding the Father
I must be in my Father's house (Luke 2:49); the works that I do in my Father's name (John 10:25); the Son can only do what he sees the Father doing (John 5:19); if I am not doing the works of my Father, do not believe me (John 10:37); I will acknowledge them before my Father who is in heaven (Matt. 10:32); I will confess his name before my Father and his angels (Rev. 3:5); I will deny them before my Father who is in heaven (Matt. 10:33); do not think that I will accuse you to the Father (John 5:45); for this reason the Father loves me, because I lay down my life (John 10:17); I have kept my Father's commandments and remain in his love (John 15:10); everything I heard from my Father I have made known to you (John 15:15); I speak of what I have seen with my Father (John 8:38); he hands over the kingdom to God the Father (1 Cor. 15:24).

D2d Father and Son alike
No one knows the Son except the Father and no one knows the Father except the Son (Matt. 11:27); as the Father raises the dead, so the Son gives life to whom he wishes (John 5:21); that all may honour the Son as they honour the Father (John 5:23); he who does not honour the Son does not honour the Father (John 5:23); that you may know that the Father is in me and I am in the Father (John 10:38; 14:10-11); if you knew me you would know my Father also (John 8:19; 14:7); as the Father knows me and I know the Father (John 10:15); he who hates me hates my Father also (John 15:23); they have seen and hated me and my Father (John 15:24).

D3 Spiritual fathers
God has made me a father to Pharaoh (Gen. 45:8); my father, my father! (2 Kgs. 2:12); I became your father through the gospel (1 Cor. 4:15); we dealt with you as a father (1 Thess. 2:11); exhort older men as fathers (1 Tim. 5:1); I am writing to you, fathers (1 John 2:13); I have written to you, fathers (1 John 2:14); do not call anyone your father on earth (Matt. 23:9).

FATHER ABRAHAM, see 169B5.

D4 Spiritual mothers
You are children of Sarah (1 Pet. 3:6); Deborah was a mother in Israel (Judg. 5:7); Jerusalem above is the mother of us all (Gal. 4:26); Babylon, mother of harlots (Rev. 17:5).

D5 Satan your father
You are of your father the devil (John 8:44); you do what you have hard from your father (John 8:38); you do what your father did (John 8:41).

CHILDREN OF EVIL, see 170B5.

170 Descendant
A Children
A1 Instructions about children
Do not give your children to Molech (Lev. 18:21; 20:2-4); in place of your fathers will be your sons (Ps. 45:16); do kings of the earth collect tax from their children or from others? (Matt. 17:25); your sons and daughters will prophesy (Joel 2:28; Acts 2:17); children should not save up for their parents, but parents for their children (2 Cor. 12:14); he who loves son or daughter more than me is not worthy of me (Matt. 10:37); whoever comes to me and does not hate his wife and children (Luke 14:26); no one who has left children for the sake of the kingdom (Luke 18:29).

A2 Teaching children
Teach your children and grandchildren (Deut. 4:9-10); that you may tell it to the next generation (Ps. 48:13); one generation will praise your works to another (Ps. 145:4); that the generation yet unborn should tell it to their children (Ps. 78:4-6); my words shall not depart out of the mouth of your children or children's children (Isa. 59:21).

A3 Children and blessing
A3a Children are a blessing
Children are a gift from the Lord (Ps. 127:3); children are like a warrior's arrows (Ps. 127:4); like olive shoots around your table (Ps. 128:3); let our sons be like plants and our daughters pillars (Ps. 144:12); grandchildren are the crown of the old (Prov. 17:6); happy is the man who has his quiver full (Ps. 127:5); Haman recounted the number of his sons (Esther 5:11).

A3b Children blessed
God will bless the fruit of your womb (Deut. 7:13); all your sons will be taught of the Lord (Isa. 54:13); I will pour out my Spirit on your descendants (Isa. 44:3); your sons and daughters will prophesy (Joel 2:28); otherwise your children would be unclean, but now they are holy (1 Cor. 7:14).

A4 Children and suffering

The fathers have eaten sour grapes and the children's teeth are set on edge (Ezek. 18:2); their little ones will be dashed in pieces (Hos. 13:16); happy he who dashes your little ones against a rock (Ps. 137:9); you will eat the flesh of your sons and daughters (Lev. 26:29; Deut. 28:53); fathers will eat their sons and sons their fathers (Ezek. 5:10); the hands of compassionate women boiled their own children for food (Lam. 4:10); the father will deliver up his child to death (Matt. 10:21; Mark 13:12); children will have parents put to death (Matt. 10:21); the king of Moab offered his eldest son as a burnt offering (2 Kgs. 3:27); he forced our fathers to expose their children so they would not survive (Acts 7:19).

A5 Daughters

When daughters were born to them (Gen. 6:1); if a man with no son dies, his daughter inherits (Num. 27:8); statutes the Lord commanded concerning fathers and daughters (Num. 30:16); when a man sells his daughter as a slave (Exod. 21:7); the king will take your daughters as perfumers, cooks and bakers (1 Sam. 8:13); daughter rises up against her mother, daughter-in-law against her mother-in-law (Mic. 7:6); the poor man's ewe lamb was like a daughter to him (2 Sam. 12:3).

A6 Better than sons

Your daughter-in-law is better than seven sons (Ruth 4:15); am I not better than ten sons? (1 Sam. 1:8).

A7 Adoption

Moses was adopted by Pharaoh's daughter (Exod. 2:10; Acts 7:21); Moses refused to be called the son of Pharaoh's daughter (Heb. 11:24); Mordecai adopted Esther (Esther 2:7); he predestined us to be adopted as sons (Eph. 1:5); you have received the Spirit of adoption as sons (Rom. 8:15); we receive adoption as sons (Gal. 4:5); we wait for adoption as sons (Rom. 8:23); the adoption of sons belongs to Israel (Rom. 9:4).

B Spiritual descendants

B1 Son of God

B1a Declared the Son by God

You are my Son, today I have begotten you (Ps. 2:7; Acts 13:33; Heb. 1:5; 5:5); I will be to him a Father and he will be to me a Son (Heb. 1:5); this is my Son, my beloved (Matt. 3:17; 17:5; Mark 1:11; 9:7; Luke 3:22; 2 Pet. 1:17); my Son, whom I have chosen (Luke 9:35); declared Son of God with power (Rom. 1:4); out of Egypt have I called my Son (Matt. 2:15); I will send my beloved son (Luke 20:13).

B1b Declared himself to be Son of God

Are you the Son of God? – I am (Luke 22:70); tell us if you are the Christ, the Son of God (Matt. 26:63); are you the Christ, the Son of the Blessed? (Mark 14:61); I am the Son of God (John 10:36); he said 'I am the Son of God' (Matt. 27:43); he made himself out to be the Son of God (John 19:7).

B1c Declared Son of God by others

Glory as of the only Son of the Father (John 1:14); I have seen and borne witness that this is the Son of God (John 1:34); you are the Christ, the Son of the living God (Matt. 16:16); Rabbi, you are the Son of God! (John 1:49); this was the Son of God! (Matt. 27:54; Mark 15:39); Son of the Most High God (Mark 5:7; Luke 1:32; 8:28); we know that the Son of God has come (1 John 5:20); I believe you are the Christ, the Son of God (John 11:27); that you may believe that Jesus is the Christ, the Son of God (John 20:31); who overcomes the world but he who believes that Jesus is the Son of God? (1 John 5:5); whoever confesses that Jesus is the Son of God (1 John 4:15); God has spoken to us by his Son (Heb. 1:2); what have we in common, O Son of God? (Matt. 8:29); unclean spirits said, 'You are the

Son of God' (Mark 3:11); demons came out of many, crying, 'You are the Son of God!' (Luke 4:41).

B1d Christ as a son

To us a child is born, a son is given (Isa. 9:6); how can they say Christ is the son of David? (Matt. 22:42-5; Mark 12:35-7; Luke 20:41-4).

B2 Children of God

B2a Mankind as children of God

We are God's offspring (Acts 17:28-9); Israel is God's firstborn son (Exod. 4:22-3); is Ephraim my dear son? (Jer. 31:20).

B2b Believers as children of God

The Spirit testifies with our spirit that we are children of God (Rom. 8:16); because you are sons, God sent the Spirit of his Son (Gal. 4:6); all who are led by the Spirit of God are sons of God (Rom. 8:14); sons of God through faith in Christ Jesus (Gal. 3:26); to those who believe in his name he gave the right to become children of God (John 1:12); you shall be my sons and daughters (2 Cor. 6:18); sons of the living God (Hos. 1:10; Rom. 9:26); you will be sons of the Most High (Luke 6:35); now we are children of God (1 John 3:2); what love, that we should be called children of God (1 John 3:1); I will be his God and he will be my son (Rev. 21:7); Jesus died to gather into one the children of God scattered abroad (John 11:52); it is not the children of the flesh who are the children of God but the children of the promise (Rom. 9:8); you are no longer a slave but a son (Gal. 4:7); the exhortation addressed to you as sons (Heb. 12:5); by this we know the children of God and the children of the devil (1 John 3:10); the peacemakers will be called sons of God (Matt. 5:9); be imitators of God as beloved children (Eph. 5:1); children of God in a crooked generation (Phil. 2:15); when God disciplines you he treats you as sons (Heb. 12:7).

B3 Children of Abraham

The promise was to Abraham's seed (Gal. 3:16); you are Abraham's seed (Gal. 3:29); those who are of faith are sons of Abraham (Gal. 3:7); a daughter of Abraham (Luke 13:16); he also is a son of Abraham (Luke 19:9); his mercy to Abraham and his offspring for ever (Luke 1:55); God is able to raise up children to Abraham from these stones (Luke 3:8); all are not Abraham's children who are descended from him (Rom. 9:7); are they descendants of Abraham? so am I (2 Cor. 11:22).

B4 Children in the faith

Paul's son in the faith, Timothy (1 Cor. 4:17; Phil. 2:22; 1 Tim. 1:2; 2 Tim. 1:2; 2:1); Titus, my true child in a common faith (Titus 1:4); my child Onesimus (Philem. 10); here am I and the children God has given me (Isa. 8:18; Heb. 2:13); the children of your elect sister (2 John 13); I admonish you as my beloved children (1 Cor. 4:14); my children, with whom I am in travail again (Gal. 4:19; 2 Tim. 2:1); my son Mark (1 Pet. 5:13); I have no greater joy than to hear that my children walk in the truth (3 John 4).

SPIRITUAL FATHERS, see 169D3.

B5 Children of evil

Children of rebellion, offspring of deceit (Isa. 57:4); you son of the devil! (Acts 13:10); you are sons of those who murdered the prophets (Matt. 23:31); the weeds are the sons of the evil one (Matt. 13:38); by this we know the children of God and the children of the devil (1 John 3:10).

SATAN YOUR FATHER, see 169D5.

C Generations

C1 Generations in general

Visiting the iniquity of the fathers on the third and fourth generations (Exod. 20:5; 34:7; Num. 14:18; Deut. 5:9); God keeps his covenant to the thousandth generation of those who love him (Deut. 7:9); the covenant he commanded for 1000 generations (1 Chr. 16:15); the illegitimate may not enter the assembly to the tenth generation (Deut. 23:2); Ammonites and Moabites may not enter the assembly to the tenth generation (Deut. 23:3); the third generation of an Edomite or Egyptian may enter the assembly (Deut. 23:8).

C2 The generations of . . .

The generations of: heaven and earth (Gen. 2:4); Adam (Gen. 5:1); Noah (Gen. 6:9); Shem, Ham, Japheth (Gen. 10:1); Shem (Gen. 11:10); Terah (Gen. 11:27); Ishmael (Gen. 25:12); Isaac (Gen. 25:19); Esau (Gen. 36:1, 9); Jacob (Gen. 37:2); Aaron and Moses (Num. 3:1); Perez (Ruth 4:18).

D Genealogies

D1 Genealogies in general

The sons of Noah according to their genealogies (Gen. 10:32); their ancestry was recorded by fathers' houses (Num. 1:18); all Israel was enrolled by genealogies (1 Chr. 9:1); the Levites were enrolled in genealogical records (2 Chr. 31:15-19); some returned exiles did not have proof of descent from Israel (Ezra 2:59, 62; Neh. 7:61-4); genealogical enrolment of the returned exiles (Ezra 8:1-14; Neh. 7:5); the book of genealogy of those who returned (Neh. 7:5-60); avoid controversies and genealogies (Titus 3:9); myths and endless genealogies (1 Tim. 1:4); this man does not have their genealogy (Heb. 7:6); Melchizedek was without genealogy (Heb. 7:3).

D2 Genealogies of various people

Genealogy of: Cain (Gen. 4:17-22); Adam to Noah's sons (Gen. 5:3-32; 1 Chr. 1:1-4); Noah's sons (Gen. 10:1-32; 1 Chr. 1:5-23); Shem to Abraham (Gen. 11:10-26; 1 Chr. 1:24-7); Abraham (1 Chr. 1:28-42); Nahor (Gen. 22:20-4); Abraham's wife Keturah (Gen. 25:1-4); Ishmael (Gen. 25:12-16; 1 Chr. 1:29-33); Isaac (1 Chr. 1:34); Jacob (Gen. 35:22-6); Esau (Gen. 36:1-19; 1 Chr. 1:35-42); Horites (Gen. 36:20-30); Ezra (Ezra 7:1-5); Jesus Christ (Matt. 1:1; Luke 3:23-38).

171 Productiveness

A Productiveness of people

A1 People multiplying

God commanded mankind to multiply (Gen. 1:28; 9:1, 7); be fruitful and multiply (Gen. 35:11); may God make you fruitful (Gen. 28:3); your wife will be like a fruitful vine (Ps. 128:3); may the Lord increase you and your children (Ps. 115:14); the barren woman has more children than she who has a husband (Isa. 54:1; Gal. 4:27); God makes the barren woman a mother (Ps. 113:9); the barren woman has borne seven children (1 Sam. 2:5); Sarah will have a son (Gen. 18:14); who would have said that Sarah would suckle children? (Gen. 21:7); none shall be barren among you (Exod. 23:26; Deut. 7:14); the Lord opened Leah's womb (Gen. 29:31); God opened Rachel's womb (Gen. 30:22); Elizabeth will bear you a son (Luke 1:13).

A2 People bearing fruit

A2a Potential of fruit

I found Israel like grapes in the wilderness (Hos. 9:10); like the gleanings of grape harvest (Isa. 24:13); Israel will fill the whole earth with fruit (Isa. 27:6); Joseph is a fruitful bough (Gen. 49:22); Judah will again take root downward and bear fruit upward (2 Kgs. 19:30; Isa. 37:31); my Father is glorified if you bear much fruit and so prove to be my disciples (John 15:8); I appointed you to go and bear fruit (John 15:16); that we might bear fruit for God (Rom. 7:4); bring forth fruit worthy of repentance (Matt. 3:8; Luke 3:8).

A2b Source of fruit

Every branch that bears fruit he prunes that it may produce more fruit (John 15:2); God has made me fruitful (Gen. 41:52); these things will keep you from being unfruitful (2 Pet. 1:8); that they may not be unfruitful (Titus 3:14); he will be like a tree bearing fruit in season (Ps. 1:3); if a grain of wheat dies it bears much fruit (John 12:24); they hear the word, accept it and bear fruit (Matt. 13:23; Mark 4:20; Luke 8:15); he who abides in me bears much fruit (John 15:5).

A2c Distinctive fruit

You will know them by their fruits (Matt. 7:20); every tree is known by its fruit (Matt. 12:33; Luke 6:44); every good tree produces good fruit but the bad tree bad fruit (Matt. 7:17-19); filled with the fruit of righteousness (Phil. 1:11); discipline yields the peaceful fruit of righteousness (Heb. 12:11); the fruit of righteousness is sown in peace (Jas. 3:18); the fruit of light is in all goodness (Eph. 5:9); the fruit of the Spirit (Gal. 5:22-3); my fruit is better than gold (Prov. 8:19); our sinful passions were bearing fruit for death (Rom. 7:5).

A2d Fruitful labour

The harvest is plentiful (Matt. 9:37; Luke 10:2); that I might have a harvest among you, as among the other Gentiles (Rom. 1:13); to continue in the flesh means fruitful labour for me (Phil. 1:22); all over the world the gospel is bearing fruit (Col. 1:6); bearing fruit in every good work (Col. 1:10); what fruit did you get from those things of which you are now ashamed? (Rom. 6:21); the fruit you get is sanctification and its end, eternal life (Rom. 6:22); I seek the fruit, not the gift (Phil. 4:17).

B Animals multiplying

God commanded all creatures to multiply (Gen. 1:22); let the waters teem with creatures (Gen. 1:20); all creatures from the ark were to multiply (Gen. 8:17); let our flocks produce tens of thousands (Ps. 144:13); when your herds and flocks multiply (Deut. 8:13).

C Productive agriculture

PEOPLE BEARING FRUIT, see 171A2.

C1 Fertile land

May God give you of the fat of the earth (Gen. 27:28); may Joseph's land give choice yield (Deut. 33:14); I brought you into a fruitful land (Jer. 2:7); he took some seed and planted it in fertile soil (Ezek. 17:5); it was planted in good soil (Ezek. 17:8); the land of a rich man bore abundantly (Luke 12:16); some fell on good soil (Matt. 13:8; Mark 4:8; Luke 8:8); the seed on good soil (Matt. 13:23; Mark 4:20; Luke 8:15); the land will yield its produce (Lev. 25:19; 26:4-5; Ps. 67:6; 85:12); blessed will be your offspring and produce (Deut. 28:4, 11; 30:9); the produce of the ground will be rich and plentiful (Isa. 30:23); may there be abundance of grain on top of the mountains (Ps. 72:16); land which bears useful vegetation is blessed by God (Heb. 6:7).

C2 Bearing fruit

When the plants grew up and bore grain (Matt. 13:26); first the blade, then the ear, then the full grain in the ear (Mark 4:28); if it bears fruit next year (Luke 13:9); the farmer waits for the precious fruit of the soil, being patient over it (Jas. 5:7); God will bless the fruit of your ground (Deut. 7:13); I will multiply the fruit of the tree and the increase of the field (Ezek. 36:30); before the sabbath year the land will give fruit for three years (Lev. 25:21); trees whose fruit is offered will yield more (Lev. 19:25); the ploughman will overtake the reaper (Amos 9:13); the desert becomes a fertile field (Isa. 32:15); Lebanon will become a fruitful field (Isa. 29:17); trees bearing fruit every month (Ezek. 47:12; Rev. 22:2); God gave you rain from heaven and fruitful seasons

(Acts 14:17); he sent his servants to collect the fruit (Matt. 21:34; Mark 12:2); he will give the vineyard to those who will hand over the fruit (Matt. 21:41); the kingdom of God will be given to a nation producing the fruit of it (Matt. 21:43).

C3 Fruit

C3a Almonds
Take almonds as a present (Gen. 43:11); Aaron's rod sprouted and bore almonds (Num. 17:8); bowls made like almonds (Exod. 25:33, 34; 37:19, 20).

C3b Apples
Refresh me with apples (S. of S. 2:5); may the scent of your breath be like apples (S. of S. 7:8); like apples of gold in settings of silver (Prov. 25:11).

C3c Figs
Take a cake of figs and lay it on the boil (2 Kgs. 20:7; Isa. 38:21); like a first-ripe fig before harvest (Isa. 28:4); two baskets of figs (Jer. 24:1-5); like bad figs which cannot be eaten (Jer. 24:8; 29:17); the figs have ripened (S. of S. 2:13); figs are not gathered from thistles (Matt. 7:16; Luke 6:44); can a vine produce figs? (Jas. 3:12); it was not the season for figs (Mark 11:13).

C3d Grapes
The vine produced ripe grapes (Gen. 40:10); a Nazirite must not eat fresh or dried grapes (Num. 6:3); they took a bunch of grapes from Eshcol (Num. 13:23); you may eat your neighbour's grapes (Deut. 23:24); grapes are not gathered from thorns (Matt. 7:16; Luke 6:44); I found Israel like grapes in the wilderness (Hos. 9:10); their grapes are grapes of poison (Deut. 32:32); the fathers have eaten sour grapes (Ezek. 18:2); he looked for grapes and it produced wild grapes (Isa. 5:2, 4); the grapes of the earth are ripe (Rev. 14:18).

C3e Pomegranates
Pomegranates on the skirt of the robe of the ephod (Exod. 28:33, 34; 39:24, 25, 26); pomegranates on the pillars (1 Kgs. 7:18, 20, 42; 2 Kgs. 25:17; 2 Chr. 3:16; 4:13; Jer. 52:22, 23); your cheeks are like pomegranates (S. of S. 4:3; 6:7).

D Firstfruits

D1 Literal firstfruits
Bring the firstfruits (Exod. 23:16, 19; 34:22, 26; Lev. 23:10-14; Deut. 26:10; Neh. 10:35); firstfruits at the Feast of Weeks (Num. 28:26); honour the Lord with the firstfruits (Prov. 3:9); firstfruits belong to the priests (Num. 18:12, 13; Deut. 18:4; Ezek. 44:30).

D2 Metaphorical firstfruits
Israel was the firstfruits of his harvest (Jer. 2:3); Christ is risen, the firstfruits of those who slept (1 Cor. 15:20, 23); that we should be the firstfruits of his creatures (Jas. 1:18); the redeemed are firstfruits (Rev. 14:4); the household of Stephanas were the firstfruits of Achaia (1 Cor. 16:15); we have the firstfruits of the Spirit (Rom. 8:23); if the firstfruits are holy, so is the whole lump (Rom. 11:16).

E Catch of fish
They could not haul in the net because of the multitude of fish (John 21:6); so many fish the nets were breaking and the boats sinking (Luke 5:6-7); amazed at the catch of fish (Luke 5:9).

172 Unproductiveness

A Childless

A1 Barrenness

A1a Barren people
The barren will one day be considered happy (Luke 23:29); sing, O barren one who did not bear (Isa. 54:1); seven brothers died childless (Matt. 22:25-6; Mark 12:20-2; Luke 20:29-31); those who were barren: Abraham and Sarah (Gen. 11:30; 15:2-3; 16:1-2; Rom. 4:19); Rebekah (Gen. 25:21); Rachel (Gen. 29:31; 30:1-2);

Manoah's wife (Judg. 13:2); Hannah (1 Sam. 1:2); Michal (2 Sam. 6:23); Elizabeth (Luke 1:7, 36).

A1b Reasons for barrenness
Sarah was past childbearing (Gen. 18:11); the Lord had closed all their wombs (Gen. 20:18); the Lord had closed Hannah's womb (1 Sam. 1:5, 6); God has withheld from you the fruit of the womb (Gen. 30:2); God has prevented me from childbearing (Gen. 16:2); those who marry near relatives will be childless (Lev. 20:20, 21).

A2 Lack of sons

A2a About lack of sons
Levirate marriage if someone dies leaving no son (Deut. 25:5; Matt. 22:24; Mark 12:19); if a man dies who has no son, the inheritance shall be his daughter's (Num. 27:8).

A2b People without sons
Does Israel have no sons? (Jer. 49:1); those who had no sons: Absalom (2 Sam. 18:18); Ahaziah (2 Kgs. 1:17); Eleazar (1 Chr. 23:22; 24:28); Jether (1 Chr. 2:32); Nadab and Abihu (Num. 3:4; 1 Chr. 24:2); Sheshan (1 Chr. 2:34); Seled (1 Chr. 2:30); Zelophehad (Num. 26:33; 27:3-4; Josh. 17:3; 1 Chr. 7:15); the Shunamite woman (2 Kgs. 4:14).

A3 Eunuchs
Eunuchs may not enter the assembly (Deut. 23:1); the eunuch should not consider himself a dry tree (Isa. 56:3); the eunuchs who keep my sabbaths will have a memorial (Isa. 56:4-5); some of your sons will be eunuchs in the palace of the king of Babylon (Isa. 39:7); eunuchs who are born so, made so by men or choose to be so for the kingdom (Matt. 19:12); would that they might castrate themselves! (Gal. 5:12).

A4 Miscarriage
If a woman is struck and has a miscarriage (Exod. 21:22); give them a miscarrying womb and dry breasts (Hos. 9:14); like a miscarriage I would not have been (Job 3:16); the miscarriages which never see the sun (Ps. 58:8); better the stillborn than that man (Eccles. 6:3); the stillborn comes in vanity and goes into darkness (Eccles. 6:4); your animals have not miscarried (Gen. 31:38); none shall miscarry (Exod. 23:26); his cow calves and does not abort (Job 21:10).

B Fruitless

B1 Infertile land
The ground will produce thorns and thistles (Gen. 3:18); the ground would not be fruitful for Cain (Gen. 4:12); the ground would not be fruitful for the disobedient Israelites (Lev. 26:20; Deut. 11:17; 28:38-40; 29:23); Esau would dwell away from fertile ground (Gen. 27:39); the land is unfruitful (2 Kgs. 2:19); the ground will no longer yield its strength (Gen. 4:12); he changes a fruitful land into a salt waste (Ps. 107:34); the fruitful land was a wilderness (Jer. 4:26); you will plant seed in vain (Lev. 26:16); ten acres will yield but a bath and a homer of seed an ephah of grain (Isa. 5:10); the vintage will fail and the fruit harvest will not come (Isa. 32:10); there will be no grapes on the vine nor figs on the fig tree (Jer. 8:13); because of you the earth has withheld its produce (Hag. 1:10); the standing grain is without heads and yields no grain (Hos. 8:7); you sow much but harvest little (Deut. 28:38; Hag. 1:6); though the fields yield no food (Hab. 3:17).

B2 Unfruitful people
The word is choked and is unfruitful (Mark 4:19); the seed among thorns gave no fruit (Mark 4:7); they bring no fruit to maturity (Luke 8:14); it produced only wild grapes (Isa. 5:2, 4); he came seeking fruit on the fig tree and found none (Luke 13:6-7); trees in autumn without fruit (Jude 12); Ephraim's root is dried up, they will bear no fruit (Hos. 9:16); you cannot bear fruit unless

you abide in me (John 15:4); take no share in the unfruitful deeds of darkness (Eph. 5:11).

B3 Response to fruitlessness
Land yielding thorns and thistles is near to being cursed (Heb. 6:8); every unproductive tree will be cut down and burnt (Matt. 3:10; 7:19; Luke 3:9); if it does not bear fruit, cut it down (Luke 13:9); every branch which bears no fruit is removed (John 15:2); the fig tree without fruit was cursed (Matt. 21:19; Mark 11:13-14); no more unfruitfulness from this water (2 Kgs. 2:21); though the produce of the olive fail (Hab. 3:17); though there be no fruit on the vines (Hab. 3:17).

C Lack of fish
They caught nothing all night (Luke 5:5; John 21:3); have you caught nothing? (John 21:5).

D Wilderness
D1 Wilderness in general
The voice of the Lord shakes the wilderness (Ps. 29:8); the wind of the Lord will come from the wilderness (Hos. 13:15); the oracle concerning the wilderness of the sea (Isa. 21:1); Egypt will become a waste, Edom a desolate wilderness (Joel 3:19); your holy cities have become a wilderness (Isa. 64:10); lifting up does not come from the wilderness (Ps. 75:6); how can one feed these people in the wilderness? (Mark 8:4); the voice of one crying in the wilderness (Isa. 40:3; Matt. 3:3; Mark 1:3; Luke 3:4; John 1:23); he leaves the 99 sheep in the wilderness (Luke 15:4); this is a desert road (Acts 8:26); in danger in the wilderness (2 Cor. 11:26); the woman fled into the wilderness (Rev. 12:6); he carried me away in the Spirit into a wilderness (Rev. 17:3).

D2 In the wilderness
He will live in parched places of the wilderness (Jer. 17:6); better to live in the desert than with a contentious woman (Prov. 21:19); may those who live in the desert bow before him (Ps. 72:9); Ishmael lived in the wilderness (Gen. 21:20, 21); John in the wilderness (Matt. 3:1; Mark 1:4; Luke 1:80; 3:2); Elijah went a day's journey into the wilderness (1 Kgs. 19:4); Jesus was led by the Spirit into the wilderness (Matt. 4:1; Mark 1:12; Luke 4:2); Jesus had to stay out in the wilderness (Mark 1:45); what did you go into the wilderness to see? (Matt. 11:7; Luke 7:24); if they say he is in the wilderness, do not go out (Matt. 24:26); Jesus withdrew to the wilderness and prayed (Luke 5:16); the one who led 4000 Assassins into the wilderness (Acts 21:38); they wandered over deserts and mountains (Heb. 11:38).

D3 Blessing in the wilderness
The wilderness will rejoice and blossom (Isa. 35:1); the Lord will make Zion's wilderness like Eden (Isa. 51:3); let the wilderness and its cities lift their voices (Isa. 42:11); he turns the wilderness into pools of water (Ps. 107:35); I will make rivers in the desert (Isa. 43:19, 20).

D4 Named wildernesses
The wilderness of: Sinai (Exod. 19:1-2; Lev. 7:38; Num. 1:1, 19; 3:14; 9:1, 5; 10:12; 26:64; 33:15-16); Beersheba (Gen. 21:14); Beth-aven (Josh. 18:12); Damascus (1 Kgs. 19:15); Edom (2 Kgs. 3:8); Engedi (1 Sam. 24:1); Etham (Num. 33:8); Gibeon (2 Sam. 2:24); Jeruel (2 Chr. 20:16); Judah (Judg. 1:16; Ps. 63:t); Judea (Matt. 3:1); Kadesh (Num. 29:8); Kedemoth (Deut. 2:26); Maon (1 Sam. 23:24-5); Moab (Deut. 2:8); Paran (Gen. 21:21; Num. 10:12; 12:16; 13:3, 26; 1 Sam. 25:1); Shur (Exod. 15:22); Sin (Exod. 16:1; 17:1; Num. 33:11-12); Tekoa (2 Chr. 20:20); Zin (Num. 13:21; 20:1; 27:14; 33:36; 34:3, 4; Deut. 32:51; Josh. 15:1); Ziph (1 Sam. 23:14, 15; 26:2).

D5 Dying in the wilderness
God will abandon them in the wilderness (Num. 32:15); have you brought us out to die in the wilderness? (Exod. 14:11; 16:3; Num. 20:4; 21:5); the Lord has

brought them out to kill them in the wilderness (Deut. 9:28); better to serve the Egyptians than die in the wilderness (Exod. 14:12); would that we had died in this wilderness! (Num. 14:2); they will die in the wilderness (Num. 14:35; 26:65); your corpses will fall in the wilderness (Num. 14:29, 32, 33); God swore that he would make them fall in the wilderness (Ps. 106:26); this is why God killed them in the wilderness (Num. 14:16); our fathers died in the wilderness (Num. 27:3); the men of war died in the wilderness (Josh. 5:4); most of them were strewn in the wilderness (1 Cor. 10:5); he was angry with those who sinned, whose bodies fell in the wilderness (Heb. 3:17); I did not annihilate them in the wilderness (Ezek. 20:17).

D6 From the wilderness to...
Your boundary shall be from the wilderness to the River (Exod. 23:31); from the wilderness and Lebanon to the River (Josh. 1:4); the land shall be yours from the wilderness (Deut. 11:24); I will make the land waste and desolate from the wilderness to Diblah (Ezek. 6:14).

D7 Like a wilderness
Have I been a wilderness to Israel? (Jer. 2:31); I will make you like a wilderness (Jer. 22:6); God led them through the deep as through the wilderness (Ps. 106:9); lest I make her like a wilderness (Hos. 2:3); he will make Nineveh a desolation, a dry waste like the wilderness (Zeph. 2:13).

173 Agency
As if a club should wield the one who lifts it (Isa. 10:15).

174 Vigour
Hebrew women are vigorous and give birth quickly (Exod. 1:19); rouse the mighty men (Joel 3:9); like a lion, who will rouse him? (Gen. 49:9).
ENTHUSIASM, see 571.

175 Inertness
SLUGGISHNESS, see 679A.

176 Violence
A Violence
A1 Violence in the earth
The earth was full of violence (Gen. 6:11, 13); men will be fierce (2 Tim. 3:3); violent men seek my life (Ps. 54:3); those that breathe out violence have risen against me (Ps. 27:12).

A2 Pursuing violence
They multiply lies and violence (Hos. 12:1); violence covers them like a garment (Ps. 73:6); their hearts devise violence (Prov. 24:2); your hands deal out violence (Ps. 58:2); violent men get riches (Prov. 11:16); the kingdom of heaven comes with violence (Matt. 11:12; Luke 16:16); woe to him who founds a city on violence (Hab. 2:12); Simeon and Levi have weapons of violence (Gen. 49:5); the priests threatened to take meat by force (1 Sam. 2:16); two men so violent no one could pass (Matt. 8:28).

A3 Avoiding violence
Do not envy a man of violence (Prov. 3:31); enough! put away violence and destruction (Ezek. 45:9); do not rob anyone by force (Luke 3:14); I hate divorce and covering one's garment with violence (Mal. 2:16); I have avoided the paths of the violent (Ps. 17:4).

A4 Rescue from violence
Preserve me from violent men (Ps. 140:1, 4); I will redeem you from the grasp of the violent (Jer. 15:21); you rescue me from violent men (2 Sam. 22:49; Ps. 18:48).

B Breaking forth
Lest the Lord break forth on them (Exod. 19:22, 24);
God has broken out against my enemies (2 Sam. 5:20; 1
Chr. 14:11); God broke out against Uzzah (2 Sam. 6:7-8;
1 Chr. 13:11; 15:13); the three mighty men broke through
at Bethlehem (2 Sam. 23:16).

C Earthquakes
C1 The earth quaking
An earthquake in the Philistine garrison (1 Sam. 14:15);
the earth quaked (2 Sam. 22:8; Ps. 18:7); three or four
things make the earth quake (Prov. 30:21); will not the
land quake because of this? (Amos 8:8); when Jesus
died the earth shook (Matt. 27:51); when the centurion
keeping watch over Jesus saw the earthquake (Matt.
27:54); there was a great earthquake (Matt. 28:2; Acts
16:26; Rev. 16:18); there was an earthquake (Rev. 6:12;
8:5; 11:13, 19); there will be earthquakes (Matt. 24:7;
Mark 13:8; Luke 21:11); the earthquake in the days of
Uzziah (Zech. 14:5); two years before the earthquake
(Amos 1:1); the Lord was not in the earthquake (1 Kgs.
19:11).
C2 God shaking the earth
When God went forth, the earth quaked (Judg. 5:4; Ps.
68:8); at his wrath the earth quakes (Jer. 10:10); God
shakes the earth (Job 9:6); you made the land quake
(Ps. 60:2); the place where they gathered was shaken
(Acts 4:31).

D Storms
A fierce storm came on the sea (Matt. 8:24; Mark 4:37;
Luke 8:23); the violent Northeaster wind (Acts 27:14);
terrify them with your storm (Ps. 83:15); Jonah in the
wind and storm (Jonah 1:4, 11, 13); his way is in
whirlwind and storm (Nahum 1:3); it will be stormy,
for the sky is red and threatening (Matt. 16:3); they are
mists driven by a storm (2 Pet. 2:17); you have not
come to darkness, gloom and tempest (Heb. 12:18).
WHIRLWIND, see 352B.

E Thunder and lightning
E1 Thunder and lightning in general
Thunder and lightning (Exod. 19:16; 20:18); thunder
and hail (Exod. 9:23, 28-9, 33-4); thunder and rain
during wheat harvest (1 Sam. 12:17, 18); his face had the
appearance of lightning (Dan. 10:6); thunder and
lightning from the throne (Rev. 4:5); thunder and
lightning from the censer (Rev. 8:5); thunder and
lightning from the temple (Rev. 11:19); there was
thunder and lightning (Rev. 16:18); Boanerges, sons of
thunder (Mark 3:17); as the lightning comes from the
east and shines as far as the west (Matt. 24:27; Luke
17:24); I saw Satan fall like lightning from heaven (Luke
10:18).
E2 God's thunder and lightning
God answered Moses with thunder (Exod. 19:19); the
Lord thundered against the Philistines (1 Sam. 7:10);
God thundered from heaven (2 Sam. 22:14; Ps. 18:13);
thunder as God's voice accompanied by lightning (Job
37:2-5; Ps. 29:3-9); he will thunder against them from
heaven (1 Sam. 2:10); can you thunder with a voice like
God? (Job 40:9); some said it thundered (John 12:29);
the seven thunders sounded (Rev. 10:3-4); a voice like
loud thunder (Rev. 14:2); the sound of many
thunderpeals (Rev. 19:6); lightning flashed from God's
right hand (Deut. 33:2); lightning was his arrows
(2 Sam. 22:15; Ps. 18:14; 77:17-18); can you send out
lightnings? (Job 38:35); do you know how God makes
the lightning of his cloud to shine? (Job 37:15); his
lightnings light up the world (Ps. 97:4); he makes
lightnings for the rain (Ps. 135:7; Jer. 10:13; 51:16).

177 Gentleness

A Gentleness of God
The wisdom from above is gentle (Jas. 3:17); your
gentleness has made me great (2 Sam. 22:36; Ps. 18:35); I
am gentle and lowly in heart (Matt. 11:29); your king
comes, gentle and on a donkey (Matt. 21:5); I exhort
you by the meekness and gentleness of Christ (2 Cor.
10:1).

B Gentleness of people
A soft answer turns away wrath (Prov. 15:1); a soft
tongue may break bones (Prov. 25:15); the fruit of the
Spirit is gentleness (Gal. 5:23); we were gentle as a
nursing mother among you (1 Thess. 2:7); the Lord's
servant must in gentleness correct those who oppose
him (2 Tim. 2:25); restore the sinner in a spirit of
gentleness (Gal. 6:1); make your defence with
gentleness (1 Pet. 3:15); put on gentleness (Col. 3:12);
pursue gentleness (1 Tim. 6:11); a bishop [overseer]
must not be violent but gentle (1 Tim. 3:3); remind
them to be gentle (Titus 3:2); a gentle and quiet spirit
(1 Pet. 3:4); let your gentleness be known to all (Phil.
4:5); blessed are the meek, for they will inherit the earth
(Matt. 5:5); walk in humility and gentleness with
patience (Eph. 4:2); let him show by his good conduct
his deeds in the meekness of wisdom (Jas. 3:13).

178 Influence

MOTIVE, see 612.

179 Tendency

INTENTION, see 617.

180 Liability

A Accountable
That the whole world may be accountable to God
(Rom. 3:19); every one will give account of himself to
God (Rom. 14:12); you required of my hand what was
stolen (Gen. 31:39).

B Without excuse
They are without excuse (Rom. 1:20); you are without
excuse (Rom. 2:1).

C Responsible to warn
The responsibility of the watchman to give warning
(Ezek. 3:17-21; 33:2-9); if anyone does not heed the
warning, his blood will be upon his own head (Ezek.
33:4-5); this generation will be held responsible for the
blood of all the prophets (Matt. 23:35; Luke 11:50); you
intend to bring this man's blood on us (Acts 5:28); your
blood will be on your own head (2 Sam. 1:16; 1 Kgs.
2:37); your blood be on your own heads! (Acts 18:6);
the Lord will return his blood on his own head (1 Kgs.
2:32); his blood will be on his own head (Ezek. 18:13);
his blood be on us and on our children (Matt. 27:25).

181 Concurrence

COOPERATION, see 706.

182 Counteraction

OPPOSITION, see 704.

183 Space

A Roominess
Rehoboth, the Lord has made room for us (Gen.
26:22); God brought me into a broad place (2 Sam.
22:20; Ps. 18:19; 31:8); from the river of Egypt to the
Euphrates (Gen. 15:18; 2 Kgs. 24:7); from the entrance
of Hamath to the brook of Egypt (1 Kgs. 8:65; 2 Chr.
7:8); from Dan to Beersheba (Judg. 20:1; 1 Sam. 3:20;
2 Sam. 3:10; 17:11; 24:2, 15; 1 Kgs. 4:25); from Beersheba
to Dan (1 Chr. 21:2; 2 Chr. 30:5); from Beersheba to the

hill country of Ephraim (2 Chr. 19:4); his dominion from sea to sea and from the River to the ends of the earth (Zech. 9:10); every place you tread on (Deut. 11:24; Josh. 1:3); to bring them to a good and spacious land (Exod. 3:8); the land is roomy enough for them (Gen. 34:21); oh, that you would bless me and enlarge my border! (1 Chr. 4:10); I will enlarge your borders (Exod. 34:24); when the Lord extends your borders (Deut. 12:20); still there is room (Luke 14:22).

B Worldwide

B1 God's dominion worldwide

From the rising of the sun to its setting my name will be great (Mal. 1:11); God summons the earth from the rising of the sun to its setting (Ps. 50:1); he makes wars to cease to the ends of the earth (Ps. 46:9); his judgements are in all the earth (Ps. 105:7); his lightning to the ends of the earth (Job 37:3); so is your praise to the ends of the earth (Ps. 48:10); that my name may be proclaimed in all the earth (Rom. 9:17).

B2 Christ's dominion worldwide

His dominion will be from sea to sea, from the river to the ends of the earth (Ps. 72:8; Zech. 9:10); I will give the ends of the earth as your possession (Ps. 2:8); he will be great to the ends of the earth (Mic. 5:4); all authority in heaven and earth has been given to me (Matt. 28:18).

B3 The gospel worldwide

Go into all the world (Mark 16:15); their voice has gone out into all the world (Ps. 19:4; Rom. 10:18); witnesses to the uttermost parts of the earth (Acts 1:8); many will come from east and west to feast in the kingdom of heaven (Matt. 8:11); many will come from east and west, north and south to the kingdom of God (Luke 13:29); that my salvation may reach to the ends of the earth (Isa. 49:6); he will gather his elect from one end of heaven to the other (Matt. 24:31; Mark 13:27); to bring salvation to the ends of the earth (Acts 13:47); your faith is proclaimed throughout the whole world (Rom. 1:8); the gospel preached to every creature under heaven (Col. 1:23); this gospel of the kingdom will be preached through the whole world (Matt. 24:14); so that we may preach the gospel in regions beyond you (2 Cor. 10:16); in all the world the gospel is bearing fruit and growing (Col. 1:6).

C No room

There was no room in the inn (Luke 2:7); there was no room even about the doorway (Mark 2:2); I have nowhere to store my crops (Luke 12:17); the world itself could not contain the books (John 21:25); there was no longer any place for the dragon and his angels in heaven (Rev. 12:8); no place was found for earth and sky (Rev. 20:11).

184 Region

A Town and country

Blessed shall you be in the town and blessed in the country (Deut. 28:3); cursed shall you be in the town and cursed in the country (Deut. 28:16).

B Lands

B1 'The land'

B1a The land given

To your offspring I will give this land (Gen. 12:7; 13:15; 15:18; 17:8; 24:7; 26:3; 28:13; 35:12; 48:4; Exod. 32:13); the land I gave to Abraham and Isaac I give to you and your descendants (Gen. 35:12); the Lord gave the land to Israel (Josh. 21:43; Ps. 135:12; 136:21-2); the Lord gave the land to Abraham's offspring (2 Chr. 20:7).

B1b Entering the land

You told them to enter and possess the land (Neh. 9:15); Joshua shall enter the land (Deut. 1:38); dwell in the land (Ps. 37:3; Jer. 25:5); Moses did not enter the land (Num. 20:12; Deut. 1:37; 3:25-6; 4:21; 32:52; 34:4); Aaron did not enter the land (Num. 20:12, 24).

B1c The land possessed

Follow the commands so that you may possess the land (Deut. 4:1; 8:1; 11:8; 1 Chr. 28:8); pursue justice, that you may possess the land (Deut. 16:20); the land is ours because we have sought the Lord (2 Chr. 14:7); the upright will inhabit the land (Prov. 2:21); the land inherited by: those blessed by the Lord (Ps. 37:22); those God exalts (Ps. 37:34); those with the blessing of Abraham (Gen. 28:4); the righteous (Ps. 37:29); he who makes God his refuge (Isa. 57:13); those who hope in the Lord (Ps. 37:9); the meek (Ps. 37:11; Matt. 5:5); your children (Deut. 1:39).

B1d Judgement on the land

I will desolate the land (Lev. 26:32-3); land, land, land, hear the word of the Lord (Jer. 22:29); the end is coming on the land (Ezek. 7:2-3); you will perish from the land (Josh. 23:13, 16); God will destroy you from the land (Josh. 23:15); the wicked will be cut off from the land (Prov. 2:22).

B1e Returning to the land

The Lord will bring you back to the land after exile (Deut. 30:5); they will come from the land of the north to the land I gave your fathers for an inheritance (Jer. 3:18); I will gather you and give you the land of Israel (Ezek. 11:17; 20:42); when I gather them they will live in the land (Ezek. 28:25).

B2 Other lands

Till I take you away to a land like your own (2 Kgs. 18:32); he who leaves lands for my name's sake (Matt. 19:29; Mark 10:29-30); he will receive lands a hundredfold (Mark 10:30); they desired a better land, a heavenly one (Heb. 11:16); they are seeking a homeland (Heb. 11:14).

C Cities

C1 Cities in general

When the righteous prosper the city rejoices (Prov. 11:10); by the blessing of the upright a city is exalted (Prov. 11:11); they must not fill the face of the world with cities (Isa. 14:21); the wild donkey scorns the tumult of the city (Job 39:7); the cities will be inhabited and the waste places rebuilt (Ezek. 36:33); the ruined cities are fortified and inhabited (Ezek. 36:35); Joseph moved the people to the cities (Gen. 47:21); there was a small city with few men in it (Eccles. 9:14); are the cities in the land open or fortified? (Num. 13:19); the cities are fortified (Num. 13:28); he went to teach in their cities (Matt. 11:1); let us go to the next towns to preach, for this is why I came out (Mark 1:38); everyone went to be registered in his own city (Luke 2:3).

C2 Cities under attack

When you attack a city, offer terms of peace (Deut. 20:10); is this the man who overthrew the world's cities? (Isa. 14:17); I will lay waste your cities (Lev. 26:31); I will destroy your cities (Mic. 5:14); Egypt's cities will be laid waste (Ezek. 30:7); destroying every fortified city (2 Kgs. 3:19, 25); the fortified city is desolate (Isa. 27:10); no city was too high for us (Deut. 2:36); the City of Destruction (Isa. 19:18); judgement on all the cities of Moab (Jer. 48:21-4; Ezek. 25:9); the forsaken cities have become a derision to the nations (Ezek. 36:4); his cities have been destroyed, without inhabitant (Jer. 2:15); the cities of Aroer will be a place for flocks (Isa. 17:2-3); to make the cities of Judah a haunt of jackals (Jer. 10:22); if I enter the city, there are the diseases of famine (Jer. 14:18); I will cut off your cities and tear down your strongholds (Mic. 5:11); the cities of the nations fell (Rev. 16:19); in danger in the city (2 Cor. 11:26).

C3 God's city
They found no way to a city to settle in (Ps. 107:4); the Lord led them to a city to settle in (Ps. 107:7); there they establish a city (Ps. 107:36); we have a strong city with salvation as walls (Isa. 26:1); to the south was a structure like a city (Ezek. 40:2); Abraham was looking for the city God built (Heb. 11:10); we are looking for a city to come (Heb. 13:14); God has prepared a city for them (Heb. 11:16).

C4 Like a city
I have made you a fortified city (Jer. 1:18); a rich man's wealth is his strong city (Prov. 18:11); a brother offended is like a strong city (Prov. 18:19); a city set on a hill cannot be hid (Matt. 5:14); like a city broken into is a man without self-control (Prov. 25:28).

FORTIFIED CITIES, see 713C.

CAPTURING CITIES, see 786C1.

C5 Cities in Israel
Cities you did not build (Deut. 6:10; Josh. 24:13); building cities (Num. 32:16-17, 24; 1 Kgs. 22:39); cities restored to Israel (1 Sam. 7:14; 1 Kgs. 20:34); Hiram did not like the cities Solomon gave him (1 Kgs. 9:11-13); they will resettle the desolate cities (Isa. 54:3); you will not have gone through all the cities of Israel before the Son of man comes (Matt. 10:23).

C6 Cities for the Levites
Cities for Aaron (Josh. 21:4, 13-19); cities for the Levites (Num. 35:2-15; Josh. 14:4; 21:2, 3-42; 1 Chr. 6:54-81); cities for the Kohathites (Josh. 21:20-6); the Gershonites (Josh. 21:27-33); the Merarites (Josh. 21:34-40).

C7 Cities of refuge
Cities of refuge (Deut. 4:41-3; 19:1-13; Josh. 20:2, 7-9; 1 Chr. 6:57-60, 67-70); six cities of refuge (Num. 35:6, 11-15); a city of refuge: Golan in Bashan (Josh. 21:27); Kedesh in Galilee (Josh. 21:32); Ramoth in Gilead (Josh. 21:38).

C8 Cities of the plain
God overthrew the cities of the plain (Gen. 19:25); God destroyed the cities of the valley where Lot lived (Gen. 19:29); Sodom and Gomorrah and the cities round them committed immorality (Jude 7).

D Place names beginning A – B
D1 Abarim – Apollonia
D1a Abel-beth-maacah [Abel] [Abel-maim]
Sheba came to Abel, to Beth-maacah (2 Sam. 20:14); they besieged Abel-beth-maacah (2 Sam. 20:15); 'ask advice at Abel' (2 Sam. 20:18); Tiglath-pileser captured Abel-beth-maacah (2 Kgs. 15:29); Ben-hadad conquered Abel (1 Kgs. 15:20; 2 Chr. 16:4).

D1b Abel-meholah
The army fled as far as Abel-meholah (Judg. 7:22); from Beth-shean to Abel-meholah (1 Kgs. 4:12); Meholathite (1 Sam. 18:19; 2 Sam. 21:8); Elisha son of Shaphat of Abel-meholah (1 Kgs. 19:16).

D1c Abilene
Lysanias was tetrarch of Abilene (Luke 3:1).

D1d Achaia
Gallio was proconsul of Achaia (Acts 18:12); Apollos wanted to cross to Achaia (Acts 18:27; 19:21); Macedonia and Achaia made a contribution to the poor saints (Rom. 15:26); the household of Stephanas were the firstfruits of Achaia (1 Cor. 16:15); with all the saints throughout Achaia (2 Cor. 1:1); I say that Achaia has been ready since last year (2 Cor. 9:2); this boast of mine will not be silenced in the regions of Achaia (2 Cor. 11:10); you became an example to all the believers in Macedonia and Achaia (1 Thess. 1:7-8).

D1e Achzib [Chezib]
Shelah was born in Chezib (Gen. 38:5); a city of Judah (Josh. 15:44); on the border of Asher (Josh. 19:29); the houses of Achzib will become a deception (Mic. 1:14); Asher did not drive out the Canaanites from Achzib (Judg. 1:31).

D1f Adam
Near Zarethan (Josh. 3:16); at Adam they broke the covenant (Hos. 6:7).

D1g Admah
The boundary of the Canaanites went by Sodom, Gomorrah, Admah, Zeboiim, as far as Lasha (Gen. 10:19); the kings of Sodom, Gomorrah, Admah, Zeboiim and Bela (Gen. 14:2, 8); like the overthrow of Sodom, Gomorrah, Admah and Zeboiim (Deut. 29:23); how can I make you like Admah and Zeboiim? (Hos. 11:8).

D1h Adullam
The king of Adullam (Josh. 12:15); a city of Judah (Josh. 15:35); the cave of Adullam (1 Sam. 22:1; 2 Sam. 23:13; 1 Chr. 11:15); Rehoboam built Adullam (2 Chr. 11:7); an Adullamite named Hirah (Gen. 38:1, 12, 20); the glory of Israel will enter Adullam (Mic. 1:15).

D1i Aenon
John was baptising at Aenon near Salim (John 3:23).

D1j Ahava
The river that runs to Ahava (Ezra 8:15, 21, 31).

D1k Ai
Ai near Beth-aven, east of Bethel (Josh. 7:2); the king of Ai (Josh. 8:1, 14, 23, 29; 10:1; 12:9); the attack on Ai (Josh. 8:1-29); Joshua had taken Ai (Josh. 10:1); men of Bethel and Ai (Ezra 2:28; Neh. 7:32); Ai is destroyed (Jer. 49:3).

D1l Aijalon of Dan
A city of Dan (Josh. 19:42); a city of the Kohathites (Josh. 21:24; 1 Chr. 6:69); the Amorites continued to live there (Judg. 1:35); the inhabitants of Aijalon put to flight the inhabitants of Gath (1 Chr. 8:13); from Michmash to Aijalon (1 Sam. 14:31); Rehoboam built Aijalon (2 Chr. 11:10); the Philistines had captured Aijalon (2 Chr. 28:18).

D1m Alexandria
Cyrenians and Alexandrians, and some from Cilicia and Asia (Acts 6:9); Apollos was an Alexandrian by birth (Acts 18:24); a ship of Alexandria (Acts 27:6; 28:11).

D1n Anathoth
A city of the Kohathites (Josh. 21:18); a city of refuge given to the sons of Aaron (1 Chr. 6:60); Abiezer the Anathothite (2 Sam. 23:27; 1 Chr. 11:28; 27:12); Jehu the Anathothite (1 Chr. 12:3); Abiathar the priest was sent home to Anathoth (1 Kgs. 2:26); priests in Anathoth in the land of Benjamin (Jer. 1:1); Benjamin lived in Anathoth (Neh. 11:32); 128 men of Anathoth (Ezra 2:23; Neh. 7:27); the men of Anathoth who seek your life (Jer. 11:21); I will bring disaster on the men of Anathoth (Jer. 11:23); why have you not rebuked Jeremiah of Anathoth? (Jer. 29:27); buying the field at Anathoth (Jer. 32:7, 8-9); poor Anathoth! (Isa. 10:30).

D1o Amphipolis
When they had passed through Amphipolis and Apollonia (Acts 17:1).

D1p Antioch of Syria
Nicolas, a proselyte from Antioch (Acts 6:5); they made their way to Phoenicia and Cyprus and Antioch (Acts 11:19); some men of Cyprus and Cyrene came to Antioch and preached to Greeks (Acts 11:20); they sent Barnabas to Antioch (Acts 11:22); in Antioch the disciples were first called Christians (Acts 11:26); prophets came from Jerusalem to Antioch (Acts 11:27); in the church at Antioch there were prophets and teachers (Acts 13:1); they sailed to Antioch (Acts 14:26); to the Gentile brethren in Antioch, Syria and Cilicia (Acts 15:23); they went down to Antioch (Acts 15:30);

Paul returned to Antioch (Acts 18:22); when Peter came to Antioch (Gal. 2:11).

D1q Antioch of Pisidia
Going on from Perga they came to Antioch of Pisidia (Acts 13:14); Jews came from Antioch and Iconium (Acts 14:19); they returned to Lystra, Iconium and Antioch (Acts 14:21); my sufferings at Antioch, Iconium and Lystra (2 Tim. 3:11).

D1r Antipatris
The soldiers brought Paul to Antipatris by night (Acts 23:31).

D1s Aphek [Aphik]
The king of Aphek (Josh. 12:18); a city of Asher (Josh. 19:30); as far as Aphek (Josh. 13:4); Asher did not drive out the Canaanites from Aphek (Judg. 1:31); the Philistines camped in Aphek (1 Sam. 4:1; 29:1); Ben-hadad went up to Aphek to fight Israel (1 Kgs. 20:26); the Arameans fled to Aphek (1 Kgs. 20:30); you will defeat the Arameans at Aphek (2 Kgs. 13:17).

D1t Apollonia
When they had passed through Amphipolis and Apollonia (Acts 17:1).

D2 Ar – Avva

D2a Ar
A city of Moab (Num. 21:15, 28; Deut. 2:29); the border of Moab (Deut. 2:18); I have given Ar to the sons of Lot (Deut. 2:9, 19); Ar of Moab is ruined in a night (Isa. 15:1).

D2b Arabia
The kings of Arabia (1 Kgs. 10:15); Arabia and all the princes of Kedar (Ezek. 27:21); Ethiopia, Put, Lud, Arabia and Lybia will fall by the sword (Ezek. 30:5); the oracle concerning Arabia (Isa. 21:13); I went away to Arabia and then returned to Damascus (Gal. 1:17); Hagar is mount Sinai in Arabia (Gal. 4:25).

D2c Aram [Syria]
From Aram Balak brought me (Num. 23:7); the king of Aram lived in Damascus (1 Kgs. 15:18); Jacob fled to the land of Aram (Hos. 12:12).

D2d Ararat
The mountains of Ararat (Gen. 8:4); Adrammelech and Sharezer escaped to the land of Ararat (2 Kgs. 19:37; Isa. 37:38); Ararat, Minni and Ashkenaz (Jer. 51:27).

D2e Armageddon
The place called in Hebrew Armageddon (Rev. 16:16).

D2f Aroer
Aroer on the edge of the Arnon valley (Deut. 2:36; 3:12; 4:48; Josh. 13:9, 16); Sihon ruled from Aroer (Josh. 12:2); given to Gad (Josh. 13:25); built by Gad (Num. 32:34); from Aroer to the entrance of Minnith (Judg. 11:33); David sent a present to Aroer (1 Sam. 30:28); the census takers camped in Aroer (2 Sam. 24:5); stand by the road and watch, inhabitant of Aroer (Jer. 48:19).

D2g Arpad
Where are the gods of Arpad? (2 Kgs. 18:34; Isa. 36:19); where is the king of Arpad? (2 Kgs. 19:13; Isa. 37:13); is not Hamath like Arpad? (Isa. 10:9); Hamath and Arpad are confounded (Jer. 49:23).

D2h Ashdod [Azotus]
The lord of Ashdod (Josh. 13:3); a city of Judah (Josh. 15:46, 47); one of the cities of the Philistines (1 Sam. 6:17); the Philistines brought the ark to Ashdod (1 Sam. 5:1-8); Uzziah broke down the walls of Ashdod (2 Chr. 26:6); the Jews had married women from Ashdod (Neh. 13:23-4); I will cut off inhabitants from Ashdod (Amos 1:8); proclaim to the strongholds in Ashdod and Egypt (Amos 3:9); Ashdod will be driven out at noon (Zeph. 2:4); Philip appeared at Azotus (Acts 8:40).

D2i Asher
The territory of Asher (Josh. 19:25-31; Ezek. 48:2); cities for Asher (Josh. 19:31).

D2j Ashkelon
The lord of Ashkelon (Josh. 13:3); taken by Judah (Judg. 1:18); where Samson killed 30 Philistines (Judg. 14:19); one of the cities of the Philistines (1 Sam. 6:17); do not proclaim it on the streets of Ashkelon (2 Sam. 1:20); the Lord has assigned his sword against Ashkelon (Jer. 47:7); Ashkelon has been ruined (Jer. 47:5); I will cut off him who holds the sceptre from Ashkelon (Amos 1:8); Ashkelon will be a desolation (Zeph. 2:4; Zech. 9:5).

D2k Asia
Residents of Asia (Acts 2:9; 6:9); forbidden by the Holy Spirit to speak the word in Asia (Acts 16:6); all who lived in Asia heard the word of the Lord (Acts 19:10); Paul stayed in Asia for a while (Acts 19:22); through almost all Asia Paul has taught (Acts 19:26); she whom all Asia and the world worship (Acts 19:27); some of the Asiarchs who were friends of Paul (Acts 19:31); Tychicus and Trophimus of Asia (Acts 20:4); so that he might not have to spend time in Asia (Acts 20:16); the first day I set foot in Asia (Acts 20:18); Jews from Asia saw him in the temple (Acts 21:27; 24:18); Epaenetus, the first convert to Christ from Asia (Rom. 16:5); the churches of Asia (1 Cor. 16:19; Rev. 1:4); to those scattered throughout Pontus, Galatia, Cappadocia, Asia and Bithynia (1 Pet. 1:1).

D2l Assos
We set sail for Assos (Acts 20:13); Paul met us as Assos (Acts 20:14).

D2m Assyria [Asshur]
He went to Assyria and built Nineveh, Rehoboth-Ir and Calah (Gen. 10:11); the Lord will whistle for the bee in Assyria (Isa. 7:18); Reuben, Gad and half Manasseh were exiled to Assyria (1 Chr. 5:26); part of Israel taken captive to Assyria (2 Kgs. 15:29); Israel taken captive to Assyria (2 Kgs. 17:6, 23; 18:11); there will be a highway from Assyria (Isa. 11:16); the Lord will gather his people from Assyria (Isa. 11:11; 27:13; Zech. 10:10); what are you doing by going to Assyria? (Jer. 2:18); they will come to you from Assyria and the cities of Egypt (Mic. 7:12); I will break Assyria (Isa. 14:25); he will stretch out his hand against the north and destroy Assyria (Zeph. 2:13); the pride of Assyria will be laid low (Zech. 10:11).

D2n Athens
Paul in Athens (Acts 17:15-34; 1 Thess. 3:1); the Athenians spent their time in nothing other than telling or hearing something new (Acts 17:21); Paul left Athens and went to Corinth (Acts 18:1).

D2o Attalia
They went down to Attalia (Acts 14:25).

D2p Avva
Men from Avva were brought to Samaria (2 Kgs. 17:24); the Avvites made Nibhaz and Tartak (2 Kgs. 17:31).

D3 Babylon

D3a Babylon, the place
Nimrod's kingdom was Babylon, Erech, Accad and Calneh in Shinar (Gen. 10:10); the city was called Babel (Gen. 11:9); from a far country, from Babylon (2 Kgs. 20:14; Isa. 39:3); the king of Assyria brought people from Babylon to Samaria (2 Kgs. 17:24); he made Daniel ruler over the whole province of Babylon (Dan. 2:48); is this not great Babylon which I have made? (Dan. 4:30); walking on the roof of the royal palace in Babylon (Dan. 4:29); I will mention Rahab [Egypt] and Babylon (Ps. 87:4); she who is in Babylon sends greetings (1 Pet. 5:13).

D3b People exiled to Babylon
Some of your sons will be officers to the king of Babylon (2 Kgs. 20:18); by the rivers of Babylon we wept (Ps. 137:1); the king and princes of Jerusalem were taken to Babylon (Ezek. 17:12); the deportation to

Babylon (Matt. 1:11-12, 17); I will remove you beyond
Babylon (Acts 7:43); exiled to Babylon: Manasseh
(2 Chr. 33:11); Jehoiakim (2 Chr. 36:6); the people (Ezra
5:12); Jeconiah (Jer. 24:1); Zedekiah (Jer. 32:5; 39:7);
Judah (2 Kgs. 24:16; 1 Chr. 9:1; 2 Chr. 36:20); the priests,
prophets and people (Jer. 29:1).

D3c Return from Babylon
The vessels of the temple will soon be brought back
from Babylon (Jer. 27:16); go forth from Babylon (Isa.
48:20; Jer. 50:8); flee from the midst of Babylon! (Jer.
51:6); Zion! escape! you who live with the daughter of
Babylon (Zech. 2:7); exiles returned from Babylon
(Ezra 1:11; 2:1; 8:1; Zech. 6:10); Ezra returned from
Babylon (Ezra 7:6, 9).

D3d Condemnation of Babylon
Oracle concerning Babylon (Isa. 13:1; Jer. 50:1);
Jeremiah wrote on a scroll all that would befall Babylon
(Jer. 51:60); Babylon the great, mother of harlots (Rev.
17:5); lamenting over Babylon (Rev. 18:9-19); the sound
of an outcry from Babylon (Jer. 51:54); heaven and
earth will shout for joy over Babylon (Jer. 51:48); the
great city spiritually called Sodom and Egypt (Rev.
11:8); the woman you saw is the great city that rules
over the kings of the earth (Rev. 17:18).

D3e Babylon destroyed
Babylon will be destroyed (Isa. 14:22-3); the destroyer is
coming against Babylon (Jer. 51:1, 56); the Lord's plan is
against Babylon to destroy it (Jer. 51:11, 55); Babylon
will be like the overthrow of Sodom and Gomorrah
(Isa. 13:19); Babylon must fall for the slain of Israel (Jer.
51:49); God remembered Babylon the great (Rev. 16:19);
Babylon has been captured (Jer. 50:2, 46); how Sheshak
has been captured! (Jer. 51:41); Babylon has fallen (Isa.
21:9; Jer. 51:8; Rev. 14:8; 18:2); so will Babylon be thrown
down (Rev. 18:21); Babylon will become a haunt of
jackals (Jer. 51:37).

D4 Bashan – Bozrah

D4a Bashan
Og ruled over Bashan (Josh. 12:5); Og king of Bashan
(Num. 32:33; Deut. 1:4); Bashan is called the land of the
Rephaim (Deut. 3:13); Bashan was given to the half
tribe of Manasseh (Deut. 3:13; Josh. 13:30; 22:7; 1 Chr.
5:23); the sons of Gad lived in Bashan (1 Chr. 5:11); Dan
is a lion's whelp which leaps from Bashan (Deut.
33:22); Israel will feed in Bashan (Jer. 50:19); oars made
from oaks of Bashan (Ezek. 27:6); you cows of Bashan
who are on the mountain of Samaria (Amos 4:1);
strong bulls of Bashan surround me (Ps. 22:12); against
the oaks of Bashan (Isa. 2:13); Bashan and Carmel lose
their foliage (Isa. 33:9); wail, oaks of Bashan (Zech.
11:2).

D4b Beersheba
Its name is Beersheba to this day (Gen. 26:33); he called
that place Beersheba (Gen. 21:31); they made a
covenant there (Gen. 21:32); Abraham planted a
tamarisk tree there (Gen. 21:33); Isaac went up there
(Gen. 26:23); Jacob came there (Gen. 46:1); Jacob left
there (Gen. 28:10; 46:5); a city of Judah (Josh. 15:28); a
city of Simeon (Josh. 19:2); Abraham lived there (Gen.
22:19); the Simeonites lived there (1 Chr. 4:28); some of
Judah lived there (Neh. 11:27); Samuel's sons judged
there (1 Sam. 8:2); Elijah came to Beersheba of Judah
(1 Kgs. 19:3); do not cross to Beersheba (Amos 5:5); as
the way of Beersheba lives (Amos 8:14).

D4c Benjamin
The territory of Benjamin (Josh. 18:11-20; Ezek. 48:23);
Benjamin lay between Judah and Joseph (Josh. 18:11);
cities for Benjamin (Josh. 18:21-8; Neh. 11:31-5); they
passed through the land of Benjamin (1 Sam. 9:4);
Jeremiah went out of Jerusalem to go to the land of
Benjamin (Jer. 37:12).

D4d Beroea [Berea]
The brethren sent Paul and Silas away to Beroea (Acts
17:10); the Jews of Thessalonica came to Beroea (Acts
17:13); Sopater of Beroea (Acts 20:4).

D4e Bethany [Ananiah]
About 15 stadia from Jerusalem (John 11:18); Jesus at
Bethany (Matt. 21:17; 26:6; Mark 14:3; John 12:1); as he
approached Bethphage and Bethany (Mark 11:1; Luke
19:29); Lazarus of Bethany, the village of Mary and
Martha (John 11:1); he led them out as far as Bethany
(Luke 24:50); he went to Bethany with the 12 (Mark
11:11-12); tBenjamin lived in Ananiah (Neh. 11:32).

D4f Bethel [Aven] [Beth-aven] [Luz]
Bethel, formerly called Luz (Gen. 28:19; Judg. 1:23);
Jacob called the place Bethel (Gen. 35:15); let us go to
Bethel (Gen. 35:3); go and live there (Gen. 35:1); Hiel
the Bethelite rebuilt Jericho (1 Kgs. 16:34); a man of
God came from Judah to Bethel (1 Kgs. 13:1); the Lord
has sent me to Bethel (2 Kgs. 2:2); Elisha went up to
Bethel (2 Kgs. 2:23); God appeared to me at Luz in
Canaan (Gen. 48:3); I am the God of Bethel where you
anointed a pillar (Gen. 31:13); the ark was at Bethel
(Judg. 20:27); Israel went to Bethel to enquire of God
(Judg. 20:18); they wept before the Lord at Bethel
(Judg. 20:26; 21:2); do not prophesy at Bethel, for it is
the king's sanctuary (Amos 7:13); one golden calf was
put in Bethel (1 Kgs. 12:29; 2 Kgs. 10:29); Jeroboam
sacrificed to the calves in Bethel (1 Kgs. 12:32-3); the
altar in Bethel (1 Kgs. 13:32; 2 Kgs. 23:15, 17); come to
Bethel and sin (Amos 4:4); do not seek Bethel (Amos
5:5); do not go to Beth-aven (Hos. 4:15); I will punish
the altars of Bethel (Amos 3:14); the high places of Aven
will be destroyed (Hos. 10:8); the inhabitants of
Samaria fear for the calf of Beth-aven (Hos. 10:5); as
the house of Israel was ashamed of Bethel (Jer. 48:13).

D4g Bethlehem of Judah [Ephratah] [Ephrath]
Rachel buried on the way to Ephrath, that is,
Bethlehem (Gen. 35:19; 48:7); Naomi and Ruth
returning to Bethlehem (Ruth 1:19, 22); Samuel came to
Bethlehem (1 Sam. 16:4); the garrison of the Philistines
was in Bethlehem (2 Sam. 23:14; 1 Chr. 11:16); a Levite
took a concubine from Bethlehem of Judah (Judg. 19:1,
2, 18); a family of Ephrathites from Bethlehem of Judah
(Ruth 1:1-2); Jesse the Bethlehemite (1 Sam. 16:1, 18;
17:58); David of Bethlehem (1 Sam. 17:12); David's city
(1 Sam. 20:6; Luke 2:4); may you prosper in Ephratah
and be renowned in Bethlehem (Ruth 4:11); water from
the well at Bethlehem (2 Sam. 23:14, 15, 16; 1 Chr.
11:16-18); David tended the flock in Bethlehem (1 Sam.
17:15); David asked leave to go to Bethlehem (1 Sam.
20:28-9); as for you, Bethlehem Ephratah, from you
will go forth a ruler (Mic. 5:2; Matt. 2:5-6); Christ
comes from Bethlehem (John 7:42); let us go to
Bethlehem (Luke 2:15); Herod sent the wise men to
Bethlehem (Matt. 2:8); he killed all boys two and under
in Bethlehem and around (Matt. 2:16); when Jesus was
born in Bethlehem of Judea (Matt. 2:1).

D4h Bethlehem of Zebulun
A city of Zebulun (Josh. 19:15); Ibzan of Bethlehem
(Judg. 12:8); Ibzan was buried in Bethlehem (Judg.
12:10).

D4i Beth-millo
The men of Beth-millo made Abimelech king (Judg.
9:6); let fire consume the men of Shechem and
Beth-millo (Judg. 9:20).

D4j Bethphage
They came to Bethphage, to the mount of Olives (Matt.
21:1); they drew near to Bethphage and Bethany (Mark
11:1; Luke 19:29).

D4k Bethsaida
Woe to you, Bethsaida! (Matt. 11:21; Luke 10:13); he
made his disciples cross by boat to Bethsaida (Mark
6:45); they came to Bethsaida (Mark 8:22); Jesus
withdrew to a city called Bethsaida (Luke 9:10); Philip
was from Bethsaida (John 1:44; 12:21).

D4l Bithynia
When they came to Mysia they tried to go into
Bithynia (Acts 16:7); to those scattered throughout
Pontus, Galatia, Cappadocia, Asia and Bithynia (1 Pet.
1:1).

D4m Bozrah
The Lord has a sacrifice in Bozrah, in the land of Edom
(Isa. 34:6); who is this who comes from Bozrah? (Isa.
63:1); Bozrah will become a horror, a reproach, a ruin
and a curse (Jer. 49:13); he will spread out his wings
against Bozrah (Jer. 49:22); judgement has come on
Kerioth and Bozrah (Jer. 48:24); fire will consume the
strongholds of Bozrah (Amos 1:12).

E Place names beginning C – E
E1 Caesarea – Cyrene
E1a Caesarea
They brought him down to Caesarea and sent him
away to Tarsus (Acts 9:30); Cornelius at Caesarea (Acts
10:1); Herod went down from Judea to Caesarea (Acts
12:19); Paul landed at Caesarea (Acts 18:22); the next
day we came to Caesarea (Acts 21:8); some disciples
from Caesarea went with us (Acts 21:16); an armed
escort to proceed to Caesarea (Acts 23:23); after three
days Festus went to Jerusalem from Caesarea (Acts
25:1); Paul was in custody at Caesarea (Acts 25:4); after
eight or ten days Festus went to Caesarea (Acts 25:6);
King Agrippa and Bernice arrived in Caesarea (Acts
25:13).

E1b Caesarea Philippi
Jesus came into the district of Caesarea Philippi (Matt.
16:13); Jesus went to the villages of Caesarea Philippi
(Mark 8:27).

E1c Cana
There was a wedding at Cana in Galilee (John 2:1); the
first of his signs Jesus did at Cana in Galilee (John 2:11);
he came again to Cana of Galilee where he made the
water wine (John 4:46); Nathanael of Cana in Galilee
(John 21:2).

E1d Canaan
I will give you the land of Canaan (Gen. 17:8; Lev. 25:38;
Deut. 32:49; 1 Chr. 16:18; Ps. 105:11); they intended to go
to the land of Canaan (Gen. 11:31); go to the land of
Canaan (Gen. 45:17); the field at Machpelah facing
Mamre, that is, Hebron, in the land of Canaan (Gen.
23:19); the grave I cut in the land of Canaan (Gen. 50:5);
Abraham dwelt in the land of Canaan (Gen. 13:12);
Jacob dwelt in Canaan (Gen. 37:1); your origin and
birth are of the land of the Canaanites (Ezek. 16:3); you
shall not do as is done in the land of Canaan (Lev.
18:3); they sacrificed to the idols of Canaan (Ps. 106:38);
the word of the Lord is against you, Canaan, land of
the Philistines (Zeph. 2:5); Simon the Canaanite (Matt.
10:4; Mark 3:18).

E1e Capernaum
Jesus left Nazareth and settled in Capernaum (Matt.
4:13); Jesus went to Capernaum (Mark 2:1; Luke 4:31;
7:1; John 2:12); he came to his own city (Matt. 9:1; Mark
6:1); he came to his home town (Matt. 13:54); he
entered Capernaum (Matt. 8:5); they came to
Capernaum (Matt. 17:24; Mark 9:33);
they came to Capernaum seeking Jesus (John 6:24);
Jesus taught in the synagogue at Capernaum (Mark
1:21; John 6:59); a sick son in Capernaum (John 4:46);
Capernaum, will you be exalted? (Matt. 11:23; Luke
10:15); what you did in Capernaum, do in your home

town too (Luke 4:23); the disciples started to cross to
Capernaum (John 6:17).

E1f Cappadocia
Residents of Mesopotamia, Judea and Cappadocia
(Acts 2:9); to those scattered throughout Pontus,
Galatia, Cappadocia, Asia and Bithynia (1 Pet. 1:1).

E1g Carmel
A city of Judah (Josh. 15:55); the majesty of Carmel and
Sharon (Isa. 35:2); Saul set up a monument to himself
in Carmel (1 Sam. 15:12); Nabal the Carmelite (2 Sam.
2:2; 3:3); they came to Abigail at Carmel (1 Sam. 25:40);
Abigail the Carmelitess (1 Sam. 27:3; 30:5; 1 Chr. 3:1).

E1h Cenchrea [Cenchreae]
In Cenchrea Paul had his hair cut (Acts 18:18); Phoebe,
a deacon of the church at Cenchrea [Cenchreae] (Rom.
16:1).

E1i Chaldea
The Lord has work to do in the land of the Chaldeans
(Jer. 50:25); I will send a destroyer against the
inhabitants of Lebkamai [Chaldea] (Jer. 51:1); I will
make the land of the Chaldeans an everlasting waste
(Jer. 25:12); the Spirit brought me in a vision to the
exiles in Chaldea (Ezek. 11:24); in the land of the
Chaldeans by the river Chebar (Ezek. 1:3); Babylonians
from Chaldea (Ezek. 23:15); she sent messengers to
them in Chaldea (Ezek. 23:16); he departed from the
land of the Chaldeans (Acts 7:4).

E1j Chorazin
Woe to you, Chorazin! (Matt. 11:21; Luke 10:13).

E1k Cilicia
Cyrenians and Alexandrians, and some from Cilicia
and Asia (Acts 6:9); to the Gentile brethren in Antioch,
Syria and Cilicia (Acts 15:23);
Paul and Silas went through Syria and Cilicia (Acts
15:41; Gal. 1:21); I am a Jew of Tarsus in Cilicia (Acts
21:39; 22:3); when the governor learned that Paul was
from Cilicia (Acts 23:34); we sailed along by Cilicia and
Pamphylia (Acts 27:5).

E1l Cnidus
We arrived off Cnidus (Acts 27:7).

E1m Colossae
To the saints and faithful brethren in Christ in
Colossae (Col. 1:2).

E1n Corinth
Paul in Corinth (Acts 18:1-18); Apollos in Corinth (Acts
19:1); to the church of God at Corinth (1 Cor. 1:2; 2 Cor.
1:1); Erastus remained at Corinth (2 Tim. 4:20).

E1o Cos
We came by a straight course to Cos (Acts 21:1).

E1p Crete [Caphtor]
This is why I left you in Crete (Titus 1:5); Cretans are
always liars (Titus 1:12); Cretans and Arabs (Acts 2:11);
the Lord will destroy the remnant of the coastland of
Caphtor (Jer. 47:4); did I not bring the Philistines from
Caphtor? (Amos 9:7); the Caphtorim (Gen. 10:14;
1 Chr. 1:12); the Caphtorim who came from Caphtor
(Deut. 2:23).

E1q Cyprus [Kittim]
Ships from Kittim will attack Assyria (Num. 24:24);
pines from the coastlands of Cyprus (Ezek. 27:6); ships
of Kittim will come against him (Dan. 11:30); Barnabas,
a Levite of Cyprus (Acts 4:36); they made their way to
Phoenicia and Cyprus and Antioch (Acts 11:19); some
men of Cyprus and Cyrene came to Antioch and
preached to Greeks (Acts 11:20); they sailed to Cyprus
(Acts 13:4; 15:39); we came in sight of Cyprus and left it
on the left (Acts 21:3); Mnason of Cyprus (Acts 21:16);
we sailed under the lee of Cyprus (Acts 27:4).

E1r Cyrene
Simon of Cyrene was forced to carry the cross (Matt.
27:32; Mark 15:21; Luke 23:26); residents of Egypt and

the parts of Libya around Cyrene (Acts 2:10); Cyrenians and Alexandrians, and some from Cilicia and Asia (Acts 6:9); some men of Cyprus and Cyrene came to Antioch and preached to Greeks (Acts 11:20); Lucius of Cyrene (Acts 13:1).

E2 Dalmatia – Derbe

E2a Dalmatia
Titus has gone to Dalmatia (2 Tim. 4:10).

E2b Damascus
You may make streets for yourself in Damascus (1 Kgs. 20:34); Jeroboam II recovered Damascus from Judah (2 Kgs. 14:28); a gift of every good thing of Damascus (2 Kgs. 8:9); Abanah and Pharpar, rivers of Damascus (2 Kgs. 5:12); Eliezer of Damascus (Gen. 15:2); the head of Damascus is Rezin (Isa. 7:8); Elisha came to Damascus (2 Kgs. 8:7); some of Judah were taken captive to Damascus (2 Chr. 28:5); Saul went to Damascus (Acts 9:2-3; 22:5-6; 26:12); they brought him into Damascus (Acts 9:8; 22:11); a disciple in Damascus called Ananias (Acts 9:10); at Damascus he preached boldly in the name of Jesus (Acts 9:27); I declared to those at Damascus first (Acts 26:20); the governor under King Aretas guarded the city of Damascus (2 Cor. 11:32); I went away to Arabia and then returned to Damascus (Gal. 1:17); oracle about Damascus (Isa. 17:1-3); concerning Damascus (Jer. 49:23); Ahaz copied the altar in Damascus (2 Kgs. 16:10); Ahaz sacrificed to the gods of Damascus (2 Chr. 28:23); the kingdom will disappear from Damascus (Isa. 17:3); for three transgressions of Damascus and for four (Amos 1:3).

E2c Dan [Laish] [Leshem]
The territory of Dan (Josh. 19:40-8; Ezek. 48:1); conquered by Ben-hadad (1 Kgs. 15:20); Dan [Leshem, Laish], a city of Dan (Josh. 19:47); Sidonians living in security there (Judg. 18:7); Danites went to spy it out (Judg. 18:14); the Danites sacked Laish (Judg. 18:27); Laish was renamed Dan (Judg. 18:29); Abraham pursued as far as Dan (Gen. 14:14); one golden calf was put in Dan (1 Kgs. 12:29; 2 Kgs. 10:29); the people went to worship as far as Dan (1 Kgs. 12:30); those who say, 'As your god lives, Dan' (Amos 8:14); Ben-hadad conquered Dan (2 Chr. 16:4).

E2d Debir [Kiriath-sepher] [Lo-debar]
Taken by Joshua (Josh. 10:38-9); Joshua cut off the Anakim from Debir (Josh. 11:21); to the one who takes Kiriath-sepher I will give my daughter as wife (Josh. 15:15-16; Judg. 1:12); a city of Judah (Josh. 15:49); a city of the Kohathites (Josh. 21:15); a city of refuge given to the sons of Aaron (1 Chr. 6:58); Judah attacked it (Judg. 1:11); Mephibosheth was in Lo-debar (2 Sam. 9:4, 5); you who rejoice in Lo-debar [a thing of nothing] (Amos 6:13).

E2e Decapolis
Crowds followed him from Decapolis, Jerusalem, Judea and beyond Jordan (Matt. 4:25); he proclaimed in Decapolis what great things Jesus had done for him (Mark 5:20); he went through the region of the Decapolis (Mark 7:31).

E2f Derbe
They fled to Lystra and Derbe, cities of Lycaonia (Acts 14:6); the next day he went with Barnabas to Derbe (Acts 14:20); Paul came to Derbe and Lystra (Acts 16:1); Gaius of Derbe (Acts 20:4).

E3 Ebenezer – Edom

E3a Ebenezer
Named by Samuel (1 Sam. 7:12); the Philistines took the ark from Ebenezer to Ashdod (1 Sam. 5:1).

E3b Eden, the garden
A garden in Eden, to the east (Gen. 2:8); the land of Nod, east of Eden (Gen. 4:16); the Lord put the man in the garden of Eden (Gen. 2:15); you were in Eden, the garden of God (Ezek. 28:13); the trees of Eden (Ezek. 31:16-18).

E3c Edom [Seir]
Over Edom I throw my shoe (Ps. 60:8; 108:9); till I come to you in Seir (Gen. 33:14); let us pass through the land of Edom (Num. 20:17); they went round the land of Edom (Num. 21:4); when the Lord went from Seir, from the field of Edom (Judg. 5:4); David put garrisons in Edom (2 Sam. 8:14); who will lead me to Edom? (Ps. 60:9; 108:10); Egypt will become a waste, Edom a desolate wilderness (Joel 3:19); I have given Mount Seir to Esau (Deut. 2:5); Esau in the land of Seir, the territory of Edom (Gen. 32:3); Esau lived in the hill country of Seir (Gen. 36:8, 9); chiefs of Edom in the land of Edom (Gen. 36:16, 17); chiefs of the Horites in the land of Edom (Gen. 36:21); chiefs of the Horites in the land of Seir (Gen. 36:30); Esau returned to Seir (Gen. 33:16); when David was in Edom (1 Kgs. 11:15); who is this who comes from Edom? (Isa. 63:1); people from Idumea came to Jesus (Mark 3:8).

E4 Egypt

E4a Egypt, the place
I will mention Rahab [Egypt] and Babylon (Ps. 87:4); Egypt called Rahab who sits still (Isa. 30:7); the land of Ham (Ps. 105:23, 27; 106:22); I gave Egypt as your ransom (Isa. 43:3); Egypt was watered by the feet (Deut. 11:10); there will be a highway from Egypt to Assyria (Isa. 19:23); the great city spiritually called Sodom and Egypt (Rev. 11:8).

E4b The affairs of Egypt
Seven years of plenty in all the land of Egypt (Gen. 41:29); seven years of famine in all the land of Egypt (Gen. 41:36); a famine came on all Egypt and Canaan (Acts 7:11); the famine was severe in Egypt (Gen. 41:55, 56; 47:13); in all the land of Egypt there was bread (Gen. 41:54); Jacob knew there was grain in Egypt (Gen. 42:1, 2; Acts 7:12); Joseph was over all the land of Egypt (Gen. 41:41, 43, 45, 46; 45:8, 9, 26; Acts 7:10); a statute in Egypt that Pharaoh should have a fifth (Gen. 47:26); five cities of Egypt speaking the language of Canaan (Isa. 19:18); the Lord will whistle for the fly in Egypt (Isa. 7:18).

E4c Going down to Egypt
Joseph was sold into Egypt (Gen. 37:36; 45:4, 5; Acts 7:9); do not be afraid to go down to Egypt (Gen. 46:3); I will go down with you to Egypt and I will bring you up (Gen. 46:4); I will send you to Egypt (Acts 7:34); woe to those who go down to Egypt for help (Isa. 31:1); they go down to Egypt without consulting me (Isa. 30:2); do not go down to Egypt (Jer. 26:2; Jer. 42:19); those who went down to Egypt: Abraham (Gen. 12:10); Ishmaelites (Gen. 37:25); Joseph (Gen. 37:28; 39:1); Joseph's brothers (Gen. 42:3; 43:15); Israel (Gen. 46:3-8; Ps. 105:23); Jacob and his offspring (Josh. 24:4; 1 Sam. 12:8; Acts 7:15); the remnant (Jer. 43:7).

E4d Fleeing to Egypt
He took the child and his mother by night and departed to Egypt (Matt. 2:13-14); those fleeing to Egypt: Hadad (1 Kgs. 11:17-18); Jeroboam (1 Kgs. 11:40; 12:2; 2 Chr. 10:2); the people (2 Kgs. 25:26); Uriah (Jer. 26:21).

E4e Living in Egypt
The land of Egypt is before you (Gen. 47:6); 70 people of the house of Jacob in Egypt (Gen. 46:27); Joseph dwelt in Egypt (Gen. 50:22); Jacob lived in Egypt 17 years (Gen. 47:28); Israel lived in Egypt for 430 years (Exod. 12:40); you were sojourners in the land of Egypt (Exod. 22:21; 23:9); Moses performed wonders and signs in Egypt (Acts 7:36); God made this people great during their stay in Egypt (Acts 13:17).

E4f Brought out of Egypt
I made myself known to them by bringing them out of the land of Egypt (Ezek. 20:9-10); I swore to them to bring them out of the land of Egypt (Ezek. 20:6); God brought Israel out of the land of Egypt (Dan. 9:15; Amos 2:10; 9:7); out of Egypt I called my son (Hos. 11:1; Matt. 2:15); bringing the Israelites out of Egypt (Exod. 3:8-17); I am the Lord who brought you up out of Egypt (Lev. 11:45); because the Lord hates us he brought us out of Egypt (Deut. 1:27); you took a vine from Egypt (Ps. 80:8); by faith Moses left Egypt (Heb. 11:27); he who saved a people out of the land of Egypt (Jude 5); the Lord will recover his people from Assyria, Egypt, Pathros (Isa. 11:11); I will bring them back from the land of Egypt (Zech. 10:10); those lost in Assyria and those scattered in Egypt will return (Isa. 27:13).

E4g Returning to Egypt
Moses returned to Egypt (Exod. 4:18, 19, 20); lest the people return to Egypt (Exod. 13:17); would it not be better to return to Egypt? (Num. 14:3, 4); they intended to go to Egypt (Jer. 41:17); they intended to return to slavery in Egypt (Neh. 9:17); the Lord will bring you back to Egypt (Deut. 28:68); in their hearts they turned back to Egypt (Acts 7:39); you will not remember Egypt any more (Ezek. 23:27).

E4h Products of Egypt
Importing horses from Egypt (1 Kgs. 10:28, 29; 2 Chr. 1:16; 9:28); let bronze be brought from Egypt (Ps. 68:31); coloured linens of Egypt (Prov. 7:16); your sail was of fine embroidered linen from Egypt (Ezek. 27:7); he will gain all the precious things of Egypt (Dan. 11:43); greater riches than all the treasures of Egypt (Heb. 11:26).

E4i Sicknesses of Egypt
He will bring on you the diseases of Egypt (Deut. 28:60); he will smite you with the boils of Egypt (Deut. 28:27); none of the diseases of Egypt will afflict you (Deut. 7:15).

E4j Defiled by Egypt
The gods your fathers served in Egypt (Josh. 24:14); do not defile yourselves with the idols of Egypt (Ezek. 20:7); they did not forsake the idols of Egypt (Ezek. 20:8); I will put an end to your harlotry from the land of Egypt (Ezek. 23:27); you must not do as is done in the land of Egypt (Lev. 18:3).

E4k God crushed Egypt
You crushed Rahab (Ps. 89:10); God did wonders in Egypt (Ps. 106:21; 135:9); he wrought wonders in the land of Egypt (Ps. 78:12, 43); did you not cut Rahab in pieces? (Isa. 51:9); he smote the firstborn of Egypt (Ps. 78:51; 135:8).

E4l Judgement on Egypt
I have given Egypt to Nebuchadnezzar as wages (Ezek. 29:20); I will give Egypt to Nebuchadnezzar as spoil (Ezek. 29:19); a sword will come upon Egypt (Ezek. 30:4); anguish will come on them in the day of Egypt's doom (Ezek. 30:9); those who support Egypt will fall (Ezek. 30:6); when I make the land of Egypt desolate (Ezek. 32:15); Egypt will become a waste (Joel 3:19); the oracle concerning Egypt (Isa. 19:1); Isaiah went naked as a sign against Egypt and Cush (Isa. 20:3); the king of Assyria will lead away captives of Egypt and Cush (Isa. 20:4); Nebuchadnezzar will strike the land of Egypt (Jer. 43:11; 46:13); the sceptre of Egypt will depart (Zech. 10:11).

E5 Ekron – Ezion-geber
E5a Ekron
One of the cities of the Philistines (1 Sam. 6:17); the ark was brought to Ekron (1 Sam. 5:10); they pursued the Philistines to the gates of Ekron (1 Sam. 17:52); enquiring of Baal-zebub god of Ekron (2 Kgs. 1:2, 3, 6,

16); I will turn my hand against Ekron (Amos 1:8); Ekron will be uprooted (Zeph. 2:4); Ekron will be like the Jebusites (Zech. 9:7).

E5b Elim
In Sinai (Num. 33:9, 10); they came to Elim (Exod. 15:27); they set out from Elim (Exod. 16:1).

E5c Emmaus
A village called Emmaus, 60 stadia from Jerusalem (Luke 24:13).

E5d Engedi [Hazazon-tamar]
Hazazon-tamar, which is Engedi (2 Chr. 20:2); the Amorites lived in Hazazon-tamar (Gen. 14:7); a city of Judah (Josh. 15:62); David was in the strongholds of Engedi (1 Sam. 23:29); David was in the wilderness of Engedi (1 Sam. 24:1).

E5e Ephesus
Paul in Ephesus (Acts 18:19-21; 19:1-20); Apollos came to Ephesus (Acts 18:24); this became known to all who lived in Ephesus (Acts 19:17); not only in Ephesus but though almost all Asia Paul has taught (Acts 19:26); great is Artemis of the Ephesians! (Acts 19:28, 34-5); if I fought with wild beasts at Ephesus (1 Cor. 15:32); Paul had decided to sail past Ephesus (Acts 20:16); from Miletus he sent to Ephesus (Acts 20:17); Trophimus the Ephesian (Acts 21:29); I will stay in Ephesus until Pentecost (1 Cor. 16:8); remain at Ephesus (1 Tim. 1:3); Tychicus I have sent to Ephesus (2 Tim. 4:12); you know the service he rendered in Ephesus (2 Tim. 1:18); to the saints who are in Ephesus (Eph. 1:1); the church in Ephesus (Rev. 1:11; 2:1-7).

E5f Ephraim
The territory of Ephraim (Josh. 16:5-8; Ezek. 48:5); the hill country of Ephraim (Judg. 17:1; 18:2, 13; 19:1, 16, 18; 1 Sam. 1:1; 9:4; 14:22; 2 Kgs. 5:22; 1 Chr. 6:67); cities for Ephraim (Josh. 21:20; 1 Chr. 7:28-9); Ephraim is my helmet (Ps. 60:7; 108:8); Jesus went to a town called Ephraim (John 11:54).

E5g Ethiopia [Cush]
I mention Philistia and Tyre with Ethiopia (Ps. 87:4); I gave Egypt as your ransom, Cush and Seba in your place (Isa. 43:3); the topaz of Ethiopia (Job 28:19); the merchandise of Cush will come to you (Isa. 45:14); let Ethiopia hasten to stretch out her hands to God (Ps. 68:31); Cush their hope and Egypt their boast (Isa. 20:5); the king of Assyria will lead away captives of Egypt and Cush (Isa. 20:4); anguish will be in Ethiopia (Ezek. 30:4).

E5h Ezion-geber
In Sinai (Num. 33:35, 36); Solomon went to Ezion-geber (2 Chr. 8:17); Solomon built ships in Ezion-geber (1 Kgs. 9:26); Jehoshaphat made ships in Ezion-geber (2 Chr. 20:36); Jehoshaphat's ships were wrecked in Ezion-geber (1 Kgs. 22:48).

F Place names beginning F – I
F1 Fair Havens – Galatia
F1a Fair Havens
A place called Fair Havens near the city of Lasea (Acts 27:8).

F1b Forum of Appius
They came as far as the Forum of Appius (Acts 28:15).

F1c Gabbatha
The Pavement, called in Hebrew Gabbatha (John 19:13).

F1d Gad
The territory of Gad (Josh. 13:24-8; Ezek. 48:27); why has Milcom taken possession of Gad? (Jer. 49:1); some crossed Jordan into the land of Gad (1 Sam. 13:7).

F1e Gadara [Gerasa] [Gergesa]
The country of the Gadarenes (Matt. 8:28; Mark 5:1; Luke 8:26, 37).

F1f Galatia
They went through the region of Phrygia and Galatia (Acts 16:6); Paul went through Galatia and Phrygia, strengthening the disciples (Acts 18:23); Crescens has gone to Galatia (2 Tim. 4:10); the churches of Galatia (1 Cor. 16:1; Gal. 1:2); you foolish Galatians! (Gal. 3:1); to those scattered throughout Pontus, Galatia, Cappadocia, Asia and Bithynia (1 Pet. 1:1).

F2 Galilee
F2a Galilee, the place
Ben-hadad conquered all Chinneroth (1 Kgs. 15:20); Galilee of the Gentiles (Isa. 9:1; Matt. 4:13-15); Tiglath-pileser captured Galilee (2 Kgs. 15:29); he came to Capernaum, a city of Galilee (Luke 4:31); Jesus decided to go to Galilee (John 1:43); when he heard that Jesus had come from Judea to Galilee (John 4:47); throughout all Judea, starting at Galilee (Acts 10:37).

F2b People from Galilee
This is the prophet Jesus, from Nazareth of Galilee (Matt. 21:11); Jesus the Galilean (Matt. 26:69); surely Christ does not come from Galilee? (John 7:41); Pilate asked whether the man was a Galilean (Luke 23:6); are you from Galilee too? no prophet is to arise from Galilee (John 7:52); Philip was from Bethsaida in Galilee (John 12:21); Nathanael of Cana in Galilee (John 21:2); when he came to Galilee the Galileans welcomed him (John 4:45); men of Galilee, why stand looking into the sky? (Acts 1:11); surely you are one of them, for you are a Galilean (Mark 14:70; Luke 22:59); are not these who are speaking Galileans? (Acts 2:7).

F2c People in Galilee
Joseph headed for Galilee (Matt. 2:22-3); after I am raised I will go before you to Galilee (Matt. 26:32; Mark 14:28); he is going before you to Galilee (Matt. 28:7; Mark 16:7); tell my brethren to go to Galilee (Matt. 28:10); the 11 disciples went to Galilee (Matt. 28:16); there was a wedding at Cana in Galilee (John 2:1); the first of his signs Jesus did at Cana in Galilee (John 2:11); he came again to Cana of Galilee where he made the water wine (John 4:46); women who had followed Jesus from Galilee (Matt. 27:55; Mark 15:41; Luke 23:49, 55); Herod was tetrarch of Galilee (Luke 3:1); the church throughout Judea, Galilee and Samaria had peace (Acts 9:31).

F3 Gath – Greece
F3a Gath
One of the cities of the Philistines (1 Sam. 6:17); tell it not in Gath (2 Sam. 1:20; Mic. 1:10); the ark was brought to Gath (1 Sam. 5:8-9); David took Gath from the Philistines (1 Chr. 18:1); the Philistines seized David in Gath (Ps. 56:t); Shimei brought back his slaves from Gath (1 Kgs. 2:39-41); Rehoboam built Gath (2 Chr. 11:8); David went to live with Achish in Gath (1 Sam. 27:2, 3); Ittai the Gittite (2 Sam. 15:19, 22; 18:2); the ark was brought to the house of Obed-edom the Gittite (2 Sam. 6:10; 1 Chr. 13:13); Goliath from Gath (1 Sam. 17:4, 23); Goliath the Gittite (2 Sam. 21:19; 1 Chr. 20:5); these were descended from the giants in Gath (2 Sam. 21:22; 1 Chr. 20:8).

F3b Gaza
A city of Judah (Josh. 15:47); Anakim remained in Gaza (Josh. 11:22); one of the cities of the Philistines (1 Sam. 6:17); Samson went to Gaza (Judg. 16:1); Samson in prison in Gaza (Judg. 16:21); before Pharaoh conquered Gaza (Jer. 47:1); baldness has come on Gaza (Jer. 47:5); for three transgressions of Gaza and for four (Amos 1:6-7); Gaza will be deserted, Ashkelon a desolation (Zeph. 2:4); Gaza will writhe in pain (Zech. 9:5); go south to the road from Jerusalem to Gaza (Acts 8:26).

F3c Gennesaret
They came to land at Gennesaret (Matt. 14:34; Mark 6:53).

F3d Gerar
Abimelech king of Gerar (Gen. 20:2); Abraham sojourned in Gerar (Gen. 20:1); Isaac went to Gerar (Gen. 26:1); Isaac lived in Gerar (Gen. 26:6); Abimelech came to him from Gerar (Gen. 26:26).

F3e Gethsamane
A place called Gethsemane (Matt. 26:36; Mark 14:32).

F3f Gibeah
A city of Judah (Josh. 15:57); a city of Benjamin (Josh. 18:28); we will attack Gibeah (Judg. 20:9); they camped against Gibeah (Judg. 20:19); Gibeah was sacked (Judg. 20:37); Saul went to his home in Gibeah (1 Sam. 10:26); Gibeah of Saul (1 Sam. 11:4; 15:34); Saul was sitting in Gibeah (1 Sam. 22:6); seven sons of Saul were to be hanged in Gibeah of Saul (2 Sam. 21:6); from the days of Gibeah you have sinned (Hos. 10:9).

F3g Gibeon
A city of the Gibeonites (Josh. 9:17); the inhabitants acted craftily (Josh. 9:3-5); the Hivites in Gibeon made peace with Israel (Josh. 10:1, 4; 11:19); Saul put the Gibeonites to death (2 Sam. 21:1); sun, stand still in Gibeon (Josh. 10:12); a city of Benjamin (Josh. 18:25); the men of Gibeon repaired the wall (Neh. 3:7); the large stone at Gibeon (2 Sam. 20:8); the great pool which is in Gibeon (Jer. 41:12); Solomon at the high place at Gibeon (1 Kgs. 3:4; 2 Chr. 1:3, 13); the Lord appeared to Solomon in Gibeon (1 Kgs. 3:5; 9:2); the tabernacle of the Lord was on the high place at Gibeon (1 Chr. 16:39; 21:29).

F3h Gilead
God showed Moses Gilead as far as Dan (Deut. 34:1); Gilead and Bashan beyond the Jordan (Josh. 17:5); the land of Gilead was suitable for livestock (Num. 32:1, 4); Gilead, land of Sihon and Og (1 Kgs. 4:19; Neh. 9:22); all Israel including the land of Gilead (Judg. 20:1); is there no balm in Gilead? (Jer. 8:22); go up to Gilead and get balm (Jer. 46:11); Og ruled half of Gilead (Josh. 12:5); Sihon ruled half of Gilead (Josh. 12:2); the Amorites had taken the land from Moab (Num. 21:26-30); Gilead is mine (Ps. 60:7; 108:8); half of Gilead was given to Manasseh (Josh. 13:31); Gilead given to Reuben, Gad and half of Manasseh (Num. 32:5, 29-42; 34:14-15; Josh. 1:13, 15); Moses gave Gilead to Machir son of Manasseh (Num. 32:40); Barzillai the Gileadite (2 Sam. 17:27; 19:31; 1 Kgs. 2:7; Ezra 2:61); Elijah the Tishbite, a settler in Gilead (1 Kgs. 17:1); our wives and children will remain in the cities of Gilead (Num. 32:26).

F3i Gilgal [Beth-gilgal] [Geliloth]
On the edge of Jericho (Josh. 4:19); where 12 stones from the Jordan were set up (Josh. 4:20); rolling away the reproach (Josh. 5:9); the angel of the Lord came from Gilgal to Bochim (Judg. 2:1); Samuel went on circuit to Gilgal (1 Sam. 7:16); go down before me to Gilgal (1 Sam. 10:8); renewing the kingdom at Gilgal (1 Sam. 11:14-15); animals to sacrifice at Gilgal (1 Sam. 15:21); Samuel hewed Agag at Gilgal (1 Sam. 15:33); Judah came to Gilgal to bring the king over Jordan (2 Sam. 19:15); Elisha went with Elijah from Gilgal (2 Kgs. 2:1); do not enter Gilgal, do not go to Beth-aven, do not swear, 'As the Lord lives' (Hos. 4:15); all their evil is in Gilgal (Hos. 9:15); surely they were in Gilgal sacrificing bulls (Hos. 12:11); Gilgal will go into captivity (Amos 5:5); come to Bethel and sin, to Gilgal and multiply transgression (Amos 4:4); do not seek Bethel or enter into Gilgal or cross to Beersheba (Amos 5:5).

F3j Golgotha

Golgotha – the place of the skull (Matt. 27:33; Mark 15:22).

F3k Gomorrah

The kings of Sodom, Gomorrah, Admah, Zeboiim and Bela (Gen. 14:2, 8); the kings of Sodom and Gomorrah (Gen. 14:10); Abraham looked down toward Sodom and Gomorrah (Gen. 19:28); they took all the food of Sodom and Gomorrah (Gen. 14:11); the outcry of Sodom and Gomorrah is great and their sin heavy (Gen. 18:20); Sodom and Gomorrah committed immorality (Jude 7); they have become like Sodom and Gomorrah to me (Jer. 23:14); their vine is the vine of Sodom and Gomorrah (Deut. 32:32); give ear, people of Gomorrah (Isa. 1:10); the Lord rained fire and brimstone on Sodom and Gomorrah (Gen. 19:24); we would have been like Sodom and Gomorrah (Isa. 1:9; Rom. 9:29); more tolerable for the land of Sodom and Gomorrah than for that town (Matt. 10:15); if God condemned Sodom and Gomorrah (2 Pet. 2:6).

F3l Goshen in Egypt

You will dwell in the land of Goshen (Gen. 45:10; 46:34); let us live in the land of Goshen (Gen. 47:4); Joseph went up to Goshen to meet his father (Gen. 46:29); Israel lived in Goshen in the land of Egypt (Gen. 47:27); I will set apart the land of Goshen where my people dwell (Exod. 8:22); in the land of Goshen there was no hail (Exod. 9:26).

F3m Greece [Javan]

The he-goat represents the king of Greece (Dan. 8:21); the prince of Greece is coming (Dan. 10:20); he will rouse the empire against Greece (Dan. 11:2); I will stir your sons, Zion, against your sons, Greece (Zech. 9:13); survivors sent to Javan (Isa. 66:19); Javan, Tubal and Meshech traded with you (Ezek. 27:13); Paul came to Greece (Acts 20:2).

F4 Hamath – Horonaim

F4a Hamath

Jeroboam II recovered Hamath from Judah (2 Kgs. 14:28); the men of Hamath made Ashima (2 Kgs. 17:30); where are the gods of Hamath? (2 Kgs. 18:34; Isa. 36:19); where is the king of Hamath? (2 Kgs. 19:13; Isa. 37:13); is not Hamath like Arpad? (Isa. 10:9); Hamath and Arpad are confounded (Jer. 49:23).

F4b Haran

They dwelt in Haran (Gen. 11:31); flee to Haran (Gen. 27:43); Jacob went towards Haran (Gen. 28:10); we are from Haran (Gen. 29:4); Abraham went out from Haran (Gen. 12:4); when Abraham was in Mesopotamia, before he lived in Haran (Acts 7:2); Abraham lived in Haran (Acts 7:4).

F4c Hebron [Kiriath-arba] [Mamre]

Sarah died in Kiriath-arba, that is, Hebron, in the land of Canaan (Gen. 23:2); the oaks of Mamre in Hebron (Gen. 13:18); Ephron's field at Machpelah, facing Mamre (Gen. 23:17; 25:9; 49:30); built seven years before Zoan in Egypt (Num. 13:22); Mamre, Kiriath-arba, that is, Hebron (Gen. 35:27); taken by Joshua (Josh. 10:36-7); a city of Judah (Josh. 15:54); given to Caleb (Josh. 14:13, 14; 15:13; 21:12; Judg. 1:20); the spies came to Hebron (Num. 13:22); Joab and his men marched to Hebron (2 Sam. 4:1); Abner died in Hebron (2 Sam. 4:1); all Israel came to David at Hebron (2 Sam. 5:1; 1 Chr. 11:1); they came to Hebron to make David king (1 Chr. 12:38); the elders of Israel made a covenant with David at Hebron (2 Sam. 5:3); David reigned in Hebron (2 Sam. 2:11; 5:5; 1 Kgs. 2:11; 1 Chr. 3:4; 29:27); say, 'Absalom is king in Hebron' (2 Sam. 15:10).

F4d Heshbon

A city of Gilead (Num. 32:3); built by Reuben (Num. 32:37); a city of Reuben (Josh. 13:17); city of Sihon (Num. 21:26, 27-8, 34; Deut. 1:4; 2:24; 3:2, 6; 4:46; 29:7; Josh. 9:10; 12:2; 13:10, 21, 27); your eyes are pools in Heshbon by the gate of Bath-rabbim (S. of S. 7:4); Heshbon is ruined (Num. 21:30); a fire has gone forth from Heshbon (Jer. 48:45).

F4e Hierapolis

Epaphras has worked hard for those in Laodicea and Hierapolis (Col. 4:13).

F4f Horonaim

On the road to Horonaim they raise a cry (Isa. 15:5; Jer. 48:5); a cry from Horonaim (Jer. 48:3); Sanballat the Horonite (Neh. 2:10, 19; 13:28).

F5 Iconium – Italy

F5a Iconium

They went to Iconium (Acts 13:51); they entered the synagogue in Iconium (Acts 14:1); Jews came from Antioch and Iconium (Acts 14:19); they returned to Lystra, Iconium and Antioch (Acts 14:21); Timothy was well spoken of by the brethren in Lystra and Iconium (Acts 16:2); my sufferings at Antioch, Iconium and Lystra (2 Tim. 3:11).

F5b Illyricum

From Jerusalem and as far round as Illyricum I have preached the gospel (Rom. 15:19).

F5c India

Ahasuerus ruled from India to Ethiopia (Esther 1:1); provinces from India to Cush (Esther 8:9).

F5d Issachar

Territory of Issachar (Josh. 19:17-23; Ezek. 48:25); 13 cities for the Gershonites from Issachar, Asher, Naphtali and half Manasseh (Josh. 21:6, 27-33); cities for Issachar (Josh. 19:23).

F5e Italy

A centurion of the Italian cohort (Acts 10:1); Aquila had come to Italy with his wife Priscilla (Acts 18:2); it was decided that we should set sail for Italy (Acts 27:1); a ship of Alexandria sailing for Italy (Acts 27:6); those from Italy greet you (Heb. 13:24).

G Place names beginning J – L

G1 Jabesh-gilead – Jericho

G1a Jabesh-gilead [Jabesh]

No one had come to Mizpah from there (Judg. 21:8-12); besieged by Nahash the Ammonite (1 Sam. 11:1; 1 Chr. 10:11-12); the inhabitants buried Saul's body (1 Sam. 31:11-13; 2 Sam. 2:4); Saul and his sons were buried in Jabesh (1 Sam. 31:12-13; 1 Chr. 10:12); David took the bones of Saul and Jonathan from the men of Jabesh-Gilead (2 Sam. 21:12).

G1b Jazer

Moses sent to spy out Jazer (Num. 21:32); a city of Gilead (Num. 32:3); the land of Jazer was suitable for livestock (Num. 32:1); a city of Gad (Josh. 13:25); I will weep for Jazer (Isa. 16:9); I weep for you more than for Jazer, O vine of Sibmah (Jer. 48:32); the branches reached as far as Jazer (Isa. 16:8).

G1c Jehovah-jireh

The Lord will provide (Gen. 22:14).

G1d Jericho

City of palm trees (Deut. 34:3; Judg. 3:13; 2 Chr. 28:15); a city of Benjamin (Josh. 18:21); spy out the land, especially Jericho (Josh. 2:1); the people crossed the Jordan at Jericho (Josh. 3:16); marching round Jericho (Josh. 6:1-15); the walls of Jericho fell down (Josh. 6:20; Heb. 11:30); cursed be he who builds Jericho (Josh. 6:26); Hiel rebuilt Jericho (1 Kgs. 16:34); do to Ai as you did to Jericho (Josh. 8:2); stay in Jericho until your beards have grown (2 Sam. 10:5; 1 Chr. 19:5); the sons of the prophets at Jericho (2 Kgs. 2:5, 15); Elisha was staying in Jericho (2 Kgs. 2:18); the Lord has sent me to Jericho (2 Kgs. 2:4); they came to Jericho (Mark 10:46; Luke 18:35); he was passing through Jericho (Luke 19:1); as they went out of Jericho (Matt. 20:29); a man was going down to Jericho when he fell among thieves (Luke 10:30).

G2 Jerusalem

G2a Jerusalem, the place

Jerusalem, that is, Jebus (1 Chr. 11:4); the border of Judah was at Jerusalem (Josh. 15:8); the border of Benjamin was at Jerusalem (Josh. 18:16); Jerusalem is built as a compact city (Ps. 122:3); this is Jerusalem, I have set her in the centre of the nations (Ezek. 5:5); you are lovely as Jerusalem (S. of S. 6:4); from Jerusalem and as far round as Illyricum I have preached the gospel (Rom. 15:19).

G2b God's city

Jerusalem which I have chosen (1 Kgs. 11:13, 32; 2 Kgs. 23:27); the city you have chosen (1 Kgs. 8:48); the Lord has chosen Zion (Ps. 132:13); Jerusalem, where I have chosen to put my name (1 Kgs. 11:36; 2 Chr. 6:6); in Jerusalem will I put my name (2 Kgs. 21:4, 7); glorious things are spoken of you, city of God (Ps. 87:3); the city of God (Ps. 46:4; 48:8); Jerusalem, the holy city (Isa. 52:1); the city of the great King (Ps. 48:2; Matt. 5:35); the God who lives in Jerusalem (Ezra 1:3; 7:15; Ps. 135:21); the holy habitation of the Most High (Ps. 46:4); the Lord will reign on Mount Zion and in Jerusalem (Isa. 24:23); the Lord roars from Zion and utters his voice from Jerusalem (Joel 3:16; Amos 1:2); the law will go forth from Zion, the word of the Lord from Jerusalem (Isa. 2:3; Mic. 4:2); his departure, to be accomplished at Jerusalem (Luke 9:31); the Lord will again comfort Zion and choose Jerusalem (Zech. 1:17); the Lord will put a shield around the inhabitants of Jerusalem (Zech. 12:8); we are witnesses to all he did in Jerusalem (Acts 10:39).

G2c Concern for Jerusalem

Pray for the peace of Jerusalem (Ps. 122:6); walk about Zion, count her towers, ramparts and palaces (Ps. 48:12-13); take no rest till he makes Jerusalem a praise in the earth (Isa. 62:7); for Zion's sake I will not keep quiet (Isa. 62:1); if I forget Jerusalem, may my right hand forget her skill (Ps. 137:5); if I do not set Jerusalem above my chief joy (Ps. 137:6); we wept when we remembered Zion (Ps. 137:1); Daniel had windows in his upper room towards Jerusalem (Dan. 6:10); Oh, that the salvation of Israel would come out of Zion! (Ps. 14:7; 53:6); may you see the prosperity of Jerusalem (Ps. 128:5); blow the trumpet in Zion (Joel 2:15); I am going to measure Jerusalem, its breadth and length (Zech. 2:2); a measuring line will be stretched over Jerusalem (Zech. 1:16).

G2d Worship in Jerusalem

Solomon stood before the ark in Jerusalem (1 Kgs. 3:15); Solomon built the house of the Lord in Jerusalem (1 Chr. 6:32); Cyrus was appointed to build a temple in Jerusalem (2 Chr. 36:23; Ezra 1:2); Zion, the city of our appointed feasts (Isa. 33:20); silence is praise for you in Zion (Ps. 65:1); in the midst of Jerusalem I fulfil my vows (Ps. 116:19); you say Jerusalem is where one should worship (John 4:20-1); the hour is coming when neither on this mountain nor in Jerusalem will you worship (John 4:21).

G2e Jerusalem and the gospel

Repentance is to be preached, beginning at Jerusalem (Luke 24:47); you will be witnesses in Jerusalem (Acts 1:8); as you have witnessed about me at Jerusalem, so you must at Rome (Acts 23:11); from Jerusalem and as far round as Illyricum I have preached the gospel (Rom. 15:19); I declared to those in Jerusalem and

throughout Judea (Acts 26:20); you have filled Jerusalem with your teaching (Acts 5:28); the number of disciples multiplied in Jerusalem (Acts 6:7); persecution arose against the church in Jerusalem (Acts 8:1); the harm he did to your saints in Jerusalem (Acts 9:13); is not this who in Jerusalem destroyed those who called on this name? (Acts 9:21); a contribution for the poor among the saints in Jerusalem (Rom. 15:26).

G2f Coming to Jerusalem

The devil took him to the holy city (Matt. 4:5; Luke 4:9); they brought him to Jerusalem (Luke 2:22); Saul wanted to bring believers bound to Jerusalem (Acts 9:2; 22:5); requesting as a favour that Paul might be brought to Jerusalem (Acts 25:3); are you willing to go to Jerusalem to be tried on these charges? (Acts 25:9); I asked whether he was willing to go to Jerusalem to trial (Acts 25:20); they will ask the way to Zion (Jer. 50:5); he must go to Jerusalem and suffer many things (Matt. 16:21); I will send those you approve with letters to Jerusalem (1 Cor. 16:3); I did not go up to Jerusalem (Gal. 1:17).

G2g Living in Jerusalem

Jebusites in Jerusalem (Josh. 15:63; Judg. 1:21); this one and that one were born in Zion (Ps. 87:5); the sons born to David in Jerusalem (2 Sam. 5:14); Ariel, the city where David encamped (Isa. 29:1); Uriah remained in Jerusalem (2 Sam. 11:12); Herod was in Jerusalem at that time (Luke 23:7); Jerusalem will be inhabited in its place (Zech. 12:6); boys and girls playing in the streets of the city (Zech. 8:5); old men and women will again sit in the streets of Jerusalem (Zech. 8:4); the inhabitants of Jerusalem have strength through the Lord (Zech. 12:5); a fountain opened for the inhabitants of Jerusalem (Zech. 13:1); he charged them not to depart from Jerusalem but to wait (Acts 1:4).

G2h The sin of Jerusalem

Jerusalem, killing the prophets (Matt. 23:37; Luke 13:34); it cannot be that a prophet perishes away from Jerusalem (Luke 13:33); the present Jerusalem is in slavery with her children (Gal. 4:25); Samaria is Oholah and Jerusalem is Oholibah (Ezek. 23:4); set your face towards Jerusalem and speak against the sanctuaries (Ezek. 21:2); what is the high place of Judah but Jerusalem? (Mic. 1:5); you build Zion with bloodshed and Jerusalem with wrong (Mic. 3:10); Jerusalem has stumbled, Judah has fallen (Isa. 3:8); Jerusalem's splendour descends into Sheol (Isa. 5:14); Jerusalem and her idols (Isa. 10:10-11).

G2i The judgement of Jerusalem

The Lord will take away from Judah and Jerusalem support and staff (Isa. 3:1); will you judge the bloody city? (Ezek. 22:2); sinners in Zion are afraid (Isa. 33:14); woe to those who are at ease in Zion (Amos 6:1); when the Lord has purged the bloodshed of Jerusalem (Isa. 4:4); the Lord has a year of recompense for the cause of Zion (Isa. 34:8); he will be a snare and a trap to the inhabitants of Jerusalem (Isa. 8:14); to make Jerusalem a horror, a hissing and a curse (Jer. 25:18); the angel was about to destroy Jerusalem (2 Sam. 24:16; 1 Chr. 21:15); I will reject Jerusalem (2 Kgs. 23:27); Jerusalem will become a heap of ruins (Jer. 9:11; Mic. 3:12); Zion will be ploughed as a field (Jer. 26:18; Mic. 3:12).

G2j Jerusalem attacked

David went up to attack Jerusalem (1 Chr. 11:4); Hazael set his face to go up to Jerusalem (2 Kgs. 12:17); Shishak came as far as Jerusalem (2 Chr. 12:4, 9); Nebuchadnezzar came to Jerusalem (2 Kgs. 25:8); Assyria besieging Jerusalem (2 Kgs. 18:17); take a brick and draw on it Jerusalem under siege (Ezek. 4:1-2); the Babylonians besieged Jerusalem (2 Kgs. 24:10, 11; 25:1; Ezek. 24:2; Dan. 1:1); Nebuchadnezzar and his armies were fighting Jerusalem (Jer. 34:1); cast up a siege against Jerusalem (Jer. 6:6); when you see Jerusalem surrounded by armies (Luke 21:20); when Jerusalem is besieged, so will Judah be (Zech. 12:2); I will gather all nations against Jerusalem to battle (Zech. 14:2).

G2k Jerusalem taken

Judah captured Jerusalem (Judg. 1:8); the king of Babylon will fight against this city and take it (Jer. 34:22); each will set his throne at the entrance of the gates of Jerusalem (Jer. 1:15); I will send fire on Judah which will destroy the strongholds of Jerusalem (Amos 2:5); when foreigners entered his gates and cast lots for Jerusalem (Obad. 11); the walls of Jerusalem were broken down (2 Kgs. 14:13; 2 Chr. 36:19; Neh. 1:3); the exile of Jerusalem (Jer. 1:3); Zion has become a wilderness (Isa. 64:10); Jerusalem will be trampled by the Gentiles (Luke 21:24).

G2l God saving Jerusalem

Do good to Zion (Ps. 51:18); you will have compassion on Zion (Ps. 102:13); the Lord will comfort Zion (Isa. 51:3); God will save Zion (Ps. 69:35); I create Jerusalem a rejoicing (Isa. 65:18); I am laying in Zion a precious cornerstone (Isa. 28:16); a redeemer will come to Zion (Isa. 59:20); I have installed my king on Zion, my holy mountain (Ps. 2:6); the Lord has redeemed Jerusalem (Isa. 52:9); they will call you the city of the Lord, Zion of the Holy One of Israel (Isa. 60:14); Jerusalem will be called the throne of the Lord (Jer. 3:17); the Lord will reign in Jerusalem (Isa. 24:23); when I restore the fortunes of Judah and Jerusalem (Joel 3:1); Zion will be redeemed with justice (Isa. 1:27); the Lord will again choose Jerusalem (Zech. 2:12); Anna spoke of Jesus to all who were looking for the redemption of Jerusalem (Luke 2:38).

G2m Jerusalem revitalised

The redeemed of the Lord will return with singing to Zion (Isa. 35:10; 51:11); Jerusalem will be called the city of Truth (Zech. 8:3); Jerusalem will be inhabited for ever (Jer. 17:25; Joel 3:20); Jerusalem will be holy, with no more strangers passing through (Joel 3:17); on Mount Zion and in Jerusalem there will be those who escape (Joel 2:32); he who is left in Zion will be called holy (Isa. 4:3); [this city] will be a name of joy, praise and glory (Jer. 33:9); bearer of good news to Zion, to Jerusalem (Isa. 40:9); I give to Jerusalem a herald of good news (Isa. 41:27); speak tenderly to Jerusalem (Isa. 40:2); Jerusalem will be inhabited like villages without walls (Zech. 2:4); Jerusalem will be inhabited and dwell in security (Zech. 14:11); living water will flow from Jerusalem (Zech. 14:8).

G2n New Jerusalem

Heavenly Jerusalem (Heb. 12:22); the Jerusalem above is free (Gal. 4:26); new Jerusalem, coming down out of heaven from God (Rev. 3:12; 21:2, 10); they surrounded the camp of the saints and the beloved city (Rev. 20:9); God will take away his share in the holy city (Rev. 22:19).

G3 Jezreel – Judah

G3a Jezreel

A city of Judah (Josh. 15:56); a city of Issachar (Josh. 19:18); David married Ahinoam of Jezreel (1 Sam. 25:43); the Philistines went up to Jezreel (1 Sam. 29:11); Abner made Ish-bosheth king over Jezreel (2 Sam. 2:9); Ahab rode to Jezreel (1 Kgs. 18:45); Elijah outran Ahab to Jezreel (1 Kgs. 18:46); Naboth the Jezreelite had a vineyard in Jezreel (1 Kgs. 21:1); dogs will eat Jezebel in Jezreel (1 Kgs. 21:23; 2 Kgs. 9:10, 36); Joram was convalescing in Jezreel (2 Kgs. 8:29; 9:15; 2 Chr. 22:6); Ahaziah visited Joram in Jezreel (2 Chr. 22:6); Jehu went to Jezreel (2 Kgs. 9:16, 30); Jehu wrote to the rulers of Jezreel (2 Kgs. 10:1); I will break the bow of

Israel in the valley of Jezreel (Hos. 1:5); I will punish the house of Jehu for the bloodshed of Jezreel (Hos. 1:4); great will be the day of Jezreel (Hos. 1:11).

G3b Joppa

Timber transported to Joppa (2 Chr. 2:16; Ezra 3:7); Jonah went down to Joppa (Jonah 1:3); in Joppa there was a disciple named Tabitha (Acts 9:36); it became known all over Joppa (Acts 9:42); I was in the city of Joppa praying (Acts 11:5); send to Joppa (Acts 10:5, 32; 11:13); some of the brethren from Joppa accompanied him (Acts 10:23).

G3c Joseph

Territory of Joseph (Josh. 16:1-4); Benjamin lay between Judah and Joseph (Josh. 18:11).

G3d Judah [Judea]

Territory of Judah (Josh. 15:1-12; Ezek. 48:7); cities for Judah (Josh. 15:21-62; Neh. 11:25-30); God will build the cities of Judah (Ps. 69:35); Judah is my sceptre (Ps. 60:7; 108:8); say to the cities of Judah, 'Behold, your God!' (Isa. 40:9); Herod king of Judea (Luke 1:5); Pontius Pilate governor of Judea (Luke 3:1); the church was scattered throughout Judea and Samaria (Acts 8:1); throughout all Judea, starting at Galilee (Acts 10:37); the disciples sent relief to the brethren living in Judea (Acts 11:29); the church throughout Judea, Galilee and Samaria had peace (Acts 9:31); let those in Judea flee to the mountains (Matt. 24:16; Mark 13:14; Luke 21:21); that I may be delivered from the disobedient in Judea (Rom. 15:31); I was unknown by sight to the churches in Judea (Gal. 1:22); the churches in Christ Jesus in Judea (1 Thess. 2:14); Naomi returned to the land of Judah (Ruth 1:7); Mary went to the hill country to a city of Judah (Luke 1:39); teaching throughout Judea, from Galilee as far as here (Luke 23:5); you will be witnesses in all Judea (Acts 1:8); I wanted you to send me on my way to Judea (2 Cor. 1:16).

G4 Kadesh-barnea – Kiriath-jearim

G4a Kadesh-barnea [Kadesh] [Kedesh]

Chedorlaomer came to En-mishpat, Kadesh (Gen. 14:7); we came to Kadesh (Deut. 1:19); when Israel came to Kadesh (Judg. 11:16); they stayed at Kadesh (Judg. 11:17); you remained there many days (Deut. 1:46); sent out from Kadesh-barnea to spy (Num. 32:8; Josh. 14:7); the word Moses spoke in Kadesh-barnea (Josh. 14:6); Kedesh, a city of Judah (Josh. 15:23).

G4b Kerioth

Judgement has come on Kerioth and Bozrah (Jer. 48:24); Kerioth has been captured (Jer. 48:41); I will send fire on Moab which will consume the strongholds of Kerioth (Amos 2:2); Judas Iscariot (Matt. 10:4; 26:14; Mark 3:19; 14:10; Luke 6:16; 22:3; John 12:4); Judas Iscariot, son of Simon (John 13:2); Simon Iscariot, father of Judas (John 6:71; 13:26).

G4c Kibroth-hattaavah

Graves of greed (Num. 11:34-5); in Sinai (Num. 33:16, 17); where they provoked the Lord (Deut. 9:22).

G4d Kir [Kir-heres] [Kir-hareseth]

The people of Damascus were taken away to Kir (2 Kgs. 16:9); Kir uncovered the shield (Isa. 22:6); Kir of Moab is ruined in a night (Isa. 15:1); they left the stones of Kir-hareseth (2 Kgs. 3:25); mourn for the raisin-cakes of Kir-hareseth (Isa. 16:7); my heart moans for Kir-hareseth (Isa. 16:11); I will mourn for the men of Kir-heres (Jer. 48:31, 36).

G4e Kiriath-jearim [Baalah] [Baale-judah] etc.

A city of the Gibeonites (Josh. 9:17); a city of Judah (Josh. 15:60; 18:14, 15); Baalah, that is Kiriath-jearim (1 Chr. 13:6); a city of Benjamin (Josh. 18:28); the ark came to Kiriath-jearim (1 Sam. 7:1-2); they went to Baalah, to Kiriath-jearim, to bring up the ark (1 Chr. 13:5, 6); David went to Baale-judah to bring up the ark

(2 Sam. 6:2); we found it in the field of Jaar (Ps. 132:6); David has brought up the ark from Kiriath-jearim (2 Chr. 1:4); Ira the Ithrite (2 Sam. 23:38; 1 Chr. 11:40); Gareb the Ithrite (2 Sam. 23:38; 1 Chr. 11:40); Uriah son of Shemaiah from Kiriath-jearim prophesied (Jer. 26:20).

G5 Lachish – Laodicea

G5a Lachish
Joshua fought Lachish (Josh. 10:31); a city of Judah (Josh. 15:39); Lachish and Azekah remained as fortified cities (Jer. 34:7); Amaziah fled to Lachish, where he was killed (2 Kgs. 14:19; 2 Chr. 25:27); Sennacherib was besieging Lachish (2 Chr. 32:9); Hezekiah sent word to the king of Assyria at Lachish (2 Kgs. 18:14); Rabshakeh was sent from Lachish to Jerusalem (2 Kgs. 18:17; Isa. 36:2); Rehoboam built Lachish (2 Chr. 11:9); harness the horses to the chariots, inhabitants of Lachish (Mic. 1:13).

G5b Laodicea
I struggle for you, and for those at Laodicea (Col. 2:1); Epaphras has worked hard for those in Laodicea and Hierapolis (Col. 4:13); greet the brethren in Laodicea (Col. 4:15); have this letter read in the church of the Laodiceans (Col. 4:16); read the letter from Laodicea (Col. 4:16); the church in Laodicea (Rev. 1:11; 3:14).

G6 Lebanon

G6a Lebanon, the place
Let me see the good hill country and the Lebanon (Deut. 3:25); all Lebanon (Josh. 13:5); streams flowing from Lebanon (S. of S. 4:15); forced labourers sent to Lebanon (1 Kgs. 5:14); Solomon built in Lebanon (1 Kgs. 9:19; 2 Chr. 8:6); he makes Lebanon skip like a calf (Ps. 29:6); does the snow of Lebanon leave the rocks of the country? (Jer. 18:14).

G6b The glory of Lebanon
The glory of Lebanon will come to you (Isa. 60:13); the glory of Lebanon will be given to it (Isa. 35:2); his appearance is like Lebanon (S. of S. 5:15); the fragrance of your garments is like Lebanon (S. of S. 4:11); may his fruit be like Lebanon (Ps. 72:16); their remembrance will be like the wine of Lebanon (Hos. 14:7); you are like the summit of Lebanon (Jer. 22:6); the bloom of Lebanon withers (Nahum 1:4).

G6c Trees of Lebanon
Lebanon would not be sufficient for fuel (Isa. 40:16); cedars of Lebanon (Judg. 9:15; 1 Kgs. 4:33; 5:6; Ps. 29:5); timber brought from Lebanon to the sea (1 Kgs. 5:9; Ezra 3:7); timber from Lebanon (2 Chr. 2:8, 14); the house of the forest of Lebanon (1 Kgs. 7:2; 10:17, 21); the cypresses and the cedars of Lebanon rejoice over you (Isa. 14:8); the thorn bush in Lebanon said to the cedar in Lebanon (2 Kgs. 14:9; 2 Chr. 25:18); a great eagle came to Lebanon and removed the top of a cedar (Ezek. 17:3); a cedar of Lebanon was taken for your mast (Ezek. 27:5); open your doors, Lebanon, that the fire may devour your cedars (Zech. 11:1).

G7 Lehi – Lystra

G7a Lehi [Ramath-lehi]
The Philistines camped at Lehi (Judg. 15:9); the Philistines gathered at Lehi (2 Sam. 23:11); the place was named (Judg. 15:17); God split the hollow place at Lehi (Judg. 15:19).

G7b Libya [Pul?]
Survivors sent to Pul [Libya?] (Isa. 66:19); Ethiopia, Put, Lud, Arabia and Libya will fall by the sword (Ezek. 30:5); residents of Egypt and the parts of Libya around Cyrene (Acts 2:10).

G7c Lycaonia
They fled to Lystra and Derbe, cities of Lycaonia (Acts 14:6).

G7d Lycia
We landed at Myra in Lycia (Acts 27:5).

G7e Lydda [Lod]
Shemed built Lod (1 Chr. 8:12); Benjamin lived in Lod (Neh. 11:35); Peter came to the saints in Lydda (Acts 9:32); all who lived at Lydda and Sharon saw him and turned to the Lord (Acts 9:35); Lydda was near Joppa (Acts 9:38).

G7f Lystra
They fled to Lystra and Derbe, cities of Lycaonia (Acts 14:6); at Lystra there was a man who could not use his feet (Acts 14:8); they returned to Lystra, Iconium and Antioch (Acts 14:21); Paul came to Derbe and Lystra (Acts 16:1); Timothy was well spoken of by the brethren in Lystra and Iconium (Acts 16:2); my sufferings at Antioch, Iconium and Lystra (2 Tim. 3:11).

H Place names beginning M – O

H1 Macedonia – Massah

H1a Macedonia
Come over to Macedonia and help us (Acts 16:9); we sought to go into Macedonia (Acts 16:10); Paul determined to pass through Macedonia and Achaia (Acts 19:21); he sent Timothy and Erastus into Macedonia (Acts 19:22); Paul set off for Macedonia (Acts 20:1); Paul decided to return through Macedonia (Acts 20:3); Macedonia and Achaia made a contribution to the poor saints (Rom. 15:26); I went on to Macedonia (2 Cor. 2:13); when we came into Macedonia (2 Cor. 7:5); the grace of God in the churches of Macedonia (2 Cor. 8:1); I boast about you to the Macedonians (2 Cor. 9:2); lest Macedonians come with me and find you unprepared (2 Cor. 9:4); when the brethren came from Macedonia they fully supplied my needs (2 Cor. 11:9); you became an example to all the believers in Macedonia and Achaia (1 Thess. 1:7-8); you love all the brethren throughout Macedonia (1 Thess. 4:10); Macedonians: Silas and Timothy (Acts 18:5); Gaius and Aristarchus (Acts 19:29); Aristarchus (Acts 27:2).

H1b Machpelah
Opposite Mamre (Gen. 23:17, 19; 25:9; 49:30; 50:13); the cave of Machpelah (Gen. 23:9).

H1c Magdala [Magadan]
He came to the district of Dalmanutha [Magadan?] (Mark 8:10); he went to the region of Magadan (Matt. 15:39); Mary Magdalene (Matt. 27:56, 61; 28:1; Mark 15:40, 47; 16:1, 9; Luke 8:2; 24:10; John 20:1, 18).

H1d Makkedah
Five kings hid in a cave (Josh. 10:16, 17); Joshua returned to camp there (Josh. 10:21); captured by Joshua (Josh. 10:28); a city of Judah (Josh. 15:41).

H1e Manasseh
Territory of Manasseh (Josh. 17:7-10; Ezek. 48:4); Manasseh is mine (Ps. 60:7; 108:8); Jephthah passed through Gilead and Manasseh (Judg. 11:29); cities for Manasseh (Josh. 17:11-12).

H1f Massah
He called that place Massah (Exod. 17:7); where they tested the Lord (Deut. 6:16); where they provoked the Lord (Deut. 9:22); as at Massah in the wilderness (Ps. 95:8).

H2 Media – Miletus

H2a Media
The officers of Persia and Media (Esther 1:3); lay siege, Media (Isa. 21:2); the ram with two horns represents the kings of Media and Persia (Dan. 8:20); Parthians and Medes and Elamites (Acts 2:9).

H2b Megiddo
A city of Manasseh (Josh. 17:11); the Manassites did not take possession (Judg. 1:27); Solomon rebuilt Megiddo (1 Kgs. 9:15); Ahaziah fled to Megiddo (2 Kgs. 9:27);

Josiah made war in the plain of Megiddo (2 Chr. 35:22); Josiah was killed at Megiddo (2 Kgs. 23:29, 30).

H2c Memphis [Noph]
The men of Noph and Tahpanhes will graze on your scalp (Jer. 2:16); the Jews living in Egypt, in Migdol, Tahpanhes, Memphis, Pathros (Jer. 44:1); proclaim in Migdol, Memphis and Tahpanhes (Jer. 46:14); the princes of Memphis are deluded (Isa. 19:13); Memphis will become a desolation (Jer. 46:19); I will put an end to the images in Memphis (Ezek. 30:13).

H2d Meribah
He called that place Meribah (Exod. 16:7); do not harden your hearts as at Meribah (Ps. 95:8); they provoked him to anger at the waters of Meribah (Ps. 106:32).

H2e Mesopotamia [Asshur]
Ships from Kittim will attack Asshur and Heber (Num. 24:24); Cushan-rishathaim king of Mesopotamia (Judg. 3:8, 10); the Ammonites hired mercenaries from Mesopotamia (1 Chr. 19:6); the servant went to Mesopotamia, to the city of Nahor (Gen. 24:10); residents of Mesopotamia, Judea and Cappadocia (Acts 2:9); when Abraham was in Mesopotamia, before he lived in Haran (Acts 7:2).

H2f Midian
Moses dwelt in the land of Midian (Exod. 2:15); God spoke to Moses in Midian (Exod. 4:19); Moses became an alien in the land of Midian (Acts 7:29).

H2g The Millo
David built from the tower of Millo (2 Sam. 5:9); Solomon built the Millo (1 Kgs. 9:15, 24; 11:27); Joash was killed at the house of Millo (2 Kgs. 12:20); Hezekiah strengthened the Millo in the city of David (2 Chr. 32:5).

H2h Miletus
The day after we came to Miletus (Acts 20:15); from Miletus he sent to Ephesus (Acts 20:17); Trophimus I left ill at Miletus (2 Tim. 4:20).

H3 Mitylene – Mysia
H3a Mitylene
We took Paul on board and came to Mitylene (Acts 20:14).

H3b Mizpah of Benjamin
A city of Benjamin (Josh. 18:26); a city of Judah (Josh. 15:38); the congregation assembled to the Lord there (Judg. 20:1, 3; 21:5, 8); Israel had sworn in Mizpah (Judg. 21:1); the Israelites had gathered at Mizpah (1 Sam. 7:7); Samuel called the people together at Mizpah (1 Sam. 10:17); Samuel went on circuit to Mizpah (1 Sam. 7:16); Asa built up Mizpah (1 Kgs. 15:22; 2 Chr. 16:6); they came to Gedaliah at Mizpah (2 Kgs. 25:23, 25; Jer. 40:12, 13); Jeremiah went to Mizpah and stayed with Gedaliah (Jer. 40:6); they came to Jeremiah at Mizpah (Jer. 40:8); Ishmael came to Mizpah (Jer. 41:1); you have been a snare at Mizpah, a net on Tabor (Hos. 5:1).

H3c Mizpah of Gilead [Mizpeh] [Galeed] [Jegar-sahadutha]
A watchtower, a heap for witness (Gen. 31:47, 49); Israel camped in Mizpah (Judg. 10:17); Jephthah's house at Mizpah (Judg. 11:34); Jephthah passed through Mizpah of Gilead (Judg. 11:29); Ramath-mizpeh, a city of Gad (Josh. 13:26).

H3d Moab
Across the Jordan in the land of Moab (Deut. 1:5); Moab is my washbowl (Ps. 60:8; 108:9); the covenant the Lord made with them in the land of Moab (Deut. 29:1); Mt Nebo in the land of Moab (Deut. 32:49); Moses died in the land of Moab (Deut. 34:5); Israel did not take the land of Moab (Judg. 11:15); Elimelech went

to sojourn in Moab (Ruth 1:1, 2); they returned from the land of Moab (Ruth 1:22; 2:6; 4:3).

H3e Moreh
The oak of Moreh (Gen. 12:6; Deut. 11:30).

H3f Moriah
Take your son Isaac to the land of Moriah (Gen. 22:2).

H3g Myra
We landed at Myra in Lycia (Acts 27:5).

H3h Mysia
When they came to Mysia they tried to go into Bithynia (Acts 16:7); passing by Mysia they came down to Troas (Acts 16:8).

H4 Nain – Nob
H4a Nain
He went to a city called Nain (Luke 7:11).

H4b Naphtali
Territory of Naphtali (Josh. 19:32-9; Ezek. 48:3); in former times he treated the land of Naphtali with contempt (Isa. 9:1); cities for Naphtali (Josh. 19:35-8, 39); he dwelt in Capernaum in the region of Zebulun and Naphtali (Matt. 4:13-15).

H4c Nazareth
Can any good thing come out of Nazareth? (John 1:46); the sect of the Nazarenes (Acts 24:5); Gabriel was sent to Nazareth in Galilee (Luke 1:26); Joseph went up from Nazareth of Galilee (Luke 2:4); Joseph settled in Nazareth (Matt. 2:23); they returned to Galilee, to their own city, Nazareth (Luke 2:39); they returned to Nazareth (Luke 2:51); Jesus came from Nazareth in Galilee (Mark 1:9); this is the prophet Jesus, from Nazareth of Galilee (Matt. 21:11); he came to Nazareth where he had been brought up (Luke 4:16); Jesus of Nazareth (Matt. 26:71; Mark 1:24; 10:47; Luke 4:34; 18:37; 24:19; John 1:45; 18:5, 7; 19:19; Acts 2:22; 10:38; 26:9); Jesus the Nazarene (Acts 22:8); Jesus left Nazareth and settled in Capernaum (Matt. 4:13); you also were with the Nazarene, Jesus (Mark 14:67); you seek Jesus of Nazareth who was crucified (Mark 16:6); Jesus Christ of Nazareth (Acts 4:10); in the name of Jesus Christ of Nazareth (Acts 3:6).

H4d Neapolis
On the next day to Neapolis (Acts 16:11).

H4e Negeb
Abraham travelled on toward the Negeb (Gen. 12:9; 20:1); Isaac was living in the Negeb (Gen. 24:62); Amalek is living in the Negeb (Num. 13:29); Moses saw the Negeb (Deut. 34:3); since you have given me the Negeb (Josh. 15:19; Judg. 1:15); the Negeb of Judah (1 Sam. 27:10); the Negeb of the Jerahmeelites (1 Sam. 27:10); the oracle of the beasts of the Negeb (Isa. 30:6); they will come from the Negeb (Jer. 17:26); prophesy against the forest land of the Negeb (Ezek. 20:46); the exiles of Israel will possess the cities of the Negeb (Obad. 20).

H4f Nicopolis
Do your best to come to me at Nicopolis (Titus 3:12).

H4g Nineveh
Nimrod built Nineveh, Rehoboth-Ir, Calah (Gen. 10:11); go to Nineveh, that great city (Jonah 1:2; 3:2); Nineveh was a very great city (Jonah 3:3); the oracle of Nineveh (Nahum 1:1); Nineveh was like a pool of water (Nahum 2:8); Nineveh is devastated (Nahum 3:7); should I not have compassion on Nineveh? (Jonah 4:11); yet forty days and Nineveh will be overthrown (Jonah 3:4); Jonah was a sign to Nineveh (Luke 11:30); the men of Nineveh will condemn this generation (Matt. 12:41; Luke 11:32).

H4h Nob
David came to Nob to Ahimelech the priest (1 Sam. 21:1; 22:9); the priests in Nob (1 Sam. 22:11); Nob, the city of the priests, was struck (1 Sam. 22:19).

H5 Ophel – Ophrah
H5a The Ophel
Jotham built the wall of the Ophel (2 Chr. 27:3);
Manasseh put a wall round the Ophel (2 Chr. 33:14);
the Nethinim living in Ophel (Neh. 3:26; 11:21).

H5b Ophir [Uphaz?]
Gold of Ophir (Job 22:24; 28:16); 420 talents of gold
were brought from Ophir (1 Kgs. 9:28); 450 talents of
gold were brought from Ophir (2 Chr. 8:18); gold
brought from Ophir (2 Chr. 9:10); gold, timber and
precious stones were brought from Ophir (1 Kgs. 10:11);
Jehoshaphat made ships to bring gold from Ophir (1
Kgs. 22:48); I will make mankind scarcer than the gold
of Ophir (Isa. 13:12); at your right hand stands the
queen in gold of Ophir (Ps. 45:9); a man girded with
gold of Uphaz [Ophir?] (Dan. 10:5).

H5c Ophrah of Benjamin [Baal-hazor] [Ephraim]
A city of Benjamin (Josh. 18:23); raiders went towards
Ophrah (1 Sam. 13:17); Baal-hazor, near Ephraim
(2 Sam. 13:23).

H5d Ophrah of Manasseh
The oak at Ophrah (Judg. 6:11); Ophrah of the
Abiezrites (Judg. 6:24); Gideon placed the ephod in
Ophrah (Judg. 8:27); Gideon was buried there (Judg.
8:32).

I Place names beginning P – R
I1 Paddan-aram – Perga
I1a Paddan-aram [Paddan]
Jacob was sent to Paddan-aram (Gen. 28:2, 6-7); Jacob
left there (Gen. 31:18; 33:18; 35:9); when I came from
Paddan (Gen. 48:7).

I1b Pamphylia
Residents of Phrygia and Pamphylia (Acts 2:10); they
set out from Paphos and came to Perga in Pamphylia
(Acts 13:13); they passed through Pisidia and came to
Pamphylia (Acts 14:24); John Mark had deserted them
in Pamphylia (Acts 15:38); we sailed along by Cilia and
Pamphylia (Acts 27:5).

I1c Paphos
They went through the island as far as Paphos (Acts
13:6); they set out from Paphos and came to Perga in
Pamphylia (Acts 13:13).

I1d Parthia
Parthians and Medes and Elamites (Acts 2:9).

I1e Patara
The next day to Rhodes and from there to Patara (Acts
21:1).

I1f Peniel [Penuel]
Named by Jacob (Gen. 32:30, 31); Gideon was refused
food there (Judg. 8:8); tearing down the tower of
Penuel (Judg. 8:9, 17); Jeroboam built Penuel (1 Kgs.
12:25).

I1g Perez-uzzah
Called that to this day (2 Sam. 6:8; 1 Chr. 13:11).

I1h Perga
They set out from Paphos and came to Perga in
Pamphylia (Acts 13:13); going on from Perga they came
to Antioch of Pisidia (Acts 13:14); when they had
spoken the word in Perga (Acts 14:25).

I2 Pergamum – Phoenix
I2a Pergamum
The church in Pergamum (Rev. 1:11); letter to the
church in Pergamum (Rev. 2:12-17).

I2b Persia
The officers of Persia and Media (Esther 1:3);
Artaxerxes king of Persia (Ezra 7:1); I will return to
fight against the prince of Persia (Dan. 10:20); in the
third year of Cyrus king of Persia (Dan. 10:1); the
prince of the kingdom of Persia withstood me (Dan.
10:13); the ram with two horns represents the kings of

Media and Persia (Dan. 8:20); three more kings will
arise in Persia (Dan. 11:2).

I2c Philadelphia
The church in Philadelphia (Rev. 1:11); letter to the
church in Philadelphia (Rev. 3:7-13).

I2d Philippi
Philippi, a leading city of the district of Macedonia
(Acts 16:12); we sailed from Philippi (Acts 20:6); to the
saints in Christ Jesus who are in Philippi (Phil. 1:1); we
had suffered and been mistreated in Philippi (1 Thess.
2:2).

I2e Philistia
I mention Philistia and Tyre with Ethiopia (Ps. 87:4);
over Philistia I shout (Ps. 108:9).

I2f Phoenicia
They made their way to Phoenicia and Cyprus and
Antioch (Acts 11:19); they passed through Phoenicia
and Samaria (Acts 15:3); we found a ship crossing to
Phoenicia and went aboard (Acts 21:2).

I2g Phoenix
Trying to reach Phoenix, a harbour of Crete (Acts
27:12).

I3 Phrygia – Puteoli
I3a Phrygia
Residents of Phrygia and Pamphylia (Acts 2:10); they
went through the region of Phrygia and Galatia (Acts
16:6); Paul went through Galatia and Phrygia,
strengthening the disciples (Acts 18:23).

I3b Pisidia
Going on from Perga they came to Antioch of Pisidia
(Acts 13:14); they passed through Pisidia and came to
Pamphylia (Acts 14:24).

I3c Pontus
Residents of Pontus and Asia (Acts 2:9); Aquila was a
native of Pontus (Acts 18:2); to those scattered
throughout Pontus, Galatia, Cappadocia, Asia and
Bithynia (1 Pet. 1:1).

I3d Ptolemais
At the end of the voyage from Tyre we arrived at
Ptolemais (Acts 21:7).

I3e Puteoli
On the second day we arrived at Puteoli (Acts 28:13).

I4 Rabbah – Reuben
I4a Rabbah of Ammon
Of the Ammonites (Deut. 3:11; 2 Sam. 17:27; Jer. 49:2);
taken by Joab and David (2 Sam. 12:26-9); Joab
besieged Rabbah (2 Sam. 11:1; 1 Chr. 20:1); cry out,
daughters of Rabbah (Jer. 49:3); I will make Rabbah a
pasture for camels (Ezek. 25:5); I will kindle a fire on
the wall of Rabbah (Amos 1:14).

I4b Ramah of Benjamin
We will spend the night in Gibeah or Ramah (Judg.
19:13); Baasha fortified Ramah (1 Kgs. 15:17; 2 Chr. 16:1);
Baasha stopped fortifying Ramah (1 Kgs. 15:21; 2 Chr.
16:5); they carried away the stones and timber of
Ramah (1 Kgs. 15:22; 2 Chr. 16:6).

I4c Ramah of Samuel [Ramathaim-zophim]
Home of Elkanah (1 Sam. 1:1, 19; 2:11); home of Samuel
(1 Sam. 7:17); David fled to Samuel at Ramah (1 Sam.
19:18); Saul came to Ramah (1 Sam. 19:22); Samuel was
buried in his house at Ramah (1 Sam. 25:1; 28:3); in
Ramah Rachel weeping for her children (Jer. 31:15;
Matt. 2:18); Joseph of Arimathea (Matt. 27:57; Mark
15:43; John 19:38); Joseph, a man from the Jewish town
of Arimathea (Luke 23:51).

I4d Rameses [Raamses]
Joseph settled them in Rameses (Gen. 47:11); storage
city built in Egypt by the Israelites (Exod. 1:11);
camping in Rameses (Num. 33:3); from Rameses to
Succoth (Exod. 12:37; Num. 33:5).

I4e Ramoth-gilead [Ramoth] [Ramah]

A city of refuge within Gad (Josh. 20:8); Ramoth-gilead belongs to us (1 Kgs. 22:3); will you go up with me to battle at Ramoth-gilead? (1 Kgs. 22:4; 2 Chr. 18:2-3); shall I go up against Ramoth-gilead? (1 Kgs. 22:6, 15; 2 Chr. 18:5, 14); who will entice Ahab to go up and fall at Ramoth-gilead? (1 Kgs. 22:20); Joram was wounded in Ramah (2 Chr. 22:6); Joram was defending Ramoth-gilead against Hazael (2 Kgs. 9:14).

I4f Reuben

Territory of Reuben (Josh. 13:15-23; Ezek. 48:6).

I5 Rhegium – Rome
I5a Rhegium

We made a circuit and arrived at Rhegium (Acts 28:13).

I5b Rhodes

The men of Rhodes traded with you (Ezek. 27:15); the next day to Rhodes and from there to Patara (Acts 21:1).

I5c Riblah

Riblah in the land of Hamath (2 Kgs. 23:33; 25:21; Jer. 39:5; 52:9, 27); Zedekiah was brought before the king of Babylon at Riblah (2 Kgs. 25:6); the chief people were brought before the king of Babylon at Riblah (2 Kgs. 25:20; Jer. 52:26); the princes of Judah were killed in Riblah (Jer. 52:10).

I5d Rogelim

Barzillai the Gileadite from Rogelim (2 Sam. 17:27; 19:31).

I5e Rome

Visitors from Rome, both Jews and proselytes (Acts 2:10); Claudius had commanded all the Jews to leave Rome (Acts 18:2); after I have been there I must see Rome (Acts 19:21); as you have witnessed about me at Jerusalem, so you must go to Rome (Acts 23:11); so we came to Rome (Acts 28:14-16); when he was in Rome he searched for me (2 Tim. 1:17); to all those beloved of God in Rome (Rom. 1:7); I am eager to preach the gospel to you also who are in Rome (Rom. 1:15); she who is in Babylon [Rome?] sends greetings (1 Pet. 5:13).

J   Place names beginning S
J1 Salamis – Salmone
J1a Salamis

When they reached Salamis they preached in the synagogues (Acts 13:5).

J1b Salim

John was baptising at Aenon near Salim (John 3:23).

J1c Salmone

We sailed under the lee of Crete off Salmone (Acts 27:7).

J2 Samaria
J2a Samaria, the place

Purchase of the hill of Samaria from Shemer (1 Kgs. 16:24); my father made streets in Samaria (1 Kgs. 20:34); food will be cheap in the gate of Samaria (2 Kgs. 7:1, 18); the head of Ephraim is Samaria (Isa. 7:9).

J2b People in Samaria

The head of Samaria is the son of Remaliah (Isa. 7:9); Elisha brought the army to Samaria (2 Kgs. 6:19, 20); Jehoshaphat went to visit Ahab in Samaria (2 Chr. 18:2); Jehu went to Samaria (2 Kgs. 10:12, 17); aliens resettled in Samaria (2 Kgs. 17:24; Ezra 4:10); Jesus had to pass through Samaria (John 4:4); you will be witnesses to me in Samaria (Acts 1:8); the church was scattered throughout Judea and Samaria (Acts 8:1); Philip preached Christ in the city of Samaria (Acts 8:5); they passed through Phoenicia and Samaria (Acts 15:3); the apostles in Jerusalem heard Samaria had received the word (Acts 8:14); the church throughout Judea, Galilee and Samaria had peace (Acts 9:31).

J2c The sin of Samaria

Samaria and her idols (Isa. 10:10-11); he has rejected your calf, Samaria (Hos. 8:5); the calf of Samaria will be broken to pieces (Hos. 8:6); Ahab built a house for Baal in Samaria (1 Kgs. 16:32); the prophets of Samaria prophesied by Baal (Jer. 23:13); the Asherah remained in Samaria (2 Kgs. 13:6); have these gods delivered Samaria? (2 Kgs. 18:34; Isa. 36:19); Samaria is Oholah and Jerusalem is Oholibah (Ezek. 23:4); the cup of your sister Samaria (Ezek. 23:33); those who swear by the shame of Samaria (Amos 8:14); the wicked deeds of Samaria are revealed (Hos. 7:1); what is the transgression of Jacob but Samaria? (Mic. 1:5).

J2d Samaria under attack

The famine was severe in Samaria (1 Kgs. 18:2); Samaria was besieged (1 Kgs. 20:1); the dust of Samaria will not suffice for my people (1 Kgs. 20:10); the spoil of Damascus and Samaria will be carried away to Assyria (Isa. 8:4); I will make Samaria a heap of ruins (Mic. 1:6).

J3 Samothrace – Sepharvaim
J3a Samothrace

We made a straight voyage to Samothrace (Acts 16:11).

J3b Sardis [Sepharad]

The church in Sardis (Rev. 1:11); letter to the church in Sardis (Rev. 3:1-6); the exiles from Jerusalem who are in Sepharad (Obad. 20).

J3c Seba

May the kings of Seba bring gifts (Ps. 72:10); I gave Egypt as your ransom, Cush and Seba in your place (Isa. 43:3).

J3d Sela

Sela was renamed Joktheel (2 Kgs. 14:7); let the inhabitants of Sela sing (Isa. 42:11).

J3e Seleucia

They went down to Seleucia (Acts 13:4).

J3f Sepharvaim

Men from Sepharvaim were brought to Samaria (2 Kgs. 17:24); the Sepharvites burned their children (2 Kgs. 17:31); Adrammelech and Anammelech, the gods of Sepharvaim (2 Kgs. 17:31); where are the gods of Sepharvaim? (2 Kgs. 18:34; Isa. 36:19).

J4 Sharon – Shunem
J4a Sharon

Gad lived in the pasture lands of Sharon (1 Chr. 5:16); Sharon shall be a pasture land for flocks (Isa. 65:10); I am the rose [crocus] of Sharon (S. of S. 2:1); the majesty of Carmel and Sharon (Isa. 35:2); Sharon is like a desert (Isa. 33:9); all who lived at Lydda and Sharon saw Aeneas and turned to the Lord (Acts 9:35).

J4b Sheba of Arabia

Caravans of Tema and Sheba (Job 6:19); the queen of Sheba visited Solomon (1 Kgs. 10:1; 2 Chr. 9:1); may gold of Sheba be given him (Ps. 72:15); may the kings of Sheba bring gifts (Ps. 72:10); those from Sheba will come bringing gold and frankincense (Isa. 60:6); traders of Sheba (Ezek. 27:22-3).

J4c Shechem

A city of refuge in the hill country of Ephraim (Josh. 20:7); Abraham came there (Gen. 12:6); the tomb Abraham purchased in Shechem (Acts 7:16); Jacob came safely there (Gen. 33:18); Jacob bought Shechem (Josh. 24:32); the oak near Shechem (Gen. 35:4); Joseph went there (Gen. 37:14); Joseph's bones were buried there (Josh. 24:32); Shechem belonged to Joseph (1 Chr. 7:28); Joshua made a covenant with the people there (Josh. 24:25); the men of Shechem made Abimelech king (Judg. 9:6); let fire consume the men of Shechem and Beth-millo (Judg. 9:20); the men of Shechem dealt treacherously with Abimelech (Judg. 9:23); Abimelech razed Shechem and sowed it with salt (Judg. 9:45);

destruction of the tower of Shechem (Judg. 9:46-9); Rehoboam went to Shechem to be made king (1 Kgs. 12:1; 2 Chr. 10:1); Jeroboam built Shechem (1 Kgs. 12:25); I will portion out Shechem (Ps. 60:6; 108:7).

J4d Shiloh
Shiloh on the north of Bethel (Judg. 21:19); the camp at Shiloh (Judg. 21:12); Israel gathered at Shiloh (Josh. 22:12); the prophet Ahijah the Shilonite (1 Kgs. 11:29; 12:15; 15:29; 2 Chr. 9:29; 10:15); Ahijah the prophet is in Shiloh (1 Kgs. 14:2); Jeroboam's wife went to Shiloh (1 Kgs. 14:4); the tent of meeting was set up there (Josh. 18:1); the house of God was at Shiloh (Judg. 18:31); go to Shiloh, where I made my name dwell at first (Jer. 7:12); he abandoned the tent at Shiloh (Ps. 78:60); I will make this house like Shiloh (Jer. 26:6, 9); Elkanah sacrificed there annually (1 Sam. 1:3); the priests ministering at Shiloh (1 Sam. 2:14); the house of Eli in Shiloh (1 Kgs. 2:27); the Lord appeared again in Shiloh (1 Sam. 3:21); the ark taken from Shiloh (1 Sam. 4:3-4).

J4e Shinar
A plain in the land of Shinar (Gen. 11:2); a beautiful robe from Shinar (Josh. 7:21); he brought the vessels to the land of Shinar (Dan. 1:2); to build a house for her in the land of Shinar (Zech. 5:11).

J4f Shunem
A city of Issachar (Josh. 19:18); Abishag the Shunammite (1 Kgs. 1:3, 15; 2:17, 21, 22); call this Shunammite (2 Kgs. 4:11); come back, O Shulammite [?] (S. of S. 6:13).

J5 Sidon – Smyrna
J5a Sidon
Great Sidon, on the border of Asher (Josh. 19:28); they served the gods of Sidon (Judg. 10:6); the Sidonians brought cedar to David (1 Chr. 22:4); merchants of Sidon (Isa. 23:2); be ashamed, Sidon (Isa. 23:4); oracle concerning Sidon (Ezek. 28:21-4); Tyre and Sidon, though they are very wise (Zech. 9:2); if the miracles had been done in Tyre and Sidon (Matt. 11:21; Luke 10:13); more bearable in the judgement for Tyre and Sidon (Matt. 11:22; Luke 10:14); Jesus withdrew to the district of Tyre and Sidon (Matt. 15:21; Mark 7:24); people from Tyre and Sidon came to Jesus (Mark 3:8); he went through Sidon to the Sea of Galilee (Mark 7:31); Zarephath in the land of Sidon (Luke 4:26); people from the seacoast of Tyre and Sidon (Luke 6:17); Herod was angry with the people of Tyre and Sidon (Acts 12:20);
the next day we put in at Sidon (Acts 27:3).

J5b Siloam
18 people on whom the tower of Siloam fell and killed them (Luke 13:4); the pool of Siloam (John 9:7, 11).

J5c Simeon
Territory of Simeon (Josh. 19:1-9; Ezek. 48:24); Simeon was in the middle of Judah (Josh. 19:1, 9); cities for Simeon (Josh. 19:2-8).

J5d Smyrna
The church in Smyrna (Rev. 1:11); letter to the church in Smyrna (Rev. 2:8-11).

J6 Sodom
J6a Sodom, the place
The boundary of the Canaanites went by Sodom, Gomorrah, Admah, Zeboiim, as far as Lasha (Gen. 10:19); they took all the food of Sodom and Gomorrah (Gen. 14:11); the men looked down toward Sodom (Gen. 18:16); Abraham looked down toward Sodom and Gomorrah (Gen. 19:28); the men went toward Sodom (Gen. 18:22); the two angels came to Sodom (Gen. 19:1); the great city spiritually called Sodom and Egypt (Rev. 11:8).

J6b The people of Sodom
The kings of Sodom, Gomorrah, Admah, Zeboiim and Bela, that is, Zoar (Gen. 14:2, 8); Lot settled in the cities of the valley, near Sodom (Gen. 13:12); when Lot went out of Sodom (Luke 17:29); if I find 50 righteous people in Sodom (Gen. 18:26).

J6c The sin of Sodom
The men of Sodom were extremely wicked (Gen. 13:13); the outcry of Sodom and Gomorrah is great and their sin heavy (Gen. 18:20); Sodom and Gomorrah and the cities round them committed immorality (Jude 7); my people's sin is greater than that of Sodom (Lam. 4:6); they display their sin like Sodom (Isa. 3:9); hear the word of the Lord, rulers of Sodom! (Isa. 1:10).

J6d The destruction of Sodom
The Lord rained fire and brimstone on Sodom and Gomorrah (Gen. 19:24); we would have been like Sodom and Gomorrah (Isa. 1:9; Rom. 9:29); if God condemned Sodom and Gomorrah (2 Pet. 2:6); more tolerable for the land of Sodom and Gomorrah than for that town (Matt. 10:15); it will be more tolerable for Sodom (Matt. 11:24; Luke 10:12).

J7 Succoth – Syrtis
J7a Succoth of Gad
Gideon asked for food there (Judg. 8:5); Gideon captured a youth from Succoth (Judg. 8:14); Gideon taught the elders of Succoth with thorns (Judg. 8:16); the valley of Succoth (Ps. 60:6; 108:7).

J7b Susa
Susa the capital (Esther 1:2, 5; 2:3; 3:15; 8:14; 9:6, 11, 12); assemble into Susa (Esther 4:16); the Jews in Susa (Esther 9:13, 15, 18); an edict issued in Susa (Esther 9:14); the city of Susa rejoiced (Esther 8:15); Susa, which is in the province of Elam (Dan. 8:2).

J7c Sychar
He came to a city of Samaria called Sychar (John 4:5).

J7d Syracuse
We stayed for three days in Syracuse (Acts 28:12).

J7e Syria
The report of him spread throughout Syria (Matt. 4:24); when Quirinius was governor of Syria (Luke 2:2); Paul set sail for Syria (Acts 18:18); Paul was about to set sail to Syria (Acts 20:3); leaving Cyprus on the left we sailed to Syria and landed at Tyre (Acts 21:3); to the Gentile brethren in Antioch, Syria and Cilicia (Acts 15:23); Paul and Silas went through Syria and Cilicia (Acts 15:41); I went into the regions of Syria and Cilicia (Gal. 1:21).

J7f Syrtis
Fearing that they might run aground on the Syrtis (Acts 27:17).

K Place names beginning T – Z
K1 Tarshish – Timnah
K1a Tarshish [Spain]
The ships of Tarshish (1 Kgs. 10:22); Solomon's ships went to Tarshish (2 Chr. 9:21); Jehoshaphat made ships to go to Tarshish (1 Kgs. 22:48; 2 Chr. 20:36); you broke the ships of Tarshish (Ps. 48:7); a day against all the ships of Tarshish (Isa. 2:16); wail, ships of Tarshish! (Isa. 23:1, 14); the ships of Tarshish bring your sons from afar (Isa. 60:9); beaten silver is brought from Tarshish (Jer. 10:9); may the kings of Tarshish bring tribute (Ps. 72:10); Tarshish traded with you (Ezek. 27:12); ships of Tarshish carried your merchandise (Ezek. 27:25); the merchants of Tarshish (Ezek. 38:13); Jonah boarded a ship bound for Tarshish (Jonah 1:3); this is why I made haste to flee to Tarshish (Jonah 4:2); I will go on by way of you to Spain (Rom. 15:28); I hope to see you in passing as I go to Spain (Rom. 15:24).

K1b Tarsus

A man from Tarsus named Saul (Acts 9:11); they brought him down to Caesarea and sent him away to Tarsus (Acts 9:30); Barnabas went to Tarsus to look for Saul (Acts 11:25); I am a Jew of Tarsus in Cilicia (Acts 21:39); I am a Jew, born in Tarsus of Cilicia (Acts 22:3).

K1c Tekoa

The wise woman of Tekoa (2 Sam. 14:2); blow a trumpet in Tekoa (Jer. 6:1); Rehoboam built Tekoa (2 Chr. 11:6); Amos, a shepherd from Tekoa (Amos 1:1).

K1d Thessalonica

They came to Thessalonica (Acts 17:1); the Jews of Thessalonica came to Berea (Acts 17:13); Aristarchus and Secundus of the Thessalonians (Acts 20:4); Aristarchus, a Macedonian of Thessalonica (Acts 27:2); even in Thessalonica you sent me help (Phil. 4:16); to the church of the Thessalonians (1 Thess. 1:1; 2 Thess. 1:1); Demas has gone to Thessalonica (2 Tim. 4:10).

K1e Thyatira

Lydia was from the city of Thyatira (Acts 16:14); the church in Thyatira (Rev. 1:11); letter to the church in Thyatira (Rev. 2:18).

K1f Tiberias

Boats from Tiberias came near (John 6:23).

K1g Timnah of Judah

A city of Judah (Josh. 15:57); a city of Dan (Josh. 19:43); Samson went down to Timnah (Judg. 14:1, 5); Samson, son-in-law of the Timnite (Judg. 15:6); the Philistines had captured Timnah (2 Chr. 28:18).

K2 Tirzah – Troas

K2a Tirzah

Jeroboam's wife came to Tirzah (1 Kgs. 14:17); Baasha became king in Tirzah (1 Kgs. 15:33); Elah became king in Tirzah (1 Kgs. 16:8); Zimri reigned in Tirzah (1 Kgs. 16:15); Omri reigned six years in Tirzah (1 Kgs. 16:23); Baasha was buried in Tirzah (1 Kgs. 16:6); Elah was at Tirzah, drinking himself drunk (1 Kgs. 16:9); Omri besieged Tirzah (1 Kgs. 16:17); Menahem went up from Tirzah (2 Kgs. 15:14).

K2b Topheth

Topheth in the valley of the son of Hinnom (2 Kgs. 23:10; Jer. 7:31); Topheth has long been prepared (Isa. 30:33); they will bury in Topheth for lack of room elsewhere (Jer. 7:32; 19:11); I will make this city like Topheth (Jer. 19:12); the houses will be defiled like Topheth (Jer. 19:13); Jeremiah came from Topheth where he had prophesied (Jer. 19:14); it will no more be called Topheth (Jer. 7:32).

K2c Trachonitis

Philip was tetrarch of Ituraea and Trachonitis (Luke 3:1).

K2d Troas

Passing by Mysia they came down to Troas (Acts 16:8); setting sail from Troas (Acts 16:11); they had gone on ahead and were waiting for us at Troas (Acts 20:5); in five days we came to them at Troas (Acts 20:6); when I came to Troas (2 Cor. 2:12); bring the cloak I left at Troas with Carpus (2 Tim. 4:13).

K3 Tyre

K3a Tyre, the place

I mention Philistia and Tyre with Ethiopia (Ps. 87:4); oracles concerning Tyre (Isa. 23:1-18; Ezek. 26:19); Tyre will be a place for spreading nets in the midst of the sea (Ezek. 26:5); Tyre will be forgotten for 70 years (Isa. 23:15); the Lord will visit Tyre (Isa. 23:17); Tyre who dwells at the entrance to the sea (Ezek. 27:3); Nebuchadnezzar's army laboured hard against Tyre (Ezek. 29:18); they will destroy the walls of Tyre (Ezek. 26:4); I will send fire on the wall of Tyre (Amos 1:10); Jesus withdrew to the district of Tyre and Sidon (Matt. 15:21); he went to the region of Tyre and Sidon (Mark

7:24); he left the region of Tyre (Mark 7:31); leaving Cyprus on the left we sailed to Syria and landed at Tyre (Acts 21:3); at the end of the voyage from Tyre we arrived at Ptolemais (Acts 21:7).

K3b The people of Tyre

Hiram was the son of a man of Tyre (1 Kgs. 7:13-14; 2 Chr. 2:14); Tyre's merchants were princes (Isa. 23:8); men of Tyre sold fish on the sabbath (Neh. 13:16); the Tyrians brought cedar (1 Chr. 22:4; Ezra 3:7); for three transgressions of Tyre (Amos 1:9-10); judgement on Tyre (Ezek. 26:2-21); take up a lamentation over Tyre (Ezek. 27:2); the prince of Tyre said he was a god (Ezek. 28:2); Tyre built herself a fortress and piled up silver like dust (Zech. 9:3); if the miracles had been done in Tyre and Sidon they would have repented (Matt. 11:21; Luke 10:13); more bearable in the judgement for Tyre and Sidon (Matt. 11:22; Luke 10:14); the daughter of Tyre will come with a gift (Ps. 45:12); people from Tyre and Sidon came to Jesus (Mark 3:8); people from the seacoast of Tyre and Sidon (Luke 6:17); Herod was angry with the people of Tyre and Sidon (Acts 12:20).

K4 Ur – Ziklag

K4a Ur

Ur of the Chaldeans (Gen. 11:28, 31; 15:7; Neh. 9:7).

K4b Zarephath

A widow of Zarephath fed Elijah (1 Kgs. 17:9-10); Zarephath in the land of Sidon (Luke 4:26).

K4c Zeboiim

The boundary of the Canaanites went by Sodom, Gomorrah, Admah, Zeboiim, as far as Lasha (Gen. 10:19); the kings of Sodom, Gomorrah, Admah, Zeboiim and Bela, that is, Zoar (Gen. 14:2, 8); like the overthrow of Sodom, Gomorrah, Admah and Zeboiim (Deut. 29:23); how can I treat you like Zeboiim? (Hos. 11:8).

K4d Zebulun

Zebulun (Josh. 19:10-16; Ezek. 48:26); in former times he treated the land of Zebulun with contempt (Isa. 9:1); cities for Zebulun (Josh. 19:16); he dwelt in Capernaum in the region of Zebulun and Naphtali (Matt. 4:13-15).

K4e Ziklag

A city of Judah (Josh. 15:31); a city of Simeon (Josh. 19:5); Achish gave it to David (1 Sam. 27:6); Ziklag was burned (1 Sam. 30:1, 4, 14); David remained in Ziklag for two days (2 Sam. 1:1); David returned to Ziklag (1 Chr. 12:20); David killed the Amalekite in Ziklag (2 Sam. 4:10).

K5 Zion [City of David]

K5a Zion, the place

David took the fortress and called it the city of David (2 Sam. 5:6-9; 1 Chr. 11:7); the city of David, which is Zion (1 Kgs. 8:1); David built houses in the city of David (1 Chr. 15:1); Manasseh built the outer wall of the city of David (2 Chr. 33:14); the steps of the city of David (Neh. 3:15; 12:37).

K5b God and Zion

The Lord loves the gates of Zion (Ps. 87:2); the Lord has founded Zion (Isa. 14:32); Mount Zion, the city of our God (Ps. 48:1-3); the Lord dwells in Zion (Ps. 9:11; Joel 3:21); the Lord is great in Zion (Ps. 99:2); the God of gods will be seen in Zion (Ps. 84:7); is the Lord not in Zion? (Jer. 8:19); God shines from Zion, the perfection of beauty (Ps. 50:2); let us go up to Zion to the Lord our God (Jer. 31:6); blessed be the Lord from Zion (Ps. 135:21); the Lord bless you from Zion (Ps. 128:5; 134:3); may he support you from Zion (Ps. 20:2); Zion, the city of our appointed feasts (Isa. 33:20); that men may declare the name of the Lord in Zion (Ps. 102:21); the Deliverer will come from Zion (Rom. 11:26); I am laying in Zion a cornerstone chosen and previous (1 Pet. 2:6).

K5c The people of Zion

This one and that one were born in Zion (Ps. 87:5); fear not, daughter of Zion (John 12:15); my people, who dwell in Zion (Isa. 10:24); I will stir your sons, Zion, against your sons, Greece (Zech. 9:13); O people in Zion who dwell in Jerusalem (Isa. 30:19); awake, O Zion (Isa. 52:1); the cry of the daughter of Zion gasping for breath (Jer. 4:31); I will cut off the daughter of Zion (Jer. 6:2); as soon as Zion was in labour she brought forth (Isa. 66:8); Zion heard this and was glad (Ps. 97:8); do not be afraid, O Zion (Zeph. 3:16); shout for joy, daughter of Zion, daughter of Jerusalem (Zeph. 3:14); say to the daughter of Zion (Matt. 21:5).

K5d Entering Zion

David did not take the ark into the city of David (1 Chr. 13:13); the ark came into the city of David (1 Chr. 15:29); the ark was brought out of the city of David, Zion (2 Chr. 5:2); Solomon brought Pharaoh's daughter into the city of David (1 Kgs. 3:1).

K6 Ziph – Zoar

K6a Ziph

A city of Judah (Josh. 15:24, 55); the wilderness of Ziph (1 Sam. 23:14, 15; 26:2); the Ziphites told Saul where David was (1 Sam. 23:19; 26:1; Ps. 54:t); they went to Ziph looking for David (1 Sam. 23:24); Rehoboam built Ziph (2 Chr. 11:8).

K6b Zoan

Hebron was built seven years before Zoan (Num. 13:22); he wrought wonders in the field of Zoan (Ps. 78:12, 43); the princes of Zoan are fools (Isa. 19:11, 13); I will set fire to Zoan (Ezek. 30:14).

K6c Zoar [Bela]

The kings of Sodom, Gomorrah, Admah, Zeboiim and Bela, that is, Zoar (Gen. 14:2, 8); like Eden, as you go to Zoar (Gen. 13:10); Zoar, a little town (Gen. 19:20, 22); Lot was afraid to live in Zoar (Gen. 19:30); Moses saw as far as Zoar (Deut. 34:3); his fugitives flee to Zoar (Isa. 15:5).

185 Place

REGION, see 184.

186 Situation

STATE, see 7.

187 Location

A Where from?

Where do you come from? what is your country? (Jonah 1:8); from what city are you? (2 Sam. 15:2); where have you been, Gehazi? (2 Kgs. 5:25); where have these men come from? (2 Kgs. 20:14; Isa. 39:3); no one knows where Christ comes from (John 7:27); I know where I have come from and where I am going (John 8:14); we know where this man comes from (John 7:27); you know me and where I am from? (John 7:28); we do not know where this man is from (John 9:29-30); where does wisdom come from? (Job 28:20); where did this man get this wisdom and these miraculous powers? (Matt. 13:54); where did this man get all this? (Matt. 13:56); where did this man get these things? (Mark 6:2); the wind blows where it wills and you do not know where it comes from or where it goes to (John 3:8).

B Where at?

B1 Where is God?

Where is the Lord? (Jer. 2:6, 8); where is the Lord, the God of Elijah? (2 Kgs. 2:14); where is your God? (Ps. 42:3, 10); where is their God? (Ps. 79:10; 115:2; Joel 2:17); where is the Lord your God? (Mic. 7:10); where is God my Maker? (Job 35:10); where is the God of justice? (Mal. 2:17); where is your Father? (John 8:19).

NO GOD, see 2A.

B2 Where are people?

Where are you? (Gen. 3:9); where is your brother Abel? (Gen. 4:9); where is the prostitute? (Gen. 38:21); where are they feeding the flock? (Gen. 37:16); where were you when I laid the foundation of the earth? (Job 38:4); woman, where are they? (John 8:10); where is he who has been born king of the Jews? (Matt. 2:2); the Jews were looking for him, saying, 'Where is he?' (John 7:11); tell me where you have laid him and I will take him away (John 20:15).

C Where to?

No one asks me, 'Where are you going?' (John 16:5); the wind blows where it wills and you do not know where it comes from or where it goes to (John 3:8); where does this man intend to go that we will not find him? (John 7:35); we do not know where you are going (John 14:5); where has your beloved gone? (S. of S. 6:1).

D There

See the place where they laid him (Mark 16:6); they will not say, 'Here it is!' or 'There it is!' (Luke 17:21); they will say, 'Look, there!' or 'Look, here!' (Luke 17:23); if anyone says, 'Here is the Christ' (Mark 13:21); where the corpse is, there the eagles will gather (Matt. 24:28); where your treasure is, there will your heart be also (Matt. 6:21).

188 Displacement

A Exile possible

You and your king will come to a nation they have not known (Deut. 28:36); you will be torn from the land (Deut. 28:63); I will uproot you from my land (2 Chr. 7:20); the Lord will uproot Israel and scatter them beyond the Euphrates (1 Kgs. 14:15); I will cut off Israel from the land (1 Kgs. 9:7); till I take you away to a land like your own (2 Kgs. 18:32; Isa. 36:17); the Chaldeans may kill us or exile us to Babylon (Jer. 43:3).

B Exile in prospect

Prepare baggage for exile (Ezek. 12:3, 4); you will go into exile beyond Damascus (Amos 5:27); they will be the first to go into exile (Amos 6:7); Israel will go into exile (Amos 7:11, 17); Judah will go into exile (Mic. 1:16); Judah will be carried into exile in Babylon (Jer. 20:4-6); you will go to Babylon (Jer. 34:3; Mic. 4:10); I will bring him to Babylon (Ezek. 17:20); I will remove you beyond Babylon (Acts 7:43); I will hurl you into another country where you were not born (Jer. 22:26-8); the one who goes into exile will never return (Jer. 22:10).

C Peoples exiled

C1 Various people exiled

Those far away in the lands where you have driven them (Dan. 9:7); Gaza carried into exile a whole people (Amos 1:6); the king of Aram took captives to Damascus (2 Chr. 28:5); Benjaminites going into exile (1 Chr. 8:6, 7); my people go into exile for lack of knowledge (Isa. 5:13).

C2 Exile of Israel to Assyria

Tiglath-pileser took captive to Assyria part of Israel (2 Kgs. 15:29); Tiglath-pileser took the two and a half tribes into exile (1 Chr. 5:26); Israel carried into exile to Assyria (2 Kgs. 17:6, 23; 18:11).

C3 Exile of Judah to Babylon

Judah carried into exile (2 Kgs. 24:14; 25:11, 21; 1 Chr. 9:1; 2 Chr. 36:20; Ezra 2:1; Jer. 13:19; 39:9; 40:1; 52:15, 27; Lam. 1:3); Nebuchadnezzar deported the people to Babylon (Ezra 5:12; Neh. 7:6); the exile of Jerusalem (Jer. 1:3); the deportation to Babylon (Matt. 1:11, 12, 17).

C4 Kings exiled

Manasseh was taken to Babylon (2 Chr. 33:11); Jehoiakim was taken taken to Babylon (2 Chr. 36:6);

Jehoiachin / Jeconiah was taken to Babylon (2 Chr. 36:10; Jer. 24:1; 27:20); Jehoiachin was led into exile with his mother, wives and officials (2 Kgs. 24:15); Zedekiah taken to Babylon (Jer. 32:5; 51:59; 52:11); the king and princes of Jerusalem were taken to Babylon (Ezek. 17:12); Jehoahaz was removed to Egypt (2 Kgs. 23:34; 2 Chr. 36:4).

C5 Others exiled
Jehozadak the priest carried into exile (1 Chr. 6:15); you, Pashhur, will go into captivity (Jer. 20:6); the priests, prophets and people exiled to Babylon (Jer. 29:1); I have found one of the exiles from Judah who will make known the interpretation (Dan. 1:15); the exiles from Jerusalem who are in Sepharad (Obad. 20); the exiles of Israel in places as far as Zarephath (Obad. 20).

D Exiled foreigners
Egypt to prepare for exile (Jer. 46:19); Chemosh will go into exile with the priests and princes of Moab (Jer. 48:7); Milcom will go into exile (Jer. 49:3); the people of Aram will be exiled to Kir (Amos 1:5); the king of Ammon will go into exile (Amos 1:15); Damascus carried into exile into Assyria (2 Kgs. 16:9); aliens resettled in Samaria (2 Kgs. 17:24; Ezra 4:10); Esarhaddon king of Assyria brought us here (Ezra 4:2); Thebes went into exile (Nahum 3:10); there will be no nation to which the outcasts of Elam will not go (Jer. 49:36).

E Not exiled
Moab has not gone into exile (Jer. 48:11); I will not remove Israel from the land if they obey (2 Kgs. 21:8; 2 Chr. 33:8); he will exile you no longer (Lam. 4:22); he begged him not to send them out of the country (Mark 5:10).

F Homeless
Foxes have holes and birds nests, but Jesus had nowhere (Matt. 8:20; Luke 9:58); we apostles are homeless (1 Cor. 4:11); a true fast is to bring the homeless poor into your house (Isa. 58:7).

189 Presence

A God's presence

A1 God is here
God is here (Gen. 28:16); God is present everywhere (Ps. 139:7-9); God is in her palaces (Ps. 48:3); the name of the city will be The Lord Is There (Ezek. 48:35); Jonah fled from the presence of the Lord (Jonah 1:3); the sailors knew that he was fleeing from the presence of the Lord (Jonah 1:10); you make him joyful with your presence (Ps. 21:6); you make me joyful with your presence (Acts 2:28); in your presence is fullness of joy (Ps. 16:11); I am Gabriel who stand in the presence of God (Luke 1:19); the sons of God presented themselves before the Lord (Job 1:6; 2:1); they rebel against his glorious presence (Isa. 3:8); do not cast me away from your presence (Ps. 51:11); Christ appears in the presence of God for us (Heb. 9:24).

A2 The presence of Christ
He stood in their midst (Luke 24:36); we ate and drank in your presence (Luke 13:26); what I have forgiven is for your sake in the presence of Christ (2 Cor. 2:10); if you had been here my brother would not have died (John 11:21, 32); he who sits on the throne will presence himself with them (Rev. 7:15).

GOD WITH US, see 89A2.

DEATH DUE TO GOD S PRESENCE, see 361C1.

A3 Bread of the Presence
The bread of the Presence [showbread] (Exod. 25:30; 35:13; 39:36; Num. 4:7; 1 Sam. 21:4; 1 Kgs. 7:48; 1 Chr. 23:29; 2 Chr. 2:4; 4:19; 13:11; Neh. 10:33; Heb. 9:2); the bread prepared by the Kohathites (1 Chr. 9:32); the

bread eaten by David (1 Sam. 21:6; Matt. 12:4; Mark 2:26; Luke 6:4).

TABLE OF SHOWBREAD, see 218G.

B Men's presence

B1 In men's presence
Though absent in body, I am present in spirit (1 Cor. 5:3-4); I who am meek when face to face to you but bold when away (2 Cor. 10:1-2); 'his bodily presence is weak' (2 Cor. 10:10); what we say by letters when absent, we do when present (2 Cor. 10:11); that when present I may not have to be severe (2 Cor. 13:10); it is good to be sought, and not only when I am present with you (Gal. 4:18); I could wish to be present with you now (Gal. 4:20); not only as in my presence, but much more now in my absence (Phil. 2:12); do you not remember that while I was with you I told you these things? (2 Thess. 2:5); when we were with you we gave you this command (2 Thess. 3:10).

B2 Inhabited
The cities will be inhabited (Ezek. 36:10, 33); the ruined cities are fortified and inhabited (Ezek. 36:35); you will be inhabited as formerly (Ezek. 36:11); Judah and Jerusalem will be inhabited for ever (Joel 3:20); Jerusalem will be inhabited and dwell in security (Zech. 14:11).

190 Absence

A God absent

A1 God not anywhere
Where is your God? (Ps. 42:3, 10); where is their God? (Ps. 79:10; 115:2; Joel 2:17); where is the Lord your God? (Mic. 7:10); where is the Lord, God of Elijah? (2 Kgs. 2:14); where is God my Maker? (Job 35:10); where is the God of justice? (Mal. 2:17); where is your Father? (John 8:19).

NO GOD, see 2A.

A2 God not with them
God would not be in their midst (Exod. 33:3); I will be with you no more unless you destroy the cursed things (Josh. 7:12); the Lord is not with you (Num. 14:42-3; Deut. 1:42); the Lord is not with Israel (2 Chr. 25:7); is there no God in Israel? (2 Kgs. 1:3, 6, 16); is it not because God is not among us? (Deut. 31:17); you do not go out with our armies (Ps. 44:9; 60:10; 108:11); I go forward and backward but he is not there (Job 23:8); while we are at home in the body we are absent from the Lord (2 Cor. 5:6); the Lord had departed from Saul (1 Sam. 16.14, 18.12, 28.15, 16); exclusion from the presence of the Lord and the glory of his power (2 Thess. 1:9).

B Gods absent
Where are their gods? (Deut. 32:37); where are your gods? (Jer. 2:28).

C People absent

C1 Leaving God's presence
Cain went out from God's presence (Gen. 4:16); Satan went out from the Lord's presence (Job 1:12; 2:7).

C2 Gone away
None of the men of the household were in the house (Gen. 39:11); Thomas was not with them (John 20:24); my husband is not at home (Prov. 7:19); my beloved had gone (S. of S. 5:6); when they saw that Jesus was not there, nor his disciples (John 6:24); for your sake I am glad I was not there (John 11:15); though absent in body, I am present in spirit (1 Cor. 5:3); we prefer to be absent from the body and at home with the Lord (2 Cor. 5:8); I who am meek when face to face to you but bold when away (2 Cor. 10:1); not only as in my presence, but much more now in my absence (Phil. 2:12).

C3 Nowhere to be found

Joseph was not in the pit (Gen. 37:29-30); when he sees that the lad is not there he will die (Gen. 44:30-1); the prostitute could not be found (Gen. 38:20, 22, 23); Saul could not be found (1 Sam. 10:21); the prisoner was gone (1 Kgs. 20:40); Enoch was not found because God took him (Heb. 11:5).

C4 No one to be found

There was no one who had been numbered before (Num. 26:64); old men are gone from the gate (Lam. 5:14); the roads of Zion are in mourning because no one comes to the feasts (Lam. 1:4); my children have gone from me and are no more (Jer. 10:20).

C5 No one available

There was no man to till the ground (Gen. 2:5); there is no man to come in to us (Gen. 19:31); there was no one to interpret (Gen. 40:8; 41:8, 15, 24); there is not a man on earth who can do what the king demands (Dan. 2:10-11); God saw that there was no one to intercede (Isa. 59:16); why was there no one when I came? (Isa. 50:2); when I look, there is no one (Isa. 41:28); I searched for a man but found no one (Ezek. 22:30); my flock has become a prey for lack of a shepherd (Ezek. 34:8); there was no one to search or seek for them (Ezek. 34:6); no one was able to open the book or look into it (Rev. 5:3-4).

D Empty

D1 Empty by nature

The earth was formless and empty (Gen. 1:2); the Lord did not create the world to be uninhabited (Isa. 45:18).

D2 Land becoming empty

I will not drive them out in one year lest the land become desolate (Exod. 23:29); I will make the land desolate because they have acted unfaithfully (Ezek. 15:8); lest I make you an uninhabited land (Jer. 6:8); the king of Babylon will cut off man and beast from this land (Jer. 36:29); the earth will be desolate because of the fruit of their deeds (Mic. 7:13); the mountains of Israel will be desolate, no one passing through (Ezek. 33:28); your land will not be called 'Desolate' (Isa. 62:4).

D3 Cities becoming empty

Your cities will be without inhabitant (Jer. 4:7; 9:11; 34:22); Jerusalem will be without inhabitant (Jer. 26:9; 33:10); until cities are devastated and without inhabitant (Isa. 6:11); Babylon will not be inhabited (Isa. 13:20; Jer. 50:3, 13, 40; 51:29, 37); Babylon will never again be inhabited (Jer. 50:39); how deserted the city is! (Jer. 49:25); how lonely the city that was full of people (Lam. 1:1); the fortified city is empty (Isa. 27:10); the populous city is empty (Isa. 32:14); their cities are laid waste without an inhabitant (Zeph. 3:6); Ashkelon will not be inhabited (Zech. 9:5).

D4 Empty things

Do not send the ark back empty (1 Sam. 6:3); the ark was empty apart from the stone tablets (1 Kgs. 8:9; 2 Chr. 5:10); set the pot empty upon the coals (Ezek. 24:11); David's place would be empty (1 Sam. 20:18, 25, 27); the pit was empty (Gen. 37:24).

D5 Empty people

I went out full and the Lord has brought me back empty (Ruth 1:21); Nebuchadnezzar has set me down like an empty vessel (Jer. 51:34); the unclean spirit finds his house empty (Matt. 12:44).

191 Inhabitant

A Born in one's house

His trained men, born in his house (Gen. 14:14); one born in my house is my heir (Gen. 15:3); one born in your house must be circumcised (Gen. 17:12, 13).

B Roman citizens

Men who are Roman citizens (Acts 16:37-8); Paul was a Roman citizen (Acts 22:25-9; 23:27); a citizen of no mean city (Acts 21:39); I bought this citizenship for a large sum (Acts 22:28).

C Citizens of heaven

Fellow-citizens with the saints (Eph. 2:19); our citizenship is in heaven (Phil. 3:20).

192 Abode

A God dwelling

A1 God's dwelling

Will God really dwell on earth? (1 Kgs. 8:27; 2 Chr. 6:18); who can build a house for him? (2 Chr. 2:6); a sanctuary that I may live among them (Exod. 25:8); until I find a dwelling place for the Lord (Ps. 132:5); I love the place where your glory dwells (Ps. 26:8); how dear are your dwelling places! (Ps. 84:1); the mountain where God will live for ever (Ps. 68:16); my house will be called a house of prayer for all peoples (Isa. 56:7); God said he would dwell in thick cloud (1 Kgs. 8:12); in my Father's house are many dwelling-places (John 14:2); what kind of a house will you build for me? (Acts 7:49); Moses was faithful in all God's house (Heb. 3:2); Christ was faithful as a Son over his house (Heb. 3:6); a great high priest over the house of God (Heb. 10:21).

A2 Building a dwelling for God

David sought a dwelling for God (2 Sam. 7:2; 1 Chr. 17:1; Ps. 132:5; Acts 7:46); David was not the one to build (2 Sam. 7:5; 1 Chr. 17:4); this is the house of the great God (1 Chr. 22:1); Solomon built (2 Sam. 7:13; 1 Chr. 22:10; 2 Chr. 6:2; Acts 7:47); he will build me a house (1 Chr. 17:12); come to your resting place (2 Chr. 6:41; Ps. 132:8); the Most High does not live in houses made with hands (Acts 7:48); God does not live in shrines made with hands (Acts 17:24).

A3 Bethel, the house of God

This is none other than the house of God (Gen. 28:17); this stone will be the house of God (Gen. 28:22); Bethel, the house of God (Gen. 35:1, 15).

A4 The house of God at Shiloh

The tent of meeting set up at Shiloh (Josh. 18:1); the house of God was at Shiloh (Judg. 18:31); the house of the Lord in Shiloh (1 Sam. 1:24).

A5 God lives in Jerusalem

The Lord dwells in Jerusalem for ever (1 Chr. 23:25); the Lord dwells in Zion (Ps. 9:11; 76:2; Joel 3:17, 21; Zech. 8:3); the Lord has chosen Zion for his habitation (Ps. 132:13); the Lord who dwells in Jerusalem (Ps. 135:21).

A6 God lives with us

I will dwell among the children of Israel (Exod. 29:45, 46; Lev. 26:11; Num. 35:34; 1 Kgs. 6:13; Ezek. 37:27; 43:7, 9); I will live among you (Zech. 2:10); the camp where I live in their midst (Num. 5:3); I live in a high and holy place, also with him who is contrite (Isa. 57:15); the dwelling place of God is with men and he will live among them (Rev. 21:3); the Word became flesh and dwelt among us (John 1:14).

A7 We live with God

Blessed is the one you choose to dwell in your courts (Ps. 65:4); the upright will dwell in your presence (Ps. 140:13); I will dwell in the house of the Lord for ever (Ps. 23:6); I will dwell in the house of the Lord all the days of my life (Ps. 27:4); let me live in your tent for ever (Ps. 61:4); you have been our dwelling-place throughout all generations (Ps. 90:1); better one day in your courts than a thousand elsewhere (Ps. 84:10); planted in the house of the Lord (Ps. 92:13); he who dwells in the shelter of the Most High (Ps. 91:1); you have made the Most High your dwelling (Ps. 91:9);

Lord, who may dwell in your tent? (Ps. 15:1); in my Father's house are many dwelling-places (John 14:2).

A8 God lives in us

The Holy Spirit who lives within us (2 Tim. 1:14); you are being built into a dwelling of God by his Spirit (Eph. 2:22); that Christ may dwell in your hearts by faith (Eph. 3:17); Christ in you, the hope of glory (Col. 1:27); we are his house (Heb. 3:6); my Father and I will make our abode with him (John 14:23); the Spirit of God lives in you (1 Cor. 3:16).

B Man's dwelling

B1 Staying temporarily

We have straw, fodder and a place to lodge (Gen. 24:25); turn aside and lodge in my house (Gen. 19:2); stay with Laban for a few days (Gen. 27:44); Jesus lodged in Bethany (Matt. 21:17); today I must stay at your house (Luke 19:5); the Samaritans asked him to stay with them (John 4:40); stay with us for it is nearly evening (Luke 24:29); Lydia urged them to stay with her (Acts 16:15); prepare a guest room for me (Philem. 22); there was no room in the inn (Luke 2:7); the Samaritan brought him to an inn and took care of him (Luke 10:34); Rabbi, where are you staying? (John 1:38-9); they asked whether Simon called Peter was staying there (Acts 10:18); Simon Peter staying at the house of Simon the tanner (Acts 10:32).

B2 Sojourning

Abraham went down to Egypt to sojourn there (Gen. 12:10); Abraham sojourned in Gerar (Gen. 20:1); Abraham sojourned in the land of the Philistines (Gen. 21:34); Canaan, the land of your sojournings (Gen. 17:8; Exod. 6:4); show kindness to the land where you are sojourning (Gen. 21:23); I have been a sojourner in a foreign land (Exod. 2:22); Elimelech went to sojourn in Moab (Ruth 1:1).

B3 Living in the land

Dwell wherever you please in my land (Gen. 20:15); let them live in the land (Gen. 34:21-3); you will dwell in the land securely (Lev. 25:18-19; 26:5); your flock settled in the land (Ps. 68:10); go to Bethel and dwell there (Gen. 35:1); living in the land of Goshen (Gen. 45:10; 47:4); Israel lived in Egypt for 430 years (Exod. 12:40).

B4 Living in particular places

Those who love his name will dwell in Zion (Ps. 69:36); Lot was living in Sodom (Gen. 14:12); Abraham lived in Beersheba (Gen. 22:19); Isaac lived in Gerar (Gen. 26:6, 17); living in the tombs (Mark 5:3; Luke 8:27); a prophet is not without honour except in his home town and in his own house (Matt. 13:57); they will receive you into the eternal dwellings (Luke 16:9); Antipas was killed among you, where Satan dwells (Rev. 2:13); I know where you dwell, where Satan's throne is (Rev. 2:13).

C Shelters

C1 Tents

C1a Tents pitched

Abraham pitched his tent (Gen. 12:8); Lot moved his tents towards Sodom (Gen. 13:12); Jacob bought the land where he had pitched his tent (Gen. 33:19); Isaac pitched his tent in Beersheba (Gen. 26:25); Absalom had a tent pitched on the roof (2 Sam. 16:22); enlarge the place of your tent (Isa. 54:2).

C1b Living in tents

He made the tribes of Israel dwell in tents (Ps. 78:55); I will make you live in tents again (Hos. 12:9); David put Goliath's weapons in his tent (1 Sam. 17:54); than to dwell in the tents of wickedness (Ps. 84:10); sounds of deliverance in the tents of the righteous (Ps. 118:15); how lovely are your tents, Israel! (Num. 24:5); your tent will be secure (Job 5:24); in them he has set a tent for the sun (Ps. 19:4); you took up the tent of Moloch (Acts 7:43); the Word became flesh and tabernacled

among us (John 1:14); as long as I am in this tent (2 Pet. 1:13); if the earthly tent we live in is destroyed we have a building from God (2 Cor. 5:1).

C1c Inside tents

The law when someone dies in a tent (Num. 19:14); Noah was uncovered within his tent (Gen. 9:21); Sarah was in the tent (Gen. 18:9); Isaac took Rebekah into the tent (Gen. 24:67); Laban went into the tents of Jacob, Leah, the two maids and Rachel (Gen. 31:33); the ark in a tent (2 Sam. 6:17; 7:2, 6; 1 Chr. 15:1; 16:1; 17:1; 2 Chr. 1:4).

C2 Tent of meeting outside the camp

Moses pitched a tent outside the camp and called it the tent of meeting (Exod. 33:7); when Moses went out to the tent (Exod. 33:8).

C3 The tabernacle inside the camp

C3a Setting up the tabernacle / tent

Make a tent for the tabernacle (Exod. 26:7); a contribution for making the tent of meeting (Exod. 35:21); the Israelites shall camp around the tent of meeting (Num. 2:2); a tabernacle was pitched (Heb. 9:2); the tabernacle of the Lord was in the high place at Gibeon (1 Chr. 16:39; 21:29; 2 Chr. 1:3).

C3b Commissioning at the tabernacle / tent

Bring them to the doorway of the tent of meeting (Exod. 29:4, 10-11); present the Levites before the tent of meeting (Num. 8:9); commissioning Joshua at the tent of meeting (Deut. 31:14); carts for use in the service of the tent of meeting (Num. 7:5); he sprinkled the tent and the vessels with the blood (Heb. 9:21).

C3c Worship at the tabernacle / tent

When the priests enter the tent of meeting (Exod. 28:43; 29:30); the Levites serving in the tent of meeting (Num. 8:22); the musicians ministered in the tent of meeting until the temple was built (1 Chr. 6:32); two lambs daily offered at the door of the tent of meeting (Exod. 29:42); bring the blood to the tent of meeting (Lev. 4:5, 16); blood brought into the tent of meeting to make atonement (Lev. 6:30).

C3d God at the tabernacle / tent

The Lord spoke to Moses from the tent of meeting (Lev. 1:1; Num. 1:1); Moses entered the tent of meeting to speak with God (Num. 7:89); the glory of the Lord appeared in the tent of meeting (Num. 14:10); the cloud covered the tent of meeting (Num. 16:42); Christ entered through the greater and more perfect tent (Heb. 9:11).

C4 Camping

C4a Camping during the exodus

You know where to camp in the wilderness (Num. 10:31); God seeks out a place for you to camp (Deut. 1:33); the camp of Israel (Exod. 14:19, 20); at the Lord's command they camped (Num. 9:18, 20, 23); where the cloud settled they would camp (Num. 9:17).

C4b Other camping

This is God's camp (Gen. 32:2); the angel of the Lord camps round those who fear him (Ps. 34:7); David came to where Saul was camped (1 Sam. 26:5); in that place will be my camp (2 Kgs. 6:8); they surrounded the camp of the saints (Rev. 20:9).

C5 Booths

Jacob made booths for his animals (Gen. 33:17); the Israelites lived in booths when they came out of Egypt (Lev. 23:43); the Feast of Booths (Lev. 23:34, 39-43; Neh. 8:14-17); three booths for Jesus, Moses and Elijah (Matt. 17:4; Mark 9:5; Luke 9:33); Jonah made a booth for himself and sat in the shade (Jonah 4:5).

D Houses

D1 Building houses

By wisdom a house is built (Prov. 24:3); unless the Lord builds the house those who build it labour in vain (Ps.

127:1); woe to him who builds a big house without righteousness (Jer. 22:13-14); each of you is busy with his own house (Hag. 1:9); is it time for you to live in your panelled houses? (Hag. 1:4); the builder of the house has more honour than the house (Heb. 3:3); every house is built by someone (Heb. 3:4).

D2 Living in houses
Consecrating your house to the Lord (Lev. 27:14); the Lord blesses the abode of the righteous (Prov. 3:33); houses which you did not fill (Deut. 6:11); he who leaves houses for my name's sake (Matt. 19:29); those leaving houses for my sake (Mark 10:29); he will receive houses a hundredfold (Mark 10:30); no one has left house or wife for the sake of the kingdom (Luke 18:29); do you not have houses in which to eat and drink? (1 Cor. 11:22).

D3 Particular houses
As you enter the house, greet it (Matt. 10:12); a prophet is not without honour except in his home town and in his own house (Matt. 13:57); I will keep the passover at your house with my disciples (Matt. 26:18); they led him away to the high priest's house (Luke 22:54); he went to the house of Mary mother of John Mark (Acts 12:12).

D4 Royal houses
I, Nebuchadnezzar, was at ease in my house (Dan. 4:4); David lived in his house (2 Sam. 7:1); a house of cedar (2 Sam. 7:2; 1 Chr. 17:1); the House of the Forest of Lebanon (1 Kgs. 7:2; 10:17; 2 Chr. 9:16); when the Queen of Sheba saw the house he had built (1 Kgs. 10:4; 2 Chr. 9:3); those who wear soft clothes are in kings' houses (Matt. 11:8); those who live in luxury are in royal palaces (Luke 7:25); they led Jesus to the praetorium (Matt. 27:27; John 18:28).

D5 Houses under attack
The Lord's curse is on the house of the wicked (Prov. 3:33); summer houses, winter houses, houses of ivory will all be destroyed (Amos 3:15); frogs in the houses (Exod. 8:3, 11, 13); swarms of insects in the houses (Exod. 8:24); leprosy in a house (Lev. 14:34-57).

D6 Metaphorical houses
The house on the rock and the house on the sand (Matt. 7:24-7; Luke 6:47-9); the house of my pilgrimage (Ps. 119:54); he finds his house empty, swept and put in order (Matt. 12:44); we have a building from God, a house not made with hands (2 Cor. 5:1).

E Dwellings of creatures
E1 Birds' nests
If you find a bird's nest with young (Deut. 22:6); birds nest in the branches (Ezek. 17:23; 31:6; Dan. 4:12, 21; Mark 4:32; Luke 13:19); the eagle makes its nest on high (Job 39:27); sparrow and swallow find a place to nest in your temple (Ps. 84:3); woe to him who puts his nest on high to be free from calamity (Hab. 2:9); though you set your nest among the stars (Obad. 4); foxes have holes and birds of the air have nests (Matt. 8:20; Luke 9:58).

E2 Other dwellings of creatures
Wild animals living in places once inhabited (Isa. 13:21-2; 32:14; 34:11, 13-17; Zeph. 2:15); where is the den of lions? (Nahum 2:11); the beast goes into its lair (Job 37:8); lions crouch in their dens (Job 38:40); badgers make homes in the rock (Prov. 30:26); the lizard is in kings' palaces (Prov. 30:28); foxes have holes and birds of the air have nests (Matt. 8:20; Luke 9:58); Babylon has become the dwelling-place of demons, the haunt of unclean spirits (Rev. 18:2).

F Synagogues
F1 Synagogues in general
Moses is read in the synagogues every sabbath (Acts 15:21); hypocrites love to stand and pray in synagogues

(Matt. 6:5); they love the chief seats in the synagogues (Matt. 23:6; Mark 12:39; Luke 11:43; 20:46); they burned all the meeting places of God in the land (Ps. 74:8); he has destroyed his appointed meeting place (Lam. 2:6); the hypocrites sound a trumpet in synagogues and in the streets (Matt. 6:2); neither in the temple nor in the synagogues did they find me discussing (Acts 24:12).

F2 Particular synagogues
The centurion built our synagogue (Luke 7:5); Jairus, a ruler of the synagogue (Mark 5:22; Luke 8:41); Sosthenes, the ruler of the synagogue (Acts 18:17); the synagogue of the Freedmen (Acts 6:9); Saul asked for letters to the synagogues in Damascus (Acts 9:2); a synagogue of Satan (Rev. 2:9; 3:9).

F3 Teaching in synagogues
Jesus taught in synagogues (Matt. 4:23; 9:35; 13:54; Mark 1:39; 6:2; Luke 4:15; 6:6; 13:10; John 18:20); Jesus preached in the synagogues of Judea (Luke 4:44); Jesus went into the synagogue (Matt. 12:9; Mark 1:21; 3:1; Luke 4:16); he taught in the synagogue at Capernaum (John 6:59); Barnabas and Paul preached in the synagogues in Salamis (Acts 13:5); on the sabbath they went to the synagogue in Pisidian Antioch (Acts 13:14); they entered the synagogue in Iconium (Acts 14:1); there was a synagogue in Thessalonica (Acts 17:1); they entered the synagogue at Berea (Acts 17:10); Paul reasoned in the synagogue at Athens (Acts 17:17); at Corinth (Acts 18:4); at Ephesus (Acts 18:19; 19:8); Apollos spoke out boldly in the synagogue at Ephesus (Acts 18:26); Saul proclaimed Jesus in the synagogues (Acts 9:20).

F4 Persecution from synagogues
They will flog you in their synagogues (Matt. 10:17; Mark 13:9); some you will scourge in your synagogues (Matt. 23:34); when they bring you before the synagogues (Luke 12:11; 21:12); in every synagogue I beat believers (Acts 22:19); in every synagogue I punished them (Acts 26:11); all in the synagogue were furious (Luke 4:28).

F5 Exclusion from synagogues
They will put you out of the synagogues (John 16:2); if any should confess Christ he would be put out of the synagogue (John 9:22); they did not confess him lest they be put out of the synagogue (John 12:42).

193 Contents
CARGO, see 795.

194 Receptacle
A Temple utensils
A1 Provision of temple utensils
The utensils made for the table (Exod. 25:29; 37:16); for the altar of burnt offering (Exod. 27:3; 38:3); the utensils made for the temple (2 Chr. 4:8, 11); the plan for the utensils of the temple (1 Chr. 28:13-18); Hiram made the basins, shovels and bowls (1 Kgs. 7:40, 45); the utensils were re-consecrated (2 Chr. 29:19).

A2 Temple utensils in use
Levites looked after the utensils (1 Chr. 9:28-9); you who bear the vessels of the Lord (Isa. 52:11); Phinehas went to war with the holy vessels (Num. 31:6).

A3 Temple utensils removed
Ahaz cut them in pieces (2 Chr. 28:24); Nebuchadnezzar cut in pieces the gold vessels (2 Kgs. 24:13); the vessels of the house of the Lord will go to Babylon (Jer. 27:21); the vessels taken away to Babylon (2 Kgs. 25:14-15; Jer. 52:18-19; Dan. 1:2); Belshazzar's guests drank from the vessels of the temple (Dan. 5:2-3, 23); the utensils restored (Ezra 1:9-10; 5:14; 6:5; 7:19).

B Containers
B1 Containers in general
Open vessels unclean due to a corpse (Num. 19:15); break any earthenware vessel touched by an unclean person (Lev. 15:12); if a dead creature falls into an earthenware vessel it must be broken (Lev. 11:33); borrow as many empty vessels as you can (2 Kgs. 4:3); Gideon's men had empty pitchers (Judg. 7:16, 19-20); bring a new jar and put salt in it (2 Kgs. 2:20); Jeremiah and the earthenware jar (Jer. 19:1-13); the deed placed in an earthenware jar (Jer. 32:14); many types of vessels, to honour and dishonour (2 Tim. 2:20); do not take a bag for your journey (Matt. 10:10; Mark 6:8; Luke 9:3); when I sent you out without purse, bag or sandals, did you lack anything? (Luke 22:35-6); an alabaster jar of expensive perfume (Matt. 26:7; Luke 7:37).

B2 Water containers
A skin of water (Gen. 21:14, 15, 19); a jar of water (1 Kgs. 19:6); let down your water jar (Gen. 24:14); Rebekah with her water jar on her shoulder (Gen. 24:15, 45); let me drink a little water from your jar (Gen. 24:17, 43); Rebekah let down her water jar (Gen. 24:18, 46); she poured her jar into the watering trough (Gen. 24:20); Jacob set the rods by the watering troughs (Gen. 30:38, 41); the water became blood in vessels of wood and vessels of stone (Exod. 7:19); go to the water jars and drink (Ruth 2:9); before the pitcher is shattered by the well (Eccles. 12:6); who can tip the water jars of heaven? (Job 38:37); a man carrying a pitcher of water (Mark 14:13; Luke 22:10); six stone jars (John 2:6); the woman left her water pot (John 4:28); Jesus poured water into a basin (John 13:5); put my tears in your bottle (Ps. 56:8).

B3 Wineskins and vats
They took worn-out wineskins (Josh. 9:4); these wineskins were new (Josh. 9:13); new wine bursts old wineskins (Matt. 9:17; Mark 2:22; Luke 5:37); new wine is put into unused wineskins (Matt. 9:17); new wine must be put into fresh wineskins (Luke 5:38); my belly is like new wineskins about to burst (Job 32:19); I am like a wineskin in the smoke (Ps. 119:83); God gathers the sea as in a wineskin (Ps. 33:7); he hewed out a wine vat (Isa. 5:2); the vats overflow, for their wickedness is great (Joel 3:13); the vats will overflow with new wine and oil (Joel 2:24).

B4 Cups
Pharaoh's cup was in my hand (Gen. 40:11); I put the cup in Pharaoh's hand (Gen. 40:11); you will put the cup in Pharaoh's hand (Gen. 40:13); he put the cup in Pharaoh's hand (Gen. 40:21); Joseph's silver cup (Gen. 44:2); is not this what my lord drinks from and divines with? (Gen. 44:5); the cup was found in Benjamin's sack (Gen. 44:12); he in whose possession the cup was found (Gen. 44:16, 17); all Solomon's drinking vessels were gold (1 Kgs. 10:21; 2 Chr. 9:20); drinks were served in golden vessels (Esther 1:7); I set before them jugs of wine and cups (Jer. 35:5); Babylon was a golden cup in the hand of the Lord (Jer. 51:7); you cleanse the outside of cup and dish (Matt. 23:25; Luke 11:39); first cleanse the inside of cup and dish (Matt. 23:26); he took a cup and gave thanks (Matt. 26:27); he took a cup, gave thanks and gave it to them (Mark 14:23); let this cup pass from me (Matt. 26:39); the woman had in her hand a gold cup (Rev. 17:4).

B5 Bowls
Those who drink wine from bowls (Amos 6:6); a bowl full of vinegar (John 19:29); seven golden bowls full of the wrath of God (Rev. 15:7); golden bowls full of incense which are the prayers of the saints (Rev. 5:8); pour out the seven bowls of the wrath of God on the earth (Rev. 16:1); the first angel poured his bowl on the earth (Rev. 16:2); the second angel poured his bowl into the sea (Rev. 16:3); the third angel poured his bowl into the rivers (Rev. 16:4); the fourth angel poured his bowl on the sun (Rev. 16:8); the fifth angel poured his bowl on the throne of the beast (Rev. 16:10); the sixth angel poured his bowl on the river Euphrates (Rev. 16:12); the seventh angel poured his bowl into the air (Rev. 16:17); one of the seven angels who had the seven bowls spoke to me (Rev. 17:1); seven bowls full of the seven last plagues (Rev. 21:9).

B6 Pots for cooking and eating
Blessed shall be your basket and your kneading-trough (Deut. 28:5); cursed shall be your basket and your kneading trough (Deut. 28:17); frogs will come into your kneading-troughs (Exod. 8:3); their kneading-troughs bound up in their clothes (Exod. 12:34); we sat by the pots of meat (Ezek. 24:3-14); I see a boiling pot (Jer. 1:13); this is the pot and we are the meat (Ezek. 11:3); this city will not be a pot for you (Ezek. 11:11); those you have slain are the meat and this city is the pot (Ezek. 11:7); woe to the bloody city, the pot with rust in it! (Ezek. 24:6); a cereal offering made in a saucepan (Lev. 2:7); on boiling the sin offering, an earthenware vessel must be broken, a bronze vessel scoured (Lev. 6:28); they break their bones and chop them up like meat in a kettle (Mic. 3:3); the sluggard buries his hand in the dish (Prov. 19:24; 26:15); John the Baptist's head on a platter (Matt. 14:8, 11; Mark 6:25, 28); every cooking pot will be holy to the Lord (Zech. 14:21); the cooking pots will be like the bowls before the altar (Zech. 14:20).

B7 Baskets
Blessed shall be your basket and your kneading-trough (Deut. 28:5); cursed shall be your basket and your kneading trough (Deut. 28:17); place some of the produce of the land in a basket (Deut. 26:2); unleavened bread in a basket (Exod. 29:3, 23, 32); do not put your neighbour's grapes in your basket (Deut. 23:24); Moses in a reed basket (Exod. 2:3, 5); Paul was lowered in a basket (Acts 9:25; 2 Cor. 11:33); 70 heads in baskets (2 Kgs. 10:7); his hands were freed from the basket (Ps. 81:6); a basket of summer fruit (Amos 8:1, 2); three baskets of white bread (Gen. 40:16, 17); the three baskets are three days (Gen. 40:18); Rachel put the teraphim in the camel basket (Gen. 31:34); like a cage [basket] full of birds their houses are full of deceit (Jer. 5:27); do you not remember how many baskets you collected? (Matt. 16:9, 10), seven baskets full of pieces left over (Mark 8:8, 20); 12 baskets of broken pieces (Mark 8:19; Luke 9:17).

B8 Quivers
Take your quiver and your bow (Gen. 27:3); in his quiver he hid me (Isa. 49:2); happy is the man whose quiver is full [of children] (Ps. 127:5).

C Rooms
C1 Rooms in great buildings
Side chambers round the temple (1 Kgs. 6:5; 1 Chr. 28:11-12); 30 side chambers in each storey (Ezek. 41:6); the porch in front of the temple (1 Kgs. 6:3); the upper rooms of the temple were overlaid with gold (2 Chr. 3:9); rooms in the temple were used to store the tithe (2 Chr. 31:11-12); a room in the temple for Tobiah (Neh. 13:5, 7); side chambers in the House of the Forest of Lebanon (1 Kgs. 7:3).

C2 Upper rooms
A large upper room (Mark 14:15; Luke 22:12; Acts 1:13); the upper room where Elijah was living (1 Kgs. 17:19); the Shunammite woman made an upper room for Elisha (2 Kgs. 4:10); Daniel had windows in his upper room open towards Jerusalem (Dan. 6:10); when they had washed her body they laid her in an upper room

(Acts 9:37-9); there were many lamps in the upper room where we gathered (Acts 20:8).

C3 Private rooms

Frogs will come into your bedroom (Exod. 8:3); frogs even in the chambers of their kings (Ps. 105:30); Tamar brought the food into Amnon's bedroom (2 Sam. 13:10); Bathsheba went to the king in the bedroom (1 Kgs. 1:15); Elisha tells the king what you say in your bedroom (2 Kgs. 6:12); even in your bedroom do not curse a rich man (Eccles. 10:20); I brought him to my mother's bedroom (S. of S. 3:4); Joash and his nurse were hidden in a bedroom (2 Kgs. 11:2; 2 Chr. 22:11); Blastus was in charge of the king's bedchamber (Acts 12:20); go to your room and pray in secret (Matt. 6:6); where is my guest room? (Mark 14:14; Luke 22:11); prepare a guest room for me (Philem. 22); what you have whispered in inner rooms will be proclaimed on housetops (Luke 12:3).

D Decks / storeys

Noah's ark had three decks (Gen. 6:16); the temple had three storeys (1 Kgs. 6:5-6, 10); three storeys of galleries (Ezek. 42:3); the chambers were in three storeys (Ezek. 41:6; 42:6); the chambers were wider with each successive storey (Ezek. 41:7).

E The ark of the covenant

E1 The ark in general

The ark of the covenant of the Lord of hosts (1 Sam. 4:4); David pitched a tent for the ark (1 Chr. 15:1); the ark: made (Exod. 25:10-16; 31:7; 35:12; 37:1-5; 39:35; Deut. 10:1, 3); covered on all sides with gold (Heb. 9:4); placed in the tent (Exod. 26:33; 40:3, 21); anointed (Exod. 30:26); containing Aaron's rod (Num. 17:10); containing the tablets (Exod. 40:20; Deut. 10:2, 5); surmounted by the propitiatory (Lev. 16:2; Num. 7:89).

E2 The ark moved around

The ark: going before the Israelites (Num. 10:33, 35; Josh. 3:3, 6, 11); crossed the Jordan (Josh. 4:11); carried round Jericho (Josh. 6:4, 6, 8, 11, 12-13); brought into the camp (1 Sam. 4:3-6); captured (1 Sam. 4:11, 17, 21-2); causing havoc among the Philistines (1 Sam. 5:1-12); restored to Israel (1 Sam. 6:1-21); bringing death to the men who look inside (1 Sam. 6:19); brought to enquire of God (1 Sam. 14:18); with the army under shelter (2 Sam. 11:11); in a tent (2 Sam. 7:2; 1 Chr. 15:1; 16:1; 17:1).

E3 The ark in Jerusalem

David brought the ark up (2 Sam. 6:2-10, 12-17; 1 Chr. 13:3; 15:3, 12, 25; 2 Chr. 1:4); David was unwilling to bring the ark into the city (2 Sam. 6:10); the Levites brought the ark after David (2 Sam. 15:24); take the ark back (2 Sam. 15:25).

E4 The ark in the temple

David wanted to build a house for the ark (1 Chr. 28:2); the ark placed in the temple (1 Kgs. 6:19; 8:1, 3; 1 Chr. 22:19; 2 Chr. 5:2-10; 6:11); Solomon stood before the ark (1 Kgs. 3:15); I have set a place for the ark (1 Kgs. 8:21); come to your resting-place, you and the ark of your might (Ps. 132:8); the ark of the covenant in the sanctuary in heaven (Rev. 11:19).

195 Size

A Big things

The temple will be great (2 Chr. 2:5, 9); Nineveh was a very great city, a city of three days' walk (Jonah 3:3); mustard is the greatest of shrubs (Matt. 13:32; Mark 4:32); the stone on the well's mouth was large (Gen. 29:2); the stone was very large (Mark 16:4); see with what large letters I am writing (Gal. 6:11); though ships are large they are directed by a very small rudder (Jas. 3:4).

B Plumpness

B1 Fat people

Jeshurun [Israel] grew fat and kicked (Deut. 32:15); their body is fat (Ps. 73:4); they are fat and sleek (Jer. 5:28); their eyes bulge from fatness (Ps. 73:7); Eglon was very fat (Judg. 3:17); why make yourselves fat with the offerings? (1 Sam. 2:29); the wicked man is very fat (Job 15:27); his body is full of fat (Job 21:24); they were fatter than the other youths (Dan. 1:15); you have fattened your hearts in a day of slaughter (Jas. 5:5).

B2 Fat animals

Seven fat cows (Gen. 41:2, 4, 18, 20); you slaughter the fat sheep but do not feed the flock (Ezek. 34:3); I will judge between the fat sheep and the lean sheep (Ezek. 34:20); the fat and the strong I will destroy (Ezek. 34:16); devouring the flesh of the fat sheep and tearing off their hooves (Zech. 11:16); bring the fattened calf and kill it (Luke 15:23).

B3 Fat things

Seven plump ears (Gen. 41:5-6, 22, 24).

C Tallness

C1 Tall people

Saul was a head taller than anyone else (1 Sam. 9:2; 10:23); do not look at his height (1 Sam. 16:7); a nation tall and smooth (Isa. 18:2, 7); the Sabeans, men of stature, will come over to you (Isa. 45:14); who by being anxious can add a cubit to his stature [or span of life]? (Matt. 6:27).

C2 Giants

There were giants in those days (Gen. 6:4); the people of the land are men of great stature (Num. 13:32); we saw the Nephilim and we seemed like grasshoppers (Num. 13:33); we saw the descendants of Anak there (Num. 13:28); the Anakim (Deut. 1:28; 9:2; Josh. 11:21-2; 14:12, 15); I destroyed before them the Amorites, tall as cedars (Amos 2:9); those descended from the giants in Gath (1 Chr. 20:8); Emim, tall as the Anakim (Deut. 2:10-11); Zamzummim, tall as the Anakim (Deut. 2:20-1); Ahiman, Sheshai and Talmai, descendants of Anak (Num. 13:22); Caleb drove out the three sons of Anak (Josh. 15:13-14; Judg. 1:20); Goliath's height was six cubits and a span (1 Sam. 17:4); Lahmi, brother of Goliath (1 Chr. 20:5); Ishbi-benob, a descendant of the giants (2 Sam. 21:16); Saph, a descendant of the giants (2 Sam. 21:18); Sippai, one of the descendants of the giants (1 Chr. 20:4); at Gath was a very tall man (2 Sam. 21:20; 1 Chr. 20:6); an Egyptian five cubits tall (1 Chr. 11:23).

D Great and small

The Lord will command that houses great and small be smashed to pieces (Amos 6:11); the great light to rule the day and the small light to rule the night (Gen. 1:16); to make the ephah small and the shekel great (Amos 8:5).

196 Littleness

A Small people

A dwarf could not serve as priest (Lev. 21:20); Zacchaeus was short in stature (Luke 19:3); we were like grasshoppers (Num. 13:33); the inhabitants of the earth are like grasshoppers (Isa. 40:22); how can Jacob stand, he is so small? (Amos 7:2, 5).

B Small creatures

Four things small but wise, ants, badgers, locusts, lizards (Prov. 30:24-8); small fish (Matt. 15:34; Mark 8:7; John 6:9).

C Small things

Zoar, a small town (Gen. 19:20, 22); a cloud as small as a man's hand (1 Kgs. 18:44); Bethlehem Ephrathah, too small to be among the clans of Judah (Mic. 5:2); mustard seed is the smallest of all seeds (Matt. 13:32;

Mark 4:31); if you have faith as a grain of mustard seed (Matt. 17:20; Luke 17:6); the kingdom of God is like a grain of mustard seed (Luke 13:19); the bed is too short and the blanket too narrow (Isa. 28:20); though ships are large they are directed by a very small rudder (Jas. 3:4); the tongue is a small member, but boasts great things (Jas. 3:5); why notice the speck in your brother's eye? (Matt. 7:3-5; Luke 6:41-2); not a jot or tittle shall pass from the law (Matt. 5:18; Luke 16:17); who has despised the day of small things? (Zech. 4:10).

197 Expansion

A Enlarging territory

You will spread out to the north, south, east and west (Gen. 28:14); you will spread abroad to right and left (Isa. 54:3); Israel's shoots will spread out (Hos. 14:6); in that day your boundary will be extended (Mic. 7:11); enlarge my border (1 Chr. 4:10); enlarge the place of your tent (Isa. 54:2-3); if God enlarges your territory (Deut. 19:8); blessed is he who enlarges Gad (Deut. 33:20); you have extended the borders of the land (Isa. 26:15).

B Spreading

If the infection spreads it is leprosy (Lev. 13:7, 8, 22, 27, 35, 36, 51, 57; 14:39, 44); if the infection has not spread (Lev. 13:5, 6, 23, 28, 32, 34, 53, 55; 14:48); Tyre will be a place for the spreading of nets (Ezek. 26:5, 14); from Engedi to Eneglaim will be a place for spreading nets (Ezek. 47:10); spreading garments and branches on the road (Matt. 21:8); let us warn them so that it may spread no further (Acts 4:17); the word of the Lord spread (Acts 13:49).

C Stretching out

Moses spread his hands out to the Lord (Exod. 9:29, 33); stretch out your hand (Exod. 7:19; 8:5; 9:22; 10:12, 21; 14:16, 26; Matt. 12:13; Mark 3:5; Luke 6:10); I [Wisdom] stretched out my hands and none heeded (Prov. 1:24); the Lord who stretched out the heavens (Zech. 12:1); he stretched out his hand to his disciples (Matt. 12:49); Jesus stretched out his hand and took hold of him (Matt. 14:31); when you are old you will stretch out your hands (John 21:18).

198 Contraction

The Lord began to reduce Israel (2 Kgs. 10:32).

199 Distance

A Distances

A1 Seeing at a distance

Abraham saw the place at a distance (Gen. 22:4); you will see the land at a distance (Deut. 32:52); women looking on from a distance (Matt. 27:55; Mark 15:40; Luke 23:49); having seen the promises from a distance (Heb. 11:13).

A2 Standing at a distance

Moses' sister stood at a distance (Exod. 2:4); the people stood at a distance (Exod. 20:18, 21); ten lepers stood at a distance (Luke 17:12); they will stand at a distance in fear of her torment (Rev. 18:10, 15).

A3 Particular distances

This far the Lord has helped us (1 Sam. 7:12); he withdrew from them about a stone's throw (Luke 22:41); every six paces David sacrificed a bull and a calf (2 Sam. 6:13); the shadow going ten steps forward or backward (2 Kgs. 20:9, 10-11); if someone forces you to go one mile, go two (Matt. 5:41).

B Far off

B1 Far away

The younger son went into a far country (Luke 15:13); a man went into a far country to receive a kingdom (Luke 19:12); I will send you far away to the Gentiles

(Acts 22:21); your eyes will behold a far-distant land (Isa. 33:17); if the place where God sets his name is too far (Deut. 12:21; 14:24); keep far from a false matter (Exod. 23:7); as far as the east is from the west, so far has he removed our transgressions (Ps. 103:12); while the other is a great way he will sue for peace (Luke 14:32); while he was far off his father ran to him (Luke 15:20); this commandment is not too hard nor far off (Deut. 30:11).

B2 People from far away

The Lord will bring against you a nation from afar, from the ends of the earth (Deut. 28:49); I am bring against you a nation from afar (Jer. 5:15); the Gibeonites said they had come from a far country (Josh. 9:6, 9, 22); the queen of the South came from the ends of the earth to hear the wisdom of Solomon (Matt. 12:42; Luke 11:31); from a far country, from Babylon (2 Kgs. 20:14; Isa. 39:3); bring my sons from afar, my daughters from the end of the earth (Isa. 43:6); your sons will come from afar (Isa. 60:4); the ships of Tarshish bring your sons from afar (Isa. 60:9); these will come from afar (Isa. 49:12); some have come from a long way (Mark 8:3).

B3 God far away

Why do you stand far off? (Ps. 10:1); why are you so far from helping me? (Ps. 22:1); do not be far from me (Ps. 35:22; 38:21; 71:12); am I a God who is near and not a God far off? (Jer. 23:23); the Lord is far from the wicked (Prov. 15:29); their heart is far from God (Matt. 15:8; Mark 7:6); you are near to their lips but far from their heart (Jer. 12:2); the promise is to those far off (Acts 2:39); you who were far off (Eph. 2:13); peace to you who were far off (Eph. 2:17); the tax collector, standing far off, would not lift up his eyes to heaven (Luke 18:13).

C Near or far

Gods of the people near you or far from you (Deut. 13:7); if they are taken into exile far or near (1 Kgs. 8:46; 2 Chr. 6:36); peace to the far and near (Isa. 57:19; Eph. 2:17).

200 Nearness

THE TIME IS NEAR, see 135A.
NEAR OR FAR, see 199C.
DRAWING NEAR, see 289.

A Near to God

A1 A God who is near

What nation has a god so near as the Lord is to us? (Deut. 4:7); the Lord is near to all who call on him (Ps. 145:18); he is not far from each of us (Acts 17:27); the Lord is at hand (Phil. 4:5); the Lord is near to the broken-hearted (Ps. 34:18); peace to those who were near (Isa. 57:19; Eph. 2:17); call on him while he is near (Isa. 55:6); draw near to God and he will draw near to you (Jas. 4:8).

A2 Face to face with God

The Lord spoke with Moses face to face (Exod. 33:11; Deut. 34:10); the Lord spoke with Moses mouth to mouth (Num. 12:8); the Lord spoke to Israel face to face (Deut. 5:4); then we will see face to face (1 Cor. 13:12).

A3 God's blessings are near

His salvation is near to those who fear him (Ps. 85:9); the kingdom is near (Matt. 3:2; 4:17; 10:7; Luke 10:9, 11; 21:31); the kingdom is at hand (Mark 1:15); you are not far from the kingdom (Mark 12:34); the word is near you (Deut. 30:14; Rom. 10:8).

A4 Brought near to God

Blessed is the one you choose and bring near (Ps. 65:4); the Lord will bring near those whom he chooses (Num. 16:5); those far off have been brought near through the blood of Christ (Eph. 2:13); the slave's master is to bring him near to God (Exod. 21:6); bring the master of the house near to God (Exod. 22:8); the priest shall bring the woman near to the Lord (Num. 5:16).

B Near to people

Come close that I might feel you (Gen. 27:21-2); come near and kiss me (Gen. 27:26-7); Jacob came near and kissed him (Gen. 27:27); I who am meek when face to face to you but bold when away (2 Cor. 10:1); we wanted to see you face to face (1 Thess. 2:17); I hope to speak with you face to face (2 John 12).

C Neighbours

Love your neighbour as yourself (Lev. 19:18; Matt. 22:39; Mark 12:31; Luke 10:27); to love one's neighbour as oneself (Mark 12:33); love your neighbour and hate your enemy (Matt. 5:43); who is my neighbour? (Luke 10:29); the Gibeonites were near neighbours (Josh. 9:16, 22).

201 Gap

Hide the waistband in the crevice of a rock (Jer. 13:4); between us and you a great chasm is fixed (Luke 16:26); you who live in the cleft of the rock (Obad. 3); he who earns wages puts them into a purse with holes (Hag. 1:6).

202 Contiguity

TOUCH, see 378.

203 Length

A Long things

The Nazirite shall let his hair grow long (Num. 6:5); the poles for the ark were so long they could be seen outside (1 Kgs. 8:8; 2 Chr. 5:9); they make the tassels of their garments long (Matt. 23:5); the scribes like to go about in long robes (Mark 12:38); a man with a limb too long could not serve as priest (Lev. 21:18); an animal with a limb too long could not be sacrificed (Lev. 22:23).

B Length and breadth

I am going to measure Jerusalem, its breadth and length (Zech. 2:2); walk through the length and breadth of the land (Gen. 13:17); the breadth and length and height and depth of the love of Christ (Eph. 3:18).

204 Shortness

An animal with a stunted limb could not be sacrificed (Lev. 22:23); is the Lord's arm shortened? (Num. 11:23); the Lord's hand is not too short to save (Isa. 59:1).

205 Breadth

A Broad

The sea, great and wide (Ps. 104:25); God's limits are broader than the sea (Job 11:9); my little finger is thicker than my father's loins (1 Kgs. 12:10; 2 Chr. 10:10); your commandment is exceedingly broad (Ps. 119:96); the gate is wide and the way is broad that leads to destruction (Matt. 7:13); they broaden their phylacteries (Matt. 23:5).

B Breadth

Make a rim a handbreadth wide round the table (Exod. 25:25); the 'sea' was a handbreadth thick (1 Kgs. 7:26; 2 Chr. 4:5); the pillars were four fingers in thickness (Jer. 52:21); I am going to measure Jerusalem, its breadth and length (Zech. 2:2); the breadth and length and height and depth of the love of Christ (Eph. 3:18).

206 Narrowness

A Thin things

My leanness witnesses against me (Job 16:8); I will judge between the fat sheep and the lean sheep (Ezek.

34:20); seven thin cows (Gen. 41:3, 4, 19-20, 27); seven thin ears (Gen. 41:6, 7, 23, 24, 27).

B Narrow things

Enter by the narrow gate (Matt. 7:13); strive to enter by the narrow door (Luke 13:24); the gate is small and the way narrow that leads to life (Matt. 7:14).

C Neck

Kids' skins on the smooth nape of the neck (Gen. 27:16); do you clothe the horse's neck with a mane? (Job 39:19); your neck is like the tower of David (S. of S. 4:4); your neck is like a tower of ivory (S. of S. 7:4); your neck is lovely with strings of jewels (S. of S. 1:10); your neck is an iron sinew (Isa. 48:4); better a millstone hung round his neck (Matt. 18:6; Mark 9:42; Luke 17:2); why put a yoke on the disciples' neck? (Acts 15:10).

D Waist

John wore a leather belt around his waist (Matt. 3:4; Mark 1:6); let your loins be girded (Luke 12:35); gird up the loins of your mind (1 Pet. 1:13); gird your loins with truth (Eph. 6:14).

207 Layer

A Boards

Boards for the tabernacle (Exod. 26:15-25; 35:11; 36:20-30; 39:33); the altar made of boards (Exod. 27:8); some got to shore on planks (Acts 27:44); your planks are made from fir trees from Senir (Ezek. 27:5).

B Flakes / scales

A fine, flake-like thing (Exod. 16:14); I will make the fish stick to your scales (Ezek. 29:4); the scales of the crocodile (Job 41:15).

C Plates

They hammered the gold into thin plates (Exod. 39:3); a plate of pure gold (Exod. 28:36); censers beaten into plates for the altar (Num. 16:38-9); an iron plate as a wall between you and the city (Ezek. 4:3).

D Stone tablets

Two tablets of stone (Exod. 31:18; Deut. 4:13; 5:22; 9:9, 10, 11, 15, 17); two stone tablets like the first (Deut. 10:1, 3); a letter written not on tablets of stone but on tablets of human hearts (2 Cor. 3:3); the tables of the covenant (Heb. 9:4).

208 Filament

A Cord / thread

He snapped the ropes like a thread (Judg. 16:12); the seal and the cord (Gen. 38:18, 25); scarlet cord tied to the window (Josh. 2:18, 21); a scarlet thread on the hand of a twin (Gen. 38:28, 30); your lips are like a scarlet thread (S. of S. 4:3); cords to the tentpegs of the tabernacle and the court (Exod. 35:18); lengthen your cords, strengthen your pegs (Isa. 54:2); before the silver cord is broken (Eccles. 12:6); the cords of the wicked surround me (Ps. 119:61); the Lord has cut the cords of the wicked (Ps. 129:4); as for your birth, your navel cord was not cut (Ezek. 16:4); I led them with cords of a man, with bonds of love (Hos. 11:4); seven fresh bowstrings (Judg. 16:7-9).

B Rope

Rahab let the spies down by a rope (Josh. 2:15); they let Jeremiah down with ropes (Jer. 38:6); Samson bound with new ropes (Judg. 15:13-14; 16:11-12); putting ropes on their heads (1 Kgs. 20:31, 32); can you put a rope in the crocodile's nose? (Job 41:2).

209 Height

A On high

A1 God is on high

God is higher than the heavens (Job 22:12); you, Lord, are on high for ever (Ps. 92:8); you, Lord, are most high over all the earth (Ps. 97:9); I saw the Lord, high and lifted up (Isa. 6:1); as the heavens are higher than the earth, so are God's ways higher than man's (Isa. 55:9); I dwell in the high and holy place (Isa. 57:15); glory to God in the highest (Luke 2:14); clothed with power from on high (Luke 24:49); the Majesty on high (Heb. 1:3).

A2 Christ is on high
I am from above (John 8:23); my servant will be high and lifted up (Isa. 52:13); he who comes from above is above all (John 3:31).

A3 People on high
The Kenites' nest is in the cliff (Num. 24:21); though you make your nest as high as the eagle's (Jer. 49:16); though you set your nest among the stars (Obad. 4); woe to him who puts his nest on high to be free from calamity (Hab. 2:9); get up on a high mountain, bearer of good news (Isa. 40:9); on top of the heights Wisdom cries out (Prov. 8:2); a city set on a hill cannot be hid (Matt. 5:14); lead me to the rock that is higher than I (Ps. 61:2).

B Mounds
B1 Cairns
Behold this heap and this pillar (Gen. 31:51-2); a heap of stones over: Achan (Josh. 7:26); the king of Ai (Josh. 8:29); Absalom (2 Sam. 18:17).

B2 Siege mounds
They cast up a mound against the city (2 Sam. 20:15); Nebuchadnezzar will cast up a mound against you (Ezek. 26:8); the Chaldeans laugh at every fortress, heaping up earth and taking it (Hab. 1:10); your enemies will cast up a bank about you (Luke 19:43).

C Towers
C1 Towers in general
A tower with its top in the heavens (Gen. 11:4-5); count her towers (Ps. 48:12); I will take my stand to watch and station myself on the tower (Hab. 2:1); he built a tower in the vineyard (Isa. 5:2; Matt. 21:33; Mark 12:1); no one builds a tower without first sitting down and counting the cost (Luke 14:28).

C2 The tower of. . .
Babel (Gen. 11:4-5); David (S. of S. 4:4); Eder (Gen. 35:21); the Furnaces (Neh. 3:11; 12:38); Hananel (Neh. 3:1; 12:39; Jer. 31:38; Zech. 14:10); the Hundred (Neh. 3:1; 12:39); Penuel (Judg. 8:9, 17); Shechem (Judg. 9:46-9); Siloam (Luke 13:4); Thebez (Judg. 9:51-2).

C3 Like a tower
The Lord is a tower of salvation (2 Sam. 22:51); you have been a strong tower (Ps. 61:3); the name of the Lord is a strong tower (Prov. 18:10).

D High places
D1 High places in general
What is the high place of Judah but Jerusalem? (Mic. 1:5); Gibeon was the great high place (1 Kgs. 3:4); the tabernacle was at the high place at Gibeon (1 Chr. 16:39; 21:29); Solomon went to the high place at Gibeon (2 Chr. 1:3); they provoked him with their high places (Ps. 78:58); your high places for sin (Jer. 17:3); they built high places (1 Kgs. 14:23; 2 Kgs. 17:9); Solomon built a high place for Chemosh and Molech (1 Kgs. 11:7); they have built the high places of Topheth (Jer. 7:31); they built the high places of Baal (Jer. 19:5; 32:35).

D2 Priests of the high places
Priests of the high places (1 Kgs. 12:32; 13:33; 2 Kgs. 17:32; 23:9); Josiah killed the priests of the high places (2 Kgs. 23:20).

D3 Sacrificing on the high places
The people sacrificed at the high places (1 Kgs. 3:2; 22:43; 2 Chr. 33:17); Solomon sacrificed at the high places (1 Kgs. 3:3); Ahaz sacrificed at the high places (2

Kgs. 16:4; 2 Chr. 28:4); they burned sacrifices on the mountains (Isa. 65:7).

D4 Destroying high places
I will destroy your high places (Lev. 26:30; Ezek. 6:3); demolish their high places (Num. 33:52); the high places of Aven, the sin of Israel, will be destroyed (Hos. 10:8); the high places were not removed (1 Kgs. 15:14; 2 Kgs. 12:3; 14:4; 15:4, 35; 2 Chr. 15:17; 20:33); those who removed the high places: Asa (2 Chr. 14:3, 5); Jehoshaphat (2 Chr. 17:6); Hezekiah (2 Kgs. 18:4, 22; 2 Chr. 31:1; 32:12); Josiah (2 Kgs. 23:8-19; 2 Chr. 34:3).

E Hill country
The Amorites forced Dan into the hill country (Judg. 1:34); the kings of the Amorites who live in the hill country (Josh. 10:6); give me the hill country of the Anakim (Josh. 14:12); the hill country is not enough for us (Josh. 17:16-18).

F About mountains / hills
F1 The mountains in general
The best things of the ancient mountains, the everlasting hills (Deut. 33:15); the everlasting heights have become our possession (Ezek. 36:2); to the boundary of the everlasting hills (Gen. 49:26); the mountains rose and the valleys sank (Ps. 104:8); the tops of the mountains were seen (Gen. 8:5); plead your case before the mountains and hills (Mic. 6:1); I lift up my eyes to the hills (Ps. 121:1); the high mountains are for the wild goats (Ps. 104:18); Jephthah's daughter bewailed her virginity on the mountains (Judg. 11:37, 38); among the tombs and on the mountains he cried out (Mark 5:5); a stone was cut out of the mountain without hands (Dan. 2:45); the stone became a mountain and filled all the earth (Dan. 2:35).

F2 The mountains and God
Who weighed the mountains in a balance? (Isa. 40:12); he who forms mountains and creates the wind (Amos 4:13); the heights of the mountains are his (Ps. 95:4); let mountains and hills praise the Lord (Ps. 148:9); let the mountains sing together for joy (Ps. 98:8); the mountains and hills will sing for joy (Isa. 55:12); mountains melt before the Lord (Ps. 97:5; Mic. 1:4); he touches the mountains and they smoke (Ps. 104:32); the mountains saw you and quaked (Hab. 3:10); oh, that the mountains might quake at your presence! (Isa. 64:1); the mountains skipped like rams (Ps. 114:4, 6); mountains quake because of him, the hills melt (Nahum 1:5); touch the mountains so that they smoke (Ps. 144:5); the Lord has a day against the lofty mountains (Isa. 2:14); I am against you, destroying mountain (Jer. 51:25); their gods are gods of the mountains (1 Kgs. 20:23, 28).

F3 Blessings from the mountains
The mountains will drip with sweet wine (Joel 3:18; Amos 9:13); on the mountains the feet of him who brings good news (Nahum 1:15); let the mountains bring peace (Ps. 72:3); may there be abundance of grain on top of the mountains (Ps. 72:16).

F4 Mountains removed
Before Zerubbabel the mountain will become a plain (Zech. 4:7); every mountain will be made low (Isa. 40:4; Luke 3:5); man overturns mountains by the roots (Job 28:9); God removes mountains (Job 9:5); if I have faith to remove mountains (1 Cor. 13:2); the mountain will move when commanded (Matt. 17:20; 21:21; Mark 11:23); every mountain was removed (Rev. 6:14); the mountains were not to be found (Rev. 16:20); he shook the nations and the eternal mountains were shattered (Hab. 3:6).

F5 Escape to the mountains
They will call on mountains and hills to cover them (Hos. 10:8; Luke 23:30; Rev. 6:15-16); flee to the

mountains! (Gen. 19:17); flee like a bird to the mountains (Ps. 11:1); they wandered over deserts and mountains (Heb. 11:38); I cannot flee to the hills (Gen. 19:19); Lot lived in the mountains (Gen. 19:30); the Israelites made dens in the mountains (Judg. 6:2); let those in Judea flee to the mountains (Matt. 24:16; Mark 13:14; Luke 21:21).

G Particular mountains

G1 Ararat – Gilboa

G1a Mt Ararat
The ark rested (Gen. 8:4).

G1b Areopagus [Mars' hill]
Mars' hill (Acts 17:19, 22); Dionysius the Areopagite (Acts 17:34).

G1c Mt Carmel
Mt Carmel (1 Kgs. 18:19, 20, 42; 2 Kgs. 2:25; 4:25); your head crowns you like Carmel (S. of S. 7:5); Bashan and Carmel wither (Nahum 1:4); the summit of Carmel withers (Amos 1:2); though they hide on the summit of Carmel I will search them out (Amos 9:3).

G1d Mt Ebal
The curse placed on Mt Ebal (Deut. 11:29; 27:13); stones set up (Deut. 27:4); Joshua built an altar (Josh. 8:30); half stood there (Josh. 8:33).

G1e Mt Esau
Every one from Mt Esau will be cut off by slaughter (Obad. 9); saviours will go up Mt Zion to govern Mt Esau (Obad. 21); those of the Negeb will possess Mt Esau (Obad. 19); will I not destroy understanding from the mountain of Esau? (Obad. 8).

G1f Mt Gerizim
The blessing placed on Mt Gerizim (Deut. 11:29; 27:12); half stood there (Josh. 8:33); Jotham shouted from there (Judg. 9:7).

G1g Mt Gilboa
Mt Gilboa (1 Sam. 31:1, 8; 2 Sam. 1:6, 21; 21:12; 1 Chr. 10:1, 8).

G2 Hermon – Seir

G2a Hermon [Baal-hermon] [Senir] [Sion] [Sirion]
From the Arnon to Mt Hermon (Deut. 3:8); Sidonians call Hermon Sirion, and Amorites Senir (Deut. 3:9); Mt Sion, that is, Hermon (Deut. 4:48); come from the summit of Senir and Hermon (S. of S. 4:8); Hermon [Sion] (Josh. 11:17; 12:1, 5; 13:5, 11; Ps. 42:6; 89:12); Hermon in the land of Mizpeh (Josh. 11:3); he makes Sirion skip like a wild ox (Ps. 29:6); like the dew of Hermon (Ps. 133:3); your planks are made from fir trees from Senir (Ezek. 27:5); Hivites living in Baal-hermon (Judg. 3:3); Manasseh lived in Baal-hermon, that is, Senir, Mt Hermon (1 Chr. 5:23).

G2b Mt Hor
On the border of Israel (Num. 34:7-8); Aaron died there (Num. 20:22-8; 33:38-9; Deut. 32:50); they set out from Mt Hor (Num. 21:4; 33:41).

G2c Mt Moriah
Offer him on a mountain in the land of Moriah (Gen. 22:2); the temple built on Mt Moriah (2 Chr. 3:1).

G2d Mt Nebo [Abarim]
Moses went up Mt Nebo (Deut. 34:1); Moses viewed the land from there (Num. 27:12; Deut. 32:49-50); they camped (Num. 33:47); the mountains of Abarim (Num. 33:48).

G2e Mt Olivet [Mount of Olives]
David went up the Mount of Olives (2 Sam. 15:30); they came to the Mount of Olives (Matt. 21:1); the mount of Olives (Matt. 24:3; 26:30; Mark 11:1; 13:3; 14:26; Luke 19:29, 37; 21:37; 22:39); Jesus went to the Mount of Olives (John 8:1); the mount called Olivet (Acts 1:12); Solomon built a high place for Chemosh on the mountain east of Jerusalem (1 Kgs. 11:7); the Mount of Olives will be split (Zech. 14:4).

G2f Peor [Baal-peor]
The top of Peor (Num. 23:28); Baal of Peor (Num. 25:3, 5); the matter of Peor (Num. 25:18; 31:16); the sin at Peor (Josh. 22:17); you have seen what the Lord did at Baal-peor (Deut. 4:3); they came to Baal-peor (Hos. 9:10).

G2g Perazim [Baal-perazim]
The Lord will rise up as at Mt Perazim (Isa. 28:21); David defeated the Philistines at Baal-perazim (2 Sam. 5:20; 1 Chr. 14:11).

G2h Pisgah
Israel came there (Num. 21:20); the field of Zophim on top of Pisgah (Num. 23:14); by the Dead Sea (Deut. 3:17; 4:49); Moses went up there (Deut. 3:27; 34:1); the slopes of Pisgah (Josh. 12:3; 13:20).

G2i The hill of Samaria
The hill of Samaria (1 Kgs. 16:24); our fathers worshipped in this mountain (John 4:20); the hour is coming when neither on this mountain nor in Jerusalem will you worship (John 4:21); woe to those who feel secure on the mountain of Samaria (Amos 6:1).

G2j Mt Seir
They circled it (Deut. 2:1); given to Esau as a possession (Deut. 2:5); Mt Seir (Josh. 15:10; 24:4; Ezek. 35:2-15); the Horites in Mt Seir (Gen. 14:6).

G3 Mt Sinai [Horeb]

G3a God appeared at Sinai
Mt Sinai (Exod. 19:2-23; 34:2-4; Neh. 9:13); Mt Horeb (Deut. 1:2; 4:10); the burning bush on Horeb, the mountain of God (Exod. 3:1-2); an angel appeared to him in the wilderness of Mt Sinai (Acts 7:30); the angel spoke to Moses on Mt Sinai (Acts 7:38); I will stand on the rock at Horeb (Exod. 17:6); the Lord will come down on Mt Sinai (Exod. 19:11); the Lord came from Sinai (Deut. 33:2); the glory of the Lord dwelt on Mt Sinai (Exod. 24:16); the mountain of God (Exod. 4:27; 18:5; 24:13); Sinai quaked at the presence of God (Ps. 68:8); make them according to the pattern shown you on the mountain (Exod. 25:40; 26:30; 27:8); they made a calf at Horeb (Ps. 106:19); at Horeb you provoked the Lord to wrath (Deut. 9:8).

G3b The covenant at Sinai
The Lord made a covenant with us at Horeb (Deut. 5:2; 29:1; 2 Chr. 5:10); the Lord commanded Moses on Mt Sinai (Lev. 7:38); what I commanded him at Horeb for all Israel (Mal. 4:4); the Lord spoke to Moses on Mt Sinai (Lev. 25:1; Num. 3:1); the statutes which the Lord decreed at Mt Sinai (Lev. 26:46); the commandments which the Lord commanded at Mt Sinai (Lev. 27:34); God spoke these words from the mountain in the midst of the fire (Deut. 5:22); tablets of stone which Moses put into the ark at Horeb (1 Kgs. 8:9); a continual burnt offering was ordained at Mt Sinai (Num. 28:6).

G3c Other references to Sinai
From Mt Horeb on they removed their ornaments (Exod. 33:6); Sinai quaked (Judg. 5:5); you have been long enough at this mountain (Deut. 1:6; 2:3); Elijah came to Horeb, the mountain of God (1 Kgs. 19:8); Mt Sinai corresponds to the present Jerusalem (Gal. 4:24-5); you have not come to a mountain burning with fire (Heb. 12:18-21); if even a beast touches the mountain it will be stoned (Heb. 12:20).

G4 Mt Tabor
Mt Tabor (Judg. 4:6, 12, 14; Ps. 89:12); one will come like Tabor among the mountains (Jer. 46:18); you have been a snare at Mizpah, a net on Tabor (Hos. 5:1).

G5 Mt Zion

G5a Zion, the holy mountain
The mountain of the Lord of hosts will be called the holy mountain (Zech. 8:3); the city of our God, his holy mountain (Ps. 48:1-2); the holy mountain at Jerusalem (Isa. 27:13); Zion, my holy mountain (Ps. 2:6; Joel 3:17); let them bring me to your holy hill (Ps. 43:3); who may live on your holy hill? (Ps. 15:1); I will bring them to my holy mountain (Isa. 56:7); he the house of Israel will serve me on my holy mountain (Ezek. 20:40); they will not hurt or destroy in my holy mountain (Isa. 65:25).

G5b God living in Zion
The mountain of the house of the Lord (Isa. 2:2-3; Mic. 4:1); Mt Zion where you dwell (Ps. 74:2); the Lord of hosts who dwells on Mt Zion (Isa. 8:18); the mountain where God chooses to live (Ps. 68:16); Mt Zion, the place of the name of the Lord (Isa. 18:7); the Lord will reign on Mt Zion and in Jerusalem (Isa. 24:23); the Lord will reign over them in Mic. (Mic. 4:7); let us go up to the mountain of the Lord, the house of the God of Jacob (Mic. 4:2); the Lamb stood on Mt Zion (Rev. 14:1).

G5c Other references to Zion
You have come to Mt Zion, the heavenly Jerusalem (Heb. 12:22); out of Mt Zion will go survivors (2 Kgs. 19:31; Isa. 37:32); on Mt Zion there will be those who escape (Joel 2:32; Obad. 17); let Mt Zion be glad (Ps. 48:11); the nations waging war against Mt Zion will be like dreamers (Isa. 29:8); the Lord will come down to wage war on Mt Zion (Isa. 31:4); the Lord will create over Mt Zion cloud by day and fire by night (Isa. 4:5); those who trust in the Lord are like Mt Zion (Ps. 125:1); like dew on the mountains of Zion (Ps. 133:3); like mountains round Jerusalem so the Lord surrounds his people (Ps. 125:2).

G6 Mountain of God
In the mount of the Lord it will be seen (Gen. 22:14); to go to the mountain of the Lord (Isa. 30:29); who may ascend the hill of the Lord? (Ps. 24:3); the hill of God (1 Sam. 10:5); Tyre, you were on the holy mountain of God (Ezek. 28:14); I cast you from the mountain of God (Ezek. 28:16).

G7 Unnamed mountains
The devil took Jesus to a high mountain (Matt. 4:8); the sermon on the mount (Matt. 5:1-7:29); the mount of transfiguration (Matt. 17:1; Mark 9:2; Luke 9:28); the holy mountain (2 Pet. 1:18); Jesus went up a mountain (Matt. 15:29; Mark 3:13; John 6:3); Jesus went up the mountain to pray (Matt. 14:23; Mark 6:46; Luke 6:12; 9:28); when he saw the crowds he went up into a mountain (Matt. 5:1); he withdrew to the mountain (John 6:15); a mountain in Galilee (Matt. 28:16); as they were coming down the mountain (Matt. 17:9; Mark 9:9; Luke 9:37); in visions the Lord set me on a very high mountain (Ezek. 40:2); he carried me away in the Spirit to a high mountain (Rev. 21:10); something like a burning mountain was thrown into the sea (Rev. 8:8).

H Deep or high
Ask a sign, as deep as Sheol or high as heaven (Isa. 7:11); blessings of heaven above and deep beneath (Gen. 49:25); as the heavens for height and the earth for depth so is the heart of kings (Prov. 25:3); neither height nor depth can separate us from the love of God (Rom. 8:39).

210 Lowness

A Underneath

A1 Things under
The firmament separated the waters above from the waters below (Gen. 1:7); underneath are the everlasting arms (Deut. 33:27); the things were in Achan's tent with the silver underneath (Josh. 7:21, 22); the crocodile's underparts are like sharp potsherds (Job 41:30); you are from below, I am from above (John 8:23).

A2 Under the sun
Nothing new under the sun (Eccles. 1:9); I have seen under the sun (Eccles. 3:16); all the works done under the sun (Eccles. 1:14); the work done under the sun (Eccles. 8:17); every deed done under the sun (Eccles. 8:9); no profit under the sun (Eccles. 1:3; 2:11); a grievous evil under the sun (Eccles. 5:13); under the sun (Eccles. 2:17, 19, 20, 22; 4:1, 7, 15; 6:1, 12; 9:6, 9, 13; 10:5); all the days of the life God has given him under the sun (Eccles. 8:15); the evil done under the sun (Eccles. 4:3); under heaven (Eccles. 1:13; 2:3; 3:1).

B Lower
You made man a little lower than God (Ps. 8:5); from his loins and downwards was like fire (Ezek. 8:2); exalt what is low and abase what is high (Ezek. 21:26); lest you begin with shame to take the lowest place (Luke 14:9); when you are invited, recline in the lowest place (Luke 14:10); you will go down lower and lower (Deut. 28:43).

C Crawling
On your belly you shall go (Gen. 3:14); let the earth bring forth creeping things (Gen. 1:24); God made every creeping thing (Gen. 1:25); man was to rule over every creeping thing (Gen. 1:26, 28); every creeping thing was given green plants for food (Gen. 1:30); insects which crawl are unclean (Lev. 11:20-3, 42); if anyone touches a creeping thing by which he may be made unclean (Lev. 22:5).

211 Depth

DEEP OR HIGH, see 209H.

A Deep things
The inward mind and heart of a man are deep (Ps. 64:6); have you explored the subterranean regions? (Job 38:16-17); put out into deep water (Luke 5:4); the well is deep (John 4:11); you will drink your sister's cup which is deep and wide (Ezek. 23:32); he descended into the lower parts of the earth (Eph. 4:9).

B The deep / the depths
Darkness was over the face of the deep (Gen. 1:2); the deeps cover them (Exod. 15:5); though they hide from my sight at the bottom of the sea (Amos 9:3); in his hands are the depths of the earth (Ps. 95:4); those who seek to destroy my life will go into the depths of the earth (Ps. 63:9); you will bring us up from the depths of the earth (Ps. 71:20); you put me in the depths of the lowest pit (Ps. 88:6); Elam went uncircumcised into the nether world (Ezek. 32:24); send them down to the nether world, to the pit (Ezek. 32:18); you will throw all their sins into the depths of the sea (Mic. 7:19).

C Spiritual depths
Can you search the depths of God? (Job 11:7); God's things are deeper than Sheol (Job 11:8); the Spirit searches the depths of God (1 Cor. 2:10); neither height nor depth can separate us from the love of God (Rom. 8:39); the depth of the riches of the wisdom and knowledge of God! (Rom. 11:33); the breadth and length and height and depth (Eph. 3:18); the rebels have gone deep in depravity (Hos. 5:2); they are deep in depravity as in the days of Gibeah (Hos. 9:9); the deep things of Satan (Rev. 2:24).

D Depthing
The water was 15 cubits deep over the mountains (Gen. 7:20); the sailors took soundings (Acts 27:28); 20 fathoms, then 15 fathoms (Acts 27:28); water ankle-deep (Ezek. 47:3); knee-deep (Ezek. 47:4); deep enough to swim in (Ezek. 47:5); water reaching to the loins (Ezek. 47:4).

E Deeper

If the infection is deeper than the skin (Lev. 13:3, 20, 25, 30); if the marks are deeper than the surface (Lev. 14:37).

212 Shallowness

If the spot is not deeper than the skin (Lev. 13:4, 21, 26, 31, 32, 34); on rocky ground there was no depth of soil (Matt. 13:5; Mark 4:5).

213 Summit

A Top

A1 Top of mountains / hills

The tops of the mountains were seen (Gen. 8:5); the Lord came down on the top of the mountain (Exod. 19:20); like fire on the top of the mountain (Exod. 24:17); David approached the summit (2 Sam. 15:32; 16:1); all the area on top of the mountain shall be most holy (Ezek. 43:12); they led him to the brow of the hill on which the city was built (Luke 4:29).

A2 Rooftop

Make a parapet for your roof (Deut. 22:8); they made an opening in the roof (Mark 2:4; Luke 5:19); twelve months later he was walking on the roof of the royal palace (Dan. 4:29); the spies were hidden on the roof (Josh. 2:6, 8); they fled to the roof of the tower (Judg. 9:51); 3000 people were on the roof (Judg. 16:27); from the roof David saw a woman bathing (2 Sam. 11:2); a tent pitched on the roof (2 Sam. 16:22); they burnt sacrifices on the rooftops to all the host of heaven (Jer. 19:13); let him on the housetop not go down (Matt. 24:17; Mark 13:15; Luke 17:31); better live in a corner of the roof than with a quarrelsome woman (Prov. 21:9; 25:24); what you hear in your ear, proclaim on the housetops (Matt. 10:27); what you have whispered in inner rooms will be proclaimed on housetops (Luke 12:3); Peter went up to the housetop to pray (Acts 10:9).

A3 Top of things

The capitals of the pillars (1 Kgs. 7:16-20, 41; 2 Chr. 4:12-13; Jer. 52:22); the devil set him on the pinnacle of the temple (Matt. 4:5; Luke 4:9).

B Heads

LIFTING HEADS, see 310C2.

B1 Heads in general

His head is like gold (S. of S. 5:11); do not swear by your head (Matt. 5:36); the head cannot say it does not need the feet (1 Cor. 12:21); he will lift up his head (Ps. 110:7); the head of the statue was of fine gold (Dan. 2:32, 38); when you fast, anoint your head and wash your face (Matt. 6:17); over his head they put the charge against him (Matt. 27:37); not my feet only, but also my hands and my head (John 13:9); angels seated where Jesus' body had been, one at the head and one at the feet (John 20:12).

B2 Damage to heads

He will bruise your head (Gen. 3:15); they plaited a crown of thorns and put it on his head (Matt. 27:29; John 19:2); they took the reed and beat him on the head (Matt. 27:30; Mark 15:19); Jael hammered a tent-peg into Sisera's temple (Judg. 4:21, 22; 5:26); my head, my head! (2 Kgs. 4:19); the whole head is sick (Isa. 1:5); the sun beat on Jonah's head so he was faint (Jonah 4:8); another servant they wounded in the head (Mark 12:4); you will heap burning coals of fire on his head (Rom. 12:20); one of the beast's heads appeared to have a mortal wound (Rev. 13:3).

B3 Covering heads

Do not uncover your heads (Lev. 10:6); the leper's head must be covered (Lev. 13:45); Haman covered his head and mourned (Esther 6:12); a man praying or prophesying with head covered dishonours his head (1

Cor. 11:4, 7); a woman praying or prophesying with head unveiled dishonours her head (1 Cor. 11:5); a woman ought to cover her head (1 Cor. 11:10, 13); a woman's hair is given to her for a covering (1 Cor. 11:15).

B4 Removing heads

Pharaoh will lift your head from you (Gen. 40:19); if Elisha's head remains on him today (2 Kgs. 6:31); see how he intends to remove my head! (2 Kgs. 6:32); ask for the head of John the baptizer (Mark 6:24); I want you to give me immediately the head of John the Baptist (Mark 6:25); they beheaded John in the prison (Mark 6:27); John I beheaded (Luke 9:9); those who had been beheaded for their testimony to Jesus (Rev. 20:4).

B5 Putting on the head

Three baskets of bread on my head (Gen. 40:16, 17); oil on the head of the cleansed leper (Lev. 14:18, 29); Moses poured oil on Aaron's head (Lev. 8:12); you anoint my head with oil (Ps. 23:5); she poured the perfume on Jesus' head (Matt. 26:7; Mark 14:3); I put a beautiful crown on your head (Ezek. 16:12); putting ropes on their heads (1 Kgs. 20:31, 32).

B6 Hands on heads

Israel put his hands on Ephraim and Manasseh's heads (Gen. 48:14, 17); laying hands on the head of a sacrificial animal (Exod. 29:10, 15, 19; Lev. 1:4; 3:2, 8, 13; 4:4, 15, 24, 29, 33); laying hands on the head of the blasphemer (Lev. 24:14); Aaron and his sons laid their hands on the head of: the sin offering (Lev. 8:14); the burnt offering (Lev. 8:18); the ram of ordination (Lev. 8:22).

B7 Animal heads

A donkey's head cost 80 shekels (2 Kgs. 6:25); a leopard with four heads (Dan. 7:6); horses with heads like lions (Rev. 9:17); the horses' tails are like serpents and have heads (Rev. 9:19); a beast with seven heads and ten horns (Rev. 12:3; 13:1; 17:3, 7).

B8 Head as chief

You will be the head and not the tail (Deut. 28:13); the alien will be the head and you the tail (Deut. 28:44); the elder and honourable man is the head (Isa. 9:15); the Lord has covered your heads, the seers (Isa. 29:10); you have kept me as head of the nations (2 Sam. 22:44; Ps. 18:43); the Lord is exalted as head over all (1 Chr. 29:11); the husband is the head of the wife as Christ is the head of the church (Eph. 5:23); Christ is the head of every man, the husband is the head of the wife, God is the head of Christ (1 Cor. 11:3); Christ is the head of all rule and authority (Col. 2:10); Christ is the head of the church (Eph. 1:22; 5:23); he is the head of the body, the church (Col. 1:18); the whole body is fitted to the head (Eph. 4:16; Col. 2:19); grow up into Christ, the head (Eph. 4:15).

214 Base

A Earth's foundation

God marked out the foundations of the earth (Prov. 8:29); God laid the foundation of the earth (Job 38:4, 6); he set the earth on its foundations (Ps. 104:5); on what were its bases sunk and who laid its cornerstone? (Job 38:6); the earth's foundations were laid bare (2 Sam. 22:16; Ps. 18:15); earth's foundations shake (Isa. 24:18); the foundations of the earth are shaken (Ps. 82:5); God stretched out the heavens and laid the foundation of the earth (Zech. 12:1).

B Foundations of buildings

Large stones for the foundation of the temple (1 Kgs. 5:17); the foundation of the house was of costly stones (1 Kgs. 7:10); laying the foundation of the temple in the time of Solomon (1 Kgs. 6:37; 2 Chr. 3:3); laying the foundation of the temple in the time of Ezra (Ezra 3:10-12; 5:16); the foundation of the temple was not yet laid (Ezra 3:6); saying of the temple, 'Your foundation will be laid' (Isa. 44:28); the foundation of the temple was laid (Hag. 2:18); Zerubbabel's hands have laid the foundation (Zech. 4:9); the house did not fall because it was founded on the rock (Matt. 7:25; Luke 6:48); after he has laid a foundation and is not able to finish (Luke 14:29); the foundations of the prison were shaken (Acts 16:26).

C Foundations of cities / nations
Laying Jericho's foundation cost the firstborn (Josh. 6:26; 1 Kgs. 16:34); on the 12 foundations were the names of the 12 apostles (Rev. 21:14); the foundation stones were adorned with precious stones (Rev. 21:19-20).

D Spiritual foundations
God's foundation stands (2 Tim. 2:19); no other foundation but Christ (1 Cor. 3:11); Christ as the cornerstone (Eph. 2:20); the stone rejected by the builders has become the head of the corner (Ps. 118:22; Matt. 21:42; Mark 12:10; Luke 20:17; Acts 4:11; 1 Pet. 2:7); I am laying in Zion a precious cornerstone (Isa. 28:16; 1 Pet. 2:6); on the foundation of the apostles and prophets (Eph. 2:20); you are Peter, and on this rock I will build my church (Matt. 16:18); I laid a foundation (1 Cor. 3:10); if the foundations are destroyed, what can the righteous do? (Ps. 11:3); that I might not build on another man's foundation (Rom. 15:20); storing up for themselves a good foundation for the future (1 Tim. 6:19); not laying again a foundation of repentance (Heb. 6:1); Abraham was looking for the city which has foundations (Heb. 11:10).

215 Vertical
STANDING UP, see 308B4.

A Plumb line
I will stretch over Jerusalem the plumb line of Samaria and Ahab (2 Kgs. 21:13); a plumb line amongst Israel (Amos 7:7-8); the plumb line in the hand of Zerubbabel (Zech. 4:10); I will make righteousness the plumb line (Isa. 28:17); the plumb line of chaos (Isa. 34:11); the Lord was standing by a wall with a plumb line in his hand (Amos 7:7-8).

B Obelisks
PILLARS FOR SUPPORT, see 218C.

B1 Sacred pillars
Do not set up a pillar (Lev. 26:1; Deut. 16:22); the oak of the pillar in Shechem (Judg. 9:6); the Lord will break down their altars and destroy their pillars (Hos. 10:2); I will cut off your images and your pillars from among you (Mic. 5:13); they built pillars on every high hill (1 Kgs. 14:23; 2 Kgs. 17:10); shatter their pillars (Exod. 34:13; Deut. 7:5; 12:3); Jehoram put away the pillar of Baal (2 Kgs. 3:2); Hezekiah broke down the pillars (2 Kgs. 18:4; 2 Chr. 31:1); Josiah cut the pillars in pieces (2 Kgs. 23:14); Asa tore down the pillars (2 Chr. 14:3).

B2 Other pillars
Jacob set up the stone as a pillar (Gen. 28:18, 22; 31:45); behold this heap and this pillar (Gen. 31:51-2); Jacob set up a pillar over Rachel's grave (Gen. 35:20); Lot's wife became a pillar of salt (Gen. 19:26); Moses set up 12 pillars (Exod. 24:4); his legs are alabaster pillars (S. of S. 5:15); the pillar of cloud and the pillar of fire (Exod. 13:21, 22; Num. 14:14; Neh. 9:12, 19); the Lord looked from the pillar of cloud and fire (Exod. 14:24); the pillar of cloud stood at the door of the tent (Exod. 33:9-10); the angel's feet were like pillars of fire (Rev. 10:1).

STONE AS PILLAR, see 344B4c.

C Standing up
Blessed is the man who does not stand in the way of sinners (Ps. 1:1); who can stand in your presence? (Ps. 76:7); who may stand in his holy place? (Ps. 24:3); stand in the holy place (2 Chr. 35:5); pray for strength to stand before the Son of man (Luke 21:36); if you tell the poor man, 'Stand there or sit at my footstool' (Jas. 2:3); the sorcerers could not stand before Moses because of the boils (Exod. 9:11).

216 Horizontal
My foot stands on a level place (Ps. 26:12); lead me in a level path (Ps. 27:11); let your good Spirit lead me on level ground (Ps. 143:10); the way of the righteous is level (Isa. 26:7); let the rough ground become level (Isa. 40:4); I will make rough places into level ground (Isa. 42:16); I will level the rough ground before you (Isa. 45:2); the farmer levels the land for planting (Isa. 28:25).

217 Hanging

A People hung to death
Cursed be every one who hangs on a tree (Deut. 21:23; Gal. 3:13); Pharaoh hanged the chief baker (Gen. 40:19, 22; 41:13); Joshua hanged the king of Ai on a tree (Josh. 8:29); Joshua hung the kings on five trees (Josh. 10:26); David had the men hanged (2 Sam. 4:12); the Gibeonites hanged Saul's sons (2 Sam. 21:6, 9); the Philistines hanged Saul and Jonathan's bodies (2 Sam. 21:12); Haman wanted to hang Mordecai (Esther 5:14; 6:4); Haman was hanged (Esther 7:9-10; 8:7); Haman's sons were hanged (Esther 9:13-14, 25); Jesus was killed by hanging him on a gibbet (Acts 5:30); they put him to death by hanging him on a tree (Acts 10:39); Ahithophel hanged himself (2 Sam. 17:23); Judas hanged himself (Matt. 27:5).

B People hanging in the air
Absalom hung by his hair in a tree (2 Sam. 18:9-10); miners hang and swing to and fro (Job 28:4); princes are hung up by their hands (Lam. 5:12).

C Things hanging
The veil was hung from pillars (Exod. 26:32-3); on the willows we hung our harps (Ps. 137:2); they will hang on him all the weight of his father's house (Isa. 22:24); can wood of the vine be used to make a peg to hang a vessel? (Ezek. 15:3); better a millstone hung round his neck (Matt. 18:6; Mark 9:42; Luke 17:2).

218 Support

A Supporting

A1 God supporting
The Lord was my support (2 Sam. 22:19; Ps. 18:18); cast your burden on the Lord and he will sustain you (Ps. 55:22); you uphold me in my integrity (Ps. 41:12); they lean on the God of Israel (Isa. 48:2); yet they lean on the Lord and say, 'Is not the Lord in our midst?' (Mic. 3:11).

A2 Other supporting
They supported Moses' hands (Exod. 17:12); the man on whose hand the king leaned (2 Kgs. 7:2, 17); leaning on her beloved (S. of S. 8:5); as if a man leans his hand against a wall and a snake bites him (Amos 5:19); it is not you who supports the root, but the root supports you (Rom. 11:18).

B Staffs / sticks

B1 Moses' staff
With his staff Moses was to perform miracles (Exod. 4:17); Moses' staff became a snake (Exod. 4:2-3; 7:9-10); take the staff that became a snake (Exod. 7:15); the staff of God (Exod. 4:20; 17:9); striking the Nile with the staff (Exod. 7:17, 20; 17:5); he struck the rock (Exod.

17:6; Num. 20:11); while he held up the staff, Israel beat Amalek (Exod. 17:9-12); he stretched out his staff: over the rivers (Exod. 8:5); over the dust (Exod. 8:16-17); to the sky (Exod. 9:23); over the land of Egypt (Exod. 10:13); over the Red Sea (Exod. 14:16).

B2 Support of a staff

With only my staff I crossed this Jordan (Gen. 32:10); eat the Passover with your staff in your hand (Exod. 12:11); each one with staff in hand because of age (Zech. 8:4); do not take a staff (Matt. 10:10; Luke 9:3); he charged them not to take anything for their journey except a staff (Mark 6:8); Jacob worshipped, leaning on his staff (Gen. 47:31; Heb. 11:21); Egypt is a staff of crushed reed (2 Kgs. 18:21; Isa. 36:6).

B3 Striking people with a staff

You will break them with a rod of iron (Ps. 2:9); he will strike the earth with the rod of his mouth (Isa. 11:4); with a rod they strike the judge of Israel on the cheek (Mic. 5:1); they beat him on the head with a reed (Mark 15:19).

B4 Shepherding with a staff

I will make you pass under the rod (Ezek. 20:37); every tenth animal to pass under the staff (Lev. 27:32); shepherd your people with your staff, the flock of your inheritance (Mic. 7:14); your rod and your staff comfort me (Ps. 23:4).

B5 Other staffs

A rod from each of the tribal leaders (Num. 17:2-10); each man took his rod (Num. 17:9); Aaron's rod that budded (Heb. 9:4); Judah's staff as security (Gen. 38:18, 25); the magicians threw down their staffs and they became snakes (Exod. 7:12); Jonathan dipped his staff in the honey (1 Sam. 14:27, 43); Elisha's staff was laid on the dead boy (2 Kgs. 4:29, 31); a stick made the iron float (2 Kgs. 6:6); the angel touched the food with his staff (Judg. 6:21); they put a reed in his hand (Matt. 27:29); a sponge put on a reed (Matt. 27:48; Mark 15:36); a sponge put on hyssop (John 19:29); two staffs, Favour and Union (Zech. 11:7, 10, 14); two sticks joined into one (Ezek. 37:16-20); a bruised reed he will not break (Isa. 42:3; Matt. 12:20); if I break the staff of bread (Ezek. 14:13); three times I was beaten with rods (2 Cor. 11:25); a measuring rod like a staff (Rev. 11:1).

B6 Beams / logs

Every one get a beam (2 Kgs. 6:2); the beams were not inserted in the wall (1 Kgs. 6:6); a beam from the house used in punishment (Ezra 6:11); a row of cedar beams (1 Kgs. 6:36; 7:12); the beams of our house are cedar (S. of S. 1:17); God lays the beams of his chambers in the waters (Ps. 104:3); the shaft of his spear was like a weaver's beam (1 Sam. 17:7; 2 Sam. 21:19; 1 Chr. 11:23; 20:5); the beam from the house will answer the stone from the wall (Hab. 2:11); you do not notice the beam in your own eye (Matt. 7:3-5); you do not notice the log in your own eye (Luke 6:41-2).

C Pillars

OBELISKS, see 215B.

C1 Pillars for the tabernacle

The Merarites looked after the frames, bars and pillars (Num. 3:36-7; 4:31-2); pillars for: the tent (Exod. 35:11; 39:33); the veil (Exod. 26:32; 36:36); the screen (Exod. 26:37; 36:38); the court (Exod. 27:10-17; 35:17; 38:10-19; 39:40); the gateway of the court (Exod. 27:16; 38:19); the tabernacle (Exod. 27:11).

C2 Pillars for Solomon's temple

Two pillars made for Solomon's temple (1 Kgs. 7:15-22, 41; 2 Kgs. 25:16; 1 Chr. 18:8; 2 Chr. 3:15-17; 4:12; Jer. 27:19; 52:20-3); the pillars were set up and named Jachin and Boaz (1 Kgs. 7:21; 2 Chr. 3:17); the pillars were broken up (2 Kgs. 25:13; Jer. 52:17); Joash was made king,

standing by the pillar (2 Kgs. 11:14; 2 Chr. 23:13); Josiah renewed the covenant near the pillar (2 Kgs. 23:3).

C3 Metaphorical pillars

God set the earth on its pillars (1 Sam. 2:8); the pillars of heaven tremble (Job 9:6; 26:11); God keeps the pillars of the earth steady (Ps. 75:3); twisdom has set up her seven pillars (Prov. 9:1); the church is the pillar and bulwark of the truth (1 Tim. 3:15); the overcomer will be made a pillar in the temple (Rev. 3:12); let our daughters be as corner pillars (Ps. 144:12); I have made you an iron pillar (Jer. 1:18); James and Cephas and John, reputed to be pillars (Gal. 2:9).

C4 Other pillars

Samson pulled the pillars of the temple (Judg. 16:29); 45 pillars for the house of the forest of Lebanon (1 Kgs. 7:3); the hall of pillars (1 Kgs. 7:6).

D Seats

An unclean person's seat and bed become unclean (Lev. 15:4, 6, 9, 20-4, 26-7); he overturned the seats of those selling doves (Matt. 21:12); they love the chief seats in the synagogues (Mark 12:39; Luke 11:43).

E Beds

E1 Beds in general

An unclean person's seat and bed become unclean (Lev. 15:4, 6, 20-4, 26-7); those who recline on beds of ivory (Amos 6:4); couches of gold and silver (Esther 1:6); snatched away with the corner of a bed and the cover of a couch (Amos 3:12); they carried on pallets those who were sick (Mark 6:55); they laid the sick on beds and couches (Acts 5:15).

E2 Particular beds

Beds were brought for David (2 Sam. 17:28); a bed for Elishah (2 Kgs. 4:10); Og had an iron bedstead (Deut. 3:11); our couch is green (S. of S. 1:16); the bed is too short to stretch oneself (Isa. 28:20); the bed of Solomon (S. of S. 3:7); rise, take up your bed (Matt. 9:6; Mark 2:9, 11-12; Luke 5:24; John 5:8-12); rise and make your bed (Acts 9:34).

E3 In bed

Aeneas had been bedridden for eight years (Acts 9:33); at evening David got out of bed (2 Sam. 11:2); the sluggard turns on his bed like a door on its hinges (Prov. 26:14); my bed will comfort me (Job 7:13); she found the child lying in bed (Mark 7:30); my children are with me in bed (Luke 11:7); in that night there will be two men in one bed (Luke 17:34).

E4 Use of beds

Israel bowed at the head of the bed (Gen. 47:31); gathered his feet up into the bed (Gen. 49:33); let them sing for joy on their beds (Ps. 149:5); he plans wickedness on his bed (Ps. 36:4); woe to those who devise wickedness on their beds (Mic. 2:1); no one lights a lamp and puts it under a bed (Mark 4:21; Luke 8:16).

F Footstool

David wanted to build a house for God's footstool (1 Chr. 28:2); let us worship at his footstool (Ps. 99:5; 132:7); the earth is God's footstool (Isa. 66:1; Matt. 5:35); the earth is my footstool (Acts 7:49); till I make your enemies your footstool (Ps. 110:1; Mark 12:36; Luke 20:43; Acts 2:35; Heb. 1:13; 10:13); sit here by my footstool (Jas. 2:3).

G Table

The table of showbread (Exod. 25:23-30; Heb. 9:2); ten tables (2 Chr. 4:8); tables to kill sacrifices (Ezek. 40:40-3); a table and chair for Elisha (2 Kgs. 4:10); you say the Lord's table may be defiled and its food despised (Mal. 1:12); you say the table of the Lord is to be despised (Mal. 1:7); dogs eat the crumbs that fall from their master's table (Matt. 15:27; Mark 7:28); Lazarus wanted to eat what fell from the rich man's table (Luke 16:21); leaving the word of God to serve tables (Acts 6:2); you cannot share in the table of the Lord and the table of demons (1 Cor. 10:21); let their table become a snare and a trap (Rom. 11:9); he overturned the tables of the money-changers (Matt. 21:12; Mark 11:15; John 2:15).

H Other supports
He took a stone to put under his head (Gen. 28:11, 18); ten stands for the lavers (1 Kgs. 7:27-39, 43; 2 Chr. 4:14; Jer. 27:19); the stands were broken up (Jer. 52:17, 20); they used supports to undergird the ship (Acts 27:17); Solomon made a bronze platform (2 Chr. 6:13); Ezra stood on a wooden podium (Neh. 8:4); the Levites stood on a platform (Neh. 9:4); Herod took his seat on the platform (Acts 12:21).

219 Parallel
OPPOSITE, see 240.

220 Tilting
I will send those to tip Moab over (Jer. 48:12); the pigs rushed down the steep bank (Matt. 8:32; Mark 5:13; Luke 8:33).

221 Turning upside down
The loaf of barley bread turned the tent upside down (Judg. 7:13); he overturned the tables of the money-changers (Matt. 21:12; Mark 11:15; John 2:15); God overturns mountains in his anger (Job 9:5); man overturns mountains by the roots (Job 28:9); I will wipe Jerusalem like a dish and turn it upside down (2 Kgs. 21:13); these men who have turned the world upside down have come here (Acts 17:6); Ephraim is a cake not turned (Hos. 7:8).

222 Crossing
A Crossing hands
Jacob crossed his hands (Gen. 48:14).
B Spinning
Spinning thread (Exod. 35:25); spinning goats' hair (Exod. 35:26); may Joab's house never be without one who holds a spindle (2 Sam. 3:29); lilies do not toil or spin (Matt. 6:28; Luke 12:27).
C Weaving
Oholiab was a weaver (Exod. 38:23); the work of a weaver (Exod. 28:39); weaving Samson's hair (Judg. 16:13-14); weaving hangings for the Asherah (2 Kgs 23:7); they weave [evil] together (Mic. 7:3); they weave spiders' webs (Isa. 59:5); he cuts me off from the loom (Isa. 38:12); his tunic was without seam, woven in one piece (John 19:23).
D Plaiting
A tunic of plaited work (Exod. 28:4, 39); plaited settings of gold for the onyx stone (Exod. 28:11); they plaited a crown of thorns (Matt. 27:29; Mark 15:17; John 19:2); not with braided hair (1 Tim. 2:9); let your adorning not be braiding of hair (1 Pet. 3:3).
E Netting
E1 Networks
Networks on the capitals of the pillars (1 Kgs. 7:17-18, 41; 2 Kgs. 25:17; 2 Chr. 4:12-13); a grating of bronze network (Exod. 27:4-5).
E2 Nets
They sacrifice to their net and burn incense to their seine (Hab. 1:16); Peter and Andrew casting their net into the sea (Matt. 4:18; Mark 1:16); James and John mending their nets (Matt. 4:21; Mark 1:19); washing nets (Luke 5:2); let down your nets for a catch (Luke 5:4); cast your net on the right side of the boat (John 21:6); at your word I will let down the nets (Luke 5:5); their nets began to break (Luke 5:6); they left their nets

and followed him (Matt. 4:20); the kingdom of heaven is like a dragnet cast into the sea (Matt. 13:47).

223 Outside
A Outside a person
Outwardly you appear righteous (Matt. 23:27-8); man looks on the outward appearance (1 Sam. 16:7); you are looking at externals (2 Cor. 10:7); did not he who made the outside make the inside also? (Luke 11:40); nothing outside a man can defile him (Mark 7:15, 18); you clean the outside of cup and dish (Matt. 23:25; Luke 11:39); being a Jew and circumcised are not truly external matters (Rom. 2:28); while our outer man is decaying, our inner man is being renewed (2 Cor. 4:16); let your adorning not be merely external (1 Pet. 3:3).
B Outside the house
Stay outside the house while the man brings the pledge (Deut. 24:11); the cleansed leper is to stay outside his tent for seven days (Lev. 14:8); his mother and brothers stood outside (Matt. 12:46; Mark 3:31-2); why stand outside? (Gen. 24:31); the sojourner has not lodged outside my door (Job 31:32); when the priests go into the outer court (Ezek. 44:19); the outer tent (Heb. 9:2); the priests go into the outer tent to perform their duties (Heb. 9:6); while the outer tent is still standing (Heb. 9:8); do not take the Passover outside the house (Exod. 12:46); do not go outside for seven days (Lev. 8:33).
C Outside the camp
Miriam outside the camp seven days (Num. 12:14-15); Nadab and Abihu carried outside the camp (Lev. 10:4-5); they brought him outside the camp and stoned him (Num. 15:36); Jesus suffered outside the gate (Heb. 13:12); let us go to him outside the camp (Heb. 13:13); outside the camp: the sin offering was burnt (Exod. 29:14; Lev. 4:12, 21; 8:17; 9:11; 16:27; Heb. 13:11); the ashes of the burnt offering are carried (Lev. 6:11); the red heifer was brought (Num. 19:3); place the ashes of the red heifer (Num. 19:9); a place to relieve themselves (Deut. 23:12).
D Outside the kingdom
Cast into outer darkness (Matt. 8:12; 22:13; 25:30); for those outside everything is in parables (Mark 4:11); conduct yourself wisely with regard to those outside (Col. 4:5); outside are the dogs and the sorcerers and the immoral (Rev. 22:15).
E Inside and out
Noah's ark covered inside and out with pitch (Gen. 6:14); the ark overlaid with gold inside and out (Exod. 25:11; 37:2); a book written inside and on the back (Rev. 5:1); first cleanse the inside that the outside also may be clean (Matt. 23:26); fighting without and fear within (2 Cor. 7:5); the four creatures were full of eyes around and within (Rev. 4:8).

224 Inside
INSIDE AND OUT, see 223E.
A Inside a person
A1 The inward being
You desire truth in the inward being (Ps. 51:6); he who made the outside also made the inside (Luke 11:40); true Jewhood and circumcision are inward matters (Rom. 2:29); give what is within for alms and all is clean (Luke 11:41); from within come evil things (Mark 7:21-3); inwardly false prophets are ravenous wolves (Matt. 7:15); inside there is robbery (Matt. 23:25; Luke 11:39); first clean the inside (Matt. 23:26-8); the Spirit of truth will be in you (John 14:17); while our outer man is decaying, our inner man is being renewed daily (2 Cor. 4:16); let your adorning be the hidden person of the heart (1 Pet. 3:4).

A2 The heart
A2a Nature of the heart
The inward mind and heart of a man are deep (Ps. 64:6); the heart is deceitful above all things (Jer. 17:9); the heart of a man reflects the man (Prov. 27:19); keep your heart diligently (Prov. 4:23); this people's heart has grown dull (Matt. 13:15; Acts 28:27); out of the heart of a person come evil things (Mark 7:21); they hold the word fast in an honest and good heart (Luke 8:15); where your treasure is, there will your heart be also (Matt. 6:21; Luke 12:34); in their hearts they turned back to Egypt (Acts 7:39); anyone who looks at a woman lustfully has committed adultery with her in his heart (Matt. 5:28).

A2b God and the heart
The Lord looks on the heart (1 Sam. 16:7); I am he who searches mind and heart (Rev. 2:23); you see the heart and mind (Jer. 20:12); Lord, who know the hearts of all men (Acts 1:24); God who knows the heart (Acts 15:8); the Lord will disclose the motives of the heart (1 Cor. 4:5); God tests the hearts (1 Thess. 2:4); their heart is far from me (Mark 7:6); your heart is not right before God (Acts 8:21); that Christ may dwell in your hearts by faith (Eph. 3:17); the peace of God will guard your hearts and minds (Phil. 4:7); may the Lord direct your hearts into the love of God (2 Thess. 3:5); by this we reassure our hearts before him (1 John 3:19); if our hearts condemn us, God is greater than our heart (1 John 3:20); if our hearts do not condemn us, we have confidence before God (1 John 3:21); God has put it into their hearts to carry out his purpose (Rev. 17:17).

A2c Worship with the heart
Your law is within my heart (Ps. 40:8); the law of his God is in his heart (Ps. 37:31); I have hidden your word in my heart (Ps. 119:11); I will put my law within them and write it on their hearts (Jer. 31:33); love the Lord your God with all your heart (Deut. 6:5; Matt. 22:37; Mark 12:30, 33; Luke 10:27).

A2d Other references to the heart
Aaron will bear the names of the sons of Israel on his heart (Exod. 28:29); Aaron will bear the judgement of the sons of Israel on his heart (Exod. 28:30); food enters not the heart but the stomach (Mark 7:19); the evil one snatches away what was sown in his heart (Matt. 13:19); their foolish heart was darkened (Rom. 1:21); the word is near you, in your mouth and in your heart (Rom. 10:8); with the heart man believes to righteousness (Rom. 10:10); the eyes of your hearts being enlightened (Eph. 1:18); a letter written not on tablets of stone but on tablets of human hearts (2 Cor. 3:3); those who boast in appearances and not in the heart (2 Cor. 5:12); in sending Onesimus back I am sending my very heart (Philem. 12); cleansing their hearts by faith (Acts 15:9); purify your hearts, you double-minded (Jas. 4:8).

A3 Kidneys
You formed my kidneys (Ps. 139:13); God tries the hearts and kidneys (Ps. 7:9; Jer. 17:10); you try the kidneys and heart (Jer. 11:20; 20:12); test my kidneys and my heart (Ps. 26:2); you are far from their kidneys (Jer. 12:2); my kidneys instruct me (Ps. 16:7); my kidneys will rejoice when you speak what is right (Prov. 23:16).

A4 Stomach
The curse will make her belly swell (Num. 5:21-2, 27); they do not serve Christ but their own stomach (Rom. 16:18); food is for the stomach and the stomach for food (1 Cor. 6:13); whatever enters the mouth passes into the stomach (Matt. 15:17; Mark 7:19); take a little wine for the sake of your stomach (1 Tim. 5:23); Jonah was three days and nights in the belly of the sea

monster (Matt. 12:40); striking in the belly: Ehud to Eglon (Judg. 3:21-2); Abner to Asahel (2 Sam. 2:23); Joab to Abner (2 Sam. 3:27); Rechab and Baanah to Ish-bosheth (2 Sam. 4:6-7); Joab to Amasa (2 Sam. 20:10).

A5 Liver
My liver is poured out on the ground (Lam. 2:11); he shakes the arrows, consults the idols, looks at the liver (Ezek. 21:21).

A6 Bowels
Amasa's bowels poured out on the ground (2 Sam. 20:10); the Lord struck Jehoram with a disease so his bowels came out (2 Chr. 21:15, 18-19); Judas' bowels gushed out (Acts 1:18).

A7 Other inner organs
You formed my inward parts (Ps. 139:13); Levi was still in the loins of his father (Heb. 7:10); piercing both joints and marrow (Heb. 4:12).

B In one another
B1 Father and Son in one another
The Father is in me and I in the Father (John 10:38; 14:10, 11); I in my Father and you in me and I in you (John 14:20); as you are in me and I in you, that they may be in us (John 17:21); I in them and you in me (John 17:23); the Father remaining in me does his works (John 14:10).

B2 Us in God
Abide in me and I in you (John 15:4); whoever eats my flesh and drinks my blood abides in me and I in him (John 6:56); to the saints in Christ Jesus who are in Philippi (Phil. 1:1); the faithful brethren in Christ in Colossae (Col. 1:2); that I may be found in him (Phil. 3:9); by this we know that we are in him (1 John 2:5; 4:13); whoever says he abides in him should walk as he walked (1 John 2:6); if what you heard remains in you, you will remain in the Son and the Father (1 John 2:24); abide in him (1 John 2:27-8); no one who abides in him continues to sin (1 John 3:6); he who keeps his commandments abides in him (1 John 3:24); there is no condemnation for those who are in Christ Jesus (Rom. 8:1); you are in Christ (1 Cor. 1:30); a man in Christ who 14 years ago was caught up to the third heaven (2 Cor. 12:2); whoever confesses that Jesus is the Son of God, God abides in him and he in God (1 John 4:15); the one who abides in love abides in God and God abides in him (1 John 4:16); we are in him who is true, in his Son Jesus Christ (1 John 5:20).

B3 God in us
That your love may be in them and I in them (John 17:26); his Spirit in the inner man (Eph. 3:16); his Spirit who dwells in you (Rom. 8:11); I will live in them and walk among them (2 Cor. 6:16); Christ in you, the hope of glory (Col. 1:27); if Christ is in you (Rom. 8:10); do you not recognize that Jesus Christ is in you? (2 Cor. 13:5); it is no longer I that live, but Christ lives in me (Gal. 2:20); I am in travail again until Christ be formed in you (Gal. 4:19); that Christ may dwell in your hearts by faith (Eph. 3:17); if we love each other, God lives in us (1 John 4:12); the one who abides in love abides in God and God abides in him (1 John 4:16); abide in me and I in you (John 15:4); whoever eats my flesh and drinks my blood abides in me and I in him (John 6:56); by this we know that we abide in him and he in us, because of the Spirit (1 John 4:13); whoever confesses that Jesus is the Son of God, God abides in him and he in God (1 John 4:15).

225 Centrality
MIDDLE, see 70.

226 Covering

A Covering God
You covered yourself with a cloud so no prayer can pass through (Lam. 3:44); you have covered yourself with anger and pursued us (Lam. 3:43).

B Covering people

B1 Entire covering of people
The water covered the chariots and horsemen (Exod. 14:28); the sea covered them (Exod. 15:5, 10); they will call on the mountains and hills to cover them (Hos. 10:8; Luke 23:30); the Lord will destroy the covering which is over all peoples (Isa. 25:7); God covered Moses with his hand (Exod. 33:22); Rahab covered the spies with flax (Josh. 2:6); Jael covered Sisera with a rug (Judg. 4:18-19); they covered Amasa's body (2 Sam. 20:12); the young men covered him up, carried him out and buried him (Acts 5:6); Joseph wrapped Jesus' body in a linen cloth (Matt. 27:59; Mark 15:46; Luke 23:53; John 19:40).

B2 Covering the body
Adam and Eve sewed fig leaves to cover themselves (Gen. 3:7); Noah's sons covered him with a garment (Gen. 9:23); they covered King David with clothes (1 Kgs. 1:1); Elijah threw his cloak over Elisha (1 Kgs. 19:19); like a shepherd wraps himself in his cloak (Jer. 43:12); wrap your cloak around you and follow me (Acts 12:8); the blanket is too narrow to wrap oneself in (Isa. 28:20).

B3 Wrapping a baby
At birth you were not wrapped in cloths (Ezek. 16:4); Mary wrapped Jesus in cloths (Luke 2:7); you will find a baby wrapped in cloths (Luke 2:12); when I made darkness the swaddling band of the sea (Job 38:9).

B4 Covering the face / head
Rebekah veiled herself before Isaac (Gen. 24:65); Tamar had covered her face like a prostitute (Gen. 38:15); Moses veiled his face after speaking with God (Exod. 34:35; 2 Cor. 3:13-16); Elijah covered his face with his mantle (1 Kgs. 19:13); they cover their heads in shame (Jer. 14:3, 4); David covered his face in mourning (2 Sam. 19:4); Haman covered his head and mourned (Esther 6:12); two wings to cover the face and two to cover the feet (Isa. 6:2); a woman's hair is given to her as a covering (1 Cor. 11:15); any man praying or prophesying with his head covered dishonours his head (1 Cor. 11:4); Peter saw the face-cloth which had been on his head (John 20:7).

C Covering things

C1 Covering the earth / sea
All the high mountains were covered by the flood (Gen. 7:19, 20); as the waters cover the sea (Hab. 2:14); that the waters may not again cover the earth (Ps. 104:9); frogs covered all the land of Egypt (Exod. 8:6); the locusts covered all the land of Egypt (Exod. 10:5, 15).

C2 Covering the tabernacle
A covering of skins for the tabernacle (Exod. 26:14; 36:19; 39:34; 40:19); the tabernacle and its furniture were to be covered before being moved (Num. 4:5-15); the Gershonites looked after the coverings (Num. 3:25).

C3 Covering the ark / mercy seat
Cherubim covered the ark (Exod. 25:20; 37:9; 1 Kgs. 8:6-7; 2 Chr. 5:8; Heb. 9:5); the cover of the ark [mercy seat]: made (Exod. 25:17; 31:7; 37:6; 39:35); put on the ark (Exod. 26:34; 40:20); sprinkled with blood (Lev. 16:14, 15).

C4 Covering swords
The angel sheathed his sword (1 Chr. 21:27); put your sword in its sheath (John 18:11); Goliath's sword was wrapped in a cloth (1 Sam. 21:9).

C5 Covering blood
Blood is to be poured out and covered with earth (Lev. 17:13); earth, do not cover my blood (Job 16:18); her blood is on the bare rock, not on the ground covered with dust (Ezek. 24:7); that the blood she shed may not be covered (Ezek. 24:8).

C6 Covering other things
Take a spade to cover your excrement (Deut. 23:13); the woman covered the well with the messengers in it (2 Sam. 17:19); they put their clothes under Jehu on the steps (2 Kgs. 9:13); they put their garments on the donkey (Matt. 21:7; Mark 11:7); they threw their garments on the colt (Luke 19:35); spreading garments and leafy branches on the road (Mark 11:8); you took your embroidered cloth and covered the images (Ezek. 16:18); the lead cover was lifted up (Zech. 5:7); nothing is covered which will not be revealed (Matt. 10:26; Luke 12:2).

D Overlaying

D1 Overlaid with gold
Overlaid with gold: the ark (Exod. 25:11-13; 37:2-4; Heb. 9:4); the table (Exod. 25:24-8; 37:11-15); the altar of incense (Exod. 30:3-5; 37:26-8; 1 Kgs. 6:22); the walls of the temple (1 Kgs. 6:21; 1 Chr. 29:4); the cherubim (1 Kgs. 6:28; 2 Chr. 3:10); the doors (1 Kgs. 6:32, 35; 2 Kgs. 18:16); the floor (1 Kgs. 6:30); Solomon's throne (1 Kgs. 10:18; 2 Chr. 9:17).

D2 Overlaid with other metals
The idol is overlaid with gold and silver (Hab. 2:19); the tops of the pillars were overlaid with silver (Exod. 38:17, 19, 28); overlaid with bronze: the altar (Exod. 27:2-6; 38:2-6); the doors for the court (2 Chr. 4:9).

D3 Overlaid with wood
The house was covered with cedar planks (1 Kgs. 6:9); the main part of the temple was overlaid with cypress wood (2 Chr. 3:5); the walls and floor were overlaid with wood (1 Kgs. 6:15-16); the altar was overlaid with cedar (1 Kgs. 6:20).

D4 Covered with pitch
Covered with pitch: Noah's ark (Gen. 6:14); the basket of reeds (Exod. 2:3).

D5 Plaster
Replace the diseased plaster (Lev. 14:41-2); cover large stones with plaster (Deut. 27:2, 4); these people plaster the wall with whitewash (Ezek. 13:10-15); fingers writing on the plaster of the wall opposite the lampstand (Dan. 5:5).

E Skins

E1 Human skin
A symptom of leprosy in his skin (Lev. 13:2); skin for skin! (Job 2:4); you clothed me with skin and flesh (Job 10:11); I will cover you with skin and put breath in you (Ezek. 37:6); can the Ethiopian change his skin? (Jer. 13:23).

E2 Animal skins
God made tunics of skin for Adam and Eve (Gen. 3:21); kids' skins on Jacob's hands and neck (Gen. 27:16); purify every article of leather (Num. 31:20); rams' skins and porpoise skins for the tabernacle (Exod. 25:5; 26:14; 35:7; 39:34; Num. 4:25); Gideon's fleece (Judg. 6:36-40); they went about in sheepskins and goatskins (Heb. 11:37).

E3 Scales
Sea creatures with fins and scales are clean (Lev. 11:9-12; Deut. 14:9-10); something like scales fell from his eyes (Acts 9:18); the crocodile's skin is like a double coat of mail (Job 41:13).

227 Lining

I will panel it with cedar (Jer. 22:14); wood panelling around the three storeys (Ezek. 41:16); the hall of the throne was panelled with cedar (1 Kgs. 7:7); is it time for you to live in your panelled houses? (Hag. 1:4). PLASTER, see 226D5.

228 Dressing

A Clothed

A1 Clothing oneself
Eat the Passover with loins girded and sandals on your feet (Exod. 12:11); bind on your turban and put your shoes on your feet (Ezek. 24:17); put your clothes on (Acts 12:8); the former demoniac was clothed and in his right mind (Mark 5:15; Luke 8:35); when he had washed their feet and taken his garments (John 13:12); Peter put on his clothes (John 21:7); when you were young you girded yourself (John 21:18); you put on clothing but no one is warm (Hag. 1:6).

A2 God clothing people
God clothed Adam and Eve in tunics of skin (Gen. 3:21); if God will give me clothes to wear (Gen. 28:20-1); do not worry about what you will wear (Matt. 6:25, 28); if God clothes weeds he will clothe you (Matt. 6:30; Luke 12:28); God gives aliens food and clothing (Deut. 10:18).

A3 Clothing others
Putting the holy garments on Aaron (Exod. 29:5-6); and his sons (Exod. 29:8-9); they put a clean turban on his head and clothed him (Zech. 3:5); Shem and Japheth covered their father with a mantle (Gen. 9:23); bring the best robe and put it on him (Luke 15:22); when you are old another will gird you (John 21:18).

A4 Clothing the needy
Clothe the naked (Isa. 58:7); if he clothes the naked (Ezek. 18:7, 16); let him who has two coats share with him who has none (Luke 3:11); from the plunder they clothed the naked prisoners (2 Chr. 28:15); if I have seen anyone perish for lack of clothing (Job 31:19-20); Dorcas made garments (Acts 9:39); I was naked and you clothed me (Matt. 25:36-8); I was naked and you did not clothe me (Matt. 25:43).

B Clothes
PRIESTS CLOTHES, see 989.

B1 Instruction about clothes
Do not wear a garment of mixed materials (Lev. 19:19; Deut. 22:11); a woman must not wear men's clothing, nor a man women's (Deut. 22:5); garments with 'leprosy' (Lev. 13:47-59; 14:55); restore a lost garment (Deut. 22:3); do not take a widow's garment in pledge (Deut. 24:17); do not take two tunics (Matt. 10:10; Mark 6:9; Luke 9:3); do not be anxious about what you shall put on (Matt. 6:31; Luke 12:22); the body is more than clothing (Matt. 6:25; Luke 12:23); your clothes did not wear out (Deut. 8:4); having food and clothing we will be content (1 Tim. 6:8).

B2 Provision of clothes

B2a People giving clothes
Abraham's servant gave garments to Rebekah (Gen. 24:53); Joseph gave garments to his brothers (Gen. 45:22); Jonathan gave his own robe to David (1 Sam. 18:4); Samson promised clothes to those who solved his riddle (Judg. 14:12, 19); Micah offered a suit of clothes per year (Judg. 17:10); Hannah made Samuel a new garment each year (1 Sam. 2:19); he must not reduce her clothing (Exod. 21:10); the Israelites asked the Egyptians for clothes (Exod. 3:22; 12:35); garments were given to Solomon (1 Kgs. 10:25); Naaman took ten changes of clothes as a present (2 Kgs. 5:5); giving two changes of clothes (2 Kgs. 5:22, 23); if anyone wants your tunic, give him your cloak also (Matt. 5:40); if he wants your cloak, give him your tunic as well (Luke 6:29).

B2b Transferred clothes
The wicked multiplies garments but the just will wear them (Job 27:16-17); I will clothe him with your robe and sash (Isa. 22:21); false prophets come in sheeps' clothing (Matt. 7:15); Saul wore other robes to disguise himself (1 Sam. 28:8); they divide my garments and cast lots for my clothing (Ps. 22:18); they divided Jesus' clothing (Matt. 27:35; Mark 15:24; Luke 23:34; John 19:23); I have not coveted any one's silver, gold or clothes (Acts 20:33).

B3 Washing clothes
He washes his clothes in wine (Gen. 49:11); purify every garment (Num. 31:20); blessed are those who wash their robes (Rev. 22:14).

B4 Changing clothes
Change your clothes (Gen. 35:2); Joseph changed his clothes (Gen. 41:14); the priest must change his clothes (Lev. 6:11); the priest shall take off the holy garments and put on others (Ezek. 42:14); the priests must put off their garments and put on others (Ezek. 44:19).

B5 Keeping clothes
Shallum the keeper of the wardrobe (2 Chr. 34:22); Paul looked after the clothes of those stoning Stephen (Acts 7:58; 22:20).

B6 Using clothes
Their kneading-troughs bound up in their clothes (Exod. 12:34); barley carried in Ruth's cloak (Ruth 3:15); they spread a garment and everyone threw into it the earrings (Judg. 8:25); good measure will be poured into the fold of your garment (Luke 6:38); they carried them in their coats (Lev. 10:5); they used worn-out clothes and rags to lift Jeremiah (Jer. 38:11-12); from your clothes you made coloured high places (Ezek. 16:16); Elijah struck the water with his mantle (2 Kgs. 2:8); Elisha struck the water with Elijah's mantle (2 Kgs. 2:13-14); they put their garments on the donkey (Matt. 21:7; Mark 11:7; Luke 19:35); they spread their garments on the road (Matt. 21:8; Mark 11:8; Luke 19:36); handkerchiefs or aprons were carried from Paul to the sick (Acts 19:12); if I only touch his garment, I will be healed (Matt. 9:21; Mark 5:27-8).

B7 Particular garments

B7a Cloaks
Tunics and cloaks which Dorcas had made (Acts 9:39); a cloak dipped in blood (Rev. 19:13); on his cloak he has a name (Rev. 19:16); bring the cloak I left at Troas (2 Tim. 4:13).

B7b Belts
Elijah wore a leather belt (2 Kgs. 1:8); as did John the Baptist (Matt. 3:4; Mark 1:6); instead of a belt, a rope (Isa. 3:24); she supplies belts to the merchants (Prov. 31:24); with belts on their loins and turbans on their heads (Ezek. 23:15); a golden girdle around his breasts (Rev. 1:13); a man dressed in linen with a gold belt (Dan. 10:5); golden girdles around their chests (Rev. 15:6); take no gold, silver or copper in your money belts (Matt. 10:9); Agabus took Paul's belt and bound his own feet and hands (Acts 21:11).

B7c Headgear
Bind on your turban and put your shoes on your feet (Ezek. 24:17); your turbans will be on your heads and shoes on your feet (Ezek. 24:23); with belts on their loins and turbans on their heads (Ezek. 23:15); my justice was like a robe and turban (Job 29:14); let them put a clean turban on his head (Zech. 3:5).

B7d Footwear
Eat the Passover with loins girded and sandals on your feet (Exod. 12:11); every warrior's boot will be fuel for the fire (Isa. 9:5); I put sandals of porpoise skin on your feet (Ezek. 16:10); over Edom I throw my shoe (Ps. 60:8; 108:9); they sell the needy for a pair of sandals

(Amos 2:6); to buy the poor for silver, the needy for a pair of sandals (Amos 8:6); the Gibeonites had patched sandals (Josh. 9:5); I am not worthy to undo his sandals (Matt. 3:11; Mark 1:7; Luke 3:16; John 1:27; Acts 13:25); do not take sandals (Matt. 10:10; Luke 10:4); he charged them to wear sandals (Mark 6:9); put sandals on his feet (Luke 15:22); when I sent you out without purse, bag or sandals, did you lack anything? (Luke 22:35); take off the shoes from your feet (Exod. 3:5; Josh. 5:15; Acts 7:33); put on your sandals (Acts 12:8).

B8 Styles of clothing

B8a Distinctive clothing
Tamar took off her widow's garments (Gen. 38:14); Tamar put on her widow's garments (Gen. 38:19); a woman dressed as a harlot (Prov. 7:10); remove her captive's clothes (Deut. 21:13); Jehoiachin changed his prison clothes (2 Kgs. 25:29; Jer. 52:33); put on mourning garments (2 Sam. 14:2); royal robes worn by the kings of Israel and Judah (1 Kgs. 22:10; 2 Chr. 18:9); royal robes worn by the king of Judah into battle (1 Kgs. 22:30; 2 Chr. 18:29); royal robes worn by Esther (Esther 5:1); royal robes worn by Mordecai (Esther 6:8, 10, 11; 8:15); royal robes worn by Herod (Acts 12:21); a garment as evidence of virginity (Deut. 22:17); can a bride forget her attire? (Jer. 2:32); festal garments (Isa. 3:22); a man without a wedding garment (Matt. 22:11, 12); praising God in holy attire (2 Chr. 20:21); an angel clothed with a cloud (Rev. 10:1).

B8b Fine clothes
Esau's best clothes for Jacob (Gen. 27:15); a long-sleeved [or multi-coloured] coat (Gen. 37:3; 2 Sam. 13:18-19); purple robes captured from Midian (Judg. 8:26); Daniel clothed in purple (Dan. 5:29); Saul clothed you in scarlet (2 Sam. 1:24); Jesus arrayed in a scarlet robe (Matt. 27:28); in a gorgeous robe (Luke 23:11); in purple (Mark 15:17; John 19:2, 5); the rich man dressed in purple and fine linen (Luke 16:19); the woman was dressed in purple and scarlet (Rev. 17:4); trading in fine clothes of blue and embroidered work (Ezek. 27:24); the princess's clothing is interwoven with gold (Ps. 45:13); a robe reaching to his feet (Rev. 1:13); bring the best robe and put it on him (Luke 15:22); Zion, put on your beautiful garments (Isa. 52:1); Achan coveted a beautiful robe (Josh. 7:21); the scribes like long robes (Mark 12:38; Luke 20:46); a rich man in fine clothes (Jas. 2:2); did you go out to see a man wearing soft clothes? (Matt. 11:8; Luke 7:25); even Solomon was not clothed like them (Matt. 6:29; Luke 12:27); let your adorning not be the wearing of robes (1 Pet. 3:3).

B8c White / bright clothes
White clothes for the Ancient of Days (Dan. 7:9); they will walk before me in white, for they are worthy (Rev. 3:4); white clothes to cover your nakedness (Rev. 3:18); the 24 elders were dressed in white (Rev. 4:4); each martyr was given a white robe (Rev. 6:11); the great multitude before the Lamb wore white robes (Rev. 7:9); who are these in white robes? (Rev. 7:13); the armies which are in heaven clothed in clean white linen (Rev. 19:14); Jesus' clothes became gleaming and white (Matt. 17:2; Mark 9:3; Luke 9:29); the angels at the tomb had white clothes (Matt. 28:3; Mark 16:5; Luke 24:4); a man in shining garments (Acts 10:30); the seven angels in clean, bright linen (Rev. 15:6); he who overcomes will be clothed in white garments (Rev. 3:5).

B8d Modest clothes
He will gird himself about and have them recline at table (Luke 12:37); gird yourself about and serve me until I have eaten and drunk (Luke 17:8); Jesus tied a towel round his waist (John 13:4); women should dress modestly (1 Tim. 2:9).

B8e Foul clothes
They gird themselves with sackcloth (Ezek. 7:18); some went about in sheepskins and goatskins (Heb. 11:37); we are poorly clothed (1 Cor. 4:11); Joshua in filthy garments (Zech. 3:3-4); if a poor man comes in in vile clothes (Jas. 2:2); your riches have rotted and your garments are moth-eaten (Jas. 5:2); hating even the garment spotted by the flesh (Jude 23).

C Figurative clothes

C1 God's clothing
The Lord is clothed with majesty (Ps. 93:1; 104:1); covering yourself with light as a cloak (Ps. 104:2); the Lord is girded with strength (Ps. 93:1); garments of vengeance for clothing (Isa. 59:17); he wrapped himself with zeal as with a mantle (Isa. 59:17); the remainder of wrath you will gird upon yourself (Ps. 76:10).

C2 Clothed with righteousness
He put on righteousness as a breastplate (Isa. 59:17); I clothed myself with righteousness (Job 29:14); righteousness and faithfulness will be his belt (Isa. 11:5); our righteous deeds are like filthy clothes (Isa. 64:6); fine clean linen, which is the righteous deeds of the saints (Rev. 19:8); he has covered me with a robe of righteousness (Isa. 61:10); let your priests be clothed with righteousness (Ps. 132:9); I have taken your iniquity from you and will clothe you with rich robes (Zech. 3:4); you have a few in Sardis who have not soiled their clothes (Rev. 3:4).

C3 Clothed with good things
Priests clothed with salvation (2 Chr. 6:41; Ps. 132:16); he has clothed me with garments of salvation (Isa. 61:10); you have clothed me with gladness (Ps. 30:11); a mantle of praise instead of a faint spirit (Isa. 61:3); clothed with a garment dipped in blood (Rev. 19:13); robes washed in the blood of the Lamb (Rev. 7:14); humility tied around you (1 Pet. 5:5); let us take off the deeds of darkness and clothe ourselves with the armour of light (Rom. 13:12); this perishable must put on the imperishable (1 Cor. 15:53-4); we long to put on our heavenly dwelling (2 Cor. 5:2-4); put on the full armour of God (Eph. 6:11); gird up the loins of your minds (1 Pet. 1:13); be belted around your waist with truth (Eph. 6:14); clothed with: strength and dignity (Prov. 31:25); Christ (Rom. 13:14; Gal. 3:27); power from on high (Luke 24:49); strength for battle (2 Sam. 22:40; Ps. 18:39); the new self (Eph. 4:24; Col. 3:10); a heart of compassion etc. (Col. 3:12); the sun (Rev. 12:1).

C4 Clothed with bad things
Clothed with cursing (Ps. 109:18-19); violence covers them like a garment (Ps. 73:6); clothed with shame (Ps. 35:26; 109:29; 132:18).

229 Uncovering

A Nakedness

A1 Naked in origin
Adam and Eve were naked and were not ashamed (Gen. 2:25); naked from his mother's womb and naked to return (Job 1:21; Eccles. 5:15).

A2 Naked in shame
Adam and Eve realised they were naked (Gen. 3:7); afraid because they were naked (Gen. 3:10-11); Saul prophesied naked before Samuel (1 Sam. 19:24); the bravest will flee naked (Amos 2:16); Isaiah went naked and barefoot (Isa. 20:2-4); the exorcists fled naked and wounded (Acts 19:16); I must go barefoot and naked (Mic. 1:8); go on your way, inhabitant of Shaphir, in nakedness and shame (Mic. 1:11); he left the linen sheet and ran away naked (Mark 14:52); that he may not go naked and men see his shame (Rev. 16:15); you do not know that you are naked (Rev. 3:17); we long to be

clothed with our new house and not be naked (2 Cor. 5:3-4).

A3 Naked in poverty
The poor are left naked (Job 24:7, 10); I was naked and you clothed me (Matt. 25:36-8); I was naked and you did not clothe me (Matt. 25:43-4); if a brother or sister is without clothing (Jas. 2:15); if he covers the naked with clothing (Ezek. 18:7, 16); nakedness will not separate us from the love of Christ (Rom. 8:35).

A4 Nakedness seen
Do not approach near relatives to uncover their nakedness (Lev. 18:6-18); do not approach a menstruating woman to uncover her nakedness (Lev. 18:19; 20:18); the Assyrians uncovered Oholah's nakedness (Ezek. 23:10); your nakedness will be uncovered and your shame seen (Isa. 47:3); Noah became drunk and was uncovered within his tent (Gen. 9:21-2); woe to him who makes his neighbours drunk so that he can gaze on their nakedness (Hab. 2:15).

B Bare parts of the body
B1 Bare feet
Take off your sandals for you are standing on holy ground (Exod. 3:5; Josh. 5:15; Acts 7:33); God makes counsellors go barefoot (Job 12:17); God makes priests go barefoot (Job 12:19); David went barefoot (2 Sam. 15:30); Isaiah went naked and barefoot as a sign (Isa. 20:2-4); keep your feet from going unshod (Jer. 2:25); a sandal removed from the man who would not marry his brother's widow (Deut. 25:9-10; Ruth 4:7-8); Ruth uncovered Boaz' feet (Ruth 3:4, 7); I am not fit to remove his sandals (Matt. 3:11); I must go barefoot and naked (Mic. 1:8).

B2 Bare headed / bald
Do not uncover your heads (Lev. 10:6); the high priest must not uncover his head (Lev. 21:10); a woman who prays or prophesies with her head uncovered dishonours her head (1 Cor. 11:5-6); is it proper for a woman to pray with head uncovered? (1 Cor. 11:13); the veil is only taken away through Christ (2 Cor. 3:14); when a man turns to the Lord the veil is taken away (2 Cor. 3:16); go up, you baldhead! (2 Kgs. 2:23); if a man becomes bald (Lev. 13:40-2); they shall not make their heads bald (Lev. 21:5); make yourselves bald because your children are exiled (Mic. 1:16); every head is bald (Isa. 15:2; Jer. 48:37; Ezek. 7:18; 29:18; Amos 8:10); instead of well-set hair, baldness (Isa. 3:24).

B3 Bare arms
Set your face toward the siege of Jerusalem with your arm bared (Ezek. 4:7); every head was made bald, every shoulder rubbed bare (Ezek. 29:18); the Lord has bared his holy arm (Isa. 52:10).

C Stripping
C1 God stripping people
Lest I strip her naked (Hos. 2:3); I will uncover her lewdness (Hos. 2:10); I will show the nations your nakedness (Nahum 3:5); I will lift your skirts up over your face and your shame will be seen (Jer. 13:26); I have stripped Esau bare (Jer. 49:10); remove the filthy garments from him (Zech. 3:4); putting off the body of flesh by the circumcision of Christ (Col. 2:11).

C2 People stripping people
They stripped Joseph of his robe (Gen. 37:23); they stripped Aaron of his garments and put them on his son (Num. 20:26, 28); the Philistines stripped Saul's dead body (1 Sam. 31:8-9; 1 Chr. 10:8-9); stripping the slain (2 Sam. 23:10); the robbers stripped him (Luke 10:30); they stripped Jesus (Matt. 27:28); they took the robe off Jesus (Matt. 27:31; Mark 15:20); the magistrates tore the clothes off them (Acts 16:22); the ten horns and the beast will strip the harlot naked (Rev. 17:16); Hanun

cut off the men's clothes at the waist (2 Sam. 10:4; 1 Chr. 19:4).

C3 People stripping off
Like one who takes off a garment on a cold day (Prov. 25:20); the high priest taking off his garments (Lev. 16:23); the priests must put off their garments and put on others (Ezek. 42:14; 44:19); Jonathan stripped off his clothes and gave them to David (1 Sam. 18:4); Jesus laid aside his clothes (John 13:4); Peter was stripped for work (John 21:7); the Lord has bared his holy arm (Isa. 52:10); daughter of Edom, you will become drunk and strip yourself naked (Lam. 4:21); my lord uncovered himself shamelessly (2 Sam. 6:20); I had taken off my garments (S. of S. 5:3); let us take off the deeds of darkness and clothe ourselves with the armour of light (Rom. 13:12); putting off the old man (Eph. 4:22; Col. 3:9); Joseph left his garment and fled (Gen. 39:12-13, 15-16); he left the linen sheet and ran away naked (Mark 14:52); whilst building the wall of Jerusalem, no one took off his clothes (Neh. 4:23).

C4 Things stripped
The voice of the Lord strips the forest bare (Ps. 29:9); I will unsheathe the sword after them (Ezek. 5:2, 12; 12:14); I will draw my sword out of its sheath (Ezek. 21:3, 5); one standing by drew his sword (Mark 14:47).

230 Surroundings

ENCLOSURE, see 235.

A God surrounding
The angel of the Lord camps round those who fear him (Ps. 34:7); God encircled his people (Deut. 32:10); you surround me behind and in front (Ps. 139:5); you surround me with songs of deliverance (Ps. 32:7); as the mountains surround Jerusalem, so the Lord surrounds his people (Ps. 125:2); I will be a wall of fire around Jerusalem (Zech. 2:5).

B Friends surrounding
Surrounding the king (2 Kgs. 11:8; 2 Chr. 23:7, 10); the righteous will surround me (Ps. 142:7); since we are surrounded by so great a cloud of witnesses (Heb. 12:1).

C Enemies surrounding
All the men of Sodom surrounded the house (Gen. 19:4); an army surrounding Dothan (2 Kgs. 6:14, 15); the Chaldeans were surrounding Jerusalem (2 Kgs. 25:4); strong bulls of Bashan surround me (Ps. 22:12); the days will come when your enemies surround you (Luke 19:43); when you see Jerusalem surrounded by armies (Luke 21:20); they surrounded the camp of the saints and the beloved city (Rev. 20:9).

231 Interposing

Meddling in a quarrel is like taking a passing dog by the ears (Prov. 26:17); the pillar and cloud came between the camps of Egypt and Israel (Exod. 14:20); they fled between the two walls (2 Kgs. 25:4; Jer. 39:4); the gate between the two walls (Jer. 52:7).

232 Circumscription

SURROUNDING, see 230.
ENCLOSURE, see 235.

233 Outline

EDGE, see 234.

234 Edge

BOUNDARY, see 236.

A River bank
The cows stood on the bank of the Nile (Gen. 41:3); Pharaoh's daughter walked by the side of the Nile (Exod. 2:5); on the sabbath we went outside the gate to the riverside (Acts 16:13).

B Seashore

Zebulun will dwell at the seashore (Gen. 49:13); Jesus went by the seashore (Mark 2:13); as day was breaking Jesus stood on the beach (John 21:4); I will multiply your seed as the sand on the seashore (Gen. 22:17); descendants innumerable as the sand by the seashore (Heb. 11:12); Simon the tanner, whose house is by the sea (Acts 10:6, 32); they noticed a bay with a beach (Acts 27:39); kneeling down on the beach we prayed (Acts 21:5); he stood on the sand of the seashore (Rev. 13:1).

C Fringe of clothes

Bells and pomegranates on the skirt of the robe of the ephod (Exod. 28:33-4); if one carries holy meat in the skirt of his garment (Hag. 2:12); tassels on clothes (Num. 15:38; Deut. 22:12); they lengthen their tassels (Matt. 23:5); take a few hairs and bind them in the skirts of your robe (Ezek. 5:3); the woman touched the fringe of his garment (Matt. 9:20; Luke 8:44); as many as touched the fringe of his garment were healed (Matt. 14:36; Mark 6:56).

235 Enclosure

A Walls

A1 Particular walls

Rahab's house was in the wall (Josh. 2:15); why go so near the wall? (2 Sam. 11:20, 21); a woman threw a millstone on Abimelech from the wall (2 Sam. 11:21); archers shot from the wall (2 Sam. 11:24); the king of Moab sacrificed his son on the city wall (2 Kgs. 3:27); the king of Israel passed by on the wall (2 Kgs. 6:26); Nehemiah inspected the walls (Neh. 2:13, 15); processions on top of the wall (Neh. 12:31); the procession went to the Broad Wall (Neh. 12:38); the wall around the temple (Ezek. 40:5); on your walls, Jerusalem, I have set watchmen (Isa. 62:6); measuring the city, its gates and its wall (Rev. 21:15).

A2 Figurative walls

They cried to the Lord, 'O wall of the daughter of Zion' (Lam. 2:18); I will be a wall of fire around Jerusalem (Zech. 2:5); you will call your walls Salvation (Isa. 60:18); a strong city with salvation for walls and bulwarks (Isa. 26:1); I searched for a man to build up the wall (Ezek. 22:30); by my God I can jump over a wall (2 Sam. 22:30; Ps. 18:29); the waters were a wall to them on the right and left (Exod. 14:22, 29); water surrounded Thebes, the sea her wall (Nahum 3:8); the men were a wall to us (1 Sam. 25:16); if she is a wall (S. of S. 8:9-10); God will strike you, you whitewashed wall! (Acts 23:3); the rich man's wealth is like a high wall in his imagination (Prov. 18:11); Christ has broken down the dividing wall between Jew and Gentile (Eph. 2:14); a man without self-control is like a city without walls (Prov. 25:28).

A3 Building walls

Solomon building the wall round Jerusalem (1 Kgs. 3:1; 9:15); Jotham built the wall of Ophel (2 Chr. 27:3); Manasseh made it higher (2 Chr. 33:14); build the walls of Jerusalem (Ps. 51:18); Hezekiah rebuilt the walls (2 Chr. 32:5); Manasseh built the outer wall of the city of David (2 Chr. 33:14); repairing the wall of Jerusalem (Neh. 3:1-32); the wall was built to half height (Neh. 4:6); the wall was completed (Neh. 6:15; 7:1); dedication of the wall (Neh. 12:27).

A4 Destroying walls

The walls of Jerusalem broken down (2 Kgs. 14:13; 2 Chr. 25:23; Neh. 1:3); the Chaldeans broke down the wall of Jerusalem (2 Kgs. 25:10; 2 Chr. 36:19; Jer. 39:8; 52:14); the wall of Jericho fell flat (Josh. 6:20); by faith (Heb. 11:30); I will set fire to the wall of Damascus (Jer.

49:27); the wall of Babylon will fall (Jer. 51:44, 58); they will break down Tyre's walls (Ezek. 26:4-12).

A5 Walled towns

Property can be transferred in walled towns (Lev. 25:29-30); cities with high walls (Deut. 3:5); the high and fortified walls in which you trusted (Deut. 28:52); the new Jerusalem had a high wall (Rev. 21:12); the wall measured 144 cubits (Rev. 21:17); the wall had 12 foundation stones (Rev. 21:14).

B Courtyards

B1 Court of the tabernacle

The courtyard of the tabernacle made (Exod. 27:9; 38:9; 40:8); the Merarites are responsible for the pillars of the court (Num. 4:32); the Gershonites looked after the hangings for the courtyard (Num. 3:26).

B2 Courts of the temple

Solomon consecrated the courtyard for making offerings (1 Kgs. 8:64; 2 Chr. 7:7); the court was filled with the brightness of the glory of the Lord (Ezek. 10:3-4); Solomon made the courtyard of the priests (2 Chr. 4:9); the court was square, 100 cubits by 100 cubits (Ezek. 40:47); Zechariah was stoned in the court of the temple (2 Chr. 24:21); Manasseh built altars for the host of heaven in the courts of the temple (2 Kgs. 21:5; 23:12).

B3 Other courtyards

Before Isaiah had gone through the middle court (2 Kgs. 20:4); Peter in the high priest's courtyard (Matt. 26:58, 69; Mark 14:54, 66); they lit a fire in the middle of the courtyard (Luke 22:55); he entered the court of the high priest with Jesus (John 18:15); do not measure the courtyard outside the temple (Rev. 11:2).

C City squares

We will spend the night in the square (Gen. 19:2); they sat in the square of the town (Judg. 19:15); do not spend the night in the open square (Judg. 19:20); I took my seat in the square (Job 29:7); Jerusalem will be built with square and moat (Dan. 9:25).

D Fields

D1 Fields in general

Give the Levites pasture lands around their cities (Num. 35:2, 4-5; Josh. 21:42); pasture fields of the Levites may not be sold (Lev. 25:34); dedicating a field to the Lord (Lev. 27:16-24); like the smell of a field which the Lord has blessed (Gen. 27:27); the king will take the best of your fields (1 Sam. 8:14); they covet fields and seize them, houses and take them (Mic. 2:2); let him in the field not return (Matt. 24:18; Mark 13:16; Luke 17:31); two men in the field, one taken and one left (Matt. 24:40; Luke 17:36).

D2 Particular fields

The field of Ephron purchased (Gen. 23:9-20; 25:10); Achsah asked Caleb for a field (Josh. 15:18; Judg. 1:14); redeeming Naomi's piece of land (Ruth 4:3-5); Judas obtained a field with the reward of wickedness (Acts 1:18); buying the potter's field (Matt. 27:7, 10); field of blood (Matt. 27:8); Jesus went through the grainfields on the sabbath (Matt. 12:1; Luke 6:1); I have bought a field and must go and see it (Luke 14:18).

D3 Figurative fields

You are God's field (1 Cor. 3:9); the kingdom of heaven is like treasure hidden in a field (Matt. 13:44); he sells all that he has and buys that field (Matt. 13:44); a man who sowed good seed in his field (Matt. 13:24); explain to us the parable of the darnel in the field (Matt. 13:36); the field is the world (Matt. 13:38).

E Sheepfolds

He who does not enter the sheepfold by the door is a thief (John 10:1); I have other sheep which are not of this fold (John 10:16).

236 Limit

A Limits in general
Can you find out the limits of the Almighty? (Job 11:7); you have appointed man's limits (Job 14:5); we will keep to the limits God has apportioned us (2 Cor. 10:13).

EDGE, see 234.

BOUNDARY MARK, see 547D.

B Borders of land
B1 God sets boundaries
I will set your boundary (Exod. 23:31); God determined the boundaries of man's habitations (Acts 17:26); he set the boundaries of the peoples (Deut. 32:8); God allotted a boundary for them (Neh. 9:22); you fixed the boundaries of the earth (Ps. 74:17).

B2 Particular borders
The border of: the land of Canaan (Num. 34:2-12); Gilead (Deut. 3:16-17); the Amorites (Judg. 1:36); Edom (Josh. 15:1); Judah (Josh. 15:1-12); Ephraim (Josh. 16:5-8); Manasseh (Josh. 17:7-10); Benjamin (Josh. 18:11-20); Zebulun (Josh. 19:10-14); Asher (Josh. 19:24-9); Naphtali (Josh. 19:32-4).

C Limits for the sea
God set limits for the sea (Job 38:10-11; Prov. 8:29); you set a boundary which the waters may not cross (Ps. 104:9); I placed the sand as the boundary of the sea (Jer. 5:22).

237 Front

A In front
I will not set any worthless thing before my eyes (Ps. 101:3); they put the stumbling-block of their iniquity before their faces (Ezek. 14:3-7); I send my messenger before your face (Matt. 11:10).

B Front of body
B1 Face
B1a Heavenly faces
Peniel – the face of God (Gen. 32:30); I have seen your face like seeing the face of God (Gen. 33:10); let your face shine on me (Ps. 31:16); the Lord lift up his face on you (Num. 6:26); his face had the appearance of lightning (Dan. 10:6); his face was like the sun (Rev. 1:16); the light of the knowledge of the glory of God in the face of Christ (2 Cor. 4:6); the angel's face was like the sun (Rev. 10:1).

B1b Faces of people
Moses' face shone (Exod. 34:29, 30, 35; 2 Cor. 3:7); laying Elisha's staff on the boy's face (2 Kgs. 4:29, 31); hypocrites neglect their face so their fasting may be noticed (Matt. 6:16-17); his face shone like the sun (Matt. 17:2); the appearance of Jesus' face changed (Luke 9:29); they spat in his face (Matt. 26:67); you bear it if someone strikes you in the face (2 Cor. 11:20); a man who looks at his face in the mirror (Jas. 1:23); the third creature had a face like a man (Rev. 4:7); the faces of the locusts were like the faces of men (Rev. 9:7).

B2 Forehead
Memorial bands between your eyes (Exod. 13:9, 16); these words shall be on your forehead (Deut. 6:8; 11:18); the plate on Aaron's forehead (Exod. 28:38); a mark on the foreheads of those who mourn the abominations (Ezek. 9:4); do not shave your forehead for the dead (Deut. 14:1); leprosy on Uzziah's forehead (2 Chr. 26:19, 20); the stone struck Goliath in the forehead (1 Sam. 17:49); until we have sealed the slaves of God on their foreheads (Rev. 7:3); to harm only people without the seal of God on their foreheads (Rev. 9:4); his name will be on their foreheads (Rev. 22:4); his name and his Father's name written on their foreheads (Rev. 14:1); a name on her forehead, Babylon the great (Rev. 17:5); a

mark on their right hand or forehead (Rev. 13:16; 14:9); they had not received the mark of the beast on their forehead or hand (Rev. 20:4).

B3 Nose
I will put my hook in your nose (2 Kgs. 19:28; Isa. 37:29); can you pierce the hippopotamus' nose? (Job 40:24); can you put a rope in the crocodile's nose? (Job 41:2); pressing the nose produces blood (Prov. 30:33); idols have noses but cannot smell (Ps. 115:6).

NOSTRIL, see 353A.

C Front and back
When Joab saw that battle was joined against him in front and at the rear (2 Sam. 10:9; 1 Chr. 19:10); the scroll was written on the front and the back (Ezek. 2:10; Rev. 5:1); four living creatures full of eyes in front and behind (Rev. 4:6).

238 Rear

FRONT AND BACK, see 237C.

A Back end
A1 One's back
I gave my back to the smiters (Isa. 50:6); with buttocks uncovered to the shame of Egypt (Isa. 20:4); bend their backs for ever (Rom. 11:10).

A2 Turning one's back
You will see my back (Exod. 33:23); I will show them my back and not my face (Jer. 18:17); our fathers have turned their backs on the Lord (2 Chr. 29:6); they have turned their back to me and not their face (Jer. 2:27; 32:33); 25 men with their backs to the temple of the Lord (Ezek. 8:16); Israel has turned their back on their enemies (Josh. 7:8); you made my enemies turn their backs to me (2 Sam. 22:41; Ps. 18:40); you will make them turn their back (Ps. 21:12); I will make all your enemies turn their backs to you (Exod. 23:27).

A3 Tails
Samson set the foxes tail to tail (Judg. 15:4); his tail swept down a third of the stars (Rev. 12:4); the Lord cuts off head and tail from Israel (Isa. 9:14); the prophet who teaches lies is the tail (Isa. 9:15); the locusts have tails like scorpions with stings (Rev. 9:10); the horses' tails are like serpents and have heads (Rev. 9:19).

A4 Stern of boat
He was in the stern of the boat (Mark 4:38); they let out four anchors from the stern (Acts 27:29); the stern was broken up (Acts 27:41).

B Behind
Jeroboam set an ambush behind Judah (2 Chr. 13:13); they cast your law behind their backs (Neh. 9:26); get behind me, Satan! (Matt. 16:23; Mark 8:33); behind you, Benjamin! (Hos. 5:8); a woman came up behind Jesus (Matt. 9:20; Mark 5:27; Luke 8:44).

C Looking back
Do not look back (Gen. 19:17); Lot's wife looked back (Gen. 19:26); Benjamin looked behind them (Judg. 20:40).

239 Side

A Side of people
Each thrust his sword into his opponent's side (2 Sam. 2:16); a soldier pierced his side (John 19:34); he showed them his hands and his side (John 20:20); put your hand in my side (John 20:27); unless I put my hand in his side (John 20:25); God made the woman from one of the man's ribs (Gen. 2:21-2).

B Cheeks
Your cheeks are like pomegranates (S. of S. 4:3; 6:7); Zedekiah struck Micaiah on the cheek (1 Kgs. 22:24); let him give his cheek to the smiter (Lam. 3:30); turn the

other cheek (Matt. 5:39; Luke 6:29); I gave my cheeks to those pluck out the beard (Isa. 50:6).

240 Opposite side

He laid each half opposite the other (Gen. 15:10); Ishmael would live opposite his brothers (Gen. 16:12; 25:18); Saul was on one side of the mountain and David on the other (1 Sam. 23:26); sitting on opposite sides of the pool (2 Sam. 2:13); the two Marys sat opposite the grave (Matt. 27:61); he sat down opposite the treasury (Mark 12:41).

PARALLEL, see 219.

241 Right side

A Right hand side

A wise man's heart inclines him to the right hand (Eccles. 10:2); the right pillar was called Jachin (1 Kgs. 7:21); all four creatures had the face of a lion on the right (Ezek. 1:10); cast your net on the right side of the boat (John 21:6); entering the tomb they saw a young man sitting on the right (Mark 16:5); the angel of the Lord standing to the right of the altar of incense (Luke 1:11).

B At the right hand

God stands at the right hand of the needy (Ps. 109:31); he is at my right hand (Ps. 16:8; Acts 2:25); the Lord is at your right hand (Ps. 110:5); the Lord is your shade on your right hand (Ps. 121:5); sit at my right hand (Ps. 110:1; Matt. 22:44; Mark 12:36; Luke 20:42; Acts 2:34; Heb. 1:13); you will see the Son of man seated at the right hand of Power (Matt. 26:64; Mark 14:62; Luke 22:69); Christ is seated at the right hand of God (Mark 16:19; Eph. 1:20; Col. 3:1; Heb. 1:3; 8:1; 10:12; 12:2); God exalted Jesus at his right hand (Acts 2:33; 5:31); Stephen saw Jesus standing at the right hand of God (Acts 7:55-6); Jesus who is at God's right hand (Rom. 8:34; 1 Pet. 3:22); he will place the sheep on his right and the goats on his left (Matt. 25:33-4); Satan standing at the right hand of Joshua the high priest to accuse him (Zech. 3:1); Bathsheba sat on Solomon's right (1 Kgs. 2:19).

C Right parts of body
C1 Right hand
C1a God's right hand
Your right hand is powerful (Exod. 15:6); in your right hand are pleasures for evermore (Ps. 16:11); save me with your right hand (Ps. 60:5; 108:6); your right hand will save me (Ps. 138:7); your right hand upholds me (Ps. 18:35; 63:8; 139:10); I will uphold you with my right hand (Isa. 41:10); my right hand spread out the heavens (Isa. 48:13); his right hand and his holy arm have gained him the victory (Ps. 98:1); the Lord has sworn by his right hand (Isa. 62:8); in the right hand of him seated on the throne (Rev. 5:1, 7).

C1b Christ's right hand
They put a reed in his right hand (Matt. 27:29); in his right hand he held seven stars (Rev. 1:16); he laid his right hand on me (Rev. 1:17).

C1c Other right hands
A mark on their right hand or forehead (Rev. 13:16); if your right hand causes you to stumble (Matt. 5:30); a man whose right hand was withered (Luke 6:6); if I forget Jerusalem, let my right hand forget (Ps. 137:5).

C2 Other right parts
Anointing their right ears, thumbs and big toes with blood (Exod. 29:20; Lev. 8:23, 24; 14:14, 25); with oil (Lev. 14:17, 28); Ehud had his sword on his right thigh (Judg. 3:16, 21); gouging out every right eye (1 Sam. 11:2); if your right eye causes you to stumble (Matt. 5:29); if anyone strikes you on the right cheek, turn to

him the other also (Matt. 5:39); Simon Peter cut off the slave's right ear (John 18:10).

D Right and left
D1 Things to right and left
The waters like a wall to right and left (Exod. 14:22, 29); Samson's right hand on one pillar and his left hand on the other (Judg. 16:29); one pillar on the right and one on the left (2 Chr. 3:17); two olive trees, one on the left and one on the right (Zech. 4:3, 11).

D2 People to right and left
Request for Zebedee's sons to sit on Christ's right and left (Matt. 20:21, 23; Mark 10:37); to sit at my right and left is not mine to grant (Mark 10:40); two robbers crucified on his right and left (Matt. 27:38; Mark 15:27; Luke 23:33); he will place the sheep on his right and the goats on his left (Matt. 25:33).

D3 Right and left hands
People who do not know their right hand from their left (Jonah 4:11); weapons of righteousness for the right hand and the left (2 Cor. 6:7); do not let your left hand know what your right hand is doing (Matt. 6:3); ambidextrous with sling and bow (1 Chr. 12:2).

D4 Turning to right and left
If you go to the left, I will go to the right, and vice versa (Gen. 13:9); he must not turn from the commandment to right or left (Deut. 17:20); no one can turn to right or left from what the king has said (2 Sam. 14:19); whether to left or right, I cannot see him (Job 23:9).

AMBIDEXTROUS, see 242B.

NOT TURN TO RIGHT OR LEFT, see 249C.

TURN TO RIGHT OR LEFT, see 282A2b.

242 Left side

RIGHT AND LEFT, see 241D.

A Left hand side
The fool's heart inclines him to the left hand (Eccles. 10:2); the left pillar was called Boaz (1 Kgs. 7:21); all four creatures had the face of a bull on the left (Ezek. 1:10); he will say to those at his left hand (Matt. 25:41).

B Left handed
Ehud was left-handed (Judg. 3:15); seven hundred soldiers who were left-handed (Judg. 20:16); ambidextrous with sling and bow (1 Chr. 12:2).

243 Form

Rachel was beautiful in form and appearance (Gen. 29:17); his form you have never seen (John 5:37).

244 Formlessness

The earth was formless and empty (Gen. 1:2; Jer. 4:23); the formless city is broken down (Isa. 24:10).

245 Symmetry

EQUAL MEASURE, see 28D.

246 Distortion

A Twisting
Who can straighten what God has bent? (Eccles. 7:13); he has made my paths crooked (Lam. 3:9); you are making crooked the straight paths of the Lord (Acts 13:10); they twisted like a deceitful bow (Ps. 78:57); the ignorant and unstable twist the scriptures to their own destruction (2 Pet. 3:16).

B Twisted ways
A twisted and crooked generation (Deut. 32:5); O unbelieving and crooked generation! (Matt. 17:17); O unbelieving and perverted generation! (Luke 9:41); in the midst of a crooked and perverse generation (Phil. 2:15); the crooked will be made straight (Luke 3:5).

C Bent over
A hunchback could not serve as priest (Lev. 21:20); I am bent and bowed down (Ps. 38:6); she could not straighten (Luke 13:11).

247 Angularity
At every corner she lies in wait (Prov. 7:12); hypocrites love to pray on street corners (Matt. 6:5).

248 Curvature
CIRCULAR, see 250.

249 Straightness
A Straightening
What is crooked cannot be straightened (Eccles. 1:15); who can straighten what God has bent? (Eccles. 7:13); the crooked will become straight (Luke 3:5); he laid his hands on her and she was made straight (Luke 13:13).

B Straight paths
Make his paths straight (Matt. 3:3; Mark 1:3; Luke 3:4); make straight in the desert a highway for our God (Isa. 40:3); make straight the way of the Lord (John 1:23); make straight paths for your feet (Heb. 12:13); make your way straight before me (Ps. 5:8); I will lead them on a straight path (Jer. 31:9); he led them by a straight way (Ps. 107:7); you are making crooked the straight paths of the Lord (Acts 13:10).

C Not turning aside
We will not turn to right or left (Num. 20:17; Deut. 2:27); do not turn aside to right or left (Deut. 5:32; 17:11, 20; 28:14; Josh. 1:7; 23:6; Prov. 4:27); every man went straight before him (Josh. 6:20); the cherubim went straight ahead (Ezek. 1:9, 12, 17; 10:11, 22); he encouraged the wicked not to turn from his wicked way (Ezek. 13:22); those who did not turn: the milch cows (1 Sam. 6:12); Asahel (2 Sam. 2:19-21); Josiah (2 Kgs. 22:2; 2 Chr. 34:2).
TURN TO RIGHT OR LEFT, see 282A2b.

250 Circularity
A Circle
God inscribes a circle on the face of the waters (Job 26:10); when God drew a circle on the face of the deep (Prov. 8:27); God sits above the circle of the earth (Isa. 40:22).
SPHERE, see 252.

B Rings
Pharaoh took off his ring and put it on Joseph's hand (Gen. 41:42); the king took his ring and gave it to Haman (Esther 3:10); the king took off his ring and gave it to Mordecai (Esther 8:2); letters sealed with the king's ring (Esther 3:12; 8:8, 10); the king and nobles sealed the den with their signet rings (Dan. 6:17); put a ring on his hand (Luke 15:22); if a man comes into your assembly with a gold ring (Jas. 2:2).

C Wheels
Problems with the chariot wheels (Exod. 14:25); each stand had four bronze wheels (1 Kgs. 7:30, 32-3); a wheel for each of the four creatures (Ezek. 1:15-21; 10:9); go in among the whirling wheels (Ezek. 10:2, 6); the wheels were called in my hearing the whirling wheels (Ezek. 10:13); the wheels were like gleaming chrysolite (Ezek. 10:9); their rims and spokes and wheels were full of eyes (Ezek. 10:12); wheels within wheels (Ezek. 1:16; 10:10); before the wheel crashes into the well (Eccles. 12:6).

D Rainbow
The rainbow was a sign of the covenant (Gen. 9:12-17); brightness round him like a rainbow (Ezek. 1:28); the rainbow on the angel's head (Rev. 10:1); a rainbow like an emerald round the throne (Rev. 4:3).

251 Convolution
A winding staircase to the chambers of the temple (1 Kgs. 6:8).

252 Sphere
The Lord will roll you up tightly like a ball (Isa. 22:18).

253 Convexity
You committed me to my mother's breasts (Ps. 22:9); let her breasts satisfy you (Prov. 5:19); their breasts were pressed (Ezek. 23:3, 8, 21); your two breasts are like two fawns (S. of S. 4:5; 7:3); your breasts are like clusters of the palm tree (S. of S. 7:7); may your breasts be like clusters of the vine (S. of S. 7:8); my breasts were like towers (S. of S. 8:10); your breasts had formed and your hair had grown (Ezek. 16:7); a golden girdle round his breasts (Rev. 1:13); blessed are the breasts you sucked (Luke 11:27); blessed are the wombs that never bore, the breasts that never nursed (Luke 23:29).

254 Prominence
A Horns
A1 Horns of animals
A ram caught by its horns (Gen. 22:13); you thrust at the weak with your horns (Ezek. 34:21); fill your horn with oil (1 Sam. 16:1).
A2 Horns of power
A2a Horns victorious
God is like the horns of the wild ox for Israel (Num. 23:22; 24:8); his horns are the horns of a wild ox (Deut. 33:17); you exalted my horn like that of the wild ox (Ps. 92:10); Zedekiah made horns of iron (1 Kgs. 22:11; 2 Chr. 18:10).
A2b Horns weakened
He will cut off the horns of the wicked (Ps. 75:10); in the fierceness of his anger he has cut down all the horn of Israel (Lam. 2:3).
A2c Horns in allegory
A little horn came up and uprooted three horns (Dan. 7:8); the other horn before which three horns fell (Dan. 7:20); a small horn which grew large (Dan. 8:9); four horns in place of the one broken (Dan. 8:8, 22); four horns which scattered Israel and Judah (Zech. 1:18-21); a he-goat with a horn between its eyes (Dan. 8:5); a ram with two horns (Dan. 8:3, 20); the beast had two horns like a lamb (Rev. 13:11); a beast with ten horns (Dan. 7:7, 20, 24); a beast with seven heads and ten horns (Rev. 12:3; 13:1; 17:3, 7); the ten horns you saw (Rev. 17:12, 16); a Lamb with seven horns and seven eyes (Rev. 5:6).
A3 Horns of altars
The altar of burnt offering with four horns (Exod. 27:2; 38:2); Adonijah clutched the horns of the altar (1 Kgs. 1:50, 51); Joab clutched the horns of the altar (1 Kgs. 2:28); the altar of incense with horns (Exod. 30:2, 3; 37:25, 26); the four horns of the golden altar (Rev. 9:13); their sin is engraved on the horns of their altars (Jer. 17:1); the horns of the altar of Bethel will be cut off (Amos 3:14).

B Tongue
Against whom do you stick out your tongue? (Isa. 57:4); I will make your tongue stick to the roof of your mouth (Ezek. 3:26); the baby's tongue cleaves to the roof of its mouth with thirst (Lam. 4:4); their tongue will rot in their mouth (Zech. 14:12); they gnawed their tongues because of pain (Rev. 16:10); Jesus spat and touched the man's tongue (Mark 7:33); his tongue was released (Mark 7:35); send Lazarus to dip the tip of his finger in water and cool my tongue (Luke 16:24); they deceive with their tongues (Rom. 3:13); the tongue is a

small member, but boasts great things (Jas. 3:5-6); no one can tame the tongue (Jas. 3:8); every tongue will confess that Jesus Christ is Lord (Phil. 2:11).

LANGUAGE, see 557.

255 Concavity

A Caves

A1 Caves for burying

The cave of Machpelah for burying (Gen. 23:9); I give you the field and the cave (Gen. 23:11); the field and the cave became Abraham's (Gen. 23:17, 20); burial place: of Sarah (Gen. 23:19); of Abraham (Gen. 25:9); of Jacob (Gen. 49:29-32; 50:13); Joseph of Arimathea had dug his own new tomb in the rock (Matt. 27:60); Jesus came to the tomb, a cave with a stone on it (John 11:38).

A2 People in caves

People will go into caves and holes from before the terror of the Lord (Isa. 2:19, 21); everyone hid in caves from the Lord (Rev. 6:15); Israel hid in caves etc. (1 Sam. 13:6); Obadiah hid prophets in a cave (1 Kgs. 18:4, 13); the cave of Adullam (1 Sam. 22:1; 2 Sam. 23:13; 1 Chr. 11:15); Lot and his daughters lived in a cave (Gen. 19:30); five kings hid in the cave at Makkedah (Josh. 10:16); Saul relieved himself in the cave (1 Sam. 24:3); David fled from Saul in the cave (Ps. 57:t); when David was in the cave (Ps. 142:t); he will have hidden himself in some cave (2 Sam. 17:9); Elijah came to a cave (1 Kgs. 19:9); they were in caves and holes in the ground (Heb. 11:38).

B Pits

TRENCH, see 262.

B1 Pits in general

Penalty for a dangerous pit (Exod. 21:33-4); he who flees from the sound of terror will fall into the pit (Isa. 24:18; Jer. 48:44); may they be cast into pits (Ps. 140:10); he was captured in their pit (Ezek. 19:4, 8); you will bring them down to the pit of destruction (Ps. 55:23); you would plunge me into a pit (Job 9:31); you put me in the lowest pit (Ps. 88:6); if a man has one sheep and it falls into a pit on the sabbath (Matt. 12:11); if a blind man leads a blind man, both will fall into a pit (Matt. 15:14; Luke 6:39); they were in caves and holes in the ground (Heb. 11:38); God kept angels who sinned in pits of darkness until the judgement (2 Pet. 2:4).

B2 Particular pits

Tar pits in the Valley of Siddim (Gen. 14:10); let us throw Joseph into a pit (Gen. 37:20-4); they threw Absalom's body into a deep pit (2 Sam. 18:17); killing a lion in a pit on a snowy day (2 Sam. 23:20; 1 Chr. 11:22); a harlot is a deep pit (Prov. 23:27); the mouth of an adulteress is a deep pit (Prov. 22:14); the key to the bottomless pit [abyss] was given to the star (Rev. 9:1); an angel had the key of the abyss (Rev. 20:1); the angel of the bottomless pit is their king (Rev. 9:11); the beast which comes out of the abyss will make war on the witnesses (Rev. 11:7); the beast is about to ascend from the bottomless pit (Rev. 17:8); the devil was thrown into the abyss (Rev. 20:3).

B3 'The pit'

B3a Going down to the pit

I am reckoned among those who go down to the pit (Ps. 88:4); lest I be like those who go down to the pit (Ps. 28:1; 143:7); what profit is it if I go down to the pit? (Ps. 30:9); send them down to the nether world, to the pit (Ezek. 32:18); do not say, 'Who will descend into the abyss?' (Rom. 10:7).

B3b Saved from the pit

He keeps back his soul from the pit (Job 33:18); he has redeemed my soul from going down to the pit (Job 33:28); he brought me up out of the pit (Ps. 40:2); you

brought up my life from the pit (Jonah 2:6); he redeems your life from the pit (Ps. 103:4).

C Valleys

C1 Valleys in general

He makes springs flow in the valleys (Ps. 104:10); the valleys shout for joy (Ps. 65:13); I am the lily of the valleys (S. of S. 2:1); though I walk through the valley dark as death (Ps. 23:4); the valleys will be split under the Lord (Mic. 1:4); every valley will be filled in (Isa. 40:4; Luke 3:5).

C2 Named valleys

The valley of: Achor (Josh. 7:24-6; 15:7; Isa. 65:10; Hos. 2:15); Ben-hinnom [son of Hinnom] (Josh. 15:8; 18:16; 2 Kgs. 23:10; 2 Chr. 28:3; 33:6; Neh. 11:30; Jer. 7:31-2; 19:2, 6; 32:35); Eshcol (Num. 13:23, 24; 32:9; Deut. 1:24); Jezreel (Josh. 17:16; Judg. 6:33; Hos. 1:5); Jordan (Gen. 13:10, 11); Kidron (2 Chr. 29:16; John 18:1).

C3 Unnamed valleys

Lot dwelt in the cities of the valley (Gen. 13:12); the Lord overthrew all that valley (Gen. 19:25); Abraham looked down all the land of the valley (Gen. 19:28); God destroyed the cities of the valley (Gen. 19:29); make this valley full of trenches (2 Kgs. 3:16); the valley of dry bones (Ezek. 37:1); the oracle concerning the valley of vision (Isa. 22:1); multitudes in the valley of decision (Joel 3:14); the mount of Olives will be split by a great valley (Zech. 14:4).

D Excavation

D1 Digging

A witness that I dug this well (Gen. 21:30); the wells Isaac's father had dug (Gen. 26:15); the well the princes dug (Num. 21:18); Isaac's servants digging wells (Gen. 26:19, 21, 22, 25); Isaac's servants dug a well and it was called Shibah (Gen. 26:32-3); the Egyptians dug around the Nile for drinking water (Exod. 7:24); dig through the wall (Ezek. 8:8); look to the quarry from which you were dug (Isa. 51:1); he who received one talent went and dug in the ground (Matt. 25:18); I am not strong enough to dig (Luke 16:3).

D2 Mines

There is a mine for silver (Job 28:1-11).

E Hollow

The altar was hollow (Exod. 27:8; 38:7); the pillars were hollow (1 Kgs. 7:15; Jer. 52:21).

256 Sharpness

A Sharp things

A1 Knives

Abraham took the fire and a knife in his hand (Gen. 22:6, 10); flint knives for circumcision (Exod. 4:25; Josh. 5:2-3); put a knife to your throat if you are a man of appetite (Prov. 23:2).

A2 Razors

Take a sharp sword and use it as a barber's razor (Ezek. 5:1); a razor hired from beyond the Euphrates, the king of Assyria (Isa. 7:20); your tongue is like a sharp razor (Ps. 52:2); no razor shall come upon the Nazirite's head (Num. 6:5; Judg. 13:5; 16:17; 1 Sam. 1:11).

A3 Swords

Pierce me through with your sword (1 Sam. 31:4); their tongue is a sharp sword (Ps. 57:4); swords are in their lips (Ps. 59:7); he made my mouth like a sharp sword (Isa. 49:2); the word of God is sharper than a two-edged sword (Heb. 4:12); out of his mouth came a sharp two-edged sword (Rev. 1:16; 2:12; 19:15).

SWORDS AS WEAPONS, see 723A4.

A4 Sharp tools

Cutting down a tree with an axe (Deut. 19:5; 20:19); a three-pronged fork (1 Sam. 2:13); they threshed Gilead with sharp iron tools (Amos 1:3); pierce his ear with an awl (Exod. 21:6; Deut. 15:17); Jael pierced Sisera's temple with a tent-peg (Judg. 4:21; 5:26); Shamgar killed Philistines with an ox-goad (Judg. 3:31); the words of the wise are like goads (Eccles. 12:11); it is hard for you to kick against the goads (Acts 26:14); can you catch the crocodile with a fishhook? (Job 41:1); can you fill his skin with harpoons or fishing spears? (Job 41:7); your arrows are sharp (Ps. 45:5); their arrows are sharp (Isa. 5:28); a camel going through the eye of a needle (Matt. 19:24; Mark 10:25; Luke 18:25); a sharp sickle (Rev. 14:14, 17, 18).

A5 Briars / thorns
For Israel, no more pricking thorn or painful briar (Ezek. 28:24); I will hedge up her way with thorns (Hos. 2:6); they plaited a crown of thorns and put it on him (Mark 15:17).

B Teeth
B1 Teeth in general
The grinders stand idle because they are few (Eccles. 12:3); I have escaped by the skin of my teeth (Job 19:20); trust in a faithless man is like a bad tooth (Prov. 25:19); some people have teeth like swords and knives (Prov. 30:14); round the teeth of the crocodile there is terror (Job 41:14); a beast with iron teeth (Dan. 7:7, 19); the locusts had teeth like those of lions (Rev. 9:8); its teeth are lions' teeth, the fangs of a lioness (Joel 1:6); I gave you cleanness of teeth and lack of bread (Amos 4:6).

B2 Gnashing teeth
God gnashes at me with his teeth (Job 16:9); they gnashed at me with their teeth (Ps. 35:16); there will be weeping and gnashing of teeth (Matt. 8:12; 13:42, 50; 22:13; 24:51; 25:30); you will weep and gnash your teeth (Luke 13:28); they gnashed their teeth at him (Acts 7:54); he foams at the mouth and grinds his teeth (Mark 9:18).

B3 Breaking teeth
Tooth for tooth (Exod. 21:24; Lev. 24:20; Matt. 5:38); knocking out a slave's tooth (Exod. 21:27); shatter their teeth (Ps. 58:6); you have shattered the teeth of the wicked (Ps. 3:7); I broke the teeth of the wicked (Job 29:17); the lions' teeth are broken (Job 4:10).

C Sharpening
If he does not sharpen the axe, he must exert more strength (Eccles. 10:10); the Israelites went to the Philistines to sharpen tools (1 Sam. 13:20); as iron sharpens iron, so one man sharpens another (Prov. 27:17); God will sharpen his sword (Deut. 32:41; Ps. 7:12); they have sharpened their tongue like a sword (Ps. 64:3); they sharpen their tongues like a serpent (Ps. 140:3).

257 Bluntness
If the iron is blunt (Eccles. 10:10).

258 Smoothness
A Smooth
I am a smooth man (Gen. 27:11); kids' skins on the smooth part of the neck (Gen. 27:16); his speech was smoother than butter (Ps. 55:21); the rough ways will become smooth (Luke 3:5).

B Slippery
Let their way be dark and slippery (Ps. 35:6); you set them in slippery places (Ps. 73:18); their way will be like slippery paths (Jer. 23:12).

259 Roughness
A Hair
A1 Body hair
A1a Hairy people
Esau was a hairy man (Gen. 27:11); Esau's body was like a hairy garment (Gen. 25:25); Jacob's hands were hairy

like the hands of Esau (Gen. 27:23); Elijah was a hairy man (2 Kgs. 1:8).

A1b The hair of the body
If the hair has turned white (Lev. 13:3-37); the hair of my flesh stood up (Job 4:15); the Lord will shave the head, the hair of the legs and the beard (Isa. 7:20).

A2 Hair of the head
A2a Appearance of hair
Your hair is like a flock of goats (S. of S. 4:1; 6:5); his hair is black as a raven (S. of S. 5:11); his hair was like pure wool (Dan. 7:9); hair white as wool (Rev. 1:14); you cannot make one hair white or black (Matt. 5:36); the hair of their head was not singed (Dan. 3:27); not with braided hair (1 Tim. 2:9; 1 Pet. 3:3).
WHITE HAIR, see 427B.
GREY HAIR, see 429.

A2b Long hair
Samson's strength lay in his hair (Judg. 16:17, 19); weaving Samson's hair (Judg. 16:13-14); his hair began to grow again (Judg. 16:22); Absalom's hair weighed two hundred shekels when it was cut (2 Sam. 14:26); if a woman has long hair it is her glory (1 Cor. 11:15); the locusts had hair like the hair of women (Rev. 9:8); the long-haired heads of the enemy (Deut. 32:42); the priests are not to grow their hair long (Ezek. 44:20); does not nature teach you that long hair is a disgrace for a man? (1 Cor. 11:14).

A2c Hair cut
Absalom's hair weighed two hundred shekels when it was cut (2 Sam. 14:26); use a sharp sword as a barber's razor on your head and beard (Ezek. 5:1); Paul cut his hair, for he had a vow (Acts 18:18); the Lord will shave the head, the hair of the legs and the beard (Isa. 7:20); priests must only trim the hair of their heads (Ezek. 44:20); do not cut your hair at the sides of your head (Lev. 19:27); the Nazirite must not cut his hair while he is under the vow (Num. 6:5); if a woman will not cover her head, let her have her hair cut off (1 Cor. 11:6); if it is a disgrace for her to have her hair cut off or shaved, let her cover her head (1 Cor. 11:6).

A2d Hairs protected
Not one of Jonathan's hairs shall fall to the ground (1 Sam. 14:45); no hair of your son's head shall fall to the ground (2 Sam. 14:11); not one of Adonijah's hairs would fall to the ground (1 Kgs. 1:52); not a hair of your head will perish (Luke 21:18; Acts 27:34).

A2e Number of hairs
The hairs of your head are all counted (Matt. 10:30; Luke 12:7); my iniquities are more than the hairs of my head (Ps. 40:12); those who hate me without cause are more than the hairs of my head (Ps. 69:4).

A2f Other references to hair
An accused woman must let her hair hang loose (Num. 5:18); burn one third of the hair at the centre of the city (Ezek. 5:2); Ezekiel was lifted by a lock of hair (Ezek. 8:3); 700 men who could sling a stone at a hair (Judg. 20:16); Mary wiped his feet with her hair (Luke 7:38, 44; John 11:2; 12:3).

A3 Facial hair
A3a Facial hair in general
David would seize the lion or bear by the beard (1 Sam. 17:35); Joab took Amasa by the beard (2 Sam. 20:9); stay in Jericho until your beards have grown (2 Sam. 10:5); Mephibosheth had not seen to his moustache (2 Sam. 19:24); the oil running down Aaron's beard (Ps. 133:2); the leper must cover his moustache (Lev. 13:45); do not cover your moustache (Ezek. 24:17); you will not cover your moustache (Ezek. 24:22).

A3b Trimming facial hair
Do not trim your beards [for the dead] (Lev. 19:27; 21:5); the cleansed leper must shave off his hair, beard

and eyebrows (Lev. 14:9); Hanun cut off half their beards (2 Sam. 10:4; 1 Chr. 19:4, 5); Ezra plucked out some of his hair and beard (Ezra 9:3); I gave my cheeks to those who pluck out the beard (Isa. 50:6); the Lord will shave the head, the hair of the legs and the beard (Isa. 7:20).

SHAVE, see 648A6.

A4 Hair garments

Elijah wore a garment of hair and a leather belt (2 Kgs. 1:8); as did John the Baptist (Matt. 3:4; Mark 1:6); the sun became black as sackcloth made of hair (Rev. 6:12).

B Wool

The king of Moab paid wool as tribute (2 Kgs. 3:4); the priests were not to wear wool (Ezek. 44:17); she looks for wool and flax (Prov. 31:13); trading in the wine of Helbon and white wool (Ezek. 27:18); you eat the fat and clothe yourselves with the wool (Ezek. 34:3); my lovers give me my wool and flax, my oil and drink (Hos. 2:5); I will take away my wool and my flax (Hos. 2:9).

260 Notch

FURROW, see 262.

261 Fold

FURROW, see 262.

262 Furrow

Elijah made a trench around the altar (1 Kgs. 18:32); make this valley full of trenches (2 Kgs. 3:16).

PIT, see 255B.

263 Opening

EYES OPENED, see 438A2.

A The act of opening

A1 Opening in general

Knock and it will be opened to you (Matt. 7:7-8; Luke 11:9-10); he who opens and no one shuts (Rev. 3:7).

A2 Opening things

A2a Opening the womb

Set apart every firstborn which opens the womb (Exod. 13:2, 12); every male that opens the womb shall be holy to the Lord (Luke 2:23).

A2b Opening pits / caves

They would roll the stone from the mouth of the well (Gen. 29:3); if a man opens a pit and leaves it uncovered (Exod. 21:33); he opened the abyss (Rev. 9:2); open the mouth of the cave (Josh. 10:22); remove the stone (John 11:39-41); the stone was rolled back (Mark 16:3-4; Luke 24:2; John 20:1); the tombs were opened (Matt. 27:52).

A2c Opening walls / roofs

A hole in the wall (Ezek. 8:7); many breaches in the wall of the city of David (Isa. 22:9); Noah removed the covering of the ark (Gen. 8:13); they made an opening in the roof (Mark 2:4).

A2d Opening gates / doors

Samuel opened the doors of the house of the Lord (1 Sam. 3:15); Hezekiah opened the doors of the temple (2 Chr. 29:3); the sanctuary in heaven was opened (Rev. 11:19; 15:5); the east gate of the inner court is to be opened on the Sabbath (Ezek. 46:1); when the prince makes an offering the gate facing east shall be opened (Ezek. 46:12); the gate opened by itself (Acts 12:10); open to me the gates of righteousness (Ps. 118:19); lift up your heads, you gates (Ps. 24:7, 9); open the gates that the righteous may enter (Isa. 26:2); do not open the gates of Jerusalem until the sun is hot (Neh. 7:3); the gates of the new Jerusalem shall never be shut (Rev. 21:25); your gates will be open day and night (Isa.

60:11); the river gates are opened (Nahum 2:6); because of her joy, Rhoda did not open the gate (Acts 12:14).

A2e Opening heaven

The heavens were opened and I saw visions of God (Ezek. 1:1); in heaven an open door (Rev. 4:1); heaven opened at Christ's baptism (Matt. 3:16; Mark 1:10; Luke 3:21; John 1:51); heaven opened to Stephen (Acts 7:56); heaven opened before Peter (Acts 10:11); I saw heaven opened (Rev. 19:11); see if I will not open for you the windows of heaven (Mal. 3:10).

A2f Opening documents

The opening of your words gives light (Ps. 119:130); who is worthy to open the book and break its seals? (Rev. 5:2-5); you are worthy to take the book and open the seals (Rev. 5:9); the court sat and the books were opened (Dan. 7:10); books were opened (Rev. 20:12); a little book open in the angel's hand (Rev. 10:2); take the book which is open in the hand of the angel (Rev. 10:8);

opening of the: first seal (Rev. 6:1); second seal (Rev. 6:3); third seal (Rev. 6:5); fourth seal (Rev. 6:7); fifth seal (Rev. 6:9); sixth seal (Rev. 6:12); seventh seal (Rev. 8:1).

A3 Opening to others

If any one hears my voice and opens the door (Rev. 3:20); that they may open to him when he knocks (Luke 12:36); to him the gatekeeper opens (John 10:3); open to me, my sister (S. of S. 5:2); I arose to open to my beloved (S. of S. 5:5-6); when they opened the door and saw Peter they were amazed (Acts 12:16); Lord, open to us! (Matt. 25:11; Luke 13:25); ephphatha – be opened (Mark 7:34); the Lord opened Lydia's heart to respond (Acts 16:14); he who opens and no one shuts (Rev. 3:7-8); an angel of the Lord opened the gates of the prison (Acts 5:19).

A4 Piercing

Pierce his ear with an awl (Exod. 21:6; Deut. 15:17); he shall be impaled on a beam from his house (Ezra 6:11); Phinehas transfixed the man and woman with a spear (Num. 25:8); Jael impaled Sisera (Judg. 4:21; 5:26); Abner struck Asahel so the butt of his spear came out at the back (2 Sam. 2:23); Joab pierced Absalom (2 Sam. 18:14); they pierced my hands and feet (Ps. 22:16); they will look on him they pierced (Zech. 12:10; John 19:37); those who pierced him (Rev. 1:7); a soldier pierced his side (John 19:34); a sword will pierce your own soul also (Luke 2:35); through love of money some have pierced themselves (1 Tim. 6:10); when they heard this they were pierced to the heart (Acts 2:37).

B Doorways

B1 Doorways of the tent / temple

B1a Presented at the doorway

Aaron and his sons to be brought to the doorway of the tent of meeting (Exod. 29:4; 40:12); remain there for seven days (Lev. 8:33, 35); do not go out from the doorway of the tent of meeting (Lev. 10:7); better to stand at the threshold of the house of God (Ps. 84:10); the cleansed leper presented (Lev. 14:11, 23); the cleansed person comes (Lev. 15:14, 29).

B1b Sacrifices at the doorway

One who offers sacrifice not at the doorway of the tent of meeting (Lev. 17:9); at the doorway: the bull to be killed (Exod. 29:11); priests eating (Exod. 29:32); the ram of ordination to be eaten (Lev. 8:31); sacrifice offered (Lev. 1:3, 5; 3:2, 13; 4:4; 12:6; 16:7; 19:21; Num. 6:10); the altar of burnt offering (Exod. 40:6, 29; Lev. 4:18); animals brought to be killed (Lev. 17:4, 5).

B1c God appearing at the doorway

The glory of the Lord went up from the cherub to the threshhold (Ezek. 10:4); the glory of the Lord went up to the threshhold of the house (Ezek. 9:3); then the glory of the Lord departed from the threshhold (Ezek. 10:18); at the doorway: the pillar of cloud would stand (Exod. 33:9, 10); pillar of cloud (Deut. 31:15); the Lord stood (Num. 12:5).

B1d Other activity at the doorway
Water flowed from under the threshold of the temple (Ezek. 47:1); I will punish all who leap over the temple threshold (Zeph. 1:9); at the doorway: the Nazirite shall shave his head (Num. 6:18); inheritances distributed (Josh. 19:51); women served (Exod. 38:8); Eli's sons lay with the serving women (1 Sam. 2:22).

B2 Other doorways
Blood on the doorposts and lintel (Exod. 12:7, 22); write these words on your doorposts (Deut. 6:9; 11:20); setting their doorpost by my doorpost with only a wall between (Ezek. 43:8); every one at the door of his tent (Exod. 33:8, 10); bring the slave to the doorpost (Exod. 21:6); the concubine was lying in the doorway with her hands on the threshold (Judg. 19:27); the whole city gathered at the door (Mark 1:33); the Judge is standing at the door (Jas. 5:9).

B3 Door of opportunity
I have placed before you an open door (Rev. 3:8); a wide door has opened for me (1 Cor. 16:9); a door was opened for me in the Lord (2 Cor. 2:12); God opened a door of faith for the Gentiles (Acts 14:27); pray that God will open a door for the word (Col. 4:3); the valley of Achor will be a door of hope (Hos. 2:15).

C Gateways
C1 Gateways
The well by the gate of Bethlehem (2 Sam. 23:15, 16); two heaps of heads at the gateway of Jezreel (2 Kgs. 10:8); the gate of Samaria (2 Kgs. 7:1, 18; 2 Chr. 18:9); the Jews watched the gates of Damascus day and night (Acts 9:24); he drew near to the gateway of the city (Luke 7:12); Peter went out into the gateway (Matt. 26:71); Lazarus lay at the rich man's gate (Luke 16:20); Solomon's portico (John 10:23; Acts 3:11; 5:12); this is the gate of heaven (Gen. 28:17); this is the gate of the Lord (Ps. 118:20); enter by the narrow gate (Matt. 7:13); the gate is wide which leads to destruction (Matt. 7:13); the gate is narrow which leads to life (Matt. 7:14); that they may enter the city by the gates (Rev. 22:14); waiting daily at Wisdom's gate (Prov. 8:34).

C2 Capturing gates
Your seed will possess the gate of their enemies (Gen. 22:17); may your seed possess the gate of those who hate them (Gen. 24:60); Abimelech and his company took the city gate (Judg. 9:44).

C3 Business at the gateway
They will speak with their enemies in the gate (Ps. 127:5); do not crush the afflicted at the gate (Prov. 22:22); establish justice in the gate (Amos 5:15); bring the evildoer to the gates and stone them (Deut. 17:5); those who lay a snare for him who reproves in the gate (Isa. 29:21); they hate him who reproves in the gate (Amos 5:10); you turn aside the poor in the gate (Amos 5:12); Hamor and Shechem spoke to the men at the gate of the city (Gen. 34:20); Joab spoke to Abner in the middle of the gate (2 Sam. 3:27); at the entrance of the gates Wisdom cries (Prov. 1:21); at the gates of the city Wisdom cries (Prov. 8:3); a fool does not open his mouth in the gate (Prov. 24:7).

C4 Sitting in the gateway
Those who sit in the gate talk about me (Ps. 69:12); sitting on thrones at the entrance of the gate of Samaria (1 Kgs. 22:10); each will set his throne at the entrance of the gates of Jerusalem (Jer. 1:15); David sat between the two gates (2 Sam. 18:24); her husband sits in the gate among the elders (Prov. 31:23); old men are gone from the gate (Lam. 5:14); those who sat in the gate: Lot

(Gen. 19:1); Tamar (Gen. 38:14); Boaz (Ruth 4:1); David (2 Sam. 19:8); Mordecai (Esther 2:19, 21; 5:9, 13; 6:10, 12); Job (Job 29:7); the lame man (Acts 3:2, 10).

D Windows
If God made windows in heaven, could this happen? (2 Kgs. 7:2, 19); Daniel had windows in his upper room open towards Jerusalem (Dan. 6:10); Eutychus was sitting in the window (Acts 20:9); Abimelech looked down through a window (Gen. 26:8); Sisera's mother looks out of the window (Judg. 5:28); Michal looked out of a window and saw David dancing (2 Sam. 6:16; 1 Chr. 15:29); Jezebel looked out of the window (2 Kgs. 9:30); Rahab lowered the spies from a window (Josh. 2:15); Michal lowered David from a window (1 Sam. 19:12).

E Keys
Eliakim will be given the key to the house of David (Isa. 22:22); Christ holds the key of David (Rev. 3:7); I have the keys of death and Hades (Rev. 1:18); I will give you the keys of the kingdom of heaven, to bind and loose (Matt. 16:19); you have taken away the key of knowledge (Luke 11:52); they took the key and opened the doors (Judg. 3:25); a star was given the key to the abyss (Rev. 9:1); he opened the abyss (Rev. 9:2); an angel had the key of the abyss (Rev. 20:1).

F The mouth
F1 Speaking with the mouth
Who made man's mouth? (Exod. 4:11); the little horn had a mouth uttering great things (Dan. 7:8); idols have mouths but cannot speak (Ps. 115:5; 135:16); God chose that by my mouth the Gentiles should hear (Acts 15:7); the word is near you, in your mouth and in your heart (Rom. 10:8); with the mouth a man confesses and is saved (Rom. 10:10).

F2 Eating with mouths
Open your mouth and I will fill it (Ps. 81:10); I open my mouth, longing for your commandments (Ps. 119:131); I opened my mouth and he gave me this scroll to eat (Ezek. 3:2); open your mouth and eat what I will give you (Ezek. 2:8).

F3 Other references to mouths
Elisha put his mouth on the boy's mouth (2 Kgs. 4:34); he touched my mouth with the coal (Isa. 6:7); the Lord touched my mouth (Jer. 1:9); your mouth is lovely (S. of S. 4:3); oh, that he would kiss me with the kisses of his mouth! (S. of S. 1:2); my God sent his angel and shut the lions' mouths (Dan. 6:22); by faith they shut the mouths of lions (Heb. 11:33); the earth opened its mouth (Gen. 4:11; Num. 16:30-4; 26:10; Ps. 106:17; Rev. 12:16); what enters the mouth does not defile a man, but what comes out of the mouth (Matt. 15:11); whatever enters the mouth passes into the stomach (Matt. 15:17); whatever comes out of the mouth comes from the heart (Matt. 15:18); the high priest Ananias ordered him to be struck on the mouth (Acts 23:2); out of his mouth came a sharp two-edged sword (Rev. 1:16; 19:15); I will make war against them with the sword of my mouth (Rev. 2:16); fire and smoke and sulphur issue from their mouths (Rev. 9:17, 18); the power of the horses is in their mouths and in their tails (Rev. 9:19); the beast's mouth was like a lion (Rev. 13:2); spirits like frogs came out of the mouths of the dragon, the beast and the false prophet (Rev. 16:13).

F4 Lips
I will put my bridle in your lips (2 Kgs. 19:28; Isa. 37:29); that your lips may guard knowledge (Prov. 5:2); your lips drip honey (S. of S. 4:11); the lips of an adulteress drip honey (Prov. 5:3); his lips are lilies (S. of S. 5:13); your lips are like a scarlet thread (S. of S. 4:3); one like a human being touched my lips (Dan. 10:16); I am of uncircumcised lips (Exod. 6:12, 30); this people

honours me with their lips (Matt. 15:8; Mark 7:6); the
fruit of lips giving thanks to his name (Heb. 13:15).

G Other openings
An opening in the robe of the ephod (Exod. 28:32;
39:23); easier for a camel to go through the eye of a
needle (Matt. 19:24; Mark 10:25; Luke 18:25).

264 Closure

A Doors

A1 Doors in general
A door for the ark (Gen. 6:16); I dug through the wall,
and there was a door (Ezek. 8:8); they came near to
breaking the door down (Gen. 19:9); they wearied
themselves trying to find the door (Gen. 19:11); he who
does not enter the sheepfold by the door is a thief
(John 10:1); he who enters by the door is the shepherd
(John 10:2); if she is a door (S. of S. 8:9); I am the door
of the sheep (John 10:7); I am the door (John 10:9); he
is near, at the very door (Matt. 24:33); I stand at the
door and knock (Rev. 3:20).

A2 Shutting doors
LOCK, see 662D.

A2a Shutting temple doors
Ahaz shut the doors of the temple (2 Chr. 28:24); let us
close the doors of the temple (Neh. 6:10); oh, that one
of you would shut the doors! (Mal. 1:10).

A2b Figurative shutting of doors
Who shut in the sea with doors? (Job 38:8); I set a bar
and doors for the sea (Job 38:10); the doors on the
street are shut (Eccles. 12:4); the way into the sanctuary
is not yet open (Heb. 9:8).

A2c Other shutting of doors
God closed up the ark (Gen. 7:16); Lot shut the door
behind him (Gen. 19:6); the angels shut the door (Gen.
19:10); Ehud shut the doors behind him (Judg. 3:23);
shut the door behind you (2 Kgs. 4:4); enter your
rooms and shut the doors behind you (Isa. 26:20);
when you pray, go into your room and shut the door
(Matt. 6:6); Elisha shut the door and prayed (2 Kgs.
4:33); the doors were shut (John 20:19, 26); the priest
shall shut up the house for seven days (Lev. 14:38);
whoever goes into a house which the priest has shut up
is unclean (Lev. 14:46); shut the door against the king's
messenger (2 Kgs. 6:32); the door is shut (Luke 11:7).

A3 Doorkeepers
King's eunuchs who were doorkeepers (Esther 6:2);
Maaseiah son of Shallum the doorkeeper (Jer. 35:4); he
commanded the doorkeeper to keep watch (Mark
13:34); I would rather be a doorkeeper in the house of
my God (Ps. 84:10).

B Gates

B1 City gates
New Jerusalem had 12 gates (Rev. 21:12-13); the 12 gates
of the city were 12 pearls (Rev. 21:21); 12 gates of the city
(Ezek. 48:30-4); the gates of Jerusalem have been
burned (Neh. 1:3; 2:3, 13, 17); doors were not yet set up
in the gateways (Neh. 6:1); setting up Jericho's gates
cost the youngest son (Josh. 6:26; 1 Kgs. 16:34); the river
gates are opened (Nahum 2:6); they watched the gates
day and night (Acts 9:24); they came to the iron gate
leading into the city (Acts 12:10); measuring the city, its
gates and its wall (Rev. 21:15).

B2 Other gates
Write these words on your gates (Deut. 6:9; 11:20); you
will call your gates Praise (Isa. 60:18); a nation without
gates or bars (Jer. 49:31); Samson uprooted the gate and
its posts (Judg. 16:3); the gates of Hades will not prevail
against the church (Matt. 16:18); Peter knocked on the
door of the gateway (Acts 12:13-14).

B3 Shutting gates
Shutting the gate at evening (Josh. 2:5, 7); Jericho was
shut up (Josh. 6:1); David has shut himself into a city
with gates and bars (1 Sam. 23:7); Nehemiah ordered
the gates of Jerusalem to be shut (Neh. 13:19); the
temple gates were shut (Acts 21:30); the gate shall not
be shut until evening (Ezek. 46:2); your gates will never
be shut (Isa. 60:11); its gates will never be shut (Rev.
21:25).

C Sealing
STONES AS STOPPERS, see 344B5.

C1 Sealing things
They sealed the tomb (Matt. 27:66); they shut the abyss
and sealed it over him (Rev. 20:3); a document which
was sealed (Neh. 10:1); God closed up the flesh where
the rib came from (Gen. 2:21); when the sky was shut
up for three years and six months (Luke 4:25); God
shut the lions' mouths (Dan. 6:22); he thrust the lead
weight on the mouth of the ephah (Zech. 5:8); do not
muzzle an ox which is threshing (1 Cor. 9:9); when you
believed you were sealed with the Holy Spirit (Eph.
1:13); you were sealed with the Holy Spirit (Eph. 4:30).

C2 Stopping wells
The Philistines stopped up the wells (Gen. 26:15, 18); a
large stone was over the mouth of the well (Gen. 29:2);
they put back the stone on the mouth of the well (Gen.
29:3).

C3 Sealing the message
Seal up the vision (Dan. 8:26); like the words of a
sealed book (Isa. 29:11); seal up the words of the scroll
(Dan. 12:4); seal up the law among my disciples (Isa.
8:16); the words are sealed up until the end time (Dan.
12:9); seal up what the seven thunders said (Rev. 10:4);
the book was sealed with seven seals (Rev. 5:1); sealed
with the king's signet ring (Esther 3:12; 8:8, 10); to seal
both vision and prophet (Dan. 9:24); do not seal up the
words of this book (Rev. 22:10).

C4 Shutting the kingdom
You shut the kingdom of heaven against men (Matt.
23:13); the door of the marriage feast was shut (Matt.
25:10); what he shuts no one will open (Isa. 22:22); he
shuts and no one opens (Rev. 3:7).

C5 Damming streams
Man dams up the streams (Job 28:11).

265 Motion

A Not still
The Spirit of God moved over the face of the waters
(Gen. 1:2); the war horse cannot stand still at the sound
of the trumpet (Job 39:24); I will not be still (Isa. 65:6);
how can the sword be still when the Lord has
commanded it? (Jer. 47:7); the dove found no
resting-place (Gen. 8:9).

B Driving
Jehu drove furiously (2 Kgs. 9:20); their chariot wheels
drove heavily (Exod. 14:25); Jacob drove his livestock
from Paddan-aram (Gen. 31:18); if the flocks are
overdriven for one day they will die (Gen. 33:13).

266 Stillness

A Motionless
FIXED, see 153.

A1 Incapable of motion
He makes an idol which cannot move (Isa. 40:20); they
fasten the idol so that it cannot move (Jer. 10:4).

A2 Coming to rest
The ark rested on the mountains of Ararat (Gen. 8:4);
stand still in the waters of Jordan (Josh. 3:8); everyone
stood still when they saw Asahel was dead (2 Sam.
2:23); Ahimaaz turned aside and stood still (2 Sam.
18:30); when they saw Amasa they stood still (2 Sam.

20:12); they stood still, looking sad (Luke 24:17); when the cherubim stood still, the wheels stood still (Ezek. 1:21; 10:17).

CEASING, see 145.

A3 Staying put
Stay with the worthy person until you depart (Matt. 10:11; Mark 6:10; Luke 9:4); remain in the same house (Luke 10:7); the people did not move on until Miriam returned to the camp (Num. 12:15); neither the ark nor Moses left the camp (Num. 14:44); Jesus stayed where he was two days longer (John 11:6); I went nowhere (2 Kgs. 5:25); some tribes stayed away from the war (Judg. 5:16-17).

A4 Undisturbed
Jerusalem, an undisturbed habitation (Isa. 33:20); they were glad because they had quiet (Ps. 107:30); in quietness and trust will be your strength (Isa. 30:15); the effect of righteousness will be quietness and trust for ever (Isa. 32:17); better a dry morsel with quiet (Prov. 17:1).

B Stilling

B1 Be still!
Be still and know that I am God (Ps. 46:10); meditate on your bed and be still (Ps. 4:4); sun and moon, stand still (Josh. 10:12-13); sword of the Lord, be at rest and stay still (Jer. 47:6).

B2 Making still
God stilled the sea by his power (Job 26:12); he stills the roaring of the seas (Ps. 65:7); you still the waves of the sea (Ps. 89:9); he stilled the storm (Ps. 107:29); Jesus rebuked the wind and sea and there was calm (Matt. 8:26; Mark 4:39; Luke 8:24); what should we do to you so that the sea will become calm? (Jonah 1:11-15); I have calmed and quieted my soul (Ps. 131:2).

267 Land travel

A Journeying
You who travel by road (Judg. 5:10); have you not asked those who travel the roads? (Job 21:29); if anyone is on a journey he may keep the Passover later (Num. 9:10); like a man going on a journey (Matt. 25:14; Mark 13:34); the Samaritan as he journeyed saw the man (Luke 10:33); Paul was on frequent journeys (2 Cor. 11:26); a three-days' journey into the wilderness (Exod. 3:18; 5:3; 8:27; Num. 33:8); Israel travelled day and night (Exod. 13:21); the Israelites set out on their journeys (Num. 10:12); they journeyed by stages (Exod. 17:1); the stages in the Israelites' journey from Egypt (Num. 21:10-20; 33:1-49); my husband has gone on a journey (Prov. 7:19); Jesus was setting out on a journey (Mark 10:17); a friend of mine has arrived on a journey (Luke 11:6).

B Wandering

TRAVELLER, see 268A.

B1 Wanderers
Cain would be a wanderer on the earth (Gen. 4:12, 14); a wandering Aramean was my father (Deut. 26:5); they will be wanderers among the nations (Hos. 9:17); Israel wandered from nation to nation (1 Chr. 16:20; Ps. 105:13); wandering over deserts and mountains (Heb. 11:38); my flock wandered over mountains and every high hill (Ezek. 34:6); they will wander from sea to sea and from north to east (Amos 8:12); you have taken account of my wanderings (Ps. 56:8); shall I make you wander with us? (2 Sam. 15:20); when God caused me to wander (Gen. 20:13); the harlot's feet do not remain at home (Prov. 7:11); itinerant Jewish exorcists tried to use the name of Jesus (Acts 19:13); Satan came from roaming about on the earth (Job 1:7; 2:2); the devil prowls like a roaring lion (1 Pet. 5:8); wandering stars

for whom darkness has been reserved for ever (Jude 13).

B2 Patrolling
These are those the Lord has sent to patrol the earth (Zech. 1:10); these seven are the eyes of the Lord which range through all the earth (Zech. 4:10); we have patrolled the earth and it is all peaceful and quiet (Zech. 1:11).

C Walking

RUNNING, see 277B.

C1 Walking in general
Four things are stately in walk, lions, cocks, goats and kings (Prov. 30:29-31); I have seen princes walking like slaves (Eccles. 10:7); talk of them when you sit and when you walk (Deut. 6:7; 11:19); I see people, but they look like trees, walking (Mark 8:24); if anyone walks in the day he does not stumble (John 11:9); when you were young you walked wherever you wished (John 21:18); I taught Ephraim to walk (Hos. 11:3); walk through the length and breadth of the land (Gen. 13:17); every place on which the sole of your foot treads is yours (Prov. 11:24; Josh. 1:3); Elisha walked to and fro (2 Kgs. 4:35); you walked in the midst of the stones of fire (Ezek. 28:14); two disciples walking to Emmaus (Luke 24:13); John looked at Jesus as he walked (John 1:36).

C2 God walking
God walking about in the garden (Gen. 3:8); God walks on the wings on the wind (Ps. 104:3); he who treads on the high places of the earth (Amos 4:13); you strode through the earth in fury (Hab. 3:12).

C3 Walking with God
That I may walk before God (Ps. 56:13); I walk before the Lord in the land of the living (Ps. 116:9); Enoch walked with God until God took him (Gen. 5:22-4).

C4 The healed walking
The lame walk (Matt. 11:5; 15:31; Luke 7:22); take up your pallet and walk (Mark 2:9; John 5:8-9, 11-12); is it easier to say, 'Your sins are forgiven' or 'Rise and walk'? (Matt. 9:5; Luke 5:23); in the name of Jesus Christ, walk (Acts 3:6); leaping up, he stood and walked (Acts 3:8); as if by our own power or piety we had made him walk (Acts 3:12); the girl got up and walked (Mark 5:42); he sprang up and walked (Acts 14:8, 10); all the people saw him walking and praising God (Acts 3:9).

C5 Procession / marching
The Israelites had to march around Jericho (Josh. 6:3-4); the Chaldeans march through the earth to seize dwellings not their own (Hab. 1:6); they have seen your procession (Ps. 68:24); I led them in procession (Ps. 42:4).

C6 Not walking
The priests of Dagon do not tread on the threshold (1 Sam. 5:5); they dogged our steps so we could not walk in the streets (Lam. 4:18); a lame man who had never walked (Acts 14:8); idols have feet but cannot walk (Ps. 115:7); idols cannot see or hear or walk (Rev. 9:20).

D Riding

D1 Riding horses
I saw in the night a man riding a red horse (Zech. 1:8); I will give you 2000 horses if you can put riders on them (2 Kgs. 18:23; Isa. 36:8); harness the horses and mount them (Jer. 46:4); we will speed on horses (Isa. 30:16); mounts were provided for Paul (Acts 23:24); I have seen slaves riding on horses (Eccles. 10:7); I will strike every rider with madness (Zech. 12:4); at God's rebuke rider and horse lay stunned (Ps. 76:6); riders on horses will be put to shame (Zech. 10:5); the number of the horsemen was 200 million (Rev. 9:16).

D2 Riding other animals
Rebekah and her maids mounted the camels (Gen. 24:61); riders on camels (Isa. 21:7); Absalom was riding on his mule (2 Sam. 18:9); Solomon was to ride on David's mule (1 Kgs. 1:33, 38, 44); the king's sons fled on mules (2 Sam. 13:29); am I not your donkey on which you have always ridden? (Num. 22:30); Abigail rode on a donkey (1 Sam. 25:20, 42); donkeys for the king's household to ride (2 Sam. 16:2); your king comes riding on a donkey (Zech. 9:9; Matt. 21:5; John 12:15); Jesus rode on the donkey (Matt. 21:7; Luke 19:35; John 12:14); Jesus sat on the donkey (Mark 11:7).

D3 God riding
God rides in the heavens (Ps. 68:33); God rides through the heavens to help you (Deut. 33:26); God rode on a cherub (2 Sam. 22:11; Ps. 18:10); God rides on a cloud (Ps. 68:4); the Lord is riding on a swift cloud (Isa. 19:1); you rode on your horses on your chariots of salvation (Hab. 3:8).

E Traversing
E1 Crossing rivers
E1a Crossing into the promised land
Crossing the Jordan (Deut. 9:1; 27:2-12; 31:2-3; 32:47; Josh. 1:2; 3:1-17; 4:1-13, 22-3; 7:7; 24:11); until I cross over Jordan (Deut. 2:29); the Lord is crossing over before you (Deut. 9:3; 31:3); Joshua will cross ahead of you (Deut. 31:3); the people crossed opposite Jericho (Josh. 3:16).

E1b Those who crossed the Jordan
Gideon and his 300 men crossed the Jordan (Judg. 8:4); Israelites crossed the Jordan to escape (1 Sam. 13:7); Gadites crossed Jordan in flood (1 Chr. 12:15); David crossed the Jordan to battle (1 Chr. 19:17); cross over with me (2 Sam. 19:33); let Chimham cross over with the king (2 Sam. 19:37-8); those who crossed the Jordan: Ammonites (Judg. 10:9); Abner and his men (2 Sam. 2:29); David (2 Sam. 10:17); David and all the people (2 Sam. 17:22; 19:18, 39, 41); Absalom (2 Sam. 17:24); Barzillai escorting David (2 Sam. 19:31, 36); Joab and the commanders (2 Sam. 24:5); Elijah and Elisha (2 Kgs. 2:8); Elisha (2 Kgs. 2:14).

E1c Fords
Jacob crossed the ford of the Jabbok (Gen. 32:22); they pursued the spies as far as the fords (Josh. 2:7); they did not allow anyone to cross the fords (Judg. 3:28); without the password (Judg. 12:5-6); David would wait at the fords (2 Sam. 15:28); do not spend the night at the fords but cross over (2 Sam. 17:16, 21); they crossed the ford to bring back the king (2 Sam. 19:18).

E2 Crossing to the other side
Let us cross over to the Philistine garrison (1 Sam. 14:1, 6); your messengers crossed the sea (Isa. 23:2); let us go across to the other side (Mark 4:35); they crossed to the other side (Luke 8:22); Jesus went to the other side of the sea of Galilee (John 6:1); Jesus and his disciples crossed the Kidron valley (John 18:1); you cross sea and land to make one proselyte (Matt. 23:15).

E3 Not crossing
Moses wanted to cross over (Deut. 3:25); God swore that Moses would not cross (Deut. 4:21-2); you will not cross over (Deut. 31:2); do not make us cross over Jordan (Num. 32:5); no one may cross between us and you (Luke 16:26); a river which could not be forded (Ezek. 47:5).

268 Traveller
A Travellers
You who travel by road (Judg. 5:10); have you not asked those who travel the roads? (Job 21:29); a traveller came to the rich man (2 Sam. 12:4); the highways are empty, travellers gone (Isa. 33:8).

WANDERER, see 267B1.

B Caravans
A caravan of Ishmaelites (Gen. 37:25); caravans follow dry watercourses and they perish (Job 6:18); caravans of Tema and Sheba (Job 6:19); O caravans of the Dedanites (Isa. 21:13); they thought he was among the caravan (Luke 2:44); in the days of Jael caravans ceased (Judg. 5:6).

269 Water travel
A Sea travel
The land who sends envoys by sea (Isa. 18:2); your messengers crossed the sea (Isa. 18:2); you cross sea and land to make one proselyte (Matt. 23:15); the voyage and shipwreck to Malta (Acts 27:2-44).
SHIP TRAVEL, see 275A5.

B Rowing
They rowed hard without avail (Jonah 1:13); they were distressed in rowing (Mark 6:48); when they had rowed about 25 or 30 stadia (John 6:19).

C Swimming
Lest any prisoners should swim away and escape (Acts 27:42); those who could swim should jump overboard (Acts 27:43); water deep enough to swim in (Ezek. 47:5).

D Walking on water
Jesus came to them walking on the sea (Matt. 14:25-6; Mark 6:48-9; John 6:19); if it is you, command me to come to you on the water (Matt. 14:28); Peter walked on the water (Matt. 14:29).

270 Mariner
Hiram sent sailors with Solomon's fleet (1 Kgs. 9:27; 2 Chr. 8:18); those who go down to the sea in ships (Ps. 107:23); the sailors on the ship to Tarshish (Jonah 1:5-16); your sailors, pilots, caulkers and merchants fall into the sea (Ezek. 27:27); all shipmasters, seagoing men and sailors stood at a distance (Rev. 18:17).

271 Flying
A Those flying
The Spirit of God hovered over the face of the waters (Gen. 1:2); God rode on a cherub and flew (2 Sam. 22:11; Ps. 18:10); seraphim used two wings to fly (Isa. 6:2); a seraph flew to me with a burning coal (Isa. 6:6); an angel flying in mid-heaven (Rev. 14:6); a flying serpent (Isa. 14:29); a flying scroll (Zech. 5:1-2); their glory will fly away like a bird (Hos. 9:11); wealth flies off like an eagle (Prov. 23:5); I would fly away and be at rest (Ps. 55:6); that she might fly into the wilderness (Rev. 12:14).

B Wings
B1 Wings of birds
Oh, for wings like a dove! (Ps. 55:6); the wings of a dove covered in silver (Ps. 68:13); I carried you on eagles' wings (Exod. 19:4); they will mount up with wings like eagles (Isa. 40:31); the woman was given the two wings of the great eagle (Rev. 12:14); wealth sprouts wings like an eagle (Prov. 23:5); a great eagle with great wings (Ezek. 17:3); another great eagle with great wings (Ezek. 17:7); the wings of the ostrich (Job 39:13); two women with wings like a stork (Zech. 5:9).

B2 God's wings
God spread his wings and caught them (Deut. 32:11); hide me in the shadow of your wings (Ps. 17:8); he will cover you with his wings (Ps. 91:4); under his wings you find refuge (Ps. 91:4); the children of men take refuge in the shadow of your wings (Ps. 36:7); in the shadow of your wings I take refuge (Ps. 57:1; 61:4); in the shadow of your wings I sing for joy (Ps. 63:7); as a

hen gathers her chicks under her wings (Matt. 23:37; Luke 13:34).

B3 Angel's wings
The wings of the cherubim (Exod. 25:20; 37:9; 1 Kgs. 6:27; 2 Chr. 3:11-13); the ark under the wings of the cherubim (1 Kgs. 8:6-7; 2 Chr. 5:7-8); seraphim with six wings (Isa. 6:2); each had four wings (Ezek. 1:6; 10:21); the cherubim appeared to have man's hands under their wings (Ezek. 10:8).

B4 Other wings
A leopard with four wings and four heads (Dan. 7:6); the lion's wings were plucked off (Dan. 7:4); on the wing of abominations will come one who makes desolate (Dan. 9:27); a spirit has wrapped them in its wings (Hos. 4:19); God walks on the wings of the wind (Ps. 104:3); if I take the wings of the dawn (Ps. 139:9); the sun of righteousness with healing in its wings (Mal. 4:2); the four living creatures, each having six wings (Rev. 4:8).

272 Transference

A Handing over

A1 Handing over people

A1a God handing over
God hands me over to the unjust (Job 16:11); God gave them up to impurity (Rom. 1:24); God gave them up to dishonourable passions (Rom. 1:26); God gave them up to a depraved mind (Rom. 1:28); he who did not spare his own Son but delivered him up for us all (Rom. 8:32); the Son of God who loved me and gave himself up for me (Gal. 2:20); Christ gave himself up for us (Eph. 5:2); he has transferred us into the kingdom of his dear Son (Col. 1:13).

A1b People handing over people
With betrayal betrayers betray (Isa. 24:16); all her friends have dealt treacherously (Lam. 1:2); do not hand over an escaped slave to his master (Deut. 23:15); lest your accuser hand you over to the judge and the judge to the assistant (Matt. 5:25); lest the judge hand you over to the officer (Luke 12:58); they will deliver you up to the councils (Matt. 10:17; Mark 13:9); they will deliver you up to the synagogues (Luke 21:12); they will hand you over to tribulation (Matt. 24:9); many will betray one another (Matt. 24:10); brother will deliver up brother to death and a father his child (Matt. 10:21; Mark 13:12); you will be delivered up even by parents, kinsmen and friends (Luke 21:16); when they deliver you up, do not be anxious what you are to say (Matt. 10:19; Mark 13:11); hand over the sons of Belial (Judg. 20:13); hand over the guilty son (2 Sam. 14:7); hand over Sheba (2 Sam. 20:21); Gaza delivered up to Edom a whole people (Amos 1:6); Tyre delivered up a whole people to Edom (Amos 1:9); do not hand over their survivors on the day of their distress (Obad. 14); will the men of Keilah hand me over to Saul? (1 Sam. 23:11, 12); we will deliver David into the king's hand (1 Sam. 23:20); the Jews will deliver Paul into the hands of the Gentiles (Acts 21:11); no one can hand me over to them (Acts 25:11); it is not the custom of the Romans to give up a man untried (Acts 25:16); deliver this man to Satan for the destruction of the flesh (1 Cor. 5:5); men will be treacherous (2 Tim. 3:4); Gentiles have given themselves over to sensuality (Eph. 4:19).

A1c Handing over Christ
Why did you not bring him? (John 7:45); the Son of man will be delivered into the hands of men (Matt. 17:22; Mark 9:31; Luke 9:44); the Son of man will be handed over to the chief priests and scribes (Matt. 20:18; Mark 10:33); they will hand him over to the Gentiles (Matt. 20:19; Mark 10:33; Luke 18:32); the Son

of man will be handed over to be crucified (Matt. 26:2); the Son of man is betrayed into the hands of sinners (Matt. 26:45; Mark 14:41); that they might deliver him up to the authority of the governor (Luke 20:20); the Son of man must be delivered into the hands of sinful men (Luke 24:7); the night he was betrayed, the Lord Jesus took bread (1 Cor. 11:23); if my kingdom were of this world, my servants would fight lest I be handed over (John 18:36); your own nation and the chief priests have handed you over to me (John 18:35); they handed him over to Pilate (Matt. 27:2; Mark 15:1); Pilate delivered Jesus to them to be crucified (Mark 15:15); if this man were not an evildoer we would not have handed him over to you (John 18:30); Pilate knew it was out of envy that they had delivered Jesus up (Matt. 27:18; Mark 15:10); Pilate delivered Jesus to them to be crucified (Matt. 27:26; John 19:16); he delivered up Jesus to their will (Luke 23:25); you delivered him up and denied him in the presence of Pilate (Acts 3:13); you have betrayed and murdered the Righteous One (Acts 7:52).

A1d Judas betrayed Christ
One of you will betray me (Matt. 26:21; Mark 14:18; John 13:21); who is going to betray you? (John 21:20); Jesus knew who would betray him (John 6:64; 13:11); the devil put it into Judas' heart to betray Jesus (John 13:2); Judas who betrayed him (Matt. 10:4; 27:3; Mark 3:19; John 12:4; 18:2, 5); Judas became a traitor (Luke 6:16); Judas went to the chief priests to betray him to them (Mark 14:10); what will you give me if I deliver him to you? (Matt. 26:15); he sought an opportunity to betray him (Matt. 26:16; Mark 14:11; Luke 22:6); he discussed how to betray Jesus (Luke 22:4); he who dips his hand in the dish with me will betray me (Matt. 26:23); the betrayer's hand is with me on the table (Luke 22:21); woe to that man by whom the Son of man is betrayed! (Matt. 26:24; Mark 14:21; Luke 22:22); my betrayer is at hand (Matt. 26:46; Mark 14:42); the betrayer had given them a sign (Matt. 26:48; Mark 14:44); do you betray the Son of man with a kiss? (Luke 22:48); I have sinned in betraying innocent blood (Matt. 27:4).

A2 Handing over authority
Abner would transfer the kingdom to David (2 Sam. 3:10); let the king give her position to another (Esther 1:19); let another take his office (Ps. 109:8; Acts 1:20); this authority has been handed over to me (Luke 4:6); he hands over the kingdom to God the Father (1 Cor. 15:24).

A3 Handing over things
All things have been handed over to me by my Father (Luke 10:22); render to Caesar the things that are Caesar's and to God the things that are God's (Luke 20:25); they have been handed over to us by those who were eyewitnesses (Luke 1:2); I received from the Lord what I delivered to you (1 Cor. 11:23).

B Sending
He sent our fathers the first time (Acts 7:12); Herod sent the wise men to Bethlehem (Matt. 2:8); John sent two disciples to Jesus (Luke 7:19-20); Jesus sent two disciples (Mark 11:1; 14:13; Luke 19:29); Jesus sent Peter and John to prepare passover (Luke 22:8); he sent servants to the tenants (Mark 12:2-5; Luke 20:10-12); the owner of the vineyard sent his son (Mark 12:6); Annas sent him bound to Caiaphas (John 18:24); Pilate sent Jesus to Herod (Luke 23:7); Herod sent Jesus back to Pilate (Luke 23:11, 15); send men to Joppa (Acts 10:5); send Lazarus to dip the tip of his finger in water (Luke 16:24); send Lazarus to my father's house (Luke 16:27); did I take advantage by those I sent to you? (2 Cor. 12:17); I hope to send Timothy to you (Phil. 2:19, 23); I

am sending Epaphroditus to you (Phil. 2:25, 28); I have
sent Tychicus to you so you may know our affairs (Col.
4:8); Tychicus I have sent to Ephesus (2 Tim. 4:12); I
am sending Onesimus back to you (Philem. 12); send
us into the pigs (Mark 5:12).

273 Carrying

A Carrying people

A1 God carrying people

God carried the Israelites on eagles' wings (Exod. 19:4;
Deut. 32:11); God carried you as a father carries his son
(Deut. 1:31); he carried them all the days of old (Isa.
63:9); he will carry the lambs in his bosom (Isa. 40:11); I
have carried you from birth and to old age I will carry
you (Isa. 46:3-4); his angels will bear you up so that you
will not hit your foot against a stone (Ps. 91:11-12; Matt.
4:6; Luke 4:11); the Spirit of the Lord will carry you
where I do not know (1 Kgs. 18:12); he carried me away
in the Spirit (Rev. 17:3; 21:10).

A2 People carrying live people

Carry him to his mother (2 Kgs. 4:19); the soldiers had
to carry Paul (Acts 21:35); they ran about and carried
on pallets those who were sick (Mark 6:55); four people
carrying on a bed a man who was paralysed (Luke 5:18);
a man lame from birth was being carried (Acts 3:2);
they carried the sick out into the streets (Acts 5:15).

A3 Carrying dead bodies

Carry me out of Egypt (Gen. 47:30); Nadab and Abihu
were carried outside the camp (Lev. 10:4, 5); Elijah
carried the boy to his own room (1 Kgs. 17:19); the
Levite placed his concubine on the donkey (Judg.
19:28); a dead man was being carried out (Luke 7:12); if
you have carried him away (John 20:15); the young
men covered him up, carried him out and buried him
(Acts 5:6); those who buried your husband will carry
you out (Acts 5:9-10).

A4 Carrying peoples' names

Aaron carried the names on his shoulders (Exod.
28:12); Aaron will carry the names of his heart (Exod.
28:29).

B Carrying things

B1 Carriers

Solomon had 70 000 carriers (1 Kgs. 5:15; 2 Chr. 2:2);
the strength of the burden bearers is failing (Neh. 4:10).

B2 Illicit carrying

Do not carry a load on the Sabbath (Jer. 17:21, 24, 27);
bringing loads into Jerusalem on the sabbath (Neh.
13:15); he would not allow anyone to carry anything
through the temple (Mark 11:16); he took up his pallet
and walked, on the sabbath (John 5:9-10).

B3 Carrying idols

Idols are loads carried by animals (Isa. 46:1); idols have
to be carried (Jer. 10:5).

B4 Bearing burdens

Issachar bowed his shoulder to bear burdens (Gen.
49:15); why should I carry the burden of all these
people? (Num. 11:11-14); the seventy were to help Moses
carry the burden of the people (Num. 11:16-17); bear
one another's burdens (Gal. 6:2); every one will carry
his own burden (Gal. 6:5); the Lord daily bears our
burden (Ps. 68:19).

B5 Carrying holy things

The Levites will carry the tabernacle (Num. 1:50); the
Levites were to carry the ark (Deut. 10:8; 31:9, 25; 1 Chr.
15:2); because you did not carry the ark the Lord broke
out against us (1 Chr. 15:13); holy things carried on their
shoulders (Num. 7:9); the Gershonites and Merarites
carried the tabernacle (Num. 10:17); the Gershonites
were to carry the curtains and coverings (Num. 4:24-5);
the Merarites were to carry the frames and posts

(Num. 4:31-2); the ark would not be carried any more
(2 Chr. 35:3); the Levites will no longer need to carry
the tabernacle (1 Chr. 23:26); you who carry the vessels
of the Lord (Isa. 52:11).

B6 Carrying the cross

Jesus went out carrying his cross (John 19:17); they
forced Simon of Cyrene to carry the cross (Matt. 27:32;
Mark 15:21; Luke 23:26).
CRUCIFIXION, see 964C.

B7 Carrying other loads

Take up your mat and go home (Mark 2:11-12; Luke
5:24-5); rise, take up your pallet and walk (John 5:8);
Samson carried the gate and posts on his shoulders
(Judg. 16:3); Abraham put the bread and the skin of
water on Hagar's shoulders (Gen. 21:14); Abraham put
the wood on Isaac (Gen. 22:6); Rebekah with her water
jar on her shoulder (Gen. 24:15, 45); a man carrying a
pitcher of water (Mark 14:13; Luke 22:10); when he has
found it, he lays it on his shoulders (Luke 15:5).
ARMOUR BEARERS, see 723A6.

B8 Carrying sin

The goat will bear their iniquities (Lev. 16:22); he bore
our griefs and carried our sorrows (Isa. 53:4); he took
our infirmities and carried our diseases (Matt. 8:17); he
will bear their iniquities (Isa. 53:11); he bore the sin of
many (Isa. 53:12); he bore our sins in his body on the
tree (1 Pet. 2:24).
ATONEMENT, see 941.

274 Vehicle

A Chariots

A1 About chariots

An imported chariot cost 600 shekels (1 Kgs. 10:29;
2 Chr. 1:17); Absalom got a chariot and horses (2 Sam.
15:1); Adonijah got himself chariots and horsemen
(1 Kgs. 1:5); Pharaoh had Joseph ride in the second
chariot (Gen. 41:43); the people of the plain had iron
chariots (Josh. 17:16, 18; Judg. 1:19); the first chariot had
red horses (Zech. 6:2); the fourth chariot had dappled
horses (Zech. 6:3); the second chariot had black horses
(Zech. 6:2); the third chariot had white horses (Zech.
6:3); cargo of cattle, sheep, horses and chariots (Rev.
18:13).

A2 Many chariots

The kings had many horses and chariots (Josh. 11:4);
when you see the enemy's many horses and chariots
(Deut. 20:1); no end to their horses and chariots (Isa.
2:7); your walls will shake at the sound of horseman,
wagons and chariots (Ezek. 26:10); your choicest valleys
were full of chariots (Isa. 22:7); with my many chariots
(2 Kgs. 19:23); 600 choice chariots (Exod. 14:7); Sisera
had 900 iron chariots (Judg. 4:3, 13); the Ammonites
hired 32 000 chariots (1 Chr. 19:7); Shishak came with
1200 chariots and 60 000 horsemen (2 Chr. 12:3);
30 000 Philistine chariots (1 Sam. 13:5); Solomon had
4000 [40 000] horses for his chariots and 12 000
horsemen (1 Kgs. 4:26; 2 Chr. 9:25); 1400 chariots and
12 000 horsemen (1 Kgs. 10:26; 2 Chr. 1:14); Jehoahaz
had no more than 50 horsemen and ten chariots (2
Kgs. 13:7); David took horses and chariots from
Hadadezer and kept horses for 100 chariots (2 Sam. 8:4;
1 Chr. 18:4).

A3 Using chariots

Harness the horses to the chariots, inhabitants of
Lachish (Mic. 1:13); both chariots and horsemen went
up with Joseph (Gen. 50:9); Rehoboam mounted his
chariot hastily (1 Kgs. 12:18; 2 Chr. 10:18); Ahab was
propped up in his chariot (1 Kgs. 22:35; 2 Chr. 18:34);
they carried Ahaziah in his chariot (2 Kgs. 9:28); they
carried Josiah's body in his chariot (2 Kgs. 23:30); they
carried Josiah in his second chariot (2 Chr. 35:24); the

Ethiopian eunuch sat in his chariot (Acts 8:28); Ahab brought Benhadad into the chariot (1 Kgs. 20:33); Jehu took Jonadab into his chariot (2 Kgs. 10:15, 16); the Ethiopian eunuch had Philip sit in his chariot (Acts 8:31); Naaman came down from the chariot (2 Kgs. 5:21); they took Josiah out of the chariot (2 Chr. 35:24).

A4 Attacking with chariots
They will come against you with chariots and wagons (Ezek. 23:24); horses and chariots pursued Saul (2 Sam. 1:6); as with the rumbling of chariots they leap on the mountaintops (Joel 2:5); the sound of their wings was like chariots and horses (Rev. 9:9); the Lord made the Arameans hear the sound of chariots and horses (2 Kgs. 7:6); galloping horse and bounding chariots! (Nahum 3:2); Nebuchadnezzar will come with horses, chariots and horsemen (Ezek. 26:7).

A5 Trusting in chariots
Some boast in horses and chariots (Ps. 20:7); with many chariots I went up the heights of the mountains (Isa. 37:24); how can you rely on Egypt for chariots and horsemen? (Isa. 36:9); woe to those who rely on horses and chariots (Isa. 31:1).

A6 Charioteers / chariot cities
The king will take your sons as charioteers (1 Sam. 8:11); Zimri, commander of half Elah's chariots (1 Kgs. 16:9); 700 Aramean charioteers were killed (2 Sam. 10:18); the Aramean chariot commanders (Isa. 22:31, 32); cities for his chariots and horsemen (1 Kgs. 9:19; 2 Chr. 8:6); chariot cities (1 Kgs. 10:26).

A7 Destroying chariots
What God did to Egypt's horses and chariots (Deut. 11:4); the chariots cast into the sea (Exod. 14:28; 15:4, 19); with you I shatter chariot and rider (Jer. 51:22); David hamstrung the chariot horses (2 Sam. 8:4); I will cut off the chariot from Ephraim, the horse from Jerusalem (Zech. 9:10).

A8 Heavenly chariots
A chariot and horses of fire took Elijah (2 Kgs. 2:11); horses and chariots of fire round Elisha (2 Kgs. 6:17); my father! the chariots and horsemen of Israel! (2 Kgs. 2:12; 13:14); with myriads of chariots the Lord came to Sinai (Ps. 68:17); the chariot of the cherubim (1 Chr. 28:18); the Lord's chariots will be like the whirlwind (Isa. 66:15); God makes the clouds his chariot (Ps. 104:3); his chariots are like the whirlwind (Jer. 4:13); you rode on your horses on your chariots of salvation (Hab. 3:8).

B Carts
Pharaoh sent carts for the children of Israel (Gen. 45:19, 21, 27; 46:5); six carts were used for carrying the tabernacle (Num. 7:3-7); the Philistines sent the ark away on a new cart (1 Sam. 6:7-8); David had the ark set on a new cart (2 Sam. 6:3-4; 1 Chr. 13:7); weighted down like a cart full of sheaves (Amos 2:13).

275 Ship

A Ships

A1 Ships in general
Solomon built ships at Ezion-geber (1 Kgs. 9:26); Huram sent Solomon ships (2 Chr. 8:18); Zebulun will be a haven for ships (Gen. 49:13); there go the ships (Ps. 104:26); the Chaldeans in the ships in which they rejoice (Isa. 43:14); though ships are great and driven by strong winds (Jas. 3:4).

A2 Ships' tackle
They threw the ship's tackle overboard (Acts 27:19); your tackle cannot hold the mast firm or spread the sail (Isa. 33:23); they slackened the ropes on the rudders and hoisted the foresail (Acts 27:40); ships guided by a small rudder (Jas. 3:4); a cedar of Lebanon was taken for your mast (Ezek. 27:5); oars made from oaks of

Bashan (Ezek. 27:6); your sail was of fine embroidered linen from Egypt (Ezek. 27:7).

A3 Ships for trading
All who had ships at sea grew rich (Rev. 18:19); cast your bread on the waters (Eccles. 11:1); the ships of Hiram brought gold from Ophir (1 Kgs. 10:11); the ships returned from sea every three years (1 Kgs. 10:22); Jehoshaphat built ships to go to Ophir for gold (1 Kgs. 22:48); Jehoshaphat built ships to go to Tarshish (2 Chr. 20:36); the ships of Tarshish carried Tyre's merchandise (Ezek. 27:25); all ships of the sea and their mariners traded for your wares (Ezek. 27:9).

A4 Ships for attacking
Ships from Kittim will attack Assyria (Num. 24:24); ships of Kittim will come against him (Dan. 11:30); the king of the north will come with chariots, horsemen and many ships (Dan. 11:40).

A5 Ship travel
The Lord will bring you back to Egypt in ships (Deut. 28:68); ships of Tarshish bring your sons from afar (Isa. 60:9); Jonah boarded a ship for Tarshish (Jonah 1:3); we found a ship crossing to Phoenicia and went aboard (Acts 21:2); we embarked in a ship of Adramyttium (Acts 27:2); a ship of Alexandria sailing for Italy (Acts 27:6); we set sail in a ship of Alexandria (Acts 28:11). SEE TRAVEL, see 269A.

A6 Disaster for ships
You broke the ships of Tarshish (Ps. 48:7); a day against all the ships of Tarshish (Isa. 2:16); wail, ships of Tarshish (Isa. 23:1, 14); a third of the ships were destroyed (Rev. 8:9); there will be no loss of life, but only of the ship (Acts 27:22).

B Boats
Vessels of papyrus (Isa. 18:2); my days go by like reed skiffs (Job 9:26); he told his disciples to have a boat ready for him (Mark 3:9); he taught from a boat (Matt. 13:2; Mark 4:1; Luke 5:3); when he got into the boat the wind stopped (Matt. 14:32; Mark 6:51); the crowd saw there had been no other boat but one (John 6:22); waves broke over the boat so it was filling with water (Mark 4:37); they were willing to receive him into the boat (John 6:21); they let down the ship's boat (Acts 27:30-2); with difficulty we secured the ship's boat (Acts 27:16).

C Noah's ark
Make an ark of gopher wood (Gen. 6:14); Noah constructed an ark (Heb. 11:7); during the building of the ark (1 Pet. 3:20); until Noah entered the ark (Matt. 24:38; Luke 17:27).

D Rafts
Timber transported by rafts (1 Kgs. 5:9; 2 Chr. 2:16); timber brought from the Lebanon by sea (Ezra 3:7).

276 Aircraft
FLYING THINGS, see 271A.

277 Swiftness

A Speed
The race is not to the swift (Eccles. 9:11); flight will perish from the swift (Amos 2:14); do not slow down for me (2 Kgs. 4:24); Jehu drove furiously (2 Kgs. 9:20); his chariots are like the whirlwind (Jer. 4:13); his horses are swifter than eagles (Jer. 4:13); our pursuers were faster than eagles (Lam. 4:19); their horses are swifter than leopards, fiercer than wolves (Hab. 1:8); the distant nation will come speedily (Isa. 5:26); Moab's calamity hastens (Jer. 48:16); those who pursue you will be swift (Isa. 30:16); the ostrich laughs at horse and rider (Job 39:18); I will be a swift witness against the sorcerers and the adulterers (Mal. 3:5); be quick to hear, slow to speak (Jas. 1:19).

RUNNING FAST, see 277B2.
HASTE, see 680.

B Running

B1 Running in general
Your sons will run before the king's chariots (1 Sam. 8:11); if you have run with men on foot and they wearied you (Jer. 12:5); the righteous man runs into the strong tower and is safe (Prov. 18:10); that he may run who reads it (Hab. 2:2); run in such a way as to win the prize (1 Cor. 9:24); I do not run aimlessly (1 Cor. 9:26).

B2 Running fast
SPEED, see 277A.

B2a Fast runners
Saul and Jonathan were swifter than eagles (2 Sam. 1:23); Asahel was as swift as a gazelle (2 Sam. 2:18); the Gadites were swift as gazelles (1 Chr. 12:8); my days are swifter than a runner (Job 9:25); they run like war horses (Joel 2:4); they run like warriors (Joel 2:7); the swift of foot will not escape (Amos 2:15).

B2b Outrunning
Ahimaaz outran the Cushite (2 Sam. 18:23); Elijah outran Ahab (1 Kgs. 18:46); the other disciple outran Peter (John 20:4).

B3 Groups running
The men in ambush ran to Ai (Josh. 8:19); they ran there on foot from all the towns (Mark 6:33); they ran about and carried on pallets those who were sick (Mark 6:55); they rushed together on him (Acts 7:57); the people ran together to them in Solomon's portico (Acts 3:11); the chiliarch took soldiers and centurions and ran down to them (Acts 21:32); the pigs rushed down the steep bank into the sea (Mark 5:13).

B4 Individuals running
Abraham ran from the doorway of the tent (Gen. 18:2); Abraham ran to the herd (Gen. 18:7); the servant ran to meet Rebekah (Gen. 24:17); Rebekah ran back to the well to draw water (Gen. 24:20); Laban ran to the man at the spring (Gen. 24:29); Laban ran to meet Jacob (Gen. 29:13); Esau ran to meet Jacob (Gen. 33:4); his father ran and embraced him and kissed him (Luke 15:20); they brought Joseph from prison at the double (Gen. 41:14); Aaron ran into the middle of the congregation (Num. 16:47); Samuel ran to Eli (1 Sam. 3:5); David ran to the battle line (1 Sam. 17:22, 48); David ran and stood over Goliath (1 Sam. 17:51); Elisha ran after Elijah (1 Kgs. 19:20); Gehazi ran after Naaman (2 Kgs. 5:20, 21); Peter ran to the tomb (Luke 24:12); a young man ran and told Moses (Num. 11:27); one ran and took a sponge (Matt. 27:48; Mark 15:36); the demoniac ran and bowed down to Jesus (Mark 5:6); a man ran up to him (Mark 10:17); Zacchaeus ran on ahead and climbed a sycamore tree (Luke 19:4); Mary Magdalene ran to Simon Peter (John 20:2); Barnabas and Paul rushed into the crowd (Acts 14:14).

B5 Running with news
The girl ran and told her mother's household (Gen. 24:28); Rachel ran to tell her father (Gen. 29:12); Manoah's wife ran to tell her husband (Judg. 13:10); a man ran from the battle to give news (1 Sam. 4:12); the Cushite ran to give David news (2 Sam. 18:21); Ahimaaz wanted to run after (2 Sam. 18:22-3); run, tell that young man (Zech. 2:4); they ran to tell his disciples (Matt. 28:8).

B6 Running after evil
Their feet run to evil and they hasten to shed blood (Prov. 1:16); their feet are swift to shed blood (Rom. 3:15); the Lord hates feet that hasten to evil (Prov. 6:18); I did not send them but they ran (Jer. 23:21).

278 Slowness
I will lead on gently (Gen. 33:14); the grasshopper drags itself along (Eccles. 12:5); we sailed along slowly and with difficulty (Acts 27:7); be slow to speak, slow to anger (Jas. 1:19).

DELAY, see 136A.

279 Impact

A Striking

A1 Beating people

A1a Regulations on beating people
He who strikes someone with a stone or his fist but does not kill him (Exod. 21:18); whoever strikes a man and kills him (Exod. 21:12); whoever strikes his own slave and kills him (Exod. 21:20); whoever strikes his father or his mother (Exod. 21:15); whoever strikes a pregnant woman (Exod. 21:22-5); you shall give blow for blow (Exod. 21:25); judicial beating should not exceed forty lashes (Deut. 25:2-3); the forty stripes minus one (2 Cor. 11:24).

A1b Advice on beating people
It is not good to strike the noble (Prov. 17:26); strike a scoffer and the simple may learn prudence (Prov. 19:25); a rebuke goes deeper into a man of understanding than 100 blows into a fool (Prov. 17:10); blows are ready for the back of fools (Prov. 19:29); though you beat the lad with a rod he will not die (Prov. 23:13); beat him with the rod and save his soul from Sheol (Prov. 23:14).

A1c God beating people
The Lord will strike Israel (1 Kgs. 14:15); the people do not turn back to him who struck them (Isa. 9:13); has he struck Israel as he struck those who struck them? (Isa. 27:7); then you will know that I am the Lord, your smiter (Ezek. 7:9); they persecute him whom you have smitten (Ps. 69:26); you have struck all my enemies on the cheek (Ps. 3:7); I will strike the shepherd (Matt. 26:31); the angel struck Peter on the side (Acts 12:7); God will strike you, you whitewashed wall! (Acts 23:3); he scourges every son whom he receives (Heb. 12:6).

A1d Others beating people
I killed a lad for hitting me (Gen. 4:23); Moses saw an Egyptian beating a Hebrew (Exod. 2:11-13); the Israelite foremen were beaten (Exod. 5:14, 16); Zedekiah slapped Micaiah in the face (1 Kgs. 22:24; 2 Chr. 18:23); Pashhur had Jeremiah beaten (Jer. 20:2); they beat Jeremiah (Jer. 37:15); a prophet ordered someone to strike him (1 Kgs. 20:35, 37); Nehemiah beat some of the men (Neh. 13:25); the watchmen beat me (S. of S. 5:7); if he beats his fellow-servants (Matt. 24:49; Luke 12:45); they beat the servants (Matt. 21:35; Mark 12:3-5; Luke 20:10-11); with a rod they strike the judge of Israel on the cheek (Mic. 5:1); the robbers stripped him and beat him (Luke 10:30); that servant who knew but did not act will receive a severe beating (Luke 12:47); the one who did not know his master's will will receive a light beating (Luke 12:48); struck down but not destroyed (2 Cor. 4:9).

A1e Beating Jesus
They will scourge him (Matt. 20:19; Mark 10:34; Luke 18:33); Pilate had Jesus flogged (Matt. 27:26; Mark 15:15; John 19:1); one of the officers struck Jesus (John 18:22-3); the guards received him with blows (Mark 14:65); the soldiers struck Jesus (John 19:3); they mocked him and beat him (Luke 22:63); they beat him on the head (Matt. 27:30; Mark 15:19); they punched him and slapped him (Matt. 26:67); prophesy, who hit you? (Luke 22:64); they struck him, saying, 'Prophesy!' (Mark 14:65); if I have spoken rightly, why strike me? (John 18:23).

A1f Beating believers

Men will scourge you in their synagogues (Matt. 10:17); men will beat you in their synagogues (Mark 13:9); some you will scourge in your synagogues (Matt. 23:34); we commend ourselves in beatings (2 Cor. 6:5); some suffered scourging (Heb. 11:36); Paul beat believers (Acts 22:19); Paul and Silas were flogged (Acts 16:22-3); the high priest ordered Paul to be struck on the mouth (Acts 23:2-3); they flogged the apostles (Acts 5:40); they have beaten us publicly (Acts 16:37); they beat Sosthenes in front of the judgement seat (Acts 18:17); they stopped beating Paul (Acts 21:32); Paul was to be examined by scourging (Acts 22:24-5); beaten numberless times (2 Cor. 11:23); three times beaten with rods (2 Cor. 11:25); we apostles are punched (1 Cor. 4:11).

A1g Beating oneself

I beat my body and make it my slave (1 Cor. 9:27); her handmaids moan like doves, beating their breasts (Nahum 2:7); the tax collector beat his breast (Luke 18:13); the crowds returned beating their breasts (Luke 23:48); strike your thigh (Ezek. 21:12); after I turned away I repented and smote on my thigh (Jer. 31:19).

A1h Striking to death

If an ox gores a person to death (Exod. 21:28); if the ox was in the habit of goring (Exod. 21:29, 36); Abner struck Asahel in the belly (2 Sam. 2:23); Joab struck Abner in the belly (2 Sam. 3:27); her little ones were dashed in pieces at the head of every street (Nahum 3:10); happy he who dashes your little ones against a rock (Ps. 137:9).

A1i Accepting beating

Let the righteous strike me and rebuke me (Ps. 141:5); you bear it if someone strikes you in the face (2 Cor. 11:20); what credit is it when you do wrong and endure a beating patiently? (1 Pet. 2:20); if someone strikes you, turn the other cheek (Matt. 5:39; Luke 6:29); let him give his cheek to the smiter (Lam. 3:30); I gave my back to those who beat me (Isa. 50:6); they beat me but I did not feel it (Prov. 23:35).

A2 Beating animals

Balaam struck his donkey (Num. 22:23, 25, 27-8, 32); the he-goat struck the ram and shattered his two horns (Dan. 8:7).

A3 Striking objects

A3a Battering rams

Lay siege, build a siege wall, build a mound, pitch camps, place battering rams (Ezek. 4:2); battering rams against Tyre (Ezek. 26:9); to set battering rams against the gates (Ezek. 21:22).

A3b Striking rocks

Moses was commanded to strike the rock (Exod. 17:6); he struck the rock (Ps. 78:20); he struck the rock when commanded to speak to it (Num. 20:11); the stone struck the statue on its feet of iron and clay (Dan. 2:34).

A3c Striking other things

Striking the Nile with the staff (Exod. 7:17, 20); striking the dust with the staff (Exod. 8:16, 17); Elisha commanded Joash to strike the ground with the arrows (2 Kgs. 13:18-19); take one third of the hair and strike it with the sword (Ezek. 5:2); I box, not as one beating the air (1 Cor. 9:26); beat your ploughshares into swords and your pruning hooks into spears (Joel 3:10); Elijah struck the water with his mantle (2 Kgs. 2:8); Elisha struck the water with Elijah's mantle (2 Kgs. 2:14).

B Trampling

B1 Trampling others

Men trample on me (Ps. 56:1, 2); you will tread down the wicked (Mal. 4:3); the official was trampled to death (2 Kgs. 7:17, 20); he trampled Jezebel under foot (2 Kgs. 9:33); I trod down the people in my wrath (Isa. 63:6); I will trample Assyria on my mountains (Isa. 14:25); Moab will be trodden down like straw (Isa. 25:10); the crown of Ephraim's drunkards is trodden under foot (Isa. 28:3); they trample the head of the poor into the dust of the earth (Amos 2:7); hear this, you who trample the needy (Amos 8:4); you trampled the nations in anger (Hab. 3:12); so many thousands had gathered that they trod on one another (Luke 12:1); he was crushed for our iniquities (Isa. 53:5); one who tramples under foot the Son of God (Heb. 10:29); the God of peace will soon crush Satan under your feet (Rom. 16:20).

B2 Trampling animals

You will tread on the lion and the snake (Ps. 91:13); I have given you authority to tread on snakes and scorpions (Luke 10:19); the ostrich forgets that a wild beast might trample her eggs (Job 39:15); the he-goat threw the ram to the ground and trampled on him (Dan. 8:7); the lion tramples and tears in pieces with none to rescue (Mic. 5:8).

B3 Trampling Jerusalem

Jerusalem will be trampled by the Gentiles (Luke 21:24); who requires of you this trampling of my courts? (Isa. 1:12); our enemies have trodden down your sanctuary (Isa. 63:18); how long are the holy place and the host to be trampled under foot? (Dan. 8:13); the Gentiles will trample the holy city for 42 months (Rev. 11:2).

B4 Trampling other things

Seed on the road was trampled under foot (Luke 8:5); tasteless salt is fit only to be trampled under foot (Matt. 5:13); lest the swine trample the pearls under foot (Matt. 7:6).

C Kicking

Jeshurun [Israel] grew fat and kicked (Deut. 32:15); why kick at my sacrifice and make yourselves fat? (1 Sam. 2:29); it is hard for you to kick against the pricks (Acts 26:14).

D Whipping

My father chastised you with whips, but I will use scorpions (1 Kgs. 12:11, 14; 2 Chr. 10:11, 14); the elders of the city shall whip that man (Deut. 22:18); a whip is for the horse (Prov. 26:3).

E Hammering

They hammered gold into thin plates (Exod. 39:3); censers made into hammered plates for the altar (Num. 16:38-9); of hammered work: two cherubim (Exod. 25:18; 37:7); the lampstand (Exod. 25:31, 36; 37:17, 22; Num. 8:4); two silver trumpets (Num. 10:2).

F Knocking

The men of Gibeah pounded the door (Judg. 19:22); my beloved was knocking (S. of S. 5:2); I stand at the door and knock (Rev. 3:20); knock and it will be opened (Matt. 7:7-8; Luke 11:9-10); to open the door when he knocks (Luke 12:36); when the householder shuts the door, you will knock (Luke 13:25); Peter knocked on the door (Acts 12:13, 16); the king's knees knocked together (Dan. 5:6).

G Clapping

Clap your hands, all peoples (Ps. 47:1); Balak struck his hands together in anger (Num. 24:10); God claps his hands at the wicked (Job 27:23); all who pass along the way clap their hands at you (Lam. 2:15); the trees of the field will clap their hands (Isa. 55:12); let the rivers clap their hands (Ps. 98:8).

H Pressing

They pressed hard on Lot (Gen. 19:9); the donkey pressed Balaam's foot against the wall (Num. 22:25); I squeezed the grapes into Pharaoh's cup (Gen. 40:11); Gideon wrung dew from the fleece (Judg. 6:38); pressing milk produces butter and pressing the nose brings blood (Prov. 30:33); lest the crowd press on him (Mark 3:9); all who were ill pressed about him to touch him (Mark 3:10); a great crowd followed him and pressed on him (Mark 5:24); the crowds pressed round him (Luke 8:42); the crowds press on you (Mark 5:31; Luke 8:45); the crowd pressed round him to hear the word of God (Luke 5:1); good measure, pressed down, shaken together (Luke 6:38).

280 Rebounding

A Evil rebounding

A1 Let evil rebound

Let the wicked fall into their own nets (Ps. 35:8; 141:10); bring the way of the wicked on his own head (1 Kgs. 8:32; 2 Chr. 6:23); let them be caught in the plots they devised (Ps. 10:2); return their reproach on their own heads (Neh. 4:4); do to her as she has done (Jer. 50:15, 29); may they be covered with the trouble their own lips have caused (Ps. 140:9); return sevenfold the reproach of our neighbours (Ps. 79:12); happy the one who repays Babylon with what they paid us (Ps. 137:8); mix a double draught in the cup she mixed (Rev. 18:6).

A2 Evil inevitably rebounds

The wicked is ensnared in the work of his own hands (Ps. 9:16); the wicked is ensnared by his own iniquities (Prov. 5:22); evil comes to the man who seeks after it (Prov. 11:27); his own scheme brings him down (Job 18:7); his mischief will return on his own head (Ps. 7:16); a cruel man brings himself harm (Prov. 11:17); those who plough iniquity and sow trouble harvest it (Job 4:8); the wicked will fall by his own wickedness (Prov. 11:3, 5); the violence of the wicked will sweep them away (Prov. 21:7); the violence done to Lebanon will overwhelm you (Hab. 2:17); you will be judged by the judgement with which you judge (Matt. 7:2); if anyone kills with the sword, with the sword he must be killed (Rev. 13:10).

A3 God makes evil rebound

The Lord will return your evil on your own head (1 Kgs. 2:44); the Lord returned Nabal's evil on his own head (1 Sam. 25:39); he has brought their wickedness back on them (Ps. 94:23); God brought the wickedness of the men of Shechem on their own heads (Judg. 9:57); the Lord will bring back his bloody deeds on his head (1 Kgs. 2:32); the Lord has returned your bloodshed on you (2 Sam. 16:8); I will bring down their way on their heads (Ezek. 9:10; 11:21); as you have done, it will be done to you (Obad. 15); their way I have brought on their heads (Ezek. 22:31); he will turn his insolence back upon him (Dan. 11:18); they shed the blood of your people and you gave them blood to drink (Rev. 16:6).

A4 Evil devices rebound

They ambush themselves (Prov. 1:18); their foot has been caught in the net they hid (Ps. 9:15); their sword will pierce their own heart (Ps. 37:15); falling into their own pit (Ps. 7:15; 9:15; 57:6; Prov. 26:27; 28:10; Eccles. 10:8); a stone will return on him who rolls it (Prov. 26:27); because you have plundered, people will plunder you (Hab. 2:8); the treacherous are taken captive by their own greed (Prov. 11:6); Haman's scheme returned on his own head (Esther 9:25); if you have been snared by your own words (Prov. 6:2); their own tongue is against them (Ps. 64:8); the talk of the foolish is a rod for his pride (Prov. 14:3); he loved to curse and curses came (Ps. 109:17-18).

B Good rebounding

Do to others as you want them to do to you (Matt. 7:12; Luke 6:31); forgive and you will be forgiven (Luke 6:37); the measure you give will be the measure you get (Matt. 7:2; Mark 4:24; Luke 6:38); a man's deeds return

to him (Prov. 12:14); the kind man does himself good (Prov. 11:17); he who waters will himself be watered (Prov. 11:25); with the kind you show yourself kind (2 Sam. 22:26-7; Ps. 18:25-6); if you do good to those who do good to you, what credit is it to you? (Luke 6:33); do not invite your friends lest they invite you back (Luke 14:12).

281 Direction

A North

A1 The north

God stretches out the north over the void (Job 26:7); black horses patrol the north country (Zech. 6:6, 8); lift up your eyes towards the north (Ezek. 8:5); I will send for the tribes of the north (Jer. 25:9); given into the hand of the people of the north (Jer. 46:24); the kings of the north (Josh. 11:2; Jer. 25:26); the king of the north (Dan. 11:6-45); Mount Zion in the far north (Ps. 48:2); kill the animal on the north side of the altar (Lev. 1:11).

A2 Out of the north

Out of the north comes cold (Job 37:9); out of the north comes gold (Job 37:22); a stormy wind from the north (Ezek. 1:4); the north wind brings rain (Prov. 25:23); out of the north evil will break forth (Jer. 1:14-15); a boiling pot facing away from the north (Jer. 1:13); I am bringing evil from the north (Jer. 4:6); a horsefly is coming from the north (Jer. 46:20); waters will rise from the north (Jer. 47:2); a people is coming from the north (Jer. 6:22); I stirred up one from the north (Isa. 41:25); Nebuchadnezzar comes upon Tyre from the north (Ezek. 26:7); God will come against Israel from the north (Ezek. 38:15; 39:2).

A3 Return from the north

They will return from the land of the north (Jer. 3:18); the Lord will bring back Israel from the north land (Jer. 16:15; 23:8; 31:8); I will drive the northerner far from you (Joel 2:20); flee from the land of the north (Zech. 2:6).

B South

God made the chambers of the south (Job 9:9); out of the south comes the storm (Job 37:9); when the south wind blows you say there will be heat (Luke 12:55); as the streams in the south (Ps. 126:4); the king of the south (Dan. 11:5-45); the queen of the south will condemn this generation (Matt. 12:42; Luke 11:31).

C East

C1 The east

The land of the sons of the east (Gen. 29:1); Abraham sent his other sons eastward from Isaac to the land of the east (Gen. 25:6); the Amalekites and the sons of the east came against Israel (Judg. 6:3, 33; 7:12); they will plunder the sons of the east (Isa. 11:14); devastate the people of the east (Jer. 49:28); the remnant of the sons of the east (Judg. 8:10); the sons of the east (1 Kgs. 4:30); I will give them to the sons of the east (Ezek. 25:4, 10); facing east, prostrating themselves to the sun, eastwards (Ezek. 8:16).

C2 To the east

Open the window toward the east (2 Kgs. 13:17); the mount of Olives lies before Jerusalem on the east (Zech. 14:4); a high place for Chemosh on the mountain east of Jerusalem (1 Kgs. 11:7); the mountain east of the city (Ezek. 11:23); Eden was to the east (Gen. 2:8); cherubim east of the garden (Gen. 3:24); Cain settled east of Eden (Gen. 4:16); we saw his star in the east [or at its rising] (Matt. 2:2, 9); Jonah went out and sat to the east of the city (Jonah 4:5); glorify the Lord in the east (Isa. 24:15).

C3 Out of the east

The glory of the God of Israel was coming from the east (Ezek. 43:2); magi from the east (Matt. 2:1); an angel ascending from the rising of the sun (Rev. 7:2); preparing the way for the kings from the east (Rev. 16:12).

D West

Moses saw as far as the western sea (Deut. 34:2); the Great Sea towards the setting of the sun (Josh. 1:4; 23:4); a very strong west wind (Exod. 10:19); they shout of the majesty of the Lord from the west (Isa. 24:14); a he-goat from the west (Dan. 8:5); his sons will come trembling from the west (Hos. 11:10); when you see a cloud rising in the west you say a shower will come (Luke 12:54).

E Combined directions

E1 North and south

Half the mountain will move toward the north and half toward the south (Zech. 14:4); whoever enters by the south gate must leave by the north and vice versa (Ezek. 46:9).

E2 East and west

Lifting up does not come from the east or west (Ps. 75:6); as far as the east is from the west (Ps. 103:12); they will fear the name of the Lord from the west, his glory from the rising of the sun (Isa. 59:19); I am going to save my people from the east and the west (Zech. 8:7); living water flowing half to the eastern sea and half to the western (Zech. 14:8); the mount of Olives will be split from east to west (Zech. 14:4); from the rising of the sun to its setting my name will be great (Mal. 1:11); many will come from east and west and recline to eat (Matt. 8:11); as the lightning comes from the east and shines as far as the west (Matt. 24:27).

E3 North, south, east and west

Look north, south, east and west (Gen. 13:14; Deut. 3:27); you will spread out to west, east, north and south (Gen. 28:14); I will gather you from east, west, north and south (Isa. 43:5-6); the Lord gathered them from east, west, north and south (Ps. 107:3); many will come from east and west, north and south to the kingdom of God (Luke 13:29); three gates on each side, east, north, south and west (Rev. 21:13).

E4 Other directions

A harbour facing southwest and northwest (Acts 27:12); a violent wind called the Northeaster (Acts 27:14).

RIGHT, see 241.

LEFT, see 242.

282 Changing direction

NOT TURNING ASIDE, see 249C.

A Those turning

A1 God turning

I [God] will turn to you (Ezek. 36:9); God turned from them (Acts 7:42).

A2 People turning

A2a Turning round

They will turn to you but you will not turn to them (Jer. 15:19); Jesus turned and saw her (Matt. 9:22); Jesus turned and saw them following (John 1:38); Jesus turned and said to Peter, 'Get behind me!' (Matt. 16:23); the Lord turned and looked at Peter (Luke 22:61); she turned around and saw Jesus (John 20:14); I turned to see the voice that was speaking to me (Rev. 1:12).

A2b Changing direction

Tell me, that I may turn to right or to left (Gen. 24:49); turn aside to right or left! (2 Sam. 2:21); whenever you turn to right or left you will hear a word (Isa. 30:21).

A2c Turning to God

Turn to me and be saved, all the ends of the earth (Isa. 45:22); I turned my feet to your testimonies (Ps. 119:59); all the ends of the earth will turn to the Lord (Ps. 22:27); lest they turn and I heal them (Matt. 13:15); lest

they should turn and be forgiven (Mark 4:12); when you have turned, strengthen your brethren (Luke 22:32); repent and turn again, that your sins may be blotted out (Acts 3:19); all who lived at Lydda and Sharon saw him and turned to the Lord (Acts 9:35); a large number who believed turned to the Lord (Acts 11:21); my judgement is that we do not trouble Gentiles who turn to God (Acts 15:19); you turned to God from idols (1 Thess. 1:9).

A2d Turning from evil

The highway of the upright is to turn aside from evil (Prov. 16:17); turn from your evil way (Jer. 25:5); turn away from evil (Prov. 3:7); let him turn away from evil and do good (1 Pet. 3:11); turn away from the path of the wicked (Prov. 4:15); perhaps they will turn from their evil way (Jer. 26:3); to turn from evil is an abomination to fools (Prov. 13:19); repent and turn from your transgressions (Ezek. 18:30); when a wicked man turns from his wickedness he will live (Ezek. 18:27, 28).

A2e Turning from the right

The turning away of the simple kills them (Prov. 1:32); when a righteous man turns from his righteousness (Ezek. 18:24, 26); Solomon's heart had turned away from the Lord (1 Kgs. 11:9); my people are bent on turning away from me (Hos. 11:7); those who turned aside to their crooked ways (Ps. 125:5); they have turned aside and gone away (Jer. 5:23); do not let me wander from your commandments (Ps. 119:10); I do not turn away from your law (Ps. 119:51); I do not turn aside from your testimonies (Ps. 119:157); I do not turn aside from your ordinances (Ps. 119:102); do not turn from my words (Prov. 4:5); you have turned aside from my statutes and not kept them (Mal. 3:7); some people have swerved from these things (1 Tim. 1:6); the ministry and apostleship from which Judas turned aside to go to his own place (Acts 1:25).

A3 Things turning

A flaming sword which turned every way (Gen. 3:24).

B Causing people to turn

They will turn your heart away after their gods (1 Kgs. 11:2); Solomon's wives turned away his heart after other gods (1 Kgs. 11:3, 4); Elymas tried to turn the proconsul away from the faith (Acts 13:8); a spirit of harlotry has led them astray (Hos. 4:12); those who turn many to righteousness will be like the stars for ever (Dan. 12:3); Levi turned many back from iniquity (Mal. 2:6); he will turn back many to the Lord (Luke 1:16); to turn the hearts of the fathers back to the children (Mal. 4:6; Luke 1:17).

C Going astray

C1 People going astray

He who rejects reproof goes astray (Prov. 10:17); cease hearing discipline only to stray from knowledge (Prov. 19:27); the Levites went far from me, going astray after idols (Ezek. 44:10); the priests had charge of the sanctuary when Israel went astray from me (Ezek. 44:15); they did not go astray as the Levites and Israelites went astray (Ezek. 48:11); woe to them, for they have strayed from me (Hos. 7:13); the more they called them the more they went astray from me (Hos. 11:2); before I was afflicted I went astray (Ps. 119:67); they always go astray in their heart (Heb. 3:10); you have turned aside from the way (Mal. 2:8); all have turned aside (Rom. 3:12); if any one strays from the truth (Jas. 5:19).

LEAD ASTRAY, see 495A.

C2 Animals going astray

If your enemy's animal strays, bring it back (Exod. 23:4); if a neighbour's animal strays, bring it back (Deut. 22:1-3); all we like sheep have gone astray (Isa.

53:6); if one of 100 sheep goes astray (Matt. 18:12-13); we were like sheep going astray (Ps. 119:176; 1 Pet. 2:25); he rejoices over it more than over the 99 that never went astray (Matt. 18:13).

283 Preceding

PRECEDENCE, see 64.

A God going before
God went before them in a pillar of cloud and fire (Exod. 13:21; Num. 14:14); the angel of the Lord had been going before them (Exod. 14:19); God goes before you to show you the way you should go (Deut. 1:33); the Lord who goes before you will fight for you (Deut. 1:30); I will go before you (Isa. 45:2); the Lord will go before you (Isa. 52:12); make us gods to go before us (Exod. 32:1, 23).

B Christ going before
Jesus was walking ahead of them (Mark 10:32); Jesus went on ahead, going up to Jerusalem (Luke 19:28); I will go before you to Galilee (Matt. 26:32); he is going before you into Galilee (Matt. 28:7; Mark 16:7).

C People going before
John would go before the Lord (Luke 1:17); I am not the Christ, but I have been sent before him (John 3:28); to prepare the way (Luke 1:76; 7:27); tax-collectors and harlots go into the kingdom of God before you (Matt. 21:31); another steps down before me (John 5:7); we who are alive will not precede those who have fallen asleep (1 Thess. 4:15); all who came before me are thieves and robbers (John 10:8); I led them in procession to the house of God (Ps. 42:4); the shepherd goes before the sheep (John 10:4).

D Things going before
The ark went ahead of the people (Num. 10:33; Josh. 3:6, 11, 14); the star went on before them (Matt. 2:9).

284 Following

A Following God
Follow the Lord your God (Deut. 13:4); Caleb followed the Lord fully (Num. 14:24; Deut. 1:36; Josh. 14:8, 9, 14); Caleb and Joshua followed the Lord fully (Num. 32:11, 12); they did not follow me fully (Num. 32:11).

B Following Christ
B1 Instructions about following
Follow me (Matt. 4:19; 8:22; 9:9; 19:21; Mark 1:17; 2:14; 10:21; Luke 5:27; 9:59; 18:22; John 1:43; 21:19, 22); the sheep follow the shepherd (John 10:4); my sheep follow me (John 10:27); if anyone serves me, let him follow me (John 12:26); whoever would come after me must take up his cross and follow me (Matt. 16:24; Mark 8:34; Luke 9:23; 14:27); he who does not take up his cross and follow me is not worthy (Matt. 10:38); he who follows me will not walk in darkness (John 8:12).
B2 Those who followed
The two disciples of John followed Jesus (John 1:37-8); they left the boat and their father and followed him (Matt. 4:22); they left everything and followed him (Mark 1:18, 20; Luke 5:11); they left their nets and followed him (Matt. 4:20); we left everything and followed you (Matt. 19:27; Mark 10:28; Luke 18:28); Matthew [Levi] rose and followed him (Matt. 9:9; Mark 2:14; Luke 5:28); blind men followed Jesus (Matt. 9:27; 20:34; Mark 10:52; Luke 18:43); I will follow you wherever you go (Matt. 8:19; Luke 9:57); I will follow you, but first let me say goodbye (Luke 9:61); Peter followed him at a distance (Matt. 26:58; Mark 14:54; Luke 22:54); Simon Peter and another disciple followed Jesus (John 18:15); women who had followed Jesus from Galilee (Matt. 27:55; Mark 15:41; Luke 23:55); his disciples followed him (Mark 6:1; Luke 22:39); we forbade him because he does not follow with us (Luke

9:49); they follow the Lamb wherever he goes (Rev. 14:4).

C Following people
The men of Shechem decided to follow Abimelech (Judg. 9:3); Israel followed Sheba, not David (2 Sam. 20:2); Elisha followed Elijah (1 Kgs. 19:21); we forbade him because he was not following us (Mark 9:38); all who followed Theudas were scattered (Acts 5:36); the followers of Judas of Galilee were scattered (Acts 5:37); do not go after them (Luke 17:23; 21:8); a stranger they will not follow (John 10:5).

285 Advance

A Going forward
The shadow going forward ten steps (2 Kgs. 20:9, 10); tell them to go forward (Exod. 14:15); they went straight forward (Ezek. 1:9, 12).

B Promotion
Lifting up does not come from the east or west (Ps. 75:6); God puts down one and lifts up another (Ps. 75:7); Ahasuerus promoted Haman (Esther 3:1; 5:11); Nebuchadnezzar promoted Shadrach, Meshach and Abednego (Dan. 3:30); the king planned to promote Daniel (Dan. 6:3); whom he would he raised up and whom he would he humbled (Dan. 5:19); he has exalted the humble (Luke 1:52); whoever exalts himself will be humbled and whoever humbles himself will be exalted (Matt. 23:12; Luke 14:11; 18:14); humble yourselves that in due time he may exalt you (1 Pet. 5:6).
GOD PROMOTING, see 310B1.

286 Backwards
Shem and Japheth walked backwards (Gen. 9:23); Eli fell backwards off his seat (1 Sam. 4:18); they went backwards and not forward (Jer. 7:24); you keep going backwards (Jer. 15:6); the shadow going backwards ten steps (2 Kgs. 20:9, 10, 11).

287 Propulsion

A Throwing
A1 Throwing stones
A time to throw stones (Eccles. 3:5); seven hundred Benjaminites could sling a stone at a hair and not miss (Judg. 20:16); David's men slung stones and shot arrows right and left-handed (1 Chr. 12:2); David took his sling (1 Sam. 17:40); David slung a stone at Goliath (1 Sam. 17:49); Shimei threw stones at David (2 Sam. 16:6, 13); engines for shooting arrows and stones (2 Chr. 26:15); God will sling out the lives of your enemies as from a sling (1 Sam. 25:29); honouring a fool is like tying a stone in a sling (Prov. 26:8); slingstones are like stubble for the crocodile (Job 41:28); if anyone is without sin let him be the first to cast a stone (John 8:7).
STONING, see 344B6e.

A2 Throwing spears
Saul hurled a spear at David (1 Sam. 18:11); Saul hurled his spear at Jonathan (1 Sam. 20:33).

A3 Throwing people
Horse and rider he threw into the sea (Exod. 15:1, 21); throwing Jonah into the sea (Jonah 1:12-15; 2:3); they wanted to throw Jesus over the cliff (Luke 4:29); thrown into a den of lions (Dan. 6:7-24); cast into a fiery furnace (Dan. 3:6-21); they will throw them into the furnace of fire (Matt. 13:42); the angels will throw the wicked into the furnace (Matt. 13:50); the Lord is about to hurl you away (Isa. 22:17); I will hurl you out of this land (Jer. 16:13; 22:26); why has Coniah been hurled into an unknown land? (Jer. 22:28); better to be cast in the sea with a millstone round his neck (Matt. 18:6; Luke 17:2); to be thrown into the eternal fire

(Matt. 18:8); cast him into the outer darkness (Matt. 22:13; 25:30); they killed him and threw him out of the vineyard (Mark 12:8).

A4 Throwing other things
If he threw something at him, lying in wait (Num. 35:20); if he threw something at him, not lying in wait (Num. 35:22); let Moses throw the soot in the air (Exod. 9:8, 10); Moses threw down the stone tablets (Deut. 9:17); Elijah threw his cloak over Elisha (1 Kgs. 19:19); cast your bread on the waters (Eccles. 11:1); if you say to this mountain, 'Be taken up and cast into the sea' (Matt. 21:21; Mark 11:23); the Lord will cast Tyre's wealth into the sea (Zech. 9:4); throw the money to the potter (Zech. 11:13); he threw the money into the temple (Matt. 27:5); Simon Peter and Andrew throwing a net into the sea (Matt. 4:18); I have come to cast fire on the earth (Luke 12:49); throwing the wheat into the sea (Acts 27:38); you will throw all their sins into the depths of the sea (Mic. 7:19); cast all your anxiety on him (1 Pet. 5:7).

B Shooting arrows
B1 God shooting arrows
God has bent his bow (Ps. 7:12-13); I will bend Judah as my bow and fill it with Ephraim [as arrow] (Zech. 9:13); he has bent his bow like an enemy (Lam. 2:4); he bent his bow and made me a target for his arrows (Lam. 3:12); God's arrows are within me (Job 6:4); he made the arrows of his quiver enter my kidneys (Lam. 3:13); your arrows have sunk deep into me (Ps. 38:2); God will shoot his arrow at them (Ps. 64:7); when I send against them my deadly arrows of famine (Ezek. 5:16); the Lord's arrow will go forth like lightning (Zech. 9:14); send out your arrows and rout them (Ps. 144:6).

GOD S BOW AND ARROWS, see 723B1c.

B2 People shooting arrows
I can bend a bow of bronze (2 Sam. 22:35; Ps. 18:34); arrows cannot make the crocodile flee (Job 41:28); you will not fear the arrow that flies by day (Ps. 91:5); Jonathan signalled by shooting arrows (1 Sam. 20:20, 36-8); taking a bow and arrows and shooting out of the window (2 Kgs. 13:15-17); whoever touches the mountain shall be stoned or shot (Exod. 19:13); shoot at Babylon, spare no arrow (Jer. 50:14); you will aim with your bow at their faces (Ps. 21:12); a man drew his bow at random (1 Kgs. 22:34; 2 Chr. 18:33); Jehu drew his bow and shot Joram (2 Kgs. 9:24); they would be shot from the wall (2 Sam. 11:20); the wicked bend the bow to shoot the upright (Ps. 11:2); they aim bitter words like arrows (Ps. 64:3); shooting from ambush at the blameless (Ps. 64:4); Ishmael became an archer (Gen. 21:20); the archers shot at Joseph (Gen. 49:23); Saul was wounded by the archers (1 Sam. 31:3; 1 Chr. 10:3); archers wounded Josiah (2 Chr. 35:23); archers shot from the wall (2 Sam. 11:24); the sons of Ulam were archers (1 Chr. 8:40); like an archer who wounds everyone is he who hires a fool (Prov. 26:10).

MEN S BOWS AND ARROWS, see 723A5.

288 Pulling
A Pulling people
They pulled Lot back into the house (Gen. 19:10); they pulled them out of the city (Gen. 19:16); they dragged Paul out of the city (Acts 14:19); they dragged Paul and Silas into the marketplace (Acts 16:19); the Jews dragged Jason before the authorities (Acts 17:6); they dragged Paul out of the temple (Acts 21:30); Saul dragged off men and women and imprisoned them (Acts 8:3); no one can come to me unless the Father draws him (John 6:44).

B Pulling things
They dragged the net full of fish (John 21:8); Peter hauled the net ashore (John 21:11); when the net was full they pulled it ashore (Matt. 13:48).

289 Approach
ARRIVE, see 295.

A Approaching God
A1 Coming to God
When shall I appear before God? (Ps. 42:2); people will stream to the mountain of the house of the Lord (Mic. 4:1); with what shall I come before the Lord? (Mic. 6:6); no one comes to the Father but by me (John 14:6); we will come to him and make our abode with him (John 14:23); Christ died for sins that he might bring us to God (1 Pet. 3:18); one of the four living creatures said, 'Come!' (Rev. 6:1, 3, 5, 7).

A2 Drawing near to God
Only Moses was to approach God (Exod. 24:2); the two sons of Aaron drew near before the Lord and died (Lev. 16:1); the sons of Zadok are the only Levites who may come near to the Lord to minister (Ezek. 40:46); the priests shall come near to minister to me (Ezek. 44:16); let us draw near to God (1 Sam. 14:36); a better hope by which we draw near to God (Heb. 7:19); those who draw near to God through him (Heb. 7:25); let us draw near (Heb. 10:22); draw near to God and he will draw near to you (Jas. 4:8); let us draw near with confidence to the throne of grace (Heb. 4:16); the sacrifices cannot perfect those who draw near (Heb. 10:1); he who draws near to God must believe he exists (Heb. 11:6).

B Approaching Christ
B1 Coming to Christ
No one can come to me unless the Father draws him (John 6:44); unless it is granted him by the Father (John 6:65); he who comes to me I will not cast out (John 6:37); all that the Father gives me will come to me (John 6:37); everyone who has heard and learned from the Father comes to me (John 6:45); you are unwilling to come to me that you may have life (John 5:40); if any one thirsts, let him come to me and drink (John 7:37); come to me! (Matt. 11:28); come, blessed of my Father (Matt. 25:34); come and see! (John 1:39, 46).

B2 Drawing near to Christ
Bring them to me (Matt. 14:18); bring him here to me (Matt. 17:17; Mark 9:19); bring your son here (Luke 9:41); they brought children to Jesus (Matt. 19:13-14; Mark 10:13-14); the blind men came to him (Matt. 9:28); when the blind man came near, Jesus questioned him (Luke 18:40); one came up to him (Matt. 19:16); he called those he wanted and they came to him (Mark 3:13); the tax collectors and sinners were drawing near to hear him (Luke 15:1); my betrayer is at hand (Mark 14:42); Judas came near to Jesus to kiss him (Luke 22:47); come to him, that living stone (1 Pet. 2:4); Jesus drew near and went with them (Luke 24:15).

C Approaching people
They will come to you from Assyria and the cities of Egypt (Mic. 7:12); nations will come to your light (Isa. 60:3); I will not leave you as orphans, I will come to you (John 14:18); him who is and was and is to come (Rev. 1:4, 8; 4:8); the beast was and is not and is to come (Rev. 17:8).

290 Recession
Move away! (Gen. 19:9).
DEPARTURE, see 296.

291 Attraction

Draw me after you, let us hurry (S. of S. 1:4); I will allure her, bring her into the wilderness and speak kindly (Hos. 2:14); if I be lifted up I will draw all to me (John 12:32).

DESIRE, see 859.

292 Repulsion

EJECTION, see 300.

293 Convergence

APPROACH, see 289.

294 Divergence

Abraham and Lot went their separate ways (Gen. 13:9-12); Ahab went one way and Obadiah went another (1 Kgs. 18:6); the king of Babylon stands at the parting of the ways (Ezek. 21:21); do not stand at the fork of the road to cut down their fugitives (Obad. 14).

DEVIATION, see 282.

295 Arrival

A Meeting

A1 Meeting God
The angels of God met Jacob (Gen. 32:1); I will meet with you at the doorway of the tent of meeting (Exod. 29:42, 43); I will meet with you at the ark (Exod. 25:22; 30:6); before the testimony, where I meet with you (Num. 17:4); the Lord met him at the lodging place on the way (Exod. 4:24); Moses brought the people out to meet God (Exod. 19:17); God met Balaam (Num. 23:4); God in his lovingkindness will meet me (Ps. 59:10); prepare to meet your God (Amos 4:12); do two walk together without an appointment? (Amos 3:3); come out to meet the bridegroom (Matt. 25:6); Jesus met them and greeted them (Matt. 28:9).

TENT OF MEETING, see 192C2.

A2 Meeting people
The king of Sodom went out to meet Abraham (Gen. 14:17); Esau is coming to meet you (Gen. 32:6); go meet Moses in the wilderness (Exod. 4:27); Moses went out to meet Pharaoh by the Nile (Exod. 7:15); Balak went out to meet Balaam (Num. 22:36); whatever comes out to meet me I will sacrifice (Judg. 11:31); his daughter came out to meet him (Judg. 11:34); let us meet in the plain of Ono (Neh. 6:2); let us meet in the temple (Neh. 6:10); death, the meeting-house for all living (Job 30:23); better meet a she-bear robbed of her cubs than a fool (Prov. 17:12); Martha went to meet Jesus while Mary sat in the house (John 11:20); the Spirit said to Philip, 'Go up and join this chariot' (Acts 8:29); the brethren came to meet us (Acts 28:15); Melchizedek met Abraham (Heb. 7:1).

B Visiting

B1 God visiting
God will surely visit you (Gen. 50:24, 25; Exod. 13:19); the Lord had visited his people and given them food (Ruth 1:6); you visit the earth (Ps. 65:9); God has visited his people (Luke 7:16); God has visited and redeemed his people (Luke 1:68); what will you do on the day of visitation? (Isa. 10:3); you did not recognise the day of your visitation (Luke 19:44); they may see your good deeds and glorify God on the day of visitation (1 Pet. 2:12).

B2 People visiting
Let your foot be seldom in your neighbour's house lest he hate you (Prov. 25:17); Dinah went to visit (Gen. 34:1); Judah went to visit Hirah the Adullamite (Gen. 38:1); Ahaziah went to see Joram who was ill (2 Kgs. 8:29; 9:16); I intended to visit you (2 Cor. 1:15); I was sick and in prison and you visited me (Matt. 25:36, 39); I was sick and in prison and you did not visit me (Matt. 25:43); I will visit you after passing through Macedonia (1 Cor. 16:5); I determined not to make another sorrowful visit to you (2 Cor. 2:1).

C Overtaking
Laban overtook Jacob (Gen. 31:23, 25); the steward overtook them (Gen. 44:6); the Egyptians overtook the Israelites by the sea (Exod. 14:9); Micah's men overtook the Danites (Judg. 18:22); Israel overtook the Benjaminites (Judg. 20:45); the Chaldean army overtook Zedekiah in the plains of Jericho (2 Kgs. 25:5; Jer. 39:5; 52:8); shall I overtake them? (1 Sam. 30:8); let the enemy pursue me and overtake me (Ps. 7:5); I pursued my enemies and overtook them (Ps. 18:37); all her pursuers have overtaken her (Lam. 1:3); the sword you fear will overtake you in Egypt (Jer. 42:16); the ploughman will overtake the reaper (Amos 9:13).

D The Lord's coming

D1 The fact of his coming
The Lord comes to judge the earth (1 Chr. 16:33; Ps. 96:13; 98:9); I believe you are the Christ who is coming into the world (John 11:27); if I had not come and spoken to them, they would not have had sin (John 15:22); I came from the Father and have come into the world (John 16:28); we made known to you the power and coming of our Lord Jesus Christ (2 Pet. 1:16); the coming of the Lord (1 Thess. 5:23; 2 Thess. 2:1); when our Lord Jesus comes with all his saints (1 Thess. 3:13); where is the promise of his coming? (2 Pet. 3:4); Maranatha – our Lord, come! (1 Cor. 16:22); I am coming to you (Rev. 2:5); him who is and was and is to come (Rev. 1:4, 8; 4:8); behold, I come! (Ps. 40:7); you proclaim the Lord's death until he comes (1 Cor. 11:26); you are our joy before the Lord Jesus at his coming (1 Thess. 2:19); the appearing of Jesus Christ (1 Pet. 1:7); come, Lord Jesus! (Rev. 22:20).

D2 The timing of his coming
When will you come to me? (Ps. 101:2); be patient until the coming of the Lord (Jas. 5:7); a little while and the coming one will come and will not delay (Heb. 10:37); Jesus is coming soon (Rev. 3:11; 22:7); I am coming soon (Rev. 2:16; 22:12, 20); the coming of the Lord is at hand (Jas. 5:8); you will not have finished the towns of Israel before the Son of man comes (Matt. 10:23); you do not know when your Lord is coming (Matt. 24:42); the Son of man comes when you do not expect (Matt. 24:44); after a long time the master returned (Matt. 25:19); wait until the Lord comes (1 Cor. 4:5).

D3 The nature of his coming
When he comes to be glorified in his saints (2 Thess. 1:10); the Son of man will come in the glory of his Father (Matt. 16:27; Mark 8:38; Luke 9:26); when the Son of man comes in his glory (Matt. 25:31); the Son of man coming on the clouds (Matt. 24:30; Mark 13:26); the Son of man coming in a cloud (Luke 21:27); he is coming with the clouds (Rev. 1:7); the Lord will slay the lawless one by his coming (2 Thess. 2:8); the coming of the Son of man will be like lightning (Matt. 24:27); like the days of Noah (Matt. 24:37); I am coming like a thief (Rev. 16:15); if you will not wake up I will come like a thief (Rev. 3:3); do not think that I came to bring peace on earth (Matt. 10:34); those who are Christ's will be raised at his coming (1 Cor. 15:23); the Lord Jesus will be revealed from heaven with his mighty angels (2 Thess. 1:7); set your hope on the grace coming to you at the appearing of Jesus Christ (1 Pet. 1:13).

296 Departure

LEAVING PLACES, see 298.

A Setting out

When the cloud lifted the Israelites set out (Exod. 40:36-7; Num. 9:17, 21, 22); they set out at the Lord's command (Num. 9:18, 23); his going forth is sure as the dawn (Hos. 6:3); depart! go out from there! (Isa. 52:11); the time of my departure has come (2 Tim. 4:6).

B Leaving

Depart from me, for I am a sinful man (Luke 5:8); they begged Jesus to leave their country (Matt. 8:34; Mark 5:17); the Philippians begged Paul and Silas to depart (Acts 16:39); leave the presence of a fool (Prov. 14:7); woe to them when I depart from them! (Hos. 9:12); the devil departed from him until an opportune time (Luke 4:13); Jesus said to the 12, 'Will you also go away?' (John 6:67); they went out one by one, beginning with the eldest (John 8:9); I am going away and you will seek me and die in your sin (John 8:21); I am going away and I will come to you (John 14:28); if I do not go away the Helper will not come (John 16:7); I am leaving the world and going to the Father (John 16:28).

ABANDONING, see 621.

C Exodus

Lest the Israelites depart from the land (Exod. 1:10); depart, do not stay! (Jer. 51:50); Joseph spoke of the exodus of Israel (Heb. 11:22); Moses and Elijah spoke with Jesus about his departure to be accomplished at Jerusalem (Luke 9:31).

297 Entrance

A Entering places

A1 Entering dwellings

A1a Entering houses

Joseph went into the house to do his work (Gen. 39:11); as she entered the house the child died (1 Kgs. 14:17); Jesus entered Peter's house (Matt. 8:14; Mark 1:29); he went into the Pharisee's house (Luke 7:36); he entered a house and would not have anyone know it (Mark 7:24); when he had entered the house his disciples questioned him privately (Mark 9:28); no one entered the house with him except Peter, James, John and the parents (Luke 8:51); wherever you enter a house, stay there till you leave (Mark 6:10; Luke 9:4); when you enter the house, greet it (Matt. 10:12); whatever house you enter, first say, 'Peace be to this house' (Luke 10:5).

A1b Breaking into houses

On earth thieves break in and steal (Matt. 6:19); in heaven thieves do not break in and steal (Matt. 6:20); he would not have let his house be broken into (Matt. 24:43; Luke 12:39); how can anyone enter a strong man's house? (Matt. 12:29; Mark 3:27); Saul entered house after house (Acts 8:3); they make their way into households and capture weak women (2 Tim. 3:6).

A1c Not entering houses

I will not enter my house until I find a place for the Lord (Ps. 132:3); do not enter a house to take a pledge (Deut. 24:10); do not go into the house to retrieve anything (Mark 13:15); I am not worthy for you to come under my roof (Matt. 8:8; Luke 7:6); he was angry and refused to go in (Luke 15:28).

A2 Entering the ark

You, your wife, your sons and their wives will enter the ark (Gen. 6:18); enter the ark with all your household (Gen. 7:1); Noah, his wife, his sons and their wives entered the ark (Gen. 7:7, 13); bring two of every creature with you into the ark (Gen. 6:19-20); until the day that Noah entered the ark (Matt. 24:38; Luke 17:27).

A3 Entering gates / doors

I will enter through the gates of righteousness (Ps. 118:19); enter his gates with thanksgiving (Ps. 100:4); he who enters by the door is the shepherd (John 10:2); he who does not enter the sheepfold by the door is a thief (John 10:1); that the king of glory may come in (Ps. 24:7, 9).

A4 Entering cities

The Jebusites thought David could not get in (2 Sam. 5:6; 1 Chr. 11:5); the kings of the earth did not believe an enemy could enter Jerusalem (Lam. 4:12); when your feet enter the city the child will die (1 Kgs. 14:12); who will bring us into the fortified city? (Ps. 60:9; 108:10); do not enter any town of the Samaritans (Matt. 10:5); whatever town or village you enter (Matt. 10:11); let not those who are in the country enter the city (Luke 21:21); rise and enter the city and you will be told what to do (Acts 9:6); when the disciples surrounded him, Paul rose up and entered the city (Acts 14:20).

ENTERING THE LAND, see 184B1b.

A5 Entering the tabernacle

When Moses entered the tent the cloud came down (Exod. 33:9); Moses and Aaron entered the tent of meeting (Lev. 9:23); how Aaron should enter the holy place (Lev. 16:3); Moses could not enter the tent of meeting because of the cloud (Exod. 40:35); do not drink wine when you enter the tent of meeting (Lev. 10:9); David entered the house of God (Matt. 12:4; Mark 2:26; Luke 6:4).

A6 Entering the temple

The priests could not enter the temple for the glory of the Lord (2 Chr. 7:2); whenever the king entered the house of the Lord (1 Kgs. 14:28); Uzziah entered the temple to burn incense (2 Chr. 26:16); Hezekiah entered the house of the Lord (Isa. 37:1); robbers will enter and profane it (Ezek. 7:22); foreign nations have entered her sanctuary (Lam. 1:10); Jesus entered the temple (Matt. 21:12, 23; Mark 11:11, 15; Luke 19:45); in the Spirit Simeon came into the temple (Luke 2:27).

THE TEMPLE ENTERED, see 990B6.

B Entering to God

B1 Access to God

We enter the sanctuary through the blood of Jesus (Heb. 10:19); we have access to the Father (Eph. 2:18); access in confidence through faith (Eph. 3:12); through Christ we have access to this grace in which we stand (Rom. 5:2).

B2 Entering life

Strive to enter by the narrow door (Luke 13:24); enter by the narrow gate that leads to life (Matt. 7:13-14); I am the door, whoever enters through me will be saved (John 10:9); that they may enter the city by the gates (Rev. 22:14); it is better to enter life maimed than with two hands to be thrown into hell (Mark 9:43); it is better to enter life lame than with two feet to be thrown into hell (Mark 9:45); they will never enter my rest (Heb. 3:11; 4:3, 5); while the promise of entering his rest remains (Heb. 4:1); those who received the good news failed to enter because of disobedience (Heb. 4:6); let us strive to enter that rest (Heb. 4:11).

B3 Entering the kingdom

How hard it is to enter the kingdom! (Mark 10:24); it is hard for the wealthy to enter (Matt. 19:23; Mark 10:23; Luke 18:24); abundant entrance into the kingdom (2 Pet. 1:11); you will not enter the kingdom unless your righteousness surpasses (Matt. 5:20); unless you become like children (Matt. 18:3; Mark 10:15); unless you are born again (John 3:5); whoever does not receive the kingdom of God like a child shall not enter it (Luke 18:17); it is better to enter maimed than not to enter (Matt. 18:8-9); better to enter the kingdom of God with one eye (Mark 9:47); easier for a camel to go through the eye of a needle than for a rich man to enter (Matt. 19:24; Mark 10:25; Luke 18:25); not everyone who says Lord! will enter (Matt. 7:21); you neither enter nor allow others to enter (Matt. 23:13; Luke 11:52); tax collectors and prostitutes enter the kingdom of God ahead of you (Matt. 21:31); enter into the joy of your master (Matt. 25:21, 23); through many tribulations we must enter the kingdom of God (Acts 14:22).

THE KINGDOM ENTERED, see 733B2e.

B4 Entering heaven
Jesus has entered within the veil (Heb. 6:19-20); Christ entered heaven itself (Heb. 9:24).

C Entering people

C1 Entering the mouth
What enters the mouth does not defile a man (Matt. 15:11, 17; Mark 7:15, 18); food enters not the heart but the stomach (Mark 7:19).

C2 Demons entering
Satan entered Judas (Luke 22:3; John 13:27); come out and do not enter him again (Mark 9:25); the demons entered the pigs (Matt. 8:32; Mark 5:12-13; Luke 8:32-3); they go in and live there (Matt. 12:45); the name was Legion because many demons had entered him (Luke 8:30); they enter the man and dwell there (Luke 11:26).

DEMONISED, see 969D3.

D Going out and coming in
A man to go out and come in before the congregation (Num. 27:17); David went out and came in before the people (1 Sam. 18:13, 16); you led Israel out and in (2 Sam. 5:2); you going out and coming in with me in the army (1 Sam. 29:6); at his command they shall go out and come in (Num. 27:21); blessed shall you be when you come in and when you go out (Deut. 28:6); cursed shall you be when you come in and when you go out (Deut. 28:19); I do not know how to go out or come in (1 Kgs. 3:7); that I may not go out and come in before this people (2 Chr. 1:10); be with the king when he goes out and comes in (2 Kgs. 11:8; 2 Chr. 23:7); Abner came to know your going out and coming in (2 Sam. 3:25); I know your going out and your coming in (2 Kgs. 19:27; Isa. 37:28); the Lord will keep your going out and your coming in (Ps. 121:8); you were the one who led out and brought in Israel (1 Chr. 11:2); he will go in and out and find pasture (John 10:9); all the time that the Lord Jesus went in and out among us (Acts 1:21); he went in and out among them in Jerusalem (Acts 9:28); none went out of Jericho and none came in (Josh. 6:1); I am no longer able to go out and come in (Deut. 31:2).

298 Emergence

GOING OUT AND COMING IN, see 297D.

A Leaving Egypt
When they came out of Egypt (Deut. 4:45, 46); when Israel went forth from Egypt (Ps. 114:1); the hosts of the Lord went out of Egypt (Exod. 12:41); remember this day when you went out of Egypt (Exod. 13:3); in the month of Abib you came out of Egypt (Exod. 23:15); they will come out and worship me in this place (Acts 7:7); with uplifted arm he led them out of Egypt (Exod. 13:17).

B Leaving other places
They went out from Ur (Gen. 11:31); go from your country and family (Gen. 12:1); you will go out with joy (Isa. 55:12); the Lord is coming out from his place (Mic. 1:3); if the manslayer goes outside the border of the city of refuge (Num. 35:26-8); Shimei was not to leave Jerusalem (1 Kgs. 2:36-7); as you go out of that house or town, shake the dust off your feet (Matt. 10:14); resurrected saints coming out of the tombs (Matt. 27:53); he led the blind man out of the village (Mark 8:23); Anna did not depart from the temple (Luke 2:37); let those in the city go out (Luke 21:21); to avoid the wicked people of the world you would need to go out

of the world (1 Cor. 5:10); they went out from us to demonstrate that they are not of us (1 John 2:19).

C Going forth
From you will go forth for me one who is ruler in Israel (Mic. 5:2); his goings forth [origin] are from eternity (Mic. 5:2); you will go out leaping like calves from the stall (Mal. 4:2).

D Going outside
Joseph fled outside (Gen. 39:12, 13, 15, 18); Jacob went out from before Pharaoh (Gen. 47:10); do not go outside until morning (Exod. 12:22); do not go outside the house (Josh. 2:19); do not go out from the doorway of the tent of meeting (Lev. 10:7); do not go out of the tent of meeting for seven days (Lev. 8:33); the high priest must not go out of the sanctuary (Lev. 21:12); Joab would not come out of the tabernacle (1 Kgs. 2:30); Shadrach, Meshach and Abednego came out of the fire (Dan. 3:26); let the bridegroom leave his room and the bride her chamber (Joel 2:16); you will not get out until you have paid the last penny (Matt. 5:26); his father came out and entreated him (Luke 15:28); Peter went out and wept bitterly (Luke 22:62); Judas went out, and it was night (John 13:30); he will never go out of the temple (Rev. 3:12).

E Coming out of people
What comes out of the mouth defiles a man (Matt. 15:11, 18; Mark 7:15, 20); out of the heart come evil things (Matt. 15:19; Mark 7:21); when the unclean spirit has gone out of a man (Matt. 12:43; Luke 11:24); the demon came out of him (Matt. 17:18); the unclean spirit came out of him (Mark 1:26); the unclean spirits came out and entered the pigs (Mark 5:13); the demon has gone out of your daughter (Mark 7:29).

F Coming out from evil
Come out of her, my people (Jer. 51:45; Rev. 18:4); go forth from Babylon (Isa. 48:20; Jer. 50:8); come out from them and be separate (2 Cor. 6:17).

299 Reception

RECEIVING, see 782.

A Receiving people

A1 Welcoming Christ
He who receives you receives me (Matt. 10:40; John 13:20); he who receives such a child receives me (Matt. 18:5; Mark 9:37; Luke 9:48); he who receives me receives him who sent me (Mark 9:37; Luke 9:48; John 13:20); you received me as an angel of God, as Christ (Gal. 4:14); those who receive him have the right to become children of God (John 1:12); when did we see you a stranger and welcome you? (Matt. 25:38); when Jesus returned, the crowd welcomed him (Luke 8:40); Martha welcomed him into her house (Luke 10:38); Zacchaeus received Jesus gladly (Luke 19:6); he has gone to be the guest of a sinner (Luke 19:7); when he came to Galilee the Galileans welcomed him (John 4:45); they were willing to receive him into the boat (John 6:21).

A2 Welcomed by God
This man receives sinners and eats with them (Luke 15:2); with such an offering, will God receive you? (Mal. 1:9); that the Israelites may be accepted (Exod. 28:38); Jesus welcomed the crowds (Luke 9:11); God has welcomed him (Rom. 14:3); welcome one another as Christ welcomed us (Rom. 15:7); touch nothing unclean and I will welcome you (2 Cor. 6:17).

A3 Welcoming believers
Welcome one another as Christ welcomed us (Rom. 15:7); receive him who is weak in the faith (Rom. 14:1); he who receives you receives me (Matt. 10:40); whoever receives me receives him who sent me (Luke 9:48); he who receives a prophet as a prophet will receive a

prophet's reward (Matt. 10:41); he who receives such a child in my name receives me (Luke 9:48); you received me as an angel of God, as Christ (Gal. 4:14); when you enter a city and they receive you (Luke 10:8); they were welcomed by the church, the apostles and the elders (Acts 15:4); Jason has welcomed them (Acts 17:7); the brethren wrote to the disciples to welcome Apollos (Acts 18:27); in Jerusalem the brethren received us gladly (Acts 21:17); they report what a welcome we had among you (1 Thess. 1:9); accept him as you would me (Philem. 17); Diotrephes puts out of the church those who receive the brethren (3 John 10).

GREETING, see 884.

B Not receiving people
B1 Not welcoming Christ
His own did not receive him (John 1:11); I come in my Father's name and you do not receive me (John 5:43); the Samaritan village would not receive him (Luke 9:53); I was a stranger and you did not welcome me (Matt. 25:43).

B2 Not welcoming people
If anyone will not receive you, shake the dust off your feet (Matt. 10:14; Luke 9:5); if you enter a town and they do not receive you (Luke 10:10); Diotrephes would not receive the brethren (3 John 10); no one took them in (Judg. 19:15, 18); if anyone does not bring this doctrine, do not receive him into the house (2 John 10).

300 Ejection
A Driving out God
They tell God to depart from them (Job 22:17).

B Driving out Christ
The Spirit drove Jesus out into the wilderness (Mark 1:12); they cast Jesus out of Nazareth (Luke 4:29); they threw the heir out of the vineyard and killed him (Matt. 21:39; Luke 20:15); away with him! (John 19:15).

C Driving out people
C1 God driving out people
C1a Driven from God's presence
Cain was driven from the ground and from the Lord's presence (Gen. 4:14, 16); the Lord removed Israel from his sight (2 Kgs. 17:18, 20, 23); removing Judah also from his sight (2 Kgs. 23:27; 24:3, 20; Jer. 52:3); I will cast you out of my sight (Jer. 7:15); the Lord would not cast them from his presence until now (2 Kgs. 13:23); I will cast you away from my presence (Jer. 23:39); I am cast out from your presence (Jonah 2:4); the sons of the kingdom will be cast out (Matt. 8:12); all the prophets in the kingdom and you thrown out (Luke 13:28); the ruler of this world will be cast out (John 12:31).

C1b Driven from God's things
He was driven out of the garden of Eden (Gen. 3:23-4); men have driven me out from the Lord's inheritance (1 Sam. 26:19); because of their wickedness I will drive them out of my house (Hos. 9:15); Israel would be uprooted from the land (2 Chr. 7:20); I will cut off Israel from the land (1 Kgs. 9:7); Uzziah was driven from the sanctuary (2 Chr. 26:18, 20); I have cast you out from God's mountain, O cherub (Ezek. 28:16).

C2 Christ driving out people
Jesus drove the traders out of the temple (Matt. 21:12; Mark 11:15; Luke 19:45; John 2:15); depart from me, you evildoers (Ps. 6:8; 119:115; Matt. 7:23; Luke 13:27); depart from me, you cursed (Matt. 25:41); he who comes to me I will not cast out (John 6:37).

C3 Driving out the people of the land
C3a The Lord will drive them out
The Lord will drive out these nations (Exod. 34:11; Deut. 6:19; 7:1; 9:3-5; 11:23); I will drive them out (Exod. 33:2; 34:24; Josh. 13:6; 23:5); I will send hornets to drive

them out (Exod. 23:28); I am casting out nations before you (Lev. 18:24); because of their wickedness the Lord is driving them out (Deut. 9:5; 18:12); driving out nations greater than you (Deut. 4:38; Josh. 23:9); I will not drive them out in one year (Exod. 23:29); I will drive them out little by little (Exod. 23:30; Deut. 7:22).

C3b The Lord drove them out
He drove out the enemy (Deut. 33:27); he drove out the nations before them (Ps. 78:55); you drove out the nations (1 Chr. 17:21; Ps. 44:2; 80:8); I sent the hornet which drove them out (Josh. 24:12); the Lord has driven the Amorites out (Josh. 24:18; Judg. 11:23; 1 Kgs. 21:26); did you not drive them out? (2 Chr. 20:7); the nations whom God drove out (Acts 7:45).

C3c Israel driving them out
Drive them out! (Exod. 23:31; Num. 33:52); though they are strong, you can drive them out (Josh. 17:18); the Lord will be with me and I will drive them out (Josh. 14:12); Caleb drove out the three sons of Anak (Josh. 15:14; Judg. 1:20).

C3d Not driving them out
If you do not drive them out they will vex you (Num. 33:55); the Israelites did not drive some of them out (Judg. 1:19, 21, 27-33); the Israelites could not drive out the Geshurites or the Maacathites (Josh. 13:13); Judah could not drive out the Jebusites (Josh. 15:63); Ephraim could not drive out the Canaanites (Josh. 16:10); Manasseh could not drive out the Canaanites (Josh. 17:12, 13); the Lord will not drive out these nations (Josh. 23:13; Judg. 2:3, 21, 23).

C4 Driven from people
C4a People sent away
Drive out a scoffer and strife will go out (Prov. 22:10); he who drives away his mother is a shameful son (Prov. 19:26); drive out the slave woman (Gen. 21:10; Gal. 4:30); Zebul drove out Gaal (Judg. 9:41); Gilead's sons drove out Jephthah (Judg. 11:2, 7); Abimelech sent Isaac away (Gen. 26:16, 27); Pharaoh drove out Moses and Aaron (Exod. 10:11, 28); Abimelech drove David away (Ps. 34:t); Amnon drove out Tamar (2 Sam. 13:15, 17); Nehemiah drove away the son-in-law of Sanballat (Neh. 13:28); Amaziah told Amos to go away (Amos 7:12); he was driven by the demon into the wilderness (Luke 8:29); they drove him out of the city (Acts 7:58); they drove Paul and Barnabas out of that district (Acts 13:50); would they now send us away secretly? (Acts 16:37); Claudius had expelled all the Jews from Rome (Acts 18:2); Gallio drove them away from the judgement seat (Acts 18:16); your brothers cast you out (Isa. 66:5); they are driven out from among men (Job 30:5); you will be driven away from among men (Dan. 4:25, 32-3).

C4b Excommunicated
They will expel you from the synagogue (John 16:2); whoever confessed that Jesus was the Christ would be put out of the synagogue (John 9:22); they did not confess him lest they be put out of the synagogue (John 12:42); blessed are you when men excommunicate you (Luke 6:22); they threw him out (John 9:34); the Jews drove us out (1 Thess. 2:15); anyone who did not come would be expelled from the assembly (Ezra 10:8); do not let the wicked drive me away (Ps. 36:11); Jehoshaphat expelled the male temple prostitutes (1 Kgs. 22:46); the one who did this should be removed from among you (1 Cor. 5:2); drive out the wicked man from among you (1 Cor. 5:13); Diotrephes puts out of the church those who receive the brethren (3 John 10); these men would shut you out (Gal. 4:17).

C5 Driving Israel out
After that Pharaoh will send you out (Exod. 3:20); with a strong hand he will drive them out (Exod. 6:1);

Pharaoh drove out all Israel (Exod. 11:1; 12:31); they had been driven out of Egypt in haste (Exod. 12:39); perhaps I can drive Israel out of the land (Num. 22:6, 11); I will drive you out of the land (Jer. 27:15); they are coming to drive us out (2 Chr. 20:11); I am slinging out the inhabitants of the land (Jer. 10:18).

C6 Disqualified
Lest after preaching to others I should be disqualified (1 Cor. 9:27).

D Casting out Satan
D1 Jesus casting out demons
Begone, Satan! (Matt. 4:10); be quiet and come out of him (Mark 1:25-6); he was casting out a dumb demon (Luke 11:14); Jesus drove out many evil spirits (Matt. 8:16; Mark 1:34); demons came out of many (Luke 4:41); Jesus was preaching and casting out evil spirits (Mark 1:39); I cast out demons today and tomorrow (Luke 13:32); come out of him! (Luke 4:35); out of the Gadarene demoniac (Matt. 8:32; Mark 5:8; Luke 8:29); out of the man's son (Mark 9:25); the Syrophoenician woman begged Jesus to cast the demon out (Mark 7:26); if you cast us out, send us into the herd of pigs (Matt. 8:31); when the demon was cast out the dumb man spoke (Matt. 9:33); Jesus had cast out seven demons from Mary Magdalene (Mark 16:9); he casts out demons by the ruler of demons (Matt. 9:34; 12:24, 27; Mark 3:22; Luke 11:15); you say I cast out demons by Beelzebul (Luke 11:18-19); how can Satan cast out Satan? (Matt. 12:26); if I cast out demons by the finger of God (Luke 11:20); if I cast out demons by the Spirit of God (Matt. 12:28).

D2 People casting out demons
Cast out demons (Matt. 10:8); he gave them authority to cast out unclean spirits (Matt. 10:1); the 12 were to have authority to cast out demons (Mark 3:15); in my name they will cast out demons (Mark 16:17); the 12 cast out many demons (Mark 6:13); unclean spirits came out of many (Acts 8:7); I command you in the name of Jesus Christ to come out of her (Acts 16:18); evil spirits went out when garments from Paul were brought (Acts 19:12); did we not cast out demons in your name? (Matt. 7:22); Teacher, we saw a man casting out demons in your name (Mark 9:38); we saw a man casting out demons in your name and we forbade him (Luke 9:49); itinerant Jewish exorcists tried to use the name of Jesus (Acts 19:13); by whom do your sons cast out demons? (Matt. 12:27; Luke 11:19); the disciples could not cast out the evil spirit (Mark 9:18; Luke 9:40); why could we not cast it out? (Matt. 17:19; Mark 9:28).

E Driving out animals
Abraham drove away the birds of prey (Gen. 15:11); there will be no one to drive away the birds and beasts from your corpses (Deut. 28:26); if an animal being kept for someone is driven away (Exod. 22:10); the goat of removal was sent into the wilderness (Lev. 16:10, 21).

F Ejecting things
F1 Sending things away
Send the ark away! (1 Sam. 5:11); they will throw their silver into the streets (Ezek. 7:19); cast away from you all your transgressions (Ezek. 18:31); cast away the detestable things of your eyes (Ezek. 20:7); they did not cast away the detestable things of their eyes (Ezek. 20:8); tasteless salt is good for nothing but to be thrown out (Matt. 5:13); if your hand causes you to stumble, cut it off and throw it from you (Matt. 5:30); do not throw away your confidence (Heb. 10:35).

F2 Emptying
As they emptied their sacks (Gen. 42:35); they have emptied out the money (2 Chr. 34:17); empty the house before the priest inspects (Lev. 14:36); will they

continue to empty the net and kill nations without mercy? (Hab. 1:17); the ship was to unload its cargo at Tyre (Acts 21:3); so may every one be shaken out and emptied who does not fulfil this promise (Neh. 5:13).

301 Food: eating and drinking

A About food
A1 Food defined
God gave mankind plants and fruit for food (Gen. 1:29; 3:18; 9:3); trees good for food (Gen. 2:9); from which they could eat (Gen. 2:16; 3:2); God gave plants to all creatures for food (Gen. 1:30); God gives animals to man as food (Gen. 9:3); these are the creatures you may eat (Lev. 11:2); distinguishing between what may be eaten and what may not (Lev. 11:47); on both banks of the river grow all kinds of trees for food (Ezek. 47:12); one man believes he may eat all things, but the weak eats only vegetables (Rom. 14:2).

A2 Food permitted
You may freely eat of every tree in the garden (Gen. 2:16); we may eat the fruit of the trees of the garden (Gen. 3:2); fruit from a tree five years old is permitted (Lev. 19:25); what a man eats does not make him unclean (Matt. 15:11; Mark 7:15); Jesus thus declared all foods clean (Mark 7:19); eat anything sold in the market (1 Cor. 10:25); no one should judge you regarding food and drink (Col. 2:16); some abstain from foods which God intended for us (1 Tim. 4:3); all food is clean, but do not eat anything which make a brother stumble (Rom. 14:20-1).

A3 Food is fitting
Do we not have a right to eat and drink? (1 Cor. 9:4); a workman deserves his food (Matt. 10:10); food is for the stomach and the stomach for food (1 Cor. 6:13); having food and clothing we will be content (1 Tim. 6:8); God satisfied your hearts with food and gladness (Acts 14:17).

A4 Limitations of food
The kingdom of God is not eating and drinking (Rom. 14:17); man does not live by bread alone (Deut. 8:3; Matt. 4:4; Luke 4:4); food will not commend us to God (1 Cor. 8:8); they serve their own stomach (Rom. 16:18); offerings under the law were only a matter of food and drink etc. (Heb. 9:10); the heart needs strengthening by grace, not food (Heb. 13:9); is not life more than food? (Matt. 6:25); all food is clean, but do not eat anything which makes a brother stumble (Rom. 14:20-1); do not destroy your brother by your food (Rom. 14:15); Esau sold his birthright for a single meal (Heb. 12:16).

B Foods
B1 Particular foods
B1a Meat
Who will give us meat? (Num. 11:4, 13, 18); no meat or wine entered my mouth (Dan. 10:3); those who eat lambs from the flock and calves from the stall (Amos 6:4); we sat by the pots of meat (Exod. 16:3); the Lord gives meat in the evening and bread in the morning (Exod. 16:8, 12); we remember the fish we ate in Egypt (Num. 11:5); five loaves and two fish (Matt. 14:17; Mark 6:38, 41; Luke 9:13, 16; John 6:9); seven loaves and a few small fish (Matt. 15:34; Mark 8:5-7); what father will give his son a snake instead of a fish? (Luke 11:11); what father will give his son a scorpion instead of an egg? (Luke 11:12); they gave him a piece of broiled fish (Luke 24:42); a charcoal fire with fish and bread on it (John 21:9); Jesus took the bread and fish and gave to them (John 21:13); it is good not to eat meat or drink wine or do anything to make your brother stumble (Rom. 14:21).

B1b Grain

God give you abundance of grain (Gen. 27:28); when they had finished eating the grain from Egypt (Gen. 43:2); give the priest the first of your coarse meal so a blessing rests on your house (Ezek. 44:30); grain will make the young men flourish and new wine the virgins (Zech. 9:17); the grain is ruined, the wine fails, the oil languishes (Joel 1:10); I called for a drought on the grain, wine, oil (Hag. 1:11); 100 measures of wheat (Luke 16:7); Satan demanded to have you all to sieve you like wheat (Luke 22:31); throwing the wheat into the sea (Acts 27:38); cargo of wine, oil, flour and wheat (Rev. 18:13).

B1c Bread

Let me fetch a morsel of bread (Gen. 18:5); Melchizedek brought bread and wine (Gen. 14:18); Lot gave the angels unleavened bread (Gen. 19:3); Abraham took bread and a skin of water (Gen. 21:14); we ate bread to the full (Exod. 16:3); three baskets of white bread (Gen. 40:16-17); baked foods for Pharaoh (Gen. 40:17); take ten loaves, cakes and a jar of honey (1 Kgs. 14:3); cakes of bread, dates and raisins (2 Sam. 6:19); five loaves and two fish (Matt. 14:17; Mark 6:38, 41; Luke 9:13, 16; John 6:9, 13); seven loaves and a few small fish (Matt. 15:34; Mark 8:5-7); you have not eaten bread or drunk wine (Deut. 29:6); the bread of the presence set on the table (Exod. 25:30; 35:13; 39:36; 40:23; Lev. 24:5-8; Num. 4:7; 1 Kgs. 7:48; Heb. 9:2); he charged them not to take any bread (Mark 6:8; Luke 9:3); shall we spend 200 denarii on bread? (Mark 6:37); he took bread, blessed and broke it (Mark 14:22); friend, lend me three loaves (Luke 11:5); a charcoal fire with fish and bread on it (John 21:9); Jesus took the bread and fish and gave to them (John 21:13); Paul ate bread among them all (Acts 27:35).

B1d Manna

God gave the Israelites bread from heaven (Exod. 16:4, 15; Neh. 9:15; Ps. 78:25; 105:40); the manna (Exod. 16:31-5; Num. 11:6-9; Deut. 8:3, 16; Neh. 9:20); which stopped when they entered Canaan (Josh. 5:11-12); he gave them bread from heaven to eat (John 6:31); in the morning you will eat bread (Exod. 16:8, 12); our fathers ate the manna in the wilderness (John 6:31, 49, 58); he rained manna on them (Ps. 78:24); all ate the same spiritual food (1 Cor. 10:3); we hate this worthless food (Num. 21:5); an omer to be kept throught the generations (Exod. 16:32, 33); a golden jar containing the manna (Heb. 9:4); to him who overcomes I will give some of the hidden manna (Rev. 2:17).

B1e Dried fruit

Israel turn to other gods and love raisin cakes (Hos. 3:1); clusters of raisins (1 Sam. 25:18; 30:12); cakes of bread, dates and raisins (2 Sam. 6:19); sustain me with raisin cakes (S. of S. 2:5); mourn for the raisin cakes of Kir-haraseth (Isa. 16:7); cakes of figs (1 Sam. 25:18; 30:12).

B1f Vegetables

Jacob gave Esau bread and lentil pottage (Gen. 25:34); take beans, lentils, millet and spelt (Ezek. 4:9); we remember the fish, cucumbers, melons, leeks, onions, garlic (Num. 11:5); let us be given vegetables to eat and water to drink (Dan. 1:12); the weak man eats only vegetables (Rom. 14:2).

B1g Other foods

Pistachio nuts and almonds (Gen. 43:11); John ate locusts and wild honey (Matt. 3:4; Mark 1:6); take these 10 cheeses to the commander (1 Sam. 17:18); cheese from the herd (2 Sam. 17:29); did you not curdle me like cheese? (Job 10:10).

B2 Clean food

All that divides the hoof and chews the cud (Lev. 11:3); water creatures which have fins and scales (Lev. 11:9); insects with jointed legs which jump (Lev. 11:21); all kinds of locusts (Lev. 11:22).

CLEAN ANIMALS, see 648B.

B3 Forbidden food

Do not eat fat (Lev. 7:23, 24, 25); do not eat blood (Gen. 9:4; Lev. 7:26-7; 17:10-14; 19:26; Deut. 12:16, 23-5; 15:23); eat neither fat nor blood (Lev. 3:17); do not eat the meat of an animal which has died (Lev. 17:15; 22:8; Deut. 14:21; Ezek. 4:14; 44:31); you must not eat the flesh of an unclean animal (Lev. 11:8, 11, 13); swarming things are not to be eaten (Lev. 11:41, 42); meat touching unclean things must not be eaten (Lev. 7:19); people who eat pork (Isa. 65:4); those who eat pork and mice (Isa. 66:17); quadrupeds, reptiles and wild animals in a sheet (Acts 10:12; 11:6); the Israelites do not eat the sinew of the thigh (Gen. 32:32); the people were sinning by eating the blood (1 Sam. 14:32, 33, 34).

CONSUMING BLOOD, see 335E2.

UNCLEAN ANIMALS, see 649C.

B4 Rich food

Asher's food will be rich (Gen. 49:20); Asher will give royal dainties (Gen. 49:20); rich food, filled with marrow (Isa. 25:6); a land flowing with milk and honey (Exod. 3:8, 17; 13:5; 33:3); honey and milk are under your tongue (S. of S. 4:11); he will eat curds and honey (Isa. 7:15); everyone will eat curds and honey (Isa. 7:22); the king allotted them a daily ration of the rich food he ate (Dan. 1:5); do not desire the ruler's delicacies (Prov. 23:3); do not desire the delicacies of an evil-eyed man (Prov. 23:6); better a meal of vegetables with love than a fatted ox with strife (Prov. 15:17); better a dry morsel with quiet than feasting and strife (Prov. 17:1).

B5 Repulsive food

The Israelites were made to drink the calf powdered (Exod. 32:20); unleavened bread, the bread of affliction (Deut. 16:3); the Gibeonites' bread was dry and crumbled (Josh. 9:5, 12); I eat ashes like bread (Ps. 102:9); I will feed them with wormwood and poisoned water (Jer. 9:15); men doomed to eat their own dung and drink their own urine (2 Kgs. 18:27; Isa. 36:12); Micaiah sentenced to eat only bread and water (1 Kgs. 22:27; 2 Chr. 18:26); they must eat what you tread down and drink what you foul (Ezek. 34:19); Nebuchadnezzar eating grass (Dan. 4:32, 33; 5:21); he would have filled his belly with the pods the pigs ate (Luke 15:16); let those who are left eat one another's flesh (Zech. 11:9); who will give his son a stone instead of bread? (Matt. 7:9); what father will give his son a snake instead of a fish? (Matt. 7:10; Luke 11:11); if a son asks for a fish, who will give him a snake? (Matt. 7:10).

BITTER FOOD, see 391B1.

B6 Offerings as food

B6a Food for God

Sacrifices as God's food (Lev. 3:11, 16; 21:6, 8, 17, 21, 22; 22:25; Num. 28:2; Mal. 1:7, 12); shall I eat the flesh of bulls? (Ps. 50:13); when you offer my food, the fat and the blood (Ezek. 44:7).

B6b Food for priests defined

The priest to have some offerings as his food (Lev. 5:13; 6:16-18; 7:6-14; Num. 5:9-10; 18:19; 1 Sam. 2:28); the remainder of the cereal offering is for the priests (Lev. 2:3, 10); the priests' portion specified (Deut. 18:3-4); the cereal offering is to be eaten in the court of the tent of meeting (Lev. 6:16); the sin offering is to be eaten in the court of the tent of meeting (Lev. 6:26); the priests were to eat the ram of ordination (Exod. 29:31-3; Lev. 8:31); the priests were to eat the bread of the presence (Lev. 24:9); every male priest may eat the sacrifices

(Lev. 6:18, 29; 7:6; 10:12-15; Num. 18:10); the priest's household could eat sacrifices (Lev. 10:14; Num. 18:11); even if deformed (Lev. 21:22); a priest's slave may eat the sacrifices (Lev. 22:11); the Levites are to eat the sacrifices (Deut. 18:1, 8); Levites given the tithe to eat (Num. 18:30-2); those who serve at the altar have their share from the altar (1 Cor. 9:13); are not those who eat the sacrifices sharers in the altar? (1 Cor. 10:18); the thank-offering must be eaten the same day (Lev. 22:30); Eli's sons despised the Lord's offerings by their practices (1 Sam. 2:13-17).

B6c Eating offerings wrongly
They sacrifice meat and eat it (Hos. 8:13); David ate the holy bread (1 Sam. 21:4-6); David ate the bread of the Presence which only the priests could eat (Matt. 12:4; Mark 2:26; Luke 6:4); add the burnt offerings to your sacrifices and eat the meat (Jer. 7:21); no one outside the priest's household could eat the sacrifices (Lev. 22:10, 13); a priest's daughter married to a non-priest may not eat the sacrifices (Lev. 22:12); unless widowed or divorced (Lev. 22:13); no one unclean may eat of it (Lev. 22:4-7); when they sacrifice to other gods and invite you to eat their sacrifices (Exod. 34:15); who ate the fat of their sacrifices? (Deut. 32:38); you who spread a table for Fortune and fill cups for Destiny (Isa. 65:11); making cakes for the queen of heaven (Jer. 7:18; 44:19); making their sons pass through the fire as food for their idols (Ezek. 23:37); eating food sacrificed to idols (1 Cor. 8:4-10; 10:19, 28; Rev. 2:14, 20).

B7 Eating one another
B7a Cannibalism
You will eat your sons and your daughters (Lev. 26:29; Deut. 28:53-7; Jer. 19:9); the hands of compassionate women boiled their own children for food (Lam. 4:10); give your son to eat today and we will eat my son tomorrow (2 Kgs. 6:28-9); they will eat one another's flesh in the siege (Jer. 19:9); fathers will eat their sons and sons their fathers (Ezek. 5:10); should women eat their offspring? (Lam. 2:20); the thin cows ate the fat cows (Gen. 41:4, 20); the fool folds his hands and eats his own flesh (Eccles. 4:5); each one eats the flesh of his own arm (Isa. 9:20); I will make them eat their own flesh (Isa. 49:26).

B7b Animals eating people
A wild beast has eaten him (Gen. 37:20, 33); the birds will eat your flesh (Gen. 40:19); I give you as food to the beasts and birds (Ezek. 29:5; 39:4); those in the open field I will give to the beasts to be eaten (Ezek. 33:27); gather the wild beasts to devour (Jer. 12:9); dogs will eat those who die in the city and birds those who die in the field (1 Kgs. 14:11; 16:4; 21:24); where dogs licked up Naboth's blood, dogs will lick up yours (1 Kgs. 21:19; 22:38); dogs will eat Jezebel (1 Kgs. 21:23-4; 2 Kgs. 9:10, 36); birds to eat the flesh of men (Ezek. 39:17-20; Rev. 19:17-18, 21); beasts of the field, come and eat! (Isa. 56:9); that the tongues of your dogs may have their portion from their foes (Ps. 68:23); the birds and beasts will eat the corpses of this people (Jer. 7:33; 16:4; 19:7; 34:20); my flock has become food for all the wild beasts (Ezek. 34:8); they became food for every beast of the field (Ezek. 34:5); the devil prowls like a lion, seeking someone to devour (1 Pet. 5:8); the dragon intended to devour her child (Rev. 12:4); the ten horns and the beast will eat the harlot's flesh and burn her up with fire (Rev. 17:16).

B8 Allegorical food and drink
B8a Wise words as food
Wisdom has prepared her food and drink (Prov. 9:2); Wisdom's invitation to eat and drink (Prov. 9:5); the lips of the righteous feed many (Prov. 10:21).

B8b God's word as food
Eating the scroll (Ezek. 2:8-10; 3:1-3); eating the scroll (Rev. 10:9-10); your words were found and I ate them (Jer. 15:16); you need milk, not solid food (1 Cor. 3:2); you need milk, not tough meat (Heb. 5:12); long for the pure spiritual milk (1 Pet. 2:2); nourished on the words of the faith and sound doctrine (1 Tim. 4:6).

B8c Right living as food
My food is to do the will of him who sent me (John 4:34); do not work for the food which perishes, but for the food which endures (John 6:27); a cheerful heart has a continual feast (Prov. 15:15); I have food to eat which you do not know about (John 4:32).

B8d Jesus as food
The bread of life (John 6:35, 48-51); the bread of God is that which comes down from heaven (John 6:32-3); the bread which came down from heaven (John 6:41, 58); the overcomer may eat from the tree of life (Rev. 2:7); as I live because of the Father, so he who eats me will live because of me (John 6:57); he who eats this bread will live for ever (John 6:58).
EATING CHRIST'S BODY, see 319A8c.

B8e Affliction as food
You have given them tears to drink (Ps. 80:5); let them drink of the wrath of the Almighty (Job 21:20); bread of adversity and water of affliction (Isa. 30:20); a cup of horror and desolation, the cup of your sister Samaria (Ezek. 23:33); I will feed them with judgement (Ezek. 34:16); if you are willing, remove this cup from me (Luke 22:42); shall I not drink the cup the Father has given me? (John 18:11).

C Getting food
C1 Seeking food
What shall we eat? (Lev. 25:20); what shall we drink? (Exod. 15:24); do not be anxious saying, 'What shall we eat or drink or wear?' (Matt. 6:31); do not be anxious about what to eat or drink (Matt. 6:25; Luke 12:22, 29); let us get grain and eat and live! (Neh. 5:2); send the crowd away to find lodging and get food (Luke 9:12); where would we get enough loaves to feed so great a crowd? (Matt. 15:33); Lazarus longed to be fed with what fell from the rich man's table (Luke 16:21).

C2 Requesting food/drink
Give us food! (Gen. 47:15); they demanded the food they craved (Ps. 78:18); give us our daily bread (Matt. 6:11; Luke 11:3); let me swallow some of that red stuff (Gen. 25:30); give me a drink (Gen. 24:14, 17, 45; John 4:7-9); friend, lend me three loaves (Luke 11:5); have you anything to eat? (Luke 24:41).

C3 Working for food
By the sweat of your brow you will eat bread (Gen. 3:19); you will eat of the labour of your hands (Ps. 128:2); all a man's labour is for his mouth (Eccles. 6:7); the ant prepares her food in summer (Prov. 6:8).

D Provision of food
D1 God provides food
He supplies seed for sowing and bread for food (Isa. 55:10; 2 Cor. 9:10); God gives aliens food and clothing (Deut. 10:18); God gives food to the hungry (Ps. 146:7); God gives food in abundance (Job 36:31); bread to sustain man's heart (Ps. 104:15); all creatures look to God for food (Ps. 104:27; 145:15-16); he gives food to every creature (Ps. 136:25); your heavenly Father feeds the birds of the air (Matt. 6:26); God feeds birds such as ravens (Luke 12:24); who gives the raven food? (Job 38:41); God causes grass to grow for cattle and plants for man (Ps. 104:14); young lions seek their food from God (Ps. 104:21); can God prepare a table in the wilderness? (Ps. 78:19); can he give bread also? (Ps. 78:20); God gives food to those who fear him (Ps. 111:5); I would feed you with the finest of wheat and honey

(Ps. 81:16); you prepare a table (Ps. 23:5); he has filled the hungry with good things (Luke 1:53); the Lord provided food for his people (Ruth 1:6); God appointed ravens to feed Elijah (1 Kgs. 17:4-6); God commanded a widow to feed Elijah (1 Kgs. 17:9).

D2 People providing food
I was hungry and you gave me food (Matt. 25:35-7); share your bread with the hungry (Isa. 58:7); if he gives his bread to the hungry (Ezek. 18:7, 16); if your enemy is hungry, give him food (Prov. 25:21; Rom. 12:20); who will give the servants food at the proper time? (Matt. 24:45; Luke 12:42); let the children be fed first (Mark 7:27); Jesus told them to give Jairus's daughter something to eat (Mark 5:43; Luke 8:55); let him who has food share with him who has none (Luke 3:11); Elisha boiled the oxen and fed the people (1 Kgs. 19:21); boil stew for the sons of the prophets (2 Kgs. 4:38); they gave the captives food and drink (2 Chr. 28:15); bring bread and water for the fugitives (Isa. 21:14); Elijah fed a hundred men with twenty loaves (2 Kgs. 4:42-4); the feeding of the five thousand (Matt. 14:15-21; Mark 6:35-44; Luke 9:12-17; John 6:5-13); the feeding of the four thousand (Matt. 15:32-8; Mark 8:1-9); has anyone brought him food? (John 4:33); I was hungry and you gave me no food (Matt. 25:42).

D3 People providing drink
He took the cup and gave thanks (Matt. 26:27; Mark 14:23); one gave Jesus a drink of vinegar (Matt. 27:48; Mark 15:36); they gave me vinegar to drink (Ps. 69:21); I was thirsty and you gave me drink (Matt. 25:35-7); when did we see you thirsty and give you drink? (Matt. 25:37); each of you unties his ox or donkey and leads it away to water it (Luke 13:15).

D4 Breast-feeding
Shall I get a nurse to suckle the child? (Exod. 2:7-9); Hannah nursed Samuel (1 Sam. 1:23); when I got up in the morning to suckle my son (1 Kgs. 3:21); as a nurse carries a nursing child (Num. 11:12); you will be nursing (Isa. 66:12); queens will be your nursing mothers (Isa. 49:23); you will suck the milk of nations and suck the breast of kings (Isa. 60:16); suck at Jerusalem's consoling breasts (Isa. 66:11); as a nursing mother cares for her children (1 Thess. 2:7); blessed are the breasts at which you nursed (Luke 11:27); blessed are the breasts which never nursed (Luke 23:29); woe to those nursing babies in those days (Matt. 24:19; Mark 13:17; Luke 21:23); can a woman forget her sucking child? (Isa. 49:15).

D5 Feeding animals
The prodigal son feeding the pigs (Luke 15:15); one opened his sack to give his donkey fodder (Gen. 42:27); should not shepherds feed the flock? (Ezek. 34:2); the shepherds fed themselves, not the flock (Ezek. 34:8); I will feed my sheep (Ezek. 34:13-16); my servant David will feed them (Ezek. 34:23); shepherds who will feed you with knowledge (Jer. 3:15); feed my lambs (John 21:15); feed my sheep (John 21:17); I will feed them with good pasture (Ezek. 34:14); you slaughter the fat sheep but do not feed the flock (Ezek. 34:3); the donkey knows its master's manger (Isa. 1:3); he will go in and out and find pasture (John 10:9).

E Consuming food
E1 Eating and drinking
Eating and drinking is God's gift to man (Eccles. 3:13); nothing better than to eat, drink and enjoy yourself (Eccles. 2:24; 5:18; 8:15); eating, drinking and rejoicing (Neh. 8:12); let us eat and drink for tomorrow we die (Isa. 22:13; 1 Cor. 15:32); eat, drink and be merry (Luke 12:19); they sat down to eat and drink and rose up to play (Exod. 32:6; 1 Cor. 10:7); the Amalekites were eating, drinking and dancing (1 Sam. 30:16); in the days

of Noah they were eating and drinking (Matt. 24:38; Luke 17:27); in the days of Lot they were eating and drinking (Luke 17:28); eat your bread with trembling and drink water with anxiety (Ezek. 12:18); they will eat bread with anxiety and drink water with horror (Ezek. 12:19); the Son of man came eating and drinking (Matt. 11:19; Luke 7:34); why do your disciples not fast but eat and drink? (Luke 5:33); that you may eat and drink at my table in my kingdom (Luke 22:30); when you eat and drink, do you not eat and drink for yourselves? (Zech. 7:6); whether you eat or drink, do all for the glory of God (1 Cor. 10:31); do you not have houses in which to eat and drink? (1 Cor. 11:22).

E2 Eating
E2a People eating
Eat what is before you (Luke 10:8; 1 Cor. 10:27); when the child died, David ate (2 Sam. 12:20-1); kill the fatted calf and let us eat and be merry (Luke 15:23); he took the fish and ate it before them (Luke 24:43); Paul took food and was strengthened (Acts 9:19); Paul encouraged them to eat (Acts 27:33-4); they were all encouraged and took food (Acts 27:36); if anyone will not work let him not eat (2 Thess. 3:10).

E2b Eating forbidden food
Fruit from one tree forbidden (Gen. 2:17); but they ate from it (Gen. 3:6); have you eaten from the tree I commanded you not to eat? (Gen. 3:11); you have eaten from the tree I commanded you not to eat (Gen. 3:17); you eat the fat and clothe yourselves with the wool (Ezek. 34:3).

E2c Eating before God
You shall eat before God (Deut. 12:7; 15:20); a tithe of produce eaten before the Lord (Deut. 12:18; 14:23-6); the elders ate bread with Jethro before God (Exod. 18:12); the elders saw God and ate and drank (Exod. 24:11); they ate and drank before the Lord with joy (1 Chr. 29:22); the prince will sit in the gate to eat bread before the Lord (Ezek. 44:3).

E2d The Lord's supper
Instructions concerning the Lord's supper (1 Cor. 11:17-34); they devoted themselves to the breaking of bread (Acts 2:42); on the first day of the week they broke bread (Acts 20:7); take, eat, this is my body (Matt. 26:26; Mark 14:22; Luke 22:19); they broke bread from house to house with glad and generous hearts (Acts 2:46); you cannot partake of the table of the Lord and the table of demons (1 Cor. 10:21); when you meet together it is not the Lord's supper that you eat (1 Cor. 11:20).

E2e Animals eating
Animals chewing the cud are clean (Lev. 11:3; Deut. 14:6-8); the camel chews the cud (Lev. 11:4); the rock badger chews the cud (Lev. 11:5); the hare chews the cud (Lev. 11:6); the pig does not chew the cud (Lev. 11:7); other animals do not chew the cud (Lev. 11:26); the oxen and donkeys will eat salted fodder (Isa. 30:24); dogs eat the crumbs that fall from the table (Matt. 15:27; Mark 7:28); the ewe lamb would eat the poor man's food (2 Sam. 12:3); the lion will eat straw like the ox (Isa. 11:7; 65:25); the serpent would eat dust (Gen. 3:14); dust will be the serpent's food (Isa. 65:25); they will lick the dust like a serpent (Mic. 7:17); he would gladly have filled his belly with the pods the pigs ate (Luke 15:16).

E3 Drinking
Those who lapped were chosen, but those who kneeled to drink were not (Judg. 7:5-7); whoever drinks this water will thirst again (John 4:13); if any one thirsts, let him come to me and drink (John 7:37); are you able to drink the cup I drink? (Matt. 20:22; Mark 10:38); you will drink my cup (Matt. 20:23; Mark 10:39); drink of it,

all of you (Matt. 26:27); he gave them the cup and they all drank from it (Mark 14:23); if this cannot pass unless I drink it (Matt. 26:42); I will not drink wine again until I do so with you in my Father's kingdom (Matt. 26:29); he would not drink the wine mixed with gall (Matt. 27:34); they all drank the same spiritual drink from the spiritual rock, Christ (1 Cor. 10:4); is not the cup of blessing a sharing in the blood of Christ? (1 Cor. 10:16); you cannot drink the cup of the Lord and the cup of demons (1 Cor. 10:21); this cup is the new covenant in my blood (1 Cor. 11:25); if they drink any deadly thing it will not harm them (Mark 16:18).

302 Excretion

A Discharges in general

The law concerning one with a discharge (Lev. 15:2-8, 32); a priest with a discharge may not eat of the sacrifices (Lev. 22:4); may Joab's house always have someone with a discharge (2 Sam. 3:29); animals with a discharge must not be sacrificed (Lev. 22:22).

B Natural functions

B1 Defecation and dung

Israelites had to relieve themselves outside the camp and cover their excrement (Deut. 23:13); they thought Eglon was relieving himself (Judg. 3:24); Saul went into the cave to relieve himself (1 Sam. 24:3); the temple of Baal was used as a latrine (2 Kgs. 10:27); the dirt came out (Judg. 3:22); what enters the mouth goes into the stomach and is evacuated (Matt. 15:17; Mark 7:19); a fourth of a kab of dove's dung (2 Kgs. 6:25); doomed to eat their own dung (2 Kgs. 18:27; Isa. 36:12); the loaf to be cooked on human dung (Ezek. 4:12); or cow's dung (Ezek. 4:15); I will spread the dung of your offerings on your faces (Mal. 2:3); as straw is trodden down in a dung heap (Isa. 25:10); I count all things as dung (Phil. 3:8); I will dig around and apply dung (Luke 13:8).

B2 Urinating

Every one who urinates against a wall (1 Sam. 25:22, 34; 1 Kgs. 14:10; 16:11; 21:21; 2 Kgs. 9:8); doomed to drink their own urine (2 Kgs. 18:27; Isa. 36:12).

C Bleeding

A menstruating woman is unclean (Lev. 15:19, 33); sexual intercourse with a menstruating woman forbidden (Lev. 18:19; 20:18); the way of women is on me (Gen. 31:35); if he does not approach a woman who is menstruating (Ezek. 18:6); they humble women unclean through their impurity (Ezek. 22:10); a longer discharge of blood makes her unclean longer (Lev. 15:25); cleansed from her flow of blood (Lev. 12:7); a woman had had a haemorrhage for 12 years (Matt. 9:20; Mark 5:25; Luke 8:43); pressing the nose produces blood (Prov. 30:33).

D Sweat

By the sweat of your brow you will eat bread (Gen. 3:19); Jesus' sweat like drops of blood falling on the ground (Luke 22:44); the priests should not wear anything which causes sweat (Ezek. 44:18).

E Semen

A man with an emission of semen is unclean (Lev. 15:16, 32; 22:4; Deut. 23:10); Onan spilled his semen on the ground (Gen. 38:9); their semen is the semen of horses (Ezek. 23:20).

F Facial excretions

F1 Saliva and spitting

If her father spat in her face she would be ashamed for seven days (Num. 12:14); if the unclean person spits on a clean person (Lev. 15:8); his brother's wife shall spit in his face (Deut. 25:9); I am one before whom men spit (Job 17:6); they spit in my face (Job 30:10); they will spit on him (Mark 10:34; Luke 18:32); they spat in his face

(Matt. 26:67); they spat on Jesus (Matt. 27:30; Mark 14:65; 15:19); I did not hide my face from shame and spitting (Isa. 50:6); Jesus spat and touched the man's tongue (Mark 7:33); Jesus spat on the man's eyes (Mark 8:23); he spat on the ground and made clay (John 9:6); David let saliva run down his beard (1 Sam. 21:13); leave me alone while I swallow my saliva (Job 7:19).

F2 Tears

Put my tears in your bottle (Ps. 56:8); she wet his feet with her tears (Luke 7:38); she wet my feet with tears (Luke 7:44); I served the Lord with tears and with trials (Acts 20:19); I admonished you night and day with tears (Acts 20:31).

MOURNING, see 836.

F3 Sneezing

The boy sneezed seven times (2 Kgs. 4:35); the crocodile's sneezes flash light (Job 41:18).

F4 Vomit

You will eat meat until it comes out of your nostrils (Num. 11:20); you will vomit the morsel (Prov. 23:8); lest you be filled with honey and vomit (Prov. 25:16); the fish vomited Jonah (Jonah 2:10); like a dog which returns to its vomit (Prov. 26:11; 2 Pet. 2:22); as a drunken man staggers in his vomit (Isa. 19:14); all tables are full of vomit (Isa. 28:8); be drunk and vomit (Jer. 25:27); make Moab drunk so he wallows in his vomit (Jer. 48:26); I will spew you out of my mouth (Rev. 3:16).

303 Insertion

A Inserting

Your deck is made of Cyprus pine inlaid with ivory (Ezek. 27:6); beams were not inserted in the walls (1 Kgs. 6:6).

B Dipping

They dipped Joseph's coat in the blood (Gen. 37:31); Jesus dipped a morsel and gave it to Judas (John 13:26); he who dips his hand in the dish with me will betray me (Matt. 26:23; Mark 14:20); I have no one to put me in the pool when the water is stirred up (John 5:7).

BAPTISM, see 988B2.

304 Extraction

A Bringing people out

A1 God bringing Israel out of Egypt

God bringing Israel out of Egypt (Exod. 3:8; 7:4-5; 12:17, 51); I will bring you up out of Egypt (Gen. 46:4); I will bring you out from under the Egyptians' burdens (Exod. 6:6, 7); why should the Egyptians say you brought them out to harm them? (Exod. 32:12); out of Egypt I called my son (Hos. 11:1; Matt. 2:15); because God hates us he brought us out of Egypt (Deut. 1:27); no longer talk of God bringing Israel up out of Egypt, but out of the north land (Jer. 16:14, 15; 23:7-8).

A2 Others bringing Israel out of Egypt

Who am I to bring the Israelites out of Egypt? (Exod. 3:11); God charged Moses and Aaron to bring the Israelites out of Egypt (Exod. 6:13, 26); this Moses who brought us out of Egypt (Exod. 32:1, 23); these are your gods who brought you up out of Egypt (Exod. 32:4, 8; 1 Kgs. 12:28; Neh. 9:18).

A3 Bringing people out of other places

Called 'woman' because she was taken out of man (Gen. 2:23); Moses, drawn out of the water (Exod. 2:10); he drew me out of the waters (2 Sam. 22:17; Ps. 18:16); he bought me up out of the miry pit (Ps. 40:2); God brought Abraham out of Ur (Gen. 15:7; 24:7; Neh. 9:7); God brought Lot out of Sodom (Gen. 19:12, 16, 29); Rahab's family brought out of the house (Josh. 6:22, 23); bringing the kings out of the cave (Josh. 10:22-3); drawing the men of Ai away from the city

(Josh. 8:6, 16); the Benjaminites were drawn away from the city (Judg. 20:31); they will gather out of his kingdom all stumbling-blocks (Matt. 13:41).

B Plucking out

I have appointed you to pluck up and to break down (Jer. 1:10); a time to uproot (Eccles. 3:2); I will uproot them from their land (Jer. 12:14); I watched over them to pluck up (Jer. 31:28); what I have planted I am uprooting (Jer. 45:4); God will uproot you from the land of the living (Ps. 52:5); every plant not planted by my Father will be rooted up (Matt. 15:13); lest in gathering the weeds you uproot the wheat (Matt. 13:29); angels will extract the wicked from the righteous (Matt. 13:49); the little horn uprooted three of the first horns (Dan. 7:8); is not this a brand plucked from the burning? (Zech. 3:2); if your eye causes you to sin, pluck it out (Matt. 5:29; 18:9; Mark 9:47); you would have plucked out your eyes and given them to me (Gal. 4:15); let me take out the speck that in is your eye (Matt. 7:4; Luke 6:42); you hypocrite, first take the log out of your own eye (Matt. 7:5; Luke 6:42); his disciples plucked ears of grain and ate (Matt. 12:1; Mark 2:23; Luke 6:1); if you say to this mountain, 'Be taken up and cast into the sea' (Matt. 21:21); be rooted up and planted in the sea (Luke 17:6); they are trees without fruit, doubly dead, uprooted (Jude 12).

C Drawing water

The one who draws your water (Deut. 29:11); women drawing water (Gen. 24:11, 13, 43, 45; 1 Sam. 9:11); I will draw water for your camels (Gen. 24:19-20, 44); they drew water and poured it out before the Lord (1 Sam. 7:6); the three mighty men drew water at Bethlehem (2 Sam. 23:16; 1 Chr. 11:18); draw some off and take it to the steward (John 2:8-9); a woman of Samaria came to draw water (John 4:7).

305 Passage: motion through

A Passing through

A firepot and torch passed through the pieces (Gen. 15:17); they passed through the halves of the calf (Jer. 34:18, 19); the Lord will pass through (Exod. 12:23); Israel passed through the Red Sea (Ps. 136:14); he caused them to pass through the sea (Ps. 78:13); they passed through the sea on dry land (Neh. 9:11); all our fathers passed through the sea (1 Cor. 10:1); they passed through the river on foot (Ps. 66:6); let us pass through your land (Num. 20:17; 21:22; Deut. 2:27; Judg. 11:17, 19); Edom refused to let them pass through (Num. 20:18-21); Jesus passed through them (Luke 4:30); he entered Jericho and was passing through (Luke 19:1).

B Passing by

All David's men passed on before him (2 Sam. 15:18); the Lord was passing by (1 Kgs. 19:11); he intended to pass them by (Mark 6:48); they heard that Jesus was passing by (Matt. 20:30); Jesus of Nazareth is passing by (Luke 18:37); is it nothing to you who pass by? (Lam. 1:12); a priest passed by on the other side (Luke 10:31); a Levite passed by on the other side (Luke 10:32); do not pass this heap and pillar (Gen. 31:52); two demoniacs so violent that no one could pass that way (Matt. 8:28).

C Passing over

When I see the blood I will pass over you (Exod. 12:13); the Lord will pass over the door (Exod. 12:23); the Lord passed over the houses of the Israelites (Exod. 12:27).

CROSSING OVER, see 222.

PASSOVER, see 988A2.

306 Overstepping

A Outdo

Solomon's wisdom surpassed that of the orientals and Egyptians (1 Kgs. 4:30); you surpass all other women

(Prov. 31:29); unless your righteousness exceeds that of the scribes and Pharisees (Matt. 5:20); what do you do more than others? (Matt. 5:47); this widow put in more than all the rest (Mark 12:43; Luke 21:3); you have acted more corruptly than they (Ezek. 16:47); outdo one another in showing honour (Rom. 12:10).

B Best of all

Wisdom exceeds folly as light exceeds darkness (Eccles. 2:13); nothing better than to eat and drink and enjoy one's work (Eccles. 2:24).

307 Shortfall

All fall short of the glory of God (Rom. 3:23).

308 Ascent

A God going up

A1 God arising

Arise, O Lord! (Num. 10:35; Ps. 3:7; 7:6; 9:19; 10:12; 17:13; 44:26; 74:22; 132:8); arise, O God! (Ps. 82:8); let God arise! (Ps. 68:1); rise up, Judge of the earth! (Ps. 94:2); you will arise and pity Zion (Ps. 102:13); I will arise (Ps. 12:5; Isa. 33:10); God has ascended with a shout (Ps. 47:5).

A2 Christ's ascension

I have not yet ascended (John 20:17); I am ascending to my Father and your Father (John 20:17); when he ascended on high he led captives in his train (Ps. 68:18; Eph. 4:8); he ascended far above the heavens (Eph. 4:10); Jesus was taken up into heaven (Mark 16:19); until the day when he was taken up (Acts 1:2); he was lifted up and a cloud received him (Acts 1:9-11); he was taken up in glory (1 Tim. 3:16); no one has ascended to heaven but he who descended from heaven (John 3:13); in saying 'he ascended' (Eph. 4:9).

B Man going up

STANDING UP, see 215C.

B1 Going up mountains

Moses went up the mountain to God (Exod. 19:20; 24:15, 18; 34:2, 4); Moses, Aaron, Nadab and Abihu went up (Exod. 24:9); the people cannot come up the mountain (Exod. 19:23, 24); who may ascend the hill of the Lord? (Ps. 24:3); let us go up to the mountain of the Lord (Isa. 2:3; Mic. 4:2).

B2 Moving upwards

The path of life leads upward for the wise (Prov. 15:24); better to be told to come up higher than to be put lower (Prov. 25:7); friend, move up higher (Luke 14:10); who knows the spirit of man which goes upward? (Eccles. 3:21).

B3 Going up to heaven

The two witnesses went up to heaven in a cloud (Rev. 11:12); God raised us up with Christ and seated us with him in the heavenlies (Eph. 2:6); do not say, 'Who will ascend into heaven?' (Rom. 10:6); you said in your heart, 'I will ascend to heaven' (Isa. 14:13); come up here (Rev. 4:1).

B4 Get up!

Rise up before the grey head (Lev. 19:32); rise up, Jerusalem (Isa. 52:2); little girl, arise! (Mark 5:41; Luke 8:54); Tabitha, arise! (Acts 9:40); young man, arise! (Luke 7:14); he said to the man with the withered hand, 'Rise' (Mark 3:3); or to say 'Rise and walk'? (Matt. 9:5-6; Mark 2:9-11; Luke 5:23-4; John 5:8); rise and make your bed (Acts 9:34); get up quickly! (Acts 12:7); stand upright! (Dan. 10:11; Acts 14:10).

B5 Getting up

The old men stood up before Job (Job 29:8); one rises up at the sound of a bird (Eccles. 12:4); though I fall, I will rise (Mic. 7:8); if the man gets up and walks around with his stick (Exod. 21:19); this child is set for the fall and rising of many in Israel (Luke 2:34).

B6 Climbing up
Jonathan climbed up on all fours (1 Sam. 14:13); Zaccheus climbed into a sycamore tree (Luke 19:4); I will climb the palm tree (S. of S. 7:8); they climb into houses, entering through the windows like a thief (Joel 2:9); they climb the wall like soldiers (Joel 2:7); he who climbs in by another way (John 10:1).

B7 Not able to get up
Do not be angry because I cannot get up (Gen. 31:35); I cannot get up and give you anything (Luke 11:7); though he will not get up because he is his friend, he will because of his persistence (Luke 11:8).

C Angels going up
An angel ascending from the rising of the sun (Rev. 7:2); angels ascending and descending the ladder (Gen. 28:12); angels ascending and descending on the Son of Man (John 1:51); the angel ascended in the flame (Judg. 13:20); the beast is about to ascend from the bottomless pit (Rev. 17:8).

D Steps
Six steps to the throne (1 Kgs. 10:19; 2 Chr. 9:18); algum wood for steps for the temple (2 Chr. 9:11); do not go up steps on to my altar (Exod. 20:26); 10 steps led up to the porch (Ezek. 40:49); its stairway had eight steps (Ezek. 40:31, 34, 37); seven steps to the gateway (Ezek. 40:22, 26); when they came to the stairs Paul had to be carried (Acts 21:35); a ladder to heaven (Gen. 28:12).

309 Descent

A Going down
A1 God going down
The Lord came down to see the city and the tower (Gen. 11:5); the Lord came down on Mt Sinai (Exod. 19:11, 18-20; 34:5); God bowed the heavens and came down (2 Sam. 22:10; Ps. 18:9); bow your heavens and come down! (Ps. 144:5); oh, that you would rend the heavens and come down! (Isa. 64:1); the Lord himself will descend from heaven (1 Thess. 4:16); the Lord will come down and tread on the high places of the earth (Mic. 1:3); the Spirit descended on Jesus like a dove (Mark 1:10); I saw the Spirit descend as a dove from heaven (John 1:32); he on whom you see the Spirit descend and remain (John 1:33).

A2 Christ going down
How can he say, 'I came down from heaven'? (John 6:42); I have come down from heaven (John 6:38); I am the bread which came down from heaven (John 6:41); no one has ascended to heaven but he who descended from heaven (John 3:13); he who descended is he who ascended (Eph. 4:10); he descended into the lower parts of the earth (Eph. 4:9).

A3 People going down
They went down like a stone (Exod. 15:5); they went down to the depths (Ps. 107:26); I went down to the roots of the mountains (Jonah 2:6); man of God, come down! (2 Kgs. 1:9-15); make haste and come down (Luke 19:5-6); let him on the housetop not go down (Matt. 24:17; Mark 13:15; Luke 17:31).

A4 Others going down
Angels ascending and descending the ladder (Gen. 28:12); angels ascending and descending on the Son of man (John 1:51); an angel of the Lord descended from heaven (Matt. 28:2); a strong angel coming down from heaven (Rev. 10:1); I saw an angel coming down from heaven (Rev. 20:1); the herd of swine rushed down into the sea (Matt. 8:32; Mark 5:13; Luke 8:33); new Jerusalem coming down out of heaven (Rev. 3:12; 21:2, 10).

A5 Kneeling
The rest kneeled to drink (Judg. 7:6); they cried before Joseph, 'Bow the knee!' (Gen. 41:43); kneeling down on the beach we prayed (Acts 21:5); let us kneel before the Lord our Maker (Ps. 95:6); before me every knee will bow (Isa. 45:23; Rom. 14:11); I bow my knees before the Father (Eph. 3:14); Solomon prayed kneeling (1 Kgs. 8:54; 2 Chr. 6:13); I fell on my knees (Ezra 9:5); Daniel knelt and prayed three times a day (Dan. 6:10); Peter knelt and prayed (Acts 9:40); Paul knelt and prayed (Acts 20:36); he knelt down and prayed (Luke 22:41); kneeling before Jesus: a leper (Matt. 8:2; Mark 1:40); a rich man (Mark 10:17); soldiers (Matt. 27:29; Mark 15:19); a [synagogue] official (Matt. 9:18); the Canaanite woman (Matt. 15:25); a man (Matt. 17:14).

B Obeisance
KNEELING, see 309A5.
B1 Obeisance before God
B1a Prostrate before God
Moses lay before the Lord (Deut. 9:18, 25); David lay on the ground (2 Sam. 12:16; 13:31); Abraham's servant bowed himself to the earth (Gen. 24:52); Job fell to the ground and worshipped (Job 1:20).

B1b Falling on one's face before God
Falling on their faces: Abraham (Gen. 17:3, 17); Balaam (Num. 22:31); Moses (Num. 16:4); Moses and Aaron (Num. 14:5; 16:22, 45; 20:6); Joshua (Josh. 5:14; 7:6, 10); Manoah and his wife (Judg. 13:20); the people (Lev. 9:24; 1 Kgs. 18:39); David and the elders (1 Chr. 21:16); Ezekiel (Ezek. 1:28; 3:23; 9:8; 11:13; 43:3; 44:4); Daniel (Dan. 8:17; 10:9); Peter, James and John (Matt. 17:6); Jesus (Matt. 26:39); the angels (Rev. 7:11); the 24 elders (Rev. 4:10; 11:16; 19:4); an unbeliever (1 Cor. 14:25).

B1c Bowing before God
Bow down to the Lord (2 Kgs. 17:36); all mankind will bow down before me (Isa. 66:23); the heavenly host bows down before you (Neh. 9:6); to him all the coastlands will bow down (Zeph. 2:11).

B2 Bowing before Messiah
Because he is your lord, bow to him (Ps. 45:11); may those who live in the desert bow before him (Ps. 72:9); let all kings bow before him (Ps. 72:11); the magi fell down and worshipped the child (Matt. 2:11); the demoniac bowed down before Jesus (Mark 5:6); the mother of Zebedee's sons bowed before Jesus (Matt. 20:20); at the name of Jesus every knee will bow (Phil. 2:10); Mary fell at his feet (John 11:32); when he said, 'I AM [he]', they fell to the ground (John 18:6); Paul fell to the ground (Acts 9:4); I fell at his feet as though dead (Rev. 1:17); the four living creatures and 24 elders fell down before the Lamb (Rev. 5:8); falling down before Jesus: Peter (Luke 5:8); Jairus (Mark 5:22; Luke 8:41); a leper (Luke 5:12; 17:16); a woman (Mark 5:33; Luke 8:47); the Syrophoenician woman (Mark 7:25); unclean spirits (Mark 3:11); a demoniac (Luke 8:28).

B3 Bowing before men
B3a Bowing before the godly
May nations and your brothers bow down (Gen. 27:29); they will bow down at your feet (Rev. 3:9); the evil bow down before the good (Prov. 14:19); those who despised you will bow down to you (Isa. 60:14).

B3b Bowing before Joseph
Your sheaves bowed down to my sheaf (Gen. 37:7); the sun, moon and stars bowed down to me (Gen. 37:9); shall I and your mother and brothers bow down to the ground before you? (Gen. 37:10); 'Bow the knee' proclaimed before Joseph (Gen. 41:43); Joseph's brothers bowing before Joseph (Gen. 42:6; 43:26, 28; 44:14; 50:18).

B3c Bowing before David
Bowing before David: Abigail (1 Sam. 25:23, 24); a man (2 Sam. 1:2); Mephibosheth (2 Sam. 9:6, 8); the wise woman (2 Sam. 14:4); Joab (2 Sam. 14:22); Absalom (2 Sam. 14:33); Ziba (2 Sam. 16:4); Ahimaaz (2 Sam.

18:28); Shimei (2 Sam. 19:18); Araunah [Ornan] (2 Sam. 24:20; 1 Chr. 21:21); Bathsheba (1 Kgs. 1:16, 31); Nathan (1 Kgs. 1:23).

B4 Bowing to false gods

Do not bow down to false gods (2 Kgs. 17:35); do not bow down to them or serve them (Exod. 20:5); do not bow down to stones (Lev. 26:1); they bow down to other gods (Jer. 13:10; 16:11); they ate and bowed down to the Moabites' gods (Num. 25:2); they bowed down to other gods (Judg. 2:12, 19; Jer. 22:9); when I bow myself in the house of Rimmon (2 Kgs. 5:18); they bow down and worship the idol (Isa. 46:6); I bow down before a block of wood (Isa. 44:19); men bowing down to the sun (Ezek. 8:16); fall down and worship the golden image (Dan. 3:5-7, 10-11); those who bow down to the host of heaven (Zeph. 1:5); all peoples, nations and languages fell down and worshipped the image (Dan. 3:7); you will no longer bow down to the work of your hands (Mic. 5:13); all these I will give you if you fall down and worship me (Matt. 4:9); I fell down to worship at the feet of the angel (Rev. 19:10; 22:8); 7000 whose knees have not bowed to Baal (1 Kgs. 19:18; Rom. 11:4).

B5 Idols bowing

Bel bows down, Nebo stoops (Isa. 46:1).

C Sitting

RECLINING TO EAT, see 309D2.

C1 Sitting in general

I know your sitting down (2 Kgs. 19:27); you know when I sit down and when I get up (Ps. 139:2); look at their sitting and rising (Lam. 3:63); talk of them when you sit and when you walk (Deut. 6:7; 11:19); whoever sits where the unclean person sat is unclean (Lev. 15:6); Peter was sitting outside in the courtyard (Matt. 26:69; Mark 14:54); two angels seated where Jesus' body had been (John 20:12); a woman was sitting in the ephah (Zech. 5:7); a woman sitting on a scarlet beast (Rev. 17:3); the seven heads are seven hills on which the woman sits (Rev. 17:9); the waters where the harlot sits are peoples (Rev. 17:15).

C2 People sitting down

Rachel sat on the camel basket and teraphim (Gen. 31:34); Moses sat by the well (Exod. 2:15); Moses sat on a stone (Exod. 17:12); David sat before the Lord (2 Sam. 7:18; 1 Chr. 17:16); David sat between the two gates (2 Sam. 18:24); David sat in the gate (2 Sam. 19:8); Jonah went out and sat to the east of the city (Jonah 4:5); the boy sat on his mother's lap (2 Kgs. 4:20); Peter sat with the guards (Matt. 26:58; Luke 22:55); Jesus, tired by the journey, sat down by the well (John 4:6); Jesus went into the hills and sat down with his disciples (John 6:3); we sat down and spoke to the women who had gathered (Acts 16:13); they sat down to eat and drink (Exod. 32:6; 1 Cor. 10:7); Job's friends sat down with him for seven days (Job 2:13); blessed is he who does not sit with scoffers (Ps. 1:1); I will not sit with the wicked (Ps. 26:4-5).

C3 Sitting in security

They will sit every one under his vine and under his fig tree (Mic. 4:4); everyone one of you will invite his neighbour to sit under his vine and under his fig tree (Zech. 3:10); old men and women will again sit in the streets of Jerusalem (Zech. 8:4); God raised us up with Christ and seated us with him in the heavenlies (Eph. 2:6).

SITTING IN THE GATEWAY, see 263C4.

C4 Sitting in dejection

Sit in the dust, daughter of Babylon! (Isa. 47:1); sit on the ground without a throne, daughter of the Chaldeans (Isa. 47:1); she will sit on the ground (Isa. 3:26); let him sit alone in silence (Lam. 3:28); they will

sit on the ground (Ezek. 26:16); the elders of Zion sit on the ground (Lam. 2:10); the people sitting in darkness have seen a great light (Matt. 4:16); to give light to those who sit in darkness and the shadow of death (Luke 1:79).

C5 Sitting to teach

Moses sat to teach the people (Exod. 18:13); the scribes and Pharisees sit on Moses' seat (Matt. 23:2); when Jesus sat down his disciples came and he taught them (Matt. 5:1); Jesus went up a mountain and sat down (Matt. 15:29); Jesus sat down in a boat and taught (Matt. 13:1-2; Mark 4:1; Luke 5:3); Jesus sat down to preach (Luke 4:20); he sat down and called the 12 (Mark 9:35); he sat down and taught them (John 8:2); day after day I sat in the temple teaching (Matt. 26:55).

C6 Sitting to learn

The demoniac at the feet of Jesus (Luke 8:35); Mary sat at the feet of Jesus (Luke 10:39); Paul at the feet of Gamaliel (Acts 22:3); they found him in the temple sitting among the teachers (Luke 2:46).

C7 Sitting in honour

God makes the poor sit in a seat of honour (1 Sam. 2:8); Bathsheba sat on Solomon's right (1 Kgs. 2:19); command that my two sons may sit to left and right of you (Matt. 20:21-3); grant us to sit on your right and left in your glory (Mark 10:37-40); to him who overcomes I will grant to sit on my throne (Rev. 3:21); the man of lawlessness takes his seat in the temple of God (2 Thess. 2:4).

C8 God sitting in glory

The Lord who sits above the cherubim (1 Sam. 4:4); God sits enthroned on the cherubim (2 Sam. 6:2); he who swears by heaven swears by God's throne and him who sits on it (Matt. 23:22); a throne in heaven and one seated on the throne (Rev. 4:2); the one seated on the throne (Rev. 4:9-10; 5:1, 7); hide us from him who sits on the throne and from the wrath of the Lamb (Rev. 6:16); salvation to our God who sits on the throne and to the Lamb (Rev. 7:10); he who sits on the throne will presence himself with them (Rev. 7:15).

C9 Christ sitting in glory

The Son of man seated at the right hand of Power (Matt. 26:64; Mark 14:62; Luke 22:69); Christ seated at God's right hand (Eph. 1:20; Col. 3:1; Heb. 1:3; 12:2); seated at the right hand of the throne of the Majesty in heaven (Heb. 8:1); Jesus sat down at the right hand of God (Mark 16:19); Christ sat down at God's right hand (Heb. 10:12); sit at my right hand (Ps. 110:1; Matt. 22:44; Mark 12:36; Luke 20:42; Acts 2:34; Heb. 1:13); the Son of man will sit on his glorious throne (Matt. 25:31); I overcame and sat down with my Father on his throne (Rev. 3:21).

D Lying down

D1 Lying down to rest

You search out my path and my lying down (Ps. 139:3); in peace I will lie down and sleep (Ps. 4:8); they will feed and lie down and no one will make them afraid (Zeph. 3:13); talk of them when you lie down and when you rise (Deut. 6:7; 11:19); when Boaz lay down (Ruth 3:4, 7); he lies down like a lion (Num. 24:9); at sunrise the lions lie down in their dens (Ps. 104:22); Issachar is a strong donkey lying down (Gen. 49:14); Balaam's donkey lay down (Num. 22:27).

D2 Reclining to eat

Jesus had them all recline (Matt. 14:19; 15:35; Mark 6:39-40; Luke 9:14-15; John 6:10); Jesus reclined at table (Matt. 9:10; 26:7; Mark 14:3; Luke 11:37; 24:30); tax collectors and sinners reclined at table with Jesus (Matt. 9:10; Mark 2:15); he appeared to the 11 as they reclined at table (Mark 16:14); they will recline to eat with Abraham, Isaac and Jacob in the kingdom of heaven (Matt. 8:11); many will recline at table in the kingdom of God (Luke 13:29); when you are invited, recline in the lowest place (Luke 14:10); come at once and recline [at table] (Luke 17:7); who is greater, he who reclines at table or he who serves? (Luke 22:27).

E Falling

E1 People falling

Bloodguilt if someone falls from your roof (Deut. 22:8); he who flees from the sound of terror will fall into the pit (Isa. 24:18); if the blind leads the blind they will both fall into a pit (Matt. 15:14; Luke 6:39); the kings fell into the tar pits (Gen. 14:10); Ahaziah fell through the lattice (2 Kgs. 1:2); Eutychus fell from the third floor (Acts 20:9); the rider falls backwards (Gen. 49:17); Mephibosheth fell (2 Sam. 4:4); Saul fell full length with fear (1 Sam. 28:20); I was frightened and fell on my face (Dan. 8:17); I fell to the ground (Acts 22:7); we all fell to the ground (Acts 26:14); Haman was falling on the couch (Esther 7:8); my son falls into the fire or the water (Matt. 17:15); the boy fell to the ground and rolled around (Mark 9:20); Shadrach, Meshach and Abednego fell into the furnace tied up (Dan. 3:23); Sisera fell between her feet dead (Judg. 5:27); the concubine fell at the doorway (Judg. 19:26); Eli fell backward off his seat (1 Sam. 4:18); Judas fell headlong (Acts 1:18); Ananias fell down and breathed his last (Acts 5:5); Sapphira fell down and breathed her last (Acts 5:10); how have the mighty fallen! (2 Sam. 1:19, 25, 27); they will fall among those who fall (Jer. 6:15; 8:12); a thousand may fall at your side (Ps. 91:7).

E2 Downfall

He who is crooked will fall (Prov. 28:18); a haughty spirit goes before a fall (Prov. 16:18); the wicked stumble in time of trouble (Prov. 24:16); the ways of the Lord are right but transgressors will stumble in them (Hos. 14:9); my adversaries stumbled and fell (Ps. 27:2); there the evildoers have fallen (Ps. 36:12); my enemies fall under my feet (2 Sam. 22:39; Ps. 18:38); do not rejoice when your enemy falls (Prov. 24:17); Jerusalem has stumbled, Judah has fallen (Isa. 3:8); Jerusalem's fall is astonishing (Lam. 1:9); Israel and Ephraim stumble in their iniquity (Hos. 5:5); to both houses of Israel he will be a rock to stumble over (Isa. 8:14); did they stumble so as to fall? (Rom. 11:11); God's severity to those who fell (Rom. 11:22).

E3 Stumbling

E3a Stumbling over Christ

A stone of stumbling (1 Pet. 2:8); everyone who falls on that stone will be broken to pieces (Luke 20:18); blessed is he who is not stumbled over me (Matt. 11:6); they were stumbled by him (Matt. 13:57; Mark 6:3); the Pharisees were stumbled when they heard this saying (Matt. 15:12).

E3b Causing others to stumble

You have caused many to stumble by your instruction (Mal. 2:8); they cannot sleep unless they make someone stumble (Prov. 4:16); if your eye causes you to stumble (Matt. 5:29, 30; 18:9; Mark 9:47); if your hand or foot causes you to stumble, cut it off (Matt. 18:8); if your hand causes you to stumble, cut it off (Mark 9:43-5); you are a stumbling-block to me (Matt. 16:23); it is inevitable that stumbling blocks come (Matt. 18:7); he who causes one of these little ones to stumble (Matt. 18:6; Mark 9:42; Luke 17:2); it is evil for a man by his eating to cause another to fall (Rom. 14:20); it is good not to eat meat or drink wine or do anything to make your brother stumble (Rom. 14:21); they will gather out of his kingdom all stumbling-blocks (Matt. 13:41).

E3c People stumbling

If anyone walks in the night he stumbles (John 11:10); before your feet stumble on the twilight mountains

(Jer. 13:16); let him who thinks he stands take heed lest he fall (1 Cor. 10:12); immediately he stumbles (Matt. 13:21); at my stumbling they rejoiced (Ps. 35:15); when my foot slips they would magnify themselves (Ps. 38:16); you will all be stumbled this night (Matt. 26:31); though all are stumbled because of you, I will not be (Matt. 26:33); let their table become a stumbling block (Rom. 11:9); they stumble because they are disobedient (1 Pet. 2:8).

E3d Recovery from stumbling

When he falls he will not go headlong (Ps. 37:24); this child is set for the fall and rising of many in Israel (Luke 2:34); if anyone walks in the day he does not stumble (John 11:9); if you do this you will never stumble (2 Pet. 1:10); God does not let our feet slip (Ps. 66:9); he will not allow your foot to slip (Ps. 121:3); to him who is able to keep you from stumbling (Jude 24); you have delivered my feet from stumbling (Ps. 56:13; 116:8); I will lead them on a straight path where they will not stumble (Jer. 31:9); if you run you will not stumble (Prov. 4:12); my feet have not slipped (2 Sam. 22:37; Ps. 17:5; 18:36); none among his tribes stumbled (Ps. 105:37); though all are stumbled because of you, I will not be (Matt. 26:33); blessed is he who is not stumbled over me (Luke 7:23); I have said these things to you that you may not be stumbled (John 16:1); they stumbled with no one to help (Ps. 107:12); the helper will stumble and the helped will fall (Isa. 31:3).

E4 Animals falling

If an ox or a donkey falls into a pit (Exod. 21:33); if an ox or donkey falls down, help lift them (Deut. 22:4); the oxen stumbled (2 Sam. 6:6); he let the birds fall in the middle of the camp (Ps. 78:28); not a sparrow falls to the ground apart from your Father (Matt. 10:29); if a man has one sheep and it falls into a pit on the sabbath (Matt. 12:11).

E5 Things falling

The wall of Jericho fell down (Josh. 6:5, 20; Heb. 11:30); the house on sand fell down (Matt. 7:27; Luke 6:49); 18 people on whom the tower of Siloam fell (Luke 13:4); the axe head fell into the water (2 Kgs. 6:5); Dagon fell before the ark (1 Sam. 5:3, 4); I will rebuild the booth of David which has fallen (Amos 9:11); no pebble will fall to the earth (Amos 9:9); they will say to mountains, 'Fall on us' (Luke 23:30); when shaken, the figs fall into the eater's mouth (Nahum 3:12); the earth will fall, never to rise again (Isa. 24:20); his sweat was like drops of blood falling on the ground (Luke 22:44).

E6 Falling from heaven

How you have fallen from heaven (Isa. 14:12); I saw Satan fall like lightning from heaven (Luke 10:18); the stars will fall from the sky (Matt. 24:29; Mark 13:25); a star fell from heaven (Rev. 8:10; 9:1); the stars fell to earth like figs (Rev. 6:13); Ephesus is the guardian of that [image] which fell from heaven (Acts 19:35).

310 Lifting up

A Christ lifted up

When you lift up the Son of man you will know (John 8:28); if I be lifted up I will draw all to me (John 12:32); how can you say that the Son of man must be lifted up? (John 12:34); so must the Son of man be lifted up (John 3:14); the days drew near for him to be received up (Luke 9:51); who will descend to bring Christ up from the dead? (Rom. 10:7); he was lifted up (Acts 1:9); until the day when he was taken up from us (Acts 1:22); David did not ascend into heaven (Acts 2:34); God has highly exalted him (Phil. 2:9).

ASCEND, see 308.

B People lifted up
B1 God lifting people
God taking Elijah to heaven (2 Kgs. 2:1); Enoch was not found because God took him up (Heb. 11:5); he made me stand upright (Dan. 8:18); lifting up does not come from east or west (Ps. 75:6); God puts one down and lifts up another (Ps. 75:7); he lifts up the poor from the dust (1 Sam. 2:8; Ps. 113:7); the Lord raises up those who are bowed down (Ps. 145:14; 146:8); I exalted you from among the people (1 Kgs. 14:7); I exalted you from the dust (1 Kgs. 16:2); the Lord lifts me above my enemies (2 Sam. 22:49; Ps. 18:48); my head will be lifted up above my enemies (Ps. 27:6); you, Lord, are the one who lifts up my head (Ps. 3:3); he brought me up out of the miry pit (Ps. 40:2); he has exalted the humble (Luke 1:52); a man in Christ who 14 years ago was caught up to the third heaven (2 Cor. 12:2).

B2 People lifting others
If one falls the other will lift him up (Eccles. 4:10); woe to him to falls and has no one to lift him up (Eccles. 4:10); they pulled Joseph out of the pit (Gen. 37:28); lifting Jeremiah out of the cistern (Jer. 38:10, 13); they took Daniel up out of the lions' den (Dan. 6:23); Jesus took him by the hand and raised him up (Mark 9:27); Jesus took her by the hand (Luke 8:54); Peter took the lame man by the hand and raised him (Acts 3:7); he gave her his hand and raised her up (Acts 9:41); Peter lifted him up (Acts 10:26).

C Body parts lifted up
C1 Lifting hands
Aaron lifted his hands and blessed the people (Lev. 9:22); when Moses lifted up his hand, Israel prevailed (Exod. 17:11); Solomon prayed with hands raised to heaven (1 Kgs. 8:22, 54; 2 Chr. 6:12-13); the people said 'Amen', lifting their hands (Neh. 8:6); I lift up my hand to heaven (Deut. 32:40); I lift up my hands (Ps. 63:4; 119:48); I lift up my hands towards your sanctuary (Ps. 28:2); may the lifting up of my hands be as the evening offering (Ps. 141:2); lift up your hands (Ps. 134:2); lift up your hands to the Lord for the life of your little ones (Lam. 2:19); we lift up heart and hands (Lam. 3:41); lifting up holy hands (1 Tim. 2:8); I stretched out my hands to the Lord (Ezra 9:5); he lifted his hands and blessed them (Luke 24:50); the angel lifted up his right hand to heaven (Rev. 10:5).

C2 Lifting heads
Lift up your heads, O gates (Ps. 24:7, 9); lift up your heads for your redemption is drawing near (Luke 21:28); the king of Babylon lifted up the head of Jehoiachin (2 Kgs. 25:27; Jer. 52:31); Pharaoh will lift up your head (Gen. 40:13, 19-20); no man lifts up his head (Zech. 1:21).

D Animals lifted up
Lift up a neighbour's animal which has fallen (Deut. 22:4); who will not lift a sheep out of a pit on the sabbath? (Matt. 12:11); who will not pull a son or an ox out of a well on the sabbath? (Luke 14:5); as Moses lifted up the snake in the wilderness (John 3:14).

311 Lowering
A Putting people down
A1 Lowering people
Rahab let the spies down the wall by a rope through the window (Josh. 2:15); Michal lowered David through a window (1 Sam. 19:12); Paul was let down the wall from the window in a basket (Acts 9:25; 2 Cor. 11:33); Jeremiah was lowered by ropes into the cistern (Jer. 38:6); the paralytic was let down through the roof (Mark 2:4; Luke 5:19); Joseph took Jesus down from the cross (Mark 15:46; Luke 23:53); they took him down

from the cross (Acts 13:29); see the place where they laid him (Mark 16:6).

A2 Throwing people down
They threw Joseph into the pit (Gen. 37:24); throwing Edomites from a cliff (2 Chr. 25:12); throwing Jezebel down (2 Kgs. 9:33); they intended to throw Jesus down the cliff (Luke 4:29); perhaps the Spirit has thrown him down (2 Kgs. 2:16); the accuser of the brethren has been thrown down (Rev. 12:10); when the demon had thrown him down in their midst (Luke 4:35).

A3 Abasing people
You bring down the haughty (2 Sam. 22:28; Ps. 18:27); a man's pride will bring him low (Prov. 29:23); better to be told to come higher than to be put lower (Prov. 25:7); the Lord brings down the wicked to the ground (Ps. 147:6); God will bring the wicked down into the pit of destruction (Ps. 55:23); God puts one down and lifts up another (Ps. 75:7); you will be thrust down to Sheol (Isa. 14:15); there is no need to bring Christ down from heaven (Rom. 10:6); you will be brought down to the depths (Matt. 11:23); he has brought down the mighty from their thrones (Luke 1:52).
PEOPLE HUMBLED, see 872A4.

B Putting things down
Exalt what is low and abase what is high (Ezek. 21:26); the horn caused some of the stars of heaven to fall to earth (Dan. 8:10); a third of the stars were thrown down to the earth (Rev. 12:4); let every mountain and hill be made low (Isa. 40:4; Luke 3:5); the mountains will be thrown down (Ezek. 38:20); your high walls will be cast down to the dust (Isa. 25:12); he brings low the lofty city (Isa. 26:5); Capernaum will be brought down to Hades (Matt. 11:23; Luke 10:15); I bring down the high tree (Ezek. 17:24); the tall trees will be felled (Isa. 10:33); you will be brought down with the trees of Eden to the nether world (Ezek. 31:18); the vine was cast down to the ground (Ezek. 19:12); he thrust the lead weight on the mouth of the ephah (Zech. 5:8); Zion's gates have sunk into the ground (Lam. 2:9); not one stone left upon another that will not be cast down (Matt. 24:2; Mark 13:2); they will raze you to the ground (Luke 19:44).

312 Leap
A People jumping
Through God I can jump over a wall (2 Sam. 22:30; Ps. 18:29); you will go forth leaping like calves from the stall (Mal. 4:2); rejoice and leap for joy, for your reward is great (Luke 6:23); Michal saw David leaping and dancing (2 Sam. 6:16; 1 Chr. 15:29); they leaped about the altar of Baal (1 Kgs. 18:26); the baby jumped in her womb (Luke 1:41, 44); the lame man walked and leaped (Acts 3:8); the lame will leap like a deer (Isa. 35:6); my beloved comes leaping on the hills (S. of S. 2:8); those who could swim should jump overboard (Acts 27:43).

B Creatures jumping
Insects which jump are clean (Lev. 11:21-2); do you make the horse leap like a locust? (Job 39:20); as with the rumbling of chariots they leap on the mountaintops (Joel 2:5); they leap on the city, they run on the walls (Joel 2:9).

C Things jumping
He makes Lebanon skip like a calf (Ps. 29:6); the mountains skipped like rams (Ps. 114:4, 6); spring up, O well! (Num. 21:17).

313 Plunge
Throw yourself down (Matt. 4:6; Luke 4:9); the herd of swine rushed down into the sea (Luke 8:33).
FALLING, see 309E.

314 Circling

They went round the land of Edom (Num. 21:4); they
went round the lands of Edom and Moab (Judg. 11:18);
they circled Mount Seir for many days (Deut. 2:1); you
have circled this mountain long enough (Deut. 2:3);
marching around the city (Josh. 6:3-4, 7, 14-15); the ark
circled the city once (Josh. 6:11); the walls of Jericho
had been encircled for seven days (Heb. 11:30); Samuel
went round a circuit, judging (1 Sam. 7:16-17).
SURROUND, see 230.

315 Rotation

A Rolling
They would roll the stone from the mouth of the well
(Gen. 29:3, 8); Jacob rolled the stone from the mouth
of the well (Gen. 29:10); roll large stones over the cave
mouth (Josh. 10:18); a stone will return on him who
rolls it (Prov. 26:27); roll a big stone to me (1 Sam.
14:33); Joseph rolled a large stone over the mouth of
the tomb (Matt. 27:60; Mark 15:46); who will roll away the
stone? (Mark 16:3); the stone had been rolled away
(Mark 16:4; Luke 24:2); the angel of the Lord rolled
away the stone (Matt. 28:2); the wheels were called in
my hearing the whirling wheels (Ezek. 10:13); the Lord
will roll you up tightly like a ball (Isa. 22:18); Peter saw
the face-cloth rolled up by itself (John 20:7); like a
mantle you will roll up the heavens and the earth (Heb.
1:12); the sky vanished like a scroll which is rolled up
(Rev. 6:14).

B Hinges
Hinges for the doors (1 Kgs. 7:50); as a door turns on its
hinges, so a sluggard on his bed (Prov. 26:14).

316 Unwinding

OPENING, see 263.

317 Oscillation

A Waving the hand
I thought he would wave his hand over the place
(2 Kgs. 5:11); the Egyptians will tremble with fear before
the hand the Lord waves over them (Isa. 19:16); he
shakes his fist at the mount of the daughter of Zion
(Isa. 10:32).

B Shaking the head
All who see me wag their heads (Ps. 22:7); all who see
them shake their heads (Ps. 64:8); everyone who passes
by will shake his head (Jer. 18:16); all who pass by hiss
and shake their heads (Lam. 2:15); those who passed by
wagged their heads (Matt. 27:39; Mark 15:29).

C Swinging / waving things
Waving the wave offering (Exod. 29:24-6; Lev. 7:30;
8:27-9; 9:21; 10:14-15; 14:12, 24; 23:20; Num. 6:20); two
loaves of bread to be waved (Lev. 23:17); he will wave
the sheaf that you may be accepted (Lev. 23:11); waving
the cereal offering (Num. 4:25); offering the Levites as a
wave offering (Num. 8:11-21); they waved their clothes
in the air (Acts 22:23).

318 Agitation: irregular motion

A Shaking
A1 God shaking
The voice of the Lord shakes the wilderness (Ps. 29:8);
the foundations of the earth are shaken (Ps. 82:5); I will
shake the heavens and the earth (Hag. 2:6, 21); the
powers of the heavens will be shaken (Luke 21:26); his
voice shook the earth (Heb. 12:26); I will shake all
nations (Hag. 2:7); he shook the nations and the eternal
mountains were shattered (Hab. 3:6); I will shake Jacob
as in a sieve (Amos 9:9); created things will be shaken
and removed so that unshakeable things will remain

(Heb. 12:27); the stars fell as a fig tree sheds its late fruit
when shaken by a wind (Rev. 6:13); the place where
they had gathered was shaken (Acts 4:31); the
foundations of the prison were shaken (Acts 16:26).
A2 Other shaking
He shakes the arrows, consults the idols, looks at the
liver (Ezek. 21:21); Paul shook the viper off (Acts 28:5);
good measure, pressed down, shaken together (Luke
6:38); I shook out my lap (Neh. 5:13); if they will not
hear, shake the dust off your feet (Matt. 10:14; Luke
9:5); he is at my right hand that I may not be shaken
(Acts 2:25); a reed shaken by the wind? (Matt. 11:7; Luke
7:24);
when shaken, the figs fall into the eater's mouth
(Nahum 3:12).
EARTHQUAKE, see 176C.

B Trembling
I will look to the man who trembles at my word (Isa.
66:2); you who tremble at my word (Isa. 66:5); all who
trembled at the word of the Lord (Ezra 9:4; 10:3); when
the Lord arises to make the earth tremble (Isa. 2:19, 21);
that the nations might tremble at your presence (Isa.
64:2); he looks at the earth and it trembles (Ps. 104:32);
the earth trembled and shook (Ps. 77:18); is this the
man who made the earth tremble? (Isa. 14:16); for fear
of the angel the guards trembled and became like dead
men (Matt. 28:4); the demons believe that God is one –
and tremble (Jas. 2:19); Isaac trembled violently (Gen.
27:33); Moses trembled and did not dare to look (Acts
7:32); the woman came in fear and trembling (Mark
5:33; Luke 8:47); the jailer was trembling with fear (Acts
16:29); I was with you in much trembling (1 Cor. 2:3);
tremble before him, all the earth (1 Chr. 16:30; Ps. 96:9;
114:7); let the peoples tremble! (Ps. 99:1); tremble, you
women at ease (Isa. 32:11); with trembling kiss his feet
(Ps. 2:11-12); eat your bread with trembling and drink
water with anxiety (Ezek. 12:18); obey your masters in
fear and trembling (Eph. 6:5).
FEAR, see 854.

C Convulsions
The demon threw him into convulsions (Mark 1:26;
9:18, 20, 26; Luke 9:39, 42).

319 Materiality

A Bodies
A1 Human bodies
You clothed me with skin and flesh (Job 10:11); we have
many limbs in one body (Rom. 12:4); God put the
members in the body as he would (1 Cor. 12:18); if they
were all one member, where would the body be? (1
Cor. 12:19); God has so arranged the body (1 Cor.
12:24); my covenant will be in your flesh (Gen. 17:13);
they want to have you circumcised that they may boast
in your flesh (Gal. 6:13); caught up to heaven, whether
in the body or out of the body (2 Cor. 12:2-3); may
your spirit, soul and body be kept blameless (1 Thess.
5:23).
A2 Varieties of bodies
With what kind of a body are the dead raised? (1 Cor.
15:35-44); sown as a natural [material] body and raised
as a spiritual body (1 Cor. 15:44); the flesh of men,
animals, birds and fish is different (1 Cor. 15:39).
A3 Limitations of the body
My spirit shall not remain in man for ever since he is
flesh (Gen. 6:3); God remembered they were but flesh
(Ps. 78:39); he knows our frame, he remembers that we
are dust (Ps. 103:14); Egyptian horses are flesh, not
spirit (Isa. 31:3); he considered his own body as good as
dead (Rom. 4:19); flesh and blood cannot inherit the
kingdom of God (1 Cor. 15:50); that which is born of
the flesh is flesh (John 3:6); the spirit is willing but the

flesh is weak (Matt. 26:41; Mark 14:38); I am speaking in human terms because of the weakness of your flesh (Rom. 6:19); though the body is dead because of sin (Rom. 8:10).

A4 Care of the body
No one hates his own flesh but nourishes and cherishes it (Eph. 5:29); pleasant words are healing to the bones (Prov. 16:24); none of his bones will be broken (Ps. 34:20; John 19:36); bodily training is only a little value (1 Tim. 4:8); your body is a temple of the Holy Spirit (1 Cor. 6:19); he will give life to your mortal bodies through his Spirit who dwells in you (Rom. 8:11); present your bodies a living sacrifice (Rom. 12:1); the body is not for immorality but for the Lord and the Lord is for the body (1 Cor. 6:13); is not the body more than clothing? (Matt. 6:25; Luke 12:22-3); we groan, waiting for the redemption of our bodies (Rom. 8:23); that the life of Jesus may be manifested in our bodies (2 Cor. 4:10).

A5 Damage to the body
Touch his bone and flesh and he will curse you (Job 2:5); if I deliver my body to be burned and have not love (1 Cor. 13:3); carrying about in our body the death of Jesus (2 Cor. 4:10); a thorn in the flesh, a messenger of Satan (2 Cor. 12:7); the tongue defiles the whole body (Jas. 3:6).

A6 Discipline over the body
Do not be afraid of those who kill the body (Luke 12:4); I beat my body and make it my slave (1 Cor. 9:27); it is better to lose a limb than have your whole body thrown into hell (Matt. 5:29, 30; Mark 9:43, 45); deliver him to Satan for the destruction of the flesh (1 Cor. 5:5); God gave them up to impurity, that their bodies be dishonoured (Rom. 1:24); do not let sin reign in your mortal body (Rom. 6:12); that Christ will be exalted in my body, by life or by death (Phil. 1:20); anyone perfect in speech is able to bridle the whole body (Jas. 3:2).

A7 One flesh
The two will become one flesh (Gen. 2:24; Matt. 19:5; Mark 10:8; 1 Cor. 6:16; Eph. 5:31); they are no longer two but one flesh (Matt. 19:6; Mark 10:8); bone of my bones and flesh of my flesh (Gen. 2:23); husband and wife do not have authority over their own bodies, but that of the spouse (1 Cor. 7:4); husbands should love their wives as their own bodies (Eph. 5:28).

A8 Christ's body
A8a The incarnation
The Word became flesh (John 1:14); every spirit which confesses that Jesus Christ has come in the flesh (1 John 4:2); deceivers do not acknowledge that Jesus Christ has come in the flesh (2 John 7); since the children have flesh and blood, he also shared in the same (Heb. 2:14); a ghost does not have flesh and bones as I have (Luke 24:39); we have known Christ according to the flesh (2 Cor. 5:16); the veil, that is, his flesh (Heb. 10:20); the temple of his body (John 2:21); a body you have prepared for me (Heb. 10:5); Christ's flesh did not suffer decay (Acts 2:31); God's Son, descended from David according to the flesh (Rom. 1:3); in him all the fullness of God dwells in a body (Col. 2:9); in the days of his flesh (Heb. 5:7); the offering of the body of Jesus Christ once for all (Heb. 10:10); he has reconciled you through his fleshly body by his death (Col. 1:22); put to death in the flesh but made alive in spirit (1 Pet. 3:18); Christ has suffered in the flesh (1 Pet. 4:1); in pouring this perfume on my body she has prepared it for burial (Matt. 26:12).

A8b The church as Christ's body
The church is Christ's body (Eph. 1:23); we are one body in Christ (Rom. 12:5); you are Christ's body (1

Cor. 12:27); as the body is one yet has many limbs, so is Christ (1 Cor. 12:12); your bodies are limbs of Christ (1 Cor. 6:15); we are members of his body (Eph. 5:30); we who are many are one body (1 Cor. 10:17); the whole body is fitted together by every joint (Eph. 4:16); building up the body of Christ (Eph. 4:12); there is one body and one Spirit (Eph. 4:4); Christ is the Saviour of the body (Eph. 5:23); he is the head of the body, the church (Col. 1:18); his body, the church (Col. 1:24); called in the one body (Col. 3:15).

A8c Eating Christ's body
This is my body (Matt. 26:26-8; Mark 14:22; Luke 22:19; 1 Cor. 11:24); sharing in the body and blood of Christ (1 Cor. 10:16); he who eats my flesh and drinks my blood has eternal life (John 6:54-6); the bread I give for the life of the world is my flesh (John 6:51-2).

B Materialism
B1 Life in a material world
My kinsmen according to the flesh (Rom. 9:3); from Israel is the Christ according to the flesh (Rom. 9:5); Gentile believers minister to the poor saints in material things (Rom. 15:27); not many wise according to the flesh (1 Cor. 1:26); a natural man does not accept the things of the Spirit of God (1 Cor. 2:14); the married woman is concerned about the things of the world (1 Cor. 7:34); if we sowed to the spirit, should we not reap material things? (1 Cor. 9:11); it is sown a natural [material] body and raised a spiritual body (1 Cor. 15:44); the spiritual is not first, but the natural [material] (1 Cor. 15:46); the first covenant had an earthly sanctuary (Heb. 9:1); remember those ill-treated, since you are also in the body (Heb. 13:3); while we are at home in the body we are absent from the Lord (2 Cor. 5:6); the life I now live in the flesh (Gal. 2:20); the flesh profits nothing (John 6:63).

B2 Hindered by materialism
I am carnal (Rom. 7:14); nothing good dwells in my flesh (Rom. 7:18); those who are in the flesh cannot please God (Rom. 8:8); God did what the law, weakened by the flesh, could not do (Rom. 8:3); the flesh lusts against the Spirit (Gal. 5:17); with my flesh I serve the law of sin (Rom. 7:25); you were fleshly, babes in Christ (1 Cor. 3:1); having begun with the Spirit are you made perfect with the flesh? (Gal. 3:3).

B3 Sins of the flesh
The deeds of the flesh (Gal. 5:19-21); while there is jealousy, are you not fleshly? (1 Cor. 3:3); while we were in the flesh our sinful passions were at work (Rom. 7:5); we formerly lived in the lusts of our flesh (Eph. 2:3); this wisdom is earthly, unspiritual, demonic (Jas. 3:15); the lust of the flesh and the lust of the eyes and the pride of life (1 John 2:16).

B4 Living for the material
Those who are of the flesh set their minds on things of the flesh (Rom. 8:5-7); they set their minds on earthly things (Phil. 3:19); he who sows to the flesh will reap corruption (Gal. 6:8); if you live according to the flesh you will die (Rom. 8:12-13); I could not speak to you as spiritual men (1 Cor. 3:1); I have reason for confidence in the flesh (Phil. 3:4); do I make plans according to the flesh? (2 Cor. 1:17); some suspect us of acting according to the flesh (2 Cor. 10:2); do not use your freedom as an opportunity for the flesh (Gal. 5:13); those who want to make a good showing in the flesh (Gal. 6:12); circumcision, made in the flesh by hands (Eph. 2:11); puffed up by his fleshly mind (Col. 2:18); Demas has loved this present world (2 Tim. 4:10); abstain from fleshly passions which war against the soul (1 Pet. 2:11); let the time past suffice for sensuality, lusts, drunkenness (1 Pet. 4:3); though judged in the flesh like men they may live in the spirit like God (1 Pet. 4:6);

those who indulge the flesh in lusts (2 Pet. 2:10); they entice by fleshly desires (2 Pet. 2:18); worldly-minded, devoid of the Spirit (Jude 19).

B5 Living not for the material
From now on we know no one according to the flesh (2 Cor. 5:16); make no provision for the flesh (Rom. 13:14); those who are Christ's have crucified the flesh (Gal. 5:24); we do not live according to the flesh but according to the Spirit (Rom. 8:4); you are not in the flesh but in the Spirit (Rom. 8:9); it is not the children of the flesh who are the children of God (Rom. 9:8); we do not put confidence in the flesh (Phil. 3:3); though we walk in the flesh we do not wage war according to the flesh (2 Cor. 10:3); our struggle is not against flesh and blood (Eph. 6:12); circumcision is nor something external in the flesh (Rom. 2:28); the unmarried woman seeks to be holy in body and spirit (1 Cor. 7:34); we prefer to be absent from the body and at home with the Lord (2 Cor. 5:8); walk by the Spirit and you will not fulfil the desires of the flesh (Gal. 5:16); you have put off the old man with its practices (Col. 3:9); living the rest of the time in the flesh not for human lusts (1 Pet. 4:2).

C Elements of the universe
We were in bondage under the elements of the universe (Gal. 4:3); you turn back to the weak and worthless elements (Gal. 4:9); according to the elements of the world rather than Christ (Col. 2:8); you have died with Christ to the elements of the world (Col. 2:20); the elements will be destroyed with fire (2 Pet. 3:10).

320 Spirituality

A That which is spiritual
God is spirit (John 4:24); the law is spiritual (Rom. 7:14); the words I have spoken are spirit and life (John 6:63); worship in spirit and in truth (John 4:23, 24); it is raised as a spiritual body (1 Cor. 15:44); that which is born of the Spirit is Spirit (John 3:6); combining spiritual things with spiritual (1 Cor. 2:13); the things of the Spirit of God are spiritually discerned (1 Cor. 2:14); the spiritual man discerns all things (1 Cor. 2:15); the weapons of our warfare are not fleshly (2 Cor. 10:4); God has blessed us with every spiritual blessing in Christ (Eph. 1:3); against spiritual wickedness in the heavenlies (Eph. 6:12).

THE HOLY SPIRIT, see 965E.

B Spirit of man
God forms the spirit of a man within him (Zech. 12:1); the God of the spirits of all flesh (Num. 16:22; 27:16); no one knows the things of a man but the spirit of the man (1 Cor. 2:11); the spirit is willing but the flesh is weak (Matt. 26:41; Mark 14:38); his spirit departs and he returns to the earth (Ps. 146:4); the spirit returns to God who gave it (Eccles. 12:7); who knows the spirit of man which goes upward? (Eccles. 3:21); Lord Jesus, receive my spirit (Acts 7:59); I will give you a new heart and a new spirit (Ezek. 36:26); destruction of the flesh that his spirit may be saved (1 Cor. 5:5); whoever is united with the Lord becomes one spirit with him (1 Cor. 6:17); if I pray in a tongue my spirit prays but my mind is unfruitful (1 Cor. 14:14-16); the spirits of prophets are subject to the prophets (1 Cor. 14:32); let us cleanse ourselves from every defilement of flesh and spirit (2 Cor. 7:1); may your spirit, soul and body be kept blameless (1 Thess. 5:23); the word of God pierces to the division of soul and spirit (Heb. 4:12); the Father of spirits (Heb. 12:9); the spirits of righteous men made perfect (Heb. 12:23); put to death in the flesh but made alive in spirit (1 Pet. 3:18); though judged in the flesh

like men they may live in the spirit like God (1 Pet. 4:6).

HEART, see 224A2.

C Spirit of particular people
Caleb has a different spirit (Num. 14:24); give me a double portion of your spirit (2 Kgs. 2:9); the spirit of Elijah rests on Elisha (2 Kgs. 2:15); Daniel had an excellent spirit (Dan. 5:12; 6:3); Father, into your hands I commit my spirit (Luke 23:46); the Lord, the God of the spirits of the prophets (Rev. 22:6).

D Living souls
Let the waters teem with living souls (Gen. 1:20); every living soul which creeps (Gen. 1:21); let the earth bring forth living souls (Gen. 1:24); all creatures having a living soul (Gen. 1:30); man became a living soul (Gen. 2:7); the soul is more than food (Matt. 6:25); they kill the body but cannot kill the soul (Matt. 10:28); God can destroy both soul and body in hell (Matt. 10:28); what profit is it to gain the world and forfeit your soul? (Matt. 16:26; Mark 8:36); what will one give in exchange for his soul? (Matt. 22:37); love the Lord your God with all your soul (Mark 8:37; 12:30; Luke 10:27); do not be anxious about your soul, what you shall eat (Luke 12:22); the soul is more than food and the body more than clothing (Luke 12:23).

E Spirit beings
A spirit said, 'I will entice him' (1 Kgs. 22:21); I will be a deceiving spirit in the mouth of his prophets (1 Kgs. 22:22); the Sadducees say there is no spirit (Acts 23:8); what if a spirit or an angel has spoken to him? (Acts 23:9); the gift of distinguishing spirits (1 Cor. 12:10); test the spirits to see whether they are from God (1 John 4:1-3); three unclean spirits like frogs (Rev. 16:13); they are demonic spirits (Rev. 16:14).

ANGEL, see 968.

EVIL SPIRIT, see 969C.

321 Universe

SUN, MOON AND STARS, see 420A.

HEAVEN AND EARTH, see 971F.

A About the universe
A1 The universe in general
What shall it profit a man if he gains the whole world? (Matt. 16:26; Mark 8:36; Luke 9:25); while I am in the world I am the light of the world (John 9:5); you are of this world, I am not of this world (John 8:23); my kingdom is not of this world (John 18:36); the world is yours (1 Cor. 3:22); to avoid the wicked people of the world you would need to go out of the world (1 Cor. 5:10); those who deal with the world should be as though they did not (1 Cor. 7:31); the creation longs for the revealing of the sons of God (Rom. 8:19); I praise you Father, Lord of heaven and earth (Luke 10:21); I call heaven and earth to witness (Deut. 30:19; 31:28); you know how to interpret the appearance of earth and sky (Luke 12:56); there are heavenly bodies and earthly bodies (1 Cor. 15:40); do not swear at all, by heaven or earth or any other oath (Jas. 5:12).

A2 The earth in general
The earth was formless and empty (Gen. 1:2); fill the earth and subdue it (Gen. 1:28); let men rule over the earth (Gen. 1:26); the earth he has given to mankind (Ps. 115:16); the world is firm and will not be moved (1 Chr. 16:30); do not store up for yourselves treasures on earth (Matt. 6:19); whatever you bind or loose on earth will be done in heaven (Matt. 16:19; 18:18); if two of you agree on earth, it will be done by my Father in heaven (Matt. 18:19); do not call anyone your father on earth (Matt. 23:9); on earth, peace among men with whom he is pleased (Luke 2:14); the Son of man has authority on earth to forgive sins (Luke 5:24); if I have told you

earthly things and you do not believe (John 3:12); he who is of the earth is from the earth and speaks of the earth (John 3:31); the first man is from the earth, made of dust (1 Cor. 15:47); if he were on earth he would not be a priest at all (Heb. 8:4); if they did not escape when they refused him who warned them on earth (Heb. 12:25); the great dragon was thrown down to the earth (Rev. 12:9); woe to you, earth and sea, for the devil has come down to you (Rev. 12:12); the Son of man in the heart of the earth (Matt. 12:40).

A3 The sky in general

It will be fair weather for the sky is red (Matt. 16:2); it will be stormy, for the sky is red and threatening (Matt. 16:3); they were gazing into the sky as Jesus went (Acts 1:10-11); a sound came from heaven like a mighty, rushing wind (Acts 2:2).

A4 Signs in the universe

I will show signs in the sky and on earth, blood, fire and columns of smoke (Joel 2:30); I will shown wonders in heaven above and signs on the earth beneath (Acts 2:19); the sign of the Son of man will appear in the sky (Matt. 24:30); the sun will be darkened and the moon not give its light (Mark 13:24); the stars will fall from the sky and the powers in the heavens will be shaken (Mark 13:25).

B Creation of the universe

B1 Creation of earth and sky

The creation of the heavens and the earth (Gen. 1:1); in six days the Lord made heaven and earth (Exod. 20:11); you made the earth and the heavens (Ps. 102:25); he who made heavens and earth (Ps. 146:6); the heavens and the earth were completed (Gen. 2:1-4); God stretched out the heavens and laid the foundation of the earth (Zech. 12:1); you made heaven and earth and sea and everything in them (Acts 4:24); a living God who made heaven and earth and sea (Acts 14:15); all things, in heaven and on earth, were created in him (Col. 1:16); through his Son God made the world (Heb. 1:2); in the beginning the Son created the earth and the heavens (Heb. 1:10); by faith we understand that the world was created by the word of God (Heb. 11:3).

B2 Creation of the earth

The dry land called 'earth' (Gen. 1:9-10); God hangs the earth on nothing (Job 26:7); the earth which he has founded for ever (Ps. 78:69); the earth was made out of water and by water (2 Pet. 3:5).

B3 Creation of the sky

God called the expanse 'heaven' (Gen. 1:8); when he established the skies above (Prov. 8:28); the creation of the heavens (Ps. 96:5); by the word of the Lord the heavens were made (Ps. 33:6); the heavens were made by the word of God (2 Pet. 3:5); can you spread out the skies like a molten mirror? (Job 37:18); God stretches out the heavens (Job 9:8); stretching out the heavens like a curtain (Ps. 104:2).

C God and the universe

C1 God of the universe

The Lord is God in heaven above and earth below (Deut. 4:39; Josh. 2:11); the Lord, God of heaven and God of the earth (Gen. 24:3); the Lord of all the earth (Josh. 3:11, 13; Zech. 4:14; 6:5); your will be done on earth as it is in heaven (Matt. 6:10); the Lord will be king of all the earth (Zech. 14:9); Lord of heaven and earth (Matt. 11:25; Acts 17:24).

C2 God's universe

All the world is mine (Exod. 19:5); the earth is my footstool (Acts 7:49); the heavens and earth belong to God (Deut. 10:14; Ps. 89:11); God most high, possessor of heaven and earth (Gen. 14:19, 22); the world is mine and all it contains (Ps. 50:12); the earth is the Lord's (Exod. 9:29; Ps. 24:1; 1 Cor. 10:26); heaven is my throne

and the earth my footstool (Isa. 66:1); the earth is God's footstool (Matt. 5:35); God fills the heaven and earth (Jer. 23:24); the lovingkindness of the Lord fills the earth (Ps. 33:5); all authority in heaven and earth has been given to me (Matt. 28:18).

C3 The universe glorifies God

The heavens declare the glory of God (Ps. 19:1); the heavens declare his righteousness (Ps. 97:6); his glory covered the heavens, the earth was full of his praise (Hab. 3:3); let heaven and earth praise him (Ps. 69:34); let the heavens be glad and the earth rejoice that the Lord reigns (1 Chr. 16:31); let heaven be glad and earth rejoice before the Lord (Ps. 96:11); shout for joy, heavens, and rejoice, earth! (Isa. 49:13); summing up all things in Christ, in heaven and on earth (Eph. 1:10).

D The universe affected

The creation was subjected to futility (Rom. 8:20); the creation will be set free from its slavery to decay (Rom. 8:21); the creation groans in travail at present (Rom. 8:22); to reconcile all things, whether on earth or in heaven (Col. 1:20); the powers of the heavens will be shaken (Matt. 24:29).

E The universe destroyed

Heaven and earth will pass away (Matt. 24:35; Mark 13:31; Luke 21:33; Rev. 21:1); I will shake heaven and earth (Hag. 2:6, 21; Heb. 12:26); the earth will be shaken from its place (Isa. 13:13); the earth will wear out like a garment (Isa. 51:6); all the earth will be consumed in the fire of his jealousy (Zeph. 1:18); the heavens will vanish like smoke (Isa. 51:6); till heaven and earth pass away, not a jot or tittle will pass from the law (Matt. 5:18); easier for heaven and earth to pass away than one tittle of the law become void (Luke 16:17); the sun and moon will be darkened and the stars will fall (Matt. 24:29); I have come to cast fire on the earth (Luke 12:49); the present heavens and earth are reserved for fire (2 Pet. 3:7); the heavens will pass away and the earth be burned up (2 Pet. 3:10); the heavens will be burned up and the elements melt with fire (2 Pet. 3:12); the sky will be rolled up like a scroll (Isa. 34:4); the sky vanished like a scroll which is rolled up (Rev. 6:14); from his presence earth and sky fled away (Rev. 20:11); a third of the earth was burned up (Rev. 8:7).

F New universe

I create new heavens and a new earth (Isa. 65:17); the new heavens and the new earth will endure (Isa. 66:22); we look for new heavens and a new earth (2 Pet. 3:13); I saw a new heaven and a new earth (Rev. 21:1).

322 Weight

A Weighing

WEIGHING SCALES, see 465A.

A1 Weighing materials

Abraham weighed out the silver for Ephron (Gen. 23:16); Ezra weighed out the silver, gold and utensils (Ezra 8:25-34); those who weigh silver in the scales for an idol (Isa. 46:6); I weighed out the silver (Jer. 32:9, 10); they weighed out thirty shekels of silver (Zech. 11:12); bread will be measured out by weight (Lev. 26:26); eat your food by weight, 20 shekels a day (Ezek. 4:10); they will eat bread by weight and with anxiety (Ezek. 4:16); weigh your hair into three parts (Ezek. 5:1-2); where is he who weighed? (Isa. 33:18); who has weighed the hills in a balance? (Isa. 40:12).

A2 Weighing the immaterial

Oh, that my vexation were weighed! (Job 6:2-3); the Lord weighs the spirit (Prov. 16:2); let God weigh me in a true balance (Job 31:6); weighed in the balances and found wanting (Dan. 5:27).

A3 Not weighed
The weight of the bronze was not determined (1 Kgs. 7:47; 2 Kgs. 25:16; 2 Chr. 4:18); more bronze than could be weighed (1 Chr. 22:3; Jer. 52:20); bronze and iron beyond weighing (1 Chr. 22:14); gold, silver, bronze and iron without reckoning (1 Chr. 22:16).

B Weights of things
Ingredients for the holy anointing oil according to the shekel of the sanctuary (Exod. 30:24); a bronze spear weighing 300 shekels (2 Sam. 21:16); an iron spear weighing 600 shekels (1 Sam. 17:7); 20 shekels weight of food per day (Ezek. 4:10); Absalom's hair weighed 200 shekels (2 Sam. 14:26); Goliath's scale armour weighed 5000 shekels (1 Sam. 17:5); hailstones about a talent in weight (Rev. 16:21); two mules' burden of earth (2 Kgs. 5:17); 100 pounds weight of myrrh and aloes (John 19:39); a pound of costly perfume of pure nard (John 12:3).

C Heavy
Eli was old and heavy (1 Sam. 4:18); a lead cover on the ephah (Zech. 5:7-8); I will make Jerusalem a heavy stone for all the peoples (Zech. 12:3); their ears are heavy of hearing (Matt. 13:15); their eyes were heavy (Matt. 26:43; Mark 14:40); they were heavy with sleep (Luke 9:32); a momentary light affliction producing an eternal weight of glory (2 Cor. 4:17).

D Burdens
D1 Heavy burdens
I will add to your yoke (1 Kgs. 12:11, 14; 2 Chr. 10:11, 14); it is good for a man to bear the yoke in his youth (Lam. 3:27); they put heavy loads on men's shoulders (Matt. 23:4); you weigh men down with burdens hard to bear (Luke 11:46); why have you put the burden of all these people on me? (Num. 11:11); you are too heavy a burden for me (Deut. 1:9, 12); you will be a burden to me (2 Sam. 15:33); the former governors laid burdens on the people (Neh. 5:15); stone and sand are heavy but a fool's anger is heavier (Prov. 27:3); anxiety weighs the heart down (Prov. 12:25); my iniquities are a heavy burden (Ps. 38:4); we have borne the burden and the heat of the day (Matt. 20:12); we were burdened beyond measure (2 Cor. 1:8); every one will carry his own burden (Gal. 6:5); lest your hearts be weighed down with dissipation, drunkenness and anxiety (Luke 21:34); weak women, burdened with sins and led by various impulses (2 Tim. 3:6).
D2 Not heavy burdens
I was never a burden to any one (2 Cor. 11:9); I was never a burden to you (2 Cor. 12:13, 16); I will not be a burden to you (2 Cor. 12:14); lest we be burdensome to you (2 Sam. 13:25); why should I be a burden to the king? (2 Sam. 19:35); working night and day so as not to burden you (1 Thess. 2:9; 2 Thess. 3:8); it seemed good to lay on you no greater burden then these essentials (Acts 15:28); I put no other burden on you (Rev. 2:24); his commandments are not burdensome (1 John 5:3); my yoke is easy and my burden light (Matt. 11:30).
D3 Sharing burdens
The 70 elders will bear the burden with you (Num. 11:17); they will carry the burden with you (Exod. 18:22); bear one another's burdens (Gal. 6:2); come to me, all who are heavy-laden (Matt. 11:28); not that others should be eased and you burdened, but that there should be equality (2 Cor. 8:13-14).
BEARING PEOPLE S BURDENS, see 273B4.
D4 Removing burdens
I will bring you out from under the burdens of the Egyptians (Exod. 6:6, 7); I removed the burden from his shoulder (Ps. 81:6); you will break the yoke of their burden (Isa. 9:4); the yoke and burden will be removed from your shoulders (Isa. 10:27); make our yoke lighter

(1 Kgs. 12:4, 9-10; 2 Chr. 10:4, 9-10); cast your burden on the Lord (Ps. 55:22); let the church not be burdened (1 Tim. 5:16).

E Sinking
They sank like lead (Exod. 15:10); so will Babylon sink (Jer. 51:64); better a millstone hung round his neck (Matt. 18:6; Mark 9:42; Luke 17:2); Peter beginning to sink (Matt. 14:30); the boats began to sink (Luke 5:7).

323 Lightness
A Light things
A1 Light as chaff
The wicked are like chaff driven away by the wind (Ps. 1:4); evildoers will be like chaff (Mal. 4:1); your enemies will be like chaff (Isa. 29:5); let them be like chaff before the wind (Ps. 35:5; 83:13); he makes them like dust and chaff (Isa. 41:2); the nations will be like chaff before the wind (Isa. 17:13); they will be like chaff from the threshing floor (Hos. 13:3); he will burn up the chaff (Matt. 3:12); the statue became like chaff (Dan. 2:35); in the balances they are lighter than a breath (Ps. 62:9); a breath will carry the idols away (Isa. 57:13).
A2 Light yoke
Make our yoke lighter (1 Kgs. 12:4, 9-10; 2 Chr. 10:4, 9-10); my yoke is easy and my burden light (Matt. 11:30); a momentary light affliction producing an eternal weight of glory (2 Cor. 4:17).
EASY BURDENS, see 701.
A3 Buoyancy
The ark floated (Gen. 7:18); Elisha made the iron float (2 Kgs. 6:6); lightening a boat by throwing out the cargo (Jonah 1:5); they jettisoned the cargo and tackle (Acts 27:18-19); they lightened the ship, throwing the wheat into the sea (Acts 27:38).

B Yeast
B1 Leavened
Peace offering with leavened bread (Lev. 7:13); loaves made with leaven as firstfruits (Lev. 23:17); yeast can be offered as firstfruits (Lev. 2:12); bring a thank-offering from what is leavened (Amos 4:5); a baker who ceases to stir the fire until the dough is leavened (Hos. 7:4); yeast which a woman hid in three measures of meal till it was all leavened (Matt. 13:33; Luke 13:21); beware of the leaven of the Pharisees (Matt. 16:6, 11-12; Mark 8:15; Luke 12:1); let us celebrate the feast, not with the old leaven of malice (1 Cor. 5:8); a little leaven leavens the whole lump (1 Cor. 5:6; Gal. 5:9).
B2 Unleavened
The Passover had to be eaten without yeast (Exod. 12:15, 18-20; 13:3, 6-7; Num. 9:11; 28:17; Deut. 16:3-4); they took the dough before it was leavened (Exod. 12:34, 39); the feast of Unleavened Bread (Exod. 34:18; Lev. 23:6; Luke 22:1); the day of Unleavened Bread on which the passover lamb was sacrificed (Luke 22:7); no leaven in your houses for seven days (Exod. 12:15, 19); eat unleavened bread for seven days (Exod. 12:15); sacrifices should not contain yeast (Exod. 34:25; Lev. 2:11); yeast should not be offered in smoke for a soothing aroma (Lev. 2:12); they ate unleavened cakes (Josh. 5:11); the medium baked unleavened bread (1 Sam. 28:24); the priests of the high places ate unleavened bread with their brethren (2 Kgs. 23:9); clean out the old leaven, that you may be fresh dough, unleavened (1 Cor. 5:7); with the unleavened bread of sincerity and truth (1 Cor. 5:8).

324 Density
HEAVINESS, see 322.

325 Tenuous
LIGHTNESS, see 323.

326 Hardness

Their horses' hooves seem like flint (Isa. 5:28); like adamant harder than flint I have made your forehead (Ezek. 3:9); the crocodile's heart is hard as stone (Job 41:24); they made their hearts like flint lest they hear the law (Zech. 7:12); I will remove your heart of stone and give you a heart of flesh (Ezek. 36:26).

OBSTINATE, see 602.

327 Softness

You will no more be called tender and delicate (Isa. 47:1); you soften the earth with showers (Ps. 65:10); I will remove your heart of stone and give you a heart of flesh (Ezek. 36:26); did you go out to see a man wearing soft clothes? (Matt. 11:8; Luke 7:25); when the shoots of the fig tree become tender (Matt. 24:32; Mark 13:28).

COMPLIANT, see 739.

328 Elasticity

REBOUNDING, see 280.

329 Toughness

The kingdom will have in it the toughness of iron (Dan. 2:41).

STRENGTH, see 162.

330 Brittleness

Like clay, part of the kingdom will be brittle (Dan. 2:42).

331 Structure

FORM, see 243.

332 Powderiness

A Grinding
A1 Grinding food
They would grind the manna (Num. 11:8); Samson ground grain in the prison (Judg. 16:21); take the millstones and grind the meal (Isa. 47:2); young men grind at the mill (Lam. 5:13); the grinders stand idle (Eccles. 12:3-4); two women grinding at the mill (Matt. 24:41; Luke 17:35); the sound of a mill will not be heard in you (Rev. 18:22).

A2 Grinding people
Crush a fool with a mortar and pestle and his folly will not leave him (Prov. 27:22); I crushed them like dust (2 Sam. 22:43; Ps. 18:42); it will devour, trample and crush the whole earth (Dan. 7:23); the beast devoured, crushed and trampled the remainder (Dan. 7:19); Ephraim is oppressed, crushed in judgement (Hos. 5:11); you will crush many peoples and devote their gain to the Lord (Mic. 4:13); if this stone falls on anyone it will crush him (Matt. 21:44; Luke 20:18); the king of Aram had made Israel like the dust at threshing (2 Kgs. 13:7); grinding the face of the poor (Isa. 3:15).

A3 Grinding other things
Beat some of the incense very small (Exod. 30:36); Moses ground the golden calf to powder (Exod. 32:20; Deut. 9:21); Josiah ground the Asherah and idols to dust (2 Kgs. 23:6; 2 Chr. 34:4); Josiah ground the high place to dust (2 Kgs. 23:15); when they crush altar stones to powder (Isa. 27:9); the statue was crushed to pieces (Dan. 2:34-5); as iron crushes and shatters all things (Dan. 2:40); it crushed the iron, bronze, clay, silver and gold (Dan. 2:45); you will thresh the mountains and pulverise them (Isa. 41:15); the ostrich forgets that her eggs might be crushed (Job 39:15).

B Dust
B1 Dust in general
The serpent would eat dust (Gen. 3:14); dust will be the serpent's food (Isa. 65:25); they will lick dust like a snake (Mic. 7:17); the nations are like dust on the scales (Isa. 40:15); he lifts up the islands like fine dust (Isa. 40:15); clouds are the dust beneath his feet (Nahum 1:3); the soot will become dust over all Egypt (Exod. 9:9); the Lord will rain powder and dust on you in the drought (Deut. 28:24); the Philistines filled up the wells with dust (Gen. 26:15); dust from the tabernacle for the water of bitterness (Num. 5:17); the dust became gnats (Exod. 8:16-17); your servants have pity on the dust of Zion (Ps. 102:14); her blood is on the bare rock, not on the ground covered with dust (Ezek. 24:7); they trample the head of the poor into the dust of the earth (Amos 2:7); he lifts up the poor from the dust (1 Sam. 2:8); I repent in dust and ashes (Job 42:6); may his enemies lick the dust (Ps. 72:9); God raises the poor from the dust (Ps. 113:7).

B2 Throwing / wiping dust
Shake the dust off your feet (Matt. 10:14; Mark 6:11; Luke 9:5); wipe the dust off your feet (Luke 10:11); they shook the dust off their feet (Acts 13:51); Shimei threw dust (2 Sam. 16:13); they were tossing dust in the air (Acts 22:23).

B3 Dust on the head
A man with dust on his head (2 Sam. 1:2); Hushai the Archite had dust on his head (2 Sam. 15:32); Joshua and the elders put dust on their heads (Josh. 7:6); Job's comforters threw dust on their heads (Job 2:12); the elders of Zion have thrown dust on their heads (Lam. 2:10); they cast dust on their heads and wallow in ashes (Ezek. 27:30); they threw dust on their heads, weeping and mourning (Rev. 18:19).

B4 Numerous as dust
Who put the dust of the earth in a measuring pot? (Isa. 40:12); the dust of Samaria will not suffice for my people (1 Kgs. 20:10); I will make your offspring like the dust of the earth in number (Gen. 13:16); your offspring will be like the dust (Gen. 28:14); a people as numerous as the dust (2 Chr. 1:9); who can count the dust of Jacob? (Num. 23:10).

B5 Creatures from dust
Man was made of the dust (Gen. 2:7); you are dust and to dust you will return (Gen. 3:19); I who am but dust and ashes (Gen. 18:27); he remembers that we are dust (Ps. 103:14); the first man is from the earth, made of dust (1 Cor. 15:47); as was the man of dust, so are those who are of the dust (1 Cor. 15:48); we have borne the image of the man of dust (1 Cor. 15:49).

B6 Creatures returning to dust
All come from dust and return to dust (Eccles. 3:20); all creatures die and return to their dust (Ps. 104:29); you turn man back to the dust (Ps. 90:3); if God withdrew his breath man would return to the dust (Job 34:14-15); would you turn me into dust again? (Job 10:9); I have become like dust and ashes (Job 30:19); will hope go down with me into the dust? (Job 17:16); will the dust praise you? (Ps. 30:9); you lay me in the dust of death (Ps. 22:15); you who lie in the dust, awake and shout for joy (Isa. 26:19); the dust will return to the earth (Eccles. 12:7).

C Soot
Soot from the kiln (Exod. 9:8, 10); the soot will be dust over all the land of Egypt (Exod. 9:9); they are blacker than soot (Lam. 4:8).

333 Friction

Job took a potsherd to scrape himself (Job 2:8); they will scrape off Tyre's soil (Ezek. 26:4); every shoulder was rubbed bare (Ezek. 29:18); his disciples plucked ears of grain and rubbed them in their hands (Luke 6:1).

GRINDING, see 332A.

334 Lubrication
Oil the shield (Isa. 21:5); Saul's shield, not anointed (2 Sam. 1:21).

OIL, see 357A.

335 Liquids
A Milk
Abraham gave curds, milk and the calf to the men (Gen. 18:8); curds of cows and milk of sheep (Deut. 32:14); because of the abundance of milk he will eat curds (Isa. 7:22); Jael gave Sisera milk (Judg. 4:19; 5:25); there will be enough goats' milk for your food (Prov. 27:27); honey and milk are under your tongue (S. of S. 4:11); his eyes are washed in milk (S. of S. 5:12); I drink my wine and milk (S. of S. 5:1); buy wine and milk without money (Isa. 55:1); do not boil a kid in its mother's milk (Exod. 23:19; 34:26; Deut. 14:21); pressing milk produces butter (Prov. 30:33); his teeth will be white from milk (Gen. 49:12); her nobles were purer than snow, whiter than milk (Lam. 4:7); they will eat your fruit and drink your milk (Ezek. 25:4); those weaned from the milk (Isa. 28:9); the hills will flow with milk (Joel 3:18); you will suck the milk of nations (Isa. 60:16); who tends a flock without drinking some of the milk? (1 Cor. 9:7); as newborn babes desire the pure milk of the word (1 Pet. 2:2); I fed you with milk, not solid food (1 Cor. 3:2); you need milk, not solid food (Heb. 5:12-13); did you not pour me out like milk and curdle me like cheese? (Job 10:10).

FLOWING WITH MILK AND HONEY, see 635D.

B Wine
DRUNKENNESS, see 949.

B1 Wine in general
Wine on the lees, well filtered (Isa. 25:6); as the wine is found in the cluster (Isa. 65:8); the firstfruits of the wine is for the priests (Num. 18:12); if a windy liar says, 'I will preach wine and strong drink' (Mic. 2:11); new wine is not put into old wineskins (Matt. 9:17; Mark 2:22; Luke 5:37-8); he washes his clothes in wine (Gen. 49:11); his eyes will be dark from wine (Gen. 49:12); your wine is mixed with water (Isa. 1:22); the cup of the wine of wrath (Jer. 25:15); the Samaritan bandaged his wounds, pouring on oil and wine (Luke 10:34).

B2 Provision of wine
B2a Plenty of wine
God give you abundance of new wine (Gen. 27:28); she does not know that I gave her the grain, wine and oil (Hos. 2:8); your vats will overflow with new wine (Prov. 3:10; Joel 2:24); the mountains will drip sweet wine (Joel 3:18; Amos 9:13); wine was plentiful (Esther 1:7); water into wine (John 2:3-10); every jug will be filled with wine (Jer. 13:12); I am giving you grain, new wine and oil (Joel 2:19); do not harm the oil and the wine (Rev. 6:6).

B2b Shortage of wine
The grain is ruined, the wine fails, the oil languishes (Joel 1:10); the new wine will fail (Hos. 9:2); the new wine mourns (Isa. 24:7); the sweet wine is cut off from your mouth (Joel 1:5); for grain and wine they gash themselves (Hos. 7:14); I called for a drought on the grain, wine, oil (Hag. 1:11); when one came to the wine vat to draw 50 measures there were only 20 (Hag. 2:16); when the wine failed his mother said, 'They have no wine' (John 2:3).

B2c Providing wine
Melchizedek brought bread and wine (Gen. 14:18); squeezing grapes into Pharaoh's cup (Gen. 40:11); Nehemiah served wine to the king (Neh. 2:1); wine for sacrifices is to be given to them (Ezra 6:9); give the Rechabites wine to drink (Jer. 35:2); the king allotted them a daily ration of the wine he drank (Dan. 1:5); how can I help? from the winepress? (2 Kgs. 6:27); they offered him wine mingled with gall (Matt. 27:34); when the steward tasted the water become wine (John 2:9-10).

B3 Use of wine
B3a Drinking wine
From the blood of grapes you drank wine (Deut. 32:14); I investigated wine (Eccles. 2:3); take a little wine for the sake of your stomach (1 Tim. 5:23); after fulfilling his vows the Nazirite may drink wine (Num. 6:20); Belshazzar drank wine in front of the 1000 nobles (Dan. 5:1); they drank the wine and praised the gods of gold and silver (Dan. 5:4); you and your nobles, wives and concubines drank wine from the vessels (Dan. 5:23); in the house of their God they drink the wine of those fined (Amos 2:8); you made the Nazirites drink wine (Amos 2:12); they will plant vineyards and drink their wine (Amos 9:14).

B3b Effect of wine
The vine would not leave its wine, which cheers God and men, to reign (Judg. 9:13); wine to make man's heart glad (Ps. 104:15); wine gladdens life (Eccles. 10:19); grain will make the young men flourish and new wine the virgins (Zech. 9:17); their hearts will be glad as from wine (Zech. 10:7); wine to make him forget his trouble (Prov. 31:6-7); wine is treacherous (Hab. 2:5); wine and new wine take away understanding (Hos. 4:11); those who try mixed wine (Prov. 23:30); they are full of sweet wine (Acts 2:13).

B3c Not drinking wine
You have not drunk wine or strong drink in the wilderness (Deut. 29:6); do not look on wine when it is red (Prov. 23:31); do not drink wine or strong drink when you come into the tent of meeting (Lev. 10:9); the Nazirite must not drink wine or strong drink (Num. 6:3); no meat or wine entered my mouth (Dan. 10:3); they will plant vineyards but not drink the wine (Zeph. 1:13); you planted pleasant vineyards but will not drink the wine (Amos 5:11); you will tread the grapes but not drink wine (Mic. 6:15); I will not drink of the fruit of the vine until the kingdom of God comes (Matt. 26:29; Mark 14:25; Luke 22:18); they offered him wine mixed with myrrh but he would not take it (Mark 15:23); it is good not to eat meat or drink wine or do anything to make your brother stumble (Rom. 14:21).

B4 Love and wine
He brought me into his house of wine (S. of S. 2:4); I would give you spiced wine (S. of S. 8:2); your mouth is like best wine (S. of S. 7:9); your love is better than wine (S. of S. 1:2; 4:10); we will extol your love more than wine (S. of S. 1:4).

B5 Metaphorical wine
You have given us wine to drink that made us stagger (Ps. 60:3); a cup of foaming wine is in the hand of the Lord (Ps. 75:8); God gave Babylon the cup of the wine of his fierce wrath (Rev. 16:19); he will drink of the wine of the wrath of God (Rev. 14:10); drunk with the wine of her immorality (Rev. 17:2); Babylon made the whole earth drink the wine of her immorality (Rev. 14:8); all nations have drunk the wine of her fornications (Rev. 18:3).

C Strong drink
Do not drink wine or strong drink when you go into the tent (Lev. 10:9); a Nazirite must not drink wine or

strong drink (Num. 6:3); drink no wine or strong drink (Judg. 13:4, 7, 14); a Nazirite must not drink vinegar made from wine or strong drink (Num. 6:3); a drink offering of strong drink (Num. 28:7); spend the money on what you desire, wine or strong drink (Deut. 14:26); I will preach of wine and strong drink (Mic. 2:11); I was the song of the drinkers of strong drink (Ps. 69:12); strong drink is a brawler (Prov. 20:1); they stagger with strong drink (Isa. 28:7); stagger, but not with strong drink (Isa. 29:9); it is not for princes to drink strong drink (Prov. 31:4); woe to those who rise early to run after strong drink (Isa. 5:11); woe to those who are strong men at mixing strong drink (Isa. 5:22); let us fill ourselves with strong drink (Isa. 56:12); strong drink is bitter to him who drinks it (Isa. 24:9); give strong drink to him who is perishing (Prov. 31:6); you have not drunk wine or strong drink (Deut. 29:6); I have drunk neither wine nor strong drink (1 Sam. 1:15).

DRUNKENNESS, see 949.

D Fruit juice
The Nazirite must not drink grape juice (Num. 6:3); from the blood of grapes you drank wine (Deut. 32:14); the juice of my pomegranates (S. of S. 8:2).

E Blood
E1 Lifeblood
FLOW OF BLOOD, see 302C.

BLOODSHED, see 362.

E1a Lifeblood in general
The life of the flesh is in the blood (Lev. 17:11); flesh with its life, its blood (Gen. 9:4); regulations concerning blood (Lev. 17:3-16); blood to be poured out and covered (Lev. 17:13); blood pollutes the land (Num. 35:33); his sweat was like drops of blood falling on the ground (Luke 22:44); you have not yet resisted to blood, striving against sin (Heb. 12:4); the sun will be turned into darkness and the moon into blood (Acts 2:20); hail and fire mixed with blood fell on the earth (Rev. 8:7).

E1b Human blood shed
Your brother's blood is crying to me (Gen. 4:10-11); they have poured out their blood like water (Ps. 79:3); your blood will be in the midst of the land (Ezek. 21:32); I will drench the land with your blood (Ezek. 32:6); her blood is on the bare rock, not on the ground covered with dust (Ezek. 24:7-8); in her was found the blood of prophets and saints (Rev. 18:24); their blood will be precious in his sight (Ps. 72:14); a woman had had a haemorrhage for 12 years (Matt. 9:20; Mark 5:25; Luke 8:43); when the blood of your witness Stephen was shed (Acts 22:20); the sprinkled blood which speaks better things than the blood of Abel (Heb. 12:24).

E1c Responsibility for blood shed
I will require your lifeblood (Gen. 9:5); his blood I will require at your hand (Ezek. 3:18, 20); whoever sheds man's blood, by man shall his blood be shed (Gen. 9:6); a man burdened with another's blood will be a fugitive until death (Prov. 28:17); I have betrayed innocent blood (Matt. 27:4); it is blood money (Matt. 27:6); his blood be on us and on our children! (Matt. 27:25); your blood be on your own heads! (Acts 18:6); the blood of all the prophets will be on this generation (Luke 11:50-1); avenging the blood of my servants the prophets (2 Kgs. 9:7); let there be vengeance for the blood of your servants (Ps. 79:10); how long before you judge and avenge our blood? (Rev. 6:10); he has avenged on her the blood of his slaves (Rev. 19:2); I am innocent of this man's blood (Matt. 27:24); I am innocent of the blood of all men (Acts 20:26).

E1d Covered with blood
They dipped Joseph's coat in goat blood (Gen. 37:31); their blood spattered my garments (Isa. 63:3); clothed in a robe dipped in blood (Rev. 19:13); a bridegroom of blood (Exod. 4:25, 26); Amasa wallowing in his blood (2 Sam. 20:12); Ahab's blood ran into the bottom of the chariot (1 Kgs. 22:35); I will make my arrows drunk with the blood of the slain (Deut. 32:42); I poured out their blood on the earth (Isa. 63:6); their land will be soaked with blood (Isa. 34:7); he will wash his feet in the blood of the wicked (Ps. 58:10); Field of Blood (Matt. 27:8; Acts 1:19); they cut themselves till the blood gushed out (1 Kgs. 18:28); Jezebel's blood splashed on the wall (2 Kgs. 9:33); pressing the nose produces blood (Prov. 30:33); the mountains will flow with their blood (Isa. 34:3); the sword of the Lord is filled with blood (Isa. 34:6); blood came out of the wine press of the wrath of God (Rev. 14:20).

E2 Consuming blood
E2a People consuming blood
You must not eat blood (Gen. 9:4; Lev. 3:17; 7:26-7; 17:10-12, 14; 19:26; Deut. 12:16, 23, 25; 15:23); abstain from blood (Acts 15:20, 29; 21:25); the people ate the animals with the blood (1 Sam. 14:32-4); you eat meat with the blood still in it (Ezek. 33:25); shall I drink the blood of these men? (2 Sam. 23:17; 1 Chr. 11:19); they poured out the blood of saints and prophets and you gave them blood to drink (Rev. 16:6); drunk with the blood of the saints and the martyrs of Jesus (Rev. 17:6); they will be drunk with their own blood (Isa. 49:26); he who eats my flesh and drinks my blood has eternal life (John 6:53-6).

BLOOD OF CHRIST, see 335E7.

E2b Creatures drinking blood
A lion drinks the blood of its prey (Num. 23:24); young eagles suck up blood (Job 39:30); assemble all birds and beasts to eat flesh and drink blood (Ezek. 39:17); drink blood until you are drunk (Ezek. 39:19); drink the blood of princes (Ezek. 39:18); dogs licking up Ahab's blood (1 Kgs. 21:19; 22:38).

E3 Turned to blood
Nile water turned to blood (Exod. 4:9; 7:17-20; Ps. 105:29); there was blood in all the land of Egypt (Exod. 7:21); he turned their rivers to blood (Ps. 78:44); a third of the sea turned into blood (Rev. 8:8); the sea turned into blood like that of a dead man (Rev. 16:3); rivers and springs became blood (Rev. 16:4); the witnesses have power to turn the waters into blood (Rev. 11:6); I will show signs in the sky and on earth, blood, fire and columns of smoke (Joel 2:30); blood, fire and vapour of smoke (Acts 2:19); the sun will be turned into darkness and the moon to blood (Joel 2:31); the moon became like blood (Rev. 6:12).

E4 Blood on the door
Blood was put on the door frame (Exod. 12:7, 22); when I see the blood I will pass over you (Exod. 12:13, 23).

E5 Blood of sacrifices
E5a Blood of sacrifices in general
Blood brought into the tent of meeting to make atonement (Lev. 6:30); the blood makes atonement (Lev. 17:11); without the shedding of blood there is no forgiveness (Heb. 9:22); under the law, all things are cleansed with blood (Heb. 9:22); when you offer my food, the fat and the blood (Ezek. 44:7); I do not delight in the blood of bulls, lambs and goats (Isa. 1:11); the high priest enters the inner tent once a year with blood (Heb. 9:7); the high priest enters the holy of holies with blood not his own (Heb. 9:25); animals whose blood is brought into the sanctuary (Heb. 13:11); it is impossible for the blood of bulls and goats to take away sins (Heb. 10:4).

E5b Blood on people / things
Blood on the horns of the altar of burnt offering (Exod. 29:12; Lev. 4:25; 8:15; 9:9); blood poured out round about the altar (Exod. 29:12; Lev. 1:15; 4:7; 8:15; 9:9); blood poured on the altar (Deut. 12:27); blood on the horns of the incense altar (Lev. 16:18); blood on the right ears, thumbs and toes for ordination (Exod. 29:20; Lev. 8:23, 24); blood on the right ears, thumbs and toes of a cleansed leper (Lev. 14:14, 25); the live bird dipped in blood (Lev. 14:6, 51).

E5c Blood sprinkled
Aaron and his sons were sprinkled with blood and oil (Exod. 29:21); he sprinkled the tent and the vessels with the blood (Heb. 9:21); sprinkling defiled people with the blood of goats and bulls (Heb. 9:13); he kept the Passover and the sprinkling of blood (Heb. 11:28); blood was sprinkled: on the altar of burnt offering (Exod. 24:6; 29:16; Lev. 1:5; 3:2; 5:9; 7:2; 8:19, 24; 9:12; Num. 18:17; 2 Chr. 29:22; Ezek. 43:18); on the altar of incense (Exod. 30:10; Lev. 4:7); on the people (Exod. 24:8); on priests (Lev. 8:30); seven times (Lev. 4:6, 17; 14:7; 16:14; Num. 19:4); by the priests (Lev. 7:14; 2 Chr. 30:16; 35:11); by Moses on the people (Heb. 9:19).

E6 Blood of the covenant
The blood of my covenant (Zech. 9:11); my blood of the covenant (Matt. 26:28; Mark 14:24); the new covenant in my blood (Luke 22:20; 1 Cor. 11:25); the blood of the covenant (Heb. 10:29); the blood of the eternal covenant (Heb. 13:20); the first covenant was not ratified without blood (Heb. 9:18); this is the blood of the covenant which God commanded you (Heb. 9:20).

E7 Blood of Christ
Redeemed by the precious blood of Christ (1 Pet. 1:19); redemption through his blood (Eph. 1:7); you were slain and by your blood ransomed men for God (Rev. 5:9); justified by his blood (Rom. 5:9); having made peace by the blood of his cross (Col. 1:20); he freed us from our sins by his blood (Rev. 1:5); taking not the blood of goats and calves but his own blood (Heb. 9:12-14); the blood of Christ cleanses the conscience (Heb. 9:14); the blood of Jesus cleanses us from all sin (1 John 1:7); for obedience to Jesus Christ and for sprinkling by his blood (1 Pet. 1:2); Jesus and the sprinkled blood (Heb. 12:24); blood and water came out (John 19:34); he who came by water and blood (1 John 5:6-8); brought near by the blood of Christ (Eph. 2:13); is not the cup a sharing in the blood of Christ? (1 Cor. 10:16); robes washed in the blood of the Lamb (Rev. 7:14); they overcame him by the blood of the Lamb (Rev. 12:11); the church of God which he purchased with his own blood (Acts 20:28); propitiation in his blood (Rom. 3:25); we enter the sanctuary through the blood of Jesus (Heb. 10:19); Jesus suffered outside the gate to sanctify the people with his own blood (Heb. 13:12).
CONSUMING BLOOD, see 335E2.

F Broth / soup
He put the broth in a pot (Judg. 6:19); pour the broth over the meat and cakes (Judg. 6:20); boil the meat, empty out the broth (Ezek. 24:10); broth of abominable things is in their vessels (Isa. 65:4).

G The cup of Jesus
Can you drink the cup I drink? (Matt. 20:22; Mark 10:38); let this cup pass from me (Matt. 26:39; Mark 14:36); shall I not drink the cup the Father has given me? (John 18:11).

336 Gaseousness
Getting treasures by lying is a driven vapour (Prov. 21:6).

AIR, see 340.

337 Liquefaction
The manna melted away (Exod. 16:21); he sends his word and melts the ice (Ps. 147:18); so that its filthiness may be melted within it (Ezek. 24:11); like wax before the fire, like water poured down a steep place (Mic. 1:4); mountains melt like wax before the Lord (Ps. 97:5); the wicked perish as wax melts before the fire (Ps. 68:2); my heart is like wax, melted within me (Ps. 22:14); the mountains will melt under the Lord (Mic. 1:4); mountains quake because of him, the hills melt (Nahum 1:5); God utters his voice and the earth melts (Ps. 46:6); the Lord touches the land and it melts (Amos 9:5); the wicked will melt away (Ps. 112:10); as metals are melted in the furnace, so I will melt you (Ezek. 22:20-2).

338 Vaporization
CLOUD, see 355.

339 Water
FLOWING WATER, see 350A.

A Water in general
The earth was made out of water and by water (2 Pet. 3:5); God separated the waters (Gen. 1:6-7); who measured the waters in the hollow of his hand? (Isa. 40:12); God measured out the waters (Job 28:25); who has wrapped the waters in his garment? (Prov. 30:4); the waters saw you and were afraid (Ps. 77:16); Moses – drawn out of the water (Exod. 2:10); he drew me out of the waters (2 Sam. 22:17; Ps. 18:16); cast your bread on the waters (Eccles. 11:1); they will throw your stones, timber and soil into the water (Ezek. 26:12); often he falls into the fire, and often into the water (Matt. 17:15; Mark 9:22); waves broke over the boat so it was filling with water (Mark 4:37); blood and water came out (John 19:34); eight people were brought safely through water (1 Pet. 3:20); the world was flooded with water and destroyed (2 Pet. 3:6).

B Supply of water
B1 God providing water
Water from the rock (Exod. 17:6; Num. 20:8-11; Deut. 8:15; Neh. 9:15; Ps. 78:15-16, 20; Isa. 48:21); he opened the rock and water gushed out (Ps. 105:41); he turned the rock into a fountain (Ps. 114:8); you gave them water for their thirst (Neh. 9:20); to give drink to my chosen people (Isa. 43:20); God gave the people water from a well at Beer (Num. 21:16); Israel will have abundant water (Num. 24:7); God split the hollow at Lehi and water came out (Judg. 15:19); the valley filled with water (2 Kgs. 3:17, 20); God opened springs and streams (Ps. 74:15); he sends springs in the valleys (Ps. 104:10); he changes the wilderness into a pool of water (Ps. 107:35); to him who thirsts I will give the water of life without cost (Rev. 21:6); out of his heart will flow rivers of living water (John 7:37); take the water of life without cost (Rev. 22:17).

B2 Man providing water
Give me a drink (Gen. 24:14, 17, 43, 45; John 4:7, 10); they gave the Egyptian water to drink (1 Sam. 30:11); giving a cup of cold water to a disciple (Matt. 10:42); he who gives you a cup of water because you bear the name of Christ (Mark 9:41); the Gibeonites became drawers of water (Josh. 9:21-7); my lovers give me my bread and water (Hos. 2:5); we will not drink your water (Num. 20:17; 21:22); if we drink water we will pay for it (Num. 20:19); how can you, a Jew, ask a drink of me, a Samaritan woman? (John 4:9); you gave me no water for my feet (Luke 7:44).

B3 Water for plants

Your mother was like a vine planted by the waters (Ezek. 19:10); he planted it beside abundant waters (Ezek. 17:5); it was planted by abundant waters (Ezek. 17:8); fruitful because of abundant waters (Ezek. 19:10); the cedar's roots extended to many waters (Ezek. 31:7); he will be like a tree planted by the water (Ps. 1:3; Jer. 17:8).

IRRIGATION, see 341C.

B4 Wells

God showed Hagar a well of water (Gen. 21:19); Abraham complained to Abimelech about a well (Gen. 21:25); a witness that I dug this well (Gen. 21:30); the Philistines had stopped up the wells (Gen. 26:15); Isaac dug again his father's wells (Gen. 26:18); Isaac's servants dug a well (Gen. 26:19, 25); Moses sat by the well in Midian (Exod. 2:15); spring up, O well! (Num. 21:17); David's messengers were hidden in the well (2 Sam. 17:18); I dug wells and drank foreign waters (2 Kgs. 19:24); a well of living water (S. of S. 4:15); with joy you will draw water from the wells of salvation (Isa. 12:3); Jesus sat by Jacob's well (John 4:6); our father Jacob gave us this well (John 4:12).

B5 Cisterns

Cisterns which you did not dig (Deut. 6:11); drink the water from your own cistern (2 Kgs. 18:31; Isa. 36:16); Uzziah hewed many cisterns (2 Chr. 26:10); they have hewn for themselves broken cisterns (Jer. 2:13); they let Jeremiah down into a cistern (Jer. 38:6-9).

C Using water

C1 Drinking water

The Egyptians dug around the Nile for drinking water (Exod. 7:24); Hezekiah brought water into the city (2 Kgs. 20:20); we have to pay for our own drinking water (Lam. 5:4); drink a sixth of a hin of water each day (Ezek. 4:11); they will drink water by measure and in horror (Ezek. 4:16); let us be given vegetables to eat and water to drink (Dan. 1:12); two or three cities would wander to another to drink water (Amos 4:8); send Lazarus to dip the tip of his finger in water (Luke 16:24); whoever drinks this water will thirst again (John 4:13); whoever drinks the water I give will never thirst again (John 4:14); no longer drink only water (1 Tim. 5:23).

C2 Water for baptism

I baptise with water (Matt. 3:11; Mark 1:8; Luke 3:16; John 1:26, 31); John baptised with water (Acts 1:5; 11:16); there was much water where John baptised (John 3:23); here is water! what is to prevent my being baptised? (Acts 8:36).

BAPTISM, see 988B2.

C3 Water for other ceremonies

Put water in the laver (Exod. 30:18); the water of cleansing (Num. 8:7); the water for impurity (Num. 19:9, 13, 20, 21; 31:23); holy water (Num. 5:17); sprinkle water over the Levites (Num. 8:7); the blood of calves and goats with water, scarlet wool and hyssop (Heb. 9:19); pass through the water what cannot stand the fire (Num. 31:23); I will sprinkle clean water on you and you will be clean (Ezek. 36:25); Pilate took water and washed his hands (Matt. 27:24); unless one is born of water and the Spirit he cannot enter the kingdom of God (John 3:5); the water for washing was made wine (John 2:6-10).

C4 Bad water

Water turned into blood (Exod. 4:9; 7:17-24; Rev. 8:8; 16:3, 4); you gave them blood to drink (Rev. 16:6); the waters of Marah were bitter (Exod. 15:23-5); Wormwood made the waters bitter (Rev. 8:11); the water is bad (2 Kgs. 2:19); Elisha purified the water with salt (2 Kgs. 2:21); the water of bitterness that brings a curse (Num. 5:18, 19, 24, 27); does a fountain put forth both fresh and bitter water? (Jas. 3:11); salt water cannot yield fresh (Jas. 3:12).

D Like water

Cursing soaked into his body like water (Ps. 109:18); pour out your heart like water before the Lord (Lam. 2:19); all hands will hang limp, all knees be like water (Ezek. 7:17); all hands will be feeble, every knee weak as water (Ezek. 21:7); wings like the sound of many waters (Ezek. 1:24); a voice like the sound of many waters (Rev. 1:15; 14:2; 19:6).

340 Atmosphere

A Air

Air cannot come between the crocodile's scales (Job 41:16); the seventh angel poured his bowl into the air (Rev. 16:17); we will meet the Lord in the air (1 Thess. 4:17).

B Weather

Predicting the weather (Luke 12:54-6); it will be fair weather for the sky is red (Matt. 16:2).

HOT WEATHER, see 379A.

COLD WEATHER, see 380A.

341 Moisture

A Moist things

A carcass falling on moist food makes it unclean (Lev. 11:34); a carcass falling on moist seed makes it unclean (Lev. 11:38); Hazael dipped the cloth in water and smothered Ben-hadad (2 Kgs. 8:15); she wet his feet with her tears (Luke 7:38); she wet my feet with tears (Luke 7:44).

B Dew

B1 Actual dew

God give you of the dew of heaven (Gen. 27:28); the heavens drop dew (Deut. 33:28); who has begotten the dew? (Job 38:28); by God's knowledge the skies drip dew (Prov. 3:20); dew in the morning (Exod. 16:13-14); the manna fell with the dew (Num. 11:9); may Joseph's land be blessed with dew (Deut. 33:13); the heavens will give their dew (Zech. 8:12); Gideon found dew on the fleece (Judg. 6:37, 38); and on the ground (Judg. 6:39, 40); my head is wet with dew (S. of S. 5:2); let him be wet with the dew of heaven (Dan. 4:15, 23, 25, 33; 5:21); because of you the heavens have withheld their dew (Hag. 1:10).

B2 Like the dew

Let my speech distill as the dew (Deut. 32:2); unity is like the dew of Hermon (Ps. 133:3); I will be like the dew to Israel (Hos. 14:5); the remnant will be like dew from the Lord (Mic. 5:7); a king's favour is like dew on the grass (Prov. 19:12); you have the dew of your youth (Ps. 110:3); your love is like the dew than vanishes (Hos. 6:4); they will be like the dew that vanishes (Hos. 13:3); like a dew-cloud in the heat of harvest (Isa. 18:4); we will fall on David like dew on the ground (2 Sam. 17:12).

C Irrigation

C1 Literal watering

A mist watered the ground (Gen. 2:6); a river watered the garden of Eden (Gen. 2:10); the Jordan valley was well-watered like Egypt (Gen. 13:10); Egypt was watered by the foot but the land of Israel drinks rain from heaven (Deut. 11:10-11); rain and snow water the earth (Isa. 55:10); the spring rains watering the earth (Hos. 6:3); a spring from the house of the Lord will water the valley of Shittim (Joel 3:18); God waters its furrows (Ps. 65:10); I water the vineyard every moment (Isa. 27:3); I made pools to water the trees (Eccles. 2:6); who sends rain on land which is unpeopled? (Job 38:26).

IRRIGATION CHANNEL, see 351.

C2 Metaphorical watering
You will be like a watered garden (Isa. 58:11); their life will be like a watered garden (Jer. 31:12); like showers that water the earth (Ps. 72:6); I planted and Apollos watered (1 Cor. 3:6-8).

342 Dryness

A Dry things
A1 Dry land
Let the dry land appear (Gen. 1:9); God called the dry land 'earth' (Gen. 1:10); all on the dry land perished (Gen. 7:22); the Israelites will cross the sea on dry ground (Exod. 14:16, 29); God turned the sea into dry land (Exod. 14:21-2; 15:19; Josh. 2:10; 4:23; Ps. 66:6); passing the Red Sea as on dry land (Neh. 9:11; Heb. 11:29); dry ground in the middle of the Jordan (Josh. 3:13, 17; 4:22-3; 5:1); Elisha and Elijah crossed the river on dry ground (2 Kgs. 2:8).

A2 Dry places
The vine is now planted in a dry and thirsty land (Ezek. 19:13); I knew you in the wilderness, in the land of drought (Hos. 13:5); I will drive the northerner into a parched and desolate land (Joel 2:20); the rebellious live in a parched land (Ps. 68:6); the wilderness, a land of drought and deep darkness (Jer. 2:6); a wilderness with no water (Deut. 8:15); in a dry and weary land with no water (Ps. 63:1); he will make Nineveh a desolation, a dry waste like the wilderness (Zeph. 2:13); you will be like a garden without water (Isa. 1:30); the pastures of the wilderness are dried up (Jer. 23:10); the unclean spirit passes through waterless places (Matt. 12:43; Luke 11:24); like a root out of dry ground (Isa. 53:2); your mother will be least of the nations, a wilderness, parched land (Jer. 50:12); her cities have become a parched land and a desert (Jer. 51:43); sit on the parched ground, inhabitant of Dibon (Jer. 48:18); pour water on the dry ground (Exod. 4:9); he turns dry land into springs of water (Ps. 107:35).
WILDERNESS, see 172D.

A3 Other dry things
The dead bones were very dry (Ezek. 37:2); what will happen when the wood is dry? (Luke 23:31); a fire will consume every green tree and every dry tree (Ezek. 20:47); I make the dry tree flourish (Ezek. 17:24); give them a miscarrying womb and dry breasts (Hos. 9:14).

B Without water
B1 Drying up
FAILING RIVERS, see 350C3.

B1a Waters drying up
When it is hot the waters vanish (Job 6:17); drought and heat consume the snow waters (Job 24:19); the water was dried up from the earth (Gen. 8:13-14); the brook Cherith dried up (1 Kgs. 17:7); the Nile will dry up (Isa. 19:5-7); the water brooks are dried up (Joel 1:20); a drought on her waters that they may be dried up (Jer. 50:38); his fountain will dry up, his spring become dry (Hos. 13:15); the depths of the Nile will dry up (Zech. 10:11); the water of the Euphrates dried up (Rev. 16:12).

B1b God drying things up
God restrains the waters and they dry up (Job 12:15); God dries up sea and rivers (Nahum 1:4); God tells the rivers to dry up (Isa. 44:27); God turns rivers into a desert (Ps. 107:33); he turns springs of water into thirsty ground (Ps. 107:33); you dried up ever-flowing streams (Ps. 74:15); God turned the sea into dry land (Exod. 14:21-2; 15:19; Josh. 2:10; 4:23; Ps. 66:6); he rebuked the Dead Sea and it dried up (Ps. 106:9); God dried up the sea (Isa. 51:10); God dried up the Jordan like the Red Sea (Josh. 4:23); I dry up the sea with my rebuke (Isa. 50:2); I will dry up the Nile (Ezek. 30:12); the Lord will

dry up the River (Isa. 11:15); I will dry up the pools (Isa. 42:15); I will dry up her sea and make her fountain dry (Jer. 51:36).

B1c People drying things up
Stopping all springs of water (2 Kgs. 3:19, 25); Hezekiah stopped the springs outside Jerusalem (2 Chr. 32:3, 4); with my foot I dried up the rivers of Egypt (2 Kgs. 19:24; Isa. 37:25); she wiped his feet with the hair of her head (Luke 7:38); she wet my feet with tears and wiped them with her hair (Luke 7:44); Jesus wiped their feet with the towel (John 13:5).

B1d Similar to things drying up
Let them vanish like water that runs away (Ps. 58:7); my friends have been like the vanishing waters of a wadi (Job 6:15); will you be to me like waters that fail? (Jer. 15:18); they say, 'Our bones are dried up, our hope lost' (Ezek. 37:11); gladness dries up from the sons of men (Joel 1:12); as a river becomes dried up so man lies down and does not rise (Job 14:11-12); springs without water (2 Pet. 2:17).

B2 No water for people
The skin of water was used up (Gen. 21:15); no water for the Israelites (Exod. 15:22; 17:1; Num. 20:2, 5; 21:5; 33:14); the army had no water (2 Kgs. 3:9); my throat is parched (Ps. 69:3); the Lord will take away the support of water from Jerusalem (Isa. 3:1); bread and water will be scarce (Ezek. 4:17).

B3 Lack of rain or dew
I will command the clouds not to rain on it (Isa. 5:6); clouds without water (Jude 12); like clouds and wind without rain is a man who boasts of non-existent gifts (Prov. 25:14); away from the dew of heaven (Gen. 27:39); let no dew or rain be on you (2 Sam. 1:21); no rain because the people have sinned (1 Kgs. 8:35; 2 Chr. 6:26); if I shut the heavens so there is no rain (2 Chr. 7:13); Elijah prayed that it would not rain and for three years and six months it did not (Jas. 5:17); when the sky was shut up for three years and six months (Luke 4:25); the two witnesses have power to stop the rain (Rev. 11:6); the showers and spring rain have been withheld (Jer. 3:3); you are a land without rain in the day of indignation (Ezek. 22:24); if they do not go up to worship, there will be no rain on them (Zech. 14:17); if the family of Egypt do not go up, there will be no rain on them (Zech. 14:18); because of you the heavens have withheld their dew (Hag. 1:10).

B4 Drought
If they do not obey, the Lord will send drought (Deut. 11:17); the Lord will strike you with drought (Deut. 28:22-4); I called for a drought (Hag. 1:11); God sent drought on some towns (Amos 4:7-8); Elijah announced the drought (1 Kgs. 17:1); Jeremiah on the drought (Jer. 14:1-6); a drought on her waters that they may be dried up (Jer. 50:38); drought and heat consume the snow waters (Job 24:19); the wilderness, a land of drought and deep darkness (Jer. 2:6); he is not anxious in a year of drought (Jer. 17:8).

B5 Seeking water
The Egyptians tired themselves trying to find water (Exod. 7:18); when the poor and needy seek water and there is none (Isa. 41:17); they have come to the cisterns and find no water (Jer. 14:3).

C Withering
C1 Limbs withered
The king's hand withered (1 Kgs. 13:4); a man with a withered hand (Matt. 12:10; Mark 3:1; Luke 6:6); he said to the man with the withered hand, 'Rise' (Mark 3:3).

C2 People withered
Their skin is shriveled on their bones, like wood (Lam. 4:8); evildoers will wither like the grass (Ps. 37:2); my heart is smitten like grass and withered (Ps. 102:4); God

has shrivelled me up (Job 16:8); scarcely are they
planted when he blows on them and they wither (Isa.
40:24); you will be like an oak whose leaf withers (Isa.
1:30); we all wither like a leaf (Isa. 64:6); I wither like
grass (Ps. 102:11); Ephraim's root is dried up, they will
bear no fruit (Hos. 9:16); his roots dry up below and
his branches above (Job 18:16); because they had no
root they withered away (Matt. 13:6; Mark 4:6); if
anyone does not abide in me he is thrown away and
withers (John 15:6).

C3 Grass withered
Evildoers will wither like the grass (Ps. 37:2); my heart
is smitten like grass and withered (Ps. 102:4); I wither
like grass (Ps. 102:11); like grass on the housetops which
withers before it grows up (Ps. 129:6); the grass is
withered (Isa. 15:6); the grass withers, the flower fades
(Isa. 40:7, 8; 1 Pet. 1:24); the sun withers the grass (Jas.
1:11).

C4 Other things withered
Without water, papyrus and rushes soon wither (Job
8:12); I will wither all their vegetation (Isa. 42:15); how
long must the vegetation wither? (Jer. 12:4); the leaf will
wither (Jer. 8:13); the fig tree withered (Matt. 21:19-20;
Mark 11:20-1); will he not pull up the vine so that it
withers? (Ezek. 17:9-10); the vine was plucked up and
withered (Ezek. 19:12); the host of heaven will wither
like a leaf from the vine (Isa. 34:4); the trees of the field
wilted on account of it (Ezek. 31:15); the grain is dried
up (Joel 1:17); the pomegranate, palm, apple tree and all
the trees dry up (Joel 1:12); the vine withers and the fig
tree fails (Joel 1:12); the worm attacked the plant and it
withered (Jonah 4:7); since it had no root it withered
away (Mark 4:6; Luke 8:6).

C5 Not withering
His leaf will not wither (Ps. 1:3); their leaves will not
wither nor their fruit fail (Ezek. 47:12).

343 Seas
A About the seas
A1 The seas in general
Have you entered the springs of the sea? (Job 38:16); he
has founded the earth upon the seas (Ps. 24:2); rivers
run into the sea yet the sea is not full (Eccles. 1:7); there
is the sea, great and wide (Ps. 104:25); do horses run on
rocks or does one plough the sea with oxen? (Amos
6:12); the deep sounded its voice (Hab. 3:10); let the sea
roar (1 Chr. 16:32); I will set his hand on the sea (Ps.
89:25); a place of two seas (Acts 27:41); though he has
escaped from the sea, justice has not allowed him to
live (Acts 28:4); do not harm the earth or sea or trees
until we have sealed the slaves of God (Rev. 7:3); woe to
you, earth and sea, for the devil has come down to you
(Rev. 12:12).

A2 Creation of the seas
In six days the Lord made heaven, earth and sea and
everything in them (Exod. 20:11); you made the seas
and all in them (Neh. 9:6); he who made the sea and
everything in it (Ps. 146:6); a living God who made
heaven and earth and sea (Acts 14:15); you made them
heaven and earth and sea and everything in them (Acts
4:24); the gathering of the waters he called 'seas' (Gen.
1:10); God brought the sea to birth (Job 38:8-9); God
pours the water of the sea on the earth (Amos 5:8; 9:6);
when God set limits for the sea (Prov. 8:29); God
covers the roots of the sea (Job 36:30); the sea is his for
he made it (Ps. 95:5); the Lord God of heaven who
made the sea and the dry land (Jonah 1:9); he who
created the heavens, earth and sea (Rev. 10:6); worship
him who made the heaven and earth, the sea and
springs of water (Rev. 14:7).
LIMITS OF THE SEA, see 236C.

A3 Expanse of the sea
If I dwell in the uttermost parts of the sea (Ps. 139:9);
the commandment is not out of reach across the sea
(Deut. 30:13); from sea to sea (Mic. 7:12); they will
wander from sea to sea and from north to east (Amos
8:12); though they hide from my sight at the bottom of
the sea (Amos 9:3); his dominion will be from sea to
sea (Zech. 9:10).

A4 In the middle of the sea
I sit in the seat of gods in the heart of the seas (Ezek.
28:2); you will throw all their sins into the depths of the
sea (Mic. 7:19); you will die the death of those slain in
the heart of the seas (Ezek. 28:8); you will be like one
who lies down in the middle of the sea (Prov. 23:34);
Tyre's borders are in the heart of the seas (Ezek. 27:4);
the Lord will cast Tyre's wealth into the sea (Ezek. 9:4);
the angel threw the stone into the sea (Rev. 18:21);
better to be cast into the sea (Matt. 18:6; Mark 9:42;
Luke 17:2); throwing Jonah into the sea (Jonah 1:12, 15;
2:3); if you say to this mountain, 'Be taken up and cast
into the sea' (Matt. 21:21; Mark 11:23; Luke 17:6); a night
and a day I have been adrift at sea (2 Cor. 11:25); in
danger at sea (2 Cor. 11:26).

A5 Sea dwellers
Let the waters teem with creatures (Gen. 1:20-2); praise
the Lord, sea monsters (Ps. 148:7); let the seas and
everything in them praise him (Ps. 69:34); four beasts
came out of the sea (Dan. 7:3); creatures with fins and
scales in the sea you may eat (Lev. 11:9, 10); Zebulun to
have the abundance of the seas (Deut. 33:19); the
abundance of the sea will be turned to you (Isa. 60:5);
those who go down to the sea (Isa. 42:10); those who go
down to the sea in ships (Ps. 107:23).

A6 Like the sea
Your judgements are like the great deep (Ps. 36:6); the
earth will be full of the knowledge of the Lord as the
waters cover the sea (Isa. 11:9); the earth will be full of
the knowledge of the glory of the Lord as the waters
cover the sea (Hab. 2:14); the wicked are like the tossing
sea (Isa. 57:20); they are wild waves of the sea (Jude 13);
he who doubts is like a wave of the sea tossed by the
wind (Jas. 1:6); your righteousness would have been
like waves of the sea (Isa. 48:18).

B Affecting the seas
B1 The sea stirred up
All the springs of the great deep were broken open
(Gen. 7:11); the wind lifted up the waves of the sea (Ps.
107:25); the four winds of heaven stirred up the sea
(Dan. 7:2); let the sea roar and all it contains (Ps. 96:11;
98:7); though the sea roars and foams (Ps. 46:3); I am
the Lord who stirs up the sea (Isa. 51:15); God stirs up
the sea so that its waves roar (Jer. 31:35); the nations
will be perplexed by the roaring of the sea (Luke 21:25);
the crocodile makes the depths boil, the sea like
ointment (Job 41:31-2); the boat was beaten by the
waves (Matt. 14:24); the sea rose because a strong wind
was blowing (John 6:18).

B2 The sea controlled
The Lord has stretched out his hand over the sea (Isa.
23:11); God treads the waves of the sea (Job 9:8); saying
to the depth of the sea, 'Be dried up!' (Isa. 44:27); here
shall your proud waves stop (Job 38:11); he will strike
the waves of the sea (Zech. 10:11); I will bring them
back from the depths of the sea (Ps. 68:22); the sea gave
up the dead in it (Rev. 20:13); I placed the sand as the
boundary of the sea (Jer. 5:22); Jesus came to them
walking on the sea (Matt. 14:25); he placed his right
foot on the sea and his left on the earth (Rev. 10:2); the
angel standing on sea and land (Rev. 10:5, 8); there was
no more sea (Rev. 21:1).

B3 The sea divided

You divided the sea (Neh. 9:11; Ps. 74:13); he divided the sea (Ps. 78:13); he divided the Red Sea (Ps. 136:13); your way was through the sea (Ps. 77:19); the Lord makes a way through the sea (Isa. 43:16); did you not make the depths of the sea a pathway for the redeemed? (Isa. 51:10).

B4 The sea stilled

They threw Jonah into the sea and the sea stopped its raging (Jonah 1:15); you still the roaring of the sea (Ps. 89:9); you still the roaring of the sea, the tumult of the peoples (Ps. 65:7); God stilled the sea by his power (Job 26:12); the springs of the deep were closed (Gen. 8:2); the waves of the sea were hushed (Ps. 107:29); he rebuked the winds and the sea (Matt. 8:26-7; Mark 4:39-41; Luke 8:24-5); that no wind might blow on earth or sea or tree (Rev. 7:1).

B5 The sea turned to blood

A burning mountain thrown into the sea and a third of the sea became blood (Rev. 8:8); the bowl was poured into the sea and it became blood (Rev. 16:3).

C Particular seas

C1 The Dead Sea

The valley of Siddim, the Salt Sea (Gen. 14:3); the sea of the Arabah (Deut. 4:49; 2 Kgs. 14:25); the sea of the Arabah, the Salt Sea [Dead Sea] (Josh. 3:16; 12:3); the waters flow into the sea and make the sea fresh (Ezek. 47:8).

C2 Sea of Galilee [Gennesaret / Tiberias / Chinnereth / Chinneroth]

Jesus settled in Capernaum by the sea (Matt. 4:13, 15); walking by the sea of Galilee (Matt. 4:18; 15:29; Mark 1:16); Jesus sat by the sea (Matt. 13:1); he was standing by the lake of Gennesaret (Luke 5:1); Jesus withdrew with his disciples to the sea (Mark 3:7); Jesus went to the other side of the sea of Galilee, the sea of Tiberias (John 6:1); Jesus appeared at the sea of Tiberias (John 21:1); Jesus was beside the sea (Mark 5:21); he went through Sidon to the Sea of Galilee (Mark 7:31).

C3 Mediterranean

The Great Sea [Mediterranean] (Josh. 15:12, 47); the coast of the Great Sea towards Lebanon (Josh. 9:1); the western sea (Deut. 11:24; 34:2); look towards the sea (1 Kgs. 18:43); fish of many kinds, like the fish of the Great Sea (Ezek. 47:10); I will drive their rear into the western sea (Joel 2:20); living water flowing half to the eastern sea and half to the western (Zech. 14:8).

C4 The Red Sea / Sea of Reeds

C4a Coming to the Red Sea

To the Red Sea (Exod. 13:18; Josh. 24:6-7; Judg. 11:16); encamping by the sea (Exod. 14:2, 9; Num. 33:10-11); turn back by the way of the Red Sea (Num. 14:25; Deut. 1:40); they went by the way of the Red Sea (Num. 21:4; Deut. 2:1); stretch out your hand over the sea (Exod. 14:16, 26-7); God did awesome things by the Red Sea (Ps. 106:22); Moses performed wonders and signs at the Red Sea (Acts 7:36); they rebelled by the Red Sea (Ps. 106:7); by faith they passed through the Red Sea (Heb. 11:29).

C4b A way through the Red Sea

Moses stretched out his hand over the sea and the Lord turned it to dry land (Exod. 14:21); the Lord dried up the water of the Red Sea (Josh. 2:10; 4:23; Ps. 106:9); he divided the Red Sea (Ps. 136:13); the sea looked and fled (Ps. 114:3, 5); did you not dry up the sea? (Isa. 51:10); they passed through the middle of the sea (Num. 33:8); all our fathers passed through the sea (1 Cor. 10:1); our fathers were all baptised into Moses in the cloud and the sea (1 Cor. 10:2).

C4c Egypt overthrown at the Red Sea

He overthrew Pharaoh and his army in the Red Sea (Ps. 136:15); horse and rider he threw into the sea (Exod. 15:1, 21); the Red Sea engulfed the Egyptians (Deut. 11:4); the sea engulfed their enemies (Ps. 78:53).

C5 Adriatic Sea

We were drifting across the sea of Adria (Acts 27:27).

C6 The 'sea'

The 'sea' made (1 Kgs. 7:23-6, 39, 44; 1 Chr. 18:8; 2 Chr. 4:2, 15; Jer. 27:19); the 'sea' for the priests to wash in (2 Chr. 4:6); the 'sea' placed on the right of the house (2 Chr. 4:10); Ahaz removed it from the oxen under it (2 Kgs. 16:17); the 'sea' broken up and taken away (2 Kgs. 25:13, 16; Jer. 52:17, 20).

C7 Sea of glass

A sea of glass (Rev. 4:6); a sea of glass mixed with fire (Rev. 15:2).

344 Land

THE EARTH, see 321A2.

A Earth

The ground cursed through Adam (Gen. 3:17); toil because of the ground the Lord has cursed (Gen. 5:29); Cain was cursed from the ground (Gen. 4:10-11); until you return to the ground for from it you were taken (Gen. 3:19); to till the ground from which he was taken (Gen. 3:23); fire consumed the great deep and began to consume the land (Amos 7:4); I will shake the land and the dry land (Hag. 2:6); make an altar of earth (Exod. 20:24); Naaman asked for two mules' burden of earth (2 Kgs. 5:17); immediately it sprang up because it had no depth of soil (Matt. 13:5; Mark 4:5); some seeds fell into good soil (Matt. 13:8; Mark 4:8; Luke 8:8); those sown on the good soil (Matt. 13:23; Mark 4:20; Luke 8:15).

DRY LAND, see 342A1.

B Stones / rocks

B1 Stones in general

You will be in league with the stones of the field (Job 5:23); water wears away stones (Job 14:19); a time to throw stones and a time to gather stones (Eccles. 3:5); a millstone is not to be taken in pledge (Deut. 24:6); God is able to raise up children to Abraham from these stones (Matt. 3:9; Luke 3:8); a stone is heavy but a fool's anger is heavier (Prov. 27:3); do horses run on rocks or does one plough the sea with oxen? (Amos 6:12); no pebble will fall to the earth (Amos 9:9); rocks are broken by him (Nahum 1:6); the stone will cry out from the wall (Hab. 2:11); the stones would cry out (Luke 19:40); woe to him who says to a dumb stone, 'Arise!' (Hab. 2:19); rocks were split when Jesus died (Matt. 27:51); Joseph of Arimathea had dug his own new tomb in the rock (Matt. 27:60; Mark 15:46; Luke 23:53); fearing that we might run on to the rocks (Acts 27:29).

PRECIOUS STONES, see 844A.

B2 Particular stones

Ebenezer – stone of help (1 Sam. 7:12); the Rock of Escape (1 Sam. 23:28); Samson lived in the cleft of the rock at Etam (Judg. 15:8, 11); Jacob set up a stone called Witness (Gen. 31:45-7); one crag was called Bozez and the other Seneh (1 Sam. 14:4).

B3 Stones for building

B3a Building with stones

Stones for the altar must not be cut (Exod. 20:25); preparing stones for the temple (1 Chr. 22:2); Solomon had 80 000 hewers of stone in the mountains (1 Kgs. 5:15); they quarried large stones (1 Kgs. 5:17); the stones were prepared at the quarry (1 Kgs. 6:7); building the temple with huge stones (Ezra 5:8); three rows of cut stone (1 Kgs. 6:36); three courses of huge stones (Ezra

6:4); costly stones, cut to measure (1 Kgs. 7:9-11); the
foundation of stones (1 Kgs. 7:10); you built
houses of hewn stone but will not live in them (Amos
5:11); he will bring forth the top stone with shouts of
'Grace, grace to it!' (Zech. 4:7); your servants hold dear
the stones of Zion (Ps. 102:14); the wise man built his
house on a rock (Matt. 7:24-5; Luke 6:48); what
wonderful stones and wonderful buildings! (Mark 13:1);
Christ Jesus himself being the cornerstone (Eph. 2:20).

B3b Building stones rejected
Tear out the diseased stones from the house (Lev.
14:40); there will not be one stone left on another
(Matt. 24:2; Mark 13:2; Luke 19:44; 21:6); they will not
take from you a stone for a corner or foundation (Jer.
51:26).

B4 Beneficial stones
B4a Stones for protection
He set my feet on a rock (Ps. 40:2); he will lift me up
on a rock (Ps. 27:5); you who live in the cleft of the
rock (Obad. 3); they climb among the rocks [to hide]
(Jer. 4:29); enter the rock from the terror of the Lord
(Isa. 2:10); they called to the rocks to fall on them and
hide them (Rev. 6:16).

B4b Provision from rock
Water out of the rock (Deut. 8:15; Isa. 48:21); he turned
the rock into a pool of water (Ps. 114:8); he brought
them streams from the rock (Ps. 78:16); he opened
the rock and water gushed out (Ps. 105:41); strike the rock
(Exod. 17:6); he struck the rock (Ps. 78:20); speak to the
rock (Num. 20:8); but he struck it twice (Num. 20:11);
they all drank from the spiritual rock (1 Cor. 10:4);
honey from the rock (Ps. 81:16); honey and oil from the
rock (Deut. 32:13); the rock poured out streams of oil
(Job 29:6); command these stones to become bread
(Matt. 4:3; Luke 4:3); if a son asks for a loaf, who will
give him a stone? (Matt. 7:9).

B4c Stones as monuments
Jacob used a stone as a pillow (Gen. 28:11); and set it up
at Bethel (Gen. 28:18); this stone will be the house of
God (Gen. 28:22); Jacob set up a pillar of stone (Gen.
35:14); they gathered stones to make a heap (Gen.
31:46); 12 stones taken from the Jordan (Josh. 4:3-9);
the 12 stones set up at Gilgal (Josh. 4:20); Joshua set up
a stone as witness (Josh. 24:26-7); write the law on large
stones (Deut. 27:2-3); a letter written not on tablets of
stone but on tablets of human hearts (2 Cor. 3:3).
HEAP OF STONES, see 209B.
PILLAR, see 218C.
MONUMENTS, see 548A.

B5 Stones as stoppers
A large stone over the well (Gen. 29:2); they roll the
stone from the mouth of the well (Gen. 29:8); Jacob
rolled the stone from the mouth of the well (Gen.
29:10); stones rolled over the mouth of the cave (Josh.
10:18, 27); a stone over the mouth of the lions' den
(Dan. 6:17); a stone rolled over the tomb (Matt. 27:60;
Mark 15:46; John 11:38); who will roll away the stone?
(Mark 16:3); the stone was rolled away from the tomb
(Matt. 28:2; Mark 16:4; Luke 24:2; John 20:1).

B6 Harmful stones
B6a Stones in the way
Clear the highway of stones (Isa. 62:10); he removed
the stones (Isa. 5:2); spoil every good piece of land with
stones (2 Kgs. 3:19, 25); some seeds fell on stony ground
(Matt. 13:5, 20; Mark 4:5, 16; Luke 8:6); fearing we
might run on the rocks (Acts 27:29); these men are
sunken reefs in your love-feasts (Jude 12).

B6b Struck with stones
He who strikes someone with a stone or his fist (Exod.
21:18); if he struck him with a stone (Num. 35:17); if he
threw a stone accidentally (Num. 35:23); lest you strike

your foot against a stone (Ps. 91:12; Matt. 4:6; Luke
4:11); night and day he was crying out and gashing
himself with stones (Mark 5:5).

B6c Killed by a rock
Abimelech killed 70 men on one stone (Judg. 9:5, 18); a
millstone was thrown down on Abimelech (Judg. 9:53;
2 Sam. 11:21); animals slaughtered on a big rock (1 Sam.
14:33-4); happy he who dashes your little ones against a
rock (Ps. 137:9); everyone who falls on that stone will
be broken to pieces (Luke 20:18); better a millstone
hung round his neck (Matt. 18:6; Mark 9:42; Luke 17:2).

B6d Slinging stones
700 men could sling a stone at a hair (Judg. 20:16);
David slung a stone (1 Sam. 17:49-50); Uzziah made
engines for shooting great stones (2 Chr. 26:14-15).

B6e Instructions about stoning
Stone the one who entices you to serve other gods
(Deut. 13:10); stone one who has served other gods
(Deut. 17:5); stone the rebellious son (Deut. 21:21);
stone the girl found not to be a virgin when married
(Deut. 22:21); stone the man and woman who commit
adultery (Deut. 22:24); in the law Moses commanded
us to stone such women (John 8:5); if even a beast
touches the mountain, it will be stoned (Heb. 12:20); he
must be stoned or shot (Exod. 19:13); stone one who
gives his children to Molech (Lev. 20:2); stone a
medium or spiritist (Lev. 20:27); all the congregation
shall stone the blasphemer (Lev. 24:14, 16); stone an ox
which gores a person to death (Exod. 21:28, 29, 32); if
anyone is without sin let him be the first to cast a stone
(John 8:7).

B6f Fear of stoning
Will the Egyptians not stone us? (Exod. 8:26); a little
more and they will stone me (Exod. 17:4); they wanted
to stone Joshua and Caleb (Num. 14:10); the people
spoke of stoning David (1 Sam. 30:6); they picked up
stones to throw at Jesus (John 8:59; 10:31-3); the
Gentiles and Jews tried to stone the apostles (Acts 14:5);
the people will stone us, for they are convinced that
John was a prophet (Luke 20:6); lest they should be
stoned (Acts 5:26).

B6g Actual stoning
They stoned the blasphemer to death (Lev. 24:23); they
stoned the sabbath-breaker to death (Num. 15:35, 36);
Achan's family were burned and stoned (Josh. 7:25);
Shimei threw stones (2 Sam. 16:6, 13); Israel stoned
Adoram to death (1 Kgs. 12:18; 2 Chr. 10:18); stoning
Naboth to death (1 Kgs. 21:10, 13, 14, 15); they stoned
Zechariah the son of Jehoiada (2 Chr. 24:21); they
stoned Stephen (Acts 7:58-9); they stoned Paul (Acts
14:19); once I was stoned (2 Cor. 11:25); some were
stoned (Heb. 11:37); killing the prophets and stoning
those sent to you! (Matt. 23:37; Luke 13:34).

B7 Various stones
They set Moses on a stone (Exod. 17:12); the ark came
to rest by a large stone (1 Sam. 6:14-15); the large stone
is a witness to this day (1 Sam. 6:18); an angel took up a
stone like a millstone (Rev. 18:21); the guardian cherub
drove you from the stones of fire (Ezek. 28:16); you
walked in the midst of the stones of fire (Ezek. 28:14);
to him who overcomes I will give a white stone with a
name written on it (Rev. 2:17).

B8 Metaphorical rocks
B8a God the rock
God the rock (Deut. 32:4); the Lord my rock (Ps. 144:1);
O Lord, my rock (Ps. 19:14); there is no rock like our
God (1 Sam. 2:2); the Lord God is an everlasting rock
(Isa. 26:4); their rock is not like our rock (Deut. 32:31);
there is no other rock (Isa. 44:8); the rock of Israel
(Gen. 49:24; 2 Sam. 23:3; Isa. 30:29); the rock of his
salvation (Deut. 32:15); the rock of my salvation (Ps.

89:26); the rock of our salvation (Ps. 95:1); the rock that begot you (Deut. 32:18); they remembered that God was their rock (Ps. 78:35); who is a rock besides our God? (2 Sam. 22:32; Ps. 18:31); God my rock (Ps. 42:9); my rock (2 Sam. 22:3; Ps. 18:2; 28:1; 31:3; 71:3; 92:15); my rock and my salvation (2 Sam. 22:2, 47; Ps. 18:46; 62:2, 6); my strong rock (Ps. 62:7); be a rock of strength to me (Ps. 31:2); be a rock of habitation to me (Ps. 71:3); my God is the rock of my refuge (Ps. 94:22).

B8b Christ the rock
The stone the builders rejected has become the head stone (Ps. 118:22; Matt. 21:42; Mark 12:10; Luke 20:17; 1 Pet. 2:7); this is the stone rejected by you builders (Acts 4:11); a stone of stumbling (Isa. 8:14; Rom. 9:33; 1 Pet. 2:8); a precious and trustworthy cornerstone (Isa. 28:16; 1 Pet. 2:6); a stone was cut out without hands (Dan. 2:34-5, 45); the rock which followed them was Christ (1 Cor. 10:4); a living stone (1 Pet. 2:4).

B8c Gods as rocks
Our rock is not like their rock (Deut. 32:31); where is the rock in which they sought refuge? (Deut. 32:37); Judah committed adultery with stones and trees (Jer. 3:9).

B8d People as rocks
Simon was named Cephas, Peter, the rock (John 1:42); you are Peter, and on this rock I will build my church (Matt. 16:18); the holy stones are poured out at the head of every street (Lam. 4:1); living stones built into a spiritual house (1 Pet. 2:5); look to Abraham, the rock from which you were hewn (Isa. 51:1-2).

C Sand and gravel
I placed the sand as the boundary of the sea (Jer. 5:22); Moses hid the Egyptian in the sand (Exod. 2:12); the foolish man built his house on sand (Matt. 7:26); I will multiply your seed as the sand of the seashore (Gen. 22:17); I will make you as the sand of the sea (Gen. 32:12); your offspring would have been like the sand (Isa. 48:19); descendants innumerable as the sand by the seashore (Heb. 11:12); Judah and Israel were as many as the sand on the seashore (1 Kgs. 4:20); as the sand of the sea cannot be measured (Jer. 33:22); though Israel be like the sand of the sea (Isa. 10:22); the number of the sons of Israel will be like the sand of the sea (Hos. 1:10); the number of their army is like the sand of the seashore (Rev. 20:8); troops like the sand of the seashore in number (Josh. 11:4; 1 Sam. 13:5); the Midianites etc. were like the sand of the seashore (Judg. 7:12); he rained birds on them like the sand of the seas (Ps. 78:27); the grain was like the sand of the sea (Gen. 41:49); God gave Solomon wisdom like the sand on the seashore (1 Kgs. 4:29); I will multiply my days like the sand (Job 29:18).

D Clay
Cast in the clay ground (1 Kgs. 7:46; 2 Chr. 4:17); the feet of the statue were partly of iron and partly of clay (Dan. 2:33-4); as the toes of the feet were partly iron and partly clay (Dan. 2:41-3, 45); you made me like clay (Job 10:9); I too have been made out of clay (Job 33:6); you are like clay in the potter's hand (Jer. 18:6); we are the clay, you are the potter (Isa. 64:8); shall the potter be regarded as equal to the clay? (Isa. 29:16); does the potter have no right over the clay? (Rom. 9:21); he will come on rulers as a potter treads clay (Isa. 41:25); we have this treasure in earthenware vessels (2 Cor. 4:7); Jesus spat on the ground and made clay (John 9:6-15).

345 Gulf: inlet
The bay which faces south (Josh. 15:2); the bay of the sea at the mouth of the Jordan (Josh. 15:5); they noticed a bay with a beach (Acts 27:39).

346 Lake
The conduit of the upper pool (2 Kgs. 18:17); Hezekiah made the pool and the conduit (2 Kgs. 20:20); you collected the waters of the lower pool (Isa. 22:9); you made a reservoir between the walls (Isa. 22:11); the artificial pool (Neh. 3:16); Nineveh was like a pool whose waters run away (Nahum 2:8); I will make the wilderness a pool of water (Isa. 41:18); the scorched land will become a pool (Isa. 35:7); the pool of Bethesda [Bethzatha, Bethsaida] (John 5:2); the pool of Siloam (John 9:7, 11); the lake of fire which burns with brimstone (Rev. 19:20); the lake of fire and brimstone (Rev. 20:10); the lake of fire is the second death (Rev. 20:14); the lake which burns with fire and brimstone, which is the second death (Rev. 21:8).

347 Marsh
The hippopotamus lies down in the marsh (Job 40:21); the crocodile spreads himself like a threshing sledge on the mire (Job 41:30); can papyrus grow without marsh? (Job 8:11); its swamps and marshes will not become fresh, but left for salt (Ezek. 47:11); Tyre amassed gold like the mire of the streets (Zech. 9:3); they will be like mighty men trampling the foe in the mud of the streets (Zech. 10:5); I trampled them like the mire of the streets (2 Sam. 22:43); I emptied them out like the mire of the streets (Ps. 18:42); he has thrown me into the mire (Job 30:19); I sink in deep mire (Ps. 69:2); Jeremiah sank into the mud at the bottom of the cistern (Jer. 38:6); now your feet are sunk in the mire your friends turn back (Jer. 38:22); deliver me from the mire (Ps. 69:14); he brought me up out of the miry bog (Ps. 40:2).

348 Plain
A The plain
Joshua struck the plain (Josh. 10:40); Joshua took the plain (Josh. 11:16); the cities of the plain (Deut. 3:10); let us fight them in the plain (1 Kgs. 20:23, 25); all the land will be turned into a plain (Zech. 14:10); they came up over the broad plain of the earth (Rev. 20:9); before Zerubbabel you will become a plain (Zech. 4:7).

B The Shephelah
Cities in the lowland [Shephelah] of Judah (Josh. 15:33-6; 2 Chr. 28:18); in the hill country and in the lowland (Deut. 1:7; Josh. 9:1; 10:40; 11:2, 16; 12:8; Judg. 1:9; Jer. 17:26); the cities of the hill country and of the Shephelah (Jer. 32:44; 33:13); the sycamore in the Shephelah (1 Kgs. 10:27;1 Chr. 27:28; 2 Chr. 1:15; 9:27).

349 Island
A Islands in general
Let the many islands be glad (Ps. 97:1); sing praise to the Lord, you islands (Isa. 42:10); the islands will wait for me (Isa. 51:5; 60:9); listen to me, you islands (Isa. 49:1); God takes up the islands like dust (Isa. 40:15); every island was moved from its place (Rev. 6:14); every island fled away (Rev. 16:20); we must run aground on some island (Acts 27:26).

B Specific islands
A small island called Cauda [Clauda] (Acts 27:16); an island called Malta (Acts 28:1); the island called Patmos (Rev. 1:9); the following day we came opposite Chios (Acts 20:15); the next day we came near to Samos (Acts 20:15); we sailed under the lee of Crete off Salmone (Acts 27:7); trying to reach Phoenix, a harbour of Crete (Acts 27:12); they sailed along Crete, close inshore (Acts 27:13); you should have listened to me and not sailed from Crete (Acts 27:21).

350 Stream

A Flowing water

WATER, see 339.

A1 Flowing water in general

Water wears away stones (Job 14:19); many waters cannot quench love (S. of S. 8:7); we went through fire and water (Ps. 66:12); the beginning of strife is like letting out water (Prov. 17:14); he leads me beside quiet waters (Ps. 23:2).

A2 Running water from God

Waters will gush in the wilderness (Isa. 35:6); he will open rivers on bare heights (Isa. 41:18); I will pour water on the thirsty land (Isa. 44:3); water flowed from under the threshold of the temple (Ezek. 47:1-12); living water will flow from Jerusalem (Zech. 14:8); everyone who thirsts, come to the water (Isa. 55:1).

A3 Pouring water

The Lord pours the waters of the sea on the earth (Amos 9:6); Rebekah emptied her jar into the trough (Gen. 24:20); pour water on the dry ground (Exod. 4:9); David poured out the water before the Lord (2 Sam. 23:16; 1 Chr. 11:18); they poured out water (1 Sam. 7:6); Elijah had water poured over the sacrifice (1 Kgs. 18:33-5); Elisha used to pour water on Elijah's hands (2 Kgs. 3:11); the serpent poured water like a river out of its mouth (Rev. 12:15); Jesus poured water into a basin (John 13:5).

A4 Flowing like water

A4a Like running water

His voice was like the sound of many waters (Ezek. 43:2); the king and princes will be like streams in a dry land (Isa. 32:2); out of his innermost being will flow rivers of living water (John 7:38); let justice flow like rivers (Amos 5:24); a wife's nagging is like a continuous dripping (Prov. 19:13; 27:15).

A4b Poured like water

We are like water spilled on the ground which cannot be gathered up (2 Sam. 14:14); I am poured out like water (Ps. 22:14); I am being poured out like a drink offering (2 Tim. 4:6); Moab has not been emptied from vessel to vessel (Jer. 48:11-12); pour out your heart like water before the Lord (Lam. 2:19); I will pour out my wrath on them like water (Hos. 5:10); I will pour out my Spirit on all flesh (Joel 2:28-9; Acts 2:17-18); Christ has poured forth what you see and hear (Acts 2:33); the Holy Spirit poured out on us richly (Titus 3:6); the love of God is poured into our hearts (Rom. 5:5); pour out the seven bowls of the wrath of God on the earth (Rev. 16:1).

A4c Other things poured out

My blood, poured out for many (Matt. 26:28; Mark 14:24); this cup which is poured out for you is the new covenant (Luke 22:20); pouring oil into the vessels (2 Kgs. 4:4-6); she poured the perfume on Jesus' head (Matt. 26:7; Mark 14:3); the ashes on the altar poured out (1 Kgs. 13:3, 5); he poured out the coins of the money-changers (John 2:15).

B Flooded

B1 Noah's flood

The flood (Gen. 6:17; 7:6-24; 2 Pet. 2:5); until the flood came and destroyed them all (Luke 17:27); the world destroyed by flood (2 Pet. 3:6); never again shall a flood destroy the earth (Gen. 9:11, 15); I swore that the waters of Noah should no more flood the earth (Isa. 54:9); they did not know until the flood swept them all away (Matt. 24:39).

B2 Other floods

God sends out waters and they flood the earth (Job 12:15); the Lord sits enthroned on the flood (Ps. 29:10); the floods lift up their pounding (Ps. 93:3); the floods

burst on that house (Matt. 7:25, 27; Luke 6:48, 49); Jordan overflows in harvest time (Josh. 3:15); Jordan overflowed as before (Josh. 4:18); the river gates are opened (Nahum 2:6); with an overflowing flood he will make an end of its place (Nahum 1:8); the serpent poured water to sweep away the woman with the flood (Rev. 12:15).

B3 Swamped

I have come into deep waters and the flood flows over me (Ps. 69:1-2); all your waves have gone over me (Ps. 42:7; Jonah 2:3); waters flowed over my head (Lam. 3:54); the boat was being swamped by the waves (Matt. 8:24; Mark 4:37; Luke 8:23); may the flood not overflow me (Ps. 69:15); deliver me from the waters (Ps. 144:7); when you pass through the rivers they will not overflow you (Isa. 43:2); when the great waters are in flood they will not reach the godly (Ps. 32:6); the waters would have swept over us (Ps. 124:4, 5).

C About rivers

C1 Rivers in general

He has established the earth upon the rivers (Ps. 24:2); stretch out your staff over the rivers, streams, ponds and pools of Egypt (Exod. 7:19; 8:5); rivers flow into the sea, then return (Eccles. 1:7); I will set his right hand on the rivers (Ps. 89:25); let the rivers clap their hands (Ps. 98:8); I will cause their rivers to run clear as oil (Ezek. 32:14); you muddy the waters with your feet and foul the rivers (Ezek. 32:2); he will drink from the brook by the way (Ps. 110:7); was your anger against the rivers or the sea? (Hab. 3:8); in danger from rivers (2 Cor. 11:26); the serpent poured water like a river out of its mouth (Rev. 12:15); the earth helped the woman by opening its mouth and swallowing the river (Rev. 12:16).

C2 God provides rivers

I am making rivers in the desert (Isa. 43:19-20); I will open rivers on the bare heights (Isa. 41:18); I will lead them by streams of water (Jer. 31:9); I will feed them by the streams (Ezek. 34:13); you cleaved the earth with rivers (Hab. 3:9); the Lord will be for us a place of rivers and wide canals (Isa. 33:21); the river of God is full of water (Ps. 65:9); you give them drink from your river of delights (Ps. 36:8); there is a river whose streams make glad the city of God (Ps. 46:4); the river of the water of life flowing from the throne of God (Rev. 22:1); out of his innermost being will flow rivers of living water (John 7:38).

C3 Failing rivers

My friends have been like the vanishing waters of a wadi (Job 6:15-18); will you be to me like a stream which fails? (Jer. 15:18); with the sole of my foot I dried up the rivers of Egypt (2 Kgs. 19:24); he turns rivers into a desert (Ps. 107:33); he dries up all the rivers (Nahum 1:4); the star fell on a third of the rivers and springs (Rev. 8:10); the rivers and springs of water became blood (Rev. 16:4).

C4 Like a river

Your peace would have been like a river (Isa. 48:18); I will extend peace to her like a river (Isa. 66:12); let your tears run down like a river day and night (Lam. 2:18); he will come like a rushing stream which the wind of the Lord drives (Isa. 59:19).

D Particular rivers

D1 Arnon

The Arnon is the border between Moab and the Amorites (Num. 21:13; Judg. 11:18); while Israel lived in cities on the banks of the Arnon (Judg. 11:26); fire devoured the heights of the Arnon (Num. 21:28); declare by the Arnon that Moab is laid waste (Jer. 48:20).

D2 Euphrates
D2a Euphrates in general
The fourth river is the Euphrates (Gen. 2:14); Pharaoh Neco went to the river Euphrates (2 Kgs. 23:29); Hadadezer went to the Euphrates (2 Sam. 8:3; 1 Chr. 18:3); by the river Euphrates (Jer. 46:6, 10); cast the book into the Euphrates (Jer. 51:63); the angel poured his bowl on the river Euphrates (Rev. 16:12); Jacob crossed the River (Gen. 31:21); the Lord is bringing on them the mighty waters of the Euphrates (Isa. 8:7); why go to Assyria to drink the waters of the Euphrates? (Jer. 2:18); go to the Euphrates and hide the waistband (Jer. 13:4); the Lord will wave his hand over the River (Isa. 11:15); four angels bound at the river Euphrates (Rev. 9:14).

D2b As far as the Euphrates
As far as the great river, the Euphrates (Gen. 15:18; Deut. 1:7; Josh. 1:4); the vine sent out its shoots to the River (Ps. 80:11); from Egypt to the Euphrates, from sea to sea and mountain to mountain (Mic. 7:12); from the river Euphrates (Deut. 11:24; 1 Kgs. 4:21; 2 Chr. 9:26); your boundary will be the River (Ps. 72:8; Zech. 9:10); from the River to the ends of the earth (Ps. 72:8; Zech. 9:10); from the river of Egypt to the Euphrates (2 Kgs. 24:7; Isa. 27:12).

D2c Beyond the Euphrates
Your fathers lived beyond the River (Josh. 24:2, 3); the gods your fathers served beyond the River (Josh. 24:14, 15); the Syrians beyond the River (2 Sam. 10:16; 1 Chr. 19:16); he will scatter them beyond the River (1 Kgs. 14:15); the province Beyond the River (Ezra 4:10-11, 16-17, 20); a razor hired from beyond the Euphrates, the king of Assyria (Isa. 7:20).

D3 Jordan
D3a Jordan in general
Jordan overflows in harvest time (Josh. 3:15); Jordan overflowed as before (Josh. 4:18); the Israelites came to the Jordan (Josh. 3:1); from the wilderness to Jordan (Judg. 11:22); they seized the fords of the Jordan (Judg. 3:28; 7:24; 12:5); the Lord has sent me to the Jordan (2 Kgs. 2:6); they searched as far as the Jordan (2 Kgs. 7:15); the waters of the Jordan cut off (Josh. 3:13; 4:7); Jordan turned back (Ps. 114:3, 5); Jesus returned from the Jordan (Luke 4:1).

D3b Crossing Jordan
With only my staff I crossed this Jordan (Gen. 32:10); do not make us cross over Jordan (Num. 32:5); why bring this people over Jordan? (Josh. 7:7); cross the Jordan (Josh. 1:2); in three days you will cross the Jordan (Josh. 1:11); they set out to cross the Jordan (Josh. 3:14); Moses would not cross the Jordan (Deut. 4:21-2; 31:2); Israel crossed Jordan on dry ground (Josh. 4:22); they crossed Jordan (Josh. 3:17; 4:1); the Ammonites crossed the Jordan to fight Judah (Judg. 10:9); Abner and his men crossed the Jordan (2 Sam. 2:29); David and the people crossed the Jordan (2 Sam. 17:22); Absalom crossed the Jordan (2 Sam. 17:24); the Gadites crossed the Jordan in flood (1 Chr. 12:15); he went across the Jordan to the place where John first baptised (John 10:40).

D3c In the Jordan
The ark is going into the Jordan (Josh. 3:11); priests to stand in the Jordan (Josh. 3:8, 13); the priests stood on dry ground in the middle of Jordan (Josh. 3:17); 12 stones taken from the middle of Jordan (Josh. 4:3, 5, 8, 20); 12 stones set up in the middle of Jordan (Josh. 4:9); washing in Jordan seven times (2 Kgs. 5:10, 14); Jesus came to the Jordan to be baptised (Matt. 3:13); baptised in the river Jordan (Matt. 3:6; Mark 1:5, 9).

D3d Beyond Jordan
The two and a half tribes inherited beyond the Jordan (Josh. 14:3); the land Moses gave you across the Jordan (Josh. 1:14, 15); Gilead and Bashan beyond the Jordan (Josh. 17:5); Amorites across the Jordan (Deut. 3:8); the good land across the Jordan (Deut. 3:25); Gilead remained across the Jordan (Judg. 5:17); from the Jordan eastward was cut off from Israel (2 Kgs. 10:33); people from beyond the Jordan came to Jesus (Matt. 4:25; Mark 3:8); he came into the region beyond the Jordan (Matt. 19:1; Mark 10:1); this took place in Bethany beyond the Jordan (John 1:28); he who was with you beyond the Jordan (John 3:26).

D3e The region of Jordan
I remember you from the land of the Jordan (Ps. 42:6); Jerusalem, all Judea and the region about Jordan went out to him (Matt. 3:5); one will come up like a lion from the jungle of Jordan (Jer. 49:19; 50:44); how will you fare in the jungle of Jordan? (Jer. 12:5); the two and a half tribes built an altar by the Jordan (Josh. 22:10, 11); he went into all the region about Jordan (Luke 3:3).

D4 Nile [Shihor]
Throw every boy into the Nile (Exod. 1:22); she set the basket in the reeds by the Nile (Exod. 2:3); Pharaoh's daughter went to bathe in the Nile (Exod. 2:5); striking the water of the Nile (Exod. 7:17); the Nile will stink (Exod. 7:18); the Nile will swarm with frogs (Exod. 8:3); you whose revenue was the grain of Shihor [the Nile] (Isa. 23:3); it will rise, be tossed about and subside like the Nile of Egypt (Amos 8:8); the land will rise like the Nile (Amos 8:8; 9:5); Egypt rises like the Nile (Jer. 46:7-8); the Nile is mine, I made it (Ezek. 29:3, 9); I will dry up the Nile (Ezek. 30:12); the depths of the Nile will dry up (Zech. 10:11); with my foot I dried up the rivers of Egypt (2 Kgs. 19:24; Isa. 37:25).

D5 Unnamed rivers
A river flowing from Eden with four tributaries (Gen. 2:10-14); whose land the rivers divide (Isa. 18:2, 7); like the streams in the south (Ps. 126:4); Jotbathah, a land of streams (Deut. 10:7); a land of streams, fountains and springs (Deut. 8:7); by the streams of Babylon we sat down and wept (Ps. 137:1).

E Springs / fountains
Give me springs of water (Josh. 15:19; Judg. 1:15); he turns dry land into springs of water (Ps. 107:35); he turns springs of water into thirsty ground (Ps. 107:33); does a fountain give both sweet and bitter water? (Jas. 3:11); the star fell on a third of the rivers and springs (Rev. 8:10); the rivers and springs of water became blood (Rev. 16:4); worship him who made the heaven and earth, the sea and springs of water (Rev. 14:7); the thirsty ground will become springs of water (Isa. 35:7); the mouth of the righteous is a fountain of life (Prov. 10:11); a fountain opened for sin and uncleanness (Zech. 13:1); God, the fountain of living waters (Jer. 2:13); with you is the fountain of life (Ps. 36:9); they have forsaken the Lord, the fountain of living water (Jer. 17:13); he would have given you living water (John 4:10); from the spring of the water of life (Rev. 21:6); a spring will flow from the house of the Lord (Joel 3:18); all my springs are in you (Ps. 87:7); he will guide them to springs of water (Isa. 49:10; Rev. 7:17); the water will be in him a spring of water (John 4:14); they make the Valley of Baca a place of springs (Ps. 84:6); understanding is a fountain of life (Prov. 16:22); they are springs without water (2 Pet. 2:17).

F Precipitation
F1 Rain
F1a Rain in general
If the clouds are full they pour rain on the earth (Eccles. 11:3); the farmer waits for the early and late

rains (Jas. 5:7); the north wind brings rain (Prov. 25:23);
a land which drinks water from the rain (Deut. 11:11);
rain for forty days and nights (Gen. 7:4, 12); the rain
fell, the floods came and the winds blew (Matt. 7:25,
27); sound of much rain (1 Kgs. 18:41); thunder and
rain during wheat harvest (1 Sam. 12:17, 18); it had
started to rain (Acts 28:2); trembling with the heavy
rain (Ezra 10:9); it is the rainy season (Ezra 10:13); rain,
hailstones and stormy wind will demolish the wall
(Ezek. 13:11); when you see a cloud rising in the west
you say a shower will come (Luke 12:54); land which
has drunk the rain which falls on it (Heb. 6:7).

F1b God sends rain
Has the rain a father? (Job 38:28); who can tip the
water-jars of heaven? (Job 38:37); God provides rain
(Ps. 147:8); the Lord gives the rain in its season (Jer.
5:24); God distills water into rain (Job 36:27-8); the
Lord has poured down the early and the latter rain
(Joel 2:23); when he utters his voice there is a tumult of
waters in the heavens (Jer. 10:13); God sends rain on
good and bad (Matt. 5:45); he gave you rain from
heaven (Acts 14:17); the Lord gives showers of rain,
vegetation in each field (Zech. 10:1); if you obey I will
send rain (Lev. 26:4; Deut. 11:14; 28:12); after Elijah's
prayer heavy rain came (1 Kgs. 18:45); Elijah prayed
again and the sky gave rain (Jas. 5:18); God will give
you rain (Isa. 30:23); ask the Lord for rain (Zech. 10:1);
send rain! (1 Kgs. 8:36; 2 Chr. 6:27); I will send rain (1
Kgs. 18:1); there will be rain and hailstones in my anger
(Ezek. 13:13).

F1c No rain
The Lord had not yet sent rain (Gen. 2:5); the rain was
restrained (Gen. 8:2); the rain no longer poured on the
earth (Exod. 9:33, 34); the rain is over and gone (S. of S.
2:11); there has been no rain on the land (Jer. 14:4);
neither dew nor rain except by Elijah's word (1 Kgs.
17:1); Elijah prayed fervently that it would not rain, and
it did not for three and a half years (Jas. 5:17); you will
not see wind and rain (2 Kgs. 3:17); rain on one city and
none on another (Amos 4:7-8).

F1d Like rain
The just ruler is like sunshine after rain (2 Sam. 23:4);
may he be like rain on the mown grass (Ps. 72:6); the
remnant of Jacob will be like showers on the grass
(Mic. 5:7); the king's favour is like clouds bringing
spring rain (Prov. 16:15); they waited for me as for the
rain (Job 29:23); let my teaching drop as the rain (Deut.
32:2); as the rain and snow come down from heaven
(Isa. 55:10); God will come like the spring rain (Hos.
6:3); I will give showers of blessing (Ezek. 34:26); until
the Lord comes to rain righteousness on you (Hos.
10:12); like rain in harvest, honour is not fitting for a
fool (Prov. 26:1); a poor man who oppresses the poor is
like driving rain which leaves no food (Prov. 28:3); the
Lord rained fire and brimstone on Sodom and
Gomorrah (Gen. 19:24); fire and brimstone rained
from heaven and destroyed Sodom (Luke 17:29).

F2 Hail
Have you seen the storehouses of hail? (Job 38:22); let
hail praise the Lord (Ps. 148:8); heavy hail (Exod. 9:18,
23-4; Rev. 11:19); large hailstones (Josh. 10:11); rain,
hailstones and stormy wind will demolish the wall
(Ezek. 13:11); hailstones a talent in weight (Rev. 16:21);
hailstones and coals of fire (Ps. 18:12, 13); hail and fire
mixed with blood fell on the earth (Rev. 8:7); I smote
you with blight, mildew and hail (Hag. 2:17); he gave
them hail for rain (Ps. 105:32); he destroyed their vines
with hail (Ps. 78:47); he gave over their cattle to hail
(Ps. 78:48); the locusts will eat what is left from the hail
(Exod. 10:5, 12, 15); the Lord's anger in cloudburst,
tempest and hailstones (Isa. 30:30); I will rain

hailstones, fire and brimstone on him (Ezek. 38:22); it
will hail when the forest comes down (Isa. 32:19); hail
will sweep away the refuge of lies (Isa. 28:17); God has
one like a storm of hail (Isa. 28:2); there has been
enough thunder and hail (Exod. 9:28); the thunder and
hail ceased (Exod. 9:29, 33, 34).

F3 Snow
Killing a lion on a snowy day (2 Sam. 23:20; 1 Chr.
11:22); as the snow comes down from heaven (Isa.
55:10); like the cold of snow in time of harvest (Prov.
25:13); like snow in summer, honour is not fitting for a
fool (Prov. 26:1); she is not afraid of snow for her
household (Prov. 31:21); God commands snow to fall
on the earth (Job 37:6); God gives snow like wool (Ps.
147:16); have you entered the storehouses of the snow?
(Job 38:22); where the snow hides itself (Job 6:16); let
snow praise the Lord (Ps. 148:8); if I wash myself with
snow (Job 9:30); his hand was leprous as snow (Exod.
4:6); Miriam was leprous, as white as snow (Num.
12:10); Gehazi went out a leper, as white as snow (2 Kgs.
5:27); wash me and I will be whiter than snow (Ps. 51:7);
though your sins be as scarlet they will be as white as
snow (Isa. 1:18); her princes were purer than snow
(Lam. 4:7); his head and hair were white as snow (Rev.
1:14); his clothing was white as snow (Dan. 7:9); the
angels' clothing was white as snow (Matt. 28:3).

351 Channel
Jerusalem was entered by way of the water tunnel
(2 Sam. 5:8); Hezekiah made the pool and the conduit
(2 Kgs. 20:20); Hezekiah directed water to the city of
David (2 Chr. 32:30); the conduit of the upper pool (2
Kgs. 18:17; Isa. 7:3; 36:2); who has made a channel for
the torrent? (Job 38:25); the king's heart is like
irrigation channels in the hand of the Lord (Prov. 21:1);
Jerusalem will be built with square and moat (Dan.
9:25); what are the two branches of the olive trees
beside the two golden pipes? (Zech. 4:12); Jacob sent
them across the wadi (Gen. 32:23); my friends have
been like the vanishing waters of a wadi (Job 6:15).

352 Wind
A Breath
A1 Breath in general
I will destroy everything in which is the breath of life
(Gen. 6:17); all died in whose nostrils was the breath of
the spirit of life (Gen. 7:22); animals in which is the
breath of life (Gen. 7:15); the breath came into them
(Ezek. 37:10); my breath is loathsome to my wife (Job
19:17); the crocodile's breath kindles coals (Job 41:21);
allowed to give breath to the image of the beast (Rev.
13:15).

A2 God's breath
By the breath of the Lord the heavens were made (Ps.
33:6); the breath of the Almighty gives me life (Job
33:4); you send forth your breath and they are created
(Ps. 104:30); when you take away your breath, they die
(Ps. 104:29); breathe on these slain, that they may live
(Ezek. 37:9); the breath of the Almighty gives a man
understanding (Job 32:8); all scripture is God-breathed
(2 Tim. 3:16); at the breath of your nostrils the waters
were piled up (Exod. 15:8); from the breath of God ice
comes (Job 37:10); at the blast of the breath of God's
nostrils (2 Sam. 22:16; Ps. 18:15); with the breath of his
lips he will slay the wicked (Isa. 11:4); scarcely are they
planted when he blows on them and they wither (Isa.
40:24); by the breath of God the wicked perish (Job
4:9); Jesus breathed on his disciples (John 20:22); the
Lord Jesus will slay the lawless one with the breath of
his mouth (2 Thess. 2:8).

A3 God gives breath

God breathed into man's nostrils the breath of life
(Gen. 2:7); God gives breath to the people on earth
(Isa. 42:5); as long as the breath of God is in my nostrils
(Job 27:3); my breath will not always remain in man
(Gen. 6:3); he gives to all men life and breath (Acts
17:25); God in whose hand is your breath (Dan. 5:23); I
will cause breath to enter you that you may live (Ezek.
37:5-6); if God were to withdraw his breath all flesh
would perish (Job 34:14-15).

A4 No breath

There is no breath in his molten images (Jer. 10:14;
51:17); there is no breath at all in the idol (Hab. 2:19);
there was no breath in them (Ezek. 37:8); there is no
breath in the mouth of idols (Ps. 135:17); there was no
breath left in the widow's son (1 Kgs. 17:17); I have no
strength left in me, and no breath in me (Dan. 10:17);
God will not let me get my breath (Job 9:18); cry of the
daughter of Zion gasping for breath (Jer. 4:31); the wild
donkeys pant for air like jackals (Jer. 14:6); Jesus
breathed his last (Luke 23:46); Ananias fell down and
breathed his last (Acts 5:5); Sapphira fell down and
breathed her last (Acts 5:10).

A5 Man a mere breath

Every man is a mere breath (Ps. 39:5, 11); man is like a
breath (Ps. 144:4); my life is a breath (Job 7:7); my days
are a breath (Job 7:16); a man's thoughts are but a
breath (Ps. 94:11).

A6 Sighing / sniffing

Jesus looked up to heaven and sighed (Mark 7:34);
Jesus sighed in his spirit (Mark 8:12); our years end like
a sigh (Ps. 90:9); you sniff at me, says the Lord (Mal.
1:13).

B Winds

B1 Winds in general

When the wind passes over the grass it is no more (Ps.
103:16); you do not know the path of the wind (Eccles.
11:5); rain, hailstones and stormy wind will demolish
the wall (Ezek. 13:11); a great wind blew down the house
(Job 1:19); the rain fell, the floods came and the winds
blew (Matt. 7:25, 27); the wind carried them away so
not a trace was found (Dan. 2:35); two women with the
wind in their wings (Zech. 5:9); they sow the wind and
reap the whirlwind (Hos. 8:7); he removed them with
fierce blast on the day of the east wind (Isa. 27:8); you
will winnow them and the wind will carry them away
(Isa. 41:16); a burning wind will be the portion of the
wicked (Ps. 11:6); when your calamity comes like a
whirlwind (Prov. 1:27); the wicked are like chaff driven
away by the wind (Ps. 1:4); I beat them fine as dust
before the wind (Ps. 18:42); the wind will sweep away
all your shepherds (Jer. 22:22); the sea rose because a
strong wind was blowing (John 6:18); though ships are
great and driven by strong winds (Jas. 3:4); as a fig tree
sheds its late fruit when shaken by a wind (Rev. 6:13);
when the south wind blows you say there will be heat
(Luke 12:55).

B2 God dispenses winds

He who forms mountains and creates the wind (Amos
4:13); God sent a wind and the flood receded (Gen. 8:1);
the Lord drove the sea back with a strong east wind
(Exod. 14:21); you blew with your wind (Exod. 15:10); a
wind from the Lord brought quails (Num. 11:31); God
raised a stormy wind (Ps. 107:25); God appointed a
scorching east wind (Jonah 4:8); the Lord sent wind
and storm on Jonah (Jonah 1:4); by God's wind the
heavens are cleared (Job 26:13); when God gave weight
to the wind (Job 28:25); who has gathered the wind in
his fists? (Prov. 30:4); he brings the wind from his
storehouses (Ps. 135:7; Jer. 10:13; 51:16); he makes his
wind blow (Ps. 147:18); stormy wind fulfilling his word

(Ps. 148:8); I will make a stormy wind break out in my
wrath (Ezek. 13:13); God makes winds his messengers
(Ps. 104:4); he makes his angels winds (Heb. 1:7); God
taking up Elijah in a whirlwind (2 Kgs. 2:1, 11); you lift
me on the wind and make me ride on it (Job 30:22); the
wind of the Lord will come from the wilderness (Hos.
13:15).

B3 God in the wind

God rode on the wind (2 Sam. 22:11; Ps. 18:10); God
rides on the wings of the wind (Ps. 104:3); his way is in
whirlwind and storm (Nahum 1:3); God answered Job
from the whirlwind (Job 38:1); the wind blows where it
will, so is everyone who is born of the Spirit [Wind]
(John 3:8); he will come like a rushing stream which
the wind of the Lord drives (Isa. 59:19); at Pentecost a
sound like a mighty wind (Acts 2:2); the Lord was not
in the wind (1 Kgs. 19:11).

B4 Wind from various directions

Scorched by the east wind (Gen. 41:6, 23, 27); the Lord
drove the sea back with a strong east wind (Exod.
14:21); an east wind which brought the locusts (Exod.
10:13); and a west wind to carry them away (Exod.
10:19); like the east wind I will scatter them before the
enemy (Jer. 18:17); the east wind carries him away (Job
27:21); where is the east wind scattered on the earth?
(Job 38:24); will it not wither when the east wind strikes
it? (Ezek. 17:10); the east wind dried up the vine's fruit
(Ezek. 19:12); though he flourishes as the reeds, an east
wind will come (Hos. 13:15); north and south winds,
blow on my garden! (S. of S. 4:16); a stormy wind from
the north (Ezek. 1:4); a fierce wind called the
Northeaster [Euraquilo] (Acts 27:14); the Lord will
march in the whirlwinds of the south (Zech. 9:14); a
south wind (Acts 28:13); a hot wind from the desert
(Jer. 4:11-12); as whirlwinds in the Negeb sweep on (Isa.
21:1); the wind blows from different directions, then
returns (Eccles. 1:6); a south wind sprang up (Acts
27:13).

B5 The four winds

Come from the four winds and breathe on these slain
(Ezek. 37:9); four horns towards the four winds of
heaven (Dan. 8:8); his kingdom will be broken and
divided to the four winds of heaven (Dan. 11:4); I have
scattered you as the four winds of heaven (Zech. 2:6);
these are the four winds of heaven (Zech. 6:5); I will
bring on Elam the four winds of heaven (Jer. 49:36);
the four winds of heaven stirred up the great sea (Dan.
7:2); he will gather his elect from the four winds (Matt.
24:31; Mark 13:27).

B6 Wind in opposition

A storm of wind arose (Mark 4:37); the wind was
against them (Matt. 14:24; Mark 6:48); the wind was
contrary (Acts 27:4); when Peter saw the wind he was
afraid (Matt. 14:30); Jesus rebuked the wind and the sea
(Matt. 8:26-7; Mark 4:39-41; Luke 8:24-5); the wind
stopped (Matt. 8:26; 14:32; Mark 6:51).

B7 No wind

The wind ceased and there was a great calm (Mark
4:39); angels held back the four winds that no wind
might blow (Rev. 7:1); each will be a refuge from the
wind (Isa. 32:2); you will not see wind and rain (2 Kgs.
3:17).

B8 Like the wind

They sweep by like the wind and pass on (Hab. 1:11);
the king of the north will rush on him like a whirlwind
(Dan. 11:40); like clouds and wind without rain is a
man who boasts of non-existent gifts (Prov. 25:14); a
reed shaken by the wind? (Matt. 11:7; Luke 7:24); to
restrain the contentious woman is to restrain the wind
(Prov. 27:16); tossed to and fro with every wind of
doctrine (Eph. 4:14); our iniquities take us away like

the wind (Isa. 64:6); let them be like chaff before the wind (Ps. 35:5); I will scatter them like chaff to the desert wind (Jer. 13:24); he who doubts is like a wave of the sea tossed by the wind (Jas. 1:6); they are waterless clouds, carried along by the winds (Jude 12).

B9 Merely wind

Man is a wind that does not return (Ps. 78:39); Ephraim herds the wind (Hos. 12:1); striving after wind (Eccles. 1:14, 17; 2:11, 17, 26; 4:4, 6, 16; 6:9); toiling for the wind (Eccles. 5:16); we brought forth as it were wind (Isa. 26:18); is the speech of a despairing man to be as wind? (Job 6:26); how long will your words be a whirling wind? (Job 8:2); should a wise man answer with windy words? (Job 15:2); is there no end to windy words? (Job 16:3); the prophets are like wind, the word is not in them (Jer. 5:13); their molten images are wind (Isa. 41:29).

C Bellows

The bellows blow fiercely (Jer. 6:29).

353 Air-pipe

A Nostrils

God breathed the breath of life into man's nostrils (Gen. 2:7); all died in whose nostrils was the breath of the spirit of life (Gen. 7:22); at the breath of your nostrils the waters were piled up (Exod. 15:8); till the meat comes out of your nostrils (Num. 11:20); out of the crocodile's nostrils comes smoke (Job 41:20).

B Chimney.

They will be like smoke from a chimney (Hos. 13:3).

354 Semiliquid

MARSH, see 347.

355 Cloud

A Clouds

A1 Clouds in general

The light is darkened by its clouds (Isa. 5:30); the sky black with clouds (1 Kgs. 18:45); if the clouds are full they pour rain on the earth (Eccles. 11:3); the clouds pour down rain (Job 36:28); the clouds are higher than you (Job 35:5); a cloud as small as a man's hand (1 Kgs. 18:44); the top of the cedar was in the clouds (Ezek. 31:3); I will cover the sun with a cloud and the moon will not give its light (Ezek. 32:7); a day of clouds and thick darkness (Ezek. 34:12); when you see a cloud rising in the west (Luke 12:54).

A2 God and clouds

A2a God dispenses clouds

Can anyone understand the spreading of the clouds? (Job 36:29); do you know about the balancing of the clouds? (Job 37:16); can you command the clouds? (Job 38:34); God covers the heavens with clouds (Ps. 147:8); he causes clouds to ascend from the end of the earth (Jer. 10:13; 51:16); the Lord makes the storm clouds (Zech. 10:1); when I bring a cloud over the earth (Gen. 9:14); I made the cloud a garment for the sea (Job 38:9); God wraps up the waters in his clouds (Job 26:8); God loads the thick cloud with moisture (Job 37:11); clouds are the dust beneath his feet (Nahum 1:3); the day of the Lord is a day of clouds and thick darkness (Joel 2:2; Zeph. 1:15); the day of the Lord will be a day of clouds (Ezek. 30:3); the Lord has covered the daughter of Zion with a cloud in his anger (Lam. 2:1); an angel clothed in a cloud (Rev. 10:1); a white cloud with one like a son of man seated on it (Rev. 14:14);

the two witnesses went up to heaven in a cloud (Rev. 11:12).

A2b The pillar of cloud

The Lord went ahead in a pillar of cloud (Exod. 13:21); a cloud by day and fire by night (Num. 9:16; 14:14;

Deut. 1:33; Isa. 4:5); with a pillar of cloud you led them (Neh. 9:12, 19); he led them with the cloud by day (Ps. 78:14); he spoke in the pillar of cloud (Ps. 99:7); the cloud of the Lord over them when they set out (Num. 10:34); when the cloud was taken up they set out (Exod. 40:36; Num. 9:17-22); the cloud was lifted (Num. 10:11); when the cloud stayed, they stayed (Exod. 40:37; Num. 9:17-22); there was cloud and darkness yet it gave light (Exod. 14:20); the Lord looked down from the pillar of cloud and fire (Exod. 14:24); the pillar of cloud stood behind them (Exod. 14:19); the pillar of cloud came to the entrance of the tent (Exod. 33:9, 10; Num. 12:5; Deut. 31:15); our fathers were all under the cloud (1 Cor. 10:1); our fathers were all baptised into Moses in the cloud and the sea (1 Cor. 10:2).

A2c God in cloud

The glory of the Lord appeared in the cloud (Exod. 16:10); I will appear in the cloud (Lev. 16:2); God came to Moses in a cloud (Exod. 19:9; Num. 11:25); the Lord came down in the cloud (Exod. 34:5); God makes the clouds his chariot (Ps. 104:3); the Lord is riding on a swift cloud (Isa. 19:1); Moses drew near to the cloud where God was (Exod. 20:21); God spoke these words from the cloud (Deut. 5:22); the cloud covered the tabernacle (Exod. 40:34, 35, 38; Num. 9:15; 16:42); the cloud filled the temple (1 Kgs. 8:10; 2 Chr. 5:13; Ezek. 10:3, 4); a great cloud with fire flashing forth and a bright light around (Ezek. 1:4); thick clouds were God's cover (2 Sam. 22:12; Ps. 18:11); he spread a cloud for a covering (Ps. 105:39); God spreads his cloud over his throne (Job 26:9); the Lord said he would dwell in a thick cloud (1 Kgs. 8:12; 2 Chr. 6:1); clouds and darkness are round him (Ps. 97:2); you wrapped yourself in a cloud so no prayer could pass through (Lam. 3:44); God does not see through the clouds (Job 22:14); the cloud of incense to cover the mercy seat (Lev. 16:13); a voice came out of the cloud (Luke 9:35).

A2d Christ in a cloud

A cloud on the mount of transfiguration (Matt. 17:5; Mark 9:7; Luke 9:34); a cloud took him out of their sight (Acts 1:9); one like a son of man, coming with the clouds of heaven (Dan. 7:13); the Son of man will come in the clouds (Matt. 24:30; 26:64; Mark 13:26; 14:62; Luke 21:27); he is coming with the clouds (Rev. 1:7); caught up to meet them in the clouds (1 Thess. 4:17).

A3 Like clouds

The king's favour is like clouds bringing rain (Prov. 16:15); you will be like a cloud covering the land (Ezek. 38:9); you will come up against Israel like a cloud covering the land (Ezek. 38:16); your steadfast love is like a morning cloud (Hos. 6:4); they will be like the morning cloud which soon vanishes (Hos. 13:3); so great a cloud of witnesses (Heb. 12:1); who are these who fly like a cloud? (Isa. 60:8); I have wiped away your transgressions like a cloud (Isa. 44:22); my prosperity has passed away like a cloud (Job 30:15); the clouds return after rain (Eccles. 12:2); as a cloud vanishes so does he who goes down to Sheol (Job 7:9); they are clouds without water (Jude 12); like clouds and wind without rain is a man who boasts of non-existent gifts (Prov. 25:14).

B Mist

A mist watered the ground (Gen. 2:6); I have wiped away your sins like mist (Isa. 44:22); you are like a mist that appears for a little while (Jas. 4:14); they are mists driven by a storm (2 Pet. 2:17); a mist and darkness fell on him (Acts 13:11).

C Foam

He foams at the mouth (Mark 9:18); he foamed at the mouth (Mark 9:20); it convulses him until he foams

(Luke 9:39); casting up the foam of their own shame (Jude 13).

356 Pulpiness

One ran and took a sponge (Matt. 27:48); one ran and filled a sponge full of vinegar (Mark 15:36); a sponge put on hyssop (John 19:29).

357 Oiliness

A Oil

A1 Oil in general

The poor have to make oil (Job 24:11); gather wine, summer fruit and oil (Jer. 40:10); you went to the king with oil (Isa. 57:9); overseeing the stores of oil (1 Chr. 27:28); the firstfruits of the oil is for the priests (Num. 18:12); a land of olive oil (Deut. 8:8); the rock gave streams of oil (Job 29:6); 20 000 baths of oil (2 Chr. 2:10); the olive tree answered, 'Should I give up my oil?' (Judg. 9:9); a handful of flour and a little oil (1 Kgs. 17:12); you ate fine flour, honey and oil (Ezek. 16:13); pour oil into the jars (2 Kgs. 4:2-7); you set on the table my incense and my oil (Ezek. 23:41); a tenth of a bath from each ten baths of oil (Ezek. 45:14); he makes a covenant with Assyria and oil is carried to Egypt (Hos. 12:1); the vats will overflow with new wine and oil (Joel 2:24); will the Lord be please with 10 000 rivers of oil? (Mic. 6:7); he who loves wine and oil will not become rich (Prov. 21:17); 100 measures of oil (Luke 16:6).

A2 Provision of oil

My lovers give me my wool and flax, my oil and drink (Hos. 2:5); she does not know that I gave her the grain, wine and oil (Hos. 2:8); the earth will answer to the grain, the wine and the oil (Hos. 2:22); I am giving you grain, new wine and oil (Joel 2:19); Asher will dip his foot in oil (Deut. 33:24); God made him suck oil out of the flinty rock (Deut. 32:13); cargo of wine, oil, flour and wheat (Rev. 18:13); there is precious treasure and oil in the house of the wise (Prov. 21:20); do not harm the oil and the wine (Rev. 6:6); the grain is ruined, the wine fails, the oil languishes (Joel 1:10); I called for a drought on the grain, wine, oil (Hag. 1:11).

A3 Oil for lamps

Oil for the lamps (Exod. 25:6; 27:20; 35:8, 14, 28; 39:37; Lev. 24:2); Eleazar has responsibility for the oil for the lamps (Num. 4:16); the two golden pipes from which the oil is poured out (Zech. 4:12); the foolish virgins took no oil with their lamps (Matt. 25:3-9).

A4 Anointing oil

The holy anointing oil (Exod. 31:11; 35:8, 15, 28; 37:29; 39:38); this shall be a holy anointing oil to me through all generations (Exod. 30:31-3); spices for the anointing oil (Exod. 25:6; 30:23-5); Eleazar looked after the anointing oil (Num. 4:16); take the anointing oil (Lev. 8:2); Hezekiah showed the Babylonians the precious oil (2 Kgs. 20:13; Isa. 39:2); take this flask of oil (2 Kgs. 9:1); dead flies make the perfumer's oil stink (Eccles. 10:1); the oil of gladness instead of mourning (Isa. 61:3).

A5 Like oil

Your name is like purified oil (S. of S. 1:3); her speech is smoother than oil (Prov. 5:3); a good name is better than good oil (Eccles. 7:1); cursing soaked like oil into his bones (Ps. 109:18); trying to restrain the contentious woman is like grasping oil (Prov. 27:16).

B Anointing

B1 Anointing kings

The trees went to anoint a king (Judg. 9:8); fill your horn with oil and go (1 Sam. 16:1); the anointing as king of: Saul (1 Sam. 9:16; 10:1; 15:1, 17); David (1 Sam. 16:3-13; 2 Sam. 2:4-7; 3:39; 5:3, 17; 12:7; 1 Chr. 11:3; 14:8); Absalom (2 Sam. 19:10); Solomon (1 Kgs. 1:34-9, 45; 5:1; 1 Chr. 29:22); Hazael king of Syria (1 Kgs. 19:15); Jehu

(1 Kgs. 19:16; 2 Kgs. 9:3-6); Joash (2 Kgs. 11:12; 2 Chr. 23:11); Jehoahaz (2 Kgs. 23:30).

B2 Anointing priests

Aaron and his sons were anointed (Exod. 28:41; 30:30; 40:13, 15; Lev. 6:20; 8:12, 30); Aaron's sons, the anointed priests (Num. 3:3); in the day he anointed them (Lev. 7:36); pour the anointing oil on Aaron's head (Exod. 29:7); Aaron and his sons were sprinkled with oil and blood (Exod. 29:21); the holy garments are for Aaron and his sons to be anointed in (Exod. 29:29); the high priest anointed with the holy oil (Lev. 21:10; Num. 35:25); the anointing oil is on them (Lev. 10:7; 21:12); they anointed Zadok as priest (1 Chr. 29:22); unity is like the precious oil on Aaron's head (Ps. 133:2).

B3 Anointing prophets

Anoint Elisha as prophet in your place (1 Kgs. 19:16).

B4 Anointing people

B4a Anointed by God

You anoint my head with oil (Ps. 23:5); you have anointed me with fresh oil (Ps. 92:10); David was anointed by God (2 Sam. 23:1; Ps. 89:20); I anointed you with oil (Ezek. 16:9); the Lord had anointed Hazael to cut off the house of Ahab (2 Chr. 22:7); it is God who anointed us (2 Cor. 1:21); you have an anointing from the Holy One (1 John 2:20); the anointing remains in you (1 John 2:27).

B4b The Lord's anointed

Saul was the Lord's anointed (1 Sam. 24:6, 10; 26:9, 11; 2 Sam. 1:14, 16); you did not guard the Lord's anointed (1 Sam. 26:16); I would not harm the Lord's anointed (1 Sam. 26:23); David, his anointed (2 Sam. 22:51; Ps. 18:50); Cyrus his anointed (Isa. 45:1); do not touch my anointed ones (1 Chr. 16:22; Ps. 105:15); he cursed the Lord's anointed (2 Sam. 19:21); the peoples plot against the Lord's anointed (Ps. 2:2); they mock your anointed one (Ps. 89:51); the breath of our nostrils, the Lord's anointed, was taken in their pits (Lam. 4:20); look on the face of your anointed (Ps. 84:9); the Lord saves his anointed (Ps. 20:6); the Lord is the saving defence of his anointed (Ps. 28:8); you went forth for the salvation of your anointed (Hab. 3:13).
CHRIST, see 357C.

B4c Anointed by people

Oil on the cleansed leper (Lev. 14:17-18, 28-9); the men of Samaria anointed the people of Judah with oil (2 Chr. 28:15); you did not anoint my head with oil (Luke 7:46); Mary anointed the feet of Jesus (John 12:3).

B4d Anointing oneself

Oil to make man's face shine (Ps. 104:15); Ruth anointed herself (Ruth 3:3); David washed and anointed himself (2 Sam. 12:20); let oil not be lacking on your head (Eccles. 9:8); when you fast, anoint your head (Matt. 6:17); those who anoint themselves with the finest of oils (Amos 6:6); you will tread olives but not anoint yourself with oil (Mic. 6:15); do not anoint yourself (2 Sam. 14:2); I did not anoint myself (Dan. 10:3).

B4e Medicinal anointing

The Samaritan bandaged his wounds, pouring on oil and wine (Luke 10:34); they anointed many who were sick (Mark 6:13); elders should anoint the sick with oil (Jas. 5:14); wounds not softened with oil (Isa. 1:6); he anointed the man's eyes with the clay (John 9:6); he made clay and anointed my eyes (John 9:11).

B5 Anointing things

Jacob anointed the pillar (Gen. 28:18; 31:13; 35:14); oil the shield (Isa. 21:5); Saul's shield, not anointed (2 Sam. 1:21); to anoint a most holy place (Dan. 9:24); the altar sprinkled seven times with oil (Lev. 8:11); anointing the tabernacle (Exod. 30:26-9; 40:9-11; Lev. 8:10-11; Num. 7:1).

C Christ [Messiah] [Anointed One]

C1 Anointed Christ

The Lord has anointed me to preach good news (Isa. 61:1; Luke 4:18); until the Anointed One [Messiah], the Prince (Dan. 9:25); God anointed Jesus with the Spirit and with power (Acts 10:38); Jesus whom you anointed (Acts 4:27); God anointed you with the oil of gladness (Ps. 45:7; Heb. 1:9); she anointed his feet with perfume (Luke 7:38, 46; John 12:3); she has anointed my body for burial (Mark 14:8); the women came to anoint Jesus' body (Mark 16:1).

C2 Jesus called Christ

Jesus called Christ (Matt. 1:16); a Saviour who is Christ the Lord (Luke 2:11); Simeon would not die before seeing the Christ (Luke 2:26); some said, 'This is the Christ' (John 7:41); are you the Christ? (Mark 14:61; Luke 23:39); if you are the Christ, tell us (Luke 22:67; John 10:24); can this be the Christ? (John 4:29); I adjure you to tell us if you are the Christ, the Son of God (Matt. 26:63); do the authorities know this is the Christ? (John 7:26); will the Christ perform more signs than this man? (John 7:31); demons knew him to be the Christ (Luke 4:41); you are the Christ (Matt. 16:16; Mark 8:29; Luke 9:20; John 11:27); Messiah, Christ, is coming (John 4:25); we have found the Messiah, Christ (John 1:41); that he may send you Jesus, the Christ foreordained for you (Acts 3:20); who is the liar but he who denies that Jesus is the Christ? (1 John 2:22); saying he is Christ, a king (Luke 23:2); Barabbas or Jesus who is called Christ? (Matt. 27:17); what shall I do with Jesus called Christ? (Matt. 27:22); prophesy to us, you Christ! (Matt. 26:68); I know who you are, the Holy One of God (Mark 1:24).

C3 Christ's origin

Where Christ should be born (Matt. 2:4); no one knows where the Christ comes from (John 7:27); surely the Christ does not come from Galilee? (John 7:41); whose son is the Christ? (Matt. 22:42; Mark 12:35; Luke 20:41); the Christ comes from David and from Bethlehem (John 7:42); from Israel is the Christ according to the flesh (Rom. 9:5); son of David according to the flesh (Rom. 1:3); this man is not from God because he does not keep the sabbath (John 9:16); we do not know where this man is from (John 9:29-30); if this man were not from God he could do nothing (John 9:33); knowing that he had come from God and was going to God (John 13:3); you have loved me and believe that I came from the Father (John 16:27-30); they know surely that I came from you (John 17:8); Jesus Christ whom you have sent (John 17:3); Abraham's seed, that is, Christ (Gal. 3:16).

C4 Christ's nature

You have one teacher, Christ (Matt. 23:10); we have heard that the Christ remains for ever (John 12:34); Christ the power of God and the wisdom of God (1 Cor. 1:24); the head of Christ is God (1 Cor. 11:3); if there is any encouragement in Christ (Phil. 2:1); let this mind be among you which was also in Christ Jesus (Phil. 2:5-9); God's mystery, which is Christ (Col. 2:2); Jesus Christ is the same yesterday, today and for ever (Heb. 13:8).

C5 Christ suffering

God foretold that Christ would suffer (Acts 3:18); was it not necessary for the Christ to suffer? (Luke 24:26); Christ had to suffer and rise again (Acts 17:3; 26:23); the prophets enquired about Christ and his suffering (1 Pet. 1:11); Christ our passover has been sacrificed (1 Cor. 5:7); if he is the Christ, let him save himself (Luke 23:35); let the Christ, the King of Israel, come

down from the cross (Mark 15:32); rulers gathered against the Lord and his Christ (Acts 4:26); we preach Christ crucified (1 Cor. 1:23); I decided to know nothing except Jesus Christ and him crucified (1 Cor. 2:2); Christ died for our sins in accordance with the scriptures (1 Cor. 15:3); as the sufferings of Christ abound for us, so our comfort abounds through Christ (2 Cor. 1:5).

C6 Believing in Christ

These are written that you might believe that Jesus is the Christ, the Son of God (John 20:31); he who gives you a cup of water because you bear the name of Christ (Mark 9:41); 'I am of Christ' (1 Cor. 1:12); for me to live is Christ (Phil. 1:21); whoever believes that Jesus is the Christ is born of God (1 John 5:1); if anyone confessed him to be the Christ, he would be expelled (John 9:22).

C7 Preaching Christ

They did not stop preaching Jesus as the Christ (Acts 5:42); God has made this Jesus both Lord and Christ (Acts 2:36); Philip preached Christ in Samaria (Acts 8:5); Saul confounded the Jews by proving that Jesus is the Christ (Acts 9:22); Paul testified that Jesus was the Christ (Acts 18:5); Apollos demonstrated that Jesus was the Christ (Acts 18:28); this Jesus is the Christ (Acts 17:3); to preach among the Gentiles the unsearchable riches of Christ (Eph. 3:8); some preach Christ from envy and strife (Phil. 1:15); these preach Christ out of contention (Phil. 1:17); Christ is proclaimed, and in that I rejoice (Phil. 1:18); we do not preach ourselves, but Christ Jesus as Lord (2 Cor. 4:5); him we proclaim (Col. 1:28).

C8 Not the Christ

False Christs will arise (Matt. 24:24; Mark 13:22); many will say, 'I am the Christ' (Matt. 24:5); do not believe one who says, 'Here is the Christ' (Matt. 24:23; Mark 13:21); whether John might be the Christ (Luke 3:15); I am not the Christ (John 1:20; 3:28); why baptise, if you are not the Christ, nor Elijah, nor the Prophet? (John 1:25); if someone preaches another Jesus (2 Cor. 11:4).

D Fat

D1 Fat of people

The wicked man is covered with fat (Job 15:27); their heart is covered with fat (Ps. 119:70); the fat closed over the blade (Judg. 3:22).

D2 Fat of animals

All fat is the Lord's (Lev. 3:16); no fat was to be eaten (Lev. 3:17; 7:23-5); though it could be used (Lev. 7:24); Eli's sons wanted the meat with the fat (1 Sam. 2:15-16); you eat the fat and clothe yourselves with the wool (Ezek. 34:3); eat fat until you are sated (Ezek. 39:19); fat is not to be kept overnight (Exod. 23:18).

D3 Fat of the sacrifices

Abel brought fat portions as an offering (Gen. 4:4); the fat is to be offered up (Lev. 7:31; 10:15); the priests were to set in order the suet of the sacrifices (Lev. 1:8, 12); the priests will offer me the fat and the blood (Ezek. 44:15); when you offer my food, the fat and the blood (Ezek. 44:7); to hearken is better than the fat of rams (1 Sam. 15:22); you have not filled me with the fat of your sacrifices (Isa. 43:24).

D4 Butter

Pressing milk produces butter (Prov. 30:33); his speech was smoother than butter (Ps. 55:21).

E Wax

Like wax before the fire, like water poured down a steep place (Mic. 1:4); mountains melt like wax before the Lord (Ps. 97:5); the wicked perish as wax melts before the fire (Ps. 68:2); my heart is like wax, melted within me (Ps. 22:14).

358 Organisms

LIFE, see 360.

359 Mineral

METALS, see 631B.

360 Life

A Life in general
A1 Nature of life
The life of every creature is its blood (Gen. 9:4; Lev. 17:11, 14; Deut. 12:23); the tree of life (Gen. 2:9; 3:22-4; Rev. 2:7; 22:2); life is more than food (Matt. 6:25); a man's life does not consist in the abundance of his possessions (Luke 12:15); from the heart are the sources of life (Prov. 4:23); the words I have spoken to you are spirit and life (John 6:63); you have made known to me the ways of life (Acts 2:28).

A2 Living things
God created every living creature (Gen. 1:20-1); let the earth bring forth living creatures (Gen. 1:24); he is not the God of the dead but of the living (Matt. 22:32); he is not God of the dead but of the living, for all live to him (Luke 20:38); a live dog is better than a dead lion (Eccles. 9:4).

B God and life
B1 God lives
The living God (Josh. 3:10; 1 Sam. 17:26, 36; Isa. 37:17; Jer. 10:10; Dan. 6:26; Rom. 9:26; 2 Cor. 3:3; 1 Tim. 4:10; Heb. 3:12; 9:14; 10:31; 12:22; Rev. 7:2); I know that my redeemer lives (Job 19:25); the well of the living One who sees me (Gen. 16:14); the Lord lives (2 Sam. 22:47; Ps. 18:46); you are the Christ, the Son of the living God (Matt. 16:16); as the Father has life in himself (John 5:26); as the living Father sent me and as I live because of the Father (John 6:57); a living God who made heaven and earth and sea (Acts 14:15); we are the temple of the living God (2 Cor. 6:16); to serve a living and true God (1 Thess. 1:9); the church of the living God (1 Tim. 3:15); he who lives for ever and ever (Rev. 4:9-10; 10:6; 15:7).

B2 Christ's life
As I live because of the Father (John 6:57); the Father has granted the Son to have life in himself (John 5:26); the originator of life (Acts 3:15); the life he lives, he lives to God (Rom. 6:10); the power of an indestructible life (Heb. 7:16); why seek the living among the dead? (Luke 24:5); a dead man, Jesus, whom Paul asserted to be alive (Acts 25:19); the eternal life which was with the Father (1 John 1:2); we are saved through his life (Rom. 5:10); I am the living bread which came down from heaven (John 6:51); I am the resurrection and the life (John 11:25); he was crucified in weakness but lives by the power of God (2 Cor. 13:4); he always lives to intercede for them (Heb. 7:25); come to him, that living stone (1 Pet. 2:4); the Word of life (1 John 1:1); the life was manifested (1 John 1:2); one of whom it is testified that he lives on (Heb. 7:8); I am the living one (Rev. 1:18); I died, and behold I am alive for evermore (Rev. 1:18).

B3 God gives life
God breathed the breath of life and man became a living being (Gen. 2:7); the breath of the Almighty gives me life (Job 33:4); he gives to all men life and breath (Acts 17:25); you give life to all things (Neh. 9:6); God who gives life to all things (1 Tim. 6:13); all that came into existence found its life in him (John 1:3-4); I put to death and give life (Deut. 32:39); the Lord kills and brings to life (1 Sam. 2:6); you will make known to me the path of life (Ps. 16:11); with you is the fountain of life (Ps. 36:9); the breath of life from God entered them

(Rev. 11:11); everything will live where the river goes (Ezek. 47:9).

C Obtaining life
C1 Seeking life
Lest man eat of the tree of life and live for ever (Gen. 3:22-4); I have set before you life and death (Deut. 30:15); choose life so that you may live (Deut. 30:19); who would love life and see good days? (Ps. 34:12; 1 Pet. 3:10); seek good and not evil that you may live (Amos 5:14); seek me and live (Amos 5:4); seek the Lord and live (Amos 5:6); show me the lovingkindness of the Lord that I may not die (1 Sam. 20:14); what must I do to get eternal life? (Matt. 19:16; Luke 10:25); what must I do to inherit eternal life? (Mark 10:17; Luke 18:18); lay hold of the eternal life to which you were called (1 Tim. 6:12); lay hold of that which is life indeed (1 Tim. 6:19); the gate leading to life is narrow (Matt. 7:14).

C2 Life by doing right
C2a Life by pursuing righteousness
The wages of the righteous is life (Prov. 10:16); one steadfast in righteousness will live (Prov. 11:19); he who pursues righteousness will find life (Prov. 21:21); if you warned the righteous man and he does not sin, he will live (Ezek. 3:21); in the way of righteousness there is life (Prov. 12:28); the righteous man will surely live (Ezek. 18:9, 17); to those who do good and seek immortality he will give eternal life (Rom. 2:7); because he has done right, he will live (Ezek. 18:19); he has done what is right and will surely live (Ezek. 33:16); the righteous go into eternal life (Matt. 25:46); sanctification and its end, eternal life (Rom. 6:22).

C2b Life through repentance
Repent and live! (Ezek. 18:32); if the wicked man turns from sin, he will live (Ezek. 18:21-2, 27, 28).

C2c Life through keeping the law
Keep the statutes that you may live (Deut. 4:1; 8:1); keep my commandments and live (Prov. 4:4; 7:2); if you would enter life, keep the commandments (Matt. 19:17); if a man observes God's ordinances he will live (Neh. 9:29; Ezek. 20:11, 13, 21); the man who keeps my statutes will live (Lev. 18:5); obeying the Lord is your life (Deut. 30:20); do all that God commands that you may live (Deut. 5:33); the man who practices the righteousness based on the law will live by it (Rom. 10:5); he who does them will live by them (Gal. 3:12); if he walks in the statutes of life he will surely live (Ezek. 33:15); I gave them bad statutes by which they could not live (Ezek. 20:25); you search the scriptures because you think that in them you have eternal life (John 5:39); if a law could give life, righteousness would be by law (Gal. 3:21); the commandment which should have brought life brought death instead (Rom. 7:10).

C2d Life by wisdom
The wise man's path leads upward to life (Prov. 15:24); wisdom will be life to your soul (Prov. 3:22); whoever finds me finds life (Prov. 8:35); good sense is a fountain of life (Prov. 16:22); the teaching of the wise is a fountain of life (Prov. 13:14); the reproofs of discipline are the way of life (Prov. 6:23).

C2e Life by fearing the Lord
The fear of the Lord is a fountain of life (Prov. 14:27); the fear of the Lord leads to life (Prov. 19:23); the rewards for humility and fear of the Lord are riches, honour and life (Prov. 22:4).

C2f Life by loving
Love the Lord with all your heart and soul that you might live (Deut. 30:6); love the Lord with all your heart and you will live (Luke 10:27-8); love the Lord and keep his commandments that you might live (Deut. 30:16); we know we have passed from death to life because we love the brothers (1 John 3:14).

C3 Life through salvation

C3a Entering life
Better to enter life maimed or lame (Matt. 18:8); better to enter life with one eye (Matt. 18:9); he who hates his life will keep it for eternal life (John 12:25); he who forsakes possessions and family for Christ's sake will inherit eternal life (Matt. 19:29; Mark 10:30; Luke 18:30); he who sows to the Spirit will reap eternal life (Gal. 6:8).

C3b Life by God's word
Listen that you may live (Isa. 55:3); holding fast the word of life (Phil. 2:16); speak to the people all the words of this life (Acts 5:20); you have the words of eternal life (John 6:68); the dead will hear the voice of the Son of God, and those who hear will live (John 5:25); if anyone keeps my word he will never see death (John 8:51-2); the Father's commandment is eternal life (John 12:50); the word of God is living and active (Heb. 4:12).

C3c Life through Christ
In the Word was life (John 1:4); I am the way, the truth and the life (John 14:6); I have come that they might have life (John 10:10); I am the bread of life (John 6:48, 51, 58); he who eats my flesh and drinks my blood has eternal life (John 6:54); God has given us eternal life, and this life is in his Son (1 John 5:11); he who has the Son has life (1 John 5:12); Christ, who is our life (Col. 3:4); for me to live is Christ (Phil. 1:21); Christ lives in me and the life I now live is by faith in the Son of God (Gal. 2:20); in Christ will all be made alive (1 Cor. 15:22); if Christ is in you your spirit is alive (Rom. 8:10); the last Adam became a life-giving spirit (1 Cor. 15:45); this is eternal life, that they know you and Jesus Christ (John 17:3); I give my sheep eternal life (John 10:28); the Son gives life to whom he wishes (John 5:21); the gift of God is eternal life in Jesus Christ (Rom. 6:23); they will reign in life through the one, Jesus Christ (Rom. 5:17); God sent his Son into the world that we might live through him (1 John 4:9); the mercy of our Lord Jesus to eternal life (Jude 21); Jesus brought life and immortality to light (2 Tim. 1:10); consider yourselves alive to God in Christ Jesus (Rom. 6:11); you are unwilling to come to me that you may have life (John 5:40).

C3d Life with Christ
When dead in sin, God brought us to life with Christ (Eph. 2:5; Col. 2:13); as Christ was raised so we might walk in newness of life (Rom. 6:4); if we died with him we will live with him (Rom. 6:8; 2 Tim. 2:11); we will live with him by the power of God (2 Cor. 13:4); whether awake or asleep, we live together with him (1 Thess. 5:10); that the life of Jesus may be manifested in our bodies (2 Cor. 4:10-11); because I live, you will live also (John 14:19).

C3e Life through faith
The righteous by faith will live (Hab. 2:4; Rom. 1:17; Gal. 3:11; Heb. 10:38); that whoever believes in him may have eternal life (John 3:15-16); he who believes in Christ has eternal life (John 3:36; 6:40, 47); those who would believe in him for eternal life (1 Tim. 1:16); he who believes in him who sent me has eternal life (John 5:24); those who believe may know that they have eternal life (1 John 5:13); that believing, you may have life in his name (John 20:31); he who believes in me will never die (John 11:26).

C3f The book of life
Those whose names are in the book of life (Phil. 4:3); another book was opened, the book of life (Rev. 20:12).

C3g The gift of eternal life
God promised eternal life (Titus 1:2; 1 John 2:25); God has granted to the Gentiles the repentance to life (Acts 11:18); ordained to eternal life (Acts 13:48); you have given him authority to grant eternal life to all you have given him (John 17:2); heirs in hope of eternal life (Titus 3:7); husbands and wives are joint heirs of the grace of life (1 Pet. 3:7); the eternal life to which you were called (1 Tim. 6:12); the Spirit gives life (John 6:63; 2 Cor. 3:6); be faithful to death and I will give you the crown of life (Rev. 2:10); the crown of life which the Lord has promised to those who love him (Jas. 1:12); his divine power has granted us everything pertaining to life and godliness (2 Pet. 1:3); to him who thirsts I will give the water of life without cost (Rev. 21:6); the river of the water of life (Rev. 22:1); a spring of water welling up to eternal life (John 4:14); take the water of life without cost (Rev. 22:17); that they may have the right to the tree of life (Rev. 22:14); God will take away his share in the tree of life (Rev. 22:19).

C3h Living the life
To set the mind on the Spirit is life and peace (Rom. 8:6); if by the Spirit you mortify the deeds of the body you will live (Rom. 8:13); I died to the law that I might live to God (Gal. 2:19); that we might die to sins and live to righteousness (1 Pet. 2:24); though judged in the flesh like men they may live in the spirit like God (1 Pet. 4:6); ask and God will give life to the one whose sin is not to death (1 John 5:16).

D Maintaining life
LONG LIFE, see 113B.

D1 Kept alive by God
God sent me before you to preserve life (Gen. 45:5); God meant it to save many people alive (Gen. 50:20); God keeps us alive (Ps. 66:9); the Lord will keep him alive (Ps. 41:2); the Lord will keep them alive in famine (Ps. 33:19); you kept me alive lest I go down to the pit (Ps. 30:3); in his hand is the life of every living thing (Job 12:10); in him we live and move and have our being (Acts 17:28); if God withdrew his breath all flesh would perish (Job 34:14-15); not a hair of your head will perish (Acts 27:34); if the Lord wills we will live and do this or that (Jas. 4:15); let my soul live that I may praise you (Ps. 119:175); sustain me that I might live (Ps. 119:116); save my life! (Ps. 116:4); you have saved my life (Gen. 19:19); you brought me up from Sheol (Ps. 30:3).

D2 Kept alive by men
Deliver our lives from death! (Josh. 2:13); have you let all the women live? (Num. 31:15); give us seed that we may live (Gen. 47:19); that we may live and not die (Gen. 43:8); you have caused us to live (Gen. 47:25); buy grain, then we will live and not die (Gen. 42:2); do this and you will live (Gen. 42:18); if it is a daughter she shall live (Exod. 1:16, 22); they let the boys live (Exod. 1:17-18); Joshua made a covenant to let the Gibeonites live (Josh. 9:15, 20-1); killing some who should not die and keeping alive some who should not live (Ezek. 13:19); Joash was not killed (2 Kgs. 11:2); he will pray for you and you will live (Gen. 20:7); perhaps we can keep the horses and mules alive (1 Kgs. 18:5); two of every creature to preserve life (Gen. 6:19, 20).

D3 Keeping oneself alive
If you go out to the Chaldeans you will live (Jer. 38:17); he who surrenders to the Chaldeans will live (Jer. 21:9); he who goes out to the Chaldeans will stay alive (Jer. 38:2); serve the king of Babylon and live (Jer. 27:12, 17); let me flee there and I will live (Gen. 19:20); save your life and Solomon's! (1 Kgs. 1:12); if you warn the righteous man, you will save yourself (Ezek. 3:21); if you warn the wicked, you will have saved yourself (Ezek. 3:19); the wicked not turning from his wicked way to save his life (Ezek. 13:22); that you may live and not die (2 Kgs. 18:32); do not be anxious about your life

(Matt. 6:25); whoever loses his life for my sake will save it (Luke 9:24); he who finds his life will lose it (Matt. 10:39); he who would save his life will lose it and he who loses his life for my sake will save it (Mark 8:35; Luke 17:33); by your endurance you will gain your lives (Luke 21:19).

D4 Still alive

D4a Living on

Let me see if my brethren are still alive (Exod. 4:18); Joseph is still alive (Gen. 45:26, 28; 46:30); is Benhadad still alive? (1 Kgs. 20:32); is your father still alive? (Gen. 43:7, 27); does my father still live? (Gen. 45:3); he is still alive (Gen. 43:28); Joshua and Caleb remained alive (Num. 14:38); see, your son is alive (1 Kgs. 17:23); his servants told him that his son was living (John 4:51); do not be troubled, for his life is in him (Acts 20:10); their lives were prolonged for a season and a time (Dan. 7:12); with their children they will live and come back (Zech. 10:9); we who remain alive until the coming of the Lord (1 Thess. 4:15); we who are alive and remain will be caught up to meet them in the clouds (1 Thess. 4:17); now we live, if you stand firm in the Lord (1 Thess. 3:8); as dying, and behold, we live (2 Cor. 6:9); present your bodies as a living sacrifice (Rom. 12:1).

D4b Living despite God's presence

I have seen God and my life is delivered (Gen. 32:30); who has heard God and still lived? (Deut. 4:33; 5:26); God speaks with man, yet he lives (Deut. 5:24); Korah's sons did not die (Num. 26:11).

D5 Whilst alive

Let them go down alive to Sheol (Ps. 55:15); they went down alive to Sheol (Num. 16:30, 33); let us swallow them alive like Sheol (Prov. 1:12); they took the king of Ai alive (Josh. 8:23); Saul captured Agag alive (1 Sam. 15:8); take them alive (1 Kgs. 20:18; 2 Kgs. 10:14); 10 000 sons of Seir were taken alive and thrown over a cliff (2 Chr. 25:12); the law has authority over a person only while he lives (Rom. 7:1); a married woman is bound to her husband as long as he lives (Rom. 7:2).

D6 Reviving

Revive us (Ps. 80:18); revive us again (Ps. 85:6); you will revive us again (Ps. 71:20); though I walk in the midst of trouble you revive me (Ps. 138:7); your word has revived me (Ps. 119:50); by your precepts you have revived me (Ps. 119:93).

D7 Not maintaining life

You judge yourselves unworthy of eternal life (Acts 13:46); no murderer has eternal life (1 John 3:15); could a man like me enter the temple and live? (Neh. 6:11); you have a name that you live but you are dead (Rev. 3:1); the father of a thief hates his own life (Prov. 29:24); why is life given to those who long for death? (Job 3:20-2); God does not keep the wicked alive (Job 36:6).

E Life and death

I set before you the way of life and the way of death (Jer. 21:8); I have set before you life and death (Deut. 30:15, 19); life and death belong to you (1 Cor. 3:22); death and life are in the power of the tongue (Prov. 18:21); whether for life or death, where the king is, there will I be (2 Sam. 15:21); whether we live or die we are the Lord's (Rom. 14:8); for this Christ died and rose, that he might be Lord of dead and living (Rom. 14:9); an aroma from life to life or from death to death (2 Cor. 2:16); death works in us but life in you (2 Cor. 4:12); that Christ will be exalted in my body, by life or by death (Phil. 1:20); God appointed Jesus as judge of the living and the dead (Acts 10:42); Jesus Christ will judge the living and the dead (2 Tim. 4:1); they will give account to the One who will judge the living and the dead (1 Pet. 4:5).

361 Death

A Nature of death

LIFE AND DEATH, see 360E.

A1 The fact of death

The rider's name was Death and Hades followed him (Rev. 6:8); if I make my bed in Sheol, you are there (Ps. 139:8); like sheep appointed for Sheol with death their shepherd (Ps. 49:14); Sheol and Abaddon are never satisfied (Prov. 27:20); Sheol is never satisfied (Prov. 30:16); greedy as Sheol, like death, never satisfied (Hab. 2:5); love is strong as death (S. of S. 8:6); jealousy is cruel as Sheol (S. of S. 8:6); since by a man came death, by a man has come resurrection of the dead (1 Cor. 15:21); him who had the power of death, the devil (Heb. 2:14).

A2 The effect of death

I would have slept and been at rest (Job 3:13); there the wicked cease from troubling and the weary are at rest (Job 3:17); there the slave is free from his master (Job 3:19); if her husband dies she is free to be married (Rom. 7:2; 1 Cor. 7:39); if her husband dies she is free from that law (Rom. 7:3); you turn man back to the dust (Ps. 90:3); you overpower him and he departs (Job 14:20); I said, 'I am cut off' (Lam. 3:54); will hope go down with me to Sheol? (Job 17:16); his own body was as good as dead (Rom. 4:19); the sting of death is sin (1 Cor. 15:56).

A3 Condition of the dead

A3a Condition of the body

The dust returns to the earth and the spirit to God (Eccles. 12:7); to dust you will return (Gen. 3:19-20); like an animal from dust and to dust (Eccles. 3:19); his breath departs and he returns to the earth (Ps. 146:4); like one dead, whose flesh is half-consumed (Num. 12:12); they lie down in the dust and worms cover them (Job 21:26); when he dies he will carry nothing away (Ps. 49:17).

A3b Condition of the spirit

Man dies and where is he? (Job 14:10); the dust returns to the earth and the spirit to God (Eccles. 12:7); man goes to his eternal home (Eccles. 12:5); the poor man died and was carried by the angels to Abraham's bosom (Luke 16:22).

A3c State of the dead

The dead tremble (Job 26:5); when the wicked dies his hope perishes (Prov. 11:7); there is no work nor thought nor wisdom in Sheol (Eccles. 9:10); the dead do not know anything (Eccles. 9:5); what does he care for his household when he is gone? (Job 21:21); the land of darkness and death-shadow (Job 10:21-2); they will never more see the light (Ps. 49:19); there is no remembrance of God in death (Ps. 6:5); the land of forgetfulness (Ps. 88:12); will the dead praise you? (Ps. 88:10-11); in Sheol who can praise you? (Ps. 6:5); the dead do not praise the Lord (Ps. 115:17); death cannot praise you (Isa. 38:18); the land of silence (Ps. 94:17); going down into silence (Ps. 115:17); lest I be like those who go down to the pit (Ps. 143:7); he made me dwell in darkness like those long dead (Ps. 143:3; Lam. 3:6); they lie still in Sheol, the uncircumcised, slain by the sword (Ezek. 32:21); you will enter into rest and rise again at the end of the age (Dan. 12:13).

A3d The dead

The time came for the dead to be judged (Rev. 11:18); the dead, great and small, stood before the throne and were judged (Rev. 20:12); Death and Hades gave up the dead which were in them (Rev. 20:13); the sea gave up the dead in it (Rev. 20:13); Sheol rouses dead leaders to greet the king of Babylon (Isa. 14:9-11); why consult the dead on behalf of the living? (Isa. 8:19); Christ is Lord of the dead and the living (Rom. 14:9); he is not God of the dead but of the living (Matt. 22:32; Mark 12:27); he is not God of the dead but of the living, for all live to him (Luke 20:38).

A4 Death is inevitable

Man is appointed to die once (Heb. 9:27); we must surely die (2 Sam. 14:14); the living know they will die (Eccles. 9:5); there is a time to die (Eccles. 3:2); you will bring me to death (Job 30:23); your fathers, where are they? and do the prophets live for ever? (Zech. 1:5); if the dead are not raised, let us eat and drink for tomorrow we die (1 Cor. 15:32); like sheep for Sheol with death their shepherd (Ps. 49:14); his day will come and he will die (1 Sam. 26:10); no one has authority over the day of death (Eccles. 8:8).

A5 Death is universal

In Adam all die (1 Cor. 15:22); death is the end of every man (Eccles. 7:2); the meeting house for all mankind (Job 30:23); the small and great are there (Job 3:19); even wise men die (Ps. 49:10; Eccles. 2:16); wise and fools alike die (Eccles. 2:16); death comes both to those who are satisfied and to those who are bitter (Job 21:23-6); what man can live and not see death? (Ps. 89:48); do not all go to the one place? (Eccles. 6:6).

A6 Death is final

He who goes down to Sheol does not come up again (Job 7:9); the dead will not live (Isa. 26:14); man lies down and cannot be awakened (Job 14:12); the way of no return (Job 16:22); if a man dies, will he live again? (Job 14:14); though a tree die it can sprout again (Job 14:8-9).

B Attitude towards death

B1 Fear of death

Through fear of death subject to lifelong bondage (Heb. 2:15); the terrors of death are on me (Ps. 55:4); the valley of the shadow of death (Ps. 23:4); those sitting in the land of the shadow of death (Matt. 4:16); he is brought to the king of terrors (Job 18:14); everyone will tremble for his own life on the day of your fall (Ezek. 32:10); Death, the strangler, has chosen the bones of my neck (Job 7:15).

B2 Prepared for death

Now let me die, since I see you are alive (Gen. 46:30); let me depart in peace, for I see your salvation (Luke 2:29-30); if they kill us, we will but die (2 Kgs. 7:4); if I welcome Sheol as my home (Job 17:13-14); the day of death is better than the day of birth (Eccles. 7:1); the sword devours this one and that one (2 Sam. 11:25); if I deserve to die, I am not trying to escape death (Acts 25:11); where you die I will die (Ruth 1:17); if I must die with you I will not deny you (Matt. 26:35; Mark 14:31); I will lay down my life for you (John 13:37); let us go that we may die with him (John 11:16); I am ready to go with you to prison and death (Luke 22:33); greater love has no one than this, that he lay down his life for his friends (John 15:13); Lord Jesus, receive my spirit (Acts 7:59); I would rather die than lose my ground for boasting (1 Cor. 9:15); be faithful to death and I will give you the crown of life (Rev. 2:10); they did not love their lives even to death (Rev. 12:11).

B3 Desire for death

Job wished he had died at birth (Job 3:11; 10:18); Jeremiah wished he had died at birth (Jer. 20:14-18); why is light given to those who long for death? (Job 3:20-2); oh, that God would crush me! (Job 6:8); oh, that God would cut me off! (Job 6:9); hide me in Sheol! (Job 14:13); Elijah asked that he might die (1 Kgs. 19:4); better for me to die than to live (Jonah 4:3, 8); men call on hills to fall on them (Luke 23:30); they will call on mountains and hills to fall on them (Hos. 10:8); men will seek death but not find it (Rev. 9:6); some long for

death but do not find it (Job 3:21); they will choose death rather than life (Jer. 8:3); I thought the dead more fortunate than the living (Eccles. 4:2); would that we had died in Egypt or in this wilderness! (Exod. 16:3; Num. 14:2); would that we had died when our brethren did! (Num. 20:3); would that I had died instead of you! (2 Sam. 18:33); some rejoice when they find the grave (Job 3:22); the hope of the wicked is to breathe their last (Job 11:20).

C Reason for death

C1 Death due to God's presence

No one can see me and live (Exod. 33:20); if we hear God more, we will die (Deut. 5:25; 18:16); he who comes near the tabernacle will die (Num. 17:12-13; 18:22); the stranger who comes near will be killed (Num. 1:51; 3:10, 38); the outsider who comes near will be put to death (Num. 18:7); lest there be a plague when they come near (Num. 8:19); Gideon feared he would die after he saw the angel (Judg. 6:22-3); we will die for we have seen God (Judg. 13:22); they have brought the ark to kill us! (1 Sam. 5:10).

C2 Death as punishment

Whoever touches the mountain must die (Exod. 19:12-13); the man who did this deserves to die (2 Sam. 12:5); for breaking the oath Jonathan must die (1 Sam. 14:44); because Abimelech took Sarah he would die (Gen. 20:3, 7); the ten spies died of a plague (Num. 14:37); Nadab and Abihu died when they offered strange fire (Lev. 10:2; 16:1; Num. 3:4; 26:61; 1 Chr. 24:2); Dathan and Abiram died an unnatural death, the earth swallowing them (Num. 16:29-33); dying of snake bite (Num. 21:6); the whole congregation would die in the desert (Num. 14:35; 26:65); your corpses will fall in the wilderness (Num. 14:29, 32, 33); 14 700 died by the plague (Num. 16:49); 24 000 died by the plague (Num. 25:9); 70 000 died of the pestilence (2 Sam. 24:15; 1 Chr. 21:14); if you are corrupt you will soon perish from the land (Deut. 4:25-6); Gideon must die for destroying the altar of Baal (Judg. 6:30); all Eli's descendants would die in the prime of life (1 Sam. 2:33); we have a law and by that law he ought to die (John 19:7); all the Jews shouted that he ought not to live any longer (Acts 25:24).

C3 Death for sin

C3a Sin produces death

When you eat of the tree you will surely die (Gen. 2:17; 3:3); the wages of sin is death (Rom. 6:23); evil will kill the wicked (Ps. 34:21); death entered the world through sin (Rom. 5:12); death reigned (Rom. 5:14); by the transgression of the one many died (Rom. 5:15); by a man came death (1 Cor. 15:21); if through the transgression of the one, death reigned through that one (Rom. 5:17); death came on all men, for all sinned (Rom. 5:12); obeying sin leads to death (Rom. 6:16); our sinful passions were bearing fruit for death (Rom. 7:5); sin deceived me and killed me (Rom. 7:11); it was sin working death through what is good (Rom. 7:13); the end of those things is death (Rom. 6:21); when sin is completed it gives birth to death (Jas. 1:15); a way which seems right to man but its end is the way to death (Prov. 14:12; 16:25); who will deliver me from the body of this death? (Rom. 7:24).

C3b Sinners will die

The soul who sins will die (Ezek. 18:4, 13, 18, 20, 24, 26); when I tell the wicked that he will surely die (Ezek. 33:14); all who have sinned without law will perish without law (Rom. 2:12); he who pursues evil will die (Prov. 11:19); each will be put to death for his own sin (2 Kgs. 14:6); there is sin unto death (1 John 5:16-17); everyone is to die for his own sin (Deut. 24:16; Jer. 31:30; Ezek. 3:18, 20).

C3c Repent lest you die

Turn from your sins, why will you die? (Ezek. 33:11); what profit is it to gain the world and forfeit your soul? (Matt. 16:26; Mark 8:36; Luke 9:25); unless you repent you will all likewise perish (Luke 13:3, 5); if he does not turn from his wickedness, he will die in his iniquity (Ezek. 3:19); if the wicked man does not turn from his way he will die (Ezek. 33:9); you will die in your sin (John 8:21); you will die in your sins (John 8:24); if you live according to the flesh you will die (Rom. 8:13).

C3d Sinners grasped by death

The loose woman's house is the way to Sheol (Prov. 7:27); the pleasure seeker is dead while she lives (1 Tim. 5:6); this is why many are ill and some have fallen asleep (1 Cor. 11:30).

C4 Death for other reasons

He dies for lack of discipline (Prov. 5:23); the desire of the sluggard kills him (Prov. 21:25); fools die for lack of understanding (Prov. 10:21); they perish because they did not love the truth (2 Thess. 2:10); all who hate wisdom love death (Prov. 8:36); he who hates reproof will die (Prov. 15:10); if God withdrew his Spirit all flesh would perish (Job 34:15).

D Expectation of death

D1 Early death

Do not take me away in the midst of my days (Ps. 102:24); his youthful frame lies in the dust (Job 20:11); wicked men were snatched away before their time (Job 22:16); why should you die before your time? (Eccles. 7:17); in the middle of my life I must enter the gates of Sheol (Isa. 38:10); the godless die in youth (Job 36:14).

D2 Death will soon happen

I am going the way of all the earth (Josh. 23:14; 1 Kgs. 2:2); the days of mourning for my father are drawing near (Gen. 27:41); I am about to die (Gen. 25:32; 48:21; 49:29; 50:5, 24); the time for Israel's death drew near (Gen. 47:29); the time is near for you to die (Deut. 31:14); the days for David's death drew near (1 Kgs. 2:1); about to lie down with your fathers (Deut. 31:16); Bathsheba's child will die (2 Sam. 12:14); when your feet enter the city the child will die (1 Kgs. 14:12); I am about to take from you the desire of your eyes (Ezek. 24:16); this night your soul is required of you (Luke 12:20); save us, Lord, we are perishing! (Matt. 8:25); Master, we are perishing! (Luke 8:24); the centurion's slave was on the point of death (Luke 7:2); Jairus' daughter was dying (Luke 8:42); his son was on the point of death (John 4:47); often near death (2 Cor. 11:23); Epaphroditus was ill, near to death (Phil. 2:27); his soul draws near to the pit (Job 33:22); this year you will die (Jer. 28:16); strengthen what remains and is about to die (Rev. 3:2).

D3 Death in peace

You will go to your fathers in peace (Gen. 15:15); you will be gathered to your people in peace (2 Chr. 34:28); you will die in peace (2 Kgs. 22:20; Jer. 34:4-5).

D4 Possibility of death

Lest Shelah also die like his brothers (Gen. 38:11); the lad cannot go lest his father die (Gen. 44:22); why bring us into the desert to die? (Exod. 14:11-12; Num. 16:13; 20:4; 21:5); give me children or I die! (Gen. 30:1); lest I die because of her (Gen. 26:9); let them return from war lest they die (Deut. 20:5, 6, 7); lest I be like those who go down to the pit (Ps. 28:1); do not return me to prison, lest I die there (Jer. 37:20); there is death in the pot (2 Kgs. 4:40); come down before my child dies (John 4:49); Teacher, do you not care if we perish? (Mark 4:38); the voyage will be with loss, not only of ship and cargo, but of our lives (Acts 27:10); they expected him to swell up and fall down dead (Acts 28:6).

E Actual deaths

E1 Death of the high priest

Until the death of the high priest (Num. 35:25, 28, 32; Josh. 20:6); before the death of the high priest (Num. 35:32).

E2 Death of Christ

KILLING CHRIST, see 362E2.

E2a Foretelling Christ's death

The Anointed One [Messiah] will be cut off (Dan. 9:26); he poured himself out to death (Isa. 53:12); his life is taken up from the earth (Acts 8:33); I lay down my life that I may take it again (John 10:17-18); Jesus indicated the kind of death by which he would die (John 12:33; 18:32); the Son of man will be three days and nights in the heart of the earth (Matt. 12:40); how can you say that the Son of man must be lifted up? (John 12:34).

E2b The fact of Christ's death

He became obedient to death, even death on a cross (Phil. 2:8); Jesus breathed his last (Matt. 27:50; Mark 15:37; Luke 23:46); Jesus gave up his spirit (John 19:30); Pilate was surprised he was already dead (Mark 15:44-5); a dead man named Jesus (Acts 25:19); Christ has suffered in the flesh (1 Pet. 4:1); Christ Jesus died and was raised (Rom. 8:34); if we believe that Jesus died and rose again (1 Thess. 4:14); put to death in the flesh but made alive in spirit (1 Pet. 3:18); I died, and behold I am alive for evermore (Rev. 1:18); the first and the last, who died and came to life (Rev. 2:8).

E2c The effect of Christ's death

Christ died for our sins (1 Cor. 15:3; 1 Pet. 3:18); he died for us (1 Thess. 5:10); greater love has no one than this, that he lay down his life for his friends (John 15:13); while we were yet sinners, Christ died for us (Rom. 5:8); while enemies of God we were reconciled by the death of his Son (Rom. 5:10); Christ died for the ungodly (Rom. 5:6); he died for all (2 Cor. 5:14-15); that he might taste death for everyone (Heb. 2:9); the good shepherd lays down his life for the sheep (John 10:11); I lay down my life for the sheep (John 10:15); expedient that one man die for the people (John 11:50-1; 18:14); he was delivered up for our transgressions (Rom. 4:25); a death for the redemption of transgressions (Heb. 9:15); the Son of man came to give his life a ransom for many (Matt. 20:28; Mark 10:45); redeemed with the precious blood of Christ (1 Pet. 1:18-19); by this we know love, that he laid down his life for us (1 John 3:16); for this Christ died and rose, that he might be Lord of dead and living (Rom. 14:9); he has reconciled you through his fleshly body by his death (Col. 1:22); when I am lifted up I will draw all men to me (John 12:32); by death he would destroy him who had the power of death (Heb. 2:14).

E3 Death of God's people

We do not want you to be ignorant about those who have fallen asleep (1 Thess. 4:13); those who have fallen asleep in Jesus (1 Thess. 4:14); those who stay alive will not precede those who have fallen asleep (1 Thess. 4:15); the dead in Christ will rise first (1 Thess. 4:16); if there is no resurrection, those who have fallen asleep in Christ have perished (1 Cor. 15:18); precious in the Lord's sight is the death of his saints (Ps. 116:15); blessed are the dead who die in the Lord (Rev. 14:13); to die is gain (Phil. 1:21); far better (Phil. 1:23); death cannot separate us from the love of God (Rom. 8:38-9); I am ready to die for the name of the Lord Jesus (Acts 21:13); we ought to lay down our lives for the brothers (1 John 3:16); perhaps for a good man one would dare to die (Rom. 5:7); if we die, we die for the Lord, not for ourselves (Rom. 14:7-8); Jesus indicated by what death Peter would glorify God (John 21:19); the laying aside of my earthly dwelling is imminent (2 Pet. 1:14); the time of my departure has come (2 Tim. 4:6).

E4 Death of other groups
Everything on the earth will die in the flood (Gen. 6:17); every living creature died (Gen. 7:21-3); all the firstborn of Egypt will die (Exod. 11:5); all the Egyptian army drowned (Exod. 14:28; 15:4-5; Heb. 11:29); your fathers ate the manna in the wilderness and died (John 6:49); not bread like the fathers ate and died (John 6:58); 18 people on whom the tower of Siloam fell and killed them (Luke 13:4); many died from the bitter waters (Rev. 8:11); a third of mankind was killed by these three plagues (Rev. 9:18).

E5 Death of creatures
When you take away their spirit they die (Ps. 104:29); if they are driven hard for one day all the flocks will die (Gen. 33:13); if an animal being kept dies (Exod. 22:10); if an animal dies it must not be eaten (Lev. 11:39-40); do not eat that which dies of itself (Lev. 22:8; Deut. 14:21); the fat of an animal which dies of itself shall not be eaten (Lev. 7:24); I have never eaten what died of itself (Ezek. 4:14); the priest must not eat bird or beast which has died or been torn (Ezek. 44:31); though the flock be cut off from the fold and no cattle in the stalls (Hab. 3:17); a third of sea creatures died (Rev. 8:9); every living thing in the sea died (Rev. 16:3).

F Spiritual death
F1 Spiritually dead
You have a name that you live but you are dead (Rev. 3:1); you were dead in trespasses and sins (Eph. 2:1); dead in sins (Eph. 2:5; Col. 2:13); the mind set on the flesh is death (Rom. 8:6); let the dead bury their dead (Matt. 8:22; Luke 9:60); if our gospel is veiled, it is veiled to those who are perishing (2 Cor. 4:3); the message of the cross is foolishness for those who are perishing (1 Cor. 1:18); the dead will hear the voice of the Son of God and will live (John 5:25); my son was dead and is alive again (Luke 15:24); your brother was dead and is alive again (Luke 15:32); he who does not love remains in death (1 John 3:14); the commandment which should have brought life brought death instead (Rom. 7:10); the letter kills but the Spirit gives life (2 Cor. 3:6); I set before you the way of life and the way of death (Jer. 21:8); when the commandment came, sin revived and I died (Rom. 7:9); the ministry of death (2 Cor. 3:7).

F2 The second death
The lake of fire is the second death (Rev. 20:14; 21:8); he who overcomes will not be hurt by the second death (Rev. 2:11); the second death has no power over those in the first resurrection (Rev. 20:6); they are trees without fruit, doubly dead, uprooted (Jude 12).

F3 Dead to sin
How can we who died to sin still live in it? (Rom. 6:2); those who are Christ's have crucified the flesh (Gal. 5:24); crucified with Christ (Gal. 2:20); our old self was crucified with him (Rom. 6:6); united with Christ in a death like his (Rom. 6:5); you have died with Christ to the elementary principles of the world (Col. 2:20); you have died and your life is hid with Christ (Col. 3:3); if we died with him we will live with him (Rom. 6:8; 2 Tim. 2:11); he who has died is freed from sin (Rom. 6:7); we were baptised into his death (Rom. 6:3); he died for all and therefore all died (2 Cor. 5:14); that we might die to sins and live to righteousness (1 Pet. 2:24); count yourselves dead to sin (Rom. 6:11); reckon your bodies as dead to immorality etc. (Col. 3:5).

F4 Self put to death
I die daily (1 Cor. 15:31); as dying, and behold, we live (2 Cor. 6:9); the sentence of death was on us (2 Cor. 1:9); carrying about in our body the death of Jesus (2

Cor. 4:10); while we live we are always being delivered over to death for Jesus' sake (2 Cor. 4:11); death works in us but life in you (2 Cor. 4:12); being conformed to his death (Phil. 3:10); he who finds his life will lose it and he who loses his life for my sake will find it (Matt. 10:39); he who would save his life will lose it and he who loses his life for my sake will find it (Matt. 16:25; Mark 8:35; Luke 17:33); he who wants to save his life will lose it (Luke 9:24); whoever loses his life for my sake will save it (Luke 9:24); he who loves his life loses it (John 12:25); he who does not take up his cross and follow me is not worthy of me (Matt. 10:38); whoever would come after me must take up his cross (Matt. 16:24); take up your cross (Mark 8:34); he must take up his cross daily (Luke 9:23); whoever does not take up his cross cannot be my disciple (Luke 14:27); put to death the deeds of the body (Rom. 8:13); I do not consider my life as of any account (Acts 20:24).

G Not dying
G1 Death averted
He would not see death before he saw the Christ (Luke 2:26); some will not taste death until they see the kingdom (Matt. 16:28; Mark 9:1; Luke 9:27); you will not die (Gen. 3:4; Judg. 6:23); we will not die (Hab. 1:12); I will not die but live (Ps. 118:17); this illness is not to death (John 11:4); Rahab did not perish with the disobedient (Heb. 11:31); the bitterness of death is past (1 Sam. 15:32); if you beat him with the rod he will not die (Prov. 23:13); the Lord has not given me over to death (Ps. 118:18); God may turn from his anger so that we do not perish (Jonah 3:9); do not let us perish for this man's life (Jonah 1:14); perhaps your God will take notice of us so we do not perish (Jonah 1:6); there will be no loss of life, but only of the ship (Acts 27:22).

G2 Death prevented
If you had been here my brother would not have died (John 11:21, 32); could he not have kept this man from dying? (John 11:37); pray for us that we will not die (1 Sam. 12:19); God has granted you all those sailing with you (Acts 27:24); he will deliver their soul from death (Ps. 33:19); the Lord releases those condemned to death (Ps. 102:20); you lift me up from the gates of death (Ps. 9:13); you have delivered my soul from death (Ps. 56:13; 116:8); God will redeem my soul from the power of Sheol (Ps. 49:15); you will not abandon me to Sheol (Ps. 16:10); you have delivered my soul from the depths of Sheol (Ps. 86:13); preserve those doomed to die (Ps. 79:11); deliver those being led away to death (Prov. 24:11).

G3 Death avoided
No one can pay a ransom to avoid dying (Ps. 49:7-8); no one can continue on for ever and never see the pit (Ps. 49:9); can man deliver his soul from the power of Sheol? (Ps. 89:48); that one may avoid the snares of death (Prov. 13:14; 14:27); what innocent man ever perished? (Job 4:7); tEnoch was not, for God took him (Gen. 5:24); Enoch did not see death (Heb. 11:5); Elijah was taken up into heaven (2 Kgs. 2:11); we will not all sleep (1 Cor. 15:51); what if he remains until I come? (John 21:22-3); sons of the resurrection, like angels, cannot die any more (Luke 20:36); whoever believes in him will not perish but have eternal life (John 3:16); this is the bread of which a man may eat and not die (John 6:50); if anyone keeps my word he will never see death (John 8:51-2); he who lives and believes in me will never die (John 11:26); their worm does not die (Mark 9:48).

G4 Death overcome
To God belongs escape from death (Ps. 68:20); righteousness delivers from death (Prov. 10:2; 11:4); I will ransom them from the power of Sheol (Hos. 13:14);

I will redeem them from death (Hos. 13:14); Christ prayed to him who was able to save him out of death (Heb. 5:7); Christ was not abandoned to Hades (Acts 2:31); Christ, raised from the dead, will never die again (Rom. 6:9); I have the keys of death and Hades (Rev. 1:18); Christ abolished death (2 Tim. 1:10); by death he would destroy him who had the power of death (Heb. 2:14); death has no more dominion over him (Rom. 6:9); the last enemy to be destroyed is death (1 Cor. 15:26); death will be swallowed up (Isa. 25:8); death is swallowed up in victory (1 Cor. 15:54-5); where is your sting, O death? (Hos. 13:14; 1 Cor. 15:55); there will be no more death (Rev. 21:4); death and Hades gave up the dead in them (Rev. 20:13); death and Hades were thrown into the lake of fire (Rev. 20:14).

362 Killing: destruction of life
A Rules about killing
A1 Murder
A1a Do not murder
Do not murder (Exod. 20:13; Deut. 5:17; Matt. 5:21; 19:18; Mark 10:19; Luke 18:20; Rom. 13:9; Jas. 2:11); do not kill the innocent (Exod. 23:7); do not shed innocent blood (Jer. 22:3); the Lord hates hands that shed innocent blood (Prov. 6:17); let none of you suffer as a murderer (1 Pet. 4:15); cursed is he who kills in secret (Deut. 27:24-5).
A1b Judged as murderers
Will you steal, murder and commit adultery? (Jer. 7:9); he who kills a thief after sunrise is guilty of bloodshed (Exod. 22:2-3); righteous men will judge them as adulteresses and murderers (Ezek. 23:45); you lift up your eyes to idols as you shed blood (Ezek. 33:25); on your skirts is found the lifeblood of the innocent poor (Jer. 2:34); you asked for a murderer to be granted you (Acts 3:14); Saul was breathing out threats and murder against the disciples (Acts 9:1); do not be afraid of those who kill the body (Luke 12:4); some kill the body but cannot kill the soul (Matt. 10:28); he who hates his brother is a murderer (1 John 3:15); this man is a murderer (Acts 28:4); the rebels had murdered in the insurrection (Mark 15:7); Barabbas had murdered in the insurrection (Luke 23:19, 25); the devil was a murderer from the beginning (John 8:44); no murderer has eternal life (1 John 3:15).
A1c Judgement on murderers
Whoever sheds man's blood, by man shall his blood be shed (Gen. 9:6); he who strikes a man to death shall be put to death (Exod. 21:12); he who kills a man shall be put to death (Lev. 24:17, 21); a murderer must be put to death (Num. 35:30-1); there is no atonement for blood except the blood of him who shed it (Num. 35:33); the avenger of blood shall put the murderer to death (Num. 35:19, 21); the murderer shall be put to death (Num. 35:16, 17, 18); the law is for patricides, matricides, murderers (1 Tim. 1:9); all who take the sword will perish by the sword (Matt. 26:52); murderers go to the lake of fire (Rev. 21:8); murderers are outside the city (Rev. 22:15).
A2 Manslaughter
Killing another unintentionally (Exod. 21:13; Num. 35:11, 15, 22-3; Deut. 4:42; 19:4); distinguishing murder from manslaughter (Exod. 21:12-13; Num. 35:16-24); cities to which the manslayer may flee (Num. 35:6).
B Anticipation of killing
B1 Possibility of killing
Whoever finds me will kill me (Gen. 4:14); Abraham feared being killed because of Sarah (Gen. 12:12; 20:11); Isaac feared being killed because of Rebekah (Gen. 26:7); lest Esau kill the mothers with the children (Gen. 32:11); this man was arrested by the Jews and was about

to be killed by them (Acts 23:27); why did you bring us out of Egypt to kill us with thirst? (Exod. 17:3).
B2 Attempting to kill
B2a Attempting to kill in general
The wicked seeks to kill the righteous (Ps. 37:32); the wicked are about to kill the upright (Ps. 37:14); let us lie in wait for blood (Prov. 1:11); an adulteress hunts for a man's precious life (Prov. 6:26); your lovers seek your life (Jer. 4:30); let us wipe out Israel as a nation (Ps. 83:4); those who sought to kill you are dead (Exod. 4:19).
B2b Attempting to kill me
Violent men seek my life (Ps. 86:14); those who seek my life (Ps. 63:9; 70:2); the wicked lie in wait to destroy me (Ps. 119:95); why does he seek my life? (1 Sam. 20:1); they seek my life (Rom. 11:3); they planned to kill me (Ps. 31:13); you know all their plots to kill me (Jer. 18:23); violent men sought my life (Ps. 54:3); those who seek my life lay snares (Ps. 38:12); the man who planned to destroy us (2 Sam. 21:5); my son seeks my life (2 Sam. 16:11); do you mean to kill me as you killed the Egyptian? (Exod. 2:14; Acts 7:28); he who seeks my life seeks your life (1 Sam. 22:23); the sword will not separate us from the love of Christ (Rom. 8:35).
B2c Attempting to kill Christ
Herod seeking to destroy Jesus (Matt. 2:13); those who sought the child's life are dead (Matt. 2:20); let us kill the heir (Matt. 21:38); they sought false testimony against Jesus to put him to death (Matt. 26:59); they persuaded the crowds to ask for Barabbas and to destroy Jesus (Matt. 27:20); they sought testimony against Jesus to put him to death (Mark 14:55).
B2d Attempting to kill specific people
Esau planned to kill Jacob (Gen. 27:41, 42); Joseph's brothers planned to kill him (Gen. 37:18, 20); Pharaoh tried to kill Moses (Exod. 2:15); Saul tried to kill David (1 Sam. 18:11; 19:10; 23:15; 24:11; 2 Sam. 4:8); men watched the house to kill him (Ps. 59:t); Solomon sought Jeroboam's death (1 Kgs. 11:40); they looked for Daniel and his companions to kill them (Dan. 2:13); the chief priests planned to killed Lazarus also (John 12:10); Herod wanted to kill John (Matt. 14:5); Herodias wanted to kill John (Mark 6:19); they wanted to kill the apostles (Acts 5:33); they tried to kill Paul (Acts 9:23-4, 29; 21:31; 23:15); they stoned Paul and thought he was dead (Acts 14:19); they vowed not to eat or drink until they had killed Paul (Acts 23:12, 14, 21); some Jews tried to put me to death (Acts 26:21); setting an ambush to kill Paul (Acts 25:3); the soldiers planned to kill the prisoners (Acts 27:42).
B3 Killing will happen
Whoever escapes Hazael, Jehu will kill and whoever escapes Jehu, Elisha will kill (1 Kgs. 19:17); they will kill you (Matt. 24:9); some they will kill and some they will persecute (Luke 11:49); some of you will be put to death (Luke 21:16); some you will kill and crucify (Matt. 23:34); if anyone would harm them, this is how he must be killed (Rev. 11:5); he will destroy those tenants and give the vineyard to others (Mark 12:9).
B4 Approval for killing
B4a Approval to kill in general
There is a time to kill (Eccles. 3:3); Death and Hades were given authority to kill with sword, famine, pestilence and wild beasts (Rev. 6:8); destroy the inhabitants of that city with the sword (Deut. 13:15); let their men be struck to death, their young men killed by the sword (Jer. 18:21); whoever has it, let him die (Gen. 31:32; 44:9); go in and kill them (2 Kgs. 10:25); put to death whoever comes between the ranks (2 Kgs. 11:8); put to death whoever follows her (2 Kgs. 11:15); slay and utterly destroy them (Jer. 50:21); cursed be he who

restrains his sword from bloodshed (Jer. 48:10); kill the one who entices you from the Lord (Deut. 13:9).

B4b Approval to kill oneself
Please kill me (Num. 11:15; 2 Sam. 1:9); kill us yourself (Judg. 8:21); kill me lest it be said a woman killed me (Judg. 9:54); if there is sin in me, kill me yourself (1 Sam. 20:8); if there is iniquity in me, let him kill me (2 Sam. 14:32); Saul asked his armour bearer to kill him (1 Sam. 31:4; 1 Chr. 10:4).

B4c Approval to kill certain people
Destroy the nations of the land (Deut. 7:2, 16, 24; 20:16); destroy the Amalekites (Deut. 25:19; 1 Sam. 15:3, 18); on taking a city, destroy all the men (Deut. 20:13); the Jews were given the right to exterminate their enemies (Esther 8:11); do not let Joab's grey hair go down to Sheol in peace (1 Kgs. 2:6); bring Shimei's grey hair down to Sheol in blood (1 Kgs. 2:9); you may kill my two sons (Gen. 42:37); let Uriah be killed (2 Sam. 11:15); seven sons of Saul were handed over to be killed (2 Sam. 21:6-9).

B5 Desire for killing
B5a Ready to kill
Men of bloodshed (Ps. 26:9); the Lord abhors the man of blood (Ps. 5:6); save me from men of blood (Ps. 59:2); depart from me, men of blood (Ps. 139:19); men of blood hate the blameless (Prov. 29:10); those who kill you will think they are offering service to God (John 16:2); from the heart come murders (Matt. 15:19; Mark 7:21); filled with murder (Rom. 1:29); you lust and do not have, so you murder (Jas. 4:2); they hasten to shed blood (Prov. 1:16); their feet swift to shed blood (Isa. 59:7; Rom. 3:15).

B5b A lifestyle of killing
One slaughters an ox and one kills a man (Isa. 66:3); if he has a violent son who sheds blood (Ezek. 18:10); righteousness lodged in her, but now murderers (Isa. 1:21); the murderer arises at dawn (Job 24:14); all of them lie in wait for bloodshed (Mic. 7:2); as robbers wait for a man, so a band of priests murder on the way to Shechem (Hos. 6:9); bloodshed follows bloodshed (Hos. 4:2); the thief comes only to steal, kill and destroy (John 10:10); the earth will reveal her bloodshed (Isa. 26:21); they did not repent of their murders (Rev. 9:21); he looked for justice, and behold, bloodshed (Isa. 5:7); for your sake we are killed all day long (Ps. 44:22; Rom. 8:36).

B5c Killing many people
The land is filled with blood (Ezek. 9:9); your hands are full of blood (Isa. 1:15); they will fill the land of Egypt with the slain (Ezek. 30:11); Saul and Jonathan did not hold back from killing (2 Sam. 1:22); Saul has slain his thousands and David his ten thousands (1 Sam. 18:7-8; 21:11; 29:5); David was a man who shed much blood (1 Chr. 22:8; 28:3); you have filled the streets with the slain (Ezek. 11:6).

B6 Restraint from killing
The Lord put a mark on Cain lest anyone kill him (Gen. 4:15); the Lord has restrained you from killing (1 Sam. 25:26, 31); you have kept me from bloodshed (1 Sam. 25:33); the centurion kept the soldiers from fulfilling their purpose (Acts 27:43); Satan was not allowed to kill Job (Job 2:6); because you have not asked for the life of those who hate you (2 Chr. 1:11).

C Means of killing
STRIKING TO DEATH, see 279A1h.
STONING, see 344B6e.

C1 Choking
The harlot lay on her child (1 Kgs. 3:19); Hazael smothered Ben-hadad (2 Kgs. 8:15); that they should abstain from what is strangled (Acts 15:20, 29; 21:25); death the strangler has chosen the bones of my neck

(Job 7:15); it binds me like the collar of my coat (Job 30:18).

C2 Animals killing
A lion killed a man of God (1 Kgs. 13:24); a lion killed a son of the prophets (1 Kgs. 20:36); lions killed the settlers in Samaria (2 Kgs. 17:25-6); two bears killed 42 youths (2 Kgs. 2:24); kill an ox which gores a person to death (Exod. 21:28, 29); wild beasts will kill your children (Lev. 26:22); if one ox kills another (Exod. 21:35-6).

C3 Killing by the sword
C3a 'The sword' in general
I have given the glittering sword (Ezek. 21:15); a sword is drawn, polished for slaughter, like lightning (Ezek. 21:28); though they go into captivity I will command the sword to slay them (Amos 9:4); fire will devour you, the sword cut you down (Nahum 3:15); if the sword comes and takes someone off (Ezek. 33:4, 6); if anyone kills with the sword, with the sword he must be killed (Rev. 13:10); all who take the sword will perish by the sword (Matt. 26:52).

C3b Killed with the sword
They will die by the sword and famine (Jer. 44:12); you will fall by the sword (Num. 14:43); the pick of his troops will fall by the sword (Ezek. 17:21); your survivors will fall by the sword (Ezek. 23:25); Ethiopia, Put, Lud, Arabia and Lybia will fall by the sword (Ezek. 30:5); Tyre's daughters on the mainland will be slain by the sword (Ezek. 26:6, 8); he will slay your people with the sword (Ezek. 26:11); they will fall in Egypt by the sword (Ezek. 30:6); by the swords of mighty ones I will cause your multitude to fall (Ezek. 32:12); your sons and daughters will fall by the sword (Ezek. 24:21); they will fall amongst those slain by the sword (Ezek. 32:20); those in the waste places will fall by the sword (Ezek. 33:27); those slain by the sword will fall in your valleys (Ezek. 35:8); they will fall by sword and flame, by captivity and by plunder (Dan. 11:33); their princes will fall by the sword (Hos. 7:16); your sons and daughters will fall by the sword (Amos 7:17); all the sinners of my people will die by the sword (Amos 9:10); they will fall by the edge of the sword (Luke 21:24); some were slain with the sword (Heb. 11:37).

D God killing
D1 God kills
The Lord kills and brings to life (Deut. 32:39; 1 Sam. 2:6); the Lord brings down to Sheol (1 Sam. 2:6); those slain by the Lord will be many (Isa. 66:16); I will kill you with the sword (Exod. 22:24); he can destroy both soul and body in hell (Matt. 10:28); fear him who after he has killed has authority to cast into hell (Luke 12:5); the Lord has given the wicked to the sword (Jer. 25:31); God will crush the head of his enemies (Ps. 68:21); kill my enemies before me (Luke 19:27); slay the wicked, O God (Ps. 139:19); with the breath of his mouth he will slay the wicked (Isa. 11:4); those slain by the Lord will be from one end of the earth to the other (Jer. 25:33); I will destroy the man who does not humble himself on the Day of Atonement (Lev. 23:30); the Lord will slay you (Isa. 65:15); though he slay me, I will trust in him (Job 13:15).

D2 God killing individuals
The Lord put Er to death (Gen. 38:7; 1 Chr. 2:3); the Lord put Onan to death (Gen. 38:10); the Lord was about to kill Moses (Exod. 4:24); the angel would have killed Balaam (Num. 22:33); God slew Sihon and Og (Ps. 135:11; 136:19-20); the Lord struck Nabal and he died (1 Sam. 25:38); the Lord will strike Saul (1 Sam. 26:10); the Lord put Saul to death (1 Chr. 10:14); the Lord struck down Uzzah (2 Sam. 6:7; 1 Chr. 13:10); the Lord struck down Jeroboam (2 Chr. 13:20); an angel of

the Lord struck down Herod (Acts 12:23); the Lord Jesus will slay the lawless one with the breath of his mouth (2 Thess. 2:8).

D3 God killing his people
D3a God might kill his people
Better to have died by the Lord's hand in Egypt (Exod. 16:3); lest I destroy you on the way (Exod. 33:3, 5); God was about to slay all the assembly (Num. 14:12; 16:21, 45; Deut. 9:14, 25); the Egyptians will say you brought them out to kill them (Exod. 32:12); he has brought them out to kill them in the wilderness (Deut. 9:28); if you kill the people as one man (Num. 14:15); God would have destroyed you (Deut. 9:8, 19; Ps. 106:23); God would have destroyed Aaron (Deut. 9:20).

D3b God will kill his people
I will cut off from you both the righteous and the wicked (Ezek. 21:3, 4); those left I will slay with the sword, so none will flee or escape (Amos 9:1); what you bring forth I will put to the sword (Mic. 6:14); he will destroy those tenants and give the vineyard to others (Matt. 21:41; Mark 12:9; Luke 20:16); he who does not listen to him will be cut off from the people (Acts 3:23); the Lord will destroy you from the land (Deut. 6:15; Josh. 23:15, 16); slaughter all who do not have the mark (Ezek. 9:6); I will destroy my people (Jer. 15:7).

D3c God killed his people
Fire from the Lord consumed the 250 men (Num. 16:35); the Lord destroyed the followers of Baal-peor (Deut. 4:3); the Lord struck Benjamin before Israel (Judg. 20:35); God struck down men of Beth-shemesh (1 Sam. 6:19); God killed the strongest of them (Ps. 78:31); he has killed all that were pleasing to the eye (Lam. 2:4); you have slain and not spared (Lam. 3:43); when he killed them, they sought him (Ps. 78:34); he destroyed those who did not believe (Jude 5); I have hewn them by the prophets, slain them with my words (Hos. 6:5); he killed them in the wilderness (Num. 14:16); you have slain them in your anger (Lam. 2:21).

D4 God killing others
D4a God killing all people
I will wipe mankind and all creatures off the face of the earth (Gen. 6:7); I will destroy them with the earth (Gen. 6:13); I will destroy all flesh (Gen. 6:17); I will destroy every living creature (Gen. 7:4); God blotted out every creature (Gen. 7:23); I will never again destroy every living creature (Gen. 8:21).

D4b God will kill the peoples
God cuts off the nations (Deut. 19:1); the Lord will shatter kings (Ps. 110:5-6); God wanted the people of the land destroyed (John. 11:20); the wicked he will destroy (Ps. 145:20); I will strike down the firstborn (Exod. 12:12); Assyria will fall by a sword not of man (Isa. 31:8); the Lord will destroy the Philistines (Jer. 47:4); I will kill her children with pestilence (Rev. 2:23); I will cut off the Cherethites (Ezek. 25:16); he will make a complete end of all the inhabitants of the earth (Zeph. 1:18); you also, O Ethiopians, will be killed by my sword (Zeph. 2:12).

D4c God killed the peoples
I have cut off nations (Zeph. 3:6); God slew great kings (Ps. 136:17, 18); God slew many nations and mighty kings (Ps. 135:10); the Lord killed the firstborn of Egypt (Exod. 4:23; 12:29; 13:15); God struck all the firstborn in the land of Egypt (Ps. 105:36); God smote the Egyptians (Exod. 12:27); the Lord threw hailstones on the Amorites and killed them (Josh. 10:11); the angel of the Lord killed 185 000 Assyrians (2 Kgs. 19:35; Isa. 37:36); he killed all the Assyrian fighting men (2 Chr. 32:21).

E People killing
E1 Killing leaders
E1a Killing priests
Saul told his guards to kill the priests (1 Sam. 22:17); his priests fell by the sword (Ps. 78:64); Seraiah et al. were killed (Jer. 52:27); should priest and prophet be slain in the temple? (Lam. 2:20); they killed Mattan priest of Baal (2 Kgs. 11:18; 2 Chr. 23:17); Jehu killed the priests and prophets of Baal (2 Kgs. 10:19-25); Josiah killed the priests of the high places (2 Kgs. 23:20).

E1b Killing prophets
Jezebel killed the prophets of the Lord (1 Kgs. 18:4, 13); they killed your prophets (1 Kgs. 19:10, 14; Neh. 9:26; Rom. 11:3); Jezebel threatened to kill Elijah (1 Kgs. 19:2); they seek my life (1 Kgs. 19:10, 14); the king seeking to kill Elisha (2 Kgs. 6:31, 32); Jehoiakim killed Uriah (Jer. 26:21-3); let Jeremiah be put to death (Jer. 38:4); they stoned Zechariah in the court of the temple (2 Chr. 24:21; Matt. 23:35); Jerusalem, killing the prophets (Matt. 23:37; Luke 13:33-4); you are sons of those who killed the prophets (Matt. 23:31; Luke 11:47-8); they killed the Lord Jesus and the prophets (1 Thess. 2:15); avenging the blood of my servants the prophets (2 Kgs. 9:7); the blood of all the prophets charged against this generation (Matt. 23:35; Luke 11:50-1); they killed those who announced the coming of the Righteous One (Acts 7:52); the beast will make war on the witnesses, overcome them and kill them (Rev. 11:7); they poured out the blood of saints and prophets (Rev. 16:6); Elijah killed the prophets of Baal (1 Kgs. 18:40; 19:1); Nebuchadnezzar will kill Ahab and Zedekiah, the false prophets (Jer. 29:21).

E2 Killing Christ
E2a Christ would be killed
He was cut off out of the land of the living (Isa. 53:8); his killing foretold (Matt. 16:21; 17:23; 20:18-19; 26:2; Mark 8:31; 9:31; 10:34; Luke 9:22; 18:33; 24:7); they plotted to kill him (Matt. 26:4); the Pharisees took counsel how to destroy him (Matt. 12:14); they took counsel against Jesus to put him to death (Matt. 27:1); they sought to kill him (Matt. 26:3-4; Mark 3:6; 14:1; Luke 22:2; John 5:18; 7:1; 8:37; 11:53); they tried to kill him (Mark 11:18; Luke 19:47); you seek to kill me (John 8:40); why do you seek to kill me? (John 7:19-20); is not this the man they are seeking to kill? (John 7:25); they picked up stones to stone him (John 8:59; 10:31); the Jews were just now seeking to stone you (John 11:8); Herod wanted to kill Jesus (Luke 13:31); let us kill him and the inheritance will be ours (Mark 12:7); he deserves death (Matt. 26:66); let him be crucified! (Matt. 27:22, 23); crucify him! (Mark 15:13-14; Luke 23:21; John 19:6, 15); they were insistent, with loud voices demanding that he be crucified (Luke 23:23); I will strike down the shepherd (Matt. 26:31); strike down the shepherd and the sheep will be scattered (Mark 14:27).

ATTEMPTING TO KILL CHRIST, see 362B2c.

E2b Christ was killed
They crucified him (Matt. 27:35; Mark 15:24; Luke 24:20); they crucified him and two others (Matt. 27:38; Mark 15:27; Luke 23:33; John 19:18); the rulers crucified the Lord of glory (1 Cor. 2:8); you are looking for Jesus who was crucified (Matt. 28:5); he was crucified in weakness (2 Cor. 13:4); we preach Christ crucified (1 Cor. 1:23); I decided to know nothing except Jesus Christ and him crucified (1 Cor. 2:2); placarded as crucified (Gal. 3:1); the city where their Lord was crucified (Rev. 11:8); this Jesus whom you crucified (Acts 2:36); you crucified him (Acts 4:10); you put him to death by hanging him on a gibbet (Acts 5:30); they killed him (Acts 2:23; 7:52; 13:28-9); you killed the

originator of life (Acts 3:15); they put him to death by hanging him on a tree (Acts 10:39); they killed the Lord Jesus and the prophets (1 Thess. 2:15); they threw him out of the vineyard and killed him (Matt. 21:39; Mark 12:8; Luke 20:15); you were slain and by your blood ransomed men for God (Rev. 5:9); worthy is the Lamb that was slain! (Rev. 5:12); as a sheep to the slaughter (Isa. 53:7; Acts 8:32); a Lamb as if it had been slain (Rev. 5:6); the Lamb who was slain from the foundation of the world (Rev. 13:8); was Paul crucified for you? (1 Cor. 1:13); they are crucifying the Son of God over again (Heb. 6:6).

E3 Killing named individuals

Cain killed his brother Abel (Gen. 4:8, 25; Matt. 23:35; 1 John 3:12); David killed Goliath (1 Sam. 17:49-51); Jael transfixed Sisera (Judg. 4:21; 5:26); Theudas was killed (Acts 5:36); Uriah was killed (2 Sam. 11:17, 21, 24); you killed Uriah with the sword of Amon (2 Sam. 12:9).

E4 Killing unnamed individuals

Benaiah killed the Egyptian with his own spear (2 Sam. 23:21; 1 Chr. 11:23); I killed a man for wounding me (Gen. 4:23); Moses killed the Egyptian (Exod. 2:12, 14; Acts 7:24, 28); Herod ordered that the sentries be executed (Acts 12:19); causing those who do not worship the image of the beast to be killed (Rev. 13:15).

E5 Killing family members

E5a Killing sons and daughters

Athaliah killed all the royal children (2 Kgs. 11:1; 2 Chr. 22:10); Zedekiah's sons were killed before him (2 Kgs. 25:7; Jer. 39:6; 52:10); making their sons pass through the fire (Ezek. 20:26, 31); blood is on their hands, they caused their sons to pass through the fire (Ezek. 23:37); the company will kill their sons and daughters (Ezek. 23:47); they slaughtered their children for their idols (Ezek. 23:39); they shed the innocent blood of their sons and daughters (Ps. 106:38); anyone prophesying falsely will be killed by his parents (Zech. 13:3); the father will deliver up his child to death (Mark 13:12); he forced our fathers to expose their children so they would not survive (Acts 7:19); Abraham took the knife to kill his son (Gen. 22:10).

E5b Killing brothers

Cain killed his brother Abel (Gen. 4:8, 25; Matt. 23:35; 1 John 3:12); everyone kill brothers, friends and neighbours (Exod. 32:27); brother will deliver up brother to death (Mark 13:12).

E5c Killing parents

Children will rise against parents and have them put to death (Matt. 10:21; Mark 13:12).

E5d Killing whole families

Lest Esau kill the mothers with the children (Gen. 32:11); Athaliah destroyed all the royal family (2 Kgs. 11:1); killing all the house of: Jeroboam by Baasha (1 Kgs. 15:29); Baasha by Zimri (1 Kgs. 16:11, 12); Ahab by Jehu (2 Kgs. 9:8; 10:11, 17); Ahaziah by Jehu (2 Kgs. 10:14).

E6 Killing groups

E6a Killing Israelites

Every Hebrew boy to be killed (Exod. 1:16, 22); Haman planned to annihilate the Jews (Esther 3:6, 9, 13; 8:5; 9:24); Herod killed all the boys (Matt. 2:16).

E6b Killing foreigners

Samson killed more at his death than during his life (Judg. 16:30); Saul slaughtered the Ammonites (1 Sam. 11:11); Saul had killed Gibeonites (2 Sam. 21:1-2); David slaughtered two thirds of the Moabites (2 Sam. 8:2); David killed Amalekites (1 Sam. 30:17); David killed Arameans (2 Sam. 10:18; 1 Chr. 18:5; 19:18); David killed Philistines (1 Sam. 18:27; 19:8; 23:5; 2 Sam. 5:25); the Jews killed their enemies (Esther 9:5); the Jews killed the ten sons of Haman (Esther 9:7-10, 12); Saul

destroyed the Amalekites (1 Sam. 15:8, 20); the Simeonites killed the remnant of the Amalekites (1 Chr. 4:43); Simeon and Levi killed every male in Shechem (Gen. 34:25); Joab killed every male in Edom (1 Kgs. 11:15, 16); Sihon and his people were wiped out (Deut. 2:34); as were Og and his people (Num. 21:35; Deut. 3:3-6); they destroyed every person (Josh. 10:40; 11:12, 14); all the Amorites (Josh. 10:20); all the Anakim (Josh. 11:21-2); the Hamites and Meunites were destroyed (1 Chr. 4:41).

E7 Killing disciples

Those killed because of the word of God and for their testimony (Rev. 6:9); is not this who destroyed those who called on this name? (Acts 9:21); when the blood of your witness Stephen was shed (Acts 22:20); when they were put to death I cast my vote against them (Acts 26:10); until the number of their brethren who were to be killed was complete (Rev. 6:11); they poured out the blood of saints and prophets (Rev. 16:6); John was beheaded in prison (Matt. 14:10; Mark 6:27; Luke 9:9); they stoned Stephen (Acts 7:58-60); Paul persecuted the Way to death (Acts 22:4); James was killed with the sword (Acts 12:2); the kind of death by which Peter would glorify God (John 21:19).

E8 Killing oneselves

E8a Killing one another

The Midianites killed each other (Judg. 7:22); the Philistines killed one another (1 Sam. 14:20); the kings must have killed one another (2 Kgs. 3:23); Ammon and Moab killed those of Mount Seir and one another (2 Chr. 20:23); every man's sword will be against his brother (Ezek. 38:21); the horses and their riders will fall by the sword of their fellows (Hag. 2:22); the hand of one will be lifted up against his fellow (Zech. 14:13); peace taken from the earth so men should kill one another (Rev. 6:4).

E8b Suicide

Samson pulled the building down on himself (Judg. 16:30); Saul fell on his sword (1 Sam. 31:4; 1 Chr. 10:4); Saul's armour bearer fell on his sword (1 Sam. 31:5; 1 Chr. 10:5); Ahithophel hanged himself (2 Sam. 17:23); Zimri burnt the palace over himself (1 Kgs. 16:18); Judas hanged himself (Matt. 27:5); the Philippian jailer was about to kill himself (Acts 16:27); will he kill himself? (John 8:22); they lie in wait for their own blood (Prov. 1:18).

E9 Killing animals

E9a Rules about killing animals

Redeem a donkey or break its neck (Exod. 13:13; 34:20); kill an ox which gores a person to death (Exod. 21:28, 29, 32); kill the animal used for bestiality (Lev. 20:15, 16); regulations for killing an animal (Lev. 17:3-4); he who kills an animal must replace it (Lev. 24:18, 21); do not kill an animal and its young on the same day (Lev. 22:28).

E9b Killing wild animals

David had killed lions and bears (1 Sam. 17:35-6); Benaiah killed a lion in a pit on a snowy day (2 Sam. 23:20; 1 Chr. 11:22); the beast was slain (Dan. 7:11).

E9c Killing sacrifices

Kill the lamb at twilight (Exod. 12:6); kill the Passover (Exod. 12:21); they killed the Passover (Ezra 6:20); killing at the doorway of the tent of meeting (Exod. 29:11; Lev. 3:2, 8, 13; 4:4); killing the burnt offering (Lev. 14:19); killing the guilt offering (Lev. 14:25); killing the sin offering (Lev. 8:15; 16:11, 15); kill the red heifer (Num. 19:3); one sacrifices a lamb and one breaks a dog's neck (Isa. 66:3).

SACRIFICES, see 981C.

363 Corpse

A Rules about corpses
What to do if a corpse is found in the country (Deut. 21:1-9); what to do if a man dies in a tent (Num. 19:14-15); touching a dead body makes one unclean (Lev. 22:4; Num. 19:11, 16); touching carcasses of unclean animals makes one unclean (Lev. 5:2); touching the carcass of a clean animal makes one unclean (Lev. 11:39); priests must not defile themselves except for a near relative (Lev. 21:1-3; Ezek. 44:25); the high priest must not go near any dead body (Lev. 21:11); a Nazirite must not touch a dead body (Num. 6:6); defiling my holy name by the corpses of their kings (Ezek. 43:7); a body must not be left hanging on a tree overnight (Deut. 21:22-3); they did not want the bodies to stay on the cross on the Sabbath (John 19:31).

B Jesus' corpse
Joseph of Arimathea asked for Jesus' body (Matt. 27:58-9; Mark 15:43; Luke 23:52; John 19:38); Pilate granted the body to Joseph (Mark 15:45); the women saw how his body was laid (Luke 23:55); two angels seated where Jesus' body had been (John 20:12).

C Corpses of other people
They took the bodies of Saul and his sons from the wall (1 Sam. 31:12); Amasa's corpse was removed from the highway (2 Sam. 20:12); the prophet took up the man of God's body (1 Kgs. 13:29); John's disciples came and took the body (Matt. 14:12; Mark 6:29); she put her dead son in my bosom (1 Kgs. 3:20); Josiah's body was brought in a chariot to Jerusalem (2 Kgs. 23:30); they washed Dorcas' body (Acts 9:37); many bodies of the saints who had fallen asleep were raised (Matt. 27:52); a dead man was being carried out (Luke 7:12); Michael disputed with the devil about the body of Moses (Jude 9); their dead bodies will lie in the street of the city (Rev. 11:8).

D Corpses en masse
Defile the house and fill the courts with the slain (Ezek. 9:7); you have filled the streets with the slain (Ezek. 11:6); dead Philistines lay as far as Gath and Ekron (1 Sam. 17:52); corpses lay like refuse in the streets (Isa. 5:25); corpses will fall like dung on the field (Jer. 9:22); they will fill the houses with corpses (Jer. 33:5); they will look on the corpses of those who transgressed (Isa. 66:24); there will be many corpses (Amos 8:3); countless corpses (Nahum 3:3); he will fill the nations with corpses (Ps. 110:6); your body is clothed with the slain (Isa. 14:19); the stench of their corpses will rise (Isa. 34:3); the valley of the dead bodies (Jer. 31:40).

E Eating corpses
Birds will eat the flesh off you (Gen. 40:19); your bodies will be food for birds and beasts (Deut. 28:26); those who die in the city will be eaten by dogs and those who die in the field will be eaten by birds (1 Kgs. 14:11; 16:4; 21:24); dogs will eat Jezebel (1 Kgs. 21:23; 2 Kgs. 9:10, 36); their corpses will be food for birds and beasts (Jer. 7:33; 16:4; 19:7; 34:20; Ezek. 39:17; Rev. 19:17-18); where the body is, there the eagles gather (Job 39:30; Matt. 24:28; Luke 17:37); birds of prey came down to the carcasses (Gen. 15:11); I will give your flesh to the birds and beasts (1 Sam. 17:44); I will give the corpses of the Philistines to the birds and beasts (1 Sam. 17:46); they have given the bodies of your servants to birds and beasts for food (Ps. 79:2).

F Parts of corpses
F1 Bones
Joseph's bones were taken from Egypt (Gen. 50:25; Exod. 13:19; Josh. 24:32; Heb. 11:22); David took the bones of Saul and Jonathan (2 Sam. 21:12); they gathered the bones of those who were hanged (2 Sam.

21:13); lay my bones beside his bones (1 Kgs. 13:31); touching Elisha's bones brought a dead man to life (2 Kgs. 13:21); if they see a man's bone they will set up a marker (Ezek. 39:15); decay enters my bones (Hab. 3:16); inside they are full of dead men's bones and uncleanness (Matt. 23:27); none of his bones shall be broken (John 19:36); bones were burned on altars to defile them (2 Kgs. 23:16; 2 Chr. 34:5); bones shall be burned on this altar (1 Kgs. 13:2); he burned to lime the bones of the king of Edom (Amos 2:1); Josiah defiled idolatrous places with human bones (2 Kgs. 23:14, 20); their bones will be spread out on the ground (Jer. 8:2); the bones of the inhabitants of Jerusalem will be brought from their graves (Jer. 8:1); your bones will be scattered around your altars (Ezek. 6:5); the valley of dry bones (Ezek. 37:1-14); these bones are the whole house of Israel (Ezek. 37:11); the jawbone of a donkey (Judg. 15:15-17).

F2 Heads / skulls
The heads of Oreb and Zeeb were brought to Gideon (Judg. 7:25); David took Goliath's head (1 Sam. 17:46, 51, 54, 57); the Philistines cut off Saul's head (1 Sam. 31:9; 1 Chr. 10:9-10); they took Ish-bosheth's head to David (2 Sam. 4:7-8); Sheba's head will be thrown to you (2 Sam. 20:21-2); if Elisha's head remains on him today (2 Kgs. 6:31-2); seventy heads were sent to Jehu (2 Kgs. 10:6-8); give me the head of John the Baptist (Matt. 14:8; Mark 6:25); John's head was brought on a platter (Matt. 14:11; Mark 6:28); the millstone crushed his skull (Judg. 9:53); they only found Jezebel's skull, feet and palms (2 Kgs. 9:35); Golgotha – the place of the skull (Matt. 27:33; Mark 15:22; John 19:17); the place called The Skull [Calvary] (Luke 23:33).

F3 Other pieces of corpses
The concubine was cut into 12 pieces (Judg. 19:29); I cut my concubine in pieces (Judg. 20:6); Saul's headless body was fixed to the wall (1 Sam. 31:10-12); they only found Jezebel's skull, feet and palms (2 Kgs. 9:35); they cut off their hands and feet (2 Sam. 4:12).

364 Interment

A Preparation for burial
40 days required for embalming (Gen. 50:3); embalming of Jacob (Gen. 50:2); embalming of Joseph (Gen. 50:26); Joseph was put in a coffin in Egypt (Gen. 50:26); Jesus' body was wrapped in linen cloths (John 19:40); they saw the wrappings (John 20:5-7); she prepared my body for burial (Matt. 26:12; John 12:7); she has anointed my body for burial (Mark 14:8); Joseph will close my eyes (Gen. 46:4); King David walked behind Abner's bier (2 Sam. 3:31); Jesus touched the bier (Luke 7:14); a pyre with fire and wood (Isa. 30:33).

B Burial places
CAVES FOR BURYING, see 255A1.

B1 One's own burial place
Asa cut out a tomb for himself (2 Chr. 16:14); all the kings lie in glory in their own tombs (Isa. 14:18); Joseph's own tomb which he had hewn (Matt. 27:60); what right do you have to hew a tomb for yourself here? (Isa. 22:16).

B2 Another's burial place
The prophet buried the man of God in his own grave (1 Kgs. 13:30-1); they threw a man in Elisha's grave (2 Kgs. 13:21); Ish-bosheth's head was buried in Abner's grave (2 Sam. 4:12); where you die I will die and there be buried (Ruth 1:17); Saul was buried in the grave of Kish his father (2 Sam. 21:14); Joseph of Arimathea laid Jesus' body in his own new tomb (Matt. 27:60).

B3 The cave of Machpelah

Give me a burying place and I will bury my dead (Gen. 23:4); let him sell it to me as a burial place (Gen. 23:9); the field and the cave became Abraham's as a burial place (Gen. 23:20; 49:30); the cave used for the burial of: Abraham (Gen. 25:9-10; 49:31); Sarah (Gen. 23:19; 49:31); Isaac (Gen. 49:31); Rebekah (Gen. 49:31); Leah (Gen. 49:31); Jacob (Gen. 47:30; 49:29; 50:5, 13); the patriarchs (Acts 7:16).

B4 Jesus' tomb

They made his grave with the wicked man (Isa. 53:9); Joseph of Arimathea laid Jesus' body in his own new tomb (Matt. 27:60); they laid Jesus in a new tomb (Mark 15:46; Luke 23:53; John 19:41-2); they laid him in a tomb (Acts 13:29); they made the tomb as secure as they could (Matt. 27:64-6); Mary Magdalene came to the tomb (Matt. 28:1; John 20:1); they came to the tomb at dawn (Luke 24:1); women went to the tomb (Luke 24:22); Peter ran to the tomb (Luke 24:12); some of us went to the tomb (Luke 24:24); the two Marys sat opposite the grave (Matt. 27:61); Mary stooped to look into the tomb (John 20:11); they went to the tomb when the sun had risen (Mark 16:2); Peter and the other disciple went to the tomb (John 20:3); entering the tomb they saw a young man sitting on the right (Mark 16:5); they fled from the tomb (Mark 16:8); returning from the tomb (Luke 24:9).

B5 Other burial places

The pillar of Rachel's grave (Gen. 35:20); Rachel's tomb (1 Sam. 10:2); they hid in tombs (1 Sam. 13:6); demoniacs coming out of the tombs (Matt. 8:28); living in the tombs (Mark 5:2-3; Luke 8:27); people who sit in tombs (Isa. 65:4); among the tombs and on the mountains he cried out (Mark 5:5); Jesus came to the tomb, a cave with a stone on it (John 11:38); David's tomb is with us to this day (Acts 2:29); Jerusalem, the city of my fathers' tombs (Neh. 2:3, 5); saints coming out of the tombs (Matt. 27:53); you build the tombs of the prophets (Matt. 23:29; Luke 11:47-8); they bought the potter's field as a burial ground for foreigners (Matt. 27:7).

C Burying people

C1 Burying in general

If you want me to bury my dead (Gen. 23:8); let me go up and bury my father (Gen. 50:5-7); permit me first to bury my father (Matt. 8:21; Luke 9:59); let the dead bury their dead (Matt. 8:22; Luke 9:60); God buried Moses (Deut. 34:6); it will take seven months to bury them all (Ezek. 39:11-16).

C2 Inadequate burial

My mother would have been my grave (Jer. 20:17); I will put your corpses on the corpses of your idols (Lev. 26:30); your body will not come to the grave of your fathers (1 Kgs. 13:22); he will have a donkey's burial (Jer. 22:19); they threw Uriah's body into the burial place of the common people (Jer. 26:23); they will bury in Topheth for lack of room elsewhere (Jer. 7:32; 19:11); Moses hid the Egyptian in the sand (Exod. 2:12); they buried Uzziah in the field of the grave because he was a leper (2 Chr. 26:23).

C3 No burial

Better the stillborn than a man without a burial (Eccles. 6:3); no one will bury Jezebel (2 Kgs. 9:10); Jehoiakim's body would not be buried (Jer. 36:30); corpses will fall like sheaves after the reaper with none to gather (Jer. 9:22); there was no one to bury them (Ps. 79:3); they will lie unburied (Jer. 25:33); their bones will not be buried (Jer. 8:2); there will be no one to bury them (Jer. 14:16); they will not be lamented or buried (Jer. 16:4, 6); their corpses lay like refuse in the streets (Isa. 5:25); dragged and thrown outside the gates

of Jerusalem (Jer. 22:19); he only of Jeroboam will come to the grave (1 Kgs. 14:13); you will not be gathered or buried (Ezek. 29:5); they will refuse to let them be placed in a tomb (Rev. 11:9).

C4 Exhumed

You have been thrown out of your tomb (Isa. 14:19-20); I will open your graves and bring you out (Ezek. 37:12-13); the tombs were opened (Matt. 27:52).

D Figurative burial

You are like unmarked tombs over which men walk (Luke 11:44); like whitewashed tombs (Matt. 23:27); their throat is an open grave (Ps. 5:9; Rom. 3:13); their quiver is like an open grave (Jer. 5:16); we were buried with Christ through baptism (Rom. 6:4; Col. 2:12).

365 Animals

A Animals in general

A1 All animals

God created all animals (Gen. 1:20-5; 2:19); sea creatures created (Gen. 1:20-2); land creatures created (Gen. 1:24-5); God gave plants as food to all creatures (Gen. 1:30); every animal of the forest and the cattle on a thousand hills are mine (Ps. 50:10); let beasts and cattle praise the Lord (Ps. 148:10); this is the law regarding animals, birds, fish and swarming things (Lev. 11:46); you are cursed more than all cattle or all beasts of the field (Gen. 3:14); I will blot out animals, creeping things and birds (Gen. 6:7); I will blot out every living thing that I have made (Gen. 7:4); two of all birds, beasts and creeping things were to be taken into the ark (Gen. 6:19-20); all birds, beasts and creeping things perished (Gen. 7:21, 23); all birds, beasts and creeping things came out of the ark (Gen. 8:17, 19); do not make an image of an animal (Deut. 4:17); images in the form of all kinds of creatures (Rom. 1:23).

A2 Wild animals

A2a Wild animals in general

God made the beasts of the earth (Gen. 1:24-5); the Lord formed every beast of the field out of the ground (Gen. 2:19); every beast according to its kind (Gen. 7:14); all beasts died (Gen. 7:21); what the poor leave the beast of the field may eat (Exod. 23:11); wild beasts and jackals will live in Babylon (Jer. 50:39); Nineveh has become a desolation, a lair of wild beasts (Zeph. 2:15); wild animals will live in places once inhabited (Isa. 13:21-2; 32:14; 34:11, 13-17); if I cause wild beasts to pass through the land (Ezek. 14:15); the oracle of the beasts of the Negeb (Isa. 30:6); all beasts of the field will be on its fallen branches (Ezek. 31:13); the beasts of the field found shade under the tree (Dan. 4:12); under which beasts of the earth dwelt (Dan. 4:21); for the wickedness of its inhabitants beasts and birds are swept away (Jer. 12:4); both birds and beasts have fled and are gone (Jer. 9:10); a covenant with you, birds, cattle and every beast (Gen. 9:10); quadrupeds, reptiles and birds in the sheet (Acts 10:12; 11:6).

A2b Wild animals as a scourge

My four severe judgements, sword, famine, wild beasts and plague (Ezek. 14:21); wild animals sent as a plague in judgement (Lev. 26:22; Deut. 32:24); I will send beasts against you (Ezek. 5:17); Death and Hades given authority to kill with sword, famine, pestilence and wild beasts (Rev. 6:8).

A2c Wild beasts subdued

You will not be afraid of wild beasts (Job 5:22); every kind of beast and bird, reptile and sea creature can be tamed (Jas. 3:7); the beasts of the field will be at peace with you (Job 5:23); I have given him the beasts of the field (Jer. 28:14); I have given the wild animals to Nebuchadnezzar to serve him (Jer. 27:6); the beasts of the field will glorify me (Isa. 43:20); Jesus was with the wild animals (Mark 1:13); she kept wild beasts from the corpses (2 Sam. 21:10); I will destroy wild beasts from the land (Lev. 26:6; Ezek. 34:25); I will not drive them out in one year lest the beasts of the field become too many for you (Exod. 23:29); lest the wild beasts become too many for you (Deut. 7:22).

A3 Men and animals
A3a Instructions regarding men and animals
Corruptible man, birds, animals or reptiles (Rom. 1:23); the flesh of men, animals, birds and fish is different (1 Cor. 15:39); the fate of men and the fate of beasts is the same – death (Eccles. 3:19); the firstborn of man and beast belong to me (Exod. 13:2; 34:19; Num. 3:13; 8:17); the firstborn of men and cattle instead of the Levites (Num. 3:41); neither man nor beast may work on the sabbath (Exod. 20:10; Deut. 5:14); Noah's covenant included every living creature (Gen. 9:10, 12, 15-17).

A3b Relation of animals to man
All creatures given into man's hand (Gen. 9:2); man was to rule over the beasts (Gen. 1:26); man is to rule all creatures (Ps. 8:7-8); man gave names to all the beasts (Gen. 2:20); beasts and birds are to fear man (Gen. 9:2); no living creature was a helper suitable for man (Gen. 2:20); do not lie with any animal (Lev. 18:23); animals given to man for food (Gen. 9:3); wherever there dwell men or beasts or birds, he has given them into your hand (Dan. 2:38); Solomon spoke of animals, birds, reptiles and fish (1 Kgs. 4:33); ask the beasts and let them teach you (Job 12:7); from every living thing I will require your lifeblood (Gen. 9:5).

A3c Men like animals
Man is like the beasts that perish (Ps. 49:12, 20); men are like beasts, for one fate comes to all (Eccles. 3:18-19); why are we treated by you as animals? (Job 18:3); like irrational animals (2 Pet. 2:12; Jude 10); I fought with wild beasts at Ephesus (1 Cor. 15:32); Cretans are evil beasts (Titus 1:12); let his mind be changed from a man's to a beast's (Dan. 4:16); your dwelling will be with the beasts of the field (Dan. 4:25, 32); he was driven out from among men and his mind was made like a beast's (Dan. 5:21).

A3d Both men and animals saved
I will multiply on you man and beast (Ezek. 36:11); I will sow Israel and Judah with the seed of man and the seed of beast (Jer. 31:27); neither you nor your cattle will be barren (Deut. 7:14); you save man and beast (Ps. 36:6).

B Small creatures
B1 Small creatures in general
Let the earth bring forth creeping things (Gen. 1:24-5); let men rule over all creeping things (Gen. 1:26); have dominion over every creeping thing (Gen. 1:28); every creeping thing will fear you (Gen. 9:2); to every creeping thing I have given plants for food (Gen. 1:30); two of every creeping thing (Gen. 6:20; 7:8); all creeping things died (Gen. 7:21, 23); insects which crawl are unclean (Lev. 11:20); creeping things which fly are unclean (Deut. 14:19).

B2 Flying insects
B2a Bee / hornet
Bees in the carcass of the lion (Judg. 14:8); the Lord will whistle for the bee in Assyria (Isa. 7:18); the Amorites chased you like bees (Deut. 1:44); they surrounded me like bees (Ps. 118:12); God will send hornets (Exod. 23:28; Deut. 7:20); I sent the hornet before you (Josh. 24:12).

B2b Fly / gnat
Dead flies make the perfumer's oil stink (Eccles. 10:1); the Lord will whistle for the fly in Egypt (Isa. 7:18); swarms [of flies] (Exod. 8:21-4, 31; Ps. 78:45; 105:31); a

gadfly [horsefly] is coming from the north (Jer. 46:20); you strain out a gnat [mosquito?] and swallow a camel (Matt. 23:24); gnat [flea?, sandfly?, louse?]: that the dust may become gnats (Exod. 8:16-18); gnats in all their territories (Ps. 105:31).

B2c Locust / grasshopper
Grasshoppers and locusts of all kinds are clean (Lev. 11:22); locusts have no king but march in rank (Prov. 30:27); John the baptist ate locusts (Matt. 3:4; Mark 1:6); the locust strips and flies away (Nahum 3:16); a plague of locusts (Exod. 10:4-20; Joel 1:4-7; Rev. 9:3); he spoke and the locusts came (Ps. 105:34); the Lord was forming locusts (Amos 7:1); if I command the grasshoppers (2 Chr. 7:13); the locust will consume your seed (Deut. 28:38); the locust will possess your trees and your produce (Deut. 28:42); he gave the fruit of their labour to the locust (Ps. 78:46); if there are locusts or grasshoppers (1 Kgs. 8:37; 2 Chr. 6:28); the locust devoured your fig trees and olive trees (Amos 4:9); I will rebuke the devourer so it will not destroy your fruit (Mal. 3:11); we seemed like grasshoppers (Num. 13:33); its inhabitants are like grasshoppers (Isa. 40:22); the grasshopper drags itself along (Eccles. 12:5); do you make the horse leap like the locust? (Job 39:20); the locusts were like horses prepared for battle (Rev. 9:7); I will restore the years that the locust has eaten (Joel 2:25).

B2d Moth
The moth will eat them (Isa. 50:9); the moth will eat them like a garment (Isa. 51:8); they are crushed before the moth (Job 4:19); you consume like a moth what is precious to man (Ps. 39:11); I am like a moth to Ephraim (Hos. 5:12); do not store up treasures on earth where moth and rust consume (Matt. 6:19-20); where no moth destroys (Luke 12:33).

B3 Worm / maggot
The worm will eat the grapes (Deut. 28:39); God appointed a worm to eat the plant (Jonah 4:7); leftover manna bred worms (Exod. 16:20); maggots are your bed and worms your covering (Isa. 14:11); my flesh is clothed with maggots (Job 7:5); Herod was eaten by worms (Acts 12:23); they lie down in the dust and worms cover them (Job 21:26); their worm will not die (Isa. 66:24; Mark 9:48); man is a maggot and a worm (Job 25:6); you worm, Jacob (Isa. 41:14); I am a worm (Ps. 22:6).

B4 Other small creatures
Ants are not strong, but provide their food (Prov. 30:25); go to the ant, you sluggard (Prov. 6:6); I am a flea (1 Sam. 24:14; 26:20); the leech has two daughters (Prov. 30:15); they weave the spider's web (Isa. 59:5); his trust is as fragile as a spider's web (Job 8:14).

C Flying creatures
C1 Flying creatures in general
C1a All kinds of birds
Flying things were created (Gen. 1:20-2); God made all birds (Gen. 2:19); pairs of birds went into the ark (Gen. 6:20; 7:8); all birds perished (Gen. 7:21); he did not cut the birds in two (Gen. 15:10); I know every bird of the mountains (Ps. 50:11); let winged birds praise the Lord (Ps. 148:10); birds were given green plants for food (Gen. 1:30); birds of the air do not sow or reap (Matt. 6:26); birds of the air nest in its branches (Ezek. 17:23; 31:6; Dan. 4:12, 21; Matt. 13:32; Luke 13:19); birds of the air nest in the shade of its mustard (Mark 4:32); birds of the air have nests (Matt. 8:20; Luke 9:58); one rises up at the sound of a bird (Eccles. 12:4); in vain is a net spread in the sight of any bird (Prov. 1:17); does a bird fall into a trap without bait? (Amos 3:5); wisdom is concealed from the birds of the air (Job 28:21); a bird will make the matter known (Eccles. 10:20).

C1b Men and birds

Man was to rule over birds (Gen. 1:26, 28); man rules over the birds of the heavens (Ps. 8:8); every bird of the air will fear you (Gen. 9:2); man gave names to all the birds (Gen. 2:20); let the birds of heaven teach you (Job 12:7); do not make an image of a bird (Deut. 4:17); distinguish between clean and unclean birds (Lev. 20:25); you may eat any clean bird (Deut. 14:11, 20); do not eat the blood of bird or beast (Lev. 7:26); do not take a mother bird with its young (Deut. 22:6).

C1c Birds eating

Birds will eat the flesh off you (Gen. 40:19); birds will eat your corpses (Deut. 28:26); I appoint birds to devour and destroy (Jer. 15:3); I will give you to all kinds of birds (Ezek. 39:4); gather every kind of bird to eat flesh and drink blood (Ezek. 39:17); those who die in the field will be eaten by birds (1 Kgs. 14:11; 16:4; 21:24); birds ate up the seed (Matt. 13:4; Mark 4:4; Luke 8:5); birds eating from the top basket (Gen. 40:17); she kept the birds of the air away from the corpses (2 Sam. 21:10).

C1d Like birds

Like hovering birds the Lord will protect Jerusalem (Isa. 31:5); the fugitives of Moab are like fluttering birds (Isa. 16:2); like a cage [basket] full of birds their houses are full of deceit (Jer. 5:27); I am against the magic bands with which you hunt souls like birds (Ezek. 13:20); my enemies hunted me like a bird (Lam. 3:52); like a bird from the snare of the fowler (Ps. 124:7); save yourself like a bird from the fowler (Prov. 6:5); flee like a bird to the mountains (Ps. 11:1); like a bird wandering from its nest is a man who wanders from home (Prov. 27:8); they will come like birds (Hos. 11:11); as a bird rushes into the snare (Prov. 7:23); like birds trapped in a snare (Eccles. 9:12); I will bring them down like the birds of the air (Hos. 7:12).

C2 Birds of prey

The birds of prey came down on the carcasses (Gen. 15:11); are the birds of prey against her? (Jer. 12:9); calling a bird of prey from the east (Isa. 46:11); they will be left to the birds of prey of the mountains (Isa. 18:6); calling all birds to the great supper of God (Rev. 19:17).

C3 Kinds of flying creatures

C3a Chickens

As a hen gathers her chicks (Matt. 23:37; Luke 13:34); the strutting cock [?] (Prov. 30:31); before the cock crows you will deny me three times (Matt. 26:34, 75; Luke 22:34, 61; John 13:38); the cock crowed (Matt. 26:74; Luke 22:60; John 18:27).

C3b Doves / pigeons

Noah sent out the dove (Gen. 8:8-12); the turtledove observes the time of its migration (Jer. 8:7); bring a turtledove and a young pigeon (Gen. 15:9); two turtledoves or two young pigeons (Lev. 5:7; 12:8; 14:22, 30; 15:14, 29; Num. 6:10; Luke 2:24); he overturned the seats of those selling doves (Matt. 21:12; Mark 11:15); selling oxen, sheep and pigeons in the temple (John 2:14); he told those who sold doves to take them away (John 2:16); a quarter of a kab of dove's dung cost five shekels (2 Kgs. 6:25); the voice of the turtledove is heard in our land (S. of S. 2:12); the wings of a dove covered in silver (Ps. 68:13); who are these who fly like doves to their windows? (Isa. 60:8); they will come like doves from the land of Assyria (Hos. 11:11); Ephraim is like a silly dove (Hos. 7:11); be like a dove that nests in the side of the gorge (Jer. 48:28); be wise as serpents and harmless as doves (Matt. 10:16); the Holy Spirit descended like a dove (Matt. 3:16; Mark 1:10; Luke 3:22; John 1:32).

C3c Eagle

The eagle [griffon vulture], an unclean bird (Lev. 11:13; Deut. 14:12); does the eagle mount up by your command? (Job 39:27); the way of an eagle in the sky (Prov. 30:19); I carried you on eagles' wings (Exod. 19:4); God stirs up the nest like an eagle (Deut. 32:11); mounting up like eagles (Isa. 40:31; Jer. 49:22); your youth is renewed like the eagle's (Ps. 103:5); his hair grew like eagle's [feathers] (Dan. 4:33); my days go by like an eagle swooping on its prey (Job 9:26); wealth flies off like an eagle (Prov. 23:5); an eagle flying in mid-heaven (Rev. 8:13); where the corpse is, the eagles will gather (Matt. 24:28; Luke 17:37); each creature had the face of an eagle (Ezek. 1:10; 10:14); the first beast had eagles' wings (Dan. 7:4); the fourth creature was like a flying eagle (Rev. 4:7); the woman was given the two wings of the great eagle (Rev. 12:14).

C3d Falcon / hawk / kite

The falcon [hawk?, kite?], an unclean bird (Lev. 11:14; Deut. 14:13); falcons will be gathered there (Isa. 34:15); no falcon's eye has seen that path (Job 28:7); the hawk [falcon?], an unclean bird (Lev. 11:16; Deut. 14:15); does the hawk soar by your discernment? (Job 39:26); the kite, an unclean bird (Lev. 11:14; Deut. 14:13).

C3e Ostrich

The ostrich, an unclean bird (Lev. 11:16; Deut. 14:15); description of the ostrich (Job 39:13-18); cruel like ostriches (Lam. 4:3); mourning like the ostriches (Mic. 1:8); I am a companion of ostriches (Job 30:29); the jackals and ostriches will glorify me (Isa. 43:20); ostriches will live there (Isa. 13:21); it will be the abode of ostriches (Isa. 34:13); ostriches will live in Babylon (Jer. 50:39).

C3f Owl

I am like an owl of the waste places (Ps. 102:6); the owl [ostrich?], an unclean bird (Lev. 11:16; Deut. 14:15); little owl, an unclean bird (Lev. 11:17; Deut. 14:16); great owl [eagle owl?, ibis?]: the great owl, an unclean bird (Lev. 11:17; Deut. 14:16); the great owl will live in Edom (Isa. 34:11); the white owl [ibis?, water-hen?, pelican?], an unclean bird (Lev. 11:18; Deut. 14:16).

C3g Partridge

A partridge on the mountains (1 Sam. 26:20); a partridge hatching eggs it has not laid (Jer. 17:11); En-hakkore – spring of the partridge (Judg. 15:19).

C3h Peafowl

The ships brought apes and peacocks (1 Kgs. 10:22; 2 Chr. 9:21).

C3i Pelican

The pelican, an unclean bird (Lev. 11:18; Deut. 14:17); the pelican will possess Edom (Isa. 34:11); the pelican will lodge in Moab (Zeph. 2:14); I am like a pelican in the wilderness (Ps. 102:6).

C3j Quail

Quail came over the camp (Exod. 16:13; Num. 11:31-2); God brought quail (Ps. 105:40); he rained birds on them (Ps. 78:27).

C3k Raven

The raven, an unclean bird (Lev. 11:15; Deut. 14:14); Noah sent out the raven (Gen. 8:7); God feeds the ravens (Ps. 147:9); who gives food to the ravens? (Job 38:41); ravens fed Elijah (1 Kgs. 17:4, 6); the raven will dwell in it (Isa. 34:11); the ravens will pluck out the eye (Prov. 30:17); ravens neither sow nor reap (Luke 12:24).

C3l Sparrow

Are not two sparrows sold for an assarion? (Matt. 10:29); five sparrows for two assaria (Luke 12:6); sparrow and swallow nest in the temple (Ps. 84:3); like a sparrow in its flitting (Prov. 26:2); I am like a sparrow on the housetop (Ps. 102:7); do not fear, you are of more value than many sparrows (Matt. 10:31).

C3m Stork
The stork, an unclean bird (Lev. 11:19; Deut. 14:18); the stork's home is the fir tree (Ps. 104:17); the stork in the sky knows her seasons (Jer. 8:7); like the wings of a stork (Zech. 5:9).

C3n Swallow
Like a swallow in its flying (Prov. 26:2); sparrow and swallow nest in the temple (Ps. 84:3).

D Water creatures
D1 Water creatures in general
God created the great sea monsters (Gen. 1:21); animals great and small are in the sea (Ps. 104:25); all water creatures with fins and scales can be eaten (Lev. 11:9-12); the hippopotamus [Behemoth] (Job 40:15-24); the crocodile is an unclean animal (Lev. 11:30); can you catch a crocodile [Leviathan] with a hook? (Job 41:1-3); Leviathan sports in the sea (Ps. 104:26); skins of the porpoise [or dugong] (Exod. 25:5; 26:14; 35:7, 23; 36:19; 39:34); a third of sea creatures died (Rev. 8:9).

D2 Fish
Man rules over the fish of the sea (Gen. 1:26, 28; Ps. 8:8); the fish of the sea are given into man's hand (Gen. 9:2); let the fish of the sea teach you (Job 12:8); do not make an image of any fish (Deut. 4:18); the fish in the Nile died (Exod. 7:18, 21; Ps. 105:29); I will make fish stick to your scales (Ezek. 29:4); the Lord appointed a fish to swallow Jonah (Jonah 1:17); Jonah was three days and nights in the belly of the sea monster (Matt. 12:40); if he asks for a fish, who will give him a snake? (Matt. 7:10; Luke 11:11); fish of many kinds, like the fish of the Great Sea (Ezek. 47:10); a dragnet which gathered fish of every kind (Matt. 13:47); seven loaves and a few small fish (Matt. 15:34); he took the seven loaves and the fish (Matt. 15:36); they had a few small fish (Mark 8:7); five loaves and two fish (Luke 9:13); their nets enclosed a great shoal of fish (Luke 5:6); bring some of the fish you have caught (John 21:10).

E Land animals
E1 Land animals A – F
E1a Bear
A bear came and took a lamb (1 Sam. 17:34); I have killed the lion and the bear (1 Sam. 17:36-7); two bears killed 42 youths (2 Kgs. 2:24); as if a man flees from a lion and a bear meets him (Amos 5:19); a beast like a bear (Dan. 7:5); the beast's feet were like a bear's (Rev. 13:2); David is like a bear robbed of her cubs (2 Sam. 17:8); I will be like a bear robbed of her cubs (Hos. 13:8); better meeting a she-bear robbed of her cubs than a fool (Prov. 17:12); a wicked ruler is like a charging bear (Prov. 28:15); the cow and the bear will graze (Isa. 11:7).

E1b Deer etc.
The deer, gazelle, roebuck, wild goat, ibex, antelope and mountain sheep are clean (Deut. 14:5); do you know when mountain goats or deer give birth? (Job 39:1); the doe abandons her newborn calf for lack of grass (Jer. 14:5); Naphtali is a doe (Gen. 49:21); Asahel was as swift as a gazelle (2 Sam. 2:18); they were swift as gazelles (1 Chr. 12:8); one's wife as a graceful deer (Prov. 5:19); my beloved is like a gazelle or a young stag (S. of S. 2:9); be like a gazelle or a young stag (S. of S. 2:17; 8:14); he makes my feet like hinds' feet (2 Sam. 22:34; Ps. 18:33); he makes my feet like hinds' feet and makes me tread on high places (Hab. 3:19); as the deer longs for the water (Ps. 42:1); like a hunted gazelle (Isa. 13:14); like an antelope in a net (Isa. 51:20); save yourself like a gazelle from the hunter (Prov. 6:5); the lame will leap like a deer (Isa. 35:6); a disciple called Tabitha, meaning Dorcas [gazelle] (Acts 9:36).

E1c Fox / jackal / hyena
Samson caught three hundred foxes (Judg. 15:4); a fox would break their wall down (Neh. 4:3); the little foxes ruin the vineyards (S. of S. 2:15); to make the cities of Judah a haunt of jackals (Jer. 10:22); I will make Jerusalem a haunt of jackals (Jer. 9:11); hyenas will howl in its towers (Isa. 13:22); jackals will howl in the palaces (Isa. 13:22); it will be a haunt of jackals (Isa. 34:13; 35:7); Babylon will become a haunt of jackals (Jer. 51:37); wild beasts and jackals will live in Babylon (Jer. 50:39); Hazor will become a haunt of jackals (Jer. 49:33); the jackals and ostriches will glorify me (Isa. 43:20); foxes have holes (Matt. 8:20; Luke 9:58); your prophets have been like foxes among the ruins (Ezek. 13:4); that fox Herod (Luke 13:32).

E1d Frog
The plague of frogs (Exod. 8:1-15; Ps. 78:45; 105:30); three unclean spirits like frogs (Rev. 16:13).

E2 Lion
E2a Lions in general
The Negeb, whence come lioness and lion (Isa. 30:6); lions suffer hunger (Ps. 34:10); young lions seek their food from God (Ps. 104:21); lions or ravenous beasts will not be found there (Isa. 35:9); the lion was standing beside the body (1 Kgs. 13:24, 28); a live dog is better than a dead lion (Eccles. 9:4).

E2b Ferocity of lions
What is stronger than a lion? (Judg. 14:18); the lion is mighty among beasts (Prov. 30:30); can you hunt prey for the lion? (Job 38:39); lions growling over their prey will not be frightened by shepherds (Isa. 31:4); as the shepherd snatches from the lion's mouth two legs (Amos 3:12); like a lion, eager to tear (Ps. 17:12; 22:13); a lion has roared! who will not fear? (Amos 3:8); as if a man flees from a lion and a bear meets him (Amos 5:19); does a lion roar in the forest if he has taken no prey? (Amos 3:4); the lion filled his caves with prey (Nahum 2:12); the roar of lions, for the majesty of the Jordan is ruined (Zech. 11:3).

E2c In danger from lions
A young lion came roaring at Samson (Judg. 14:5); Daniel was thrown into the lions' den (Dan. 6:7, 16); a lion from the forest will kill them (Jer. 5:6); a lion killed the man of God (1 Kgs. 13:24-5); a lion killed a son of the prophets (1 Kgs. 20:36); the Lord sent lions among them (2 Kgs. 17:25-6); the Lord has given him to the lion (1 Kgs. 13:26); the lions have roared at him (Jer. 2:15); Israel is a flock driven away by lions (Jer. 50:17); the sluggard says, 'There is a lion outside!' (Prov. 22:13; 26:13).

E2d Deliverance from lions
Save me from the lion's mouth (Ps. 22:21); rescue me from the lions (Ps. 35:17); tear out the fangs of the young lions (Ps. 58:6); the Lord who delivered me from the paw of the lion (1 Sam. 17:37); he has delivered Daniel from the power of the lions (Dan. 6:27); my God sent his angel and shut the lions' mouths (Dan. 6:22); the lion will eat straw like the ox (Isa. 11:6-7; 65:25); Samson tore the lion like a kid (Judg. 14:6); David had killed lions (1 Sam. 17:34-6); Benaiah killed a lion in a pit on a snowy day (2 Sam. 23:20; 1 Chr. 11:22); you will tread on lions and snakes (Ps. 91:13); by faith they shut the mouths of lions (Heb. 11:33); lions are quelled by God's anger (Job 4:10-11); I was delivered from the lion's mouth (2 Tim. 4:17); a sword will devour your young lions (Nahum 2:13).

E2e Sculpted lions
Lions, oxen and cherubim round the stands (1 Kgs. 7:29); cherubim, lions and palm trees on the stands (1 Kgs. 7:36); two lions beside the arms of the throne (1

Kgs. 10:19; 2 Chr. 9:18); 12 lions beside the steps of the throne (1 Kgs. 10:20; 2 Chr. 9:19).

E2f God like a lion
The Lord has left his hiding-place like a lion (Jer. 25:38); the Lord will roar like a lion (Hos. 11:10); I will be a lion to Israel (Hos. 5:14); I will be like a lion or leopard to them (Hos. 13:7); I will devour them like a lion, as a wild beast would tear them (Hos. 13:8); one will come up like a lion from the jungle of Jordan (Jer. 49:19; 50:44); like a lion he breaks all my bones (Isa. 38:13); he is like a lion in hiding (Lam. 3:10); you hunt me like a lion (Job 10:16).

E2g Creatures like lions
Each cherub had a lion's face (Ezek. 1:10; 10:14; 41:19); the first living creature was like a lion (Rev. 4:7); a beast like a lion with the wings of an eagle (Dan. 7:4); the locusts had teeth like those of lions (Rev. 9:8); horses with heads like lions (Rev. 9:17); the beast's mouth was like a lion (Rev. 13:2).

E2h Others like lions
The wrath of a king is like the growling of a lion (Prov. 20:2); a wicked ruler is like a roaring lion (Prov. 28:15); the righteous are bold as a lion (Prov. 28:1); where is the den of lions? [Nineveh] (Nahum 2:11); the lion of Judah (Rev. 5:5); Jerusalem's princes are roaring lions (Zeph. 3:3); one of her cubs became a lion (Ezek. 19:3, 5); they are like a roaring lion tearing the prey (Ezek. 22:25); the devil prowls like a roaring lion (1 Pet. 5:8).

E3 Land animals L – R

E3a Leopards
A leopard is watching them (Jer. 5:6); can the leopard change its spots? (Jer. 13:23); a leopard with four wings and four heads (Dan. 7:6); the beast was like a leopard (Rev. 13:2); I will be like a lion or leopard to them (Hos. 13:7); the leopard will lie down with the kid (Isa. 11:6); their horses are swifter than leopards, fiercer than wolves (Hab. 1:8).

E3b Mouse
The mouse, an unclean animal (Lev. 11:29); five golden mice (1 Sam. 6:4-5, 11, 18); they eat mice (Isa. 66:17).

E3c Rock badger
The rock badger chews the cud but does not divide the hoof so it is unclean (Lev. 11:5; Deut. 14:7); the rocks are a refuge for the rock badger (Ps. 104:18); the rock badgers are not mighty but make houses in the rock (Prov. 30:26).

E4 Snake

E4a Snakes in general
The Lord sent fiery snakes (Num. 21:6); fiery snakes and scorpions in the wilderness (Deut. 8:15); they were destroyed by serpents (1 Cor. 10:9); I am sending against you adders which cannot be charmed (Jer. 8:17); a snake will bite him who breaks through a wall (Eccles. 10:8); a man leans against a wall and a snake bites him (Amos 5:19); Moses' staff became a snake (Exod. 4:3; 7:9-10); the magicians' staffs became snakes (Exod. 7:12); if he asks for a fish, who will give him a snake? (Matt. 7:10; Luke 11:11); the way of a serpent on a rock (Prov. 30:19); Moses put a snake on a pole (Num. 21:8-9; John 3:14); the bronze snake Moses made, called Nehushtan (2 Kgs. 18:4); a viper came out of the sticks (Acts 28:3).

E4b Power over snakes
You will tread on lions and snakes (Ps. 91:13); they will pick up snakes and if they drink poison it will not harm them (Mark 16:18); I have given you authority to tread on snakes and scorpions (Luke 10:19); the toddler will put his hand on the viper's den (Isa. 11:8); the infant will play by the cobra's hole (Isa. 11:8).

E4c The ancient serpent
The snake was more crafty than any beast of the field (Gen. 3:1); the great dragon, the serpent, Satan (Rev. 12:9; 20:2); the serpent deceived me and I ate (Gen. 3:13); the snake deceived Eve (2 Cor. 11:3); the serpent was cursed more than all other animals (Gen. 3:14); the serpent poured water like a river out of its mouth (Rev. 12:15).

E4d Like snakes
They will lick dust like a snake (Mic. 7:17); like a deaf cobra (Ps. 58:4); they sharpen their tongues like a snake (Ps. 140:3); viper's poison is under their lips (Ps. 140:3); the poison of asps is under their lips (Rom. 3:13); you brood of vipers (Matt. 3:7; 12:34; 23:33; Luke 3:7); the horses' tails are like serpents (Rev. 9:19); wise as serpents and harmless as doves (Matt. 10:16); wine bites like a serpent and stings like an adder (Prov. 23:32).

E5 Land animals S – W

E5a Scorpion
I will chastise you with scorpions (1 Kgs. 12:11, 14; 2 Chr. 10:11, 14); he led you through the wilderness with serpents and scorpions (Deut. 8:15); though you sit on scorpions (Ezek. 2:6); locusts given authority like scorpions (Rev. 9:3); they have tails like scorpions (Rev. 9:10); like the sting of a scorpion (Rev. 9:5); I have given you authority to tread on snakes and scorpions (Luke 10:19); what father will give his son a scorpion instead of an egg? (Luke 11:12).

E5b Wolf
The hireling sees the wolf coming and flees (John 10:12); their horses are swifter than leopards, fiercer than wolves (Hab. 1:8); Benjamin is a wolf (Gen. 49:27); her judges are wolves at evening (Zeph. 3:3); ravenous wolves, not sparing the flock (Acts 20:29); her princes are like wolves tearing the prey (Ezek. 22:27); false prophets as wolves (Matt. 7:15); sheep among wolves (Matt. 10:16); lambs among wolves (Luke 10:3); the wolf will dwell with the lamb (Hab. 11:6); the wolf and the lamb will feed together (Isa. 65:25).

E6 Wild cattle

E6a Wild donkey
Who set the wild donkey free? (Job 39:5-8); does the wild donkey bray over grass? (Job 6:5); the wild donkeys quench their thirst (Ps. 104:11); a fool will be wise when a wild donkey's foal is born a man (Job 11:12); the wild donkeys pant for air like jackals (Jer. 14:6); hill and watch-tower have become a delight for wild donkeys (Isa. 32:14).

E6b Wild goat
The Rocks of the Wild Goat (1 Sam. 24:2); the mountains are for the wild goats (Ps. 104:18); the wild goat will cry to its fellow (Isa. 34:14).

E6c Wild ox
Will the wild ox [aurochs] serve you? (Job 39:9-12); like the horns of the wild ox (Num. 23:22; 24:8); his horns are the horns of a wild ox (Deut. 33:17); save me from the horns of the wild oxen (Ps. 22:21); many bulls have surrounded me (Ps. 22:12).

F Cattle, sheep and goats

F1 Cattle, sheep and goats in general
Jabal was the father of those who keep stock (Gen. 4:20); cargo of cattle, sheep, horses and chariots (Rev. 18:13); they will go with their flocks and herds to seek the Lord (Hos. 5:6); those who eat lambs from the flock and calves from the stall (Amos 6:4); the beasts groan, the flocks of sheep suffer (Joel 1:18); selling oxen, sheep and pigeons in the temple (John 2:14-15).

F2 Sacrificing cattle, sheep and goats
I will offer rams, bulls and he-goats (Ps. 66:15); bulls, rams and lambs for sacrifice are to be given to them (Ezra 6:9); buy bulls, rams and lambs for sacrifice (Ezra

7:17); sprinkling defiled people with the blood of goats and bulls (Heb. 9:13); Moses took the blood of calves and goats (Heb. 9:19); not by the blood of goats and calves (Heb. 9:12); it is impossible for the blood of bulls and goats to take away sins (Heb. 10:4).

F3 Cattle

F3a Cattle in general

Let the earth bring forth cattle (Gen. 1:24); God made the cattle (Gen. 1:25); let men rule over the cattle (Gen. 1:26); cattle are clean animals (Deut. 14:4); all cattle died (Gen. 7:21); a covenant with you, birds, cattle and every beast (Gen. 9:10); do not covet your neighbour's ox (Exod. 20:17); the ox knows its master (Isa. 1:3); if an ox or a donkey falls into a pit (Exod. 21:33); who will not pull a son or an ox out of a well on the sabbath? (Luke 14:5); on the sabbath each of you unties his ox or donkey (Luke 13:15); do horses run on rocks or does one plough the sea with oxen? (Amos 6:12); if one ox kills another (Exod. 21:35); restitution for stealing an ox (Exod. 22:1); if an ox gores someone to death (Exod. 21:28-36); do not muzzle an ox which is threshing (Deut. 25:4; 1 Cor. 9:9; 1 Tim. 5:18); Saul was coming from the field behind the oxen (1 Sam. 11:5); Saul cut up a yoke of oxen (1 Sam. 11:7); ploughing with 12 pair of oxen (1 Kgs. 19:19); the Philistines used two cows to draw the ark (1 Sam. 6:7); does the ox low over its fodder? (Job 6:5); the oxen and donkeys will eat salted fodder (Isa. 30:24).

F3b Eating cattle

Oxen for food (1 Kgs. 4:23); Abraham took a calf tender and good (Gen. 18:7); the woman took a fattened calf (1 Sam. 28:24); killing the fattened calf (Luke 15:23, 27, 30).

F3c Sculpted cattle

A molten bull calf (Exod. 32:4, 8); you had made a molten calf (Deut. 9:16); they made a calf of molten metal (Neh. 9:18); they made a calf in Horeb (Ps. 106:19); they made a calf and offered a sacrifice to the idol (Acts 7:41); an image of an ox that eats grass (Ps. 106:20); when Moses saw the calf he was angry (Exod. 32:19-20); Jeroboam made two golden calves (1 Kgs. 12:28; 2 Kgs. 10:29; 2 Chr. 13:8); Jeroboam appointed priests for the calves he had made (2 Chr. 11:15); they made molten images of two calves (2 Kgs. 17:16); he has rejected your calf, Samaria (Hos. 8:5); the calf of Samaria will be broken to pieces (Hos. 8:6); let those who sacrifice kiss the calves (Hos. 13:2); the inhabitants of Samaria fear for the calf of Beth-aven (Hos. 10:5); 12 oxen supporting the 'sea' (1 Kgs. 7:25, 44; 2 Chr. 4:3-4, 15; Jer. 52:20); Ahaz removed the 'sea' from the oxen (2 Kgs. 16:17); lions, oxen and cherubim round the frames (1 Kgs. 7:29).

F3d Like cattle

Nebuchadnezzar would be like cattle (Dan. 4:15, 23, 25, 32, 33; 5:21); I was chastened like an untrained calf (Jer. 31:18); you cows of Bashan (Amos 4:1); Israel is like a stubborn heifer (Hos. 4:16); Ephraim is a heifer that loves to thresh (Hos. 10:11); Egypt is a pretty heifer (Jer. 46:20); you will go forth leaping like calves from the stall (Mal. 4:2); if you had not ploughed with my heifer (Judg. 14:18); God's concern is not for oxen, is it? (1 Cor. 9:9); the calf, lion and fatling together (Isa. 11:6); the cow and the bear will graze (Isa. 11:7); the second creature was like a calf (Rev. 4:7); their feet were like calves' hooves (Ezek. 1:7); each creature had the face of a bull (Ezek. 1:10).

F4 Sheep and goats

Arabia and the princes of Kedar traded lambs, rams and goats (Ezek. 27:21); where is the lamb [or kid] for a burnt offering? (Gen. 22:7-8); if his offering is from the flock, sheep or goats (Lev. 1:10; 3:6); a female sheep or

goat for a sin offering (Lev. 5:6; Num. 6:14); every house is to take a lamb [or goat] (Exod. 12:3-10, 21); take it from the sheep or the goats (Exod. 12:5); the sheep and the goats (Matt. 25:32).

F5 Sheep

F5a Sheep in general

Sheep are clean animals (Deut. 14:4); restitution for stealing a sheep (Exod. 22:1); a sheep from every 200 for the prince (Ezek. 45:15); if a man has one sheep and it falls into a pit on the sabbath (Matt. 12:11); three flocks of sheep (Gen. 29:2); Abraham set apart seven ewe lambs (Gen. 21:28-30); all speckled, spotted and discoloured animals (Gen. 30:32, 33, 35); rams' skins (Exod. 25:5; 26:14; 35:7, 23; 36:19; 39:34); 100 000 lambs and the wool of 100 000 rams (2 Kgs. 3:4); 250 000 sheep (1 Chr. 5:21); the lambs will provide your clothing (Prov. 27:26); a ram with two horns (Dan. 8:3, 20); the fire of God burnt up the sheep (Job 1:16).

F5b Possessing sheep

Abel was a keeper of sheep (Gen. 4:2); Abraham had sheep (Gen. 12:16; 24:35); Lot had sheep (Gen. 13:5); Isaac had flocks and herds (Gen. 26:14); Job had 7000 sheep (Job 1:3); Jacob had many sheep (Gen. 30:43; 32:5); 200 ewes and 20 rams for Esau (Gen. 32:14); 675 sheep (Num. 31:37); 337 500 sheep (Num. 31:36, 43); 675 000 sheep (Num. 31:32); Judah sent a kid from the flock (Gen. 38:17, 20); send lambs to the ruler of the land (Isa. 16:1); Joseph gave them food in exchange for their flocks (Gen. 47:17); the poor man had only little ewe lamb (2 Sam. 12:3).

F5c Sacrificing sheep

Where is the lamb [or kid] for a burnt offering? (Gen. 22:7-8); a ram caught by its horns (Gen. 22:13); two lambs as a daily burnt offering (Exod. 29:38; Num. 28:3; Ezek. 46:13); does the Lord take delight in thousands of rams? (Mic. 6:7); redeem a donkey with a lamb (Exod. 13:13).

F5d Like sheep

We are the sheep of his hand (Ps. 95:7); the sheep of his pasture (Ps. 100:3); little flock (Luke 12:32); lost sheep (Jer. 50:6; Matt. 10:6; 15:24; 18:12-14; Luke 15:4-7); gone astray like sheep (Ps. 119:176; Isa. 53:6; 1 Pet. 2:25); I am sending you as sheep among wolves (Matt. 10:16; Luke 10:3); like sheep for the slaughter (Ps. 44:22; Jer. 11:19; 12:3; Rom. 8:36); like a lamb to slaughter or a sheep to shearing (Isa. 53:7); as a sheep to slaughter or a lamb before its shearers (Acts 8:32); like sheep without a shepherd (Matt. 9:36); like sheep with none to gather them (Isa. 13:14); I will strike the shepherd and the sheep will be scattered (Zech. 13:7; Matt. 26:31); wolves in sheep's clothing (Matt. 7:15); he will place the sheep on his right and the goats on his left (Matt. 25:33); sheep cared for by the good shepherd (John 10:2-16); I will gather them like sheep in the fold (Mic. 2:12); I have other sheep which are not of this fold (John 10:16); feed my lambs (John 21:15); tend my sheep (John 21:16); feed my sheep (John 21:17); a beast with two horns like a lamb (Rev. 13:11); the mountains skipped like rams, the hills like lambs (Ps. 114:4, 6).

F5e The Lamb of God

The Lamb of God (John 1:29, 36); the Lamb (Rev. 5:6-13; 14:1); they will make war on the Lamb (Rev. 17:14); as of a lamb without blemish (1 Pet. 1:19); the Lamb opened the first seal (Rev. 6:1); hide us from him who sits on the throne and from the wrath of the Lamb (Rev. 6:16); salvation to our God who sits on the throne and to the Lamb (Rev. 7:10); they overcame him by the blood of the Lamb (Rev. 12:11); the Lamb who was slain from the foundation of the world (Rev. 13:8); they sang the song of the Lamb (Rev. 15:3); the marriage of the Lamb has come (Rev. 19:7); I will show you the bride, the wife of the Lamb (Rev. 21:9); the Lord God Almighty and the Lamb are its temple (Rev. 21:22); its lamp is the Lamb (Rev. 21:23); the river flowing from the throne of God and of the Lamb (Rev. 22:1); the throne of God and of the Lamb will be in it (Rev. 22:3).

F6 Goats

F6a Goats in general

Goats are clean animals (Deut. 14:4); the he-goat is stately in walk (Prov. 30:31); do not boil a kid in its mother's milk (Exod. 34:26); you never gave me a kid to make merry with my friends (Luke 15:29); Gideon prepared a kid (Judg. 6:19); Samson took a young goat to his wife (Judg. 15:1).

F6b Like goats

Your hair is like a flock of goats come down from Gilead (S. of S. 6:5); the Israelites were like two little flocks of goats (1 Kgs. 20:27); like a flock of goats moving down Mount Gilead (S. of S. 4:1); the leopard will lie down with the kid (Isa. 11:6); a he-goat from the west (Dan. 8:5, 21); he will place the sheep on his right and the goats on his left (Matt. 25:33).

G Other domesticated animals

G1 Domesticated animals in general

The law on animals which gore people or are killed (Exod. 21:28-36); if a man gives a neighbour an animal to keep (Exod. 22:10); if your neighbour's animal strays, bring it back (Deut. 22:1-4); the animals were taken for booty (Deut. 2:35; 3:7); Joseph bartered food for the Egyptians' livestock (Gen. 47:16, 17); Abraham was rich in livestock (Gen. 13:2); you have much livestock (Deut. 3:19); the Lord will make a distinction between the livestock of Israel and of Egypt (Exod. 9:4); the Egyptians' livestock died (Exod. 9:6); your flocks and herds must remain behind (Exod. 10:24); take your flocks and herds and go (Exod. 12:32); flocks and herds and very many livestock went with them (Exod. 12:38); Saul spared the animals (1 Sam. 15:9); the rich man had many flocks and herds (2 Sam. 12:2); the horses, mules, camels and donkeys of those returning from exile (Neh. 7:68-9); food brought on donkeys, camels, mules and oxen (1 Chr. 12:40); bring an offering from the herd or the flock (Lev. 1:2); firstborn domestic animals are not to be redeemed (Num. 18:17).

G2 Camels

The camel chews the cud but does not divide the hoof and so is unclean (Lev. 11:4; Deut. 14:7); Abraham had camels (Gen. 12:16); the Lord has given Abraham camels (Gen. 24:35); I will also water your camels (Gen. 24:14, 19-20, 44-6); Camels without number (Judg. 7:12); ornaments on the camels' necks (Judg. 8:21, 26); the servant took ten camels (Gen. 24:10); treasures carried on camels' humps (Isa. 30:6); Rebekah and her maids mounted the camels (Gen. 24:61); Isaac looked and saw the camels coming (Gen. 24:63); a caravan of camels (Gen. 37:25); camels carrying spices (2 Chr. 9:1); camels used in warfare (Judg. 6:5); riders on camels (Isa. 21:7); 400 men escaped on camels (1 Sam. 30:17); 30 milch camels and their young for Esau (Gen. 32:15); 50 000 camels (1 Chr. 5:21); Obil had charge of the camels (1 Chr. 27:30); 435 camels (Ezra 2:67; Neh. 7:69); the Chaldeans took the camels (Job 1:17); they carried off many camels (2 Chr. 14:15); John wore a garment of camel's hair (Matt. 3:4; Mark 1:6); it is easier for a camel to go through the eye of a needle (Matt. 19:24; Mark 10:25; Luke 18:25); you strain out a gnat and swallow a camel (Matt. 23:24).

G3 Dogs

G3a Dogs in general

A live dog is better than a dead lion (Eccles. 9:4); against Israel not even a dog will bark (Exod. 11:7); dogs licked his sores (Luke 16:21); those who die in the city will be eaten by dogs (1 Kgs. 14:11; 16:4; 21:24); dogs will eat Jezebel (1 Kgs. 21:23; 2 Kgs. 9:10, 36); where dogs licked Naboth's blood dogs will lick yours (1 Kgs. 21:19); dogs licked up Ahab's blood (1 Kgs. 22:38); I would have disdained to set their fathers with the dogs of my flock (Job 30:1); one sacrifices a lamb and one breaks a dog's neck (Isa. 66:3).

G3b Like dogs

Do not give what is holy to dogs (Matt. 7:6); it is not good to throw the children's bread to the dogs (Matt. 15:26; Mark 7:27); dogs eat the crumbs (Matt. 15:27; Mark 7:28); like a dog who returns to his vomit (Prov. 26:11; 2 Pet. 2:22); meddling in a quarrel is like taking a passing dog by the ears (Prov. 26:17); everyone who laps like a dog will go (Judg. 7:5); am I a dog that you come to me with sticks? (1 Sam. 17:43); I am a dead dog (1 Sam. 24:14); this dead dog (2 Sam. 16:9); why regard a dead dog like me? (2 Sam. 9:8); I am only a dog (2 Kgs. 8:13); the earnings of a dog [male prostitute] (Deut. 23:18); many dogs have surrounded me (Ps. 22:16); save me from the power of the dog (Ps. 22:20); outside are the dogs (Rev. 22:15); beware of the dogs (Phil. 3:2).

G4 Donkeys

G4a Donkeys in general

Redeem the firstborn of a donkey or break its neck (Exod. 13:13; 34:20); do not covet your neighbour's donkey (Exod. 20:17); the donkey knows its master's manger (Isa. 1:3); if your enemy's donkey lies under its burden (Exod. 23:5); restore a lost donkey (Deut. 22:3); some drive away the donkey of the orphans (Job 24:3); do not plough with an ox and a donkey (Deut. 22:10); the donkeys were feeding (Job 1:14); Balaam's donkey (Num. 22:22-33); a donkey spoke with a man's voice (2 Pet. 2:16); a donkey's head cost 80 shekels (2 Kgs. 6:25); Jehdeiah had charge of the donkeys (1 Chr. 27:30); riches carried on the backs of donkeys (Isa. 30:6); they put their feeble ones on donkeys (2 Chr. 28:15); Issachar is a strong donkey (Gen. 49:14); Ishmael a wild donkey (Gen. 16:12); he ties his donkey to the vine (Gen. 49:11); he will have a donkey's burial (Jer. 22:19).

G4b Multitudes of donkeys

Abraham had donkeys (Gen. 12:16); Jacob had donkeys (Gen. 30:43; 32:5); ten he-donkeys and 20 she-donkeys for Esau (Gen. 32:15); ten loaded he-donkeys and ten loaded she-donkeys (Gen. 45:23); 30 sons on 30 donkeys (Judg. 10:4); 40 sons and 30 grandsons on 70 donkeys (Judg. 12:14); Job had 500 female donkeys (Job 1:3); 2000 donkeys (1 Chr. 5:21); 6720 donkeys (Ezra 2:67; Neh. 7:69); 30 500 donkeys (Num. 31:39, 45); 61 000 donkeys (Num. 31:34).

G4c Loss of donkeys

They took the Hivites' donkeys (Gen. 34:28); Joseph gave them food in exchange for their donkeys (Gen. 47:17); the Sabeans took Job's donkeys (Job 1:15); I have taken not even a donkey from them (Num. 16:15); whose donkey have I taken? (1 Sam. 12:3); a king will take your donkeys (1 Sam. 8:16); the brothers feared Joseph would take their donkeys (Gen. 43:18); the donkeys of Kish were lost (1 Sam. 9:3).

G4d Using donkeys

Abigail loaded the food on donkeys (1 Sam. 25:19); they loaded the grain on their donkeys (Gen. 42:26; 44:13); loading sacks of grain on their donkeys (Neh. 13:15); Ziba brought David provisions and donkeys (2 Sam. 16:1-2); send me one of the donkeys (2 Kgs. 4:22); you will find a donkey tied up and a colt with her (Matt. 21:2); Moses put his family on a donkey (Exod. 4:20); Abigail rode on a donkey (1 Sam. 25:20, 42); a donkey standing by the lion (1 Kgs. 13:24, 28); he laid the man of God's body on the donkey (1 Kgs. 13:29); your king is coming to you, humble and seated on a donkey (Zech. 9:9); your king comes to you mounted on a donkey (Matt. 21:5); they brought the donkey and the colt and put their garments on them (Matt. 21:7); Jesus rode on a donkey (Mark 11:2-7; Luke 19:30-5; John 12:14-15); Samson killed 1000 men with the jawbone of a donkey (Judg. 15:15, 16).

G5 Horses
G5a Horses in general
God does not delight in the strength of a horse (Ps. 147:10); do horses run on rocks or does one plough the sea with oxen? (Amos 6:12); I will strike every horse with panic (Zech. 12:4); hamstring their horses (Josh. 11:6); he hamstrung their horses (Josh. 11:9); inscribed on the bells of the horses, 'Holy to the Lord' (Zech. 14:20); a red horse (Zech. 1:8; Rev. 6:4); a white horse (Rev. 6:2; 19:11); white horses (Rev. 19:14); the white horses go to the west country (Zech. 6:6); the dappled horses go to the south country (Zech. 6:6); a black horse (Rev. 6:5); the black horses go to the north country (Zech. 6:6); a greenish horse (Rev. 6:8); Pharaoh's horses (Exod. 14:9, 23); the snorting of his horses is heard from Dan (Jer. 8:16); perhaps we can keep the horses and mules alive (1 Kgs. 18:5); his horses are swifter than eagles (Jer. 4:13); the noise of the hooves of his stallions (Jer. 47:3); 736 horses (Ezra 2:66; Neh. 7:68).

G5b Acquiring horses
The king must not make the people return to Egypt to multiply horses (Deut. 17:16); their land is filled with horses (Isa. 2:7); Joseph gave them food in exchange for their horses (Gen. 47:17); Solomon imported horses from Egypt and Kue (1 Kgs. 10:28-9; 2 Chr. 1:16-17); horses were brought to Solomon from Egypt (2 Chr. 9:28); horses, war horses and mules were traded (Ezek. 27:14); Solomon had thousands of horses (1 Kgs. 4:26); horses were given to Solomon (1 Kgs. 10:25); he sought horses and numerous troops from Egypt (Ezek. 17:15).

G5c Using horses
The horse is made ready for the day of battle (Prov. 21:31); we put bits in horses' mouths (Jas. 3:3); a whip is for the horse (Prov. 26:3); the war horse (Job 39:19-25); how will you compete with horses? (Jer. 12:5); a horse is a vain hope for victory (Ps. 33:17); I will not deliver them by bow, sword, battle, horses or horsemen (Hos. 1:7); eat the flesh of horses and their riders (Rev. 19:18); Mordecai was paraded on the king's horse (Esther 6:8, 10-11); kings riding in chariots and on horses (Jer. 17:25); couriers riding on horses bred from the royal mares (Esther 8:10, 14); I have seen slaves riding on horses (Eccles. 10:7); horse and rider he threw into the sea (Exod. 15:1, 21); I will give you 2000 horses if you can put riders on them (2 Kgs. 18:23); with you I shatter horse and rider (Jer. 51:21).

G5d Like horses
He will make his flock, Judah, like a battle horse (Zech. 10:3); the horses' tails are like serpents (Rev. 9:19); horses with heads like lions (Rev. 9:17); the locusts were like war horses (Joel 2:4; Rev. 9:7); well-fed lusty stallions neighing after their neighbours' wives (Jer. 5:8); you skip like a heifer and neigh like stallions (Jer. 50:11); like a horse charging into battle (Jer. 8:6); like a horse in the wilderness they did not stumble (Isa. 63:13); you are like my mare (S. of S. 1:9); do not be like the horse or mule (Ps. 32:9).

G6 Mules
The king's sons mounted their mules and fled (2 Sam. 13:29); Absalom was riding on his mule (2 Sam. 18:9); Solomon rode on David's mule (1 Kgs. 1:33, 38, 44); mules were given to Solomon (1 Kgs. 10:25); perhaps we can keep the horses and mules alive (1 Kgs. 18:5);

horses, war horses and mules were traded (Ezek. 27:14); 245 mules (Ezra 2:66; Neh. 7:68); do not be like the horse or mule (Ps. 32:9); a plague on the horses, mules, camels, donkeys and cattle (Zech. 14:15).

G7 Pigs
The pig has cloven hoof but does not chew the cud and so is unclean (Lev. 11:7; Deut. 14:8); the boar from the forest ravages it (Ps. 80:13); one offers a grain offering and one offers pig's blood (Isa. 66:3); a gold ring in a pig's snout (Prov. 11:22); do not throw pearls before swine (Matt. 7:6); the sow is washed only to wallow in the mire (2 Pet. 2:22); a great herd of pigs was feeding (Matt. 8:30-1; Mark 5:11-12); the demons entered the pigs (Matt. 8:32; Luke 8:32-3); he sent him into the fields to feed pigs (Luke 15:15).

H Cosmic creatures
Four living creatures (Ezek. 1:5-14; Rev. 4:6-8; 14:3; 15:7; 19:4); living creatures identified as cherubim (Ezek. 10:6-22); the cherubim are the living creatures I saw by the river Chebar (Ezek. 10:15, 20); four great beasts (Dan. 7:3-8, 17); the he-goat represents the king of Greece (Dan. 8:21); the ram with two horns represents the kings of Media and Persia (Dan. 8:20); a great red dragon (Rev. 12:3); the dragon and his angels waged war (Rev. 12:7); the great dragon, the serpent, Satan (Rev. 12:9; 20:2); the beast from the abyss (Rev. 11:7); a beast out of the sea (Rev. 13:1-4); another beast out of the earth (Rev. 13:11-18); the beast spoke like a dragon (Rev. 13:11); a beast with seven heads and ten horns (Rev. 17:7); the beast which was and is not is an eighth king (Rev. 17:11); the beast was and is not and is about to ascend from the bottomless pit (Rev. 17:8); the beast was captured (Rev. 19:20); the mark of the beast (Rev. 16:2; 19:20; 20:4); the lake of fire and brimstone where the beast and false prophet are (Rev. 20:10).

366 Plants
A Plants in general
No shrub of the field was yet in the earth (Gen. 2:5); let the earth sprout vegetation (Gen. 1:11-12); every plant bearing seed was given to man for food (Gen. 1:29); every green plant was given to all creatures for food (Gen. 1:30; 9:3); God overthrew all that sprouted from the ground (Gen. 19:25); hail on every plant of the field (Exod. 9:22, 25); the locusts ate every plant (Exod. 10:12, 15; Ps. 105:35); there is no vegetation (Jer. 14:6); God appointed a plant to shade Jonah (Jonah 4:6); let our sons be like full-grown plants (Ps. 144:12); I made you numerous like plants of the field (Ezek. 16:7); every plant not planted by my Father will be uprooted (Matt. 15:13); Judah will take root downward and bear fruit upward (2 Kgs. 19:30).

B Parts of plants
B1 Roots
A branch will grow out of his roots (Isa. 11:1); the root of Jesse will stand as an ensign to the peoples (Isa. 11:10); the root of Jesse will come (Rom. 15:12); the cedar's roots extended to many waters (Ezek. 31:7); leave the stump with its roots in the ground (Dan. 4:15); the axe is laid at the root of the trees (Matt. 3:10; Luke 3:9); the fig tree was withered to its roots (Mark 11:20); if the root is holy, so are the branches (Rom. 11:16); it is not you who supports the root, but the root supports you (Rom. 11:18); that no root of bitterness spring up (Heb. 12:15); the lion of the tribe of Judah, the root of David (Rev. 5:5); the root and the offspring of David (Rev. 22:16); they have no root (Luke 8:13).

B2 Foliage
Foliage for the Feast of Booths (Lev. 23:40; Neh. 8:15); branches cut from trees (Judg. 9:48-9; Matt. 21:8; Mark 11:8); the righteous will flourish like a green leaf (Prov.

11:28); its leaf does not wither (Ps. 1:3); their leaves will not wither nor their fruit fail (Ezek. 47:12); strip off its leaves and scatter its fruit (Dan. 4:14); the tree whose foliage was beautiful and fruit abundant (Dan. 4:21); when the fig tree has tender branches and puts forth leaves (Mark 13:28); when they put forth leaves, you know that summer is near (Luke 21:30); the fig tree had nothing but leaves (Matt. 21:19; Mark 11:13); first the blade, then the ear, then the full grain in the ear (Mark 4:28); their leaves will be for healing (Ezek. 47:12); the leaves of the tree are for the healing of the nations (Rev. 22:2).

B3 Flowers
The flowers appear on the earth (S. of S. 2:12); the vines are in blossom (S. of S. 2:13, 15); I went down to see the blossoms (S. of S. 6:11); let us see whether the vine has blossomed (S. of S. 7:12); the vine has budded, arrogance has blossomed (Ezek. 7:10); the wilderness will blossom (Isa. 35:1); though the fig tree should not blossom (Hab. 3:17).

B4 Fruiting
Joseph is a fruitful bough (Gen. 49:22); first the blade, then the ear, then the full grain in the ear (Mark 4:28); he would gladly have filled his belly with the pods the pigs ate (Luke 15:16).
FRUIT, see 171C3.

B5 Seeds
If a carcass falls on seed for sowing it remains clean (Lev. 11:37); if a carcass falls on wet seed for sowing it is unclean (Lev. 11:38); do not sow two different kinds of seed in one field (Lev. 19:19; Deut. 22:9); the value of a field is in proportion to the seed for sowing it (Lev. 27:16); mustard seed is the smallest of all seeds (Matt. 13:32); if you have faith as a grain of mustard seed (Matt. 17:20; Luke 17:6); the kingdom of heaven is like a grain of mustard seed (Matt. 13:31; Mark 4:31); the good seed are the sons of the kingdom (Matt. 13:38); the seed is the word of God (Luke 8:11); you sow a bare grain of wheat (1 Cor. 15:37); he who supplies seed to the sower will multiply your seed for sowing (2 Cor. 9:10).

C Herbaceous plants
C1 Grass / reeds / flax
C1a Grass
God makes grass grow (Ps. 147:8); God will give grass for your beasts (Deut. 11:15); searching for grass for the animals (1 Kgs. 18:5); you will eat grass like an ox (Dan. 4:25, 32); Nebuchadnezzar ate grass like an ox (Dan. 5:21); if God so clothes the grass (Luke 12:28); all green grass was burned up (Rev. 8:7); they were told not to harm grass, green thing or tree (Rev. 9:4).

C1b Reeds
Grass becomes reeds and rushes (Isa. 35:7); the fat cows fed in the reeds (Gen. 41:2, 18); a chest of papyrus reeds (Exod. 2:3); the basket in the reeds (Exod. 2:5); sending ambassadors in vessels of papyrus (Isa. 18:2); reeds and rushes will rot (Isa. 19:6); can papyrus grow without marsh? (Job 8:11); though he flourishes as the reeds, an east wind will come (Hos. 13:15); as a reed is shaken in water (1 Kgs. 14:15); Egypt a staff of reed to Israel (Ezek. 29:6); a reed shaken by the wind? (Matt. 11:7; Luke 7:24); a bruised reed he will not break (Matt. 12:20); they put a reed in his right hand (Matt. 27:29); they took the reed and beat him on the head (Matt. 27:30; Mark 15:19); a sponge on a reed (Matt. 27:48; Mark 15:36).

C1c Darnel [tares]
While men were asleep his enemy sowed darnel among the wheat (Matt. 13:25-7); lest in gathering the darnel you root up the wheat (Matt. 13:29-30); explain to us the parable of the darnel in the field (Matt. 13:36); the

darnel are the sons of the evil one (Matt. 13:38); the darnel are gathered and burned (Matt. 13:40).

C1d Like grass
All flesh is grass, soon withering (Isa. 40:6-8); all flesh is like grass (1 Pet. 1:24); man's days are like grass (Ps. 103:15); they will wither like grass and herbs (Ps. 37:2); like grass sprouting in the morning and withering by evening (Ps. 90:5-6); the rich man will pass away like grass (Jas. 1:10-11); like showers on the mown grass (Ps. 72:6).

C1e Flax
Rahab had covered the spies with flax (Josh. 2:6); she seeks wool and flax (Prov. 31:13); the ropes became like flax burned with fire (Judg. 15:14).

C2 Cereals / pulses
A land of wheat and barley (Deut. 8:8); does he not plant wheat, barley and rye? (Isa. 28:25); seven ears of grain on one stalk (Gen. 41:5, 22); the flax in bud and the barley with fresh ears were ruined (Exod. 9:31); wheat and spelt are later than flax and barley (Exod. 9:32); gather the wheat into my barn (Matt. 13:30); Absalom set Joab's field of barley on fire (2 Sam. 14:30); a plot of ground full of barley (1 Chr. 11:13); a field of lentils (2 Sam. 23:11).

C3 Other herbaceous plants
C3a Crocus / rose
The wilderness will blossom like the crocus (Isa. 35:1); I am the rose [crocus] of Sharon (S. of S. 2:1).

C3b Cucumber
We remember the cucumbers in Egypt (Num. 11:5); like a hut in a cucumber field (Isa. 1:8); like a post [scarecrow] in a cucumber field (Jer. 10:5).

C3c Cummin and dill
Does he not sow dill and cummin? (Isa. 28:25); they do not roll a cart wheel over cummin (Isa. 28:27); dill is not threshed with a threshing sledge (Isa. 28:27); you tithe mint and dill and cummin (Matt. 23:23).

C3d Gourds
Gourds among the herbs (2 Kgs. 4:39); gourds moulded around the 'sea' (1 Kgs. 7:24).

C3e Hyssop
Hyssop (Exod. 12:22; Lev. 14:4, 6, 49, 51-2; Num. 19:6, 18; 1 Kgs. 4:33); purify me with hyssop (Ps. 51:7); the blood of calves and goats with water, scarlet wool and hyssop (Heb. 9:19); a sponge put on hyssop (John 19:29).

C3f Lily
I am the lily of the valleys (S. of S. 2:1); like a lily among thorns (S. of S. 2:2); the capitals were of lily design (1 Kgs. 7:19, 22); the brim of the 'sea' was like a lily blossom (1 Kgs. 7:26; 2 Chr. 4:5); the lilies of the field do not toil or spin (Matt. 6:28); Israel will blossom as the lily (Hos. 14:5).

C3g Mandrakes
Reuben found mandrakes (Gen. 30:14-16); the mandrakes are fragrant (S. of S. 7:13).

C3h Mustard
Mustard is the greatest of shrubs and becomes a tree (Matt. 13:32); mustard has the smallest seed but is the biggest garden plant (Mark 4:31-2); the grain of mustard seed grew and became a tree (Luke 13:19).
MUSTARD seed, see 366B5.

C3i Nettles / thistles
The ground will produce thorns and thistles (Gen. 3:18); if the ground produces thorns and thistles (Heb. 6:8); the sluggard's vineyard was overgrown with thistles and nettles (Prov. 24:31); nettles and thistles will come up in its fortresses (Isa. 34:13); are grapes gathered from thorns or figs from thistles? (Matt. 7:16).

D Trees
D1 Trees in general
D1a About trees
The Lord made all kinds of trees in Eden (Gen. 2:9); let the earth bring forth fruit trees bearing fruit in which is their seed (Gen. 1:11-12); every tree bearing fruit in which is their seed given for food (Gen. 1:29); man could eat from every tree but one (Gen. 2:16); we may eat the fruit of the trees of the garden (Gen. 3:2); a tree cut down will sprout again (Job 14:7); when you plant all kinds of trees for food (Lev. 19:23); are there trees in the land? (Num. 13:20); a tree made the waters sweet (Exod. 15:25); the trees of the fields will clap their hands (Isa. 55:12); the tree bears its fruit (Joel 2:22); every good tree produces good fruit but the bad tree bad fruit (Matt. 7:17); a good tree does not bear bad fruit nor a bad tree good fruit (Luke 6:43); every tree which does not bear good fruit will be cut down and burnt (Matt. 7:19); every tree is known by its fruit (Matt. 12:33); the burning bush (Exod. 3:2-4); he who dwelt in the bush (Deut. 33:16); an angel appeared in fire in a bush (Acts 7:30); in the passage about the bush (Mark 12:26; Luke 20:37).

D1b Worship at trees
You shall not plant a tree as an Asherah (Deut. 16:21); Ahaz sacrificed under every green tree (2 Kgs. 16:4; 2 Chr. 28:4); they sacrificed at every leafy tree (Ezek. 20:28); they made Asherim under every green tree (2 Kgs. 17:10); altars under every green tree (Ezek. 6:13); Judah committed adultery with stones and trees (Jer. 3:9); Israel was a harlot on every high hill and under every green tree (Jer. 2:20; 3:6); destroy worship places under every green tree (Deut. 12:2); their Asherim by green trees on the high hills (Jer. 17:2).

D1c Harming trees
Do not destroy the trees when besieging a town (Deut. 20:19-20); is a tree a man that you should besiege it? (Deut. 20:19); non-fruit trees may be felled in a siege (Deut. 20:20); felling every good tree (2 Kgs. 3:19, 25); God shattered the trees of the Egyptians (Ps. 105:33); every tree was shattered by the hail (Exod. 9:25); the locusts will eat every tree (Exod. 10:5, 15); a fire will consume every green tree and every dry tree (Ezek. 20:47); the axe is laid to the root of the trees (Luke 3:9); the flame has burned up all the trees of the field (Joel 1:19); the pomegranate, palm, apple tree and all the trees dry up (Joel 1:12); the Lord will destroy the glory of his forest (Isa. 10:18); I will kindle a fire in her forest (Jer. 21:14); you could tell this tree to be uprooted (Luke 17:6); wail, oaks of Bashan, for the thick forest has been felled (Zech. 11:2); a third of the trees were burned up (Rev. 8:7); do not harm the earth or sea or trees until we have sealed the slaves of God (Rev. 7:3); they were told not to harm grass, green thing or tree (Rev. 9:4).

D1d Forests
Going into the forest to cut wood (Deut. 19:5); go up to the forest and clear a place (Josh. 17:15); the forest devoured more than the sword (2 Sam. 18:8); the fruitful field will be regarded as a forest (Isa. 29:17); until the fertile field is considered a forest (Isa. 32:15); Asaph, the keeper of the king's forest (Neh. 2:8); the trees of the forest will sing for joy (1 Chr. 16:33; Ps. 96:12); how will you fare in the jungle of Jordan? (Jer. 12:5); one will come up like a lion from the jungle of Jordan (Jer. 49:19; 50:44); they will not need to gather firewood from the forests (Ezek. 39:10); I will make them a forest and the beasts of the field will devour them (Hos. 2:12); the mountain of the house will be a wooded height (Mic. 3:12); the people who live alone in a forest (Mic. 7:14); how big a forest is set ablaze by a small fire (Jas. 3:5).

D1e People as trees
He will be like a tree planted by water (Ps. 1:3; Jer. 17:8); a violent man like a luxuriant tree (Ps. 37:35); I see men like trees, walking (Mark 8:24); Nebuchadnezzar pictured as a huge tree cut down (Dan. 4:10-15, 20-3); a shoot from the stump of Jesse (Isa. 11:1); they will blossom like the vine (Hos. 14:7); Israel as a vine (Isa. 5:1-6; Hos. 10:1); I planted you as a choice vine (Jer. 2:21); a vine from Egypt (Ps. 80:8); parable of the two eagles and a vine (Ezek. 17:3-10); I am the vine (John 15:1-5); your mother was like a vine in your vineyard (Ezek. 19:10); your wife will be like a vine, your children like olive shoots (Ps. 128:3); Jerusalem is like a useless vine (Ezek. 15:2-8); how have you degenerated into a wild vine? (Jer. 2:21); their vine is of Sodom (Deut. 32:32); the vine of Sibmah has withered (Isa. 16:8-9); I weep for you, vine of Sibmah (Jer. 48:32).

D1f Metaphorical trees
The tree of the knowledge of good and evil (Gen. 2:9, 17; 3:2-7); the tree of life (Gen. 2:9; 3:22, 24; Rev. 2:7; 22:2, 14, 19); wisdom is a tree of life (Prov. 3:18); the fruit of the righteous is a tree of life (Prov. 11:30); desire fulfilled is a tree of life (Prov. 13:12); a soothing tongue is a tree of life (Prov. 15:4); trees on both banks of the river (Ezek. 47:7, 12); the trees went to anoint a king (Judg. 9:8-15); the tree which grew, whose height reached the sky, visible to all the earth (Dan. 4:20); the shoot of my planting, the work of my hands (Isa. 60:21); dream of a vine (Gen. 40:9).

D2 Trees A – C
D2a Aloe
Trees of frankincense, myrrh and aloes (S. of S. 4:14); like aloes planted by the Lord (Num. 24:6).

D2b Apple
Under the apple tree I awakened you (S. of S. 8:5); my beloved is like an apple tree (S. of S. 2:3); the pomegranate, palm, apple tree and all the trees dry up (Joel 1:12).

D2c Almond
Jacob took rods of fresh poplar and almond and plane (Gen. 30:37); Aaron's rod produced ripe almonds (Num. 17:8); I see a rod of almond (Jer. 1:11); cups like almond blossoms on the lampstand (Exod. 25:33, 34; 37:19, 20).

D2d Broom
Coals of the broom tree (Ps. 120:4); they pick mallow and the root of the broom shrub (Job 30:4).

D2e Cedar
The cedar of Lebanon (1 Kgs. 4:33; Ps. 104:16); cutting cedars of Lebanon for the temple (1 Kgs. 5:6); I cut down the cedars and cypresses of Lebanon (Isa. 37:24); the top of a cedar of Lebanon plucked off (Ezek. 17:3-4, 22); they will cut down your cedars and throw them on the fire (Jer. 22:7); like cedars beside the waters (Num. 24:6); like a cedar they bring forth fruit in old age (Ps. 92:12-14); the cypresses and the cedars of Lebanon rejoice over you (Isa. 14:8); I will place in the wilderness cedar, acacia, olive tree, juniper, box, cypress (Isa. 41:19); Assyria as a huge cedar (Ezek. 31:3-9); the voice of the Lord breaks the cedars of Lebanon (Ps. 29:5); the Lord will lop the boughs and cut down Lebanon (Isa. 10:33-4); against the cedars of Lebanon and the oaks of Bashan (Isa. 2:13); it will become a stately cedar (Ezek. 17:23); a cedar of Lebanon was taken for your mast (Ezek. 27:5); the cedars in the garden of Eden could not match it (Ezek. 31:8); Israel's fragrance will be like Lebanon (Hos. 14:6); the Amorites, tall as cedars and strong as oaks (Amos 2:9); open your doors, Lebanon, that the fire may

devour your cedars (Zech. 11:1); wail, O cypress, for the cedar has fallen (Zech. 11:2).

D2f Cypress [fir?] [pine?]

The cypress and the myrtle instead of thorns (Isa. 55:13); the juniper, box tree and cypress (Isa. 60:13); the cypresses and the cedars of Lebanon rejoice over you (Isa. 14:8); I will place in the wilderness cedar, acacia, olive tree, juniper, box, cypress (Isa. 41:19); the stork lives in the cypress trees (Ps. 104:17); your planks are made from cypress trees from Senir (Ezek. 27:5); I cut down the cypresses of Lebanon (2 Kgs. 19:23; Isa. 37:24); cypresses could not compare with its branches (Ezek. 31:8); I am like a luxuriant cypress, from me comes your fruit (Hos. 14:8); wail, O cypress, for the cedar has fallen (Zech. 11:2).

D3 Trees F – O

D3a Fig

Fig leaves for clothing (Gen. 3:7); a land of vines and fig trees (Deut. 8:8); every man under his vine and under his fig tree (1 Kgs. 4:25; 2 Kgs. 18:31; Mic. 4:4); everyone one of you will invite his neighbour to sit under his vine and under his fig tree (Zech. 3:10); when you were under the fig tree I saw you (John 1:48, 50); the trees wanted the fig tree to reign over them (Judg. 9:10-11); the parable of the fig tree (Matt. 24:32; Mark 13:28; Luke 13:6; 21:29); Jesus cursed the fig tree (Matt. 21:19-21); when he came to the fig tree he found nothing but leaves (Mark 11:13); the vine withers and the fig tree fails (Joel 1:12); I will destroy her vines and fig trees (Hos. 2:12); though the fig tree should not blossom (Hab. 3:17); the vine, fig tree, pomegranate and olive have not yet borne fruit (Hag. 2:19); can a fig tree produce olives? (Jas. 3:12); the stars fell as a fig tree sheds its late fruit when shaken by a wind (Rev. 6:13).

D3b Fir / pine

He plants a fir (Isa. 44:14); your deck is made of Cyprus pine inlaid with ivory (Ezek. 27:6).

D3c Myrtle

I will put in the wilderness the myrtle (Isa. 41:19); the cypress and the myrtle instead of thorns (Isa. 55:13); olive, myrtle and palm branches (Neh. 8:15); the angel of the Lord was standing among the myrtle trees (Zech. 1:11); the man standing among the myrtle trees (Zech. 1:8, 10).

D3d Oaks

Oaks of Mamre (Gen. 13:18; 14:13; 18:1); Allon-bacuth – oak of weeping (Gen. 35:8); Absalom's head stuck in a great oak (2 Sam. 18:9-10); the man of God sitting under an oak (1 Kgs. 13:14); they will be called oaks of righteousness (Isa. 61:3); you will be like an oak whose leaf withers (Isa. 1:30); oars made from oaks of Bashan (Ezek. 27:6); altars under every leafy oak (Ezek. 6:13); you will be ashamed of the oaks (Isa. 1:29).

D3e Olives

Vineyards and olive trees (Neh. 9:25); a land of olive trees and honey (Deut. 8:8; 2 Kgs. 18:32); I will put in the wilderness the olive (Isa. 41:19); overseeing the olive trees (1 Chr. 27:28); the olives will drop from the olive trees (Deut. 28:40); do not beat your olive trees twice (Deut. 24:20); the dove brought an olive leaf (Gen. 8:11); the trees wanted the olive tree to reign over them (Judg. 9:8-9); I am like an olive tree in the house of God (Ps. 52:8); your wife will be like a vine, your children like olive shoots (Ps. 128:3); the Lord called you a green olive tree (Jer. 11:16); the two olive trees (Zech. 4:3); two olive trees and two lampstands (Rev. 11:4); Israel's beauty will be like the olive tree (Hos. 14:6); though the produce of the olive fail (Hab. 3:17); you, a wild olive shoot, grafted in (Rom. 11:17).

D4 Trees P – W

D4a Palm trees

70 date palms at Elim (Exod. 15:27; Num. 33:9); Jericho, the city of palm trees (Deut. 34:3; Judg. 1:16; 3:13; 2 Chr. 28:15); the righteous flourish like the palm tree (Ps. 92:12); your stature is like a palm tree (S. of S. 7:7-8); the Lord cuts off palm branch and reed from Israel (Isa. 9:14); olive, myrtle and palm branches (Neh. 8:15); take palm branches for the feast of booths (Lev. 23:40); they took branches of palm trees (John 12:13); palm branches in their hands (Rev. 7:9); palm trees carved in the temple (1 Kgs. 6:29, 32, 35); the walls were decorated with palm trees and chains (2 Chr. 3:5); cherubim, lions and palm trees on the stands (1 Kgs. 7:36); carved with cherubim and palm trees (Ezek. 41:18, 20, 25).

D4b Pomegranate

A land of pomegranates (Deut. 8:8); pomegranates on the skirt of the robe of the ephod (Exod. 28:33; 39:24); pomegranates on the capitals of the pillars (1 Kgs. 7:18, 20, 42; 2 Kgs. 25:17; 2 Chr. 3:16; 4:13); Saul was under the pomegranate tree (1 Sam. 14:2); your shoots are an orchard of pomegranates (S. of S. 4:13); seeing whether the pomegranate has bloomed (S. of S. 6:11; 7:12).

D4c Poplar

Jacob took rods of poplar, almond and plane (Gen. 30:37); they will spring up like poplars (Isa. 44:4); they burn incense under oak, poplar and terebinth (Hos. 4:13).

D4d Sycamore

Overseeing the sycamore trees (1 Chr. 27:28); he destroyed their sycamores with frost (Ps. 78:47); the sycamores are cut down but we will replace them with cedars (Isa. 9:10); I am a herdsman and a dresser of sycamore trees (Amos 7:14); Zacchaeus ran on ahead and climbed a sycamore tree (Luke 19:4).

D4e Tamarisk

Abraham planted a tamarisk tree in Beersheba (Gen. 21:33); the tamarisk tree at Gibeah (1 Sam. 22:6); Saul's bones were buried under a tamarisk tree (1 Sam. 31:13); that you may be like a tamarisk in the wilderness (Jer. 48:6).

D4f Vines

Vineyards and olive trees (Neh. 9:25); every man under his vine and under his fig tree (1 Kgs. 4:25; 2 Kgs. 18:31; Isa. 36:16; Mic. 4:4); everyone one of you will invite his neighbour to sit under his vine and under his fig tree (Zech. 3:10); to see whether the vines had budded (S. of S. 6:11; 7:12); can you use wood of the vine? (Ezek. 15:2-6); though there be no fruit on the vines (Hab. 3:17); the vine will yield its fruit (Zech. 8:12); your vine will not drop its grapes (Mal. 3:11); can a vine produce figs? (Jas. 3:12); he ties his donkey to the vine (Gen. 49:11); your wife will be like a fruitful vine (Ps. 128:3); the trees wanted the vine to reign over them (Judg. 9:12-13); the Nazirite must not eat anything from the vine (Num. 6:4); she may not eat anything which comes from the vine (Judg. 13:14).

PEOPLE AS VINES, see 366D1e.

D4g Willow

Take willows of the brook for the feast of booths (Lev. 23:40); the willows of the brook surround him (Job 40:22); we hung our harps on the willows (Ps. 137:2); he set it like a willow (Ezek. 17:5).

D5 Thorns and briars

The ground producing thorns and thistles (Gen. 3:18; Heb. 6:8); if fire catches in thorns (Exod. 22:6); the laughter of fools is like the crackling of thorns under a pot (Eccles. 7:6); the trees wanted the bramble to reign over them (Judg. 9:14); do not sow among thorns (Jer. 4:3); some seed fell among thorns (Matt. 13:7, 22; Mark 4:7, 18; Luke 8:7, 14); they have sown wheat and reaped thorns (Jer. 12:13); are grapes gathered from thorns or figs from thistles? (Matt. 7:16); figs are not gathered from thorns nor grapes from briars (Luke 6:44); thrashing the men of Succoth with thorns (Judg. 8:7, 16); a briar sent to a cedar (2 Kgs. 14:9); briars and thorns will grow up (Isa. 5:6; 7:23-5; 32:13); thorns will come up in its strongholds (Isa. 34:13); the thorn bush said to the cedar (2 Chr. 25:18); a crown of thorns (Matt. 27:29; Mark 15:17; John 19:2, 5); Paul's thorn in the flesh (2 Cor. 12:7).

367 Zoology
ANIMALS, see 365.

368 Botany
PLANTS, see 366.

369 Animal husbandry
A Owning livestock
Abraham had oxen (Gen. 12:16); Lot had oxen (Gen. 13:5); Isaac had flocks and herds (Gen. 26:14); Jacob had oxen (Gen. 32:5); Uzziah had much livestock (2 Chr. 26:10); Job had 500 yoke of oxen (Job 1:3); Job had thousands of sheep, camels, oxen and donkeys (Job 42:12); I had herds and flocks larger than those before me (Eccles. 2:7); the sons of Reuben and Gad had many livestock (Num. 32:1-4); our livestock must go too (Exod. 10:26); whose ox have I taken? (1 Sam. 12:3); some take the widow's ox in pledge (Job 24:3); they took the Hivites' herds (Gen. 34:28); they took the Hagrites' cattle (1 Chr. 5:21); I have bought five yoke [pairs] of oxen and must try them out (Luke 14:19); Joseph gave them food in exchange for their herds (Gen. 47:12); Mesha king of Moab was a sheep-breeder (2 Kgs. 3:4).
B Tending livestock
Overseeing the animals (1 Chr. 27:29-31); building sheepfolds (Num. 32:16, 24, 36); though you stay among the sheepfolds (Ps. 68:13); a righteous man has regard for the life of his beasts (Prov. 12:10); he who enters by the door is the shepherd (John 10:2); know well the condition of your flocks and herds (Prov. 27:23); shepherds are abominations to the Egyptians (Gen. 46:34); woe to the worthless shepherd who deserts the flock (Zech. 11:17); the herdsmen fled and went into the city (Matt. 8:33; Luke 8:34); strife between Abraham's and Lot's herdsmen (Gen. 13:7); the herdsmen of Gerar quarrelled with Isaac's herdsmen (Gen. 26:20); lions growling over their prey will not be afraid of shepherds (Isa. 31:4); the Lord took me from following the flock (Amos 7:15); I took you from following the sheep (2 Sam. 7:8; 1 Chr. 17:7); he took David from the sheepfolds (Ps. 78:70); David left the flock with a keeper (1 Sam. 17:20); with whom have you left the sheep? (1 Sam. 17:28); shepherds will not make their flocks lie down there (Isa. 13:20); the shepherds returned, glorifying and praising God (Luke 2:20).
C Shepherding people
C1 God shepherding people
God who has been my shepherd (Gen. 48:15); the Lord is my shepherd (Ps. 23:1); shepherd of Israel (Gen. 49:24; Ps. 80:1); he will lead Israel as a shepherd keeps his flock (Jer. 31:10); he will tend his flock like a shepherd (Isa. 40:11); he leads his people like a flock of sheep (Ps. 78:52); you led your people like a flock (Ps. 77:20); you who lead Joseph like a flock (Ps. 80:1); he is their God and they are his flock (Ps. 95:7; Ezek. 34:31); they are the flock of his people (Zech. 9:16); the sheep of your pasture (Ps. 74:1; 79:13); I will shepherd my sheep (Ezek. 34:12); be their shepherd (Ps. 28:9); shepherd your people (Mic. 7:14); I will shepherd my

flock (Ezek. 34:15); [the Messiah] will stand and shepherd his flock (Mic. 5:4); out of Bethlehem will come a shepherd for Israel (Mic. 5:2-4; Matt. 2:6); I am the good shepherd (John 10:11, 14); one flock, one shepherd (John 10:16); the great Shepherd of the sheep (Heb. 13:20); the Shepherd and Guardian of your souls (1 Pet. 2:25); when the chief Shepherd appears (1 Pet. 5:4); the Lamb will be their shepherd (Rev. 7:17); you will shepherd them with a rod of iron (Ps. 2:9).
C2 People shepherding people
David will shepherd Israel (2 Sam. 5:2; 1 Chr. 11:2; Ps. 78:71); they will have one shepherd, David (Ezek. 34:23; 37:24); Cyrus is God's shepherd (Isa. 44:28); they will shepherd the land of Assyria with the sword (Mic. 5:6); he will separate them as a shepherd separates sheep from goats (Matt. 25:32); I will give you shepherds after my own heart (Jer. 3:15); I will raise up shepherds to tend them (Jer. 23:4); tend my sheep (John 21:16); he gave some to be shepherds [pastors] and teachers (Eph. 4:11); shepherd the church of God (Acts 20:28); shepherd the flock of God (1 Pet. 5:2); who tends a flock without using the milk? (1 Cor. 9:7); shepherd the flock doomed to slaughter (Zech. 11:4, 7).
C3 Inadequate shepherding
Woe to the shepherds who scatter the sheep (Jer. 23:1); I will raise up a shepherd who will not care for the flock (Zech. 11:16-17); woe to the shepherds who only take care of themselves (Ezek. 34:2-10); shepherding only themselves (Jude 12); I destroyed the three shepherds in one month (Zech. 11:8); my anger is kindled against the shepherds (Zech. 10:3); their own shepherds have no pity on them (Zech. 11:5); the shepherds have become stupid and their flock is scattered (Jer. 10:21); the people wander and are afflicted for want of a shepherd (Zech. 10:2-3); sheep without a shepherd (Num. 27:17; 1 Kgs. 22:17; 2 Chr. 18:16; Matt. 9:36; Mark 6:34); strike the shepherd and the sheep will be scattered (Zech. 13:7; Matt. 26:31; Mark 14:27); they were scattered without a shepherd (Ezek. 34:5); death will be their shepherd (Ps. 49:14).
D Sheep-shearing
Do not shear the firstborn of your flock (Deut. 15:19); give the priest the first shearing of your flock (Deut. 18:4); like a sheep that before its shearers is dumb (Isa. 53:7); as a lamb before its shearers is dumb (Acts 8:32); sheep-shearing time: for Laban (Gen. 31:19); for Judah (Gen. 38:12, 13); for Nabal (1 Sam. 25:2, 4, 7); for Absalom (2 Sam. 13:23, 24).

370 Agriculture
A Laws about agriculture
When you reap, leave gleanings (Lev. 19:9, 10; 23:22); laws on planting fruit trees (Lev. 19:23-5); do not sow or reap in the seventh year (Lev. 25:4-5, 11); or in the year of Jubilee (Lev. 25:11).
B Farmers
Adam had to till the garden (Gen. 2:15); Cain tilled the soil (Gen. 4:2); Noah began farming (Gen. 9:20); Uzziah loved the soil (2 Chr. 26:10); I am a herdsman and a dresser of sycamore trees (Amos 7:14); the farmer and those who wander with the flocks (Jer. 31:24); with you I shatter farmer and his team (Jer. 51:23); they call the farmers to mourning (Amos 5:16); they went off, one to his farm and another to his business (Matt. 22:5); the farmer waits for the precious fruit of the soil, being patient over it (Jas. 5:7).
C Products of agriculture
C1 Gardens
FIELD, see 235D.

C1a Gardens in general

Plant gardens and eat their produce (Jer. 29:5, 28); they will make gardens and eat their fruit (Amos 9:14); I made gardens and parks (Eccles. 2:5); those who sanctify themselves to go to the gardens (Isa. 66:17); they sacrifice in gardens (Isa. 65:3); you will be ashamed of the gardens you have chosen (Isa. 1:29); I smote your gardens and vineyards (Amos 4:9).

C1b Particular gardens

The Lord planted a garden in Eden (Gen. 2:8); God put man in the garden of Eden (Gen. 2:15); you were in Eden, the garden of God (Ezek. 28:13); he was sent out of the garden of Eden (Gen. 3:23); all the trees in Eden, the garden of God, were jealous of it (Ezek. 31:8-9); the tree of life which is in the paradise of God (Rev. 2:7); Manasseh was buried in the garden of Uzza (2 Kgs. 21:18); Amon was buried in the garden of Uzza (2 Kgs. 21:26); the king's garden (2 Kgs. 25:4; Neh. 3:15); the palace gardens (Esther 7:7); there was a garden which he and his disciples entered (John 18:1); the garden of the tomb (John 19:41); did I not see you in the garden with him? (John 18:26).

C1c Like gardens

The Jordan valley was like the garden of the Lord (Gen. 13:10); the desolate land in exile has become like the garden of Eden (Ezek. 36:35); the land is like the garden of Eden before them (Joel 2:3); like gardens beside the river (Num. 24:6); my beloved is a locked garden (S. of S. 4:12); you will be like a watered garden (Isa. 58:11); their life will be like a watered garden (Jer. 31:12); you will be like a garden without water (Isa. 1:30).

C2 Vineyards

PRUNING, see 46F4a.

C2a Vineyards in general

The king will take the best of your vineyards (1 Sam. 8:14); Ahab wanted Naboth's vineyard (1 Kgs. 21:1-18); I will give her her vineyards (Hos. 2:15); will David give you fields and vineyards? (1 Sam. 22:7); let your vineyard lie fallow the seventh year (Exod. 23:11); overseeing the vineyards (1 Chr. 27:27); some of the poorest people were left to be ploughmen and vinedressers (Jer. 52:16); foreigners will be your vinedressers (Isa. 61:5); they made me a keeper of vineyards but I neglected my own (S. of S. 1:6); I passed by the vineyard of the man without sense (Prov. 24:30).

C2b Planting vineyards

Noah planted a vineyard (Gen. 9:20); the good wife plants a vineyard (Prov. 31:16); again you will plant vineyards (Jer. 31:5); I planted vineyards (Eccles. 2:4); in the third year, sow, reap, plant vineyards (2 Kgs. 19:29; Isa. 37:30); they will build houses and plant vineyards (Ezek. 28:26); Samaria will be a place for planting vineyards (Mic. 1:6); he who has planted a vineyard and not yet tasted the fruit (Deut. 20:6); they will plant vineyards and eat the fruit (Isa. 65:21); who plants a vineyard without eating the fruit? (1 Cor. 9:7); they will plant vineyards and drink their wine (Amos 9:14); they will plant vineyards but not drink the wine (Amos 5:11; Zeph. 1:13); you will plant a vineyard and not have the fruit (Deut. 28:30, 39); vineyards you did not plant (Deut. 6:11; Josh. 24:13); the Rechabites were not to plant a vineyard (Jer. 35:7, 9).

C2c Metaphorical vineyards

A song about a vineyard (Isa. 5:1-7; 27:2-3); the Lord's vineyard is the house of Israel (Isa. 5:7); a householder hiring labourers for his vineyard (Matt. 20:1-16); go and work in the vineyard today (Matt. 21:28); they threw the heir out of the vineyard and killed him (Matt. 21:39-40); my Father is the vinedresser (John 15:1).

C3 Orchards

I planted all kinds of fruit trees (Eccles. 2:5); you will plant olive trees and have no oil (Deut. 28:40); olive orchards you did not plant (Deut. 6:11; Josh. 24:13); overseeing the olive and sycamore trees (1 Chr. 27:28); let your olive orchard lie fallow the seventh year (Exod. 23:11); like the shaking of an olive tree (Isa. 24:13); he who tends a fig tree will eat its fruit (Prov. 27:18); an orchard of pomegranates (S. of S. 4:13); I went down to the nut orchard (S. of S. 6:11).

D Processes of agriculture

D1 Tilling

D1a Tilling the soil

Adam had to till the garden (Gen. 2:15); to till the ground from which he was taken (Gen. 3:23); Cain tilled the soil (Gen. 4:2); agriculture would be through toil (Gen. 3:17-19); he who tills his land will have plenty of bread (Prov. 12:11; 28:19); the desolate land will be tilled (Ezek. 36:34); an advantage to a land is a king over cultivated fields (Eccles. 5:9); you will be tilled and sown (Ezek. 36:9); they will beat their swords into ploughshares (Mic. 4:3); the oxen were ploughing (Job 1:14); do not plough with an ox and a donkey (Deut. 22:10); does the farmer plough continually? (Isa. 28:24); the sluggard does not plough in autumn (Prov. 20:4); do horses run on rocks or does one plough the sea with oxen? (Amos 6:12); when you till the ground it will not yield its strength (Gen. 4:12); for five years there will be neither ploughing nor harvesting (Gen. 45:6).

D1b Ploughmen

Not yet a man to till the ground (Gen. 2:5); the ploughman should plough in hope (1 Cor. 9:10); he who puts his hand to the plough and looks back (Luke 9:62); in ploughing time, rest on the sabbath (Exod. 34:21); Elisha was ploughing (1 Kgs. 19:19); the ploughman will overtake the reaper (Amos 9:13); the king will appoint men to plough and harvest for him (1 Sam. 8:12); I am not a prophet, I am a tiller of the soil (Zech. 13:5).

D1c Metaphorical ploughing

Those who plough iniquity and trouble harvest it (Job 4:8); you have ploughed wickedness and reaped injustice (Hos. 10:13); the ploughers ploughed on my back (Ps. 129:3); you will be tilled and sown (Ezek. 36:9); Judah will plough, Jacob will harrow (Hos. 10:11); Zion will be ploughed as a field (Jer. 26:18; Mic. 3:12); if you had not ploughed with my heifer (Judg. 14:18); break up your fallow ground (Jer. 4:3).

D2 Planting

D2a Literal planting

The Lord planted a garden in Eden (Gen. 2:8); Isaac planted crops and reaped a hundredfold (Gen. 26:12); give us seed that we may live (Gen. 47:19); for six years sow your field (Exod. 23:10; Lev. 25:3); in the third year, sow, reap, plant vineyards (2 Kgs. 19:29; Isa. 37:30); in the days of Lot they bought, they sold, they planted, they built (Luke 17:28).

D2b Metaphorical planting

You will be tilled and sown (Ezek. 36:9); I will plant a twig of cedar on a high and lofty mountain (Ezek. 17:22); you will plant them in your own mountain (Exod. 15:17); I will plant my people Israel (1 Chr. 17:9); I will build them and plant them (Jer. 24:6); I will watch over them to build and to plant (Jer. 31:28); I will plant them in this land (Jer. 32:41); I will plant you and not uproot you (Jer. 42:10); you have planted them and they take root (Jer. 12:2); the planting of the Lord that he may be glorified (Isa. 61:3); I planted and Apollos watered (1 Cor. 3:6-8); scarcely are they planted when he blows on them and they wither (Isa. 40:24).

D3 Harvesting
GLEANING, see 41B3.

D3a Harvest time
Seedtime and harvest will not cease (Gen. 8:22); a faithful messenger is like the cold of snow in harvest-time (Prov. 25:13); harvest time (2 Sam. 23:13); wheat harvest (Gen. 30:14; Judg. 15:1; Ruth 2:23; 1 Sam. 6:13; 12:17); barley harvest (Ruth 1:22; 2:23; 2 Sam. 21:9); in harvest time, rest on the sabbath (Exod. 34:21); they rejoice with the joy of harvest (Isa. 9:3); he who watches the clouds will not reap (Eccles. 11:4); he who sleeps in harvest brings shame (Prov. 10:5); the ant gathers food in harvest (Prov. 6:8); Jordan overflows at harvest time (Josh. 3:15); soon the time of harvest will come for the daughter of Babylon (Jer. 51:33); for you also, Judah, there is a harvest appointed (Hos. 6:11); let them grow together until harvest (Matt. 13:30); the harvest has come (Mark 4:29); when harvest time came he sent his servants (Matt. 21:34); the harvest is the end of the age (Matt. 13:39); the fields are white for harvest (John 4:35); put in the sickle, for the harvest is ripe (Joel 3:13); the hour to reap has come because the harvest of the earth is ripe (Rev. 14:15).

D3b Feast of harvest
The Feast of Harvest (Exod. 23:16); the Feast of Ingathering (Exod. 23:16); count seven weeks from the time you put sickle to the grain (Deut. 16:9); seven days from harvest to the Feast of Booths (Deut. 16:13); the firstfruits of the wheat harvest (Exod. 34:22); when you harvest your land, bring the sheaf of firstfruits (Lev. 23:10).

D3c Reaping / the harvest
For six years sow your land and gather its produce (Exod. 23:10); in the third year, sow, reap, plant vineyards (2 Kgs. 19:29; Isa. 37:30); when you reap your harvest, leave gleanings (Lev. 19:9-10; Deut. 24:19-21); would not grape-gatherers leave gleanings? (Obad. 5); your sheaves bowed down to my sheaf (Gen. 37:7); the disciples plucked ears of grain (Matt. 12:1; Mark 2:23; Luke 6:1); the harvest is plentiful (Matt. 9:37; Luke 10:2); he will gather the wheat into the barn (Matt. 3:12; Luke 3:17); he who sat on the cloud swung his sickle over the earth (Rev. 14:16); if we sowed to the spirit, should we not reap material things? (1 Cor. 9:11); they sow the wind and reap the whirlwind (Hos. 8:7); those who sow trouble harvest it (Job 4:8); he who sows iniquity will reap vanity (Prov. 22:8); you have ploughed wickedness and reaped injustice (Hos. 10:13); what a man sows, that will he reap (Gal. 6:7-9); he who sows sparingly will reap sparingly and he who sows bountifully will reap bountifully (2 Cor. 9:6); in due season we shall reap (Gal. 6:9); he will increase the harvest of your righteousness (2 Cor. 9:10).

D3d Not reaping what is sown
For five years there will be neither ploughing nor harvesting (Gen. 45:6); wail for the wheat and barley because the harvest is destroyed (Joel 1:11); harvest is past, summer is ended and we are not saved (Jer. 8:20); you will sow but not reap (Mic. 6:15); he gave their crops to the grasshopper and the locust (Ps. 78:46); the fool's harvest is eaten up by others (Job 5:5); they have sown wheat and reaped thorns (Jer. 12:13); he who looks at the clouds will not reap (Eccles. 11:4); the birds do not sow, nor reap or gather into barns (Matt. 6:26; Luke 12:24); you reap what you did not sow (Luke 19:21-2); I sent you to reap where you have not laboured (John 4:38).

D3e Reapers
Pray the Lord of the harvest to send workers (Matt. 9:38; Luke 10:2); those who sow in tears will reap in joy (Ps. 126:5-6); he who sows and he who reaps will

rejoice together (John 4:36); the ploughman will overtake the reaper (Amos 9:13); the farmer is the first to have a share of the crops (2 Tim. 2:6); the reapers are angels (Matt. 13:39); he who reaps gets wages (John 4:36); one sows and another reaps (John 4:37); the pay of the labourers who mowed your fields (Jas. 5:4).

D3f Threshing / winnowing
Ornan was threshing wheat (1 Chr. 21:20); Gideon was threshing wheat in the winepress (Judg. 6:11); do not muzzle an ox when threshing (Deut. 25:4; 1 Cor. 9:9; 1 Tim. 5:18); threshing sledges for firewood (2 Sam. 24:22; 1 Chr. 21:23); dill and cummin are not threshed with a sledge (Isa. 28:27); they threshed Gilead with sharp iron tools (Amos 1:3); threshing the men of Succoth with thorns (Judg. 8:7); the thresher should thresh in hope of a share of the crop (1 Cor. 9:10); the Lord will thresh in that day (Isa. 27:12); I have made you into a threshing sledge (Isa. 41:15); a just king winnows evil with his eyes (Prov. 20:8); a wise king winnows the wicked (Prov. 20:26); O my threshed and winnowed one! (Isa. 21:10); I will winnow them with a winnowing fork (Jer. 15:7); his winnowing fork is in his hand (Matt. 3:12); you will winnow them and the wind will carry them away (Isa. 41:16); foreigners will winnow Babylon (Jer. 51:2); a scorching wind, not to winnow or cleanse (Jer. 4:11).

D3g Threshing floors
The threshing floor of Araunah [Ornan] (2 Sam. 24:16; 1 Chr. 21:15, 18, 28); the threshing floor bought and an altar erected there (2 Sam. 24:18-25; 1 Chr. 21:18-28); the temple was built there (2 Chr. 3:1); Boaz at the threshing floor (Ruth 3:2-14); the threshing floor at the gate of Samaria (1 Kgs. 22:10; 2 Chr. 18:9); the daughter of Babylon is like a threshing floor (Jer. 51:33); he will clear his threshing floor (Matt. 3:12).

D3h Treading grapes
Harvesting and treading grapes (Judg. 9:27); treading the wine press on the sabbath (Neh. 13:15); thirsty, they tread the wine press (Job 24:11); the grapes of the earth are ripe for harvesting and treading (Joel 3:13); why are your garments like one who treads in the wine press? (Isa. 63:2-3); the Lord will shout like those who tread the grapes (Jer. 25:30); the Lord has trodden Judah as in a wine press (Lam. 1:15); the wine press of the wrath of God (Rev. 14:19-20); the treader of grapes will overtake him who sows seed (Amos 9:13); you will tread the grapes but not drink wine (Mic. 6:15).

D4 Fallow land
This year and next year eat what grows of itself (2 Kgs. 19:29; Isa. 37:30); it will not be pruned or hoed (Isa. 5:6); break up your fallow ground (Jer. 4:3; Hos. 10:12).

E Parables of agriculture
Parables of: the sower (Matt. 13:3-9, 18-23; Mark 4:3-9, 14-20; Luke 8:4-8, 11-15); the leaven (Matt. 13:31-2); the growing seed (Mark 4:26-9); the mustard seed (Mark 4:31-2; Luke 13:18-19); the vineyard and tenants (Matt. 21:33-41; Mark 12:1-11; Luke 20:9-18).

371 Mankind

A Man in general
A1 What man is
NATURE OF PEOPLE, see 5C.
MAN S KNOWLEDGE, see 490E.

A1a Man's nature
The first man is from the earth, the second from heaven (1 Cor. 15:47); to till the ground from which he was taken (Gen. 3:23); God created mankind from dust (Gen. 2:7); dust you are and to dust you will return (Gen. 3:19); God forms the spirit of a man within him (Zech. 12:1); no one knows the things of a man but the spirit of the man within him (1 Cor. 2:11); man created

in the likeness of God (Gen. 1:26-7; 5:1-2; 9:6); man
who dies (Isa. 51:12); God tests men for them to see that
they are but animals (Eccles. 3:18); man is like the
beasts that perish (Ps. 49:12, 20); God teaches us more
than the beasts or birds (Job 35:11); the voice of a god
and not man! (Acts 12:22); you are a man and not a god
(Ezek. 28:2, 9); men do not warrant worship (Acts
10:26); behold, the man! (1 Sam. 9:17; John 19:5).

A1b Man's relation to God

God created mankind (Deut. 4:32); from dust (Gen.
2:7); the breath of all mankind is in God's hands (Job
12:10); the life was the light of men (John 1:4); God
named them Man (Gen. 5:2); man created in the
likeness of God (Gen. 1:26-7; 5:1-2; 9:6); a little lower
than God, crowned with glory (Ps. 8:5); as the heavens
are higher than the earth, so are God's thoughts and
ways compared with man's (Isa. 55:8-9); I am God and
not man (Hos. 11:9); God is greater than man (Job
33:12); a man like me cannot answer him (Job 9:32); can
man be more righteous than God? (Job 4:17); God is
true though every man a liar (Rom. 3:4); am I God to
kill and make alive? (2 Kgs. 5:7); with men this is
impossible but with God all things are possible (Matt.
19:26; Mark 10:27); what is impossible with men is
possible with God (Luke 18:27); who are you, O man,
to answer back to God? (Rom. 9:20); no man can see
God and live (Exod. 33:20).

A1c Man's relation to nature

Man's function to rule all creatures (Gen. 1:26); to
subdue the earth (Gen. 1:28); to till the ground (Gen.
2:5); all creatures given into man's hand (Gen. 9:2);
every kind of animal has been tamed by man (Jas. 3:7).

A1d Man's sinful nature

Out of the heart of a person come evil things (Mark
7:21); all flesh had corrupted their way on the earth
(Gen. 6:12); man [unlike God] lies and changes his
mind (Num. 23:19; 1 Sam. 15:29); all men are liars (Ps.
116:11); man is born for trouble as the sparks fly upward
(Job 5:7); what is man that he should be pure? (Job
15:14).

A2 Man's value

MAN A MERE BREATH, see 352A5.
GREATNESS OF MAN, see 638B.

A2a What value is man?

Of what account is man? (Isa. 2:22); what is man that
you care about him? (Job 7:17; Ps. 8:4; 144:3; Heb. 2:6);
of how much more value is a man than a sheep! (Matt.
12:12); do not fear, you are of more value than many
sparrows (Matt. 10:31; Luke 12:7); how much more
valuable are you than the birds! (Luke 12:24); the
precious sons of Zion, worth their weight in fine gold
(Lam. 4:2).

A2b Mere men

We also are men, of the same nature as you (Acts
14:15); the son of man who is made like grass (Isa.
51:12); surely the people are grass (Isa. 40:7); all flesh is
grass (Isa. 40:6); all men are but a breath (Ps. 62:9);
man is like a breath (Ps. 144:4); let no one boast about
men (1 Cor. 3:21); let the nations know that they are but
men (Ps. 9:20); the sheep of my pasture, you are men
(Ezek. 34:31); man is a maggot and a worm (Job 25:6); I
am a worm and no man (Ps. 22:6).

A3 Like men

The shadows of the mountains looking like men (Judg.
9:36); he makes the idol in form like a man (Isa. 44:13);
each living creature had a man's face (Ezek. 1:10; 10:14;
41:19); the four living creatures had human form (Ezek.
1:5); the third creature had a face like a man (Rev. 4:7);
the faces of the locusts were like the faces of men (Rev.
9:7); on the throne was a figure resembling that of a
man (Ezek. 1:26); the lion was made to stand on two

feet like a man and given a man's mind (Dan. 7:4); the
little horn had eyes like the eyes of a man (Dan. 7:8);
one like a human being touched my lips (Dan. 10:16);
standing before me was someone like a man (Dan.
8:15); I see people, but they look like trees, walking
(Mark 8:24); the gods have come down in human form
(Acts 14:11); are you not acting like mere men? (1 Cor.
3:4); in the middle of the lampstands was one like a son
of man (Rev. 1:13); a white cloud with one like a son of
man seated on it (Rev. 14:14).

A4 Christ's human nature

He emptied himself, born in the likeness of men (Phil.
2:7-8); the Word became flesh (John 1:14); the last
Adam became a life-giving spirit (1 Cor. 15:45); one
mediator between God and man, the man Christ Jesus
(1 Tim. 2:5); you, a man, make yourself out to be God
(John 10:33); they gave glory to God who had given
such authority to men (Matt. 9:8).

A5 'Son of man'

A5a Ministry of the Son of man

Who do men say the Son of man is? (Matt. 16:13); who
is this Son of man? (John 12:34); God gave him
authority to judge because he is the Son of man (John
5:27); the Son of man came eating and drinking (Matt.
11:19; Luke 7:34); he did not come to be served but to
serve (Matt. 20:28; Mark 10:45); he has come to seek
and save (Matt. 18:11; Luke 19:10); the Son of man will
be a sign to this generation (Luke 11:30); the hour has
come for the Son of man to be glorified (John 12:23);
now is the Son of man glorified (John 13:31); if you
were to see the Son of man ascending (John 6:62); no
one has ascended to heaven but he who descended
from heaven, the Son of man (John 3:13); the Son of
man in the heart of the earth three days and three
nights (Matt. 12:40); do you believe in the Son of man?
(John 9:35).

A5b Activity of the Son of man

The Son of man: is Lord of the Sabbath (Matt. 12:8;
Mark 2:28; Luke 6:5); has authority to forgive sins
(Matt. 9:6; Mark 2:10; Luke 5:24); sowing the good seed
(Matt. 13:37); has nowhere to lay his head (Matt. 8:20);
suffering (Matt. 17:12; Mark 9:12); being betrayed and
killed (Matt. 17:22; 20:18; 26:2, 24, 45; Mark 8:31; 9:31;
10:33; 14:21, 41; Luke 9:22, 44; 22:22; 24:7); being lifted
up (John 3:14; 8:28; 12:34); rising from the dead (Matt.
17:9; Mark 9:9); being given a kingdom (Dan. 7:13-14);
being seated in heaven (Matt. 19:28; Mark 14:62; Luke
22:69); seated at the right hand of Power (Matt. 26:64);
standing in heaven (Acts 7:56); sending forth his angels
(Matt. 13:41); returning (Matt. 10:23; Luke 12:40; 17:30;
18:8); coming in glory (Matt. 16:27; 24:27, 30, 37-40, 44;
25:31; 26:64; Mark 8:38; 13:26; Luke 9:26; 17:24; 21:27).

A5c Relations with the Son of man

Pray for strength to stand before the Son of man (Luke
21:36); blessed are you when they spurn your name as
evil for the sake of the Son of man (Luke 6:22); do you
betray the Son of man with a kiss? (Luke 22:48);
speaking against the Son of man will be forgiven (Matt.
12:32; Luke 12:10); eat the flesh of the Son of man (John
6:53); the Son of man confessing his own before the
Father (Luke 12:8).

A6 Dealings with men

TRUSTING IN MEN, see 485D.
FEAR OF MEN, see 854D.

A6a Danger from men

Beware of men (Matt. 10:17); cursed is the man who
trusts in man (Jer. 17:5); trust in the Lord, not in man
(Ps. 146:3); better to take refuge in the Lord than to
trust in man (Ps. 118:8); with him is an arm of flesh
(2 Chr. 32:8); with God helping me, what can man do?
(Ps. 56:4, 11; 118:6; Heb. 13:6); fear of men is a snare

(Prov. 29:25); the Son of man is to be delivered into the hands of men (Matt. 17:22; Mark 9:31; Luke 9:44); the anger of man does not work the righteousness of God (Jas. 1:20).

A6b Seen by man

Do not practise your religious acts before men to be seen by them (Matt. 6:1); hypocrites pray to be seen by men (Matt. 6:5); hypocrites look gloomy so their fasting may be seen by men (Matt. 6:16); they do all their works to be seen by men (Matt. 23:5); man looks at the outside but the Lord looks at the heart (1 Sam. 16:7); you outwardly appear righteous to men (Matt. 23:28); take thought for what is good in the sight of all men (Rom. 12:17); obey your masters, not with eyeservice as pleasing men (Col. 3:22).

A6c Man's teaching

You are not setting your mind on God's things, but on man's (Matt. 16:23; Mark 8:33); according to the teaching of men (Col. 2:22); teaching as doctrines the traditions of men (Matt. 15:9; Mark 7:7-8); the baptism of John, was it from heaven or from men? (Matt. 21:25-6; Mark 11:30-2; Luke 20:4-6); the gospel I preached was not man's (Gal. 1:11-12); flesh and blood did not reveal this to you (Matt. 16:17); the message is not the word of men, but of God (1 Thess. 2:13); if this movement is of men it will fail (Acts 5:38); he who rejects is not rejecting man but God (1 Thess. 4:8); we must obey God rather than men (Acts 5:29).

A6d Pleasing men

I do not receive glory from men (John 5:41); if I pleased men I would not be a slave of Christ (Gal. 1:10); not trying to please men but God (1 Thess. 2:4); not as men-pleasers (Eph. 6:6); they loved the praise of men more than praise from God (John 12:43); I did not look for glory from men (1 Thess. 2:6); what is highly valued among men is an abomination before God (Luke 16:15); obey your masters, not with eyeservice as pleasing men (Col. 3:22); submit yourself for the Lord's sake to every human institution (1 Pet. 2:13); we seek what is honourable not only before the Lord but also before men (2 Cor. 8:21).

A6e Witness before men

Everyone who acknowledges me before men, I will acknowledge before my Father (Matt. 10:32-3; Luke 12:8-9); Jesus increased in favour with God and man (Luke 2:52); I will make you fishers of men (Matt. 4:19); I try to keep a clear conscience before God and before men (Acts 24:16).

B Israel and the Gentiles
B1 Israel and the Jews
B1a Israel in general

Who is like God's people Israel? (2 Sam. 7:23); Israel dwells alone, not reckoned among the nations (Num. 23:9); of all families on earth God chose Israel (Amos 3:2); Israel is my firstborn son (Exod. 4:22); my people, the sons of Israel (Exod. 3:10); no other god has taken one nation for himself (Deut. 4:34); blessed more than all peoples (Deut. 7:14); Israel will not cease from being a nation before me (Jer. 31:36-7); what advantage has the Jew? (Rom. 3:1); salvation is from the Jews (John 4:22); your people shall be my people (Ruth 1:16); many became Jews for fear of the Jews (Esther 8:17); ten men will grasp the garment of a Jew (Zech. 8:23); Jeshurun grew fat and kicked (Deut. 32:15); the Jew is also a sinner (Rom. 2:17-29).

B1b Jews under threat

Haman sought to destroy all Jews (Esther 3:6); Haman's plot against the Jews (Esther 8:3, 7); let us wipe out Israel as a nation (Ps. 83:4).

B1c Particular Jews

These men are Jews and they are disturbing our city (Acts 16:20); when they recognised that Alexander was a Jew (Acts 19:34); Esther did not make her people known (Esther 2:10, 20); Mordecai had told them he was a Jew (Esther 3:4); if Mordecai is a Jew (Esther 6:13); there are certain Jews whom you set over the province of Babylon (Dan. 3:12); Nathanael was a true Israelite (John 1:47); Zacchaeus was a son of Abraham (Luke 19:9); I am a Jew, born in Tarsus of Cilicia (Acts 22:3); I am an Israelite (Rom. 11:1); are they Israelites? so am I (2 Cor. 11:22); of the nation of Israel, of the tribe of Benjamin, a Hebrew of Hebrews (Phil. 3:5); we are Jews, not Gentile sinners (Gal. 2:15).

B1d Salvation for Israel

Oh that the salvation of Israel would come out of Zion! (Ps. 14:7); will you at this time restore the kingdom to Israel? (Acts 1:6); where is he who has been born king of the Jews? (Matt. 2:2); are you the king of the Jews? (Luke 23:3, 37-8); for this reason I came baptising, that he might be manifested to Israel (John 1:31); the word which he sent to Israel by Jesus Christ (Acts 10:36); they spoke the word to no one except Jews (Acts 11:19); let the children be fed first (Mark 7:27); Paul testified to the Jews that Jesus was the Christ (Acts 18:5); the Jewish believers were zealous for the law (Acts 21:20); after three days Paul called the leaders of the Jews (Acts 28:17); for the sake of the hope of Israel I am bound with this chain (Acts 28:20); my heart's desire for Israel is that they be saved (Rom. 10:1); Christ became a servant to the circumcision (Rom. 15:8); Paul became like a Jew to win Jews (1 Cor. 9:20); he will turn back many of the sons of Israel to the Lord (Luke 1:16); God grants repentance to Israel and forgiveness of sins (Acts 5:31).

B1e Israel hardened

I will destroy Israel and make of Moses a great nation (Exod. 32:10); Israel pursued righteousness based on law but did not attain that law (Rom. 9:31); Israel is hardened until the full complement of the Gentiles comes in (Rom. 11:25); the kingdom of God will be taken away from you (Matt. 21:43); the sons of the kingdom will be cast out (Matt. 8:12); they are not his people and God is not their God (Hos. 1:9); Paul was in anguish about his kinsmen, the people of Israel (Rom. 9:3); the full inclusion of the Jews will bring great richness (Rom. 11:12); God has not rejected his people whom he foreknew (Rom. 11:2); what Israel sought it did not obtain, and the rest were hardened (Rom. 11:7).

B2 Jew and Gentile
B2a Blessings for Jew and Gentile

All people on earth will be blessed through Abraham (Gen. 22:18; 28:14; Acts 3:25); in you all the families of the earth will be blessed (Gen. 12:3); a light of revelation to the Gentiles and for glory to your people Israel (Luke 2:32); is God only the God of the Jews and not the God of the Gentiles? (Rom. 3:29).

B2b Jews separate from Gentiles

Jews have no dealings with Samaritans (John 4:9); you know how unlawful it is for a Jew to associate with a foreigner (Acts 10:28); am I a Jew? (John 18:35); if you, a Jew, live like a Gentile, why compel Gentiles to live like Jews? (Gal. 2:14).

B2c The gospel to Jew and Gentile

To the Jew first and also to the Greek (Rom. 1:16; 2:9-10); Jews and Greeks are all under sin (Rom. 3:9); Christ became a servant for the circumcision and the Gentiles (Rom. 15:8-9); Jesus came, with his people (Rom. 15:10); to carry my name before the Gentiles and kings and sons of Israel (Acts 9:15); Paul was persuading Jews and Greeks (Acts 18:4); testifying both to Jews and Greeks of repentance and faith (Acts 20:21); they hear you teach the Jews among the Gentiles to forsake Moses (Acts 21:21); Christ would announce light both to the people and to the Gentiles (Acts 26:23); God justifies both circumcised and uncircumcised through faith (Rom. 3:30); Abraham was the father of circumcised and uncircumcised who believe (Rom. 4:11-12); those who are the called, both Jews and Greeks (1 Cor. 1:24); one body, Jews or Greeks, slave or free (1 Cor. 12:13); Paul with the gospel to the uncircumcised and Peter to the circumcised (Gal. 2:7-9).

B2d Antagonism from Jew and Gentile

Jews require signs and Greeks seek wisdom (1 Cor. 1:22); both Gentiles and Israel gathered against Jesus (Acts 4:27); an attempt was made by both Gentiles and Jews to stone them (Acts 14:5); delivering you from the [Jewish] people and from the Gentiles (Acts 26:17); give no offence to Jews or Greeks or the church of God (1 Cor. 10:32); in danger from my countrymen, in danger from Gentiles (2 Cor. 11:26); you suffered the same things from your countrymen as they did from the Jews (1 Thess. 2:14).

B2e The new Israel

Not all descended from Israel belong to Israel (Rom. 9:6); peace and mercy be on all who walk by this rule, on the Israel of God (Gal. 6:16); God can raise up children for Abraham even from stones (Matt. 3:9; Luke 3:8); Abraham is the father of those who copy his faith (Rom. 4:12); he is not a real Jew who is one outwardly (Rom. 2:28); some claim to be Jews and are not (Rev. 2:9; 3:9); Gentiles are now members of the same body with the Jews (Eph. 3:6); fellow-citizens (Eph. 2:19); those whom he has called, not only from the Jews but also from the Gentiles (Rom. 9:24); Christ has made Jew and Gentile one (Eph. 2:14); Gentiles have been brought near through the blood of Christ (Eph. 2:11-13); there is no distinction between Jew and Greek (Rom. 10:12; Col. 3:11); there is neither Jew nor Greek (Gal. 3:28); those who were not God's people have become his people (Hos. 1:10; 2:23; Rom. 9:25); those who were no people have become the people of God (1 Pet. 2:10).

B3 Tribes and kingdoms of Israel

B3a The 12 tribes

The 12 tribes of Israel (Gen. 49:28; Exod. 28:21; 39:14; Rev. 21:12); the number of the tribes of Israel (Josh. 4:5, 8); Israel camping tribe by tribe (Num. 24:2); 144 000 were sealed from every tribe of Israel (Rev. 7:4); you will sit on thrones judging the 12 tribes of Israel (Matt. 19:28).

B3b Judah and Israel

To establish the throne of David over Israel and Judah (2 Sam. 3:10); David reigned 33 years over Israel and Judah (2 Sam. 5:5); contention between Israel and Judah over the king (2 Sam. 19:41-3); Israel followed Sheba but Judah followed David (2 Sam. 20:2); Solomon was king over Israel and Judah (1 Kgs. 1:35; 4:1); breaking the brotherhood between Judah and Israel (Zech. 11:14); since the day Ephraim separated from Judah (Isa. 7:17); Israel took people and spoil from Judah (2 Chr. 28:8); Ephraim and Judah will no longer be jealous of one another (Isa. 11:13); in those days the house of Judah will walk with the house of Israel (Jer. 3:18); Israel and Judah will be gathered together (Hos. 1:11); Judah and Israel will be reunited (Ezek. 37:16-20, 22).

B3c Northern kingdom of Israel

Abner made Ish-bosheth king over all Israel (2 Sam. 2:9); I will give you ten tribes (1 Kgs. 11:31); Israel rebelled against the house of David (2 Chr. 10:19);

Hezekiah sent letters to Ephraim and Manasseh inviting them to the Passover (2 Chr. 30:1); the head of Ephraim is Samaria (Isa. 7:9); woe to the proud crown of the drunkards of Ephraim (Isa. 28:1); within 65 years Ephraim will no longer be a people (Isa. 7:8); I will take Joseph, Ephraim and the Israelites with him (Ezek. 37:19); Ephraim is a trained heifer that loves to thresh (Hos. 10:11); for three transgressions of Israel and for four (Amos 2:6).

B3d Reuben, Gad and half Manasseh

Reuben, Gad and half Manasseh (Num. 32:1-42; 34:14; Deut. 29:8; Josh. 1:12-18; 4:12-13; 12:6; 13:8; 22:1-34; 1 Chr. 5:18; 26:32); half the hill country of Gilead given to Reuben and Gad (Deut. 3:12); the rest of Gilead and all Bashan given to half Manasseh (Deut. 3:13); Reuben, Gad and half Manasseh exiled to Assyria (1 Chr. 5:26); the land of Gad, Reuben and Manasseh was cut off from Israel (2 Kgs. 10:33).

B3e Various tribes

Why should one tribe be missing from Israel? (Judg. 21:3); is it better to be a priest to one man or to a tribe? (Judg. 18:19); Christ belongs to another tribe, from which no one has ever served at the altar (Heb. 7:13); Simeon, Levi, Judah, Issachar, Joseph, Benjamin to bless from Mount Gerizim (Deut. 27:12); Reuben, Gad, Asher, Zebulun, Dan, Naphtali to curse from Mount Ebal (Deut. 27:13).

B4 Tribes Asher – Gad

B4a Tribe of Asher

Asher is more blessed than sons (Deut. 33:24); gifts of the leader of Asher (Num. 7:72); the lot of the tribe of Asher (Josh. 19:24-31); Asher did not drive out all the Canaanites (Judg. 1:31); Asher remained at the seashore (Judg. 5:17); 12 000 sealed from the tribe of Asher (Rev. 7:6).

B4b Tribe of Benjamin in general

There is Benjamin the youngest (Ps. 68:27); prophecy concerning Benjamin (Deut. 33:12); Joab did not number Benjamin (1 Chr. 21:6); Benjamin did not drive out the Jebusites (Judg. 1:21); no one shall give his daughter in marriage to Benjamin (Judg. 21:1); 12 000 sealed from the tribe of Benjamin (Rev. 7:8).

B4c Particular Benjaminites

A man of Benjamin ran with the news (1 Sam. 4:12); the family of the Matrites (1 Sam. 10:21); Cush, a Benjaminite (Ps. 7:t); Abner made Ish-bosheth king over Benjamin (2 Sam. 2:9); the sons of Benjamin gathered behind Abner (2 Sam. 2:25); Abner spoke in the hearing of Benjamin (2 Sam. 3:19); this Benjaminite seeks my life (2 Sam. 16:11); chief officer for Benjamin (1 Chr. 27:21); I am a descendant of Abraham, of the tribe of Benjamin (Rom. 11:1); Paul was of the tribe of Benjamin (Phil. 3:5); am I not a Benjaminite? (1 Sam. 9:21); of Bela, the Belaites (Num. 26:38); of Ashbel, the Ashbelites (Num. 26:38); of Ahiram, the Ahiramites (Num. 26:38); of Shephupham, the Shuphamites (Num. 26:39); of Hupham, the Huphamites (Num. 26:39); of Ard, the Ardites (Num. 26:40); of Naaman, the Naamites (Num. 26:40); of Benjamin: Abidan (Num. 1:11; 2:22; 10:24); Elidad (Num. 34:21); Kish (1 Sam. 9:1); Palti (Num. 13:9); Sheba (2 Sam. 20:1); Shimei (2 Sam. 19:16).

B4d Tribe of Dan

Dan is a lion's whelp (Deut. 33:22); Dan shall judge as one of the tribes of Israel (Gen. 49:16); the Amorites forced the Danites into the hill country (Judg. 1:34); why did Dan stay in the ships? (Judg. 5:17); the tribe of Dan was seeking an inheritance (Judg. 18:1).

B4e Tribe of Ephraim

He did not choose the tribe of Ephraim (Ps. 78:67); the ten thousands of Ephraim (Deut. 33:17); the

Ephraimites were archers (Ps. 78:9); Ephraim did not drive out the Canaanites from Gezer (Josh. 16:10; Judg. 1:29); the Ephraimites criticised Gideon (Judg. 8:1); Ephraimites could not say 'shibboleth' (Judg. 12:5-6).

B4f Tribe of Gad
Blessed is he who enlarges Gad (Deut. 33:20); 12 000 sealed from the tribe of Gad (Rev. 7:5).

B5 Tribes Issachar – Judah

B5a Tribe of Issachar
Rejoice, Issachar, in your tents (Deut. 33:18); 12 000 sealed from the tribe of Issachar (Rev. 7:7).

B5b Joseph [Ephraim and Manasseh]
Prophecy concerning Joseph (Deut. 33:13-17); you who lead Joseph like a flock (Ps. 80:1); he rejected the tent of Joseph (Ps. 78:67); the sons of Joseph, Manasseh and Ephraim (Num. 26:28); the sons of Joseph were two tribes, Manasseh and Ephraim (Josh. 14:4); the tribe of Joseph complained at receiving only one lot (Josh. 17:14); Joseph shall have two portions (Ezek. 47:13); 12 000 sealed from the tribe of Joseph (Rev. 7:8).

B5c Tribe of Judah in general
He chose the tribe of Judah (Ps. 78:68); God has chosen Judah to be leader (1 Chr. 28:4); Lord, hear the voice of Judah (Deut. 33:7); for three transgressions of Judah and for four (Amos 2:4); do not rejoice over Judah's ruin (Obad. 12); none was left except the tribe of Judah (2 Kgs. 17:18); Judah did not keep the Lord's commandments (2 Kgs. 17:19); I will remove Judah as I removed Israel (2 Kgs. 23:27); Bethlehem in the land of Judah (Matt. 2:6); our Lord was descended from Judah (Heb. 7:14); the lion of the tribe of Judah, the root of David (Rev. 5:5); 12 000 sealed from the tribe of Judah (Rev. 7:5).

B6 Tribe of Levi

B6a Tribe of Levi in general
The Levites do not have an inheritance (Deut. 10:9; 12:12; Josh. 13:14, 33; 14:3; 18:7); prophecy concerning Levi (Deut. 33:8-11); that my covenant with Levi may continue (Mal. 2:4); O house of Levi, bless the Lord! (Ps. 135:20); he will refine the sons of Levi (Mal. 3:3); bring near the tribe of Levi to serve Aaron (Num. 3:6; 18:2); I have taken the Levites instead of the firstborn (Num. 3:12); Levites start work at 25 and retire at 50 (Num. 8:24-5); the Levites were set apart to carry the ark (Deut. 10:8); none but the Levites must carry the ark (1 Chr. 15:2); the sons of Zadok are the only Levites who may come near to the Lord to minister (Ezek. 40:46); the Levites explained the law to the people (Neh. 8:7); the Levites shall recite the curse and the blessing (Deut. 27:14); Jehoshaphat appointed Levites and priests to be judges (2 Chr. 19:8); 12 000 sealed from the tribe of Levi (Rev. 7:7); a Levite and his concubine (Judg. 19:1-29); a Levite passed by on the other side (Luke 10:32).

B6b Care of the Levites
Do not neglect the Levite (Deut. 12:19; 14:27); invite Levites to the Feast of Booths (Deut. 16:14); let the Levite eat the tithe with you (Deut. 12:18); let the Levite eat the Feast of Weeks with you (Deut. 16:11); Levites given: food (Deut. 14:29); firstfruits (Deut. 26:11); tax of the booty (Num. 31:30, 47); the tithe (Deut. 26:12-13; Neh. 10:37-8).

B6c Gershom / Gershon
The Gershonites looked after the hangings of the tabernacle (Num. 3:25-6; 4:24-8); two carts and four oxen were given to the Gershonites (Num. 7:7).

B6d Kohath
The Kohathites camped south of the tabernacle (Num. 3:29); the Kohathites looked after the furniture of the tabernacle (Num. 3:31); the Kohathites carried the holy

things (Num. 4:15; 10:21); no carts were given to the Kohathites (Num. 7:9).

B6e Merari
The Merarites camped on the north side of the tabernacle (Num. 3:35); the Merarites looked after the frames of the tabernacle (Num. 3:36-7); four carts and eight oxen were given to the Merarites (Num. 7:8).

B7 Tribes Manasseh – Zebulun

B7a Tribe of Manasseh
The Manassites did not take possession of some cities (Judg. 1:27); my clan is the least in Manasseh (Judg. 6:15); 12 000 sealed from the tribe of Manasseh (Rev. 7:6).

B7b Tribe of Naphtali
Naphtali, satisfied with favour (Deut. 33:23); Naphtali did not drive out all the Canaanites (Judg. 1:33); Naphtali risked their lives (Judg. 5:18); 12 000 sealed from the tribe of Naphtali (Rev. 7:6).

B7c Tribe of Reuben
May Reuben live and not die! (Deut. 33:6); there were searchings of heart among Reuben (Judg. 5:15-16); 12 000 sealed from the tribe of Reuben (Rev. 7:5).

B7d Tribe of Simeon
Simeon and Levi will be scattered in Israel (Gen. 49:7); 12 000 sealed from the tribe of Simeon (Rev. 7:7).

B7e Tribe of Zebulun
Rejoice, Zebulun, in your going out! (Deut. 33:18); Zebulun risked their lives (Judg. 5:18); 12 000 sealed from the tribe of Zebulun (Rev. 7:8).

C Groupings of men

C1 The nations

C1a The nations in general
The people were separated by languages and family into the nations (Gen. 10:5); the nations are a drop from the bucket (Isa. 40:15); let the nations know they are but men (Ps. 9:20); the nations of the world seek food and drink (Luke 12:30); you will be father of a multitude of nations (Gen. 17:4, 5); I will make nations of you (Gen. 17:6); Abraham will become a great and mighty nation (Gen. 18:18); I will make you a great nation (Gen. 12:2); a company of nations will come from you (Gen. 35:11); I will make you a company of peoples (Gen. 48:4); he will become a multitude of nations (Gen. 48:19); Sarah will be a mother of nations (Gen. 17:16); you may take slaves from the nations around you (Lev. 25:44); let all nations serve him (Ps. 72:11); they mingled with the nations (Ps. 106:35); nation will rise against nation (Mark 13:8).

C1b All nations
They came from all peoples to hear Solomon's wisdom (1 Kgs. 4:34); the devil showed him all the kingdoms of the world (Matt. 4:8; Luke 4:5); the beast was given authority over every tribe, people, tongue and nation (Rev. 13:7); Jews, devout men from every nation under heaven (Acts 2:5).

C1c God rules the nations
God made all nations from one man (Acts 17:26); God allotted the territories of the nations (Deut. 32:8; Acts 17:26); he will judge between many peoples and decide for many nations far off (Mic. 4:3); I will shake all nations (Hag. 2:7); all nations will be gathered before him (Matt. 25:32); the Lord is high above all nations (Ps. 113:4); I will give you the nations as your inheritance (Ps. 2:8); that the living may know that the Most High rules the kingdom of men (Dan. 4:17); that all peoples, nations and languages should serve the Son of man (Dan. 7:14); he shook the nations and the eternal mountains were shattered (Hab. 3:6); you trampled the nations in anger (Hab. 3:12); the Lord has his eye on all men as on the tribes of Israel (Zech. 9:1); I have appointed you over the nations (Jer. 1:10); I

appointed you a prophet to the nations (Jer. 1:5); God will call for a foreign nation (Isa. 5:26-30).

C1d The nations before God

Why do the nations rage against the Lord? (Ps. 2:1-2); the peoples, inhabitants of many cities, will seek the Lord (Zech. 8:20); many nations will join themselves to the Lord (Zech. 2:11); my name will be great among the nations (Mal. 1:11); let all the ends of the earth fear him (Ps. 67:7); the nations will fear the name of the Lord (Ps. 102:15); tell of his glory among the nations (Ps. 96:3); all peoples have seen his glory (Ps. 97:6); all nations will come and worship before you (Ps. 86:9).

C1e The gospel to the nations

The salvation you have prepared in the presence of all peoples (Luke 2:31); go into all the world and preach the gospel to the whole creation (Mark 16:15); repentance and forgiveness should be preached to all nations (Luke 24:47); the gospel will be preached as a witness to all nations (Matt. 24:14); the gospel must first be preached to all nations (Mark 13:10); make disciples of all nations (Matt. 28:19); a great multitude from every nation (Rev. 7:9); a gospel to preach to every nation, tribe, tongue and people (Rev. 14:6); all nations will come and worship you (Rev. 15:4); all nations would be blessed in Abraham (Gal. 3:8); you ransomed them from every tribe, tongue, people and nation (Rev. 5:9); many nations will come seeking God (Jer. 16:19; Mic. 4:2; Zech. 8:22); all the nations called by my name (Amos 9:12; Acts 15:16); the ends of the earth will turn to the Lord (Ps. 22:27); that your salvation may be known among all nations (Ps. 67:2); all the ends of the earth will see the salvation of God (Isa. 52:10).

C1f God's people

Your city and your people are called by your name (Dan. 9:19); many nations will become my people (Zech. 2:11); he will save his people from their sins (Matt. 1:21); God took from the Gentiles a people for his name (Acts 15:14); where it was said 'You are not my people' they will be called sons of God (Rom. 9:26); they will be God's people and he will be their God (Exod. 6:7; Lev. 26:12; Deut. 29:13; Jer. 11:4; 24:7; 30:22; 32:38; Ezek. 11:20; 14:11; 37:23, 27; Zech. 8:8; 13:9; Rev. 21:3); he will be their God and they will be his people (Jer. 7:23; 31:33; 2 Cor. 6:16; Heb. 8:10); God's own people (Exod. 33:13; Deut. 27:9; 2 Sam. 7:24; 1 Chr. 17:22; Titus 2:14); a people for himself (1 Sam. 12:22); you will be my special possession among all the peoples (Exod. 19:5; Deut. 14:2); by your presence we are distinct from all other peoples (Exod. 33:16); a covenant that they should be the Lord's people (2 Kgs. 11:17; 2 Chr. 23:16); the people of his pasture (Ps. 95:7); blessed are the people whose God is the Lord (Ps. 144:15).

C2 Amalekites – Babylonians

C2a Amalekites

Amalek was the first of the nations (Num. 24:20); the Lord will war against Amalek from generation to generation (Exod. 17:16); I will blot out the memory of Amalek (Exod. 17:14); blot out the memory of Amalek (Deut. 25:19); oracle concerning Amalek (Num. 24:20); I delivered you from the Amalekites (Judg. 10:12); remember what Amalek did (Deut. 25:17); I will punish Amalek (1 Sam. 15:2-3); Saul defeated the Amalekites (1 Sam. 14:48); destroy the Amalekites (1 Sam. 15:3, 18); I have destroyed the Amalekites (1 Sam. 15:20); the Amalekites had raided Ziklag (1 Sam. 30:1); the remnant of Amalek destroyed (1 Chr. 4:43).

C2b Ammonites

Oracles concerning Ammon (Jer. 49:1-6; Ezek. 21:28-32; 25:2-7); Israel did not take the land of the Ammonites (Judg. 11:15); that the sons of Ammon may not be remembered among the nations (Ezek. 25:10); the Lord

sold them into the hands of the Ammonites (Judg. 10:7); Nahash the Ammonite besieged Jabesh-gilead (1 Sam. 11:1); Moab will be like Sodom and the Ammonites like Gomorrah (Zeph. 2:9); afterwards I will restore the fortunes of Ammon (Jer. 49:6); for three transgressions of the Ammonites and for four (Amos 1:13); I have heard the taunts of Moab, the revilings of the Ammonites (Zeph. 2:8); Ammonites are not to enter the assembly to the tenth generation (Deut. 23:3-6); no Ammonite should enter the assembly (Neh. 13:1); the Israelites have not separated themselves from the Ammonites (Ezra 9:1); do not provoke the Ammonites (Deut. 2:19); Ammon help the children of Lot (Ps. 83:8); the Ammonites were put to forced labour (2 Sam. 12:31); the Ammonites brought tribute (2 Chr. 26:8; 27:5); Solomon loved Ammonite women (1 Kgs. 11:1); the Jews had married women from Ammon (Neh. 13:23); they served the gods of the Ammonites (Judg. 10:6; 1 Kgs. 11:5-7).

C2c Amorites

The Amorites live in the hill country (Num. 13:29; Josh. 10:6); the Amorites, tall as cedars and strong as oaks (Amos 2:9); Mamre the Amorite (Gen. 14:13); Sihon and Og, the kings of the Amorites (Deut. 31:4; Josh. 2:10); I will drive out the Amorites (Exod. 33:2; 34:11); God will dispossess the Amorites (Josh. 3:10); Balak saw what Israel did to the Amorites (Num. 22:2); I delivered you from the Amorites (Judg. 10:11); exterminate the Amorites (Deut. 20:17); Solomon put the Amorites to forced labour (1 Kgs. 9:20-1; 2 Chr. 8:7-8); the Amorites chased you like bees (Deut. 1:44); the Amorites chased Dan into the hill country (Judg. 1:34); peace between Israel and the Amorites (1 Sam. 7:14); the Gibeonites were the remnant of the Amorites (2 Sam. 21:2); the iniquity of the Amorites is not yet complete (Gen. 15:16); the Israelites have not separated themselves from the Amorites (Ezra 9:1).

C2d Anakim

The Anakim are part of the Nephilim (Num. 13:33); Anakim are reckoned as Rephaim (Deut. 2:11); the Nephilim were on the earth in those days (Gen. 6:4); we saw the descendants of Anak there (Num. 13:28; Deut. 1:28); Ahiman, Sheshai and Talmai, descendants of Anak (Num. 13:22); Caleb drove out the three sons of Anak, Sheshai, Ahiman and Talmai (Josh. 15:14; Judg. 1:20); Joshua cut off the Anakim in the hill country (Josh. 11:21).

C2e Arabs

The Arabs brought tribute to Jehoshaphat (2 Chr. 17:11); the Lord stirred up the Arabs who bordered the Ethiopians (2 Chr. 21:16); the Lord helped Uzziah against the Arabians of Gur-baal (2 Chr. 26:7); the Arab will not pitch his tent in Babylon (Isa. 13:20); Geshem the Arab (Neh. 2:19; 6:1); when the Arabs heard (Neh. 4:7); by the road you sat like an Arab in the desert (Jer. 3:2); Cretans and Arabs (Acts 2:11).

C2f Arameans / Syrians

They served the gods of Aram (Judg. 10:6); the head of Aram is Damascus (Isa. 7:8); spoil from Aram (2 Sam. 8:12); the remnant of Aram will be like the glory of Israel (Isa. 17:3); the people of Aram will be exiled to Kir (Amos 1:5); Bethuel the Aramean (Gen. 25:20); Laban the Aramean (Gen. 25:20; 28:5; 31:20, 24); my father was a wandering Aramean (Deut. 26:5); Naaman the Aramean (2 Kgs. 5:20); anoint Hazael king over Aram (1 Kgs. 19:15); the Arameans gathered against Israel (2 Sam. 10:15); the Arameans on the east and the Philistines on the west devour Israel (Isa. 9:12); going to the camp of the Arameans (2 Kgs. 7:4-5); 100 000 Aramean infantry were killed (1 Kgs. 20:29); with these horns you will push the Arameans (1 Kgs. 22:11; 2 Chr.

18:10); you will defeat the Arameans at Aphek (2 Kgs. 13:17); the Arameans did not raid Israel again (2 Kgs. 6:23).

C2g Assyrians

Oracle concerning Assyria (Isa. 14:24-7); the king of Assyria as God's razor (Isa. 7:20); Assyria the rod of my anger (Isa. 10:5); the Assyrian oppressed my people (Isa. 52:4); the Assyrian will fall by a sword not of man (Isa. 31:8); blessed be Assyria the work of my hands (Isa. 19:25); the Egyptians will worship with the Assyrians (Isa. 19:23); Israel will be the third with Egypt and Assyria (Isa. 19:24); Ephraim is like a silly dove, calling to Egypt, going to Assyria (Hos. 7:11); Assyria will not save us, we will not ride on horses (Hos. 14:3); he will deliver us from the Assyrian when he invades our land (Mic. 5:6); when the Assyrian comes into our land (Mic. 5:5).

C2h Babylonians

Oracles concerning Babylon (Isa. 13:1; Jer. 25:12-14; 50:1); a sword against the inhabitants of Babylon (Jer. 50:35); Egypt will be destroyed by Nebuchadnezzar king of Babylon (Ezek. 30:10); I will bring on Tyre Nebuchadnezzar king of Babylon (Ezek. 26:7); in the first year of Belshazzar king of Babylon (Dan. 7:1).
CHALDEANS, see 371C3b.

C3 Canaanites – Greeks

C3a Canaanites

Canaan was the ancestor of the Jebusites, Amorites, Girgashites, Hivites, Arkites, Sinites, Arvadites, Zemarites and Hamathites (Gen. 10:15-18); the Canaanites and Perizzites were then in the land (Gen. 12:6; 13:7); hornets will drive out the Canaanites (Exod. 23:28); I will drive out the Canaanites (Exod. 33:2; 34:11); the Canaanites have iron chariots (Josh. 17:16); God will dispossess the Canaanites (Josh. 3:10); exterminate the Canaanites (Deut. 20:17); Ephraim did not drive out the Canaanites from Gezer (Josh. 16:10); the Manassites could not drive out the Canaanites (Josh. 17:1); do not take a wife from the daughters of the Canaanites (Gen. 24:3, 37; 28:1, 6); Esau took wives from the Canaanites (Gen. 36:2); the Canaanites continued living among Israel (Judg. 1:27-33); the Israelites have not separated themselves from the Canaanites (Ezra 9:1); a Canaanite woman from the region of Tyre and Sidon (Matt. 15:22).

C3b Chaldeans

Ur of the Chaldeans (Gen. 15:7); Babylon, the glory of the Chaldeans (Isa. 13:19); Chaldea, the land of merchants (Ezek. 16:29); the captives of Judah sent into the land of the Chaldeans (Jer. 24:5); the oracle concerning Babylon, the land of the Chaldeans (Jer. 50:1); the king had them taught the letters and language of the Chaldeans (Dan. 1:4); the Lord sent the Chaldeans against Judah (2 Kgs. 24:2; 2 Chr. 36:17); the Chaldeans had been besieging Jerusalem (Jer. 37:5); I will give you into the hands of the Chaldeans (Jer. 22:25); he who surrenders to the Chaldeans will live (Jer. 21:9).
BABYLONIANS, see 371C2h.

C3c Cherethites

We raided the Negeb of the Cherethites (1 Sam. 30:14); the Cherethites and Pelethites and all the mighty men (2 Sam. 20:7); Benaiah was over the Cherethites and the Pelethites (2 Sam. 8:18; 20:23; 1 Chr. 18:17); the Cherethites and Pelethites who had come with David from Gath (2 Sam. 15:18); the Cherethites and the Pelethites went down with Solomon (1 Kgs. 1:38, 44); I will cut off the Cherethites (Ezek. 25:16); woe to the nation of the Cherethites (Zeph. 2:5).

C3d Edomites

Esau father of the Edomites (Gen. 36:9, 43); oracles concerning Edom (Isa. 21:11-17; Jer. 49:7-22; Ezek. 35:2-15; Obad. 1-21); do not hate an Edomite or an Egyptian (Deut. 23:7); the sons of Esau live in Seir (Deut. 2:4, 8, 22, 29); for three transgressions of Edom and for four (Amos 1:11); Solomon loved Edomite women (1 Kgs. 11:1); Edom refused to let the Israelites pass through their land (Num. 20:14-21); David killed 18 000 Edomites (2 Sam. 8:13); the Edomites became servants to David (2 Sam. 8:14); Joab killed every male in Edom (1 Kgs. 11:15, 16); Joab smote 12 000 of Edom (Ps. 60:t); Edom revolted against Judah (2 Kgs. 8:20; 2 Chr. 21:8, 10); Abishai slew 18 000 Edomites (1 Chr. 18:12); 10 000 Edomites were killed in the Valley of Salt (2 Kgs. 14:7); 10 000 sons of Seir were struck down (2 Chr. 25:11-12); Amaziah slaughtered the Edomites (2 Chr. 25:14); Jehoram struck down the Edomites (2 Chr. 21:9); I will punish Edom (Jer. 9:26); rejoice and be glad, daughter of Edom, dweller in the land of Uz (Lam. 4:21).

C3e Egyptians

Oracles concerning Egypt (Isa. 19:1-25; Jer. 46:2-26; Ezek. 29:2); Ephraim is like a silly dove, calling to Egypt, going to Assyria (Hos. 7:11); Moses was taught all the wisdom of the Egyptians (Acts 7:22); are you not the Egyptian who stirred up a revolt? (Acts 21:38); Hebrew woman are not like Egyptians (Exod. 1:19); Solomon's wisdom surpassed the wisdom of Egypt (1 Kgs. 4:30); Egypt rises like the Nile (Jer. 46:8); it is an abomination to the Egyptians to eat with Hebrews (Gen. 43:32); shepherds are an abomination to the Egyptians (Gen. 46:34); our sacrifices would be an abomination to the Egyptians (Exod. 8:26); do not hate an Edomite or an Egyptian (Deut. 23:7); Egypt was glad when they departed (Ps. 105:38); how I made sport of the Egyptians (Exod. 10:2); the Lord saved Israel from the hand of the Egyptians (Exod. 14:30); I will punish the Egyptians (Jer. 9:26); the Egyptians you see today you will never see again (Exod. 14:13); you are relying on Egypt (Isa. 36:6); how can you rely on Egypt for chariots and horsemen? (Isa. 36:9); the Israelites have not separated themselves from the Egyptians (Ezra 9:1); Israel will be the third with Egypt and Assyria (Isa. 19:24).

C3f Ethiopians

Oracle concerning Ethiopia (Isa. 18:1-7); Ethiopia will stretch out her hands to God (Ps. 68:31); can the Ethiopian change his skin? (Jer. 13:23); Moses had married a Cushite woman (Num. 12:1); Ebed-melech the Ethiopian, a eunuch (Jer. 38:7-16); Ethiopia and Put, who handle the shield (Jer. 46:9); Ethiopia, Put, Lud, Arabia and Lybia will fall by the sword (Ezek. 30:5); messengers will go from me in ships to frighten Ethiopia (Ezek. 30:9); you also, O Ethiopians, will be killed by my sword (Zeph. 2:12); an Ethiopian eunuch, a minister of Candace queen of the Ethiopians (Acts 8:27).

C3g Gog

Gog, with Magog, symbolic leader of the forces against Christ (Rev. 20:8).

C3h Greeks

You sold the people of Judah and Jerusalem to the Greeks (Joel 3:6); I will stir your sons, Zion, against your sons, Greece (Zech. 9:13); will he go to the Dispersion among the Greeks and teach the Greeks? (John 7:35); among those who went up to worship at the feast were some Greeks (John 12:20); Saul disputed with the Hellenists (Acts 9:29); some men of Cyprus and Cyrene came to Antioch and preached to Greeks (Acts 11:20); a great multitude of both Jews and Greeks believed (Acts 14:1); many of the devout Greeks joined Paul and Silas (Acts 17:4); he brought Greeks into the temple and defiled this holy place (Acts 21:28); I am a debtor both to Greeks and barbarians (Rom. 1:14); to the Jew first and also to the Greek (Rom. 1:16); there is no distinction between Jew and Greek (Rom. 10:12); Jews require signs and Greeks seek wisdom (1 Cor. 1:22); those who are the called, both Jews and Greeks (1 Cor. 1:24); give no offence to Jews or Greeks or the church of God (1 Cor. 10:32); one body, Jews or Greeks, slave or free (1 Cor. 12:13); Titus, though a Greek, was not compelled to be circumcised (Gal. 2:3).

C4 Hamites – Kedar
C4a Hamites
Hamites formerly lived in Gedor (1 Chr. 4:40).

C4b Hazor
Oracles about Kedar and Hazor (Jer. 49:28-33).

C4c Hebrews
Abraham the Hebrew (Gen. 14:13); he has brought a Hebrew to mock us (Gen. 39:14); the Hebrew slave you brought (Gen. 39:17); in the seventh year a Hebrew slave shall be set free (Exod. 21:2; Deut. 15:12); Hebrew slaves, male and female, must be set free (Jer. 34:9); Egyptians do not eat with Hebrews (Gen. 43:32); the Hebrew midwives (Exod. 1:15); this is one of the Hebrews' children (Exod. 2:6); the Lord, the God of the Hebrews (Exod. 3:18); Hebrews are coming out of their homes (1 Sam. 14:11); what are these Hebrews doing here? (1 Sam. 29:3); I am a Hebrew (Jonah 1:9); are they Hebrews? so am I (2 Cor. 11:22); Paul was a Hebrew of Hebrews (Phil. 3:5).

C4d Hittites
The Hittites are living in the hill country (Num. 13:29); Abraham spoke to the sons of Heth (Gen. 23:3); the field and the cave were bought from the sons of Heth (Gen. 23:20); to bring them to the land of the Hittites (Exod. 3:8, 17; 13:5; 23:23); hornets will drive out the Hittites (Exod. 23:28); I will drive out the Hittites (Exod. 33:2; 34:11); exterminate the Hittites (Deut. 20:17); Israel lived among the Hittites (Judg. 3:5); Solomon put the Hittites to forced labour (1 Kgs. 9:20-1; 2 Chr. 8:7-8); Solomon loved Hittite women (1 Kgs. 11:1); the Israelites have not separated themselves from the Hittites (Ezra 9:1); your father was an Amorite and your mother a Hittite (Ezek. 16:3, 45).

C4e Hivites
Shechem the son of Hamor the Hivite (Gen. 34:2); the people of Gibeon were Hivites (Josh. 9:7; 11:19); the Hivites who live in Mount Lebanon (Judg. 3:3); the land of the Hivites (Josh. 12:8); hornets will drive out the Hivites (Exod. 23:28); God will dispossess the Hivites (Josh. 3:10); exterminate the Hivites (Deut. 20:17); Israel lived among the Hivites (Judg. 3:5); Solomon put the Hivites to forced labour (1 Kgs. 9:20-1; 2 Chr. 8:7-8).

C4f Ishmaelites
I will make Ishmael a nation (Gen. 21:13, 18); the sons of Ishmael by their settlements and tribes (Gen. 25:16); a caravan of Ishmaelites from Gilead (Gen. 37:25); they sold Joseph to the Ishmaelites (Gen. 37:28); they had gold earrings because they were Ishmaelites (Judg. 8:24).

C4g Jebusites
Jebus [Jerusalem], the city of the Jebusites (Judg. 19:11); I will drive out the Jebusites (Exod. 33:2; 34:11); exterminate the Jebusites (Deut. 20:17); the sons of Judah could not drive out the Jebusites (Josh. 15:63); Benjamin did not drive out the Jebusites (Judg. 1:21); Israel lived among the Jebusites (Judg. 3:5); the Jebusites thought David could not enter Jerusalem (2 Sam. 5:6); Solomon put the Jebusites to forced

labour (1 Kgs. 9:20-1; 2 Chr. 8:7-8); the Israelites have not separated themselves from the Jebusites (Ezra 9:1).

C4h Kedar
The villages that Kedar inhabits (Isa. 42:11); the princes of Kedar traded with you (Ezek. 27:21); I dwell among the tents of Kedar (Ps. 120:5); black as the tents of Kedar (S. of S. 1:5); within one year the glory of Kedar will come to an end (Isa. 21:16-17); oracles about Kedar and Hazor (Jer. 49:28-33).

C5 Kenites – Perrizites
C5a Kenites
The Kenites' dwelling-place was enduring (Num. 24:21); the sons of the Kenite, Moses' father-in-law (Judg. 1:16; 4:11); David told the Kenites to depart out of Amalek (1 Sam. 15:6); David sent a present to the Kenites (1 Sam. 30:29).

C5b Medes
Israel was exiled to the cities of the Medes (2 Kgs. 17:6; 18:11); lay siege, Media (Isa. 21:2); I am stirring up the Medes against them (Isa. 13:17); the law of the Medes and Persians cannot be revoked (Dan. 6:8, 12, 15); your kingdom is divided and given to the Medes and Persians (Dan. 5:28); Darius the Mede (Dan. 5:31; 9:1; 11:1).

C5c Meshech
Gog of the land of Magog, chief prince of Meshech and Tubal (Ezek. 38:2-3; 39:1); Meshech and Tubal are in Sheol with their graves around them (Ezek. 32:26).

C5d Midianites
Midianite traders (Gen. 37:28); the Midianites sold Joseph to Potiphar (Gen. 37:36); the priest of Midian, Reuel [Jethro] (Exod. 2:16); the two princes of Midian, Oreb and Zeeb (Judg. 7:25; 8:3); Zebah and Zalmunna, the kings of Midian (Judg. 8:5, 12); an Israelite man and a Midianite woman (Num. 25:6, 14); take vengeance on the Midianites (Num. 31:2); they killed every male Midianite (Num. 31:7); the Lord gave them into the hand of Midian (Judg. 6:1-6, 13); the Israelites cried to the Lord because of the Midianites (Judg. 6:7); Gideon delivered you from Midian (Judg. 9:17); Midian was subdued (Judg. 8:28); you have broken the rod of the oppressor as on the day of Midian (Isa. 9:4).

C5e Moabites
The Moabites live in Ar (Deut. 2:29); Moabites are not to enter the assembly to the tenth generation (Deut. 23:3-6); no Moabite should enter the assembly (Neh. 13:1); Solomon loved Moabite women (1 Kgs. 11:1); Israel played the harlot with the daughters of Moab (Num. 25:1); the Jews had married women from Moab (Neh. 13:23); Moab rebelled against Israel (2 Kgs. 1:1); they served the gods of Moab (Judg. 10:6); Solomon built a high place for Chemosh the abomination of Moab (1 Kgs. 11:7; 2 Kgs. 23:13); the Lord sold them into the hand of the king of Moab (1 Sam. 12:9); I will execute judgements on Moab (Ezek. 25:11); I will send fire on Moab which will consume the strongholds of Kerioth (Amos 2:2); David defeated the Moabites (2 Sam. 8:2; 1 Chr. 18:2); a ruler from Israel will crush Moab (Num. 24:17); Moab was subdued by Israel (Judg. 3:30); oracles concerning Moab (Isa. 15:1; Jer. 48:1-47; Ezek. 25:8-11); Moab has been at ease since his youth (Jer. 48:11); for three transgressions of Moab and for four (Amos 2:1); we have heard of the pride of Moab (Isa. 16:6); Moab will be destroyed from being a people (Jer. 48:42); I will restore the fortunes of Moab in the latter days (Jer. 48:47).

C5f Nicolaitans
You hate the deeds of the Nicolaitans, which I also hate (Rev. 2:6); you have some who hold the teaching of the Nicolaitans (Rev. 2:15).

C5g Pelethites
Benaiah was over the Cherethites and the Pelethites (2 Sam. 8:18; 20:23; 1 Chr. 18:17); the Cherethites and the Pelethites who had come with David from Gath (2 Sam. 15:18); the Cherethites and the Pelethites and all the mighty men (2 Sam. 20:7).

C5h Perizzites
The Canaanites and Perizzites were then in the land (Gen. 13:7); you have made me stink among the Canaanites and the Perizzites (Gen. 34:30); I will drive out the Perizzites (Exod. 33:2; 34:11); exterminate the Perizzites (Deut. 20:17); Israel lived among the Perizzites (Judg. 3:5); the Israelites have not separated themselves from the Perizzites (Ezra 9:1); Solomon put the Perizzites to forced labour (1 Kgs. 9:20-1; 2 Chr. 8:7-8).

C6 Persians – Tubal
C6a Persians
The law of the Persians and Medes (Esther 1:19); the law of the Medes and Persians cannot be revoked (Dan. 6:8, 12, 15); your kingdom is divided and given to the Medes and Persians (Dan. 5:28).

C6b Philistines
Oracles concerning Philistia (Isa. 14:29-32; Jer. 47:1-7; Ezek. 25:15-17); did I not bring the Philistines from Caphtor, the Arameans from Kir? (Amos 9:7); the ark had been in the country of the Philistines for seven months (1 Sam. 6:1); the Philistines ruled over Israel (Judg. 14:4); Samson saw one of the daughters of the Philistines (Judg. 14:1); Philistines brought tribute to Jehoshaphat (2 Chr. 17:11); they served the gods of the Philistines (Judg. 10:6); I will stretch out my hand against the Philistines (Ezek. 25:16); Shamgar killed 600 Philistines with an ox-goad (Judg. 3:31); 100 Philistine foreskins (1 Sam. 18:25; 2 Sam. 3:14); all the days of Saul there was war with the Philistines (1 Sam. 14:52); David defeated the Philistines (2 Sam. 8:1; 1 Chr. 18:1); I delivered you from the Philistines (Judg. 10:11); by David I will save Israel from the Philistines (2 Sam. 3:18); the Lord stirred up the Philistines against Judah (2 Chr. 21:16); the Lord gave Israel into the hand of the Philistines for 40 years (Judg. 13:1); the Philistines seized David in Gath (Ps. 56:t); David was about to go to battle alongside the Philistines (1 Chr. 12:19); Goliath the Philistine (1 Sam. 21:9; 22:10); the garrison of the Philistines was in Bethlehem (2 Sam. 23:14).

C6c Rechabites
Give the Rechabites wine to drink (Jer. 35:2); Jeremiah commended the Rechabites (Jer. 35:18).

C6d Romans
The Romans will take away our place and our nation (John 11:48); customs which it is not lawful for Romans to accept (Acts 16:21); we who are Roman citizens (Acts 16:37); they were afraid when they heard that they were Romans (Acts 16:38); is it lawful for you to scourge a Roman and uncondemned? (Acts 22:25); this man is a Roman (Acts 22:26-9); I rescued him, having learned that he was a Roman (Acts 23:27); it is not the custom of the Romans to give up a man untried (Acts 25:16); I was delivered prisoner from Jerusalem into the hands of the Romans (Acts 28:17).

C6e Samaritans
The mixed practices of the Samaritans (2 Kgs. 17:28-41); Jews have no dealings with the Samaritans (John 4:9); the Samaritans would not receive him (Luke 9:52-3); the Samaritan had compassion on the man (Luke 10:33); the leper who gave thanks was a Samaritan (Luke 17:16); are we not right in saying you are a Samaritan and have a demon? (John 8:48); do not enter any town of the Samaritans (Matt. 10:5); a woman of Samaria came to draw water (John 4:7); many

Samaritans believed because of the woman's testimony (John 4:39-40); they preached the gospel in many villages of the Samaritans (Acts 8:25).

C6f Sidonians
Oracle concerning Sidon (Ezek. 28:21-4); I will drive out all the Sidonians (Josh. 13:6); Sidonians were left in the land (Judg. 3:3); no one knows how to cut timber like the Sidonians (1 Kgs. 5:6); the Sidonians and Tyrians brought cedar from Lebanon (Ezra 3:7); Solomon loved Sidonian women (1 Kgs. 11:1); Solomon went after Ashtoreth goddess of the Sidonians (1 Kgs. 11:5).

SIDON, see 184J5a.

C6g Syrophoenicians
The woman was a Gentile, a Syrophoenician (Mark 7:26).

C6h Tubal
Oracles about Meshech and Tubal (Ezek. 38:2-39:1); Gog of the land of Magog, chief prince of Meshech and Tubal (Ezek. 38:2); Gog, chief prince of Meshech and Tubal (Ezek. 38:3; 39:1).

D Individuals A
D1 Individuals Aaron – Abimelech
D1a Aaron
Moses' elder brother (Exod. 4:14); son of Amram (Exod. 6:20; Num. 26:59; 1 Chr. 6:3; 23:13); the sons of Aaron (1 Chr. 6:50; 24:1); Nadab and Abihu his sons (Lev. 10:1); Eleazar and Ithamar his sons (Lev. 10:6); Miriam was his sister (Exod. 15:20); the genealogy of Aaron (Num. 3:1-4); went to meet Moses (Exod. 4:27); Aaron will be your prophet (Exod. 7:1); Moses and Aaron went to Pharaoh (Exod. 5:1); Moses and Aaron did all these wonders before Pharaoh (Exod. 11:10); went up to the Lord with Moses, Nadab and Abihu (Exod. 24:1, 9); spoke against Moses (Num. 12:1); made a calf of gold (Exod. 32:3-5); holy garments made for him (Exod. 39:1, 41); anointed as priest (Exod. 30:30; 40:13; Lev. 8:2-36); no one takes this honour to himself, but is called by God, as Aaron was (Heb. 5:4); Aaron's rod that budded (Num. 17:8; Heb. 9:4); what is Aaron that you grumble against him? (Num. 16:11); death of Aaron (Num. 20:24-9).

D1b Abednego [Azariah]
Name given to Azariah (Dan. 1:6-7); ate vegetables (Dan. 1:11); did not worship the golden image (Dan. 3:12); set over the province of Babylon (Dan. 2:49); brought before Nebuchadnezzar (Dan. 3:13); Shadrach, Meshach and Abednego came out of the fire (Dan. 3:26); the king promoted Shadrach, Meshach and Abednego in the province of Babylon (Dan. 3:30).

D1c Abel
Second son of Adam and Eve, a shepherd (Gen. 4:2, 4); killed by Cain (Gen. 4:8-9, 25); Abel offered a more acceptable sacrifice (Heb. 11:4); the blood of Abel (Matt. 23:35; Luke 11:51; Heb. 12:24).

D1d Abiathar
Son of Ahimelech the priest, fled to David (1 Sam. 22:20); sending word to David (2 Sam. 15:35); succeeded Ahithophel (1 Chr. 27:34); when Abiathar was high priest (Mark 2:26).

D1e Abigail
Wife of Nabal (1 Sam. 25:3, 14); wife of David (1 Sam. 25:39-42; 27:3; 30:5; 2 Sam. 2:2).

D1f Abihu
Second son of Aaron (Exod. 6:23); went up Sinai (Exod. 24:1, 9); offered unholy fire (Lev. 10:1; Num. 3:4; 26:61); died childless before his father (1 Chr. 24:2).

D1g Abijah [Abijam]
King of Judah, son of Rehoboam (1 Kgs. 14:31; 1 Chr. 3:10; 2 Chr. 11:20); died (2 Chr. 14:1).

D1h Abimelech [1]
King of the Philistines in Gerar who took Sarah (Gen. 20:2-18); made a covenant with Abraham (Gen. 21:22-4); Abraham complained to him at Beer-sheba (Gen. 21:25-32).

D1i Abimelech [2]
King of the Philistines in Gerar (Gen. 26:1); saw Rebekah was Isaac's wife (Gen. 26:6-11); made a covenant with Isaac (Gen. 26:26-31).

D1j Abimelech [3]
Son of Gideon (Judg. 8:31); made king by the men of Shechem (Judg. 9:1-6, 22); fell out with the men of Shechem (Judg. 9:23-49); killed besieging Thebez (Judg. 9:50-7).

D2 Abishag – Achsah
D2a Abishag
Shunammite maiden, David's nurse (1 Kgs. 1:3, 15); Adonijah asked for her as his wife (1 Kgs. 2:17, 21-2).

D2b Abishai
Brother of Joab (1 Sam. 26:6; 2 Sam. 2:18; 1 Chr. 2:16); chief of the 30 (2 Sam. 23:18; 1 Chr. 11:20-1); slew 18 000 in the Valley of Salt (1 Chr. 18:12-13); led the fight against the Ammonites (2 Sam. 10:10; 1 Chr. 19:11); with Joab, killed Abner (2 Sam. 3:30); wanted to kill Shimei (2 Sam. 16:9-11; 19:21-2); led one third of the army (2 Sam. 18:2); ordered to be gentle with Absalom (2 Sam. 18:5); sent to pursue Sheba (2 Sam. 20:6); saved David from the giant (2 Sam. 21:17).

D2c Abner
Son of Ner, Saul's uncle, and commander of Saul's army (1 Sam. 14:50); brought David before Saul (1 Sam. 17:57); lay sleeping by Saul in the camp (1 Sam. 26:5); installed Ish-bosheth as king (2 Sam. 2:8-9); challenged Joab to a contest of the young men (2 Sam. 2:12-17); pursued by Asahel, whom he killed (2 Sam. 2:19-23); accused over Saul's concubine, defected to David (2 Sam. 3:7-21); killed by Joab (2 Sam. 3:22-30; 1 Kgs. 2:5, 32); mourned by David (2 Sam. 3:31-9).

D2d Abraham in general
Married Sarai [Sarah] (Gen. 11:29); travelled from Ur to Haran (Gen. 11:31); called by the Lord to leave country and kindred (Gen. 12:1-3); went with Lot to Canaan (Gen. 12:4-9); separated from Lot (Gen. 13:1-13); recovered captive Lot (Gen. 14:12-17); received covenant promises from God (Gen. 15:1-21); took Hagar as wife (Gen. 16:1-6); name changed from Abram to Abraham (Gen. 17:1-8; Neh. 9:7); received covenant of circumcision (Gen. 17:9-14, 22-7); welcomed three visitors (Gen. 18:1-22); prayed for Sodom (Gen. 18:23-33; 19:29); went to sacrifice Isaac (Gen. 22:1-19); bought the cave of Machpelah (Gen. 23:1-20); took Keturah as wife (Gen. 25:1-6); the people [of Israel] are descended from Abraham (Heb. 7:5); look to Abraham your father (Isa. 51:2); Abraham is our father (John 8:39); do not say Abraham is your father (Matt. 3:9; Luke 3:8); what shall we say about Abraham our forefather? (Rom. 4:1); all are not Abraham's children who are descended from him (Rom. 9:7); God is able to raise up children to Abraham from these stones (Matt. 3:9).

D2e Abraham and God
Your father Abraham rejoiced to see my day (John 8:56); you are not yet 50 years old, and have you seen Abraham? (John 8:57); before Abraham was, I AM (John 8:58); the God of glory appeared to our father Abraham (Acts 7:2); the father of those who have faith (Gal. 3:6-14); by faith Abraham obeyed when he was called (Heb. 11:8-9); by faith Abraham offered up Isaac (Heb. 11:17); Abraham believed God and it was reckoned to him as righteousness (Jas. 2:23); Abraham was called the friend of God (Jas. 2:23); the God before

whom Abraham walked (Gen. 48:15); the poor man died and was carried by the angels to Abraham's bosom (Luke 16:22-31); the God of Abraham (Matt. 22:32; Mark 12:26; Luke 20:37; Acts 3:13; 7:32).

D2f Absalom
Hated Amnon for raping Tamar (2 Sam. 13:22); arranged Amnon's death (2 Sam. 13:23-33); fled (2 Sam. 13:34-9); brought back to Jerusalem (2 Sam. 14:1-27); brought before David (2 Sam. 14:28-33); stole the hearts of Israel (2 Sam. 15:1-6); set himself up as king (2 Sam. 15:7-37); went after David (2 Sam. 17:24-6); David fled from him (Ps. 3:1); killed by Joab (2 Sam. 18:9-18); mourned by David (2 Sam. 18:33; 19:1-4).

D2g Achan [Achar]
Took devoted things (Josh. 7:1; 22:20; 1 Chr. 2:7); confessed his crime (Josh. 7:18-21); stoned and burned (Josh. 7:22-6).

D2h Achish
King of Gath to whom David fled (1 Sam. 21:10-15; 27:2); David went to war alongside him (1 Sam. 28:1-2); dismissed David (1 Sam. 29:2-11).

D2i Achsah
Daughter of Caleb promised to conqueror of Kiriath-sepher (Josh. 15:16; Judg. 1:12); given to Othniel as wife (Josh. 15:17-19).

D3 Adam – Ahasuerus
D3a Adam
The first man on earth (Gen. 5:1-5; 1 Chr. 1:1); son of God (Luke 3:38); created from dust (Gen. 2:7); of the earth, a man of dust (1 Cor. 15:47-9); made before Eve (1 Tim. 2:13); placed in the garden of Eden (Gen. 2:8-17); Eve made from his side (Gen. 2:18-25); sinned (Gen. 3:6-19); was not deceived as Eve was (1 Tim. 2:14); sin entered the world through him and death reigned (Rom. 5:12-21); in him all die (1 Cor. 15:22); clothed by God (Gen. 3:21); driven out of Eden (Gen. 3:22-4); had children by Eve (Gen. 4:1-2, 25); was the father of Seth (Gen. 5:3); the first man Adam and the last Adam (1 Cor. 15:45).

D3b Adonijah
David's fourth son (2 Sam. 3:4); son of David by Haggith (1 Chr. 3:2); attempted to become king (1 Kgs. 1:5-27); sought sanctuary (1 Kgs. 1:41-53); sought Abishag as wife (1 Kgs. 2:13-22); killed by Benaiah (1 Kgs. 2:23-5).

D3c Adoniram [Adoram, Hadoram]
In charge of the forced labour (2 Sam. 20:24; 1 Kgs. 4:6; 5:14); stoned to death by Israel (1 Kgs. 12:18; 2 Chr. 10:18).

D3d Aeneas
A paralysed man healed by Peter (Acts 9:33-5).

D3e Agabus
Prophesied a famine (Acts 11:28); prophesied Paul's arrest (Acts 21:10-11).

D3f Agag
King of the Amalekites, spared by Saul (1 Sam. 15:8-9, 20); hewn in pieces by Samuel (1 Sam. 15:32-3).

D3g Agrippa
Arrived in Caesarea and heard of Paul (Acts 25:13-22); came to the audience hall (Acts 25:23-7); heard Paul speak (Acts 26:1-23); appealed to by Paul (Acts 26:27-8); justified Paul (Acts 26:32).

D3h Ahab
Son of Omri and wicked king of Israel (1 Kgs. 16:28-33); warned of famine by Elijah (1 Kgs. 17:1); met with Elijah at Mount Carmel (1 Kgs. 18:1-19:1); seized Naboth's vineyard (1 Kgs. 21:1-29); made a marriage alliance with Jehoshaphat (2 Chr. 18:1); died after the battle at Ramoth-gilead (1 Kgs. 22:1-40; 2 Chr. 18:2-34).

D3i Ahasuerus [Xerxes]
King of the Persian empire (Esther 1:1; 3:6-7; 10:1); gave a banquet (Esther 1:2-12); deposed Vashti and sought a replacement (Esther 1:13-2:4); chose Esther (Esther 2:12-18); a plot against him (Esther 2:21; 6:2); promoted Haman (Esther 3:1); gave permission to destroy the Jews (Esther 3:8-12); gave the Jews' enemies into Mordecai's hands (Esther 8:1-2, 7-9:30; 10:3).

D4 Ahaz – Ahithophel
D4a Ahaz
Son of Jotham and wicked king of Judah (2 Kgs. 15:38; 16:1-20; 1 Chr. 3:13; 2 Chr. 27:9; 28:1-27); died (2 Chr. 28:27).

D4b Ahaziah [1]
Son of Ahab and wicked king of Israel (1 Kgs. 22:40, 51-3); Jehoshaphat allied himself with him (2 Chr. 20:35); fell through a lattice and sent to enquire of Baal-zebub (2 Kgs. 1:2-16); died (2 Kgs. 1:17).

D4c Ahaziah [2] [Jehoahaz]
Son of Jehoram and wicked king of Judah (2 Kgs. 8:24-7; 9:29; 1 Chr. 3:11; 2 Chr. 21:17; 22:1); went up with Joram to Ramoth-gilead (2 Kgs. 8:28); visited Joram (2 Kgs. 8:29; 9:16); caught up in Jehu's attack (2 Kgs. 9:21, 23); killed by Jehu (2 Kgs. 9:27-8; 2 Chr. 22:9).

D4d Ahijah
The Shilonite prophet who met Jeroboam (1 Kgs. 11:29-31); going to Shiloh to Ahijah the prophet (1 Kgs. 14:2-16).

D4e Ahimaaz
Carried news to David from Jerusalem (2 Sam. 17:17-21); carried news to David of the battle (2 Sam. 18:19-23, 27-30).

D4f Ahimelech
Priest and son of Ahitub, helping the fleeing David (1 Sam. 21:1-9); Doeg told Saul that David had come to Ahimelech (Ps. 52:t); killed by Doeg (1 Sam. 22:9-23).

D4g Ahithophel
A counsellor esteemed by David and Absalom (2 Sam. 16:23; 1 Chr. 27:33-4); went over to Absalom (2 Sam. 15:12, 31); counselled Absalom to lie with his father's concubines (2 Sam. 16:20-2); Hushai's counsel overruled his (2 Sam. 17:1-15); hanged himself (2 Sam. 17:23).

D5 Agrippa – Amon
D5a Alexander [1]
Son of Simon of Cyrene (Mark 15:21).

D5b Alexander [2]
A member of the high priest's family (Acts 4:6).

D5c Alexander [3]
An accuser of Paul (Acts 19:33).

D5d Alexander [4]
Made shipwreck of his faith (1 Tim. 1:20).

D5e Alexander [5]
The coppersmith and opponent of Paul (2 Tim. 4:14-15).

D5f Amasa
Chief of Absalom's army (2 Sam. 17:25); promised the leadership of David's army (2 Sam. 19:13); killed by Joab (2 Sam. 20:4-12; 1 Kgs. 2:5, 32).

D5g Amaziah
Son of Joash and king of Judah (2 Kgs. 12:21; 14:1-3; 1 Chr. 3:12; 2 Chr. 24:27; 25:1-2); killed those who murdered his father (2 Kgs. 14:6-7; 2 Chr. 25:3-4); fought with Edom (2 Chr. 25:5-13); worshipped the gods of Edom (2 Chr. 25:14-16); Jehoahaz fought him (2 Kgs. 13:12); fought with Joash king of Israel (2 Kgs. 14:8-14; 2 Chr. 25:17-24); captured by Jehoash (2 Kgs. 14:13); assassinated (2 Kgs. 14:17-20; 2 Chr. 25:25-8).

D5h Amnon
David's firstborn, born in Hebron (2 Sam. 3:2; 1 Chr. 3:1); raped Tamar, Absalom's sister (2 Sam. 13:1-22); killed by Absalom (2 Sam. 13:28-33).

D5i Amon [Amos]
Son of Manasseh and wicked king of Judah (2 Kgs. 21:18-22; 1 Chr. 3:14; 2 Chr. 33:20-3); killed by his own servants (2 Kgs. 21:23-6; 2 Chr. 33:24-5).

D6 Amos – Apelles
D6a Amos
A shepherd of Tekoa (Amos 1:1).

D6b Ampliatus
'My beloved in the Lord' (Rom. 16:8).

D6c Ananias [1]
With his wife Sapphira, held back part of the proceeds of selling property (Acts 5:1-10).

D6d Ananias [2]
A disciple in Damascus who laid hands on Paul (Acts 9:10-17); Ananias went to Paul in Damascus (Acts 22:12-16).

D6e Andrew
Brother of Simon Peter (Matt. 4:18-20; Mark 1:16-20; John 1:40); a disciple of John the Baptist who brought Peter to Christ (John 1:35-42); one of the 12 apostles (Matt. 10:2; Mark 3:18; Luke 6:14; Acts 1:13); told Christ about the boy with five loaves and two fish (John 6:8-9); with Philip, told Jesus about the Greeks (John 12:22); asked Christ about the destruction of the temple (Mark 13:3); Jesus entered his house (Mark 1:29).

D6f Anna
Daughter of Phanuel of Asher who acknowledged Christ (Luke 2:36-8).

D6g Annas
High priest with Caiaphas (Luke 3:2; Acts 4:6); interrogated Christ (John 18:13-24).

D6h Antipas
'My witness, my faithful one' (Rev. 2:13).

D6i Apelles
'Approved in Christ' (Rom. 16:10).

D7 Apollos – Artemas
D7a Apollos
A Jew who came to Ephesus, instructed by Priscilla and Aquila (Acts 18:24-6); greatly helped the believers (Acts 18:27-19:1); some say, 'I am of Apollos' (1 Cor. 1:12; 3:4); Apollos watered (1 Cor. 3:6); I urged him to visit you (1 Cor. 16:12); speed Zenas and Apollos on their way (Titus 3:13); while Apollos was in Corinth (Acts 19:1).

D7b Apphia
'Our sister' (Philem. 2).

D7c Aquila
A Christian Jew, husband of Priscilla (Acts 18:2); sailed with Paul (Acts 18:18); expounded the way of God more accurately to Apollos (Acts 18:26); greet Prisca and Aquila (Rom. 16:3; 2 Tim. 4:19); Aquila and Prisca send greetings (1 Cor. 16:19).

D7d Araunah [Ornan]
A Jebusite who owned a threshing floor (2 Chr. 3:1); David bought his threshing floor (2 Sam. 24:16-18; 1 Chr. 21:15-25).

D7e Archelaus
Ruler of Judea (Matt. 2:22).

D7f Aretas
King over the governor of Damascus (2 Cor. 11:32).

D7g Aristarchus
A Macedonian of Thessalonica who accompanied Paul (Acts 19:29; 20:4; 27:2); fellow-worker with Paul (Philem. 24); fellow-prisoner of Paul (Col. 4:10).

D7h Artaxerxes
King of Persia, to whom a letter was written (Ezra 4:7-16); the king sent a letter back (Ezra 4:17-23); by his decree the temple was built (Ezra 6:14); he gave Ezra a

letter of support (Ezra 7:11-26); Nehemiah was his
cupbearer (Neh. 2:1); he approved Nehemiah's journey
to Jerusalem (Neh. 2:2-9).

D7i Artemas
To be sent by Paul to Titus (Titus 3:12).

D8 Asa – Azariah
D8a Asa
Son of Abijah and good king of Judah (1 Kgs. 15:8-15; 1
Chr. 3:10; 2 Chr. 14:1-8; Matt. 1:7); made a cistern (Jer.
41:9); prayed when attacked by Zerah the Ethiopian
(2 Chr. 14:9-14); encouraged by Oded the prophet to
seek God (2 Chr. 15:1-19); war between Asa and Baasha
(1 Kgs. 15:32); made a league with Ben-hadad king of
Syria (1 Kgs. 15:16-22; 2 Chr. 16:1-11); diseased in his feet
in old age (1 Kgs. 15:23; 2 Chr. 16:12); died (1 Kgs. 15:24;
2 Chr. 16:13-14).

D8b Asahel
Son of Zeruiah (2 Sam. 2:18; 1 Chr. 2:16); one of the 30
mighty men (2 Sam. 23:24; 1 Chr. 11:26); pursued Abner
(2 Sam. 2:19-23); was killed (2 Sam. 2:23).

D8c Asenath
Daughter of Potiphera, priest of On, who married
Joseph (Gen. 41:45); bore Manasseh and Ephraim
(Gen. 41:50-2; 46:20).

D8d Asher
Jacob's son by Zilpah (Gen. 30:13); Asher's food shall
be rich (Gen. 49:20).

D8e Athaliah
Mother of Ahaziah (2 Kgs. 8:26; 2 Chr. 22:2); killed all
the royal family (2 Kgs. 11:1; 2 Chr. 22:10); taken out of
the temple and killed (2 Kgs. 11:13-16; 2 Chr. 23:12-15).

D8f Augustus
Caesar Augustus (Luke 2:1).

D8g Azariah [Uzziah]
Son of Amaziah and good king of Judah (2 Kgs. 14:21;
1 Chr. 3:12; 2 Chr. 26:1-15; Isa. 1:1; Hos. 1:1; Amos 1:1;
Zech. 14:5); became a leper (2 Chr. 26:16-22); died
(2 Kgs. 15:7; 2 Chr. 26:23; Isa. 6:1).

E Individuals B – D
E1 Baanah – Bartholomew
E1a Baanah
Son of Rimmon the Beerothite who killed Ish-bosheth
(2 Sam. 4:2, 5-12); killed by David's young men (2 Sam.
4:12).

E1b Baasha
Son of Ahijah who conspired against Nadab and killed
him (1 Kgs. 15:27-30); ruled over Israel (1 Kgs. 15:33-4;
Jer. 41:9); Jehu prophesied against him (1 Kgs. 16:1-4, 7,
12-13); war between Asa and Baasha (1 Kgs. 15:16, 32);
built Ramah (1 Kgs. 15:17; 2 Chr. 16:1); stopped building
Ramah (1 Kgs. 15:21); died (1 Kgs. 16:5-6).

E1c Balaam
Son of Beor, summoned by Balak to curse Israel (Num.
22:4-6; Deut. 23:4; Josh. 24:9); refused to go (Num.
22:7-14); heeded the second summonse (Num.
22:15-20); beat his ass who saw an angel and spoke
(Num. 22:35; 2 Pet. 2:16); blessed Israel (Num.
22:41-23:12; 23:13-26, 27-24:9); final prophecy (Num.
24:10-25); he loved gain from wrongdoing (2 Pet. 2:15);
Balaam's error (Jude 11); advised the Midianites to lure
the Israelites into sin (Num. 31:16; Rev. 2:14); killed
with the sword (Num. 31:8; Josh. 13:22); remember
Balaam son of Beor (Mic. 6:5).

E1d Balak
Son of Zippor and king of Moab (Num. 22:2-4; Judg.
11:25); summoned Balaam to curse Israel for him
(Num. 22:4-14, 15-18; 23:7; Josh. 24:9; Mic. 6:5); was
indignant with Balaam (Num. 23:11; 24:10-13, 25); was
taught by Balaam to lure Israel into sin (Rev. 2:14).

E1e Barabbas
A murderer who was released instead of Jesus (Matt.
27:16-26; Mark 15:7-15; Luke 23:18-19, 25; John 18:40).

E1f Barak
Son of Abinoam, who fought Sisera (Judg. 4:6-10, 12-16;
5:12); sang with Deborah (Judg. 5:1); the Lord sent
Barak (1 Sam. 12:11); time would fail to tell of Barak
(Heb. 11:32).

E1g Bar-jesus [Elymas]
A Jewish false prophet and magician (Acts 13:6-11).

E1h Barnabas
A Levite of Cyprus, son of encouragement (Acts 4:36);
cousin of Mark (Col. 4:10); sold a field and gave the
proceeds (Acts 4:37); brought Paul before the disciples
(Acts 9:27); was sent to Antioch (Acts 11:22-4); brought
Paul to Antioch (Acts 11:25-6); took relief to Judea
(Acts 11:30); returned from Jerusalem (Acts 12:25); one
of the church leaders in Antioch (Acts 13:1); sent out
with Paul (Acts 13:2-4); faced opposition (Acts 13:46);
called Zeus at Lystra (Acts 14:12-14); accompanied Paul
to Jerusalem (Acts 14:20; Gal. 2:1, 9); opposed the
circumcision party (Acts 15:2); went with
representatives to Antioch (Acts 15:22, 25); was misled
by the Jews (Gal. 2:13); disagreed with Paul and left
with John Mark (Acts 15:36-9).

E1i Bartholomew
An apostle (Matt. 10:3; Mark 3:18; Luke 6:14; Acts 1:13).

E2 Bartimaeus – Ben-hadad
E2a Bartimaeus
A blind beggar whom Jesus healed (Mark 10:46-52).

E2b Baruch
Son of Neriah and secretary to Jeremiah (Jer. 32:12-16);
wrote at Jeremiah's dictation and read from it (Jer.
36:4-19, 27); wrote again (Jer. 36:32); led away into
Egypt with Jeremiah (Jer. 43:3, 6); prophecy to him
from Jeremiah (Jer. 45:1-5).

E2c Barzillai
A Gileadite from Rogelim who brought supplies to
David (2 Sam. 17:27-9); escorted David back over the
Jordan (2 Sam. 19:31-9); kindness to be shown to his
sons (1 Kgs. 2:7).

E2d Bathsheba [Bath-shua]
Daughter of Eliam and wife of Uriah the Hittite
(2 Sam. 11:3); taken and pregnant by David (2 Sam.
11:4-5); David went in to her (Ps. 51:1); married by
David (2 Sam. 11:26-7); wife of David who bore four
children (1 Chr. 3:5); bore Solomon (2 Sam. 12:24; Matt.
1:6); pleaded for Solomon as king (1 Kgs. 1:11-31);
pleaded for Adonijah to have Abishag as wife (1 Kgs.
2:13-21).

E2e Belshazzar
Made a feast (Dan. 5:1); drank from the temple vessels
(Dan. 5:2-4); called Daniel to interpret the writing on
the wall (Dan. 5:5-29); killed (Dan. 5:30).

E2f Benaiah
Son of Jehoiada, over the Cherethites and Pelethites
(2 Sam. 8:18; 20:23; 1 Chr. 18:17); a renowned member
of the 30 mighty men (2 Sam. 23:20-3; 1 Chr. 11:22-5);
king's counsellor (1 Chr. 27:34); did not join in
Adonijah's rebellion (1 Kgs. 1:8); in charge of the army
(1 Kgs. 2:35; 4:4); killed Adonijah (1 Kgs. 2:25); killed
Joab (1 Kgs. 2:29-34); killed Shimei (1 Kgs. 2:46).

E2g Ben-ammi
Son of Lot by his youngest daughter (Gen. 19:38).

E2h Ben-hadad
Son of Tabrimmon and king of Damascus (1 Kgs.
15:18-20); entered into a league with Asa king of Judah
(2 Chr. 16:2-4).

E2i Ben-hadad [2]
King of Syria who besieged Samaria (1 Kgs. 20:1-12);
fled on horseback (1 Kgs. 20:19-21); fought again in the

spring (1 Kgs. 20:26-30); spared by King Ahab (1 Kgs. 20:31-4); besieged Samaria again (2 Kgs. 6:24); died by the hand of Hazael (2 Kgs. 8:7-15).

E2j Ben-hadad [3]
Son of Hazael king of Syria (2 Kgs. 13:3, 24); Jehoash recovered cities from him (2 Kgs. 13:25); under God's judgement (Jer. 49:27; Amos 1:4).

E3 Benjamin – Boaz
E3a Benjamin [Ben-oni]
Son of Jacob by Rachel (Gen. 35:24; 46:19-21; Exod. 1:3; 1 Chr. 2:2); called Ben-oni by Rachel (Gen. 35:18); was not sent to Egypt the first time (Gen. 42:4); Joseph had him brought to Egypt (Gen. 42:13-20); his portion was five times the others (Gen. 43:34); Joseph's cup in his sack (Gen. 44:2, 12); Joseph greeted him (Gen. 45:14); a ravenous wolf dividing the plunder (Gen. 49:27).

E3b Bernice
Sister of Agrippa (Acts 25:13, 23; 26:30).

E3c Bethuel
Father of Rebekah (Gen. 22:23); an Aramean of Paddan-aram (Gen. 25:20; 28:5); received Abraham's servant (Gen. 24:50).

E3d Bezalel
Filled with God's Spirit for work on the tabernacle (Exod. 31:3-5; 35:30-5); the Lord gave skill to him (Exod. 36:1); summoned by Moses (Exod. 36:2); Bezalel made the tabernacle furniture (Exod. 37:1; 38:22; 2 Chr. 1:5).

E3e Bildad
A Shuhite and friend of Job (Job 2:11; 42:9); made a speech (Job 8:1-22; 18:1-21; 25:1-6).

E3f Bilhah
Rachel's maid (Gen. 29:29; 35:25; 46:25); became Jacob's concubine and bore children (Gen. 30:3-8; 37:2; 1 Chr. 7:13); Reuben lay with her (Gen. 35:22).

E3g Blastus
The king's chamberlain (Acts 12:20).

E3h Boanerges
The name Jesus gave to James and John, 'sons of thunder' (Mark 3:17).

E3i Boaz
Kinsman of Naomi, of Elimelech's family (Ruth 2:1, 19-23); visited his field (Ruth 2:3-16); winnowing barley (Ruth 3:2-15); marrying Ruth (Ruth 4:1-13).

E4 Caiaphas – Chimham
E4a Caiaphas
The high priest (Matt. 26:3; Luke 3:2; John 18:13); prophesied of Jesus' death (John 11:49-51; 18:14); Jesus appeared before him (Matt. 26:57; John 18:24, 28); a member of the Sanhedrin (Acts 4:6).

E4b Cain
Son of Adam by Eve (Gen. 4:1); sacrificed produce of the ground (Gen. 4:2-7); by faith Abel offered a better sacrifice than Cain (Heb. 11:4); killed his brother Abel (Gen. 4:8, 25; 1 John 3:12); sentenced by God (Gen. 4:9-16); the Lord put a mark on Cain (Gen. 4:15); avenged sevenfold (Gen. 4:15, 24); built a city called Enoch after his son (Gen. 4:17); walking in the way of Cain (Jude 11).

E4c Caleb
Son of Jephunneh (1 Chr. 4:15); sent to spy out Canaan (Num. 13:6); was sure of victory (Num. 13:30; 14:6-10); would enter the promised land (Num. 14:24, 30; Deut. 1:36); survived (Num. 14:38; 26:65; 32:12); divided the land (Num. 34:19); claimed Hebron as his inheritance (Josh. 14:6-14; 15:13-14; 21:12; Judg. 1:20; 1 Chr. 6:56).

E4d Canaan
Son of Ham (Gen. 9:18); his sons (Gen. 10:15-19; 1 Chr. 1:13-16); he was cursed (Gen. 9:25-7).

E4e Candace
Title of the queen of Ethiopia (Acts 8:27).

E4f Carpus
Bring the cloak I left at Troas with Carpus (2 Tim. 4:13).

E4g Chedorlaomer
King of Elam (Gen. 14:1).

E4h Chimham
Let Chimham go over with the king (2 Sam. 19:37); Chimham shall go over with me (2 Sam. 19:38); Chimham went with him (2 Sam. 19:40).

E5 Chloe – Cozbi
E5a Chloe
Her people reported information to Paul (1 Cor. 1:11).

E5b Chuza
Herod's steward (Luke 8:3).

E5c Claudius [1]
Claudius Caesar (Acts 11:28); ejected Jews from Rome (Acts 18:2).

E5d Claudius [2]
Claudius Lysias, a Roman tribune (Acts 23:26).

E5e Clement
A fellow-worker with Paul (Phil. 4:3).

E5f Cleopas
One of those walking to Emmaus (Luke 24:18).

E5g Cornelius
A centurion of the Italian Cohort who believed (Acts 10:1-48).

E5h Cozbi
Daughter of Zur prince of Midian (Num. 25:15, 18); brought into an Israelite house (Num. 25:6-8).

E6 Crescens – Cyrus
E6a Crescens
Went to Galatia (2 Tim. 4:10).

E6b Crispus
Ruler of the synagogue who believed (Acts 18:8); baptised by Paul (1 Cor. 1:14).

E6c Cushan-rishathaim
King of Mesopotamia who oppressed Israel (Judg. 3:8-10).

E6d Cyrus
King of Persia, commanded the return to Jerusalem (2 Chr. 36:22-3; Ezra 1:1-4; 4:3; 5:13); gave back the things from the temple (Ezra 1:7-8; 5:14-15; 6:5); commanded the rebuilding of the temple (Ezra 6:3-4, 14); made a grant to the returned exiles (Ezra 3:7); subject of prophecy by Isaiah (Isa. 44:28; 45:1).

E7 Damaris – David
E7a Damaris
A Greek woman who believed (Acts 17:34).

E7b Dan
Son of Jacob by Bilhah (Gen. 30:6; Exod. 1:4; 1 Chr. 2:2); prophecy concerning him (Gen. 49:16-17).

E7c Daniel [Belteshazzar]
An exile from the tribe of Judah (Dan. 1:6); named Belteshazzar (Dan. 1:7; 4:8; 5:12); would not defile himself with the king's food (Dan. 1:8-16); understood visions and dreams (Dan. 1:17); excellent in wisdom (Dan. 1:19-21); a man greatly beloved (Dan. 10:19); interpreted the king's dream of an image (Dan. 2:13-47); interpreted the king's dream of a tree (Dan. 4:8-27); interpreted the writing on the wall (Dan. 5:11-29); cast into a den of lions (Dan. 6:1-28); the desolation spoken of by Daniel (Matt. 24:15); Noah, Daniel and Job would only save themselves (Ezek. 14:14, 20); you are wiser than Daniel (Ezek. 28:3); O Belteshazzar, chief of the magicians (Dan. 4:9); Daniel was distinguished over all the commissioners and satraps (Dan. 6:3); Daniel was one of the three commissioners (Dan. 6:2).

E7d Darius [1]
King of Persia (Ezra 4:5; Neh. 12:22; Hag. 1:1, 15; Zech. 1:1; 7:1); a letter sent to him (Ezra 5:5-17); made a decree to build the temple (Ezra 6:1-15).

E7e Darius [2]
Darius the Mede, ruler of Babylon (Dan. 5:31; 6:1; 9:1; 11:1).

E7f Dathan
Son of Eliab who rebelled against Moses (Num. 16:1, 12; 26:9); swallowed up by the ground (Num. 16:24-33; Deut. 11:6; Ps. 106:17).

E7g David's life
Youngest son of Jesse (Ruth 4:17; 1 Sam. 16:11; 17:14); keeping sheep (1 Sam. 16:11); anointed by Samuel (1 Sam. 16:12-13); played the lyre before Saul (1 Sam. 16:20-3); killed Goliath (1 Sam. 17:17-54); in peril from Saul (1 Sam. 18:6-27:1); feigned madness (1 Sam. 21:11-15); took his parents to the king of Moab (1 Sam. 22:3-4); poured out water from the well of Bethlehem (1 Chr. 11:15-19); went with Achish to battle (1 Sam. 28:1-2; 29:2-11); pursued the Amalekites (1 Sam. 30:1-31); showed kindness to Mephibosheth (2 Sam. 9:1-13); conquered Jerusalem (2 Sam. 5:6-10; 1 Chr. 11:4-9); brought up the ark to Jerusalem (2 Sam. 6:1-23; 1 Chr. 13:1-14; 15:2-16:43); wanted to build the temple (2 Sam. 7:1-29; 1 Chr. 17:1-27; 22:7-8); sinned over Bathsheba (2 Sam. 11:1-27); was rebuked by Nathan (2 Sam. 12:1-14); suffered from Absalom (2 Sam. 13:1-19:1); was nearly killed by Ishbi-benob (2 Sam. 21:15-17); numbered Israel (2 Sam. 24:1-25; 1 Chr. 21:1-22:1); made Solomon king (1 Kgs. 1:1-48; 1 Chr. 23:1); his last words (2 Sam. 23:1); the prayers of David are ended (Ps. 72:20); died (1 Kgs. 2:1-11; 1 Chr. 29:28).

E7h David's importance
David my servant will be their prince for ever (Ezek. 37:25); I will set over them one shepherd, my servant David (Ezek. 34:23); I have found David my servant (Ps. 89:20); he chose David his servant (Ps. 78:70); I have sworn a covenant to David my chosen one (Ps. 89:3); he shows love to David and his descendants for ever (Ps. 18:50); blessed is the kingdom of our father David (Mark 11:10); the Lord swore to David to set his son on the throne (Ps. 132:11); God will give him the throne of his father David (Luke 1:32); David the man of God (Neh. 12:36); afterwards Israel will seek the Lord and David their king (Hos. 3:5); I will rebuild the booth of David which has fallen (Amos 9:11); David prophesied of Christ (Acts 2:29-31); time would fail to tell of David (Heb. 11:32); I have found David the son of Jesse a man after my heart (Acts 13:22); I chose David to be over my people Israel (1 Kgs. 8:16).

E7i Christ the Son of David
Jesus, Son of David (Mark 10:47); have mercy on us, son of David! (Matt. 9:27); this can't be the son of David, can it? (Matt. 12:23); have mercy on me, Son of David! (Matt. 15:22; 20:30-1; Mark 10:48; Luke 18:38-9); Hosanna to the Son of David! (Matt. 21:9, 15); Christ is the Son of David (Matt. 22:42; Mark 12:35; Luke 20:41); how is it that David calls him Lord? (Matt. 22:43; Mark 12:37; Luke 20:44); Christ is descended from David and comes from Bethlehem, David's village (John 7:42); from the posterity of David God has brought a Saviour, Jesus (Acts 13:23); God's Son, descended from David according to the flesh (Rom. 1:3); Jesus Christ, descended from David (2 Tim. 2:8); he who has the key of David (Rev. 3:7); the lion of the tribe of Judah, the root of David (Rev. 5:5); the root and the offspring of David (Rev. 22:16).

E8 Deborah – Drusilla
E8a Deborah [1]
Rebekah's nurse (Gen. 35:8).
E8b Deborah [2]
Prophetess and wife of Lappidoth (Judg. 4:4-10, 14); awake, Deborah! (Judg. 5:12); sang with Barak (Judg. 5:1).
E8c Delilah
A woman in Philistine territory who enticed Samson (Judg. 16:4-20).
E8d Demas
Travelling companion of Paul (Col. 4:14; Philem. 24); in love with this present world (2 Tim. 4:10).
E8e Demetrius
A silversmith (Acts 19:24, 38).
E8f Dinah
Daughter of Jacob by Leah (Gen. 30:21; 46:15); raped and sought in marriage by Shechem (Gen. 34:1-31); brought out of Shechem's house (Gen. 34:26).
E8g Dionysius
An Areopagite who believed (Acts 17:34).
E8h Diotrephes
Did not acknowledge John's authority (3 John 9).
E8i Doeg
An Edomite, chief of Saul's herdsmen (1 Sam. 21:7); told Saul that Ahimelech had helped David (1 Sam. 22:9; Ps. 52:t); killed the priests (1 Sam. 22:18-22).
E8j Dorcas [Tabitha]
A disciple full of good works (Acts 9:36); raised from the dead by Peter (Acts 9:37-42).
E8k Drusilla
Jewish wife of Felix (Acts 24:24).

F Individuals E – G
F1 Ebed-melech – Eliakim
F1a Ebed-melech
An Ethiopian eunuch who lifted Jeremiah out of the cistern (Jer. 38:7-13); was promised deliverance (Jer. 39:16-18).
F1b Eglon
King of Moab who oppressed Israel (Judg. 3:12-14); killed by Ehud (Judg. 3:15-23).
F1c Ehud
Son of Gera of Benjamin, who delivered Israel from Eglon (Judg. 3:15-30); died (Judg. 4:1).
F1d Elah
Son of Baasha and king of Israel (1 Kgs. 16:6, 8-10).
F1e Eldad
One of 70 elders who remained in the camp and prophesied (Num. 11:26-7).
F1f Eleazar
Son of Aaron (Exod. 6:23; 1 Chr. 6:3-4); served as priest (Num. 3:4; Deut. 10:6; Josh. 17:4; 19:51; 21:1; 1 Chr. 24:2); wore Aaron's garments (Num. 20:25-8); in charge of the Levites (Num. 3:32); in charge of the oil (Num. 4:16); took up the censers of the rebels (Num. 16:37, 39); slaughtered the red heifer (Num. 19:3); helped divide out the land (Num. 34:17; Josh. 14:1); Moses was angry with him (Lev. 10:16).
F1g Eli
The priest in Shiloh (1 Sam. 1:9); rebuked Hannah (1 Sam. 1:12-18); rebuked his sons (1 Sam. 2:22-5); looked after Samuel (1 Sam. 1:25); was rebuked by a man of God (1 Sam. 2:27-36); advised Samuel when God spoke (1 Sam. 3:2-18); died when the ark was captured (1 Sam. 4:13-18); prophecy concerning his house fulfilled (1 Kgs. 2:27).
F1h Eliakim
Son of Hilkiah (2 Kgs. 18:18; Isa. 36:3; 37:2); given the key of the house of David (Isa. 22:20-4).

F2 Eliashib – Elisha

F2a Eliashib
The high priest in Nehemiah's time (Neh. 3:1); prepared a chamber for Tobiah (Neh. 13:4-5, 7).

F2b Eliezer [1]
Abraham's servant (Gen. 15:2-4).

F2c Eliezer [2]
Son of Dodavahu of Mareshah who prophesied against Jehoshaphat (2 Chr. 20:37).

F2d Elihu
Son of Barachel the Buzite (Job 32:2, 6); his speeches (Job 32:6-33:33; 34:1-37; 35:1-16; 36:1-37:24).

F2e Elijah
The prophet from Tishbe who prophesied drought (1 Kgs. 17:1); fed by ravens (1 Kgs. 17:2-7); stayed with a widow of Zarephath (1 Kgs. 17:8-24; Luke 4:25-6); showed himself to Ahab (1 Kgs. 18:1-18); confronted the prophets of Baal on Mount Carmel (1 Kgs. 18:20-40); prayed for rain (1 Kgs. 18:41-6); fled to the wilderness (1 Kgs. 19:1-18); called Elisha (1 Kgs. 19:19-21); confronted Ahab about Naboth's vineyard (1 Kgs. 21:17-29); prophesied Ahaziah's death (2 Kgs. 1:3-17); wrote to King Jehoram of Judah (2 Chr. 21:12-15); taken up to heaven (2 Kgs. 2:1-18); appeared at the transfiguration (Matt. 17:3-4; Mark 9:4-5; Luke 9:30-3); I will send you Elijah the prophet (Mal. 4:5); John the Baptist was Elijah who was to come (Matt. 11:14; 17:10-12; Mark 9:11-13); John the Baptist will go before him in the spirit and power of Elijah (Luke 1:17); some said that Jesus was Elijah (Matt. 16:14; Mark 8:28; Luke 9:8, 19); some said he was calling for Elijah (Matt. 27:47-9; Mark 15:35-6); do you not know what the Scripture says of Elijah? (Rom. 11:2); Elijah was a man like us (Jas. 5:17).

F2f Elimelech
Husband of Naomi of Bethlehem (Ruth 1:2); kinsman of Boaz (Ruth 2:1).

F2g Eliphaz
The Temanite friend of Job (Job 2:11; 4:1; 15:1; 22:1; 42:7, 9).

F2h Elisha
Son of Shaphat, anointed as prophet by Elijah (1 Kgs. 19:16, 19-21); saw Elijah taken up into heaven (2 Kgs. 2:1-18); healed the spring of water with salt (2 Kgs. 2:19-22); cursed the youths (2 Kgs. 2:23-5); prophesied the defeat of Moab (2 Kgs. 3:11-19); miracle of the jar of oil (2 Kgs. 4:1-7); raised to life the Shunammite woman's son (2 Kgs. 4:8-37); healing the pottage containing wild gourds (2 Kgs. 4:38-41); feeding 100 men (2 Kgs. 4:42-4); healing Naaman the Syrian (2 Kgs. 5:1-27); making the iron swim (2 Kgs. 6:1-7); bringing the army of Syria to Samaria (2 Kgs. 6:11-23); prophesying plenty when Samaria was besieged (2 Kgs. 6:31-7:2; 7:18-20); Elisha's great deeds told to the king (2 Kgs. 8:1-6); prophesying the reign of Hazael (2 Kgs. 8:7-15); anointing Jehu (2 Kgs. 9:1-3); final illness and death (2 Kgs. 13:14-20); resurrection of a man touching his bones (2 Kgs. 13:20-1).

F3 Elizabeth – Er

F3a Elizabeth
Descendant of Aaron and wife of Zechariah (Luke 1:5); righteous (Luke 1:6); old and barren (Luke 1:7, 18); to bear a son (Luke 1:13); conceived (Luke 1:24-5, 36); visited by Mary (Luke 1:40); blessed Mary (Luke 1:41-5); bore John the Baptist (Luke 1:57).

F3b Elkanah
Husband of Hannah (1 Sam. 1:2); worshipped annually at Shiloh (1 Sam. 1:3-8, 21-3; 2:11, 19); father of Samuel (1 Chr. 6:34).

F3c Enoch
Father of Methuselah (Gen. 5:21; 1 Chr. 1:3; Luke 3:37); walked with God until God took him (Gen. 5:22-4); by faith Enoch was taken up so he should not see death (Heb. 11:5); prophesied (Jude 14).

F3d Epaphras
Paul's fellow-servant (Col. 1:7); a slave of Christ Jesus (Col. 4:12); Paul's fellow-prisoner (Philem. 23).

F3e Epaphroditus
Messenger from the Philippian church to Paul (Phil. 2:25; 4:18).

F3f Epaenetus
The first convert to Christ in Asia (Rom. 16:5).

F3g Ephraim
Joseph's second son (Gen. 41:52; 46:20; Num. 26:28); given pre-eminence over Manasseh by Jacob (Gen. 48:1-20); his right hand on the head of Ephraim, the younger (Gen. 48:13-14).

F3h Er
Son of Judah (Gen. 38:3); wicked, slain by the Lord (Gen. 38:6-7; 1 Chr. 2:3).

F4 Erastus – Ezra

F4a Erastus
City treasurer who sent greetings to Rome (Rom. 16:23); Paul's helper, sent into Macedonia (Acts 19:22); remained at Corinth (2 Tim. 4:20).

F4b Esau
Isaac's firstborn twin by Rebekah (Gen. 25:25-6; 1 Chr. 1:34); Esau was called Edom (Gen. 25:30); father of the Edomites (Gen. 36:43); a hunter, loved by Isaac (Gen. 25:27-8); sold his birthright for pottage (Gen. 25:29-34; Heb. 12:16-17); married foreign women (Gen. 26:34; 28:6-9; 36:2-3); Jacob stole his blessing (Gen. 27:1-40); planned to kill Jacob (Gen. 27:41-2; 35:1); came out to meet Jacob (Gen. 32:3-33:1); dwelt in Seir (Gen. 36:6-8; Josh. 24:4); hated by God (Mal. 1:3; Rom. 9:13).

F4c Esther [Hadassah]
Cousin whom Mordecai adopted (Esther 2:7); became queen of King Ahasuerus (Esther 2:8-18); revealed a plot (Esther 2:20-2); sought the welfare of the Jews (Esther 4:4-5:8; 6:14-7:8; 8:1-8; 9:29-32).

F4d Eunice
Daughter of Lois and mother of Timothy (2 Tim. 1:5).

F4e Euodia
Christian woman at Philippi (Phil. 4:2-3).

F4f Eutychus
A youth who fell asleep when Paul preached (Acts 20:9).

F4g Eve
Formed from Adam's side (Gen. 2:18-23); Adam's wife (Gen. 4:1, 25); fell into sin (Gen. 3:1-16; 2 Cor. 11:3; 1 Tim. 2:13-14); named by Adam as mother of all living (Gen. 3:20).

F4h Ezekiel
Son of Buzi and priest (Ezek. 1:3); a sign to you (Ezek. 24:24).

F4i Ezra
The priest and scribe, son of Seraiah (Ezra 7:1; Neh. 12:26, 33, 36); returned from Babylon (Ezra 7:6); set his heart to study the law (Ezra 7:10); given a letter by King Artaxerxes (Ezra 7:11-26); prayed and fasted over the faithlessness of the people (Ezra 10:1-16); read the law (Neh. 8:1-13).

F5 Felix – Festus

F5a Felix
Governer at Caesarea to whom Paul was taken (Acts 23:24-35); Paul appeared before him (Acts 24:1-23); left Paul in prison (Acts 24:24-7; 25:14).

F5b Festus [Porcius Festus]
Succeeded Felix as governor (Acts 24:27); went up to Jerusalem (Acts 25:1-5); agreed to send Paul to Caesar (Acts 25:6-12); heard Paul with Agrippa and Bernice (Acts 25:13-26:3); said Paul was out of his mind (Acts 26:24-5).

F6 Gaal – Gallio

F6a Gaal
Son of Ebed who reviled Abimelech (Judg. 9:26-31); ambushed by Abimelech (Judg. 9:35-41).

F6b Gad [1]
Son of Jacob by Zilpah (Gen. 30:10-11; 1 Chr. 2:2); went down into Egypt (Gen. 46:16; Exod. 1:4); Jacob prophesied about him (Gen. 49:19).

F6c Gad [2]
A prophet, David's seer (1 Sam. 22:5; 2 Chr. 29:25); warned David after the census (2 Sam. 24:11-14; 1 Chr. 21:9-13); told David to erect an altar (2 Sam. 24:18-19; 1 Chr. 21:18-19); wrote a book of chronicles (1 Chr. 29:29).

F6d Gaius [1]
A Macedonian and companion of Paul (Acts 19:29).

F6e Gaius [2]
A man of Derbe who went on ahead of Paul (Acts 20:4-5).

F6f Gaius [3]
Paul's host in Corinth who sent greetings (Rom. 16:23); Paul baptised him (1 Cor. 1:14).

F6g Gaius [4]
One beloved by the elder (3 John 1).

F6h Gallio
Proconsul of Achaia who heard Paul's case (Acts 18:12-17).

F7 Gamaliel – Gomer

F7a Gamaliel
A teacher of the law (Acts 5:34-40); taught Paul (Acts 22:3).

F7b Gedaliah
Son of Ahikam, appointed governor by Nebuchadnezzar (2 Kgs. 25:22-4; Jer. 40:5-12); looked after Jeremiah (Jer. 39:14; 43:6); killed by Ishmael (2 Kgs. 25:25; Jer. 40:13-41:18).

F7c Gehazi
Servant of Elisha (2 Kgs. 4:12; 8:4-5); suffered the leprosy of Naaman (2 Kgs. 5:20-7).

F7d Gershon [Gershom]
Son of Levi (Gen. 46:11; Exod. 6:16; Num. 3:17; 1 Chr. 6:1; 23:6).

F7e Geshem
The Arab who opposed work on Jerusalem (Neh. 2:19; 6:1-2, 6).

F7f Gideon [Jerubbaal]
Son of Joash the Abiezrite, to whom an angel appeared (Judg. 6:11-24); cut down the altar of Baal (Judg. 6:25-32); was called Jerubbaal (Judg. 6:32); called out Israel (Judg. 6:34-5); tested God with a fleece (Judg. 6:36-40); defeated Midian (Judg. 7:1-8:21); made an idol (Judg. 8:22-7); his last days (Judg. 8:28-35); the Lord sent Jerubbaal (1 Sam. 12:11); time would fail to tell of Gideon (Heb. 11:32).

F7g Gog
Chief prince of Meshech and Tubal (Ezek. 38:2-39:16).

F7h Goliath
A Philistine giant from Gath (1 Sam. 17:4-7; 22:10); challenged Israel (1 Sam. 17:8-11, 23-7); killed by David (1 Sam. 17:31-57; 21:9); killed by Elhanan (2 Sam. 21:19; 1 Chr. 20:5).

F7i Gomer
Daughter of Diblaim and wife of Hosea (Hos. 1:3).

G Individuals H – I

G1 Habakkuk – Hananiah

G1a Habakkuk
The prophet (Hab. 1:1; 3:1).

G1b Hadadezer
Son of Rehob and king of Zobah (2 Sam. 8:3-12; 1 Kgs. 11:23); kings were his servants (2 Sam. 10:19); gathered his army against Israel (2 Sam. 10:16); defeated by David (1 Chr. 18:3-10); his servants made peace with David (1 Chr. 19:19).

G1c Hagar
Sarah's Egyptian maid (Gen. 16:1); bore Ishmael to Abraham (Gen. 16:2-16; 25:12); cast out (Gen. 21:9-21); the one from Mount Sinai is Hagar (Gal. 4:24-5).

G1d Haggai
The prophet (Ezra 5:1; 6:14; Hag. 1:1, 3, 12-13; 2:1, 10-14, 20).

G1e Ham
Son of Noah (Gen. 5:32; 1 Chr. 1:4); saw Noah's nakedness (Gen. 9:22).

G1f Haman
Sought to destroy the Jews (Esther 3:1-15; 4:7; 9:24); invited to Queen Esther's banquet (Esther 5:4-12; 6:14-7:1); planned to kill Mordecai (Esther 5:13-14; 6:4); forced to honour Mordecai (Esther 6:5-13); defeated before Esther and Mordecai (Esther 7:6-8:7).

G1g Hamor
Father of Shechem, the Hivite (Gen. 33:19); spoke with Jacob about Dinah (Gen. 34:6, 8-10); deceived by Jacob's sons (Gen. 34:13-24); killed by Simeon and Levi (Gen. 34:26).

G1h Hananiah
Son of Azzur from Gibeon, a false prophet (Jer. 28:1-17).

G2 Hannah – Herod

G2a Hannah
Wife of Elkanah (1 Sam. 1:2-18); mother of Samuel (1 Sam. 1:19-28); prophesied (1 Sam. 2:1-10); bore other children (1 Sam. 2:21).

G2b Hanun
Son of Nahash and king of the Ammonites (2 Sam. 10:1; 1 Chr. 19:2); cut off the garments and beards of David's men (2 Sam. 10:2-4; 1 Chr. 19:3-4); hired mercenaries (1 Chr. 19:6).

G2c Haran
Son of Terah and brother of Abraham (Gen. 11:26-9); father of Lot (Gen. 11:31).

G2d Hazael
To be anointed king of Syria (1 Kgs. 19:15); he who escapes from his sword will be slain by Jehu (1 Kgs. 19:17); sent to Elisha (2 Kgs. 8:8-14); killed Ben-hadad (2 Kgs. 8:15); attacked by Joram and Ahaziah (2 Kgs. 8:28-9; 2 Chr. 22:5); defeated Israel (2 Kgs. 10:32); the Lord gave them into his hand (2 Kgs. 13:3); took Gath (2 Kgs. 12:17); paid by Jehoash not to attack Jerusalem (2 Kgs. 12:18); I will send fire on the house of Hazael (Amos 1:4).

G2e Hermogenes
Turned away from Paul (2 Tim. 1:15).

G2f Herod [1] [Herod the Great]
Massacred the children in Bethlehem (Matt. 2:1-20; Luke 1:5); died (Matt. 2:19).

G2g Herod [2] [Herod Antipas]
Tetrarch of Galilee (Luke 3:1); beheaded John the Baptist (Matt. 14:1-12; Mark 6:14-29; Luke 3:19-20; 9:7-9); beware of his leaven (Mark 8:15); wanted to kill Jesus (Luke 13:31); Pilate sent Jesus to him (Luke 23:6-15); opposed Jesus (Acts 4:27).

G2h Herod [3] [Herod Agrippa I]
Attacked the church (Acts 12:1-19); was eaten by worms for his pride (Acts 12:20-3).

G2i Herod [4] [Herod Agrippa II]
In whose praetorium Paul was imprisoned (Acts 23:35).

G3 Herodias – Hoshea

G3a Herodias
Wife of Herod and former wife of Philip (Matt. 14:3-4; Mark 6:17-19; Luke 3:19); advised her daughter to ask for John's head (Matt. 14:6-11; Mark 6:22-8).

G3b Hezekiah
Son of Ahaz and good king of Judah (2 Kgs. 16:20; 1 Chr. 3:13; Matt. 1:9); attacked by Sennacherib king of Assyria (2 Kgs. 18:13-19:3; 2 Chr. 32:1-23; Isa. 36:1-37:21); recovered from illness (2 Kgs. 20:1-11; 2 Chr. 32:24-6; Isa. 38:1-22); welcomed the envoys from Babylon (2 Kgs. 20:12-19; 2 Chr. 32:27-31; Isa. 39:1-8); died (2 Kgs. 20:20-1; 2 Chr. 32:32-3).

G3c Hiel
Of Bethel, who rebuilt Jericho (1 Kgs. 16:34).

G3d Hilkiah
High priest during Josiah's reign (2 Kgs. 22:4-14; 2 Chr. 34:9-22; 35:8); son of Shallum and father of Azariah (1 Chr. 6:13; Ezra 7:1).

G3e Hiram [Huram]
King of Tyre who supplied timber (2 Sam. 5:11; 1 Kgs. 5:1-18; 1 Chr. 14:1; 2 Chr. 2:3); disappointed with the cities Solomon gave him (1 Kgs. 9:11-14); gave cities to Solomon (2 Chr. 8:2); sent his servants to sea with Solomon's (1 Kgs. 9:27; 10:22; 2 Chr. 8:18; 9:10).

G3f Hophni
Son of Eli (1 Sam. 1:3; 2:34; 4:4, 11, 17).

G3g Hosea
Son of Beeri, the prophet (Hos. 1:1-2); as he says in Hosea (Rom. 9:25).

G3h Hoshea
Son of Elah, became king of Israel (2 Kgs. 15:30; 17:1-6).

G4 Huldah – Hymenaeus
G4a Huldah
The prophetess, wife of Shallum (2 Kgs. 22:14-20; 2 Chr. 34:22-8).

G4b Hur
Son of Caleb by Ephrath (1 Chr. 2:19, 50; 4:4); held up Moses' hands (Exod. 17:10-12); in charge when Moses was up the mountain (Exod. 24:14).

G4c Huram [Hiram] [Huram-abi]
From Tyre, skilled workman for Solomon (1 Kgs. 7:13-45; 2 Chr. 4:13-16).

G4d Hushai
The Archite, defeated the counsel of Ahithophel (2 Sam. 15:32-7; 16:16-19; 17:5-16); the king's friend (1 Chr. 27:33).

G4e Hymenaeus
Made shipwreck of his faith (1 Tim. 1:20); swerved from the truth (2 Tim. 2:17).

G5 Ibzan – Issachar
G5a Ibzan
Of Bethlehem, judged Israel (Judg. 12:8-10).

G5b Ichabod
Son of Phinehas and grandson of Eli (1 Sam. 4:21-2; 14:3).

G5c Iddo
The seer (2 Chr. 9:29; 12:15; 13:22).

G5d Isaac
His birth foretold (Gen. 17:19-21); son of Abraham by Sarah (Gen. 21:3-7; 1 Chr. 1:28; Matt. 1:2; Acts 7:8); sole heir of Abraham (Gen. 21:8-12; 25:5-6; Rom. 9:7; Gal. 4:28); led to be sacrificed on Mount Moriah (Gen. 22:1-18; Heb. 11:17-19; Jas. 2:21); married Rebekah (Gen. 24:2-67; 25:20); buried Abraham (Gen. 25:9-11); father of Jacob and Esau (Gen. 25:21-8; Josh. 24:4; Matt. 1:2; Luke 3:34; Acts 7:8; Rom. 9:10); was grieved by Esau's wives (Gen. 26:35; 27:46); loved Esau because he ate of his game (Gen. 25:28); blessed Jacob and Esau (Gen. 27:1-40; Heb. 11:20); sent Jacob away (Gen. 27:46-28:6); died and was buried (Gen. 35:28-9; 49:31); they will recline to eat with Abraham, Isaac and Jacob in the kingdom of heaven (Matt. 8:11); when you see Abraham, Isaac and Jacob in the kingdom (Luke 13:28); I am the God of Abraham, Isaac and Jacob (Matt. 22:32; Acts 3:13); I am the God of Isaac (Mark 12:26); he calls God the God of Isaac (Luke 20:37); the God before whom Isaac walked (Gen. 48:15); I am the God of your fathers, of Abraham, Isaac and Jacob (Acts 7:32); through Isaac your descendants will be reckoned (Heb. 11:18).

G5e Isaiah
The prophet, son of Amoz (Isa. 1:1); they came to Isaiah (2 Kgs. 19:5); wrote about Uzziah (2 Chr. 26:22); wrote about Hezekiah (2 Chr. 32:32); prophesied about the king of Assyria (Isa. 19:2-7, 20-34; 2 Chr. 32:20; Isa. 37:1-35); prophesied Hezekiah's death and healing (2 Kgs. 20:1-11; Isa. 38:1-8, 21-2); prophesied about the envoys from Babylon (2 Kgs. 20:14-19; Isa. 39:1-8); the prophet Isaiah (Matt. 3:3; 4:14; 8:17; 12:17; 13:14; John 1:23; 12:38-41); well did Isaiah prophesy about you (Matt. 15:7; Mark 7:6); as it is written in Isaiah the prophet (Mark 1:2; Luke 3:4); he was given the book of the prophet Isaiah (Luke 4:17); he was reading the prophet Isaiah (Acts 8:28, 30); the Holy Spirit spoke rightly through Isaiah the prophet (Acts 28:25); Isaiah cries out (Rom. 9:27); as Isaiah predicted (Rom. 9:29); Isaiah says (Rom. 10:16; 15:12); Isaiah is so bold as to say (Rom. 10:20).

G5f Ish-bosheth [Esh-baal]
Son of Saul, made king by Abner (2 Sam. 2:8-12; 1 Chr. 8:33; 9:39); accused Abner (2 Sam. 3:7-11); restored Michal to David (2 Sam. 3:14-15); killed (2 Sam. 4:1-12).

G5g Ishmael [1]
Son of Abraham by Hagar (Gen. 16:4-16; 1 Chr. 1:28); Abraham pleaded for him (Gen. 17:18-20); was circumcised (Gen. 17:23-7); buried Abraham (Gen. 25:9).

G5h Ishmael [2]
Son of Nethaniah (2 Kgs. 25:23; Jer. 40:8); assassinated Gedaliah (2 Kgs. 25:25; Jer. 40:14-41:18).

G5i Issachar
Son of Jacob by Leah (Gen. 30:18; 35:23; Exod. 1:3; 1 Chr. 2:1); subject of prophecy (Gen. 49:14-15).

H Individuals J
H1 Jabez – James
H1a Jabez
More honourable than his brethren (1 Chr. 4:9-10).

H1b Jacob
Son of Isaac by Rebekah, twin brother of Esau (Gen. 25:21-6; 1 Chr. 1:34; Matt. 1:2; Luke 3:34; Acts 7:8); a quiet man, loved by Rebekah (Gen. 25:27-8); bought Esau's birthright with pottage (Gen. 25:29-34); stole Esau's blessing by deception (Gen. 27:5-30); Isaac blessed Jacob and Esau (Heb. 11:20); fled to Haran from Esau (Gen. 27:41-28:5); slept at Bethel (Gen. 28:10-22); married Leah and Rachel (Gen. 29:21-30); fled from Laban (Gen. 31:1-55); met angels at Mahanaim (Gen. 32:1-2); prepared to meet Esau (Gen. 32:3-23; 33:1-17); strove with God (Gen. 32:24-31); was called Israel (Gen. 32:28; 35:10; 1 Kgs. 18:31); God appeared to him (Gen. 35:9-15); buried Isaac his father (Gen. 35:27-9); made Joseph his favourite (Gen. 37:1-14); came to Egypt (Gen. 45:26-46:7); appeared before Pharaoh (Gen. 47:7-10); blessed Ephraim and Manasseh (Gen. 48:1-22; Heb. 11:21); prophesied about his sons (Gen. 49:1-28); died and was buried (Gen. 49:29-50:11; Acts 7:15-16); God loved Jacob (Mal. 1:2; Rom. 9:13).

H1c Jael
Wife of Heber the Kenite (Judg. 4:17; 5:6); killed Sisera with a tent peg (Judg. 4:18-22; 5:24-7).

H1d Jairus
A ruler of the synagogue whose daughter was dying (Mark 5:22; Luke 8:41).

H1e Jambres
An Egyptian magician who opposed Moses (2 Tim. 3:8).

H1f James [1]
Son of Zebedee and brother of John, called by Jesus (Matt. 4:21-2; Mark 1:19-20; Luke 5:10-11); one of the 12 apostles (Matt. 10:2; Mark 3:17; Luke 6:14; Acts 1:13); went up the mount of transfiguration (Matt. 17:1; Mark 9:2; Luke 9:28); asked to sit by Jesus in his glory (Mark 10:35-41); wanted fire to come down (Luke 9:54-5); killed by Herod (Acts 12:2).

H1g James [2]
Brother of Jesus (Matt. 13:55; Mark 6:3; Gal. 1:19); a leader in the church at Jerusalem (Acts 12:17; 21:18; 1 Cor. 15:7; Gal. 2:9); at the Council of Jerusalem (Acts 15:13-21); writer of the epistle (Jas. 1:1).

H1h James [3]
Son of Alphaeus and one of the 12 apostles (Matt. 10:3; Mark 3:18; Luke 6:15; Acts 1:13); son of Mary, James the less (Matt. 27:56; Mark 15:40; Luke 24:10).

H2 Jannes – Jehoash
H2a Jannes
An Egyptian magician who opposed Moses (2 Tim. 3:8).

H2b Japheth
Son of Noah (Gen. 5:32; 1 Chr. 1:4); helped Shem cover his father (Gen. 9:23-7).

H2c Jason
A Christian of Thessalonica (Acts 17:5-9); a kinsman of Paul who sent greetings (Rom. 16:21).

H2d Jeduthun
A Levite (1 Chr. 9:16); musician (1 Chr. 16:41-2; 25:6; 2 Chr. 5:12); psalms written for him (Ps. 39:t; 62:t; 77:t); the king's seer (2 Chr. 35:15).

H2e Jehoahaz [1] [Joahaz]
Son of Jehu who became king of Israel (2 Kgs. 10:35; 13:1-9); Hazael took cities from him (2 Kgs. 13:25).

H2f Jehoahaz [2] [Shallum]
Son of Josiah who became king of Judah (2 Kgs. 23:30-4; 1 Chr. 3:15; 2 Chr. 36:1-4; Jer. 22:11-17).

H2g Jehoash [1] [Joash]
Son of Ahaziah, kept secretly (2 Kgs. 11:2-3; 1 Chr. 3:11; 2 Chr. 22:11-12); crowned king of Judah (2 Kgs. 11:4-12:3; 2 Chr. 23:3-24:3); repaired the temple (2 Kgs. 12:4-7; 2 Chr. 24:4-8); forsook the Lord (2 Chr. 24:17-22); sent gifts to the king of Syria (2 Kgs. 12:17-18); defeated by the Syrians (2 Chr. 24:23); was assassinated (2 Kgs. 12:19-21; 2 Chr. 24:25-7).

H2h Jehoash [2]
Son of Jehoahaz and king of Israel (2 Kgs. 13:10-13); Amaziah sent messengers to him (2 Kgs. 14:8; 2 Chr. 25:17); captured Amaziah (2 Kgs. 14:13; 2 Chr. 25:23); died (2 Chr. 25:25).

H3 Jehoiachin – Jemimah
H3a Jehoiachin [Coniah, Jeconiah]
Son of Jehoiakim and king of Judah (2 Kgs. 24:6-9; 1 Chr. 3:16-17; 2 Chr. 36:8-9; Jer. 22:24; 37:1); taken into exile (2 Kgs. 24:10-15; 2 Chr. 36:10; Esther 2:6; Jer. 22:28; 24:1; 27:20; 29:2); freed from prison (2 Kgs. 25:27-30; Jer. 52:31-4); his return from exile prophesied (Jer. 28:4).

H3b Jehoiada
The priest who made Joash king (2 Kgs. 11:4-17; 2 Chr. 23:1-21); his wife brought up Joash (2 Chr. 22:11); instructed Joash (2 Kgs. 12:2); he advised the king and got wives for him (2 Chr. 24:2-3); collected money for the repair of the temple (2 Kgs. 12:7-9; 2 Chr. 24:6-14); died (2 Chr. 24:15-17).

H3c Jehoiakim [Eliakim]
Son of Josiah and king of Judah (2 Kgs. 23:34-24:6; 1 Chr. 3:15-16; 2 Chr. 36:4-8; Jer. 1:3); prophecy

concerning him (Jer. 22:18-19); killed Uriah the prophet (Jer. 26:20-3); burned Jeremiah's scroll (Jer. 36:20-31); given into the hand of Nebuchadnezzar (Dan. 1:2).

H3d Jehoram [Joram]
Son of Jehoshaphat and king of Judah (1 Kgs. 22:50; 2 Kgs. 1:17; 8:16-19; 12:18; 1 Chr. 3:11; 2 Chr. 21:1-7; Matt. 1:8); killed his brothers (2 Chr. 21:4); Edom revolted against his rule (2 Kgs. 8:20-2; 2 Chr. 21:8-10); was diseased in the bowels, as prophesied (2 Chr. 21:11-19); died (2 Chr. 21:18-20).

H3e Jehoshaphat
Son of Asa and king of Judah (1 Kgs. 15:24; 22:41-6; 2 Kgs. 12:18; 1 Chr. 3:10; 2 Chr. 17:1-7; 20:31-4; Matt. 1:8); went with Ahab to battle at Ramoth-gilead (1 Kgs. 22:2-33; 2 Chr. 18:1-19:3); went with Joram against Moab (2 Kgs. 3:7-14); routed enemies by God's help (2 Chr. 20:1-30); made ships (1 Kgs. 22:48-9; 2 Chr. 20:35-7); appointed teachers and judges (2 Chr. 19:4-11); died (1 Kgs. 22:50; 2 Chr. 21:1).

H3f Jehu
Son of Hanani, the prophet (1 Kgs. 16:1-4; 2 Chr. 19:2-3; 25:17); wrote a book of chronicles (2 Chr. 20:34).

H3g Jehu [2]
Son of Nimshi and king of Israel (1 Kgs. 19:16-17); anointed king (2 Kgs. 9:1-13); attacked Joram and Ahaziah at Jezreel (2 Kgs. 9:14-37; 2 Chr. 22:7-9); was punished for the bloodshed at Jezreel (Hos. 1:4); killed Ahab's descendants (2 Kgs. 10:1-17); killed the followers of Baal (2 Kgs. 10:18-28); continued in the sins of Jeroboam (2 Kgs. 10:20-31); the Lord's promise to him fulfilled (2 Kgs. 15:12); died (2 Kgs. 10:34-6).

H3h Jemimah
Daughter of Job (Job 42:14-15).

H4 Jephthah – Jesse
H4a Jephthah
Illegitimate son of Gilead (Judg. 11:1-3); sent by the Lord to deliver Israel (1 Sam. 12:11; Heb. 11:32); defeated the Ammonites (Judg. 11:5-33); sacrificed his daughter (Judg. 11:34-40); fought the men of Ephraim (Judg. 12:1-6); died (Judg. 12:7).

H4b Jeremiah
The prophet, son of Hilkiah, a priest from Anathoth (Jer. 1:1); Jeremiah of Anathoth (Jer. 29:27); composed a lament for Josiah (2 Chr. 35:25); stood and prophesied in the temple (Jer. 7:1-4); hid a linen waistband near the Euphrates (Jer. 13:1-11); went to the potter's house (Jer. 18:1-4); broke a potter's vessel (Jer. 19:1-15); was beaten and put in the stocks (Jer. 20:1-6); wore thongs and yoke-bars (Jer. 27:1-28:1); bought a field at Anathoth (Jer. 32:6-16); offered the Rechabites wine (Jer. 35:1-19); wrote his words on a scroll (Jer. 36:1-32); Zedekiah did not humble himself before him (2 Chr. 36:12); some said that Jesus was Jeremiah or one of the prophets (Matt. 16:14); Jeremiah the prophet (Dan. 9:2); his prophecy was fulfilled (2 Chr. 36:21, 22; Ezra 1:1; Matt. 2:17; 27:9).

H4c Jeroboam [1]
Rebelled against Solomon (2 Chr. 13:6); returned from Egypt (1 Kgs. 12:2; 2 Chr. 10:2); received prophecy from Ahijah (1 Kgs. 11:28-40; 12:15; 2 Chr. 10:15); was spokesman before Rehoboam (1 Kgs. 12:3, 12; 2 Chr. 10:3, 12); made king Rehoboam I over Israel (1 Kgs. 12:20; 2 Kgs. 17:21); invented false worship (1 Kgs. 12:25-33; 13:33-4); made war with Judah (1 Kgs. 14:30; 15:6; 2 Chr. 12:15; 13:3-20); Iddo prophesied about him (2 Chr. 9:29); received prophecy against him (1 Kgs. 13:1-9; 14:1-18); died (1 Kgs. 14:19-20; 2 Chr. 13:20); he made Israel to sin (2 Kgs. 23:15).

H4d Jeroboam [2]
Son of Joash and king Jeroboam II of Israel (2 Kgs. 13:13; 14:16, 23-9; Hos. 1:1); prophecy against him (Amos 7:9-11); Jeroboam will die by the sword (Amos 7:11).

H4e Jesse
Son of Obed and father of David (Ruth 4:17, 22; 1 Sam. 17:58; 1 Chr. 2:12-15; Ps. 72:20; Matt. 1:5-6; Luke 3:32; Acts 13:22); Samuel chose David from his sons (1 Sam. 16:1-13); Saul requested David from him (1 Sam. 16:18-22); sent David to the battle (1 Sam. 17:12-20); a rod will come from the stem of Jesse (Isa. 11:1); the root of Jesse (Isa. 11:10; Rom. 15:12).

H5 Jesus
H5a Jesus' nature
Son of Mary (Matt. 1:16, 25; Luke 1:31); son of David (Matt. 1:1; Luke 3:23-38); Son of God (Matt. 3:17; Mark 1:1; Luke 1:32; John 20:31); the only Son who is in the bosom of the Father (John 1:18); the Christ (Matt. 16:13-20; Mark 8:27-30; Luke 9:18-21; John 3:27-30; 20:31); the prophet Jesus, from Nazareth of Galilee (Matt. 21:11); Jesus the Galilean (Matt. 26:69); Jesus of Nazareth (Matt. 26:71; Luke 18:37; Acts 26:9); the Nazarene, Jesus (Mark 14:67).

H5b Jesus' life
Named by the angel (Matt. 1:21; Luke 1:31; 2:21); his birth (Matt. 1:18); circumcised (Luke 2:21); sought by the wise men (Matt. 2:1-12); grew (Luke 2:40, 52); stayed behind in Jerusalem (Luke 2:41-51); baptised by John (Matt. 3:13-17; Mark 1:9-11; Luke 3:21-2; John 1:29-34); tempted in the wilderness (Matt. 4:1-11; Mark 1:12-13; Luke 4:1-13); transfigured (Matt. 17:1-13; Mark 9:1-13; Luke 9:28-36); choosing 12 apostles (Luke 6:13-16); paying tax (Matt. 17:24-7); receiving children (Matt. 19:13-15; Mark 10:13-16; Luke 18:15-17); entering Jerusalem (Matt. 21:1-11; Mark 11:1-11; Luke 19:28-45; John 12:12-15); sending out disciples (Matt. 10:5; 28:18-20; Mark 6:7; 16:15-17; Luke 9:1-6; 10:1); driving traders from the temple (Matt. 21:12-13; Mark 11:15-19; Luke 19:45-6; John 2:13-24); anointed with ointment (Matt. 26:6-13; Mark 14:3-9; John 12:1-8); washing the disciples' feet (John 13:1-20); keeping passover at the last supper (Matt. 26:20-9; Mark 14:12-25; Luke 22:7-23); dealing with the woman caught in adultery (John 8:2-11).

H5c Latter end of Jesus' life
Arrested in the garden of Gethsemane (Matt. 26:45-56; Mark 14:40-50; Luke 22:47-53; John 18:1-12); before the high priest (Matt. 26:57-68; Mark 14:53-65; Luke 22:54-71; John 18:13, 19-24); before Pilate (Matt. 27:1-2, 11-26; Mark 15:1-15; Luke 23:1-6, 11-25; John 18:28-19:15); before Herod (Luke 23:7-12); crucified (Matt. 27:27-66; Mark 15:16-47; Luke 23:26-53; John 19:16-42); risen from the dead (Matt. 28:5-10, 16-17; Mark 16:6-14; Luke 24:1-53; John 20:1-29); final instructions before his ascension (Acts 1:4-8); his ascension (Mark 16:19; Acts 1:9-11).

H5d Jesus' miracles
Stilling wind and sea (Matt. 8:23-7; Mark 4:35-41); walking on water (Mark 6:47-52; John 6:19-21); miraculous catch of fish (Luke 5:3-10; John 21:4-14); turning water into wine (John 2:1-11); feeding crowds (Matt. 14:13-21; 15:32-9; Mark 6:30-44; 8:1-10; Luke 9:10-17; John 6:3-15); cursing the fig tree (Matt. 21:18-22; Mark 11:12-14, 20-5); healing (Matt. 4:23-5; 8:28-34; 9:1-8, 18-36; 12:9-22; 14:34-6; 15:21-31; 17:14-18; 19:1-2; 20:29-34; 21:14; Mark 1:21-34; 3:1-12; 5:1-43; 6:5-6, 53-6; 7:24-37; 8:22-6; 9:14-29; 10:46-52; Luke 4:33-41; 5:12-15, 17-26; 6:6-11, 17-19; 7:1-23; 8:26-56; 9:37-43; 11:14; 13:10-17; 14:1-6; 17:11-19; 18:35-43; John 4:46-5:9; 9:1-12; 11:4-44).

H6 Jethro – Job
H6a Jethro [Reuel]
Moses' father-in-law (Exod. 2:18-21; Num. 10:29); priest of Midian (Exod. 2:16-21; 18:1-12).

H6b Jezebel
Daughter of Ethbaal king of the Sidonians and wife of Ahab (1 Kgs. 16:31); killed the prophets of the Lord (1 Kgs. 18:4, 13; 2 Kgs. 9:7); false prophets ate at her table (1 Kgs. 18:19); threatened Elijah (1 Kgs. 19:1-2); her harlotries and sorceries (2 Kgs. 9:22); encouraged Ahab to do evil (1 Kgs. 21:5-15, 25); painted her eyes (2 Kgs. 9:30); eaten by dogs (1 Kgs. 21:23; 2 Kgs. 9:10, 33-7); you tolerate that woman Jezebel (Rev. 2:20).

H6c Joab
Son of Zeruiah (2 Sam. 2:13); Asahel was his brother (2 Sam. 23:24); Naharai was his armour-bearer (2 Sam. 23:37; 1 Chr. 11:39); first to invade Jerusalem (1 Chr. 11:6); repaired Jerusalem (1 Chr. 11:8); killed Abner (2 Sam. 3:22-31; 1 Kgs. 2:5); in charge of the army (2 Sam. 8:16; 20:23; 1 Kgs. 11:15; 1 Chr. 18:15; 27:34); arranged Uriah's death (2 Sam. 11:14-25); engineered Absalom's recall (2 Sam. 14:1-33); killed Absalom (2 Sam. 18:10-16); sent a messenger to David (2 Sam. 18:20-3); rebuked David for mourning Absalom (2 Sam. 19:1-7); was deposed in favour of Amasa (2 Sam. 19:13); killed Amasa (2 Sam. 20:8-13; 1 Kgs. 2:5); pursued Bichri (2 Sam. 20:15-22); killed the Edomites (1 Kgs. 11:15-16; Ps. 60:t); dedicated gifts to the Lord (1 Chr. 26:28); pursued Sheba (2 Sam. 20:7); was commanded to number the people (2 Sam. 24:2-9; 1 Chr. 21:2-6; 27:24); supported Adonijah (1 Kgs. 1:7, 19, 25, 41; 2:22); sought sanctuary in the tabernacle and was killed there (1 Kgs. 2:28-35).

H6d Joanna
Wife of Chuza, Herod's steward (Luke 8:3; 24:10).

H6e Joash [1]
The Abiezrite and father of Gideon (Judg. 6:11); refused to deliver up Gideon (Judg. 6:30-1).

H6f Joash [2]
Son of King Ahab of Israel (1 Kgs. 22:26; 2 Chr. 18:25); visited Elisha on his death bed (2 Kgs. 13:14); died (2 Kgs. 13:13).

H6g Job
A man living in the land of Uz (Job 1:1-5); feared God (Job 1:8-2:10); his speeches (Job 3:2-26; 6:1-7:21; 9:1-10:22; 12:1-14:2; 16:1-17:1; 19:1-29; 21:1-34; 23:1-24:2; 27:1-28:28; 29:1-31:40); justified himself (Job 32:1-4); answered by God (Job 38:1; 40:1-6); answered the Lord (Job 40:3); restored (Job 42:1-16); died (Job 42:17); Noah, Daniel and Job could only deliver themselves (Ezek. 14:14, 20); you have heard of the patience of Job (Jas. 5:11).

H7 Joel – Joram
H7a Joel
The prophet, son of Pethuel (Joel 1:1; Acts 2:16).

H7b John [1]
Son of Zebedee, called by Jesus (Matt. 4:21-2; Mark 1:19-20; Luke 5:10-11); one of the 12 apostles (Matt. 10:2; Mark 3:17; Luke 6:14; Acts 1:13); present at the transfiguration (Matt. 17:1; Mark 9:2; Luke 9:28); forbade an exorcist (Mark 9:38; Luke 9:49); wanted fire to come down from heaven (Luke 9:54); wanted to sit at Jesus' side in glory (Mark 10:35-41); the disciple whom Jesus loved (John 13:23-5; 19:26; 20:2; 21:7, 20); bore witness (John 21:24); healed the lame man (Acts 3:1-11); before the council (Acts 4:13-19); was sent to Samaria (Acts 8:14-17); recognised Paul's gift (Gal. 2:9); John to the seven churches (Rev. 1:4); exiled to Patmos (Rev. 1:9).

H7c John [2] [John the Baptist]
Son of Zechariah by Elizabeth (Luke 1:13-17, 57-63); preaching and baptising in the wilderness (Matt. 3:1-12;

Mark 1:4-8; Luke 3:2-18; John 3:23-4; 4:1; 10:40; Acts 1:5, 22; 10:37; 11:16; 13:24-5; 19:3-4); John did no sign, but all he said about this man was true (John 10:41); baptised Jesus (Matt. 3:13-15; Mark 1:9; Luke 3:21); arrested (Matt. 4:12; Mark 1:14; Luke 3:19-20); questions about his disciples fasting (Matt. 9:14; Mark 2:18; Luke 5:33); taught his disciples to pray (Luke 11:1); sent his disciples to Jesus (Matt. 11:2-6; Luke 7:18-23); Jesus' view of John (Matt. 11:7-19; 17:13; Mark 11:30-3; Luke 7:24-35; 20:4-8); the baptism of John, was it from heaven or from men? (Matt. 21:25); some thought Jesus was John (Matt. 14:2; 16:14; Mark 6:14-16; 8:28; Luke 9:7, 19); they all hold John to be a prophet (Matt. 21:26; Luke 20:6); John came to you in the way of righteousness (Matt. 21:32); Apollos knew only the baptism of John (Acts 18:25); beheaded (Matt. 14:3-12; Mark 6:16-29; Luke 9:9).

H7d Jonah
Son of Amittai, the prophet (2 Kgs. 14:25; Jonah 1:1); fled to Tarshish (Jonah 1:3-15); swallowed by a big fish (Jonah 1:17-2:10); preached in Nineveh (Jonah 3:1-4); sulked (Jonah 4:1-11); no sign will be given except the sign of the prophet Jonah (Matt. 12:39; 16:4; Luke 11:29); Nineveh repented at the preaching of Jonah (Matt. 12:41; Luke 11:32).

H7e Jonathan [1]
Son of King Saul (1 Sam. 13:2; 1 Chr. 8:33-4); defeated the Philistines (1 Sam. 14:1-17); ate honey (1 Sam. 14:27-30); loved David (1 Sam. 18:1-4); warned David about Saul (1 Sam. 19:1-7; 20:1-42); strengthened David's hand in God (1 Sam. 23:16-18); killed by the Philistines (1 Sam. 31:2; 2 Sam. 1:4-5; 1 Chr. 10:2); mourned by David (2 Sam. 1:12, 17-26); buried by David (2 Sam. 21:12-14).

H7f Jonathan [2]
Son of Abiathar the high priest (2 Sam. 15:27, 36); took David news secretly (2 Sam. 17:17-21); gave Adonijah news of Solomon's kingship (1 Kgs. 1:42-3).

H7g Joram
Son of Ahab and king of Israel (2 Kgs. 1:17; 3:1; 8:16, 25; 9:29); went with Jehoshaphat to fight Moab (2 Kgs. 3:6-27); went with Ahaziah to fight Hazael (2 Kgs. 8:28-9; 2 Chr. 22:5-6); Jehu conspired against him (2 Kgs. 9:14-24; 2 Chr. 22:7).

H8 Joseph – Josiah
H8a Joseph [1] [Zaphenath-paneah]
Son of Jacob by Rachel (Gen. 30:23-5; 1 Chr. 2:2); at 17, Jacob's favourite son (Gen. 37:2-4); dreamed of supremacy (Gen. 37:5-11); sold into Egypt by his brothers (Gen. 37:13-36; Ps. 105:17-22; Acts 7:9); accused by Potiphar's wife (Gen. 39:1-19); imprisoned (Gen. 39:20-3); interpreted the dreams of Pharaoh's butler and baker (Gen. 40:4-23; 41:12-13); interpreted Pharaoh's dream (Gen. 41:14-36); was over all Egypt (Gen. 41:38-57; 47:13-26; Acts 7:10); called Zaphenath-paneah by Pharaoh (Gen. 41:45); made himself known to his brothers (Gen. 45:1-28; Acts 7:13); received his father and brothers (Gen. 46:28-34; Acts 7:14); brought his brothers and father before Pharaoh (Gen. 47:1-12); took Ephraim and Manasseh to Jacob (Gen. 48:1-22; Heb. 11:21); Jacob gave him a field (John 4:5); received prophecy (Gen. 49:22-6); buried his father (Gen. 47:29-31; 50:1-14); reassured his brothers (Gen. 50:15-21); died (Gen. 50:22-6; Exod. 1:6); his bones were taken to the promised land (Exod. 13:19; Josh. 24:32; Heb. 11:22).

H8b Joseph [2]
Husband of Mary (Matt. 1:16; Luke 1:27); a righteous man (Matt. 1:19); visited by an angel (Matt. 2:13-14, 19-23); went to Bethlehem (Luke 2:4); with Mary and the baby (Luke 2:16); supposedly Jesus' father (Luke

3:23; John 1:45; 6:42); is not this Joseph's son? (Luke 4:22).

H8c Joseph [3] [Joses]
Brother of Jesus (Matt. 13:55; Mark 6:3).

H8d Joseph [4] [Joses]
Son of Mary and brother of James the younger (Matt. 27:56; Mark 15:40, 47).

H8e Joseph [5]
A rich man of Arimathea (Matt. 27:57-60; Mark 15:43-5; Luke 23:50-3; John 19:38-42).

H8f Joseph [6] [Barsabbas] [Justus]
Barsabbas surnamed Justus (Acts 1:23).

H8g Joshua [1] [Hoshea]
The son of Nun and Moses' servant (Exod. 33:11; Num. 11:28); originally called Hoshea (Num. 13:16); one of the 12 spies (Num. 13:8; 14:6-10); went up Sinai with Moses (Exod. 24:13; 32:17); led the fight against Amalek (Exod. 17:9-14); replaced Moses as leader (Num. 27:18-23; Deut. 1:38); led the people over Jordan (Josh. 1:10-18; 3:1-4:24); sent out spies (Josh. 2:1, 23-4); conquered Jericho (Josh. 5:13-6:21; 1 Kgs. 16:34); conquered Ai after initial setback (Josh. 7:2-8:29); read the law of Moses (Josh. 8:30-5); was deceived by the Gibeonites (Josh. 9:6-27); defeated the kings of the land (Josh. 10:1-12:2); was old (Josh. 13:1; 23:1); received his inheritance (Josh. 19:49-50); encouraged the people to follow the Lord (Josh. 23:2-24:2); died (Josh. 24:29-30); Israel served the Lord all his days (Josh. 24:31; Judg. 2:6-7); did not conquer some nations (Judg. 2:21, 23); did not give the people true rest (Heb. 4:8).

H8h Joshua [2] [Jeshua]
Son of Jehozadak [Jozadak] and high priest (Ezra 3:2; Neh. 12:1; Hag. 1:1); accused by Satan (Zech. 3:1-9); crowned (Zech. 6:12-14).

H8i Josiah
Son of Amon and king of Judah (2 Kgs. 21:24-22:2; 1 Chr. 3:14; 2 Chr. 33:25-34:2; Jer. 25:3; Matt. 1:10); his coming was prophesied (1 Kgs. 13:2); found the book of the law (2 Kgs. 22:3-20; 2 Chr. 34:14-32); destroyed tokens of false religion (2 Kgs. 23:1-20, 24-5; 2 Chr. 34:3-7, 33); kept passover (2 Kgs. 23:21-3; 2 Chr. 35:1-19); was killed by Pharaoh Neco (2 Kgs. 23:28-30; 2 Chr. 35:20-7).

H9 Jotham – Justus
H9a Jotham [1]
Youngest son of Gideon [Jerubbaal] (Judg. 9:5); shouted a parable to the men of Shechem (Judg. 9:7-21); his curse came on the men of Shechem (Judg. 9:57).

H9b Jotham [2]
Son of King Uzziah who governed as regent (2 Kgs. 15:5; 1 Chr. 3:12; 2 Chr. 26:21; Matt. 1:9); became king of Judah (2 Kgs. 15:7, 32-7; 2 Chr. 26:23-27:8); died (2 Kgs. 15:38; 2 Chr. 27:9).

H9c Judah
Son of Jacob by Leah (Gen. 29:35; 35:23; 1 Chr. 2:1; Matt. 1:2; Luke 3:33); suggested selling Joseph (Gen. 37:26-7); bore children by Tamar, his daughter-in-law (Gen. 38:1-26); became surety for Benjamin (Gen. 43:3-10; 44:14-34); was strong among his brethren (1 Chr. 5:2); received prophecy (Gen. 49:8-12).

H9d Judas [1] [Judas Iscariot]
The apostle who betrayed Jesus (Matt. 10:4; Mark 3:19; Luke 6:16; John 6:71; 13:2); stole from the money box (John 12:4-6); received money from the chief priests (Matt. 26:14-16; Mark 14:10-11); Satan entered him (Luke 22:3); asked who the betrayer was (Matt. 26:25); received the morsel from Jesus (John 13:26-31); betrayed Jesus (Matt. 26:47-9; Mark 14:43-5; Luke 22:47-8; John 18:2-5); hanged himself (Matt. 27:3-5); his

bowels gushed out (Acts 1:18); he was replaced (Acts 1:16-20).

H9e Judas [2] [Jude]
Brother of Jesus (Matt. 13:55; Mark 6:3); brother of James (Jude 1).

H9f Judas [3] [Barsabbas]
Named Barsabbas (Acts 15:22, 27); a prophet who exhorted the people (Acts 15:32).

H9g Judas [4] [Judas of Galilee]
He rose up in the days of the census (Acts 5:37).

H9h Justus [1] [Titius Justus]
A worshipper of God (Acts 18:7).

H9i Justus [2] [Jesus Justus]
Jesus called Justus (Col. 4:11).

I Individuals K – M

I1 Keren-happuch – Korah

I1a Keren-happuch
Daughter of Job (Job 42:14-15).

I1b Keturah
Wife of Abraham (Gen. 25:1-4; 1 Chr. 1:32-3).

I1c Keziah
Daughter of Job (Job 42:14-15).

I1d Kish
Son of Abiel and father of Saul of Benjamin (1 Sam. 9:1-2); his asses were lost (1 Sam. 9:3).

I1e Korah
Rebelled against Moses (Num. 16:1-49; 26:9-11; 27:3); swallowed up by the ground (Num. 16:24-33); they perish in Korah's rebellion (Jude 11).

I2 Laban – Lo-ammi

I2a Laban
Brother of Rebekah and son of Bethuel (Gen. 25:20; 28:5); received Abraham's servant (Gen. 24:29-32, 50); Jacob fled to him (Gen. 27:43); made Jacob serve for Leah and Rachel as wives (Gen. 29:15-30; 46:18, 25); let Jacob work for the mottled animals (Gen. 30:25-31:1); was outwitted by Jacob who fled (Gen. 31:19-24); agreed to let Jacob go (Gen. 31:25-55).

I2b Lamech
Son of Methushael (Gen. 4:18); took two wives, Adah and Zillah (Gen. 4:19-22); boasted of killing a man (Gen. 4:23); Lamech will be avenged seventy-sevenfold (Gen. 4:24).

I2c Lazarus [1]
A beggar in a parable (Luke 16:20-5).

I2d Lazarus [2]
Brother of Martha and Mary of Bethany (John 11:1); Jesus raised him from the dead (John 11:3-44); in danger of death (John 12:9-11); loved by Jesus (John 11:5).

I2e Leah
Laban's elder daughter (Gen. 29:16-17); married to Jacob (Gen. 29:23-5); unloved (Gen. 29:30-1); bore sons (Gen. 29:31-5; 30:14-20; 35:23; 46:15); gave her maid Zilpah to Jacob (Gen. 30:9-13); buried in the field of Ephron (Gen. 49:31).

I2f Levi
Son of Jacob by Leah (Gen. 29:34; 1 Chr. 2:1); with Simeon, massacred the Shechemites (Gen. 34:25-31; 49:5-7); father of Gershon, Kohath and Merari (Exod. 6:16; Num. 3:17; 1 Chr. 6:1); Levi, who receives tithes, paid tithes (Heb. 7:9-10).

I2g Lo-ammi
'Not my people', son of Hosea by Gomer (Hos. 1:9).

I3 Lois – Lysanias

I3a Lois
Grandmother of Timothy and mother of Eunice (2 Tim. 1:5).

I3b Lo-ruhamah
'Not pitied', son of Hosea by Gomer (Hos. 1:6, 8).

I3c Lot
Son of Haran (Gen. 11:27); went with Abraham (Gen. 11:31); separated from Abraham (Gen. 13:5-14); captured by the kings (Gen. 14:12); received the angels (Gen. 19:1-10); fled from Sodom (Gen. 19:12-29); was seduced by his daughters (Gen. 19:30-6); as in the days when Lot went out of Sodom (Luke 17:28-9); remember Lot's wife (Luke 17:32); God rescued righteous Lot (2 Pet. 2:7).

I3d Luke
The beloved physician (Col. 4:14); the only one with Paul (2 Tim. 4:11); Paul's fellow-worker (Philem. 24).

I3e Lydia
A seller of purple goods from Thyatira (Acts 16:14-15); they visited Lydia (Acts 16:40).

I3f Lysanias
Tetrarch of Abilene (Luke 3:1).

I4 Maacah – Manasseh

I4a Maacah [Abishalom] [Micaiah]
Daughter of Abishalom, wife of Rehoboam and mother of Abijah (1 Kgs. 15:2; 2 Chr. 11:20-2); [grand]mother of Asa (1 Kgs. 15:10);
deposed from being queen mother (1 Kgs. 15:13; 2 Chr. 15:16).

I4b Magog
With Gog, symbolic leader of the forces against Christ (Rev. 20:8).

I4c Maher-shalal-hash-baz
'The spoil speeds, the prey hastens', son of Isaiah (Isa. 8:1, 3).

I4d Mahlon
Son of Elimelech by Naomi (Ruth 1:2); husband of Ruth (Ruth 4:10); died (Ruth 1:5); all his possessions bought by Boaz (Ruth 4:9).

I4e Malachi
The prophet (Mal. 1:1).

I4f Malchus
Slave of the high priest (John 18:10).

I4g Mamre
A friend of Abraham (Gen. 14:13, 24); the oaks of Mamre (Gen. 13:17; 18:1).

I4h Manasseh [1]
Joseph's firstborn son (Gen. 41:51; 46:20; Num. 26:28-34; Josh. 17:2); made second to Ephraim (Gen. 48:1-20); Ephraim and Manasseh are mine as Reuben and Simeon are (Gen. 48:5); Manasseh in his left hand toward Israel's right hand (Gen. 48:13-14).

I4i Manasseh [2]
Son of Hezekiah and evil king of Judah (2 Kgs. 20:21; 21:1-16; 1 Chr. 3:13; 2 Chr. 32:33-33:9; Jer. 15:4; Matt. 1:10); humbled himself when exiled to Babylon for a time (2 Chr. 33:10-19, 23); died (2 Kgs. 21:17-18; 2 Chr. 33:20).

I5 Manoah – Mary

I5a Manoah
A Danite from Zorah, father of Samson (Judg. 13:2; 16:31); encountered the angel (Judg. 13:8-22).

I5b Mark [John Mark]
Son of Mary (Acts 12:12); cousin of Barnabas (Col. 4:10); taken by Barnabas and Paul to Antioch (Acts 12:25); left Paul and Barnabas and went home to Jerusalem (Acts 13:13); Barnabas separated from Paul over Mark (Acts 15:37-40); Paul found him useful and wanted him (2 Tim. 4:11); Paul's fellow-worker (Philem. 24); my son Mark (1 Pet. 5:13).

I5c Martha
Served Jesus with anxiety, unlike her sister Mary (Luke 10:38-42); sister of Lazarus and Mary (John 11:1, 19); came to seek Jesus about Lazarus (John 11:20-39); served Jesus with a meal (John 12:2); loved by Jesus (John 11:5).

15d Mary [1]
Wife of Joseph and mother of Jesus (Matt. 1:16); visited by the angel Gabriel (Luke 1:26-38); visited Elizabeth (Luke 1:39-56); discovered to be pregnant when engaged to Joseph (Matt. 1:18); Mary, engaged to Joseph, went to be enrolled (Luke 2:5); gave birth in Bethlehem (Luke 2:4-7); married by Joseph (Matt. 1:20-5); the child Jesus with his mother (Matt. 2:11; Luke 2:16); she pondered on these things (Luke 2:19); Simeon prophesied to her (Luke 2:34-5); Jesus' mother, brothers and sisters (Matt. 13:55-6); Mary at the wedding at Cana in Galilee (John 2:1-5); his mother was standing by his cross (John 19:25-6).

15e Mary [2]
Mother of James and Joseph [Joses] (Matt. 27:56, 61; 28:1; Mark 15:40, 47; 16:1; Luke 24:10); wife of Clopas (John 19:25).

15f Mary [3]
Magdalene [of Magdala] (Matt. 27:56, 61; 28:1; Mark 15:40, 47; 16:1; Luke 24:10; John 19:25; 20:1); Jesus had cast out seven demons from her (Mark 16:9; Luke 8:2); Jesus appeared to her (Mark 16:9; John 20:11-18).

15g Mary [4]
Sister of Lazarus and Martha in Bethany (John 11:1, 19-20); sat at Jesus' feet and listened (Luke 10:39-42); went out to Jesus (John 11:28-32, 45); anointed the Lord with ointment and wiped his feet with her hair (John 11:2; 12:3).

15h Mary [5]
Mother of John Mark (Acts 12:12).

15i Mary [6]
Worked hard among the Romans (Rom. 16:6).

16 Mattan – Merab

16a Mattan
Priest of Baal, killed by Jehoiada (2 Kgs. 11:18; 2 Chr. 23:17).

16b Matthew [Levi]
Son of Alphaeus and a tax collector called by Jesus (Matt. 9:9; Mark 2:14; Luke 5:27-8); made a feast for Jesus (Luke 5:29); one of the 12 apostles (Matt. 10:3; Mark 3:18; Luke 6:15; Acts 1:13).

16c Matthias
Chosen to fill Judas' place in the 12 apostles (Acts 1:23-6).

16d Medad
Prophesied in the camp (Num. 11:26-7).

16e Melchizedek
King of Salem who blessed Abraham (Gen. 14:18-20; Heb. 7:1-10); a priest for ever, after his order (Ps. 110:4; Heb. 5:6, 10; 6:20; 7:17); what need was there for another priest after the order of Melchizedek? (Heb. 7:11); if another priest arises in his likeness (Heb. 7:15).

16f Menahem
Son of Gadi who reigned over Israel (2 Kgs. 15:14-21); died (2 Kgs. 15:22).

16g Mephibosheth [Merib-baal]
Son of Jonathan, crippled through a fall (2 Sam. 4:4; 9:3; 1 Chr. 8:34; 9:40); restored to eat at David's table (2 Sam. 9:5-13); slandered by his servant Ziba (2 Sam. 16:1-4; 19:24-30); spared by David (2 Sam. 21:7).

16h Merab
Saul's elder daughter (1 Sam. 14:49); offered to David as wife then married to Adriel (1 Sam. 18:17-19); her five sons handed over to the Gibeonites (2 Sam. 21:8).

17 Mesha – Mordecai

17a Mesha
King of Moab and a sheep breeder (2 Kgs. 3:4).

17b Meshach [Mishael]
An exile, called Meshach by the king (Dan. 1:6-7); ate vegetables, with Daniel (Dan. 1:11-16); outstanding in wisdom (Dan. 1:17-19); promoted on Daniel's request

(Dan. 2:49); refused to worship the image (Dan. 3:12-18); thrown into the fiery furnace (Dan. 3:19-30); came out of the fire (Dan. 3:26); the king promoted Shadrach, Meshach and Abednego in the province of Babylon (Dan. 3:30).

17c Methuselah
Son of Enoch and father of Lamech (Gen. 5:21-7; 1 Chr. 1:3; Luke 3:37).

17d Micah [1]
An Ephraimite and an idolater (Judg. 17:1-6); installed a Levite as his priest (Judg. 17:8-13); visited by Danites (Judg. 18:2-4); lost his gods and priest to the Danites (Judg. 18:13-31).

17e Micah [2]
The prophet of Moresheth (Jer. 26:18; Mic. 1:1).

17f Micaiah
The prophet, son of Imlah (1 Kgs. 22:8-9, 13-28; 2 Chr. 17:7; 18:7-8, 12-27).

17g Michal
Saul's younger daughter (1 Sam. 14:49); loved David (1 Sam. 18:20); married David (1 Sam. 18:27-8); helped David escape (1 Sam. 19:11-17); given as wife to Palti (1 Sam. 25:44); was returned to David (2 Sam. 3:13-16); despised David (2 Sam. 6:16, 20-3; 1 Chr. 15:29).

17h Miriam
Daughter of Amram by Jochebed and sister of Aaron and Moses (Exod. 15:20-1; Num. 26:59; 1 Chr. 6:3; Mic. 6:4); watched Moses in the reeds (Exod. 2:4-8); spoke against Moses (Num. 12:1-5); became leprous (Num. 12:10-15; Deut. 24:9); died (Num. 20:1).

17i Mnason
An early disciple of Cyprus (Acts 21:16).

17j Mordecai
Son of Jair of Benjamin, exiled to Susa (Esther 2:5-6); had adopted Esther (Esther 2:7, 15); sought to know how Esther fared (Esther 2:10-11); reported the plot against King Ahasuerus (Esther 2:19-22; 6:2); would not bow before Haman (Esther 3:2-6; 5:9); mourned in sackcloth and ashes (Esther 4:1-4); told Esther of Haman's plot (Esther 4:5-17); his death plotted by Haman (Esther 5:13-14; 7:9-10); honoured by the king at the hands of Haman (Esther 6:3-13); given authority by the king (Esther 8:1-2, 7-9, 15; 9:3-4; 10:2-3); wrote to the Jews (Esther 9:20-31).

18 Moses

18a Moses' life
Son of Amram by Jochebed (Exod. 6:20; Num. 26:59; 1 Chr. 6:3; 23:13); was hidden (Exod. 2:2-9; Heb. 11:23); adopted by Pharaoh's daughter (Exod. 2:10; Acts 7:20-2; Heb. 11:24-6); killed an Egyptian (Exod. 2:11-14; Acts 7:23-8); fled to Midian (Exod. 2:15-22; Acts 7:29); met God at the burning bush (Exod. 3:1-4:17; Acts 7:30-4); was appointed to bring Israel out of Egypt (1 Sam. 12:6, 8; Ps. 105:26; Mic. 6:4; Acts 7:35-6); dealt with Pharaoh (Exod. 5:1-11:1); Moses and Aaron did all these wonders before Pharaoh (Ps. 78:11; Heb. 11:10); Jannes and Jambres withstood him (2 Tim. 3:8); struck the rock (Exod. 17:2-7; Num. 20:6-12); spoke rash words (Ps. 106:32-3); held up the rod of God while Israel fought Amalek (Exod. 17:9-16); went up Sinai (Exod. 19:3-25; 24:1-18; 34:1-28); erected the tabernacle (Exod. 40:18); spoken against by Miriam and Aaron (Num. 12:1); stood in the breach (Ps. 106:23); his face shone (Exod. 34:29-35; 2 Cor. 3:7-13); men were jealous of him (Ps. 106:16); put a bronze serpent on a pole (Num. 21:8-9; 2 Kgs. 18:4; John 3:14); saw the land from the top of Pisgah (Deut. 34:1-5); died (Deut. 34:5; Josh. 1:1-2).

18b Moses' significance
Moses the man of God (Deut. 33:1); he was humble (Num. 12:3); he was very great in the land of Egypt (Exod. 11:3); he spoke with God face to face (Num.

12:6-8; Deut. 34:10); God made known his ways to him (Ps. 103:7); he was one of God's priests (Ps. 99:6); he appeared at the transfiguration (Matt. 17:3-4; Mark 9:4-5; Luke 9:30-3); our fathers were all baptised into Moses in the cloud and the sea (1 Cor. 10:2); we are disciples of Moses (John 9:28); Moses was instructed by God when he was about to erect the tabernacle (Heb. 8:5); we know that God has spoken to Moses (John 9:29); Moses sprinkled the people with blood (Heb. 9:19); Moses was faithful in all God's house (Heb. 3:2); as a servant (Heb. 3:5); the scribes and Pharisees sit on Moses' seat (Matt. 23:2); death reigned from Adam to Moses (Rom. 5:14); Michael disputed with the devil about the body of Moses (Jude 9); they sang the song of Moses the slave of God (Rev. 15:3); though Moses and Samuel stood before me (Jer. 15:1); Jesus is counted worthy of more honour than Moses (Heb. 3:3).

18c Moses' writings
The law of Moses (Mal. 4:4; Luke 2:22; 1 Cor. 9:9; Heb. 10:28); did not Moses give you the law? (John 7:19); the law was given through Moses (John 1:17); Moses gave you circumcision (John 7:22); unless you are circumcised according to the custom of Moses you cannot be saved (Acts 15:1); circumcision is not from Moses but from the fathers (John 7:22); in the law Moses commanded us to stone such women (John 8:5); present the offering Moses commanded (Matt. 8:4; Mark 1:44; Luke 5:14); why did Moses command us to give her a certificate of divorce? (Matt. 19:7-8); beginning with Moses and all the prophets (Luke 24:27); everything written about me in the law of Moses and the prophets and the psalms (Luke 24:44); we have found him of whom Moses wrote in the law, Jesus of Nazareth (John 1:45); Moses accuses you, on whom you set your hope (John 5:45); Moses said, 'The Lord will raise up a prophet' (Acts 3:22); we have heard him speak blasphemy against Moses and against God (Acts 6:11); Jesus will alter the customs Moses handed down to us (Acts 6:14); Moses has in every city those who preach him (Acts 15:21); saying nothing but what the prophets and Moses said would come to pass (Acts 26:22).

J Individuals N – O
J1 Naaman – Naomi
J1a Naaman
Commander of the army of Syria and a leper (2 Kgs. 5:1); went to Elisha to be healed (2 Kgs. 5:2-14); gave gifts to Gehazi (2 Kgs. 5:15-27); Naaman the Syrian (Luke 4:27).
J1b Nabal
A Calebite of Maon with business in Carmel (1 Sam. 25:2-3); husband of Abigail (1 Sam. 27:3; 30:5; 2 Sam. 2:2; 3:3); refused to recompense David (1 Sam. 25:4-34); died (1 Sam. 25:36-9).
J1c Naboth
Refused to let Ahab have his vineyard (1 Kgs. 21:1-4); died through Jezebel's plan (1 Kgs. 21:5-16).
J1d Nadab
Son of Aaron by Elisheba (Exod. 6:23; 28:1; Num. 3:2; 1 Chr. 6:3; 24:1); went up to see the God of Israel (Exod. 24:1, 9); offered unholy fire and died (Lev. 10:1-2; Num. 3:4; 26:61; 1 Chr. 24:2).
J1e Nahash
King of the Ammonites (1 Sam. 11:1; 12:12); wanted to gouge out the eyes of the men of Jabesh (1 Sam. 11:2); died, and David dealt kindly with his son Hanun (2 Sam. 10:1-2; 1 Chr. 19:1-2).
J1f Nahum
The prophet from Elkosh (Nahum 1:1).

J1g Naomi
Wife of Elimelech (Ruth 1:2-3); returned to Bethlehem with Ruth (Ruth 1:6-22; 2:6); advised Ruth about Boaz (Ruth 2:18-3:6).
J2 Naphtali – Nehemiah
J2a Naphtali
Son of Jacob by Bilhah (Gen. 30:8; 1 Chr. 2:2); received prophecy (Gen. 49:21).
J2b Nathan
Prophesied to David about the temple (2 Sam. 7:2-17; 1 Chr. 17:1-15); rebuked David over Bathsheba (2 Sam. 12:1-15; Ps. 51:t); brought God's message about Solomon (2 Sam. 12:25); cooperated with Bathsheba to depose Adonijah (1 Kgs. 1:10-14, 22-7); participated in Solomon's crowning (1 Kgs. 1:32-45); gave commandment about the temple worship (2 Chr. 29:25); wrote a book (1 Chr. 29:29; 2 Chr. 9:29).
J2c Nathanael
Brought to Jesus by Philip (John 1:45-51); from Cana in Galilee (John 21:2).
J2d Nebuchadnezzar [Nebuchadrezzar]
King of Babylon (2 Kgs. 24:1; 25:8); attacked Judah and Jerusalem (2 Kgs. 24:10-11; Jer. 21:2; Dan. 1:1); attacked the kingdoms (Jer. 46:2, 13; 49:28-30; Ezek. 29:18); took Judah into exile (1 Chr. 6:15; 2 Chr. 36:6, 10; Ezra 2:1; 5:12; Neh. 7:6; Esther 2:6; Jer. 24:1; 29:1; 52:28); carried away the vessels of the temple (2 Chr. 36:7; Ezra 1:7; 5:14; 6:5; Jer. 27:19-22; 28:3; Dan. 5:2); made Zedekiah king (Jer. 37:1); left people in the land (2 Kgs. 25:22); gave instructions concerning Jeremiah (Jer. 39:11); he would set his throne in Tahpanhes (Jer. 43:10); his yoke would be broken (Jer. 28:11); Daniel and his friends were brought before him (Dan. 1:18); his dream interpreted by Daniel (Dan. 2:1-49); the Most High gave him the kingdom (Dan. 5:18); humbled and made like a beast (Dan. 4:1-37).
J2e Nebuzaradan
The captain of the guard of the king of Babylon (2 Kgs. 25:8); took away people into exile (2 Kgs. 25:11, 20; Jer. 39:9; 52:12-15, 26); left some in the land (Jer. 39:10; 52:16); looked after Jeremiah (Jer. 39:11-14; 40:1); committed people to Gedaliah (Jer. 41:10; 43:6).
J2f Neco
Pharaoh of Egypt, killed Josiah (2 Kgs. 23:29; 2 Chr. 35:20-3); bound Jehoahaz and taxed the land (2 Kgs. 23:33-5; 2 Chr. 36:3-4); defeated by Nebuchadnezzar (Jer. 46:2).
J2g Nehemiah
Son of Hacaliah (Neh. 1:1); cupbearer to King Artaxerxes (Neh. 1:11); the governor (Neh. 12:26); governor who set his seal to the covenant (Neh. 10:1).
J3 Nicanor – Noah
J3a Nicanor
One of the seven administrators (Acts 6:5).
J3b Nicodemus
A Pharisee, ruler of the Jews, who came to Jesus (John 3:1-9; 7:50-2); brought myrrh and aloes (John 19:39).
J3c Nicolas
One of the seven administrators (Acts 6:5).
J3d Nimrod
Son of Cush and a mighty hunter (Gen. 10:8-12; 1 Chr. 1:10).
J3e Noadiah
The prophetess opposed to Nehemiah (Neh. 6:14).
J3f Noah
Son of Lamech (Gen. 5:28-30; Luke 3:36); found favour in the eyes of the Lord (Gen. 6:8-9); made an ark (Gen. 6:13-22; Heb. 11:7; 1 Pet. 3:20); went into the ark (Gen. 7:1-24; Matt. 24:37-8; Luke 17:26-7); a preacher of righteousness (2 Pet. 2:5); blessed by God and given meat to eat (Gen. 9:1-7); received the covenant of the

rainbow (Gen. 9:8-17; Isa. 54:9); got drunk (Gen. 9:20-7); died (Gen. 9:29); he, Daniel and Job would only save themselves (Ezek. 14:14, 20).

J4 Obadiah – Othniel

J4a Obadiah
The prophet (Obad. 1).

J4b Obed-edom [1]
The Hittite in whose house the ark stayed (2 Sam. 6:10-12; 1 Chr. 13:13-14; 15:25); the vessels in the house of God with Obed-edom (2 Chr. 25:24).

J4c Og
King of Bashan, defeated and killed by Israel (Num. 21:33-5; Deut. 1:4; Josh. 2:10; 1 Kgs. 4:19; Neh. 9:22; Ps. 135:11; 136:20).

J4d Omri
King of Israel (1 Kgs. 16:16-17, 21-7); died (1 Kgs. 16:28).

J4e Onan
Son of Judah by Shua (Gen. 38:4; Num. 26:19; 1 Chr. 2:3); shed his semen on the ground and was killed by the Lord (Gen. 38:8-10).

J4f Onesimus
A runaway slave on whose behalf Paul appealed (Philem. 10-18); sent to Colossae (Col. 4:9).

J4g Onesiphorus
His household refreshed Paul (2 Tim. 1:16); his household greeted by Paul (2 Tim. 4:19).

J4h Orpah
Moabite wife of Chilion (Ruth 1:4); kissed Naomi and returned home (Ruth 1:14-15).

J4i Othniel
Son of Kenaz who captured Kiriath-sepher (Josh. 15:17; Judg. 1:13); one of the judges (Judg. 3:9); died (Judg. 3:11).

K Individuals P – R

K1 Paltiel – Parmenas

K1a Paltiel [Palti]
Son of Laish and husband of Michal (1 Sam. 25:44); Michal was taken from him and returned to David (2 Sam. 3:15-16).

K1b Parmenas
One of the seven chosen for administration (Acts 6:5).

K2 Paul

K2a Paul [Saul] – his life
Saul, also known as Paul (Acts 13:9); witnesses laid garments at his feet (Acts 7:58); approved Stephen's death (Acts 8:1); persecuted the church (Acts 8:3); struck down on the road to Damascus (Acts 9:1-9; 22:6-11; 26:12-18); Ananias went to him (Acts 9:10-19; 22:12-16); proclaimed Jesus as the son of God (Acts 9:20-2); escaped over the wall (Acts 9:24-5); was brought to the apostles by Barnabas (Acts 9:26-30); set apart for work (Acts 13:1-3); summoned by the proconsul (Acts 13:7); the Jews reviled Paul (Acts 13:45-6); they drove Paul and Barnabas out of that district (Acts 13:50); stoned at Lystra (Acts 14:19-20); related what God had done (Acts 15:12); quarrelled with Barnabas (Acts 15:36-41); joined with Timothy (Acts 16:1-3); cast out the spirit of divination (Acts 16:16-18); in and out of prison in Philippi (Acts 16:19-40); addressing the Ephesian elders (Acts 20:17-38); arrested in the temple (Acts 21:18-36); addressing the crowd (Acts 21:37-22:2); before the council (Acts 22:30-23:1); escaping ambush by the Jews (Acts 23:12-35); before Felix (Acts 24:1-27); appealing to Caesar (Acts 25:1-26:3).

K2b Paul's travels
Was brought by Barnabas to Antioch (Acts 11:25-6); took relief to Jerusalem (Acts 11:30); returned from Jerusalem (Acts 12:25; 15:30-5); in Salamis (Acts 13:4-12); in Antioch of Pisidia (Acts 13:13-52); in Iconium (Acts 14:1-6); preached and was stoned in Lystra (Acts

14:6-20); returned to Antioch (Acts 14:21-8; 18:22); attended the council of Jerusalem (Acts 15:1-29); went with representatives to Antioch (Acts 15:22, 25); in Philippi (Acts 16:11-15); in Thessalonica (Acts 17:1-9); in Beroea (Acts 17:10-14); in Athens (Acts 17:16-34); in Corinth (Acts 18:1-18); in Ephesus (Acts 18:19-21; 19:1-15, 21-30); in Galatia and Phrygia (Acts 18:23); in Macedonia and Greece (Acts 20:1-3); in Troas, reviving Eutychus (Acts 20:6-12); by ship to Miletus (Acts 20:13-16); to Jerusalem despite warnings (Acts 21:1-17); shipwrecked (Acts 27:1-44); in Malta (Acts 28:1-10); in Rome (Acts 28:11-31).

K2c Paul's ministry
What is Paul? (1 Cor. 3:5); an apostle (Rom. 1:1; 1 Cor. 1:1; 2 Cor. 1:1; Gal. 1:1; Eph. 1:1; Col. 1:1; 1 Tim. 1:1; 2 Tim. 1:1; Titus 1:1); a slave of Christ (Rom. 1:1; Phil. 1:1); a servant of the gospel (Col. 1:23); a slave of God (Titus 1:1); a prisoner for Christ Jesus (Eph. 3:1; Philem. 1); our beloved brother (2 Pet. 3:15); I write this in my own handwriting (1 Cor. 16:21; Col. 4:18; 2 Thess. 3:17; Philem. 19); I, Paul, say to you (Gal. 5:2); Paul was called Hermes because he was the chief speaker (Acts 14:12-14); I adjure you by Jesus whom Paul preaches (Acts 19:13); Paul, an ambassador and a prisoner of Christ Jesus (Philem. 9); was he crucified for you or were you baptized in his name? (1 Cor. 1:13).

K3 Paulus – Persis

K3a Paulus [Sergius Paulus]
The proconsul at Paphos (Acts 13:7).

K3b Pekah
Son of Remaliah who killed Pekahiah (2 Kgs. 15:25); reigned over Israel (2 Kgs. 15:27-32); attacked Judah (2 Kgs. 15:37; 16:5; 2 Chr. 28:6; Isa. 7:1).

K3c Pekahiah
Son of Menahem and king of Israel (2 Kgs. 15:22-4); killed by Pekah (2 Kgs. 15:25-6).

K3d Pelatiah
Son of Benaiah (Ezek. 11:1); died when Ezekiel prophesied (Ezek. 11:13).

K3e Persis
Worked hard in the Lord, greeted by Paul (Rom. 16:12).

K4 Peter

K4a Peter [Cephas] [Simon Peter]
Brother of Andrew and a fisherman (Matt. 4:18; Mark 1:16; John 6:8); from Bethsaida (John 1:44); brought to Jesus by Andrew (John 1:40-2); astonished by the catch of fish (Luke 5:3-11); one of the 12 apostles (Matt. 10:2; Mark 3:16; Luke 6:14; Acts 1:13); an apostle of Jesus Christ (1 Pet. 1:1; 2 Pet. 1:1); Jesus entered Peter's house (Matt. 8:14; Mark 1:29; Luke 4:38); Jesus healed his mother-in-law (Matt. 8:14-15); pointed out the fig tree (Mark 11:21); walked on water (Matt. 14:28-31); confessed Jesus as the Christ (Matt. 16:16; Mark 8:29; Luke 9:20; John 6:68-9); was called the rock (Matt. 16:17-19); rebuked Jesus (Matt. 16:22); was rebuked by Jesus (Mark 8:32-3); at the transfiguration (Matt. 17:1-4; Mark 9:2-6; Luke 9:28-33); fished for the half-shekel tax (Matt. 17:24-7); asked how often to forgive (Matt. 18:21); asked what they would have (Matt. 19:27; Mark 10:28; Luke 18:28); asked about the destruction of the temple (Mark 13:3); prepared the passover (Luke 22:8); had problems over foot-washing (John 13:6-9); beckoned to John (John 13:24).

K4b Peter and Christ's death
Declared he would not fall away (Matt. 26:33-5; Mark 14:29-31; Luke 22:33-4; John 13:37-8); slept (Matt. 26:40; Mark 14:37); cut off the slave's ear (John 18:10-11); followed at a distance (Matt. 26:58; Mark 14:54; Luke 22:54; John 18:15-16); denied Christ three times (Matt. 26:69-75; Mark 14:66-72; Luke 22:55-62; John 18:17-18, 25-7); ran to the tomb (Luke 24:12; John 20:2-7); tell his

disciples and Peter (Mark 16:7); went fishing (John 21:2-3); jumped into the sea (John 21:7); hauled the net ashore (John 21:11); was commissioned to feed the sheep (John 21:15-19); told to strengthen his brothers (Luke 22:31-2); what of this man? (John 21:20-1); the Lord has risen indeed and has appeared to Simon (Luke 24:34); Simon Peter said, 'Lord, where are you going?' (John 13:36); he appeared to Cephas (1 Cor. 15:5).

K4c Peter in the church
Choosing a successor to Judas (Acts 1:15-22); preaching on the day of Pentecost (Acts 2:14-40); healing the lame man (Acts 3:1-7); preaching in the temple (Acts 3:11-26); bold before the council (Acts 4:8-13, 19-20; 5:29-32); dealing with Ananias and Sapphira (Acts 5:3-4, 8-9); his shadow falling on the sick (Acts 5:15); bringing the Holy Spirit to Samaria (Acts 8:14-23); healing Aeneas (Acts 9:32-4); healing Tabitha (Acts 9:36-41); teaching Cornelius (Acts 10:5-48); countering criticism over Cornelius (Acts 11:2-17); imprisoned (Acts 12:3-5); released by an angel (Acts 12:6-18); at the council of Jerusalem (Acts 15:7-11); Simeon [Symeon] has related how God visited the Gentiles (Acts 15:14); Paul visited him (Gal. 1:18; 2:6-10); opposed by Paul in Antioch (Gal. 2:11-14); Peter was entrusted with the gospel to the circumcised (Gal. 2:7-8); 'I am of Cephas' (1 Cor. 1:12); Paul, Apollos, Cephas, all are yours (1 Cor. 3:22); a believer as wife, as the rest of the apostles, the Lord's brothers and Cephas? (1 Cor. 9:5); James and Cephas and John, reputed to be pillars (Gal. 2:9).

K5 Philemon – Phinehas
K5a Philemon
Paul wrote to him (Philem. 1).

K5b Philetus
Swerved from the truth (2 Tim. 2:17-18).

K5c Philip [1]
One of the 12 apostles (Matt. 10:3; Mark 3:18; Luke 6:14; Acts 1:13); from Bethsaida (John 1:44); called to follow Jesus (John 1:43); told Nathanael about Jesus (John 1:45-6, 48); questioned about bread for the multitude (John 6:5-7); Greeks came to him wanting to see Jesus (John 12:21-2); wanted to see the Father (John 14:8-9).

K5d Philip [2]
Brother of Herod and husband of Herodias (Matt. 14:3); brother of Herod (Mark 6:17; Luke 3:19).

K5e Philip [3]
Brother of Herod and tetrarch of Ituraea and Trachonitis (Luke 3:1).

K5f Philip [4]
Selected for administration (Acts 6:5); preached in Samaria (Acts 8:5-13); taught the Ethiopian eunuch (Acts 8:26-40); the evangelist with four daughters (Acts 21:8-9).

K5g Phinehas [1]
Son of Eleazar (Exod. 6:25; Num. 31:6; Judg. 20:28; 1 Chr. 6:4, 50; 9:20; Ezra 7:5); impaled Zimri and Cozbi (Num. 25:7-13; Ps. 106:30); his town was Gibeah (Josh. 24:33).

K5h Phinehas [2]
Son of Eli (1 Sam. 1:3; 2:34; 4:4; 14:3); was killed (1 Sam. 4:11, 17); his wife gave birth to Ichabod (1 Sam. 4:19-22).

K6 Phoebe – Publius
K6a Phoebe
Ministered in the church at Cenchreae (Rom. 16:1).

K6b Phygelus
Turned away from Paul (2 Tim. 1:15).

K6c Pilate [Pontius Pilate]
The Roman governor of Judea (Matt. 27:2; Luke 3:1); mixed Galileans' blood with their sacrifices (Luke 13:1); Jesus before him (Matt. 27:11-14; Mark 15:1-5; Luke 23:1-4; John 18:29-38; 19:8-11; 1 Tim. 6:13); sending Jesus

to Herod (Luke 23:6-12); exonerating Jesus (Luke 23:13-16; John 18:38-19:6; 19:4-7, 12-15; Acts 3:13); desired to release Jesus (Luke 23:20); releasing Barabbas (Matt. 27:15-22; Mark 15:6-15); had Jesus flogged (John 19:1); delivering Jesus to be crucified (Matt. 27:22-6; Mark 15:12-15; John 19:16; Acts 13:28); opposed Jesus (Acts 4:27); writing a title for the cross (John 19:19-22); gave permission for the legs to be broken (John 19:31); handed over Jesus' body (Matt. 27:58; Mark 15:43-5; Luke 23:52; John 19:38); approved a guard (Matt. 27:62-5).

K6d Potiphar
Captain of Pharaoh's guard who bought Joseph (Gen. 37:36; 39:1-20).

K6e Priscilla [Prisca]
Wife of Aquila (Acts 18:2, 18); taught Apollos (Acts 18:26); greeted by Paul (Rom. 16:3; 2 Tim. 4:19); sent greetings to the Corinthians (1 Cor. 16:19).

K6f Prochorus
One of the seven chosen for administration (Acts 6:5).

K6g Publius
Chief man of Malta (Acts 28:7-8).

K7 Rachel – Ruth
K7a Rachel
Younger daughter of Laban (Gen. 29:6, 16-17); Jacob met and kissed her (Gen. 29:9-12); Jacob served seven years for her (Gen. 29:18-20, 25); Jacob married her (Gen. 29:28-30); was barren (Gen. 29:31; 30:1-2); bore children through Bilhah (Gen. 30:3-8); wanted mandrakes (Gen. 30:14-15); bore Joseph (Gen. 30:22-5); stole Laban's gods (Gen. 31:19, 33-5); died giving birth to Benjamin (Gen. 35:16-19; 48:7); her tomb (Gen. 35:20; 1 Sam. 10:2); weeping for her children (Jer. 31:15; Matt. 2:18).

K7b Rahab
A prostitute of Jericho (Josh. 2:1); hid the spies and was saved (Josh. 2:3-21; 6:17, 22-5; Heb. 11:31; Jas. 2:25).

K7c Rebekah
Daughter of Bethuel by Milcah (Gen. 22:23; 28:5); returned with Abraham's servant (Gen. 24:55-61); became Isaac's wife (Gen. 24:64-7; 25:20); bore twins (Gen. 25:21-4; Rom. 9:10-12); mother of Jacob (Gen. 29:12); loved Jacob (Gen. 25:28); was said to be Isaac's sister (Gen. 26:7-11); was grieved by Esau's wives (Gen. 26:35; 27:46); led Jacob in deceiving Isaac (Gen. 27:5-17); buried in the field at Machpelah (Gen. 49:31).

K7d Rechab
Son of Rimmon of Benjamin (2 Sam. 4:2); killed Ish-bosheth (2 Sam. 4:5-11); killed by David's young men (2 Sam. 4:12).

K7e Rehoboam
Son of Solomon who reigned after him (1 Kgs. 11:43; 14:21; 1 Chr. 3:10; 2 Chr. 9:31; Matt. 1:7); threatened to make the yoke heavier (1 Kgs. 12:1-14; 2 Chr. 10:1-14); reigned over Judah only (1 Kgs. 12:17-20; 2 Chr. 10:17-19); tried to fight against Israel (1 Kgs. 12:21-4; 2 Chr. 11:1-4); built up the kingdom wisely (2 Chr. 11:5-23); war between him and Jeroboam (1 Kgs. 14:30; 15:6; 2 Chr. 12:15); invaded by Shishak (1 Kgs. 14:25-7; 2 Chr. 12:1-12); died (1 Kgs. 14:29-31; 2 Chr. 12:13-16).

K7f Reuben
Firstborn son of Jacob by Leah (Gen. 29:32; 1 Chr. 2:1; 5:1); found mandrakes (Gen. 30:14); lay with Bilhah his father's concubine (Gen. 35:22; 49:4; 1 Chr. 5:1); saved Joseph from being killed by his brothers (Gen. 37:21-2); horrified when Joseph had been sold (Gen. 37:29-30); said, 'Slay my two sons' (Gen. 42:37).

K7g Rezin
King of Syria who attacked Judah (2 Kgs. 15:37; 16:5; Isa. 7:1, 4, 8; 8:6; 9:11); killed by the king of Assyria (2 Kgs. 16:9).

K7h Rhoda
A maid who did not open the gate to Peter (Acts 12:13).

K7i Rizpah
Daughter of Aiah and concubine of Saul (2 Sam. 3:7); her sons were given to the Gibeonites to be killed (2 Sam. 21:8-9); she kept predators from the bodies (2 Sam. 21:10-11).

K7j Ruth
Moabite wife of Mahlon (Ruth 1:4); would not leave Naomi (Ruth 1:14, 16-18); returned to Bethlehem with Naomi (Ruth 1:19, 22); went gleaning (Ruth 2:2); was treated kindly by Boaz (Ruth 2:8-23); lay by Boaz at the threshing-floor (Ruth 3:7-18); redeemed and married by Boaz (Ruth 4:5, 10, 13).

L Individuals S – T
L1 Salome – Sceva
L1a Salome
A woman who watched the crucifixion (Mark 15:40); she brought spices (Mark 16:1).

L1b Samson
Son of Manoah (Judg. 13:24-5); wanted to marry a Philistine of Timnah (Judg. 14:1-4); tore a lion and later ate honey from its carcase (Judg. 14:5-9); set a riddle at the wedding feast (Judg. 14:10-20); set foxes loose with torches (Judg. 15:1-8); burst new ropes (Judg. 15:10-14); killed Philistines with the jawbone of an ass (Judg. 15:15-20); removed the gates of Gaza (Judg. 16:1-3); courted Delilah (Judg. 16:4-22); pulled down the pillars of the house (Judg. 16:23-31); time would fail to tell of him (Heb. 11:32).

L1c Samuel
Son of Elkanah by Hannah (1 Sam. 1:20; 1 Chr. 6:33-4); lent to the Lord after he was weaned (1 Sam. 1:22-8; 2:18-20); grew (1 Sam. 2:26); heard the Lord speak (1 Sam. 3:1-4:1); the victory of Ebenezer (1 Sam. 7:3-17); was asked for a king (1 Sam. 8:1-22); anointed Saul (1 Sam. 9:14-10:9; 10:14-16); challenged the people (1 Sam. 12:1-25); rebuked Saul (1 Sam. 13:8-15; 15:10-35); instructed Saul to smite Amalek (1 Sam. 15:1-3); anointed David (1 Sam. 16:1-13; 1 Chr. 11:3); David fled to him (1 Sam. 19:18-24); died (1 Sam. 25:1; 28:3); Saul brought up his spirit (1 Sam. 28:11-20); his book of chronicles (1 Chr. 29:29); he was among those who called on the name of the Lord (Ps. 99:6); though he stood before the Lord, it would be in vain for the people (Jer. 15:1); time would fail to tell of him (Heb. 11:32).

L1d Sanballat
Opposed the work of Israel (Neh. 2:10, 19; 4:1, 7-8; 6:1-14); a priest was his son-in-law (Neh. 13:28).

L1e Sapphira
Wife of Ananias (Acts 5:1-10).

L1f Sarah [Sarai]
Abraham's wife (Gen. 11:29, 31; 12:5); obeyed Abraham, calling him Lord (1 Pet. 3:6); was barren (Gen. 11:30; 16:1-2; Rom. 4:19); was passed off as Abraham's sister (Gen. 12:11-20; 20:2-18); gave Abraham her maid as wife (Gen. 16:2-9; 25:12); the Lord changed her name (Gen. 17:15); was promised a child (Gen. 17:16-21; 18:9-15; Rom. 9:9); prepared food for the guests (Gen. 18:6); bore Isaac (Gen. 21:1-7; 24:36; Heb. 11:11); had Abraham cast out Ishmael (Gen. 21:9-12); died (Gen. 23:1-2); was buried in the field of Machpelah (Gen. 23:19; 25:10; 49:31).

L1g Saul
Son of Kish, a Benjaminite (1 Sam. 9:2; Acts 13:21); looked for Kish's asses (1 Sam. 9:3-5; 10:14-16); received by Samuel (1 Sam. 9:6-27); anointed by Samuel (1 Sam. 10:1); prophesied (1 Sam. 10:10-13; 19:20-4); reigned (1 Sam. 10:21-7; 13:1); delivered Jabesh-gilead (1 Sam. 11:5-15); fought the Philistines (1 Sam. 13:2-7, 15-16;

14:17-46; 17:19); sacrificed the offerings (1 Sam. 13:8-14); cursed anyone who ate (1 Sam. 14:24-45); partially slaughtered Amalek (1 Sam. 15:1-35); was soothed by David's playing (1 Sam. 16:14-23); angry with David (1 Sam. 18:6-9); tried to kill David (1 Sam. 18:10-11; 19:1-17; 20:30-1; 23:7-28; 24:1-2; 26:1-3; 1 Chr. 12:1); killed the priests (1 Sam. 22:6-19); spared by David (1 Sam. 24:3-22; 26:6-25); visited the medium (1 Sam. 28:3-25); overrun by the Philistines (1 Chr. 10:2); fell on his own sword (1 Sam. 31:4-6; 1 Chr. 10:4-6); his bones buried in the tomb of Kish (2 Sam. 21:12-14).

L1h Sceva
A Jewish high priest whose sons practised exorcism (Acts 19:14).

L2 Sennacherib – Shechem
L2a Sennacherib
King of Assyria who invaded Judah (2 Kgs. 18:13; 2 Chr. 32:1-2; Isa. 36:1); sent a message to Hezekiah (2 Chr. 32:9-15); Hezekiah prayed about him (2 Kgs. 19:16, 20; Isa. 37:17, 21); went home and was killed by his sons (2 Kgs. 19:36-7; 2 Chr. 32:21-2; Isa. 37:37-8).

L2b Seth
Son of Adam by Eve (Gen. 4:25; 5:3; Luke 3:38).

L2c Shadrach [Hananiah]
Brought into the king's court (Dan. 1:6); renamed by King Nebuchadnezzar (Dan. 1:7); ate vegetables (Dan. 1:11-16); set over the province of Babylon (Dan. 2:49; 3:12); cast into the furnace (Dan. 3:13-30); came out of the fire (Dan. 3:26); promoted in the province of Babylon (Dan. 3:30).

L2d Shallum
Son of Jabesh who killed Zechariah and ruled Israel (2 Kgs. 15:10); killed by Menahem (2 Kgs. 15:13-15).

L2e Shalmaneser
King of Assyria who attacked Israel (2 Kgs. 17:3); took the northern kingdom into exile (2 Kgs. 18:9-11).

L2f Shamgar
Son of Anath who killed 600 Philistines (Judg. 3:31; 5:6).

L2g Shaphan
Son of Azaliah (2 Kgs. 22:3; 2 Chr. 34:8); took the book of the law to Josiah (2 Kgs. 22:8-10; 2 Chr. 34:15-18); went to enquire of the Lord (2 Kgs. 22:12-14; 2 Chr. 34:20-2).

L2h Sheba
Son of Bichri of Benjamin who rebelled against David (2 Sam. 20:1-21); his head was cut off and thrown over the wall (2 Sam. 20:22).

L2i Shechem
Son of Hamor and a prince of the Hivites (Gen. 33:19; Josh. 24:32; Judg. 9:28); raped Dinah (Gen. 34:2-7); wanted to marry Dinah (Gen. 34:8-12); agreed to be circumcised (Gen. 34:13-24); killed by Simeon and Levi (Gen. 34:26).

L3 Shelah – Simeon
L3a Shelah
Son of Judah by Shua (Gen. 38:5; 46:12; Num. 26:20; 1 Chr. 2:3); remain in my house until Shelah grows up (Gen. 38:11); I did not give her to my son Shelah (Gen. 38:26).

L3b Shem
Son of Noah (Gen. 5:32; 6:10; 1 Chr. 1:4; Luke 3:36); entered the ark (Gen. 7:13); covered his naked father (Gen. 9:23); blessed by the Lord (Gen. 9:26-7).

L3c Sheshbazzar [Shenazzar]
A descendant of King Jehoiachin (1 Chr. 3:18); he was given the vessels from the temple (Ezra 1:8, 11; 5:14); laid the foundation of the temple (Ezra 5:16).

L3d Shimei
Son of Gera, a Benjaminite, who cursed David (2 Sam. 16:5-13); begged forgiveness (2 Sam. 19:16, 18-23); brought down by Solomon (1 Kgs. 2:8-9, 36-46).

L3e Shishak
King of Egypt (1 Kgs. 11:40); attacked Jerusalem (1 Kgs. 14:25-6; 2 Chr. 12:2-9).

L3f Shobach [Shophach]
Commander of the Syrian army (2 Sam. 10:16; 1 Chr. 19:16); was wounded and died (2 Sam. 10:18; 1 Chr. 19:18).

L3g Silas [Silvanus]
Sent with Paul and Barnabas to Antioch (Acts 15:22, 27); a prophet who exhorted the people (Acts 15:32); accompanied Paul (Acts 15:40; 17:4; 2 Cor. 1:19); arrested with Paul in Philippi (Acts 16:19); released with Paul from prison (Acts 16:25-34); sent away with Paul to Berea (Acts 17:10); remained in Berea with Timothy (Acts 17:14-15); came from Macedonia to Corinth (Acts 18:5); joined in writing letters (1 Thess. 1:1; 2 Thess. 1:1; 1 Pet. 5:12).

L3h Simeon [1]
Son of Jacob by Leah (Gen. 29:33; 48:5; Exod. 1:2; 1 Chr. 2:1); killed the men of Shechem (Gen. 34:25-31; 49:5-7); imprisoned by Joseph (Gen. 42:24, 36; 43:23).

L3i Simeon [2]
He recognised the child Jesus as the Christ (Luke 2:25-35).

L3j Simeon [3] [Niger] [Symeon]
One of the prophets and teachers in Antioch (Acts 13:1).

L4 Simon – Sisera
L4a Simon [1]
The Zealot, one of the 12 disciples (Matt. 10:4; Luke 6:15; Acts 1:13); the Canaanean, one of the 12 (Mark 3:18).

L4b Simon [2]
Brother of Jesus (Matt. 13:55; Mark 6:3).

L4c Simon [3]
The leper (Matt. 26:6; Mark 14:3).

L4d Simon [4]
A man of Cyrene compelled to carry the cross (Matt. 27:32; Mark 15:21; Luke 23:26).

L4e Simon [5]
A Pharisee who invited Jesus to a meal (Luke 7:36-46).

L4f Simon [6]
A sorcerer in Samaria (Acts 8:9-24).

L4g Simon [7]
A tanner in Joppa (Acts 9:43; 10:6, 17, 32).

L4h Sisera
The commander of the army of Jabin (Judg. 4:2, 7; 1 Sam. 12:9); to be defeated by a woman (Judg. 4:9); routed before Israel (Judg. 4:12-15; Ps. 83:9); killed by Jael wife of Heber (Judg. 4:17-22; 5:24-7); the stars fought against him (Judg. 5:20); his mother awaiting his return (Judg. 5:28-30).

L5 Solomon
L5a Solomon's life
Son of David by Bathsheba, born in Jerusalem (2 Sam. 5:14; 1 Kgs. 1:11-12; 1 Chr. 3:5; Matt. 1:6); called Jedidiah (2 Sam. 12:25); was not invited by Adonijah (1 Kgs. 1:10, 19, 26); was king (1 Kgs. 1:33-48; 1 Chr. 23:1); was charged by David (1 Kgs. 2:1; 1 Chr. 22:5-19; 28:9-21); had Adonijah killed (1 Kgs. 2:13-25); expelled Abiathar from being priest (1 Kgs. 2:26-7); had Joab killed (1 Kgs. 2:28-35); had Shimei killed (1 Kgs. 2:36-46); married Pharaoh's daughter (1 Kgs. 3:1; 9:24; 2 Chr. 8:11); judged between the two harlots (1 Kgs. 3:16-28); built the temple (1 Kgs. 5:1-6:38; 2 Kgs. 24:13; 1 Chr. 6:10; 2 Chr. 2:1-5:1; Jer. 52:20; Acts 7:47); built other houses (1 Kgs. 7:1-8); dedicated the temple (1 Kgs. 8:1-66; 2 Chr.

5:2-7:11; Neh. 12:45); sent a fleet of ships to sea (1 Kgs. 9:26-8; 10:11, 22; 2 Chr. 8:17-18); received the queen of Sheba (1 Kgs. 10:1-13; 2 Chr. 9:1-12; Luke 11:31); the queen of the South came to hear the wisdom of Solomon (Matt. 12:42); turned away from the Lord (1 Kgs. 11:1-13, 31-6; 2 Chr. 23:13; Neh. 13:26); died (1 Kgs. 11:41-3; 2 Chr. 9:29-31).

L5b Solomon's affairs
David prayed for him (1 Chr. 29:19); Solomon asked the Lord for wisdom (1 Kgs. 3:3-15; 2 Chr. 1:2-13); warned by the Lord (1 Kgs. 9:1-9; 2 Kgs. 21:7-8; 2 Chr. 7:12-22; 33:7-8); displeased Hiram (1 Kgs. 9:10-14); psalms for him (Ps. 72:t; 127:t); his proverbs (Prov. 1:1; 10:1; 25:1); his song of songs (S. of S. 1:1); in all his glory (Matt. 6:29; Luke 12:27).

L6 Sosthenes – Syntyche
L6a Sosthenes [1]
Ruler of the synagogue in Corinth (Acts 18:17).

L6b Sosthenes [2]
Paul's amanuensis (1 Cor. 1:1).

L6c Stephanas
His household were the first converts in Achaia (1 Cor. 16:15); Paul baptised his household (1 Cor. 1:16); his coming encouraged Paul (1 Cor. 16:17).

L6d Stephen
Chosen for administration (Acts 6:5); performed signs and wonders (Acts 6:8); was accused before the council (Acts 6:9-7:53); stoned to death (Acts 7:54-8:2; 22:20).

L6e Susanna
Provided for Jesus and his disciples (Luke 8:3).

L6f Syntyche
A woman who laboured with Paul in the gospel (Phil. 4:2-3).

L7 Tamar – Thaddaeus
L7a Tamar [1]
Wife of Judah's sons (Gen. 38:6-11); pregnant through Judah (Gen. 38:13-26).

L7b Tamar [2]
Daughter of David raped by Amnon (2 Sam. 13:1-22, 32; 1 Chr. 3:9); sent by David to prepare food for Amnon (2 Sam. 13:7).

L7c Terah
Son of Nahor and father of Abraham (Gen. 11:24-8; Luke 3:34); died in Haran (Gen. 11:31-2; Josh. 24:2; 1 Chr. 1:26).

L7d Tertius
Amanuensis for the letter to the Romans (Rom. 16:22).

L7e Tertullus
A spokesman who accused Paul (Acts 24:1-2).

L7f Thaddaeus [Judas]
One of the 12 disciples (Matt. 10:3; Mark 3:18; John 14:22).

L8 Theophilus – Tiglath-pileser
L8a Theophilus
Luke dedicated his books to him (Luke 1:3; Acts 1:1).

L8b Theudas
An insurrectionist who was killed (Acts 5:36).

L8c Thomas [Didymus]
One of the 12 disciples (Matt. 10:3; Mark 3:18; Luke 6:15; John 21:2); urged the disciples to go to Jerusalem to die (John 11:16); did not know where Jesus was going (John 14:5); doubted the resurrection (John 20:24-9); present in the upper room (Acts 1:13).

L8d Tiberius
In the 15th year of his reign as Caesar (Luke 3:1).

L8e Tibni
Son of Ginath and contender as king of Israel (1 Kgs. 16:21-2).

L8f Tiglath-pileser [Tiglath-pilneser, Pul]
King of Assyria hired by the king of Judah (2 Kgs. 15:19; 16:7-10; 2 Chr. 28:20-1); carried away Israel into exile (2 Kgs. 15:29; 1 Chr. 5:6, 26).

L9 Timon – Tychicus
L9a Timon
One of the seven administrators (Acts 6:5).

L9b Timothy
Son of a Greek father and a Jewish woman (Acts 16:1-3); accompanied Paul (Acts 20:4; 2 Cor. 1:19); was sent to the churches (1 Cor. 4:17; 16:10; Phil. 2:19; 1 Thess. 3:2); reported back to Paul (1 Thess. 3:6); joined with Paul in writing (2 Cor. 1:1; Phil. 1:1; Col. 1:1; 1 Thess. 1:1; 2 Thess. 1:1; Philem. 1); was sent letters by Paul (1 Tim. 1:2, 18; 6:20; 2 Tim. 1:2); was set free (Heb. 13:23).

L9c Titus
Accompanied Paul to Jerusalem (Gal. 2:1); a Greek who was not compelled to be circumcised (Gal. 2:3); Paul could not rest without him (2 Cor. 2:13); brought word from Corinth (2 Cor. 7:6-7, 13-14); was to raise funds in Corinth (2 Cor. 8:6); was concerned for the Corinthians (2 Cor. 8:16); Paul's fellow-worker (2 Cor. 8:23); Paul sent him to Corinth (2 Cor. 12:18); Paul wrote to him (Titus 1:4); went to Dalmatia (2 Tim. 4:10).

L9d Tobiah
An Ammonite who opposed Nehemiah (Neh. 2:10, 19; 4:3, 7; 6:1, 12, 14); sent and received many letters (Neh. 6:17, 19); related to Eliashib the priest (Neh. 13:4); had a chamber prepared in the temple (Neh. 13:5, 7-8).

L9e Trophimus
An Ephesian who accompanied Paul (Acts 20:4); supposed to have entered the temple (Acts 21:29); Paul left him ill at Miletus (2 Tim. 4:20).

L9f Tychicus
An Asian who accompanied Paul (Acts 20:4); sent by Paul to young churches (Eph. 6:21-2; Col. 4:7-9); sent by Paul to Ephesus (2 Tim. 4:12); to be sent to Titus (Titus 3:12).

M Individuals U – Z
M1 Uriah – Vashti
M1a Uriah [Urijah]
The Hittite, husband of Bathsheba (2 Sam. 11:3; 12:15); one of the 30 mighty men (2 Sam. 23:39; 1 Chr. 11:41); would not go to his house (2 Sam. 11:6-13); killed by David (2 Sam. 11:14-26; 12:9-10; 1 Kgs. 15:5); David was the father of Solomon by the wife of Uriah (Matt. 1:6).

M1b Vashti
Queen of King Ahasuerus (Esther 1:9); refused to come before the king (Esther 1:10-12; 2:1); deposed and replaced (Esther 1:15-19; 2:4, 17).

M2 Zacchaeus – Zechariah
M2a Zacchaeus
A tax collector who met Jesus (Luke 19:2-8).

M2b Zadok
Son of Ahitub, a priest (2 Sam. 8:17; 1 Kgs. 2:35; 1 Chr. 6:8); a brave young man (1 Chr. 12:28); sent back with the ark (2 Sam. 15:24-9); sending word to David (2 Sam. 15:35-6; 17:15); did not follow Adonijah (1 Kgs. 1:8, 26); anointed Solomon king (1 Kgs. 1:32-9, 44-5); the sons of Zadok are the only Levites who may come near to the Lord to minister (Ezek. 40:46).

M2c Zalmunna
King of Midian pursued by Gideon (Judg. 8:5-7, 10-12, 15); killed by Gideon (Judg. 8:18-21); make their princes like them (Ps. 83:11).

M2d Zebah
King of Midian pursued by Gideon (Judg. 8:5-7, 10-12, 15); killed by Gideon (Judg. 8:18-21); make their princes like them (Ps. 83:11).

M2e Zebulun
Son of Jacob by Leah (Gen. 30:20; 1 Chr. 2:1); prophecy concerning him (Gen. 49:13).

M2f Zechariah [1]
Son of Jeroboam and king of Israel (2 Kgs. 14:29; 15:8-9); killed by Shallum (2 Kgs. 15:10-12).

M2g Zechariah [2]
Son of Jehoiada the priest, killed in the temple (2 Chr. 24:20-2; 26:5; Matt. 23:35; Luke 11:51).

M2h Zechariah [3]
Son of Berechiah and grandson of Iddo, the prophet (Ezra 5:1; 6:14; Zech. 1:1).

M2i Zechariah [4] [Zacharias]
A priest of the division of Abijah (Luke 1:5); Zechariah, father of John the Baptist (Luke 3:2); saw an angel in the temple (Luke 1:8-20); emerged dumb (Luke 1:21-3); Mary entered his house (Luke 1:40); insisted that his child be named John (Luke 1:59-64); was filled with the Holy Spirit and prophesied (Luke 1:67-79).

M3 Zedekiah – Zerubbabel
M3a Zedekiah [1]
Son of Chenaanah, a false prophet (1 Kgs. 22:11; 2 Chr. 18:10); struck Micaiah (1 Kgs. 22:24; 2 Chr. 18:23).

M3b Zedekiah [2] [Mattaniah]
Uncle of Jehoiachin and king of Judah (2 Kgs. 24:17-19; 2 Chr. 36:10-12); rebelled against Nebuchadnezzar (2 Kgs. 24:20; 2 Chr. 36:13; Jer. 52:3); sent to Jeremiah (Jer. 21:1-7; 37:3, 17-21; 38:14-26); would be made a horror (Jer. 24:8); envoys came to him (Jer. 27:3); should obey the king of Babylon (Jer. 27:12-15); sent a letter to Nebuchadnezzar (Jer. 29:3); imprisoned Jeremiah (Jer. 32:3-5); gave up Jeremiah to his enemies (Jer. 38:5); would be taken captive (Jer. 34:2-6, 21); I will deliver Zedekiah into the hand of Nebuchadnezzar (Jer. 21:7); made proclamation to free Hebrew slaves (Jer. 34:8); his sons were killed and he was blinded (2 Kgs. 25:4-7; Jer. 39:4-7; 44:30; 52:8-11); went to Babylon (Jer. 51:59).

M3c Zeeb
Prince of Midian killed at his wine press (Judg. 7:25; 8:3); make their nobles like him (Ps. 83:11).

M3d Zelophehad
Son of Hepher of Manasseh, with five daughters (Num. 26:33; 27:1, 7; 36:2, 6, 10-11; Josh. 17:3; 1 Chr. 7:15).

M3e Zenas
A lawyer (Titus 3:13).

M3f Zerubbabel
Son of Pedaiah (1 Chr. 3:19); son of Shealtiel and governor of Judah (Ezra 3:2; Matt. 1:12; Luke 3:27); returned from exile (Ezra 2:2; Neh. 7:7; 12:1); encouraged by prophecy (Hag. 1:1, 12, 14; 2:2, 4, 21, 23; Zech. 4:6-10); refused to work with his enemies (Ezra 4:2-3); gave the Levites their portions (Neh. 12:47).

M4 Ziba – Zophar
M4a Ziba
Saul's servant who served Mephibosheth (2 Sam. 9:2-4, 9-12); brought provisions for David (2 Sam. 16:1-4); greeted David on his return (2 Sam. 19:17); slandered Mephibosheth (2 Sam. 19:26-30).

M4b Zilpah
Maid to Leah (Gen. 29:24); given to Jacob as wife (Gen. 30:9-12).

M4c Zimri [1]
Son of Salu of Simeon, impaled by Phinehas (Num. 25:14).

M4d Zimri [2]
Elah's captain who killed his master and reigned over Israel (1 Kgs. 16:9-12; 2 Kgs. 9:31); committed suicide when besieged (1 Kgs. 16:15-20).

M4e Zipporah
Daughter of Jethro and wife of Moses (Exod. 2:21; 4:25; 18:2).

M4f Zophar
A Naamathite, friend of Job (Job 2:11; 11:1; 20:1; 42:9).

372 Male

A Males

A1 Males in general
Can a male bear a child? (Jer. 30:6); valuation of males (Lev. 27:3-7); every male must be circumcised (Gen. 17:10, 14; 34:15, 22); every male eight days old (Gen. 17:12); Abraham circumcised every male (Gen. 17:23); every male in Shechem was circumcised (Gen. 34:24); all a sojourner's males must be circumcised before he can keep the Passover (Exod. 12:48); a woman bearing a male child is unclean seven days (Lev. 12:2); firstborn males belong to the Lord (Exod. 13:12); every male that opens the womb shall be holy to the Lord (Luke 2:23); sacrifice every firstborn male animal and redeem firstborn sons (Exod. 13:15); a man shall not wear woman's clothing (Deut. 22:5); men with men committing shameless acts (Rom. 1:27); the head of every man is Christ (1 Cor. 11:3); a man praying or prophesying with head covered dishonours his head (1 Cor. 11:4); a man ought not to have his head covered since he is the image and glory of God (1 Cor. 11:7); man was not from woman but woman from man (1 Cor. 11:8); does not nature teach you that long hair is a disgrace for a man? (1 Cor. 11:14); she gave birth to a male son (Rev. 12:5); the dragon persecuted the woman who gave birth to the male son (Rev. 12:13).

A2 Men worshipping
Pharaoh was prepared to let the men go to worship (Exod. 10:11); three times a year your males shall appear before God (Exod. 23:17; 34:23; Deut. 16:16); I want the men to pray (1 Tim. 2:8).

A3 Death of all males
If the baby is a boy, kill him (Exod. 1:16); throw every boy into the Nile (Exod. 1:22); kill all the males (Num. 31:17; Deut. 20:13); they killed every male (Gen. 34:25); they killed every male in Midian (Num. 31:7); David intended to kill everyone who urinated against a wall (1 Sam. 25:22, 34); Joab killed every male in Edom (1 Kgs. 11:15, 16); I will cut off every male from Jeroboam (1 Kgs. 14:10); not a male left of the house of Baasha (1 Kgs. 16:11); I will cut off every male from Ahab (1 Kgs. 21:21; 2 Kgs. 9:8); Herod killed all boys up to two years old (Matt. 2:16); all the males had died in the wilderness (Josh. 5:4).

A4 Reprieving males
They let the boys live (Exod. 1:17); why have you let the boys live? (Exod. 1:18).

B Male and female

B1 Relationship of men and women
God made them male and female (Gen. 1:27; 5:2; Matt. 19:4; Mark 10:6); I have found one man among a thousand, but not a woman (Eccles. 7:28); the man is the head of the woman (1 Cor. 11:3); man was not from woman but woman from man (1 Cor. 11:8); man was not created for woman, but woman for man (1 Cor. 11:9); in the Lord woman is not independent of man nor man of woman (1 Cor. 11:11); as woman was made from man, now man is born of woman (1 Cor. 11:12); the way of a man with a maiden (Prov. 30:19); you shall not lie with a male as with a female (Lev. 18:22); men abandoned natural relations with women (Rom. 1:27).

B2 Regulations for men and women
Neither male nor female may work on the sabbath (Exod. 20:10; Deut. 5:14); when the ox gores a son or a daughter, the same rule applies (Exod. 21:31); the law for an unclean person, whether male or female (Lev. 15:33); the law after bearing a child, whether male or female (Lev. 12:7); unclean people, male or female, sent out (Num. 5:3); Hebrew slaves, male and female, must be set free (Jer. 34:9, 10); male and female servants may choose to stay in service (Deut. 15:17); do not make an image in the likeness of male or female (Deut. 4:16).

B3 Men and women killed
Slay old men, young men, maidens, little children and women (Ezek. 9:6); we destroyed men, women and children (Deut. 2:34; 3:6); they destroyed both men and women in Jericho (Josh. 6:21); they killed both the men and the women of Ai (Josh. 8:25); 1000 men and women were burned to death (Judg. 9:49); 3000 Philistine men and women were on the roof (Judg. 16:27); kill both men and women in Jabesh-gilead (Judg. 21:10, 11); destroy both men and women of Amalek (1 Sam. 15:3); both men and women were killed in Nob (1 Sam. 22:19); whoever did not seek the Lord should be killed, whether male or female (2 Chr. 15:13); with you I shatter man and woman (Jer. 51:22); maidens and young men have fallen by the sword (Lam. 2:21).

B4 Men and women in the church
Multitudes of both men and women were added to their number (Acts 5:14); men and women alike were baptised (Acts 8:12); any belonging to the Way, men or women, might be bound (Acts 9:2); in Christ it is not a case of male and female (Gal. 3:28).

B5 Male and female animals
Male and female of every living creature was to be brought into the ark (Gen. 6:19; 7:2, 3, 9, 16).

373 Female

MALE AND FEMALE, see 372B.

A Woman's place
God made woman as man's helper (Gen. 2:21-3); woman was created for man (1 Cor. 11:9); God made man's rib into a woman (Gen. 2:22); called 'woman' because she came from man (Gen. 2:23); the woman you gave me to be with me (Gen. 3:12); God sent his Son, born of a woman (Gal. 4:4); among those born of women none is greater than John the Baptist (Matt. 11:11); his disciples were amazed that he was talking to a woman (John 4:27); a woman praying or prophesying with head uncovered dishonours her head (1 Cor. 11:5); if a woman has long hair it is her glory (1 Cor. 11:15); woman is the glory of man (1 Cor. 11:7); man was not from woman but woman from man (1 Cor. 11:8); do not give your strength to women (Prov. 31:3).

B Instructions about women
If it is a daughter she shall live (Exod. 1:16, 22); a woman bearing a female child is unclean two weeks (Lev. 12:5); valuation of females (Lev. 27:4-7); female slaves shall not go free like males (Exod. 21:7); take the women of the city as booty (Deut. 20:14); do not go near a woman (Exod. 19:15); a woman's vows may be annulled by her father (Num. 30:3-5); or her husband (Num. 30:6-15); a woman shall not wear man's clothing (Deut. 22:5); a woman should have her head covered (1 Cor. 11:3-16); women should adorn themselves modestly (1 Tim. 2:9; 1 Pet. 3:3-5); let the women keep silent (1 Cor. 14:34-6); women are to learn in silence (1 Tim. 2:11); I do not allow a woman to teach or to have authority over men (1 Tim. 2:12); requirements for a woman involved in the activities of a deacon (1 Tim. 3:11); women should have authority on their heads because of the angels (1 Cor. 11:10).

C Women and warfare
A wench or two for every warrior (Judg. 5:30); the women from the palace will be led out to the Chaldean

officers (Jer. 38:22); the women have been destroyed from Benjamin (Judg. 21:16); the women will go into captivity (Ezek. 30:17); the women of Midian: captured (Num. 31:9); spared (Num. 31:15, 18); killed (Num. 31:17).

D Excellent women
Description of the excellent wife (Prov. 31:10-31); all the city knows you are an excellent woman (Ruth 3:11); most blessed of women is Jael (Judg. 5:24); blessed are you among women (Luke 1:42); the holy women who hoped in God adorned themselves like that (1 Pet. 3:5).

E Weak women
Give honour to the woman as the weaker vessel (1 Pet. 3:7); the Lord will sell Sisera into the hands of a woman (Judg. 4:9); lest they say a woman killed me (Judg. 9:53-4); the Egyptians will be like women (Isa. 19:16); your troops will be like women (Nahum 3:13); the foreign troops within her will become women (Jer. 50:37); the mighty men have become like women (Jer. 51:30); these people capture weak women (2 Tim. 3:6).

F Women doing wrong
The woman gave me the fruit of the tree (Gen. 3:6, 12); consequences of the fall for the woman (Gen. 3:16); I will put enmity between you and the woman (Gen. 3:15); rise up you women who are at ease (Isa. 32:9); you cows of Bashan who are on the mountain of Samaria (Amos 4:1); women weeping for Tammuz (Ezek. 8:14); the scribes and Pharisees brought a woman caught in adultery (John 8:3); women exchanged natural relations for unnatural (Rom. 1:26); give ear to my word, you complacent daughters (Isa. 32:9); the woman who snares is more bitter than death (Eccles. 7:26).

G Women in prophecy
A woman was sitting in the ephah (Zech. 5:7); two women with the wind in their wings (Zech. 5:9); a woman clothed with the sun (Rev. 12:1); a woman sitting on a scarlet beast (Rev. 17:3); I will tell you the mystery of the woman and the beast that carries her (Rev. 17:7); the locusts had women's hair (Rev. 9:8).

374 Physical sensibility
FEELING, see 818.

375 Physical insensibility
A Anaesthetic
Jesus refused wine and gall (Matt. 27:34); wine and myrrh (Mark 15:23); God gave them a spirit of stupefaction (Rom. 11:8).

B Absence of feeling
They beat me but I did not feel it (Prov. 23:35); idols have hands but cannot feel (Ps. 115:7); Gentiles have become callous (Eph. 4:19).

C Fainting
Your sons faint (Isa. 51:20); children faint like wounded men in the streets of the city (Lam. 2:12); little ones and infants faint on the streets of the city (Lam. 2:11); your little ones faint with hunger at the head of every street (Lam. 2:19); woe is me, for I faint before murderers (Jer. 4:31); the beautiful virgins and young men will faint from thirst (Amos 8:13); the sun beat on Jonah's head so he was faint (Jonah 4:8); when I was fainting I remembered the Lord (Jonah 2:7); lest they faint on the way (Matt. 15:32); men fainting with fear (Luke 21:26).

376 Physical pleasure
PLEASURABLENESS, see 826.

377 Physical pain
Pain in childbirth would be increased (Gen. 3:16); in painful toil you will eat (Gen. 3:17); man is chastened

with pain (Job 33:19); I would rejoice in pain unsparing (Job 6:10); the wicked man writhes in pain all his life (Job 15:20); Jehoram died in great pain (2 Chr. 21:19); my servant is lying paralysed, in terrible pain (Matt. 8:6); on the third day they were sore (Gen. 34:25); they gnawed their tongues because of pain (Rev. 16:10-11); the wicked have no pains (Ps. 73:4); there will be no more mourning or crying or pain (Rev. 21:4).

378 Touch
A Touching
A1 Touching in general
Darkness which may be felt (Exod. 10:22).

A2 Touching holy things
Whatever touches them will be holy (Exod. 30:29); whatever touches the altar will be holy (Exod. 29:37); whatever touches the offerings becomes holy (Lev. 6:18, 27); Uzzah took hold of the ark and was struck down (2 Sam. 6:6; 1 Chr. 13:9-10); whoever touches the mountain will be killed (Exod. 19:12-13); if even a beast touches the mountain it will be stoned (Heb. 12:20); if his skirt touches bread, cooked food, wine or oil (Hag. 2:12); you have not come to what may be touched, a burning fire (Heb. 12:18).

A3 Touching unclean things
Touching unclean things (Lev. 5:2-3; 15:27); touch nothing unclean (Isa. 52:11); meat touching unclean things must not be eaten (Lev. 7:19); he who touches what is unclean and eats the peace offering will be cut off (Lev. 7:21); you must not touch the carcasses of unclean animals (Lev. 11:8, 24, 27; Deut. 14:8); he who touches an unclean animal becomes unclean (Lev. 11:26, 36); he who touches the carcass of a clean animal will be unclean until evening (Lev. 11:39); he who touches a corpse will be unclean seven days (Num. 19:11, 13); whoever touches a corpse in the open (Num. 19:16); touching an unclean person makes one unclean (Lev. 15:7, 11); whatever an unclean person touches becomes unclean (Num. 19:22); touching a menstruating woman makes one unclean (Lev. 15:19); touching the bed on which an unclean person has lain (Lev. 15:5, 21, 23); touching anything on which an unclean person has been (Lev. 15:10, 22, 23); an unclean woman must not touch any holy thing (Lev. 12:4); Jesus touched the bier (Luke 7:14).

A4 Touching to recognise
Perhaps my father will feel me (Gen. 27:12); come close so that I might feel you (Gen. 27:21); Isaac felt Jacob to see who he was (Gen. 27:22); Laban groped through all the things but found nothing (Gen. 31:34, 37); let me feel the pillars (Judg. 16:26); we grope for the wall like the blind (Isa. 59:10); you will grope at noon like the blind (Deut. 28:29); they grope at noon as at night (Job 5:14); that which our hands have handled (1 John 1:1); touch me and see (Luke 24:39); unless I put my finger in the mark of the nails (John 20:25); put your finger in my hands (John 20:27).

A5 Touching to raise / strengthen / lead
Men whose hearts God had touched (1 Sam. 10:26); he touched me and made me stand (Dan. 8:18); a hand touched me and set me on my hands and knees (Dan. 10:10); he touched me and strengthened me (Dan. 10:18); the Lord stretched out his hand and touched my mouth (Jer. 1:9); Jesus came and touched them saying, 'Arise' (Matt. 17:7).

A6 Touching for healing / blessing
This [coal] has touched your lips (Isa. 6:7); he touched my lips (Dan. 10:16); the one like a human being touched me again and strengthened me (Dan. 10:18); the woman touched the fringe of Jesus' garment (Matt. 9:20-1; Mark 5:27-31; Luke 8:44-7); the crowd tried to

touch him (Luke 6:19); they begged to touch the edge of his garment (Matt. 14:36; Mark 6:56); they begged him to touch the blind man (Mark 8:22); they were bringing children that he might touch them (Mark 10:13-16; Luke 18:15); he put his fingers in the deaf man's ears (Mark 7:33); all who were ill pressed about him to touch him (Mark 3:10); Jesus spat and touched the man's tongue (Mark 7:33); Jesus touched: the leper (Matt. 8:3; Mark 1:41; Luke 5:13); the blind men's eyes (Matt. 9:29; 20:34); the slave's ear (Luke 22:51).

A7 Touching to harm
Touch all that Job has and he will curse you (Job 1:11); touch his bone and his flesh and he will curse you (Job 2:5); the man touched Jacob's thigh (Gen. 32:25, 32); the Lord touches the land and it melts (Amos 9:5); he who touches you touches the apple of his eye (Zech. 2:8); whoever touches this man or his wife will surely die (Gen. 26:11); whoever touches his neighbour's wife will not go unpunished (Prov. 6:29).

A8 Not touching
Do not eat from it or touch it lest you die (Gen. 3:3); touch nothing unclean (Isa. 52:11); the Kohathites must not touch the holy things (Num. 4:15); no hand must touch the offender (Exod. 19:13); touch nothing belonging to these wicked men (Num. 16:26); my soul refuses to touch them (Job 6:7); do not touch my anointed ones (Ps. 105:15); I did not let you touch her (Gen. 20:6); we have not touched you (Gen. 26:29); have I not commanded the young men not to touch you? (Ruth 2:9); bring him to me and he will not touch you again (2 Sam. 14:10); 'Keep away! Do not touch!' they cry of themselves (Lam. 4:15); so defiled with blood that no one could touch their garments (Lam. 4:14); it is good for a man not to touch a woman (1 Cor. 7:1); 'handle not, taste not, touch not' (Col. 2:21); you burden men but do not touch the burdens with a finger (Luke 11:46).

B Laying on hands
B1 Laying on hands in general
Instructions about the laying on of hands (Heb. 6:2); they will lay their hands on you and persecute you (Luke 21:12).

B2 Laying hands on sacrifices
Laying hands on the head of the sacrificial animal (Exod. 29:10; Lev. 1:4; Num. 8:12; 2 Chr. 29:23); Aaron and his sons laid their hands on the head of: the sin offering (Lev. 8:14); the burnt offering (Lev. 8:18); the ram of ordination (Lev. 8:22).

B3 Laying on hands to commission
The Israelites laid hands on the Levites (Num. 8:10); Moses laid hands on Joshua (Num. 27:18, 23); the apostles prayed and laid hands on the seven (Acts 6:6); a gift given to Timothy through the laying on of hands (1 Tim. 4:14; 2 Tim. 1:6); do not lay hands on anyone hastily (1 Tim. 5:22); when they had fasted and prayed and laid their hands on them (Acts 13:3).

B4 Laying on hands for the Holy Spirit
Joshua was filled with the spirit of wisdom because Moses laid his hands on him (Deut. 34:9); Peter and John laid hands on the Samaritans and they received the Holy Spirit (Acts 8:17-19); Ananias laid hands on Saul (Acts 9:17); Paul laid hands on the Ephesians and the Holy Spirit came on them (Acts 19:6).

B5 Laying on hands to heal / bless
Elisha put his hands on the boy's hands (2 Kgs. 4:34); you have laid your hand on me (Ps. 139:5); he laid his right hand on me (Rev. 1:17); Jesus laid hands on a blind man (Mark 8:23); he laid his hands upon his eyes (Mark 8:25); he laid his hands on her and she was made straight (Luke 13:13); he laid his hands on a few sick people (Mark 6:5); he laid his hands on every one of

the sick (Luke 4:40); he laid hands on children (Matt. 19:13, 15); Ananias laying hands on Saul that he might regain his sight (Acts 9:12, 17); they begged him to lay his hands on him (Mark 7:32); lay your hands on her (Matt. 9:18; Mark 5:23); they will lay hands on the sick and they will recover (Mark 16:18); Paul prayed and laid hands on Publius' father (Acts 28:8); Israel's hands laid on Ephraim and Manasseh's heads (Gen. 48:14); put your right hand on his head (Gen. 48:18).

B6 Laying on hands for evil
When I was with you daily in the temple you did not lay hands on me (Luke 22:53); no one laid hands on him because his hour had not yet come (John 7:30); they wanted to arrest him, but no one laid hands on him (John 7:44); Herod the king laid violent hands on some of the church (Acts 12:1).

C Other contact
C1 Taking by the hand
The men seized the hands of Lot and his family (Gen. 19:16); arise, take the lad by the hand (Gen. 21:18); a boy held Samson's hand (Judg. 16:26); Elisha laid his hands on the king's hands (2 Kgs. 13:16); Jehonadab gave Jehu his hand (2 Kgs. 10:15); Jesus touched her hand (Matt. 8:15); he took Peter's mother-in-law by the hand (Mark 1:31); Jesus took Jairus' daughter by the hand (Matt. 9:25); Jesus took her by the hand (Mark 5:41; Luke 8:54); Jesus took the boy by the hand (Mark 9:27); Jesus reached out and took hold of Peter (Matt. 14:31); I will hold you by the hand (Isa. 42:6); Peter seized him by the hand and raised him up (Acts 3:7); he gave her his hand and raised her (Acts 9:41); the chiliarch took him by the hand and led him aside (Acts 23:19); you hold my right hand (Ps. 73:23).

C2 Hands under thigh to swear
The servant put his hand under Abraham's thigh (Gen. 24:9); put your hand under my thigh (Gen. 24:2; 47:29).

C3 Embracing
Elijah stretched himself on the child three times (1 Kgs. 17:21); Elisha stretched himself on the child (2 Kgs. 4:34-5); I took them up in my arms (Hos. 11:3); Paul threw his arms around him (Acts 20:10).

C4 Clinging to
They took hold of Jesus' feet (Matt. 28:9); do not cling to me (John 20:17).

379 Heat
FIRE, see 381.

A Hot weather
Cold and heat will not cease (Gen. 8:22); nothing is hidden from the sun's heat (Ps. 19:6); like glowing heat in sunshine (Isa. 18:4); sitting at the tent door in the heat of the day (Gen. 18:1); in the heat of the day Ish-bosheth rested (2 Sam. 4:5); by day the heat consumed me (Gen. 31:40); my strength was dried up like the heat of summer (Ps. 32:4); your garments are hot due to the south wind (Job 37:17); we have borne the scorching heat (Matt. 20:12); God appointed a scorching east wind (Jonah 4:8); a scorching wind from the wilderness (Jer. 4:11); when it is hot the waters vanish (Job 6:17); when the sun grew hot the manna melted (Exod. 16:21); by the time the sun is hot you will be saved (1 Sam. 11:9); like heat in drought you subdue the noise of the aliens (Isa. 25:5); like a dew-cloud in the heat of harvest (Isa. 18:4); do not open the gates until the sun is hot (Neh. 7:3); the sun beat on Jonah's head so he was faint (Jonah 4:8); when the south wind blows you say there will be heat (Luke 12:55); the sun rises with scorching heat (Jas. 1:11); the sun will not beat on them nor any heat (Rev. 7:16); a shade from the

heat by day (Isa. 4:6); he does not fear when heat comes (Jer. 17:8).

B Hot things

The furnace was made seven times hotter (Dan. 3:19); so hot that the flame killed the soldiers (Dan. 3:22); I see a boiling pot (Jer. 1:13); make the pot boil (Ezek. 24:5); set the pot on the coals so that the bronze will be hot (Ezek. 24:11); a smouldering wick he will not extinguish (Isa. 42:3; Matt. 12:20); my bones burn with heat (Job 30:30); they are all hot as an oven (Hos. 7:7); our skin is as hot as an oven because of the heat of famine (Lam. 5:10); a viper came out because of the heat (Acts 28:3).

380 Cold

COOLING, see 382A.

A Cold weather

Cold and heat will not cease (Gen. 8:22); out of the north comes cold (Job 37:9); she is not afraid of snow for her household is clothed in double [scarlet?] (Prov. 31:21); like the cold of snow at harvest time is a faithful messenger (Prov. 25:13); he who sings songs to a heavy heart is like one who takes off a garment on a cold day (Prov. 25:20); like locusts settling on walls on a cold day (Nahum 3:17); who has given birth to ice and frost? (Job 38:29); he sends forth his ice (Ps. 147:17); from the breath of God ice comes and the waters freeze (Job 37:10); water becomes hard as stone (Job 38:30); God says to the snow, 'Fall on the earth' (Job 37:6); who can stand before his cold? (Ps. 147:17); God scatters frost like ashes (Ps. 147:16); waters dark with ice and snow (Job 6:16); he destroyed their sycamores with frost (Ps. 78:47); frost by night (Gen. 31:40); manna fine as hoar-frost (Exod. 16:14); it was cold (John 18:18; Acts 28:2); killing a lion on a snowy day (2 Sam. 23:20; 1 Chr. 11:22); the poor have no covering in the cold (Job 24:7); in cold and exposure (2 Cor. 11:27); David could not keep warm (1 Kgs. 1:1); in that day there will be neither cold nor frost [?] (Zech. 14:6).

B Cool of the day

God walked in the garden in the cool of the day (Gen. 3:8); a cool roof chamber (Judg. 3:20); until the cool of the day (S. of S. 2:17; 4:6).

C Cold things

Like cold water to a weary soul (Prov. 25:25); most people's love will grow cold (Matt. 24:12).

381 Heating

A Fire in general

A1 About fire

Fire never says, 'Enough!' (Prov. 30:16); as fire causes water to boil (Isa. 64:2); let fire praise the Lord (Ps. 148:8); you who kindle a fire, walk by the light of your fire (Isa. 50:11); heap on the logs, kindle the fire (Ezek. 24:10); breastplates the colour of fire and jacinth and brimstone (Rev. 9:17); fire and smoke come from the crocodile's mouth (Job 41:19-21); fire and smoke and sulphur issue from their mouths (Rev. 9:17, 18); the angel's feet were like pillars of fire (Rev. 10:1); the angel who has power over fire (Rev. 14:18).

A2 Using fire

Metal objects should be purified by fire (Num. 31:22-3); gold is tested by fire (1 Pet. 1:7); buy from me gold refined by fire (Rev. 3:18); even fire will not drive out the rust (Ezek. 24:12); putting fire in the censers (Num. 16:7, 18); a seraph flew with a burning coal and touched my mouth (Isa. 6:6-7); coals of broom for the deceitful tongue (Ps. 120:4); burning an infected garment (Lev. 13:52, 55, 57); a large fire was made for Asa's funeral (2 Chr. 16:14); they did not make a fire for Jehoram (2 Chr. 21:19).

A3 Fire of evil

The tongue is a fire, set on fire by hell (Jas. 3:5); the words of a son of Belial are like a scorching fire (Prov. 16:27); the beast made fire come down from heaven (Rev. 13:13); can a man take fire in his bosom and his clothes not be burned? (Prov. 6:27); can a man walk on hot coals and his feet not be scorched? (Prov. 6:28); like a madman who throws firebrands (Prov. 26:18); wickedness burns like a fire (Isa. 9:18); the flaming darts of the evil one (Eph. 6:16); the tongue is a fire, set on fire by hell (Jas. 3:6).

A4 Saved from fire

Snatch some out of the fire (Jude 23); you were like a brand plucked from the burning (Amos 4:11); is this not a brand plucked from the fire? (Zech. 3:2); we went through fire and water (Ps. 66:12); I see four men loose, walking unharmed in the fire (Dan. 3:25); by faith they quenched the power of fire (Heb. 11:34); when you walk through the fire you will not be burned (Isa. 43:2).

B God and fire

B1 God is fire

Our God is a consuming fire (Deut. 4:24; 9:3; Heb. 12:29); I will be a wall of fire around Jerusalem (Zech. 2:5); his appearance was like fire (Ezek. 1:27; 8:2); he is like a refiner's fire and fuller's soap (Mal. 3:2); the Lord has burned in Jacob like a flaming fire (Lam. 2:3); lest the Lord break out like a fire (Amos 5:6).

B2 Fire of Christ

The Son of God who has eyes like a flame of fire (Rev. 2:18); his eyes were like flaming fire (Rev. 1:14; 19:12); I have come to cast fire on the earth (Luke 12:49); when the Lord Jesus is revealed in flaming fire (2 Thess. 1:7).

B3 Fire of the Spirit

Seven torches of fire which are the seven spirits of God (Rev. 4:5); baptism with the Holy Spirit and with fire (Matt. 3:11); tongues of fire, distributed and resting on each one of them (Acts 2:3).

B4 God dwelling in fire

B4a God appearing in fire

A sea of glass mixed with fire (Rev. 15:2); a pillar of fire by night (Exod. 13:21; Neh. 9:12); cloud by day and fire by night (Num. 14:14; Deut. 1:33; Ps. 78:14; 105:39; Isa. 4:5); a firepot and a flaming torch (Gen. 15:17); God appeared in a burning bush (Exod. 3:2-3; Acts 7:30); his throne blazed with fire (Dan. 7:9); the Lord spoke from the fire (Deut. 4:12); you heard his words from the fire (Deut. 4:36; 5:26); the Lord descended on Mount Sinai in fire (Exod. 19:18); you have not come to what may be touched, a burning fire (Heb. 12:18); the glory of the Lord was like consuming fire on the top of the mountain (Exod. 24:17); the Lord will come in fire (Isa. 66:15); fire devours before God (Ps. 50:3); from God's brightness coals were kindled (2 Sam. 22:13; Ps. 18:12); the Lord was not in the fire (1 Kgs. 19:12).

B4b Others in God's fire

Who can live with the consuming fire? (Isa. 33:14); the angel ascended in the flame from the altar (Judg. 13:20); the Lord's fire is in Zion, his furnace in Jerusalem (Isa. 31:9); a chariot of fire and horses of fire (2 Kgs. 2:11); horses and chariots of fire round Elisha (2 Kgs. 6:17); in the midst of the creatures were coals of fire (Ezek. 1:13); the fire between the cherubim (Ezek. 10:7); fill your hands with burning coals from between the cherubim (Ezek. 10:2); take fire from between the whirling wheels (Ezek. 10:6); you [Tyre] walked in the midst of the stones of fire (Ezek. 28:14); the guardian cherub drove you from the stones of fire (Ezek. 28:16).

B5 Fire from God

B5a Fire emanating from God

Smoke from his nostrils and fire from his mouth (2 Sam. 22:9; Ps. 18:8); a river of fire streamed from him

(Dan. 7:10); fire came forth from the Lord (Num. 16:35); the mountain burned with fire (Deut. 4:11; 5:23; 9:15); a great cloud with fire flashing forth and a bright light around (Ezek. 1:4); you were afraid of the fire (Deut. 5:5); this great fire will consume us (Deut. 5:25); let me not see this great fire any more (Deut. 18:16); all flesh will see that I the Lord have kindled the fire (Ezek. 20:48); the voice of the Lord hews out flames of fire (Ps. 29:7); his tongue is like a consuming fire (Isa. 30:27); I will send fire upon Magog (Ezek. 39:6); I will show signs in the sky and on earth, blood, fire and columns of smoke (Joel 2:30); blood, fire and vapour of smoke (Acts 2:19); a fire is kindled in my anger (Deut. 32:22).

B5b Fire from heaven
Fire ran down to the earth (Exod. 9:23); the fire of the Lord burned among them at Taberah [Burning] (Num. 11:1, 3); fire from the Lord burned up the offering (Lev. 9:24; Judg. 6:21; 1 Kgs. 18:38; 1 Chr. 21:26; 2 Chr. 7:1); fire from heaven consumed them (2 Kgs. 1:10, 12, 14; Rev. 20:9); do you want us to call down fire from heaven? (Luke 9:54); fire from the altar was cast on the earth (Rev. 8:5); hail and fire mixed with blood fell on the earth (Rev. 8:7); I will rain hailstones, fire and brimstone on him (Ezek. 38:22); the God who answers by fire (1 Kgs. 18:24).

B5c Fire from God's servants
Cherubim with a flaming sword (Gen. 3:24); God makes flame and fire his servants (Ps. 104:4); he makes his ministers a flame of fire (Heb. 1:7); fire comes from the mouth of the witnesses (Rev. 11:5); scattering coals from among the cherubim (Ezek. 10:2-7).

B5d Fire of God's word
God's word is a fire (Jer. 20:9); is not my word like fire? (Jer. 23:29); I am making my words in your mouth a fire (Jer. 5:14).

B5e Fire of God's anger
Lest my wrath go forth like fire with none to quench it (Jer. 4:4); lest my wrath go forth like fire (Jer. 21:12); by the wrath of the Lord of hosts the land is burned up (Isa. 9:19); God's anger will be seen in devouring fire (Isa. 30:30); the Lord will render his anger with flames of fire (Isa. 66:15); I have consumed them with the fire of my wrath (Ezek. 22:31); I will blow on you with the fire of my wrath (Ezek. 21:31); in the tent of the daughter of Zion he has poured out his wrath like fire (Lam. 2:4); his wrath is poured out like fire (Nahum 1:6); in the fire of my jealousy I spoke against the nations (Ezek. 36:5); all the earth will be consumed in the fire of his jealousy (Zeph. 1:18; 3:8).

B6 Fire of judgement
The Lord will execute judgement with fire (Isa. 66:16; Amos 7:4); by the spirit of judgement and the spirit of burning (Isa. 4:4); I will set a fire in Egypt and her helpers will be broken (Ezek. 30:8); I will kindle a fire on the wall of Rabbah (Amos 1:14); I will bring the third part through the fire (Zech. 13:9); he will be saved, but as by fire (1 Cor. 3:15); each man's work will be revealed with fire (1 Cor. 3:13); a fearful expectation of judgement and fire (Heb. 10:27); fire devours before them and behind them a flame burns (Joel 2:3); the fiery ordeal comes on you to test you (1 Pet. 4:12); the elements will be destroyed with fire and the earth burned up (2 Pet. 3:10); I will rain hailstones, fire and brimstone on him (Ezek. 38:22); hail and fire mixed with blood fell on the earth (Rev. 8:7); the heavens and earth are reserved for fire (2 Pet. 3:7); the heavens will be burned up and the elements melt (2 Pet. 3:12); I will send fire on: the house of Hazael (Amos 1:4); the wall of Gaza (Amos 1:7); the wall of Tyre (Amos 1:10);

Teman (Amos 1:12); Moab (Amos 2:2); Judah (Amos 2:5).

B7 Fire of hell
The angels will throw the wicked into the furnace (Matt. 13:50); to be thrown into the eternal fire (Matt. 18:8); the eternal fire prepared for the devil and his angels (Matt. 25:41); the punishment of eternal fire (Jude 7); the hell of fire (Matt. 5:22; 18:9); I am in anguish in this flame (Luke 16:24); hell, the unquenchable fire (Mark 9:43); their fire will not be quenched (Isa. 66:24); where their fire is not quenched (Mark 9:48); the beast and false prophet were thrown into the lake of fire (Rev. 19:20); with the devil (Rev. 20:10); those whose names were not in the book of life were thrown into the lake of fire (Rev. 20:15); the lake of fire is the second death (Rev. 20:14; 21:8); worshippers of the beast will be tormented with fire and brimstone (Rev. 14:10).

C Effects of fire
SOOT, see 332C.

C1 Smoke
C1a Smoke in general
Smoke from his nostrils and fire from his mouth (2 Sam. 22:9; Ps. 18:8); the temple was filled with smoke (Isa. 6:4; Rev. 15:8); the smoke went up as from a furnace (Gen. 19:28); the mountain smoked when God descended on it in fire (Exod. 19:18); he touches the mountains and they smoke (Ps. 104:32); touch the mountains so that they smoke (Ps. 144:5); the smoke of Ai went up (Josh. 8:20-1); a column of smoke from Gibeah was the signal (Judg. 20:38-40); the forests roll upwards in a column of smoke (Isa. 9:18); the mountain smoking (Exod. 20:18); thick is the Lord's smoke (Isa. 30:27); smoke comes from the north (Isa. 14:31); smoke went up from the abyss (Rev. 9:2); its smoke will go up for ever (Isa. 34:10); the smoke from her goes up for ever (Rev. 19:3); the smoke of their torment goes up for ever (Rev. 14:11); I will show signs in the sky and on earth, blood, fire and columns of smoke (Joel 2:30); blood, fire and vapour of smoke (Acts 2:19); I will burn her chariots in smoke (Nahum 2:13); out of the smoke came locusts (Rev. 9:3); fire and smoke and sulphur issue from their mouths (Rev. 9:17, 18); when they see the smoke of Babylon's burning (Rev. 18:9); as they saw the smoke of her burning (Rev. 18:18).

C1b Sacrifices in smoke
Offering up sacrifices in smoke (Lev. 1:9); the smoke of the incense went up before God (Rev. 8:4); do not offer up honey or yeast in smoke (Lev. 2:11, 12).

C1c Like smoke
I am like a wineskin in the smoke (Ps. 119:83); a lazy man is like smoke to the eyes (Prov. 10:26); the wicked will vanish like smoke (Ps. 37:20); as smoke is driven away, so drive them away (Ps. 68:2); my days pass away like smoke (Ps. 102:3); they will be like smoke from a chimney (Hos. 13:3); they are smoke in my nostrils (Isa. 65:5); who is this like pillars of smoke? (S. of S. 3:6); the heavens will vanish like smoke (Isa. 51:6).

C2 Ashes
C2a Ashes of sacrifices
The ashes are to be taken to a clean place (Lev. 6:11); removing the ashes from the altar (Num. 4:13); beside the altar to the east, the place of the ashes (Lev. 1:16); take the ashes from the burnt offering and put them beside the altar (Lev. 6:10); the ashes of a red heifer (Num. 19:9-10, 17; Heb. 9:13); the ashes on the altar poured out (1 Kgs. 13:3, 5).

C2b Ashes of humiliation
They cast dust on their heads and wallow in ashes (Ezek. 27:30); Tamar put ashes on her head (2 Sam.

13:19); Mordecai put ashes on his head (Esther 4:1); Job sat among the ashes (Job 2:8); the king of Nineveh sat in the ashes (Jonah 3:6); I repent in dust and ashes (Job 42:6); he has made me cower in ashes (Lam. 3:16); those reared in purple lie on ash heaps (Lam. 4:5); prayer with fasting, sackcloth and ashes (Dan. 9:3); repenting in sackcloth and ashes (Matt. 11:21; Luke 10:13); put on sackcloth and roll in ashes (Jer. 6:26); is a fast just to lie on sackcloth and ashes? (Isa. 58:5); I eat ashes like bread (Ps. 102:9); he feeds on ashes (Isa. 44:20); God lifts the needy from the ash heap (Ps. 113:7); to give to those who mourn a garland instead of ashes (Isa. 61:3); God turned Sodom and Gomorrah to ashes (2 Pet. 2:6).

C2c Like ashes
I have turned you to ashes (Ezek. 28:18); I who am but dust and ashes (Gen. 18:27); I have become like dust and ashes (Job 30:19); the wicked will be ashes under your feet (Mal. 4:3); your maxims are proverbs of ashes (Job 13:12); he scatters frost like ashes (Ps. 147:16).

C3 Lime
The people will be burned to lime (Isa. 33:12); he burned to lime the bones of the king of Edom (Amos 2:1).

C4 Warming
They lit a fire (Luke 22:55; Acts 28:2); the king had a fire burning in a brazier (Jer. 36:22); Peter warmed himself at the fire (Mark 14:54, 67; John 18:18, 25); he takes a part of the tree and warms himself (Isa. 44:15-16); a virgin to keep David warm (1 Kgs. 1:2); if two lie together they keep warm (Eccles. 4:11); the boy's flesh became warm (2 Kgs. 4:34); the ostrich leaves her eggs to be warmed in the dust (Job 39:14); be warmed and filled! (Jas. 2:16).

C5 Scorching
Scorched by the east wind (Gen. 41:6, 23, 27); the plants on rocky ground were scorched (Matt. 13:6; Mark 4:6); scorched like grass on the housetops (2 Kgs. 19:26; Isa. 37:27); the flame will wither his shoots (Job 15:30); if vine wood has been used for fuel, both ends burnt and the middle charred (Ezek. 15:4-5); the sun has scorched me (S. of S. 1:6); with consciences cauterised [seared as with an iron] (1 Tim. 4:2); the sun scorched people with fire (Rev. 16:8); men were scorched by the heat (Rev. 16:9).

C6 Baking / cooking
C6a Baking bread / cakes
Baking unleavened bread (Exod. 12:39); bake 12 loaves (Lev. 24:5); ten women will bake your bread in one oven (Lev. 26:26); the king will take your daughters as cooks and bakers (1 Sam. 8:13); the medium baked unleavened bread (1 Sam. 28:24); Tamar baked cakes for Amnon (2 Sam. 13:8); the cake to be baked on dung (Ezek. 4:12); I baked bread on its coals and roasted meat (Isa. 44:19); a cereal offering baked on a fire-pot (Lev. 2:4); the cereal offering must not be baked with leaven (Lev. 6:17); a cereal offering baked on a griddle (Lev. 2:5; 6:21); a cake baked on hot stones (1 Kgs. 19:6); Ephraim is a cake not turned (Hos. 7:8); like an oven heated by the baker (Hos. 7:4).

C6b Baking / cooking other things
Baking bricks (Gen. 11:3); roasted ears of grain (Lev. 2:14); a charcoal fire with fish and bread on it (John 21:9); cook the Passover (Deut. 16:7); eat the lamb roasted (Exod. 12:8-9); they roasted the Passover (2 Chr. 35:13); these are kitchens for boiling the people's sacrifices (Ezek. 46:24); all who sacrifice will use the cooking pots to boil the meat (Zech. 14:21); do not eat the lamb raw or boiled (Exod. 12:9); bake or boil the manna (Exod. 16:23); boiling manna (Num. 11:8); Jacob boiled some pottage (Gen. 25:29); boiling

the sin offering (Lev. 6:28); boil the ram of ordination (Exod. 29:31; Lev. 8:31); places for baking and boiling the offerings (Ezek. 46:20-4); the priest will not have boiled meat, but raw (1 Sam. 2:15); do not boil a kid in its mother's milk (Exod. 23:19; 34:26; Deut. 14:21); he boiled the oxen (1 Kgs. 19:21); compassionate women boil their own children (Lam. 4:10); we boiled my son and ate him (2 Kgs. 6:29); seethe the bones in the pot (Ezek. 24:5).

D Burning
D1 Burning people
D1a Burning people in general
The worthless will be burned like thorns (2 Sam. 23:7); evildoers will be set on fire like stubble (Mal. 4:1); fire goes before him and burns up his enemies (Ps. 97:3); everyone will be salted with fire (Mark 9:49); fire will devour your enemies (Ps. 21:9; Isa. 26:11); a fire will spread to all the house of Israel (Ezek. 5:4); they will fall by sword and flame, by captivity and by plunder (Dan. 11:33); fire will devour you, the sword cut you down (Nahum 3:15); your survivors will be consumed by the fire (Ezek. 23:25); the rust of your gold and silver will eat your flesh like fire (Jas. 5:3); the man and his work will burn with none to quench them (Isa. 1:31); fire devoured his young men (Ps. 78:63); fire from the Lord consumed the 250 men (Num. 16:35); the fire of God burned up Job's sheep and servants (Job 1:16); let an unfamed fire devour him (Job 20:26); may burning coals fall on them (Ps. 140:10); let the bones be burned (Ezek. 24:10); the beast's body was destroyed and given over to be burned (Dan. 7:11); fire burns them like stubble (Isa. 47:14).

D1b Judicial burning
You shall give burning for burning (Exod. 21:25); if a priest's daughter becomes a prostitute she must be burned (Lev. 21:9); let her be burned (Gen. 38:24); if a man marries a woman and her mother they shall all be burned (Lev. 20:14).

D1c Individuals burned
Fire consumed Dathan and Abiram (Ps. 106:18); fire from the Lord consumed them (Lev. 10:2); all Israel will mourn the burning of Nadab and Abihu (Lev. 10:6); Josiah burned the bones of the priests on their altars (2 Chr. 34:5); he burned to lime the bones of the king of Edom (Amos 2:1); often he falls into the fire, and often into the water (Matt. 17:15); it has often cast him into the fire and into the water (Mark 9:22); you will heap burning coals of fire on his head (Prov. 25:22; Rom. 12:20); if I deliver my body to be burned and have not love (1 Cor. 13:3); the ten horns and the beast will eat the harlot's flesh and burn her up with fire (Rev. 17:16); she will be burned with fire (Rev. 18:8); let fire consume Abimelech and his followers (Judg. 9:20); we will burn your house down on you (Judg. 12:1); we will burn you and your house (Judg. 14:15); Zimri burned the king's house over himself (1 Kgs. 16:18); they burned her and her father (Judg. 15:6); they burned the bodies of Saul and his sons (1 Sam. 31:12); they burned Achan's family (Josh. 7:15, 25); Zedekiah and Ahab whom the king of Babylon roasted in the fire (Jer. 29:22).

D1d Burning children in sacrifice
Burning children as sacrifices (Deut. 12:31; 2 Chr. 28:3; 33:6; Jer. 7:31; 19:5); making son or daughter pass through the fire (Deut. 18:10; 2 Kgs. 21:6; 2 Chr. 33:6); making their sons pass through the fire (Ezek. 20:26, 31; 23:37); they make their children pass through the fire to Molech (Jer. 32:35); you offered up my children to idols, making them pass through the fire (Ezek. 16:21); Ahaz made his son pass through the fire (2 Kgs. 16:3); they made their children pass through the fire (2 Kgs.

17:17, 31); Josiah defiled Topheth so it could not be used for making children pass through the fire (2 Kgs. 23:10).

D2 Burning cities

The Lord rained fire and brimstone on Sodom and Gomorrah (Gen. 19:24); fire and brimstone rained from heaven and destroyed Sodom (Luke 17:29); the king set their city on fire (Matt. 22:7); burn that unfaithful city with its booty (Deut. 13:16); they burned Jericho (Josh. 6:24); set Ai on fire (Josh. 8:8, 19, 28); they burned Hazor (Josh. 11:11, 13); a fire went out from Heshbon which devoured Ar (Num. 21:28); the city of Laish was burnt (Judg. 18:27); the Amalekites had burnt Ziklag (1 Sam. 30:1, 3, 14); Pharaoh burned Gezer (1 Kgs. 9:16); I will set fire to the wall of Damascus (Jer. 49:27); Memphis will be burned down (Jer. 46:19); they did not burn cities on their mounds (Josh. 11:13); Tyre will be consumed with fire (Zech. 9:4); Babylon's high gates will be burned (Jer. 51:58); when they see the smoke of Babylon's burning (Rev. 18:9, 18).

D3 Burning Jerusalem / Judah

The king of Babylon will burn Jerusalem (Jer. 21:10); Jerusalem was burnt (Judg. 1:8); the Chaldeans will set this city on fire (Jer. 32:29); the Lord kindled a fire in Zion which consumed its foundations (Lam. 4:11); I will kindle a fire in the gates of Jerusalem (Jer. 17:27); he set fire to the temple of the Lord (2 Kgs. 25:9; 2 Chr. 36:19; Jer. 52:13); our holy and beautiful house has been burned (Isa. 64:11); they burned your sanctuary (Ps. 74:7); they burned all the meeting places (Ps. 74:8).

D4 Burning sacrifices

Fire from the Lord burned up the offering (Lev. 9:24; Judg. 6:21; 1 Kgs. 18:38; 1 Chr. 21:26; 2 Chr. 7:1); Abraham took fire for the sacrifice (Gen. 22:6-7); fire for burning the sacrifice (Lev. 1:7); the fire must burn continuously on the altar (Lev. 6:12, 13); the fire for the burnt offering must burn all night (Lev. 6:9); the sin offering must be burned (Lev. 6:30); burn the sin offering outside the camp (Exod. 29:14; Lev. 4:12); the bodies of sin offerings are burned outside the camp (Heb. 13:11); burn the red heifer (Num. 19:5); the Nazirite must burn his hair with the peace offerings (Num. 6:18); a pan of coals for the incense (Lev. 16:12); Nadab and Abihu offered unauthorised fire (Lev. 10:1; Num. 3:4; 26:61); that you might not kindle fire on my altars in vain (Mal. 1:10); the priests' portion had been burned (Lev. 10:16); before the fat was burned (1 Sam. 2:15); they burn sacrifices on bricks (Isa. 65:3); they burned sacrifices on the mountains (Isa. 65:7); burn the remainder of: the passover lamb (Exod. 12:10); the ram of ordination and the bread (Exod. 29:34; Lev. 8:32); the peace offering (Lev. 7:17; 19:6-7).

D5 Burning idolatrous things

Moses burned the calf (Exod. 32:20; Deut. 9:21); burn their graven images (Deut. 7:5, 25); burn their Asherim (Deut. 12:3); David burned the Philistines' gods (1 Chr. 14:12); Asa burned the horrible idol (1 Kgs. 15:13; 2 Chr. 15:16); Josiah burned the Asherah (2 Kgs. 23:6); they have cast their gods into the fire (2 Kgs. 19:18; Isa. 37:19); burning the pillar of the house of Baal (2 Kgs. 10:26); they burned the vessels made for Baal (2 Kgs. 23:4); the chariots of the sun burned (2 Kgs. 23:11); the temples of the gods of Egypt will be burned (Jer. 43:12, 13).

D6 Burning plants

Fire burning grain or field (Exod. 22:6); Samson used foxes to set fire to the grain (Judg. 15:4-5); Joab's field was set on fire (2 Sam. 14:30); fire has devoured the pastures of the wilderness (Joel 1:19, 20); as a tongue of fire devours stubble (Isa. 5:24); like the crackling of a flame of fire devouring the stubble (Joel 2:5); he will

burn the chaff with unquenchable fire (Matt. 3:12; Luke 3:17); tie the weeds in bundles to be burned (Matt. 13:30); land bearing thorns and thistles will be burned (Heb. 6:8); a third of the earth, trees and all the grass were burned up (Rev. 8:7); your vine is burned with fire (Ps. 80:16); as fire consumes the forest (Ps. 83:14); I will kindle a fire in her forest (Jer. 21:14); if I had briars and thorns to battle I would burn them (Isa. 27:4); let fire from the bramble consume the cedars of Lebanon (Judg. 9:15); open your doors, Lebanon, that the fire may devour your cedars (Zech. 11:1); they will cut down your cedars and throw them on the fire (Jer. 22:7); how great a forest is kindled by a small fire! (Jas. 3:5); with the noise of a great tumult he will set fire to the olive tree (Jer. 11:16); every unfruitful tree is thrown into the fire (Matt. 3:10; 7:19; Luke 3:9); the withered branches are burned up (John 15:6).

D7 Burning other things

Paul shook the creature off into the fire (Acts 28:5); I threw the gold into the fire and out came this calf (Exod. 32:24); fire consumes the tents of the wicked (Job 15:34); burning chariots (Josh. 11:6, 9; Ps. 46:9; Nahum 2:13); fire has consumed your gate bars (Nahum 3:13); Jehoiakim burned Jeremiah's scroll (Jer. 36:22-3); many who had practised magic burnt their books (Acts 19:19); something like a burning mountain was thrown into the sea (Rev. 8:8); take some hairs and burn them in the fire (Ezek. 5:4); fire has consumed the abundance of the wicked (Job 22:20); burning shields, bucklers, bows, arrows and spears (Ezek. 39:9); all her earnings will be burned (Mic. 1:7).

382 Refrigeration

A Cooling

Most people's love will grow cold (Matt. 24:12); send Lazarus to dip the tip of his finger in water and cool my tongue (Luke 16:24).

B Extinguishing

For lack of wood the fire goes out (Prov. 26:20); the fire was quenched (Num. 11:2); they will extinguish the coal which is left (2 Sam. 14:7); they were extinguished like a fire of thorns (Ps. 118:12); by faith they quenched fire (Heb. 11:34); the shield of faith can extinguish the flaming darts of the evil one (Eph. 6:16); they have put out the lamps (2 Chr. 29:7); our lamps are going out (Matt. 25:8); the lamp of the wicked goes out (Job 18:6; Prov. 13:9); the lamp of the wicked will be put out (Prov. 24:20); he who curses his parents, his light will be put out in darkness (Prov. 20:20); horse and army are extinguished like a wick (Isa. 43:17).

C Not extinguishing

Do not put out the light of Israel (2 Sam. 21:17); many waters cannot quench love (S. of S. 8:7); the man and his work will burn with none to quench them (Isa. 1:31); my anger will burn and not be quenched (Jer. 7:20); let his fire consume with none to quench it for Bethel (Amos 5:6); a dimly burning wick he will not extinguish (Isa. 42:3; Matt. 12:20); do not quench the Spirit (1 Thess. 5:19).

D No fire

Do not light your fire on the sabbath (Exod. 35:3); do not put any fire under the oxen (1 Kgs. 18:23, 25).

383 Heater

A Furnace

A furnace is for gold (Prov. 17:3; 27:21); as they melt metals in the furnace (Ezek. 22:20, 22); they are bronze and tin and iron and lead in the furnace (Ezek. 22:18); whoever does not worship will be cast into a fiery furnace (Dan. 3:6-26); grass alive today and tomorrow thrown into the furnace (Matt. 6:30; Luke 12:28); his feet were as if they burned in a furnace (Rev. 1:15); the smoke of Sinai went up like that of a furnace (Exod. 19:18); smoke from the pit like the smoke of a great furnace (Rev. 9:2); evildoers will be cast into the fiery furnace (Matt. 13:42); the day comes, burning like a furnace (Mal. 4:1); the smoke went up as from a kiln (Gen. 19:28); soot from the kiln (Exod. 9:8, 10); David made the Ammonites pass through the brick kiln (2 Sam. 12:31); out of the iron furnace of Egypt (Deut. 4:20; 1 Kgs. 8:51; Jer. 11:4); the Lord's furnace is in Jerusalem (Isa. 31:9); my bones burn like a furnace (Ps. 102:3).

B Oven

Frogs will come into your ovens (Exod. 8:3); an oven on which a carcass falls must be smashed (Lev. 11:35); like an oven neglected by the baker (Hos. 7:4); they are hot as an oven (Hos. 7:6-7); our skin is hot as an oven from the heat of famine (Lam. 5:10); you will make your enemies like a blazing oven (Ps. 21:9); they are all hot as an oven (Hos. 7:7).

C Hearth / kitchen

Each of the four courts had hearths (Ezek. 46:23); the altar hearth will be 12 cubits square (Ezek. 43:16); the altar hearth will be four cubits (Ezek. 43:15); these are kitchens for boiling the people's sacrifices (Ezek. 46:24).

384 Refrigerator

COOLING, see 382A.

385 Fuel

A Firewood / charcoal

A1 Firewood in general

Women make a fire of the branches (Isa. 27:11); using the wood of the vine for fuel (Ezek. 15:4-6); heap on the logs, kindle the fire (Ezek. 24:10); Elijah boiled the oxen with the implements (1 Kgs. 19:21); the Asherah was used as fuel for the altar (Judg. 6:26); the cart was used as fuel for the altar (1 Sam. 6:14); threshing sledges and yokes used for fuel (2 Sam. 24:22; 1 Chr. 21:23); putting the ox on the wood (1 Kgs. 18:23, 33); I burned half of it in the fire (Isa. 44:19).

A2 Provision of firewood

Abraham took wood for the sacrifice (Gen. 22:3, 6-7); the priest must put wood on the altar every morning (Lev. 6:12); a man gathering wood on the sabbath (Num. 15:32); pile wood under the pot (Ezek. 24:5); a widow gathering sticks (1 Kgs. 17:10, 12); the children gather wood (Jer. 7:18); young men grind at the mill and boys stagger under loads of wood (Lam. 5:13); Paul gathered a bundle of sticks and put them on the fire (Acts 28:3); they will not need to gather firewood from the forests (Ezek. 39:10); the Gibeonites became hewers of wood (Josh. 9:21, 23, 27); the one who chops your wood (Deut. 29:11); casting lots for the people to bring firewood (Neh. 10:34); Nehemiah provided for the supply of wood (Neh. 13:31); the wood we get must be paid for (Lam. 5:4); Lebanon would not suffice for fuel (Isa. 40:16); for lack of wood the fire goes out (Prov. 26:20).

A3 Charcoal

Charcoal to hot embers and wood to a fire (Prov. 26:22); they had made a charcoal fire (John 18:18); a charcoal fire with fish and bread on it (John 21:9).

B Oil for fuel

Bring oil of olives for the light (Exod. 27:20).

C Dung for fuel

The cake to be baked on human dung (Ezek. 4:12); or cow's dung (Ezek. 4:15).

D Weapons for fuel

Weapons will be used for fuel (Ezek. 39:9-10); every warrior's boot and bloody cloak will be fuel (Isa. 9:5).

E Sulphur

It rained fire and brimstone on Sodom and Gomorrah (Gen. 19:24; Luke 17:29); the land will be brimstone and salt (Deut. 29:23); its streams will be turned into pitch and its soil brimstone (Isa. 34:9); the breath of the Lord is like a stream of brimstone (Isa. 30:33); brimstone is scattered on his habitation (Job 18:15); on the wicked he will rain fire and sulphur (Ps. 11:6); I will rain hailstones, fire and brimstone on him (Ezek. 38:22); breastplates the colour of fire and jacinth and brimstone (Rev. 9:17); fire and smoke and sulphur issue from their mouths (Rev. 9:17, 18); worshippers of the beast will be tormented with fire and brimstone (Rev. 14:10); the lake of fire which burns with brimstone (Rev. 19:20); the lake of fire and brimstone (Rev. 20:10); the lake which burns with fire and brimstone, which is the second death (Rev. 21:8).

F Like fuel

As fire kindles brushwood (Isa. 64:2); I will make Judah like a flaming torch among sheaves (Zech. 12:6); I will make the clans of Judah like a firepot among wood (Zech. 12:6); the arrogant and evildoers will be like stubble set ablaze (Mal. 4:1); like the wood of the vine, given up for fuel, so are Jerusalem's inhabitants (Ezek. 15:6); a contentious man is like fuel to a fire (Prov. 26:21); the people are like fuel for the fire (Isa. 9:19); I will make this people the wood (Jer. 5:14); you will be fuel for the fire (Ezek. 21:32); like thorns burned in the fire (Isa. 33:12); these two smouldering stumps of firebrands (Isa. 7:4); the house of Jacob will be a fire and the house of Esau stubble (Obad. 18).

386 Taste

A Flavour

The manna tasted like wafers made with honey (Exod. 16:31); like cakes baked with oil (Num. 11:8); Moab's taste remains in him (Jer. 48:11).

B Tasting

The steward tasted the water become wine (John 2:9); when Belshazzar tasted the wine (Dan. 5:2); when he tasted the wine mixed with gall he would not drink it (Matt. 27:34); the ear tastes words as the palate tastes food (Job 12:11; 34:3); cannot my palate discern calamity? (Job 6:30); those who have tasted the heavenly gift (Heb. 6:4); those who have tasted the good word of God (Heb. 6:5); taste and see that the Lord is good (Ps. 34:8); tasting the kindness of the Lord (1 Pet. 2:3); 'do not taste' (Col. 2:21).

387 Insipidness

A Tasteless

If salt has become tasteless (Matt. 5:13; Luke 14:34); if salt has lost its saltness (Mark 9:50); is there any taste in the white of an egg [slime of the purslane?] (Job 6:6); can something tasteless be eaten without salt? (Job 6:6).

B Unable to taste

Barzillai could no longer taste his food (2 Sam. 19:35).

388 Pungency

SOURNESS, see 393.

389 Salt

Lot's wife became a pillar of salt (Gen. 19:26); he turns a fruitful land into a salt waste (Ps. 107:34); the land brimstone and salt (Deut. 29:23); an uninhabited salt land (Jer. 17:6); Abimelech sowed Shechem with salt (Judg. 9:45); its swamps and marshes will not become fresh, but left for salt (Ezek. 47:11); a place possessed by nettles and salt pits (Zeph. 2:9); make the incense, salted, pure and holy (Exod. 30:35); salt for sacrifices is to be given to them (Ezra 6:9; 7:22); at birth you were not rubbed with salt (Ezek. 16:4); Elisha threw salt into the spring (2 Kgs. 2:20-2); salt water cannot yield fresh (Jas. 3:12); the priests shall throw salt on them and offer them as a burnt offering (Ezek. 43:24); everyone will be salted with fire (Mark 9:49); if salt has become tasteless, how can you season it? (Matt. 5:13; Mark 9:50; Luke 14:34); the salt of the covenant on cereal offerings (Lev. 2:13); an everlasting covenant of salt (Num. 18:19; 2 Chr. 13:5); we eat the salt of the palace (Ezra 4:14); the oxen and donkeys will eat salted fodder (Isa. 30:24); can something tasteless be eaten without salt? (Job 6:6); you are the salt of the earth (Matt. 5:13); have salt in yourselves (Mark 9:50); let your speech be seasoned with salt (Col. 4:6).

390 Savouriness

Savoury food such as he loves (Gen. 27:4-31); I did not eat any tasty food (Dan. 10:3); those that ate delicacies are desolate in the streets (Lam. 4:5); the words of a whisperer are like tasty morsels (Prov. 18:8; 26:22).

391 Unsavouriness

A Inedible

Figs so bad they could not be eaten (Jer. 24:2, 3, 8).

B Bitter

UNPLEASANT, see 825D2.

B1 Bitter food

Eat the lamb with bitter herbs (Exod. 12:8; Num. 9:11); they gave me gall for my food (Ps. 69:21); strong drink is bitter to those who drink it (Isa. 24:9); to a hungry man the bitter is sweet (Prov. 27:7); those who turn justice into wormwood (Amos 5:7); you have turned the fruit of righteousness into wormwood (Amos 6:12); the scroll making the stomach bitter (Rev. 10:9-10); a root bearing poisonous fruit and wormwood (Deut. 29:18); I will feed them with wormwood (Jer. 9:15; 23:15); he has filled me with bitterness, he has made me drunk with wormwood (Lam. 3:15); remember my affliction and wandering, the wormwood and bitterness (Lam. 3:19).

B2 Bitter water

Marah, bitter water (Exod. 15:23); wormwood made the waters bitter (Rev. 8:11); the water of bitterness (Num. 5:18-27).

C Bitter and sweet

Woe to those who put bitter for sweet and sweet for bitter (Isa. 5:20); does a fountain give both sweet water and bitter? (Jas. 3:11).

392 Sweetness

A Sweet

Out of the strong came something sweet (Judg. 14:14); the fig tree would not leave its sweetness to reign (Judg. 9:11); why does sweet cane come to me from a distant land? (Jer. 6:20); you bought me no sweet cane (Isa. 43:24); the waters of the sea became fresh (Ezek. 47:8); where the waters go the sea becomes fresh (Ezek. 47:9); does a fountain give both sweet and bitter water? (Jas. 3:11); he threw the tree into the water and the water became sweet (Exod. 15:25); its swamps and marshes will not become fresh, but left for salt (Ezek. 47:11); to a hungry man the bitter is sweet (Prov. 27:7); what is sweeter than honey? (Judg. 14:18); honey is sweet, as is wisdom (Prov. 24:13-14); pleasant words are a honeycomb (Prov. 16:24); your words are sweeter than honey (Ps. 19:10; 119:103); the scroll was sweet as honey (Ezek. 3:3); the scroll sweet as honey in the mouth (Rev. 10:9, 10); desire fulfilled is sweet to the soul (Prov.

13:19); his fruit was sweet to my taste (S. of S. 2:3); bread gained by deceit is sweet to a man (Prov. 20:17); evil is sweet in his mouth (Job 20:12).

BITTER AND SWEET, see 391C.

B Honey

B1 Honey in general

Take some honey (Gen. 43:11); take a jar of honey (1 Kgs. 14:3); a land of olive trees and honey (Deut. 8:8; 2 Kgs. 18:32); bees and honey in the carcass of the lion (Judg. 14:8-9); you ate fine flour, honey and oil (Ezek. 16:13); honey on the floor of the forest (1 Sam. 14:25-9); honey provided for David and the people (2 Sam. 17:29); the manna was like wafers with honey (Exod. 16:31); I have eaten my honeycomb and my honey (S. of S. 5:1); John the baptist ate locusts and wild honey (Matt. 3:4; Mark 1:6); they traded with wheat, olives, early figs, honey, oil and balm (Ezek. 27:17); he fed them honey from the rock (Deut. 32:13); with honey from the rock I would not satisfy you (Ps. 81:16); your lips drip honey (S. of S. 4:11); the lips of an adulteress drip honey (Prov. 5:3); honey was not to be used in a fire-offering (Lev. 2:11); honey must not be offered as a soothing aroma (Lev. 2:12); honey could be offered as firstfruits (Lev. 2:12); my bread, fine flour, oil and honey you offered to the images (Ezek. 16:19); it is not good to eat too much honey (Prov. 25:27); do not eat too much honey lest you vomit it (Prov. 25:16); a sated man loathes honey (Prov. 27:7).

B2 Sweetness of honey

The scroll was sweet as honey in my mouth (Ezek. 3:3); the scroll sweet as honey in the mouth (Rev. 10:9, 10); what is sweeter than honey? (Judg. 14:18); your words are sweeter than honey (Ps. 19:10; 119:103); pleasant words are a honeycomb (Prov. 16:24); honey is sweet, as is wisdom (Prov. 24:13-14).

B3 Milk and honey

A land flowing with milk and honey (Exod. 3:8, 17; 13:5; 33:3; Lev. 20:24; Num. 13:27; 14:8; 16:14; Deut. 6:3; 11:9; 26:9, 15; 27:3; 31:20; Josh. 5:6; Jer. 11:5; 32:22; Ezek. 20:6, 15); rivers flowing with honey and curds (Job 20:17); you brought us from a land flowing with milk and honey (Num. 16:13).

393 Sourness

A Vinegar

The Nazirite must not drink vinegar (Num. 6:3); dip your bread in the vinegar (Ruth 2:14); they offered Christ vinegar to drink (Matt. 27:48; Mark 15:36; Luke 23:36; John 19:29-30); they gave me vinegar to drink (Ps. 69:21); undue cheerfulness is like vinegar on soda (Prov. 25:20); a lazy man is like vinegar to the teeth (Prov. 10:26).

B Sour grapes

The fathers have eaten sour grapes (Jer. 31:29; Ezek. 18:2); everyone who eats sour grapes, his teeth will be set on edge (Jer. 31:30).

394 Odour

A Smelling

God smelled the soothing aroma (Gen. 8:21); I will not smell your soothing aromas (Lev. 26:31); Isaac smelled his son's garments (Gen. 27:27); a wild donkey sniffing the wind in her heat (Jer. 2:24); the horse smells battle from afar (Job 39:25); whoever makes incense like this to smell (Exod. 30:38).

B Sense of smell

If all were hearing, where would be the sense of smell? (1 Cor. 12:17).

395 Without smell
Idols cannot smell (Deut. 4:28); idols have noses but cannot smell (Ps. 115:6).

396 Fragrance
A Perfume and spices
A1 Perfume and spices in general
Oil and perfume make the heart glad (Prov. 27:9); let its fragrance be wafted abroad (S. of S. 4:16); be like a gazelle on the mountains of spices (S. of S. 8:14); Israel's fragrance will be like Lebanon (Hos. 14:6); the finest spices (S. of S. 4:13-14); my beloved has gone down to the beds of spices (S. of S. 6:2); Hezekiah showed them the spices (2 Kgs. 20:13; Isa. 39:2); sons of the priests mixed the spices (1 Chr. 9:30).

A2 Particular spices
Bdellium in Havilah (Gen. 2:12); the manna looked like bdellium (Num. 11:7); 500 shekels of free-flowing myrrh (Exod. 30:23); 250 shekels of sweet-smelling cane (Exod. 30:23); 500 shekels of cassia (Exod. 30:24); 250 shekels of sweet-smelling cinnamon (Exod. 30:23); equal parts of stacte, onycha, galbanum and frankincense (Exod. 30:34); nard, saffron, calamus and cinnamon (S. of S. 4:14); cassia and sweet cane (Ezek. 27:19); trees of frankincense, myrrh and aloes (S. of S. 4:14); my beloved is a bag of myrrh (S. of S. 1:13); my beloved is a cluster of henna blossoms (S. of S. 1:14); perfumed with myrrh and frankincense (S. of S. 3:6); to the mountains of myrrh and incense (S. of S. 4:6); gum, balm and myrrh from Gilead (Gen. 37:25); aromatic gum and myrrh (Gen. 43:11); why does sweet cane come to me from a distant land? (Jer. 6:20); you set on the table my incense and my oil (Ezek. 23:41).

A3 Provision of perfume
An alabaster jar of expensive perfume (Matt. 26:7-9; Mark 14:3; Luke 7:37-8); a pound of costly perfume of pure nard (John 12:3); dealing in spices, precious stones and gold (Ezek. 27:22); they traded with wheat, olives, early figs, honey, oil and balm (Ezek. 27:17); cargo of cinnamon, spice, incense, myrrh and frankincense (Rev. 18:13); the Queen of Sheba brought a large quantity of spices (1 Kgs. 10:2, 10; 2 Chr. 9:1, 9); spices were given to Solomon (1 Kgs. 10:25); why does frankincense come to me from Sheba? (Jer. 6:20); they will bring gold and frankincense (Isa. 60:6); gold, frankincense and myrrh were given to Jesus (Matt. 2:11); they offered him wine mixed with myrrh (Mark 15:23); they brought the spices (Luke 24:1); spices were prepared to anoint Jesus' body (Mark 16:1); the women prepared spices and perfumes (Luke 23:56); Nicodemus and Joseph wrapped his body with myrrh and aloes (John 19:39-40); Asa was buried with spices (2 Chr. 16:14); they will burn spices at your funeral (Jer. 34:5).

A4 Anointed with perfume
Mary anointed the Lord with ointment (John 11:2); in pouring this perfume on my body she has prepared it for burial (Matt. 26:12); while the king was at his table my nard gave out its fragrance (S. of S. 1:12); the smell of Esau's garments was like the smell of a field blessed by the Lord (Gen. 27:27); your garments are fragrant as myrrh, aloes and cassia (Ps. 45:8); the fragrance of your garments is like Lebanon (S. of S. 4:11); my hands dripped with myrrh (S. of S. 5:5); his lips drip liquid myrrh (S. of S. 5:13); I have sprinkled my bed with myrrh, aloes and cinnamon (Prov. 7:17); six months of myrrh and six months (Esther 2:12); the fragrance of your oils is better than all spices (S. of S. 4:10); his cheeks are like a bed of spices (S. of S. 5:13); you increased your perfumes (Isa. 57:9); your oils are fragrant (S. of S. 1:3).

A5 Perfumed anointing oil
The perfumed anointing oil (Exod. 30:25); spices for the anointing oil (Exod. 25:6; 30:23-4; 35:8, 28).

B Incense
B1 Holy incense
The holy incense (Exod. 30:34-8; 31:11; 35:8; 37:29; 39:38); the incense of spices (Exod. 25:6); Eleazar looked after the incense (Num. 4:16); incense burnt on the gold altar (Exod. 40:27); morning and evening (Exod. 30:7-9); and when making atonement (Lev. 16:12-13; Num. 16:46-7); incense on the grain offering (Lev. 2:1, 15-16; 6:15); frankincense on the 12 loaves (Lev. 24:7); no incense on a sin offering (Lev. 5:11); nor on grain offering of jealousy (Num. 5:15); gold pans full of incense (Num. 7:14-86); in every place incense is offered to my name (Mal. 1:11); the golden altar of incense (Heb. 9:4); an angel holding a golden censer (Rev. 8:3); only priests could burn incense (Num. 16:40; 1 Sam. 2:28; 1 Chr. 23:13; 2 Chr. 26:18); the Levites will offer incense (Deut. 33:10); some Levites looked after the incense (1 Chr. 9:29); Nadab and Abihu put incense in their censers (Lev. 10:1); Solomon burned incense with his sacrifices (1 Kgs. 9:25); Zechariah was chosen by lot to burn incense (Luke 1:9); a temple in which to burn incense (2 Chr. 2:4).

B2 Incense and prayer
Golden bowls of incense which are the prayers of the saints (Rev. 5:8); incense was mixed with the prayers of the saints (Rev. 8:3-4); may my prayer be as incense (Ps. 141:2); people praying at the hour of incense (Luke 1:10); the smoke of the incense went up with the prayers of the saints (Rev. 8:4).

B3 Incense offered amiss
Do not offer strange incense on the altar (Exod. 30:9); Nadab and Abihu took their censers (Lev. 10:1); Korah and his men were to present incense (Num. 16:6-39); Uzziah entered the temple to burn incense (2 Chr. 26:16); each man with his censer in his hand (2 Chr. 8:11); incense is an abomination to me (Isa. 1:13); Nebuchadnezzar commanded that incense be offered to Daniel (Dan. 2:46); they sacrifice to their net and burn incense to their seine (Hab. 1:16); Solomon burned incense at the high places (1 Kgs. 3:3); Ahaz burned incense at the high places (2 Kgs. 16:4; 2 Chr. 28:4); the people burned incense at the high places (1 Kgs. 22:43; 2 Kgs. 12:3); Jeroboam burned incense on the altar (1 Kgs. 12:33; 13:1); burning incense to other gods (1 Kgs. 11:8; 2 Kgs. 22:17; Jer. 18:15); they will cry to the gods to whom they burn incense (Jer. 11:12); burning incense to Baal (2 Kgs. 23:5; Jer. 11:13; 32:29); Ahaz burned incense in the valley of Ben-hinnom (2 Chr. 28:3); offering incense to idols (Ezek. 8:11); you offered my oil and my incense to the images (Ezek. 16:18).

B4 No incense
I will cut down your incense altars (Lev. 26:30); I will make an end of the Moabite who burns incense to his gods (Jer. 48:35); Asa removed the incense altars (2 Chr. 14:5); they have not burned incense (2 Chr. 29:7).

C Aroma of sacrifices
God smelled the soothing aroma of the burnt offerings (Gen. 8:21); sacrifices are a soothing aroma to God (Exod. 29:41; Lev. 1:9; Num. 15:3); the burnt offering is a soothing aroma (Exod. 29:18); it is a fire offering, a soothing aroma (Exod. 29:25); where they offered soothing aroma to all their idols (Ezek. 6:13); you made offerings to the images for a soothing aroma (Ezek. 16:19); the sacrifice of Christ is a fragrant aroma (Eph. 5:2); the gifts you sent are a fragrant aroma, an acceptable sacrifice (Phil. 4:18); he spreads the aroma of the knowledge of Christ (2 Cor. 2:14); we are the

fragrance of Christ to God (2 Cor. 2:15-16); as a
soothing aroma I will accept you (Ezek. 20:41); they
sent up their soothing aroma at every hill or tree (Ezek.
20:28); yeast must not be offered as a soothing aroma
(Lev. 2:12); I will not smell your pleasant aromas (Lev.
26:31).

397 Stench

You have made me stink before the inhabitants of the
land (Gen. 34:30); you have made us stink in the eyes of
Pharaoh and his servants (Exod. 5:21); dead flies make
the perfumer's oil stink (Eccles. 10:1); Egypt's canals
will stink (Isa. 19:6); their fish stink for lack of water
(Isa. 50:2); the Nile stank (Exod. 7:18); the land stank
(Exod. 8:14); the leftover manna stank (Exod. 16:20); I
made the stench of your camp rise in your nostrils
(Amos 4:10); Lazarus, dead for four days, would stink
(John 11:39); the stench of their corpses will rise (Isa.
34:3); his stench and foul smell will rise (Joel 2:20); the
leftover manna did not stink on the sabbath (Exod.
16:24); their clothes were not harmed and no smell of
fire was on them (Dan. 3:27).

398 Sound

There is the sound of heavy rain (1 Kgs. 18:41); more
than the sound of many waters the Lord is mighty (Ps.
93:4); his voice was like the sound of many waters
(Ezek. 43:2); the sound of his words was like the noise
of a crowd (Dan. 10:6); Ahijah heard the sound of her
feet (1 Kgs. 14:6); the sound of his master's feet is
behind him (2 Kgs. 6:32); Athaliah heard the sound of
the coronation (2 Kgs. 11:13; 2 Chr. 23:12); the Lord
made the Arameans hear the sound of chariots and
horses (2 Kgs. 7:6); the noise of the hooves of his
stallions (Jer. 47:3); the sound of marching in the tops
of the balsam trees (1 Chr. 14:15); the noise of battle is
in the land (Jer. 50:22); the sound of the living
creatures' wings (Ezek. 1:24; 3:13; 10:5); I heard behind
me the sound of a great earthquake (Ezek. 3:12-13); a
sound like a snake (Jer. 46:22); a sound came from
heaven like a mighty, rushing wind (Acts 2:2); the
sound of the locusts' wings was like the sound of
chariots (Rev. 9:9); the Lord will make Babylon's loud
noise vanish from her (Jer. 51:55).

399 Silence

Silence in heaven for about half an hour (Rev. 8:1); the
Lord will make Babylon's loud noise vanish from her
(Jer. 51:55); I will silence the sound of your songs (Ezek.
26:13); groan silently (Ezek. 24:17).

400 Loudness

A Noisy

Joseph wept so loudly that the Egyptians heard it (Gen.
45:2); the earth shook with their noise (1 Kgs. 1:40); the
sound of the trumpet grew louder and louder (Exod.
19:19); the harlot is loud and wayward (Prov. 7:11); the
foolish woman is noisy (Prov. 9:13); he who blesses
loudly early in the morning will be reckoned as a curse
(Prov. 27:14); call Pharaoh loudmouth who has missed
his opportunity (Jer. 46:17); the sound of a great
commotion out of the north (Jer. 10:22); the
commander could not hear because of the uproar (Acts
21:34); a noisy gong or clanging cymbal (1 Cor. 13:1);
your walls will shake at the sound of horseman, wagons
and chariots (Ezek. 26:10); a noisy multitude of the
peoples (Mic. 2:12); people weeping and wailing loudly
(Mark 5:38); one turned back, praising God with a loud
voice (Luke 17:15).

B Shout

B1 Shout of God

The Lord will roar from on high (Jer. 25:30); the Lord
will shout (Isa. 42:13); the Lord will shout like those
who tread the grapes (Jer. 25:30); God has ascended
with a shout (Ps. 47:5); over Philistia I shout (Ps. 60:8);
the Lord himself will descend from heaven with a
shout (1 Thess. 4:16); a loud voice came out of the
sanctuary, from the throne (Rev. 16:17).

B2 Shout!

Shout! (Josh. 6:16); shout to the Lord with a voice of
joy (Ps. 47:1); call out to Baal with a loud voice (1 Kgs.
18:27); cry loudly, raise your voice like a trumpet,
declare to my people their sins (Isa. 58:1).

B3 Shouting to the Lord

Shout to the Lord with a voice of joy (Ps. 47:1); praising
the Lord with a very loud voice (2 Chr. 20:19); the
people shouted for joy when they praised the Lord
(Ezra 3:11-13); the Levites cried to the Lord with a loud
voice (Neh. 9:4); they made an oath to the Lord with
shouting (2 Chr. 15:14); the enemies shouted in the
house of the Lord as on an appointed feast (Lam. 2:7).

B4 Individuals shouting

Solomon blessed all the assembly with a loud voice
(1 Kgs. 8:55); the voice of one shouting in the
wilderness (Matt. 3:3; Mark 1:3; Luke 3:4); Elizabeth
cried out with a loud voice (Luke 1:42); send her away,
for she is shouting after us (Matt. 15:23); two blind men
cried out (Matt. 20:30-1); he began to cry out, 'Jesus,
have mercy!' (Mark 10:47-8); the unclean spirit
convulsed him, cried out with a loud voice and came
out of him (Mark 1:26); the demoniac shouted out
(Mark 1:23; 5:7; Luke 4:33); night and day he was crying
out and gashing himself with stones (Mark 5:5); when
he saw Jesus he cried out (Luke 8:28); a spirit seizes
him and he suddenly cries out (Luke 9:39); the woman
cried out in labour pains (Rev. 12:2); Jesus cried out
(Matt. 27:46, 50; Mark 15:34, 37; Luke 23:46; John 11:43;
12:44); Paul said with a loud voice, 'Stand upright!'
(Acts 14:10); Paul cried out with a loud voice (Acts
16:28).

B5 Groups shouting

Joshua heard the people shout (Exod. 32:17-18); the
shout of a king is among them (Num. 23:21); when
Samson came the Philistines shouted (Judg. 15:14); all
the city shouted (1 Sam. 4:13); the prophets of Baal
shouted (1 Kgs. 18:28); crowds before and behind were
shouting out (Matt. 21:9); the crowd shouted, 'Crucify
him!' (Matt. 27:23; Mark 15:13-14; Luke 23:23); they
thought it was a ghost and they cried out (Mark 6:49);
those who went before and those who came after cried
out (Mark 11:9); they cried out with a loud voice (Acts
7:57); unclean spirits came out of many, shouting with
a loud voice (Acts 8:7); some shouted one thing and
some another (Acts 19:32; 21:34); they shouted and
waved their garments in the air (Acts 22:23); they called
out with a loud voice (Rev. 6:10); they cry out with a
loud voice (Rev. 7:10); the loud voice of a great
multitude in heaven (Rev. 19:1); when the ark came
into the camp, the Israelites raised a great shout (1 Sam.
4:5-6); they brought up the ark with shouting and
trumpet sound (2 Sam. 6:15); the people shouted, 'Long
live the king!' (1 Sam. 10:24).

B6 No shouting

Do not shout until you are told (Josh. 6:10); the words
of the wise in quiet are better than the shouting of a
ruler (Eccles. 9:17); my servant will not quarrel or shout
out (Matt. 12:19); if they kept quiet, the stones would
cry out (Luke 19:40).

C Battle cry

Around Jericho, all the people shouted (Josh. 6:5, 16, 20); Gideon's men shouted (Judg. 7:20); shouting the war cry (1 Sam. 17:20; 2 Chr. 13:15); to lift up the voice with a battle cry (Ezek. 21:22); Moab will die with war cries and the sound of the trumpet (Amos 2:2); shouting on the day of battle (Amos 1:14).

D Hailing

Jotham shouted from the top of Mount Gerizim (Judg. 9:7); David shouted from a distant mountain (1 Sam. 26:13-14); Goliath shouted to Israel (1 Sam. 17:8); Micah and his men shouted to the Danites (Judg. 18:23); the Rabshakeh cried with a loud voice (2 Kgs. 18:28); wisdom calls out (Prov. 8:1); wisdom shouts in the streets (Prov. 1:20); a voice says 'Shout!' (Isa. 40:6); like children calling to others (Matt. 11:16).

401 Faintness

The words of the wise in quiet are better than the shouting of a ruler (Eccles. 9:17); they could only whisper a prayer (Isa. 26:16); David's servants were whispering (2 Sam. 12:19); how faint a whisper do we hear of him! (Job 26:14); you were the talk and whispering of the people (Ezek. 36:3); what you hear in your ear, proclaim on the housetops (Matt. 10:27); what you have whispered in inner rooms will be proclaimed on housetops (Luke 12:3); the sound of the grinding is low (Eccles. 12:4).

402 Bang

The crack of the whip, the rumble of the wheel (Nahum 3:2); there will be a loud crash from the hills (Zeph. 1:10).

403 Roar

A Lion's roar

Young lions roar after their prey (Ps. 104:21); a young lion came roaring towards him (Judg. 14:5); the lions have roared at him (Jer. 2:15); the lion has roared (Amos 3:8); does a lion roar without prey? (Amos 3:4); the Lord will roar like a lion (Hos. 11:10); the Lord roars from Zion (Joel 3:16; Amos 1:2); the land was appalled at the sound of his roaring (Ezek. 19:7); the roar of lions, for the majesty of the Jordan is ruined (Zech. 11:3); they are like a roaring lion tearing the prey (Ezek. 22:25); a loud voice like a lion roaring (Rev. 10:3); a king's anger is like a lion's roar (Prov. 19:12; 20:2); a wicked ruler is like a roaring lion (Prov. 28:15); their roaring is like a lion (Isa. 5:29); they will roar together like lions (Jer. 51:38); my inheritance is like a lion roaring against me (Jer. 12:8); the devil prowls like a roaring lion (1 Pet. 5:8); the heavens will pass away with a roar (2 Pet. 3:10).

B Rumble / growl

Listen to the thunder of his voice, the rumbling from his mouth (Job 37:2); the rumble of his chariot wheels (Jer. 47:3); as with the rumbling of chariots they leap on the mountaintops (Joel 2:5); we growl like bears (Isa. 59:11); they growl if they are not satisfied (Ps. 59:15); the crack of the whip, the rumble of the wheel (Nahum 3:2).

404 Resonance

ROAR, see 403.

405 Nonresonance

FAINTNESS, see 401.

406 Hissing

God hisses at the wicked (Job 27:23); I will make them a horror and a hissing (Jer. 25:9); I will make this city a desolation and a hissing (Jer. 19:8); to make Jerusalem a horror, a hissing and a curse (Jer. 25:18); they will be a curse, a horror and a hissing (Jer. 29:18); Babylon will become a horror and a hissing (Jer. 51:37); those who pass by Babylon will hiss because of her wounds (Jer. 50:13); everyone who passes by Edom will hiss (Jer. 49:17); all who pass by hiss and shake their heads (Lam. 2:15); your enemies hiss and gnash their teeth (Lam. 2:16); their land will be a place to be hissed at for ever (Jer. 18:16); the merchants hiss at you (Ezek. 27:36); everyone who passes Nineveh will hiss and shake his hand (Zeph. 2:15).

407 Squeak

Your speech will squeak from the dust (Isa. 29:4).

408 Human cry

Lest you groan at the end of your life (Prov. 5:11); all her people groan seeking bread (Lam. 1:11); her priests groan (Lam. 1:4); my groans are poured out like water (Job 3:24); my groans are many and my heart is faint (Lam. 1:22); Pharaoh will groan like a stricken man (Ezek. 30:24); when the wounded groan (Ezek. 26:15); I have heard their groans (Acts 7:34); the creation groans in travail (Rom. 8:22); we groan, waiting for the redemption of our bodies (Rom. 8:23); the Spirit intercedes for us with groans too deep for words (Rom. 8:26); here indeed we groan (2 Cor. 5:2); while we are in this tent we groan (2 Cor. 5:4).

409 Animal sounds

LION S ROAR, see 403A.

A Barking and howling

They howl like a dog (Ps. 59:6, 14); not even a dog will bark against Israel (Exod. 11:7); they are dumb dogs, unable to bark (Isa. 56:10).

B Lowing and bleating

The cows lowed as they went (1 Sam. 6:12); what is this bleating and lowing? (1 Sam. 15:14); does the ox low over his fodder? (Job 6:5); the lowing of cattle is not heard (Jer. 9:10).

C Neighing and braying

The horse's shrill neigh terrifies (Job 39:20); well-fed lusty stallions neighing after their neighbours' wives (Jer. 5:8); I have seen your adulteries and your neighings (Jer. 13:27); at the neighing of his stallions the whole land quakes (Jer. 8:16); you neigh like stallions (Jer. 50:11); the snorting of his horses is heard from Dan (Jer. 8:16); does the wild donkey bray over his grass? (Job 6:5).

D Bird sounds

One rises up at the sound of a bird (Eccles. 12:4); before the cock crows you will deny me (Matt. 26:34, 75; Mark 14:30, 72; Luke 22:34, 61; John 13:38); the cock crowed (Matt. 26:74; Mark 14:72; Luke 22:60; John 18:27); we moan like doves (Isa. 59:11); none moved a wing, opened its beak or chirped (Isa. 10:14).

410 Melody

Making melody with your heart to the Lord (Eph. 5:19).

411 Discord

DISSENSION, see 709.

412 Music

A Music to celebrate

The righteous sings and rejoices (Prov. 29:6); sing aloud with gladness for Jacob (Jer. 31:7); sing, O barren one who did not bear (Isa. 54:1); the sound of singing in the camp (Exod. 32:18); rejoicing with singing and instrumental music (1 Sam. 18:6; 1 Chr. 13:8); the elder brother heard music and dancing (Luke 15:25); they sing to tambourine, lyre and pipe (Job 21:12); tambourines and dancing (Judg. 11:34); playing flutes (1 Kgs. 1:40); we played the flute for you and you did not dance (Luke 7:32).

B Singing praise

B1 Sing praise!

Sing! (Judg. 5:10); sing to the Lord, all the earth (1 Chr. 16:23); sing to him (Ps. 105:2); sing to his name (Ps. 135:3); sing to the Lord, praise the Lord! (Jer. 20:13); sing praises to God's name (Ps. 68:4); sing praise to the Lord (Ps. 12:5); sing to God, kingdoms of the earth (Ps. 68:32); sing for joy to the Lord (Ps. 95:1); sing praise to him! (1 Chr. 16:9); sing to the Lord with thanksgiving (Ps. 147:7); sing with psalms, hymns and spiritual songs (Eph. 5:19; Col. 3:16); come before him with singing (Ps. 100:2); when you come together, each one has a song etc. (1 Cor. 14:26); let them sing for joy on their beds (Ps. 149:5); let the mountains sing before the Lord (Ps. 98:8-9); let my tongue sing of your word (Ps. 119:172); if anyone is cheerful he should sing praises (Jas. 5:13); sing for joy, daughter of Zion (Zech. 2:10).

B2 I will sing praise

My tongue will sing of your righteousness (Ps. 51:14); I will sing to the Lord (Ps. 13:6); I will sing praise (2 Sam. 22:50; Ps. 18:49; 57:7; 108:1); I will sing praises to you (Ps. 27:6); I will praise the name of God with a song (Ps. 69:30); I will sing of lovingkindness and justice (Ps. 101:1); I will sing of the lovingkindness of the Lord for ever (Ps. 89:1); I will sing to the Lord as long as I live (Ps. 104:33); I will sing of your strength (Ps. 59:16); I will sing with the spirit and sing with the mind (1 Cor. 14:15); in the shadow of your wings I sing for joy (Ps. 63:7); with my song I thank him (Ps. 28:7); we will sing and praise your power (Ps. 21:13); I will praise you among the Gentiles, I will sing to your name (Rom. 15:9).

B3 Those singing praise

Singing praise to the Lord (Ezra 3:11); singing to the Lord (Exod. 15:1, 21; 2 Sam. 22:1; Ps. 18:1); singing a song of thanksgiving (Ps. 26:7); thanksgiving and song will be found in Zion (Isa. 51:3); they sang his praise (Ps. 106:12); Deborah and Barak sang that day (Judg. 5:1); the Levites sang praises to the Lord with the words of David and Asaph (2 Chr. 29:30); while the assembly worshipped, the singers sang and the trumpets sounded (2 Chr. 29:28); when they had sung a hymn they went out to the Mount of Olives (Matt. 26:30; Mark 14:26); Paul and Silas were singing hymns of praise in prison (Acts 16:25); the priest and Levites praised the Lord with loud music (2 Chr. 30:21); kings will sing of the ways of the Lord (Ps. 138:5); the trees of the forest will sing for joy before the Lord (Ps. 96:12).

C Songs

C1 Songs in general

I would have sent you away with joy and with songs (Gen. 31:27); when the burnt offering began the song began (2 Chr. 29:27); you will have a song as in the night (Isa. 30:29); our captors demanded songs (Ps. 137:3); sing us one of the songs of Zion (Ps. 137:3); how can we sing the Lord's song in a foreign land? (Ps. 137:4); he who sings songs to a heavy heart is like vinegar on soda (Prov. 25:20); those who sing idle songs to the harp (Amos 6:5); better to listen to the rebuke of the wise than the song of fools (Eccles. 7:5); they listen to you as to a love song (Ezek. 33:32); I am [the theme of] their mocking song (Lam. 3:63); I have become their [mocking] song all the day (Lam. 3:14); the Lord is my strength and song (Isa. 12:2); shout joyfully with psalms (Ps. 95:2); your statutes are my

songs (Ps. 119:54); the Lord is my strength and my song (Exod. 15:2; Ps. 118:14); you surround me with songs of deliverance (Ps. 32:7); at night his song is with me (Ps. 42:8).

C2 Writing songs

David says in the Book of Psalms (Luke 20:42); everything written about me in the law of Moses and the prophets and the psalms (Luke 24:44); those who improvise on the harp and like David compose songs (Amos 6:5); Solomon made 1005 songs (1 Kgs. 4:32); write this song (Deut. 31:19); Moses wrote this song (Deut. 31:22); Moses spoke the words of this song (Deut. 31:30; 32:44); they sang the song of Moses (Deut. 32:1-44; Rev. 15:3); the song of Deborah and Barak (Judg. 5:1-31); the song of songs, which is Solomon's (S. of S. 1:1).

C3 Particular songs

Moses and Israel sang this song (Exod. 15:1); Israel sang the song of the well (Num. 21:17-18); this song will be sung in Judah (Isa. 26:1); the song of the vineyard (Isa. 5:1-6); a vineyard! sing of it! (Isa. 27:2); the song of the harlot (Isa. 23:15-16); they sang the song of the Lamb (Rev. 15:3).

C4 A new song

Sing to him a new song (Ps. 33:3; 96:1; 98:1; 149:1; Isa. 42:10); he put a new song in my mouth (Ps. 40:3); I will sing a new song to you (Ps. 144:9); they sang a new song (Rev. 5:9; 14:3).

D Sad music

I am the song of drunkards (Ps. 69:12); they will ridicule you and taunt you with a mournful song (Mic. 2:4); this is a lamentation to be chanted (Ezek. 32:16).

E No music

Young men have quit their music (Lam. 5:14); I will turn your festivals into mourning, your songs into lamentation (Amos 8:10); his maidens had no wedding songs (Ps. 78:63); the music of your harps has been brought down to Sheol (Isa. 14:11); the sound of harpists, minstrels, flute-players and trumpeters will not be heard in you (Rev. 18:22); I will silence the sound of your songs (Ezek. 26:13); take away from me the noise of your songs (Amos 5:23).

413 Musician

A Singers

Singers appointed by David (1 Chr. 15:16); singers appointed by Jehoshaphat (2 Chr. 20:21); singers appointed by Nehemiah (Neh. 12:31); the singers were appointed (Neh. 7:1); the singers of the palace will become mourners (Amos 8:3); the singers (1 Chr. 9:33-4; 15:17-18; 2 Chr. 35:15; Neh. 7:44, 67); singers and pipe-players (Ps. 87:7); I accumulated male and female singers (Eccles. 2:8); the Levitical singers, Asaph, Heman, Jeduthun (2 Chr. 5:12); the singers, sons of Asaph (Ezra 2:41); the children of Asaph were the temple singers (Neh. 11:22); leaders of the singers (Neh. 12:46); Jezrahiah the leader of the singers (Neh. 12:42); no tax to be levied on the singers (Ezra 7:24); can I hear the voice of singing men and women? (2 Sam. 19:35); 200 singing men and women (Ezra 2:65); 288 trained in singing to the Lord (1 Chr. 25:7); the singers were assembled (Neh. 12:28-9); the singers went up to Jerusalem (Ezra 7:7); singers and musicians in procession (Ps. 68:25); Chenaniah was over the singing (1 Chr. 15:22, 27); the daughters of song are brought low (Eccles. 12:4).

B Instrumentalists

Play skilfully with shouts of joy (Ps. 33:3); Jubal was the father of all who play the lyre and pipe (Gen. 4:21); the priests are to blow the trumpets (Num. 10:8); we played the flute for you and you did not dance (Matt. 11:17);

the sound of harpists, minstrels, flute-players and trumpeters will not be heard in you (Rev. 18:22); let a skilful harp-player be found (1 Sam. 16:16-18, 17); David played his harp before Saul (1 Sam. 16:23; 18:10; 19:9); Elisha called for someone to play the harp (2 Kgs. 3:15); the voice was like harpists playing on their harps (Rev. 14:2); the foremen were skilful musicians (2 Chr. 34:12); flute-players at a funeral (Matt. 9:23).

414 Musical instruments

A **Instruments in general**
The instruments of David (2 Chr. 29:26, 27; Neh. 12:36); David made musical instruments for praising the Lord (2 Chr. 7:6); when you hear the musical instruments you must fall down and worship (Dan. 3:5-15).

B **Particular instruments**
B1 **Percussion**
B1a **Bells**
Gold bells were made for the high priest's robe (Exod. 28:33; 39:25); inscribed on the bells of the horses, 'Holy to the Lord' (Zech. 14:20).

B1b **Tambourine**
Singing to God with tambourines (Exod. 15:20); with tambourines (Gen. 31:27; 1 Sam. 10:5; 2 Sam. 6:5; 1 Chr. 13:8); at their banquets they have lyre, harp, tambourine and flute (Isa. 5:12).

B1c **Cymbals and other percussion**
Prophesying with lyres, harps and cymbals (1 Chr. 25:1); praise him with resounding cymbals (Ps. 150:5); cymbals of bronze (1 Chr. 15:19); singing in the temple with cymbals, harps and lyres (1 Chr. 25:6); the Levites were stationed with cymbals, harps and lyres (2 Chr. 29:25); on harps, lyres and cymbals (1 Chr. 15:16); cymbals, harps and lyres (2 Chr. 5:12); the sound of horn, flute, lyre, trigon, harp, bagpipe (Dan. 3:5-15); with lyres, harps, tambourines, castanets and cymbals (2 Sam. 6:5); with lyres, harps, tambourines, cymbals and trumpets (1 Chr. 13:8); the horn, trumpets, cymbals, harps and lyres (1 Chr. 15:28); I am a noisy gong or a clanging cymbal (1 Cor. 13:1).

B2 **Stringed instruments**
B2a **Strings in general**
Stringed instruments made you glad (Ps. 45:8); we will sing to stringed instruments (Isa. 38:20); praise him with stringed instruments (Ps. 150:4).

B2b **Harp**
Lyres and harps were made of algum wood (1 Kgs. 10:12; 2 Chr. 9:11); prophets with harp, tambourine, flute and lyre (1 Sam. 10:5); prophesying with lyres, harps and cymbals (1 Chr. 25:1); praise him with harp and lyre (Ps. 150:3); singing in the temple with cymbals, harps and lyres (1 Chr. 25:6); cymbals, harps and lyres (2 Chr. 5:12); with the ten-stringed harp (Ps. 33:2; 92:3; 144:9); the flute and harp need to give distinct notes (1 Cor. 14:7); the sound of horn, flute, lyre, trigon, harp, bagpipe (Dan. 3:5-15); we hung our harps on the willows (Ps. 137:2); those who improvise on the harp and like David compose songs (Amos 6:5); the sound of your harps will be heard no more (Ezek. 26:13); with lyres, harps, tambourines, castanets and cymbals (2 Sam. 6:5); with lyres, harps, tambourines, cymbals and trumpets (1 Chr. 13:8); the horn, trumpets, cymbals, harps and lyres (1 Chr. 15:28); on harps, lyres and cymbals (1 Chr. 15:16); playing harps and lyres (1 Chr. 16:5); with harps and lyres and trumpets (2 Chr. 20:28); the living creatures and elders had each one a harp (Rev. 5:8); the voice was like harpists playing on their harps (Rev. 14:2); standing on the sea of glass, holding harps of God (Rev. 15:2).

B2c **Lyre**
Lyres and harps were made of algum wood (1 Kgs. 10:12; 2 Chr. 9:11); Jubal was the father of those who handle the lyre and pipe (Gen. 4:21); prophesying with lyres, harps and cymbals (1 Chr. 25:1); praise him with harp and lyre (Ps. 150:3); singing in the temple with cymbals, harps and lyres (1 Chr. 25:6); prophets with harp, tambourine, flute and lyre (1 Sam. 10:5); the Levites were stationed with cymbals, harps and lyres (2 Chr. 29:25); with tambourine and lyre (Gen. 31:27); cymbals, harps and lyres (2 Chr. 5:12); the sound of horn, flute, lyre, trigon, harp, bagpipe (Dan. 3:5, 7, 10, 15); at their banquets they have lyre, harp, tambourine and flute (Isa. 5:12); with lyres, harps, tambourines, castanets and cymbals (2 Sam. 6:5); with lyres, harps, tambourines, cymbals and trumpets (1 Chr. 13:8); the horn, trumpets, cymbals, harps and lyres (1 Chr. 15:28); on harps, lyres and cymbals (1 Chr. 15:16); playing harps and lyres (1 Chr. 16:5); with harps and lyres and trumpets (2 Chr. 20:28).

B3 **Trumpets**
B3a **Trumpets for signalling**
The war horse responds to the trumpet (Job 39:24-5); Two trumpets to be made of silver (Num. 10:2); a voice like a trumpet (Rev. 1:10; 4:1); when you give alms, do not sound a trumpet (Matt. 6:2); the ram's horn sounded for them to go up the mountain (Exod. 19:13-19); the blast of a trumpet (Exod. 20:18; Heb. 12:19); when the trumpet is blown, hear it (Isa. 18:3); listen to the sound of the trumpet (Jer. 6:17); wherever you hear the sound of the trumpet, rally there (Neh. 4:20); the trumpet sounded as a warning of invasion (Jer. 4:5; Hos. 5:8); priests with trumpets to sound the alarm (2 Chr. 13:12, 14); trumpets for the alarm (Num. 31:6); the watchman sounds the trumpet (Ezek. 33:3, 6); put the trumpet to your lips (Hos. 8:1); if a trumpet is blown in a city will the people not tremble? (Amos 3:6); cry loudly, raise your voice like a trumpet (Isa. 58:1); Joab sounded the trumpet for the troops to stop fighting (2 Sam. 2:28; 18:16; 20:22); the trumpet blown to summon the people: by Ehud (Judg. 3:27); by Gideon (Judg. 6:34); by Saul (1 Sam. 13:3); by Sheba (2 Sam. 20:1).

B3b **Trumpets for battle**
If the trumpet gives an uncertain sound, who will prepare for battle? (1 Cor. 14:8); when you go into battle the priests should sound the trumpets (Num. 10:9); I will cause the trumpet blast of war to be heard (Jer. 49:2); a day of trumpet blast and battle cry (Zeph. 1:16); the sound of the trumpet, the alarm of war (Jer. 4:19); they have blown the trumpet but no one goes to battle (Ezek. 7:14); in Egypt we will not see war or hear the trumpet (Jer. 42:14); Moab will die with war cries and the sound of the trumpet (Amos 2:2); the Lord God will sound the trumpet (Zech. 9:14); circling Jericho with the priests blowing trumpets (Josh. 6:4-20); Gideon's men blew their trumpets (Judg. 7:18-22).

B3c **Trumpets for celebration**
The trumpet to sound the year of Jubilee (Lev. 25:9); a day for blowing the trumpets (Num. 29:1); blow the trumpet for your feasts (Num. 10:10); blow the trumpet to proclaim a solemn assembly (Joel 2:15); blow the trumpet at the new moon (Ps. 81:3); 120 priests blowing trumpets (2 Chr. 5:13); priests blowing trumpets (2 Chr. 7:6; Neh. 12:35, 41); bringing up the ark with trumpet sound (2 Sam. 6:15); the Lord has ascended with the sound of a trumpet (Ps. 47:5); the trumpet was sounded for the coronation of: Absalom (2 Sam. 15:10); Solomon (1 Kgs. 1:34, 39); Jehu (2 Kgs. 9:13); Joash (2 Kgs. 11:14; 2 Chr. 23:13).

B3d Trumpets at the end
A great trumpet will sound to gather the exiles (Isa. 27:13); with a loud trumpet call the angels will gather the elect (Matt. 24:31); as the alarm for the day of the Lord (Joel 2:1); at the last trumpet (1 Cor. 15:52); the Lord will descend with the trumpet of God (1 Thess. 4:16); the trumpet will sound and the dead will be raised imperishable (1 Cor. 15:52).

B3e Seven trumpets
Seven trumpets of ram's horns (Josh. 6:4, 6, 8, 13); seven angels with seven trumpets (Rev. 8:2); the seven angels prepared to sound the seven trumpets (Rev. 8:6); sounding: the first trumpet (Rev. 8:7); the second trumpet (Rev. 8:8); the third trumpet (Rev. 8:10); the fourth trumpet (Rev. 8:12); the fifth trumpet (Rev. 9:1); the sixth trumpet (Rev. 9:13); the seventh trumpet (Rev. 11:15).

B4 Pipe / flute
Jubal was the father of those who handle the lyre and pipe (Gen. 4:21); for the flutes (Ps. 5:1); at their banquets they have lyre, harp, tambourine and flute (Isa. 5:12); prophets with harp, tambourine, flute and lyre (1 Sam. 10:5); the flute and harp need to give distinct notes (1 Cor. 14:7); the sound of horn, flute, lyre, trigon, harp, bagpipe (Dan. 3:5-15).

415 Hearing
PAYING ATTENTION, see 455.

A Hearing in general
A1 The faculty of hearing
God made hearing ears (Prov. 20:12); God opens the ears of men (Job 33:16); God opens their ear to instruction (Job 36:10); the Lord has opened my ear (Isa. 50:5); my ears you have dug (Ps. 40:6); your ears will hear a word behind you (Isa. 30:21); if all was hearing, where would be the sense of smell? (1 Cor. 12:17); if the whole body were an eye, where would the hearing be? (1 Cor. 12:17); he who planted the ear, does he not hear? (Ps. 94:9); the ear is not satisfied with hearing (Eccles. 1:8).

A2 Hear and understand!
Hear, O Israel! (Deut. 6:4; Mark 12:29); look with your eyes, hear with your ears and pay attention (Ezek. 40:4); hear this dream of mine (Gen. 37:6); hear and understand! (Matt. 15:10; Mark 7:14); he who has ears, let him hear (Matt. 11:15; 13:9, 43; Mark 4:9, 23; 7:16; Luke 8:8); he who has an ear, let him hear what the Spirit says to the churches (Rev. 2:7, 11, 17, 28; 3:6, 13, 22); he who has an ear, let him hear (Rev. 13:9); you will indeed hear but never understand (Matt. 13:14; Mark 4:12; Luke 8:10; Acts 28:26); when one hears but does not understand (Matt. 13:19); take heed what you hear (Mark 4:24); take care how you hear (Luke 8:18); let every one be quick to hear (Jas. 1:19); blessed are your ears, for they hear (Matt. 13:16); many desired to hear what you hear (Matt. 13:17).

A3 The deaf hearing
Hear, you deaf! (Isa. 42:18); the ears of the deaf will be unstopped (Isa. 35:5); the deaf will hear the words of a book (Isa. 29:18); Jesus healed a deaf man (Mark 7:32-7); the deaf hear (Matt. 11:5; Luke 7:22).

B Ears
He who planted the ear, does he not hear? (Ps. 94:9); if the ear should say, 'I am not an eye' (1 Cor. 12:16); idols have ears but cannot hear (Ps. 115:6; 135:17); they will cut off your nose and your ears (Ezek. 23:25); they stopped up their ears (Acts 7:57); having itching ears (2 Tim. 4:3); the ears of all who hear it will tingle (1 Sam. 3:11; 2 Kgs. 21:12; Jer. 19:3); the ear is not satisfied with hearing (Eccles. 1:8); blood on right ear (Exod. 29:20; Lev. 8:23, 24; 14:14, 25); oil on right ear

(Lev. 14:17, 28); the slave's ear is pierced at the doorpost (Exod. 21:6; Deut. 15:17); my ear you have pierced (Ps. 40:6); I put earrings in your ears (Ezek. 16:12); Jesus put his fingers in the man's ears (Mark 7:33); Peter cut off the ear of the high priest's slave (Matt. 26:51; Mark 14:47; Luke 22:50; John 18:10).

C God hearing
He who planted the ear, does he not hear? (Ps. 94:9); O Lord, hear! (Dan. 9:19); incline your ear and hear! (Dan. 9:18); Samuel repeated their words in the ears of the Lord (1 Sam. 8:21); God heard the voice of the lad (Gen. 21:17); the Lord has heard the sound of my weeping (Ps. 6:8); the Lord heard their grumbling (Exod. 16:2-9); you will know that I have heard your revilings against Israel (Ezek. 35:12); I have heard what the prophets who prophesy falsely have said (Jer. 23:25); whatever the Spirit hears he will speak (John 16:13).

D Hearing God
D1 Hearing God's voice
They heard the sound of the Lord walking in the garden (Gen. 3:8); I heard the sound of you in the garden (Gen. 3:10); I heard the voice of the Lord (Isa. 6:8); I come in a cloud so that the people may hear when I speak to you (Exod. 19:9); you heard the voice out of the darkness (Deut. 5:23); has any other people heard the voice of God? (Deut. 4:33); out of heaven he let you hear his voice (Deut. 4:36); you heard God's voice but saw no form (Deut. 4:12); Moses heard a voice from between the two cherubim (Num. 7:89); I heard one speaking to me from the house (Ezek. 43:6); when I heard the sound of his voice I fell on my face in a deep sleep (Dan. 10:9); no one has heard or seen a God besides you (Isa. 64:4); I heard a man's voice between the banks of the Ulai (Dan. 8:16); today, if you hear his voice (Heb. 3:7, 15-16; 4:7); we heard this voice from heaven (2 Pet. 1:18).

D2 Hearing Christ
That which we have heard, which we have seen with our eyes (1 John 1:1-3); we cannot but speak of what we have seen and heard (Acts 4:20); you will be a witness to all men of what you have seen and heard (Acts 22:15); go and tell John what you hear and see (Matt. 11:4; Luke 7:22); he who hears my words and does them (Matt. 7:24; Luke 6:47); he who hears my words and does not do them (Matt. 7:26; Luke 6:49); Mary sat at his feet and listened to his teaching (Luke 10:39); he who hears my word and believes in him who sent me (John 5:24); crowds gathered to hear him and be healed (Luke 5:15); they came to hear him and to be healed of their diseases (Luke 6:17); you have heard his blasphemy (Matt. 26:65); we have heard for ourselves (John 4:42); the tax collectors and sinners were drawing near to hear him (Luke 15:1); the dead will hear the voice of the Son of God and those who hear will live (John 5:25); they heard the voice but saw no one (Acts 9:7); if any one hears my voice and opens the door (Rev. 3:20).

D3 Hearing God's word
He hears the word and receives it with joy (Matt. 13:20; Mark 4:16; Luke 8:13); those among thorns hear the word but are choked (Matt. 13:22; Mark 4:18; Luke 8:14); they hear the word and hold it fast (Luke 8:15); they hear the word, accept it and bear fruit (Mark 4:20); my mother and brothers are those who hear God's word and do it (Luke 8:21); everyone who has heard and learned from the Father comes to me (John 6:45); he has appointed you to hear a word from his mouth (Acts 22:14); be doers of the word and not merely hearers (Jas. 1:22-5); it is not the hearers of the law but the doers who are just (Rom. 2:13); have they

not all heard? (Rom. 10:18); a famine of hearing the
words of the Lord (Amos 8:11).

E Hearing others
Joseph wept so loudly that the Egyptians heard it (Gen.
45:2); bells so that Aaron might be heard (Exod. 28:35);
do you not hear how many things they testify against
you? (Matt. 27:13); when Herod heard John he was
puzzled, yet he heard him gladly (Mark 6:20); when
Elizabeth heard Mary's greeting the baby leaped in her
womb (Luke 1:41); Jesus was listening to them and
asking them questions (Luke 2:46); the prisoners were
listening to Paul and Silas (Acts 16:25); go down to the
camp and hear what they say (Judg. 7:10-11); Sarah was
listening at the tent door (Gen. 18:10); Rebekah was
listening when Isaac spoke to Esau (Gen. 27:5, 6).

F Hearing information
F1 Hearing about God
Have you not heard? (Isa. 37:26; 40:21, 28); they have
heard that you are in the midst of this people (Num.
14:14); I had heard of you by the hearing of the ear (Job
42:5); our ears have heard what you did in days of old
(Ps. 44:1); the peoples have heard and tremble (Exod.
15:14); Lord, I have heard the report of you and I fear
(Hab. 3:2).

F2 Hearing about Christ
When Herod heard this he was agitated, and all
Jerusalem too (Matt. 2:3); Herod heard of all that
happened (Luke 9:7); John heard of the works of the
Christ (Matt. 11:2); a great crowd, hearing all he did,
came to him (Mark 3:8); she had heard about Jesus
(Mark 5:27); they heard that Jesus was passing by
(Matt. 20:30); Herod the tetrarch heard about Jesus
(Matt. 14:1); if the governor hears about this (Matt.
28:14).

F3 Hearing about other things
When Jesus heard this, he withdrew (Matt. 14:13); Jesus
overheard [or ignored] what was said (Mark 5:36);
what you have said in the dark will be heard in the light
(Luke 12:3); when you hear of wars and disturbances
(Luke 21:9); I have heard of your faith (Eph. 1:15); Jacob
heard that Shechem had defiled Dinah (Gen. 34:5);
Jacob heard that Reuben had lain with Bilhah (Gen.
35:22); Pharaoh heard of it (Exod. 2:15); the Egyptians
will hear of it (Num. 14:13); the Canaanites will hear of
it (Josh. 7:9); Eli heard what his sons did (1 Sam. 2:22);
when Saul hears of it he will kill me (1 Sam. 16:2);
Ebed-melech heard that they had put Jeremiah in the
cistern (Jer. 38:7); all Israel will hear and be afraid
(Deut. 13:11).

G Hearing things
He who hears the trumpet and does not heed the
warning (Ezek. 33:4, 5); what is this bleating and lowing
which I hear? (1 Sam. 15:14); the Lord made the
Arameans hear the sound of an army (2 Kgs. 7:6); when
you hear the sound of marching (2 Sam. 5:24); Ahijah
heard the sound of her feet (1 Kgs. 14:6); Adonijah and
his guests heard the rejoicing (1 Kgs. 1:41); Athaliah
heard the sound of the coronation (2 Kgs. 11:13; 2 Chr.
23:12).

416 Deafness

NOT PAYING ATTENTION, see 456.

A Deaf
It is God who makes man deaf (Exod. 4:11); do not
curse the deaf (Lev. 19:14); can I hear the voice of
singing men and women? (2 Sam. 19:35); who is deaf as
my messenger? (Isa. 42:19); do not be deaf to me (Ps.
28:1); you deaf and dumb spirit! (Mark 9:25); the deaf
cobra which stops up its ears (Ps. 58:4-5); people who
are deaf yet have ears (Isa. 43:8); hear, you deaf! (Isa.
42:18); the ears of the deaf will be unstopped (Isa. 35:5);

the deaf will hear the words of a book (Isa. 29:18); the
deaf hear (Matt. 11:5; Mark 7:37; Luke 7:22).

B Unhearing
Idols have ears but cannot hear (Ps. 115:6; 135:17); idols
do not hear (Deut. 4:28); idols cannot see or hear or
walk (Rev. 9:20); people who are deaf yet have ears
(Isa. 43:8); make their ears dull and their eyes dim (Isa.
6:10); this people have ears but hear not (Jer. 5:21; Ezek.
12:2); hearing they do not hear (Matt. 13:13-15; Mark
8:18); let us hear no more about the holy One of Israel
(Isa. 30:11); their voice is not heard (Ps. 19:3); how can
they hear without a preacher? (Rom. 10:14); refusing to
listen to the Lord's instruction (Isa. 30:9); your ears are
open but no one hears (Isa. 42:20); they stopped up
their ears (Acts 7:57); they turned a stubborn shoulder
and stopped their ears (Zech. 7:11); you have become
dull of hearing (Heb. 5:11); their ears are heavy of
hearing (Acts 28:27); eyes to see not and ears to hear
not (Rom. 11:8); God has not given you ears to hear
(Deut. 29:4); they will turn away their ears from the
truth (2 Tim. 4:4); the time will come when they will
not endure sound doctrine (2 Tim. 4:3); if you will not
listen my soul will weep in secret (Jer. 13:17); if they will
not listen, I will uproot that nation (Jer. 12:17).

417 Light

LIGHT SOURCE, see 420.

A Light in general
God saw the light that it was good (Gen. 1:4); light is
pleasant (Eccles. 11:7); where is the way to where light
dwells? (Job 38:19); man cannot look at the brightness
of the sky (Job 37:21); I could not see because of the
brightness of the light (Acts 22:11); light makes things
become visible (Eph. 5:13); what becomes visible is light
(Eph. 5:13); evildoers hate the light (John 3:20); some
rebel against the light (Job 24:13).

B The light of God
GOD IS A LIGHT, see 420C1.

B1 God is light
God is light (1 John 1:5); there was a radiance around
him (Ezek. 1:27-8); from his loins upwards was
brightness like gleaming metal (Ezek. 8:2); my
judgement goes forth as the light (Hos. 6:5); my justice
will be a light to the peoples (Isa. 51:4); the glory of the
Lord shone round about them (Luke 2:9); the court
was filled with the brightness of the glory of the Lord
(Ezek. 10:4); his radiance is like the light (Hab. 3:4); a
flaming torch passed between the pieces (Gen. 15:17);
from God's brightness fire was kindled (2 Sam. 22:13;
Ps. 18:12); while he was speaking a bright cloud
overshadowed them (Matt. 17:5).

B2 God dwells in light
God dwells in unapproachable light (1 Tim. 6:16);
covering yourself with light as with a cloak (Ps. 104:2);
the light dwells with him (Dan. 2:22).

B3 The light of Christ
I am the light of the world (John 8:12; 9:5); a light to
illuminate the Gentiles (Isa. 42:6); a light of revelation
to the Gentiles (Luke 2:32); I have come as light into
the world (John 12:46); light has come into the world
(John 3:19); the light that enlightens every man (John
1:9); the life was the light of men (John 1:4); daylight
from on high dawns on us (Luke 1:78); the true light is
already shining (1 John 2:8); walk while you have light
(John 12:35); believe in the light to become sons of light
(John 12:36); Christ would be the first to announce
light (Acts 26:23); the light is with you for a little longer
(John 12:35); the light of the gospel of the glory of
Christ (2 Cor. 4:4); the light of the knowledge of the
glory of God in the face of Christ (2 Cor. 4:6); his face
shone like the sun (Matt. 17:2); his garments became as

white as light (Matt. 17:2); John came to bear witness to the light (John 1:7, 8); those with me saw the light but did not understand the voice (Acts 22:9); his face was like the sun shining in its strength (Rev. 1:16).

C The light of people
C1 God gives light
The Lord is my light (Ps. 27:1); the Lord will be your everlasting light (Isa. 60:19-20); the Lord will be my light (Mic. 7:8); the Lord make his face shine upon you (Num. 6:25); let your face shine on me (Ps. 31:16; 80:3, 7, 19; 119:135); may God make his face shine upon us (Ps. 67:1); lift up the light of your face upon us (Ps. 4:6); the Lord lights my darkness (2 Sam. 22:29; Ps. 18:28); the eyes of your hearts being enlightened (Eph. 1:18); those who have been once enlightened (Heb. 6:4); after you were enlightened (Heb. 10:32); in your light we see light (Ps. 36:9); the Lord has given us light (Ps. 118:27); God will be their light (Rev. 22:5); by his light I walked (Job 29:3); let us walk in the light of the Lord (Isa. 2:5); those who walk in the light of your countenance (Ps. 89:15); our secret sins in the light of your countenance (Ps. 90:8); he will bring me out into the light and I will see his righteousness (Mic. 7:9); arise from the dead and Christ will shine on you (Eph. 5:14); let your light and truth lead me (Ps. 43:3); the commandment of the Lord enlightens the eyes (Ps. 19:8); the commandment is light (Prov. 6:23); your word is a light to my path (Ps. 119:105); the entrance of your words gives light (Ps. 119:130).

C2 Light of God's people
You are the light of the world (Matt. 5:14); let your light shine before men (Matt. 5:16); believe in the light to become sons of light (John 12:36); you are children of the light (1 Thess. 5:5); I have set you as a light for the Gentiles (Acts 13:47); you are sure you are a light to those in darkness (Rom. 2:19); nations will come to your light (Isa. 60:3); he will bring forth your righteousness as the light (Ps. 37:6); shine, for your light has come (Isa. 60:1); if your whole body is full of light with no part dark (Luke 11:36); we share in the inheritance of the saints in light (Col. 1:12); light dawns for the righteous (Ps. 97:11); then your light will break out like dawn (Isa. 58:8); your light will rise in darkness (Isa. 58:10); light rises in the darkness for the upright (Ps. 112:4); Moses' face shone (Exod. 34:29-30, 35; 2 Cor. 3:7); they looked to him and were radiant (Ps. 34:5); a man's wisdom makes his face shine (Eccles. 8:1); the light of my face they did not cast down (Job 29:23); those who are wise will shine like the sky (Dan. 12:3); the light of the righteous shines brightly (Prov. 13:9); the path of the righteous is like dawn, increasing in brightness (Prov. 4:18); the righteous will shine like the sun (Matt. 13:43).

PEOPLE AS LIGHTS, see 420C3.

C3 Living in the light
He who does the truth comes to the light (John 3:21); live as children of light, exhibiting the fruit of the light (Eph. 5:8-9); he who walks in the day does not stumble because he sees this world's light (John 11:9); he who loves his brother abides in the light (1 John 2:10); if we walk in the light as he is in the light we have fellowship ·(1 John 1:7); if the eye is good the whole body is full of light (Matt. 6:22; Luke 11:34-6); take care that the light in you may not be darkness (Luke 11:35); the light of the wicked will be extinguished (Job 18:5).

C4 From darkness to light
The people who walked in darkness have seen a great light (Isa. 9:2); to give light to those who sit in darkness and the shadow of death (Luke 1:79); the people sitting in darkness have seen a great light (Matt. 4:16); the light shines in darkness (John 1:5); God who

commanded light to shine out of darkness has shone in our hearts the light of the knowledge of God (2 Cor. 4:6); he called you out of darkness into his marvellous light (1 Pet. 2:9); once you were darkness but now you are light in the Lord (Eph. 5:8); he who follows me shall not walk in darkness but will have the light of life (John 8:12); Paul was sent to turn them from darkness to light (Acts 26:18).

D The light of things
D1 Light in the world
Let there be light (Gen. 1:3); God put the lights in the firmament to light up the earth (Gen. 1:15-18); God called the light 'day' (Gen. 1:5); on whom does God's light not rise? (Job 25:3); the Lord gives light to both the poor and the oppressor (Prov. 29:13); the Israelites had light (Exod. 10:23); the pillar of fire brought light to Israel (Exod. 13:21; 14:20); a pillar of fire to light their way (Neh. 9:12, 19); there was a light from heaven (Acts 9:3; 22:6; 26:13); light shone in the prison (Acts 12:7).

D2 Light of lamps
Moses lit the lamps (Exod. 40:25); the lamps will give light before the lampstand (Num. 8:2); a lamp is placed on a lampstand so that the light may be seen (Luke 8:16); those who light a lamp put it on a lampstand that those who enter may see the light (Luke 11:33); as when a lamp gives you light (Luke 11:36); the light of a lamp will not shine in you again (Rev. 18:23).

E Light and darkness
God makes light and darkness (Isa. 45:7); darkness and light are alike to you (Ps. 139:12); God separated light from darkness (Gen. 1:4); God gave sun, moon and stars to divide light from darkness (Gen. 1:18); the boundary between light and darkness (Job 26:10); wisdom exceeds folly as light exceeds darkness (Eccles. 2:13); woe to those who put darkness for light and light for darkness (Isa. 5:20); he turns deep darkness into morning and darkens day into night (Amos 5:8); what fellowship has light with darkness? (2 Cor. 6:14); as to a lamp shining in a dark place (2 Pet. 1:19); he who says he is in the light and hates his brother is in darkness still (1 John 2:9).

418 Darkness

LIGHT AND DARKNESS, see 417E.

A Darkness over the earth
A1 Darkness in general
Where is the place of darkness? (Job 38:19-20); darkness was upon the face of the deep (Gen. 1:2); I made darkness the swaddling band of the sea (Job 38:9); God separated the light from the darkness (Gen. 1:4).

A2 Darkness during daytime
The earth will mourn and the heaven be dark (Jer. 4:28); I will darken the earth at noon (Amos 8:9); a day of clouds and thick darkness (Ezek. 34:12); the land darkened with the locusts (Exod. 10:15); the sky grew black with clouds and rain (1 Kgs. 18:45); darkness over the land at the crucifixion (Matt. 27:45; Mark 15:33; Luke 23:44); the sun and the air were darkened by the smoke from the pit (Rev. 9:2).

A3 Darkness at the end
The sun will be darkened and the moon not give light (Matt. 24:29; Mark 13:24); the sun will be turned into darkness and the moon into blood (Acts 2:20); the stars and their constellations will not give their light (Isa. 13:10); the moon will not shed its light (Isa. 13:10); the sun will be dark when it rises (Isa. 13:10); I will cover the heavens and darken the stars (Ezek. 32:7); the sun will be turned into darkness and the moon to blood (Joel 2:31); in that day there will be no light (Zech. 14:6); a third of sun, moon and stars were darkened

(Rev. 8:12); a third of the day and a third of the night were darkened (Rev. 8:12).

B God and darkness

God makes light and darkness (Isa. 45:7); God called the darkness 'night' (Gen. 1:5); God made darkness his canopy (2 Sam. 22:12; Ps. 18:11); darkness under his feet (2 Sam. 22:10; Ps. 18:9); clouds and darkness are round him (Ps. 97:2); the day of the Lord is a day of darkness (Joel 2:2; Amos 5:18, 20; Zeph. 1:15); there is no darkness where evildoers may hide from God (Job 34:22); even the darkness is not dark to you (Ps. 139:12); God knows what is in darkness (Dan. 2:22); in God there is no darkness (1 John 1:5); the Lord lights my darkness (2 Sam. 22:29; Ps. 18:28); he put darkness between you and the Egyptians (Josh. 24:7); the plague of darkness over Egypt (Exod. 10:21-3); God sent darkness (Ps. 105:28); God spoke from the darkness (Deut. 5:23); I will give you the treasures of darkness (Isa. 45:3); you have not come to darkness, gloom and tempest (Heb. 12:18).

C People and darkness

C1 People in darkness

C1a Acting in the dark

Men prospect for metals in deep darkness (Job 28:3); do you see what the elders of Israel are doing in the dark? (Ezek. 8:12); in the dark they dig through houses (Job 24:16); what you have said in the dark will be heard in the light (Luke 12:3); he who walks in darkness does not know where he goes (John 12:35); if any one walks in the night he stumbles because the light is not in him (John 11:10); who among you walks in darkness and has no light? (Isa. 50:10).

C1b Overtaken by darkness

Terror and darkness fell on Abraham (Gen. 15:12); a mist and darkness fell on him (Acts 13:11); we look for light, and behold, darkness (Isa. 59:9); lest the darkness overtake you (John 12:35); their foolish heart was darkened (Rom. 1:21); Gentiles darkened in their understanding (Eph. 4:18); some dwelt in darkness and the shadow of death (Ps. 107:10); the land of darkness and death-shadow (Job 10:21-2); remember the days of darkness, for they will be many (Eccles. 11:8); darkness and distress in the land (Isa. 5:30); darkness will cover the earth and the peoples (Isa. 60:2); if they do not speak according to this word they have no light of dawn (Isa. 8:20); chiefs grope in darkness without light (Job 12:25); before the sun, light, moon and stars are darkened (Eccles. 12:2); 'surely the darkness will cover me' (Ps. 139:11); to bring those who sit in darkness from the prison (Isa. 42:7).

C2 Darkness of evil

The power of darkness (Luke 22:53); men loved darkness rather than light (John 3:19); when your eye is bad your whole body is full of darkness (Matt. 6:23; Luke 11:34-5); those whose deeds are done in the dark (Isa. 29:15); have nothing to do with the unfruitful deeds of darkness (Eph. 5:11); throw off the deeds of darkness (Rom. 13:12); if we say we have fellowship with him and walk in darkness, we lie (1 John 1:6); those who walk in the paths of darkness (Prov. 2:13); he who hates his brother is in darkness (1 John 2:9, 11); the way of the wicked is like darkness (Prov. 4:19); the fool walks in darkness (Eccles. 2:14); they walk about in darkness (Ps. 82:5); the pestilence that stalks in darkness (Ps. 91:6); the wicked shoot the upright in the dark (Ps. 11:2); we wrestle against the world rulers of this present darkness (Eph. 6:12); the dark places of the land are full of the habitations of violence (Ps. 74:20).

C3 Out of darkness

Those who sat in darkness saw a great light (Isa. 9:2; Matt. 4:16); to give light to those who sit in darkness

and the shadow of death (Luke 1:79); the light shines in the darkness (John 1:5); he has delivered us from the domain of darkness (Col. 1:13); God called you out of darkness (1 Pet. 2:9); he brought them out of darkness (Ps. 107:14); you are not in darkness (1 Thess. 5:4-5); he who follows me will not walk in darkness but will have the light of life (John 8:12); that whoever believes in me may not remain in darkness (John 12:46); formerly you were darkness but now are light (Eph. 5:8); though I sit in darkness the Lord will be my light (Mic. 7:8); the Lord will bring to light the things hidden in darkness (1 Cor. 4:5); the darkness is passing away and the true light is already shining (1 John 2:8).

C4 Outer darkness

The wicked are silenced in darkness (1 Sam. 2:9); they will be driven away into darkness (Isa. 8:22); thrown into outer darkness (Matt. 8:12; 22:13; 25:30); black darkness has been reserved for them (2 Pet. 2:17); those for whom darkness has been reserved for ever (Jude 13); the land where light is as darkness (Job 10:22); he knows a day of darkness is at hand (Job 15:23); he is driven from light into darkness (Job 18:18); let darkness be laid up for his treasures (Job 20:26); the wicked will not escape from darkness (Job 15:30); angels in everlasting bonds in darkness (Jude 6); the kingdom of the beast was in darkness (Rev. 16:10); God kept angels who sinned in pits of darkness until the judgement (2 Pet. 2:4).

D Shadow

D1 Shadow of God

Abiding in the shadow of the Almighty (Ps. 91:1); he hid me in the shadow of his hand (Isa. 49:2); I have hidden you in the shadow of my hand (Isa. 51:16); they take refuge in the shadow of your wings (Ps. 36:7); a cloud overshadowed them (Mark 9:7; Luke 9:34); while he was speaking a bright cloud overshadowed them (Matt. 17:5); the power of the Most High will overshadow you (Luke 1:35); the cherubim of glory overshadowing the mercy seat (Heb. 9:5); the Lord is your shade (Ps. 121:5); you have been a shade from the heat (Isa. 25:4); the Father of lights with whom is no shifting shadow (Jas. 1:17).

D2 Other shadows

The shadow of the mountains looks like men (Judg. 9:36); the shadow went back ten steps (2 Kgs. 20:9-11; Isa. 38:8); the Lord appointed a plant to grow up and be a shade (Jonah 4:5-6); the mountains were covered with the vine's shadow (Ps. 80:10); birds of the air nest in the shade of mustard (Mark 4:32); birds of the air will nest in the shade of its branches (Ezek. 17:23); the beasts of the field found shade under the tree (Dan. 4:12); all great nations lived under the cedar's shadow (Ezek. 31:6); under oak, poplar and terebinth because their shade is pleasant (Hos. 4:13); you have covered us with the shadow of death (Ps. 44:19); my eyelids are sunk in dark shadows (Job 16:16); they wanted Peter's shadow to fall on the sick (Acts 5:15).

D3 Like a shadow

Our days on earth are like a shadow (1 Chr. 29:15; Job 8:9); man's life is like a shadow (Eccles. 6:12); man's days are like a passing shadow (Ps. 144:4); my days are like a lengthened shadow (Ps. 102:11); the sinner will not lengthen his days like a shadow (Eccles. 8:13); man flees like a shadow (Job 14:2); my members are like a shadow (Job 17:7); I am gone like a lengthening shadow (Ps. 109:23); the king and princes will be like the shade of a great rock (Isa. 32:2).

419 Dimness

Those who look through the windows grow dim (Eccles. 12:3); how dim the gold has become! (Lam. 4:1).

420 Light source

A Sun, moon and stars

A1 Sun, moon and stars in general

Sun, moon and stars differ in splendour (1 Cor. 15:41); the sun like a bridegroom (Ps. 19:5); the sun rises, sets and rises again (Eccles. 1:5); God makes his sun rise on good and bad (Matt. 5:45); when the sun rose, the plant was scorched (Matt. 4:6); the sun rises with scorching heat (Jas. 1:11); at noon I saw a light brighter than the sun (Acts 26:13); neither sun nor stars appeared for many days (Acts 27:20); the sun will not beat on them nor any heat (Rev. 7:16); the sun, moon and 11 stars bowed down to Joseph (Gen. 37:9).

A2 The stars

Count the stars if you are able (Gen. 15:5); as the host of heaven cannot be counted (Jer. 33:22); God counts the stars and names them (Ps. 147:4; Isa. 40:26); see how high the distant stars are! (Job 22:12); though you set your nest among the stars (Obad. 4); the stars fought against Sisera (Judg. 5:20); we saw the star at its rising (Matt. 2:2); Herod found what time the star appeared (Matt. 2:7); the star stood over where the child lay (Matt. 2:9); I will give him the morning star (Rev. 2:28); the star of the god Rephan (Acts 7:43); till day dawns and the morning star rises in your hearts (2 Pet. 1:19).

A3 Sun, moon and stars before God

Creation of sun, moon and stars (Gen. 1:14-16; Ps. 136:7-9); he made the stars also (Gen. 1:16); he made the Pleiades and Orion (Amos 5:8); God makes the Bear, Orion and the Pleiades (Job 9:9); God gave sun, moon and stars for light (Jer. 31:35); you established light and sun (Ps. 74:16); he made the moon for the seasons and the sun to set (Ps. 104:19); when I consider the heavens, the moon and stars which you have made (Ps. 8:3); the moon has no brightness in his sight (Job 25:5); the stars are not pure in his sight (Job 25:5); praise him, sun, moon and stars (Ps. 148:3); the heavenly host bows down before you (Neh. 9:6).

A4 Worshipping sun, moon and stars

Do not worship sun, moon and stars (Deut. 4:19; 17:3); they worshipped all the host of heaven (2 Kgs. 17:16); Manasseh worshipped all the host of heaven (2 Kgs. 21:3; 2 Chr. 33:3); and made altars for them (2 Kgs. 21:5; 2 Chr. 33:5); vessels made for the host of heaven (2 Kgs. 23:4); burning incense to sun, moon and stars (2 Kgs. 23:5); 25 men worshipping the sun (Ezek. 8:16); the sun, moon and stars which they have served (Jer. 8:2); they burnt sacrifices on the rooftops to all the host of heaven (Jer. 19:13); horses and chariots for the sun (2 Kgs. 23:11); God gave them up to serve the host of heaven (Acts 7:42); if I have looked at the sun or moon (Job 31:26); those who bow down on rooftops to the host of heaven (Zeph. 1:5); those who predict by the stars and the new moons (Isa. 47:13).

A5 Controlling sun, moon and stars

Can you bind the Pleiades or loose Orion? (Job 38:31); can you guide the Bear? (Job 38:32); do you know the ordinances of the heavens? (Job 38:33); God seals up the stars (Job 9:7); the sun will not smite you by day nor the moon by night (Ps. 121:6); heat or sun will not smite them (Isa. 49:10); the sun and moon stood still (Josh. 10:12-13).

A6 Darkening sun, moon and stars

The stars, sun and moon will not give their light (Isa. 13:10); God tells the sun not to shine (Job 9:7); the sun and moon grow dark and the stars no longer shine (Joel 2:10); I will make the sun go down at noon (Amos 8:9); before sun, moon and stars are darkened (Eccles. 12:2); the stars, sun and moon will be darkened (Ezek. 32:7-8); the sun and moon grow dark and the stars are dimmed (Joel 3:15); the sun and moon will be darkened and the stars will fall (Matt. 24:29); the sun will be darkened and the moon not give its light (Mark 13:24); the sun will be turned to darkness and the moon to blood (Joel 2:31; Acts 2:20); the sun turned black as sackcloth and the moon like blood (Rev. 6:12); the sun failed (Luke 23:45); I will cover the sun and the moon will not give its light (Ezek. 32:7); I will darken the stars (Ezek. 32:7); all the bright lights in the heavens I will darken over you (Ezek. 32:8).

A7 Affecting sun, moon and stars

A third of sun, moon and stars was struck (Rev. 8:12); the fourth bowl was poured on the sun (Rev. 16:8); the horn threw stars down (Dan. 8:10); the dragon's tail swept a third of the stars from the sky (Rev. 12:4); the host of heaven will rot away (Isa. 34:4); a star from heaven fell to earth (Rev. 9:1); the stars will fall from the sky (Mark 13:25); the stars of the sky fell to the earth (Rev. 6:13).

A8 New role for sun, moon and stars

Your sun will set no more, nor your moon wane (Isa. 60:20); the light of the moon will be as the sun and the sun seven times brighter (Isa. 30:26); no more sun and moon for light (Isa. 60:19-20); the city has no need of sun or moon, for God's glory shines on it (Rev. 21:23).

A9 Like sun, moon or stars

The Lord God is a sun and shield (Ps. 84:11); those who turn to righteousness will be like the stars for ever (Dan. 12:3); a star will come from Jacob (Num. 24:17); fair as the moon, flawless as the sun (S. of S. 6:10); his throne will be established like the sun and moon (Ps. 89:36-7); let those who love God be like the rising sun (Judg. 5:31); the righteous will shine like the sun in the kingdom of their Father (Matt. 13:43); his face shone like the sun (Matt. 17:2); his face was like the sun shining in its strength (Rev. 1:16); in his right hand he held seven stars (Rev. 1:16); the one who holds the seven stars in his hand (Rev. 2:1); he who has the seven stars (Rev. 3:1); the seven stars are the angels of the seven churches (Rev. 1:20); the angel's face was like the sun (Rev. 10:1); wandering stars for whom darkness has been reserved for ever (Jude 13).

B Lamps / torches

B1 Various lamps / torches

A firepot and a flaming torch (Gen. 15:17); Gideon's men had torches in the pitchers (Judg. 7:16, 20); Samson fastened torches to the foxes (Judg. 15:4-5); a woman lights a lamp and sweeps the house (Luke 15:8); Judas came with lanterns, torches and weapons (John 18:3); the jailer called for lights (Acts 16:29); there were many lamps where we were gathered (Acts 20:8); I will search Jerusalem with lamps (Zeph. 1:12); her lamp does not go out at night (Prov. 31:18); a dimly burning wick he will not extinguish (Matt. 12:20); no one lights a lamp and covers it or puts it under a bed (Luke 8:16); no one lights a lamp and puts it in a cellar or under a measure (Luke 11:33); the eye is the lamp of the body (Luke 11:34); as when a lamp gives you light (Luke 11:36); the wise and foolish virgins with their lamps (Matt. 25:3-8); I will take from them the light of the lamp (Jer. 25:10).

B2 The gold lampstand
The lampstand placed on the south side (Exod. 26:35); the lamp of God had not yet gone out (1 Sam. 3:3); the gold lampstand: made (Exod. 25:31-40; 31:8; 35:14; 37:17-24; 39:37; Heb. 9:2); set up (Exod. 40:4, 24-5; Num. 8:2-4); anointed (Exod. 30:27); looked after by Aaron (Lev. 24:3-4); looked after by the Kohathites (Num. 3:31); covered with a blue cloth (Num. 4:9).

B3 Other lampstands
Ten gold lampstands for the temple (1 Kgs. 7:49; 1 Chr. 28:15; 2 Chr. 4:7, 20-1); Zechariah saw a gold lampstand (Zech. 4:2); silver lampstands for the temple (1 Chr. 28:15); seven lamps to give light (Exod. 25:37); seven golden lampstands (Rev. 1:12-13); the seven lampstands are the seven churches (Rev. 1:20); the one who walks among the seven golden lampstands (Rev. 2:1); these are the two olive trees and the two lampstands (Rev. 11:4); a lamp is put on a lampstand (Matt. 5:15; Mark 4:21; Luke 8:16; 11:33); I will remove your lampstand unless you repent (Rev. 2:5).

C Metaphorical lights
C1 God is a light
You are my lamp, O Lord (2 Sam. 22:29); seven lamps which are the seven spirits of God (Rev. 4:5); the Father of lights (Jas. 1:17); no need of lamp or sun, for God will give them light (Rev. 22:5); its lamp is the Lamb (Rev. 21:23).
GOD IS LIGHT, see 417B1.

C2 The word is a light
Your word is a lamp to my feet (Ps. 119:105); the commandment is a lamp (Prov. 6:23); a lamp shining in a dark place (2 Pet. 1:19).

C3 People as lights
You light my lamp (Ps. 18:28); you appear as lights in the world (Phil. 2:15); John was a shining lamp (John 5:35); do not put out the lamp of Israel (2 Sam. 21:17); his eyes were like flaming torches (Dan. 10:6); let your lamps be burning (Luke 12:35); the spirit [breath] of a man is the lamp of the Lord (Prov. 20:27); the lamp of the body is the eye (Matt. 6:22); haughty eyes and proud heart, the lamp of the wicked (Prov. 21:4).
THE LIGHT OF PEOPLE, see 417C.

421 Screen
A Curtains
Hangings of the tabernacle of linen (Exod. 26:1-6; 36:8-13); hangings of the tabernacle of goat's hair (Exod. 26:7-13; 36:14-18); hangings of the court (Exod. 27:9-15; 35:17; 38:9-16); the screen for the gateway (Exod. 27:16; 35:17; 38:18); the screen for the doorway (Exod. 26:36-7; 35:15; 36:37-8); Gershonites responsible for the hangings (Num. 3:25; 4:25-6); black as the curtains of Solomon (S. of S. 1:5); he spreads out the heavens like a curtain (Ps. 104:2; Isa. 40:22).

B The veil of the tabernacle / temple
The veil of the tabernacle (Exod. 26:31-5; 35:12; 36:35-6; 39:34; 40:3; Heb. 9:3); Kohathites looked after the veil (Num. 3:31); the ark was screened with the veil (Exod. 40:3, 21; Num. 4:5); the veil of the testimony (Lev. 24:3); the veil of the temple (2 Chr. 3:14); Jesus entered within the veil (Heb. 6:19); we enter the sanctuary through the veil, his flesh (Heb. 10:20); the veil of the temple was torn in two (Matt. 27:51; Mark 15:38; Luke 23:45).

C Other veils
Rebekah took a veil and covered herself (Gen. 24:65); Tamar covered herself with a veil (Gen. 38:14); why should I be like one who veils herself? (S. of S. 1:7); woe to the women who make veils for those of every stature (Ezek. 13:18); the Lord will destroy the veil over all nations (Isa. 25:7); Moses put a veil over his face (Exod. 34:33-5; 2 Cor. 3:13-15).

422 Transparency
A platform gleaming like crystal (Ezek. 1:22); a sea of glass like crystal (Rev. 4:6); a sea of glass (Rev. 15:2); the street was pure gold, like transparent glass (Rev. 21:21); the river of the water of life, clear as crystal (Rev. 22:1); gold and glass cannot equal wisdom (Job 28:17); coral and crystal cannot equal wisdom (Job 28:18); I will cause their rivers to run clear as oil (Ezek. 32:14); new Jerusalem like a jasper, clear as crystal (Rev. 21:11); the city was pure gold, like clear glass (Rev. 21:18).

423 Opacity
Neither man nor beast will muddy the waters any more (Ezek. 32:13).

424 Semitransparency
TRANSPARENT, see 422.

425 Colour
Dyed embroidered material (Judg. 5:30); coloured linens of Egypt (Prov. 7:16); from your clothes you made coloured high places (Ezek. 16:16); who comes from Bozrah with garments of vivid colour? (Isa. 63:1).

426 Colourless
Why has every face turned pale? (Jer. 30:6); before them people are in anguish, all faces turn pale (Joel 2:6); all faces grow pale (Nahum 2:10).

427 White
PALE, see 426.
A White cloth
The garment of the Ancient of Days was white as snow (Dan. 7:9); at the transfiguration Jesus' garments were shining white (Matt. 17:2; Luke 9:29); clothes whiter than any launderer could whiten them (Mark 9:3); the angels' clothing was white as snow (Matt. 28:3); a young man wearing a white robe (Mark 16:5); two angels in white (John 20:12); two men in white clothing (Acts 1:10); royal robes of blue and white (Esther 8:15); curtains of white and violet linen (Esther 1:6); let your clothes be always white (Eccles. 9:8); they will walk with me in white (Rev. 3:4); he who overcomes will be clothed in white (Rev. 3:5); buy from me white garments (Rev. 3:18); 24 elders clothed in white (Rev. 4:4); white robes given to the martyrs (Rev. 6:11); a multitude clothed in white robes (Rev. 7:9); who are these in white robes? (Rev. 7:13); armies clothed in fine linen, white and clean (Rev. 19:14).

B White hair / wool
His head and hair were white like wool, like snow (Rev. 1:14); the almond tree blossoms (Eccles. 12:5); you cannot make one hair white or black (Matt. 5:36); leprosy turns hairs white (Lev. 13:3-26); leprous, like snow (Num. 12:10; 2 Kgs. 5:27); trading in the wine of Helbon and white wool (Ezek. 27:18); your sins will be like wool (Isa. 1:18).

C White spots
If the bright spot is white (Lev. 13:4-43); his hand was leprous as snow (Exod. 4:6).

D Various white things
Every animal with white in it (Gen. 30:35); white horses (Zech. 1:8; 6:3, 6; Rev. 6:2; 19:11, 14); three baskets of white bread (Gen. 40:16); his teeth will be white with milk (Gen. 49:12); the manna was white (Exod. 16:31); her nobles were purer than snow, whiter than milk (Lam. 4:7); the fields are white for harvest (John 4:35); I saw a great white throne (Rev. 20:11); the bark is stripped off and the branches left white (Joel 1:7); to

him who overcomes I will give a white stone (Rev.
2:17).

E Made white

E1 Washed white
Wash me and I will be whiter than snow (Ps. 51:7);
your sins will be white as snow (Isa. 1:18); your sins will
be like wool (Isa. 1:18); robes washed and made white
in the blood of the Lamb (Rev. 7:14).

E2 Whitewashing
The false prophets whitewash any wall (Ezek. 13:10-15);
her prophets have daubed whitewash (Ezek. 22:28); I
will spend my wrath on the wall and those who
plastered it with whitewash (Ezek. 13:15); I will tear
down the wall you plastered with whitewash (Ezek.
13:14); tell those who whitewash the wall that it will fall
(Ezek. 13:11); you whitewashed wall! (Acts 23:3);
whitewashed tombs (Matt. 23:27).

428 Black

A Black people
My skin turned black (Job 30:30); I am black but
comely (S. of S. 1:5-6); I am blackened but not by the
sun (Job 30:28); they are blacker than soot (Lam. 4:8).

B Black animals
Every black lamb (Gen. 30:32-5); all the black in
Laban's flock (Gen. 30:40); black horses (Zech. 6:2, 6;
Rev. 6:5).

C Black hair
If there is no black hair in it (Lev. 13:31); if black hair
has grown in it (Lev. 13:37); his hair is black as a raven
(S. of S. 5:11); you cannot make one hair white or black
(Matt. 5:36).

D Various black things
The sky grew black with clouds and rain (1 Kgs. 18:45);
the sun became black as sackcloth (Rev. 6:12); like
blackness is spread over the mountains a great people
(Joel 2:2).

429 Grey

Rise up before the grey head (Lev. 19:32); a grey head is
a crown of glory (Prov. 16:31); the glory of old people is
their grey hair (Prov. 20:29); even to grey hairs I will
carry you (Isa. 46:4); you will bring down my hoary
head in sorrow to Sheol (Gen. 42:38; 44:29, 31); the man
of grey hair will be killed (Deut. 32:25); I am old and
grey (1 Sam. 12:2); do not cast me off when I am old
and grey (Ps. 71:18); do not let Joab's grey hair go down
to Sheol in peace (1 Kgs. 2:6); bring his grey hair down
to Sheol with blood (1 Kgs. 2:9).

430 Brown

Sorrel horses (Zech. 1:8).

431 Red

A Red people

A1 Red body
Esau was red at birth (Gen. 25:25); called Edom [red]
through his desire for red stew (Gen. 25:30); they were
more ruddy in body than corals (Lam. 4:7).

A2 Red face
They did not know how to blush (Jer. 6:15; 8:12); David
was ruddy (1 Sam. 16:12; 17:42); my beloved is ruddy (S.
of S. 5:10); my face is red with weeping (Job 16:16); who
has redness of the eyes but the drunkard? (Prov.
23:29-30); his eyes will be red with wine (Gen. 49:12).

B Red animals
A red heifer (Num. 19:2); red horses (Zech. 1:8; 6:2;
Rev. 6:4); a great red dragon (Rev. 12:3); a woman
sitting on a scarlet beast (Rev. 17:3).

C Red cord
Scarlet thread tied to one twin (Gen. 38:28, 30); scarlet
cord dipped in blood (Lev. 14:6, 49, 51-2); scarlet cord
tied in the window (Josh. 2:18, 21); your lips are like a
scarlet thread (S. of S. 4:3).

D Red material
Rams' skins dyed red (Exod. 25:5; 35:7, 23; 36:19); a
cover of scarlet cloth (Num. 4:8); scarlet stuff (Num.
19:6); cargo of fine linen, purple, silk and scarlet (Rev.
18:12); the blood of calves and goats with water, scarlet
wool and hyssop (Heb. 9:19); blue, purple and scarlet
material (Exod. 25:4; 2 Chr. 2:7).

E Red clothes
Saul clothed you in scarlet (2 Sam. 1:24); her household
are clothed in scarlet (Prov. 31:21); though you dress in
scarlet (Jer. 4:30); why are your garments red? (Isa.
63:2); the soldiers are clothed in scarlet (Nahum 2:3);
they put a scarlet robe on Jesus (Matt. 27:28); the
woman was clothed in purple and scarlet (Rev. 17:4);
she who was clothed in purple and scarlet (Rev. 18:16).

F Various red things
Let me swallow some of that red stuff (Gen. 25:30); I
will paint it bright red (Jer. 22:14); the water looked red
like blood (2 Kgs. 3:22); do not look on wine when it is
red (Prov. 23:31); the sky is red (Matt. 16:2, 3);
breastplates the colour of fire (Rev. 9:17); she saw
Chaldeans painted on the wall with vermilion (Ezek.
23:14); the shields of the mighty men are red, the
soldiers clothed in scarlet (Nahum 2:3); though your
sins be as scarlet, as red as crimson (Isa. 1:18).

432 Orange

BROWN, see 430.

433 Yellow

If there is thin yellow hair in it (Lev. 13:30-6);
breastplates the colour of brimstone (Rev. 9:17).

434 Green

Full of sap and green in old age (Ps. 92:14); its leaves
remain green (Jer. 17:8); if the mark is greenish (Lev.
13:49; 14:37); a yellowish green horse (Rev. 6:8); our
couch is green (S. of S. 1:16); if they do this when the
wood is green (Luke 23:31); his branch will not be green
(Job 15:32).

435 Blue

A Blue cloth
The robe of the ephod was blue (Exod. 28:31; 39:22);
trading in fine clothes of blue and embroidered work
(Ezek. 27:24); royal robes of blue and white (Esther
8:15); an awning of blue and purple (Ezek. 27:7); blue,
purple and scarlet material (Exod. 25:4; 2 Chr. 2:7);
blue cloths covering: the ark (Num. 4:6); the table
(Num. 4:7); the lampstand (Num. 4:9); the golden altar
(Num. 4:11-12).

B Blue cords
Loops of blue joining the curtains (Exod. 26:4; 36:11);
joining the breastpiece to the ephod with a blue cord
(Exod. 28:28; 39:21); the holy crown fastened with a
blue cord (Exod. 28:37; 39:31); cords of blue on tassels
of garments (Num. 15:38).

C Blue armour
Breastplates the colour of jacinth (Rev. 9:17).

436 Purple

A Purple cloth
Purple cloth over the altar (Num. 4:13); the seat made
of purple cloth (S. of S. 3:10); cords of purple linen
(Esther 1:6); purple was traded (Ezek. 27:16); Lydia was
a dealer in purple cloth (Acts 16:14); your flowing locks

are like purple (S. of S. 7:5); cargo of fine linen, purple, silk and scarlet (Rev. 18:12); violet hangings (Esther 1:6); an awning of blue and purple (Ezek. 27:7); blue, purple and scarlet material (Exod. 25:4; 2 Chr. 2:7).

B Purple clothes
Purple robes of the kings of Midian (Judg. 8:26); a garment of fine linen and purple (Esther 8:15); her clothing is fine linen and purple (Prov. 31:22); those reared in purple lie on ash heaps (Lam. 4:5); the Assyrians were clothed in purple (Ezek. 23:6); whoever reads this writing will be clothed in purple (Dan. 5:7, 16); they clothed Daniel in purple (Dan. 5:29); a rich man dressed in purple (Luke 16:19); they dressed Jesus with purple (Mark 15:17; John 19:5); the woman was clothed in purple and scarlet (Rev. 17:4); she who was clothed in purple and scarlet (Rev. 18:16); idols clothed in violet and purple (Jer. 10:9).

437 Variegation

A Black and white
Jacob exposed white stripes in the rods (Gen. 30:37-8); every speckled and spotted animal (Gen. 30:32-9; 31:8-12); can the leopard change its spots? (Jer. 13:23); dappled horses (Zech. 6:3, 6).

B Multi-coloured
Joseph wore a multi-coloured [or long-sleeved] coat (Gen. 37:3, 23, 32); virgin daughters of the king wore a multi-coloured [or long-sleeved] robe (2 Sam. 13:18); the work of a weaver of variegations (Exod. 26:36; 27:16); an eagle with plumage of many colours (Ezek. 17:3); carpets of many colours (Ezek. 27:24).

C Blue and purple
An awning of blue and purple (Ezek. 27:7).

D Blue, purple and scarlet
Blue, purple and scarlet material (Exod. 25:4; 2 Chr. 2:7).

438 Vision

A Sight in general

A1 The faculty of sight
It is God who gives man sight (Exod. 4:11); God made seeing eyes (Prov. 20:12); take the log out of your own eye, then you will see clearly (Luke 6:42); blessed are the eyes which see what you see (Luke 10:23); you will indeed see but never perceive (Matt. 13:14; Acts 28:26); that seeing they may not see (Luke 8:10); who hopes for what he already sees? (Rom. 8:24); what is seen was made out of things that do not appear (Heb. 11:3); eyesalve to anoint your eyes that you may see (Rev. 3:18); we walk by faith, not by sight (2 Cor. 5:7).

A2 Receiving sight
God opened Hagar's eyes (Gen. 21:19); the Lord opened Balaam's eyes (Num. 22:31); Lord, open his eyes (2 Kgs. 6:17); open their eyes (2 Kgs. 6:20); Paul was sent to open their eyes (Acts 26:18); we want our eyes to be opened (Matt. 20:33); I want to receive my sight (Mark 10:51; Luke 18:41).

THE BLIND HEALED, see 439C.

B Eyes

B1 Eyes in general
If the whole body were an eye, where would be the hearing? (1 Cor. 12:17); 'because I am not an eye I am not part of the body' (1 Cor. 12:16); the eye cannot say it does not need the hand (1 Cor. 12:21); a just king winnows evil with his eyes (Prov. 20:8); he who formed the eye, does he not see? (Ps. 94:9); having eyes, do you not see? (Mark 8:18); blessed are your eyes, for they see (Matt. 13:16; Luke 10:23); it is better to enter with one eye than with two eyes be thrown into hell (Mark 9:47); the crocodile's eyes are like the eyelids of the dawn (Job 41:18); their eyes bulge from fatness (Ps. 73:7); you will

be as eyes for us (Num. 10:31); you would have plucked out your eyes and given them to me (Gal. 4:15); I made a covenant with my eyes (Job 31:1).

B2 Eyes in prophecy
The eyes of the Lord range to and fro through the earth (2 Chr. 16:9); his eyes were like flaming fire (Rev. 1:14); his eyes are a flame of fire (Rev. 2:18; 19:12); the cherubim and the wheels were full of eyes (Ezek. 10:12); the rims of the wheels were covered with eyes (Ezek. 1:18); the horn had eyes (Dan. 7:8, 20); four living creatures full of eyes in front and behind (Rev. 4:6); the four creatures were full of eyes around and within (Rev. 4:8); his eyes were like flaming torches (Dan. 10:6).

B3 Eyes cared for
You bathed, painted your eyes and put on ornaments (Ezek. 23:40); Jesus spat on the man's eyes (Mark 8:23); he anointed the man's eyes with the clay (John 9:6, 11); Elisha put his eyes on the boy's eyes (2 Kgs. 4:34); something like scales fell from his eyes (Acts 9:18); let me take the speck out of your eye (Matt. 7:4); keep my teaching as the pupil of your eye (Prov. 7:2); keep me as the pupil of your eye (Ps. 17:8); he kept him as the pupil of his eye (Deut. 32:10); he who touches you touches the apple of his eye (Zech. 2:8).

B4 Eyes harmed
Destroying a slave's eye (Exod. 21:26); the eye which mocks parents will be plucked out (Prov. 30:17); if your eye makes you stumble, pluck it out (Matt. 5:29; 18:9; Mark 9:47); will you gouge out the eyes of these men? (Num. 16:14); they gouged out Samson's eyes (Judg. 16:21, 28); Nahash wanted to gouge out their right eyes (1 Sam. 11:2); an eye for an eye (Exod. 21:24; Lev. 24:20; Deut. 19:21; Matt. 5:38); the people of the land will be pricks to your eyes (Num. 33:55; Josh. 23:13); I will bring on you illnesses that waste the eyes (Lev. 26:16); those who look through the windows grow dim (Eccles. 12:3); because of these things my eyes have grown dim (Lam. 5:17); who has redness of eyes but the drunkard? (Prov. 23:29-30); a man with a defect in his eye could not serve as priest (Lev. 21:20); may the sword strike his arm and his right eye (Zech. 11:17); their eyes will rot in their sockets (Zech. 14:12); the Lord has closed your eyes, the prophets (Isa. 29:10); though his eyes were open he could see nothing (Acts 9:8); why notice the speck in your brother's eye and not the beam in your own? (Matt. 7:3-5; Luke 6:41-2).

B5 Good eyes
Moses' eye was not dim at 120 (Deut. 34:7); David had beautiful eyes (1 Sam. 16:12); your eyes are like doves (S. of S. 1:15; 4:1); his eyes are like doves (S. of S. 5:12); your eyes are like pools in Heshbon (S. of S. 7:4); his eyes will be dark from wine (Gen. 49:12); Jonathan's eyes brightened after the honey (1 Sam. 14:27, 29); the eye is the lamp of the body (Matt. 6:22; Luke 11:34).

B6 Evil eyes
Cast away the detestable things of your eyes (Ezek. 20:7-8); there is no fear of God before their eyes (Rom. 3:18); they have eyes full of adultery (2 Pet. 2:14); the lust of the flesh and the lust of the eyes and the pride of life (1 John 2:16); playing the harlot after your own eyes (Num. 15:39); seductive eyes (Isa. 3:16); the Lord hates haughty eyes (Prov. 6:17); the wicked man winks with his eyes (Prov. 6:13); he who winks the eye causes trouble (Prov. 10:10); do not let her catch you with her eyelids (Prov. 6:25); the eye is not satisfied with seeing (Eccles. 1:8); Leah had weak eyes (Gen. 29:17); if your eye is not healthy, your whole body will be full of darkness (Matt. 6:23); is your eye evil [envious] because I am good? (Matt. 20:15); from the heart comes

an evil eye [envy] (Mark 7:22); idols have eyes but cannot see (Ps. 115:5; 135:16).

C Those seeing

PAYING ATTENTION, see 455.

C1 God seeing

C1a God sees all the earth

God of seeing (Gen. 16:13); have you eyes of flesh to see as man sees? (Job 10:4); he who formed the eye, does he not see? (Ps. 94:9); the eyes of the Lord range through the earth (2 Chr. 16:9; Zech. 4:10); the Lord looks down on heaven and earth (Ps. 113:6); the Lord looks down from heaven (Ps. 33:13; 102:19); I will quietly look from my dwelling (Isa. 18:4); until the Lord looks down from heaven and sees (Lam. 3:50); God saw all that he had made and it was very good (Gen. 1:31); I will look at the bow in the cloud (Gen. 9:16); the eyes of the Lord are always on the land to care for it (Deut. 11:12); the eyes of the Lord keep watch over knowledge (Prov. 22:12); God looks to the ends of the earth and sees everything (Job 28:24).

C1b God sees all people

The Lord looks down from heaven to see if any one seeks him (Ps. 14:2; 53:2); the eyes of the Lord are everywhere, watching the evil and the good (Prov. 15:3); the Lord has his eye on all men as on the tribes of Israel (Zech. 9:1); his eyes keep watch on the nations (Ps. 66:7); God sees all a man's steps (Job 34:21); his eyes are on all their ways (Job 24:23); the well of the living One who sees me (Gen. 16:14); does he not see my ways? (Job 31:4); he watches all my paths (Job 33:11); the Lord's eyes test the sons of men (Ps. 11:4); the Lord sees all the sons of men (Ps. 33:13, 14); a man's ways are before the Lord's eyes (Prov. 5:21); your eyes are open to all the ways of men (Jer. 32:19); my eyes are on all their ways (Jer. 16:17); you watcher of men (Job 7:20); will you never look away from me? (Job 7:19); you watch all my paths (Job 13:27); my enemy looks daggers at me with his eyes (Job 16:9); your eyes have seen my unformed substance (Ps. 139:16).

C1c God sees the wicked

God saw that man's wickedness was great (Gen. 6:5); God looked on the earth, and lo, it was corrupt (Gen. 6:12); the Lord came down to see the city and the tower (Gen. 11:5); I have come down to see whether they have done according to their outcry (Gen. 18:21); the eyes of the Lord are on the sinful kingdom (Amos 9:8); the Lord saw it and rejected them (Deut. 32:19); I have seen this people, that they are stiff-necked (Exod. 32:9; Deut. 9:13).

C1d God sees the righteous

The eyes of the Lord are on those who fear him (Ps. 33:18); the eyes of the Lord are on the righteous (Ps. 34:15; 1 Pet. 3:12); God keeps his eyes on the righteous (Job 36:7); I will set my eyes on them for good (Jer. 24:6); your Father who sees in secret will reward you (Matt. 6:4, 6, 18).

C1e God sees their affliction

God has seen my affliction and toil (Gen. 31:42); Reuben – the Lord has seen my affliction (Gen. 29:32); the Lord saw that Leah was hated (Gen. 29:31); I have seen all that Laban has done to you (Gen. 31:12); God saw the Israelites (Exod. 2:25); I have seen the affliction of my people (Exod. 3:7; Acts 7:34); perhaps the Lord will see my affliction (2 Sam. 16:12); the Lord saw the affliction of Israel (2 Kgs. 14:26).

C1f God, see!

Let your eyes look with justice (Ps. 17:2); look on my affliction (Ps. 25:18; 119:153); look on my enemies (Ps. 25:19); open your eyes and see! (2 Kgs. 19:16; Dan. 9:18); come to my help and see! (Ps. 59:4); look down from heaven and see! (Ps. 80:14; Isa. 63:15); see, O Lord, for I

am despised! (Lam. 1:11); see, O Lord, my affliction! (Lam. 1:9); may God see and judge (1 Chr. 12:17).

C2 Christ seeing

The Lord turned and looked at Peter (Luke 22:61); Jesus saw two brothers, Simon Peter and Andrew (Matt. 4:18); Jesus looked at Simon Peter (John 1:42); Jesus saw Nathanael coming to him (John 1:47); before Philip called you, I saw you (John 1:48, 50); when Jesus saw his mother and the disciple whom he loved (John 19:26); when he saw the crowds he had compassion on them (Matt. 9:36); he looked around at them with anger (Mark 3:5); Jesus looking at him loved him (Mark 10:21); when Jesus saw the city he wept over it (Luke 19:41); Jesus turned and saw them following (John 1:38); Jesus saw a great crowd coming to him (John 6:5); when he saw the crowds he went up into a mountain (Matt. 5:1).

D What is seen

D1 Seeing God's things

D1a About seeing God

In my flesh I will see God (Job 19:26-7); I will see your face in righteousness (Ps. 17:15); we will see him as he is (1 John 3:2); the pure in heart will see God (Matt. 5:8); they will see his face (Rev. 22:4); to behold the beauty of the Lord (Ps. 27:4); your eyes will see the king in his beauty (Isa. 33:17); holiness, without which no one will see the Lord (Heb. 12:14); the upright will behold his face (Ps. 11:7); the God of gods will be seen in Zion (Ps. 84:7); all flesh will see the Lord's glory (Isa. 40:5); the people must not force their way through to see the Lord (Exod. 19:21); his eternal power and deity have been clearly seen in what is made (Rom. 1:20); the mountains saw you and quaked (Hab. 3:10); the waters saw you and were afraid (Ps. 77:16); seeing Esau was like seeing the face of God (Gen. 33:10).

NOT seeing God, see 439D2.

D1b Those who saw God

I saw the Lord, high and lifted up (Isa. 6:1); my eyes have seen the Lord (Isa. 6:5); I have beheld you in the sanctuary (Ps. 63:2); now my eye sees you (Job 42:5); I saw the Lord standing by the altar (Amos 9:1); have I remained alive after seeing God? (Gen. 16:13); Jacob saw God at Peniel (Gen. 32:30); Moses saw God's form (Num. 12:8); Moses endured as seeing him who is invisible (Heb. 11:27); the seventy elders saw God (Exod. 24:10, 11); we will die for we have seen God (Judg. 13:22); in heaven their angels always behold the face of my Father (Matt. 18:10); he who is from God has seen the Father (John 6:46); he who sees me sees him who sent me (John 12:45); he who has seen me has seen the Father (John 14:9); you know him and have seen him (John 14:7); they have seen and hated me and my Father (John 15:24).

D1c Seeing angels

David saw the angel (2 Sam. 24:17); the donkey saw the angel (Num. 22:23-33); Balaam saw the angel (Num. 22:31).

D1d Looking at God's works

Now you will see what I will do to Pharaoh (Exod. 6:1); you saw with your own eyes what God did in Egypt (Deut. 29:2; Josh. 24:7); your eyes have seen all God did (Deut. 3:21; 11:7); your eyes have seen what the Lord did to the followers of Baal-peor (Deut. 4:3); all flesh will see the salvation of God (Luke 3:6); my eyes have seen your salvation (Luke 2:30-1); men see God's work from afar (Job 36:25); you will see it with your own eyes but you will not eat of it (2 Kgs. 7:2, 19); all flesh will see that I the Lord have kindled the fire (Ezek. 20:48); see this great thing which the Lord will do (1 Sam. 12:16); they will see who had never been told of him (Rom. 15:21); blessed are your eyes, for they see (Matt. 13:16);

many desired to see what you see (Matt. 13:17); see the works of the Lord (Ps. 66:5); they have seen the works of the Lord (Ps. 107:24).

D2 Seeing Christ

D2a First sight of Christ

Simeon would not die before seeing the Lord's Christ (Luke 2:26); they came into the house and saw the child with Mary his mother (Matt. 2:11); we want to see Jesus (John 12:21); Herod sought to see Jesus (Luke 9:9); when Herod saw Jesus he was very glad (Luke 23:8); Zacchaeus wanted to see who Jesus was (Luke 19:3); when he saw him the spirit threw him into convulsions (Mark 9:20); when he saw Jesus he cried out (Luke 8:28).

D2b Watching Christ

They watched him to see whether he would heal on the sabbath (Mark 3:2; Luke 6:7); the eyes of all in the synagogue were on him (Luke 4:20); the people stood by, watching (Luke 23:35); the women were looking on (Mark 15:47; Luke 23:49, 55).

D2c Seeing Jesus the Lord

Your father Abraham rejoiced to see my day (John 8:56); he who sees me sees him who sent me (John 12:45); he who has seen me has seen the Father (John 14:9); that which we have seen with our eyes (1 John 1:1); that which we have seen we proclaim (1 John 1:3); have I not seen Jesus our Lord? (1 Cor. 9:1); he has appointed you to see the righteous One (Acts 22:14); beholding as in a mirror the glory of the Lord (2 Cor. 3:18); they shall look on the one they pierced (Zech. 12:10; John 19:37); what if you were to see the Son of man ascending where he was before? (John 6:62); go and tell John what you hear and see (Matt. 11:4); you will be a witness to all men of what you have seen and heard (Acts 22:15); we cannot but speak of what we have seen and heard (Acts 4:20); a witness to the things you have seen (Acts 26:16); we see Jesus, made for a little while lower than the angels (Heb. 2:9); looking to Jesus (Heb. 12:2).

D2d Seeing the risen Christ

Mary Magdalene told the disciples, 'I have seen the Lord' (John 20:18); when they heard that he was alive and had been seen by her (Mark 16:11); they had not believed those who saw him after he had risen (Mark 16:14); the disciples were glad when they saw the Lord (John 20:20); we have seen the Lord (John 20:25); have you believed because you have seen me? (John 20:29); he told how Saul had seen the Lord on the road (Acts 9:27); they will see the Son of man coming in clouds (Mark 13:26; Luke 21:27); every eye will see him (Rev. 1:7).

D3 Looking at people

D3a Seeing people

They saw Joseph afar off (Gen. 37:18); I have seen your face (Gen. 46:30); I did not think I would see your face (Gen. 48:11); God has let me see your children too (Gen. 48:11); Balaam saw Israel camping tribe by tribe (Num. 24:2); all the people saw him walking and praising God (Acts 3:9); seeing the man who had been healed standing beside them (Acts 4:14); that no one may think more of me than he sees in me or hears from me (2 Cor. 12:6); he who does not love his brother whom he has seen cannot love God whom he has not seen (1 John 4:20); so shine so that they may see your good works (Matt. 5:16); beware of practising your righteousness before men to be seen by them (Matt. 6:1); hypocrites pray so as to be seen by men (Matt. 6:5); they do all their deeds to be seen by men (Matt. 23:5); that your fasting may not be seen by men (Matt. 6:18).

D3b Looking intently at people

A maidservant looked intently at Peter (Luke 22:56); Peter and John fixed their gaze on the lame man (Acts 3:4); look at us! (Acts 3:4); why stare at us as if by our own power we made this man walk? (Acts 3:12); Paul fixed his gaze on Elymas (Acts 13:9); Paul fixed his gaze on him and saw that he had faith to be made well (Acts 14:9); Paul looked intently on the council (Acts 23:1).

D3c Looking at people for evil

Looking at a woman in lust (Matt. 5:28); Potiphar's wife cast eyes on Joseph (Gen. 39:7); his eyes stealthily watch for the hapless (Ps. 10:8); they watch my steps (Ps. 56:6); men watched David's house to kill him (Ps. 59:t).

D4 Looking at things

UNDERSTANDING, see 516.

D4a Looking and seeing

Do you see what the elders of Israel are doing? (Ezek. 8:12); what do you see, Amos? (Amos 7:8; 8:2); what have they seen in your house? (Isa. 39:4); what did you go into the wilderness to see? (Matt. 11:7); when the herdsmen saw what happened (Luke 8:34); let us see this thing which the Lord has made known to us (Luke 2:15); he looked around to see who had done it (Mark 5:32); he looked intently and saw everything clearly (Mark 8:25).

D4b Seeing places

Lot looked out over the Jordan valley (Gen. 13:10); the men looked down toward Sodom (Gen. 18:16); Abraham looked down the valley (Gen. 19:28); Moses viewed the land (Num. 27:12; Deut. 32:49; 34:1-4); Hiram went to see the cities Solomon had given him (1 Kgs. 9:12); I have bought a field and must go and see it (Luke 14:18); see the place where he lay (Matt. 28:6).

D4c Seeing other things

When the woman saw that the tree was good for food (Gen. 3:6); when Laban saw the ring and the bracelets (Gen. 24:30); everyone who looked on the bronze snake lived (Num. 21:8, 9); when they saw the star, they rejoiced (Matt. 2:10); when Peter saw the wind he was afraid (Matt. 14:30); the Kohathites must not go in to look at the holy things (Num. 4:20); they died because they had looked into the ark of the Lord (1 Sam. 6:19).

D4d Looking back

Do not look back (Gen. 19:17); Lot's wife looked back (Gen. 19:26); the men of Benjamin looked behind them (Judg. 20:40); let not your eyes look with regret on your stuff (Gen. 45:20).

D4e Inspecting

Nehemiah inspected the city walls (Neh. 2:13); when the king came in to look over the guests (Matt. 22:11); the priest examines: suspected leprosy (Lev. 13:2-44); someone healed of leprosy (Lev. 14:3); a leprous garment (Lev. 13:50-7); a leprous house (Lev. 14:36-7, 39, 44, 48).

E Dreams

E1 Dreams in general

God speaks in a dream (Job 33:15); I speak to prophets in dreams (Num. 12:6); your old men will dream dreams (Joel 2:28; Acts 2:17); God spoke to Israel in visions of the night (Gen. 46:2); a dream comes with much business (Eccles. 5:3); the dream is true and the interpretation sure (Dan. 2:45); you terrify me with dreams (Job 7:14); they are dreamers who love to sleep (Isa. 56:10); God did not answer Saul by dreams (1 Sam. 28:6, 15).

E2 Those who dreamed

Jacob had a dream at Bethel (Gen. 28:12); I saw in a dream the goats mating (Gen. 31:10); God came to Abimelech in a dream (Gen. 20:3, 6); God came to Laban in a dream (Gen. 31:24); Joseph had dreams

(Gen. 37:5-7, 9); this dreamer! (Gen. 37:19-20); Joseph remembered his dreams (Gen. 42:9); the butler and the baker each had a dream (Gen. 40:5-17; 41:11); Pharaoh's dream (Gen. 41:1-32); the Amalekite's dream of Gideon (Judg. 7:13-14); Solomon's vision was a dream (1 Kgs. 3:5, 15); Nebuchadnezzar's dream of the statue (Dan. 2:31-5); Nebuchadnezzar's dream of the tree (Dan. 4:10-18); Daniel's dream of the four beasts (Dan. 7:1-8); Eliphaz received a message in a dream (Job 4:12-21); Nebuchadnezzar had dreams (Dan. 2:1, 3; 4:5); this is the dream which I, King Nebuchadnezzar, saw (Dan. 4:18); Joseph's dreams (Matt. 1:20; 2:13, 19, 22); God spoke to the wise men in a dream (Matt. 2:12); Pilate's wife suffered much in a dream (Matt. 27:19).

E3 Dreams interpreted
It is said that when you hear a dream you can interpret it (Gen. 41:15); Daniel understood visions and dreams (Dan. 1:17); the mystery was revealed to Daniel in a vision of the night (Dan. 2:19); are you able to make known the dream and its interpretation? (Dan. 2:26); this was your dream and the visions in your head (Dan. 2:28); let not the dream or its interpretation alarm you (Dan. 4:19); this was the dream, and now here is the interpretation (Dan. 2:36).

E4 Misleading dreams
If a dreamer of dreams arises to mislead you (Deut. 13:1); do not listen to the dreamer of dreams (Deut. 13:3); do not listen to the dreams which they dream (Jer. 29:8); do not listen to your diviners, dreamers, soothsayers or sorcerers (Jer. 27:9); that dreamer of dreams shall be put to death (Deut. 13:5); I had a dream, I had a dream (Jer. 23:25); let the prophet who had a dream tell the dream (Jer. 23:28); I am against those who prophesy false dreams (Jer. 23:32); they want to make my people forget my name by their dreams (Jer. 23:27); in many dreams and many words there is futility (Eccles. 5:7); the dreamers see false dreams (Zech. 10:2); these men in their dreamings defile the flesh (Jude 8).

E5 Like a dream
The wicked vanishes like a dream (Job 20:8); those who attack Jerusalem will be like a dream (Isa. 29:8); those who wage war against her will be like a dream (Isa. 29:7); like the hungry dreaming of food (Isa. 29:8); like a dream when one awakes they are dismissed (Ps. 73:20); it was like a dream! (Ps. 126:1).

F Visions

F1 Visions from God
I reveal myself to prophets in visions (Num. 12:6); I spoke to the prophets and gave numerous visions (Hos. 12:10); once you spoke in a vision to your faithful ones (Ps. 89:19); your young men will see visions (Joel 2:28; Acts 2:17); I will go on to visions and revelations of the Lord (2 Cor. 12:1); I was not disobedient to the heavenly vision (Acts 26:19); the valley of vision (Isa. 21:1; 22:5); he brought me in visions of God to Jerusalem (Ezek. 8:3); the Spirit brought me in a vision to the exiles in Chaldea (Ezek. 11:24); he brought me in visions of God to the land of Israel (Ezek. 40:2); I was left alone and saw this great vision (Dan. 10:8); it was a great struggle but he understood the vision (Dan. 10:1); men of violence among your people will lift themselves up to fulfil the vision (Dan. 11:14); my spirit was distressed and the visions alarmed me (Dan. 7:15); the vision of the evenings and mornings is true (Dan. 8:26); to seal both vision and prophet (Dan. 9:24); do not tell anyone about the vision (Matt. 17:9); they said they had seen a vision of angels (Luke 24:23); the one who sees the vision of the Almighty (Num. 24:16); the vision will not turn back (Ezek. 7:13).

F2 Those who saw visions
I, Daniel, alone saw the vision (Dan. 10:7); the vision of Obadiah (Obad. 1); the Lord spoke to Paul by night in a vision (Acts 18:9); Peter thought he was seeing a vision (Acts 12:9); those who saw visions: Abraham (Gen. 15:1); Nathan (2 Sam. 7:17); Zechariah (2 Chr. 26:5); Isaiah (2 Chr. 32:32; Isa. 1:1); Ezekiel (Ezek. 1:1); Daniel (Dan. 8:1-8); Zechariah (Luke 1:22); Ananias (Acts 9:10); Paul, of Ananias (Acts 9:12); Peter (Acts 10:10-13; 11:5); Cornelius (Acts 10:3); Paul, of a man of Macedonia (Acts 16:9); Paul, in a trance (Acts 22:17-18).

F3 False visions
The proverb, 'Time passes, every vision fails' (Ezek. 12:22); prophets of Israel who see visions of peace when there is no peace (Ezek. 13:16); your prophets have seen for you false and deceptive visions (Lam. 2:14); the prophets who see false visions (Ezek. 13:9; 21:29; 22:28); there will be no more false vision or flattering divination (Ezek. 12:24); let no one disqualify you, taking his stand on visions (Col. 2:18).

F4 No visions
Visions were infrequent (1 Sam. 3:1); her prophets find no vision from the Lord (Lam. 2:9); the prophets' visions are from their own imagination (Jer. 23:16); you will no longer see false visions (Ezek. 13:23); woe to the foolish prophets who follow their own spirit and have seen nothing (Ezek. 13:3); where there is no vision the people run wild (Prov. 29:18); they say to the seers, 'You must not see visions' (Isa. 30:10); the men with me did not see the vision (Dan. 10:7); it will be night for you with no vision (Mic. 3:6); every prophet will be ashamed of his vision (Zech. 13:4).

G Seers
The prophet used to be called a seer (1 Sam. 9:9); are you not a seer? (2 Sam. 15:27); the words of the seers (2 Chr. 33:18); the Lord has covered your heads, the seers (Isa. 29:10); the seers and diviners will be ashamed and cover their lips (Mic. 3:7); Samuel the seer (1 Chr. 9:22; 26:28; 29:29); Gad the seer (1 Chr. 29:29); Gad, David's seer (2 Sam. 24:11; 1 Chr. 21:9; 2 Chr. 29:25); Heman the king's seer (1 Chr. 25:5); Iddo the seer (2 Chr. 9:29; 12:15); Hanani the seer (2 Chr. 16:7); Jehu son of Hanani the seer (2 Chr. 19:2); Asaph the seer (2 Chr. 29:30); Jeduthun the king's seer (2 Chr. 35:15); O seer! (Amos 7:12).

PROPHET, see 579C.

439 Blindness

A Those who were blind

A1 Blind people
When he entered the house, the blind men came to him (Matt. 9:28); they brought to him the blind (Matt. 15:30); a certain blind man sitting by the roadside begging (Luke 18:35); the Jews did not believe that he had been born blind (John 9:18-20); you do not know that you are blind (Rev. 3:17); he who lacks these things is blind or short-sighted (2 Pet. 1:9); people who are blind yet have eyes (Isa. 43:8); you blind! (Matt. 23:19); you blind Pharisee! (Matt. 23:26); his watchmen are blind, knowing nothing (Isa. 56:10); are we also blind? (John 9:40); you will grope like a blind man at noon (Deut. 28:29); we grope for the wall like the blind (Isa. 59:10); who is blind like the servant of the Lord? (Isa. 42:19-20); people who were blind through old age: Isaac (Gen. 27:1); Israel (Gen. 48:10); Ahijah (1 Kgs. 14:4); Eli (1 Sam. 3:2; 4:15).

A2 Dealing with the blind
Do not place a stumbling-block before the blind (Lev. 19:14); cursed is he who misleads the blind (Deut. 27:18); I was eyes to the blind (Job 29:15); I will lead the blind in a way they do not know (Isa. 42:16); invite the

blind (Luke 14:13, 21); if a blind man leads a blind man they will both fall into a pit (Matt. 15:14; Luke 6:39); if you are sure you are a guide to the blind (Rom. 2:19); blind guides (Matt. 15:14; 23:16, 24); blind men could not serve as priests (Lev. 21:18); the blind and the lame will keep you out (2 Sam. 5:6, 8).

B Blinded

B1 God blinding

It is God who makes man blind (Exod. 4:11); God will strike you with blindness (Deut. 28:28); the angels struck the men with blindness (Gen. 19:11); Elisha asked the Lord to strike the soldiers with blindness (2 Kgs. 6:18); let their eyes be darkened so that they cannot see (Ps. 69:23); on the Damascus road Saul was blinded (Acts 9:8-9; 22:11); Elymas was struck blind (Acts 13:11); God gave them eyes that do not see (Rom. 11:8); God has not given you eyes to see (Deut. 29:4); I have come that those who see may become blind (John 9:39); he has shut their eyes so that they cannot see (Isa. 44:18); he has blinded their eyes and hardened their heart (John 12:40); let their eyes be darkened so that they cannot see (Rom. 11:10).

B2 Other blinding

Will you gouge out the eyes of these men? (Num. 16:14); the Philistines gouged out Samson's eyes (Judg. 16:21); Nahash wanted to gouge out every right eye (1 Sam. 11:2); the king of Babylon put out Zedekiah's eyes (2 Kgs. 25:7; Jer. 39:7; 52:11); I will bring him to Babylon but he will not see it (Ezek. 12:13); the god of this world has blinded their minds (2 Cor. 4:4); the darkness has blinded his eyes (1 John 2:11); blind yourselves and be blind (Isa. 29:9); a bribe blinds the seeing (Exod. 23:8; Deut. 16:19); have I taken a bribe to blind my eyes? (1 Sam. 12:3); their eyes were prevented from recognising him (Luke 24:16); they blindfolded Jesus (Mark 14:65; Luke 22:64); the eyes of those who see will not be blinded (Isa. 32:3).

C The blind healed

RECEIVING SIGHT, see 438A2.

C1 Healing of the blind

God opens the eyes of the blind (Ps. 146:8); the eyes of the blind will be opened (Isa. 35:5); the eyes of the blind will see (Isa. 29:18); look, you blind, that you may see (Isa. 42:18); I appoint you to open the eyes of the blind (Isa. 42:7); the blind receive their sight (Luke 7:22); he has sent me to preach recovery of sight to the blind (Luke 4:18); I have come that those who do not see may see (John 9:39); from the beginning it has never been known for a man born blind to be healed (John 9:32); can a demon open the eyes of the blind? (John 10:21); Paul was sent to open their eyes (Acts 26:18).

C2 Blind individuals healed

Two blind men called out to Jesus (Matt. 9:27-31; 20:30); blind Bartimaeus (Mark 10:46-52); the man born blind (John 9:1-7); the blind received sight (Matt. 11:5; 15:31; 21:14; Luke 7:21); he healed a blind and dumb demoniac (Matt. 12:22); they brought a blind man to Jesus to be healed (Mark 8:22-6); receive your sight! (Luke 18:42); Ananias laying hands on Saul that he might regain his sight (Acts 9:12); the Lord Jesus has sent me that you might regain your sight (Acts 9:17); he regained his sight (Acts 9:18); brother Saul, receive your sight! (Acts 22:13).

D Not seeing

NOT PAYING ATTENTION, see 456.

D1 God not seeing

The Lord does not see (Ps. 94:7); the Lord does not see us (Ezek. 8:12); 'The Lord has forsaken the land, the Lord does not see' (Ezek. 9:9); God will never see it (Ps. 10:11); he will not see our latter end (Jer. 12:4).

D2 Not seeing God

You saw no form when the Lord spoke to you (Deut. 4:12, 15); you cannot see my face for no man can see God and live (Exod. 33:20); you will see my back but not my face (Exod. 33:23); you say you do not see him (Job 35:14); no one has ever seen God (John 1:18; 1 John 4:12); you have never heard his voice or seen his form (John 5:37); no man has ever seen God or can see him (1 Tim. 6:16); no one has seen the Father except he who is from God (John 6:46); the one who does evil has not seen God (3 John 11); no one who sins has seen him or known him (1 John 3:6); he who does not love his brother whom he has seen cannot love God whom he has not seen (1 John 4:20); I shall not see the Lord in the land of the living (Isa. 38:11); Moses was afraid to look at God (Exod. 3:6); Moses trembled and did not dare to look (Acts 7:32).

D3 Idols not seeing

Gods which do not see nor understand (Dan. 5:23); idols have eyes but cannot see (Ps. 115:5; 135:16); idols do not see (Deut. 4:28); idols cannot see or hear or walk (Rev. 9:20).

D4 People not seeing

D4a Not seeing in general

Faith is the certainty of things not seen (Heb. 11:1); if we hope for what we do not see, we wait patiently for it (Rom. 8:25).

D4b Not seeing spiritual things

The men with me did not see the vision (Dan. 10:7); they heard the voice but saw no one (Acts 9:7); what no eye has seen nor ear heard (1 Cor. 2:9); many desired to see what you see and did not see it (Matt. 13:17; Luke 10:24); we do not yet see all things in subjection to him (Heb. 2:8); this people have eyes but see not (Jer. 5:21; Ezek. 12:2); seeing they do not see (Matt. 13:13; Luke 8:10); seeing they do not perceive (Mark 4:12); having eyes, do you not see? (Mark 8:18); your hand is lifted up but they do not see it (Isa. 26:11); the wicked does not see the majesty of the Lord (Isa. 26:10); God's judgements are out of sight of the wicked (Ps. 10:5); they have closed their eyes lest they should see (Matt. 13:15; John 12:40; Acts 28:27).

NOT UNDERSTANDING, see 517.

D4c Not seeing Christ

They found it as the women had said, but him they did not see (Luke 24:24); blessed are those who have not seen yet have believed (John 20:29); yet a little while and the world will see me no more (John 14:19); I go to the Father and you will see me no more (John 16:10); a little while and you will see me, and again a little while and you will see me no more (John 16:16-19); a cloud took him out of their sight (Acts 1:9); though you do not now see him, you believe in him (1 Pet. 1:8); you will not see me again until you say, 'Blessed is he' (Matt. 23:39).

D4d Not seeing people

Shem and Japheth went backward so as not to see (Gen. 9:23); do not let me see the boy die (Gen. 21:16); I will not see your face again (Exod. 10:29); you will not see my face again (Acts 20:25, 38); you will never see the Egyptians again (Exod. 14:13); Samuel did not see Saul again (1 Sam. 15:35); I struggle for all those who have not seen my face (Col. 2:1); the adulterer says, 'No eye will see me' (Job 24:15); 'Who can see us?' (Ps. 64:5); who sees us? (Isa. 29:15).

440 Defective vision

We see dimly, as in a mirror (1 Cor. 13:12); because of these things my eyes have grown dim (Lam. 5:17); he who lacks these things is blind or short-sighted (2 Pet. 1:9); make their ears dull and their eyes dim (Isa. 6:10); I see men like trees, walking (Mark 8:24); do not look at the speck in your brother's eye when you have a log in your own (Matt. 7:3-5; Luke 6:41-2).

441 Spectator
Those who from the beginning were eyewitnesses (Luke 1:2); eyewitnesses of his majesty (2 Pet. 1:16).

442 Mirror
The mirrors of the serving women (Exod. 38:8); a man who looks at his face in a mirror (Jas. 1:23); the Lord will take away the mirrors (Isa. 3:23); we behold the glory of the Lord as in a mirror (2 Cor. 3:18); now we see dimly as in a mirror (1 Cor. 13:12); the skies spread out like a molten mirror (Job 37:18).

443 Visibility
Light makes things become visible (Eph. 5:13); the tops of the mountains were seen (Gen. 8:5); the bow will be seen in the cloud (Gen. 9:14); a visible God [a God of seeing] (Gen. 16:13); the tree was visible to the ends of the earth (Dan. 4:11); the tree which grew, whose height reached the sky, visible to all the earth (Dan. 4:20); God granted him to become visible (Acts 10:40); all things, visible and invisible, were created in him (Col. 1:16).

444 Invisibility
A Invisible God
Moses endured as seeing him who is invisible (Heb. 11:27); Christ is the image of the invisible God (Col. 1:15); God's invisible attributes are clearly seen (Rom. 1:20); were God to pass by, I would not see him (Job 9:11); immortal, invisible, the only God (1 Tim. 1:17).
B Invisible things
By faith we understand that the visible things were made out of invisible (Heb. 11:3); we look at what is unseen and eternal (2 Cor. 4:18); all things, visible and invisible, were created in him (Col. 1:16).

445 Appearance
A Appearances
Do not look at his appearance or his height (1 Sam. 16:7); do not judge by the appearance (John 7:24); you judge according to the flesh (John 8:15); he will not judge by what his eyes see (Isa. 11:3); those who take pride in appearance (2 Cor. 5:12); observe our appearance and that of the youths who eat the king's rich food (Dan. 1:13-15); you outwardly appear righteous to men (Matt. 23:28); the appearance of the likeness of the glory of the Lord (Ezek. 1:28).
B Appearing
B1 God appearing
The Lord appeared to Abraham (Gen. 12:7; 17:1; 18:1; Acts 7:2); the Lord appeared to David (2 Chr. 3:1); the Lord appeared to Isaac (Gen. 26:2, 24); the Lord appeared to Jacob (Gen. 35:1, 7, 9; 48:3); the Lord appeared to Solomon (1 Kgs. 3:5; 9:2; 2 Chr. 1:7; 7:12); the Lord had appeared to Solomon twice (1 Kgs. 11:9); the Lord appeared to Joseph (Matt. 1:20; 2:13, 19); I appear in the cloud over the mercy seat (Lev. 16:2); the Lord will appear over them (Zech. 9:14); the God of our fathers appeared to me (Exod. 3:16); that they may believe that the Lord has appeared to you (Exod. 4:5); the Lord appeared again in Shiloh (1 Sam. 3:21); the angel of the Lord appeared to Moses (Exod. 3:2); the angel of the Lord appeared to Gideon (Judg. 6:12); the angel of the Lord appeared to Zechariah (Luke 1:11); an angel of the Lord appeared to the shepherds (Luke 2:9); what if they say, 'The Lord has not appeared to you'? (Exod. 4:1); the angel of the Lord appeared no more to Manoah and his wife (Judg. 13:21).

B2 Christ appearing
I have appeared to you for this purpose (Acts 26:16); a witness to the things in which I will appear to you (Acts 26:16); by his appearing and his kingdom (2 Tim. 4:1); the Lord will give the crown to all who have loved his appearing (2 Tim. 4:8); he appeared once for all to put away sin (Heb. 9:26); he appeared in order to take away sin (1 John 3:5); when Christ, your life, appears, you also will appear with him (Col. 3:4); when he appears we will be like him (1 John 3:2); waiting for the appearing of our great God and Saviour Jesus Christ (Titus 2:13); keep the commandment until the appearing of our Lord Jesus Christ (1 Tim. 6:14); that when he appears we may have confidence (1 John 2:28); the appearing of our Saviour (2 Tim. 1:10); after his resurrection he appeared to Mary Magdalene (Mark 16:9); the Lord Jesus who appeared to you on the road (Acts 9:17); he appeared: to two walking in the country (Mark 16:12); to the apostles (Mark 16:14; 1 Cor. 15:7); to the 12 (1 Cor. 15:5); to Simon Peter (Luke 24:34); to Cephas (1 Cor. 15:5); to his disciples (John 21:1, 14); to more than 500 brethren (1 Cor. 15:6); to James (1 Cor. 15:7); to Paul (1 Cor. 15:8).
B3 People appearing
Elijah and Moses appeared to them (Matt. 17:3; Mark 9:4; Luke 9:30-1); resurrected saints appeared to many (Matt. 27:53); John the Baptist appeared in the wilderness (Mark 1:4).
C Spectacle
Apostles have become a spectacle to the world (1 Cor. 4:9); you were made a spectacle (Heb. 10:33); I will make you a spectacle (Nahum 3:6).

446 Disappearance
Christ vanished from their sight (Luke 24:31); the angel of the Lord vanished (Judg. 6:21); the sky will vanish like smoke (Isa. 51:6); friendship vanishes like the waters of a wadi (Job 6:15-18); the wicked will fly away like a dream (Job 20:8); the wicked will vanish like smoke (Ps. 37:20); you are like a mist that appears for a little while and then vanishes (Jas. 4:14); as a cloud vanishes so does the one who goes down to Sheol (Job 7:9); the idols will utterly vanish (Isa. 2:18).

447 Intellect
A Nature of the heart / mind
What goes out of the mouth comes from the heart (Matt. 15:18); from the abundance of the heart the mouth speaks (Matt. 12:34; Luke 6:45); with the heart man believes (Rom. 10:10).
B Searching the heart
The Lord searches all hearts (1 Chr. 28:9); you test the heart (1 Chr. 29:17); the hearts of men lie open before the Lord (Prov. 15:11).
C Evil hearts
God gave them over to a depraved mind (Rom. 1:28); the heart is deceitful (Jer. 17:9); puffed up by his fleshly mind (Col. 2:18); their mind and conscience are defiled (Titus 1:15); their heart is far from me (Matt. 15:8); out of the heart come evil thoughts etc. (Matt. 15:19); Nebuchadnezzar was given the mind of an animal (Dan. 4:16).
D Receptive hearts
These words which I command you shall be on your heart (Deut. 6:6); I will write my laws on their heart (Jer. 31:33; Heb. 8:10); I will put my laws in their heart (Heb. 10:16); I will take from them their heart of stone and give them a heart of flesh (Ezek. 11:19; 36:26); I will give them one heart (Ezek. 11:19); oh, that they always had such a heart (Deut. 5:29); make yourselves a new heart and a new spirit (Ezek. 18:31); love the Lord with

all your heart and soul and strength and mind (Deut. 6:5; Matt. 22:37; Mark 12:30, 33; Luke 10:27); have this mind in Christ (Phil. 2:5).

448 Absence of intellect
Like unreasoning animals (2 Pet. 2:12; Jude 10).

449 Thought
A **God's thoughts**
My thoughts are not your thoughts, says the Lord (Isa. 55:8); as the heavens are higher than the earth so are my thoughts than your thoughts (Isa. 55:9); your thoughts are very deep (Ps. 92:5); God declares his thoughts to men (Amos 4:13); they do not know the thoughts of the Lord (Mic. 4:12); who has known the mind of the Lord? (Rom. 11:34; 1 Cor. 2:16); many are your thoughts toward us (Ps. 40:5); how precious are your thoughts to me, O God (Ps. 139:17); what is man that you think of him? (Ps. 144:3).

B **Man's thoughts**
B1 God knows man's thoughts
The Lord knows that the thoughts of a man are a mere breath (Ps. 94:11); I know their thoughts (Isa. 66:18); I know your thoughts (Ezek. 11:5); try me and know my thoughts (Ps. 139:23); you know my thoughts from afar (Ps. 139:2); Jesus knew their thoughts (Matt. 12:25; Luke 6:8); the thoughts of many hearts will be revealed (Luke 2:35); Jesus was aware of their reasonings (Luke 5:22); God's word discerns the thoughts and intentions of the heart (Heb. 4:12); all the churches will know that I am he who searches mind and heart (Rev. 2:23).

B2 Thoughts of the righteous
The thoughts of the righteous are just (Prov. 12:5); the righteous ponders how to answer (Prov. 15:28); those who are of the Spirit set their minds on the things of the Spirit (Rom. 8:5); to set the mind on the Spirit is life and peace (Rom. 8:6); be transformed by the renewal of your mind (Rom. 12:2); we have the mind of Christ (1 Cor. 2:16); the peace of God will guard your hearts and minds (Phil. 4:7).

B3 Thoughts of the wicked
Man's frame of mind is evil from his youth (Gen. 8:21); why do you think evil in your hearts? (Matt. 9:4); you are not setting your mind on God's things, but on man's (Matt. 16:23; Mark 8:33); he has scattered the proud in the thoughts of their heart (Luke 1:51); those who kill you will think they are offering service to God (John 16:2); those who are of the flesh set their minds on things of the flesh (Rom. 8:5); to set the mind on the flesh is death (Rom. 8:6); men depraved in mind (1 Tim. 6:5; 2 Tim. 3:8); every thought was evil (Gen. 6:5); from the heart come evil thoughts (Matt. 15:19; Mark 7:21); their thoughts are thoughts of iniquity (Isa. 59:7); all their thoughts are against me for evil (Ps. 56:5); how long will your wicked thoughts lodge within you? (Jer. 4:14); a rebellious people who follow their own thoughts (Isa. 65:2); their thoughts run riot (Ps. 73:7); they became futile in their reasoning (Rom. 1:21); God gave them over to a depraved mind (Rom. 1:28); on that day his thoughts perish (Ps. 146:4); their thoughts accusing or defending them (Rom. 2:15).

B4 Thinking aright
Apply your mind to my knowledge (Prov. 22:17); think of what is true, honourable, right etc. (Phil. 4:8); set your mind on things above (Col. 3:2); consider the wonders of God (Job 37:14); let the unrighteous forsake his thoughts (Isa. 55:7); to him who thinks anything is unclean, it is unclean (Rom. 14:14); when I was a child, I thought as a child (1 Cor. 13:11); I will pray with my spirit and also with my mind (1 Cor. 14:15); I will sing with my spirit and sing with my mind (1 Cor. 14:15); I

would rather speak five words with my mind to instruct others (1 Cor. 14:19); in thinking be mature (1 Cor. 14:20); renewed in the spirit of your minds (Eph. 4:23); let this mind be among you which was also in Christ Jesus (Phil. 2:5); let those who are mature think like this (Phil. 3:15); think over what I say (2 Tim. 2:7); since Christ has suffered in the flesh, arm yourselves with the same thought (1 Pet. 4:1).

B5 Meditating
Meditate on the law day and night (Josh. 1:8); in his law he meditates day and night (Ps. 1:2); your law is my meditation all the day (Ps. 119:97); I meditate on your word through the night watches (Ps. 119:148); I meditate on you in the night watches (Ps. 63:6); evening, morning and noon I meditate (Ps. 55:17); I meditate on your precepts (Ps. 119:15, 78); I meditate on your statutes (Ps. 119:23, 48); I will meditate on all your work (Ps. 77:12); I meditate on your doings (Ps. 143:5); I meditate on your wonders (Ps. 119:27; 145:5); your testimonies are my meditation (Ps. 119:99); all men wondered in their hearts about John (Luke 3:15); while Peter was pondering on the vision (Acts 10:19); consider him, lest you grow weary (Heb. 12:3); Isaac went out to meditate in the field (Gen. 24:63); let my meditation be acceptable (Ps. 19:14); let my meditation be pleasing to him (Ps. 104:34); she pondered what kind of greeting this was (Luke 1:29); Mary pondered these things in her heart (Luke 2:19); his mother kept these things in her heart (Luke 2:51).

B6 Philosophy
Epicurean and Stoic philosophers (Acts 17:18); see that you are not carried off through philosophy (Col. 2:8).

450 Absence of thought
Swearing thoughtlessly (Lev. 5:4); they do not consider that I remember all their wickedness (Hos. 7:2); if I pray in a tongue my spirit prays but my mind is unfruitful (1 Cor. 14:14).

451 Idea
A **Opinion**
I give my opinion (1 Cor. 7:25; 2 Cor. 8:10); I also will declare my opinion (Job 32:17).
B **Invention**
For all inventive designs in gold, silver and bronze (Exod. 31:4); inventors of evil (Rom. 1:30).

452 Topic
He explained in all the scriptures the things concerning himself (Luke 24:27).

453 Curiosity
ATTENTIVE, see 455.

454 Incuriosity
INATTENTIVE, see 456.

455 Attention
A **God attentive**
A1 Pay attention, O God!
Hear, O Lord (Ps. 27:7; 30:10; Dan. 9:19); hear, O Lord, the voice of Judah (Deut. 33:7); let your eyes be open and your ears attentive to prayer here (1 Kgs. 8:29-30; 2 Chr. 6:20, 40); hear your people's prayer (1 Kgs. 8:33-52; 2 Chr. 6:21-39); hear the foreigner's prayer (1 Kgs. 8:42-3; 2 Chr. 6:33); incline your ear and hear (2 Kgs. 19:16; Isa. 37:17; Dan. 9:18); O Lord, listen and act! (Dan. 9:19); listen to the prayer of your servant (Dan. 9:17); incline your ear to me (Ps. 31:2; 71:2; 86:1; 102:2); give heed to me (Jer. 18:19); give heed to my cry (Ps. 17:1; 142:6); give ear to my cry (Ps. 39:12); give ear

to my words (Ps. 5:1; 17:6); let my cry come before you (Ps. 119:169); hear my supplications (Ps. 140:6); O God, hear how we are despised! (Neh. 4:4); do not shut your ear to my cry for help (Lam. 3:56); look, and see our reproach! (Lam. 5:1); see, O Lord, and look (Lam. 2:20); see, O Lord, for I am in distress (Lam. 1:20); may God lift up his countenance upon you (Num. 6:26).

A2 Will God pay attention?

Perhaps the Lord will hear the words of the Rabshakeh (2 Kgs. 19:4; Isa. 37:4); perhaps your God will take notice of us so we do not perish (Jonah 1:6); listen to me that God may listen to you (Judg. 9:7); he would give heed to me (Job 23:6).

A3 God pays attention

Ishmael – 'God hears' (Gen. 16:11, 15); you who hear prayer (Ps. 65:2); my eyes will be open and my ears attentive (2 Chr. 7:15); my eyes and heart will always be there (1 Kgs. 9:3; 2 Chr. 7:16); you will pray to me and I will listen to you (Jer. 29:12); God hears the cry of the orphan and widow (Exod. 22:23); God hears the cry of the poor (Exod. 22:27); the Lord hears the needy (Ps. 69:33); the Lord hears the prayer of the righteous (Prov. 15:29); if anyone is God-fearing and does his will, God listens to him (John 9:31); while they are still speaking I will hear (Isa. 65:24); you will incline your ear (Ps. 10:17); my God will hear me (Mic. 7:7); I knew that you always hear me (John 11:42); God will hear me (Ps. 77:1); in the morning you hear my voice (Ps. 5:3); I love the Lord for he hears my voice (Ps. 116:1); he who made ears and eyes hears and sees (Ps. 94:9); I am watching over my word to do it (Jer. 1:12); if I sin you take note of me (Job 10:14).

A4 God paid attention

A4a God paid attention to them

The Lord has heeded your affliction (Gen. 16:11); I have surely paid attention to you (Exod. 3:16); they heard that the Lord paid attention to them (Exod. 4:31); he looked on their distress when he heard their cry (Ps. 106:44); God heard the groaning of the Israelites (Exod. 2:24); God heeded their cry (Exod. 3:7); you saw their affliction and heard their cry (Neh. 9:9); the Lord saw (Isa. 59:15); I have heard their groaning (Exod. 6:5); the Lord heard our voice and saw our affliction (Deut. 26:7); God heard us and brought us out of Egypt (Num. 20:16); when he cried for help, God heard (Ps. 22:24); he heard the desire of the meek (Ps. 10:17); the Lord heard their grumblings (Num. 11:1); the Lord has heard your grumblings (Exod. 16:8, 9); I have heard their grumbling (Exod. 16:12); I have heard what the people said (Deut. 5:28); the Lord heard your words and was angry (Deut. 1:34); when God heard he was filled with anger (Ps. 78:59); the Lord heard and was angry with them (Ps. 78:21); your words have been heard (Dan. 10:12); the Lord regarded the prayer of the destitute (Ps. 102:17); when they cried to you, you heard them (Neh. 9:27, 28).

A4b God paid attention to me

You have heard my vows (Ps. 61:5); he heard my cry (Ps. 40:1); you heard my voice (Lam. 3:56; Jonah 2:2); he heard my voice (Gen. 30:6; 2 Sam. 22:7; Ps. 18:6); he inclined his ear to me (Ps. 116:2); he has heard my supplication (Ps. 28:6); you heard my supplication (Ps. 31:22); the Lord has heard my prayer (Ps. 6:8); God has heard and heeded my prayer (Ps. 66:19); the Lord has heard the sound of my weeping (Ps. 6:8); this poor man cried and the Lord heard him (Ps. 34:6); Father, thank you that you heard me (John 11:41-2); the Lord has heard that I was hated (Gen. 29:33); at the acceptable time I listened to you (2 Cor. 6:2); I have heard you about Ishmael (Gen. 17:20); because you prayed I have heard you (2 Kgs. 19:20); I have heard

your prayer (2 Kgs. 20:5; 2 Chr. 34:27; Isa. 38:5); the Lord listened to a man's voice (Josh. 10:14).

A4c God heard individuals

God had regard for Abel and his offering (Gen. 4:4); God heard Ishmael (Gen. 21:17); God heard Leah (Gen. 30:17); God heard Rachel and opened her womb (Gen. 30:22); the Lord heard Miriam and Aaron's criticism (Num. 12:2); God heard Moses (Deut. 9:19; 10:10); God listened to Manoah (Judg. 13:9); the Lord listened to Jehoahaz (2 Kgs. 13:4); the Lord heard Elijah's voice (1 Kgs. 17:22); the Lord heard Hezekiah (2 Chr. 30:20).

B Attentive to God

B1 Pay attention to God!

Hear, O Israel, the Lord our God is one (Deut. 6:4; Mark 12:29); hear what the Lord is saying (Mic. 6:1); hear, O tribe and assembly of the city! (Mic. 6:9); give me a hearing heart (1 Kgs. 3:9); in all your ways acknowledge him (Prov. 3:6); heed the Lord and you will escape the Egyptians' diseases (Exod. 15:26); to hearken is better than the fat of rams (1 Sam. 15:22); coastlands, listen to me! (Isa. 41:1); listen to me, you islands (Isa. 49:1); hear, heaven and earth (Isa. 1:2); let all the earth hear (Isa. 34:1); listen to me, my people (Isa. 51:4); listen to me, Israel (Isa. 48:12); listen, Jacob my servant (Isa. 44:1); listen to me, house of Jacob (Isa. 46:3); listen to me, you stubborn of heart (Isa. 46:12); all the words I speak to you take into your heart and hear with your ears (Ezek. 3:10); set these words on your heart and soul (Deut. 11:18); today if you hear his voice (Ps. 95:7; Heb. 3:7); let the woman pay attention to all I said (Judg. 13:13).

B2 Paying attention to God

Who has stood in the council of the Lord to hear his word? (Jer. 23:18); he who is of God hears the words of God (John 8:47); if they hear him they will have prosperity (Job 36:11); afterward you will listen to me (Ezek. 20:39); the other sheep will hear my voice (John 10:16); is it right to pay attention to you rather than to God? (Acts 4:19); the Lord will cause his voice to be heard (Isa. 30:30); our eyes look to the Lord as servants to their masters (Ps. 123:2);
I will hear what God will say (Ps. 85:8); they heard the Lord's word and went home (1 Kgs. 12:24); he wakens my ear to listen (Isa. 50:4); I will hear what the Lord commands (Num. 9:8); speak, Lord, for your servant is listening (1 Sam. 3:9-10); I have listened to the Lord's voice (Deut. 26:14).

B3 Heeding Christ

Mary was listening to the Lord's word (Luke 10:39); this is my Son, hear him (Matt. 17:5; Mark 9:7; Luke 9:35); everyone who hears these words of mine and does them (Matt. 7:24; Luke 6:47); let these words sink into your ears (Luke 9:44); if any one hears my voice and opens the door (Rev. 3:20); listen to the prophet who is like Moses (Deut. 18:15); to him you should give heed (Acts 3:22); we must pay closer attention to what we have heard (Heb. 2:1); everyone who is of the truth hears my voice (John 18:37); he who listens to you listens to me (Luke 10:16); all the people hung on his words (Luke 19:48); hear and understand! (Matt. 15:10); looking to Jesus (Heb. 12:2).

B4 Heeding the word

B4a Hear God's word!

Land, land, land, hear the word of the Lord (Jer. 22:29); hear this, you who trample the needy (Amos 8:4); hear now, heads of Jacob (Mic. 3:1); hear this, heads of the house of Jacob (Mic. 3:9); hear, O Israel! (Deut. 6:4; 9:1); hear this word (Jer. 28:7); give ear, people of Gomorrah (Isa. 1:10); hear the word of the Lord, rulers of Sodom! (Isa. 1:10); listen, for the Lord has spoken (Jer. 13:15); listen to my instruction (Ps. 78:1); give ear, heaven and earth! (Deut. 32:1); oh, that my people would listen to me! (Ps. 81:13); listen, that you may live (Isa. 55:3); those who [falsely] say, 'Hear the word of the Lord' (Ezek. 13:2).

B4b Hear wisdom!

Make your ear attentive to wisdom (Prov. 2:2); be attentive to my words (Prov. 4:20; 5:7; 7:24); be attentive to my wisdom (Prov. 5:1); hear instruction and be wise (Prov. 8:33); listen, my son, and be wise (Prov. 23:19); hear the words of the wise (Prov. 22:17); listen to advice (Prov. 19:20); blessed is he who listens to me (Prov. 8:34); he who listens to me will dwell in security (Prov. 1:33); if you receive my sayings (Prov. 2:1).

B4c Those who hear God's word

He who hears instruction is on the path to life (Prov. 10:17); he who listens to reproof will dwell among the wise (Prov. 15:31); he who heeds the word will find good (Prov. 16:20); faith comes from hearing and hearing by the preaching of Christ (Rom. 10:17); the hearing of faith (Gal. 3:2, 5); mark well, see with your eyes and hear with your ears (Ezek. 44:5); they have Moses and the prophets, let them hear them (Luke 16:29); the Gentiles will hear (Acts 28:28); do you not listen to the law? (Gal. 4:21); you will do well to pay attention to this (2 Pet. 1:19); blessed are those who heed the words of the prophecy (Rev. 1:3); will you not receive instruction and listen to my words? (Jer. 35:13); hear the statutes and ordinances (Deut. 5:1); the blessing if you hear the commandments (Deut. 11:27); the people were attentive to the book of the law (Neh. 8:3); if only you had heeded my commandments! (Isa. 48:18); be doers of the word, not just hearers (Jas. 1:22).

C Attentive to people

C1 About paying attention to people

If you listen to the words of my servants the prophets (Jer. 26:5); if he had taken warning he would have saved his life (Ezek. 33:5); if he listens to you, you have gained your brother (Matt. 18:15); he who heeds reproof is prudent (Prov. 15:5); he who heeds reproof gains understanding (Prov. 15:32); whether they will hear or not (Ezek. 2:5, 7; 3:11); the elders will listen to you (Exod. 3:18); how will Pharaoh listen to me? (Exod. 6:30); that all the congregation may heed Joshua (Num. 27:20); the king will hear and deliver me (2 Sam. 14:16).

C2 Pay attention to people!

Listen to me, Adah and Zillah (Gen. 4:23); listen to me that God may listen to you (Judg. 9:7); listen to whatever Sarah says to you (Gen. 21:12); listen to me as I command you (Gen. 27:8); only listen to me and do as I say (Gen. 27:13); my son, listen to me (Gen. 27:43); hear your father's instruction (Prov. 1:8; 4:1); heed your parents (Prov. 6:20; 23:22); listen to Jacob your father (Gen. 49:2); listen to the voice of the people (1 Sam. 8:7, 9, 22); I beg you to grant us a brief hearing (Acts 24:4); I beg you to listen to me patiently (Acts 26:3); you should have listened to me (Acts 27:21).

C3 Those who paid attention

They all listened to Hamor and Shechem (Gen. 34:24); the Israelites listened to Joshua (Deut. 34:9); David listened to Abigail (1 Sam. 25:35); the brothers listened to Judah (Gen. 37:27); Saul listened to the voice of Jonathan (1 Sam. 19:6); Benhadad listened to Asa (1 Kgs. 15:20; 2 Chr. 16:4); the king of Aram listened to the voice of his servants (1 Kgs. 20:25); the king of Assyria listened to Ahaz (2 Kgs. 16:9); he fixed his attention on them (Acts 3:5); he listened to Paul as he spoke (Acts 14:9); the Lord opened Lydia's heart to respond (Acts 16:14); the crowds with one accord gave heed to what Philip said (Acts 8:6); he who knows God listens to us (1 John 4:6).

C4 Paying attention to evil people

Because you listened to your wife and ate from the tree (Gen. 3:17); Joash listened to the officials to do evil (2 Chr. 24:17); lying to my people who listen to your lies (Ezek. 13:19); an evildoer listens to wicked lips (Prov. 17:4); the Samaritans gave heed to Simon Magus (Acts 8:10-11); is it right to pay attention to you rather than to God? (Acts 4:19); the world listens to them (1 John 4:5).

D Paying attention to other things

Pay attention to the state of your herds (Prov. 27:23-7); some will give heed to deceitful spirits and doctrines of demons (1 Tim. 4:1).

456 Inattention

A God not heeding

God does not pay heed (Ps. 94:7); the Lord would not listen to me (Deut. 3:26); God would not listen to Balaam (Deut. 23:5); will God hear the cry of the godless? (Job 27:9); do not pray for them for I will not hear you (Jer. 7:16); I will not listen when they call to me (Jer. 11:11, 14); though they cry in my ears with a loud voice, I will not listen (Ezek. 8:18); how long will I call and God will not hear? (Hab. 1:2); I will not listen to the sound of your harps (Amos 5:23); I will not look at your peace offerings (Amos 5:22); as I called and they would not listen, so they called and I would not listen (Zech. 7:13); they did not keep my covenant so I regarded them not (Heb. 8:9); if I regard sin, the Lord will not hear (Ps. 66:18); God does not listen to sinners (John 9:31); though you make many prayers I will not listen (Isa. 1:15); why have we fasted and you do not see it? (Isa. 58:3); fasting like this will not make your voice heard on high (Isa. 58:4); when they fast I will not hear their cry (Jer. 14:12); for Cain and his offering God had no regard (Gen. 4:5); do not regard their offering (Num. 16:15); the Lord did not listen to you (Deut. 1:45); God's ear is not too dull to hear (Isa. 59:1).

B Refusing to heed the word

B1 What if they do not listen to the word

What if they do not listen to me? (Exod. 4:1); the curse if you do not hear the commandments (Deut. 11:28); if you do not listen I will send the curse on you (Mal. 2:2); if anyone will not recognise this, he is not recognised (1 Cor. 14:38); he who does not listen to him will be cut off from the people (Acts 3:23); if they will not hear, shake the dust off your feet (Matt. 10:14; Mark 6:11).

B2 They will not listen

How will Pharaoh listen? (Exod. 6:12); the Israelites will be unwilling to listen (Ezek. 3:7); he who hears these words of mine and does not do them (Matt. 7:26); this nation will not listen to my voice (Judg. 2:20); the reason why you do not hear God's words is that you are not of God (John 8:47); why listen to him? (John 10:20); I will speak by men of strange tongues and yet they will not listen to me (1 Cor. 14:21); whoever will not hear the words of the prophet (Deut. 18:19); the Israelites would not listen (Exod. 6:9, 12; 2 Kgs. 18:12); they would not listen (Isa. 28:12); they said, 'We will not listen' (Jer. 6:17); they have stiffened their neck so as not to heed my words (Jer. 19:15); they will not listen to you because they will not listen to me (Ezek. 3:7).

B3 Those who would not listen

Pharaoh did not listen (Exod. 7:4, 13, 22; 8:15, 19; 9:12; 11:9); those who disregarded the word left people and animals outside (Exod. 9:21); they did not listen to the voice of the Lord (Ps. 106:25); they did not listen to Moses (Exod. 16:20); they refused to listen (Neh. 9:17); we will not listen (Jer. 44:16); they would not listen to your commandments (Neh. 9:16, 29); they did not listen to the words the Lord had spoken (Jer. 37:2); we have not paid attention to your commandments (Neh. 9:34); Jehu was heedless of the law of the Lord (2 Kgs. 10:31); I spoke but they did not listen (Jer. 35:17); I told you and you did not listen (John 9:27); my people did not listen to my voice (Ps. 81:11); my God will cast them away because they have not listened to him (Hos. 9:17); as I called and they would not listen, so they called and I would not listen (Zech. 7:13); they made their hearts like flint lest they hear the law (Zech. 7:12); their heart is dull, their ears heavy and they have closed their eyes (Matt. 13:15); because you have not listened to the voice of the Lord, a lion will kill you (1 Kgs. 20:36).

B4 Not listening, despite all
They saw the signs I did but they have not listened to me (Num. 14:22); the Lord spoke, but they paid no attention (2 Chr. 33:10); they do not regard the deeds of the Lord (Isa. 5:12); though prophets testified, they would not listen (2 Chr. 24:19; Neh. 9:30).

C Not heeding people
C1 Not listening to people
The poor man's words are not heeded (Eccles. 9:16); a scoffer does not listen to rebuke (Prov. 13:1); a fool rejects his father's discipline (Prov. 15:5); he who hears the trumpet and does not heed the warning (Ezek. 33:4, 5); a prudent man ignores an insult (Prov. 12:16); if he does not listen, take one or two others along (Matt. 18:16); if he refuses to listen to the church (Matt. 18:17); if anyone will not recognise this, he is not recognised (1 Cor. 14:38).

C2 Do not listen!
Do not listen to the false prophets (Jer. 23:16); do not listen to the words of the prophets (Jer. 27:14, 16); do not listen to your prophets and diviners (Jer. 27:9); do not listen to the dreamer of dreams (Deut. 13:3); do not listen to one who entices you to serve other gods (Deut. 13:8); do not listen to Hezekiah (2 Kgs. 18:31, 32; Isa. 36:16); do not listen or consent to the king of Aram (1 Kgs. 20:8); do not listen to them (Acts 23:21); do not pay attention to Jewish myths (Titus 1:14).

C3 Those not listening to people
We would not listen when we saw his distress (Gen. 42:21-2); he would not listen to her to lie with her (Gen. 39:10); Amnon would not listen to Tamar (2 Sam. 13:14, 16); Rehoboam did not listen to the people (1 Kgs. 12:15-16; 2 Chr. 10:15-16); Rehoboam rejected the elders' advice (1 Kgs. 12:8); Irijah would not listen to Jeremiah (Jer. 37:14); Daniel, one of the exiles from Judah, pays no attention (Dan. 6:13); we have not listened to your servants the prophets (Dan. 9:6); the sheep did not listen to them (John 10:8); the centurion took more notice of the captain and the owner than of Paul (Acts 27:11); the king of Ammon disregarded Jephthah's message (Judg. 11:28); Amaziah would not listen to Joash (2 Kgs. 14:11; 2 Chr. 25:20); I know God plans to destroy you because you have not listened to me (2 Chr. 25:16); if I counsel you you will not listen to me (Jer. 38:15); they did not listen to the judges (Judg. 2:17); Eli's sons would not listen to him (1 Sam. 2:25); the people would not listen to Samuel (1 Sam. 8:19); let us not give heed to anything Jeremiah says (Jer. 18:18); no one takes it to heart (Jer. 12:11); they called to Baal but no one paid attention (1 Kgs. 18:29).

457 Carefulness
A Taking care
What is man that you care for him? (Ps. 8:4); taking care of his victim (Exod. 21:19); the Samaritan brought him to an inn and took care of him (Luke 10:34-5); he who takes care of his master will be honoured (Prov. 27:18); take care of Jeremiah and look after him (Jer.

39:12); the Lord will care for them (Zeph. 2:7); take care that the light in you may not be darkness (Luke 11:35); that the members should have the same care of one another (1 Cor. 12:25); they consecrated Eleazar to keep the ark (1 Sam. 7:1); ten concubines to look after the house (2 Sam. 15:16).

B Beware
Beware the leaven of the Pharisees and Sadducees (Matt. 16:6, 11-12; Mark 8:15); beware of the leaven of the Pharisees, hypocrisy (Luke 12:1); beware of the scribes (Mark 12:38; Luke 20:46); beware of dogs, evil workers, mutilators (Phil. 3:2); beware of covetousness (Luke 12:15); beware of men (Matt. 10:17); beware of Alexander (2 Tim. 4:15); beware lest you be carried away (2 Pet. 3:17); take heed that no one misleads you (Matt. 24:4); take heed what you hear (Mark 4:24); take heed (Mark 13:23); take care how you hear (Luke 8:18); be on your guard (Luke 17:3); take care lest there be an unbelieving heart in any of you (Heb. 3:12); take heed to yourself and do not be faithless (Mal. 2:16); take heed to yourselves that you may receive a full reward (2 John 8); be careful how you walk (Eph. 5:15); let him who thinks he stands take heed lest he fall (1 Cor. 10:12); see that no one misleads you (Mark 13:5); take care what you do with these men (Acts 5:35).

C Keep watch
C1 Keep watch!
Be on your guard (Mark 13:9); be alert! (Acts 20:31); watch out for those who create dissensions (Rom. 16:17); in prayer keep watch with thanksgiving (Col. 4:2); be sober, be watchful (1 Pet. 5:8); be on your guard concerning all I have said (Exod. 23:13); keep watch, for you do not know when your Lord is coming (Matt. 24:42-3); keep watch, for you do not know the time (Matt. 25:13; Mark 13:33-7); keep watch at all times (Luke 21:36); be on guard lest the day come suddenly (Luke 21:34); he commanded the doorkeeper to keep watch (Mark 13:34); watch and pray that you may not enter into temptation (Matt. 26:41; Mark 14:38); keep watch with me (Matt. 26:38); could you not keep watch for one hour? (Matt. 26:40; Mark 14:37); keep watch (Mark 13:37; 14:34); keep watch, stand firm in the faith (1 Cor. 16:13); watch yourself and your teaching (1 Tim. 4:16); keep your soul diligently (Deut. 4:15); keep your soul diligently lest you forget (Deut. 4:9); watch yourself lest you forget (Deut. 4:23); guard your heart diligently (Prov. 4:23); be on guard for yourselves and the flock (Acts 20:28); let everyone be on guard against his neighbour (Jer. 9:4).

C2 God keeping watch
May the Lord watch between us (Gen. 31:49); God guarded Israel as the apple of his eye (Deut. 32:10); the days gone by when God watched over me (Job 29:2); the Lord's eyes are always on the land to care for it (Deut. 11:12); the eyes of the Lord are toward the righteous (Ps. 34:15); I will counsel you with my eye upon you (Ps. 32:8); the eye of the Lord is on those who fear him (Ps. 33:18); the Lord keeps all his bones (Ps. 34:20); I am watching over my word (Jer. 1:12).

C3 Man keeping watch
This is a night of watching for Israel (Exod. 12:42); I will take my stand to watch and station myself on the tower (Hab. 2:1); if the householder had known he would have watched (Matt. 24:43); shepherds keeping watch over their flock by night (Luke 2:8); they watched the gates day and night (Acts 9:24); your leaders keep watch over your souls (Heb. 13:17); he who guards his way preserves his life (Prov. 16:17); our eyes failed, watching vainly for help (Lam. 4:17); we watched for a nation which could not save (Lam. 4:17); we

prayed to God and set a guard (Neh. 4:9); they sat down and kept watch over him (Matt. 27:36).

D Watchmen

On your walls I have appointed watchmen (Isa. 62:6); I set watchmen over you (Jer. 6:17); when I choose someone and make him a watchman (Ezek. 33:2-6); I have made you a watchman (Ezek. 3:17; 33:7); set a watchman (Isa. 21:6); the prophet is the watchman of Ephraim (Hos. 9:8); watchmen on the hills of Ephraim (Jer. 31:6); a watcher, a holy one, came down from heaven (Dan. 4:13, 23); this sentence is by decree of the watchers, the holy ones (Dan. 4:17); the day you post watchmen has come, the day God visits you (Mic. 7:4); the watchman stands continually on the watchtower (Isa. 21:8); Saul's watchmen looked (1 Sam. 14:16); the watchman saw people coming (2 Sam. 13:34; 18:24-7; 2 Kgs. 9:17); watchman, what of the night? (Isa. 21:11); your watchmen shout joyfully together (Isa. 52:8); his watchmen are blind, knowing nothing (Isa. 56:10); when the watchmen of the house tremble (Eccles. 12:3); the watchmen found me (S. of S. 3:3; 5:7); my soul waits for the Lord more than watchmen for the morning (Ps. 130:6); those sent to patrol the earth (Zech. 1:10-11; 6:7).

458 Negligence

A Neglecting people

You must not neglect the Levite (Deut. 14:27); he who shuts his ear to the cry of the poor will cry and not be answered (Prov. 21:13); he who shuts his eyes [to the poor] will have many a curse (Prov. 28:27); no one cares for my soul (Ps. 142:4); it is Zion, no one cares for her (Jer. 30:17); a shepherd who will not care for the perishing (Zech. 11:16); Levi disregarded parents, brothers and children (Deut. 33:9); the Hellenist widows were neglected in the daily distribution (Acts 6:1); do not neglect to show hospitality (Heb. 13:2); do not neglect to do good and share (Heb. 13:16).

B Neglecting duties

Do not be negligent in carrying out the king's business (Ezra 4:22); my own vineyard I have neglected (S. of S. 1:6); no negligence was found in Daniel (Dan. 6:4); these you ought to have done without neglecting the others (Matt. 23:23; Luke 11:42).

C Neglecting God's things

You neglected the rock that begot you (Deut. 32:18); we will not neglect the house of our God (Neh. 10:39); the Pharisees tithed herbs but neglected weightier matters (Matt. 23:23); you neglect justice and the love of God (Luke 11:42); hear instruction and do not neglect it (Prov. 8:33); how shall we escape if we neglect such a great salvation? (Heb. 2:3); you neglected all my counsel (Prov. 1:25); it is not desirable that we should neglect the word of God to serve tables (Acts 6:2); do not neglect the gift you have (1 Tim. 4:14).

459 Enquiry

A Asking

REQUESTING, see 761.

A1 God enquiring

I will ask you and you instruct me! (Job 38:3; 40:7; 42:4); is not this so? (Amos 2:11).

A2 Christ enquiring

Jesus was asking the teachers questions (Luke 2:46); who do men say I am? (Matt. 16:13; Mark 8:27; Luke 9:18); who do you say I am? (Matt. 16:15; Mark 8:29; Luke 9:20); Jesus asked the Pharisees a question (Matt. 22:41); if I ask you a question you will not answer (Luke 22:68); if you answer my question I will answer yours (Matt. 21:24; Mark 11:29); I also will ask you a question (Luke 20:3); he asked them what they were discussing

on the way (Mark 9:33); is it lawful on the sabbath to do good? (Luke 6:9); when the blind man came near, Jesus questioned him (Luke 18:40).

A3 Enquiring of God

They came to Moses to enquire of God (Exod. 18:15); enquire of God for us (Judg. 18:5; 2 Kgs. 22:13; Jer. 21:2); when a man went to enquire of God (1 Sam. 9:9); elders came to enquire of the Lord (Ezek. 20:1); they enquired of the Lord where Saul was (1 Sam. 10:22); Ahimelech enquired of the Lord for David (1 Sam. 22:10-15); enquire of the Lord through Elisha (2 Kgs. 8:8); Zedekiah sent to enquire of the Lord by Jeremiah (Jer. 37:7); enquire first for the word of God (1 Kgs. 22:5; 2 Kgs. 3:11; 2 Chr. 18:4); enquire of the Lord for me (2 Chr. 34:21); the advice of Ahithophel was like enquiring from God (2 Sam. 16:23); should I be consulted by such people? (Ezek. 14:3); enquiring by Urim (Num. 27:21); using an ephod to enquire (1 Sam. 23:9-12; 30:7-8); enquiring at the ark (Judg. 20:27); Saul called for the ark (1 Sam. 14:18-19); the bronze altar is for me to enquire by (2 Kgs. 16:15); the prophets enquired about this salvation (1 Pet. 1:10).

A4 Questioning Christ

They asked him about the parables (Mark 4:10; 7:17); his disciples asked him what this parable meant (Luke 8:9); the disciples asked him why they could not cast it out (Matt. 17:19; Mark 9:28); Peter, John and James questioned him (Mark 13:3); they asked him, 'Is it right to heal on the sabbath?' (Matt. 12:10); why ask me about what is good? (Matt. 19:17); the Sadducees asked him a question (Matt. 22:23; Mark 12:18; Luke 20:28); in the house the disciples questioned him about divorce (Mark 10:10); Pharisees questioned him about divorce (Mark 10:2); the Pharisees asked Jesus when the kingdom of God was coming (Luke 17:20); a Pharisee asked him a question to test him (Matt. 22:35); the scribes and Pharisees assailed him with questions (Luke 11:53); one of the scribes asked him, 'Which is the greatest commandment?' (Matt 12:28); Pilate asked him, 'Are you the king of the Jews?' (Luke 23:3); when they persisted in asking him (John 8:7); Jesus knew that they wanted to ask him (John 16:19); they asked him, 'Will you now restore the kingdom to Israel?' (Acts 1:6).

A5 Asking people

I was only asking (1 Sam. 17:29); when your children ask you about these things (Exod. 12:26; 13:14; Deut. 6:20; Josh. 4:6, 21); ask your father and he will tell you (Deut. 32:7); enquire of past generations (Job 8:8); I am going to ask you a question (Jer. 38:14); we will send for the girl and ask her (Gen. 24:57); ask him, he is of age (John 9:21, 23); they ask me about things I do not know (Ps. 35:11); the elder son asked a servant what was happening (Luke 15:26); the blind man asked what was happening (Luke 18:36); let women ask their husbands at home (1 Cor. 14:35); the Queen of Sheba came with difficult questions (1 Kgs. 10:1; 2 Chr. 9:1); ask the priests for a ruling (Hag. 2:11); Esther sent to enquire why Mordecai was mourning (Esther 4:5); Herod enquired where the Christ was to be born (Matt. 2:4); they made signs to Zechariah asking what he wanted him called (Luke 1:62); Pilate asked whether he were already dead (Mark 15:44); I asked them about Jerusalem (Neh. 1:2); they will ask the way to Zion (Jer. 50:5).

A6 Enquiring of other things

Enquiring of Baal-zebub instead of God (2 Kgs. 1:2-3, 6, 16); Saul enquired of a medium, not of the Lord (1 Chr. 10:13-14); when they say consult mediums, should not a people consult their God? (Isa. 8:19); they enquire of a thing of wood (Hos. 4:12).

A7 Not asking

They did not enquire of God about the Gibeonites (Josh. 9:14); we did not enquire of God about the ark (1 Chr. 15:13); David dared not enquire of God at the tabernacle (1 Chr. 21:30); I will not have you enquire of me (Ezek. 20:3, 31); those who have not sought the Lord or enquired of him (Zeph. 1:6); they were afraid to ask him (Mark 9:32; Luke 9:45); no one dared ask him any more questions (Matt. 22:46; Mark 12:34; Luke 20:40); in that day you will ask me no questions (John 16:23); you know all things and have no need for anyone to question you (John 16:30);

no one dared ask, 'Who are you?' (John 21:12); eat anything without asking questions for conscience' sake (1 Cor. 10:25-7).

B Exploring

B1 Investigating

I have come down to see whether they have done according to their outcry (Gen. 18:21); investigate reports that some are following other gods (Deut. 13:14; 17:4); the priests and judges shall investigate for false witness (Deut. 19:18); investigate how this sin happened (1 Sam. 14:38); we have investigated it (Job 5:27); as though you were going to investigate his case more thoroughly (Acts 23:15, 20); by investigating him yourself you will learn these things (Acts 24:8); after the investigation I may have something to write (Acts 25:26).

B2 Interrogating

Gideon interrogated a youth from Succoth (Judg. 8:14); Hezekiah questioned the priests and Levites about the heaps of tithe (2 Chr. 31:9); the officials questioned Jeremiah (Jer. 38:27); the governor interrogated Jesus (Matt. 27:11; Mark 15:2); Herod questioned Jesus at some length (Luke 23:9); the high priest questioned Jesus about his disciples and teaching (John 18:19); why question me? (John 18:21); the high priest questioned them (Acts 5:27); Paul was to be examined by scourging (Acts 22:24); the commander asked Paul who he was and what he had done (Acts 21:33); this is my defence to those who would question me (1 Cor. 9:3).

B3 Spying

The wicked spies on the righteous (Ps. 37:32); you are spies (Gen. 42:9-34); Moses sent men to spy out the land (Num. 13:2; 14:36; 32:8; Deut. 1:22-5; Josh. 14:7); Moses sent men to spy out Jazer (Num. 21:32); Joshua sent out two spies (Josh. 2:1-3; 6:22, 25); Rahab welcomed the spies (Heb. 11:31); Joshua sent men to spy out Ai (Josh. 7:2); men were sent to spy our Bethel (Judg. 1:23-4); the Danites sent five men to spy out the land (Judg. 18:2); David sent out spies (1 Sam. 26:4); Abner came to find out all you are doing (2 Sam. 3:25); the Ammonites suspected David of sending spies (2 Sam. 10:3; 1 Chr. 19:3); Absalom sent spies throughout the land (2 Sam. 15:10); the priests sent spies to watch Jesus (Luke 20:20); false brethren who slipped in to spy out our liberty in Christ (Gal. 2:4).

C Searching / seeking

C1 Seeking in general

There is a time to seek (Eccles. 3:6); the preacher was seeking out everything done under heaven (Eccles. 1:13); the glory of kings is to seek things out (Prov. 25:2); do not your eyes look for truth? (Jer. 5:3); seek and you will find (Matt. 7:7-8; Luke 11:9-10).

C2 God searching

C2a God searches hearts

God searches minds and hearts (1 Chr. 28:9; Rev. 2:23); he who searches the hearts knows what the mind of the Spirit is (Rom. 8:27); Lord, you have searched me and known me (Ps. 139:1); search and know my heart (Ps. 139:23); I the Lord search the heart (Jer. 17:10).

C2b God searches for people

I myself will search for my sheep (Ezek. 34:11); seek me like a lost sheep! (Ps. 119:176); I will seek the lost (Ezek. 34:16); the Son of man has come to seek and to save what was lost (Luke 19:10); searching for the straying sheep (Matt. 18:12); you will be called, 'Sought out, a city not forsaken' (Isa. 62:12); the Father seeks such to worship him (John 4:23); though they hide on the summit of Carmel I will search them out (Amos 9:3); I will search Jerusalem with lamps (Zeph. 1:12).

C3 Seeking God

C3a Seek God!

Seek God! (Job 8:5); seek my face! (Ps. 27:8); seek the Lord while he may be found (Isa. 55:6); seek the Lord at the place he chooses to put his name (Deut. 12:5); seek the Lord and live (Amos 5:4, 6); seek the Lord, all you humble of the earth (Zeph. 2:3); seek the Lord and his strength (1 Chr. 16:11; Ps. 105:4); set your heart to seek the Lord (1 Chr. 22:19); let us go to seek the Lord (Zech. 8:21-2); let us seek the Lord (Zech. 8:22); it is time to seek the Lord (Hos. 10:12); Asa commanded them to seek the Lord (2 Chr. 14:4); seek first God's kingdom (Matt. 6:33; Luke 12:31); seek the things above, where Christ is (Col. 3:1); if my people humble themselves and seek my face (2 Chr. 7:14).

C3b It is good to seek God

The Lord is good to those who seek him (Lam. 3:25); those who seek the Lord will not lack (Ps. 34:10); the hand of our God is on all who seek him (Ezra 8:22); as long as Uzziah sought the Lord, he prospered (2 Chr. 26:5); I sought the Lord and he answered he (Ps. 34:4); let those who seek the Lord rejoice (1 Chr. 16:10; Ps. 105:3); let those who seek you rejoice (Ps. 40:16; 70:4); happy are those who seek him (Ps. 119:2); those who seek him will praise him (Ps. 22:26); those who seek the Lord understand all things (Prov. 28:5); you have not forsaken those who seek you (Ps. 9:10); you who seek God, let your heart revive (Ps. 69:32); the Lord whom you seek will suddenly come to his temple (Mal. 3:1).

C3c Those seeking God

I seek you (Ps. 63:1); your face I will seek (Ps. 27:8); with my whole heart I have sought you (Ps. 119:10); I would seek God (Job 5:8); like you, we seek your God (Ezra 4:2); that they may seek your name (Ps. 83:16); listen, you who seek the Lord (Isa. 51:1); I set my face to seek the Lord (Dan. 9:3); the proconsul sought to hear the word of God (Acts 13:7); that the rest of mankind may seek the Lord (Acts 15:17); those who sought God went to the tent of meeting (Exod. 33:7); a covenant to seek the Lord (2 Chr. 15:12-13); Jehoshaphat sought the Lord (2 Chr. 17:4; 19:3; 20:3; 22:9); Hezekiah sought the Lord (2 Chr. 31:21); Josiah began to seek God (2 Chr. 34:3); Judah gathered to seek the Lord (2 Chr. 20:4); in the day of my trouble I sought the Lord (Ps. 77:2); for my people who seek me (Isa. 65:10); Israel and Judah will come weeping, seeking the Lord (Jer. 50:4); may those who seek you not be dishonoured through me (Ps. 69:6); those who set their heart on seeking the Lord (2 Chr. 11:16); this is the generation of those who seek him (Ps. 24:6); afterwards Israel will seek the Lord (Hos. 3:5).

C3d Unsatisfactory seeking of God

In their distress they seek me (Hos. 5:15); in distress they sought you (Isa. 26:16); when he killed them they sought him (Ps. 78:34); they will seek the Lord but not find him (Hos. 5:6); yet they seek me day by day (Isa. 58:2); they will seek the word of the Lord but not find it (Amos 8:12).

C3e Seeking and finding God

If you seek him, he will be found by you (1 Chr. 28:9; 2 Chr. 15:2); you will seek him and find him when you seek with all your heart (Deut. 4:29; Jer. 29:13); that men would seek him and find him (Acts 17:27); they sought God and he was found by them (2 Chr. 15:4, 15); he must believe God rewards those who seek him (Heb. 11:6); if I only knew where to find him! (Job 23:3).

C3f Not seeking God
The Lord looks to see if any seek after God (Ps. 14:2; 53:2); no one seeks for God (Rom. 3:11); the wicked does not seek God (Ps. 10:4); they do not seek the Lord (Isa. 9:13; 31:1); the shepherds do not seek the Lord (Jer. 10:21); they have not sought him (Hos. 7:10); they do not seek your statutes (Ps. 119:155); I was found by those who did not seek me (Isa. 65:1; Rom. 10:20); I will sweep away those who do not seek the Lord (Zeph. 1:6); I will go to my place until they seek me (Hos. 5:15); Rehoboam did not set his heart to seek the Lord (2 Chr. 12:14); he who did not seek the Lord should be killed (2 Chr. 15:13).

C4 Seeking Christ
Herod searched for the child Jesus (Matt. 2:8, 13); Mary and Joseph searched for Jesus (Luke 2:44-9); the disciples searched for Jesus (Mark 1:36); they were seeking Jesus (John 11:56); the crowds were searching for him (Luke 4:42); they went to Capernaum, seeking Jesus (John 6:24); everyone is seeking you (Mark 1:37); you seek me not because you saw signs, but because you ate bread (John 6:26); you are looking for Jesus who was crucified (Matt. 28:5; Mark 16:6); you will seek me but not find me (John 7:34, 36); you will seek me and die in your sin (John 8:21); you will seek me and not be able to come (John 13:33); his mother and brothers sought to speak with him (Matt. 12:46); Herod sought to see Jesus (Luke 9:9); why seek the living among the dead? (Luke 24:5); the Jews were looking for him, saying, 'Where is he?' (John 7:11); if you seek me, let these people go (John 18:8).

C5 Seeking people
C5a Those looking for people
Joseph seeking his brothers (Gen. 37:15-16); they sought the spies but did not find them (Josh. 2:22); they searched but could not find the messengers (2 Sam. 17:20); Saul searched daily for David (1 Sam. 23:14); Shimei went to look for his servants (1 Kgs. 2:40); Ahab searched for Elijah (1 Kgs. 18:10); the prophets searched for Elijah (2 Kgs. 2:16-17); I will show you the man you seek (Judg. 4:22); three men were looking for Peter (Acts 10:19); when Onesiphorus was in Rome he searched for me and found me (2 Tim. 1:17); they searched for a beautiful young virgin for David (1 Kgs. 1:2, 3); let beautiful young virgins be sought for the king (Esther 2:2); search whether any servants of the Lord are here (2 Kgs. 10:23); they looked for Daniel and his companions to kill them (Dan. 2:13); my counsellors and nobles sought me (Dan. 4:36); search out the one who is worthy in that place (Matt. 10:11); Barnabas went to Tarsus to look for Saul (Acts 11:25); the devil prowls like a lion, seeking someone to devour (1 Pet. 5:8).

C5b Seeking but not finding people
I looked for my beloved but did not find him (S. of S. 3:1; 5:6); Herod searched for Peter and did not find him (Acts 12:19); I sought for the wicked but he could not be found (Ps. 37:36); you will seek those who contend with you but not find them (Isa. 41:12); she will seek her lovers but not find them (Hos. 2:7).

C5c Not seeking people
Do not seek mediums or spiritists (Lev. 19:31); Saul no longer searched for David (1 Sam. 27:4); your lovers do not seek you (Jer. 30:14); a shepherd who will not seek the strayed (Zech. 11:16); my shepherds did not search

for my flock (Ezek. 34:8); there was no one to search or seek for them (Ezek. 34:6); you have not sought the lost (Ezek. 34:4).

C6 Searching for things
C6a Seeking for concrete things
Moses searched diligently for the sin offering (Lev. 10:16); they will search for human remains left unburied (Ezek. 39:14); how Esau will be ransacked, his treasures searched out! (Obad. 6); the Gentiles seek all these things (Matt. 6:32); the kingdom of heaven is like a merchant seeking fine pearls (Matt. 13:45); do not seek what you are to eat and drink (Luke 12:29-30); he came seeking fruit on the fig tree and found none (Luke 13:6); for three years I have come seeking fruit and found none (Luke 13:7); searching for the straying sheep (Luke 15:4); she searches diligently until she finds the coin (Luke 15:8); they are seeking a homeland (Heb. 11:14); searching for stubble as straw (Exod. 5:12); all her people groan seeking bread (Lam. 1:11); the ark went before to seek out a resting place for them (Num. 10:33); Laban searched the tent (Gen. 31:34, 35); the steward searched their sacks (Gen. 44:12); Saul looked for the donkeys (1 Sam. 9:3; 10:14); none who seek the donkey need weary themselves (Jer. 2:24); a search was made in the royal archives (Ezra 5:17; 6:1); search in the books (Ezra 4:15); a search has been made (Ezra 4:19).

C6b Seeking for abstract things
He who seeks good seeks favour (Prov. 11:27); seek good and not evil (Amos 5:14); seek righteousness, seek humility (Zeph. 2:3); seek wisdom like silver (Prov. 2:4); those who seek for me [Wisdom] will find me (Prov. 8:17); they will seek Wisdom but not find her (Prov. 1:28); the mind of the intelligent seeks knowledge (Prov. 15:14); do you seek the priesthood also? (Num. 16:10); do you seek great things for yourself? (Jer. 45:5); he sought an opportunity to betray him (Matt. 26:16); the chief priests and council sought false false testimony against Jesus (Matt. 26:59); it seeks a sign but no sign will be given it (Luke 11:29); you search the scriptures because you think that in them you have eternal life (John 5:39); seeking to establish their own righteousness (Rom. 10:3); what Israel sought it did not obtain (Rom. 11:7).

460 Answer
A About answering
An apt answer is a joy (Prov. 15:23); a right answer is a kiss on the lips (Prov. 24:26); a soft answer turns away wrath (Prov. 15:1); the answer of the tongue is from the Lord (Prov. 16:1); the heart of the righteous ponders how to answer (Prov. 15:28); it is folly to give an answer before hearing (Prov. 18:13); that you may give a true answer to him who sent you (Prov. 22:21); that I may answer him who reproaches me (Prov. 27:11); do not answer a fool according to his folly (Prov. 26:4); answer a fool according to his folly (Prov. 26:5); the rich man answers roughly (Prov. 18:23); one of the scribes saw that he answered well (Mark 12:28); when Jesus saw that he answered wisely (Mark 12:34); let us have an answer for those who sent us (John 1:22).

B God answering
B1 God, answer me!
Answer me when I call! (Ps. 4:1); make haste to answer me (Ps. 69:17); save me and answer me (Ps. 108:6); answer me in your faithfulness (Ps. 143:1); may the King answer us in the day we call (Ps. 20:9); let the Almighty answer me! (Job 31:35); let me speak and you reply to me (Job 13:22); I would learn what he would answer (Job 23:5); answer me with your sure salvation (Ps. 69:13).

B2 God will answer

Call to me and I will answer you (Jer. 33:3); I call on you for you will answer me (Ps. 17:6); it is I who answer and look after you (Hos. 14:8); may the Lord answer you in the day of trouble (Ps. 20:1); I the Lord will answer him myself (Ezek. 14:7); if he comes to the prophet, I the Lord will answer him myself (Ezek. 14:4); you will answer (Ps. 38:15; 86:7); he will answer him from his holy heaven (Ps. 20:6); I will answer them (Zech. 10:6; 13:9); you will call and the Lord will answer (Isa. 58:9); the God who answers by fire is God (1 Kgs. 18:24); when he hears your cry he will answer you (Isa. 30:19); before they call I will answer (Isa. 65:24).

B3 God answered

I cry to the Lord and he answers me (Ps. 3:4); I sought the Lord and he answered me (Ps. 34:4); I called to the Lord and he answered me (Ps. 118:5; 120:1; Jonah 2:2); they called to the Lord and he answered them (Ps. 99:6); on the day I called you answered me (Ps. 138:3); then the Lord answered me (Hab. 2:2); the Lord answered the angel with gracious and comforting words (Zech. 1:13); God who answered me in the day of trouble (Gen. 35:3); Moses spoke and God answered him (Exod. 19:19); the Lord answered Samuel (1 Sam. 7:9); God answered David with fire (1 Chr. 21:26); the Lord answered Job out of the whirlwind (Job 38:1); in a favourable time I have answered you (Isa. 49:8); by awesome deeds you answer us in righteousness (Ps. 65:5); I answered you in the secret place of thunder (Ps. 81:7); if I called and he answered me (Job 9:16).

C Answering God

He will call and I will answer him (Ps. 91:15); you would call and I would answer (Job 14:15); there she will answer as in the days of her youth (Hos. 2:15); answer me! (Mic. 6:3); I will see how I may reply (Hab. 2:1); how can I answer him? (Job 9:14); what will I answer to God? (Job 31:14); I called but no one answered (Isa. 65:12; 66:4); I called but they did not answer (Jer. 35:17); a man like me cannot answer him (Job 9:32); he could not answer God once in 1000 times (Job 9:3); who are you to answer back to God? (Rom. 9:20).

D Answering people

Be prepared to give an answer to everyone who asks for a reason (1 Pet. 3:15); to know how to reply to each one (Col. 4:6); if you answer my question I will answer yours (Matt. 21:24; Mark 11:29); I will have an answer for him who reproaches me (Ps. 119:42); everyone was amazed at his understanding and his answers (Luke 2:47); Solomon answered all the Queen of Sheba's questions (1 Kgs. 10:3; 2 Chr. 9:2); is that how you answer the high priest? (John 18:22); the earth will answer to the grain, the wine and the oil (Hos. 2:22).

E No answer

E1 God not answering

The Lord will not answer you in that day (1 Sam. 8:18); I cry but you do not answer (Ps. 22:2); is there anyone who will answer? (Job 5:1); God does not answer (Job 35:12); God did not answer him (2 Sam. 22:42; Ps. 18:41); God did not answer Saul that day (1 Sam. 14:37); the Lord did not answer him by dreams or Urim or prophets (1 Sam. 28:6, 15); the seers are ashamed because there is no answer from God (Mic. 3:7); I cry out to you but you do not answer me (Job 30:20); he who neglects the poor will cry and not be answered (Prov. 21:13); they will cry to the Lord but he will not answer them (Mic. 3:4); I cry, 'Violence!', but there is no answer (Job 19:7).

E2 Others not answering

They will call, but wisdom will not answer (Prov. 1:28); he did not answer her a word (Matt. 15:23); when

accused by the chief priests and elders, he made no answer (Matt. 27:12); he was silent and made no answer (Mark 14:61); he gave no answer even to a single charge (Matt. 27:14); do you make no answer? (Matt. 26:62; Mark 14:60; 15:4); Jesus did not answer Herod (Luke 23:9); if I ask you a question you will not answer (Luke 22:68); you will call but they will not answer you (Jer. 7:27); why was there no answer when I called? (Isa. 50:2); I called you but you did not answer (Jer. 7:13); I called but no one answered (Isa. 65:12; 66:4); I called but they did not answer (Jer. 35:17); Joseph's brothers could not answer him (Gen. 45:3); Ish-bosheth could not answer Abner (2 Sam. 3:11); they were silent and did not answer the Rabshakeh (2 Kgs. 18:36; Isa. 36:21); a man like me cannot answer him (Job 9:32); he could not answer God once in 1000 times (Job 9:3); when they called on Baal no one answered (1 Kgs. 18:26, 29); though you cry to an idol it cannot answer (Isa. 46:7).

461 Experiment

TEMPTATION, see 612B.

A Testing in general

Count it all joy when you fall into testings (Jas. 1:2); that the proving of your faith may result in glory (1 Pet. 1:7); the fiery ordeal comes on you to test you (1 Pet. 4:12); a man is tested by his praise (Prov. 27:21); the Lord knows how to rescue the godly from trial (2 Pet. 2:9).

B God testing people

B1 God tests people

Test me, O Lord (Ps. 26:2); try me and know my thoughts (Ps. 139:23); I test the mind (Jer. 17:10); God tries the heart (1 Chr. 29:17; Ps. 7:9); God who tests our hearts (1 Thess. 2:4); you test the feelings and heart (Jer. 11:20); his eyes test the sons of men (Ps. 11:4); the Lord tests the righteous and the wicked (Ps. 11:5); God tests men for them to see that they are but animals (Eccles. 3:18); God tests like one refining silver (Ps. 66:10; Prov. 17:3); what is man that you examine him every moment? (Job 7:17-18); I have tested you in the furnace of affliction (Isa. 48:10); I will refine and assay them (Jer. 9:7); when he has tested me, I will come forth like gold (Job 23:10); I will test them as gold is tested (Zech. 13:9); the fire will test what kind of work each has done (1 Cor. 3:13); the testing of your faith produces endurance (Jas. 1:3); you test the righteous (Jer. 20:12); God knows men without needing further investigation (Job 34:23-4).

B2 God tested people

You have tested me and found nothing (Ps. 17:3); God tested Abraham (Gen. 22:1); Abraham, when he was tested, offered up Isaac (Heb. 11:17); God tested Gideon's soldiers (Judg. 7:4); the word of the Lord tested Joseph (Ps. 105:19); I tested you at the waters of Meribah (Ps. 81:7); you proved Levi at Massah and Meribah (Deut. 33:8); God has come to test you (Exod. 20:20); God fed them manna to test them (Deut. 8:16); the Lord left nations in the land to test Israel (Judg. 3:1); God left Hezekiah alone to test him (2 Chr. 32:31); he said this to test Philip (John 6:6); God tested the Israelites to see whether: they would walk in his law (Exod. 16:4); they would follow his commands (Deut. 8:2; Judg. 3:4); they would keep the way of the Lord (Judg. 2:22); they loved the Lord (Deut. 13:3).

C Testing God

Test me now (Mal. 3:10); do not put the Lord to the test (Deut. 6:16; Matt. 4:7; Luke 4:12); your fathers tested me (Ps. 95:9; Heb. 3:9); why put God to the test? (Exod. 17:2; Acts 15:10); they put God to the test (Exod. 17:7; Num. 14:22; Ps. 78:18, 41, 56; 106:14); Massah – testing (Exod. 17:7); as on the day of testing in the wilderness (Heb. 3:8); why have you agreed together to put the Spirit of the Lord to the test? (Acts 5:9); we should not test the Lord as some of them did (1 Cor. 10:9); I will not test the Lord (Isa. 7:12); evildoers put God to the test and escape (Mal. 3:15).

D Testing Christ
They asked for a sign to test Jesus (Matt. 16:1; Mark 8:11; Luke 11:16); a Pharisee asked Jesus a question to test him (Matt. 22:35); Pharisees tested him about divorce (Matt. 19:3; Mark 10:2); a lawyer put Jesus to the test (Luke 10:25); they said this to test him (John 8:6); why put me to the test? (Matt. 22:18; Mark 12:15).

E People testing
E1 People testing people
Deacons must first be tested (1 Tim. 3:10); you have put to the test those who claim to be apostles (Rev. 2:2); I wrote to test you (2 Cor. 2:9); to prove by the earnestness of others that your love is genuine (2 Cor. 8:8); we are sending the brother whom we have often tested (2 Cor. 8:22); the devil will throw some of you into prison that you may be tested (Rev. 2:10); the hour of trial which is coming to test those who dwell on the earth (Rev. 3:10); I have made you an assayer and tester among my people (Jer. 6:27); Joseph's brothers were to be tested (Gen. 42:15-16); test us for ten days (Dan. 1:12, 14); the Queen of Sheba came to test Solomon with hard questions (1 Kgs. 10:1; 2 Chr. 9:1).

E2 Testing oneself
Let us test and examine our ways (Lam. 3:40); I said 'I will test myself with pleasure' (Eccles. 2:1); test yourselves to see whether you are in the faith (2 Cor. 13:5); let a man examine himself before eating and drinking (1 Cor. 11:28); let each one test his own work (Gal. 6:4).

E3 Testing other things
Test everything (1 Thess. 5:21); test the spirits to see whether they are from God (1 John 4:1); the ear tests words as the palate tastes food (Job 12:11; 34:3); I tested all this with wisdom (Eccles. 7:23); examining the scriptures daily so see if these things were so (Acts 17:11); I have bought five yoke [pairs] of oxen and must try them out (Luke 14:19).

462 Comparison

A Comparing
Some compare themselves with themselves (2 Cor. 10:12); to what shall I compare this generation? (Matt. 11:16); to what shall I compare the men of this generation? (Luke 7:31); with what shall we compare the kingdom of God? (Mark 4:30).

B Beyond compare
To whom will you compare God? (Isa. 40:18); to whom will you compare me? (Isa. 40:25; 46:5); the present sufferings are not worth comparing with the glory to come (Rom. 8:18).

463 Discrimination

A Discernment in general
The spiritual man discerns all things (1 Cor. 2:15); whoever is discerning, let him know these things (Hos. 14:9); to give to the youth knowledge and discretion (Prov. 1:4); let Pharaoh look for a discerning and wise man (Gen. 41:33); there is no one so discerning and wise as you (Gen. 41:39); I have filled Bezalel with discernment (Exod. 31:3); everyone to whom the Lord has given discernment (Exod. 36:1); the king is like an angel of God to discern good and evil (2 Sam. 14:17); until he knows how to refuse evil and choose good (Isa. 7:15); youths without blemish, handsome, intelligent, discerning (Dan. 1:4); the discernment of their

discerning men will be hidden (Isa. 29:14); God takes away discernment from the elders (Job 12:20).

B Discerning God's things
How will we know a message which the Lord has not spoken? (Deut. 18:21); if one prophesies peace and it happens, the Lord has sent him (Jer. 28:9); the God who answers by fire, he is God (1 Kgs. 18:24); help me discern between good and evil (1 Kgs. 3:9); the gift of distinguishing spirits (1 Cor. 12:10); that your love may abound in knowledge and discernment (Phil. 1:9); if anyone is willing to do his will, he will know whether the teaching is from God (John 7:17); the things of the Spirit of God are spiritually discerned (1 Cor. 2:14).

C Distinguishing
Let me feel you to know whether you are Esau or not (Gen. 27:21); see whether it is your son's coat or not (Gen. 37:32); if the cart goes straight to Beth-shemesh we will know it was the Lord (1 Sam. 6:9); the word 'Shibboleth' used to discriminate (Judg. 12:5-6); you will know them by their fruits (Matt. 7:16, 20); a tree is known by its fruit (Matt. 12:33); by this you will know that God sent me (Num. 16:28-30); by this we know the children of God and the children of the devil (1 John 3:10); every tree is known by its fruit (Luke 6:44); they sorted the good fish into containers but threw the bad away (Matt. 13:48); by this will all know that you are my disciples, if you love one another (John 13:35); by this we know that we are in him (1 John 2:5); by this you know the Spirit of God (1 John 4:2); by this we know the spirit of truth and the spirit of error (1 John 4:6); by this we know that we love the children of God (1 John 5:2).

464 Lack of discrimination

A Without discernment
A beautiful woman without discernment is like a gold ring in a pig's snout (Prov. 11:22); the spiritual man discerns all things but is discerned by no one (1 Cor. 2:15); condemnation if one does not discern the Lord's body (1 Cor. 11:29).

B Indiscriminate judgement
Will you sweep away the righteous with the wicked? (Gen. 18:23); far be it from you to treat the righteous and the wicked alike (Gen. 18:25).

C Confounding opposites
Woe to those who confound good and evil, light and darkness, bitter and sweet (Isa. 5:20); they could not distinguish the sounds of joy and grief (Ezra 3:13); you strain out a gnat and swallow a camel (Matt. 23:24).

465 Measurement

A Weights and measures
A1 Right measures
Use honest weights and measures (Lev. 19:35; Ezek. 45:10); a just ephah and a just hin (Lev. 19:36); you shall have a just ephah and a just bath (Ezek. 45:10); a just balance and scales are the Lord's (Prov. 16:11); the Levites are to assist the priest over measures of volume and size (1 Chr. 23:29); by the measure you measure it will be measured to you (Matt. 7:2; Mark 4:24; Luke 6:38); the rider had a pair of scales (Rev. 6:5); the shekel of the sanctuary (Exod. 30:13); the homer will be the standard measure (Ezek. 45:11).
A2 Comparative measures
A shekel is 20 gerahs (Exod. 30:13; Lev. 27:25; Ezek. 45:12); the maneh will be 20 plus 25 plus 15 [60] shekels (Ezek. 45:12); a beka is half a shekel (Exod. 38:26); a homer of barley seed corresponds to 50 shekels of silver (Lev. 27:16); an ephah is equal to a bath, a tenth of a homer (Ezek. 45:11, 14); an omer is a tenth of an ephah

(Exod. 16:36); the kor [cor] is ten baths (Ezek. 45:14); a homer of seed yields only an ephah of grain (Isa. 5:10).

A3 Dishonest measures

Do not have different sets of weights and measures (Deut. 25:13-15); differing weights and measures are an abomination to the Lord (Prov. 20:10, 23); false scales are not good (Prov. 20:23); a trader with false balances (Hos. 12:7); cheating with dishonest scales (Amos 8:5; Mic. 6:11); the Lord hates dishonest scales (Prov. 11:1); to make the ephah small and the shekel great (Amos 8:5); can I acquit the man with wicked scales and a bag of deceitful weights? (Mic. 6:11); the scant measure that is cursed (Mic. 6:10).

UNEQUAL WEIGHTS AND MEASURES, see 29C.

B Measuring

B1 Measuring in general

God measured out the waters (Job 28:25); who has measured the waters in his palm? (Isa. 40:12); who has put the dust of the earth in a measure? (Isa. 40:12); who stretched the measuring line over the earth? (Job 38:5); he stood and measured the earth (Hab. 3:6); who marked off the heavens with a span? (Isa. 40:12); if the heavens above can be measured (Jer. 31:37); I will make justice the measuring line (Isa. 28:17); the measuring line will go out further (Jer. 31:39); I will measure recompense into their bosom (Isa. 65:7); they will drink water by measure and in horror (Ezek. 4:16); your land will be parcelled out by line (Amos 7:17).

B2 Measuring lengths

B2a Measuring implements

The cubit of a man (Deut. 3:11); measuring the temple with a measuring rod (Rev. 11:1); measuring the city with a gold measuring rod (Rev. 21:15-17); measuring Jerusalem with a measuring line (Zech. 1:16); a man with a measuring line in his hand (Zech. 2:1); you will have no one to use the measuring line by lot (Mic. 2:5); the Lord has stretched out a line over Zion (Lam. 2:8); a line of flax and a measuring reed in his hand (Ezek. 40:3); a measuring reed six cubits long (Ezek. 40:5); a full reed of six long cubits (Ezek. 41:8); each [long] cubit was a cubit and a handbreadth (Ezek. 40:5; 43:13).

B2b Measuring the temple

He brought me to the nave and measured the pillars (Ezek. 41:1); he measured the most holy place, 20 cubits square (Ezek. 41:4); he measured the nave, 40 cubits by 20 cubits (Ezek. 41:2); he measured the side pillars of the porch, five cubits on each side (Ezek. 40:48); he measured the temple round about (Ezek. 42:15); measuring the gate of the outer court which faced north (Ezek. 40:20); when he had finished measuring the interior of the house (Ezek. 42:15).

B2c Measuring Jerusalem and the land

I am going to measure Jerusalem, its breadth and length (Zech. 2:2); he measured the four sides (Ezek. 42:20); he measured each side with the measuring reed, 500 reeds (Ezek. 42:16-19); dimensions of the special area of the land (Ezek. 48:8-21); each side of the city, 4500 cubits (Ezek. 48:30-4); he measured another 1000 cubits (Ezek. 47:4, 5); the man with a line in his hand measured 1000 cubits (Ezek. 47:3); the city measured 1600 stadia (Rev. 21:16); he measured the wall as 144 cubits (Rev. 21:17).

B2d Measuring other lengths

Who by being anxious can add a cubit to his span of life? (Matt. 6:27; Luke 12:25); God gave him not even a foot length of land (Acts 7:5); measuring to the nearest city from a corpse (Deut. 21:2-3); David measured Moab with a line (2 Sam. 8:2).

B3 Measuring quantities

When they measured the manna with an omer (Exod. 16:18); the ephah measure with Wickedness inside (Zech. 5:6-8).

B4 Immeasurable

The grain was beyond measuring (Gen. 41:49); as the sand of the sea cannot be measured (Jer. 33:22); God gives his Spirit without measure (John 3:34); do not measure the courtyard outside the temple (Rev. 11:2).

C Volumes

Keep an omer of manna throughout your generations (Exod. 16:32, 33); an omer of manna per head (Exod. 16:16); two omers per head on the sixth day (Exod. 16:22); a quarter of a kab of dove's dung (2 Kgs. 6:25); when one came to a heap of 20 measures there were only ten (Hag. 2:16); when one came to the wine vat to draw 50 measures there were only 20 (Hag. 2:16); a choenix [quart] of wheat for a denarius and three of barley for a denarius (Rev. 6:6); given six measures of barley (Ruth 3:15, 17); three measures of meal (Matt. 13:33); 100 measures of oil (Luke 16:6); 100 measures of wheat (Luke 16:7); each jar contained 20 or 30 measures (John 2:6); take your bill, sit down quickly and write 50 measures (Luke 16:6); take your bill and write 80 measures (Luke 16:7).

466 Evidence

A Witness in general

Two or three witnesses are needed for a conviction (Num. 35:30; Deut. 17:6; 19:15; 1 Tim. 5:19); by the mouth of two or three witnesses every word may be confirmed (Matt. 18:16); the testimony of two men is true (John 8:17); every word is to be confirmed by the evidence of two or three witnesses (2 Cor. 13:1); one who violates the law of Moses dies on the evidence of two or three witnesses (Heb. 10:28); a witness must testify (Lev. 5:1); a faithful witness will not lie (Prov. 14:5); a truthful witness saves lives (Prov. 14:25); what your eyes have seen do not hastily bring into court (Prov. 25:7-8); why do we still need witnesses? (Matt. 26:65); what is it that these men testify against you? (Matt. 26:62); the testimony I receive is not from man (John 5:34); what you heard from me in the presence of many witnesses (2 Tim. 2:2); this testimony is true (Titus 1:13).

B God bearing witness

B1 The witness of God

The Lord is witness (Judg. 11:10; 1 Sam. 12:5); I am witness, says the Lord (Jer. 29:23); the Lord be witness! (1 Sam. 20:12); God is my witness (Rom. 1:9; Phil. 1:8; 1 Thess. 2:5); you are witnesses and so is God (1 Thess. 2:10); I call God to witness (2 Cor. 1:23); God is witness between me and you (Gen. 31:50); God testifies against his people (Ps. 50:7); my witness is in heaven (Job 16:19); God has not left himself without witness (Acts 14:17); God bore witness to the Gentiles by giving them the Spirit (Acts 15:8); God bore witness to Abel's sacrifice (Heb. 11:4); I will be a swift witness against the sorcerers and the adulterers (Mal. 3:5); the Lord was a witness between you and the wife of your youth (Mal. 2:14); there is another who bears witness to me, and I know his testimony is true (John 5:32); God testified about David (Acts 13:22); if we receive the witness of men, the witness of God is greater (1 John 5:9); he has not believed the testimony that God bore to his Son (1 John 5:10); God bore witness to his word with signs and wonders (Acts 14:3; Heb. 2:4); God confirmed the word by the signs which followed (Mark 16:20).

B2 The witness of Christ

I testify against the world that its deeds are evil (John 7:7); Jesus testified the good confession before Pilate

(1 Tim. 6:13); for this I came into the world, to bear witness to the truth (John 18:37); he gave many proofs that he was alive (Acts 1:3); Jesus Christ the faithful witness (Rev. 1:5); the faithful and true witness (Rev. 3:14); he bears witness of what he has seen and heard (John 3:32); whoever bears witness to me before men, I will bear witness to them before my Father (Matt. 10:32); Jesus himself testified that a prophet has no honour in his own country (John 4:44); the blood of the martyrs [witnesses] of Jesus (Rev. 17:6); I, Jesus, have sent my angel with this testimony to the churches (Rev. 22:16); I will confess his name before my Father and his angels (Rev. 3:5).

B3 The witness of the Spirit
We are witnesses and so is the Holy Spirit (Acts 5:32); the Spirit bears witness with our spirit (Rom. 8:16); my conscience bears me witness in the Holy Spirit (Rom. 9:1); the Holy Spirit bears witness to us (Heb. 10:15); there are three that bear witness, the Spirit, the water and the blood (1 John 5:8); he who believes in the Son of God has the witness in himself (1 John 5:10).

C Those bearing witness
C1 Bearing witness to Christ
C1a God bearing witness to Christ
There is another who bears witness to me, and I know his testimony is true (John 5:32); God bore witness to Jesus (Acts 17:31); Jesus, attested by God with mighty works, wonders and signs (Acts 2:22); the Father who sent me has himself borne witness to me (John 5:37); the Father bears witness to me (John 8:18); God has borne witness to his Son (1 John 5:9); the Spirit will bear witness to me (John 15:26; Acts 5:32; 1 John 5:7).

C1b Scriptures bearing witness to Christ
The Scriptures bear witness to me (John 5:39); Moses bore witness to the things which were to be spoken later (Heb. 3:5); all the prophets bear witness to him (Acts 10:43).

C1c Contemporary witness to Christ
John bearing witness to Jesus (John 1:7, 32; 3:26; 5:33-4); John came to bear witness to the light (John 1:8); John bore witness to him (John 1:15); this is John's testimony (John 1:19); I have borne witness that this is the Son of God (John 1:34); many Samaritans believed because of the woman's testimony (John 4:39); the crowd who had seen him raise Lazarus from the dead bore witness (John 12:17); he became visible to witnesses chosen beforehand by God (Acts 10:41); a witness of the sufferings of Christ (1 Pet. 5:1); he who has seen has borne witness (John 19:35); this Jesus God raised up, and of that we are witnesses (Acts 2:32); one of these should become with us a witness to his resurrection (Acts 1:22); witnesses to the resurrection (Acts 3:15; 5:32; 13:31); with great power the apostles bore witness to the resurrection (Acts 4:33); we are witnesses to all that he did (Acts 10:39).

C1d Subsequent witness to Christ
Whoever bears witness to me before men, I will bear witness to them before my Father (Matt. 10:32); this will lead to you bearing testimony (Luke 21:13); he commanded us to testify that he is judge of the living and the dead (Acts 10:42); Paul testified to the Jews that Jesus was the Christ (Acts 18:5); they will not accept your testimony about me (Acts 22:18); the testimony to Christ was confirmed among you (1 Cor. 1:6); witness to Christ's ransom was borne at the proper time (1 Tim. 2:6); do not be ashamed of testifying to our Lord (2 Tim. 1:8); we have seen and bear witness that the Father sent the Son (1 John 4:14); you will be a witness of what you have seen and heard (Acts 22:15); we bear witness to what we have seen (John 3:11); we bear witness to the life (1 John 1:2); on Patmos because of

the testimony of Jesus (Rev. 1:9); Antipas, my witness (Rev. 2:13); they overcame him by the blood of the Lamb and the word of their testimony (Rev. 12:11); those slain for their testimony (Rev. 6:9); those beheaded for their testimony to Jesus (Rev. 20:4); those who bear testimony to Jesus (Rev. 12:17); the testimony of Jesus is the spirit of prophecy (Rev. 19:10); you will be witnesses to me to the ends of the earth (Acts 1:8).

C1e Other witness to Christ
The works which the Father has given me to accomplish bear witness to me (John 5:36); the works bear witness to me (John 10:25); if I bear witness to myself, my testimony is not true (John 5:31); I bear witness to myself (John 8:18); the Pharisees said, 'You are bearing witness to yourself' (John 8:13); even if I do bear witness to myself, my witness is true (John 8:14).

C2 Witness to the gospel
You will be witnesses before kings and governors (Matt. 10:18; Mark 13:9; Luke 21:12-13); the gospel will be preached as a witness to all nations (Matt. 24:14); offer what Moses commanded, as a testimony (Matt. 8:4; Mark 1:44; Luke 5:14); you are witnesses of these things (Luke 24:48); you will bear witness for you have been with me from the beginning (John 15:27); we know this disciple's testimony is true (John 21:24); John bore witness to the word of God and to the testimony of Jesus Christ (Rev. 1:2); Paul was appointed a witness (Acts 26:16); as you have witnessed about me at Jerusalem, so you must at Rome (Acts 23:11); you made the good confession before many witnesses (1 Tim. 6:12); two witnesses prophesying for 1260 days clothed in sackcloth (Rev. 11:3); since we are surrounded by so great a cloud of witnesses (Heb. 12:1); testifying both to Jews and Greeks of repentance and faith (Acts 20:21); the ministry I received, to testify to the gospel of the grace of God (Acts 20:24); I stand here testifying to small and great (Acts 26:22); the law and the prophets bear witness to imputed righteousness (Rom. 3:21); proclaiming to you the testimony of God (1 Cor. 2:1); our testimony to you was believed (2 Thess. 1:10); what further need of testimony? (Luke 22:71).

C3 Witness to other things
C3a People as witnesses
I have made David a witness to the peoples (Isa. 55:4); you are my witnesses (Isa. 43:10, 12; 44:8); what further need do we have of witnesses? (Mark 14:63); you are witnesses to the deeds of your fathers (Luke 11:48); you yourselves bear me witness (John 3:28); the witnesses laid their garments at Paul's feet (Acts 7:58); I bear them witness that they have a zeal for God (Rom. 10:2); I bear you witness that you would have plucked out your eyes (Gal. 4:15); you are witnesses and so is God (1 Thess. 2:10); I rejoiced when some bore witness that you are walking in the truth (3 John 3); they bear witness to your love before the church (3 John 6); let them present their witnesses to justify them (Isa. 43:9); I got faithful witnesses (Isa. 8:2); I got witnesses [to the sale] (Jer. 32:10); men will sign, seal and witness deeds (Jer. 32:44); you are witnesses (Ruth 4:9, 10-11); bear witness against me if I have defrauded you (1 Sam. 12:3); while you are speaking, I will confirm your words (1 Kgs. 1:14); Demetrius has received a good testimony from everyone (3 John 12); we also bear witness, and you know our witness is true (3 John 12).

C3b Things as witnesses
Seven lambs as a witness (Gen. 21:30); let the covenant be a witness between you and me (Gen. 31:44); the stone heap was a witness (Gen. 31:48); this heap is a witness and the pillar is a witness (Gen. 31:52); the two and a half tribes built an altar as a witness (Josh.

22:27-8, 34); Joshua took a stone as a witness (Josh.
24:27); their conscience also bears witness (Rom. 2:15);
the testimony of our conscience (2 Cor. 1:12); heaven
and earth witness against people (Deut. 4:26; 30:19;
31:28); this song witnesses against people (Deut. 31:19,
21); the book of the law witnesses against people (Deut.
31:26).

C4 False witnesses
You shall not bear false witness (Exod. 20:16; 23:1-3;
Deut. 5:20; Matt. 19:18; Mark 10:19; Luke 18:20); do not
join hands with the wicked as a witness (Exod. 23:1); do
not witness against your neighbour without cause
(Prov. 24:28); the Lord hates false witness (Prov. 6:19);
a false witness will not go unpunished (Prov. 19:5, 9); a
false witness will perish (Prov. 21:28); a man who bears
false witness is like a club, a sword, an arrow (Prov.
25:18); I will be a witness against those who swear
falsely (Mal. 3:5); the investigation of a false witness
(Deut. 19:16-21); from the heart comes false witness
(Matt. 15:19); will you commit false witness? (Jer. 7:9);
false witnesses have risen against me (Ps. 27:12; 35:11);
the chief priests and Council sought false testimony
against Jesus (Matt. 26:59); many false
witnesses came forward against Jesus (Matt. 26:60;
Mark 14:56-7); many false witnesses came forward
against Stephen (Acts 6:13); two worthless men to
testify against Naboth (1 Kgs. 21:10, 13); If Christ did
not rise, we are false witnesses against God (1 Cor.
15:15).

D The 'testimony'
Two tablets of the testimony (Exod. 31:18; 32:15; 34:29);
'the testimony' (Num. 17:4-10); the testimony put into
the ark (Exod. 25:16, 21; 40:20); the ark of the testimony
(Exod. 25:22); the tabernacle of the testimony (Exod.
38:21; Num. 1:50); they gave Joash the testimony (2 Kgs.
11:12; 2 Chr. 23:11); our fathers had the tent of witness in
the wilderness (Acts 7:44); the temple of the tent of
witness in heaven was opened (Rev. 15:5).

467 Counterevidence
A Witness against people
They sought testimony against Jesus (Mark 14:55); how
many things they testify against you! (Matt. 27:13);
what is it that these men testify against you? (Mark
14:60); this day I have testified against you (Jer. 42:19);
your own lips testify against you (Job 15:6); shake off
the dust from your feet as a testimony against them
(Mark 6:11; Luke 9:5); I testify against the world that its
deeds are evil (John 7:7).

B Witness against oneself
You are witnesses against yourselves (Josh. 24:22); your
own mouth is witness against you (2 Sam. 1:16); you
testify against yourselves (Matt. 23:31); our sins testify
against us (Isa. 59:12); our iniquities testify against us
(Jer. 14:7); the rust of your gold and silver will be
witness against you (Jas. 5:3).

468 Qualification
EXCUSES, see 614.

469 Possibility
A Possible for God
Is anything beyond God's power? (Gen. 18:14); nothing
is too difficult for you (Jer. 32:17); with man this is
impossible, but with God all things are possible (Matt.
19:26; Mark 10:27); what is impossible with men is
possible with God (Luke 18:27); with God nothing will
be impossible (Luke 1:37); all things are possible for
you (Mark 14:36); I know you can do all things (Job
42:2); if it be possible, let this cup pass (Matt. 26:39);

that if it were possible, the hour might pass from him
(Mark 14:35).

B Possible for people
Nothing will be impossible for them (Gen. 11:6);
nothing will be impossible for you (Matt. 17:20);
everything is possible to him who believes (Mark 9:23);
I can do all things through him who strengthens me
(Phil. 4:13); as far as possible, be at peace with all men
(Rom. 12:18).

470 Impossibility
A Impossible for God
It is impossible for God to lie (Heb. 6:18); God cannot
lie (Titus 1:2); he cannot deny himself (2 Tim. 2:13); if
God made windows in heaven, could this happen?
(2 Kgs. 7:2, 19).
GOD S IMPOTENCE, see 161A.

B Impossible for people
If anyone can count the dust, your offspring can be
counted (Gen. 13:16); count the stars if you are able to
count them (Gen. 15:5); your offspring will be too
many to count (Gen. 16:10); like the sand of the sea
which cannot be counted (Gen. 32:12); the grain was
like the sand of the sea and could not be measured
(Gen. 41:49); it is impossible to restore to repentance
those who have been enlightened (Heb. 6:4); it is
impossible for the blood of bulls and goats to take
away sins (Heb. 10:4); without faith it is impossible to
please God (Heb. 11:6); you cannot see my face for no
man can see me and live (Exod. 33:20); who can build a
house for him? (2 Chr. 2:6); we cannot build the wall
(Neh. 4:10); with men it is impossible (Matt. 19:26;
Mark 10:27); what is impossible with men is possible
with God (Luke 18:27).

471 Probability
CERTAIN, see 473.

472 Improbability
UNCERTAIN, see 474.

473 Certainty
A Sure knowledge
How can I know I will possess the land? (Gen. 15:8);
how can I be sure of this? (Luke 1:18); know of a
certainty (Gen. 15:13); let every one be fully convinced
in his own mind (Rom. 14:5); the testimony to Christ
was confirmed among you (1 Cor. 1:6); our gospel
came in power and in the Holy Spirit and full
conviction (1 Thess. 1:5); faith is the certainty of things
not seen (Heb. 11:1); every word of God is proved
(Prov. 30:5); the gifts and calling of God are irrevocable
(Rom. 11:29); the dream is true and the interpretation
sure (Dan. 2:45); since these things are undeniable
(Acts 19:36).

B Faithful sayings
It is a faithful saying that Christ came to save sinners
(1 Tim. 1:15); this is a faithful saying (1 Tim. 3:1); the
saying is sure, deserving full acceptance (1 Tim. 4:9);
the saying is sure (2 Tim. 2:11; Titus 3:8).

474 Uncertainty
A Uncertain things
Your life will hang in doubt (Deut. 28:66); refuse
foolish controversies (2 Tim. 2:23); the disciples were
uncertain of whom he was speaking (John 13:22); not to
trust in uncertain riches (1 Tim. 6:17).

B Puzzlement
The Lord confused the Egyptian camp (Exod. 14:24); I
will confuse the peoples to whom you come (Exod.
23:27); confuse their tongues (Ps. 55:9); Susa was in

confusion (Esther 3:15); when Herod heard John he was perplexed (Mark 6:20); Herod was perplexed about Jesus (Luke 9:7); the king's nobles were perplexed (Dan. 5:9); she was greatly perplexed at this saying (Luke 1:29); while they were perplexed about this (Luke 24:4); they were bewildered, because each one heard them speak in his own language (Acts 2:6); they were amazed and puzzled, saying, 'What does this mean?' (Acts 2:12); the captain of the guard and the chief priests were very perplexed (Acts 5:24); Peter was perplexed as to what the vision might mean (Acts 10:17); I was at a loss how to investigate these matters (Acts 25:20); perplexed but not despairing (2 Cor. 4:8); I am perplexed about you (Gal. 4:20).

475 Reasoning

A Reasoned argument

I would present my case before him (Job 13:3, 15; 23:4); hear my argument (Job 13:6); come, let us reason together (Isa. 1:18); scribes reasoning in their hearts about who could forgive sins (Mark 2:6, 8); Saul disputed with the Hellenists (Acts 9:29); where is the debater of this age? (1 Cor. 1:20); they became futile in their reasoning (Rom. 1:21); the Lord knows that the reasonings of the wise are useless (1 Cor. 3:20); when I was a child, I reasoned as a child (1 Cor. 13:11).

B Discussions

What were you discussing on the way? (Mark 9:33); they discussed among themselves (Matt. 21:25; Mark 11:31; Luke 20:5); they discussed it with one another (Mark 8:16); discussing what rising from the dead might mean (Mark 9:10); what are you discussing with them? (Mark 9:16); they had discussed who was the greatest (Mark 9:34); he discussed with the chief priests and officers how to betray Jesus (Luke 22:4); a discussion between John's disciples and a Jew (John 3:25); Paul conducted discussions (Acts 17:2; 18:19; 19:8); Paul reasoned in the synagogue at Athens (Acts 17:17); Paul reasoned in the synagogue every sabbath (Acts 18:4); Paul reasoned daily in the school of Tyrannus (Acts 19:9); the Jews then argued among themselves (John 6:52); they conferred with one another (Acts 4:15); neither in the temple nor in the synagogues did they find me discussing (Acts 24:12); some have turned to fruitless discussion (1 Tim. 1:6).

476 Intuition: absence of reason

Creatures of instinct (2 Pet. 2:12); the things they know by instinct (Jude 10).

477 Sophistry

We destroy sophistries (2 Cor. 10:5).

478 Proof

Proving that this Jesus is the Christ (Acts 9:22); which of you convicts me of sin? (John 8:46); the Spirit will convict the world of sin, righteousness and judgement (John 16:8); he showed himself alive after his suffering with many proofs (Acts 1:3); they cannot prove the charges they make against me (Acts 24:13); they brought many serious charges which they could not prove (Acts 25:7); give proof of your love (2 Cor. 8:24); you desire proof that Christ is speaking in me (2 Cor. 13:3).

479 Confuting

If it is not so, who can prove me a liar? (Job 24:25); no one refuted Job (Job 32:12); refute me if you can (Job 33:5); Apollos completely refuted the Jews (Acts 18:28); a mouth and wisdom which your adversaries cannot resist or refute (Luke 21:15); Saul confounded the Jews

by proving that Jesus is the Christ (Acts 9:22); convince those who doubt (Jude 22).

480 Judgement: conclusion

MAGISTRATE, see 957.

A Judge rightly

Judge your neighbour in righteousness (Lev. 19:15; Deut. 1:16); the judges shall judge the people with righteous judgement (Deut. 16:18); by the judgement you judge you will be judged (Matt. 7:2); do not judge according to appearance (John 7:24); you judge according to the flesh (John 8:15); why do you not judge what is right? (Luke 12:57); does our law judge a man without first hearing him? (John 7:51); make judgements which are true and make for peace in your gates (Zech. 8:16).

B God judges

B1 God, judge!

Judge the earth, O God (Ps. 82:8); let the nations be judged (Ps. 9:19); hear in heaven and judge (1 Kgs. 8:32); may the Lord judge between us (Gen. 16:5; 1 Sam. 24:12, 15); the God of Abraham and Nahor judge between us (Gen. 31:53); judge me (Ps. 35:24); judge my case! (Lam. 3:59); may my judgement come forth from before you (Ps. 17:2); when will you judge my persecutors? (Ps. 119:84); may the Lord judge you (Exod. 5:21); will you not judge them? (2 Chr. 20:12).

B2 God judges

It is God who judges (Ps. 75:7); judgement belongs to God (Deut. 1:17); with him deeds are weighed (1 Sam. 2:3); God will bring every act to judgement (Eccles. 12:14); you bring men to judgement (Job 14:3); the Lord judges the peoples (Ps. 7:8); the Lord will judge the earth (1 Sam. 2:10; 1 Chr. 16:33); there is a God who judges the earth (Ps. 58:11).

B3 God judges righteously

You will judge the peoples with righteousness (Ps. 67:4); you judge righteously (Jer. 11:20); you sit on your throne judging righteously (Ps. 9:4); he will judge the world in righteousness (Ps. 9:8; 96:13; 98:9); I judge with equity (Ps. 75:2); he will judge the peoples with equity (Ps. 96:10); if God be unjust, how will he judge the world? (Rom. 3:6); will not the Judge of all the earth do right? (Gen. 18:25); this is evidence of the righteous judgement of God (2 Thess. 1:5); the Father judges each one impartially according to his deeds (1 Pet. 1:17); he trusted in him who judges righteously (1 Pet. 2:23); his judgements are true and righteous (Rev. 19:2).

B4 God judges his people

The Lord will judge his people (Ps. 135:14; Heb. 10:30); the Lord stands to judge his people (Isa. 3:13); it is time for judgement to begin with the household of God (1 Pet. 4:17); we must all stand before the judgement seat of God (Rom. 14:10-11); we must all stand before the judgement seat of Christ (2 Cor. 5:10); if we sin wilfully there is a fearful expectation of judgement (Heb. 10:27); God summons heaven and earth to judge his people (Ps. 50:4); when we are judged, we are disciplined by the Lord (1 Cor. 11:32); teachers will be judged more strictly (Jas. 3:1); speak and act like those who will be judged by the law of liberty (Jas. 2:12); the Lord is the one to judge me (1 Cor. 4:4).

B5 God judges all people

All who sin under the law will be judged by the law (Rom. 2:12); God will judge fornicators and adulterers (Heb. 13:4); God will judge those outside (1 Cor. 5:13); God has judged her (Rev. 18:20); the ruler of this world has been judged (John 16:11); all nations will see my judgement which I have executed (Ezek. 39:21); though judged in the flesh like men they may live in the spirit like God (1 Pet. 4:6); I will judge the nation which they serve (Acts 7:7); I will judge that nation (Gen. 15:14); the Lord who judges her is strong (Rev. 18:8); I will execute judgements against all the gods of Egypt (Exod. 12:12); when your judgements are on the earth the world learns righteousness (Isa. 26:9); he will judge the nations (Isa. 2:4; Joel 3:2, 12; Mic. 4:3).

C Christ judging

The king's son will judge the people in righteousness (Ps. 72:2); with righteousness he will judge (Isa. 11:3-4); the Father has committed all judgement to the Son (John 5:22); as I hear, I judge, and my judgement is just (John 5:30); my judgement is true (John 8:16); for judgement I have come into the world (John 9:39); God will judge the world by the man he has appointed (Acts 17:31); God will judge men through Jesus Christ (Rom. 2:16); he gave him authority to execute judgement (John 5:27); Jesus Christ will judge the living and the dead (2 Tim. 4:1); if anyone hears my sayings and does not keep them, I do not judge him (John 12:47); in righteousness he judges and wages war (Rev. 19:11); who made me a judge? (Luke 12:14); I judge no one (John 8:15); I did not come to judge but to save (John 12:47); this is the judgement, that light has come into the world (John 3:19); the word that I have spoken will judge him (John 12:48); now is the judgement of this world (John 12:31); God did not send the Son to judge the world (John 3:17); he who believes in him is not judged (John 3:18); he who does not believe is judged already (John 3:18); whoever believes does not come into judgement (John 5:24).

D The final judgement

Those who have done evil will come forth to the resurrection of judgement (John 5:29); the dead were judged according to what they had done (Rev. 20:11-13); man dies once, and after that comes judgement (Heb. 9:27); Paul spoke on the judgement to come (Acts 24:25); he will convict the world regarding judgement (John 16:8); the queen of the South will arise at the judgement (Matt. 12:42; Luke 11:31); the men of Nineveh will arise at the judgement (Matt. 12:41; Luke 11:32); it will be more bearable in the judgement for Tyre and Sidon (Luke 10:14); the time came for the dead to be judged (Rev. 11:18); the dead were judged according to what was written in the books, by what they had done (Rev. 20:12); they were judged according to their deeds (Rev. 20:13); he will judge the living and the dead (1 Pet. 4:5); the Lord comes to judge everyone (Jude 15); the hour of his judgement has come (Rev. 14:7).

E People judging

E1 Judge!

Take him and judge him by your own law (John 18:31); you must judge whether it is right to pay attention to you rather than to God (Acts 4:19); Dan will judge (Gen. 49:16); is there no one among you wise enough to decide between the brethren? (1 Cor. 6:5); judge for yourselves what I say (1 Cor. 10:15); let prophets speak and the others judge (1 Cor. 14:29).

E2 People involved in judgement

Priests are to judge (Ezek. 44:24); let them judge the people (Exod. 18:22); the priests and the judge will decide (Deut. 17:9); the congregation shall judge between the killer and the avenger (Num. 35:24); you have appointed them to judge (Hab. 1:12); Moses judged disputes (Exod. 18:13, 16); by the word of the Levites every dispute shall be settled (Deut. 21:5); they judged the people (Exod. 18:26); thrones for judgement stand in Jerusalem (Ps. 122:5); the Lord is a spirit of judgement to him who sits in judgement (Isa. 28:6); give us a king to judge us (1 Sam. 8:6); give me a

hearing heart to judge your people (1 Kgs. 3:9); the hall of the throne where he was to judge (1 Kgs. 7:7); may the king judge your people with justice (Ps. 72:1-2); do you judge uprightly, you rulers? (Ps. 58:1); Paul appealed to be held in custody for the decision of the emperor (Acts 25:21); if we judged ourselves we would not be judged (1 Cor. 11:31).

E3 Judging Israel

In the days when the judges judged (Ruth 1:1); Samuel judging on circuit (1 Sam. 7:15-17); those who judged Israel: Othniel (Judg. 3:10); Deborah (Judg. 4:4-5); Tola (Judg. 10:2); Jair (Judg. 10:3); Jephthah (Judg. 12:7); Ibzan (Judg. 12:8); Elon (Judg. 12:11); Abdon (Judg. 12:13-14); Samson (Judg. 15:20; 16:31); Samuel (1 Sam. 7:6); Samuel's sons (1 Sam. 8:2).

E4 Believers judging

You will sit on thrones judging the 12 tribes of Israel (Matt. 19:28; Luke 22:30); thrones on which those given authority to judge were seated (Rev. 20:4); the saints will judge the world (1 Cor. 6:2); what have I to do with judging outsiders? (1 Cor. 5:12); should you not judge those inside the church? (1 Cor. 5:12); is there no one among you wise enough to decide between the brethren? (1 Cor. 6:5); I have already judged him as though present (1 Cor. 5:3); judge for yourselves what I say (1 Cor. 10:15); let prophets speak and the others judge (1 Cor. 14:29); we will judge angels, so how much more matters of this life (1 Cor. 6:3).

F Reckoning

God reckoned his faith as righteousness (Gen. 15:6; Rom. 4:3-6, 9-11, 22; Jas. 2:23); Abraham believed God and it was reckoned to him as righteousness (Gal. 3:6); reckoned righteous by faith (Rom. 4:24); Phinehas' intervention was reckoned to him for righteousness (Ps. 106:31); faith is reckoned as righteousness (Rom. 4:5-6); blessed is the man whose sin the Lord will not reckon against him (Rom. 4:8); sin is not reckoned where there is no law (Rom. 5:13); will not his uncircumcision be reckoned as circumcision? (Rom. 2:26); I reckon the present sufferings not worth comparing with the glory (Rom. 8:18); may it not be reckoned against them (2 Tim. 4:16); does our father not reckon us as foreigners? (Gen. 31:15); he was reckoned with the transgressors (Mark 15:28; Luke 11:50); reckon yourselves dead to sin and alive to God (Rom. 6:11).

G Not judging

Do not judge lest you be judged (Matt. 7:1); do not judge and you will not be judged (Luke 6:37); do not complain against one another, that you might not be judged (Jas. 5:9); let us not judge one another (Rom. 14:13); who are you to judge your neighbour? (Jas. 4:11-12); if we judged ourselves we would not be judged (1 Cor. 11:31); do not judge before the time (1 Cor. 4:5); I refuse to be a judge of these matters (Acts 18:15); let no one judge you regarding food and drink (Col. 2:16); he who abstains should not pass judgement on him who eats (Rom. 14:3); who are you to judge another man's servant? (Rom. 14:4); why do you judge your brother? (Rom. 14:10); I do not judge myself (1 Cor. 4:3); I did not come to judge but to save (John 12:47); God did not send the Son to judge the world (John 3:17); I judge no one (John 8:15); the Father judges no one, but has committed all judgement to the Son (John 5:22).

481 Misjudgement. Prejudice

God shows no partiality (Deut. 10:17; Job 34:19; Acts 10:34; Rom. 2:11; Gal. 2:6; Eph. 6:9; Col. 3:25); God covers the face of the judges (Job 9:24); does our law judge a man without first hearing him and knowing what he is doing? (John 7:51); show no injustice in judgement (Lev. 19:15); do not regard faces [persons] when judging (Deut. 1:17); do not show partiality (Deut. 16:19); either to small or great (Deut. 1:17); do not show partiality to the great (Lev. 19:15); do not show partiality to a poor man (Exod. 23:3; Lev. 19:15); do not pervert justice due to the poor in his law suit (Exod. 23:6); follow these instructions without bias or partiality (1 Tim. 5:21); do not show partiality as believers (Jas. 2:1-4); if you show partiality you are committing sin (Jas. 2:9); you are not partial to any one (Matt. 22:16; Mark 12:14; Luke 20:21); let me not show partiality (Job 32:21).

BRIBERY, see 612C.

482 Overestimation
Let no one think more highly of himself than he ought (Rom. 12:3); if anyone thinks he is something when he is nothing (Gal. 6:3); do not be wise in your own eyes (Rom. 12:16); that no one may think more of me than he sees in me or hears from me (2 Cor. 12:6).

483 Underestimation
You thought it an easy thing to go up and fight (Deut. 1:41); the people underestimated Ai (Josh. 7:3); do not let our hardship seem little to you (Neh. 9:32); do not regard lightly the discipline of the Lord (Heb. 12:5).

484 Discovery
A Finding God
You will find God if you seek with all your heart (Deut. 4:29); you will seek me and find me when you seek with all your heart (Jer. 29:13); I will be found by you (Jer. 29:14); I was found by those who did not seek me (Rom. 10:20); can you find out the deep things of God? (Job 11:7); Jacob found him at Bethel and there he spoke with us (Hos. 12:4); that men would seek him and find him (Acts 17:27); then you will find the knowledge of God (Prov. 2:5).

B Finding people
God found his people in the wilderness (Deut. 32:10); I found Israel like grapes in the wilderness (Hos. 9:10); I have found David my servant (Ps. 89:20); have you found me, my enemy? (1 Kgs. 21:20); when you have found him, bring me word (Matt. 2:8); when they had found Jesus (Mark 1:37); after three days they found him in the temple (Luke 2:46); we have found the Messiah, Christ (John 1:41); we have found him of whom Moses and the prophets wrote, Jesus of Nazareth (John 1:45); he was lost and is found (Luke 15:24); an excellent wife who can find? (Prov. 31:10); he who finds a wife finds a good thing (Prov. 18:22).

C Finding things
Seek and you will find (Matt. 7:7-8; Luke 11:9-10); we have found water (Gen. 26:32); we found this coat (Gen. 37:32); the cup was found in Benjamin's sack (Gen. 44:12); if someone finds something and lies about it (Lev. 6:3); the donkeys which were lost are found (1 Sam. 9:20; 10:2, 16); when he finds the sheep which went astray (Matt. 18:13); rejoice with me, for I have found my sheep which was lost (Luke 15:6); Hilkiah found the book of the law in the temple (2 Chr. 34:14); few find the narrow gate leading to life (Matt. 7:14); whoever loses his life for my sake will find it (Matt. 16:25); he who finds his life will lose it and he who loses his life for my sake will find it (Matt. 10:39); treasure which a man found and covered up (Matt. 13:44); she searches diligently until she finds the coin (Luke 15:8-9).

D Found out
God has found out our iniquity (Gen. 44:16); men cannot find out all of God's work (Eccles. 3:11; 8:17); what wrong did your fathers find in me? (Jer. 2:5); be sure your sin will find you out (Num. 32:23); he who perverts his ways will be found out (Prov. 10:9); this woman has been caught in adultery, in the very act (John 8:4); I will find out not the words of these arrogant people but their power (1 Cor. 4:19).

E Not finding
He could not find the prostitute (Gen. 38:20, 22-3); I sought my beloved but did not find him (S. of S. 3:1, 2); they searched but could not find the messengers (2 Sam. 17:20); they did not find Elijah (2 Kgs. 2:17); they wearied themselves trying to find the door (Gen. 19:11); they will seek the word of the Lord but not find it (Amos 8:12); few find the narrow gate leading to life (Matt. 7:14); when they did not find Jesus they returned to Jerusalem (Luke 2:45); when they entered the tomb they did not find Jesus' body (Luke 24:3, 23); you will seek me and you will not find me (John 7:34-6); the officers did not find them in the prison (Acts 5:22); Herod searched for Peter and did not find him (Acts 12:19); when they could not find Paul and Silas (Acts 17:6); Laban did not find his gods (Gen. 31:33-7); they did not find a city to dwell in (Ps. 107:4); the Almighty – we cannot find him (Job 37:23); they will seek the Lord but not find him (Hos. 5:6); they will seek me [Wisdom] but not find me (Prov. 1:28); what exists is far off and very deep, who can discover it? (Eccles. 7:24).

485 Belief
A Faith in general
A1 About faith
Faith is the assurance of things hoped for, the certainty of things not seen (Heb. 11:1); faith, hope and love remain (1 Cor. 13:13); love believes all things (1 Cor. 13:7); the law is not of faith (Gal. 3:12); boasting is excluded by the principle of faith (Rom. 3:27); weightier matters of the law, justice and mercy and faith (Matt. 23:23); he who comes to God must believe that he exists (Heb. 11:6); by faith we understand that the world was created by the word of God (Heb. 11:3); the righteousness of God is revealed from faith to faith (Rom. 1:17); the shield of faith can extinguish flaming darts (Eph. 6:16); faith and love as a breastplate (1 Thess. 5:8); faith working through love is what counts (Gal. 5:6); we walk by faith, not by sight (2 Cor. 5:7); our aim is sincere faith (1 Tim. 1:5); the obedience of faith (Rom. 16:26); now faith has come we are no longer under a custodian (Gal. 3:25).

A2 How faith comes
Faith comes by hearing (Rom. 10:17); the teaching of God which is by faith (1 Tim. 1:4); Jesus is the author and finisher of faith (Heb. 12:2); the spiritual gift of faith (1 Cor. 12:9); the faith and love which are in Christ Jesus (1 Tim. 1:14).

A3 Have faith!
Stand firm in the faith (1 Cor. 16:13); resist the devil, firm in your faith (1 Pet. 5:9); let us draw near in full assurance of faith (Heb. 10:22); if you had faith as a grain of mustard seed (Luke 17:6).

A4 Those who had faith
The heroes of faith (Heb. 11:4-40); Abraham is the father of the circumcised who also believe (Rom. 4:12); those who are of faith are sons of Abraham (Gal. 3:7); those who are of faith are blessed with Abraham, who had faith (Gal. 3:9); your steadfastness and faith in all your persecutions and afflictions (2 Thess. 1:4); let us do good to all men, especially those of the household

of faith (Gal. 6:10); the word of God is at work in you who believe (1 Thess. 2:13); the Lord is coming to be marvelled at in those who have believed (2 Thess. 1:10); those who believe and know the truth (1 Tim. 4:3); many priests were obedient to the faith (Acts 6:7); Simon himself believed (Acts 8:13); an elder's children should be believers (Titus 1:6); they were attested by their faith (Heb. 11:39); what has a believer in common with an unbeliever? (2 Cor. 6:15).

A5 The Faith
One Lord, one faith, one baptism (Eph. 4:5); test yourselves to see whether you are in the faith (2 Cor. 13:5); I have kept the faith (2 Tim. 4:7); fight the good fight of the faith (1 Tim. 6:12); with one mind striving side by side for the faith of the gospel (Phil. 1:27); contend for the faith once for all delivered to the saints (Jude 3); you did not deny my faith (Rev. 2:13); Timothy, my true child in the faith (1 Tim. 1:2); Titus, my true child in a common faith (Titus 1:4); I will remain for your progress and joy in the faith (Phil. 1:25); build yourselves up in your most holy faith (Jude 20); nourished on the words of the faith (1 Tim. 4:6); they encouraged the disciples to continue in the faith (Acts 14:22); established in the faith (Col. 2:7); rebuke them sharply that they may be sound in the faith (Titus 1:13); some will depart from the faith (1 Tim. 4:1); if any one will not provide for his family, he has denied the faith (1 Tim. 5:8); by craving for money some have wandered from the faith (1 Tim. 6:10); unapproved as regards the faith (2 Tim. 3:8).

A6 Maintaining faith
That we may be mutually encouraged by each other's faith (Rom. 1:12); the churches were being strengthened in the faith (Acts 16:5); let each think according to the measure of faith which God has allotted (Rom. 12:3); prophecy should be according to one's faith (Rom. 12:6); I am reminded of your sincere faith (2 Tim. 1:5); you have followed my faith (2 Tim. 3:10); the faith of God's elect (Titus 1:1); set the believers an example in love, faith and purity (1 Tim. 4:12); keeping faith and a good conscience (1 Tim. 1:19); continue in the things you have learned and have firmly believed (2 Tim. 3:14); older men are to be sound in faith, love and perseverance (Titus 2:2); your work of faith, labour of love and steadfastness of hope (1 Thess. 1:3); a drink offering on the sacrificial offering of your faith (Phil. 2:17); imitate the faith of your leaders (Heb. 13:7); the testing of your faith produces endurance (Jas. 1:3); God chose the poor to be rich in faith (Jas. 2:5); those who have obtained a faith of equal standing with ours (2 Pet. 1:1); I know your love and faith and service (Rev. 2:19); keep sound words in the faith and love which are in Christ Jesus (2 Tim. 1:13); here is a call for the perseverance and faith of the saints (Rev. 13:10); pursue faith (1 Tim. 6:11; 2 Tim. 2:22).

A7 Deficient faith
If Christ is not raised, our preaching is in vain and your faith is in vain (1 Cor. 15:14); if Christ has not been raised, your faith is worthless (1 Cor. 15:17); they are upsetting the faith of some (2 Tim. 2:18); do not show partiality in your faith in the Lord Jesus Christ (Jas. 2:1); do not throw away your confidence (Heb. 10:35).

B Believing God
B1 Trust in God!
Trust in God (Ps. 4:5; 37:3, 5; 115:9; Prov. 3:5); O house of Aaron, trust in the Lord (Ps. 115:10); you who fear the Lord, trust in the Lord (Ps. 115:11); have faith in God (Mark 11:22); trust in him at all times (Ps. 62:8); trust in the Lord for ever (Isa. 26:4); let him trust in the name of the Lord (Isa. 50:10); trust in the Lord and you will be established (2 Chr. 20:20); that your faith not be

in the wisdom of men but the power of God (1 Cor. 2:5); I have taught you so that your trust may be in the Lord (Prov. 22:19); that you may know and believe me (Isa. 43:10); let your widows trust in me (Jer. 49:11); believe in God, believe also in me (John 14:1).

B2 Belief in God
Faith toward God (Heb. 6:1); your faith and hope are in God (1 Pet. 1:21); the king trusts in the Lord (Ps. 21:7); our fathers trusted in you and you delivered them (Ps. 22:4, 5); the eyes of all look to you (Ps. 145:15); you are the trust of all the earth (Ps. 65:5); many will see and fear and trust in the Lord (Ps. 40:3); faith in God who raised Jesus from the dead (Rom. 4:24; Col. 2:12); your faith in God has gone forth so we do not need to say anything (1 Thess. 1:8); that those who have believed in God might be careful to do good deeds (Titus 3:8); through Christ you are believers in God (1 Pet. 1:21); he trusted in him who judges righteously (1 Pet. 2:23); those who know your name will trust you (Ps. 9:10); he will not fear for he trusts in the Lord (Ps. 112:7); in quietness and trust will be your strength (Isa. 30:15); do not let your God in whom you trust deceive you (2 Kgs. 19:10; Isa. 37:10); do not let Hezekiah make you trust in the Lord (Isa. 36:15).

B3 I / we trust in God
In God I put my trust (Ps. 56:4, 11); my God, in whom I trust (Ps. 91:2); my eyes are toward you (Ps. 141:8); I have trusted in the Lord (Ps. 26:1); you are my trust from my youth (Ps. 71:5); we trust in his holy name (Ps. 33:21); so that we might trust in God (2 Cor. 1:9); save your servant who trusts in you (Ps. 86:2); I will trust and not be afraid (Isa. 12:2); I know whom I have believed (2 Tim. 1:12); God, our eyes are on you (2 Chr. 20:12); I will put my trust in him (Heb. 2:13); we know and believe the love God has for us (1 John 4:16); though he slay me I will trust him (Job 13:15); I believed, even when afflicted (Ps. 116:10); when I am afraid I will put my trust in you (Ps. 56:3).

B4 Others believing in God
Stephen was full of faith and of the Holy Spirit (Acts 6:5); Barnabas was full of the Holy Spirit and of faith (Acts 11:24); the demons believe that God is one – and tremble (Jas. 2:19); those who believed God: Abraham (Rom. 4:20); Daniel (Dan. 6:23); Hezekiah (2 Kgs. 18:5); the people of Israel (Exod. 4:5, 31; 14:31); the house of Israel (Isa. 10:20); Jesus (Matt. 27:43); Mary (Luke 1:45); the people of Nineveh (Jonah 3:5); Shadrach, Meshach and Abednego (Dan. 3:28).

C Believing in Christ
C1 Believe in Christ!
The work of God is to believe in the one he sent (John 6:29); this is his commandment, that we believe on Jesus Christ (1 John 3:23); that they may believe that you sent me (John 11:42); do not be unbelieving but believing (John 20:27); repent and believe the gospel (Mark 1:15); that they may be one in us, that the world may believe (John 17:21); John came to bear witness that all might believe through him (John 1:7); John told people to believe in the one coming after him, Jesus (Acts 19:4); believe in God, believe also in me (John 14:1); believe in the light that you may become sons of light (John 12:36); believe me that I am in the Father and the Father in me (John 14:11); for your sake I am glad I was not there, that you may believe (John 11:15); I told you beforehand so when it happens you may believe (John 14:29); to bring about obedience of faith among the Gentiles (Rom. 1:5).

C2 Benefits of faith in Christ
He who believes in me, though he die, shall yet live (John 11:25-6); if you believe you will see the glory of God (John 11:40); when you believed you were sealed

with the Holy Spirit (Eph. 1:13); those sanctified by faith in me (Acts 26:18); the gospel is the power of God for salvation to everyone who believes (Rom. 1:16); the righteousness of God through faith in Jesus Christ for all who believe (Rom. 3:22); propitiation in his blood through faith (Rom. 3:25); we have believed in Christ in order to be justified by faith (Gal. 2:16); that the promise by faith in Christ Jesus might be given to those who believe (Gal. 3:22); sons of God through faith in Christ Jesus (Gal. 3:26); the power at work in us who believe (Eph. 1:19); we have boldness and access in confidence through our faith in him (Eph. 3:12); that Christ may dwell in your hearts by faith (Eph. 3:17); those who would believe in him for eternal life (1 Tim. 1:16); whoever believes that Jesus is the Christ is born of God (1 John 5:1); who overcomes the world but he who believes that Jesus is the Son of God? (1 John 5:5); he who believes in the Son of God has the witness in himself (1 John 5:10).

C3 Faith in Christ in general

He was believed on in the world (1 Tim. 3:16); a large number who believed turned to the Lord (Acts 11:21); a great multitude of both Jews and Greeks believed (Acts 14:1); they committed them to the Lord in whom they had believed (Acts 14:23); God chose that by my mouth the Gentiles should hear and believe (Acts 15:7); prophecy is a sign for those who believe (1 Cor. 14:22); whether it was I or they, so we preach and so you believed (1 Cor. 15:11); if we believe that Jesus died and rose again (1 Thess. 4:14); though you do not now see him, you believe in him (1 Pet. 1:8); to you who believe he is precious (1 Pet. 2:7); those who keep the commandments of God and the faith of Jesus (Rev. 14:12); whoever believes in me believes in him who sent me (John 12:44); repentance toward God and faith in our Lord Jesus Christ (Acts 20:21); Paul spoke of faith in Christ (Acts 24:24); if we let him go on like this, every one will believe in him (John 11:48).

C4 Those who believed in Christ

I know whom I have believed (2 Tim. 1:12); Lord, I believe! (Mark 9:24; John 9:38); we have believed and come to know that you are the holy One of God (John 6:69); you have loved me and believe that I came from the Father (John 16:27); we believe that you came from God (John 16:30); they have believed that you sent me (John 17:8); he saw and believed (John 20:8); the man believed the word that Jesus spoke to him (John 4:50); he believed and all his household (John 4:53); those who believed: his disciples (John 2:11); many people (John 2:23; 7:31; 8:30; Acts 4:4); many Samaritans (John 4:39, 41); the man born blind (John 9:35-8); many across Jordan (John 10:42); many Jews (John 11:45; 12:11); many rulers (John 12:42); the proconsul (Acts 13:12); Gentiles appointed for eternal life (Acts 13:48); Pharisees (Acts 15:5); the jailer and all his house (Acts 16:34); many Bereans (Acts 17:12); some Athenians (Acts 17:34); many Corinthians (Acts 18:8).

C5 Strong faith in Christ

Your faith is spoken of all over the world (Rom. 1:8); I have heard of your faith (Eph. 1:15); we heard of your faith in Christ (Col. 1:4); I hear of your faith in the Lord Jesus (Philem. 5); you have received a faith like ours (2 Pet. 1:1); your faith is more precious than gold (1 Pet. 1:7); I rejoice to see the stability of your faith (Col. 2:5); sincere faith which your grandmother and mother also had (2 Tim. 1:5); I have prayed for you that your faith fail not (Luke 22:32).

C6 Reasons for faith in Christ

Because I said I saw you under the fig tree do you believe? (John 1:50); it is no longer because of what you said that we believe (John 4:42); what sign do you do,

that we may see and believe you? (John 6:30); have you believed because you have seen me? (John 20:29); let him come down from the cross and we will believe in him (Matt. 27:42; Mark 15:32).

D Trusting people

D1 Trusting oneself

So that we might not trust in ourselves but in God (2 Cor. 1:9); they trusted in themselves that they were righteous (Luke 18:9); if a man trusts in his own righteousness (Ezek. 33:13); he who trusts in his own heart is a fool (Prov. 28:26); you trusted in your beauty (Ezek. 16:15); do not lean on your own understanding (Prov. 3:5).

D2 Believing prophets

The people trusted the Lord and Moses (Exod. 14:31); that they may believe in Moses for ever (Exod. 19:9); if you believed Moses you would believe me (John 5:46); believe in the Lord and in his prophets (2 Chr. 20:20); believing everything in the law and the prophets (Acts 24:14); they believed the scripture and Jesus' word (John 2:22); how slow you are to believe all the prophets have spoken! (Luke 24:25); who has believed what we have heard? (Isa. 53:1; John 12:38); do you believe the prophets, King Agrippa? (Acts 26:27); the tax-collectors and harlots believed John (Matt. 21:32).

D3 Trusting other people

Cursed is he who trusts in man (Jer. 17:5); we put no confidence in the flesh (Phil. 3:3); do not trust in princes or men (Ps. 146:3); better to trust in the Lord than to put confidence in men (Ps. 118:8); better to trust in the Lord than to put confidence in princes (Ps. 118:9); my friend in whom I trusted has lifted up his heel against me (Ps. 41:9); trust in a faithless man is like a bad tooth (Prov. 25:19); the men of Shechem trusted Gaal (Judg. 9:26); they relied on the men in ambush (Judg. 20:36); you are relying on Egypt (2 Kgs. 18:21-4; Isa. 36:6); how can you rely on Egypt for chariots and horsemen? (Isa. 36:9); woe to those who rely on Egyptian horses and chariots (Isa. 31:1); Egypt will never again be the confidence of Israel (Ezek. 29:16); you relied on the king of Aram (2 Chr. 16:7); Achish trusted David (1 Sam. 27:12);

I hear there are divisions among you and in part I believe it (1 Cor. 11:18); I have great confidence in you (2 Cor. 7:4); I have complete confidence in you (2 Cor. 7:16); he is now more earnest because of his great confidence in you (2 Cor. 8:22); her husband's heart trusts in the good wife (Prov. 31:11).

E Trusting things

E1 Trusting deceptive things

Let him not trust in emptiness (Job 15:31); do not trust in deceptive words (Jer. 7:4); you are trusting in deceptive words (Jer. 7:8); you trusted in lies (Jer. 13:25); you made this people trust in a lie (Jer. 28:15); he made you trust in a lie (Jer. 29:31); they believe what is false (2 Thess. 2:11).

E2 Trusting idols

Everyone who trusts in idols will become like them (Ps. 115:8; 135:18); those who trust in idols will be put to shame (Isa. 42:17); the idolater trusts in his own creation (Hab. 2:18).

E3 Trusting riches

If I have trusted in gold (Job 31:24); you trust in your own achievements and riches (Jer. 48:7); he who trusts in his riches will fall (Prov. 11:28); the man who trusted in his wealth (Ps. 52:7); those who trust in their wealth (Ps. 49:6); do not trust in extortion, robbery or riches (Ps. 62:10); not to trust in uncertain riches (1 Tim. 6:17).

E4 Trusting other things

The high and fortified walls in which you trusted (Deut. 28:52); the house called by my name in which you trust (Jer. 7:14); they will demolish the fortified cities in which you trusted (Jer. 5:17); since you put your trust in oppression and what is perverted (Isa. 30:12); they were disappointed because they had trusted in the dry watercourses (Job 6:20); Israel was ashamed of Bethel, their confidence (Jer. 48:13); I will not trust in bow or sword (Ps. 44:6); he takes away his armour in which he trusted (Luke 11:22); if you call yourself a Jew and rely on the law (Rom. 2:17); if you do not believe me, believe the works (John 10:38; 14:11).

F Results of faith

F1 Miracles and faith

Your faith has healed you (Matt. 9:22; Mark 5:34; 10:52; Luke 8:48; 17:19; 18:42); let it be done for you as you have believed (Matt. 8:13); according to your faith be it done to you (Matt. 9:29); faith in Jesus has healed this man (Acts 3:16); he had faith to be healed (Acts 14:9); if you have faith as a grain of mustard seed (Matt. 17:20); whatever you ask in prayer, believing, you will receive (Matt. 21:22); whatever you ask for in prayer, believe that you have received them and you will (Mark 11:23-4); the name of Jesus, by faith in his name, has made this man strong (Acts 3:16); faith to move mountains (Matt. 21:21; Mark 11:23; 1 Cor. 13:2); faith to uproot a tree (Luke 17:6); everything is possible to him who believes (Mark 9:23); he who believes in me will do the works I do (John 14:12); I have not found such faith even in Israel (Matt. 8:10; Luke 7:9); great is your faith! (Matt. 15:28); increase our faith (Luke 17:5); your faith is growing (2 Thess. 1:3); you excel in faith (2 Cor. 8:7); the prayer of faith will heal the sick (Jas. 5:15); he must ask in faith, not doubting (Jas. 1:6); I believe, help my unbelief! (Mark 9:24).

F2 Righteous by faith

Abraham believed God and it was reckoned to him as righteousness (Gen. 15:6; Rom. 4:3, 9; Gal. 3:6; Jas. 2:23); the father of all who believe unto righteousness (Rom. 4:11); the righteous by faith shall live (Hab. 2:4; Rom. 1:17; Gal. 3:11; Heb. 10:38); faith is reckoned as righteousness (Rom. 4:5); the righteousness of God through faith in Jesus Christ for all who believe (Rom. 3:22); the righteousness which is by faith (Rom. 9:30; Phil. 3:9); the righteousness for all who believe (Rom. 10:4); the righteousness based on faith (Rom. 10:6); with the heart man believes to righteousness (Rom. 10:10); a man is justified by faith (Rom. 3:28); since we are justified by faith (Rom. 5:1); a man is justified by faith in Jesus Christ (Gal. 2:16); God will justify both circumcised and uncircumcised by faith (Rom. 3:30); God justifies him who believes in Jesus (Rom. 3:26); the scripture, foreseeing that God would justify the Gentiles by faith (Gal. 3:8); that we might be justified by faith (Gal. 3:24); Noah became an heir of the righteousness by faith (Heb. 11:7).

F3 Saved by faith

Believe in the Lord Jesus and you will be saved (Acts 16:31); God saves those who believe (1 Cor. 1:21); we are of those who believe and are saved (Heb. 10:39); saved by grace through faith (Eph. 2:8); he who believes and is baptised will be saved (Mark 16:16); if you believe God raised him you will be saved (Rom. 10:9); whoever believes in him will have eternal life (John 3:15-16); he who believes in the Son has eternal life (John 3:36); he who believes has eternal life (John 5:24; 6:40); to those who believe in his name he gave the right to become children of God (John 1:12); that believing you may have life in his name (John 20:31); every one who believes in him receives forgiveness (Acts 10:43);

everyone who believes is freed from all things (Acts 13:39); salvation through sanctification by the Spirit and belief in the truth (2 Thess. 2:13); God is the Saviour of all people, especially of those who believe (1 Tim. 4:10); salvation of your souls as the outcome of your faith (1 Pet. 1:9); the devil takes away the word that they may not believe and be saved (Luke 8:12).

F4 Exploits of faith

Exploits by faith (Heb. 11:5-33); these all died in faith (Heb. 11:13); by faith they conquered kingdoms (Heb. 11:33).

F5 The effects of faith

Judah conquered because they trusted the Lord (2 Chr. 13:18; 16:8); you will be delivered because you trusted in me (Jer. 39:18); the Spirit which those who believed in him were to receive (John 7:39); that we might receive the promise of the Spirit through faith (Gal. 3:14); those who through faith and patience inherit the promises (Heb. 6:12); he who believes in me will not thirst (John 6:35); he who believes in him will not be put to shame (1 Pet. 2:6); the one who believes: is blessed (Ps. 40:4; 84:12; Prov. 16:20; Jer. 17:7); is radiant (Ps. 34:5); is like Mount Zion (Ps. 125:1); will not be moved (Isa. 28:16); will not be disappointed (Rom. 9:33; 10:11); has prayers heard (1 Chr. 5:20); will prosper (Prov. 28:25); will be exalted (Prov. 29:25); is surrounded by lovingkindness (Ps. 32:10); is kept in perfect peace (Isa. 26:3); does not remain in darkness (John 12:46); out of his innermost being will flow rivers of living water (John 7:38).

F6 A faith that works

Faith without works is dead (Jas. 2:17, 26); faith without works is useless (Jas. 2:20); what use is it if a man says he has faith but has not works? (Jas. 2:14); show me faith without works and I will show you my faith by my works (Jas. 2:18); faith was made complete by works (Jas. 2:22); a man is justified by works and not by faith alone (Jas. 2:24); that God may fulfil your good pleasure and work of faith in power (2 Thess. 1:11).

G Entrusting

The keeper of the prison entrusted everything to Joseph (Gen. 39:22); Pharaoh entrusted everything to Joseph (Gen. 41:41); you entrusted to me five talents (Matt. 25:20); you entrusted to me two talents (Matt. 25:22); who will entrust to you the true riches? (Luke 16:11); the glorious gospel with which I have been entrusted (1 Tim. 1:11); they saw I had been entrusted with the gospel to the uncircumcised (Gal. 2:7); I entrust you to God and to the word of his grace (Acts 20:32); guard what has been entrusted to you (1 Tim. 6:20); entrust these things to faithful men who will be able to teach others also (2 Tim. 2:2); I was entrusted with the preaching of his word (Titus 1:3); Jesus did not entrust himself to them (John 2:24).

486 Unbelief. Doubt

A Unbelief in general

Whatever is not of faith is sin (Rom. 14:23); he who doubts is like a wave driven by the sea (Jas. 1:6); some have made shipwreck of their faith (1 Tim. 1:19); he has denied the faith and is worse than an unbeliever (1 Tim. 5:8); without faith it is impossible to please God (Heb. 11:6); they were unable to enter because of unbelief (Heb. 3:19); the message was not combined with faith (Heb. 4:2); not all men have faith (2 Thess. 3:2); take care lest there be an unbelieving heart in any of you (Heb. 3:12).

B God doubting

God puts no trust in his servants (Job 4:18; 15:15).

C Doubting God

You did not trust the Lord (Deut. 1:32; 9:23); how long will they not believe in me? (Num. 14:11); they did not believe in God (Ps. 78:22); like their fathers, they did not believe in the Lord (2 Kgs. 17:14); Jerusalem did not trust in the Lord (Zeph. 3:2); they did not believe his word (Ps. 106:24); they did not believe in his wonders (Ps. 78:32); I am doing something which you will never believe (Hab. 1:5; Acts 13:41); who has believed our report? (Isa. 53:1; Rom. 10:16); he has not believed the testimony that God bore to his Son (1 John 5:10); he who does not believe God has made him a liar (1 John 5:10); he destroyed those who did not believe (Jude 5); no strong trust, no trusty stronghold (Isa. 7:9); the branches were broken off through unbelief (Rom. 11:20); does their unbelief nullify God's faithfulness? (Rom. 3:3); because you did not believe me you will not bring the people into the land (Num. 20:12).

D Not believing in Jesus

O unbelieving generation! (Matt. 17:17; Mark 9:19; Luke 9:41); O you of little faith! (Matt. 6:30; 8:26; 14:31; 16:8; Luke 12:28); because of your little faith (Matt. 17:20); why have you no faith? (Mark 4:40); where is your faith? (Luke 8:25); he marvelled at their unbelief (Mark 6:6); even his brothers did not believe in him (John 7:5); none of the rulers or Pharisees have believed, have they? (John 7:48); some of you do not believe (John 6:64); he will convict of sin because they do not believe in me (John 16:9); he has not believed in the name of the only begotten Son of God (John 3:18); if I tell the truth, why do you not believe me? (John 8:46); if I tell you, you will not believe (Luke 22:67); therefore they could not believe (John 12:39); do you not believe that I am in the Father and the Father in me? (John 14:10); you have seen me yet do not believe (John 6:36); you do not believe the one he has sent (John 5:38); because I speak the truth you do not believe me (John 8:45); when the Son of man comes, will he find faith on the earth? (Luke 18:8); if you do not believe Moses' writings, how will you believe my words? (John 5:47); how can you believe when you seek glory from each other? (John 5:44).

E Not believing the gospel

Whoever does not believe will be condemned (Mark 16:16); he who does not believe is condemned already (John 3:18); you do not believe because you are not of my sheep (John 10:26); the unbelieving will end up in the lake of fire (Rev. 21:8); tongues are a sign for unbelievers (1 Cor. 14:22); some would not believe (Acts 28:24); I told you and you do not believe (John 10:25); how shall they believe in the one of whom they have not heard? (Rom. 10:14); they have not all heeded the gospel (Rom. 10:16); the unbelieving husband is sanctified through his wife (1 Cor. 7:14); if unbelieving spouses leave, let them (1 Cor. 7:15); if an unbeliever invites you to a meal (1 Cor. 10:27); if uninitiated [enquirers] or unbelievers enter (1 Cor. 14:23, 24); do not be unequally yoked with unbelievers (2 Cor. 6:14); what has a believer in common with an unbeliever? (2 Cor. 6:15); all will be condemned who did not believe the truth but took pleasure in wickedness (2 Thess. 2:12); to the defiled and unbelieving nothing is pure (Titus 1:15); convince those who doubt (Jude 22); I received mercy because I acted ignorantly in unbelief (1 Tim. 1:13).

F Doubting the resurrection

At the resurrection, some doubted (Matt. 28:17); they did not believe it (Mark 16:11, 13); they did not believe the women (Luke 24:11); they had not believed those who saw him after he had risen (Mark 16:14); they did not believe it through joy (Luke 24:41); Thomas refused

to believe (John 20:25); do not be unbelieving but believing (John 20:27); he reproached them for their unbelief (Mark 16:14); why do doubts arise in your hearts? (Luke 24:38); why is it thought incredible that God raises the dead? (Acts 26:8).

G Not believing people

The people might not believe Moses (Exod. 4:1); the Queen of Sheba did not believe until she came and saw it (1 Kgs. 10:7; 2 Chr. 9:6); Gedaliah did not believe Johanan (Jer. 40:14); you did not believe John (Matt. 21:32); he will say, 'Why did you not believe him?' (Matt. 21:25; Mark 11:31; Luke 20:5); Zacharias did not believe Gabriel (Luke 1:20); the Jews did not believe that he had been born blind (John 9:18); they will not accept your testimony about me (Acts 22:18); do not trust neighbour or brother (Jer. 9:4); if they say the Christ is here, do not believe it (Matt. 24:23, 26; Mark 13:21).

H Unbelief and signs

If they do not believe these two signs (Exod. 4:9); unless you see signs and wonders you will not believe (John 4:48); if I am not doing the works of my Father, do not believe me (John 10:37); if you do not believe me, believe the works (John 10:38); after so many signs they did not believe in him (John 12:37); he did not work many miracles because of their lack of faith (Matt. 13:58).

487 Credulity

The simple man believes everything (Prov. 14:15).

488 Assent

A Assenting

Let your word be 'Yes, yes' or 'No, no' (Matt. 5:37); let your Yes be Yes and your No be No (Jas. 5:12); do I say yes, yes and no, no? (2 Cor. 1:17-19); all the promises of God are Yes in Christ (2 Cor. 1:20); you have said it (Matt. 26:25, 64; 27:11; Mark 15:2; Luke 22:70; 23:3; John 18:37).

B Amen!

The woman shall say, 'Amen, amen!' (Num. 5:22); all the people shall say, 'Amen!' (Deut. 27:15-26); how will the other person say 'Amen' if he does not understand? (1 Cor. 14:16); our amen is through Christ (2 Cor. 1:20); the Amen, the faithful and true witness (Rev. 3:14); amen and amen! (Ps. 41:13; 72:19; 89:52); even so, amen (Rev. 1:7).

489 Dissent

Peter denied it (Mark 14:68, 70); Zechariah said, 'Not so' (Luke 1:60); let your word be 'Yes, yes' or 'No, no' (Matt. 5:37); do I say yes, yes and no, no? (2 Cor. 1:17-19); let your Yes be Yes and your No be No (Jas. 5:12).

490 Knowledge

A Knowledge in general

A1 Knowing

The tree of the knowledge of good and evil (Gen. 2:9, 17); 'we all have knowledge' (1 Cor. 8:1); if someone sees you who have knowledge at table in an idol's temple (1 Cor. 8:10); you abound in faith, utterance, knowledge, earnestness and love for us (2 Cor. 8:7); the new man is being renewed in knowledge (Col. 3:10); who is wise and endued with knowledge among you? (Jas. 3:13); you know the truth and know that no lie is of the truth (1 John 2:21); if I have all knowledge (1 Cor. 13:2); the Lord will be a store of salvation, wisdom and knowledge (Isa. 33:6).

A2 Acquiring knowledge

To give to the youth knowledge (Prov. 1:4); give me wisdom and knowledge (2 Chr. 1:10, 11); I have filled Bezalel with knowledge (Exod. 31:3); many will run to and fro and knowledge will increase (Dan. 12:4); shepherds who will feed you with knowledge and understanding (Jer. 3:15); add to your virtue knowledge (2 Pet. 1:5); how do I benefit you unless I bring revelation, knowledge, prophecy or teaching? (1 Cor. 14:6); that your love may abound in knowledge and discernment (Phil. 1:9); a wise man will increase in learning (Prov. 1:5); when the wise is instructed he receives knowledge (Prov. 21:11); then I shall know fully as I am fully known (1 Cor. 13:12).

A3 Valuing knowledge

The wise seek knowledge (Prov. 15:14; 18:15); wise men store up knowledge (Prov. 10:14); he who loves discipline loves knowledge (Prov. 12:1); that your lips may guard knowledge (Prov. 5:2); knowledge is an advantage (Eccles. 7:12); take knowledge rather than choice gold (Prov. 8:10); having in the law the embodiment of knowledge and truth (Rom. 2:20); the lips of a priest should guard knowledge (Mal. 2:7); you have rejected knowledge so I reject you from being priest (Hos. 4:6).

A4 Despising knowledge

They hated knowledge (Prov. 1:29); how long will fools hate knowledge? (Prov. 1:22); you have taken away the key of knowledge (Luke 11:52).

A5 Benefits of knowledge

A man of knowledge increases power (Prov. 24:5); through knowledge the righteous are delivered (Prov. 11:9); by knowledge the rooms are filled with riches (Prov. 24:4); knowledge will be pleasant to your soul (Prov. 2:10); you will know the truth and the truth will set you free (John 8:32); you were enriched in him with all speech and knowledge (1 Cor. 1:5); God wants all men to come to a knowledge of the truth (1 Tim. 2:4).

A6 Drawbacks to knowledge

Knowledge puffs up but love builds up (1 Cor. 8:1); no one has yet known as he should (1 Cor. 8:2); knowledge will cease (1 Cor. 13:8); through your knowledge a weak brother is destroyed (1 Cor. 8:11); we know in part (1 Cor. 13:9, 12); knowledge falsely so-called (1 Tim. 6:20); increasing knowledge increases sorrow (Eccles. 1:18); your wisdom and knowledge deceived you (Isa. 47:10).

B God's knowledge

B1 God knows all things

God knows all things (1 John 3:20); the wonders of him who is perfect in knowledge (Job 37:16); a God of knowledge (1 Sam. 2:3); the riches of the wisdom and knowledge of God! (Rom. 11:33); like God, knowing good and evil (Gen. 3:5, 22); God knows the place of wisdom (Job 28:23); God knows what is in the darkness (Dan. 2:22); he who searches the hearts knows what the mind of the Spirit is (Rom. 8:27); no one knows of that day except the Father (Matt. 24:36; Mark 13:32); your Father knows what you need (Matt. 6:8, 32; Luke 12:30); I know the plans I have for you (Jer. 29:11); how does God know? (Ps. 73:11); you say, 'What does God know?' (Job 22:13); from God's mouth come knowledge and understanding (Prov. 2:6); in Christ are hid all the treasures of knowledge (Col. 2:3); God gives knowledge to those who have understanding (Dan. 2:21).

B2 God knows the heart

Search me and know my heart (Ps. 139:23); God knows the hearts of all men (1 Kgs. 8:39; 2 Chr. 6:30); Lord, who knows the hearts of all men (Acts 1:24); God who knows the heart (Acts 15:8); God knows your hearts (Luke 16:15); God knows the secrets of the heart (Ps. 44:21); the Lord knows the thoughts of man (Ps. 94:11);

the Lord understands every intention of the thoughts (1 Chr. 28:9); I know your thoughts (Ezek. 11:5); I know their thoughts (Isa. 66:18); before a word is on my tongue, you know it (Ps. 139:4); you know me (2 Sam. 7:20; 1 Chr. 17:18; Jer. 12:3); Lord, you know my folly and my sins (Ps. 69:5); I know your sitting down and going out and coming in (2 Kgs. 19:27; Isa. 37:28); you know my thoughts from afar (Ps. 139:2); the Lord knows the haughty from afar (Ps. 138:6); you know all about me (Ps. 139:1-6); now I know you fear God (Gen. 22:12); the Lord knows that the reasonings of the wise are useless (1 Cor. 3:20).

B3 God knowing his people

I know you by name (Exod. 33:12, 17); if anyone loves God he is known by him (1 Cor. 8:3); the Lord knows those who are his (2 Tim. 2:19); you have come to be known by him (Gal. 4:9); before I formed you in the womb I knew you (Jer. 1:5); I know Abraham (Gen. 18:19); I know Israel (Hos. 5:3); I know my own and my own know me (John 10:14); I know my sheep (John 10:27); I know whom I have chosen (John 13:18); you only have I known of all the families of the earth (Amos 3:2); the Lord knows those who take refuge in him (Nahum 1:7); no one knows the Son except the Father (Matt. 11:27); as the Father knows me and I know the Father (John 10:15); then I will know fully, as I have been fully known (1 Cor. 13:12).

C Christ's knowledge

C1 Christ knowing all things

We know that you know all things (John 16:30); you know all things, you know I love you (John 21:17).

C2 Christ knowing God

The Father knows me and I know the Father (John 10:15); I know him (John 7:29; 8:55); no one knows the Father except the Son and those to whom the Son reveals him (Matt. 11:27; Luke 10:22); I know you and they know you have sent me (John 17:25).

C3 Christ knowing about himself

Jesus, knowing all that was going to befall him (John 18:4); Jesus perceived that power had gone forth from him (Mark 5:30); he himself knew what he intended to do (John 6:6); I know where I came from and where I am going (John 8:14); knowing that he had come from God and went to God (John 13:3); knowing that the Father had given all things into his hands (John 13:3); knowing that his hour had come (John 13:1).

C4 Christ knowing about people

He perceived their cunning (Luke 20:23); Jesus knew their malice (Matt. 22:18); knowing their hypocrisy (Mark 12:15); he knew what was in man (John 2:25); see a man who told me all the things I have done (John 4:29, 39); I know that you do not have the love of God within you (John 5:42); you know that I love you (John 21:15, 16); I know your tribulation and poverty (Rev. 2:9); I know where you dwell (Rev. 2:13); I know your deeds (Rev. 2:2, 19; 3:1, 8, 15); Jesus knew their thoughts (Matt. 9:4; 12:25; Luke 5:22; 6:8; 9:47; 11:17); Jesus knew who did not believe (John 6:64); he knew who was going to betray him (John 13:11); if he were a prophet he would know what kind of woman she is (Luke 7:39).

D Knowledge of God

D1 Knowing about God

D1a Knowing that the Lord is God

Let it be known that you are God (1 Kgs. 18:36, 37); that everyone may know that you are God (2 Kgs. 19:19; Isa. 37:20); know that the Lord is God (Deut. 4:39; Ps. 100:3); that you might know that the Lord is God (Deut. 4:35); that you may all know that I am the Lord your God (Deut. 29:6); then Manasseh knew that the Lord was God (2 Chr. 33:13); that all the earth may know there is a God in Israel (1 Sam. 17:46); now I know there is no God except in Israel (2 Kgs. 5:15); that they may know that you alone are the Most High (Ps. 83:18); may all peoples know that the Lord is God (1 Kgs. 8:60).

D1b Recognizing God's activity

That your way may be known on earth (Ps. 67:2); let me know your ways (Exod. 33:13); make known his deeds among the nations (Isa. 12:4, 5); that you might know the righteous deeds of the Lord (Mic. 6:5); I know that your works are wonderful (Ps. 139:14); that all men may know his work (Job 37:7); Manoah and his wife knew it was the angel of the Lord (Judg. 13:20); that this assembly may know that the Lord does not save by sword or spear (1 Sam. 17:47); you will know it was the Lord who brought you out of Egypt (Exod. 16:6); I know the Lord has given you the land (Josh. 2:9); that they may see and know that the Lord has done this (Isa. 41:20); the elders who had known God's deeds (Josh. 24:31); the great know the way of the Lord (Jer. 5:5); we know that God has spoken to Moses (John 9:29); by this we know he abides in us, by the Spirit he has given us (1 John 3:24); now I know that the Lord has sent his angel (Acts 12:11); all the churches will know that I am he who searches mind and heart (Rev. 2:23).

D1c Knowing God's character

That all peoples may know your name (1 Kgs. 8:43; 2 Chr. 6:33); he has known my name (Ps. 91:14); that you may know there is none like me (Exod. 9:14); if you know his will (Rom. 2:18); I knew you to be a hard man (Matt. 25:24-6; Luke 19:22); I knew that you are a gracious and merciful God (Jonah 4:2); no one knows who the Father is except the Son and those to whom the Son reveals him (Luke 10:22); what is to be known about God is evident to men (Rom. 1:19); who has known the mind of the Lord? (Rom. 11:34; 1 Cor. 2:16); asking that you may be filled with the knowledge of his will (Col. 1:9); now I know that the Lord is greater than all the gods (Exod. 18:11); I know that you can do all things (Job 42:2); that you may know that there is no one like the Lord our God (Exod. 8:10).

D1d Knowing about God's kingdom

That you might know the truth about the things you have been taught (Luke 1:4); to give knowledge of salvation by the forgiveness of sins (Luke 1:77); to you it is given to know the secrets of the kingdom of God (Luke 8:10); if you knew the gift of God (John 4:10); that you might know what is the hope of his calling (Eph. 1:18); that you may know and understand that the Father is me and I am in the Father (John 10:38); you will know that I am in my Father and you in me and I in you (John 14:20); we know that we are of God (1 John 5:19); we know that the Son of God has come (1 John 5:20); they will know that I have loved you (Rev. 3:9); that we might know the things given to us by God (1 Cor. 2:12).

D1e Knowing God's truth

Those who believe and know the truth (1 Tim. 4:3); God may grant them repentance and knowledge of the truth (2 Tim. 2:25); the knowledge of the truth which accords with godliness (Titus 1:1); if we sin after we received the knowledge of the truth (Heb. 10:26); all who know the truth (2 John 1).

D2 Knowing God

D2a Knowing God in general

The earth will be full of the knowledge of the Lord (Isa. 11:9); the earth will be filled with the knowledge of the glory of the Lord (Hab. 2:14); the light of the knowledge of the glory of God (2 Cor. 4:6); knowledge of the Holy One is understanding (Prov. 9:10); that God may give you a spirit of wisdom and revelation in the knowledge of him (Eph. 1:17); know the God of your father (1 Chr. 28:9); let us press on to know the Lord (Hos. 6:3); they will not teach each other, 'Know the Lord!' (Jer. 31:34; Heb. 8:11); I will give them a heart to know me (Jer. 24:7); grace and peace in the knowledge of God and of Jesus our Lord (2 Pet. 1:2); through the knowledge of him who called us to his own glory and excellence (2 Pet. 1:3); we are of God and he who knows God listens to us (1 John 4:6); he who loves is born of God and knows God (1 John 4:7); let him who boasts boast that he knows me (Jer. 9:24); I desire the knowledge of God and not sacrifice (Hos. 6:6); we demolish everything against the knowledge of God (2 Cor. 10:5); growing in the knowledge of God (Col. 1:10); if you had known me, you would have known my Father also (John 14:7).

D2b Those who know God

God is known in Judah (Ps. 76:1); the Egyptians will know the Lord (Isa. 19:21); Rahab and Babylon are among those who know me (Ps. 87:4); we Israel know you (Hos. 8:2); those who know your name trust in you (Ps. 9:10); you have come to know God, or rather be known by him (Gal. 4:9); the people who know God will stand firm and take action (Dan. 11:32); we worship what we know, for salvation is from the Jews (John 4:22); you know him and have seen him (John 14:7); you know the Spirit, for he dwells with you and will be in you (John 14:17); I know whom I have believed (2 Tim. 1:12); I have written to you, children, because you know the Father (1 John 2:13); you all know (1 John 2:20); though they knew God, they did not glorify him (Rom. 1:21); they profess to know God but deny him by their deeds (Titus 1:16); no one who sins has seen him or known him (1 John 3:6).

D3 Knowing Christ

D3a Knowing about Christ

Knowing the love of Christ (Eph. 3:18-19); that you may know that the Son of man has authority to forgive sins (Matt. 9:6; Mark 2:10; Luke 5:24); Teacher, we know that you are true (Mark 12:14); Rabbi, we know you are a teacher come from God (John 3:2); I know that whatever you ask of God, God will give you (John 11:22); they know that everything you have given me is from you (John 17:7); did you not know that I must be in my Father's house? (Luke 2:49); they know surely that I came from you (John 17:8); now we know you have a demon (John 8:52); we know this man is a sinner (John 9:24).

D3b Knowing who Christ is

Knowledge of God's mystery, that is, Christ (Col. 2:2); is not this Jesus, whose father and mother we know? (John 6:42); you know me and where I am from? (John 7:27-8); if you knew me you would know my Father also (John 8:19; 14:7); I know who you are, the Holy One of God (Mark 1:24; Luke 4:34); we have believed and come to know that you are the Holy One of God (John 6:69); the demons knew him (Mark 1:34; Luke 4:41); no one knows who the Son is except the Father (Luke 10:22); we know that this is the Saviour of the world (John 4:42); do the authorities know this is the Christ? (John 7:26); when you lift up the Son of man you will know that I AM [he] (John 8:28); they recognised him by the breaking of bread (Luke 24:35); they knew it was the Lord (John 21:12); the sheep know his voice (John 10:4); he spreads the fragrance of the knowledge of Christ through us (2 Cor. 2:14); Jesus I know and Paul I know, but who are you? (Acts 19:15).

D3c Knowing Christ personally

That I may know Christ (Phil. 3:10); this is eternal life, that they know you and Jesus Christ (John 17:3); the excellence of knowing Christ (Phil. 3:8); that we may know him who is true (1 John 5:20); grow in knowledge of our Lord Jesus Christ (2 Pet. 3:18); by this we know that we know him, if we keep his commands (1 John 2:3); I know my own and my own know me (John 10:14); until we reach the knowledge of the Son of God (Eph. 4:13); the cock will not crow until you three times deny that you know me (Luke 22:34); he who says he knows him but does not keep his commands is a liar (1 John 2:4).

E Man's knowledge

E1 People with knowledge

Man became like God, knowing good and evil (Gen. 3:22); youths endowed with knowledge (Dan. 1:4, 17); you are filled with all knowledge (Rom. 15:14); the word of knowledge (1 Cor. 12:8); I am not unskilled in knowledge (2 Cor. 11:6); we commend ourselves in knowledge (2 Cor. 6:6); how does this man have learning when he never studied? (John 7:15); one who is complete in knowledge is among you (Job 36:4); a prudent man conceals his knowledge (Prov. 12:23).

E2 People with general knowledge

We speak of what we know (John 3:11); we are not ignorant of Satan's devices (2 Cor. 2:11); you know where to camp in the wilderness (Num. 10:31); you, though evil, know how to give good gifts to your children (Matt. 7:11); you know that the rulers of the Gentiles lord it over them (Matt. 20:25); Felix had an accurate knowledge of the Way (Acts 24:22); the king knows about these matters (Acts 26:26).

E3 Knowing facts

The one who knew his master's will but did not obey will be punished severely (Luke 12:47); he has appointed you to know his will (Acts 22:14); they laughed at him, knowing that she was dead (Luke 8:53); know that Jerusalem's desolation is at hand (Luke 21:20); the servants who drew the water knew where it came from (John 2:9); Ananias, with his wife's knowledge, kept back part of the proceeds (Acts 5:2); the plot became known to Saul (Acts 9:24); by this all men will know that you are my disciples (John 13:35).

E4 Self-knowledge

They knew that they were naked (Gen. 3:7); through the law comes knowledge of sin (Rom. 3:20); we know our wickedness (Jer. 14:20); I know my transgression (Ps. 51:3); that you may know that you have eternal life (1 John 5:13); one thing I know, that I was blind and now I see (John 9:25); the woman, knowing what had happened to her (Mark 5:33); do you know what I have done to you? (John 13:12).

E5 Knowing people

Do you know Laban? (Gen. 29:5); you know the man and his talk (2 Kgs. 9:11); he will know that there is a prophet in Israel (2 Kgs. 5:8); they will know that a prophet has been among them (Ezek. 33:33); Nathanael said, 'How do you know me?' (John 1:48); we know this is our son and that he was born blind (John 9:20); the other disciple was known to the high priest (John 18:15, 16); from now on we know no one according to the flesh (2 Cor. 5:16); as unknown and yet well-known (2 Cor. 6:9); Jesus I know and Paul I know, but who are you? (Acts 19:15); the ox knows its master (Isa. 1:3).

E6 Recognising people

They recognised him as the one who sat begging (Acts 3:10); they recognised them as men who had been with Jesus (Acts 4:13); Rhoda recognised Peter's voice (Acts 12:14); Joseph recognised his brothers (Gen. 42:7, 8); Saul knew that it was Samuel (1 Sam. 28:14); Obadiah recognised Elijah (1 Kgs. 18:7); Ahab recognised the prophet (1 Kgs. 20:41); they recognized Jesus (Matt. 14:35; Mark 6:54; Luke 24:31); they recognised him by the breaking of bread (Luke 24:35).

E7 Recognising things

Judah recognised the seal and staff (Gen. 38:26); the voice is the voice of Jacob (Gen. 27:22); they recognised the Levite's voice (Judg. 18:3); Saul recognised David's voice (1 Sam. 26:17); every tree is known by its fruit (Luke 6:44).

491 Ignorance

A Being ignorant

A1 About ignorance

If you plead ignorance, does not God know it? (Prov. 24:12); blood for the sins of the people committed in ignorance (Heb. 9:7); God overlooked the time of ignorance (Acts 17:30); a high priest can deal gently with the ignorant (Heb. 5:2); it is God's will that by doing right you silence the ignorance of foolish men (1 Pet. 2:15).

A2 The dangers of ignorance

It is not good for a person to be without knowledge (Prov. 19:2); my people are destroyed for lack of knowledge (Hos. 4:6); my people go into exile for lack of knowledge (Isa. 5:13); they will die without knowledge (Job 36:12).

A3 Those who were ignorant

Every man is stupid and without knowledge (Jer. 51:17); who is this who is in the dark without counsel or knowledge? (Job 38:2; 42:3); have the workers of iniquity no knowledge? (Ps. 14:4; 53:4); idolaters have no knowledge (Isa. 45:20); the stillborn never knows anything (Eccles. 6:5); your children who do not know good and evil (Deut. 1:39); the dead do not know anything (Eccles. 9:5); Israel does not know (Isa. 1:3); you know nothing at all (John 11:49); God has not given you a heart to know (Deut. 29:4); Job speaks without knowledge (Job 34:35); I was stupid and ignorant (Ps. 73:22); we are but of yesterday and know nothing (Job 8:9); I decided to know nothing except Christ and him crucified (1 Cor. 2:2).

A4 God not knowing

Is there knowledge in the Most High? (Ps. 73:11); who knows us? (Isa. 29:15); I never knew you (Matt. 7:23); I do not know you (Matt. 25:12); I do not know where you come from (Luke 13:25-7).

B Ignorant of God

B1 Not knowing God

There is no knowledge of God in the land (Hos. 4:1); the world neither sees nor knows the Spirit of truth (John 14:17); the world has not known you (John 17:25); we destroy every lofty obstacle to the knowledge of God (2 Cor. 10:5); the Gentiles who do not know God (1 Thess. 4:5); the world through wisdom did not know God (1 Cor. 1:21); they did not see fit to acknowledge God (Rom. 1:28); they refuse to know me (Jer. 9:6); punishment for those who do not know God (2 Thess. 1:8); pour out your wrath on the nations who do not know you (Ps. 79:6; Jer. 10:25); this is the place of him who does not know God (Job 18:21); separated from the life of God because of ignorance (Eph. 4:18); he who does not love does not know God (1 John 4:8).

B2 Those ignorant of God

I do not know the Lord (Exod. 5:2); I do not have knowledge of the Holy (Prov. 30:3); those who handle the law did not know me (Jer. 2:8); another generation who did not know the Lord (Judg. 2:10); the sons of Eli did not know the Lord (1 Sam. 2:12); Samuel did not yet know the Lord (1 Sam. 3:7); there are those who have no knowledge of God (1 Cor. 15:34); you worship what you do not know (John 4:22); you do not know God (John 8:55); I gird you though you have not known me (Isa. 45:5); no one knows the Father except the Son and those to whom the Son reveals him (Matt.

11:27; Luke 10:22); if I said I do not know him I should be a liar like you (John 8:55); when you did not know God (Gal. 4:8); you know neither me nor my Father (John 8:19); they have known neither the Father nor me (John 16:3); the one who sent me you do not know (John 7:28); they do not know him who sent me (John 15:21).

B3 Not knowing about God

No one knows the things of God but the Spirit of God (1 Cor. 2:11); God is here and I did not know it (Gen. 28:16); Manoah did not know it was the angel of the Lord (Judg. 13:16); Samson's parents did not know it was the Lord (Judg. 14:4); Samson did not know the Lord had left him (Judg. 16:20); they have not known my ways (Ps. 95:10; Heb. 3:10); zealous for God, but not according to knowledge (Rom. 10:2); they do not know the thoughts of the Lord (Mic. 4:12); do not be conformed to the lusts of your former ignorance (1 Pet. 1:14); always learning but never coming to a knowledge of the truth (2 Tim. 3:7); their children who have not known will hear and learn (Deut. 31:13).

B4 Ignorant of God's doings

You have not let me know whom you will send (Exod. 33:12); your children have not known God's discipline (Deut. 11:2); she does not know that I gave her the grain, wine and oil (Hos. 2:8); my people do not know the ordinance of the Lord (Jer. 8:7); you know neither the scriptures nor the power of God (Matt. 22:29); no other nation has known his ordinances (Ps. 147:20); the ignorant and unstable twist the scriptures to their own destruction (2 Pet. 3:16); they did not know until the flood swept them all away (Matt. 24:39); being ignorant of the righteousness which comes from God (Rom. 10:3); they did not know that I healed them (Hos. 11:3); the Spirit of the Lord will carry you where I do not know (1 Kgs. 18:12); you do not know what you are asking (Matt. 20:22; Mark 10:38); we do not know about John's authority (Matt. 21:27; Mark 11:33; Luke 20:7); not all have this knowledge (1 Cor. 8:7); I do not want you to be ignorant about spiritual gifts (1 Cor. 12:1); what has not entered into the heart of man, God has prepared (1 Cor. 2:9).

C Ignorant of Christ

C1 Not knowing about Christ

No one knows where the Christ comes from (John 7:27; 8:14; 9:29-30); among you stands one you do not know (John 1:26); you know neither me nor my Father (John 8:19; 16:3); the world did not know him (John 1:10; 1 John 3:1); they did not recognise either him or the words of the prophets (Acts 13:27); no one knows the Son except the Father (Matt. 11:27; Luke 10:22); we do not know where you are going, how can we know the way? (John 14:5); he has a name written which no one knows but himself (Rev. 19:12); John did not recognise Jesus (John 1:31, 33); their eyes were prevented from recognising him (Luke 24:16); I made it my ambition to preach the gospel where Christ was unknown (Rom. 15:20); are you the only visitor to Jerusalem not to know of these things? (Luke 24:18).

C2 Ignorant of Christ's return

You do not know when the master of the house will return (Mark 13:35); I will come like a thief and you will not know at what hour (Rev. 3:3); be alert, for you do not know when he is coming (Matt. 24:42; Mark 13:33); neither people, angels nor the Son know the time (Matt. 24:36; Mark 13:32); it is not for you to know times and seasons (Acts 1:7); his master will come at an hour he does not know (Matt. 24:50); you know neither the day nor the hour (Matt. 25:13).

D Ignorant of people

D1 Not knowing people

A king who did not know of Joseph (Exod. 1:8; Acts 7:18); Abner did not know who David was (1 Sam. 17:55); you are our Father though Abraham does not know us (Isa. 63:16); you will call a nation you do not know (Isa. 55:5); you came to a people you did not know before (Ruth 2:11); I heard a voice I had not known (Ps. 81:5); some entertained angels unawares (Heb. 13:2); the world does not know us because it did not know him (1 John 3:1); as unknown and yet well-known (2 Cor. 6:9); Paul was unknown by sight to the Judean churches (Gal. 1:22); I never knew you (Matt. 7:23); I do not know you (Matt. 25:12).

D2 Not recognising people

Isaac did not recognise Jacob (Gen. 27:23); Judah did not know it was his daughter-in-law (Gen. 38:16); Joseph's brothers did not recognise him (Gen. 42:8); Job's friends did not recognise him (Job 2:12); Elijah came but they did not recognise him (Matt. 17:12).

D3 Not knowing about people

Cain said he did not know where Abel was (Gen. 4:9); we do not know what has become of Moses (Exod. 32:1, 23; Acts 7:40); I did not know that he was the high priest (Acts 23:5); no one knows the things of a man but the spirit of the man within him (1 Cor. 2:11).

E Ignorant of things

E1 Not knowing how

You do not know how bones grow in the womb (Eccles. 11:5); he does not know how the seed sprouts (Mark 4:27); we do not know how he now sees nor who opened his eyes (John 9:21); they do not know how to do good (Jer. 4:22).

E2 Not knowing where

I will lead the blind in a way they do not know (Isa. 42:16); Abraham went out not knowing where he was going (Heb. 11:8); a fool's toil wearies him so he does not know the way to the city (Eccles. 10:15); you do not know the path of the wind (Eccles. 11:5); the wind blows where it will and you do not know where it comes from or where it goes to (John 3:8); the steward did not know where the wine had come from (John 2:9); he who walks in darkness does not know where he goes (John 12:35); he who hates his brother does not know where he is going (1 John 2:11); they did not recognise the land (Acts 27:39).

E3 Not knowing the future

You do not know what a day may bring forth (Prov. 27:1); you do not know about tomorrow (Jas. 4:14); I do not know the day of my death (Gen. 27:2); man does not know his time (Eccles. 9:12); man heaps up and does not know who will gather (Ps. 39:6); not knowing what will happen to me in Jerusalem (Acts 20:22).

E4 Ignorant of evil

Instructions concerning one who sins through ignorance (Lev. 5:17; Ezek. 45:20); if the whole congregation sins and it is hidden from the eyes of the assembly (Lev. 4:13); touching unclean carcasses unwittingly (Lev. 5:2); touching human uncleanness unwittingly (Lev. 5:3); I know that you acted in ignorance (Acts 3:17); I received mercy because I acted ignorantly in unbelief (1 Tim. 1:13); forgive them for they do not know what they are doing (Luke 23:34); those who do not know the deep things of Satan (Rev. 2:24).

E5 Ignorant of facts

A slave does not know what his master is doing (John 15:15); people who do not know their right hand from their left (Jonah 4:11); do not let your left hand know what your right hand is doing (Matt. 6:3); you do not know that you are poor and blind and naked (Rev.

275

3:17); Moses did not know that his face shone (Exod. 34:29); grey hairs come and he does not know it (Hos. 7:9); David does not know that Adonijah is king (1 Kgs. 1:11, 18); David did not know that Abner and Amasa were being killed (1 Kgs. 2:32); his wife came in, not knowing what had happened (Acts 5:7); he did not know that what the angel was doing was real (Acts 12:9); Jacob did not know Rachel had stolen the gods (Gen. 31:32); most in the theatre did not know why they had come together (Acts 19:32).

F What is unknown

F1 Unknown gods
Other gods which you have not known (Deut. 11:28; 13:2, 6, 13; 28:64); they served gods which you had not known (Deut. 29:26); they sacrificed to other gods which they had not known (Jer. 19:4; 44:3); an altar to an unknown god (Acts 17:23).

F2 Unknown things
I will show you great and mighty things which you do not know (Jer. 33:3); they did not know what the manna was (Exod. 16:15); manna which neither you nor your fathers knew (Deut. 8:3, 16); he did not know what the wild gourds were (2 Kgs. 4:39); the path no bird of prey knows (Job 28:7); the love of Christ which passes knowledge (Eph. 3:19); a name written on the stone which no one knows but the one who receives it (Rev. 2:17).

492 Scholar
Agrippa was an expert in Jewish customs (Acts 26:3); if you are instructed in the law (Rom. 2:18).

493 Ignoramus
How has this man learning since he never studied? (John 7:15); they saw that Peter and John were uneducated men (Acts 4:13); those who do not know the law are accursed (John 7:49).

494 Truth

A Truth in general
What is truth? (John 18:38); buy truth and do not sell it (Prov. 23:23); lovingkindness and truth have met (Ps. 85:10); truth springs from the earth (Ps. 85:11); whatever is true, think about it (Phil. 4:8); bind lovingkindness and truth around your neck (Prov. 3:3); you will know the truth and the truth will set you free (John 8:32); love truth and peace (Zech. 8:19); they perish because they do not love the truth and so be saved (2 Thess. 2:10); you know the truth and know that no lie is of the truth (1 John 2:21); by this we know that we are of the truth (1 John 3:19); truth is lacking (Isa. 59:15).

B God and truth

B1 God is true
God is true (John 3:33); he who sent me is true (John 7:28; 8:26); God of truth (Ps. 31:5; Isa. 65:16); he who is true (Rev. 3:7); the Spirit of truth (John 14:17; 15:26; 16:13); the Spirit is the truth (1 John 5:7); Christ came to maintain the truth of God in fulfilling the promises (Rom. 15:8); to serve a living and true God (1 Thess. 1:9); the only true God (John 17:3); the faithful and true witness (Rev. 3:14); O Lord, holy and true (Rev. 6:10); just and true are your ways (Rev. 15:3); true and righteous are your judgements (Rev. 16:7; 19:2); I am the truth (John 14:6); truth is in Jesus (Eph. 4:21); the Word, full of grace and truth (John 1:14); grace and truth came through Jesus Christ (John 1:17); we are in him who is true, in his Son Jesus Christ (1 John 5:20); the rider is called Faithful and True (Rev. 19:11).

B2 God's word is true
All your word is truth (Ps. 119:160); your words are truth (2 Sam. 7:28); your word is truth (John 17:17); the judgements of the Lord are true (Ps. 19:9); all your commandments are true (Ps. 119:151); we commend ourselves in the word of truth (2 Cor. 6:7); your law is truth (Ps. 119:142); you teach the way of God in truth (Matt. 22:16; Mark 12:14; Luke 20:21); I came to bear witness to the truth (John 18:37); having in the law the embodiment of knowledge and truth (Rom. 2:20); that the truth of the gospel might be preserved for you (Gal. 2:5); the word of truth, the gospel (Eph. 1:13; Col. 1:5); a new commandment which is true in him and in you (1 John 2:8); write, for these words are faithful and true (Rev. 21:5); these words are trustworthy and true (Rev. 22:6).

B3 God's truth
The Lord, abounding in truth (Exod. 34:6); your truth is great to the clouds (Ps. 57:10); abounding in lovingkindness and truth (Ps. 86:15); send out your light and your truth (Ps. 43:3); your truth reaches to the clouds (Ps. 108:4); the truth of the Lord is eternal (Ps. 117:2); he will guide you into all truth (John 16:13); lead me in your truth (Ps. 25:5); I will walk in your truth (Ps. 86:11); I have walked in your truth (Ps. 26:3); by this we know the spirit of truth and the spirit of error (1 John 4:6); gird your loins with truth (Eph. 6:14); the unleavened bread of sincerity and truth (1 Cor. 5:8).

B4 The truth of the gospel
As the truth of Christ is in me (2 Cor. 11:10); that the truth of the gospel might be preserved for you (Gal. 2:5); the word of truth, the gospel (Eph. 1:13; Col. 1:5); God wants all men to come to a knowledge of the truth (1 Tim. 2:4); those who believe and know the truth (1 Tim. 4:3); God may grant them repentance and knowledge of the truth (2 Tim. 2:25); always learning but never coming to a knowledge of the truth (2 Tim. 3:7); they will turn away their ears from the truth (2 Tim. 4:4); if we sin after we received the knowledge of the truth (Heb. 10:26); having purified your souls by obedience to the truth (1 Pet. 1:22); you are established in the truth (2 Pet. 1:12); all who know the truth (2 John 1); I rejoiced to find some of your children walking in truth (2 John 4); I rejoiced when some bore witness that you are walking in the truth (3 John 3-4); Demetrius has received a good testimony from the truth itself (3 John 12); that you might know the truth (Luke 1:4); the truth which lives in us and will be with us for ever (2 John 2); the knowledge of the truth which accords with godliness (Titus 1:1).

C Acting on truth

C1 Christ telling the truth
Teacher, we know that you are truthful and teach God's way in truth (Matt. 22:16); even if I do bear witness to myself, my witness is true (John 8:14); you seek to kill me, a man who has told you the truth I heard from God (John 8:40); because I speak the truth you do not believe me (John 8:45); if I tell the truth, why do you not believe me? (John 8:46).

C2 Others telling the truth
He is telling the truth that they may believe (John 19:35); John has borne witness to the truth (John 5:33); all that John said about this man was true (John 10:41); we know this disciple's testimony is true (John 21:24); I am telling the truth in Christ (Rom. 9:1); by the manifestation of the truth we commend ourselves to every one's conscience (2 Cor. 4:2); speaking the truth in love (Eph. 4:15); I am telling the truth (1 Tim. 2:7); this testimony is true (Titus 1:13).

C3 Performing the truth
Teacher, we know that you are true (Mark 12:14); he
who practises the truth comes to the light (John 3:21);
my judgement is true (John 8:16); dedicate them in the
truth (John 17:17); I dedicate myself that they may be
dedicated in truth (John 17:19); everyone who is of the
truth hears my voice (John 18:37); those who are selfish
and do not obey the truth (Rom. 2:8); who hindered
you from obeying the truth? (Gal. 5:7); the church is
the pillar and bulwark of the truth (1 Tim. 3:15).

C4 Against the truth
Men suppress the truth (Rom. 1:18); we can do nothing
against the truth, only for it (2 Cor. 13:8); there is no
truth in the devil (John 8:44); truth was dragged in the
mud (Dan. 8:12); they exchanged the truth about God
for a lie (Rom. 1:25); these people oppose the truth (2
Tim. 3:8); do not heed commandments of men who
reject the truth (Titus 1:14); if we say we have no sin we
deceive ourselves and the truth is not in us (1 John 1:8).

495 Error
A Misleading
The way of the wicked leads them astray (Prov. 12:26);
have you also been led astray? (John 7:47); Jezebel
misleads my servants into immorality (Rev. 2:20); your
leaders mislead you (Isa. 3:12; 9:16); they mislead my
people, saying 'Peace' when there is no peace (Ezek.
13:10); their shepherds have led them astray (Jer. 50:6);
they will lead many astray (Mark 13:6); we found this
man misleading our nation (Luke 23:2); you brought
me this man as one misleading the people (Luke 23:14);
he is leading the people astray (John 7:12); by this we
know the spirit of truth and the spirit of error (1 John
4:6); you err, not knowing the scriptures or God's
power (Matt. 22:29; Mark 12:24); men speaking
perverse things will seek to draw away the disciples
(Acts 20:30); false Christs will lead many astray (Matt.
24:5, 24); they will turn aside to myths (2 Tim. 4:4);
signs and wonders to lead astray, if possible, the elect
(Matt. 24:24; Mark 13:22).

B No misleading
Cursed is the one who leads a blind person astray
(Deut. 27:18); see that no one misleads you (Matt. 24:4;
Mark 13:5; Luke 21:8); have nothing to do with worldly
old women's tales (1 Tim. 4:7); do not pay attention to
Jewish myths (Titus 1:14); do not be carried away by the
error of lawless men (2 Pet. 3:17); our exhortation is not
from error (1 Thess. 2:3); we did not follow clever
myths (2 Pet. 1:16).

496 Maxim
A Wise proverbs
To understand a proverb and a satire (Prov. 1:6); a
proverb in the mouth of fools is like lame legs (Prov.
26:7); a proverb is like a thorn in a drunkard's hand
(Prov. 26:9); your maxims are proverbs of ashes (Job
11:12); proverbs about Heshbon (Num. 21:27-30);
Solomon spoke three thousand proverbs (1 Kgs. 4:32); I
will listen to a proverb (Ps. 49:4); the proverbs of
Solomon (Prov. 1:1; 10:1; 25:1); the Preacher arranged
many proverbs (Eccles. 12:9).

B Old sayings
It is said, 'Like Nimrod a mighty hunter before the
Lord' (Gen. 10:9); 'Saul among the prophets' became a
proverb (1 Sam. 10:12; 19:24); 'from the wicked comes
wickedness' – a proverb (1 Sam. 24:13); a saying, 'the
blind or lame will not enter the house' (2 Sam. 5:8);
'ask advice at Abel' (2 Sam. 20:18); 'skin for skin' (Job
2:4); the proverb, 'Time passes, every vision fails'
(Ezek. 12:22); 'like mother, like daughter' (Ezek. 16:44);
'fathers eat sour grapes and the children's teeth are set

on edge' (Ezek. 18:2); 'physician, heal yourself' (Luke
4:23); ' a dog returns to its vomit' (2 Pet. 2:22); the
saying is true, 'One sows and another reaps' (John
4:37).

497 Absurdity
Do horses run on rocks or does one plough the sea
with oxen? (Amos 6:12).

498 Intelligence. Wisdom
WISE PEOPLE, see 500.

A Wisdom in general
A1 About wisdom
I considered wisdom, madness and folly (Eccles. 1:17;
2:12); where does wisdom come from? (Job 28:20); who
has put wisdom in the mind? (Job 38:36); where can
wisdom be found? (Job 28:12); God knows where
wisdom is to be found (Job 28:23); I have taught you
the way of wisdom (Prov. 4:11); Wisdom personified
cries out (Prov. 1:20-33; 8:1-36; 9:1-6); who is wise and
understanding? (Jas. 3:13); wisdom is with the aged (Job
12:12); many years should teach wisdom (Job 32:7);
wisdom will die with you! (Job 12:2); with the humble
is wisdom (Prov. 11:2); wisdom is justified by her deeds
(Matt. 11:19); wisdom is justified by her children (Luke
7:35).

A2 Acquiring wisdom
Get wisdom! (Prov. 4:5); consider the ant's ways and be
wise (Prov. 6:6); hear instruction and be wise (Prov.
8:33); seek for wisdom as for silver (Prov. 2:4); buy
wisdom (Prov. 23:23); teach us to number our days that
we may get a heart of wisdom (Ps. 90:12); teach and
admonish one another in all wisdom (Col. 3:16); to
know wisdom and instruction (Prov. 1:2); Joseph
taught the elders of Egypt wisdom (Ps. 105:22); I set my
heart to know wisdom (Eccles. 8:16).

A3 Benefits of wisdom
Wisdom strengthens a wise man (Eccles. 7:19); wisdom
brings success (Eccles. 10:10); wisdom is protection just
as money is (Eccles. 7:12); better to get wisdom than
gold (Prov. 16:16); wisdom is sweet to the soul (Prov.
24:14); a poor wise lad is better than an old foolish king
(Eccles. 4:13); the wisdom from above is pure,
peaceable etc. (Jas. 3:17); he who gets sense loves
himself (Prov. 19:8); wisdom is better than: coral (Job
28:18); crystal (Job 28:18); glass (Job 28:17); gold (Job
28:15, 16, 17, 19); silver (Job 28:15); silver and gold (Prov.
3:13); jewels (Prov. 3:15; 8:11); onyx (Job 28:16); pearls
(Job 28:18); sapphire (Job 28:16); strength (Eccles. 9:16);
weapons of war (Eccles. 9:18); topaz (Job 28:19).

A4 Drawbacks to wisdom
In the wisdom of God the world could not know God
by wisdom (1 Cor. 1:21); that your faith not be in the
wisdom of men (1 Cor. 2:5); in much wisdom there is
much grief (Eccles. 1:18).
FALSE WISDOM, see 498E.

B God's wisdom
B1 God is wise
God is wise in heart (Job 9:4); with God are wisdom
and power (Job 12:13, 16); wisdom and power belong to
God (Dan. 2:20); the Lord is great in wisdom (Isa.
28:29); God's wisdom and insight (Eph. 1:8); the riches
of the wisdom and knowledge of God! (Rom. 11:33); the
only wise God (Rom. 16:27); by wisdom the Lord
founded the earth (Prov. 3:19); the Lord established the
world by his wisdom (Jer. 51:15); in wisdom you made
them all (Ps. 104:24); the Spirit of wisdom and
understanding (Isa. 11:2); God's hidden wisdom (1 Cor.
2:7); that the manifold wisdom of God might be made
known (Eph. 3:10); in the wisdom of God the world
could not know God by wisdom (1 Cor. 1:21).

B2 God gives wisdom

The fear of the Lord is wisdom (Job 28:28); the fear of the Lord is the beginning of wisdom (Ps. 111:10; Prov. 1:7; 9:10); it is sound wisdom to fear your name (Mic. 6:9); the Lord gives wisdom (Prov. 2:6); that God may give you a spirit of wisdom and revelation (Eph. 1:17); to the man who pleases him God gives wisdom, knowledge and joy (Eccles. 2:26); would that God would show you the secrets of wisdom! (Job 11:6); God gives wisdom to the wise (Dan. 2:21); those I have filled with the spirit of wisdom (Exod. 28:3); Bezalel was filled with the Spirit in wisdom (Exod. 35:31); if any one lacks wisdom, let him ask God (Jas. 1:5); the word of wisdom (1 Cor. 12:8); you have given me wisdom and power (Dan. 2:23); I will give you a mouth and wisdom (Luke 21:15); God gave him favour and wisdom before Pharaoh king of Egypt (Acts 7:10); we do speak wisdom among those who are mature (1 Cor. 2:6); Paul wrote according to the wisdom given him (2 Pet. 3:15); not taught by human wisdom but taught by the Spirit (1 Cor. 2:13); a wisdom not of this age nor its rulers (1 Cor. 2:6); filled with the knowledge of his will in all spiritual wisdom and understanding (Col. 1:9).

B3 God's word gives wisdom

Keeping the statutes is wisdom (Deut. 4:6); your commandments make me wiser than my enemies (Ps. 119:98); the law of the Lord makes the simple wise (Ps. 19:7); proverbs giving prudence to the simple (Prov. 1:4); the scriptures make one wise to salvation (2 Tim. 3:15); rejecting the Lord's word, what wisdom is theirs? (Jer. 8:9).

C Christ's wisdom

Christ the wisdom of God (1 Cor. 1:24, 30); all the treasures of wisdom and knowledge are hidden in Christ (Col. 2:3); Jesus was filled with wisdom (Luke 2:40); Jesus increased in wisdom (Luke 2:52); where did this man get this wisdom? (Matt. 13:54); what is the wisdom given to him? (Mark 6:2).

D Man's wisdom

D1 About man's wisdom

The mouth of the righteous utters wisdom (Ps. 37:30); give [instruction] to a wise man and he will be still wiser (Prov. 9:9); those who are wise will give understanding to many (Dan. 11:33); a man's wisdom causes his face to shine (Eccles. 8:1); he who walks with wise men will be wise (Prov. 13:20); by wisdom a house is built (Prov. 24:3); those who are wise will shine (Dan. 12:3); be silent and let that be your wisdom (Job 13:5); when the scoffer is punished the simple becomes wise (Prov. 21:11); a wise man will know the time and the way (Eccles. 8:5); him we proclaim, warning and teaching every man in all wisdom (Col. 1:28); let him show by his good conduct his deeds in the meekness of wisdom (Jas. 3:13).

D2 Be wise!

Be wise as serpents (Matt. 10:16); be wise as to good, innocent as to evil (Rom. 16:19); conduct yourself wisely toward outsiders (Col. 4:5); be sober, be watchful (1 Pet. 5:8); act according to your wisdom (1 Kgs. 2:6); let him become foolish that he may become wise (1 Cor. 3:18).

D3 Wisdom of individuals

The queen of the South came to hear the wisdom of Solomon (Luke 11:31); Rehoboam acted wisely (2 Chr. 11:23); by your wisdom and understanding you have gained riches (Ezek. 28:4-5); the king of Tyre was full of wisdom (Ezek. 28:12); on all matters of wisdom and understanding they were ten times better than the magicians (Dan. 1:20); when Jesus saw that he answered wisely (Mark 12:34); the master commended

the dishonest steward for his shrewdness (Luke 16:8); you, being so wise, gladly bear with fools! (2 Cor. 11:19).

E False wisdom

The tree was desirable to make one wise (Gen. 3:6); the wisdom of this world is folly with God (1 Cor. 3:19); the Greeks seek wisdom (1 Cor. 1:22); do not make yourself overwise (Eccles. 7:16); to preach not in wise words (1 Cor. 1:17); the wisdom of the wise will perish (Isa. 29:14); I will destroy the wisdom of the wise (1 Cor. 1:19); the wise are put to shame (Jer. 8:9); God captures the wise in their cunning (Job 5:13); God turns the knowledge of the wise to foolishness (Isa. 44:25); lest you be wise in your own estimation (Rom. 11:25); God has made foolish the wisdom of the world (1 Cor. 1:20); not in fleshly wisdom but by the grace of God (2 Cor. 1:12); this wisdom is not from above, but is earthly (Jas. 3:15); do not be wise in your own eyes (Prov. 3:7; Rom. 12:16); the rich man is wise in his own eyes (Prov. 28:11); there is more hope for a fool than for a man who is wise in his own eyes (Prov. 26:12); do you limit wisdom to yourself? (Job 15:8); by my own wisdom I did this (Isa. 10:13); let not the wise man boast in his wisdom (Jer. 9:23); how can you say, 'We are wise'? (Jer. 8:8); he has ceased to be wise (Ps. 36:3).

499 Unintelligence. Folly

FOOL, see 501.

A Folly in general

I set myself to consider wisdom, madness and folly (Eccles. 1:13, 17); wisdom exceeds folly as light exceeds darkness (Eccles. 2:13); a fool speaks nonsense (Isa. 32:6); the mouth of fools pours out folly (Prov. 15:2); the mouths of fools feed on folly (Prov. 15:14); every mouth speaks folly (Isa. 9:17); folly is joy to one without sense (Prov. 15:21); a little foolishness outweighs wisdom (Eccles. 10:1); do not be foolish (Eph. 5:17); refuse foolish controversies (2 Tim. 2:23); avoid stupid controversies (Titus 3:9); fools despise wisdom (Prov. 1:7); wisdom is too high for a fool (Prov. 24:7).

B Foolishness of God

The foolishness of God is wiser than men (1 Cor. 1:25); Christ crucified is foolishness to the Gentiles (1 Cor. 1:23); the message of the cross is foolishness for those who are perishing (1 Cor. 1:18); the foolishness of what is preached (1 Cor. 1:21); to the natural man the things of the Spirit are foolishness (1 Cor. 2:14); God has chosen foolish things to shame the wise (1 Cor. 1:27).

C Foolishness of men

C1 Widespread folly

Claiming to be wise, they became fools (Rom. 1:22); the wisdom of this world is folly with God (1 Cor. 3:19); they are senseless (Rom. 1:31); God has made foolish the wisdom of the world (1 Cor. 1:20); the shepherds have become stupid and their flock is scattered (Jer. 10:21); their folly will become apparent to all (2 Tim. 3:9); idolaters are foolish (Jer. 10:8; 51:17); my people are foolish (Jer. 4:22); Ephraim is like a silly dove (Hos. 7:11); you foolish Galatians! (Gal. 3:1); the Lord knows that the reasonings of the wise are useless (1 Cor. 3:20); God has chosen foolish things to shame the wise (1 Cor. 1:27).

C2 The folly of sin

Loss of virginity before marriage is folly in Israel (Deut. 22:21); the one who commits adultery lacks sense (Prov. 6:32); a man of quick temper acts foolishly (Prov. 14:17); a hasty temper exalts folly (Prov. 14:29); he who hates reproof is stupid (Prov. 12:1); their foolish heart was darkened (Rom. 1:21); from the heart comes foolishness (Mark 7:22).

500 Wise person

WISDOM, see 498.

A Wise people in general

A1 About wise people

A wise man is strong (Prov. 24:5); the wise man will hear and increase in learning (Prov. 1:5); give [instruction] to a wise man and he will be still wiser (Prov. 9:9); the words of the wise in quiet are better than the shouting of a ruler (Eccles. 9:17); the excellent woman speaks wisdom (Prov. 31:26); the wise will inherit honour (Prov. 3:35); the fool will be servant to the wise (Prov. 11:29); he who loves wisdom makes his father glad (Prov. 29:3); a wise son makes a glad father (Prov. 10:1; 15:20; 23:24).

A2 Be wise!

Be wise, my son, and make my heart glad (Prov. 27:11); walk not as unwise but as wise (Eph. 5:15); who is the faithful and wise servant? (Matt. 24:45).

A3 The work of the wise

He who is wise wins souls (Prov. 11:30); the wise woman builds her house (Prov. 14:1); the wise man built his house on the rock (Matt. 7:24); a poor wise man delivered the city with wisdom (Eccles. 9:15); he who gathers in summer is a wise son (Prov. 10:5); the faithful and sensible steward who gives the servants food (Luke 12:42).

A4 Disadvantages of the wise

If you are wise, you are wise for yourself (Prov. 9:12); where is the wise man? where is the scribe? (1 Cor. 1:20); he catches the wise in their cunning (1 Cor. 3:19); you hid these things from the wise and prudent (Matt. 11:25; Luke 10:21); even the wise die (Ps. 49:10); the wise men are put to shame (Jer. 8:9); bread is not to the wise (Eccles. 9:11); oppression makes a wise man mad (Eccles. 7:7); a fool who keeps silent is considered wise (Prov. 17:28).

B People who were wise

B1 Solomon

Solomon prayed for wisdom (1 Kgs. 3:9; 2 Chr. 1:10, 11); wisdom would be given him (1 Kgs. 3:12; 2 Chr. 1:12); God gave Solomon surpassing wisdom (1 Kgs. 4:29-31; 5:12); he was greater in wisdom than all other kings (1 Kgs. 10:23; 2 Chr. 9:22); Solomon's wisdom exceeded what the Queen of Sheba had heard (1 Kgs. 10:7; 2 Chr. 9:6); she came to hear the wisdom of Solomon (1 Kgs. 10:4; 2 Chr. 9:3; Matt. 12:42); they came to hear Solomon's wisdom (1 Kgs. 4:34; 10:24); God has given David a wise son (1 Kgs. 5:7; 2 Chr. 2:12).

B2 Wise men

Pharaoh sent for his wise men (Gen. 41:8); the wise men, sorcerers and magicians of Egypt (Exod. 7:11, 22; 8:7); the seven wise men of Ahasuerus (Esther 1:13-14); the magicians, conjurers, sorcerers and Chaldeans (Dan. 2:2; 5:7); the visit of the magi (Matt. 2:1-12); Elymas the magus (Acts 13:6, 8); I called for all the wise men of Babylon (Dan. 4:6); O Belteshazzar, chief of the magicians (Dan. 4:9); Daniel was appointed chief of the magicians, sorcerers, Chaldeans and diviners (Dan. 5:11); the king spoke to the wise men of Babylon (Dan. 5:7); the magicians, enchanters, Chaldeans and diviners came (Dan. 4:7); the wise men of my kingdom cannot make known to me the interpretation (Dan. 4:18); the king's wise men could not read the inscription or interpret it (Dan. 5:8); the wise men and enchanters could not read the writing (Dan. 5:15).

B3 Wise men in the church

I send you prophets, wise men and scribes (Matt. 23:34); choose men full of the Spirit and wisdom (Acts 6:3); they could not withstand Stephen's wisdom (Acts 6:10); not many wise men were called (1 Cor. 1:26); as a

wise master-builder I laid a foundation (1 Cor. 3:10); you are wise in Christ (1 Cor. 4:10); is there no one among you wise enough to decide between the brethren? (1 Cor. 6:5).

B4 Various wise people

Let Pharaoh look for a discerning and wise man (Gen. 41:33); no one was so wise as Joseph (Gen. 41:39); God gave him favour and wisdom before Pharaoh king of Egypt (Acts 7:10); provide wise men as leaders of the tribes (Deut. 1:13, 15); Joshua was filled with the spirit of wisdom (Deut. 34:9); Abigail was intelligent (1 Sam. 25:3); the wise woman from Tekoa (2 Sam. 14:2); a wise woman of Abel-beth-maacah (2 Sam. 20:16); Jonadab was very wise (2 Sam. 13:3); David had wisdom like an angel of God (2 Sam. 14:20); God gave the four youths wisdom (Dan. 1:17, 20); Sergius Paulus was an intelligent man (Acts 13:7); five of the virgins were wise (Matt. 25:2-9).

C Wise creatures

Four types of creature are small but wise (Prov. 30:24).

D Wise man or fool

Who knows whether he will be a wise man or a fool? (Eccles. 2:19); what advantage has the wise man over the fool? (Eccles. 6:8); wise and fools alike die (Eccles. 2:16); the wise and the fools perish alike (Ps. 49:10); no lasting remembrance of wise or fools (Eccles. 2:16); better to listen to the rebuke of the wise than the song of fools (Eccles. 7:5); claiming to be wise, they became fools (Rom. 1:22); God chose the foolish things to shame the wise (1 Cor. 1:27); I am a debtor to both wise and foolish (Rom. 1:14).

501 Fool

FOLLY, see 499.

WISE MAN OR FOOL, see 500D.

A Nature of fools

The characteristics of a fool (Prov. 26:1-12); this is the way of the foolish (Ps. 49:13); crush a fool with a pestle and mortar and his folly will not leave him (Prov. 27:22); wisdom is too high for a fool (Prov. 24:7); fools despise wisdom (Prov. 1:7); the fool walks in darkness (Eccles. 2:14); anger is in the bosom of fools (Eccles. 7:9); the fool folds his hands and eats his own flesh (Eccles. 4:5); the fool encounters problems (Job 5:3-5); fools get disgrace (Prov. 3:35); a fool filled with food is unbearable (Prov. 30:22); the foolish woman is noisy (Prov. 9:13); any fool will quarrel (Prov. 20:3); the fool will be servant to the wise (Prov. 11:29).

B God and fools

B1 God's attitude to fools

God said, 'You fool!' (Luke 12:20); hear this, foolish and senseless people (Jer. 5:21); you fools and blind! (Matt. 23:17); God takes no delight in fools (Eccles. 5:4); God makes fools of judges (Job 12:17); it is God's will that by doing right you silence the ignorance of foolish men (1 Pet. 2:15); the Lord preserves the foolish (Ps. 116:6).

B2 Fools' attitude to God

The fool says in his heart, 'There is no God' (Ps. 14:1; 53:1); a foolish people reviles your name (Ps. 74:18); the foolish man reviles you all the day (Ps. 74:22).

C Foolish people

I am more stupid than any man (Prov. 30:2); I was stupid and ignorant (Ps. 73:22); my wounds fester because of my folly (Ps. 38:5); I have acted foolishly (2 Sam. 24:10; 1 Chr. 21:8); I have played the fool (1 Sam. 26:21); Lord, you know my folly (Ps. 69:5); I have been a fool, you forced me to it (2 Cor. 12:11); are you so foolish? (Gal. 3:3); once we were foolish (Titus 3:3); let him become foolish that he may become wise (1 Cor. 3:18); let no one think me foolish, or accept me as a fool that I too may boast (2 Cor. 11:16); I am saying this as a fool (2 Cor. 11:17); Nabal's name meant Fool (1 Sam. 25:25); the princes of Zoan are fools (Isa. 19:11, 13); in the end he will be a fool (Jer. 17:11); five of the virgins were foolish (Matt. 25:2-8); you fools! (Luke 11:40); you fool! (1 Cor. 15:36); whatever anyone else dares, I speak as a fool, I also dare (2 Cor. 11:21); if I boast I will not be a fool for I will be telling the truth (2 Cor. 12:6); foolish and unwise people (Deut. 32:6); fools through their sinful ways (Ps. 107:17); I will provoke them to anger with a foolish people (Deut. 32:21); by a foolish nation I will anger you (Rom. 10:19).

D Counted as fools
Should Abner die like a fool? (2 Sam. 3:33); you will be like a fool (2 Sam. 13:13); you speak like a foolish woman (Job 2:10); fools and slow of heart to believe! (Luke 24:25); we are fools for Christ's sake (1 Cor. 4:10).

E Work of fools
The foolish man built his house on the sand (Matt. 7:26); draw near to listen rather than offer the sacrifice of fools (Eccles. 5:1); the heart of fools is in the house of pleasure (Eccles. 7:4); folly is set in exalted places (Eccles. 10:6); a poor wise lad is better than an old foolish king (Eccles. 4:13).

F Fools becoming wise
To give prudence to the simple (Prov. 1:4); fools, learn wisdom! (Prov. 8:5); leave fools and live! (Prov. 9:6); do not be a fool (Eccles. 7:17); how long will you love being simple? (Prov. 1:22); if you are a corrector of the foolish (Rom. 2:20); walk not as unwise but as wise (Eph. 5:15).

502 Sanity

A Sane
If we are sane, it is for you (2 Cor. 5:13); I am not mad, most noble Festus (Acts 26:25).

B Regaining sanity
Nebuchadnezzar's sanity returned (Dan. 4:34, 36); the man possessed by legion was clothed and in his right mind (Mark 5:15; Luke 8:35).

503 Insanity

MADMAN, see 504.

A People acting madly
The beginning of his talk is folly and the end is wicked madness (Eccles. 10:13); madness is in men's hearts (Eccles. 9:3); if we are beside ourselves, it is for God (2 Cor. 5:13); I am speaking like a madman (2 Cor. 11:23); a dumb donkey restrained the prophet's insanity (2 Pet. 2:16).

B Studying insanity
I set myself to know madness and folly (Eccles. 1:17; 2:12); I sought to know the evil of folly and the folly of madness (Eccles. 7:25); I said of laughter, 'It is madness' (Eccles. 2:2).

C Striking insane
The Lord will strike you with madness (Deut. 28:28); you will be driven mad by what you see (Deut. 28:34); I will strike every rider with madness (Zech. 12:4); oppression makes a wise man mad (Eccles. 7:7); the nations will drink and stagger and go mad (Jer. 25:16); the nations drink Babylon's wine and go mad (Jer. 51:7).

D Reckoned insane
David pretended to be insane (1 Sam. 21:13-15; Ps. 34:t); why did this madman come to you? (2 Kgs. 9:11); they said Jesus was out of his mind (Mark 3:21); he has a demon and is mad (John 10:20); Festus said Paul was out of his mind (Acts 26:24-5); they said Rhoda was out of her mind (Acts 12:15); every madman who prophesies (Jer. 29:26); the man of the Spirit is mad

(Hos. 9:7); if all speak in tongues, outsiders will say you are mad (1 Cor. 14:23).

504 Madman

See, he is acting like a madman (1 Sam. 21:14-15); like a madman who throws firebrands, arrows and death (Prov. 26:18); every madman who prophesies (Jer. 29:26); why did this madman come to you? (2 Kgs. 9:11).

INSANITY, see 503.

505 Memory

A Reminders

A1 Memorials
This name is my memorial to all generations (Exod. 3:15); this day will be a memorial for you (Exod. 12:14); the Feast of Trumpets is a reminder (Lev. 23:24); names on the shoulders as a memorial (Exod. 28:12; 39:7); bearing the names on the breastpiece as a memorial (Exod. 28:29); the half-shekel tax will be a memorial for the children of Israel (Exod. 30:16); the tassels are a reminder of the Lord's commands (Num. 15:39-40); it will be a reminder on your forehead (Exod. 13:9); the trumpets a memorial before God (Num. 10:10); the beaten plates were a reminder to the Israelites (Num. 16:40); the gold was a memorial for the Israelites before the Lord (Num. 31:54); these stones are a memorial for Israel (Josh. 4:7); the crown will be in the temple as a reminder (Zech. 6:14).

A2 Reminders of the gospel
I have written boldly to remind you (Rom. 15:15); I want to remind you (Jude 5); I think it right to stir you up by way of reminder (2 Pet. 1:13); I will see to it that after my departure you will be able to remember these things (2 Pet. 1:15); remind them of these things (2 Tim. 2:14); remind them to be subject to rulers and authorities (Titus 3:1); Timothy will remind you of my ways in Christ (1 Cor. 4:17); I stir up your mind by a reminder (2 Pet. 3:1); I have said these things that you may remember (John 16:4).

A3 Reminders of sin
The sacrifices are a reminder of sins year by year (Heb. 10:3); this day I remember my sins (Gen. 41:9).

A4 Memorials for people
I will give eunuchs a memorial in my house (Isa. 56:5); a book of remembrance was written for those who feared the Lord (Mal. 3:16); wherever the gospel is preached, what she has done will be told in memory of her (Matt. 26:13; Mark 14:9); the righteous will be remembered for ever (Ps. 112:6); you have no memorial in Jerusalem (Neh. 2:20).

B Remembering

B1 Remember!
Remember all the way the Lord has led you (Deut. 8:2); remember this day (Exod. 13:3); remember Lot's wife (Luke 17:32); remember what God did to Miriam (Deut. 24:9); remember what Moses said to you (Josh. 1:13); call to mind the blessing and the curse when you are exiled (Deut. 30:1); remember the days of darkness, for they will be many (Eccles. 11:8); remember the law of Moses (Mal. 4:4); remember the sabbath day (Exod. 20:8); remember what he told you when he was still in Galilee (Luke 24:6); remember the word I spoke to you (John 15:20); do you not remember that while I was with you I told you these things? (2 Thess. 2:5); remember the predictions of the holy prophets (2 Pet. 3:2); remember from what you have fallen (Rev. 2:5); remember the former things (Isa. 46:9); remember the former days (Heb. 10:32); remember what you have received (Rev. 3:3); remember the words of the apostles

(Jude 17); the memory of Purim should not cease (Esther 9:28).

B2 God remembering

B2a Remember, O God!

Lord God, remember me! (Judg. 16:28); remember me, O God (Neh. 5:19; 13:14, 22, 31; Ps. 106:4); remember how I walked before you in truth! (Isa. 38:3); remember Abraham, Isaac and Israel! (Exod. 32:13; Deut. 9:27); remember the word you spoke to Moses! (Neh. 1:8); remember your covenant with us (Jer. 14:21); remember your word to me (Ps. 119:49); according to your lovingkindness remember me (Ps. 25:7); remember me and visit me (Jer. 15:15); in wrath remember mercy (Hab. 3:2); remember how I walked before you in truth! (2 Kgs. 20:3); remember David's affliction (Ps. 132:1); remember the day of Jerusalem (Ps. 137:7); remember the reproach of your servants (Ps. 89:50); remember what has befallen us (Lam. 5:1); remember how short my life is (Ps. 89:47); remember how the foolish reviles you (Ps. 74:22); remember that the enemy scoffs (Ps. 74:18); let the iniquity of his fathers be remembered before the Lord (Ps. 109:14); you who remind the Lord, take no rest (Isa. 62:6); remind me (Isa. 43:26).

B2b God remembers his people

God remembering Noah and all the animals with him (Gen. 8:1); God remembered Abraham (Gen. 19:29); God remembered Rachel (Gen. 30:22); God remembered Hannah (1 Sam. 1:19); God remembered Ephraim (Jer. 31:20); he remembered his promise to Abraham (Ps. 105:42).

B2c God remembers his covenant

God remembered his covenant (Gen. 9:15, 16; Exod. 2:24; 6:5; Lev. 26:42, 45; Deut. 4:31; Ps. 106:45; Ezek. 16:60); he has remembered his covenant for ever (Ps. 105:8); he remembers his covenant for ever (1 Chr. 16:15); I will remember my covenant with you in your youth (Ezek. 16:60); to remember his holy covenant (Luke 1:72).

B2d God remembers devotion

Did not the Lord remember your sacrifices? (Jer. 44:21); your prayers and alms have ascended as a memorial before God (Acts 10:4); your alms have been remembered before God (Acts 10:31); God will not forget your work and love (Heb. 6:10); I remember the love of your youth (Jer. 2:2).

B2e God remembers the needy

What is man, that you remember him? (Heb. 2:6); he remembered that they were but flesh (Ps. 78:39); he remembers that we are dust (Ps. 103:14); he remembered us in our low estate (Ps. 136:23); though a mother may forget, I will not forget you (Isa. 49:15); you will not be forgotten by me (Isa. 44:21); the needy will not always be forgotten (Ps. 9:18); God does not forget the cry of the afflicted (Ps. 9:12); not one sparrow is forgotten by God (Luke 12:6).

B2f God remembers sin

I remember their wickedness (Hos. 7:2); he will remember their iniquity (Jer. 14:10; Hos. 8:13; 9:9); God remembered Babylon the great (Rev. 16:19); God has remembered her iniquities (Rev. 18:5).

B3 Remembering God

B3a Remember God!

Remember the Lord your God (Deut. 8:18); remember the Lord (Neh. 4:14; Jer. 51:50); remember your Creator (Eccles. 12:1); remember his wonderful deeds (1 Chr. 16:12); remember the wonders he has done (Ps. 105:5); remember his covenant (1 Chr. 16:15-17).

B3b Those who remember God

I will remember the deeds of the Lord (Ps. 77:11); after he was raised they remembered his word (John 2:22);

we have not forgotten you (Ps. 44:17); they remembered that God was their rock (Ps. 78:35); when I remember you on my bed (Ps. 63:6); I remember your name in the night (Ps. 119:55); I remembered the Lord (Jonah 2:7); I remember you from the land of Jordan (Ps. 42:6); they will remember me in far countries (Zech. 10:9); those who escape will remember me among the nations (Ezek. 6:9); all the ends of the earth will remember and turn to the Lord (Ps. 22:27).

B3c Reminders of God

Everywhere I cause my name to be remembered (Exod. 20:24); I will cause your name to be remembered for all generations (Ps. 45:17); I will remind you of these things (2 Pet. 1:12); he has caused his wonders to be remembered (Ps. 111:4); the Holy Spirit will bring to your remembrance all I said (John 14:26).

B4 Remembering Christ

Remember Jesus Christ (2 Tim. 2:8); do this in remembrance of me (Luke 22:19; 1 Cor. 11:24-5); Peter remembered Jesus' word (Matt. 26:75; Luke 22:61); they remembered his words (Luke 24:8); when Jesus was glorified they remembered that this had been written of him (John 12:16); I remembered the word of the Lord (Acts 11:16); remember the words of the Lord Jesus (Acts 20:35).

B5 Remembering people

Joseph asked the butler to remember him (Gen. 40:14); when the Lord deals well with you, remember me (1 Sam. 25:31); remember me when you come into your kingdom (Luke 23:42); remember those in prison as if in prison with them (Heb. 13:3); remember your leaders (Heb. 13:7); sing songs that you may be remembered (Isa. 23:16); he asked us to remember the poor (Gal. 2:10); making remembrance of you in my prayers (Eph. 1:16); I thank my God on every remembrance of you (Phil. 1:3); we remember your work of faith (1 Thess. 1:3); you remember us kindly (1 Thess. 3:6); I remember you in my prayers night and day (2 Tim. 1:3); I remember your tears (2 Tim. 1:4); I am reminded of your sincere faith (2 Tim. 1:5).

B6 People remembering

The memory of the righteous is a blessing (Prov. 10:7); these things I remember (Ps. 42:4); I remember the days of old (Ps. 143:5); this I call to mind and therefore have hope (Lam. 3:21); we remember the fish we ate in Egypt (Num. 11:5); we wept when we remembered Zion (Ps. 137:1); if you are making an offering and remember that your brother has something against you (Matt. 5:23); we remember what that impostor said (Matt. 27:63); his disciples remembered that it was written (John 2:17); Joseph remembered his dreams (Gen. 42:9); you will remember your ways (Ezek. 16:63; 20:43); their children remember their altars and their Asherim (Jer. 17:2); can a maid forget her ornaments or a bride her attire? (Jer. 2:32).

C Not forgetting

This song will not be forgotten (Deut. 31:21); that they should not forget the works of God (Ps. 78:7); do not forget all his benefits (Ps. 103:2); do not forget the covenant (2 Kgs. 17:38); I have not forgotten your commandments (Deut. 26:13); do not forget the afflicted (Ps. 10:12; 74:19); the needy will not always be forgotten (Ps. 9:18); everlasting shame which will not be forgotten (Jer. 23:40); their disgrace will never be forgotten (Jer. 20:11); the Lord has sworn, 'I will never forget any of their deeds' (Amos 8:7).

506 Forgetfulness

NOT FORGETTING, see 505C.

A God forgetting

The Lord has forgotten me (Isa. 49:14); I will forget your children (Hos. 4:6); I am like the dead whom you remember no more (Ps. 88:5); I will forget you (Jer. 23:39); why have you forgotten me? (Ps. 42:9); why do you forget our affliction? (Ps. 44:24); will you forget me for ever? (Ps. 13:1); has God forgotten to be gracious? (Ps. 77:9); do not remember the sins of my youth (Ps. 25:7); do not remember against us the sins of our forefathers (Ps. 79:8); do not remember iniquity for ever (Isa. 64:9); their sins I will remember no more (Heb. 8:12; 10:17); I will not remember your sins (Isa. 43:25); none of his sins will be remembered (Ezek. 33:16); none of his righteous deeds will be remembered (Ezek. 33:13).

B Forgetting God

B1 Do not forget God

Do not forget the Lord (Deut. 6:12; 8:11, 14); keep your soul lest you forget what you have seen (Deut. 4:9); lest you forget the covenant (Deut. 4:23); if you forget the Lord your God (Deut. 8:19); those who forget God will perish (Job 8:13).

B2 They forgot God

The Israelites forgot the Lord their God (Judg. 3:7); they forgot the Lord (1 Sam. 12:9; Jer. 3:21); you forgot the God who gave you birth (Deut. 32:18); you have forgotten the Lord your maker (Isa. 51:13); they forgot God their Saviour (Ps. 106:21); they did not remember the Lord (Judg. 8:34); you have forgotten God (Isa. 17:10); you who forget God (Ps. 50:22); they forgot me (Hos. 13:6); you have forgotten me (Jer. 13:25; Ezek. 22:12; 23:35); you did not remember me (Isa. 57:11); my people have forgotten me (Jer. 2:32; 18:15); all the nations who forget God return to Sheol (Ps. 9:17); Israel has forgotten his Maker and built palaces (Hos. 8:14); they did not remember your wonderful deeds (Neh. 9:17); they forgot his deeds (Ps. 78:11); they soon forgot his works (Ps. 106:13); they did not remember his power (Ps. 78:42); our fathers did not remember your lovingkindness (Ps. 106:7); their fathers forgot my name because of Baal (Jer. 23:27); you who forget my holy mountain (Isa. 65:11); my foes forget your words (Ps. 119:139); the adulteress forgets the covenant of her God (Prov. 2:17).

C Forgetting people

The butler forgot Joseph (Gen. 40:23); Joash did not remember Jehoiada's kindness (2 Chr. 24:22); no one remembered the poor man who delivered the city (Eccles. 9:15); take your harp, forgotten harlot (Isa. 23:16); your lovers have forgotten you (Jer. 30:14); Tyre will be forgotten for 70 years (Isa. 23:15); can a woman forget her sucking child? (Isa. 49:15); forget your people and your father's house (Ps. 45:10); no lasting remembrance of wise or fools (Eccles. 2:16); that his name be remembered no more (Jer. 11:19); those who are dead are forgotten (Eccles. 9:5); I am forgotten like a dead man (Ps. 31:12); I would have removed the memory of Israel (Deut. 32:26); let us wipe out Israel that their name not be remembered (Ps. 83:4); you will make their name perish (Deut. 7:24); the Lord will cut off the memory of evildoers (Ps. 34:16); you have no memorial in Jerusalem (Neh. 2:20).

D Forgetting things

The abundance will be forgotten when famine comes (Gen. 41:30); I have forgotten what happiness is (Lam. 3:17); the Lord has caused to be forgotten appointed feast and sabbath (Lam. 2:6); they did not remember the covenant of brotherhood (Amos 1:9); have you forgotten the exhortation? (Heb. 12:5); he has forgotten he was cleansed from his old sins (2 Pet. 1:9); he forgets what his face is like (Jas. 1:24-5); they will not

remember the ark of the covenant (Jer. 3:16); if I forget Jerusalem, let my right hand forget (Ps. 137:5); if I do not remember Jerusalem (Ps. 137:6); lest they drink and forget what has been decreed (Prov. 31:5); let him drink and forget his poverty (Prov. 31:7); God has made me forget my trouble (Gen. 41:51); he will not overmuch remember the days of his life (Eccles. 5:20); forgetting what lies behind (Phil. 3:13); I forget to eat my bread (Ps. 102:4).

E Blotted out

I will blot out the memory of Amalek (Exod. 17:14); blot out the memory of Amalek (Deut. 25:19); you blot out their name for ever and ever (Ps. 9:5); blot me out of your book (Exod. 32:32); whoever has sinned I will blot out of my book (Exod. 32:33).

507 Expectation

A God waiting

The Lord waits to be gracious (Isa. 30:18); God's patience waited in the days of Noah (1 Pet. 3:20).

B Waiting for God

B1 Wait for God!

Wait for the Lord (Ps. 27:14; 37:34); wait patiently for him (Ps. 37:7); it is good for one to wait quietly for the Lord's salvation (Lam. 3:26); if it is slow, wait for it (Hab. 2:3); he charged them to wait for the promise of the Father (Acts 1:4).

B2 Those who wait for God

I wait for the Lord more than watchmen wait for the morning (Ps. 130:6); I waited patiently for the Lord (Ps. 40:1); my eyes fail with waiting for God (Ps. 69:3); I wait for God my Saviour (Mic. 7:7); I wait for your deliverance, Lord (Gen. 49:18); Joseph of Arimathea was waiting for the kingdom of God (Mark 15:43).

B3 About waiting for God

Those who wait for the Lord renew their strength (Isa. 40:31); those who wait for the Lord will inherit the land (Ps. 37:9); none who wait for you will be ashamed (Ps. 25:3); those who wait for me will not be put to shame (Isa. 49:23); the Lord is good to those who wait for him (Lam. 3:25); you work on behalf of those who wait for you (Isa. 64:4); waiting until his enemies should be made his footstool (Heb. 10:13); this is our God for whom we have waited (Isa. 25:9); why should I wait for the Lord? (2 Kgs. 6:33).

B4 Waiting for the second coming

We wait for a Saviour from heaven (Phil. 3:20); we wait for the revealing of the Lord Jesus (1 Cor. 1:7); we wait for the appearing of our God and Saviour (Titus 2:13); we wait for his Son from heaven (1 Thess. 1:10); wait for the mercy of our Lord Jesus to eternal life (Jude 21); we wait for the redemption of our bodies (Rom. 8:23); waiting for and hastening the coming of the day of God (2 Pet. 3:12); according to his promise we wait for new heavens and a new earth (2 Pet. 3:13); be like men waiting for their master (Luke 12:36); through the Spirit, by faith, we wait for the hope of righteousness (Gal. 5:5); the creation waits for the sons of God to be revealed (Rom. 8:19).

C People waiting

Noah waited seven days (Gen. 8:10, 12); Saul waiting seven days for Samuel (1 Sam. 10:8; 13:8); if he lay in wait and threw something at him (Num. 35:20); one who lies in wait to kill his neighbour (Deut. 19:11); they wait for my life (Ps. 56:6); the wicked lie in wait to destroy me (Ps. 119:95); if I bore sons would you wait until they grew up? (Ruth 1:13); David would wait until word came (2 Sam. 15:28); the people were waiting for Zechariah (Luke 1:21); the crowd were waiting for Jesus (Luke 8:40); while Paul waited for them in Athens (Acts 17:16); they had gone on ahead and were waiting for us at Troas (Acts 20:5); they are ready, waiting for the promise from you (Acts 23:21); if we hope for what we do not see, we wait patiently for it (Rom. 8:25); when you come together to eat, wait for one another (1 Cor. 11:33).

508 Lack of expectation

When you did wonders which we did not expect (Isa. 64:3); the coming of the Son of man will be unexpected (Matt. 24:37-41; Luke 12:40); at an hour you do not think (Matt. 24:44); lest the day come unexpectedly like a trap (Luke 21:34-5); the master will come on a day the slave does not expect (Matt. 24:50; Luke 12:46); let ruin come on him unawares (Ps. 35:8); if he threw something without lying in wait (Num. 35:22); I have said these things that you may not be taken by surprise (John 16:1); this was not as we expected (2 Cor. 8:5).

509 Disappointment

They were disappointed in the dry watercourses (Job 6:20); they trusted in you and were not disappointed (Ps. 22:5); he who believes in him will not be disappointed (Rom. 9:33; 10:11); hope does not disappoint us (Rom. 5:5).

510 Foreknowledge

A **Knowing beforehand**
Before a word is on my tongue, you know it (Ps. 139:4); your Father knows what you need before you ask him (Matt. 6:8); delivered up by the predetermined plan and foreknowledge of God (Acts 2:23); David foresaw and spoke of the resurrection of Christ (Acts 2:31); the scripture, foreseeing that God would justify the Gentiles by faith (Gal. 3:8).

B **Christ foreknown**
Christ was foreknown before the foundation of the world (1 Pet. 1:20).

C **The elect foreknown**
Chosen according to the foreknowledge of God (1 Pet. 1:2); those whom he foreknew he also predestined (Rom. 8:29); God has not rejected those he foreknew (Rom. 11:2).

511 Prediction

A **Predicting the future**
God has made known what will happen in the future (Dan. 2:45); taking the 12 he began to tell them what would happen to him (Mark 10:32); that when these things happen you will remember that I told you of them (John 16:4); as Isaiah predicted (Rom. 9:29); we told you beforehand that we would be afflicted (1 Thess. 3:4); remember the predictions of the holy prophets (2 Pet. 3:2); write the things which will take place hereafter (Rev. 1:19); I will show you what must take place after these things (Rev. 4:1); the Holy Spirit will declare things to come (John 16:13); God has told Pharaoh what he is about to do (Gen. 41:25, 28); Jacob told his sons what would happen to them in days to come (Gen. 49:1); I have told you in advance (Matt. 24:25; Mark 13:23; John 13:19; 14:29); declaring the end from the beginning (Isa. 46:10); Agabus predicted the famine (Acts 11:28).

B **Predicting Christ**
The Spirit predicted the sufferings of Christ (1 Pet. 1:11); God foretold by the prophets that Christ would suffer (Acts 3:18); they killed those who predicted the coming of the Righteous One (Acts 7:52); saying nothing but what the prophets and Moses said would come to pass (Acts 26:22); the gospel promised beforehand through his prophets in the holy scriptures (Rom. 1:2).

512 Supposition

Jesus was supposedly the son of Joseph (Luke 3:23); they supposed Mary was going to the tomb to weep there (John 11:31); myths and endless genealogies which lead to speculation (1 Tim. 1:4).

513 Imagination

The prophets' visions are from their own imagination (Jer. 23:16); why did the Gentiles rage and the peoples imagine futile things? (Acts 4:25).

514 Meaning

We want to know what these things mean (Acts 17:20); what does this great shout mean? (1 Sam. 4:6); what does this noise mean? (1 Sam. 4:14); I desired to know the meaning of the fourth beast (Dan. 7:19); his disciples asked him what this parable meant (Luke 8:9); what does he mean by this? (John 7:36); what does he mean by 'a little while'? (John 16:18); they were amazed and puzzled, saying, 'What does this mean?' (Acts 2:12); many languages in the world, and none without meaning (1 Cor. 14:10-11).

515 Lack of meaning

They honour me with their lips but their heart is far from me (Isa. 29:13; Matt. 15:8; Mark 7:6); you are near to their lips but far from their heart (Jer. 12:2); they show love with their lips but their heart goes after gain (Ezek. 33:31); in prayer do not use meaningless babbling (Matt. 6:7); they do not cry to me from the heart (Hos. 7:14); the women's words seemed like nonsense (Luke 24:11); avoid empty chatter (1 Tim. 6:20; 2 Tim. 2:16); he says, 'Eat and drink', but his heart is not with you (Prov. 23:7).

516 Intelligibility

EXPLANATION, see 520C.

A **About understanding**
A1 Understanding in general
Knowledge of the Holy One is understanding (Prov. 9:10); men who understood the times (1 Chr. 12:32); to understand a proverb and a satire (Prov. 1:6); do not lean on your own understanding (Prov. 3:5); to love God with all the understanding (Mark 12:33).

A2 Proper understanding
What they had not heard they will understand (Isa. 52:15); what I do now you will understand later (John 13:7); in the last days you will understand it (Jer. 23:20; 30:24); those who have understanding will shine like the firmament (Dan. 12:3); they understood that he did not tell them to beware of the leaven of bread (Matt. 16:12); the disciples understood that he had spoken about John the Baptist (Matt. 17:13); they understood that he spoke this parable against them (Mark 12:12; Luke 20:19); if I understand all mysteries (1 Cor. 13:2); you will see my insight into the mystery of Christ (Eph. 3:4); that you may be able to understand with all the saints (Eph. 3:18).

A3 Understand!
Hear and understand! (Matt. 15:10; Mark 7:14); incline your heart to understanding (Prov. 2:2); let the reader understand (Matt. 24:15; Mark 13:14); I have come to give you understanding (Dan. 10:14); whoever is wise, let him understand these things (Hos. 14:9); I want you to understand this mystery (Rom. 11:25); understand what the will of the Lord is (Eph. 5:17).

B **God has understanding**
By understanding the Lord established the heavens (Prov. 3:19); God understands all their works (Ps. 33:15); his understanding is beyond measure (Ps. 147:5);

his understanding is fathomless (Isa. 40:28); who taught God the way of understanding? (Isa. 40:14); they were amazed at Jesus' understanding (Luke 2:47).

C God gives understanding
The breath of the Almighty gives a man understanding (Job 32:8); the Lord will give you understanding (2 Tim. 2:7); those who seek the Lord understand all (Prov. 28:5); a good understanding have all who practise wisdom (Ps. 111:10); give me understanding that I might live (Ps. 119:144); from your precepts I get understanding (Ps. 119:104); the unfolding of your word gives understanding (Ps. 119:130); we have received the Spirit of God that we might understand what God has given us (1 Cor. 2:12); filled with the knowledge of his will in all spiritual wisdom and understanding (Col. 1:9); I have more understanding than my teachers (Ps. 119:99); I understand more than the aged (Ps. 119:100).

D Able to understand
D1 Understanding God's word
Open my eyes to see wonders in your law (Ps. 119:18); he opened their minds to understand the scriptures (Luke 24:45); they celebrated because they had understood the words (Neh. 8:12); they who have not heard of him will understand (Rom. 15:21); since the day you heard and understood the grace of God in truth (Col. 1:6); the riches of assurance of understanding and knowledge (Col. 2:2).
D2 Making the message clear
Unless you speak intelligible words, how will the message be understood? (1 Cor. 14:9); write it with common characters (Isa. 8:1); I write nothing but what you can read and understand (2 Cor. 1:13); that I may make it clear (Col. 4:4).
D3 Eyes opened
Your eyes will be opened, knowing good and evil (Gen. 3:5); their eyes were opened and they knew they were naked (Gen. 3:7); their eyes were opened through the breaking of bread (Luke 24:31); the eyes of your hearts being enlightened (Eph. 1:18).
D4 People understanding
They did not know that Joseph understood them (Gen. 42:23).

517 Unintelligibility

A Without understanding
Seeing, they do not see, hearing, they do not hear, nor do they understand (Matt. 13:13-15); they will hear but never understand (Isa. 6:9-10; Mark 4:12; Luke 8:10; Acts 28:26-7); lest they understand with their hearts (John 12:40); are you without understanding? (Matt. 15:16; Mark 7:18; 8:17); gods which do not see nor understand (Dan. 5:23); there is no understanding of it (Obad. 7); comparing themselves with one another, they are without understanding (2 Cor. 10:12); no one understands (Rom. 3:11); my people do not understand (Isa. 1:3); he has shut their hearts so that they cannot understand (Isa. 44:18); Gentiles darkened in their understanding (Eph. 4:18); it is hard to explain because you are dull of hearing (Heb. 5:11); are you a teacher of Israel yet you do not understand? (John 3:10); they want to be teachers of the law though they do not understand (1 Tim. 1:7); they revile whatever they do not understand (Jude 10).

B Unintelligible
The peace of God passes all understanding (Phil. 4:7); the love of Christ passes knowledge (Eph. 3:19); how inscrutable are his ways! (Rom. 11:33); his greatness is unsearchable (Ps. 145:3); God does great and unfathomable things (Job 9:10); God does great things which we cannot understand (Job 37:5); who can

understand the heart? (Jer. 17:9); three or four things I do not understand (Prov. 30:18-19); no one understands him who speaks in tongues, but he utters mysteries (1 Cor. 14:2).

C Not understanding words
C1 Not understanding sayings
The disciples did not understand (Matt. 16:8-11; Mark 9:32; Luke 9:45; 18:34; John 8:27; 12:16; 20:9); when anyone hears the word of the kingdom and does not understand it (Matt. 13:19); Paul wrote some things hard to understand (2 Pet. 3:16); I heard but did not understand (Dan. 12:8); those with me saw the light but did not understand the voice (Acts 22:9); how can he say 'Amen' when he does not understand what you are saying? (1 Cor. 14:16); Jesus' parents did not understand the saying (Luke 2:50); it was concealed from them so that they should not perceive it (Luke 9:45); why do you not understand what I say? (John 8:43).
C2 Not understanding language
They will not understand one another's language (Gen. 11:7); a nation whose language you do not understand (Deut. 28:49; Jer. 5:15); you are not sent to a people whose speech you cannot understand (Ezek. 3:6); you will no longer see a people of unintelligible language (Isa. 33:19).

D Not understanding God's things
They do not understand the Lord's purpose (Mic. 4:12); you err, not understanding the scriptures or the power of God (Matt. 22:29; Mark 12:24); the darkness did not comprehend the light (John 1:5); what I do you do not know now (John 13:7); the natural man cannot understand the things of the Spirit (1 Cor. 2:14); none of the rulers understood this mystery (1 Cor. 2:8); the Israelites did not understand (Acts 7:25).

E Not understanding other things
I do not understand my actions (Rom. 7:15); how can man understand his way? (Prov. 20:24); you do not understand that it is expedient that one man die (John 11:50).

518 Ambiguity
DOUBLE-MINDED, see 601A.

519 Metaphor

A Use of parables
A1 Jesus using parables
Jesus told them many things in parables (Matt. 13:3; Mark 4:2); he began to speak to them in parables (Mark 12:1); Jesus spoke to them again in parables (Matt. 22:1); he spoke to them in parables (Mark 3:23); this is why I speak to them in parables (Matt. 13:13); he did not say anything to them without a parable (Matt. 13:34; Mark 4:34); why speak to them in parables? (Matt. 13:10-13); for those outside everything is in parables (Mark 4:11; Luke 8:10); I have said these things in figures (John 16:25); this figure of speech Jesus used with them (John 10:6); explain the parable to us (Matt. 15:15); they asked him about the parables (Mark 4:10); how will you understand all the parables? (Mark 4:13); are you telling this parable for us or for all? (Luke 12:41); when the chief priests and the Pharisees heard his parables (Matt. 21:45); they understood that he spoke this parable against them (Mark 12:12; Luke 20:19).
A2 Others using parables
Is he not a maker of parables? (Ezek. 20:49); through the prophets I gave parables (Hos. 12:10); I will open my mouth in parables (Ps. 78:2; Matt. 13:35).

B Actual parables

B1 Old testament parables

Jotham's parable of the trees choosing a king (Judg. 9:8-15); Nathan's parable of the poor man's ewe lamb (2 Sam. 12:1-4); Jehoash's parable of the thorn bush and the cedar (2 Kgs. 14:9; 2 Chr. 25:18); parable of the vineyard (Isa. 5:1-7); parable of the two eagles and the vine (Ezek. 17:2-10); parable of the cedar (Ezek. 17:22-4); parable of Oholah and Oholibah (Ezek. 23:2-45); parable of the boiling pot (Ezek. 24:3-14); this is an allegory (Gal. 4:24); Abraham received Isaac back from the dead in parable (Heb. 11:19).

B2 Jesus' parables

Parable of the: blind leading the blind (Matt. 15:14; Luke 6:39); drag-net (Matt. 13:47-50); fig tree (Matt. 24:32-3; Mark 13:28; Luke 13:6-8; 21:29-31); good Samaritan (Luke 10:30-7); good shepherd (John 10:1-5); guests choosing places (Luke 14:7-11); houses on rock and sand (Matt. 7:24-7; Luke 6:48-9); importunate neighbour (Luke 11:5-8); invitations to the feast (Matt. 22:2-14; Luke 14:16-24); king settling accounts (Matt. 18:23-34); labourers in the vineyard (Matt. 20:1-16); lamp and lampstand (Luke 8:16); leaven (Matt. 13:33); lost coin (Luke 15:8-10); lost sheep (Matt. 18:12-14; Luke 15:3-7); master returning from the wedding feast (Luke 12:36-40); mustard seed (Matt. 13:31-2; Mark 4:31-2; Luke 13:18-19); patched garments (Luke 5:36); pearl (Matt. 13:45-6); Pharisee and tax collector (Luke 18:9-14); prodigal son (Luke 15:11-32); rich fool (Luke 12:16-21); rented vineyard (Matt. 21:33-41; Mark 12:1-12; Luke 20:9-13); rich man and Lazarus (Luke 16:19-31); sheep and goats (Matt. 25:31-46); sower (Matt. 13:3-9; Mark 4:3-9; Luke 8:4-8); sprouting seed (Mark 4:26-9); talents (Matt. 25:14-30); ten minas (Luke 19:11-27); ten virgins (Matt. 25:1-13); treasure (Matt. 13:44); two debtors (Luke 7:41-3); two sons (Matt. 21:28-32); unjust judge (Luke 18:1-8); unjust steward (Luke 16:1-9); wheat and tares (Matt. 13:24-30); wineskins (Luke 5:37-8).

520 Interpretation

A Interpreting dreams

A1 Able to interpret dreams

It is said that when you hear a dream you can interpret it (Gen. 41:15); do not interpretations belong to God? (Gen. 40:8); Daniel had an excellent spirit, knowledge, insight, interpretation of dreams (Dan. 5:12).

A2 Interpreting particular dreams

He interpreted to us according to each man's dream (Gen. 41:12); no one could interpret the dreams (Gen. 41:8, 15; Dan. 4:6-7); this is the interpretation (Gen. 40:12, 18); Gideon heard the dream and its interpretation (Judg. 7:15); Daniel interpreted Nebuchadnezzar's dreams (Dan. 2:24-45; 4:18-26); Daniel interpreted the inscription (Dan. 5:16-28); Daniel asked the king for time, that he might show the interpretation (Dan. 2:16); I have found one of the exiles from Judah who will make known the interpretation (Dan. 2:25); the wise men of my kingdom cannot make known to me the interpretation (Dan. 4:18); tell the dream and we will show the interpretation (Dan. 2:4); the wise men could not interpret the inscription (Dan. 5:8).

B Interpreting language

Joseph used an interpreter (Gen. 42:23); the gift of interpretation (1 Cor. 12:10); not all interpret, do they? (1 Cor. 12:30); interpretation is necessary when one speaks in tongues (1 Cor. 14:5, 27-8); let him who speaks in tongues pray for an interpretation (1 Cor. 14:13); this is the interpretation of the inscription (Dan. 5:26); Immanuel translated means 'God with us' (Matt. 1:23); Golgotha means 'the place of the skull' (Matt.

27:33; Mark 15:22); 'Eli, lama sabachthani' means 'My God, why have you forsaken me?' (Matt. 27:46; Mark 15:34); 'Talitha cumi' means 'Little girl, I say to you, arise' (Mark 5:41); 'ephphatha' means 'be opened' (Mark 7:34); Melchizedek, by translation of his name, is king of righteousness (Heb. 7:2).

C Explanation

To whom will he interpret the message? (Isa. 28:9); you know how to interpret the appearance of the sky, but cannot interpret the present time (Matt. 16:3; Luke 12:56); he explained in all the scriptures the things concerning himself (Luke 24:27); did not our hearts burn when he explained the scriptures to us? (Luke 24:32); he opened their minds to understand the scriptures (Luke 24:45); explaining and demonstrating that the Christ had to suffer (Acts 17:3); the Levites gave the meaning of the Law (Neh. 8:7-8); explain to us the parable (Matt. 13:36; 15:15); he explained the parables privately to his disciples (Mark 4:34); no scripture is a matter of private interpretation (2 Pet. 1:20).

521 Misinterpretation

NOT UNDERSTAND, see 517.

522 Manifestation

A God manifest

Show me your glory! (Exod. 33:18); what is to be known about God is evident to men (Rom. 1:19-20); Jesus Christ was placarded as crucified (Gal. 3:1); Jesus manifested his glory (John 2:11); to each is given the manifestation of the Spirit for the common good (1 Cor. 12:7).

GOD APPEARING, see 445B1.

B Things manifest

Everything is uncovered before God's eyes (Heb. 4:13); Sheol and Abaddon lie open before God, how much more men's hearts (Prov. 15:11); the sins of some men are evident (1 Tim. 5:24); good deeds are evident (1 Tim. 5:25); the weeds appeared (Matt. 13:26); Sanballat sent an open letter (Neh. 6:5); I have always spoken openly (John 18:20); it is useless to spread a net in the bird's sight (Prov. 1:17); he showed them his hands and feet (Luke 24:40).

523 Hiding oneself

A God hiding

I will hide my face from them (Deut. 31:17-18; 32:20); he will hide his face from them (Mic. 3:4); I hid my face from them (Ezek. 39:23, 24); I hid my face and was angry (Isa. 57:17); I hid my face from you for a moment (Isa. 54:8); you hid your face (Ps. 30:7; Isa. 64:7); I have hidden my face from this city (Jer. 33:5); God has hidden his face (Ps. 10:11); the Lord is hiding his face from the house of Jacob (Isa. 8:17); you are a God who hides yourself (Isa. 45:15); how long will you hide your face? (Ps. 13:1); will you hide yourself for ever, O Lord? (Ps. 89:46); why do you hide your face? (Job 13:24; Ps. 44:24; 88:14); you hide your face and they are dismayed (Ps. 104:29); when God hides his face, who can behold him? (Job 34:29); your sins have hidden his face from you (Isa. 59:2); hide your face from my sins (Ps. 51:9); Cain would be hidden from God's face (Gen. 4:14); he has not hidden his face from the afflicted (Ps. 22:24); do not hide yourself from my supplication (Ps. 55:1); your Teacher will no longer hide himself (Isa. 30:20); I will not hide my face from them any more (Ezek. 39:29).

B Hiding from God

Adam and Eve hid from the Lord (Gen. 3:8, 10); Moses hid his face (Exod. 3:6); Daniel's companions ran to hide themselves (Dan. 10:7); hide in the dust from the fear of the Lord (Isa. 2:10); hide until wrath is past (Isa. 26:20); they hid in the caves and among the rocks (Rev. 6:15); can a man hide so that I cannot see him? (Jer. 23:24); there is no darkness where evildoers may hide (Job 34:22); they are not hidden from me (Jer. 16:17); though they hide from my sight at the bottom of the sea (Amos 9:3); though they hide on the summit of Carmel I will search them out (Amos 9:3); then I will not hide from your face (Job 13:20).

C Hiding from people

The spies hid themselves in the hill country (Josh. 2:16); Jonathan and Ahimaaz hid in a well (2 Sam. 17:18); five kings hid in a cave (Josh. 10:16-17); Israel hid in caves and pits (1 Sam. 13:6); the Benjaminites hid in the vineyards (Judg. 21:20); the king thought the Arameans were hiding (2 Kgs. 7:12); Jotham hid himself (Judg. 9:5); Saul hid among the baggage (1 Sam. 10:22); David hid from Saul (1 Sam. 19:2; 26:1; Ps. 54:t); David hid himself in the field (1 Sam. 20:5, 19, 24); Ahaziah was hiding in Samaria (2 Chr. 22:9); hide by the brook Cherith (1 Kgs. 17:3); go hide yourself (Jer. 36:19); Jesus hid himself (John 8:59; 12:36); when the wicked rise, men hide themselves (Prov. 28:28); you will go into an inner room to hide yourself (1 Kgs. 22:25; 2 Chr. 18:24); one from whom men hide their face (Isa. 53:3); Elizabeth hid herself for five months (Luke 1:24).

D Not hiding oneself

I uncovered his hiding places so he cannot conceal himself (Jer. 49:10); he could not be hid (Mark 7:24).

524 Informing

A Telling of God

The heavens are telling the glory of God (Ps. 19:1); I will tell of your name to my brethren (Ps. 22:22); Moses told Aaron all the words with which the Lord had sent him (Exod. 4:28); Aaron told the elders all that the Lord had said to Moses (Exod. 4:30); Moses told Jethro all that the Lord had done for them (Exod. 18:8); Samuel told Eli all that God said (1 Sam. 3:18); I told the exiles all that the Lord had shown me (Ezek. 11:25); he described how the Lord had brought him out of prison (Acts 12:17); they reported all that God had done with them (Acts 15:4).

B Telling of Jesus

Go and tell John what you hear and see (Matt. 11:4; Luke 7:22); Anna spoke of Jesus to all who were looking for the redemption of Jerusalem (Luke 2:38); news about Jesus spread through all the surrounding country (Luke 4:14, 37); the news about him went abroad all the more (Luke 5:15); this report about him went throughout Judea (Luke 7:17); the herdsmen told what had happened to the demoniacs and pigs (Matt. 8:33; Mark 5:14-16; Luke 8:34-6); he told how much Jesus had done for him (Luke 8:39); the man told the Jews that it was Jesus who had healed him (John 5:15); some went to the Pharisees and told them what Jesus had done (John 11:46); go tell his disciples and Peter (Mark 16:7); tell his disciples that he has risen (Matt. 28:7); Mary Magdalene told those who had been with him (Mark 16:10); the women reported these things to the disciples (Luke 24:9-10); they ran to tell his disciples (Matt. 28:8); tell my brethren to go to Galilee, there they will see me (Matt. 28:10).

C Telling of people

C1 Telling what people did

Potiphar's wife told him what Joseph had done (Gen. 39:17-18, 19); all Ruth did was told to Boaz (Ruth 2:11); they told David what Rizpah had done (2 Sam. 21:11); they told the old prophet what the man of God had done (1 Kgs. 13:11); Abiathar told David that Saul had killed the priests (1 Sam. 22:21); Ahab told Jezebel what

Elijah had done (1 Kgs. 19:1); Gehazi told the king all that Elisha had done (2 Kgs. 8:4-5); the apostles told Jesus all they had done and taught (Mark 6:30; Luke 9:10); what she has done will be told in memory of her (Matt. 26:13; Mark 14:9).

C2 Telling what people said

Rebekah was told what Esau said (Gen. 27:42); tell me what Samuel said to you (1 Sam. 10:15); Saul's servants told him what David said (1 Sam. 18:24); Moses reported the words of the people to the Lord (Exod. 19:9); Naaman told his master what the girl said (2 Kgs. 5:4); they told Mordecai what Esther had said (Esther 4:12).

C3 Telling of people's situations

Who told you that you were naked? (Gen. 3:11); Ham told his two brothers of their father's nakedness (Gen. 9:22); Judah was told Tamar was pregnant (Gen. 38:24); afraid to tell David the child was dead (2 Sam. 12:18); Chloe's people have reported that there is quarrelling among you (1 Cor. 1:11); Epaphras has made known to us your love in the Spirit (Col. 1:8); Tychicus will tell you all about my affairs (Col. 4:7); they will tell you about the situation here (Col. 4:9).

D Telling of happenings

A fugitive told Abraham about Lot's capture (Gen. 14:13); Joab sent a report to David about the war (2 Sam. 11:18); the guards reported to the chief priests what had happened (Matt. 28:11); Abiathar told David that Saul killed the priests (1 Sam. 22:21); when Jesus heard that John had been arrested (Matt. 4:12).

E Giving information

Cause her to know her abominations (Ezek. 22:2); I have told you in advance (Matt. 24:25); I have told you everything beforehand (Mark 13:23); you will be told what to do (Acts 9:6; 22:10); Samson told his wife and she told the men (Judg. 14:17); the lepers told the people in the city (2 Kgs. 7:9-10); Jonathan told David all he found out (1 Sam. 19:3, 7; 20:12-13); whatever you hear, tell to the priests (2 Sam. 15:35); the Jews who lived near told us ten times (Neh. 4:12); Mordecai gave information about the plot (Esther 2:22).

525 Concealment

HIDING ONESELF, see 523.

A Hidden from God

I will be hidden from your face (Gen. 4:14); they called on mountains and rocks to hide them (Rev. 6:16); perhaps you will be hidden on the day of the Lord's anger (Zeph. 2:3); my way is hidden from the Lord (Isa. 40:27); no creature is hidden from his sight (Heb. 4:13).

B Hidden people

B1 People hiding people

Do not hide one who entices you from the Lord (Deut. 13:8); Moses' mother hid him for three months (Exod. 2:2; Heb. 11:23); she has hidden her son (2 Kgs. 6:29); Joash was hidden for six years (2 Kgs. 11:2-3; 2 Chr. 22:11-12); Rahab hid the spies (Josh. 2:4, 6; 6:17, 25); a woman covered the mouth of the well containing Jonathan and Ahimaaz (2 Sam. 17:19); Obadiah hid a hundred prophets (1 Kgs. 18:4, 13); hide the outcasts! (Isa. 16:3-4); hide the wicked in the dust (Job 40:13).

B2 God hiding people

In trouble he will hide me in his tent (Ps. 27:5); you hide them in the secret place of your presence (Ps. 31:20); hide me in the shadow of your wings (Ps. 17:8); hide me from the scheming of evildoers (Ps. 64:2); oh, that you would hide me in Sheol! (Job 14:13); in his quiver he hid me (Isa. 49:2); God hid Jeremiah and Baruch (Jer. 36:26); your life is hid with Christ in God (Col. 3:3).

C Hidden things

Jacob buried the earrings (Gen. 35:4); Achan hid the things in his tent (Josh. 7:21-2); the lepers hid valuables (2 Kgs. 7:8); he hid his talent in the ground (Matt. 25:18, 25); here is your mina which I kept put away in a face-cloth (Luke 19:20); hide the waistcloth in a crevice of rock (Jer. 13:4); hide stones in the mortar of Pharaoh's palace in Tahpanhes (Jer. 43:9); yeast which a woman hid in three measures of meal (Matt. 13:33; Luke 13:21); the kingdom of heaven is like treasure which a man found and covered up (Matt. 13:44); nothing is hidden which will not be known (Matt. 10:26; Luke 12:2); nothing is concealed which will not be revealed (Mark 4:22; Luke 8:17); to him who overcomes I will give some of the hidden manna (Rev. 2:17); the proud have hidden a trap for me (Ps. 140:5); their foot has been caught in the net they hid (Ps. 9:15).

D Hiding information

D1 God's things concealed

Shall I hide from Abraham what I am going to do? (Gen. 18:17); the Lord has hidden it from me (2 Kgs. 4:27); it is the glory of God to conceal a matter (Prov. 25:2); you hid these things from the wise and revealed them to babes (Matt. 11:25; Luke 10:21); the mystery hidden for ages in God (Eph. 3:9); I will utter things hidden since the foundation of the world (Matt. 13:35); it was concealed from them so that they should not perceive it (Luke 9:45); this saying was hidden from them (Luke 18:34); the mystery was not made known to previous generations (Eph. 3:5); do not hide from me what God said (1 Sam. 3:17); if our gospel is veiled, it is veiled to those who are perishing (2 Cor. 4:3); the things that make for peace are hidden from you (Luke 19:42).

D2 Christ concealing things

Jesus would not let the demons say who he was (Mark 1:34; 3:12; Luke 4:41); see that you tell no one (Matt. 8:4); he charged the leper not to tell anyone (Mark 1:44; Luke 5:14); also the blind men (Matt. 9:30); he gave strict orders that no one should know of this (Mark 5:43); he told them to tell no one what had happened (Luke 8:56); Jesus warned them not to make him known (Matt. 12:16); he charged them to tell no one (Mark 7:36); to say no one to say he was the Christ (Matt. 16:20; Mark 8:30; Luke 9:21); not to tell anyone about the transfiguration (Matt. 17:9; Mark 9:9; Luke 9:36); Jesus did not want anyone to know he was in a house (Mark 7:24); he would not have anyone know he was in Galilee (Mark 9:30); neither will I tell you by what authority I do these things (Matt. 21:27; Mark 11:33; Luke 20:8).

D3 Hiding sins

He who conceals his transgressions will not prosper (Prov. 28:13); if I have hidden my transgressions like Adam (Job 31:33); he who conceals hatred has lying lips (Prov. 10:18); clear me from hidden faults (Ps. 19:12); do not hide from me what you have done (Josh. 7:19); their iniquity is not concealed from my eyes (Jer. 16:17); woe to those who hide their plans from the Lord (Isa. 29:15).

D4 Not telling

D4a Do not tell

A prudent man conceals his knowledge (Prov. 12:23); he who is trustworthy keeps a secret (Prov. 11:13); our life for yours if you do not tell (Josh. 2:14); let it not be known that a woman came here (Ruth 3:14); tell it not in Gath (2 Sam. 1:20; Mic. 1:10); do not tell anyone (Acts 23:22); do not reveal another's secret (Prov. 25:9).

D4b Those who did not tell

For fear of the Pharisees they did not confess their faith in Christ (John 12:42); Samson did not tell his parents

about the lion (Judg. 14:6-16); Samuel was afraid to tell Eli (1 Sam. 3:15); Saul did not tell his uncle about the kingship (1 Sam. 10:16); we are keeping quiet on a day of good news (2 Kgs. 7:9); no one tells me when my son makes a covenant (1 Sam. 22:8); Jacob did not tell Laban he was fleeing (Gen. 31:20); Esther did not make her people known (Esther 2:10, 20); the women said nothing to anyone (Mark 16:8).

SECRET, see 530.

KEEP SILENT, see 582.

526 Disclosure

A Disclosure in general

The secret things belong to the Lord but the things revealed belong to us (Deut. 29:29); I will utter what has been hidden from the foundation of the world (Matt. 13:35); nothing is concealed which will not be revealed (Matt. 10:26; Mark 4:22; Luke 8:17; 12:2); what you have whispered in inner rooms will be proclaimed on housetops (Luke 12:3); a bird will make the matter known (Eccles. 10:20); the Lord will bring to light the things hidden in darkness (1 Cor. 4:5); man brings what is hidden into the light (Job 28:11); what I tell you in the dark, speak in the light (Matt. 10:27); nothing is secret except to come to light (Mark 4:22); a city on a hill cannot be hid (Matt. 5:14); do not seal up the words of this book (Rev. 22:10); a light of revelation to the Gentiles (Luke 2:32); no one acts in secret if he seeks to be known openly (John 7:4).

B Revelation of God

B1 God revealed

God has shown to man what can be known about God (Rom. 1:19); the glory of the Lord will be revealed (Isa. 40:5); the Lord of hosts has revealed himself in my ears (Isa. 22:14); to whom has the arm of the Lord been revealed? (Isa. 53:1; John 12:38); you have begun to show me your goodness (Deut. 3:24); the Lord revealed himself to Samuel (1 Sam. 3:21); I made myself known to them by bringing them out of the land of Egypt (Ezek. 20:9); I will magnify myself, sanctify myself and make myself known (Ezek. 38:23); show us the Father and we will be satisfied (John 14:8-9); God will make himself known to the Egyptians (Isa. 19:21); no one knows the Father except those to whom the Son reveals him (Matt. 11:27; Luke 10:22); everything I heard from my Father I have made known (John 15:15); I manifested your name to them (John 17:6); I made known your name to them and I will make it known (John 17:26); the only begotten God has made the Father known (John 1:18).

B2 God's things revealed

The Lord has revealed his salvation (Ps. 98:2); God made known his ways to Moses (Ps. 103:7); the wrath of God is revealed from heaven (Rom. 1:18); I will make known my holy name in the midst of Israel (Ezek. 39:7); in the midst of the years make your work known (Hab. 3:2); at the proper time he manifested his word (Titus 1:3); the Father shows the Son all that he is doing (John 5:20); I declare to the world what I have heard from him (John 8:26); you have made known to me the ways of life (Acts 2:28); the Lord has made these things known from of old (Acts 15:18); the day when God's righteous judgement will be revealed (Rom. 2:5); God does nothing without revealing it to the prophets (Amos 3:7).

B3 God revealing mysteries

There is a God who reveals mysteries (Dan. 2:28); your God is a revealer of mysteries (Dan. 2:47); God reveals mysteries out of darkness (Dan. 12:22); God reveals hidden things (Dan. 2:22); I will show you great and unknown things (Jer. 33:3); he who reveals mysteries has made known to you what will take place (Dan. 2:29); to make known the mystery of the gospel (Eph. 6:19); he made known the mystery of his will (Eph. 1:9); he made known among the Gentiles the riches of this mystery (Col. 1:27); it has been given to you to know the mysteries of the kingdom (Matt. 13:11; Mark 4:11; Luke 8:10); the mystery hid for ages but now made known to the saints (Col. 1:26); the mystery made known to apostles and prophets by the Spirit (Eph. 3:5); the mystery now made known (Rom. 16:25-6); the mystery was made known to me by revelation (Eph. 3:3).

B4 God revealed through the gospel
When Christ comes he will show us all things (John 4:25); how do I benefit you unless I bring revelation, knowledge, prophecy or teaching? (1 Cor. 14:6); when you come together, each one has a revelation etc. (1 Cor. 14:26); I will go on to visions and revelations of the Lord (2 Cor. 12:1); because of the abundance of revelations (2 Cor. 12:7); that the manifold wisdom of God might be made known through the church (Eph. 3:10); the stewardship given me to make the word of God fully known (Col. 1:25); grace now revealed through the appearing of our Saviour (2 Tim. 1:10); a partaker of the glory to be revealed (1 Pet. 5:1); the revelation of Jesus Christ which God gave him (Rev. 1:1); the mystery was made known to me by revelation (Eph. 3:3); in the gospel the righteousness of God is revealed (Rom. 1:17); you have revealed these things to babes (Matt. 11:25; Luke 10:21); my Father revealed it to you (Matt. 16:17); God has revealed them to us (1 Cor. 2:10); that God may give you a spirit of wisdom and revelation (Eph. 1:17); I went up by revelation (Gal. 2:2).

B5 God's deeds revealed
Make known God's deeds among the peoples (1 Chr. 16:8; Ps. 105:1; Isa. 12:4, 5); tell among the people his deeds (Ps. 9:11); they will speak of your deeds (Ps. 145:6); I will tell of the deeds of the Lord (Ps. 118:17); I will make known your faithfulness to all generations (Ps. 89:1); this was that the works of God might be displayed in him (John 9:3); they reported all that God had done (Acts 14:27); your righteous deeds have been revealed (Rev. 15:4).

C Revelation of Christ
C1 Making Christ known
Christ was revealed in these last times (1 Pet. 1:20); for this reason I came baptising, that he might be manifested to Israel (John 1:31); you are going to disclose yourself to us, and not to the world? (John 14:22); show yourself to the world (John 7:4); on the day when the Son of man is revealed (Luke 17:30); I will love him and will manifest myself to him (John 14:21); Jesus revealed himself again to his disciples (John 21:1); that you may rejoice when his glory is revealed (1 Pet. 4:13); God revealed his Son in me (Gal. 1:15-16); the Spirit will take what is mine and declare it to you (John 16:14-15); revelation of Jesus Christ (Gal. 1:12; 1 Pet. 1:13); at the revelation of Jesus Christ (1 Pet. 1:7); you wait for the revealing of our Lord Jesus Christ (1 Cor. 1:7); when Christ is revealed, you will be revealed with him (Col. 3:4).

C2 Acknowledging Christ
Every tongue will confess that Jesus is Lord (Phil. 2:11); if you confess with your mouth that Jesus is Lord (Rom. 10:9-10); everyone who acknowledges me before men, I will acknowledge before my Father (Matt. 10:32; Luke 12:8); announce to your family what the Lord has done for you (Mark 5:19); he who confesses the Son has the Father also (1 John 2:23); every spirit which confesses that Jesus Christ has come in the flesh (1 John

4:2); whoever confesses that Jesus is the Son of God (1 John 4:15).

D People revealed
Joseph made himself known to his brethren (Gen. 45:1; Acts 7:13); bring out the men who came to you (Josh. 2:3); I will show you the man you seek (Judg. 4:22); do not make yourself known to the man until he has finished eating and drinking (Ruth 3:3); reveal yourself to Ahab (1 Kgs. 18:1); I will show myself to Ahab today (1 Kgs. 18:15); Jehoiada showed them the king's son (2 Kgs. 11:4); the man of lawlessness will be revealed (2 Thess. 2:3-8); the creation longs for the revealing of the sons of God (Rom. 8:19); when Christ is revealed, you will be revealed with him (Col. 3:4).

E Things revealed
God had revealed Saul's coming to Samuel (1 Sam. 9:15); God revealed to Simeon that he would see the Christ (Luke 2:26); many came disclosing their practices (Acts 19:18); Paul's nephew told him of the ambush (Acts 23:16); each man's work will be manifest, for the day will disclose it (1 Cor. 3:13); Tychicus will make everything known to you (Eph. 6:21); if you think differently, God will reveal this to you (Phil. 3:15); my death is near, as our Lord Jesus Christ showed me (2 Pet. 1:14); Hezekiah showed the Babylonians all he had (2 Kgs. 20:13; Isa. 39:2); the devil showed him all the kingdoms of the world (Luke 4:5); the thoughts of many hearts will be revealed (Luke 2:35).

F Sin revealed
F1 Sin made known
Let the heavens reveal his iniquity (Job 20:27); my sins are not hidden from you (Ps. 69:5); make known to Jerusalem her abominations (Ezek. 16:2); declare to them their abominations (Ezek. 23:36); I have power to make known to Israel his sin (Mic. 3:8); take no share in the unfruitful deeds of darkness but rather expose them (Eph. 5:11); elders who sin are to be rebuked in the presence of all (1 Tim. 5:20); the secrets of his heart are disclosed (1 Cor. 14:25); your prophets have not exposed your iniquity (Lam. 2:14).

F2 Sin confessed
The guilty person must confess his sin (Lev. 5:5; Num. 5:7); Achan had to confess his sin (Josh. 7:19-21); tell me what you have done (1 Sam. 14:43); I prayed and confessed (Dan. 9:4); I will confess my transgressions (Ps. 32:5); I confess my iniquity (Ps. 38:18); he who confesses will find mercy (Prov. 28:13); they confessed and worshipped for one quarter of the day (Neh. 9:3); confessing their sins, they were baptised by John (Matt. 3:6; Mark 1:5); the Ephesians confessed their deeds (Acts 19:18); confess your sins to each other (Jas. 5:16); if we confess our sins he will forgive us (1 John 1:9).

527 Disguising
A Disguise
The adulterer disguises his face (Job 24:15); those who disguised themselves: Jacob (Gen. 27:15-23); Tamar (Gen. 38:14); Joseph (Gen. 42:7); Saul (1 Sam. 28:8); Jeroboam's wife (1 Kgs. 14:2); a prophet (1 Kgs. 20:38); the king of Israel in battle (1 Kgs. 22:30; 2 Chr. 18:29); king Josiah (2 Chr. 35:22); wolves in sheep's clothing (Matt. 7:15); false apostles as apostles of Christ (2 Cor. 11:13); Satan as an angel of light (2 Cor. 11:14); Satan's servants as servants of righteousness (2 Cor. 11:15).

B Ambush
Let us ambush the innocent (Prov. 1:11); the Lord is to me like a bear lying in wait (Lam. 3:10); those who eat your bread set an ambush for you (Obad. 7); they set an ambush behind Ai (Josh. 8:2-9, 12-21); the men of Shechem set an ambush against Abimelech (Judg. 9:25); Abimelech set an ambush for the men of

Shechem (Judg. 9:32-5, 43); Israel set an ambush against Gibeah (Judg. 20:29-38); Saul set an ambush against Amalek (1 Sam. 15:5); Jeroboam had set an ambush behind Judah (2 Chr. 13:13); prepare ambushes against Babylon (Jer. 51:12); they lay in wait for Samson all night (Judg. 16:2); the Jews wanted to set an ambush for Paul (Acts 23:21; 25:3); the son of Paul's sister heard of their ambush (Acts 23:16); they ambush their own lives (Prov. 1:18).

528 Publication

A Preachers / evangelists

The words of the Preacher (Eccles. 1:1); Noah, a preacher of righteousness (2 Pet. 2:5); do the work of an evangelist (2 Tim. 4:5); he gave some as evangelists (Eph. 4:11); Philip the evangelist (Acts 21:8); how can they hear without a preacher? (Rom. 10:14-15); elders who work hard at preaching and teaching (1 Tim. 5:17); I was appointed a preacher and apostle and teacher (2 Tim. 1:11); I was entrusted with the preaching of his word (Titus 1:3).

B Preaching

B1 Preach!

Declare this in Judah (Jer. 5:20); proclaim the message I tell you (Jonah 3:2); proclaim good news of salvation (1 Chr. 16:23); preach as you go (Matt. 10:7); preach the word (2 Tim. 4:2); proclaim his salvation (Ps. 96:2); feet shod with the preparation of the gospel of peace (Eph. 6:15); the apostles were sent out to preach (Mark 3:14; Luke 9:2); go and preach the kingdom of God (Luke 9:60); preach the gospel to all creation (Mark 16:15); repentance and forgiveness should be preached to all nations (Luke 24:47); this gospel must be preached to all nations (Matt. 24:14; Mark 13:10); he commanded us to preach to the people (Acts 10:42); Christ did not send me to baptise but to preach the gospel (1 Cor. 1:17); woe is me if I do not preach the gospel (1 Cor. 9:16); God called us to preach the gospel to them (Acts 16:10); that you may declare the excellence of him who called you out of darkness (1 Pet. 2:9).

B2 Christ preaching

Jesus began to preach (Matt. 4:17); Jesus preached the good news of the kingdom in Galilee (Matt. 4:23); Jesus preached the good news of God (Mark 1:14); in all the towns (Matt. 9:35; Luke 8:1); I must preach the good news in other towns also (Mark 1:38; Luke 4:43); the kingdom of God is preached (Luke 16:16); Jesus was preaching the gospel in the temple (Luke 20:1); Christ preached to the spirits in prison (1 Pet. 3:19); this salvation was declared at first by the Lord (Heb. 2:3).

B3 Many preaching

They preached that men should repent (Mark 6:12); they preached the gospel and healed (Luke 9:6); they will declare my glory among the nations (Isa. 66:19); to preach among the Gentiles the riches of Christ (Eph. 3:8); to preach Christ among the Gentiles (Gal. 1:16); that by me the message be proclaimed to all the Gentiles (2 Tim. 4:17); my ambition has been to preach the gospel where Christ was unknown (Rom. 15:20); so that we may preach the gospel in regions beyond you (2 Cor. 10:16); the Lord has anointed me to preach good news to the poor (Isa. 61:1; Luke 4:18); good news is preached to the poor (Matt. 11:5; Luke 7:22); the brother who is famous among all the churches for preaching the gospel (2 Cor. 8:18); we had courage in our God to declare the gospel (1 Thess. 2:2); they went out and preached everywhere (Mark 16:20); those scattered preached the message (Acts 8:4); Paul preached the kingdom of God (Acts 28:31); many women proclaim the good news (Ps. 68:11); he who

persecuted us is now preaching the faith (Gal. 1:23); I did not shrink from proclaiming the whole purpose of God (Acts 20:27); I have fully preached the gospel of Christ (Rom. 15:19).

B4 The gospel preached

They preached the gospel in many villages of the Samaritans (Acts 8:25); they continued to preach the gospel (Acts 14:7); we preach the gospel that you should turn from these vain things (Acts 14:15); the word of faith which we preach (Rom. 10:8); by the foolishness of what is preached God saves those who believe (1 Cor. 1:21); that when I preach the gospel I may make it free of charge (1 Cor. 9:18); the gospel which I preached to you (1 Cor. 15:1); what has happened to me has caused the gospel to progress (Phil. 1:12); thankful for your partnership in the gospel (Phil. 1:5); we were ready to share not only the gospel but also our own selves (1 Thess. 2:8); we preached to you the gospel of God (1 Thess. 2:9); those who preached the gospel to you (1 Pet. 1:12); the scripture preached the gospel beforehand to Abraham (Gal. 3:8); day to day pours forth speech (Ps. 19:2); the gospel was proclaimed in all creation (Col. 1:23); the word of the Lord has sounded forth from you (1 Thess. 1:8); wherever the gospel is preached, what she has done will be told (Matt. 26:13; Mark 14:9).

B5 Preaching Christ

Christ is proclaimed, and in that I rejoice (Phil. 1:18); him we proclaim (Col. 1:28); we do not preach ourselves but Christ as Lord (2 Cor. 4:5); they never stopped preaching Jesus as the Christ (Acts 5:42); Philip preached Jesus to him (Acts 8:35); he was preached among the nations (1 Tim. 3:16); we proclaim the mystery of Christ (Col. 4:3); in the Lord's supper you proclaim the Lord's death (1 Cor. 11:26); they spoke to Greeks, preaching the Lord Jesus (Acts 11:20); faith comes from hearing and hearing by the preaching of Christ (Rom. 10:17); according to the preaching of Jesus Christ (Rom. 16:25); we preach Christ crucified (1 Cor. 1:23); if Christ is preached as raised from the dead (1 Cor. 15:12); the Son of God, Christ Jesus, whom we preached among you (2 Cor. 1:19); we proclaim to you the eternal life which was with the Father (1 John 1:2); some preach Christ from envy and strife (Phil. 1:15-17); if someone preaches another Jesus (2 Cor. 11:4).

B6 Other preaching

If a windy liar says, 'I will preach wine and strong drink' (Mic. 2:11); 'Do not preach' – so they preach (Mic. 2:6); if I preach circumcision, why am I still persecuted? (Gal. 5:11); Nineveh repented at the preaching of Jonah (Matt. 12:41); the scribes and Pharisees preach but do not practise (Matt. 23:3); John the Baptist preached (Matt. 3:1; Mark 1:4); John preached a baptism of repentance (Luke 3:3); John preached good news to the people (Luke 3:18).

C Spreading stories

When my enemy goes out he tells it abroad (Ps. 41:6); he who goes about as a talebearer reveals secrets (Prov. 11:13; 20:19); going about as a talebearer (Jer. 6:28); he who spreads slander is a fool (Prov. 10:18); the more he told them not to tell anyone, the more they proclaimed it (Mark 7:36); this story spread among the Jews (Matt. 28:15).

529 News

SPOKEN WORD, see 579.

A God's word

THE BIBLE, see 975.

A1 About the word of God

A1a The nature of the word of God

The word of our God stands for ever (Isa. 40:8); the word of the Lord remains for ever (1 Pet. 1:25); heaven and earth will pass away, but my words will not (Matt. 24:35; Luke 21:33); the word of the Lord is tested (2 Sam. 22:31; Ps. 18:30); the word of the Lord is upright (Ps. 33:4); the words of the Lord are pure (Ps. 12:6); is not my word like a hammer? (Jer. 23:29); is not my word like fire? (Jer. 23:29); in praise of the word of God (Ps. 19:7-11; 119:1-176); the sword of the Spirit, which is the word of God (Eph. 6:17); the word of God is living and active (Heb. 4:12); in the beginning was the Word (John 1:1); the Word of life (1 John 1:1); his name is the Word of God (Rev. 19:13).

A1b The effect of the word of God

My word will accomplish what I purpose (Isa. 55:11); the worlds were made by the word of God (Ps. 33:6; Heb. 11:3); the heavens were made by the word of God (2 Pet. 3:5); he spoke and it was done (Ps. 33:9); he upholds all things by the word of his power (Heb. 1:3); I have hewn them by the prophets, slain them with my words (Hos. 6:5).

A2 God's word through people

The word of the Lord came through Jehu (1 Kgs. 16:1, 7); the word of the Lord was with Elisha (2 Kgs. 3:12); the word of the Lord came to Solomon (1 Kgs. 6:11); when you hear a word from my mouth you must give them warning (Ezek. 33:7); this took place to fulfil what the Lord had spoken by the prophet (Matt. 1:22; 2:15); I have given them your word (John 17:14); I pray for all who will believe through their word (John 17:20); it is not desirable that we should neglect the word of God to serve tables (Acts 6:2); we will devote ourselves to prayer and the ministry of the word (Acts 6:4); they spoke the word of the Lord to him and all in his house (Acts 16:32).

A3 Receiving God's word

Let the word of Christ dwell in you richly (Col. 3:16); if you remain in my word you are truly my disciples (John 8:31); if you abide in me and my words abide in you, ask what you will (John 15:7); receive the implanted word which can save your souls (Jas. 1:21); born again of imperishable seed, the living and abiding word of God (1 Pet. 1:23); he gave us birth by the word of truth (Jas. 1:18); you received God's message not as the word of men but as the word of God (1 Thess. 2:13); the word of his grace is able to build you up (Acts 20:32); a workman correctly handling the word of truth (2 Tim. 2:15); do not my words do good to him who walks uprightly? (Mic. 2:7); you are clean through the word I have spoken to you (John 15:3);
we refuse to tamper with God's word (2 Cor. 4:2); holding fast the word of life (Phil. 2:16); you are strong and the word of God abides in you (1 John 2:14); those slain because of the word of God (Rev. 6:9); man lives by every word from the mouth of God (Deut. 8:3; Matt. 4:4); your words were found and I ate them (Jer. 15:16); whoever is ashamed of me and my words (Luke 9:26); famine of hearing the words of the Lord (Amos 8:11-12).

A4 Progress of God's word

The seed is the word of God (Luke 8:11); the sower sows the word (Mark 4:14); grant your servants to speak your word with all boldness (Acts 4:29-31); the word of God had to be spoken to you first (Acts 13:46); the word of God continued to grow (Acts 12:24); that the word of the Lord may run on (2 Thess. 3:1); the word of the Lord spread (Acts 13:49); the word of the Lord was growing (Acts 19:20); did not my words which I commanded my servants the prophets

overtake your fathers? (Zech. 1:6); it is not as though the word of God has failed (Rom. 9:6).

A5 The gospel

A5a Characteristics of the gospel

I bring you good news of great joy (Luke 2:10); the word of truth, the gospel (Col. 1:5); I am not ashamed of the gospel for it is the power of God (Rom. 1:16); the gospel promised beforehand through the prophets (Rom. 1:1-2); the terms of the gospel (1 Cor. 15:1-7); the gospel I preached is not of man (Gal. 1:11); I set before them the gospel I preach (Gal. 2:2); the glorious gospel of the blessed God (1 Tim. 1:11); the message of reconciliation (2 Cor. 5:19); the gospel of the grace of God (Acts 20:24); the light of the gospel of the glory of Christ (2 Cor. 4:4); the word of truth, the gospel of your salvation (Eph. 1:13); Christ brought life and immortality to light through the gospel (2 Tim. 1:10); punishment for those who do not obey the gospel (2 Thess. 1:8); what will be the end of those who do not obey the gospel? (1 Pet. 4:17).

A5b The gospel preached

The feet of him who brings good news (Isa. 52:7; Nahum 1:15; Rom. 10:15); John preached good news to the people (Luke 3:18); preaching the good news of the kingdom (Matt. 4:23; 9:35); Jesus preached the gospel of God (Mark 1:14); I was sent to bring you this good news (Luke 1:19); the Lord has anointed me to preach good news to the poor (Luke 4:18); good news came to us as to them (Heb. 4:2); the gospel of the kingdom of God is preached (Luke 16:16); those who proclaim the gospel should get their living by the gospel (1 Cor. 9:14); he has committed to us the message of reconciliation (2 Cor. 5:19); we speak as men approved by God to be entrusted with the gospel (1 Thess. 2:4); Paul was entrusted with the gospel to the uncircumcised (Gal. 2:7); Peter was entrusted with the gospel to the circumcised (Gal. 2:7); of this gospel I was made a minister [servant] (Eph. 3:7).

A5c The purity of the gospel

That the truth of the gospel might be preserved for you (Gal. 2:5); I saw they were not being straightforward about the truth of the gospel (Gal. 2:14); let your conduct be worthy of the gospel of Christ (Phil. 1:27); with one mind striving side by side for the faith of the gospel (Phil. 1:27); I am here for the defence of the gospel (Phil. 1:16); not shifting from the hope of the gospel (Col. 1:23); a different gospel from the one you accepted (2 Cor. 11:4); you are turning to a different gospel (Gal. 1:6); some want to distort the gospel of Christ (Gal. 1:7); though we or an angel should preach a contrary gospel, let him be accursed (Gal. 1:8, 9).

B Other news

B1 Good news

Good news makes the bones fat (Prov. 15:30); good news is like cold water to the thirsty (Prov. 25:25); Timothy has brought us good news of your faith and love (1 Thess. 3:6); he thought Saul's death was good news (2 Sam. 4:10); the Philistines sent the good news to their idols and people (1 Sam. 31:9; 1 Chr. 10:9); this is a day of good news (2 Kgs. 7:9); a man running alone brings good news (2 Sam. 18:25-7, 26); the Lord has anointed me to bring good news to the afflicted (Isa. 61:1).

B2 Bad news

They brought an evil report (Num. 13:32); lest the evil report about you have no end (Prov. 25:10); news from the east and the north will alarm him (Dan. 11:44).

B3 Rumour

David was told that all his sons were dead (2 Sam. 13:30); he will hear a rumour and return home (2 Kgs. 19:7; Isa. 37:7); rumour comes on rumour (Ezek. 7:26);

it is reported (Neh. 6:6); when you hear rumours of wars (Matt. 24:6; Mark 13:7); the rumour spread that John would not die (John 21:23).

C Messengers
ANGELS, see 968.

C1 About messengers
A faithful messenger is like the cold of snow at harvest time (Prov. 25:13); a wicked messenger causes trouble (Prov. 13:17); he cuts off his own feet who sends a message by a fool (Prov. 26:6); the voice of your messengers will be heard no more (Nahum 2:13).

C2 Messengers of the Lord
The Lord sent to Judah by his messengers (2 Chr. 36:15-16); Malachi – 'my messenger' (Mal. 1:1); I will send my messenger, the messenger of the covenant (Mal. 3:1); I send my messenger before you (Matt. 11:10; Mark 1:2; Luke 7:27); a priest is a messenger of the Lord (Mal. 2:7); God makes winds his messengers (Ps. 104:4).

C3 Other messengers
Gideon sent messengers to summon others to war (Judg. 6:24, 35); Israel sent men throughout Benjamin (Judg. 20:12); Jabesh-gilead sent messengers throughout Israel (1 Sam. 11:3-4); send news by Ahimaaz and Jonathan (2 Sam. 15:36); Hushai sent news by Ahimaaz and Jonathan (2 Sam. 17:15-21); the messenger with news about Absalom (2 Sam. 18:20-3); a thorn in the flesh, a messenger of Satan (2 Cor. 12:7); Epaphroditus, your messenger (Phil. 2:25).

530 Secret

A Secrets
A1 God and secrets
The secret things belong to the Lord our God (Deut. 29:29); the secret of the Lord is with those who fear him (Ps. 25:14); your Father who sees in secret (Matt. 6:4, 6, 18); your Father who is in secret (Matt. 6:6, 18); keep the vision sealed up (Dan. 8:26); you have put our secret sins in the light of your countenance (Ps. 90:8); God will bring hidden things to judgement (Eccles. 12:14); God will judge the secrets of men through Christ Jesus (Rom. 2:16); no secret is hidden from you (Ezek. 28:3).

A2 Information in secret
A secret message for King Eglon (Judg. 3:19); Joab spoke with Abner privately (2 Sam. 3:27); the king questioned Jeremiah secretly (Jer. 37:17); Johanan spoke with Gedaliah secretly (Jer. 40:15); Herod called the magi secretly (Matt. 2:7); the gospel I preach I set before them privately (Gal. 2:2); do not reveal another's secret (Prov. 25:9).

A3 Acting in secret
It is disgraceful even to speak of the things they do in secret (Eph. 5:12); see what the elders of Israel are doing in the dark (Ezek. 8:12); bread eaten in secret is pleasant (Prov. 9:17); they spend the night in secret places (Isa. 65:4); threshing wheat in the wine press (Judg. 6:11); Joshua sent out two men secretly (Josh. 2:1); you did it in secret (2 Sam. 12:12); I was made in secret (Ps. 139:15); do not let your left hand know what your right hand is doing (Matt. 6:3); Jesus went up to the feast secretly (John 7:10); Joseph wanted to divorce Mary secretly (Matt. 1:19); so that your alms may be in secret (Matt. 6:4).

A4 Avoid secrecy
Nothing is secret except to come to light (Mark 4:22; Luke 8:17); no one acts in secret if he seeks to be known openly (John 7:4); I have said nothing in secret (John 18:20); would they now send us away secretly? (Acts 16:37); this has not been done in a corner (Acts 26:26);

we have renounced disgraceful, underhanded ways (2 Cor. 4:2).

B Mysteries
B1 Man's mysteries
Mystery: Babylon the Great (Rev. 17:5); the mystery of lawlessness is at work (2 Thess. 2:7); the secrets of his heart are disclosed (1 Cor. 14:25); I will tell you the mystery of the woman and the beast that carries her (Rev. 17:7).

B2 God and mysteries
The mystery of Christ (Eph. 3:4; Col. 4:3); God's mystery, which is Christ (Col. 2:2); the mystery of godliness (1 Tim. 3:16); the mystery was revealed to Daniel in a vision of the night (Dan. 2:19); no mystery is too difficult for you (Dan. 4:9); your God is a revealer of mysteries (Dan. 2:47); God reveals deep and mysterious things (Dan. 2:22); I want you to understand this mystery (Rom. 11:25); stewards of the mysteries of God (1 Cor. 4:1); if I understand all mysteries (1 Cor. 13:2); no one understands him who speaks in tongues, but he utters mysteries (1 Cor. 14:2); I tell you a mystery (1 Cor. 15:51); the mystery made known to apostles and prophets by the Spirit (Eph. 3:5); the mystery hidden for ages in God (Eph. 3:9); the mystery hidden for ages but now made known (Col. 1:26); it is a great mystery, but I speak of Christ and the church (Eph. 5:32); the riches of the glory of this mystery (Col. 1:27); to you it has been given to know the secrets of the kingdom (Matt. 13:11); the mystery was made known by revelation (Eph. 3:3); we speak God's wisdom in a mystery (1 Cor. 2:7); the mystery of God is completed (Rev. 10:7).

C Riddles
Samson's riddle (Judg. 14:12-18); I will expound my riddle with the harp (Ps. 49:4); propound a riddle (Ezek. 17:2); Daniel could explain riddles and solve problems (Dan. 5:12).

531 Communications
PUBLICATION, see 528.

532 Affirmation

A Oaths
A1 Swearing oaths
When a man swears an oath in this temple (1 Kgs. 8:31; 2 Chr. 6:22); an oath is final for confirmation (Heb. 6:16); putting a hand under the thigh and swearing (Gen. 24:2-3, 9); he swears to his own hurt and does not change (Ps. 15:4); an oath to the Lord between the two parties (Exod. 22:11).

A2 Swearing by . . .
Men swear by one greater than themselves (Heb. 6:16); you shall swear by the name of the Lord (Deut. 6:13; 10:20); if they swear by my name (Jer. 12:16); he who swears will swear by the God of truth (Isa. 65:16); those who bow down and swear to the Lord yet swear by Milcom (Zeph. 1:5); they taught my people to swear by Baal (Jer. 12:16); they have sworn by those who are not gods (Jer. 5:7); if one swears, whether by the temple, its gold, the altar or the sacrifice, it is binding (Matt. 23:16-22); the man in linen swore by him who lives for ever (Dan. 12:7); the angel swore by the Creator of all (Rev. 10:6).

A3 God swearing oaths
A3a God swearing to give them the land
God swore to give the land (Gen. 24:7; Exod. 6:8; Num. 11:12; Deut. 1:8; Josh. 1:6; Judg. 2:1; Neh. 9:15; Jer. 11:5; Ezek. 20:5-6); the land I swore to give them (Ezek. 20:28); the land I swore to give to your fathers (Ezek. 20:42); God swore to enlarge their territory (Deut. 19:8).

A3b God swearing to bless them

God swore to the patriarchs that he would multiply their descendants (Exod. 32:13); as he swore to Abraham, Isaac and Jacob that he would be your God (Deut. 29:13); God swore by himself to bless Abraham (Gen. 22:16-17; Heb. 6:13-14); the oath which he swore to Abraham (Luke 1:73); I swore that the waters of Noah should not again flood the earth (Isa. 54:9); I swore to them to bring them out of the land of Egypt (Deut. 7:8; Ezek. 20:6); I have sworn to David my servant (Ps. 89:3); God swore to make David king (2 Sam. 3:9); God swore to David that one of his descendants would reign (Ps. 132:11-12; Acts 2:30); the Lord has sworn, 'You are a priest for ever' (Ps. 110:4; Heb. 7:20-1); God showed the unchangeableness of his purpose by an oath (Heb. 6:17).

A3c God swearing harm

I swore in my anger they would not enter my rest (Ps. 95:11; Heb. 3:11); God swore that those men would not enter the land (Num. 14:21-2; Deut. 1:34-5); God swore to make them fall in the wilderness (Ps. 106:26); I have sworn that the iniquity of Eli's house will not be atoned for (1 Sam. 3:14).

A4 People swearing oaths

Swear that you will not kill me (Judg. 15:12; 1 Sam. 30:15); let Solomon swear not to kill me (1 Kgs. 1:51); the woman must swear with the oath of the curse (Num. 5:19-21); swear to me that you will not deal falsely (Gen. 21:23); Joseph made the Israelites swear an oath (Gen. 50:25; Exod. 13:19); Israel took an oath about those who did not come to fight (Judg. 21:5); did I not make you swear by the Lord not to go anywhere? (1 Kgs. 2:42); Ezra bound Israel with an oath (Ezra 10:5); the men of Israel had taken an oath (Judg. 21:1); Saul bound the people by oath not to eat (1 Sam. 14:24); Nehemiah made the people swear not to intermarry (Neh. 13:25); the Jews bound themselves by an oath to kill Paul (Acts 23:12-14, 21); Ahab made people swear Elijah was not with him (1 Kgs. 18:10); Abraham lifted up his hand to God that he would take nothing from the king of Sodom (Gen. 14:22); Israel swore to the Gibeonites (Josh. 9:15, 18-20); Herod promised his daughter with an oath (Matt. 14:7; Mark 6:23); Peter swore that he did not know Jesus (Matt. 26:72, 74; Mark 14:71).

A5 Not swearing oaths

Do not swear falsely (Lev. 19:12); do not swear by their gods (Josh. 23:7); do not swear at all, by anything (Matt. 5:34-6); do not swear at all, by heaven or earth or any other oath (Jas. 5:12); let your Yes be Yes and your No be No (Matt. 5:37; Jas. 5:12); do not enter Gilgal, do not go to Beth-aven, do not swear, 'As the Lord lives' (Hos. 4:15); former priests took office without an oath (Heb. 7:21).

B Vows

B1 Making vows

I will fulfil my vows (Ps. 22:25; 61:8; 66:13; 116:14, 18); a vow must be fulfilled (Num. 30:2; Deut. 23:23; Matt. 5:33); pay your vows to the Most High (Ps. 50:14); make your vows to the Lord and fulfil them (Ps. 76:11); perform your vows (Judg. 11:35-6); better not vow than vow and not repay (Deut. 23:21; Eccles. 5:4); do not delay in fulfilling a vow (Deut. 23:21; Eccles. 5:4); do not make vows rashly (Prov. 20:25); vows made by a dependant woman may be countermanded (Num. 30:3-16).

B2 People who made vows

Jacob made a vow to God at Bethel (Gen. 28:20; 31:13); Jephthah swore to sacrifice the first to greet him (Judg. 11:30-1, 35); Hannah vowed to give her son to the Lord (1 Sam. 1:11); Absalom had vowed to worship at Hebron (2 Sam. 15:7-8); David vowed to find a dwelling

for God (Ps. 132:2-5); Paul had his hair cut because of a vow (Acts 18:18); four men were under a vow (Acts 21:23).

B3 Not vowing

Not to vow is no sin (Deut. 23:22); better not vow than vow and not repay (Eccles. 5:5).

C Adjuring

If someone hears an adjuration (Lev. 5:1); he hears the adjuration but says nothing (Prov. 29:24); how often must I adjure you to speak only the truth? (1 Kgs. 22:16); I adjure you to tell us whether you are the Christ (Matt. 26:63); I adjure you to have this letter read (1 Thess. 5:27); I adjure you by Jesus whom Paul preaches (Acts 19:13).

533 Negation

A God denying

God cannot deny himself (2 Tim. 2:13); if we deny him, he will deny us (2 Tim. 2:12).

B Denying Christ

This very night you will deny me three times (Matt. 26:34-5; Mark 14:30-1, 72; Luke 22:34, 61; John 13:38); as he did (Matt. 26:70-5; Mark 14:68-71; Luke 22:57-61; John 18:17, 25-7); whoever denies me before men, I will deny before my Father (Matt. 10:33); whoever denies me before men, I will deny before the angels of God (Luke 12:9); if we deny him, he will deny us (2 Tim. 2:12); denying the Master who bought them (2 Pet. 2:1); they deny our only Master and Lord (Jude 4); they deny him by their deeds (Titus 1:16); you delivered him up and denied him in the presence of Pilate (Acts 3:13-14); this is the antichrist who denies the Father and the Son (1 John 2:22); no one who denies the Son has the Father (1 John 2:23); you have a little strength and have not denied my name (Rev. 3:8).

C Denying oneself

Whoever would come after me must deny himself (Matt. 16:24; Mark 8:34; Luke 9:23).

D Contradicting

You will certainly not die! (Gen. 3:4); God forbid! this will never happen to you! (Matt. 16:22); the Jews contradicted what Paul said (Acts 13:45); avoid the contradictions of so-called knowledge (1 Tim. 6:20); that he may be able to refute those who contradict the doctrine (Titus 1:9).

534 Teaching

A About teaching

Teach a righteous man and he will increase his learning (Prov. 9:9); when a disciple is fully taught he will be like his teacher (Luke 6:40); a slave will not be instructed by words alone (Prov. 29:19).

B Teaching and God

B1 Teaching God

Who has taught God? (Isa. 40:14); who has known the mind of the Lord so as to teach him? (1 Cor. 2:16); shall anyone teach God knowledge? (Job 21:22).

B2 God teaching

I will instruct you what to say (Exod. 4:12); whom will he teach knowledge? (Isa. 28:9); God teaches man knowledge (Ps. 94:10); I have taught you statutes and ordinances (Deut. 4:5); happy is the man whom you teach (Ps. 94:12); his God teaches him (Isa. 28:26); all your children will be taught by the Lord (Isa. 54:13); you have taught me from my youth (Ps. 71:17); you have taught me (Ps. 119:102); I do nothing of myself but speak as the Father taught me (John 8:28); he will teach us his ways (Isa. 2:3; Mic. 4:2); I will teach you in the way you should go (Ps. 32:8); teach me to do your will (Ps. 143:10); teach me your way, O Lord (Ps. 25:4-5; 27:11; 86:11); teach me the way I should go (Ps. 143:8);

teach us to number our days (Ps. 90:12); he trains my
hands for battle (2 Sam. 22:35; Ps. 18:34; 144:1); they
shall all be taught by God (John 6:45); you are taught
by God to love one another (1 Thess. 4:9).

B3 The Spirit teaching
You gave your Spirit to instruct them (Neh. 9:20); the
Holy Spirit will teach you all things (John 14:26); you
have no need for anyone to teach you because the
anointing teaches you (1 John 2:27).

B4 Christ teaching
Jesus taught in the temple (Matt. 21:23; 26:55; Mark
12:35; Luke 19:47; 20:1; 21:37; John 7:14, 28; 8:2, 20;) day
after day I was with you in the temple teaching (Mark
14:49); teaching in synagogues (Matt. 4:23; 9:35; 13:54;
Mark 1:21; 6:2; Luke 4:15-16, 31-3; 6:6; 13:10); I always
taught in synagogues and in the temple (John 18:20);
teaching in the towns and villages (Matt. 9:35; 11:1;
Mark 6:6; Luke 13:22); he taught his disciples (Matt.
5:2); teach us to pray (Luke 11:1); what Jesus began to
do and to teach (Acts 1:1); when Jesus had finished
instructing his 12 disciples (Matt. 11:1); they were
amazed at his teaching (Matt. 7:28; 22:33; Mark 1:22;
11:18; Luke 4:32); we know you teach the way of God in
truth (Matt. 22:16; Mark 12:14; Luke 20:21); Mary sat at
his feet and listened to his teaching (Luke 10:39); you
taught in our streets (Luke 13:26); teaching throughout
Judea, from Galilee as far as here (Luke 23:5); will he go
to the Dispersion among the Greeks and teach the
Greeks? (John 7:35).

B5 Scripture teaching
These things were written for our instruction (1 Cor.
10:11); all scripture is profitable for teaching (2 Tim.
3:16); his teachings which he gave us by his servants the
prophets (Dan. 9:10); everything written in the past
was written for our instruction (Rom. 15:4); all
scripture is profitable for training in righteousness
(2 Tim. 3:16).

B6 Teaching the way of God
Levi teaches God's ordinances to Jacob (Deut. 33:10);
let one of the priests teach them (2 Kgs. 17:27-8); priests
are to teach the difference between holy and profane
(Ezek. 44:23); the Levites taught all Israel (2 Chr. 35:3);
they will not teach each other, 'Know the Lord' (Jer.
31:34; Heb. 8:11); whoever practises and teaches will be
called great (Matt. 5:19); they were teaching the people
and proclaiming the resurrection (Acts 4:2); they
charged them not to speak or teach in the name of
Jesus (Acts 4:18); the men you put in prison are
standing in the temple teaching the people (Acts 5:25);
we ordered you not to teach in this name (Acts 5:28);
you have filled Jerusalem with your teaching (Acts
5:28); Apollos taught accurately the things concerning
Jesus (Acts 18:25); if you have been taught the truth
which is in Jesus (Eph. 4:21); we know you teach the
way of God in truth (Matt. 22:16; Mark 12:14; Luke
20:21); him we proclaim, warning and teaching every
man in all wisdom (Col. 1:28).

B7 Teaching in the church
The apostles taught the people (Acts 5:21); Barnabas
and Paul taught great numbers (Acts 11:26); Paul,
Barnabas and others taught the word (Acts 15:35); Paul
taught the word of God in Corinth for 18 months (Acts
18:11); I taught you in public and in from house to
house (Acts 20:20); as I teach everywhere in every
church (1 Cor. 4:17); I would rather speak five words
with my mind to instruct others (1 Cor. 14:19); teach
and admonish one another in all wisdom (Col. 3:16);
stand firm to the traditions you were taught, whether
by word of mouth or letter (2 Thess. 2:15); teach and
urge these things (1 Tim. 6:2); I was appointed a
preacher and apostle and teacher (2 Tim. 1:11); reprove,

rebuke, exhort with all longsuffering and teaching
(2 Tim. 4:2); older women are to teach what is good
(Titus 2:3-4); teach them to observe all I have
commanded you (Matt. 28:20); teach these things
(1 Tim. 4:11); teach all nations (Matt. 28:19); entrust
these things to faithful men who will be able to teach
others also (2 Tim. 2:2); if your gift is teaching, use it in
your teaching (Rom. 12:7); I do not permit a woman to
teach (1 Tim. 2:12); attend to teaching (1 Tim. 4:13); you
need teaching the elementary principles over again
(Heb. 5:12).

C Other teaching
The Preacher taught the people knowledge (Eccles.
12:9); the scribes and Pharisees sit in Moses' seat (Matt.
23:2); I will teach transgressors your ways (Ps. 51:13); if
you are sure you are a teacher of the immature (Rom.
2:20-1); teaching as doctrines the precepts of men
(Mark 7:7); bodily training is only a little value (1 Tim.
4:8).

D Doctrine
D1 Doctrine in general
Listen to my instruction (Ps. 78:1); pay attention to
your teaching (1 Tim. 4:16); they were astonished at his
teaching (Matt. 7:28; 22:33; Mark 1:22; 11:18; Luke 4:32);
a new teaching! (Mark 1:27); the high priest questioned
Jesus about his disciples and teaching (John 18:19); the
proconsul was amazed at the teaching of the Lord (Acts
13:12); may we know what this new teaching is? (Acts
17:19); you were obedient to the kind of teaching to
which you were committed (Rom. 6:17); that the name
of God and the teaching not be spoken against (1 Tim.
6:1); keep my teaching as the apple of your eye (Prov.
7:2); you have followed my teaching (2 Tim. 3:10);
Alexander strongly opposed our teaching (2 Tim. 4:15);
let us leave the elementary teaching (Heb. 6:1).

D2 Sound doctrine
Keep the form of sound words (2 Tim. 1:13); nourished
on sound doctrine (1 Tim. 4:6); I give you good
teaching (Prov. 4:2); you say, 'My doctrine is pure' (Job
11:4); the law is for whatever else is contrary to sound
doctrine (1 Tim. 1:10); if anyone does not agree with the
sound words of our Lord Jesus Christ (1 Tim. 6:3); the
teaching which accords with godliness (1 Tim. 6:3); the
time will come when they will not endure sound
doctrine (2 Tim. 4:3); an elder [overseer] must keep to
the faithful word in accordance with the teaching
(Titus 1:9); they devoted themselves to the apostles'
teaching (Acts 2:42); speak the things fitting to sound
doctrine (Titus 2:1); show purity in doctrine (Titus 2:7);
that they may adorn the doctrine of God (Titus 2:10);
my teaching is not mine but his who sent me (John
7:16-17); he who abides in the doctrine has both the
Father and the Son (2 John 9).
UNSOUND DOCTRINE, see 535.

E Nurture / training
Sons I have reared (Isa. 1:2); Pharaoh's daughter
brought up Moses as her son (Acts 7:21); Mordecai
brought up Esther (Esther 2:7); those whom I dandled
and reared my enemy annihilated (Lam. 2:22); he came
to Nazareth, where he had been brought up (Luke
4:16); an enrolled widow should have brought up
children (1 Tim. 5:10); train a child in the way he
should go (Prov. 22:6); bring your children up in the
instruction of the Lord (Eph. 6:4).

535 Misteaching
Blown to and fro by every wind of doctrine (Eph. 4:14);
do not be carried away by strange teachings (Heb.
13:9); many are teaching things they ought not to teach
(Titus 1:11); doctrines of demons (1 Tim. 4:1); you have
some who hold the teachings of Balaam (Rev. 2:14); the

teaching of the Nicolaitans (Rev. 2:15); beware of the teaching of the Pharisees and Sadducees (Matt. 16:12); teaching as doctrines the traditions of men (Matt. 15:9; Mark 7:7); whoever looses the least of the commandments and teaches others so (Matt. 5:19); teaching that one must be circumcised to be saved (Acts 15:1); they hear you teach the Jews among the Gentiles to forsake Moses (Acts 21:21); this man teaches against our people and the law and this place (Acts 21:28); those who create hindrances contrary to the doctrine you have learned (Rom. 16:17); instruct some not to teach strange doctrines (1 Tim. 1:3); bringing destructive heresies (2 Pet. 2:1); Jezebel teaches my servants to commit immorality (Rev. 2:20); if anyone does not bring this teaching, do not receive him (2 John 10); he who does not abide in the doctrine of Christ does not have God (2 John 9).

536 Learning
A Learning from God
Learn to do good (Isa. 1:17); Ezra determined to study the law of the Lord (Ezra 7:10); that I might learn your statutes (Ps. 119:71); that I might learn your commandments (Ps. 119:73); if they will really learn the ways of my people (Jer. 12:16); let a woman learn in silence (1 Tim. 2:11); take my yoke and learn from me (Matt. 11:29); you did not so learn Christ (Eph. 4:20); everyone who has heard and learned from the Father comes to me (John 6:45); you can all prophesy that all may learn and be exhorted (1 Cor. 14:31); try to learn what is pleasing to the Lord (Eph. 5:10); what you have learned and received and heard and seen in me (Phil. 4:9); continue in the things you have learned (2 Tim. 3:14).

B Fruitless learning
Their fear of me is a commandment of men learned by rote (Isa. 29:13); always learning but never coming to a knowledge of the truth (2 Tim. 3:7); do not learn the way of the nations (Jer. 10:2); much study is wearying to the flesh (Eccles. 12:12); they will never learn war again (Mic. 4:3); they have hearts trained in greed (2 Pet. 2:14); no one could learn that song except the redeemed (Rev. 14:3).

537 Teacher
A About teachers
They want to be teachers of the law, but are ignorant (1 Tim. 1:7); are you a teacher and do not understand? (John 3:10); a disciple is not above his teacher (Matt. 10:24-5; Luke 6:40); it is enough for the disciple to be like his teacher (Matt. 10:25); they love being called Rabbi (Matt. 23:7-8); do not be called teacher, for you have one Teacher, the Christ (Matt. 23:10); I have more insight than my teachers (Ps. 119:99); the heir is under tutors and governors (Gal. 4:2); they will accumulate teachers after their own lusts (2 Tim. 4:3).

B God the teacher
I am the Lord your God who teaches you to profit (Isa. 48:17); who is a teacher like God? (Job 36:22); your Teacher will no longer hide himself (Isa. 30:20).

C Christ the teacher
You call me Teacher and Lord, and so I am (John 13:13); do not be called Rabbi, for you have one Teacher (Matt. 23:8); do not be called teacher, for you have one Teacher, the Christ (Matt. 23:10); Rabbi, we know you are a teacher come from God (John 3:2); if I, your Lord and Teacher, have washed your feet (John 13:14); does your teacher not pay the two-drachma tax? (Matt. 17:24); why trouble the Teacher any further? (Mark 5:35; Luke 8:49); the Teacher is here and is calling for you (John 11:28); Teacher, we know that you are true

(Mark 12:14); Rabboni, let me receive my sight (Mark 10:51); Mary called out Rabboni! meaning Teacher (John 20:16).
D Teachers in the church
God appointed teachers in the church (1 Cor. 12:28); he gave some pastors and teachers (Eph. 4:11); in the church there were prophets and teachers (Acts 13:1); you ought by this time to be teachers (Heb. 5:12); the Lord's slave should be an able teacher (2 Tim. 2:24); a bishop [overseer] must be apt to teach (1 Tim. 3:2); not many of you should be teachers (Jas. 3:1); let him who is taught share with him who teaches (Gal. 6:6); not all are teachers, are they? (1 Cor. 12:29); there will be false teachers among you (2 Pet. 2:1).

538 Learner
A Discipleship
A disciple is not above his teacher (Matt. 10:24-5; Luke 6:40); the Lord has given me the tongue of those who are taught (Isa. 50:4); if you remain in my word you are truly my disciples (John 8:31); make disciples of all nations (Matt. 28:19); whoever does not hate his father and mother cannot be my disciple (Luke 14:26); whoever does not take up his cross cannot be my disciple (Luke 14:27); whoever does not give up all he has cannot be my disciple (Luke 14:33); by this all men will know that you are my disciples (John 13:35).
B Disciples of Christ
B1 Christ with his disciples
Jesus called his 12 disciples (Matt. 10:1; Luke 6:13); Jesus revealed himself again to his disciples (John 21:1); this was the third time that Jesus appeared to his disciples (John 21:14).
B2 Actions of disciples
His disciples plucked ears of grain (Matt. 12:1-2; Mark 2:23; Luke 6:1); some of his disciples ate bread with defiled, unwashed, hands (Mark 7:2); it was not Jesus who baptised, but only his disciples (John 4:2); I brought him to your disciples and they could not cure him (Matt. 17:16; Mark 9:18; Luke 9:40); many of his disciples withdrew and did not walk with him (John 6:66); the disciples forsook him and fled (Matt. 26:56); lest his disciples steal him and say he has risen from the dead (Matt. 27:64); his disciples came by night and stole him away while we were sleeping (Matt. 28:13).
B3 Disciples' reactions
When the disciples heard this they were astonished (Matt. 19:25); when the disciples saw him walking on the sea they were terrified (Matt. 14:26); when the disciples saw the fig tree they were amazed (Matt. 21:20); the disciples were amazed at his words (Mark 10:24); his disciples were amazed that he was talking to a woman (John 4:27); when the disciples saw it, they were indignant (Matt. 26:8); his disciples believed in him (John 2:11); the disciples were glad when they saw the Lord (John 20:20); the disciples praised God for the great works they had seen (Luke 19:37); the disciples rebuked those bringing children to Jesus (Mark 10:13; Luke 18:15); the disciples wanted to send the crowds away (Matt. 14:15); the disciples wanted to send the woman away (Matt. 15:23).
B4 Other disciples of Christ
Joseph of Arimathea was a disciple (Matt. 27:57); but secretly, for fear of the Jews (John 19:38); another of the disciples wanted leave to bury his father (Matt. 8:21); do you want to become his disciples? (John 9:27); a disciple in Damascus called Ananias (Acts 9:10); the disciples did not think that Paul was a disciple (Acts 9:26); in Joppa there was a disciple named Tabitha (Acts 9:36); they made many disciples (Acts 14:21).

C Disciples of John the Baptist
Why do the disciples of John fast but not your disciples? (Matt. 9:14; Mark 2:18; Luke 5:33); teach us how to pray as John taught his disciples (Luke 11:1); a discussion between John's disciples and a Jew (John 3:25); John's disciples came and took the body (Matt. 14:12; Mark 6:29); disciples who knew nothing of the Holy Spirit (Acts 19:1-7).

D Disciples of others
Seal up the law among my disciples (Isa. 8:16); you are his disciples, but we are disciples of Moses (John 9:28); the Pharisees sent their disciples to him (Matt. 22:16); the disciples of the Pharisees fast (Mark 2:18; Luke 5:33).

539 School
Paul discussed in the school of Tyrannus (Acts 19:9).

540 Truthfulness

A God is truthful
God cannot lie (Titus 1:2); if through my lie God's truthfulness abounds to his glory (Rom. 3:7).

B Speaking truth
Speak the truth to one another (Zech. 8:16; Eph. 4:25); who may sojourn in your tent? He who speaks the truth (Ps. 15:2); speaking the truth in love (Eph. 4:15); by manifestation of the truth we commend ourselves to everyone's conscience (2 Cor. 4:2); all that John said about this man was true (John 10:41); write, for these words are faithful and true (Rev. 21:5); these words are trustworthy and true (Rev. 22:6); have I become your enemy by telling you the truth? (Gal. 4:16).
THE TRUTH, see 494.

541 Falseness

A False ways
I hate every false way (Ps. 119:104, 128); they see false visions, divining lies (Ezek. 21:29); blessed are you when they say all kinds of evil against you falsely (Matt. 5:11); you must not make false vows (Matt. 5:33); do not accuse anyone falsely (Luke 3:14); in their greed they will exploit you with false words (2 Pet. 2:3).

B False people
False Christs and false prophets will arise (Matt. 24:24; Mark 13:22); false prophets come in sheeps' clothing (Matt. 7:15); false prophets arose among the people (2 Pet. 2:1); false prophets (1 John 4:1); false apostles (2 Cor. 11:13; Rev. 2:2); false brethren (2 Cor. 11:26; Gal. 2:4); false teachers (2 Pet. 2:1).
HYPOCRITES, see 542C2.

C Pretending
Israel pretended to be beaten (Josh. 8:15); the Gibeonites pretended to be from a far country to deceive Joshua (Josh. 9:3-13, 22); David pretended to be mad (1 Sam. 21:13; Ps. 34:t); Amnon pretended to be ill (2 Sam. 13:5, 6); the wise woman of Tekoa pretended to be in mourning (2 Sam. 14:2); one pretends to be rich but has nothing, and vice versa (Prov. 13:7); for a pretence they offer long prayers (Mark 12:40); pretending to lay out anchors from the bow (Acts 27:30); they sent spies who pretended to be sincere (Luke 20:20).

542 Deception

A Deceit

A1 God and deceit

A1a God deceiving
Do not let your God deceive you (2 Kgs. 19:10; Isa. 37:10); Lord, you deceived me and I was deceived (Jer. 20:7); you have utterly deceived this people (Jer. 4:10); if the prophet be deceived and speak, I the Lord have deceived him (Ezek. 14:9); God sends them a delusion (2 Thess. 2:11); God put a deceiving spirit in the mouths of the prophets (1 Kgs. 22:22-3; 2 Chr. 18:21-2).

A1b Deceiving God
Will you deceive God? (Job 13:9); they deceived him and lied to him (Ps. 78:36).

A1c Christ and deceit
There was no deceit in his mouth (Isa. 53:9; 1 Pet. 2:22); 'that deceiver' (Matt. 27:63); the last deception will be worse than the first (Matt. 27:64).

A2 Men and deceit

A2a Men deceive
A man who deceives as a joke is like a madman (Prov. 26:18-19); everyone deceives his neighbour (Jer. 9:5); your close friends have deceived you (Jer. 38:22); from the prophet to the priest everyone practises deceit (Jer. 8:10); impostors will go from bad to worse (2 Tim. 3:13); many deceivers have gone out into the world (2 John 7); he harbours deceit in his heart (Prov. 26:24); you are full of deceit and fraud (Acts 13:10); filled with deceit (Rom. 1:29); they deceive the hearts of the unsuspecting (Rom. 16:18); bread gained by deceit is sweet at first (Prov. 20:17); he will act deceitfully and become strong with few people (Dan. 11:23); false apostles, deceitful workers (2 Cor. 11:13); empty talkers and deceivers (Titus 1:10); I have written this to you about those who would deceive you (1 John 2:26); false prophets will deceive many (Matt. 24:11); your prophets have seen for you false and deceptive visions (Lam. 2:14).

A2b Deceitful tongues
The tongue frames deceit (Ps. 50:19); deceitful tongue! (Ps. 52:4; 120:3); whose mouths speak deceit (Ps. 144:8, 11); they devise deceitful words (Ps. 35:20); his words are deceit (Ps. 36:3); his mouth is full of curses and deceit (Ps. 10:7); their tongue speaks with deceit (Jer. 9:8); they deceive with their tongues (Rom. 3:13); their tongue is deceitful in their mouth (Mic. 6:12).

A2c Deceiving oneself
The heart is deceitful above all things (Jer. 17:9); from the heart comes deceit (Mark 7:22); your wisdom and knowledge deceived you (Isa. 47:10); let no one deceive himself (1 Cor. 3:18); do not deceive yourselves (Jer. 37:9); deceiving themselves (Gal. 6:3; Jas. 1:22); you have deceived yourselves (Jer. 42:20); if anyone deceives his own heart, his religion is in vain (Jas. 1:26); if we say we have no sin, we deceive ourselves (1 John 1:8); do not be deceived (1 Cor. 15:33); let him not trust in emptiness, deceiving himself (Job 15:31); the pride of your heart has deceived you (Jer. 49:16; Obad. 3).

A2d Those who deceived
Jacob deceived Isaac (Gen. 27:11-24); Jacob deceived Laban (Gen. 31:20, 26-7); Jacob was deceived over Rachel (Gen. 29:25); Michal deceived her father with an idol (1 Sam. 19:13, 17); Zibah deceived Mephibosheth (2 Sam. 16:2); the wise men tricked Herod (Matt. 2:16); I was crafty and took you in by deceit (2 Cor. 12:16-18); nations were deceived by the sorcery of Babylon (Rev. 18:23); the false prophet had deceived those who had received the mark of the beast (Rev. 19:20).

A2e Avoiding deceit
The law concerning a man who deceives his neighbour (Lev. 6:2); blessed is the man in whose spirit there is no deceit (Ps. 32:2); he who practises deceit will not dwell in my house (Ps. 101:7); keep your lips from speaking deceit (Ps. 34:13; 1 Pet. 3:10); put aside all guile (1 Pet. 2:1); put off the old man, corrupt through deceitful lusts (Eph. 4:22); once we were deceived (Titus 3:3); do not let Hezekiah deceive you (2 Kgs. 18:29; 2 Chr. 32:15); do not be deceived (Gal. 6:7); let no one deceive

you (Eph. 5:6; 2 Thess. 2:3; 1 John 3:7); that no one delude you with plausible arguments (Col. 2:4); our exhortation is not from deceit (1 Thess. 2:3); as deceivers and yet we are true (2 Cor. 6:8); see that no one takes you captive through deception (Col. 2:8); do not let the prophets deceive you (Jer. 29:8); he will not put on a hairy garment in order to deceive (Zech. 13:4).

A3 Satan and deceit
The serpent deceived me and I ate (Gen. 3:13); the woman was deceived (1 Tim. 2:14); the serpent deceived Eve by its craftiness (2 Cor. 11:3); the working of Satan with all wicked deception (2 Thess. 2:10); the beast deceives those who dwell on earth by its signs (Rev. 13:14); so that he should not deceive the nations until the 1000 years were over (Rev. 20:3); Satan will go out to deceive the nations (Rev. 20:8); Satan deceives the whole world (Rev. 12:9); deceitful spirits (1 Tim. 4:1); the devil who had deceived them (Rev. 20:10).

B Lying
LIES, see 543A.

B1 About lying
Do not lie to one another (Lev. 19:11; Col. 3:9); do not be arrogant and lie against the truth (Jas. 3:14); save me from lying lips (Ps. 120:2); laying aside falsehood (Eph. 4:25); let lying lips be dumb (Ps. 31:18); put the way of falsehood from me (Ps. 119:29); a lying tongue is but for a moment (Prov. 12:19); he who tells lies will not escape (Prov. 19:5); he who tells lies will perish (Prov. 19:9); a lying tongue hates its victims (Prov. 26:28); if through my lie God's truthfulness abounds to his glory (Rom. 3:7).

B2 God and lying
B2a God does not lie
God is not a man to lie (Num. 23:19; 1 Sam. 15:29); it is impossible for God to lie (Heb. 6:18); I will not lie to David (Ps. 89:35).

B2b God hates lying
Lying lips are an abomination to the Lord (Prov. 12:22); the Lord hates a lying tongue (Prov. 6:17); Ananias lied not to men but to the Holy Spirit (Acts 5:3-4).

B3 People lying
B3a Prophesying lies
They are prophesying lies (Jer. 27:16); the old prophet was lying (1 Kgs. 13:18); they see false visions, divining lies (Ezek. 21:29; 22:28); if a windy liar says, 'I will preach wine and strong drink' (Mic. 2:11); the working of Satan with all lying power and signs and wonders (2 Thess. 2:9); the teraphim speak iniquity and the diviners see lies (Zech. 10:2).

B3b Not lying
No lie was found in their mouth (Rev. 14:5); the remnant of Israel will tell no lies (Zeph. 3:13); God knows I am not lying (2 Cor. 11:31).

C Hypocrisy
C1 Showing hypocrisy
Knowing their hypocrisy (Mark 12:15); the Jews joined Peter in his hypocrisy (Gal. 2:13); the leaven of the Pharisees is hypocrisy (Luke 12:1); within you are full of hypocrisy (Matt. 23:28); the hypocrisy of liars with seared consciences (1 Tim. 4:2); let love be without hypocrisy (Rom. 12:9); the wisdom from above is without hypocrisy (Jas. 3:17); put aside hypocrisy (1 Pet. 2:1).

C2 Hypocrites
Hypocrites sound a trumpet when they give alms (Matt. 6:2); hypocrites love to stand and pray in synagogues and on street corners (Matt. 6:5); hypocrites look gloomy when they fast (Matt. 6:16); give him a place with the hypocrites (Matt. 24:51); scribes and Pharisees, hypocrites! (Matt. 23:13-29; Mark 7:6; Luke 6:42; 12:56; 13:15).

D Trapping
HUNTING, see 619A.

D1 Trapping in general
Does a bird fall into a trap without bait? (Amos 3:5); in vain is a net spread in the sight of any bird (Prov. 1:17).

D2 Fishing
Peter and Andrew casting their net into the sea (Matt. 4:18; Mark 1:16); James and John mending their nets (Matt. 4:21); washing nets (Luke 5:2); let down your nets for a catch (Luke 5:4-6); fishing with a hook (Matt. 17:27); I am going fishing (John 21:3); Tyre will be a place for spreading nets (Ezek. 26:5, 14); from Engedi to Eneglaim will be a place for spreading nets (Ezek. 47:10); they left their nets and followed him (Matt. 4:20); the kingdom of heaven is like a dragnet cast into the sea (Matt. 13:47); from now on you will be catching men (Luke 5:10).

D3 God trapping
The Lord will become a snare and a trap (Isa. 8:14); I will spread my net over him and he will be caught in my snare (Ezek. 12:13; 17:20); he spread a net for my feet (Lam. 1:13); God has closed his net around me (Job 19:6); lest that day come on you suddenly like a trap (Luke 21:34).

D4 Man trapping
How long will this man be a snare to us? (Exod. 10:7); Saul wanted Michal to be a snare for David (1 Sam. 18:21); the woman whose heart is a snare and a trap (Eccles. 7:26); the fowler's snare is on all the prophet's ways (Hos. 9:8); the survivors of the nations will be a snare and a trap for you (Josh. 23:13); wicked men set a trap to catch men (Jer. 5:26); they planned to trap him in his talk (Matt. 22:15; Mark 12:13).

D5 Trapping oneself
A fool's lips are a snare to him (Prov. 18:7); lest you entangle yourself with a snare (Prov. 22:25); their own foot has been caught in the net they hid (Ps. 9:15).

D6 Evil trapping
Their gods will be a snare to you (Exod. 23:33; Deut. 7:16; Judg. 2:3); be careful you are not ensnared to follow the nations (Deut. 12:30); the ephod was a snare for Gideon (Judg. 8:27); idolatry became a snare to them (Ps. 106:36); the fear of man brings a snare (Prov. 29:25); lest a covenant with the people of the land be a snare to you (Exod. 34:12); wanting to be rich is a snare (1 Tim. 6:9); they may escape from the snare of the devil (2 Tim. 2:26); lest he fall into the reproach and snare of the devil (1 Tim. 3:7); if they are again entangled and overcome (2 Pet. 2:20).

D7 Escaping the trap
Keep me from the snares of the wicked (Ps. 141:9); he will deliver you from the snare (Ps. 91:3); they may escape from the snare of the devil (2 Tim. 2:26); you will pull me out of the net (Ps. 31:4); he will pluck my feet out of the net (Ps. 25:15); the snare is broken and we have escaped (Ps. 124:7).

543 Untruth
A Lies
Let them not listen to words of falsehood (Exod. 5:9); a righteous man hates falsehood (Prov. 13:5); no lie is of the truth (1 John 2:21); the devil is the father of lies (John 8:44); they exchanged the truth about God for a lie (Rom. 1:25); you have agreed together to speak lying and corrupt words (Dan. 2:9); they will speak lies at the same table (Dan. 11:27); what good is an image, a teacher of lies? (Hab. 2:18).
MISLEAD, see 495.
TELL LIES, see 542B.

B Myths

Have nothing to do with silly myths (1 Tim. 4:7); not to pay heed to myths (1 Tim. 1:4); not paying heed to Jewish myths (Titus 1:14); they will turn aside to myths (2 Tim. 4:4); we did not follow cleverly devised myths (2 Pet. 1:16).

544 Dupe

FOOL, see 501.

545 Deceiver

A Those who are liars

Men speak lies to one another (Ps. 12:2); all men are liars (Ps. 116:11); let God be true though every man a liar (Rom. 3:4); Cretans are always liars (Titus 1:12); if I said I do not know him I would be a liar like you (John 8:55); he who claims to love God yet hates his brother is a liar (1 John 4:20); who is the liar but he who denies that Jesus is the Christ? (1 John 2:22); do not add to God's words, lest you be found a liar (Prov. 30:6); he who says he knows him but does not keep his commands is a liar (1 John 2:4); who can prove me a liar? (Job 24:25); when the devil lies, he speaks from his own, for he is a liar and the father of lies (John 8:44). LIES, see 543A.

B Making God a liar

He who does not believe God has made him a liar (1 John 5:10); if we say we have not sinned, we make him a liar (1 John 1:10).

C The end of liars

The mouths of liars will be stopped (Ps. 63:11); liars will end in the lake of fire (Rev. 21:8); all who love lying will be outside the city (Rev. 22:15); the law is for liars and perjurers (1 Tim. 1:10).

546 Exaggeration

OVERESTIMATE, see 482.

547 Indication

A Signs

MIRACLES, see 864B.

A1 Signs from God

A1a Signs from God in general

This will be the sign that I have sent you (Exod. 3:12); the Lord will give you a sign (Isa. 7:14); signs for Moses to perform (Exod. 4:1-9); God did great signs (Josh. 24:17); the sign that God had sent Moses (Num. 16:28-30); the Lord gave Hezekiah a sign (2 Chr. 32:24).

A1b Rites as signs

Circumcision will be the sign of the covenant (Gen. 17:11); Abraham received the sign of circumcision (Rom. 4:11); the feast of unleavened bread would be a sign (Exod. 13:9); the consecration of the firstborn will be as a sign on your hand (Exod. 13:16); the Sabbath is a sign between me and you (Exod. 31:13; Ezek. 20:12).

A1c Signs in the sky / heaven

Lights in the sky will be signs to mark the seasons (Gen. 1:14); the rainbow would be the sign of the covenant (Gen. 9:12-17); there will be great signs from heaven (Luke 21:11); do not be afraid of the signs in the heavens (Jer. 10:2); a great sign appeared in heaven (Rev. 12:1-3); I will show signs in the sky and on earth, blood, fire and columns of smoke (Joel 2:30); there will be signs in sun, moon and stars (Luke 21:25); the sign of the Son of man in the sky (Matt. 24:30); a great and marvellous sign in heaven (Rev. 15:1).

A1d Things as signs

The blood will be a sign for you (Exod. 12:13); keep Aaron's rod as a sign (Num. 17:10); let the beaten plates be a sign to the Israelites (Num. 16:38); the sign of the

fleece (Judg. 6:36-40); the pillar will be a sign and witness to the Lord (Isa. 19:20).

A1e People as signs

Ezekiel will be a sign to you (Ezek. 24:24); Jonah was a sign to the men of Nineveh (Luke 11:30); the Son of man will be a sign to this generation (Luke 11:30).

A2 Signs of the Christ

A2a Signs performed by Christ

Scribes and Pharisees wanted to see a sign (Matt. 12:38); they asked Jesus for a sign (Matt. 16:1; Mark 8:11; Luke 11:16; John 2:18; 6:30); Herod wanted to see a sign (Luke 23:8); Jesus, attested by God with mighty works, wonders and signs (Acts 2:22); Jesus performed the first of his signs (John 2:11); the second sign (John 4:54); the sign of the feeding of the 5000 (John 6:14); no one could do these signs unless God were with him (John 3:2); how can a sinner perform such signs? (John 9:16); many believed when they saw the signs he did (John 2:23); though he performed many signs, they did not believe (John 12:37); the crowds followed him because they saw the signs he did (John 6:2); will the Christ do more signs than this? (John 7:31); this man performs many signs (John 11:47); Jesus did many other signs in the presence of his disciples (John 20:30).

A2b Signs attending Christ

The sign of Immanuel (Isa. 7:11-16); the sign will be the baby wrapped in cloths (Luke 2:12); the betrayer used a kiss as the sign (Matt. 26:48; Mark 14:44); unless I see in his hands the print of the nails (John 20:25); I bear in my body the marks of Jesus (Gal. 6:17).

A3 Signs and wonders

A3a Signs and wonders before Christ

Moses performed wonders and signs (Acts 7:36); he has shown signs and wonders in the land of Egypt (Jer. 32:20); I will multiply my signs and wonders (Exod. 7:3); you brought your people out of Egypt with signs and wonders (Jer. 32:21); how great are his signs! (Dan. 4:3); I will declare the signs and wonders which God has done for me (Dan. 4:2); he delivers and rescues and works signs and wonders (Dan. 6:27); I and my children are for signs and wonders (Isa. 8:18).

A3b Signs and wonders of the gospel

Jesus, attested by God with mighty works, wonders and signs (Acts 2:22); God confirmed the word with the signs that followed (Mark 16:20); the Lord bore witness to his word with signs and wonders (Acts 14:3); God bore witness with signs and wonders (Heb. 2:4); many signs and wonders were done through the apostles (Acts 2:43; 5:12); Paul and Barnabas recounted the signs and wonders God had done through them (Acts 15:12); signs and wonders, the signs of a true apostle (2 Cor. 12:12); signs and wonders in the power of the Spirit (Rom. 15:19); what Christ has done through me by the power of signs and wonders (Rom. 15:18-19); grant that signs and wonders take place in the name of Jesus (Acts 4:30); a noteworthy sign has been done through them (Acts 4:16); Stephen performed great wonders and signs (Acts 6:8); they saw the signs Philip performed (Acts 8:6); Simon saw signs and great miracles performed (Acts 8:13); these signs will accompany those who believe (Mark 16:17); tongues are a sign for unbelievers, prophecy for believers (1 Cor. 14:22); not being afraid of them is a sign to them of destruction (Phil. 1:28).

A4 Seeking a sign

The servant asked for a sign to indicate the right girl (Gen. 24:14, 43-4); what will be the sign that the Lord will heal me? (2 Kgs. 20:8-11); what is the sign? (Isa. 38:22); show me a sign of good (Ps. 86:17); ask a sign, as deep as Sheol or high as heaven (Isa. 7:11); give me a sign that it is you speaking to me (Judg. 6:17); Gideon

asked for signs on the fleece (Judg. 6:36-9); scribes and
Pharisees wanted to see a sign (Matt. 12:38); they asked
Jesus for a sign (Matt. 16:1; Mark 8:11; Luke 11:16); what
sign do you perform? (John 2:18; 6:30); Herod wanted
to see a sign (Luke 23:8); a wicked and adulterous
generation asks for a sign (Matt. 12:39; 16:4); the Jews
require signs (1 Cor. 1:22); unless you see signs and
wonders you will not believe (John 4:48).

A5 Signs of evil
The beast performed great signs (Rev. 13:13-14); false
Christs and false prophets will show great signs and
wonders (Matt. 24:24); the working of Satan with all
lying power and signs and wonders (2 Thess. 2:9); they
are demonic spirits performing signs (Rev. 16:14); the
false prophet who performed the signs (Rev. 19:20).

A6 Not believing signs
If they do not believe the first sign they may believe the
latter (Exod. 4:8); if they do not believe these two signs
(Exod. 4:9); they will not believe in me despite the
signs I performed (Num. 14:11); the saw the signs I did
yet have not listened to me (Num. 14:22); though he
performed many signs, they did not believe (John
12:37).

A7 No signs
I will not ask a sign (Isa. 7:12); John did no sign (John
10:41); no sign will be given to this generation (Mark
8:12); no sign will be given except the sign of Jonah
(Matt. 12:39; 16:4; Luke 11:29); the kingdom of God is
not coming with signs to be observed (Luke 17:20).

B Signals
B1 Flags
Tribes camping by their banners (Num. 1:52; 2:2-34);
awesome as [an army] with banners (S. of S. 6:4, 10); in
the name of our God we will set up our banners (Ps.
20:5); the Lord is my banner (Exod. 17:15); you have
given a banner to those who fear you (Ps. 60:4); his
banner over me is love (S. of S. 2:4); he will lift up an
ensign to the nations (Isa. 5:26; 11:12; 49:22); the root of
Jesse will stand as an ensign (Isa. 11:10); you will be left
like a banner on a hill top (Isa. 30:17); the enemy set up
their own signs for signs (Ps. 74:4).

B2 Signalling
Two silver trumpets for signalling (Num. 10:2-10); they
signalled to their partners to come and help them
(Luke 5:7); stretch out your javelin towards Ai (Josh.
8:18); a column of smoke was the signal (Judg. 20:38).

B3 Gesturing
Zechariah made signs to them (Luke 1:22); they made
signs to Zechariah (Luke 1:62); Peter gestured to the
disciple lying by Jesus (John 13:24); Peter motioned
with his hand for them to be quiet (Acts 12:17);
Alexander motioned with his hand (Acts 19:33); Paul
motioned with his hand (Acts 13:16; 21:40; 26:1); the
governor nodded for Paul to speak (Acts 24:10).

B4 Winking
The wicked man winks and points (Prov. 6:13); he who
winks the eye causes trouble (Prov. 10:10); he who
winks the eye plans perverse things (Prov. 16:30).

B5 Whistling
The Lord will whistle for a distant nation (Isa. 5:26);
the Lord will whistle for the fly in Egypt (Isa. 7:18).

C Personal marks
C1 Marks on people
Memorial bands [phylacteries] between your eyes
(Exod. 13:9, 16); a sign on your hand (Exod. 13:9, 16);
bind these words as a sign on your hand and forehead
(Deut. 6:8; 11:18); a mark on all those who mourn over
Jerusalem (Ezek. 9:4); the Lord put a mark on Cain
(Gen. 4:15); the mark of the beast on the right hand or
forehead (Rev. 13:16-17; 14:9-11; 16:2; 19:20); do not
tattoo yourselves in mourning the dead (Lev. 19:28).

C2 Seals
Judah's seal and cord given to Tamar (Gen. 38:18, 25);
you were sealed with the Holy Spirit (2 Cor. 1:22; Eph.
1:13; 4:30); an angel with the seal of God (Rev. 7:2-3); to
harm only people without the seal of God on their
foreheads (Rev. 9:4); circumcision was the seal of
righteousness by faith (Rom. 4:11); you are the seal of
my apostleship in the Lord (1 Cor. 9:2); God's
foundation stands, having this seal (2 Tim. 2:19).

C3 Signet rings
Pharaoh gave Joseph his signet ring (Gen. 41:42); the
king gave his signet ring to Haman (Esther 3:10, 12); the
king gave his signet ring to Mordecai (Esther 8:2-10);
the stone was sealed with a signet ring (Dan. 6:17);
engraved like signets (Exod. 39:6, 14, 30); I will make
Zerubbabel like my signet ring (Hag. 2:23); even if
Jehoiachin were a signet ring (Jer. 22:24); put a ring on
his hand (Luke 15:22).

D Boundary marks
Do not move a boundary mark (Deut. 19:14; Prov.
22:28; 23:10); cursed is he who moves his neighbour's
boundary mark (Deut. 27:17); set up road signs (Jer.
31:21); make a signpost (Ezek. 21:19).

548 Record
A Monuments
Jacob set up a pillar at Bethel (Gen. 28:18; 31:13; 35:14);
Jacob set up a pillar at Mizpah (Gen. 31:45-9); Jacob set
up a pillar near Bethlehem (Gen. 35:19-20); Moses set
up twelve stone pillars (Exod. 24:4); Saul set up a
monument to himself (1 Sam. 15:12); Absalom had set
up a pillar as a monument to himself (2 Sam. 18:18);
you adorn the monuments of the righteous (Matt.
23:29).

B Written records
B1 Tablets
Moses was given two tablets of stone (Exod. 24:12; 31:18;
32:15; Deut. 4:13; 5:22; 9:9-11); he wrote on the tablets
the ten commandments (Exod. 34:28-9); he threw
down the tablets (Exod. 32:19; Deut. 9:17); hew two
stone tablets like the first (Exod. 34:1, 4; Deut. 10:1-5);
the tablets were put into the ark (Deut. 10:5); nothing
in the ark except the two stone tablets (1 Kgs. 8:9;
2 Chr. 5:10).

B2 Bills of divorce
He who divorces his wife must give her a certificate of
divorce (Deut. 24:1; Matt. 5:31); Moses commanded us
to give her a certificate of divorce (Matt. 19:7); I gave
faithless Israel her certificate of divorce (Jer. 3:8); where
is your mother's certificate of divorce? (Isa. 50:1).

B3 Names written in heaven
Rejoice that your names are written in heaven (Luke
10:20); the firstborn enrolled in heaven (Heb. 12:23);
when the Lord registers the peoples he will record who
was born in Zion (Ps. 87:6); everyone recorded for life
in Jerusalem (Isa. 4:3).

549 Recorder
Jehoshaphat was recorder (2 Sam. 8:16; 1 Chr. 18:15);
Joah the recorder (2 Kgs. 18:18; 2 Chr. 34:8; Isa. 36:3).

550 Obliteration
Blot me out of the book you have written (Exod.
32:32-3); may they be blotted out of the book of life (Ps.
69:28).

551 Representation
Jerusalem drawn on a brick (Ezek. 4:1).

552 Misrepresentation
Say you are my sister (Gen. 12:13); she is my sister (Gen. 20:2-5); he said of his wife, 'She is my sister' (Gen. 26:7).

553 Painting
Oholibah saw Chaldeans painted on the wall (Ezek. 23:14).

554 Sculpture
IDOL, see 982.

A Sculpting
Aaron fashioned a molten calf with a graving tool (Exod. 32:4); make a fiery snake and put it on a pole (Num. 21:8-9); lions by the throne (1 Kgs. 10:19-20; 2 Chr. 9:18-19); five golden tumours and five golden mice (1 Sam. 6:4-5); animals and creeping things and idols carved round the wall (Ezek. 8:10); every man in his room of images (Ezek. 8:12); King Nebuchadnezzar made an image of gold (Dan. 3:1); what profit is an idol when its maker has carved it (Hab. 2:18); the twin boys as figurehead (Acts 28:11); making an image of the beast (Rev. 13:14-15); Bezalel was skilled in carving wood (Exod. 35:33); The carved work was smashed with hatchets and hammers (Ps. 74:6); carvings in the temple: cherubim, palm trees and flowers on the walls (1 Kgs. 6:23-35; 2 Chr. 3:7, 10-13; Ezek. 41:18-20); palm trees and chains (2 Chr. 3:5); gourds and flowers (1 Kgs. 6:18); flowers on the lampstand (2 Chr. 4:21); pomegranates on the capitals (1 Kgs. 7:18; 2 Chr. 3:16; Jer. 52:22-3); lilies at the top of the pillars (1 Kgs. 7:22); gourds round the 'sea' (1 Kgs. 7:24); the 'sea' standing on 12 oxen (1 Kgs. 7:25; 2 Chr. 4:3-4; Jer. 52:20); lions, oxen and cherubim around the stands (1 Kgs. 7:29); palm trees (Ezek. 40:16-37).

B Castings
The sea was made of cast metal (1 Kgs. 7:23); the wheels and axles for the stands were cast (1 Kgs. 7:33); they were cast in the clay ground (1 Kgs. 7:46; 2 Chr. 4:17); the idol! a workman casts it (Isa. 40:19).

555 Engraving
See 586D4.

556 Artist
SCULPTORS, see 554A.
SKILLED PEOPLE, see 696.

557 Language

A Languages of the earth
A1 All languages
There are many languages in the world (1 Cor. 14:10); they heard them speak in their own languages (Acts 2:6, 8-11); all peoples, nations and languages (Dan. 3:4, 7; 4:1; 5:19; 6:25; 7:14; Rev. 5:9; 7:9; 11:9; 13:7; 14:6; 17:15).
A2 Languages separated
God confused their language (Gen. 11:1-9); the nations were separated according to their languages (Gen. 10:5); confuse and divide their tongues (Ps. 55:9).
A3 Unknown languages
When Israel went forth from a people of a strange language (Ps. 114:1); a nation of unknown language will swoop on you (Deut. 28:49); a nation whose language you do not understand (Jer. 5:15); through foreign languages God will speak to this people (Isa. 28:11; 1 Cor. 14:21); you will no longer see a people with unintelligible language (Isa. 33:19); you are not sent to a people of unintelligible language (Ezek. 3:5-6).

B Particular languages
Messages were sent to every people in their own language (Esther 1:22; 3:12; 8:9); five cities in Egypt will speak the language of Canaan (Isa. 19:18); the king had them taught the letters and language of the Chaldeans (Dan. 1:4); half of them spoke the language of Ashdod, and none could speak the language of Judah (Neh. 13:24); Rabshakeh shouted in the language of Judah (Isa. 36:11-13); Christ spoke to Paul in Hebrew (Acts 26:14); Paul spoke to them in Hebrew (Acts 21:40); when they heard him speak in Hebrew they were quieter (Acts 22:2); please speak in Aramaic, not Hebrew (2 Kgs. 18:26; Isa. 36:11); the letter was written in Aramaic (Ezra 4:7); the Chaldeans spoke to the king in Aramaic (Dan. 2:4); dispute between the Hebrews and Hellenists in the church (Acts 6:1); Saul disputed with the Hellenists (Acts 9:29); do you know Greek? (Acts 21:37); the Assyrians called out in Hebrew (2 Chr. 32:18); the inscription was in Hebrew, Latin and Greek (John 19:20); they spoke in the Lycaonian language (Acts 14:11).

C Speaking in tongues
They will speak in new tongues (Mark 16:17); they spoke in other languages (Acts 2:4); they heard them speaking in tongues and exalting God (Acts 10:46); they spoke in tongues and prophesied (Acts 19:6); the gift of speaking in tongues (1 Cor. 12:10-30); if I come speaking in tongues, how do I benefit you? (1 Cor. 14:2-6); five words with my mind rather than 10 000 words in a tongue (1 Cor. 14:19); I speak in tongues more than you all (1 Cor. 14:18); if all speak in tongues, will they not say you are mad? (1 Cor. 14:23); the one who prophesies is greater than he who speaks in tongues unless he interprets (1 Cor. 14:5); if I pray in a tongue my spirit prays but my mind is unfruitful (1 Cor. 14:14); if I speak with the tongues of men and angels and have not love (1 Cor. 13:1); tongues, prophecy and knowledge will cease (1 Cor. 13:8); when you come together, each one has a tongue etc. (1 Cor. 14:26); do not forbid speaking in tongues (1 Cor. 14:39); let him who speaks in tongues pray for an interpretation (1 Cor. 14:13); two or three may speak in tongues if someone interprets (1 Cor. 14:27).

558 Letter
To every province in its own script (Esther 1:22; 3:12; 8:9); write it in ordinary characters (Isa. 8:1); see with what large letters I am writing (Gal. 6:11); the king had them taught the letters and language of the Chaldeans (Dan. 1:4); not a yod nor tittle will pass from the law (Matt. 5:18; Luke 16:17).

559 Word
All the earth had one language and one set of words (Gen. 11:1); he cast out the demons with a word (Matt. 8:16); it is a matter about words and names and your own law (Acts 18:15); disputes about words (1 Tim. 6:4); charge them not to quarrel about words (2 Tim. 2:14); there are no words (Ps. 19:3).
MESSAGE, see 529.

560 Neology
DIALECT, see 580A.

561 Names

A God's name
A1 What is God's name?
What is your name? (Gen. 32:29; Judg. 13:17); what is his name? (Exod. 3:13); what is his name or his son's name? (Prov. 30:4); why ask my name, seeing it is

wonderful? (Judg. 13:18); he did not tell me his name (Judg. 13:6).

A2 The name of God

A2a God's great and holy name

You made a name for yourself (Jer. 32:20; Dan. 9:15); to make for himself an everlasting name (Isa. 63:12); you have exalted your name and your word (Ps. 138:2); as is your name, so is your praise (Ps. 48:10); holy and awesome is his name (Ps. 111:9); my name will be great among the nations (Mal. 1:11); glory in his holy name! (1 Chr. 16:10); we trust in his holy name (Ps. 33:21); may your name be hallowed (Matt. 6:9; Luke 11:2); holy is his name (Luke 1:49); the Lord will not abandon his people for the sake of his great name (1 Sam. 12:22); my people will know my name (Isa. 52:6); foreigners will hear of your great name (1 Kgs. 8:41-2).

A2b His name is the Lord

The name of God is I AM (Exod. 3:14-15); by my name the Lord [Yahweh] I did not make myself known (Exod. 6:3); Yahweh is his name (Exod. 15:3; Jer. 33:2); I am the Lord, that is my name (Isa. 42:8); the Lord is his name (Amos 5:8; 9:6); the Lord of hosts is his name (Jer. 31:35); the Lord will be one and his name one (Zech. 14:9).

A2c Other references to God's name

She called the name of the Lord 'God of seeing' (Gen. 16:13); the Lord whose name is Jealous (Exod. 34:14); it is sound wisdom to fear your name (Mic. 6:9); they will take refuge in the name of the Lord (Zeph. 3:12); glorify your name (John 12:28); I have manifested your name to the people you gave me (John 17:6); God took from the Gentiles a people for his name (Acts 15:14); the God of Abraham, Isaac and Jacob, this is my name for ever (Exod. 3:15).

A3 Proclaiming God's name

I have raised you up that my name might be proclaimed in all the earth (Exod. 9:16); God proclaimed his name, the Lord, before Moses (Exod. 33:19; 34:5); I will proclaim the name of the Lord (Deut. 32:3); I will proclaim your name to my brethren (Ps. 22:22; Heb. 2:12); that my name may be proclaimed in all the earth (Rom. 9:17); hush! we must not mention the name of the Lord (Amos 6:10).

A4 Called by God's name

You are called by the name of the Lord (Deut. 28:10); my people who are called by my name (2 Chr. 7:14); everyone who is called by my name (Isa. 43:7); all the Gentiles who are called by my name (Acts 15:17); we are called by your name (Jer. 14:9); I am called by your name (Jer. 15:16); they will put my name on the sons of Israel (Num. 6:27); I will write on him the name of my God (Rev. 3:12); his name and his Father's name written on their foreheads (Rev. 14:1).

A5 In God's name

Keep them in your name which you gave me (John 17:11-12); blessed is he who comes in the name of the Lord (Matt. 21:9; 23:39; Mark 11:9; Luke 13:35; 19:38; John 12:13); in your name we have come (2 Chr. 14:11); I come in my Father's name and you do not receive me (John 5:43); the works that I do in my Father's name (John 10:25); anointing the sick one with oil in the name of the Lord (Jas. 5:14); we will walk in the name of the Lord our God (Mic. 4:5); in his name they will walk (Zech. 10:12); in the name of our God we will set up our banners (Ps. 20:5); the name of the Lord is a strong tower (Prov. 18:10).

A6 A place for God's name

The place chosen as a dwelling for his name (Deut. 12:5; 1 Kgs. 14:21; 1 Chr. 22:19; 2 Chr. 6:6; Neh. 1:9); a house for the name of the Lord (1 Kgs. 5:3; 2 Chr. 2:1); the house I have built for your name (1 Kgs. 8:20); I have

consecrated this house by putting my name there for ever (1 Kgs. 9:3; 2 Chr. 7:16); in this house I will put my name (2 Chr. 33:7); they have built a sanctuary for your name (2 Chr. 20:8); my name will be there (1 Kgs. 8:29; 2 Kgs. 23:27; 2 Chr. 33:4); in Jerusalem will I put my name (2 Kgs. 21:4, 7); I have chosen Jerusalem for my name (2 Chr. 6:6); the city called by your name (Dan. 9:18); Shiloh, where I made my name dwell at first (Jer. 7:12); the name of the city will be, The Lord is There (Ezek. 48:35).

A7 Profaning God's name

Do not take the name of the Lord in vain (Exod. 20:7; Deut. 5:11); do not profane the name of the Lord (Lev. 18:21); whoever blasphemes the name of the Lord must be put to death (Lev. 24:16); a man blasphemed the name and cursed (Lev. 24:11); my name is blasphemed all day long (Isa. 52:5); you will profane my holy name no longer (Ezek. 20:39); you profane the Lord's name (Mal. 1:12); the name of God is blasphemed among the Gentiles because of you (Rom. 2:24); that the name of God and the teaching not be spoken against (1 Tim. 6:1); blaspheming God's name and dwelling, that is, those who dwell in heaven (Rev. 13:6); they blasphemed the name of God (Rev. 16:9); profaning God's name by: swearing falsely (Lev. 19:12); giving children to Molech (Lev. 20:3); being unholy priests (Lev. 21:6).

B The name of Christ

B1 Christ's name

The man named the Branch (Zech. 6:12); the Lord our righteousness (Jer. 23:6); his name will be Wonderful Counsellor, Mighty God, Everlasting Father, Prince of Peace (Isa. 9:6); his name is the Word of God (Rev. 19:13); he will be called a Nazarene (Matt. 2:23); you shall name him Jesus (Matt. 1:21; Luke 1:31); he was called Jesus (Matt. 1:25; Luke 2:21); God has given him the name above all names (Phil. 2:9-10); he has a name written which no one knows but himself (Rev. 19:12); his name shall be called Immanuel (Matt. 1:23); he has obtained a far more excellent name than that of angels (Heb. 1:4); he has a name written, 'King of kings and lord of lords' (Rev. 19:16); the disciples were first called Christians (Acts 11:26); suffering as a Christian (1 Pet. 4:16); I will write on him my new name (Rev. 3:12); his name and his Father's name written on their foreheads (Rev. 14:1); his name will be on their foreheads (Rev. 22:4); the name of the Lord Jesus was magnified (Acts 19:17); I thought I should do many things opposing the name of Jesus of Nazareth (Acts 26:9); do not the rich blaspheme that worthy name by which you were called? (Jas. 2:7).

B2 In the name of Christ

Many will come in my name (Matt. 24:5; Mark 13:6); we saw a man casting out demons in your name (Mark 9:38; Luke 9:49); in my name they will cast out demons (Mark 16:17); even the demons are subject to us in your name (Luke 10:17); did we not cast out demons in your name? (Matt. 7:22); did we not do many mighty works in your name? (Matt. 7:22); no one who does a miracle in my name can soon speak evil of me (Mark 9:39); by the name of Jesus Christ this man stands healed (Acts 4:10); there is no other name by which we must be saved (Acts 4:12); he who receives one such child in my name receives me (Matt. 18:5; Mark 9:37; Luke 9:48); where two or three are gathered in my name (Matt. 18:20); in the name of Jesus Christ of Nazareth, walk (Acts 3:6); the name of Jesus, by faith in his name, has made this man strong (Acts 3:16); do all in the name of the Lord Jesus (Col. 3:17); signs and wonders through the name of your holy servant Jesus (Acts 4:30); itinerant Jewish exorcists named the name of the Lord Jesus over those demonised (Acts 19:13); I command you in the name of Jesus Christ to come out of her (Acts 16:18); we command you in the name of our Lord Jesus Christ (2 Thess. 3:6).

B3 Believing on the name of Christ
To those who believe in his name he gave the right to become children of God (John 1:12); I have written to you who believe in the name of the Son of God (1 John 5:13); he has not believed in the name of the only begotten Son of God (John 3:18); in his name will the Gentiles hope (Matt. 12:21).

B4 Baptised in Christ's name
Be baptised in the name of Jesus Christ (Acts 2:38); they had been baptised in the name of the Lord Jesus (Acts 8:16); they were baptised in the name of the Lord Jesus (Acts 19:5); be baptised, calling on his name (Acts 22:16).

B5 For the sake of Christ's name
He who gives you a cup of water because you bear the name of Christ (Mark 9:41); your sins have been forgiven for his name's sake (1 John 2:12); you will be hated by all for my name's sake (Mark 13:13; Luke 21:17); you will be brought before kings and governors for my name's sake (Luke 21:12); all this they will do to you for my name's sake (John 15:21); they rejoiced that they were worthy to suffer for the name (Acts 5:41); I will show him how much he must suffer for my name's sake (Acts 9:16); if you are reviled for the name of Christ, you are blessed (1 Pet. 4:14); you have endured for my name's sake (Rev. 2:3); they went out for the sake of the name (3 John 7); I am ready to die for the name of the Lord Jesus (Acts 21:13); men who have risked their lives for the name of the Lord Jesus (Acts 15:26).

B6 Calling in Christ's name
Is not this who destroyed those who called on this name? (Acts 9:21); whoever calls on the name of the Lord will be saved (Acts 2:21; Rom. 10:13); those who call on the name of our Lord Jesus Christ (1 Cor. 1:2); whatever you ask in my name, I will do it (John 14:13-14); that whatever you ask in my name, the Father may give you (John 15:16; 16:23-6).

B7 Speaking in Christ's name
Did we not prophesy in your name? (Matt. 7:22); repentance and forgiveness should be preached in his name (Luke 24:47); Philip preached good news about the name of Jesus Christ (Acts 8:12); they warned them not to speak any more in this name (Acts 4:17-18; 5:28, 40); at Damascus he preached boldly in the name of Jesus (Acts 9:27-8); he is my chosen instrument to carry my name to the Gentiles (Acts 9:15).

C Names of people
C1 Names of people in general
A good name is better than good oil (Eccles. 7:1); rejoice that your names are written in heaven (Luke 10:20); whose names are in the book of life (Phil. 4:3); those whose names are not written in the book of life of the Lamb (Rev. 13:8); he calls his own sheep by name and leads them out (John 10:3); the names of the sons of Israel engraved upon stones (Exod. 28:9-11); Aaron bore the stones before the Lord (Exod. 28:12); a name on her forehead, Babylon the great (Rev. 17:5).

C2 God naming people
God named them 'Man' (Gen. 5:2); you shall name him Ishmael (Gen. 16:11); name him Jezreel (Hos. 1:4); from birth he named me (Isa. 49:1); Israel – striving with God (Gen. 32:28); you will call him John (Luke 1:13); call him Isaac – he laughs (Gen. 17:19); Solomon – man of peace (1 Chr. 22:9); Maher-shalal-hash-baz – the spoil speeds, the prey hastes (Isa. 8:3); Lo-ruhamah – no pity (Hos. 1:6); Lo-ammi – not my people (Hos.

1:9); Ammi – my people (Hos. 2:1); Ruhamah – pitied (Hos. 2:1).

C3 God renaming people
You will be called by a new name (Isa. 62:2); I will give him a new name written on the stone (Rev. 2:17); your name will be no more Abram but Abraham (Gen. 17:5); no more Sarai but Sarah (Gen. 17:15); no more Jacob, but Israel (Gen. 32:28).

D Names of things
D1 God naming things
God called the light 'day' and the darkness 'night' (Gen. 1:5); God called the expanse 'heaven' (Gen. 1:8); God called the dry land 'earth' and the gathering of waters 'seas' (Gen. 1:10); God names all the stars (Ps. 147:4).

D2 People naming things
The man named all the living creatures (Gen. 2:19-20); whatever exists has already been named (Eccles. 6:10); they named lands after their own names (Ps. 49:11); manna – what is it? (Exod. 16:15, 31); lest the city be called by my name (2 Sam. 12:28).

E Other names
The name of the demons was Legion (Mark 5:9; Luke 8:30); it is a matter about words and names and your own law (Acts 18:15); Christ is far above every name that is named (Eph. 1:21); I will write on him the name of the city of my God (Rev. 3:12); they call themselves after the holy city (Isa. 48:2); the mark of the beast is his name or the number of his name (Rev. 13:17; 14:11; 15:2); all the peoples walk each in the name of his god (Mic. 4:5); do not let the names of other gods be on your lips (Exod. 23:13); do not mention the names of their gods (Josh. 23:7); I will not take their names on my lips (Ps. 16:4); blasphemous names on the beast's heads (Rev. 13:1).

F Names blotted out
Levirate marriage so that the name not be blotted out (Deut. 25:6); the Lord will blot out his name (Deut. 29:20); the Lord did not say that he would blot out the name of Israel (2 Kgs. 14:27); that the name of Israel be remembered no more (Ps. 83:4); may their name be blotted out (Ps. 109:13); I will not rub out his name from the book of life (Rev. 3:5).

562 Misnomer
NAMES, see 561.

563 Phrase
WORD, see 559.

564 Grammar
LANGUAGE, see 557.

565 Solecism
DIALECT, see 580A.

566 Style
ELEGANCE, see 575.

567 Perspicuity
INTELLIGIBLE, see 516.

568 Imperspicuity
NOT UNDERSTANDING, see 517.

569 Conciseness
I have written to you briefly (Eph. 3:3; Heb. 13:22; 1 Pet. 5:12); the law is summed up as 'love your neighbour as yourself' (Rom. 13:9).

570 Diffuseness

Of these we cannot now speak in detail (Heb. 9:5).

571 Vigour

Whatever you do, do it with all your might (Eccles. 9:10).

STRENGTH, see 162.

572 Feebleness

WEAK, see 163.

573 Plainness

How effective is straight talking! (Job 6:25); I speak to Moses openly, not in dark sayings (Num. 12:8); write the words of this law very plainly (Deut. 27:8); he was stating the matter plainly (Mark 8:32); if you are the Christ, tell us plainly (John 10:24); Jesus said to them plainly (John 11:14); I will tell you plainly of the Father (John 16:25); now you are speaking plainly (John 16:29); he spoke plainly (Mark 7:35).

574 Ornament

ELOQUENCE, see 579A3.

575 Elegance

The smooth tongue of the adulteress (Prov. 6:24); her speech is smoother than oil (Prov. 5:3).

576 Inelegance

SPEECH DEFECT, see 580.

577 Voice

A Voices in general

I am the voice of one crying in the wilderness (John 1:23); the friend of the bridegroom rejoices at the bridegroom's voice (John 3:29); the sheep recognise the shepherd's voice (John 10:3-5, 16); the voice is the voice of Jacob (Gen. 27:22); they recognised the Levite's voice (Judg. 18:3); Saul recognised David's voice (1 Sam. 26:17).

B God's voice

As Moses drew near there came the voice of the Lord (Acts 7:31); Moses heard a voice from between the cherubim (Num. 7:89); I fell on my face and heard a voice speaking (Ezek. 1:28); after the fire, a still small voice (1 Kgs. 19:12); the power of the voice of the Lord (Ps. 29:3-9); the voice of the Lord like the sound of many waters (Ezek. 43:2); his voice was like the sound of many waters (Rev. 1:15); a voice like a trumpet (Rev. 1:10; 4:1); a voice came from heaven (Dan. 4:31; Matt. 3:17; Mark 1:11; Luke 3:22; John 12:28-30); we heard this voice from heaven (2 Pet. 1:18); a voice from the cloud (Matt. 17:5; Mark 9:7; Luke 9:35); his voice shook the earth (Heb. 12:26); a voice came from the throne (Rev. 19:5); I heard a loud voice from the throne (Rev. 21:3); his voice you have never heard (John 5:37).

C Cry of distress

C1 Cry of distress to God

In my trouble I cried to the Lord (Ps. 120:1); out of the depths I cried to you (Ps. 130:1); God remembers the cry of the afflicted (Ps. 9:12); if the orphan or widow cries out to me, I will hear their cry (Exod. 22:23); if the man without a cloak cries out to me, I will hear him (Exod. 22:27); your brother's blood cries out from the ground (Gen. 4:10); I have heard their cry (Exod. 2:23); I have heard their cry (Exod. 3:7-9); though they cry in my ears with a loud voice, I will not listen (Ezek. 8:18).

C2 Other cry of distress

The girl cried out but there was no one to save her (Deut. 22:27); a woman attacked in a city should cry out (Deut. 22:23-4); Tamar cried aloud (2 Sam. 13:19); after crying out, the demon came out (Mark 9:26); Esau cried out with a loud and bitter cry (Gen. 27:34); a great outcry throughout Egypt (Exod. 11:6; 12:30); David wailed with a loud voice (2 Sam. 19:4); they wept with a loud voice (Ezra 3:12).

578 Voicelessness

A Dumb

God makes man dumb (Exod. 4:11); Zacharias was struck dumb (Luke 1:20-2); a demonised dumb man was brought to him (Matt. 9:32); a dumb spirit (Mark 9:17); they brought to him the dumb (Matt. 15:30); you deaf and dumb spirit! (Mark 9:25); he was casting out a demon which was dumb (Luke 11:14); the dumb spoke (Matt. 9:33; 12:22; 15:31; Mark 7:35; Luke 11:14); he makes the dumb speak (Mark 7:37); the tongue of the dumb will sing for joy (Isa. 35:6); a dumb donkey spoke (2 Pet. 2:16); dumb idols (Hab. 2:18); woe to him who says to a dumb stone, 'Arise!' (Hab. 2:19); they are dumb dogs, unable to bark (Isa. 56:10); you were led astray to dumb idols (1 Cor. 12:2).

B Silenced

KEEPING QUIET, see 582.

B1 Silencing in general

These men must be silenced (Titus 1:11); by doing right you will silence the ignorance of foolish men (1 Pet. 2:15); the law speaks that every mouth may be closed (Rom. 3:19); he heard things a man is not permitted to speak (2 Cor. 12:4); kings will shut their mouths because of him (Isa. 52:15).

B2 Those silenced

He would not permit the demons to speak (Mark 1:34); Jesus told the unclean spirit to be silent (Mark 1:25; Luke 4:35); when they heard this they were silenced (Acts 11:18); the man was speechless (Matt. 22:12); no one could answer him a word (Matt. 22:46); they had nothing to say (Acts 4:14); do not speak to Jacob either good or evil (Gen. 31:24); Paul's companions stood speechless (Acts 9:7); Jesus had silenced the Sadducees (Matt. 22:34); they warned them not to speak any more in this name (Acts 4:17-18; 5:28, 40); they told the blind men to be quiet (Matt. 20:31; Mark 10:48; Luke 18:39); Paul motioned to them to be quiet (Acts 12:17); the town clerk quieted the crowd (Acts 19:35).

C Under one's breath

Hannah was praying without a sound (1 Sam. 1:12-13); they could only whisper a prayer (Isa. 26:16); how faint a whisper do we hear of him! (Job 26:14); what you hear in your ear, proclaim on the housetops (Matt. 10:27); what you have whispered in inner rooms will be proclaimed on housetops (Luke 12:3); a whisperer separates close friends (Prov. 16:28); the words of a whisperer are tasty morsels (Prov. 18:8).

D Without speech

There is no speech nor words (Ps. 19:3); the Spirit intercedes for us with groans too deep for words (Rom. 8:26); your faith in God has gone forth so we do not need to say anything (1 Thess. 1:8).

579 Speech

A Faculty of speech

A1 Power of speech

Life and death are in the power of the tongue (Prov. 18:21); from the fullness of the heart the mouth speaks (Matt. 12:34-6; Luke 6:45); there is a time to speak (Eccles. 3:7); with the mouth a man confesses and is saved (Rom. 10:10); when I was a child, I spoke as a child (1 Cor. 13:11); the tongue is a small member, but boasts great things (Jas. 3:5); the tongue is a fire, a world of evil (Jas. 3:6); the tongue is a restless evil, full of deadly poison (Jas. 3:8).

A2 The dumb speaking
Zechariah's tongue was loosed and he could speak (Luke 1:64); the dumb spoke (Matt. 9:33; 12:22; 15:31; Mark 7:35; Luke 11:14); he makes the dumb speak (Mark 7:37); the Lord opened the mouth of the donkey (Num. 22:28); a dumb donkey spoke (2 Pet. 2:16).

A3 Eloquence
Sweet speech increases persuasiveness (Prov. 16:21); his speech was smoother than butter (Ps. 55:21); not in wisdom of words lest the cross of Christ be nullified (1 Cor. 1:17); even if I am unskilled in speech (2 Cor. 11:6); pray that utterance may be given me (Eph. 6:19); Aaron could speak well (Exod. 4:14); Apollos was eloquent (Acts 18:24); Moses had never been eloquent (Exod. 4:10); I do not know how to speak (Jer. 1:6); Paul came not with eloquence (1 Cor. 2:1); or with persuasive words (1 Cor. 2:4); the kingdom of God is not words but power (1 Cor. 4:20).

A4 Good speech
A4a The effect of good speech
On the lips of the discerning wisdom is found (Prov. 10:13); the lips of the wise spread knowledge (Prov. 15:7); the lips of the wise will preserve them (Prov. 14:3); words from the mouth of a wise man are gracious (Eccles. 10:12); the mouth of the righteous is a fountain of life (Prov. 10:11); the mouth of the righteous speaks wisdom and justice (Ps. 37:30); the lips of the righteous feed many (Prov. 10:21); the mouth of the upright will deliver them (Prov. 12:6); a healing tongue is a tree of life (Prov. 15:4); the tongue of the wise brings healing (Prov. 12:18); lips of knowledge are more precious than gold (Prov. 20:15); a word fitly spoken is like apples of gold (Prov. 25:11); truthful lips endure for ever (Prov. 12:19).

A4b Let your speech be good
Let your talking be edifying, imparting grace to those who hear (Eph. 4:29); let your speech always be gracious, seasoned with salt (Col. 4:6); speak and act as those to be judged by the law of liberty (Jas. 2:12); the lips of a priest should guard knowledge (Mal. 2:7); set the believers an example in speech and conduct (1 Tim. 4:12); talk of these things when you sit, walk, lie down and rise (Deut. 6:7; 11:19).

A4c People speaking what is good
All marvelled at the gracious words which proceeded from his mouth (Luke 4:22); teacher, you have spoken well (Luke 20:39); Jesus of Nazareth, a prophet mighty in deed and word (Luke 24:19); the words I have spoken to you are spirit and life (John 6:63); you have the words of eternal life (John 6:68); Abel, though dead, still speaks (Heb. 11:4); the blood which speaks better things than that of Abel (Heb. 12:24); that I might speak boldly, as I ought to speak (Eph. 6:20); the fruit of lips giving thanks to his name (Heb. 13:15); not everyone who says, 'Lord, Lord' will enter the kingdom (Matt. 7:21); how can you speak what is good when you are evil? (Matt. 12:34).

A5 Evil speech
A5a Unsatisfactory speech
O deceitful tongue! (Ps. 52:4); the tongue that speaks great things (Ps. 12:3-4); they flatter with their tongue (Ps. 5:9); their throat is an open grave (Ps. 5:9; Rom. 3:13); their lips talk of mischief (Prov. 24:2); the sin of their mouth (Ps. 59:12); under his tongue are mischief and wickedness (Ps. 10:7); their tongue is a sharp sword (Ps. 57:4); swords are in their lips (Ps. 59:7); rash speaking is like sword thrusts (Prov. 12:18); your

tongue is like a sharp razor (Ps. 52:2); they make their tongues sharp as a serpent's (Ps. 140:3); their tongue is a deadly arrow (Jer. 9:8); they bend their tongue like a bow (Jer. 9:3); better a poor man with integrity than one perverse in speech (Prov. 19:1); the perverted tongue will be cut out (Prov. 10:31); let us attack him with our tongue (Jer. 18:18); all your enemies have opened their mouths against you (Lam. 2:16); this man never ceases to speak against this holy place and the law (Acts 6:13); what would this idle babbler say? (Acts 17:18); 'his speech is contemptible' (2 Cor. 10:10).

A5b Speaking against God
Their speech and actions are against the Lord (Isa. 3:8); they speak against you [God] (Ps. 139:20); your words have been hard against me, says the Lord (Mal. 3:13).

A5c Evil speech from evil people
Evildoers pour out arrogant words (Ps. 94:4); the lips of an adulteress drip honey (Prov. 5:3); the mouth of an adulteress is a deep pit (Prov. 22:14); the words of a son of Belial are like scorching fire (Prov. 16:27); by the mouth of the wicked a city is torn down (Prov. 11:11); the mouth of fools pours out folly (Prov. 15:2); an evil man is ensnared by the transgression of his lips (Prov. 12:13); the lips of the fool consume him (Eccles. 10:12); in the mouth of the foolish is a rod for his pride (Prov. 14:3); they could not speak peaceably to Joseph (Gen. 37:4).

A5d Evil done by evil speech
Their talk will spread like gangrene (2 Tim. 2:17); in their greed they will exploit you with false words (2 Pet. 2:3); talking nonsense against us with wicked words (3 John 10); a fool's lips bring strife (Prov. 18:6); the beast was given a mouth speaking arrogant words and blasphemies (Rev. 13:5).

A5e Avoid evil speech
Let him keep his tongue from evil and his lips from speaking guile (Ps. 34:13; 1 Pet. 3:10); do not let your mouth lead you into sin (Eccles. 5:6); let no unwholesome talk come out of your mouth (Eph. 4:29); avoid empty chatter (1 Tim. 6:20; 2 Tim. 2:16); that I may not sin with my tongue (Ps. 39:1); if I have spoken wrongly, bear witness to the wrong (John 18:23).

A5f Kept from evil speech
You hide them from the strife of tongues (Ps. 31:20); put a deceitful mouth and devious talk far from you (Prov. 4:24); blessed are you when they say all kinds of evil against you falsely (Matt. 5:11).

A6 Beware of your speech
Trying to catch him in what he said (Matt. 22:15; Mark 12:13; Luke 11:54; 20:26); he who guards his mouth guards his life (Prov. 13:3); Lord, set a guard over my mouth (Ps. 141:3); before a word is on my tongue, you know it (Ps. 139:4); do not be anxious how or what you are to speak (Matt. 10:19); from the abundance of the heart the mouth speaks (Matt. 12:34); whatever comes out of the mouth comes from the heart (Matt. 15:18); what you have said in the dark will be heard in the light (Luke 12:3); if anyone does not stumble in what he says he is perfect (Jas. 3:2); a fool's lips are a snare to him (Prov. 18:7); if you have been snared by your own words (Prov. 6:2); men will render account for every careless word (Matt. 12:36-7); I will judge you out of your own mouth (Luke 19:22).

A7 Mere talk
Mere talk tends only to poverty (Prov. 14:23); this people honours me with their lips (Isa. 29:13; Matt. 15:8; Mark 7:6); the Pharisees say but do not do (Matt. 23:3); let us not love in word but in deed (1 John 3:18); our gospel did not come to you in word only (1 Thess. 1:5); a slave will not be instructed by words alone (Prov.

29:19); they show love with their lips but their heart goes after gain (Ezek. 33:31); they utter mere words (Hos. 10:4); the obedience of the Gentiles by word and deed (Rom. 15:18); I will find out not the words of these arrogant people but their power (1 Cor. 4:19); the kingdom of God does not consist of words but of power (1 Cor. 4:20); if I speak with the tongues of men and angels but have not love (1 Cor. 13:1); if he says, 'Go in peace', without giving anything (Jas. 2:16); you will be speaking into the air (1 Cor. 14:9); let no one deceive you with empty talk (Eph. 5:6); empty talkers and deceivers (Titus 1:10); whoever says he abides in him should walk as he walked (1 John 2:6); he who says he is in the light and hates his brother is in darkness still (1 John 2:9).

B Speech and God
B1 God speaking
God said, 'Let there be ...' and there was (Gen. 1:3-24); God said, 'Let us make man' (Gen. 1:26); I will speak and my word will be performed (Ezek. 12:25); I have spoken to you from heaven (Exod. 20:22); the doorway of the tent of meeting where I will speak with you (Exod. 29:42); I will speak to you from the mercy seat (Exod. 25:22); he spoke to them in the pillar of cloud (Ps. 99:7); would that God might speak! (Job 11:5); the Lord roars from Zion and utters his voice from Jerusalem (Joel 3:16); the Lord has spoken! who can but prophesy? (Amos 3:8); God has spoken to us in his Son (Heb. 1:2); God speaks once or twice, but no one notices (Job 33:14-16); let not God speak to us lest we die (Exod. 20:19); words which made the hearers beg that no more be spoken to them (Heb. 12:19); God spoke by the mouth of his holy prophets (Acts 3:21).
B2 Christ speaking
I have spoken openly to the world (John 18:20); no man ever spoke like this man (John 7:46); speak the word and my servant will be healed (Matt. 8:8; Luke 7:7); he whom God has sent speaks the word of God (John 3:34).
B3 The Spirit speaking
The Spirit said to Philip, 'Go up and join this chariot' (Acts 8:29); the Lord said to him in a vision, 'Ananias' (Acts 9:10); the Spirit said to him, 'Three men are looking for you' (Acts 10:19); the Spirit told me to go with them (Acts 11:12); the Holy Spirit said, 'Set apart for me Barnabas and Saul' (Acts 13:2).
B4 Speaking to God
I have undertaken to speak to the Lord (Gen. 18:27-32); we will render the fruit of our lips (Hos. 14:2).
PRAYER, see 761A.
B5 Speaking God's words
B5a Speaking the word God gives
I will be with your mouth and teach you what to say (Exod. 4:12, 15); say to Pharaoh all that I say to you (Exod. 6:29); only speak the word I speak to you (Num. 22:35); speak all I command you (Jer. 1:7, 17); whatever God shows me I will tell you (Num. 23:3); I will put my words in his mouth (Deut. 18:18); I have put my words in your mouth (Isa. 51:16; Jer. 1:9); I must speak the word God puts in my mouth (Num. 22:38; 23:12, 26; 24:13; 2 Chr. 18:13); I must speak what God says to me (1 Kgs. 22:14); I will give you words that no one can withstand (Luke 21:15); what to say will be given you (Matt. 10:19); the Holy Spirit will teach you what to say (Luke 12:12); it is not you speaking, but the Holy Spirit (Matt. 10:20; Mark 13:11); I do nothing of myself but speak as the Father taught me (John 8:28); the Father has given me commandment what to speak (John 12:49); the words I say to you are not of my own speaking (John 14:10); the word you hear is not mine

but the Father's who sent me (John 14:25); the words you gave me I gave them (John 17:8).
B5b Speaking as from God
You will be as my mouth (Jer. 15:19); the Lord has given me the tongue of those who are taught (Isa. 50:4); he made my mouth like a sharp sword (Isa. 49:2); whoever speaks, as the oracles of God (1 Pet. 4:11); the prophets spoke in your name to our kings and all the people (Dan. 9:6); I speak of what I have seen with my Father (John 8:38); our words are not by human wisdom but taught by the Spirit (1 Cor. 2:13); the prophets who spoke in the name of the Lord (Jas. 5:10).

C Prophecy
C1 About prophecy
The Lord, the God of the spirits of the prophets (Rev. 22:6); they will know that a prophet has been among them (Ezek. 2:5; 33:33).
C2 God sending prophets
C2a God spoke by the prophets
You have commanded by your servants the prophets (Ezra 9:11); God spoke to our forefathers by the prophets (Heb. 1:1); as he spoke by the mouth of his holy prophets (Luke 1:70; Acts 3:21); the Lord warned Israel through the prophets (2 Kgs. 17:13); the Lord has raised up prophets for us in Babylon (Jer. 29:15); this took place to fulfil what the Lord had spoken by the prophet (Matt. 1:22); what God foretold by the mouth of all the prophets (Acts 3:18); I have hewn them by the prophets (Hos. 6:5).
C2b God sends prophets
I will send you prophets and wise men and scribes (Matt. 23:34); I will send prophets and apostles (Luke 11:49); when the Israelites cried to the Lord, he sent a prophet (Judg. 6:8).
C2c Prophets who were not sent
I have not sent them (Jer. 27:15; 29:9); I have not sent them or commanded them or spoken to them (Jer. 14:14); they say, 'Says the Lord', when the Lord has not sent them (Ezek. 13:6, 7); the Lord has not sent you (Jer. 28:15); I did not send them, but they ran, I did not speak to them yet they prophesied (Jer. 23:21); Shemaiah prophesied though God had not sent him (Neh. 6:10-13; Jer. 29:31).
UNGODLY PROPHETS, see 579C5.
C3 Prophesying
C3a Prophesying in general
Would that all the Lord's people were prophets! (Num. 11:29); the word will not perish from the prophets (Jer. 18:18); do not despise prophesyings (1 Thess. 5:20); I speak to prophets in visions (Num. 12:6); the Lord does nothing without revealing it to the prophets (Amos 3:7); a man praying or prophesying with head covered dishonours his head (1 Cor. 11:4-5); he who prophesies edifies the church (1 Cor. 14:4-6); we have the prophetic word made more sure (2 Pet. 1:19); no prophecy of scripture is a matter of one's own interpretation (2 Pet. 1:20); blessed are those who hear the words of the prophecy (Rev. 1:3); blessed is he who keeps the words of the prophecy of this book (Rev. 22:7); the prophets who prophesied of the grace that was to be yours (1 Pet. 1:10); the prophets and the law prophesied until John (Matt. 11:13).
C3b Prophesy!
Prophesy against them! (Ezek. 11:4); prophesy to the dry bones (Ezek. 37:4); prophesy to the breath (Ezek. 37:9); you must again prophesy about many peoples and tongues and kings (Rev. 10:11); prophesy! who hit you? (Matt. 26:68; Mark 14:65; Luke 22:64).
C3c Particular prophesyings
The seventy elders prophesied (Num. 11:25-7); Saul prophesied (1 Sam. 10:6-11; 19:23-4); as I prophesied,

Pelatiah son of Benaiah fell dead (Ezek. 11:13); as I prophesied there was a noise and the bones came together (Ezek. 37:7); the two witnesses will prophesy (Rev. 11:10); two witnesses prophesying for 1260 days clothed in sackcloth (Rev. 11:3).

C3d Oracles

The oracle concerning: Amalek (Num. 24:20); Ammon (Jer. 49:1-6; Ezek. 21:28-32; 25:2-7); Arabia (Isa. 21:13); Damascus (Isa. 17:1); Dumah [Edom] (Isa. 21:11); Egypt (Isa. 19:1); Moab (Isa. 15:1); Tyre (Isa. 23:1); the wilderness of the sea (Isa. 21:1); the valley of vision (Isa. 22:1); beasts of the Negeb (Isa. 30:6).

C3e Written in the prophets

The law and the prophets were until John (Luke 16:16); they have Moses and the prophets, let them hear them (Luke 16:29); beginning with Moses and all the prophets (Luke 24:27); everything written about me in the law of Moses and the prophets and the psalms (Luke 24:44); we have found him of whom Moses and the prophets wrote, Jesus of Nazareth (John 1:45); Paul spoke about Jesus from the law of Moses and the prophets (Acts 28:23); after the reading of the law and the prophets (Acts 13:15); they did not understand the utterances of the prophets, read every sabbath (Acts 13:27); believing everything in the law and written in the prophets (Acts 24:14); saying nothing but what the prophets and Moses said would come to pass (Acts 26:22); the gospel promised beforehand through his prophets in the holy scriptures (Rom. 1:2); the law and the prophets bear witness to imputed righteousness (Rom. 3:21); the gospel now made known by the scriptures of the prophets (Rom. 16:26); remember the predictions of the holy prophets (2 Pet. 3:2); on these two commandments depend all the law and the prophets (Matt. 22:40).

C3f Prophesying in the church

Your sons and your daughters will prophesy (Joel 2:28; Acts 2:17-18); the gift of prophecy (1 Cor. 12:10); earnestly desire to prophesy (1 Cor. 14:1, 39); prophecy is a sign for believers (1 Cor. 14:22); a gift bestowed on Timothy by prophetic utterance (1 Tim. 4:14); if I have the gift of prophecy and have not love (1 Cor. 13:2); he who prophesies speaks to men for edification, exhortation and comfort (1 Cor. 14:3); you can all prophesy one by one (1 Cor. 14:31); if all prophesy, the unbeliever is called to account (1 Cor. 14:24); let two or three prophets speak and the others judge (1 Cor. 14:29); they spoke in tongues and prophesied (Acts 19:6); prophecy should be according to one's faith (Rom. 12:6); the testimony of Jesus is the spirit of prophecy (Rev. 19:10); we prophesy in part (1 Cor. 13:9); prophecy will cease (1 Cor. 13:8).

C4 Prophets of God

SEER, see 438G.

C4a The prophets in general

Rejoice over her, heaven, saints, apostles and prophets (Rev. 18:20); I am the only one left of the prophets of the Lord (1 Kgs. 18:22); is there not a prophet of the Lord here? (1 Kgs. 22:7); I am not a prophet nor a son of the prophets (Amos 7:14); when you see all the prophets in the kingdom (Luke 13:28); time would fail to tell of the prophets (Heb. 11:32); the prophets enquired about this salvation (1 Pet. 1:10); the time has come for rewarding your slaves the prophets (Rev. 11:18).

C4b Individual prophets

No prophet has arisen like Moses (Deut. 34:10); Aaron would be Moses' prophet (Exod. 7:1); is Saul also among the prophets? (1 Sam. 10:11-12; 19:24); there were many lepers in Israel in the time of Elisha the prophet (Luke 4:27); you will be called prophet of the Most

High (Luke 1:76); the people considered John a prophet (Matt. 14:5; 21:26; Mark 11:32; Luke 20:6); John was more than a prophet (Matt. 11:9; Luke 7:26); Moses and Elijah appeared to them (Matt. 17:3-4; Mark 9:4; Luke 9:30); I also am a prophet like you (1 Kgs. 13:18); John was more than a prophet (Matt. 11:9; Luke 7:26); an old prophet of Bethel (1 Kgs. 13:11; 2 Kgs. 23:18); a prophet (1 Kgs. 20:13, 22); some said that Jesus was Jeremiah or one of the prophets (Matt. 16:14); these two prophets had tormented those who dwell on the earth (Rev. 11:10).

C4c Jesus the prophet

The Lord will raise up for you a prophet like me (Deut. 18:15, 18; Acts 3:22; 7:37); this is the prophet Jesus (Matt. 21:11); a great prophet has arisen (Luke 7:16); I can see you are a prophet (John 4:19); the people considered him a prophet (Matt. 21:46); are you the Prophet? (John 1:21); this is the Prophet who is to come into the world (John 6:14); this is really the Prophet (John 7:40); he is a prophet (John 9:17); a prophet, mighty in word and deed (Luke 24:19); he is a prophet, like one of the prophets of old (Mark 6:15); some said Jesus was one of the prophets (Mark 8:28; Luke 9:8); some said he was one of the old prophets risen (Luke 9:19); why baptise, if you are not the Christ, nor Elijah, nor the Prophet? (John 1:25); a prophet does not come from Galilee (John 7:52); if this man were a prophet (Luke 7:39); no prophet is accepted in his home town (Luke 4:24); prophesy! who hit you? (Matt. 26:68; Mark 14:65; Luke 22:64).

C4d Prophets in the church

God appointed prophets in the church (1 Cor. 12:28; Eph. 4:11); built on the foundation of apostles and prophets (Eph. 2:20); the mystery now revealed to his apostles and prophets (Eph. 3:5); he who receives a prophet as a prophet will receive a prophet's reward (Matt. 10:41); in the church there were prophets and teachers (Acts 13:1); if anyone thinks he is a prophet or spiritual (1 Cor. 14:37); Judas and Silas were prophets (Acts 15:32); prophets came from Jerusalem to Antioch (Acts 11:27); the spirits of prophets are subject to the prophets (1 Cor. 14:32); not all are prophets, are they? (1 Cor. 12:29).

C5 Ungodly prophets

PROPHETS WHO WERE NOT SENT, see 579C2c.

C5a Wicked prophets

The prophets are prophesying lies (Jer. 5:31; 14:14; 27:10, 14, 16); they prophesy falsely (Jer. 27:15); your prophets have seen false and deceptive visions (Jer. 14:14); her prophets divine for money (Mic. 3:11); both prophet and priest are polluted (Jer. 23:11); from prophet to priest everyone deals falsely (Jer. 6:13); from the prophet to the priest everyone practises deceit (Jer. 8:10); because of the sins of prophets and priests (Lam. 4:13); priest and prophet reel from strong drink (Isa. 28:7); the prophets committed adultery (Jer. 23:14; 29:23); her prophets are faithless (Zeph. 3:4).

C5b False prophets

Beware of false prophets (Matt. 7:15); false prophets will arise (Matt. 24:11, 24; Mark 13:22); false prophets arose among the people (2 Pet. 2:1); many false prophets have gone out into the world (1 John 4:1); the prophets who see false visions and speak lying divinations (Ezek. 13:9); the prophets who prophesy falsely in my name (Jer. 23:25); Pashhur had prophesied falsely (Jer. 20:6); Ahab and Zedekiah prophesied falsely (Jer. 29:21); a false prophet called Bar-jesus (Acts 13:6); Jezebel calls herself a prophetess (Rev. 2:20); out of the mouths of the dragon, the beast and the false prophet (Rev. 16:13); the beast and the false prophet were captured (Rev. 19:20); the lake of fire and brimstone where the beast and false prophet are (Rev. 20:10); false prophets denounced (Jer. 23:9-40; Mic. 3:5-7); anyone prophesying falsely will be killed by his parents (Zech. 13:3); prophesy against the prophets who prophesy out of their own minds (Ezek. 13:2); woe to the foolish prophets who follow their own spirit and have seen nothing (Ezek. 13:3); a prophet speaking false words must die (Deut. 18:20); do not listen to your prophets (Jer. 27:9); do not listen to the words of the prophets (Jer. 27:14).

C5c Prophets of other gods
450 prophets of Baal (1 Kgs. 18:19, 22); prophets of Baal (1 Kgs. 18:25); Elijah killed the prophets of Baal (1 Kgs. 18:40; 19:1); summon the prophets of Baal (2 Kgs. 10:19); 400 prophets of the Asherah (1 Kgs. 18:19); 400 prophets, not of the Lord (1 Kgs. 22:6-7; 2 Chr. 18:5-6); go to the prophets of your father and mother (2 Kgs. 3:13); a Cretan prophet (Titus 1:12); I will remove the prophets and unclean spirits from the land (Zech. 13:2); the prophets prophesied by Baal (Jer. 2:8); the prophets of Samaria prophesied by Baal (Jer. 23:13).

C6 Hindered prophecy
C6a Prophecy muzzled
They commanded the prophets not to prophesy (Amos 2:12; Mic. 2:6); do not prophesy in the name of the Lord lest we kill you (Jer. 11:21); do not prophesy at Bethel (Amos 7:13); they tell the prophets not to prophesy truth (Isa. 30:10); you say, 'Do not prophesy against Israel' (Amos 7:16); if I say I will not speak any more in his name (Jer. 20:9).

C6b Prophecy ignored
They mocked God's prophets (2 Chr. 36:16); we have not listened to your servants the prophets (Dan. 9:6); the prophet is a fool, the man of the spirit is mad (Hos. 9:7); a prophet is not without honour except in his home town (Matt. 13:57; Mark 6:4; John 4:44).

C6c Prophets suffering
The prophets were an example of suffering and patience (Jas. 5:10); which one of the prophets did your fathers not persecute? (Acts 7:52); this is how they persecuted the prophets (Matt. 5:12); so their fathers did to the prophets (Luke 6:23).

C6d Prophets killed
They killed the prophets and you build their tombs (Luke 11:48); it cannot be that a prophet perishes away from Jerusalem (Luke 13:33); you are sons of those who killed the prophets (Matt. 23:31); killing the prophets and stoning those sent to you! (Matt. 23:37); they have killed your prophets (Rom. 11:3); they killed the Lord Jesus and the prophets (1 Thess. 2:15); they poured out the blood of saints and prophets (Rev. 16:6); Jezebel destroyed the prophets of the Lord (1 Kgs. 18:4, 13); should priest and prophet be slain in the temple? (Lam. 2:20); that I may avenge the blood of my servants the prophets (2 Kgs. 9:7); the blood of all the prophets will be on this generation (Luke 11:50-1).

D Spokesmen
Aaron will be your mouth (Exod. 4:16); Joab put words in the wise woman's mouth (2 Sam. 14:3); I will speak for you to the king (1 Kgs. 2:18); Paul was called Hermes because he was the chief speaker (Acts 14:12).

E Reading
E1 Reading the Scriptures
Read this law before the people at the Feast of Booths (Deut. 31:11); Moses read the book of the covenant to the people (Exod. 24:7); Joshua read all the law (Josh. 8:34); Shaphan read the book of the law (2 Kgs. 22:8, 10; 2 Chr. 34:18); the king must read the law (Deut. 17:19); Josiah read it to all the people (2 Kgs. 23:2; 2 Chr. 34:30); Ezra read the book of the law before the people (Neh. 8:1-3, 18); Baruch read from the scroll (Jer.

36:6-15); Jehudi read the scroll to the king (Jer. 36:21, 23); when you come to Babylon, read all these words (Jer. 51:61); the eunuch was reading Isaiah (Acts 8:28-30); reading the law and the prophets (Acts 13:15); Moses is read in the synagogues every sabbath (Acts 15:21); the prophets are read every sabbath (Acts 13:27); blessed is he who reads the words of this prophecy (Rev. 1:3); attend to the public reading of Scripture (1 Tim. 4:13); Jesus stood up to read (Luke 4:16); when reading the old covenant the veil remains (2 Cor. 3:14-15).

E2 Reading other matter
Zephaniah read the letter to Jeremiah (Jer. 29:29); they read the letter to the congregation (Acts 15:31); when this letter is read, read it to the Laodiceans also (Col. 4:16); have this letter read to all the brethren (1 Thess. 5:27); many Jews read the inscription (John 19:20); you are our letter, known and read by all men (2 Cor. 3:2); the book of the chronicles was read to the king (Esther 6:1); letters were read out (Ezra 4:18, 23); I cannot read (Isa. 29:12).

580 Speech defect
A Accent
The Gileadites could not say Shibboleth (Judg. 12:6); your speech gives you away (Matt. 26:73).

B Speech impediment
I am slow of speech and of tongue (Exod. 4:10); with stammering lips he will speak to this people (Isa. 28:11); a man with an impediment in his speech (Mark 7:32); the tongue of the stammerers will speak clearly (Isa. 32:4); you will no longer see a people stammering in an unintelligible language (Isa. 33:19).

581 Talkativeness
A Eager to speak
My tongue is the pen of a ready writer (Ps. 45:1); I will praise you and not be silent (Ps. 30:12); all day and all night they will never be silent (Isa. 62:6); I have many things to say but you cannot bear them yet (John 16:12); he testified with many other words (Acts 2:40); Paul prolonged his speech until midnight (Acts 20:7); they think they will be heard for their many words (Matt. 6:7).

B Too many words
Is there no end to windy words? (Job 16:3); shall a multitude of words go unanswered? (Job 11:2); you have multiplied your words against me (Ezek. 35:13); the more words, the more vanity (Eccles. 6:11); when words are many, transgression is inevitable (Prov. 10:19); a fool multiplies words (Eccles. 10:14); a fool's voice comes with many words (Eccles. 5:3); there is more hope for a fool than for a man hasty in speech (Prov. 29:20); Job multiplies words without knowledge (Job 35:16).

KEEPING SILENT, see 582A.

582 Not speaking
SILENCED, see 578B.
A About keeping silent
A1 Silence is wise
He who restrains his lips is wise (Prov. 10:19); a silent fool is considered wise (Prov. 17:28); be silent and let that be your wisdom (Job 13:5); he who guards his tongue guards his soul from evil (Prov. 21:23); there is a time to be silent (Eccles. 3:7); when words abound, sin is not wanting (Prov. 10:19); if anyone does not bridle his tongue his religion is vain (Jas. 1:26).

TOO MANY WORDS, see 581B.

A2 Curbing speech

Be slow to speak (Jas. 1:19); let your words be few before God (Eccles. 5:2); be silent before the Lord (Zeph. 1:7); be silent, all flesh, before the Lord (Zech. 2:13); let him keep his tongue from evil and his lips from speaking guile (1 Pet. 3:10); I will not speak of anything except what Christ has wrought though me (Rom. 15:18); they may be won without a word by the conduct of their wives (1 Pet. 3:1); if there is no interpreter, the speaker in tongues should keep silent (1 Cor. 14:28); if a revelation comes to another, let the first prophet be silent (1 Cor. 14:30); let women keep silent in the churches (1 Cor. 14:34-5); women are to be quiet (1 Tim. 2:11-12); do not let immorality, impurity or covetousness even be named among you (Eph. 5:3); it is disgraceful even to speak of the things they do in secret (Eph. 5:12).

A3 Unduly silent

Do not keep silent (Ps. 35:22); if a woman's father says nothing on hearing of her vow (Num. 30:4); if a woman's husband says nothing on hearing of her vow (Num. 30:7, 11, 14); if one hears an adjuration but does not speak (Lev. 5:1); he hears the adjuration but tells nothing (Prov. 29:24); if they kept quiet, the stones would cry out (Luke 19:40); do not be silent (Acts 18:9).

B Those who kept silent

B1 God silent

These things you did and I kept silence (Ps. 50:21); will you keep silence? (Isa. 64:12); why are you silent when the wicked swallows up the righteous? (Hab. 1:13); when God keeps silent, who can condemn? (Job 34:29); from eternity I have kept silent (Isa. 42:14); was I not silent for a long time? (Isa. 57:11); he will be silent in his love (Zeph. 3:17); do not be silent to me (Ps. 28:1); O God, do not keep silent (Ps. 83:1; 109:1); for Zion's sake I will not keep silent (Isa. 62:1).

B2 Christ silent

God's servant will not cry out (Isa. 42:2; Matt. 12:19); he did not open his mouth (Isa. 53:7; Acts 8:32); Jesus kept silent (Matt. 15:23; 26:63; 27:12, 14; Mark 14:61; 15:5; Luke 23:9; John 19:9); his voice will not be heard in the streets (Matt. 12:19); will you not speak to me? (John 19:10); as a lamb before its shearers is dumb (Acts 8:32).

B3 People silent

My heart waits in silence for God (Ps. 62:1, 5); it is good for one to wait quietly for the Lord's salvation (Lam. 3:26); let all the earth be silent before him (Hab. 2:20); if we were to be made slaves, I would have kept quiet (Esther 7:4); the servant gazed at Rebekah in silence (Gen. 24:21); the people did not answer Elijah (1 Kgs. 18:21); the people did not answer the Assyrians (2 Kgs. 18:36; Isa. 36:21); the Pharisees kept silent (Luke 14:4); the spies were silenced (Luke 20:26); they listened in silence (Acts 15:12); when they heard him speak in Hebrew they were quieter (Acts 22:2); after I spoke they did not speak again (Job 29:22); Job's friends did not speak for seven days (Job 2:13); these three men stopped answering Job (Job 32:1).

583 Addressing someone

God spoke with Moses mouth to mouth (Num. 12:8); speak to the rock (Num. 20:8); let me speak to the people (Acts 21:39).

584 Conversation

After that his brothers talked with him (Gen. 45:15); Moses and Elijah talking with him (Matt. 17:3; Mark 9:4; Luke 9:30); they discussed what had happened (Luke 24:14-15); those who feared the Lord spoke to one another (Mal. 3:16); his mother and brothers sought to speak with him (Matt. 12:46); Paul talked

with them until daybreak (Acts 20:11); Felix often sent for Paul and conversed with him (Acts 24:26); I hope to speak with you face to face (2 John 12).

585 Soliloquy

He says, 'I will return to my house from which I came' (Matt. 12:44); I will say to my soul, 'Soul, you have ample goods' (Luke 12:19); if there is no interpreter, the speaker in tongues should speak to himself and God (1 Cor. 14:28); the fool says in his heart, 'There is no God' (Ps. 14:1).

586 Writing

A The Scriptures written

THE BIBLE, see 975.

A1 The scripture in general

A1a Scripture says

The scripture preached the gospel beforehand to Abraham (Gal. 3:8); attend to the public reading of Scripture (1 Tim. 4:13); today this scripture has been fulfilled in your hearing (Luke 4:21).

A1b It is written

It is written in their law (John 15:25); in the law it is written (1 Cor. 14:21); it is written in the law of Moses (1 Cor. 9:9); in your law it is written (John 8:17); it is written in the prophets (John 6:45); it is written in the book of Psalms (Acts 1:20); as it is written in the law of Moses (2 Kgs. 14:6; 2 Chr. 23:18); as it is written in the second psalm (Acts 13:33); as it is written in the book of the words of Isaiah (Luke 3:4); as it is written in the book of the prophets (Acts 7:42); what is written in the law of Moses (1 Kgs. 2:3); what is written in the law? (Luke 10:26); is it not written in your law (John 10:34).

A1c Written about Christ

In the scroll of the book it is written of me (Ps. 40:7; Heb. 10:7); this is he of whom it is written (Matt. 11:10; Luke 7:27); how is it written of the Son of man? (Mark 9:12); the Son of man goes as it is written of him (Matt. 26:24; Mark 14:21); everything written about the Son of man will be fulfilled (Luke 18:31); what is written about me has its fulfilment (Luke 22:37); his disciples remembered that it was written (John 2:17); when Jesus was glorified they remembered that this had been written of him (John 12:16); David says concerning Christ (Acts 2:25); we have found the one about whom Moses wrote in the law (John 1:45); Moses wrote about me (John 5:46).

A1d Other scriptures fulfilled

It was written not just for his sake but for ours (Rom. 4:23-4); everything written in the past was written for our sake (Rom. 15:4); it was written for our sake (1 Cor. 9:10); these things were written for our instruction (1 Cor. 10:11); these are days of vengeance to fulfil all that is written (Luke 21:22); they did to Elijah as it was written of him (Mark 9:13).

A2 Writing the law

The first tablets of stone were engraved with God's writing (Exod. 32:16; Deut. 5:22); he wrote them on two stone tablets (Deut. 4:13); written with the finger of God (Exod. 31:18; Deut. 9:10); the second set were God's writing (Exod. 34:1; Deut. 10:2-4); but in Moses' hand (Exod. 34:27-8); Moses wrote down the law (Exod. 24:4; Deut. 31:9, 24); the king was to write a copy of the law for himself (Deut. 17:18); Samuel wrote out the ordinances of the kingdom (1 Sam. 10:25); Moses wrote the stages of the Israelites' journeys (Num. 33:2); Joshua wrote this in the book of the law of God (Josh. 24:26); the ministry of death, in letters engraved on stone (2 Cor. 3:7); the law was to be written on plastered stones on Mount Ebal (Deut. 27:3, 8); Joshua wrote on the stones a copy of the law (Josh.

8:32); we serve in the new life of the Spirit, not the old written code (Rom. 7:6); the letter kills but the Spirit gives life (2 Cor. 3:6).

A3 Writing other scriptures
Write it on a tablet and a scroll (Isa. 30:8); write the vision on tablets (Hab. 2:2); written in the book of the Kings of Israel (1 Chr. 9:1); as God says in Hosea (Rom. 9:25); a writing of Hezekiah (Isa. 38:9); Jeremiah had to write his prophecy on a scroll (Jer. 36:2); Baruch wrote at Jeremiah's dictation (Jer. 36:4; 45:1); they are written in Lamentations (2 Chr. 35:25); Daniel wrote down the dream (Dan. 7:1); believing everything in the law and written in the prophets (Acts 24:14).

A4 Psalms
The Levites sang praises with the words of David and Asaph (2 Chr. 29:30); David says in the book of Psalms (Luke 20:42); everything written about me in the law of Moses and the prophets and the psalms (Luke 24:44); as it is written in the book of psalms (Acts 1:20); as it is written in the second psalm (Acts 13:33).

A5 Writing the New Testament
These have been written that you may believe (John 20:31); these things we write that our joy may be complete (1 John 1:4); this is the disciple who has written these things (John 21:24); I am writing this to you that you may not sin (1 John 2:1); write what you see (Rev. 1:11, 19); if everything about Jesus was written, the world could not contain the books (John 21:25); it seemed good for me to write an account (Luke 1:3); Peter wrote by Silvanus (1 Pet. 5:12); the letter was written by Tertius (Rom. 16:22).

B Other written matter
B1 Judgements written
Fingers wrote on the plaster of the wall (Dan. 5:5); curses written down and washed off into the water of bitterness (Num. 5:23); write in a book that the Amalekites are to be wiped out (Exod. 17:14); to execute God's written judgement (Ps. 149:9); a hand was stretched out to me with a written scroll in it (Ezek. 2:9).

B2 Writing letters
We should write to the Gentiles to abstain from pollutions (Acts 15:20); I have written to you very boldly (Rom. 15:15); concerning the matters about which you wrote (1 Cor. 7:1); I write nothing but what you can read and understand (2 Cor. 1:13); I am writing these things when absent (2 Cor. 13:10); in what I am writing to you, before God, I am not lying (Gal. 1:20); as I have written briefly (Eph. 3:3); I am writing these things to you (1 Tim. 3:14); confident of your obedience, I write to you (Philem. 21); I have written to you briefly (Heb. 13:22); I write to you, not because you do not know the truth, but because you do (1 John 2:21); I have written this to you about those who would deceive you (1 John 2:26); I have written to you who believe in the name of the Son of God (1 John 5:13); I wrote something to the church (3 John 9); I was eager to write to you of our common salvation (Jude 3); letters to the seven churches (Rev. 2:1-3:22).
LETTERS, see 588.

B3 Other writings
Oh, that my words were written in a book! (Job 19:23); write it with common characters (Isa. 8:1); write down this song and teach the Israelites (Deut. 31:19); a written survey of the land (Josh. 18:4); writing the names of the leaders of Succoth (Judg. 8:14); Zechariah wrote, 'His name is John' (Luke 1:63); rejoice that your names are written in heaven (Luke 10:20); I heard a voice from heaven saying, 'Write!' (Rev. 14:13); he said to me, 'Write this' (Rev. 19:9); write, for these words are

faithful and true (Rev. 21:5); bring the books, especially the parchments (2 Tim. 4:13).

C Secretaries
C1 The scribes
Where is the wise man? where is the scribe? (1 Cor. 1:20); the scribes were summoned (Esther 3:12; 8:9); I send your prophets and wise men and scribes (Matt. 23:34); beware of the scribes (Mark 12:38; Luke 20:46); unless your righteousness exceeds that of the scribes and Pharisees (Matt. 5:20); the lying pen of the scribes has made the law a lie (Jer. 8:8); they stirred up the people, the elders and the scribes (Acts 6:12); the rulers, elders and scribes were gathered in Jerusalem (Acts 4:5).

C2 Particular scribes
Ezra was a scribe skilled in the law of Moses (Ezra 7:6); a man clothed in linen with a writing case at his side (Ezek. 9:2-11); one of the scribes asked him, 'Which is the greatest commandment?' (Mark 12:28).

C3 Christ and the scribes
C3a Christ and scribes in general
He taught with authority, not as their scribes (Matt. 7:29; Mark 1:22); a scribe offered to follow him (Matt. 8:19); every scribe trained for the kingdom of heaven (Matt. 13:52); how can the scribes say that Christ is the son of David? (Mark 12:35); scribes and Pharisees wanted to see a sign (Matt. 12:38); woe to you, scribes and Pharisees, hypocrites! (Matt. 23:13-29); the scribes and Pharisees brought a woman caught in adultery (John 8:3).

C3b Opposition to Christ from scribes
The scribes said he blasphemed (Matt. 9:3); scribes from Jerusalem said he was possessed by Beelzebub (Mark 3:22); the scribes questioned how a man could forgive sins (Mark 2:6-7); the chief priests and scribes were indignant (Matt. 21:15); scribes and Pharisees watched to see if he would heal on the sabbath (Luke 6:7); the scribes of the Pharisees saw that he ate with sinners (Mark 2:16); the Pharisees and scribes grumbled at Jesus receiving sinners (Luke 15:2); the chief priests, the scribes and the elders asked him of his authority (Mark 11:27-8); the scribes and Pharisees assailed him with questions (Luke 11:53); he must suffer many things from the elders, chief priests and scribes (Matt. 16:21; Luke 9:22); rejected by the elders and chief priests and scribes (Mark 8:31); he will be delivered to the chief priests and scribes (Matt. 20:18; Mark 10:33); the chief priests and scribes sought to kill him (Mark 11:18; 14:1; Luke 19:47; 22:2); the scribes and chief priests tried to lay hands on Jesus (Luke 20:19); the chief priests and scribes accused Jesus (Luke 23:10); the chief priests, scribes and elders mocked him (Matt. 27:41; Mark 15:31).

D The act of writing
D1 Signatures
Here is my signature (Job 31:35); men will sign, seal and witness deeds (Jer. 32:44); I signed and sealed the deed (Jer. 32:10); the witnesses signed the deed of purchase (Jer. 32:12); King Darius signed the document (Dan. 6:9, 10).

D2 Writing on objects
Write these words on your doorposts (Deut. 6:9; 11:20); Jesus wrote on the ground with his finger (John 8:6, 8); writing on two sticks (Ezek. 37:16-17); he called for a writing tablet (Luke 1:63); a white stone with a name written on it (Rev. 2:17).

D3 Writing on people
I will write my law on their hearts (Jer. 31:33; Heb. 8:10); I will write my laws on their mind (Heb. 10:16); the work of the law is written on their hearts (Rom. 2:15); write the teachings on the tablet of your heart

(Prov. 7:3); a letter from Christ written by the Spirit on human hearts (2 Cor. 3:3); their sin is engraved on the tablet of their hearts (Jer. 17:1); on her forehead was written a name (Rev. 17:5); on his robe and on his thigh he has a name written (Rev. 19:16); I will write on him the name of my God and the name of the city and my new name (Rev. 3:12); his name and his Father's name written on their foreheads (Rev. 14:1); one will write on his hand, 'The Lord's' (Isa. 44:5); I have engraved you on the palms of my hands (Isa. 49:16).

D4 Engraving

Engraving the names of Israel on two onyx stones (Exod. 28:9-11; 39:6); engraving the names of Israel on twelve stones (Exod. 28:21; 39:14); the ministry of death, in letters engraved on stone (2 Cor. 3:7); the names of the twelve tribes were inscribed on the gates (Rev. 21:12); 'Holy to the Lord' was to be engraved on a gold plate (Exod. 28:36; 39:30); oh, that my words were engraved with an iron stylus and lead! (Job 19:24); the sin of Judah is written with an iron pen, engraved with a diamond (Jer. 17:1).

587 Print

WRITING, see 586.

588 Correspondence

WRITING LETTERS, see 586B2.

A Paul's letters

As our brother Paul wrote to you (2 Pet. 3:15); Paul's letters contain some things hard to understand (2 Pet. 3:16); his letters are weighty and strong (2 Cor. 10:10); have this letter read to all the brethren (1 Thess. 5:27); see this letter is read by the Laodiceans, and read the letter from Laodicea (Col. 4:16); do not be shaken by a letter supposed to be from us (2 Thess. 2:2); I wrote to you in my letter (1 Cor. 5:9); I am not writing to gain any such provision (1 Cor. 9:15); I wrote to you that your zeal for us might be revealed (2 Cor. 7:12); what we say by letters when absent, we do when present (2 Cor. 10:11); if anyone does not obey what we say in this letter (2 Thess. 3:14); my own handwriting is the mark in every letter (2 Thess. 3:17); I wrote to you with many tears (2 Cor. 2:3-4); I caused you sorrow by my letter (2 Cor. 7:8); I do not want to appear to frighten you by my letters (2 Cor. 10:9); hold fast to the traditions whether taught by word of mouth or letter (2 Thess. 2:15).

B Letters to churches

A letter sent to the church at Antioch (Acts 15:23-9); I will give letters to the men carrying your gift (1 Cor. 16:3); do we need letters of recommendation? (2 Cor. 3:1); the brethren wrote to the disciples to welcome Apollos (Acts 18:27); you are a letter from Christ written on human hearts (2 Cor. 3:2-3); this is my second letter to you (2 Pet. 3:1); I wrote to the church (3 John 9); we wrote to the Gentiles who believed (Acts 21:25); the letter to the church of: Ephesus (Rev. 2:1-7); Smyrna (Rev. 2:8-11); Pergamum (Rev. 2:12-17); Thyatira (Rev. 2:18-29); Sardis (Rev. 3:1-6); Philadelphia (Rev. 3:7-13); Laodicea (Rev. 3:14-22).

C Other letters

David wrote to Joab (2 Sam. 11:14); Jezebel wrote letters in Ahab's name (1 Kgs. 21:8); Sennacherib wrote letters insulting the Lord (2 Chr. 32:17); the king of Babylon sent Hezekiah letters (Isa. 39:1); Hezekiah spread the letter before the Lord (2 Kgs. 19:14; Isa. 37:14); Berodach-baladan sent letters to Hezekiah (2 Kgs. 20:12); we have received no letters from Judea about you (Acts 28:21); the enemies of Judah sent a letter to Artaxerxes (Ezra 4:6-16); Artaxerxes sent a reply (Ezra 4:17-22); Tattenai sent a letter to Darius (Ezra 5:6-17);

Sanballat sent his servant with an open letter (Neh. 6:5); Tobiah sent letters to frighten me (Neh. 6:19); Saul [Paul] asked for letters to Damascus (Acts 9:2); I received letters from the high priest and the Council (Acts 22:5).

589 Book

A Books in general

Of the writing of books there is no end (Eccles. 12:12); the world could not contain all the books (John 21:25); bring the books, especially the parchments (2 Tim. 4:13); the deaf will hear the words of a book (Isa. 29:18); at the judgement the books were opened (Dan. 7:10; Rev. 20:12); write what you see in a book (Rev. 1:11); the sky vanished like a scroll which is rolled up (Rev. 6:14); books of magic were burned (Acts 19:19).

B Historical books

The book of the generations of Adam (Gen. 5:1); the book of the Wars of the Lord (Num. 21:14); the book of Jashar (Josh. 10:13; 2 Sam. 1:18); the book of the Chronicles of the Kings of Israel (1 Kgs. 14:19; 2 Kgs. 1:18); the book of the Chronicles of the Kings of Judah (1 Kgs. 14:29; 2 Kgs. 8:23); the book of the Kings of Judah and Israel (2 Chr. 16:11); the book of the Kings of Israel (1 Chr. 9:1; 2 Chr. 20:34); the book of the Kings (2 Chr. 24:27); the chronicles of Samuel the seer (1 Chr. 29:29); the chronicles of Nathan the prophet (1 Chr. 29:29; 2 Chr. 9:29); the chronicles of Gad the seer (1 Chr. 29:29); the book of the deeds of Solomon (1 Kgs. 11:41); the book of the Chronicles of the Kings of Media and Persia (Esther 10:2); the book of the Chronicles (Esther 2:23; 6:1); the annals of Jehu son of Hanani (2 Chr. 20:34); they wrote the description of the land in a book (Josh. 18:9); search in the record books (Ezra 4:15); search was made in the house of the books (Ezra 6:1); a scroll was found in Ecbatana (Ezra 6:2); the customs for Purim were written in the book (Esther 9:32); many have compiled narratives (Luke 1:1).

C Books registering people

The number was not entered in David's chronicles (1 Chr. 27:24); the Levites were registered in the book of the chronicles (Neh. 12:23); the book of the genealogy of returned exiles (Neh. 7:5); false prophets will not be written in the register of Israel (Ezek. 13:9).

D Book of the covenant

Moses read the book of the covenant (Exod. 24:7); Josiah read the book of the covenant (2 Kgs. 23:2); as it is written in the book of the covenant (2 Kgs. 23:21).

E Book of the law

Moses wrote the law in a book (Deut. 31:24); Joshua wrote this in the book of the law of God (Josh. 24:26); the book of the law of Moses (Josh. 8:31; Neh. 8:1); the law in the book of Moses (2 Chr. 25:4); the book of Moses (2 Chr. 35:12; Ezra 6:18; Neh. 13:1); take this book of the law (Deut. 31:26); this book of the law shall not depart out of your mouth (Josh. 1:8); Hezekiah found the book of the law in the temple (2 Kgs. 22:8-10; 2 Chr. 34:14-16); have you not read in the book of Moses (Mark 12:26).

LAW, see 953.

F Books of prophecy

Write this in a book, that I will blot out Amalek (Exod. 17:14); as it is written in the book of the words of Isaiah the prophet (Luke 3:4); the book of the prophet Isaiah (Luke 4:17); it is written in the book of Psalms (Acts 1:20); blessed is he who keeps the words of the prophecy of this book (Rev. 22:7); those who keep the words of this book (Rev. 22:9); do not seal up the words of the prophecy of this book (Rev. 22:10); the words of the prophecy of this book (Rev. 22:18); oh, that my words were written in a book! (Job 19:23); I observed in the books the years for Jerusalem (Dan. 9:2); as it is written in the book of the prophets (Acts 7:42); they are written in Lamentations (2 Chr. 35:25).

G Books in prophecy

A book in the hand of the one on the throne (Rev. 5:1); a scroll written on both sides (Ezek. 2:10); a hand was stretched out to me with a written scroll in it (Ezek. 2:9); I opened my mouth and he gave me this scroll to eat (Ezek. 3:2-3); a little book in the angel's hand (Rev. 10:2); take the book from the angel (Rev. 10:8-10); a flying scroll (Zech. 5:1-2); he took the book from the right hand of him who was seated on the throne (Rev. 5:7).

H God's book

Seek and read in the book of the Lord (Isa. 34:16); blot me out of your book (Exod. 32:32); whoever has sinned I will blot them out of my book (Exod. 32:33); may they be blotted out of the book of life (Ps. 69:28); a book of remembrance for those who fear the Lord (Mal. 3:16); everyone found written in the book will be saved (Dan. 12:1); fellow-workers whose names are in the book of life (Phil. 4:3); I will not rub out his name from the book of life (Rev. 3:5); those whose names are not written in the book of life of the Lamb (Rev. 13:8); their names not written in the book of life from the foundation of the world (Rev. 17:8); another book was opened, the book of life (Rev. 20:12); if anyone's name was not found written in the book of life (Rev. 20:15); only those whose names are written in the Lamb's book of life (Rev. 21:27); those enrolled in heaven (Heb. 12:23); the days ordained for me were written in your book (Ps. 139:16); are my tears not in your book? (Ps. 56:8).

590 Description

A Inscription

The inscription Mene, Mene, Tekel, Parsin (Dan. 5:7-25); whose likeness and inscription are these? (Matt. 22:20; Mark 12:16; Luke 20:24); there was an inscription above the cross (Luke 23:38; John 19:19); the inscription of the charge against him read, 'The King of the Jews' (Mark 15:26); an altar with this inscription, 'To an unknown god' (Acts 17:23).

B Description

Write a description of the land (Josh. 18:4); they wrote the description in a book (Josh. 18:9); describe the temple that they may be ashamed (Ezek. 43:10).

591 Dissertation

BOOK, see 589.

592 Summary

CONCISENESS, see 569.

593 Poetry. Prose

As some of your own poets have said (Acts 17:28).

594 Drama

SPECTACLE, see 445C.

595 Will

WILLING, see 597.

A God's will

A1 What God's will is

By your will all things existed and were created (Rev. 4:11); by that will we have been sanctified through the offering of Jesus Christ (Heb. 10:10); it is God's will that by doing right you silence the ignorance of foolish men (1 Pet. 2:15); by his will he gave birth to us by the word of truth (Jas. 1:18); Christ delivers us according to the will of God the Father (Gal. 1:4); those born not of

the will of the flesh nor of the will of man but of God (John 1:13); this is the will of God, your sanctification (1 Thess. 4:3); it is not God's will that any little one perish (Matt. 18:14); in everything give thanks, for this is God's will (1 Thess. 5:18); this is his will, that I lose nothing of what he has given me (John 6:39); this is the will of my Father, that every who believes in the Son should have eternal life (John 6:40); Paul, an apostle by the will of God (1 Cor. 1:1; 2 Cor. 1:1; Eph. 1:1; Col. 1:1; 2 Tim. 1:1).

A2 God works his will

He works all things according to the counsel of his will (Eph. 1:11); who can resist his will? (Rom. 9:19); he has mercy on whom he will and hardens whom he will (Rom. 9:18); he predestined us according to the purpose of his will (Eph. 1:5); God is at work in you both to will and to work (Phil. 2:13); gifts distributed by the Spirit as he wills (1 Cor. 12:11); gifts of the Holy Spirit distributed according to his will (Heb. 2:4); if we ask anything according to his will, he hears us (1 John 5:14).

B Man and God's will

B1 Knowing God's will

Prove what the will of God is (Rom. 12:2); understand what the will of the Lord is (Eph. 5:17); filled with the knowledge of his will (Col. 1:9); if you know his will (Rom. 2:18); he made known to us the mystery of his will (Eph. 1:9); that servant who knew his master's will but did not act in accord with his will (Luke 12:47); that you might know his will (Acts 22:14); praying that you may be mature, fully assured in all the will of God (Col. 4:12).

B2 Doing God's will

Not as I will, but as you will (Matt. 26:39; Mark 14:36; Luke 22:42); I do not seek my own will, but the will of the him who sent me (John 5:30); I came not to do my own will, but the will of him who sent me (John 6:38); my food is to do the will of him who sent me (John 4:34); if any man is willing to do his will, he will know of the teaching (John 7:17); he who does the will of God abides for ever (1 John 2:17); not everyone who says 'Lord' but he who does the will of my Father (Matt. 7:21); David, a man who will do all my will (Acts 13:22); slaves of Christ, doing the will of God from the heart (Eph. 6:6); I come to do your will (Heb. 10:7-9); that after you have done the will of God you might receive what is promised (Heb. 10:36); God will equip you with everything good to do his will (Heb. 13:21); living the rest of the time in the flesh for the will of God (1 Pet. 4:2); the Lord's will be done (Acts 21:14); your will be done (Matt. 6:10; 26:42); suffering according to the will of God (1 Pet. 4:19); if the Lord wills we shall do this and that (Jas. 4:15); I will return if God wills (Acts 18:21); I will come to you soon if the Lord wills (1 Cor. 4:19).

C The will of men

Which son did the will of his father? (Matt. 21:31); Elijah has come and they did to him whatever they wished (Mark 9:13); he delivered up Jesus to their will (Luke 23:25); those born not of the will of the flesh nor of the will of man but of God (John 1:13).

596 Necessity

A Necessary

Only a few things are necessary, or only one (Luke 10:42); did you not know that I had to be in my Father's house? (Luke 2:49); was it not necessary for the Christ to suffer? (Luke 24:26); explaining and demonstrating that the Christ had to suffer and rise again (Acts 17:3); for me to remain in the flesh is more necessary for you (Phil. 1:24); it is necessary that stumbling blocks come (Matt. 18:7); it is necessary to circumcise Gentiles who believe (Acts 15:5); it seemed good to lay on you no greater burden than these essentials (Acts 15:28).

B Destiny
You who set a table for Fortune and Destiny (Isa. 65:11); I will destine you to the sword (Isa. 65:12); we were destined for affliction (1 Thess. 3:3); God has not destined us for wrath but to obtain salvation (1 Thess. 5:9).

597 Willingness
WILL, see 595.

A God willing
If the Lord wills we will live and do this or that (Jas. 4:15); God is willing for all men to be saved (1 Tim. 2:4); if you are willing, remove this cup from me (Luke 22:42).

B Christ willing
If you are willing, you can make me clean (Matt. 8:2-3; Mark 1:40-1; Luke 5:12); if you are willing, I will make three booths (Matt. 17:4).

C People willing
Everyone who is of a willing heart, let him bring a contribution (Exod. 35:5); some volunteered to live in Jerusalem (Neh. 11:2); if someone forces you to go one mile, go with him two (Matt. 5:41); I did not shrink from declaring to you anything that was profitable (Acts 20:20); I did not shrink from proclaiming the whole purpose of God (Acts 20:27); if I do this willingly, I have a reward (1 Cor. 9:17); that your goodness might not be by compulsion but of your own free will (Philem. 14); tend the flock of God, not under compulsion but willingly (1 Pet. 5:2); the spirit is willing but the flesh is weak (Matt. 26:41; Mark 14:38); your people will volunteer freely in the day of your power (Ps. 110:3).

598 Unwillingness
A God unwilling
It is not your Father's will that one of these little ones should perish (Matt. 18:14); the Lord was unwilling to destroy you (Deut. 10:10); the Lord does not willingly afflict men (Lam. 3:33); the Lord was unwilling to destroy the house of David (2 Chr. 21:7).

B Christ unwilling
Jesus would not drink the wine mixed with gall (Matt. 27:34); I am unwilling to send them away hungry (Matt. 15:32).

C People unwilling
What if the woman is unwilling to come back here? (Gen. 24:5); you would not go up to the land (Deut. 1:26); the man who is unwilling to take his brother's wife (Deut. 25:7, 8); David was unwilling to bring the ark of the Lord in (2 Sam. 6:10); Herod was unwilling to refuse her (Mark 6:26); the judge was unwilling (Luke 18:4); Joseph was unwilling to put Mary to shame (Matt. 1:19); you are unwilling to come to me that you may have life (John 5:40); do not give grudgingly or under compulsion (2 Cor. 9:7); I would gather you as a hen gathers her chicks, and you would not (Matt. 23:37; Luke 13:34); the son said, 'I will not' (Matt. 21:29).

599 Resolution
A God resolute
I will not change my mind (Jer. 4:28); the Lord has sworn and will not change his mind (Ps. 110:4; Heb. 7:21).

B Whole-hearted
Love the Lord with all your heart, soul, might (Deut. 6:5; Matt. 22:37; Mark 12:30; Luke 10:27); unite my heart to fear your name (Ps. 86:11); you will seek the Lord and find him if you seek with all your heart (Deut. 4:29; Jer. 29:13); with my whole heart I have sought you (Ps. 119:10); do these statutes with all your heart and soul (Deut. 26:16); they gave their offering with a whole heart (1 Chr. 29:9); they helped David with an undivided heart (1 Chr. 12:33); David followed me with all his heart (1 Kgs. 14:8); Asa's heart was wholly true to the Lord (1 Kgs. 15:14); Josiah turned to the Lord with all his heart, soul and might (2 Kgs. 23:25); Hezekiah did everything with all his heart (2 Chr. 31:21); he exhorted them to remain true to the Lord with resolute heart (Acts 11:23); Jehoshaphat sought the Lord with all his heart (2 Chr. 22:9); you will keep in perfect peace him whose mind is stayed on you (Isa. 26:3); I have set my face like a flint (Isa. 50:7); Hazael set his face to go to Jerusalem (2 Kgs. 12:17); Jesus set his face to go to Jerusalem (Luke 9:51).

600 Perseverance
A God enduring
You bore with them for many years (Neh. 9:30); how long must I endure you? (Mark 9:19; Luke 9:41); God endured with much patience the vessels of wrath (Rom. 9:22); Jesus for the joy set before him endured the cross (Heb. 12:2).

B Standing firm
If you do this you will be able to stand (Exod. 18:23); continue in the faith, stable and steadfast (Col. 1:23); stand against the devil's wiles (Eph. 6:11); resist the devil, standing firm in the faith (1 Pet. 5:9); stand firm in the faith (1 Cor. 16:13); you stand firm in the faith (2 Cor. 1:24); we must hold fast our confidence (Heb. 3:6, 14; 4:14); hold fast the confession of our hope (Heb. 10:23); realize the full assurance of hope until the end (Heb. 6:11); stand firm in the teaching (2 Thess. 2:15); stand firm in one spirit (Phil. 1:27); stand firm in the Lord (Phil. 4:1); that you may be able to resist in the evil day, and having done all to stand (Eph. 6:13).

C Enduring
Love bears all things, endures all things (1 Cor. 13:7); for all endurance and patience with joy (Col. 1:11); you have endured for my name's sake (Rev. 2:3); he who endures to the end will be saved (Matt. 10:22; 24:13; Mark 13:13); by your endurance you will gain your lives (Luke 21:19); that through endurance and the encouragement of the scriptures we might have hope (Rom. 15:4); God will provide the way of escape that you may be able to endure temptation (1 Cor. 10:13); endure hardship (2 Tim. 4:5); you have need of endurance (Heb. 10:36); let endurance have its full effect (Jas. 1:4); this is grace, if one endures pain whilst suffering unjustly (1 Pet. 2:19); blessed is the man who perseveres under trial (Jas. 1:12); we count those blessed who endured (Jas. 5:11); if we endure we will reign with him (2 Tim. 2:12); we endure all things (1 Cor. 9:12); we commend ourselves by much endurance (2 Cor. 6:4); when persecuted we endure (1 Cor. 4:12); it is for discipline that you have to endure (Heb. 12:7); I endure all things for the sake of the elect (2 Tim. 2:10); Moses endured as seeing him who is invisible (Heb. 11:27); the endurance of Job (Jas. 5:11); the testing of your faith produces endurance (Jas. 1:3).

D Persevering
Be steadfast, unmoveable (1 Cor. 15:58); pursue perseverance (1 Tim. 6:11); add to self-control perseverance (2 Pet. 1:6); here is a call for the perseverance and faith of the saints (Rev. 13:10); here is

the perseverance of the saints (Rev. 14:12); his heart is steadfast, trusting in the Lord (Ps. 112:7); persevering in tribulation (Rom. 12:12); you have followed my perseverance (2 Tim. 3:10); your work of faith, labour of love and steadfastness of hope (1 Thess. 1:3); older men are to be sound in faith, love and perseverance (Titus 2:2); we boast of your perseverance (2 Thess. 1:4); they bear fruit with perseverance (Luke 8:15); he who keeps my works to the end (Rev. 2:26); I want to complete my course and ministry (Acts 20:24); those who persevere in doing good (Rom. 2:7); the marks of a true apostle were wrought among you with perseverance (2 Cor. 12:12); your partner in the tribulation and kingdom and perseverance in Jesus (Rev. 1:9); pray with all perseverance (Eph. 6:18); I know your perseverance (Rev. 2:2, 19); may the Lord direct your hearts into the steadfastness of Christ (2 Thess. 3:5); tribulation produces perseverance (Rom. 5:3); perseverance produces character (Rom. 5:4).

E Persisting
Because of his friend's persistence he will give him what he needs (Luke 11:8); she will wear me out with her persistence (Luke 18:5).

601 Irresolution

A Double-minded
A double-minded man, unstable in all his ways (Jas. 1:8); purify your hearts, you double-minded (Jas. 4:8); they speak with a double heart (Ps. 12:2); I hate the double-minded (Ps. 119:113); how long will you limp between two opinions? (1 Kgs. 18:21).

B Yes and no
Was I vacillating, saying yes, yes and no, no? (2 Cor. 1:17-18); Christ Jesus is not yes and no (2 Cor. 1:19).

C Not whole-hearted
Solomon's heart was not wholly true to the Lord as David's had been (1 Kgs. 11:4, 6); Abijam's heart was not wholly true to the Lord as David's had been (1 Kgs. 15:3); Amaziah did right, but not with a whole heart (2 Chr. 25:2); Judah did not return to me with all her heart (Jer. 3:10); he endures only for a while (Matt. 13:21).

602 Obstinacy

A God hardening people
The Lord hardened Pharaoh's heart (Exod. 4:21; 7:3; 9:12; 10:1, 20, 27; 11:10; 14:4, 8); I will harden the heart of the Egyptians (Exod. 14:17); the Lord made Sihon's heart obstinate (Deut. 2:30); the Lord hardened the hearts of the Canaanites (Josh. 11:20); you will give them hardness of heart (Lam. 3:65); why do you harden our heart? (Isa. 63:17); he has blinded their eyes and hardened their heart (John 12:40); he hardens whom he will (Rom. 9:18).

B Obstinate people
B1 An obstinate nation
I know that you are obstinate (Isa. 48:4); a disobedient and obstinate people (Rom. 10:21); a stubborn generation (Ps. 78:8); stubborn children (Ezek. 2:4); Israel is like a stubborn heifer (Hos. 4:16); they made their faces harder than rock (Jer. 5:3); the house of Israel are strong of forehead and hard of heart [obstinate] (Ezek. 3:7); divorce was permitted because of their hardness of heart (Matt. 19:8; Mark 10:5); the Israelites were a stiff-necked people (Exod. 32:9; Deut. 9:6; 2 Kgs. 17:14; Neh. 9:16-17); you stiff-necked people (Acts 7:51).

B2 Obstinate individuals
If a man has a stubborn, rebellious son (Deut. 21:18); our son is stubborn (Deut. 21:20); they turned a stubborn shoulder and stopped their ears (Zech. 7:11);

Jesus was grieved at their hardness of heart (Mark 3:5); daring and self-willed (2 Pet. 2:10); Pharaoh hardened his heart (Exod. 8:15, 32; 9:34); why harden your hearts as Pharaoh did? (1 Sam. 6:6); they did not understand about the loaves, but their hearts were hardened (Mark 6:52); are your hearts hardened? (Mark 8:17); when some became hardened and disobeyed (Acts 19:9); their minds were hardened (2 Cor. 3:14); I know your rebellion and stubbornness (Deut. 31:27).

B3 Avoid obstinacy
Do not be stiff-necked (Deut. 10:16; 2 Chr. 30:8); do not harden your hearts (Ps. 95:8; Heb. 3:8, 15; 4:7); lest any of you be hardened by the deceitfulness of sin (Heb. 3:13); an elder [overseer] must not be self-willed (Titus 1:7); they will not walk in the stubbornness of their evil heart (Jer. 3:17); a man stiff-necked after much reproof will suddenly be broken (Prov. 29:1); because of your stubborn, unrepentant heart you store up wrath (Rom. 2:5); Jesus reproached them for their hardness of heart (Mark 16:14).

603 Change of mind

A God changing his mind
God is not man, that he should change his mind (Num. 23:19); God does not change his mind like a man (1 Sam. 15:29); the Lord does not take back his words (Isa. 31:2); the Son of God was not Yes and No (2 Cor. 1:19); I knew that you were a God who repented of evil (Jonah 4:2); change your mind about harming your people (Exod. 32:12-14); God changed his mind (Amos 7:3, 6; Jonah 3:9-10); if the nation turns from evil, I will repent of the evil (Jer. 18:8); the Lord repented of the evil he pronounced (Jer. 26:19); the Lord repented from the evil (2 Sam. 24:16); if it does evil, I will repent of the good (Jer. 18:10).

B People changing their minds
The Egyptians changed their minds (Exod. 14:5); they turned around and took back their slaves (Jer. 34:11); lest the people change their minds when they see war (Exod. 13:17); they changed their minds and said Paul was a god (Acts 28:6); he changed his mind and went to work (Matt. 21:29); you did not change your minds and believe John (Matt. 21:32).

REPENTANCE, see 939.

C Change of allegiance
C1 Turning from God
C1a Do not turn from God
Do not turn away from following the Lord (1 Sam. 12:20-1); lest any turn away from the Lord (Deut. 29:18).

C1b Many turned from God
They have quickly turned aside from the way (Exod. 32:8); they have all turned aside (Ps. 14:3; 53:3); they have turned away from the Holy One of Israel (Isa. 1:4); they have strayed from me (Hos. 7:13); their apostasies are many (Jer. 5:6); an unbelieving heart to fall away from the living God (Heb. 3:12); Saul has turned back from following me (1 Sam. 15:11); many of his disciples withdrew and did not walk with him (John 6:66); forsaking the right way they have gone astray (2 Pet. 2:15); some have strayed from the faith (1 Tim. 6:21); some have strayed from the truth (2 Tim. 2:18); through love of money some have wandered from the faith (1 Tim. 6:10); some have turned aside to follow Satan (1 Tim. 5:15); they turn away from the holy commandment (2 Pet. 2:21); our backslidings are many (Jer. 14:7); why has this people turned away in perpetual apostasy? (Jer. 8:5).

C1c Many will turn from God
You will all fall away this night (Matt. 26:31; Mark 14:27); many will fall away (Matt. 24:10); when

persecution comes he falls away (Matt. 13:21; Mark 4:17); they believe for a while and in time of temptation they fall away (Luke 8:13); the day of the Lord will be preceded by apostasy (2 Thess. 2:3); in the last days some will fall away from the faith (1 Tim. 4:1).

C1d Judgement on backsliders
No one who puts his hand to the plough and looks back is fit for the kingdom (Luke 9:62); cursed is the man whose heart turns away from the Lord (Jer. 17:5); I hate the work of those who fall away (Ps. 101:3); if they fall away it is impossible to bring them to repentance (Heb. 6:4-7).

C1e Not turning from God
We will not turn back from you (Ps. 80:18); our steps have not departed from your way (Ps. 44:18); I will put the fear of me in their hearts so they will not turn away (Jer. 32:40); even if all fall away, I will not (Matt. 26:33; Mark 14:29).

C2 Turning against men
You are defecting to the Chaldeans! (Jer. 37:13); the people who had deserted to Nebuchadnezzar (Jer. 39:9); the deserters who had deserted to the king of Babylon (Jer. 52:15); I fear the Jews who have deserted to the Chaldeans (Jer. 38:19); my friend has lifted up his heel against me (Ps. 41:9); the Hebrews who had been with the Philistines turned against them (1 Sam. 14:21).

604 Caprice
IRRATIONAL, see 448.

605 Choice

A God's choice

A1 God chooses
Blessed is the man you choose (Ps. 65:4); many are called but few chosen (Matt. 22:14); the rod of the one I choose will sprout (Num. 17:5); your king shall be the one God chooses (Deut. 17:15); no one knows the Father except the one to whom the Son chooses to reveal him (Matt. 11:27); he became visible to witnesses chosen beforehand by God (Acts 10:41); he chooses our inheritance for us (Ps. 47:4); he did not choose Ephraim (Ps. 78:67).

A2 God's chosen nation
God chose Israel (Deut. 10:15); God chose you as his own people (Deut. 14:2); the Lord has chosen Israel for himself (Ps. 135:4); blessed is the people he chose for his inheritance (Ps. 33:12); you only have I chosen (Amos 3:2); Israel whom I have chosen (Isa. 44:1); Israel, my chosen one (Isa. 45:4); Jacob whom I have chosen (Isa. 41:8); Jeshurun whom I have chosen (Isa. 44:2); the God of Israel chose our fathers (Acts 13:17); the Lord will again choose Israel (Isa. 14:1); God chose you to be a people for himself (Deut. 7:6); he led forth his chosen ones with joy (Ps. 105:43); you are a chosen race (1 Pet. 2:9).

A3 God's chosen city
God choosing a place for his name (Deut. 12:5; Josh. 9:27; 2 Kgs. 21:7; 2 Chr. 12:13; Neh. 1:9); the place the Lord chooses (Deut. 15:20); God chose the temple (2 Chr. 7:12); the city you have chosen (1 Kgs. 8:44); Jerusalem which I have chosen (1 Kgs. 11:13; 2 Kgs. 23:27; 2 Chr. 33:7); I have chosen Jerusalem for my name (2 Chr. 6:6); God chose Zion (Ps. 132:13); the Lord will again choose Jerusalem (Zech. 1:17).

A4 God's chosen individuals
A4a Chosen Son
I have chosen him to be my son (1 Chr. 28:6); this is my Son, my chosen one (Luke 9:35); my servant, my chosen one (Isa. 42:1; 43:10; Matt. 12:18); the Holy One of Israel has chosen you (Isa. 49:7); if he is the Christ of

God, his chosen One (Luke 23:35); rejected by men but chosen and precious in God's sight (1 Pet. 2:4-6).

A4b The elect [chosen ones]
For the sake of the elect the days will be shortened (Matt. 24:22; Mark 13:20); misleading, if possible, even the elect (Matt. 24:24; Mark 13:22); I endure all things for the sake of the elect (2 Tim. 2:10); God's elect ones (Col. 3:12); angels will gather his elect from the four winds (Matt. 24:31; Mark 13:27); will God not bring justice for his elect? (Luke 18:7); who will bring a charge against God's elect? (Rom. 8:33);
what Israel sought only the elect found (Rom. 11:7); the faith of God's elect (Titus 1:1); the elder to the elect lady and her children (2 John 1).

A4c Chosen disciples
Jesus called his disciples and chose 12 whom he named apostles (Luke 6:13); you did not choose me but I chose you (John 15:16); I have chosen you out of the world (John 15:19); I know the ones I have chosen (John 13:18); I chose you and one of you is a devil (John 6:70); show which of these two you have chosen (Acts 1:24); Jesus gave orders to the apostles whom he had chosen (Acts 1:2);
Paul is my chosen instrument (Acts 9:15); chosen in him before the foundation of the world (Eph. 1:4); we know he chose you (1 Thess. 1:4); God chose you from the beginning for salvation (2 Thess. 2:13); God chose the poor to be rich in faith (Jas. 2:5); God chose the low-born, despised and non-entities (1 Cor. 1:28); make your calling and election sure (2 Pet. 1:10); those with him are called, chosen and faithful (Rev. 17:14); God's purpose in choosing (Rom. 9:11); God has chosen the weak and foolish things (1 Cor. 1:27); a remnant chosen by grace (Rom. 11:5); chosen according to the foreknowledge of God (1 Pet. 1:1-2).

B People choosing

B1 Choosing God's way
Choose this day whom you will serve (Josh. 24:15); choose life (Deut. 30:19); God will instruct him in the way he should choose (Ps. 25:12); decide in your hearts not to prepare what to answer (Luke 21:14); Moses chose to endure ill-treatment with the people of God (Heb. 11:26).

B2 Choosing people
I will follow the one the Lord and this people have chosen (2 Sam. 16:18); which of the two do you want me to release for you? (Matt. 27:21); select seven men of good reputation (Acts 6:3); they chose men to send to Antioch with Paul and Barnabas (Acts 15:22); choose a man for single combat (1 Sam. 17:8).

B3 Choosing things
Choose one of these three things (2 Sam. 24:12; 1 Chr. 21:10); Lot chose the valley of Jordan (Gen. 13:11); Gad chose the best for himself (Deut. 33:21).

C Choice by instrument

C1 By casting lots
C1a About casting lots
The lot is cast into the lap, but the decision is from the Lord (Prov. 16:33); the lot puts an end to disputes (Prov. 18:18); they called these days Purim after Pur – the lot (Esther 9:26); the lines have fallen for me in pleasant places (Ps. 16:6).

C1b Urim and Thummim
Urim and Thummim (Exod. 28:30; Lev. 8:8; Deut. 33:8; Ezra 2:63; Neh. 7:65); the judgement of the Urim (Num. 27:21); if it is me or Jonathan give Urim, but if it is the people give Thummim (1 Sam. 14:41); God did not answer Saul by Urim (1 Sam. 28:6).

C1c Lots being cast
Casting lots: over the two goats (Lev. 16:8); for tribal allocations (Num. 26:55; Josh. 14:2; Ezek. 45:1); for

towns for the Levites (Josh. 21:4; 1 Chr. 6:65); for attackers of Benjamin (Judg. 20:9); for who had broken the oath (1 Sam. 14:41-2); for divisions of the priests (1 Chr. 24:5); for divisions of the Levites (1 Chr. 24:31); for duties of the musicians (1 Chr. 25:8-31); for gates for the gatekeepers (1 Chr. 26:13-19); for people to bring firewood (Neh. 10:34); for who should live in Jerusalem (Neh. 11:1); for a day and month to destroy the Jews (Esther 3:7; 9:24); for my people (Joel 3:3); over Jerusalem (Obad. 11); to decide the troublemaker (Jonah 1:7); for the priest to burn incense (Luke 1:9); for a replacement for Judas (Acts 1:26); for Jesus' garments (Ps. 22:18; Matt. 27:35; Mark 15:24; Luke 23:34; John 19:24).

CASTING LOTS TO GAMBLE, see 618B.

C2 By inspecting omens
The king of Babylon consults omens to choose the way (Ezek. 21:21-2); frustrating the omens of boasters (Isa. 44:25).

606 Absence of choice
How long will you limp between two opinions? (1 Kgs. 18:21); you did not choose me but I chose you (John 15:16); I do not know which to choose [life or death] (Phil. 1:22).

607 Rejection
A Rejecting people
I have rejected these (1 Sam. 16:7-10); he did not choose Ephraim (Ps. 78:67); the Lord has rejected those in whom you trust (Jer. 2:37); he who rejects you rejects me and rejects the one who sent me (Luke 10:16).

B Rejecting the Christ
He was despised and rejected by men (Isa. 53:3); the Son of man must be rejected (Mark 8:31; Luke 9:22); the stone which the builders rejected (Ps. 118:22; Matt. 21:42; Mark 12:10; Luke 20:17; 1 Pet. 2:7); this is the stone rejected by your builders (Acts 4:11); a living stone rejected by men (1 Pet. 2:4); rejected by this generation (Luke 17:25); he who rejects me has one who judges him (John 12:48); away with this man and release Barabbas (Luke 23:18); much less shall we escape if we reject him who warns from heaven (Heb. 12:25); he who rejects you rejects me and rejects the one who sent me (Luke 10:16).

C Rejecting things
They did not choose the fear of the Lord (Prov. 1:29); they would have none of my [Wisdom's] counsel (Prov. 1:30); they have rejected my law (Jer. 6:19); they have rejected the law of the Lord (Amos 2:4); they have rejected my ordinances (Ezek. 5:6); do not reject the discipline of the Lord (Prov. 3:11); he has rejected your calf, Samaria (Hos. 8:5); we have renounced disgraceful, underhanded ways (2 Cor. 4:2); he who rejects this is not rejecting man but God (1 Thess. 4:8); nothing is to be rejected if it is received with thanksgiving (1 Tim. 4:4).

D Throw away
Every one will throw away his idols (Isa. 31:7); Moses threw the tablets from his hands (Exod. 32:19); they sorted the good fish into containers but threw the bad away (Matt. 13:48); if anyone does not abide in me he is thrown away as a branch (John 15:6).

RELINQUISH, see 621.

608 Predetermination
A Predestined plan
The peoples did whatever your hand predestined to occur (Acts 4:28); the hidden wisdom which God predestined (1 Cor. 2:7); God prepared our good works beforehand (Eph. 2:10); delivered up by the predetermined plan and foreknowledge of God (Acts 2:23); that he may send you Jesus, the Christ foreordained for you (Acts 3:20); they stumble because they are disobedient, as they were appointed (1 Pet. 2:8); a man's lifespan is predetermined (Job 14:5).

B Predestined people
Whom he knew, he also predestined to become conformed to the image of his Son (Rom. 8:29-30); he predestined us to adoption (Eph. 1:5); predestined according to his purpose (Eph. 1:11); as many as were ordained to eternal life believed (Acts 13:48); God chose you from the beginning for salvation (2 Thess. 2:13); vessels of mercy prepared beforehand for glory (Rom. 9:23); God has not destined us for wrath but to obtain salvation (1 Thess. 5:9); their names not written in the book of life before the foundation of the world (Rev. 13:8; 17:8).

609 Spontaneity
UNPREMEDITATED, see 618A.

610 Habit
If the ox was in the habit of goring (Exod. 21:29, 36); Daniel prayed and gave thanks to God three times a day as formerly (Dan. 6:10); not neglecting to meet together, as is the habit of some (Heb. 10:25).

TRADITION, see 127C.

611 Weaning
The day Isaac was weaned (Gen. 21:8); Samuel stayed with his mother until he was weaned (1 Sam. 1:22-4); my soul is like a weaned child (Ps. 131:2); will he teach those just weaned? (Isa. 28:9).

612 Motive
A Urging
A1 God urging
God was like an eagle stirring up the nest (Deut. 32:11); have you forgotten the exhortation? (Heb. 12:5); I will arouse your lovers against you (Ezek. 23:22); the Lord incited David to take a census (2 Sam. 24:1); the angels urged Lot (Gen. 19:15).

A2 Exhort others
If your gift is exhortation, use it in your exhortation (Rom. 12:8); stirring up one another to love and good works (Heb. 10:24); attend to exhortation (1 Tim. 4:13); teach and urge these things (1 Tim. 6:2); reprove, rebuke, exhort with all longsuffering and teaching (2 Tim. 4:2); exhort one another every day (Heb. 3:13); he who prophesies speaks to men for edification, exhortation and comfort (1 Cor. 14:3); you can all prophesy that all may learn and be exhorted (1 Cor. 14:31); if you have any word of exhortation for the people, say it (Acts 13:15).

A3 Exhorting people to good
Paul exhorted the disciples (Acts 20:1); I urge you by the mercy of God (Rom. 12:1); I urge you by our Lord Jesus Christ and by the love of the Spirit (Rom. 15:30); I urge you, brethren (Rom. 16:17; 1 Cor. 1:10; 4:16); we urge you in the Lord Jesus (1 Thess. 4:1); we urge you to love one another more and more (1 Thess. 4:10); I thought it necessary to urge the brethren to go on ahead (2 Cor. 9:5); I urge you by the meekness and gentleness of Christ (2 Cor. 10:1); our exhortation does not spring from error or uncleanness or deceit (1 Thess. 2:3); we exhorted and encouraged you (1 Thess. 2:11); we command and exhort such people in the Lord Jesus (2 Thess. 3:12); I urged you when I left for Macedonia (1 Tim. 1:3); I urge that prayers be made for all men (1 Tim. 2:1); encouraging one another all the more as you

see the day drawing near (Heb. 10:25); I urge you to do this (Heb. 13:19); bear with this word of exhortation (Heb. 13:22); I exhort the elders among you (1 Pet. 5:1); knowing the fear of the Lord, we persuade men (2 Cor. 5:11); Paul tried to persuade them about Jesus (Acts 28:23); Paul was persuading Jews and Greeks (Acts 18:4).

A4 Inciting to evil
Jezebel incited Ahab to do evil (1 Kgs. 21:25); Satan incited God against Job (Job 2:3); Satan moved David to number Israel (1 Chr. 21:1); the chief priests persuaded the crowds (Matt. 27:20; Mark 15:11); the Jews incited the devout women of high standing (Acts 13:50); the unbelieving Jews stirred up the Gentiles (Acts 14:2); having persuaded the crowds they stoned Paul (Acts 14:19); they stirred up the crowd (Acts 17:8); the Jews stirred up and incited the crowds in Berea (Acts 17:13); Jews from Asia stirred up all the crowd (Acts 21:27).

B Tempting
TESTING, see 461.

B1 Being tempted
No temptation has overtaken you except what is common to man (1 Cor. 10:13); come together again lest Satan tempt you (1 Cor. 7:5); do not lead us into temptation (Matt. 6:13; Luke 11:4); pray that you might not enter into temptation (Matt. 26:41; Mark 14:38; Luke 22:40, 46); look to yourself lest you also be tempted (Gal. 6:1); those wanting to be rich fall into temptation and a snare (1 Tim. 6:9); God cannot be tempted with evil and tempts no one (Jas. 1:13); let no one say he is tempted by God (Jas. 1:13-14); the seduction of riches (Matt. 13:22); I was afraid the tempter might have tempted you (1 Thess. 3:5).

B2 Christ's temptation
Jesus was tempted by the devil (Matt. 4:1; Mark 1:13; Luke 4:2); we have a high priest who has been tempted in every way as we are (Heb. 4:15); since he was tempted, he is able to help those who are tempted (Heb. 2:18).

B3 Enticing
Sweet speech increases persuasiveness (Prov. 16:21); wisdom adds persuasiveness to the lips (Prov. 16:23); with patience a ruler may be persuaded (Prov. 25:15); they entice unstable souls (2 Pet. 2:14); they entice by fleshly desires (2 Pet. 2:18); if a man seduces a virgin (Exod. 22:16); if sinners entice you, do not consent (Prov. 1:10); the harlot entices him (Prov. 7:21).

C Bribing
C1 Taking bribes
You take bribes (Amos 5:12); everyone loves a bribe (Isa. 1:23); they acquit the guilty for a bribe (Isa. 5:23); leaders give judgement for a bribe (Mic. 3:11); they have taken bribes to shed blood (Ezek. 22:12); the prince and the judge ask for a bribe (Mic. 7:3); Samuel's sons took bribes (1 Sam. 8:3); the priests bribed the soldiers (Matt. 28:12); Felix hoped Paul would give him a bribe (Acts 24:26).

C2 Effect of bribes
A man's gift makes room for him (Prov. 18:16); a gift in secret averts anger (Prov. 21:14); a bribe corrupts the heart (Eccles. 7:7); a bribe blinds the seeing (Exod. 23:8); a bribe perverts the cause of the righteous (Exod. 23:8); cursed is he who accepts a bribe to kill (Deut. 27:25).

C3 Avoid bribes
Do not accept a bribe (Exod. 23:8; Deut. 16:19); he who hates bribes will live (Prov. 15:27); from whom have I taken a bribe? (1 Sam. 12:3); he who shakes his hands lest they hold a bribe (Isa. 33:15); God does not take a

bribe (Deut. 10:17); there is no bribery with God (2 Chr. 19:7).

613 Dissuasion
The people were restrained from giving more (Exod. 36:6); with difficulty they restrained the people from sacrificing to them (Acts 14:18).

614 Pretext
They began to make excuses (Luke 14:18).

615 Good
GOODNESS, see 644.

616 Evil
BADNESS, see 645.

617 Intention
PLAN, see 623.

A God's purposes
Shall I hide from Abraham what I am about to do? (Gen. 18:17); you meant evil but God meant it for good (Gen. 50:20); in accord with God's eternal purpose (Eph. 3:11); according to his purpose which he set forth in Christ (Eph. 1:9); the Pharisees and lawyers rejected God's purpose for themselves (Luke 7:30); those called according to his purpose (Rom. 8:28); not according to works but according to his own purpose (2 Tim. 1:9).
GOD S WILL, see 595A.
GOD S PLANS, see 623A.

B Man's purposes
The word of God is able to discern the intentions of the heart (Heb. 4:12); you did well that it was in your heart (1 Kgs. 8:18; 2 Chr. 6:8); Ezra set his heart to study the law (Ezra 7:10); repent and pray that the intent of your heart may be forgiven (Acts 8:22); let each one do as he has purposed in his heart (2 Cor. 9:7); God has put it into their hearts to carry out his purpose (Rev. 17:17); Assyria does not intend so (Isa. 10:7).
THE WILL OF MEN, see 595C.

C Target
Shooting at a target (1 Sam. 20:20); make love your aim (1 Cor. 14:1); the aim of our instruction is love (1 Tim. 1:5).

618 Nondesign. Gamble

A Unintentional
Sinning unintentionally (Lev. 4:2); if anyone eats a sacrifice unintentionally (Lev. 22:14); instructions concerning one who kills another unintentionally (Exod. 21:13; Deut. 4:42; Josh. 20:3).
BY CHANCE, see 159.

B Gambling
They divided his garments by casting lots (Matt. 27:35; Mark 15:24; Luke 23:34); for my garments they cast lots (Ps. 22:18; John 19:24).

619 Pursuit

A Hunting
A1 Hunting game
Nimrod was a mighty hunter before the Lord (Gen. 10:9); Esau became a skilful hunter (Gen. 25:27); go hunt game for me (Gen. 27:3); can you hunt prey for the lion? (Job 38:39).

A2 Hunting people
I am against the magic bands with which you hunt souls like birds (Ezek. 13:20-1); each of them hunts his brother with a net (Mic. 7:2); fishermen will fish for them and hunters will hunt for them (Jer. 16:16); my enemies hunt me down like a bird (Lam. 3:52); like

hunting a partridge in the mountains (1 Sam. 26:20); you hunt me like a lion (Job 10:16).

B Pursuing people

B1 God pursuing people

You have pursued us (Lam. 3:43); you will pursue them (Lam. 3:66); he will pursue his enemies into darkness (Nahum 1:8).

B2 Pursuing people in general

Five of you will chase 100 and 100 chase 10 000 (Lev. 26:8); one puts to flight 1000 (Josh. 23:10); how could one chase 1000 and two put 10 000 to flight unless the Lord had given them up (Deut. 32:30); 1000 will flee from one (Isa. 30:17); faint yet pursuing (Judg. 8:4); your pursuers will be swift (Isa. 30:16); our pursuers were swifter than eagles (Lam. 4:19); how long will you pursue your brothers? (2 Sam. 2:26).

B3 Pursuing specific people

Abraham pursued the kings (Gen. 14:14, 15); Barak pursuing Sisera (Judg. 4:16, 22); Edom pursued his brother with the sword (Amos 1:11); Laban pursued Jacob (Gen. 31:23); Pharaoh pursued the Israelites (Exod. 14:4, 8); the Amorites chased you like bees (Deut. 1:44); the men of Ai pursued the Israelites (Josh. 7:5; 8:16); Saul pursued by chariots and horsemen (2 Sam. 1:6); Saul pursued David (1 Sam. 23:25-8); Asahel pursued Abner (2 Sam. 2:19); Joab and Abishai pursued Abner (2 Sam. 2:24); let me choose 12 000 men to pursue David (2 Sam. 17:1).

C Pursuing good

Pursue righteousness, faith, love and peace (2 Tim. 2:22); seek peace and pursue it (Ps. 34:14; 1 Pet. 3:11); pursue peace with all men and holiness (Heb. 12:14); Gentiles who did not pursue righteousness attained it (Rom. 9:30-1); let us pursue what makes for peace and mutual upbuilding (Rom. 14:19); I press on to make it my own (Phil. 3:12); I press on toward the goal (Phil. 3:14); pursue righteousness etc. (1 Tim. 6:11).

620 Avoidance

A Fleeing

A1 Fleeing in general

The wicked flee when no one pursues (Prov. 28:1); like those ashamed who flee in battle (2 Sam. 19:3); the hireling sees the wolf and flees (John 10:12); he who flees from the terror will fall into the pit (Isa. 24:18; Jer. 48:44); three months fleeing from your enemies? (2 Sam. 24:13; 1 Chr. 21:12); flight will perish from the swift (Amos 2:14); your enemies will flee seven ways from you (Deut. 28:7); you will flee seven ways from your enemies (Deut. 28:25); they put foreign armies to flight (Heb. 11:34); as if a man flees from a lion and a bear meets him (Amos 5:19); do not stand at the fork of the road to cut down their fugitives (Obad. 14); I cannot flee to the hills (Gen. 19:19).

A2 Fleeing from God

Jonah ran away from the Lord (Jonah 1:3, 10); where can I flee from your presence? (Ps. 139:7); who warned you to flee from the wrath to come? (Matt. 3:7; Luke 3:7); at your rebuke the waters fled (Ps. 104:7); the sea looked and fled (Ps. 114:3, 5); earth and sky fled from his presence (Rev. 20:11).

A3 Flee!

Get up and get out of this place! (Gen. 19:14); flee from Babylon (Isa. 48:20; Jer. 50:8; 51:6); flee from the land of the north (Zech. 2:6-7); flee to Egypt (Matt. 2:13); flee like a bird to the mountain (Ps. 11:1); let those who hate him flee before him (Ps. 68:1); should a man like me flee? (Neh. 6:11); let those in Judea flee to the mountains (Matt. 24:16; Mark 13:14; Luke 21:21); when they persecute you, flee to the next town (Matt. 10:23).

A4 Peoples who fled

Those who feared the Lord made their servants and livestock flee into the house (Exod. 9:20); the Egyptians were fleeing into the water (Exod. 14:27); Edom have fled from the sword and bow (Isa. 21:15); a sound of fugitives from Babylon (Jer. 50:28).

A5 Israel fleeing

Pharaoh was told that the people had fled (Exod. 14:5); Israel fled before the men of Ai (Josh. 7:4); the people fled from the Philistines (1 Sam. 31:1; 2 Sam. 23:11; 1 Chr. 10:1; 11:13); Judah fled from Israel (2 Chr. 25:22); Joshua pretended to flee (Josh. 8:5-6, 15); Israel fled to draw Benjamin out (Judg. 20:32); people in Thebez fled into the tower (Judg. 9:51); you are fugitives from Ephraim, you Gileadites (Judg. 12:4); 600 Benjaminites fled (Judg. 20:47); the Israelites fled to their tents (1 Sam. 4:10; 2 Sam. 18:17; 19:8; 2 Kgs. 8:21); Judah fled to their tents (2 Kgs. 14:12); the Israelites fled from the battle (1 Sam. 4:17; 2 Sam. 1:4); the Israelites fled before Goliath (1 Sam. 17:24).

A6 Individuals fleeing

A6a Those who fled from people

Those who fled from people: Absalom from David (2 Sam. 13:34, 37-8); Ahaziah from Jehu (2 Kgs. 9:27); David from Absalom (2 Sam. 19:9; 1 Kgs. 2:7; Ps. 3:t); David and his men from Absalom (2 Sam. 15:14); David from Saul (1 Sam. 19:10-18; 20:1; 21:10; 27:4; Ps. 57:t); Elijah from Jezebel (1 Kgs. 19:3); Gaal from Abimelech (Judg. 9:40); Hagar from Sarah (Gen. 16:6-8); Jacob from Esau (Gen. 27:43; 35:1, 7); Jacob from Laban (Gen. 31:21); Jephthah from his brothers (Judg. 11:3); Jeroboam from Solomon (1 Kgs. 11:40; 12:2; 2 Chr. 10:2); Joseph from Potiphar's wife (Gen. 39:12-18); Jotham from Abimelech (Judg. 9:21); Lot from Sodom (Gen. 19:17-20); Moses from Pharaoh (Exod. 2:15; Acts 7:29); Rezon from his master (1 Kgs. 11:23); Uriah the prophet from Jehoiakim (Jer. 26:21).

A6b Those who fled

The herdsmen fled and told what had happened (Luke 8:34); the exorcists fled naked and wounded (Acts 19:16); Jesus dodged their grasp (John 10:39); we who have fled for refuge (Heb. 6:18); those who fled: Adoni-bezek (Judg. 1:6); Amaziah (2 Kgs. 14:19); Benhadad (1 Kgs. 20:30); Hadad to Egypt (1 Kgs. 11:17); Mephibosheth's nurse (2 Sam. 4:4); Paul and Barnabas to Lystra (Acts 14:6); Rehoboam to Jerusalem (1 Kgs. 12:18; 2 Chr. 10:18); Sisera (Judg. 4:15, 17); Zebah and Zalmunna (Judg. 8:12); Zedekiah and his men (Jer. 39:4); the king's sons (2 Sam. 13:29); the prophet (2 Kgs. 9:10); the people to Egypt (2 Kgs. 25:26); the herdsmen (Matt. 8:33; Mark 5:14); the disciples (Matt. 26:56; Mark 14:50); a naked man (Mark 14:52); the women from the tomb (Mark 16:8); the woman into the wilderness (Rev. 12:6).

A7 Refuge for those fleeing

I will appoint a place where he may flee (Exod. 21:13); the cities of refuge to which the manslayer could flee (Num. 35:6, 11-34; Deut. 4:42; 19:3-5; Josh. 20:4).

A8 Evil fleeing

Resist the devil and he will flee from you (Jas. 4:7); God's hand has pierced the fleeing serpent (Job 26:13); the sun rises and the locusts flee to an unknown place (Nahum 3:17).

B Avoiding evil

Flee from youthful lusts (2 Tim. 2:22); flee immorality (1 Cor. 6:18); flee from idolatry (1 Cor. 10:14); abstain from every kind of evil (1 Thess. 5:22); flee from these things (1 Tim. 6:11); abstain from iniquity (2 Tim. 2:19); Gentiles should abstain from pollutions (Acts 15:20, 29); they should abstain from meat sacrificed to idols (Acts 21:25); have nothing to do with worldly old women's tales (1 Tim. 4:7); avoid empty chatter (2 Tim. 2:16); be free from the love of money (Heb. 13:5); abstain from fleshly passions which war against the soul (1 Pet. 2:11).

C Leaving alone

C1 Leaving God alone

Leave me alone that my anger may burn among them (Exod. 32:10); leave me alone that I might destroy them (Deut. 9:14).

C2 Leave us alone

Leave us alone to serve the Egyptians (Exod. 14:12); leave us alone for seven days (1 Sam. 11:3); do not bother me (Luke 11:7); turn your gaze from me (Ps. 39:13); leave me alone for two months (Judg. 11:37); 'Keep away! Unclean!' they cry of themselves (Lam. 4:15).

C3 Leave them alone

Leave them alone (Matt. 15:14); Ephraim is joined to idols – let him alone (Hos. 4:17); leave him alone, let us see whether Elijah will come to save him (Matt. 27:49); leave him alone and let him curse (2 Sam. 16:11); leave her alone (2 Kgs. 4:27; Mark 14:6; John 12:7); have nothing to do with that righteous man (Matt. 27:19); leave these men alone (Acts 5:38); do nothing to these men (Gen. 19:8); do not stretch out your hand against the lad (Gen. 22:12).

C4 Leaving people alone

Two men in the field, one taken and one left (Matt. 24:40); two women grinding at the mill, one taken and one left (Matt. 24:41); in past generations he allowed all nations to walk in their own ways (Acts 14:16); the spirit will hardly leave him alone (Luke 9:39); God left him alone to test him (2 Chr. 32:31).

C5 Having no dealings

Do not associate with a hot-tempered man (Prov. 22:24); keep away from those who cause divisions (Rom. 16:17); have nothing to do with a factious man after a first and second warning (Titus 3:10); keep away from every brother living in idleness (2 Thess. 3:6); do not associate with those who do not obey these instructions (2 Thess. 3:14); have nothing to do with these people (2 Tim. 3:5); get away from all that belongs to these wicked men (Num. 16:26).

621 Relinquishment

A God forsaking

A1 God will forsake

God will abandon them in the wilderness (Num. 32:15); I will forsake them (Deut. 31:17); I will abandon you (Jer. 23:33); I will reject this temple (1 Kgs. 9:7; 2 Chr. 7:20); I will reject Jerusalem and this temple (2 Kgs. 23:27); I will abandon the remnant of my inheritance (2 Kgs. 21:14); he will give Israel up (1 Kgs. 14:16); I reject you as my priests (Hos. 4:6); will the Lord reject us for ever? (Ps. 77:7); he leaves the 99 to search for the one (Matt. 18:12; Luke 15:4).

A2 Do not forsake us!

Do not forsake me (Ps. 27:9; 38:21; 119:8); do not turn away the face of your anointed (Ps. 132:10); do not cast me from your presence (Ps. 51:11); do not cast me off in old age (Ps. 71:9, 18); do not forsake me when my strength fails (Ps. 71:9); do not forsake the work of your hands (Ps. 138:8); do not reject us for ever (Ps. 44:23).

A3 God has forsaken

Have you utterly rejected Judah? (Jer. 14:19); the Lord rejected Israel (Deut. 32:19; 2 Kgs. 17:20; Ps. 78:59); you have abandoned your people (Isa. 2:6); these two families the Lord chose, he has now rejected (Jer. 33:24); Zion said, 'The Lord has forsaken me' (Isa. 49:14); you abandoned them to their enemies (Neh. 9:28); because you have forsaken the Lord, he has

forsaken you (2 Chr. 24:20); you have rejected us (Ps. 44:9; 60:1, 10; 74:1); he rejected the tent of Joseph (Ps. 78:67); the Lord has forsaken the land (Ezek. 8:12); you have rejected your anointed one (Ps. 89:38); reject silver, because the Lord has rejected them (Jer. 6:30); God had rejected them (Ps. 53:5); unless the Lord had given them up (Deut. 32:30); the Lord has rejected his altar (Lam. 2:7); the Lord has abandoned his sanctuary (Lam. 2:7); he abandoned the tent at Shiloh (Ps. 78:60); I have forsaken my house (Jer. 12:7); why do you forsake us so long? (Lam. 5:20); for a brief moment I forsook you (Isa. 54:7); if the rejection of the Jews led to the reconciliation of the world (Rom. 11:15).

A4 God abandoning individuals

Afterwards Esau was rejected (Heb. 12:17); Samson did not know that the Lord had left him (Judg. 16:20); he has rejected you from being king (1 Sam. 15:23); the Spirit of God left Saul (1 Sam. 16:14); I have rejected Saul from being king (1 Sam. 16:1); my God, why have you forsaken me? (Ps. 22:1; Matt. 27:46; Mark 15:34); God has forsaken him (Ps. 71:11).

A5 God not forsaking

How can I give you up? (Hos. 11:8); God will not reject a blameless man (Job 8:20); I will not reject them (Lev. 26:44); the Lord will not reject for ever (Lam. 3:31); the Lord will not forsake his inheritance (Ps. 94:14); you will not abandon me to Sheol (Ps. 16:10); the Lord will not leave him in the hand of the wicked (Ps. 37:33); I am old yet have I not seen the righteous forsaken (Ps. 37:25); the Lord does not forsake his godly ones (Ps. 37:28); the Lord will not abandon his people (1 Sam. 12:22; Ps. 94:14); God will not forsake you (Deut. 4:31); God will never leave you or forsake you (Deut. 31:6; Josh. 1:5; 1 Chr. 28:20); I will never leave you or forsake you (Heb. 13:5); I will not leave you (Gen. 28:15); I will not forsake my people (1 Kgs. 6:13); I will not leave you as orphans (John 14:18); God has not forsaken us (Ezra 9:9); Israel and Judah have not been forsaken by God (Jer. 51:5); God has not rejected his people (Rom. 11:1); you did not forsake them (Neh. 9:17, 19, 31); you have not forsaken those who seek you (Ps. 9:10); we are persecuted but not forsaken (2 Cor. 4:9); God has not rejected his people whom he foreknew (Rom. 11:2).

B People forsaking

B1 Forsaking God

B1a Those who forsake God

Why does the wicked renounce God? (Ps. 10:13); the land commits harlotry, forsaking the Lord (Hos. 1:2); they have forsaken the Lord to pay heed to harlotry (Hos. 4:10); they played the harlot, deserting their God (Hos. 4:12); you have played the harlot, forsaking your God (Hos. 9:1); forsaking the right way they have gone astray (2 Pet. 2:15); you have rejected your God who saves you (1 Sam. 10:19); you have forsaken the Lord (2 Chr. 13:11; Jer. 2:17); you have forsaken me (Jer. 5:19; 15:6); they have forsaken me (2 Chr. 34:25; Jer. 1:16); they have rejected me as king (1 Sam. 8:7); our fathers have forsaken him (2 Chr. 29:6); your fathers have forsaken me (Jer. 16:11); your children have forsaken me (Jer. 5:7); they will forsake me (Deut. 31:16); they have forsaken the Lord (Isa. 1:4; Jer. 19:4); they have forsaken me (1 Kgs. 11:33; 2 Kgs. 22:17); they have forsaken me and served other gods (1 Sam. 8:8); they have forsaken the spring of living water (Jer. 2:13; 17:13); he forsook the God who made him (Deut. 32:15); you have cast me behind your back (1 Kgs. 14:9); you are deserting him who called you (Gal. 1:6).

B1b Consequences of forsaking God

Those who forsake the Lord will perish (Isa. 1:28); you will be destroyed because you have forsaken me (Deut. 28:20); God's anger is against all who forsake him (Ezra

8:22); all who forsake you will be put to shame (Jer. 17:13); if you forsake him, he will harm you (Josh. 24:20); because you rejected him, he has rejected you (1 Sam. 15:23); if you forsake him, he will forsake you (1 Chr. 28:9; 2 Chr. 15:2); you have forsaken me so I have forsaken you (2 Chr. 12:5).

B1c Forsaking God's things
They abandoned the temple (2 Chr. 24:18); he abandoned the law of the Lord (2 Chr. 12:1); they rejected his statutes and covenant (2 Kgs. 17:15); forsaking his commandments (1 Kgs. 18:18; 2 Kgs. 17:16; Ezra 9:10); you leave the commandment of God and hold fast the tradition of men (Mark 7:8); they have forsaken my law (Jer. 9:13); the wicked forsake your law (Ps. 119:53); they have rejected the word of the Lord (Jer. 8:9); you have abandoned your first love (Rev. 2:4); they have forsaken your covenant (1 Kgs. 19:10, 14).

B2 Abandoning for God
Go forth from your country, your kin and your home (Gen. 12:1); Ruth left her parents and her land (Ruth 2:11); they left their nets (Matt. 4:20-2; Mark 1:18-20); Matthew left everything and followed him (Luke 5:28); they left everything and followed him (Luke 5:11); we have left everything and followed you (Matt. 19:27; Mark 10:28; Luke 18:28); whoever does not forsake everything cannot be my disciple (Luke 14:33); he who leaves houses, family, children or lands for my name's sake (Matt. 19:29; Mark 10:29; Luke 18:29).

B3 People abandoning people
For this reason a man will leave his father and mother (Gen. 2:24; Matt. 19:5; Mark 10:7; Eph. 5:31); my father and mother forsake me (Ps. 27:10); the adulteress leaves the companion of her youth (Prov. 2:17); the disciples forsook him and fled (Matt. 26:56; Mark 14:50); the hireling leaves the sheep and flees (John 10:12); woe to the shepherd who deserts the flock (Zech. 11:17); everyone has deserted me (2 Tim. 1:15); at my first defence everyone deserted me (2 Tim. 4:16); John Mark left them in Pamphylia (Acts 13:13; 15:38); Demas has deserted me (2 Tim. 4:10); Paul agreed to be left behind in Athens (1 Thess. 3:1); like a wife forsaken and rejected (Isa. 54:6).

B4 Abandoning things
There is a time to throw away (Eccles. 3:6); put away the gods your fathers served (Josh. 24:14); put away the foreign gods (Josh. 24:23); they put away the foreign gods (Judg. 10:16); he left his garment in her hand (Gen. 39:12-13); he left the linen sheet and ran away naked (Mark 14:52); Bartimaeus threw aside his cloak (Mark 10:50); they jettisoned the cargo (Acts 27:18); they threw the ship's tackle overboard (Acts 27:19); they threw the wheat into the sea (Acts 27:38); leave your gift there before the altar (Matt. 5:24); the Philistines abandoned their idols (2 Sam. 5:21; 1 Chr. 14:12); the woman left her water pot (John 4:28).

622 Business

Danger that this trade of ours may fall into disrepute (Acts 19:27).

623 Plan

A God's plans
No plan of yours can be thwarted (Job 42:2); the Lord has planned and who can annul it? (Isa. 14:27); the plans of the Lord stand for ever (Ps. 33:11); I will accomplish all my purpose (Isa. 46:10); God planned it long ago (2 Kgs. 19:25; Isa. 22:11; 25:1; 37:26); the Lord planned it (Isa. 23:9); you devised evil against me but God devised good (Gen. 50:20); I have purposed to do good to Jerusalem and Judah (Zech. 8:15); I know the

plans I have for you, plans for welfare (Jer. 29:11); a plan for the fullness of time (Eph. 1:10); who planned this against Tyre? (Isa. 23:8); hear the Lord's plan against Edom (Jer. 49:20); hear the Lord's plan against Babylon (Jer. 50:45); the Lord's plan is against Babylon to destroy it (Jer. 51:11); God has planned to destroy you (2 Chr. 25:16).

INTENTION, see 617.

B Others' plans

B1 Plans in general
Man was made upright, but seeks many devices (Eccles. 7:29); a plan in the heart of a man is like deep water (Prov. 20:5); commit your works to the Lord and your plans will be established (Prov. 16:3); man plans his way but the Lord directs his steps (Prov. 16:9); the plans are man's but the answer is the Lord's (Prov. 16:1); man plans much, but the Lord's purposes will stand (Prov. 19:21); the noble man devises noble plans (Isa. 32:8); may he fulfil all your plans (Ps. 20:4); woe to those who hide their plans from the Lord (Isa. 29:15).

B2 Designs
Able to design for work in gold, silver and bronze (Exod. 31:4; 35:32); David gave Solomon the plans for the temple (1 Chr. 28:11-12); show them the design of the house (Ezek. 43:11).

B3 Evil plans

B3a Evil plans in general
With perverse heart he devises evil (Prov. 6:14); why do the peoples plot in vain? (Ps. 2:1); they devise treachery all day long (Ps. 38:12); they plot evil against you (Ps. 21:11); one who plots evil against the Lord (Nahum 1:11); the knave devises wicked schemes (Isa. 32:7); the wicked plots against the righteous (Ps. 37:12); he plans wickedness on his bed (Ps. 36:4); the counsels of the wicked are deceitful (Ps. 12:5); deceit is in the heart of those who devise evil (Prov. 12:20); do they not err who devise evil? (Prov. 14:22); though I trained and strengthened their arms they devise evil against me (Hos. 7:15); do not devise evil in your hearts against one another (Zech. 7:10; 8:17); the Lord hates hearts that devise wicked plans (Prov. 6:18); evil plans are an abomination to the Lord (Prov. 15:26); woe to those who carry out a plan, but not mine (Isa. 30:1); he will devise plans against strongholds, but only for a time (Dan. 11:24); Aram and Ephraim have planned evil against you (Isa. 7:5).

B3b Specific evil plans
They plot to take my life (Ps. 31:13); they plotted to kill Joseph (Gen. 37:18); you devised evil against me but God devised good (Gen. 50:20); they plotted to kill Jeremiah (Jer. 11:19); let us make plots against Jeremiah (Jer. 18:18); the Jews plotted how to kill Jesus (Matt. 12:14; 26:4; 27:1; Mark 3:6); the chief priests planned to killed Lazarus also (John 12:10); they plotted how to kill Paul (Acts 9:23-4; 23:12-15, 20-1, 30); tears and trials befell me through the plots of the Jews (Acts 20:19).

B3c Counteracting evil plans
We are not ignorant of Satan's schemes (2 Cor. 2:11); the Lord frustrates the plans of the people (Ps. 33:10); God frustrates the plots of the cunning (Job 5:12); whatever you devise against the Lord, he will put a stop to it (Nahum 1:9); let them be caught in the plots they devise (Ps. 10:2); you hide them from the plots of men (Ps. 31:20).

B4 Conspiracies
They have conspired together (Ps. 83:5); do not call conspiracy what this people call conspiracy (Isa. 8:12); Ahithophel was one of the conspirators (2 Sam. 15:31); Zimri's conspiracy is written in the book of the Chronicles of the Kings of Israel (1 Kgs. 16:20); Amos has conspired against you (Amos 7:10); there is a

conspiracy of prophets in her midst (Ezek. 22:25); they planned together to kill him (John 11:53).

624 Way

A Ways and means

A1 Ways in general

The way of an eagle in the sky (Prov. 30:19); the way of a serpent on a rock (Prov. 30:19); the way of a ship on the sea (Prov. 30:19); how have we despised your name? (Mal. 1:6); how have we polluted you? (Mal. 1:7); how have we robbed you? (Mal. 3:8); how have we wearied him? (Mal. 2:17); how have you loved us? (Mal. 1:2); how shall we return? (Mal. 3:7); how can Satan cast out Satan? (Mark 3:23); how am I to know this? (Gen. 15:8); how can this be, seeing I have no husband? (Luke 1:34); how can this be? (John 3:9); how were your eyes opened? (John 9:10-26); Jesus indicated by what death he was to die (John 18:32); by what kind of death he would glorify God (John 21:19); if we are on trial concerning the means whereby a cripple was healed (Acts 4:9).

A2 God's ways

A2a The nature of God's ways

God's way is perfect (2 Sam. 22:31; Ps. 18:30); the ways of the Lord are right (Hos. 14:9); your way is holy (Ps. 77:13); just and true are your ways (Rev. 15:3); all his works are true and his ways are just (Dan. 4:37); my ways are not your ways (Isa. 55:8); my ways are right but yours are not (Ezek. 18:25, 29); as the heavens are higher than the earth, so are God's ways than our ways (Isa. 55:9); how unsearchable are his judgements, how unfathomable his ways! (Rom. 11:33); the way of the Lord is not right (Ezek. 33:17).

A2b Preparing God's way

I send my messenger to prepare the way before me (Mal. 3:1); he will prepare your way before you (Matt. 11:10; Mark 1:2; Luke 7:27).

A2c Knowing God's ways

Teach me your way, O Lord (Ps. 27:11); teach me your ways (Exod. 33:13; Ps. 25:4; 86:11); that he may teach us his ways (Isa. 2:3; Mic. 4:2); God teaches the humble his way (Ps. 25:9); that your way may be known on earth (Ps. 67:2); God made known his ways to Moses (Ps. 103:7); you know the way where I am going (John 14:4); they have not known my ways (Ps. 95:10; Heb. 3:10); we do not know where you are going, how can we know the way? (John 14:5).

A2d Walking in God's ways

Oh that Israel would walk in my ways! (Ps. 81:13); if you will walk in my ways and keep my charge (Zech. 3:7); walk in God's ways all your days (Deut. 19:9); that we might walk in his paths (Mic. 4:2); they walk in his ways (Ps. 119:3); happy are those who walk in his ways (Ps. 128:1); keep to the Lord's ways (Ps. 37:34).

A3 Man's ways

The ways of a man are before the Lord (Prov. 5:21); a man's steps are ordered by the Lord (Prov. 20:24); he knows the way I take (Job 23:10); a man's way is not in himself (Jer. 10:23); consider your ways (Hag. 1:5, 7); I considered my ways (Ps. 119:59); you search out my paths (Ps. 139:3); their way I have brought on their heads (Ezek. 22:31); I will judge you according to your ways and your doings (Ezek. 24:14); I judged them according to their ways and their deeds (Ezek. 36:19).

A4 Evil ways

There is a way which seems right to a man but its end is the way of death (Prov. 14:12; 16:25); every man's way is right in his own eyes (Prov. 21:2); blessed is he who does not stand in the way of sinners (Ps. 1:1); let the wicked forsake his way (Isa. 55:7); the way of the wicked ends in ruin (Ps. 1:6); God brings the way of the wicked to ruin (Ps. 146:9); return from your evil ways and deeds (Zech. 1:4).

A5 The right way

A5a About the right way

The path of the righteous is like the dawn (Prov. 4:18); in the way of righteousness there is life (Prov. 12:28); the path of the upright is a highway (Prov. 15:19); the highway of the upright is to turn aside from evil (Prov. 16:17); in his heart are the highways [to Zion] (Ps. 84:5); the Lord knows the way of the righteous (Ps. 1:6); the Lord delights in his way (Ps. 37:23); wisdom's ways are ways of pleasantness (Prov. 3:17); I am the way (John 14:6); we enter by a new and living way (Heb. 10:20); the wise man's path leads upward to life (Prov. 15:24); John came to you in the way of righteousness (Matt. 21:32); they have not known the way of peace (Rom. 3:17).

A5b Learning the right way

How can a young man keep his way pure? (Ps. 119:9); ask for the ancient paths, where the good way is (Jer. 6:16); I will give heed to the blameless way (Ps. 101:2); commit your way to the Lord (Ps. 37:5); ponder the path of your feet and all your ways will be sure (Prov. 4:26); teach them the way they are to go (Exod. 18:20); I will teach you the way you should go (Ps. 32:8); I have taught you the way of wisdom (Prov. 4:11); you make known to me the path of life (Ps. 16:11); to guide our feet into the way of peace (Luke 1:79); this is the way, walk in it (Isa. 30:21); God makes my way perfect (Ps. 18:32); he led them by a straight way (Ps. 107:7); he instructs sinners in the way (Ps. 25:8); make straight paths for your feet (Heb. 12:13); he leads me in the paths of righteousness (Ps. 23:3); lead me in the way everlasting (Ps. 139:24).

A6 'The Way'

'The Way' (Acts 9:2; 19:9, 23; 22:4; 24:14, 22); because of them the way of truth will be maligned (2 Pet. 2:2); better not to have known the way of righteousness (2 Pet. 2:21).

B Paths

B1 Specific roads

The Philistia road was more direct (Exod. 13:17); the Lord led them by the wilderness road (Exod. 13:18); the Arabah road (Deut. 2:8); one highway goes up to Bethel and one to Gibeah (Judg. 20:31); the highway from Bethel to Shechem (Judg. 21:19); you may make streets for yourself in Damascus (1 Kgs. 20:34); you have as many altars as there are streets in Jerusalem (Jer. 11:13); do not return by the way you came (1 Kgs. 13:9); by the way he came he will return (2 Kgs. 19:28, 33; Isa. 37:34); the prince shall enter by the porch of the gate and go out the same way (Ezek. 46:8); they will ask the way to Zion (Jer. 50:5); go to the road from Jerusalem to Gaza (Acts 8:26); go to the street called Straight (Acts 9:11).

B2 Tragedy on the streets

Amasa wallowing in his blood in the middle of the highway (2 Sam. 20:12); the holy stones are poured out at the head of every street (Lam. 4:1); they lie at the head of every street (Isa. 51:20); they push the poor off the road (Job 24:4); the highways were deserted (Judg. 5:6); the highways are empty, travellers gone (Isa. 33:8); I have laid waste their streets with none passing by (Zeph. 3:6); the roads of Zion are in mourning because no one comes to the feasts (Lam. 1:4).

B3 Making roads

Prepare roads to the cities of refuge (Deut. 19:3); in the desert prepare a highway for our God (Isa. 40:3; Matt. 3:3; John 1:23); prepare the way of the Lord, make his paths straight (Mark 1:3; Luke 3:4); the Lord who made a way through the sea (Isa. 43:16); is making a highway in the wilderness (Isa. 43:19); you made the depths of the sea a pathway for the redeemed (Isa. 51:10); there will be a highway from Assyria (Isa. 11:16; 19:23); a highway will be there called the Way of Holiness (Isa. 35:8).

B4 Using roads
You taught in our streets (Luke 13:26); they spread garments on the road (Matt. 21:8; Mark 11:8; Luke 19:36); they carried the sick out into the streets (Acts 5:15); two blind men sitting by the roadside (Matt. 20:30); Bartimaeus was sitting by the roadside (Mark 10:46); a certain blind man sitting by the roadside begging (Luke 18:35); by the road you sat like an Arab in the desert (Jer. 3:2); Tamar sat by the roadside (Gen. 38:14); they found a colt tied at the door outside in the street (Mark 11:4); boys and girls playing in the streets of the city (Zech. 8:5); old men and women will again sit in the streets of Jerusalem (Zech. 8:4); you built your high place at the top of every street (Ezek. 16:25); you built your shrine at the head of every street (Ezek. 16:31); hypocrites love to pray on street corners (Matt. 6:5); the hypocrites sound a trumpet in synagogues and in the streets (Matt. 6:2); if a town does not receive you, go into its streets and wipe off the dust (Luke 10:10); go out into the streets and lanes of the city (Luke 14:21); go to the highways and invite as many as you can find (Matt. 22:9); they went into the streets and gathered all they could (Matt. 22:10); go to the highways and hedges and compel them to come in (Luke 14:23); man the ramparts, watch the road (Nahum 2:1); the chariots dash through the streets and squares (Nahum 2:4); with the hooves of his horses he will trample all your streets (Ezek. 26:11); some seed fell by the path (Matt. 13:4, 19; Mark 4:4, 15; Luke 8:5); those along the path are those who have heard (Luke 8:12); his voice will not be heard in the streets (Matt. 12:19).

B5 Pavements
The judgement seat at a place called The Pavement (John 19:13); under God's feet there appeared to be a pavement of sapphire (Exod. 24:10); the street of the city was pure gold (Rev. 21:21); a mosaic pavement (Esther 1:6).

625 Middle way
MODERATION, see 177.

626 Circuit
CIRCLING, see 314.

627 Requirement
A God's needs
God is not served by human hands as though he needed anything (Acts 17:25); what does the Lord require of you? (Deut. 10:12; Mic. 6:8); the Lord has need of them (Matt. 21:3); the Lord has need of it (Mark 11:3; Luke 19:31, 34).
B Man's needs
What do I lack? (Matt. 19:20); one thing you lack (Mark 10:21; Luke 18:22); I need to be baptised by you, and do you come to me? (Matt. 3:14); your Father knows what you need before you ask him (Matt. 6:8); your heavenly Father knows that you need these things (Matt. 6:32); those who are well do not need a doctor, but those who are ill (Matt. 9:12); he had to pass through Samaria (John 4:4); the eye cannot say it has no need of the hand (1 Cor. 12:21); the head cannot say it has no need of the feet (1 Cor. 12:21); the members which seem to be feeble are necessary (1 Cor. 12:22).

628 Instrumentality
TOOL, see 630.

629 Means
REMEDY, see 658.

630 Equipment
A Tools in general
No tool used on the altar (Exod. 20:25; Deut. 27:5); no iron tool was heard at the site when the temple was being built (1 Kgs. 6:7); machines for shooting arrows and stones (2 Chr. 26:15); do not present your limbs to sin as instruments of wickedness (Rom. 6:13); present your limbs to God as instruments of righteousness (Rom. 6:13).
B Agricultural tools
Sharpening ploughshares, mattocks, axes and hoes (1 Sam. 13:20-1); beat your ploughshares into swords and your pruning hooks into spears (Joel 3:10); do not use a sickle in your neighbour's grainfield (Deut. 23:25); put in the sickle, for the harvest is ripe (Joel 3:13); a sharp sickle (Rev. 14:14, 17-18); have a spade among your tools to cover your excrement (Deut. 23:13); his winnowing fork is in his hand (Matt. 3:12; Luke 3:17).
C Cutting tools
Pierce his ear with an awl (Exod. 21:6; Deut. 15:17); swinging an axe to cut down a tree (Deut. 19:5; 20:19); the axe-head fell into the water (2 Kgs. 6:5); sharpening ploughshares, mattocks, axes and hoes (1 Sam. 13:20-1); David made the Ammonites work with saws and iron axes (2 Sam. 12:31; 1 Chr. 20:3); the carved work smashed with hatchets and hammers (Ps. 74:6); neither hammer nor axe was heard in the temple (1 Kgs. 6:7); the axe is laid at the root of the trees (Matt. 3:10; Luke 3:9); does the axe or saw boast over the one who uses them? (Isa. 10:15); the carpenter uses compasses (Isa. 44:13); Jael took a tent-peg and a hammer (Judg. 4:21; 5:26); neither hammer nor axe was heard in the temple (1 Kgs. 6:7); the man shapes the idol with hammers (Isa. 44:12); the idol is smoothed with a hammer (Isa. 41:7); the idol is fastened with hammer and nails (Jer. 10:4); is not my word like a hammer? (Jer. 23:29); the hammer of the whole earth is broken (Jer. 50:23); the carpenter shapes it with planes (Isa. 44:13); costly stones, sawed with saws (1 Kgs. 7:9); does the axe or saw boast over the one who uses them? (Isa. 10:15).
D Other tools
She puts her hand to the distaff (Prov. 31:19); her hand holds the spindle (Prov. 31:19); Aaron fashioned the calf with a graving tool (Exod. 32:4); they made your oars of oaks of Bashan (Ezek. 27:6); tongs [snuffers] for the lampstand (Exod. 25:38); a burning coal taken from the altar with tongs (Isa. 6:6); Solomon made the snuffers (1 Kgs. 7:50; 2 Chr. 4:22); they did not make snuffers (2 Kgs. 12:13); they took away the snuffers (2 Kgs. 25:14; Jer. 52:18); my days are swifter than a weaver's shuttle (Job 7:6).

631 Materials
A Materials in general
Materials for making the tabernacle (Exod. 25:3-7; 35:5-9); materials for the temple (1 Chr. 22:14; 29:2); you have seen their idols, wood, stone, silver and gold (Deut. 29:17); that day will show what materials have been used, gold, silver, precious stones, wood, hay, stubble (1 Cor. 3:12).

B Metals
B1 Metals in general
There is a place for mining and refining metals (Job 28:1-11); something like glowing metal in the midst of the fire (Ezek. 1:4); from his loins upward was the appearance of gleaming metal (Ezek. 1:27; 8:2).

B2 Combinations of metals
B2a Metals of different kinds
That day will show what materials have been used, gold, silver, precious stones, wood, hay, stubble (1 Cor. 3:12); work in gold, silver and bronze (Exod. 31:4; 35:32); sending a skilled man to work in gold, silver, brass and iron (2 Chr. 2:7, 14); silver, iron, tin and lead were exchanged for goods (Ezek. 27:12); I will make the sky like iron and earth like bronze (Lev. 26:19); gold instead of bronze, silver instead of iron, bronze instead of wood, iron instead of stones (Isa. 60:17); the head of gold, chest of silver, belly of bronze, legs of iron, feet of iron and clay (Dan. 2:32-5); as silver, bronze, iron, lead and tin are melted (Ezek. 22:20); they are bronze and tin and iron and lead in the furnace (Ezek. 22:18); objects of gold, silver, bronze, iron, tin and lead passed through the fire (Num. 31:22-3); they praised the gods of gold, silver, bronze, iron, wood, stone (Dan. 5:4); you praised the gods of silver, gold, bronze, iron, wood, stone (Dan. 5:23).

B2b Amassing mixed metals
Gold, silver, bronze and iron without limit (1 Chr. 22:16); David provided gold, silver, bronze and iron for the temple (1 Chr. 29:2); David gave 3000 talents of gold and 7000 talents of silver for the temple (1 Chr. 29:4); the leaders gave 5000 talents and 10 000 darics of gold, 10 000 of silver, 18 000 of brass and 100 000 of iron (1 Chr. 29:7); David planned the weight for the gold and silver vessels of the temple (1 Chr. 28:14-18); gold, silver and bronze to be given for the tabernacle (Exod. 25:3; 35:5); put the silver, gold and things of bronze and iron into the Lord's treasury (Josh. 6:19, 24); Asa brought silver and gold into the Lord's house (1 Kgs. 15:15; 2 Chr. 15:18); I accumulated silver and gold (Eccles. 2:8).

B2c Like silver and gold
The Almighty will be your gold and silver (Job 22:25); we should not think that God is like silver and gold (Acts 17:29); wisdom is more profitable than silver or gold (Prov. 3:14); a word fitly spoken is like apples of gold in settings of silver (Prov. 25:11).

B3 Gold
B3a Gold in general
The gold of Havilah is good (Gen. 2:11-12); the gold was gold of Parvaim (2 Chr. 3:6); gold is brought from Uphaz (Jer. 10:9); its dust contains gold (Job 28:6); Solomon made gold as common as stones (2 Chr. 1:15); if one swears by the gold of the temple he is obligated (Matt. 23:16-17); there is a place for refining gold (Job 28:1); a furnace is for gold (Prov. 17:3; 27:21); gold is tested by fire (1 Pet. 1:7).

B3b Amassing gold
29 talents and 730 shekels of gold (Exod. 38:24); Hiram sent Solomon 120 talents of gold (1 Kgs. 9:14); Hiram king of Tyre provided Solomon with gold (1 Kgs. 9:11); they brought 420 talents of gold from Ophir (1 Kgs. 9:28); 450 talents of gold from Ophir (2 Chr. 8:18); the Queen of Sheba brought 120 talents of gold (1 Kgs. 10:10; 2 Chr. 9:9); 666 talents of gold in one year (1 Kgs. 10:14; 2 Chr. 9:13); 100 000 talents of gold (1 Chr. 22:14); Tyre amassed gold like the mire of the streets (Zech. 9:3).

B3c Gold transferred
Tear off the gold rings from your ears (Exod. 32:2); whoever has any gold, let them tear it off (Exod. 32:24);

give me the gold earrings (Judg. 8:24); buy from me gold refined by fire (Rev. 3:18); gold and silver vessels carried off from the temple (Dan. 5:2); they presented him with gifts, gold, frankincense and myrrh (Matt. 2:11); cargo of gold, silver and precious stones (Rev. 18:12).

B3d Overlaid with gold
Overlaid with gold: the ark (Exod. 25:11; 37:2; Heb. 9:4); the altar of incense (Exod. 30:3; 37:26; 39:38; 40:5, 26; 1 Kgs. 7:48; 2 Chr. 4:19; Heb. 9:4; Rev. 9:13); poles for the incense altar (Exod. 37:28); the table of showbread (Exod. 25:24; 37:11; Lev. 24:6); poles (Exod. 25:13, 28; 30:5; 37:4, 15); boards and bars (Exod. 26:29; 36:34); pillars (Exod. 26:32, 37; 36:36); the holy of holies (1 Kgs. 6:20; 2 Chr. 3:8); the cherubim (1 Kgs. 6:28; 2 Chr. 3:10); the porch of the temple (2 Chr. 3:4); the main part of the temple (2 Chr. 3:5); the inside of the temple (1 Kgs. 6:21, 22); the walls of the temple (1 Chr. 29:4; 2 Chr. 3:7); the floor of the temple (1 Kgs. 6:30); the altar (1 Kgs. 6:22); the doors of the temple (1 Kgs. 6:32, 35; 2 Kgs. 18:16; 2 Chr. 4:22); the upper rooms (2 Chr. 3:9); Solomon's throne (1 Kgs. 10:18; 2 Chr. 9:17); molten images (Isa. 30:22); the idol (Isa. 40:19).

B3e Gold ornaments
A gold ring and two gold bracelets (Gen. 24:22); a gold ring in a pig's snout (Prov. 11:22); Saul put gold ornaments on you (2 Sam. 1:24); the princess's clothing is interwoven with gold (Ps. 45:13); a man girded with pure gold of Uphaz (Dan. 10:5); he will be clothed in purple and have a necklace of gold (Dan. 5:7); women should not adorn themselves with gold or pearls (1 Tim. 2:9); let your adorning not be gold jewels (1 Pet. 3:3); the woman was adorned with gold, jewels and pearls (Rev. 17:4); she who was adorned with gold and precious stones and pearls (Rev. 18:16); if a man comes into your assembly with a gold ring (Jas. 2:2); you set a crown of gold on his head (Ps. 21:3); a golden crown on his head (Rev. 14:14); elders with golden crowns (Rev. 4:4); a golden girdle around his breasts (Rev. 1:13); golden girdles around their chests (Rev. 15:6).

B3f Like gold
The Lord's words are more desirable than gold (Ps. 19:10); I love your commandments more than fine gold (Ps. 119:127); take knowledge rather than choice gold (Prov. 8:10); it is much better to get wisdom than gold (Prov. 16:16); a wise reprover is like gold ornaments (Prov. 25:12); before the golden bowl is broken (Eccles. 12:6); the precious sons of Zion, worth their weight in fine gold (Lam. 4:2); how dim the gold has become! (Lam. 4:1); Babylon was a golden cup in the hand of the Lord (Jer. 51:7); I will make mankind scarcer than the gold of Ophir (Isa. 13:12); I will test them as gold is tested (Zech. 13:9); when he has tested me I will come forth as gold (Job 23:10).

B4 Silver
B4a Silver in general
There is a mine for silver (Job 28:1); beaten silver is brought from Tarshish (Jer. 10:9); the crucible is for silver (Prov. 17:3; 27:21); take the dross from the silver and the smith has material for a vessel (Prov. 25:4); silver was not esteemed in Solomon's time (1 Kgs. 10:21; 2 Chr. 9:20); Solomon made silver as common as stones (1 Kgs. 10:27; 2 Chr. 9:27); your gold and silver have rusted (Jas. 5:3); nettles will take over their treasures of silver (Hos. 9:6).

B4b Silver amassed
100 talents and 1775 shekels of silver (Exod. 38:25); 1 000 000 talents of silver (1 Chr. 22:14); he will gain the treasures of gold and silver (Dan. 11:43); cargo of gold, silver and precious stones (Rev. 18:12).

B4c Overlaid with silver
Overlaid with silver: the tops of the pillars (Exod. 38:17, 19, 28); the wings of a dove (Ps. 68:13); graven images (Isa. 30:22).

B4d Like silver
Seek for wisdom as for silver (Prov. 2:4); the Lord's words are pure as silver refined seven times (Ps. 12:6); understanding is to be chosen rather than silver (Prov. 16:16); take my instruction instead of silver (Prov. 8:10); the tongue of the righteous is choice silver (Prov. 10:20); I have refined you, but not like silver (Isa. 48:10); as silver is melted in the furnace so I will melt you (Ezek. 22:22); he will sit as a smelter and refiner of silver (Mal. 3:3); I will refine them as silver is refined (Zech. 13:9); like one refining silver (Ps. 66:10); your silver has become dross (Isa. 1:22); reject silver because the Lord has rejected them (Jer. 6:30); they are the dross of silver (Ezek. 22:18); before the silver cord is broken (Eccles. 12:6).

B5 Copper / bronze
B5a Copper / bronze in general
A land where you can dig copper out of the hills (Deut. 8:9); copper is smelted from the rock (Job 28:2); shiny bronze, fine as gold (Ezra 8:27); can one break iron from the north, and bronze? (Jer. 15:12); I will shatter doors of bronze (Isa. 45:2); he shatters doors of bronze (Ps. 107:16); the crocodile regards bronze as rotten wood (Job 41:27); set the pot on the coals so that the bronze will be hot (Ezek. 24:11); Hiram was skilled in working bronze (1 Kgs. 7:14); Tubal-cain worked in bronze and iron (Gen. 4:22); bronze from the mirrors of the serving women (Exod. 38:8).

B5b Bronze amassed
Let bronze be brought from Egypt (Ps. 68:31); David took much bronze from Hadadezer (2 Sam. 8:8; 1 Chr. 18:8); the weight of the bronze could not be determined (1 Kgs. 7:47); bronze beyond weight (2 Kgs. 25:16); David prepared bronze beyond weight (1 Chr. 22:3); cargo of bronze, iron and marble (Rev. 18:12).

B5c Overlaid with bronze
Overlaid with bronze: the bronze altar (Exod. 27:2; 38:2, 30; 39:39); poles for the altar (Exod. 27:6; 38:6); doors for the court (2 Chr. 4:9).

B5d Like bronze
Heaven above will be bronze (Deut. 28:23); is my flesh bronze? (Job 6:12); his bones are tubes of bronze (Job 40:18); your forehead is bronze (Isa. 48:4); his arms and feet were like the gleam of burnished bronze (Dan. 10:6); his feet like burnished bronze (Rev. 1:15; 2:18); they gleamed like burnished bronze (Ezek. 1:7); your locks will be iron and bronze (Deut. 33:25); they are bronze and iron (Jer. 6:28); I have made you walls of bronze (Jer. 1:18); I will make you a fortified wall of bronze (Jer. 15:20); a man whose appearance was like bronze (Ezek. 40:3); a third kingdom of bronze (Dan. 2:39).

B6 Iron
B6a Iron in general
A land whose stones are iron (Deut. 8:9); iron is taken from the dust (Job 28:2); David prepared much iron for nails (1 Chr. 22:3); David prepared iron beyond weight (1 Chr. 22:14); the crocodile regards iron as straw (Job 41:27); he cuts bars of iron (Ps. 107:16).

B6b Iron objects
The iron head of an axe (Deut. 19:5); iron picks and iron axes (2 Sam. 12:31); Og had an iron bedstead (Deut. 3:11); to bind their nobles with fetters of iron (Ps. 149:8); I will cut through iron bars (Isa. 45:2); you have broken wooden yokes, but have made yokes of iron (Jer. 28:13); the Canaanites had iron chariots (Josh. 17:16-18; Judg. 1:19); Sisera had 900 iron chariots (Judg.

4:3, 13); Zedekiah made horns of iron (1 Kgs. 22:11; 2 Chr. 18:10); the sin of Judah is written with an iron pen (Jer. 17:1); get an iron plate and set it as an iron wall between you and the city (Ezek. 4:3); the legs of the statue were of iron (Dan. 2:33); a beast with large iron teeth (Dan. 7:7); an altar on which no one has lifted an iron tool (Josh. 8:31); you will shepherd them with a rod of iron (Ps. 2:9); a son who was to rule the nations with a rod of iron (Rev. 12:5); he will rule them with a rod of iron (Rev. 2:27; 19:15).

B6c Like iron
The earth below will be iron (Deut. 28:23); your neck is an iron sinew (Isa. 48:4); I have made you an iron pillar (Jer. 1:18); their breastplates were like breastplates of iron (Rev. 9:9); a fourth kingdom as strong as iron (Dan. 2:40); as iron crushes and shatters all things (Dan. 2:40); the kingdom will have in it the toughness of iron (Dan. 2:41); as iron sharpens iron (Prov. 27:17).

B7 Lead
They sank like lead (Exod. 15:10); the lead is consumed by the fire (Jer. 6:29); engraved with an iron stylus and lead (Job 19:24); he thrust the lead weight on the mouth of the ephah (Zech. 5:7-8).

C Stone / ceramics
C1 Wood and stone
The water became blood in vessels of wood and vessels of stone (Exod. 7:19); vessels of wood and earthenware (2 Tim. 2:20); cutting stones and timber (Exod. 31:5); they will throw your stones, timber and soil into the water (Ezek. 26:12); they carried away the stones and timber of Ramah (1 Kgs. 15:22; 2 Chr. 16:6); timber and stone prepared for the temple (1 Chr. 22:14); timber and stone for repairing the temple (2 Kgs. 12:12; 22:6); they were no gods but only wood and stone (2 Kgs. 19:18; Isa. 37:19); you will serve other gods, wood and stone (Deut. 28:36, 64); let us be like the nations, serving wood and stone (Ezek. 20:32); they praised the gods of gold, silver, bronze, iron, wood, stone (Dan. 5:4, 23); idols of gold, silver, brass, stone and wood (Rev. 9:20).

C2 Stone items
Stone tablets of the law (Exod. 24:12; 31:18; 34:1, 4; 1 Kgs. 8:9); the bricks have fallen down but we will build with dressed stones (Isa. 9:10); make flint knives for circumcision (Josh. 5:2-3); Zipporah took a flint (Exod. 4:25); like adamant harder than flint I have made your forehead (Ezek. 3:9); marble pillars (Esther 1:6); a pavement of porphyry, marble, mother-of-pearl and precious stones (Esther 1:6); four tables of hewn stone for the burnt offering (Ezek. 40:42); his legs are alabaster pillars (S. of S. 5:15); an alabaster jar of expensive perfume (Matt. 26:7; Mark 14:3); six stone jars (John 2:6); we should not think that God is like stone (Acts 17:29); cargo of bronze, iron and marble (Rev. 18:12).

C3 Bricks and mortar
They used bricks for stone and tar for mortar (Gen. 11:3); he will come on rulers as on mortar (Isa. 41:25); hide stones in the mortar of Pharaoh's palace in Tahpanhes (Jer. 43:9); tread the mortar, take hold of the brick mould (Nahum 3:14); hard labour with mortar and bricks (Exod. 1:14); no straw to make bricks (Exod. 5:7-18); David set the Ammonites to making bricks (2 Sam. 12:31); they burn sacrifices on bricks (Isa. 65:3); take a brick and draw Jerusalem on it (Ezek. 4:1).

C4 Earthenware
Holy water in an earthenware vessel (Num. 5:17); an earthenware vessel which becomes unclean must be broken (Lev. 11:33; 15:12); buy a potter's earthenware jar (Jer. 19:1); you will shatter them like earthenware (Ps.

2:9); we have this treasure in earthenware vessels
(2 Cor. 4:7).

D Wood
WOOD AND STONE, see 631C1.

D1 Wood in general
A wooden vessel must be rinsed with water (Lev. 15:12);
purify every article of wood (Num. 31:20); you have
broken wooden yokes, but have made yokes of iron
(Jer. 28:13); their idol is wood! (Jer. 10:8); an idol is
wood cut from the forest (Jer. 10:3); I bow down before
a block of wood (Isa. 44:19); those who carry their
wooden idols (Isa. 45:20); my people enquire of a thing
of wood (Hos. 4:12); woe to him who says to a piece of
wood, 'Awake!' (Hab. 2:19); if they do this when the
wood is green (Luke 23:31); that day will show what
materials have been used, gold, silver, precious stones,
wood, hay, stubble (1 Cor. 3:12); carving of wood
(Exod. 35:33); David prepared wood for the temple
(1 Chr. 29:2); timber from Lebanon (2 Chr. 2:16); no
one knows how to cut timber like the Sidonians (1 Kgs.
5:6); cutting timber at the Jordan (2 Kgs. 6:2-4); timber
for gates of the city (Neh. 2:8).

D2 Acacia wood
Acacia wood contributed (Exod. 25:5; 35:7); anyone
who had acacia wood brought it (Exod. 35:24); made of
acacia wood: the ark (Exod. 25:10; Deut. 10:3); poles for
the ark (Exod. 25:13); the table of showbread (Exod.
25:23); poles for the table (Exod. 25:28); the altar of
burnt offering (Exod. 27:1); poles for the altar of burnt
offering (Exod. 27:6); the incense altar (Exod. 30:1);
poles for the altar of incense (Exod. 30:5); boards
(Exod. 26:15); bars (Exod. 26:26); pillars (Exod. 26:32).

D3 Cedar wood
Taking cedar wood (Lev. 14:4); large amounts of cedar
timber (1 Chr. 22:4); Hiram sent cedar for David's
house (2 Sam. 5:11; 1 Chr. 14:1; 2 Chr. 2:3); I live in a
house of cedar (2 Sam. 7:2; 1 Chr. 17:1); why have you
not built me a house of cedar? (2 Sam. 7:7; 1 Chr. 17:6);
cedar wood for the temple (1 Kgs. 5:6-10); the temple
was panelled with boards of cedar (1 Kgs. 6:9, 15-16); all
was cedar, with no stone seen (1 Kgs. 6:18); the altar
was overlaid with cedar (1 Kgs. 6:20); a row of cedar
beams for the court (1 Kgs. 6:36; 7:12); cedar pillars and
beams (1 Kgs. 7:2); cedar and cypress timber for
Solomon's palace and the temple (1 Kgs. 5:6-10; 9:11; 2
Chr. 2:8-9); the hall of the throne was panelled in cedar
(1 Kgs. 7:7); the houses were made of stone and cedar (1
Kgs. 7:11); the beams of our house are cedar (S. of S.
1:17); boards of cedar (S. of S. 8:9); I will panel it with
cedar (Jer. 22:14); he made cedar as plentiful as
sycamore (1 Kgs. 10:27; 2 Chr. 1:15; 9:27); the sycamores
are cut down but we will replace them with cedars (Isa.
9:10); cedar wood from Lebanon (Ezra 3:7); a cedar of
Lebanon for a mast (Ezek. 27:5); her cedar work is laid
bare (Zeph. 2:14).

D4 Other woods
Algum trees (2 Chr. 9:10-11); send me algum timber (2
Chr. 2:8); almug wood from Ophir (1 Kgs. 10:11-12);
cargo of citron [thyine] wood, ivory, costly wood (Rev.
18:12); cypress timber for the temple (1 Kgs. 5:8, 10); the
main part of the temple was overlaid with cypress (2
Chr. 3:5); the temple was floored with cypress (1 Kgs.
6:15); cedar and cypress timber for Solomon's palace
and the temple (1 Kgs. 9:11; 2 Chr. 2:8-9); our rafters are
cypress (S. of S. 1:17); ivory tusks and ebony were
traded (Ezek. 27:15); instruments made of fir wood (2
Sam. 6:5); planks of fir from Senir (Ezek. 27:5); make
an ark of gopher wood (Gen. 6:14); oars from oaks of
Bashan (Ezek. 27:6); of olive wood: two cherubim
(1 Kgs. 6:23); doors (1 Kgs. 6:31, 32); doorposts (1 Kgs.
6:33); decks of Cyprus pine inlaid with ivory (Ezek.

27:6); he made cedar as plentiful as sycamore (1 Kgs.
10:27; 2 Chr. 1:15; 9:27); can wood be taken from the
vine to make anything? (Ezek. 15:2-6).
TREES, see 366D.

E Straw / hay
We have both straw and fodder (Gen. 24:25); straw and
fodder for the camels (Gen. 24:32); barley and straw for
the horses (1 Kgs. 4:28); no straw to make bricks (Exod.
5:7-18); that day will show what materials have been
used, gold, silver, precious stones, wood, hay, stubble
(1 Cor. 3:12).

F Cloth
F1 Cloth in general
No one sews a path of unshrunk cloth on an old
garment (Mark 2:21); you took your embroidered cloth
and covered the images (Ezek. 16:18); she wrapped him
in cloths (Luke 2:7); you will find a baby wrapped in
cloths (Luke 2:12).

F2 Linen
F2a Linen cloth and flax
Those making linen from combed flax (Isa. 19:9); cargo
of fine linen, purple, silk and scarlet (Rev. 18:12); a sail
of linen from Egypt (Ezek. 27:7); the priests shall wear
linen turbans and undergarments (Ezek. 44:18); the
priests shall wear linen, not wool (Ezek. 44:17); do not
wear a garment of wool and linen mixed (Deut. 22:11);
a line of flax and a measuring reed in his hand (Ezek.
40:3); a young man followed dressed only in a linen
sheet (Mark 14:51); Jesus' body was wrapped in linen
cloths (Matt. 27:59; Mark 15:46; Luke 23:53; John 19:40);
Peter saw the linen wrappings (Luke 24:12); stooping
and looking in he saw the linen cloths (John 20:5).

F2b Clothed in linen
Pharaoh clothed Joseph in fine linen (Gen. 41:42); a
man clothed in linen (Ezek. 9:2-3, 11; 10:2-7); I said to
the man clothed in linen (Dan. 12:6-7); a rich man
dressed in purple and fine linen (Luke 16:19); the great
city clothed in fine linen (Rev. 18:16); the bride was
clothed in fine linen, which is the righteous deeds of
the saints (Rev. 19:8); the armies which are in heaven
clothed in fine linen (Rev. 19:14); the seven angels in
clean, bright linen (Rev. 15:6).

F2c Linen items
Samuel wore a linen ephod (1 Sam. 2:18); buy a linen
waistband (Jer. 13:1); linen for: the curtains of the
tabernacle (Exod. 26:1); hangings of the court (Exod.
27:9; 38:9); clothing of the priests (Exod. 28:39, 42;
39:27-8; Lev. 16:4); clothes to be worn whilst taking up
the ashes (Lev. 6:10).

F3 Wool
The priests shall wear linen, not wool (Ezek. 44:17);
garments of wool or linen (Lev. 13:47-59); do not wear
a garment of wool and linen mixed (Deut. 22:11).

F4 Silk
I clothed you with linen and silk (Ezek. 16:10); your
clothing was of fine linen, silk and embroidered cloth
(Ezek. 16:13); cargo of fine linen, purple, silk and scarlet
(Rev. 18:12).

F5 Sackcloth
F5a Sackcloth in general
Put on sackcloth and mourn (2 Sam. 3:31; Isa. 22:12; Jer.
4:8; 49:3; Joel 1:13); let us wear sackcloth (1 Kgs. 20:31);
when they were ill, my clothing was sackcloth (Ps.
35:13); instead of fine robes, sackcloth (Isa. 3:24); I
made sackcloth my clothing (Ps. 69:11); they put on
sackcloth (1 Kgs. 20:32; Isa. 15:3; Ezek. 7:18; 27:31; Jonah
3:5-8); the king wore sackcloth underneath (2 Kgs.
6:30); the leaders were covered with sackcloth (2 Kgs.
19:2); the elders of the priests covered with sackcloth
(Isa. 37:2); Israel fasted and put sackcloth with dirt on
them (Neh. 9:1); no one in sackcloth could enter the

---

king's gate (Esther 4:2-4); spreading sackcloth on the rock (2 Sam. 21:10); lament like a virgin in sackcloth for the bridegroom of her youth (Joel 1:8); pass the night in sackcloth (Joel 1:13); I will bring sackcloth on all loins and baldness on all heads (Amos 8:10); there is sackcloth on all the loins (Jer. 48:37); you have loosed my sackcloth (Ps. 30:11); the sun became black as sackcloth (Rev. 6:12).

F5b Sackcloth and ashes
Put on sackcloth and roll in ashes (Jer. 6:26); Mordecai put on sackcloth and ashes (Esther 4:1); many Jews lay in sackcloth and ashes (Esther 4:3); repenting in sackcloth and ashes (Matt. 11:21; Luke 10:13).

F5c Those who wore sackcloth
Those who wore sackcloth: Ahab (1 Kgs. 21:27); Daniel (Dan. 9:3); David and the elders (1 Chr. 21:16); Hezekiah (2 Kgs. 19:1; Isa. 37:1); Isaiah (Isa. 20:2); Jacob (Gen. 37:34); Job (Job 16:15); Moab (Isa. 15:2-3); Mordecai (Esther 4:1-4); the king of Israel (2 Kgs. 6:30); the Israelites (Neh. 9:1); the elders of Zion (Lam. 2:10); the king of Nineveh (Jonah 3:6); two witnesses (Rev. 11:3).

F6 Haircloth
Goats' hair for the tabernacle (Exod. 25:4; 35:6, 23); spinning goats' hair (Exod. 35:26); purify every article of goats' hair (Num. 31:20); a pillow of goats' hair (1 Sam. 19:13); Elijah wore a garment of haircloth (2 Kgs. 1:8); a prophet will not put on a hairy mantle (Zech. 13:4); John wore a garment of camel's hair (Matt. 3:4).

G Other materials

G1 Ivory
The ships brought gold, silver and ivory (1 Kgs. 10:22; 2 Chr. 9:21); cargo of ivory (Rev. 18:12); ivory tusks and ebony were traded (Ezek. 27:15); a throne of ivory (1 Kgs. 10:18; 2 Chr. 9:17); an ivory house (1 Kgs. 22:39); out of the ivory palaces (Ps. 45:8); the houses of ivory will perish (Amos 3:15); his trunk is ivory work (S. of S. 5:14); your neck is like an ivory tower (S. of S. 7:4); those who recline on beds of ivory (Amos 6:4).

G2 Leather
I put sandals of porpoise skin on your feet (Ezek. 16:10); Elijah had a leather belt around his waist (2 Kgs. 1:8); so did John (Matt. 3:4; Mark 1:6).
SKINS, see 226E.

G3 Coral and crystal
Coral and crystal cannot equal wisdom (Job 28:18).
GLASS, see 422.

G4 Pitch / tar
The ark was covered inside and outside with pitch (Gen. 6:14); they used bricks for stone and tar for mortar (Gen. 11:3); the valley of Siddim was full of tar pits (Gen. 14:10); a basket covered with tar and pitch (Exod. 2:3); streams turned into pitch (Isa. 34:9).

632 Store

A Stores of food
Store up every kind of food (Gen. 6:21); Joseph stored up the food of Egypt (Gen. 41:35, 48-9); Rehoboam put stores of food in the fortresses (2 Chr. 11:11); we have stores of wheat, barley, oil and honey hidden in the field (Jer. 41:8); I have nowhere to store my crops (Luke 12:17-19); the Lord will bless your barns (Deut. 28:8); your barns will be filled with plenty (Prov. 3:10); let our garners be full (Ps. 144:13); the birds do not gather into barns (Matt. 6:26); ravens have neither storehouse nor barn (Luke 12:24).

B God's storehouses
The Lord will open his good storehouse, the heavens, to give rain (Deut. 28:12); God's storehouses of snow and hail (Job 38:22); he brings the wind from his storehouses (Ps. 135:7; Jer. 10:13; 51:16); he gathers the deeps in storehouses (Ps. 33:7); the Lord will be a store of salvation, wisdom and knowledge (Isa. 33:6); gather the wheat into my barn (Matt. 13:30); he will gather his wheat into the barn (Matt. 3:12; Luke 3:17).

C Storing treasure on earth
Do not store up treasure on earth (Matt. 6:19-20); hoarded riches are a grievous evil (Eccles. 5:13); I will demolish my barns and build bigger ones (Luke 12:18); he who lays up treasure for himself but is not rich toward God (Luke 12:21); children should not save up for their parents, but parents for their children (2 Cor. 12:14); you have stored up treasure in the last days (Jas. 5:3).

D Storing other things
You are storing up wrath for yourself (Rom. 2:5); the first day of the week everyone is to store something (1 Cor. 16:2); storing up for themselves a good foundation for the future (1 Tim. 6:19).

633 Provision

A God providing
God richly supplies us with everything to enjoy (1 Tim. 6:17); he satisfies the thirsty one (Ps. 107:9); God will equip you with everything good to do his will (Heb. 13:21); the provision of the Spirit (Phil. 1:19); his divine power has granted us everything pertaining to life and godliness (2 Pet. 1:3); the Lord will provide a lamb (Gen. 22:8, 14).

B People providing
Joseph promised to provide for his relatives in Egypt (Gen. 45:11); Rehoboam provided abundant food for his sons (2 Chr. 11:23); Jehoshaphat had large supplies in Judah (2 Chr. 17:13); let the widow's children make some return to their parents (1 Tim. 5:4); if any one will not provide for his family, he has denied the faith (1 Tim. 5:8); your abundance will supply their need, then their abundance will supply your need (2 Cor. 8:14); when the brethren came from Macedonia they fully supplied my needs (2 Cor. 11:9); that we may supply what is lacking in your faith (1 Thess. 3:10); see that Zenas and Apollos lack nothing (Titus 3:13); Barzillai provided for the king (2 Sam. 19:32-3); David provided materials for the temple (1 Chr. 29:2-5); twelve governors provided for the king for each month (1 Kgs. 4:7, 27-8).

634 Waste
Why this waste? (Matt. 26:8; Mark 14:4); the unjust steward was squandering his master's possessions (Luke 16:1); the younger son squandered his property (Luke 15:13); the wine is lost and so are the skins (Mark 2:22).
WASTE TIME, see 136.

635 Sufficiency

A Plenty in general
I know how to face abundance and want (Phil. 4:12); as you abound in everything, abound in giving too (2 Cor. 8:7); he who tills his land will have plenty of food (Prov. 12:11; 28:19); work so you may not be in need (1 Thess. 4:12); your barns will be filled with plenty (Prov. 3:10); Esau had plenty (Gen. 33:9); Jacob had plenty (Gen. 33:11); Sodom had pride, abundant food and careless ease (Ezek. 16:49); when we practised idolatry we had plenty of food (Jer. 44:17); when I fed them to the full they committed adultery (Jer. 5:7); how many of my father's hired men have bread enough and to spare! (Luke 15:17); wine was plentiful (Esther 1:7); the material was enough to build the sanctuary and more (Exod. 36:7).
MORE THAN ENOUGH, see 637.

B Plenty in Egypt
In Egypt we ate bread to the full (Exod. 16:3); seven years of plenty (Gen. 41:29); grain like the sand of the sea (Gen. 41:49); you brought us from a land flowing with milk and honey (Num. 16:13).

C Plenty in the wilderness
These forty years you have not lacked anything (Deut. 2:7); they ate and were filled (Ps. 78:29); they did not thirst when he led them through the deserts (Isa. 48:21).

D Plenty in the land
A land flowing with milk and honey (Exod. 3:8; 13:5; 33:3; Lev. 20:24; Num. 13:27; Deut. 6:3; Josh. 5:6; Ezek. 20:6); a land of grain and new wine (Deut. 33:28); a land where there is no lack (Judg. 18:10); the priests had plenty to eat and to spare (2 Chr. 31:10); they ate, were filled and grew fat (Neh. 9:25); you crown the year with your bounty (Ps. 65:11); you will be satisfied with Jerusalem's consoling breasts (Isa. 66:11); when you have eaten and are satisfied (Deut. 8:10-12).

E Plenty for the poor
He fills the hungry with good things (Ps. 107:9; Luke 1:53); the poor will eat and be satisfied (Ps. 22:26); I will satisfy her poor with bread (Ps. 132:15); the widow's flour and oil will not run out until rain comes (1 Kgs. 17:14-16); the oil flowed until all the vessels were full (2 Kgs. 4:5-6); he who gives to the poor will not want (Prov. 28:27); there was no needy person among them (Acts 4:34).

F Plenty through God
You satisfy the desire of every living thing (Ps. 145:16); he fulfils the desire of all who fear him (Ps. 145:19); those who fear him lack nothing (Ps. 34:9-10); satisfied with favour and full of the blessing of the Lord (Deut. 33:23); they feast on the abundance of your house (Ps. 36:8); we will be satisfied with the goodness of your house (Ps. 65:4); I will not want (Ps. 23:1); my cup overflows (Ps. 23:5); my soul is feasted as with fat (Ps. 63:5); the abundance of the sea will be turned to you (Isa. 60:5); not that we are sufficient of ourselves, our sufficiency is of God (2 Cor. 3:5); good measure, pressed down, shaken together, running over (Luke 6:38); there will be overflowing threshing floors and vats (Joel 2:24); my cities will again overflow with prosperity (Zech. 1:17).

G Plenty through Christ
Whoever drinks the water I give will never thirst (John 4:14); he who comes to me will not hunger and he who believes in me will not thirst (John 6:35); those who hunger and thirst after righteousness will be satisfied (Matt. 5:6); you do not lack any gift (1 Cor. 1:7); God is able to make all grace abound so that you always have enough of everything (2 Cor. 9:8); God will supply all your needs according to his riches in Christ (Phil. 4:19); my grace is sufficient for you (2 Cor. 12:9); a treasure in heaven which is inexhaustible (Luke 12:33); they will not hunger or thirst (Isa. 49:10; Rev. 7:16).

636 Insufficiency
LACK OF WATER, see 342B2.

A Shortage in general
One withholds what is due yet suffers want (Prov. 11:24); the sluggard craves and gets nothing (Prov. 13:4); at harvest the sluggard will have nothing (Prov. 20:4); lest I be in want and steal (Prov. 30:9); TEKEL – weighed in the balances and found wanting (Dan. 5:27); he began to be in need (Luke 15:14); when I sent you out without purse, bag or sandals, did you lack anything? (Luke 22:35); when I was in need I was not a burden to any one (2 Cor. 11:9); not that I speak of

want (Phil. 4:11); if anyone sees his brother in need (1 John 3:17).

B No food
There is no pasture for the flocks (Gen. 47:4); have you brought us out to die of hunger in the wilderness? (Exod. 16:3); there is no food (Num. 21:5); little ones ask for bread but no one breaks it for them (Lam. 4:4); her princes have become like deer that find no pasture (Lam. 1:6); a friend has arrived and I have nothing to set before him (Luke 11:6); I perish here with hunger (Luke 15:17); the grain is ruined, the wine fails, the oil languishes (Joel 1:10); the sweet wine is cut off from your mouth (Joel 1:5); I have made the wine cease (Jer. 48:33); when the wine failed his mother said, 'They have no wine' (John 2:3); may Joab's house always have someone who lacks bread (2 Sam. 3:29); the lion perishes for lack of prey (Job 4:11); lions lack and suffer hunger (Ps. 34:10).

C Famine
C1 Famine in general
Our skin is like an oven from the heat of famine (Lam. 5:10); the doe abandons her newborn calf for lack of grass (Jer. 14:5-6); children faint from hunger (Lam. 2:19); better those slain by the sword than those slain with hunger (Lam. 4:9); I gave you cleanness of teeth and lack of bread (Amos 4:6); devastation and destruction, famine and sword (Isa. 51:19); sword, famine and pestilence (Jer. 32:24); their honourable men die of hunger (Isa. 5:13); those who are gaunt from want and famine (Job 30:3); the city defeated by sword, famine and pestilence (Jer. 32:36).

C2 Particular famines
Seven years of famine (Gen. 41:27-57); there was famine in the land of Canaan (Gen. 42:5; 47:4-20); the famine was heavy in the land (Gen. 43:1); famine in the time of: Abraham (Gen. 12:10; 26:1); Isaac (Gen. 26:1); Joseph (Gen. 45:6; Ps. 105:16; Acts 7:11); the judges (Ruth 1:1); David (2 Sam. 21:1); Elijah (1 Kgs. 18:2; Luke 4:25); Elisha (2 Kgs. 4:38; 6:25; 7:4; 8:1); Zedekiah (2 Kgs. 25:3; Jer. 52:6); Nehemiah (Neh. 5:3); the prodigal son (Luke 15:14); Claudius (Acts 11:28).

C3 Famine will come
David was given the option of three years of famine (2 Sam. 24:13; 1 Chr. 21:12); they will be wasted by famine (Deut. 32:24); bread and water will be scarce (Ezek. 4:17); they will eat bread by weight and with anxiety (Ezek. 4:16); they will eat but not have enough (Hos. 4:10); her plagues will come, pestilence and mourning and famine (Rev. 18:8); ten women will bake your bread in one oven (Lev. 26:26); there will be famines (Matt. 24:7; Mark 13:8; Luke 21:11); those who are intended for famine, let them go to famine (Jer. 15:2); famine will follow close after you to Egypt (Jer. 42:16); famine, sword and pestilence will come (Jer. 14:12-16); the Lord will remove the supply of bread and water (Isa. 3:1); I will send sword, famine and pestilence among them (Jer. 24:10); I will send famine against Jerusalem (Ezek. 14:21); I will increase the famine on you (Ezek. 5:16); I will send famine and wild beasts against you (Ezek. 5:17); when I send against them my deadly arrows of famine (Ezek. 5:16); I will punish them with sword, famine and pestilence (Jer. 44:13); I will kill your root with famine (Isa. 14:30); I am sending among them the sword, famine and pestilence (Jer. 29:17-18); I will punish with sword, famine and pestilence (Jer. 27:8).

C4 No more famine
They will no longer be subject to famine (Ezek. 34:29; 36:29); we will not see sword or famine (Jer. 5:12); in Egypt we will not hunger for bread (Jer. 42:14); the prophets say they will not see sword or famine (Jer.

14:13, 15); no longer the disgrace of famine (Ezek. 36:30).

D Shortage other than food

The women were not sufficient for the Benjaminites (Judg. 21:14); men will be scarcer than gold (Isa. 13:12); the water in the skin was spent (Gen. 21:15); all the money in Egypt and Canaan was used up (Gen. 47:15-18); why have you given us only one portion of land? (Josh. 17:14-16); the dust of Samaria will not suffice for my people (1 Kgs. 20:10); there will not be enough oil for us and you (Matt. 25:9); Lebanon's beasts would not be enough for a burnt offering (Isa. 40:16); there will be a famine of hearing the Lord's word (Amos 8:11).

E Empty-handed

They sent him away empty-handed (Mark 12:3; Luke 20:10-11); you would have sent me away empty-handed (Gen. 31:42); do not go to your mother-in-law empty-handed (Ruth 3:17); he has sent the rich away empty-handed (Luke 1:53); you will not go empty-handed (Exod. 3:21); none will come before me empty-handed (Exod. 23:15; 34:20; Deut. 16:16); do not send away a slave empty-handed (Deut. 15:13).

F Help in shortage

When famine comes and your people pray (1 Kgs. 8:37; 2 Chr. 6:28; 20:9); famine will not separate us from the love of Christ (Rom. 8:35); in famine God will redeem you from death (Job 5:20); he will keep them alive in famine (Ps. 33:19); you will laugh at famine (Job 5:22); I know how to face abundance and want (Phil. 4:12); if a brother or sister is without food (Jas. 2:15).

637 Excess

A More than enough

The people brought more than enough for the tabernacle (Exod. 36:5-7); I have had enough of burnt offerings (Isa. 1:11); enough of your abominations (Ezek. 44:6); it is not good to eat too much honey (Prov. 25:27); a sated man loathes honey (Prov. 27:7); eat only enough honey, lest you be sated and vomit it (Prov. 25:16); the full stomach of the rich does not let him sleep (Eccles. 5:12).

B Surplus

They contributed from their surplus (Mark 12:44; Luke 21:4); your vats will overflow with new wine (Prov. 3:10); it is superfluous for me to write to you (2 Cor. 9:1); those who gathered much had nothing over (Exod. 16:18; 2 Cor. 8:15).

638 Importance

A Greatness of God

The Lord is a great God (Ps. 95:3); great is the Lord (1 Chr. 16:25; Ps. 48:1; 96:4; 145:3); great is our lord (Ps. 147:5); you are great (Ps. 86:10); you are very great (Ps. 104:1); you are great and your name is great in might (Jer. 10:6); what god is great like our God? (Ps. 77:13); the Lord is greater than all gods (Exod. 18:11; 2 Chr. 2:5); he that is in you is greater than he that is in the world (1 John 4:4); he who comes from heaven is above all (John 3:31); he [Christ] will be great to the ends of the earth (Mic. 5:4); I am a great king (Mal. 1:14); from the rising of the sun to its setting my name will be great (Mal. 1:11).

B Greatness of man

B1 Intrinsic importance of man

Man is worth more than many sparrows (Matt. 10:31; Luke 12:7); worth more than the birds (Luke 12:24); worth more than a sheep (Matt. 12:12).

B2 Men relatively great

An argument arose as to who was the greatest (Luke 22:24); whoever practises and teaches will be called

great (Matt. 5:19); whoever would be great among you must be your servant (Matt. 20:26-7; Mark 10:43); if anyone wants to be first he must be last of all and servant of all (Mark 9:35); the greatest among you will be your servant (Matt. 23:11); let the greatest become as the youngest (Luke 22:26-7); lest a more important man than you be invited (Luke 14:8); he who prophesies is greater than he who speaks in tongues (1 Cor. 14:5); men swear by one greater than themselves (Heb. 6:16).

C Great things

Every major matter they will bring to you (Exod. 18:22); which is the great commandment in the law? (Matt. 22:36-8; Mark 12:28-31); I am doing a great work (Neh. 6:3); do you seek great things for yourself? (Jer. 45:5); which is greater, the gold or the temple? (Matt. 23:17); which is greater, the offering or the altar? (Matt. 23:19); is not life more than food and the body more than clothing? (Matt. 6:25); I delivered to you as of first importance that Christ died for our sins (1 Cor. 15:3).

D Great and small

From the least to the greatest they will all know me (Jer. 31:34; Heb. 8:11); from the least to the greatest everyone is greedy for gain (Jer. 6:13; 8:10); judge the small and great alike (Deut. 1:17); from the greatest to the least they called a fast and put on sackcloth (Jonah 3:5); everyone, from the least to the greatest, gave heed to Simon (Acts 8:10); I stand here testifying to small and great (Acts 26:22); those who fear your name, small and great (Rev. 11:18); all, small and great, rich and poor, free and slave, must have a mark (Rev. 13:16); you who fear him, small and great (Rev. 19:5); eat the flesh of all men, free and slaves, small and great (Rev. 19:18); the dead, great and small, stood before the throne (Rev. 20:12).

639 Unimportance

A Unimportant people

A1 I am unimportant

Who am I? (Exod. 3:11; 2 Sam. 7:18; 2 Kgs. 8:13; 1 Chr. 17:16; 29:14; 2 Chr. 2:6); what are we that you grumble about us? (Exod. 16:7-8); who is David? (1 Sam. 25:10); who am I to be the king's son-in-law? (1 Sam. 18:18); a dead dog like me? (2 Sam. 9:8); who are you pursuing? a dead dog, one flea? (1 Sam. 24:14); I am dust and ashes (Gen. 18:27); my family is least in Benjamin (1 Sam. 9:21); if I have not love I am nothing (1 Cor. 13:2, 3); I am not inferior to these superlative apostles, even though I am nothing (2 Cor. 12:11).

A2 Other unimportant people

The Most High gives dominion to the lowliest of men (Dan. 4:17); as you did it to the least of my brethren you did it to me (Matt. 25:40); neither he who plants nor he who waters is anything (1 Cor. 3:7); who are you to answer back to God? (Rom. 9:20); all the nations are as nothing before him (Isa. 40:17); all the inhabitants of the earth are as nothing (Dan. 4:35); he brings princes to nought (Isa. 40:23-4); God has chosen things that are not (1 Cor. 1:28).

B Unimportant things

Does it seem a light thing to become the king's son-in-law? (1 Sam. 18:23); is it too small a thing that God has brought you near himself? (Num. 16:9); it is too small a thing that you should be my servant (Isa. 49:6); whoever swears by the temple, it is nothing (Matt. 23:16); if one swears by the altar it is nothing (Matt. 23:18); does not this temple seem as nothing in comparison? (Hag. 2:3); Bethlehem is by no means least (Matt. 2:6); the least commandment (Matt. 5:19); it is a small thing to be judged by you (1 Cor. 4:3);

neither circumcision nor uncircumcision is anything (1 Cor. 7:19).

640 Usefulness

A Useful people
You will be neither useless nor unfruitful (2 Pet. 1:8); a vessel useful for the master (2 Tim. 2:21); can a man be profitable to God? (Job 22:2); Onesimus – 'Useful' (Philem. 10-11); Mark is useful to me (2 Tim. 4:11).

B Useful things
All scripture is profitable for correction etc. (2 Tim. 3:16); it is expedient that one man die (John 11:50; 18:14); it is to your advantage that I go away (John 16:7); I did not shrink from declaring to you anything that was profitable (Acts 20:20); training in godliness is of value in every way (1 Tim. 4:8); these things are good and profitable for men (Titus 3:8); land which brings forth useful vegetation receives a blessing from God (Heb. 6:7).

641 Uselessness

A Useless people
Remember for what vanity you have created mankind (Ps. 89:47); God knows useless men (Job 11:11); you are worthless physicians (Job 13:4); God says to a king, 'Worthless one!' (Job 34:18); let them be like this waistband, which is useless (Jer. 13:10); we have become the scum of the earth, the offscouring of all things (1 Cor. 4:13); you have made us offscouring and refuse (Lam. 3:45); formerly Onesimus was useless to you (Philem. 11); they are the dross of silver (Ezek. 22:18); woe to the worthless shepherd who deserts the flock (Zech. 11:17); cast the worthless servant into the outer darkness (Matt. 25:30); together they have become useless (Rom. 3:12); Gentiles walk in the futility of their minds (Eph. 4:17); they are worthless for any good deed (Titus 1:16); they went after worthless things and became worthless (Jer. 2:5).

B Useless idols
Who has shaped an idol which is profitable for nothing? (Isa. 44:10); his images are worthless (Jer. 10:15; 51:18); an idol is nothing in the world (1 Cor. 8:4); we preach the gospel that you should turn from these vain things (Acts 14:15).

C Useless things
C1 Useless things in general
Not all things are profitable (1 Cor. 6:12; 10:23); how long will you love what is worthless? (Ps. 4:2); our fathers inherited nothing but worthless things (Jer. 16:19); you who rejoice in Lo-debar [a thing of nothing] (Amos 6:13); the weak and worthless elements (Gal. 4:9).

C2 Useless words
Controversies are unprofitable (Titus 3:9); some have turned to fruitless discussion (1 Tim. 1:6); they speak swollen discourses of vanity (2 Pet. 2:18); it is not an unprofitable word but your life (Deut. 32:47).

C3 Rubbish
For Christ I count all things as rubbish (Phil. 3:8); houses made a rubbish heap (Ezra 6:11; Dan. 2:5; 3:29); take away dross from silver (Prov. 25:4); your silver has become dross (Isa. 1:22); there is much rubbish (Neh. 4:10); he lifts the needy from the ash-heap (1 Sam. 2:8).

C4 Other useless things
I said of pleasure, 'What use is it?' (Eccles. 2:2); what use is a birthright to me? (Gen. 25:32); tasteless salt is good for nothing (Matt. 5:13); he will burn the chaff with unquenchable fire (Luke 3:17); why did the Gentiles rage and the peoples imagine futile things? (Acts 4:25); the temple of the great goddess Artemis may be considered worthless (Acts 19:27); if you let

yourselves be circumcised, Christ will be of no value to you (Gal. 5:2); if it bears thorns and thistles it is worthless and close to being cursed (Heb. 6:8); cities called Cabul – as good as nothing (1 Kgs. 9:13); the waistcloth was worthless (Jer. 13:7); your anger consumes them like chaff (Exod. 15:7); the storm carries them off like stubble (Isa. 40:24).

D Useless endeavour
D1 Useless endeavour in general
Vanity, vanity, everything is vanity (Eccles. 1:2; 12:8); all is vanity (Eccles. 3:19); all comes to vanity (Eccles. 11:8); vanity, chasing after wind (Eccles. 1:14); vanity under the sun (Eccles. 4:7); the creation was subjected to futility (Rom. 8:20); they followed vanity and became vain (2 Kgs. 17:15); redeemed from the futile way of life inherited from your fathers (1 Pet. 1:18).

D2 Useless labour
Why should I toil in vain? (Job 9:29); in vain have I guarded all that belongs to him (1 Sam. 25:21); your strength will be spent uselessly (Lev. 26:20); the peoples toil for nothing (Jer. 51:58); in vain you rise early and retire late (Ps. 127:2); you will sow seed in vain (Lev. 26:16); in vain is a net spread in the sight of any bird (Prov. 1:17); I am afraid I have laboured over you in vain (Gal. 4:11); I have laboured in vain (Isa. 49:4); after defilement, the former days as a Nazirite shall be void (Num. 6:12); for fear I was running in vain (Gal. 2:2); lest our labour should be in vain (1 Thess. 3:5); did you suffer so much in vain? (Gal. 3:4); I did not run in vain or labour in vain (Phil. 2:16); I do not run aimlessly (1 Cor. 9:26); I box, not as one beating the air (1 Cor. 9:26); your labour is not in vain in the Lord (1 Cor. 15:58); our coming to you was not in vain (1 Thess. 2:1).

D3 Useless religion
That you might not kindle fire on my altars in vain (Mal. 1:10); you say it is vain to serve God (Mal. 3:14); unless you believed in vain (1 Cor. 15:2); his grace toward me was not in vain (1 Cor. 15:10); what use is it if a man says he has faith but has not works? (Jas. 2:14-20); unless the Lord builds the house the builders labour in vain (Ps. 127:1); unless the Lord guards the city the watchmen keep awake in vain (Ps. 127:1); if Christ is not raised, our preaching is in vain and your faith is in vain (1 Cor. 15:14-17); if righteousness is by the law, then Christ died in vain (Gal. 2:21); lest the cross of Christ should be made void (1 Cor. 1:17); in vain do they worship me (Matt. 15:9; Mark 7:7); if anyone does not bridle his tongue his religion is vain (Jas. 1:26); do not receive the grace of God in vain (2 Cor. 6:1).

D4 Useless words and thinking
Do not take the name of the Lord in vain (Exod. 20:7); men will render account for every idle word (Matt. 12:36); quarrelling about words is a useless activity (2 Tim. 2:14); the Lord knows that the reasonings of the wise are futile (1 Cor. 3:20); they became futile in their thinking (Rom. 1:21); why do the peoples plot a vain thing? (Ps. 2:1); their deceitfulness is useless (Ps. 119:118).

642 Good policy
UTILITY, see 640.

643 Inexpedience
HARMFUL, see 645.

644 Goodness
A God is good
The Lord is good (Ps. 100:5; 135:3; Jer. 33:11; Nahum 1:7); how great is your goodness! (Ps. 31:19); taste and see that the Lord is good (Ps. 34:8); I will make my

goodness pass before you (Exod. 33:19); my people will be satisfied with my goodness (Jer. 31:14); One there is who is good – God (Matt. 19:17; Mark 10:18; Luke 18:19); give thanks to the Lord for he is good (Ps. 106:1; 107:1; 118:1, 29); I will see the goodness of the Lord in the land of the living (Ps. 27:13).

B Good people

Good teacher (Mark 10:17; Luke 18:18); good and faithful servant (Matt. 25:21-3); well done, good servant! (Luke 19:17); the good man out of the good treasure of his heart produces good (Luke 6:45); why call me good? (Mark 10:18; Luke 18:19); I am the good shepherd (John 10:11, 14); perhaps for a good man one would dare to die (Rom. 5:7); the fruit of the Spirit is goodness (Gal. 5:22); Barnabas was a good man (Acts 11:24).

C Good things

C1 Good in general

Why ask me about what is good? (Matt. 19:17); he has told you, O man, what is good (Mic. 6:8); cling to what is good (Rom. 12:9); the old is good (Luke 5:39); to each is given the manifestation of the Spirit for the common good (1 Cor. 12:7); that you may approve the things which are excellent (Phil. 1:10); take thought for what is good in the sight of all men (Rom. 12:17); if there is any excellence, think about it (Phil. 4:8); hold fast to what is good (1 Thess. 5:21); I would have you wise as to what is good, simple as to evil (Rom. 16:19); do not let what is for you a good thing be spoken of as evil (Rom. 14:16); this is good and acceptable in the sight of God our Saviour (1 Tim. 2:3); an elder [overseer] must love what is good (Titus 1:8); these things are good and profitable for men (Titus 3:8).

C2 Good activity

It seemed good to the Holy Spirit and to us (Acts 15:28); it is good for us to be here (Matt. 17:4; Mark 9:5; Luke 9:33); it is good for a man to remain as he is (1 Cor. 7:26); it is good for a man not to touch a woman (1 Cor. 7:1); it is good to give thanks to the Lord (Ps. 92:1); how good it is when brothers dwell in unity (Ps. 133:1); 'let us do evil that good may come' (Rom. 3:8).

C3 Things which are good

God saw that the light was good (Gen. 1:4); God saw that what he had made was good (Gen. 1:10-25); it was very good (Gen. 1:31); everything created by God is good (1 Tim. 4:4); the woman saw that the tree was good for food (Gen. 3:6); an exceedingly good land (Num. 14:7); the Lord is bringing you into a good land (Deut. 8:7); some seed fell on good soil (Matt. 13:8, 23; Mark 4:8, 20; Luke 8:8, 15); a man who sowed good seed in his field (Matt. 13:24-7); he who sows the good seed is the Son of man (Matt. 13:37); a good tree bears good fruit (Matt. 7:17-18; Luke 6:43); every tree which does not bear good fruit will be cut down and burnt (Matt. 7:19); every man serves the good wine first (John 2:10); a basket of good figs (Jer. 24:2, 5); they desire a better country, a heavenly one (Heb. 11:16).

C4 Giving good things

The Lord will give what is good (Ps. 85:12); every good and perfect gift is from the Father (Jas. 1:17); you open your hand and they are satisfied with good (Ps. 104:28); no good thing does he withhold from them who walk uprightly (Ps. 84:11); how much more will your Father in heaven give good things to those who ask him (Matt. 7:11); those who seek the Lord will not lack any good thing (Ps. 34:10); you, though evil, know how to give good gifts to your children (Matt. 7:11; Luke 11:13).

C5 Good words

If you utter what is precious rather than what is worthless (Jer. 15:19); your ordinances are good (Ps. 119:39); the law is holy and the commandment holy and righteous and good (Rom. 7:12); did that which is good bring death to me? (Rom. 7:13); the law is good (Rom. 7:16); the law is good if one uses it lawfully (1 Tim. 1:8). GOOD SPEECH, see 579A4.

D Doing good

D1 God doing good

You are good and do good (Ps. 119:68); the Lord is good to all (Ps. 145:9); do good, Lord, to those who are good (Ps. 125:4); in all things God works for good to those who love him (Rom. 8:28); God sends sun and rain on all (Matt. 5:45); God did good and gave you rain from heaven (Acts 14:17); Jethro rejoiced at all the good the Lord had done to Israel (Exod. 18:9); the Lord has promised good to Israel (Num. 10:29); I have purposed to do good to Jerusalem and Judah (Zech. 8:15); I will rejoice over them to do them good (Jer. 32:41); all nations will fear when they see the good I do to Jerusalem (Jer. 33:9); I am bringing on them all the good I promised (Jer. 32:42); I will do you more good than before (Ezek. 36:11); God is good to Israel (Ps. 73:1); do good to Zion (Ps. 51:18); you meant evil but God meant it for good (Gen. 50:20); surely goodness and mercy will follow me (Ps. 23:6); apart from you I have no good thing (Ps. 16:2); I will repent of the good I intended (Jer. 18:10).

D2 Do good!

Do good! (Ps. 37:3, 27); do good to Zion (Ps. 51:18); do good or evil, that we may fear (Isa. 41:23); depart from evil and do good (Ps. 34:14); do not withhold good from those to whom it is due (Prov. 3:27); let us do good to all men (Gal. 6:10); it is right to do good on the sabbath (Matt. 12:12); seek to do good to one another and to all men (1 Thess. 5:15); do not grow weary in doing good (2 Thess. 3:13); they should do good, be rich in good works (1 Tim. 6:18); be ready for any good deed (Titus 3:1); that those who have believed in God might be careful to do good deeds (Titus 3:8); let our people engage in good deeds (Titus 3:14); stirring up one another to love and good works (Heb. 10:24); do not neglect to do good and share (Heb. 13:16); let him turn away from evil and do good (1 Pet. 3:11); do good to your enemies (Luke 6:35); do good to those who hate you (Luke 6:27).

D3 People doing good

D3a About doing good

Teacher, what good thing must I do to have eternal life? (Matt. 19:16); is it right on the sabbath to do good or do harm? (Mark 3:4; Luke 6:9); whenever you wish you can do good to the poor (Mark 14:7); those who have done good will come forth to the resurrection of life (John 5:29); those who persevere in doing good (Rom. 2:7); there will be glory and honour and peace to everyone who does good (Rom. 2:10); a people zealous for good deeds (Titus 2:14); the fruit of light is in all that is good and right and true (Eph. 5:9).

D3b Those who did good

Jesus went about doing good (Acts 10:38); he who does good is of God (3 John 11); she has done a good thing to me (Matt. 26:10; Mark 14:6); Dorcas was always doing good (Acts 9:36).

E Nothing good

My days flee away and see no good (Job 9:25); many say, 'Who will show us any good?' (Ps. 4:6); there is no one who does good (Ps. 53:1, 3); nothing good dwells in me (Rom. 7:18); how can you do good who are accustomed to do evil? (Jer. 13:23); how can you speak what is good when you are evil? (Matt. 12:34); can any good thing come out of Nazareth? (John 1:46); men will be haters of good (2 Tim. 3:3).

F Good or bad

Do good or evil, that we may fear (Isa. 41:23); they cannot do evil and they cannot do good (Jer. 10:5); is it not from the mouth of the Most High that both good and evil go forth? (Lam. 3:38); 'the Lord will not do either good or evil' (Zeph. 1:12); they had done nothing either good or bad (Rom. 9:11).

645 Badness

A Badness in general

I would have you wise as to what is good, simple as to evil (Rom. 16:19); how can you speak what is good when you are evil? (Matt. 12:34); the evil man out of his evil treasure brings forth evil (Matt. 12:35; Luke 6:45). THE WICKED, see 938.

B Bad things

B1 Bad items

No cattle so bad in all Egypt (Gen. 41:19); a basket of very bad figs (Jer. 24:2); make the tree bad and its fruit bad (Matt. 12:33); every tree which does not bear good fruit is cut down (Matt. 3:10); a good tree does not bear bad fruit nor a bad tree good fruit (Luke 6:43); when men have drunk freely the poor wine is served (John 2:10).

B2 Bad situations

It is not good for the man to be alone (Gen. 2:18); what you are doing is not good (Exod. 18:17); this is an evil, that one fate comes to all men (Eccles. 9:3); Lazarus in his lifetime received evil things (Luke 16:25).

B3 Calamity

A disaster, a unique disaster comes! (Ezek. 7:5; disaster comes on disaster (Ezek. 7:26); he who is at ease is contemptuous of calamity (Job 12:5); we commend ourselves in afflictions, hardships, calamities (2 Cor. 6:4).

C Doing evil

C1 God doing evil

C1a God can harm people

I will heap misfortune on them (Deut. 32:23); shall we accept good from God and not accept evil? (Job 2:10); God causes peace and creates calamity (Isa. 45:7); does evil befall a city and the Lord has not done it? (Amos 3:6); is it not from the mouth of the Most High that both good and evil go forth? (Lam. 3:38); I will set my eyes against them for evil and not for good (Amos 9:4).

C1b God will bring harm

If you serve other gods, he will harm you (Josh. 24:20); I purposed to do evil to you (Zech. 8:14); I will raise up evil from your own household (2 Sam. 12:11); I will bring evil in his son's days (1 Kgs. 21:29); I am bringing evil on this place (2 Kgs. 22:16; 2 Chr. 34:24); I am bringing evil on all flesh (Jer. 45:5); I am bringing evil on this people (Jer. 6:19); I am watching over them for evil and not for good (Jer. 44:27); I am bringing on them all the evil about which I spoke (Jer. 35:17; 36:31); I am beginning to work evil in the city called by my name (Jer. 25:29).

C1c God harmed them

The Lord brought evil on Absalom (2 Sam. 17:14); this evil is from the Lord (2 Kgs. 6:33); evil has come down from the Lord to the gate of Jerusalem (Mic. 1:12); God smote the people because they made the calf (Exod. 32:35); you have seen all the evil I brought on Jerusalem (Jer. 44:2); wherever they went, the Lord's hand was against them for evil (Judg. 2:15).

C2 People doing evil

SIN, see 914.

C2a People harming others

Pharaoh has harmed this people (Exod. 5:23); the Egyptians ill-treated us (Num. 20:15); Alexander the coppersmith did me much harm (2 Tim. 4:14); the

harm he did to your saints in Jerusalem (Acts 9:13); if he has harmed you (Philem. 18); they were ill-treated (Heb. 11:37); remember those ill-treated, since you are also in the body (Heb. 13:3).

C2b Harming oneself

Afraid David would do himself harm (2 Sam. 12:18); do not harm yourself, for we are all here! (Acts 16:28).

C3 Not doing evil

He does not do evil to his neighbour (Ps. 15:3); love does no wrong to anyone (Rom. 13:10); though I have afflicted you I will afflict you no more (Nahum 1:12); if they drink any deadly thing it will not harm them (Mark 16:18); the demon had done him no harm (Luke 4:35); no man will attack you to harm you (Acts 18:10); who will harm you if you are zealous for what is right? (1 Pet. 3:13); do not harm the earth or sea or trees (Rev. 7:3); they were told not to harm grass, green thing or tree (Rev. 9:4); God did not allow Laban to harm me (Gen. 31:7); do not harm my prophets (1 Chr. 16:22; Ps. 105:15); we have wronged no one (2 Cor. 7:2).

D No evil

Oh, that you would keep me from harm! (1 Chr. 4:10); no evil will befall you (Ps. 91:10); no harm befalls the righteous (Prov. 12:21); they will not hurt or destroy in my holy mountain (Isa. 11:9; 65:25).

646 Perfection

A God is perfect

Your heavenly Father is perfect (Matt. 5:48); the law of the Lord is perfect (Ps. 19:7); God's way is perfect (2 Sam. 22:31; Ps. 18:30); his work is perfect (Deut. 32:4); the will of God which is good, acceptable and perfect (Rom. 12:2).

B Christ made perfect

The author of salvation was made perfect through suffering (Heb. 2:10); having been made perfect (Heb. 5:9); a Son, made perfect for ever (Heb. 7:28); such a high priest, holy, innocent, undefiled (Heb. 7:26).

C People made perfect

The spirits of righteous men made perfect (Heb. 12:23); without us they should not be made perfect (Heb. 11:40); if you want to be perfect (Matt. 19:21); be perfect as your heavenly Father is (Matt. 5:48); that you may be perfect (Jas. 1:4); not that I am already perfect (Phil. 3:12); by one offering he has perfected those who are sanctified (Heb. 10:14); if perfection was through the Levitical priesthood (Heb. 7:11); the king of Tyre had the seal of perfection (Ezek. 28:12); perfect in beauty (Ezek. 27:3); is this the city they called the perfection of beauty? (Lam. 2:15); if anyone does not stumble in speech he is perfect (Jas. 3:2).

D Unblemished

The animals for sacrifice must be without defect (Lev. 9:2-3; 14:10; 22:19-21; Num. 28:19); as of a lamb without blemish (1 Pet. 1:19); he offered himself without blemish to God (Heb. 9:14); presenting the church without spot or blemish (Eph. 5:27); that you may be children of God without blemish (Phil. 2:15); be zealous to be found by him without spot or blemish (2 Pet. 3:14); he is able to present you without blemish in the presence of his glory (Jude 24); no lie was found in their mouth, for they are without blemish (Rev. 14:5); there was no defect in Absalom (2 Sam. 14:25); Nebuchadnezzar sought youths without a defect (Dan. 1:4); there is no blemish in you (S. of S. 4:7).

647 Imperfection

A Blemished people

No one with a defect could act as priest (Lev. 21:17-20, 21); a swelling, scab or bright spot (Lev. 13:2; 14:56); my flesh is clothed with maggots and scabs (Job 7:5); the

Lord will smite their heads with scabs (Isa. 3:17); the scab and the itch (Deut. 28:27); his appearance was marred (Isa. 52:14); they are blots and blemishes (2 Pet. 2:13).

B Blemished creatures

Every speckled and spotted animal (Gen. 30:32-9); if he offered speckled ones, all the flock were speckled (Gen. 31:8-12); an animal with a blemish or defect was not to be sacrificed (Lev. 22:20-5; Deut. 15:21; 17:1); cursed be the cheat who vows a male animal yet sacrifices a blemished animal (Mal. 1:14).

C Perfection limited

There is a limit to all perfection (Ps. 119:96); the law made nothing perfect (Heb. 7:19); the law cannot perfect those who draw near (Heb. 10:1).

648 Cleanness

A Clean people

A1 Purifying

A1a Means of purifying

A bronze laver for washing (Exod. 30:18); ten basins for washing (1 Kgs. 7:38; 2 Chr. 4:6); the 'sea' was for the priests to wash in (2 Chr. 4:6); ashes for the purifying of sin (Num. 19:9); six stone jars for purification (John 2:6); Moab is my washbasin (Ps. 60:8; 108:9).

A1b Purifying oneself

33 days for purifying the mother of a male child (Lev. 12:4); 66 days for purifying the mother of a female child (Lev. 12:5); instructions about washings (Heb. 6:2); offer for your cleansing what Moses commanded (Mark 1:44); the time for their purification according to the law of Moses (Luke 2:22); Bathsheba purified herself from her uncleanness (2 Sam. 11:4); they do not eat unless they purify themselves (Mark 7:4); cleansing the flesh with the blood and ashes of animals (Heb. 9:13); the worshippers, being cleansed, would no longer be conscious of sin (Heb. 10:2); many went up to Jerusalem before passover to purify themselves (John 11:55); Paul purified himself along with the four men (Acts 21:26); six stone jars for purification (John 2:6); John's disciples argued with a Jew over purification (John 3:25); purify yourself with the four men (Acts 21:24); baptism is not the removal of dirt from the body (1 Pet. 3:21).

A1c Purification of others

If you are willing, you can make me clean [from leprosy] (Matt. 8:2-3; Mark 1:40-1; Luke 5:12-13); cleanse the lepers (Matt. 10:8); only Naaman the Syrian was cleansed (Luke 4:27); lepers are cleansed (Luke 7:22); you are clean, but not all of you (John 13:10); he will purify the sons of Levi (Mal. 3:3).

A1d Ritual purification

Priests must wash before they minister, lest they die (Exod. 30:20-1); cleansed with the water on the third and seventh days (Num. 19:2); for seven months Israel will be burying them to cleanse the land (Ezek. 39:12-16); the days of purification when a sacrifice would be offered for each man (Acts 21:26); they found me purified in the temple (Acts 24:18); the healed leper is declared clean (Lev. 14:7); what God has cleansed, do not call common (Acts 10:15; 11:9); give what is within for alms and all is clean (Luke 11:41); cleansing their hearts by faith (Acts 15:9).

A2 Bathing

Pharaoh's daughter went to bathe in the Nile (Exod. 2:5); David saw Bathsheba bathing (2 Sam. 11:2); at birth you were not washed with water (Ezek. 16:4); I bathed you with water and washed off your blood (Ezek. 16:9); he who has bathed only needs to wash his feet (John 13:10); you bathed, painted your eyes and put on ornaments (Ezek. 23:40); they do not eat unless they

baptise themselves (Mark 7:4); the high priest had to bathe (Lev. 16:4, 24); bathing for ritual cleansing (Lev. 14:8-9; 15:5-27; 17:15-16; Num. 19:7-8; Deut. 23:11); Naaman washing himself in Jordan seven times (2 Kgs. 5:10, 14).

A3 Clean face

Joseph washed his face (Gen. 43:31); Ruth washed and anointed herself (Ruth 3:3); David washed and anointed himself (2 Sam. 12:20); when you fast, anoint your head and wash your face (Matt. 6:17).

A4 Clean hands

The elders shall wash their hands (Deut. 21:6); I wash my hands in innocence (Ps. 26:6); Pilate washed his hands (Matt. 27:24); in vain have I washed my hands (Ps. 73:13); the Pharisees, and all Jews, do not eat without washing their hands (Mark 7:3); wash your hands and purify your hearts (Jas. 4:8); he who has clean hands and a pure heart (Ps. 24:4); though I wash my hands with snow and lye (Job 9:30); though you wash with lye and use much soap (Jer. 2:22); they did not wash when they ate (Matt. 15:2; Luke 11:38).

A5 Clean feet

Water to wash their feet (Gen. 24:32); Joseph's brothers washed their feet (Gen. 43:24); Abraham offered to have the men's feet washed (Gen. 18:4); Lot offered to have the men wash their own feet (Gen. 19:2); the woman washed Jesus' feet with her tears (Luke 7:38, 44); Jesus washed the disciples' feet (John 13:5-14); an enrolled widow should have washed the saints' feet (1 Tim. 5:10); I am a maid to wash your feet (1 Sam. 25:41).

A6 Shaving

The Nazirite must shave off his hair at his dedication (Num. 6:18-19); Levites must shave their whole bodies (Num. 8:7); shaving heads on completion of a vow (Acts 21:24); a cleansed leper must shave (Lev. 14:8-9); the woman must shave her head and pare her nails (Deut. 21:12); it is as if her head were shaved (1 Cor. 11:5-6); Joseph shaved (Gen. 41:14); Samson's hair was shaved off (Judg. 16:19); half of each man's beard was shaved off (2 Sam. 10:4; 1 Chr. 19:4); their beards shaved off and clothes torn (Jer. 41:5); the king of Assyria will be the razor to shave your head and legs (Isa. 7:20); Ezekiel had to shave off his hair and beard (Ezek. 5:1); Job shaved his head (Job 1:20); priests must not shave their heads (Lev. 21:5; Ezek. 44:20); the Nazirite must not shave (Num. 6:5); no razor shall come on Samson's head (Judg. 13:5); a razor has never come on my head (Judg. 16:17); Samuel's head would not be shaved (1 Sam. 1:11); do not shave your forehead for the dead (Deut. 14:1); no one will gash himself or shave his head for them (Jer. 16:6).

B Clean animals

Lists of clean and unclean animals (Lev. 11:2-47; Deut. 14:3-21); seven pairs of every clean animal (Gen. 7:2); clean animals and birds sacrificed (Gen. 8:20); criteria for clean or unclean creatures (Lev. 11:3-21; Deut. 14:6-10).

C Clean things

C1 Clean clothes

The people had to wash their clothes (Exod. 19:10, 14); washing clothes for ritual cleansing (Lev. 11:25; Num. 8:7); washing an infected garment (Lev. 13:54, 58); purify every garment and article of leather, goats' hair and wood (Num. 31:20); he washes his garments in wine (Gen. 49:11); they put a clean turban on his head and clothed him (Zech. 3:5); Joseph wrapped Jesus' body in a clean linen cloth (Matt. 27:59); Jacob told his household to purify themselves and change their clothes (Gen. 35:2); Joseph changed his clothes (Gen. 41:14); David changed his clothes (2 Sam. 12:20); you have a few who have not soiled their clothes (Rev. 3:4); they have washed their robes in the blood of the Lamb (Rev. 7:14); he is like fuller's soap (Mal. 3:2); clothes whiter than any launderer could whiten them (Mark 9:3); the heavens and the earth will wear out and be changed like a garment (Ps. 102:26; Heb. 1:10-12).

C2 Clean objects
All things are clean (Rom. 14:20); nothing is unclean of itself (Rom. 14:14); Jesus declared all foods clean (Mark 7:19); place the ashes in a clean place (Lev. 6:11; Num. 19:9); scouring and rinsing bronze vessels (Lev. 6:28); you cleanse the outside of cup and dish (Matt. 23:25); cleansing of utensils (Mark 7:4; Luke 11:39-41); they washed the chariot (1 Kgs. 22:38); the temple was purified (2 Chr. 29:15); they cleansed the rooms Tobiah had had (Neh. 13:9); Moses purified the altar with blood (Lev. 8:15); cleansing the altar by sprinkling blood (Lev. 16:19); according to the law, all things are cleansed with blood (Heb. 9:22); I will wipe Jerusalem like a dish (2 Kgs. 21:13); I will smelt away your dross as with lye (Isa. 1:25).

C3 Sieving
He will shake the nations in a sieve (Isa. 30:28); I will shake Jacob as in a sieve (Amos 9:9); Satan has demanded to have you all to sieve you like wheat (Luke 22:31); straining out a gnat and swallowing a camel (Matt. 23:24).

C4 Sweeping
I will sweep it with the broom of destruction (Isa. 14:23); he finds his house empty, swept and put in order (Matt. 12:44; Luke 11:25); she lights a lamp and sweeps the house (Luke 15:8).

D Cleansing from sin
D1 Be clean from sin!
Wash yourselves (Isa. 1:16); wash your heart from evil (Jer. 4:14); be baptized and wash away your sins (Acts 22:16); let us cleanse ourselves from every defilement of flesh and spirit (2 Cor. 7:1); if a man cleanses himself from these things he will be a vessel for honour (2 Tim. 2:21); blessed are those who wash their robes (Rev. 22:14); everyone who has this hope in him purifies himself as he is pure (1 John 3:3); true religion is to keep yourself unspotted from the world (Jas. 1:27).

D2 Being cleansed from sin
Wash me from my sin (Ps. 51:2); cleanse me with hyssop and I will be clean (Ps. 51:7); create in me a clean heart (Ps. 51:10); the day of atonement to cleanse from sin (Lev. 16:30); the Lord will wash away the filth of the daughters of Zion (Isa. 4:4); water for the removal of sin (Num. 19:9); I will sprinkle clean water on you and you will be clean (Ezek. 36:25); to redeem us from lawlessness and cleanse for himself a people (Titus 2:14); after he had made purification for sins, he sat down (Heb. 1:3); he is faithful to forgive our sins and to cleanse us from all unrighteousness (1 John 1:9); having purified your souls by obedience to the truth (1 Pet. 1:22); he has forgotten he was cleansed from his old sins (2 Pet. 1:9); a fountain will be opened to cleanse sin (Zech. 13:1); the blood of Christ cleanses our consciences (Heb. 9:14); the blood of Jesus purifies us from all sin (1 John 1:7); the washing of regeneration (Titus 3:5); our hearts sprinkled from an evil conscience and our bodies washed with pure water (Heb. 10:22); you are clean through the word I have spoken to you (John 15:3); you were washed, you were sanctified (1 Cor. 6:11); Christ cleansed the church by the washing of water with the word (Eph. 5:26).

E Clean and unclean
Make a distinction between clean and unclean (Lev. 10:10; 11:47; 20:25); the law for a garment being clean or unclean (Lev. 13:59); to teach when it is clean and when

unclean (Lev. 14:57); they made no distinction between holy and profane, clean and unclean (Ezek. 22:26); priests must teach how to distinguish between unclean and clean (Ezek. 44:23); pairs of clean and unclean animals went into the ark (Gen. 7:8); lists of clean and unclean animals (Lev. 11:2-47; 20:25; Deut. 14:3-21); criteria for clean or unclean creatures (Lev. 11:3-42; Deut. 14:6-10).

649 Uncleanness

A Unclean people
A1 What makes people unclean
A woman who gives birth is unclean (Lev. 12:2-5); a leper is unclean (Lev. 13:3-46); discharges from the body make people unclean (Lev. 15:2-33); sexual intercourse with your neighbour's wife makes you unclean (Lev. 18:20); sexual intercourse with an animal makes you unclean (Lev. 18:23); when a man dies in a tent all who enter become unclean (Num. 19:14); Jerusalem sinned and so became unclean (Lam. 1:8); they became unclean by their deeds (Ps. 106:39); what comes out of a man makes him unclean (Matt. 15:11, 18-20; Mark 7:15, 20-3); becoming unclean by touching: human uncleanness (Lev. 5:3); a dead body (Num. 19:11; 31:19); unclean animals (Lev. 11:24-8, 31-8, 39-40); the carcass of a clean animal which dies (Lev. 11:39; 17:15).

A2 People being unclean
I am a man of unclean lips (Isa. 6:5); at the New Moon David must be unclean (1 Sam. 20:26); we have all become like one unclean (Isa. 64:6); both prophet and priest are polluted (Jer. 23:11); you are not all clean (John 13:11); let the one who is filthy still be filthy (Rev. 22:11); God has shown me not to call any man common or unclean (Acts 10:28); otherwise your children would be unclean, but now they are holy (1 Cor. 7:14); that no root of bitterness spring up and through it many be defiled (Heb. 12:15); the tongue defiles the whole body (Jas. 3:6); if any one touches what is unclean he becomes unclean (Lev. 5:2).

A3 People unwashed
Some of his disciples ate bread with defiled, unwashed, hands (Mark 7:2); they do not wash their hands when they eat (Matt. 15:2); to eat with unclean hands does not defile anyone (Matt. 15:20); when hypocrites fast, they neglect [to wash] their face (Matt. 6:16).

A4 Consequences of uncleanness
Anyone unclean must be sent out of the camp (Num. 5:2; Deut. 23:10); the unclean could not enter the temple (2 Chr. 23:19); the unclean will not travel on the highway of holiness (Isa. 35:8); the leper must shout, 'Unclean!' (Lev. 13:45); an unclean person touching food defiles it (Hag. 2:13); if any one is unclean he must eat the Passover on another day (Num. 9:6-10); some attending the Passover were unclean (2 Chr. 30:17-19); the Jews did not want to be unclean and unable to eat the Passover (John 18:28).

B Unclean spirits
When the unclean spirit has gone out of a man (Matt. 12:43); a man with an unclean spirit (Mark 1:23; 5:2); with authority he commands even the unclean spirits (Mark 1:27); unclean spirits fell down before him (Mark 3:11); they said Jesus had an unclean spirit (Mark 3:30); he gave the 12 authority over the unclean spirits (Mark 6:7).

C Unclean animals
Two of every unclean animal (Gen. 7:2); valuation of unclean animals (Lev. 27:11-12); redeeming unclean animals (Lev. 27:27); Peter had never eaten anything unclean (Acts 10:14-15; 11:8-9); Babylon has become the

haunt of every unclean bird (Rev. 18:2); lists of clean and unclean animals (Lev. 11:2-47; Deut. 14:3-21).

D Unclean things

A leprous garment is unclean (Lev. 13:51-9); a leprous house is unclean (Lev. 14:36); bringing every unclean thing out of the temple (2 Chr. 29:16); the bed on which an unclean person lies becomes unclean (Lev. 15:4); that on which an unclean person sits becomes unclean (Lev. 15:4); Joshua was clothed in filthy garments, standing before the angel (Zech. 3:3); you say the Lord's table may be defiled and its food despised (Mal. 1:12); inside they are full of dead men's bones and uncleanness (Matt. 23:27); hating even the garment spotted by the flesh (Jude 23); a gold cup full of abominations and the impurity of her fornications (Rev. 17:4); who can bring a clean thing from an unclean? (Job 14:4); he who regards the blood of the covenant as unclean (Heb. 10:29); to him who thinks anything is unclean, it is unclean (Rom. 14:14).

E Pollution

E1 Polluting holy places

He defiled my sanctuary (Lev. 20:3); the unclean who do not cleanse themselves defile the tabernacle (Num. 19:13, 20); lest they die by defiling my tabernacle (Lev. 15:31); they have defiled your holy temple (Ps. 79:1); he has defiled this holy place (Acts 21:28); they defiled my sanctuary (Ezek. 23:38); I will profane my sanctuary, the pride of your power (Ezek. 24:21).

E2 Polluting the land

They defiled the land by their ways and their deeds (Ezek. 36:17); they defiled the land with their idols (Ezek. 36:18); the land was polluted with the blood (Ps. 106:38); the earth is polluted by its inhabitants (Isa. 24:5); they have polluted my land (Jer. 16:18); the land became defiled (Lev. 18:25, 27); if a divorced wife returns to her husband the land will be polluted (Jer. 3:1); you have polluted the land with your harlotry (Jer. 3:2); Judah polluted the land and committed adultery (Jer. 3:9); do not pollute the land by bloodshed (Num. 35:33).

E3 Polluting other things

How have we polluted you [God]? (Mal. 1:7); they have defiled my holy name by their abominations (Ezek. 43:7-8); you muddy the waters with your feet and foul the rivers (Ezek. 32:2); must you foul the rest of the water with your feet? (Ezek. 34:18); like a muddied spring or a polluted fountain is the righteous who gives way to the wicked (Prov. 25:26).

650 Health

A Health promised

The Lord will remove sickness from you (Exod. 23:25; Deut. 7:15); I will not give you any of the Egyptians' diseases (Exod. 15:26; Deut. 7:15); no one will say they are sick (Isa. 33:24).

B Health achieved

Faith in Jesus has given him this perfect health (Acts 3:16); my words are health to all their body (Prov. 4:22); a tranquil [healed] heart is health to the body (Prov. 14:30); if your eye is healthy your whole body will be full of light (Matt. 6:22); I pray you may be in good health (3 John 2); those who are well do not need a doctor (Matt. 9:12; Mark 2:17; Luke 5:31).

651 Ill health

A Illness in general

There is no health in me because of my sin (Ps. 38:3-8); if God's people disobey he will bring on them diseases (Lev. 26:16; Deut. 28:21-2, 59-61); this is why many of you are weak and ill (1 Cor. 11:30); the skin of the wicked is devoured by disease (Job 18:13); heal me, for I

have sinned (Ps. 41:4); I will make you sick, striking you because of your sins (Mic. 6:13); the Lord will put disease on those who hate you (Deut. 7:15); if your eye is not healthy, your whole body will be full of darkness (Matt. 6:23); he carried our sicknesses (Isa. 53:4; Matt. 8:17); this illness is so that the Son of God may be glorified (John 11:4).

B Particular diseases

B1 Boils / sores

Boils breaking out in blisters (Exod. 9:9-10); the Lord will strike you with boils (Deut. 28:35); a cake of figs applied to the boil (Isa. 38:21); Job had painful sores (Job 2:7); those with the mark of the beast had painful sores (Rev. 16:2); Lazarus was full of sores (Luke 16:20); dogs licked his sores (Luke 16:21); they blasphemed the God of heaven for their pain and sores (Rev. 16:11).

B2 Fever

The Lord will strike you with fever (Deut. 28:22); I will bring on you fever that wastes the eyes (Lev. 26:16); Peter's mother-in-law had fever (Matt. 8:14; Mark 1:30); a high fever (Luke 4:38); Publius' father had fever and dysentery (Acts 28:8).

B3 Diseased hands

A man with a broken hand could not serve as priest (Lev. 21:19); Jeroboam's hand dried up (1 Kgs. 13:4); a man with a withered hand (Matt. 12:10; Mark 3:1; Luke 6:6); strengthen the weak hands (Heb. 12:12).

B4 Leprosy

Instructions over leprosy (Lev. 13:2-59; 14:2-57; Deut. 24:8); send lepers out of the camp (Num. 5:2); priests with leprosy may not eat of the offerings (Lev. 22:4); Naaman was a leper (2 Kgs. 5:1); Naaman's leprosy was on Gehazi (2 Kgs. 5:27); there were many lepers in Israel (Luke 4:27); four men with leprosy (2 Kgs. 7:3); Moses' hand became leprous (Exod. 4:6); the Lord struck Uzziah with leprosy (2 Kgs. 15:5; 2 Chr. 26:19-21); a man full of leprosy (Luke 5:12); the ten lepers (Luke 17:12); Miriam was leprous (Num. 12:10; Deut. 24:9); a leper (Matt. 8:2; Mark 1:40); Simon the leper (Matt. 26:6; Mark 14:3); may Joab's house never be without a leper (2 Sam. 3:29).

B5 Pestilence / plague

The Lord will make pestilence cling to you (Deut. 28:21); a third of you will die by plague and famine (Ezek. 5:12); famine and plague will devour those in the city (Ezek. 7:15); the house of Israel will fall by sword, famine and plague (Ezek. 6:11); my four severe judgements, sword, famine, wild beasts and plague (Ezek. 14:21); with pestilence and bloodshed I will enter into judgement with him (Ezek. 38:22); pestilence goes before him and plague follows (Hab. 3:5); there will be famines and plagues (Luke 21:11); I will kill her children with pestilence (Rev. 2:23); Death and Hades given authority to kill with sword, famine, pestilence and wild beasts (Rev. 6:8); a third of mankind was killed by these three plagues (Rev. 9:18); those who were not killed by these plagues (Rev. 9:20); the witnesses have authority to smite the earth with every plague (Rev. 11:6); her plagues will come, pestilence and mourning and famine (Rev. 18:8).

B6 Paralysis

The centurion's servant was paralysed (Matt. 8:6); a paralytic (Matt. 9:2; Mark 2:3; Luke 5:18); they brought to him demoniacs, epileptics and paralytics and he healed them (Matt. 4:24); many invalids lay there, blind, lame, paralysed (John 5:3); many who were paralysed or lame were healed (Acts 8:7); Aeneas was paralysed (Acts 9:33).

B7 Other illnesses

The Lord will strike you with consumption (Deut. 28:22); a man with dropsy (Luke 14:2); the Lord struck

Jehoram with a disease of his bowels (2 Chr. 21:15, 18); Publius' father had fever and dysentery (Acts 28:8); my son is moon-struck [epileptic] (Matt. 17:15); they brought to him demoniacs, epileptics and paralytics and he healed them (Matt. 4:24); it is eczema [tetter] (Lev. 13:39); their talk will spread like gangrene (2 Tim. 2:17); the Lord will strike you with inflammation (Deut. 28:22); the Lord will strike you with tumours (Deut. 28:27); the Lord struck the Philistines with tumours (1 Sam. 5:6-12; 6:4-17); he gave them what they asked but sent a wasting disease (Ps. 106:15); the Lord will send a wasting disease among his warriors (Isa. 10:16).

C Sick people

C1 Sick people in general

They brought to him all who were sick (Matt. 4:24; 14:35; Mark 1:32; 6:55; Luke 4:40); all who were ill pressed about him to touch him (Mark 3:10); they carried the sick out into the streets (Acts 5:15-16); those who are well do not need a doctor, but those who are ill (Matt. 9:12; Mark 2:17; Luke 5:31); he healed all who were sick (Matt. 8:16); Jesus healed every kind of disease and sickness (Matt. 9:35); he gave his disciples authority to heal every kind of disease and sickness (Matt. 10:1); I was sick and you visited me (Matt. 25:36); this is why many of you are weak and ill (1 Cor. 11:30); if anyone is ill he should call for the elders of the church (Jas. 5:14); the people who had diseases were coming to Paul and being healed (Acts 28:9); Paul first preached the gospel to the Galatians through illness (Gal. 4:13); the sick you have not healed (Ezek. 34:4).

C2 Sick individuals

Joseph heard that his father was ill (Gen. 48:1); Michal said David was ill (1 Sam. 19:14); the Lord struck Bathsheba's child with an illness (2 Sam. 12:15); Elisha had the illness from which he died (2 Kgs. 13:14); Daniel was ill for several days (Dan. 8:27); Amnon made himself ill over Tamar (2 Sam. 13:2); at Capernaum there was an official whose son was ill (John 4:46); a man was there who had been ill for 38 years (John 5:5); he whom you love is ill (John 11:3); Paul left Trophimus ill at Miletus (2 Tim. 4:20); Epaphroditus had been sick, near to death (Phil. 2:26-7); Timothy's frequent ailments (1 Tim. 5:23); those who fell ill: Abijah (1 Kgs. 14:1); the son of the woman of Zarephath (1 Kgs. 17:17); Benhadad king of Aram (2 Kgs. 8:7); Hezekiah (2 Kgs. 20:1; 2 Chr. 32:24; Isa. 38:1); Lazarus (John 11:1).

652 Salubrity

HEALTH, see 650.

653 Insalubrity

Meat of the peace offering left until the third day is foul (Lev. 7:18).

654 Improvement

A People improved

He enquired the hour when his son began to get better (John 4:52); that all may see your progress (1 Tim. 4:15); if you are a corrector of the foolish (Rom. 2:20); we pray for your improvement (2 Cor. 13:9).

B People refined

Trying to refine the people like silver (Jer. 6:29-30); I will smelt away your dross (Isa. 1:25); I will refine and assay them (Jer. 9:7); I have refined you but not like silver (Isa. 48:10); he will refine the sons of Levi (Mal. 3:3); I will refine them as silver is refined (Zech. 13:9).

C Things improved

The Lord's words are like silver refined seven times (Ps. 12:6); your word is well refined (Ps. 119:140); you

refined us like one refining silver (Ps. 66:10); the sycamores are cut down but we will replace them with cedars (Isa. 9:10).

655 Deterioration

A Worse

The last state is worse than the first (Matt. 12:45; Luke 11:26; 2 Pet. 2:20); evil men will go from bad to worse (2 Tim. 3:13); the woman was no better but rather worse (Mark 5:26); the last deception will be worse than the first (Matt. 27:64); a patch of unshrunk cloth tears away from an old garment and a worse tear results (Matt. 9:16); stop sinning or something worse will happen to you (John 5:14).

B Wearing out

B1 People wearing out

After I am worn out, shall I have pleasure? (Gen. 18:12); they will all wear out and be moth-eaten like a garment (Isa. 50:9); the moth will eat them like a garment (Isa. 51:8); you will wear yourself out (Exod. 18:18).

B2 Things wearing out

Moth and rust destroy (Matt. 6:19); during forty years in the desert your clothes did not wear out (Deut. 8:4; 29:5; Neh. 9:21); the Gibeonites wore worn-out clothes (Josh. 9:4-5); water wears away stones (Job 14:19); the earth will wear out like a garment (Ps. 102:26; Isa. 51:6).

C Wounds

C1 About wounds

The law on injuries (Exod. 21:12-27); he who injures a man must so be injured (Lev. 24:19-20); bruises, sores and raw wounds (Isa. 1:6); these wounds I received in the house of my friends (Zech. 13:6); your wound is incurable (Jer. 30:12; Nahum 3:19); my wound is incurable (Jer. 10:19); he has wounded us but he will bind us up (Hos. 6:1); I wound and I heal (Deut. 32:39); God wounds but he binds up (Job 5:18); who has wounds without cause but the drunkard? (Prov. 23:29-30); like an archer who wounds everyone is he who hires a fool (Prov. 26:10); blows that wound cleanse away evil (Prov. 20:30); faithful are the wounds of a friend (Prov. 27:6).

C2 Christ's wounds

He was wounded for our transgressions (Isa. 53:5); by his wounds you were healed (1 Pet. 2:24); he will bruise your head and you will bruise his heel (Gen. 3:15); I bear in my body the marks of Jesus (Gal. 6:17).

C3 Others wounded

Lamech killed a man for wounding him (Gen. 4:23); Gideon promised to tear their flesh with briers (Judg. 8:7); a woman dropped a millstone on Abimelech's head (Judg. 9:53); they gouged out Samson's eyes (Judg. 16:21); Nahash wanted to gouge out every right eye (1 Sam. 11:2); Ahaziah fell through the lattice and injured himself (2 Kgs. 1:2); Peter cut off the slave's ear (Matt. 26:51; Mark 14:47; Luke 22:50; John 18:10); the horses' tails wound like snakes (Rev. 9:19); the Samaritan bandaged his wounds (Luke 10:34); the jailer washed their wounds (Acts 16:33); a prophet asked another to wound him (1 Kgs. 20:35, 37); the man cut himself with stones (Mark 5:5); they fled naked and wounded (Acts 19:16); a mortal wound which was healed (Rev. 13:3, 12-14).

C4 Snakebite / stings

If the serpent bites before being charmed (Eccles. 10:11); everyone who is bitten will live when he sees the brazen serpent (Num. 21:8); Dan will be a serpent which bites the horse's heels (Gen. 49:17); wine bites like a serpent and stings like an adder (Prov. 23:32); like the sting of a scorpion (Rev. 9:5, 10).

D Lameness

D1 The lame in general

Lame men could not serve as priests (Lev. 21:18-19); that the lame joint may not be dislocated (Heb. 12:13); it is better to enter life lame or crippled (Matt. 18:8); the blind and the lame could defend Jerusalem (2 Sam. 5:6); the lame will take the plunder (Isa. 33:23); I am feet to the lame (Job 29:15); the lame will leap like a deer (Isa. 35:6); the lame walk (Matt. 11:5; Luke 7:22); the crippled were healed and the lame walked (Matt. 15:31); the lame came to him and he healed them (Matt. 15:30-1; 21:14); many who were paralysed or lame were healed (Acts 8:7); many invalids lay there, blind, lame, paralysed (John 5:3); invite the lame (Luke 14:13, 21); I will assemble the lame and gather the outcasts (Mic. 4:6); how long will you limp between two opinions? (1 Kgs. 18:21).

D2 Lame individuals

Jacob limped (Gen. 32:31); Mephibosheth was lame in both feet (2 Sam. 4:4; 9:3); Asa was diseased in his feet (1 Kgs. 15:23; 2 Chr. 16:12); I am lame (2 Sam. 19:26); a man lame from birth (Acts 3:2); a lame man at Lystra (Acts 14:8).

D3 Hamstringing

In their self-will they hamstrung an ox (Gen. 49:6); David hamstrung chariot horses (2 Sam. 8:4; 1 Chr. 18:4); hamstring their horses (Josh. 11:6, 9).

656 Restoring

A Healing

A1 God heals

There is a time to heal (Eccles. 3:3); the Lord heals all your diseases (Ps. 103:3); I am the Lord your healer (Exod. 15:26); I wound and I heal (Deut. 32:39); God wounds and heals (Job 5:18); God heals the broken-hearted (Ps. 147:3); he restores my soul (Ps. 23:3); he has torn, but let him heal us (Hos. 6:1); they did not know that I healed them (Hos. 11:3); lest they turn and I heal them (Matt. 13:15; Acts 28:27); heal my soul, for I have sinned (Ps. 41:4); he sent out his word and healed them (Ps. 107:20); the sun of righteousness will rise with healing in its wings (Mal. 4:2); I will heal their backsliding (Hos. 14:4); I will heal your faithlessness (Jer. 3:22); by his scourging we are healed (Isa. 53:5); their leaves are for healing (Ezek. 47:12); the leaves of the tree are for the healing of the nations (Rev. 22:2).

A2 Jesus healing

Jesus healed all who were ill (Matt. 4:23-4; 8:16; 12:15; 14:14, 36; 15:30; 21:14; Luke 4:40; 5:17; 9:11); Jesus healed every kind of disease and sickness (Matt. 9:35); all who touched his cloak were healed (Mark 6:56); those troubled with unclean spirits were cured (Luke 6:18); Jesus healed all who were oppressed by the devil (Acts 10:38); Jesus healed a few sick people (Mark 6:5); he makes the deaf hear and the dumb speak (Mark 7:37); I cast out demons and cure today and tomorrow (Luke 13:32); Jesus Christ heals you (Acts 9:34); by his wounds you were healed (Isa. 53:5; 1 Pet. 2:24); they brought to him demoniacs, epileptics and paralytics and he healed them (Matt. 4:24); power came forth from him and healed them all (Luke 6:19); physician, heal yourself! (Luke 4:23); they watched him to see whether he would heal on the sabbath (Mark 3:2; Luke 6:7).

A3 Those Jesus healed

Jesus healed: the leper (Matt. 8:2-3; Mark 1:40-2; Luke 5:12-14); ten lepers (Luke 17:12-19); the man with the withered hand (Matt. 12:13; Mark 3:5; Luke 6:10); the centurion's servant (Matt. 8:13; Luke 7:2-10); Peter's mother-in-law (Matt. 8:15; Mark 1:31; Luke 4:39); the ruler's daughter (Matt. 9:18, 25; Mark 5:41-2; Luke 8:41,

54-5); a dumb demoniac (Matt. 9:33; Luke 11:14); a blind and dumb demoniac (Matt. 12:22); a deaf man with a speech impediment (Mark 7:32-5); the Canaanite woman's daughter (Matt. 15:28; Mark 7:30); a demoniac in the synagogue (Luke 4:35); the Gadarene demoniac (Matt. 8:28-34; Mark 5:8-20; Luke 8:29-35); the blind (Matt. 9:29-30; 20:34; Mark 8:22-6; 10:46-52; Luke 18:35-43; John 9:1-7); an invalid (John 5:8-9); the widow's son (Luke 7:14-15); a woman bent over (Luke 13:13); the woman with the flow of blood (Matt. 9:22; Mark 5:29; Luke 8:44); several women (Luke 8:2); an official's son (John 4:47-53); the paralytic (Matt. 9:2-7; Mark 2:5-12; Luke 5:18-25); the epileptic boy (Matt. 17:18; Mark 9:25-7; Luke 9:42); the man with dropsy (Luke 14:4); the slave's ear (Luke 22:51).

A4 How healing came

Your faith has healed you (Matt. 9:22; Mark 5:34; Luke 8:48; 17:19); your faith has made you well (Luke 18:42); only believe and she will be made well (Luke 8:50); Paul fixed his gaze on him and saw that he had faith to be made well (Acts 14:9); she said, 'If I just touch his garments I shall be healed' (Mark 5:28-9); she declared why she had touched him and how she had been healed (Luke 8:47); lay your hands on her that she may be healed and live (Mark 5:23); handkerchiefs or aprons from Paul were used to heal the sick (Acts 19:12); by the name of Jesus Christ this man stands healed (Acts 4:10).

A5 Healing through disciples

He gave them authority to heal diseases (Matt. 10:1; Luke 9:1); gifts of healings (1 Cor. 12:9, 28); not all have gifts of healing, do they? (1 Cor. 12:30); they will lay hands on the sick and they will recover (Mark 16:18); the prayer of faith will heal the sick (Jas. 5:15-16); he sent them out to heal (Luke 9:2); heal the sick (Matt. 10:8; Luke 10:9); stretch out your hand to heal! (Acts 4:30); they preached the gospel and healed (Luke 9:6); they anointed the sick with oil and healed them (Mark 6:13); all were healed (Acts 5:16); many were healed (Acts 8:7); all the people on the island came to be cured (Acts 28:9); those who were healed: the lame man (Acts 3:1-10); blind Paul (Acts 9:17-18; 22:13); a cripple in Lystra (Acts 14:8-10); Publius' father and the rest of the sick (Acts 28:8-9).

A6 People / creatures healed

He who struck him must see him healed (Exod. 21:19); the tongue of the wise brings healing (Prov. 12:18); a healing tongue is a tree of life (Prov. 15:4); pleasant words are healing to the bones (Prov. 16:24); a faithful envoy brings healing (Prov. 13:17); that what is lame might be healed (Heb. 12:13); a mortal wound which was healed (Rev. 13:3, 12).

A7 No healing

The Lord will strike you with diseases from which you cannot be healed (Deut. 28:27); the Lord will strike you with boils from which you cannot be healed (Deut. 28:35); the wicked will be broken with no healing (Prov. 6:15); why is there no healing for my people? (Jer. 8:22); why have you stricken us beyond healing? (Jer. 14:19); why is my wound incurable? (Jer. 15:18); my wound is incurable (Jer. 10:19); your wound is incurable (Jer. 30:12-13); they have healed my people superficially (Jer. 6:14; 8:11); lest they return and be healed (Isa. 6:10); lest they be converted and I heal them (John 12:40); the sick you have not healed (Ezek. 34:4); Samaria's wound is incurable and it has come to Judah (Mic. 1:9); a shepherd who will not heal the maimed (Zech. 11:16); I brought him to your disciples and they could not cure him (Matt. 17:16); the woman could not be healed by any one (Luke 8:43).

B Resurrection

B1 About resurrection

Instruction about the resurrection of the dead (Heb. 6:2); they proclaimed in Jesus the resurrection of the dead (Acts 4:2); Paul was preaching 'Jesus' and 'Resurrection' (Acts 17:18); by a man came resurrection (1 Cor. 15:21); in the resurrection they neither marry nor are given in marriage (Matt. 22:30; Mark 12:25; Luke 20:35); the body is sown in dishonour and raised in glory (1 Cor. 15:43).

B2 Are the dead raised?

If a man dies, will he live again? (Job 14:14); can these bones live? (Ezek. 37:3); they discussed what rising from the dead meant (Mark 9:10); the Sadducees say there is no resurrection (Matt. 22:23; Mark 12:18; Luke 20:27; Acts 23:8); why should it be thought incredible that God raises the dead? (Acts 26:8); when they heard of the resurrection of the dead, some mocked (Acts 17:32); if there is no resurrection then Christ has not been raised (1 Cor. 15:13-32).

B3 The dead are raised

Abraham reckoned that God could raise the dead (Heb. 11:19); that the dead are raised even Moses showed (Luke 20:37); we trust in God who raises the dead (2 Cor. 1:9); God gives life to the dead (Rom. 4:17); you will not abandon me to Sheol (Ps. 16:10); as a Pharisee, Paul is on trial concerning the resurrection of the dead (Acts 23:6; 24:21); I hope in God that there will be a resurrection of both righteous and wicked (Acts 24:15); this is the first resurrection (Rev. 20:5); they came to life and stood on their feet, a great army (Ezek. 37:10); the men of Nineveh will arise at the judgement (Matt. 12:41; Luke 11:32); the queen of the South will arise at the judgement (Matt. 12:42; Luke 11:31); in Christ will all be made alive (1 Cor. 15:22); the rest of the dead did not come to life until after the 1000 years (Rev. 20:5-6); some said the resurrection has already happened (2 Tim. 2:18).

B4 Resurrection of Christ

B4a Christ would rise

Moses said that Christ would suffer and be the first to rise (Acts 26:23); Christ had to suffer and rise again (Acts 17:3); David spoke of the resurrection of Christ (Acts 2:31); he would be crucified and on the third day would rise (Luke 24:7); on the third day he would be raised (Matt. 16:21; 17:23; 20:19; Mark 8:31; Luke 9:22; 18:33; 24:46); after three days he would rise again (Matt. 27:63; Mark 9:31; 10:34); they did not yet understand the scripture that he must rise (John 20:9); lest his disciples steal him and say he has risen from the dead (Matt. 27:64); I lay down my life that I may take it again (John 10:17-18); God raised the Lord and will raise us also by his power (1 Cor. 6:14); if there is no resurrection then Christ has not been raised (1 Cor. 15:13-17).

B4b Christ is risen

He has risen (Matt. 28:6-7; Mark 16:6); the Lord has risen indeed! (Luke 24:34); Jesus Christ, risen from the dead (2 Tim. 2:8); Christ has risen, the firstfruits of those who slept (1 Cor. 15:20); the firstborn of the dead (Rev. 1:5); he who died and came to life (Rev. 2:8); he showed himself alive after his suffering with many proofs (Acts 1:3); one of these should become with us a witness to his resurrection (Acts 1:22); with power the apostles bore witness to his resurrection (Acts 4:33); Christ, raised from the dead, will never die again (Rom. 6:9); put to death in the flesh but made alive in spirit (1 Pet. 3:18); for this Christ died and rose, that he might be Lord of dead and living (Rom. 14:9); that you might belong to another, who has been raised from the dead (Rom. 7:4); declared Son of God with power by

the resurrection (Rom. 1:4); I was dead and now I am alive for evermore (Rev. 1:18).

B4c God raised Christ

God raised him from the dead (Acts 2:24; 3:15; 4:10; 5:30; 10:40; 13:30, 34; Rom. 4:24; Gal. 1:1; 1 Pet. 1:21); this Jesus God raised up, and of that we are witnesses (Acts 2:32); God raised up his Servant (Acts 3:26); Christ was raised from the dead by the glory of the Father (Rom. 6:4); God brought from the dead the great Shepherd (Heb. 13:20); God bore witness to him by raising him from the dead (Acts 17:31); God fulfilled the promise in raising Jesus (Acts 13:33).

B4d Christ's resurrection for us

God works in us with the power which raised Christ from the dead (Eph. 1:20); that I may know the power of his resurrection (Phil. 3:10); born again through the resurrection of Christ (1 Pet. 1:3); he was raised for our justification (Rom. 4:25); he died and rose again for them (2 Cor. 5:15); an appeal to God for a good conscience through the resurrection of Jesus Christ (1 Pet. 3:21).

B5 Our resurrection

B5a Present resurrection

If you have been raised with Christ (Col. 3:1); he raised us up with Christ (Eph. 2:6; Col. 2:13); you were raised with him in baptism by faith in God who raised him (Col. 2:12); arise from the dead and Christ will shine on you (Eph. 5:14); he who raised Christ from the dead will give life to your mortal bodies (Rom. 8:11); God raised the Lord and will raise us also by his power (1 Cor. 6:14); present yourselves to God as those alive from the dead (Rom. 6:13); if we died with him we will live with him (2 Tim. 2:11); as the Father raises the dead, so the Son gives life to whom he wishes (John 5:21-5).

B5b Future resurrection

I am the resurrection and the life (John 11:25); we will be united with him in his resurrection (Rom. 6:5); as Jesus died and rose, so God will bring those who have fallen asleep (1 Thess. 4:14); you will enter into rest and rise again at the end of the age (Dan. 12:13); he who believes in me, though he die, shall yet live (John 11:25); he who raised the Lord Jesus will also raise us with Jesus (2 Cor. 4:14); those who are Christ's will be raised at his coming (1 Cor. 15:23); Lazarus will rise in the resurrection (John 11:24); I will raise him up at the last day (John 6:40, 44, 54); all in the tombs will hear his voice and come forth (John 5:28-9); the resurrection of the just (Luke 14:14); those who sleep in the dust of the earth will awake (Dan. 12:2); the dead in Christ will rise first (1 Thess. 4:16); that I may attain the resurrection from the dead (Phil. 3:11); how are the dead raised? (1 Cor. 15:35); the dead will be raised imperishable (1 Cor. 15:52); the sons of the resurrection cannot die any more (Luke 20:36); the resurrection of life and the resurrection of judgement (John 5:29).

B6 People raised

B6a People in general raised

Women received their dead raised to life (Heb. 11:35); the bodies of many saints were raised to life (Matt. 27:52); if someone goes to them from the dead they will repent (Luke 16:30-1); the breath of life from God came into them (Rev. 11:11); the beast which was wounded yet came to life (Rev. 13:14); they came to life and reigned with Christ for 1000 years (Rev. 20:4); the dead are raised (Matt. 11:5; Luke 7:22); raise the dead (Matt. 10:8); what will the acceptance of the Jews be but life from the dead? (Rom. 11:15).

B6b Individuals raised

Elijah prayed and the boy revived (1 Kgs. 17:21-3); the man whose body touched Elisha's bones revived

(2 Kgs. 13:21); can I bring the child back to life again? (2 Sam. 12:23); this is John the Baptist risen from the dead (Matt. 14:2; Mark 6:14, 16; Luke 9:7); your brother will rise (John 11:23); he was dead and is alive again (Luke 15:24); bring up Samuel for me (1 Sam. 28:11); those who were raised: the Shunammite's son (2 Kgs. 4:35; 8:1); the widow of Nain's son (Luke 7:11-16); Jairus' daughter (Matt. 9:23-5; Mark 5:38-43; Luke 8:49-56); Lazarus (John 11:43-4; 12:1-17); Tabitha (Acts 9:36-42); Eutychus (Acts 20:10-12).

C Restoration

C1 Repairing

Repairing the altar (1 Kgs. 18:30; 2 Chr. 15:8); repairing the temple (2 Kgs. 12:5; 22:5-6; 2 Chr. 24:4-13; 34:8); the priests agreed that they should not repair the house (2 Kgs. 12:8); the money was given to the workmen who were repairing the house (2 Kgs. 12:14); Hezekiah repaired the doors of the temple (2 Chr. 29:3); repairing the wall (2 Chr. 32:5; Neh. 3:1-32); they will repair the ruined cities (Isa. 61:4); the repairer of the breech, the restorer of streets to dwell in (Isa. 58:12); mending nets (Matt. 4:21; Mark 1:19); the Gibeonites had patched sandals (Josh. 9:5); patching garments (Matt. 9:16, 16; Luke 5:36); as a broken potter's vessel cannot be repaired (Jer. 19:11); I will repair the breaches of the booth of David (Amos 9:11); I will rebuild its ruins and restore the tabernacle (Acts 15:16).

C2 Restoring things

Abraham brought back the goods taken by the kings (Gen. 14:16); David recovered all that was taken (1 Sam. 30:18); David would restore Saul's land to Mephibosheth (2 Sam. 9:7); how can the saltness of salt be restored? (Matt. 5:13); Elijah restores all things (Matt. 17:11; Mark 9:12); the time for the restoration of all things (Acts 3:21); in the regeneration, when the Son of man sits on his throne (Matt. 19:28).

C3 Reinstating people

Pharaoh restored Sarah to Abraham (Gen. 12:19); Abimelech restored Sarah to Abraham (Gen. 20:14); Pharaoh would restore his butler (Gen. 40:13); bring back Absalom (2 Sam. 14:21); God does not take away the life of him who plans to bring back his banished one (2 Sam. 14:14); if the Lord brings me back (2 Sam. 15:8); Israel will restore my father's kingdom to me (2 Sam. 16:3); why are you silent about bringing the king back? (2 Sam. 19:10-12); trying to restore the kingdom to Rehoboam (1 Kgs. 12:21); the Lord restored the fortunes of Job (Job 42:10); Nebuchadnezzar was re-established in his kingdom (Dan. 4:36).

C4 Restoring nations

Restore us! (Ps. 80:3; 85:4); restore our fortunes! (Ps. 126:4); the Lord will restore the splendour of Jacob (Nahum 2:2); when God restores the fortunes of his people, Israel will be glad (Ps. 14:7; 53:6); will you now restore the kingdom to Israel? (Acts 1:6); restoration of Israel promised (Jer. 33:6-13); I will restore your fortunes (Jer. 29:14); I will hear from heaven and heal their land (2 Chr. 7:14); the service of the temple was restored (2 Chr. 29:35); you restored the fortunes of Jacob (Ps. 85:1); revive your work (Hab. 3:2); will you not revive us again? (Ps. 85:6); after two days he will revive us (Hos. 6:2); I will restore to you double (Zech. 9:12).

C5 Restoring sinners

He will turn back many to the Lord (Luke 1:16); Jehoshaphat brought people back to the Lord (2 Chr. 19:4); restore the sinner gently (Gal. 6:1); if one wanders from the truth and someone brings him back (Jas. 5:19); the law of the Lord restores the soul (Ps. 19:7); one to restore my soul is far from me (Lam. 1:16).

657 Relapse

If the mark breaks out again in the house (Lev. 14:43).

658 Remedy

A Medicines

There is no medicine to cure you (Jer. 30:13); in vain you have used many medicines (Jer. 46:11); a poultice of figs (2 Kgs. 20:7; Isa. 38:21); flour counteracted the poisonous gourds (2 Kgs. 4:41); anointing the sick with oil (Mark 6:13; Jas. 5:14); pouring oil and wine on wounds (Luke 10:34); not pressed out nor bandaged nor softened with oil (Isa. 1:6); making clay with saliva to put on a man's eyes (John 9:6, 11); he put clay on my eyes and I washed and I see (John 9:15); the jailer washed their wounds (Acts 16:33); is there no balm in Gilead? (Jer. 8:22); go up to Gilead and get balm (Jer. 46:11); bring balm for her pain, perhaps she may be healed (Jer. 51:8); buy salve to put on your eyes (Rev. 3:18); drink a little wine for your stomach's sake (1 Tim. 5:23); a cheerful heart is good medicine (Prov. 17:22).

B Doctors

B1 God as doctor

I, the Lord, am your healer (Exod. 15:26); the Lord binds up their wounds (Ps. 147:3); those who are well do not need a doctor (Matt. 9:12; Mark 2:17; Luke 5:31); doctor, heal yourself! (Luke 4:23); he has wounded us but he will bind us up (Hos. 6:1).

B2 Human doctors

Joseph told his servants the physicians to embalm his father (Gen. 50:2); Asa sought help from doctors, not the Lord (2 Chr. 16:12); you are worthless physicians (Job 13:4); is there no physician in Gilead? (Jer. 8:22); the woman had suffered much from many doctors (Mark 5:26); Luke, the beloved doctor (Col. 4:14).

C Midwives

The midwife told Rachel not to fear (Gen. 35:17); the midwife tied a scarlet thread on the twin's hand (Gen. 38:28); the Hebrew midwives Shiphrah and Puah (Exod. 1:15).

659 Bane

A Plagues

A1 The plagues in Egypt

These are the gods who struck the Egyptians with plagues (1 Sam. 4:8); I send a plague on you as on Egypt (Amos 4:10); the plagues: water turned to blood (Exod. 7:17-25; Ps. 78:44; 105:29); frogs (Exod. 8:2-15; Ps. 78:45; 105:30); gnats [or lice] (Exod. 8:16-19; Ps. 105:31); flies (Ps. 78:45; 105:31); swarms of insects (Exod. 8:21-32; Ps. 78:46); pestilence on livestock (Exod. 9:3-7; Ps. 78:48); boils (Exod. 9:8-12); hail (Exod. 9:18-35; Ps. 78:47-8; 105:32); locusts (Exod. 10:4-20; Ps. 78:46; 105:34); darkness (Exod. 10:21-9; Ps. 105:28); death of the firstborn (Exod. 11:5; Ps. 78:51; 105:36).

A2 Other plagues

The Lord struck Pharaoh with plagues because of Sarah (Gen. 12:17); the plague has started (Num. 16:46); three days of plague? (2 Sam. 24:13; 1 Chr. 21:12); if I send a plague on the land (Ezek. 14:19); the ten spies died from a plague (Num. 14:37); seven angels with seven plagues (Rev. 15:6); the seven last plagues (Rev. 15:1); seven bowls full of the seven last plagues (Rev. 21:9); God who had power over these plagues (Rev. 16:9); do not share in her sins lest you share in her plagues (Rev. 18:4); if anyone adds to the words, God will add to him the plagues written in this book (Rev. 22:18); her plagues will overtake her in one day (Rev. 18:8).

B Poisons and pests

There were poisonous gourds in the stew (2 Kgs. 4:39-40); the Lord has given us poisonous water to drink (Jer. 8:14); I will give them poisonous water to drink (Jer. 9:15; 23:15); you have turned justice into poison (Amos 6:12); if they drink any deadly thing it will not harm them (Mark 16:18); a root bearing poison and wormwood (Deut. 29:18); the tongue is full of poison (Jas. 3:8); snake's poison is under their lips (Ps. 140:3; Rom. 3:13); my spirit drinks the poison of God's arrows (Job 6:4); they have venom like a serpent (Ps. 58:4).

660 Safety

A Safety through God
A1 God, keep safe!
Keep them from the evil one (John 17:15); protect us from this generation (Ps. 12:7); guard my soul (Ps. 25:20); protect my life (Ps. 64:1); protect me from those who rise against me (Ps. 59:1).
A2 God will keep safe
Judah will be saved and Jerusalem dwell in safety (Jer. 33:16); I will set him in safety (Ps. 12:5); the Lord will protect him (Ps. 41:2); the Lord will be your confidence (Prov. 3:26); he will strengthen and protect you (2 Thess. 3:3); they will be secure in their land (Ezek. 34:27-8); I will send an angel before you to guard you along the way (Exod. 23:20); his angels will guard you (Ps. 91:11); he will give his angels charge of you to guard you (Luke 4:10).
A3 God keeps safe
You alone make me dwell in safety (Ps. 4:8); God gives them security (Job 24:23); the righteous man runs into the strong tower and is safe (Prov. 18:10); the eye of God was on the Jew (Ezra 5:5); like hovering birds the Lord will protect Jerusalem (Isa. 31:5); unless the Lord guards the city the watchman keeps awake in vain (Ps. 127:1); you who are guarded by the power of God (1 Pet. 1:5); I have guarded them (John 17:12); the peace of God will guard your hearts and minds (Phil. 4:7); he who was born of God keeps him and the evil one does not touch him (1 John 5:18); he is able to guard what I have committed to him (2 Tim. 1:12).
REFUGE, see 662.

B Man keeping safe
Guard through the Holy Spirit what has been entrusted (2 Tim. 1:14); guard what has been entrusted to you (1 Tim. 6:20); wisdom is a protection as money is (Eccles. 7:12); do not forsake wisdom and she will guard you (Prov. 4:6); a woman protects a man! (Jer. 31:22); Herod kept John safe (Mark 6:20); when a strong man, fully armed, guards his own home (Luke 11:21); bringing Paul safely to Felix the governor (Acts 23:24); the men were a wall to us by day and night (1 Sam. 25:16); I will make you my bodyguard for life (1 Sam. 28:2); the king charged you to protect Absalom (2 Sam. 18:12); the temple guards guarding the king's son Joash (2 Kgs. 11:8; 2 Chr. 23:7); let the tomb be made secure (Matt. 27:64-5).

661 Danger

A Risking
Zebulun and Naphtali risked their lives (Judg. 5:18); Gideon risked his life for them (Judg. 9:17); I took my life in my hands (Judg. 12:3; 1 Sam. 28:21); David took his life in his hands (1 Sam. 19:5); the mighty men risked their lives to bring David water (2 Sam. 23:17; 1 Chr. 11:19); we get our bread at the risk of our lives (Lam. 5:9); Paul and Barnabas risked their lives for the Lord Jesus (Acts 15:26); Prisca and Aquila risked their necks for Paul (Rom. 16:4); Epaphroditus risked his life to complete your service to me (Phil. 2:30); they did not love their lives even to death (Rev. 12:11).

B In danger
Place Uriah in the thick of the battle (2 Sam. 11:15); in danger from robbers, countrymen, Gentiles etc. (2 Cor. 11:26); the voyage was now dangerous (Acts 27:9); they were being swamped and were in danger (Luke 8:23); danger will not separate us from the love of Christ (Rom. 8:35); why are we in danger every hour? (1 Cor. 15:30).

662 Refuge
DEFENCE, see 713.

A Refuge
A1 God our refuge
A1a God is a refuge
God is a refuge (Ps. 62:8; 71:7); the Lord is a refuge (Joel 3:16); a rock of refuge (Ps. 71:3; 94:22); God is our refuge and strength (Ps. 46:1); my refuge in the day of trouble (Jer. 16:19); we have fled for refuge (Heb. 6:18); the Lord is the refuge of the poor (Ps. 14:6; Isa. 25:4); my refuge is God (Ps. 62:7); you are my refuge (Ps. 59:16; 61:3; 142:5; Jer. 17:17); my refuge (Ps. 91:2); the Lord is the refuge of my life (Ps. 27:1).

A1b Taking refuge in God
Blessed are those who take refuge in him (Ps. 2:12; 34:8); let the righteous take refuge in the Lord (Ps. 64:10); the Lord knows those who take refuge in him (Nahum 1:7); he delivers them because they take refuge in him (Ps. 37:40); let all who take refuge in you be glad (Ps. 5:11); none who take refuge in him will be condemned (Ps. 34:22); he who takes refuge in me will inherit the land (Isa. 57:13); better to take refuge in the Lord than trust in man (Ps. 118:8); better to take refuge in the Lord than trust in princes (Ps. 118:9); I take refuge in God (Ps. 7:1); my God in whom I take refuge (2 Sam. 22:3; Ps. 18:2); I have made the Lord my refuge (Ps. 73:28); you have made the Lord your refuge (Ps. 91:9); the man who would not make God his refuge (Ps. 52:7).

A1c Refuge under God's wings
Under God's wings you have sought refuge (Ruth 2:12); in the shadow of your wings men find refuge (Ps. 36:7); in the shadow of your wings I take refuge (Ps. 57:1; 61:4); under his wings you will seek refuge (Ps. 91:4); in the shadow of your wings I sing for joy (Ps. 63:7).

A2 Sanctuary of refuge
The Lord will become a sanctuary (Isa. 8:14); those clutching the horns of the altar: Adonijah (1 Kgs. 1:50-1); Joab (1 Kgs. 2:28); not even the altar will be a sanctuary for a crafty killer (Exod. 21:14).
CITIES OF REFUGE, see 184C7.

A3 Other refuge
They have come under the shadow of my roof-tree (Gen. 19:8); I would hasten to find a shelter from the storm (Ps. 55:8); there will be a refuge and a shelter (Isa. 4:6); the king and princes will be like a refuge from the wind (Isa. 32:2); we sailed under the lee of Cyprus (Acts 27:4); we sailed under the lee of Crete off Salmone (Acts 27:7); running under the lee of a small island called Cauda (Acts 27:16); take refuge in Pharaoh (Isa. 30:2-3); the rich man's wealth is his fortress (Prov. 10:15); we have made lies our refuge (Isa. 28:15-17).

B Strongholds
B1 Strongholds in general
The Lord has torn down the strongholds of the daughter of Judah (Lam. 2:2); I will cut off your cities and tear down your strongholds (Mic. 5:11); they will come trembling out of their strongholds (Mic. 7:17); our weapons are mighty through God for the destruction of strongholds (2 Cor. 10:4-5); fire will consume the strongholds of: Ben-hadad (Amos 1:4);

Bozrah (Amos 1:12); Gaza (Amos 1:7); Rabbah (Amos 1:14); Tyre (Amos 1:10); Kerioth (Amos 2:2); Jerusalem (Amos 2:5).

B2 God is a stronghold
God is my fortress (2 Sam. 22:33); the Lord is my fortress (2 Sam. 22:2; Ps. 18:2); you are my fortress (Ps. 31:3); a fortress and stronghold (Ps. 9:9); God is a stronghold (Ps. 48:3; 62:2); the God of Jacob is our stronghold (Ps. 46:7); the Lord has been my stronghold (Ps. 94:22); the Lord is a stronghold in the day of trouble (Nahum 1:7).

B3 Other strongholds
The Israelites made shelters in caves and strongholds (Judg. 6:2); the strongholds of Engedi (1 Sam. 23:29); David went to the stronghold (2 Sam. 5:17); David was in the stronghold (1 Sam. 22:4; 2 Sam. 23:14; 1 Chr. 11:16); Gadites joined David in the stronghold in the wilderness (1 Chr. 12:8); some from Benjamin and Judah came to David in the stronghold (1 Chr. 12:16); do not stay in the stronghold (1 Sam. 22:5); David captured the stronghold of Zion (2 Sam. 5:7; 1 Chr. 11:5); the stronghold was called the city of David (2 Sam. 5:9; 1 Chr. 11:7).

C Defensive armour
C1 Shields
C1a Shields through God
God is a shield (Gen. 15:1; 2 Sam. 22:3, 31; Ps. 3:3; 18:2; Prov. 2:7; 30:5); the Lord is my shield (Ps. 28:7); he is our help and shield (Ps. 33:20); he is their help and shield (Ps. 115:9-11); the shield of faith (Eph. 6:16); the shield of your salvation (2 Sam. 22:36; Ps. 18:35); his faithfulness is a shield (Ps. 91:4); you surround the righteous with favour like a shield (Ps. 5:12); the Lord will put a shield around the inhabitants of Jerusalem (Zech. 12:8).

C1b Other shields
The shield of Saul, not anointed with oil (2 Sam. 1:21); David took Hadadezer's gold shields (2 Sam. 8:7; 1 Chr. 18:7); 300 shields of beaten gold (1 Kgs. 10:17; 2 Chr. 9:16); 200 large shields of beaten gold (1 Kgs. 10:16; 2 Chr. 9:15); 1000 shields hung on the tower of David (S. of S. 4:4); all the shields were taken away by Shishak (1 Kgs. 14:26; 2 Chr. 12:9); Rehoboam made shields of bronze (1 Kgs. 14:27; 2 Chr. 12:10); the wicked charges at God with his shield (Job 15:26).

C2 Helmets
Goliath wore a bronze helmet (1 Sam. 17:5); Saul put a bronze helmet on David (1 Sam. 17:38); Ephraim is my helmet (Ps. 60:7; 108:8); the helmet of salvation (Isa. 59:17; Eph. 6:17); as a helmet the hope of salvation (1 Thess. 5:8).

D Locks and bars
He has strengthened the bars of your gates (Ps. 147:13); Asher's locks will be iron and bronze (Deut. 33:25); Ehud locked the doors (Judg. 3:23); lock the door behind her (2 Sam. 13:17-18); the prison was locked but empty (Acts 5:23); a garden locked is my sister, my bride (S. of S. 4:12); Samson lifted the gates, bar and all (Judg. 16:3).

663 Pitfall
DANGER, see 661.

664 Warning
A Warning the people
Warn the people not to break through (Exod. 19:21); who warned you to flee from the wrath to come? (Matt. 3:7; Luke 3:7); I admonished you night and day with tears (Acts 20:31); him we proclaim, warning and teaching every man in all wisdom (Col. 1:28); as we solemnly warned you (1 Thess. 4:6); if they did not

escape when they refused him who warned them on earth (Heb. 12:25); Ezekiel was made a watchman to warn the people (Ezek. 3:17-21; 33:7-9); Samuel had to warn the people about kings (1 Sam. 8:9); kings of the earth, be warned (Ps. 2:10); I warned the merchants (Neh. 13:21); the Lord warned Israel and Judah through the prophets (2 Kgs. 17:13); I write to admonish you (1 Cor. 4:14); let us warn them not to speak any more to anyone in this name (Acts 4:17); Jesus warned them not to make him known (Matt. 12:16; Mark 8:30); these things were written down as examples for us (1 Cor. 10:6); God made Sodom and Gomorrah an example (2 Pet. 2:6; Jude 7).

B Warning individuals
Laban was warned in a dream (Gen. 31:24, 29); the magi were warned in a dream (Matt. 2:12); Joseph was warned in a dream (Matt. 2:22); Elisha warned the king of Israel about the Arameans (2 Kgs. 6:9, 10); the rich man wanted someone to warn his five brothers (Luke 16:28); I warn you as I warned you before (Gal. 5:21); Noah was warned about things not yet seen (Heb. 11:7); warn those who are unruly (1 Thess. 5:14); warn him as a brother (2 Thess. 3:15); shun a factious man after two warnings (Titus 3:10); you are able to admonish one another (Rom. 15:14); the disciples warned Paul not to go to Jerusalem (Acts 21:4, 11).

665 Danger signal
WARNING, see 664.

666 Preservation
A God keeping
Preserve me, O God, for I take refuge in you (Ps. 16:1); let your lovingkindness and truth preserve me (Ps. 40:11); keep me as the pupil of your eye (Ps. 17:8); preserve those doomed to die (Ps. 79:11); keep them in your name which you gave me (John 17:11); the Lord bless and keep you (Num. 6:24); while I was with them I kept them in your name (John 17:12); an inheritance reserved in heaven for you (1 Pet. 1:4); God preserved Noah (2 Pet. 2:5); beloved in God the Father and kept for Jesus Christ (Jude 1); I will keep you from the hour of trial which is coming on the whole world (Rev. 3:10); I will keep you (Gen. 28:15); if God will keep me (Gen. 28:20); the Lord is your keeper (Ps. 121:5); you preserve me from trouble (Ps. 32:7); he will keep you from all evil (Ps. 121:7); he who keeps you will not sleep (Ps. 121:3-4); the Lord keeps all those who love him (Ps. 145:20); the Lord preserves the faithful (Ps. 31:23); the righteous will be preserved for ever (Ps. 37:28); wandering stars for whom darkness has been reserved for ever (Jude 13).

B People keeping
Let them guard the food (Gen. 41:35); if someone gives his neighbour money or things to keep for him (Exod. 22:7); why have you not guarded the king? (1 Sam. 26:15).

667 Escape
RUN AWAY, see 620A.

A Escaping from people
Do not hand back an escaped slave (Deut. 23:15); many slaves are breaking away from their masters (1 Sam. 25:10); in Jerusalem there will be those who escape (Joel 2:32); those who have barely escaped from those who live in error (2 Pet. 2:18); if Esau attacks one company the remaining company will escape (Gen. 32:8); whoever escapes from Hazael, Jehu will kill (1 Kgs. 19:17); whoever escapes from Jehu, Elisha will kill (1 Kgs. 19:17); Ehud escaped (Judg. 3:26); Jotham escaped from Abimelech (Judg. 9:21); David escaped

(1 Sam. 18:11; 19:10, 18; 23:13; 27:1); the Rock of Escape (1 Sam. 23:28); flee, or no one will escape from Absalom (2 Sam. 15:14); Ishmael escaped from Johanan (Jer. 41:15); Zion! escape! you who live with the daughter of Babylon (Zech. 2:7); the jailer supposed that the prisoners had escaped (Acts 16:27); the army of Aram has escaped out of your hand (2 Chr. 16:7); I escaped from the camp of Israel (2 Sam. 1:3); why have you let my enemy escape? (1 Sam. 19:17); 400 men escaped on camels (1 Sam. 30:17); Adrammelech and Sharezer escaped to the land of Ararat (2 Kgs. 19:37).

B Escaping evil

I have escaped by the skin of my teeth (Job 19:20); the sailors tried to escape from the ship (Acts 27:30); lest any prisoners should swim away and escape (Acts 27:42); pray that you will have strength to escape these things (Luke 21:36); they may escape from the devil (2 Tim. 2:26); how shall we escape if we ignore this great salvation? (Heb. 2:3); how shall we escape if we turn from him who speaks from heaven? (Heb. 12:25); on Mount Zion will be those who escape and it will be holy (Obad. 17); though he has escaped from the sea, justice has not allowed him to live (Acts 28:4); you may escape the corruption that is in the world (2 Pet. 1:4); after they have escaped the defilements of the world (2 Pet. 2:20); with the temptation God will provide the way of escape (1 Cor. 10:13); if it be possible, let this cup pass from me (Matt. 26:39); let no one escape (2 Kgs. 9:15; 10:25); the swift of foot will not escape (Amos 2:15).

C Escaping through God

We have escaped like a bird from a snare (Ps. 124:7); oh, for wings like a dove, to fly away! (Ps. 55:6); by faith they escaped the edge of the sword (Heb. 11:34); with the temptation God will provide the way of escape (1 Cor. 10:13); if it be possible, let this cup pass from me (Matt. 26:39).

D Escaping from God

How will you escape being sentenced to hell? (Matt. 23:33); do you hope to escape the judgement of God? (Rom. 2:3); if I deserve to die, I am not trying to escape death (Acts 25:11); there will be no escape (1 Thess. 5:3); if they did not escape when they refused him who warned them on earth (Heb. 12:25).

668 Deliverance

A God saving

A1 Deliverance is of God

A1a God my salvation

O Lord, my salvation (Ps. 38:22); God is our salvation (Ps. 68:19); God of our salvation (Ps. 65:5; 79:9; 85:4); God of my salvation (Ps. 25:5; 27:9; 88:1); he only is my rock and my salvation (Ps. 62:2, 6); the Lord has become my salvation (Exod. 15:2; Isa. 12:2); the Lord is my light and my salvation (Ps. 27:1); my deliverer (2 Sam. 22:2; Ps. 144:2); I will rejoice in the God of my salvation (Hab. 3:18).

A1b Can God save?

Many say God will not deliver me (Ps. 3:2); let God deliver him (Ps. 22:8; Matt. 27:43); do not believe Hezekiah that the Lord can deliver you (2 Kgs. 18:32); what god can deliver you out of my hands? (Dan. 3:15); has your God been able to deliver you from the lions? (Dan. 6:20); who then can be saved? (Luke 18:26); the Lord is not limited in saving by many or by few (1 Sam. 14:6); he saved others, let him save himself (Luke 23:35); it is difficult for the righteous to be saved (1 Pet. 4:18).

A1c God will save

Deliverance is from the Lord (Ps. 3:8; Jonah 2:9); our God is able to save us (Dan. 3:17); God will deliver us (2 Cor. 1:10); no other god can save like this (Dan.

3:29); God is a God of deliverance (Ps. 68:20); it is I who have declared and saved and proclaimed (Isa. 43:12); on God rests my deliverance (Ps. 62:7); you save man and beast (Ps. 36:6); God is able to save and to destroy (Jas. 4:12); in returning and rest you will be saved (Isa. 30:15).

A1d Save us!

Save us, O God! (1 Chr. 16:35); save us, Lord! (Matt. 8:25); save me! (Ps. 3:7; Matt. 14:30); hosanna! [save, Lord!] (Ps. 118:25; Matt. 21:15; Mark 11:9, 10; John 12:13); hosanna in the highest! (Matt. 21:9); deliver us! (Ps. 79:9; 106:47); save your people! (Ps. 28:9); deliver us from the evil one (Matt. 6:13); save yourself and us! (Luke 23:39).

A1e God the Saviour

My Saviour (2 Sam. 22:3; Ps. 18:2); a righteous God and a saviour (Isa. 45:21); God is the Saviour of all men (1 Tim. 4:10); the holy One of Israel, your Saviour (Isa. 43:3); God of Israel, Saviour (Isa. 45:15); I rejoice in God my Saviour (Luke 1:47); by command of God our Saviour (1 Tim. 1:1; Titus 1:3); God our Saviour wants all men to be saved (1 Tim. 2:3); that they may adorn the doctrine of God our Saviour (Titus 2:10); the glory of our great God and Saviour Jesus Christ (Titus 2:13); when the kindness and love of God our Saviour appeared (Titus 3:4); they forgot God their Saviour (Ps. 106:21).

A1f Christ the Saviour

A Saviour, Christ the Lord (Luke 2:11); this is the Saviour of the world (John 4:42); a Saviour, Jesus (Acts 13:23); Christ is the Saviour of the body (Eph. 5:23); the Father sent the Son to be the Saviour of the world (1 John 4:14); God exalted him as Leader and Saviour (Acts 5:31); the Deliverer will come from Zion (Rom. 11:26); the appearing of our Saviour Christ Jesus (2 Tim. 1:10); God the Father and Christ Jesus our Saviour (Titus 1:4); by the righteousness of our God and Saviour Jesus Christ (2 Pet. 1:1); our Lord and Saviour Jesus Christ (2 Pet. 1:11); through the knowledge of our Lord and Saviour Jesus Christ (2 Pet. 2:20).

A1g Christ saves

I did not come to judge but to save (John 12:47); the Son of Man came to seek and to save (Luke 19:10); there is no other name by which we may be saved (Acts 4:12); I am the door, whoever enters through me will be saved (John 10:9); God sent the Son that the world might be saved (John 3:17); Jesus who saves us from the wrath to come (1 Thess. 1:10); the source of eternal salvation (Heb. 5:9); my eyes have seen your salvation (Luke 2:30); he will appear a second time for salvation (Heb. 9:28); he saved others but he cannot save himself (Matt. 27:42; Mark 15:31); through the grace of the Lord Jesus we are saved (Acts 15:11); much more, being justified, we will be saved from God's wrath by him (Rom. 5:9); he is able for ever to save those who draw near to God through him (Heb. 7:25).

A2 Those whom God saves

A2a Reasons for God saving

I will save you because you trust in me (Jer. 39:18); save your servant who trusts in you (Ps. 86:2); he who believes and is baptised will be saved (Mark 16:16); believe in the Lord Jesus and you will be saved (Acts 16:31); the angel of the Lord delivers those who fear him (Ps. 34:7); you save those who take refuge in you from their foes (Ps. 17:7); call upon me and I will deliver you (Ps. 50:15); whoever calls on the name of the Lord will be saved (Joel 2:32; Acts 2:21; Rom. 10:13); deliver me according to your word (Ps. 119:170); save me because of your steadfast love (Ps. 6:4); because he loves me I will rescue him (Ps. 91:14); he rescued me because he delighted in me (2 Sam. 22:20; Ps. 18:19); he saved them for his name's sake (Ps. 106:8); the Lord saves the upright in heart (Ps. 7:10); through knowledge the righteous are delivered (Prov. 11:9); everyone found written in the book will be delivered (Dan. 12:1); he who endures to the end will be saved (Matt. 10:22; 24:13; Mark 13:13).

A2b God wants to save all
Turn to me and be saved, all the ends of the earth (Isa. 45:22); all Israel will be saved (Rom. 11:26); will just a few be saved? (Luke 13:23); God wants all men to be saved (1 Tim. 2:4).

A2c God saves the needy
He will deliver the needy (Ps. 72:12); he delivers the soul of the needy (Jer. 20:13); the Lord delivered this poor man out of all his troubles (Ps. 34:6); you save an afflicted people (2 Sam. 22:28; Ps. 18:27); you deliver the afflicted (Ps. 35:10); the Lord saves those crushed in spirit (Ps. 34:18); I will save the lame and gather the outcast (Zeph. 3:19); woman will be saved through the bearing of children (1 Tim. 2:15).

A2d God saves his people
I will defend this city and save it (2 Kgs. 19:34); God will save Zion (Ps. 69:35); I will put salvation in Zion (Isa. 46:13); Judah will be saved and Jerusalem dwell in safety (Jer. 33:16); Israel is saved by the Lord with everlasting salvation (Isa. 45:17); I am with you to deliver you (Jer. 15:20); I will save you from afar (Jer. 46:27); you will call your walls Salvation (Isa. 60:18); oh, that the salvation of Israel would come from Zion! (Ps. 53:6); in his days Judah will be saved (Jer. 23:6); I will deliver my flock (Ezek. 34:10, 22); may your God whom you serve constantly deliver you (Dan. 6:16); the Lord will save them in that day, the flock of his people (Zech. 9:16); we worship what we know, for salvation is from the Jews (John 4:22); only a remnant will be saved (Rom. 9:27); my heart's desire for Israel is that they be saved (Rom. 10:1).

A3 What God saves from
A3a God saves from enemies in general
God saved them from their enemies (Judg. 2:18; 1 Sam. 12:11; 2 Sam. 18:19); he delivered me from my strong enemy (2 Sam. 22:18; Ps. 18:17); deliverance from our enemies (Luke 1:71, 74); you rescue me from the violent man (2 Sam. 22:49; Ps. 18:48); the Lord delivers them from the wicked (Ps. 37:40; 97:10); I delivered you from the nations (Judg. 10:11-12); when I deliver them from those who enslave them (Ezek. 34:27); that I may be delivered from the disobedient in Judea (Rom. 15:31); delivering you from the [Jewish] people and from the Gentiles (Acts 26:17); God saves the poor from the mighty (Job 5:15).

A3b Save us from enemies!
Deliver me from Esau (Gen. 32:11); deliver us from his hand (2 Kgs. 19:19; Isa. 37:20); save me from all who pursue me (Ps. 7:1); deliver me from evildoers (Ps. 59:2); deliver me from my enemies (Ps. 31:15; 59:1; 69:14; 143:9); deliver me from my persecutors (Ps. 142:6); rescue me from evil men (Ps. 140:1); deliver me from the unjust (Ps. 43:1); pray that we may be delivered from evil men (2 Thess. 3:2); deliver us from evil (Matt. 6:13).

A3c God saves from particular foes
I have come down to deliver them from the Egyptians (Exod. 3:8); the Lord saved Israel from the Egyptians (Exod. 14:30; 18:9, 10); I delivered you from the hand of Saul (2 Sam. 12:7); I will deliver you from the king of Assyria (2 Kgs. 20:6; Isa. 38:6); the Lord rescued me from Herod (Acts 12:11); the Lord will deliver me from this Philistine (1 Sam. 17:37).

A3d God saves from trouble
The Lord will deliver him in the day of trouble (Ps. 41:1); in trouble I will rescue him and honour him (Ps. 91:15); he will pluck my feet out of the net (Ps. 25:15); you will pull me out of the net (Ps. 31:4); I was in distress and the Lord gave me room (Ps. 4:1); you called in trouble and I rescued you (Ps. 81:7); God rescued him from all his afflictions (Acts 7:10); I was delivered from the lion's mouth (2 Tim. 4:17); the Lord rescued me from persecutions (2 Tim. 3:11); the Lord will rescue me from every evil (2 Tim. 4:18); this will turn out for my deliverance (Phil. 1:19).

A3e God saves from sin and death
You have delivered my soul from death (Ps. 56:13; 86:13; 116:8); who will save me from this body of death? (Rom. 7:24-5); he will save his people from their sins (Matt. 1:21); Christ gave himself for our sins to rescue us from this evil age (Gal. 1:4); Christ Jesus came into the world to save sinners (1 Tim. 1:15); to give knowledge of salvation by the forgiveness of sins (Luke 1:77); God saved us and called us with a holy calling (2 Tim. 1:9); he saved us by the washing of regeneration (Titus 3:5); now is the day of salvation (2 Cor. 6:2); he has delivered us from the domain of darkness (Col. 1:13); to deliver those who through fear of death were subject to lifelong bondage (Heb. 2:15); baptism now saves you (1 Pet. 3:21).

A4 The salvation of God
A4a God's salvation made known
Proclaim his salvation (Ps. 96:2); my mouth will speak of your salvation all day long (Ps. 71:15); all the ends of the earth will see the salvation of God (Isa. 52:10); all flesh will see the salvation of God (Luke 3:6); that my salvation may reach to the ends of the earth (Isa. 49:6); to bring salvation to the ends of the earth (Acts 13:47); he has clothed me with garments of salvation (Isa. 61:10); the helmet of salvation (Eph. 6:17; 1 Thess. 5:8); he has raised up a horn of salvation for us (Luke 1:69-71).

A4b The gospel of salvation
God has destined us for salvation (1 Thess. 5:9); today salvation has come to this house (Luke 19:9); these men are proclaiming to you the way of salvation (Acts 16:17); this salvation of God is sent to the Gentiles (Acts 28:28); the gospel is the power of God for salvation (Rom. 1:16); the word of truth, the gospel of your salvation (Eph. 1:13); God chose you from the beginning for salvation (2 Thess. 2:13); how shall we escape if we neglect such a great salvation? (Heb. 2:3); Christ is the originator of our salvation (Heb. 2:10); salvation of your souls as the outcome of your faith (1 Pet. 1:9); the grace of God that brings salvation to all men (Titus 2:11); the scriptures are able to make you wise to salvation (2 Tim. 3:15); by grace you have been saved (Eph. 2:5, 8); if you confess Jesus as Lord and believe God raised him you will be saved (Rom. 10:9-10); the message of salvation has been sent to us (Acts 13:26); what must I do to be saved? (Acts 16:30); the gospel by which you are saved (1 Cor. 15:2).

A4c Final salvation
Consider the Lord's forbearance as salvation (2 Pet. 3:15); salvation is nearer now than when we first believed (Rom. 13:11); salvation to be revealed in the last time (1 Pet. 1:5); now the salvation, the power and the kingdom of our God have come (Rev. 12:10).

B People saving
B1 Saving people in general
Deliver those being led away to death (Prov. 24:11); rescue the weak and needy (Ps. 82:4); save some, snatching them out of the fire (Jude 23); whoever turns a sinner back will save his soul from death (Jas. 5:20);

how do you know, wife, whether you will save your husband? (1 Cor. 7:16); I want to make my fellow Jews jealous and so save some of them (Rom. 11:14); I have become all things to all men that by all means I might save some (1 Cor. 9:22).

B2 Individuals saving others

Noah built an ark for the saving of his household (Heb. 11:7); Reuben rescued Joseph out of their hand (Gen. 37:21-2); God sent Joseph in order to save lives (Gen. 45:5, 7; 50:20); Moses was sent to be a deliverer (Acts 7:25, 35); Jonathan brought great deliverance (1 Sam. 14:45); David rescued his two wives (1 Sam. 30:18); pray that he will deliver us from the Philistines (1 Sam. 7:8); Saul will deliver them from the Philistines (1 Sam. 9:16); Saul delivered Israel (1 Sam. 14:48); by David I will save Israel from the Philistines (2 Sam. 3:18); David delivered Keilah from the Philistines (1 Sam. 23:5); until sunset he set his mind on delivering Daniel (Dan. 6:14); I rescued him, having learned that he was a Roman (Acts 23:27); a poor wise man delivered the city with wisdom (Eccles. 9:15).

B3 The deliverers [judges]

The judges delivered them from the plunderers (Judg. 2:16); the Lord raised up Othniel as deliverer (Judg. 3:9); the Lord raised up Ehud as deliverer (Judg. 3:15); Shamgar saved Israel (Judg. 3:31); Deborah was judging Israel (Judg. 4:4); Gideon was told to save Israel (Judg. 6:14); Gideon delivered Israel from Midian (Judg. 8:22; 9:17); Tola rose to save Israel (Judg. 10:1); Samson would begin to deliver Israel (Judg. 13:5).

THE JUDGES IN ISRAEL, see 957C3.

B4 Saving oneself

Noah, Daniel and Job would only save themselves (Ezek. 14:14-20); save yourself! (Matt. 27:40; Mark 15:30; Luke 23:35, 37, 39); he cannot save himself (Isa. 44:20; Matt. 27:42; Mark 15:31); save yourselves from this perverse generation (Acts 2:40); he who would save his life will lose it (Matt. 16:25); work out your own salvation with fear and trembling (Phil. 2:12).

C Salvation by other things

Has any nation's god delivered them? (2 Kgs. 18:33; 2 Chr. 32:13-17; Isa. 36:18); let your gods arise and save you, if they can (Jer. 2:28); why serve the gods who did not deliver their people? (2 Chr. 25:15); let your idols deliver you! (Isa. 57:13); the idol cannot save one from trouble (Isa. 46:7); silver and gold cannot deliver them (Zeph. 1:18); a king is not saved by his large army nor a warrior by his great strength (Ps. 33:16); in a son of man there is no salvation (Ps. 146:3); man's deliverance is in vain (Ps. 60:11); a horse cannot save anyone by its strength (Ps. 33:17); righteousness delivers from death (Prov. 10:2; 11:4); the righteousness of the upright delivers them (Prov. 11:6); evil will not deliver those who practise it (Eccles. 8:8); I will not deliver them by bow, sword, battle, horses or horsemen (Hos. 1:7); unless you are circumcised according to the custom of Moses you cannot be saved (Acts 15:1).

D Not delivered

D1 God not saving

You have not delivered your people at all (Exod. 5:23); why are you like a mighty man who cannot save? (Jer. 14:9); I will deliver you no more (Judg. 10:13); if [he does] not [deliver us], we will not serve our gods (Dan. 3:18); I cry out 'Violence!' but you do not save (Hab. 1:2); I will not deliver them (Zech. 11:6).

D2 No one can save

Lest I tear in pieces and there be none to deliver (Ps. 50:22); they looked, but there was no one to save (2 Sam. 22:42); they cried for help, but there was no one to save (Ps. 18:41); there is no one to deliver (Ps. 71:11); there is no one to save you (Isa. 47:15); how can

this man save us? (1 Sam. 10:27); Hezekiah will not be able to deliver you (2 Kgs. 18:29); no beast could stand before the ram or rescue from his power (Dan. 8:4); no one could rescue the ram from the power of the he-goat (Dan. 8:7); no one will rescue her out of my hand (Hos. 2:10); the lion tramples and tears in pieces with none to rescue (Mic. 5:8); there is salvation in no one else (Acts 4:12).

D3 Things which cannot save

We watched for a nation which could not save (Lam. 4:17); their gods will not save them in time of trouble (Jer. 11:12); their silver and gold cannot save them in the day of the Lord's wrath (Ezek. 7:19); a righteous man's righteousness will not deliver him when he sins (Ezek. 33:12); Assyria will not save us, we will not ride on horses (Hos. 14:3); where now is your king that he might save you? (Hos. 13:10); can faith without works save him? (Jas. 2:14).

D4 Those not saved

Harvest is past, summer is ended and we are not saved (Jer. 8:20); we were in our sins a long time and shall we be saved? (Isa. 64:5); if those days had not been shortened no one would be saved (Matt. 24:22; Mark 13:20); he cannot save himself (Isa. 44:20; Matt. 27:42; Mark 15:31); unless these men stay in the ship you cannot be saved (Acts 27:31); they perish because they do not love the truth and so be saved (2 Thess. 2:10).

669 Preparation

A Preparing for action

A1 Preparing for action in general

The Passover had to be eaten with loins girded (Exod. 12:11); Elijah girded up his loins (1 Kgs. 18:46); gird up your loins like a man (Job 38:3; 40:7); gird up the loins of your minds (1 Pet. 1:13); the Lord has bared his holy arm (Isa. 52:10); Peter was stripped for work (John 21:7); Uzziah prepared weapons (2 Chr. 26:14); man the ramparts, watch the road (Nahum 2:1); the wise virgins took flasks of oil with their lamps (Matt. 25:4); be ready for any good deed (Titus 3:1); the four angels had been prepared for the hour, day, month and year (Rev. 9:15).

A2 Preparing to travel

Joseph prepared his chariot (Gen. 46:29); Pharaoh made ready his chariot (Exod. 14:6); they made Joram's chariot ready (2 Kgs. 9:21); get your baggage ready for exile (Jer. 46:19); now take purse, bag and sword (Luke 22:36); he told his disciples to have a boat ready for him (Mark 3:9).

A3 Preparing to build

David prepared for building the temple (1 Chr. 22:5); stones and timbers were prepared for the temple (1 Kgs. 5:18); the stones for the temple were prepared at the quarry (1 Kgs. 6:7).

A4 Prepared for burial

The women prepared spices and perfumes (Luke 23:56); she has prepared my body for burial (Matt. 26:12); they took the spices which they had prepared (Luke 24:1).

B Prepared people

B1 Prepared for God

Make ready a people prepared for the Lord (Luke 1:17); prepare to meet your God (Amos 4:12); vessels of mercy prepared beforehand for glory (Rom. 9:23); those who were ready went in to the marriage feast (Matt. 25:10); new Jerusalem made ready as a bride adorned for her husband (Rev. 21:2); his bride has made herself ready (Rev. 19:7); that the man of God may be equipped for every good work (2 Tim. 3:17); the equipping of the saints for service (Eph. 4:12); let your loins be girded and your lamps burning (Luke 12:35); be ready in season and out of season (2 Tim. 4:2); be ready, for he is coming when you least expect (Matt. 24:44); the fields are white for harvest (John 4:35).

B2 Ready to speak

That the words of the wise may be ready on your lips (Prov. 22:18); gird up your loins and speak to them (Jer. 1:17); feet shod with the preparation of the gospel of peace (Eph. 6:15); ready to make a defence to anyone who calls you to account (1 Pet. 3:15).

C Prepared things

C1 Preparing food

They prepared their present for Joseph (Gen. 43:25); the disciples made preparations for the Passover in the upper room (Matt. 26:17-19; Mark 14:12-16; Luke 22:8-13); prepare something for me to eat (Luke 17:8); prepare provisions (Josh. 1:11); I have prepared my dinner (Matt. 22:4); preparing food for Peter (Acts 10:10); ants prepare their food in summer (Prov. 6:8; 30:25).

C2 A way prepared

I send my messenger to prepare the way (Mal. 3:1; Matt. 11:10; Mark 1:2; Luke 7:27); prepare the way of the Lord (Isa. 40:3; Matt. 3:3; Mark 1:3; Luke 3:4; John 1:23); you will prepare the way for him (Luke 1:76).

C3 A place prepared

My angel will bring you to the place I have prepared (Exod. 23:20); the places are for those for whom they have been prepared (Mark 10:40); I go to prepare a place for you (John 14:2); what neither eye has seen nor ear heard, God has prepared (1 Cor. 2:9); inherit the kingdom prepared for you from the foundation of the world (Matt. 25:34); God has prepared a city for them (Heb. 11:16); the woman has a place prepared by God in which to be nourished (Rev. 12:6); the eternal fire prepared for the devil and his angels (Matt. 25:41).

670 Unpreparedness

A Unprepared

Gideon attacked the Midianites when they were unsuspecting (Judg. 8:11); do not think beforehand what to say (Matt. 10:19-20; Luke 12:11-12; 21:14-15); that servant who knew his master's will but did not make ready (Luke 12:47); they had not prepared provisions (Exod. 12:39); lest Macedonians come with me and find you unprepared (2 Cor. 9:4).

B Not equipped

Those sent out had to take no extra equipment (Matt. 10:9-10; Mark 6:8; Luke 9:3; 10:4); when I sent you out without purse, bag or sandals, did you lack anything? (Luke 22:35); the foolish virgins took no oil with them (Matt. 25:3).

C Raw

Do not eat the lamb raw or boiled (Exod. 12:9); the priest will not have boiled meat, but raw (1 Sam. 2:15).

671 Attempt

EXPERIMENT, see 461.

672 Undertaking

WORK, see 676.

673 Use

USEFUL, see 640.

674 Nonuse

USELESS, see 641.

675 Misuse

ABUSE, see 735B.

676 Action

A God's works

A1 What God does

Our God does whatever he pleases (Ps. 115:3); I act and who can hinder it? (Isa. 43:13); his work is perfect (Deut. 32:4); great are the works of the Lord (Ps. 111:2); the Lord has done great things for us (Ps. 126:2-3); how awesome are your deeds! (Ps. 66:3-5); how great are your works! (Ps. 92:5); great and marvellous are your works (Rev. 15:3); I am doing a work which you would not believe if you were told (Hab. 1:5; Acts 13:41); my Father has never stopped working and I work (John 5:17); the word of God is living and active (Heb. 4:12); all his works are true and his ways are just (Dan. 4:37); this is the Lord's doing and it is marvellous in our eyes (Ps. 118:23; Matt. 21:42; Mark 12:11); there are varieties of workings, but the same God (1 Cor. 12:6); he spoke and it was done (Ps. 33:9); do as you have said (2 Sam. 7:25).

A2 Revealing God's work

The Father shows the Son all that he is doing (John 5:20); we hear them telling in our own languages of the mighty works of God (Acts 2:11); he related what God had done among the Gentiles (Acts 21:19); see the works of the Lord (Ps. 46:8); all men will tell what God has done (Ps. 64:9); our fathers have told us what you did in days of old (Ps. 44:1); I will tell what God has done for my soul (Ps. 66:16).

A3 God's work in us

Of Israel it will be said, See what God has done! (Num. 23:23); the Father living in me does his works (John 14:10); we are God's workmanship (Eph. 2:10); God works in you to will and to work (Phil. 2:13); God works in us what is pleasing to him (Heb. 13:21); you work on behalf of those who wait for you (Isa. 64:4); tell them how much the Lord has done for you (Mark 5:19; Luke 8:39); he who worked in Peter among the circumcised worked in me to the Gentiles (Gal. 2:8); the word of God is at work in you who believe (1 Thess. 2:13).

A4 Christ's work

My Father has never stopped working and I work (John 5:17); Jesus, a prophet mighty in deed and word (Luke 24:19); John heard of the works of the Christ (Matt. 11:2); go to Judea that your disciples may see the works you are doing (John 7:3); he told how much Jesus had done for him (Mark 5:20; Luke 8:39).

B Man's works

B1 Doing one's work

Six days to do all your work (Exod. 20:9; Lev. 23:3); there are six days on which work should be done (Luke 13:14); she works with willing hands (Prov. 31:13); whatever was done in prison, he was the doer of it (Gen. 39:22); work with your hands, as we commanded you (1 Thess. 4:11); such people should do their work in quietness and eat their own bread (2 Thess. 3:12).

B2 One's deeds

I know your deeds (Rev. 2:2, 19; 3:1, 8, 15); it is by his deeds that the lad makes himself known (Prov. 20:11); let her works praise her in the gates (Prov. 31:31); do to others as you want them to do to you (Matt. 7:12); to him who works his wages are not a gift but his due (Rom. 4:4); the evil I do not want is what I do (Rom. 7:19); you cannot do what you would (Gal. 5:17); each man's work will be manifest, for the day will disclose it (1 Cor. 3:13); are you not my work in the Lord? (1 Cor. 9:1); whatever you do, do everything in the name of the Lord Jesus (Col. 3:17); whatever you do, work heartily, as to the Lord (Col. 3:23); women should adorn themselves with good deeds (1 Tim. 2:10); stirring up one another to love and good works (Heb. 10:24); be doers of the word, not just hearers (Jas. 1:22-5); let him show by his good conduct his deeds in the meekness of wisdom (Jas. 3:13); repent and do the works you did at first (Rev. 2:5); their deeds follow them (Rev. 14:13); fine linen stands for the righteous deeds of the saints (Rev. 19:8).

B3 Repaid for deeds
He will reward every man according to his deeds (Matt. 16:27); I give every man according to his deeds (Jer. 17:10); he will render to every one according to his deeds (Prov. 24:12; Rom. 2:6); my reward is with me and I will give to everyone according to what he has done (Rev. 22:12); each one will receive according to what he has done (2 Cor. 5:10); the Lord will requite Jacob according to his deeds (Hos. 12:2); those who have done evil will come forth to the resurrection of judgement (John 5:29); those who have done good will come forth to the resurrection of life (John 5:29); each will receive a reward according to his work (1 Cor. 3:8); their end will be according to their deeds (2 Cor. 11:15); the Lord will repay him according to his deeds (2 Tim. 4:14); God is not so unjust as to overlook your work (Heb. 6:10); the Father judges each one impartially according to his deeds (1 Pet. 1:17); I will give to each of you according to your deeds (Rev. 2:23); the dead were judged according to what was written in the books, by what they had done (Rev. 20:12-13).

B4 Bad deeds
The deeds of the flesh (Gal. 5:19-21); by their deeds they deny God (Titus 1:16); the unfruitful works of darkness (Eph. 5:11); I do not do what I want, but what I hate (Rom. 7:15-25); they were eager to make all their deeds corrupt (Zeph. 3:7); once you were doing evil deeds (Col. 1:21); the blood of Christ cleanses the conscience from dead works (Heb. 9:14).

B5 Works of the law
The man who does them shall live (Lev. 18:5; Neh. 9:29; Ezek. 20:11; Rom. 10:5; Gal. 3:12); not the hearers of the law but the doers who are justified (Rom. 2:13); they did not pursue righteousness by faith but as if it were based on works (Rom. 9:32); do this and you will live (Luke 10:28); if Abraham was justified by works, he has something to boast about (Rom. 4:2); by grace you are saved, not by works (Eph. 2:8-9); not by righteous deeds which we have done (Titus 3:5); not according to our works (2 Tim. 1:9); by the works of the law no one is justified (Rom. 3:20; Gal. 2:16); justified by faith apart from works of the law (Rom. 3:28); to the one who does not work but believes (Rom. 4:5); the man to whom God reckons righteousness apart from works (Rom. 4:6); all who rely on works of the law are under a curse (Gal. 3:10); the one who enters God's rest rests from his own works (Heb. 4:10); repentance from dead works (Heb. 6:1); God's choice is not because of works (Rom. 9:11-12); did you receive the Spirit by the works of the law? (Gal. 3:2); if the choice is by grace it is no longer on the basis of works (Rom. 11:6).

B6 Doing God's works
What shall we do to do the works of God? (John 6:28); good deeds which God prepared for us to do (Eph. 2:10); what must I do to be saved? (Acts 16:30); what must I do to inherit eternal life? (Matt. 19:16; Mark 10:17; Luke 10:25; 18:18); he who hears my words and does them (Matt. 7:24; Luke 6:47); not everyone who says 'Lord' but he who does the will of my Father (Matt. 7:21); do to others as you would have them do to you (Matt. 7:12; Luke 6:31); the work of God is to believe in the one he sent (John 6:29); my food is to do the will of him who sent me and to accomplish his work (John 4:34); the works which the Father has given

me to accomplish bear witness to me (John 5:36); we must work the works of him who sent me while it is day (John 9:4); I have shown you many good works from the Father (John 10:32); if I am not doing the works of my Father, do not believe me (John 10:37); if I had not done among them the works which no one else did (John 15:24); I have finished the work you gave me to do (John 17:4); God did mighty works, wonders and signs through Jesus (Acts 2:22); Timothy is doing the Lord's work, as I am (1 Cor. 16:10); to him who keeps my works to the end (Rev. 2:26).

B7 Works of faith
What use is faith without works? (Jas. 2:14); faith without works is dead (Jas. 2:17-26); if a man will not work he shall not eat (2 Thess. 3:10); perform deeds fitting repentance (Acts 26:20); that God may fulfil your good pleasure and work of faith in power (2 Thess. 1:11); work out your own salvation with fear and trembling (Phil. 2:12); command them to be rich in good deeds (1 Tim. 6:18); careful to devote themselves to good deeds (Titus 3:8, 14); women should be decked with good deeds (1 Tim. 2:9-10); they may see your good deeds and glorify God (Matt. 5:16; 1 Pet. 2:12); deeds wrought in God (John 3:21); blessed is the servant whom his master finds so doing (Matt. 24:46; Luke 12:43); we remember your work of faith and labour of love (1 Thess. 1:3); always abounding in the work of the Lord (1 Cor. 15:58); a believer will do the works I do, and greater (John 14:12).

C Man-made
Their idols are the work of men's hands (2 Kgs. 19:17; Ps. 115:4; 135:15; Isa. 37:19); the idols your hands have made (Isa. 31:7); can a man make gods for himself? such are no gods (Jer. 16:20); saying that gods made with hands are no gods (Isa. 2:8; Jer. 1:16; Acts 19:26); a workman made it, it is not God (Hos. 8:6); you will no longer bow down to the work of your hands (Mic. 5:13); what profit is an idol when its maker has carved it? (Hab. 2:18); men will not have regard for their man-made altars (Isa. 17:8); I will destroy this temple made with hands and build another not made with hands (Mark 14:58); they rejoiced in the works of their hands (Acts 7:41); the Most High does not live in houses made with hands (Acts 7:48); God does not live in shrines made with hands (Acts 17:24); we have a building from God, a house not made with hands (2 Cor. 5:1); the more perfect tent not made with hands (Heb. 9:11); Christ did not enter a sanctuary made with hands (Heb. 9:24).

677 Inaction

A No work on feast days
No work to be done on: the sabbath (Exod. 20:10; Lev. 23:3; Deut. 5:14); days one and seven of the Passover (Exod. 12:16; Lev. 23:7-8; Num. 28:25; Deut. 16:8); the Day of Atonement (Lev. 16:29; 23:28-32; Num. 29:7); the Feast of Weeks (Lev. 23:21; Num. 28:26); the Feast of Trumpets (Lev. 23:25; Num. 29:1); the Feast of Booths (Lev. 23:35-6; Num. 29:12, 35).
SABBATH REST, see 683A.

B Lack of activity
A land and cities on which you have not laboured (Deut. 6:10-11; Josh. 24:13); do not work with the firstling of your herd (Deut. 15:19); you make them cease from their labours (Exod. 5:4-5); they hear your words but do not do them (Ezek. 33:31-2); the scribes and Pharisees preach but do not practise (Matt. 23:3); night comes when no one can work (John 9:4); I can wish to do good, but the doing is not present in me (Rom. 7:18-19); sit still, my daughter (Ruth 3:18).

C God inactive
Lest their enemies should say the Lord has not done all this (Deut. 32:27); why do you keep your hand in your bosom? (Ps. 74:11); 'The Lord will not do either good or evil' (Zeph. 1:12); I withheld my hand (Ezek. 20:22).

678 Activity

A Industriousness
The hand of the diligent makes rich (Prov. 10:4); the soul of the diligent is made fat (Prov. 13:4); the plans of the diligent lead to abundance (Prov. 21:5); the hand of the diligent will rule (Prov. 12:24); she does not eat the bread of idleness (Prov. 31:27); Solomon saw that Jeroboam was industrious (1 Kgs. 11:28); Martha was distracted with all her serving (Luke 10:40).

B Sleeplessness
My sleep fled from me (Gen. 31:40); the king could not sleep (Esther 6:1; Dan. 6:18); I lie awake (Ps. 102:7); I am tossing until dawn (Job 7:4); at night his mind does not rest (Eccles. 2:23); you hold my eyelids open (Ps. 77:4); the full stomach of the rich does not let him sleep (Eccles. 5:12); Nebuchadnezzar had dreams, was troubled and his sleep left him (Dan. 2:1); they cannot sleep unless they do evil (Prov. 4:16); though one does not sleep night or day (Eccles. 8:16); we commend ourselves in sleeplessness (2 Cor. 6:5); through many a sleepless night (2 Cor. 11:27); God neither slumbers nor sleeps (Ps. 121:3-4).

C Waking up
C1 God waking up
Awake, Lord! (Ps. 35:23; 44:23; 59:5); awake, arm of the Lord! (Isa. 51:9); the Lord awoke (Ps. 78:65).
C2 Christ waking up
They woke Jesus up (Matt. 8:25; Mark 4:38; Luke 8:24); Jesus woke up and rebuked the wind (Mark 4:39).
C3 Others waking up
C3a Wake up!
Awake, Deborah! (Judg. 5:12); awake, Zion! (Isa. 52:1); rouse yourself, Jerusalem! (Isa. 51:17); awake, sleeper! (Eph. 5:14); wake up! (Rev. 3:2); it is time for you to wake from sleep (Rom. 13:11); awake, drunkards, and weep (Joel 1:5); woe to him who says to a piece of wood, 'Awake!' (Hab. 2:19).
C3b About others waking
Perhaps Baal is asleep and needs to be awakened (1 Kgs. 18:27); blessed are whose whom the master finds awake when he comes (Luke 12:37-9); let us keep awake and be self-controlled (1 Thess. 5:6); whether awake or asleep we live with him (1 Thess. 5:10); if you will not wake up I will come like a thief (Rev. 3:3); I woke, and my sleep was pleasant to me (Jer. 31:26); I woke, the Lord sustains me (Ps. 3:5); morning by morning he awakens me (Isa. 50:4); when I awake I am still with you (Ps. 139:18); I will be satisfied when I awake in your likeness (Ps. 17:15); the captain woke Jonah up (Jonah 1:6); I am going to wake Lazarus out of sleep (John 11:11); when the jailer woke up (Acts 16:27).

D Restlessness
I am restless (Ps. 55:2); the wicked are like the sea which cannot rest (Isa. 57:20); when you grow restless you will break his yoke (Gen. 27:40); take no rest and give God no rest (Isa. 62:6-7); let none of you suffer as a busybody (1 Pet. 4:15).

679 Inactivity

A Idleness
The sluggard craves and gets nothing (Prov. 13:4); the sluggard says there is a lion outside (Prov. 22:13; 26:13); the sluggard turns on his bed like a door on its hinges (Prov. 26:14); the sluggard buries his hand in the dish (Prov. 19:24; 26:15); the sluggard does not plough in

autumn (Prov. 20:4); the sluggard's field is neglected (Prov. 24:30-4); how long will you lie, sluggard? (Prov. 6:9); go to the ant, you sluggard (Prov. 6:6); keep away from every brother living in idleness (2 Thess. 3:6); we were not idle when we were with you (2 Thess. 3:7); that you may not be sluggish (Heb. 6:12); through idleness the roof sags (Eccles. 10:18); he who is slack in his work is brother to him who destroys (Prov. 18:9); a lazy man is like vinegar or smoke to him who sends him (Prov. 10:26); Pharaoh said the Israelites were lazy (Exod. 5:8, 17); shall your brothers go to war while you sit here? (Num. 32:6); some among you are idle (2 Thess. 3:11); Cretans are lazy gluttons (Titus 1:12); younger widows learn to be idle (1 Tim. 5:13); people standing idle (Matt. 20:3); you lazy slave! (Matt. 25:26).

B Sleep
B1 Ones sleeping
Jacob fell asleep at Bethel (Gen. 28:11); without his cloak, what will he sleep in? (Exod. 22:27); Sisera was asleep (Judg. 4:21); Saul lay asleep in the camp (1 Sam. 26:7); Elijah slept under a juniper tree (1 Kgs. 19:5); I fell into a deep sleep (Dan. 8:18; 10:9); Jonah fell into a deep sleep (Jonah 1:5-6); Jesus was asleep in the boat (Matt. 8:24; Mark 4:38; Luke 8:23); the disciples were sleeping (Matt. 26:40, 43-5; Mark 14:37, 40; Luke 9:32; 22:45); his disciples stole him while we were sleeping (Matt. 28:13); Peter was sleeping between two soldiers (Acts 12:6); Eutychus fell into a deep sleep (Acts 20:9); perhaps Baal is asleep (1 Kgs. 18:27); when the bridegroom was delayed they slept (Matt. 25:5); whether awake or asleep we live with him (1 Thess. 5:10).
B2 Wholesome sleep
The sleep of a labourer is sweet (Eccles. 5:12); in peace I will lie down and sleep (Ps. 4:8); my sleep was pleasant to me (Jer. 31:26); your sleep will be sweet (Prov. 3:24); if he has fallen asleep, he will recover (John 11:12).
B3 Putting people to sleep
God put Adam into a deep sleep (Gen. 2:21); the Lord has poured on you a spirit of deep sleep (Isa. 29:10); the Lord put them into a deep sleep (1 Sam. 26:12); God gives sleep to his beloved (Ps. 127:2); Delilah made Samson sleep on her knees (Judg. 16:19).
B4 Visions in sleep
Visions of the night when deep sleep falls on men (Job 4:13); God speaks when sound sleep falls on men (Job 33:15); Peter fell into a trance (Acts 10:10); in a trance I saw a vision (Acts 11:5).
B5 Sleep instead of work
Do not love sleep lest you come to poverty (Prov. 20:13); a little sleep, a little slumber, and poverty comes like a robber (Prov. 6:10; 24:33); he who sleeps in harvest brings shame (Prov. 10:5).
B6 Sleep of death
Man dies and cannot be roused out of his sleep (Job 14:12); that they may sleep a perpetual sleep and not wake (Jer. 51:39, 57); lest I sleep the sleep of death (Ps. 13:3); the girl is not dead but sleeping (Matt. 9:24; Mark 5:39; Luke 8:52); Lazarus has fallen asleep (John 11:11); those who sleep in Jesus (1 Thess. 4:14); the firstfruits of those who slept (1 Cor. 15:20); we will not all sleep (1 Cor. 15:51); many who sleep in the dust of the earth will awake (Dan. 12:2); Jesus spoke of his death, but they thought he meant taking rest in sleep (John 11:13).
B7 Not sleeping
Watch, lest he find you asleep (Mark 13:36); let us not sleep as others do (1 Thess. 5:6); Uriah did not sleep at home (2 Sam. 11:9, 13); how can you sleep? (Jonah 1:6); awake, sleeper! (Eph. 5:14); blessed is he who keeps awake (Rev. 16:15); why do you sleep, Lord? (Ps. 44:23).

680 Haste

A Acting hurriedly

A1 Hasty action in general

He who makes haste errs (Prov. 19:2); feet that make haste to evil (Prov. 1:16; Isa. 59:7); a man with evil eye hastens after wealth (Prov. 28:22); he who hastens to get rich will not go unpunished (Prov. 28:20); wealth hastily gotten will dwindle (Prov. 13:11); an inheritance gained hastily will not be blessed (Prov. 20:21); what your eyes have seen do not hastily bring into court (Prov. 25:7-8); let him hasten his work that we may see it (Isa. 5:19); in its time I will hasten it (Isa. 60:22).

A2 Particular hasty actions

Rebekah hastened to let down her jar (Gen. 24:18); Joseph hurried to find a place to weep (Gen. 43:30); eat the Passover in haste (Exod. 12:11); you came out of Egypt in haste (Deut. 16:3); the king's business required haste (1 Sam. 21:8); Rehoboam mounted his chariot hastily (1 Kgs. 12:18; 2 Chr. 10:18); the Arameans threw away their garments in their haste (2 Kgs. 7:15); the king went in haste to the lions' den (Dan. 6:19); Mary went in haste to the hill country (Luke 1:39); the shepherds went with haste (Luke 2:16); she came in haste before the king (Mark 6:25); Zaccheus made haste and came down (Luke 19:6); Paul was hurrying to be in Jerusalem for Pentecost (Acts 20:16).

B Hurrying others on

Lord, hasten to me! (Ps. 141:1); make haste to help me! (Ps. 22:19); hurry up, flee there (Gen. 19:22); the Egyptians urged them to leave in haste (Exod. 12:33); come down quickly! (2 Kgs. 1:11); bring Haman quickly (Esther 5:5); make haste and come down (Luke 19:5); make haste and get out of Jerusalem (Acts 22:18); hastening the coming of the day of God (2 Pet. 3:12).

C Not in haste

He who believes will not hurry about (Isa. 28:16); you will not go out in haste (Isa. 52:12).

681 Leisure

REST, see 683.

682 Exertion

A Working hard

A1 The fact of toil

Through toil you will eat (Gen. 3:17); by the sweat of your brow (Gen. 3:19); the span of life is but toil and sorrow (Ps. 90:10); a man goes to work to labour until evening (Ps. 104:23); there is profit in all labour (Prov. 14:23); others have laboured, and you have entered into their labour (John 4:38); we commend ourselves in labours (2 Cor. 6:5); in labour and hardship (2 Cor. 11:27); by hard work we must help the weak (Acts 20:35); we toil and strive because we set our hope on the living God (1 Tim. 4:10); the hard-working farmer should have first share of the crops (2 Tim. 2:6); I know your toil and perseverance (Rev. 2:2); Noah will give us rest in our toil (Gen. 5:29); come to me, you who labour and are heavy-laden (Matt. 11:28).

A2 Those who toiled

Greet Mary who has worked hard among you (Rom. 16:6); Persis who has worked hard in the Lord (Rom. 16:12); Jacob's toil for Laban (Gen. 31:42); Ruth has worked from morning until now (Ruth 2:7); to this end I toil (Col. 1:29); you remember our toil, working night and day (1 Thess. 2:9; 2 Thess. 3:8); we toiled, working with our hands (1 Cor. 4:12); in far more labours (2 Cor. 11:23).

A3 Not toiling

You pitied the plant for which you did not toil (Jonah 4:10); the lilies of the field do not toil or spin (Matt. 6:28; Luke 12:27); I sent you to reap that for which you have not laboured (John 4:38).

A4 Toiling in vain

I am afraid I have laboured over you in vain (Gal. 4:11); what does man get from his toil? (Eccles. 1:3; 2:22); the peoples toil for nothing (Jer. 51:58).

B Forced labour

The lazy will be put to forced labour (Prov. 12:24); conquered citizens will be put to forced labour (Deut. 20:11); Issachar submits to forced labour (Gen. 49:15); gang drivers afflicted them with hard labour (Exod. 1:11); the Gibeonites became slaves, hewers of wood and drawers of water (Josh. 9:21-7); the Canaanites were put to forced labour (Josh. 16:10; Judg. 1:28-35); David put the Ammonites to forced labour (2 Sam. 12:31); Solomon levied forced labourers (1 Kgs. 5:13; 9:15); Solomon made the Canaanites forced labourers (2 Chr. 8:8).

C Struggle

Strive to enter by the narrow door (Luke 13:24); strive together with me in your prayers to God for me (Rom. 15:30); I want you to know how greatly I struggle on your behalf (Col. 2:1); you have not yet resisted to blood, striving against sin (Heb. 12:4).

683 Repose

A The sabbath

A1 Sabbaths instituted

On the seventh day God rested (Gen. 2:2-3; Exod. 20:11; 31:17; Heb. 4:4); a sabbath of rest (Exod. 31:15; 35:2-3); on the seventh day you shall rest (Exod. 34:21; Lev. 23:3); you shall not do any work (Exod. 20:10; 23:12); I gave them my sabbaths as a sign (Ezek. 20:12); the sabbaths of the Lord (Lev. 23:38).

A2 On the sabbath

Every sabbath the showbread is to be set out (Lev. 24:8); every sabbath two lambs as a burnt offering (Num. 28:9-10); on the sabbath they went to the synagogue (Matt. 12:9-10; Luke 4:16; Acts 13:14); on the sabbath he taught in the synagogue (Mark 1:21; 6:2; Luke 4:31-3; 6:6; 13:10); Paul reasoned in the synagogue every sabbath (Acts 18:4); the people begged that these things might be told them the next sabbath (Acts 13:42); on the sabbath we went outside the gate to the riverside (Acts 16:13); for three sabbaths he discussed with him (Acts 17:2); the prophets are read every sabbath (Acts 13:27); Moses is read in the synagogues every sabbath (Acts 15:21); they went through the grainfields on the sabbath (Matt. 12:1; Mark 2:23; Luke 6:1); should not this woman be loosed on the sabbath day? (Luke 13:16); he went to eat in a Pharisee's house on the sabbath (Luke 14:1); it was the day of preparation, and the Sabbath was dawning (Luke 23:54).

A3 Sabbath observed

Observe the sabbath day (Exod. 20:8; Deut. 5:12); blessed is the man who keeps the sabbath (Isa. 56:2); the eunuchs who keep my sabbaths will have a memorial (Isa. 56:4-5); keep the sabbath day holy (Jer. 17:22-7); if you call the sabbath a delight (Isa. 58:13); the priest shall sanctify my sabbaths (Ezek. 44:24); no manna on the sabbath (Exod. 16:25-9); pray that your flight may not be on the sabbath (Matt. 24:20); the bodies were not to remain on the cross on the sabbath (John 19:31).

A4 Sabbath violated

You bring wrath on Israel by profaning the sabbath (Neh. 13:18); when will the sabbath be over that we may trade? (Amos 8:5); a man gathered wood on the sabbath (Num. 15:32); men trod winepresses on the sabbath (Neh. 13:15-16).

A5 The sabbath and Christ

Your disciples are doing what is unlawful on the sabbath (Matt. 12:2; Mark 2:24); why do you do what is not proper on a sabbath? (Luke 6:2); on the sabbath the priests profane the sabbath (Matt. 12:5); is it lawful to heal on the sabbath? (Matt. 12:10; Luke 14:3); is it lawful to do good or to harm on the sabbath? (Mark 3:4; Luke 6:9); they watched him to see if he would heal on the sabbath (Mark 3:2; Luke 6:7); for this reason the Jews persecuted Jesus, because he healed on the sabbath (John 5:16); the official was indignant because Jesus had healed on the sabbath (Luke 13:14); he not only broke the sabbath but called God his Father (John 5:18); this man is not from God because he does not keep the sabbath (John 9:16); why be angry because I made a made a whole man well on the sabbath? (John 7:23); it is lawful to do good on the sabbath (Matt. 12:12); the sabbath was made for man, not man for the sabbath (Mark 2:27); the Son of man is Lord of the sabbath (Matt. 12:8; Mark 2:28; Luke 6:5); let no one judge you with regard to a festival, New Moon or sabbath (Col. 2:16).

B Rest

B1 God and rest

God rested from all his works (Heb. 4:4); my presence will go with you and I will give you rest (Exod. 33:14); when the Lord gives you rest (Isa. 14:3); God has given rest to his people (1 Kgs. 8:56); this is rest, give rest to the weary (Isa. 28:12); come to me, all who are weary, and I will give you rest (Matt. 11:28); you will find rest for your souls (Jer. 6:16; Matt. 11:29); in returning and rest you will be saved (Isa. 30:15); while the promise of entering his rest remains (Heb. 4:1-3); there remains a Sabbath rest for the people of God (Heb. 4:9-10).

B2 Those at ease

Issachar saw that rest was good (Gen. 49:15); the wicked are always at ease (Ps. 73:12); woe to those who are at ease in Zion (Amos 6:1); Moab has been at ease from his youth (Jer. 48:11).

B3 No rest

The dove found no resting-place (Gen. 8:9); among the nations you will find no rest (Deut. 28:65); they will never enter my rest (Ps. 95:11; Heb. 3:11; 4:3-5); take no rest and give him no rest (Isa. 62:6-7); I had no rest in my spirit (2 Cor. 2:13); our flesh had no rest (2 Cor. 7:5); the unclean spirit seeks rest and does not find it (Matt. 12:43; Luke 11:24); the man will not rest until he has finished the matter today (Ruth 3:18).

684 Fatigue

A Fatigue and God

A1 God growing weary

The Lord does not grow weary or tired (Isa. 40:28); you have wearied the Lord (Mal. 2:17); it is too little a thing for you to weary men, that you will weary God? (Isa. 7:13); I am weary with bearing your festivals (Isa. 1:14); you have wearied me with your iniquities (Isa. 43:24).

A2 Weary of God

You have been weary of me (Isa. 43:22); how have I wearied you? (Mic. 6:3); you say, 'How wearisome it is!' (Mal. 1:13).

B Tired out

B1 Tired in general

Even youths grow weary (Isa. 40:30); all things are wearisome (Eccles. 1:8); the sluggard is too tired to bring his hand back to his mouth (Prov. 26:15); Moses' hands grew heavy (Exod. 17:12); he will wear out the saints of the Most High (Dan. 7:25); the land mourns

and everyone in it languishes (Hos. 4:3); he found them sleeping, for their eyes were very heavy (Mark 14:40); you and the people will wear yourselves out (Exod. 18:18).

B2 Tired in activity

If you ran with men on foot and they wearied you (Jer. 12:5); I am weary with holding in God's word (Jer. 20:9); the strength of the burden bearers is failing (Neh. 4:10); Eleazar struck the Philistines till his hand was weary (2 Sam. 23:10); David became exhausted fighting the Philistines (2 Sam. 21:15); much study is wearying to the flesh (Eccles. 12:12); Jesus was tired from his journey (John 4:6); they wearied themselves trying to find the door (Gen. 19:11); the Egyptians tired themselves trying to find water (Exod. 7:18); a fool's toil wearies him so he does not know the way to the city (Eccles. 10:15); Gideon and his men were exhausted yet pursuing (Judg. 8:4); some of David's men were too exhausted to continue the pursuit (1 Sam. 30:10, 21).

B3 Do not grow weary

Do not grow weary in doing good (2 Thess. 3:13); consider him, lest you grow weary (Heb. 12:3); they will walk and run and not get tired (Isa. 40:31); you have not grown weary (Rev. 2:3); in due season we will reap if we do not grow weary (Gal. 6:9).

685 Refreshment

A Refreshment and God

On the seventh day God was refreshed (Exod. 31:17); that times of refreshing may come from the Lord (Acts 3:19); that I might know how to sustain him who is weary (Isa. 50:4); the fear of the Lord will be refreshment to your bones (Prov. 3:8).

B People refreshed

Good news is like cold water to a weary soul (Prov. 25:25); Jonathan's eyes brightened after the honey (1 Sam. 14:27-9); Saul was refreshed by David's playing (1 Sam. 16:23); David refreshed himself (2 Sam. 16:14); come home with me and refresh yourself (1 Kgs. 13:7); Onesiphorus often refreshed me (2 Tim. 1:16); the hearts of the saints have been refreshed (Philem. 7); refresh my heart (Philem. 20); they have refreshed my spirit (1 Cor. 16:18).

686 Worker

A Workers

Pray that the Lord of the harvest will send out workers (Matt. 9:38; Luke 10:2); hiring workers for his vineyard (Matt. 20:1); be a workman who does not need to be ashamed (2 Tim. 2:15); the workman deserves his food (Matt. 10:10); fellow-workers in Christ (Rom. 16:3-21).

B Occupations

B1 Occupations in general

What is your occupation? (Gen. 46:33; 47:3; Jonah 1:8); they were craftsmen (1 Chr. 4:14); no craftsman of any craft will be found in you (Rev. 18:22).

B2 Food occupations

The king of Egypt's baker (Gen. 40:1-23); the king will take your daughters as cooks and bakers (1 Sam. 8:13); Samuel spoke to the cook (1 Sam. 9:23-4); the king of Egypt's butler (Gen. 40:1-23); Nehemiah was cupbearer to the king (Neh. 1:11); Solomon's waiters and cupbearers (1 Kgs. 10:5).

B3 Manufacturing occupations

B3a Carpenter / mason

Carpenters and stonemasons sent by Hiram (2 Sam. 5:11; 1 Chr. 14:1); carpenters, builders, masons and stonecutters (2 Kgs. 12:11-12; 22:6; 1 Chr. 22:15; 2 Chr. 34:10-11); the carpenter stretches out a line (Isa. 44:13); is not this the carpenter? (Mark 6:3); is not this the carpenter's son? (Matt. 13:55).

B3b Potter
A lesson from the potter (Jer. 18:1-6); shall the potter be regarded as equal to the clay? (Isa. 29:16); will the vessel question the potter? (Isa. 45:9); the potter (Rom. 9:21); throw the money to the potter (Zech. 11:13); they bought the potter's field as a burial ground for foreigners (Matt. 27:7).

B3c Smiths
Tubal-cain forged implements (Gen. 4:22); Israel had no blacksmith (1 Sam. 13:19); four smiths to cast down the horns (Zech. 1:20-1); the goldsmiths (Neh. 3:32); they hire a goldsmith to make an idol (Isa. 46:6); she gave the silver to a silversmith (Judg. 17:4); Demetrius the silversmith (Acts 19:24); Alexander the coppersmith (2 Tim. 4:14).

B3d Other manufacturers
Simon the tanner (Acts 9:43; 10:6, 32); Aquila, Priscilla and Paul were tentmakers (Acts 18:3); linen workers (1 Chr. 4:21); the workers in combed flax and the weavers of white cotton (Isa. 19:9); as a jeweller engraves signets (Exod. 28:11).

B4 Other occupations
SAILOR, see 270.
FARMER, see 370D1.

B4a Fisherman
The fishermen were washing their nets (Luke 5:2); Simon and Andrew were fishermen (Matt. 4:18; Mark 1:16); I will make you fishers of men (Matt. 4:19; Mark 1:17; Luke 5:10).

B4b Gardener
She thought Jesus was the gardener (John 20:15); the vinedresser (Luke 13:7); my Father is the vinedresser (John 15:1); be ashamed, O tillers of the soil, wail, O vinedressers (Joel 1:11).

B4c Perfumer
The work of a perfumer (Exod. 37:29); holy anointing oil blended as by the perfumer (Exod. 30:25); incense blended as by the perfumer (Exod. 30:35); the king will take your daughters as perfumers (1 Sam. 8:13).

687 Workshop
KITCHEN, see 383C.

688 Conduct
Oh, that Israel would walk in my ways! (Ps. 81:13); conduct yourselves in a manner worthy of the gospel (Phil. 1:27); walk worthy of God who calls you to his own kingdom and glory (1 Thess. 2:12); how one ought to conduct himself in the church (1 Tim. 3:15); whoever says he abides in him should walk as he walked (1 John 2:6); as you received Christ, so walk in him (Col. 2:6); we will walk in the name of the Lord our God for ever (Mic. 4:5); you yourselves know how I lived among you (Acts 20:18); my manner of life from my youth is known to all Jews (Acts 26:4); let each one walk as God has assigned and as God has called (1 Cor. 7:17); in these things you once walked (Col. 3:7); you learned from us how you ought to walk and please God (1 Thess. 4:1); you have followed my conduct (2 Tim. 3:10); let him show by his good conduct his deeds in the meekness of wisdom (Jas. 3:13); maintain good conduct among the Gentiles (1 Pet. 2:12); they may be won without a word by the conduct of their wives (1 Pet. 3:1); as they see your pure behaviour (1 Pet. 3:2); that those who revile your good conduct in Christ may be put to shame (1 Pet. 3:16).

689 Guiding
A Guiding in general
Bits in horses' mouths direct their whole bodies (Jas. 3:3); ships are guided by a small rudder (Jas. 3:4); the

integrity of the upright guides them (Prov. 11:3); when you walk about, the teaching will guide you (Prov. 6:22); where there is no guidance the people fall (Prov. 11:14); how can I understand unless someone guides me? (Acts 8:31); the gift of administrations (1 Cor. 12:28).

B God guiding
B1 God guides
You will guide me (Ps. 31:3); lead me in your truth (Ps. 25:5); the Lord will guide you continually (Isa. 58:11); with your counsel you will guide me (Ps. 73:24); I will lead the blind by a way they do not know (Isa. 42:16); he leads me beside still waters (Ps. 23:2); he will lead them to springs of water (Isa. 49:10); the Lord directs his steps (Prov. 16:9); however far away I go, your hand leads me (Ps. 139:10); let your light and truth lead me to your holy hill (Ps. 43:3); he leads me in the paths of righteousness (Ps. 23:3); do not lead us into temptation (Matt. 6:13).

B2 God has guided
God went before them to lead them in the way (Exod. 13:21); I led them with cords of love (Hos. 11:4); the Lord has guided me (Gen. 24:27, 48); you led your people (Isa. 63:14); you led them to your holy habitation (Exod. 15:13); the pillar of cloud to guide them (Neh. 9:12); the day I took them by the hand to lead them out of Egypt (Heb. 8:9); he led them through the deep as through the wilderness (Ps. 106:9).

B3 The Spirit guiding
Jesus was led by the Spirit into the wilderness (Matt. 4:1; Luke 4:1); the Spirit drove him out into the wilderness (Mark 1:12); all who are led by the Spirit of God are sons of God (Rom. 8:14); let your good Spirit lead me (Ps. 143:10); he will guide you into all truth (John 16:13); if you are led by the Spirit you are not under the law (Gal. 5:18).

C People guiding
He led the blind man out of the village (Mark 8:23); he calls his own sheep by name and leads them out (John 10:3); Cornelius was directed by a holy angel to send for you (Acts 10:22); those conducting Paul brought him as far as Athens (Acts 17:15).

D Inadequate guiding
There is none to guide her among the sons she has borne (Isa. 51:18); it is not in a man who walks to direct his own steps (Jer. 10:23); they are blind guides (Matt. 15:14); blind guides! (Matt. 23:16, 24); the blind leading the blind (Matt. 15:14; Luke 6:39).

690 Director
A Human guides
Skilled men of Zemer were your pilots (Ezek. 27:8); your sailors, pilots, caulkers and merchants fall into the sea (Ezek. 27:27); Judas was a guide to those who arrested Jesus (Acts 1:16); if you are sure you are a guide to the blind (Rom. 2:19); though you have many guides in Christ (1 Cor. 4:15).

B The law our guide
The law was our guide to lead us to Christ (Gal. 3:24); now faith has come we are no longer under a guide (Gal. 3:25).

691 Advice
A Need for advice
A wise man listens to advice (Prov. 12:15); what king goes to war without first taking counsel? (Luke 14:31); in many counsellors there is safety (Prov. 11:14); with many counsellors plans succeed (Prov. 15:22); in abundance of counsellors there is victory (Prov. 24:6).

B God's counsel
You guide me with your counsel (Ps. 73:24); I bless the Lord who counsels me (Ps. 16:7); I will counsel you with my eye upon you (Ps. 32:8); his name will be called wonderful counsellor (Isa. 9:6); he works all things according to the counsel of his will (Eph. 1:11); they spurned the counsel of the Most High (Ps. 107:11); they did not wait for his counsel (Ps. 106:13); they go down to Egypt without consulting me (Isa. 30:2).

C Advising God
Who has been counsellor to the Lord? (Isa. 40:13; Rom. 11:34).

D Man's counsel
Counsel will not perish from the wise (Jer. 18:18); 'ask advice at Abel' (2 Sam. 20:18); the counsel of Balaam (Num. 31:16); shall we follow Ahithophel's counsel? (2 Sam. 17:6); the counsel of Hushai (2 Sam. 17:11-14); Rehoboam sought counsel from the elders (1 Kgs. 12:6-8; 2 Chr. 10:6); Rehoboam sought counsel from the young men (1 Kgs. 12:8-9; 2 Chr. 10:8); let us take counsel together (Neh. 6:7); rulers take counsel against the Lord's anointed (Ps. 2:2); the Pharisees took counsel how to trap him in his talk (Matt. 22:15); the chief priests and elders took counsel (Matt. 27:1; 28:12); the Pharisees and Herodians took counsel how to destroy him (Mark 3:6).

E Counsellors
Artaxerxes had seven counsellors (Ezra 7:14); have we made you a royal counsellor? (2 Chr. 25:16); God makes counsellors go barefoot (Job 12:17); I will restore your counsellors as at the beginning (Isa. 1:26); Ahaziah's mother was his counsellor to do evil (2 Chr. 22:3-4); Ahithophel was a counsellor (2 Sam. 15:12; 1 Chr. 27:33).

F Failing counsel
Without counsel plans go wrong (Prov. 15:22); an old and foolish king who will no long take advice (Eccles. 4:13); take counsel together, but it will come to nought (Isa. 8:10); blessed is the man who does not walk in the counsel of the wicked (Ps. 1:1); how you have counselled one without wisdom! (Job 26:3); I did not consult with flesh and blood (Gal. 1:16); if I counsel you you will not listen to me (Jer. 38:15).

692 Council

A Councils of men
The council assembled (Mark 15:1; Luke 22:66; John 11:47; Acts 5:21; 22:30); Joseph of Arimathea was a member of the council (Mark 15:43; Luke 23:50); whoever says 'Raca' to his brother will be guilty before the sanhedrin (Matt. 5:22); they brought Stephen before the council (Acts 6:12); asking for Paul to be brought to the council (Acts 23:15, 20); Festus conferred with his council (Acts 25:12); they will deliver you up to the councils (Matt. 10:17; Mark 13:9).

B The Lord's council
Who has stood in the council of the Lord? (Jer. 23:18); if they had stood in my council (Jer. 23:22).

693 Precept

PROVERB, see 496A.

694 Skill

SKILLED PEOPLE, see 696.

695 Unskilfulness

Solomon was young and inexperienced (1 Chr. 22:5; 29:1); I do not know how to speak (Jer. 1:6); even if I am unskilled in speech (2 Cor. 11:6); everyone who lives only on milk is unskilled in the word of righteousness (Heb. 5:13).

696 Proficient person

A Skilled people in general
In all skilled people God has put skill (Exod. 31:6; 36:1, 2); the scriptures make the man of God proficient (2 Tim. 3:17); skilled women spun materials (Exod. 35:25); do you see a man skilled in his work? (Prov. 22:29); the Lord will take away the skilled craftsman (Isa. 3:3); I will give you into the hand of brutal men, skilled to destroy (Ezek. 21:31); they are skilled in evil (Jer. 4:22).

B Particular skilled people
Skilled people had to make the priests' garments (Exod. 28:3; 39:3); Bezalel was an expert craftsman (Exod. 31:2-5); Oholiab was a skilful worker (Exod. 38:23); God filled Bezalel and Oholiab with skill (Exod. 35:35); Huram-abi was a skilled man (2 Chr. 2:13); Hiram was skilled in working with bronze (1 Kgs. 7:14); 700 men could sling a stone at a hair and not miss (Judg. 20:16).

697 Bungler

FAILURE, see 728.

698 Cunning

The serpent was more crafty than any beast of the field (Gen. 3:1); the Gibeonites acted craftily (Josh. 9:4); when Herod saw he had been tricked by the wise men (Matt. 2:16); they plotted to arrest him by stealth (Matt. 26:4); he perceived their cunning (Luke 20:23); he catches the wise in their cunning (1 Cor. 3:19); we will not walk in cunning (2 Cor. 4:2); I was crafty and took you in by deceit (2 Cor. 12:16); by the craftiness of men in deceitful schemes (Eph. 4:14); stand against the wiles of the devil (Eph. 6:11).

699 Artlessness

SINGLE-HEARTED, see 44B.

700 Difficulty

IMPOSSIBLE, see 470.

A Hard tasks
They brought hard matters to Moses (Exod. 18:26); you have asked a hard thing (2 Kgs. 2:10); with difficulty they restrained the people from sacrificing to them (Acts 14:18); it is hard to explain because you are dull of hearing (Heb. 5:11); the chariots met difficulty (Exod. 14:25); we sailed slowly and with difficulty (Acts 27:7); in the last days there will be difficult times (2 Tim. 3:1).

B Hard to be saved
It is hard for a rich man to enter the kingdom (Matt. 19:23; Mark 10:23-4; Luke 18:24); easier for a camel to go through the eye of a needle (Luke 18:25); it is difficult for the righteous to be saved (1 Pet. 4:18); the gate is small and the way narrow that leads to life (Matt. 7:14).

701 Facility

Is anything too hard for the Lord? (Gen. 18:14); is anything too hard for me? (Jer. 32:27); nothing is too hard for you (Jer. 32:17); lighten the heavy yoke (1 Kgs. 12:4-10; 2 Chr. 10:4-10); my yoke is easy and my burden light (Matt. 11:30); this commandment is not too difficult for you (Deut. 30:11); The people of the land are bread for us (Num. 14:9); you thought it easy to go up and fight (Deut. 1:41).

702 Hindrance

A Hindering in general
A1 Do not hinder
Do not put a stumbling block before the blind (Lev. 19:14); determine not to put an obstacle or stumbling block in a brother's way (Rom. 14:13); it is not good to

do anything which makes your brother stumble (Rom. 14:21); if food makes my brother stumble I will never eat meat again (1 Cor. 8:13); we do not cause anyone to stumble (2 Cor. 6:3); take care your liberty does not become a stumbling block to the weak (1 Cor. 8:9); let the children come to me and do not hinder them (Matt. 19:14; Mark 10:14; Luke 18:16).

A2 Avoid being hindered
Watch out for those who cause divisions and hindrances (Rom. 16:17); let nothing hinder you from coming (Num. 22:16); so that the rain does not stop you (1 Kgs. 18:44); let us lay aside every hindrance (Heb. 12:1); if your hand or foot causes you to stumble, cut it off (Matt. 18:8); if your eye causes you to stumble, pluck it out (Matt. 18:9); who hindered you from obeying the truth? (Gal. 5:7); we do not cause a hindrance to the gospel (1 Cor. 9:12); give honour to your wife so that your prayers are not hindered (1 Pet. 3:7).

A3 Woe to hinderers
Woe to the world for stumbling blocks! (Matt. 18:7); woe to the one through whom stumbling blocks come (Luke 17:1); whoever causes one of these little ones to stumble (Matt. 18:6; Mark 9:42); they will extract from his kingdom all stumbling blocks (Matt. 13:41).

B Hindrance to God
Whatever God does, who can hinder him? (Job 11:10); you are a stumbling block to me (Matt. 16:23).

C Hindrance to people
C1 God hindering
The Lord has kept you back from honour (Num. 24:11); he has walled up my way (Job 19:8); he has blocked my way with hewn stones (Lam. 3:9); the Lord clogged their chariot wheels (Exod. 14:25); God ordained that Ahithophel's advice should be thwarted (2 Sam. 17:14); God had frustrated their plan (Neh. 4:15).

C2 Stumbled by Christ
Christ crucified was a stumbling block to the Jews (1 Cor. 1:23); if I preach circumcision the stumbling block of the cross is removed (Gal. 5:11); Israel stumbled over the stone of stumbling (Rom. 9:32-3); blessed is he who is not stumbled over me (Matt. 11:6; Luke 7:23); they stumble because they are disobedient (1 Pet. 2:8).

C3 Other hindrances
Fathers, do not provoke your children lest they become discouraged (Col. 3:21); you did not enter and you hindered those that did (Luke 11:52); who is stumbled and I do not burn with indignation? (2 Cor. 11:29); Balaam taught Balak to put a stumbling block before the Israelites (Rev. 2:14); Paul had been hindered from coming to Rome (Rom. 1:13); I have often been hindered from coming to you (Rom. 15:22); the Jews hinder us from speaking to the Gentiles (1 Thess. 2:16); Satan hindered us (1 Thess. 2:18).

703 Aid
A God helping
A1 God, help!
Help, Lord! (Ps. 12:1); help me, O Lord my God! (Ps. 109:26); Lord, help me! (Matt. 15:25); have pity on us and help us (Mark 9:22); give us help against the enemy (Ps. 60:11; 108:12); make haste to help me! (Ps. 38:22); O my help, hasten to my aid! (Ps. 22:19); may he send you help from the sanctuary (Ps. 20:2).

A2 God helps
Eliezer, God was my help (Exod. 18:4); God is my helper (Ps. 54:4); the Lord is my helper (Heb. 13:6); my help is from the Lord (Ps. 121:2); with us is the Lord to help us (2 Chr. 32:8); you are my help and my deliverer

(Ps. 40:17; 70:5); your help made me great (2 Sam. 22:36; Ps. 18:35); the Lord who will help you (Isa. 44:2); I will again praise him, my help (Ps. 33:20; 42:5; 115:9-11); a very present help in trouble (Ps. 46:1); our help is in the name of the Lord (Ps. 124:8); God will help her at break of day (Ps. 46:5); Ebenezer, this far has the Lord helped us (1 Sam. 7:12); I have had the help which comes from God (Acts 26:22); on the day of salvation I helped you (2 Cor. 6:2); the earth helped the woman by opening its mouth and swallowing the river (Rev. 12:16).

A3 People helped by God
The Lord helped David wherever he went (2 Sam. 8:6, 14; 1 Chr. 18:6, 13); Uzziah was marvellously helped (2 Chr. 26:15); he has helped his servant Israel (Luke 1:54); the wall had been built with the help of God (Neh. 6:16); Jehoshaphat cried out and the Lord helped him (2 Chr. 18:31).

A4 Christ the helper
Christ is able to help those who are tempted (Heb. 2:18); we have an advocate with the Father, Jesus Christ the righteous (1 John 2:1).

A5 The Spirit, the helper
The Father will give you another helper (John 14:16); the helper, the Holy Spirit, whom the Father will send (John 14:26); the helper whom I will send from the Father (John 15:26); the Spirit helps us in our weakness (Rom. 8:26); I will send the helper to you (John 16:7).

B People helping
B1 People helping in general
I will make a helper suitable for man (Gen. 2:18); I hope to be helped on my way by you (Rom. 15:24); you helping us by your prayers (2 Cor. 1:11); help the weak (1 Thess. 5:14); the gift of helps (1 Cor. 12:28); a believer should assist a relative who is a widow (1 Tim. 5:16); the disciples wanted to help the brethren in Judea (Acts 11:29); help Phoebe, for she has helped many (Rom. 16:2); help these women (Phil. 4:3); we ought to help such people (3 John 8); come to Macedonia and help us (Acts 16:9); should you help the wicked? (2 Chr. 19:2).

B2 Individuals helping
Michael, one of the chief princes, came to help me (Dan. 10:13); they had John [Mark] to assist them (Acts 13:5); Apollos greatly helped those who through grace had believed (Acts 18:27); Aaron and Hur supported Moses' hands (Exod. 17:12); tell my sister to help me (Luke 10:40).

C No help
No animal was a helper suitable for man (Gen. 2:20); if the Lord does not help, how can I? (2 Kgs. 6:27); that of mine by which you might have been helped is a gift [to God] (Matt. 15:5); they will not move the loads with so much as a finger (Matt. 23:4; Luke 11:46); I have no one to put me in the pool when the water is stirred up (John 5:7); how you have helped him who is weak! (Job 26:2).

704 Opposition
A God opposing
God opposes the proud (Jas. 4:6); God opposes the proud but gives grace to the humble (1 Pet. 5:5); the hand of the Lord was against Israel (Judg. 2:15); the hand of the Lord was against the Philistines (1 Sam. 7:13); the face of the Lord is against those who do evil (Ps. 34:16; 1 Pet. 3:12); I have set my face against Jerusalem (Jer. 21:10; Ezek. 15:7); I will set my face against the idolater (Ezek. 14:8); I am against you, destroying mountain (Jer. 51:25); is the law against the promises of God? (Gal. 3:21); the flesh and the Spirit are in opposition (Gal. 5:17).

B Opposing God

You may be fighting against God (Acts 5:39); he who opposes a ruler opposes God (Rom. 13:2); the wicked man acts in opposition to God (Job 15:25-6); the mind set on the flesh is hostile to God (Rom. 8:7); who was I that I could withstand God? (Acts 11:17); once you were hostile to God (Col. 1:21).

C Opposing Christ

A sign that is spoken against (Luke 2:34); rulers set themselves against the Lord and his anointed (Ps. 2:2; Acts 4:26); he who is not with me is against me (Matt. 12:30; Luke 11:23); I thought I should oppose the name of Jesus (Acts 26:9); consider him who endured such hostility from sinful men (Heb. 12:3); the Pharisees were very hostile (Luke 11:53).

D Opposing people

The well was called Sitnah – opposition (Gen. 26:21); we told you the gospel amid much opposition (1 Thess. 2:2); division will be caused within families (Matt. 10:35; Luke 12:52-3); whoever is not against you is for you (Luke 9:50); they understood that he had spoken this parable against them (Luke 20:19); everyone who makes himself a king sets himself against Caesar (John 19:12); the Lord's slave must in gentleness correct those who oppose him (2 Tim. 2:25); if God be for us, who is against us? (Rom. 8:31); I will not be afraid of tens of thousands who set themselves against me (Ps. 3:6); all these things are against me (Gen. 42:36); Elymas the sorcerer opposed them (Acts 13:8); as Jannes and Jambres opposed Moses, so these people oppose the truth (2 Tim. 3:8); Alexander strongly opposed our teaching (2 Tim. 4:15); the Jews are hostile to all men (1 Thess. 2:15); Paul opposed Peter to his face (Gal. 2:11).

705 Opponent

A God as enemy

The Lord has become your enemy (1 Sam. 28:16); God turned and became their enemy (Isa. 63:10); God counts me as an enemy (Job 19:11; 33:10); God has bent his bow like an enemy (Lam. 2:4-5); I will be an enemy to your enemies (Exod. 23:22); the angel of the Lord stood in the road as Balaam's adversary (Num. 22:22, 32).

B Enemies of God

Many live as enemies of the cross of Christ (Phil. 3:18); while we were enemies to God we were reconciled (Rom. 5:10); whoever is a friend of the world is an enemy of God (Jas. 4:4); he must reign until all his enemies are put under his feet (1 Cor. 15:25); the last enemy to be destroyed is death (1 Cor. 15:26); sit at my right hand till I make your enemies your footstool (Heb. 1:13); many antichrists have appeared (1 John 2:18); the man of lawlessness is the opposer (2 Thess. 2:4); a door for service has opened and there are many adversaries (1 Cor. 16:9); they are enemies of God for your sake (Rom. 11:28); you enemy of all righteousness! (Acts 13:10); his enemy sowed tares (Matt. 13:25); the enemy is the devil (Matt. 13:39).

C Enemies of people

C1 Enemies in general

How my enemies have increased! (Ps. 3:1); the enemies of Judah heard of the rebuilding of the temple (Ezra 4:1); lead me in your righteousness because of my enemies (Ps. 5:8); do not rejoice over me, O my enemy (Mic. 7:8); he that is not against us is for us (Mark 9:40); a man's enemies will be from his own family (Mic. 7:6; Matt. 10:36); have you found me, my enemy? (1 Kgs. 21:20); have I become your enemy by telling you the truth? (Gal. 4:16).

C2 Particular enemies

Saul was David's enemy (1 Sam. 18:29); Haman the enemy of the Jews (Esther 3:10; 8:1; 9:10, 24); your adversary the devil is like a roaring lion (1 Pet. 5:8).

C3 Overcoming enemies

Your seed will possess the gate of their enemies (Gen. 22:17); I would quickly subdue their enemies (Ps. 81:14); sit at my right hand till I make your enemies your footstool (Mark 12:36; Acts 2:34-5); that we, being delivered from the hand of our enemies (Luke 1:74); a mouth and wisdom which your adversaries cannot resist or refute (Luke 21:15); you prepare a table in the presence of my enemies (Ps. 23:5); the Jews rid themselves of their enemies (Esther 9:22); he delivered me from my enemies (2 Sam. 22:18; Ps. 18:17); deliverance from our enemies (Luke 1:71).

C4 Attitudes to enemies

Hate your enemy (Matt. 5:43); love your enemies (Matt. 5:44; Luke 6:27, 35); if your enemy's animal wanders, take it back (Exod. 23:4); if your enemy's donkey is lying under its burden, help him (Exod. 23:5); if your enemy is hungry, feed him (Prov. 25:21; Rom. 12:20); do not regard him as an enemy (2 Thess. 3:15); do not rejoice when your enemy falls (Prov. 24:17).

706 Cooperation

A God for us

God is for me (Ps. 56:9); the Lord is for me (Ps. 118:6, 7); if it had not been the Lord who was on our side (Ps. 124:1, 2); if God be for us, who can be against us? (Rom. 8:31).

B For God

Whoever is for the Lord (Exod. 32:26); working together with him (2 Cor. 6:1).

C For people

You will be in league with the stones of the field (Job 5:23); we are with you, David (1 Chr. 12:18); who is on my side? (2 Kgs. 9:32); let us build with you (Ezra 4:2); serving the Lord shoulder to shoulder (Zeph. 3:9); he who is not with me is against me (Luke 11:23); whoever is not against us is for us (Mark 9:40); whoever is not against you is for you (Luke 9:50); do not join hands with the wicked in testimony (Exod. 23:1); are you for us or for our enemies? (Josh. 5:13).

707 Co-worker

We are the fellow-workers of God (1 Cor. 3:9); we would not have been partners with our fathers in killing the prophets (Matt. 23:30); if you consider me as your partner (Philem. 17); you were partners with those so treated (Heb. 10:33); we ought to help such people, to be fellow-workers in the truth (3 John 8).

708 Party

A Factions

Factions are deeds of the flesh (Gal. 5:20).

B Pharisees and Sadducees

B1 Pharisees and Sadducees combined

Pharisees and Sadducees coming for baptism (Matt. 3:7); the Council was part Sadducees, part Pharisees (Acts 23:6); a dissension arose between the Pharisees and Sadducees (Acts 23:7); the chief priests and Pharisees understood he meant them (Matt. 21:45); beware of the leaven [teaching] of the Pharisees and Sadducees (Matt. 16:6, 11-12).

B2 Pharisees

B2a Characteristics of Pharisees

The Pharisees acknowledge resurrection, angels and spirits (Acts 23:8); the scribes and Pharisees sit on Moses' seat (Matt. 23:2); the Pharisees fast (Matt. 9:14;

Mark 2:18); the Pharisees were lovers of money (Luke 16:14); beware of the leaven of the Pharisees, hypocrisy (Luke 12:1); unless your righteousness exceeds that of the scribes and Pharisees (Matt. 5:20); two men went up into the temple to pray, a Pharisee and a tax collector (Luke 18:10-12); the Pharisees and lawyers rejected God's purpose for them (Luke 7:30).

B2b Pharisees concerned about Christ

Pharisees asked the disciples why he ate with tax collectors and sinners (Matt. 9:11; Mark 2:16; Luke 15:2); the Pharisees asked when the kingdom of God was coming (Luke 17:20); the Pharisees were divided about Jesus (John 9:16); the Pharisees accused the disciples over the sabbath (Matt. 12:2; Mark 2:24; Luke 6:2); scribes and Pharisees watched to see whether he would heal on the sabbath (Luke 6:7); Pharisees and scribes came to ask about hand-washing (Matt. 15:1-2); Pharisees tested him about divorce (Matt. 19:3; Mark 10:2); scribes and Pharisees wanted to see a sign (Matt. 12:38; Mark 8:11).

B2c Pharisees in opposition to Christ

The Pharisees plotted how to destroy Jesus (Matt. 12:14); the Pharisees wanted to trap him in his words (Matt. 22:15; Mark 12:13); the Pharisees tested him by asking for a sign (Mark 8:11); the Pharisees took counsel with the Herodians (Mark 3:6); the chief priests and Pharisees sent officers to seize him (John 7:32); the chief priests and Pharisees convened the council (John 11:47); woe to you, scribes and Pharisees, hypocrites! (Matt. 23:13-29); the Pharisees said he cast out demons by the prince of demons (Matt. 9:34; 12:24); the Pharisees were offended (Matt. 15:12); you blind Pharisee! (Matt. 23:26).

B2d Particular Pharisees

A Pharisee called Nicodemus (John 3:1); a Pharisee called Gamaliel (Acts 5:34); a Pharisee invited him to a meal (Luke 7:36; 11:37; 14:1); I am a Pharisee, a son of Pharisees (Acts 23:6); I lived as a Pharisee, the strictest party of our religion (Acts 26:5); as to the law, a Pharisee (Phil. 3:5); some of the party of the Pharisees who believed (Acts 15:5); some of the scribes of the Pharisees found nothing wrong in Paul (Acts 23:9).

B3 Sadducees

The Sadducees say there is no resurrection (Matt. 22:23; Mark 12:18; Luke 20:27); no resurrection nor an angel nor a spirit (Acts 23:8); the priests and Sadducees came on them (Acts 4:1); the high priest rose up and his associates, the Sadducees (Acts 5:17).

C Christians

We have found this man to be a ringleader of the sect of the Nazarenes (Acts 24:5); the Way, which they call a sect (Acts 24:14); this sect is everywhere spoken against (Acts 28:22); suffering as a Christian (1 Pet. 4:16); in Antioch the disciples were first called Christians (Acts 11:26); you want to make me a Christian (Acts 26:28).

D Other factions

4000 men of the Assassins (Acts 21:38); those of the circumcision (Titus 1:10); the circumcision party – the concision (Gal. 2:12; Phil. 3:2-3); fellow-workers from the circumcision (Col. 4:11); they sent Pharisees and Herodians to entrap him in his talk (Mark 12:13); they sent their disciples along with the Herodians (Matt. 22:16); the Pharisees took counsel with the Herodians (Mark 3:6); Epicurean and Stoic philosophers (Acts 17:18); Simon the Zealot (Matt. 10:4; Luke 6:15; Acts 1:13).

709 Dissension

A About quarrels

If men quarrel and one strikes the other (Exod. 21:18); disputes and dissensions are deeds of the flesh (Gal.

5:20); foolish controversies produce quarrels (2 Tim. 2:23); out of controversies arises strife (1 Tim. 6:4); meddling in a quarrel is like taking a passing dog by the ears (Prov. 26:17); what causes conflicts among you? (Jas. 4:1); pressing anger produces strife (Prov. 30:33); hatred stirs up strife (Prov. 10:12); filled with strife (Rom. 1:29); the wicked man spreads strife (Prov. 6:14); a greedy man stirs up strife (Prov. 28:25); the Lord hates those who spread strife among brothers (Prov. 6:19); better a dry morsel with quiet than feasting with strife (Prov. 17:1).

B Avoid quarrels

Stop the quarrel before it breaks out (Prov. 17:14); avoid disputes about the law (Titus 3:9); avoid disputes about words (1 Tim. 6:4); a bishop [overseer] must not be quarrelsome (1 Tim. 3:3); warn them not to dispute about words (2 Tim. 2:14); the Lord's slave must not be quarrelsome (2 Tim. 2:24); watch those who cause dissensions (Rom. 16:17); not in strife or jealousy (Rom. 13:13); do all things without grumblings or disputings (Phil. 2:14); slaves are not to be argumentative (Titus 2:9); avoid quarrelling (Titus 3:2); avoid stupid controversies (Titus 3:9).

C People quarrelling

C1 Cases of quarrelling

Abraham's herdsmen quarrelled with Lot's (Gen. 13:7); the herdsmen of Gerar quarrelled with Isaac's herdsmen (Gen. 26:20, 21); those of the circumcision took issue with Peter (Acts 11:2); Michael the archangel disputed with the devil (Jude 9); Meribah – quarrel (Exod. 17:7); an argument arose as to who was the greatest (Luke 9:46; 22:24); Paul and Barnabas had great dissension with the circumcisers (Acts 15:2); if anyone is contentious, we have no other practice (1 Cor. 11:16); the Pharisees argued with Jesus (Mark 8:11); scribes arguing with his disciples (Mark 9:14); some argued with Stephen (Acts 6:9); a dissension arose between the Pharisees and Sadducees (Acts 23:7); I fear there may be quarrelling (2 Cor. 12:20); I hear there are quarrels among you (1 Cor. 1:11).

C2 Quarrelsome wives

Rather than live with a quarrelsome wife it is better to live on a housetop (Prov. 21:9; 25:24); better to live in a desert (Prov. 21:19); a quarrelsome wife is like constant dripping on a day of rain (Prov. 27:15).

710 Concord

A Agreeing with God

David was a man after God's own heart (1 Sam. 13:14; Acts 13:22); I will give you shepherds after my own heart (Jer. 3:15).

B Agreeing with one another

All Israel were of one mind to make David king (1 Chr. 12:38); be likeminded (2 Cor. 13:11; Phil. 2:2); live in harmony (1 Pet. 3:8); I exhort you all to agree with one another (1 Cor. 1:10); may God grant you to be of the same mind (Rom. 15:5); I urge Euodia and Syntyche to agree in the Lord (Phil. 4:2); those who believed were of one heart and soul (Acts 4:32); be of the same mind toward one another (Rom. 12:16); with one mind striving side by side for the faith of the gospel (Phil. 1:27); be of one mind (Phil. 2:2); lovingkindness and truth have met, justice and peace have kissed (Ps. 85:10).

C Agreeing for evil

They are of one mind (Rev. 17:17); why have you agreed together to put the Spirit of the Lord to the test? (Acts 5:9); the Jews with one accord rose up against Paul (Acts 18:12); these are of one mind (Rev. 17:13).

711 Defiance

Goliath defied the armies of Israel (1 Sam. 17:10); you have exalted yourself against the Lord of heaven (Dan. 5:23); who has defied God with impunity? (Job 9:4).

712 Attack

FIGHT, see 716.

A The nations attacked

How to conduct a siege (Deut. 20:19-20); a small city besieged and saved by wisdom (Eccles. 9:14-15); draw water for the siege! (Nahum 3:14); through God I can attack a troop (2 Sam. 22:30; Ps. 18:29); attack the Midianites (Num. 25:17); I give my daughter to the man who attacks Kiriath-sepher (Josh. 15:16; Judg. 1:12); Jonathan attacked the Philistines (1 Sam. 13:3-4); attack the Philistines (1 Sam. 23:2); besieging Gibbethon of the Philistines (1 Kgs. 15:27; 16:15); Joab besieged Rabbah of the Ammonites (2 Sam. 11:1; 12:26-9); the kings of Israel and Judah attacked Ramoth-gilead (1 Kgs. 22:29; 2 Chr. 18:2-3); siege walls against Tyre (Ezek. 26:8); the king of the north will besiege a fortified city (Dan. 11:15).

B Nations attacking Israel

Gad, raiders will raid him (Gen. 49:19); the archers attacked Joseph (Gen. 49:23); the Canaanites will attack me (Gen. 34:30); Nahash besieged Jabesh-gilead (1 Sam. 11:1); Benhadad attacked Israel (1 Kgs. 15:20); Shalmaneser besieged Samaria (2 Kgs. 18:9); Dothan was surrounded (2 Kgs. 6:14); Sennacherib was besieging Lachish (2 Chr. 32:9); the Amalekites attacked the Israelites (Exod. 17:8); the king of Arad attacked the Israelites (Num. 21:1); Sennacherib attacked the cities of Judah (2 Kgs. 18:13; Isa. 36:1); the nations have invaded your inheritance (Ps. 79:1); I am bringing a nation from afar against you (Jer. 5:15); a great army will advance against my people Israel (Ezek. 38:8-9).

C Attacks on Jerusalem

C1 Attacks on Jerusalem foretold

Prophecies concerning the siege of Jerusalem (Isa. 29:1-3; Jer. 4:16; 6:4-6; Ezek. 4:2-3; Luke 21:20); the kingdoms of the north will set their thrones round Jerusalem (Jer. 1:15); the omens are for besieging Jerusalem (Ezek. 21:22); I will gather all nations against Jerusalem to battle (Zech. 14:2); when Jerusalem is besieged, so will Judah be (Zech. 12:2).

C2 Actual attacks on Jerusalem

Shishak king of Egypt attacked Jerusalem (1 Kgs. 14:25; 2 Chr. 12:2); the Lord sent Rezin king of Aram and Pekah king of Israel against Jerusalem (2 Kgs. 15:37); Rezin and Pekah besieged Jerusalem (2 Kgs. 16:5); Assyria besieging Jerusalem (2 Kgs. 18:17; 2 Chr. 32:2); the king of Babylon besieged Jerusalem (2 Kgs. 24:10-11; 25:1-2; Jer. 32:2; 39:1; 52:4-5; Ezek. 24:2; Dan. 1:1); Nebuchadnezzar and his armies were fighting Jerusalem (Jer. 34:1); the army of the king of Babylon was fighting against Jerusalem (Jer. 34:7).

D Attacked by evil

Though a host camp against me (Ps. 27:3); no man will attack you to harm you (Acts 18:10).

713 Defence

A Defending

The Lord will plead the case of the poor (Prov. 22:23; 23:11); he will plead their cause (Jer. 50:34); I will defend Jerusalem (Isa. 37:35; 38:6); the three mighty men defended the plot of barley (1 Chr. 11:14); defend the rights of the poor and needy (Prov. 31:9); do not prepare beforehand how to defend yourselves (Luke 21:14); Paul stretched out his hand and made his defence (Acts 26:1); this is my defence to those who

would question me (1 Cor. 9:3); have you been thinking we have been defending ourselves? (2 Cor. 12:19); I am here for the defence of the gospel (Phil. 1:16); at my first defence everyone deserted me (2 Tim. 4:16).

B Defensive armour

B1 Material armour

Let not him who puts on his armour boast like him who takes it off (1 Kgs. 20:11); Goliath wore bronze scale armour weighing 5000 shekels (1 Sam. 17:5-6); Saul's armour was too heavy for David (1 Sam. 17:38-9); Jonathan gave David his armour (1 Sam. 18:4); when a strong man, fully armed, guards his own home (Luke 11:21-2); their breastplates were like breastplates of iron (Rev. 9:9); breastplates the colour of fire and jacinth and brimstone (Rev. 9:17).

B2 Spiritual armour

Put on the armour of light (Rom. 13:12); put on the full armour of God (Eph. 6:11-17); put on the breastplate of faith and love (1 Thess. 5:8); righteousness as a breastplate (Isa. 59:17); take the helmet of salvation (Eph. 6:17); as a helmet the hope of salvation (1 Thess. 5:8); the breastplate of righteousness (Eph. 6:14).

SHIELDS, see 662C1.

C Fortified cities

Are the cities open or fortified? (Num. 13:19); the cities are fortified and very large (Num. 13:28; Deut. 1:28); cities fortified to heaven (Deut. 9:1); the high and fortified walls in which you trusted (Deut. 28:52); our little ones will live in the fortified cities (Num. 32:17); let us go into the fortified cities (Jer. 4:5; 8:14); though Babylon fortify her strong height (Jer. 51:53); the ruined cities are fortified and inhabited (Ezek. 36:35); Judah has multiplied fortified cities (Hos. 8:14).

714 Retaliation

AVENGING, see 910.

715 Resistance

A Resisting

Resist the devil and he will flee from you (Jas. 4:7); resist the devil, firm in your faith (1 Pet. 5:9); you have not yet resisted to blood, striving against sin (Heb. 12:4); he who resists the authorities resists what God has appointed (Rom. 13:2); you always resist the Holy Spirit (Acts 7:51).

B Not resisting

Do not resist one who is evil (Matt. 5:39); the righteous man does not resist (Jas. 5:6); a mouth and wisdom which your adversaries cannot resist or refute (Luke 21:15); they could not stand before their enemies (Josh. 7:12-13; Judg. 2:14).

716 Contention

WAR, see 718.

A God fighting

A1 God fighting people

The Lord will fight against you (Jer. 21:5); I will contend with you (Jer. 2:9); God fought against them (Isa. 63:10); my spirit will not strive with man for ever (Gen. 6:3); a man wrestled with Jacob (Gen. 32:24).

A2 God fighting for people

The Lord fights for you (Exod. 14:14; Deut. 1:30; Josh. 23:3, 10); the Lord fights our battles (2 Chr. 32:8); our God fights for us (Neh. 4:20); the battle is the Lord's (1 Sam. 17:47); the battle is not yours but God's (2 Chr. 20:15); Lord, fight against those who fight me (Ps. 35:1); you do not go out with our armies (Ps. 60:10).

B Fighting God

The wicked charges at God in full armour (Job 15:26); Israel, you have striven with God and men (Gen.

32:28); he strove with God (Hos. 12:3-4); do not fight against the Lord (2 Chr. 13:12).

C Fighting people

C1 Fighting enemies
You are fighting the Lord's battles (1 Sam. 25:28); fight the Lord's battles (1 Sam. 18:17); fighting without and fear within (2 Cor. 7:5); fight for your families (Neh. 4:14).

C2 Fighting one another
You must not fight your brethren (1 Kgs. 12:24); the children struggled within her (Gen. 25:22); two Hebrews fighting (Exod. 2:13); Moses found them fighting one another (Acts 7:26); Abner and Joab's young men fought (2 Sam. 2:16-17); the citizens of Shechem fought Abimelech (Judg. 9:39); the Gileadites fought the men of Ephraim (Judg. 12:4); the men of Israel fought the Benjaminites (Judg. 20:20); do not fight your brothers (2 Chr. 11:4); Joash king of Israel fought Amaziah king of Judah (2 Kgs. 13:12; 14:15); I set every one against his neighbour (Zech. 8:10); since there is jealousy and strife among you, are you not of the flesh? (1 Cor. 3:3); strife is a deed of the flesh (Gal. 5:20); some preach Christ from envy and strife (Phil. 1:15); you are envious and cannot obtain, so you fight (Jas. 4:2).

D Fighting for the faith
Shall we strike with the sword? (Luke 22:49); if my kingdom were of this world, my servants would be fighting (John 18:36); contend for the faith (Phil. 1:27; Jude 3); fight the good fight (1 Tim. 1:18); fight the good fight of faith (1 Tim. 6:12); I have fought the good fight (2 Tim. 4:7).

E Competitive sports
Let us run the race before us (Heb. 12:1); in a race only one receives the prize (1 Cor. 9:24); an athlete must compete according to the rules (2 Tim. 2:5); the race is not to the swift (Eccles. 9:11); I have finished the race (2 Tim. 4:7); a man wrestled with Jacob (Gen. 32:24, 25); Jacob wrestled with the angel and prevailed (Hos. 12:4); we do not wrestle against flesh and blood (Eph. 6:12).

717 Peace

MAKING PEACE, see 719.

A Peace in general
There is a time for peace (Eccles. 3:8); all her paths are peace (Prov. 3:17); love truth and peace (Zech. 8:19); there will be glory and honour and peace to everyone who does good (Rom. 2:10).

B God and peace

B1 God of peace
The Lord is Peace (Judg. 6:24); God is not a God of disorder but of peace (1 Cor. 14:33); the God of peace be with you all (Rom. 15:33); the God of peace (Rom. 16:20; 2 Cor. 13:11; Phil. 4:9; Heb. 13:20); the Lord of peace (2 Thess. 3:16); his name will be Prince of Peace (Isa. 9:6).

B2 Peace with God
The good news of peace (Acts 10:36); be at peace with God (Job 22:21); we have peace with God (Rom. 5:1); he is our peace (Eph. 2:14); peace in heaven (Luke 19:38); on earth, peace among men with whom he is pleased (Luke 2:14); the feet of him who proclaims peace (Nahum 1:15); peace to those far and near (Isa. 57:19); he preached peace to those far away and to those near (Eph. 2:17); feet shod with the preparation of the gospel of peace (Eph. 6:15).

B3 Peace of God
The Lord will bless his people with peace (Ps. 29:11); may the Lord of peace give you peace (2 Thess. 3:16); the peace of God (Phil. 4:7); the Lord give you peace

(Num. 6:26); I will extend peace to her like a river (Isa. 66:12); let the peace of God rule in your hearts (Col. 3:15); great peace have they who love your law (Ps. 119:165); the mind set on the Spirit is life and peace (Rom. 8:6); the kingdom of God is peace in the Holy Spirit (Rom. 14:17); the fruit of the Spirit is peace (Gal. 5:22); may God fill you with joy and peace in believing (Rom. 15:13); the effect of righteousness will be peace (Isa. 32:17-18); to guide our feet into the way of peace (Luke 1:79); you will keep in perfect peace him who trusts in you (Isa. 26:3).

C Peace among people

C1 Time of peace
The land had rest from war (Josh. 11:23; 14:15); the land had peace (Judg. 3:11, 30; 5:31; 8:28; 2 Chr. 14:1); in this place I will give peace (Hag. 2:9); her warfare has ended (Isa. 40:2); Solomon had peace on all sides (1 Kgs. 4:24; 5:4); there was no more war (2 Chr. 15:19); the kingdom was at peace (2 Chr. 20:30); there will be peace in my lifetime (2 Kgs. 20:19; Isa. 39:8); great will be the peace of your children (Isa. 54:13); the church had peace (Acts 9:31); we have patrolled the earth and it is all peaceful and quiet (Zech. 1:11).

C2 Men of peace
The man of peace will have a posterity (Ps. 37:37); Solomon would be a man of peace (1 Chr. 22:9); Melchizedek was king of peace (Heb. 7:2); discipline yields the peaceful fruit of righteousness (Heb. 12:11); if a son of peace is there (Luke 10:6).

C3 Peace to you
Peace be on Israel (Ps. 125:5; 128:6); peace to you (3 John 14); peace be with you (Dan. 10:19; John 20:19, 21, 26); peace to all who are in Christ (1 Pet. 5:14); peace I leave with you, my peace I give you (John 14:27); I have said this to you that in me you may have peace (John 16:33); peace and mercy be on all who walk by this rule (Gal. 6:16); go in peace and be healed of your disease (Mark 5:34); go in peace, be warmed and filled! (Jas. 2:16).

C4 Going in peace
We have sent you away in peace (Gen. 26:29); let me now depart in peace, according to your word (Luke 2:29); go in peace (Luke 8:48); send Timothy on his way in peace (1 Cor. 16:11); you will go out with joy and be led forth with peace (Isa. 55:12).

C5 Seek peace
Seek peace and pursue it (Ps. 34:14); as far as possible, be at peace with all men (Rom. 12:18); preserving the unity of the Spirit in the bond of peace (Eph. 4:3); be at peace with one another (Mark 9:50; 1 Thess. 5:13); live in peace and the God of love and peace will be with you (2 Cor. 13:11); God has called us to peace (1 Cor. 7:15); be diligent to be found by him in peace (2 Pet. 3:14); pursue peace (2 Tim. 2:22; Heb. 12:14); seek peace and pursue it (1 Pet. 3:11); the wisdom from above is peaceable (Jas. 3:17); pray for kings, that we may have a quiet life (1 Tim. 2:2); pray for the peace of Jerusalem (Ps. 122:6).

D No peace
Joseph's brothers could not speak to him peaceably (Gen. 37:4); they do not speak peace (Ps. 35:20); they speak peace while evil is in their hearts (Ps. 28:3); there is no peace for the wicked (Isa. 48:22; 57:21); they have not known the way of peace (Isa. 59:8; Rom. 3:17); I have lived too long among those who hate peace (Ps. 120:6); they seek peace but there will be none (Ezek. 7:25); if you only knew the things that make for peace! (Luke 19:42); if the house is not worthy, let your peace return to you (Matt. 10:13); men will be implacable (2 Tim. 3:3); the prophets prophesy peace falsely (Jer. 14:13); 'peace', when there is no peace (Jer. 6:14; 8:11; Ezek. 13:10, 16); when a prophet prophesies peace and it

comes to pass you will know (Jer. 28:9); when they say 'Peace and security' destruction will come (1 Thess. 5:3); I did not come to bring peace, but a sword (Matt. 10:34); do you think I came to give peace on earth? No, rather, division (Luke 12:51).

718 War

KILLED BY THE SWORD, see 362C3.

FIGHTING, see 716.

A Concerning war
There is a time for war (Eccles. 3:8); when you go to war, sound the trumpets (Num. 10:9); though war rise against me I will be confident (Ps. 27:3); the war was of God (1 Chr. 5:22); evil men continually stir up wars (Ps. 140:2); when the people see war they might change their minds (Exod. 13:17); lest in war they join our enemies (Exod. 1:10); when you go to war, do not be afraid (Deut. 20:1); when you hear of wars, do not be afraid (Matt. 24:6; Mark 13:7; Luke 21:9); when your people go to war and they pray (1 Kgs. 8:44; 2 Chr. 6:34); we do not wage war according to the flesh (2 Cor. 10:3); there is no discharge in the war [against death] (Eccles. 8:8); I find another principle in my limbs, warring against the principle of my mind (Rom. 7:23); abstain from fleshly passions which war against the soul (1 Pet. 2:11).

B Ready for war
What king goes to war without first considering? (Luke 14:31); in the spring kings go to war but David did not (2 Sam. 11:1; 1 Chr. 20:1); shall your brethren go to war and you sit here? (Num. 32:6); prepare for war! (Joel 3:9); he trains my hands for war (Ps. 144:1); I am for peace, but they are for war (Ps. 120:7); David was a man of warfare (2 Sam. 17:8); so could not build the temple (1 Kgs. 5:3; 1 Chr. 28:3); war a good warfare (1 Tim. 1:18); they became mighty in war (Heb. 11:34); I will make war against them with the sword of my mouth (Rev. 2:16); who is able to wage war on the beast? (Rev. 13:4); if the trumpet sound an unclear sound, who will prepare for battle? (1 Cor. 14:8); the horse is made ready for the day of battle (Prov. 21:31).

C Various wars
C1 Wars in general
The book of the Wars of the Lord (Num. 21:14); from now on you will have wars (2 Chr. 16:9); nation will rise against nation (Matt. 24:7; Luke 21:10); the prophets have prophesied war, calamity and pestilence (Jer. 28:8); the horn waged war against the saints (Dan. 7:21); the beast which comes out of the abyss will make war on the witnesses (Rev. 11:7); the beast was allowed to wage war against the saints (Rev. 13:7); gathering the kings of the world for war on the great day of God (Rev. 16:14); there was war in heaven (Rev. 12:7); they waged war against the rider and his army (Rev. 19:19); they will make war on the Lamb (Rev. 17:14); in righteousness he wages war (Rev. 19:11).

C2 Specific wars
Four kings went to war against five (Gen. 14:1-9); Og king of Bashan went to battle against Israel (Num. 21:33; Deut. 3:1); the Canaanites made war on Israel (Josh. 9:2); Moab and Ammon made war on Jehoshaphat (2 Chr. 20:1); Aram warred against Israel (2 Kgs. 6:8); Rezin of Aram and Pekah of Israel made war on Jerusalem (2 Kgs. 16:5); war against the Philistines (1 Sam. 14:52; 28:1; 2 Sam. 21:18; 1 Chr. 20:4; 2 Chr. 26:6); Ahaziah and Joram made war against Hazael (2 Kgs. 8:28; 2 Chr. 22:5); the Reubenites made war on the Hagrites (1 Chr. 5:10); Neco making war on Carchemish (2 Chr. 35:20); the kings gathered for battle at Armageddon (Rev. 16:16).

ATTACK, see 712.

C3 Civil war
Civil war in Israel (Josh. 22:12); Benjamin went to battle against Israel (Judg. 20:14); war between the houses of Saul and David (2 Sam. 3:1, 6); Rehoboam was about to make war with Israel (1 Kgs. 12:21; 2 Chr. 11:1); war between Rehoboam and Jeroboam (1 Kgs. 14:30; 15:6; 2 Chr. 12:15); war between Abijam [Abijah] and Jeroboam (1 Kgs. 15:7; 2 Chr. 13:2); war between Asa and Baasha (1 Kgs. 15:16, 32); Egyptians will fight Egyptians (Isa. 19:2); if Satan has risen up against himself, he cannot stand (Mark 3:26).

719 Pacification

A God makes peace
He makes wars cease (Ps. 46:9); he makes even his enemies at peace with him (Prov. 16:7); let them make peace with me (Isa. 27:5); they will never again learn war (Isa. 2:4; Mic. 4:3).

B Peace made through Christ
God reconciled us to himself through Christ (2 Cor. 5:18-20); through Christ God reconciles all things to himself (Col. 1:20); while enemies of God we were reconciled by the death of his Son (Rom. 5:10-11); reconciled through Christ's death (Col. 1:22); if the rejection of the Jews led to the reconciliation of the world (Rom. 11:15); having made peace through the blood of his cross (Col. 1:20); he is our peace, who made both one (Eph. 2:14); he reconciles Jew and Gentile in one body through the cross (Eph. 2:16); do not think that I came to bring peace on earth (Matt. 10:34).

C People making peace
Blessed are the peacemakers (Matt. 5:9); we have been given the ministry of reconciliation (2 Cor. 5:18-19); whatever house you enter, first say, 'Peace be to this house' (Luke 10:5-6); if the house is worthy, let your peace come on it (Matt. 10:13); when slandered we try to conciliate (1 Cor. 4:13); pursue what makes for peace (Rom. 14:19); pursue peace with all men (Heb. 12:14); righteousness is sown in peace by those who make peace (Jas. 3:18); they will beat their swords into ploughshares (Isa. 2:4; Mic. 4:3); when you attack a city, offer terms of peace (Deut. 20:10); he will ask for terms of peace (Luke 14:32); go and be reconciled with your brother (Matt. 5:24); be reconciled with your accuser (Matt. 5:25; Luke 12:58).

720 Mediation

A Mediator with God
Moses was to be between the people and God (Exod. 18:19); I stood between the Lord and you (Deut. 5:5); Aaron stood between the living and the dead (Num. 16:48); if one man sins against another, God will mediate (1 Sam. 2:25); if only there were an arbitrator between God and man (Job 9:33); God sought for a man to stand in the gap (Ezek. 22:30); there is one mediator between God and man (1 Tim. 2:5); Jesus is the mediator of a better covenant (Heb. 8:6); Jesus is the mediator of a new covenant (Heb. 9:15; 12:24); the law was mediated by angels (Acts 7:53); the law was given through a mediator (Gal. 3:19); a mediator implies more than one party (Gal. 3:20).

B Mediator between men
The wise woman of Tekoa mediated between Absalom and David (2 Sam. 14:1-20); no one is deputed to listen to you on behalf of the king (2 Sam. 15:3).

721 Submission

A Submit to God
We should submit to the Father of spirits (Heb. 12:9); submit yourselves to God (Jas. 4:7); the church submits

to Christ (Eph. 5:24); they did not submit to God's righteousness (Rom. 10:3).

B Submit to others

Be subject to one another (Eph. 5:21); submit to such men and to every fellow-worker (1 Cor. 16:16); servants, be submissive to your masters (1 Pet. 2:18); submit to your leaders (Heb. 13:17); the younger should be submissive to their elders (1 Pet. 5:5); Hagar had to submit to her mistress (Gen. 16:9); wives, be submissive to your husbands (Eph. 5:22; Col. 3:18; 1 Pet. 3:1); as the church is subject to Christ, so wives ought to be subject to their husbands (Eph. 5:24); they should be subject to their husbands (Titus 2:5); holy women in the past were submissive to their husbands (1 Pet. 3:5); a woman should learn in submission (1 Cor. 14:34-5; 1 Tim. 2:11).

722 Combatant

A God as a warrior

The Lord is a man of war (Exod. 15:3); the Lord will go forth like a warrior (Isa. 42:13); the Lord is with me like a warrior (Jer. 20:11); he runs at me like a warrior (Job 16:14); the Lord at the head of his army (Joel 2:11); the commander of the army of the Lord (Josh. 5:14); the Lord your God is in your midst, a warrior of victory (Zeph. 3:17); the Lord of Sabaoth [armies] (Jas. 5:4).

B Warriors

Jephthah was a mighty warrior (Judg. 11:1); Kish was a mighty man of valour (1 Sam. 9:1); Goliath was a champion (1 Sam. 17:4, 23); David could not build the temple because he was a man of war (1 Chr. 28:3); Jeroboam was a valiant warrior (1 Kgs. 11:28); Asa had an army of brave warriors (2 Chr. 14:8); I have called my mighty warriors (Isa. 13:3); how can you say, 'We are mighty warriors'? (Jer. 48:14).

C The mighty men

David's mighty men (2 Sam. 16:6; 23:8-39; 1 Chr. 11:10-47; 12:1-22; 19:8); Benaiah had charge of the 30 (1 Chr. 27:6); the mighty men did not follow Adonijah (1 Kgs. 1:8); the mighty men were not invited (1 Kgs. 1:10).

D Officers

D1 Centurions

A centurion begged him to heal his servant (Matt. 8:5-6; Luke 7:2); the centurion keeping watch over Jesus on the cross (Matt. 27:54; Mark 15:39; Luke 23:47); Pilate summoned the centurion and asked if Jesus were already dead (Mark 15:44-5); a centurion of the Italian cohort (Acts 10:1, 22); a centurion named Julius of the Augustan cohort (Acts 27:1).

D2 Chiliarchs

A report came to the chiliarch of the cohort (Acts 21:31); Lysias, the chiliarch of the Roman cohort (Acts 22:24); take this young man to the chiliarch (Acts 23:17-19); chiliarchs hid themselves in caves in fear of God's wrath (Rev. 6:15-17).

D3 Various officers

The officers shall address the people before battle (Deut. 20:5); Phicol, commander of the army of Abimelech (Gen. 21:22); Sisera was the commander of Jabin's army (Judg. 4:2, 7); Saul set David over the men of war (1 Sam. 18:5); Abner son of Ner was commander of Saul's army (1 Sam. 14:50; 2 Sam. 2:8); Omri, commander of the army of Israel (1 Kgs. 16:16); Ish-bosheth had two commanders, Baanah and Rechab (2 Sam. 4:2); Joab was over the army (2 Sam. 8:16); Absalom set Amasa over the army in place of Joab (2 Sam. 17:25); Benaiah was over the Cherethites and Pelethites (2 Sam. 8:18); Joab, Abishai and Ittai were over thirds of David's army (2 Sam. 18:2); Sisera, captain of the army of Hazor (1 Sam. 12:9); Naaman

was captain of the army of Aram (2 Kgs. 5:1); Shobach [Shophach] commanded Hadadezer's army (2 Sam. 10:16); Nebuzaradan captain of the guard (2 Kgs. 25:8).

E Armies

E1 Armies in general

A king is not saved by a big army (Ps. 33:16); God's great army of locusts (Joel 2:5); they came to life and stood on their feet, a great army (Ezek. 37:10); after some years he will come with a great army (Dan. 11:13); the king was angry and sent his armies (Matt. 22:7); the name of the demons was Legion (Mark 5:9); I saw the beast and the kings of the earth with their armies (Rev. 19:19).

E2 Earthly armies

Pharaoh with his mighty army will not help him (Ezek. 17:17); the armies of the Lord went out of Egypt (Exod. 12:41); the Lord of hosts is mustering an army for battle (Isa. 13:4); Saul chose 3000 men for a standing army (1 Sam. 13:2); the army of Judah (2 Chr. 17:14-19); David put garrisons in Damascus (2 Sam. 8:6); David put garrisons in Edom (2 Sam. 8:14; 1 Chr. 18:13); Uzziah had a prepared army (2 Chr. 26:11); the garrison of the Philistines was in Bethlehem (2 Sam. 23:14); there was a great army with David (1 Chr. 12:22); David sent Joab and all the army (2 Sam. 10:7); an army surrounded Dothan (2 Kgs. 6:14-15).

E3 The armies of heaven

The armies of heaven (1 Kgs. 22:19; 2 Chr. 18:18); the armies which are in heaven (Rev. 19:14); the Father would send Jesus more than twelve legions of angels (Matt. 26:53); they waged war against the rider and his army (Rev. 19:19); the number of their army is like the sand of the seashore (Rev. 20:8).

F Soldiers

F1 Soldiers in general

A man newly married shall not go to war (Deut. 24:5); who serves as a soldier at his own expense? (1 Cor. 9:7); no soldier gets entangled in civilian affairs (2 Tim. 2:4); men 20 and up are able to go to war (Num. 1:3); a census was taken of men able to serve in the army (Num. 1:3); armed men from Gilead must fight beyond the Jordan (Num. 32:20; Deut. 3:18); Saul enlisted any mighty man he saw (1 Sam. 14:52); I am a man under authority with soldiers under me (Matt. 8:9; Luke 7:8); soldiers asked, 'What shall we do?' (Luke 3:14).

F2 Soldiers' treatment of Christ

Judas took a band of soldiers (John 18:3); the band of soldiers arrested Jesus and bound him (John 18:12); the soldiers took him inside the palace and called together the whole cohort (Mark 15:16); they gathered the whole cohort (Matt. 27:27); Herod and his soldiers treated him with contempt (Luke 23:11); the governor's soldiers mocked Jesus (Matt. 27:28-31; Mark 15:17-20); the soldiers plaited a crown of thorns (John 19:2).

F3 Soldiers of Christ

A good soldier of Jesus Christ (2 Tim. 2:3); Epaphroditus, my fellow-soldier (Phil. 2:25); Archippus our fellow-soldier (Philem. 2).

F4 Other soldiers

The men of war came to make David king (1 Chr. 12:23-38); Amaziah hired soldiers from Israel (2 Chr. 25:6); they gave a sum of money to the soldiers (Matt. 28:12); there was no small stir among the soldiers over what had become of Peter (Acts 12:18); the soldiers planned to kill the prisoners (Acts 27:42); Paul stayed by himself with the soldier guarding him (Acts 28:16).

723 Weapons

A Literal weapons

A1 Weapons in general
Half of the people carried arms (Neh. 4:16); a weapon
in one hand and a load in the other (Neh. 4:17); Judas
came with lanterns, torches and weapons (John 18:3);
David put Goliath's weapons in his tent (1 Sam. 17:54);
the king will have people make his weapons (1 Sam.
8:12); Rehoboam put shields and spears in every city
(2 Chr. 11:12); Uzziah prepared spears (2 Chr. 26:14);
Hezekiah provided many weapons and shields (2 Chr.
32:5); beat ploughshares into swords and pruning
hooks into spears (Joel 3:10); the Philistines did not
want Israel to make weapons (1 Sam. 13:19); here are
two swords – enough! (Luke 22:38).

A2 Clubs
The crowd armed with swords and clubs (Matt. 26:47;
Mark 14:43; Luke 22:52); have you come with swords
and clubs to arrest me? (Matt. 26:55; Mark 14:48); as if a
club should wield the one who lifts it (Isa. 10:15).

A3 Spears and javelins
Phinehas transfixed the couple with a spear (Num.
25:7-9); Joshua held out his javelin towards Ai (Josh.
8:18); Goliath had a bronze javelin (1 Sam. 17:6); the
shaft of his spear was like a weaver's beam (1 Sam. 17:7;
2 Sam. 21:19; 1 Chr. 11:23; 20:5); you come to me with a
sword, a spear and a javelin (1 Sam. 17:45); Saul threw a
spear at David (1 Sam. 18:11; 19:10); Saul threw a spear
at Jonathan (1 Sam. 20:33); they took Saul's spear
(1 Sam. 26:11-12); Saul was leaning on his spear (2 Sam.
1:6); Joab pierced Absalom with three spears (2 Sam.
18:14); Abishai killed 300 with his spear (2 Sam. 23:18);
Benaiah snatched the Egyptian's spear and killed him
with it (2 Sam. 23:21); a soldier pierced his side with a
spear (John 19:34).

A4 Swords
SWORDS AS SHARP OBJECTS, see 256A3.

A4a 'The sword'
I appoint the sword to slay (Jer. 15:3); if I make the
sword pass through that land (Ezek. 14:17); a third of
you will fall by the sword (Ezek. 5:12); he who is in the
field will die by the sword (Ezek. 7:15); he who is near
will fall by the sword (Ezek. 6:12); you have feared the
sword so I will bring the sword on you (Ezek. 11:8); all
who take the sword will perish by the sword (Matt.
26:52); you will fall by the sword (Ezek. 11:10); my four
severe judgements, sword, famine, wild beasts and
plague (Ezek. 14:21); by faith they escaped the edge of
the sword (Heb. 11:34).
KILLED BY THE SWORD, see 362C3.
GOD S SWORD, see 723B1b.

A4b Swords in general
Simeon and Levi's swords are weapons of violence
(Gen. 49:5); if only there had been a sword in my hand
(Num. 22:29); the sword of the king of Babylon will
come upon you (Ezek. 32:11); if I bring a sword on the
land (Ezek. 33:2-3); use a sharp sword as a barber's
razor (Ezek. 5:1); I will make you like a warrior's sword
(Zech. 9:13); I did not come to bring peace but a sword
(Matt. 10:34); a sword will pierce your own soul also
(Luke 2:35).

A4c Particular swords
Jonathan gave David his sword and bow and belt
(1 Sam. 18:4); Ehud had made a two-edged sword
(Judg. 3:16); Goliath's sword (1 Sam. 17:51); the Field of
Sword-edges (2 Sam. 2:16); bring me a sword (1 Kgs.
3:24); one with Jesus drew his sword (Matt. 26:51-2);
Peter, having a sword, cut off the slave's ear (John
18:10); the jailer drew his sword to kill himself (Acts
16:27); the rider was given a great sword (Rev. 6:4).

A5 Other weapons
I can bend a bow of bronze (2 Sam. 22:35; Ps. 18:34); let
a bronze arrow pierce him (Job 20:24); burning shields,
bucklers, bows, arrows and spears (Ezek. 39:9); arrows
cannot make the crocodile flee (Job 41:28); you will not
fear the arrow that flies by day (Ps. 91:5); the fiery darts
of the evil one (Eph. 6:16); they twisted like a deceitful
bow (Ps. 78:57); children are like a warrior's arrows (Ps.
127:4-5); they bend their tongue like a bow (Jer. 9:3);
the rider had a bow (Rev. 6:2); each with his shattering
weapon in his hand (Ezek. 9:2); Samson used the
jaw-bone of a donkey (Judg. 15:15).
PEOPLE SHOOTING ARROWS, see 287B2.

A6 Armour bearers
Abimelech was killed by his armour bearer (Judg. 9:54);
Jonathan's armour bearer (1 Sam. 14:1); David became
Saul's armour bearer (1 Sam. 16:21); Goliath had a
shield bearer (1 Sam. 17:7); Saul's armour bearer was
afraid to kill him (1 Sam. 31:4; 1 Chr. 10:4); ten men
who carried Joab's armour (2 Sam. 18:15).

A7 Inadequate weapons

A7a Useless weapons
No weapon will succeed against you (Isa. 54:17); neither
sword, spear, dart nor javelin can harm the crocodile
(Job 41:26-9); I will not deliver them by bow, sword,
battle, horses or horsemen (Hos. 1:7); not by your
sword or your bow (Josh. 24:12); the Lord does not
deliver by sword or spear (1 Sam. 17:47); I will not trust
in bow or sword (Ps. 44:6); they did not win the land
by their own sword (Ps. 44:3); God broke all the
weapons of war (Ps. 76:3); the bows of the mighty are
broken (1 Sam. 2:4); swords into ploughshares and
spears into pruning hooks (Isa. 2:4; Mic. 4:3).

A7b Lacking weapons
Lack of arms in Israel (Judg. 5:8; 1 Sam. 13:22); Samson
tore the lion with nothing in his hand (Judg. 14:6);
David had no sword (1 Sam. 17:50); David was without
weapons (1 Sam. 21:8).

B Spiritual weapons

B1 Weapons of God

B1a God's weapons in general
The Lord has prepared deadly weapons (Ps. 7:13); the
Lord and his weapons of wrath, to destroy all the land
(Isa. 13:5); the Lord has brought out weapons and
wrath from his armoury (Jer. 50:25); six men with
shattering weapons to slay at God's command (Ezek.
9:2).

B1b God's sword
A flaming sword at the garden of Eden (Gen. 3:24); the
Lord will execute judgement by his sword (Isa. 66:16);
the commander of the Lord's army with a drawn sword
(Josh. 5:13); three days of the sword of the Lord,
pestilence (1 Chr. 12:12); the angel with his sword
drawn (Num. 22:23; 1 Chr. 21:16); rest, sword of the
Lord! (Jer. 47:6); I will draw my sword out of its sheath
(Ezek. 21:3); the sword of the Spirit, which is the word
of God (Eph. 6:17); the word of God is sharper than a
two-edged sword (Heb. 4:12); the rider was given a
great sword (Rev. 6:4).

B1c God's bow and arrows
The Lord's arrow of victory over Aram (2 Kgs. 13:17);
lightning is God's arrows (2 Sam. 22:15; Ps. 18:14); when
I send against them my deadly arrows of famine (Ezek.
5:16); the Lord's arrow will go forth like lightning
(Zech. 9:14); God makes his arrows fiery shafts (Ps.
7:13); your arrows are sharp in the heart of the king's
enemies (Ps. 45:5); arrows against the deceitful tongue
(Ps. 120:4); he made me a polished arrow (Isa. 49:2); I
will bend Judah as my bow (Zech. 9:13-14); God's
arrows are within me (Job 6:4); he made the arrows of

his quiver enter my kidneys (Lam. 3:13); your arrows
have sunk deep into me (Ps. 38:2).
GOD SHOOTING ARROWS, see 287B1.

B1d Other weapons of God
Assyria, the rod of God's anger (Isa. 10:5); Babylon is
his war-club (Jer. 51:20).

B2 Weapons of Christ
Out of his mouth came a sharp two-edged sword (Rev.
1:16; 19:15); he who has the sharp two-edged sword in
his mouth (Rev. 2:12); I will make war against them
with the sword of my mouth (Rev. 2:16); gird your
sword on your thigh (Ps. 45:3).

B3 Weapons of the believer
The weapons of righteousness (2 Cor. 6:7); weapons
with divine power (2 Cor. 10:4); a two-edged sword in
their hands (Ps. 149:6); let him who has no sword sell
his mantle and buy one (Luke 22:36); the sword of the
Spirit, which is the word of God (Eph. 6:17); wisdom is
better than weapons of war (Eccles. 9:18).

724 Arena
They rushed together into the theatre (Acts 19:29-31).

725 Completion

A Work finished

A1 God's work finished
The heavens and the earth were finished (Gen. 2:1-2;
Heb. 4:3); I have finished the work you gave me to do
(John 17:4); it is finished! (John 19:30); Jesus, knowing
that all was accomplished (John 19:28); he who began a
good work in you will complete it (Phil. 1:6); as I have
planned, so it will happen (Isa. 14:24); I will accomplish
all I purpose (Isa. 46:10-11); it is done! (Rev. 16:17; 21:6);
Jesus, the originator and finisher of our faith (Heb.
12:2).

A2 Man's work finished
Complete the quota of bricks (Exod. 5:13-18); the
tabernacle was completed (Exod. 39:32); the temple was
finished (1 Kgs. 6:14; 2 Chr. 5:1); Zerubbabel will
complete the temple (Zech. 4:9); the rebuilt temple
finished (Ezra 6:14-15); the wall of Jerusalem was
completed (Neh. 6:15); counting the cost, whether he
has enough to complete it (Luke 14:28); as Titus had
made a beginning, he should complete this gracious
work (2 Cor. 8:6); complete what you began a year ago
(2 Cor. 8:10-11); fulfil your ministry (2 Tim. 4:5); tell
Archippus to complete his work in the Lord (Col. 4:17);
that I may finish my course (Acts 20:24); I have
finished the race (2 Tim. 4:7).

B Words fulfilled

B1 God's words fulfilled

B1a Future fulfilment of God's words
Who speaks and it comes to pass unless the Lord
commanded it? (Lam. 3:37); you will see whether my
word will come to pass or not (Num. 11:23); whatever
word I speak will be performed (Ezek. 12:25); my word
will accomplish what I purpose (Isa. 55:11); convinced
that God had power to do what he promised (Rom.
4:21); has he spoken and will he not do it? (Num.
23:19); I have spoken, it will come to pass (Ezek. 24:14);
I will do it (Ezek. 17:24; 36:36); my
words will be fulfilled in their time (Luke 1:20); do as
you have said (2 Sam. 7:25; 1 Chr. 17:23); that the Lord
may fulfil his promise (1 Kgs. 2:4); I believe God that it
will be exactly as I have been told (Acts 27:25); the Lord
will execute his word, finishing it and cutting it short
(Rom. 9:28); until the words of God should be fulfilled
(Rev. 17:17); let it be to me according to your word
(Luke 1:38); the days approach and the fulfilment of
every vision (Ezek. 12:23).

B1b Past fulfilment of God's words
The Lord did to Sarah as he had said (Gen. 21:1); you
have fulfilled your promise to Abraham (Neh. 9:8); not
one word has failed of all his promise (1 Kgs. 8:56);
every one of God's promises was fulfilled (Josh. 21:45;
23:14); the Lord has fulfilled his word (1 Kgs. 8:20); he is
risen, as he said (Matt. 28:6); what God promised he
has fulfilled by raising Jesus (Acts 13:33).

B2 Scriptures fulfilled
What is written about me must be fulfilled (Luke 22:37;
24:44); I have not come to abolish the law and the
prophets but to fulfil them (Matt. 5:17); not a jot or
tittle will pass from the law till all is fulfilled (Matt.
5:18); that the scripture may be fulfilled (John 13:18);
today this scripture has been fulfilled in your hearing
(Luke 4:21); God fulfilled the words of the prophets
(Acts 3:18); days of vengeance, that everything written
might be fulfilled (Luke 21:22); with them is fulfilled
the prophecy of Isaiah (Matt. 13:14); this had been
written of him and had been done to him (John 12:16);
when they had fulfilled all that was written of him
(Acts 13:29); he who loves his neighbour has fulfilled
the law (Rom. 13:8); love is the fulfilment of the law
(Rom. 13:10); that the requirement of the law might be
fulfilled in us (Rom. 8:4).

B3 Vows fulfilled
Vows must be fulfilled (Num. 30:2-15); fulfil your vows
(Matt. 5:33); better not to vow than to vow and not pay
(Eccles. 5:5); Jephthah did according to his vow (Judg.
11:39); a sacrifice to fulfil a vow (Num. 15:3); we will
perform our vows to the queen of heaven (Jer. 44:25).

726 Non-completion

A Incomplete works
Why have you not completed the quota of bricks?
(Exod. 5:14); I have not found your works completed
(Rev. 3:2); Joab began the count but did not finish (1
Chr. 27:24); if he is not able to finish the tower (Luke
14:29-30).

B Unfulfilled word
Then we will see what will become of his dreams (Gen.
37:20); if a prophet's word does not happen, it is not
from the Lord (Deut. 18:22); what comes into your
mind will never happen (Ezek. 20:32); pray for me that
nothing of what you have said may happen (Acts 8:24).

727 Success
NOT DEFEATED, see 728D.

A God overcoming
Victory belongs to the Lord (Prov. 21:31); his right hand
and his holy arm have gained him the victory (Ps. 98:1);
the Lord will prevail over his enemies (Isa. 42:13); do
not let men prevail against you (2 Chr. 14:11); the Lord
your God is in your midst, a warrior of victory (Zeph.
3:17).

B Overcoming through God

B1 Success through God
Abraham's servant prayed for success (Gen. 24:12); the
Lord will make your way successful (Gen. 24:40); the
Lord has prospered my way (Gen. 24:56); grant me
success this day (Neh. 1:11); the God of heaven will give
us success (Neh. 2:20); keep the law that you may have
success (Josh. 1:7, 8; 1 Kgs. 2:3; 1 Chr. 22:13); the Lord be
with you that you may be successful (1 Chr. 22:11); God
was with Joseph so he was successful (Gen. 39:2, 23).

B2 Victory through God
When Moses held his hand up, Israel prevailed, and
when he let it down, Amalek prevailed (Exod. 17:11);
Judah conquered because they relied on the Lord
(2 Chr. 13:18); David defeated his enemies when the
Lord broke out against them (2 Sam. 5:20; 1 Chr. 14:11);

you are of God and have overcome them (1 John 4:4); through God we shall do valiantly (Ps. 60:12; 108:13); I will make your enemies turn their backs to you (Exod. 23:27); I will subdue all your enemies (1 Chr. 17:10); through you we will push back our foes (Ps. 44:5); you subdued under me my assailants (2 Sam. 22:40; Ps. 18:39); God subdues peoples under me (2 Sam. 22:48; Ps. 18:47); he gives great victories to his king (Ps. 18:50); God defeats your enemies (Deut. 23:14; 33:29); God will tread down our enemies (Ps. 60:12; 108:13); God commands victories for Jacob (Ps. 44:4); victory over enemies through God (2 Sam. 22:38-43; Ps. 18:37-42); by faith they conquered kingdoms (Heb. 11:33).

C Christ overcoming
I have overcome the world (John 16:33); he triumphed over authorities in the cross (Col. 2:15); the Lamb will overcome them (Rev. 17:14); his enemies will become his footstool (Ps. 110:1; Matt. 22:44; Mark 12:36; Luke 20:43; Acts 2:34-5; Heb. 1:13; 10:13); he must reign until his enemies are put under his feet (1 Cor. 15:25); ride on victoriously for truth (Ps. 45:4); I overcame and sat down with my Father on his throne (Rev. 3:21); the lion of the tribe of Judah has overcome (Rev. 5:5); the darkness did not overcome the light (John 1:5).

D Overcoming through Christ
We are more than conquerors through him who loved us (Rom. 8:37); he gives us the victory through our Lord Jesus Christ (1 Cor. 15:57); God leads us in triumph in Christ (2 Cor. 2:14); death is swallowed up in victory (1 Cor. 15:54-5); God will soon crush Satan under your feet (Rom. 16:20); you have overcome the evil one (1 John 2:13, 14); they overcame him by the blood of the Lamb (Rev. 12:11); whatever is born of God overcomes the world (1 John 5:4); overcome evil with good (Rom. 12:21); this is the victory that overcomes the world, our faith (1 John 5:4-5).

E People overcoming
E1 People overcoming in general
Fill the earth and subdue it (Gen. 1:28); five will chase 100 and 100 will chase 10 000 (Lev. 26:8); Israel will do valiantly (Num. 24:18); my enemies fell under my feet (2 Sam. 22:39; Ps. 18:38); my enemies stumbled and fell (Ps. 27:2).

E2 Particular victories
Abraham defeated the kings (Gen. 14:15); Hadad king of Edom defeated the Midianites (Gen. 36:35); Joshua overcame Amalek (Exod. 17:13); the Amorites had defeated Moab (Num. 21:26-30); Joshua defeated Horam (Josh. 10:33); Gideon routed Zebah and Zalmunna (Judg. 8:12); the Gileadites defeated Ephraim (Judg. 12:4); David defeated the Philistines (2 Sam. 8:1; 1 Chr. 18:1); David defeated the Moabites (2 Sam. 8:2; 1 Chr. 18:2); Hezekiah defeated the Philistines (2 Kgs. 18:8); you will defeat the Arameans at Aphek (2 Kgs. 13:17); Nebuchadnezzar defeated Pharaoh Neco (Jer. 46:2); Abimelech took Thebez (Judg. 9:50).

F Various victories
The rider on the white horse went out conquering and to conquer (Rev. 6:2); the beast will make war on the witnesses, overcome them and kill them (Rev. 11:7); the horn waged war against the saints and overpowered them (Dan. 7:21); the beast was allowed to wage war against the saints and overcome them (Rev. 13:7); lest Satan gain the advantage over us (2 Cor. 2:11).

728 Failure

A Prospect of defeat
When Israel has been defeated by an enemy because they have sinned (1 Kgs. 8:33; 2 Chr. 6:24); you cannot stand before your enemies until you get rid of the

things under the ban (Josh. 7:13); if you fight the Chaldeans you will not succeed (Jer. 32:5); if this movement is of men it will fail (Acts 5:38); unless you fail the test (2 Cor. 13:5-7); it is defeat for you to go to law with one another (1 Cor. 6:7).

B God causing defeat
B1 God will cause defeat
Three months being defeated by your enemies? (2 Sam. 24:13; 1 Chr. 21:12); the Lord gave them into the hands of Midian (Judg. 6:1); the Lord delivered Israel into the hands of the Philistines (Judg. 13:1; 1 Sam. 28:19); I will deliver them into the hand of Nebuchadnezzar (Jer. 29:21).

B2 God caused defeat
He gave them into the hand of the nations (Ps. 106:41); God gave Israel into their hands (2 Chr. 13:16); he delivered his people to the sword (Ps. 78:62); the Lord delivered them into the hands of Joash (2 Chr. 25:20); the Lord has delivered Judah into your hands (2 Chr. 28:9); the Lord gave them into the hand of Nebuchadnezzar (Ezra 5:12); I gave them into the hand of their enemies and they all fell by the sword (Ezek. 39:23); God overthrew Pharaoh and his army in the Red Sea (Ps. 136:15); I will give Egypt into the hand of Nebuchadnezzar (Jer. 46:26).

C Defeat of God's people
Israel were defeated by the Amalekites and Canaanites (Num. 14:45); Israel were defeated by Moab, Ammon and Amalek (Judg. 3:13); the Israelites were defeated (1 Sam. 4:10); Israel were routed by the men of Ai (Josh. 7:4); Israel has been routed by their enemies (Josh. 7:8); Hazael defeated Israel (2 Kgs. 10:32); Israel were beaten by Benjamin (Judg. 20:21, 25); Israel were defeated by David's men (2 Sam. 2:17; 18:7); Judah was routed by Israel (2 Kgs. 14:12; 2 Chr. 25:22); if their failure be riches for the Gentiles (Rom. 11:12).

D Not defeated
The enemy does not triumph over me (Ps. 41:11); they will fight against you but will not overcome you (Jer. 1:19); it is not as though the word of God has failed (Rom. 9:6).

729 Trophy
BOOTY, see 790.

730 Prosperity

A Prosperity in general
My cities will again overflow with prosperity (Zech. 1:17); when Jerusalem was inhabited and prosperous (Zech. 7:7); you know that from this business we have our prosperity (Acts 19:25); let each one set something aside as he may prosper (1 Cor. 16:2).

B The righteous prosper
He who fears the Lord will prosper (Ps. 25:13); he who trusts in the Lord will prosper (Prov. 28:25); prosperity rewards the righteous (Prov. 13:21); whatever he does, he prospers (Ps. 1:3); keep the covenant that you may prosper (Deut. 29:9); may you see the prosperity of Jerusalem (Ps. 128:5); meditate on this book of the law that your way may be prosperous (Josh. 1:8); prosperity for those who hear and serve God (Job 36:11); the generous man will be prosperous (Prov. 11:25); the Lord will make you abound in prosperity (Deut. 28:11; 30:9); the Lord caused all in Joseph's hand to prosper (Gen. 39:3); David always prospered, for God was with him (1 Sam. 18:14); Solomon prospered (1 Chr. 29:23); wherever Hezekiah went he prospered (2 Kgs. 18:7); as long as Uzziah sought the Lord, God prospered him (2 Chr. 26:5).

C **The wicked prosper**
The wicked prosper (Ps. 10:5); I saw the prosperity of the wicked (Ps. 73:3); evildoers prosper (Mal. 3:15); why does the way of the wicked prosper? (Jer. 12:1); do not fret over him who prospers (Ps. 37:7).

731 Adversity
I will laugh at your calamity (Prov. 1:26-7); disaster on disaster (Jer. 4:20); God made the day of adversity as well as the day of prosperity (Eccles. 7:14); do not lead us into trial (Matt. 6:13).

732 Averageness
AVERAGE, see 30.

733 Authority
A **Authority in general**
A1 **About authority**
God removes kings and sets up kings (Dan. 2:21); by me princes rule (Prov. 8:16); I gave you a king and took him away (Hos. 13:11); the Most High decides who should rule (Dan. 4:17; 5:21); you would have no authority unless you were given it from above (John 19:11); there is no authority except from God (Rom. 13:1); God gave Nebuchadnezzar sovereignty (Dan. 5:18); great men of the Gentiles exercise authority over them (Mark 10:42); husband and wife do not have authority over their own bodies, but that of the spouse (1 Cor. 7:4); the king does whatever he pleases (Eccles. 8:3); the word of the king is supreme (Eccles. 8:4); the king who observes the law will rule for a long time (Deut. 17:20); when someone rules in righteousness he is like the light of sunshine (2 Sam. 23:3-4); if a king judges the poor in truth, his throne will last for ever (Prov. 29:14).
A2 **Unsuitable rule**
The sceptre of wickedness will not rest on the land of the righteous (Ps. 125:3); to turn them from the authority of Satan to God (Acts 26:18); the beast exercised authority for 42 months (Rev. 13:5); authority over all peoples and nations (Rev. 13:7); it is not fitting for a slave to rule over princes (Prov. 19:10); when a land transgresses it has many rulers (Prov. 28:2); foreign kings rule over us (Neh. 9:37); children would rule over them (Isa. 3:4); woe to the land whose king is a boy (Eccles. 10:16); women rule over them (Isa. 3:12); I do not permit a woman to have authority over a man (1 Tim. 2:12); those who hate you will rule over you (Lev. 26:17); those who hated them ruled over them (Ps. 106:41); slaves rule over us (Lam. 5:8); we do not want this man to rule over us (Luke 19:14); do you want to lord it over us? (Num. 16:13); the rulers of the Gentiles lord it over them (Matt. 20:25; Mark 10:42; Luke 22:25); do not lord it over the flock (1 Pet. 5:3); we do not lord it over your faith (2 Cor. 1:24).
A3 **Sin / death ruling**
Sin desires you, but you must master it (Gen. 4:7); do not let sin reign in your mortal body (Rom. 6:12); sin will not rule over you (Rom. 6:14); I will not be mastered by anything (1 Cor. 6:12); death reigned from Adam to Moses (Rom. 5:14); if through the transgression of the one, death reigned through that one (Rom. 5:17); Death and Hades were given authority over a quarter of the earth (Rev. 6:8).
B **Authority of God**
B1 **God's reign**
B1a **God reigns**
The Lord reigns (1 Chr. 16:31; Ps. 93:1); your God reigns (Isa. 52:7); sovereign Lord (Acts 4:24); I saw the Lord sitting on a throne (Isa. 6:1); enthroned above the cherubim (2 Kgs. 19:15; 1 Chr. 13:6; Ps. 99:1); enthroned

in the heavens (Ps. 123:1); you are enthroned on the praises of Israel (Ps. 22:3); the Father has fixed times by his own authority (Acts 1:7); fear him who has authority to cast into hell (Luke 12:5); your kingdom will be sure after you recognise that Heaven rules (Dan. 4:26).
B1b **God reigns over people**
God rules over mankind (Dan. 4:17, 25, 32; 5:21); men are in the hand of God (Eccles. 9:1); the Lord rules over the nations (Ps. 22:28); God reigns over the nations (Ps. 47:8); he rules over all the kingdoms (2 Chr. 20:6); the head of Christ is God (1 Cor. 11:3); let the peace of God rule in your hearts (Col. 3:15).
B1c **God reigns for ever**
The Lord reigns for ever (Exod. 15:18; Ps. 66:7; 146:10; Lam. 5:19); he will reign for ever and ever (Rev. 11:15); his kingdom is an everlasting kingdom (Dan. 4:3); your throne is from generation to generation (Lam. 5:19); an eternal dominion (Dan. 4:34); enthroned for ever (Ps. 29:10); of the Son he says, 'Your throne, O God, is for ever' (Heb. 1:8); his kingdom will never be destroyed (Dan. 6:26); glory and dominion are his for ever (1 Pet. 4:11); to him be dominion for ever and ever (1 Pet. 5:11); to him be glory and dominion for ever and ever (Rev. 1:6).
B2 **Kingdom of God [/heaven]**
B2a **Kingdom of God in general**
A sceptre of righteousness is the sceptre of your kingdom (Ps. 45:6); the kingdom of God is not food and drink but righteousness, peace and joy in the Holy Spirit (Rom. 14:17); the kingdom of God does not consist of words but of power (1 Cor. 4:20); a kingdom which cannot be shaken (Heb. 12:28); the kingdom of heaven suffers violence (Matt. 11:12); are you at this time restoring the kingdom to Israel? (Acts 1:6); to you it has been given to know the secrets of the kingdom of God (Matt. 13:11; Mark 4:11; Luke 8:10).
B2b **People of the kingdom**
You will be to me a kingdom of priests (Exod. 19:6); the good seed are the sons of the kingdom (Matt. 13:38); he has made us a kingdom (Rev. 1:6); the greatness of the kingdoms under heaven will be given to the saints of the Most High (Dan. 7:27); you have made them a kingdom and priests (Rev. 5:10); blessed are the poor in spirit, for theirs is the kingdom of heaven (Matt. 5:3); the kingdom of God is to the poor (Luke 6:20); God chose the poor to be heirs of the kingdom (Jas. 2:5); the kingdom of heaven belongs to those persecuted for righteousness (Matt. 5:10); the kingdom of heaven belongs to the childlike (Matt. 19:14); to such as these children belongs the kingdom of God (Mark 10:14); the kingdom of God belongs to such as these (Luke 18:16); the kingdom prepared for you from the creation (Matt. 25:34); your Father's pleasure is to give you the kingdom (Luke 12:32); I give you a kingdom (Luke 22:29); he has transferred us into the kingdom of his dear Son (Col. 1:13); the Lord will save me for his heavenly kingdom (2 Tim. 4:18); God calls you into his own kingdom (1 Thess. 2:12).
B2c **The coming kingdom**
The kingdom of God [/heaven] is near (Matt. 3:2; 4:17; 10:7; Mark 1:15; Luke 10:9, 11; 21:31); they thought the kingdom of God would appear immediately (Luke 19:11); Joseph of Arimathea was waiting for the kingdom of God (Mark 15:43; Luke 23:51); the Pharisees asked when the kingdom of God was coming (Luke 17:20); the kingdom of God has come upon you (Matt. 12:28; Luke 11:20); the kingdom of God is in your midst (Luke 17:21); the kingdom of God is not coming with signs to be observed (Luke 17:20); your kingdom come (Matt. 6:10; Luke 11:2); seek first God's kingdom (Matt.

6:33; Luke 12:31); he hands over the kingdom to God the Father (1 Cor. 15:24); the kingdom of the world has become the kingdom of our Lord and of his Christ (Rev. 11:15); now the salvation, the power and the kingdom of our God have come (Rev. 12:10).

B2d Preaching the kingdom

Jesus was preaching the good news of the kingdom (Matt. 4:23; 9:35); preaching the kingdom of God (Luke 8:1); he spoke to them of the kingdom of God (Luke 9:11); he sent them to preach the kingdom of God and to heal (Luke 9:2); go and preach the kingdom of God (Luke 9:60); the kingdom of God is preached (Luke 16:16); this gospel of the kingdom will be preached in all the world (Matt. 24:14); Philip preached the good news of the kingdom of God (Acts 8:12); Paul testified to the kingdom of God (Acts 28:23); I must preach the kingdom of God to other cities also (Luke 4:43); Paul reasoned and persuaded them about the kingdom of God (Acts 19:8).

B2e Entering the kingdom

That you may be worthy of the kingdom of God (2 Thess. 1:5); no one who looks back is fit for the kingdom of God (Luke 9:62); unless one is born again he cannot see the kingdom of God (John 3:3); unless one is born of water and the Spirit he cannot enter the kingdom of God (John 3:5); unless your righteousness exceeds you will not enter the kingdom of heaven (Matt. 5:20); unless you become like children you will not enter the kingdom (Matt. 18:3; Mark 10:15); whoever does not receive the kingdom of God like a child will not enter it (Luke 18:17); not everyone who says 'Lord' will enter (Matt. 7:21); better to enter the kingdom of God with one eye (Mark 9:47); how hard it is to enter the kingdom of God! (Mark 10:24); it is hard for the rich to enter the kingdom (Matt. 19:23; Mark 10:23; Luke 18:24); easier for a camel to go through the eye of a needle than for a rich man to enter (Matt. 19:24; Mark 10:25; Luke 18:25); harlots enter the kingdom of God before you (Matt. 21:31); through many tribulations we must enter the kingdom of God (Acts 14:22); I give you the keys of the kingdom of heaven (Matt. 16:19); you shut the kingdom of heaven against men (Matt. 23:13).

B2f Bereft of the kingdom

The kingdom of God will be taken away from you (Matt. 21:43); those who will not inherit the kingdom of God: the unrighteous (1 Cor. 6:9-10); those who do the deeds of the flesh (Gal. 5:21); the immoral or covetous (Eph. 5:5); flesh and blood (1 Cor. 15:50).

C Authority of Christ

C1 Christ's authority

By what authority are you doing these things? (Matt. 21:23-7; Mark 11:28-33; Luke 20:2-8); I have authority to lay down my life and authority to take it again (John 10:18); Jesus taught with authority (Matt. 7:29; Mark 1:22; Luke 4:32); with authority he commands unclean spirits (Mark 1:27; Luke 4:36); given all authority in heaven and on earth (Matt. 28:18); the government will rest upon his shoulders (Isa. 9:6-7); the Father gave the Son authority to judge (John 5:27); you gave him authority over all flesh to grant eternal life (John 17:2); authority to forgive sins (Matt. 9:6; Mark 2:10; Luke 5:24); the Father gave all things into his hands (John 13:3); the authority of Christ has come (Rev. 12:10); the Son of man is Lord of the sabbath (Matt. 12:8; Mark 2:28; Luke 6:5); they glorified God who had given such authority to men (Matt. 9:8).

C2 Christ's kingdom

Your throne, O God, is for ever (Ps. 45:6); of the Son he says, 'Your throne, O God, is for ever' (Heb. 1:8); he must reign until all enemies are put under his feet (1 Cor. 15:25); the root of Jesse who rises to rule the Gentiles (Rom. 15:12); a son who was to rule the nations with a rod of iron (Rev. 12:5); he will rule them with a rod of iron (Rev. 2:27; 19:15); remember me when you come in your kingdom (Luke 23:42); a man went into a far country to receive a kingdom (Luke 19:12); he will rule from sea to sea (Ps. 72:8; Zech. 9:10); your kingdom is an everlasting kingdom (Ps. 145:13); his kingdom will never end (Luke 1:33); when you come in your kingdom (Matt. 20:21); by his appearing and his kingdom (2 Tim. 4:1); the righteous sceptre is the sceptre of your kingdom (Heb. 1:8); when the Son of man sits on his glorious throne (Matt. 19:28; 25:31); my kingdom is not of this world (John 18:36).

D Authority of people

D1 Authority of people in general

Man was to rule all living things (Gen. 1:26); to subdue the earth (Gen. 1:28); God appointed man over all creation (Ps. 8:6-8; Heb. 2:7-8); your husband will rule over you (Gen. 3:16); the man is the head of the woman (1 Cor. 11:3); every man should be master in his own house (Esther 1:22).

D2 Authority delegated to people

Potiphar put everything in Joseph's hands (Gen. 39:4-8); Pharaoh set Joseph over all the land of Egypt (Gen. 41:41-6); Ahasuerus set Mordecai over the house of Haman (Esther 8:2); rule over ten cities (Luke 19:17); rule over five cities (Luke 19:19); you would have no authority unless you were given it from above (John 19:11); I am a man under authority (Matt. 8:9; Luke 7:8); he has authority from the chief priests to bind all who call on your name (Acts 9:14); I received authority from the chief priests (Acts 26:10, 12).

D3 The kingdom of David

God established David's kingdom for the sake of his people Israel (2 Sam. 5:12); the throne of David will be established for ever (1 Kgs. 2:45); there will be no end to his reign on the throne of David (Isa. 9:7); The Lord will make a house for you (2 Sam. 7:11-13; 1 Chr. 17:10); I will build you a house (2 Sam. 7:27; 1 Chr. 17:25); David's dynasty would last for ever (2 Sam. 7:16; 2 Chr. 13:5; Ps. 89:4); David will never lack a man to sit on the throne of Israel (Jer. 33:17, 21); blessed is the kingdom of our father David (Mark 11:10); God will give him the throne of his father David (Luke 1:32-3); I tore the kingdom from the house of David (1 Kgs. 14:8).

D4 Authority of disciples

He gave his disciples authority over evil spirits (Matt. 10:1; Mark 6:7; Luke 9:1); the 12 were to have authority to cast out demons (Mark 3:15); I have given you authority over all the power of the enemy (Luke 10:19); to those who believe in his name he gave the authority to become children of God (John 1:12); the authority the Lord gave me for building up (2 Cor. 10:8; 13:10); give me this authority, that everyone on whom I lay my hands may receive the Spirit (Acts 8:19); they will reign on the earth (Rev. 5:10); they reigned with Christ 1000 years (Rev. 20:4); if we endure we will reign with him (2 Tim. 2:12); you will sit on 12 thrones (Matt. 19:28); they will reign for ever (Rev. 22:5); they will reign in life through the one, Jesus Christ (Rom. 5:17); would that you did reign, so that we might reign with you! (1 Cor. 4:8); Diotrephes does not acknowledge my authority (3 John 9); they have authority to shut up the sky (Rev. 11:6); a woman should have authority on her head (1 Cor. 11:10).

E Other authority

Lights to govern day and night (Gen. 1:16-18); the sun to rule by day (Ps. 136:8); the moon and stars to rule by night (Ps. 136:9); an angel coming from heaven with great authority (Rev. 18:1); authority was given to the locusts as scorpions have authority (Rev. 9:3); the dragon gave the beast his authority (Rev. 13:2); giving over their kingly authority to the beast (Rev. 17:17); it exercises all the authority of the first beast (Rev. 13:12); the ten kings give their authority to the beast (Rev. 17:13); to you I will give all this authority and their glory (Luke 4:6); raised far above all rule and authority (Eph. 1:21); the wisdom of God made known to the rulers and authorities in the heavenlies (Eph. 3:10).

734 Anarchy

A No king

There was no king in Israel (Judg. 18:1; 19:1); no king, so everyone did what was right in his own eyes (Judg. 17:6; 21:25); there was no king in Edom (1 Kgs. 22:47); Israel will have no king for many days (Hos. 3:4); we have no king (Hos. 10:3); as sheep without a shepherd, these have no master (1 Kgs. 22:17; 2 Chr. 18:16).

B Not ruled

Who is lord over us? (Ps. 12:4); the ant has no chief or ruler (Prov. 6:7); those who despise authority (2 Pet. 2:10); these men reject authority (Jude 8); we have become like those you have never ruled (Isa. 63:19).

735 Severity

A Strictness

A harsh word stirs up anger (Prov. 15:1); the rich man answers roughly (Prov. 18:23); the ostrich treats her young cruelly (Job 39:16); the daughter of my people has become as cruel as an ostrich (Lam. 4:3); that servant who knew but did not act will receive a severe beating (Luke 12:47); I lived as a Pharisee, the strictest party of our religion (Acts 26:5); that when present I may not have to be severe (2 Cor. 13:10); fathers, do not provoke your children lest they become discouraged (Col. 3:21); consider the kindness and the severity of God (Rom. 11:22); I knew you to be a hard man (Matt. 25:24; Luke 19:21-2).

B Oppression

B1 Oppressors in general

I saw the oppressions done under the sun (Eccles. 4:1); a ruler who lacks understanding is a great oppressor (Prov. 28:16); oppression makes a wise man mad (Eccles. 7:7); because he practised oppression he will die (Ezek. 18:18); if he oppresses the poor and needy (Ezek. 18:12); they have oppressed the alien in your midst (Ezek. 22:7); they have practised oppression and robbery (Ezek. 22:29); a merchant with false balances, Ephraim loves to oppress (Hos. 12:7); they seized his servants and mistreated them (Matt. 22:6); the king ill-treated our fathers (Acts 7:19); I have seen the ill-treatment of my people (Acts 7:34); if you bite and devour one another take care you are not consumed by one another (Gal. 5:15); is it not the rich who oppress you? (Jas. 2:6).

B2 Those oppressed in general

When they are brought low by oppression (Ps. 107:39); he was oppressed and afflicted (Isa. 53:7); why do I go mourning because of the oppression of the enemy? (Ps. 42:9; 43:2); Israel has been persecuted from youth (Ps. 129:1-3); you will have nothing but oppression (Deut. 28:33); they would be enslaved and afflicted for 400 years (Gen. 15:13; Acts 7:6).

B3 Specific oppression

Sarah ill-treated Hagar (Gen. 16:6); Joseph spoke harshly to his brothers (Gen. 42:7); slave drivers oppressed the Israelites (Exod. 1:11-14); Sisera cruelly oppressed the Israelites (Judg. 4:3); Solomon was to deal harshly with Joab (1 Kgs. 2:6); Solomon was to deal harshly with Shimei (1 Kgs. 2:9); Rehoboam spoke harshly to the people (1 Kgs. 12:10-14; 2 Chr. 10:10-14);

Asa oppressed some of the people (2 Chr. 16:10); Hazael king of Aram oppressed Israel (2 Kgs. 13:22).

B4 Attitude under oppression

Pray for those who mistreat you (Luke 6:28); servants should be submissive even to harsh masters (1 Pet. 2:18).

B5 Avoiding oppression

Do not oppress your neighbour (Lev. 19:13); do not rule harshly over an Israelite (Lev. 25:43); do not oppress the widow, the orphan, the stranger or the poor (Zech. 7:10); no oppressor will overrun them any more (Zech. 9:8); my princes will no longer oppress my people (Ezek. 45:8).

C Persecution

C1 Persecuting

They will persecute you (Luke 21:12); a hundred times more, with persecutions (Mark 10:30); if they persecute me, they will persecute you (John 15:20); which prophet did your fathers not persecute? (Acts 7:52); so they persecuted the prophets (Matt. 5:12); you will persecute them from town to town (Matt. 23:34); the one born according to the flesh persecutes the one of the Spirit (Gal. 4:29); the dragon persecuted the woman (Rev. 12:13); some they will kill and some they will persecute (Luke 11:49); for this reason the Jews persecuted Jesus, because he healed on the sabbath (John 5:16); as to zeal, a persecutor of the church (Phil. 3:6); I was once a persecutor (1 Tim. 1:13); I persecuted them even to foreign cities (Acts 26:11); why do you persecute me? (Acts 9:4-5; 22:7-8; 26:14-15); I persecuted the church (Acts 22:4; 1 Cor. 15:9; Gal. 1:13); persecution arose against the church in Jerusalem (Acts 8:1); the Jews stirred up persecution (Acts 13:50; 14:5).

C2 Persecuted

Many are my persecutors (Ps. 119:157); princes persecute me without cause (Ps. 119:161); they persecuted him whom you have smitten (Ps. 69:26); deliver me from those who persecute me (Ps. 31:15); blessed are those who are persecuted for righteousness' sake (Matt. 5:10-11); those scattered because of the persecution that arose over Stephen (Acts 11:19); will persecution separate us from the love of Christ? (Rom. 8:35); I am content with persecutions (2 Cor. 12:10); what persecutions I endured (2 Tim. 3:11); you have followed my persecutions (2 Tim. 3:11); all who would live godly will be persecuted (2 Tim. 3:12); if I preach circumcision, why am I still persecuted? (Gal. 5:11); that they may not be persecuted for the cross of Christ (Gal. 6:12); when persecution comes he falls away (Matt. 13:21; Mark 4:17); your steadfastness and faith in all your persecutions and afflictions (2 Thess. 1:4); pray for those who persecute you (Matt. 5:44); bless those who persecute you (Rom. 12:14); when persecuted, we endure (1 Cor. 4:12); we are persecuted but not forsaken (2 Cor. 4:9); when they persecute you in one town, flee to the next (Matt. 10:23).

736 Leniency

A Soft treatment

Deal gently with Absalom (2 Sam. 18:5); his father never pained him by asking what he did (1 Kgs. 1:6); he who pampers a slave will find him his heir (Prov. 29:21).

B Less punishment

The one who did not know his master's will will receive a light beating (Luke 12:48); it will be more tolerable for Tyre and Sidon (Matt. 11:22); it will be more tolerable for Sodom than for you (Matt. 11:24); it will be more bearable for Sodom and Gomorrah than for them (Matt. 10:15).

GENTLE, see 177.

737 Command

A Ordering

A1 God's orders

God commanded the man concerning the trees (Gen. 2:16-17); all that the Lord has commanded you though Moses (Num. 15:23); as the Lord commanded Moses (Num. 29:40); the Lord commanded this through his prophets (2 Chr. 29:25); to the married I give command, not I but the Lord (1 Cor. 7:10); by command of God our Saviour (1 Tim. 1:1; Titus 1:3); at the Lord's command they camped and set out (Num. 9:18-23); the Lord commanded the fish and it vomited Jonah on to dry land (Jonah 2:10); I have no command of the Lord but I give my opinion (1 Cor. 7:25).

A2 Christ's orders

Jesus gave orders by the Holy Spirit to the apostles (Acts 1:2); what I am writing is a command from the Lord (1 Cor. 14:37); he who has my commandments and keeps them is the one who loves me (John 14:21); you are my friends if you do what I command you (John 15:14); this is my commandment, that you love one another (John 15:12, 17); a new commandment, that you love one another (John 13:34); love one another, as he commanded us (1 John 3:23); with authority he commands even the unclean spirits (Mark 1:27); he charged them not to depart from Jerusalem (Acts 1:4); he commanded us to preach to the people (Acts 10:42); remember the commandment of the Lord and Saviour by your apostles (2 Pet. 3:2).

A3 The king's orders

Pharaoh commanded his men concerning Abraham (Gen. 12:20); Abimelech commanded them not to touch Isaac or Rebekah (Gen. 26:11); Pharaoh commanded his people to kill the boys (Exod. 1:22); David ordered them to deal gently with Absalom (2 Sam. 18:5); David charged Solomon (1 Kgs. 2:1-9); David charged Solomon to build the temple (1 Chr. 22:6); King Cyrus issued a decree to rebuild the temple (2 Chr. 36:22-3; Ezra 1:1-4); King Darius made a decree (Ezra 6:1); Artaxerxes' decree (Ezra 7:11-26); an edict to destroy the Jews (Esther 3:9-15); a decree from Caesar Augustus for a census (Luke 2:1); because of his oath and his guests he commanded the head to be given (Matt. 14:9).

A4 Men's orders

Isaac charged Jacob (Gen. 28:1); Jacob charged his sons (Gen. 49:29); Boaz commanded his servants not to touch Ruth (Ruth 2:9); Moses commanded the people (Deut. 27:11); what did Moses command you? (Mark 10:3); I say to my slave, 'Do this' and he does it (Luke 7:8); they charged them not to speak or teach in the name of Jesus (Acts 4:18); we command you in the name of our Lord Jesus Christ (2 Thess. 3:6); when we were with you we gave you this command (2 Thess. 3:10); we command and exhort such people in the Lord Jesus (2 Thess. 3:12); command and teach these things (1 Tim. 4:11); command these things so that they may be without reproach (1 Tim. 5:7); I charge you in the presence of God and of Christ Jesus (1 Tim. 5:21); do not heed commandments of men who reject the truth (Titus 1:14).

B Summoning

B1 Called by God

B1a Called to salvation

Many are called but few chosen (Matt. 22:14); I did not come to call the righteous but sinners (Matt. 9:13; Luke 5:32); those whom he predestined he called and those he called he justified (Rom. 8:30); called according to his purpose (Rom. 8:28); not because of works but of God's call (Rom. 9:11); God calls you into his own

kingdom (1 Thess. 2:12); the promise is for all whom the Lord will call to himself (Acts 2:39); you were called in one hope of your calling (Eph. 4:4); the prize of the upward call of God in Christ Jesus (Phil. 3:14); faithful is he who calls you (1 Thess. 5:24); partakers of a heavenly calling (Heb. 3:1); the God of all grace who called you to his eternal glory in Christ (1 Pet. 5:10); that those who are called may receive the promised inheritance (Heb. 9:15); through the knowledge of him who called us to his own glory and excellence (2 Pet. 1:3); the gifts and calling of God are irrevocable (Rom. 11:29); those with him are called and chosen and faithful (Rev. 17:14); God called me through his grace (Gal. 1:15); he called you through our gospel so as to obtain the glory of our Lord (2 Thess. 2:14); the hope of his calling (Eph. 1:18); to those who are the called (1 Cor. 1:24; Jude 1); you are the called of Jesus Christ (Rom. 1:6).

B1b Consider your call to salvation

Consider your calling (1 Cor. 1:26); you were called into fellowship with his Son (1 Cor. 1:9); you were called to freedom (Gal. 5:13); the peace of God, to which you were called in the one body (Col. 3:15); walk worthy of the calling with which you have been called (Eph. 4:1); God did not call us to impurity but to sanctification (1 Thess. 4:7); lay hold of the eternal life to which you were called (1 Tim. 6:12); God saved us and called us with a holy calling (2 Tim. 1:9); as he who called you is holy (1 Pet. 1:15); to this you have been called (1 Pet. 2:21); you were called that you might inherit a blessing (1 Pet. 3:9); confirm your calling and election (2 Pet. 1:10).

B1c Called to service

I have called you by name, you are mine (Isa. 43:1); that you may know that it is the Lord who calls you by name (Isa. 45:3); for Israel's sake I have called you by your name (Isa. 45:4); I have called him (Isa. 48:15); I have called by name Bezalel (Exod. 31:2); the Lord has called by name Bezalel (Exod. 35:30); I will call my servant Eliakim son of Hilkiah (Isa. 22:20); from the womb the Lord called me (Isa. 49:1); out of Egypt I called my son (Hos. 11:1; Matt. 2:15); set apart Barnabas and Paul for the work to which I have called them (Acts 13:2); we concluded that God had called us to preach the gospel in Macedonia (Acts 16:10); Paul was called an apostle of Jesus Christ by the will of God (1 Cor. 1:1); let each one walk as God has assigned and as God has called (1 Cor. 7:17); no one takes this honour to himself, but is called by God (Heb. 5:4).

B1d Others called by God

By faith Abraham obeyed when he was called (Heb. 11:8); 'Moses, Moses' (Exod. 3:4); God called to Samuel (1 Sam. 3:4-10); God called to the man clothed in linen (Ezek. 9:3); Israel, whom I called (Isa. 48:12); you will call and I will answer you (Job 14:15); then call and I will answer (Job 13:22).

B2 Christ summoning

Jesus called James and John (Matt. 4:21); he called them and they left their father Zebedee (Mark 1:20); he called to him his 12 disciples (Matt. 10:1); he summoned the 12 and sent them out (Mark 6:7); he called his disciples to him (Matt. 15:32; Mark 8:1); he called a child and put him in the midst of them (Matt. 18:2); Jesus called the children to him (Luke 18:16); rise, he is calling you! (Mark 10:49); Jesus stopped and called them (Matt. 20:32); he called those he wanted and they came to him (Mark 3:13); he calls his own sheep by name and leads them out (John 10:3).

B3 People summoning

Pharaoh summoned his magicians and wise men (Gen. 41:8; Exod. 7:11); Pharaoh summoned Joseph (Gen.

41:14); Pharaoh called Moses and Aaron (Exod. 8:8); the king summoned the midwives (Exod. 1:18); David called for Absalom (2 Sam. 14:33); David summoned Bathsheba (1 Kgs. 1:28); David summoned Zadok, Nathan and Benaiah (1 Kgs. 1:32); Solomon summoned Shimei (1 Kgs. 2:42); Ahab called Obadiah (1 Kgs. 18:3); King Joash called for Jehoiada the priest (2 Kgs. 12:7); Herod summoned the wise men secretly (Matt. 2:7); Jacob summoned Rachel and Leah to the flock (Gen. 31:4); Jacob summoned his sons (Gen. 49:1); Moses sent to call Dathan and Abiram (Num. 16:12); the girl called Moses' mother (Exod. 2:8); Eli called Samuel (1 Sam. 3:16); Pilate summoned the centurion and asked if Jesus were already dead (Mark 15:44); Absalom summoned Joab (2 Sam. 14:29, 32); Absalom summoned Hushai (2 Sam. 17:5); Jesus' mother and brothers called him (Mark 3:31); he called the steward (Luke 16:2); call your husband (John 4:16); she went and called her sister Mary (John 11:28); calling the saints and widows, he presented her alive (Acts 9:41).

738 Disobedience

A Disobedient

A1 Disobedient to God

Those who were disobedient in the days of Noah (1 Pet. 3:20); Moses and Aaron did not obey God's command (Num. 20:24; 27:14); they disobeyed in the desert (Num. 14:22; Deut. 9:7); they disobeyed in the land (Judg. 2:2); this is the nation which did not obey the voice of the Lord (Jer. 7:28); all Israel has transgressed your law, refusing to obey your voice (Dan. 9:11); our fathers refused to obey him (Acts 7:39); you were once disobedient to God (Rom. 11:30).

A2 Disobedient to the gospel

The sons of disobedience (Eph. 2:2; 5:6); if any husbands are disobedient to the word (1 Pet. 3:1); those who do not obey the gospel (2 Thess. 1:8); those who do not obey the truth but obey unrighteousness (Rom. 2:8); when some became hardened and disobeyed (Acts 19:9); that I may be delivered from the disobedient in Judea (Rom. 15:31); if anyone does not obey what we say in this letter (2 Thess. 3:14); once we also were disobedient (Titus 3:3).

A3 Disobedient to people

A rebellious son must be stoned to death (Deut. 21:18-21); an elder must not have disobedient children (Titus 1:6); disobedient to parents (Rom. 1:30; 2 Tim. 3:2); they are acting against the decrees of Caesar (Acts 17:7).

A4 Results of disobedience

The disastrous consequences of disobedience (Lev. 26:14-39; Deut. 30:17-18); by one man's disobedience many were made sinners (Rom. 5:19); if every transgression and disobedience received a just recompense (Heb. 2:2); they stumble because they are disobedient (1 Pet. 2:8); if you rebel, the Lord will be against you (1 Sam. 12:15); if you do not obey, curses will come upon you (Deut. 28:15); Israel was exiled through disobedience (2 Kgs. 18:11-12); those who were disobedient would not enter his rest (Heb. 3:18; 4:6); he who does not obey the Son will not see life (John 3:36); what will be the end of those who do not obey the gospel? (1 Pet. 4:17); you have received mercy because of their disobedience (Rom. 11:30); they have been disobedient so that by the mercy shown to you they may receive mercy (Rom. 11:31); God's wrath is coming on the sons of disobedience (Col. 3:6).

B Rebelling

B1 Rebellion against God

B1a Rebellion against God in general

Do not rebel against the angel (Exod. 23:21); do not rebel against the Lord (Num. 14:9; Josh. 22:19); rebellion is like the sin of divination (1 Sam. 15:23); the law is not for the righteous but for the lawless and rebellious (1 Tim. 1:9); they perish in Korah's rebellion (Jude 11).

B1b People rebellious against God

Say to the rebellious house (Ezek. 17:12); O rebellious house! (Ezek. 12:25); the house of Israel, the rebellious house (Ezek. 12:9); woe to the rebellious children (Isa. 30:1); all of them are stubbornly rebellious (Jer. 6:28); rebellious from the day I knew you (Deut. 9:24); I will purge the rebels from you (Ezek. 20:38).

B1c Those who rebelled against God

They have rebelled against you (Ps. 5:10); they rebelled against the Most High God (Ps. 78:56); Samaria has rebelled against her God (Hos. 13:16); do not harden your hearts as in the rebellion (Heb. 3:8, 15); who were those who heard and yet were rebellious? (Heb. 3:16); they rebelled in being unwilling to go up (Deut. 1:26; 9:23); they rebelled in going up (Num. 14:41; Deut. 1:43); they rebelled against the Most High (Ps. 78:17); they rebelled against God's Spirit (Ps. 106:33); they rebelled and grieved his Holy Spirit (Isa. 63:10); prisoners because they rebelled against God (Ps. 107:11); I raised up children but they rebelled (Isa. 1:2).

B2 Rebellion against men

The kings rebelled against Chedorlaomer (Gen. 14:4); Absalom's conspiracy against David (2 Sam. 15:7-12); Sheba has lifted his hand against King David (2 Sam. 20:21); Jeroboam rebelled against Solomon (1 Kgs. 11:26-7; 2 Chr. 13:6); Israel rebelled against the house of David (1 Kgs. 12:19; 2 Chr. 10:19); Moab rebelled against Israel (2 Kgs. 1:1; 3:5-7); Edom rebelled against Judah (2 Kgs. 8:20-2; 2 Chr. 21:8-10); Libnah revolted against Judah (2 Kgs. 8:22; 2 Chr. 21:10); Hezekiah rebelled against the king of Assyria (2 Kgs. 18:7); Jehoiakim rebelled against Nebuchadnezzar (2 Kgs. 24:1); Zedekiah rebelled against Nebuchadnezzar (2 Kgs. 24:20; 2 Chr. 36:13; Jer. 52:3; Ezek. 17:15); are you not the Egyptian who stirred up a revolt? (Acts 21:38); this is a rebellious city (Ezra 4:12, 15); the Jews are planning to rebel (Neh. 6:6); Barabbas committed insurrection (Mark 15:7; Luke 23:19, 25).

739 Obedience

A Obey!

Moses commanded them to do all the Lord had said (Exod. 34:32); why say 'Lord' and do not do what I say? (Luke 6:46); not everyone who says 'Lord' but he who does the will of my Father (Matt. 7:21); he who hears my words and does them is like a wise man (Matt. 7:24; Luke 6:47); if you know these things, blessed are you if you do them (John 13:17); as obedient children (1 Pet. 1:14); remind them to be obedient (Titus 3:1); whatever he says to you, do it (Gen. 41:55; John 2:5); confident of your obedience, I write to you (Philem. 21); obey your leaders and submit to them (Heb. 13:17); for obedience to Jesus Christ and for sprinkling by his blood (1 Pet. 1:2).

B We obey

All God has said we will do (Exod. 19:8; 24:3, 7); I have obeyed the voice of the Lord (1 Sam. 15:20); I do what the Father commanded (John 14:31); I have kept my Father's commandments (John 15:10); I come to do your will (Ps. 40:8); my food is to do the will of him who sent me (John 4:34); not disobedient to the heavenly vision (Acts 26:19); we must obey God rather than men (Acts 5:29).

C Those obeying

C1 Obeying God
Noah did all that God commanded (Gen. 6:22; 7:5); Abraham obeyed God (Gen. 22:18; 26:5; Heb. 11:8); Moses and Aaron did all that the Lord commanded them (Exod. 7:6, 10, 20); Joshua did all that the Lord commanded Moses (Josh. 11:15); David went up as the Lord commanded (2 Sam. 24:19); all dominions will serve and obey him (Dan. 7:27); the people obeyed the voice of the Lord and the words of Haggai (Hag. 1:12); angels obeying the voice of God (Ps. 103:20); he did as the angel of the Lord commanded him (Matt. 1:24); through one man's obedience many are made righteous (Rom. 5:19); Christ was obedient to death (Phil. 2:8); though a Son, he learned obedience by what he suffered (Heb. 5:8).

C2 Obeying Christ
If you love me, you will keep my commandments (John 14:15); he who has my commandments and keeps them is the one who loves me (John 14:21); if anyone loves me he will keep my word (John 14:23); taking every thought captive to obey Christ (2 Cor. 10:5); obedience to Jesus Christ (1 Pet. 1:2); to him shall be the obedience of the peoples (Gen. 49:10); the source of salvation to all who obey him (Heb. 5:9); even winds and sea obey him (Matt. 8:27; Luke 8:25); unclean spirits obeyed Jesus (Mark 1:27).

C3 Obeying people
Keep the king's command (Eccles. 8:2); children, obey your parents (Eph. 6:1; Col. 3:20); slaves, obey your masters (Eph. 6:5; Col. 3:22); I say, 'Go', 'Come' or 'Do this' and my soldiers do it (Matt. 8:9); I say to my slave, 'Do this' and he does it (Luke 7:8); I never disobeyed your command (Luke 15:29); you have kept all that Moses commanded you (Josh. 22:2); as we obeyed Moses, we will obey you (Josh. 1:17); Sarah obeyed Abraham (1 Pet. 3:6); Ruth did all her mother-in-law commanded her (Ruth 3:6); Esther did all that Mordecai commanded her (Esther 2:20); Mordecai did as Esther had commanded him (Esther 4:17); the Jews did as Mordecai had written (Esther 9:23); all Israel obeyed Solomon (1 Chr. 29:23); we have obeyed Jonadab son of Rechab (Jer. 35:8-10); obey the Pharisees (Matt. 23:3); Jesus was obedient to Mary and Joseph (Luke 2:51).

C4 Obeying the gospel
Many priests were obedient to the faith (Acts 6:7); as you have always obeyed (Phil. 2:12); having purified your souls by obedience to the truth (1 Pet. 1:22); the obedience of faith (Rom. 1:5; 16:26); obedience to your confession of the gospel (2 Cor. 9:13); you were obedient to the teaching (Rom. 6:17); the obedience of the Gentiles (Rom. 15:18); who hindered you from obeying the truth? (Gal. 5:7).

C5 Obeying evil
For those who obey wickedness there will be wrath (Rom. 2:8); do not let sin reign, to obey its lusts (Rom. 6:12); you are slaves of the one you obey, whether sin or obedience (Rom. 6:16).

D Blessings of obedience
Obeying God's commands brings blessing (Lev. 26:3-10; Deut. 6:24; 28:1-2; 30:2, 9-10; 1 Chr. 28:8); the man who keeps them will live (Lev. 18:5); if he observes my statutes he will live (Ezek. 18:21); if you do all I command I will establish your throne (1 Chr. 28:7; 2 Chr. 7:17-18); if you pay attention to my commands your peace would be like a river (Isa. 48:18); if you obey you will eat the best of the land (Isa. 1:19); God gives

the Holy Spirit to those who obey him (Acts 5:32); to obey is better than sacrifice (1 Sam. 15:22).

740 Compulsion

A Compelled
If any one forces you to go one mile, go two (Matt. 5:41); Simon of Cyrene was forced to bear Christ's cross (Matt. 27:32; Mark 15:21; Luke 23:26); compel them to come in (Luke 14:23); they were going to make Jesus king by force (John 6:15); they try to compel you to be circumcised (Gal. 6:12); I am under compulsion to preach the gospel (1 Cor. 9:16); the Lord has spoken! who can but prophesy? (Amos 3:8); I was compelled to appeal to Caesar (Acts 28:19).

B Not compelled
There was no compulsion over drinking (Esther 1:8); giving should not be by compulsion (2 Cor. 9:7); tend the flock of God, not under compulsion but willingly (1 Pet. 5:2); why compel Gentiles to live like Jews? (Gal. 2:14); Titus, though a Greek, was not compelled to be circumcised (Gal. 2:3); that your goodness might not be by compulsion but of your own free will (Philem. 14).

741 Master

A About kings

A1 Nature of kings
The heart of kings is unsearchable (Prov. 25:3); it is the glory of kings to seek things out (Prov. 25:2); in the spring when kings go out to war (2 Sam. 11:1); tell them what a king will do (1 Sam. 8:9); an advantage to a land is a king over cultivated fields (Eccles. 5:9); we do not fear the Lord, and what could a king do for us? (Hos. 10:3); those who wear soft clothes are in kings' houses (Matt. 11:8); the ruler is God's servant for your good (Rom. 13:4); a wisdom not of this age nor of the rulers of this age (1 Cor. 2:6); God sends governors to punish evildoers and praise those who do right (1 Pet. 2:14); I dwelt like a king (Job 29:25); Caesar's likeness and inscription (Matt. 22:20-1; Mark 12:16; Luke 20:24).

A2 Kings and wisdom
By me [Wisdom] kings reign (Prov. 8:15); wisdom strengthens a wise man more than ten rulers in a city (Eccles. 7:19); a wise king winnows the wicked (Prov. 20:26); a poor wise lad is better than an old foolish king (Eccles. 4:13); a ruler who lacks understanding is a great oppressor (Prov. 28:16); Solomon was greater than the kings of the earth in riches and wisdom (1 Kgs. 10:23).

A3 Kings and justice
By justice a king gives stability to the land (Prov. 29:4); a king who rules in justice winnows evil with his eyes (Prov. 20:8); if a king judges the poor with truth his throne will last for ever (Prov. 29:14); a king will rule in righteousness (Isa. 32:1); it is an abomination for kings to do evil (Prov. 16:12); a wicked ruler over a poor people is like a roaring lion or a charging bear (Prov. 28:15); if a ruler listens to falsehood all his ministers become wicked (Prov. 29:12).

A4 Kings and pride
In the multitude of people is a king's glory (Prov. 14:28); a king is not saved by a big army (Ps. 33:16); a slave who becomes king is unbearable (Prov. 30:22); the kings lie in glory, each in his own tomb (Isa. 14:18).

A5 Favour of kings
A king's favour is like dew (Prov. 19:12); the king favours a wise servant (Prov. 14:35); he who loves purity will have the king as his friend (Prov. 22:11); the man skilled in his work will stand before kings (Prov. 22:29); kings will come to the brightness of your rising (Isa. 60:3); you will suck the breast of kings (Isa. 60:16).

A6 Attitudes towards kings

Prayer should be made for kings (1 Tim. 2:2); submit yourselves to the king (1 Pet. 2:13); honour the king (1 Pet. 2:17); give to Caesar what is Caesar's (Matt. 22:21; Mark 12:17); do not speak evil of a ruler (Acts 23:5); let everyone be subject to the governing authorities (Rom. 13:1); remind them to be subject to rulers and authorities (Titus 3:1); they were not afraid of the king's edict (Heb. 11:23); Moses did not fear the anger of the king (Heb. 11:27); the Chaldeans scoff at kings and laugh at rulers (Hab. 1:10).

A7 Kings before God

A7a God rules over kings

Surely your God is Lord of kings (Dan. 2:47); the king's heart is like irrigation channels in the hand of the Lord (Prov. 21:1); let kings of the earth praise the Lord (Ps. 148:11); let all kings bow before him (Ps. 72:11); he is feared by the kings of the earth (Ps. 72:11); all the kings of the earth will give thanks to you (Ps. 138:4); the Lord will give strength to his king (1 Sam. 2:10); O Lord, in your strength the king rejoices (Ps. 21:1); give the king your judgements (Ps. 72:1); the king will rejoice in God (Ps. 63:11); the kings of the earth will bring their glory into new Jerusalem (Rev. 21:24).

A7b Kings opposed by God

None of the rulers of this age has understood this (1 Cor. 2:8); kings and great men hid themselves in caves in fear of God's wrath (Rev. 6:15-17); gathering the kings of the world for war on the great day of God (Rev. 16:14); the kings of the earth committed fornication with her (Rev. 17:2); the kings of the earth have committed immorality with her (Rev. 18:3); I saw the beast and the kings of the earth with their armies (Rev. 19:19); the kings of the earth set themselves against the Lord's anointed (Ps. 2:2); he reproved kings for their sake (1 Chr. 16:21; Ps. 105:14); the Lord will punish the kings of the earth on earth (Isa. 24:21); God says to a king, 'Worthless one!' (Job 34:18); to bind their kings in chains and fetters (Ps. 149:8); when the Almighty scattered the kings (Ps. 68:14); the Lord will shatter kings on the day of his wrath (Ps. 110:5).

A8 Making kings

May the Lord appoint a man over the congregation (Num. 27:16); appoint a king over us like all the nations (Deut. 17:14-16; 1 Sam. 8:5-6, 19-20); the Lord has set a king over you (1 Sam. 12:13); Tyre, the bestower of crowns (Isa. 23:8); they made kings, but not by me (Hos. 8:4); they put the crown on Joash (2 Kgs. 11:12); they were going to make Jesus king by force (John 6:15); the trees went forth to anoint a king (Judg. 9:8); everyone who makes himself a king sets himself against Caesar (John 19:12); the authorities which exist have been instituted by God (Rom. 13:1); without us you have become kings! (1 Cor. 4:8).

See also 733A1.

B God the ruler

B1 God is King

The Lord is king (Ps. 10:16); my king and my God! (Ps. 5:2); the King, the Lord (Ps. 98:6); the King whose name is the Lord of hosts (Jer. 48:15; 51:57); the Lord is a great king above all gods (Ps. 95:3); God is the king of all the earth (Ps. 47:2, 7; Zech. 14:9); king of the nations (Jer. 10:7); the king of glory (Ps. 24:7-10); the Lord, the king of Israel (Isa. 44:6); the Lord is the everlasting king (Jer. 10:10); the king eternal (1 Tim. 1:17); your eyes will see the king in his beauty (Isa. 33:17); Jerusalem is the city of the great King (Matt. 5:35); the King of Israel, the Lord, is in your midst (Zeph. 3:15); I am a great king (Mal. 1:14); King of the nations (Rev. 15:3); they have rejected me as king (1 Sam. 8:7).

B2 Christ as Lord

B2a Christ is king of Israel

A ruler will come out of Jacob (Num. 24:17, 19); from Judah will come a ruler over Israel (Mic. 5:2); from Bethlehem will come a ruler over Israel (Matt. 2:6); you are the king of Israel! (John 1:49); king of Israel (John 12:13); let the Christ, the king of Israel, come down from the cross (Mark 15:32); if you are the king of the Jews, save yourself (Luke 23:37); where is he who has been born king of the Jews? (Matt. 2:2); are you the king of the Jews? (Matt. 27:11); hail, king of the Jews! (Matt. 27:29; John 19:3); will you have me release the King of the Jews? (John 18:39); I have installed my king on Zion (Ps. 2:6); your king is coming to you, humble and seated on a donkey (Zech. 9:9); he is the King of Israel (Matt. 27:42).

B2b Christ is king of all

King of kings and Lord of lords (1 Tim. 6:15; Rev. 19:16); the Lamb is Lord of lords and King of kings (Rev. 17:14); Christ, the ruler of the kings of the earth (Rev. 1:5); the only sovereign (1 Tim. 6:15); saying there is another king, Jesus (Acts 17:7); the righteous Branch will reign as king (Jer. 23:5); so you are a king? (John 18:37); behold, your king! (John 19:14-15); your king is coming to you riding on a donkey (Matt. 21:5; John 12:15); saying he is Christ, a king (Luke 23:2); everyone who makes himself a king opposes Caesar (John 19:12); the King will say to those at his right hand (Matt. 25:34); the King will answer them (Matt. 25:40).

B2c Christ is Lord

God has made this Jesus both Lord and Christ (Acts 2:36); King of kings and Lord of lords (1 Tim. 6:15; Rev. 17:14; 19:16); Jesus Christ is lord of all (Acts 10:36); the same Lord is Lord of all (Rom. 10:12); Christ is Lord both of the dead and the living (Rom. 14:9); you call me Teacher and Lord, and so I am (John 13:13-14); those who call on the name of our Lord Jesus Christ, their Lord and ours (1 Cor. 1:2); one God, the Father and one Lord, Jesus Christ (1 Cor. 8:6); one Lord, one faith, one baptism (Eph. 4:5); Christ Jesus our Lord (1 Tim. 1:2); the Son of man is Lord of the sabbath (Luke 6:5); reverence Christ as Lord (1 Pet. 3:15); not everyone who says, 'Lord, Lord' will enter (Matt. 7:21); why call me Lord and do not do what I say? (Luke 6:46); they deny our only Master and Lord, Jesus Christ (Jude 4).

B2d Christ is my Lord

If you confess with your mouth that Jesus is Lord (Rom. 10:9); no one can say, 'Jesus is Lord' except by the Holy Spirit (1 Cor. 12:3); we do not preach ourselves but Christ Jesus as Lord (2 Cor. 4:5); every tongue will confess that Jesus Christ is Lord (Phil. 2:11); my Lord and my God! (John 20:28).

B2e Christ as ruler

God exalted him as Leader and Saviour (Acts 5:31); that in all things he might have the pre-eminence (Col. 1:18); the head of every man is Christ (1 Cor. 11:3); Christ is the head of the church (Eph. 1:22; 4:15; 5:23; Col. 2:19); he is the head of the body, the church (Col. 1:18); the head of all rule and authority (Col. 2:10).

C Rulers of Israel

C1 Rulers of northern kingdom

Those who reigned over Israel: Ish-bosheth (2 Sam. 2:10); Jeroboam I (1 Kgs. 12:20); Nadab (1 Kgs. 14:20); Baasha (1 Kgs. 15:16; 2 Chr. 16:1); Elah (1 Kgs. 16:6); Zimri (1 Kgs. 16:10); Omri (1 Kgs. 16:16; 2 Kgs. 8:26); Tibni [over half Israel] (1 Kgs. 16:21); Ahab (1 Kgs. 16:28-9; 2 Kgs. 21:3); Ahaziah (1 Kgs. 22:40; 2 Kgs. 1:2-3; 2 Chr. 20:35); Jehoram [Joram] (2 Kgs. 1:17); Jehu (2 Kgs. 9:6); Jehoahaz (2 Kgs. 10:35); Joash [Jehoash] (2 Kgs. 13:9); Jeroboam II (2 Kgs. 13:13; 1 Chr. 5:17); Zechariah (2 Kgs. 14:29); Shallum (2 Kgs. 15:10);

Menahem (2 Kgs. 15:14); Pekahiah (2 Kgs. 15:22); Pekah son of Remaliah (2 Kgs. 15:25; Isa. 7:1); Hoshea (2 Kgs. 15:30).

C2 Rulers of Judah

Those who reigned over Judah: Abimelech (Judg. 9:1-6); David (2 Sam. 2:4); Solomon (1 Kgs. 2:12; 1 Chr. 29:23); Rehoboam (1 Kgs. 12:17; 2 Chr. 9:31); Abijam [Abijah] (1 Kgs. 14:31; 2 Chr. 12:16); Asa (1 Kgs. 15:8; 2 Chr. 14:1; Jer. 41:9); Jehoshaphat (1 Kgs. 15:24; 2 Kgs. 3:1; 2 Chr. 17:1); Jehoram [Joram] (1 Kgs. 22:50; 2 Kgs. 1:17; 2 Chr. 21:1); Ahaziah [Jehoahaz] (2 Kgs. 8:24; 2 Chr. 22:1); Athaliah (2 Kgs. 11:3); Joash [Jehoash] (2 Kgs. 11:12; 2 Chr. 24:1); Amaziah (2 Kgs. 12:21; 2 Chr. 24:27); Azariah [Uzziah] (2 Kgs. 14:21; 2 Chr. 26:1; Isa. 6:1); Jotham (2 Kgs. 15:7; 1 Chr. 5:17; 2 Chr. 26:23); Ahaz (2 Kgs. 15:38; 2 Chr. 27:9); Hezekiah (2 Kgs. 16:20; 1 Chr. 4:41; 2 Chr. 28:27); Manasseh (2 Kgs. 20:21; 2 Chr. 32:33); Amon (2 Kgs. 21:18; 2 Chr. 33:20); Josiah (2 Kgs. 21:24; 2 Chr. 33:25); Jehoahaz [Shallum] (2 Kgs. 23:30, 31; 2 Chr. 36:1); Jehoiakim [Eliakim] (2 Kgs. 23:34; 2 Chr. 36:4); Jehoiachin [Jeconiah, Coniah] (2 Kgs. 24:6; 2 Chr. 36:8); Zedekiah [Mattaniah] (2 Kgs. 24:17; 2 Chr. 36:10).

D Earthly masters

D1 Masters in general

If the slave says, 'I love my master' (Exod. 21:5); a slave is not above his master (Matt. 10:24-5); let the leader become as the servant (Luke 22:26); masters, do not threaten (Eph. 6:9); masters, show justice (Col. 4:1); masters, you too have a master in heaven (Col. 4:1); like servant, like master, like maid, like mistress (Isa. 24:2); do not curse a ruler of your people (Exod. 22:28); if a ruler sins (Lev. 4:22); I have seen princes walking like slaves (Eccles. 10:7); would the governor be pleased with your offering? (Mal. 1:8); who made you a prince and a judge? (Exod. 2:14); who made you a ruler and a judge? (Acts 7:27).

D2 Leaders in Israel

Provide wise men from your tribes and I will appoint them as your heads (Deut. 1:13); the 12 heads, one from each tribe (Num. 1:4-16); 12 rods from the leaders of the tribes (Num. 17:2); the 70 elders (Num. 11:24); 250 leaders of the congregation (Num. 16:2); the leaders have been foremost in unfaithfulness (Ezra 9:2); take the leaders of the people and hang them (Num. 25:4); leaders of thousands, hundreds, fifties, tens (Exod. 18:21; Deut. 1:15); the king will appoint commanders of thousands and fifties (1 Sam. 8:12); the leaders of thousands are to assemble if only one trumpet is blown (Num. 10:4).

E Elders

E1 Elders of Israel

70 of the elders of Israel (Exod. 24:1; Num. 11:16); the elders of the congregation put their hands on the head of the bull (Lev. 4:15); bring the rebellious son to the elders of the city at the gate (Deut. 21:19); take the evidence of virginity to the elders of the city at the gate (Deut. 22:15); his brother's wife shall go to the elders at the gate (Deut. 25:7); the manslayers shall speak to the elders of the city (Josh. 20:4).

E2 Jewish elders and Christianity

He must suffer many things from the elders (Matt. 16:21; Luke 9:22); rejected by the elders and chief priests and scribes (Mark 8:31); the chief priests and elders of the people took counsel (Matt. 26:3; 27:1; 28:12; Mark 15:1); the scribes and elders had gathered (Matt. 26:57; Mark 14:53); when accused by the chief priests and elders, he made no answer (Matt. 27:12); the chief priests and elders persuaded the crowds (Matt. 27:20); they stirred up the people, the elders and the scribes (Acts 6:12); the chief priests, scribes and elders mocked

him (Matt. 27:41); Judas brought back the money to the chief priests and elders (Matt. 27:3); the chief priests and elders brought charges against him (Acts 25:15).

E3 Elders in the church

Going up to Jerusalem to the apostles and elders over this question (Acts 15:2-6); the apostles, elders and the whole church chose men to send to Antioch (Acts 15:22-3); they delivered the decisions of the apostles and elders in Jerusalem (Acts 16:4); all the elders were present (Acts 21:18); the laying on of hands by the elders (1 Tim. 4:14); appoint elders in every town (Titus 1:5); they appointed elders in every church (Acts 14:23); Paul called together the elders of the church (Acts 20:17); requirements for bishops [overseers] (1 Tim. 3:1-7); requirements for elders [overseers] (Titus 1:6-9); elders who rule well should be given double honour (1 Tim. 5:17); accusations against elders (1 Tim. 5:19-20); let the sick one call for the elders of the church (Jas. 5:14); I exhort the elders among you as a fellow-elder (1 Pet. 5:1).

E4 Elders in heaven

24 elders (Rev. 4:4, 10; 11:16); the four living creatures and 24 elders fell down before the Lamb (Rev. 5:8); one of the elders spoke to me (Rev. 7:13).

742 Servant

A Service of God

A1 Serving God

Serve the Lord (Exod. 23:25; Deut. 10:12; Josh. 24:14); him only shall you serve (Deut. 6:13; Matt. 4:10; Luke 4:8); we will serve the Lord (Josh. 24:15-24); serve the Lord with gladness (Ps. 100:2); to serve him without fear (Luke 1:74); to serve a living and true God (1 Thess. 1:9); I served the Lord with all humility (Acts 20:19); according to the Way I serve the God of our fathers (Acts 24:14); God whom I serve with my spirit in the gospel of his Son (Rom. 1:9); we serve in the new life of the Spirit, not the old written code (Rom. 7:6); they serve God day and night (Rev. 7:15); those who kill you will think they are offering service to God (John 16:2); David rendered service to God in his own generation (Acts 13:36); there are varieties of ministry, but the same Lord (1 Cor. 12:5); cleansing the conscience from dead works to serve the living God (Heb. 9:14); I know your love and faith and service (Rev. 2:19); he is not served by human hands (Acts 17:25); it is vain to serve God (Mal. 3:14); who is the Almighty, that we should serve him? (Job 21:15).

A2 Servants of God

The Israelites are my servants (Lev. 25:42); a thousand thousands served him (Dan. 7:10); slaves of God (Rom. 6:22; 1 Pet. 2:16); on my menservants and maidservants I will pour out my Spirit (Joel 2:29; Acts 2:18); these men are slaves of the Most High God (Acts 16:17); the ruler is God's servant for your good (Rom. 13:4-6); we commend ourselves as servants of God (2 Cor. 6:4); he makes his servants a flame of fire (Heb. 1:7); I am the handmaid of the Lord (Luke 1:38); Satan's servants disguise themselves as servants of righteousness (2 Cor. 11:15); Abraham his servant (Ps. 105:6); fear not, Jacob my servant (Jer. 30:10); remember Abraham, Isaac and Israel, your servants! (Exod. 32:13); Joshua the servant of the Lord (Judg. 2:8); Moses the Lord's servant (Exod. 14:31); Moses was faithful as a servant (Heb. 3:5); my servant Job (Job 1:8); I have found David my servant (Ps. 89:20); my servant Eliakim son of Hilkiah (Isa. 22:20); Nebuchadnezzar king of Babylon, my servant (Jer. 27:6); Zerubbabel my servant (Hag. 2:23); he has helped his servant Israel in remembrance of his mercy (Luke 1:54); Timothy, servant of God (1 Thess.

3:2); I am a fellow-slave with you (Rev. 10:10); you are no longer a slave but a son (Gal. 4:7).

A3 Christ the Servant of the Lord
Behold, my servant (Isa. 42:1; Matt. 12:18); my servant, the Branch (Zech. 3:8); the Lord formed me from the womb to be his servant (Isa. 49:5-6); who is blind but my servant? (Isa. 42:19); my servant will prosper (Isa. 52:13); the righteous one, my servant (Isa. 53:11); God has glorified his servant Jesus (Acts 3:13); your holy servant Jesus whom you anointed (Acts 4:27); signs and wonders through the name of your holy servant Jesus (Acts 4:30); the Son of Man came not to be served but to serve (Matt. 20:28; Mark 10:45); I am among you as one who serves (Luke 22:27); Christ became a servant to the circumcision (Rom. 15:8); Christ took the form of a slave (Phil. 2:7).

A4 Not serving God
They worshipped and served the creature rather than the Creator (Rom. 1:25); you cannot serve God and mammon (Luke 16:13).

B Service of Christ
That all peoples, nations and languages should serve the Son of man (Dan. 7:14); angels ministered to Jesus (Matt. 4:11; Mark 1:13); women who ministered to him in Galilee (Matt. 27:55; Mark 15:41); Martha was distracted with all her serving (Luke 10:40); Martha served at the meal (John 12:2); if your gift is service, use it in your serving (Rom. 12:7); fervent in Spirit, serving the Lord (Rom. 12:11); he who thus serves Christ is acceptable to God and approved by men (Rom. 14:18); serving the Lord Christ (Col. 3:24); if any one serves me, let him follow me (John 12:26); when did we see you in need and did not minister to you? (Matt. 25:44); they do not serve Christ but their own stomach (Rom. 16:18); the free man is Christ's slave (1 Cor. 7:22); to appoint you a servant and a witness (Acts 26:16); are they servants of Christ? I am a better one (2 Cor. 11:23); if I were trying to please men I would not be a slave of Christ (Gal. 1:10); slaves of Christ, doing the will of God from the heart (Eph. 6:6); you will be a good servant of Christ Jesus (1 Tim. 4:6); James, a slave of God and of the Lord Jesus Christ (Jas. 1:1); Paul and Apollos are servants through whom you believed (1 Cor. 3:5); of this gospel I was made a minister [servant] (Eph. 3:7).

C Service of people
C1 Serving people
I have given him all his brothers as servants (Gen. 27:37); the older will serve the younger (Gen. 25:23; Rom. 9:12); no one can serve two masters (Matt. 6:24; Luke 16:13); who is greater, he who reclines at table or he who serves? (Luke 22:27); let them serve all the more because those who benefit are believers and beloved (1 Tim. 6:2); Timothy and Erastus ministered to Paul (Acts 19:22); whoever serves, by the strength that God supplies (1 Pet. 4:11); through love serve one another (Gal. 5:13); use your gift in serving one another (1 Pet. 4:10); I am going to Jerusalem, serving the saints (Rom. 15:25); that my service for Jerusalem may be acceptable to the saints (Rom. 15:31); the love you showed in serving the saints (Heb. 6:10); they devoted themselves to serving the saints (1 Cor. 16:15); it was revealed to them that they were not serving themselves but you (1 Pet. 1:12); those who will serve the king of Babylon will remain in the land (Jer. 27:11-17); I will serve you seven years for Rachel (Gen. 29:18-20); serve me for her for another seven years (Gen. 29:27-30); Mark is useful in serving me (2 Tim. 4:11); that Onesimus might serve me on your behalf (Philem. 13).

C2 Servants
C2a Servants of people in general
As the eyes of servants look to the hand of their master (Ps. 123:2); do not covet your neighbour's male or female servant (Exod. 20:17; Deut. 5:21); Satan's servants disguise themselves as servants of righteousness (2 Cor. 11:15); a king will take your male and female servants (1 Sam. 8:16); a wise servant will rule over a son who acts shamefully (Prov. 17:2); the fool will be servant to the wise (Prov. 11:29); like servant, like master, like maid, like mistress (Isa. 24:2); even on menservants and maidservants I will pour out my Spirit (Joel 2:29; Acts 2:18); who are you to judge another man's servant? (Rom. 14:4); servants, be submissive to your masters (1 Pet. 2:18); if you speak kindly to these people, they will be your servants (1 Kgs. 12:7; 2 Chr. 10:7); whoever would be great must be your servant (Matt. 20:26-7; Mark 10:43); the greatest among you will be your servant (Matt. 23:11); if any one would be first, he must be the servant of all (Mark 9:35); let the leader become as the servant (Luke 22:26).

C2b Particular servants of people
The oldest servant in Abraham's house (Gen. 24:2); Joseph became Potiphar's chief servant (Gen. 39:4); Joshua, Moses' servant (Exod. 24:13; Num. 11:28; Josh. 1:1); Elisha was Elijah's servant (1 Kgs. 19:21; 2 Kgs. 3:11); Ziba the servant of Mephibosheth (2 Sam. 16:1); Gehazi, Elisha's servant (2 Kgs. 4:12); the tribe of Levi is to serve Aaron and the tabernacle (Num. 3:6-8).

C2c Deacons
Requirements for deacons (1 Tim. 3:8-13); Phoebe was a deacon of the church at Cenchrea (Rom. 16:1).

C3 Maidservants
A maidservant who supplants her mistress is unbearable (Prov. 30:23); like servant, like master, like maid, like mistress (Isa. 24:2); Hagar was Sarah's Egyptian maidservant (Gen. 16:1; 25:12); Laban gave Zilpah as Leah's maidservant (Gen. 29:24); Laban gave Bilhah as Rachel's maidservant (Gen. 29:29); a maidservant went to tell Jonathan and Ahimaaz (2 Sam. 17:17); a captive Israelite girl served Naaman's wife (2 Kgs. 5:2); a servant girl accused Peter of being with Jesus (Matt. 26:69); the maid told other bystanders, 'This is one of them' (Mark 14:69); a maid, seeing Peter as he sat in the firelight (Luke 22:56); the maid who kept the door spoke to Peter (John 18:17); Rhoda, a servant-girl (Acts 12:13).

C4 Slaves
SLAVERY, see 745B.
C4a Slaves in general
If an ox gores a male or female slave (Exod. 21:32); if I have despised the rights of my slaves (Job 31:13); slaves, whether native-born or bought, must be circumcised (Gen. 17:12-13, 13); slaves should be subject to their masters (Titus 2:9); slaves should honour their masters (1 Tim. 6:1); a slave is not above his master (Matt. 10:24; John 13:16; 15:20); it is enough for the slave to be like his master (Matt. 10:25); which of you will tell his slave to eat and drink first? (Luke 17:7-8); whoever would be first among you must be your slave (Matt. 20:27; Mark 10:44); while the heir is a child he is no different from a slave (Gal. 4:1); slaves, obey your masters (Eph. 6:5; Col. 3:22); masters, treat your slaves justly and fairly (Col. 4:1); do not slander a slave to his master (Prov. 30:10); the slave who becomes king is unbearable (Prov. 30:22); I have seen slaves riding and princes walking (Eccles. 10:7); the slave is Christ's free man (1 Cor. 7:22); in Christ there is neither slave nor free (Gal. 3:28; Col. 3:11); I do not call you slaves (John

15:15); you are no longer a slave but a son (Gal. 4:7); were you a slave when called? (1 Cor. 7:21).

C4b Individual slaves
I am Abraham's slave (Gen. 24:34); Abraham had two sons, one by the slave-girl (Gal. 4:22); drive out the slave woman (Gen. 21:10); Issachar became a slave at forced labour (Gen. 49:15); is Israel a slave? (Jer. 2:14); Peter cut off the ear of the high priest's slave (Matt. 26:51); a centurion had a slave who was valued (Luke 7:2); ourselves your slaves for Jesus' sake (2 Cor. 4:5); Onesimus is no longer a slave but a beloved brother (Philem. 16); a slave girl with a spirit of divination (Acts 16:16).

C4c Groups of slaves
Abraham had male and female slaves (Gen. 12:16); Abimelech gave Abraham male and female slaves (Gen. 20:14); the Lord has given Abraham menservants and maidservants (Gen. 24:35); Jacob had male and female slaves (Gen. 30:43; 32:5); you will always be slaves, hewers of wood and drawers of water (Josh. 9:23); I bought male and female slaves (Eccles. 2:7); we will be slaves to Pharaoh (Gen. 47:19); remember you were slaves in Egypt (Deut. 5:15); they would be enslaved and afflicted for 400 years (Gen. 15:13; Acts 7:6); Israel came out of the land of slavery (Exod. 13:3; Deut. 6:12); you will be the king's slaves (1 Sam. 8:17); you will offer yourselves as slaves (Deut. 28:68); we are slaves (Ezra 9:9; Neh. 9:36); cargo of bodies, and souls of men (Rev. 18:13).

C5 Slave or free
I will cut off every male, slave or free (1 Kgs. 21:21); he who was called in the Lord as a slave is the Lord's freedman (1 Cor. 7:22); he who was called whilst free is a slave of Christ (1 Cor. 7:22); one body, Jews or Greeks, slave or free (1 Cor. 12:13); he will receive back the good done, whether slave or free (Eph. 6:8); they promise freedom, though they are slaves of corruption (2 Pet. 2:19); slave and free hid themselves in caves in fear of God's wrath (Rev. 6:15-17); all, small and great, rich and poor, free and slave, must have a mark (Rev. 13:16); eat the flesh of all men, free and slaves, small and great (Rev. 19:18).

D Serving false gods
Do not serve their gods (Exod. 23:24); do not bow down to them or serve them (Exod. 20:5).

743 Badge of rule

A Thrones

A1 God's throne

A1a The throne of God
Your throne is from generation to generation (Lam. 5:19); something like a throne above a platform (Ezek. 1:26); heaven is my throne (Isa. 66:1); heaven is God's throne (Matt. 5:34; Acts 7:49); he who swears by heaven swears by God's throne (Matt. 23:22); Jerusalem will be called the Throne of the Lord (Jer. 3:17); this is the place of my throne (Ezek. 43:7); the throne of God and of the Lamb will be in the city (Rev. 22:3); a throne of sapphire (Ezek. 10:1); there was a throne in heaven (Rev. 4:2); let us draw near to the throne of grace (Heb. 4:16); a great white throne (Rev. 20:11).

A1b God seated on his throne
God sits on his holy throne (Ps. 47:8); God is enthroned on the cherubim (Isa. 37:16); I saw the Lord sitting on his throne (1 Kgs. 22:19; 2 Chr. 18:18); I overcame and sat down with my Father on his throne (Rev. 3:21); seated at the right hand of the throne of the Majesty in heaven (Heb. 8:1); Jesus sat down at the right hand of the throne of God (Heb. 12:2); hide us from him who sits on the throne and from the wrath of the Lamb (Rev. 6:16); salvation to our God who sits on

the throne and to the Lamb (Rev. 7:10); he who sits on the throne will presence himself with them (Rev. 7:15); God who sits on the throne (Rev. 19:4).

A2 Christ's throne
When the Son of man sits on his glorious throne (Matt. 19:28; 25:31); the throne of God and of the Lamb will be in the city (Rev. 22:3); the river flowing from the throne of God and of the Lamb (Rev. 22:1); your throne is for ever (Heb. 1:8); to him who overcomes I will grant to sit on my throne (Rev. 3:21).
CHRIST ON GOD S THRONE, see 743A1b.

A3 Other thrones
Pharaoh who sits on his throne (Exod. 11:5); Solomon made a great throne (1 Kgs. 10:18; 2 Chr. 9:17); the hall of the throne (1 Kgs. 7:7); the kings were sitting on their thrones (1 Kgs. 22:10; 2 Chr. 18:9); he set Jehoiachin's throne above the thrones of the other kings (Jer. 52:32); they set Joash on the throne (2 Kgs. 11:19; 2 Chr. 23:20); Ahasuerus sat on his throne (Esther 1:2; 5:1); Nebuchadnezzar will set his throne over these stones (Jer. 43:10); you will sit on 12 thrones (Matt. 19:28; Luke 22:30); thrones were placed (Dan. 7:9); thrones on which those given authority to judge were seated (Rev. 20:4); the elders on 24 thrones (Rev. 4:4); the dragon gave the beast his throne (Rev. 13:2); the fifth angel poured his bowl on the throne of the beast (Rev. 16:10); Satan's throne (Rev. 2:13).

B Crowns / diadems

B1 Crowns for Christ
They put a crown of thorns on Jesus' head (Matt. 27:29; Mark 15:17; John 19:2, 5); on his head are many diadems (Rev. 19:12).

B2 Priest's crown
A plate of pure gold (Exod. 28:36); the holy crown (Exod. 29:6; Lev. 8:9); the plate of the holy crown (Exod. 39:30); make a crown and set it on the head of Joshua the high priest (Zech. 6:11).

B3 Crowns on creatures
A crown for the king's horse (Esther 6:8); on the heads were seven diadems (Rev. 12:3); on its horns were ten diadems (Rev. 13:1); the locusts had what looked like golden crowns (Rev. 9:7).

B4 Crowns for God's people
The Lord will become a crown of glory for his people (Isa. 28:5); the crown of righteousness is laid up for me (2 Tim. 4:8); the crown of life which the Lord has promised to those who love him (Jas. 1:12); the crown of life (Rev. 2:10); you will receive the unfading crown of glory (1 Pet. 5:4); lest any one take your crown (Rev. 3:11); 24 elders with golden crowns (Rev. 4:4); a crown was given to the rider (Rev. 6:2); the woman had a crown of 12 stars (Rev. 12:1); who is our hope or joy or crown of boasting but you? (1 Thess. 2:19); my joy and crown (Phil. 4:1).

B5 Other crowns
You set a crown of fine gold on the king's head (Ps. 21:3); the Amalekite took Saul's crown and armlet (2 Sam. 1:10); David took the crown of the king of Rabbah (2 Sam. 12:30; 1 Chr. 20:2); they put the crown on Joash (2 Kgs. 11:12; 2 Chr. 23:11); Queen Vashti with her royal crown (Esther 1:11); the king put a crown on Esther's head (Esther 2:17); Mordecai had a gold crown (Esther 8:15); no athlete is crowned unless he competes according to the rules (2 Tim. 2:5); the crown of the wise is their riches (Prov. 14:24); a grey head is a crown of glory (Prov. 16:31); grandchildren are the crown of old men (Prov. 17:6); an excellent wife is her husband's crown (Prov. 12:4).

C Sceptres
The sceptre will not depart from Judah (Gen. 49:10); Judah is my sceptre (Ps. 60:7; 108:8); a sceptre will rise

from Israel (Num. 24:17); a sceptre of righteousness is the sceptre of your kingdom (Ps. 45:6; Heb. 1:8); unless the king extends the golden sceptre (Esther 4:11).

D Gold chains
Pharaoh put a gold chain round Joseph's neck (Gen. 41:42); you will have a chain of gold for your neck (Dan. 5:16); they put a chain of gold around Daniel's neck (Dan. 5:29).

744 Freedom
FREED, see 746.

A Freedom in general
Happy the land whose king is the son of free men (Eccles. 10:17); we have never been in bondage to anyone (John 8:33); in the year of jubilee proclaim liberty through the land (Lev. 25:10); you were called to freedom (Gal. 5:13); live as free men (1 Pet. 2:16).

B Freedom from the law
If her husband dies, the woman is free from the law of marriage (Rom. 7:2-3); free to be married to whom she wishes (1 Cor. 7:39); then the sons are free (Matt. 17:26); do not use your freedom as an opportunity for the flesh (Gal. 5:13); do not use your freedom as a cover for evil (1 Pet. 2:16); the law of liberty (Jas. 1:25; 2:12).

C Freedom in the gospel
Where the Spirit of the Lord is, there is freedom (2 Cor. 3:17); for freedom Christ has set us free (Gal. 5:1); Jerusalem above is free (Gal. 4:26); we are children of the free woman (Gal. 4:31); am I not free? (1 Cor. 9:1); the word of God is not imprisoned (2 Tim. 2:9); take care your liberty does not become a stumbling block to the weak (1 Cor. 8:9); though I am free from all men, I have made myself a slave to all (1 Cor. 9:19); my freedom should not be condemned because of another man's conscience (1 Cor. 10:29); false brethren who slipped in to spy out our liberty in Christ (Gal. 2:4).

745 Subjection

A Being subject
A1 Subject to God
The Son will be subject to God (1 Cor. 15:28); the Son can do nothing of himself (John 5:19, 30); I have come not to do my own will (John 6:38); I do not speak from myself (John 12:49; 14:10); slaves of God (Rom. 6:22); till I make your enemies your footstool (Ps. 110:1; Matt. 22:44; Mark 12:36; Luke 20:43; Acts 2:35; Heb. 1:13); he must reign until he has put all his enemies under his feet (1 Cor. 15:25).

A2 Subject to Christ
Angels, authorities and powers are subjected to Christ (1 Pet. 3:22); he is able to subject all things to himself (Phil. 3:21); he has put all things under his feet (Ps. 8:6; 1 Cor. 15:27; Eph. 1:22); you have led captives (Ps. 68:18).

A3 Subject to people
A3a Subjection to people
We do not yet see everything subject to man (Heb. 2:8); he subdues people under us (Ps. 47:3); even the demons are subject to us in your name (Luke 10:17-20); we did not yield in subjection to them for one hour (Gal. 2:5); he did not subject to angels the world to come (Heb. 2:5).

A3b Be subject to people
Let everyone be subject to the governing authorities (Rom. 13:1-5); be subject to rulers and authorities (Titus 3:1; 1 Pet. 2:13); slaves should be subject to their masters (Titus 2:9); I make myself a slave to all men (1 Cor. 9:19).

A4 Subject to evil
We were in slavery to the elemental principles of the world (Gal. 4:3); through fear of death they were in

lifelong bondage (Heb. 2:15); when you were slaves of sin you were free with regard to righteousness (Rom. 6:20); everyone who sins is a slave to sin (John 8:34); though you were slaves of sin (Rom. 6:17); what overcomes a man enslaves him (2 Pet. 2:19); you are slaves of the one you obey, whether sin or obedience (Rom. 6:16); you are in the bond of iniquity (Acts 8:23); once we were in slavery to various lusts (Titus 3:3); the present Jerusalem is in slavery with her children (Gal. 4:25); you desire to be enslaved once more (Gal. 4:9); false brethren bringing us into bondage (Gal. 2:4); do not take on a yoke of slavery (Gal. 5:1); no longer slaves to sin (Rom. 6:6); you have not received a spirit of slavery (Rom. 8:15).

B Slavery
SLAVES, see 742C4.

B1 The law on slavery
The law on slavery (Exod. 21:2; Lev. 25:39-55; Deut. 15:12); do not become slaves of men (1 Cor. 7:23); do not hand back an escaped slave (Deut. 23:15); the slave does not remain in the house for ever (John 8:35).

B2 Enslaved
B2a Making slaves in general
You may take male and female slaves from the nations (Lev. 25:44-5); the borrower becomes the lender's slave (Prov. 22:7); you bear it if someone makes slaves of you (2 Cor. 11:20); if we were to be made slaves I would have kept quiet (Esther 7:4); one is from Mount Sinai, bearing children for slavery (Gal. 4:24); the Israelites cried out because of their slavery (Exod. 2:23); they turned around and took back their slaves (Jer. 34:11); they appointed a leader to return to slavery in Egypt (Neh. 9:17).

B2b Enslaving particular people
May Canaan be Shem's slave (Gen. 9:26-7); Judah asked to be a slave in place of Benjamin (Gen. 44:33); the men of Israel intended to make slaves of the people of Judah (2 Chr. 28:10); our sons and daughters are being forced into slavery (Neh. 5:5); Joseph was sold as a slave (Ps. 105:17); the creditor coming to make the two sons slaves (2 Kgs. 4:1).
FORCED LABOUR, see 682B.

C Taming
Every kind of animal has been tamed by man (Jas. 3:7); no one can tame the tongue (Jas. 3:8).

746 Liberation

A God releasing
A1 God freeing Israel
Let my people go (Exod. 5:1); let my son go (Exod. 4:23); I will deliver you from your bondage (Exod. 6:6); God delivered the people from under the hand of the Egyptians (Exod. 18:10); I have come down to free them (Acts 7:34); I broke the bars of your yoke (Lev. 26:13); I relieved his shoulder of the burden (Ps. 81:6); I brought you out of the land of bondage (Deut. 5:6); when the Lord brought back the captives of Zion (Ps. 126:1); I will break the yoke of the king of Babylon (Jer. 28:4); he will let my exiles go free (Isa. 45:13).

A2 God freeing captives
The Lord releases those condemned to death (Ps. 102:20); you have broken the yoke of his burden (Isa. 9:4); God broke their bonds (Ps. 107:14); God loosens the bond of kings (Job 12:18); God sets the prisoners free (Ps. 146:7); God released him from the agony of death (Acts 2:24); Peter's chains fell off (Acts 12:7); everyone's chains were unfastened (Acts 16:26); the angel opened the prison doors and brought them out (Acts 5:19).

A3 Freedom through Christ

If the Son sets you free you will be free indeed (John 8:36); the truth will make you free (John 8:32-3); freed from sin (Rom. 6:7, 18, 22); set free from the principle of sin and death (Rom. 8:2); everyone who believes is freed from all things (Acts 13:39); he has freed us from our sins by his blood (Rev. 1:5); the Lord sent me to proclaim release to the captives (Isa. 61:1; Luke 4:18); to set at liberty those who are downtrodden (Luke 4:18); the glorious freedom of the children of God (Rom. 8:21); for freedom Christ has set us free (Gal. 5:1); woman, you are freed from your infirmity (Luke 13:12-16); unbind him and let him go (John 11:44); whatever you loose on earth will be loosed in heaven (Matt. 16:19; 18:18); the creation will be released from bondage (Rom. 8:21).

A4 Freed from the law

We have been released from the law (Rom. 7:6); if her husband dies, the woman is free from the law of marriage (Rom. 7:2, 3); free to be married to whom she wishes (1 Cor. 7:39).

B People releasing

B1 People freeing captives

The fast I choose is to break every yoke (Isa. 58:6); I have authority to release you and authority to crucify you (John 19:10); it was the governor's custom to release a prisoner (Matt. 27:15-21; Mark 15:6-9; John 18:39); Pilate desired to release Jesus (Luke 23:16-22; Acts 3:13); if you release this man you are no friend of Caesar's (John 19:12); when they had threatened them further they let them go (Acts 4:21-3); the apostles were flogged, warned and released (Acts 5:40); Herod intended to bring Peter out after the passover (Acts 12:4); Paul and Silas were to be released from prison (Acts 16:35-7); when they had taken a pledge from Jason and the others they released them (Acts 17:9); Paul could have been set free if he had not appealed (Acts 26:32); when they examined me they wanted to release me (Acts 28:18); Timothy has been released (Heb. 13:23); Jehoiachin was released from prison (2 Kgs. 25:27; Jer. 52:31); some refused to accept release that they might rise to a better life (Heb. 11:35).

B2 People freeing slaves

In the seventh year the Hebrew slave must go free (Exod. 21:2; Deut. 15:12; Jer. 34:14); the female slave will go out for nothing (Exod. 21:11); if a slave is injured, he or she should be freed (Exod. 21:26-7); an Israelite slave must be released in the year of Jubilee (Lev. 25:54); Hebrew slaves had to be set free (Jer. 34:8-10); if you can become free, do so (1 Cor. 7:21); I will not go out free (Exod. 21:5; Deut. 15:16); a female slave shall not go free like males (Exod. 21:7).

B3 Freeing animals

Let the live bird go free (Lev. 14:7, 53); let the mother bird go (Deut. 22:7); the goat released in the wilderness (Lev. 16:22); on the sabbath each of you unties his ox or donkey (Luke 13:15); Samson let the foxes go (Judg. 15:5).

B4 Untying things

Untie her hair (Num. 5:18); I am not worthy to loose his sandals (Mark 1:7; Luke 3:16; John 1:27).

C Evil and freedom

At the end of the 1000 years Satan will be released from prison (Rev. 20:7); after the 1000 years the devil must be released for a little while (Rev. 20:3); the four angels were released (Rev. 9:14-15); they promise freedom, though they are slaves of corruption (2 Pet. 2:19); let us break their fetters and bonds from us! (Ps. 2:3); I proclaim a release to sword, pestilence and famine (Jer. 34:17); there is no discharge in the war [against death]

(Eccles. 8:8); you will not get out until you have paid the last penny (Matt. 5:26).

747 Restraint

A Restraining

I will not let you go unless you bless me (Gen. 32:26); before faith came we were in custody under the law (Gal. 3:23); a dumb donkey restrained the prophet's insanity (2 Pet. 2:16); you know what restrains the man of sin now (2 Thess. 2:6-7).

B Arresting

B1 Arresting Christ

Jesus' family sought to seize him, saying he was mad (Mark 3:21); they looked for a way to arrest Jesus (Matt. 21:46; Mark 12:12; Luke 20:19; John 7:30-2; 11:57); they tried to seize him (John 10:39); they plotted to arrest him by stealth (Matt. 26:4; Mark 14:1); the one I kiss is the man, seize him (Matt. 26:48; Mark 14:44); have you come with swords and clubs to arrest me? (Matt. 26:55; Mark 14:48-9); they arrested him (Matt. 26:50; Mark 14:46; Luke 22:54; John 18:12); if you seek me, let these people go (John 18:8).

B2 Arresting others

When they arrest you, do not be anxious what to say (Mark 13:11); Herod had arrested John (Matt. 14:3; Mark 6:17); they arrested Peter and John (Acts 4:3); Herod arrested some of the church (Acts 12:1); Herod arrested Peter (Acts 12:3); this man was arrested by the Jews and was about to be killed by them (Acts 23:27); some Jews seized me in the temple (Acts 26:21); the governor guarded Damascus in order to seize me (2 Cor. 11:32); like creatures of instinct, born to be caught and killed (2 Pet. 2:12); the beast and the false prophet were captured (Rev. 19:20).

C Binding

C1 Tying up

Abraham bound Isaac (Gen. 22:9); binding Samson (Judg. 15:10-13; 16:6-13); Ezekiel would be tied with ropes (Ezek. 3:25); Shadrach, Meshach and Abednego were tied up (Dan. 3:20-4); Lazarus was bound hand and foot with wrappings (John 11:44); bind him hand and foot (Matt. 22:13); they bound Jesus (Matt. 27:2; Mark 15:1; John 18:12); Annas sent him bound to Caiaphas the high priest (John 18:24); Saul took believers bound to Jerusalem (Acts 9:2); he has authority from the chief priests to bind all who call on your name (Acts 9:14); did he not come here to bring them bound before the high priests? (Acts 9:21); Paul would be bound in Jerusalem (Acts 21:11); Paul was tied up with the thongs (Acts 22:25); the commander was afraid because he had bound a Roman citizen (Acts 22:29); angels in everlasting bonds in darkness (Jude 6); the devil was bound for 1000 years (Rev. 20:2); unless he first binds the strong man (Matt. 12:29; Mark 3:27; Luke 11:22); whatever you bind on earth will be bound in heaven (Matt. 16:19; 18:18).

C2 Binding animals

Bind the sacrifice to the horns of the altar (Ps. 118:27); he ties his donkey to the vine (Gen. 49:11); you will find a donkey tied up (Matt. 21:2; Mark 11:2-4; Luke 19:30); do not muzzle an ox which is threshing (Deut. 25:4; 1 Cor. 9:9; 1 Tim. 5:18); we put bits in horses' mouths (Jas. 3:3); the horse and mule need bit and bridle (Ps. 32:9); anyone perfect in speech is able to bridle the whole body (Jas. 3:2).

C3 Fettering and shackling

Joseph was shackled (Ps. 105:18); Samson was bound with bronze shackles (Judg. 16:21); Manasseh was bound with bronze shackles (2 Chr. 33:11); Zedekiah was bound with bronze shackles (2 Kgs. 25:7; Jer. 39:7; 52:11); Jehoiakim was bound with bronze shackles (2

Chr. 36:6); Jeremiah was put in the stocks (Jer. 20:2); the demoniac had been chained (Mark 5:3-4; Luke 8:29); Peter was bound with chains (Acts 12:6); Paul and Silas were put in the stocks (Acts 16:24); Paul was chained (Acts 21:33); Paul wore bonds (2 Tim. 2:9); for the sake of the hope of Israel I am bound with this chain (Acts 28:20); they suffered chains and imprisonment (Heb. 11:36); to bind their kings with chains and fetters (Ps. 149:8).

C4 Yoked
Make a yoke and put it on your neck (Jer. 27:2); Hananiah broke Jeremiah's yoke (Jer. 28:10-12); yokes of iron made (Jer. 28:13-14); it is good for a man to bear the yoke in his youth (Lam. 3:27); take my yoke upon you (Matt. 11:29-30); why put a yoke on the disciples which we ourselves could not bear? (Acts 15:10); do not be unequally yoked together with unbelievers (2 Cor. 6:14).

D Imprisoning
D1 Imprisoning in general
God imprisons and there is no release (Job 12:14); lest you be put in prison (Matt. 5:25; Luke 12:58); he had his fellowservant imprisoned (Matt. 18:30); John had not yet been put in prison (John 3:24).

D2 Believers imprisoned
Some were chained and imprisoned (Heb. 11:36); you will be thrown into prison (Matt. 5:25); the devil is about to throw some of you into prison (Rev. 2:10); the Holy Spirit testifies that imprisonment and affliction await me (Acts 20:23); I was in prison and you came to me (Matt. 25:36-44); remember those in prison as if in prison with them (Heb. 13:3); remember my fetters (Col. 4:18); we commend ourselves in imprisonment (2 Cor. 6:5); in far more imprisonments (2 Cor. 11:23); they think to afflict me in my imprisonment (Phil. 1:17); an ambassador in chains (Eph. 6:20); my imprisonment in Christ (Phil. 1:13); the mystery of Christ, for which I was imprisoned (Col. 4:3).

D3 Others imprisoned
Pharaoh Neco imprisoned Jehoahaz (2 Kgs. 23:33); Barabbas had been thrown into prison for insurrection (Luke 23:19); the rest of you will be imprisoned (Gen. 42:16); those imprisoned: Joseph (Gen. 39:20; 40:3); the butler and baker (Gen. 40:3); Joseph's brothers for three days (Gen. 42:17); Simeon (Gen. 42:19); Micaiah (1 Kgs. 22:27; 2 Chr. 18:26); Hoshea (2 Kgs. 17:4); a seer (2 Chr. 16:10); Jeremiah (Jer. 32:2; 37:15); Zedekiah (Jer. 52:11); John the Baptist (Matt. 4:12; 14:3; Mark 1:14; 6:17; Luke 3:20).

PRISON, see 748.

E Taking captive
Let those intended for captivity go into captivity (Jer. 15:2; 43:11); if anyone is to be taken captive, to captivity he will go (Rev. 13:10); they will be taken captive (Isa. 28:13); they will be led captive among all nations (Luke 21:24); they will take their captors captive (Isa. 14:2); your enemies will go into captivity (Jer. 30:16); Joash captured Amaziah (2 Kgs. 14:13; 2 Chr. 25:23); Israel took 200 000 of Judah captive (2 Chr. 28:8); those taken captive: Lot (Gen. 14:12); the Kenites (Num. 24:22); the women of Midian (Num. 31:9); the king of Ai (Josh. 8:23); Agag (1 Sam. 15:8); the women of Ziklag (1 Sam. 30:2); a young girl from Israel (2 Kgs. 5:2); Jehoiachin (2 Kgs. 24:12); Zedekiah (2 Kgs. 25:6); Zebah and Zalmunna (Judg. 8:12); Judah (2 Kgs. 25:21; Jer. 52:27); Bel and Nebo (Isa. 46:2).

748 Prison
Joseph was put in prison (Gen. 39:20); imprisoned in the house of the captain of the bodyguard (Gen. 40:3, 7; 41:10); the house of Jonathan was made the prison (Jer.

37:15, 20); Jeremiah was imprisoned in the court of the guard (Jer. 37:21; 38:13, 28); Jeremiah came to the dungeon (Jer. 37:16); Christ preached to the spirits in prison (1 Pet. 3:19); John was beheaded in the prison (Matt. 14:10; Mark 6:27); I am ready to go with you to prison and death (Luke 22:33); they sent to the prison for the apostles to be brought (Acts 5:21); sentries guarded the door of the prison (Acts 12:6); the jailer put them into the inner prison (Acts 16:24); the foundations of the prison were shaken (Acts 16:26).

749 Jailer
Joseph found grace in the eyes of the jailer (Gen. 39:21-2); our captors demanded songs (Ps. 137:3); Peter sat with the guards (Matt. 26:58; Mark 14:54); for fear of the angel the guards trembled and became like dead men (Matt. 28:4); some of the guard went into the city and told the chief priests (Matt. 28:11); soldiers guarding Peter (Acts 12:4); sentries guarded the door of the prison (Acts 12:6); they passed the first and second guards (Acts 12:10); Herod ordered that the sentries be executed (Acts 12:19); the jailer was commanded to keep them securely (Acts 16:23); Paul stayed by himself with the soldier guarding him (Acts 28:16).

750 Prisoner
IMPRISON, see 747D.

A Prisoners
The Lord does not despise his own who are prisoners (Ps. 69:33); he does not willingly crush under foot all the prisoners of the earth (Lam. 3:34); let the groaning of the prisoner come before you (Ps. 79:11); Joseph was imprisoned with the king's prisoners (Gen. 39:20); the jailer committed all the prisoners to Joseph (Gen. 39:22); a well-known prisoner called Barabbas (Matt. 27:16); the governor used to free for the crowd one prisoner at the feast (Matt. 27:15); the soldiers planned to kill the prisoners (Acts 27:42); you showed sympathy on the prisoners (Heb. 10:34); Joash took hostages (2 Kgs. 14:14; 2 Chr. 25:24).

B Prisoners for Christ
The prisoner of Christ (Eph. 3:1; Philem. 1; 9); the prisoner of the Lord (Eph. 4:1); Andronicus and Junias, my fellow-prisoners (Rom. 16:7); Aristarchus my fellow-prisoner (Col. 4:10); Epaphras, my fellow-prisoner in Christ (Philem. 23); do not be ashamed of me, his prisoner (2 Tim. 1:8).

751 Commission
A God commissioning
A1 God appointing
A1a God appointing his Son
Who gave you this authority? (Matt. 21:23; Mark 11:28; Luke 20:2); the Father judges no one, but has committed all judgement to the Son (John 5:22); God appointed Jesus as judge of the living and the dead (Acts 10:42); Jesus was faithful to the one who appointed him (Heb. 3:2); he will judge the world in righteousness by a man whom he has appointed (Acts 17:31).

A1b God appointing others
The authorities which exist have been instituted by God (Rom. 13:1); Aaron and his sons were ordained as priests (Exod. 28:41; Lev. 8:2-36); ordain yourselves to the Lord today (Exod. 32:29); the Lord appointed Moses and Aaron (1 Sam. 12:6); God commissioned Bezalel (Exod. 31:2); and Oholiab (Exod. 31:6); let the Lord appoint a leader for the community (Num. 27:16); I will commission Joshua (Deut. 31:14); commission Joshua (Num. 27:19); he commissioned Joshua (Deut. 31:23); I appointed you a prophet to the nations (Jer.

1:5); the Lord appointed a great fish (Jonah 1:17); the Lord appointed a plant to be a shade (Jonah 4:6); God appointed a worm (Jonah 4:7); God appointed a scorching east wind (Jonah 4:8); the God of our fathers has appointed you (Acts 22:14).

A2 God sending

A2a God sending his Son
God sent his Son into the world that we might live through him (1 John 4:9); the Father sent the Son to be the Saviour of the world (1 John 4:14); he sent his Son to be the propitiation for our sins (1 John 4:10); God sent his Son (John 3:17; Gal. 4:4); he whom God has sent (John 3:34); these people know that you sent me (John 17:25); that the world may know that you sent me (John 17:21-3); I was sent only to the lost sheep of the house of Israel (Matt. 15:24); as the Father sent me, so I send you (John 20:21); as you sent me into the world, I have sent them (John 17:18); I was sent for this purpose (Luke 4:43); you do not believe the one he has sent (John 5:38); the work of God is to believe in the one he sent (John 6:29); as the living Father sent me and as I live because of the Father (John 6:57); I know him for I am from him and he sent me (John 7:29); I did not come of myself, but he sent me (John 8:42); he whom the Father sanctified and sent into the world (John 10:36); that they may believe that you sent me (John 11:42); Jesus Christ whom you have sent (John 17:3); they have believed that you sent me (John 17:8); that he may send you Jesus, the Christ foreordained for you (Acts 3:20).

A2b The one who sent Christ
He who receives me receives him who sent me (Matt. 10:40; Mark 9:37; Luke 9:48; John 13:20); he who rejects me rejects the one who sent me (Luke 10:16); he who does not honour the Son does not honour the Father who sent him (John 5:23-4); I do not seek my own will, but the will of him who sent me (John 5:30); the Father who sent me (John 5:37; 8:18); this is the will of him who sent me (John 6:39); my teaching is not mine but his who sent me (John 7:16); he who seeks the glory of him who sent him is true (John 7:18); he who sent me is true (John 7:28; 8:26); I will go to him who sent me (John 7:33); it is not alone [I judge], but I and he who sent me (John 8:16); he who sent me is with me (John 8:29); we must work the works of him who sent me while it is day (John 9:4); he who sees me sees him who sent me (John 12:45); the Father who sent me has given me commandment (John 12:49); the word you hear is not mine but the Father's who sent me (John 14:25); they do not know him who sent me (John 15:21); I am going to him who sent me (John 16:5).

A2c God sending prophets
God sent his prophets to you repeatedly (Jer. 25:4); I will send them prophets and apostles (Luke 11:49); I send my messenger before your face (Mal. 3:1; Matt. 11:10; Mark 1:2).

A2d God sending others
It was not you who sent me here but God (Gen. 45:8); God sent Moses and Aaron (Ps. 105:26); I will send you to Egypt (Acts 7:34); I am sending you to Pharaoh (Exod. 3:10); the God of your fathers has sent me (Exod. 3:13-15); please send someone else (Exod. 4:13); why did you send me? (Exod. 5:22); here am I, send me! (Isa. 6:8); the Lord sent Nathan to David (2 Sam. 12:1); the Lord has sent me and his Spirit (Isa. 48:16); then you will know that the Lord of hosts has sent me (Zech. 2:9); my Father would send more than 12 legions of angels (Matt. 26:53); the helper, the Holy Spirit, whom the Father will send in my name (John 14:26); there was a man sent from God, named John (John 1:6); God sent his angel to show his slaves what

must soon take place (Rev. 22:6); he will send out his angels (Mark 13:27); I was sent to bring you this good news (Luke 1:19); the angel Gabriel was sent from God to Nazareth (Luke 1:26); pray the Lord of the harvest to send out workers (Matt. 9:38); being sent out by the Holy Spirit (Acts 13:4).

A2e God not sending
I did not send the prophets (Jer. 23:21); Shemaiah prophesied though I did not send him (Jer. 29:31); God had not sent him (Neh. 6:12).

B Christ commissioning

B1 Christ appointing
The 12 apostles were appointed (Matt. 10:1-4; Mark 3:14-19); the Lord appointed 70 others and sent them two by two (Luke 10:1); I appointed you to go and bear fruit (John 15:16); God appointed first apostles, second prophets (1 Cor. 12:28); I was appointed an apostle (2 Tim. 1:11); we have received grace and apostleship (Rom. 1:5); you are the seal of my apostleship (1 Cor. 9:2); to appoint you a servant and a witness (Acts 26:16); I have a commission entrusted to me (1 Cor. 9:17).

B2 Christ sending
Jesus sent out the 12 apostles (Matt. 10:5); Jesus sent out the 12 two by two (Mark 6:7); I send you out as sheep among wolves (Matt. 10:16; Luke 10:3); as the Father sent me, so I send you (John 20:21); as you sent me into the world, I have sent them (John 17:18); he sent them out to preach (Luke 9:2); the Lord sent 70 ahead of him (Luke 10:1); when I sent you out without purse, bag or sandals, did you lack anything? (Luke 22:35); the Lord Jesus has sent me to you (Acts 9:17); he who receives one I send receives me (John 13:20); if I go I will send the Helper to you (John 16:7); I will send you to the Gentiles (Acts 22:21; 26:17); how will they preach unless they are sent? (Rom. 10:15); Christ did not send me to baptise but to preach the gospel (1 Cor. 1:17); the Lord has sent his angel and rescued me (Acts 12:11); I, Jesus, have sent my angel to you (Rev. 22:16); the Son of man will send out his angels (Matt. 13:41; 24:31).

C Man commissioning

C1 Man appointing
Jethro taught Moses how to delegate responsibility (Exod. 18:19-22); appoint judges and officials in all your towns (Deut. 16:18); oh, that they would make me a judge! (2 Sam. 15:4); he has been appointed by the churches to travel with us in this gracious work (2 Cor. 8:19); Joab assigned Uriah to a place with valiant men (2 Sam. 11:16); set apart Barnabas and Paul for the work (Acts 13:2); at Antioch they had been commended to the grace of God for the work (Acts 14:26); Paul and Barnabas appointed elders (Acts 14:23); appoint elders in every town (Titus 1:5); Paul, Barnabas and others were appointed to go up to Jerusalem (Acts 15:2); Paul went to Damascus with the commission of the high priests (Acts 26:12).

C2 Man sending

C2a People sending people
I say to one, 'Go' and he goes (Luke 7:8); he who is sent is not greater than he who sent him (John 13:16); Jacob sent Joseph to Shechem (Gen. 37:13-14); wherever you send us we will go (Josh. 1:16); it pleased the king to send me (Neh. 2:6); they sent Barnabas to Antioch (Acts 11:22); when they had fasted and prayed and laid hands on them they sent them off (Acts 13:3); being sent on their way by the church (Acts 15:3); they chose men to send to Antioch with Paul and Barnabas (Acts 15:22-5); Judas and Silas were sent back to those who had sent them (Acts 15:33); he sent Timothy and Erastus into Macedonia (Acts 19:22); I have sent Timothy to you (1 Cor. 4:17); that you may send me on

my way (1 Cor. 16:6); send Timothy on his way in peace
(1 Cor. 16:11); I wanted you to send me on my way to
Judea (2 Cor. 1:16); we are sending the brother whom
we have often tested (2 Cor. 8:22).

C2b People sending creatures
Noah sent out the raven (Gen. 8:7); Noah sent out the
dove (Gen. 8:8-12).

752 Abrogation

A Deposing
God removes kings and sets up kings (Dan. 2:21); I gave
you a king in my anger and took him away in my wrath
(Hos. 13:11); he has put down the mighty from their
thrones (Luke 1:52); when he has nullified all rule and
authority and power (1 Cor. 15:24); he has rejected you
from being king (1 Sam. 15:23-6); I will depose you
from your office (Isa. 22:19); another king who is
different will put down three kings (Dan. 7:24); you
have rejected knowledge so I reject you from being
priest (Hos. 4:6); after God removed Saul (Acts 13:22); I
removed Saul (2 Sam. 7:15); Asa removed Maacah from
being queen mother (1 Kgs. 15:13; 2 Chr. 15:16); the king
of Egypt dethroned Jehoahaz (2 Chr. 36:3); Vashti
would no longer be queen (Esther 1:19);
Nebuchadnezzar was deposed (Dan. 5:20); danger that
Artemis may be deposed (Acts 19:27).

B Cancelling
The former commandment is set aside (Heb. 7:18); if
those of the law are heirs, the promise is void (Rom.
4:14); I do not nullify the grace of God (Gal. 2:21); he
cancelled the bill of debt (Col. 2:14); does their unbelief
nullify God's faithfulness? (Rom. 3:3); lest the cross of
Christ be nullified (1 Cor. 1:17); no one annuls a man's
will or adds to it (Gal. 3:15); you nullify the word of
God for the sake of your traditions (Matt. 15:6; Mark
7:9); do we nullify the law by faith? (Rom. 3:31); the law
does not invalidate the covenant (Gal. 3:17); a woman's
vows may be annulled by her father (Num. 30:3-5); or
husband (Num. 30:6-15); let Haman's letters be
countermanded (Esther 8:5); letters sealed with the
king's ring may not be revoked (Esther 8:8); your
covenant with death will be cancelled (Isa. 28:18); he
has blessed and I cannot revoke it (Num. 23:20); the
laws of the Medes and Persians cannot be repealed
(Esther 1:19; Dan. 6:8); whoever annuls the least
commandment will be least in the Kingdom (Matt.
5:19); I have not come to abolish the law and the
prophets but to fulfil them (Matt. 5:17-18).

753 Resignation
DEPARTURE, see 296.

754 Nominee

A Apostles
A1 Apostles in general
Jesus, the apostle and high priest (Heb. 3:1); Jesus chose
12 whom he named apostles (Luke 6:13); God
appointed in the church first apostles (1 Cor. 12:28); he
gave some as apostles (Eph. 4:11); built on the
foundation of apostles and prophets (Eph. 2:20); the
mystery now revealed to his apostles and prophets
(Eph. 3:5); the marks of a true apostle, signs and
wonders (2 Cor. 12:12); I will send them prophets and
apostles (Luke 11:49); they devoted themselves to the
apostles' teaching (Acts 2:42); all are not apostles, are
they? (1 Cor. 12:29); Jesus gave orders to the apostles
whom he had chosen (Acts 1:2); remember the
commandment of the Lord and Saviour by your
apostles (2 Pet. 3:2); remember the words of the
apostles of our Lord Jesus Christ (Jude 17); he appeared
to all the apostles (1 Cor. 15:7); rejoice over her, heaven,

saints, apostles and prophets (Rev. 18:20); we might
have used authority as apostles of Christ (1 Thess. 2:6);
the foundations have the names of the 12 apostles of
the Lamb (Rev. 21:14); God has exhibited us apostles
last of all (1 Cor. 4:9); those who were apostles before
me (Gal. 1:17).

A2 The apostles in action
The apostles said, 'Increase our faith!' (Luke 17:5);
many wonders and signs were done through the
apostles (Acts 2:43; 5:12); with great power the apostles
bore witness to the resurrection (Acts 4:33); they
brought them to the apostles who prayed and laid
hands on them (Acts 6:6); they laid hands on the
apostles and put them in jail (Acts 5:18); the apostles
were flogged (Acts 5:40); going up to Jerusalem to the
apostles and elders over this question (Acts 15:2-6); the
apostles, elders and the whole church chose men to
send to Antioch (Acts 15:22); the apostles and elders to
the brethren in Antioch (Acts 15:23); they delivered the
decisions of the apostles and elders in Jerusalem (Acts
16:4); a believer as wife, as the rest of the apostles, the
Lord's brothers and Cephas? (1 Cor. 9:5).

A3 Particular apostles
Matthias was numbered with the eleven apostles (Acts
1:26); to take the ministry and apostleship from which
Judas turned aside (Acts 1:25); Paul was called as an
apostle (Rom. 1:1; 1 Cor. 1:1); Paul, an apostle (Gal. 1:1;
Titus 1:1); Paul, an apostle of Christ Jesus (2 Cor. 1:1;
Eph. 1:1; 1 Tim. 1:1; 2 Tim. 1:1); Paul, an apostle of Jesus
Christ (Col. 1:1); for this I was appointed an apostle
(1 Tim. 2:7; 2 Tim. 1:11); am I not an apostle? (1 Cor.
9:1); I am the least of the apostles (1 Cor. 15:9); I am an
apostle to the Gentiles (Rom. 11:13); if to others I am
not an apostle, at least I am to you (1 Cor. 9:2); you are
the seal of my apostleship (1 Cor. 9:2); the apostles
Barnabas and Paul (Acts 14:14); Peter, an apostle of
Jesus Christ (1 Pet. 1:1; 2 Pet. 1:1); Andronicus and
Junias, of note among the apostles (Rom. 16:7); these
brethren are the apostles of the churches (2 Cor. 8:23).

A4 False apostles
False apostles, disguising themselves as apostles of
Christ (2 Cor. 11:13); you test those who call themselves
apostles but are not (Rev. 2:2); I am not inferior to
these superlative apostles (2 Cor. 11:5; 12:11).

B Ambassadors
We are ambassadors for Christ (2 Cor. 5:20); I am an
ambassador in chains (Eph. 6:20); he sent ambassadors
to Egypt (Ezek. 17:15); Paul, an ambassador and a
prisoner of Christ Jesus (Philem. 9).

C Stewards
It is required of stewards that they be found
trustworthy (1 Cor. 4:2); a rich man who had a steward
(Luke 16:1-8); who is the faithful and wise steward?
(Luke 12:42); stewards of the mysteries of God (1 Cor.
4:1); the child is under guardians and stewards (Gal.
4:2); an overseer must be blameless, as God's steward
(Titus 1:7); Erastus the steward of the city greets you
(Rom. 16:23).

755 Deputy
Aaron and Hur are here, whoever has a matter, go to
them (Exod. 24:14).

756 Permission
Without your permission no one will lift hand or foot
(Gen. 41:44); Pharaoh permitted Joseph to go and bury
his father (Gen. 50:6); permit me first to bury my
father (Matt. 8:21); Jesus permitted the demons to enter
the pigs (Matt. 8:32; Mark 5:13; Luke 8:32); let the
children come to me (Matt. 19:14; Mark 10:14; Luke
18:16); this we will do if God permits (Heb. 6:3); Moses

permitted a man to write a certificate of divorce (Mark 10:4); Pilate gave leave for Joseph to take the body (John 19:38); in past generations he allowed all nations to walk in their own ways (Acts 14:16); if unbelieving spouses leave, let them (1 Cor. 7:15); I hope to stay with you for some time, if the Lord permits (1 Cor. 16:7); do not grant the desires of the wicked (Ps. 140:8).

757 Prohibition

A God forbidding
God commanded them not to eat of the tree (Gen. 3:11); the Lord had forbidden them to serve idols (2 Kgs. 17:12); God commands the sun not to shine (Job 9:7); God will not allow you to be tempted beyond your ability (1 Cor. 10:13); do not go down to Egypt (Gen. 26:2); God did not allow Laban to harm Jacob (Gen. 31:7); he did not permit anyone to oppress them (1 Chr. 16:21; Ps. 105:14); God would not let Balaam go (Num. 22:12-13).

B Christ forbidding
He would not permit the demons to speak (Mark 1:34); he did not allow any to follow him except Peter, James and John (Mark 5:37; Luke 8:51); he would not allow people to carry anything through the temple (Mark 11:16); we found this man forbidding us to pay taxes to Caesar (Luke 23:2).

C The Holy Spirit forbidding
They were forbidden by the Holy Spirit to speak the word in Asia (Acts 16:6); the Spirit of Jesus did not allow them to enter Bithynia (Acts 16:7).
PREVENT, see 702.

D People forbidding
If a dependant woman is forbidden to fulfil a vow (Num. 30:5-15); the Rechabites were commanded not to drink wine (Jer. 35:14); men who forbid marriage (1 Tim. 4:3); you commanded the prophets not to prophesy (Amos 2:12); you neither enter nor allow others to enter (Matt. 23:13); who can forbid water for baptising these people? (Acts 10:47); Paul wanted to go in among the crowd but the disciples would not let him (Acts 19:30); I do not allow a woman to teach or to have authority over men (1 Tim. 2:12); Moses, my lord, stop them! (Num. 11:28); David did not permit his men to attack Saul (1 Sam. 24:7); her father did not let Samson go in to his wife (Judg. 15:1); make these men stop work (Ezra 4:21); Pharaoh will not let you go (Exod. 3:19); the Amorites would not allow the Danites into the valley (Judg. 1:34); John tried to stop Jesus from being baptised (Matt. 3:14); we forbade him because he was not following us (Mark 9:38-9; Luke 9:49-50); do not forbid speaking in tongues (1 Cor. 14:39).

758 Consent

A Concession
I say this by way of concession, not command (1 Cor. 7:6).

B Consent
Only on this condition will we consent (Gen. 34:15); I did not want to do anything without your consent (Philem. 14); none of us will withhold his grave from you (Gen. 23:6).

759 Offer
I offer you three things (2 Sam. 24:12; 1 Chr. 21:10); Naaman offered Elisha a present (2 Kgs. 5:15); they brought him to Jerusalem to present him to the Lord (Luke 2:22).

760 Refusal

A Refusing God
Pharaoh will not let the people go (Exod. 4:21); he did not let them go (Exod. 9:7); if you refuse to let them go (Exod. 8:2; 9:2; 10:4); how long will you refuse to humble yourself? (Exod. 10:3); they refuse to know me (Jer. 9:6); they refused to return to me (Hos. 11:5); if they did not escape when they refused him who warned them on earth (Heb. 12:25); she refuses to repent of her immorality (Rev. 2:21).

B Refusing people
B1 Refusing to come to people
Dathan and Abiram would not come (Num. 16:12-14); Balaam refused to come (Num. 22:14); Joab refused to come to Absalom (2 Sam. 14:29); Queen Vashti refused to come (Esther 1:12, 17); those invited to the king's wedding feast would not come (Matt. 22:3).
B2 Refusing people in other ways
If sinners entice you, do not consent (Prov. 1:10); Jacob refused to be comforted (Gen. 37:35); Joseph refused to lie with her (Gen. 39:8); Edom refused to let them pass through (Num. 20:18); Moab would not let them pass through (Judg. 11:17); Sihon refused to let them pass through (Num. 21:23); Saul refused to accept food (1 Sam. 28:23); David refused to eat (2 Sam. 12:17); Amnon refused to eat (2 Sam. 13:9); we will not drink wine (Jer. 35:6); the man refused to strike the prophet (1 Kgs. 20:35); Elisha refused a present from Naaman (2 Kgs. 5:16); Moses refused to be called the son of Pharaoh's daughter (Heb. 11:24); some refused to accept release that they might rise to a better life (Heb. 11:35); they will refuse to let them be placed in a tomb (Rev. 11:9).

C Not refusing
No good thing will he withhold from those who walk uprightly (Ps. 84:11); he did not withhold anything except you, because you are his wife (Gen. 39:9); let husband and wife not refuse one another (1 Cor. 7:5); the king will not withhold me from you (2 Sam. 13:13); do not refuse my request (1 Kgs. 2:20); see that you do not refuse him who speaks (Heb. 12:25); do not refuse him who wants to borrow from you (Matt. 5:42); because of his oaths and his guests he did not want to refuse her (Mark 6:26).

761 Request

A Prayer
A1 About prayer
A1a Prayer in general
My house will be called a house of prayer for all nations (Isa. 56:7; Matt. 21:13; Mark 11:17; Luke 19:46); may my prayer be like incense (Ps. 141:2); golden bowls full of incense which are the prayers of the saints (Rev. 5:8); incense with the prayers of the saints (Rev. 8:3-4).
A1b Pray!
Call on me in the day of trouble (Ps. 50:15); call on him while he is near (Isa. 55:6); call to me and I will answer you (Jer. 33:3); ask me and I will give the nations as your inheritance (Ps. 2:8); watch and pray that you may not enter into temptation (Matt. 26:41; Mark 14:38); ask and you will receive, that your joy may be full (John 16:24); if any one lacks wisdom, let him ask God (Jas. 1:5); pray for one another that you may be healed (Jas. 5:16); they ought always to pray (Luke 18:1); pray constantly (1 Thess. 5:17); men should pray, lifting up holy hands (1 Tim. 2:8); devote yourselves to prayer (Col. 4:2); prayer should be made for everyone (1 Tim. 2:1); in everything, by prayer and supplication, make known your requests to God (Phil. 4:6); persist in prayer (Rom. 12:12); pray at all times in the Spirit (Eph.

6:18); pray in the Holy Spirit (Jude 20); you do not have because you do not ask (Jas. 4:2); if anyone is suffering, let him pray (Jas. 5:13); if my people humble themselves and pray (2 Chr. 7:14).

A1c How to pray
Teach us how to pray (Luke 11:1); we do not know how to pray, but the Spirit helps us (Rom. 8:26); do not pray to be seen by men (Matt. 6:5-6); do not pray with meaningless babbling like the heathen (Matt. 6:7); if I pray in a tongue my spirit prays but my mind is unfruitful (1 Cor. 14:14-15); if you abide in me and my words abide in you, ask what you will (John 15:7); in that day you will ask in my name (John 16:26); those that call on the Lord from a pure heart (2 Tim. 2:22); 'our Father' (Matt. 6:9-13; Luke 11:2-4); abstinence to devote oneself to prayer (1 Cor. 7:5); prayer and fasting (Matt. 17:21; Acts 13:3; 14:23); this kind comes out only by prayer and fasting (Mark 9:29); when you pray, forgive (Mark 11:25); if two agree in what they ask, it shall be done (Matt. 18:19); let them pray over him, anointing him with oil (Jas. 5:14); when you pray, believe that you have received (Mark 11:24); whatever you ask in prayer, believing, you will receive (Matt. 21:22); how shall they call on him in whom they do not believe? (Rom. 10:14); be sober for your prayers (1 Pet. 4:7); be considerate with your wives lest your prayers be hindered (1 Pet. 3:7).

A1d When to pray
In the morning I will pray (Ps. 5:3); evening, morning and noon I meditate (Ps. 55:17); Daniel prayed three times a day (Dan. 6:10); going up to the temple at the ninth hour, the hour of prayer (Acts 3:1); Cornelius prayed at the ninth hour (Acts 10:30); the people were praying at the hour of incense (Luke 1:10).

A1e Calling on God
Men began to call on the name of the Lord (Gen. 4:26); everyone who calls on the name of the Lord will be saved (Joel 2:32; Acts 2:21; Rom. 10:13); you call on the name of your god and I will call on mine (1 Kgs. 18:24); Naaman thought Elisha would call on the name of the Lord (2 Kgs. 5:11); those who call on the name of our Lord Jesus (1 Cor. 1:2).

A2 God hearing prayer
A2a God answers prayer
Ask and it will be given you (Matt. 7:7-8; Luke 11:9-10); ask and you will receive, that your joy may be full (John 16:24); God gives to all men liberally (Jas. 1:5); you will pray and he will hear (Job 22:27); he will call to me and I will answer him (Ps. 91:15); you who hear prayer (Ps. 65:2); how much more will your Father give good things to those who ask him (Matt. 7:11); whatever you ask in my name, I will do it (John 14:13, 14); that whatever you ask in my name, the Father may give you (John 15:16); if you ask the Father for anything, he will give it in my name (John 16:23); ask what you wish and it will be given you (John 15:7); the prayer of a righteous man accomplishes much (Jas. 5:16); whatever you ask in prayer, believing, you will receive (Matt. 21:22); if we ask anything according to his will, he hears us (1 John 5:14); if we know that he hears us, whatever we ask, we know we have our requests (1 John 5:15); the Lord is rich to all who call on him (Rom. 10:12); he is able to do far more than all we ask or think (Eph. 3:20).

A2b God answered prayer
I called on God and he answered me (Job 12:4); my prayer came to you into your holy temple (Jonah 2:7); you called and I rescued you (Ps. 81:7); when they cried to you they heard them (Neh. 9:27); this poor man cried and the Lord heard him (Ps. 34:6); because he inclined his ear to me I will call on him as long as I live

(Ps. 116:2); I have heard your prayer (1 Kgs. 9:3; 2 Kgs. 20:5; Isa. 38:5); your prayer has been heard (Acts 10:31); he asked you for life and you gave it (Ps. 21:4); God answered prayer for the land again (2 Sam. 21:14; 24:25); he answered their prayers because they trusted in him (1 Chr. 5:20); God hears the cry of the righteous (Ps. 34:15); his ears are open to their prayer (1 Pet. 3:12); your prayers have been heard (Luke 1:13); your prayers and alms have ascended as a memorial before God (Acts 10:4); God granted Jabez what he requested (1 Chr. 4:10); Christ was heard because of his godliness (Heb. 5:7); Elijah prayed fervently that it would not rain, and it did not for three and a half years (Jas. 5:17).

A2c Prayer not answered
The Lord will not answer you (1 Sam. 8:18); when you pray I will hide my eyes from you (Isa. 1:15); though they cry to me I will not listen to them (Jer. 11:11); they cried to the Lord but he did not answer them (Ps. 18:41); if Moses and Samuel stood before me I would not turn to this people (Jer. 15:1); as I called and they would not listen, so they called and I would not listen (Zech. 7:13); if anyone will not listen to the law, even his prayer is an abomination (Prov. 28:9); you ask and do not receive because you ask amiss (Jas. 4:3); if I regard iniquity in my heart the Lord will not hear me (Ps. 66:18); the Lord does not answer because of man's pride (Job 35:12).

A3 Praying for people
A3a Praying for sinners
Pray for those who harm you (Luke 6:28); pray for those who persecute you (Matt. 5:44); ask and God will give life to the one whose sin is not to death (1 John 5:16); Abraham prayed for Sodom (Gen. 18:23-32); Abraham prayed for Abimelech (Gen. 20:7); pray to the Lord for me (Exod. 8:24); Moses asked God not to destroy the people (Exod. 32:11-13; Num. 11:2; Deut. 9:18-19); Moses prayed for Miriam to be healed (Num. 12:13); Moses prayed for Aaron (Deut. 9:20); Job prayed for his friends (Job 42:8-9).

A3b Praying for God's people
The Israelites won whilst Moses held up his hands (Exod. 17:11-12); Peter prayed for dead Tabitha (Acts 9:40); they prayed for Peter in prison (Acts 12:5); they will pray for you because of the surpassing grace of God in you (2 Cor. 9:14); Epaphras always prays that you may stand mature (Col. 4:12); they prayed and laid hands on them (Acts 6:6; 13:3); Peter and John prayed for them to receive the Holy Spirit (Acts 8:15); I remember you in my prayers (Rom. 1:9-10; Eph. 1:16; 2 Tim. 1:3); we have not stopped praying for you (Col. 1:9); we thank God when we pray for you (Col. 1:3; 1 Thess. 1:2); I thank God when I pray for you (Philem. 4); praying for their spiritual maturity (Eph. 3:14-19; Col. 1:9-12); we pray to God that you do not do wrong (2 Cor. 13:7-9); this I pray, that your love may abound (Phil. 1:9); we pray that God may count you worthy of his calling (2 Thess. 1:11); always making my prayer for you with joy (Phil. 1:4).

A3c Pray for us
Do not cease to cry to the Lord for us (1 Sam. 7:8; 12:19); pray to the Lord for us (Jer. 37:3); entreat the Lord for me (Exod. 8:8); pray to the Lord for me (Acts 8:24); pray for me that my hand may be restored (1 Kgs. 13:6); Esther asked the Jews to fast (Esther 4:16); Daniel asked his friends to pray (Dan. 2:17-18); pray for us (1 Thess. 5:25; 2 Thess. 3:1; Heb. 13:18); help us by your prayers (2 Cor. 1:11); strive together with me in your prayers to God for me (Rom. 15:30); through your prayers I will be delivered (Phil. 1:19); I hope to be freed through your prayers (Philem. 22); pray for us, that God may open a door for the word (Col. 4:3).

A3d Praying against people

Your poor brother may cry to the Lord against you (Deut. 15:9); lest the poor hireling cry to the Lord against you (Deut. 24:15); Elijah pleads with God against Israel (Rom. 11:2).

A4 Praying about needs

A4a Praying for God's kingdom

Pray the Lord of the harvest to send out labourers (Matt. 9:38; Luke 10:2); your kingdom come (Matt. 6:10; Luke 11:2); they devoted themselves to prayer (Acts 1:14; 2:42); we will devote ourselves to prayer and the ministry of the word (Acts 6:4); my prayer for Israel is that they be saved (Rom. 10:1); your heavenly Father will give the Holy Spirit to those who ask him (Luke 11:13).

A4b Praying for healing

Hezekiah cried to the Lord when mortally ill (2 Kgs. 20:2; 2 Chr. 32:24; Isa. 38:2-3); Elijah praying for the child's healing (1 Kgs. 17:21); Peter prayed for Tabitha (Acts 9:40); blind Saul was praying (Acts 9:11); Paul prayed God to remove the thorn in the flesh (2 Cor. 12:8); Paul prayed and laid hands on Publius' father (Acts 28:8).

A4c Praying for various needs

In my distress I called on the Lord (2 Sam. 22:7; Ps. 18:6; 118:5); they cried to the Lord in their trouble (Ps. 107:6); praying about the lack of water (Exod. 17:4); Samuel – asked of God (1 Sam. 1:20); one thing have I asked of the Lord (Ps. 27:4); open his eyes! (2 Kgs. 6:17); open their eyes! (2 Kgs. 6:20); blind this people! (2 Kgs. 6:18); pray for the welfare of the city to which you are exiled (Jer. 29:7); pray that you may not enter into temptation (Luke 22:40-6); pray that you will escape what is going to happen (Luke 21:36); pray that your flight will not be in winter (Matt. 24:20; Mark 13:18); ask rain from the Lord in the season of spring rain (Zech. 10:1); they asked for a king (Acts 13:21); let him who speaks in tongues pray for an interpretation (1 Cor. 14:13).

A5 Those who prayed

A5a Jesus praying

During Jesus' earthly life he prayed (Heb. 5:7); he prayed at his baptism (Luke 3:21); at the transfiguration (Luke 9:28-9); in the hills (Matt. 14:23; Mark 6:46; Luke 6:12); in solitary places (Mark 1:35; Luke 5:16; 9:18); at Gethsemane (Matt. 26:36-44; Mark 14:32-9; Luke 22:41-5); in a certain place (Luke 11:1); that he might lay his hands on the children and pray (Matt. 19:13); I have prayed for you that your faith fail not (Luke 22:32); he interceded for the transgressors (Isa. 53:12); he always lives to intercede for them (Heb. 7:25); Christ intercedes for us (Rom. 8:34); Jesus' prayer (John 17:1-25).

A5b The Spirit praying

The Spirit intercedes for the saints according to the will of God (Rom. 8:27); with groans too deep for words (Rom. 8:26).

A5c Named individuals who prayed

David's prayer for God to confirm his word (2 Sam. 7:18-29; 1 Chr. 17:16-17); David's prayer for the temple to be built (1 Chr. 29:10-20); Elijah prayed for rain (1 Kgs. 18:42-4; Jas. 5:18); Elijah praying for the child's healing (1 Kgs. 17:21); Ezra prayed in shame over Israel (Ezra 10:1); Hannah prayed for a child (1 Sam. 1:10-17); Jonah prayed from the belly of the fish (Jonah 2:1); Habakkuk prayed (Hab. 3:1); Hezekiah prayed when besieged (2 Kgs. 19:14-19; 2 Chr. 32:20; Isa. 37:15-20); Manasseh prayed in prison (2 Chr. 33:12-13); Moses cried to the Lord about the bitter water (Exod. 15:25); Moses implored God's favour (Deut. 3:23); Nehemiah prayed and set a guard (Neh. 4:9); Paul and Silas

prayed in prison (Acts 16:25); Paul prayed God to remove the thorn in the flesh (2 Cor. 12:8); Peter prayed for Tabitha (Acts 9:40); Samson prayed for strength (Judg. 16:28); Samuel prayed about their request for a king (1 Sam. 8:6); Solomon's prayer of dedication of the temple (1 Kgs. 8:22-54; 2 Chr. 6:14-42).

A6 Praying amiss

You ask and do not receive because you ask amiss (Jas. 4:3); cry to the gods you have chosen (Judg. 10:14); praying to a graven image (Isa. 44:17); praying to a god who cannot save (Isa. 45:20); they called on the name of Baal (1 Kgs. 18:26-9); each cried to his god (Jonah 1:5).

A7 Not praying

Why cry to me? (Exod. 14:15); do not pray for this people (Jer. 7:16; 11:14; 14:11); anyone who prays will be thrown into the den of lions (Dan. 6:7, 12); you have not called on me, Jacob (Isa. 43:22); a nation which did not call on my name (Isa. 65:1); they do not call on God (Ps. 14:4; 53:4); there is no one who calls on your name (Isa. 64:7); none of them calls on me (Hos. 7:7); the nations which do not call on your name (Ps. 79:6).

B Requesting Jesus

The demons begged him to send them into the pigs (Matt. 8:31; Mark 5:10-12; Luke 8:31-2); they begged him to depart (Matt. 8:34; Mark 5:17; Luke 8:37); Zebedee's wife made request for her sons (Matt. 20:20-1); Teacher, we want you to do for us whatever we ask (Mark 10:35); a leper came beseeching him (Mark 1:40; Luke 5:12); Jairus begged Jesus to come and heal his daughter (Mark 5:23; Luke 8:41); she begged Jesus to cast the demon out of her daughter (Mark 7:26); they begged him to lay his hands on him (Mark 7:32); they begged him to touch the blind man (Mark 8:22); they besought Jesus on her behalf (Luke 4:38); requesting Jesus to come and heal his slave (Luke 7:3); you would have asked him and he would have given you living water (John 4:10); give me this water (John 4:15); Lord, give us this bread always (John 6:34); he begged him to come down and heal his son (John 4:47); they begged to be able to touch the fringe of his garment (Matt. 14:36); the man begged to accompany Jesus (Mark 5:18); Lord Jesus, receive my spirit (Acts 7:59).

C Requesting from people

C1 Begging

Your descendants will beg for money and bread (1 Sam. 2:36); may his children beg (Ps. 109:10); the blind man used to sit and beg (John 9:8); a blind beggar called Bartimaeus (Mark 10:46); the blind man sat begging (Luke 18:35); the lame man begged for money (Acts 3:2-10, 10); I have not seen the righteous begging bread (Ps. 37:25); I am ashamed to beg (Luke 16:3).

C2 Asking people for things

The people cried out to Pharaoh for bread (Gen. 41:55); give me some of your son's mandrakes (Gen. 30:14); he asked for water and she gave him milk (Judg. 5:25); if your son asks for a loaf (Matt. 7:9); if his son asks for a fish (Matt. 7:10; Luke 11:11); the Israelites asked the Egyptians for silver and gold (Exod. 3:22; 11:2; 12:35); Gideon asked for the gold earrings (Judg. 8:24); Achsah asked her father for a field (Josh. 15:18; Judg. 1:14); the woman appealed to the king for her house and land (2 Kgs. 8:3, 5); David asked for a gift from Nabal (1 Sam. 25:8); give us some of your oil, for our lamps are going out (Matt. 25:8).

C3 Asking people

Adonijah requested Abishag as wife (1 Kgs. 2:16-21); my life and my people are my request (Esther 7:3); Pilate used to release any prisoner for which they asked

(Mark 15:6); they persuaded the crowds to ask for Barabbas (Matt. 27:20); you asked for a murderer to be granted you (Acts 3:14); Nicodemus asked for the body of Jesus (Matt. 27:58); Joseph of Arimathea asked Pilate for the body of Jesus (Mark 15:43; Luke 23:52; John 19:38).

C4 Appealing to people
Esther was to beg the king for mercy (Esther 4:8); Haman begged for his life from Esther (Esther 7:7); Esther implored the king again (Esther 8:3); Joseph pleaded for mercy from us (Gen. 42:21); his father came out and entreated him (Luke 15:28); the people begged that these things might be told them the next sabbath (Acts 13:42); they begged them to leave the city (Acts 16:39); we begged Paul not to go up to Jerusalem (Acts 21:12); for love's sake I would rather appeal to you (Philem. 9-10); Nehemiah requested leave from the king (Neh. 13:6); we appeal to you on Christ's behalf to be reconciled (2 Cor. 5:20); they begged to be allowed to contribute (2 Cor. 8:4); Paul appealed to Caesar (Acts 25:11-12).

C5 Inviting
The king sent his servants to call those invited (Matt. 22:3); those who were invited were not worthy (Matt. 22:8); go to the highways and invite as many as you can find (Matt. 22:9); when you are invited to a marriage feast (Luke 14:8-13); Jesus was invited to the wedding with his disciples (John 2:2); blessed are those invited to the wedding supper of the Lamb (Rev. 19:9).

762 Deprecation
PRAYING AGAINST PEOPLE, see 761A3d.

763 Petitioner
REQUEST, see 761.

764 Promise
A God's promises
None of God's good promises have failed (Josh. 21:45; 23:14; 1 Kgs. 8:56); the promises of God are Yes in Christ (2 Cor. 1:20); what God had promised he was able to do (Rom. 4:21); God promised the gospel through the scriptures (Rom. 1:2); has his promise ceased for all time? (Ps. 77:8); he who promised is faithful (Heb. 10:23); by faith they received promises (Heb. 11:33); he has promised to shake not only the earth but also heaven (Heb. 12:26); the crown of life which the Lord has promised to those who love him (Jas. 1:12); the Lord is not slow about his promise (2 Pet. 3:9); according to his promise we wait for new heavens and a new earth (2 Pet. 3:13); the first commandment with a promise (Eph. 6:2).

B Promise to Abraham
The promise to Abraham (Rom. 4:13); God granted the inheritance to Abraham by promise (Gal. 3:18); Abraham patiently endured and obtained the promise (Heb. 6:15); the promises were to Abraham and his seed (Gal. 3:16); one son was born through promise (Gal. 4:23); to Israel belong the promises (Rom. 9:4); Christ came to confirm the promise made to the fathers (Rom. 15:8); God promised to give the land to him and to his posterity (Acts 7:5); if those of the law are heirs, the promise is void (Rom. 4:14); if the inheritance is by law it is no longer by promise (Gal. 3:18); is the law against the promises of God? (Gal. 3:21); Melchizedek blessed him who had the promises (Heb. 7:6); Abraham, Isaac and Jacob, fellow-heirs of the same promise (Heb. 11:9); he who received the promises offered up his only begotten son (Heb. 11:17); you are children of promise (Gal. 4:28); the children of

the promise are reckoned as the seed (Rom. 9:8); the Gentiles share in the promise (Eph. 3:6).

C Promise of eternal life
God promised eternal life ages ago (Titus 1:2); this is what he has promised us, eternal life (1 John 2:25); precious and very great promises to become partakers of God's nature (2 Pet. 1:4); having these promises (2 Cor. 7:1); according to the promise of life in Christ Jesus (2 Tim. 1:1); while the promise of entering his rest remains (Heb. 4:1); a better covenant, enacted on better promises (Heb. 8:6); those who through faith and patience inherit the promises (Heb. 6:12).

D Promise of the Spirit
I send the promise of my Father (Luke 24:49); they had to wait for what the Father had promised (Acts 1:4); Christ received from the Father the promise of the Holy Spirit (Acts 2:33); the promise is to you and to your children (Acts 2:39); the Holy Spirit of promise (Eph. 1:13); the promise of the Spirit through faith (Gal. 3:14).

765 Covenant
A God's covenants
KEEPING COVENANT, see 768C.

A1 God's covenant with Noah
God made a covenant with Noah and his sons (Gen. 6:18; 9:9-17).

A2 God's covenant with the patriarchs
The Lord made a covenant with Abraham (Gen. 15:18); the holy covenant sworn to Abraham (Luke 1:72-3); I make my covenant between me and you, circumcision (Gen. 17:2-13); the covenant of circumcision (Acts 7:8); I will establish my covenant with Isaac (Gen. 17:19); a covenant to give his descendants the land (Exod. 6:4); you are heirs of the covenant God made with your fathers (Acts 3:25); theirs are the covenants (Rom. 9:4); the law 430 years later does not annul the covenant (Gal. 3:17).

A3 Covenant at Sinai
I am making a covenant with you (Exod. 34:10); the Lord made a covenant with us at Horeb (Deut. 5:2); one covenant is from Mount Sinai (Gal. 4:24); my covenant with Levi (Mal. 2:4-5); he wrote the words of the covenant, the ten commandments (Exod. 34:28); he declared his covenant, the ten commandments (Deut. 4:13); the tablets [tables] of the covenant (Deut. 9:9; Heb. 9:4); the ark containing the covenant (1 Kgs. 8:21; 2 Chr. 6:11); the book of the covenant (Exod. 24:7; 2 Chr. 34:30); let them keep the sabbath as an everlasting covenant (Exod. 31:16); this is the blood of the covenant (Exod. 24:8; Heb. 9:20); the first covenant was not ratified without blood (Heb. 9:18-20); do not omit the salt of the covenant of your God from grain offerings (Lev. 2:13); a covenant of salt (2 Chr. 13:5); it is an everlasting covenant of salt (Num. 18:19); when reading the old covenant the veil remains (2 Cor. 3:14).

A4 Later covenants with God
Covenant made in the land of Moab (Deut. 29:1); God made a covenant of peace with Phinehas (Num. 25:12); God made an everlasting covenant with David (2 Sam. 23:5); the kingdom given to David by a covenant of salt (2 Chr. 13:5); I will not violate my covenant [with David] (Ps. 89:34); Jehoiada made a covenant between the Lord, the king and the people (2 Kgs. 11:17; 2 Chr. 23:3); Josiah renewed the covenant (2 Kgs. 23:3; 2 Chr. 34:31-2); they made a covenant to seek the Lord (2 Chr. 15:12); Hezekiah wanted to make a covenant with the Lord (2 Chr. 29:10); let us make a covenant to send away these women (Ezra 10:3); I will make an everlasting covenant (Isa. 55:3; 61:8; Jer. 32:40; Ezek.

16:60; 37:26); gather those who have made a covenant with me by sacrifice (Ps. 50:5).

A5 The new covenant
I will make a new covenant with the house of Israel (Jer. 31:31; Heb. 8:8-13); he is the mediator of a new covenant (Heb. 9:15; 12:24); these women are two covenants (Gal. 4:24); this cup is the new covenant in my blood (Luke 22:20; 1 Cor. 11:25); this is my blood of the covenant (Matt. 26:28; Mark 14:24); the blood of the covenant (Heb. 10:29); the blood of the eternal covenant (Heb. 13:20); this is my covenant, when I remove their sins (Rom. 11:27); servants of a new covenant (2 Cor. 3:6); a better covenant (Heb. 7:22; 8:6); this is my covenant, my Spirit will not depart from you (Isa. 59:21).

B People's covenants
B1 Agreements between people
Joshua made a covenant with the people (Josh. 24:25); with empty oaths they make covenants (Hos. 10:4); they did not remember the covenant of brotherhood (Amos 1:9); you had made a covenant before me to release Hebrew slaves (Jer. 34:15); Abner made a covenant with David (2 Sam. 3:12-13); he will make a strong covenant with many for one week (Dan. 9:27); those who make an alliance but not of my Spirit (Isa. 30:1); those who made a covenant: Abraham, Mamre, Eshcol and Aner (Gen. 14:13); Abraham and Abimelech (Gen. 21:27); Ahab and Ben-Hadad (1 Kgs. 20:34); Hiram and Solomon (1 Kgs. 5:12); Isaac and Abimelech (Gen. 26:28); Jacob and Laban (Gen. 31:44); Jonathan and David (1 Sam. 18:3); David and the people (2 Sam. 5:3; 1 Chr. 11:3); the king of Babylon and Zedekiah (Ezek. 17:13-14).

B2 Last will and covenant
No one annuls a man's will once it has been ratified (Gal. 3:15); a will only comes into effect when one dies (Heb. 9:16-17).

C Agreements with evil
Do not make a covenant with these people or their gods (Exod. 23:32; 34:12; Judg. 2:2); do not make a covenant with them (Deut. 7:2); Israel made a covenant with the Gibeonites (Josh. 9:6; 2 Sam. 21:2); the men of Jabesh Gilead asked for a covenant with Nahash the Ammonite (1 Sam. 11:1); will the crocodile make a covenant with you? (Job 41:4); I made a covenant with my eyes (Job 31:1); we have made a covenant with death (Isa. 28:15).

766 Conditions
Then John permitted Jesus to be baptised (Matt. 3:15).

767 Security
A Pledges
Do not take a widow's cloak as a pledge (Deut. 24:17); do not take a millstone in pledge (Deut. 24:6); do not go into your neighbour's house to get a pledge (Deut. 24:10-11); return the pledge by sunset (Exod. 22:26; Deut. 24:12-13); Judah giving a pledge (Gen. 38:17-20); be surety for your servant for good (Ps. 119:122); we are given the Spirit as a pledge (2 Cor. 1:22; 5:5; Eph. 1:14); they took security from Jason (Acts 17:9); do not give pledges (Prov. 22:26-7); a senseless man gives a pledge (Prov. 17:18); he who gives surety for a stranger will suffer for it (Prov. 11:15); woe to him who loads himself with pledges (Hab. 2:6); you have taken pledges needlessly (Job 22:6); some take the widow's ox in pledge (Job 24:3); they take a pledge against the poor (Job 24:9); they lie beside altars on garments taken in pledge (Amos 2:8).

B Guarantees
Judah would be surety for Benjamin (Gen. 43:9; 44:32); this makes Jesus the guarantor of a better covenant (Heb. 7:22); O Lord, be my surety (Isa. 38:14).

768 Observance
A Keeping Passover
A night to be observed by all Israelites (Exod. 12:42); observe the Passover (Num. 9:2); keep this service in this month (Exod. 13:5); keep this statute at its appointed time (Exod. 13:10).

B Keeping the sabbath
Let them keep the sabbath through all generations (Exod. 31:16); keep my sabbaths (Lev. 19:3); the Lord commanded you to keep the sabbath (Deut. 5:15); the eunuchs who keep my sabbaths will have a memorial (Isa. 56:4-5).

C Keeping covenant
C1 God keeps covenant
I will keep my covenant with you (Lev. 26:9); God keeps covenant (Neh. 1:5); God remembers his covenant (Exod. 2:24; Lev. 26:42); I will never break my covenant (Judg. 2:1); if you can break my covenant with day and night then my covenant with David will be broken (Jer. 33:20-1).

C2 Man keeping covenant
You and your offspring must keep my covenant (Gen. 17:9); keep my covenant (Exod. 19:5); keep the words of this covenant (Deut. 29:9); his lovingkindness is to those who keep his covenant (Ps. 103:18); the inhabitants of Jerusalem did according to the covenant (2 Chr. 34:32); eunuchs who keep my covenant will have a memorial (Isa. 56:4-5).

D Keeping commandments
D1 Keep the commandments!
Keep the commandments (Lev. 22:31; Deut. 6:1-2; Josh. 1:7; 1 Kgs. 2:3; 2 Kgs. 17:13; 1 Chr. 22:12; 2 Chr. 14:4; Matt. 19:17-19); fear God and keep his commandments (Eccles. 12:13); oh, that they would keep my commandments! (Deut. 5:29); the Lord commanded us to do all these statutes (Deut. 6:24); keep the commandments that you may live long in the land (Deut. 4:40); converted Gentiles must observe the law of Moses (Acts 15:5); they would see that Paul kept the law (Acts 21:24); what matters is keeping the commandments (1 Cor. 7:19); blessed are those who hear the word of God and keep it (Luke 11:28); keep the commandment unstained and without reproach (1 Tim. 6:14); this is the love of God, that we keep his commandments (1 John 5:3); be doers of the word (Jas. 1:22); if the uncircumcised man keeps the law he will be regarded as circumcised (Rom. 2:26); circumcision is only of value if you keep the law (Rom. 2:25).

D2 I keep the commandments
I keep your law (Ps. 119:55); I have carried out the Lord's commands (1 Sam. 15:13); I have kept the ways of the Lord (2 Sam. 22:22-3; Ps. 18:21-2); I have not departed from his commands (Job 23:12); all these I have observed (Matt. 19:20); all these I have observed from my youth (Mark 10:20; Luke 18:21); I know him and I keep his word (John 8:55); I have kept my Father's commandments and remain in his love (John 15:10).

D3 Those who kept the commandments
David kept my commands (1 Kgs. 11:34); Hezekiah kept the commandments (2 Kgs. 18:6); Josiah's devotion according to all written in the law of the Lord (2 Chr. 35:26); Zechariah and Elizabeth walked blamelessly in all the commandments (Luke 1:6); we keep his commandments and do what pleases him (1 John 3:22); he who is physically uncircumcised but keeps the law

will condemn you (Rom. 2:27); those who keep the commandments of God and the faith of Jesus (Rev. 14:12).

D4 Results of keeping the commandments
In keeping your words there is great reward (Ps. 19:11); if one observes the statutes and ordinances he will live (Ezek. 20:11); he who keeps the commandment keeps his soul (Prov. 19:16); keep the commandments that you may live long in the land (Deut. 4:40); if you heed God's commandments and statutes you will avoid the diseases of the Egyptians (Exod. 15:26); God shows lovingkindness to those who keep his commandments (Exod. 20:6; Deut. 5:10).

D5 Keeping Christ's commands
Teaching them to observe all that I have commanded you (Matt. 28:20); you are my friends if you do what I command you (John 15:14); if you love me, you will keep my commandments (John 14:15); if anyone loves me he will keep my word (John 14:23-4); he who has my commandments and keeps them is the one who loves me (John 14:21); if you keep my commandments you will abide in my love (John 15:10); we know that we know him if we keep his commandments (1 John 2:3); this is love, that we walk according to his commands (2 John 6); if anyone keeps my word he will never see death (John 8:51, 52); he who says he knows him but does not keep his commands is a liar (1 John 2:4); whoever keeps his word, in him the love of God is made perfect (1 John 2:5).

769 Nonobservance
A Breaking the covenant
Breaking the covenant (Gen. 17:14; Lev. 26:15; Ezek. 16:59); you have not kept my covenant (1 Kgs. 11:11); they did not continue in my covenant (Heb. 8:9); they violated the covenant (Josh. 7:11); they have forsaken your covenant (1 Kgs. 19:10); my covenant which they broke (Jer. 31:32); like Adam they broke the covenant (Hos. 6:7); you have corrupted the covenant of Levi (Mal. 2:8); cursed is the one who does not obey the covenant (Jer. 11:3); the adulteress forgets the covenant of her God (Prov. 2:17).

B Not keeping commands
B1 If you do not keep commands . . .
If a man turns away from the law, even his prayer is an abomination (Prov. 28:9); you will be destroyed if you do not keep the commandments (Deut. 28:45); one who violates the law of Moses dies on the evidence of two or three witnesses (Heb. 10:28); if anyone hears my sayings and does not keep them, I do not judge him (John 12:47); if you break the law your circumcision becomes uncircumcision (Rom. 2:25).

B2 They do not keep commands
How long will you refuse to keep my commands? (Exod. 16:28); none of you keeps the law (John 7:19); they did not keep your word (Ps. 119:158); they have not kept my law (Jer. 16:11); you have turned aside from my statutes and not kept them (Mal. 3:7); you have not even observed the ordinances of the nations around you (Ezek. 5:7); Saul has not obeyed my commands (1 Sam. 15:11); Solomon did not observe what the Lord commanded (1 Kgs. 11:10); this man is not from God because he does not keep the sabbath (John 9:16); he who does not love me does not keep my words (John 14:24); if they kept my word they will keep yours also (John 15:20); you who boast in the law, do you dishonour God by breaking the law? (Rom. 2:23); you who have the letter [of the law] and circumcision but break the law (Rom. 2:27); those who are circumcised do not keep the law (Gal. 6:13); to turn away from the holy commandment delivered to them (2 Pet. 2:21).

BREAKING THE LAW, see 954.

C Not keeping Passover
Whoever does not keep the Passover will be cut off (Num. 9:13).

770 Compromise
MODERATION, see 177.

771 Acquisition
A Inheriting
A1 About inheriting
An inheritance gained hastily will not be blessed (Prov. 20:21); if the inheritance is by law it is no longer by promise (Gal. 3:18); the Spirit is a pledge of our inheritance (Eph. 1:14); work as to the Lord and you will receive the inheritance as a reward (Col. 3:24); you were called that you might inherit a blessing (1 Pet. 3:9).

A2 Who inherits
Daughters can inherit (Num. 27:4; Josh. 17:3-6); Job gave his daughters inheritance (Job 42:15); if a man with no children dies, another relative shall inherit (Num. 27:9-11); if those of the law are heirs, the promise is void (Rom. 4:14); those who do such things will not inherit the kingdom of God (Gal. 5:21); the Gentiles are fellow-heirs (Eph. 3:6); those who through faith and patience inherit the promises (Heb. 6:12); that those who are called may receive the promised inheritance (Heb. 9:15).

HEIR, see 776A.

INHERITANCE, see 777.

A3 Inheriting the land
He gave them their land as an inheritance (Acts 13:19); the promise that Abraham's descendants would inherit the world (Rom. 4:13); Abraham went to the place he was to receive as an inheritance (Heb. 11:8); Joshua will cause Israel to inherit the land (Deut. 1:38); my chosen ones will inherit my mountains (Isa. 65:9); I will cause them to inherit the desolate heritages (Isa. 49:8); the land will be inherited by: those who wait for the Lord (Ps. 37:9, 34); the humble (Ps. 37:11); those blessed by him (Ps. 37:22); the righteous (Ps. 37:29); him who takes refuge in me (Isa. 57:13); the seed of those who fear the Lord (Ps. 25:13); those who keep the commandments (Deut. 11:8).

B Taking possession
They took possession of houses full of good things (Neh. 9:25); they took possession of the fruit of the peoples' toil (Ps. 105:44); woe to those who add house to house and field to field (Isa. 5:8); I press on to make it my own, because Christ has made me his own (Phil. 3:12-13).

C Gain
C1 What gain?
What does a man gain from his toil? (Eccles. 1:3; 3:9); what gain do we have if we pray to God? (Job 21:15); what do I gain by not sinning? (Job 35:3); what will it profit a man if he gains the whole world? (Matt. 16:26; Mark 8:36; Luke 9:25); what profit is it if I go down to the pit? (Ps. 30:9); ill-gotten gains do not profit (Prov. 10:2); wealth gained hastily will dwindle (Prov. 13:11); getting treasures by a lying tongue is a fleeting vapour (Prov. 21:6); gain by violence leads to loss of life (Prov. 1:19); my people have changed their glory for that which does not profit (Jer. 2:11); they went after things which do not profit (Jer. 2:8); 'it profits a man nothing to delight in God' (Job 34:9); whatever was gain, I counted loss for the sake of Christ (Phil. 3:7); the man with a good wife will have no lack of gain (Prov. 31:11).

C2 Unjust gain
They think godliness is a means of gain (1 Tim. 6:5); does Job fear God for nothing? (Job 1:9); shepherding the flock not for shameful gain (1 Pet. 5:2); teaching for the sake of shameful gain (Titus 1:11); they show love with their lips but their heart goes after gain (Ezek. 33:31); the slave girl brought her owners much gain from soothsaying (Acts 16:16); for gain they have rushed into Balaam's error (Jude 11); deacons must not be greedy for gain (1 Tim. 3:8); an elder [overseer] should not seek shameful gain (Titus 1:7).

C3 True gain
The gain from wisdom is better than from silver (Prov. 3:14); I am the Lord who teaches you to profit (Isa. 48:17); godliness is great gain with contentment (1 Tim. 6:6); to die is gain (Phil. 1:21).

772 Loss

A Loss in general
Whoever does not have will lose what he has (Matt. 25:29; Mark 4:25; Luke 8:18); if anyone's work is burned up, he will suffer loss (1 Cor. 3:15); a time to give up as lost (Eccles. 3:6); I count all things as loss because of the worth of knowing Christ Jesus (Phil. 3:8); for him I have suffered the loss of all things (Phil. 3:8).

B Losing specific things
Earning wages to put into a bag with holes (Hag. 1:6); a woman who loses one of her 10 drachma (Luke 15:8); the donkeys of Kish were lost (1 Sam. 9:3); he goes to find the sheep which was lost (Luke 15:4); there will be no loss of life, but only of the ship (Acts 27:22); take heed that you may not lose what you have accomplished (2 John 8).

C Losing one's life
He who seeks to keep his life will lose it but whoever loses his life will find it (Matt. 10:39; 16:25; Mark 8:35; Luke 9:24; 17:33); he who loves his life loses it (John 12:25); to gain the whole world and forfeit your soul (Matt. 16:26; Mark 8:36; Luke 9:25).

D Lost people
My people have become lost sheep (Jer. 50:6); seek me, for I have gone astray like a lost sheep (Ps. 119:176); the Son of man came to seek and save the lost (Luke 19:10); the lost sheep of the house of Israel (Matt. 10:6; 15:24); he was lost and is found (Luke 15:24); this is his will, that I lose nothing of what he has given me (John 6:39); I will seek the lost (Ezek. 34:16); you have not sought the lost (Ezek. 34:4); no one is lost except the son of perdition (John 17:12).

E Bereavement
You have bereaved me of my children (Gen. 42:36); if I am bereaved, I am bereaved (Gen. 43:14); Naomi was bereaved of husband and sons (Ruth 1:5); David will be like a bear bereaved (2 Sam. 17:8); I will be like a bear robbed of her cubs (Hos. 13:8); better meeting a she-bear robbed of her cubs than a fool (Prov. 17:12).

773 Possession
POSSESSIONS, see 777.

A Possessing in general
He who has will be given more (Matt. 13:12; 25:29; Mark 4:25; Luke 8:18; 19:26); I would have received what was my own with interest (Matt. 25:27); if you have not been faithful with another's, who will give you your own? (Luke 16:12).

B God possessing

B1 God possessing in general
Render to God the things that are God's (Matt. 22:21; Mark 12:17; Luke 20:25); all that the Father has is mine (John 16:15).

B2 All things belong to God
The highest heaven, earth and all in it belong to the Lord (Deut. 10:14); God most high, possessor of heaven and earth (Gen. 14:19); the earth is the Lord's (Exod. 9:29); the earth is the Lord's and everything in it (Ps. 24:1; 1 Cor. 10:26); the mountains are his (Ps. 95:4); the sea is his (Ps. 95:5); the cattle on a thousand hills are mine (Ps. 50:10); firstlings of animals belong to the Lord (Lev. 27:26); all the tithe of the land is the Lord's (Lev. 27:30); the silver is mine and the gold is mine (Hag. 2:8); all fat is the Lord's (Lev. 3:16).

B3 People belong to God
All souls are mine (Ezek. 18:4); the firstborn of men and beast belong to me (Exod. 13:2); all firstborn males belong to the Lord (Exod. 13:12); I have separated you from the peoples to be mine (Lev. 20:26); I have called you by name, you are mine (Isa. 43:1); Gilead is mine and Manasseh is mine (Ps. 60:7; 108:8); the Levites are mine (Num. 3:45); yours they were and you gave them to me (John 17:6); the God to whom I belong and whom I worship (Acts 27:23); among whom you are called to belong to Jesus Christ (Rom. 1:6); until the redemption of God's own possession (Eph. 1:14); we are his (Ps. 100:3); I am praying for those you have given me, for they are yours (John 17:9); whether we live or die we are the Lord's (Rom. 14:8); you are Christ's and Christ is God's (1 Cor. 3:23).

C Christ possessing
You are Christ's and Christ is God's (1 Cor. 3:23); if anyone is confident that he is Christ's, let him remind himself that so are we (2 Cor. 10:7); yours they were and you gave them to me (John 17:6); I am praying for those you have given me, for they are yours (John 17:9).

D People possessing

D1 People possessing in general
All things are yours (1 Cor. 3:21-2); render to Caesar the things that are Caesar's (Matt. 22:21; Mark 12:17; Luke 20:25); when it was unsold, did it not remain your own? (Acts 5:4); be content with what you have (Heb. 13:5); no one claimed that anything was his own (Acts 4:32).

D2 Possessing through God
The land as an everlasting possession (Gen. 17:8); every place that the sole of your foot treads on is yours (Deut. 11:24); the house of Jacob will possess their possessions (Obad. 17); as having nothing yet possessing all things (2 Cor. 6:10); if you have not been faithful with another's, who will give you your own? (Luke 16:12); we have left everything, what shall we have? (Matt. 19:27).

D3 Priests possessing
The guilt offering shall belong to the priest who makes atonement with it (Lev. 7:7); the skin of the burnt offering shall belong to the priest who offers it (Lev. 7:8); every cereal offering shall belong to the priest who offers it (Lev. 7:9); the breast shall belong to Aaron and his sons (Lev. 7:31); the right thigh shall belong to the one who offers the blood and the fat (Lev. 7:33).

D4 People possessing other things
The field and the cave at Machpelah were established as Abraham's (Gen. 23:17-18); the daughters, children and flocks are mine (Gen. 31:43); I will bring the worst of the nations to take possession of their houses (Ezek. 7:24); the land belonged to Pharaoh (Gen. 47:20); am I not your donkey? (Num. 22:30); your most beautiful wives and children are mine (1 Kgs. 20:3); Ephraim and Manasseh are mine as Reuben and Simeon are mine (Gen. 48:5); my beloved is mine and I am his (S. of S. 2:16); I am my beloved's and he is mine (S. of S. 6:3); the one this people has chosen, his will I be (2 Sam. 16:18).

774 Nonownership

A Not possessing
From him who has not, what he has will be taken away (Matt. 13:12; 25:29; Mark 4:25; Luke 8:18); to sit at my right and left is not mine to give (Matt. 20:23; Mark 10:40); you are not your own (1 Cor. 6:19); you are envious and cannot obtain, so you fight (Jas. 4:2).

B No earthly inheritance
God gave Abraham no inheritance in the land (Acts 7:5); there was no inheritance for the priests (Num. 18:20); as having nothing, yet possessing all things (2 Cor. 6:10).

C No heavenly inheritance
You have no portion in the Lord (Josh. 22:25); the unrighteous will not inherit the kingdom of God (1 Cor. 6:9); no immoral or covetous man can inherit the kingdom (Eph. 5:5); flesh and blood cannot inherit the kingdom of God (1 Cor. 15:50).

775 Joint possession

A Sharing material things
Let Aner, Eshcol and Mamre take their share (Gen. 14:24); all that is mine is yours (Luke 15:31); the thresher should thresh in hope of a share of the crop (1 Cor. 9:10); those who believed had all things in common (Acts 2:44; 4:32).

B Sharing in Christ
The cup and the bread are a sharing in the blood and body of Christ (1 Cor. 10:16); we are partakers in Christ (Heb. 3:14); the Gentiles share in the promise of Christ (Eph. 3:6); I John share with you the tribulation and the kingdom (Rev. 1:9); Gentile believers have shared in spiritual things (Rom. 15:27); rejoice as you share the sufferings of Christ (1 Pet. 4:13); that you may become partakers of the divine nature (2 Pet. 1:4); those who became partakers of the Holy Spirit (Heb. 6:4); husbands and wives are joint heirs of the grace of life (1 Pet. 3:7).

C Sharing evil
He who greets him shares in his evil deeds (2 John 11); I do not want you to be sharers with demons (1 Cor. 10:20); do not share in her sins lest you share in her plagues (Rev. 18:4).

776 Possessor

POSSESSING, see 773.

A Heirs of God
Heirs of God and fellow-heirs with Christ (Rom. 8:17); this is the heir, let us kill him and take his inheritance (Matt. 21:38; Mark 12:7; Luke 20:14); God appointed his Son heir of all things (Heb. 1:2); if a son, then an heir (Gal. 4:7); heirs according to the hope of eternal life (Titus 3:7); heirs according to the promise (Gal. 3:29); Noah became an heir of the righteousness by faith (Heb. 11:7); Abraham, Isaac and Jacob, fellow-heirs of the same promise (Heb. 11:9); God chose the poor to be heirs of the kingdom (Jas. 2:5); husbands and wives are joint heirs of the grace of life (1 Pet. 3:7).

B Heirs of men
The heir of my house is Eliezer (Gen. 15:2-4); your own son will be your heir (Gen. 15:4); they will kill the heir (2 Sam. 14:7); the son of the slave woman shall not be heir with Isaac (Gen. 21:10).

777 Property

A Owning property in general
The law on property rights (Exod. 22:1-4); is it not right for me to do as I wish with what is mine? (Matt. 20:15); a good man leaves an inheritance for his children's children (Prov. 13:22); house and wealth are inherited from fathers (Prov. 19:14); a man's life does not consist in the abundance of his possessions (Luke 12:15); I will build bigger barns to store all my goods (Luke 12:18); sell your possessions and give to the poor (Matt. 19:21); you accepted the seizure of your goods, knowing you have a better possession (Heb. 10:34).

B God's possession
You will be my special possession among the nations (Exod. 19:5); a people for his own possession (Deut. 4:20; 7:6); God's special possession (Deut. 14:2; 26:18; Ps. 135:4; 1 Pet. 2:9); God's inheritance (Deut. 4:20); take us as your possession (Exod. 34:9); they will be mine when I make up my own possession (Mal. 3:17); my inheritance, Israel (Joel 3:2); the riches of the glory of his inheritance in the saints (Eph. 1:18).

C Man's possession

C1 God is my portion
God is my portion for ever (Ps. 73:26); you are my portion (Ps. 142:5); the Lord is my portion (Ps. 119:57; Lam. 3:24); the Lord is my allotted portion and my cup (Ps. 16:5); the Lord is the inheritance of Levi (Deut. 10:9); I am your inheritance (Num. 18:20).

C2 Inheritance from God
You have given me the inheritance of those who fear your name (Ps. 61:5); the meek will inherit the earth (Matt. 5:5); I will give you the nations as your inheritance (Ps. 2:8); that they may obtain an inheritance (Acts 26:18); we have obtained an inheritance in Christ (Eph. 1:11); an imperishable inheritance in heaven (1 Pet. 1:4); come, inherit the kingdom prepared for you (Matt. 25:34); he has qualified us to share the inheritance of the saints (Col. 1:12); what shall I do to inherit eternal life? (Mark 10:17; Luke 10:25; 18:18); the word of God is able to give you the inheritance (Acts 20:32).

C3 Priestly inheritance
The priests' offerings are their inheritance (Deut. 18:1; Josh. 13:14); this is the priests' portion from the fire-offerings (Lev. 7:35); the priesthood is their inheritance (Josh. 18:7).

THE LORD THEIR INHERITANCE, see 777C1.

C4 The land an inheritance
The land was divided for an inheritance (Num. 26:53); Joshua gave them the land as their inheritance (Josh. 11:23); the land you gave us for an inheritance (2 Chr. 20:11); the land on which Caleb's foot trod was to be his inheritance (Josh. 14:9).

D Baggage
Prepare baggage for exile (Jer. 46:19; Ezek. 12:3-7); David left his things with the baggage keeper (1 Sam. 17:22); 200 men stayed with the baggage (1 Sam. 25:13); those who stay with the baggage have the same share as those in the battle (1 Sam. 30:24); Saul hid among the baggage (1 Sam. 10:22).

778 Retention

There is a time to keep (Eccles. 3:6); Ananias kept back a part of the price (Acts 5:2); the pay of your labourers which you kept back by fraud (Jas. 5:4); keep your gifts for yourself and give your rewards to another (Dan. 5:17); if you hold fast the gospel (1 Cor. 15:2); hold fast what you have until I come (Rev. 2:25); hold fast what you have (Rev. 3:11).

779 Nonretention

A Orphans
We have become orphans without a father (Lam. 5:3); Esther [Hadassah] had neither father nor mother (Esther 2:7); your children will become orphans (Exod. 22:24); I will not leave you as orphans (John 14:18); the Lord supports the fatherless (Ps. 146:9); God is a father

of the fatherless (Ps. 68:5); in you the orphan finds
mercy (Hos. 14:3); the Lord does not pity their orphans
or widows (Isa. 9:17); give the tithe to the fatherless
(Deut. 26:12-13); use the tithe to feed the orphan (Deut.
14:29); invite the orphan to the Feast of Booths (Deut.
16:14); let the orphans eat the Feast of Weeks with you
(Deut. 16:11); leave the forgotten sheaf and gleanings
for the fatherless (Deut. 24:19-21); true religion is to
visit orphans and widows (Jas. 1:27); do not oppress
widows or orphans (Exod. 22:22-4); do not pervert the
justice due to the fatherless (Deut. 24:17; 27:19); I will
be a witness against those who oppress the widow and
the orphan (Mal. 3:5).

B Putting away
Put away the foreign gods (Gen. 35:2); cut off your hair
and throw it away (Jer. 7:29).

780 Transfer [of property]

A man who has toiled leaves a legacy to those who have
not (Eccles. 2:21); I must leave it to the man who comes
after me (Eccles. 2:18); the sinner's wealth is laid up for
the righteous (Prov. 13:22).

781 Giving

A Giving in general
The leech has two daughters, 'Give, give!' (Prov. 30:15);
give to him who asks you (Matt. 5:42; Luke 6:30); give
and it will be given you (Luke 6:38); Jesus said, 'It is
more blessed to give than to receive' (Acts 20:35); God
loves a cheerful giver (2 Cor. 9:7); you know how to
give good gifts to your children (Matt. 7:11); give as
God has blessed (Deut. 15:14); everyone is a friend to
him who gives gifts (Prov. 19:6).

B God giving
B1 God giving to the Son
All things have been handed over to me by my Father
(Matt. 11:27; Luke 10:22); the Father has given all things
into the Son's hands (John 3:35; 13:3); all authority in
heaven and earth has been given to me (Matt. 28:18);
the Father has granted the Son to have life in himself
(John 5:26); the Father gave the Son authority to judge
(John 5:27); my Father has given them to me (John
10:29); they know that everything you have given me is
from you (John 17:7); your name which you gave me
(John 17:12); the glory you have given me (John 17:22,
24); shall I not drink the cup the Father has given me?
(John 18:11); the revelation of Jesus Christ which God
gave him (Rev. 1:1); all that the Father gives to me will
come to me (John 6:37); you have given him authority
to grant eternal life to all you have given him (John
17:2); the people you gave me out of the world (John
17:6); I am praying for those you have given me (John
17:9); you have given them to me (John 17:24); this is
his will, that I lose nothing of what he has given me
(John 6:39); of those you gave me I did not lose one
(John 18:9); yours they were and you gave them to me
(John 17:6).
B2 God giving freely
God gives generously to all (Jas. 1:5); your Father in
heaven gives good gifts (Matt. 7:11); every good and
perfect gift is from the Father (Jas. 1:17); he will give
you the desires of your heart (Ps. 37:4); the Lord has
much more to give you (2 Chr. 25:9); he gives to all life
and breath and all things (Acts 17:25); he who did not
spare his own Son will with him freely give us all things
(Rom. 8:32); ask and it will be given you (Matt. 7:7;
Luke 11:9); not as the world gives do I give to you (John
14:27); you thought you could obtain the gift of God
with money! (Acts 8:20); grace was given to each
according to the measure of Christ's gift (Eph. 4:7); the
Lord gave and the Lord has taken away (Job 1:21); he

gave them what they asked but sent a disease (Ps.
106:15).
CHILDREN A GIFT OF GOD, see 170A3a.
B3 What God gives
B3a What God gives in general
What will you give me? (Gen. 15:2); the gifts of God are
irrevocable (Rom. 11:29); peace I leave with you, my
peace I give you (John 14:27); you give him authority to
grant eternal life to all you have given him (John 17:2);
the glory you have given me I have given them (John
17:22); you would have no authority unless you were
given it from above (John 19:11); the Most High gives
dominion to whom he will (Dan. 4:17); you will receive
power when the Holy Spirit has come on you (Acts
1:8).
B3b God giving his Son
If you knew the gift of God (John 4:10); God so loved
the world that he gave his only son (John 3:16); thanks
be to God for his inexpressible gift (2 Cor. 9:15).
B3c God giving his Spirit
God gives his Spirit without measure (John 3:34); God
gave the Gentiles the Holy Spirit just as he did to us
(Acts 15:8); God gave the same gift to them as to us
(Acts 11:17); the Holy Spirit given to us (Rom. 5:5); he
who gives the Spirit to you (Gal. 3:5); how much more
will your heavenly Father give the Holy Spirit (Luke
11:13); God gave us the Spirit as a pledge (2 Cor. 1:22;
5:5); God gives the Holy Spirit to those who obey him
(Acts 5:32).
B3d God giving new life
The gift of God is eternal life (Rom. 6:23); being saved
is the gift of God (Eph. 2:8); God grants repentance
and forgiveness of sins (Acts 5:31); to the Gentiles also
God has granted repentance (Acts 11:18); they are
justified by his grace as a gift (Rom. 3:24); the grace
which he freely bestowed on us in the Beloved (Eph.
1:6).
B3e Spiritual gifts
When he ascended he gave gifts to men (Eph. 4:8);
concerning spiritual gifts (1 Cor. 12:1-31); we have gifts
that differ according to the grace given to us (Rom.
12:6); every one has his own gift from God (1 Cor. 7:7);
do not neglect the spiritual gift within you (1 Tim.
4:14); rekindle the gift of God (2 Tim. 1:6); whoever has
a gift should use it in serving (1 Pet. 4:10); gifts of the
Holy Spirit (Heb. 2:4); you are not lacking in any gift
(1 Cor. 1:7); I long to impart some spiritual gift to you
(Rom. 1:11).
B3f God giving the land
To your offspring I will give this land (Gen. 12:7; 13:15;
15:18); I will give you the land to possess (Lev. 20:24); I
brought you out of Ur to give you this land (Gen. 15:7);
to your seed I will give this land (Gen. 24:7; 28:13); I will
given you the land of Israel (Ezek. 11:17); I will give
your descendants this land as an everlasting possession
(Gen. 48:4); the land the Lord will give them across the
Jordan (Deut. 3:20); every place the sole of your foot
treads on I have given you (Josh. 1:3); I know the Lord
has given you the land (Josh. 2:9); I am giving you the
land of Canaan (Lev. 14:34; 25:38); the land I swore to
give to the descendants of Abraham, Isaac and Jacob
(Exod. 33:1; Deut. 6:10); he gave them their land as an
inheritance (Acts 13:19); God promised to give the land
to him and to his posterity (Acts 7:5).
B3g Other gifts of God
He gave him the covenant of circumcision (Acts 7:8);
the Lord has given you the sabbath (Exod. 16:29); I
have given you the blood on the altar to make
atonement (Lev. 17:11); they were entrusted with the
oracles of God (Rom. 3:2); eating and drinking are

God's gift to man (Eccles. 3:13); children are a gift of the Lord (Ps. 127:3).

B4 Those to whom God gives
Only those to whom it is given can accept this (Matt. 19:11); a man can only receive what has been given him from heaven (John 3:27); to him who has will more be given (Matt. 13:12; 25:29; Mark 4:25; Luke 8:18; 19:26); from him who is given much will much be required (Luke 12:48); to you it is given to know the secrets of the kingdom (Matt. 13:11; Mark 4:11; Luke 8:10); why is this given to me, that the mother of my Lord should come to me? (Luke 1:43); no one can come to me unless it is granted him by the Father (John 6:65).

C People giving
C1 Giving to God
C1a Giving to God in general
Who has given to God that God should repay him? (Rom. 11:35); if you are righteous, what do you give to God? (Job 35:7); what shall I render to the Lord? (Ps. 116:12); give to God what is God's (Matt. 22:21; Mark 12:17; Luke 20:25); everything comes from you and from your hand we have given to you (1 Chr. 29:14, 16); they brought gifts of gold, incense and myrrh (Matt. 2:11); when you ascended you received gifts from men (Ps. 68:18).

C1b Giving for the sanctuary
The Israelites were to make a contribution of materials (Exod. 25:2; 35:5); everyone whose heart moved him brought a contribution (Exod. 35:21); David and the leaders gave materials for the temple (1 Chr. 29:3-9); the temple was adorned with beautiful stones and votive gifts (Luke 21:5); the crowd put money in the treasury (Mark 12:41); he saw the rich put money in the treasury (Luke 21:1); some gave of their wealth, but the widow put in all she had (Mark 12:44; Luke 21:4).

C1c Giving oneself to God
The people offered themselves willingly (Judg. 5:2); they gave themselves first to the Lord, then to us (2 Cor. 8:5); present yourselves to God as those alive from the dead (Rom. 6:13).

C2 Giving to other people
C2a Giving to others in general
Give to Caesar the things that are Caesar's (Matt. 22:21; Mark 12:17; Luke 20:25); Herod promised to give her whatever she asked (Matt. 14:7); may the kings of Sheba and Seba bring gifts (Ps. 72:10); the Moabites brought tribute to David (2 Sam. 8:2); the Arameans brought tribute to David (2 Sam. 8:6); send lambs as tribute to the ruler (Isa. 16:1).

C2b Gifts given to people
Jonathan gave David his clothes and armour (1 Sam. 18:4); perhaps I can appease Esau with my present (Gen. 32:20); the brothers gave their gifts to Joseph (Gen. 43:25-6); Abigail brought a present for David and his men (1 Sam. 25:27); Ahaz sent a gift to the king of Assyria (2 Kgs. 16:8); Berodach-baladan sent gifts to Hezekiah (2 Kgs. 20:12);
the gift you promised beforehand (2 Cor. 9:5); I seek the fruit, not the gift (Phil. 4:17); no church except you shared with me in giving and receiving (Phil. 4:15).

C2c Giving food and drink
The woman gave fruit to her husband and he ate (Gen. 3:6); the woman gave me fruit and I ate (Gen. 3:12); you give them something to eat (Matt. 14:16); he gave the loaves to the disciples and the disciples gave them to the crowd (Matt. 14:19; 15:36; Luke 9:16); Jesus dipped the morsel and gave it to Judas (John 13:26).

C2d Giving to the poor
If I give away all I have and have not love (1 Cor. 13:3); the righteous is gracious and gives (Ps. 37:21); your prayers and alms have ascended as a memorial before

God (Acts 10:4); give what is within for alms and all is clean (Luke 11:41); they thought Jesus was telling Judas to give something to the poor (John 13:29); if you do not give them what they need, what use is it? (Jas. 2:16); when you give alms, do not sound a trumpet (Matt. 6:2-4); he who gives should do so with all his heart (Rom. 12:8); sell your possessions and give to the poor (Matt. 19:21; Mark 10:21; Luke 12:33; 18:22); freely you have received, freely give (Matt. 10:8); contribute to the needs of the saints (Rom. 12:13); let the former thief work so that he can give (Eph. 4:28); I give half my possessions to the poor (Luke 19:8); Macedonia and Achaia made a contribution to the poor saints (Rom. 15:26); Macedonia gave beyond their means (2 Cor. 8:3); begging us for the favour of taking part in the relief of the saints (2 Cor. 8:4); I came to give alms to my nation (Acts 24:17); the perfume could have been sold and the money given to the poor (Matt. 26:9; Mark 14:5; John 12:5).

782 Receiving

WELCOME, see 299.

A God receiving
If God wanted to kill us, he would not have received an offering (Judg. 13:23); should I receive that from your hand? (Mal. 1:13); the Lord no longer regards your offering or receives it with favour (Mal. 2:13); I will not receive an offering from you (Mal. 1:10).

B Receiving from God
B1 Receiving the Spirit
Receive the Holy Spirit (John 20:22); the Spirit which those who believed in him were to receive (John 7:39); Christ received from the Father the promise of the Holy Spirit (Acts 2:33); you will receive the gift of the Holy Spirit (Acts 2:38); Peter and John prayed for them to receive the Holy Spirit (Acts 8:15-17); that we might receive the promise of the Spirit through faith (Gal. 3:14); did you receive the Holy Spirit when you believed? (Acts 19:2); did you receive the Spirit by works or by faith? (Gal. 3:2).

B2 Other receiving from God
Everyone who asks receives (Matt. 7:8; Luke 11:10); whatever you ask in prayer, believing, you will receive (Matt. 21:22); freely you have received, freely give (Matt. 10:8); he hears the word and immediately receives it with joy (Matt. 13:20); not everyone can receive this word but only those to whom it is given (Matt. 19:11-12); a man cannot receive anything unless it is given him from heaven (John 3:27); whoever has forsaken for Christ will receive a hundredfold (Matt. 19:29; Mark 10:30); I received from the Lord what I delivered to you (1 Cor. 11:23); the gospel which you received (1 Cor. 15:1); the Gentiles had received the word of God (Acts 11:1); the Bereans received the word eagerly (Acts 17:11); as you received Christ, so walk in him (Col. 2:6); of his fullness we have all received (John 1:16); what do you have that you did not receive? (1 Cor. 4:7).

C Receiving from man
Sinners lend to sinners, to receive back the same amount (Luke 6:34); Jesus said, 'It is more blessed to give than to receive' (Acts 20:35); concerning the collection for the saints (1 Cor. 16:1).

D Not receiving
Abraham would take nothing from the king of Sodom (Gen. 14:22-4); Elisha would take nothing from Naaman (2 Kgs. 5:16); is it a time to receive presents? (2 Kgs. 5:26); they did not receive what was promised (Heb. 11:39); let that man not expect to receive anything from the Lord (Jas. 1:7); you ask and do not receive because you ask amiss (Jas. 4:3).

783 Apportioning

A Sharing in general
Do not neglect to do good and share (Heb. 13:16); sell all you have and distribute to the poor (Luke 18:22); the one with two tunics or food should share with him who has none (Luke 3:11); they sold their possessions and shared with any who had need (Acts 2:45); the proceeds of sales were distributed to those in need (Acts 4:35); he who is taught must share with his teacher (Gal. 6:6); tell my brother to divide the inheritance with me (Luke 12:13-14).

B Dividing food
Jehoiachin had a regular allowance every day (2 Kgs. 25:30); David distributed food to the people (1 Chr. 16:3); Jesus and the disciples distributed the food (Matt. 14:19; 15:36; John 6:11); a true fast is to share your bread with the hungry (Isa. 58:7); the king allotted them a daily ration of the rich food he ate (Dan. 1:5); take this and divide it among yourselves (Luke 22:17); he divided up the two fish among them all (Mark 6:41).

C Dividing out land
Apportioning the land (Num. 26:53-6; 34:13-29; Ezek. 47:13-23; 48:29); apportioning this land among the nine tribes (Josh. 13:7; 14:1-2); I will portion out Shechem and Succoth (Ps. 60:6; 108:7).

D Dividing plunder
In the evening Benjamin shares out the spoil (Gen. 49:27); all share alike in the plunder (1 Sam. 30:22-5); Jesus' garments were divided by casting lots (Matt. 27:35; Mark 15:24; Luke 23:34; John 19:23-4); they divided my garments between them (Ps. 22:18).

E Dividing spiritual blessings
Judas received his share in this ministry (Acts 1:17); tongues of fire, distributed and resting on each one of them (Acts 2:3); spiritual gifts are distributed by the Spirit (1 Cor. 12:11); gifts of the Holy Spirit distributed according to his will (Heb. 2:4).

784 Lending

A Lend!
Lend, expecting nothing (Luke 6:35); lend generously to the poor (Deut. 15:8); do not refuse one who wants to borrow (Matt. 5:42); the righteous is gracious and lends (Ps. 37:26); do not just lend to those from whom you hope to receive (Luke 6:34).

B Lending to the Lord
Samuel was lent to the Lord (1 Sam. 1:28; 2:20); he who is kind to the poor lends to the Lord (Prov. 19:17).

C Lending to others
If you lend, do not charge interest (Exod. 22:25); if you lend to your neighbour, do not enter his house to get his pledge (Deut. 24:10); in the seventh year the item loaned shall be released (Deut. 15:2-3); the alien will lend to you, and not you to him (Deut. 28:44).
borrowing, see 785.

D Lending and borrowing
You will lend to many nations but not borrow (Deut. 15:6; 28:12); like lender, like borrower (Isa. 24:2); I have neither lent nor borrowed yet everyone curses me (Jer. 15:10).

785 Borrowing
You will lend to many nations but not borrow (Deut. 15:6; 28:12); the wicked borrow and do not repay (Ps. 37:21); the borrower becomes a slave to the lender (Prov. 22:7); give to him who wants to borrow (Matt. 5:42); borrow as many vessels as you can (2 Kgs. 4:3); a borrowed axe-head (2 Kgs. 6:5); we borrowed money to pay the king's tax (Neh. 5:4).
lending and borrowing, see 784D.

786 Taking
keeping, see 778.

A Taking in general
The Lord gave and the Lord has taken away (Job 1:21); from him who has not, what he has will be taken away (Matt. 13:12; 25:29; Mark 4:25; Luke 8:18; 19:26).

B Taking people
They captured their children and their wives (Gen. 34:29); Lysias with great violence took him out of our hands (Acts 24:7); catching wives from those dancing (Judg. 21:21, 23); Abimelech sent and took Sarah (Gen. 20:2); they took away Dinah (Gen. 34:26); you have taken my husband (Gen. 30:15); no one can snatch them out of my hand (John 10:28-9); Enoch was no more because God took him (Gen. 5:24); the Lord is going to take your master from you today (2 Kgs. 2:3, 5); one will be taken and the other left (Matt. 24:40-1; Luke 17:34-6).

C Taking objects
stealing, see 788.

C1 Capturing cities
David captured the stronghold of Zion (1 Chr. 11:5); David captured Jerusalem (2 Sam. 5:6-9); Joab and David captured Rabbah (2 Sam. 12:26, 29); David took Gath from the Philistines (1 Chr. 18:1); Solomon captured Hamath-zobah (2 Chr. 8:3); the king of Assyria captured Damascus (2 Kgs. 16:9); the king of Assyria captured Samaria (2 Kgs. 17:6; 18:10); Jerusalem was captured (Jer. 39:1); Babylon has been captured (Jer. 50:2, 46; 51:41); he who rules his spirit is better than he who takes a city (Prov. 16:32).

C2 Taking treasures
The ark was captured (1 Sam. 4:11); the things in the temple were carried off to Babylon (2 Kgs. 25:13-15; 2 Chr. 36:7); Shishak carried off temple treasures to Egypt (1 Kgs. 14:26; 2 Chr. 12:9); Ahaz took some things from the temple to give to the king of Assyria (2 Chr. 28:21); Nebuchadnezzar took away all the treasure of the temple (2 Kgs. 24:13; Ezra 1:7).

C3 Taking animals
God has taken away your father's livestock and given them to me (Gen. 31:9); he took the poor man's ewe lamb (2 Sam. 12:4); the Sabeans took Job's oxen and donkeys (Job 1:14-15); the Chaldeans took Job's camels (Job 1:17).

C4 Taking possessions
The king will take the best of your fields and orchards for his servants (1 Sam. 8:14); Jacob has taken all our father's property (Gen. 31:1); I will take away my wool and my flax (Hos. 2:9); taking possession of Naboth's vineyard (1 Kgs. 21:15-16); the Midianites took all the produce of the land (Judg. 6:3-5); the Philistines were plundering (1 Sam. 23:1); my servants will take whatever they want (1 Kgs. 20:6); everything in your house will be carried off to Babylon (2 Kgs. 20:17).

D Taking intangible things
D1 Taking God's things
The evil one takes away the word (Matt. 13:19; Mark 4:15; Luke 8:12); you have taken away the key of knowledge (Luke 11:52); do not take your Holy Spirit from me (Ps. 51:11); I will remove your lampstand from its place (Rev. 2:5); the kingdom of God will be taken from you (Matt. 21:43).

D2 Taking away evil
The goat of removal [scapegoat, or goat for Azazel] (Lev. 16:8-26); take away all iniquity (Hos. 14:2); he took our infirmities and carried away our diseases (Matt. 8:17).
atonement, see 941.

D3 Taking other intangible things

I will tear the kingdom from Solomon (1 Kgs. 11:11-13, 31); the Romans will take away our place and our nation (John 11:48); if you are willing, remove this cup from me (Luke 22:42); Jacob took birthright and blessing (Gen. 27:35-6).

E Grasping

Lest man put forth his hand and take of the tree of life (Gen. 3:22); Jacob grasped Esau's heel (Gen. 25:26); she seized him by his garment (Gen. 39:12); grasp the snake by the tail (Exod. 4:4); if a wife seizes her husband's assailant by the private parts (Deut. 25:11); he did not consider equality with God a thing to be grasped (Phil. 2:6); holding fast the word of life (Phil. 2:16); happy are those who hold wisdom fast (Prov. 3:18).

CLING, see 48.

TOUCH, see 378.

787 Restitution

A Law of restitution

Restitution for violation of property (Exod. 22:1-15); restitution for stealing an animal (2 Sam. 12:6); a sinner must make restitution, adding one fifth (Lev. 5:16; 22:14; Num. 5:7); a thief must repay sevenfold (Prov. 6:31).

B About restitution

What I did not steal must I now restore? (Ps. 69:4); I will pay back for the years the locust has eaten (Joel 2:25); if I have cheated anyone, I will repay it fourfold (Luke 19:8).

788 Stealing

THIEF, see 789.

A Robbing

You rob God (Mal. 3:8-9, 9); I robbed other churches, taking pay from them (2 Cor. 11:8); Rachel stole the household gods (Gen. 31:19); they took the image, teraphim and ephod (Judg. 18:17-18); do you rob temples? (Rom. 2:22); do not store up treasure on earth where thieves break in and steal (Matt. 6:19); they robbed all who passed by (Judg. 9:25); why not rather be defrauded? (1 Cor. 6:7-8); from him who takes things from you do not ask for them again (Luke 6:30); whoever takes your coat, give him your shirt too (Matt. 5:40; Luke 6:29); you took joyfully the plundering of your goods (Heb. 10:34).

B Things stolen

B1 About stealing

Regulations concerning the theft of property (Exod. 22:1-13); guilt offering for theft (Lev. 6:2-7); what is stolen must be restored plus one fifth (Lev. 6:4-5); from the heart comes theft (Matt. 15:19; Mark 7:21); there is swearing, lying, murder, stealing and adultery (Hos. 4:2); inside they are full of robbery (Matt. 23:25; Luke 11:39); the scribes devour widows' houses (Mark 12:40); lest I be needy and steal (Prov. 30:9); stolen water is sweet (Prov. 9:17); they did not repent of their thefts (Rev. 9:21).

B2 Stealing people / bodies

The law is for kidnappers (1 Tim. 1:10); a kidnapper must be executed (Exod. 21:16; Deut. 24:7); Joseph was kidnapped (Gen. 40:15); his disciples might steal the body (Matt. 27:64); his disciples came by night and stole him away while we were sleeping (Matt. 28:13).

B3 Stealing property

What was stolen by day or night you required of me (Gen. 31:39); you bring what was taken by robbery as an offering (Mal. 1:13); having the money box, he used to take what was put into it (John 12:6); I took the 1100 pieces of silver (Judg. 17:2).

C No stealing

C1 Do not steal

Do not steal (Exod. 20:15; Lev. 19:11; Deut. 5:19; Matt. 19:18; Mark 10:19; Luke 18:20; Rom. 13:9); do not rob the poor because he is poor (Prov. 22:22); will you steal, murder and commit adultery? (Jer. 7:9); do not take money by force (Luke 3:14); you who preach against stealing, do you steal? (Rom. 2:21); let him who stole steal no more (Eph. 4:28); not pilfering (Titus 2:10); do not defraud (Mark 10:19).

C2 Nothing is stolen

Whose ox or donkey have I stolen? (1 Sam. 12:3); the shepherds did not miss anything when they were with us (1 Sam. 25:7); what I did not steal must I now restore? (Ps. 69:4); these men are neither temple robbers nor blasphemers of our goddess (Acts 19:37); treasure in heaven, where no thief comes (Luke 12:33).

789 Thief

STEALING, see 788.

A About thieves

He who climbs in another way is a thief and a robber (John 10:1); all who came before me are thieves and robbers (John 10:8); the thief comes only to steal, kill and destroy (John 10:10); thank you that I am not like other men, swindlers, unjust, adulterers (Luke 18:11); I did not mean the covetous, robbers or idolaters (1 Cor. 5:10); do not associate with a 'brother' who is a swindler (1 Cor. 5:11); let none of you suffer as a thief (1 Pet. 4:15); thieves will not inherit the kingdom of God (1 Cor. 6:10); in danger from robbers (2 Cor. 11:26); a thief is not despised who steals through hunger (Prov. 6:30); you made my house a den of robbers (Jer. 7:11; Matt. 21:13; Mark 11:17; Luke 19:46).

B Actual thieves

Judas was a thief (John 12:6); Barabbas was a robber (John 18:40); two thieves crucified with Jesus (Matt. 27:38, 44; Mark 15:27); a man fell among robbers (Luke 10:30).

C The Lord as a thief

The day of the Lord will come like a thief (1 Thess. 5:2; 2 Pet. 3:10); I come like a thief (Rev. 3:3; 16:15); if the householder had known when the thief was coming (Matt. 24:43; Luke 12:39); have you come with swords and clubs to arrest me like a thief? (Matt. 26:55; Mark 14:48; Luke 22:52).

790 Booty

A Rules about booty

Regulations concerning the taking of plunder (Deut. 20:14); apportioning booty (Num. 31:26-54); count the booty (Num. 31:26); divide the plunder with your brothers (Josh. 22:8); all share in the booty (1 Sam. 30:22-5); the Jews were given the right to plunder their enemies (Esther 8:11).

B Given as plunder

Tyre will become spoil for the nations (Ezek. 26:5); the spoil of Damascus and Samaria will be carried away to Assyria (Isa. 8:4); Chaldea will become plunder (Jer. 50:10); the houses of Jerusalem will be plundered (Zech. 14:2); the Jews' possessions to be taken as booty (Esther 3:13); our wives and children will be taken as plunder (Num. 14:3); your little ones whom you thought would be booty (Deut. 1:39); Maher-shalal-hash-baz – the spoil hastes, the prey speeds (Isa. 8:1, 3); those who plunder you will become plunder (Jer. 30:16).

C Specific plundering

Israel plundered the Egyptians (Exod. 3:22; 12:36); David took plunder from his raids (1 Sam. 27:9); the lepers carried off silver, gold and clothes (2 Kgs. 7:8);

Israel took the plunder from: Shechem (Gen. 34:27-9); Midian (Num. 31:9); Sihon (Deut. 2:35); Bashan (Deut. 3:7); Ai (Josh. 8:2); the cities of the land (Josh. 11:14); the Philistines (1 Sam. 17:53); the Hagrites (1 Chr. 5:21); Rabbah (2 Sam. 12:30; 1 Chr. 20:2); the camp of the Arameans (2 Kgs. 7:16); the Ethiopians (2 Chr. 14:13); Ammon, Moab and Mount Seir (2 Chr. 20:25); Gerar (2 Chr. 14:14-15); Judah (2 Chr. 25:13; 28:8).

D Dividing the spoil

He will divide the spoil with the strong (Isa. 53:12); he divides his spoil (Luke 11:22); they will rejoice like those who divide the spoil (Isa. 9:3); Sisera is delayed, dividing the spoils (Judg. 5:30); spoil dedicated to the Lord (2 Sam. 8:11-12); some plunder was given for the repair of the temple (1 Chr. 26:27).

E Metaphorical plundering

I rejoice at your word as one who finds great spoil (Ps. 119:162); he will have his life as booty (Jer. 21:9); he who goes out to the Chaldeans will have his life as booty (Jer. 38:2); bind the strong man and you can plunder his house (Matt. 12:29; Mark 3:27).

791 Trade

A Trading in general

Trade with us (Gen. 34:10); you can trade in the land (Gen. 42:34); the land shall not be sold or exchanged for it is holy to the Lord (Ezek. 48:14); they went off, one to his farm and another to his business (Matt. 22:5); you shall not make my Father's house a house of trade (John 2:16); we will spend a year there and trade (Jas. 4:13); the one with five talents traded with them (Matt. 25:16); trade with these till I return (Luke 19:13).

B Trading specific items

They gave their livestock in exchange for food (Gen. 47:16-17); they have given their valuables for food (Lam. 1:11); horses and chariots imported and exported (1 Kgs. 10:29; 2 Chr. 1:16-17); Ahab would have exchanged a vineyard for Naboth's (1 Kgs. 21:2, 6).

C Trading for a soul

What will one give in exchange for his soul? (Matt. 16:26; Mark 8:37).

792 Purchase

A Buying

A1 About buying

Those who buy should live as if they had no possessions (1 Cor. 7:30); why does the fool have the price in his hand to buy wisdom? (Prov. 17:16); no one could buy or sell without the mark of the beast (Rev. 13:17); the buyer says it is bad, but boasts of the bargain (Prov. 20:14); why spend money on what is not bread? (Isa. 55:2).

A2 Buying land

Houses, fields and vineyards will again be bought (Jer. 32:15); she considers a field and buys it (Prov. 31:16); Abraham bought the field at Machpelah (Gen. 23:8-16); Jacob bought a plot of ground near Shechem (Gen. 33:19); Joseph bought all the land of Egypt for Pharaoh (Gen. 47:20); buying Araunah's [Ornan's] threshing floor (2 Sam. 24:21; 1 Chr. 21:22-5); Omri bought the hill of Samaria (1 Kgs. 16:24); Ahab wanted to buy Naboth's vineyard (1 Kgs. 21:2); Jeremiah bought the field at Anathoth (Jer. 32:7-15); they bought the potter's field (Matt. 27:7); Judas bought a field (Acts 1:18).

A3 Buying other things

All the earth came to buy grain (Gen. 41:57); Egypt and Canaan bought grain from Joseph (Gen. 47:15); send the crowds away to buy food (Matt. 14:15; Mark 6:36); how are we to buy bread so that these people may eat? (John 6:5); go to the dealers and buy oil (Matt. 25:9); the centurion had bought his citizenship (Acts 22:28);

his disciples had gone away into the city to buy food (John 4:8).

A4 Buying God's gift

Buy wine and milk without money (Isa. 55:1); buy truth and do not sell it (Prov. 23:23); I counsel you to buy from me gold, garments and eyesalve (Rev. 3:18); you thought to obtain the gift of God with money! (Acts 8:20); he sells all that he has and buys that field (Matt. 13:44); he sold all that he had and bought that pearl (Matt. 13:46).

B Hiring

A hired man may not eat the Passover (Exod. 12:45); or the sacrifices (Lev. 22:10); the hireling flees (John 10:12-13); the Moabites hired Balaam (Deut. 23:4; Neh. 13:2); Ephraim has hired lovers (Hos. 8:9-10); like an archer who wounds everyone is he who hires a fool (Prov. 26:10); a landowner hiring workers for his vineyard (Matt. 20:1); how many of my father's hired men have bread enough and to spare! (Luke 15:17).

C Redeeming

C1 About redeeming

I redeem every firstborn son (Exod. 13:15); every firstborn offspring is to be redeemed (Exod. 34:20; Num. 18:15-16); a female slave is to be redeemed (Exod. 21:8); redeeming an Israelite slave (Lev. 25:48-52); the rich man's wealth is his ransom (Prov. 13:8).

C2 People who redeemed

Redeeming Naomi's field and Ruth (Ruth 4:3-9); we redeemed our brethren who were sold to the nations (Neh. 5:8); Jeremiah redeeming his uncle's field (Jer. 32:7-15); the kinsman-redeemer is to buy back the land (Lev. 25:25); Boaz was a kinsman-redeemer (Ruth 3:9); the Lord has not left you without a kinsman-redeemer (Ruth 4:14).

C3 God redeeming

C3a God the redeemer

My rock and my redeemer (Ps. 19:14); your redeemer is the holy One of Israel (Isa. 41:14); our redeemer, the Lord of hosts, is the holy One of Israel (Isa. 47:4); I am your redeemer (Isa. 60:16); I the Lord am your Saviour and your redeemer (Isa. 49:26); their redeemer is strong (Prov. 23:11; Jer. 50:34).

C3b God redeems

With him is abundant redemption (Ps. 130:7); the Lord redeems the soul of his servants (Ps. 34:22); he redeems your life from the pit (Ps. 103:4); until the redemption of God's own possession (Eph. 1:14); you were sold for nothing and you will be redeemed without money (Isa. 52:3); the Lord will redeem Israel from their iniquities (Ps. 130:8).

C3c God redeemed

I redeemed you from the house of slavery (Mic. 6:4); Israel was the people God redeemed (Exod. 6:6; 1 Chr. 17:21; Neh. 1:10; Ps. 74:2); the Lord has redeemed his servant Jacob (Isa. 48:20); the Lord has ransomed Jacob (Jer. 31:11); the Lord redeemed you from the house of slavery (Deut. 7:8); God bought his people (Exod. 15:16); I have given Egypt as your ransom (Isa. 43:3); return to me, for I have redeemed you (Isa. 44:22); the Lord has redeemed Jerusalem (Isa. 52:9); the angel who redeemed me from all evil (Gen. 48:16).

C3d The redeemed of the Lord

They will call them the redeemed of the Lord (Isa. 62:12); let the redeemed of the Lord say so (Ps. 107:2); the redeemed of the Lord will return (Isa. 35:10; 51:11); the redeemed of the Lord will walk on the highway (Isa. 35:9).

C4 Redemption in Christ

You will be redeemed without money (Isa. 52:3); redeemed not with silver or gold but with the blood of Christ (1 Pet. 1:18-19); you have been bought with a

price (1 Cor. 6:20; 7:23); with your blood you
purchased men for God (Rev. 5:9); the church of God
which he purchased with his own blood (Acts 20:28);
in him we have redemption through his blood (Eph.
1:7); he gave himself as a ransom for all (1 Tim. 2:6); to
give his life a ransom for many (Matt. 20:28; Mark
10:45); the 144 000 redeemed from the earth (Rev.
14:3-4); God has redeemed his people (Luke 1:68);
Anna spoke of Jesus to all who were looking for the
redemption of Jerusalem (Luke 2:38); we hoped he
would be the one to redeem Israel (Luke 24:21); Christ
Jesus is made to us redemption (1 Cor. 1:30); in him we
have redemption, the forgiveness of sins (Col. 1:14); I
know that my redeemer lives (Job 19:25); eternal
redemption (Heb. 9:12); he redeemed us from
lawlessness (Titus 2:14); Christ redeemed us from the
curse of the law (Gal. 3:13); that he might redeem those
under the law (Gal. 4:5); denying the master who
bought them (2 Pet. 2:1).

D Buying and selling
Like buyer, like seller (Isa. 24:2); buy or sell according
to the number of years to jubilee (Lev. 25:15); let not
the buyer rejoice nor the seller mourn (Ezek. 7:12);
Jesus drove out all who were buying and selling in the
temple (Matt. 21:12); in the days of Lot they bought,
they sold, they planted, they built (Luke 17:28); he sells
all that he has and buys that field (Matt. 13:44); he sold
all that he had and bought that pearl (Matt. 13:46).

793 Sale
BUYING AND SELLING, see 792D.

A About selling
Selling should be according to the years before the
Jubilee (Lev. 25:14-16); the land may not be sold in
perpetuity (Lev. 25:23); anything under a ban may not
be sold (Lev. 27:28).

B Selling things
Ephron sold the cave of Machpelah to Abraham (Gen.
23:9); Ornan sold the threshing floor to David (1 Chr.
21:22-5); Barnabas sold his field (Acts 4:37); Ananias
sold some property (Acts 5:1); sell all you have and give
to the poor (Mark 10:21; Luke 18:22); sell your
possessions and give to the poor (Matt. 19:21; Luke
12:33); they sold their possessions and shared with any
who had need (Acts 2:45); those owning land or houses
would sell them (Acts 4:34); the widow sold the oil to
pay her debts (2 Kgs. 4:7); Esau sold his birthright to
Jacob (Gen. 25:33); Esau sold his birthright for a single
meal (Heb. 12:16); why was this perfume not sold for
300 denarii? (John 12:5).

C Selling people
Israelites are not to be sold as slaves (Lev. 25:42); if
your brother sells himself to you (Lev. 25:39); if your
brother, a Hebrew, is sold to you (Deut. 15:12); if your
brother sells himself to a sojourner (Lev. 25:47); if
someone steals and sells him (Exod. 21:16); a
female slave may not be sold to a foreign people (Exod.
21:8); you may not sell a captive woman whom you
married (Deut. 21:14); he shall be sold for his theft
(Exod. 22:3); his lord ordered him to be sold (Matt.
18:25); they sell a girl for wine (Joel 3:3); they sell the
righteous for silver (Amos 2:6); Joseph's brothers sold
him (Gen. 37:28); Joseph was sold into Egypt (Acts 7:9);
Joseph was sold as a slave (Ps. 105:17); you sell your
people cheaply (Ps. 44:12); you were sold for nothing
and you will be redeemed without money (Isa. 52:3).

D Sold to evil
How could one chase a thousand unless their rock had
sold them? (Deut. 32:30); he sold them into the hands
of their enemies (Judg. 2:14; 1 Sam. 12:9); Ahab sold
himself to do evil (1 Kgs. 21:20); they sold themselves to

do evil (2 Kgs. 17:17); I am carnal, sold under sin (Rom.
7:14).

794 Merchant
Merchants and traders camped outside Jerusalem
(Neh. 13:20); he overturned the tables of the
money-changers and the seats of those selling pigeons
(Matt. 21:12; Mark 11:15; John 2:15); you increased your
traders more than the stars of heaven (Nahum 3:16);
there will no longer be a Canaanite [trader] in the
house of the Lord (Zech. 14:21); the kingdom of heaven
is like a merchant seeking fine pearls (Matt. 13:45); go
to the dealers and buy oil (Matt. 25:9); merchants weep
over her because no one buys their cargo (Rev. 18:11);
we are not peddlers of God's word (2 Cor. 2:17).

795 Merchandise
Ten donkeys loaded with the good things of Egypt
(Gen. 45:23); the merchandise of Tyre (Ezek. 27:12-24);
the merchandise of Babylon (Rev. 18:12-13); the
merchandise of Egypt and Ethiopia will be yours (Isa.
45:14); now you are wrecked in the sea your
merchandise has sunk with you (Ezek. 27:34); they
jettisoned the cargo (Acts 27:18).

796 Market
You may make bazaars for yourself in Damascus
(1 Kgs. 20:34); they love salutations in the market place
(Matt. 23:7; Mark 12:38; Luke 11:43; 20:46); men
standing idle in the market place (Matt. 20:3); Paul
reasoned in the market place (Acts 17:17); we came to
the Forum Appii [Forum of Appius] (Acts 28:15); we
came to the Tres Tabernae [Three Taverns] (Acts
28:15); eat anything sold in the market (1 Cor. 10:25).

797 Money
GOLD, see 631B3.

A Denominations of money
A1 Small denominations
A shekel is 20 gerahs (Exod. 30:13); you will not get out
until you have paid the last lepton (Luke 12:59); the
widow put in two lepta which make one quadrans
[quarter of an as] (Luke 21:2); you will not get out until
you have paid the last quadrans (Matt. 5:26); are not
two sparrows sold for an assarion [as]? (Matt. 10:29);
are not five sparrows sold for two assaria? (Luke 12:6);
if a woman with ten drachmas loses one drachma
(Luke 15:8); the half-shekel tax (Exod. 30:13); a beka,
half a shekel, a head (Exod. 38:26); the two-drachma
tax (Matt. 17:24); in the fishes mouth you will find a
stater [= four drachmas, one shekel] (Matt. 17:27); the
shekel of the sanctuary (Exod. 30:13); a denarius a day
(Matt. 20:2); a quart of wheat for a denarius (Rev. 6:6);
three quarts of barley for a denarius (Rev. 6:6); he gave
two denarii to the innkeeper (Luke 10:35).

A2 Large denominations
Each one gave Job a qesita (Job 42:11); Jacob bought the
land for 100 qesitas (Gen. 33:19; Josh. 24:32); your mina
shall be 50 shekels (Ezek. 45:12); he gave his ten servants
ten minas (Luke 19:13); one man owed 10 000 talents
(Matt. 18:24); to one he gave five talents, to another
two, to another one (Matt. 25:15).

B Use of money
B1 Indeterminate sums of money
The silver is mine and the gold is mine (Hag. 2:8); may
gold of Sheba be given to him (Ps. 72:15); they will
bring gold and frankincense (Isa. 60:6); they gave gold,
frankincense and myrrh (Matt. 2:11); he poured out the
coins of the money-changers (John 2:15); he threw the
money into the temple (Matt. 27:5); they gave a sum of
money to the soldiers (Matt. 28:12).

B2 Money for the temple

Money for the guilt offering and sin offering was for the priests (2 Kgs. 12:16); silver and gold to buy offerings (Ezra 7:15-18); he watched how the crowd put money into the treasury (Mark 12:41); collect all the money for the temple (2 Kgs. 12:4; 2 Chr. 24:5); they counted the money in the chest (2 Kgs. 12:10); the leaders gave 61 000 gold drachmas and 5000 silver minas (Ezra 2:69); the leaders gave 20 000 gold drachmas and 2200 silver minas (Neh. 7:71); the widow put in two lepta which make a quadrans (Mark 12:42).

B3 Supplied with money

Abraham was very rich in silver and gold (Gen. 13:2); the Lord has given Abraham silver and gold (Gen. 24:35); I accumulated silver and gold (Eccles. 2:8); were Balak to give me his house full of silver and gold (Num. 22:18; 24:13); their land is filled with silver and gold (Isa. 2:7).

C Attitude towards money

WEALTH, see 800.

C1 Money as protection

Money is a protection as wisdom is (Eccles. 7:12); money is the answer to everything (Eccles. 10:19); if I have put my trust in gold (Job 31:24); get rid of your gold and the Almighty will be your gold and silver (Job 22:24-5).

C2 Love of money

Whoever loves money will not be satisfied with money (Eccles. 5:10); men will be lovers of money (2 Tim. 3:2); the love of money is the root of all evil (1 Tim. 6:10); the Pharisees loved money (Luke 16:14); Balaam loved the wages of unrighteousness (2 Pet. 2:15); I have not coveted any one's silver, gold or clothes (Acts 20:33); be free from the love of money (Heb. 13:5); a bishop [overseer] must be free from love of money (1 Tim. 3:3).

C3 Money's deficiencies

Neither silver nor gold will be able to deliver them (Zeph. 1:18); their silver and gold cannot save them in the day of the Lord's wrath (Ezek. 7:19); you were not redeemed with silver and gold (1 Pet. 1:18); Simon offered them money for power to confer the Holy Spirit (Acts 8:18-19).

C4 Alternatives to money

Wisdom is much better than gold or silver (Prov. 16:16); favour is better than silver or gold (Prov. 22:1); a good name is better than riches (Prov. 22:1); choose my instruction rather than silver or gold (Prov. 8:10); the Lord's words are better than much gold (Ps. 19:10); I love your commandments more than fine gold (Ps. 119:127); your law is better than thousands of gold and silver pieces (Ps. 119:72); I counsel you to buy gold refined in the fire (Rev. 3:18); get rid of your gold and the Almighty will be your gold and silver (Job 22:24-5).

D Lacking money

I have no silver or gold (Acts 3:6); take no gold, silver or copper in your money belts (Matt. 10:9); do not take money (Mark 6:8; Luke 9:3); carry no purse (Luke 10:4).

POVERTY, see 801.

798 Treasurer

Judas had the moneybox (John 13:29); the Ethiopian eunuch had charge of all the queen's treasure (Acts 8:27);

Erastus was the city treasurer (Rom. 16:23); you ought to have taken my money to the bankers (Matt. 25:27).

799 Treasury

A Treasure house

Hezekiah showed the Babylonians his treasure house (2 Kgs. 20:13); let a search be made in the king's treasure house (Ezra 5:17); he said these things in the treasury (John 8:20); the silver, gold and things of bronze and iron were put into the Lord's treasury (Josh. 6:19); the things dedicated by David were put in the treasuries of the temple (1 Kgs. 7:51); gifts put in the treasuries of the temple (2 Chr. 5:1); why did you not put my money in the bank? (Luke 19:23).

B Money-box

A money chest was made for the upkeep of the temple (2 Kgs. 12:9; 2 Chr. 24:8); he who earns wages puts them into a purse with holes (Hag. 1:6); take no gold, silver or copper in your money belts (Matt. 10:9); carry no purse, no bag, no sandals (Luke 10:4); make for yourselves purses which do not grow old (Luke 12:33); let him who has a purse take it with him (Luke 22:36); we will all have one purse (Prov. 1:14); the Lord will take away purses (Isa. 3:22); Judas had the money-box (John 12:6).

C Heart's treasure

The good man brings good out of his treasure and the evil man evil (Matt. 12:35); he brings out of his treasure things new and old (Matt. 13:52).

800 Wealth

MONEY, see 797.

A Getting rich

A man with evil eye hastens after wealth (Prov. 28:22); Tyre amassed gold like the mire of the streets (Zech. 9:3); he who lays up treasure for himself but is not rich toward God (Luke 12:21); you have stored up treasure in the last days (Jas. 5:3); Balak offered to make Balaam rich (Num. 22:17-18); violent men get riches (Prov. 11:16); a fortune unjustly made will flee (Jer. 17:11); do not toil to gain wealth (Prov. 23:4); the wicked swallow riches but vomit them up (Job 20:15); he who hastens to get rich will not go unpunished (Prov. 28:20); the king must not accumulate silver and gold (Deut. 17:17); do not lay up treasures on earth (Matt. 6:19); he who loves wine and oil will not become rich (Prov. 21:17).

B The source of riches

B1 God gives wealth

Your God has given you hidden treasure (Gen. 43:23); God gives you the power to make wealth (Deut. 8:18); the Lord makes poor and rich (1 Sam. 2:7); riches and honour come from you (1 Chr. 29:12); I will give you riches and honour (2 Chr. 1:12); God gave Hezekiah great wealth (2 Chr. 32:29); a man to whom God has given wealth (Eccles. 5:19; 6:2); give me neither poverty nor riches (Prov. 30:8).

B2 Wisdom gives wealth

In Wisdom's left hand are riches and honour (Prov. 3:16); wisdom fills the treasuries of those who love her (Prov. 8:21); by your wisdom you have acquired wealth (Ezek. 28:4); by knowledge the rooms are filled with riches (Prov. 24:4).

B3 People giving wealth

Merchants grew rich by Babylon's wealth (Rev. 18:3); with the abundance of your merchandise you enriched kings (Ezek. 27:33); lest you should say you have made Abraham rich (Gen. 14:23).

B4 Various sources of wealth

You might say your own strength brought you wealth (Deut. 8:17); the blessing of the Lord is what makes rich (Prov. 10:22); riches are a reward for humility and fear of the Lord (Prov. 22:4); the hand of the diligent makes rich (Prov. 10:4); riches are not to the intelligent

(Eccles. 9:11); he who gains wealth by interest will lose it (Prov. 28:8); he who oppresses the poor to increase his wealth will come to poverty (Prov. 22:16).

C Wealthy people
He was wealthy in his death (Isa. 53:9); those who live in luxury are in royal palaces (Luke 7:25); do not invite your relatives or rich neighbours (Luke 14:12); let the rich man boast in his humiliation (Jas. 1:10); those who were wealthy: Abraham (Gen. 13:2; 24:35); Ahasuerus (Esther 1:4); Barzillai (2 Sam. 19:32); Boaz (Ruth 2:1); David (1 Chr. 29:28); Ephraim (Hos. 12:8); Esau (Gen. 36:7); Haman (Esther 5:11); Hezekiah (2 Chr. 32:27); Isaac (Gen. 26:13); Jacob (Gen. 30:43; 32:5; 36:7); Jehoshaphat (2 Chr. 17:5; 18:1); Job (Job 1:3); Joseph of Arimathea (Matt. 27:57); Nabal (1 Sam. 25:2); Solomon (1 Kgs. 3:13; 10:7, 23; 2 Chr. 1:12; 9:22); Zacchaeus (Luke 19:2); the rich young ruler (Matt. 19:22; Mark 10:22; Luke 18:23).

D Attitudes towards wealth
D1 Satisfied with riches
Those who trust in their wealth (Ps. 49:6); he who trusts in his riches will fall (Prov. 11:28); the rich man's wealth is his fortress (Prov. 10:15); a rich man's wealth is his strong city (Prov. 18:11); the rich man's wealth is his ransom (Prov. 13:8); I am rich, I have need of nothing (Rev. 3:17); let not a rich man boast of his riches (Jer. 9:23); direct the rich not to be conceited (1 Tim. 6:17); because of your wealth your heart has become proud (Ezek. 28:5); the deceitfulness of riches chokes the word (Matt. 13:22; Mark 4:19; Luke 8:14); weep and howl, you rich (Jas. 5:1); woe to you rich, for you have received your comfort (Luke 6:24); if riches increase, do not set your heart on them (Ps. 62:10).

D2 The rich lording it
Is it not the rich who oppress you? (Jas. 2:6); the rich rule over the poor (Prov. 22:7); if a man comes into your assembly with a gold ring and fine clothes (Jas. 2:2); even in your bedroom do not curse a rich man (Eccles. 10:20); parable of the rich man and poor man (2 Sam. 12:1-4).

D3 Right use of wealth
Honour the Lord with your wealth (Prov. 3:9); make friends by means of unrighteous mammon (Luke 16:9); wealth brings friends (Prov. 19:4); worthy is the Lamb to receive riches (Rev. 5:12); he who gives to the rich will come to poverty (Prov. 22:16).

E Drawbacks to riches
It is hard for the rich to enter the kingdom of God (Matt. 19:23; Mark 10:23; Luke 18:24); easier for a camel to go through the eye of a needle (Mark 10:25; Luke 18:25); he has sent the rich away empty-handed (Luke 1:53); you cannot serve God and mammon (Matt. 6:24); riches do not profit in the day of wrath (Prov. 11:4); your riches have rotted and your garments are moth-eaten (Jas. 5:2); in one hour this wealth has been laid waste (Rev. 18:17); wealth takes wings and flies away (Prov. 23:5); riches do not last for ever (Prov. 27:24); the rich man will fade away (Jas. 1:10-11); those who want to get rich fall into a temptation and a snare (1 Tim. 6:9); they leave their wealth to others (Ps. 49:10); man heaps up and does not know who will gather (Ps. 39:6); better a poor man who walks in integrity than a perverse rich man (Prov. 28:6).

F True treasure
F1 True treasure in God
I delight in your testimonies as much as in riches (Ps. 119:14); your law is better than thousands of gold and silver pieces (Ps. 119:72); search for wisdom as for hidden treasure (Prov. 2:4); the Lord is rich to all who call on him (Rom. 10:12); where your treasure is, there will your heart be also (Matt. 6:21; Luke 12:34); lay up

treasure in heaven (Matt. 6:20); you will have treasure in heaven (Matt. 19:21; Mark 10:21; Luke 12:33; 18:22); true riches (Luke 16:11); rich in good works (1 Tim. 6:18); God chose the poor to be rich in faith (Jas. 2:5); the reproach of Christ considered greater riches than all the treasures of Egypt (Heb. 11:26); the man who is not rich toward God (Luke 12:21).

F2 The riches of Christ
You were enriched in Christ (1 Cor. 1:5); though he was rich, he became poor that we might be rich (2 Cor. 8:9); according to the riches of his glory (Eph. 3:16); riches in glory in Christ Jesus (Phil. 4:19); you will be enriched in every way (2 Cor. 9:11); the treasures of wisdom and knowledge are hidden in Christ (Col. 2:3); the treasure of a good foundation for the future (1 Tim. 6:19); the kingdom of heaven is like treasure hidden in a field (Matt. 13:44); to preach the unsearchable riches of Christ (Eph. 3:8); we have this treasure in earthenware vessels (2 Cor. 4:7); if their transgression be riches for the world (Rom. 11:12); buy from me gold refined by fire that you may become rich (Rev. 3:18); the riches of the glory of his inheritance (Eph. 1:18).

G Poor or rich
The Lord sends poverty and wealth (1 Sam. 2:7); give me neither poverty nor riches (Prov. 30:8); as poor yet making many rich (2 Cor. 6:10); though he was rich, yet for your sake he became poor (2 Cor. 8:9); that you through his poverty might be made rich (2 Cor. 8:9); I know your poverty but you are rich! (Rev. 2:9); you say you are rich, but you do not realise you are poor (Rev. 3:17).

801 Poverty
POOR OR RICH, see 800G.

A Being poor
The Lord sends poverty and wealth (1 Sam. 2:7); give me neither poverty nor riches (Prov. 30:8); better to be poor than a liar (Prov. 19:22); the poverty of the poor is their ruin (Prov. 10:15); let him drink and forget his poverty (Prov. 31:7); the poor shall not give less than half a shekel (Exod. 30:15).

B Poor people
There will be no poor among you if you obey (Deut. 15:4); there will always be poor people (Deut. 15:11); you will always have the poor with you (Matt. 26:11; Mark 14:7; John 12:8); a poor man loses his friends (Prov. 19:4, 7); a poor man is hated by his brothers (Prov. 19:7); the poor man is disliked even by his neighbour (Prov. 14:20); the poor man's wisdom is despised (Eccles. 9:16); if a poor man comes in in vile clothes (Jas. 2:2); a poor widow (Mark 12:42; Luke 21:2-3); parable of a rich man and a poor man (2 Sam. 12:1-4); the poor man Lazarus lay at the rich man's gate (Luke 16:20); a contribution for the poor among the saints in Jerusalem (Rom. 15:26).

C Becoming poor
Do not love sleep lest you come to poverty (Prov. 20:13); poverty will come on you like an armed man (Prov. 6:11; 24:34); a negligent hand causes poverty (Prov. 10:4); he who loves pleasure will become poor (Prov. 21:17); the drunkard and the glutton will come to poverty (Prov. 23:21).

D Helping the poor
D1 God helps the poor
The Lord maintains justice for the poor (Ps. 140:12); he lifts up the poor from the dust (1 Sam. 2:8; Ps. 113:7); God saves the poor (Job 5:15); the cry of the poor came to God (Job 34:28); he raises the needy out of affliction (Ps. 107:41).

D2 People helping the poor
D2a Help the poor!

Let your land lie fallow that the poor may eat (Exod. 23:11); leave gleanings for the poor and alien (Lev. 19:10; 23:22; Deut. 24:19-21); do not be stingy with the poor (Deut. 15:7-8); sell your possessions and give to the poor (Matt. 19:21); sell all you have and give to the poor (Mark 10:21); when you give a feast, invite the poor (Luke 14:13); bring in the poor (Luke 14:21); send portions to those who have nothing (Neh. 8:10); we should continue to remember the poor (Gal. 2:10); why was this perfume not sold and given to the poor? (John 12:5); visit orphans and widows in their affliction (Jas. 1:27); bring the homeless poor into your house (Isa. 58:7); do not deny justice to the poor (Exod. 23:6); whenever you wish you can do good to the poor (Mark 14:7).

D2b Those helping the poor

She stretches out her hand to the poor (Prov. 31:20); I was a father to the poor (Job 29:16); was not my soul grieved for the poor? (Job 30:25); half of my possessions I give to the poor (Luke 19:8); they sold their possessions and shared with any who had need (Acts 2:45); he gives to the poor (Ps. 112:9; 2 Cor. 9:9); the poor have good news preached to them (Matt. 11:5; Luke 7:22); anointed to preach the gospel to the poor (Luke 4:18).

D2c Blessings for those who help the poor

He who is kind to the poor lends to the Lord (Prov. 19:17); happy he who is kind to the poor (Prov. 14:21); he who gives to the poor will not want (Prov. 28:27).

D3 Not helping the poor

He who oppresses the poor insults his Maker (Prov. 14:31); he who oppresses the poor will come to poverty (Prov. 22:16); a poor man who oppresses the poor is like driving rain (Prov. 28:3); what do you mean by grinding the face of the poor? (Isa. 3:15); to buy the poor for silver, the needy for a pair of sandals (Amos 8:6); do not oppress the widow, the orphan, the stranger or the poor (Zech. 7:10); he did not say this because he was concerned about the poor (John 12:6); do you humiliate those who have nothing? (1 Cor. 11:22); Sodom's sin was that she did not help the poor and needy (Ezek. 16:49); they do not defend the rights of the poor (Jer. 5:28); he has oppressed the poor (Job 20:19); the poor are pushed off the road (Job 24:4); you have dishonoured the poor man (Jas. 2:6).

D4 Unfairly helping the poor

Do not be partial to a poor man (Exod. 23:3; Lev. 19:15).

E Blessings of the poor

Their poverty overflowed in liberality (2 Cor. 8:2); God has chosen the poor to be rich in faith (Jas. 2:5); as poor yet making many rich (2 Cor. 6:10); that you through his poverty might be made rich (2 Cor. 8:9); I know your poverty but you are rich! (Rev. 2:9); one pretends to be poor but has great wealth (Prov. 13:7); better the little of the righteous than the wealth of the wicked (Ps. 37:16); blessed are you poor (Luke 6:20); blessed are the poor in spirit, for theirs is the kingdom of heaven (Matt. 5:3); a poor wise lad is better than an old foolish king (Eccles. 4:13).

802 Credit

To which of my creditors have I sold you? (Isa. 50:1); like creditor, like debtor (Isa. 24:2).
LENDING, see 784.

803 Debt

A Being in debt

Owe no one anything except to love one another (Rom. 13:8); he put him in prison until he should pay the debt (Matt. 18:30); husband and wife should give each other what is owed (1 Cor. 7:3); I am a debtor to Greeks and barbarians (Rom. 1:14); we are debtors, but not to the flesh (Rom. 8:12); the Gentiles are indebted to minister to the Jerusalem church (Rom. 15:27).

B People in debt

Anyone in debt joined David (1 Sam. 22:2); a prophet's widow was in debt (2 Kgs. 4:1-7); a man owed 10 000 talents (Matt. 18:24); the parable of the two debtors, one owing 500 denarii, the other 50 (Luke 7:41-3); how much do you owe my master? (Luke 16:5-7); we are mortgaging our fields (Neh. 5:3).

C Charging interest

Do not charge your brother interest (Exod. 22:25; Lev. 25:36-7; Deut. 23:19-20; Neh. 5:10); he who increases wealth by interest will lose it (Prov. 28:8); you may charge a foreigner interest (Deut. 23:20); I would have received my money with interest (Matt. 25:27; Luke 19:23).

D Cancelling debts

At the end of every seven years you are to cancel debts (Deut. 15:1); we will remit debts (Neh. 10:31); I forgave you all your debt because you besought me (Matt. 18:32); forgive us our debts as we forgive our debtors (Matt. 6:12; Luke 11:4); God cancelled the bill of debt (Col. 2:14); if he owes you anything, charge it to me (Philem. 18).

804 Payment

A Paying dues
A1 Settling accounts

A king wanted to settle accounts (Matt. 18:23); the master came to settle accounts (Matt. 25:19); be patient and I will repay (Matt. 18:26, 29); you will not get out till you have paid the last coin (Matt. 5:26; Luke 12:59); do not invite your friends lest they repay you (Luke 14:12); their reward has been paid in full (Matt. 6:2, 5, 16); men will render account for every idle word (Matt. 12:36); who has given to God that God should repay him? (Rom. 11:35).
ACCOUNTS, see 808.

A2 Paying for goods

If anyone drinks water we will pay for it (Num. 20:19); we have to pay for our own drinking water and firewood (Lam. 5:4); whatever more you spend I will repay you (Luke 10:35); I will repay what Onesimus owes (Philem. 19); pay the expenses for the four men (Acts 21:24); Paul stayed two years at his own expense (Acts 28:30).

A3 Paying wages
A3a Being paid wages

Pay a hired man before sunset (Lev. 19:13; Deut. 24:15); the labourer deserves his wages (Luke 10:7); the workman is worthy of his wages (1 Tim. 5:18); wages are not a favour but a right (Rom. 4:4); nurse this baby and I will pay you your wages (Exod. 2:9); they paid the workmen who worked in the temple (2 Kgs. 12:11-12; 2 Chr. 24:12); they agreed to pay Judas money (Luke 22:5); be content with your wages (Luke 3:14); Laban changed my wages ten times (Gen. 31:7); the pay of the labourers who mowed your fields cries out against you (Jas. 5:4).

A3b Wages of a prostitute

The wages of a prostitute are not to be offered to God (Deut. 23:18); her harlot's wages will be set apart to the Lord (Isa. 23:18); from a prostitute's earnings she gathered them and to a prostitute's earnings they will return (Mic. 1:7); a kid for a prostitute (Gen. 38:17); they sell a girl for wine (Joel 3:3); these are the wages my lovers have given me (Hos. 2:12).

A3c Wages for spiritual work

Preachers should receive payment (1 Cor. 9:7-14); elders who rule well deserve a double stipend (1 Tim. 5:17); I robbed other churches, taking pay from them to serve you (2 Cor. 11:8); your Father will repay you (Matt. 6:4, 6, 18).

A3d Wages for evil

The wages of sin is death (Rom. 6:23); the income of the wicked is punishment (Prov. 10:16); trouble is in the income of the wicked (Prov. 15:6); suffering harm as the wages of doing harm (2 Pet. 2:13); Balaam loved the wages of unrighteousness (2 Pet. 2:15); the wicked man earns deceptive wages (Prov. 11:18).

A4 Paying tribute

Let the kings of the isles bring tribute (Ps. 72:10); tribute sent by Ehud to Eglon (Judg. 3:15); the king of Moab paid lambs and wool as tribute (2 Kgs. 3:4); the Moabites brought tribute to David (1 Chr. 18:2); if this city is built, no more tax or duty will be paid (Ezra 4:13); the priests should not pay tax or tribute (Ezra 7:24).

A5 Paying tax

A5a Tax to be paid

In a census, every Israelite is to pay half a shekel (Exod. 30:13); does your teacher not pay the two-drachma tax? (Matt. 17:24); is it right to pay taxes to Caesar? (Matt. 22:17; Mark 12:14-15; Luke 20:22); we found this man forbidding us to pay taxes to Caesar (Luke 23:2); from whom do kings collect tax? (Matt. 17:25); you ought to pay taxes, for the authorities are servants of God (Rom. 13:6); pay tax to whom tax is due, revenue to whom revenue is due (Rom. 13:7).

A5b Tax collectors

The collectors of the two-drachma tax (Matt. 17:24); tax collectors and sinners reclined at table with Jesus (Matt. 9:10-11; Mark 2:15-16; Luke 5:29-30); a friend of tax collectors and sinners (Luke 7:34); the tax collectors and sinners were drawing near to hear him (Luke 15:1); tax collectors and prostitutes enter the kingdom of God ahead of you (Matt. 21:31); the tax collectors and prostitutes believed John (Matt. 21:32); tax collectors came to be baptised (Luke 3:12); let him be to you as a Gentile or a tax-collector (Matt. 18:17); two men went up into the temple to pray, a Pharisee and a tax collector (Luke 18:10-13); Matthew [Levi] sitting in the tax office (Matt. 9:9; Mark 2:14; Luke 5:27); a chief tax collector called Zaccheus (Luke 19:2).

B Requiting

B1 God requiting

Requite them for their deeds (Ps. 28:4); may the Lord repay the evildoer for his evil (2 Sam. 3:39); give her back double for her deeds (Rev. 18:6); the Lord will repay everyone for his righteousness (1 Sam. 26:23); the Lord requites those who act proudly (Ps. 31:23); according to their deeds, so he will repay (Isa. 59:18); the Lord will repay him according to his deeds (2 Tim. 4:14); God will repay everyone for his works (Matt. 16:27); he will render to every one according to his deeds (Rom. 2:6); I will give each of you according to his deeds (Rev. 2:23); we will be recompensed for what we have done, good or bad (2 Cor. 5:10); whatever good anyone does, he will receive back from the Lord (Eph. 6:8); vengeance is mine, I will repay (Rom. 12:19); I will punish them for their ways and repay them for their deeds (Hos. 4:9); the Lord will requite Jacob according to his deeds (Hos. 12:2); you will see the recompense of the wicked (Ps. 91:8); God will repay with affliction those who afflict you (2 Thess. 1:6); you will be repaid at the resurrection of the just (Luke 14:14); if the righteous is paid back, how much more

the sinner? (Prov. 11:31); every transgression and disobedience received a just recompense (Heb. 2:2).

B2 Repaying evil for evil

Do not repay evil for evil (Rom. 12:17; 1 Thess. 5:15; 1 Pet. 3:9); do not resist one who is evil but turn the other cheek (Matt. 5:39); we have come to do to him as he did to us (Judg. 15:10-11); do not say, 'I will do to him as he has done to me' (Prov. 24:29); do not say, 'I will repay evil' (Prov. 20:22).

C Repaying God

How can I repay the Lord? (Ps. 116:12); are you paying me back for something? (Joel 3:4); is that how you repay the Lord? (Deut. 32:6).

805 Nonpayment

If I have eaten fruit from the land without payment (Job 31:39); woe to him who does not pay his neighbour's wages (Jer. 22:13); we did not eat anyone's bread without paying (2 Thess. 3:8); you will be blessed because they cannot repay you (Luke 14:14).

806 Expenditure

I will gladly spend and be spent for you (2 Cor. 12:15).

807 Receipt

RECEIVING, see 782.
INCOME, see 804A3.

808 Accounts

They did not require an account from the workmen (2 Kgs. 12:15; 22:7); the servants were called to give account of what they had gained (Luke 19:15); give an account of your stewardship (Luke 16:2); your leaders watch over your souls as those who will have to give account (Heb. 13:17); every one will give account of himself to God (Rom. 14:12); they will give account to the One who will judge the living and the dead (1 Pet. 4:5).

809 Price

A Price of things

A1 Price of sparrows

Are not two sparrows sold for an assarion? (Matt. 10:29); are not five sparrows sold for two assaria? (Luke 12:6).

A2 Price of food

A donkey's head for 80 shekels and dove's dung for five shekels (2 Kgs. 6:25); a measure of flour for a shekel and two measures of barley for a shekel (2 Kgs. 7:1); a measure of wheat for a denarius and three measures of barley for a denarius (Rev. 6:6); shall we spend 200 denarii on bread? (Mark 6:37; John 6:7).

A3 Price of land

Valuation of property (Lev. 27:14-25); Ephron set the price of the field at 400 shekels (Gen. 23:15-16); a piece of land bought for 100 qesitas (Gen. 33:19; Josh. 24:32); the field at Anathoth bought for 17 shekels of silver (Jer. 32:9); tell me whether you sold the land for such a price (Acts 5:8).

A4 Price of wisdom

Man does not know the price of wisdom (Job 28:13); the price of wisdom is beyond gold and pearls (Job 28:15-19); why does a fool have the price in his hand to buy wisdom? (Prov. 17:16).

A5 Price of other things

No one builds a tower without first sitting down and counting the cost (Luke 14:28); David paid 600 gold shekels for Ornan's threshing floor (1 Chr. 21:25); David paid 50 shekels for the threshing floor (2 Sam. 24:24); Samaria bought for two talents of silver (1 Kgs. 16:24); a chariot imported for 600 shekels of silver (1

Kgs. 10:29; 2 Chr. 1:17); a horse imported for 150 shekels of silver (1 Kgs. 10:29; 2 Chr. 1:17); this perfume might have been sold for 300 denarii (Mark 14:5; John 12:5); the price of the books of magic was 50 000 pieces of silver (Acts 19:19).

B Price of a person
B1 Price of people in general
The precious sons of Zion, worth as much as gold (Lam. 4:2); are you not worth much more than the birds? (Matt. 6:26); you are of more value than many sparrows (Matt. 10:31; Luke 12:7); you are of more value than a sheep (Matt. 12:12); the worth of a good wife exceeds jewels (Prov. 31:10); you have been bought with a price (1 Cor. 7:23).

B2 Valuation of people
Valuation of a person (Lev. 27:2-8); five shekels a head for ransoming the firstborn (Num. 3:47; 18:16); Jehoiakim taxed people according to their valuation (2 Kgs. 23:35).

B3 Price set on individuals
30 shekels of silver for the death of a slave (Exod. 21:32); 30 shekels of silver paid to Zechariah and thrown to the potter (Zech. 11:12-13); they paid 30 pieces of silver for Jesus (Matt. 26:15); 30 pieces of silver, the price set on him by the sons of Israel (Matt. 27:9); Joseph was sold for 20 pieces of silver (Gen. 37:28); I bought her for 15 shekels of silver and a homer and a half of barley (Hos. 3:2); they sell a girl for wine (Joel 3:3); they sell the needy for a pair of sandals (Amos 2:6; 8:6).

C Dowry
I will serve you seven years for Rachel (Gen. 29:18); he shall pay the equivalent of a dowry for a virgin (Exod. 22:17); 50 shekels of silver as a bride price (Deut. 22:29); ask what you will as a bridal price (Gen. 34:12); as bridal price, 100 Philistine foreskins (1 Sam. 18:25; 2 Sam. 3:14); Pharaoh gave Gezer as dowry (1 Kgs. 9:16).

D Fee
The elders of Moab and Midian took with them the fee for divination (Num. 22:7); 200 pieces of silver to make an image (Judg. 17:4); two thirds of a shekel for sharpening tools (1 Sam. 13:21); they gave Abimelech 70 pieces of silver (Judg. 9:4); the Philistine rulers offered Delilah 1100 pieces of silver each (Judg. 16:5); a quarter of a shekel to give Samuel (1 Sam. 9:8); Joab would have given ten pieces of silver for the killing of Absalom (2 Sam. 18:11); if you gave me 1000 pieces of silver I would not harm Absalom (2 Sam. 18:12); Naaman took ten talents of silver and 6000 shekels of gold (2 Kgs. 5:5); Gehazi accepted two talents of silver (2 Kgs. 5:22-3); 1000 talents of silver to buy off the king of Assyria (2 Kgs. 15:19); 1000 talents of silver to hire mercenaries (1 Chr. 19:6); warriors of Israel hired for 100 talents of silver (2 Chr. 25:6, 9); a denarius a day (Matt. 20:2); Haman would pay 10 000 talents of silver (Esther 3:9); Jonah paid the fare (Jonah 1:3); her priests teach for a fee (Mic. 3:11); her prophets divine for money (Mic. 3:11); what will you give me if I deliver him to you? (Matt. 26:15); who serves as a soldier at his own expense? (1 Cor. 9:7).

E Fine as penalty
It is not good to fine the righteous (Prov. 17:26); 100 shekels of silver for defaming a wife (Deut. 22:19); a talent of silver as fine for losing a prisoner (1 Kgs. 20:39); Pharaoh Neco fined them 100 talents of silver and a talent of gold (2 Kgs. 23:33).

810 Discount
CHEAPNESS, see 812.

811 Dearness
A Expensive
The dearness of a donkey's head and dove's dung in Samaria (2 Kgs. 6:25); the dearness of wheat and barley (Rev. 6:6); very expensive perfume (Matt. 26:7; Mark 14:3; John 12:3); he found one pearl of great value (Matt. 13:46).

B Precious
A centurion had a slave who was valued (Luke 7:2); how much more valuable are you than the birds! (Luke 12:24); rejected by men but chosen and precious in God's sight (1 Pet. 2:4-7); a gentle and quiet spirit is previous in God's sight (1 Pet. 3:4); his precious and very great promises (2 Pet. 1:4); the death of his saints is precious to the Lord (Ps. 116:15).

812 Cheapness
A Inexpensive
The cheapness of flour and barley in Samaria (2 Kgs. 7:1, 16, 18); two sparrows are sold for an assarion (Matt. 10:29); five sparrows sold for two assaria (Luke 12:6).

B Free of charge
Should you serve me for nothing because you are a relative? (Gen. 29:15); in the seventh year the slave shall go free for nothing (Exod. 21:2); you were sold for nothing and you will be redeemed without money (Isa. 51:3); the fish we ate in Egypt for nothing (Num. 11:5); that when I preach the gospel I may make it free of charge (1 Cor. 9:18); I preached the gospel of God to you free of charge (2 Cor. 11:7); freely you received, freely give (Matt. 10:8); I will give the water of life without cost (Rev. 21:6); buy wine and milk without price (Isa. 55:1); come and take the water of life without cost (Rev. 22:17); I will not offer burnt offerings which cost nothing (2 Sam. 24:24; 1 Chr. 21:24).

813 Liberality
A Generous
Give generously to the poor (Deut. 15:8-11); direct the rich to be generous (1 Tim. 6:18); God gives his Spirit without measure (John 3:34); God gives to all men generously, without reproach (Jas. 1:5); he has given freely to the poor (Ps. 112:9); the generous man will prosper (Prov. 11:25); their joy and poverty overflowed in liberality (2 Cor. 8:2-3); he who sows bountifully will reap bountifully (2 Cor. 9:6); the generosity of your contribution (2 Cor. 9:13).

B Hospitality
Show hospitality to strangers, for some have entertained angels unawares (Heb. 13:2); a bishop / elder must be hospitable (1 Tim. 3:2; Titus 1:8); be hospitable (Rom. 12:13; 1 Pet. 4:9); if she has shown hospitality to strangers (1 Tim. 5:10); those who gave hospitality: Abraham to the angels (Gen. 18:1-7); Lot to the two angels (Gen. 19:1-3); Laban to Abraham's servant (Gen. 24:31-3); Reuel to Moses (Exod. 2:20-1); the concubine's father to the Levite (Judg. 19:4-9); the old man of Ephraim to the Levite (Judg. 19:16-21).

814 Economy
FRUGALITY, see 816.

815 Prodigality
Parable of the prodigal son (Luke 15:11-32).

816 Parsimony
A Do not be stingy
Do not close your hand towards your poor brother (Deut. 15:7-9); do not withhold good from those to whom it is due (Prov. 3:27).

B Stingy people

One withholds what is due yet suffers want (Prov. 11:24); he will begrudge food to his brother, wife and children (Deut. 28:54); a man with evil eye hastens after wealth (Prov. 28:22); he who sows sparingly will reap sparingly (2 Cor. 9:6).

817 Affections

David longed for Absalom (2 Sam. 13:39); I long for you with all the affection of Christ (Phil. 1:8); if there is any affection (Phil. 2:1); having an affection for you (1 Thess. 2:8).

818 Feeling

A Emotion

Joseph was deeply moved over his brother (Gen. 43:30); David was deeply moved (2 Sam. 18:33); Jesus wept (John 11:35); when Jesus saw Mary and the Jews weeping, he was deeply moved (John 11:33); Jesus, deeply moved again (John 11:38); they were pierced in their hearts (Acts 2:37).

B Sympathy

You know the soul of a sojourner (Exod. 23:9); rejoice with those who rejoice and weep with those who weep (Rom. 12:15); we do not have a high priest who is unable to sympathise with our weaknesses (Heb. 4:15); you showed sympathy on the prisoners (Heb. 10:34); have sympathy (1 Pet. 3:8).

C Zeal

C1 About zeal

Who will harm you if you are zealous for what is right? (1 Pet. 3:13); the fervent prayer of a righteous man accomplishes much (Jas. 5:16); do not be lacking in zeal (Rom. 12:11); a people zealous for good deeds (Titus 2:14); love one another fervently (1 Pet. 1:22); tend the flock of God, not for shameful gain but eagerly (1 Pet. 5:2); be all the more zealous to confirm your call and election (2 Pet. 1:10); be zealous and repent (Rev. 3:19); be zealous to be found by him in peace (2 Pet. 3:14); fervent in spirit, serving the Lord (Rom. 12:11); I wrote to you that your zeal for us might be revealed (2 Cor. 7:12); eager to preserve the unity of the Spirit (Eph. 4:3).

C2 God's zeal

Let them see your zeal for your people and be ashamed (Isa. 26:11); where are your zeal and your might? (Isa. 63:15); the zeal of the Lord will do this (2 Kgs. 19:31; Isa. 9:7; 37:32); he wrapped himself with zeal as with a mantle (Isa. 59:17).

C3 Those who were zealous

I have been very zealous for the Lord (1 Kgs. 19:10); come and see my zeal for the Lord (2 Kgs. 10:16); zeal for your house has consumed me (Ps. 69:9; John 2:17); your zeal has stirred up most of them (2 Cor. 9:2); Elijah prayed fervently that it would not rain (Jas. 5:17); Apollos was fervent in spirit (Acts 18:25); a zeal for God but not according to knowledge (Rom. 10:2); the Jewish believers were zealous for the law (Acts 21:20); I was brought up strictly under the law, zealous for God (Acts 22:3); I was zealous for the traditions (Gal. 1:14); as to zeal, a persecutor of the church (Phil. 3:6); being in agony, he prayed more fervently (Luke 22:44); since you are zealous for spiritual gifts (1 Cor. 14:12); your longing, your mourning, your zeal for me (2 Cor. 7:7).

C4 Selfish ambition

If you have bitter jealousy and selfish ambition in your heart (Jas. 3:14); where there are jealousy and selfish ambition there will be disorder (Jas. 3:16).

819 Sensibility

FEELING, see 818.

820 Insensibility

Make their ears dull and their eyes dim (Isa. 6:10); this people's heart has grown dull (Matt. 13:15; Acts 28:27).

821 Excitement

Do not stir up love until it please (S. of S. 2:7; 3:5; 8:4); you have aroused my heart (S. of S. 4:9); my feelings were aroused (S. of S. 5:4); the Lord stirred up the spirit of Zerubbabel and Joshua (Hag. 1:14); he stirs up the people (Luke 23:5).

822 Excitability

A Excited

Weak women, burdened with sins and led by various impulses (2 Tim. 3:6); all the city was stirred (Ruth 1:19; Matt. 21:10).

B Impatient

Now it touches you and you are impatient (Job 4:5); why should I not be impatient? (Job 21:4); is the Spirit of the Lord impatient? (Mic. 2:7).

823 Inexcitability

A Patience in general

Love is patient and kind (1 Cor. 13:4); the fruit of the Spirit is patience (Gal. 5:22); your comfort when you patiently endure the same sufferings we suffer (2 Cor. 1:6); for all endurance and patience with joy (Col. 1:11).

B God's patience

God is slow to anger (Neh. 9:17; Ps. 103:8; 145:8; Joel 2:13; Jonah 4:2; Nahum 1:3); God endured with patience the vessels of wrath (Rom. 9:22); God's patience waited in the days of Noah (1 Pet. 3:20); the Lord is patient towards you (2 Pet. 3:9); in me Christ demonstrated his patience (1 Tim. 1:16); the riches of his forbearance and longsuffering (Rom. 2:4); consider the Lord's forbearance as salvation (2 Pet. 3:15); for 40 years he put up with them in the wilderness (Acts 13:18).

C Be patient!

Put on patience (Col. 3:12); be patient with everyone (1 Thess. 5:14); walk with patience and forbearance in love (Eph. 4:2); be patient until the Lord's coming (Jas. 5:7); the Lord's slave must be patient (2 Tim. 2:24); reprove, rebuke, exhort with all longsuffering and teaching (2 Tim. 4:2); you also be patient (Jas. 5:8); if when you do right and suffer for it you take it patiently, this is approved by God (1 Pet. 2:20).

D Patient people

Abraham patiently endured and obtained the promise (Heb. 6:15); the prophets were an example of suffering and patience (Jas. 5:10); you have heard of the patience of Job (Jas. 5:11); those who through faith and patience inherit the promises (Heb. 6:12); we commend ourselves in patience (2 Cor. 6:6); you have followed my patience (2 Tim. 3:10); the farmer waits for the precious fruit of the soil, being patient over it (Jas. 5:7). WAIT FOR, see 507.

E Self-control

The fruit of the Spirit is self-control (Gal. 5:23); if they do not have self-control, let them marry (1 Cor. 7:9); competitors in the games exercise self-control (1 Cor. 9:25); Paul spoke about righteousness, self-control and judgement (Acts 24:25); add to knowledge self-control (2 Pet. 1:6); he who rules his spirit is better than he who takes a city (Prov. 16:32); God has given us a spirit of self-control (2 Tim. 1:7); lest Satan tempt you through lack of self-control (1 Cor. 7:5); the spirits of prophets are subject to the prophets (1 Cor. 14:32); let us keep awake and be self-controlled (1 Thess. 5:7); since we belong to the day, let us be self-controlled (1 Thess. 5:8); an elder [overseer] must be self-controlled (Titus

1:8); urge the young men to be self-controlled (Titus 2:6); be sober (1 Pet. 1:13); Joseph could not control himself (Gen. 45:1); men will be without self-control (2 Tim. 3:3).

824 Joy

A Rejoicing

Rejoice always (1 Thess. 5:16); rejoice in hope (Rom. 12:12); rejoice with those who rejoice (Rom. 12:15); sing for joy, daughter of Zion (Zech. 2:10); rejoice (2 Cor. 13:11); a good word makes the heart glad (Prov. 12:25); oil and perfume make the heart glad (Prov. 27:9); for all endurance and patience with joy (Col. 1:11); presenting you in the presence of his glory with great joy (Jude 24); we write this that our joy may be complete (1 John 1:4); eat your good things and rejoice before the Lord (Deut. 12:7); eat and be joyful! (1 Kgs. 21:7); they were eating, drinking and rejoicing (1 Kgs. 4:20; 1 Chr. 12:40); a rich man who enjoyed himself every day (Luke 16:19); eat, drink and be merry (Luke 12:19); kill the fatted calf and let us eat and be merry (Luke 15:23).

B God rejoicing

May the Lord rejoice in his works (Ps. 104:31); God will rejoice over you (Deut. 30:9; Zeph. 3:17); as the bridegroom rejoices over the bride so your God will rejoice over you (Isa. 62:5); I will rejoice over Jerusalem and be glad in my people (Isa. 65:19); I will rejoice over them to do them good (Jer. 32:41); more joy in heaven over one sinner who repents (Luke 15:7); there is joy before the angels of God over one sinner who repents (Luke 15:10).

C Christ rejoicing

God has anointed you with the oil of gladness (Ps. 45:7; Heb. 1:9); for the joy set before he him endured the cross (Heb. 12:2); I have told you this that my joy may be in you and your joy may be full (John 15:11); that they may have my joy fulfilled (John 17:13); Jesus rejoiced in the Holy Spirit (Luke 10:21).

D Creation rejoicing

You make the dawn and the sunset sing for joy (Ps. 65:8); the valleys sing for joy (Ps. 65:13); heaven and earth rejoice for the Lord reigns (1 Chr. 16:31; Ps. 96:11-13); let the earth rejoice (Ps. 97:1); the trees of the forest will sing for joy for the Lord comes (1 Chr. 16:33).

E Causes for rejoicing

E1 Rejoicing due to God

E1a Rejoicing in the Lord

God my exceeding joy (Ps. 43:4); I rejoice greatly in the Lord (Isa. 61:10); you make him joyful in your presence (Ps. 21:6); the king will rejoice in God (Ps. 63:11); there we rejoiced in him (Ps. 66:6); the needy will find fresh joy in the Lord (Isa. 29:19); in your name they rejoice all the day (Ps. 89:16); Tabor and Hermon shout for joy at your name (Ps. 89:12); there is a river whose streams make glad the city of God (Ps. 46:4); I will rejoice in your lovingkindness (Ps. 31:7); I will rejoice in the Lord (Ps. 104:34); my heart rejoices in the Lord (1 Sam. 2:1); I rejoice in God my Saviour (Luke 1:47); my heart is glad because the Lord is at my right hand (Ps. 16:9); the disciples were glad when they saw the Lord (John 20:20); you make me joyful with your presence (Acts 2:28); in your presence is fullness of joy (Ps. 16:11); the joy of the Lord is your strength (Neh. 8:10).

E1b Rejoice in the Lord!

Rejoice in the Lord (Joel 2:23; Phil. 3:1; 4:4); rejoice, Gentiles, with his people (Deut. 32:43); let those who seek the Lord rejoice (1 Chr. 16:10; Ps. 70:4); let the hearts of those who seek the Lord rejoice (Ps. 105:3); let all who seek you rejoice and be glad in you (Ps. 40:16); let all who take refuge in you sing for joy (Ps. 5:11);

shout for joy to the Lord (Ps. 81:1; 100:1); sing for joy to the Lord (Ps. 95:1; 98:4-6); make a joyful noise to God (Ps. 66:1).

E1c Rejoicing in God's word

I rejoice at your word (Ps. 119:162); the precepts of the Lord give joy to the heart (Ps. 19:8); your testimonies are the joy of my heart (Ps. 119:111); your words were the joy of my heart (Jer. 15:16); one immediately receives the word with joy (Matt. 13:20; Mark 4:16; Luke 8:13); I bring you good news of great joy (Luke 2:10); Christ is proclaimed, and in that I rejoice (Phil. 1:18).

E1d Rejoicing in God's works

You have made me glad by your work (Ps. 92:4); they were joyful for all God had done (1 Kgs. 8:66; 2 Chr. 7:10); Hezekiah and the people rejoiced at what God had done (2 Chr. 29:36); the Lord has done great things for us and we are glad (Ps. 126:3); when the Lord restores their fortunes Israel will be glad (Ps. 14:7; 53:6); God richly supplies us with everything to enjoy (1 Tim. 6:17); all the crowd rejoiced at all the glorious things done by him (Luke 13:17); for the Jews it was a time of joy (Esther 8:16, 17); they rejoiced with Elizabeth over God's mercy (Luke 1:58); they disbelieved for joy (Luke 24:41); this joy of mine is now full (John 3:29); if you loved me you would rejoice because I go to the Father (John 14:28); they broke bread from house to house with glad and generous hearts (Acts 2:46); when Barnabas saw the grace of God he rejoiced (Acts 11:23).

E1e Rejoicing in Jerusalem

There was great joy in Jerusalem for what had happened (2 Chr. 30:25-6); joy and gladness will be found in Zion (Isa. 51:3); I create Jerusalem a rejoicing (Isa. 65:18-19); Zion is the joy of the whole earth (Ps. 48:2); [this city] will be a name of joy, praise and glory (Jer. 33:9); rejoice with Jerusalem (Isa. 66:10); the voice of joy, of bridegroom and bride, will be heard in her again (Jer. 33:11); is this the city called a joy to all the earth? (Lam. 2:15).

E1f Rejoicing in serving God

I will offer sacrifices with shouts of joy (Ps. 27:6); the Lord led forth his people with joy (Ps. 105:43); you will go out with joy (Isa. 55:12); you did not serve the Lord with joy (Deut. 28:47).

E2 Rejoicing in conditions

E2a Rejoicing in prosperity

Happy is the man who has his quiver full [of children] (Ps. 127:5); she does not remember the anguish for joy that a child is born (John 16:21); when you eat of the labour of your hands you will be happy (Ps. 128:2); those who sow in tears will reap in joy (Ps. 126:5-6); the wilderness will rejoice and blossom (Isa. 35:1); if one member suffer, all suffer, if one is honoured, all rejoice (1 Cor. 12:26).

E2b Rejoicing over justice

Justice done is a joy to the righteous (Prov. 21:15); when the wicked perish there are shouts of joy (Prov. 11:10); let those who desire my vindication shout for joy (Ps. 35:27); the righteous will rejoice when he sees the vengeance (Ps. 58:10); heaven and earth will shout for joy over Babylon (Jer. 51:48); rejoice over her, heaven, saints, apostles and prophets (Rev. 18:20); do not rejoice when your enemy falls (Prov. 24:17-18).

E3 Rejoicing in salvation

E3a Rejoice in salvation!

Shout for joy for the Lord has redeemed us (Isa. 44:23); let us rejoice and be glad in his salvation (Isa. 25:9); rejoice that your names are written in heaven (Luke 10:20); may God fill you with all joy and peace in believing (Rom. 15:13).

E3b You will rejoice in salvation

The fruit of the Spirit is joy (Gal. 5:22); the kingdom of God is joy in the Holy Spirit (Rom. 14:17); joy unspeakable and full of glory (1 Pet. 1:8); we rejoice in hope of the glory of God (Rom. 5:2); in this salvation you rejoice (1 Pet. 1:6); with joy you will draw water from the wells of salvation (Isa. 12:3); you will have joy and gladness (Luke 1:14); as sorrowful yet always rejoicing (2 Cor. 6:10); the ransomed of the Lord will return with everlasting joy on their heads (Isa. 35:10; 51:11); you have increased their joy (Isa. 9:3); your sorrow will be turned to joy (John 16:20); the oil of gladness instead of mourning (Isa. 61:3); no one will take your joy from you (John 16:22); ask and you will receive, that your joy may be full (John 16:24); that you may rejoice when his glory is revealed (1 Pet. 4:13); restore to me the joy of your salvation (Ps. 51:12).

E3c Those who rejoiced in salvation

Abraham rejoiced to see my day (John 8:56); many would rejoice at John's birth (Luke 1:14); the baby in Elizabeth's womb leaped for joy (Luke 1:44); in his joy he goes and sells all that he has (Matt. 13:44); when the Gentiles heard this they rejoiced (Acts 13:48); their joy and poverty overflowed in liberality (2 Cor. 8:2); when they saw the star, they rejoiced (Matt. 2:10); they went from the tomb in fear and great joy (Matt. 28:8); they returned with great joy (Luke 24:52); they rejoiced to hear of the conversion of the Gentiles (Acts 15:3); we rejoice before God because of you (1 Thess. 3:9); the jailer rejoiced, believing in God (Acts 16:34); there was much rejoicing in Samaria (Acts 8:8); the eunuch went on his way rejoicing (Acts 8:39); the disciples were filled with joy and with the Holy Spirit (Acts 13:52).

E4 Rejoicing in people

After Titus' report of you, I rejoiced even more (2 Cor. 7:7); we rejoiced for the joy of Titus (2 Cor. 7:13); always making my prayer for you with joy (Phil. 1:4); fulfil my joy by being of the same mind (Phil. 2:2); my joy and crown (Phil. 4:1); I rejoice to see your orderliness (Col. 2:5); who is our hope or joy or crown of boasting but you? (1 Thess. 2:19); I long to see you that I may be filled with joy (2 Tim. 1:4); I have much joy and comfort in your love (Philem. 7); let your leaders give account with joy, not grief (Heb. 13:17); rejoice in the wife of your youth (Prov. 5:18).

E5 Rejoicing in trial

Rejoice when you are persecuted (Matt. 5:12; Luke 6:23); rejoice as you share the sufferings of Christ (1 Pet. 4:13); count it all joy when you face testings (Jas. 1:2); rejoicing that they were found worthy to suffer shame (Acts 5:41); you took joyfully the plundering of your goods (Heb. 10:34); though all fails, yet I will rejoice in the Lord (Hab. 3:17-18); we glory in tribulations (Rom. 5:3); I rejoice in my sufferings for you (Col. 1:24); in much affliction with joy of the Holy Spirit (1 Thess. 1:6).

E6 Rejoicing in evil

Do not let my enemies exult over me (Ps. 25:2); lest the daughters of the Philistines rejoice (2 Sam. 1:20); at my calamity they rejoiced (Ps. 35:15); as you rejoiced over the desolation of Israel, so I will do to you (Ezek. 35:15); they were glad and promised Judas money (Mark 14:11; Luke 22:5); you will weep and lament but the world will rejoice (John 16:20); they rejoiced in the works of their hands (Acts 7:41); those on earth will rejoice over them (Rev. 11:10).

E7 Rejoicing in other things

E7a Rejoicing in wisdom

A wise son makes a glad father (Prov. 10:1); be wise, my son, and make my heart glad (Prov. 27:11); if your heart is wise my heart will be glad (Prov. 23:15); let your father and mother be glad (Prov. 23:25).

E7b Joy at a marriage

They will be led with joy and gladness (Ps. 45:15); we will rejoice and delight in you (S. of S. 1:4); the friend of the bridegroom rejoices at the bridegroom's voice (John 3:29).

F Lack of rejoicing

Love does not rejoice in wrong (1 Cor. 13:6); those who rejoice should live as though they did not (1 Cor. 7:30); let not the buyer rejoice nor the seller mourn (Ezek. 7:12); I will take from them the voice of joy and gladness (Jer. 25:10); are not gladness and joy cut off from the house of our God? (Joel 1:16); you did not serve the Lord with joy (Deut. 28:47); do not rejoice that the spirits are subject to you (Luke 10:20); let your laughter be turned to mourning, your joy to dejection (Jas. 4:9).

825 Suffering

A God suffering

God could not bear Israel's misery (Judg. 10:16); in all their affliction he was afflicted (Isa. 63:9).

B Christ suffering

We esteemed him stricken, smitten by God and afflicted (Isa. 53:4); he bore our griefs (Isa. 53:4); was it not necessary for the Christ to suffer? (Luke 24:26); Christ had to suffer and rise (Luke 24:46; Acts 17:3; 26:23); he must suffer many things from the elders and the chief priests (Matt. 16:21; Mark 8:31; Luke 9:22); the Son of man will suffer at their hands (Matt. 17:12); he must suffer many things (Luke 17:25); he learned obedience by what he suffered (Heb. 5:8); he was made perfect through suffering (Heb. 2:10); the prophets predicted the sufferings of Christ (Acts 3:18; 1 Pet. 1:11); Christ suffered for you (1 Pet. 2:21); Christ suffered in the flesh (1 Pet. 4:1); being in agony, he prayed more fervently (Luke 22:44); now is my soul troubled (John 12:27); he was troubled in spirit (John 13:21); Jesus suffered outside the gate to sanctify the people with his own blood (Heb. 13:12); a witness of the sufferings of Christ (1 Pet. 5:1).

C People suffering

C1 God's people suffering

C1a God's people suffer

Many are the afflictions of the righteous (Ps. 34:19); though the Lord has given you bread of adversity and water of affliction (Isa. 30:20); I have tested you in the furnace of affliction (Isa. 48:10); when affliction or persecution arises because of the word, they fall away (Mark 4:17); do not lose heart at my tribulations for you (Eph. 3:13); he comforts us in our affliction (2 Cor. 1:4); God is just to give relief to those afflicted (2 Thess. 1:7); is anyone suffering? let him pray (Jas. 5:13).

C1b Particular people suffering

The thing distressed Abraham (Gen. 21:11-12); Lot's soul was tormented by their lawless deeds (2 Pet. 2:8); son of my sorrow (Gen. 35:18); you will bring down my hoary head in sorrow to Sheol (Gen. 42:38); Samuel was distressed over Saul (1 Sam. 15:11); God had seen their affliction (Exod. 4:31).

C1c Suffering with Christ

Christ suffered leaving us an example (1 Pet. 2:21); since Christ suffered, arm yourselves with the same mind (1 Pet. 4:1); you share in the sufferings of Christ (1 Pet. 4:13); that I may know the fellowship of his sufferings (Phil. 3:10); I fill up what is lacking in Christ's afflictions (Col. 1:24); if we suffer with him that we may be glorified with him (Rom. 8:17).

C1d Christ's disciples will suffer

Endure hardship (2 Tim. 4:5); endure hardship as a soldier of Christ (2 Tim. 2:3); how much he must suffer for my name's sake (Acts 9:16); it is given to you not only to believe on Christ but also to suffer for him (Phil. 1:29); taking up one's cross (Matt. 10:38; 16:24; Mark 8:34; Luke 9:23; 14:27); we were destined for affliction (1 Thess. 3:3); we told you beforehand that we would be afflicted (1 Thess. 3:4); join me in suffering for the gospel (2 Tim. 1:8); they will hand you over to tribulation (Matt. 24:9); for a little while you may have to suffer (1 Pet. 1:6); it is better to suffer for doing right than for doing wrong (1 Pet. 3:17); suffer as a Christian (1 Pet. 4:15-17); suffer according to God's will (1 Pet. 4:19); after you have suffered a little, God will strengthen you (1 Pet. 5:10); we glory in tribulations knowing that tribulation produces perseverance (Rom. 5:3); we commend ourselves in afflictions, hardships, calamities (2 Cor. 6:4); we are afflicted but not crushed (2 Cor. 4:8); this momentary light affliction (2 Cor. 4:17); as you share in our suffering so you share in our comfort (2 Cor. 1:7); do not fear what you are about to suffer (Rev. 2:10); you will have tribulation for ten days (Rev. 2:10).

C1e Christ's disciples suffering

What we suffered in Asia (2 Cor. 1:8); in Philippi (1 Thess. 2:2); in Antioch, Iconium and Lystra (2 Tim. 3:11); I suffer because I teach the gospel (2 Tim. 1:11-12); we were afflicted on all sides (2 Cor. 7:5); you received the word in much tribulation (1 Thess. 1:6); you endured the same sufferings (1 Thess. 2:14); you endured much suffering (Heb. 10:32); it was good of you to share with me in my affliction (Phil. 4:14); I rejoice in my sufferings for you (Col. 1:24); your steadfastness and faith in all your persecutions and afflictions (2 Thess. 1:4); worthy of the kingdom of God for which you are suffering (2 Thess. 1:5); the gospel for which I suffer hardship, even to being imprisoned (2 Tim. 2:9); your brethren throughout the world share the same experience of suffering (1 Pet. 5:9); your partner in the tribulation and kingdom and perseverance in Jesus (Rev. 1:9); I know your tribulation and your poverty (Rev. 2:9).

C2 The ungodly suffering

Many are the sorrows of the wicked (Ps. 32:10); who has woe and sorrow but the drunkard? (Prov. 23:29-30); those who run after other gods will have multiplied sorrows (Ps. 16:4); the day of the Lord is a day of distress and anguish (Zeph. 1:15); weep and howl, you rich, for the miseries that are coming (Jas. 5:1); I will throw those who committed adultery with her into great tribulation (Rev. 2:22).

C3 Various suffering

Jabez – born in pain (1 Chr. 4:9); a foolish son is a grief to his father and mother (Prov. 17:25); when he heard this the king was deeply distressed (Dan. 6:14); I have suffered much over him today in a dream (Matt. 27:19); the woman had suffered much from many doctors (Mark 5:26); I am in anguish in this flame (Luke 16:24); everyone in distress joined David (1 Sam. 22:2); why is light given to one who suffers? (Job 3:20); the heart knows its own bitterness (Prov. 14:10); the present sufferings are not worth comparing with the glory to come (Rom. 8:18).

D Sorrow

D1 About sorrow

Sorrow is better than laughter (Eccles. 7:3); the end of joy may be grief (Prov. 14:13); in much wisdom there is much grief (Eccles. 1:18); he came to his disciples and found them sleeping from sorrow (Luke 22:45); a woman in travail has sorrow because her hour has come (John 16:21); I have great sorrow in my heart over my kinsmen (Rom. 9:2-4); if I give you sorrow, who is there to make me glad but the one I have pained? (2 Cor. 2:2-8).

D2 Bitterness of heart

The heart knows its own bitterness (Prov. 14:10); I will speak in the bitterness of my soul (Job 7:11); remember the wormwood and bitterness (Lam. 3:19); their grapes are bitter (Deut. 32:32); the gall of bitterness (Acts 8:23); a root bearing poison and wormwood (Deut. 29:18); that no root of bitterness spring up (Heb. 12:15); put away all bitterness (Eph. 4:31); if you have bitter jealousy and selfish ambition in your heart (Jas. 3:14); their mouth is full of cursing and bitterness (Rom. 3:14); the adulteress in the end is bitter as wormwood (Prov. 5:4); they brought bitterness of spirit to Isaac and Rebekah (Gen. 26:35); the Egyptians made their lives bitter (Exod. 1:14); call me Mara for the Lord has dealt bitterly (Ruth 1:20); remember my affliction and wandering, the wormwood and bitterness (Lam. 3:19); all who were bitter of soul joined David (1 Sam. 22:2); husbands, do not be bitter towards your wife (Col. 3:19); the bitterness of death is past (1 Sam. 15:32).

D3 God healing sorrow

God has made me forget my trouble (Gen. 41:51); God has made me fruitful in the land of my affliction (Gen. 41:52); God heals the broken-hearted (Ps. 147:3); he has anointed me to bind up the broken-hearted (Isa. 61:1); the Lord saves the broken-hearted (Ps. 34:18); he adds no sorrow with his blessing (Prov. 10:22); you will be sorrowful, but your sorrow will be turned to joy (John 16:20).

E Anxiety

E1 About anxiety

Anxiety weighs the heart down (Prov. 12:25); anxieties of the world choke the word (Matt. 13:22; Mark 4:19; Luke 8:14); Mary was worried about many things (Luke 10:41); my anxiety for the churches (2 Cor. 11:28-9); I am in labour until Christ is formed in you (Gal. 4:19); lest my father be anxious about us (1 Sam. 9:5).

E2 Do not be anxious

Do not fret over evildoers (Ps. 37:1; Prov. 24:19); do not worry about what to eat or drink or wear (Matt. 6:25-31); do not be anxious about what to eat (Luke 12:22); why are you troubled? (Luke 24:38); be anxious for nothing (Phil. 4:6); do not be anxious for tomorrow (Matt. 6:34); do not be anxious about what to say (Matt. 10:19; Mark 13:11; Luke 12:11); who by being anxious can add a cubit to his life? (Matt. 6:27; Luke 12:25-6); lest your hearts be weighed down with dissipation, drunkenness and anxiety (Luke 21:34); do not let your heart be troubled (John 14:1); do not be anxious (Luke 12:29); I want you to be free from anxiety (1 Cor. 7:32); cast all your anxiety on him (1 Pet. 5:7).

826 Pleasurableness

A God pleased

A1 God's pleasure

God does whatever he pleases (Ps. 115:3; 135:6); this was well-pleasing in your sight (Matt. 11:26; Luke 10:21); it pleased the Lord to crush him (Isa. 53:10); does the Lord take delight in thousands of rams? (Mic. 6:7); it pleased God to save those who believe (1 Cor. 1:21); the Lord was pleased to magnify the law (Isa. 42:21); it pleased the Lord to kill them (1 Sam. 2:25); God's delight: a just weight (Prov. 11:1); those who act faithfully (Prov. 12:22); the blameless (Prov. 11:20); the prayer of the upright (Prov. 15:8); lovingkindness, justice and righteousness (Jer. 9:24).

A2 Christ pleasing God

This is my Son with whom I am well pleased (Matt. 3:17; 17:5; Mark 1:11; Luke 3:22); my beloved in whom I am well pleased (Matt. 12:18; 2 Pet. 1:17); my chosen one in whom my soul delights (Isa. 42:1); I always do the things that please him (John 8:29); in him all the fullness of God was pleased to dwell (Col. 1:19); let God deliver him if he delights in him (Ps. 22:8; Matt. 27:43).

A3 God pleased with people

The Lord takes pleasure in those who fear him (Ps. 147:11); the Lord takes pleasure in his people (Ps. 149:4); as a father reproves the son in whom he delights (Prov. 3:12); on earth, peace among men with whom he is pleased (Luke 2:14); if the Lord is pleased with us, he will give them the land (Num. 14:8); God gave them the land because he delighted in them (Ps. 44:3); to the man who pleases him God gives wisdom, knowledge and joy (Eccles. 2:26); God is pleased to give you the kingdom (Luke 12:32); God took pleasure in David to make him king (1 Chr. 28:4); he delighted in me (2 Sam. 22:20; Ps. 18:19); God took pleasure in Solomon to make him king (2 Chr. 9:8); Enoch pleased God (Heb. 11:5); Samuel grew in favour with God and man (1 Sam. 2:26); you finding favour in God's eyes: Noah (Gen. 6:8); Moses (Exod. 33:12-17; Num. 11:15); Gideon (Judg. 6:17); David (2 Sam. 15:25; Acts 7:46).

A4 Doing what pleases God

Learn what is pleasing to the Lord (Eph. 5:10); how you ought to live and please God (1 Thess. 4:1); we do what pleases him (1 John 3:22); to please the Lord in every way (Col. 1:10); the unmarried man is concerned to please the Lord (1 Cor. 7:32); whether home or away, we want to please him (2 Cor. 5:9); a soldier wants to please the one who enlisted him (2 Tim. 2:4); God works in you what is pleasing in his sight (Heb. 13:21); I delight in steadfast love and the knowledge of God (Hos. 6:6); present your bodies as a living sacrifice, holy and pleasing to God (Rom. 12:1); God works in you to will and to work for his good pleasure (Phil. 2:13); making a return to one's parents is pleasing to God (1 Tim. 5:4); do good and share, for God is pleased with such sacrifices (Heb. 13:16); you will delight in right sacrifices (Ps. 51:19); thanksgiving will please the Lord better than an ox (Ps. 69:31); without faith it is impossible to please him (Heb. 11:6); not pleasing men but God (1 Thess. 2:4); it pleased God that Solomon asked this (1 Kgs. 3:10); children, obey your parents, for this is pleasing to the Lord (Col. 3:20); your sacrifice was well-pleasing to God (Phil. 4:18).

A5 Not pleasing God

God takes no pleasure in the death of the wicked (Ezek. 18:23; 33:11); God takes no delight in fools (Eccles. 5:4); God does not delight in the strength of a horse or a man's legs (Ps. 147:10); you are not pleased with burnt offering (Ps. 51:16; Heb. 10:6-8); has the Lord as much delight in sacrifice as in obeying? (1 Sam. 15:22); is it any pleasure to the Almighty if you are righteous? (Job 22:3); those who are in the flesh cannot please God (Rom. 8:8); with most of them God was not pleased (1 Cor. 10:5); they are not pleasing to God (1 Thess. 2:15).

B People pleased

B1 Pleasure in God

Delight yourself in the Lord (Ps. 37:4); they drink from your river of delights (Ps. 36:8); the works of the Lord are studied by all who delight in them (Ps. 111:2); they delight to know my ways (Isa. 58:2); all nations will call you blessed, for you will be a land of delight (Mal. 3:12).

B2 Pleasure in God's law

He delights in the law of the Lord (Ps. 1:2); I delight in your law (Ps. 119:70); happy the man who delights in

his commandments (Ps. 112:1); they do not delight in the word of the Lord (Jer. 6:10).

B3 Pleasing other people

B3a Pleasing people in general

I please all men (1 Cor. 10:33); let each of us please his neighbour for his good (Rom. 15:2); the married person is concerned to please his spouse (1 Cor. 7:33-4); if I were trying to please men I would not be a slave of Christ (Gal. 1:10); would the governor be pleased with your offering? (Mal. 1:8); a soldier wants to please the one who enlisted him (2 Tim. 2:4).

B3b Pleasing particular people

The messenger of the covenant in whom you delight (Mal. 3:1); when Herod saw it pleased the Jews, he arrested Peter too (Acts 12:3); Shechem delighted in Jacob's daughter (Gen. 34:19); the woman looked agreeable to Samson (Judg. 14:3, 7); the king delights in you (1 Sam. 18:22); Jonathan delighted in David (1 Sam. 19:1); let the one who pleases the king be queen (Esther 2:4).

B4 Pleasures

B4a Evil pleasures

All will be condemned who did not believe the truth but took pleasure in wickedness (2 Thess. 2:12); those who delight in doing evil (Prov. 2:14); the pleasure in riches chokes the word (Mark 4:19; Luke 8:14); the pleasures of sin (Heb. 11:25); your pleasures wage war in your members (Jas. 4:1); you have lived a life of pleasure (Jas. 5:5); men will be lovers of pleasure rather than lovers of God (2 Tim. 3:4); in slavery to pleasures (Titus 3:3); if you turn from seeking your own pleasure on the sabbath (Isa. 58:13); the pleasure seeker is dead while she lives (1 Tim. 5:6).

B4b Other pleasures

The trees in the garden were pleasing to the eye (Gen. 2:9); the woman saw that the fruit was pleasing to the eye (Gen. 3:6); wisdom's ways are ways of pleasantness (Prov. 3:17); the lines have fallen for me in pleasant places (Ps. 16:6); that God may fulfil your good pleasure and work of faith in power (2 Thess. 1:11); enjoy life with the wife you love (Eccles. 9:9); when I am worn out and my husband is old, shall I have pleasure? (Gen. 18:12); Issachar saw that the land was pleasant (Gen. 49:15); many concubines – men's delight (Eccles. 2:8).

B5 Not pleasing people

It greatly displeased Jonah (Jonah 4:1); we ought to bear with the failings of the weak and not please ourselves (Rom. 15:1); even Christ did not please himself (Rom. 15:3); not pleasing men but God (1 Thess. 2:4); the cities in Galilee did not please Hiram (1 Kgs. 9:12).

827 Painfulness

A Trouble

A1 Trouble in general

Man is born for trouble (Job 5:7); man's life is full of trouble (Job 14:1); trouble does not sprout out of the ground (Job 5:6); Achor – trouble (Josh. 7:24, 26); trouble is near (Ps. 22:11); days of affliction confront me (Job 30:27); before the sad days come in which you have no delight (Eccles. 12:1); lest they also come to this place of torment (Luke 16:28); pain in childbirth was greatly increased (Gen. 3:16); those who marry will have trouble (1 Cor. 7:28); may the Lord answer you in the day of trouble (Ps. 20:1); the Lord is a stronghold in the day of trouble (Nahum 1:7); in view of the present distress it is good for a man to remain as he is (1 Cor. 7:26); great distress in the land (Luke 21:23); there will be weeping and gnashing of teeth (Matt. 13:42, 50; 22:13; 24:51; 25:30; Luke 13:28); a time of distress unknown

since the beginning of the world (Dan. 12:1; Matt. 24:21;
Mark 13:19); a sword will pierce your own soul (Luke
2:35).

A2 Trouble for the believer
Do not be surprised at the fiery trial (1 Pet. 4:12); in a
severe ordeal of affliction (2 Cor. 8:2); through many
tribulations we must enter the kingdom of God (Acts
14:22); persevere in tribulation (Rom. 12:12); shall
trouble, hardship or persecution separate us from the
love of Christ? (Rom. 8:35); Paul lists his afflictions
(2 Cor. 11:23-7); his thorn in the flesh (2 Cor. 12:7); I
bear in my body the marks of Jesus (Gal. 6:17).

A3 No trouble
The wicked are not in trouble like others (Ps. 73:5);
there the wicked cease from troubling (Job 3:17); I will
keep you from the hour of trial which is coming on the
whole world (Rev. 3:10); they have come out of the
great tribulation (Rev. 7:14); henceforth let no one
trouble me (Gal. 6:17).

B Troubling

B1 Grieving God
It grieved God that he had made man (Gen. 6:6); they
grieved him in the desert (Ps. 78:40); David's census
displeased God (1 Chr. 21:7); they rebelled and grieved
his Holy Spirit (Isa. 63:10); do not grieve the Holy
Spirit (Eph. 4:30).

B2 God troubling
You have made your people experience hardship (Ps.
60:3); God troubled them with all hardship (2 Chr.
15:6); why have you brought trouble on this people?
(Exod. 5:22); the Almighty has dealt bitterly with me
(Ruth 1:20); if he causes grief, he will have compassion
(Lam. 3:32); worshippers of the beast will be tormented
with fire and brimstone (Rev. 14:10); as she glorified
herself, to that extent give her torment and mourning
(Rev. 18:7); God is just to afflict those who afflict you (2
Thess. 1:6); there will be tribulation for every one who
does evil (Rom. 2:9); they were afflicted because of
their iniquities (Ps. 107:17); it will be more bearable for
Sodom than for them (Matt. 10:15; 11:22-2; Luke
10:12-14); have you come here to torment us before the
time? (Matt. 8:29); do not torment us! (Mark 5:7; Luke
8:28).

B3 People troubling
Do not afflict orphans or widows (Exod. 22:22); do not
oppress a sojourner (Exod. 22:21; 23:9); do not oppress
an escaped slave (Deut. 23:16); they were permitted to
torture them for five months (Rev. 9:5); Achar
[Achan], the troubler of Israel (1 Chr. 2:7); is it you,
you troubler of Israel? (1 Kgs. 18:17-18); David had
become odious to the Israelites (1 Sam. 27:12); the
inhabitants of the land will become pricks in your eyes
and thorns in your sides (Num. 33:55); he who is
troubling you will bear his judgement (Gal. 5:10-12);
some were tortured (Heb. 11:35); Esau's wives brought
grief to Isaac and Rebekah (Gen. 26:35); the daughters
of Canaan displeased Isaac (Gen. 28:8); Simeon and
Levi brought trouble on Jacob (Gen. 34:30); Delilah
nagged Samson to death (Judg. 16:16); Hannah's rival
provoked her (1 Sam. 1:6); why trouble the Teacher any
further? (Mark 5:35; Luke 8:49); why do you trouble
her? (Mark 14:6); they think to afflict me in my
imprisonment (Phil. 1:17); because this widow bothers
me I will get her justice (Luke 18:5); my judgement is
that we do not trouble the Gentiles who turn to God
(Acts 15:19).

C Discipline

C1 About discipline
Whoever loves discipline loves knowledge (Prov. 12:1);
apply your heart to discipline (Prov. 23:12); he who
loves his son is careful to discipline him (Prov. 13:24);

discipline your son (Prov. 19:18; 29:17); do not withhold
discipline from a child (Prov. 23:13); a wise son takes
his father's discipline (Prov. 13:1); what son is there
whom his father does not discipline? (Heb. 12:7-10); no
discipline seems joyful but rather painful (Heb. 12:11).

C2 God's discipline
Do not despise the Lord's discipline (Job 5:17; Prov.
3:11-12; Heb. 12:5-7); happy is the man you discipline
(Ps. 94:12); when he sins, I will correct him with the
rod (2 Sam. 7:14); when we are judged, we are
disciplined by the Lord (1 Cor. 11:32); before I was
afflicted I went astray (Ps. 119:67); in faithfulness you
have afflicted me (Ps. 119:75); he does not willingly
afflict the sons of men (Lam. 3:33); he disciplines us for
our good, that we may share his holiness (Heb. 12:10).

C3 Lack of discipline
His father had never pained him by challenging what
he did (1 Kgs. 1:6); you hate discipline (Ps. 50:17);
poverty and shame come to him who ignores discipline
(Prov. 13:18).

D Unbearable things
There are four unbearable things (Prov. 30:21-3); a yoke
which neither we nor our fathers were able to bear
(Acts 15:10); the Lord could no longer bear the evil of
your deeds (Jer. 44:22); they could not bear the
command (Heb. 12:20).

828 Content

A Contentment
I will be satisfied when I awake in your likeness (Ps.
17:15); I have learned to be content in all circumstances
(Phil. 4:11); I am well-pleased with weakness, insults
etc. (2 Cor. 12:10); godliness with contentment is great
gain (1 Tim. 6:6); if we have food and clothing we will
be content (1 Tim. 6:8); show us the Father and we will
be satisfied (John 14:8); God satisfied your hearts with
food and gladness (Acts 14:17).

B Be content!
Be content with your wages (Luke 3:14); be content
with what you have (Heb. 13:5).

829 Discontent

A Dissatisfaction
Cain's face fell (Gen. 4:5-6); all this does me no good
when I see Mordecai (Esther 5:13); the eye is not
satisfied with seeing nor the ear with hearing (Eccles.
1:8); his eyes are not satisfied with riches (Eccles. 4:7-8);
annoyed because they were proclaiming resurrection
(Acts 4:2); I fear I may come and find you not what I
wish (2 Cor. 12:20).

B Grumbling

B1 Grumbling in general
They made all the congregation grumble (Num. 14:36);
they grumbled against their leaders (Josh. 9:18); they
grumbled in their tents (Deut. 1:27; Ps. 106:25); Jesus,
knowing in himself that his disciples grumbled at this
(John 6:61); these men are grumblers, finding fault
(Jude 16).

B2 Grumbling at God
Why do you complain against him? (Job 33:13); they
grumbled against the Lord (Exod. 16:7-9; Num. 14:27);
I have heard their grumbling (Exod. 16:12).

B3 Grumbling at people
The Israelites complained against Moses (Exod. 15:24;
17:3); they complained against Moses and Aaron (Exod.
16:2; Num. 14:2; 16:41); what are we that you grumble
about us? (Exod. 16:7-8; Num. 16:11); the workmen
grumbled at the landowner (Matt. 20:11); the Pharisees
and scribes grumbled at Jesus receiving sinners (Luke
15:2); they grumbled at Jesus going to Zaccheus' house
(Luke 19:7); the Jews grumbled at him (John 6:41);

there was much grumbling about him among the people (John 7:12); the Hellenists complained against the Hebrews (Acts 6:1).

B4 Do not grumble
Do all things without grumbling (Phil. 2:14); do not complain against one another (Jas. 5:9); do not grumble among yourselves (John 6:43); do not grumble as some of them did (1 Cor. 10:10).

830 Regret

A Regretting
God was sorry that he had made man and all creatures (Gen. 6:6-7); God regretted that he made Saul king (1 Sam. 15:11); I do not regret causing you sorrow, though I did regret it (2 Cor. 7:8); godly sorrow produces repentance without regret leading to salvation (2 Cor. 7:10); Judas was filled with remorse (Matt. 27:3); Jehoram went without anyone regretting it (2 Chr. 21:20).

B Woe to...

B1 Woe to Israel and Jerusalem
Woe to you, Jerusalem! (Jer. 13:27); woe to the bloody city, the pot with rust in it! (Ezek. 24:6); woe to those who are at ease in Zion (Amos 6:1); woe, shepherds of Israel (Ezek. 34:2); woe to the worthless shepherd who deserts the flock (Zech. 11:17); woe to the shepherds who scatter my sheep (Jer. 23:1); woe to the proud crown of the drunkards of Ephraim (Isa. 28:1); woe to the rebellious children (Isa. 30:1); woe to the women who make veils for those of every stature (Ezek. 13:18); woe to the foolish prophets who follow their own spirit and have seen nothing (Ezek. 13:3).

B2 Woe to the wicked
Woe to you, Chorazin and Bethsaida (Matt. 11:21; Luke 10:13); woe to those who devise evil on their beds (Mic. 2:1); woe to him who builds a city with bloodshed (Hab. 2:12); woe to him who heaps up what is not his (Hab. 2:6); woe to those who are heroes at drinking wine (Isa. 5:22); woe to him who makes his neighbours drunk (Hab. 2:15); woe to those who add house to house! (Isa. 5:8); woe to those who build a house by unrighteousness (Jer. 22:13); woe to those who call evil good (Isa. 5:20); woe to those who decree evil decrees (Isa. 10:1); woe to those who are wise in their own eyes (Isa. 5:21); woe to those who hide their plans from the Lord (Isa. 29:15); woe to the world for stumbling blocks (Matt. 18:7); woe to that man by who the Son of man is betrayed (Mark 14:21; Luke 22:22); woe to him who quarrels with his maker (Isa. 45:9).

B3 Woe to the prosperous
Woe to those who are rich (Luke 6:24-5); woe to you who laugh now (Luke 6:25); woe to you when all speak well of you (Luke 6:26).

B4 Woe for disaster
Woe, woe, woe because of the last three trumpet blasts (Rev. 8:13); the first woe is past, two more to come (Rev. 9:12); the second woe is past, the third comes quickly (Rev. 11:14).

B5 Woe to people
Woe is me, for I am ruined (Isa. 6:5); woe is me if I do not preach the gospel (1 Cor. 9:16); woe to them! (Jude 11); woe to you, earth and sea, for the devil has come down to you (Rev. 12:12); woe to you, scribes and Pharisees (Matt. 23:13-29; Luke 11:42-52); woe to you, blind guides (Matt. 23:16); woe to those who are pregnant in those days (Matt. 24:19; Mark 13:17; Luke 21:23).

831 Comfort

A God comforting
A1 God will comfort
As one whom his mother comforts, so will I comfort you (Isa. 66:13); the Lord will comfort Zion (Isa. 51:3; Zech. 1:17); God will wipe away every tear (Isa. 25:8; Rev. 7:17; 21:4); you will comfort me again (Ps. 71:21); may he comfort you (2 Thess. 2:17); in anxiety your consolations cheer me (Ps. 94:19); comfort my people, says your God (Isa. 40:1); the Father of mercies and God of all comfort (2 Cor. 1:3); blessed are those who mourn for they will be comforted (Matt. 5:4); the Father will give you a Comforter to be with you for ever (John 14:16); the Comforter, the Holy Spirit, whom the Father will send in my name (John 14:26); God has sent me to comfort those who mourn (Isa. 61:2); he comforts us so we may be able to comfort others with the comfort with which he comforts us (2 Cor. 1:4); as the sufferings of Christ abound for us, so our comfort abounds through Christ (2 Cor. 1:5); if we are comforted, it is for your comfort (2 Cor. 1:6-7); if there is any comfort in love (Phil. 2:1); eternal comfort (2 Thess. 2:16).

A2 God has comforted
The Lord has comforted his people (Isa. 49:13; 52:9); your rod and your staff comfort me (Ps. 23:4); God who comforts the downcast comforted us (2 Cor. 7:6); Simeon was looking for the consolation of Israel (Luke 2:25); the poor man was carried by the angels to Abraham's bosom (Luke 16:22-3); the church was walking in the comfort of the Holy Spirit (Acts 9:31).

B Human comfort
The rich receive their comfort now (Luke 6:24); if I say, 'My bed will comfort me' (Job 7:13); he who prophesies speaks to men for edification, exhortation and comfort (1 Cor. 14:3); he comforts us so we may be able to comfort others with the comfort with which he comforts us (2 Cor. 1:4); you ought to forgive and comfort him (2 Cor. 2:7); comfort one another with these words (1 Thess. 4:18); I am filled with comfort (2 Cor. 7:4); for this reason we are comforted (2 Cor. 7:13); be comforted (2 Cor. 13:11); in our distress and affliction we were comforted through your faith (1 Thess. 3:7); I have had much comfort from your love (Philem. 7).

C Relief
God is just to give relief to those afflicted (2 Thess. 1:7); to give him relief from the days of trouble (Ps. 94:13).

D No comfort
Storm-tossed and not comforted (Isa. 54:11); I looked for comforters and there were none (Ps. 69:20); there is none to comfort (Lam. 1:2); Jacob would not be comforted (Gen. 37:35); Rachel refuses to be comforted for her children (Jer. 31:15; Matt. 2:18); miserable comforters! (Job 16:2).

832 Aggravation
DETERIORATION, see 655.

833 Cheerfulness
A glad heart makes a cheerful face (Prov. 15:13); a cheerful heart has a continual feast (Prov. 15:15); a cheerful heart is a good medicine (Prov. 17:22); is anyone cheerful? let him sing praise (Jas. 5:13); God loves a cheerful giver (2 Cor. 9:7); use your gift in showing mercy with cheerfulness (Rom. 12:8).

834 Sadness
MOURNING, see 836.

A About sadness

A sad heart crushes the spirit (Prov. 15:13); a broken spirit dries up the bones (Prov. 17:22); he who sings songs to a heavy heart is like vinegar on soda (Prov. 25:20); let your laughter be turned to mourning, your joy to dejection (Jas. 4:9); if I make you sad, who is there to make me glad? (2 Cor. 2:2).

B Benefits in sadness

The Lord is near to those who are broken-hearted and saves those crushed in spirit (Ps. 34:18); God who comforts the downcast comforted us (2 Cor. 7:6); a broken and a contrite heart you will not despise (Ps. 51:17); godly sorrow produced repentance (2 Cor. 7:9-11); as sorrowful yet always rejoicing (2 Cor. 6:10); those who weep now shall laugh (Luke 6:21); sorrow and sighing will flee away (Isa. 35:10).

C Sad people

Jesus was grieved at their hardness of heart (Mark 3:5); Jesus was grieved to the point of death (Matt. 26:38; Mark 14:34); my life is spent with sorrow (Ps. 31:10); my soul is cast down within me (Ps. 42:6); why do you despair, O my soul? (Ps. 42:5, 11; 43:5); out of the depths I cry to you (Ps. 130:1); in anguish of heart I wrote to you (2 Cor. 2:4); I have great sorrow about my kinsmen (Rom. 9:2-3); God had mercy on me, lest I should have sorrow on sorrow (Phil. 2:27); why are your faces sad today? (Gen. 40:7); their hearts sank (Gen. 42:28); Amnon was continually depressed (2 Sam. 13:4); Nehemiah was sad before the king (Neh. 2:1-3); Herod was grieved about John (Mark 6:26); they stood still, looking sad (Luke 24:17); he was downcast because you heard he was ill (Phil. 2:26); the disciples were very sad (Matt. 17:23); grieved that one of them would betray him (Matt. 26:22; Mark 14:19); sorrow has filled your heart (John 16:6); the rich young man went away grieved (Matt. 19:22; Mark 10:22; Luke 18:23).

835 Signs of joy

JOY, see 824.

A Laughter

There is a time to laugh (Eccles. 3:4); our tormentors demanded mirth (Ps. 137:3); even in laughter the heart may be sad (Prov. 14:13); I said laughter was mad (Eccles. 2:2); the laughter of fools is like the crackling of thorns (Eccles. 7:6); woe to you who laugh now (Luke 6:25); let your laughter be turned to mourning, your joy to dejection (Jas. 4:9); Abraham laughed (Gen. 17:17); call him Isaac – he laughs (Gen. 17:19; 21:3); Sarah laughed (Gen. 18:12-15); you who weep will laugh (Luke 6:21); he who sits in the heavens laughs (Ps. 2:4); sorrow is better than laughter (Eccles. 7:3).

B Dancing

There is a time to dance (Eccles. 3:4); you have turned my mourning into dancing (Ps. 30:11); our dancing has been turned to mourning (Lam. 5:15); we played the flute and you did not dance (Matt. 11:17; Luke 7:32); the elder brother heard music and dancing (Luke 15:25); the people sat down to eat and drink and rose up to dance (1 Cor. 10:7); praise his name with dancing (Ps. 149:3); praise him with timbrel and dancing (Ps. 150:4); you will go forth to the dances of the merrymakers (Jer. 31:4); Miriam with tambourines and dancing (Exod. 15:20); Jephthah's daughter with tambourines and dancing (Judg. 11:34); the daughters of Shiloh dancing (Judg. 21:21); the women came out singing and dancing (1 Sam. 18:6); David danced before the Lord (2 Sam. 6:14-16; 1 Chr. 15:29); the daughter of Herodias danced (Matt. 14:6; Mark 6:22).

836 Mourning

A Mourning in general

A1 About mourning

There is a time to mourn (Eccles. 3:4); better to go to the house of mourning than to the house of feasting (Eccles. 7:2); blessed are those who mourn (Matt. 5:4); blessed are you who weep now (Luke 6:21); weeping may last for a night but joy comes in the morning (Ps. 30:5); those who sow in tears will reap in joy (Ps. 126:5); those who weep should live as if they did not (1 Cor. 7:30).

A2 Accompaniments of mourning

Do not trim your hair or your beards in mourning (Lev. 19:27; 21:5); do not cut your bodies or tattoo yourselves in mourning (Lev. 19:28; 21:5); do not cut yourselves or shave your foreheads for the dead (Deut. 14:1); the priest shall not let his hair hang loose or tear his garments (Lev. 21:10).

TEARS, see 302F2.

A3 Mourn!

Mourn and weep, you sinners (Jas. 4:9); weep and howl, you rich, for the miseries that are coming (Jas. 5:1); weep for yourselves and your children (Luke 23:28); weep with those who weep (Rom. 12:15); gird on sackcloth and lament, O priests (Joel 1:13); let the priests, the ministers of the Lord, weep (Joel 2:17); wail, you shepherds, for your day of slaughter has come (Jer. 25:34).

B Mourning and God

The people mourned because God would not go with them (Exod. 33:4); they mourned because they could not go up (Num. 14:39; Deut. 1:45); Israel wept before the Lord when Benjamin beat them (Judg. 20:23); return to me with fasting, weeping and mourning (Joel 2:12); should I mourn and fast in the fifth month, as I have for many years? (Zech. 7:3); what is the good of us walking in mourning before the Lord? (Mal. 3:14); the people wept over the angel's rebuke (Judg. 2:4-5); the people of Israel mourned after the Lord (1 Sam. 7:2); Ezra was mourning over the unfaithfulness of the exiles (Ezra 10:6); the people wept when they heard the book of the law (Neh. 8:9); my eyes stream with tears because they do not keep your law (Ps. 119:136); Israel and Judah will go in tears to seek the Lord (Jer. 50:4); a mark on the foreheads of those who groan over the abominations (Ezek. 9:4).

C Reasons for mourning

C1 Mourning a death

C1a Mourning death in general

Mourners go about the streets (Eccles. 12:5); the captive woman shall mourn her parents one month (Deut. 21:13); lament like a virgin in sackcloth the bridegroom of her youth (Joel 1:8); I will make it like the mourning for an only son (Amos 8:10); like one who grieves for a friend or relative (Ps. 35:14); Allon-bacuth – oak of weeping (Gen. 35:8); Abel-mizraim – mourning of the Egyptians (Gen. 50:11); Rachel weeping for her children (Jer. 31:15; Matt. 2:18).

C1b Mourning the death of Christ

The disciples mourned for Jesus (Mark 16:10); they mourned and wailed for Jesus (Luke 23:27); Mary stood weeping outside the tomb (John 20:11); you will weep and lament but the world will rejoice (John 16:20); they beat their breasts (Luke 23:48); they will look on him they have pierced and mourn for him (Zech. 12:10); all tribes of the earth will wail because of him (Rev. 1:7).

C1c Mourning the death of others

Abraham mourned for Sarah (Gen. 23:2); Jacob mourned for Joseph (Gen. 37:34-5); Joseph mourned for Jacob (Gen. 50:1); David mourned for Saul and

Jonathan (2 Sam. 1:12, 17); David wept for Abner (2 Sam. 3:32); David's household mourned for Amnon (2 Sam. 13:36); David wept for Absalom (2 Sam. 18:33); all Judah mourned Josiah (2 Chr. 35:24-5); they mourned over Jairus's daughter (Mark 5:38-9; Luke 8:52); Jesus wept for Lazarus (John 11:35); lamentation over Stephen (Acts 8:2); the widows stood beside him weeping (Acts 9:39); the women mourned for Tammuz (Ezek. 8:14).

C2 Mourning catastrophe

C2a People mourning catastrophe
Elisha wept over what Hazael would do (2 Kgs. 8:11-12); mourning when the Jews heard the edict (Esther 4:3); the priests, the ministers of the Lord, mourn (Joel 1:9); every family will mourn by itself (Zech. 12:12); Jephthah's daughter bewailed her virginity (Judg. 11:37-8); Hezekiah wept because he was due to die (2 Kgs. 20:3); mariners will weep over Tyre (Ezek. 26:17-18); lamentation over Babylon (Rev. 18:9-19).

C2b Mourning due to catastrophe
The roads of Zion are in mourning because no one comes to the feasts (Lam. 1:4); the pastures of the shepherds mourn (Amos 1:2); there will be weeping and gnashing of teeth (Matt. 13:42, 50; 25:30; Luke 13:28); all the tribes of the earth will mourn (Matt. 24:30); her plagues will come, pestilence and mourning and famine (Rev. 18:8).

C3 Mourning oppression
Why do I go mourning, oppressed by the enemy? (Ps. 42:9; 43:2); I saw the tears of the oppressed (Eccles. 4:1); put my tears in your bottle (Ps. 56:8); you fed them with the bread of tears (Ps. 80:5).

C4 Mourning parting
Naomi, Ruth and Orpah wept at parting (Ruth 1:9); David and Jonathan wept at parting (1 Sam. 20:41); Paltiel wept over his wife Michal (2 Sam. 3:16); they wept and embraced Paul and kissed him (Acts 20:37); why weep and break my heart? (Acts 21:13).

C5 Mourning over Israel
Some wept when the foundation of the temple was laid (Ezra 3:12); Nehemiah mourned at the fate of Jerusalem (Neh. 1:4); Jesus wept over Jerusalem (Luke 19:41); we wept when we remembered Zion (Ps. 137:1); Paul's grief over his kinsmen, the Israelites (Rom. 9:2-4); who will mourn for you? (Isa. 51:19).

C6 Mourning in regret
The people wept for meat (Num. 11:4); the people wept for tasty food (Num. 11:10); Samuel mourned over Saul (1 Sam. 15:35; 16:1); the king of Israel wept to see Elisha ill (2 Kgs. 13:14); Peter wept after denying Jesus (Matt. 26:75; Mark 14:72; Luke 22:62); the people will mourn for the calf of Beth-aven (Hos. 10:5); your longing, your mourning, your zeal for me (2 Cor. 7:7); I tell you in tears, many live as enemies of the cross of Christ (Phil. 3:18); Esau found no place for repentance, though he sought it with tears (Heb. 12:17); I wept that no one was worthy to open the book (Rev. 5:4).

D No mourning
Do not enter a house of mourning or lament (Jer. 16:5); do not mourn when your wife dies (Ezek. 24:16); do not mourn the dead (Jer. 22:10); do not mourn or weep (Neh. 8:9-11); do not weep (Luke 7:13; 8:52; Rev. 5:5); daughters of Jerusalem, do not weep for me (Luke 23:28); that you may not grieve like those without hope (1 Thess. 4:13); those who weep should live as if they did not (1 Cor. 7:30); they have not grieved over the ruin of Joseph (Amos 6:6); I sit as a queen and will never see mourning (Rev. 18:7); can the bridegroom's attendants mourn when the bridegroom is with them? (Matt. 9:15); he will wipe away every tear from their eyes (Isa. 25:8; Rev. 21:4); you will weep no more (Isa.

30:19); your days of mourning will be finished (Isa. 60:20); you have delivered my eyes from tears (Ps. 116:8); to comfort all who mourn (Isa. 61:2-3); the voice of weeping will no more be heard in her (Isa. 65:19); there will be no more mourning or crying or pain (Rev. 21:4); you have turned mourning into dancing (Ps. 30:11).

837 Amusement

A Playing
Boys and girls playing in the streets of Jerusalem (Zech. 8:5); they rose up to play [dance] (Exod. 32:6; 1 Cor. 10:7); let the young men make sport (2 Sam. 2:14); will you play with the crocodile as with a bird? (Job 41:5); competitors in the games exercise self-control (1 Cor. 9:25); I box, not as one beating the air (1 Cor. 9:26); I do not run aimlessly (1 Cor. 9:26).

B Making fun
Bring out Samson to amuse us (Judg. 16:25); lest these uncircumcised make fun of me (1 Sam. 31:4); the Chaldeans laugh at every fortress, heaping up earth and taking it (Hab. 1:10); the Chaldeans scoff at kings and laugh at rulers (Hab. 1:10).
JOKE, see 839.
MOCKING, see 851.

838 Tedium
FATIGUE, see 684.

839 Wit
Lot's sons-in-law thought he was joking (Gen. 19:14); a man who deceives as a joke is like a madman (Prov. 26:19); coarse jokes are not fitting (Eph. 5:4).

840 Dullness
SADNESS, see 834.

841 Beauty

A Beauty of God
The Lord will be a beautiful crown (Isa. 28:5); the Lord will display his beauty in Israel (Isa. 44:23); your eyes will see the King in his beauty (Isa. 33:17); to behold the beauty of the Lord (Ps. 27:4); the Branch of the Lord will be beautiful and glorious (Isa. 4:2); you are fairer than the sons of men (Ps. 45:2).

B Beauty of people

B1 Beauty of people in general
Wisdom will put a crown of beauty on your head (Prov. 4:9); a grey head is a crown of beauty (Prov. 16:31); how beautiful are the feet of those who bring good news (Isa. 52:7; Rom. 10:15).

B2 Beauty of women
When you see a beautiful woman among the captives (Deut. 21:11); a beautiful woman without discretion is like a gold ring in a pig's snout (Prov. 11:22); charm is deceitful, beauty is vain (Prov. 31:30); your most beautiful wives and children are mine (1 Kgs. 20:3); a search was made for beautiful young virgins (Esther 2:2); is not her younger sister more beautiful? (Judg. 15:2); the king will desire your beauty (Ps. 45:11); most beautiful of women (S. of S. 1:8); beautiful women: Sarah (Gen. 12:11, 14); Rebekah (Gen. 24:16; 26:7); Rachel (Gen. 29:17); Abigail (1 Sam. 25:3); Bathsheba (2 Sam. 11:2); Tamar (2 Sam. 13:1); Absalom's daughter Tamar (2 Sam. 14:27); Abishag (1 Kgs. 1:4); Queen Vashti (Esther 1:11); Esther (Esther 2:7); Job's daughters (Job 42:15).

B3 Beauty of men
The beauty of young men is their strength (Prov. 20:29); the beauty of old men is their grey hair (Prov. 20:29); Moses was lovely before God (Acts 7:20); when

she saw he was a fair child (Exod. 2:2); Moses was a beautiful child (Heb. 11:23); the king brought youths who were good-looking (Dan. 1:4); how handsome you are! (S. of S. 1:16); handsome men: Joseph (Gen. 39:6); Saul (1 Sam. 9:2); David (1 Sam. 16:12; 17:42); Absalom (2 Sam. 14:25); Adonijah (1 Kgs. 1:6).

C Beauty of nations / cities
How beautiful are your tents, Jacob (Num. 24:5); Mount Zion is beautiful in elevation (Ps. 48:2); Zion, the perfection of beauty (Ps. 50:2); the most beautiful inheritance of the nations (Jer. 3:19); is this the city which was called the perfection of beauty? (Lam. 2:15); Tyre, perfect in beauty (Ezek. 27:3-4); Egypt, whom do you surpass in beauty? (Ezek. 32:19).

D Beauty of things
He has made everything beautiful in its time (Eccles. 3:11); whatever is lovely, think about it (Phil. 4:8); trees pleasing to the sight (Gen. 2:9; 3:6); no tree in God's garden could compare with it in beauty (Ezek. 31:8); the temple was adorned with beautiful stones (Luke 21:5); garments for glory and beauty (Exod. 28:2); whitewashed tombs appear beautiful outwardly (Matt. 23:27).

E No beauty
The fading flower of the beauty of Ephraim (Isa. 28:1, 4); he has no beauty or comeliness that we should desire him (Isa. 53:2); the beauty of the grass perishes (Jas. 1:11).

842 Ugliness
NO BEAUTY, see 841E.

843 Beautification
The women had cosmetics given to them (Esther 2:3); Jezebel painted her eyes and adorned her head (2 Kgs. 9:30); you painted your eyes (Ezek. 23:40); though you enlarge your eyes with paint (Jer. 4:30); he will beautify the afflicted with salvation (Ps. 149:4); in vain you beautify yourself (Jer. 4:30).

844 Ornamentation

A Jewellery
A1 Provision of jewellery
A1a Jewellery in general
The Queen of Sheba brought precious stones (1 Kgs. 10:2; 2 Chr. 9:1); precious stones brought from Ophir (1 Kgs. 10:11; 2 Chr. 9:10); that day will show what materials have been used, gold, silver, precious stones, wood, hay, stubble (1 Cor. 3:12); dealing in spices, precious stones and gold (Ezek. 27:22); cargo of gold, silver and precious stones (Rev. 18:12); Abraham's servant took a gold ring and two gold bracelets (Gen. 24:22); the cutting of stones for setting (Exod. 35:33); the crown contained a precious stone (2 Sam. 12:30; 1 Chr. 20:2); each one gave Job a gold ring (Job 42:11); we will make you ornaments of gold (S. of S. 1:11); I adorned you with ornaments (Ezek. 16:11-13); whoever reads the writing will have a chain of gold for his neck (Dan. 5:7); I put bracelets on your hands and a chain round your neck (Ezek. 16:11-12).

A1b Types of precious stones
Onyx stone in Havilah (Gen. 2:12); two onyx stones engraved with names (Exod. 28:9); its stones are the place of sapphires (Job 28:6); their polishing was like lapis lazuli (Lam. 4:7); the wheels were like gleaming chrysolite (Ezek. 10:9); I will make your gates of crystal (Isa. 54:12); they traded with emeralds, coral and rubies (Ezek. 27:16); ruby, topaz, diamond, beryl, onyx, jasper, lapis lazuli, turquoise, emerald (Ezek. 28:13); I will lay your stones in antimony and sapphires (Isa. 54:11); I will make your battlements of rubies (Isa. 54:12); the

wheels' appearance was like chrysolite [topaz] (Ezek. 1:16); the wall was of jasper (Rev. 21:18); the foundation stones of the city (Rev. 21:19-20).

A2 Value of jewellery
Do not cast pearls before swine (Matt. 7:6); wisdom is above pearls (Job 28:18); wisdom cannot be purchased with onyx or sapphire (Job 28:16); the topaz of Ethiopia cannot equal wisdom (Job 28:19); with an iron pen with a diamond point (Jer. 17:1); the kingdom of heaven is like a merchant seeking fine pearls (Matt. 13:45-6); the 12 gates were 12 pearls (Rev. 21:21).

A3 Wearing jewellery
Saul put gold ornaments on you (2 Sam. 1:24); as a bride adorns herself with jewels (Isa. 61:10); the woman was adorned with gold, jewels and pearls (Rev. 17:4); she who was adorned with gold and precious stone and pearls (Rev. 18:16); you bathed, painted your eyes and put on ornaments (Ezek. 23:40); she would adorn herself with rings and jewellery and follow her lovers (Hos. 2:13); let your adorning not be gold jewels (1 Pet. 3:3); Aaron used their gold earrings to make the calf (Exod. 32:2); Gideon used gold earrings to make an ephod (Judg. 8:24-7); can a maid forget her ornaments? (Jer. 2:32); your rounded thighs are like jewels (S. of S. 7:1).

A4 Removing jewellery
Jacob buried the earrings (Gen. 35:4); the Israelites took off their ornaments at Mount Horeb (Exod. 33:4-6); I took the bracelet from his arm (2 Sam. 1:10); the Lord will take away all the ornaments (Isa. 3:18-21); your lovers will take away your jewellery (Ezek. 16:39).

A5 Jewellery and God
They brought brooches, earrings, signet rings and bracelets of gold to the Lord as an offering (Exod. 35:22); jewellery from the war as an offering (Num. 31:50-4); the names of the sons of Israel were engraved on two onyx stones (Exod. 39:6-7, 10-14); four rows of stones on the breastpiece with the names of the sons of Israel (Exod. 28:17-21); a pavement of sapphire (Exod. 24:10); something like a sapphire resembling a throne (Ezek. 10:1); above the platform was a throne like sapphire [lapis lazuli] (Ezek. 1:26); the one on the throne was like a jasper and a sardius (Rev. 4:3); a rainbow like an emerald (Rev. 4:3); the temple adorned with precious stones (2 Chr. 3:6); the new Jerusalem shone like a precious stone, like jasper (Rev. 21:11).

B Embroidery
To do all the work of an embroiderer (Exod. 35:35); cherubim embroidered on the veil (2 Chr. 3:14); I clothed you with embroidered cloth (Ezek. 16:10); they traded with embroidered work and fine linen (Ezek. 27:16); trading in fine clothes of blue and embroidered work (Ezek. 27:24); your sail was of fine embroidered linen from Egypt (Ezek. 27:7).

C Internal adornment
Your adornment should not be external but internal (1 Pet. 3:3-4); women should not adorn themselves with gold or pearls (1 Tim. 2:9); wisdom is more precious than jewels (Prov. 3:15; 8:11); lips of knowledge are more precious than gold or jewels (Prov. 20:15); to give to those who mourn a garland instead of ashes (Isa. 61:3); they should adorn the doctrine (Titus 2:10); the holy women who hoped in God adorned themselves like that (1 Pet. 3:5); new Jerusalem made ready as a bride adorned for her husband (Rev. 21:2).

845 Blemish
DEFECT, see 647.

846 Good taste

Our unpresentable parts are treated with greater decorum (1 Cor. 12:23-4).

847 Bad taste

BADNESS, see 645.

848 Fashion

ORNAMENTS, see 844.

849 Ridiculousness

RIDICULE, see 851.

850 Affectation

DECEPTION, see 542.

851 Ridicule

DESPISING, see 922.

A About mocking

He who mocks the poor insults his Maker (Prov. 17:5); fools mock at guilt (Prov. 14:9); the innocent mock the wicked (Job 22:19); the eye that mocks parents will be plucked out (Prov. 30:17); the ostrich laughs at horse and rider (Job 39:18).

B Mocking and God

The words of Sennacherib, sent to mock the living God (Isa. 37:17); God is not mocked (Gal. 6:7); the Lord laughs at the wicked (Ps. 2:4; 37:13; 59:8); he scoffs at the scoffers (Prov. 3:34); when Jesus said the girl was not dead they laughed at him (Matt. 9:24; Mark 5:40; Luke 8:53); they will mock the Son of Man (Matt. 20:19; Mark 10:34; Luke 18:32); they ridiculed and mocked him (Matt. 27:29, 31; Mark 15:20; Luke 22:63); the chief priests mocked him (Matt. 27:41; Mark 15:31); Herod and his soldiers mocked him (Luke 23:11); the soldiers mocked him (Luke 23:36); when they heard of the resurrection, some mocked (Acts 17:32).

C Mocking people

In the last days there will be scoffers (2 Pet. 3:3; Jude 18); hear the word of the Lord, you scoffers (Isa. 28:14); when the scoffer is punished the simple becomes wise (Prov. 21:11); drive out a scoffer and strife will go out (Prov. 22:10); blessed is the man who does not sit in the seat of scoffers (Ps. 1:1); behold, you scoffers, and marvel, and perish (Acts 13:41); the Lord scoffs at the scoffers (Prov. 3:34); the scoffer will cease (Isa. 29:20); lest we become a laughing-stock (Gen. 38:23); you have made a mockery of me (Num. 22:29); I am a joke to my friends (Job 12:4); our enemies mocked us (Neh. 2:19); we are mocked by those around us (Ps. 79:4); all who see me mock me (Ps. 22:7); the word of the Lord has become a reproach and derision for me (Jer. 20:8); Ishmael mocked Isaac (Gen. 21:9); Elijah mocked the prophets of Baal (1 Kgs. 18:27); the people of Ephraim mocked the couriers from Judah (2 Chr. 30:10); Sanballat mocked the Jews (Neh. 4:1); all who see it begin to mock him (Luke 14:29); youths mocked Elisha (2 Kgs. 2:23); they mocked at Pentecost (Acts 2:13); some were mocked and scourged (Heb. 11:36); how the king of Israel honoured himself today! (2 Sam. 6:20).

MAKING FUN, see 837B.

852 Hope

A About hope

There is hope for all who are joined to the living (Eccles. 9:4); love hopes all things (1 Cor. 13:7); faith, hope and love remain (1 Cor. 13:13); hope that is seen is not hope (Rom. 8:24-5); hope deferred makes the heart sick (Prov. 13:12); character produces hope (Rom. 5:4);

my flesh will dwell in hope (Acts 2:26); hope does not disappoint us (Rom. 5:5); the creation was subjected to futility in hope (Rom. 8:20); the ploughman should plough in hope and the thresher thresh in hope (1 Cor. 9:10); on God we have set our hope that he will deliver us (2 Cor. 1:10); since we have such a hope we are very bold (2 Cor. 3:12); charge the rich not to set their hopes on uncertain riches (1 Tim. 6:17); faith is the assurance of things hoped for (Heb. 11:1).

B The hope of Israel

Israel, hope in the Lord (Ps. 131:3); you hope of Israel! (Jer. 14:8); O Lord, the hope of Israel (Jer. 17:13); this I call to mind and therefore have hope (Lam. 3:21); in his word I hope (Ps. 130:5); for the hope of Israel I am chained (Acts 28:20); the valley of Achor will be a door of hope (Hos. 2:15); Moses accuses you, on whom you set your hope (John 5:45); I am on trial for the hope and resurrection of the dead (Acts 23:6); having a hope in God that there will be a resurrection (Acts 24:15); I stand on trial for hope in the promise God made to our fathers (Acts 26:6-7); in hope Abraham believed against hope (Rom. 4:18).

C Hope in Christ

C1 The hope of the gospel

Christ in you, the hope of glory (Col. 1:27); Christ Jesus, our hope (1 Tim. 1:1); in his name will the Gentiles hope (Matt. 12:21; Rom. 15:12); God gave us good hope through grace (2 Thess. 2:16); we have our hope set on the living God (1 Tim. 4:10); your faith and hope are in God (1 Pet. 1:21); not shifting from the hope of the gospel (Col. 1:23); in hope of eternal life (Titus 1:2); in hope we were saved (Rom. 8:24); by his mercy we have been born anew to a living hope (1 Pet. 1:3); as a helmet, the hope of salvation (1 Thess. 5:8); ready to make a defence for the hope that is in you (1 Pet. 3:15); we rejoice in hope of the glory of God (Rom. 5:2); that we might seize the hope set before us (Heb. 6:18); everyone who has this hope in him purifies himself as he is pure (1 John 3:3); the God of hope fill you with joy and peace so that you may overflow with hope (Rom. 15:13); that you might know what is the hope of his calling (Eph. 1:18); this hope is an anchor of the soul (Heb. 6:19); a better hope through which we draw near to God (Heb. 7:19); a true widow has fixed her hope on God (1 Tim. 5:5); charge the rich to set their hopes on God (1 Tim. 6:17); if for this life only we have hope, we are pitiable (1 Cor. 15:19).

C2 Steadfast in hope

Let us hold fast the confession of our hope without wavering (Heb. 10:23); if we hold fast our boast in our hope firm to the end (Heb. 3:6); realize the full assurance of hope until the end (Heb. 6:11); your steadfastness of hope (1 Thess. 1:3).

853 Hopelessness

My days end without hope (Job 7:6); the hope of the wicked perishes (Prov. 10:28); when a wicked man dies his hope perishes (Prov. 11:7); what is the hope of the godless when he is cut off? (Job 27:8); that you may not grieve like others without hope (1 Thess. 4:13); having no hope and without God in the world (Eph. 2:12); all hope of our being saved was abandoned (Acts 27:20); we despaired of life itself (2 Cor. 1:8); perplexed but not despairing (2 Cor. 4:8); there is more hope for a fool than for a man wise in his own eyes (Prov. 26:12); there is more hope for a fool than for a man hasty in his words (Prov. 29:20).

854 Fear

TREMBLING, see 318B.

A Fear in general

A1 Fear will come
Men will faint with fear (Luke 21:26); conflicts without and fears within (2 Cor. 7:5); they will eat bread by weight and with anxiety (Ezek. 4:16); all Israel will hear and will be afraid (Deut. 13:11); Pashhur renamed Terror on every side (Jer. 20:3); terror on every side (Ps. 31:13; Jer. 6:25; Lam. 2:22); there will be terrors and great signs from heaven (Luke 21:11); in the evening there is terror (Isa. 17:14); he who flees from the terror will fall into the pit (Isa. 24:18; Jer. 48:44).

A2 Fear is due
He who does evil has reason to fear (Rom. 13:3-4); the people will hear and be afraid and not do such a thing (Deut. 19:20); justice done is terror to evildoers (Prov. 21:15); what the wicked fears will come on him (Prov. 10:24); a lion has roared! who will not fear? (Amos 3:8); rebuke them in the presence of all that the rest may fear (1 Tim. 5:20).

A3 People fearing
They were afraid when they heard that they were Romans (Acts 16:38); the commander was afraid because he had bound a Roman citizen (Acts 22:29); when the crowds saw it they were afraid (Matt. 9:8); why are you afraid? (Mark 4:40); they were afraid and amazed (Luke 8:25); they were terrified and bowed their faces to the ground (Luke 24:5); the soldiers were afraid at the crucifixion (Matt. 27:54); fear fell on those who saw the witnesses come to life (Rev. 11:11); I was with you in weakness and fear (1 Cor. 2:3); see what fear, what longing, what zeal this godly sorrow has produced (2 Cor. 7:11); fear has to do with punishment (1 John 4:18).

A4 Do not fear
Do not be afraid (Matt. 17:7; 24:6; 28:5, 10; Luke 1:13, 30; 2:10; 5:10; 12:32; John 14:27; Rev. 1:17); do not be afraid of what you have heard (2 Kgs. 19:6; Isa. 37:6); rulers are not a cause of fear for good conduct (Rom. 13:3); you are Sarah's children if you do good and fear nothing (1 Pet. 3:6); do not fear what they fear (Isa. 8:12); do not fear their fear (1 Pet. 3:14); do not fear when you hear of wars (Mark 13:7; Luke 21:9); do not fear what you will soon suffer (Rev. 2:10); do not fear because God will undertake (Gen. 15:1; 21:17; 46:3; Exod. 14:13; Judg. 6:23; 2 Kgs. 6:16; 2 Chr. 32:7; Prov. 3:25-6; Acts 27:24); do not be afraid for I am with you (Gen. 26:24; Isa. 41:10; 43:5; Jer. 42:11; 46:28; Acts 18:9-10); do not fear for I will help you (Isa. 41:13-14); do not be afraid, only believe (Mark 5:36; Luke 8:50).

B Fear of God

B1 The fear of the Lord
The fear of the Lord is wisdom (Job 28:28); the fear of the Lord is the beginning of wisdom (Ps. 111:10; Prov. 9:10); fear of the Lord is the beginning of knowledge (Prov. 1:7); the fear of the Lord lengthens life (Prov. 10:27); the fear of the Lord is a fountain of life (Prov. 14:27); in the fear of the Lord there is security (Prov. 14:26); better a little with the fear of the Lord (Prov. 15:16); blessed are those who fear the Lord (Ps. 112:1; 128:1); to fear the Lord is to hate evil (Prov. 8:13); the fear of the Lord will keep you from sinning (Exod. 20:20); the fear of the Lord is clean (Ps. 19:9); is not the fear of the Lord your confidence? (Job 4:6); obey your masters in singleness of heart, fearing the Lord (Col. 3:22); I will teach you the fear of the Lord (Ps. 34:11).

B2 God is to be feared
The Lord is to be feared (Ps. 47:2); he is to be feared above all gods (1 Chr. 16:25; Ps. 96:4); who would not fear you? (Jer. 10:7); to fear this great and awesome name (Deut. 28:58); it is a terrifying thing to fall into the hands of the living God (Heb. 10:31); my name is feared among the nations (Mal. 1:14).

B3 Fear God!
Fear God (Lev. 19:14; Deut. 8:6; Eccles. 5:7; 1 Pet. 2:17; Rev. 14:7); fear the Lord (Deut. 6:13; Josh. 4:24; 1 Sam. 12:14; 2 Kgs. 17:36; Ps. 34:9; Prov. 3:7); serve the Lord with fear (Ps. 2:11); the Lord is the one you are to fear (Isa. 8:13); fear him who can destroy body and soul in hell (Matt. 10:28); fear him who has authority to cast into hell (Luke 12:5); tremble before him, all the earth (1 Chr. 16:30; Ps. 114:7); let all the ends of the earth fear him (Ps. 67:7); work out your own salvation with fear and trembling (Phil. 2:12); perfecting holiness in the fear of God (2 Cor. 7:1); since you call on an impartial Father, live your lives in fear (1 Pet. 1:17); let us fear lest any fail to enter his rest (Heb. 4:1); fear, lest God not spare you (Rom. 11:20-1); let us offer acceptable worship with reverence and awe (Heb. 12:28).

B4 People fearing God
I will put the fear of me in their hearts (Jer. 32:40); God has done it so that man should fear him (Eccles. 3:14); the one who fears God is acceptable to him (Acts 10:35); unite my heart to fear your name (Ps. 86:11); now I know that you fear God (Gen. 22:12); I fear God (Gen. 42:18); the midwives feared God (Exod. 1:17); Obadiah feared the Lord (1 Kgs. 18:3); I have feared the Lord from my youth (1 Kgs. 18:12); the people feared the Lord and Samuel (1 Sam. 12:18); I fear the Lord God of heaven (Jonah 1:9); those who feared the Lord talked with one another (Mal. 3:16); come and hear, all you who fear God (Ps. 66:16); you who you who fear the Lord, trust in the Lord (Ps. 115:11); you who fear the Lord, praise him (Ps. 22:23); you who fear him, small and great (Rev. 19:5); who among you fears the Lord? (Isa. 50:10); I am a companion of all who fear you (Ps. 119:63); the time for rewarding those who fear your name (Rev. 11:18); fear came upon everyone (Acts 2:43); the church went on in the fear of the Lord (Acts 9:31); they feared the Lord and served their own gods (2 Kgs. 17:33); their fear of me is a commandment of men learned by rote (Isa. 29:13).

B5 Results of the fear of God
A woman who fears the Lord is to be praised (Prov. 31:30); knowing the fear of the Lord, we persuade men (2 Cor. 5:11); fear fell on all and the name of the Lord Jesus was magnified (Acts 19:17); the Lord takes pleasure in all who fear him (Ps. 147:11); the eye of the Lord is on those who fear him (Ps. 33:18); the angel of the Lord camps round those who fear him (Ps. 34:7); the secret of the Lord is with those who fear him (Ps. 25:14); you have given me the inheritance of those who fear your name (Ps. 61:5); so great is his lovingkindness to those who fear him (Ps. 103:11); the goodness you have stored up for those who fear you (Ps. 31:19); he fulfils the desire of all who fear him (Ps. 145:19); by the fear of the Lord a man avoids evil (Prov. 16:6); God will instruct the one who fears him (Ps. 25:12); his mercy is on those who fear him (Luke 1:50).

B6 Frightened of God
The terrors of God are arrayed against me (Job 6:4); at the day of the Lord men will be terrified (Isa. 13:6-8); enter the rock from the terror of the Lord (Isa. 2:10); do not be a terror to me (Jer. 17:17); if we sin wilfully there is a fearful expectation of judgement (Heb. 10:27); the terror of God fell on the towns round about (Gen. 35:5; 2 Chr. 14:14); the fear of the Lord fell on the kingdoms around (2 Chr. 17:10; 20:29); the rest were terrified and gave glory to the God of heaven (Rev. 11:13); Adam was afraid because he was naked (Gen. 3:10); terror and darkness fell on Abraham (Gen. 15:12); Sarah was afraid because she had laughed (Gen. 18:15);

Moses was afraid to look at God (Exod. 3:6); Moses was full of fear and trembling (Heb. 12:21); stop terrifying me with your dread (Job 13:21); David was afraid of the Lord that day (2 Sam. 6:9; 1 Chr. 13:12); the kings were panic-stricken (Ps. 48:5-6); the sailors feared the Lord (Jonah 1:16); the shepherds were frightened (Luke 2:9); fear with Ananias and Sapphira died (Acts 5:5, 11).

B7 Fearing God's word
I am afraid of your judgements (Ps. 119:120); I will look to the one who trembles at my word (Isa. 66:2); the king was not afraid of the scroll (Jer. 36:24).

B8 No fear of God
There is no fear of God here (Gen. 20:11); Amalek did not fear God (Deut. 25:18); at first the Samaritans did not fear the Lord (2 Kgs. 17:25); there is no fear of God before their eyes (Ps. 36:1; Rom. 3:18); you still do not fear the Lord (Exod. 9:30); you do away with the fear of God (Job 15:4); do you not fear God? (Luke 23:40); there was a judge who did not fear God (Luke 18:2); we do not fear the Lord, and what could a king do for us? (Hos. 10:3).

C Fear of Christ
May they fear you while the sun endures (Ps. 72:5); the chief priests were afraid of Jesus (Mark 11:18); they were afraid when the widow's son was raised (Luke 7:16); they were afraid when they saw the demoniac healed (Mark 5:15; Luke 8:35, 37); they were afraid when they saw the paralytic walking (Luke 5:26); the woman who was healed was afraid (Mark 5:33); Pilate was the more afraid (John 19:8); be subject to one another in the fear of Christ (Eph. 5:21); the disciples were afraid: to ask (Luke 9:45); when Jesus stilled the wind and sea (Mark 4:41); at the transfiguration (Matt. 17:6; Mark 9:6); when Jesus appeared (Luke 24:37); seeing Jesus walking on the sea (Matt. 14:26; Mark 6:50; John 6:19).

D Fear of people
D1 The fear of man
The fear of man brings a snare (Prov. 29:25); who are you to be afraid of mortal man? (Isa. 51:12); if you do evil, be afraid (Rom. 13:4); obey your masters in fear and trembling (Eph. 6:5).

D2 Fear of men
The Egyptians were in dread of the Israelites (Exod. 1:12; Ps. 105:38); the Israelites were afraid of the Egyptians (Exod. 14:10); fear of the Jews fell on them (Esther 8:17); for fear of the Pharisees they did not confess their faith in Christ (John 12:42); Gideon was afraid of his family (Judg. 6:27); Saul was afraid of the people (1 Sam. 15:24); Herod was afraid of the people (Matt. 14:5); the Jews feared the people, who said John was a prophet (Matt. 21:26; Mark 11:32); they wanted to arrest Jesus but were afraid of the people (Matt. 21:46; Mark 12:12; Luke 20:19; 22:2); they brought the apostles out without force because they feared the people (Acts 5:26); whoever is afraid may go home (Deut. 20:8; Judg. 7:3); if you are afraid to attack, go down into the camp (Judg. 7:10); he was hired so that I might be frightened (Neh. 6:13); Peter was afraid of the circumcision party (Gal. 2:12); no one spoke openly of him for fear of the Jews (John 7:13); his parents were afraid of the Jews (John 9:22); a secret disciple for fear of the Jews (John 19:38); doors shut for fear of the Jews (John 20:19).

D3 Fear of individuals
Jacob was afraid of Laban (Gen. 31:31); Jacob was afraid of Esau (Gen. 32:7); Joseph's brothers were afraid of him (Gen. 45:3); Samuel was afraid to tell Eli (1 Sam. 3:15); people feared the Lord and Samuel (1 Sam. 12:18); Saul was afraid of David (1 Sam. 18:12); the Israelites were afraid of Goliath (1 Sam. 17:11); David was afraid of Achish (1 Sam. 21:12); the fear of David fell on all lands (1 Chr. 14:17); Ish-bosheth was afraid of Abner (2

Sam. 3:11); Adonijah was afraid of King Solomon (1 Kgs. 1:51); they were afraid of Jehu (2 Kgs. 10:4); Tobiah sent letters to frighten me (Neh. 6:19); Haman was terrified before the king and queen (Esther 7:6); the people were afraid of Mordecai (Esther 9:3); all peoples, nations and languages feared Nebuchadnezzar (Dan. 5:19); Herod feared John (Mark 6:20); the disciples were afraid of Paul (Acts 9:26).

D4 Do not fear men
Do not be afraid of any man (Deut. 1:17); do not fear the prophet who speaks presumptuously (Deut. 18:22); do not be scared by your opponents (Phil. 1:28); do not be afraid of the people of the land (Num. 14:9; Deut. 1:29; Josh. 10:8); do not be afraid of the Chaldeans (2 Kgs. 25:24); do not be afraid of fellow Israelites (2 Kgs. 1:15; Jer. 1:8; Ezek. 2:6); fear neither them nor their words (Ezek. 2:6); do not be afraid of your enemies (Deut. 20:1; Neh. 4:14); do not be afraid of them (Matt. 10:26); do not fear those who kill the body (Matt. 10:28; Luke 12:4).

E Fear of things
The fear of death (Heb. 2:15); the terrors of death are on me (Ps. 55:4); the terrors of Sheol came on me (Ps. 116:3); the diseases of Egypt which you feared (Deut. 28:60); I am afraid of all my sufferings (Job 9:28); you have feared the sword so I will bring the sword on you (Ezek. 11:8); I had a dream which made me fearful (Dan. 4:5); my thoughts alarmed me and my colour changed (Dan. 7:28); the inhabitants of Samaria fear for the calf of Beth-aven (Hos. 10:5); on some have mercy with fear (Jude 23); the kings will stand at a distance in fear of her torment (Rev. 18:10); the merchants will stand at a distance in fear of her torment (Rev. 18:15).

F Horror
I sat appalled among them for seven days (Ezek. 3:15); everyone who passes by Babylon will be horrified (Jer. 50:13); the land was appalled at the sound of its roaring (Ezek. 19:7); a cup of horror and desolation (Ezek. 23:33); all who know you are appalled at you (Ezek. 28:19); the inhabitants of the coastlands are appalled at you (Ezek. 27:35); I will make many peoples appalled at you (Ezek. 32:10); I was appalled at the vision and did not understand it (Dan. 8:27); I will make you a terror to yourself and your friends (Jer. 20:4); I will make them a horror and a hissing (Jer. 25:9); to make Jerusalem a horror, a hissing and a curse (Jer. 25:18); the land has become a horror and a curse (Jer. 44:22); Babylon will become a horror and a hissing (Jer. 51:37); Babylon has become an object of horror among the nations (Jer. 51:41); Bozrah will become a horror (Jer. 49:13); Edom will become a horror (Jer. 49:17); Moab has become a horror to all around (Jer. 48:39).

855 Courage
A Boldness
A1 Be courageous!
Be strong and courageous (Deut. 31:6-7; Josh. 1:6-9; 2 Sam. 10:12; 13:28; 1 Chr. 22:13; 2 Chr. 32:7; Dan. 10:19); be strong and take courage (Ps. 27:14; 31:24); be of good courage and act (Ezra 10:4); quit you like men! (1 Sam. 4:9; 1 Cor. 16:13); let us not lose heart (Gal. 6:9); do not lose heart at my tribulations (Eph. 3:13).

A2 Being strong
The righteous are bold as a lion (Prov. 28:1); through God we will do valiantly (Ps. 60:12); we do not lose heart (2 Cor. 4:1, 16); they spoke the word of God boldly (Acts 4:31); they saw the boldness of Peter and John (Acts 4:13); they spoke boldly for the Lord (Acts 14:3); we have boldness and access in confidence

through our faith in him (Eph. 3:12); we had courage in our God to declare the gospel (1 Thess. 2:2).

B Encouraging

B1 God encouraging
God gives encouragement (Rom. 15:5); the Lord caused the king of Assyria to encourage them (Ezra 6:22); that through endurance and the encouragement of the scriptures we might have hope (Rom. 15:4); that by two unchangeable things we might have strong encouragement (Heb. 6:18).

B2 People encouraging
Encourage the faint-hearted (1 Thess. 5:14); encourage one another (1 Thess. 5:11); encourage one another daily (Heb. 3:13); encourage and reprove with all authority (Titus 2:15); be of good courage, for I believe God (Acts 27:25); Jonathan strengthened David's hand in God (1 Sam. 23:16); Barnabas – 'son of encouragement' (Acts 4:36); Barnabas encouraged them to go on (Acts 11:23); they encouraged the disciples to continue in the faith (Acts 14:22); they rejoiced at the encouragement of the letter (Acts 15:31-2); they were all encouraged and took food (Acts 27:36); that we may be mutually encouraged by each other's faith (Rom. 1:12); that their hearts might be encouraged (Col. 2:2); I have sent Tychicus so he may encourage you (Col. 4:8); these fellowworkers from the circumcision have been an encouragement to me (Col. 4:11); we exhorted and encouraged you (1 Thess. 2:11); the brethren have been encouraged to speak the word (Phil. 1:14); when Paul saw the believers he took courage (Acts 28:15); if there is any encouragement in Christ (Phil. 2:1).

B3 Not discouraged
He will not falter or be discouraged (Isa. 42:4); Joseph of Arimathea took courage and asked Pilate for the body of Jesus (Mark 15:43); they ought always to pray and not to lose heart (Luke 18:1); we are always of good courage (2 Cor. 5:6); we are of good courage (2 Cor. 5:8).

C Not fearing
I will not be afraid (Ps. 56:4, 11; Heb. 13:6); I will trust and not be afraid (Isa. 12:2); I will not be afraid of tens of thousands (Ps. 3:6); though a host camp against me, I will not fear (Ps. 27:3); I will fear no evil (Ps. 23:4); the Lord is my light, whom shall I fear? (Ps. 27:1); I will not fear, what can man do to me? (Ps. 118:6); when I am afraid I will put my trust in you (Ps. 56:3); he delivered me from all my fears (Ps. 34:4); we are not those who shrink back (Heb. 10:38-9); we will not fear though the earth change (Ps. 46:2); you will not fear the terror by night (Ps. 91:5); that we might serve him without fear (Luke 1:74); you have not received a spirit of slavery leading to fear (Rom. 8:15); fear will not come near you (Isa. 54:14); perfect love casts out fear (1 John 4:18); the brethren have courage to speak the word of God without fear (Phil. 1:14); they were not afraid of the king's edict (Heb. 11:23); Moses did not fear the anger of the king (Heb. 11:27); God has not given us a spirit of timidity (2 Tim. 1:7).
DO NOT FEAR, see 854A4.

856 Cowardice
No one dared ask him any more questions (Mark 12:34; Luke 20:40); no one dared ask, 'Who are you?' (John 21:12); Moses trembled and did not dare to look (Acts 7:32); encourage the faint-hearted (1 Thess. 5:14); consider him, lest you grow weary and lose heart (Heb. 12:3); do not lose heart when you are reproved by him (Heb. 12:5); cowards will go to the lake of fire (Rev. 21:8); why are you cowardly, men of little faith? (Matt.

8:26); do not be faint-hearted (Deut. 20:3); no one dared join them (Acts 5:13).

857 Rashness
It is folly to give an answer before hearing (Prov. 18:13); he who pleads his case first seems right until the other examines him (Prov. 18:17); there is more hope for a fool than for one hasty in his words (Prov. 29:20); every one who is hasty comes to poverty (Prov. 21:5); do not be hasty in word before God (Eccles. 5:2); do not lay hands on anyone hastily (1 Tim. 5:22); you ought to be calm and do nothing rash (Acts 19:36); men will be reckless (2 Tim. 3:4); Reuben, reckless as water (Gen. 49:4); the heart of the hasty will discern the truth (Isa. 32:4); a fool is careless (Prov. 14:16).
HASTE, see 680.

858 Caution
A wise man is cautious (Prov. 14:16).
CAREFUL, see 457.

859 Desire

A Desires in general

A1 About desires
Desire fulfilled is a tree of life (Prov. 13:12); desire fulfilled is sweet to the soul (Prov. 13:19); whatever my eyes desired I did not refuse them (Eccles. 2:10); the desire of the sluggard kills him (Prov. 21:25-6); better is the sight of the eyes than the wandering of desire (Eccles. 6:9).

A2 Right desires
Who is the man who desires life? (Ps. 34:12); I have earnestly desired to eat this passover with you (Luke 22:15); I have longed to come to you (Rom. 15:23); we eagerly desired to see you (1 Thess. 3:6); I long to see you (Rom. 1:11; 2 Tim. 1:4); longing to see us as we long to see you (1 Thess. 3:6); I wish you all spoke in tongues, but even more that you prophesied (1 Cor. 14:5); we long to put on our heavenly dwelling (2 Cor. 5:2); your longing, your mourning, your zeal for me (2 Cor. 7:7); a year ago you began not only to do this but to desire it (2 Cor. 8:10); that you may complete what you were ready to desire (2 Cor. 8:11); be it done for you as you desire (Matt. 15:28); my heart's desire for Israel is that they be saved (Rom. 10:1).

A3 Desires for evil

A3a Evil desires in general
The soul of the wicked desires evil (Prov. 21:10); the desires for other things choke the word (Mark 4:19); do not let sin reign, to obey its lusts (Rom. 6:12); walk by the Spirit and you will not fulfil the desires of the flesh (Gal. 5:16-17); put off the old man, corrupt through deceitful lusts (Eph. 4:22); foolish and hurtful desires which plunge men into ruin and destruction (1 Tim. 6:9); teaching us to renounce worldly passions (Titus 2:12); you desire and do not have (Jas. 4:2); sinful desires were awakened by the law (Rom. 7:5); they entice by fleshly desires (2 Pet. 2:18); flee youthful passions (2 Tim. 2:22); one is tempted when enticed by his own desire (Jas. 1:14); when desire has conceived it gives birth to sin (Jas. 1:15); sin's desire is for you (Gen. 4:7).

A3b Lusts
Fleshly lusts war against the soul (1 Pet. 2:11); the corruption that is in the world through lust (2 Pet. 1:4); those who are Christ's have crucified the flesh with its passions and desires (Gal. 5:24); we formerly followed the lusts of our flesh (Eph. 2:3); the lust of the flesh and the lust of the eyes (1 John 2:16); we should not lust for evil things as they did (1 Cor. 10:6); once we were in slavery to various lusts (Titus 3:3); you ask wrongly, to

spend it on your lusts (Jas. 4:3); do not be conformed
to the lusts of your former ignorance (1 Pet. 1:14); living
the rest of the time in the flesh not for human lusts
(1 Pet. 4:2); let the time past suffice for sensuality, lusts,
drunkenness (1 Pet. 4:3); those who indulge the flesh in
lusts (2 Pet. 2:10); scoffers following their own lusts
(2 Pet. 3:3); following their own lusts (Jude 16; 18); the
world and its lusts are passing away (1 John 2:17).

A3c Specific evil desires
An evil and adulterous generation seeks for a sign
(Matt. 12:39); Herod wanted to put John to death
(Matt. 14:5); by craving for money some have
wandered from the faith (1 Tim. 6:10); she saw the tree
was desirable to make one wise (Gen. 3:6).

A4 Greed
Greed, which is idolatry (Col. 3:5); everyone is greedy
for gain (Jer. 6:13); greed should not even be named
(Eph. 5:3); consider your members dead to greed (Col.
3:5); Gentiles practice impurity with greed (Eph. 4:19);
filled with greed (Rom. 1:29); deacons must not be
greedy for gain (1 Tim. 3:8); in their greed they will
exploit you with false words (2 Pet. 2:3); they have
hearts trained in greed (2 Pet. 2:14); their god is the
belly (Phil. 3:19); Kibroth-hattaavah – graves of greed
(Num. 11:34); why look with greedy eye at the
sacrifices? (1 Sam. 2:29); we never came with a pretext
for greed (1 Thess. 2:5).

A5 Coveting
Do not covet (Exod. 20:17; Deut. 5:21; Rom. 7:7; 13:9);
beware of all covetousness (Luke 12:15); from the heart
come covetings (Mark 7:22); if riches increase, do not
set your heart on them (Ps. 62:10); I would have not
have known coveting except for the law (Rom. 7:7-8);
the covetous will not inherit the kingdom (1 Cor. 6:10;
Eph. 5:5); do not associate with a 'brother' who is
covetous (1 Cor. 5:11); Achan coveted things (Josh.
7:21); I have not coveted any one's silver, gold or
clothes (Acts 20:33); no one will covet your land when
you go to the feast (Exod. 34:24).

B Desires and God
B1 God's desires
You desire truth in the inward being (Ps. 51:6); I desire
mercy and not sacrifice (Hos. 6:6; Matt. 9:13; 12:7); the
desires of the Spirit are against the flesh (Gal. 5:17);
sacrifice and offering you did not desire (Ps. 40:6).

B2 Christ's desires
I desire that they may be with me (John 17:24); Jesus
said, 'I thirst' (John 19:28); I was thirsty and you gave
me drink (Matt. 25:35); I was hungry and you gave me
food (Matt. 25:35).

B3 Desire for God
My soul thirsts for God (Ps. 42:2; 63:1; 143:6); my soul
longs for you (Ps. 42:1); there is nothing on earth that I
desire but you (Ps. 73:25); you will long to see one of
the days of the Son of man (Luke 17:22); I desire to
depart and be with Christ (Phil. 1:23).

B4 Desires satisfied in God
The Lord will fulfil all my desires (2 Sam. 23:5); he will
give you the desires of your heart (Ps. 37:4); may he
grant your heart's desire! (Ps. 20:4); you have given
him his heart's desire (Ps. 21:2); you satisfy the desires
of every living thing (Ps. 145:16); he fulfils the desire of
all who fear him (Ps. 145:19); come, every one who
thirsts (Isa. 55:1); if any one thirsts, let him come to me
and drink (John 7:37); to him who thirsts I will give the
water of life without cost (Rev. 21:6); whoever is thirsty,
let him come (Rev. 22:17); whoever drinks the water I
give will never thirst again (John 4:14); those who
hunger and thirst after righteousness will be satisfied
(Matt. 5:6); blessed are you who hunger now, for you
will be satisfied (Luke 6:21); he who comes to me will

not hunger and he who believes in me will not thirst
(John 6:35); he has filled the hungry with good things
(Luke 1:53); earnestly desire spiritual gifts (1 Cor. 12:31;
14:1).

C Physical desires
C1 Hunger
C1a Hungering
A worker's appetite works for him (Prov. 16:26); to a
hungry man the bitter is sweet (Prov. 27:7); a thief is
not despised if he steals to satisfy his hunger (Prov.
6:30); these men serve their own stomach (Rom. 16:18);
those who are full now will be hungry (Luke 6:25); God
caused you to hunger (Deut. 8:3); when they are
hungry they will curse the king and their God (Isa.
8:21); the Lord will not let the righteous go hungry
(Prov. 10:3); there he lets the hungry dwell (Ps. 107:36);
my servants will eat but you will be hungry (Isa. 65:13);
if your enemy is hungry, give him food (Prov. 25:21;
Rom. 12:20); if you pour yourself out for the hungry
(Isa. 58:10); one is hungry and another is drunk (1 Cor.
11:21); if anyone is hungry let him eat at home (1 Cor.
11:34); silver and gold cannot satisfy their appetite
(Ezek. 7:19); they will hunger no more and thirst no
more (Rev. 7:16).

C1b Hungry people
Esau was famished (Gen. 25:29-30); the people were
hungry and thirsty in the wilderness (2 Sam. 17:29);
after Jesus fasted he was hungry (Matt. 4:2; Luke 4:2);
on his way to Jerusalem he was hungry (Matt. 21:18;
Mark 11:12); Jesus did not want to send the crowd
home hungry (Matt. 15:32; Mark 8:3); Paul had known
hunger and thirst, often without food (2 Cor. 11:27);
Peter was hungry (Acts 10:10); his disciples were
hungry and plucked ears of grain (Matt. 12:1); he would
gladly have filled his belly with the pods the pigs ate
(Luke 15:16-17); Lazarus longed to be fed with what fell
from the rich man's table (Luke 16:21); if I were hungry
I would not tell you (Ps. 50:12); I was hungry and you
gave me food (Matt. 25:35); I have learned the secret of
being filled and going hungry (Phil. 4:12); we apostles
hunger and thirst (1 Cor. 4:11); we commend ourselves
in hunger (2 Cor. 6:5).

C2 Thirst
The people were thirsty (Exod. 17:3); they are parched
with thirst (Isa. 5:13); Sisera was thirsty (Judg. 4:19);
Samson was thirsty (Judg. 15:18); when you are thirsty,
drink from the water jars (Ruth 2:9); David longed for
water from the well at Bethlehem (2 Sam. 23:15; 1 Chr.
11:17); if your enemy is thirsty give him a drink (Prov.
25:21; Rom. 12:20); as the deer longs for water (Ps. 42:1);
they will hunger no more and thirst no more (Rev.
7:16); Jesus said, 'I thirst' (John 19:28); I was thirsty and
you gave me drink (Matt. 25:35); whoever drinks this
water will thirst again (John 4:13).

C3 Sexual desire
Woman's desire will be for her husband (Gen. 3:16);
the king will desire your beauty (Ps. 45:11); I am my
beloved's and his desire is for me (S. of S. 7:10); you
burn with lust under every green tree (Isa. 57:5); you
are like a wild donkey in heat (Jer. 2:24); like well-fed
lusty stallions (Jer. 5:8); he who looks at a woman
lustfully has committed adultery (Matt. 5:28); I made a
covenant with my eyes, so how could I look at a maid?
(Job 31:1); not in the lusts of passion like the Gentiles
(1 Thess. 4:5); younger widows feel sensual desires (1
Tim. 5:11); better to marry than to burn (1 Cor. 7:9);
Potiphar's wife desired Joseph (Gen. 39:7); Amnon
desired Tamar (2 Sam. 13:1); God gave them over to
dishonourable passions (Rom. 1:26); men burning with
passion for men (Rom. 1:27).

860 Indifference

Pharaoh did not take this to heart either (Exod. 7:23); is it nothing to you who pass by? (Lam. 1:12); do you not care if we perish? (Mark 4:38); Lord, do you not care that my sister has left me to serve alone? (Luke 10:40); Gallio was not concerned (Acts 18:17); what is that to us? (Matt. 27:4); he flees because he is a hireling and does not care about the sheep (John 10:13); you are lukewarm, neither cold nor hot (Rev. 3:15-16).

861 Dislike

We do not want this man to rule over us (Luke 19:14); the evil I do not want is what I do (Rom. 7:19-20).

862 Fastidiousness

The tender and delicate man will be hostile to his kin (Deut. 28:54); the tender and delicate woman will be hostile to her husband (Deut. 28:56).
DISCRIMINATION, see 463.

863 Satiety

EXCESS, see 637.

864 Wonder

A Amazed

A1 Amazed by God
This is the Lord's doing and it is marvellous in our eyes (Ps. 118:23; Matt. 21:42; Mark 12:11); be astonished and wonder! (Hab. 1:5); Moses marvelled at the sight (Acts 7:31); behold, you scoffers, and marvel, and perish (Acts 13:41).

A2 Amazed by Jesus
Many were astonished at him (Isa. 52:14); they were amazed at his understanding (Luke 2:47); astonished that the wind stopped (Mark 6:51); amazed to see him (Mark 9:15; Luke 2:48); amazed to see he was talking to a woman (John 4:27); amazed that he was going to Jerusalem (Mark 10:32); amazed that he did not wash before eating (Luke 11:38); Pilate was amazed that he said nothing (Matt. 27:14; Mark 15:5); all marvelled at the gracious words which proceeded from his mouth (Luke 4:22); when the disciples heard this they were astonished (Matt. 19:25).

A3 Amazed by miracles
They were amazed by healings (Matt. 9:33; 12:23; 15:31; Mark 2:12; 5:42; 7:37; Luke 4:36; 5:26; 8:56; 11:14; Acts 3:10-12); I did one deed and you all marvel (John 7:21); amazed at the fig tree withering (Matt. 21:20); amazed at his authority over demons (Mark 1:27); amazed at the catch of fish (Luke 5:9); greater works will he show him, that you may marvel (John 5:20); trembling and astonishment had gripped them (Mark 16:8); amazed at the empty tomb (Luke 24:12); amazed to see him risen (Luke 24:41); amazed at Pentecost (Acts 2:7); amazed that the Spirit was poured out on the Gentiles (Acts 10:45); amazed at miracles (Acts 8:13); amazed that Paul had believed (Acts 9:21); when they opened the door and saw Peter they were amazed (Acts 12:16).

A4 Amazed by teaching
The proconsul was amazed at the teaching (Acts 13:12); do not marvel that I said, 'You must be born again' (John 3:7); they were amazed at Jesus' teaching (Matt. 7:28; 13:54; 22:22, 33; Mark 1:22; 6:2; 10:24, 26; 11:18; 12:17; Luke 4:32; 20:26; John 7:15).

A5 Jesus amazed
Jesus marvelled at their unbelief (Mark 6:6); Jesus marvelled at the centurion's faith (Matt. 8:10; Luke 7:9).

A6 Amazed by people
Jacob was stunned to hear that Joseph was ruler of Egypt (Gen. 45:26); the people were surprised that Zechariah was delayed in the temple (Luke 1:21); when they saw they were uneducated men, they marvelled (Acts 4:13); Simon astonished the people of Samaria (Acts 8:9); when I saw her I marvelled greatly (Rev. 17:6); I am amazed that you are turning from the gospel (Gal. 1:6); they were amazed at Zechariah (Luke 1:63); all who heard it marvelled at what the shepherds said (Luke 2:18); his father and mother were amazed at the things said about him (Luke 2:33).

B Miracles
SIGNS, see 547A.

B1 God's miracles
I will see this great marvel, why the bush is not consumed (Exod. 3:3); I will strike Egypt with my wonders (Exod. 3:20); he sent signs and wonders upon Egypt (Deut. 4:34; Ps. 135:9); he did wonders in driving out the nations (Exod. 34:10-11; 1 Chr. 17:21); thank the Lord for his wonders to the sons of men (Ps. 107:8, 15, 21, 31); I will declare all your wonders (Ps. 26:7); who is like God, working wonders? (Exod. 15:11); he performs signs and wonders (Dan. 6:27); I will show you miracles (Mic. 7:15); you are the God who works wonders (Ps. 77:14); God alone works wonders (Ps. 72:18; 136:4); he who works miracles among you (Gal. 3:5); perhaps the Lord will do wonderful things for us (Jer. 21:2); when you did wonders which we did not expect (Isa. 64:3); I will show wonders in heaven and on earth (Joel 2:30; Acts 2:19); they forgot his miracles (Ps. 78:11); where are all his miracles? (Judg. 6:13).

B2 Jesus' miracles
If the miracles had been done in Tyre and Sidon they would have repented (Matt. 11:21; Luke 10:13); many believed when they saw the signs he did (John 2:23); no one could do these signs if God were not with him (John 3:2); Jesus did many other signs in the presence of his disciples (John 20:30); Jesus, attested by God with mighty works, wonders and signs (Acts 2:22); they praised God for all the miracles they had seen (Luke 19:37); when the chief priests and scribes saw the wonders he did (Matt. 21:15); where did this man get these deeds of power? (Matt. 13:54); what are these miracles performed by his hands? (Mark 6:2); it must be John, resurrected, and so able to work miracles (Matt. 14:2); unless you see signs and wonders you will not believe (John 4:48); Jesus did not do many miracles there because of their unbelief (Matt. 13:58; Mark 6:5).

B3 Other miracles
The gift of miracles (1 Cor. 12:10, 28); no one who does a miracle in my name can soon speak evil of me (Mark 9:39); you will not only do what has been done to the fig tree (Matt. 21:21); I and my children are for signs and wonders (Isa. 8:18); many wonders and signs were done through the apostles (Acts 2:43; 5:12); an outstanding miracle has taken place (Acts 4:16); may signs and wonders take place though the name of Jesus (Acts 4:30); Stephen did great wonders and signs (Acts 6:8); Simon was amazed at the signs and miracles (Acts 8:13); the Lord bore witness with signs and wonders (Acts 14:3); God did extraordinary miracles by Paul (Acts 19:11); Barnabas and Paul related the signs and wonders God had done (Acts 15:12); what Christ has done through me by the power of signs and wonders (Rom. 15:18-19); the marks of a true apostle, signs, wonders and miracles (2 Cor. 12:12); God bore witness by signs and wonders and various miracles (Heb. 2:4); not all are miracle workers, are they? (1 Cor. 12:29).

B4 False miracles

If a false prophet shows a sign or wonder (Deut. 13:1-2); false Christs and false prophets will show great signs and wonders (Matt. 24:24; Mark 13:22); the working of Satan with all lying power and signs and wonders (2 Thess. 2:9); did we not perform mighty works in your name? (Matt. 7:22).

865 Lack of wonder

Do not marvel at this (John 5:28).
UNCONCERNED, see 860.

866 Repute

A Glory in general

The priests' clothes were for glory and beauty (Exod. 28:2, 40); the latter glory of this house will be greater than the former (Hag. 2:9); glorious things are spoken of Zion (Ps. 87:3); what wonderful stones and wonderful buildings! (Mark 13:1); the glory of heavenly bodies differs from that of earthly bodies (1 Cor. 15:40-1); what had glory now has no glory because of the glory that surpasses it (2 Cor. 3:10-11); they were to be a people for renown, praise and glory (Jer. 13:11); when the righteous triumph there is great glory (Prov. 28:12); the devil offered Jesus all kingdoms and their glory (Matt. 4:8; Luke 4:6); he who seeks the glory of him who sent him is true (John 7:18); the kings of the earth will bring their glory into new Jerusalem (Rev. 21:24).

B God's glory

B1 God is glorious

Great is the glory of the Lord (Ps. 138:5); may the glory of the Lord endure for ever (Ps. 104:31); the Lord is clothed with majesty (Ps. 93:1); the king of glory (Ps. 24:7-10); the God of glory appeared to our father Abraham (Acts 7:2); all have sinned and fall short of the glory of God (Rom. 3:23); the God of our Lord Jesus Christ, the Father of glory (Eph. 1:17); according to the riches of his glory (Eph. 3:16).

B2 God exalted

Be exalted, O Lord! (Ps. 21:13); be exalted above the heavens (Ps. 57:5; 108:5); exalted be the God of my salvation (2 Sam. 22:47; Ps. 18:46); my soul exalts the Lord (Luke 1:46); I will be exalted in the earth (Ps. 46:10); the Lord is exalted (Exod. 15:21; Ps. 47:9; 138:6; Isa. 5:16; 33:5); the Lord is highly exalted (Exod. 15:1); the Lord alone will be exalted (Isa. 2:11, 17); he is exalted above the peoples (Ps. 99:2); you are exalted far above all gods (Ps. 97:9); his glory is above earth and heavens (Ps. 148:13); the Lord is high above all nations (Ps. 113:4); you are on high for ever (Ps. 92:8).

B3 Giving God the glory

B3a To God be the glory

To God be the glory for ever! (Rom. 11:36; 16:27); to God be honour and glory for ever and ever (1 Tim. 1:17); to him be honour and eternal dominion (1 Tim. 6:16); to him be glory for ever and ever (2 Tim. 4:18); blessing and glory and honour be to our God (Rev. 7:12); salvation and glory and power be to our God (Rev. 19:1); give to the Lord glory and strength (Ps. 96:7); give to the Lord the glory of his name (Ps. 96:8); glorify your name (John 12:28); may the whole earth be filled with his glory (Ps. 72:19); do all for the glory of God (1 Cor. 10:31); everyone whom I have created for my glory (Isa. 43:7); the planting of the Lord that he may be glorified (Isa. 61:3); the beasts of the field will glorify me (Isa. 43:20).

B3b Give glory to God

Sing to the glory of his name (Ps. 66:2); you whose glory is chanted above the heavens (Ps. 8:1); let them give glory to the Lord (Isa. 42:12); they gave glory to

God who had given such authority to men (Matt. 9:8); glorify your Son that the Son may glorify you (John 17:1); in the name of Christian let him glorify God (1 Pet. 4:16); with one accord glorify the God and Father of our Lord (Rom. 15:6); the rest were terrified and gave glory to the God of heaven (Rev. 11:13); fear God and give him glory (Rev. 14:7); give glory to the Lord your God (Jer. 13:16); glorify God in your body (1 Cor. 6:20); let us rejoice and give him the glory (Rev. 19:7); magnify the Lord with me and let us exalt his name together (Ps. 34:3).

B3c Glorifying God by one's actions

Those who honour me I will honour (1 Sam. 2:30); honour the Lord with your wealth (Prov. 3:9); he who is kind to the needy honours his Maker (Prov. 14:31); I will deliver you and you will honour me (Ps. 50:15); he who offers thanksgiving as his sacrifice honours me (Ps. 50:23); I glorified you on earth (John 17:4); I honour my Father (John 8:49); by what kind of death he would glorify God (John 21:19); that in everything God may be glorified through Jesus Christ (1 Pet. 4:11); confessing Jesus is Lord, to the glory of God the Father (Phil. 2:11).

B3d Not giving God glory

They did not repent and give him glory (Rev. 16:9); God in whose hand is your breath you have not glorified (Dan. 5:23); Herod did not give God the glory (Acts 12:23); if you do not lay it to heart to give honour to God (Mal. 2:2); who will not glorify your name? (Rev. 15:4); they did not honour him as God (Rom. 1:21).

B4 God's glory manifested

B4a God's glory in the world

Let your glory be over all the earth (Ps. 57:5; 108:5); may the whole earth be filled with his glory (Ps. 72:19); all the earth will be filled with the glory of God (Num. 14:21); the earth will be filled with the knowledge of the glory of the Lord (Hab. 2:14); the earth is full of his glory (Isa. 6:3); how majestic is your name in all the earth! (Ps. 8:1); the heavens are telling the glory of God (Ps. 19:1); the glory of the Lord will be revealed (Isa. 40:5); if you believe you will see the glory of God (John 11:40); I have glorified my name and will glorify it again (John 12:28); no need of sun or moon in the city, for God's glory shines on it (Rev. 21:23).

B4b God's glory in Israel

The glory of the Lord appeared in the cloud (Exod. 16:10; Num. 16:42); the glory of the Lord filled the tabernacle (Exod. 40:34-5); the glory of the Lord filled the temple (1 Kgs. 8:11; 2 Chr. 5:14; 7:1-3; Ezek. 43:5); the glory of the Lord dwelt on Mount Sinai (Exod. 24:16); I love the place where your glory dwells (Ps. 26:8); I will fill this house with glory (Hag. 2:7); the court was filled with the brightness of the glory of the Lord (Ezek. 10:4); I will glorify my glorious house (Isa. 60:7).

B4c God's glory seen in the Son

In the Son of man God is glorified (John 13:31); I will answer prayer, that the Father may be glorified in the Son (John 14:13); my Father is glorified if you bear much fruit (John 15:8); Christ was raised from the dead by the glory of the Father (Rom. 6:4); welcome one another as Christ welcomed us, for the glory of God (Rom. 15:7); Stephen saw the glory of God (Acts 7:55); our amen is through Christ, to the glory of God (2 Cor. 1:20); the light of the knowledge of the glory of God in the face of Christ (2 Cor. 4:6).

B4d God's glory to people

A man is the image and glory of God (1 Cor. 11:7); to make known the riches of his glory on vessels of mercy (Rom. 9:23); they will glorify God for your obedience (2 Cor. 9:13); the fruit of righteousness is to the glory and praise of God (Phil. 1:11); the glory of the Lord shone about them (Luke 2:9); beholding your power and glory (Ps. 63:2); show me your glory (Exod. 33:18); the glory of the Lord has risen on you (Isa. 60:1-2).

B5 Glory through God

B5a God bestowing glory

The holy One of Israel has glorified you (Isa. 60:9); your God will be your glory (Isa. 60:19); all kings will see your glory (Isa. 62:2); the glory you have given me I have given them (John 17:22); there will be glory and honour and peace to everyone who does good (Rom. 2:10); a light of revelation to the Gentiles and for glory to your people Israel (Luke 2:32); to Israel belongs the glory (Rom. 9:4).

B5b Glory through the gospel

Vessels of mercy prepared beforehand for glory (Rom. 9:23); the wisdom God predestined before the ages for our glory (1 Cor. 2:7); the ministry of the Spirit must have more glory (2 Cor. 3:8-9); walk worthy of God who calls you to his own kingdom and glory (1 Thess. 2:12); in bringing many sons to glory (Heb. 2:10); joy unspeakable and full of glory (1 Pet. 1:8); the Spirit of glory and of God rests on you (1 Pet. 4:14); the God of all grace who called you to his eternal glory in Christ (1 Pet. 5:10); through the knowledge of him who called us to his own glory and excellence (2 Pet. 1:3).

B5c Future glory for people

That the elect may obtain salvation and eternal glory (2 Tim. 2:10); that you may obtain the glory of our Lord Jesus Christ (2 Thess. 2:14); if we suffer with him that we may be glorified with him (Rom. 8:17); if anyone serves me, the Father will honour him (John 12:26); the glory to be revealed to us (Rom. 8:18); those whom he justified he also glorified (Rom. 8:30); an eternal weight of glory beyond all comparison (2 Cor. 4:17); you will receive the unfading crown of glory (1 Pet. 5:4); we rejoice in hope of the glory of God (Rom. 5:2); Christ in you, the hope of glory (Col. 1:27); when Christ appears, you will appear with him in glory (Col. 3:4); a partaker of the glory to be revealed (1 Pet. 5:1); new Jerusalem had the glory of God (Rev. 21:11).

C Christ's glory

C1 Christ's own glory

We saw his glory, the glory of the only begotten of the Father (John 1:14); the Son is the radiance of God's glory (Heb. 1:3); Isaiah saw his glory and spoke of him (John 12:41); Jesus manifested his glory (John 2:11); if I glorify myself, my glory is nothing (John 8:54); gird your sword on your thigh in your glory and majesty (Ps. 45:3); worthy of more honour than Moses (Heb. 3:3); they saw his glory and the two men standing with him (Luke 9:32); we were eyewitness of his majesty (2 Pet. 1:16); when he received honour and glory from God the Father (2 Pet. 1:17); worthy to be the Lamb to receive honour and glory (Rev. 5:12); if they had understood they would not have crucified the Lord of glory (1 Cor. 2:8); the light of the gospel of the glory of Christ (2 Cor. 4:4); the glory of our great God and Saviour Jesus Christ (Titus 2:13); Jesus Christ, to whom be glory for ever and ever (Heb. 13:21); the Lord Jesus Christ, the glory (Jas. 2:1).

C2 Christ given glory by God

Glorify your Son (John 17:1); the glory you have given me (John 17:22, 24); my Father glorifies me (John 8:54); Jesus was not yet glorified (John 7:39); the hour has come for the Son of man to be glorified (John 12:23); now is the Son of man glorified (John 13:31); when Jesus was glorified they remembered that this had been written of him (John 12:16); God will glorify the Son of man in himself, and that at once (John 13:32); God raised him from the dead and gave him glory (1 Pet.

1:21); God has glorified his servant Jesus (Acts 3:13); the suffering of Christ and the glory following (1 Pet. 1:11); crowned with glory and honour because he suffered and died (Heb. 2:9); it was necessary for him to suffer and enter his glory (Luke 24:26); he was obedient to death, therefore God exalted him (Phil. 2:9); God exalted him to his own right hand (Acts 5:31); the Spirit will glorify Christ (John 16:14).

C3 Other references to Christ's glory

The Son of man will come with great power and glory (Matt. 24:30; Mark 13:26; Luke 21:27); when the Son of man comes in his glory (Luke 9:26); that you may rejoice when his glory is revealed (1 Pet. 4:13); I do not seek my own glory (John 8:50); I do not receive glory from men (John 5:41); if I glorify myself, my glory is nothing (John 8:54); that all may honour the Son as they honour the Father (John 5:23); I am glorified in them (John 17:10); that Christ will be exalted in my body (Phil. 1:20); this illness is so that the Son of God may be glorified (John 11:4).

D Man's honour

GIVE HONOUR, see 923.

D1 People have honour

Man is crowned with glory and honour (Ps. 8:5; Heb. 2:7); they were mighty men of renown (Gen. 6:4); vessels for honour (Rom. 9:21; 2 Tim. 2:20); you are our glory and joy (1 Thess. 2:20); woman is the glory of man (1 Cor. 11:7); a woman's long hair is her glory (1 Cor. 11:15); the body is sown in dishonour and raised in glory (1 Cor. 15:43).

D2 Honoured people

David made a name for himself (2 Sam. 8:13); the fame of David spread (1 Chr. 14:17); Solomon's fame was known all around (1 Kgs. 4:31); the queen of Sheba heard of the fame of Solomon (1 Kgs. 10:1; 2 Chr. 9:1); Solomon in all his glory was not arrayed like one of these (Matt. 6:29); Jabez was more honourable than his brothers (1 Chr. 4:9); Jehoshaphat had riches and honour (2 Chr. 17:5; 18:1); Uzziah's fame reached afar (2 Chr. 26:8, 15); Hezekiah had riches and honour (2 Chr. 32:27); Mordecai's fame spread abroad (Esther 9:4); those who were of high reputation in the church (Gal. 2:9); Gamaliel was held in honour by all the people (Acts 5:34).

D3 Giving people honour

D3a Honour others

Honour your father and mother (Exod. 20:12; Deut. 5:16; Matt. 15:4; 19:19; Mark 7:10; 10:19; Luke 18:20; Eph. 6:2); a son honours his father and a servant his master (Mal. 1:6); honour widows who are widows indeed (1 Tim. 5:3); let slaves regard their masters as worthy of all honour (1 Tim. 6:1); pay honour to whom it is due (Rom. 13:7); honour the king (1 Pet. 2:17); esteem them highly in love because of their work (1 Thess. 5:13); outdo one another in showing honour (Rom. 12:10).

D3b People being honoured

Tell my father of all my glory in Egypt (Gen. 45:13); you will be honoured in the sight of all (Luke 14:10); Cornelius, well spoken of by all the Jews (Acts 10:22); they honoured us with many honours (Acts 28:10).

D3c Good reputation

Having favour among all the people (Acts 2:47); the people held them in high honour (Acts 5:13); an elder must have a good reputation with those outside (1 Tim. 3:7); we commend ourselves in honour and dishonour (2 Cor. 6:8); select seven men of good reputation (Acts 6:3); Timothy was well spoken of by the brethren in Lystra and Iconium (Acts 16:2); Ananias was well spoken of by all in Damascus (Acts 22:12); a good name is better than riches (Prov. 22:1); a good name is better than good oil (Eccles. 7:1); the glory has departed from Israel (1 Sam. 4:21-2).

D4 Seeking honour
He who speaks from himself seeks his own glory (John 7:18); let us make a name for ourselves (Gen. 11:4); if you have been foolish, exalting yourself (Prov. 30:32); Ahasuerus displayed the riches of his glory (Esther 1:4); Haman recounted his own glory (Esther 5:11); the scribes and Pharisees love places of honour in synagogues at feasts (Matt. 23:6; Mark 12:39; Luke 20:46); you love the chief seats in the synagogues (Luke 11:43); Jesus saw how they chose places of honour for themselves (Luke 14:7-10); Christ did not glorify himself to become high priest (Heb. 5:5); no one takes this honour to himself, but is called by God (Heb. 5:4); how can you believe when you seek glory from each other? (John 5:44); nor did we seek glory from men (1 Thess. 2:6).

D5 Source of honour
Wisdom will honour you (Prov. 4:8); a gracious woman gets honour (Prov. 11:16); he who heeds reproof will be honoured (Prov. 13:18); humility comes before honour (Prov. 15:33; 18:12); it is an honour for a man to keep away from strife (Prov. 20:3); he who pursues righteousness finds life, righteousness and honour (Prov. 21:21); in the multitude of people is a king's glory (Prov. 14:28); riches and honour come from God (1 Chr. 29:12); God brings low and exalts the poor and needy (1 Sam. 2:7).

867 Disrepute
SHAME, see 872B.

A Dishonour

A1 God dishonoured
How long will my honour suffer shame? (Ps. 4:2); by breaking the law you dishonour God (Rom. 2:23); he who does not honour the Son does not honour the Father who sent him (John 5:23); a man praying or prophesying with head covered dishonours his head (1 Cor. 11:4); that the word of God may not be dishonoured (Titus 2:5).

A2 Dishonour for people
Only at home is a prophet without honour (Matt. 13:57); a prophet is not without honour except in his home town (Mark 6:4); no prophet is accepted in his home town (Luke 4:24); a prophet has no honour in his own country (John 4:44); I honour my father and you dishonour me (John 8:49); we commend ourselves in honour and dishonour (2 Cor. 6:8); you have dishonoured the poor man (Jas. 2:6); impurity, the dishonouring of their bodies (Rom. 1:24); vessels for honour and dishonour (2 Tim. 2:20); apostles are without honour (1 Cor. 4:10); less honourable members are given more honour (1 Cor. 12:23); the body is sown in dishonour and raised in glory (1 Cor. 15:43); a woman praying or prophesying with head uncovered dishonours her head (1 Cor. 11:5).

B Disgrace
When pride comes, then comes disgrace (Prov. 11:2); wickedness brings dishonour and disgrace (Prov. 18:3); giving our sister to the uncircumcised would be a disgrace (Gen. 34:14); disgrace will not overtake us (Mic. 2:6); I will show the kingdoms your disgrace (Nahum 3:5).

C Disreputable
Danger that this trade of ours may fall into disrepute (Acts 19:27); do you make those least esteemed in the church your judges? (1 Cor. 6:4).

868 Nobility
The king had Israelites of the royal family and the nobility brought (Dan. 1:3); the king and his nobles, wives and concubines drank from the vessels (Dan. 5:2-3); a nobleman went into a far country (Luke 19:12); the Bereans were more noble than the Thessalonicans (Acts 17:11); most noble Felix (Acts 24:3); most noble Festus (Acts 26:25); not many noble people were called (1 Cor. 1:26).
MASTER, see 741.

869 Common
If one of the common people sins (Lev. 4:27); let the lowly brother boast in his exaltation (Jas. 1:9); a vessel for common use (Rom. 9:21); God chose the base things of the world (1 Cor. 1:28); we have this treasure in earthenware vessels (2 Cor. 4:7).

870 Title
HONOUR, see 866.

871 Pride
HUMBLING AND EXALTING, see 872A4d.

A Pride in general
The proud are an abomination to the Lord (Prov. 16:5); arrogance is like idolatry (1 Sam. 15:23); the pride of your heart has deceived you (Obad. 3); from the heart comes pride (Mark 7:22); they are insolent, arrogant (Rom. 1:30); men will be arrogant (2 Tim. 3:2); conceited (2 Tim. 3:4); he is conceited (1 Tim. 6:4); the lust of the flesh and the lust of the eyes and the pride of life (1 John 2:16); the contempt of the proud (Ps. 123:4); when pride comes, disgrace follows (Prov. 11:2); haughty eyes and a proud heart are sin (Prov. 21:4); 'scoffer' is the name of the proud man (Prov. 21:24); henceforth we call the arrogant blessed (Mal. 3:15); knowledge puffs up but love builds up (1 Cor. 8:1); love is not arrogant (1 Cor. 13:4).

B Do not be proud
Do not be proud (Jer. 13:15); do not think of yourself more highly than you ought (Rom. 12:3); do nothing out of vain conceit (Phil. 2:3); do not be arrogant towards the branches (Rom. 11:18); do not be conceited (Rom. 11:20); do not become arrogant (1 Cor. 4:6); do not be arrogant and lie against the truth (Jas. 3:14); charge those who are rich not to be proud (1 Tim. 6:17); not a new convert, lest he become conceited (1 Tim. 3:6); do not take the place of honour (Luke 14:8); that the king's heart may not be lifted up above his brethren (Deut. 17:20); you boast in your arrogance and such boasting is evil (Jas. 4:16).

C Pride and externals
When riches increase, your heart will become proud (Deut. 8:14); charge those who are rich not to be proud (1 Tim. 6:17); the women of Zion are proud in their finery (Isa. 3:16); your heart was proud because of your beauty (Ezek. 28:17); those who pride themselves on appearance and not on the Lord (2 Cor. 5:12); Sodom was arrogant and did not help the poor (Ezek. 16:49).

D Proud people
You have defeated Edom and now you are proud (2 Kgs. 14:10; 2 Chr. 25:19); when Uzziah became strong, he became proud (2 Chr. 26:16); Hezekiah's heart was proud (2 Chr. 32:25); Zedekiah did not humble himself (2 Chr. 36:12); some of you have become arrogant (1 Cor. 4:18); we have heard of the pride of Moab (Isa. 16:6; Jer. 48:29); Diotrephes loves to be first (3 John 9); you have become arrogant (1 Cor. 5:2); I fear there may be arrogance among you (2 Cor. 12:20).

E Fate of the proud

The proud, God knows from afar (Ps. 138:6); I hate pride and arrogance (Prov. 8:13); I am against you, arrogant one (Jer. 50:31); the Lord hates haughty eyes (Prov. 6:17); I loathe the pride of Jacob (Amos 6:8); God opposes the proud (Jas. 4:6; 1 Pet. 5:5); God will abase the proud (Isa. 2:12); those who walk in pride he is able to humble (Dan. 4:37); he has scattered the proud (Luke 1:51); all the proud of the earth will bow down before him (Ps. 22:29); pride goes before destruction, a haughty spirit before a fall (Prov. 16:18); the arrogant one will stumble and fall (Jer. 50:32); a man's pride brings him low (Prov. 29:23); the proud crown of Ephraim's drunkards is trodden under foot (Isa. 28:3); the pride of Assyria will be laid low (Zech. 10:11); the arrogant and evildoers will be like stubble set ablaze (Mal. 4:1); whoever exalts himself will be humbled (Matt. 23:12; Luke 14:11).

872 Humility. Humiliation

A Humility

A1 About humility

With the humble is wisdom (Prov. 11:2); humility goes before honour (Prov. 15:33; 18:12); the humble will inherit the land (Ps. 37:11); blessed are the meek, for they will inherit the earth (Matt. 5:5); the humble will receive honour (Prov. 29:23); the humble will hear of it and be glad (Ps. 34:2).

A2 Be humble!

Live with humility and gentleness (Eph. 4:2); in humility reckon others better than yourselves (Phil. 2:3); put on humility (Col. 3:12); be clothed with humility (1 Pet. 5:5); humble yourselves under the mighty hand of God (1 Pet. 5:6); walk humbly with your God (Mic. 6:8); do not be haughty, but associate with the lowly (Rom. 12:16); in humility accept the implanted word (Jas. 1:21); at a feast, take the lowest place (Luke 14:10); the arrogance of man will be brought low (Isa. 2:11, 17); better to be of humble spirit than to divide spoil with the proud (Prov. 16:19); insistence on self-abasement (Col. 2:18, 23); be humble in spirit (1 Pet. 3:8).

A3 God and the humble

The Lord is on high yet regards the lowly (Ps. 138:6); I dwell with the lowly and contrite in spirit (Isa. 57:15); I look to him who is humble and contrite (Isa. 66:2); God gives grace to the humble (Jas. 4:6; 1 Pet. 5:5); God teaches the humble his way (Ps. 25:9); he has regarded the humble state of his maidservant (Luke 1:48).

A4 People being humbled

PEOPLE ABASED, see 311A3.

A4a Those who were humbled

God led you these forty years to humble you (Deut. 8:2, 3); he fed you manna to humble you (Deut. 8:16); he is able to humble those who walk in pride (Dan. 4:37); whom he would he raised up and whom he would he humbled (Dan. 5:19); the arrogance of man will be brought low (Isa. 2:11, 17); so man has been humbled (Isa. 2:9); the Lord will lay low the pride of Moab (Isa. 25:11); God makes counsellors walk barefoot (Job 12:17); God makes priests walk barefoot (Job 12:19); man is humbled (Isa. 5:15).

A4b Humbling oneself

Humble yourselves on the Day of Atonement (Lev. 16:29; 23:27; Num. 29:7); if my people humble themselves and pray (2 Chr. 7:14); whoever humbles himself like this child is the greatest (Matt. 18:4); from the first day you humbled yourself before your God (Dan. 10:12); whoever would be great among you must be your servant (Matt. 20:26-7); Ahab humbled himself (1 Kgs. 21:29); because you humbled yourself, I have heard you (2 Kgs. 22:19; 2 Chr. 34:27); since they

humbled themselves, I will not destroy them (2 Chr. 12:7); why have we humbled ourselves and you do not notice? (Isa. 58:3); Hezekiah humbled the pride of his heart (2 Chr. 32:26); Manasseh humbled himself (2 Chr. 33:12); I humbled my soul with fasting (Ps. 35:13); is a fast just a day for a man to humble himself? (Isa. 58:5); how long will you refuse to humble yourself (Exod. 10:3); you, Belshazzar, have not humbled yourself (Dan. 5:22); Amon did not humble himself (2 Chr. 33:23).

A4c Christ humbled himself

Jesus was made for a little while lower than the angels (Heb. 2:9); he emptied himself (Phil. 2:7); I am gentle and lowly of heart (Matt. 11:29); your king is coming to you, humble and seated on a donkey (Zech. 9:9).

A4d Humbling and exalting

Whoever exalts himself will be humbled and whoever humbles himself will be exalted (Matt. 23:12; Luke 14:11; 18:14); he has brought down rulers and exalted the humble (Luke 1:52); humble yourselves and he will exalt you (Jas. 4:10; 1 Pet. 5:6).

B Humiliation

DISGRACE, see 867B.

B1 Shame

B1a Shame has come

Shame has covered my face (Ps. 44:15); to us belongs confusion of face (Dan. 9:8); I was ashamed to ask the king for soldiers (Ezra 8:22); Sennacherib returned home in shame (2 Chr. 32:21); you chose David to your own shame (1 Sam. 20:30); casting up the foam of their own shame (Jude 13).

B1b Shame of bad conduct

The Philistines were ashamed of your lewd conduct (Ezek. 16:27); you will remember your ways and be ashamed (Ezek. 16:61); the things of which you are now ashamed (Rom. 6:21); if they are ashamed of all that they have done (Ezek. 43:11); Aaron had let them run loose to their shame (Exod. 32:25); sin is a disgrace to a people (Prov. 14:34); he who sleeps in harvest brings shame (Prov. 10:5); I am ashamed to beg (Luke 16:3); it is shameful for a woman to speak in church (1 Cor. 14:35); does not nature teach you that long hair is a disgrace for a man? (1 Cor. 11:14); it is disgraceful even to speak of the things they do in secret (Eph. 5:12).

B1c Shame of idolatry

All who worship images will be put to shame (Ps. 97:7); those who trust in idols will be put to shame (Isa. 42:17); those who make idols will be put to shame (Isa. 44:9); they will be ashamed because of their sacrifices (Hos. 4:19); you will be ashamed of the oaks (Isa. 1:29); Moab will be ashamed of Chemosh (Jer. 48:13); as the house of Israel was ashamed of Bethel (Jer. 48:13).

B1d Shame of nakedness

I stripped your skirts so your shame would be seen (Jer. 13:26); our unpresentable parts are treated with greater modesty (1 Cor. 12:23); white garments that the shame of your nakedness may not be seen (Rev. 3:18); that he may not go naked and men see his shame (Rev. 16:15); with buttocks uncovered to the shame of Egypt (Isa. 20:4); the servants were humiliated by Hanun (2 Sam. 10:5; 1 Chr. 19:5); your nakedness will be uncovered and your shame seen (Isa. 47:3).

B1e Enjoying shame

They glory in their shame (Phil. 3:19); let the rich man boast in his humiliation (Jas. 1:10); they rejoiced that they were counted worthy of suffering shame (Acts 5:41).

B2 Ashamed

B2a Shaming people

If her father spat in her face she would be in shame seven days (Num. 12:14); do you humiliate those who have nothing? (1 Cor. 11:22); the farmers are put to shame through lack of rain (Jer. 14:4); the wise men are put to shame (Jer. 8:9); God chose the foolish and weak things to shame the wise and strong (1 Cor. 1:27); may those who seek my life be put to shame (Ps. 35:4; 40:14-15; 70:2); may all who hate Zion be put to shame (Ps. 129:5); those who oppose us will be ashamed (Titus 2:8); that those who revile your conduct may be put to shame (1 Pet. 3:16); have nothing to do with him that he may be ashamed (2 Thess. 3:14); Nahash wanted to bring reproach on all Israel (1 Sam. 11:2); you have covered David with shame (Ps. 89:45); they urged Elisha until he was ashamed (2 Kgs. 2:17); lest I be put to shame by your unpreparedness (2 Cor. 9:4); I say this to your shame (1 Cor. 6:5; 15:34); they stole into the city like those humiliated (2 Sam. 19:3).

B2b Christ and shaming
In his humiliation justice was taken away (Acts 8:33); they crucify the Son of God afresh and put him to shame (Heb. 6:6); if anyone is ashamed of me, the Son of man will be ashamed of him (Mark 8:38; Luke 9:26).

B3 Not ashamed
B3a Not put to shame
May those who seek you not be put to shame (Ps. 69:6); Joseph did not want to put Mary to shame (Matt. 1:19); I do not write these things to shame you (1 Cor. 4:14); my hope that I will not be put to shame (Phil. 1:20); whoever believes in him will not be put to shame (Rom. 10:11; 1 Pet. 2:6); if I boast too much of our authority, I will not be put to shame (2 Cor. 10:8).

B3b Not shamed
He endured the cross, despising the shame (Heb. 12:2); God is not ashamed to be called their God (Heb. 11:16); Jesus is not ashamed to call them brothers (Heb. 2:11); Adam and his wife were naked yet not ashamed (Gen. 2:25); their faces were not ashamed (Ps. 34:5); I am not ashamed (2 Tim. 1:12); I am not ashamed of the gospel (Rom. 1:16); do not be ashamed to testify (2 Tim. 1:8); Onesiphorus was not ashamed of my chains (2 Tim. 1:16); a workman who does not need to be ashamed (2 Tim. 2:15); that we may not shrink in shame from him at his appearing (1 John 2:28).

873 Vanity
USELESSNESS, see 641.

874 Modesty
Women should dress modestly (1 Tim. 2:9).
HUMILITY, see 872.

875 Ostentation
A For appearance sake
Do not practise your religion to be seen by men (Matt. 6:1, 2); hypocrites pray to be seen by men (Matt. 6:5); do not look gloomy when you fast (Matt. 6:16); the Pharisees do everything to be seen by men (Matt. 23:5); for appearance they offer long prayers (Mark 12:40; Luke 20:47).
OUTWARD APPEARANCE, see 445A.

B Pomp
Man in his pomp cannot endure (Ps. 49:12, 20); Agrippa and Bernice came with great pomp (Acts 25:23).

876 Celebration
A Feasts in general
Better to go to the house of mourning than to the house of feasting (Eccles. 7:2); they love the places of honour at banquets (Matt. 23:6; Mark 12:39; Luke 20:46); when you give a feast, do not invite your friends (Luke 14:12-14).

B Wedding feasts
Laban made a wedding feast (Gen. 29:22); Samson gave a wedding feast (Judg. 14:10); a king who gave a wedding feast (Matt. 22:2); those who were ready went in to the marriage feast (Matt. 25:10).

C Feasting in the kingdom
Feasting in the kingdom of God (Matt. 8:11; Luke 14:15); many will recline at table in the kingdom of God (Luke 13:29); you will eat and drink at my table in my kingdom (Luke 22:30); blessed are those invited to the wedding supper of the Lamb (Rev. 19:9).

D Other feasts
Lot made a feast for the angels (Gen. 19:3); feast for Isaac's weaning (Gen. 21:8); Nabal was having a feast (1 Sam. 25:36); Solomon gave a feast for his servants (1 Kgs. 3:15); each son held a feast in turn (Job 1:4); the king of Israel made a feast for the army of Aram (2 Kgs. 6:23); Ahasuerus gave a banquet (Esther 1:3); Queen Vashti gave a banquet for the women (Esther 1:9); the king gave a banquet for Esther (Esther 2:18); may the king and Haman come to the banquet (Esther 5:4); he brought me to the banqueting hall (S. of S. 2:4); Belshazzar gave a feast for his nobles (Dan. 5:1); Herod gave a banquet on his birthday (Mark 6:21); a man gave a big dinner (Luke 14:16); Matthew made him a big feast in his house (Luke 5:29); kill the fatted calf and let us eat and be merry (Luke 15:23).

877 Boasting
A Those who boast
A1 Boasters in general
Men will be boastful (2 Tim. 3:2); they are boastful (Rom. 1:30); those who boast of their riches (Ps. 49:6); you who boast in the law (Rom. 2:23); those who boast in appearances and not in the heart (2 Cor. 5:12); the circumcisers want to boast in your flesh (Gal. 6:13); his reason for boasting will then be in himself alone (Gal. 6:4); those who boast that they work on the same terms as we do (2 Cor. 11:12); let the lowly brother boast in his exaltation (Jas. 1:9); the tongue is a small member, but boasts great things (Jas. 3:5); a man who boasts of non-existent gifts is like clouds without rain (Prov. 25:14).

A2 Boasting in God
Let him who boasts, boast in the Lord (Jer. 9:23-4; 1 Cor. 1:31; 2 Cor. 10:17); I will boast in the Lord (Ps. 34:2); in God we boast (Ps. 44:8); I boast in things regarding God (Rom. 15:17); if you are a Jew and boast of God (Rom. 2:17); in me you may have ample cause to boast in Christ Jesus (Phil. 1:26); if we hold our boast in our hope firm to the end (Heb. 3:6); we glory in Christ Jesus (Phil. 3:3); I will not boast except in the cross (Gal. 6:14).

A3 Paul's boasting
By my boasting in you (1 Cor. 15:31); we boast of you among the churches of God (2 Thess. 1:4); if I have boasted to Titus about you, I was not put to shame (2 Cor. 7:14); I boast about you to the Macedonians (2 Cor. 9:2); I sent the brethren that our boasting about you may not prove vain (2 Cor. 9:3); of such a man I will boast (2 Cor. 12:5-6); our boast is this (2 Cor. 1:12); I would rather die than lose my ground for boasting (1 Cor. 9:15); this boast of mine will not be silenced in the regions of Achaia (2 Cor. 11:10); let me boast of my endeavours (2 Cor. 11:17-18); if I boast too much of our authority (2 Cor. 10:8); we will not boast beyond our limit (2 Cor. 10:13); I will boast of my weakness (2 Cor. 11:30; 12:1).

B Against boasting
B1 Do not boast
Do not boast (1 Sam. 2:3; Ps. 75:4); let us not be boastful (Gal. 5:26); your boasting is not good (1 Cor. 5:6); do not boast of wisdom, strength or riches (Jer. 9:23-4); let no one boast about men (1 Cor. 3:21); love is not boastful (1 Cor. 13:4); why do you boast of evil? (Ps. 52:1); do not boast about tomorrow (Prov. 27:1); you boast in your arrogance and such boasting is evil (Jas. 4:16); too many soldiers, lest Israel boast (Judg. 7:2); let not him who puts on his armour boast like him who takes it off (1 Kgs. 20:11).

B2 Boasting excluded
Boasting is excluded by the principle of faith (Rom. 3:27); no one may boast before God (1 Cor. 1:29); why boast, as if you have something you did not receive? (1 Cor. 4:7); Abraham has no reason to boast before God (Rom. 4:2); salvation is not of works, lest any one should boast (Eph. 2:9); if I preach the gospel I have nothing to boast about (1 Cor. 9:16); without boasting of work accomplished in another's field (2 Cor. 10:16); of myself I will not boast (2 Cor. 12:5).

878 Insolence
If a man kills another presumptuously (Exod. 21:14); keep me back from presumptuous sins (Ps. 19:13); their princes will die because of the insolence of their tongue (Hos. 7:16); do not presume to say Abraham is your father (Matt. 3:9).
ARROGANCE, see 871.

879 Servility
SUBJECTION, see 745.

880 Friendship
LOVE, see 887.
A About friends
There is a friend who sticks closer than a brother (Prov. 18:24); a friend loves at all times (Prov. 17:17); faithful are the wounds of a friend (Prov. 27:6); I went about as if mourning for my friend or brother (Ps. 35:14); make friends quickly with your opponent (Matt. 5:25); greater love has no one than this, that he lay down his life for his friends (John 15:13); friendship of the world is enmity with God (Jas. 4:4).

B Friends of God
The friendship of God (Job 29:4); my Father, the friend of my youth (Jer. 3:4); Abraham your friend (2 Chr. 20:7); Abraham my friend (Isa. 41:8); Abraham was called the friend of God (Jas. 2:23); God spoke to Moses as to a friend (Exod. 33:11); you are my friends if you do what I command you (John 15:14); I have called you friends, for everything I heard from my Father I made known to you (John 15:15).

C Human friends
He who loves purity will have the king as his friend (Prov. 22:11); Hiram was a friend of David (1 Kgs. 5:1); Hushai was David's friend (2 Sam. 15:37; 1 Chr. 27:33); Amnon's friend Jonadab (2 Sam. 13:3); Zabud, Solomon's friend (1 Kgs. 4:5); Herod and Pilate became friends (Luke 23:12); Job's three friends (Job 2:11); Paul's friends ministered to him (Acts 24:23); Paul went to his friends (Acts 27:3); some of the Asiarchs who were friends of Paul (Acts 19:31); a friend of taxmen and sinners (Matt. 11:19; Luke 7:34); these wounds I received in the house of my friends (Zech. 13:6); make friends by means of unrighteous mammon (Luke 16:9).

D Friends failing
Friends desert a poor man (Prov. 19:4); if your friend entices you to serve other gods, kill him (Deut. 13:6-10);

my close friend has lifted up his heel against me (Ps. 41:9); my familiar friend reproaches me (Ps. 55:13); all her friends have dealt treacherously (Lam. 1:2); your close friends have deceived you (Jer. 38:22); friend, do what you have come for (Matt. 26:50); you will be delivered up even by parents, kinsmen and friends (Luke 21:16); if you release this man you are no friend of Caesar's (John 19:12).

881 Enmity
Enmity is a deed of the flesh (Gal. 5:20); Herod and Pilate had formerly been at enmity (Luke 23:12); having put to death the enmity (Eph. 2:16); enmity between the serpent and the woman (Gen. 3:15).
ENEMY, see 705.

882 Sociality
A Eating together
Be careful when you sit down to eat with a ruler (Prov. 23:1); he who eats my bread has lifted his heel against me (Ps. 41:9; John 13:18); he who dips his hand in the dish with me will betray me (Matt. 26:23; Mark 14:20; Luke 22:21); you will eat with me today (1 Sam. 9:19); the man of God ate and drank with the prophet (1 Kgs. 13:19); the king and Haman sat down to drink (Esther 3:15); Jesus ate with tax-collectors and sinners (Matt. 9:10-11; Mark 2:15-17; Luke 5:29-30); the scribes of the Pharisees saw that he ate with sinners (Mark 2:16); why does your teacher eat with tax collectors and sinners? (Matt. 9:11); this man receives sinners and eats with them (Luke 15:2); Peter used to eat with Gentiles (Gal. 2:12); you ate with the uncircumcised (Acts 11:3); a Pharisee invited him to a meal (Luke 7:36; 11:37); he went in to eat in the house of a Pharisee (Luke 14:1); while eating with them he charged them (Acts 1:4); they ate and drank with Jesus after he rose (Acts 10:41); I will come in and eat with him (Rev. 3:20); while they were eating together Ishmael killed Gedaliah (Jer. 41:1-2).

B Saying goodbye
Moses said goodbye to Jethro (Exod. 18:27); one man wanted first to say goodbye to those at home (Luke 9:61).

883 Unsociability. Seclusion
A No dealings
Egyptians would not eat bread with Hebrews (Gen. 43:32); Jews have no dealings with Samaritans (John 4:9); the man of God was commanded not to eat or drink there (1 Kgs. 13:8-9); do not associate with them (1 Kgs. 11:2); do not associate with immoral people (1 Cor. 5:9); do not associate with those who disobey this letter (2 Thess. 3:14); do not even eat with a disorderly 'brother' (1 Cor. 5:11); Absalom did not see the king (2 Sam. 14:24); Joseph ate by himself (Gen. 43:32); they stand aloof from me (Job 30:10).
DO NOT GREET, see 884D.

B Isolation
I am lonely and afflicted (Ps. 25:16); David will not spend the night with the people (2 Sam. 17:8); you would have stood aloof (2 Sam. 18:13); my loved ones stand aloof (Ps. 38:11); you stood aloof from the destruction of Jerusalem (Obad. 11); they went away by boat to a lonely place by themselves (Mark 6:32); this is a lonely place (Mark 6:35); Jesus withdrew to a lonely place (Matt. 14:13; Luke 4:42); Jesus went out to a lonely place and prayed (Mark 1:35; Luke 5:16); Jesus withdrew into the hills by himself (John 6:15); come away by yourselves to a lonely place and rest (Mark 6:31); Jesus took the man aside (Mark 7:33); he took the blind man out of the village (Mark 8:23); he withdrew from them

about a stone's throw (Luke 22:41); Paul withdrew and took the disciples away (Acts 19:9); Peter withdrew from the Gentiles (Gal. 2:12); Paul went into Arabia (Gal. 1:17).

884 Courtesy

WELCOMING PEOPLE, see 299A.

A Who to greet
If you greet only your brothers, what do you do more than others? (Matt. 5:47); show every courtesy to all men (Titus 3:2); as you enter the house, greet it (Matt. 10:12).

B How to greet
Greet one another with a holy kiss (Rom. 16:16; 1 Cor. 16:20; 2 Cor. 13:12; 1 Thess. 5:26); greet one another with a kiss of love (1 Pet. 5:14).

C Spoken greetings
Boaz greeted his reapers (Ruth 2:4); Saul went out to greet Samuel (1 Sam. 13:10); hail, favoured one! (Luke 1:28); she pondered what kind of greeting this was (Luke 1:29); Mary greeted Elizabeth and the baby leaped (Luke 1:40-1); Judas said, 'Hail, Rabbi' (Matt. 26:49); hail, king of the Jews! (Matt. 27:29; Mark 15:18; John 19:3); Jesus met them and greeted them (Matt. 28:9); they love salutations in the market place (Matt. 23:7; Mark 12:38; Luke 11:43; 20:46).

D Do not greet
If anyone does not bring this teaching, do not give him a greeting (2 John 10-11); greet no one on the way (Luke 10:4); neither greet nor return a greeting (2 Kgs. 4:29).

885 Discourtesy

NOT WELCOMING PEOPLE, see 299B.
CONTEMPT, see 922.

886 Congratulation

CELEBRATION, see 876.

887 Love

A Love in general
A1 About love
The characteristics of love (1 Cor. 13:1-13); there is a time for love (Eccles. 3:8); love is strong as death (S. of S. 8:6); love covers all transgressions (Prov. 10:12); love covers a multitude of sins (1 Pet. 4:8); love is the fulfilment of the law (Rom. 13:10); many waters cannot quench love (S. of S. 8:7); perfect love casts out fear (1 John 4:18); knowledge puffs up but love builds up (1 Cor. 8:1); better a meal of vegetables where love is (Prov. 15:17); greater love has no one than this, that he lay down his life for his friends (John 15:13); faith working through love is what counts (Gal. 5:6); if there is any comfort in love (Phil. 2:1); your work of faith, labour of love and steadfastness of hope (1 Thess. 1:3); you have followed my love (2 Tim. 3:10); the one who abides in love abides in God and God abides in him (1 John 4:16-17).

A2 Aim at love
Over all things put on love which is the bond of unity (Col. 3:14); make love your aim (1 Cor. 14:1); the aim of this command is love (1 Tim. 1:5); let all that you do be done in love (1 Cor. 16:14); this I pray, that your love may abound (Phil. 1:9); let love be sincere (Rom. 12:9); pursue love (1 Tim. 6:11; 2 Tim. 2:22); let us not love in word and speech but in deed and truth (1 John 3:18); that we should be holy and blameless before him in love (Eph. 1:4); walk in love, as Christ loved us (Eph. 5:2); set the believers an example in love, faith and purity (1 Tim. 4:12); older men are to be sound in faith,

love and perseverance (Titus 2:2); stirring up one another to love and good works (Heb. 10:24).

B God and love
B1 God's love
God is love (1 John 4:8, 16); the God of love and peace (2 Cor. 13:11); love is from God (1 John 4:7); he will be silent in his love (Zeph. 3:17); the love of God be with you all (2 Cor. 13:14); may the Lord direct your hearts to the love of God (2 Thess. 3:5); in this is love, not that we loved God but that he loved us (1 John 4:10); the Lord loves righteousness (Ps. 11:7); I the Lord love justice (Isa. 61:8).

B2 Love between Father and Son
The Father loves the Son (John 3:35; 5:20); you loved me before the foundation of the world (John 17:24); the Father loves me because I lay down my life (John 10:17); the Beloved (Eph. 1:6); my beloved in whom I am well-pleased (Matt. 12:18); my beloved Son (Matt. 3:17; 17:5; Mark 1:11; 9:7; Luke 3:22); as the Father loved me, so have I loved you (John 15:9); that the love you have for me may be in them (John 17:26); you have loved them even as you loved me (John 17:23); I have kept my Father's commandments and remain in his love (John 15:10); that the world may know that I love the Father (John 14:31).

B3 God's love for people
LOVINGKINDNESS, see 897.

B3a Nature of God's love
God loves you (Deut. 23:5); I loved you with an everlasting love (Jer. 31:3); her who was not beloved I will call beloved (Rom. 9:25); I will love them freely (Hos. 14:4); God loves aliens (Deut. 10:18); the Lord loves the righteous (Ps. 146:8); God loves a cheerful giver (2 Cor. 9:7); he whom the Lord loves he reproves (Prov. 3:12); he whom the Lord loves he disciplines (Heb. 12:6); those whom I love I reprove and discipline (Rev. 3:19); keep yourselves in the love of God (Jude 21).

B3b God's love for Israel
Jacob I loved but Esau I hated (Mal. 1:2-3; Rom. 9:13); the Lord loved Israel for ever (1 Kgs. 10:9); when Israel was a child I loved him (Hos. 11:1); Israel are beloved for the sake of their forefathers (Rom. 11:28); the Lord did not love you because of your numbers (Deut. 7:7); it was because the Lord loved you (Deut. 7:8); love her as the Lord loves the Israelites (Hos. 3:1); the Lord loves the gates of Zion (Ps. 87:2); Mount Zion which he loves (Ps. 78:68).

B3c God's love for individuals
The Lord loved Solomon (2 Sam. 12:24; Neh. 13:26); O Daniel, man greatly beloved (Dan. 10:11, 19); you are greatly beloved (Dan. 9:23).

B3d God's love for the church
We know and believe the love God has for us (1 John 4:16); be imitators of God as beloved children (Eph. 5:1); as God's chosen ones, holy and beloved (Col. 3:12); brethren beloved by God (1 Thess. 1:4); brethren beloved by the Lord (2 Thess. 2:13); God loved us and gave us eternal comfort (2 Thess. 2:16); if God so loved us, we ought to love one another (1 John 4:11); to those who are the called, beloved in God the Father (Jude 1); they will know that I have loved you (Rev. 3:9).

B3e God's love in Christ
God so loved the world that he gave his Son (John 3:16); God shows his love in that Christ died for us (Rom. 5:8); the Father himself loves you (John 16:27); when the love of God our Saviour appeared, he saved us (Titus 3:4-5); what manner of love the Father has bestowed upon us (1 John 3:1); nothing can separate us from the love of God in Christ (Rom. 8:35-9); he who loves me will be loved by my Father (John 14:21); the

love of God has been poured into our hearts (Rom. 5:5); you being rooted and grounded in love (Eph. 3:17); in this the love of God was manifested, that he sent his Son (1 John 4:9); God, because of his great love, raised us with Christ (Eph. 2:4-5); more than conquerors through him who loved us (Rom. 8:37); those beloved of God (Rom. 1:7); if anyone loves me, my Father will love him (John 14:23); you have loved them even as you loved me (John 17:23); the faith and love which are in Christ Jesus (1 Tim. 1:14).

B4 Christ's love
Jesus loved the rich young ruler (Mark 10:21); Jesus loved Martha, Mary and Lazarus (John 11:5); he whom you love is ill (John 11:3); see how he loved him! (John 11:36); the disciple whom Jesus loved (John 13:23; 19:26; 20:2; 21:7, 20); as the Father loved me, so have I loved you (John 15:9); if you keep my commandments you will remain in my love (John 15:10); the Son of God who loved me (Gal. 2:20); Christ loved us and gave himself up for us (Eph. 5:2); by this we know love, that he laid down his life for us (1 John 3:16); to know the love of Christ which surpasses knowledge (Eph. 3:18-19); having loved his own, he loved them to the end (John 13:1); Christ loved the church and gave himself up for her (Eph. 5:25); you love righteousness (Ps. 45:7); to him who loves us and freed us from our sins by his blood (Rev. 1:5); the love of Christ constrains us (2 Cor. 5:14).

B5 Loving God
B5a The need to love God
Love the Lord your God (Deut. 6:5; Josh. 22:5; 23:11; Mark 12:30); love the Lord your God with all your heart, soul and mind (Matt. 22:37; Luke 10:27); to love him with all the heart (Mark 12:33); this is the love of God, that we keep his commandments (1 John 5:3); this is love, that we walk according to his commandments (2 John 6); whoever keeps his word, in him the love of God is made perfect (1 John 2:5); we love because he first loved us (1 John 4:19).

B5b The need to love Christ
He who loves father or mother more than me is not worthy of me (Matt. 10:37); Simon, do you love me? (John 21:15-16); the Father himself loves you because you have loved me and believe (John 16:27); if you loved me you would rejoice because I go to the Father (John 14:28); he who has my commandments and keeps them is the one who loves me (John 14:21); grace be with all who love our Lord Jesus Christ with incorruptible love (Eph. 6:24).

B5c Results of loving God
Because he loves me I will deliver him (Ps. 91:14); if anyone loves God he is known by him (1 Cor. 8:3); showing lovingkindness to those who love me (Exod. 20:6); he keeps covenant to the thousandth generation of those who love him (Deut. 7:9); O Lord who keeps his covenant and steadfast love for those who love him (Dan. 9:4); the Lord keeps all who love him (Ps. 145:20); in all things God works for good to those who love him (Rom. 8:28); what God has prepared for those that love him (1 Cor. 2:9); God promised the kingdom to those who love him (Jas. 2:5); the crown of life which the Lord has promised to those who love him (Jas. 1:12); her sins are forgiven, for she loved much (Luke 7:47); he who loves me will keep my word (John 14:23).

C Loving people
C1 About loving other people
A friend loves at all times (Prov. 17:17); many people love the rich (Prov. 14:20); if the slave says, 'I love my master, my wife and my children' (Exod. 21:5); which debtor will love him more? (Luke 7:42); he will hate the

one master and love the other (Matt. 6:24; Luke 16:13); let them serve all the more because those who benefit are believers and beloved (1 Tim. 6:2); everyone who loves is born of God (1 John 4:7); if we love each other, God lives in us and his love is perfected in us (1 John 4:12); he who loves his brother remains in the light (1 John 2:10); the fruit of the Spirit is love (Gal. 5:22); God has given us a spirit of love (2 Tim. 1:7); the breastplate of faith and love (1 Thess. 5:8); we love because he first loved us (1 John 4:19); we commend ourselves in genuine love (2 Cor. 6:6); we know we have passed from death to life because we love the brethren (1 John 3:14); if you were of the world the world would love its own (John 15:19); may the Lord cause you to increase in love for one another and for all men (1 Thess. 3:12); whoever loves the parent loves the child (1 John 5:1); we know that we love the children of God when we love God (1 John 5:2).

C2 Love other people!
C2a Love your neighbour!
Love your neighbour as yourself (Lev. 19:18; Matt. 19:19; 22:39; Mark 12:31; Luke 10:27); the law is summed up as 'love your neighbour as yourself' (Rom. 13:9; Gal. 5:14); the royal law to love your neighbour as yourself (Jas. 2:8); he who loves his neighbour has fulfilled the law (Rom. 13:8); love your neighbour and hate your enemies (Matt. 5:43); love your enemies (Matt. 5:44; Luke 6:27, 35); love aliens (Deut. 10:19); love an alien as yourself (Lev. 19:34); to love one's neighbour as oneself (Mark 12:33); owe no one anything except to love one another (Rom. 13:8).

C2b Love fellow-Christians!
A new commandment to love one another as I have loved you (John 13:34; 15:12); this I command you, to love one another (John 15:17); if God so loved us, we ought to love one another (1 John 4:11); this is his commandment, that we love one another (1 John 3:23; 2 John 5); by this will all know that you are my disciples (John 13:35); he who loves God should love his brother also (1 John 4:21); fulfil my joy by having the same love (Phil. 2:2); through love serve one another (Gal. 5:13); showing forbearance in love (Eph. 4:2); speaking the truth in love (Eph. 4:15); be devoted to one another in brotherly love (Rom. 12:10); love one another fervently (1 Pet. 1:22; 4:8); love the brotherhood (1 Pet. 2:17); let brotherly love continue (Heb. 13:1); we should love one another (1 John 3:11); let us love one another (1 John 4:7); have love of the brethren (1 Pet. 3:8); add to brotherly kindness love (2 Pet. 1:7); about brotherly love we do not need to write to you (1 Thess. 4:9-10); esteem them highly in love because of their work (1 Thess. 5:13); the body builds itself up in love (Eph. 4:16); for love's sake I would rather appeal to you (Philem. 9); reaffirm your love for the one who did wrong (2 Cor. 2:8).

C3 Love exists between people
Your love for all the saints (Eph. 1:15; Col. 1:4); you had become very dear to us (1 Thess. 2:8); I thank God for your love (Philem. 5); your love for one another is growing (2 Thess. 1:3); knit together in love (Col. 2:2); not to cause you sorrow but to show you the love I have for you (2 Cor. 2:4); you abound in faith, utterance, knowledge, earnestness and love for us (2 Cor. 8:7); the love you showed in serving the saints (Heb. 6:10); the elect lady and her children whom I love in the truth (2 John 1); these men are sunken reefs in your love-feasts (Jude 12).

C4 Those loved
The centurion loves our nation (Luke 7:5); your only son whom you love (Gen. 22:2); Isaac loved Esau but Rebekah loved Jacob (Gen. 25:28); Israel loved Joseph

more than his other sons (Gen. 37:3); Jacob loved Benjamin (Gen. 44:20); Ruth loved Naomi (Ruth 4:15); Saul loved David (1 Sam. 16:21); all Israel loved David (1 Sam. 18:16); Jonathan loved David (1 Sam. 18:1; 20:17); your love for me was more than the love of women (2 Sam. 1:26).

FAVOURITE, see 890.

C5 Loving oneself
He who gets wisdom loves himself (Prov. 19:8); men will be lovers of self (2 Tim. 3:2); he who loves his life loses it (John 12:25); they did not love their lives even to death (Rev. 12:11).

C6 Love of man and woman
Husbands, love your wives (Eph. 5:25; Col. 3:19); husbands should love their wives as their own bodies (Eph. 5:28); let everyone love his wife as himself (Eph. 5:33); they should teach young women to love their husbands and children (Titus 2:4); be intoxicated with your wife's love (Prov. 5:19); enjoy life with the wife you love (Eccles. 9:9); his banner over me is love (S. of S. 2:4); love a woman beloved of a paramour, an adulteress (Hos. 3:1); two wives, one loved and one hated (Deut. 21:15).

C7 Men and women who loved
Isaac loved Rebekah (Gen. 24:67); Jacob loved Rachel (Gen. 29:18); seven years seemed like a few days because of his love for her (Gen. 29:20); Jacob loved Rachel more than Leah (Gen. 29:30); Shechem loved Dinah (Gen. 34:3, 8); Samson loved Delilah (Judg. 16:4); Michal loved David (1 Sam. 18:20); Amnon loved Tamar (2 Sam. 13:1); Amnon hated Tamar more than he had loved her (2 Sam. 13:15); Solomon loved many foreign women (1 Kgs. 11:1-2).

D Loving things
D1 Loving good
He who loves discipline loves knowledge (Prov. 12:1); love Wisdom and she will guard you (Prov. 4:6); hate evil, love good (Amos 5:15); what does the Lord require of you but to love kindness (Mic. 6:8); love truth and peace (Zech. 8:19); they perish because they do not love the truth and so be saved (2 Thess. 2:10); an elder [overseer] must love what is good (Titus 1:8); you have loved righteousness and hated lawlessness (Heb. 1:9).

D2 Loving evil
You who hate good and love evil (Mic. 3:2); you love evil more than good (Ps. 52:3); do not love the world (1 John 2:15); Demas has loved this present world (2 Tim. 4:10); men loved darkness rather than light (John 3:19); they became detestable like the thing they loved (Hos. 9:10); men will be lovers of pleasure rather than lovers of God (2 Tim. 3:4); everyone who loves and practises lying is outside the city (Rev. 22:15).

D3 Loving money
Whoever loves money will not be satisfied with money (Eccles. 5:10); men will be lovers of money (2 Tim. 3:2); the love of money is the root of all evil (1 Tim. 6:10); the Pharisees loved money (Luke 16:14); Balaam loved the wages of unrighteousness (2 Pet. 2:15); be free from the love of money (Heb. 13:5); a bishop [overseer] must be free from love of money (1 Tim. 3:3).

D4 Loving other things
Savoury food such as I love (Gen. 27:4); they love the places of honour at feasts (Matt. 23:6); you love the chief seats in the synagogues and salutations in the market place (Luke 11:43); they loved the praise of men more than praise from God (John 12:43); the Lord will give the crown to all who have loved his appearing (2 Tim. 4:8).

E Lack of love
E1 Unloving
They are unloving (Rom. 1:31); men will be unloving (2 Tim. 3:3); you have abandoned your first love (Rev. 2:4); if I do not have love I am nothing (1 Cor. 13:2-3); he who does not love remains in death (1 John 3:14); if anyone closes his heart against his brother, how does God's love abide in him? (1 John 3:17); he who does not love his brother whom he has seen cannot love God whom he has not seen (1 John 4:20); if your brother is hurt by what you eat, you are not walking in love (Rom. 14:15); he who does not love his brother is not of God (1 John 3:10); he who does not love does not know God (1 John 4:8); an unloved woman who marries is unbearable (Prov. 30:23).

E2 Not loving God
The love of many will grow cold (Matt. 24:12); you do not have the love of God within you (John 5:42); if God were your Father you would love me (John 8:42); men will be lovers of pleasure rather than lovers of God (2 Tim. 3:4); if anyone loves the world, the love of the Father is not in him (1 John 2:15); if anyone does not love the Lord let him be accursed (1 Cor. 16:22); you neglect justice and the love of God (Luke 11:42); he who does not love me does not keep my words (John 14:24); he who does not love his brother whom he has seen cannot love God whom he has not seen (1 John 4:20); he who says, 'I love God', and hates his brother, is a liar (1 John 4:20).

888 Hatred

A Hating in general
There is a time to hate (Eccles. 3:8); hatred stirs up strife (Prov. 10:12); he who hates disguises it with his lips (Prov. 26:24); those who hate you will rule over you (Lev. 26:17); he who spares the rod hates his son (Prov. 13:24); a man of evil devices is hated (Prov. 14:17); the poor is hated even by his neighbour (Prov. 14:20); the nations will abhor him who tells the wicked they are righteous (Prov. 24:24); they became detestable like the thing they loved (Hos. 9:10).

LACK OF LOVE, see 887E.

B God hating
B1 God hating people
Because of these customs God abhorred them (Lev. 20:23); you hate all workers of iniquity (Ps. 5:5); whoever does these things is detestable to the Lord (Deut. 18:12); the Lord detests those who wear clothing of the opposite sex (Deut. 22:5); the Lord hates him that loves violence (Ps. 11:5); Jacob I loved but Esau I hated (Mal. 1:2-3; Rom. 9:13); because God hates us he brought us out of Egypt (Deut. 1:27); God abhorred his heritage (Ps. 106:40); at Gilgal I began to hate them (Hos. 9:15); have you loathed Zion? (Jer. 14:19).

B2 God hating things
Six or seven things which the Lord hates (Prov. 6:16-19); the Lord hates a false balance (Prov. 11:1); you hate the deeds of the Nicolaitans, which I also hate (Rev. 2:6); the Lord detests different weights and measures (Deut. 25:16); unclean animals are detestable (Lev. 11:10-12); sacrificing blemished animals is detestable to the Lord (Deut. 17:1); I hate your feasts and offerings (Isa. 1:13-14); I hate the pride of Jacob (Amos 6:8); I hate false oaths (Zech. 8:17); I hate your festivals (Amos 5:21); I hate divorce and covering one's garment with violence (Mal. 2:16).

B3 Abominations
B3a Abominations in general
Do not imitate the abominations of the nations (Deut. 18:9); because you have defiled my sanctuary with your detestable things (Ezek. 5:11); go in and see the

abominations they are committing (Ezek. 8:9); make known to Jerusalem her abominations (Ezek. 16:2); you have multiplied your abominations (Ezek. 16:51); you made your sisters appear righteous by your abominations (Ezek. 16:51); abomination has been committed in Israel and in Jerusalem (Mal. 2:11); let them know the abominations of their fathers (Ezek. 20:4); on the wing of abominations will come one who makes desolate (Dan. 9:27); the abomination of desolation (Dan. 11:31; 12:11; Matt. 24:15); a gold cup full of abominations and the impurity of her fornications (Rev. 17:4); Babylon, the mother of prostitutes and of earth's abominations (Rev. 17:5).

B3b Particular abominations

It is an abomination for kings to do evil (Prov. 16:12); if a man turns away from the law, even his prayer is an abomination (Prov. 28:9); you made my inheritance an abomination (Jer. 2:7); what is exalted among men is an abomination to God (Luke 16:15); an abomination to the Lord: the perverse man (Prov. 3:32); the proud of heart (Prov. 16:5); he who justifies the wicked (Prov. 17:15); lying lips (Prov. 12:22); the sacrifice of the wicked (Prov. 15:8); prostitution (Deut. 23:18); male prostitution (Deut. 23:18); graven images (Deut. 7:25-6); an idol (Deut. 27:15); the one who chooses idols (Isa. 41:24); differing weights (Prov. 20:23); remarrying the wife you divorced (Deut. 24:4).

B3c Repenting of abominations

Turn your faces from all your abominations (Ezek. 14:6); mark the foreheads of those who mourn the abominations being committed (Ezek. 9:4); if you put away your abominations from my presence (Jer. 4:1).

C Hating God

Haters of God (Rom. 1:30); God will repay those who hate him with destruction (Deut. 7:10); punishing those who hate me (Exod. 20:5); I will repay those who hate me (Deut. 32:41); visiting the iniquity of the fathers on the children of those who hate me (Deut. 5:9); let those who hate you flee before you (Num. 10:35; Ps. 68:1); he who hates me hates my Father also (John 15:23); do I not hate those who hate you? (Ps. 139:21); the world hates me because I testify against it (John 7:7); if the world hates you, it hated me before it hated you (John 15:18); they have seen and hated me and my Father (John 15:24); once we were hateful and hating (Titus 3:3).

D Hating people

D1 About hating people

Do not hate your brother (Lev. 19:17); he who hates his brother is in darkness (1 John 2:9-11); he who hates his brother is a murderer (1 John 3:15); he who says, 'I love God', and hates his brother, is a liar (1 John 4:20); love your neighbour and hate your enemy (Matt. 5:43); may your seed possess the gate of those who hate them (Gen. 24:60); I will give you into the hands of those you hate (Ezek. 23:28); he will hate the one master and love the other (Matt. 6:24; Luke 16:13); lest in war they join those who hate us (Exod. 1:10); many will betray and hate each other (Matt. 24:10).

D2 Hating the righteous

They hate him who speaks the truth (Amos 5:10); do not reprove a scoffer lest he hate you (Prov. 9:8); they hate him who reproves in the gate (Amos 5:10); men of bloodshed hate the blameless (Prov. 29:10).

D3 Hating peoples

It is an abomination to the Egyptians to eat with Hebrews (Gen. 43:32); shepherds are detestable to the Egyptians (Gen. 46:34); the sacrifices would be detestable to the Egyptians (Exod. 8:26); Israel had become odious to the Philistines (1 Sam. 13:4); the Ammonites had become odious to David (2 Sam. 10:6;

1 Chr. 19:6); the Jews overmastered those who hated them (Esther 9:1).

D4 Hating individuals

The Lord saw that Leah was hated (Gen. 29:31); the Lord has heard that I was hated (Gen. 29:33); Amnon hated Tamar more than he had loved her (2 Sam. 13:15); Absalom hated Amnon (2 Sam. 13:22); I thought you hated her (Judg. 15:2); his brothers hated Joseph (Gen. 37:4); you hate those who love you (2 Sam. 19:6); I hate Micaiah because he prophesies evil (1 Kgs. 22:8; 2 Chr. 18:7); the beast and the ten horns will hate the harlot (Rev. 17:16).

D5 Hating without a cause

Many hate me wrongfully (Ps. 38:19); those who hate me without a cause (Ps. 35:19); those who hate me without a cause are more than the hairs of my head (Ps. 69:4); they hated me without a cause (John 15:25).

D6 Being hated

D6a People being hated

You have made me an abomination to my friends (Ps. 88:8); my enemies hate me with violent hatred (Ps. 25:19); your brothers who hate you cast you out (Isa. 66:5); all men will hate you because of me (Matt. 10:22); you will be hated by all for my name's sake (Matt. 24:9; Mark 13:13; Luke 21:17); blessed are you when men hate you (Luke 6:22); if the world hates you, it hated me before it hated you (John 15:18); the world has hated them (John 17:14); do not be surprised if the world hates you (1 John 3:13); I chose you out of the world, therefore the world hates you (John 15:19).

D6b Reaction when hated

I will look [in triumph] on those who hate me (Ps. 118:7); God delivered me from those who hated me (2 Sam. 22:18; Ps. 18:17); that we should be delivered from the hand of those who hate us (Luke 1:71); you have put to shame those who hate us (Ps. 44:7); lift up the ass of him who hates you (Exod. 23:5); do good to those who hate you (Luke 6:27).

E Hating things

E1 Hating evil

The fear of the Lord is to hate evil (Prov. 8:13); let those who love the Lord hate evil (Ps. 97:10); hate evil, love good (Amos 5:15); hate what is evil, hold fast what is good (Rom. 12:9); I hate falsehood (Ps. 119:163); I hate the work of those who fall away (Ps. 101:3); he who hates bribes will live (Prov. 15:27); you love righteousness and hate iniquity (Ps. 45:7; Heb. 1:9); I do not do what I want, but what I hate (Rom. 7:15); hating even the garment spotted by the flesh (Jude 23); you hate the deeds of the Nicolaitans, which I also hate (Rev. 2:6); do I not hate those who hate you? (Ps. 139:21-2).

E2 Hating uncleanness

These of the birds you shall detest (Lev. 11:13); do not make yourselves detestable through swarming things (Lev. 11:43); the practice of homosexuality is an abomination (Lev. 18:22; 20:13); do not perform abominable practices (Lev. 18:30).

E3 Hating good

You who hate good and love evil (Mic. 3:2); men will be haters of good (2 Tim. 3:3); they hated knowledge (Prov. 1:29); how I hated discipline! (Prov. 5:12); he who hates reproof is stupid (Prov. 12:1); you who abhor justice and twist everything which is straight (Mic. 3:9).

E4 Hating life

I loathe my life (Job 9:21); I loathe my life because of the daughters of Heth (Gen. 27:46); I hated life (Eccles. 2:17); he who hates his life in this world will keep it (John 12:25).

E5 Hating food
We hate this worthless food (Num. 21:5); they hated all kinds of food (Ps. 107:18); his soul loathes food (Job 33:20); until the meat becomes loathsome to you (Num. 11:20).

F Not hating
Do not abhor an Edomite or an Egyptian (Deut. 23:7); he who does not hate father, mother etc. cannot be my disciple (Luke 14:26); the world cannot hate you but it hates me (John 7:7).

889 Endearment

A Kissing
A1 Good kissing
A right answer is a kiss on the lips (Prov. 24:26); greet one another with a holy kiss (Rom. 16:16; 1 Cor. 16:20; 2 Cor. 13:12; 1 Thess. 5:26); greet one another with a kiss of love (1 Pet. 5:14); justice and peace have kissed (Ps. 85:10).

A2 Evil kissing
Every mouth that has not kissed Baal (1 Kgs. 19:18); if my mouth kissed my hand (Job 31:27); the harlot kisses him (Prov. 7:13); the kisses of an enemy are profuse (Prov. 27:6).

A3 People kissing
Let him kiss me with the kisses of his mouth (S. of S. 1:2); if I met you outside I would kiss you (S. of S. 8:1); the father kissed the prodigal (Luke 15:20); let me kiss my father and mother (1 Kgs. 19:20); the elders kissed Paul (Acts 20:37); Jacob kissed Rachel (Gen. 29:11); Joseph kissed his brothers (Gen. 45:15); Joseph fell on Jacob's neck (Gen. 46:29); Naomi kissed her daughters-in-law (Ruth 1:9); Orpah kissed Naomi (Ruth 1:14); Samuel kissed Saul (1 Sam. 10:1); Jonathan and David kissed each other (1 Sam. 20:41); you did not permit me to kiss my sons and daughters (Gen. 31:28).

A4 Kissing Christ
Judas came to kiss Jesus (Luke 22:47); the one I kiss is the man (Matt. 26:48-9; Mark 14:44-5); do you betray the Son of Man with a kiss? (Luke 22:48); this woman kissed my feet (Luke 7:45); kiss his feet, lest he be angry (Ps. 2:12).

B Embracing
A time to embrace and a time to refrain from embracing (Eccles. 3:5); the poor man's ewe lamb would lie in his bosom (2 Sam. 12:3); Abimelech saw Isaac caressing his wife Rebekah (Gen. 26:8); let his right hand embrace me (S. of S. 2:6; 8:3); wisdom will honour you if you embrace her (Prov. 4:8); his father embraced him and kissed him (Luke 15:20); Paul embraced Eutychus (Acts 20:10); they wept and embraced Paul and kissed him (Acts 20:37).

890 Darling. Favourite

A God's favourite
The Lord loves the gates of Zion more than all the dwelling places of Jacob (Ps. 87:2).

B Man's favourite
Isaac loved Esau but Rebekah loved Jacob (Gen. 25:28); Jacob loved Rachel more than Leah (Gen. 29:30); Israel loved Joseph more than all his sons (Gen. 37:3-4); Elkanah gave Hannah a double portion for he loved her (1 Sam. 1:5); Rehoboam loved Maacah more than all his other wives and concubines (2 Chr. 11:21); the king loved Esther more than all the women (Esther 2:17); she is her mother's favourite (S. of S. 6:9).

891 Anger

A Anger in general
A harsh word stirs up anger (Prov. 15:1); pressing anger produces strife (Prov. 30:33); the wrath of men will

praise you (Ps. 76:10); do not let the sun go down on your anger (Eph. 4:26).

B God's anger
B1 God's anger in general
B1a God has anger
God has indignation every day (Ps. 7:11); who can stand before you when you are angry? (Ps. 76:7); who can stand before his indignation? (Nahum 1:6); at his wrath the earth quakes (Jer. 10:10); should we say God is unjust to inflict wrath on us? (Rom. 3:5); God overturns the mountains in his anger (Job 9:5); the earth shook because God was angry (2 Sam. 22:8; Ps. 18:7); God willing to show his wrath and make known his power (Rom. 9:22); the law brings wrath (Rom. 4:15).

B1b Will God be angry?
Will you be angry for ever? (Ps. 79:5; 85:5); would you not be angry? (Ezra 9:14); will you be angry with the whole assembly? (Num. 16:22); how long will you be angry with the prayer of your people? (Ps. 80:4).

B1c God will be angry
Leave me alone that my anger may burn against them (Exod. 32:10); arise, O Lord, in your anger (Ps. 7:6); the Lord did not turn from his fierce anger (2 Kgs. 23:26); if you rebel today, tomorrow the Lord will be angry with all Israel (Josh. 22:18); if you serve other gods, the Lord will be angry (Deut. 7:4); the Lord will shatter kings in the day of his wrath (Ps. 110:5); God's anger will burn against you (Josh. 23:16); in anger and wrath I will execute vengeance (Mic. 5:15).

B1d Speed of God's anger
God is slow to anger (Exod. 34:6; Num. 14:18; Neh. 9:17; Ps. 86:15; 103:8; 145:8; Joel 2:13); the Lord is slow to anger and great in power (Nahum 1:3); his anger lasts for a moment, but his favour is for a lifetime (Ps. 30:5); in a little while my anger will be spent (Isa. 10:25); he does not retain his anger for ever but delights in steadfast love (Mic. 7:18); his anger is quickly kindled (Ps. 2:12).

B2 God angry with his people
B2a God will be angry with his people
The anger of the Lord will be kindled against you (Deut. 6:15); I will vent my fury on you (Ezek. 16:42); wrath will be on this people (Luke 21:23).

B2b God is angry with his people
Why does your anger burn against your people? (Exod. 32:11); or are you exceedingly angry with us? (Lam. 5:22); his anger is not turned away (Isa. 5:25; 9:12, 17, 21; 10:4); the fierce anger of the Lord has not turned back from us (Jer. 4:8); great is the wrath of the Lord poured out on us (2 Chr. 34:21); I have consumed them in my anger (Ezek. 43:8); my anger burns against them (Hos. 8:5); my anger is kindled against the shepherds (Zech. 10:3); my wrath burns against this place (2 Kgs. 22:17); great wrath burns against us (2 Kgs. 22:13); the burning anger of the Lord is against you (2 Chr. 28:11); Assyria, the rod of my anger (Isa. 10:5); my wrath is against all their multitude (Ezek. 7:14); wrath is on all their multitude (Ezek. 7:12); be ashamed of your harvest because of the Lord's anger (Jer. 12:13); he has kindled his anger against me (Job 19:11); you have kindled a fire in my anger which will burn for ever (Jer. 17:4); you increase your anger towards me (Job 10:17); God's anger is against all those who forsake him (Ezra 8:22); the wrath of God has come upon them (1 Thess. 2:16); full of the wrath of the Lord (Isa. 51:20).

B2c God was angry with his people
When the Lord heard what you said, he was angry (Deut. 1:34); the anger of the Lord burned against Israel (Num. 25:3); the Lord's anger burned against Israel because of Achan (Josh. 7:1); wrath came on them for

serving the Asherim (2 Chr. 24:18); the Lord's anger burned against his people (Num. 11:33; Judg. 2:14); I was angry with that generation (Heb. 3:10); I was angry with my people (Isa. 47:6); as I swore in my wrath, they will never enter my rest (Ps. 95:11; Heb. 3:11; 4:3); he was angry with those who sinned, whose bodies fell in the wilderness (Heb. 3:17); I gave you a king in my anger and took him away in my wrath (Hos. 13:11).

B3 God angry with all the earth

In anger put down the peoples (Ps. 56:7); the Lord is angry with all nations (Isa. 34:2); I am very angry with the nations who are at ease (Zech. 1:15); you trampled the nations in anger (Hab. 3:12); pour out your wrath on the nations which do not know you (Ps. 79:6; Jer. 10:25); the nations were angry, and your wrath has come (Rev. 11:18); the Lord overthrew the cities of the plain in his anger (Deut. 29:23); to pour out on the nations my burning anger (Zeph. 3:8); the day of God's wrath (Zeph. 2:2; Rom. 2:5); the day of the Lord's wrath (Zeph. 1:18); the day of the Lord is a day of wrath (Zeph. 1:15); the day of the Lord will come with burning anger (Isa. 13:9); the cup of God's anger (Isa. 51:22); the cup of the wine of wrath (Jer. 25:15; Rev. 16:19); the wine of the wrath of God, poured unmixed in the cup of his anger (Rev. 14:10); pour out the seven bowls of the wrath of God on the earth (Rev. 16:1); the winepress of the wrath of God (Isa. 63:1-6; Rev. 14:19; 19:15); fleeing from the wrath to come (Luke 3:7).

B4 God angry with people

The wrath of God is against all wickedness of men (Rom. 1:18); for those who follow evil there will be wrath and anger (Rom. 2:8); the ruler is God's servant to execute his wrath on the wrongdoer (Rom. 13:4); vessels of wrath designed for destruction (Rom. 9:22); we were by nature children of wrath (Eph. 2:3); God's wrath comes on the disobedient (Eph. 5:6); the wrath of God remains on him (John 3:36); because of these things, God's wrath is coming (Col. 3:6); the Lord's anger against Moses (Exod. 4:14; Deut. 1:37); the anger of the Lord burned against Aaron and Miriam (Num. 12:9); the Lord's anger broke out against Uzzah (2 Sam. 6:7-8; 1 Chr. 13:10); the Lord was angry with Solomon (1 Kgs. 11:9); wrath came on Hezekiah because he was proud (2 Chr. 32:25); God was angry with Amaziah (2 Chr. 25:15); God was angry with Job's friends (Job 42:7); do not rebuke me in your anger (Ps. 6:1; 38:1); do not turn me away in anger (Ps. 27:9).

B5 Provoking God to anger

They provoked the Lord to anger (Judg. 2:12; 2 Kgs. 21:15; Ps. 106:29, 32); they provoked him to anger with their abominations (Deut. 32:16); they provoked me to anger with their idols (Deut. 32:21); they provoked the Lord to anger with their Asherim (1 Kgs. 14:15); at Horeb you provoked the Lord to wrath (Deut. 9:8); Ahaz provoked the Lord to anger (2 Chr. 28:25); Manasseh provoked the Lord to anger (2 Kgs. 33:6); Ahaziah provoked the Lord to anger (1 Kgs. 22:53); you multiplied your harlotry to provoke me to anger (Ezek. 16:26); our fathers angered the God of heaven (Ezra 5:12).

B6 Averting God's anger

In anger remember mercy (Hab. 3:2); turn from your burning anger (Exod. 32:12); put away your indignation towards us (Ps. 85:4); do not let your anger burn (Judg. 6:39); God may turn from his anger so that we do not perish (Jonah 3:9); the priests shall camp around the congregation so that there will not be wrath on the congregation (Num. 1:53); hang the leaders that the Lord's anger may turn away (Num. 25:4); Phinehas has turned away my wrath (Num. 25:11); Moses stood in the breach to turn God away from his wrath (Ps.

106:23); when Rehoboam humbled himself the anger of the Lord turned away (2 Chr. 12:12); a covenant to turn his burning anger from us (2 Chr. 29:10); I have sworn not to be angry with you (Isa. 54:9); will he be angry for ever? (Jer. 3:5); I will not always be angry (Isa. 57:16); he will not keep his anger for ever (Ps. 103:9); we are saved from God's wrath (Rom. 5:9); God did not appoint us to wrath but to salvation (1 Thess. 5:9); my anger has turned away from them (Hos. 14:4); seven last plagues, for with them the wrath of God is ended (Rev. 15:1); God will not turn back his anger (Job 9:13); the anger of the Lord will not turn back (Jer. 23:20).

C Christ's anger

Jesus looked round at them with anger (Mark 3:5); Jesus was indignant at the disciples (Mark 10:14); hide us from him who sits on the throne and from the wrath of the Lamb (Rev. 6:16).

D People's anger

D1 People's anger in general

A king's wrath is like a lion's roar (Prov. 19:12); a king's wrath is like messengers of death (Prov. 16:14); anger is in the bosom of fools (Eccles. 7:9); Edom kept his fury for ever (Amos 1:11); be subject to rulers, not just because of wrath but for conscience' sake (Rom. 13:5); who is stumbled and I do not burn with indignation? (2 Cor. 11:29); Moses did not fear the anger of the king (Heb. 11:27); I will provoke them to anger with a foolish nation (Deut. 32:21); by a foolish nation I will anger you (Rom. 10:19).

D2 Angry people

Cain was angry about his sacrifices (Gen. 4:5-6); cursed be their anger (Gen. 49:7); Samson's anger burned (Judg. 14:19); Saul was angry about Jabesh-gilead (1 Sam. 11:6); Saul was angry about David's success (1 Sam. 18:8); David was angry at Perez-uzzah (2 Sam. 6:8); David was angry at Nathan's story (2 Sam. 12:5); David was angry about Amnon (2 Sam. 13:21); Ahab was sullen and angry (1 Kgs. 20:43); Naaman went away angry (2 Kgs. 5:11); the troops from Ephraim were furious to be sent home (2 Chr. 25:10); Sanballat was angry that the wall was being rebuilt (Neh. 4:1, 7); Nehemiah was angry (Neh. 5:6); Jonah was angry (Jonah 4:1, 4); when Herod saw he had been tricked, he became enraged (Matt. 2:16); Paul's spirit was provoked when he saw the idols (Acts 17:16); they were filled with rage (Acts 19:28).

D3 Angry with God

Why are you angry? (Gen. 4:6); the fool rages against the Lord (Prov. 19:3); David was angry because the Lord broke out against Uzzah (1 Chr. 13:11); I have a right to be angry, even to death (Jonah 4:9); why did the Gentiles rage and the peoples imagine futile things? (Acts 4:25); the nations were angry, and your wrath has come (Rev. 11:18).

D4 Angry with Christ

The people in the synagogue were furious with Jesus (Luke 4:28); they were angry because he healed on the Sabbath (Luke 6:11; 13:14); why are you angry with me for healing on the Sabbath? (John 7:23); the priests were indignant (Matt. 21:15); they were infuriated (Acts 5:33).

D5 People angry with others

Jacob was angry with Laban (Gen. 31:36); Jacob's sons were furious about Shechem (Gen. 34:7); Potiphar was angry with Joseph (Gen. 39:19); what if Joseph holds a grudge against us? (Gen. 50:15); Moses was angry with Pharaoh (Exod. 11:8); Moses was angry with the people (Exod. 16:20; 32:19); Moses was angry with Aaron's sons (Lev. 10:16); Balaam was angry with his donkey (Num. 22:27); Balak was angry with Balaam (Num. 24:10); Saul was angry with Jonathan (1 Sam. 20:30);

Jonathan was very angry with his father (1 Sam. 20:34); Abner was angry with Ish-bosheth (2 Sam. 3:8); Asa was angry with the seer (2 Chr. 16:10); Uzziah was enraged with the priest (2 Chr. 26:19); King Ahasuerus was furious with Queen Vashti (Esther 1:12); Haman was filled with rage against Mordecai (Esther 3:5; 5:9); Herodias bore a grudge against John (Mark 6:19); Herod was angry with the people of Tyre and Sidon (Acts 12:20); some indignantly said, 'Why this waste of perfume?' (Mark 14:4); the ten were indignant with James and John (Matt. 20:24; Mark 10:41); they were furious with Stephen (Acts 7:54); the prodigal's older brother was angry (Luke 15:28).

E Avoiding anger
Cease from anger (Ps. 37:8); get rid of anger (Eph. 4:31; Col. 3:8); do not be quick to anger (Eccles. 7:9); be slow to anger (Jas. 1:19); the anger of man does not work the righteousness of God (Jas. 1:20); outbursts of anger are deeds of the flesh (Gal. 5:20); everyone who is angry with his brother will be liable to judgement (Matt. 5:22); an elder [overseer] must not be quick-tempered (Titus 1:7); a soft answer turns away wrath (Prov. 15:1); a gift in secret averts anger (Prov. 21:14); fathers, do not provoke your children to anger (Eph. 6:4); do not be angry because I cannot get up (Gen. 31:35); until your brother's anger subsides (Gen. 27:44); do not let the sun go down on your anger (Eph. 4:26).

892 Quick temper

A Quick-tempered
A man of quick temper acts foolishly (Prov. 14:17); a hasty temper exalts folly (Prov. 14:29); a fool loses his temper (Prov. 29:11); a hot-tempered man abounds in transgression (Prov. 29:22); a hot-tempered man stirs up strife (Prov. 15:18); if you rescue a man of great temper you will only have to do it again (Prov. 19:19); do not associate with a hot-tempered man (Prov. 22:24).

B Fierce men
Cursed be Simeon and Levi's anger for it is fierce (Gen. 49:7); Benjamin is a ravening wolf (Gen. 49:27); David and his men are fierce (2 Sam. 17:8); fierce wolves will come, not sparing the flock (Acts 20:29).
VIOLENCE, see 176.

893 Sullenness
Ahab was sullen and angry (1 Kgs. 20:43; 21:4); when you fast do not put on a sullen face (Matt. 6:16).

894 Marriage

A Marriage in general
A1 About marriage
Do not break faith with the wife of your youth (Mal. 2:14-15); the husband and wife should fulfil their duty to each other (1 Cor. 7:3); let marriage be held in honour and the marriage bed be undefiled (Heb. 13:4); younger widows want to marry (1 Tim. 5:11).
A2 Rules about marriage
A2a Marriage allowed
The sons of this age marry and are given in marriage (Luke 20:34); do we not have a right to take a believer as wife? (1 Cor. 9:5); each man should have his own wife and each woman her husband (1 Cor. 7:2); if they do not have self-control, let them marry (1 Cor. 7:9); if you marry you do not sin, and if a virgin marries, she does not sin (1 Cor. 7:28); let them marry, it is no sin (1 Cor. 7:36); I want younger widows to marry (1 Tim. 5:14); marriage to a captive woman is permitted (Deut. 21:11).

A2b Marriage controlled
Do not covet your neighbour's wife (Exod. 20:17; Deut. 5:21); a man must not marry his father's wife (Deut. 22:30); a man must not marry a woman and her sister (Lev. 18:18); a man must not marry a woman and her mother (Lev. 20:14); someone has his father's wife (1 Cor. 5:1); if a man takes his brother's wife, it is impurity (Lev. 20:21); it is not lawful for you to have your brother's wife (Matt. 14:4; Mark 6:18); a man will leave his father and mother and will be joined to his wife (Matt. 19:5; Mark 10:7); if such is the relationship of man and wife, it is better not to marry (Matt. 19:10); the wife should not leave her husband (1 Cor. 7:10); priests must not marry prostitutes or divorcees (Lev. 21:7); the high priest must take a wife in her virginity (Lev. 21:13-14); he who marries a divorced woman commits adultery (Matt. 5:32); a bishop [elder, overseer] must be the husband of one wife (1 Tim. 3:2; Titus 1:6); as must a deacon (1 Tim. 3:12); an enrolled widow should have been the wife of one man (1 Tim. 5:9); a widow is free to marry but only in the Lord (1 Cor. 7:39); a married woman is bound to her husband as long as he lives (Rom. 7:2; 1 Cor. 7:39); a man recently married must not go to war (Deut. 24:5).

A2c Remarriage
A divorced woman must not re-marry her first husband (Deut. 24:4); if the divorced woman becomes another man's wife (Deut. 24:2); he who divorces his wife and marries another commits adultery against her (Mark 10:11); if she divorces her husband and marries another, she commits adultery (Mark 10:12); if she remarries after her husband's death she is not an adulteress (Rom. 7:3).

A2d Levirate marriage
The husband's brother must marry the widow (Deut. 25:5; Matt. 22:24; Mark 12:19; Luke 20:28); raise up children for your brother (Gen. 38:8).

A2e Rules about multiple marriages
A king must not take many wives (Deut. 17:17); if a man has two wives, one loved and one not (Deut. 21:15-17); on taking a second wife, marriage rights must not be reduced (Exod. 21:10).

A2f Intermarriage
Do not intermarry with them (Exod. 34:16; Deut. 7:3; Josh. 23:12; 1 Kgs. 11:2; Ezra 9:12); do not be unequally yoked together with unbelievers (2 Cor. 6:14); do not take a wife from the Canaanites (Gen. 24:3); foreign wives will turn away your sons from following me (Deut. 7:4); we promise not to intermarry with them (Neh. 10:30); daughters who inherit should not marry men from other tribes (Num. 36:3); intermarry with us (Gen. 34:9).

B Particular marriages
B1 Individuals marrying
She will be led to the king (Ps. 45:14); a believer as wife, as the rest of the apostles, the Lord's brothers and Cephas? (1 Cor. 9:5); there was a wedding at Cana in Galilee (John 2:1); I have married a wife and therefore I cannot come (Luke 14:20); Judah married a Canaanite (Gen. 38:2); a man of Levi took a woman of Levi (Exod. 2:1); the daughters of Zelophehad married their cousins (Num. 36:11); Abraham married Sarah and Nahor married Milcah (Gen. 11:29); Isaac married Rebekah (Gen. 24:67); Amram married his father's sister Jochebed (Exod. 6:20); Aaron married Elisheba (Exod. 6:23); Boaz married Ruth (Ruth 4:13); Saul offered his daughter Merab to David in marriage (1 Sam. 18:17); but she was given to Adriel instead (1 Sam. 18:19); Solomon married Pharaoh's daughter (1 Kgs. 3:1; 2 Chr. 8:11); Ahab married Jezebel (1 Kgs. 16:31); Jehoshaphat allied himself with Ahab by marriage (2 Chr. 18:1);

Jehoram married Ahab's daughter (2 Kgs. 8:18; 2 Chr. 21:6); Joseph married Mary (Matt. 1:24).

B2 Particular multiple marriages
Lamech married two wives, Adah and Zillah (Gen. 4:19); Sarah gave Hagar to Abraham as wife (Gen. 16:3); Abraham took another wife, Keturah (Gen. 25:1); Esau married two Hittite women, Judith and Basemath (Gen. 26:34); Esau married Adah and Oholibamah (Gen. 36:2); Esau also married Mahalath daughter of Ishmael (Gen. 28:9); Jacob married Leah (Gen. 29:21-5); Rachel (Gen. 29:28-30); Bilhah (Gen. 30:4); and Zilpah (Gen. 30:9); Gideon had many wives (Judg. 8:30); Elkanah had two wives (1 Sam. 1:2); Solomon had 700 wives (1 Kgs. 11:3); Rehoboam had 18 wives and 60 concubines (2 Chr. 11:21); Abijah took 14 wives (2 Chr. 13:21); Jehoiada took two wives for Joash (2 Chr. 24:3); if you take other wives besides my daughters (Gen. 31:50); seven women saying, 'Let us be called by your name!' (Isa. 4:1).

B3 Particular intermarriage
They intermarried with them (Judg. 3:6; Ezra 9:2); they had married foreign women (Neh. 13:23); lists of those who had married foreign wives (Ezra 10:18-44); Jews were linked to Tobiah by marriage (Neh. 6:18); as iron mixed with clay, they will join together in marriage (Dan. 2:43); the sons of God took to wife the daughters of men whom they chose (Gen. 6:2); Esau married Hittites (Gen. 26:34); Shechem wanted Dinah as his wife (Gen. 34:4); Joseph married Asenath (Gen. 41:45); Moses married Zipporah (Exod. 2:21); Moses had married a Cushite (Num. 12:1); Samson married a Philistine woman (Judg. 14:2); Naomi's sons married Moabite women (Ruth 1:4); Judah married a Canaanite (Gen. 38:2).

B4 Giving in marriage
I gave my daughter to this man as his wife (Deut. 22:16); it is better to give her to you than to anyone else (Gen. 29:19); give Dinah to him as wife (Gen. 34:8); Tamar had not been given to Shelah as wife (Gen. 38:14, 26); Reuel [Jethro] gave Zipporah his daughter to Moses (Exod. 2:21); Caleb gave his daughter in marriage to the one who took Kiriath-sepher (Josh. 15:16-17; Judg. 1:12-13); the king will give his daughter in marriage to the man who kills Goliath (1 Sam. 17:25); Saul gave David his daughter Michal in marriage on payment of 100 Philistine foreskins (1 Sam. 18:27); Sarah gave her maid Hagar to Abraham as wife (Gen. 16:3); Rachel gave her maid Bilhah to Jacob as wife (Gen. 30:4); Leah gave her maid Zilpah to Jacob as wife (Gen. 30:9); do not give your daughters to their sons nor take their daughters for your sons (Deut. 7:3).

B5 Taking a wife
Take a wife for my son from my land (Gen. 24:4); Ibzan took 30 women of another clan for his 30 sons (Judg. 12:9); take to yourself a wife of harlotry (Hos. 1:2); do not be afraid to take Mary your wife (Matt. 1:20); let each one know how to possess his vessel in holiness and honour (1 Thess. 4:4).

C Husbands and wives
C1 Husbands and wives in general
Statutes the Lord commanded concerning a man and his wife (Num. 30:16); husbands, live considerately with your wives (1 Pet. 3:7); whoever comes to me and does not hate his wife and children (Luke 14:26); the voice of bridegroom and bride will cease (Jer. 7:34); the voice of joy, of bridegroom and bride, will be heard again (Jer. 33:11).

C2 Husbands / bridegrooms
Husbands, love your wives (Eph. 5:25; Col. 3:19); the head of a woman is her husband (1 Cor. 11:3); a husband may annul his wife's vows (Num. 30:6-15);

you are a bridegroom of blood (Exod. 4:25); do wedding guests mourn when the bridegroom is with them? (Matt. 9:15; Mark 2:19; Luke 5:34); ten virgins who went out to meet the bridegroom (Matt. 25:1-10); the friend of the bridegroom rejoices at the bridegroom's voice (John 3:29); the unbelieving husband is sanctified through his wife (1 Cor. 7:14); the married man is concerned to please his wife (1 Cor. 7:33); Joseph was the husband of Mary (Matt. 1:16); call your husband (John 4:16).

C3 Wives
C3a About wives
An excellent wife is her husband's crown (Prov. 12:4); your wife will be like a fruitful vine (Ps. 128:3); a prudent wife is from the Lord (Prov. 19:14); description of an excellent wife (Prov. 31:10-31); he who finds a wife finds a good thing (Prov. 18:22); rejoice in the wife of your youth (Prov. 5:18); drink water from your own cistern (Prov. 5:15); wives, be subject to your husbands (Eph. 5:22; Col. 3:18; 1 Pet. 3:1); teach wives to love their husbands (Titus 2:4); be considerate to your wives (1 Pet. 3:7); as a bride adorns herself with jewels (Isa. 61:10); no one has left house or wife for the sake of the kingdom (Luke 18:29); if your wife entices you to serve other gods, kill her (Deut. 13:6-10).

C3b David's wives
David married Abigail (1 Sam. 25:39-42; 1 Chr. 3:1); David also married Ahinoam (1 Sam. 25:43; 1 Chr. 3:1); Maacah the daughter of Talmai king of Geshur (2 Sam. 3:3; 1 Chr. 3:2); Haggith (2 Sam. 3:4; 1 Chr. 3:2); Abital (2 Sam. 3:4; 1 Chr. 3:3); Eglah (2 Sam. 3:5; 1 Chr. 3:3); Bath-shua (1 Chr. 3:5); David took more wives (2 Sam. 5:13; 1 Chr. 14:3); David married Bathsheba (2 Sam. 11:27); give me my wife Michal (2 Sam. 3:13-15).

C3c Other wives
Lot's wife looked back (Gen. 19:26); Potiphar's wife cast eyes on Joseph (Gen. 39:7); I have acquired Ruth to be my wife (Ruth 4:10); David was the father of Solomon by the wife of Uriah (Matt. 1:6).

C3d Wives for Benjamin
No one will give his daughter in marriage to a Benjaminite (Judg. 21:1); how will we provide wives? (Judg. 21:7, 16); seize a wife from the girls of Shiloh (Judg. 21:21).

C3e Transferring wives
Well-fed lusty stallions neighing after their neighbours' wives (Jer. 5:8); another will lie with your wives in broad daylight (2 Sam. 12:11); you said, 'She is my sister', so I took her for my wife (Gen. 12:19); you will die for taking a married woman (Gen. 20:3); Samson's wife was given to his friend (Judg. 14:20); David's wife Michal given to Palti (1 Sam. 25:44); Michal was taken from Paltiel and given back to David (2 Sam. 3:15); you took Uriah's wife to be your wife (2 Sam. 12:9-10); I gave your master's wives into your bosom (2 Sam. 12:8); Absalom went in to his father's concubines (2 Sam. 16:21-2); Adonijah wanted Abishag as his wife (1 Kgs. 2:17); your most beautiful wives are mine (1 Kgs. 20:3); their wives will be turned over to others (Jer. 6:12); Herod had married Herodias, his brother Philip's wife (Mark 6:17-18); having no children he left his wife to his brother (Matt. 22:25); all seven had her as wife (Matt. 22:28; Mark 12:23; Luke 20:33).

D Marriage to God
Your Maker is your husband (Isa. 54:5); the Lord will take delight in you and your land will be married (Isa. 62:4); you will call me 'my husband' (Hos. 2:16); that you might belong to another, who has been raised from the dead (Rom. 7:4); I remember how as a bride you loved me (Jer. 2:2); return, for I am your husband (Jer. 3:14); I betrothed you to one husband, to Christ (2

Cor. 11:2); I will betroth you to me in righteousness (Hos. 2:19-20); the marriage of the Lamb has come (Rev. 19:7); blessed are those invited to the wedding supper of the Lamb (Rev. 19:9); I will show you the bride, the wife of the Lamb (Rev. 21:9); new Jerusalem as a bride adorned for her husband (Rev. 21:2).

E No marriage
E1 Not marrying
Some forbid marriage (1 Tim. 4:3); you must not marry in this place (Jer. 16:2); I am too old to have a husband (Ruth 1:12); 'it is better not to marry' (Matt. 19:10); it is good for a man not to touch a woman (1 Cor. 7:1); he who marries does well but he who does not marry does better (1 Cor. 7:38); she is not my wife and I am not her husband (Hos. 2:2); those who have wives should live as though they had none (1 Cor. 7:29).

E2 Marriage no more
In the resurrection they will not marry (Matt. 22:30; Mark 12:25; Luke 20:35); in the days of Noah they were marrying and giving in marriage until the flood came (Matt. 24:38; Luke 17:27); the voice of bridegroom and bride will be heard in you no more (Rev. 18:23).

F Betrothal
An engaged man should return from war (Deut. 20:7); Lot spoke to his sons-in-law who were to take his daughters (Gen. 19:14); Mary was pledged in marriage to Joseph (Matt. 1:18; Luke 1:27; 2:5); I betrothed you to one husband, to Christ (2 Cor. 11:2); I will betroth you to me in righteousness (Hos. 2:19-20).
BRIDE PRICE, see 809C.

895 Celibacy

A Unmarried
The unmarried person is concerned with the things of the Lord (1 Cor. 7:32-4); if he came in single, he shall go out single (Exod. 21:3); it is good for them to remain as I am [unmarried] (1 Cor. 7:8); if you are unmarried, do not seek for a wife (1 Cor. 7:27); if he decides not to marry he will do well (1 Cor. 7:37); how can this be, seeing I have no husband? (Luke 1:34); if a wife leaves her husband she should remain single or be reconciled (1 Cor. 7:11).
EUNUCHS, see 172A3.
NO MARRIAGE, see 894E.

B Virgins
Proof of a woman's virginity on marriage (Deut. 22:13-21); virgin princesses wore a long-sleeved robe (2 Sam. 13:18); the high priest must marry a virgin (Lev. 21:13, 14); a priest shall marry a virgin or a widow of a priest (Ezek. 44:22); a priest may defile himself on the death of his virgin sister (Lev. 21:3); spare those women who have not known man (Num. 31:18); a virgin is concerned with the things of the Lord (1 Cor. 7:34); Lot's daughters had never had relations with a man (Gen. 19:8); Jephthah's daughter would remain a virgin (Judg. 11:37-9); they sought a virgin to keep David warm (1 Kgs. 1:2); beautiful young virgins were sought for Ahasuerus (Esther 2:2); a virgin will conceive (Isa. 7:14; Matt. 1:23); a virgin called Mary betrothed to Joseph (Luke 1:27); Philip had four virgin daughters (Acts 21:9); Paul wanted to present them to Christ as a pure virgin (2 Cor. 11:2); the parable of the ten virgins (Matt. 25:1-12).

C Chastity
They have not been defiled by women for they are virgins (Rev. 14:4); do not refuse one another except by agreement for a season (1 Cor. 7:5); they may eat holy bread if they have kept themselves from women (1 Sam. 21:4).

896 Divorce. Widowhood

A Divorce
A1 Divorce permitted
Is it lawful for a man to divorce his wife? (Matt. 19:3; Mark 10:2); he who divorces his wife must give her a certificate of divorce (Deut. 24:1; Matt. 5:31; 19:7; Mark 10:4); Moses permitted you to divorce your wives because your hearts were hard (Matt. 19:8).
BILLS OF DIVORCE, see 548B2.

A2 About divorce
He who divorces his wife, except for unchastity and marries another commits adultery (Matt. 19:9); he who divorces his wife, except for unchastity, makes her an adulteress (Matt. 5:32); he who divorces his wife and marries another commits adultery (Mark 10:11; Luke 16:18); he who marries a divorced woman commits adultery (Matt. 5:32; Luke 16:18); if she divorces her husband and marries another, she commits adultery (Mark 10:12); if a wife leaves her husband she should remain single or be reconciled (1 Cor. 7:11); if a divorced wife returns to her former husband (Jer. 3:1); a priest must not marry a divorcee (Lev. 21:7, 14).

A3 Actual divorces
Shaharaim sent away his two wives Hushim and Baara (1 Chr. 8:8); separate yourselves from these foreign wives (Ezra 10:11); Joseph wanted to divorce Mary privately (Matt. 1:19).

A4 Divorce from the Lord
I gave faithless Israel her certificate of divorce (Jer. 3:8); where is your mother's certificate of divorce? (Isa. 50:1); as a faithless wife leaves her husband so you have dealt with me (Jer. 3:20).

A5 Avoid divorce
What God has joined together, let not man separate (Mark 10:9); I hate divorce, says the Lord (Mal. 2:16); a wife should not leave her husband (1 Cor. 7:10); a believer should not divorce an unbelieving partner willing to live with them (1 Cor. 7:12-13); if you are bound to a wife, do not seek to be released (1 Cor. 7:27).

B Widowhood
B1 About widows
A widow's vow will stand (Num. 30:9); a priest's daughter widowed may eat the offerings (Lev. 22:13); when you buy the land you acquire the dead man's widow (Ruth 4:5); rules for enrolling widows (1 Tim. 5:3-16); younger widows want to marry (1 Tim. 5:11); the high priest must not marry a widow (Lev. 21:14); a priest shall marry a virgin or a widow of a priest (Ezek. 44:22); I say to unmarried and widows that it is good for them to remain as I am [single] (1 Cor. 7:8); there were many widows in Israel (Luke 4:25).

B2 Actual widows
Naomi was bereft of husband and sons (Ruth 1:5); Abigail the widow of Nabal (1 Sam. 27:3; 30:5; 2 Sam. 2:2); Uriah's widow (2 Sam. 12:15); I am a widow (2 Sam. 14:5); a widow looked after Elijah (1 Kgs. 17:9-16); Anna lived as a widow until she was 84 (Luke 2:37); Elijah was sent to a widow of Zarephath (Luke 4:26); the only son of a widow (Luke 7:12); Tamar was to live as a widow (Gen. 38:11); the ten concubines lived as widows (2 Sam. 20:3).

B3 Helping widows
God judges for orphans and widows (Deut. 10:18); the Lord supports the widow (Ps. 146:9); his brother must marry the widow (Matt. 22:24); honour widows who are widows indeed (1 Tim. 5:3); do not pervert the justice due to a widow (Deut. 27:19); a widow kept coming to the judge (Luke 18:3); plead for the widow (Isa. 1:17); do not take a widow's garment in pledge

(Deut. 24:17); do not afflict a widow (Exod. 22:22); give the tithe to the widow (Deut. 14:29; 26:12-13); invite the widow to the Feast of Booths (Deut. 16:14); let the widow eat the Feast of Weeks with you (Deut. 16:11); leave a forgotten sheaf and gleanings for the widow (Deut. 24:19); true religion is to visit orphans and widows (Jas. 1:27).

B4 Not helping widows

Evildoers murder widows and orphans (Ps. 94:6); you have sent widows away empty (Job 22:9); they devour widows' houses (Mark 12:40; Luke 20:47); they do no good to the widow (Job 24:21); they have wronged the fatherless and widows (Ezek. 22:7); I will be a witness against those who oppress the widow and the orphan (Mal. 3:5); the Hellenist widows were neglected in the daily distribution (Acts 6:1).

897 Benevolence

A Blessing

A1 About blessing

The blessing of the Lord makes rich (Prov. 10:22); blessings accompanying obedience (Deut. 28:2-14); the lesser is blessed by the greater (Heb. 7:7); this is how you are to bless the children of Israel (Num. 6:23); henceforth we call the arrogant blessed (Mal. 3:15); two staffs, called Favour and Union (Zech. 11:7).

A2 God blessing

A2a May God bless!

May your blessing be on your people (Ps. 3:8); bless your heritage (Ps. 28:9); bless your people Israel (Deut. 26:15); oh, that you would bless me indeed! (1 Chr. 4:10); may God almighty bless you (Gen. 28:3); may you be blessed by the Lord (Ruth 3:10); the Lord bless you and keep you (Num. 6:24); the Lord be gracious to you (Num. 6:25); may you be blessed by the Lord (Ps. 115:15); I will not let you go unless you bless me (Gen. 32:26).

A2b God will bless

I will give showers of blessing (Ezek. 34:26); you will be blessed above all peoples (Deut. 7:14); they may curse, but you will bless (Ps. 109:28); he will receive a blessing from the Lord (Ps. 24:5); you will be blessed because they cannot repay you (Luke 14:14); stay in this land and I will bless you (Gen. 26:3); the Lord blesses his people with peace (Ps. 29:11); from this day on I will bless you (Hag. 2:19); I will pour out for you an overflowing blessing (Mal. 3:10); I will surely bless you (Heb. 6:14).

A2c God blesses

Our God blesses us (Ps. 67:6); I will come in the fullness of the blessing of Christ (Rom. 15:29); you were called that you might inherit a blessing (1 Pet. 3:9); do not put a curse on this people, for they are blessed (Num. 22:12); when the kindness and love of God our Saviour appeared (Titus 3:4); land which brings forth useful vegetation receives a blessing from God (Heb. 6:7).

A2d Blessed by God

God blessed the seventh day (Gen. 2:3; Exod. 20:11); like the smell of a field which the Lord has blessed (Gen. 27:27); God has blessed you for ever (Ps. 45:2); God blessed mankind (Gen. 1:28); God blessed Noah and his sons (Gen. 9:1); I will bless Ishmael (Gen. 17:20); the Lord had blessed Abraham (Gen. 24:1); God blessed Isaac (Gen. 25:11); God blessed Jacob (Gen. 35:9); Naphtali, full of the blessing of the Lord (Deut. 33:23); he has blessed and I cannot change it (Num. 23:20); they are a people whom the Lord has blessed (Isa. 61:9); come, blessed of my Father (Matt. 25:34); Jael was most blessed among women (Judg. 5:24); Mary

was blessed among women (Luke 1:42); all generations will call me blessed (Luke 1:48).

A2e Blessed are . . .

Blessed is the man who trusts in the Lord (Jer. 17:7); blessed are those who dwell in your house (Ps. 84:4); blessed is the fruit of your womb! (Luke 1:42); the beatitudes (Matt. 5:3-12; Luke 6:20-3); blessed is she who believed for there will be a fulfilment (Luke 1:45); blessed are those who hear the word of God and keep it (Luke 11:28); if you know these things, blessed are you if you do them (John 13:17); blessed is the people whose God is the Lord (Ps. 33:12; 144:15); blessed are those who take refuge in him (Ps. 2:12; 34:8); blessed is the one you choose (Ps. 65:4); blessed are those who dwell in your house (Ps. 84:4); blessed is he whose transgression is forgiven (Ps. 32:1-2; Rom. 4:7-8); blessed are those who will eat in the kingdom of God (Luke 14:15); blessed are those invited to the wedding supper of the Lamb (Rev. 19:9); blessed and holy is he who has a part in the first resurrection (Rev. 20:6); blessed are the dead who die in the Lord (Rev. 14:13); blessed are those who have not seen yet have believed (John 20:29); blessed is he who reads and they who hear and heed (Rev. 1:3); blessed is the man who fears the Lord (Ps. 112:1; 128:1); blessed is the man who does not walk in the counsel of the wicked (Ps. 1:1).

A3 People blessing

A3a Blessing through God's people

I will bless those who bless you (Gen. 12:3); all nations will be blessed through you (Gen. 12:3; 18:18; 22:18; 26:4; Acts 3:25); in you and your seed all families of the earth will be blessed (Gen. 28:14); Israel will be a blessing in the midst of the earth (Isa. 19:24-5); the Lord blessed Laban because of Jacob (Gen. 30:27, 30); the Lord blessed Potiphar because of Joseph (Gen. 39:5); let your talking be edifying, imparting grace to those who hear (Eph. 4:29).

A3b About people blessing

Bless those who persecute you (Rom. 12:14); bless those who curse you (Luke 6:28); do not repay reviling with reviling but rather bless (1 Pet. 3:9); when reviled we bless (1 Cor. 4:12); bless me also, my father! (Gen. 27:38); we bless you in the name of the Lord (Ps. 129:8); her children rise and bless her (Prov. 31:28); he who blesses with a loud voice early in the morning will be reckoned as a curse (Prov. 27:14); that I may bless you before I die (Gen. 27:4); your brother took away your blessing (Gen. 27:35); have you not reserved a blessing for me? (Gen. 27:36).

A3c People who blessed others

Melchizedek blessed Abraham (Gen. 14:19; Heb. 7:1); Melchizedek blessed him who had the promises (Heb. 7:6); Isaac blessed Jacob (Gen. 27:23; Heb. 11:20); Jacob blessed Joseph's sons (Gen. 48:9; Heb. 11:21); Jacob blessed Joseph (Gen. 48:15); Jacob blessed all his sons (Gen. 49:28); Eli blessed Elkanah (1 Sam. 2:20); Samuel will bless the sacrifice (1 Sam. 9:13); David blessed Barzillai (2 Sam. 19:39); David returned to bless his household (2 Sam. 6:20; 1 Chr. 16:43); Hezekiah blessed the people (2 Chr. 31:8); Simeon blessed them (Luke 2:34); blessing the people: Moses (Exod. 39:43; Deut. 33:1); Aaron (Lev. 9:22); Moses and Aaron (Lev. 9:23); David (2 Sam. 6:18; 1 Chr. 16:2); Solomon (1 Kgs. 8:14, 55; 2 Chr. 6:3).

B Lovingkindness / steadfast love

B1 About God's lovingkindness

With the Lord there is lovingkindness (Ps. 130:7); lovingkindness is yours, O Lord (Ps. 62:12); I am the Lord who practises lovingkindness (Jer. 9:24); the Lord is great in lovingkindness (Ps. 145:8); abounding in lovingkindness (Ps. 103:8); according to the multitude

of his lovingkindnesses (Lam. 3:32); God shows
lovingkindness to thousands (Deut. 5:10); he does not
retain his anger for ever but delights in lovingkindness
(Mic. 7:18); the earth is full of the lovingkindness of the
Lord (Ps. 33:5); how precious is your lovingkindness
(Ps. 36:7); your lovingkindness is better than life (Ps.
63:3); your lovingkindness is great to the heavens (Ps.
57:10); your lovingkindness reaches to the heavens (Ps.
36:5); as high as the heavens, so great is his
lovingkindness (Ps. 103:11); lovingkindness and truth
go before you (Ps. 89:14); all the paths of the Lord are
lovingkindness and truth (Ps. 25:10); he will send forth
his lovingkindness and truth (Ps. 57:3); lovingkindness
and truth have met together (Ps. 85:10).

B2 God's lovingkindness is eternal

God's lovingkindness endures for ever (1 Chr. 16:34;
2 Chr. 5:13; 7:3; Ps. 106:1; 107:1; 118:1; 136:1-26; Jer. 33:11);
his lovingkindness to Israel endures for ever (Ezra 3:11);
his lovingkindness is everlasting (Ps. 100:5; 138:8); his
lovingkindness is from everlasting to everlasting (Ps.
103:17); the Lord's lovingkindnesses never cease (Lam.
3:22); has his lovingkindness ceased for ever? (Ps. 77:8).

B3 God showing lovingkindness

Show us your lovingkindness (Ps. 85:7); let your
lovingkindness be on us (Ps. 33:22); satisfy us in the
morning with your lovingkindness (Ps. 90:14);
continue your lovingkindness to those who know you
(Ps. 36:10); be gracious to me according to your
lovingkindness (Ps. 51:1); show lovingkindness to my
master Abraham (Gen. 24:12); he has remembered his
lovingkindness (Ps. 98:3); your lovingkindness is great
towards me (Ps. 86:13); blessed be God who has not
removed his lovingkindness from me (Ps. 66:20); I am
unworthy of all the lovingkindness you have shown me
(Gen. 32:10); the Lord showed Joseph lovingkindness
(Gen. 39:21); you show lovingkindness to thousands
(Jer. 32:18); he crowns you with lovingkindness (Ps.
103:4); where are your former lovingkindnesses? (Ps.
89:49).

B4 Responding to God's lovingkindness

Consider the lovingkindness of the Lord (Ps. 107:43);
we have thought on your lovingkindness (Ps. 48:9); to
declare your lovingkindness in the morning (Ps. 92:2);
I will sing of the lovingkindness of the Lord for ever
(Ps. 89:1); I will recount the lovingkindnesses of the
Lord (Isa. 63:7); thank the Lord for his lovingkindness
(Ps. 107:8); I will rejoice in your lovingkindness (Ps.
31:7); will your lovingkindness be declared in the grave?
(Ps. 88:11).

B5 Man's lovingkindness

I desire lovingkindness rather than sacrifice (Hos. 6:6);
your lovingkindness is like a morning cloud (Hos. 6:4);
he did not remember to show lovingkindness (Ps.
109:16); let there be no one to show lovingkindness to
him (Ps. 109:12).

C Grace and favour

C1 God's favour

May God be gracious to us and bless us (Ps. 67:1); the
Lord has shown his favour (Luke 1:25); greetings,
favoured one! (Luke 1:28); may the favour of the Lord
our God be on us (Ps. 90:17); he who finds a wife
obtains favour from the Lord (Prov. 18:22); let us
entreat the favour of the Lord (Zech. 8:22); entreat
God's favour that he may be gracious to us (Mal. 1:9);
the favour of God was on Jesus (Luke 2:40); great grace
was on them all (Acts 4:33); am I seeking the favour of
men or of God? (Gal. 1:10); his mercies are very great
(1 Chr. 21:13); the Lord is gracious and compassionate
(2 Chr. 30:9).

C2 Grace through Christ

C2a Grace be to you

The grace of the Lord Jesus be with you (Rom. 16:20,
24; 1 Cor. 16:23; 1 Thess. 5:28; 2 Thess. 3:18; Rev. 22:21);
the grace of the Lord Jesus be with your spirit (Gal.
6:18; Phil. 4:23; Philem. 25); grace be with you all (Titus
3:15; Heb. 13:25); grace to you and peace from God our
Father and the Lord Jesus Christ (Rom. 1:7; 1 Cor. 1:3; 2
Cor. 1:2; Gal. 1:3; Phil. 1:2); grace and peace to you (Col.
1:2; 1 Thess. 1:1; 2 Thess. 1:2; Titus 1:4; Philem. 3; 2 Pet.
1:2; Rev. 1:4); grace, mercy and peace (1 Tim. 1:2; 2 Tim.
1:2; 2 John 3); grace be with those who love our Lord
Jesus (Eph. 6:24); grace to you and peace from God
(Eph. 1:2); may grace and peace be yours (1 Pet. 1:2).

C2b The grace of God

The God of all grace (1 Pet. 5:10); this is the true grace
of God (1 Pet. 5:12); the manifold grace of God (1 Pet.
4:10); the gospel of the grace of God (Acts 20:24); when
Barnabas saw the grace of God he rejoiced (Acts 11:23);
since the day you heard and understood the grace of
God in truth (Col. 1:6); I entrust you to God and to the
word of his grace (Acts 20:32); the grace of God and the
gift by the grace of that one man Jesus Christ (Rom.
5:15); those who receive the abundance of grace and the
gift of righteousness (Rom. 5:17); Apollos greatly
helped those who through grace had believed (Acts
18:27); when God called me through his grace (Gal.
1:15); do you not know that God's kindness is to lead
you to repentance? (Rom. 2:4); God's kindness, if you
remain in his kindness (Rom. 11:22); in coming ages he
will show the riches of his kindness to us (Eph. 2:7); the
riches of his kindness and forbearance (Rom. 2:4);
tasting the kindness of the Lord (1 Pet. 2:3); the Spirit
of grace (Heb. 10:29); with the kind you show yourself
kind (2 Sam. 22:26; Ps. 18:25); you have fallen from
grace (Gal. 5:4); people who pervert the grace of God
into licentiousness (Jude 4).

C2c The grace of Christ

The Word, full of grace and truth (John 1:14); grace and
truth came through Jesus Christ (John 1:17); the grace
of God and the gift by the grace of that one man Jesus
Christ (Rom. 5:15); you know the grace of our Lord
Jesus Christ (2 Cor. 8:9); from his fullness we all
received, grace upon grace (John 1:16); through the
grace of the Lord Jesus we are saved (Acts 15:11); the
grace of our Lord was poured out on me (1 Tim. 1:14);
you are deserting him who called you by the grace of
Christ (Gal. 1:6).

C2d Justified by grace

They are justified by his grace as a gift through
redemption in Christ (Rom. 3:24); it is by faith that it
might be according to grace (Rom. 4:16); tit is no
longer on the basis of works, otherwise grace would no
longer be grace (Rom. 11:6); forgiveness according to
the riches of his grace (Eph. 1:7); the grace of God that
brings salvation to all men (Titus 2:11); that being
justified by his grace (Titus 3:7); we are not under law
but under grace (Rom. 6:14); by grace you have been
saved (Eph. 2:5); through faith (Eph. 2:8); where sin
increased, grace abounded (Rom. 5:20); so grace might
reign in righteousness to eternal life through Jesus
Christ (Rom. 5:21); God gave us good hope through
grace (2 Thess. 2:16); a remnant chosen by grace, not
works (Rom. 11:5-6).

C2e The grace given to men

Through him we have received grace and apostleship
(Rom. 1:5); we have gifts that differ according to the
grace given to us (Rom. 12:6); I thank my God for the
grace of God given you in Christ Jesus (1 Cor. 1:4); not
in fleshly wisdom but by the grace of God (2 Cor. 1:12);
God is able to make all grace abound to you (2 Cor.

9:8); the stewardship of God's grace given to me for you (Eph. 3:2); the grace given to me according to the working of his power (Eph. 3:7); grace was given to each according to the measure of Christ's gift (Eph. 4:7); you are partakers with me of grace (Phil. 1:7); God gives grace to the humble (Jas. 4:6); set your hope on the grace coming to you at the appearing of Jesus Christ (1 Pet. 1:13); God opposes the proud but gives grace to the humble (1 Pet. 5:5); the grace which he bestowed on us in the Beloved (Eph. 1:6); this grace was given us in Christ from all eternity (2 Tim. 1:9); by the grace of God I am what I am (1 Cor. 15:10); my grace is sufficient (2 Cor. 12:9); be strong in the grace that is in Christ Jesus (2 Tim. 2:1); the heart needs strengthening by grace, not food (Heb. 13:9); Stephen, full of grace and power (Acts 6:8); see that no one misses the grace of God (Heb. 12:15).

C3 Kindness through people
The fruit of the Spirit is kindness (Gal. 5:22); he who is kind to the poor lends to the Lord (Prov. 19:17); Julius treated Paul kindly (Acts 27:3); the people showed us unusual kindness (Acts 28:2); we commend ourselves in kindness (2 Cor. 6:6); some preach Christ from goodwill (Phil. 1:15); let your graciousness be known to all men (Phil. 4:5); put on kindness (Col. 3:12); let your speech always be gracious, seasoned with salt (Col. 4:6); you remember us kindly (1 Thess. 3:6); the Lord's slave must be kind to all (2 Tim. 2:24); be kindhearted (1 Pet. 3:8); add to godliness brotherly kindness (2 Pet. 1:7); David showed kindness to Mephibosheth (2 Sam. 9:1, 7); Evil-merodach spoke kindly to Jehoiachin (2 Kgs. 25:28).

D Blessing and curse
I am setting before you a blessing and a curse (Deut. 11:26-8; 30:19); the blessing and the curse (Deut. 30:1); blessing on Mt Gerizim and curse on Mt Ebal (Deut. 11:29; 27:12-13); Joshua read the blessings and the curses (Josh. 8:34); bless those who curse you (Luke 6:28); bless and do not curse those who persecute you (Rom. 12:14); I brought you to curse and you have done nothing but bless (Num. 23:11; 24:10); neither curse them at all nor bless them at all (Num. 23:25); blessed is everyone who bless you and cursed everyone who curses you (Num. 24:9); from the same mouth come blessing and cursing (Jas. 3:10); I will curse your blessings (Mal. 2:2).

898 Malevolence
Men will be brutal (2 Tim. 3:3); filled with malice (Rom. 1:29); put away malice (Eph. 4:31; Col. 3:8; 1 Pet. 2:1); Nabal was churlish (1 Sam. 25:3); Jesus knew their malice (Matt. 22:18); Cretans are evil beasts (Titus 1:12).

899 Curse
BLESSING AND CURSE, see 897D.

A About cursing
A curse without cause does not alight (Prov. 26:2); him whom you curse is cursed (Num. 22:6); bless those who curse you (Luke 6:28); I brought you to curse and you have done nothing but bless (Num. 23:11); he who blesses with a loud voice early in the morning will be reckoned as a curse (Prov. 27:14); there will be no more curse (Zech. 14:11).

B God cursing
God cursed the serpent (Gen. 3:14); cursed is the ground (Gen. 3:17); the ground which the Lord has cursed (Gen. 5:29); never again will I curse the ground (Gen. 8:21); the one who curses you I will curse (Gen. 12:3); lest I come and smite the land with a curse (Mal. 4:6); if it bears thorns and thistles it is worthless and close to being cursed (Heb. 6:8); I could wish that I

were accursed from Christ for the sake of my kinsmen (Rom. 9:3); depart from me, you cursed (Matt. 25:41).

C The curse of the law
If you do not obey, these curses will come on you (Deut. 28:15-20); the curse written in the law of Moses is poured out on us (Dan. 9:11); cursed be he who does not do the law (Deut. 27:26); you are cursed for robbing me (Mal. 3:9); all who rely on works of the law are under a curse (Gal. 3:10); he who is hanged is accursed by God (Deut. 21:23); cursed be every one who hangs on a tree (Gal. 3:13); Christ redeemed us from the curse of the law, becoming a curse for us (Gal. 3:13); there will no longer be any curse (Rev. 22:3).

D People cursing
D1 Cursing God
Do not curse God or a ruler of your people (Exod. 22:28); he blasphemed the Name and cursed (Lev. 24:11); if anyone curses his God he will bear his sin (Lev. 24:15); testify that he has cursed both God and the king (1 Kgs. 21:10, 13); no one speaking by the Spirit of God can say 'Jesus is cursed' (1 Cor. 12:3); Job will curse you to your face (Job 1:11; 2:5); curse God and die! (Job 2:9); when they are hungry they will curse the king and their God (Isa. 8:21).

D2 Cursing Israel
Curse Israel for me (Num. 22:11); put a curse on these people, for those you curse are cursed (Num. 22:6); God turned the curse into a blessing (Deut. 23:5; Josh. 24:9-10; Neh. 13:2); whoever curses you I will curse (Gen. 12:3); cursed be those who curse you (Gen. 27:29; Num. 24:9); how can I curse whose whom God has not cursed? (Num. 23:8); lest you bring cursing on the camp of Israel (Josh. 6:18).

D3 Ungodly cursing
They bless with their mouths, but in their hearts they curse (Ps. 62:4); with the tongue we curse men (Jas. 3:9); from the same mouth come blessing and cursing (Jas. 3:10); their mouth is full of curses and bitterness (Rom. 3:14); anyone who curses father or mother must be put to death (Exod. 21:17; Lev. 20:9); do not curse the deaf (Lev. 19:14); do not curse the king even in private (Eccles. 10:20); he loved cursing, so it came on him (Ps. 109:17); Goliath cursed David by his gods (1 Sam. 17:43).

D4 Cursing people
Cursed be the one who gives a wife to Benjamin (Judg. 21:18); cursed be the man who rebuilds Jericho (Josh. 6:26); curse Meroz because they did not help the Lord (Judg. 5:23); cursed be he who is negligent in the Lord's work (Jer. 48:10); the curse of Jotham came on them (Judg. 9:57); Elisha called down a curse on the youths (2 Kgs. 2:24); Shimei cursed David (2 Sam. 16:5-9); Nehemiah called down curses on those who married foreign women (Neh. 13:25); if anyone preaches a different gospel, let him be accursed (Gal. 1:8-9); if anyone does not love the Lord, let him be accursed (1 Cor. 16:22).

D5 Cursing oneself
I will bring a curse on myself rather than a blessing (Gen. 27:12); Peter called down a curse on himself (Matt. 26:74; Mark 14:71); the Jews bound themselves with a curse to kill Paul (Acts 23:21).

D6 Cursing things
Job cursed the day of his birth (Job 3:1); cursed be the day I was born! (Jer. 20:14); the fig tree you cursed has withered (Mark 11:21).

E People cursed
People will curse him who tells the wicked they are righteous (Prov. 24:24); do not slander a slave lest he curse you (Prov. 30:10); depart from me, you cursed (Matt. 25:41); this crowd who do not know the law are

accursed (John 7:49); accursed children! (2 Pet. 2:14); Cain was under a curse (Gen. 4:11); cursed be Canaan (Gen. 9:25); Eli's sons brought a curse on themselves (1 Sam. 3:13); I could wish that I were accursed from Christ for the sake of my kinsmen (Rom. 9:3).

F Under the ban
Do not take a cursed thing into your house (Deut. 7:26); do not take things under the ban (Josh. 6:18); the city shall be under the ban (Josh. 6:17); Achan took things under the ban (Josh. 7:1); every devoted thing belongs to the priests (Num. 18:14).

900 Threat
The Danites threatened Micah with death (Judg. 18:25); Saul was breathing out threats and murder against the disciples (Acts 9:1); Lord, note their threats (Acts 4:29); when they had threatened them further they let them go (Acts 4:21); masters, do not threaten your slaves (Eph. 6:9); Jesus did not threaten (1 Pet. 2:23).

901 Philanthropy
BENEVOLENCE, see 897.

902 Misanthropy
MALEVOLENCE, see 898.

903 Benefactor
PEOPLE BLESSING, see 897A3.

904 Evildoer
THE WICKED, see 938.

905 Pity
A God's mercy
A1 Be merciful!
According to your abundant mercy blot out my transgressions (Ps. 51:1); have pity on your servants! (Ps. 90:13); God be merciful to me, the sinner! (Luke 18:13); in wrath remember mercy (Hab. 3:2); may the Lord grant mercy to the household of Onesiphorus (2 Tim. 1:16); Son of David, have mercy! (Matt. 9:27; 15:22; 20:30-1; Mark 10:47-8; Luke 18:38-9); Jesus, have mercy! (Luke 17:13); lord, have mercy on my son! (Matt. 17:15).
A2 God is merciful
God is merciful (Deut. 4:31); God is rich in mercy (Eph. 2:4); your Father is merciful (Luke 6:36); the Father of mercies (2 Cor. 1:3); the Lord is merciful and forgiving (Dan. 9:9); the Lord is compassionate and gracious (Exod. 34:6; Ps. 103:8; 111:4; 145:8; Joel 2:13); the Lord is compassionate and merciful (Jas. 5:11); as a father has compassion on his children, so the Lord has compassion (Ps. 103:13); in you the orphan finds mercy (Hos. 14:3); the Lord will have compassion (Lam. 3:32); his compassions are new every morning (Lam. 3:22-3).
A3 God will show mercy
God has mercy on whom he will have mercy (Exod. 33:19; Rom. 9:15, 18); God will have mercy on all (Rom. 11:32); to make known the riches of his glory on vessels of mercy (Rom. 9:23); his mercy is on generations of those who fear him (Luke 1:50); I will betroth you to me in lovingkindness and in compassion (Hos. 2:19); the Lord will have pity on his people (Joel 2:18); you will arise and have compassion on Zion (Ps. 102:13); wait for the mercy of our Lord Jesus to eternal life (Jude 21); should I not have compassion on Nineveh? (Jonah 4:11); the Lord grant him to find mercy on that day (2 Tim. 1:18).
A4 God showed mercy
Because of the tender mercy of our God (Luke 1:78); in the clemency of God he passed over former sins (Rom.

3:25); to show mercy to our fathers (Luke 1:72); God had mercy on me, lest I should have sorrow on sorrow (Phil. 2:27); for this reason I found mercy (1 Tim. 1:16); he saved us according to his mercy (Titus 3:5); according to his great mercy we have been born anew (1 Pet. 1:3); God had compassion (Judg. 2:18); he was compassionate and forgave them (Ps. 78:38); the father had compassion for the prodigal (Luke 15:20); that slave's master felt compassion for him (Matt. 18:27); Ruhamah – pitied (Hos. 2:1).
A5 Receiving God's mercy
Tell your family how the Lord has had mercy on you (Mark 5:19); he has remembered to be merciful to Abraham (Luke 1:54-5); I was shown mercy because I acted in ignorance (1 Tim. 1:13); once you had not received mercy, but now you have (1 Pet. 2:10); let us approach the throne of grace that we may find mercy (Heb. 4:16); you have received mercy because of their disobedience (Rom. 11:30-1); as we have received mercy (2 Cor. 4:1); peace and mercy be on all who walk by this rule (Gal. 6:16).
B Christ has compassion
Jesus had compassion on the crowds (Matt. 9:36; 14:14; 15:32; Mark 6:34; 8:2); Jesus was filled with compassion for the leper (Mark 1:41); Jesus had compassion on the widow of Nain (Luke 7:13); moved with compassion, he touched the blind men (Matt. 20:34); a merciful and faithful high priest (Heb. 2:17).
C Merciful people
Blessed are the merciful, for they will receive mercy (Matt. 5:7); I desire mercy, not sacrifice (Matt. 9:13; 12:7); you should have had mercy on your fellow-servant as I had mercy on you (Matt. 18:33); clothe yourselves with compassion (Col. 3:12); be merciful as your Father is merciful (Luke 6:36); be kind, tender-hearted, forgiving (Eph. 4:32); use your gift in showing mercy with cheerfulness (Rom. 12:8); mercy triumphs over judgement (Jas. 2:13); what does the Lord require of you but to love kindness? (Mic. 6:8); weightier matters of the law, justice and mercy and faith (Matt. 23:23); love is kind (1 Cor. 13:4); the wisdom from above is full of mercy and good fruits (Jas. 3:17); on some have mercy with fear (Jude 23); Pharaoh's daughter had pity on the baby (Exod. 2:6); the mother of the child was deeply stirred over her son (1 Kgs. 3:26); we have heard that the kings of Israel are merciful (1 Kgs. 20:31); the Samaritan had compassion (Luke 10:33); you pitied the plant for which you did not toil (Jonah 4:10); I will pour on the inhabitants of Jerusalem a spirit of compassion and supplication (Zech. 12:10); the one who showed mercy on him (Luke 10:37); Father Abraham! have mercy on me (Luke 16:24).

906 Pitilessness
A God without mercy
Show them no mercy (Deut. 7:2); my eye will have no pity and I will not spare (Ezek. 5:11; 7:9); I have taken away my peace, lovingkindness and compassion (Jer. 16:5); judgement without mercy will be shown to him who is not merciful (Jas. 2:13); Lo-ruhamah – I will no longer have pity (Hos. 1:6); I will no longer have pity on the inhabitants of the land (Zech. 11:6); their Maker will not have compassion on them (Isa. 27:11).
B People without mercy
People are unmerciful (Rom. 1:31); the Medes will have no mercy (Isa. 13:18); Nebuchadnezzar will not pity them or spare them (Jer. 21:7); you did not show mercy to my people (Isa. 47:6); if anyone sees his brother in need and closes his heart (1 John 3:17); we saw his distress but we would not listen (Gen. 42:21); there is

no faithfulness or kindness in the land (Hos. 4:1); judgement without mercy will be shown to him who is not merciful (Jas. 2:13); no one is sorry for me (1 Sam. 22:8).

C Show no mercy

Your eye shall not pity peoples whom the Lord delivers to you (Deut. 7:16); your eye shall not pity one who entices you from the Lord (Deut. 13:6); do not pity the murderer (Deut. 19:13); do not pity the false witness (Deut. 19:21); show no pity, cut off her hand (Deut. 25:12); do not let your eye have pity and do not spare (Ezek. 9:5).

907 Gratitude

A Thanks to God

A1 About thanking God

It is good to give thanks to the Lord (Ps. 92:1); thanksgiving will please the Lord better than an ox (Ps. 69:30-1); he who offers a sacrifice of thanksgiving honours me (Ps. 50:23); the fruit of lips which give thanks to his name (Heb. 13:15).

A2 Thank God!

Give thanks to the Lord (1 Chr. 16:8; Ps. 97:12; Isa. 12:4); give thanks to the God of heaven (Ps. 136:26); give thanks to the God of gods (Ps. 136:2-3); let them give thanks to the Lord for his lovingkindness (Ps. 107:8); be thankful (Col. 3:15); give thanks in everything (1 Thess. 5:18); by prayer and supplication with thanksgiving (Phil. 4:6); sing with thankfulness in your hearts to God (Col. 3:16); blessing and glory and thanksgiving be to our God (Rev. 7:12); come before him with thanksgiving (Ps. 95:2); enter his gates with thanksgiving (Ps. 100:4); offer a sacrifice of thanksgiving (Ps. 50:14; 107:22); thanks be to God through Jesus Christ! (Rom. 7:25); thanks be to God! (Rom. 6:17; 1 Cor. 15:57; 2 Cor. 2:14; 8:16); sing to the Lord with thanksgiving (Ps. 147:7); giving thanks for all things to the Father (Eph. 5:20); giving thanks to the Father through Jesus (Col. 3:17); no coarse jokes, but rather thanksgiving (Eph. 5:4); in prayer keep watch with thanksgiving (Col. 4:2); overflowing with thanksgiving (Col. 2:7).

A3 Those thanking God

I will give thanks to the Lord (2 Sam. 22:50; Ps. 9:1; Isa. 12:1); I will give thanks to you for ever (Ps. 30:12; 52:9); with my mouth I will give thanks to the Lord (Ps. 109:30); at midnight I rise to thank you (Ps. 119:62); we give you thanks, Lord God Almighty (Rev. 11:17); I will give thanks in the great congregation (Ps. 35:18); I will give thanks to you among the peoples (Ps. 57:9); I thank you that I am not like other men (Luke 18:11); Father, thank you that you heard me (John 11:41); I thank God that I speak in tongues more than you all (1 Cor. 14:18); for this we thank God, that you received the message as God's word (1 Thess. 2:13); you are giving thanks well enough, but the other man is not edified (1 Cor. 14:17); many will give thanks for blessings granted through the prayers of many (2 Cor. 1:11); when the living creatures give glory and honour and thanks to him seated on the throne (Rev. 4:9).

A4 Thanking God for food

Jesus gave thanks and broke the loaves (Matt. 14:19; 15:36; 26:26; Mark 6:41; 8:6-7; Luke 9:16; 22:19; 24:30; John 6:11); Jesus gave thanks and broke the bread (Mark 14:22; 1 Cor. 11:24); Paul gave thanks and broke bread (Acts 27:35); if I eat with thankfulness, why am I slandered? (1 Cor. 10:30); those who eat or do not eat give thanks to God (Rom. 14:6); food which God created to be received with thanksgiving (1 Tim. 4:3); he took a cup and gave thanks (Matt. 26:27; Luke

22:17); Jesus said a blessing for the fish (Mark 8:7); the place where they ate the bread after the Lord gave thanks (John 6:23); nothing is to be rejected if it is received with thanksgiving (1 Tim. 4:4).

A5 Thanking God for people

That prayers and thanksgivings be made for all men (1 Tim. 2:1); I thank my God for you (Rom. 1:8; 1 Cor. 1:4); what thanks can we render to God for you? (1 Thess. 3:9); I do not cease to give thanks for you (Eph. 1:16); I thank my God on every remembrance of you (Phil. 1:3); I thank God when I pray for you (2 Tim. 1:3; Philem. 4); we give thanks to God as we pray for you (Col. 1:3; 1 Thess. 1:2; 2 Thess. 2:13); Paul thanked God for the brothers meeting him (Acts 28:15); thankful for your partnership in the gospel (Phil. 1:5); we ought always to give thanks for you (2 Thess. 1:3).

B Thanks for Christ

Thanks be to God for his inexpressible gift! (2 Cor. 9:15); Anna gave thanks to God for Jesus (Luke 2:38); one leper fell at Jesus' feet, giving him thanks (Luke 17:16); I thank him who has strengthened me, Christ Jesus our Lord (1 Tim. 1:12).

C Thanks to people

They were thankful to Felix (Acts 24:3); does he thank the slave for doing what was commanded? (Luke 17:9); not only I, but all the churches give thanks to Prisca and Aquila (Rom. 16:4).

908 Ingratitude

Men will be ungrateful (2 Tim. 3:2); they neither glorified God nor gave thanks (Rom. 1:21); God is kind to the ungrateful (Luke 6:35); was there no one to give glory to God except this foreigner? (Luke 17:18).

909 Forgiveness

A Means of forgiveness

A1 Who can forgive sins?

Who is this who forgives sins? (Luke 7:49); who can forgive sins but God? (Mark 2:7; Luke 5:21); the Son of Man has authority to forgive sins (Mark 2:10; Luke 5:24).

A2 Forgiveness by atonement

The priest will make atonement and they will be forgiven (Lev. 4:20; Num. 15:25); in him we have redemption, the forgiveness of sins (Eph. 1:7; Col. 1:14); my blood, poured out for many for the forgiveness of sins (Matt. 26:28); without the shedding of blood there is no forgiveness (Heb. 9:22); where sins have been forgiven, there is no more sacrifice (Heb. 10:18).

A3 Forgiveness through repentance

A baptism of repentance for the forgiveness of sins (Mark 1:4; Luke 3:3); repent and be baptised, that your sins may be forgiven (Acts 2:38); repent, that your sins may be blotted out (Acts 3:19); he gives repentance and forgiveness of sins to Israel (Acts 5:31).

B God forgiving

B1 A forgiving God

God forgives iniquity, transgression and sin (Exod. 34:7); the Lord forgives sin and rebellion (Num. 14:18); you forgive our transgressions (Ps. 65:3); you are a forgiving God (Neh. 9:17; Ps. 99:8); you are kind and forgiving (Ps. 86:5); with you there is forgiveness (Ps. 130:4); the Lord forgives all your sins (Ps. 103:3); I am he who blots out your transgressions (Isa. 43:25); he is faithful to forgive our sins (1 John 1:9); our God will freely pardon (Isa. 55:7); who is a God like you, forgiving sin? (Mic. 7:18).

B2 God, forgive!

Forgive their sin (Exod. 32:32; Num. 14:19); forgive our sins (Ps. 79:9); when you hear, forgive (1 Kgs. 8:30; 2 Chr. 6:21); may the good Lord pardon everyone who seeks God (2 Chr. 30:18-19); forgive my iniquity, though it is great (Ps. 25:11); blot out my iniquities (Ps. 51:9); blot out my transgressions (Ps. 51:1); forgive all my sins (Ps. 25:18); clear me from hidden faults (Ps. 19:12); do not remember the sins of my youth (Ps. 25:7); Father, forgive them (Luke 23:34); Lord, do not hold this sin against them (Acts 7:60); O Lord, forgive! (Dan. 9:19); Lord, please forgive! (Amos 7:2); forgive us our debts as we forgive (Matt. 6:12); forgive us our sins for we forgive every one who is indebted to us (Luke 11:4).

B3 God will forgive
I will remember their sins no more (Jer. 31:34; Heb. 8:12; 10:17); I will pardon their iniquities (Jer. 33:8); I will forgive their sin and heal their land (2 Chr. 7:14); perhaps the Lord will forgive you (Acts 8:22); if you forgive others' transgressions, your heavenly Father will forgive you (Matt. 6:14); every sin and blasphemy will be forgiven (Matt. 12:31); all sins can be forgiven the sons of men (Mark 3:28); speaking against the Son of man will be forgiven (Matt. 12:32; Luke 12:10); my covenant when I take away their sins (Rom. 11:27); knowledge of salvation through the forgiveness of their sins (Luke 1:77); forgiveness of sins will be preached to all nations (Luke 24:47); everyone who believes receives forgiveness of sins (Acts 10:43); the forgiveness of sins is proclaimed (Acts 13:38); that they may receive forgiveness of sins (Acts 26:18); if the sick person has sinned, he will be forgiven (Jas. 5:15); if you forgive anyone's sins, they are forgiven (John 20:23).

B4 God has forgiven
The Lord has taken away your sin (2 Sam. 12:13); you forgave the guilt of my sin (Ps. 32:5); God forgave their iniquity (Ps. 78:38); I have forgiven them (Num. 14:20); her iniquity is pardoned (Isa. 40:2); so far he has removed our transgressions from us (Ps. 103:12); I have swept away your sins like the morning mist (Isa. 44:22); you have cast all my sins behind your back (Isa. 38:17); God was not counting their trespasses against them (2 Cor. 5:19); your sins have been forgiven for his name's sake (1 John 2:12); he forgave us our sins (Col. 2:13); in his forbearance he passed over former sins (Rom. 3:25); forgive one another, as God in Christ forgave you (Col. 3:13).

B5 God not forgiving
The angel will not forgive (Exod. 23:21); God will never forgive one whose heart turns away (Deut. 29:20); God will not forgive your rebellion and your sins (Josh. 24:19); this iniquity will not be forgiven you (Isa. 22:14); the Lord would not forgive (2 Kgs. 24:4); we transgressed and rebelled and you have not pardoned (Lam. 3:42); blasphemy against the Spirit will not be forgiven (Matt. 12:31, 32; Mark 3:29; Luke 12:10); if you do not forgive, your Father will not forgive you (Matt. 6:15; Mark 11:26); I will no longer have pity on the house of Israel to forgive them (Hos. 1:6); if you retain the sins of any, they are retained (John 20:23).

C Christ forgiving
Your sins are forgiven (Matt. 9:2; Mark 2:5; Luke 5:20; 7:48); who is this who forgives sins? (Luke 7:49); the Son of Man has authority to forgive sins (Mark 2:10; Luke 5:24).

D People forgiving
Shall I forgive my brother as many as seven times? (Matt. 18:21-2); if seven times he says, 'I repent', you must forgive him (Luke 17:4); you must forgive your brother from the heart (Matt. 18:35); forgive and you will be forgiven (Matt. 6:14; Mark 11:25; Luke 6:37); forgive one another, as God in Christ forgave you (Eph. 4:32; Col. 3:13); you ought to forgive and comfort him (2 Cor. 2:7); when you stand praying, forgive if

you have anything against anyone (Mark 11:25); Joseph was asked to forgive his brothers (Gen. 50:17); Abigail asked David to forgive Nabal (1 Sam. 25:28); forgive me that I did not burden you! (2 Cor. 12:13); love does not keep account of wrong (1 Cor. 13:5); love covers a multitude of sins (1 Pet. 4:8); it is man's glory to overlook an offence (Prov. 19:11); forgive us our debts as we forgive our debtors (Matt. 6:12; Luke 11:4); at the end of seven years, a year of remission of debts (Deut. 15:1); whoever you forgive, I forgive also (2 Cor. 2:10); what I have forgiven is for your sake in the presence of Christ (2 Cor. 2:10); if you do not forgive, your Father will not forgive you (Matt. 6:15; Mark 11:26).

910 Revenge

A God avenging
Vengeance is mine, I will repay (Deut. 32:35; Rom. 12:19; Heb. 10:30); the Lord is a God of retribution (Jer. 51:56); the Lord is a jealous and avenging God (Nahum 1:2); God of vengeance (Ps. 94:1); an avenger of wrongdoing (Ps. 99:8); taking vengeance on the disobedient (2 Thess. 1:8); shall I not avenge myself? (Jer. 5:29; 9:9); they will know I am the Lord, when I take vengeance (Ezek. 25:17); to declare in Zion the vengeance of the Lord (Jer. 50:28); he put on garments of vengeance for clothing (Isa. 59:17); in anger and wrath I will execute vengeance (Mic. 5:15); a day of vengeance to avenge himself on his foes (Jer. 46:10); to proclaim the day of vengeance of our God (Isa. 61:2); these are days of vengeance (Luke 21:22); May the Lord avenge me on you, but I will not harm you (1 Sam. 24:12); God performs vengeance for me (2 Sam. 22:48; Ps. 18:47); take vengeance for me on my persecutors (Jer. 15:15); he will avenge the blood of his servants (Deut. 32:43; 2 Kgs. 9:7); how long before you avenge our blood? (Rev. 6:10); the Lord is an avenger in all these things (1 Thess. 4:6); he has avenged on her the blood of his slaves (Rev. 19:2).

B Man avenging
The avenger of blood shall put the murderer to death (Num. 35:19-21; Deut. 19:12); cities of refuge from the avenger (Num. 35:12; Josh. 20:3); an eye for an eye (Deut. 19:21; Matt. 5:38); Samson wanted to take revenge (Judg. 15:7); avenged for my two eyes (Judg. 16:28); take vengeance on the Midianites (Num. 31:2); the Jews were to avenge themselves (Esther 8:13); Moses took vengeance for the oppressed (Acts 7:24); if anyone kills Cain, he will suffer vengeance seven times (Gen. 4:15); if Cain is avenged seven times, then Lamech seventy-seven times (Gen. 4:24).

C Not avenging
Do not seek revenge (Lev. 19:18); do not avenge yourselves (Rom. 12:19); do not say, 'I will repay evil' (Prov. 20:22); never repay evil for evil (Rom. 12:17; 1 Pet. 3:9); you have kept me from taking my own revenge (1 Sam. 25:33); praise from the mouth of infants to still the avenger (Ps. 8:2).

911 Jealousy

ENVY, see 912.

A Jealousy in general
Jealousy enrages a man (Prov. 6:34); jealousy is hard as Sheol (S. of S. 8:6); who can stand before jealousy? (Prov. 27:4); if you have bitter jealousy and selfish ambition in your heart (Jas. 3:14); where there are jealousy and selfish ambition there will be disorder (Jas. 3:16).

B God is jealous
The Lord is a jealous God (Exod. 20:5; Deut. 4:24; Josh. 24:19); the Lord, whose name is Jealous, is a jealous God (Exod. 34:14); all the earth will be consumed by

the fire of my jealousy (Zeph. 3:8); all the earth will be consumed in the fire of his jealousy (Zeph. 1:18); I will be jealous for my holy name (Ezek. 39:25); the Lord will be jealous for his land (Joel 2:18); I am very jealous for Jerusalem (Zech. 1:14; 8:2); he yearns jealously over the spirit he has made to dwell in us (Jas. 4:5); they made him jealous with their foreign gods (Deut. 32:16; Ps. 78:58); they made me jealous with what is not God (Deut. 32:21); they provoked the Lord to jealousy (1 Kgs. 14:22); the image of jealousy which provokes to jealousy (Ezek. 8:3); do we make the Lord jealous? (1 Cor. 10:22); will your jealousy burn like fire? (Ps. 79:5).

C Jealous people
Phinehas was jealous with my jealousy (Num. 25:11); he was jealous for his God (Num. 25:13); I will make you jealous by what is not a nation (Deut. 32:21; Rom. 10:19); I want to make my fellow Jews jealous and so save some of them (Rom. 11:14); salvation has come to the Gentiles to make Israel jealous (Rom. 11:11); the Sadducees were filled with jealousy (Acts 5:17); the Jews were jealous (Acts 13:45; 17:5); I am jealous for you with a godly jealousy (2 Cor. 11:2); regulations concerning a jealous husband (Num. 5:12-31); are you jealous for my sake? (Num. 11:29); Rachel was jealous of Leah (Gen. 30:1); his brothers were jealous of Joseph (Gen. 37:11; Acts 7:9).

D Avoiding jealousy
Since there is jealousy among you, are you not worldly? (1 Cor. 3:3); I fear there may be strife and jealousy (2 Cor. 12:20); jealousy is a deed of the flesh (Gal. 5:20); love is not jealous (1 Cor. 13:4); not in strife and jealousy (Rom. 13:13).

912 Envy
JEALOUSY, see 911.

A Nature of envy
All achievement springs from envy (Eccles. 4:4); envy is a deed of the flesh (Gal. 5:21); from the heart comes envy (Mark 7:22); filled with envy (Rom. 1:29); you are envious and cannot obtain, so you fight (Jas. 4:2); out of controversies arises envy (1 Tim. 6:4).

B Those who envied
The Philistines envied Isaac (Gen. 26:14); the people grew envious of Moses (Ps. 106:16); it was out of envy that Jesus was handed over to Pilate (Matt. 27:18; Mark 15:10); some preach Christ out of envy and selfish ambition (Phil. 1:15); I was envious of the arrogant (Ps. 73:3); we once spent our days in malice and envy (Titus 3:3).

C Avoid envy
Put aside envy (1 Pet. 2:1); do not envy one another (Gal. 5:26); do not envy the wicked (Ps. 37:1; Prov. 24:1); do not envy a violent man (Prov. 3:31).

913 Righteousness

A About righteousness
A1 Righteousness in general
Let the skies pour down righteousness (Isa. 45:8); righteousness guards him whose way is blameless (Prov. 13:6); better a little with righteousness than much gain with injustice (Prov. 16:8); then you will understand righteousness and justice (Prov. 2:9); wealth and righteousness are with me [Wisdom] (Prov. 8:18); when your judgements are on the earth the world learns righteousness (Isa. 26:9); scripture is profitable for training in righteousness (2 Tim. 3:16); to bring in everlasting righteousness (Dan. 9:24); blessed are those who are persecuted for righteousness' sake (Matt. 5:10); weightier matters of the law, justice and mercy and faith (Matt. 23:23); because this widow bothers me I

will get her justice (Luke 18:5); he will bring justice to them speedily (Luke 18:8); though he has escaped from the sea, justice has not allowed him to live (Acts 28:4); present your limbs to God as instruments of righteousness (Rom. 6:13); Noah, a preacher of righteousness (2 Pet. 2:5); better not to have known the way of righteousness (2 Pet. 2:21); new heavens and a new earth in which righteousness dwells (2 Pet. 3:13).

A2 Distinctives of righteousness
When the righteous prosper, the city rejoices (Prov. 11:10); righteousness exalts a nation (Prov. 14:34); the throne is established in righteousness (Prov. 16:12); righteousness delivers from death (Prov. 10:2; 11:4); the fruit of righteousness will be peace (Isa. 32:17); the effect of righteousness will be quietness and trust for ever (Isa. 32:17); in righteousness you will be established (Isa. 54:14); the righteousness of the blameless smooths his way (Prov. 11:5); the righteousness of the upright delivers them (Prov. 11:6); is it any pleasure to God if you are righteous? (Job 22:3).

A3 Righteous by obedience
If we obey all the law, that will be our righteousness (Deut. 6:25); his intervention was credited to Phinehas as righteousness (Ps. 106:31); you have become slaves of righteousness (Rom. 6:18); Abel was attested righteous because of his sacrifice (Heb. 11:4).

A4 Imputed righteousness
Abraham believed God and it was reckoned to him as righteousness (Gen. 15:6; Rom. 4:3, 9, 22; Gal. 3:6; Jas. 2:23); faith is reckoned as righteousness (Rom. 4:5); a righteousness from God, by faith (Rom. 3:21-2; Phil. 3:9); the righteousness of faith (Rom. 4:13); righteousness reckoned to all who believe (Rom. 4:11; 10:4); God reckons righteousness apart from works (Rom. 4:6, 24); Gentiles attained righteousness by faith (Rom. 9:30); Noah became an heir of the righteousness by faith (Heb. 11:7); the righteous by faith will live (Hab. 2:4; Rom. 1:17; Gal. 3:11; Heb. 10:38); those who receive the abundance of grace and the gift of righteousness (Rom. 5:17); being ignorant of the righteousness which comes from God (Rom. 10:3); the righteousness based on faith (Rom. 10:6); a robe of righteousness (Isa. 61:10); righteousness as a breastplate (Isa. 59:17; Eph. 6:14); the crown of righteousness (2 Tim. 4:8).

A5 Christ our righteousness
Christ has become our righteousness (1 Cor. 1:30); the righteousness of God is revealed from faith to faith (Rom. 1:17); we become the righteousness of God in him (2 Cor. 5:21); the Lord our righteousness (Jer. 23:6; 33:16); Melchizedek, king of righteousness (Heb. 7:2); seek first his righteousness (Matt. 6:33); he will proclaim justice to the Gentiles (Matt. 12:18).

B Righteousness of God
B1 God is righteous
The Lord is righteous (2 Chr. 12:6; Ps. 11:7; 129:4; 145:17; Lam. 1:18; Zeph. 3:5); the righteous God (Ps. 7:9); righteous and upright is he (Deut. 32:4); good and upright is the Lord (Ps. 25:8); a righteous God and a Saviour (Isa. 45:21); just and the justifier of him who believes (Rom. 3:26); the Lord is a God of justice (Isa. 30:18); God is not unjust (Heb. 6:10); with God there is no injustice (2 Chr. 19:7); where is the God of justice? (Mal. 2:17); righteous Father (John 17:25); only in the Lord are righteousness and strength (Isa. 45:24); your righteousness endures for ever (Ps. 111:3; 119:142); your righteousness is like great mountains (Ps. 36:6); your righteousness reaches to the heavens (Ps. 71:19); righteousness and justice are the foundation of God's

throne (Ps. 89:14; 97:2); he put on righteousness as a breastplate (Isa. 59:17).

B2 God's word is righteous
Wwhat nation has statutes so righteous? (Deut. 4:8); the precepts of the Lord are right (Ps. 19:8-9); your testimonies are righteous for ever (Ps. 119:144); the law is holy and the commandment holy and righteous and good (Rom. 7:12).

B3 Showing that God is just
My tongue will speak of your righteousness (Ps. 35:28; 71:15); my tongue will sing of your righteousness (Ps. 51:14); I have proclaimed your righteousness (Ps. 40:9-10); I will speak of your righteousness, yours alone (Ps. 71:16); they will declare his righteousness to a people yet unborn (Ps. 22:31); the heavens declare his righteousness (Ps. 97:6); every morning he shows forth his justice (Zeph. 3:5); if our unrighteousness demonstrates the righteousness of God (Rom. 3:5).

B4 God does what is right
Will not the Judge of all the earth do right? (Gen. 18:25); I am the Lord who practises justice and righteousness (Jer. 9:24); he will not falter till he establishes justice (Isa. 42:4); he will bring justice to the nations (Isa. 42:1); the righteous acts of the Lord (1 Sam. 12:7); that you might know the righteous deeds of the Lord (Mic. 6:5); just and true are your ways (Rev. 15:3); your righteous deeds have been revealed (Rev. 15:4); the Holy Spirit will convict the world of righteousness (John 16:8); Paul spoke of righteousness, self-control and judgement (Acts 24:25); the anger of man does not work the righteousness of God (Jas. 1:20); God's righteous judgement (2 Thess. 1:5); the Lord judges the people with righteousness and equity (Ps. 9:8); just are you in your judgements (Rev. 16:5); true and righteous are your judgements (Rev. 16:7); you are righteous when you speak and blameless when you judge (Ps. 51:4); his judgements are true and righteous (Rev. 19:2); he will judge the world in righteousness by a man whom he has appointed (Acts 17:31); will God not bring justice for his elect? (Luke 8:7); God is just to afflict those who afflict you (2 Thess. 1:6); this was to show God's righteousness in passing over former sins (Rom. 3:25).

C Righteousness of Christ
The righteous one, my servant (Isa. 53:11); Jesus Christ the righteous (1 John 2:1); a sceptre of righteousness is the sceptre of your kingdom (Ps. 45:6; Heb. 1:8); as he is righteous, so every one who does right is born of him (1 John 2:29); the one who does righteousness is righteous as he is righteous (1 John 3:7); you love righteousness (Ps. 45:7; Heb. 1:9); may he judge the people with righteousness (Ps. 72:2); ride victoriously for truth, humility and righteousness (Ps. 45:4); you denied the holy and righteous one (Acts 3:14); they killed those who predicted the coming of the righteous one (Acts 7:52); he has appointed you to see the righteous one (Acts 22:14); by the righteousness of our God and Saviour Jesus Christ (2 Pet. 1:1); in righteousness he judges and wages war (Rev. 19:11).

D Righteousness of people
GOOD PEOPLE, see 937.

D1 Do right!
Justice, justice shall you pursue (Deut. 16:20); pursue righteousness (1 Tim. 6:11; 2 Tim. 2:22); seek justice (Isa. 1:17); they shall judge with righteous judgement (Deut. 16:18); administer justice every morning (Jer. 21:12); let justice flow like a river, righteousness like a stream (Amos 5:24); do not deny justice to the poor (Exod. 23:6); do not deprive the alien or fatherless of justice (Deut. 24:17); perform justice for the needy (Ps. 82:3); I will make justice the measuring-line and

righteousness the plumbline (Isa. 28:17); sow for yourselves in righteousness (Hos. 10:12); masters, show justice (Col. 4:1); seek righteousness, seek humility (Zeph. 2:3); he has made you king to maintain justice and righteousness (1 Kgs. 10:9).

D2 Doing right
The Lord has rewarded me according to my righteousness (2 Sam. 22:21; Ps. 18:20); she is more righteous than I (Gen. 38:26); you are more righteous than I (1 Sam. 24:17); beware of practising your righteousness before men (Matt. 6:1); that we might serve him in holiness and righteousness (Luke 1:75); those who do what is right are acceptable to God (Acts 10:35); obedience leads to righteousness (Rom. 6:16); yield your limbs as slaves to righteousness (Rom. 6:19); the man who practices the righteousness based on the law will live by it (Rom. 10:5); the fruit of light is in all that is good and right and true (Eph. 5:9); all scripture is profitable for training in righteousness (2 Tim. 3:16); by faith they wrought righteousness (Heb. 11:33); he who does right is righteous as he is righteous (1 John 3:7); Noah was a righteous and blameless man (Gen. 6:9; 7:1); David did what was just and right (2 Sam. 8:15; 1 Chr. 18:14); Job did not sin (Job 1:22; 2:10); Simeon was righteous (Luke 2:25); John came to you in the way of righteousness (Matt. 21:32).

D3 Man's righteousness
D3a People in righteousness
I hold fast to my righteousness (Job 27:6); I will behold your face in righteousness (Ps. 17:15); his righteousness endures for ever (Ps. 112:3; 2 Cor. 9:9); let uprightness preserve me (Ps. 25:21); your righteousness would have been like waves of the sea (Isa. 48:18); faithless Israel has shown herself more righteous than false Judah (Jer. 3:11); the righteousness of the righteous will be on himself (Ezek. 18:20); a righteous man's righteousness will not deliver him when he sins (Ezek. 33:12); Israel pursued righteousness based on law but did not attain that law (Rom. 9:31); an elder [overseer] must be just (Titus 1:8).

D3b Self-righteousness
It is not because of your righteousness that the Lord is bringing you into the land (Deut. 9:4-6); doing what is right in one's own eyes (Deut. 12:8; Judg. 17:6; 21:25); those who trusted in themselves that they were righteous (Luke 18:9); can man be more righteous than God? (Job 4:17); how can man born of woman be righteous? (Job 15:14; 25:4-6); all our righteousnesses are as filthy rags (Isa. 64:6); they sought to establish their own righteousness, and did not submit to God's (Rom. 10:3); Gentiles did not pursue righteousness (Rom. 9:30); Job was righteous in his own eyes (Job 32:1; 33:9; 34:5); they way of a fool is right in his own eyes (Prov. 12:15); every man's way is right in his own eyes (Prov. 21:2); not having a righteousness of my own based on law (Phil. 3:9); do not be too righteous (Eccles. 7:16).

D4 A righteous people
Your righteousness must exceed that of the Pharisees (Matt. 5:20); what does the Lord require of you but to act justly? (Mic. 6:8); to do what is right and just is better to the Lord than sacrifice (Prov. 21:3); thus it becomes us to fulfil all righteousness (Matt. 3:15); the kingdom of God is a matter of righteousness (Rom. 14:17); created like God in true righteousness (Eph. 4:24); filled with the fruit of righteousness (Phil. 1:11); to live upright lives (Titus 2:12); he will increase the harvest of your righteousness (2 Cor. 9:10); blessed are those who hunger and thirst for righteousness (Matt. 5:6); you will be called the City of Righteousness (Isa. 1:26); they will be called oaks of righteousness (Isa.

61:3); the nations will see your righteousness (Isa. 62:2); open the gates that the righteous nation may enter (Isa. 26:2); I will betroth you to me in righteousness and justice (Hos. 2:19); he leads me in the paths of righteousness (Ps. 23:3); discipline yields the peaceful fruit of righteousness (Heb. 12:11); the fruit of righteousness is sown in peace (Jas. 3:18).

E No justice

We look for justice but there is none (Isa. 59:11); those who deprive the needy of justice (Isa. 10:2); cursed is the man who withholds justice (Deut. 27:19); they do not know how to do what is right (Amos 3:10); those who turn justice into wormwood and cast righteousness to the earth (Amos 5:7); you have turned justice into poison (Amos 6:12); justice is not upheld (Hab. 1:4); in his humiliation justice was taken away (Acts 8:33); they have beaten us publicly without trial (Acts 16:37).

F Right and wrong

The tree of the knowledge of good and evil (Gen. 2:9); you will be like God, knowing good and evil (Gen. 3:5); the man has become like us, knowing good and evil (Gen. 3:22); you hate good and love evil (Mic. 3:2); when you were slaves of sin you were free with regard to righteousness (Rom. 6:20); Cain's deeds were evil and his brother's righteous (1 John 3:12); what fellowship has righteousness with lawlessness? (2 Cor. 6:14); woe to those who call evil good and good evil (Isa. 5:20).

914 Wrong

RIGHT AND WRONG, see 913F.

A About sin

A1 Nature of sin

All unrighteousness is sin (1 John 5:17); sin is lawlessness (1 John 3:4); the devising of folly is sin (Prov. 24:9); through one man sin entered the world (Rom. 5:12); through the law comes knowledge of sin (Rom. 3:20); the sting of death is sin and the power of sin is the law (1 Cor. 15:56); lest any of you be hardened by the deceitfulness of sin (Heb. 3:13); there is sin to death and sin not to death (1 John 5:16-17); to know the right thing and not to do it is sin (Jas. 4:17); I would sin if I ceased to pray for you (1 Sam. 12:23); sin is a disgrace to a people (Prov. 14:34); evil will not deliver those who practise it (Eccles. 8:8).

A2 The entrance of sin

Sin is crouching at the door (Gen. 4:7); your first forefather sinned (Isa. 43:27); through one man sin entered the world (Rom. 5:12); if your right eye causes you to stumble (Matt. 5:29); if your right hand causes you to stumble (Matt. 5:30); anything more than 'yes' or 'no' comes from evil (Matt. 5:37); from the heart comes wickedness (Mark 7:22); before the law, sin was in the world (Rom. 5:13); if it had not been for the law I would not have known sin (Rom. 7:7); it is no longer I that do it but sin which dwells within me (Rom. 7:17, 20); through the commandment sin might become sinful beyond measure (Rom. 7:13); the love of money is the root of all evil (1 Tim. 6:10).

A3 All have sinned

The earth was corrupt before God (Gen. 6:11); all flesh had corrupted their way on the earth (Gen. 6:12); there is no one who does not sin (1 Kgs. 8:46; 2 Chr. 6:36); there is no righteous man who never sins (Eccles. 7:20); there is none righteous, not one (Rom. 3:10); there is no one who does good (Ps. 14:1; 53:1); no one is righteous before you (Ps. 143:2); Jews and Gentiles are all under sin (Rom. 3:9); all have sinned and fall short of the glory of God (Rom. 3:23); the scripture has shut

up all men under sin (Gal. 3:22); you, being evil (Matt. 7:11; Luke 11:13); evil things come out of the heart of man (Matt. 15:18-19); man who is corrupt and drinks iniquity like water (Job 15:16); though you were slaves of sin (Rom. 6:17); the devil has sinned from the beginning (1 John 3:8).

A4 Thoroughly sinful

The law came in to increase the transgression (Rom. 5:20); our sins prevail over us (Ps. 65:3); sin reigned in death (Rom. 5:21); if you should mark iniquities, who could stand? (Ps. 130:3); now they sin more and more (Hos. 13:2); adding sin to sin (Isa. 30:1); they sinned still more against him (Ps. 78:17); they are corrupt and do abominable things (Ps. 14:1); their feet run to evil (Prov. 1:16; Isa. 59:7); men are filled with every kind of wickedness (Rom. 1:29); the wickedness of man was great, every thought being evil (Gen. 6:5); man's thoughts are evil from youth (Gen. 8:21); I was conceived and born in sin (Ps. 51:5); the works of the flesh are plain (Gal. 5:19-21); you have done evil more than your fathers (Jer. 16:12); my sins are more than the hairs of my head (Ps. 40:12); my iniquities have gone over my head (Ps. 38:4); our iniquities have risen above our heads (Ezra 9:6); your iniquity and hatred are great (Hos. 9:7); the vats overflow, for their wickedness is great (Joel 3:13); weak women, burdened with sins and led by various impulses (2 Tim. 3:6).

A5 Hidden sins

The sins of some men are obvious, the sins of others not so (1 Tim. 5:24); who can discern his errors? forgive my hidden faults (Ps. 19:12); be sure your sin will find you out (Num. 32:23); men loved darkness rather than light because their deeds were evil (John 3:19); every one who does evil does not come to the light lest his deeds be exposed (John 3:20).

A6 Continuing in sin

Shall we continue in sin that grace may abound? (Rom. 6:1); 'let us do evil that good may come' (Rom. 3:8); no one who abides in him continues to sin (1 John 3:6); no one born of God goes on sinning (1 John 3:9; 5:18); how can we who died to sin still live in it? (Rom. 6:2); if we are found to be sinners, is Christ a minister of sin? (Gal. 2:17); if we sin after we received the knowledge of the truth, there is no sacrifice for sins (Heb. 10:26); the wicked will continue to be wicked (Dan. 12:10); let him who does wrong continue to do wrong (Rev. 22:11).

A7 Results of sin

A7a Sin brings death

The soul who sins will die (Ezek. 18:4); the wages of sin is death (Rom. 6:23); all who sin without law will perish without law (Rom. 2:12); you will die in your sin (John 8:21); sin deceived me and killed me (Rom. 7:11); you were dead in trespasses and sins (Eph. 2:1); when we were dead in sins (Eph. 2:5).

A7b Sin brings sickness

They suffered affliction because of their iniquities (Ps. 107:17); there is no health in my bones because of my sin (Ps. 38:3); who sinned, this man or his parents, that he was born blind? (John 9:2); I will make you sick, striking you because of your sins (Mic. 6:13).

A7c Sin brings impoverishment

When there is no rain because your people have sinned (1 Kgs. 8:35); he turns fruitful land into salt waste because of the iniquity of its inhabitants (Ps. 107:34); the earth will be desolate because of the fruit of their deeds (Mic. 7:13).

A7d Sin brings judgement

One transgression brought condemnation to all (Rom. 5:18); God drove out the people of the land because of their wickedness (Deut. 9:4-5); Israel was exiled because they had sinned (2 Kgs. 17:7); he will remember their iniquity and punish their sins (Hos. 8:13); there will be tribulation and distress for everyone who does evil (Rom. 2:9); he was angry with those who sinned, whose bodies fell in the wilderness (Heb. 3:17).

A7e Sin separates from God
He will hide his face from them because they have done evil deeds (Mic. 3:4); your iniquities have separated you and your God (Isa. 59:2); whoever has sinned I will blot out of my book (Exod. 32:33).

B God and evil
B1 Is God unjust?
God has denied me justice (Job 19:6; 27:2); God has taken away my right (Job 34:5); the way of the Lord is not just (Ezek. 18:25; 33:17); there is no justice (Job 19:7); is God unjust in bringing his wrath upon us? (Rom. 3:5); far be it from God to do wrong (Job 34:10); shall one who hates justice rule? (Job 34:17); God will not act wickedly (Job 34:12); there is no unrighteousness in him (Ps. 92:15); there is no injustice in God (Rom. 9:14); what wrong did your fathers find in me? (Jer. 2:5).

B2 God's attitude to sin
If you sin, how does that affect him? (Job 35:6); if I sinned, you would be watching me (Job 10:14); if I regard wickedness in my heart the Lord will not hear (Ps. 66:18); you are not a God who takes pleasure in evil (Ps. 5:4); the Lord was displeased that there was no justice (Isa. 59:15); against you only have I sinned (Ps. 51:4); the Lord against whom we have sinned (Isa. 42:24); they do not consider that I remember all their wickedness (Hos. 7:2); the wrath of God is revealed against all ungodliness and unrighteousness of men (Rom. 1:18); you hate evil (Ps. 45:7); the Holy Spirit will convict the world of sin because they do not believe (John 16:8–9).

C People who did evil
C1 God's people sinning
This people is set on evil (Exod. 32:22); the iniquity of my people is greater than the sin of Sodom (Lam. 4:6); the iniquity of Israel and Judah is very great (Ezek. 9:9); Judah did wrong in the eyes of the Lord (1 Kgs. 14:22); the Israelites did evil in the eyes of the Lord (Judg. 2:11; 3:7, 12; 4:1; 6:1; 10:6; 13:1); you have committed a great sin (Exod. 32:30); your wickedness is great in asking for a king (1 Sam. 12:17); the people are sinning by eating blood (1 Sam. 14:32–4); lie on your left side for the sin of the house of Israel (Ezek. 4:4); lie on your right side for the sin of the house of Judah (Ezek. 4:6); the eyes of the Lord are on the sinful kingdom (Amos 9:8); the sin of the priests was very great before the Lord (1 Sam. 2:17); because of the sins of prophets and priests (Lam. 4:13); priests commit villainy (Hos. 6:9); the more [the priests] multiplied, the more they sinned (Hos. 4:7).

C2 Individuals sinning
Why did you [Aaron] bring such great sin on them? (Exod. 32:21); what David did was evil in the eyes of the Lord (2 Sam. 11:27); David sinned in the matter of Uriah the Hittite (1 Kgs. 15:5); Abijah committed all the sins of his father (1 Kgs. 15:3); Ahab sold himself to do evil (1 Kgs. 21:25); Baasha caused Israel to sin (1 Kgs. 16:2); Jehoshaphat acted wickedly in making an alliance with Ahaziah (2 Chr. 20:35); he who delivered me up has the greater sin (John 19:11).

C3 Various nations sinning
The sin of Sodom and Gomorrah is grievous (Gen. 18:20); Nineveh's wickedness has come up against me (Jonah 1:2); Samaria did not commit half your sins (Ezek. 16:51); the iniquity of the Amorites is not yet complete (Gen. 15:16); [Edom] will be called the wicked country (Mal. 1:4); Babylon has sinned against the Lord (Jer. 50:14); for three transgressions and for four: of

Damascus (Amos 1:3); of Gaza (Amos 1:6); of Tyre (Amos 1:9); of Edom (Amos 1:11); of Ammon (Amos 1:13); of Moab (Amos 2:1); of Judah (Amos 2:4); of Israel (Amos 2:6).

C4 We / I have sinned
We sinned when we spoke against the Lord (Num. 21:7); if they say, 'We have sinned' (1 Kgs. 8:47); I and my son Solomon will be considered sinners (1 Kgs. 1:21); I am the one who has sinned (1 Chr. 21:17); heal my soul, for I have sinned (Ps. 41:4); I have sinned against heaven and before you (Luke 15:18, 21); I have sinned, said by: Achan (Josh. 7:20); Balaam (Num. 22:34); David (2 Sam. 12:13; 24:10; 1 Chr. 21:8); Hezekiah to Sennacherib (2 Kgs. 18:14); Job (Job 7:20); Judas (Matt. 27:4); Pharaoh (Exod. 9:27; 10:16); Saul (1 Sam. 15:24, 30; 26:21); Shimei (2 Sam. 19:20).

C5 Wronging other people
Do not wrong one another (Lev. 25:14); the butler and the baker sinned against the king of Egypt (Gen. 40:1); do not sin against the lad (Gen. 42:22); do not sin against David (1 Sam. 19:4–5); forgive your brothers' transgression and sin against you (Gen. 50:17); Queen Vashti has wronged both king and people (Esther 1:17); how have I sinned against you that you put me in prison? (Jer. 37:18); if you forgive people their transgressions (Matt. 6:14–15); if your brother sins against you, reprove him privately (Matt. 18:15); how many times shall my brother sin and I forgive? (Matt. 18:21); if he sins against you seven times in a day (Luke 17:4); you are brethren, why wrong one another? (Acts 7:26); why not rather be wronged? (1 Cor. 6:7); you wrong and defraud your brethren (1 Cor. 6:8); sinning against the brethren you sin against Christ (1 Cor. 8:12).

D No evil
D1 Removing sin
He appeared to take away sins and in him there is no sin (1 John 3:5); he was stricken for the transgression of my people (Isa. 53:8); he who knew no sin God made to be sin for us (2 Cor. 5:21); he was wounded for our transgressions (Isa. 53:5); the Lord has laid on him the iniquity of us all (Isa. 53:6); he will bear their iniquities (Isa. 53:11); he bore the sin of many (Isa. 53:12); that the body of sin might be destroyed (Rom. 6:6); the death that he died, he died to sin (Rom. 6:10); though your sins are as scarlet they will be as white as snow (Isa. 1:18); I will remove the sin of this land in a single day (Zech. 3:9).

SIN OFFERING, see 981D5.

D2 Avoiding sin
Turn your foot from evil (Prov. 4:27); my brothers, do not act wickedly (Gen. 19:7; Judg. 19:23); be angry and do not sin (Ps. 4:4); do not follow a crowd to do evil (Exod. 23:2); depart from evil (Ps. 34:14; 37:27); stop sinning (1 Cor. 15:34); I write this that you may not sin (1 John 2:1); do not let sin reign in your mortal body (Rom. 6:12); let us lay aside sin which entangles us (Heb. 12:1); if your brother sins, reprove him (Luke 17:3); that the fear of God might keep you from sinning (Exod. 20:20); your word have I hid in my heart that I might not sin (Ps. 119:11); thank you that I am not like other men, swindlers, unjust, adulterers (Luke 18:11); he who has died is freed from sin (Rom. 6:7); sin will not rule over you (Rom. 6:14); having been freed from sin (Rom. 6:18, 22); love does not rejoice in unrighteousness (1 Cor. 13:6); you have not yet resisted to blood, striving against sin (Heb. 12:4); if you warned the righteous man and he does not sin, he will live (Ezek. 3:21); do not be too wicked (Eccles. 7:17).

D3 What sin?
How have I sinned against you? (Gen. 20:9); what is my crime? (Gen. 31:36; 1 Sam. 20:1); what wrong am I guilty

of? (1 Sam. 26:18); what sin have I committed? (1 Kgs. 18:9); show me how I have erred (Job 6:24); make my sin known to me (Job 13:23); what is our sin? (Jer. 16:10); what crime has he committed? (Matt. 27:23; Mark 15:14; Luke 23:22); what have you done? (John 18:35); let these men say what misdeed they found (Acts 24:20); if there is anything wrong about the man, let them accuse him (Acts 25:5).

915 Dueness
A Worthy
A1 God is worthy
You are worthy to receive honour (Rev. 4:11); who will not fear you? for this is your due (Jer. 10:7); praise is fitting (Ps. 147:1); send them on their way in a manner worthy of God (3 John 6).
A2 Christ is worthy
Who is worthy to open the book and break its seals? (Rev. 5:2); you are worthy to take the scroll (Rev. 5:9); worthy is the Lamb that was slain! (Rev. 5:12).
A3 Worthy people
When you enter a town, ask who is worthy in it (Matt. 10:11); he is worthy for you to do this (Luke 7:4); those considered worthy to attain to that age and the resurrection (Luke 20:35); live a life worthy of your calling (Eph. 4:1); we pray that God may count you worthy of your calling (2 Thess. 1:11); worthy of the gospel (Phil. 1:27); worthy of the Lord (Col. 1:10); live lives worthy of God who calls you (1 Thess. 2:12); that you may be made worthy of the kingdom of God (2 Thess. 1:5); they rejoiced that they were worthy to suffer shame (Acts 5:41); not that we are worthy in ourselves (2 Cor. 3:5); they are worthy (Rev. 3:4).
B What is due
B1 Due rights
It is your due from the offerings (Lev. 10:13-15); a workman deserves his food (Matt. 10:10); the workman is worthy of his wages (1 Tim. 5:18); render to all what is due (Rom. 13:7); render to Caesar the things that are Caesar's and to God the things that are God's (Matt. 22:21; Mark 12:17; Luke 20:25); defend the rights of the needy (Prov. 31:9); those who rob the poor of my people of their rights (Isa. 10:2); until he comes whose right it is (Ezek. 21:27); to him who works his wages are not a gift but his due (Rom. 4:4); do we not have a right to eat and drink? (1 Cor. 9:4-5); the husband and wife should fulfil their duty to each other (1 Cor. 7:3); do only Barnabas and I have no right to stop working? (1 Cor. 9:6); we did not use this right (1 Cor. 9:12); that they may have the right to the tree of life (Rev. 22:14).
B2 Due return
We are receiving our just deserts (Luke 23:41); he deserves death (Matt. 26:66); the labourer deserves his wages (Luke 10:7); if I have done anything for which I deserve to die (Acts 25:11); he had done nothing deserving death (Acts 25:25; 26:31); the judgement of God rightly falls on those who do such things (Rom. 2:2); it is their due (Rev. 16:6).
C What is right / proper / lawful
It is fitting for us to fulfil all righteousness (Matt. 3:15); it was fitting for God to perfect Christ through suffering (Heb. 2:10); it was fitting for us to have such a high priest (Heb. 7:26); a word fitly spoken is like apples of gold in settings of silver (Prov. 25:11); it is right to do good on the sabbath (Matt. 12:12); the body is not for immorality but for the Lord and the Lord is for the body (1 Cor. 6:13); is it proper for a woman to pray with head uncovered? (1 Cor. 11:13); as is fitting among saints (Eph. 5:3); wives, be submissive to your husbands, as is fitting in the Lord (Col. 3:18); good deeds befit women who profess godliness (1 Tim. 2:10);

all things are proper but not all are useful (1 Cor. 6:12; 10:23); is it right to pay taxes to Caesar? (Matt. 22:17; Mark 12:14; Luke 20:22); is it right to heal on the sabbath? (Matt. 12:10; Mark 3:4; Luke 14:3); is it proper on the sabbath to do good or to harm, to save life or to destroy it? (Luke 6:9); is it lawful for a man to divorce his wife? (Matt. 19:3; Mark 10:2); is it not proper for me to do what I want with my own? (Matt. 20:15).

916 Undueness
A Unworthy
I am unworthy of all the kindness you have shown (Gen. 32:10); his sandals I am not worthy to untie (Matt. 3:11; Mark 1:7; Luke 3:16; John 1:27; Acts 13:25); I am not worthy for you to enter my house (Matt. 8:8; Luke 7:6-7); I am no longer worthy to be called your son (Luke 15:19, 21); those who were invited were not worthy (Matt. 22:8); no one who looks back is fit for the kingdom (Luke 9:62); you judge yourselves unworthy of eternal life (Acts 13:46); whoever loves father or mother more than me is not worthy of me (Matt. 10:37); he who does not take up his cross and follow me is not worthy of me (Matt. 10:38); the world was not worthy of them (Heb. 11:38); if the house is not worthy, let your peace return to you (Matt. 10:13); I am not fit to be called an apostle (1 Cor. 15:9); no one was worthy to open the book (Rev. 5:3-4); we are unworthy slaves (Luke 17:10); whoever eats the bread or drinks the cup of the Lord in an unworthy manner (1 Cor. 11:27).
B Without cause
Let us ambush the innocent without cause (Prov. 1:11); the Assyrian oppressed my people without cause (Isa. 52:4); Joab shed blood without cause (1 Kgs. 2:31); they attack me without a cause (Ps. 109:3); princes persecute me without cause (Ps. 119:161); they hated me without a cause (John 15:25); those who hate me without a cause are more than the hairs of my head (Ps. 69:4); many hate me wrongfully (Ps. 38:19); I have done nothing to deserve being imprisoned (Gen. 40:15); a curse without cause does not alight (Prov. 26:2).
C Not fitting
C1 Unfitting action
Such a thing ought not to be done (Gen. 34:7); killing some who should not die and keeping alive some who should not live (Ezek. 13:19); to eat on such a day would not have been fitting (Lev. 10:19-20); your disciples are doing what is not proper on a sabbath (Matt. 12:2; Mark 2:24); why do you do what is not proper on a sabbath? (Luke 6:2); it is not proper for you to carry your pallet on the sabbath (John 5:10); David ate the bread of the presentation, which was not proper (Matt. 12:4; Mark 2:26; Luke 6:4); it is not right for you to have your brother's wife (Matt. 14:4; Mark 6:18); it is not right to put the money in the treasury (Matt. 27:6); God gave them over to do things which are not fitting (Rom. 1:28); love does not act in an unseemly fashion (1 Cor. 13:5).
C2 Unfitting things
Honour is not fitting for a fool (Prov. 26:1); luxury is not fitting for a fool (Prov. 17:7); it is not for a slave to rule over princes (Prov. 19:10); do not give what is holy to dogs or pearls to swine (Matt. 7:6); the body is not for immorality but for the Lord (1 Cor. 6:13); filthiness, silly talk and coarse jokes are not fitting (Eph. 5:4).

917 Duty
A Conscience
A1 Good conscience
Keeping faith and a good conscience (1 Tim. 1:19); deacons must hold the mystery of the faith with a good

conscience (1 Tim. 3:9); I have lived my life in all good
conscience (Acts 23:1); I try to keep a clear conscience
(Acts 24:16); my heart does not reproach me (Job 27:6);
I serve God with a clear conscience (2 Tim. 1:3); we are
sure we have a good conscience (Heb. 13:18); keep a
good conscience (1 Pet. 3:16); my conscience bears me
witness in the Holy Spirit (Rom. 9:1); eat anything sold
in the market without asking questions for conscience'
sake (1 Cor. 10:25-7); do not eat, for the sake of
conscience (1 Cor. 10:28-9); my freedom should not be
condemned because of another man's conscience
(1 Cor. 10:29); the testimony of our conscience (2 Cor.
1:12); the aim of our instruction is a good conscience (1
Tim. 1:5); be subject to rulers for conscience' sake
(Rom. 13:5); commending ourselves to every one's
conscience (2 Cor. 4:2).

A2 Bad conscience
David's heart smote him (1 Sam. 24:5); David was
conscience-stricken for counting the fighting men
(2 Sam. 24:10); some eat food as offered to an idol and
their weak conscience is defiled (1 Cor. 8:7); someone's
weak conscience may be emboldened to eat food
sacrificed to idols (1 Cor. 8:10); by wounding their weak
consciences you sin against Christ (1 Cor. 8:12); some
have rejected conscience (1 Tim. 1:19); consciences
seared as with an iron (1 Tim. 4:2); their minds and
consciences are defiled (Titus 1:15).

A3 Cleansing the conscience
The blood of Christ cleanses the conscience (Heb.
9:14); our hearts sprinkled from an evil conscience
(Heb. 10:22); an appeal to God for a good conscience
(1 Pet. 3:21); gifts are offered which cannot perfect the
conscience (Heb. 9:9).

B Knowing right and wrong
The tree of the knowledge of good and evil (Gen. 2:9,
17; 3:3-7); the man has become like one of us, knowing
good and evil (Gen. 3:22); your children who do not
know good and evil (Deut. 1:39).

918 Undutifulness
NEGLIGENCE, see 458.

919 Exemption

A Spared
Joshua spared Rahab and her family (Josh. 6:17); they
spared the man and his family (Judg. 1:25); they spared
the Midianite women (Num. 31:15); spare those who
are virgins (Num. 31:18); Saul spared Agag and the best
of the animals (1 Sam. 15:9); the king spared
Mephibosheth (2 Sam. 21:7); if the king extends the
gold sceptre and spares her life (Esther 4:11); do not
touch any one on whom is the mark (Ezek. 9:6); it was
to spare you that I did not come (2 Cor. 1:23); whom he
would he killed and whom he would he spared (Dan.
5:19); spare your people and do not make your
inheritance a reproach (Joel 2:17); I will spare them as a
man spares his son who serves him (Mal. 3:17).

B Unpunished
If the man gets up, he who struck him will go
unpunished (Exod. 21:19); if the slave survives a day or
two his master will go unpunished (Exod. 21:21); the
owner of an ox which gores a man is to go unpunished
(Exod. 21:28); those who buy them slay them and go
unpunished (Zech. 11:5).

C Pass over
I will pass over you (Exod. 12:13); God passed over their
houses and spared them (Exod. 12:27); God passed over
former sins (Rom. 3:25).
PASSOVER, see 988A2.

D Exempt
He will exempt his father's house from taxes (1 Sam.
17:25); the sons are exempt (Matt. 17:26); my master let
Naaman off lightly (2 Kgs. 5:20); no one was exempt
(1 Kgs. 15:22).

E Not sparing
You did not withhold your son (Gen. 22:12, 16); he who
did not spare his own Son (Rom. 8:32); fierce wolves
will come, not sparing the flock (Acts 20:29); I warn
those who sin that I will not spare them (2 Cor. 13:2);
will you not spare the place for the 50 righteous? (Gen.
18:24); do not spare the one who entices you from the
Lord (Deut. 13:8); do not let your eye have pity and do
not spare (Ezek. 9:5); if God did not spare the natural
branches, neither will he spare you (Rom. 11:21); if God
did not spare the angels who sinned (2 Pet. 2:4); if God
did not spare the ancient world (2 Pet. 2:5).

920 Respect
Respect your God (Lev. 19:32); have reverence for my
sanctuary (Lev. 26:2); honour your father and mother
(Exod. 20:12; Lev. 19:3; Deut. 5:16; Matt. 15:4; Mark 7:10;
10:19; Eph. 6:2); honour men like Epaphroditus (Phil.
2:29); respect those who are over you in the Lord
(1 Thess. 5:12); husbands, treat your wives with honour
(1 Pet. 3:7); let the wife respect her husband (Eph. 5:33);
those who have believing masters should not be
disrespectful to them (1 Tim. 6:2); show respect for the
elderly (Lev. 19:32; Matt. 21:37); they will respect my
son (Mark 12:6; Luke 20:13); we had earthly fathers to
discipline us and we respected them (Heb. 12:9); win
the respect of outsiders (1 Thess. 4:12).
HONOUR, see 866D.

921 Disrespect
REVILING, see 924.

A Insulting God
Sennacherib wrote letters insulting the Lord (2 Chr.
32:17); you have insulted the Holy One of Israel (2 Kgs.
19:22; Isa. 37:23); the insults of those who insult you fall
on me (Ps. 69:9).

B Insulting Christ
They insulted Jesus (Matt. 27:39, 44); they hurled abuse
at him (Mark 15:29); those crucified with him also
insulted him (Mark 15:32); the man who has trampled
under foot the Son of God and insulted the Spirit of
grace (Heb. 10:29); the insults of those who insult you
fall on me (Ps. 69:9).

C Insulting people
Cursed is he who dishonours his father or mother
(Deut. 27:16); whoever says 'Raca' to his brother will be
guilty before the sanhedrin (Matt. 5:22); a prudent man
ignores an insult (Prov. 12:16); Nabal hurled insults at
David's servants (1 Sam. 25:14); would you insult God's
high priest? (Acts 23:4); Teacher, in saying this you
insult us also (Luke 11:45); blessed are you if you are
reviled for the name of Christ (1 Pet. 4:14); blessed are
you when you are insulted (Matt. 5:11); blessed are you
when men revile you (Luke 6:22); I am content with
insults (2 Cor. 12:10).

922 Contempt
MOCKING, see 851.

A Contempt and God
A1 Despising God
He who is crooked in his ways despises the Lord (Prov.
14:2); they have treated the Lord with contempt (Num.
16:30); the servants of the king of Assyria have reviled
me (Isa. 37:6); those who despise me will be disdained
(1 Sam. 2:30); you have despised me (2 Sam. 12:10); O

priests, you despise my name (Mal. 1:6); you sniff at me, says the Lord (Mal. 1:13).

A2 Despising God's things

He has despised the word of the Lord (Num. 15:31); the word of the Lord has become an object of scorn to them (Jer. 6:10); you have despised the Lord's word (2 Sam. 12:9); do not despise the Lord's chastening (Job 5:17); you say the Lord's table may be defiled and its food despised (Mal. 1:12); do you despise the riches of his kindness? (Rom. 2:4); do you despise the church of God? (1 Cor. 11:22); they treated the Lord's offering with contempt (1 Sam. 2:17); you have despised my holy things (Ezek. 22:8).

B Contempt for Christ

The Son of man will be treated with contempt (Mark 9:12); Herod and his soldiers treated him with contempt (Luke 23:11).

C Contempt for people

C1 Despising people in general

He who despises his neighbour lacks sense (Prov. 11:12); in his eyes a reprobate is despised (Ps. 15:4); he will cling to one master and despise the other (Matt. 6:24; Luke 16:13).

C2 Specific contempt for others

My adversaries revile me (Ps. 42:10); even young children despise me (Job 19:18); they despise my people as no longer a nation (Jer. 33:24); a son treats his father with contempt (Mic. 7:6); Hagar despised her mistress (Gen. 16:4); they despised Saul (1 Sam. 10:27); Goliath despised David (1 Sam. 17:42); Michal despised David in her heart (2 Sam. 6:16; 1 Chr. 15:29); women will despise their husbands (Esther 1:17); see, O Lord, for I am despised! (Lam. 1:11); those who trusted in themselves that they were righteous and despised others (Luke 18:9); he was despised and forsaken by men (Isa. 53:3); some will awake to everlasting life, others to everlasting contempt (Dan. 12:2); God has chosen those who are despised (1 Cor. 1:28).

D Contempt for things

Esau despised his birthright (Gen. 25:34); they despised the pleasant land (Ps. 106:24); one who is at ease is contemptuous of calamity (Job 12:5); who has despised the day of small things? (Zech. 4:10); do not treat prophecies with contempt (1 Thess. 5:20); you have despised the rod with everything of wood (Ezek. 21:10).

E Not despising

Do not despise one of these little ones (Matt. 18:10); do not let anyone despise your youth (1 Tim. 4:12); do not despise your mother when she is old (Prov. 23:22); do not let anyone disregard you (Titus 2:15); the one who eats should not despise the one who does not (Rom. 14:3); why do you look down on your brother? (Rom. 14:10); let no one despise Timothy (1 Cor. 16:11); do not despise the Lord's chastening (Job 5:17); you did not despise me (Gal. 4:14).

923 Approval

A Praising God

A1 Praise to God is fitting

Great is the Lord and worthy of praise (Ps. 145:3); the Lord is worthy of praise (2 Sam. 22:4; Ps. 18:3); great is the Lord and greatly to be praised (Ps. 96:4); from the lips of children you have ordained praise (Ps. 8:2; Matt. 21:16); all day long the name of the Lord is to be praised (Ps. 113:3); every tongue will give praise to God (Rom. 14:11); with the tongue we bless the Lord and Father (Jas. 3:9); worthy is the Lamb to receive power, riches, wisdom, might, honour, glory and blessing. (Rev. 5:12); you are enthroned on the praises of Israel (Ps. 22:3).

A2 Praise God!

A2a Praise the Lord!

Praise the Lord! (Ps. 105:45); let the high praises of God be in their mouth (Ps. 149:6); you who fear the Lord, praise him (Ps. 22:23); let all the peoples praise you (Ps. 67:3); enter his courts with praise (Ps. 100:4); offer to God a sacrifice of praise (Heb. 13:15); praise the Lord, all creation (Ps. 148:2-5, 7-13); praise the Lord, all you Gentiles (Rom. 15:11); praise our God, all you his slaves (Rev. 19:5); let everything that has breath praise the Lord (Ps. 150:6); hallelujah! (Rev. 19:1, 3, 4, 6); sing to the Lord, praise his name (Ps. 96:2); sing praises to God (Ps. 47:6, 7; 105:2); sing praises to God on the lyre (Ps. 147:7); is anyone cheerful? let him sing praise (Jas. 5:13); bless the Lord! (Ps. 103:1); bless the Lord your God (1 Chr. 29:20); blessed be God! (Ps. 66:20); blessed be the God and Father of our Lord Jesus Christ (2 Cor. 1:3; Eph. 1:3; 1 Pet. 1:3); Christ is God over all, blessed for ever (Rom. 9:5).

A2b Glory to God!

To the only God and Saviour be glory, majesty, dominion and authority (Jude 25); to him who sits on the throne and to the Lamb be praise, honour, glory and power (Rev. 5:13); to our God and Father be glory (Phil. 4:20); to whom be glory for ever and ever (Gal. 1:5); glory to the righteous One (Isa. 24:16); to him be glory in the church (Eph. 3:21); blessing and glory be to our God (Rev. 7:12); ascribe to the Lord glory and strength (1 Chr. 16:28); glory to God in the highest (Luke 2:14); not to us but to your name be glory (Ps. 115:1).

A3 Those praising God

A3a Praising God in general

Levites were appointed to give praise before the ark (1 Chr. 16:4); Jehoshaphat appointed those to praise God before the army (2 Chr. 20:21); one generation will praise your works to another (Ps. 145:4); a people yet unborn will praise the Lord (Ps. 102:18); all the earth will sing praises to your name (Ps. 66:4); all flesh will bless his holy name (Ps. 145:21); with the tongue we both praise God and curse men (Jas. 3:9); the wrath of men will praise you (Ps. 76:10).

A3b Specific praising of God

Daniel blessed the God of heaven (Dan. 2:19); I, Nebuchadnezzar, praise, exalt and honour the King of heaven (Dan. 4:37); Zechariah spoke, praising God (Luke 1:64); the shepherds glorified and praised God for all they had heard and seen (Luke 2:20); he took him in his arms and blessed God (Luke 2:28); he rose up before them and went home, glorifying God (Luke 5:25); she was made straight and praised God (Luke 13:13); one turned back, praising God with a loud voice (Luke 17:15); when the centurion saw this he praised God (Luke 23:47); walking and leaping and praising God (Acts 3:8); Paul and Silas were singing hymns of praise in prison (Acts 16:25); when they heard it they glorified God (Acts 21:20); he grew strong in his faith as he gave glory to God (Rom. 4:20); they may see your good deeds and glorify God (1 Pet. 2:12); when the living creatures give glory and honour and thanks to him seated on the throne (Rev. 4:9); the heavenly host praising God (Luke 2:13); they praised the God of Israel (Matt. 15:31); the disciples praised God for the great works they had seen (Luke 19:37); they glorified God because of me (Gal. 1:24).

A3c I will praise you

I will praise you, O Lord (Ps. 9:2; 145:1-2); he is my God and I will praise him (Exod. 15:2); because your lovingkindness is better than life I will praise you (Ps. 63:3); I will praise the Lord while I live (Ps. 146:2); this time I will praise the Lord (Gen. 29:35); I will again praise him (Ps. 42:5, 11; 43:5); in the midst of the congregation I will praise you (Heb. 2:12); I praise you, Father (Matt. 11:25; Luke 10:21); my tongue will declare your praise (Ps. 35:28); I will sing praise to my God while I have my being (Ps. 104:33); he put a new song into my mouth, praise to our God (Ps. 40:3); I will praise you among the Gentiles, I will sing to your name (Rom. 15:9); I will praise God's name in song (Ps. 69:30); I will sing praise to you (Ps. 101:1); I will sing praises to you among the peoples (Ps. 108:3); will praise you with harp and lyre (Ps. 71:22); my soul magnifies the Lord (Luke 1:46).

A3d Praise God for his benefits
Praise the Lord your God for the good land (Deut. 8:10); that the people offered themselves willingly, praise the Lord (Judg. 5:2); bless the Lord and forget not all his benefits (Ps. 103:2); you will have plenty to eat and praise the name of the Lord (Joel 2:26); for the Gentiles to glorify God for his mercy (Rom. 15:9).

A3e Showing forth his praise
That we might be to the praise of his glory (Eph. 1:12); that you may declare the excellence of him who called you out of darkness (1 Pet. 2:9); the name of the Lord Jesus was magnified (Acts 19:17); to the praise of the glory of his grace (Eph. 1:6); to the praise of his glory (Eph. 1:14); may result in praise, glory and honour at the appearing of Jesus Christ (1 Pet. 1:7); that the name of the Lord Jesus may be glorified in you (2 Thess. 1:12); when he comes to be glorified in his saints (2 Thess. 1:10); that men may see your good deeds and glorify your Father in heaven (Matt. 5:16); they saw Jesus healing and glorified God (Matt. 15:31); the fruit of righteousness is to the glory and praise of God (Phil. 1:11); named Judah – praise (Gen. 29:35); Judah, your brothers will praise you (Gen. 49:8).

A4 Not praising God
The dead do not praise the Lord (Ps. 115:17); will the dead praise you? (Ps. 88:10-11); will the dust praise you? (Ps. 30:9); in Sheol who can praise you? (Ps. 6:5); this people honours me with their lips but their heart is far from me (Matt. 15:8); was there no one to give glory to God except this foreigner (Luke 17:18).

B Praising people
HONOUR, see 866D.

B1 People commended by God
From you comes my praise (Ps. 22:25); one who is a Jew inwardly has praise from God (Rom. 2:29); by faith the men of old received approval (Heb. 11:2); they were attested by their faith (Heb. 11:39); it is not he one who commends himself who is approved, but the one the Lord commends (2 Cor. 10:18); we speak as men approved by God (1 Thess. 2:4); show yourself approved to God (2 Tim. 2:15); food will not commend us to God (1 Cor. 8:8); greet Apelles, approved in Christ (Rom. 16:10); every man will receive his praise from God (1 Cor. 4:5); the Lord had regard to Abel and his offering (Gen. 4:4).

B2 People commended by people
A woman who fears the Lord is to be praised (Prov. 31:30); one who is a Jew inwardly has praise from God (Rom. 2:29); he who serves Christ like this is approved by men (Rom. 14:18); give him no rest until he makes Jerusalem a praise in the earth (Isa. 62:7); do good and you will receive the ruler's approval (Rom. 13:3); God sends governors to praise those who do right (1 Pet. 2:14); people turn and praise the wicked (Ps. 73:10); they loved the praise of men more than praise from God (John 12:43); woe to you when all men speak well of you (Luke 6:26); what honour has been given to Mordecai for this? (Esther 6:3-7); I should have been commended by you (2 Cor. 12:11); the officials praised

Sarah to Pharaoh (Gen. 12:15); the man fell to the ground to pay David honour (2 Sam. 1:2); he taught in their synagogues, being praised by all (Luke 4:15); all spoke well of him (Luke 4:22); I will send those you approve with letters to Jerusalem (1 Cor. 16:3); the Jews spoke highly of Tobiah (Neh. 6:19); in the following instructions I do not commend you (1 Cor. 11:17); Mordecai would not pay homage to Haman (Esther 3:2).

B3 Commending oneself
While he lives he congratulates himself (Ps. 49:18); let another praise you, not your own mouth (Prov. 27:2); it is not the one who commends himself who is approved, but the one the Lord commends (2 Cor. 10:18); we are not commending ourselves to you again (2 Cor. 5:12); we do not compare ourselves with those who commend themselves (2 Cor. 10:12); are we beginning to commend ourselves again? (2 Cor. 3:1); we commend ourselves in every way by the hardships we endure (2 Cor. 6:4); we commend ourselves to everyone's conscience (2 Cor. 4:2).

C Praising / approving things
They praised the gods of gold, silver, bronze, iron, wood, stone (Dan. 5:4); you approve what your forefathers did (Luke 11:48); they not only do such things, but approve those who practise them (Rom. 1:32); Paul approved of Stephen's death (Acts 8:1; 22:20); that you may approve the things which are excellent (Phil. 1:10); if you approve the things that really matter (Rom. 2:18); blessed is he who does not condemn himself in what he approves (Rom. 14:22); if there is anything worthy of praise, think about it (Phil. 4:8).

924 Disapproval
A Reproving God
Reproaching the living God (2 Kgs. 19:4); you have reproached the Lord (Ps. 19:23); let him who reproves God answer him! (Job 40:2); he who oppresses the poor reproaches his Maker (Prov. 14:31); the reproaches of those who reproached you fell on me (Rom. 15:3).

B Reproving Christ
The reproaches of those who reproached you fell on me (Rom. 15:3); let us go out to him, bearing his reproach (Heb. 13:13); Moses considered the reproach of Christ greater riches than the treasures of Egypt (Heb. 11:26); when reviled, he did not revile back (1 Pet. 2:23); Peter rebuked Jesus (Matt. 16:22; Mark 8:32).

C Reproving people
C1 God reproving
You rebuke the nations (Ps. 9:5); he reproved kings for their sake (1 Chr. 16:21; Ps. 105:14); last night God rebuked you (Gen. 31:42); do not add to his words, lest he rebuke you (Prov. 30:6); the Lord rebuke you! (Zech. 3:2; Jude 9); do not lose heart when you are reproved by him (Heb. 12:5); he whom the Lord loves he reproves (Prov. 3:12); those whom I love I reprove and discipline (Rev. 3:19); happy is the man whom God reproves (Job 5:17).

C2 Christ reproving
Jesus turned and rebuked the disciples (Luke 9:55); Jesus rebuked the eleven for their lack of faith (Mark 16:14); Jesus rebuked evil spirits (Mark 1:25; 9:25; Luke 4:35, 41; 9:42); Jesus rebuked him and the demon came out (Matt. 17:18); Jesus reproached the cities (Matt. 11:20); Teacher, rebuke your disciples (Luke 19:39); Jesus rebuked Peter (Mark 8:33); Jesus rebuked the wind and the sea (Matt. 8:26; Mark 4:39; Luke 8:24); he rebuked the fever (Luke 4:39).

C3 Reproving others

The rod and reproof give wisdom (Prov. 29:15); better an open rebuke than concealed love (Prov. 27:5); elders who sin are to be rebuked in the presence of all (1 Tim. 5:20); rebuke them sharply (Titus 1:13); do not rebuke an older man harshly (1 Tim. 5:1); if your brother sins, reprove him (Matt. 18:15; Luke 17:3); reprove, rebuke (2 Tim. 4:2); all scripture is profitable for reproof (2 Tim. 3:16); admonish the unruly (1 Thess. 5:14); respect those who admonish you (1 Thess. 5:12); he who heeds reproof will be honoured (Prov. 13:18); reprove a man of understanding and he will gain knowledge (Prov. 19:25); a rebuke goes deeper into a wise man than blows into a fool (Prov. 17:10); they hate him who reproves in the gate (Amos 5:10); John reproved Herod (Luke 3:19); why have you not rebuked Jeremiah of Anathoth? (Jer. 29:27); the crowd rebuked them, telling them to be quiet (Matt. 20:31); they rebuked the blind man, telling him to be quiet (Luke 18:39);

the other criminal rebuked him (Luke 23:40); the disciples rebuked those bringing children to Jesus (Matt. 19:13; Mark 10:13; Luke 18:15); they rebuked the woman who poured perfume on Jesus' head (Mark 14:5).

DISCIPLINE, see 827C.

C4 Being reproved

It is not an enemy who reproaches me, but my friend (Ps. 55:12-13); reproach has broken my heart (Ps. 69:20); this sect is spoken against everywhere (Acts 28:22); do not fear the reproach of man (Isa. 51:7); that I may answer him who reproaches me (Prov. 29:11); for your sake I endure reproach (Jer. 15:15); when reviled, we bless (1 Cor. 4:12); lest he fall into the reproach and snare of the devil (1 Tim. 3:7); Balaam was rebuked for his transgression (2 Pet. 2:16).

C5 Reviling

Do not associate with a 'brother' who is a reviler (1 Cor. 5:11); revilers will not inherit the kingdom of God (1 Cor. 6:10); they said many other things against him, reviling him (Luke 22:65); they reviled him (John 9:28); when reviled, he did not revile back (1 Pet. 2:23); do not repay reviling with reviling but rather bless (1 Pet. 3:9); the Jews reviled Paul (Acts 13:45); reviling the glorious ones (2 Pet. 2:10); even angels do not bring reviling accusations (2 Pet. 2:11); they revile whatever they do not understand (Jude 10).

D Reproving things

He rebuked the Red Sea and it dried up (Ps. 106:9); at your rebuke the waters fled (Ps. 104:7); at the Lord's rebuke earth's foundations were laid bare (2 Sam. 22:16; Ps. 18:15); Jesus rebuked the wind and the sea (Matt. 8:26; Mark 4:39; Luke 8:24); he rebuked the fever (Luke 4:39).

E Avoiding reproof

He who rejects reproof goes astray (Prov. 10:17); he who hates reproof is stupid (Prov. 12:1); a scoffer does not like to be reproved (Prov. 15:12); Eli did not rebuke his sons (1 Sam. 3:13); when reviled, he did not revile back (1 Pet. 2:23); sound speech that is beyond reproach (Titus 2:8); we want to avoid criticism in administering this gift (2 Cor. 8:20); God gives to all men generously, without reproach (Jas. 1:5); God has removed my reproach (Gen. 30:23); the Lord has taken away my reproach among men (Luke 1:25); today I have rolled away the reproach of Egypt from you (Josh. 5:9); do not repay reviling with reviling but rather bless (1 Pet. 3:9).

925 Flattery

They flatter with their tongue (Ps. 5:9); a flattering mouth works ruin (Prov. 26:28); with smooth and

flattering speech they deceive (Rom. 16:18); flattering to gain advantage (Jude 16); he who flatters his neighbour spreads a net (Prov. 29:5); I do not know how to flatter (Job 32:21-2); let me not flatter any one (Job 32:21); we never came with flattering speech (1 Thess. 2:5); he who rebukes will find more favour than he who flatters (Prov. 28:23); may the Lord cut off all flattering lips (Ps. 12:2); there will be no more false vision or flattering divination (Ezek. 12:24).

926 Calumny

A Slandering

From the heart comes slander (Matt. 15:19; Mark 7:22); a whisperer separates close friends (Prov. 16:28); with his mouth the godless destroys his neighbour (Prov. 11:9); he who spreads slander is a fool (Prov. 10:18); one of the criminals hurled abuse at him (Luke 23:39); out of controversies arises slander (1 Tim. 6:4); men will be revilers (2 Tim. 3:2); the harsh things which ungodly sinner have spoken against him (Jude 15); Miriam and Aaron spoke against Moses (Num. 12:1); Ziba slandered Mephibosheth (2 Sam. 19:27); come, denounce Israel (Num. 23:7); some spoke evil of the Way (Acts 19:9); the Assyrians spoke against the Lord and Hezekiah (2 Chr. 32:16); the way of truth will be maligned (2 Pet. 2:2); reviling the glorious ones (Jude 8); reviling without knowledge (2 Pet. 2:12); they are gossips, slanderers (Rom. 1:29-30); men will be slanderers (2 Tim. 3:3); the words of a whisperer are like delicious titbits (Prov. 18:8; 26:22); the devil – 'slanderer' (Matt. 4:1).

B Being slandered

My enemies have spoken against me (Ps. 71:10); as some people slanderously charge us with saying (Rom. 3:8); if I eat with thankfulness, why am I slandered? (1 Cor. 10:30); I know the slander of those who say they are Jews and are not (Rev. 2:9); blessed are you when they say all kinds of evil against you falsely (Matt. 5:11); they malign you for not sharing in dissipation (1 Pet. 4:4); when slandered we conciliate (1 Cor. 4:13); we commend ourselves by bad report and good report (2 Cor. 6:8).

C Not being slandered

Give the enemy no opportunity for slander (1 Tim. 5:14); that they may be ashamed of their slander (1 Pet. 3:16); no one performing a miracle in my name can soon speak evil of me (Mark 9:39); do not let what is for you a good thing be spoken of as evil (Rom. 14:16); that the name of God and the teaching not be spoken against (1 Tim. 6:1); no one spoke against the Israelites (Josh. 10:21); not a dog will growl against Israel (Exod. 11:7).

D Not slandering

Do not spread slander (Lev. 19:16); do not slander a slave to his master (Prov. 30:10); speak evil of no one (Titus 3:2); do not speak against one another (Jas. 4:11); he who speaks evil of parents must die (Matt. 15:4); do not speak evil of a ruler (Acts 23:5); put away slander (Eph. 4:31; Col. 3:8; 1 Pet. 2:1); I fear there may be gossip (2 Cor. 12:20); deacons must not be double-tongued (1 Tim. 3:8); women must not be slanderers (1 Tim. 3:11); older women must not be slanderers (Titus 2:3); they become gossips and busybodies (1 Tim. 5:13); how can I denounce whom the Lord has not denounced? (Num. 23:8).

927 Vindication

A God vindicates

God has vindicated me (Gen. 30:6); vindicate me, O Lord (Ps. 7:8; 26:1; 43:1; 54:1); I know that my vindicator lives (Job 19:25); it is God who justifies (Rom. 8:33); will not God vindicate his elect? (Luke 18:7); their vindication is from me (Isa. 54:17); he was vindicated in the Spirit (1 Tim. 3:16).

B Justified by grace

Justified freely by his grace (Rom. 3:24; Titus 3:7); by his knowledge my servant will justify many (Isa. 53:11); justified by his blood (Rom. 5:9); the free gift following many trespasses brought justification (Rom. 5:16); the result of one act of righteousness was justification bringing life for all (Rom. 5:18); he was raised for our justification (Rom. 4:25); those he called he also justified (Rom. 8:30); you were justified (1 Cor. 6:11); he is just and the justifier of him who believes (Rom. 3:26); God justifies the ungodly (Rom. 4:5); this man went home justified rather than the other (Luke 18:14); by the obedience of one many will be made righteous (Rom. 5:19); the scripture, foreseeing that God would justify the Gentiles by faith (Gal. 3:8); justified by faith (Rom. 5:1; Gal. 3:24); God justifies both circumcised and uncircumcised by faith (Rom. 3:30).

C Justified by works

Was not Abraham justified by works? (Jas. 2:21); as was Rahab (Jas. 2:25); a man is justified by works and not by faith alone (Jas. 2:24); wisdom is justified by her deeds (Matt. 11:19); it is not the hearers of the law but the doers who are justified (Rom. 2:13); no one is justified before God by the law (Gal. 3:11); if a law could bring life, righteousness would be by the law (Gal. 3:21); a man is not justified by works of the law but by faith (Gal. 2:16); justified by faith apart from works of the law (Rom. 3:28); by the works of the law no one will be justified (Rom. 3:20); in seeking to be justified by the law you are severed from Christ (Gal. 5:4); if Abraham was justified by works, he has something to boast about (Rom. 4:2).

D Man vindicates

It is your vindication (Gen. 20:16); I desire to justify you (Job 33:32); I am not aware of anything against myself, but I am not by this acquitted (1 Cor. 4:4); you are those who justify yourselves before men (Luke 16:15); the lawyer wished to vindicate himself (Luke 10:29).

928 Accusation

A About accusations

Do not accuse a man for no reason (Prov. 3:30); do not receive an accusation against an elder except on the evidence of two or three witnesses (1 Tim. 5:19); do not accuse anyone falsely (Luke 3:14); I wanted to know the charge on which they accused him (Acts 23:28); their thoughts accuse or excuse them (Rom. 2:15).

B Accusing Christ

They looked for a reason to accuse Jesus (Matt. 12:10; Mark 3:2; Luke 6:7; John 8:6); what charges are you bringing? (John 18:29); the chief priests accused him (Matt. 27:12; Mark 15:3); the leaders accused him (Luke 23:2); the chief priests and scribes accused him (Luke 23:10); above the head was the charge (Matt. 27:37); the charge read, 'The king of the Jews' (Mark 15:26); see how many charges they bring against you! (Mark 15:4); he gave no answer even to a single charge (Matt. 27:14).

C Accusing people

The Lord is bringing a charge against Israel (Mic. 6:2); your accuser is Moses (John 5:45); listen, you mountains, to the indictment of the Lord (Mic. 6:2); I have this against you, that you have abandoned your first love (Rev. 2:4); I have a few things against you (Rev. 2:14); I have this against you, that you tolerate the woman Jezebel (Rev. 2:20); Satan stood to accuse the high priest (Zech. 3:1); the accuser of the brethren, who accuses them day and night (Rev. 12:10); in return for

my love they accuse me (Ps. 109:4); they tried to find grounds to accuse Daniel (Dan. 6:4-5); Abner was accused over a woman (2 Sam. 3:7-8); let them bring charges against these men (Acts 19:38); they brought their charges against Paul (Acts 24:1; 25:2, 7); for this hope I am accused by Jews! (Acts 26:7); we will not find grounds to accuse Daniel except for the law of his God (Dan. 6:5); who will bring a charge against God's elect? (Rom. 8:33); I had no accusation against my nation (Acts 28:19); Felix had no charge to write about (Acts 25:27); make friends quickly with your accuser (Matt. 5:25).

929 Faithfulness

A God is faithful

God is faithful (1 Cor. 1:9; 10:13); the Lord is faithful (2 Thess. 3:3); the faithful God (Deut. 7:9); a God of faithfulness and without injustice (Deut. 32:4); his faithfulness is to all generations (Ps. 100:5); God keeps faith for ever (Ps. 146:6); your faithfulness reaches to the clouds (Ps. 36:5); the one who calls you is faithful (1 Thess. 5:24); he who promised is faithful (Heb. 10:23); great is your faithfulness (Lam. 3:23); Sarah considered him faithful who had promised (Heb. 11:11); if we are faithless, he remains faithful (2 Tim. 2:13); he is faithful to forgive our sins (1 John 1:9); I will betroth you to me in faithfulness (Hos. 2:20); does their unbelief nullify God's faithfulness? (Rom. 3:3); as surely as God is faithful (2 Cor. 1:18); in faithfulness you have afflicted me (Ps. 119:75).

B Christ is faithful

Jesus was faithful to the one who appointed him (Heb. 3:2); the rider is called Faithful and True (Rev. 19:11); the faithful and true witness (Rev. 3:14).

C Faithful people

C1 The need to be faithful

The fruit of the Spirit is faithfulness (Gal. 5:22); do not be faithless to the wife of your youth (Mal. 2:15); the women likewise must be faithful in all things (1 Tim. 3:11); it is required that stewards must prove trustworthy (1 Cor. 4:2); an overseer [elder] must be above reproach (1 Tim. 3:2; Titus 1:6, 7); be faithful to death (Rev. 2:10); I have chosen the way of faithfulness (Ps. 119:30).

C2 Faithful people in general

My eyes will be on the faithful in the land (Ps. 101:6); the workmen acted with complete honesty (2 Kgs. 12:15; 22:7); sons who will not deal falsely (Isa. 63:8); good and faithful servant (Matt. 25:21, 23); the faithful and sensible steward who gives the servants food (Luke 12:42); entrust these things to faithful men who will be able to teach others also (2 Tim. 2:2); to the saints who are faithful in Christ Jesus (Eph. 1:1); those with him are called, chosen and faithful (Rev. 17:14); you have been faithful in a few things (Matt. 25:21, 23); you have been faithful in a very little (Luke 19:17); he who is faithful in a little is faithful also in much (Luke 16:10-12).

C3 Faithful individuals

By this I will know that you are honest men (Gen. 42:33); you found Abraham's heart to be faithful (Neh. 9:8); Moses was faithful in all God's house (Num. 12:7); I will raise up a faithful priest (1 Sam. 2:35); who is as faithful as David? (1 Sam. 22:14); Asa was blameless all his days (2 Chr. 15:17); Job was blameless and upright (Job 1:1); Zechariah and Elizabeth were blameless in the sight of God (Luke 1:6); Christ considered me faithful (1 Tim. 1:12); you do a faithful thing in rendering service to the brethren (3 John 5); the Bereans were more noble than the Thessalonians (Acts 17:11); you will be called the faithful city (Isa. 1:26); who is the

faithful and wise servant? (Matt. 24:45); if you have
judged me to be faithful to the Lord (Acts 16:15); I give
my opinion as one who by the Lord's mercy is
trustworthy (1 Cor. 7:25); Moses was faithful in all
God's house (Heb. 3:2); Antipas, my faithful one (Rev.
2:13).

930 Unfaithfulness
BETRAYING, see 272A1.

A Unfaithful
The harlot increases the faithless among men (Prov.
23:28); they are unfaithful sons (Deut. 32:20); the
Israelites acted unfaithfully (Josh. 7:1); if a land sins
against me by acting unfaithfully (Ezek. 14:13); they
were unfaithful to the Lord (2 Chr. 12:2; 30:7); as a
faithless wife leaves her husband, so you have been
faithless to me (Jer. 3:20); Judah exiled for their
unfaithfulness (1 Chr. 9:1); you treacherous one with
whom none has been treacherous (Isa. 33:1); if we are
faithless, he remains faithful (2 Tim. 2:13); they are
untrustworthy (Rom. 1:31); at Adam they dealt
faithlessly with me (Hos. 6:7); why do you countenance
faithless men? (Hab. 1:13); her prophets are faithless
(Zeph. 3:4); he who eats my bread has lifted his heel
against me (John 13:18); Saul died for his unfaithfulness
(1 Chr. 10:13); treason! (2 Kgs. 11:14; 2 Chr. 23:13).

B Cheating
Your father has cheated me (Gen. 31:7); if anyone
cheats his neighbour (Lev. 6:2); whom have I cheated?
(1 Sam. 12:3-4); if I have cheated anyone, I will repay it
fourfold (Luke 19:8); cursed be the cheat who vows a
male animal yet sacrifices a blemished animal (Mal.
1:14).

931 Unselfishness
None of us lives or dies for himself (Rom. 14:7); even
Christ did not please himself (Rom. 15:3); my own
vineyard I neglected (S. of S. 1:6); the Son can do
nothing of himself, but only what he sees the Father
doing (John 5:19); I can do nothing of myself (John
5:30); my teaching is not mine but his who sent me
(John 7:16); I have not come of myself (John 7:28); I do
nothing of myself but speak as the Father taught me
(John 8:28); I have not spoken on my own account
(John 12:49); the words I say to you are not of my own
speaking (John 14:10); the word you hear is not mine
but the Father's who sent me (John 14:25); the Spirit
will not speak on his own initiative (John 16:13).

932 Selfishness
SELF, see 80.

A Selfish people
People will be lovers of self (2 Tim. 3:2); we have
turned every one to his own way (Isa. 53:6); they have
all turned to their own way (Isa. 56:11); everyone looks
to his own things, not those of Jesus Christ (Phil. 2:21);
he who speaks from himself seeks his own glory (John
7:18); those who are selfish and do not obey the truth
(Rom. 2:8); each one eats his own meal first (1 Cor.
11:21); Diotrephes loves to be first (3 John 9); they feast,
looking after themselves (Jude 12); if you have selfish
ambition (Jas. 3:14); where there is selfish ambition
there is disorder (Jas. 3:16).

B Do not be selfish
Let no one seek his own good but the good of his
neighbour (1 Cor. 10:24); not looking to one's own
things, but also to the things of others (Phil. 2:4); those
who live should no longer live for themselves (2 Cor.
5:15); do nothing through selfishness (Phil. 2:3); we
ought not merely to please ourselves (Rom. 15:1); if I

have eaten my morsel alone (Job 31:17); love does not
seek its own (1 Cor. 13:5).
NOT ACTING ALONE, see 89E.

933 Virtue
Perseverance produces character and character hope
(Rom. 5:4).

934 Wickedness
WRONG, see 914.

935 Innocence
A The need for innocence
Who may sojourn in your tent? he whose walk is
blameless (Ps. 15:2); blessed are those whose ways are
blameless (Ps. 119:1); be wise as serpents and innocent
as doves (Matt. 10:16); be wise as to good, innocent as
to evil (Rom. 16:19); make every effort to be found
spotless and blameless (2 Pet. 3:14); you will be
blameless on the day of our Lord Jesus (1 Cor. 1:8); God
is able to make you stand blameless (Jude 24); sincere
and blameless until the day of Christ (Phil. 1:10); may
he establish your hearts unblameable in holiness
(1 Thess. 3:13); that the church should be holy and
blameless (Eph. 5:27); he has chosen us to be holy and
blameless (Eph. 1:4); that you may be blameless and
innocent (Phil. 2:15); may your spirit, soul and body be
kept blameless (1 Thess. 5:23); to present you holy and
blameless (Col. 1:22).

B Innocence of Christ
This man has done nothing wrong (Luke 23:41); he
committed no sin (1 Pet. 2:22); tempted in every way,
yet without sin (Heb. 4:15); such a high priest, holy,
innocent, undefiled (Heb. 7:26); which of you convicts
me of sin? (John 8:46); I find no guilt in this man (Luke
23:4, 14-15, 22; John 18:38; 19:4, 6); surely this man was
innocent (Luke 23:47); I have sinned in betraying
innocent blood (Matt. 27:4); they found no charge
deserving death (Acts 13:28); Christ died for sins, the
just for the unjust (1 Pet. 3:18); he appeared to take
away sins and in him there is no sin (1 John 3:5).

C Plea of innocence
Our hands have not shed this blood (Deut. 21:7); Lord,
will you destroy an innocent nation? (Gen. 20:4-6);
who, being innocent, has ever perished? (Job 4:7); I
wash my hands in innocence (Ps. 26:6); though I am
innocent, my mouth would condemn me (Job 9:20);
how blamelessly we behaved towards you believers
(1 Thess. 2:10); I am innocent of the blood of Abner (2
Sam. 3:28); I am innocent (Job 34:5; Dan. 6:22); I am
innocent of this man's blood (Matt. 27:24); I am
innocent of the blood of all men (Acts 20:26); I have
done nothing wrong (Acts 25:8); you show yourself to
be innocent (2 Cor. 7:11).

D Innocence of people
God has not seen iniquity in Israel (Num. 23:21); Noah
was blameless in his generation (Gen. 6:9); the priests
profane the sabbath and are innocent (Matt. 12:5); you
would not have condemned the innocent (Matt. 12:7);
we find nothing wrong in this man (Acts 23:9); he has
done nothing deserving death (Acts 25:25); this man is
not doing anything deserving death or imprisonment
(Acts 26:31); there were no grounds for putting me to
death (Acts 28:18); if you were blind you would have no
sin (John 9:41).

E Who is innocent?
All a man's ways seem innocent to him, but the Lord
weighs motives (Prov. 16:2); if anyone is without sin let
him be the first to cast a stone (John 8:7); if we say we
have no sin we deceive ourselves (1 John 1:8); if we say
we have not sinned we make God a liar (1 John 1:10); if

I had not come and spoken to them, they would not have had sin (John 15:22); if I not done unique works among them, they would not have had sin (John 15:24).

936 Guilt

A Found guilty
We are guilty (Gen. 42:21; Ezra 9:15); the woman shall bear her guilt (Num. 5:31); whoever keeps the whole law but breaks one point is guilty of all (Jas. 2:10); mankind is without excuse (Rom. 1:20); guilty enough for the hell of fire (Matt. 5:22); whoever is angry with his brother will be guilty before the court (Matt. 5:22); whoever says 'Raca' to his brother will be guilty before the sanhedrin (Matt. 5:22); you are without excuse (Rom. 2:1).

B Incurring guilt
Bloodguilt if blood is not offered (Lev. 17:4); bloodguilt if someone falls from your roof (Deut. 22:8); he who curses his God shall bear his sin (Lev. 24:15); he has cursed father or mother, his blood is on him (Lev. 20:9); those who engage in illicit sex, their blood is on them (Lev. 20:11-16); if the anointed priest sins and brings guilt on the people (Lev. 4:3); if the whole congregation sins and becomes guilty (Lev. 4:13); if a leader sins unintentionally and becomes guilty (Lev. 4:22); if one of the common people sins unintentionally and becomes guilty (Lev. 4:27); if a person sins unwittingly he will bear his iniquity (Lev. 5:17); if a man becomes unclean unwittingly he will be guilty (Lev. 5:2-4); if a witness does not testify he will bear his iniquity (Lev. 5:1); if a person does not cleanse himself he will bear his iniquity (Lev. 17:16); the one who does not keep Passover shall bear his sin (Num. 9:13); guilty of the body and blood of the Lord (1 Cor. 11:27); if I do not bring him back I will be guilty before you for ever (Gen. 43:9; 44:32); now they have no excuse for their sin (John 15:22); he who is troubling you will bear his judgement (Gal. 5:10).

C Removal of guilt
Deliver me from bloodguilt (Ps. 51:14); remove the guilt of innocent blood (Deut. 21:9); the guilt of Eli's house will never be atoned for (1 Sam. 3:14).
GUILT OFFERING, see 981D6.

937 Good person

A The righteous
A1 The righteous in general
The Lord loves the righteous (Ps. 146:8); tell the righteous it will be well with him (Isa. 3:10); in his days may the righteous man flourish (Ps. 72:7); let the righteous rejoice in the Lord (Ps. 33:1; 68:3); the righteous will flourish like a green leaf (Prov. 11:28); he who receives a righteous man as a righteous man will receive a righteous man's reward (Matt. 10:41); the good man out of his good treasure brings forth good (Matt. 12:35); the righteous will shine in the kingdom of their Father (Matt. 13:43); the resurrection of the just (Luke 14:14); one will hardly die for a righteous man (Rom. 5:7); the fervent prayer of a righteous man accomplishes much (Jas. 5:16).

A2 Numbers of righteous people
99 righteous persons who need no repentance (Luke 15:7); if there are in the city 50 righteous (Gen. 18:24).

A3 Particular righteous people
Zechariah and Elizabeth were righteous in the sight of God (Luke 1:6); Simeon was righteous and devout (Luke 2:25); Cornelius, a centurion, a righteous and God-fearing man (Acts 10:22); God rescued righteous Lot (2 Pet. 2:7-8); Noah, Daniel and Job would only deliver themselves by their righteousness (Ezek. 14:14-20); Joseph, Mary's husband, was a righteous

men (Matt. 1:19); Herod knew John was a righteous man (Mark 6:20); some said Jesus was a good man (John 7:12); Joseph of Arimathea was a good man (Luke 23:50).

B The righteous perishing
The godly person has perished from the earth (Mic. 7:2); the righteous man perishes and no one takes it to heart (Isa. 57:1); there are righteous to whom it happens according to the deeds of the wicked (Eccles. 8:14); there is a righteous man who perishes in his righteousness (Eccles. 7:15); you have condemned and put to death the righteous man (Jas. 5:6).

C Righteous and wicked
God will judge both the righteous and the wicked (Eccles. 3:17); one fate comes to the righteous and the wicked (Eccles. 9:2); will you destroy the righteous with the wicked? (Gen. 18:23); I will cut off from you both the righteous and the wicked (Ezek. 21:3); you will again distinguish between the righteous and the wicked (Mal. 3:18); the angels will separate the wicked from the righteous (Matt. 13:49); he sends rain on the just and the unjust (Matt. 5:45); I came not to call the righteous but sinners (Matt. 9:13; Mark 2:17; Luke 5:32); a resurrection of both just and unjust (Acts 24:15).

938 Bad person
THE RIGHTEOUS AND THE WICKED, see 937C.

A Wicked people
A1 Wicked people in general
How can you who are evil say anything good? (Matt. 12:34); you who are evil (Matt. 7:11; Luke 11:13); the law is not for the righteous but for the lawless and rebellious (1 Tim. 1:9); outside are dogs, sorcerers, fornicators, murderers, idolaters (Rev. 22:15);this evil generation (Matt. 12:45); an evil and adulterous generation (Matt. 16:4); this is a wicked generation (Luke 11:29); from the wicked comes wickedness (1 Sam. 24:13); every one is godless and an evildoer (Isa. 9:17); you brood of vipers! (Matt. 3:7); tax collectors and sinners reclined at table with Jesus and his disciples (Matt. 9:10-11); the scribes of the Pharisees saw that he ate with sinners (Mark 2:16); he was numbered with transgressors (Isa. 53:12; Mark 15:28; Luke 22:37).

A2 Specific wicked people
The woman was deceived and became a transgressor (1 Tim. 2:14); the men of Sodom were wicked (Gen. 13:13); Judah's firstborn was wicked (Gen. 38:7; 1 Chr. 2:3); Abimelech hired worthless men (Judg. 9:4); worthless men gathered to Jephthah (Judg. 11:3); you wicked slave! (Matt. 18:32); you wicked and lazy servant! (Matt. 25:26); a woman who was a sinner (Luke 7:37); depart from me, for I am a sinful man (Luke 5:8); he has gone to be the guest of a sinner (Luke 19:7); we know that this man is a sinner (John 9:24); two criminals were led out to be put to death with him (Luke 23:32); you nailed him to a cross by the hands of lawless men (Acts 2:23); the Jews took wicked men from the market place (Acts 17:5); you were born in sin, and would you teach us? (John 9:34); do you think these were worse sinners than all the others? (Luke 13:2, 4).

B Ways of the wicked
The wicked forsake your law (Ps. 119:53); the wicked are like the tossing sea (Isa. 57:20); one sinner destroys much good (Eccles. 9:18); do not even the tax collectors love those who love them? (Matt. 5:46); even sinners love those who love them (Luke 6:32-4); do not even pagans greet their brethren? (Matt. 5:47); the unjust knows no shame (Zeph. 3:5); the evil man out of his evil treasure brings forth evil (Matt. 12:35); an evil

generation seeks for a sign (Matt. 12:39; 16:4; Luke 11:29).

C Avoiding the wicked
Blessed is the man who does not walk in the counsel of the wicked (Ps. 1:1); I will not sit with the wicked (Ps. 26:5); rescue me out of the hand of the wicked (Ps. 71:4); do not resist one who is evil (Matt. 5:39); does anyone dare to go to law against a brother before the unrighteous? (1 Cor. 6:1); pray that we may be delivered from evil men (2 Thess. 3:2); Job walks with the wicked (Job 34:8).

D Judgement on the wicked
The wicked are like chaff driven away by the wind (Ps. 1:4); the way of the wicked will perish (Ps. 1:6); the dawn shakes the wicked out of the skirts of the earth (Job 38:13); we know that God does not listen to sinners (John 9:31); the unrighteous will not inherit the kingdom of God (1 Cor. 6:9); there is no peace for the wicked (Isa. 48:22; 57:21); tell the wicked it will go badly for them (Isa. 3:11); a little while and the wicked will be no more (Ps. 37:9-10); the lamp of the wicked will be snuffed out (Job 18:5); God has made even the wicked for the day of evil (Prov. 16:4); the wicked he will destroy (Ps. 145:20); you destroy the wicked (Ps. 9:5); when I say to the wicked, 'You shall surely die' (Ezek. 3:18); though the wicked sprout like grass they will be destroyed for ever (Ps. 92:7); depart from me, you evildoers (Matt. 7:23); depart from me, you workers of iniquity (Luke 13:27); they will gather out of his kingdom all who commit lawlessness (Matt. 13:41); the face of the Lord is against those who do evil (1 Pet. 3:12); the Lord knows how to keep the unrighteous under punishment until the day of judgement (2 Pet. 2:9); the wicked will not stand in the judgement (Ps. 1:5).

E Prosperity of the wicked
Why do the wicked live on? (Job 21:7-13); there is a wicked man who prolongs his life in wickedness (Eccles. 7:15); how long will the wicked exult? (Ps. 94:3); how often is the lamp of the wicked snuffed out? (Job 21:17); the wicked goes to his end unpunished (Job 21:30-3); the earth is given into the hand of the wicked (Job 9:24); I saw the prosperity of the wicked (Ps. 73:3-9); why does the way of the wicked prosper? (Jer. 12:1); there are sinners who experience what is due to the righteous (Eccles. 8:14); why are you silent when the wicked swallow up those more righteous? (Hab. 1:13); evildoers prosper (Mal. 3:15); the joy of the wicked is short (Job 20:5); the wicked man is in pain all his life (Job 15:20-4); though the wicked sprout like grass they will be destroyed for ever (Ps. 92:7).

F Sinners saved
He instructs sinners in the way (Ps. 25:8); the tax collectors and prostitutes believed John (Matt. 21:32); tax collectors and prostitutes enter the kingdom of God ahead of you (Matt. 21:31); I have not come to call the righteous, but sinners (Matt. 9:13; Mark 2:17; Luke 5:32); God be merciful to me, the sinner (Luke 18:13); the tax collectors and sinners were drawing near to hear him (Luke 15:1); a friend of tax collectors and sinners (Matt. 11:19; Luke 7:34); Christ Jesus came into the world to save sinners, of whom I am chief (1 Tim. 1:15-16); the Most High is kind to the ungrateful and wicked (Luke 6:35); while we were yet sinners Christ died for us (Rom. 5:8).

RESTORING SINNERS, see 656C5.

939 Repentance

A Repentance in general
If the wicked turns from his sins he will live (Ezek. 18:21); the men of Nineveh repented at the preaching of Jonah (Luke 11:32); more joy in heaven over one sinner who repents (Luke 15:7); if someone goes to them from the dead they will repent (Luke 16:30); if your brother repents, forgive him (Luke 17:3-4); John proclaiming a baptism of repentance (Acts 13:25); I will remove your lampstand unless you repent (Rev. 2:5); the Lord repents of evil (Joel 2:13).

B Repent!
Turn from your evil ways! (Ezek. 33:11); if my people will turn from their wicked ways (2 Chr. 7:14); if they repent (1 Kgs. 8:47); let each turn from his evil way and from violence (Jonah 3:8); repent and pray that the intent of your heart may be forgiven (Acts 8:22); stop sinning or something worse will happen to you (John 5:14); go and sin no more (John 8:11); unless you repent you will all likewise perish (Luke 13:3, 5); repent and do the first works (Rev. 2:5); repent, or I will come (Rev. 2:16); remember what you have heard, keep it and repent (Rev. 3:3); be zealous and repent (Rev. 3:19); I will throw them into great tribulation unless they repent (Rev. 2:22).

C Repentance and forgiveness
I have not come to call the righteous, but sinners to repentance (Luke 5:32); repent and believe the gospel (Mark 1:15); they preached that men should repent (Mark 6:12); repentance and forgiveness should be preached (Luke 24:47); there is joy before the angels of God over one sinner who repents (Luke 15:10); repent and turn to God (Acts 3:19); he commands all people everywhere to repent (Acts 17:30); testifying of repentance toward God and faith in our Lord Jesus Christ (Acts 20:21); they must turn to God in repentance (Acts 26:20); repentance from dead works (Heb. 6:1).

D God gives repentance
God gives repentance to Israel (Acts 5:31); God has granted to the Gentiles repentance unto life (Acts 11:18); God may grant them repentance (2 Tim. 2:25); God's kindness leads you to repentance (Rom. 2:4); he wants all to come to repentance (2 Pet. 3:9).

CHANGE OF MIND, see 603.

E Signs of repentance
I repent in dust and ashes (Job 42:6); a baptism of repentance (Matt. 3:11; Mark 1:4; Luke 3:3; Acts 13:24; 19:4); repent and be baptised (Acts 2:38); when God saw their deeds, how they turned from their wicked way (Jonah 3:10); godly sorrow produces repentance without regret leading to salvation (2 Cor. 7:10); bring forth fruit fitting repentance (Matt. 3:8; Luke 3:8); perform deeds fitting repentance (Acts 26:20).

940 Impenitence
A stubborn, unrepentant heart (Rom. 2:5); if you warn the wicked and he does not turn from his wickedness (Ezek. 3:19); Jesus upbraided the cities because they did not repent (Matt. 11:20); the rest of mankind did not repent (Rev. 9:20-1); they refused to repent (Jer. 5:3; Rev. 16:9); they did not repent of their deeds (Rev. 16:11); she refuses to repent of her immorality (Rev. 2:21); you did not afterwards repent and believe him (Matt. 21:32); it is impossible to restore to repentance some who have fallen away (Heb. 6:6); those who have sinned and not repented (2 Cor. 12:21); Esau found no place for repentance (Heb. 12:17); no one repented of his wickedness (Jer. 8:6); 99 righteous persons who need no repentance (Luke 15:7).

941 Atonement

A God atoning
The Lord making atonement for Aaron (Lev. 8:34); he will atone for his land and his people (Deut. 32:43); I

have taken your iniquity from you and will clothe you with rich robes (Zech. 3:4); I will remove the iniquity of that land in one day (Zech. 3:9).

B Priests atoning
The priest makes atonement (Lev. 4:20; Num. 6:11); Aaron's descendants make atonement for Israel (1 Chr. 6:49); the priests made atonement for all Israel (2 Chr. 29:24); the high priest makes atonement for himself (Lev. 16:6); make atonement for your self and for the people (Lev. 9:7); the priest makes atonement for: the holy place (Lev. 16:16); the altar (Lev. 16:18); the tent of meeting (Lev. 16:20); the priests (Lev. 16:33).

C Christ atoning
The Lamb of God who takes away the sin of the world (John 1:29); Christ died for our sins in accordance with the scriptures (1 Cor. 15:3); God displayed him as a propitiation in his blood (Rom. 3:25); we have redemption through his blood (Eph. 1:7); after he had made purification for sins, he sat down (Heb. 1:3); he is the propitiation for our sins (1 John 2:2); he sent his Son to be the propitiation for our sins (1 John 4:10); he appeared to take away sins (1 John 3:5); he will save his people from their sins (Matt. 1:21); to make propitiation for the sins of the people (Heb. 2:17); he appeared in order to put away sin by the sacrifice of himself (Heb. 9:26); Christ died for sins, the just for the unjust, that he might bring us to God (1 Pet. 3:18); Christ gave himself for our sins (Gal. 1:4); to him who loves us and freed us from our sins by his blood (Rev. 1:5).
CLEANSING OF SIN, see 648D.

D Day of atonement
Regulations for the Day of Atonement (Lev. 16:29-34; 23:27-32; Num. 29:7-11); only the high priest goes into the second tent once a year (Heb. 9:7); the high priest enters the holy of holies every year with blood not his own (Heb. 9:25); the 'fast' was already past (Acts 27:9).

E Propitiatory [mercy seat]
A propitiatory [mercy seat] (Exod. 25:17; 31:7; 35:12; 37:6; 39:35); put the propitiatory on top of the ark (Exod. 25:21; 26:34; 30:6; 40:20); I will speak to you from the propitiatory (Exod. 25:22; 37:9); the cloud of incense is to cover the propitiatory of the testimony (Lev. 16:13); the cherubim of glory overshadowing the mercy seat (Heb. 9:5); blood sprinkled before the propitiatory (Lev. 16:14, 15); Moses heard a voice from above the propitiatory (Num. 7:89).
MERCY SEAT, see 226C3.

F Atoning by sacrifices
The burnt offering will make atonement (Lev. 1:4; Num. 28:30); the sin offering to make atonement (Num. 28:22; 29:5; Neh. 10:33); blood brought into the tent of meeting to make atonement (Lev. 6:30); cereal, burnt and peace offerings to make atonement (Ezek. 45:15); sin offering, cereal offering, burnt offering, peace offering to make atonement (Ezek. 45:17); every high priest offers gifts and sacrifices for sins (Heb. 5:1); he offers sacrifices for his own sins as well as for the sins of the people (Heb. 5:3; 7:27); the high priest offers blood for his own sins and the sins of the people (Heb. 9:7); the ram of atonement (Num. 5:8); priests offer repeatedly sacrifices which can never take away sin (Heb. 10:11); it is impossible for the blood of bulls and goats to take away sins (Heb. 10:4).
BEARING SIN, see 273B8.
TAKING AWAY SIN, see 786D2.

G Various atoning
Aaron offered incense to make atonement (Num. 16:46-7); the half-shekel tax to make atonement (Exod. 30:15, 16); an offering of jewellery to make atonement (Num. 31:50); perhaps I can make atonement for your

sin (Exod. 32:30); atone for your people (Deut. 21:8); Phinehas made atonement with his spear (Num. 25:13); through love and faithfulness sin is atoned for (Prov. 16:6); your sin is atoned for (Isa. 6:7); by exile Jacob's iniquity will be atoned for (Isa. 27:9); seventy sevens are decreed to atone for wickedness (Dan. 9:24); the sin of Eli's house will never be atoned for (1 Sam. 3:14).

942 Temperance
GENTLENESS, see 177.
SOBRIETY, see 948.

943 Intemperance
A man without self-control is like a city broken into (Prov. 25:28); inside they are full of robbery and self-indulgence (Matt. 23:25); men will be without self-control (2 Tim. 3:3); you have lived in luxury and pleasure (Jas. 5:5).

944 Sensualism
These things are no use against fleshly indulgence (Col. 2:23).

945 Asceticism
Severe treatment of the body (Col. 2:23).

946 Fasting
A Vowing to fast
David took an oath not to eat before the sun set (2 Sam. 3:35); cursed be the man who eats food before evening (1 Sam. 14:24); they vowed not to eat or drink until they had killed Paul (Acts 23:12).

B Conditions of fasting
B1 How to fast
Instructions for times of fasting and mourning (Esther 9:31); is not this the kind of fasting I have chosen? (Isa. 58:5, 6); I humbled my soul with fasting (Ps. 35:13); when you fast, do not look gloomy (Matt. 6:16); on the day of fasting, you do as you please (Isa. 58:3); when you fasted, was it for me? (Zech. 7:5); you fast to quarrel and fight (Isa. 58:4).

B2 Who will fast
How is it that John's disciples fast but yours do not? (Matt. 9:14; Mark 2:18; Luke 5:33); can the wedding guests fast while the bridegroom is with them? (Mark 2:19; Luke 5:34); on that day they will fast (Matt. 9:15; Mark 2:20; Luke 5:35).

B3 Fasting regularly
Anna fasted and prayed (Luke 2:37); John came neither eating nor drinking (Matt. 11:18; Luke 7:33); I fast twice a week (Luke 18:12); the 'fast' was already past (Acts 27:9); fasting in the fifth and seventh months (Zech. 7:3, 5); the fasts of the fourth, fifth, seventh and tenth month will become joy (Zech. 8:19).

B4 Fasting for long periods
Moses did not eat or drink for 40 days (Exod. 34:28; Deut. 9:9); and for another 40 days (Deut. 9:18); Elijah did not eat or drink for 40 days (1 Kgs. 19:8); Jesus fasted for 40 days (Matt. 4:2; Luke 4:2).

C Reasons for fasting
C1 Prayer and fasting
They fasted and confessed their sin (1 Sam. 7:6); the men of Israel fasted and presented burnt offerings (Judg. 20:26); David pleaded with God for the child and fasted (2 Sam. 12:16-22); we fasted and prayed to our God (Ezra 8:21); gather all the Jews and fast for me (Esther 4:16); Nehemiah was fasting and praying (Neh. 1:4); fasting and in sackcloth to confess their sin (Neh. 9:1); prayer and supplication with fasting (Dan. 9:3); the men of Nineveh declared a fast and put on sackcloth (Jonah 3:5); while they were ministering to

the Lord and fasting (Acts 13:2); prayer and fasting (Matt. 17:21; Mark 9:29); they fasted and prayed and laid their hands on them (Acts 13:3); with prayer and fasting they committed the elders to the Lord (Acts 14:23).

C2 Fasting in mourning
Hannah wept and would not eat (1 Sam. 1:7-8); Jonathan ate nothing that day (1 Sam. 20:34); I was reproached for weeping and fasting (Ps. 69:10); return to me with fasting, weeping and mourning (Joel 2:12); the men of Jabesh fasted seven days, mourning Saul (1 Sam. 31:13; 1 Chr. 10:12); they fasted until evening for Saul and Jonathan (2 Sam. 1:12); he ate no food and drank no water, mourning over their unfaithfulness (Ezra 10:6).

C3 Pointless fasting
Now the child is dead, why should I fast? (2 Sam. 12:23); why have we fasted and you did not see it? (Isa. 58:3); fasting like this will not make your voice heard on high (Isa. 58:4); when they fast I will not listen (Jer. 14:12).

D Going without food
Saul had eaten nothing all that day (1 Sam. 28:20); the Egyptian had not eaten or drunk for three days (1 Sam. 30:12); Ahab would not eat (1 Kgs. 21:4-5); the king spent the night without eating (Dan. 6:18); I will not eat the passover until it is fulfilled (Luke 22:16); Paul did not eat or drink for three days (Acts 9:9); for fourteen days you have not eaten anything (Acts 27:33); I forget to eat my bread (Ps. 102:4); he loathes food (Job 33:20); they hated all kinds of food (Ps. 107:18); a crowd gathered so they could not even eat (Mark 3:20); they did not have time to eat (Mark 6:31); if food makes my brother stumble I will never eat meat again (1 Cor. 8:13).

947 Gluttony
The glutton will come to poverty (Prov. 23:21); a companion of gluttons shames his father (Prov. 28:7); our son is a glutton and a drunkard (Deut. 21:20); they called Jesus a glutton and a drunkard (Matt. 11:19; Luke 7:34); Cretans are lazy gluttons (Titus 1:12).

948 Sobriety
AVOIDING ALCOHOL, see 949B3.

A Drinking no wine
Aaron and his sons were not to drink wine or other fermented drink (Lev. 10:9); John the Baptist had to drink no wine (Luke 1:15); John the Baptist came eating no bread and drinking no wine (Luke 7:33); a Nazirite must not consume anything from the vine (Num. 6:3-4); Samson's mother had to drink no wine or liquor (Judg. 13:4); I will not drink of the fruit of the vine (Luke 22:18); he would not drink the wine mixed with myrrh (Mark 15:23); the Rechabites do not drink wine (Jer. 35:14).

B Not too much wine
Deacons must not be addicted to much wine (1 Tim. 3:8); a bishop [elder] must not be addicted to wine (1 Tim. 3:3; Titus 1:7); older women must not be slaves to much wine (Titus 2:3); do not join those who drink too much wine (Prov. 23:20-1).

C Not drunk
Hannah was not drunk (1 Sam. 1:15); in the morning when he had sobered up (1 Sam. 25:37); these men are not drunk (Acts 2:15).
DRUNKENNESS, see 949.

949 Drunkenness
A Intoxicating drink
Wine is a mocker and beer a brawler (Prov. 20:1); wine is treacherous (Hab. 2:5); do not gaze at wine when it is red (Prov. 23:29-35); 'I will preach of wine and strong drink' (Mic. 2:11); wine to make him forget his trouble (Prov. 31:6-7); new wine (Matt. 9:17; Mark 2:22); it is not for kings to drink wine or crave beer (Prov. 31:4); woe to those who rise early to run after drink (Isa. 5:11); woe to those who are heroes at drinking wine (Isa. 5:22).

WINE, see 335B.

B Being drunk
B1 Drunken people
Description of the drunkard (Prov. 23:29-35); the drunkard will come to poverty (Prov. 23:21); one is hungry and another is drunk (1 Cor. 11:21); they reeled like drunken men (Ps. 107:27); like a drunken man staggers in his vomit (Isa. 19:14); priests and prophets stagger from beer (Isa. 28:7); woe to the land whose princes feast in the morning (Eccles. 10:16-17); princes sick with the heat of wine (Hos. 7:5); woe to the pride of Ephraim's drunkards (Isa. 28:1); you who say to your husbands, 'Bring, that we may drink' (Amos 4:1); he begins to beat his fellow-servants and to eat and drink with drunkards (Matt. 24:49; Luke 12:45); do not associate with a 'brother' who is a drunkard (1 Cor. 5:11); drunkards will not inherit the kingdom of God (1 Cor. 6:10); let the time that is past suffice for drunkenness (1 Pet. 4:3); Noah drank wine and became drunk (Gen. 9:21); Nabal was very drunk (1 Sam. 25:36); when Amnon is merry with wine (2 Sam. 13:28); Elah was getting drunk (1 Kgs. 16:9); Benhadad and the kings were getting drunk (1 Kgs. 20:12, 16); Ahasuerus was merry with wine (Esther 1:10).

B2 Accused of drunkenness
Our son is a glutton and a drunkard (Deut. 21:20); Eli thought Hannah was drunk (1 Sam. 1:13-14); they said Jesus was a glutton and a drunkard (Matt. 11:19; Luke 7:34); they are full of sweet wine (Acts 2:13).

B3 Do not get drunk
Those who get drunk, get drunk at night (1 Thess. 5:7); not in carousing and drunkenness (Rom. 13:13); drunkenness and carousing are deeds of the flesh (Gal. 5:21); lest your hearts be weighed down with dissipation, drunkenness and anxiety (Luke 21:34); put your wine from you (1 Sam. 1:14); do not be drunk with wine but be filled with the Spirit (Eph. 5:18).

C Making others drunk
C1 God making drunk
In the hand of the Lord is a cup full of foaming wine (Ps. 75:8); I took the cup from the Lord's hand and made all the nations drink (Jer. 25:17); drink the cup in the Lord's hand (Hab. 2:16); you who have drunk the cup of his wrath (Isa. 51:17); I will make Jerusalem a cup which causes reeling to the people around (Zech. 12:2); I made the peoples drunk in my wrath (Isa. 63:6); they will drink and stagger and go mad (Jer. 25:16); drink and be drunk (Jer. 25:27-8); be drunk, but not from wine (Isa. 29:9); you who are drunk, but not with wine (Isa. 51:21); I will make them drunk (Jer. 51:39); I will fill with drunkenness all who live in this land (Jer. 13:13); I will make her priests and wise men drunk (Jer. 51:57); the wine of the wrath of God (Rev. 14:10); you gave us wine that made us reel (Ps. 60:3); the earth reels like a drunkard (Isa. 24:20); they will become drunk with their own blood (Isa. 49:26).

C2 People making drunk
Lot's daughters made their father drunk (Gen. 19:32-5); David made Uriah drunk (2 Sam. 11:13); give the

Rechabites wine to drink (Jer. 35:2-6); you made the Nazirites drink wine (Amos 2:12); woe to those who make others drunk to look at their nakedness (Hab. 2:15).

C3 Evil making drunk
Babylon made the whole earth drunk (Jer. 51:7); the woman was drunk with the blood of the saints and the martyrs of Jesus (Rev. 17:6); drunk with the wine of her immorality (Rev. 17:2).

950 Purity

A God is pure
To the pure you show yourself pure (2 Sam. 22:27; Ps. 18:26); your eyes are too pure to look on evil (Hab. 1:13); the wisdom from above is pure (Jas. 3:17); the Lord's words are pure words (Ps. 12:6); the commandment of the Lord is pure (Ps. 19:8).

B Pure people
He who has clean hands and a pure heart (Ps. 24:4); how can a young man keep his way pure? (Ps. 119:9); led astray from singleness and purity towards Christ (2 Cor. 11:3); set the believers an example in love, faith and purity (1 Tim. 4:12); treat younger women as sisters, in all purity (1 Tim. 5:2); keep yourself pure (1 Tim. 5:22); as they see your pure behaviour (1 Pet. 3:2); blessed are the pure in heart for they shall see God (Matt. 5:8); God is good to those who are pure in heart (Ps. 73:1); our aim is love from a pure heart (1 Tim. 1:5); with those that call on the Lord from a pure heart (2 Tim. 2:22); that you may become blameless and pure (Phil. 2:15); we commend ourselves in purity (2 Cor. 6:6); to the pure all things are pure (Titus 1:15); all the ways of a man are pure in his own eyes (Prov. 16:2); in vain have I kept my heart pure (Ps. 73:13).

SINGLENESS OF HEART, see 44B.

C Pure things
Whatever is pure, think about it (Phil. 4:8); pure beaten olive oil for the lamp (Exod. 27:20); incense, pure and holy (Exod. 30:35); a pound of costly perfume of pure nard (John 12:3).

951 Impurity

A Immorality

A1 About immorality
From the heart comes fornication (Matt. 15:19; Mark 7:21); immorality and impurity are deeds of the flesh (Gal. 5:19); from the heart comes licentiousness (Mark 7:22); Lot was distressed with the licentiousness of the wicked (2 Pet. 2:7); God will judge fornicators and adulterers (Heb. 13:4); fornicators will not inherit the kingdom of God (1 Cor. 6:9); outside are fornicators (Rev. 22:15); no immoral man has any inheritance in the kingdom of Christ (Eph. 5:5); our exhortation is not from uncleanness (1 Thess. 2:3); if a man lies with a virgin not pledged to be married (Exod. 22:16).

DEATH PENALTY FOR SEXUAL SIN, see 963F5.

A2 They committed immorality
The men of Israel played the harlot with Moabite women (Num. 25:1); Eli's sons lay with the serving women (1 Sam. 2:22); a stumbling block before Israel to commit immorality (Rev. 2:14); God gave them over to impurity (Rom. 1:24); they pervert the grace of God into licentiousness (Jude 4); they indulge in every kind of impurity (Eph. 4:19); Jezebel teaches my servants to commit immorality (Rev. 2:20); they did not repent of their immorality (Rev. 9:21); he squandered his property with loose living (Luke 15:13); you once yielded your limbs to impurity (Rom. 6:19); many will follow her licentiousness (2 Pet. 2:2); she refuses to repent of her immorality (Rev. 2:21); the kings of the earth who committed immorality with her will lament

(Rev. 18:9); the inhabitants of the earth were intoxicated with the wine of her fornication (Rev. 17:2); she held a golden cup filled with the filth of her fornications (Rev. 17:4); all nations have drunk the wine of her fornications (Rev. 18:3); the kings of the earth have committed immorality with her (Rev. 18:3); Babylon made the whole earth drink the wine of her immorality (Rev. 14:8); he has judged the great harlot who corrupted the earth with her fornication (Rev. 19:2).

A3 Avoid immorality
They should abstain from fornication (Acts 15:20, 29; 21:25); not in sexual promiscuity (Rom. 13:13); flee immorality (1 Cor. 6:18); we should not commit immorality as some of them did (1 Cor. 10:8); that you abstain from sexual immorality (1 Thess. 4:3); do not let immorality, impurity or covetousness even be named among you (Eph. 5:3); God did not call us to impurity but to sanctification (1 Thess. 4:7); see that no one is immoral (Heb. 12:16); the body is not for immorality (1 Cor. 6:13); reckon your members dead to immorality, impurity etc. (Col. 3:5); I wrote to you not to associate with immoral people (1 Cor. 5:9-11); some in the church who have not repented of immorality (2 Cor. 12:21); do not associate with a 'brother' who is immoral (1 Cor. 5:11); because immorality abounds, each man should have his own wife (1 Cor. 7:2).

B Adultery
ADULTERERS, see 952A.

B1 About adultery
From the heart come adulteries (Matt. 15:19; Mark 7:21); adultery is a fire which consumes to Abaddon (Job 31:12); anyone who looks at a woman lustfully has already committed adultery (Matt. 5:28); adulterers will not inherit the kingdom of God (1 Cor. 6:9); sex with your neighbour's wife is forbidden (Lev. 18:20); if he defiles his neighbour's wife (Ezek. 18:11); if a man is found lying with a married woman, both shall die (Deut. 22:22); if a man's wife lies with another and it is hidden from him (Num. 5:12-14).

B2 Divorce and adultery
Anyone divorcing his wife, except for unchastity, makes her commit adultery, and anyone marrying a divorced woman commits adultery (Matt. 5:32); he who divorces his wife, except for unchastity, and marries another, commits adultery (Matt. 19:9); he who divorces his wife and marries another commits adultery against her (Mark 10:11); if either husband or wife divorces and remarries, they commit adultery (Luke 16:18); if she lives with another man she will be called an adulteress (Rom. 7:3); if she divorces her husband and marries another, she commits adultery (Mark 10:12).

B3 Those who committed adultery
They committed adultery (Jer. 5:7); they are all adulterers (Hos. 7:4); they brought in a woman caught in adultery (John 8:3); with eyes full of adultery (2 Pet. 2:14); stolen water is sweet (Prov. 9:17); take a wife of adultery (Hos. 1:2); you who forbid adultery, do you commit adultery? (Rom. 2:22); there is swearing, lying, murder, stealing and adultery (Hos. 4:2); your daughters play the harlot and your brides commit adultery (Hos. 4:13); David was the father of Solomon by the wife of Uriah (Matt. 1:6); this woman has been caught in adultery, in the very act (John 8:4); those who committed adultery with her (Rev. 2:22).

B4 Avoid adultery
Do not commit adultery (Exod. 20:14; Deut. 5:18; Matt. 5:27; 19:18; Mark 10:19; Luke 18:20; Rom. 13:9; Jas. 2:11); why embrace the bosom of a stranger? (Prov. 5:20); why be infatuated with an adulteress? (Prov. 5:20);

should your springs be scattered abroad? (Prov. 5:16); thank you that I am not like other men, swindlers, unjust, adulterers (Luke 18:11).

B5 Adultery towards God
Like a woman unfaithful to her husband, so you have been unfaithful to me (Jer. 3:20); they committed adultery with their idols (Ezek. 23:37); on a high and lofty mountain you made your bed (Isa. 57:7); the land is guilty of adultery in departing the Lord (Hos. 1:2); you have been unfaithful to your God (Hos. 9:1); Judah committed adultery with stones and trees (Jer. 3:9); all of them are adulterers (Jer. 9:2); you adulteresses! (Jas. 4:4); you adulterous wife! (Ezek. 16:32); an evil and adulterous generation (Matt. 12:39; 16:4); this adulterous and sinful generation (Mark 8:38).

C Bestiality
Cursed is he who lies with an animal (Deut. 27:21); whoever lies with an animal shall be put to death (Exod. 22:19); you shall not have intercourse with an animal (Lev. 18:23); if a man or woman has intercourse with an animal, both shall be killed (Lev. 20:15-16).

D Homosexuality
You shall not lie with a male as one lies with a female (Lev. 18:22); if a man lies with a man as one lies with a woman, both shall be put to death (Lev. 20:13); male prostitution is an abomination to the Lord (Deut. 23:18); women exchanged natural relations for unnatural (Rom. 1:26); men were consumed with passion for men, committing shameful acts (Rom. 1:27); neither the effeminate nor homosexuals will inherit the kingdom of God (1 Cor. 6:9); the law is for the immoral, homosexuals and whatever else is contrary to sound doctrine (1 Tim. 1:10); bring out the men that we may know them (Gen. 19:5; Judg. 19:22); Sodom and Gomorrah engaged in unnatural lust (Jude 7).

E Incest
Cursed be he who lies with his father's wife (Deut. 27:20); Lot's daughters lay with their father (Gen. 19:31-6); Reuben lay with his father's concubine (Gen. 35:22); Absalom went in to his father's concubines (2 Sam. 16:22); father and son use the same girl (Amos 2:7); sexual immorality of a kind unknown to pagans: a man has his father's wife (1 Cor. 5:1); cursed is the man who lies with his sister (Deut. 27:22); cursed is the man who lies with his mother-in-law (Deut. 27:23); sexual intercourse with a close relative is forbidden (Lev. 18:6-18; Ezek. 22:11).

F Prostitution
PROSTITUTES, see 952C.

F1 Going with prostitutes
They thronged to the houses of the prostitutes (Jer. 5:7); he who goes with harlots wastes his wealth (Prov. 29:3); because of a harlot a man is brought to a loaf of bread (Prov. 6:26); this son has devoured your wealth with harlots (Luke 15:30); Samson went in to a prostitute in Gaza (Judg. 16:1); they have forsaken the Lord to pay heed to harlotry (Hos. 4:10); they will play the harlot but not multiply (Hos. 4:10); your daughters play the harlot and your brides commit adultery (Hos. 4:13); they have given a boy for a harlot (Joel 3:3).

F2 Avoid prostitution
Do not make your daughter a prostitute (Lev. 19:29); prostitution is an abomination to the Lord (Deut. 23:18); if a priest's daughter becomes a prostitute, she must be burned (Lev. 21:9); a priest is not to marry a prostitute (Lev. 21:7, 14); the earnings of a male or female prostitute are not to be brought to the Lord's house (Deut. 23:18); should he treat our sister like a prostitute? (Gen. 34:31); shall I take the limbs of Christ

and make them limbs of a prostitute? (1 Cor. 6:15); let her put her harlotry from her face (Hos. 2:2).

F3 Prostitution to other gods
A spirit of harlotry (Hos. 4:12; 5:4); Oholah and Oholibah played the harlot (Ezek. 23:3-19); though you play the harlot, Israel, do not let Judah become guilty (Hos. 4:15); you have played the harlot, forsaking your God (Hos. 9:1); the faithful city has become a harlot (Isa. 1:21); under every green tree you lay as a harlot (Jer. 2:20); Israel was a harlot on every high hill and under every green tree (Jer. 3:6); Judah was a harlot also (Jer. 3:8); Ephraim, you have played the harlot (Hos. 5:3); they played the harlot, deserting their God (Hos. 4:12); you have played the harlot with the nations (Ezek. 23:30); the Babylonians defiled her with their harlotry (Ezek. 23:17); this people will play the harlot with the gods of the land (Deut. 31:16); when they prostituted themselves to their gods (Exod. 34:15-16); they prostituted themselves to other gods (Judg. 2:17; 1 Chr. 5:25); they prostituted themselves to the Baals (Judg. 8:33); playing the harlot after Molech (Lev. 20:5); they played the harlot after their idols (Ezek. 6:9); playing the harlot after mediums and spiritists (Lev. 20:6); they prostituted themselves by worshipping the ephod (Judg. 8:27); let them put away their harlotry (Ezek. 43:9).

G Rape
If a man rapes a girl pledged to be married (Deut. 22:25); a virgin not pledged to be married (Deut. 22:28-9); you will be betrothed to a woman and another will rape her (Deut. 28:30); Shechem raped Dinah (Gen. 34:2, 5); do to my virgin daughters as seems good to you (Gen. 19:8); rape my virgin daughter and his concubine (Judg. 19:24); Amnon raped Tamar (2 Sam. 13:12-14); they raped women in Zion (Lam. 5:11); the women of Jerusalem will be raped (Zech. 14:2); their wives will be raped (Isa. 13:16); will he even assault the queen? (Esther 7:8).

952 Libertine

A The adulteress / adulterer
Description of the adulteress (Prov. 5:3-23; 6:24-35); the mouth of an adulteress is a deep pit (Prov. 22:14); an adulteress hunts for a man's life (Prov. 6:26); an adulteress says she has done no wrong (Prov. 30:20); love a woman beloved of a paramour, an adulteress (Hos. 3:1); God will judge fornicators and adulterers (Heb. 13:4); the immoral will end in the lake of fire (Rev. 21:8); the land is full of adulterers (Jer. 23:10).
ADULTERY, see 951B.

B Concubines
I got many concubines – man's delight (Eccles. 2:8); David took more concubines (2 Sam. 5:13); David left ten concubines to keep the house (2 Sam. 15:16); Absalom went in to them (2 Sam. 16:21); David shut them up like widows (2 Sam. 20:3); Solomon had 300 concubines (1 Kgs. 11:3); Rehoboam had 60 concubines (2 Chr. 11:21); 80 concubines (S. of S. 6:8); the eunuch in charge of the king's concubines (Esther 2:14).

C Prostitutes
PROSTITUTION, see 951F.

C1 About prostitutes
Description of the prostitute (Prov. 7:6-27); in scorning payment, you were not like a harlot (Ezek. 16:31); a prostitute is a deep pit (Prov. 23:27); the earnings of a male or female prostitute are not to be brought into the Lord's house (Deut. 23:18); the song of the harlot (Isa. 23:15); harlots enter the kingdom of God before you (Matt. 21:31); shall I take the limbs of Christ and make them limbs of a prostitute? (1 Cor. 6:15).

C2 Specific prostitutes

Judah thought Tamar was a prostitute (Gen. 38:15); Rahab the prostitute (Josh. 2:1; Heb. 11:31; Jas. 2:25); Jephthah's mother was a prostitute (Judg. 11:1); two prostitutes came before Solomon (1 Kgs. 3:16); harlots bathed in the pool of Samaria (1 Kgs. 22:38); your wife will be a harlot in the city (Amos 7:17); their mother has played the harlot (Hos. 2:5); a woman of the city who was a sinner (Luke 7:37).

C3 Male prostitutes

The sons of Israel shall not be cult prostitutes (Deut. 23:17); they go aside with harlots and sacrifice with cult prostitutes (Hos. 4:14); there were male cult prostitutes in the land (1 Kgs. 14:24); Asa removed the male cult prostitutes (1 Kgs. 15:12); Jehoshaphat expelled the male cult prostitutes (1 Kgs. 22:46); Josiah tore down the quarters of the male cult prostitutes (2 Kgs. 23:7); the earnings of a male or female prostitute are not to be brought into the Lord's house (Deut. 23:18).

C4 Nations as prostitutes

Tyre will return to her hire as a prostitute (Isa. 23:17); you have lived as a prostitute with many lovers (Jer. 3:1); Babylon, the mother of prostitutes (Rev. 17:5); the great harlot (Rev. 17:1); O harlot, hear the word of the Lord (Ezek. 16:35); you multiplied your harlotry with Chaldea, the land of merchants (Ezek. 16:29); you played the harlot with the Assyrians (Ezek. 16:28); you played the harlot with the Egyptians, your lustful neighbours (Ezek. 16:26); the waters where the harlot sits are peoples (Rev. 17:15); he has judged the great harlot who corrupted the earth with her fornication (Rev. 19:2).

953 Law

IS IT LAWFUL (PROPER)? see 915C.

A The law in general

A1 The law given

A1a The law given through Moses

Moses wrote this law (Deut. 31:9); Moses wrote on the tablets the Ten Commandments (Exod. 34:28); this is the law Moses set before the Israelites (Deut. 4:44); the book of the law of Moses (Josh. 8:31); the law of Moses (1 Kgs. 2:3; 2 Chr. 30:16); God's law given through Moses (Neh. 10:29); the law was given through Moses (John 1:17); Moses gave you the law (John 7:19); Hilkiah found the book of the law of the Lord given by Moses (2 Chr. 34:14); Moses received living oracles to give to us (Acts 7:38).

A1b The law given by God

I gave them my statutes and ordinances (Ezek. 20:11); the Lord is our lawgiver (Isa. 33:22); there is one Lawgiver and Judge (Jas. 4:12); the Lord spoke the ten commandments (Exod. 20:2-17; Deut. 5:6-21); he declares his statutes and ordinances to Israel (Ps. 147:19).

A1c The law given to Israel

To Israel is the giving of the law (Rom. 9:4); the law will go out from Zion (Isa. 2:3; Mic. 4:2); on these two commandments depend all the law and the prophets (Matt. 22:40); you received the law as delivered by angels (Acts 7:53); the law 430 years later does not annul the covenant (Gal. 3:17); under the Levitical priesthood the people received the law (Heb. 7:11); it is a statute for Israel (Ps. 81:4); the laws of the Jews are different (Esther 3:8).

A2 Written in the law

It is written in the law of Moses (2 Kgs. 14:6; 2 Chr. 23:18; 25:4; Ezra 3:2; Dan. 9:13; 1 Cor. 9:9); as it is written in the law of the Lord (2 Chr. 31:3); as it is written in the law of the Lord (Luke 2:23, 24); everything written about me in the law of Moses and the prophets and the

psalms (Luke 24:44); we have found him of whom Moses wrote in the law, Jesus of Nazareth (John 1:45); in your law it is written, 'The testimony of two men is true' (John 8:17).

A3 Copying the law

Joshua copied on stones the law of Moses (Josh. 8:32); the king must write a copy of the law (Deut. 17:18).

A4 The law proclaimed

The law of the Lord is to be on your lips (Exod. 13:9); teach them the decrees and the laws (Deut. 18:20); do not let this Book of the Law depart out of your mouth (Josh. 1:8); the prophets and the law prophesied until John (Matt. 11:13); the law and the prophets were until John (Luke 16:16); Moses has in every city those who preach him (Acts 15:21); they want to be teachers of the law (1 Tim. 1:7).

A5 Excellent law

The law of the Lord is perfect (Ps. 19:7); what other nation has such righteous decrees? (Deut. 4:8); you gave them regulations and laws that are just and right (Neh. 9:13); to the law and to the testimony! (Isa. 8:20); having in the law the embodiment of knowledge and truth (Rom. 2:20); the law is spiritual (Rom. 7:14); the law is good (Rom. 7:16); the law is good if one uses it lawfully (1 Tim. 1:8); the law is holy and the commandment holy and righteous and good (Rom. 7:12).

A6 Purpose of the law

Why the law? It was added because of transgressions (Gal. 3:19); the law came in to increase the transgression (Rom. 5:20); the law has only a shadow of good things to come (Heb. 10:1); the law is not for the righteous but for lawbreakers (1 Tim. 1:9); the law was our schoolteacher to bring us to Christ (Gal. 3:24); the law speaks to those under the law that every mouth may be stopped (Rom. 3:19); through the law comes knowledge of sin (Rom. 3:20).

A7 Effect of the law

The law brings wrath (Rom. 4:15); anyone who violated the law of Moses died without mercy (Heb. 10:28); the letter kills (2 Cor. 3:6); Moses accuses you, on whom you set your hope (John 5:45); when the commandment came, sin revived and I died (Rom. 7:9); the commandment which should have brought life brought death instead (Rom. 7:10); sin took opportunity through the commandment (Rom. 7:11); the man who practices the righteousness based on the law will live by it (Rom. 10:5); the law is not of faith (Gal. 3:12); sinful passions were awakened by the law (Rom. 7:5); I would not have known coveting except through the law (Rom. 7:7); apart from the law sin is dead (Rom. 7:8); the power of sin is the law (1 Cor. 15:56); freed from all things from which you could not be freed by the law of Moses (Acts 13:39).

B Using the law

B1 Taking the law to heart

His delight is in the law of the Lord (Ps. 1:2); the law of his God is in his heart (Ps. 37:31); your law is within my heart (Ps. 40:8); a people in whose heart is my law (Isa. 51:7); they have Moses and the prophets, let them hear them (Luke 16:29); the Jewish believers were zealous for the law (Acts 21:20); I was brought up strictly under the law, zealous for God (Acts 22:3); believing everything in the law and written in the prophets (Acts 24:14); the work of the law is written on their hearts (Rom. 2:15); I agree with the law (Rom. 7:16); I agree with the law in my inner man (Rom. 7:22); as to the law, a Pharisee (Phil. 3:5).

PLEASURE IN GOD'S LAW, see 826B2.

B2 Studying the law
Ezra determined to study the law of the Lord (Ezra 7:10); Ezra read from the book of the law of Moses (Neh. 8:1-3); after the reading of the law and the prophets (Acts 13:15); Paul spoke about Jesus from the law of Moses and the prophets (Acts 28:23); if you are instructed in the law (Rom. 2:18).

B3 Fulfilling the law
God commanded you to follow these decrees and laws (Deut. 26:16); you know the commandments (Mark 10:19; Luke 18:20); if he walks in the statutes of live he will surely live (Ezek. 33:15); they came to do for him according to the custom of the law (Luke 2:27); as to righteousness under the law, blameless (Phil. 3:6); there are priests who offer gifts according to the law (Heb. 8:4); sacrifices are offered according to the law (Heb. 10:8); if you fulfil the royal law according to the scripture (Jas. 2:8); which commandment is first and foremost? (Mark 12:28); the law is fulfilled by loving your neighbour (Gal. 5:14); love is the fulfilment of the law (Rom. 13:10); I have not come to abolish the law and the prophets but to fulfil them (Matt. 5:17); we establish the law through faith (Rom. 3:31); that the requirement of the law might be fulfilled in us (Rom. 8:4); I will put my Spirit in you and cause you to walk in my statutes (Ezek. 36:27); he who loves has fulfilled the law (Rom. 13:8); I will put my laws in their minds and write them on their hearts (Jer. 31:33; Heb. 8:10); I will put my laws in their heart and write them on their mind (Heb. 10:16).

B4 Under the law
You who want to be under the law (Gal. 4:21); if you receive circumcision you are obliged to keep the whole law (Gal. 5:3); if you call yourself a Jew and rely on the law (Rom. 2:17); Jesus was born under the law (Gal. 4:4); the law has authority over a person only while he lives (Rom. 7:1); the law speaks to those under the law that every mouth may be stopped (Rom. 3:19); before faith came we were in custody under the law (Gal. 3:23); that he might redeem those under the law (Gal. 4:5); under the law, all things are cleansed with blood (Heb. 9:22); all who rely on works of the law are under a curse (Gal. 3:10); all who sin under the law will be judged by the law (Rom. 2:12); though not under the law, Paul became as under the law to win others (1 Cor. 9:20).

WORKS OF THE LAW, see 676B5.

THE CURSE OF THE LAW, see 899C.

B5 Without the law
Where there is no law there is no transgression (Rom. 4:15); sin is not reckoned where there is no law (Rom. 5:13); when the Gentiles who have not the law do what the law requires (Rom. 2:14); all who have sinned without law will perish without law (Rom. 2:12); the righteousness of God apart from the law has been manifested (Rom. 3:21); justified by faith apart from works of the law (Rom. 3:28); if her husband dies, the woman is free from the law of marriage (Rom. 7:2); you are not under the law but under grace (Rom. 6:14); if you are led by the Spirit you are not under the law (Gal. 5:18); we have been released from the law (Rom. 7:6); you have died to the law through the body of Christ (Rom. 7:4); Christ is the end of the law (Rom. 10:4); there is no law against the fruit of the Spirit (Gal. 5:23); shall we sin because we are not under law but under grace? (Rom. 6:15); Paul became as without law to win others (1 Cor. 9:21).

B6 Blessing not through the law
No one will be justified by works of the law (Rom. 3:20; Gal. 2:16); if righteousness was through the law, Christ died in vain (Gal. 2:21); if a law could bring life,

righteousness would be by the law (Gal. 3:21); I gave them bad statutes by which they could not live (Ezek. 20:25); the law made nothing perfect (Heb. 7:19); it was not through the law that Abraham received the promise (Rom. 4:13); did you receive the Spirit by works of law? (Gal. 3:2); does God work miracles among you because you keep the law? (Gal. 3:5); God did what the law, weakened by the flesh, could not do (Rom. 8:3); no one is justified before God by the law (Gal. 3:11); if the inheritance is by law it is no longer by promise (Gal. 3:18); you who would be justified by the law are severed from Christ (Gal. 5:4); not having a righteousness of my own based on law (Phil. 3:9); a change in the priesthood requires a change in the law (Heb. 7:12).

B7 Rejecting the law
They have rejected the law of the Lord (Isa. 5:24); you have neglected the weightier matters of the law (Matt. 23:23); since you forget the law of God I will forget your children (Hos. 4:6); do not think that I came to abolish the law and the prophets (Matt. 5:17); this man never ceases to speak against this holy place and the law (Acts 6:13); they hear you teach Jews to forsake Moses (Acts 21:21); the former commandment is set aside (Heb. 7:18); he who speaks against his brother speaks against the law and judges the law (Jas. 4:11); Jesus abolished the enmity, the law (Eph. 2:15).

LAWLESSNESS, see 954A.

C The law of Christ
I am under the law of Christ (1 Cor. 9:21); fulfil the law of Christ (Gal. 6:2); the law of liberty (Jas. 2:12); the perfect law, the law of liberty (Jas. 1:25).

D Human law
Woe to those who enact unjust decrees (Isa. 10:1); Joseph made it a statute that Pharaoh should have a fifth (Gen. 47:26); the law of the Persians and Medes (Esther 1:19); the law of the Medes and Persians cannot be revoked (Dan. 6:8, 12, 15); why do you still submit to regulations? (Col. 2:20).

E Commandments
Which is the great commandment in the law? (Matt. 22:36-8); which commandment is first and foremost? (Mark 12:28); whoever annuls the least commandment (Matt. 5:19); you know the commandments (Mark 10:19; Luke 18:20); his commandments are not burdensome (1 John 5:3); this is his commandment, that we believe on Jesus Christ and love one another (1 John 3:23); a new commandment (John 13:34; 1 John 2:8).

954 Illegality

A Lawlessness
Sin is lawlessness (1 John 3:4); they have rejected my law (Jer. 6:19); if a man turns away from the law, even his prayer is an abomination (Prov. 28:9); lawlessness will increase (Matt. 24:12); inwardly you are full of lawlessness (Matt. 23:28); the man of lawlessness will be revealed (2 Thess. 2:3); the mystery of lawlessness (2 Thess. 2:7); the lawless one will be revealed (2 Thess. 2:8-9); they will gather out of his kingdom all who commit lawlessness (Matt. 13:41); they have rejected the law of the Lord (Amos 2:4); her priests do violence to the law (Zeph. 3:4); this man teaches against our people and the law and this place (Acts 21:28); you once yielded your limbs to impurity leading to lawlessness (Rom. 6:19); if I build again what I once destroyed I prove myself to be a law-breaker (Gal. 2:18); you have loved righteousness and hated lawlessness (Heb. 1:9); Lot's soul was tormented by their lawless deeds (2 Pet. 2:8); do not be carried away by the error of lawless men

(2 Pet. 3:17); he was reckoned with the lawless (Isa. 53:12; Luke 22:37).

WITHOUT LAW, see 953B5.

B Breaking God's law

They disobeyed the law (Isa. 24:5; Jer. 9:13; Acts 7:53); we have not kept your law (Neh. 1:7; 9:34); the law is ignored (Hab. 1:4); they cast your law behind their backs (Neh. 9:26); it is time for the Lord to act for they have broken your law (Ps. 119:126); my eyes stream with tears because they do not keep your law (Ps. 119:136); why do you transgress God's commandment for the sake of your tradition? (Matt. 15:3); whoever does not keep the law is to be executed (Ezra 7:26); if his children forsake my law (Ps. 89:30-1); whoever breaks one part of the law is guilty of all (Jas. 2:10-11); the lying pen of the scribes has made the law a lie (Jer. 8:8); they rebelled against my law (Hos. 8:1); contrary to the law you order me to be struck (Acts 23:3); if you show partiality you are convicted by the law as transgressors (Jas. 2:9); if you do not commit adultery but do kill you have become a transgressor of the law (Jas. 2:11); the priests profane the sabbath and are innocent (Matt. 12:5); this man persuades people to worship God contrary to the law (Acts 18:13); some ate the Passover other than prescribed (2 Chr. 30:18).

C Breaking man's law

Why do your disciples transgress the tradition of the elders? (Matt. 15:2); they proclaim customs which it is not lawful for Romans to accept (Acts 16:21); you know how unlawful it is for a Jew to associate with a foreigner (Acts 10:28); is it lawful for you to scourge a Roman and uncondemned? (Acts 22:25); they do not observe the king's laws (Esther 3:8).

D Illegitimate children

If you are without discipline, you are illegitimate children (Heb. 12:8); the illegitimate may not enter the assembly (Deut. 23:2); we were not born of fornication (John 8:41).

955 Jurisdiction

AUTHORITY, see 733.

956 Tribunal

A Court sessions

Why are not times of judgement kept by the Almighty? (Job 24:1); the court sat and the books were opened (Dan. 7:10); make friends with your opponent while you are going to court (Matt. 5:25); the courts are in session (Acts 19:38); I am standing before Caesar's tribunal where I ought to be tried (Acts 25:10); whether he was willing to go to Jerusalem to be tried (Acts 25:20).

B Judgement seat

Pilate was on the judgement seat (Matt. 27:19; John 19:13); they brought Paul before the judgement seat of Gallio (Acts 18:12-17); we must all stand before the judgement seat of God (Rom. 14:10); of Christ (2 Cor. 5:10).

957 Magistrate

JUDGING, see 480.

A God the Judge

Shall not the Judge of all the earth do right? (Gen. 18:25); rise up, Judge of the earth! (Ps. 94:2); God is a righteous judge (Ps. 7:11); you have come to God, the judge of all men (Heb. 12:23); the Lord is our Judge (Isa. 33:22); there is one Lawgiver and Judge (Jas. 4:12); the Judge is standing at the door (Jas. 5:9).

B Christ the judge

Jesus is the one God has appointed as judge of the living and the dead (Acts 10:42); who made me a judge over you? (Luke 12:14).

C Human judges

C1 Judges in general

Have them serve as judges (Exod. 18:22); appoint judges and officials (Deut. 16:18); Jehoshaphat appointed judges (2 Chr. 19:5-7, 8-11); with a rod they strike the judge of Israel on the cheek (Mic. 5:1); her judges are wolves at evening that leave nothing for the morning (Zeph. 3:3); your sons will be your judges (Matt. 12:27; Luke 11:19); do you make those least esteemed in the church your judges? (1 Cor. 6:4); have you not made distinctions and become judges with evil thoughts? (Jas. 2:4); let all judges praise the Lord (Ps. 148:11); if only I were made judge! (2 Sam. 15:4).

C2 Judges judged

God makes fools of judges (Job 12:17); be warned, judges of the earth (Ps. 2:10); the parable of the unjust judge (Luke 18:2); I will cut off the judge from her midst (Amos 2:3); the Lord will take away the judge and the prophet (Isa. 3:2).

C3 Judges in Israel

Moses took his seat to serve as judge (Exod. 18:13); who made you ruler and judge? (Exod. 2:14; Acts 7:27, 35); the Lord raised up judges (Judg. 2:16); the judges: Othniel (Judg. 3:9-11); Ehud (Judg. 3:15-30); Shamgar (Judg. 3:31; 5:6); Deborah (Judg. 4:4-24); Gideon (Judg. 6:32); Abimelech (Judg. 9:1-57); Tola (Judg. 10:1-2); Jair (Judg. 10:3-5); Jephthah (Judg. 11:7); Ibzan (Judg. 12:8-10); Elon (Judg. 12:11-12); Abdon (Judg. 12:13-15); Samson (Judg. 15:20; 16:31); Eli (1 Sam. 4:18); Samuel (1 Sam. 7:6, 15-17); Samuel's sons (1 Sam. 8:1).

C4 Other human judges

Lot wants to be the judge! (Gen. 19:9); they brought them to the magistrates (Acts 16:20); the magistrates sent to release them (Acts 16:35-6); for many years you have been judge over this nation (Acts 24:10).

958 Lawyer

A lawyer asked him a question to test him (Matt. 22:35); a lawyer tested him (Luke 10:25); the Pharisees and lawyers rejected God's purpose for them (Luke 7:30); Jesus spoke to the lawyers and Pharisees (Luke 14:3); a lawyer said he insulted them also (Luke 11:45); woe to you, lawyers! (Luke 11:46, 52); help Zenas the lawyer (Titus 3:13).

959 Litigation

ACCUSATION, see 928.

CONDEMNATION, see 961.

A God suing

God will bring to judgement both the righteous and the wicked (Eccles. 3:17); for all these things God will bring you to judgement (Eccles. 11:9); the wicked will not stand in the judgement (Ps. 1:5); the Lord will plead the case of the poor (Prov. 22:23; 23:11); the Lord who pleads the cause of his people (Isa. 51:22); whoever is angry with his brother will be subject to judgement (Matt. 5:22); that you might succeed when you enter into judgement (Rom. 3:4); the court will sit in judgement (Dan. 7:26); do not bring your servant into judgement (Ps. 143:2).

B Suing God

I would argue my case with God (Job 13:3); I would present my cause before God (Job 5:8); woe to him who quarrels with his maker (Isa. 45:9); in a dispute with God one could not answer him (Job 9:3); we cannot go to court together (Job 9:32).

C Human lawsuits

When men have a dispute, they are to take it to court (Deut. 25:1); the first to plead his case seems right (Prov. 18:17); any one with a dispute went to the king for judgement (2 Sam. 15:2); if anyone wants to sue you and take your tunic, let him have your cloak as well (Matt. 5:40); is it not the rich who drag you into court? (Jas. 2:6); anyone who commits murder will be brought to court (Matt. 5:21); anyone who is angry with his brother will be brought to court (Matt. 5:22); make friends with your accuser before it comes to court (Matt. 5:25; Luke 12:58); if we are on trial concerning the means whereby a cripple was healed (Acts 4:9); are you sitting to judge me according to the law? (Acts 23:3); for the resurrection of the dead I am on trial (Acts 24:21); are you willing to go to Jerusalem to be tried on these charges? (Acts 25:9); does anyone dare to go to law against a brother before the unrighteous? (1 Cor. 6:1); brother goes to law with brother, and that before unbelievers (1 Cor. 6:6).

960 Acquittal

NOT PUNISH, see 919B.

VINDICATION, see 927.

A Acquitting the just

Justify the righteous (1 Kgs. 8:32; 2 Chr. 6:23); I would be acquitted for ever by my Judge (Job 23:7); by your words you will be justified or condemned (Matt. 12:37).

B Acquitting the guilty

I will not acquit the guilty (Exod. 23:7); he who justifies the wicked is an abomination to the Lord (Prov. 17:15); he who tells the wicked they are innocent will be cursed (Prov. 24:24); woe to those who acquit the guilty for a bribe (Isa. 5:23); can I acquit the man with wicked scales and a bag of deceitful weights? (Mic. 6:11).

961 Condemnation

HANDS LAID ON TO CONDEMN, see 378B6.

A Condemning the wicked

A1 Condemnation of the wicked in general

May they not be acquitted (Ps. 69:27); when he is tried, let him be found guilty (Ps. 109:7); God condemns the one who devises evil (Prov. 12:2); he who eats and drinks brings judgement on himself (1 Cor. 11:29); I will judge you out of your own mouth (Luke 19:22); the judgement of God rightly falls on those who do such things (Rom. 2:2); do you hope to escape the judgement of God? (Rom. 2:3); Noah by faith condemned the world (Heb. 11:7); the ministry of condemnation (2 Cor. 3:9); judgement following one trespass brought condemnation (Rom. 5:16); the result of one trespass was condemnation for all (Rom. 5:18); God, sending his Son, condemned sin in the flesh (Rom. 8:3).

A2 Final condemnation of the wicked

The men of Nineveh will condemn this generation (Matt. 12:41; Luke 11:32); the queen of the South will condemn this generation (Matt. 12:42; Luke 11:31); whoever does not believe will be condemned (Mark 16:16); whoever does not believe is condemned already (John 3:18); all will be condemned who did not believe the truth but took pleasure in wickedness (2 Thess. 2:12); they will receive greater condemnation (Mark 12:40; Luke 20:47).

B Condemning the innocent

They condemn the innocent to death (Ps. 94:21); he who condemns the innocent is an abomination to the Lord (Prov. 17:15); you would not have condemned the innocent (Matt. 12:7); you have condemned and put to death the righteous man (Jas. 5:6).

C Condemning Jesus

They will condemn the Son of Man to death (Matt. 20:18; Mark 10:33); they all condemned him as worthy of death (Mark 14:64); when Judas saw Jesus was condemned (Matt. 27:3); they fulfilled the prophets by condemning him (Acts 13:27).

D Condemning ourselves

Though I am innocent, my own mouth will condemn me (Job 9:20); in judging another, you condemn yourself (Rom. 2:1); blessed is he who does not condemn himself in what he approves (Rom. 14:22); if our hearts condemn us, God is greater than our hearts (1 John 3:20); such a man is self-condemned (Titus 3:11).

E Being condemned

By your words you will be justified or condemned (Matt. 12:37); you are under the same condemnation (Luke 23:40); requesting that he be condemned (Acts 25:15); those who resist authorities will incur condemnation (Rom. 13:2); in Antioch Peter stood condemned (Gal. 2:11); lest he fall into the condemnation of the devil (1 Tim. 3:6); younger widows incur condemnation, forsaking their pledge (1 Tim. 5:12); their condemnation has long been hanging over them (2 Pet. 2:3); their condemnation is just (Rom. 3:8); people long ago marked out for condemnation (Jude 4); the prince of this world stands condemned (John 16:11).

F No condemnation

The Lord helps me, who is to condemn me? (Isa. 50:9); it is God who justifies, who is he that condemns? (Rom. 8:33-4); no one who takes refuges in him will be condemned (Ps. 34:22); there is no condemnation for those who are in Christ (Rom. 8:1); the Lord will not let them be condemned (Ps. 37:33); that we might not be condemned along with the world (1 Cor. 11:32); do not swear, that you may not be condemned (Jas. 5:12); if our hearts do not condemn us, we have confidence before God (1 John 3:21); do not condemn and you will not be condemned (Luke 6:37); does our law judge a man without first hearing him? (John 7:51); has no one condemned you? (John 8:10); neither do I condemn you (John 8:11); God did not send his Son to condemn the world (John 3:17).

962 Reward

A Reward from God

I am your shield, your reward will be very great (Gen. 15:1); the Lord has rewarded me for my righteousness (2 Sam. 22:21; Ps. 18:20); my reward is with my God (Isa. 49:4); his reward is with him (Isa. 40:10; 62:11); children are a reward from the Lord (Ps. 127:3); man's reward is to eat, drink and enjoy himself (Eccles. 5:18); the time has come for rewarding your slaves the prophets (Rev. 11:18); pray in secret and your Father will reward you (Matt. 6:6); he must believe God rewards those who seek him (Heb. 11:6).

B Reward for works

God will reward everyone according to what he has done (Ps. 62:12; Rom. 2:6); each will receive a reward according to his work (1 Cor. 3:8); my reward is with me and I will give to everyone according to what he has done (Rev. 22:12); if what he has built survives, he will receive his reward (1 Cor. 3:14); work as to the Lord and you will receive the inheritance as a reward (Col. 3:24); if I do this willingly, I have a reward (1 Cor. 9:17); God has rewarded me for giving my maidservant to my husband (Gen. 30:18); he who receives a righteous man as a righteous man will receive a righteous man's reward (Matt. 10:41); he who gives a cup of cold water will not lose his reward (Matt. 10:42; Mark 9:41);

whoever receives a prophet as a prophet will receive a prophet's reward (Matt. 10:41); do good and your reward will be great (Luke 6:35); run in such a way as to get the prize (1 Cor. 9:24).

C Men rewarding

Come home with me and I will reward you (1 Kgs. 13:7); if you show the dream you will receive gifts, a reward and great honour (Dan. 2:6).

D No reward

You will have no reward from your Father in heaven (Matt. 6:1); if you love those who love you, what reward will you have? (Matt. 5:46); the Lord has kept you from being rewarded (Num. 24:11); keep your gifts for yourself and give your rewards to another (Dan. 5:17).

963 Punishment

A Punishment in general

Why should a living man complain about the punishment of his sins? (Lam. 3:39); at the time of Israel's final punishment (Ezek. 35:5); Ephraim will become a desolation on the day of punishment (Hos. 5:9); the days of punishment have come (Hos. 9:7); I went to Damascus to bring them to Jerusalem to be punished (Acts 22:5); this punishment by the majority is sufficient (2 Cor. 2:6); as punished and yet not put to death (2 Cor. 6:9); ready to punish all disobedience when your obedience is complete (2 Cor. 10:6); fear has to do with punishment (1 John 4:18); they found no way to punish them (Acts 4:21).

B God punishing

B1 God will punish evildoers

Shall I not punish them for these things? (Jer. 9:9); I will punish them for their sin (Exod. 32:34); I will punish the world for its evil (Isa. 13:11); he does not leave the guilty unpunished (Exod. 34:7); the income of the wicked is punishment (Prov. 10:16); the Lord knows how to keep the unrighteous under punishment (2 Pet. 2:9); the Lord will punish the powers in heaven and the kings on earth (Isa. 24:21); the Lord is coming to punish the people of the earth for their sins (Isa. 26:21); they receive the penalty of their perversion (Rom. 1:27); awake to punish all the nations (Ps. 59:5); I will punish them for their ways and repay them for their deeds (Hos. 4:9); he will remember their iniquity and punish their sins (Hos. 8:13; 9:9); you have appointed [the Chaldeans] as a judgement and a chastisement (Hab. 1:12).

B2 God punishing specific evildoers

God punished Israel (1 Chr. 21:7); the punishment of your iniquity is completed, daughter of Zion (Lam. 4:22); the Lord will punish Jacob according to his deeds (Hos. 12:2); you only have I chosen, therefore I will punish you for all your sins (Amos 3:2); I will punish the Amalekites (1 Sam. 15:2); the Lord will punish Leviathan (Isa. 27:1); the Lord will punish Assyria (Isa. 10:12); I will punish the king of Babylon (Jer. 25:12); this will be the punishment of Egypt (Zech. 14:19); he will punish your iniquity, daughter of Edom (Lam. 4:22); I will visit punishment on the he-goats [leaders] (Zech. 10:3); my punishment is more than I can bear (Gen. 4:13).

B3 God not punishing

The rod of God does not fall on the wicked (Job 21:9); because sentence is delayed, men are devoted to evil (Eccles. 8:11).

C Scale of punishment

He who knew his master's will will receive a severe beating (Luke 12:47); one who did not know will receive a light beating (Luke 12:48); I will not make an end of you but will not leave you unpunished (Jer.

46:28); how much more severe punishment for him who tramples the Son of God (Heb. 10:29); God exacts less than your guilt deserves (Job 11:6); he has not dealt with us according to our sins (Ps. 103:10).

LESS PUNISHMENT, see 736B.

D Judicial punishment

God sends governors to punish evildoers (1 Pet. 2:14); rulers do not bear the sword for nothing (Rom. 13:4); in anger his lord handed him over to the torturers (Matt. 18:34); I will punish him and release him (Luke 23:16, 22); the elders shall take the man and punish him (Deut. 22:18); anyone under a ban must be put to death (Lev. 27:29); life for life, eye for eye, tooth for tooth (Exod. 21:23-5; Lev. 24:19-20; Deut. 19:21; Matt. 5:38).

CORPORAL PUNISHMENT, see 279A1a.

E Fines

A man causing miscarriage shall be fined (Exod. 21:22); the king of Egypt fined them 100 talents of silver and one talent of gold (2 Chr. 36:3); you will not go out until you have paid the last penny (Matt. 5:26).

FINE AS PENALTY, see 809E.

F Death penalty

DEATH AS PUNISHMENT, see 361C2.

F1 Death penalty for killing

Whoever sheds man's blood, by man shall his blood be shed (Gen. 9:6); he who kills a man shall be put to death (Exod. 21:12; Lev. 24:17; Num. 35:30); the murderer shall be put to death by the avenger of blood (Num. 35:16-19); take him even from my altar to die (Exod. 21:14); whoever kills Cain will meet sevenfold vengeance (Gen. 4:15); death penalty if anyone harmed Isaac or his wife (Gen. 26:11); it is not lawful for us to put anyone to death (John 18:31).

F2 Death penalty for violence

The death penalty for cursing one's parents (Exod. 21:17; Lev. 20:9; Mark 7:10); he who speaks evil of parents must be put to death (Matt. 15:4); death penalty for: striking one's parents (Exod. 21:15); a rebellious son (Deut. 21:18-21); one who shows contempt for judge or priest (Deut. 17:12); kidnapping (Exod. 21:16; Deut. 24:7); sinning defiantly (Num. 15:30).

F3 Death penalty for profanity

The Lord will not allow a man who takes his name in vain to go unpunished (Exod. 20:7; Deut. 5:11); do not allow a sorceress to live (Exod. 22:18); the death penalty for: desecrating the sabbath (Exod. 31:14; Num. 15:35-6); not being circumcised (Gen. 17:14); not observing the Day of Atonement (Lev. 23:29-30); not observing the Passover (Num. 9:13); not purifying oneself after touching a dead body (Lev. 19:13, 20); eating offerings whilst unclean (Lev. 7:20-1; 22:3); eating the fat of an animal suitable for sacrifice (Lev. 7:25); eating blood (Lev. 7:27; 17:10); eating a peace offering on the third day (Lev. 19:8); using holy anointing oil (Exod. 30:33); making sacred incense illegally (Exod. 30:38); making a sacrifice other than at the Tent of Meeting (Lev. 17:4); coming near the sanctuary illegally (Num. 18:7); cursing the Lord's anointed (2 Sam. 19:21).

F4 Death penalty for heresy

They will condemn the Son of man to death (Matt. 20:18); he deserves death (Matt. 26:66); they all condemned him as worthy of death (Mark 14:64); the death penalty for: blaspheming God's name (Lev. 24:16); urging people to worship other gods (Deut. 13:1-15); worshipping other gods (Exod. 22:20); serving other gods (Deut. 17:2-7); giving one's children to Molech (Lev. 20:2); turning to mediums and spirits (Lev. 20:6); being a medium or spiritist (Lev. 20:27); a false prophet or a dreamer of dreams (Deut. 13:5); a prophet speaking false words (Deut. 18:20); not seeking the Lord (2 Chr. 15:13).

F5 Death penalty for sexual sin
The death penalty for adultery (Gen. 38:24; Lev. 20:10; Deut. 22:22; John 8:5); the death penalty for homosexual acts (Lev. 20:13); the death penalty for not being a virgin on marriage (Deut. 22:21); whoever lies with an animal shall be put to death (Exod. 22:19); the death penalty for sexual relations with: a betrothed woman (Deut. 22:23-4); a near relative (Lev. 20:11); an animal (Lev. 20:15-16); a menstruating woman (Lev. 20:18).

G Final punishment
The eternal fire (Matt. 18:8); the punishment of eternal fire (Jude 7); eternal destruction (2 Thess. 1:9); how will you escape being condemned to hell? (Matt. 23:33); the smoke of their torment goes up for ever (Rev. 14:11); its smoke will go up for ever (Isa. 34:10); eternal chains in the lower darkness (Jude 6); eternal judgement (Heb. 6:2); their worm will not die, nor will their fire be quenched (Isa. 66:24; Mark 9:48); the eternal fire prepared for the devil and his angels (Matt. 25:41); the devil was thrown into the lake of fire and sulphur (Rev. 20:10); shared by: the rebellious (Jude 13); those led into sin (Matt. 18:8); the uncaring (Matt. 25:46); those who do not obey the gospel (2 Thess. 1:9); those who blaspheme the Holy Spirit (Mark 3:29); the cowardly, faithless, polluted, murderers, fornicators, sorcerers, idolators and liars (Rev. 21:8).

964 Means of punishment

A The rod / whip
A rod is for the back of fools (Prov. 26:3); he who spares the rod hates his son (Prov. 13:24); shall I come to you with a rod? (1 Cor. 4:21); you have despised the rod with everything of wood (Ezek. 21:10); Assyria, the rod of my anger (Isa. 10:5); God will strike Assyria with the rod (Isa. 30:31-2); he made a whip of cords (John 2:15).

BEATING, see 279.

B Gallows
The two officials were hanged on a gallows (Esther 2:23); a gallows 50 cubits high (Esther 5:14; 7:9).

C Crucifixion
C1 Christ crucified
C1a Christ's crucifixion foretold
The Son of man will be handed over to be crucified (Matt. 26:2); he will be mocked and scourged and crucified (Matt. 20:19); that he must be crucified and on the third day rise (Luke 24:7); even so must the Son of man be lifted up (John 3:14); when you have lifted up the Son of man (John 8:28); when I am lifted up from the earth (John 12:32).

C1b Crucifixion of Christ
They were insistent, with loud voices demanding that he be crucified (Luke 23:23); let him be crucified! (Matt. 27:22-3); crucify him! (Mark 15:13-14; Luke 23:21; John 19:6); Pilate delivered Jesus to them to be crucified (Matt. 27:26; Mark 15:15); Jesus carrying his own cross (John 19:17); carrying Jesus' cross (Matt. 27:32; Mark 15:21; Luke 23:26); they crucified him (Matt. 27:35; Mark 15:24; Luke 24:20; John 19:18); he endured the cross (Heb. 12:2); you nailed him to a cross by the hands of lawless men (Acts 2:23); this Jesus whom you crucified (Acts 2:36); you put him to death by hanging him on a gibbet (Acts 5:30); they put him to death by hanging him on a tree (Acts 10:39).

C1c Significance of Christ's crucifixion
Lest the cross of Christ be nullified (1 Cor. 1:17); we preach Christ crucified (1 Cor. 1:23); he was crucified in weakness (2 Cor. 13:4); Jesus Christ was placarded as

crucified (Gal. 3:1); he became obedient to death, even death on a cross (Phil. 2:8); having made peace through the blood of his cross (Col. 1:20); our bill of debt was nailed to the cross (Col. 2:14); he bore our sins in his own body on the tree (1 Pet. 2:24); reconciled to God through the cross (Eph. 2:16); no boasting except in the cross (Gal. 6:14); the world has been crucified to me and I to the world (Gal. 6:14); I decided to know nothing except Jesus Christ and him crucified (1 Cor. 2:2); the message of the cross is foolishness to those who are perishing (1 Cor. 1:18); the stumbling block of the cross (Gal. 5:11); that they may not be persecuted for the cross of Christ (Gal. 6:12); enemies of the cross of Christ (Phil. 3:18).

C2 Others crucified
Some prophets you will kill and crucify (Matt. 23:34); two thieves were crucified with him (Matt. 27:38; Mark 15:27; Luke 23:33; John 19:18).

C3 Our crucifixion
He who does not take up his cross and follow me is not worthy of me (Matt. 10:38); whoever would come after me must take up his cross (Matt. 16:24); take up the cross (Mark 8:34; Luke 9:23); our old self was crucified with him (Rom. 6:6); I have been crucified with Christ (Gal. 2:20).

965 God

A God in general
A1 About God
A1a Nature of God
God is spirit (John 4:24); God is light (1 John 1:5); God is love (1 John 4:8, 16); the Lord is peace (Judg. 6:24); your heavenly Father is perfect (Matt. 5:48); his deity is seen in what is made (Rom. 1:20); before the world was formed, from everlasting to everlasting you are God (Ps. 90:2); the God in whose hand is your breath (Dan. 5:23); the Lord of all the earth (Josh. 3:11, 13); Lord of heaven and earth (Matt. 11:25); the Holy One (1 John 2:20); the Lord is the true God (Jer. 10:10); this is the true God and eternal life (1 John 5:20).

GOD AS FIRE, see 381B1.

GOD IS LIGHT, see 417B1.

A1b God as trinity
Baptised in the name of the Father, Son and Holy Spirit (Matt. 28:19); the grace of the Lord Jesus Christ, the love of God, the fellowship of the Spirit (2 Cor. 13:14); same Spirit . . . same Lord . . . same God (1 Cor. 12:4-6); one Spirit . . . one Lord . . . one God and Father (Eph. 4:4-6); foreknowledge of the Father, sanctification of the Spirit, to obey Jesus Christ (1 Pet. 1:2).

THE TRINITY, see 93A.

A1c The Lord [Yahweh] is God
The Lord is God (Deut. 4:35; Josh. 22:34; 1 Kgs. 18:39; Ps. 118:27); I am who I am (Exod. 3:14); know that the Lord is God (Ps. 100:3); the mighty One, God the Lord (Ps. 50:1); the Lord is God in heaven and earth (Deut. 4:39; Josh. 2:11); I am the Lord, the God of all flesh (Jer. 32:27); the Lord is the true God (Jer. 10:10); if the Lord is God, serve him (1 Kgs. 18:21); who is God besides the Lord? (2 Sam. 22:32; Ps. 18:31); Lord, you alone are God (2 Kgs. 19:15; Isa. 37:16, 20).

GOD IS UNIQUE, see 21A.

A1d God in relation to man
He is not a man like me (Job 9:32); God is greater than man (Job 33:12); do you see as man sees? (Job 10:4); are your years man's? (Job 10:5); I am God and not man (Hos. 11:9); God is not a man that he should lie or repent (Num. 23:19); we must obey God rather than men (Acts 5:29); give to God the things which are

God's (Matt. 22:21); he is not the God of the dead but of the living (Matt. 22:32; Mark 12:27; Luke 20:38).

A2 God Almighty
I am God Almighty (Gen. 17:1; 35:11); God Almighty appeared to me (Gen. 48:3); I appeared to Abraham, Isaac and Jacob as God Almighty (Exod. 6:2); wonderful Counsellor, mighty God, everlasting Father, Prince of peace (Isa. 9:6); the Lord is the great King above all gods (Ps. 95:3); your God is the God of gods and Lord of kings (Dan. 2:47); God of gods and Lord of lords (Deut. 10:17).

GOD IS GREAT, see 34A.

A3 God of his people
A3a Their God
I will be their God (Gen. 17:8; Exod. 29:45; Lev. 26:45; Ezek. 14:11; Zech. 8:8; 2 Cor. 6:16; Heb. 8:10); they will be my people and I will be their God (Jer. 32:38; Ezek. 11:20; 37:23); I will be his God (Rev. 21:7); I will be the God of all the families of Israel (Jer. 31:1); I am the Lord your God (Exod. 20:2; Isa. 41:13; Ezek. 20:5); I brought you out of Egypt to be your God (Lev. 11:45; Num. 15:41); I have been the Lord your God since the land of Egypt (Hos. 12:9); I am ascending to my Father and your Father, to my God and your God (John 20:17); this God is our God (Ps. 48:14); this is our God (Isa. 25:9); say to the cities of Judah, 'Behold, your God!' (Isa. 40:9); blessed is the people whose God is the Lord (Ps. 33:12; 144:15); God is not ashamed to be called their God (Heb. 11:16); if he will look after me, the Lord will be my God (Gen. 28:21).

A3b God of particular people
The God of our Lord Jesus Christ, the Father of glory (Eph. 1:17); the God of Shem (Gen. 9:26); I am the God of Abraham (Gen. 26:24); the God of your father [Isaac] (Gen. 31:29); the God of Abraham and Isaac (Gen. 28:13; 32:9); God of Abraham, Isaac and Jacob (Exod. 3:6; Matt. 22:32; Mark 12:26; Luke 20:37; Acts 3:13; 7:32); the God of your fathers (Gen. 43:23; Exod. 3:13); the God of our fathers (Acts 5:30; 22:14); the Lord, the God of the Hebrews (Exod. 3:18); the God of this people Israel (Acts 13:17); the God of both Jews and Gentiles (Rom. 3:29); the God of the spirits of all flesh (Num. 16:22; 27:16).

A3c Man of God
Moses the man of God (Deut. 33:1; 2 Chr. 30:16; Ps. 90:1); David the man of God (Neh. 12:36); Shemaiah the man of God (1 Kgs. 12:22; 2 Chr. 11:2); Elisha the man of God (2 Kgs. 4:21); a man of God came to Eli (1 Sam. 2:27); a man of God in this city (1 Sam. 9:6); a man of God came from Judah to Bethel (1 Kgs. 13:2; 2 Kgs. 23:16-17); a man of God came to Amaziah (2 Chr. 25:7); O man of God! (1 Kgs. 17:18; 2 Kgs. 1:9); if I am a man of God (2 Kgs. 1:10); this is a holy man of God (2 Kgs. 4:9); a man of God spoke to the king of Israel (1 Kgs. 20:28); Hanan son of Igdaliah the man of God (Jer. 35:4).

A4 Names involving God
Jehovah-jireh – the Lord will provide (Gen. 22:14); Jehovah-rophekhah – the Lord your healer (Exod. 15:26); Jehovah-nissi – the Lord my banner (Exod. 17:15); Jehovah-shalom – the Lord is peace (Judg. 6:24); Jehovah-tsidhkenu – the Lord our righteousness (Jer. 23:6; 33:16); Jehovah-shammah – the Lord is there (Ezek. 48:35).

B God the Father
GOD OUR FATHER, see 169D1.

B1 The Father
There is but one God, the Father, and one Lord, Jesus Christ (1 Cor. 8:6); God the Father (John 6:27; Gal. 1:1); the Father from which every family is named (Eph. 3:14-15); the Father (Matt. 11:27; John 4:21; Acts 1:4;

Rom. 6:4; Eph. 2:18; Col. 1:12; Jas. 3:9; 1 Pet. 1:17; 1 John 1:2; 2 John 4); the heavenly Father (Luke 11:13); the Father of glory (Eph. 1:17); the Father of spirits (Heb. 12:9); the Father of lights (Jas. 1:17).

B2 Our Father in heaven
Have we not all one Father? (Mal. 2:10); one God and Father of all (Eph. 4:6); God our Father (Rom. 1:7; 1 Cor. 1:3; 2 Cor. 1:2; Gal. 1:4; Eph. 1:2; Phil. 1:2; Col. 1:2; 1 Thess. 1:3; 2 Thess. 1:1; Philem. 3); our Father in heaven (Matt. 6:9); your Father (Matt. 5:16; Luke 6:36); your heavenly Father (Matt. 6:14); your Father in heaven (Matt. 7:11; Mark 11:25); I will be a Father to you (2 Cor. 6:18); we cry, Abba, Father! (Rom. 8:15; Gal. 4:6); if God were your Father (John 8:42).

C The Father and the Son
C1 Relationship of Father and Son
He called God his Father (John 5:18); the God and Father of our Lord Jesus Christ (Rom. 15:6; 2 Cor. 1:3; Eph. 1:3; Col. 1:3; 1 Pet. 1:3); his God and Father (Rev. 1:6); God the Father and Jesus Christ the Father's Son (2 John 3); I will be to him a Father (Heb. 1:5); my Father in heaven (Matt. 7:21); my heavenly Father (Matt. 15:13); my Father (Matt. 11:27; Luke 22:29; John 2:16; Rev. 2:27); my Father and your Father, my God and your God (John 20:17); his Father (Rev. 14:1); Father! (Matt. 11:25; Luke 10:21; John 11:41); Abba, Father! (Mark 14:36); holy Father! (John 17:11); righteous Father! (John 17:25); I and the Father are one (John 10:30); the Father is in me and I am in the Father (John 10:38); I am in the Father and the Father in me (John 14:10); the only Son from the Father (John 1:14); the only Son in the bosom of the Father (John 1:18); the Father is greater than I (John 14:28).

C2 Interaction of Father and Son
I must be in my Father's house (Luke 2:49); of that day and hour not even the Son knows but only the Father (Matt. 24:36; Mark 13:32); baptising them in the name of the Father, the Son and the Holy Spirit (Matt. 28:19); the Son of man will come in the glory of the Father (Matt. 16:27; Mark 8:38; Luke 9:26); no one knows who the Father is except the Son and those to whom the Son reveals him (Luke 10:22); the Son can only do what he sees the Father doing (John 5:19); I do as the Father has commanded me (John 14:31); the Father has borne witness to me (John 5:37); the Father had given all things into his hands (John 13:3); the Father has committed judgement to the Son (John 5:22); that all may honour the Son as they honour the Father (John 5:23); the Father loves the Son (John 3:35; 5:20); all that the Father gives to me will come to me (John 6:37); he hands over the kingdom to God the Father (1 Cor. 15:24); the head of Christ is God (1 Cor. 11:3); the Son will be subject to him who subjected all things to him (1 Cor. 15:28).

D God the Son
The Word was God (John 1:1); the only begotten God who is in the bosom of the Father (John 1:18); of the Son he says, 'Your throne, O God, is for ever' (Heb. 1:8); Christ is God over all, blessed for ever (Rom. 9:5); our great God and Saviour, Jesus Christ (Titus 2:13); he was in the form of God (Phil. 2:6); my Lord and my God! (John 20:28); he called God his Father, making himself equal with God (John 5:18); in him all the fullness of God dwells in a body (Col. 2:9); baptising them in the name of the Father, the Son and the Holy Spirit (Matt. 28:19); by the righteousness of our God and Saviour Jesus Christ (2 Pet. 1:1); truly you are the Son of God! (Matt. 14:33); tell us if you are the Christ, the Son of God (Matt. 26:63); Jesus, Son of the Most High God! (Mark 5:7); he claimed to be the Son of God (John 19:7); surely he was the Son of God (Mark 15:39);

the gospel of Jesus Christ, the Son of God (Mark 1:1); you are the Christ, the Son of God (Matt. 16:16; Luke 9:20; John 11:27); are you the Christ, the Son of the Blessed? (Mark 14:61).

ANOINTED CHRIST, see 357C.

CHRIST S LIFE, see 360B2.

DEATH OF CHRIST, see 361E2.

HUMAN NATURE OF CHRIST, see 371A4.

E God the Holy Spirit

E1 The Spirit in general

The Spirit of truth (John 14:17; 15:26; 16:13); the Spirit is the truth (1 John 5:7); the Spirit of holiness (Rom. 1:4); the Spirit of grace (Heb. 10:29); the Spirit of your Father (Matt. 10:20); the Spirit of Christ (1 Pet. 1:11); the Spirit of God hovering over the waters (Gen. 1:2); where can I go from your Spirit? (Ps. 139:7); the seven spirits of God (Rev. 1:4); the seven horns and seven eyes are the seven spirits of God sent out into the earth (Rev. 5:6); blasphemy against the Spirit will not be forgiven (Matt. 12:31; Mark 3:29; Luke 12:10); baptising them in the name of the Father, the Son and the Holy Spirit (Matt. 28:19); no one knows the things of God but the Spirit of God (1 Cor. 2:11); there is one body and one Spirit (Eph. 4:4); by this you know the Spirit of God (1 John 4:2); God sent the Spirit of his Son into our hearts (Gal. 4:6); the Holy Spirit who lives within us (2 Tim. 1:14).

E2 The Spirit on people

E2a The Spirit on Christ

The Spirit descended on Jesus like a dove (Matt. 3:16; Mark 1:10; Luke 3:22; John 1:32); he on whom the Spirit descends and remains, he baptises with the Holy Spirit (John 1:33); Jesus returned in the power of the Spirit (Luke 4:14); full of the Holy Spirit (Luke 4:1); the Spirit of the Lord will rest on him (Isa. 11:2); the Spirit of the Lord is upon me (Isa. 61:1; Luke 4:18); I will put my Spirit in him (Matt. 12:18); I have put my Spirit upon him (Isa. 42:1); God anointed Jesus of Nazareth with the Holy Spirit (Acts 10:38); if I cast out demons by the Spirit of God (Matt. 12:28); by the finger of God (Luke 11:20); Jesus gave orders to the apostles by the Holy Spirit (Acts 1:2); Jesus rejoiced in the Holy Spirit (Luke 10:21).

E2b The Spirit poured out

I will pour out my Spirit on your offspring (Isa. 44:3); I will pour out my Spirit on the house of Israel (Ezek. 39:29); I will pour out my Spirit on all flesh (Joel 2:28-9; Acts 2:17-18); until the Spirit is poured on us from on high (Isa. 32:15); while he was still speaking the Holy Spirit fell on them (Acts 10:44); the Holy Spirit poured out on us richly (Titus 3:6); I [Wisdom] will pour out my spirit on you (Prov. 1:23); even on menservants and maidservants I will pour out my Spirit (Joel 2:29); God gives his Spirit without measure (John 3:34); Christ has received from the Father the promise of the Holy Spirit and poured it forth (Acts 2:33); he charged them to wait for the promise of the Father (Acts 1:4); amazed that the Spirit was poured out on the Gentiles (Acts 10:45); the Holy Spirit sent from heaven (1 Pet. 1:12).

PROMISE OF THE HOLY SPIRIT, see 764D.

E2c The gift of the Spirit

Those who believed in him were to receive the Spirit (John 7:39); the Father will give you a Comforter to be with you for ever, the Spirit of truth (John 14:16-17); if I go I will send him to you (John 16:7); the Spirit had not been given as Jesus was not yet glorified (John 7:39); receive the Holy Spirit (John 20:22); we have the firstfruits of the Spirit (Rom. 8:23); we know that he lives in us, because he has given us his Spirit (1 John 4:13); Peter and John prayed for them to receive the Holy Spirit (Acts 8:15); when Paul laid hands on them

the Holy Spirit came on them (Acts 19:6); they received the Holy Spirit just as we have (Acts 10:47); the Holy Spirit fell on them, just as on us (Acts 11:15); they received the Holy Spirit just as we have (Acts 15:8); did you receive the Holy Spirit when you believed? (Acts 19:2); did you receive the Spirit by law or by believing? (Gal. 3:2); we receive the promise of the Spirit by faith (Gal. 3:14); you will receive the gift of the Holy Spirit (Acts 2:38); how much more will your heavenly Father give the Holy Spirit (Luke 11:13); God who gives his Holy Spirit (1 Thess. 4:8); God has given us the Spirit as a deposit (2 Cor. 1:22; 5:5).

E2d Filled with the Spirit

The Spirit had not yet fallen on any of them (Acts 8:16); Peter and John laid hands on them and they received the Holy Spirit (Acts 8:17); give me this authority, that everyone on whom I lay my hands may receive the Spirit (Acts 8:19); he has sent me that you may be filled with the Holy Spirit (Acts 9:17); be filled with the Spirit (Eph. 5:18); the seven men should be full of the Spirit (Acts 6:3); those filled with the Holy Spirit: Bezalel (Exod. 31:3; 35:31); John, from his mother's womb (Luke 1:15); Elizabeth (Luke 1:41); Zechariah (Luke 1:67); Jesus (Luke 4:1); the disciples in Jerusalem (Acts 2:4; 4:31); Peter (Acts 4:8); Stephen (Acts 6:5; 7:55); Paul (Acts 13:9); Barnabas (Acts 11:24); the disciples in Antioch of Pisidia (Acts 13:52).

E2e The Spirit in people

I will put my Spirit in you (Ezek. 36:27); I was in the Spirit on the Lord's day (Rev. 1:10); you are God's temple and God's Spirit lives in you (1 Cor. 3:16); your body is a temple of the Holy Spirit who is in you (1 Cor. 6:19); those who became partakers of the Holy Spirit (Heb. 6:4); the Spirit of glory and of God rests on you (1 Pet. 4:14).

E3 Activity of the Spirit

SPIRITUAL GIFTS, see 781B3e.

E3a Activity of the Spirit in general

The Spirit of God has made me (Job 33:4); the Spirit set me on my feet (Ezek. 2:2); the Spirit of the Lord caught up Philip (Acts 8:39); the Spirit will carry you somewhere else (1 Kgs. 18:12); the flock of which the Holy Spirit has made you overseers (Acts 20:28); the Spirit searches the depths of God (1 Cor. 2:10); to another is given gifts of healing by the one Spirit (1 Cor. 12:9); all these are the work of the one Spirit (1 Cor. 12:11); where the Spirit of the Lord is, there is freedom (2 Cor. 3:17); through him we have access in one Spirit to the Father (Eph. 2:18); salvation through sanctification by the Spirit and belief in the truth (2 Thess. 2:13); through the sanctification of the Spirit (1 Pet. 1:2); God's love is poured into our hearts by the Holy Spirit (Rom. 5:5); the kingdom of God is righteousness, peace and joy in the Holy Spirit (Rom. 14:17).

E3b The power of the Spirit

Not by might nor by power but by my Spirit (Zech. 4:6); you will receive power when the Holy Spirit has come on you (Acts 1:8); signs and wonders in the power of the Spirit (Rom. 15:19); demonstration of the Spirit and of power (1 Cor. 2:4); abound in hope by the power of the Holy Spirit (Rom. 15:13).

E3c Life by the Spirit

We have rebirth and renewal by the Holy Spirit (Titus 3:5); unless one is born of water and the Spirit he cannot enter the kingdom of God (John 3:5); so is everyone who is born of the Spirit (John 3:8); the Spirit gives life (2 Cor. 3:6); we commend ourselves in the Holy Spirit (2 Cor. 6:6); you are a letter written not with ink but with the Spirit (2 Cor. 3:3); the principle of the Spirit of life in Christ Jesus (Rom. 8:2); if we live by the Spirit let us walk by the Spirit (Gal. 5:25); sealed with the Holy Spirit as a pledge (2 Cor. 1:22; Eph. 1:13-14); do not grieve the Holy Spirit by whom you were sealed (Eph. 4:30).

E3d Baptism in the Spirit
He will baptise you with the Holy Spirit (Matt. 3:11; Mark 1:8; Luke 3:16; John 1:33); you will be baptised with the Holy Spirit (Acts 1:5; 11:16); by one Spirit we were all baptised and all drink of one Spirit (1 Cor. 12:13).

E3e Taught by the Spirit
God has revealed them to us by his Spirit (1 Cor. 2:10); the mystery made known to apostles and prophets by the Spirit (Eph. 3:5); you gave your good Spirit to teach them (Neh. 9:20); the Holy Spirit had revealed to Simeon that he would see the Christ (Luke 2:26); the Holy Spirit testifies that imprisonment and affliction await me (Acts 20:23); not taught by human wisdom but taught by the Spirit (1 Cor. 2:13); the Spirit expressly says that some will depart from the faith (1 Tim. 4:1); as the Holy Spirit says (Heb. 3:7); the Holy Spirit indicates that the way into the sanctuary is not yet open (Heb. 9:8); the Holy Spirit bears witness to us (Heb. 10:15).

E3f Led by the Spirit
Let your good Spirit lead me (Ps. 143:10); led by the Spirit (Rom. 8:14; Gal. 5:18); the Spirit led Jesus out into the wilderness (Matt. 4:1); the Spirit drove Jesus out into the wilderness (Mark 1:12); in the Spirit Simeon came into the temple (Luke 2:27); the Spirit said to Philip, 'Go up and join this chariot' (Acts 8:29); the Spirit said to him, 'Three men are looking for you' (Acts 10:19-20); the Holy Spirit said, 'Set apart for me Barnabas and Saul' (Acts 13:2); it seemed good to the Holy Spirit and to us (Acts 15:28); they were forbidden by the Holy Spirit to speak the word in Asia (Acts 16:6); the Spirit of Jesus did not allow them to enter Bithynia (Acts 16:7); Paul determined in the Spirit to go to Jerusalem (Acts 19:21); I am going to Jerusalem, bound in the Spirit (Acts 20:22).

E3g Living by the Spirit
We do not live according to the flesh but according to the Spirit (Rom. 8:4-13); walk by the Spirit (Gal. 5:16); if we live by the Spirit let us walk by the Spirit (Gal. 5:25); he who sows to the Spirit will reap eternal life (Gal. 6:8); those who are of the Spirit set their minds on the things of the Spirit (Rom. 8:5); the fruit of the Spirit (Gal. 5:22-3); the gifts of the Spirit (1 Cor. 12:4-11); the church was walking in the comfort of the Holy Spirit (Acts 9:31); we serve in the new life of the Spirit, not the old written code (Rom. 7:6); the Spirit helps us in our weakness (Rom. 8:26); may you be strengthened through his Spirit in the inner man (Eph. 3:16); pray at all times in the Spirit (Eph. 6:18); pray in the Holy Spirit (Jude 20); we are the true circumcision who worship by the Spirit of God (Phil. 3:3); in much affliction with joy of the Holy Spirit (1 Thess. 1:6).

E3h Speaking by the Spirit
The Spirit of the Lord spoke through me (2 Sam. 23:2); the Holy Spirit will teach you what to say (Luke 12:12); it is not you who speak but the Spirit (Matt. 10:20; Mark 13:11); we are witnesses and so is the Holy Spirit (Acts 5:32); the Spirit and the bride say 'Come' (Rev. 22:17); no one can say 'Jesus is Lord' except by the Spirit (1 Cor. 12:3); they could not withstand the wisdom and Spirit with which he spoke (Acts 6:10); through the Spirit they told Paul not to go to Jerusalem (Acts 21:4); this is what the Holy Spirit says (Acts 21:11); to one is given the word of wisdom through the Spirit (1 Cor. 12:8); to another is given the word of knowledge by the same Spirit (1 Cor. 12:8); the sword of the Spirit,

which is the word of God (Eph. 6:17); our gospel came not in word only but in power and in the Holy Spirit (1 Thess. 1:5).

E4 Defying the Spirit
You always resist the Holy Spirit (Acts 7:51); do not quench the Spirit (1 Thess. 5:19); do not grieve the Holy Spirit by whom you were sealed (Eph. 4:30); why have you agreed together to put the Spirit of the Lord to the test? (Acts 5:9); they rebelled and grieved his Holy Spirit (Isa. 63:10); a natural man does not accept the things of the Spirit (1 Cor. 2:14); blasphemy against the Spirit will not be forgiven (Matt. 12:32; Mark 3:29; Luke 12:10).

F Without God
The Spirit of the Lord had departed from Saul (1 Sam. 16:14); do not take your Holy Spirit from me (Ps. 51:11); you are not my people and I am not your God (Hos. 1:9); having no hope and without God in the world (Eph. 2:12); Gentiles alienated from the life of God (Eph. 4:18); he who does not abide in the doctrine of Christ does not have God (2 John 9); if anyone does not have the Spirit of Christ he does not belong to him (Rom. 8:9); devoid of the Spirit (Jude 19).

966 Deities in general

A Many 'gods'
There are many 'gods' and many 'lords' (1 Cor. 8:5); you were slaves to what are no gods (Gal. 4:8); you have as many gods as cities (Jer. 2:28; 11:13); all the peoples walk each in the name of his god (Mic. 4:5); I will cut off idol and image from the house of your gods (Nahum 1:14); an altar to an unknown god (Acts 17:23); the man of lawlessness exalts himself against every so-called god or object of worship (2 Thess. 2:4); the Lord is greater than all the gods (Exod. 18:11); the Lord is above all gods (Ps. 135:5); he is to be feared above all gods (1 Chr. 16:25); who is like you among the gods? (Exod. 15:11); there is none like you among the gods (Ps. 86:8); worship him, all gods (Ps. 97:7); I will praise you before the gods (Ps. 138:1); has a nation changed its gods, even though they are no gods? (Jer. 2:11); the gods of the people are idols (1 Chr. 16:26; Ps. 96:5); can a man make gods for himself? such are no gods (Jer. 16:20); the gods who did not make heaven and earth will perish from heaven and earth (Jer. 10:11); I will execute judgements against the gods of Egypt (Exod. 12:12); Goliath cursed David by his gods (1 Sam. 17:43).

B Hand-made gods
You will serve gods made by human hands (Deut. 4:28); the gods of the nations, the work of men's hands (2 Chr. 32:19); Rachel stole her father's teraphim (Gen. 31:19); why steal my gods? (Gen. 31:30); you have stolen the gods I made (Judg. 18:24); do not make gods of silver and gold (Exod. 20:23); make us gods to go before us (Exod. 32:1); they made a god of gold (Exod. 32:31); golden calves which Jeroboam made for gods (2 Chr. 13:8); every people still made gods of their own (2 Kgs. 17:29); they praised the gods of silver and gold (Dan. 5:4, 23); those who say to molten images, 'You are our gods' (Isa. 42:17); they were not gods but only wood and stone, the work of men's hands (2 Kgs. 19:18; Isa. 37:19); saying that gods made with hands are no gods (Acts 19:26); we will no more say 'Our God' to the work of our hands (Hos. 14:3).

C Men as gods
You will be like God (Gen. 3:5); man has become like one of us (Gen. 3:22); the gods have come down in human form (Acts 14:11); they said Paul was a god (Acts 28:6); the king of Tyre said he was a god (Ezek. 28:2); the voice of a god and not man! (Acts 12:22); am I in place of God? (Gen. 30:2; 50:19); you will be like

God to Aaron (Exod. 4:16); I have made you like God to Pharaoh (Exod. 7:1); if he called them gods to whom the word of God came (John 10:35).

D Serving gods

BOWING TO FALSE GODS, see 309B4.
PROPHETS OF OTHER GODS, see 579C5c.
PRAYING TO OTHER GODS, see 761A6.
PROSTITUTION TO OTHER GODS, see 951F3.

D1 Serving one's own gods

Your forefathers worshipped other gods (Josh. 24:2); the gods your fathers served beyond the river and in Egypt (Josh. 24:14); the sailors were afraid and every one cried to his god (Jonah 1:5); he brought the vessels to the house of his god (Dan. 1:2); Solomon's wives sacrificed to their gods (1 Kgs. 11:8); they feared the Lord and served their own gods (2 Kgs. 17:33); their god is the belly (Phil. 3:19).

D2 Serving foreign gods

They worshipped other gods (Deut. 29:26; 2 Kgs. 17:7); they served the gods of the peoples (Judg. 2:12; 3:6); they served other gods (Judg. 2:19; 1 Sam. 8:8; 1 Kgs. 9:9); they worshipped and served other gods (2 Chr. 7:22; Jer. 22:9); they have gone after other gods to serve them (Jer. 11:10); they feared other gods (2 Kgs. 17:7); they will serve other gods (Deut. 31:20); there you will serve other gods day and night (Jer. 16:13); if you serve other gods and bow down to them (Josh. 23:16; 1 Kgs. 9:6; 2 Chr. 7:19); will you go after other gods which you have not known? (Jer. 7:9); Israel turn to other gods and love raisin cakes (Hos. 3:1); if we had spread our hands to a strange god (Ps. 44:20); serve the gods of the Amorites in whose land you are (Josh. 24:15); foreign wives will cause you to follow other gods (Deut. 7:4); they will turn your heart away after their gods (1 Kgs. 11:2); Solomon's wives turned his heart after other gods (1 Kgs. 11:4); you may be enticed to worship other gods (Deut. 11:16); let us follow other gods (Deut. 13:2); they will teach you the detestable things they do in worshipping their gods (Deut. 20:18); 'advocating foreign gods' because he preached Jesus and Resurrection (Acts 17:18).

D3 No help in other gods

Have the gods of the nations delivered them? (2 Chr. 32:13, 14, 15); did their gods deliver them? (2 Kgs. 19:12-13; Isa. 36:18-20; 37:12); let those gods help you! (Deut. 32:38); the sorrows of those will increase who run after other gods (Ps. 16:4); what god can deliver you out of my hands? (Dan. 3:15); the Lord will starve all the gods of the earth (Zeph. 2:11).

D4 No other gods

D4a Do not have other gods

You shall have no other gods before me (Exod. 20:3; Deut. 5:7); you shall have no foreign god among you (Ps. 81:9); do not enquire after their gods (Deut. 12:30); do not follow other gods (Deut. 6:14); do not worship any other god (Exod. 34:14); do not fear other gods (2 Kgs. 17:38); do not worship their gods (Exod. 23:24); do not serve their gods (Deut. 7:16); do not worship sun, moon and stars, which the Lord has allotted to the nations (Deut. 4:19); do not make a covenant with their gods (Exod. 23:32).

D4b Penalties for serving other gods

A curse if you follow other gods (Deut. 11:28); death penalty for following other gods (Deut. 17:2-7); if you bow down to other gods and worship them you will be destroyed (Deut. 30:17); if you serve other gods it will be a snare for you (Exod. 23:33); the prophet who speaks in the name of other gods must die (Deut. 18:20).

D4c Putting away other gods

Put away your foreign gods (Gen. 35:2); put away the gods your forefathers worshipped (Josh. 24:14); rid yourselves of the foreign gods (1 Sam. 7:3); Nebuchadnezzar will burn the temples of the gods of Egypt (Jer. 43:12-13); the images of her gods are shattered on the ground (Isa. 21:9).

967 Pagan gods

A Asherah / Astarte / Ashtoreh

Ashtoreth goddess of the Sidonians (1 Kgs. 11:5, 33); do not set up an Asherah (Deut. 16:21); remove the Ashtaroth from among you (1 Sam. 7:3); Baal and Ashtaroth (Judg. 2:13; 10:6; 1 Sam. 12:10); Baals and Asheroth (Judg. 3:7); Solomon built high places for Ashtoreth (2 Kgs. 23:13); they made their Asherim (1 Kgs. 14:15; 2 Kgs. 17:10); an image as an Asherah (1 Kgs. 15:13); Ahab made an Asherah (1 Kgs. 16:33); they served the Asherim and the idols (2 Chr. 24:18); 400 prophets of the Asherah (1 Kgs. 18:19); anasseh made an Asherah (2 Kgs. 21:3; 2 Chr. 33:3); making cakes for the queen of heaven (Jer. 7:18); burning sacrifices to the queen of heaven (Jer. 44:17-19, 25); Cut down their Asherim (Exod. 34:13; Deut. 7:5); burn their Asherim (Deut. 12:3); Gideon demolished the Asherah (Judg. 6:25-32); they removed the Ashtaroth (1 Sam. 7:4); Asa cut down the Asherim (2 Chr. 14:3; 15:16); Jehoshaphat removed the Asherim (2 Chr. 17:6; 19:3); Hezekiah cut down the Asherah (2 Kgs. 18:4; 2 Chr. 31:1); the Asherah removed from the house of the Lord (2 Kgs. 23:6); Josiah cut down the Asherim (2 Kgs. 23:14; 2 Chr. 34:3).

B Baal

B1 Serving Baal

Baals and Ashtaroth (Judg. 2:13; 10:6; 1 Sam. 12:10); if Baal is God, serve him (1 Kgs. 18:21); we have forsaken our God and served the Baals (Judg. 10:10); they played the harlot with Baals and made Baal-berith their god (Judg. 8:33); Israelites were linked with Baal of Peor (Num. 25:3; Ps. 106:28); the prophets prophesied by Baal (Jer. 2:8); enquire of Baal-zebub (2 Kgs. 1:2); they called on the name of Baal (1 Kgs. 18:26); he casts out demons by Beelzebul the ruler of demons (Luke 11:15-19); they called the master of the house Beelzebul (Matt. 10:25); Ahaz made molten images for the Baals (2 Chr. 28:2); Manasseh made altars for Baal (2 Kgs. 21:3; 2 Chr. 33:3); the holy things of the temple had been used for the Baals (2 Chr. 24:7); how can you say, 'I have not gone after the Baals'? (Jer. 2:23); Jehoshaphat did not seek the Baals (2 Chr. 17:3).

B2 Followers of Baal

450 prophets of Baal (1 Kgs. 18:19, 22); summon the prophets and priests of Baal (2 Kgs. 10:18-21); the prophets of Samaria prophesied by Baal (Jer. 23:13); Ahab served Baal (1 Kgs. 16:31-2; 18:18).

B3 Not worshipping Baal

Do not set up a pillar [for Baal] (Deut. 16:22); will you offer sacrifices to Baal? (Jer. 7:9); Gideon demolished the altar of Baal (Judg. 6:25-32); they removed the Baals (1 Sam. 7:4); they tore down the altars of Baal before Josiah (2 Chr. 34:4); Jehoram put away the pillar of Baal (2 Kgs. 3:2); they tore down the house of Baal and killed Mattan the priest of Baal (2 Kgs. 11:18; 2 Chr. 23:17); Elijah killed the prophets of Baal (1 Kgs. 18:40; 19:1); the followers of Baal-peor were killed (Deut. 4:3); Jehu destroyed Baal out of Israel (2 Kgs. 10:28); you will no longer call me 'My Baal' (Hos. 2:16); every knee that has not bowed to Baal and every mouth that has not kissed him (1 Kgs. 19:18); 7000 who have not bowed the knee to Baal (Rom. 11:4).

C **Bel [Marduk, Nebo]**
Bel bows down, Nebo stoops (Isa. 46:1); Bel has been shamed, Marduk shattered (Jer. 50:2); I will punish Bel in Babylon (Jer. 51:44).

D **Chemosh**
Chemosh god of Ammon (Judg. 11:24); Moabites worshipped Chemosh (Num. 21:29); Chemosh the abomination of Moab (1 Kgs. 11:7; 2 Kgs. 23:13); Moab will be ashamed of Chemosh (Jer. 48:13).

E **Dagon**
Dagon god of the Philistines (Judg. 16:23; 1 Sam. 5:2-5); the hand of the God of Israel is heavy on Dagon our god (1 Sam. 5:7).

F **Molech [Milcom, Moloch]**
Milcom the abomination of the Ammonites (1 Kgs. 11:5, 33; 2 Kgs. 23:13); Molech the abomination of the Ammonites (1 Kgs. 11:7); making children pass through the fire for Molech (2 Kgs. 23:10; Jer. 32:35); do not give your children to Molech (Lev. 18:21; 20:2-5); you took up the tent of Moloch (Acts 7:43); those who bow down and swear to the Lord yet swear by Milcom (Zeph. 1:5).

G **National deities**
Nisroch god of the king of Assyria (2 Kgs. 19:37; Isa. 37:38); Naaman bowing in the house of Rimmon (2 Kgs. 5:18); the men of Babylon made Succoth-benoth, the men of Cuth made Nergal and the men of Hamath made Ashima (2 Kgs. 17:30); the Avvites made Nibhaz and Tartak (2 Kgs. 17:31); Sepharvites burned their children to Adrammelech and Anammelech, the gods of Sepharvaim (2 Kgs. 17:31); where are the gods of Hamath, Arpad and Sepharvaim? (Isa. 36:19); where are the gods of Hamath, Arpad, Sepharvaim, Hena, Ivvah? (2 Kgs. 18:34); do not serve the gods of the Amorites (Judg. 6:10); the gods of Aram, Sidon, Moab, the Ammonites, the Philistines (Judg. 10:6); Ahaz offered sacrifices to the gods of Damascus (2 Chr. 28:23); they had sought the gods of Edom (2 Chr. 25:20); they do not know the way of the god of the land (2 Kgs. 17:26).

H **Various other deities**
The temple of El-berith (Judg. 9:46); Demetrius made silver shrines of Artemis [Diana] (Acts 19:24-35); the star of the god Rephan [Rompha?] (Acts 7:43); I am going to punish Amon of Thebes (Jer. 46:25); why has Apis [Haf] fled? (Jer. 46:15); you carried Sakkuth and Kaiwan, your images (Amos 5:26); women weeping for Tammuz (Ezek. 8:14); Daniel called Belteshazzar after the name of my god (Dan. 4:8); vessels for the host of heaven (2 Kgs. 23:4); those who bow down on rooftops to the host of heaven (Zeph. 1:5); like the mourning for Hadad-rimmon in the plain of Megiddo (Zech. 12:11); these are your gods who brought you out of Egypt (Exod. 32:4; 1 Kgs. 12:28); the god of this world (2 Cor. 4:4); the man of lawlessness sets himself up as being God (2 Thess. 2:4); they called Barnabas Zeus and Paul Hermes (Acts 14:12-13).

968 Angel

EVIL ANGELS, see 969C2.

WORSHIPPING ANGELS, see 981B1.

A **About angels**
Angels are more powerful than men (2 Pet. 2:11); angels are not to be worshipped (Col. 2:18; Rev. 19:10; 22:8-9); men ate the food of angels (Ps. 78:25); the guardian cherub drove you from the stones of fire (Ezek. 28:16); to which of the angels has he said, 'Sit at my right hand'? (Heb. 1:13); who among the sons of God is like the Lord? (Ps. 89:6); the Son is much higher than the angels (Heb. 1:4); I will confess his name before my Father and his angels (Rev. 3:5); he did not subject to angels the world to come (Heb. 2:5); not even angels know of that day and hour (Matt. 24:36; Mark 13:32); things angels desire to look into (1 Pet. 1:12); we will judge angels (1 Cor. 6:3); he is not concerned with angels (Heb. 2:16); man was made for a little while lower than the angels (Heb. 2:7); Jesus was made for a little while lower than the angels (Heb. 2:9); angels are fellow-slaves with the brethren (Rev. 19:10; 22:9); are not angels ministering spirits? (Heb. 1:14); Sadducees say there is no angel (Acts 23:8).

B **Varieties of angels**
B1 **The angel of the Lord**
The angel of the Lord destroying in Israel (1 Chr. 21:12); the angel of the Lord killed 185 000 Assyrians (2 Kgs. 19:35); the angel of the Lord pursuing them (Ps. 35:5-6); my angel will go before you (Exod. 23:23); the angel of the Lord camps round those who fear him (Ps. 34:7); alas, for I have seen the angel of the Lord! (Judg. 6:22); an angel of the Lord spoke to me (1 Kgs. 13:18); Joshua the high priest standing before the angel of the Lord (Zech. 3:1); the angel of the Lord charged Joshua (Zech. 3:6); he did as the angel of the Lord commanded him (Matt. 1:24); the angel of the Lord dealing with: Abraham (Gen. 22:11, 15); Balaam (Num. 22:22-6); David (1 Chr. 21:16); Elijah (2 Kgs. 1:3, 15); Gad (1 Chr. 21:18); Gideon (Judg. 6:11); Hagar (Gen. 16:7; 21:17); Jacob (Gen. 31:11); Joseph (Matt. 1:20; 2:13, 19); Manoah and his wife (Judg. 13:3, 6, 9, 16, 21); Moses (Exod. 3:2); Zechariah the prophet (Zech. 1:12); Zechariah the priest (Luke 1:11); the camp of Israel (Exod. 14:19); the Israelites (Judg. 2:1).

B2 **Cherubim /seraphim**
Cherubim were placed on the east side of Eden (Gen. 3:24); God rode on a cherub (2 Sam. 22:11; Ps. 18:10); the living creatures were cherubim (Ezek. 10:2-22); God is enthroned on the cherubim (2 Sam. 6:2; 2 Kgs. 19:15; 1 Chr. 13:6; Ps. 80:1; Isa. 37:16); the Lord is enthroned on the cherubim (Ps. 99:1); two cherubim of gold (Exod. 25:18; 37:7-9); the cherubim of glory overshadowing the mercy seat (Heb. 9:5); the ark under the wings of the cherubim (1 Kgs. 8:6-7; 2 Chr. 5:7-8); the Lord sits above the cherubim (1 Sam. 4:4); I will speak to you from between the two cherubim (Exod. 25:22); cherubim embroidered on the curtains (Exod. 26:1; 36:8); and on the veil (Exod. 26:31; 36:35; 2 Chr. 3:14); carved cherubim in the temple (1 Kgs. 6:23; 2 Chr. 3:7, 10; Ezek. 41:18); seraphs in the temple (Isa. 6:2).

CHERUBIM S WINGS, see 271B3.

B3 **Archangels**
The Lord will descend with the voice of the archangel (1 Thess. 4:16); Michael the archangel (Jude 9).

C **Work of angels**
C1 **Angels before God**
Bless the Lord, you his angels (Ps. 103:20); praise him, all his angels (Ps. 148:2); at the creation the sons of God shouted for joy (Job 38:7); a multitude of the heavenly host praising God (Luke 2:13); the angels around the throne fell on their faces and worshipped God (Rev. 7:11); let all God's angels worship [Christ] (Heb. 1:6); I heard the voice of many angels around the throne praising the Lamb (Rev. 5:11-12); you have come to tens of thousands of angels (Heb. 12:22); their angels in heaven always behold the face of my Father (Matt. 18:10); the sons of God came to present themselves before the Lord (Job 1:6; 2:1).

C2 **Angels sent by God**
The two angels came to Sodom (Gen. 19:1); God will send his angel before you (Gen. 24:7, 40); I am sending an angel ahead of you (Exod. 23:20; 32:34; 33:2); God sent an angel and brought us out of Egypt (Num.

20:16); my God sent an angel and shut the mouths of the lions (Dan. 6:22); God sent the angel Gabriel to Mary (Luke 1:26); God sent his angel to show his slaves what must soon take place (Rev. 22:6); I, Jesus, have sent my angel to you (Rev. 22:16); would my Father not send more than 12 legions of angels? (Matt. 26:53); the angels of God were ascending and descending the stairway (Gen. 28:12); the angels of God ascending and descending on the Son of man (John 1:51).

C3 Angels doing God's work
An angel of the Lord rolled away the stone (Matt. 28:2-7); an angel of the Lord opened the prison (Acts 5:19); an angel of the Lord released Peter (Acts 12:7-10); an angel of the Lord struck Herod (Acts 12:23); the angel who has power over fire (Rev. 14:18); seven angels with the seven last plagues (Rev. 15:1); four angels holding back the winds (Rev. 7:1); an angel having the seal of God (Rev. 7:2); seven angels with seven trumpets (Rev. 8:2, 6); an angel clothed in a cloud (Rev. 10:1); an angel flying in mid-heaven (Rev. 14:6); an angel coming from heaven with great authority (Rev. 18:1); angels were involved in the giving of the law (Acts 7:53; Gal. 3:19); the angel spoke to Moses on Mount Sinai (Acts 7:38); the word spoken through angels (Heb. 2:2); he will give his angels charge of you (Ps. 91:11; Matt. 4:6; Luke 4:10); angels attended Jesus (Matt. 4:11; Mark 1:13); an angel strengthened him (Luke 22:43); an angel fed Elijah (1 Kgs. 19:5, 7); an angel of the Lord directed Philip (Acts 8:26); if there is an angel as mediator (Job 33:23); he sent his angel and delivered his servants who trusted in him (Dan. 3:28); the poor man died and was carried by the angels to Abraham's bosom (Luke 16:22).

C4 Angels coming with Christ
The Son of man will come with his angels (Matt. 16:27; Mark 8:38); when the Son of man comes in glory and all the angels with him (Matt. 25:31); in the glory of the angels (Luke 9:26); the Lord Jesus will be revealed from heaven with his mighty angels (2 Thess. 1:7); the Lord came with myriads of his holy ones (Jude 14); he will send his angels to gather the elect (Matt. 24:31; Mark 13:27); the Son of man will send out his angels (Matt. 13:41); the reapers are angels (Matt. 13:39); the angels will separate the wicked from the righteous (Matt. 13:49).

D Particular angels
The man Gabriel (Dan. 8:16; 9:21); I am Gabriel (Luke 1:19); the angel Gabriel (Luke 1:26); Michael the archangel (Jude 9); Michael and his angels (Rev. 12:7).

E Angels and people
Cornelius saw an angel of God in a vision (Acts 10:3); an angel appeared to Paul (Acts 27:23-4); Joshua was clothed in filthy garments, standing before the angel (Zech. 3:3); an angel appeared to him in the wilderness of Mount Sinai (Acts 7:30); the angel who appeared to him in the bush (Acts 7:35); he showed it by his angel to his slave John (Rev. 1:1); there were two angels seated where Jesus' body had been (John 20:12); an angel of the Lord appeared to the shepherds (Luke 2:9); a vision of angels (Luke 24:23); men with white clothes at the resurrection (Mark 16:5-7; Luke 24:4-7); two men in white clothing at the ascension (Acts 1:10); Christ was seen by angels (1 Tim. 3:16); some entertained angels unawares (Heb. 13:2); whoever confesses me before men, I will confess before the angels of God (Luke 12:8-9); they said it was Peter's angel (Acts 12:15); we have become a spectacle to angels and men (1 Cor. 4:9); women should have authority on their heads because of the angels (1 Cor. 11:10); if an angel from heaven should preach a different gospel (Gal. 1:8); the seven stars are the angels of the seven churches (Rev. 1:20).

F Like angels
The king is like an angel of God (2 Sam. 14:17; 19:27); you are good in my eyes like an angel of God (1 Sam. 29:9); my lord is wise as an angel of God (2 Sam. 14:20); in the resurrection people are like angels (Matt. 22:30; Mark 12:25; Luke 20:36); his face was like an angel's (Acts 6:15); you received me like an angel of God (Gal. 4:14); Satan disguises himself as an angel of light (2 Cor. 11:14).

969 Devil

A Nature of the devil
The dragon, that ancient serpent, who is the devil, or Satan (Rev. 12:9; 20:2); Beelzebul the prince of demons (Matt. 12:24, 27); the ruler of the world (John 12:31; 14:30; 16:11); the god of this world (2 Cor. 4:4); the prince of the power of the air (Eph. 2:2); the devil was a murderer from the beginning (John 8:44); he who does what is sinful is of the devil, because the devil has sinned from the beginning (1 John 3:8); there is no truth in him (John 8:44); when he lies, he speaks from his own, for he is a liar and the father of lies (John 8:44); Satan disguises himself as an angel of light (2 Cor. 11:14); the devil had the power of death (Heb. 2:14); Satan appeared before God (Job 1:6; 2:1); if Satan is divided against himself, how can his kingdom stand? (Matt. 12:26; Mark 3:26; Luke 11:18); how can Satan cast out Satan? (Mark 3:23); what agreement has Christ with Belial? (2 Cor. 6:15); the demons believe that God is one – and tremble (Jas. 2:19).

B Activity of the devil
B1 The devil tempting people
The serpent deceived Eve by its craftiness (2 Cor. 11:3); Jesus tempted by the devil (Matt. 4:1; Mark 1:13); Luke 4:2); come together again lest Satan tempt you (1 Cor. 7:5); for fear the tempter might have tempted you (1 Thess. 3:5); why has Satan filled your heart to lie to the Holy Spirit? (Acts 5:3); Satan urged David to number Israel (1 Chr. 21:1); the devil put it into Judas' heart to betray Jesus (John 13:2).

B2 The devil opposing people
Satan demanded to have you all to sieve you like wheat (Luke 22:31); the shield of faith can extinguish the flaming darts of the evil one (Eph. 6:16); the devil is about to throw some of you into prison (Rev. 2:10); the dragon persecuted the woman who gave birth to the male son (Rev. 12:13); condemnation of the devil (1 Tim. 3:6); the snare of the devil (1 Tim. 3:7; 2 Tim. 2:26); Satan has bound this woman for 18 years (Luke 13:16); we wanted to come but Satan hindered us (1 Thess. 2:18); the thorn in the flesh was a messenger of Satan (2 Cor. 12:7); your enemy the devil prowls round like a roaring lion (1 Pet. 5:8); the devil has come down to the earth in great wrath (Rev. 12:12); Satan accusing Joshua (Zech. 3:1); the accuser of the brethren, who accuses them day and night (Rev. 12:10); the god of this world has blinded their minds (2 Cor. 4:4); the evil one snatches away the seed (Matt. 13:19; Mark 4:15; Luke 8:12); the enemy who sows the weeds is the devil (Matt. 13:39); that Satan may gain no advantage, for we are not ignorant of his devices (2 Cor. 2:11).

C Demons
C1 Evil spirits
Unclean spirits like frogs came out of the mouths of the dragon, the beast and the false prophet (Rev. 16:13); you deaf and dumb spirit! (Mark 9:25); the demons begged him to send them into the pigs (Matt. 8:31); the unclean spirits came out and entered the pigs (Mark 5:13; Luke 8:33); seven other spirits more evil than himself (Matt. 12:45; Luke 11:26); come out of the man, you unclean spirit! (Mark 5:8); he was driven by the

demon into the wilderness (Luke 8:29); the name was legion because many demons had entered him (Luke 8:30); he was casting out a demon which was dumb (Luke 11:14); the evil spirit answered, 'Jesus I know and Paul I know, but who are you?' (Acts 19:15); Babylon has become the dwelling-place of demons, the haunt of unclean spirits (Rev. 18:2); they are demonic spirits (Rev. 16:14); an evil spirit from the Lord came on Saul (1 Sam. 16:14-15; 18:10; 19:9).

C2 Evil angels
Angels cannot separate us from the love of God (Rom. 8:38-9); the dragon and his angels waged war (Rev. 12:7); God did not spare angels who sinned (2 Pet. 2:4); angels who left their proper dwelling have been kept in eternal chains (Jude 6); Satan's angels were thrown down with him (Rev. 12:9); the eternal fire prepared for the devil and his angels (Matt. 25:41); Satan disguises himself as an angel of light (2 Cor. 11:14); the angel of the abyss is king over them, Abaddon or Apollyon (Rev. 9:11).

C3 Principalities and powers
Principalities and powers were created through Christ (Col. 1:16); our struggle is against principalities and powers (Eph. 6:12); principalities cannot separate us from the love of God (Rom. 8:38-9); he disarmed principalities and powers (Col. 2:15); angels, authorities and powers are subject to Christ (1 Pet. 3:22); the wisdom of God made known to the principalities and powers in the heavenlies (Eph. 3:10); the prince of the kingdom of Persia withstood Gabriel (Dan. 10:13, 20); the prince of Greece is coming (Dan. 10:20); the Lord will punish the host of heaven in heaven (Isa. 24:21).

D People ruled by the devil
D1 Following the devil
The whole world is in the power of the evil one (1 John 5:19); you live where Satan's throne is (Rev. 2:13); the synagogue of Satan (Rev. 2:9; 3:9); the Gentiles sacrifice to demons, not to God (1 Cor. 10:20-1); they sacrificed to demons (Deut. 32:17); they sacrificed sons and daughters to demons (Ps. 106:37); they did not turn from worshipping demons (Rev. 9:20); deceitful spirits and doctrines of demons (1 Tim. 4:1); some have turned away to follow Satan (1 Tim. 5:15); this wisdom is earthly, unspiritual, demonic (Jas. 3:15); those who do not know the deep things of Satan (Rev. 2:24).
WORSHIPPING THE DEVIL, see 981B2.

D2 Children of the devil
You son of the devil! (Acts 13:10); sons of the evil one (Matt. 13:38); you are of your father the devil (John 8:44); one of you is a devil (John 6:70); by this we know the children of God and the children of the devil (1 John 3:10).

D3 Those demonised
A man in the synagogue with an unclean spirit (Mark 1:23; Luke 4:33); Gadarene demoniacs from the tombs (Matt. 8:28; Luke 8:27); a man with an unclean spirit (Mark 5:2); a man who was demonised and dumb (Matt. 9:32); a boy possessed by a spirit (Matt. 17:18; Mark 9:17); the Canaanite woman's daughter was demonised (Matt. 15:22; Mark 7:25); they brought to him many who were demonised (Matt. 8:16); demonised, blind and dumb (Matt. 12:22); they brought to him demoniacs, epileptics and paralytics and he healed them (Matt. 4:24); they brought to him all who were sick or demonised (Mark 1:32); they brought people who were sick or troubled with unclean spirits (Acts 5:16); they enter the man and dwell there (Luke 11:26); Satan entered Judas (Luke 22:3; John 13:27); naming the name of the Lord Jesus over those who had evil spirits (Acts 19:13).
DEMONS ENTERING, see 297C2.

D4 Accused of being demonised
They said John had an evil spirit (Matt. 11:18); you say John the Baptist has a demon (Luke 7:33); they said Jesus had an unclean spirit (Mark 3:30); they said he had Beelzebul (Mark 3:22); it is by the prince of demons that he drives out demons (Matt. 9:34; 12:24; Mark 3:22; Luke 11:15); they called the master of the house Beelzebul (Matt. 10:25); you have a demon (John 7:20; 8:48-9); he has a demon and is mad (John 10:20-1).

D5 Handed over to the devil
Hand him over to Satan for the destruction of the flesh (1 Cor. 5:5); Hymenaeus and Alexander, whom I have handed over to Satan (1 Tim. 1:20).

E Authority over the devil
CASTING OUT DEMONS, see 300D.

E1 God's authority over the devil
He commands even the unclean spirits and they obey him (Mark 1:27; Luke 4:36); he cast out many demons and would not permit the demons to speak (Mark 1:34); unclean spirits fell down before him (Mark 3:11); angels, authorities and powers are subject to Christ (1 Pet. 3:22); preaching in their synagogues and casting out demons (Mark 1:39); Jesus rebuked the unclean spirit (Mark 9:25); I cast out demons and cure today and tomorrow (Luke 13:32); to turn them from the authority of Satan to God (Acts 26:18); God will protect you from the evil one (2 Thess. 3:3); the reason the Son of God appeared was to destroy the works of the devil (1 John 3:8); Jesus healed all who were oppressed by the devil (Acts 10:38); the ruler of this world is judged (John 16:11); the ruler of this world will be cast out (John 12:31).

E2 Man's authority over the devil
The 12 were to have authority to cast out demons (Mark 3:15); he gave the disciples authority over unclean spirits (Matt. 10:1; Mark 6:7; Luke 9:1); I have given you authority over all the power of the enemy (Luke 10:19); the 12 cast out many demons (Mark 6:13); cast out demons (Matt. 10:8); in my name they will cast out demons (Mark 16:17); even the demons are subject to us (Luke 10:17); young men, you have overcome the evil one (1 John 2:13, 14); resist the devil and he will flee from you (Jas. 4:7); do not give the devil an opportunity (Eph. 4:27); stand against the wiles of the devil (Eph. 6:11); the God of peace will soon crush Satan under your feet (Rom. 16:20); I saw Satan fall like lightning from heaven (Luke 10:18); unclean spirits came out of many (Acts 8:7); evil spirits went out went out when garments from Paul were brought (Acts 19:12).

970 Ghost
The spirits of the dead greet the king of Babylon (Isa. 14:9); your voice will come from the ground like that of a ghost (Isa. 29:4); Samuel appeared (1 Sam. 28:11-12); they thought Jesus was a ghost (Matt. 14:26; Mark 6:49; Luke 24:37); a ghost does not have flesh and bones (Luke 24:39).

971 Heaven
A God and heaven
A1 God in heaven
Our God is in the heavens (Ps. 115:3); God is in heaven and you on earth (Eccles. 5:2); there is a God in heaven who reveals mysteries (Dan. 2:28); the God of heaven (Ps. 136:26; Rev. 11:13; 16:11); are you not God in heaven? (2 Chr. 20:6); hear from heaven your dwelling place (2 Chr. 6:30); he who sits in the heavens (Ps. 2:4); enthroned in the heavens (Ps. 123:1); the Lord has established his throne in the heavens (Ps. 103:19);

heaven is my throne (Isa. 66:1; Acts 7:49); a throne in heaven and one seated on the throne (Rev. 4:2); do not swear by heaven, for it is God's throne (Matt. 5:34); he who swears by heaven swears by God's throne and him who sits on it (Matt. 23:22); our Father in heaven (Matt. 6:9); if I ascend to heaven, you are there (Ps. 139:8); whom have I in heaven but you? (Ps. 73:25); the highest heaven cannot contain God (1 Kgs. 8:27; 2 Chr. 2:6; 6:18).

A2 God speaks from heaven
I have spoken to you from heaven (Exod. 20:22); out of heaven he let you hear his voice (Deut. 4:36); you spoke from heaven with them (Neh. 9:13); you uttered judgement from heaven (Ps. 76:8); a voice from heaven (Dan. 4:31; Mark 1:11; Luke 3:22; John 12:28; 2 Pet. 1:18; Rev. 14:2); the angel of God called to Hagar from heaven (Gen. 21:17); the angel of the Lord called to him from heaven (Gen. 22:11, 15); much less shall we escape if we reject him who warns from heaven (Heb. 12:25).

A3 God acts from heaven
I saw the Spirit descend as a dove from heaven (John 1:32); do you want us to call down fire from heaven? (Luke 9:54); he gave them bread from heaven to eat (John 6:31-2); there will be terrors and great signs from heaven (Luke 21:11); the wrath of God is revealed from heaven (Rom. 1:18).

B Christ and heaven
He who comes from heaven is above all (John 3:31); I have come down from heaven (John 6:38); the bread which came down from heaven (John 6:33); no one has ascended into heaven but he who descended from heaven (John 3:13); this Jesus who was taken up from you into heaven (Acts 1:11); whom heaven must receive until the time for restoring everything (Acts 3:21); the second man is from heaven (1 Cor. 15:47-9); Christ is seated at God's right hand in the heavenlies (Eph. 1:20); seated at the right hand of the throne of the Majesty in heaven (Heb. 8:1); their Master and yours is in heaven (Eph. 6:9); from heaven we await a Saviour, the Lord Jesus Christ (Phil. 3:20); the Lord himself will descend from heaven with a shout (1 Thess. 4:16); when the Lord Jesus is revealed from heaven (2 Thess. 1:7); Christ entered not a man-made sanctuary but heaven itself (Heb. 9:24); we have a great high priest who has passed into the heavens (Heb. 4:14); Jesus has gone into heaven (1 Pet. 3:22).

C Other activity in heaven
Your will be done on earth as it is in heaven (Matt. 6:10); joy in heaven over one sinner who repents (Luke 15:7); silence in heaven for half an hour (Rev. 8:1); peace in heaven and glory in the highest! (Luke 19:38); you whose glory is chanted above the heavens (Ps. 8:1); every knee will bow, in heaven, on earth and under the earth (Phil. 2:10); the armies which are in heaven clothed in clean white linen (Rev. 19:14); he has promised to shake not only the earth but also heaven (Heb. 12:26); the powers of the heavens will be shaken (Luke 21:26); against spiritual wickedness in the heavenlies (Eph. 6:12); the wisdom of God made known to the rulers and authorities in the heavenlies (Eph. 3:10); there was no longer any place for the dragon and his angels in heaven (Rev. 12:8).

D Heaven opened
This is the gate of heaven (Gen. 28:17); oh that you would rend the heavens and come down! (Isa. 64:1); the heavens were opened and I saw visions of God (Ezek. 1:1); the heavens were opened and the Holy Spirit descended (Matt. 3:16; Mark 1:10; Luke 3:21-2); you will see the heavens opened (John 1:51); an open door in heaven (Rev. 4:1); I saw heaven opened (Rev. 19:11); if God made windows in heaven, could this

happen? (2 Kgs. 7:2, 19); Stephen saw heaven opened (Acts 7:55-6).

HEAVEN OPENED, see 263A2e.

E Heaven for us
E1 Belonging to heaven
God blessed us in the heavenlies (Eph. 1:3); God seated us in the heavenlies (Eph. 2:6); our citizenship is in heaven (Phil. 3:20); partakers of a heavenly calling (Heb. 3:1); those who have tasted the heavenly gift (Heb. 6:4); you have come to the heavenly Jerusalem (Heb. 12:22); the assembly of the firstborn enrolled in heaven (Heb. 12:23); whatever you bind or loose on earth will be done in heaven (Matt. 16:19; 18:18); rejoice that your names are written in heaven (Luke 10:20); as is the man of heaven, so are those who are of heaven (1 Cor. 15:48); you will have treasure in heaven (Matt. 19:21; Mark 10:21; Luke 18:22); lay up treasure in heaven (Matt. 6:20; Luke 12:33); great is your reward in heaven (Luke 6:23).

E2 Taken to heaven
God taking Elijah up to heaven (2 Kgs. 2:1, 11); the Lord will save me for his heavenly kingdom (2 Tim. 4:18); an inheritance reserved in heaven for you (1 Pet. 1:4); they desire a better country, a heavenly one (Heb. 11:16); in the resurrection people are like angels in heaven (Matt. 22:30; Mark 12:25); we have a building from God, eternal in the heavens (2 Cor. 5:1); we long to put on our heavenly dwelling (2 Cor. 5:2); the hope laid up for you in heaven (Col. 1:5); the two witnesses went up to heaven in a cloud (Rev. 11:12); the loud voice of a great multitude in heaven (Rev. 19:1); I know a man in Christ who was caught up to the third heaven (2 Cor. 12:2); today you will be with me in paradise (Luke 23:43); eating of the tree of life in the paradise of God (Rev. 2:7); afterwards you will take me to glory (Ps. 73:24); the beggar died and the angels carried him to Abraham's bosom (Luke 16:22).

GOING UP TO HEAVEN, see 308B3.

COMING DOWN FROM HEAVEN, see 309A1.

KINGDOM OF HEAVEN, see 733B2.

F Heaven and earth
Heaven is my throne and the earth my footstool (Isa. 66:1); there are heavenly bodies and earthly bodies (1 Cor. 15:40); do not swear at all, by heaven or earth or any other oath (Jas. 5:12); there may be so-called gods in heaven or on earth (1 Cor. 8:5); from whom all fatherhood in heaven and on earth is named (Eph. 3:15); to reconcile all things, whether on earth or in heaven (Col. 1:20); every knee will bow, in heaven, on earth and under the earth (Phil. 2:10); summing up all things in Christ, in heaven and on earth (Eph. 1:10).

972 Hell

A Hell of fire
It is better to lose one limb than for your whole body to be thrown into hell (Matt. 5:29-30; 18:8-9; Mark 9:43-7); fear him who can destroy soul and body in hell (Matt. 10:28); fear him who has authority to cast into hell (Luke 12:5); the rich man was in torment in Hades (Luke 16:23); guilty enough for the hell of fire (Matt. 5:22); how will you escape being sentenced to hell? (Matt. 23:33); thrown into the fiery furnace (Matt. 13:42, 50); God cast angels into hell (2 Pet. 2:4); lest they also come to this place of torment (Luke 16:28).

SECOND DEATH, see 361F2.

FIRE OF HELL, see 381B7.

B Bottomless pit
The demons entreated him not to command them to depart into the abyss (Luke 8:31); God consigned angels to pits of darkness (2 Pet. 2:4); the abyss was opened with a key (Rev. 9:1-2); the angel of the abyss is king

over them (Rev. 9:11); the beast that comes up out of the abyss (Rev. 11:7; 17:8); the angel sealed the devil in the abyss (Rev. 20:1-3); who will descend into the abyss? (Rom. 10:7).

973 Religion

A Religious
I see that you are very religious (Acts 17:22); some disagreement about their own religion (Acts 25:19); religion with unbridled tongue is worthless (Jas. 1:26); pure religion is to visit the needy (Jas. 1:27); beware of practising your righteousness before men to be seen by them (Matt. 6:1); Simeon was righteous and devout (Luke 2:25); Jews, devout men from every nation under heaven (Acts 2:5); devout men buried Stephen (Acts 8:2); Cornelius was a devout man (Acts 10:2); the Jews incited the devout women of high standing (Acts 13:50); Ananias, a devout man according to the law (Acts 22:12); the children of a widow should learn their religious duty to their own family (1 Tim. 5:4); having a form of religion but denying the power of it (2 Tim. 3:5).

B Godliness
Train yourself in godliness (1 Tim. 4:7-8); the teaching which accords with godliness (1 Tim. 6:3); they think godliness is a means of gain (1 Tim. 6:5-6); pursue godliness (1 Tim. 6:11); the knowledge of the truth which accords with godliness (Titus 1:1); teaching us to live godly lives (Titus 2:12); Christ was heard because of his godliness (Heb. 5:7); his divine power has granted us everything pertaining to life and godliness (2 Pet. 1:3); add to perseverance godliness (2 Pet. 1:6); all who desire to live godly will be persecuted (2 Tim. 3:12); the Lord knows how to rescue the godly from trial (2 Pet. 2:9); what sort of people ought you to be in holiness and godliness? (2 Pet. 3:11).

C Judaism
My former life in Judaism (Gal. 1:13-14); I lived as a Pharisee, the strictest party of our religion (Acts 26:5).

974 Irreligion

A The world without God
All that is in the world is not of the Father (1 John 2:16); I have overcome the world (John 16:33); I chose you out of the world, therefore the world hates you (John 15:18-19); if you were of the world the world would love its own (John 15:19); that they may be one that the world may know that you sent me (John 17:23); the world does not know us because it did not know him (1 John 3:1); they are of the world and the world listens to them (1 John 4:5); whatever is born of God overcomes the world (1 John 5:4); who overcomes the world but he who believes that Jesus is the Son of God? (1 John 5:5); the whole world is in the power of the evil one (1 John 5:19); friendship of the world is enmity with God (Jas. 4:4); if anyone loves the world, the love of the Father is not in him (1 John 2:15); Demas has loved this present world (2 Tim. 4:10); they are not of the world just as I am not (John 17:14, 16); the world has not known you (John 17:25).

B Godless
God justifies the ungodly (Rom. 4:5); Christ died for the ungodly (Rom. 5:6); the law is for the ungodly and sinners (1 Tim. 1:9); empty chatter leads to more and more ungodliness (2 Tim. 2:16); teaching us to renounce ungodliness (Titus 2:12); that there be no immoral or godless person like Esau (Heb. 12:16); if the righteous are saved with difficulty, what about the ungodly and the sinner? (1 Pet. 4:18); God made Sodom and Gomorrah an example to the ungodly (2 Pet. 2:6); the day of judgement and the destruction of ungodly

men (2 Pet. 3:7); ungodly people who pervert the grace of God (Jude 4); to convict the ungodly of ungodly deeds done in an ungodly way (Jude 15); he will remove ungodliness from Jacob (Rom. 11:26).

C Uncircumcised
C1 About the uncircumcised
An uncircumcised male shall be cut off from his people (Gen. 17:14); no uncircumcised man may eat the Passover (Exod. 12:48); no foreigner, uncircumcised in heart and flesh, may enter the temple (Ezek. 44:9); Gentiles, the 'uncircumcision' (Eph. 2:11); you were dead in the uncircumcision of your flesh (Col. 2:13); Paul was entrusted with the gospel to the uncircumcised (Gal. 2:7).

C2 Specific uncircumcised people
We cannot give in marriage to the uncircumcised (Gen. 34:14); why take a wife from the uncircumcised Philistines? (Judg. 14:3); shall I fall into the hands of the uncircumcised? (Judg. 15:18); let us cross over to the garrison of the uncircumcised (1 Sam. 14:6); this uncircumcised Philistine (1 Sam. 17:26, 36); lest these uncircumcised make sport of me (1 Sam. 31:4; 1 Chr. 10:4); lest the daughters of the uncircumcised Philistines rejoice (2 Sam. 1:20); you went to the uncircumcised and ate with them (Acts 11:3).

C3 Uncircumcised in heart
I am a man of uncircumcised lips (Exod. 6:12, 30); if their uncircumcised heart is humbled (Lev. 26:41); Israel are uncircumcised in heart (Jer. 9:26); you brought foreigners, uncircumcised in heart and flesh, into the temple (Ezek. 44:7); I will punish all who are circumcised yet uncircumcised (Jer. 9:25); uncircumcised in heart and ears (Acts 7:51).

C4 Uncircumcision irrelevant
If you break the law your circumcision becomes uncircumcision (Rom. 2:25); he who is physically uncircumcised but keeps the law will condemn you (Rom. 2:27); God justifies both circumcised and uncircumcised through faith (Rom. 3:30); is this blessing only for the circumcised or for the uncircumcised as well? (Rom. 4:9); Abraham is the father of those who believe without being circumcised (Rom. 4:11); if anyone was uncircumcised when called, let him not be circumcised (1 Cor. 7:18); neither circumcision nor uncircumcision is anything (Gal. 5:6; 6:15); there is no distinction between circumcised and uncircumcised (Col. 3:11); if the uncircumcised man keeps the law he will be regarded as circumcised (Rom. 2:26); Abraham was justified while uncircumcised (Rom. 4:10).

975 Scriptures

THE WORD OF GOD, see 529A.
THE SCRIPTURES WRITTEN, see 586A.
BOOKS OF SCRIPTURE, see 589.
THE LAW, see 953A.

A Authority of the scriptures
The scriptures cannot be broken (John 10:35); all scripture is God-breathed and profitable (2 Tim. 3:16); no scripture is of private interpretation (2 Pet. 1:20); believing everything in the law and the prophets (Acts 24:14); speaking only what the prophets and Moses said (Acts 26:22); they have Moses and the prophets, let them hear them (Luke 16:29); slow of heart to believe all that the prophets have spoken! (Luke 24:25); they believed the scripture and Jesus' word (John 2:22); men moved by the Holy Spirit spoke from God (2 Pet. 1:21).
THE SCRIPTURES FULFILLED, see 725B2.

B Christ and the scriptures
The scriptures bear witness to me (John 5:39); Moses wrote of me (John 5:46); we have found him of whom

Moses and the prophets wrote (John 1:45); everything written about me in the law of Moses and the prophets and the psalms (Luke 24:44); he explained in all the scriptures the things concerning himself (Luke 24:27); Paul spoke about Jesus from the law of Moses and the prophets (Acts 28:23); Christ died for our sins according to the scriptures (1 Cor. 15:3-4); I did not come to abolish the law and the prophets, but to fulfil (Matt. 5:17); did not our hearts burn when he explained the Scriptures to us? (Luke 24:32).

C The gospel in the scriptures
The gospel was promised in the holy scriptures (Rom. 1:2); the gospel is made known by the scriptures of the prophets (Rom. 16:26); the law and the prophets testify of righteousness through faith (Rom. 3:21-2).

D Use of the scriptures
These things were written in earlier times so that through the encouragement of the scriptures we might have hope (Rom. 15:4); he opened their minds to understand the scriptures (Luke 24:45); beginning with this scripture he told him the good news of Jesus (Acts 8:35); the scripture has shut up all men under sin (Gal. 3:22); the ignorant and unstable twist the scriptures to their own destruction (2 Pet. 3:16); the Jews are entrusted with the oracles of God (Rom. 3:2); from a child you have known the holy scriptures (2 Tim. 3:15); Apollos was powerful in the scriptures (Acts 18:24); you do not perceive the scriptures nor the power of God (Matt. 22:29; Mark 12:24); the Bereans examined the scriptures daily to see if these things were so (Acts 17:11).

976 Orthodoxy
SOUND DOCTRINE, see 534D2.

977 Heterodoxy
MISTEACHING, see 535.

978 Sectarianism
PARTIES, see 708.

979 Holiness
A God's holiness
A1 God is holy
He is a holy God (Josh. 24:19); holy is he! (Ps. 99:3, 5); you are holy (Ps. 22:3); the Lord our God is holy (Ps. 99:9); holy, holy, holy is the Lord of hosts (Isa. 6:3); holy, holy, holy is the Lord God Almighty (Rev. 4:8); the holy One (Isa. 40:25; 1 John 2:20; Rev. 16:5); the holy God shows himself holy in righteousness (Isa. 5:16); holy Father (John 17:11); he who is holy and true (Rev. 3:7); O Lord, holy and true (Rev. 6:10); there is no one holy like the Lord (1 Sam. 2:2); you alone are holy (Rev. 15:4); who is like you, majestic in holiness? (Exod. 15:11); his name is holy (Isa. 57:15; Luke 1:49); holy and awesome is his name (Ps. 111:9).

A2 God shows his holiness
I will show myself holy (Lev. 10:3); I will show myself holy in you in the sight of the nations (Ezek. 20:41); the Spirit of holiness (Rom. 1:4); the Lord Almighty is the one you are to regard as holy (Isa. 8:13); hallowed be your name (Matt. 6:9; Luke 11:2); I will be sanctified among Israel (Lev. 22:32); they will sanctify my name (Isa. 29:23); I will vindicate the holiness of my great name (Ezek. 36:23).

A3 Christ is holy
The child to be born will be called holy, the Son of God (Luke 1:35); the holy One of God (Mark 1:24; Luke 4:34); we have believed and come to know that you are the holy One of God (John 6:69); your holy servant Jesus (Acts 4:27, 30); he whom the Father sanctified

and sent into the world (John 10:36); such a high priest, holy, innocent, undefiled (Heb. 7:26); you denied the holy and righteous One (Acts 3:14).

A4 Be holy for I am holy
Be holy because I am holy (Lev. 11:44-5; 19:2; 20:26; 1 Pet. 1:16); as he who called you is holy, be holy yourselves (1 Pet. 1:15); priests are to be considered holy because I, the Lord, who makes you holy, am holy (Lev. 21:8); your camp must be holy because God walks there (Deut. 23:14).

B Holy people
B1 A holy nation
A people holy to the Lord (Exod. 22:31; Deut. 7:6; 26:19; 28:9); you are holy to the Lord (Deut. 14:2; Ezra 8:28); a holy people (Exod. 19:6; Isa. 62:12); a holy nation (1 Pet. 2:9); all the congregation is holy (Num. 16:3); the temple of God is holy, which temple you are (1 Cor. 3:17); that the church should be without spot or blemish, holy and blameless (Eph. 5:27).

B2 Holy people in general
The tassels are to remind you to be holy to your God (Num. 15:40); he whom the Lord chooses is holy (Num. 16:7); that we should be holy and blameless before him (Eph. 1:4); as God's chosen ones, holy and beloved (Col. 3:12); the unmarried woman seeks to be holy in body and spirit (1 Cor. 7:34); men should pray, lifting up holy hands (1 Tim. 2:8); he will be a vessel for honour, sanctified, useful (2 Tim. 2:21); an elder [overseer] must be holy (Titus 1:8); blessed and holy is he who has a part in the first resurrection (Rev. 20:6); let the one who is holy still be holy (Rev. 22:11); the Nazirite will be holy to the Lord (Num. 6:5); he disciplines us that we may share his holiness (Heb. 12:10); that we might serve him in holiness and righteousness (Luke 1:75); let each one know how to possess his vessel in holiness and honour (1 Thess. 4:4); perfecting holiness in the fear of God (2 Cor. 7:1); present your bodies as a living sacrifice, holy and pleasing to God (Rom. 12:1); God saved us and called us with a holy calling (2 Tim. 1:9); without holiness no one will see the Lord (Heb. 12:14); what sort of people ought you to be in holiness and godliness? (2 Pet. 3:11).

B3 Making people holy
I am the Lord who sanctifies you (Exod. 31:13; Lev. 20:8; Ezek. 20:12); a priest is holy to his God (Lev. 21:7); sanctify yourselves (2 Chr. 35:6); holiness befits your house (Ps. 93:5); worship the Lord in holy adornment (1 Chr. 16:29); I the Lord sanctify Israel (Ezek. 37:28); levery male that opens the womb shall be holy to the Lord (Luke 2:23); Aaron and his descendants were set apart (1 Chr. 23:13); the priests consecrated themselves (Exod. 19:22; 1 Chr. 15:14; 2 Chr. 5:11); the Levites consecrated themselves in holiness (2 Chr. 31:18); Job sanctified his children (Job 1:5); otherwise your children would be unclean, but now they are holy (1 Cor. 7:14); the unbelieving wife is sanctified through her believing husband (1 Cor. 7:14).

B4 Sanctification in Christ
This is God's will, your sanctification (1 Thess. 4:3); God did not call us to impurity but to sanctification (1 Thess. 4:7); Christ is made to us sanctification (1 Cor. 1:30); sanctification by the Spirit (2 Thess. 2:13); presenting your limbs as slaves to righteousness produces sanctification (Rom. 6:19); the fruit you get is sanctification and its end, eternal life (Rom. 6:22); through the sanctification of the Spirit (1 Pet. 1:2); may God sanctify you wholly (1 Thess. 5:23); Christ sanctified the church (Eph. 5:26); he has reconciled you to present you holy in his sight (Col. 1:22); to give you the inheritance among all those who are sanctified (Acts 20:32); he who sanctifies and they who are

sanctified are all of one (Heb. 2:11); by that will we have been sanctified through the offering of Jesus Christ (Heb. 10:10); by one offering he has perfected those who are sanctified (Heb. 10:14); the blood of the covenant by which he was sanctified (Heb. 10:29); Jesus suffered outside the gate to sanctify the people with his own blood (Heb. 13:12); those sanctified by faith in me (Acts 26:18); you were sanctified (1 Cor. 6:11).

B5 The saints

B5a The saints in general
The saints on earth are the noble ones (Ps. 16:3); fear the Lord, you his saints (Ps. 34:9); many bodies of the saints were raised (Matt. 27:52); the saints of the Most High will possess the kingdom for ever (Dan. 7:18); the perseverance of the saints (Rev. 14:12); God's inheritance in the saints (Eph. 1:18); the prayers of the saints (Rev. 5:8; 8:3-4); fine linen is the righteous deeds of the saints (Rev. 19:8); the coming of our Lord Jesus with his saints (1 Thess. 3:13); when he comes to be glorified in his saints (2 Thess. 1:10).

B5b All believers are saints
Called to be saints (Rom. 1:7); called saints (1 Cor. 1:2); to all the saints (2 Cor. 1:1; Col. 1:2); to the saints (Eph. 1:1); to the saints in Christ Jesus who are in Philippi (Phil. 1:1); the churches of the saints (1 Cor. 14:33); the faith delivered to the saints (Jude 3); that you may be able to understand with all the saints (Eph. 3:18); we share in the inheritance of the saints in light (Col. 1:12); as is fitting among saints (Eph. 5:3); pray for all the saints (Eph. 6:18); the Spirit intercedes for the saints (Rom. 8:27).

B5c Practical dealings with the saints
I imprisoned many of the saints (Acts 26:10); I am the least of the saints (Eph. 3:8); why go to law before the unrighteous and not before the saints? (1 Cor. 6:1); the saints will judge the world (1 Cor. 6:2); the collection for the saints (1 Cor. 16:1); the support of the saints (2 Cor. 8:4); service to the saints (2 Cor. 9:1; Heb. 6:10); for equipping the saints (Eph. 4:12); your love for all the saints (Eph. 1:15; Col. 1:4; Philem. 5); you have refreshed the hearts of the saints (Philem. 7); washing the saints' feet (1 Tim. 5:10); that my service may be acceptable to the saints (Rom. 15:31).

B5d Warfare against the saints
The horn waged war against the saints (Dan. 7:21); making war on the saints (Rev. 13:7); they surrounded the camp of the saints (Rev. 20:9); in her was found the blood of prophets and saints (Rev. 18:24); the blood of the saints (Rev. 16:6; 17:6).

C Holy things
C1 About holy things
Make a distinction between holy and profane (Lev. 10:10); a wall, 500 reeds long and 500 broad, to divide holy from profane (Ezek. 42:20); priests must teach the difference between holy and profane (Ezek. 44:23); they made no distinction between holy and profane, clean and unclean (Ezek. 22:26); the priests must change their clothes lest they transmit holiness to the people (Ezek. 44:19); holiness is not imparted by touching holy things (Hag. 2:12); do not give dogs what is holy (Matt. 7:6); if the firstfruits are holy, so is the whole lump (Rom. 11:16); if the root is holy, so are the branches (Rom. 11:16).

CARRYING HOLY THINGS, see 273B5.

C2 Consecrating things
You told us to consecrate the mountain (Exod. 19:23); the tabernacle and its contents were consecrated (Exod. 30:29; 40:9; Lev. 8:10; Num. 7:1); sanctify my sabbaths (Ezek. 20:20); which is greater, the gold or the temple which sanctified the gold? (Matt. 23:17); which is greater, the gift or the altar which sanctifies the gift?

(Matt. 23:19); it is sanctified by the word of God and prayer (1 Tim. 4:5); I have consecrated this house by putting my name there for ever (1 Kgs. 9:3); consecrating one's house as holy to the Lord (Lev. 27:14); consecrating a field to the Lord (Lev. 27:16, 22).

C3 Holy places
Holy ground (Exod. 3:5; Josh. 5:15); the place where you are standing is holy ground (Acts 7:33); the holy portion of land for priests' houses and the sanctuary (Ezek. 45:4); a holy portion of land for the Lord (Ezek. 45:1; 48:10-20); who may stand in his holy place? (Ps. 24:3); the holy place (Heb. 9:2); the abomination of desolation standing in the holy place (Matt. 24:15); aliens have entered the holy places of the Lord's house (Jer. 51:51); Jerusalem, the holy city (Isa. 52:1); Zion, my holy mountain (Ps. 2:6); Jerusalem will be holy, with no more strangers passing through (Joel 3:17); hear the Lord from his holy temple (Mic. 1:2); the Lord is in his holy temple (Hab. 2:20); the mountain of the Lord of hosts will be called the holy mountain (Zech. 8:3); on Mount Zion will be those who escape and it will be holy (Obad. 17); the holy way (Isa. 35:8); when we were with him on the holy mountain (2 Pet. 1:18).

C4 Other holy things
The holy anointing oil (Exod. 30:25; 37:29); the incense is holy (Exod. 30:35); holy garments for glory and beauty (Exod. 28:2); holy water (Num. 5:17); the silver, gold, bronze and iron from Jericho were sacred to the Lord (Josh. 6:19); the censers of Nadab's company became holy (Num. 16:37-8); 'Holy to the Lord' engraved on a plate (Exod. 28:36; 39:30); 'Holy to the Lord' on the bells of the horses (Zech. 14:20); the holy scriptures (Rom. 1:2; 2 Tim. 3:15).

C5 Most holy things
The most holy place [holy of holies] (Exod. 26:34; Ezek. 41:4; Heb. 9:3); the veil separates between the holy and the most holy (Exod. 26:33); it shall be a most holy place by the territory of the Levites (Ezek. 48:12); the Levites shall not come near the most holy things (Ezek. 44:13); the Kohathites were to take care of the most holy things (Num. 4:4); to anoint a most holy place (Dan. 9:24); build yourselves up in your most holy faith (Jude 20); things that were most holy: the temple area (Ezek. 43:12); the bronze altar (Exod. 29:37; 40:10); the altar of incense (Exod. 30:10); the furniture of the tabernacle (Exod. 30:29; Num. 4:4, 19); the incense (Exod. 30:36); the sacrifices (Lev. 6:17, 25, 29; 7:1, 6; 10:17; 14:13; 24:9; Num. 18:9, 10; Ezek. 42:13); the cereal offering (Lev. 2:3, 10; 6:17; 10:12); the sin offering (Lev. 6:25, 29; 10:17); the guilt offering (Lev. 7:1, 6; 14:13); the bread of the Presence (Lev. 24:9); things under a ban of destruction (Lev. 27:28).

HOLY OF HOLIES, see 990B7.

D Holy sabbaths
God sanctified the seventh day (Gen. 2:3; Exod. 20:11); the sabbath is holy (Exod. 31:14); remember the sabbath day to keep it holy (Exod. 20:8; Deut. 5:12); your holy sabbath (Neh. 9:14); the Year of Jubilee is holy (Lev. 25:12).

980 Impiety
A Lack of holiness
Men will be unholy (2 Tim. 3:2); her priests profane what is holy (Zeph. 3:4); priests on the sabbath profane the sabbath (Matt. 12:5); I have never eaten anything common or unclean (Acts 10:14-15; 11:8-9); these men are neither sacrilegious nor blasphemers of our goddess (Acts 19:37); he tried to desecrate the temple (Acts 24:6); the law is for the unholy and profane (1 Tim. 1:9); everyone who profanes the sabbath must die (Exod. 31:14).

B Blasphemy

He will speak against the God of gods (Dan. 11:36); the beast opened his mouth to blaspheme God (Rev. 13:6); blasphemous names on the beast's heads (Rev. 13:1); the scarlet beast was covered with blasphemous names (Rev. 17:3); blasphemy against the Holy Spirit will not be forgiven (Matt. 12:31-2; Mark 3:28-9; Luke 12:10); when the Jews blasphemed, Paul shook out his garments (Acts 18:6); these men are neither temple robbers nor blasphemers of our goddess (Acts 19:37); the name of God is blasphemed among the Gentiles because of you (Rom. 2:24); do not the rich blaspheme that worthy name by which you were called? (Jas. 2:7); they blasphemed the name of God (Rev. 16:9); they blasphemed the God of heaven for their pain and sores (Rev. 16:11); we have heard Stephen speak blasphemy against Moses and against God (Acts 6:11); Paul tried to force the believers to blaspheme (Acts 26:11); I was formerly a blasphemer (1 Tim. 1:13); I delivered them to Satan that they may be taught not to blaspheme (1 Tim. 1:20); they said Jesus was blaspheming (Matt. 9:3; 26:65; Mark 2:7; 14:64; Luke 5:21; John 10:33, 36).

C Set apart for evil

Do not come near, for I am holier than you (Isa. 65:5); those who sanctify themselves to eat pork and mice (Isa. 66:17).

981 Worship

A Worship of God

A1 Worship God!

Worship God (Rev. 19:10; 22:9); worship the Lord your God (Deut. 6:13; Matt. 4:10; Luke 4:8); worship the Lord in holiness (Ps. 96:9); worship the Lord in holy array (1 Chr. 16:29; Ps. 29:2); let us offer acceptable worship with reverence and awe (Heb. 12:28); worship him who made the heaven and earth, the sea and springs of water (Rev. 14:7).

A2 How to worship God

The Father seeks those who will worship him in spirit and truth (John 4:23); we are the circumcision who worship by the Spirit of God (Phil. 3:3); you say Jerusalem is where one should worship (John 4:20-1); we worship what we know, for salvation is from the Jews (John 4:22); present your bodies as a living sacrifice, which is your spiritual worship (Rom. 12:1); the first covenant had regulations for worship (Heb. 9:1).

A3 How not to worship

In vain do they worship me, teaching the precepts of men (Matt. 15:9; Mark 7:7); they sacrificed to Baal and burned incense to idols (Hos. 11:2); do not worship or serve their gods (Exod. 23:24); do not worship another god (Exod. 34:14); you worship what you do not know (John 4:22); what you worship in ignorance, this I proclaim to you (Acts 17:23); this man persuades people to worship God contrary to the law (Acts 18:13).

A4 Those who worshipped God

We will worship and return (Gen. 22:5); Israel worshipped, leaning on his staff (Gen. 47:31; Heb. 11:21); Moses made haste to bow to the earth and worship (Exod. 34:8); Gideon worshipped God (Judg. 7:15); Saul worshipped the Lord (1 Sam. 15:31); David went into the house of the Lord and worshipped (2 Sam. 12:20); Hezekiah bowed down and worshipped (2 Chr. 29:29); Job fell to the ground and worshipped (Job 1:20); while they were worshipping the Lord and fasting (Acts 13:2); I went up to Jerusalem to worship (Acts 24:11); the Ethiopian eunuch had come to Jerusalem to worship (Acts 8:27); the God to whom I belong and whom I worship (Acts 27:23); the 24 elders fell on their faces and worshipped God (Rev. 11:16; 19:4); the angels fell on their faces and worshipped (Rev. 7:11).

A5 Worshipping Christ

We saw his star in the east and have come to worship him (Matt. 2:2); tell me that I may go and worship him (Matt. 2:8); they fell down and worshipped him (Matt. 2:11); they worshipped him (Matt. 14:33); they clasped his feet and worshipped him (Matt. 28:9); they worshipped him, but some doubted (Matt. 28:17); let all God's angels worship him (Heb. 1:6); the man born blind worshipped Jesus (John 9:38).

B Worshipping others

B1 Worshipping angels

I fell down to worship at the feet of the angel (Rev. 19:10; 22:8-9); insisting on the worship of angels (Col. 2:18).

B2 Worshipping the devil

All this I will give you if you will bow down and worship me (Matt. 4:9; Luke 4:7); men worshipped the dragon and the beast (Rev. 13:4); all inhabitants of the earth will worship the beast (Rev. 13:8); it makes all the earth worship the first beast (Rev. 13:12); if anyone worships the beast and his image (Rev. 14:9); they did not turn from worshipping demons (Rev. 9:20); those who worship the beast and its image (Rev. 14:11); they had not worshipped the beast (Rev. 20:4).

B3 Worshipping men

Nebuchadnezzar made an offering with incense to Daniel (Dan. 2:46); the crowd wanted to offer sacrifices to Barnabas and Paul (Acts 14:13); Cornelius tried to worship Peter (Acts 10:25-6); with difficulty they restrained the people from sacrificing to them (Acts 14:18).

B4 Worshipping material things

They have worshipped the molten calf and sacrificed to it (Exod. 32:8); they worshipped the creature rather than the creator (Rom. 1:25); she whom all Asia and the world worship (Acts 19:27); do not worship idols (Exod. 20:5); they sacrifice to their net (Hab. 1:16). WORSHIPPING ON THE HIGH PLACES, see 209D3. WORSHIPPING SUN, MOON AND STARS, see 420A4. WORSHIPPING OTHER GODS, see 966D.

C Sacrifices

C1 Regulating sacrifices

Bring an offering from the herd or the flock (Lev. 1:2); the types of sacrificial offerings listed (Lev. 7:37); from eight days old an animal may be sacrificed (Lev. 22:27); set apart to the Lord every firstborn male animal (Exod. 13:2); offer on an altar of earth your burnt offering, peace offering and cattle (Exod. 20:24); every grain offering, sin offering and guilt offering was for the priests (Num. 18:9); money from burnt offerings and sin offerings was for the priests (2 Kgs. 12:16); the offerings are the inheritance of the tribe of Levi (Josh. 13:14); a deformed animal is acceptable as a freewill offering (Lev. 22:23); that they may present right offerings to the Lord (Mal. 3:3); be reconciled to your brother and then present your offering (Matt. 5:24).

C2 About sacrifices

We must have animals to sacrifice (Exod. 10:25); I will offer sacrifices with shouts of joy (Ps. 27:6); I will sacrifice to you with the voice of thanksgiving (Jonah 2:9); those who have made a covenant with me by sacrifice (Ps. 50:5); present the offering Moses commanded (Matt. 8:4; Luke 5:14); did you bring me sacrifices for 40 years in the wilderness? (Amos 5:25; Acts 7:42); if the Lord has stirred you up against me, let him accept an offering (1 Sam. 26:19); the gifts you sent are a fragrant aroma, an acceptable sacrifice (Phil. 4:18).

C3 About offering sacrifices

Every high priest offers gifts and sacrifices for sins (Heb. 5:1); he offers sacrifices for his own sins as well as for the sins of the people (Heb. 5:3); the same sacrifices offered continually (Heb. 10:1); are not those who eat the sacrifices sharers in the altar? (1 Cor. 10:18); which is greater, the gift or the altar which sanctifies the gift? (Matt. 23:19); what you would have gained from me is Corban, an offering (Mark 7:11).

C4 Those offering sacrifices

Cain brought an offering of the fruit of the ground (Gen. 4:3); Abel brought some of the firstborn of his flocks and their fat portions (Gen. 4:4); by faith Abel offered a better sacrifice than Cain (Heb. 11:4); Jacob offered a sacrifice (Gen. 31:54); Israel offered sacrifices (Gen. 46:1); let us take a three-day journey into the desert to offer sacrifices (Exod. 3:18; 5:3); Balaam and Balak offered a bull and a ram on each altar (Num. 23:2); Elkanah went to sacrifice to the Lord in Shiloh (1 Sam. 1:3); Samuel went to sacrifice (1 Sam. 9:12); Absalom offered sacrifices (2 Sam. 15:12); Solomon and the people offered sacrifices (2 Chr. 7:4); Solomon offered sacrifices on the high places (1 Kgs. 3:3-4); Elisha sacrificed the oxen (1 Kgs. 19:21); they have saved the best animals to sacrifice (1 Sam. 15:15, 21); the Egyptians will worship with sacrifice and burnt offering (Isa. 19:21).

C5 Large numbers of sacrifices

Every six steps he sacrificed a bull and a calf (2 Sam. 6:13); they offered innumerable sacrifices (1 Kgs. 8:5; 2 Chr. 5:6); Solomon offered 22 000 oxen and 120 000 sheep (1 Kgs. 8:62-3; 2 Chr. 7:5); Judah sacrificed 700 oxen and 7000 sheep (2 Chr. 15:11); 1000 bulls, 1000 rams and 1000 lambs sacrificed (1 Chr. 29:21).

C6 Right sacrifices

Offer right sacrifices and trust in the Lord (Ps. 4:5); you will delight in right sacrifices (Ps. 51:19); a drink offering on the sacrificial offering of your faith (Phil. 2:17); the heavenly things themselves needed better sacrifices (Heb. 9:23); he appeared in order to put away sin by the sacrifice of himself (Heb. 9:26); the sacrifices of God are a broken spirit (Ps. 51:17); to do what is right and just is more acceptable to the Lord than sacrifice (Prov. 21:3); has the Lord as great delight in sacrifice as in obedience? (1 Sam. 15:22); I desire compassion rather than sacrifice (Matt. 9:13; 12:7); to obey is better than sacrifice (1 Sam. 15:22); I desire steadfast love and the knowledge of God, not sacrifice (Hos. 6:6); to love God and one's neighbour is more than all sacrifices (Mark 12:33); to do good and to share are sacrifices which please God (Heb. 13:16); he who offers a sacrifice of thanksgiving honours me (Ps. 50:23); thanksgiving will please the Lord better than an ox (Ps. 69:31); bring a sacrifice of praise and thanksgiving (Heb. 13:15); present your bodies as living sacrifices (Rom. 12:1); offering spiritual sacrifices acceptable to God (1 Pet. 2:5); priestly service that the offering of the Gentiles might be acceptable (Rom. 15:16).

C7 Alternative sacrifices

C7a Human sacrifices

Shall I give my firstborn for my transgression? (Mic. 6:7); Jephthah offered up his daughter as a burnt offering (Judg. 11:31-9); the king of Moab sacrificed his son on the city wall (2 Kgs. 3:27); they burned their sons in the fire to Baal (Jer. 19:5); they burned their children in the fire to the gods of Sepharvaim (2 Kgs. 17:31); they slaughtered their children for their idols (Ezek. 23:39); the blood of your children whom you gave to the idols (Ezek. 16:36); you slaughtered my children and offered them to idols (Ezek. 16:21); they

sacrificed sons and daughters to demons (Ps. 106:37-8); Pilate mixed their blood with their sacrifices (Luke 13:1); God's great sacrifice, for birds and beasts to eat men (Ezek. 39:17-20); offer your son Isaac as a burnt offering (Gen. 22:2); by faith Abraham offered Isaac as a sacrifice (Heb. 11:17); when Abraham offered up Isaac on the altar (Jas. 2:21).

C7b Sacrificing amiss

Do not offer burnt offering, cereal offering or libation on the incense altar (Exod. 30:9); offering a burnt offering not at the tent of meeting (Lev. 17:8-9); they burnt sacrifices on the rooftops to all the host of heaven (Jer. 19:13); Saul offered the burnt offering (1 Sam. 13:9-12); the people sacrificed on the high places (1 Kgs. 3:2; 2 Kgs. 12:3); they burned sacrifices on the mountains (Isa. 65:7); Ahaz sacrificed on the high places and under every green tree (2 Kgs. 16:4; 2 Chr. 28:4); they sacrifice in gardens (Isa. 65:3); Ahaz sacrificed on the altar from Damascus (2 Kgs. 16:12-15); cursed be the cheat who vows a male animal yet sacrifices a blemished animal (Mal. 1:14).

C7c Sacrificing to other gods

Do not sacrifice to other gods (2 Kgs. 17:35); they shall no longer sacrifice to satyrs (Lev. 17:7); they sacrificed to other gods which they had not known (Jer. 19:4); burning sacrifices and pouring out libations to the queen of heaven (Jer. 44:17-18); sacrifices and burnt offerings to Baal (2 Kgs. 10:24); a sacrifice to Dagon (Judg. 16:23); the Gentiles sacrifice to demons, not to God (1 Cor. 10:20); if anyone says, 'This has been offered in sacrifice' (1 Cor. 10:28).

C8 Enough of sacrifices

C8a Sacrifices not needed

Sacrifice and offering you did not desire (Ps. 40:6; Heb. 10:5); you do not delight in sacrifice (Ps. 51:16); you took no pleasure in burnt offering (Heb. 10:6, 8); I have no need of a bull from your stall (Ps. 50:9); I have more than enough of burnt offerings (Isa. 1:11-13); add your burnt offerings to the sacrifices and eat the meat (Jer. 7:21-3); I desire mercy and not sacrifice (Matt. 12:7).

C8b Sacrifices not effective

Gifts and sacrifices are offered which cannot make the consciences perfect (Heb. 9:9); your sacrifices are not acceptable to me (Jer. 6:20); I will not accept your offerings (Amos 5:22); I will accept no offering from your hands (Mal. 1:10); God no longer regards your offering (Mal. 2:13); the Lord detests the sacrifice of the wicked (Prov. 15:8); the Lord had no regard for Cain and his offering (Gen. 4:5); Eli's iniquity will not be atoned for by sacrifice (1 Sam. 3:14); one fate comes to him who sacrifices and him who does not (Eccles. 9:2).

C8c Sacrifices terminated

For half of the week he will put an end to sacrifice and offering (Dan. 9:27); Israel will be many days without king, sacrifice or pillar (Hos. 3:4); where there is forgiveness there is no longer any offering for sin (Heb. 10:18); if we sin wilfully there no longer remains a sacrifice for sins (Heb. 10:26).

D Types of sacrifice

D1 Fire-offerings

It is a burnt offering, a fire-offering (Exod. 29:18); a fire-offering of soothing aroma (Lev. 2:2); leaven and honey must not be used in a fire-offering (Lev. 2:11); it is the priests' share of the fire-offerings (Lev. 6:17-18).

D2 Burnt offerings

D2a Regulations for the burnt offering

The law of burnt offerings (Lev. 1:3-17; 6:8-13; 7:37); a burnt offering must be without defect (Lev. 1:3-17; 7:37); bring your burnt offerings to the place God will choose (Deut. 12:6); offering the burnt offering with song (2 Chr. 29:27-8).

D2b The regular burnt offerings

The continual burnt offering (Exod. 29:42; Num. 28:23; Neh. 10:33; Ezek. 46:15); each morning (Ezek. 46:13-15); two lambs as a daily burnt offering, morning and evening (Exod. 29:38-42; Num. 28:3-8; 2 Chr. 8:13; Ezra 3:3); he will abolish the daily sacrifice (Dan. 11:31; 12:11); the continual burnt offering was taken away (Dan. 8:11-12); for how long does the vision about the regular burnt offering apply? (Dan. 8:13); may the lifting of my hands be as the evening offering (Ps. 141:2); each sabbath two extra lambs (Num. 28:9-10; 2 Chr. 8:13); a burnt offering at the start of every month (Num. 28:11-14; 2 Chr. 8:13); new moon (Neh. 10:33).

D2c Other references to burnt offerings

God will provide a lamb for a burnt offering (Gen. 22:8); I will come into your house with burnt offerings (Ps. 66:13); Solomon offered 1000 burnt offerings (2 Chr. 1:6); Solomon offered daily burnt offerings (2 Chr. 8:12-13); you took no pleasure in burnt offerings and sin offerings (Heb. 10:6, 8); Lebanon's beasts would not be enough for a burnt offering (Isa. 40:16).

D3 Cereal offerings and libations

Instructions on the cereal offering (Lev. 2:1-16; 6:14-18); cereal offerings belong to the priests (Lev. 7:9-10; 10:12-13; Num. 18:9); the continual cereal offering (Num. 4:16); a cereal offering morning by morning (Ezek. 46:14); Solomon offered cereal offerings (1 Kgs. 8:64); one offers a grain offering and one offers pig's blood (Isa. 66:3); they poured out their libations at every hill or tree (Ezek. 20:28); Jacob poured a drink offering on the pillar (Gen. 35:14); perhaps he will leave a cereal offering and libation (Joel 2:14); I will not pour out their libations of blood (Ps. 16:4); I am being poured out like a drink offering (Phil. 2:17; 2 Tim. 4:6).

D4 Peace offerings

Instructions on the peace offering (Lev. 3:1-17; 7:11-21, 29-34); a portion of peace offerings to be eaten by the priests (Exod. 29:28; Lev. 10:14); animals killed for food are to be sacrificed as peace offerings (Lev. 17:5); I will not look at your peace offerings (Amos 5:22).

THANK-OFFERINGS, see 907A.

D5 Sin offerings

D5a About the sin offering

Regulations for the sin offering (Lev. 4:1-35; 5:6-13; 6:25-30); the sin offering to make atonement for Israel (Neh. 10:33); burn the sin offering outside the camp (Exod. 29:14); a pair of turtledoves or two young pigeons (Luke 2:24); you took no pleasure in burnt offerings and sin offerings (Heb. 10:6); you did not desire burnt offerings and sin offerings (Heb. 10:8); blood of the sin offering brought into the holy place by the high priest (Heb. 13:11); the high priest offers sacrifices for his own sins as well as for the sins of the people (Heb. 5:3).

D5b Christ the sin offering

God sent his own Son to be a sin offering (Rom. 8:3); he offered himself as a sacrifice for sins once for all (Heb. 7:27); Christ was once offered to take away sins (Heb. 9:28); Christ offered one sacrifice for sins (Heb. 10:12); Christ gave himself for us, a sacrifice to God (Eph. 5:2); the offering of the body of Jesus Christ (Heb. 10:10); Christ offered himself without blemish to God (Heb. 9:14).

D6 Guilt offerings

Instructions on the guilt offering (Lev. 7:1-7); guilt offerings belong to the priests (Num. 18:9); guilt offering for sin (Lev. 5:15-16); for a cleansed leper (Lev. 14:12-14); for a defiled Nazirite (Num. 6:12); the suffering servant will be a guilt offering (Isa. 53:10).

D7 Wave offerings

The wave offering (Exod. 29:24); the Levites were presented as a wave offering (Num. 8:11); wave the sheaf of firstfruits (Lev. 23:11); waving the cereal offering of jealousy (Num. 5:25); loaves for a wave offering (Lev. 23:17); wave offerings to be eaten by the priests (Lev. 10:15).

982 Idolatry

A Idols

A1 Nature of idols

Gods of wood and stone (Deut. 28:36); he nails down an idol so that it will not topple (Isa. 41:7); he says gods made with hands are no gods (Acts 19:26); their idols are silver and gold, made by the hands of men (Ps. 115:4-8; 135:15); we should not think that God is like silver and gold, an image made by man (Acts 17:29); the idol is made of materials by men (Isa. 40:19-20; 44:12-17; 46:6; Jer. 10:3-5, 8-9); they have worshipped the works of their own hands (Jer. 1:16); a workman made it, it is not God (Hos. 8:6); with part of the wood he makes a god and worships it (Isa. 44:15, 17); they hire a goldsmith to make an idol (Isa. 46:6); idols skilfully made of silver, the work of a craftsman (Hos. 13:2); we will no more say 'Our God' to the work of our hands (Hos. 14:3).

MAN-MADE GODS, see 966B.

A2 Idols are useless

Their idols are borne by beasts of burden (Isa. 46:1-2); all who make idols are nothing and the things they treasure are worthless (Isa. 44:9-10); of what value is an idol, since man has carved it? (Hab. 2:18-19); their molten images are empty wind (Isa. 41:29); his images are worthless (Jer. 10:15); his molten images are false, there is no breath in them (Jer. 10:14; 51:17); you were led astray to dumb idols (1 Cor. 12:2); can idols give rain? (Jer. 14:22); they can do no harm, nor can they do good (Jer. 10:3-5); surely they were in Gilead with a worthless idol (Hos. 12:11); we preach the gospel that you should turn from these vain things (Acts 14:15); an idol has no real existence (1 Cor. 8:4); do I mean that an idol is anything? (1 Cor. 10:19).

TRUSTING IN IDOLS, see 485E2.

A3 Particular idols

Idols of gold, silver, brass, stone and wood (Rev. 9:20); Rachel took Laban's household gods (Gen. 31:34-7); Aaron made an idol in the form of a calf (Exod. 32:4); they made a molten image (Deut. 9:12); they made a calf and offered a sacrifice to the idol (Acts 7:41); Gideon made an ephod of gold (Judg. 8:27); Micah made an ephod and teraphim (Judg. 17:3-5); Jeroboam made two golden calves (1 Kgs. 12:28-9; 2 Chr. 13:8); they made molten images and two calves (2 Kgs. 17:16); Samaria and her idols (Isa. 10:10-11); Ahaz made molten images for the Baals (2 Chr. 28:2); King Nebuchadnezzar made an image of gold (Dan. 3:1).

B Idol-worship

B1 Nature of idolatry

Idolaters have no knowledge (Isa. 45:20); they exchanged the glory of God for an image (Ps. 106:20; Rom. 1:23); idolatry is a deed of the flesh (Gal. 5:20); some, accustomed to idols, eat food as really offered to an idol (1 Cor. 8:7); the covetous are idolaters (Eph. 5:5); greed is idolatry (Col. 3:5); disobedience is as idolatry (1 Sam. 15:23); you who abhor idols, do you rob temples? (Rom. 2:22).

B2 Idolatry in general

If he lifts up his eyes to the idols (Ezek. 18:12); let every one of you serve his idols (Ezek. 20:39); let us be like the nations, serving wood and stone (Ezek. 20:32); those who cling to vain idols will abandon their loyalty to them (Jonah 2:8); if someone sees you who have knowledge at table in an idol's temple (1 Cor. 8:10); there you will worship man-made gods of wood and stone (Deut. 4:28).

B3 Specific idolatry
They feared the Lord and served their idols (2 Kgs. 17:41); they played the harlot after their idols (Ezek. 6:9); you sacrificed your sons and daughters to the idols (Ezek. 16:20-1); these men have set up their idols in their hearts (Ezek. 14:3-4); he shakes the arrows, consults the idols, looks at the liver (Ezek. 21:21); they consult a wooden idol (Hos. 4:12); they worshipped the works of their own hands (Jer. 1:16); their land is full of idols (Isa. 2:8); they set up an image in honour of the beast (Rev. 13:14); those who had worshipped the image of the beast (Rev. 19:20); they did not forsake the idols of Egypt (Ezek. 20:8); the Danites set up the graven image (Judg. 18:30-1); they made a calf and offered a sacrifice to the idol (Acts 7:41); the worship of the golden calves at Bethel and Dan (2 Kgs. 10:29); Manasseh put the image he had made in God's temple (2 Kgs. 21:7; 2 Chr. 33:7); Molech and Rephan, the idols you made to worship (Acts 7:42-3); Paul was provoked to see Athens full of idols (Acts 17:16); they did not repent of their idolatry (Rev. 9:20).

B4 Food offered to idols
Instructions concerning food offered to idols (1 Cor. 8:1-13; 10:14-33); Gentiles warned to abstain from food sacrificed to idols (Acts 15:20, 29; 21:25); making their sons pass through the fire as food for their idols (Ezek. 23:37); eating sacrifices to other gods (Exod. 34:15; Num. 25:2); idolaters, sitting down to eat and drink (Exod. 32:6; 1 Cor. 10:7); teaching God's servants to eat food offered to idols (Rev. 2:14, 20).

B5 Not worshipping idols
He does not lift up his eyes to the idols (Ezek. 18:15); causing those who do not worship the image of the beast to be killed (Rev. 13:15); they neither serve your gods nor worship the image of gold (Dan. 3:12); you will no longer profane my name with your idols (Ezek. 20:39); let the time that is past suffice for idolatries (1 Pet. 4:3).

C Against idolatry

C1 God opposes idolatry
They made him jealous with their graven images (Ps. 78:58); the image of jealousy, which provokes to jealousy (Ezek. 8:3); they provoked the Lord to anger with their idols (1 Kgs. 16:13); the hearts of Israel are estranged from me through their idols (Ezek. 14:5); shall I not do to Jerusalem and her images as I did to Samaria and her images? (Isa. 10:11); I hate those who cling to worthless idols (Ps. 31:6); I will cut off the name of the idolatrous priests along with the priests (Zeph. 1:4).

C2 Avoiding idolatry
Do not make idols (Exod. 20:4; Lev. 19:4; Deut. 4:16); do not make molten gods (Exod. 34:17; Lev. 19:4); do not defile yourselves with their idols (Ezek. 20:18); I will cleanse you from your filthiness and your idols (Ezek. 36:25); these men do not serve your gods or worship the golden image (Dan. 3:12); those who had not worshipped the image of the beast (Rev. 20:4); do not worship idols (Exod. 20:5; Deut. 5:9); keep yourselves from idols (1 John 5:21); do not be idolaters as some of them were (1 Cor. 10:7); flee from idolatry (1 Cor. 10:14); what agreement has the temple of God with idols? (2 Cor. 6:16); how you turned to God from idols (1 Thess. 1:9); do not associate with a 'brother' who is an idolater (1 Cor. 5:11).

C3 Abandoning idols
The images of their gods you are to burn in the fire (Deut. 7:25); Asa removed the idols (1 Kgs. 15:12; 2 Chr. 15:8); Hezekiah broke in pieces the bronze snake Moses had made (2 Kgs. 18:4); Josiah removed the horses that the kings of Judah had dedicated to the sun (2 Kgs. 23:11); Josiah removed the teraphim and idols (2 Kgs. 23:24); Manasseh removed the idol (2 Chr. 33:15); all her idols will be smashed (Mic. 1:7); the Philistines abandoned their idols (2 Sam. 5:21); men will throw away their idols of silver and gold (Isa. 2:20); every one of you will reject the idols your hands have made (Isa. 31:7); the images of Babylon's gods are shattered (Isa. 21:9); I will destroy the idols of Egypt (Ezek. 30:13); I will cut off the names of idols from the land (Zech. 13:2).

BURNING IDOLS, see 381D5.

C4 Fate of idolaters
I will put your corpses on the corpses of your idols (Lev. 26:30); I will lay the dead bodies of the sons of Israel in front of their idols (Ezek. 6:5); those who trust in idols will be put to shame (Isa. 42:17); all makers of idols will be put to shame (Isa. 45:16); let idolaters be ashamed (Ps. 97:7); cursed is the man who carves an image or casts an idol (Deut. 27:15); if anyone worships the beast and his image (Rev. 14:9, 11); sores on those who worshipped the image of the beast (Rev. 16:2); idolaters will not inherit the kingdom of God (1 Cor. 6:9); idolaters will end in the lake of fire (Rev. 21:8); idolaters will be outside the city (Rev. 22:15).

983 Sorcery

A Sorcery in general
Sorcery is a deed of the flesh (Gal. 5:20); rebellion is as the sin of divination (1 Sam. 15:23); sorcerers will end in the lake of fire (Rev. 21:8); outside the city are sorcerers (Rev. 22:15).

B Practice of sorcery

B1 Divination
I have learned by divination that the Lord has blessed me through you (Gen. 30:27); is not this the cup my master uses for divination? (Gen. 44:5); do you not know I can find things out by divination? (Gen. 44:15); Balaam the diviner (Josh. 13:22); they took the fee for divination to Balaam (Num. 22:7); they practised divination and enchantments (2 Kgs. 17:17); Manasseh practised sorcery and divination (2 Kgs. 21:6; 2 Chr. 33:6); they practise divination like the Philistines (Isa. 2:6); he shakes the arrows, consults the idols, looks at the liver (Ezek. 21:21); the Philistines called for priests and diviners (1 Sam. 6:2-9); let your astrologers save you (Isa. 47:13); the Lord will take away the soothsayer and the elder (Isa. 3:2); a girl with a spirit of divination (Acts 16:16).

B2 Magic
Pharaoh called his magicians (Gen. 41:8); I told my magicians (Gen. 41:24); the Egyptian magicians did the same by their secret arts (Exod. 7:11, 22; 8:7); the magicians tried to produce gnats by their magic (Exod. 8:18); the king summoned the magicians, enchanters, sorcerers and astrologers (Dan. 2:2); Daniel chief of the magicians, enchanters, Chaldeans and diviners (Dan. 5:11); for a long time Simon has astonished them with his magic (Acts 8:11); many who had practised magic burnt their books (Acts 19:19); magi from the east (Matt. 2:1); Elymas the magician (Acts 13:8); nations were deceived by the sorcery of Babylon (Rev. 18:23); they did not repent of their sorceries (Rev. 9:21); in spite of your sorceries and spells (Isa. 47:9).

C Avoid sorcery

Do not allow a sorceress to live (Exod. 22:18); do not practise divination or sorcery (Lev. 19:26; Deut. 18:10); woe to the women who sew magic charms on their wrists (Ezek. 13:18); how can there be peace as long as the witchcraft of Jezebel abounds? (2 Kgs. 9:22); who has bewitched you? (Gal. 3:1); do not listen to your diviners, dreamers, soothsayers or sorcerers (Jer. 27:9).

D Sorcery ineffective

There is no sorcery against Jacob, no divination against Israel (Num. 23:23); the sorcerers could not stand before Moses because of the boils (Exod. 9:11); Balaam did not resort to sorcery as at other times (Num. 24:1); no wise men, enchanters, magicians nor diviners can reveal the mystery (Dan. 2:27); it will be darkness for you, without divination (Mic. 3:6); God makes fools of diviners (Isa. 44:25).

984 Occultism

The Egyptians will consult the spirits of the dead, the mediums and spiritists (Isa. 19:3); Saul calling up the dead through a medium (1 Sam. 28:7-14; 1 Chr. 10:13); Manasseh dealt with mediums and spiritists (2 Kgs. 21:6; 2 Chr. 33:6); do not turn to mediums or seek out spiritists (Lev. 19:31; 20:6); mediums and spiritists are to be stoned (Lev. 20:27); let no one be a medium or spiritist or consult the dead (Deut. 18:11); why consult the dead on behalf of the living? (Isa. 8:19); I have not offered the tithe to the dead (Deut. 26:14); Saul had expelled the mediums and spiritists (1 Sam. 28:3, 9); Josiah got rid of the mediums and spiritists (2 Kgs. 23:24).

985 The church

A The church universal

On this rock I will build my church (Matt. 16:18); the assembly of the firstborn (Heb. 12:23); Christ is the head of the church (Eph. 1:22; 5:23; Col. 1:18); his body, the church (Col. 1:24); Christ loved the church and gave himself up for her (Eph. 5:25); everyone nourishes and cherishes his own flesh, as Christ does the church (Eph. 5:29); the church of God which he purchased with his own blood (Acts 20:28); the wisdom of God made known to principalities through the church (Eph. 3:10); God has appointed in the church apostles etc. (1 Cor. 12:28); Christ cleansed the church with the washing of water with the word (Eph. 5:26-7); the household of God, the church of the living God (1 Tim. 3:15); I persecuted the church of God (1 Cor. 15:9; Gal. 1:13); as to zeal, a persecutor of the church (Phil. 3:6); Paul laid the church waste (Acts 8:3); the church throughout Judea, Galilee and Samaria had peace (Acts 9:31); prayer was made by the church (Acts 12:5); do you despise the church of God? (1 Cor. 11:22); give no offense to the church of God (1 Cor. 10:32).

THE CHURCH AS CHRIST S BODY, see 319A8b.

B The local church

B1 All local churches

All the churches will know that I am he who searches mind and heart (Rev. 2:23); the churches of God have no other practice (1 Cor. 11:16); as I teach in every church (1 Cor. 4:17); as I direct in every church (1 Cor. 7:17); as in all the churches (1 Cor. 14:33); I, Jesus, have sent my angel with this testimony to the churches (Rev. 22:16); Paul strengthened the churches (Acts 15:41); the churches were strengthened (Acts 16:5); concern for all the churches (2 Cor. 11:28); let the women keep silence in the churches (1 Cor. 14:34); not only I, but all the churches give thanks to Prisca and Aquila (Rom. 16:4); the brother who is famous among all the churches for preaching the gospel (2 Cor. 8:18); he has been appointed by the churches to travel with us in this gracious work (2 Cor. 8:19); I robbed other churches, taking pay from them (2 Cor. 11:8); we boast of you among the churches of God (2 Thess. 1:4); how were you less favoured than the other churches? (2 Cor. 12:13); no church except you shared with me in giving and receiving (Phil. 4:15).

B2 Each local church

They appointed elders in every church (Acts 14:23); call for the elders of the church (Jas. 5:14); if a man cannot manage his own household, how can he care for the church of God? (1 Tim. 3:5); when you come together as a church (1 Cor. 11:18); he who prophesies edifies the church (1 Cor. 14:4); seek to excel in building up the church (1 Cor. 14:12); it is shameful for a woman to speak in church (1 Cor. 14:35); let the church not be burdened (1 Tim. 5:16); if he refuses to listen to the church (Matt. 18:17).

B3 Particular local churches

The churches in Judea (Gal. 1:22; 1 Thess. 2:14); the churches of the Gentiles (Rom. 16:4); the grace of God in the churches of Macedonia (2 Cor. 8:1); the seven churches in Asia (Rev. 1:4, 11); the church in Jerusalem (Acts 11:22); the apostles, elders and the whole church chose men to send to Antioch (Acts 15:22); the church in Antioch (Acts 11:26); Paul greeted the church in Caesarea (Acts 18:22); the church in Cenchrea (Rom. 16:1); the church of the Laodiceans (Col. 4:16); as I directed the churches of Galatia (1 Cor. 16:1); greet Nympha and the church in her house (Col. 4:15); the church in their house (Rom. 16:5; 1 Cor. 16:19); to the church in your house (Philem. 2).

986 Priests

A Priests in general

A1 About priests

Regulations for the priests (Lev. 21:1-24; Ezek. 44:15-31); the priesthood is the inheritance of the Levites (Josh. 18:7); no tax to be levied on priests or Levites (Ezra 7:24); Nob, the city of priests (1 Sam. 22:19); a count of the priests (Ezra 2:36-9; Neh. 7:39-42); God makes priests go barefoot (Job 12:19); no one with a defect could act as priest (Lev. 21:17-20, 21); a priest must not defile himself by going near a dead body (Lev. 21:1; Ezek. 44:25); I will raise up for myself a faithful priest (1 Sam. 2:35); may your priests be clothed with salvation (2 Chr. 6:41); may your priests be clothed with righteousness (Ps. 132:9); I will clothe her priests with salvation (Ps. 132:16); I will fill the soul of the priests with abundance (Jer. 31:14); a change in the priesthood requires a change in the law (Heb. 7:12); the former priests were prevented by death from continuing in office (Heb. 7:23).

ANOINTING PRIESTS, see 357B2.

KILLING PRIESTS, see 362E1a.

PRIESTLY INHERITANCE, see 777C3.

A2 Aaron chosen as priest

Aaron and his sons will serve me as priests (Exod. 28:1); anoint Aaron and his sons and consecrate them to serve me as priests (Exod. 30:30); only the descendants of Aaron could burn incense (Num. 16:40); a covenant of perpetual priesthood (Exod. 40:15; Num. 25:13); Aaron's sons make atonement (1 Chr. 6:49); do you seek the priesthood, Korah? (Num. 16:10); the priests of the sons of Zadok (Ezek. 48:11).

A3 Work of the priests

A3a Work of the priests in the sanctuary

The Levitical priests will never lack a man to offer burnt offerings (Jer. 33:18); temple workers eat food of the temple and those who serve at the altar have their share from the altar (1 Cor. 9:13); there are priests who

offer gifts according to the law (Heb. 8:4); the priests
go into the outer tent to perform their duties (Heb.
9:6); Eleazar had responsibility for the oil, the incense
and all the tabernacle (Num. 4:16); only the priests
could eat the bread of the presentation (Matt. 12:4;
Mark 2:26).

SACRIFICES AS FOOD FOR THE PRIESTS, see 301B6b.

A3b Other work of the priests
The priests were to blow the trumpets (Num. 10:8); the
priest had to address the people going to war (Deut.
20:2-4); priests collect the tithe (Heb. 7:5); priests were
given tax of the booty (Num. 31:28-9, 41); restitution
goes to the priest in the absence of anyone else (Num.
5:8); the priest shall enquire of the Lord by the Urim
(Num. 27:21); a teaching priest (2 Chr. 15:3); Moses
gave the law to the priests and elders (Deut. 31:9); the
law will not perish from the priests (Jer. 18:18); the
priests shall settle every dispute (Deut. 21:5); when a
man has leprosy, bring him to the priest (Lev. 13:9);
show yourself to the priest (Matt. 8:4; Mark 1:44; Luke
5:14; 17:14); the priest is to value a poor man (Lev. 27:8);
the priest is to value unclean animals (Lev. 27:12); the
priest is to value a house (Lev. 27:14); the priest is to
value the field (Lev. 27:23); the priests repaired the wall
of Jerusalem (Neh. 3:22, 28); the lips of a priest should
guard knowledge (Mal. 2:7).

A4 Particular priests
The Levite became his priest (Judg. 17:12-13); you have
stolen the priest (Judg. 18:24); let one of the priests
teach them (2 Kgs. 17:27-8); 12 of the leading priests
(Ezra 8:24); many of the priests were obedient to the
faith (Acts 6:7).

A5 Bad priests
The priests rule by their own authority (Jer. 5:31); the
priests were unfaithful (2 Chr. 36:14); they have defiled
the priesthood (Neh. 13:29); the priests did not say,
'Where is the Lord?' (Jer. 2:8); from prophet to priest
everyone deals falsely (Jer. 6:13); priest and prophet reel
from strong drink (Isa. 28:7); her priests profane what
is sacred (Zeph. 3:4); the law will be lost to the priest
and counsel from the elders (Ezek. 7:26); the life of a
priest ought to preserve knowledge (Mal. 2:7); a priest
passed by on the other side (Luke 10:31); her priests
have done violence to my law (Ezek. 22:26); like people,
like priest (Isa. 24:2; Hos. 4:9); her priests teach for a
fee (Mic. 3:11); O priests, you despise my name (Mal.
1:6).

A6 Deposed priests
The priests were slaughtered (1 Sam. 22:17-19);
Solomon removed Abiathar from the priesthood (1
Kgs. 2:27); the Lord has made Zephaniah high priest
instead of Jehoiada (Jer. 29:26); priests without proof
of descent were removed from the priesthood (Ezra
2:62; Neh. 7:64).

B High priests
B1 About the high priest
Regulations for the high priest (Lev. 21:10-15); Aaron
was to bear the guilt of the priesthood (Num. 18:1); the
priest makes atonement for the priests (Lev. 16:33);
every high priest acts on behalf of men in relation to
God (Heb. 5:1); every high priest is appointed to offer
gifts and sacrifices (Heb. 8:3); only the high priest goes
into the second tent once a year (Heb. 9:7); the high
priest offers sacrifices first for his own sins then for the
sins of the people (Heb. 7:27); blood of the sin offering
brought into the holy place by the high priest (Heb.
13:11); manslayers remain in the city of refuge until the
death of the high priest (Num. 35:25; Josh. 20:6); the
Lord has made Zephaniah high priest instead of
Jehoiada (Jer. 29:26).

B2 Particular high priests
B2a Unnamed high priests
They led Jesus away to the high priest (Mark 14:53;
Luke 22:54); the high priest questioned Jesus (Mark
14:60; John 18:19); the high priest adjured him (Matt.
26:63); the high priest tore his clothes (Matt. 26:65); the
high priest questioned them (Acts 5:27); the high priest
said, 'Are these things so?' (Acts 7:1); Saul went to the
high priest to ask for letters (Acts 9:1); the high priest
rose up and his associates, the Sadducees (Acts 5:17);
the high priest and his associates summoned the
council (Acts 5:21); would you revile God's high priest?
(Acts 23:4); is that how you answer the high priest?
(John 18:22).

B2b Named high priests
Those who were high priests: Aaron (Exod. 31:10; Lev.
1:7); Abiathar (1 Kgs. 2:35; Mark 2:26); Amariah (2 Chr.
19:11); Ananias (Acts 23:2); Annas and Caiaphas (Luke
3:2; Acts 4:6); Azariah son of Zadok (1 Kgs. 4:2; 1 Chr.
6:10; 2 Chr. 26:17); Caiaphas (Matt. 26:3; John 11:49;
18:13); Eleazar (Num. 20:26-8; Deut. 10:6; Josh. 14:1); Eli
(1 Sam. 1:9); Eliashib (Neh. 3:1); Hilkiah (2 Kgs. 22:4;
2 Chr. 34:9); Jehoiada (2 Kgs. 11:9; 1 Chr. 27:5; 2 Chr.
22:11; Jer. 29:26); Joshua son of Jehozadak (Hag. 1:1;
Zech. 3:1); Seraiah (2 Kgs. 25:18; Jer. 52:24); Zadok
(1 Kgs. 2:35; 1 Chr. 29:22).

B3 High-priestly family
B3a The chief priests condemning Christ
He must suffer many things from the chief priests
(Matt. 16:21; Luke 9:22); he will be delivered to the chief
priests (Matt. 20:18; Mark 10:33); rejected by the elders
and chief priests and scribes (Mark 8:31); the chief
priests and Pharisees sent officers to seize him (John
7:32); the scribes and chief priests tried to lay hands on
Jesus (Luke 20:19); Judas went to the chief priests to
betray him (Matt. 26:14; Mark 14:10; Luke 22:4); Judas
took officers from the chief priests and Pharisees (John
18:3); a mob from the chief priests and elders (Matt.
26:47; Mark 14:43); Pilate knew that the chief priests
had delivered up Jesus out of envy (Mark 15:10); when
accused by the chief priests and elders, he made no
answer (Matt. 27:12); our chief priests and rulers
delivered him up to the sentence of death (Luke 24:20);
your own nation and the chief priests have handed you
over to me (John 18:35); the chief priests and officers
cried, 'Crucify him' (John 19:6); some of the guard
went into the city and told the chief priests (Matt.
28:11).

B3b The chief priests against believers
All of the high-priestly family (Acts 4:6); they reported
what the chief priests and elders had said (Acts 4:23);
the captain of the guard and the chief priests were very
perplexed (Acts 5:24); he has authority from the chief
priests to bind all who call on your name (Acts 9:14); I
received authority from the chief priests (Acts 26:10,
12); did he not come here to bring them bound before
the high priests? (Acts 9:21); the chief priests and
leading Jews brought charges against Paul (Acts 25:2).

B3c Actions of the chief priests
The chief priests: were indignant (Matt. 21:15); asked
him of his authority (Matt. 21:23; Mark 11:27-8); plotted
to kill him (Matt. 26:3; Mark 11:18; 14:1; Luke 22:2);
sought to kill him (Luke 19:47); planned to kill Lazarus
also (John 12:10); took counsel against Jesus (Matt.
27:1); accused Jesus (Matt. 27:12; Mark 15:3; Luke 23:10);
persuaded the crowds (Matt. 27:20; Mark 15:11);
mocked him (Matt. 27:41; Mark 15:31); asked Pilate to
set a guard (Matt. 27:62-4); took counsel together
(Matt. 28:12).

B4 Christ the high priest

You are a priest for ever after the order of Melchizedek (Ps. 110:4; Heb. 5:6; 6:20; 7:17); designated by God a high priest after the order of Melchizedek (Heb. 5:10); a priest for ever (Heb. 7:3, 21); the man called the Branch will be a priest on his throne (Zech. 6:13); Jesus, the apostle and high priest of our confession (Heb. 3:1); we have a great high priest (Heb. 4:14); a great high priest over the house of God (Heb. 10:21); we have a high priest who has been tempted, yet without sin (Heb. 4:15); the law appoints weak men as high priests, but the oath appoints the Son (Heb. 7:28); Christ did not glorify himself to become high priest (Heb. 5:5); I will raise up a faithful priest (1 Sam. 2:35); a merciful and faithful high priest (Heb. 2:17); a high priest of the good things to come (Heb. 9:11); we have a high priest who sat down in heaven (Heb. 8:1); it was fitting that we should have such a high priest (Heb. 7:26).

C Non-Levitical priests

C1 Various other priests

Melchizedek was priest of God most high (Gen. 14:18; Heb. 7:1); Potiphera priest of On (Gen. 41:45); Reuel [Jethro] priest of Midian (Exod. 2:16; 3:1; 18:1); Amaziah priest of Bethel (Amos 7:10); the priest of Zeus wanted to offer sacrifices (Acts 14:13); Micah made his own son a priest (Judg. 17:5); Jeroboam appointed non-Levitical priests (1 Kgs. 12:31; 2 Chr. 11:15); Josiah sacrificing the priests of the high places (1 Kgs. 13:2; 2 Kgs. 23:20); Mattan the priest of Baal (2 Kgs. 11:18; 2 Chr. 23:17).

C2 A kingdom of priests

You will be called priests of the Lord (Isa. 61:6); he has made us a kingdom and priests (Rev. 1:6); you have made them a kingdom and priests (Rev. 5:10); a kingdom of priests (Exod. 19:6); a royal priesthood (1 Pet. 2:9); a holy priesthood (1 Pet. 2:5); they will be priests of God and of Christ (Rev. 20:6).

LEVITES, see 371B6.

987 Non-priests

A non-priest may not eat the ram of ordination (Exod. 29:33); a non-priest may not eat the sacrifices (Lev. 22:10); no non-priest could come near to burn incense (Num. 16:40); a priest's daughter married to a non-priest may not eat the sacrifices (Lev. 22:12).

GOD S PEOPLE, see 965A3.

988 Ritual

A Festivals

A1 Festivals in general

Three times a year you are to celebrate a festival (Exod. 23:14; 2 Chr. 8:13); three times a year, for the feasts of Unleavened Bread, Weeks and Booths (Deut. 16:16); three times a year your males are to appear before the Lord (Exod. 23:17); these are my appointed feasts (Lev. 23:2); Zion, city of our appointed feasts (Isa. 33:20); let no one judge you with regard to a festival, New Moon or sabbath (Col. 2:16); joy and thanksgiving in time of festival (Ps. 42:4); Jesus went up to Jerusalem for a feast of the Jews (John 5:1); I am not going up to the feast (John 7:8); Jesus went up to the feast secretly (John 7:10); no one comes to Zion's appointed feasts (Lam. 1:4); I will put an end to all her feasts, new moons and sabbaths (Hos. 2:11); the Lord has caused to be forgotten appointed feast and sabbath (Lam. 2:6); I hate your festivals (Amos 5:21); I hate your new moon festivals and your appointed feasts (Isa. 1:14).

A2 Passover

KEEPING PASSOVER, see 768A.

A2a Regulations for Passover

The regulations for the Passover (Exod. 12:43-9); the Passover begins on the fourteenth day of the first month (Lev. 23:5; Num. 28:16; Ezek. 45:21); those who are unclean or on a journey may eat it in the second month (Num. 9:10-12); leftovers of the Passover are not to be kept overnight (Exod. 34:25); celebrate the feast of Unleavened Bread (Exod. 12:17); celebrate the Passover (Num. 9:2; Deut. 16:1; 2 Kgs. 23:21).

NOT KEEPING PASSOVER, see 769C.

A2b Passovers in the Old Testament

By faith Moses kept the Passover (Heb. 11:28); they left Rameses the day after the Passover (Num. 33:3); at Gilgal the Israelites celebrated the Passover (Josh. 5:10); Hezekiah sent invitations to celebrate the Passover (2 Chr. 30:1); a crowd assembled to celebrate the Feast of Unleavened Bread (2 Chr. 30:13); Josiah celebrated the Passover (2 Chr. 35:1); the exiles celebrated the Passover (Ezra 6:19).

A2c Passover in the New Testament

His parents went to Jerusalem every year at the feast of the Passover (Luke 2:41); the Passover was at hand (John 2:13; 6:4; 11:55); the feast of Unleavened Bread, called Passover, was approaching (Luke 22:1); before the feast of the Passover (John 13:1); I will keep the Passover at your house with my disciples (Matt. 26:18); on the first day of Unleavened Bread the disciples made preparations (Matt. 26:17; Mark 14:12); the day of preparation for the Passover (John 19:14); the day of Unleavened Bread on which the passover lamb was sacrificed (Luke 22:7); I have eagerly desired to eat this Passover with you (Luke 22:15); not during the feast, or the people may riot (Matt. 26:5; Mark 14:2); the governor used to free for the crowd one prisoner at the feast (Matt. 27:15, 17; Mark 15:6; John 18:39); Herod arrested Peter during the Feast of Unleavened Bread (Acts 12:3); we sailed from Philippi after the days of Unleavened Bread (Acts 20:6).

A2d Christ our Passover

Christ our passover has been sacrificed (1 Cor. 5:7); let us celebrate the feast, not with the old leaven of malice and evil (1 Cor. 5:8); the Passover fulfilled in the kingdom of God (Luke 22:16).

A3 Feast of Weeks [Pentecost]

Celebrate the feast of harvest with the firstfruits (Exod. 23:16; Lev. 23:10-14); celebrate the Feast of Weeks with the firstfruits of the wheat harvest (Exod. 34:22); count off fifty days to the day after the seventh sabbath (Lev. 23:15-16); when the day of Pentecost came (Acts 2:1); Paul tried to reach Jerusalem by Pentecost (Acts 20:16); I will stay in Ephesus until Pentecost (1 Cor. 16:8).

A4 Feast of Booths [Tabernacles]

Celebrate the feast of ingathering at the end of the year (Exod. 23:16); on the fifteenth day of the seventh month is the Feast of Tabernacles (Lev. 23:34-6; Num. 29:12-38; Deut. 16:13-15); the feast in the seventh month (1 Kgs. 8:2; 2 Chr. 5:3); they celebrated the Feast of Tabernacles (Ezra 3:4; Neh. 8:14-18); the nations will go up to Jerusalem to celebrate the Feast of Tabernacles (Zech. 14:16-19); I will make you live in tents, as at the festival (Hos. 12:9); the plague with which the Lord smites those not attending the Feast of Booths (Zech. 14:18); the Feast of Tabernacles was at hand (John 7:2); on the last day of the feast, the great day, Jesus stood up (John 7:37).

A5 Year of Jubilee

The fiftieth year will be a year of Jubilee (Lev. 25:8-12); when the year of Jubilee comes (Num. 36:4); the year of liberty (Ezek. 46:17); release from service at the year of Jubilee (Lev. 25:40); the price of a field is proportional to the time from the year of Jubilee (Lev. 27:17-18).

A6 Other festivals
Tomorrow is the New Moon festival (1 Sam. 20:5); the fourteenth and fifteenth days of the month Adar were to be celebrated annually (Esther 9:21); on the first day of the seventh month is the Feast of Trumpets (Lev. 23:24-5; Num. 29:1-6); Solomon observed the festival [of dedication of the temple] (2 Chr. 7:8-10); dedication of the rebuilt temple (Ezra 6:16); the feast of Dedication at Jerusalem (John 10:22).
DAY OF ATONEMENT, see 941D.
SABBATH, see 683A.

B Rites
B1 Circumcision
B1a About circumcision
Every eight-day old male shall be circumcised (Gen. 17:10-13); circumcised on the eighth day (Lev. 12:3); he gave him the covenant of circumcision (Acts 7:8); you circumcise on the sabbath (John 7:22-3); circumcision is not from Moses but from the fathers (John 7:22); if you receive circumcision you are obliged to keep the whole law (Gal. 5:3); the circumcision party (Gal. 2:12; Titus 1:10).

B1b Circumcision performed
Abraham circumcised every male in his household (Gen. 17:23); 'bridegroom of blood' because of the circumcision (Exod. 4:26); the believers from among the circumcised were amazed (Acts 10:45); Titus, though a Greek, was not compelled to be circumcised (Gal. 2:3); those who were circumcised: Isaac (Gen. 21:4; Acts 7:8); the men of Shechem (Gen. 34:24); Moses' son (Exod. 4:25-6); the Israelites at Gilgal (Josh. 5:2, 7-8); John the Baptist (Luke 1:59); Jesus (Luke 2:21); Timothy (Acts 16:3); Paul (Phil. 3:5).

B1c Necessity of circumcision
Only on this condition, that you be circumcised like us (Gen. 34:15); unless you are circumcised you cannot be saved (Acts 15:1); the Gentiles must be circumcised (Acts 15:5); those who want to make a good impression compel you to be circumcised (Gal. 6:12); circumcision is only of value if you keep the law (Rom. 2:25-7); if I preach circumcision the stumbling block of the cross is removed (Gal. 5:11); Paul was said to teach Jews to forsake circumcision (Acts 21:21); what is the benefit of circumcision? (Rom. 3:1); called the uncircumcision by what is called the circumcision (Eph. 2:11); neither circumcision nor uncircumcision is anything (1 Cor. 7:19; Gal. 5:6; 6:15); Abraham was the father of the circumcised and uncircumcised who believe (Rom. 4:11-12); there is no distinction between circumcised and uncircumcised (Col. 3:11); God justifies both circumcised and uncircumcised through faith.(Rom. 3:30); if anyone was uncircumcised when called, let him not be circumcised (1 Cor. 7:18); if you let yourselves be circumcised, Christ will be of no value to you (Gal. 5:2-3).

B1d True circumcision
The Lord will circumcise your hearts (Deut. 30:6); circumcise your hearts (Deut. 10:16; Jer. 4:4); in him you were circumcised with a circumcision made without hands (Col. 2:11); I will punish all who are circumcised yet uncircumcised (Jer. 9:25); circumcision is not something external in the flesh (Rom. 2:28); we are the true circumcision (Phil. 3:3); if the uncircumcised man keeps the law he will be regarded as circumcised (Rom. 2:26); putting off the body of flesh by the circumcision of Christ (Col. 2:11).

B2 Baptism
B2a John baptising
John the baptiser (Matt. 3:1); John the Baptist (Matt. 14:2, 8); John was baptising at Aenon near Salim (John 3:23); confessing their sins, they were baptised by John

(Matt. 3:6); John preached a baptism of repentance (Mark 1:4; Luke 3:3; Acts 13:24; 19:4); John baptised with water (Matt. 3:11; Mark 1:8; Luke 3:16; John 1:26; Acts 1:5); he who sent me to baptise with water (John 1:33); was John's baptism from heaven or from men? (Matt. 21:25; Mark 11:30; Luke 20:4); Apollos knew only the baptism of John (Acts 18:25); the disciples in Ephesus knew only John's baptism (Acts 19:3); tax-collectors came to be baptised (Luke 3:12); Pharisees and Sadducees coming for baptism (Matt. 3:7); they were baptised by John in the river Jordan (Mark 1:5); the Pharisees and scribes had not been baptised by John (Luke 7:30).

B2b Christ's baptism
Jesus came to be baptised by John (Matt. 3:13; Mark 1:9); John tried to prevent Jesus being baptised (Matt. 3:14); I have a baptism to undergo (Luke 12:50); can you drink the cup I drink or be baptised with the baptism I undergo? (Mark 10:38-9).

B2c Christian baptism
Jesus remained in Judea and baptised (John 3:22); Jesus is baptising and everyone is going to him (John 3:26); it was not Jesus who baptised, but his disciples (John 4:2); make disciples, baptising them in the name of Father, Son and Spirit (Matt. 28:19); they were baptised in the name of the Lord Jesus (Acts 19:5); repent and be baptised in the name of Jesus Christ (Acts 2:38); those who received his word were baptised (Acts 2:41); here is water! what is to prevent my being baptised? (Acts 8:36); rise, be baptised and wash away your sins (Acts 22:16); who can forbid these people being baptised with water since they have received the Holy Spirit (Acts 10:47); they had been baptised in the name of the Lord Jesus (Acts 8:16); I baptised none of you except Crispus and Gaius (1 Cor. 1:14); that no one should say you were baptised in my name (1 Cor. 1:15); I did baptise the household of Stephanas (1 Cor. 1:16); Christ did not send me to baptise but to preach the gospel (1 Cor. 1:17); what will those do who are baptised for the dead? (1 Cor. 15:29); those who were baptised: Lydia and her household (Acts 16:15); Samaritans (Acts 8:12); Saul [Paul] (Acts 9:18); Simon (Acts 8:13); the Philippian jailer.(Acts 16:33).

B2d Baptised into Christ
We were baptised into his death (Rom. 6:3-4); buried with him in baptism (Col. 2:12); by one spirit we were all baptised into one body (1 Cor. 12:13); you who have been baptised into Christ have put on Christ (Gal. 3:27); were you baptised in the name of Paul? (1 Cor. 1:13); this water symbolises baptism that now saves you (1 Pet. 3:21); he who believes and is baptised will be saved (Mark 16:16); one Lord, one faith, one baptism (Eph. 4:5); I need to be baptised by you, and do you come to me? (Matt. 3:14).

B2e Baptised in the Spirit
He is the one who will baptise with the Holy Spirit (John 1:33); he will baptise you with the Holy Spirit (Mark 1:8); and fire (Matt. 3:11; Luke 3:16); you will be baptised with the Holy Spirit (Acts 1:5; 11:16); by one Spirit we were all baptised and all drink of one Spirit (1 Cor. 12:13).
BAPTISM IN THE SPIRIT, see 965E3d.

989 Priests' garments
A Priests' garments in general
Holy garments for glory and for beauty (Exod. 28:2, 40); a contribution of materials for making the holy garments (Exod. 35:21); making the garments (Exod. 31:10); putting on the garments (Lev. 8:7-9); put the holy garments on Aaron (Exod. 40:13); blood and oil were sprinkled on the garments to consecrate them

(Exod. 29:21; Lev. 8:30); the oil running down the edge of Aaron's robes (Ps. 133:2); the priest has to wear them for seven days when ordained (Exod. 29:30); Aaron's garments shall be for his sons after him (Exod. 29:29); strip Aaron of his garments and put them on Eleazar his son (Num. 20:26).

B Breastpiece
The breastpiece (Exod. 25:7; 28:15-30); put the Urim and Thummim in the breastpiece (Exod. 28:30; Lev. 8:8).

C Ephods
The ephod (Exod. 25:7; 28:6-14; Lev. 8:7); I chose the priests to wear an ephod (1 Sam. 2:28); Doeg killed 85 men who wore a linen ephod (1 Sam. 22:18); Samuel wore a linen ephod (1 Sam. 2:18); Ahijah was wearing an ephod (1 Sam. 14:3); Abiathar fled with an ephod in his hand (1 Sam. 23:6); ephod used to enquire of God (1 Sam. 23:9; 30:7-8); David wore a linen ephod (2 Sam. 6:14); the robe of the ephod (Exod. 28:4, 31-5; Lev. 8:7); Micah made an ephod and a teraphim (Judg. 17:5).

D Tunics
The tunic (Exod. 28:4, 39; Lev. 8:7); tunics for Aaron's sons (Exod. 28:40; Lev. 8:13); they carried Nadab and Abihu, still in their tunics, out of the camp (Lev. 10:5).

E Turban and caps
The turban (Exod. 28:4; Lev. 8:9); caps for Aaron's sons (Exod. 28:40; Lev. 8:13); the priests shall wear linen turbans and undergarments (Ezek. 44:18).

F Priests' girdles
The girdle (Exod. 28:4; Lev. 8:7; 16:4); girdles for Aaron's sons (Exod. 28:40; Lev. 8:13).

G Undergarments
Linen undergarments (Exod. 28:42; Lev. 6:10; Ezek. 44:18).

990 Temple

A Tents
A1 The tent of meeting
Moses pitched a tent and called it the tent of meeting (Exod. 33:7); light in the tent of meeting (Exod. 27:21); the Israelites are to camp round the tent of meeting (Num. 2:2).
A2 The tabernacle
Make a sanctuary for me (Exod. 25:8); make this tabernacle according to the pattern I will show you (Exod. 25:9); skilled men made the tabernacle (Exod. 35:10-11); Moses erected the tabernacle (Exod. 40:18); setting up the tabernacle (Exod. 40:17-33); anointing it (Exod. 30:26; Lev. 8:10); the Gershonites were responsible for the tent and its coverings (Num. 3:25-6; 4:21-8); the Kohathites were responsible for the furniture (Num. 3:27-32; 4:1-20); the Merarites were responsible for the frames (Num. 3:36-7; 4:29-33); the first covenant had an earthly sanctuary (Heb. 9:1); our forefathers had the tabernacle of testimony in the wilderness (Acts 7:44); we have an altar from which those who minister at the tabernacle have no right to eat (Heb. 13:10); Solomon went to God's tent of meeting at Gibeon (2 Chr. 1:3); the holy things of the tent of meeting were brought up to the temple (1 Kgs. 8:4); the true tent which God pitched (Heb. 8:2).

B The temple
B1 The temple in general
B1a About the temple
Judah became his sanctuary (Ps. 114:2); at your holy temple I bow in reverence (Ps. 5:7); praise God in his sanctuary (Ps. 150:1); to enquire in his temple (Ps. 27:4); until I came into the sanctuary of God (Ps. 73:17); in the courts of the Lord's house I fulfil my vows (Ps. 116:19); let us go to the house of the Lord (Ps. 122:1); you who stand in the house of the Lord (Ps. 135:2); you

who stand by night in the house of the Lord (Ps. 134:1); I will appoint the Levites to have charge of the temple (Ezek. 44:14); a spring from the house of the Lord will water the valley of Shittim (Joel 3:18); I will again look on your holy temple (Jonah 2:4); Jesus taught in the temple (Luke 20:1); day after day I was with you in the temple teaching (Mark 14:49).
B1b Status of the temple
Do not trust in deceptive words, saying, 'The temple of the Lord!' (Jer. 7:4); whoever swears by the temple, it is nothing (Matt. 23:16); which is greater, the gold or the temple which sanctified the gold? (Matt. 23:17); he who swears by the temple swears by it and him who dwells in it (Matt. 23:21); has this house become a den of robbers? (Jer. 7:11; Matt. 21:13; Mark 11:17; Luke 19:46); the Lord you seek will suddenly come to his temple (Mal. 3:1); Jesus stood on the pinnacle of the temple (Matt. 4:5; Luke 4:9); the disciples pointed out the temple buildings to Jesus (Matt. 24:1); what wonderful stones and wonderful buildings! (Mark 13:1); the temple was beautifully adorned (Luke 21:5); zeal for your house will consume me (John 2:17); I will fill this house with glory (Hag. 2:7); my house will be called a house of prayer (Matt. 21:13).

B2 The temple at Shiloh
The house of God was in Shiloh (Judg. 18:31); bringing offerings to the house of the Lord in Shiloh (Jer. 41:5); Eli sat by a doorpost of the temple in Shiloh (1 Sam. 1:9); Samuel was lying in the temple of the Lord where the ark was (1 Sam. 3:3).

B3 Solomon's temple
I intend to build a temple for the name of the Lord (1 Kgs. 5:5); I have built a magnificent temple, a place for you to dwell for ever (1 Kgs. 8:13); in this house will I put my name for ever (2 Kgs. 21:7); the Levites helped Aaron's descendants in the service of the temple (1 Chr. 23:28).

B4 Damage to the temple
B4a Desecrating the temple
Manasseh put an Asherah in the temple (2 Kgs. 21:7); Manasseh built altars in the temple for all the host of heaven (2 Chr. 33:4-5); defile the house and fill the courts with the slain (Ezek. 9:7); pagan nations entered her sanctuary (Lam. 1:10); the enemy has destroyed everything in the sanctuary (Ps. 74:3); they entered my temple to profane it (Ezek. 23:39); they have defiled your temple (Ps. 79:1); he tried to desecrate the temple (Acts 24:6); because you said 'Aha!' when my sanctuary was profaned (Ezek. 25:3); how long are the holy place and the host to be trampled under foot? (Dan. 8:13); Judah has profaned the sanctuary of the Lord, which he loves (Mal. 2:11); you shall not make my Father's house a house of trade (John 2:16); this man never ceases to speak against this holy place and the law (Acts 6:13); this man teaches against our people and the law and this place (Acts 21:28); you brought foreigners, uncircumcised in heart and flesh, into the temple (Ezek. 44:7); he brought Greeks into the temple and defiled this holy place (Acts 21:28); Josiah had all the articles made for Baal and Asherah removed from the temple (2 Kgs. 23:4); start at my sanctuary (Ezek. 9:6). THE TEMPLE A MARKET, see 796.
B4b Destroying the temple
I will do to the house called by my name as I did to Shiloh (Jer. 7:14); I will desolate your sanctuaries (Lev. 26:31); the people of the coming prince will destroy the city and the sanctuary (Dan. 9:26); the place of the sanctuary was overthrown (Dan. 8:11); the temple was burned (2 Kgs. 25:9; 2 Chr. 36:19; Jer. 52:13); our holy temple has been burned with fire (Isa. 64:11); your house is left to you desolate (Matt. 23:38); destroy this

temple and in three days I will raise it up (John 2:19); I can destroy the temple and rebuild it in three days (Matt. 26:61; Mark 14:58); you who would destroy the temple and rebuild it in three days (Matt. 27:40; Mark 15:29); the veil of the temple was torn in two from top to bottom (Mark 15:38).

B5 Rebuilding the temple
Cyrus' order to rebuild the temple (2 Chr. 36:23; Ezra 1:2-3; 6:3-5); the foundation laid (Ezra 3:10-11); the building stopped (Ezra 4:24); the building resumed (Ezra 5:2-5); the house of the great God is being built (Ezra 5:8); building completed (Ezra 6:14-15); the man called the Branch will build the temple of the Lord (Zech. 6:12, 13); destroy this temple and in three days I will raise it up (John 2:19); I can destroy the temple and rebuild it in three days (Matt. 26:61; Mark 14:58); you who would destroy the temple and rebuild it in three days (Matt. 27:40; Mark 15:29).

B6 Entering the temple
B6a Various people in the temple
Aaron to wear bells when entering the holy place (Exod. 28:35); Zechariah was chosen by lot to enter the temple (Luke 1:9); David entered the house of God (Matt. 12:4; Mark 2:26; Luke 6:4); Simeon came into the temple in the Spirit (Luke 2:27); Anna did not depart from the temple (Luke 2:37); two men went up into the temple to pray (Luke 18:10).

B6b Christ in the temple
They found boy Jesus in the temple (Luke 2:46); he was walking in the temple (Mark 11:27); Jesus walked in the temple in Solomon's portico (John 10:23); the blind and lame came to him in the temple and he healed them (Matt. 21:14); Jesus taught in the temple (Mark 12:35; John 7:28; 8:20); I always taught in the synagogue and in the temple (John 18:20); when I was with you daily in the temple you did not lay hands on me (Luke 22:53).

B6c Disciples in the temple
The disciples were continually in the temple, praising God (Luke 24:53); they met in the temple day by day (Acts 2:46); Peter and John went up to the temple at the ninth hour (Acts 3:1); speak to the people in the temple all the words of this life (Acts 5:20-1); when I returned to Jerusalem and was praying in the temple (Acts 22:17); they found me purified in the temple (Acts 24:18); Jews from Asia saw Paul in the temple (Acts 21:27).

B6d Interlopers in the temple
Aliens have entered the holy places of the Lord's house (Jer. 51:51); robbers will enter and profane it (Ezek. 7:22); Uzziah entered the temple to burn incense (2 Chr. 26:16); could one like me enter the temple and live? (Neh. 6:11); they supposed that Paul brought Trophimus the Ephesian into the temple (Acts 21:29); the man of lawlessness takes his seat in the temple of God (2 Thess. 2:4).

B7 The holy of holies
He built the holy of holies (2 Chr. 3:8); within the temple was an inner sanctuary, the holy of holies (1 Kgs. 6:16, 19-20); the priests brought the ark to its place in the holy of holies (1 Kgs. 8:6; 2 Chr. 5:7); behind the second curtain was a tent called the holy of holies (Heb. 9:3); the veil separated the holy place from the holy of holies (Exod. 26:33); Christ entered the holy of holies once for all by his own blood (Heb. 9:12); our hope enters the inner sanctuary where Jesus entered for us (Heb. 6:19-20); we enter the sanctuary through the blood of Jesus (Heb. 10:19-20).

B8 The perfect temple
B8a The temple in heaven
God does not live in shrines made with hands (Acts 17:24); Christ entered not a man-made sanctuary, a copy of the true one, but heaven itself (Heb. 9:24); Christ went through the perfect tabernacle which is not man-made (Heb. 9:11); the true tent set up not by man but by God (Heb. 8:2); they serve a copy and shadow of the heavenly tabernacle (Heb. 8:5); the Lord is in his temple in heaven (Ps. 11:4); God's sanctuary in heaven was opened (Rev. 11:19); the temple of the tent of witness in heaven was opened (Rev. 15:5); I saw no temple, because the Lord God Almighty and the Lamb are its temple (Rev. 21:22).

B8b Plans for a new temple
Ezekiel's vision of the temple being measured (Ezek. 40:31); measuring the temple (Ezek. 40:5-41:6); measure the sanctuary of God (Rev. 11:1); describe the temple that they may be ashamed (Ezek. 43:10); the glory of the Lord filled the house of the Lord (Ezek. 44:4); water for the trees flows from the sanctuary (Ezek. 47:12).

B8c The living temple
The temple of his body (John 2:21); something greater than the temple is here (Matt. 12:6); you are God's temple and God's Spirit lives in you (1 Cor. 3:16); the temple of God is holy, which temple you are (1 Cor. 3:17); your body is a temple of the Holy Spirit (1 Cor. 6:19); we are the temple of the living God (2 Cor. 6:16); the whole building is growing into a holy temple (Eph. 2:21); I will make him a pillar in the temple of my God (Rev. 3:12); what agreement has the temple of God with idols? (2 Cor. 6:16).

C Foreign temples
The ark was carried into Dagon's temple (1 Sam. 5:2); the temple of El-berith (Judg. 9:46); Sennacherib worshipping in the house of Nisroch his god (2 Kgs. 19:37; 2 Chr. 32:21; Isa. 37:38); Nebuchadnezzar put things from the temple in his temple in Babylon (2 Chr. 36:7; Ezra 1:7; 5:14); Ahab built a house for Baal in Samaria (1 Kgs. 16:32); the house of Baal was used as a latrine (2 Kgs. 10:27); Demetrius made silver shrines of Artemis (Acts 19:24); the temple of the great goddess Artemis (Acts 19:27); you who abhor idols, do you rob temples? (Rom. 2:22); if someone sees you who have knowledge at table in an idol's temple (1 Cor. 8:10).

D Altars
D1 Altars in general
Make an altar of earth (Exod. 20:24); not an altar of cut stone (Exod. 20:25); no steps to the altar (Exod. 20:26); leave your gift there before the altar (Matt. 5:24); Christ belongs to another tribe, from which no one has ever served at the altar (Heb. 7:13).

D2 Altar of burnt offering
Build an altar of acacia wood (Exod. 27:1); the bronze altar (Exod. 39:39); building the altar of burnt offering (Exod. 31:9); censers beaten into plates for the altar (Num. 16:38-9); setting up the altar of burnt offering (Exod. 40:6; Ezra 3:3); dedication of the altar (Num. 7:10-11); bring the sacrifice, bound, to the horns of the altar (Ps. 118:27); burnt offerings are only to be offered on the Lord's altar (Deut. 12:27); put blood on the horns of the altar (Exod. 29:12; Lev. 4:25); sprinkle blood around the altar (Exod. 29:16); Gershonites looked after the altar (Num. 3:26); the bronze altar was too small for all the offerings (1 Kgs. 8:64; 2 Chr. 7:7); which is greater, the gift or the altar which sanctifies the gift? (Matt. 23:19-20); water flowed from south of the altar (Ezek. 47:1); Zechariah, murdered between the temple and the altar (Matt. 23:35; Luke 11:51); the bronze altar was removed from in front of the temple (2 Kgs. 16:14); Adonijah took hold of the horns of the

altar (1 Kgs. 1:50-3); Joab took hold of the horns of the altar (1 Kgs. 2:28); take him even from my altar (Exod. 21:14); the sparrow and swallow nest in your altar (Ps. 84:3); the Lord has rejected his altar (Lam. 2:7).

D3 Altar of incense

Make an altar of acacia wood for burning incense (Exod. 30:1); the golden altar (Exod. 39:38; 1 Kgs. 7:48; 2 Chr. 4:19; Rev. 9:13); the altar of incense (Heb. 9:4); making the altar of incense (Exod. 31:8); the altar of incense set up (Exod. 40:26); the altar anointed (Exod. 30:27); Moses sprinkled blood on the altar (Exod. 24:6); the altar atoned for (Lev. 16:18-19); blood on the horns of the incense altar (Lev. 4:7, 18); the Kohathites looked after the altar of incense (Num. 3:31); the altar was covered with a blue cloth (Num. 4:11); the golden altar before the throne (Rev. 8:3); Uzziah entered the temple to burn incense on the altar of incense (2 Chr. 26:16); the angel of the Lord to the right of the altar of incense (Luke 1:11); a burning coal from the altar (Isa. 6:6).

D4 The heavenly altar

We have an altar from which those who minister at the tabernacle have no right to eat (Heb. 13:10); under the altar were the souls of those martyred (Rev. 6:9); I heard the altar say (Rev. 16:7); measure the sanctuary, the altar and those who worship (Rev. 11:1); the angel filled the censer with fire from the altar and threw it on the earth (Rev. 8:5); the angel who has power over fire came out from the altar (Rev. 14:18).

D5 Various altars

Abraham laid Isaac on the altar (Gen. 22:9); an altar for witness, not for sacrifice (Josh. 22:23); there will be an altar to the Lord in Egypt (Isa. 19:19); build an altar at Bethel (Gen. 35:1); build an altar on Mt Ebal (Deut. 27:5); build an altar to the Lord your God (Judg. 6:26); the altar in Bethel (1 Kgs. 13:1); O altar, altar! (1 Kgs. 13:2); build an altar on the threshing-floor of Araunah [Ornan] the Jebusite (2 Sam. 24:18; 1 Chr. 21:18); Manasseh made altars for Baal (2 Kgs. 21:3); Manasseh made altars to the host of heaven (2 Kgs. 21:4-5); Ahab set up an altar for Baal in the temple of Baal (1 Kgs. 16:32); King Ahaz copied an altar in Damascus (2 Kgs. 16:10-11); Ahaz made altars all over Jerusalem (2 Chr. 28:24); Ephraim multiplied altars for sinning (Hos. 8:11); an altar to an unknown god (Acts 17:23).

D6 Destroying altars

Break down their altars (Deut. 7:5); tear down your father's altar to Baal (Judg. 6:25); Asa removed the foreign altars (2 Chr. 14:3); they removed the altars and incense altars (2 Chr. 30:14; 31:1); isn't he the one whose altars Hezekiah removed? (2 Kgs. 18:22; 2 Chr. 32:12; Isa. 36:7); Manasseh removed the altars (2 Chr. 33:15); Josiah destroyed the altars Manasseh had made (2 Kgs. 23:12); Josiah destroyed the altar at Bethel (2 Kgs. 23:15, 16); the altar will be split apart (1 Kgs. 13:3); they have torn down your altars (1 Kgs. 19:10; Rom. 11:3).

Index

Aaron 371D1a
Abaddon 168
  the grave 361
abandon 621
abandon hope 853
Abarim
  Mt Nebo 209G2d
abase
  bring down 311A3
abash
  frighten 854
  humiliate 872
abate 37
Abba
  father 169D1a
abdomen 224A4
abduct 786B
Abednego 371D1b
Abel 371D1c
  Abel-beth-maacah
  184D1a
Abel-beth-maacah
184D1a
Abel-maim
  Abel-beth-maacah
  184D1a
Abel-meholah 184D1b
aberration 282
abet 703
abettor 703
abeyance 145
abhor 888
abhorrence 888
Abia
  Abijah 371D1g
Abiah
  Abijah 371D1g
Abiathar 371D1d
Abib
  first month 108G2
abide
  dwell 192
  remain 144
abide by
  observe 768
Abigail 371D1e
Abihu 371D1f
Abijah 371D1g
Abijam
  Abijah 371D1g
  king of Judah 741C2
Abilene 184D1c
ability 160F
  possibility 469
Abimelech 371D1h
  king of Israel 741C2
Abiner
  Abner 371D2c
Abishag 371D2a
Abishai 371D2b
Abishalom
  Maacah 371I4a
ablaze 381
able 160F
  able people 696
  skilful 696

ablutions 648
Abner 371D2c
abnormal 84
abnormality 84
aboard 275
abode 192
abolish 752B
  abrogate 752
  destroy 165
abominable 888
abomination 888B3
abort 172A4
abortion
  miscarriage 172A4
abound 635
abounding 635
about
  concerning 9
about-turn 282
above
  higher 209
  more important 638
  superior 34
above average 34
above suspicion 935
Abraham 371D2d
Abram
  Abraham 371D2d
abrogate 752
abrogation 752
abrupt
  sudden 116
Absalom 371D2f
abscess 651B1
abscond
  escape 667
  run away 620A
absence 190
absent 190
absolution
  acquittal 960
  forgiveness 909
absolve
  acquit 960
  forgive 909
abstain 620B
abstainer
  teetotal 948
abstemious 948
abstention 620B
abstinence
  avoidance 620B
  teetotal 948
abstract
  take away 786
absurd 497
absurdity 497
abundance 635
  much 32
abundant
  many 104
abuse
  be severe 735
  curse 899
  detraction 926
  ill-treat 645

abyss
  hell 972B
  pit 255B2
acacia
  acacia wood 631D2
academic
  scholar 492
accede
  consent 758
accent 580A
  dialect 557
accept
  receive 782
  welcome 299A
acceptable
  acceptable time 108D1
accepted 782
access 297B
accident
  chance 159
acclaim
  praise 923
accolade
  praise 923
accommodation
  quarters 192
accompaniment 89
accompany 89
accomplice 707
accomplish
  complete 725
  do 676
accomplished
  skilful 696
accord
  agreement 24
  concord 710
according to 12
  according to the
    number 85
  in rank 73
accost
  address 583
account 808
  description 590B
accountability 180
accountable 180
accounts 808
accoutred
  dressed 228
accredited
  credible 485
accumulate
  store up 632
accuracy
  truthfulness 494
accurate
  true 494
accursed 899
accusation 928
accuse 928
accuser 928
accustom 610
accustomed 610
Aceldama
  field of blood 335E1d

Achaia 184D1d
Achan 371D2g
Achar
  Achan 371D2g
Achaz
  Ahaz 371D4a
ache 377
achievable
  possible 469
achieve
  accomplish 725
achievement
  completion 725
aching 377
Achish 371D2h
Achor
  valley of 255C2
Achsa
  Achsah 371D2i
Achsah 371D2i
Achzib 184D1e
acknowledge
  approve 923
  assent 488
acknowledgement
  assent 488
acme 213
acquaintance
  friend 880
acquainted
  knowing 490
acquiesce 488
acquiescence 488
acquire 771
acquisition 771
acquisitive
  greedy 859A4
acquit 960
acquittal 960
acreage 183
acrimony
  malevolence 898
across 222
Acsah
  Achsah 371D2i
act
  do 676
acting
  drama 542C
action 676
  lawsuit 959
active
  vigorous 174
activist 678A
activity
  action 676
actor
  player 542C
actress 542C
actual
  authentic 494
acuity
  wisdom 498
acumen
  wisdom 498

acute
  intelligent 498
Aczib
  Achzib 184D1e
adage 496
Adam
  the person 371D3a
  the place 184D1f
adapt
  conform 83
adaptable 83
Adar
  twelfth month 108G4
add 38
adder 365E4
adding 38
addition 38
address
  speak to 583
  speech 579
adept
  skilful 696
  skilled person 696
adequate
  sufficient 635
adhere 48
adherent
  follower 284
adhesion 48
adjacent 200
adjudge 480
adjudicate 480
adjuration 532C
adjure 532C
adjust
  conform 83
Admah 184D1g
administer
  manage 689
administration 689A
admirable 923
admiration 923
admirer 887
admission
  disclosure 526
  reception 299
admit
  let in 299
admittance
  entrance 297
admonish
  reprove 924
  warn 664
admonition
  reprimand 924
  warning 664
adolescence 130
adolescent 132
Adonijah 371D3b
Adoniram 371D3c
adopt
  rear 170A7
adoption 170A7
Adoram
  Adoniram 371D3c
adoration
  worship 981
adore
  worship 981
adorn 844

Adrammelech 967G
Adria
  Adriatic Sea 343C5
Adriatic 343C5
adrift
  shipwrecked 165C7
adulation
  flattery 925
  praise 923
Adullam 184D1h
Adullamite 184D1h
adult 134
adulterate
  mix 43
adulterer 952
adulteress 952A
adulterous 951B
adultery 951B
adultness 134
adultress 952A
advance 285
advantage 34D
advent
  approach 289
  arrival 295
adversary 705
adverse
  hindering 702
  opposing 704
adversity
  calamity 731
  harm 645
advice 691
advise 691
adviser 691A
advocate 958
Aeneas 371D3d
Aenon 184D1i
aeon 110
aesthetic 841
afar 199
affair
  topic 452
affection 817
affectionate 817
affections 817
affiliation
  relation 9
affinity 9
  no affinity 10
affirm 532
affirmation 532
affirmative 532
afflict
  hurt 827
affliction
  suffering 825
  tribulation 827
affluence 800
affluent 800
affordable 812
affray 716
afire 381
aflame 381
afloat 275
aforetime 125
afraid 854
afresh 126

after
  afterwards 120
  born after 67
afterbirth 167B4a
afternoon 129B
afterwards 120
Agabus 371D3e
Agag 371D3f
again
  repetition 106
against
  opposing 704
against the law 954
Agar
  Hagar 371G1c
agate 844A1b
age
  ages ago 125
  days old 131
  long duration 113
  of age 134B
  old age 131C
  period 110
  years old 131
aged
  old person 133
agency 173
agenda
  topic 452
agent 173
aggravate
  annoy 827
aggravating 827
aggression 712
aggrieved 829
aghast
  fearful 854
agitate
  excite 821
  shake 318A
agitated
  nervous 854
agitation
  excitation 821
  shaking 318A
aglow 417
agnostic
  doubter 486
ago
  formerly 125
agog
  expectant 507
agonise
  suffer 825
agony
  pain 377
  suffering 825
agree 24
  be of one mind 710
  not agree 25
agreement 24
  concord 710
  covenant 765
agriculture 370
Agrippa 371D3g
aground 344A
Ahab 371D3h
  king of Israel 741C1
Ahasuerus 371D3i
Ahava 184D1j

Ahaz 371D4a
  king of Judah 741C2
Ahaziah 371D4b
  king of Israel 741C1
  king of Judah 741C2
ahead 237A
  go on ahead 283
Ahijah 371D4d
Ahimaaz 371D4e
Ahimelech 371D4f
Ahiramite 371B4c
Ahithophel 371D4g
Aholah
  Oholah 184J2c
Aholibah
  Oholibah 184G2h
Ai 184D1k
aid 703
Aijalon 184D1l
ailing 651
ailment 651
aim 617C
air 340
Ajalon
  Aijalon 184D1l
ajar 263
Akeldama
  field of blood 335E1d
alabaster
  precious stone
    844A1b
  the material 631C1
alarm
  signal 547
  warning 664
alarming
  frightening 854
alas! 830B
alcohol
  alcoholic drink 335B
alcoholic
  drunkard 949
ale 335C
alert
  vigilant 457
Alexander 371D5a
Alexandria 184D1m
Alexandrian 184D1m
algum wood 631D4
alias
  nickname 561
alien 59
alienated 46B1
alienation
  enmity 881
alike
  identical 16
  similar 18
alive 360
all
  all kinds 82
  all things to all men
    83B
  all ways 281E4
  at all times 146
  everything 79
  fullness 54
  whole of 52
all at once 116
all day 146

allegation
accusation 928
allegiance 739
change of allegiance
603C
allegorical 519
allegory 519
alleluia 923
alleviate 831
all eyes 455
alliance 765B1
allied 765B1
all-knowing 490B1
allocation 783
allocution 583
Allon-bachuth
Allon-bacuth 836C1a
Allon-bacuth 836C1a
allot 783
allow
not allow 757
permit 756
allowance 783
alloy
mix 43
all-powerful 160A1
allure
attract 291
all-wise 498B
ally 707
Almighty
God 965A2
almighty
powerful 160A1
almond
almond tree 366D2c
almonds 171C3a
alms 781C2d
alms-giving 781C2d
almug
almug wood 631D4
aloe 366D2a
spice 396A
alone 88B4
not alone 89E
alongside
near 200
along with 89
aloof 883B
alopecia 229B2
aloud
loudly 400A
alpha
Alpha and Omega 68F
alphabet 558
altar 990D
bronze altar 990D2
altar of burnt offering
990D2
altar of incense 990D3
alter 147
altercation
quarrel 709
alternate
different 15
always
unceasing 146

am
am present 189
exist 1
I AM 1
identity 13
who am? 13
Amalek
Amalekites 371C2a
Amalekites 371C2a
amanuensis 586C
Amasa 371D5f
amass 632
amaze 864
amazed 864
amazement 864
Amaziah 371D5g
king of Judah 741C2
ambassador 754B
amber
yellow 433
ambidextrous 242B
ambition 818C4
ambush 527B
ameliorate 654
amen 488B
amenable 597
amend 656
amendment
restoration 656
amends
atonement 941
amethyst 844A1b
amity
friendship 880
Ammi 561C2
Ammon
Ammonites 371C2b
Ammonites 371C2b
amnesia 506
amnesty
peace 717
Amnon 371D5h
Amon 371D5i
king of Judah 741C2
among 89
Amorites 371C2c
amorous 887
amorphous 244
Amos 371D6a
Amon 371D5i
amount
big amount 32
quantity 26
Amphipolis 184D1o
ample 635
Amplias
Ampliatus 371D6b
Ampliatus 371D6b
amputate 46E3
amuse 837
amusement 837
anaemia 651B7
anaesthesia 375A
anaesthetic 375A
Anak
Anakim 371C2d
Anakim 371C2d
giants 195C2
analgesic 375A
analogy 462

Anammelech 967G
Ananiah
Bethany 184D4e
Ananias 371D6c
anarchic 734
anarchist 734
anarchy 734
anathema 899
anathematise 899
Anathoth 184D1n
Anathothite 184D1n
anatomy 319
ancestor 169B1
ancestral 169
ancestry 170D
anchor
fastening 47A
ancient 127
ancillary 703
Andrew 371D6e
Anethothite
Anathothite 184D1n
anew 126
angel 968
angelic 968
anger 891
angle 247
angry 891
angular 247
angularity 247
animal 365
men and animals 365A3
wild animals 365A2
ankle
ankle-deep 211D
anklet 844
Anna 371D6f
annals 589
Annas 371D6g
annex 786
annihilate 362E6b
anniversary 141D1
announce 528
announcement 528
annoy 827B3
annoyance 827B3
annoyed 829
annoying 827
annual 141D1
annually 141D1
annul 752B
annular 250
annulled 752B
annulment 752B
anoint 357B
anointed 357B
anointing 357B
another
different one 15
answer 460
no answer 460E
not answer 460E
ant 365B4
antagonism 881
antagonist 881
antelope 365E1b
anterior 237
Antichrist 969
anticipate 507

anticipation 507
antidote 658A
antimony 844A1b
Antioch
of Pisidia 184D1q
of Syria 184D1p
Antipas 371D6h
Herod Antipas 371G2g
antipathy 881
Antipatris 184D1r
antiquated 127
antique 127
antiquity 125
antiseptic 658A
antisocial 883
antitype 23
antler
horn 254A
Antothite
Anathothite 184D1n
anxiety 825E
anxious 825E
apace 277
apart 46
apartment 194C
Apelles 371D6i
aperture 263
apex 213
aphasia 580
Aphek 184D1s
Aphik
Aphek 184D1s
aphorism 496
Apis 967H
Apollonia 184D1t
Apollos 371D7a
Apollyon 168
apostasy 603C1
apostate 603C1
apostle 754A
apostolic 754A
appal 854F
appalled 854F
apparel 228
apparent
appearing 445A
obvious 522
apparition 445B
ghost 970
appeal 761
appear 445B
appearance 445A
for appearance sake
875A
appease
pacify 719
appelation
name 561
appetite 859C1
Apphia 371D7b
Appii Forum 184F1b
applaud
approve 923
applause
clapping 279G
apple 366D2b
apple of the eye 438B3
apples 171C3b
appliance
tool 630

appoint 751
appointee 754
apportion 783
apprehend
  arrest 747B
  understand 516
apprehension
  anxiety 825E
apprehensive
  anxious 825E
apprise
  inform 524
approach 289
  draw near 289
approvable 923
approval 923
approve 923
aqueous 339
Aquila 371D7c
Ar 184D2a
Arabah
  sea of the Arabah 343C1
Arabia 184D2b
Arabian 371C2e
Arabs 371C2e
Aram
  Arameans 371C2f
  the country 184D2c
Aramaic
  Aramaic language 557B
Arameans 371C2f
Ararat
  Mt Ararat 209G1a
  the land 184D2d
Araunah 371D7d
arbiter 720
arbitrate 720
arbitrator 720
archaic 127
archangel 968B3
Archelaus 371D7e
archer 287B2
archetype 23B
archives 548B
Arcturus
  the Bear 420A3
ardent 818
Ardite 371B4c
ardour 818
arduous 682
are
  are present 189
  exist 1
  identity 13
  who are? 13
area
  region 184
  space 183
  territory 183A
arena 724
are not
  do not exist 2
Areopagite 209G1b
Areopagus 209G1b
Aretas 371D7f
argue 709
argument 709
arid 172
Ariel
  Jerusalem 184G2

Arimathea
  Ramathaim-zophim
    184I4c
arise 310
Aristarchus 371D7g
aristocrat 868
ark
  ark of the covenant 194E
  Noah's ark 275C
arm
  limb 53D2
Armageddon 184D2e
armlet 844A
armour
  defensive armour 713B1
  weapons 723
armour bearer 723A6
arms
  weapons 723
army 722E
Arnon 350D1
Aroer 184D2f
Aroerite 184D2f
aroma 396
aromatic 396
around 230
  encircle 314
arouse
  excite 821
aroused
  stirred up 174
Arpad 184D2g
Arphad
  Arpad 184D2g
arrange
  put in order 62
arrears
  debt 803
arrest
  seize 747B
arrival 295
arrive 295
arrogance 871
arrogant 871
arrow 723
  shooting 287B
arson 381
art 551
Artaxerxes 371D7h
Artemas 371D7i
Artemis 967H
artful
  cunning 698
articulate
  join 45
artifice
  stratagem 698
artless
  simple 44
as
  assarion 797A1
  equality 28
  like 18
Asa 371D8a
  king of Judah 741C2
Asahel 371D8b
ascend 308
ascent 308
ascertain
  discover 484

ascetic 945
asceticism 945
ascribe
  attribute 158
Asenath 371D8c
Aser
  Asher 371D8d
as for me 80A2
ash 381C2
ashamed 872B
  not ashamed 872B3
Ashbelite 371B4c
Ashdod 184D2h
Ashdodite 184D2h
Asher
  territory of 184D2i
  the person 371D8d
  tribe of 371B4a
Asherah 967A
Asherim 967A
ashes 381C2
ash-heap 641C3
Ashima 967G
Ashkelon 184D2j
Ashtoreth 967A
Asia 184D2k
Asiarchs 184D2k
aside
  stand aside! 290
as is 7
ask
  ask questions 459A
  request 761
asleep 679B
asperity 892
asphyxiate 362C1
aspirate
  breathe 352A
aspiration
  hope 852
aspire
  hope 852
ass 365G4
assail 712
assailant 712
assarion 797A1
Assassins 708D
assault 712
assay
  test 461
assemblage 74
assemble 74
assembly 74
assent 488
assert
  affirm 532
assertion
  affirmation 532
assessment
  tax 809
Asshur
  Assyria 184D2m
  Assyrians 371C2g
  Mesopotamia 184H2e
assign
  commission 751
assimilate
  conform 83
assimilation
  conformity 83

assistance 703
assistant 707
assizes 956
associate
  accompany 89
  colleague 707
Assos 184D2l
assuage 266B
assume
  suppose 512
assumption
  supposition 512
assurance
  affirmation 532
assured
  convinced 485
Assyria 184D2m
  Assyrians 371C2g
Assyrians 371C2g
Astarte 967A
astonish 864
astonishing 864
astonishment 864
astound 864
astray
  go astray 282C
astrologer 983B1
astute
  intelligent 498
asunder 46
as well 38
asylum 662
at ease 683
at fault 936
Athaliah 371D8e
  queen of Judah
    741C2
at hand 200
atheism 486
atheist 486
Athens 184D2n
athlete 716E
athletics 716E
atmosphere 340
at night 129C
at no time 109
at once 116
atone 941
atonement 941
at peace 717
at present 121
at rest
  relaxing 683
  still 266
at sea 269A
at short notice 135
attach 45
attack 712
attacker 712
Attalia 184D2o
attempt 617
attend
  accompany 89
attention 455
attentive 455
attest 461
at the beginning 68
at the ready 669
at the same time 123
at this moment 121

attorney
lawyer 958
attract 291
attraction 291
attractive
beautiful 841
at war 718
at work 676
audacity
courage 855
audit
accounts 808
augment
increase 36
augur 511
augury 983B1
Augustus 371D8f
aurochs 365E6c
auspicious 511
austerity
asceticism 945
authentic 494
authenticate 488
authenticity 494
author 589
authority 733
autumn 129D
Ava
Avva 184D2p
avarice 816
avenge 910
avenger 910
Aven [Beth-aven] 184D4f
aver 532
average 30
aversion 861
avoid 620
avoidance 620
avouch 532
Avva 184D2p
Avvite 184D2p
await 507
awake 678C
awaken 678C3
aware
knowing 490
awareness 490
away
absent 190
far off 199
move away! 290
awe
fear 854
awesome 854
awkward
noncomforming 84C
awl 630C
sharp thing 256A4
awning 421A
axe 630C
sharp thing 256A4
Azariah 371D8g
Abednego 371D1b
king of Judah 741C2
Azazel 786D2
Azotus
Ashdod 184D2h
azure 435
Azzah
Gaza 184F3b

Baal 967B
Baal-berith 967B
Baal-peor 967B
Baal-zebub 967B
Baalah
Kiriath-jearim 184G4e
Baal-berith 967B
Baale
Baale-judah 184G4e
Baale-judah 184G4e
Baal-hazor
Ophrah 184H5c
Baal-hermon
Mt Hermon 209G2a
Baal-peor 967B
the place 209G2f
Baal-perazim 209G2g
Baal-zebub 967B
Baanah 371E1a
Baasha 371E1b
king of Israel 741C1
babble 515
babe 132
Babel
Babylon 184D3
tower of 209C2
baby 132
Babylon 184D3
Babylonia
Chaldea 184E1i
Babylonians 371C2h
bachelor 895
back 238A
front and back 237C
backlash
recoil 280
backslide 603C1
backwards 286
bad 645
bad person 938
bad to worse 655
bad conscience 917A2
badger
rock badger 365E3c
badness 645
baffle
puzzle 474B
baggage 777D
bagpipe 414B4
bake 381C6
baker 895
Balaam 371E1c
Balac
Balak 371E1d
Balak 371E1d
balance
scales 465A
bald 229B2
bald locust 365B2c
baldness 229B2
plain speaking 573
ball 252
balm 658A
ban
curse 899F
band
fastening 47B
bandit 789
bane 659

bangle
bracelet 844A
banish
eject 300
bank
edge 234A
treasury 799A
banker 798
banned
cursed 899F
banner 547B1
ban of destruction 165A3
baptise 988B2
baptism 988B2
baptism in the Spirit 965E3d
Baptist
John the Baptist 371H7c
Barabbas 371E1e
Barak 371E1f
barbarian
foreigner 59
barber
haircut 46E4
bard
musician 413
bare 229
barefoot 229B1
bareheaded 229B2
bargain 791
Bar-jesus 371E1g
bark
like a dog 409A
barley 366C2
grain 301B1b
barn 632
Barnabas 371E1h
barren 172A1
barrier
wall 235A
bars
locks 662D
Barsabbas
Joseph Barsabbas 371H8f
Judas 371H9f
barter 791
Bartholomew 371E1i
Bartimaeus 371E2a
Baruch 371E2b
Barzillai 371E2c
base
bottom 214
baseless 916B
basement
cellar 194C
bash
hit 279A
Bashan 184D4a
basin
washbasin 648A1a
basket 194B7
bastard 954D
bastion
fortification 713
bath
measure 465
bathe 648A2
bathing 648A2
Bathsheba 371E2d

Bath-shua
Bathsheba 371E2d
baton
stick 218B
batter
strike 279A
battering ram 279A3a
battle 718
battle cry 400C
bawd 952
bawdy 951
bawl
shout 400B
bay 345
bazaar 796
bdellium 396A
be
exist 1
identity 13
not to be 2
beach
seashore 234B
beam
timber 218B6
bear
animal 365E1a
carry 273
endure 823
Bear
the Bear 420A3
beard 259A3a
bereaved 772E
bearer 273
armour bearer 723A6
bearing
direction 281
beast
creature 365
beat
defeat 727
hit 279A
beating
beating with a rod 964A
hitting 279A
beat small 332A3
beautiful 841
make beautiful 843
beautify 843
beauty 841
because 156B
beckon 547
bed 218E
sexual intercourse 45C1a
bedazzle 417
bedchamber 194C3
bedew 341B
bedroom 194C3
bee 365B2a
Beelzebub
Baal-zebub 967B
beer 335C
intoxicating drink 949A
Beersheba 184D4b
befitting 915B
befool
puzzle 474B

before
  beforehand 125C
  go before 283
  going before 64
  in front 237A
  of time 119C
  previous 125
beforehand 125C
befriend 880
befuddle
  puzzle 474B
beg 761C
  request 761
beget 167B1
beggar 761C
begging 761C
begin 68
beginning 68
begotten 167B1
  only begotten 88B2
begrime 649
begrudge 816
beguile
  deceive 542A
behaviour 688
behead 46E3
Behemoth 365D1
behest 737
behind 238B
behind bars 747D
behindhand 136
behold
  see 438
behove
  be due 915B
being
  existence 1
beka 465
Bel 967C
Bela
  Zoar 184K6c
Belaite 371B4c
belated 136
belief 485
believable 485
believe 485
  not believe 486
believer 485
belittle 926
bell 414B1a
belle 841
bellicose 716
belligerent 716
bellow
  shout 400B
bellows
  wind pump 352C
belly 224A4
belong 773
belongings 777
beloved 887
below 210A1
Belshazzar 371E2e
belt 228B7b
Belteshazzar
  Daniel 371E7c
bemoan
  lament 836
Benaiah 371E2f
Ben-ammi 371E2g

bench
  seat 218D
bend
  stoop 309A5
bend the knee 309A5
beneath
  under 210
benediction
  blessing 897
beneficial 644
benefit
  do good 644
benevolence 897
benevolent 897
Ben-hadad 371E2h
Ben-hinnom
  valley of 255C2
Benjamin
  territory of 184D4c
  the person 371E3a
  tribe of 371B4b
Ben-oni
  Benjamin 371E3a
bent
  twisted 246C
be present 189
bequeath 780
berate 924
Berea
  Beroea 184D4d
bereave 772E
bereavement 772E
bereft 772
Berith
  Baal-berith 967B
Bernice 371E3b
Beroea 184D4d
beryl 844A1b
beseech 761
beset
  besiege 712
besiege 712
besom 648C4
best
  excelling 306B
bestial
  animal 365
bestiality 951C
bestow 781
bet
  gamble 618B
Beth-abara
  Bethany 184D4e
Bethany 184D4e
Beth-aven
  Bethel 184D4f

Bethel 184D4f
  house of God 192A3
Bethelite 184D4f
Bethesda
  Pool of Bethesda 346
Beth-gilgal
  Gilgal 184F3i
Bethlehem
  Bethlehem Ephratah
    184D4g
  Bethlehem of Judah
    184D4g
  of Zebulun 184D4h

Bethlehemite 184D4g
Beth-maacah
  Abel-beth-maacah
    184D1a
Beth-millo 184D4i
Bethphage 184D4j
Bethsaida
  Pool of Bethsaida 346
  the town 184D4k
Bethuel 371E3c
Bethzatha
  Pool of Bethzatha 346
betide
  happen 154
betray 272A
betrayal 272A
betrothal 894F
betrothe 894F
better
  get better 654
better off 34D
betting
  gambling 618B
between 231
  in the middle 70
betwixt 231
beverage 301E3
bewail 836
beware 457C
bewilder 474B
bewildered 474B
bewitch 983
bewitched 983
bewitchment 983
beyond
  beyond comparison
    462B
Bezaleel
  Bezalel 371E3d
Bezalel 371E3d
bias
  prejudice 481
Bible 975
biblical 975
bid
  offer 759
bier 364A
big
  large 195B
Bildad 371E3e
Bilhah 371E3f
bill
  bill of divorce 548B2
billhook 630B
billow
  wave 343
billy goat 365F
bin
  vessel 194A
bind
  restrain 747C
  tie 45
bird 365C
bird of prey 365C2
birth 167B4a
  from birth 130C2
birthdays 141D2
birthright
  firstborn 119A3

bisect
  halve 92
bishop
  overseer 741E3
bit
  bit by bit 27
  bridle 747C2
bit and bridle 747C2
bite
  snakebite 655C4
Bithynia 184D4l
bitter 391B1
  unpleasant 825D2
bitterness 391B1
  unpleasantness
    825D2
bitumen
  pitch 631C3
bivouac 192C1
black 428
black and white 437A
blacksmith 686B3c
blade
  sharp edge 256A
blain 651B1
blame
  accuse 928
blameless 935
blameworthy 936
blanched
  pale 426
blandishments
  flattery 925
blanket 226B2
blaspheme 980B
blasphemy 980B
Blastus 371E3g
blaze 381
bleach 427E
bleat 409B
bleed 335E
bleeding 651B7
blemish 647
  without blemish 646
blemished 647
blend
  mix 43
bless 897
blessed
  happy 824
blessing 897
blind 439
blinded 439B
blindfold 439B
blindness 439
bliss 824
blissful 824
blithe 824
blood 335E
  bloodshed 362
  flow of blood 302C
  menstrual flow 302C
bloodguilt 936B
blood of Christ 335E7
blood on his head 180
bloodshed 362
bloodthirsty 362B5
blossom 366B3
blot
  blot out 550

blot out
forget 506E
blow
hit 279A
impact 279A
blow away 352A
blue 435
blueprint 23A
bluff
deceive 542A
blunt 257
blush 431A2
Boanerges 371E3h
boar 365G7
board 207A
boast 877
boastful 877
boasting 877
boat 275B
Boaz 371E3i
a pillar 218C2
bodily 319
body 319
dead body 363
body life
fellowship 9
bog 347
bogus 541
boil
blain 651B1
cook 381C6b
boiling
hot 379B
bold
courageous 855
boldness
courage 855
plain speaking 573
bolster
cushion 218E
bond 47
bones
bones broken 46E6a
dead bones 363F1
flesh and bones 319
bonfire 381
book 589
boomerang
rebound 280
boost
augment 36
boot 228B7d
booth 192C5
Feast of Booths 988A4
booty 790
Booz
Boaz 371E3i
border
boundary 236
edge 234
bore
perforate 263A4
born
born again 167B5b
born in one's house
191A
never born 2C
borrow 785
boss 741
bothersome 827

both sides 91E
bottle 194A
bottom 214
buttocks 238A
bottomless pit 255B2
bough
branch 53B
boulder 344B
bound 747C
boundary 236B
boundary mark 547D
bounty 813
bow
bow down 309
rainbow 250D
shooting 287B
weapon 723
bowels 224A6
bowl 194A
bowman 287B2
bowstring 208A
box 194A
Bozez 344B2
Bozrah 184D4m
bracelet 844A
bracket 218
bradawl 630C
brag
boast 877
braid
plait 222D
brainy
intelligent 498
bramble 366D5
branch
bough 53B
foliage 366B2
brand
mark 547C1
branded 547
brand new 126
brass
bronze 631B5
brave 855
bray
sound of donkey 409C
breach
division 46
gap 201
opening 263A2a
bread 301B1c
bread of the Presence
189A3
breadth 205B
length and breadth
203B
break
break agreements 769
break bones 46E6a
break of day 128A2
break out against 176B
divide 46
not observe 769
breaker
wave 343
breaking forth 176B
breast 253
breast-feeding 301D4
breastpiece 989B

breath 352A
under one's breath
578C
breathe 352A
breed 167
breeze 352B
brethren
brothers 11
fellow-Christians 985
brevity 114
briar 366D5
sharp thing 256A5
bribe 612C
bribery 612C
brick 631C3
bride 894
bridegroom 894
bride price 809C
bridle 747C2
brief 114
concise 569
briefly 569
brier 366D5
sharp thing 256A5
bright 417
brightness 417
brimstone
sulphur 385E
bring 272B
bring back 656C3
bring down 311A3
bring near 200A4
bring out 304A
bring forth
reproduce 167
bring up
adopt 170A7
rear 534E
brittle 330
brittleness 330
broad 205A
roomy 183A
broadcast
scatter 75
broaden
enlarge 197
broil
cook 381C6
broken 46
broken-hearted 834
bronze 631B5
brooch 844A5
brood
children 170
meditate 449B5
brook
river 350C
broom 648C4
the tree 366D2d
broth 335F
brother 11
brotherhood
family 11
the church 985
brow
face 237B1
brown 430
bruise 655C1
brush
broom 648C4

brutal 735
brute
animal 365
buckler 662C1
bud
flower 366B3
budge
move 265
buffoon
fool 501
bugle
trumpet 414B3
build 164
builder 164
building 192
built on rock 153
built on sand 152
bulky 195B
bull 365F
wild bull 365E6c
bull-headed 602
bullock 365F
bully
threaten 900
bulrush 366C1b
bulwark 713
buoyant 323A3
burden 322D
carrying burdens 273
burdensome 682
burgher 191
burglar 789
burial 364
burial place 364B
buried 364
burn 381
be hot 379B
burn for burn 28C6
burning 381
burnt 381
burnt offering 981D2
burst 46
bury 364
hide 525
bush 366D
burning bush 366D1a
bushel 465
business 622
trade 791
buss
kiss 889A
bust
break 46
busy 678A
busybody 678D
butcher 362
butler 686B2
butter 357D4
buttocks 238A
buttress 218
buy 792
buzzard
red kite? 365C3d
by
nearby 200
pass by 305B
by chance 159
by day 128
by degrees 27
by force 740

bygone 125
by instinct 476
by oneself 88B4
byre
  stable 192
byway 624
cable
  rope 208B
cackle
  laugh 835A
cad 938
cadaver 363
cadge 761
Caesar
  Caesar Augustus 371D8f
  Claudius Caesar 371E5c
Caesarea 184E1a
Caesarea Philippi 184E1b
cage
  basket 194B7
Caiaphas 371E4a
Cain 371E4b
cairn 209B1
cajole
  flatter 925
cake
  raisin cakes 301B1e
calamitous 731
calamity 731
calculate
  reckon 480F
Caleb 371E4c
calf 365F
  idol 982
call
  call out 577
  hail 400D
  name 561
  pray 761A1e
  summon 737B1
called
  named 561
  summoned 737B1
calling
  occupation 686B1
  summoning 737B1
call in question 486
callous
  pitiless 906
calm 266A4
  to still 266B
calumny 926
Calvary 363F2
camel 365G2
camel load 26
camels' hair 631F6
camp 192C4
camping 192C4
Cana 184E1c
Canaan
  Canaanites 371C3a
  the land 184E1d
  the person 371E4d
Canaanites 371C3a
cancel 752B
cancer 651B7
Candace 371E4e
candelabra 420B
candid 494
candle 420B

cane
  sweet cane 392A
  sweet-smelling cane 396A
canine 365G3
cannibal 301B7a
cannibalism 301B7a
cannot 161
cannot move 266A1
canonicals 989
canopy 226C6
canyon 255C
cap
  the priests' caps 989E
cape
  cloak 228B7a
Caphtor
  Crete 184E1p
Caphtorim 184E1p
capital
  top 213A3
  capital punishment 963F
Cappadocia 184E1f
captain 741
captive 747E
captivity 747D
captor 749
capture 747E
caravan 268B
carcass 363
care
  anxiety 825E
  take care of 457A
careful 457
careless
  negligent 458
  rash 857
caress 889B
cargo 795
Carmel 184E1g
  Mt Carmel 209G1c
Carmelite 184E1g
Carmelitess 184E1g
carnage 362
carnal 319B
carnality 319B
carnelian 844A1b
carousal 949
carouse
  get drunk 949
carouser
  drunkard 949
carpenter 686B3a
Carpus 371E4f
carriage 274
carrier 273
carry 273
carry off 786B
cart 274B
carve 46
  sculpt 554
carving 554
case
  argument 475A
cash
  money 797
cask 194A
casket 194A
cassia 396A

cast
  cast out 300
  mould 554B
  throw 287
castanets 414B1c
casting 554B
castrate 172A3
castrated
  eunuch 172A3
catch 747E
  catch of fish 171E
caterer
  cook 686B2
cattle 365F
  wild cattle 365E6c
Cauda 349B
cause
  reason 156
  what cause? 158
  without cause 916B
causeless 916B
caution 858
cautious 858
cavalry 722
cave 255A
  burial place 364B
cavern 255A
cease 145
  cease to exist 2D
ceaseless 115
cedar 366D2e
cedar wood 631D3
Cedron
  Kidron 255C2
celebrate 876
celebrated
  renowned 866
celebration 876
celibacy 895
celibate 895
cellar 194C
Cenchrea 184E1h
Cenchreae
  Cenchrea 184E1h
censer 396B
censure
  reprove 924
census 86C1
central 70
centre 70
centurion 722D1
Cephas
  Peter 371K4
ceramics 631C4
cereal
  cereal offering 981D3
cerebral 447
ceremonial 875B
ceremony
  pomp 875B
  ritual 988
certain 473
certainty 473
certificate 548B2
chafe
  rub 333
chaff 641C3
  light 323A

chain
  fastening 47C
  gold chain 743D
chair 218D
chalcedony 844A1b
Chaldea 184Eii
Chaldeans 371C3b
chamber
  room 194C
champion 722
chance 159
change 143
  change clothes 228B4
  change direction 282
  change one's mind 603
  conversion 147
  exchange 150
changeable 152
changed 147
changeless
  secure 153D
channel 351
chant
  sing 413A
chaos 61
chaotic 61
char 381C5
character
  nature 5
  virtue 933
charcoal 385A3
charge
  command 737
  commission 751
charger
  warhorse 365G5
chariot 274A
charity
  benevolence 897
charm
  talisman 983C
charred 381C5
chase
  pursue 619
chasm
  cavity 255B
  gap 201
chaste 895C
chasten 827C
chastening 827C
chastise
  punish 963
chastisement 963
chastity 895C
chatter 581
cheap 812
cheat 930B
check
  halt 145
  test 461
Chedorlaomer 371E4g
cheek
  side of face 239B
cheer 831B
cheerful 833
cheerfulness 833
cheese 301B1g

chef
  cook 686B2
chela 538
Chemosh 967D
Cherethites 371C3c
cherub 968B2
cherubim 968B2
chest
  money-box 799A
Chezib
  Achzib 184D1e
chicken 365C3a
chide
  reprove 924
chief
  master 741D
  supreme 34
child
  descendant 170
  young one 132
childhood 130
childless 172A1
childlike 132
children
  descendants 170
  young people 132
chiliarch 722D2
chill 382A
chilly 380A
Chimham 371E4h
chimney 353B
chin 237B1
Chinnereth
  Galilee 184F2
  Sea of Galilee 343C2
Chinneroth
  Galilee 184F2
  Sea of Chinneroth
    343C2
Chios 349B
chirp 409D
chisel
  sculpt 554
Chittim
  Cyprus 184E1q
Chiun
  Kaiwan 967H
Chloe 371E5a
choenix 465C
choice 605
choinix
  choenix 465C
choir 413A
choke
  smother 362C1
choose 605
  not choose 606
choosy
  fastidious 862
chop
  divide 46
Chorazin 184E1j
chore 682
chosen 605
Christ
  anointed one 357C
  Jesus Christ 371H5
Christian 708C
chronic
  lasting 113

chrysolite 844A1b
chrysoprase 844A1b
chubby
  plump 195B
chuckle 835A
chum
  friend 880
church 985
Chushan-rishathaim
  Cushan-rishathaim
    371E6c
Chuza 371E5b
Cilicia 184E1k
cinders 381
cinnamon 396A
Cinneroth
  Galilee 184F2
circle 250
  encircle 314
circuit 250
  go round 314
circular 250A
circumcise 988B1
circumcision 988B1
  circumcision party
    708D
circumspect 457
circumstances 8A
cistern 339B5
citizen 191
citizenship 191
citron wood 631D4
city 184C
  city of refuge 184C7
  fortified city 713C
City of David 184G2

civil war 718C3
  killing one another
    362E8a
clad 228
clairvoyant 984
clan 11
clap 279G
clasp
  fastening 47D
  hug 378C
class
  kind 77
  species 77
Clauda
  Cauda 349B
Claudius 371E5c
clay 344D
clean 648
clean conscience 917A1
cleanness 648
cleanse 648
cleansed 648
cleansing 648
clear
  transparent 422
clearness
  transparency 422
cleave
  chop 46
  cling 48
cleft
  cleft of a rock 46F5
  divided 46

clemency 905
Clement 371E5e
Cleopas 371E5f
clever
  intelligent 498
climb 308B6
cling 378C4
  stick 48A
clinging
  cohesive 48
cloak 228B7a
close
  near 200
  shut 264
closeness
  nearness 200
closure 264
cloth 631F
  covering 226B3
clothe 228
clothed 228
clothes 228
clothing 228
cloud 355A
clout
  strike 279A
cloven
  divided 46
club
  cudgel 723A2
  war-club 723
cluster 74
clutch
  cling 378C4
  grasp 786E
Cnidus 184E1l
coal
  charcoal 385
coast 234B
coastal 234B
coat
  cover 226B2
coating 226D
coax 612
cobra 365E4
cobweb 222C
cock 365C3a
coequal 28
coerce 740
coercion 740
coffin 364A
cogent
  powerful 160
cogitate 449B5
cognition 490
cohere 48
cohesion 48
cohesive 48
cohort 722
coinage 797
coins 797A
coition 45C1a
coitus 45C1a
cold 380
  making cold 382A

colleague 707
collect
  gather 74
Colossae 184E1m
colossal 195A
colossus 195A
colour 425
  dye 425
colt 365G5
  young animal 132B
column 215B2
combat
  fight 716
combatant 722
combination
  mixture 43
combined
  mixed 43
combustion 381
come
  approach 289
  arrive 295
  things to come 124
come down 309
comely
  beautiful 841
come to one's senses 502
come to rest 266A2
comfort 831
comfortable
  content 828
comforter 831
comforting 831
coming 295D
  future 124
  second coming 295D
command 737
  authority 733
  give orders 737
commandment 953E
commemorate 505
commemoration 505
commemorative 505
commence 68
commend 923
  commend oneself 923B3
commendable 923
commendation 923
commerce
  trade 791
commercial 791
commission 751
commit
  do 676
  give 781
committee 692
commodious 183A
commodity
  merchandise 795
common
  common people 869
  general 79
  in common 775
  what in common? 10A
commonalty 869
common cause
  cooperation 706
commoner 869
common ownership 775
commonplace 79

commotion 61
communal 775
communicate 524
communion
  fellowship 9
companion 89
  friend 880
company
  assembly 74
  fellowship 9
compare 462
  liken 18
comparison 462
  beyond comparison 462B
compasses 630C
compassion 905
  no compassion 906
compass point 281
compel 740
compensate 804B
compensation 804B
compete 716E
competence
  skill 696
competent
  skilful 696
competition
  contest 716E
complacency 483
complacent
  underestimating 483
complain
  grumble 829
complainer 829
complaint
  grumble 829
complete
  entire 52
  fulfil 725
  full 54
  perfect 646
completed 725
completion 725
compliance
  observance 768
compliant
  willing 597
comply
  obey 739
composite
  mixture 43
composition
  proportions 56A
composure
  inexcitability 823
compound
  mixture 43
comprehend
  understand 516
compress 279H
  compress the lips 547B3
compulsion 740
compunction 905
compute
  count 86
conceal 525
concealed 525
concealment 525

concede
  permit 756
conceit
  pride 871
conceited
  proud 871
conceive
  become pregnant 167B1
conception
  becoming pregnant 167B1
concern
  not concerned 860
concession 758A
concise 569
concision
  mutilators 46E3
conclave 74B
conclusion
  end 69
concord
  in harmony 710
concrete 319
concubine 952B
concur 24
concurrent 123
condemn 961
condemnation 961
condemned 961
condescend 872
condescension 872
condiment 389
condition
  circumstances 8
  state 7
conduct 688
conduit 351
confer
  discuss 475B
confess 526F2
  bear witness 466
confession
  disclosure 526
  testimony 466
confidence 660
confirm 473
conflagration 381
conform 83
conforming 83
conformity 83
confound
  confute 479
  fail to discriminate 464
confuse
  bewilder 474B
  derange 63A
confute 479
congratulate 923
congratulation 923
congregate 74B
congregation 74B
Coniah
  Jehoiachin 371H3a
connect 45
connection
  relation 9
conquer 786C1
conscience 917
conscript 740
consecrate 979B3

consent 758
  not consent 760
consequence 156
conserve 666
consider 449B5
consist
  exist 1C
  hold together 48A
consistency
  uniformity 16
consistent
  not consistent 25B
consolation 831
console 831
conspicuous 522
conspiracy 623B4
conspirator 623B4
conspire 623B3
constancy 153
constant
  unchanging 153
constellations 420A3
consternation
  fear 854
constituency
  proportions 56A
constraint
  compulsion 740
construct 164
construction 164
construe
  interpret 520
consult 691
consultant
  adviser 691
consume
  destroy 165
  eat 301
consumption
  disease 651B7
  eating 301
contact
  touch 378A
contagion
  illness 651
container 194
contemplation
  meditation 449B5
contempt 922
contend
  fight 716
contender 716
content 828
contention
  fight 716
  quarrel 709
contentment 828
contest 716E
continual burnt offering
  981D2
continually 146
continuous 146
contract 198
  agreement 765
  reduce 198
contraction 198
contradict 533D
contradiction 533
contrary
  opposite 14

contribute
  give 781
contribution
  giving 781
contrite
  penitent 830
contrition
  penitence 830
control
  self-control 823E
controlled
  self-controlled 823
controversy 709
contumely 926
conversation 584
converse
  opposite 14
  talk 584
conversely 14
conversion 147
convert 147
converted 147
converts 147B
convey
  transfer 272
convince 485
convinced 485
convulsion 318C
cook 381C6
  chef 686B2
cool
  cold 380
  cool spirit 823
  making cool 382A
cooling 382A
cooperate 706
cooperation 706
cooperative 706
copper 631B5
coppersmith 686B3c
copulation 45C1a
copy
  imitate 20
  make a copy 22
cor 465
coral
  precious stone 844A1b
  the material 631G3
cord 208A
Corinth 184E1n
corn
  grain 301B1b
  plant 366C2
cornelian
  carnelian 844A1b
Cornelius 371E5g
corner
  angle 247
cornerstone
  foundation 214
corporal punishment
  279A1a
corporeal 319
corpse 363
corpulence 195B
correct
  reprove 924
  true 494
correlation 12

correspondence 588
corrosion 51
corrupt
  make worse 655
  wicked 914
corruptible 51
corruption
  bribery 612C
  decay 51
  making worse 655
Cos 184E10
cosh
  club 723
cosmetics 843
cosmos 321
cost
  price 809
costly 811
cot
  bed 218E
cottage 192
couch 218E
council 692
counsel 691
counsellor 691A
count
  enumerate 86
countenance 237B1
counter
  contrary 14
counterevidence 467
counterfeit 541
countermand 752B
countless 104
count on 485
country
  countryside 184A
  land 184
countryside 184A
couple
  join 45
courage 855
courageous 855
court
  courtyard 235B
  law court 956
courtesy 884
courtyard 235B
cousin 11
covenant 765
cover 226
covering 226
covet 859A5
covetous 859A5
cow 365F
coward 856
cowardice 856
cowardly 856
co-worker 707
Cozbi 371E5h
crack
  break 46
  sharp noise 402
cradle
  bed 218E
craft
  ship 275A
craftsmanship 696
crafty 698
crag 209

cramped
  no room 183C
cranium 213B
crash
  sharp noise 402
crave 859C1
craven 856
crawl 210C
crazy
  mad 503
create 164
creation
  making 164
creator 164
creature
  animal 365
credence 485
credible 485
credit
  thanks 907C
creditable 923
creditor 802
credulous 487
creep 210C
  creeping things 365B
creeping 210C
cremation
  burning 381
  interment 364
Crescens 371E6a
crestfallen
  disappointed 509
Cretan 184E1p
Crete 184E1p
  the island 349B
crevasse 201
crevice 201
crew
  sailors 270
cricket 365B2c
crime 914
criminal 938
crimson
  red 431
crippled 655D
Crispus 371E6b
criticism 926
crocodile 365D1
crocus 366C3a
crooked 246B
crop
  agriculture 370
Cross
  cross hands 222A
  cross over 267E
  gallows 964C
crossing
  passage 305
crow
  crowing 409D
crowd 74B
crowing 409D
crown 743B
crucifixion 964C
crucify 964C
cruel 735
cruelty 735
crumb
  leftover 41B1

crush 332A
  crushed in spirit 834
  press 279H
  trample 279B
crushed
  no room 183C
cry
  battle cry 400C
  cry of distress 577C
  weep 836
crystal
  precious stone 844A1b
  the material 631G3
  transparent 422
cube 28D3
cubicle 194C
cubit
  distance measure 199A3
  measure 465B2
cucumber 366C3b
  food 301B1f
cud
  chewing the cud 301E2e
cudgel 723A2
cuff
  hit 279A
culpable
  guilty 936
cultivate 370
cultivation 370
cummin 366C3c
cunning 698
cup 194A
  drinking 301E3
cupbearer 686B2
curds 301B4
cure 656A
currency 797
curse 899
cursed 899
curtain 421A
curvature 250
curve 250
Cush
  Ethiopia 184E5g
Cushan-rishathaim
371E6c
cushion 218E3
Cushite
  Ethiopian 371C3f
custom
  habit 610
  tradition 127C
cut 46
  cut hair 46E4
  cut in pieces 46E1
cut off
  kill 362
Cuza
  Chuza 371E5b
cymbals 414B1c
cynic
  unbeliever 486
cypress 366D2f
  cypress timber 631D4
Cyprus 184E1q
Cyrene 184E1r
Cyrus 371E6d
dad
  father 169B

daft 499
dagger 723A5
Dagon 967E
daily 141A2
  all day 146
dais
  platform 218H
dale
  valley 255C
dally
  be late 136
Dalmanutha
  Magadan? 184H1c
Dalmatia 184E2a
dam 264C5
  dam up 264C5
damage
  destroy 165
Damaris 371E7a
Damascus 184E2b
damn
  condemn 961
damned
  condemned 961
damp 341A
dampness 341A
Dan
  territory of 184E2c
  the city 184E2c
  the person 371E7b
  tribe of 371B4d
dance 835B
danger 661
Daniel 371E7c
dappled 437
dare 855A2
  not dare 856
daric 797A1
daring 855
Darius 371E7d
dark 418
darken 418
darkness 418
  from darkness to light
    417C4
  outer darkness 418C4
darling 890
darnel 366C1c
dart
  shooting 287B
dash
  move fast 277
date
  calendar 108
  fruit 366D4a
dated
  old 127
dates 301B1e
Dathan 371E7f
daughter 170A5
daunt
  frighten 854
dauntless 855
David 371E7g
  City of David 184K5
  king of Judah 741C2
  tower of 209C2
dawdle 136
dawn 128A2

day
day after day 106
day and night 128F1
day of the Lord 108D2a
days old 131
daytime 128
first day 108F1a
period 110
short time 114
time 108
today 121B
to this day 121D
daybreak 128A2
day by day
repeatedly 106
daylight
daytime 128
day of rest 683A
days
period 110
daysman 720
dazzle 417
deacon 742C2c
dead 361
Dead Sea 343C1
living and dead 360E
dead body 363
deaf 416
deafness 416
dealer
merchant 794
dealings
avoid dealings 620C5
no dealings 883A
dear
expensive 811
loved 887
dearest
darling 890
dearness 811
death 361
life and death 360E
put to death 362
deathbed 361
deathless
eternal 115
death penalty 963F
death sentence 963F
debar
prohibit 757
debase
dishonour 867
debatable
uncertain 474
debate 475A
debater 475A
debauch 951
debauched 951
debauchery 951
debilitate
weaken 163
debility
ill-health 651
weakness 163
Debir
the city 184E2d
debit
debt 803
debonair
cheerful 833

Deborah 371E8a
debris
rubbish 641C3
debt 803
debtor 803
decade 110E2
decamp 296
decapitate 46E3
Decapolis 184E2e
decay 51
decease 361
deceit 542A
deceitful 542A
deceive 542A
deceiver 545
deception 542A
deceptive 542
decide 617
decision 617
deck
deck of ship 194D
declaim 579
declamation
oration 579
declare
affirm 532
divulge 526
reveal 526
decline
go down 309
refuse 760
decompose 51
decomposition 51
decorum 846
decrease 37
decree 737
decry 926
deduct
subtract 39
deed
action 676
deep 211
deeper 211E
deer 365E1b
defamation 926
defame 926
defeat 728
defeated 728
defecate 302B1
defecation 302B1
defect
speech defect 580B
defection 930
defective vision 440
defence 713
defend 713
plead a cause 927
defer
delay 136
deference 920
deferential 920
defiance 711
defiant 711
deficiency 636
deficient 636
defile
make unclean 649
profane 980
defiled 649

deflower
rape 951G
defraud 788
defrayment
payment 804
deft
skilful 696
defy 711
degenerate
deteriorate 655
deities 966
deity 965
dejected 834
dejection 834
delay 136
no delay 135B
delayed
dawdled 136
late 136
delete
obliterate 550
delicacy 390
delicate 327
delicious 390
delight 826
delighted 824
delightful 826
Delilah 371E8c
deliver
childbirth 167
hand over 272
rescue 668
deliverance 668
deliver up
hand over 272
delude 542A
deluge
flood 350B
delusion 542A
delve
dig 255D1
demand
order 737
demanding
difficult 700
demarcate
limit 236
demeanour
conduct 688
demented
insane 503
dementia
insanity 503
Demetrius 371E8e
demise
death 361
demolish 165
demolition 165
demon 969C
demonised 969D3
demon-possessed 969D3
demoniac 969D3
demonised 969D3
demonstrate
prove 478
demoralised 856
demote 752A
den 192E2
denarius 797A1

denial 533
denizen
citizen 191
denounce
accuse 928
defame 926
dental 256B
denude
uncover 229C
denunciation
accusation 928
deny 533
depart 296
go out and come in
297D
departure 296C
depend 485
dependable 929
dependent
interdependent 12
depict 551
depleted 636
deplore
regret 830
deport 188
deportation 188A
deportment
conduct 688
depose 752A
deposit
security 767
depot
store 632
deprecate 924
depression
low spirits 834
depth 211
no depth 212
sounding depths
211D
depthing 211D
deputy 755
derange 63
deranged
insane 503
Derbe 184E2f
deride 851
derision 851
descend 309
descendant 170
descent 309
describe 590B
description 590B
desecrate 980
desert
abandon 621
wilderness 172D1
deserted
uninhabited 190D
deserts
due return 915B
deserve 915B
design
pattern 23A
plan 623B2
designation
name 561
desire 859
sexual desire 859C3

desist
  cease 145
desolate
  empty 190D
desolation
  destruction 165
despair 853
despairing 853
despatch
  send 272B
despise 922
despoil 165
despot
  dictator 741
dessication 342
destine 596B
destined 596B
destiny 596B
destitute 801
destroy 165
destroyer 168
destruction 165
  ban of destruction 165A3
destructive 165
detail
  no detail 570
detain
  imprison 747D
detect 484
detection 484
detention 747D
deter
  hinder 702
deteriorate 655
deterioration 655
determination 599
determine 617
determined
  resolute 599
detest 888
dethrone 752A
detraction 926
devastate
  destroy 165
deviant 84
deviate 282
devil 969
  slanderer 926A
devious 282
devise 623
devoted
  devoted thing 899F
devour
  destroy 165
  eat 301
devout 979
dew 341B
dexterity
  skill 696
dexterous
  skilful 696
diaconate 742C2c
diadem 743B
dialect 580A
dialogue 584
diamond 844A1b
Diana
  Artemis 967H
diarrhoea 651B7

diatribe
  censure 924
dice 618B
dictator 741
didactic 534
Didymus
  Thomas Didymus
    371L8c
die 361
  die of itself 361E5
diet 301
differ
  be unlike 19
difference 15
  no difference 16
different 15
  diverse 17
  not different 16
  unlike 19
differentiate 15D
difficult 700
difficulty 700
dig 255D1
digest 301
digger 255D1
digit
  toes 53E6
dignity
  honour 866
digress
  go astray 282
diligence 678A
diligent 678A
dill 366C3c
dilly-dally 136
dim 419
  see dimly 440
  unintelligent 499
dime 797
diminish 198
dimness 419
din
  noise 400A
Dinah 371E8f
dine 301
dinghy 275B
dinner 301
Dionysius 371E8g
Diotrephes 371E8h
dip 303B
  baptise 988B2
direct
  guide 689
  straight 249
direction
  guidance 689
  heading 281
directive
  command 737
directly
  immediately 116
  straight 249
directness
  plain speaking 573
director 690
dirge
  lament 836
dirt 649
  dung 302B1
dirty 649

dirty joke 839
disagree 25
disagreement
  quarrel 709
disallow
  prohibit 757
disappear 446
disappearance 446
disappoint 509
disappointed 509
  not disappointed 509
disapproval 924
disapprove 924
disarm 719
disarranged 63
disarray 61
disaster 645
disastrous 645
disbelief 486
disbelieve 486
disburse
  pay 804
discard 779
discern 463
discerning 463
discernment 463
discharge
  discharge of blood 302C
  excretion 302A
disciple 538
discipleship 538A
discipline 827C
disclaim 533
disclose 526
disclosure 526
discomfort 825
discontent 829
discontented 829
discontinuance 145
discontinue 145
discord
  disagreement 25
  quarrelling 709
discount
  underestimate 483
discourage
  hinder 702
discouragement 853
discourse
  address 579
discover 484
discovery 484
discredit
  cast doubt 486
discretion 463
discriminate 463
discrimination 463
  lack of discrimination
    464
discuss 475B
discussion 475B
disease 651
disengaged
  at leisure 683
disfavour 924
disgrace 867
  humiliation 872B
disguise 527

dish 194A
  basin 194B6
  food 301
disharmony
  dissension 709
dishearten
  discourage 702
dishonest
  false 541
dishonour 867
dishonourable 867
disinclination
  unwillingness 598
disintegrate 46
dislike 861
dislocate 46
disloyal 930
disloyalty 603C
dismay
  fear 854
dismember 46E3
disobedience 738
disobedient 738
disobey 738
disorder 61
disorderly 61
disorganised 61
disown 533
disparage 926
disparaging 926
disparity 29
dispassionate 823
dispatch
  send 272B
dispersal 75
disperse 75
dispersion 75
displace 188
displaced person 188
displacement 188
display
  ostentation 875
displease 827
displeased
  discontented 829A
  distressed 825
dispraise 924
disputation
  argument 709
  discussion 475
dispute 709
  debate 475
disqualification 300
disqualified 300C6
disqualify 300
disregard 458
disrepair 655
disreputable 867C
disrepute 867
disrespect 921
disrespectful 921
disrobe 229C
dissatisfaction 829A
dissatisfy 827
dissemble 541
dissembler 545
disseminate 528
dissension 709
dissent 489

dissident
  malcontent 829
dissimilar 19
dissimilarity 19
dissipate
  disperse 75
dissipation 943
dissociate oneself 883
dissolute 951
dissuade 613
dissuasion 613
distaff 630D
distance
  at a distance 199A
  in space 199
distant
  in space 199
distend 197
distinct 80
distinction
  difference 15
  importance 638
  no distinction 16
distinguish
  differentiate 15D
distort 246
distortion 246
distracted
  excited 821
distress 827
  being distressed 825
  cause distress 827
distressed 825
distressing 827
distribute 783
distribution 783
district 184
distrust 486
disturb
  trouble 827
disturbance
  commotion 61
disunited 46
ditch 262
divan 218E
dive
  plunge 313
diverge 294
diverse 17
diversion
  amusement 837
diversity 17
divert
  turn someone away 282B
divide 46
  divide into two 92
  divide up 100
  share out 783
divided 46
divination 983B1
divine
  God 965
diviner 983B1
divining 983B1
division
  subdivision 53A
divorce 896A
  bill of divorce 548B2
divulge 526

do 676
  do as you would be done
    by 280B
  obey 739
  what have I to do with
    you? 10A
dock
  court 956
docket
  certificate 548B2
doctor 658B1
doctrine 534D
document 548B2
dodge
  avoid 620
doe 365E1b
Doeg 371E8i
doer 676
doff 229C
dog 365G3
  pursue 619
dogged
  persevering 600
dogma
  doctrine 534D
dogmatic
  certain 473
dog-tired 684
doing
  action 676
doing well
  prosperous 730
dole out
  apportion 783
do likewise
  imitate 20
dolour
  suffering 825
dolt
  dunce 501

domestic
  servant 742
domesticated
  domesticated animals
    365G
domicile
  abode 192
dominate 733
domination 733
domineering 735
dominion
  authority 733
  land 184
don
  wear 228
donate 781
donation 781
done
  completed 725
donkey 365G4
  nonconformist 84C
  wild donkey 365E6a
donor 781
door 264A
  doorway 263B
doorkeeper 264A3
doorpost 263B
doorway 263B
Dorcas 371E8j

dorsal 238
dot
  small thing 33A
double 91
  double-minded 601A
double-cross 542A
doubled 91
double-minded 601A
  changeable 152A
doubly 91
doubt
  in doubt 474
  unbelief 486
doubtless 473
dough 301B1c
dove 365C3b
down 309
downcast
  sad 834
downfall 309E2
down payment 767
downpour 350F1
downtrodden 745
dowry 809C
doze
  sleep 679B
dozen 99F3
drachma 797A1
draconian 735
drag
  pull 288
dragon 365H
drag on
  prolong 113
drama 542C
dramatic 542C
drape
  curtain 421A
draught
  wind 352B
draw
  attract 291
  depict 551
  draw water 304C
  pull 288
draw back 290
drawing
  picture 551
drawl
  accent 580A
drawn out
  protracted 113
dread 854F
dreadful
  frightening 854
dream 438E
dregs
  lees 41B4
drench 341C
dress
  clothe 228
dressed 228
dressing
  bandage 658A
dressing down
  reprimand 924
dried fruit 301B1e
dried out 342
dried up 342
drift 282

drink 301
  eat and drink 301E1
drinkable 301E3
drinker
  drunkard 949
drinking 301
drinking water 339C1
drip 350A4a
dripping
  dripping wet 341A
  water dropping
    350A4a
drive 265B
  drive back 715
  drive out 300
  energy 160
drivel 515
drizzle 350F1
droll
  witty 839
drop
  small amount 33A
droplet 33A
droppings
  excrement 302B1
dropsy 651B7
dross
  rubbish 641C3
drought 342B4
drove
  flock 74C1
drown 361
drowse
  sleep 679B
drudge
  servant 742
drunk 949
  not drunk 948C
drunkard 949
drunken 949
drunkenness 949
Drusilla 371E8k
dry 342
  dry up 342B1
dryness 342
dual
  double 91
dub
  name 561
dubious
  uncertain 474
due 915B
dueness 915B
dues
  tax 809
due to
  caused by 158
duffer
  ignoramus 493
dug 255D1
dugong 365D1
dull
  insensitive 820
dumb
  unintelligent 499
  voiceless 578A
dumpy
  plump 195B
dun
  brown 430

dunce 493
dune 209
dung
  dung for fuel 385C
  excreta 302B1
  rubbish 641C3
dungeon
  prison 748
duo 90
dupe
  deceive 542A
duplicate
  copy 22
  duplicating words 91D3
duplicity 541
durable 144
duration
  long duration 113
dusk
  evening 129B
dust 332B
  numerous as dust 104
dusty 332
duty 917
dwarf 196A
dwell 192
dwelling 192
dwelling-place 192
dwindle 37
dye 425
dyeing 425
dying 361
  dying of itself 361E5
dynamism
  energy 160
dynasty 733D3
dysentery 651B7

each other
  correlation 12
eager 818C
  eager to speak 581A
eagle 365C3c
ear 415B
earlier 119
early
  promptly 135
  rise early 128B
earn 771C
earnest
  down-payment 767
  fervent 818
earnings 771C
earring 844A
earshot 415
ear-splitting 400A
earth 321
  ground 344
earthenware 631C4
  common things 869
earthquake 176C1
earthworm 365B3
ease
  rest 683
east 281C
eastern 281C
eastern sea 343C1
eat 301
  eat and drink 301E1
  eat together 882
  not eat 946D

eating 301
eaves
  roof 213A2
Ebal
  Mt Ebal 209G1d
Ebed-melech 371F1a
Ebenezer 184E3a
ebony wood 631D4
ecstasy 824
ecstatic 824
eczema 651B7
Eden
  the garden 184E3b
Eder
  tower of 209C2
edge 234
edible 301
edict 737
edification 164
edifice 164
edify 164
Edom
  Edomites 371C3d
  Esau 371F4b
  the land 184E3c
Edomites 371C3d
educate 534
education 534
educator
  teacher 537
efface 550
effect
  consequence 156
effects
  property 777
effort
  exertion 682
Eglon 371F1b
ego
  self 80
egocentric
  selfish 932
egoism
  selfishness 932
egotist 932
egress 298
Egypt 184E4
  Egyptians 371C3e
Egyptians 371C3e
Ehud 371F1c
eight 99D
  day eight 108F4
  eight days old 131B1
eighth
  eighth day 108F4
eject 300
ejection 300
Ekron 184E5a
Ekronites 184E5a
Elah 371F1d
  king of Israel 741C1
elated
  rejoicing 824
El-berith 967H
Eldad 371F1e
elder
  chief 741E
  old person 133
elderly
  old people 133

eldest
  firstborn 119A
Eleazar 371F1f
elect
  chosen 605A
elegy
  lament 836
elemental spirits 319C
elementary
  simple 44
elements 319C
  elementary components 319C
  the weather 340B
elevate 310
elevated 310
elevation 209
eleven 99F2
eleventh 99F2
  eleventh hour 108E4f
Eli 371F1g
Eliakim 371F1h
  Jehoiakim 371H3c
Elias
  Elijah 371F2e
Eliashib 371F2a
Eliezer 371F2b
Elihu 371F2d
Elijah 371F2e
Elim 184E5b
Elimelech 371F2f
Eliphaz 371F2g
Elisabeth
  Elizabeth 371F3a
Eliseus
  Elisha 371F2h
Elisha 371F2h
Elizabeth 371F3a
Elkanah 371F3b
elocution
  eloquence 579A3
elongate
  lengthen 203
eloquence 579A3
eloquent 579A3
else
  someone else 15B
elucidate
  explain 520
elude
  avoid 620
  escape 667
Elymas
  Bar-jesus 371E1g
emaciated 206
emancipation 746
embalm 364A
embittered 891
embody 319
embolden
  give courage 855
embrace 889B
embroider 844B
embroidery 844B
emerald 844A1b
emerge 298
emetic 302F4
emissary 754
Emmanuel
  Immanuel 89A2a

Emmaus 184E5c
Emmor
  Hamor 371G1g
emollient
  balm 658A
emotion 818
empathy 818B
employment 686
emptiness
  uselessness 641
empty
  empty out 300F2
  pour 350A3
  useless 641
  vacant 190D
empty-handed 636E
empty talk 515
emulate
  imitate 20
encamp 192C1
enchanter 983B2
encircle 314
enclosure 235
encourage 855B
encouragement 855B
end 69
  the ends of the earth 183B
endanger 661
endearment 889
endeavour
  attempt 617
endless 115
endow
  give 781
endowment
  gift 781
endurance 600
endure 600
  cannot endure 827D
  stand firm 153C
enduring
  changeless 153C
Eneas
  Aeneas 371D3d
enemy 705
energetic 160
energy 160
enervate 163
enfeeble 163
enforce
  compel 740
engaged
  betrothed 894F
engagement
  battle 718
  betrothal 894F
Engedi 184E5d
engrave 586D4
engraving 586D4
enigma 530
enjoy 826
enjoyment 826
enlarge 197A
enliven
  revive 360
En-mishpat
  Kadesh-barnea 184G4a
enmity 881
Enoch 371F3c

enormous 195A
enough
  long enough 113A4
  sufficient 635
  too much 637
enquire 459
enrich
  make rich 800
ensconce
  place 187
ensign 547B1
enslave 745B
enslaved 745B
ensnare 542D
enter 297
  enter the temple 990B6
  go out and come in 297D
entertainment 837
enthroned 743A
enthusiasm 818
enthusiastic 818
entice 612B
entire 54
  all of 52
entrails 224A7
entrance 263C
  entering 297
entrap 542D
entreat 761
entrust 485G
enumerate 86
envious 912
envoy
  messenger 529C
envy 912
Epaenetus 371F3f
Epaphras 371F3d
Epaphroditus 371F3e
Epenetus
  Epaenetus 371F3f
ephah 465
ephemeral 114
Ephesian 184E5e
Ephesus 184E5e
ephod
  the ephod 989C
Ephraim
  northern kingdom
    371B3c
  Ophrah 184H5c
  territory of 184E5f
  the person 371F3g
  tribe of 371B4e
Ephratah
  Bethlehem 184D4g
Ephrath
  Bethlehem 184D4g
Ephrathah
  Bethlehem 184D4g
Ephrathite 184D4g
Epicureans
  party 708D
  philosophers 449B6
epilepsy 651B7
epistle
  letter 588
epoch 110
equal 28
  not equal 29

equality 28
  equivalent 28C1
equine 365G5
equip
  prepare 669
equipment 630
equipped
  prepared 669
equity
  justice 913
equivalent 28
Er 371F3h
era 110
erase 550
Erastus 371F4a
erect
  build 164
  vertical 215
Esaias
  Isaiah 371G5e
Esau 371F4b
  Edomites 371C3d
  Mt Esau 209G1e
escape 667
eschatology 69
eschew
  avoid 620
escort
  accompany 89
Esh-baal
  Ish-bosheth 371G5f
Eshcol
  valley of 255C2
Eshkalonites
  Ashkelonites 184D2j
espionage 459B3
established
  unchanging 153
esteem
  respect 920
Esther 371F4c
estimate 480F
estranged 46B1
estrangement
  enmity 881
eternal 115
  eternal life 360B3
eternity 115
Ethanim 108G3
Ethiopia 184E5g
  Ethiopians 371C3f
Ethiopians 371C3f
eulogise
  praise 923
Eunice 371F4d
eunuch 172A3
Euodia 371F4e
Euodias
  Euodia 371F4e
Euphrates 350D2
Euraquilo
  Northeaster 352B4
Euroclydon
  Northeaster 352B4
Eutychus 371F4f
evacuate
  defecate 302B1
  exile 188
evacuee 188

evade
  avoid 620
evanescent 114
evangelist 528A
evasion
  avoidance 620
evasive
  avoiding 620
Eve 371F4g
even
  equal 28
evening 129
event 154
even temper 823
ever
  for ever 115
everlasting 115
every
  every day 141A2
  every direction 281E4
  every kind 82
everyone 79
everything 79
  all circumstances 8A
evict 300
eviction 300
evidence 466
  evidence against 467
evident 522
evil
  badness 645
  wrongdoing 914
evildoer 938
evil eye
  parsimony 816
evil spirit 969C
ewe 365F
exaction
  tax 809
exalt 310
  promote 285B
exalted
  honoured 866B2
examine 438D4e
  interrogate 459B2
example 83C1
  warning 664
excavate 255D2
excavation 255D2
exceed
  outdo 306
exceeding 306
excel 306
excellence
  superiority 34
excess 637
excessive
  superfluous 637
exchange
  substitute 150
  swap 151
excise
  tax 809
excited 822A
excitement 821
exciting 821
exclude
  dam up 264C5
excommunicate 300C4b
excrement 302B1

excreta 302B1
excrete 302
excuse
  without excuse 180B
excuses 614
execute
  carry out 725
  kill 362
execution
  capital punishment
    963F
exemplify 83C1
exempt 919
exemption 919
exertion 682
exhalation 352A
exhale 352A
exhaust
  tire 684
exhausted 684
exhaustion 684
exhibition
  spectacle 445C
exhort 612
exhortation 612
exile 188A
exist 1
  cease to exist 2D
  not exist 2
existence 1
exit
  egress 298
exodus 296C
exonerate
  acquit 960
exorbitant
  expensive 811
exorcise 300D
exorcism 300D
expand 197
expanse 183A
expansion 197
expect 507
expectancy 507
expectation 507
  hope 852
expectorate 302F1
expedient
  useful 640
expedite
  hasten 680
expeditious
  hasty 680
expel 300
expend
  spend 806
expenditure 806
expense 806
expensive 811
experienced
  expert 696
experiment 461
expert
  scholar 492
  skilled person 696
expertise 696
expire
  breathe out 352A
  die 361
explanation 520C

exploit
action 676
expose
disclose 526
exposition
explanation 520
exposure
cold 380A
expound
interpret 520
expulsion 300
extend
enlarge 197A
extension
expansion 197
extensive
spacious 183A
exterior 223
exterminate 362
extermination 362
external 223
extinguish 382B
extol
praise 923
extort 788
extortionate 788
extra 38
extract 304
extradition
exile 188
extraneous 59
extraordinary 84
extravagance 815
extravagant 815
extricate 304
exult 824
eye 438B
eye for eye 28C6
eyes opened to
understand 516D3
paint eyes 843
eyeball 438B
eyebrow 259A3a
eyes
right in own eyes 913D3
eyeshot
visibility 443
eyewitness 441
Ezekias
Hezekiah 371G3b
Ezekiel 371F4h
Ezel 344B2
Ezion-gaber
Ezion-geber 184E5h
Ezion-geber 184E5h
Ezra 371F4i
fable 496
falsehood 543B
fabric 631F
fabricate
make 164
fabrication
falsehood 542B
facade
exterior 223
face 237B1
regard faces 481
set face against 704
face-cloth 648A3

face fall
one's face fall 829A
facial
facial hair 259A3a
fact
truth 494
faction 708
factional 708
factious
quarrelsome 709
facts
evidence 466
fade 114C
fading 114C
faeces 302B1
fagged out
fatigued 684
faggot 385
fail 728
failure 728
faint
be insensible 375C
weak 163
faint-hearted 856
faintness
weakness 163
fair
just 913
Fair Havens 184F1a
faith 485
little faith 486
no faith 486
faithful 929
faithful saying 473B
faithfulness 929
faithless 930
fake 542A
falcon 365C3d
fall 309E
autumn 129D

fall on one's face 309B1a
fall short 307
fallow 370D4
false 541A
false people 541B
falsehood 543
tell a lie 542B
false witness 466C4
fame 866
family 11
famine 636
diseases of famine 651B7
famished
hungry 859C1
famous 866
fancy
imagination 513
fanfare 412
fang
tooth 256B
fantasy
imagination 513
far 199
far away 199B
not far 200
farewell 882B
farmer 370D1

fast
not eat 946
speedy 277A
fasten
close 264
fastening
clasp 47
fastidious 862
fasting 946
fat
fat of meat 357D
plump 195B
prosperous 730
fate
destiny 596B
fated
predetermined 608
father 169
ancestor 169B1
God the Father 965B
the Father 965B
fatherless 779A
fathom
measure 465
understand 516
fathomless 211
fatigue 684
fatness
obesity 195B
fat of the land
plenty 635
fatten 195B
fault
defect 647
faultfinder 924
faultless
perfect 646
faulty
imperfect 647
fauna 365
favour
grace 897
favourite 890
fear 854
not fear 855C
fearful 854
fearless 855
fearlessness 855
feasible
possible 469
feast
religious feast 988
feat
deed 676
febrile
fevered 651B2
fed up
discontented 829
fee 809D
feeble 161
feed 301
breast-feeding 301D4
feel
have emotion 818
no feeling 375B
touch 378A
feeling
emotion 818
touching 378A
zeal 818C

feet 53E4
hands and feet 53C3
feign
dissemble 541
felicity
happiness 824
Felix 371F5a
fell
chop trees 46F4a
fellow
colleague 707
fellow-citizen 191
fellow-heir 776
fellowship 9
no fellowship 10
fellow-worker 707
felt
touched 378A1
female 373
male and female 372B
feminine 373
fen 347
fence 235A

ferment
turmoil 61
fertile 171C1
fertility 171C1
fervent 818C
fervid 818
fervour 818
festival 988
festivity 988
Festus 371F5b
fetch
carry 273
fetish
talisman 983C
fetter
bond 748
fettered 747C3
feud
enmity 881
fever 651B2
few 105
few days 114
few words 569
fib
untruth 543
fibber
liar 545
fibre 208
fickle
changeable 152A
fidelity
faithfulness 929
field 235D
fierce
irate 892B
violent 176
fifth
fifth part 102A
fifties 99F4d
fiftieth
fiftieth part 102C
fifty 99F4d
fig
tree 366D3a
fight 716

fighting man
soldier 722
figs
cakes of figs 301B1e
fruit 171C3c
figurative 519
figuratively 519
figure
figure of speech 519
filament 208
filigree
plaited 222D
fill 54
filled 54
filth 649
fin 53F
final
last 69
finance 797
find
discover 484
find out 484
find fault 924
fine
fine speech 575
penalty 809E
punishment 963E
small 196C
finger 53D4
thickness 205B
finish
complete 725
the end 69
fir
the tree 366D3b
the wood 631D4
fire 381
hellfire 972
lake of fire 346
no fire 382D
fire-offering 981D1
firepot 420B
firewood 385A
firm
stable 153B2
first 119
beginning 68
first and last 68F
first day 108F1b
first month 108G2
firstborn 119A
first 68A2
firstborn rights 119A3
firstfruits 171D
first 68A2
first of all 68
fiscal 797
fish 365D2
catch fish 542D2
catch of fish 171E
food 301B1a
no fish 172C
fisher 686B4a
fisherman 686B4a
fishhook 256A4
fishing-spear 256A4
fishnet 542D
fist 53D3a
shake the fist 317A

fit
convulsions 318C
due 915B
healthy 650
fitting 915B
not fitting 916
five 99A
five hundredth 102C
five o'clock 108E4f
five thousand 99H4
fix
affix 45
fixed
unchanging 153
flag
banner 547B1
be tired 684
be weak 163
flake 207B
flaked out
be tired 684
flame 381
flaming 381
flannel
empty talk 515
flat
level 216
smooth 258
flatter 925
flatterer 925
flattery 925
flautist 413B
flavour 386A
flavouring
condiment 389
flavourless 387A
flaw
defect 647
flawed
imperfect 647
flawless
perfect 646
flax 366C1e
flea 365B4
flee 620A
fleece
skin 226E2
fleet
navy 275A
speedy 277
fleeting
short 114
flesh
carnality 319B
flesh and blood 319
meat 319
one flesh 45C1a
flesh and blood 319
fleshly 319
fleshly indulgence 944
flexed
curved 250
flight
fleeing 620A
put to flight 619
flimsy 163C
fling
throw 287
flint 631C1

flinty
hard 326
float 323A3
flock
sheep and goats 365F
flog
beat 279A1a
flogging
beating 279A1a
punishment 963D
flood 350B
flooded 350B
flop
failure 728
flora 366
floral 366B3
flourish
prosper 730
flout
disobey 738
flow
flowing water 350
flower 366B3
flowing water 350
fluid 335
flute 414B4
flute-player 413B
fly
flying 271
insect 365B2b
run away 620A
flying creature 365C
foam 355C
fodder 301D5
foe 705
fog 355B
fold
enclosure 235E
foliage 366B2
follow
go after 284
imitate 20
sequel 67
follower
disciple 538
folly 499
fondle
caress 889B
food 301
no food 636B
foodstuffs 301
fool 501
foolish 499
foolishness 499
foot 53E4
bottom 214
foot for foot 28C6
on foot 267C
footpath 624
footsore
tired 684
footstool 218F
footwear 228B7d
for
cooperating 706
instead of 150
foray
attack 712
forbear 823
forbearance 823

forbid 757
force 176
compel 740
rape 951G
without force 177
forced labour
toil 682B
ford 267E1c
forearmed 669
forebear 169
forebode
predict 511
forecast
predict 511
forehead 237B2
foreign 59
foreigner 59
foreknow 510
foreknowledge 510
foreknown 510
foremost
leading 34
foreordain 608
forerunner 66
foresail 275A2
foresee 510
foreshadow
typify 23B
foresight 510
foreskin 167A3
forest 366D1d
foretell 511
forethought
preparation 669
for ever 115
forewarn 664
forfeit
lose 772
forgather 74B
forget 506
not forget 505C
forgetful 506
forgive 909
forgiveness 909
forgotten 506
fork
parting 294
sharp tool 256A4
form
shape 243
former 125
formerly 125
formless 244
fornication 951A
fornicator 952
for nothing
for free 812
for oneself 88B5
forsake 621
forsaken
empty 190D
for sure
certainly 473
fort
fortress 713
forties 99F4c
fortification 713
fortified
fortified city 713C
fortress 662B

fortune
destiny 596B
fortune-teller 983B1
forty 99F4c
Forum of Appius 184F1b
forward 285A
foster
rear 534E
foul 653
found
discovered 484
foundation 214
fountain 350E
four 96
four thousand 99H4
four times 97
three or four 93F
fourfold 97
foursquare 28D2
fourth
quarter 98
fowl 365C3a
fox 365E1c
fraction 102
fracture 46
fracture for fracture 28C6
fragile
frail 163
fragment
small thing 33A
fragrance 396
frail
weak 163
frame
body 319
frank
plain speaking 573
frankincense 396A
frankness 573
fraternal
brotherly 11
fratricide 362E5b
fraudulent 541
fray
fight 716
free 744
exempt 919
free of charge 812B
set free 746
slave or free 742C5
freeborn 744
freedom 744
freely 744
freeze
be cold 380A
refrigerate 382A
freezing
cold 380A
freight
merchandise 795
freighter 275A3
frequency
how often 141
frequent 139
frequently 139
fresh 126D
sweet 392A
freshness 126

fret
worry 825E
friction 333
friend 880
friendless 883
friendly
kind 897
friendship 880
fright
fear 854
frighten 854
frightened 854
frightening 854
fringe 234C
fritter away
waste 634
frog 365E1d
from ... to ... 183A
front 237
front and back 237C
in front 237A
frost 380A
frosty 380A
froth 355C
frothy 355C
frozen 380A
frugal 816
frugality 816
fruit 171C3
consequence 171A2
dried fruit 301B1e
part of plant 366B4
producing fruit 171C1
productiveness 171
fruitful 171
fruition
completion 725
fruitless
useless 641
fuel 385
fugitive 620A
fulfil 725
fulfilled 725
not fulfilled 726B
fulfilment 725
full
complete 54
not full 55
fuller
laundryman 648C1
fullness 54
fully
completely 54
fun
make fun 837B
make fun of 851
funeral 364
fur
skin 226E2
furious
angry 891
furnace 383A
Furnaces
tower of 209C2
furrow 262
fury
anger 891
futile 641
future 124
Gaal 371F6a

Gabbatha 184F1c
gabble
empty talk 515
Gabriel
the angel 968D
Gad
Reuben, Gad and half Manasseh 371B3d
the person 371F6b
the territory 184F1d
tribe of 371B4f
Gadara 184F1e
Gadarene 184F1e
gag
silence 578B
gain
profit 771C
Gaius 371F6d
Galatia 184F1f
Galatian 184F1f
gale
wind 352B
Galeed
Mizpah 184H3c
Galilean 184F2b
Galilee 184F2
Judas of Galilee 371H9g
Sea of Galilee 343C2
gall
anaesthetic 375A
gall bladder 224A7
Gallio 371F6h
gallows 964B
Gamaliel 371F7a
gamble 618B
gambler 618B
gambling 618B
game
meat 301B1a
gang 74B
gangrene 651B7
gaol 748
gaoler 749
gap 201
garb
clothing 228
garbage
rubbish 641C3
garden 370C1
gardener 686B4b
gardening 370C1
garland 844
garlic 301B1f
garment 228
holy garments 989
garner
storehouse 632
garnish
decorate 844
garrison 713
garrulous 581
gas 336
gaseous 336
gash
cut 46E5
gate 264B
gateway 263C
gateway 263C
Gath 184F3a

gather 74
harvest 370D3
gathering 74
gay
homosexual 951D
Gaza 184F3b
Gazathites 184F3b
gaze 438
gazelle 365E1b
Dorcas 371E8j
Gazites 184F3b
Gedaliah 371F7b
Gedeon
Gideon 371F7f
Gehazi 371F7c
Gehenna
hell 972
Geliloth
Gilgal 184F3i
gem 844A
geminate
double 91
gender
male and female 372B
genealogy 170D
generation 170C
generosity 813
generous 813
genesis
beginning 68A
genial
benevolent 897
genitalia 167A2
genitals 167A2
Gennesaret 184F3c
Sea of Galilee 343C2
genocide 362E6b
Gentile
foreigner 59
gentle 177
lenient 736
gentleness 177
genuflect
bow the knee 309A5
genuine 494
genuineness 494
genus
kind 77
gerah
coin 797A1
the weight 465
Gerar 184F3d
Gerasa
Gadara 184F1e
Gerasene
Gadarene 184F1e
Gergesa
Gadara 184F1e
Gergesene
Gadarene 184F1e
Gerizim
Mt Gerizim 209G1f
Gershom
Gershon 371F7d
Gershonites 371B6c
Gershon
Gershonites 371B6c
the person 371F7d
Gershonites 371B6c
Geshem 371F7e

gestation
  gestation period 110A3
gesture 547B3
get
  acquire 771
get away
  escape 667
Gethsamane 184F3e
ghost 970
giant 195C2
gibbet
  gallows 964B
Gibeah 184F3f
Gibeath
  Gibeah 184F3f
Gibeathite 184F3f
Gibeon 184F3g
Gibeonite 184F3g
Gideon 371F7f
gift 781
gigantic 195A
Gilboa
  Mt Gilboa 209G1g
gilded 226D1
Gilead
  the place 184F3h
Gilgal 184F3i
  Geliloth 184F3i
gilt
  gilded 226D1
gimlet 630C
gird
  clothe 228
  gird loins 669
girdle 228B7b
  the priest's girdle 989F
girl 132
Gittite 184F3a
Gittith 184F3a
give 781
  give in marriage 894B4
  give up, abandon 621
give into the hands
  defeat 728
giver 781
give way 601A
giving 781
glacial
  cold 380
glad 824
gladden
  please 826
glance
  look 438
glass
  transparency 422
glean 41B3
gleaning 41B3
glee
  delight 824
glen
  valley 255C
glib
  talkative 581
glimmer
  shine 417
glimpse
  see 438
glitter
  shine 417

gloat 877
global
  worldwide 183A
gloom
  darkness 418
glorify
  praise 923
glorious 866
glory 866
  boast 877
glossolalia
  speaking in tongues 557C
glow
  shine 417
glum
  sad 834
glut
  excess 637
glutton 947
gluttonous 947
gluttony 947
gnash
  gnashing teeth 256B2
gnat 365B2b
go
  go around 314
  go away 296
  go back 148
  go home 148
  go in 297
  go out 298
  go out and come in 297D
  go up 308
  pass away 2D
go! 290
goad 256A4
goal
  objective 617C
goat 365F
  wild goat 365E6b
goats' hair 631F6
goatskin 226E2
God 965
  God the Father 965B
  God the Son 965D
  man of God 965A3c
  no God 2A
God-breathed 352A2
godless 974B
godliness 973B
godly 973B
go down 309A
gods 966
God the Holy Spirit 965E1
Gog 371F7g
  the people 371C3g
go in
  sexual intercourse 45C1a
gold 631B3
  money 797
  yellow 433
golden 433
golden rule
  do as you would be done
    by 280B
goldsmith 686B3c
Golgotha 184F3j
Goliath 371F7h
Gomer 371F7i
Gomorrah 184F3k

gone
  absent 190
gong 414B1c
good 644
  good person 937
goodbye 882B
good deed 676
good health 650
good-looking 841B3
good looks
  beauty 841
good name
  reputation 866
goodness 644
good person 937
goods
  property 777
good taste 846
goof
  fool 501
goofy
  foolish 499
gopher wood 631D4
gore
  blood 335E
  goring 279A1h
Goshen
  in Egypt 184F3l
gospel 529A5
gossip 528C
  slanderer 926
gourd 366C3d
govern 733
government 733
governor 741
grab 786E
grace
  kindness 897
gracious 897
gradual 27
gradually
  little by little 27
graduate
  scholar 492
graft
  bribery 612C
  join 45
grain 301B1b
  fruit 366B4
  grain offering 981D3
grandfather 169B
grandmother 169C
grandparents 169
grant
  give 781
  permit 756
grape
  fruit 171C3d
  grape juice 335D
  vines 366D4f
grapes 171C3d
  tread grapes 370D3h
grapple
  struggle 716
grasp 786E
grass 366C1a
grasshopper 365B2c
  tiny 196B
grateful 907
gratis 812B

gratitude 907
grave 364
  the grave 361
gravel 344C
graveyard 364
graving tool 630D
gravy 335F
gray 429
grease
  fat 357D
great
  great owl 365C3f
  Great Sea 343C3
  important 638
  large 195A
  superior 34
greater
  superior 34
greatness
  superiority 34
Greece 184F3m
greed 859A4
greedy 859A4
Greek
  foreigner 59
  Greek language 557B
  the people 371C3h
green 434
  green plant 366A
greet 884
greeting 884
grey 429
grief 825
grieve 836
griffon vulture 365C3c
grill
  interrogate 459B2
grime
  dirt 649
grind 332A
grip
  grasp 778
grit
  courage 855
groan 408
grope 378A
ground 344
groundless 916B
  causeless 159
group 74B
grouse
  grumble 829
grouser
  grumbler 829
grow 36
  expand 197
growl 403B
growth 36
grow up
  come of age 134
grub
  worm 365B3
grumble 829
guarantee 767B
guard 660
  be on your guard
    457C
  jailer 749
  preserve 666
  safeguard 660

guardian 749
guess
  conjecture 512
guidance 691
guide 689
  director 690
guile
  cunning 698
guilt 936
  guilt offering 981D6
guiltless 935
guilty 936
guitar
  harp 414B2b
gulf
  gap 201
gullible 487
gully
  valley 255C
gum
  aromatic gum 396A
gush
  flow 350
gust
  wind 352B
guts
  courage 855
Habakkuk 371G1a
habit
  custom 610
  tradition 127C
habitation 192
habitual 610
  repeated 106
hack
  cut 46
Hadadezer 371G1b
Hadad-rimmon 967H
Hadarezer
  Hadadezer 371G1b
Hadassah
  Esther 371F4c
Hades 361
Hadoram
  Adoniram 371D3c
haemorrhage
  discharge of blood 302C
  illness 651B7
Haf
  Apis 967H
Hagar 371G1c
Haggai 371G1d
Hai
  Ai 184D1k
hail
  hailstones 350F2
  salute 400D
hailstones 350F2
hair 259A
  camels' hair 631F6
  facial hair 259A3a
  goats' hair 631F6
  without hair 229B2
haircloth 631F6
haircut 46E4
hairless
  bald 229B2
hairy 259A1
Hakeldama
  field of blood 335E1d

hale
  healthy 650
half 92
  half an hour 110B1
  nine and a half 99E
  two and a half 90I
halfpenny 797A1
half-wit
  fool 501
hallelujah 923A
halt 145
halve 92
Ham
  land of Egypt 184E4
  the Egyptians 371C3e
  the person 371G1e
Haman 371G1f
Hamath 184F4a
Hamites 371C4a
hammer
  hammered work 279E
  hit 279A
  tool 630C
hammered 279E
Hamor 371G1g
hamstring 655D3
hamstrung 655D3
Hananeel
  Hananel 209C2
Hananel
  tower of 209C2
Hananiah 371G1h
  Shadrach 371L2c
hand 53D3a
  hand for hand 28C6
  hands and feet 53C3
  left hand 242
  lift hands 310C1
  right hand 241
  take by the hand 378C1
  wave the hand 317A
handbreadth 205B
handcuff
  fetter 747C3
handful 26
handicap
  hindrance 702
handkerchief 648A1a
handle 378A
hand-made 676C
handmaid 742C3
hand over 272A
hands
  lay on 378B
  stretch out hands 197C
handsome 841B3
handwriting 586
handy
  useful 640
hang 217
hanged 217A
hanging 217
  curtain 421A
Hannah 371G2a
Hanun 371G2b
happen 154
  not happen 109
happening 154
happiness 824
happy 824

Haran
  the person 371G2c
  the place 184F4b
harass
  torment 827
harassed
  suffering 825
harbour 662A3
hard
  difficult 700
  hard-hearted 906
  hardness of heart 602
  hard work 682
  inflexible 326
harden
  harden the heart 602
hard labour 682
hardly
  with difficulty 700
hardness 326
hard of hearing 416
hardship
  difficulty 700
hard up
  poor 801
hard work 682
Hareth
  Hereth 366D1d
harlot 952C
harlotry 951F
harm 645
  harmful 645
harmony
  agreement 24
harp 414B2b
harper 413B
harpist 413B
harpoon 256A4
harp-player 413B
harrow
  cultivate 370
harsh 735
harvest 370D3
has
  possesses 773
haste 680
hasten 680
  go quickly 277
hasty
  rash 857
hat 228B7c
hatchet 630C
hate 888
hateful 888
hatred 888
haul
  drag 288
have
  possess 773
haven 662A3
have none of
  reject 621
havoc
  destruction 165
  disorder 61
hawk 365C3d
hay 631E
Hazael 371G2d
hazard 661A

Hazazon-tamar
  Engedi 184E5d
haze
  cloud 355A
Hazezon-tamar
  Engedi 184E5d
Hazor
  the people 371C4b
he
  himself 80
head 213B
  forehead 237B2
  head cut off 46E3
  lift heads 310C2
  most important 638
  on his own head 280A2
  severed head 363F2
heading
  direction 281
headstrong
  wilful 602
heal 656A
healer 658B1
healing 656A
health 650
healthy 650
heap 209B
hear 415
  not hear 416B
  not listen to 456
  pay attention 455
hearing 415
hearken
  hear 415
  obey 739
  pay attention 455
heart 224A2
  affection 817
  conscience 917
  mind 447
  with all your heart 599B
heartbroken 825
hearten
  encourage 855
hearth 383C
heartless
  pitiless 906
hearty
  vigorous 174
heat 379
  heating 381
  hot weather 379
heathen 974
  foreigner 59
heaven 971
  host of heaven 967H
  names written in
    heaven 548B3
  sky 321
heavens
  sky 321
heavy 322C
  difficult 700
heavy-hearted 825
Hebrew
  Hebrew language 557B
  Hebrew people 371C4c
Hebrews 371C4c
Hebron
  the city 184F4c

heed 455
  not heed 456
heedless 456
heel 53E5
  take by the heel 150C
he-goat 365F
heifer 365F
height 209
  tallness 195C
heights 209
heir 776
hell 972
Hellenist
  Greek person 371C3h
  Greek speaker 557B
hellfire 972
helmet 662C2
help 703
helper 703
helpless
  weak 163
hem 234C
Hemath
  Hamath 184F4a
hen 365C3a
henna
  the perfume 396A
herald
  forerunner 66
herb 366A
herbage 366A
herd 365F
herdsman 369
here 187D
  present 189
heresy 535
Hereth
  forest of Hereth 366D1d
heritage 777
Hermes
  Mercury 967H
Hermogenes 371G2e
Hermon
  Mt Hermon 209G2a
Hermonites 209G2a
Herod
  Herod Agrippa I 371G2h
  Herod Agrippa II 371G2i
  Herod the Great 371G2f
Herodians 708D
Herodias 371G3a
herself 80
Heshbon 184F4d
hesitate 601
hesitation 601
heterogeneous 43
Heth
  Hittites 371C4d
hew
  cut 46
Hezekiah 371G3b
  king of Judah 741C2
hidden
  concealed 525
  remain hidden 523
hide
  conceal 525
  hide oneself 523
hiding place
  refuge 662

Hiel 371G3c
Hierapolis 184F4e
high 209
  high place 209
high day
  holy day 988
higher 209
highly
  think too highly 482
highness 209
high noon 108E4d
high place
  high place for worship 209D2
high priest 986B1
highroad 624
high seas 343A
high street 624
high temperature 379
highway 624
hilarious 833
Hilkiah 371G3d
hill 209F
  hill country 209E
hillock 209
hillside 220
hilltop 213A1
hilly 209
himself 80
hin 465
hind
  back 238A1
  deer 365E1b
hinder 702
hinderer 702
hindquarters 238A1
hindrance 702
hinges 315B
hippopotamus 365D1
Hiram 371G3e
  Huram 371G4c
hire 792B
  wage 804A3
hireling 792B
hirsute 259A1
his
  his possession 773
hiss 406
hit 279A
hitch
  difficulty 700
  tie 45
Hittites 371C4d
Hivites 371C4e
hoard
  store 632
hoar-frost 380A
hoary
  grey 429
hoax 542A
hobble
  limp 655D
hoe 630B
hog
  pig 365G7
hoist 310
hold
  clasp 378C
  clutch 786E
hold fast 778

hold sway 733
hold together
  exist 1C
hole 201
holiness 979
hollow 255E
holy 979
  set apart for evil 980C
holy of holies 990B7
homage 920
home 192
  not at home 190C2
homeless 188F
homer
  measure 465
homicide 362
homosexual 951D
homosexuality 951D
hone
  sharpen 256C
honest 929
honey 392B
honeycomb 392B
honour 866
  respect 920
hoof 53E4g
hook
  fastening 47D1
hope 852
  without hope 853
hopeful 852
hopeless 853
hopelessness 853
Hophni 371G3f
Hor
  Mt Hor 209G2b
Horeb
  Mt Horeb 209G3
horizontal 216
horn 254A
  musical instrument 414B4
hornet 365B2a
Horonaim 184F4f
Horonite 184F4f
horrify
  frighten 854
horror 854F
horse 365G5
horseback 267D1
hosanna 668A1d
Hosea 371G3g
Hoshea 371G3h
  Joshua 371H8g
  king of Israel 741C1
hospitable 813B
hospitality 813B
host
  army 722E
hostage 750
hostile 704
host of heaven 967H
hot 379
  hot-tempered 892
hotel 192B1
hotheaded
  excitable 822A
hot-tempered
  irascible 892

hound
  dog 365G3
  pursue 619
hour
  period 110B
house
  dwelling 192
  dynasty 733D3
  house of God 990
household
  family 11
housetop 213A2
hover? 265A
how?
  in what way? 624A1
howl 409A
how long? 136C
how many? 86
how often
  frequency 141
hubbub 400A
hue
  colour 425
hug 889B
huge 195A
Huldah 371G4a
human 371
humanity
  mankind 371
human sacrifices 981C7a
humble 872
humid 341A
humidity 341A
humiliation 872B
humility 872
hummock 209
humorous 839
humour
  sense of humour 839
hump 209
hunch
  supposition 512
hunchback 246C
hundred 99G1
  hundred thousand 99H6
  six hundred 99G4
  three hundred 99G3
  tower of the 209C2
  two hundred 99G2
hundredth
  hundredth part 102C
hundredweight 465
hung 217A
hunger 859C1
hungry 859C1
hunt 619A
hunter 619A
hunting 619
Huphamite 371B4c
Hur 371G4b
Huram 371G4c
  Hiram 371G3e
Huram-abi
  Huram 371G4c
hurdle
  obstacle 702
hurl 287
hurricane 176

hurried
  hasty 680
hurry 680
hurt
  injured 655C1
husband 894
husbandry
  animal husbandry 369
hush
  quiet 399
  quieten 578B
Hushai 371G4d
hustle
  hasten 680
hut 192
hybrid
  mixture 43
hyena 365E1c
hygiene 648
Hymenaeus 371G4e
hymn 412C
hyperbole
  exaggeration 482
hypocrisy 542C
hypocrite 542C2
hypothermia 380A
hyssop 366C3e
I
  I am ... 13
  myself 80
I AM 1
I am the ... 13B5
ibex 365E1b
ibis 365C3f
Ibzan 371G5a
ice 380A
Ichabod 371G5b
icy
  cold 380A
Iddo 371G5c
idea
  thought 449
identical 16
identity 13
idiot 501
idiotic
  foolish 499
idle 679A
idleness 679A
idol 982
idolater 982
idolatrous 982
idolatry 982
Idumaea
  Edom 184E3c
Idumea
  Edom 184E3c
ignite
  kindle 381
ignoble
  dishonourable 867
ignoramus 493
ignorance 491
ignorant 493
ignore 458
ill
  unwell 651
ill-considered
  unwise 499

ill-disposed
  malevolent 898
illegal 954
illegality 954
illegitimate
  illegitimate children
  954D
ill-health 651
illicit 954
illiterate
  ignorant person 493
illness 651
ill-timed 138
ill-treat 645
illuminate 417
illumination 417
ill-use 645
illustration
  metaphor 519
illustrious 866
ill will
  malevolence 898
Illyricum 184F5b
image
  idol 982
  likeness 18
  metaphor 519
imagination 513
imagine 513
imbecile
  fool 501
imbibe 301E3
imitate 20
imitation 20
Immanuel 89A2a
immaterial
  unimportant 639
immature
  youthful 130
immaturity 130
immeasurable 465B4
immediate 116
immediately 116
immense 195A
immerse 303B
immersion 303B
  baptism 988B2
immigrant
  foreigner 59
immobile 153B4
immobility 153
immoral 951
immorality 951
immortal
  eternal 115
immortality 115
immoveable 153B4
impact 279A
impair 655
impairment 655
impale 263A4
impart
  give 781
impartial 480A
impartiality 480A
impassive 820
impatience 822A
impatient 822B
impecunious 801

impediment
  hindrance 702
  speech impediment
  580B
impel 287
impenitence 940
impenitent 940
imperative
  compelling 740
imperfect 647
imperfection 647
imperil
  endanger 661
imperishable
  everlasting 115
impetuosity 857
impetuous 680A
impiety 980
impious 980
implement
  tool 630
implore 761
importance 638
important 638
importunity 600E
imposition
  tax 809
impossibility 470
impossible 470
impostor 545
imposture
  deception 542A
impotent 161
impoverish 801
imprison 747D
imprisoned 747D
imprisonment 747D
improbity 929
improper 916
improve 654
improvement 654
imprudence
  folly 499
imprudent
  foolish 499
impulsive
  hasty 680
impure 951
impurity 951
in
  inside 224
  inside and out 223E
  in the midst 89
inability 161
inaction 677
inactive 677
inactivity 679
in addition 38
inadequate
  insufficient 636
inalterable 153
in and out 223E
inappropriate 916
in arrears 803
inattention 456
inattentive 456
inaugurate 876
inauguration 876
incapable 161
incapacity 161

incarnate 319A8a
incarnation 319A8a
incautious
  rash 857
incense 396B
incentive 612
incessant 146
incest 951E
inch 465
incident
  event 154
incinerate 381
incinerator 383A
incise
  cut 46
incite 612
incitement 612
income tax 809
in common 775
incomparable 21
incomplete 726
  partial 55
inconsistent 25B
inconsolable 830
inconstant 601
incontestable 473
incorrigible
  obstinate 602
incorruptible
  pure 950
increase
  addition 38
  make many 36
incredible
  unbelievable 486
incredulous
  unbelieving 486
inculpate
  accuse 928
incurable 651
incursion
  attack 712
in custody
  imprisoned 747D
indebted
  grateful 907
  in debt 803
indecisive 601A
indefatigable 600
independence 744
independent 744
  not independent 89E
India 184F5c
indication 547
indict
  accuse 928
indictment
  accusation 928
indifference 860
indifferent 860
in difficulties 700
indigent
  poor 801
indignant 891
indignation 891
indignity
  humiliation 872
indiscriminate 464
indoctrinate
  teach 534

indolence 679A
indolent 679A
indomitable
  courageous 855
in dribs and drabs 27
indubitable 473
induce 612
inducement 612
industrious 678A
inebriated 949
inebriation 949
inedible 391A
ineffective 161
ineffectual 161
inept 695
inequality 29
inerrant 473
inexcitable 823
inexcusable
  guilty 936
inexhaustible 635
inexpensive 812
inexperienced 695
inexpert 695
infallible
  certain 473
infancy 130
infant 132
infanticide 362E5a
infection 651
inferior 35
inferiority 35
infertile 172
infidel 486
infirm
  unhealthy 651
  weak 163
inflame
  excite 821
inflammation 651B7
inflexible 326
influence
  motivate 612
inform 524
information 524
infrequency 140
infrequent 140
infringement
  law-breaking 954
in front 237A
infuriate 891
ingathering
  harvest 370D3
ingratitude 908
ingress 297
inhabit 192
inhabitant 191
inherit 771A1
inheritance 777
  no inheritance 774
inhospitable 299B
inimical 881
inimitable 21
iniquity 914
initial
  beginning 68
initiate
  begin 68
injudicious
  unwise 499

injure 655
injured 655C1
injury 655C1
injustice 914
inlay 303A
inlet 345
in lieu
  instead 150
in memoriam 505
inn 192B1
innards
  insides 224
inner
  interior 224
inner man
  spirit 447
innocence 935
innocent 935
innovation 126
innumerable
  many 104
  uncountable 86E
in order
  in sequence 65
  put in sequence 73
  tidiness 60
in perpetuity 115
in place of 150
in proportion to 12
inquire 459
insane 503
insanity 503
inscribe 586
inscription 590A
inscrutable 517
insect 365B
insensible 375C
insert 303
inside 224
  inside and out 223E
insides 224
insight 490
insincere 515
insincerity 541A
insipid 387A
insolence 878
  pride 871
insolent 878
  proud 871
insolvency 805
insolvent 803
insomnia 678B
inspect 438D4e
inspection 438D4e
instability 152
instant
  time 108
instantaneous
  sudden 116
instantly 116
instead of 150
instinct 476
instinctive 476
instruct 534
instruction 534D
instructor 537
instrument
  musical instruments 414
  tool 630
instrumentalist 413B

insubordinate
  disobedient 738
insufficiency 636
insufficient 636
insult 921
intangible 320
intellect 447
intellectual 447
intelligence 498
intelligent 498
intelligible 516
intemperance 943
intend 617
intent
  attentive 455
intention 617
  will 595
inter 364
intercede 720
intercession 761
interchange 151
intercourse
  sexual intercourse 45C1a
interdependent 12
interdict
  prohibition 757
interest
  attention 455
  charge interest 803C
interfere 231
interior 224
intermarriage 894A2f
intermarry 894A2f
intermediary 720
interment 364
interminable 115
intermingle
  mix 43
intermittent 141
internal 224
international 371C1b
internment 747D
interpose 231
interpret 520
interpretation 520
interpreter 520
interrogate 459B2
intersperse
  mix 43
interval
  period 110
intervene
  interfere 231
  mediate 720
intervention 720
interweave 222C
interwoven 222C
intestines 224A6
in the distance 199
in the red
  in debt 803
intimidate
  frighten 854
intolerable 827D
intoxicated 949
intrigue
  plot 623B3
intrinsic 5
intuition 476
in turn 65

inundate 350B
inundation 350B
invade 712
in vain 641
invalidate 752B
invaluable 811
invariable 153
invasion 712
invent 623B2
invention 451B
  design 623B2
inverse
  opposite 240
invert 221
investigate 459B1
invigorate 162
invisibility 444
invisible 444
invitation 761C5
invite 761C5
inward 224
  inward parts 224A7
inwardly 224
in writing 586
iod
  yod 558
iota
  small amount 33A
irate
  angry 891
ire 891
iridescent 437
iron 631B6
irons
  fetters 748
irrational 448
irreconcilable 881
irrecoverable 772
irrefutable 473
irreligious 974
irresolute 601
irresolution 601
irreversible
  fixed 153
irrevocable
  certain 473
  fixed 153
irrigate 341C
irrigation 341C
irritant 827
irritate 827
irritation 827
is
  as is 7
  does not exist 2
  exists 1
  identity 13
  is present 189
  nature 5
  who is? 13
Isaac 371G5d
Isaiah 371G5e
Iscariot
  Judas 371H9d
  man of Kerioth
  184G4b
Ish-bosheth 371G5f
Ishmael 371G5g
  Ishmaelites 371C4f
Ishmaelites 371C4f

island 349
isle 349
isolated 883B
  alone 88B4
isolation 883B
Israel 371B1
  Jacob 371H1b
Israelites 371B1
Issachar
  territory of 184F5d
  the person 371G5i
  tribe of 371B5a
issue
  emerge 298
Italian 184F5e
Italy 184F5e
itch
  disease 651B7
iterate
  repeat 106
Ithrites 184G4e
ivory 631G1
Jaar
  Kiriath-jearim 184G4e
Jaazer
  Jazer 184G1b
Jabesh
  Jabesh-gilead 184G1a
Jabesh-gilead 184G1a
Jabez
  the person 371H1a
Jachin
  a pillar 218C2
jacinth 844A1b
jackal 365E1c
Jacob 371H1b
  supplanter 150C
Jael 371H1c
Jah
  Yahweh 13A
Jahweh
  the I AM 13A
  Yahweh 561A2b
jail 748
jailer 749
Jairus 371H1d
jamb
  doorpost 218C
Jambres 371H1e
James 371H1f
Jannes 371H2a
Japheth 371H2b
Japho
  Joppa 184G3b
jar 194A
  water jar 194B2
Jason 371H2c
jasper 844A1b
Javan
  Greece 184F3m
javelin 723A3
jaws 263F
Jazer 184G1b
jealous 911
jealousy 911
Jebus
  Jerusalem 184G2
Jebusites 371C4g
Jechoniah
  Jeconiah 371H3a

Jechonias
  Jehoiachin 371H3a
Jeconiah
  Jehoiachin 371H3a
Jedidiah
  Solomon 371L5
Jeduthun
  the person 371H2d
jeer
  despise 922
Jegar-sahadutha
  Mizpah 184H3c
Jehoahaz 371H2e
  Ahaziah 371D4c
  king of Israel 741C1
  king of Judah 741C2
Jehoash 371H2g
Jehoiachin 371H3a
  king of Judah 741C2
Jehoiada 371H3b
Jehoiakim 371H3c
  king of Judah 741C2
Jehoram 371H3d
  Joram king of Israel
    371H7g
  king of Israel 741C1
  king of Judah 741C2
Jehoshaphat 371H3e
  king of Judah 741C2
Jehoshua
  Joshua 371H8g
Jehovah 13A
  God 965A1c
  Jehovah-jireh 965A4
  Jehovah-nissi 965A4
  Jehovah-rophekhah
    965A4
  Jehovah-shalom 965A4
  Jehovah-shammah
    965A4
  Jehovah-tsidhkenu
    965A4
  name of God 561A2b
  the I AM 13A
Jehovah-jireh 184G1c
Jehu 371H3f
  king of Israel 741C1
Jemimah 371H3h
jeopardy 661A
Jephthae
  Jephthah 371H4a
Jephthah 371H4a
Jeremiah 371H4b
Jericho 184G1d
Jeroboam I 371H4c
Jeroboam II 371H4d
  king of Israel 741C1
Jerubbaal
  Gideon 371F7f
Jerubbesheth
  Gideon 371F7f
Jeruel 172D4
Jerusalem 184G2
Jeshua
  Joshua 371H8h
Jeshurun
  Israel 371B1
Jesse 371H4e
jest 839

Jesus
  Jesus Christ 371H5
  Jesus Justus 371H9h
  Joshua 371H8g
Jethro 371H6a
jettison 621B4
jewel 844A
jeweller 686B3d
jewellery 844A
Jewry 371B1
Jews 371B1
Jezebel 371H6b
Jezreel
  the city 184G3a
  valley of 255C2
Jezreelite 184G3a
jibe 922
jitters
  nervousness 854
Joab 371H6c
Joahaz
  Jehoahaz 371H2e
Joanna 371H6d
Joash 371H6e
  Jehoash 371H2g
  king of Israel 741C1
  king of Judah 741C2
Joatham
  Jotham 371H9a
Job 371H6g
job
  occupation 686B1
jobless 677
jocular 839
Joel 371H7a
John 371H7b
  John Mark 371I5b
join 45
joiner 686B3a
joint
  limb 53
joke 839
Jonah 371H7d
Jonas
  Jonah 371H7d
Jonathan 371H7e
Joppa 184G3b
Joram 371H7g
  Jehoram king of Judah
    371H3d
Jordan
  river Jordan 350D3
  valley of 255C2
Josaphat
  Jehoshaphat 371H3e
Jose
  Joshua 371H8g
Joseph 371H8a
  Ephraim and Manasseh
    371B5b
  Joseph Barnabas 371E1h
  territory of 184G3c
Joses
  brother of James
    371H8d
  Joseph Jesus' brother
    371H8c
josh
  ridicule 851
Joshua 371H8g

Josiah 371H8i
  king of Judah 741C2
jot
  letter 558
  small thing 33A
Jotham 371H9a
  king of Judah 741C2
journal 589
journey 267A
joy 824
joyful 824
joyous 824
jubilant 824
jubilation 835A
Jubilee 988A5
Juda
  Judah 371H9c
Judah
  the person 371H9c
  the territory 184G3d
  tribe of 371B5c
Judaism 973C
Judas 371H9d
  Judah 371H9c
  Thaddaeus 371L7f
Jude
  Judas 371H9e
Judea 184G3d
judge
  arbitrate 480
  magistrate 957
judgement 480
  condemnation 961
judgement seat 956B
judging 480
judiciary 957
judicious
  discriminating 463
jug
  prison 748
  vessel 194A
juice
  fruit juice 335D
jumble
  confusion 61
jump 312
juncture
  joining 45
jungle 366D1d
junk
  rubbish 641C3
Jupiter
  Zeus 967H
jurisdiction
  authority 733
just
  righteous 913
just deserts 915B
justice
  righteousness 913
justice of the peace
  magistrate 957
justification 927
justified 927
justifier 927
justify 927
  acquit 960
Justus 371H9h
  Joseph Barsabbas
    371H8f

kab 465C
Kadesh
  Kadesh-barnea 184G4a
Kadesh-barnea 184G4a
Kain
  Kenites 371C5a
Kaiwan 967H
Kedar 371C4h
Kedesh
  Kadesh-barnea 184G4a
  of Judah 184G4a
Kedorlaomer
  Chedorlaomer 371E4g
keen
  lament 836
  sharp 256
keep
  observe 768
  preserve 666
  protect 660
  retain 778
keep from
  avoid 620
ken
  knowledge 490
Kenites 371C5a
kerchief
  headgear 228B7c
Keren-happuch 371I1a
Kerioth 184G4b
kesita
  qesita 797A2
Keturah 371I1b
key 263E
Kezia
  Keziah 371I1c
Keziah 371I1c
Kezib
  Chezib 184D1e
Kibroth-hattaavah 184G4c
kick 279C
kick out
  expel 300
kid
  child 132
  young goat 365F
kidnap 788B2
kidney 224A3
Kidron
  valley of 255C2
kill 362
  kill oneself 362E8b
killer 362
killing 362
kiln 383A
Kimham
  Chimham 371E4h
kin 11
kind
  all kinds 82
  class 77
  gracious 897
  nature 5
kindle 381
  not kindle 382D
kindly 897
kindness 897
kindred 11
king 741
  no king 734

kingdom 733
kingship 733
Kinnereth
  Galilee 184F2
  Sea of Chinnereth 343C2
kinship 11
kinsman 11
kinsman-redeemer 792C2
Kir 184G4d
Kir-haraseth
  Kir 184G4d
Kir-hareseth
  Kir 184G4d
Kir-haresh
  Kir 184G4d
Kir-heres
  Kir 184G4d
Kiriath
  Kiriath-jearim 184G4e
Kiriath-arba
  Hebron 184F4c
Kiriath-arim
  Kiriath-jearim 184G4e
Kiriath-baal
  Kiriath-jearim 184G4e
Kiriath-jearim 184G4e
Kiriath-sannah
  Debir 184E2d
Kiriath-sepher
  Debir 184E2d
Kirioth
  Kerioth 184G4b
Kish 371I1d
kiss 889A
kitchen 383C
kite 365C3d
Kittim
  Cyprus 184E1q
knave 938
kneading-trough 194B6
knee 53E3
  bend the knee 309A5
  knee-deep 211D
kneel 309A5
knife 256A1
knit 45
knock 279F
know 490
  not know 491
knowledge 490
  no knowledge 491
known
  make known 526
Kohath
  Kohathites 371B6d
Kohathites 371B6d
Korah 371I1e
Korazin
  Chorazin 184E1j
kowtow
  make obeisance 309A5
Laban 371I2a
laborious 682
labour
  forced labour 682B
  labour pains 167B4b
  toil 682
labourer 686
lacerate 46E5
Lachish 184G5a

lachrymatory 194B2
lack
  go short 636
lacking
  people missing 190C4
lack of discrimination 464
ladder 308D
laden 322D
lag
  delay 136
laggard
  lateness 136
  lazy 679A
lair 192E2
Laish
  city of Dan 184E2c
laity 987
lake 346
lamb 365F
lame 655D
Lamech 371I2b
lament 836
lamentation 836
lamina 207
lamp 420B
lampstand 420B2
lance
  spear 723A3
land
  country 184
  soil 344
landmark 547D
lane 624
language 557
Laodicea 184G5b
Laodiceans 184G5b
lap
  drink 301E3
lapis lazuli 844A1b
lard
  fat 357D
large 195A
  numerous 104
largesse
  liberality 813
lash
  punish 963D
  strike 279A
last
  endure 113
  final 69
  last in sequence 67
late
  delayed 136
  late hour 136B
lateness 136
later 136B
lather 355C
Latin 557B
latrine 302B1
latter 136B
laud
  praise 923
laugh 835A
  laugh at 851
laughingstock 851
laughter 835A
launder 648C1
laundry 648C1

laundryman
  cleaner 648C1
lavatory 302B1
laver 648A1a
law 953
  principle 81
law-breaking 954
lawful 953
  proper 915C
lawless 954
lawlessness 954
lawsuit 959
lawyer 958
lax 734
laxity 734
lay 311B
  lay hands on 378B
  make to lie 311A
  non-priest 987
layer 207
laying
  laying hands on 378B
Lazarus 371I2c
laziness 679A
lazy 679A
lead
  go before 283
  guide 689
  lead astray 495A
  the metal 631B7
leaden 631B7
leader 741D
leadership 733
leaf 366B2
league
  compact 765
Leah 371I2e
leak 341A
lean
  gain support 218A
  thin 206
lean on
  trust 485
leap 312
learn 536
learner 538
learning 536
  knowledge 490
least
  lowliest 35
leather 631G2
leave
  abandon 621
  come out 298
  depart 296B
leave alone 620C
leaven 323B
leavened 323B
leaves 366B2
leavings
  leftovers 41B1
Lebanon 184G6
Lebkamai
  Chaldea 184E1i
lecture 579
lecturer
  teacher 537
lee
  shelter 662
leech 365B4

leek 301B1f
lees
  dregs 41B4
left
  left side 242
  remaining 41
  right and left 241D
left-handed 242B
left over
  remainder 41
leftovers 41B1
leg 53E1
legacy 777
legal 953
legality 953
legate
  messenger 529C
legation
  envoy 754
legion 722
legionary 722
legislate
  decree 737
Lehi 184G7a
leisure 683
lend 784
length 203
  length of life 113B
  length of time 110
lengthy 203
leniency 736
lenient 736
lentils 366C2
  food 301B1f
leopard 365E3a
leper 651B4
leprosy 651B4
lepton 797A1
lesbian
  homosexual 951D
Leshem
  city of Dan 184E2c
less
  lowlier 35
lesson 534
let
  permit 756
let alone 620C
let down
  lower 311A1
lethargic 679A
lethargy 679A
let off
  acquit 960
letter
  alphabet 558
  epistle 588
level 216
Levi 371I2f
  Matthew 371I6b
  tribe of 371B6
Leviathan 365D1
Levirate marriage 894A2d
Levites 371B6
levy
  tax 809
lewd 951
liability 180
liable
  responsible 180

liar 545
libation 981D3
liberal
  generous 813
liberality 813
liberate 746
liberation 746
libertine 952
liberty 744
libido 859C3
Libya 184G7b
licentious 951
licentiousness 951
lid
  stopper 264C
lie
  lie in wait 527B
  lying down 309D
  sexual intercourse
    45C1a
  tell a falsehood 542B
  untruth 543
life 360
  life and death 360E
  life for life 28C6
  station in life 7
lifeblood 335E1
life-giving 360B3
lifeless 361
lifelong 113A6
lifespan 131A
lifetime
  lifelong 113A6
  lifespan 131A
lift
  lift up 310
  promote 285B
lift up
  be crucified 964C1a
ligament 47
light
  brightness 417
  from darkness to light
    417C4
  insignificant 33A
  lamp 420B
  not heavy 323
  source of light 420
lighten 323A3
lightness 323
lightning 176E
lightweight 323
like
  conformed to 83
  desire 859
  none is like 21
  same as 16
  similar 18
  unlike 19
  what sort 5
  who is like? 21
liken
  compare 462
  make similar 18
likeness
  similarity 18
liking 859
lily 366C3f
limbs 53C1
lime 381C3

limit 236
limitation 161A
limp
  lame 655D
  weak 163
line
  lineage 169
  line by line 27
  measure 465B2
  plumb line 215A
lineage 169
linen 631F2
  linen worker 686B3d
link
  bond 47
  join 45
lintel 263B2
lion 365E2
lips 263F4
  compress the lips 547B3
liquefy 337
liquid 335
liquor 949
  strong drink 335C
lisp 580B
listen
  hear 415
  not listen to 456
  pay attention 455
litigation 959
little
  little by little 27
  little faith 486
  little ones 132
  little owl 365C3f
  little while 114
  not much 33
  short 196
liturgy 988
live 360
  dwell 192
liver 224A5
livestock 365G
living 360
  living and dead 360E
load 322D
  carrying loads 273
loaf 301B1c
Lo-ammi 371I2g
loan 784
loathe 888
loathing 888
loathsome 888
locality 187
locate 187
location 187
lock
  bars 662D
locks
  hair 259A2
locust 365B2c
Lod
  Lydda 184G7e
Lo-debar
  Debir 184E2d
lodge 192B1
lofty 209
log
  beam 218B6
logic 475A

loins 224A7
  thighs 53E2
  waist 206D
Lois 371I3a
lonely 883B
  alone 88B4
long 203
  long life 113B
  long time 113
  too long 203A
longer 203
longevity 113B
longsuffering 823
long way 199
longwinded 581
look
  look down on 922
  pay attention 455
  see 438
look like
  resemble 18
loom 222C
loose
  running loose 61
loose woman 952A
loot
  booty 790
lop 46
loquacity 581
Lord
  God 965
lord
  lord it 733A2
  master 741B2c
lording
  lording it 733A2
lore
  tradition 127C
Lo-ruhamah 371I3b
lose 772
  be defeated 728
  lose one's life 772C
lose one's temper 891
loser
  defeated 728
loss 772
lost 772
Lot 371I3c
lot
  cast lots 605C1
  fate 596B
  gamble 618B
loud 400A
loudly 400A
loudness 400A
louse 365B2b
love 887
  covenant love 897B
lovely 841
lover
  friend 880C
lovingkindness 897B
low 210
  lowing 409B
  small 196C
lower 210B
  lowering 311
lowing 409B
lowland 348B

lowliness 35
  humility 872
lowly 35
  humble 872
lowness 210
loyal 929
lubricant 334
lubricate 334
Lucas
  Luke 371I3d
lucre 797
lug
  pull 288
luggage 777D
Luke 371I3d
lukewarm
  indifferent 860
  mediocre 30
lull
  cessation 145
lumber
  rubbish 641C3
luminary 420
luminous 417
lunacy
  insanity 503
lunar 420A
lunatic 504
  epileptic 651B7
lure
  tempt 612
lurk 523C
luscious 390
lust 859A3b
  sexual desire 859C3
lustful 859C3
lusty
  strong 162
lute 414B2b
Luz
  Bethel 184D4f
Lycaonia 184G7c
Lycaonian 557B
Lycia 184G7d
Lydda 184G7e
Lydia 371I3e
lye 648C1
lying
  telling lies 542B
lying down 309D
lynch 362
lyre 414B2c
Lysanias 371I3f
Lysias
  Claudius Lysias 371E5d
Lystra 184G7f
Maacah 371I4a
Macedonia 184H1a
machination
  plot 623B3
machine 630A
Machpelah 184H1b
  cave for burying 364B3
mad 503
madman 504
Magadan
  Magdala 184H1c
Magdala 184H1c

Magdalene
  Mary Magdalene 371I5f
  of Magdala 184H1c
maggot 365B3
  corruption 51
magi 500B2
magic 983B2
magician
  sorcerer 983B2
  wise man 500B2
magistrate 957
Magog 371I4b
magus 500B2
Maher-shalal-hash-baz
  371I4c
Mahlon 371I4d
maid
  servant 742C3
  virgin 895B
maiden
  virgin 895B
maidservant 742C3
mail
  correspondence 588
maim 655
maimed 655
maintain
  provide 633
  support 218
majesty
  authority 733
major
  superior 34
make 164
make amends
  atone 941
make a profit 771C
make known 526
make money 800
maker 164
make up one's mind 605
Makkedah 184H1d
Malachi 371I4e
malady
  disease 651
Malchus 371I4f
malcontent 829
male 372
  male and female 372B
  male member 167A2
malediction 899
male member 167A2
male prostitute 952C3
malevolent 898
malice 898
malign 926
malignant
  malevolent 898
mallet 630C
malnutrition 636
Malta 349B
maltreat 645
Mammon 800
mammoth
  huge 195A
Mamre 371I4g
  Hebron 184F4c

man
  male 372A
  mankind 371
  men and animals 365A3
  old man 127B
  Son of man 371A5
manacle
  bind 747C
  handcuffs 747C3
manage
  guide 689
management 689
manager 690
Manasseh
  king of Judah 741C2
  Reuben, Gad and half
    Manasseh 371B3d
  territory of 184H1e
  the person 371I4h
  tribe of 371B7a
Manasses
  Manasseh 371I4h
mandate
  command 737
  permit 756
mandatory 737
mandrake 366C3g
mane
  hair 259A
maneh 465
manful
  courageous 855
manger 301D5
manhood
  adulthood 134
manhunt 619
maniac
  madman 504
manifest 522
manifestation
  appearance 445B
manifold 82
mankind 371
manly
  courageous 855
man-made 676C
manna 301B1d
manner
  manner of life 688
  way 624A1
Manoah 371I5a
manservant 742
manslaughter 362A2
manslayer 362A2
mantelet 662B1
mantle 228B7a
manure
  fertiliser 171
many 104
  many days 113
  not many 105
mar
  destroy 165
Mara
  Naomi 371J1g
Marah
  bitter 391B2
Maranatha 295D1

marble
  precious stone
    844A1b
  the material 631C1
march 267C5
marching 267C5
Marcus
  Mark 371I5b
Marduk 967C
mare 365G5
margin
  edge 234
marine 343A
mariner 270
marital 894
Mark 371I5b
mark 547C1
  boundary mark
    547D
marker 547
market place 796
marriage 894
  intermarriage
    894A2f
  Levirate marriage
    894A2d
  remarriage 894A2c
married 894
marrow 224A7
marry 894
  intermarry 894A2f
  remarry 894A2c
Mars
  Mars' hill 209G1b
marsh 347
marshy 347
Martha 371I5c
marvel 864
  not marvel 865
Mary 371I5d
masculine 372
mason
  stonemason 686B3a
Massah 184H1f
massive 195A
master 741
match
  be similar 18
  not match 19
mate
  unite with 45C1a
material 319
materialism 319B
materials 631
maternal 169
maternity 169
Mathusala
  Methuselah 371I7c
mating 45C1a
Matri 371B4c
matricide 362E5c
Matrite 371B4c
Mattan 371I6a
Mattaniah
  Zedekiah 371M3b
matter
  material 319
Matthew 371I6b
Matthias 371I6c
mattock 630B

mature 134
maturity 134A
maxim 496
meal
    repast 301
mean
    average 30
    imply 514
    intend 617
    stingy 816
meaning 514
meaningless 515
means
    way 624A1
meant 617
measure 465
    weights and measures
    465A
measurement 465
meat 301B1a
meatpot 194B6
Medad 371I6d
meddle 231
meddler 231
Mede
    of Media 184H2a
Medes 371C5b
Media 184H2a
    Medes 371C5b
Median
    Mede 371C5b
mediation 720
mediator 720
medic
    doctor 658B1
medication 658A
medicine 658A
mediocre 30
meditate 449B5
meditation 449B5
meditative 449B5
Mediterranean 343C3
medium
    middle 30
    spiritist 984
meek
    gentle 177
meet 295A
meeting 295A
meeting house 192F
meeting place 192F
Megiddo 184H2b
Megiddon
    Megiddo 184H2b
Meholathite 184D1b
melancholic 834
melancholy 834
Melchisedec
    Melchizedek 371I6e
Melchizedek 371I6e
Melita
    Malta 349B
melon 301B1f
melt 337
member
    limb 53C1
    male member 167A2
memorial 505
memory 505
Memphis 184H2c

men
    males 372A
    mankind 371
    men and animals 365A3
    men and women 372B
Menahem 371I6f
    king of Israel 741C1
mend
    repair 656
menstrual 302C
menstruate 302C
menstruation 302C
mensuration
    measurement 465
mental 447
mental illness 503
mentality 447
Mephibosheth 371I6g
Merab 371I6h
Merari
    Merarites 371B6e
Merarites 371B6e
merchandise 795
merchant 794
merciful 905
merciless 906
Mercurius
    Mercury 967H
Mercury
    Hermes 967H
mercy 905
    no mercy 906
mercy seat
    cover for the ark 226C3
mere words 579A7
merge
    mix 43
Meribah 184H2d
Meribah-kadesh
    Meribah 184H2d
Meribath
    Meribah 184H2d
Meribath-kadesh
    Meribath-kadesh
    184H2d
Merib-baal
    Mephibosheth 371I6g
merit
    be due 915
    virtue 933
Merodach
    Marduk 967C
merriment 835A
merry 824
Mesha
    the person 371I7a
Meshach 371I7b
Meshech 371C5c
Mesopotamia 184H2e
message 529
messenger 529C
Messiah
    anointed one 357C
Messias
    Messiah 357C
metal 631B
metals 631B
metalworker 686B3c
metamorphose 147A
metamorphosis 147A

metaphor 519
metaphorical 519
metereology 340B
Methuselah 371I7c
mettle
    courage 855
Micah 371I7d
Micaiah 371I7f
    Maacah 371I4a
mice 365E3b
Michael 968D
Michah
    Micah 371I7d
Michaiah
    Micaiah 371I7f
Michal 371I7g
mid
    middle 70
midday 108E4d
midden 641C3
middle 70
    in the middle 70
middling 30
midge 365B2b
midget 196A
Midian
    Midianites 371C5d
    the land of 184H2f
Midianites 371C5d
midnight 108E3
midst
    in the midst 89
    middle 70
    presence 189
midway 70
midwife 658C
midwinter 129E
might 160
    be possible 469
    do it with your might
    571
mighty 160
mighty man 722C
Milcom 967F
mild
    gentle 177
mildness
    gentleness 177
Miletus 184H2h
milk 335A
mill 332A
millenium 110E4
million 99H7
Millo 184H2g
millstone
    grinding 332A
    stone 344B
mimic
    imitate 20
mina 797A2
mind 447
    change one's mind 603
    right mind 502
mindful
    attentive 455
mindless
    irrational 448
mine
    excavation 255D2
    my possession 773

miner 255D2
mineral 631B
mingle
    mix 43
mining 631B
minister
    servant 742
minor
    child 132
    unimportant 639
minority
    childhood 130
miracle 864B
miraculous 864
mire 347
Miriam 371I7h
mirror 442
mirth 835A
miry 347
misbehave
    disobey 738
miscalculate
    misjudge 481
miscarriage 172A4
misdeed 914
misdoing 914
miser 816
miserly 816
misery 825
misfortune 645
Mishael
    Meshach 371I7b
misinterpret 517
misjudge 481
mislay
    lose 772
mislead 495A
misled 495A
mismatched 29B
misrepresent 552
miss
    lose 772
    remember 505
missing
    absent 190
    lost 772
    people missing 190C4
missionary
    apostle 754A
mist 355B
misteach 535
misteaching 535
mistreat 735
mistress
    concubine 952
mistrust 486
misty 355B
misunderstand 517
misuse 735
mite
    coin 797A1
Mitylene 184H3a
mixture 43
Mizpah
    of Benjamin 184H3b
    of Gilead 184H3c
Mizpeh
    Mizpah 184H3c
Mizraim
    Egypt 184E4

Mnason 371I7i
Moab
  land of 184H3d
  Moabites 371C5e
Moabites 371C5e
moan
  cry 408
  lament 836
moat 351
mob 74B
mock 851
model
  design 23A
  example 83C1
  pattern 23
modest
  humble 872
modesty
  humility 872
moiety
  half 92
moist 341A
moisture 341A
Molech 967F
Moloch 967F
moment
  short time 114
  time 108
momentarily 116
momentary 114
monarch 741
monarchy 733
monetary 797
money 797
  money-box 799B
money-box 799
monster 365H
monstrous
  huge 195A
month
  month one 108G2
  month seven 108G3
  month twelve 108G4
  period 110
  time 108G1
monthly 141B
monument 548A
moon 420A
  new moon 108G1
moon-struck 651B7
Mordecai 371I7j
more
  addition 38
  excelling 306
  more than 34E
Moreh 184H3e
Moriah 184H3f
  Mt Moriah 209G2c
morn
  morning 128C
morning 128
morning star 420A
moron
  fool 501
morose 834
mortality 361
mortar
  bricks and mortar 631C3
  mortar and pestle 332A
mortgage 803B

mortify
  humiliate 872B
Moses 371I8
mosquito 365B2b
most holy place 990B7
mote
  small thing 33A
moth 365B2d
moth-eaten 51B
mother 169
  mother-in-law 169C2
motherhood 169C
mother-of-pearl
  precious stone 844A1b
  the material 631C1
motion 265
  gesture 547B3
motionless 266A
motive 612
mottled 437
mould
  cast 554B
  decay 51
mouldy 51
mound 209B
mount
  climb 308
  mountain 209
mountain 209F
mourn 836
mourner 836
mourning 836
mouse 365E3b
moustache 259A3a
mouth 263F
mouthpiece
  spokesman 579D
move 265
  move away! 290
moved
  emotional 818
movement 265
mow
  harvest 370
much 32
  not much 33
  too much 637
muck
  dirt 649
  dung 302B1
  rubbish 641C3
mud 347
muddle
  confusion 61
muddy
  marshy 347
mug
  cup 194A
mule 365G6
  mule's burden 322B
mull over 449B5
multi-coloured 437B
multiplicity 82
multiply
  increase 36
  make numerous 36
  procreate 171A1
multisection 100

multitude
  crowd 74B
  many 104
mum
  mother 169C
  silent 582
murder 362
murderer 362
murmur
  grumble 829B
murmurer
  grumbler 829B
muse
  meditate 449B5
music 412
  musical instruments 414
musical instruments 414
musician 413
must
  necessity 596
  new wine 335B
mustard 366C3h
muster
  gather 74B
mute
  dumb 578A
mutilate
  cut 46
mutinous 738
mutiny 738
mutton 301B1a
mutual 12
mutually
  mutually dependent 12
muzzle 747C2
Myra 184H3g
myriad
  myriads 104B
  ten thousand 99H5
myrrh 396A
  anaesthetic 375A
myrtle 366D3c
myself 80
mystery 530
myth
  falsehood 543B
  misleading story 495A
Naaman 371J1a
Naamite 371B4c
Nabal 371J1b
Naboth 371J1c
Nadab 371J1d
  king of Israel 741C1
nag
  pester 709C2
nagging 709C2
Nahash 371J1e
Nahum 371J1f
nail
  fastening 47D2
Nain 184H4a
naive
  naive person 501
naked 229
nakedness
  private parts 167A
name 561
  reputation 866D3c
naming 561
Naomi 371J1g

nap
  sleep 679B
Naphtali
  territory of 184H4b
  the person 371J2a
  tribe of 371B7b
napkin 226B4
nard 396A
narrow 206
nasal 237B3
Nathan 371J2b
Nathanael 371J2c
nation
  the nations 371C1
national 371C1
nationality 371
natural
  normal 83A
nature
  character 5
  material world 319B
  old nature 127B
nautical 275
naval 275A
Nazarene 184H4c
Nazareth 184H4c
Nazarite
  Nazirite 46B2
Nazirite 46B2
Neapolis 184H4d
near 200
  bring near 200A4
  draw near 289
  in time 135A
  near or far 199C
nearby 200
nearness 200
Nebo 967C
  Mt Nebo 209G2d
Nebuchadnezzar
371J2d
Nebuchadrezzar
  Nebuchadnezzar
  371J2d
Nebuzaradan 371J2e
necessary 596
necessity 596
  requirement 627
Necho
  Neco 371J2f
Nechoh
  Neco 371J2f
neck 206C
  stiff-necked 602B
necklace 844A
Neco 371J2f
necromancy 984
need 627
  shortage 636
needful 627
needle 256A4
negate 533
negation 533
negative 533
Negeb 184H4e
Negev
  Negeb 184H4e
neglect 458
neglectful 458
negligence 458

negligent 458
negotiate
  bargain 791
Nehemiah 371J2g
Nehushtan 365E4a
neigh 409C
neighbour 200C
Nephilim
  Anakim 371C2d
  giants 195C2
Nephtalim
  Naphtali 184H4b
Nergal 967G
nerve
  courage 855
nervous
  fearful 854
nest 192E1
net 222E2
  trap 542D
netting 222E
nettles 366C3i
network 222E1
neuter
  spay 172A3
never 109
never been 2C
never born 2C
new 126
  new moon 108G1
  nothing new 126C5
new Jerusalem 184G2n
newness 126
news 529
  bad news 529B2
  good news 529B1
New Testament writings
586A5
new wine 335B
next of kin 11
Nibhaz 967G
Nicanor 371J3a
nickname 561
Nicodemus 371J3b
Nicolaitans 371C5f
Nicolas 371J3c
Nicopolis 184H4f
Niger
  Simeon 371L3j
niggardly 816
nigh
  near 200
night
  day and night 128F1
  night time 129
night-hag 129C1
nighthawk
  owl 365C3f
night-monster 129C1
nil
  zero 103
Nile 350D4
nimble 277A
Nimrod 371J3d
nine 99E
  nine am 108E4b
  nine and a half 99E
  nine pm 108E4i
nineties 99F4g
ninety 99F4g

Nineve
  Nineveh 184H4g
Nineveh 184H4g
Ninevites 184H4g
ninth
  ninth hour 108E4e
Nisan
  first month 108G2
Nisroch 967G
no 489
  yes and no 601B
Noadiah 371J3e
Noah 371J3f
no answer 460E
Nob 184H4h
nobility 868
noble
  nobility 868
nobody 190C4
  nonentity 639A
no compassion 906
nocturnal 129C2
nod
  nod the head 547B3
no dealings 883A
no depth 212
no difference 16
no distinction 16
Noe
  Noah 371J3f
no feeling 375B
no fellowship 10
no fire 382D
no food 636B
no God 2A
no inheritance 774
noise 398
noisy 400A
no king 734
nomad 267B
nomenclature 561
no mercy 906
no more
  not exist 2D
nonconformist 84
nonconformity 84
none
  have none of 621
  none is like 21
  no one 190C4
nonentity 639A
nonexistence 2
non-existent 2
nonpayment 805
non-priest 987
nonsense 515
nonstop 146
non-uniform 17
noon 108E4d
no one 190C4
Noph
  Memphis 184H2c
normal 83A
no room 183C
north 281A
northeast 281E4
Northeaster 281E4
northern 281A
northwest 281E4

no ruler 734
nose 237B3
  nostril 353A
nostril 353A
not agree 25
not allow 757
not alone 89E
not answer 460E
not ashamed 872B3
not a soul 190C4
no taste 387A
not at home 190C2
not care
  indifferent 860
not change one's mind
  599
not choose
  no choice 606
  reject 607
not concerned 860
not consent 760
not different 16
not disappointed 509
not drink wine 948A
not drunk 948C
not equal 29
not exist 2
not far 200
not fear 855C
not fitting 916
not forget 505C
not fruitful 172
not fulfilled 726B
not guilty 935
not happen 109
not hear 416B
not heed 456
not here
  absent 190
nothing 103
  nothing to do with
    620C5
  unimportant 639
nothing to do with 10
notion
  idea 451
not know 491
not listen
  inattentive 456
not many 105
not match 19
not mind
  indifferent 860
not much 33
not observe 769
not own 774
not pay 805
not permit 757
not possess 774
not prepared 670
not ready 670
not real 2B
not relate 10
not remember 506
not resemble 19
not respect 921
not see 439D
not sharp 257
not similar 19
not so! 489

not spare 919E
not speak 582
  unable to speak 578A
not there
  absent 190
not the time 138
not turn 249C
not understand 517
not welcome 299B
not with
  absent 190
nourish 301
now
  at this time 121
no water 342
nude 229
nudity 229
nuisance 827
nullify 752B
numb 375B
number
  count 86
  numbers 99
  total 85
numerals 99
numeration
  counting 86
numerous 104
nurse
  breast-feed 301D4
nurture 534E
nut 301B1g
nutrition 301
o'clock 108E4
oak 366D3d
  oak timber 631D4
oar
  ship's tackle 275A2
  tool 630D
oath 532A
Obadiah 371J4a
Obed-edom 371J4b
obedience 739
obeisance 309B
obelisk 215B
obese 195B
obesity 195B
obey 739
objective
  goal 617C
oblation
  sacrifice 981C
obligation
  compulsion 740
obliged
  compelled 740
  grateful 907
obliterate 550
obliteration 550
oblivion 506
oblivious 506
obloquy 926
obnoxious
  hateful 888
obscene 951
observance 768
observe
  keep 768
  see 438
obstacle 702

obstinacy 602
obstinate 602
obstruct 702
obstruction 702
obstructive 702
obtain
  acquire 771
obtuse
  unintelligent 499
occasion
  right time 137
occult 984
occupation 686B1
occur 154
occurrence 154
ocean 343
odd
  unusual 84
odious
  hateful 888
odorous 394
odour 394
of age 134B
of all sorts 82
offal 224A7
offer 759
offering
  burnt offering 981D2
  cereal offering 981D3
  guilt offering 981D6
  peace offering 981D4
  sacrifice 981C
  sin offering 981D5
officer 722
official 741D
off one's head 503
offspring 170
of old 125
of one mind 710
often 139
  repeatedly 106
Og 371J4c
Oholah
  Samaria 184J2c
Oholibah
  Jerusalem 184G2h
oil 357A
  lubricate 334
  oil for fuel 385B
ointment 357B
old 127
  old man 127B
  old nature 127B
  old person 133
  years old 131
old age 131C
olden 127
olden days 125
olden times 125
older 131
oldness 127
olfactory 394A
olive 366D3e
  Mount of Olives 209G2e
  olive oil 357A
  olive wood 631D4
Olivet 209G2e
ombudsman
  mediator 720

omega
  Alpha and Omega 68F
omen 605C2
omer 465
omission
  negligence 458
omnipotence 160A1
omnipotent 160A1
omnipresence 189A
omniscience 490B1
  omniscience of Christ
   490C1
Omri 371J4d
  king of Israel 741C1
Onan 371J4e
once 88
  once a day 141A2
  once for all 88F
one 88
  day one 108F1b
  month one 108G2
  one flesh 45C1a
  oneself 80
one after another 65
one and all 52
one and only 21
one by one 65
oneness
  singleness 88
  unity 88
one or two
  few 105
oneself 80
  by oneself 88B4
  commend oneself 923B3
  say to oneself 585
one-sided
  biased 481
Onesimus 371J4f
Onesiphorus 371J4g
on high 209
onion 301B1f
only
  only begotten 88B2
  only once 88F
  simply 44
on one's own 88B4
on purpose 617
onset
  beginning 68
on time 137
onyx 844A1b
open 263
  manifest 522
  open letter 522B
open arms
  welcoming 299A
open-handed
  generous 813
opening 263
openly 522B
  plainly 573
open the eyes
  heal the blind 438A2
operator 173
Ophel 184H5a
Ophir
  the place 184H5b

Ophrah
  of Benjamin 184H5c
  of Manasseh 184H5d
ophthalmic 438B
opinion 451A
opponent 705
opportune 137
opportunity 137
oppose 704
opposite
  contrary 14
  over against 240
opposition 704
oppress 735B
oppression 735B
oppressive 735
oppressor 735
optimism
  hope 852
option
  choice 605
opulence 800
opulent 800
oracle 579C3d
orator 579
oratory
  eloquence 579A3
orb
  circle 250
orchard 370C3
ordain 751
ordeal
  suffering 825
order
  command 737
  sequence 65
  set in order 62
  sort into order 73
  system 60
orderly
  tidy 60
ordinary
  ordinary people 869
ordination 751
ordure 302B1
ore 631B
organ
  internal organ 224A7
  limb 53
origin 68
originate 68A2
originator 68A2
Orion 420A3
ornament 844
ornamental 844
ornamentation 844
Ornan
  Araunah 371D7d
Orpah 371J4h
orphan 779A
oscillate 317
Osee
  Hosea 371G3g
Oshea
  Hoshea 371G3h
  Joshua 371H8g
ostentation 875
ostentatious 875
ostracise 300
ostracism 300

ostrich 365C3e
other
  different 15
Othniel 371J4i
ourselves 80
oust
  depose 752A
  eject 300
out
  inside and out 223E
  outside 223
outcast 883A
outdated 127
outdistance 306
outdo 306A
outdoors 223
outer
  exterior 223
outer darkness 418C4
outermost 223
outfit
  clothing 228
outflow 350
outgoings
  expenditure 806
outlay
  expenditure 806
outline
  summary 570
outrank 34
outside 223
  inside and out 223E
outsider
  alien 59
outsize
  huge 195A
outstretched 205
outstrip 306
outward 223
oven 383B
over
  pass over 305C
over against 240
over and over
  repetition 106
overcome
  triumph 727
overcoming 727
overdue
  late 136
overeat 947
overestimate 482
overflow 637
  flood 350B
overhear 416B
overindulgence
  gluttony 947
overlaid 226D
overlay 226D
overloaded
  burdened 322D
overlook
  forgive 909
  neglect 458
overlord 741
overmaster 727
overseer 741E3
overshadow 418
oversight
  negligence 458

overtake 295C
overthrow
  conquer 727
  destruction 165
overturn 221
overweight 195B
overwork 682
owe 803
owing to 158
owl 365C3f
  great owl 365C3f
  little owl 365C3f
  white owl 365C3f
own
  not own 774
  one's own 80
  right in own eyes 913D3
owner 776
ownership 773
ox 365F
  wild ox 365E6c
oxen 365F3
ox-goad 256A4
pace
  distance measure 199A3
pacification 719
pacify 719
pact
  compact 765
Padam-aram
  Paddan-aram 184I1a
Padan
  Paddan-aram 184I1a
Paddan
  Paddan-aram 184I1a
Paddan-aram 184I1a
padlock 662D
pagan 974
  foreigner 59
paid 804
pail 194A
pain
  cause pain 827
  physical pain 377
painful 827
paint 553
  paint eyes 843
painted 553
painting 553
pair 90
palace 192D4
pale 426
palisade 235A
pallet 218E
palm 366D4a
palsy
  paralysis 651B6
Palti
  Paltiel 371K1a
Paltiel 371K1a
pamper 736
Pamphylia 184I1b
pan 194A
panel 227
panelling 227
pang
  suffering 825
panic
  fear 854

panoply
  armour 713
pant
  gasp 352A
Paphos 184I1c
papyrus 366C1b
parable 519
Paradise
  heaven 971
paralysed 651B6
paralysis 651B6
paralytic 651B6
paramour 952B
parapet 235A
parched 342
pardon 909
pare
  cut 46
parent 169
parental 169
parenthood 169
parity
  equality 28
Parmenas 371K1b
paroxysm
  convulsion 318C
parsimony 816
part
  component 53
Parthia 184I1d
Parthian 184I1d
partial
  biased 481
partiality
  bias 481
particular
  fastidious 862
parting
  fork 294
partner 707
partnership
  fellowship 9
partridge 365C3g
party
  faction 708
Paschal 988A2
pass
  pass away 2D
  pass by 305B
  pass over 305C
  pass through 305A
  pass water 302B2
passage
  passing 305A
pass away
  not exist 2D
passer-by 305B
passion
  fervour 818
  lust 859C3
  suffering 825
  zeal 818C
pass out
  faint 375C
Passover 988A2
pass over
  exempt 919C
past
  past time 125
pastor [shepherd] 369C2

pasture 301D5
Patara 184I1e
patch 45D
  repair 656C1
paternal 169B
paternity 169B
path 624
pathetic
  pitiable 905
pathless 624A1
patience 823
patient
  longsuffering 823
Patmos 349B
patriarch 169B
patricide 362E5c
patrol
  walk 267B2
  watchman 457D
pattern 23A
  example 83C1
  orderly pattern 60
Paul 371K2
Paulus
  Sergius Paulus 371K3a
pause 145
pavement 624B5
pavilion 192
paw 53
pay 804
  not pay 805
  pay attention 455
  requite 804B
pay attention 455
pay heed 455
payment 804
pay no attention 456
peace 717
  pacification 719
peaceful 717
peacemaker
  mediator 720
peace offering 981D4
peacock 365C3h
peafowl 365C3h
peahen 365C3h
peak
  summit 213A1
peal of bells 412
pearl 844A2
  mother-of-pearl 631C1
pebble 344B
peculiar
  special 80
peddler 794
pedlar 794
peep 438
peer
  equal 28
  gaze 438
peg 47D3
  tent peg 47D3
Pekah 371K3b
  king of Israel 741C1
Pekahiah 371K3c
  king of Israel 741C1
Pelatiah 371K3d
Pelethites 371C5g
pelican 365C3i
  white owl 365C3f

pelt
  skin 226E2
  throw 287
pen
  enclosure 235A
penalty
  death penalty 963F
pendant 217
Peniel 184I1f
penis 167A2
penitence 939
penitent 939
penny 797A1
pensive
  thoughtful 449
Pentecost 988A3
Penuel
  Peniel 184I1f
  tower of 209C2
penury
  poverty 801
people
  mankind 371
  nation 371C1
Peor 209G2f
Perazim 209G2g
perceive
  understand 516
peremptory 680B
Perez-uzzah 184I1g
perfect 646
perfection 646
perfidious 930
perfidy 930
perform
  do 676
performer
  actor 542C
perfume 396
perfumer 686B4c
Perga 184I1h
Pergamos
  Pergamum 184I2a
Pergamum 184I2a
peril 661
perilous 661
period
  menstruation 302C
  time 110
periodical 141
periodicity 141
perish
  die 361
perishable
  fleeting 114
Perizzites 371C5h
perjurer
  liar 545
perjury
  falsehood 542B
permanence 144
permanent
  endless 115
  unchanging 144
permission 756
permit 756
  not permit 757
permitted
  legal 953

perpetual
eternal 115
perpetually
continually 146
perpetuity
in perpetuity 115
perplex 474B
persecute 735C
persecution 735C
persecutor 735
perseverance 600
persevere 600
Persia 184I2b
Persians 371C6a
Persians 371C6a
Persis 371K3e
persist 600E
persevere 600
persistent 600
person 371
regarding persons 481
perspire 302D
persuade 612
persuasion 612
persuasive 612
perverse 246B
perversion 84B
derangement 63B
pervert
derange 63B
perverted 84B
pest 659B
pester
torment 827
pestilence 659B
illness 651B5
pestle 332A
Peter 371K4
petition
request 761
petty
unimportant 639
Phalti
Paltiel 371K1a
Phaltiel
Paltiel 371K1a
phantom
ghost 970
Pharaoh
Pharaoh Neco 371J2f
Pharisee 708B
Phebe
Phoebe 371K6a
Phenice
Phoenicia 184I2f
Phoenix 184I2g
Phenicia
Phoenicia 184I2f
Philadelphia 184I2c
Philemon 371K5a
Philetus 371K5b
Philip 371K5c
Philippi 184I2d
Philippians 184I2d
Philistia 184I2e
Philistines 371C6b
Philistim
Philistines 371C6b
Philistines 371C6b
philosophy 449B6

Phinehas 371K5g
phobia
fear 854
Phoebe 371K6a
Phoenicia 184I2f
Phoenix 184I2g
Phrygia 184I3a
Phygellus
Phygelus 371K6b
Phygelus 371K6b
phylactery 547C1
box 194B1
physical 319
physician 658B1
pick
choose 605
picked
chosen 605
picture
drawing 551
piece 53
piece of silver 797B
pierce 263A4
piercing 263A4
piety
holiness 979
pig 365G7
pigeon 365C3b
Pilate 371K6c
pillar
monument 548A
obelisk 215B
support 218C
pillow 218E
pilot
guide 690
sailor 270
pine
cypress 366D2f
pine timber 631D4
the tree 366D3b
pinnacle 213A3
pioneer 68A2
pipe
musical instrument 414B4
tube 351
pipes
bagpipe 414B4
Pisgah 209G2h
Pisidia 184I3b
pistachio nuts 301B1g
pit 255B
bottomless pit 972B
the Pit 361
pitch 631C3
pitiable 905
pitiful
pitiable 905
pitiless 906
pitilessness 906
pity 905
placard 522
place
circumstances 8A
in place of 150
where? 187
placenta
afterbirth 167B4a

plague 659
illness 651B5
plain
flat land 348
plain speaking 573
plainly 573
plait 222D
plan 623
pattern 23A
plane
tool 630C
planet 420A
plank 207A
plant
leafy plant 366
planting 370
root firmly 153B5
plaster
stucco 226D5
plate
dinner plate 194B6
sheet 207
slab 207C
platform 218H
platter 194B6
play
play musical instruments 413B
sport 837A
play-acting 542C
plaza 235C
plea
request 761
plead
plead a cause 927
pleasant
pleasing 826
please 826
pleased 826
pleasurable 826
pleasure 826
amusement 837
pledge 767A
pledge in marriage 894F
Pleiades 420A3
plenty 635
much 32
plot 623B4
plotter 623B4
plough 370D1
ploughman 370D1
ploughshare 630B
plowshare 630B
pluck
courage 855
pluck hair 46E4
pluck out 304C
plumb line 215A
plump 195B
plunder
booty 790
plunge 313
pod 366B4
podium
platform 218H
poem 593
poet 593
poetic 593
poetry 593

point
sharp point 256
pointless
useless 641
poison 659B
poisonous 659B
polite 884
politeness 884
pollute 649E
pollution 649E
polygamy 894A2e
polygyny 894A2e
pomegranate
the fruit 171C3e
the tree 366D4b
pomp 875B
pond 346
ponder 449B5
ponderous
heavy 322C
pong
stench 397
Pontius
Pontius Pilate 371K6c
Pontus 184I3c
pool
lake 346
poor 801
poor or rich 800G
poorly
ill 651
poplar 366D4c
popular 923
populate 167
population 371
porch 194C
Porcius
Porcius Festus 371F5b
pork 301B3
porphyry
precious stone 844A1b
the material 631C1
porpoise 365D1
portent 547A
portion
part 53
property 777
share 775
positive
affirmative 532
possess 773
not possess 774
take possession 771
possessed
demonised 969D3
possession 773
possessions 777
possessor 776
possibility 469
possible 469
post
pillar 215B
posterity 170
pot 194B6
potent
powerful 160
Potiphar 371K6d

pottage 301B1f
potter 686B3b
poultice 658A
poultry 365C3a
pound
  knock 279F
  weight 322B
pour
  pouring water 350A3
  pour like water 350A4b
poverty 801
powder 332
powdery 332
power 160
powerful 160
powerless 161
practice
  doing 676
praetorium 192D4
praise 923
  praise oneself 923B3
pray 761
prayer 761
preach
  proclaim 528
preacher 528
precede
  forerunner 66
  go before 283
precedence 64
precious 644
  expensive 811
  good 644B
  precious stone 844
precipitation 350F
precognition
  foreknowledge 510
preconceived
  biased 481
precursor
  forerunner 66
predestination 608
predestine 608
predetermination 608
predetermined 608
predict 511
prediction 511
pregnancy 167B2
pregnant 167B2
  become pregnant 167B1
prejudge 481
premature 138
  premature death 114B3
  untimely birth 138B
preordain
  predestine 608
preparation 669
prepare 669
prepared 669
  not prepared 670
prerequisite
  requirement 627
prescient
  foreseeing 510
presence 189
  bread of the Presence
    189A3

present
  gift 781
  in attendance 189
  present time 121
preservation 666
preserve 666
press 279H
  crowd 74B
pressing
  compelling 740
prestige 866
presume 878
presumption 878
presumptuous 878
pretence 541C
pretend 541C
pretentious
  ostentatious 875
pretext 614
pretty 841
prevent
  hinder 702
previous 125
previously 125
prevision
  foresight 510
prey
  bird of prey 365C2
  booty 790
price 809
prick
  sharp point 256
pricy
  expensive 811
pride 871
priest 986
  high priest 986B1
  priest's garments 989
primacy
  superiority 34
prime
  prime of life 134B
prince 741D
principalities and powers
  969C3
principle 81
Prisca
  Priscilla 371K6e
Priscilla 371K6e
prison 748
  imprison 747D
prisoner 750
private
  private parts 167A
privately 883B
probity 929
procession 267C5
Prochorus 371K6f
proclaim 528
proclamation 528
Procorus
  Prochorus 371K6f
procrastinate 136
procreation 171A1
procure
  acquire 771
prodigal 815
produce
  make 164
productive 171

profane
  make unclean 649E
  unholy 980
profess
  affirm 532
profession 622
proffer
  offer 759
proficiency 696
profit
  gain 771C
profitable
  useful 640
profligacy 815
profligate 815
prohibit 757
prohibition 757
prolific 171
prolong 113
promiscuity 951A
promiscuous 951A
promise 764
promote 285B
prompt
  early 135
pronunciation 580
proof 478
prop
  prop up 218A
propagate 167
propagation 167
propel 287
proper 915C
property 777
prophecy 579C
prophesying 579C
prophet 579C
prophetic
  predicting 511
propitiate 941
propitiation 941
propitiatory
  cover for the ark 226C3
proportion
  in proportion to 12
propulsion 287
proscribe
  prohibit 757
prosecute
  accuse 928
proselyte 147C
prospect
  future 124
prosper 730
prosperity 730
prosperous 730
prostitute 952C
prostitution 951F
prostrate 309B1a
protect 660
protection
  protecting 660
  refuge 662
protector 660
prototype 23
protract 113
proud 871
prove 478
proved
  certain 473

provender 301D5
proverb 496
provide 633
provision 633
provisions
  food 301
provocation
  annoyance 827
  quarrel 709
provoke
  annoy 827B3
  quarrel 709
proximity 200
prudent
  wise person 500
pruning hook 630B
psalm 412C
psalms 586A4
Ptolemais 184I3d
public
  in public 522B
publication 528
public convenience
  latrine 302B1
publicly 522B
publish 528
Publius 371K6g
pudenda 167A2
puffed up
  proud 871
Pul
  Libya? 184G7b
  Tiglath-pileser 371L8f
pull 288
pull out
  pull out hair 46E4
pulpit
  platform 218H
punch 279A
punctual 135
punish 963
  punish less 736B
punishment 963
  less punishment 736B
  means of punishment
    964
punitive 963
puny
  weak 163
pupil
  pupil of the eye 438B3
Pur
  casting lots 605C1
purchase 792
pure 950
purification 648
purify 648
Purim
  casting lots 605C1
purity 950
purple 436
purpose
  intention 617
  plan 623
  will 595
purposeful 599B
purse 799B
pursue 619
pursuit 619

push
  press 279H
put
  put out flame 382B
put away 779B
put down
  depose 752A
Puteoli 184I3e
put off
  delay 136
put on
  wear 228
putrefaction 51
putrefy 51
puzzle 474B
  riddle 530C
pyre 364A
qesita 797A2
quadrans 797A1
quadrisection 98
quadruplicate 97
quagmire 347
quail
  be afraid 854
  bird 365C3j
quake
  be afraid 854
  earthquake 176C1
quantity
  amount 26
  small quantity 33
quarrel 709
quarry 344B3
  mine 255D2
quarter
  fourth 98
quartered 98
quartering 98
quartet 96
quaternion 96C
quaternity 96
queen of heaven 967A
query 459
question
  ask questions 459A
questioner 459
quick
  speedy 277A
quicken
  give life 360D6
quickly 277
  promptly 135
quick temper 892
quiescent 266
quiet
  calm 266A4
  lack of noise 399
  not speaking 582
  stillness 266
quieten 578B
quip 839
quit
  depart 296
quiver
  be agitated 318
  container for arrows 194B8
quiz
  interrogate 459B2

quota
  number 85
Raamses
  Rameses 184I4d
Rabbah
  of Ammon 184I4a
Rabbath
  Rabbah 184I4a
rabbi
  teacher 537
rabble 74B
race
  run race 716E
  speed 277A
Rachab
  Rahab 371K7b
Rachel 371K7a
racket
  noise 400A
radiant
  luminous 417
raft 275D
rafter 213A2
rag 228B8e
rage 891
rags 228B8e
Rahab 371K7b
  Egypt 184E4
Rahel
  Rachel 371K7a
raid 712
raider 712
rain 350F1
rainbow 250D
rainy 350F1
raise
  adopt 170A7
  bring up 534E
  elevate 310
  resurrect 656B
raised
  resurrected 656B
raisins 301B1e
rally
  assemble 74
ram 365F
  battering ram 279A3a
Ramah
  of Benjamin 184I4b
  Ramathaim-zophim 184I4c
  Ramoth-gilead 184I4e
Ramathaim-zophim 184I4c
Ramathite 184I4c
Ramath-lehi
  Lehi 184G7a
Ramath-mizpeh 184H3c
Rameses 184I4d
Ramoth
  Ramoth-gilead 184I4e
Ramoth-gilead 184I4e
random 159
range
  patrol 267B2
rank 73
ransack
  lay waste 165
ransom 792C
rape 951G

rapid 277A
rapture
  joy 824
rare
  infrequent 140
rash
  incautious 857
rashness 857
rattle
  shake 318A
ravage
  lay waste 165
raven 365C3k
ravish
  rape 951G
raw 670C
  live flesh 360A2
ray
  light 417
raze
  destroy 165
razor 256A2
read 579E
reader 579E
readiness 669
reading 579E
ready
  not ready 670
  prepared 669
real 1
  not real 2B
reality 1
reap
  harvest 370D3
rear
  adopt 170A7
  back 238
  bring up the rear 238B
  raise 534E
reason
  cause 156
  reasoned argument 475
reasoning 475
Rebecca
  Rebekah 371K7c
Rebekah 371K7c
rebel 738B
rebellion 738B
rebellious 738
rebound 280
rebuild 164B2
rebuke 924
Recab
  Rechab 371K7d
recall
  remember 505
recede
  abate 37
receive 782
  welcome 299
receiving 782
recent
  recent convert 130B
receptacle 194
reception
  welcome 299
Rechab 371K7d
Rechabites 371C6c
reciprocal 12
reckless 857

reckon 480F
recline 309D2
recognise 490E6
  not recognise 491D2
recognition
  knowing 490E6
recoil 280
recommend 923
recommendation 923
recompense
  reward 962
reconcile 719
reconciliation 719
record 548
recorder 549
records 548B
recount 590B
recover
  get well 656
recovery
  getting well 656
recurrence
  relapse 657
red 431
  Red Sea 343C4
redeem 792C
redemption 792C
reduce 198
  decrease 37
reduction
  decrease 37
  subtraction 39
reed 366C1b
  measure 465B2
  Sea of Reeds 343C4
  staff 218B2
reef 344B6a
reel
  stagger 152C
re-establish 656C3
referee
  mediator 720
refine
  improve 654
reflection 18
reform 654
refrain
  avoid 620A
  cease 145
refresh 685
refreshing 685
refreshment 685
refuge 662
  city of refuge 184C7
refugee 188
refusal 760
refuse
  decline 760
  rubbish 641C3
refutation 479
refute 479
regard
  look 438
regeneration 360D6
regime 733
region 184
register 548B
regress 286
regret 830

regular
  regular periods 141
regularly 141
regulations
  rules 737
Rehoboam 371K7e
  king of Judah 741C2
reign 733
reimburse 804
reinstate 656C3
reject 607
  forsake 621
rejection 607
  forsaking 621
rejoice 824
rejoicing 824
rejoinder
  reply 460
relapse 657
relate
  describe 590B
  have fellowship 9
  not relate 10
related 11
relations
  relatives 11
relationship
  fellowship 9
relatives
  kin 11
relax 683
release
  setting free 746
relentless
  pitiless 906
reliable
  trustworthy 929
relief 831C
relieve
  bring relief 831
  relieve oneself 302B1
religion 973
religious 973
relinquish 621
relinquishment 621
reluctance 598
reluctant 598
rely on 485
remain
  leftover 41
  stay 144
remainder 41
remarkable 864
remarriage 894A2c
remarry 894A2c
remedial 658
remedy 658
remember 505
  not remember 506
remembrance 505
remind 505
reminder 505
remission
  forgiveness 909
Remmon
  Rimmon 967G
remnant 41A
remorse 830A
remorseful 830A

remote
  far off 199
remove
  depose 752A
  displace 188
  subtract 39
  take 786
removed
  not exist 2D
Remphan
  Rephan 967H
remuneration 804A3
rename 561C3
rend 46
render
  give 781
renew 126
renewal 126
renounce
  relinquish 621
renovate 656
renown 866
renunciation
  relinquishment 621
repair 656C1
repast
  meal 301
repatriate 188
repay 804B
repeat 106
repeatedly 106
repel 715
repent 939
repentance 939
repentant 939
repetition 106
repetitive 106
Rephan 967H
replenish 54
replica 22
reply 460
report 524
repose 683
represent
  stand for 720
representative
  mediator 720
reprieve
  forgive 909
reprimand 924
reprisal
  revenge 910
reproach 924
reprobate 938
reproduce 167
reproduction 167
  procreation 171A1
reproof 924
reprove 924
repugnance
  hatred 888
reputable 866
reputation 866D3c
repute 866
request 761
require
  demand 737
  need 627
requirement 627

requisite
  needful 627
requite 804B
rescue 668
resemble
  be similar 18
  not resemble 19
resent
  hate 888
resentful
  angry 891
reservoir 346
resettle
  deport 188
residue
  remainder 41
resilient
  tough 329
resist 715
resistance 715
resolute 599
resolution 599
resolve
  decide 605
  intend 617
respect 920
respectful 920
respiration 352A
respire 352A
respite 145A3
respond
  reply 460
response
  reply 460
responsibility 180
responsible
  liable 180
rest
  come to rest 266A2
  day of rest 683A
  remainder 41
  repose 683
resting-place 266
restitution 787
restless 678D
restoration 656
restore 656
  reinstate 656C3
restrain 747
  dissuade 613
restraint 747
  self-restraint 823E
restrict
  hinder 702
  prohibit 757
resurrect 656B
resurrection 656B
retain 778
retaliation
  equality in 28C6
retch
  vomit 302F4
retention 778
retire
  stop work 145A1
retort
  reply 460
retribution
  punishment 963

return 148
  rebound 280
Reuben
  Reuben, Gad and half
    Manasseh 371B3d
  territory of 184I4f
  the man 371K7f
  tribe of 371B7c
Reubenites 371B7c
Reuel
  Jethro 371H6a
reveal
  disclose 526
  show 522
revelation
  disclosure 526
revenge 910
revere
  respect 920
reverence
  respect 920
reversion 148D1
revert 148D1
revile 924C5
reviler 924C5
revive 360D6
  restore 656C4
revoke 752B
revolt 738B
revolution
  revolt 738
revolve 315
revulsion
  hatred 888
reward 962
Rezin 371K7g
Rhegium 184I5a
rhetoric 579A3
Rhoda 371K7h
Rhodes 184I5b
rib 239A
Riblah 184I5c
rich 800
  poor or rich 800G
riches
  wealth 800
riddle 530C
ride 267D
rider 267D
ridicule 851
riding 267D
rigging
  ship's rigging 275A2
right
  due rights 915B1
  right and left 241D
  righteousness 913
  right in own eyes 913D3
  right mind 502
  right side 241
righteous 913
  self-righteous 913D3
  the righteous 937
righteousness 913
right-handed 241C1
rights 915
right time 108C
  opportunity 137
rigid 326
Rimmon 967G

ring 250B
  earring 844A
  gold ring 844A
  signet 547C3
riot 61
rip 46E5
  rip open 263A2a
ripe
  ready 669C
rise
  live again 656B
  rise early 128B
  rise up 308
risen
  resurrected 656B
risk 661A
risky
  dangerous 661
rite 988
ritual 988
river 350C
  the River 350D2
Rizpah 371K7i
road 624
road sign 547D
roam 267B
roar 403
rob 788
robber 789
robbery 788
robbing 788
rock 344B
rock badger 365E3c
rod
  measure 465B2
  staff 218B
roebuck 365E1b
Rogelim 184I5d
roll 315A
roll-call
  count 86
rolling 315A
Roman
  Roman citizen 191B
  Romans 371C6d
Rome 184I5e
Rompha 967H
roof 213A2
room
  chamber 194C
  no room 183C
  space 183A
  upper room 194C2
roomy 183A
roost 192
rooster 365C3a
root 366B1
  bottom 214
  take root 153B5
  without root 152B
rootless 152B
root out 304B
rope 208B
rose
  flower 366C3a
rostrum 218H
rosy
  red 431
rot
  decay 51

rotate 315
rough 259
roughness 259
round
  circular 250
  surrounding 230
rouse
  stir up 174
  wake up 678C3
rout
  defeat 727
route 624B
rove
  wander 267B
rover
  wanderer 267B1
row
  quarrel 709
  row a boat 269B
rowing
  boating 269B
royal 733
rub 333
  rub out 550
rubbish 641C3
  nonsense 515
ruby 844A1b
rudder 275A2
ruddy
  red 431
rudiments 68
ruin 165
ruined 165
rule 733
  not ruled 734B
  principle 81
  reign 733
ruler 741
  no ruler 734
rumble
  roar 403B
rumour 529B3
run 277B
  run away 620A
  running water 350
  run race 716E
run loose
  riot 61
running water 350
rural 184A
rush
  run 277B
rust 51B
Ruth 371K7j
rye 366C2
sabaoth
  armies 722
sabbath 683A
sackcloth 631F5
sacred 979
sacred writings 975
sacrifice
  human sacrifices 981C7a
  offering 981C
sacrificial 981C
sacrilege 980
sacrilegious 980
sad 825
  dejected 834
  unhappy 825

saddle
  seat 218D
Sadducee 708B
sadness
  dejection 834
  depression 834
  suffering 825
  unhappiness 825
Sadoc
  Zadok 371M2b
safe 660
safeguard
  keep safe 660
  refuge 662
safety 660
sage
  wise person 500
sail
  sail a boat 269A
  ship's sail 275A2
sailor 270
saint 979B5
sake
  for the sake of 156C
Sakkuth 967H
Salamis 184J1a
salary 804A3
sale 793
Salem
  Jerusalem 184G2
Salim 184J1b
saliva 302F1
Salmone 184J1c
Salome 371L1a
salt 389
  Salt Sea 343C1
salted 389
salty 389
salute
  greet 884
salvation 668
salve 658A
salver
  plate 194A
Samaria
  hill of 209G2i
  Samaritans 371C6e
Samaritans 371C6e
same
  equal 28
  identical 16
  same time 123
  same words 106A
  unchanging 144
same as
  conformed to 83
Samos 349B
Samothrace 184J3a
Samothracia
  Samothrace 184J3a
sample
  example 83C1
Samson 371L1b
Samuel 371L1c
Sanballat 371L1d
sanctification 979B4
sanctified 979
sanctify 979
  set apart for evil 980C

sanctuary
  holy place 990
  refuge 662A2
sanctum sanctorum
  990B7
sand 344C
  numerous as sand
  104
sandal 228B7d
sandfly 365B2b
sane 502
Sanhedrin
  council 692A
sanitation 648
sanity 502
sapient
  wise 498
Sapphira 371L1e
sapphire 844A1b
Sarah 371L1f
Sarai
  Sarah 371L1f
sarcasm 851
sarcastic 851
Sardis 184J3b
sardius 844A5
sardonyx 844A1b
Sarepta
  Zarephath 184K4b
Saron
  Sharon 184J4a
Satan
  adversary 705B
  the devil 969
sate 637A
sated 637A
satire
  ridicule 851
satisfaction
  content 828
  dissatisfaction 829A
satisfied 635
  content 828
  not satisfied 636
satisfy 633
saucepan 194B6
Saul 371L1g
  Paul 371K2
save
  rescue 668
savings 632C
saviour 668A1e
savoury 390
  savoury food 301B1a
saw
  proverb 496
  tool 630C
say 579
saying
  proverb 496
scab 647
scabbard 226C4
scabby 647
scaffold 964B
scale
  plate 207
scales
  balance 465A
scarce 105

scarlet
red 431
scatter 75
scattering 75
scent
perfume 396A
smell 394
sceptre 743C
Sceva 371L1h
scheme 623B3
schemer 623B3
schism 46
scholar 492
school 539
scoff 851
scoffer 851
scoffing 851
scold 924
scorch 381C5
scorched 381C5
scorching 379
scorn 922
scornful 922
scorpion 365E5a
scourge
beat 279A1e
scourings
rubbish 641C3
scrape 333
scraps
leftovers 41B1
screen 421
scribe 586C
script 558
scripture 586A
Scriptures 975
scroll 589
sculpt 554
sculpture 554
sea 343
Dead Sea 343C1
Great Sea 343C3
Mediterranean Sea 343C3
Red Sea 343C4
sea creatures 365D
Sea of Chinneroth 343C2
Sea of Galilee 343C2
Sea of Gennesaret 343C2
Sea of Tiberias 343C2
seah 465C
seal
seal up 264C3
sign 547C2
sealed
sealed up 264C3
seaman 270
seance 984
search 459C
seashore 234B
season
in season 137
period 110A3
seat 218D
judgement seat 956B
Seba
the place 184J3c
seclusion 883

second
second coming 295D
second death 361F2
second time 91D
second thoughts 603
secrecy 530
secret 530
secretary 586C
secretly 530
sect 708
sectarian 708
section
subdivision 53
secure
unchanging 153
security
pledge 767A
safety 660
seduce 612B3
see 438
not see 439D
pay attention 455
see dimly 440
seed
seed for sowing 366B5
seeing 438A
seek 459C
seemingly
supposedly 512
seen
to be seen by men 875
seer 438G
Seir
Edomites 371C3d
Mt Seir 209G2j
the land of Edom 184E3c
seize 786E
arrest 747B
Sela 184J3d
select
choose 605
pick 605A
selected 605
selection
choosing 605
Seleucia 184J3e
self 80
oneself 80A
self-centred 932
self-condemned 961D
self-control 823E
no self-control 943
self-indulgence 943
selfish 932
selfishness 932
self-restraint 823E
self-righteous 913D3
self-seeking 932
sell 793
Sem
Shem 371L3b
semblance
similarity 18
semen 302E
send
commission 751
dispatch 272B
send away 300

send forth
publish 528
send-off 296A
Seneh 344B2
Senir
Mt Hermon 209G2a
Sennacherib 371L2a
sense
sense of smell 394B
sensible 498
senseless
foolish 499
sense of humour 839
sensible 498
sensual 944
separate
divide 46
separate ways 294
separation
breach 46
Sepharad
Sardis 184J3b
Sepharvaim 184J3f
Sepharvites 184J3f
sequel 67
sequence 65
put in order 73
seraph 968B2
seraphim 968B2
Sergius
Sergius Paulus 371K3a
serif
part of letter 558
sermon 579
serpent 365E4
servant 742
serve 742
set
sunset 129
Seth 371L2b
set in order 62
set one's face 599B
set out 296A
settle
dwell 192B3
settle accounts 804A1
seven 99C
day seven 108F3
month seven 108G3
sevenfold 99C6
seven o'clock 108E4h
seven thousand 99H4
seven times 99C5
seven times a day 141A1
sevenfold 99C6
seventh
seventh day 108F3
seventh hour 108E4h
seventh month 108G3
seventies 99F4f
seventy 99F4f
seventy years 110E2c
severe 735
severity 735
sew 45D
sex
intercourse 45C1a
male and female 372B
sexual
sexual desire 859C3

sexual intercourse 45C1a
shackle
fetter 747C3
shade 418D
shadow 418D
protection 662A3
type 23B
Shadrach 371L2c
shaft
pit 255B
shake
agitate 318A
shake the hand 317A
shake the head 317B
swing 317C
tremble 318B
shallow 212
Shallum 371L2d
Jehoahaz 371H2f
king of Israel 741C1
Shallun
Shallum 371L2d
Shalmaneser 371L2e
shame 872B
not ashamed 872B3
Shamgar 371L2f
shape 243
shapeless 244
Shaphan 371L2g
shard
piece 53
share 775
no share with them 620C5
share out 783
Sharon 184J4a
Sharonite 184J4a
sharp 256
not sharp 257
sharpen 256C
sharpness 256
Shaul
Saul 371L1g
shave 648A6
shear
sheep-shearing 369D
sheath
scabbard 226C4
sheathe 226C4
Sheba 371L2h
of Arabia 184J4b
Shechem
the person 371L2i
the place 184J4c
tower of 209C2
shed
barn 192
shed blood 362
sheep 365F
numerous as sheep 104
sheep-shearing 369D
sheepfold 235E
sheepskin 226E2
sheet
layer 207
shekel 465
coin 797A1
weight 322B
Shelah 371L3a
shelter 662B

Shem 371L3b
Shenazar
  Sheshbazzar 371L3c
Shenazzar
  Sheshbazzar 371L3c
Shenir
  Senir 209G2a
Sheol
  the grave 361
Shephelah 348B
shepherd 369
Sheshach
  Sheshak 184D3
Sheshak
  Babylon 184D3
Sheshbazzar 371L3c
Sheth
  Seth 371L2b
shewbread 189A3
shibboleth 580A
shield 662C1
Shihor
  the Nile 350D4
Shiloh 184J4d
Shiloni
  Shilonite 184J4d
Shilonite 184J4d
Shimei 371L3d
Shinar 184J4e
shine 417
ship 275A
shipmaster 270
shipwreck 165C7
Shishak 371L3e
Shobach 371L3f
shod 228B7d
shoe 228B7d
shoot 287B
shop 796
Shophach
  Shobach 371L3f
shore
  seashore 234B
short
  fall short 307
  feeble 161A
  in a short time 116
  short people 196A
  short things 204
  short time 114
shortage 636
shortcoming 307
shorten 204
shortened 204
shortfall 307
shortness 204
short-sighted 440
shot 287B
shoulder 53D1
shout 400B
shovel 194A
show
  reveal 522
showbread 189A3
shower
  rain 350F1
show off
  boast · 877
shrewd 498
shrine 990

shrivel 342C
shroud
  grave clothes 364A
shrub 366A
Shulamite
  Shulammite 184J4f
Shulammite
  of Shunem 184J4f
Shunammite
  of Shunem 184J4f
Shunem 184J4f
Shuphamite 371B4c
Shushan
  Susa 184J7b
shut 264A2a
shuttle
  loom 222C
sibboleth 580A
sibling 11
Sichem
  Shechem 184J4c
sick
  ill 651
  vomit 302F4
sickle 630B
side 239
  two-sided 91E
Sidon 184J5a
  Sidonians 371C6f
Sidonian 184J5a
Sidonians 371C6f
siege 712
sieve 648C3
sift 648C3
sigh 352A6
sight 438A
sign 547A
  road sign 547D
  signs and wonders 547A3
signal 547B
signalling 547B
signature 586D1
signet 547C3
significance 514
signify 514
signpost 547D
Sihor
  Shihor 350D4
Silas 371L3g
silence
  deprive of speech 578B
  lack of noise 399
silenced 578B
silent
  be silent! 578B
  not speak 582
silk 631F4
silly
  foolish 499
Siloam 184J5b
  Pool of Siloam 346
  tower of 209C2
Silvanus
  Silas 371L3g
silver 631B4
  money 797
silversmith 686B3c

Simeon
  territory of 184J5c
  the person 371L3h
  tribe of 371B7d
Simeonites 371B7d
similar 18
  conformed to 83
  identical 16
  not similar 19
similarity 18
simile 519
Simon 371L4a
  Simon Peter 371K4
simple
  simpleton 501
  unmixed 44
simpleton 501
simultaneous 123
sin 914
  sin offering 981D5
Sina
  Sinai 209G3
Sinai
  Mt Sinai 209G3
sing 412B
singer 413A
singing 412B
single
  one 88
  unmixed 44
single-hearted 44
single-minded
  resolute 599
singly 88
sink 322E
sinless 935
sinner 938
sin offering 981D5
Sion
  Mt Hermon 209G2a
Sirion
  Mt Hermon 209G2a
sirocco 352B
Sisera 371L4h
sister 11
sit
  sit down 309C1
six
  six am 108E4a
  six hundred 99G4
  six o'clock pm 108E4g
sixth
  sixth hour am 108E4a
  sixth hour pm 108E4g
sixties 99F4e
sixty 99F4e
size 195
skiff
  boat 275B
skilful 696
skill 696
  skilled person 696
skilled 696
skin 226E
  wineskin 194B3
skinny
  thin 206
skirt
  edge 234C
skull 363F2

sky 321
slab
  plate 207C
slack
  not work 677B
slander 926
slanderer 926
slap 279A
slash
  cut 46
slaughter 362
slave 742C4
  enslaved 745B
slave-girl 742C3
slave or free 742C5
slavery 745B
slay 362
slayer 362
sledge
  threshing sledge
    370D3f
sleep 679B
  die 361
  not sleep 678B
  sexual intercourse
    45C1a
  sleep in death 679B6
sleepless 678B
sleeplessness 678B
sleepy 679B
slender 206
slide
  feet slide 309E3
sling
  for stones 287A1
slip
  feet slip 309E3
  not slip 309E3d
slippery 258B
slope 220
slow 278
  not slow 135B
  tardy 136
slowly 278
slowness 278
slow to anger 823
sluggard 679A
slumber 679B
slur
  calumny 926
sly
  cunning 698
smack
  hit 279A
small 196B
  few in number 105
  unimportant 639
smash
  destroy 165
smell
  fragrance 396
  odour 394
  sniff 394A
  stench 397
  unable to smell 395
smelling
  sense of smell 394B
smile 835A
smite 279A

smith
  blacksmith 686B3c
smoke 381C1
smooth 258
  smooth tongued 575
  smooth-tongued 925
smooth-tongued 925
smother 362C1
smoulder 381
Smyrna 184J5d
snag
  difficulty 700
snake 365E4
  snakebite 655C4
snakebite 655C4
snare 542D
snatch 786
sneeze 302F3
sniff 352A6
  smell 394A
snip 46F2d
snow 350F3
  cold of snow 380A
snuffers 630D
so
  in the same way 28
soap 648C1
sober 948
sobriety 948
social 882
Sodom 184J6
sodomy 951D
soft 327
  gentle 177
  lenient 736
soften 327
soil 344A
  dung 302B1
sojourn 192B2
sojourner
  foreigner 59
solace
  comfort 831
soldier 722
sole
  only 88
soliloquy
  talk to oneself 585
solitary 88B4
Solomon 371L5
  king of Judah 741C2
  wise man 500B1
someone else 15B
son 170
  God the Son 965D
  no sons 172A2
  Son of man 371A5
  the Son 965D
song 412C
sons of God
  angels 968
soon 135A
  near the time 135
  promptly 135
  suddenly 116
soot 332C
soothe
  comfort 831
  refresh 685

soothing
  comforting 831
  refreshing 685
soothsayer 983B1
soothsaying 983B1
sophistry 477
sorcerer 983
sorcery 983
sore
  sore spot 651B1
sorrel
  brown 430
sorrow
  depression 834
  suffering 825
sorry
  regretting 830
sort
  all sorts 82
  class 77
  nature 5
  put in order 73
so-so
  average 30
Sosthenes 371L6a
sotto voce 578C
soul 320D
sound
  noise 398
  sound doctrine 534D2
  sound the depth 211D
soup 335F
sour 393
  sour wine 393A
sourness 393
south 281B
southeast 281E4
southern 281B
southwest 281E4
sovereign 741
sow
  pig 365G7
  plant 370
  scatter 75C
sowing 75C
space 183
  interval 201
  room 183A
spacious 183A
spade 630B
Spain
  Tarshish 184K1a
span
  handbreadth 465B2
  span of life 131A
spare
  exempt 919
  not spare 919E
  remaining 41
spared 919
sparrow 365C3l
sparse
  few 105
speak 579
  not speak 582
  unable to speak 578A
speak against 926
speak in tongues 557C
spear 723A3
  fishing-spear 256A4

species
  kind 77
speckled 437A
spectacle 445C
spectator 441
spectre
  ghost 970
speculation 512
speech 579
  language 557
  without speech 578D
speech impediment 580B
speechless 578B
speed 277A
speedily
  without delay 135B
spelt 366C2
spend 806
spent 806
spew
  vomit 302F4
sphere 252
spherical 252
spices 396A
spider 365B4
spies 459B3
spill
  pour 350A3
spin
  spin thread 222B
spindle 630D
spinster 895
spirit
  ghost 970
  God the Holy Spirit 965E1
  not material 320
  spirit being 320E
  the Spirit 965E1
spiritism 984
spiritual 320
spiritualist 984
spit 302F1
spite
  malevolence 898
spitting 302F1
spittle 302F1
splice 45
split
  divide 46
spoil
  booty 790
  lay waste 165
spoken 579
spokesman 579D
sponge 356
spoon 194A
sport
  play 837A
spot
  blemish 647
spotless 646
spotted
  blemished 647
  speckled 437A
spotty
  blemished 647
spread 197B
  disperse 75

spring
  fountain 350E
  leap 312
  spring of year 128G
spring up
  sprout 36B
sprinkle 75D
sprinkling 75D
sprout 36B
spurn
  forsake 621
spy 459B3
spying 459B3
squall 176D
squander 815
  waste 634
square
  plaza 235C
  square thing 28D2
squashed
  no room 183C
squeak 407
squeal 407
squeeze 279H
squirm
  struggle 682C
stab 263A4
stability 153
stable
  fixed 153
stack 209B
staff
  stick 218B
stage
  journey stage 267A
stagger 152C2
staircase 308D
stairs 308D
stallion 365G5
stammer 580B
stand
  be stable 153B
  stand firm 600
  standing up 215C
  stand still 266A2
  support 218H
  take one's stand 153B1
standard
  flag 547B1
stand aside! 290
standstill 145
star 420A
stare
  gaze 438
stars
  numerous as stars 104
start 68
starve
  be hungry 859C1
state
  condition 7
  state of affairs 8
stater 797A1
station
  state 7
stationary 266A
statue 554
stature
  tallness 195C

status
status quo 7
stay
dwell 192
remain 144
stay put 266A3
stead
in their stead 150
steadfast 600
steadfast love
lovingkindness 897B
steady
unchanging 153
steal 788
stealing 788
stealth 542D4
steed 365G5
steep 220
steer
cattle 365F
guide 689
steersman 690
stellar 420A
stench 397
step
distance measure 199A3
Stephanas 371L6c
Stephen 371L6d
steps 308D
sterile 172
stew 301B1a
steward
guide 690
overseer 754C
stick
join 48A
staff 218B
stick to 48
stiff-necked 602B
still 266
not still 265A
stillborn 172A4
stilling 266B
stillness 266
sting 655C4
stingy 816
stink 397
stipend 804A3
stir
arouse 174
stir up 612
stirred
excited 822A
stir up
excite 821
stock
livestock 365G
stocks
shackled 747C3
Stoicks
Stoics 708D
Stoics
party 708D
philosophers 449B6
stomach 224A4

stone 344B
not one stone on
another 165C5
precious stone 844
stone's throw 199A3
stone to death 344B6
stone work 631C
stoned
killed 344B6
stonemason 686B3a
stood 215C
stool
footstool 218F
stoop 309A
stop
cease 145
come to rest 266A2
stop up 264C2
store 632
storehouse 632
storey
storey of house 194D
stork 365C3m
storm 176D
stormwind 176D
story
news 529
stout-hearted 855
stove 383B
straight 249
straight talking 573
straighten
make straight 249A
straightness 249
stranger
foreigner 59
strangle 362C1
strangulation 362C1
straw 631E
light as a straw 323A
stray 282C
stream
river 350C
street 624
strength 162
strengthen 162
stretch
stretch out hands 197C
strict 735
strictness 735
stricture
reprimand 924
strife 709
strike
hit 279A
string 208A
stringed instruments
414B2
strip
undress 229C
stripe
blow 279A
striped 437A
strong 162
strong drink 335C
stronghold 662B
struggle 682C
stubble
rubbish 641C3
the material 631E

stubborn 602
stucco
plaster 226D5
student 538
study 536
stumble 309E3
not stumble 309E3d
stumbling block 702
stump
of tree 41C
stunted 204
stupefaction 375A
stupefy 375A
stupid
foolish 499
stutter 580B
subdivision 53A
subdue 745
subdued 745
subject
in subjection 745
topic 452
subjection 745
subjugation 745
submission 721
submissive
willing 597
submit 721
subside 37
substance 3
substantiality 3
substitute 150
substitution 150
subtract 39
subtraction 39
succeed 727
success 727
successful 727
Succoth
of Gad 184J7a
Succoth-benoth 967G
succour 703
succulent
tasty 390
suck
breast-feed 301D4
suckle 301D4
sudden 116A
suddenly 116A
sue 959
suet 357D
suffer 825
suffering 825
pain 377
sufficiency 635
sufficient 635
suffocate 362C1
suicide 362E8b
suit
lawsuit 959
suitable 915B
suitable time 137
sulfur
sulphur 385E
sulk 893
sulking 893
sulky 893
sullen 893
sulphur 385E

summer 128H1
summer and winter
128H2
summit 213
summon 737B1
sun 420A
sunburnt 381C5
sunday 108F1a
sunder
divide 46
sundown 129
sunrise 128A2
sunset 129
sup
eat 301
superabundance 637
superfluous 637
superintend 689
superior 34
superiority 34
superlative 34
supplant 150C
supplanter 150C
supple 327
supply
provide 633
support 218
cooperate 706
give support 218A
suppose 512
supposedly 512
suppress
overmaster 727
sure
certain 473
surety 767A
surmount 308
surpass 306
surplus 637
surprising
unexpected 508
surround 230
surroundings 230
survivor 41A
Susa 184J7b
Susanchites 184J7b
Susanna 371L6e
sustain 218A
swaddling clothes
226B3
swag
booty 790
swallow
bird 365C3n
swamp
marsh 347
swamped 350B3
swank
boast 877
swap 151
swarm
accumulation 74C1
swarms of flies
365B2b
teem 104C
swarming 74C1
swarming things
365B1
swear
swear an oath 532A

sweat 302D
sweep 648C4
sweet 392
sweetness 392
swell
  grow 36A2
swift
  quick 277
  swiftly gone 114B3
swim 269C
swimming 269C
swindle 542A
swindler 545
swine 365G7
swing 317C
swoon 375C
swop 151
sword 723A4
  killing by the sword
  362C3
  sharp thing 256A3
sycamore 631D4
  the tree 366D4d
Sychar 184J7c
Sychem
  Shechem 184J4c
symbolic
  figurative 519
sympathetic 818
sympathise 818
sympathy 818B
synagogue 192F
synchronised 123
Syntyche 371L6f
Syracuse 184J7d
Syria 184J7e
  Aram 184D2c
  Syrians 371C2f
Syriac
  Aramaic 557B
Syrian
  Aramaic 557B
Syrians 371C2f
Syrophenician
  Syrophoenician 371C6g
Syrophoenician 371C6g
Syrtis 184J7f
tabernacle
  booth 192C5
  Feast of Tabernacles
  988A4
  God in the tabernacle
  192A1
  the tabernacle 990A2
Tabitha
  Dorcas 371E8j
table 218G
tablet 548B1
  stone tablet 207D
Tabor
  Mt Tabor 209G4
tackle
  ship's tackle 275A2
tail 238A3
  turn tail 238A2

take
  conquer 786C1
  steal 788
  take away 786
  take captive 747E
  take hold of 786E
take care of 457A
take heart 855
take heed
  take care 457A
talebearer 528C
talent
  coin 797A2
  weight 322B
talisman 983C
talk 579
talkative 581
tall 195C
  high 209
tallness 195C
tally
  agree 24
  not tally 25B
Tamar
  the person 371L7a
tamarisk 366D4e
tambourine 414B1b
tame 745C
taming 745C
Tammuz 967H
tangible 378A1
tank
  cistern 339B5
tanner 686B3d
tar 631C3
tardy 136
tares [darnel] 366C1c
target 617C
Tarshish
  the place 184K1a
Tarsus 184K1b
Tartak 967G
tassel 234C
taste
  flavour 386A
  no taste 387A
  to taste 386B
  unable to taste 387B
tasteless 387A
tasting 386B
tasty
  savoury 390
tattoo 547C1
taunt 579A5
tax 804A5
teach 534
teacher 537
teaching 534
  doctrine 534D
tear
  rip 46
tears 302F2
  bottle of tears 194B2
teem
  be numerous 104C
teens 131
teeth 256B
  teeth broken 46E6c
teetotal 948A
Tekoa 184K1c

Tekoah
  Tekoa 184K1c
Tekoite 184K1c
tell
  inform 524
  order 737
temper
  bad temper 892
tempest 176D
temple
  side of head 213B2
  the sanctuary 990
tempt 612B
temptation 612B
ten 99F1
  ten am 108E4c
  ten thousand 99H5
  ten times 99F1c
tend
  tend animals 369
tender 327
tenfold 99F1c
ten-stringed
  ten-stringed harp
  414B2b
tent 192C1
  tent of meeting 990A1
tenth
  tenth hour 108E4c
  tenth part 102B1
tentmaker 686B3d
Ten Towns
  Decapolis 184E2e
tent peg 47D3
tent-peg
  sharp item 256A4
Terah
  the person 371L7c
teraphim 982
tergiversate 603
terminate
  end 69
termination 69
terrible
  frightening 854
terrified 854
terrify 854
territory 183A
terror 854
Tertius 371L7d
Tertullus 371L7e
test 461
testament
  will 765B2
tested
  approved 923
testicle 167A2
testify 466
  testify against 467
testimony 466
testing 461
  trouble 827
tether 47
tetter 651B7
textile 631F
  textile worker 686B3d
Thaddaeus 371L7f
Thamar
  Tamar 371L7a
thank 907

thankful 907
thank-offering 907
thanks 907
  no thanks 908
thanksgiving 907
Tharshish
  Tarshish 184K1a
thaw 337
theatre
  arena 724
Thebez
  tower of 209C2
Theophilus 371L8a
therapist 658B1
therapy 658
there 187D
  present 189
Thessalonian 184K1d
Thessalonica 184K1d
Theudas 371L8b
thick
  broad 205A
thickness 205
thief 789
thieve 788
thieving 788
thigh 53E2
Thimnathath
  Timnah 184K1g
thin 206
think 449
  think too highly 482
thinking 449
third
  one third 95A
  third day 108F2
  third hour 108E4b
thirst 859C2
  desire 859
thirsty 859C2
thirties 99F4b
thirty 99F4b
this day 121B
thistle 366C3i
Thomas 371L8c
thorn 366D5
  sharp thing 256A5
thorns
  difficulty 700A
thought 449
thoughtless 450
thousand 99H
  hundred thousand 99H6
  thousand years 110E4
thrash
  strike 279A
thread 208A
threat 900
threaten 900
three 93
  day three 108F2
  three hundred 99G3
  three pm 108E4e
  three thousand 99H3
  three times 94
  three times a day 141A1
  three times a year 141C
  trinity 93A
  two or three 90J
threefold 94

three or four 93F
thresh 370D3f
threshhold 263B
threshing 370D3f
thrice 94
  thrice daily 141A1
  thrice yearly 141C
thrift 816
thriftless 815
thrive
  prosper 730
throat 263F
throne 743A
throng
  crowd 74B
throttle 362C1
through
  pass through 305A
throw 287
  throw oneself down 313
  throw out 300
throw away 607D
throw down 311A3
thumb 53D4
Thummim
  Urim and Thummim
  605C1b
thunder 176E
thunderbolt 176E
thunderstorm 176E
thwart
  hinder 702
Thyatira 184K1e
thyine
  citron wood 631D4
Tiberias 184K1f
  Sea of Tiberias 343C2
Tiberius 371L8d
Tibni 371L8e
  king of Israel 741C1
tidiness 60
tidings 529
tidy
  orderly 60
tie
  bind 747C
  bond 47
  join 45
tight-fisted 816
Tiglath-pileser 371L8f
Tiglath-pilneser
  Tiglath-pileser 371L8f
Tilgath-pilneser
  Tiglath-pileser 371L8f
till
  plough 370D1
tilt 220
timber 631D
time 108
  long time 113
  period 110
  same time 123
  time past 125
timeliness 137
timely 137
timid
  fearful 854
Timnah
  of Judah 184K1g
Timnite 184K1g

Timon 371L9a
Timotheus
  Timothy 371L9b
Timothy 371L9b
tint 425
tiny 196B
tip
  tilt 220
tire 684
tired 684
Tirzah
  the place 184K2a
Tishri
  seventh month 108G3
titbit 390
tithe 102B3a
Titius
  Titius Justus 371H9h
tittle
  part of letter 558
  small thing 33A
Titus 371L9c
Tobiah 371L9d
today 121B
toe 53E6
together
  together with 89
toil 682
told 524
tolerance 823
tomb 364
tomorrow 124B2
tongs 630D
tongue
  in mouth 254B
  language 557
tongues
  speaking in tongues 557C
tool 630
too long
  in length 203A
  in time 113A5
too many 104
too much 637
tooth 256B
  tooth for tooth 28C6
top 213A
topaz 844A1b
Tophet
  Topheth 184K2b
Topheth 184K2b
topic 452
torch 420B
torment 827D
torn 46E2
torrent 350
torture 735
to this day 121D
tot up
  count 86
touch 378A
  not touch 378A8
tough
  resilient 329
towel 648
tower 209C
town 184C
toy
  caress 889B
Trachonitis 184K2c

track
  path 624
  pursue 619
tracker
  hunter 619
trackless 624A1
trade
  business 622
  occupation 686B1
  trading 791
trader 794
tradition 127C
trail
  path 624
  pursue 619
train
  teach 534
trained men 696
training 534
traitor 272A
trample 279B
tranquil
  peaceful 717
transcript
  copy 22
transfer 272
  transfer property 780
transfiguration 147A
transfigure 147A
transfix 263A4
transform 147A
transient
  fleeting 114
translate 520B
translation 520B
transparent 422
transpose
  interchange 151
trap 542D
trash 641C3
travail
  labour pains 167B4b
travel
  land travel 267
  water travel 269
traveller 268
tray 194B6
treacherous 272A
treachery 272A
tread 267C
  tread down 279B
  tread grapes 370D3h
treason 930A
treasure 800
treasure house 799A
treasurer 798
treasury 799
treaty 765B1
tree 366D
tremble 318B
trench 262
trespass 914
triad 93
  trinity 93A
trial
  test 461
  trouble 827
tribal 371B3
tribe 371B3
tribulation 827

tribunal 956
tribute
  tax 804A4
trick 698
trigon 414B1c
trim
  trim lamps 62
trinity 93A
Trinity
  triune God 965A1b
trip 309E3
  cause to trip 309E3b
  make someone trip
  311A3
triple
  three 93
triplicate 94
triumph 727
triumphal 727
triumphant 727
triune God 965A1b
Troas 184K2d
trodden 279B
Trophimus 371L9e
trouble 827
  misfortune 645
trough 194B2
  kneading-trough
  194B6
trounce
  defeat 727
true 494
trumpet 414B3
  Feast of Trumpets
  988A6
trumpeter 413B
trust 485
trustful 485
trustworthy 929
truth 494
truthful 540
try
  judge 480
  test 461
Tubal 371C6h
tubby 195B
tuberculosis 651B7
tug
  pull 288
tuition 534
tumble 309E
tumour 651B7
tumult 61
tune 412
tunic
  the priest's tunic
  989D
tunnel 351
turban 228B7c
  the priest's turban
  989E
turbulent 61
turmoil 61

turn
backslide 603C1
change direction 282
in turn 65
not turn 249C
repent 939
turn away 282
turn round 282
turn to 282A2c
turn upside down 221
turn into 147
turn tail 238A2
turquoise 844A1b
turtledove 365C3b
tutor
teacher 537
tweet 409D
twelfth
twelfth month 108G4
twelve 99F3
month twelve 108G4
twelve noon 108E4d
twelve thousand 99H5
twenty 99F4a
twenty thousand 99H5
twice 91D
twice a week 141A3
twig
branch 53B
twilight 108E2
twin 90B4
twine
string 208B
twinkle
shine 417
twinkling
instantaneous 116
twins 90B4
twist 246
twisted 246
twitter 409D
two 90
divide into two 92
two and a half 90I
two hundred 99G2
two or three 90J
two thousand 99H2
two times 91D
two-edged 91E
two-faced
hypocritical 542C
two-sided 91E
Tychicus 371L9f
type
archetype 23B
sort 77
typical 79
typology 23B
tyrannical 735
tyranny 735
tyrant 735
Tyre 184K3
Tyrian 184K3b
Tyrus
Tyre 184K3
ubiquitous 189A
ultimatum
warning 664
umpire
mediator 720

unable 161
unable to hear 416B
unable to smell 395
unable to speak 578A
unable to taste 387B
unadulterated 44
unafraid 855C
unalloyed 44
unalterable 153
unawares 508
unbearable 827
unbeaten 727
unbelief 486
unbeliever 486E
unbending 326
unbiased 913
unbind 746
unblemished 646
unborn
never born 2C
unceasing 146
uncertain 474
uncertainty 474
unchangeable 153
unchanging
permanent 144
stable 153
uncircumcised 974C
unclean 649
uncleanness 649
unclothed 229
uncomfortable
no comfort 831D
uncomforted 831D
uncompleted 726
unconcerned 860
unconquerable 727
unconscious 375C
uncooked 670C
uncountable 86E
uncover 229
uncovered
manifest 522
unction 357B
uncut 126A
undecided 601A
undefeated 727
undeniable 473
under 210A1
under arrest 747B
underclothes 989G
under cover 525
underestimate 483
underfed 636
undergarments 989G
underneath 210A1
undernourished 636
under one's breath 578C
understand 516
not understand 517
understanding 516
undertaker 364
underwear 989G
undisturbed 266A4
undressed 229
undue 916
undying
eternal 115
uneatable 391A
uneducated 493

unendurable 827D
unequal 29
unequally yoked 29B
unexpected 508
unfailing 153
unfaithful 930
unfaithfulness 930
unfamiliar 491
unfasten 746
unfathomable
unintelligible 517
unfeeling
pitiless 906
unfettered 744
unfitting 916
unflinching 855
unforeseen 508
unforgiving 919E
unforgotten 505
unfruitful 172
unfulfilled 726B
ungodly 974B
ungrateful 908
unhappy 825
unhearing 416B
unheeding 456
unholy 980
unified 88
uniformity 16
unify
make one 88D3
unimportant 639
unimpressed 860
uninhabited 190D
unintelligent 499
unintelligible 517
unintended 618A
unintentional 618A
uninterested 860
union 45
unique 21
one 88
unison
agreement 24
unite 45
gather together 74
united 45
unity
joining 45
one 88
universe 321
unjust 914
unknown 491D
unlawful 954
unleavened 323B2
Feast of Unleavened
Bread 988A2
unlike 19
unload 300F2
unlock 263E
unloose 746
unloved 887E1
unloving 887E1
unmarried 895
unmatching
dissimilar 19
unmerciful 906
unmerited 916B
unmindful
negligent 458

unmixed 44
unmoveable
steadfast 600D
unmoved
stable 153B4
unnatural 84B
unoccupied
empty 190D
unpalatable 391
unpitying 906
unprejudiced 913
unprepared 670
unproductive 172
unpunished 919B
unready
not prepared 670
unreasoning 448
unrecognised 491D1
unrelated 10
have no dealings 620C5
unrepentant 940
unrighteous 914
unrighteousness 914
unruly 61
unsafe 661
unsavoury 391
unsearchable
unintelligible 517
unseeable 444
unseeing 439D
unselfish 931
unselfishness 931
unshaken 153
unsheathe 229C4
unshifting 144
unshod 229B1
unskilled 695
unsleeping 678B
unsociable 883
unsound doctrine 535
unstable 152
unsteady 152
unsuspecting 670
unthankful 908
untie 746
untimely 138
untried 126A
untruth 543
unused 126A
unvarying 144
unwashed 649
unwavering 600
unweighable 322A3
unwell 651
unwilling 598
unwillingness 598
unworthy 916
unyielding 599
up 209
Uphaz
Ophir 184H5b
uphold 218
upper
upper room 194C2
upright
just 913
vertical 215
uproar
disorder 61
uproot 304B

upside down
  turn upside down 221
Ur
  the place 184K4a
urge 612
Uriah 371M1a
Urias
  Uriah 371M1a
Urijah
  Uriah 371M1a
Urim and Thummim
  605C1b
urinate 302B2
urine 302B2
urn 194A
us
  ourselves 80
use
  usefulness 640
useful 640
usefulness 640
useless 641
uselessness 641
usurer 803C
usury
  interest 803C
utensils 194A
uterus
  womb 167A
utility
  usefulness 640
Uzziah
  Azariah 371D8g
  king of Judah 741C2
vacant
  empty 190D
vacillate 601B
vain
  in vain 641
  proud 871
vale 255C
valiant 855
valiantly 855
valley 255C
valour 855
valuable 644
valuables 644C3
valuation 809
value
  price 809
valued 644
valueless
  inexpensive 812
  worthless 641
van
  front 237
vanish 446
  pass away 2D
vanity
  pride 871
  uselessness 641
vapour 336
varied 17
variegated 437
variety 17
various
  diverse 17
Vashti 371M1b
vassal
  servant 742

vast
  huge 195A
vat 194B3
vegetable 301B1f
vegetation 366A
vehicle 274
veil 421B
  veil the face 226B4
veneer
  covering 226D
venerate
  respect 920
vengeance 910
vengeful 910
venom 659B
venomous 659B
venture
  at a venture 159
veracious 540
verbiage
  empty talk 515
verbose 581
verbosity 581
verdict 480
verdure 366A
verge
  edge 234
verily 494
verity 494
vernacular 557
vertical 215
very
  that very time 123
vessel
  container 194
  ship 275
vestibule 194C
vestments 989
vesture 228
vex
  torment 827
vicarious 150D
victory 727
viewpoint 451A
vigorous 174
  enthusiastic 571
vigour 174
  enthusiasm 571
vilify 926
village 184C
villain 938
vindicate 927
vindication 927
vindictive 898
vindictiveness 898
vine 366D4f
  wood of the vine 631D4
vinedresser 686B4b
vinegar 393A
vineyard 370C2
violate
  rape 951G
violence 176
violent 176
violet 436
viper 365E4
virgin 895B
  unused 126A
virginity 895B

virtue
  character 933
visage
  face 237B1
visible 443
vision 438F
  defective vision 440
  sight 438
visit 295B
visitation 295B
vocation
  call 737B1
  occupation 686B1
voice 577
void
  empty space 190D
  null and void 752B
volume
  quantity 26
volunteer 597C
vomit 302F4
voracious
  gluttonous 947
votive
  for a vow 532B
vow 532B
vowing 532B
voyage 269A
vulture
  griffon vulture 365C3c
wadi 351
wafer
  sheet 207
wag
  wag the head. 317B
wage 804A3
wages 804A3
wage war 718
waggon 274B
wagon 274B
wail
  lament 836
waist 206D
wait
  lie in wait 527B
  wait for 507
waiter 686B2
wakeful 678B
wake up 678C3
walk 267C
  conduct 688
  walk on water 269D
  walk with 89
wall 235A
wander 267B
wanderer 267B1
want
  desire 859
  not want 861
war 718
  civil war 718C3
war-club 723
wardrobe 228B5
warfare 718
warm 381C4
warming 381C4
warmth 379
warn 664
warning 664
warrior 722

wary
  cautious 858
was
  existed 1
wash 648
washbasin 648A1a
waste 634
wasting disease 651B7
watch
  keep watch 457C
  period 110B6
watchful 457C
watchman 457D
watchtower 457C3
water 339
  drinking water 339C1
  irrigate 341C
  no water 342
  urine 302B2
  water container
    194B2
  water creatures 365D
water hen
  white owl? 365C3f
waters 339
wave
  gesture 547B3
  swing 317C
  wave-offering 981D7
  wave the hand 317A
waves
  waves of the sea
    343A6
wax 357E
  wax melting 337
way 624
  tradition 127C
  way of life 688
  way of women 302C
we
  ourselves 80
weak 163
weakness 163
wealth 800
wean 611
weapon 723
  weapons for fuel
    385D
wear
  wear clothes 228
wearied 684
weariness 684
wear out 655B2
weary 684
weather 340B
weave 222C
weaver 686B3d
wed 894
wedding 894
weed 366A
week 110C4
  Feast of Weeks
    988A3
weep 836
weigh 322A
  beyond weighing
    322A3
  weighed down 322D
weight 322B
  weights and

measures 465A
weighty 322C
welcome 299
   not welcome 299B
welfare 8B
well
   as well 38
   good 644
   well of water 339B4
well-known 490E6
well-timed 137
welter
   squirm 682C
were
   existed 1
west 281D
westerly 352B
western 281D
western sea 343C3
wet 341A
wetness 341A
what
   what in common? 10A
   what kind? 77B
   what nature 5
what? 5
what is
   what nature 5
what sort
   what nature 5
wheat 366C2
   grain 301B1b
wheel 250C
when? 108B
   how long? 136C
whence? 187
where? 187
   where is? [nowhere] 190
   where is God? 2A
while
   at that time 123B
whip
   punishment 964A
   strike 279D
whipping
   punishment 963D
whirl 315A
whirlwind 352B
whiskers 259A3a
whisper
   faint speech 401
   slander 926
   under one's breath
      578C
whisperer 578C
   slanderer 926
whistle 547B5
white 427
   black and white 437A
   white owl 365C3f
whiten 427E
whitewash 427E2
who
   who is like? 21
who?
   identity 13
   what sort of person 5
whole
   all of 52

whole-hearted 599B
   not whole-hearted 601C
whore 952C
whoredom 951F
why
   reason why 156
why? 158
wick
   lamp 420B
wicked 914
   the wicked 938
wickedness 914
wide 205A
widow 896B
widowhood 896B
width 205
wield 173
wife 894
wild
   nonconformist 84C
   wild cattle 365E6c
   wild donkey 365E6a
   wild goat 365E6b
   wild ox 365E6c
wild animals 365A2
wilderness 172D1
will 595
   will and testament
      765B2
willing 597
willingness 597
willow 366D4g
wilt
   wither 342C4
wily
   cunning 698
win
   succeed 727
wind
   gale 352
   twist 251
winding 251
window 263D
windy
   breezy 352B
   talkative 581
wine 335B
   intoxicating drink 949A
   medicinal use 658A
   not drink wine 948A
wine-bibber 949
wine press
   treading grapes 370D3h
wineskin 194B3
winevat 194B3
wing 271B
   under God's wings
      662A1c
wink 547B4
   in a wink 116
winnow 370D3f
winter 129E
   summer and winter
      128H2
wintering 129E
wipe 333
wisdom 498
wise 498
   wise person 500
wise men 500B2

wish
   desire 859
wit 839
witch 983
witchcraft 983
with
   along with 89
   cooperating 706
   not with 190
withdraw
   be aloof 883B
   draw back 290
   pluck out 304B
wither 342C
withhold 778
   refuse 760
   spare 919
within 224
without
   outside 223
without cause 916B
without excuse 180B
without honour 867
without hope 853
without mercy 906
without reason 916B
without speech 578D
without taste 387A
withstand 704
witness 466
   eyewitness 441
   false witness 466C4
   witness against 467
witty 839
wizard 983
woe
   sorrow 825
woe! 830B
wolf 365E5b
woman 373
womb 167A4
   from the womb 130C1
women 373
   men and women 372B
wonder 864
   not wonder 865
wood
   firewood 385A
   forest 366D1d
   timber 631D
wooden 631D
woodworker 686B3a
wool 259B
   woollen cloth 631F3
word
   message 529
   single word 559
   word of God 529A
wordless 578
words
   mere words 579A7
wordy 581
work
   deed 676
   not work 677
   no work 677
   work hard 682
worker 686
   fellow-worker 707
working 676

workman 686
works
   deeds 676
world 321
   world without God
      974A
worldly 319B
worldwide 183B
worm 365B3
worms
   decay 51
wormwood 825D2
   bitterness 391B1
worn
   dilapidated 655B2
worn-out 655B2
worried 825E
worry 825E
worse
   bad to worse 655
worsen 655
worship 981
worth
   goodness 644
worthless
   useless 641
worthy 915A
wound 655C1
   wound for wound 28C6
wounded 655C1
woven 222C
wrap
   cover 226
wrappings 226
wrath 891
wreath
   crown 743B
wreck
   destroy 165
   shipwreck 165C7
wrestle 716E
wretched 825
wring 279H
write 586
   written in heaven 548B3
writing 586
writing case 586D2
wrong
   wrongdoing 914
wrongdoing 914
Xerxes
   Ahasuerus 371D3i
Yah
   Yahweh 13A
Yahweh 13A
   God 965A1c
   name of God 561A2b
yard
   courtyard 235B
yarn
   news 529
   thread 208A
year
   date 108H
   period 110
   Year of Jubilee 988A5
   years of age 131
yearly 141D1
yearn 859
yearning 859

yeast 323B
 without yeast 323B2
yell
 shout 400B
yellow 433
 cowardly 856
yes 488
yes and no 601B
yesterday 125C
yod
 letter 558
yoke
 burden 322D
 join 45
 yoked 747C4
you
 yourself 80
young
 the younger 132
 young person 132
 youthful 130
younger
 the younger one 132

youngest 132
yourself 80
youth
 from youth 130C3
 young person 132
 youthfulness 130
youthful 130
Zabulon
 Zebulun 371M2e
Zacchaeus 371M2a
Zachariah
 Zechariah 371M2f
Zacharias
 Zechariah 371M2i
Zadok 371M2b
Zalmunna 371M2c
Zaphenath-paneah
 Joseph 371H8a
Zaphnath-paaneah
 Zaphenath-paneah
  371H8a
Zarephath 184K4b
zeal 818C

Zealots 708D
zealous 818C
Zebah 371M2d
Zeboiim 184K4c
Zeborim
 Zeboiim 184K4c
Zebulonites 371B7e
Zebulun
 territory of 184K4d
 the person 371M2e
 tribe of 371B7e
Zechariah 371M2f
 king of Israel 741C1
Zedekiah 371M3a
 king of Judah 741C2
Zeeb 371M3c
Zelophehad 371M3d
Zelotes
 Zealots 708D
Zenas 371M3e
zero 103
Zerubbabel 371M3f
Zeus 967H

Ziba 371M4a
Zidon
 Sidon 184J5a
Zidonians
 Sidonians 184J5a
Ziklag 184K4e
Zilpah 371M4b
Zimri
 king of Israel 741C1
 the person 371M4c
Zion 184K5
 Mt Zion 209G5
Ziph 184K6a
Ziphites 184K6a
Zipporah 371M4e
Zoan 184K6b
Zoar 184K6c
Zophar 371M4f
Zorobabel
 Zerubbabel 371M3